The *South* in *Perspective*

An Anthology of Southern Literature

Edward Francisco
Robert Vaughan
Linda Francisco

Upper Saddle River, New Jersey 07458

Library of Congress Cataloging-in-Publication Data

The South in perspective : an anthology of southern literature / [compiled by] Edward Francisco, Linda Francisco, Robert Vaughan.

    p. cm.

Includes bibliographical references and index.

ISBN 0-13-011490-1

    1. American literature—Southern States.   2. Southern States—Literary collections.   I. Francisco, Edward. II. Francisco, Linda. III. Vaughan, Robert.

PS551 .S553 2001

810.8'0975—dc21

                                                   00-025048

VP, Editorial Director: Laura Pearson
Editor in Chief: Leah Jewell
Sr. Acquisitions Editor: Carrie Brandon
Editorial Assistant: Sandy Hrasdzira
Managing Editor: Mary Rottino
Production Liaison: Fran Russello
Project Manager: Pine Tree Composition
Prepress and Manufacturing Buyer: Mary Ann Gloriande
Cover Designer: Robert Farrar-Wagner
Cover Art: USDA US Agricultural Department
Marketing Manager: Rachel Falk

Acknowledgments appear on pages 1377–1382, which constitute a continuation of the copyright page.

This book was set in 9/11 Century Book by Pine Tree Composition, Inc., and was printed and bound by Courier Companies. The cover was printed by Phoenix Color Corp.

 © 2001 by Prentice-Hall, Inc.
A Division of Pearson Education
Upper Saddle River, New Jersey 07458

Printed in the United States of America

10 9 8 7 6 5 4 3 2 1

ISBN 0-13-011490-1

Prentice-Hall International (UK) Limited, *London*
Prentice-Hall of Australia Pty. Limited, *Sydney*
Prentice-Hall Canada Inc., *Toronto*
Prentice-Hall Hispanoamericana, S.A., *Mexico*
Prentice-Hall of India Private Limited, *New Delhi*
Prentice-Hall of Japan, Inc., *Tokyo*
Pearson Education Asia Pte Ltd., *Singapore*
Editora Prentice-Hall do Brasil, Ltda., *Rio de Janeiro*

This anthology is dedicated to Professor Louis Henry of Clemson University, who kindled in countless students a deep and abiding affection for the literature and culture of the South, and to Gabriel Francisco and Carla, Hannah, and Michael Vaughan, whose love and support made the completion of this project possible.

Contents

❦

II   The Rise of the Confederacy and the Civil War (1815–1865)   131

III   Reconstruction and the Rise
of the New South (1865–1925)   354

IV   Renaissance (1925–1960)   553

Upper South   562

V   Tradition and Identity Reevaluated (1960–1980)   854

Upper South   *862*

Lower South   *926*

VII   The Postmodern South (1980–Present)   **1161**

Upper South   *1170*

Lower South   *1281*

Genre Table of Contents

VII   The Postmodern South (1980–Present)   1161

Upper South   1170

Preface

At the dawn of the twenty-first century, the American South remains one of the most anomalous places on earth. Few regions showcase with such unabashed enthusiasm what Pat Conroy once described as those "delightful ambiguities" characteristic of the South and of Southerners. In the most extreme cases, these celebrated features metamorphose into schizophrenic polarities, showing the South to be a place wreathed in ironies, a cultural "island" where the best and worst often sit side by side. A mile in any direction may find the astute observer encountering near-Gothic extremes: antebellum mansions and mobile home parks; family values and families ranking lowest in the U.S. in caring for their children; numerous churches dotting the landscape and abiding racial intolerance; politeness and a proliferation of firearms.

Despite worries in some quarters that a new generation of Southerners will forget or cease to care about all the best qualities the South has managed to offer, few serious students of the region's history are ready to sound the death knell for Southern identity, recalling instead George Tindall's observation that "the Vanishing South has staged one of the most prolonged disappearing acts since the decline of the Roman Empire." Neither Internet globalism nor classes designed to eradicate Southern speech can extinguish Morris Dees's claim that the South is still a "separate country," one with a history for displaying innumerable paradoxes.

One of the greatest of these paradoxes is that the region most educationally disadvantaged has produced one of the most vital and sustained literary traditions in the world's history. If, in his vitriolic essay "The Sahara of the Bozart," H. L. Mencken had maintained that the South had produced no first-class physicists, he would have received little opposition to his claim. It was when he argued that the South was devoid of storytellers and of stories *worth telling* that Southerners rose up to defend the accomplishments of numerous literary sons and daughters devoted to the task of depicting the region in all its irreducible complexity.

People have long speculated on the reasons for the South's rich and diverse literary heritage, citing influences as disparate as the Civil War and the front porch rocking chair as factors contributing to significant literary production. However, few scholars will deny the debt Southern literature owes to the inextricable trinity of race, class, and gender—themes originating as early as 1585 and continuing to the present. Of course, these preoccupations fan out into an ever-widening web of concerns, including such features of Southern experience as family, geography, climate, settlement patterns and history, economics, regional and national politics, industry and commerce, education, religion, music, food, recreation, and language varieties.

Although comprising an intricate constellation of concerns for more than four hundred years, these themes have undergone significant transformations in most cases. Often literature has provided the impetus for such changes. Thus, history for Southerners has always been a dynamic occurrence reflecting many of the tensions, conflicts, and contradictions mirrored in Southern literature. This inseparable relationship between the South's history and its literature was a major reason for our dividing *The South in Perspective* into six chronologically inspired sections: Colonial South (1585–1815), Rise of the Confederacy and the Civil War (1815–1865), Reconstruction and the New South (1865–1925), Renaissance (1925–1960), Tradition and Identity Reevaluated (1960–1980), and Postmodern South (1980–present). As we saw it, these divisions reflected a phenomenological relationship in which significant historical events informed the sort of literature produced in each period, just as the literature of each period distilled a complex and variegated treatment of recurring historical themes. Given this approach, we were able to *discover* genuinely diverse voices without imposing an agenda of "diversity" that would, in actuality, minimize the richness and complexity of Southern literary expression.

As a result, the reader will have an opportunity to examine "voices" not usually found in close proximity. For example, the passionate logic of African American slave Harriet Jacobs finds its shadowy antithesis in the pro-slavery rhetoric of George Fitzhugh. Mary Chesnut's Civil War diaries questioning the justness of the Southern war effort stand in stark contrast to the defense of the Lost Cause offered by Asia Booth Clarke in her memoirs detailing the life of her infamous brother, John Wilkes Booth. These are two of the numerous selections showing the South to be anything but monolithic in its approach to "traditional" subjects.

Even a cursory examination of the Table of Contents will reveal inclusions rarely found in previous anthologies of Southern literature. Among these novel or underrepresented selections are Robert Munford's political farce entitled *The Candidates* from the Colonial section; entries from battlefield nurse Kate Cumming's *A Journal of Hospital Life in the Confederate Army of Tennessee* from the Rise of the Confederacy and Civil War section; portions of anti-

Romantic author Corra Harris's *The Recording Angel* from the section on Reconstruction and Rise of the New South; excerpts from the disarmingly witty and dramatic Scopes Trial Transcripts from the Renaissance section; Robert Penn Warren's interview with Malcolm X in *Who Speaks for the Negro?* from the section on Tradition and Identity Reevaluated; and portions of Maya Angelou's inaugural poem "On the Pulse of the Morning" from the Postmodern section. These and other strategically positioned works reawaken our awareness of the many-voiced and multi-layered literature produced by a region often serving as a showcase of traits defining the American character.

Although we have been careful not to weave a "metanarrative" out of the people and events influencing Southern literature, we know the advantages students receive from a "story" comprised of more than discrete units of information. We have thus attempted to suggest meaningful, engaging connections where they exist. At the same time, we have avoided generalizations that reduce the tensions and paradoxes that Southern literature has always had a gift for displaying. The introductions to the various chronological sections are our efforts at offering both original insights and the time-tested observations of other scholars and critics.

Consonant with our desire to celebrate the complexity of the region's literature, we have further divided each chronological section into works written by writers from both the Upper South and Lower South. A unique feature of *The South in Perspective*, this organization offers the broadest possible view of diversity, emphasizing the need to acknowledge the existence of many Souths rather than a single South. Readers will notice at once a pattern of differences exhibited by Upper South and Lower South writers in their treatment of similar themes. Commenting on our particular geographical arrangement of selections, Southern dialectologist Guy H. Bailey notes that "the organization of literature by Upper and Lower South recognizes a division that emerged with initial settlement patterns, was sustained by economic and social developments, and is evident of a wide variety of material and non-material cultural patterns."

Realizing that no clear agreement exists concerning the precise boundary between the Upper and Lower South, we relied on the socio-historical research of Edward L. Ayers and John Shelton Reed to help settle the issue. For our purposes, then, the literature of the Upper South includes selections by writers from Virginia, Maryland, West Virginia, North Carolina, Kentucky, Tennessee, and Arkansas. The literature of the Lower South includes work by writers from South Carolina, Georgia, Florida, Alabama, Mississippi, Louisiana, and Texas. Some geographical purists may quibble with our particular form of literary gerrymandering; however, such disagreements simply underscore the complex nuances of cultural and historical expression found throughout the South. Similarly, literature, as we define it, does not refer exclusively to the *belles lettres*. We have made room for as many genres as possible when situations permitted.

It is with pride that we also include in this anthology a section entitled Appalachia Recognized. For too long now, the literature of Southern Appalachia has been regarded as a subspecies of regional folk expression—neither fish nor fowl in the taxonomic classifications of Southern letters. Consequently, we have focused on the distinctiveness of the fourteen Appalachian writers represented here while, at the same time, suggesting the contributions they have made both to our Southern and national literature. On the doorstep of the new millennium, we owe an inestimable debt to writers willing to show us how to balance the difficult demands of tradition and change often reflected in Appalachian culture.

Indebtedness has been a frequent theme in our conversations as editors, and we gratefully acknowledge all of those scholars and critics on whose works we have relied in editing this anthology. In particular, we note the following sources that benefitted our approach and that we offer as indispensable aids to Southern literary studies: Richard Beale Davis's *Intellectual Life in the Colonial South*, Samuel Eliot Morison's *The Oxford History of the American People*, Lewis P. Simpson's *Mind and the American Civil War*, Eugene D. Genovese's *The Slaveholders' Dilemma*, John Hope Franklin's *Reconstruction After the Civil War*, Erik Foner's *Reconstruction: America's Unfinished Revolution 1863–1867*, Edward L. Ayers's *The Promise of the New South*, B. C. Hall and C. T. Wood's *The South: A Two-Step Odyssey on the Backroads of the Enchanted Land*, Carol S. Manning's *The Female Tradition in Southern Literature*, *The History of Southern Literature* edited by Louis D. Rubin et. al., and *The Literature of the South* edited by R. C. Beatty, Floyd C. Watkins, and Thomas Daniel Young

No work of this scope could have survived the initial stages of planning without the recommendations of a core group of supporters. Each of the following individuals contributed to this anthology in singularly beneficial ways. Shirley A. Lumpkin, Professor of English at Marshall University and Co-Director of the Center for the Study of Gender and Ethnicity in Appalachia, enriched our selections by her considerable knowledge of both African American and Appalachian literature. Guy H. Bailey, Professor of English and Dean of the Graduate School at The University of Texas at San Antonio, offered keen insights about music, dialects, and the Southern film genre. Edward W. Bratton, Professor Emeritus of The University of Tennessee, shaped our approach to the section on Tradition and Identity Reevaluated (1960–1980), in particular. Homer Kemp, Professor of English at Tennessee Technological University and Director of the Upper Cumberland Institute, reinforced our principle of organization by reminding us of the innumerable subregions that have long existed in the South. The late Richard Marius, Director of Expository Writing and Senior Lecturer in English at Harvard University, gave his moral support to our project and helped us envision all the ways we could offer a genuinely diverse collection of literature. Richard's death in November of 1999 was an occasion of great sadness for the many people who knew him and who appreciated his tireless contributions to the cultural life of the South. A special note of thanks goes to friend and colleague Michael K. Smith whose acute critical sense and good judgment we consulted on numerous occasions.

Finally, to Prentice Hall Publishers we owe unqualified gratitude for the opportunity to produce this book. In particular, Brandy Dawson nudged us to accept this project more than three and half years ago. Fran Russello smoothed out inevitable wrinkles in production. And Carrie Brandon, our editor, shepherded us through the process of bringing this text to completion. Despite her geographical origins, Carrie is a Southerner at heart. We thank her for all her support and generosity of spirit.

To you, the students and teachers of Southern literature for whom this text was intended, we now offer *The South in Perspective.*

The Editors

I

Colonial Period

Many white settlers saw the American South as soil in which the values of Englishness, particularly individual freedom and political independence, could take root and flourish. Early on, then, white Southerners felt more affinity for region than for nation.[1] Viewing the South as a place apart, some colonists wished to revive traditions that were on the wane in England, invoking a spirit of enterprise that had once been embodied in the yeoman farmer but that was only a fond memory by the time Jamestown was settled in 1607.[2] In England, middle-class landowners had never gained a foothold solid enough to challenge the prerogatives of nobility, a small but admired class wielding great power.

It was the nobility, rather than the yeoman class, that many Southern colonists sought to emulate, giving rise to the myth of a landed aristocracy. A few prominent families actually qualified as British nobility whose "holdings" included land in the New World. Other families simply fabricated aristocratic connections, the sort designed to produce ready-made "gentlemen." Whether by birthright or manufacture, gentlemen nurtured a sense of entitlement that provided obstacles to easy settlement and economic productivity. Students of the period will recall John Smith's famous complaint that Jamestown's early denizens contained far too many gentlemen and too few workers. Smith's quip recognizes the sense of perpetuating a tradition of nobility that had outlived its day and that was scarcely suitable to the harsh requirements of living imposed by the New World.

The notion that gentlemen were entitled to leisure nonetheless became widespread—a source of justification for the rise of the planter aristocracy, many of whom believed themselves superior to perfunctory tasks and mundane labors. The complaint by New Englanders that antebellum Southerners were lazy and hedonistic probably had its origin in the assumption held by a good many Southerners that too much work was coarse and degrading, unbecoming of a gentle people.[3] Unlike New England, the South never wholeheartedly embraced the Calvinistic work ethic.[4] John

Smith put it more bluntly: "They [the Jamestown settlers] would rather starve than work." A more generous interpretation is that colonial Southerners tended to "culti-vate the amenities," emphasizing manners, chivalry, and noblesse oblige, as well as vestiges of a medieval tradition rooted in feudal, precapitalistic society.[5]

For white Southerners, ownership of land and the attendant prestige accorded to landowners were more important than money. Southerners, who tended to scorn what they saw as the acquisitive tendencies of New Englanders, refused to equate materialistic wealth with salvation of either the secular or the heavenly sort. Eugene Genovese notes that "Southern ideals constituted a rejection of the crass, vulgar, in-humane elements of capitalistic society," so that even slaveholders "could not accept the idea that the cash nexus offered a permissible basis for human relations."[6] As dif-ficult as it may be for us to grasp, Southerners believed themselves on solid moral ground in rejecting the unfettered capitalist spirit and practices of New Englanders, whose economic calculus was viewed by antebellum Southerners as a cynical contra-diction. Let them preach morality, some Southerners pointed out: Money was their bottom line. Besides, a good name was of significantly greater and more lasting value for planter class Southerners, an idea straight out of the Middle Ages with that epoch's penchant for such aristocratic trappings as genealogy and the obligatory coat of arms.

Such a view offered its own blind spot, creating a contradiction that Southerners would be hard pressed to reconcile or defend, for it was difficult to sustain devotion to leisure without large numbers of people willing to support a vast agricultural econ-omy. If assumed privilege and benevolent paternalism generated the problem, they also provided the solution, at least in the eyes of many colonial Southerners. The sense of entitlement promoted by class distinctions and the social doctrine that "infe-rior" classes were part of an arrangement benefiting everyone—even those in virtual peonage—enabled Southerners to perpetuate a caste system that had been familiar to Europeans for centuries. Although this system was never viewed as ideal, it was con-sidered by many as necessary for maintaining social order and averting chaos. Anar-chy was a sin among people given to defending rigid social stratification. Part of the Southern colonists' disgust with New England Puritans stemmed from a belief that the Puritans had gone to radical extremes in separating themselves from the institu-tional church and its socially cohesive functions.[7]

Important to note, however, is that the early South did not simply seek to reclaim "some refurbished medievalism."[8] Early Southerners were too practical for that. They might observe rituals and appreciate the role of institutions such as the Roman Catholic Church in preserving order, but they would never have identified themselves with an ethos that included "unprogressive" elements.[9] Colonial Southerners never doubted their progressiveness in matters social and economic. Because of an eco-nomic autonomy that let them produce almost everything they wanted on their own plantations, Virginia planters of the seventeenth and early eighteenth centuries en-joyed, in Richard Gray's words, "feelings of pride and independence and a manner that was frequently equated, and perhaps was meant to be equated, with the arrogant self-will of the aristocrat."[10] It was just one of the dualities that compelled colonial Southerners to believe they could embrace tradition and be forward-looking at the same time. Such was the origin of what writer W. J. Cash would call the Savage Ideal: the South's stubborn refusal to accept changes in the imported social order while si-multaneously adapting to new requirements for survival.

And adapt the South did—by embracing tensions and paradoxes that the absolutist North would have deemed irreconcilable. From their earliest colonial history, Southerners found life anomalous, rife with contradictions that had to be tolerated. Even the climate and geography offered excruciating extremes. Thus, it was a small stretch for Virginia planters to shun the vulgarity attached to work and money while realizing the necessity of both. The planter plutocracy, especially, believed that it had found a creative solution to the problem of work, a solution upholding vaunted traditions and the status quo. The nature of this solution was to insist on prestige and privilege for the planter class, understanding that a stable society could not exist without a few to lead the many. As long as those of rank treated underlings as benevolently as conditions permitted, this arrangement could be justified on both moral and practical grounds.

It little mattered that the New World Cavaliers sought to create a myth about their own aristocratic status. Myth, after all, could be a potent social force. Still, the reality behind the plantation aristocrat was that he was all too often a pretender and a deprived beneficiary of the laws of English primogeniture that prevented third and fourth sons from inheriting largely middle-class estates. Consequently, dispossessed offspring sought their fortunes in America, taking pains to elevate their status by skillful propagandizing and mutual cooperation among the self-styled elite. Not even the affected nonchalance of the would-be aristocrat could disguise his hunger for legitimacy and the baronial claims he made for himself and his family. Money was a feature of those claims, and despite his disgust for the taint of commerce, he set about to acquire as much cash as possible by exploiting land and labor.

With land, the possibility of cash was always available. What began as outpost settlements, such as Roanoke Island (1587) and Jamestown (1607) in Virginia, eventually became colonies in which settlers gained control of increasingly larger parcels of land. Thanks to a new broad-leafed plant grown by Native Americans and coveted by Europeans, Virginia colonists were able to secure a substantial livelihood by cultivating what Spanish explorers as early as 1552 had called *tabaco* (tobacco). Similarly, settlers in Upper and Lower Carolina (designated by Royal decree as North Carolina and South Carolina in 1727) acquired colonial status and began to explore possibilities offered by a somewhat different geography and climate.

For instance, although North Carolinians found their soil every bit as conducive to growing cash-crop tobacco as did Virginia settlers, the Carolinians were plagued with a treacherous shoreline, making it difficult to haul products to market.[11] Only a few cities sprang up on the North Carolina coast, and small interior farms, rather than plantations, tended to be the rule. It was one example of the way geography influenced, even ratified, the emerging class system in the Old South. By contrast, South Carolina, with its swampy lowlands and accessible coast, discovered the commercial possibilities of rice and indigo, the latter plant grown for the deep blue dye it produced. These crops were best cultivated on immense tracts; hence, the plantation system evolved, as the sprawling tracts of the best land were accumulated by the wealthiest planters.

By 1860, these planters had established their own port capital at Charles Town, later Charleston. Given the wealth and luxurious ease of living enjoyed by the growing class of planters, Charleston came to represent the flowering of high Southern culture, prompting the nineteenth-century writer William Gilmore Simms to declare to a Northern visitor: "Charleston, sir, was the finest city in the world . . . the flower of modern civilization." Simms is nostalgically recalling the gilded colonial age in which the old feudal privileges, coupled with vast wealth, created a sense of entitlement among would-be aristocrats who saw themselves as heirs to the high culture of the "grandees," the noble families of Spain and Portugal.

It would be grossly inaccurate to characterize the Old South as a land comprising mostly elite, aristocratic-seeking land barons. There was always "in the antebellum era a substantial and genuine middle class—independent people, neither rich nor poor. . . ."[12] However, it was the planter class that largely set the prevailing cultural tone and standards of aspiration in the colonial South. Moreover, leisure and wealth were the benchmarks of a society willing to perpetuate the plantation myth at any cost.

The cost of this myth could be ascertained in the "labor" required to support a complex network of economic and social relations. Put simply, labor meant slaves. As early as 1619, African slaves were introduced into Virginia, where trading posts became colonies for the production of tobacco. Given that the colonial South's economy tended to be agriculturally based, slavery was seen as an economic imperative. Some white Southerners argued that an economy rooted in the soil necessitated large numbers of laborers to propagate a social system benefiting everyone. In the early history of the single-crop colonies, this workforce had included indentured servants whose term of indenture usually lasted no more than seven years, after which time the workers constituted free, and therefore expensive, labor. Slavery seemed a solution, albeit hardly an ideal one. The ambivalence with which some white Southern colonists viewed slavery is best distilled in a statement made by Thomas Jefferson, third U.S. president and architect of the *Declaration of Independence*, who acknowledged that slavery was like holding a wolf by the ears. No one liked it, but no one dared let go of it.

Jefferson's grim quip suggests that if Southern planters were frequently uncomfortable with slavery, they weren't uncomfortable enough. Numbers bear out this condition. Statistics on the growing slave population indicate that close to ten million Africans were brought to the New World between the sixteenth and nineteenth centuries. As slavery grew, the need to defend the institution grew, as well. Mounting a polemical assault, the magnitude of which had never been experienced in the New World, Southerners set about to defend the indefensible institution, invoking authorities as disparate as John Locke and resorting to sophistic appeals and casuistical gymnastics that would turn the body politic on its head in absurd gestures of defiance. The caricature of the rhetoric-prone, hotheaded Southerner, existing for no other reason but to defend lost causes, comes from a desire to preserve the sclerotic practice of slaveholding while presenting a facade of enlightenment.

The slaveholders' best defense was paradoxically the one they had put forth earlier to justify stealing lands from Native Americans. Commenting on the historical precedent for sanctioning slavery and the slave trade, John Blassingame notes that "the enslavement of Africans was intimately related to the history of Indian-white relations in the New World and to certain historical and anthropological principles."[13] A key phrase in understanding strenuous efforts to justify slavery is "certain historical and anthropological principles." For as Eugene Genovese observes, "the word *equality* does not appear anywhere in the Constitution of the United States—except for a reference to equality among the states."[14] Genovese adds that "rights asserted were, first and foremost, the rights of historically evolved communities to which an individual owed loyalty and obedience."[15] Not being members of historically evolved communities as defined by the European tradition, Native Americans and African slaves possessed no rights that white colonists felt obliged to acknowledge. What Southern colonists did consider necessary was protecting the Western Christian tradition against the disintegrating tendencies of modernity.[16] Decimation of Native American tribes and enslavement of African peoples came under the aegis of this obligation. Colonists even pitted African slaves and Native Americans against one another, striking bargains with Native Americans to hunt down and return runaway slaves while simultaneously arming slaves to fight hostile Indians.

The situation was hardly endemic to the South. From the earliest records of the seventeenth century, New England's history was one of constant encroachment on Native American lands with battles designed to secure a foothold in the New World. Old World philosophic and theological assumptions implicitly supported the actions of settlers who evinced no evidence of a troubled conscience in dividing Native Americans from their habitations. As for slavery, New Englanders experienced little difficulty initially in accepting the practice, importing slaves into Connecticut as early as 1629 and into Massachusetts by 1637. By mid–seventeenth century, New England ships were actively involved in the slave trade.

For the same reasons offered by the plantation class in the South, many in New England saw slavery as an acceptable practice, even adding a religious cache in justifying it. Elevating an inferior race was considered a Christian obligation, the exploitative effects of which can be seen in the tragic life of Phyllis Wheatley, the most celebrated New England slave of the eighteenth century. Kidnapped from Africa at age seven, Wheatley was sold in Boston to well-to-do John and Suzannah Wheatley, who quickly recognized Phyllis's prodigious talents and therefore tutored her in Latin and the Bible. Wheatley became famous in the colonies, though largely as a curiosity, an exception to the conventional notion that African Americans were incapable of learning to read and write, let alone of producing complex metaphysical poetry of the sort Wheatley produced. Wheatley's accomplishments were seen as providing a partial answer to a question that Henry Louis Gates, Jr., summarizes as follows:

> At least since 1600, Europeans had wondered aloud whether or not the "African species of men," as they most commonly put it, could ever create formal literature, could ever master the arts and sciences. If they could, then the argument ran, the African variety of humanity and the European variety were fundamentally related. If not, then it seemed clear that the African was destined by nature to be a slave.[17]

The implications of Wheatley's achievements were eclipsed by a desire to show the role of Christian charity in contributing to her "conversion" and subsequent production of pietistic verses. While few took her seriously as a poet, many praised religion for its role in prompting her humanity and refining her sensibilities. This view was perhaps best articulated by Thomas Jefferson, who said, "Religion indeed has produced a Phyllis Whately [sic]; but it could not produce a poet. The compositions published under her name are below the dignity of criticism."

Jefferson's prejudices were as prevalent in slaveholding New England as they were in the slaveholding South. Only the Quakers had expressed consistent opposition to slavery as early as the first quarter of the seventeenth century. In both the Northern and the Southern colonies, Quakers were derided for their beliefs and often referred to as a "pestilential sect" and "an unruly and turbulent sort of people." In

1659, the Virginia Assembly banished all Quakers from the colony. Puritans in New England simply hanged them.

These examples demonstrate some of the reasons why slaveholding Southerners leveled accusations of hypocrisy at those New Englanders who were willing to condemn the Southern way of life and its "peculiar institution" of slavery. A more exact phrase might have been "increasingly peculiar," since changing economic circumstances made slavery less profitable in the industrial North than in the agrarian South. The morality of slavery did become a concern in the North, but many planter-class Southerners viewed the North's shift in sympathies as something less than an authentic regard for the plight of African Americans. If slavery was gradually decreasing in the North, the reasons for the decrease, Southerners posited, were economic rather than ethical. Southern colonists complained that Northerners were envious of the superior culture and economic prosperity enjoyed by the South. Moreover, a majority of Southern landowners could not imagine a slackening of their roles as feudal patriarchs. Thus, the stage was set for an ideological conflict that would cast a shadow over America's efforts to become a country, rather than to remain a loose aggregate of colonies, in the face of growing external pressures and threats.

Throughout the colonial era, white Southerners continued to defend a way of life that increasingly came under attack. They believed their social and economic habits made "life more manageable, more amenable, and quite simply, more human."[18] Many distrusted what they perceived to be the inhumane qualities of capitalism that encouraged "the growth of a servile urban proletariat and an avaricious, amoral capitalist class."[19] Unrestrained commerce and manufacturing were regarded as antithetical to civilized virtues. Agriculture was viewed as salvation.

This discussion would serve only as a brief history of a moribund socioeconomic system were it not that this system gave rise to a literature both political and polemical in nature. Colonial Southern literature tended to be a literature of defense in twin senses of the word. On the one hand, Southern literary production often distilled a self-conscious apologia, or defense, of Southern practices and habits of mind. These features suggested a New World effort to transplant Old World values onto Southern soil. On the other hand, Southern letters were forced to address criticisms that were urgent and topical, leveled with sharp focus at the absence of an egalitarian ideal in the South. One irony of the colonial age is that the leisure engendered by the prosperous plantation system produced anything but a favorable climate for the belles lettres. At best, the imaginative efforts of the period reflect a superficiality and an imitation of the dominant genteel literary practices of Europe, in general, and of England, in particular. Southerners like William Byrd, for example, never ceased seeing themselves as Englishmen, "and a considerably large number of great planters were sent across the Atlantic in their youth in order to study at English schools, universities, and inns of court."[20]

It was further assumed that a Southern writer would share the dominant Southern views about race and other issues that made it unlikely for him to disagree with members of his community.[21] His identity was bound up in being a member of a community whose social and political structure he did not feel bound to criticize. The literature he produced, then, was doctrinaire and unavoidably political. This ongoing state of affairs would prompt one nineteenth-century Southern author to proclaim, "No periodical can well succeed in the South which does not include the political constituent. The mind of the South is active chiefly in the direction of politics."

With a few striking exceptions, the literature of the early South is best seen in its historical and anthropological contexts. Its value is in teaching us about the circumstances that shaped our country's history and contributed to a literature exceeding the tidewater of mediocrity about which a good many later Southern writers complained. By the same token, we can scarcely expect the literature of the Southern colonies to have been other than what it was. Just as the early literature of New England contained an inevitable focus on religious concerns, the literature of the colonial South was unabashedly, and, some would say, unavoidably political.

Notes

1. Richard Gray, *Writing the South* (Baton Rouge: Louisiana State University Press, 1986), 3.
2. Gray, 3.
3. Louis D. Rubin, *The Writer in the South* (Athens: University of Georgia Press, 1972), 27.
4. Rubin, 27.
5. Rubin, 27.
6. Rubin, 27.
7. For a comprehensive discussion of Southern colonial religion and its comparative stance with New England religious experience, see Chapter Five, "Religion: Established, Evangelical, and Individual," in Richard Beale Davis's *Intellectual Life in the Colonial South, 1585–1763*, Vol. 2, (Knoxville: University of Tennessee Press, 1978).
8. Eugene Genovese, *The Slaveholders' Dilemma* (Columbia: University of South Carolina Press, 1992), 7.
9. Genovese, 6.
10. Gray, 14.
11. Tim Jacobson, *Heritage of the South* (New York: Crescent Books, 1992), 29.
12. Jacobson, 33.
13. John Blassingame, *The Slave Community: Plantation Life in the Antebellum South* (New York: Oxford University Press, 1979), 4–5.
14. Genovese, 15.
15. Genovese, 15.
16. Genovese, 7.
17. Henry Louis Gates Jr., *The Signifying Monkey* (New York: Oxford University Press, 1988), 129.
18. Genovese, 5.
19. Genovese, 5.
20. Gray, 15.
21. Rubin, 23.

From its beginnings, the literature of the Upper South was countercultural, opposing trends the rest of the country was willing to embrace. Perhaps no one expressed the South's resistance to emerging New World values more forcefully than John Randolph of Roanoke, who isolated what he perceived as threats to the specifically rural way of life that he and other Virginia planters advocated. Among these threatening forces were "fanatical and preposterous theories about the rights of man; puritanical jargon; and high-strained Calvinistic theory." In an address to Congress, Randolph expressed a belief that "no government extending from the Atlantic to the Pacific, can be fit to govern me or the people I represent." Randolph's chauvinism was indicative of a tendency to defend Virginia and its prerogatives at the expense of an emerging national identity.

Possibly Richard Beale Davis understood this tendency and the intellectual propensities that contributed to it better than any other scholar in recent times. In his flawlessly researched *Intellectual Life in the Colonial South, 1585–1763* (1978), Professor Davis not only corrects many misconceptions about "unlettered" Southerners but also shows the extent to which colonial Southerners appreciated Old World literature, particularly romance with its omnipresent themes of honor and chivalry. Davis specifically challenges such scholars as Perry Miller, who describes the early South as a backwater region of illiterate, untutored provincials, thereby perpetuating a stereotype that has continued to the present. Davis is careful to show the origins of a literary tradition that appealed to the Old World sensibilities of the planter class, reinforcing their sense of clan and regional identification. He stresses that a literature of the colonial South was never lacking but that it shared similarities with the literature produced by New Englanders, who also engendered a considerable output that scarcely constituted the belles lettres: promotion literature, exploration accounts, political tracts, and sermons.

The class of Southerners receiving Davis's chief focus includes such early chroniclers as Robert Beverly, whose *The History and Present State of Virginia* (1705) offers an account of the Jamestown settlement that is vigorous and unflinching. Beverly describes the harsh circumstances encountered by the Virginia Company and their leader, Captain John Smith, who "were at last reduced to such Extremity, as to eat the very Hides of their Horses, and the Bodies of the Indians they had killed . . ." In addition to cannibalism, Beverly's narrative focuses on the saga of Pocahontas, John Smith, and John Rolfe, whose mutually considered solution of intermarriage brought peace for a time to Southern settlers and Native Americans, who had been waging ferocious warfare. Throughout Beverly's *History*, Smith is lionized as a prudent and an industrious savior of the Jamestown colonists, who are seen as ungrateful, haughty, and lacking in ambition.

Conditions like those at Jamestown tended to be the rule rather than the exception. Internecine squabbling is at a premium in the literature of the Old South, nor were early Southern writers reluctant "to throw its [the region's] flaws and blemishes into literary image," as has been argued.[1] The literature of class distinctions naturally invites acid wit and stinging satire, with name-calling enjoying special privilege. Nowhere is this satirical impulse more evident than in the poetical works of Ebenezer Cook, whose "The Sotweed Factor," subtitled "Voyage to Maryland" (1708), is one of the earliest examples of Hudibrastic, or mock-epic, verse written in the American colonies. An Old World "gentleman," Cook's narrator finds nothing good about the

Maryland colony and its inhabitants, satirizing both the countryside and the "Sot-weed [tobacco] Planters" who "Crowd the Shoar . . . with neither Stockings, Hat, nor Shooe." The frequency of coarse planters, barbaric Indians, execrable slaves, and foul tobacco expands into a full-blown catalogue of complaints from which few people escape ridicule and censure: Quakers, physicians, lawyers, sailors, and peasants. This excessive and indiscriminate attack on everything Maryland has to offer alerts us to the double-edged nature of Cook's satire, which exposes the pretensions of the visiting narrator with as much verve as it pokes fun at the Marylanders.

No less pointed than Cook's description, William Byrd's *History of the Dividing Line* and *Secret History of the Dividing Line* are subtler and more scurrilous, prompting the need for coded names that simultaneously conceal and reveal the targets of Byrd's barbs. Purporting to offer "history," Byrd's narratives describe his experiences, both public and private, as one of three Virginia commissioners appointed by George II to settle a boundary dispute between Virginia and North Carolina. Sectional and class rivalry surface early in both versions, with Byrd, the Virginia aristocrat, self-consciously patronizing the rude yeoman swain of interior Carolina. Carolinians, according to Byrd, are a tribe of unbaptized denizens given to drinking wine and rum on the Sabbath—nor do they give much thought to working the rest of the week. Debauchery is their chief pastime, and Byrd relates an especially frank incident in which survey camp members invite a "tallow-faced wench" to drink with them, after which they "examined her hidden Charms, and played a great many gay pranks." What Byrd finds most offensive about his backcountry companions are their porcine features and swinish behavior, doubtless the result of eating too much pork. Byrd's material is a peculiar mix of ribaldry and reporting that points to a later fiction meant to amuse readers by recording the antics and foibles of folk deprived of civilizing influences.

If Byrd expresses jocular concern about the lack of religion displayed by the rabble of North Carolina, Samuel Davies takes that concern more seriously in his *Miscellaneous Poems* (1752), published just after the peak years of the famed religious revival known as the Great Awakening. From its earliest days, New England had experienced religious foment and upheaval, with confrontations occurring between Puritans and Separatists, Presbyterians and Congregationalists, Barrowists and Brownists.[2] Although New England's religious turmoil may have been more dramatic and received more attention, the colonial South was not without its fair share of doctrinal struggles, spawning hostilities between Puritans and Anglo-Catholics in Maryland, strife between Anglicans and Presbyterians in Virginia, and persecution of Quakers almost everywhere. A Calvinist and friend of the famous New England Puritan divine Jonathan Edwards, Davies struck a middle ground between the humanitarian revolt that conceived of God as desiring the happiness of all creatures and the strict Puritan view holding that "God's moral honor compels him to insist on infinite punishment for infinite evil."[3] As can be seen in his stylized verses characteristic of the period, Davies finds a resolution of religious tensions in the mediating influence of Jesus Christ, whose love alone, Davies asserts, can stay the wrathful hand of a just God.

As for championing religion, the South has always stood on *terra firma*, with a majority of Southerners congregating under the umbrella of Protestantism as early as the seventeenth century. However, the colonial South was preoccupied more with politics than with religion, given an impetus for protecting "property," which included slaves, and guaranteeing a way of life that planter-class Southerners were more than willing to defend. It is safe to say that without some assurance their interests would be protected, Southern colonials never would have agreed to ally themselves with the North in declaring independence from Great Britain.

As beneficiaries of the Enlightenment, sons of Virginia (and later, four of our first five U.S. presidents) such as George Washington, James Madison, Thomas Jefferson, and James Monroe proved instrumental in fashioning the American system of government. It is no exaggeration to say that America was a country founded on paper. Our nation's premises of a government instituted "by the people" are encapsulated in such documents as the *U.S. Constitution, The Federalist Papers*, and *Declaration of Independence*. All of these reflect a basic suspicion of government and a need to establish social contracts that recognize the desirability of a union created by equals. Only when citizens stood in a relationship of political equality could government offer necessary checks that would deter despotism. Although what Southern statesmen meant by "equality" has been the subject of ongoing debate, one conclusion can be drawn with a fair degree of certainty: Southern spokesmen were attempting to ensure that their rights and interests would be equal to those of people in other parts of the country. That such rights included owning slaves was an assumption held by the aforementioned Virginians. If and when the time came that the rights of Virginia landowners were violated or ignored, so argued the emerging states' rightists, Virginia could legally withdraw from whatever alliance it had formerly entered. The very documents drawn up by the Southerners would offer this guarantee.

The circumscribed role of government is a key concern of Thomas Jefferson's *Declaration of Independence* (1776), one of several Revolutionary-era documents embodying the view of Virginian Richard Henry Lee that "the United Colonies are, and of right ought to be, free and independent states." It was the sovereign status of states, according to Jefferson, that enabled them to enter into a compact, or union, from which they could freely extricate themselves at any time, an assumption invoked almost a century later to justify Southern secession. The equality to which Jefferson alludes in the *Declaration* is the sort necessary for maintaining a balance of power among the politically enfranchised, whose rights must be recognized as equal to the imperatives of government lest tyranny result. Jefferson assumes that the colonies are every bit as "sovereign" in their claim as Great Britain is, just as he assumes that Virginia is equal in political authority to all the other colonies.

What Jefferson does not address in the *Declaration of Independence* is the notion of personal equality. Without question he shared many of the racial attitudes of his time, believing African Americans to be inferior to whites of European origin. This presumed inequality was the basis for Jefferson's idea that relations between African Americans and whites would never succeed and that slavery would continue to be an evil, a "burden" that threatened dissolution of the Union before it had time to become firmly established. Proof that slavery would eventually unravel the fabric of Jefferson's agrarian society was evident in the wrangling that occurred over the wording of the *Declaration*. In his original draft, Jefferson denounced King George III for waging "cruel war against human nature itself, violating its most sacred rights of life and liberty in the persons of a distant people who never offended him, captivating and carrying them into slavery in another hemisphere, or to incur miserable death in their transportation thither."

By suggesting that the British king was responsible for perpetuating the slave trade in colonial America, Jefferson not only offered a criticism of the "peculiar institution," as it would later be called, but also implied a possible end to slavery once

America had secured its independence. Because delegates from South Carolina and Georgia objected to any statements hinting at the termination of slavery, Jefferson deleted the passage, postponing an inevitable sectional showdown.[4]

As of this writing, DNA evidence substantiates a claim that was made as early as 1802 and that was resurrected as a serious inquiry by Fawn Brodie in 1974, that Jefferson conducted a long-term affair with Sally Hemmings, the quadroon half sister of his late wife, Martha, and that he fathered a child, Eston, with Hemmings. It is one of the bitter ironies of the age and the man, that the "paradoxical patriot," as Jefferson has been called, could be so staunch in his views about the incompatibility of the races while demonstrating obvious affection, even devotion, for his slave mistress, who tragically had no rights that Jefferson was obliged to respect. For all his ideological convictions, Jefferson's actions betrayed what William Faulkner later described as "the heart in conflict with itself." Although Jefferson's affair with Hemmings may teach us many things about ourselves as a nation, one thing it shows is the extent to which the South has always been a place of tremendous and humbling contradictions, a place where all ties are ultimately familial and where a person's lineage can include a president, as well as a slave.

For whatever reasons, George Washington has escaped much of the personal scrutiny that has exposed tensions and contradictions in the character and thought of Thomas Jefferson. A slaveholder like Jefferson, Washington is remembered, in Richard Shenkman's aphoristic assessment, "not for what he was but for what he should have been."[5] Washington's life is steeped in folklore, demonstrating the American public's need not only to create myths about civic figures but also to believe in those myths. Washington could not have asked for a better publicist and mythmaker than Mason Locke Weems, the man almost singularly responsible for making Washington the Father of His Country. In his sentimentalized *The Life of Washington* (1799), Weems targets Washington's uncommon probity and wisdom as traits worthy of national emulation. Weems's account meets the patriotic requirements of the hour by supplying often historically inaccurate details or outright fictions about the first U.S. president.

If politics tends to inspire privileged myths, political advancement and partisan antics offer a chance to debunk those myths and deflate personal character. Few sacred cows can survive a genuine political contest, as seen in Robert Munford's *The Candidates* (1777), perhaps America's first political comedy. Written for possible public presentation, this farce contains numerous local allusions to persons and places familiar to voters in the southside region of Virginia. Though the setting is local, the themes are universal, suggesting the extremes that politicians will go to create a facade of respectability while behaving roguishly.

Even a writer with serious literary pretensions would find colonial Southern politics a tempting vehicle for the type of satire produced by transplanted Virginian William Wirt. As with Weems, Wirt was originally from Maryland but came to Virginia at age twenty, where he prospered as an attorney who nonetheless desired "to awaken the taste of the people for literary attainments." His series of essays entitled *The Old Bachelor* (1814) includes selections by prominent friends, though most of the collection was written by Wirt himself. Lewis Leary identifies the subjects of the essays as "education, manners, gambling, and the all-usurping desire among Virginians for public office."[6] Wirt's tone was intended to be gently mocking; however, some readers perceived his ripostes and raillery as thinly veiled personal attacks. Still,

Leary praises Wirt, concluding that *The Old Bachelor* "contained some of the most effective writing of its kind to appear in the United States before Washington Irving's *Sketch Book* half a dozen years later."[7]

Notes

1. Louis D. Rubin, *The Writer in the South* (Athens: University of Georgia Press, 1972), 23.
2. Herbert W. Schneider, *The Puritan Mind* (Ann Arbor: University of Michigan Press, 1958), 95.
3. Schneider, 232.
4. Richard Matthews, *The Radical Politics of Thomas Jefferson* (Lawrence: University Press of Kansas, 1984), 66.
5. Richard Shenkman, *Legends, Lies, and Cherished Myths of American History* (New York: Harper Collins, 1988), 27.
6. Lewis Leary, "1776–1815," *The History of Southern Literature*, ed. Louis Rubin et al. (Baton Rouge: Louisiana State University Press, 1985), 79.
7. Leary, 80.

Richard Beale Davis

(1907–1981)

Richard Beale Davis devoted most of his long and productive career to correcting what he perceived to be an imbalance in the historical record of early America. The history of colonial America, he contended, had been written by New Englanders, highlighting their own achievements and neglecting the substantial contributions of the colonial South. *Intellectual Life in the Colonial South*, which won the National Book Award in 1979, thoroughly documents the South's literary and cultural life, demolishing the stereotype of the Southerner who cared only for drinking, hunting, and card playing, and revealing a substantial Southern influence on the development of the new nation's culture and consciousness.

from *Intellectual Life in the Colonial South*

The Five Colonies in the Eighteenth Century

Promotion literature *per se*, and even accounts of exploration, became much less frequent in the eighteenth century for the four now established southern colonies. South Carolina within two decades became a royal province, and in 1729 North Carolina was purchased from the Proprietors by the Crown. Maryland, which had one fairly brief royal period, was returned to the Proprietor and remained his until the Revolution. Virginia had since 1624 been a Crown province. The Chesapeake colonies, which had by the 1730s (Maryland earlier) printing presses of their own, still welcomed immigrants, especially those who would settle on their western frontier. But they did little direct advertising in print in Great Britain, and only a little in their own gazettes. They were concerned, at least until the French and Indian War, with internal affairs of government, church, and education. South and North Carolina, which set up their own presses in 1732 and 1749 respectively, continued with colonization schemes and some promotion literature. And the Georgia colony, the youngest, in this period developed propaganda writing roughly comparable, but with distinctive qualities, to that of her elder sisters in the preceding century.

In the older colonies there was some self-assessment, or stocktaking, in the form of brief histories, the most significant remaining unpublished until the nineteenth century; and the present-state reports were still sent frequently, usually annually, to the Board of Trade and Plantations. In Maryland appeared an anti-utopian or anti-promotional poem, a savage satire designed to show things as they were. Much of the propaganda in favor of the colonies has a religious cast, consisting of letters and tracts begging for church libraries and more clergy. A great deal of this centers in the Carolinas, to which in 1701 the newly organized Society for the Propagation of the Gospel in Foreign Parts began to devote a great deal of attention.

In 1705, when the establishment of the Church of England in South Carolina outraged an apparent majority, who were dissenters, a major English writer was drawn into writing about that colony as John Locke had done for different reasons a generation before. Daniel Defoe, using the manuscript accounts of the situation by two Carolina emissaries to the Proprietors, John Ash and Joseph Boone, composed tracts more political than promotional, *Party-Tyranny, or an Occasional Bill in Miniature; as now Practiced in Carolina. Humbly offered to the Consideration of both Houses of Parliament* and *The Case of the Protestant Dissenters in Carolina* (both London, 1705 and 1706).

The two sources for Defoe were present-state, socio-political reports. Ash, whose work was being printed when he died (only two pages actually were set up), left in manuscript *The Present State of Affairs in Carolina*, which was published in part the next year, 1706. This is a prejudiced account significant largely as representative of the troubled times.

A fairer account of Carolina at the turn of the century, an attempt at reconciliation of warring elements, is John Archdale's *A New Description of that Fertile and Pleasant Province of Carolina: with a Brief Account of its Discovery, Settling, and the Government thereof to this Time. With Several Remarkable Passages of Divine Providence during my Time* (London, 1707). The author, a Quaker, had been governor and was a proprietor of the province. He was also a man of ability and tact. His "Description of Carolina" near the beginning is an effective piece of writing, perhaps most distinguished for its piety and such remarks as that concerning "the first Settlement of Carolina, where the Hand of God was eminently seen in thining the Indians, to make room for the English." He traces American history to the Cabots, tells some good stories, extols Carolina climate and topography, suggests means of educating the Indians in the faith, and documents with letters the struggles of his own time. His design, he declares, is to make Carolina "a suitable Bulwark to our American Colonies." It is not accidental that "Divine Providence" is alluded to in this tract more than in any other from the colonial South. His is the puritan spirit manifested by most early Quakers—in practice, and practical.

The Whig historian John Oldmixon in *The British Empire in America* (2 vols., London, 1708, 1741 and rev. ed.) attempted a comprehensive survey of the English

New World in a work drawing upon many sources. It was remarkably influential in shaping Europe's, especially Great Britain's, concept of her American possessions. The Virginia chapter drew the indignation of Robert Beverley and the assistance of William Byrd, the latter in what was probably a revision before first printing. Oldmixon claims that he had read every chapter of his book to inhabitants of the colonies treated therein. If so, says one modern historian, the reader or listener to the two chapters on South Carolina must have indeed been ignorant of the facts of his home region. What Oldmixon used, and perhaps carelessly, in these two were several promotion pieces and early brief histories of the province or of America in general. He is confused and confusing in his first chapter on colonial history. The second chapter, on the geography and natural attractions of the country, is interesting and useful, though it still has to be used with caution. He concludes with some observations on a French dancing master who in Craven Country was teaching the Indians to play on the flute and hautboy, and with regret that the red men have learned one of the whites' worst vices, drinking. Oldmixon actually devoted more care and space to the southern colonies than did other "imperialists" among the British historians, as the later William Douglass and John Mitchell.

But by 1710 the two Carolinas had officially separate governments and were recognized for what they had long been, distinct political and economic entities. Several promotion pieces from the more southern colony came out in the generation after the legal separation. In 1712 John Norris, probably at some time a resident of the province, published in London a promotional pamphlet rather unusual in form, *Profitable Advice for Rich and Poor, In a Dialogue, or Discourse between James Freeman, a Carolina Planter, and Simon Question, a West-Country Farmer, Containing a Description, or True Relation of South Carolina*. Dedicated to town and country shopkeepers, parish clerks, innkeepers, or masters of public houses, it contains a quantity of information on every subject the author thought might be pertinent. Though datelined in 1710, Thomas Nairne's *A Letter from South Carolina; Giving an Account of the Soil, Air, Product, Trade, Government, Laws, Religion, People, Military Strength, &c. of that Province* (London) was not published until 1718. It includes useful statistics regarding the relative proportion of various religious sects. Covering much more territory, including the Mississippi Basin, is Daniel Coxe's *A Description of the English Province of Carolana, by the Spaniards call'd Florida and by the French la Louisianne. . . . And a Preface Containing Some Considerations on the Consequences of the French Making Settlements there* (London, 1722). Descriptive of a vast territory later to become part of the South, it is one of our earliest printed records of direct concern with the French as southern neighbors and rivals. Much narrower in scope is a work of provincial agent and councilor under the royal government Francis Yonge, *A View of the Trade of South-Carolina, with Proposals Humbly Offer'd for Improving the same* (London, 1722). This treats of economic difficulties in the early 1720s, especially resulting from the Yamassee War in 1715, hardships from customs duties, and remedies proposed, none very original nor feasible.

Jean Pierre Purry's proposals to Swiss Protestants in 1731, to produce happy results in the founding of Purrysburgh, were translated from the French and appeared in the *Gentleman's Magazine* during 1732 as "A Description of the Province of South Carolina, Drawn Up at Charles Town, in September 1731." Purry tried for ten years under the Proprietors to establish a Swiss colony, but he succeeded only when the Crown took over and the new government approved his plan.

Perhaps even more significant is governor James Glen's *A Description of South Carolina; Containing, Many curious and interesting particulars relating to the Civil, Natural and Commercial History of the Colony* (London, 1761), finished originally in 1749 but adulterated with additional material before publication. Yet it remains a well-written, even moving account, beginning with the usual descriptions of the country and its products. More unusual are the tables showing climate and rainfall and above all the survey of the Indian and frontier country and the forts built there, with some account of tribes and trade. Begun as an answer to queries from the Board of Trade, this careful description by the ablest of South Carolina's colonial governors is a modest forerunner, as is one of the more formal histories noted below, of Jefferson's *Notes on the State of Virginia*, which also originated in a series of inquiries.

Composed in 1763 but not published until 1770 is Dr. George Milligen-Johnston's *A Short Description of the Province of South-Carolina, with an Account of the Air, Weather, and Diseases, at Charles-Town* (London). The author was once confusing to historians because, under the name of Dr. George Milligen, he was a surgeon in military service in South Carolina and Georgia for a number of years and then a prominent Charleston physician. This fresh, hopeful account of Carolina and the Cherokee War is in marked contrast to his pessimistic observations in 1775, when he was compelled as a Loyalist to leave America forever. As his editor notes, there is a poignancy in Milligen-Johnston's final remark that "South Carolina was at this period [1763?] the most thriving Country perhaps on the Globe and might have been the happiest. . . . At last the Demon of rebellion took possession of their hearts, and almost banished humanity among them, with every other virtue." Thus South Carolina's promotion-description literature, written up to the very first years of rebellion, ends for the British Loyalist on a note of disillusionment, even though it is private disillusionment expressed in a manuscript note to a printed volume designed to advertise this thriving country.

One must glance back briefly to the beginnings of the eighteenth century in North Carolina. Some of the tracts just noted were used to advertise both colonies, or the two as one, as did Daniel Coxe's work. For North Carolina alone very little promotion-discovery literature exists. There was Hugh Meredith's "An Account of the Cape Fear Country 1731," printed in two issues of the *Pennsylvania Gazette*. A former printer and partner of Franklin, Meredith had sold out and moved to North Carolina, from whence he sent the two-installment account. He describes topography, a canoe trip, eighteen-foot-high Indian corn, and the areas of fertile land. A typical governor's answer to official query, probably by Arthur Dobbs himself, is the reply to "Quere I." in 1761 as to the general state of the province from the Lords Commissioners of Trade and the Plantations. The answer, in first person, is a useful survey of Indians, government, French and Spanish settlements, and quitrents and other taxes, with answers to sixteen other queries as well.

But far more significant as history, literature, and scientific observation than any other writings from North or South Carolina are two books intended for promotion purposes, though the first has at times been considered primarily as serious history. The second, in large part a blatant plagiarizing of the first and of other books, is still valuable for its original scientific materials. Both will be considered again for various reasons in Chapters II and VII.

The earlier of these accounts is the only book composed both in and of Carolina during the Proprietary period. John Lawson's *A New Voyage to Carolina* (London, 1709) went through several editions in the eighteenth century and in the twentieth, sometimes under the title *A History of Carolina*. The latter title is a misnomer, for the book is essentially a promotion-discovery tract, albeit the greatest of them, dedicated to the Lords Proprietors in the latter years of their control of the twin colonies. The author, an educated gentleman and scientist, lived in the Carolinas, principally in the northern province, from 1700 to 1708/9, was surveyor-general of North Carolina and a cofounder as well as planner of two of its important towns. He returned to England and brought out his book, went back to the colonies, became a commissioner of the Virginia-Carolina boundary line, and in 1711 was tortured and executed by some of the Indians he had befriended while he was on an exploring expedition with the Baron von Graffenreid to discover a more convenient route to Virginia.

The book is in five parts, several of which will be considered in different chapters for the evidence they afford of intellectual and cultural interests of the colonists. The full title of *A New Voyage* claims that his journey covered one thousand miles. More exactly it was about 550 from Charleston, where he landed, by a circuitous horseshoe-shaped route to the plantation of one Richard Smith, on Pamlico River, in the vicinity of the present Washington, North Carolina. His small party had crossed swamps, paddled treacherous rivers, and visited Indians of several tribes and a number of isolated white settlers, all in winter with only the aid of Indian guides. Part One is the journal of this remarkable trek. The second part, "A Description of North Carolina," traces history, topography, coastal outline, geology, and products in detail, with learned and usually quite accurate comments on plants and animals. In Part Three, "The Present State of Carolina," he explains location of settlements, the colony's situation in relation to Virginia, its fine livestock and other natural and cultivated assets, with the usual come-hither tract's emphasis on abundance and ease of living but also with a number of perceptive comments on the longevity of the natives, trade with the Indians, and freedom from frontier fears, the last tragically ironic in the light of his own painful death. Perhaps most useful has been the fourth part, "The Natural History of Carolina," in which he displays acute observational powers and an immense knowledge of fauna and flora, really giving his reader a comparative treatise on European and American wild life. His concluding fifth division is valuable for its data: "An Account of the Indians of North Carolina" is a concise encyclopedia of aboriginal life to be considered in more detail in Chapter II. He ends with a plea that the red man be converted to Christianity not through the Spanish way of a field of blood, but through mild inducements to schooling and to learning crafts.

This is but a bare outline of his substance. He writes with an earthy humor resembling William Byrd's but not quite so sophisticated in tone, and the two men share love of a good story of life in the woods. Lawson depicts or discusses the droll or ridiculous appearance of a noseless Indian witch-doctor, the appetite shared by white men and red women for bedfellows of another race, even the sex life of the opossum. Indian religion and conjurations, the burial of a warrior struck by lightning, and native medicines and remarkable cures are among matters discussed with sympathy and at times dry wit.

Certainly one if not two of the ablest colonial southern writers after Lawson borrowed liberally and without acknowledgment from his book. In 1737 a physician of Edenton in North Carolina, Dr. John Brickell, "plagiarized" extensively from *A New Voyage* in his own *The Natural History of North Carolina* (Dublin). A great portion—about animals, plants, topography, and Indians—is straight from Lawson, though Brickell, himself a scientist, adds some new and useful information (even though at times inaccurate) in every category. His preface acknowledges the book as "a compendious Collection," and claims the double purpose of satisfying the curiosity of the European intellectual and supplying vital information for those inclined to live in Carolina. Thus it remains in the promotion-tract tradition. In style it suffers badly in comparison with Lawson, and it lacks his humorous observations.

At least two scholars consider the German-language promotion piece, *Neugefundenes Eden* (Bern, 1737), an even more amazing plagiarism. In recent years this tract, aimed at obtaining Swiss settlers for William Byrd's backcountry lands, has been translated into English and its authorship assigned to Byrd himself, though from internal evidence it seems fairly clearly to have been put together by a European land speculator named Samuel Jenner, probably from materials supplied by Byrd. The little compendium is a series of extracts straight from Lawson (perhaps taken from either one of the German versions or any of the several English), concluding with two documents or letters concerning his 40,000-acre tract signed by William Byrd. Whether Byrd actually furnished all of the material or not, the natural descriptions which simply substitute the name *Virginia* for *Carolina* were, for most eighteenth-century writers, in the public domain in a wider sense than they would be today. Throughout the seventeenth and early eighteenth centuries, at least, such borrowing for such a purpose and even for genuine histories was as frequent without acknowledgment of source as with casual recognition of indebtedness. The use of John Smith's writings up to at least 1750 is a classic case in point. The material in the present instance was used purely for propaganda purposes, with no announced author, just as advertising still carries none. The *Neu-gefundenes Eden* must remain of interest, however, not as a brazen plagiarism, but as an evidence of Lawson's repute as an accurate reporter and of the fairly late use, for the upper southern colonies, of promotion pamphlets. As already noted, this is not a colony advertising, but one or two individuals advertising for their private gain.

Perhaps the greatest of all literary productions of the colonial South designed to promote the sale of lands and attract settlers was written by William Byrd II, probably between 1732 and 1740. But it had absolutely no influence on prospective emigrants from the Old World, for it remained unpublished until 1841. This was the masterpiece of the owner of Westover, his *History of the Dividing Line betwixt Virginia and North Carolina Run in the Year of Our Lord 1728*. Byrd's *Secret History of the Line*, a shorter and quite different version which remained in manuscript until 1929, was written for entertainment, and probably earlier than the *History*. But employing the same materials as went into the *Secret History*—notes, diaries, documents, and letters—Byrd "fleshed out" (his own term) his story, adding materials which pointed to Virginia as the Eden among American colonies (he disparages directly North Carolina, Maryland, and New England). And he composed it during a decade when he was absorbed in attempting to populate his vast landholdings. The *History* is far more than a come-hither pamphlet or even a travel account or a present-state report, but it is aimed at extolling the abundant natural and human or humane virtues of his native province. This book will be considered in greater detail later, but it must be registered as perhaps the last and greatest of the Virginia literature of discovery and promotion beginning a century and a half earlier with Hariot and Smith and Strachey.

As writers and explorers on and in Virginia gave the first glimpses in literature of what became North Carolina, so pamphleteers ostensibly discussing South Carolina promoted the land of Georgia long before that last of the southern colonies was chartered or settled. Thomas Nairne, Indian agent for South Carolina, had in the 1710 *Letter* noted above urged the establishment of a settlement west of the Savannah to check Spanish Florida and develop fur trade. *A Discourse Concerning the design'd Establishment of a New Colony to the South of Carolina, in the Most delightful Country of the Universe* (London, 1717), Sir Robert Montgomery's dream of a real utopia in an area about that of modern Georgia indicates that the British mind seems to have been forming the concept of a new colony combining altruism with economic gain and the political strategy of a buffer state guarding against the Spaniards and Indians. The Scottish baronet's proposals to establish the Margravate of Azilia in what is now Georgia were made to the Lords Proprietors in June 1717 and were readily accepted. The scheme included two stages of settlement: the immediate setting up of the first District of Azilia, a manufacturing-ship-trade unit, which would be the exclusive property of subscribers who would realize quick profits—under the most feudal of American governments; the second, more utopian stage, which would include a second, smaller district, with the Margrave's residence and government houses in a kind of fort, in turn surrounded by a city, in turn surrounded by square-mile estates of the landed gentry, and outside this a strip of settlement for former indentured servants who had completed their time. Every subscriber of five hundred pounds would be entitled to a square-mile estate, to be developed independently by himself. Much of all this scheme derived from earlier English utopian literature such as Harrington's *Oceana* (1656) and even perhaps More's *Utopia*, from Bacon's *Of Plantations*, and from the example of the baronies of South Carolina established under Locke's Fundamental Constitutions.

Though Montgomery apparently raised £30,000, sufficient to carry five or six hundred settlers to his margravate, the politico-economic difficulties and technicalities were never solved or overcome. For some years the baronet and his friends advertised a revised Azilian scheme of settlement for "the Golden Islands," just off the Georgia coast. But Proprietors, Crown, and Crown advisors could never agree, and the great dream faded. Sir Robert died in 1731, just two years before the actual successful planting of Georgia began. His scheme remains of interest as the most ambitious and highly organized colonization plan proposed by a private person, and in many respects the most visionary, though it came very close to some sort of realization. Above all, it reflects vividly and directly the utopian atmosphere in which Georgia was to be conceived and as far as possible implemented.

Another dreamer, the Jean Pierre Purry mentioned above, before his South Carolina promotion and settlement, proposed "a perfect bulwark against the French and Spaniards," to be called Georgia or Georgiana, in *A Memorial Presented to . . . the Duke of Newcastle* (1724); but, despite a friendly Board of Trade, by 1726 this scheme had collapsed. A London merchant, Joshua Gee, in *The Trade and Navigation of Great Britain Considered* (London, 1729), urged in a widely read and often-reprinted pamphlet that the region must be settled, perhaps by convicts and the unemployed. These tracts are hardly American in authorship or origin of ideas, but they did anticipate in one way or another much of what went into the economic and political planning and practice for Georgia when it was chartered in 1732 and settled in 1733. For here is the idea of a utopian society, of a haven for the underprivileged and distressed of the European continent as well as of Great Britain, and of a buffer state protecting the older colonies against the French, Spanish, and Indians. Here, too, long beforehand are the extravagant claims for soil and climate which were to produce an unusual degree of disenchantment among an appreciable number of early Georgians.

But most interesting is that here is something, though not all, of the philanthropic idealism which was actually to go into the shaping of government and society which, for a time at least, worked. For Georgia did become the haven of many people from many lands, and from several British prisons.

The Georgia charter was granted by the King on June 9, 1732, to General James Oglethorpe, Lord Perceval (later Lord Egmont), and nineteen other prominent men for "settling poor persons of London" on a tract to the southwest of Carolina. The group of recipients of the charter had grown out of Dr. Bray's Associates, a religio-philanthropic body interested largely in the educational aspects of missionary endeavor. These twenty-one formed the first board of Trustees to manage the colony and were given definite powers. A smaller body called the Common Council, requiring a quorum of only eight, could act on smaller matters. The "trust" was limited to twenty-one years with the design by the Crown of its taking over with little expense to itself. The British government was motivated by self-interest of several kinds, such as protection for South Carolina and increased imperial trade. The board of Trustees had quite different motivations and designs. Oglethorpe, Perceval, and Benjamin Martyn (London secretary throughout the life of the board) were attempting the greatest philanthropic and social experiment of the age. They ruled largely through "regulations," which were not subject to the King's veto, rather than through enacted laws. For all these and other reasons all Britain became interested in Georgia, and the advertising and promotion literature, much of it written entirely in England by men who had not been to America, resembles somewhat in volume that of the initial Anglo-American undertakings of 150 or 125 years earlier, though it lacks the stately and sinewy Elizabethan-Jacobean rhetorical style. The Trustees' ideal state and even plans differed not too much in some respects from those of the earlier Azilia, and the intense conviction that they were doing good caused them to be obstinate and to ignore the facts of life in what they liked to think was at least a natural demiparadise. The rigidity of some of their rules was to bring their eventual downfall.

Much of the promotion material was written by Secretary Benjamin Martyn, poet and playwright and a man of inflexible integrity. His *Reasons for Establishing the Colony of Georgia with Regard to the Trade of Great Britain* (London, 1733) hews the line the Trustees were usually to follow: Georgia would make England independent of foreign sources for wine, hemp, flax, and potash; she would produce more than enough silk to supply England (actually she did produce more silk than any other colony but not in marketable quantities); she would give new opportunities to the poor and unfortunate and relieve overpopulation in England; and she would offer refuge to oppressed Protestants anywhere in Europe. The arguments differ little from those used by the older colonies, but there is a great difference in emphasis. Martyn also was probably the author of the most famous of these pamphlets, *A New and Accurate Account of the Provinces of South Carolina and Georgia* (London, 1732), which rhapsodizes on Georgia air and soil and points out proof of the healthfulness of the place in that one Florida Indian king was 300 years old and his father 350. Another Martyn pamphlet, once attributed to Oglethorpe, is *Some Account of the Designs of the Trustees for Establishing the Colony of Georgia* (London, 1732), a beautiful prospectus with elaborate engravings. Within the first year or two of settlement several tracts appeared. *A Brief Account of the Establishment of the Colony of Georgia, under Gen. James Oglethorpe, February 1, 1733* includes proceedings of the Trustees, a list of designs for the colony and an announcement of the arrival of the first settlers at the port of Charleston and their gradual movement toward their future home, together with Oglethorpe's conference with the Indians and his speech before the General Assembly of South Carolina.

After 1733 and before 1740 Georgia publicity dwindled but did not disappear entirely. One interesting feature is the poetic tributes. In 1736 appeared "Georgia, a Poem," "Tomo Chachi, an Ode," and "A Copy of Verses on Mr. Oglethorpe's Second Voyage to Georgia," all long ascribed to Samuel Wesley, but more recently on good evidence shown to have been written by Wesley's friend and colleague, the Reverend Thomas Fitzgerald. Journals of the day, such as the *Scot's Magazine* and the *Gentleman's Magazine*, frequently carried poems on Oglethorpe and Georgia. James Thomson and Aaron Hill were among the well-known poets who praised the enterprise in their verse. The whole concept had caught the imagination and gained the sympathy of the British public.

In 1740 a new era of propaganda literature began, not all of it praise. Many colonists, dissatisfied with the land-tenure system and the prohibition of rum and slaves, were criticizing the Trustees and Oglethorpe caustically. This period is marked by one famous antipromotion tract, actually written in Georgia and South Carolina by a group of disgruntled colonists who had fled to Charleston. This is the oft-cited *A True and Historical Narrative of the Colony of Georgia in America* (Charles Town, S.C., 1741) by Patrick Tailfer, Hugh Anderson, David Douglas, and other former planters. Prefaced by a bitingly satiric dedication to Oglethorpe with scathing language about the whole administration of the colony, the main text is more temperate in tone but loaded with abuse and alleged evidences of failure and mistake, and buttressed by documents and letters, including some to Oglethorpe and Martyn. In conclusion it summarizes the grievances, taking Trustees to task for misrepresenting the country in glowing terms, for oppressive land-tenure practices, for denying the lawful liberties of Englishmen, for neglecting manufactures such as silk—twelve in all. The dedication belongs to a long tradition of satiric political writing in the colonial South, and the main text to an equally long tradition of declaration of rights, both to be considered later, in Chapter IX. But more immediately the tract was a culmination of a series of criticisms the Trustees had been facing at home and in Georgia for some years.

In a pamphlet printed in December 1740, *An Impartial Inquiry into the State and Utility of Georgia* (London), Benjamin Martyn had already anticipated or faced much of the criticism, and the Earl of Egmont (Perceval) saw to it that Parliament, the King, and the royal family received copies. A second answer was in the better-known folio, *An Account Shewing the Progress of the Colony of Georgia in America from Its First Establishment* (London, 1741; Annapolis, 1742), some copies at least including an engraved map of the coast from Carolina to St. Augustine. When the Tailfer attack arrived, Egmont led the Trustees in denouncing it before the British Cabinet. Also as an antidote the three-volume *A Journal of the Proceedings in Georgia, beginning October 20, 1737* (1741?) was printed in a small edition for the information of the Trustees. While William Stephens, the Trustees' resident secretary in Georgia, continued to support his own and the Trustees' policies in *A State of the Province of Georgia, attested upon Oath in the Court of Savannah. November 10, 1740* (London, 1742), his son Thomas attacked the establishment in *A Brief Account of the Causes that have retarded the Progress of the Colony of Georgia* (London, 1743). Thomas presumably thought himself an economic realist, or perhaps he and those for whom he was agent were simply greedy.

Such was the controversial "promotion" writing produced by British and British-born proadministration and antiadministration elements. As already noted, most was written in England and published there; but all of it used letters and data straight from the colony. William Stephens, Tailfer et al., and perhaps others wrote in or near Georgia, and at least two tracts were published in other southern colonies. But there was an additional segment of Georgia propaganda writing often overlooked, the Swiss-German accounts of the settlement. Most of these were in German, but some were translated contemporaneously and used to buttress one position or the other, usually the Proprietors'. In recent years several other German letters, tracts, and questionnaires originating in Georgia or advertising it have been translated and published in English. Since they too reflect the early southern mind, they should at least be noted. Nor should Whitefield's pleas throughout America and Great Britain for his orphanage at Bethesda be overlooked as a facet of Georgia promotion.

The Salzburgers, Lutherans persecuted in their native mountains in central Europe, began arriving in Georgia eleven months after Oglethorpe's first party set out. Led by John Martin Bolzius and the younger Baron Von Reck, they landed at Savannah but soon removed to a spot on the bank of the river they named Ebenezer, later moving to a healthier location bearing the same name. They continued to arrive in small numbers until by the 1740's there were 1,200, the largest single population element in early Georgia. Moravians came a little later but soon departed, to be followed by Scottish Highland and Puritan groups. Though all of these and a fine Jewish enclave in Savannah left their mark on early Georgia life, only the Salzburgers left it in literary form.

The best-known of these German-Swiss writings translated into English and published at the direction of the Society for Promoting Christian Knowledge is *An Extract of the Journals of Mr. Commissary Von Reck, Who Conducted the First Transport of Salzburgers to Georgia: and of Reverend Mr. Bolzius, One of their Ministers. Giving an Account of their Voyage to, and happy Settlement in that Province* (London, 1734). This orthodox voyage-promotion tract appealed to potential colonists and to those philanthropists who might contribute funds for sending more of "our persecuted Protestant Brethren" to the colony. It is in journal style, succinct enough to be choppy but it could and should have been effective as a simple testimony of fact. The recently published *Henry Newman's Salzburger Letterbooks* covers the period 1732 to 1735. Only in the letters from such men as Bolzius is there anything resembling propaganda, but the whole volume reveals much of the history of these admirable people in the southernmost colony. Some time before 1740, perhaps in 1734, Bolzius sent home a report on the religious situation in Georgia, viewing it realistically, lamenting present but not despairing of future religious education for all Protestants there. Bolzius is the principal author in the Reverend Samuel Urlsperger's *Der ausführlichen Nachrichten von der Königlich-Gross-Britannischen Colonie Saltzburgischer Emigranten in America . . .* (in 19 parts, 3 vols., Halle, 1735–1752) and in other tract series or collections on America and Georgia. Embedded in this lengthy work are two questionnaires of about 1751 with answers, "vivid and earthy," now recently translated. They are by Bolzius, and they reveal as much of Georgia life, including Indians, agriculture, white servants, blacks, and manufactures as any promotion tract could. They form an optimistic yet realistic and temperate report on affairs which should have been an inducement to keep the Salzburgers and others coming. Today, literature in German on all the southern colonies from Maryland to Georgia is gradually being translated and printed. In the main, it differs from most other promotion material in that it seems to convey a deep, underlying gratitude for the *freedom* the American colonies afforded and a sturdy determination to make the most of it.

Perhaps the story of voyage-promotion-travel writing in the southern colonies before 1763 would not be complete without some notice of the prose, and the verse for that matter, of Edward Kimber (1719–1769), young English journalist and man of letters who published in the *London Magazine*, of which his father was editor, his "Itinerant Observations in America." Kimber had reached New York in 1742, traveled immediately by ship to Maryland, from thence proceeded slowly through the Chesapeake Bay colonies, taking ship again to Georgia, and then on to South Carolina. From Charleston he returned to Europe. Kimber thus observed, and had something to say about, four of the five southern colonies. While in America he also wrote verse published in various colonial gazettes as well as in Great Britain. His account continues a tradition of descriptive travel, but it is much more specific than most earlier southern observations, giving even details of buildings in such villages as York Town, Virginia, and of harbors and estates, with mention by name of prominent citizens. Though he is probably aiming more to satisfy the curiosity of the British reader than to encourage emigration, Kimber is in some respects the beginning of a new tradition in outsiders' observations on America, that which is more fully developed in the decade just before the Revolution and the first generation of the new republic. The travelers in this new tradition were residents of other colonies, of Great Britain, or of Europe, and they wrote to inform, to entertain, and perhaps to prejudice, depending upon their own views or their readers'.

Though promotion writing in one form or another was to continue well into the national period and, in specific situations or cases into our own time, it has ceased to be a form of literature in any esthetic sense. The account of exploration has remained alive, as the American people themselves have become its avid readers, most notably in the early national period in the journals of the Lewis and Clark expedition and of other great western treks, and in our own century in accounts of journeys to the arctic and antarctic poles. The moon explorers have been seen rather than read. But southern Americans' interest in faraway places, as their own land once was to their ancestors, has continued, perhaps merged with a general national curiosity about strange places and stranger imagined beings. The peculiarly southern search for a paradise, or a potential paradise, in his own region is still represented in the individual southerner's hedonism and perhaps in the savage-wistful yearnings of author and personae in Faulkner's "The Bear" or Warren's *All the King's Men*. Disillusioned as the modern southern writer may appear, he often seems still to be asking why there cannot be, for one brief shining moment or for ages, a Camelot located in his own land. And he often supplies his own answer.

History and Major Historians

As the reader will already have observed, where the writing of the literature of promotion and discovery ends and the writing of history begins is in many instances difficult if not impossible to determine. Often it is a matter of emphasis more than of point of view or subject matter. If society and the development of social institutions are the true matter of history, the works discussed above are only in certain instances, or portions, and often only incidentally, history. During the period from 1585 to 1763 there were, however, if one accepts a fairly broad definition of social institutions, a few writings by southern colonials which were actual histories. These differ in primary intention or total effect from the writings of Hariot or Strachey or Lawson. They are all concerned with one colony, Virginia, though sometimes with a glance at her nearer neighbors. A few are pamphlets, but most are full-length books, each reflecting among other things the stylistic fashions of its own time and in more or less degree the historical methodology of particular periods.

They are not imperial histories reflecting the aspirations for national expansion which the British such as Ogilby and Oldmixon wrote. They are not God's remembrancers, as the New England histories and historians were. Though three of the more prominent southern historians were clergymen, they were not recording or analyzing their spiritual evolution in America, albeit the conversion of the Indians may be an incidental theme and church as related to state a prominent element. Rather, they were looking at what transplanted Europeans along the south Atlantic coast had done, were doing, and might do in developing a new society in an exciting environment. Even John Smith, the earliest of them, is more than half-conscious of this formation of a new society. The last of them, William Stith, is fully aware of what the society he chronicles has led to, and what it should become.

It has been suggested that the New Englanders wrote more history because they had more dramatic confrontations, such as the Anne Hutchinson controversy, the Roger Williams case, or the Half-Way Covenant dispute, which were inciting or exciting themes. But surely the southern colonies had enough of this raw material of history, for there were dramatic confrontations of Puritan and Proprietor and Puritan and Catholic in Maryland Dissenters vs. Church of England in South Carolina, Berkeley vs. Bacon in Virginia, and a dozen lesser tense and complex socio-political-religious facedowns. Any look at colonial insurrections and movements, down to the Regulators of the two Carolinas and the Pistole Fee and Parson's Cause controversies in Virginia, will show that the South throughout the period had its share of involved and dramatic controversy. Yet, so far as is yet known, only one of these, Bacon's Rebellion, incited genuine historical interpretation.

The focus of the Puritan colonial historian is on the people as they build their city upon a hill in this howling or mighty wilderness, a spiritual city for a spiritually chosen people. "Wilderness" and "Providence" are pervasive terms in New England's chronicles. God had always provided for His people in the scriptural deserts. The focus of the southern colonial was on the place, the natural paradise or the potential Garden of Eden and what men might become within it or make of it if they were wise. "Canaan," "paradise," and "Eden" are the recurrent southern terms, biblical enough in their origin, but carrying in their connotations as much of Renaissance and Enlightenment classicism or secularism as of Christianity. The southerner's terrain was somewhat different, but the way he looked at it made the real difference. He did indeed identify with his environment. Except for the weather, the shore of the James was almost as bleak and desolate in 1607 as was the rockbound Massachusetts coast in 1620. Yet John Smith refers rarely, perhaps only once or twice, to "the desolate wilderness," and then hardly in the New England sense. No fitter place for man's habitation, he suggests, exists in the physical world. As Roanoke Island had been to Lane and Hariot, so was Virginia—in its natural state—to Smith, Beverley, Jones, and Stith, and even to the less emotionally attached Hartwell, Blair, and Chilton. "Providence" is noted many times in Smith, but without the moral complacency usually present in a Bradford, a Winthrop, or a Cotton Mather. Later Virginians use it rarely, and then more or less as a vague figure of speech.

Unlike the relatively considerable number of diaries, verses, plays, and prose satires by southerners discovered in manuscript only within the past century, the southern histories, except for two relatively brief pamphlets to be considered, were read in print by the contemporaries of their authors. The intention was to explain, to demonstrate, their region for these contemporaries, usually those in Great Britain but certainly in the later period for their neighbors as well. Britons did read them, but so did southern colonists. The inventories of almost all fair-sized libraries in Virginia and Maryland, and sometimes in the two Carolinas, include the works of John Smith, Robert Beverley, Hugh Jones, and William Stith, and sometimes the smaller books of Hartwell, Blair, and Chilton.

Lying undiscovered or irretrievably lost are the histories of Virginia written by such able and intelligent men as William Fitzhugh, William Byrd, and Sir John Randolph, though the last never completed his. Their manuscripts were read by at least a few of their contemporaries, and all three intended some day to publish. Probably many other southerners had the urge to write, and perhaps did write, the stories of their respective colonies, for by the earlier eighteenth century these people were conscious of their possible or probable place in the history of the western world.

Captain John Smith

John Smith (1580–1631), "President of Virginia and Admiral of New England," has received more attention for his historical writing than has any other colonial American, Cotton Mather not excepted. Part of the reason is that he has been a controversial figure, denounced for supreme egotism and mendacity and equally praised as the last knight-errant or the first gallant southern gentleman. If he did not himself create a myth, he gave the materials from which one of the most American of our myths was formed, the story of his rescue by the Indian princess Pocahontas. He prepared the way for or gave examples of other American traits, or traits Americans like to think of as theirs, such as the equality of men of every degree faced with the problems of self-preservation. The America he anticipated by his own example was not for the lily-fingered or the blue-blooded, but for the aggressive, resourceful, and courageous. And he recorded a persistent southern trait, one which Robert Beverley and Hugh Jones agreed existed—laziness—with its remedy. Sheer indolence, sloth, was a major cause of the first catastrophes of starvation and Indian attack at Jamestown, as they have been on a larger scale a regional characteristic down to the twentieth century.

Two of his major writings, *A True Relation* and *A Map of Virginia*, have been noted above. Both have elements of history, and perhaps *A True Relation* is, with the work here to be discussed, one of his two genuinely historical works. *A Map of Virginia* became part of the *Generall Historie*, slightly edited from its original to fit somewhat different aims. The later *True Travels* is autobiography. *The Generall Historie of Virginia, New-England, and the Summer Isles* (London, 1624), in six large books, is Smith's major claim to serious consideration as a historian in an age of great events. It has been read, borrowed from, assailed, and admired through three and a half centuries. As mentioned above, promotion literature owed much to him. Succeeding Virginia historians all acknowledged their indebtedness, as did almost every British historian of empire. In the nineteenth century American historians, especially but not entirely New England ones, believed they had proved him a contemptible liar in his belatedly recorded Pocahontas-rescue episode. They had no evidence either way on the story, but they cited the "proved" falsehoods of his *True Travels* in eastern Europe and concluded that, if he were proved a liar once, he was always a liar. By 1891 the distinguished historian J. Franklin Jameson could say that the legend of Pocahontas must go! He was but following such historians as Charles Deane and Henry Adams, the latter having mounted a prejudiced, perhaps unethical attack with inaccurate data to get himself started in the profession. Even though today a few cautious historians disbelieve, most admit the episode could well have taken place. This is largely the result of the pioneering investigations of Bradford Smith and Laura Polanyi Striker, together with the imaginative researches and real proofs unearthed by Philip L. Barbour, which prove what can be proved—that in every instance which has been checked (and there are hundreds) Smith told nothing but the truth in his *True Travels*. Thus historians, sometimes grudgingly, admit that Smith was probably or surely telling the truth in his account of Virginia, most surely of course in the part of the *Generall Historie* which concerns Virginia while he was in the colony. In other words, what the sometime president, councilor, and explorer had to say about the first two years at Jamestown is to be taken seriously.

The paragraph above is a drastic condensation of a long and complex critical controversy, here perhaps oversimplified. The other major charge against Smith, and it of course has relation to his veracity, is his alleged inordinate egotism. The egocentricity is there, in the accounts of actual events in Virginia or the explorations in New England in which he had a personal part, and in other sections. It is particularly evident in his continual reminders that, had his advice been followed in the governing of Virginia and the treatment of the Indians, the miseries of that first settlement might never have come upon it. But throughout the *Generall Historie* there is the sometimes haunting suggestion that this is a story of and by a man who realized he never quite achieved what he sought to achieve, a man of damaged ego. As Philip Barbour has suggested, this most ambitious in scale of Smith's works was the author's apologia, or defense, and his memoirs. The twentieth-century reader is not likely to find Smith objectionably egotistic, though he will note a total lack of modesty.

The *Generall Historie* is indeed Smith's apologia, but it is also much more. Its origin, as at least two recent scholars think, may lie in a motion of April 12, 1621, in a meeting of the Virginia Company of London by another John Smith who was to go to Virginia, to the effect that "a faire and perspicuous history" be compiled of that colony, "and to have the memory and fame of many of her worthies though they be dead to live and be transmitted to all posterities." This our Smith may have been suggesting at the beginning of Book III, when he mentions "the eternizing of the memory of those that effected [established] it," though he is here saying that so many calamities have occurred that only now is the eternizing taking place. Strachey's earlier plan for a general history may have been in Smith's mind. And in September 1622 he may have conferred with Purchas on the idea, or with someone else of the Council for Virginia who was interested in such a literary project. At the conclusion of Book IV Smith asserts that he wrote at the request of the Company, though no record of such a request exists and the explicit and implicit criticism of the Company's administration is frequent in Books II–IV. Perhaps he means that the old Company thought he might bring together a book which would show the progress of the colony, however slow or halting, and that the Company unofficially sponsored the beginning of his writing in 1621–1622. After the massacre of 1622 he was still writing and did not finish until the Commission appointed by the Crown to investigate the Company was already at work, as he observes. In other words, Smith's motivations may have changed as he wrote. There were severe critics of the Company's policies who remained loyal to that organization, notably Governor Sir Francis Wyatt and Treasurer George Sandys in Virginia, officials who wrote scathing letters about the measures of their London relative Sir Edwin Sandys and their friend Deputy John Ferrar. It is quite clear that Wyatt and George Sandys by no means wanted a complete takeover by the Crown. Smith, though later he was to appear to approve royal government (he could hardly do anything else in print) was probably in much the same mood or temper as the two officials in the colony, that of a friendly critic within the family.

But to return to the *Generall Historie*'s history. Smith found a printer, Michael Sparkes, and he began to collect his materials, including copper plates of maps. Then he proceeded rapidly. He added, shaped, rephrased various sources. Of the six books, one was soon completed. Then Smith issued a prospectus and sought a patron. He found this patron, or patroness, in the great Duchess of Lennox and Richmond, a proud and powerful lady whose portrait adorns most copies of the *Generall Historie*. With her help he was able to publish a handsome folio with engraved title page, four engraved maps, and in some copies portraits of Pocahontas as well as of the duchess. Two printers worked simultaneously on different parts of the book, a fact which accounts for certain missing signatures within the volume and for some paddings of commendatory verses at inappropriate places.

The *Generall Historie* is not quite history in the modern sense, but it is history more nearly in that sense than is Francis Bacon's writing on English kings or Hakluyt's on English voyages and discoveries. In general outline it is somewhat like Hakluyt, a compendium of facts held together by the author's egocentric point of view. Even when he quotes long passages from his companions in peril in Virginia, his reader soon realizes that, as in *A Map of Virginia* the companions see through Smith's eyes, they see as Smith does. Certainly even as early as *A Map of Virginia* Smith was rephrasing his sources and even his own quoted letters, and he continues to do so here.

Book I is Smith's condensed and edited gathering of pre-Jamestown New World history from Hakluyt, John Brereton, and manuscripts Purchas was also then using for his *Pilgrimes*. Nothing is new here, but it formed a handy and necessary introduction for Books II–IV. Probably after he had written his first book Smith took a careful look at George Sandys' *A Relation of a Journey begun . . . 1610* (London, 1615), the most popular seventeenth-century travel account in English (on Mediterranean countries, including the Holy Land) by a poet-traveler who was at the moment (1622–1623), as Smith knew, Treasurer of the colony in Virginia. Barbour makes a strong case for Smith's adoption of Sandys' form and general style, including plentiful engravings and quotations from ancient authors, borrowings from contemporary guidebooks and from geographers, historians, and philosophers. Barbour also points out Smith's extensive use of Martin Fotherby's *Atheomastix* as a source for many of his poetic quotations. Though these quoted embellishments are not always so apt as Sandys', the *Generall Historie* is much the more vigorous and readable of the two books. Whether the Virginia treasurer's travel volume was the specific model or not, Smith's later five books indicate an attempt at learned and literary ornament, at extensive use of older authorities, at smoothness of style.

Book II is principally from "A Description of Virginia" in his own *A Map of Virginia*, with few revisions but with some of the polishing and ornamentation just noted. Based on the "Proceedings" or second section of the 1612 *A Map of Virginia* and employing the narratives of his old Virginia compatriots but with considerable rewriting and addition, Book III is generally considered the best of the whole volume and the part on which Smith's reputation as a historian must largely rest. It is primarily a recounting of events during the author's 1607–1609 sojourn in Virginia. Book IV continues a roughly chronological tracing of events from a variety of contemporary narrative sources, with interspersed documents such as Smith's letter to Queen Anne on Pocahontas, and lists of adverturers. Included are the best existing account of the 1622 massacre based upon a number of sources but composed by Smith himself and his offer to the Company to go to the colony and clean up the mess; also his "brief relation" to the commissioners appointed by the King, with his answers to their questions, all with seeming candor and some tactful avoidance of placing blame on any particular person—only on policies—for the troubles of the colony.

Book V is concerned with the Bermudas and is based primarily on Nathaniel Butler's unpublished manuscript. Book VI is a reprint with variations of Smith's *Description of New England* (1616) and *New England's Trials* (1620) with extracts from such pamphlets as *Mourt's Relation* (1622) and Winslow's *Good News from New England* (1624). As has often been observed, at the end of the *Generall Historie* there is no peroration, no real conclusion on a high or low note of enthusiasm, despair, or encouragement. Actually the last two parts are in most respects quite detached from the first four, in effect forming a sort of double appendix. The *True Travels* (London, 1630) does include a brief "continuation" of the *Historie*, but it is a mere filling in of events between 1624 and 1629, which comprise short chapters on the three colonies.

Thus the *Generall Historie* is no unified work. But there are relative unities within the work, if one will take the first four books as an account of Virginia from 1584 to 1624, or II and III as the Virginia Smith and his friends knew, or simply Book III as the kernel, the genuine recorded history of the province in a crucial two-year period. A great deal is to be said for taking the first four books as the most accurate and comprehensive history—in its coverage of all features and activities—of a seventeenth-century American colony. Smith concludes Book IV with his remark, "Thus far I have travelled in this Wildernesse of Virginia," and the final words: "But here I must leave all to the triall of time, both my selfe, *Virginia's* preparations, proceedings and good events; praying to that great God the protector of all goodnesse to send them as good successe as the goodnesse of the action and Countrey deserveth, and my heart desireth."

Book II describes topography, commodities, and aborigines. The Indian section is especially varied and dramatic, giving the details of the manner of life, including hunting, which were to be borrowed by many later writers. What today one might call the romanticizing of Pocahontas is begun here with several brief appearances, no longer Powhatan's preadolescent daughter, but the fawnlike child of nature who adores Captain Smith and many times—not simply in the rescue scene—saves the colonists from starvation or more brutal annihilation. The new Indian princess, who continues through books III and IV, is emphasized by the author's phrasing: "His dearest daughter *Pocahontas*"; "*Pocahontas*, his dearest jewell and daughter, in that darke night came through the irksome woods, and told our *Captaine*"; "Pocahontas hid [Wyffin] for a time, and sent them who pursued him the clean contrary way"; "Pokahontas the Kings daughter saved a boy called Henry Spilman"; "the poore innocent *Pocahontas* [and her perfidious capture]"; and "the Lady *Rebecca*, alias *Pocahontas*." These are a few of the phrases and clauses denoting her presence and its significance. One should note that she saves at least two other individuals besides Smith and also that the almost casual mention of her intercession is in easily believable terms. In his letter to Queen Anne, incidentally often criticized as an entirely unnecessary intrusion into the narrative, Smith is chronologically perfectly in order and offers as gallant a tribute to womanhood as colonial American literature presents. It was but eminently fitting that he should implore Her Majesty to receive this regal wife of a poor English commoner, "seeing this Kingdome may rightly have a Kingdome by her meanes." Thus "the Mother of us all" was prepared for American mythology through history. For, as Smith later commented, "History is the memory of time, the life of the dead, and the happiness of the living." The copper-colored spirit of the time and place was to become in future centuries the symbol of the brave new world and, dressed in crinoline, the ideal of southern womanhood. She represented all at once a region, a nation, and a state of mind.

The Pocahontas relationship, the stern measures taken with indolent and profane loiterers among the colonists, the hand-to-hand combat with an Indian chief, are among the many autobiographical elements of the *Historie*. This personal quality gives the book interest and at the same time subjects it to suspicion as prejudiced writing, or special pleading. Yet that Smith was accurate whenever he wrote from firsthand observation or participation has been abundantly proved by Philip Barbour, as already noted.

As personal narrative, collection of voyages and travels, chronicle of the English settlement of North America, the *Generall Historie* suggests at least three major facts: America, southern branch particularly, was a natural paradise; unfit and evil men, red and white, threatened to spoil this Eden; and the author alone knew what to do to prevent catastrophe. There is also pervasive patriotism and full realization as to what "this deare bought Land with so much bloud and cost" should become beyond a natural paradise. That is, the author had a sense of high destiny for British America, especially Virginia, a sense that most of the major Virginia historians to be discussed below shared with him, and in their case with more palpable evidence of that promise before them. But he more than they is the participant-historian.

Smith's style, in those parts of the *Historie* pretty clearly of his composition, is for his age and despite the borrowed poetic embellishments, plain, unadorned, though in his dramatizing he becomes perforce somewhat rhetorical. His changes in mood are reflected in changes in style—from the indignation of the Hotspur rhetoric replying to early Company criticisms, to grim and sober rhythms of sadness at the loss of good and brave friends, to irritation with inept Captain Newport in mocking or sardonic terms, to soaring sanguinity in his again rhetorical exhortations to adventure. In his polishings for the *Historie* he often becomes sententious, but he is often too most effective in the axiomatic rhetoric of these later observations. For the Jacobean-Caroline British nation he seems to be saying, as he expressed it in 1631, that this work is the record of the nation's ideals and aspirations: "Seeing honour is our lives ambition, and our ambition after death, to have an honourable memory of our life: and seeing by no meanes we would be abated of the dignitie and glory of our predecessors, let us imitate their vertues to be worthily their successors."

Partly because he spent only two years in that colony of which he principally wrote and derived his materials for other periods at secondhand, Smith has sometimes been labeled the precursor, rather than the first, of New World colonial historians. He is radically unlike the Puritan historians of that land of which he liked to call himself Admiral. But he shares with later southern historians from Beverley to Stith, and actually on to Jefferson and Ulrich B. Phillips, a preoccupation with environment and external nature. With most of them he shares an interest in the Indians, both good and bad, and in the implementation of laws in society, the good and evil of local government and government from across the seas. Like most of them, he is in some way even in his strictures promoting what he considers to be the welfare of the colony. He sees that in such a natural paradise the combination of hedonism and laziness will produce infinite, perhaps fatal, ills: like later southerners and critics of southerners, he argued that "heaven and earth never agreed better to frame a place for mans habitation . . . were it fully manured and inhabited by industrious people."

Robert Beverley

(1673–1722)

Robert Beverley, Jr., was born in Middlesex County, Virginia, in 1673. His father, Major Robert Beverley, had emigrated from England ten years earlier, settling at Jamestown, where he became a stout supporter of Governor William Berkeley in the dispute that led to Bacon's Rebellion of 1676. A tobacco planter and attorney as well as a militia officer, Berkeley's father died in 1687, leaving a 6,000-acre plantation, which Beverley inherited when he came of age. In 1697, he married Ursula Byrd, the sister of William Byrd of Westover. She died in childbirth a year later, leaving a son, William; Beverley never remarried. From 1699 until 1715, he held a number of public posts, including the clerkship of King and Queen County, and he represented Jamestown in the 1699, 1700–1702, and 1705–1706 assemblies of the House of Burgesses. In 1703, Beverley sailed to England to defend his interests in a land dispute; from there he wrote scathing letters home, criticizing Governor Francis Nicholson and other members of Virginia's ruling party. The accusations leveled in those letters made an enemy of the governor, who removed Beverley from his clerkship in 1705. With his involvement in public affairs now sharply curtailed because of his political adversaries, Beverley retired to his plantation for good in 1715 and was buried on its grounds when he died in 1722.

During his time in London, Beverley read the manuscript of John Oldmixon's *The British Empire in America*. Angered by what he considered the work's irredeemable errors in its history of Virginia, Beverley determined to compose his own work. His *History and Present State of Virginia* was published in 1705, a spirited account that combined vivid description and sharp satire in equal parts. Throughout his *History*, Beverley contrasts natural laws, exemplified by idealized portraits of Virginia's Native American inhabitants, with the "laws of Englishmen." In fact, in his preface he claims to be "an *Indian* . . . [who doesn't] pretend to be too exact" in his language. Because of this very directness and lack of pretension, Beverley's work has survived as a notable historical source.

from *The History and Present State of Virginia*

Chap. III. *"Shewing what happen'd after the Alteration of the Government from an Elective President to a Commissionated Governour, until the Dissolution of the Company.*

❡ **20.**   In the mean while the Treasurer, Council, and Company of *Virginia* Adventurers in *London*, not finding that Return and Profit from the Adventures they expected; and rightly judging that this Disappointment, as well as the idle Quarrels in the Colony, proceeded from a Mismanage of the Government; petition'd his Majesty, and got a new Patent with Leave to appoint a Governour.

Upon this new Grant they sent out Nine Ships, and plentiful Supplies of Men and Provisions; and made Three Joint Commissioners or Governours in equal Power, *viz.* Sir *Thomas Gates*, Sir *George Summers*, and Capt. *Newport*. They agreed to go all together in one Ship.

This Ship, on Board of which the Three Governours had embarqued, being separated from the Rest, was put to great Distress in a severe Storm; and after Three Days and Nights constant Baling and Pumping, was at last cast Ashore at *Bermudas*, and there staved, but by good Providence the Company was preserved.

Notwithstanding this Shipwreck, and Extremity they were put to, yet could not this common Misfortune make them agree. The Best of it was, they found Plenty of Provisions in that Island, and no *Indians* to annoy them: But still they quarrell'd amongst themselves, and none more than the Two Knights; who made their Parties, built each of them a Cedar Vessel, one call'd the *Patience*, the other the *Deliverance*, and used what they gather'd of the Furniture of the old Ship for Rigging, and Fish-Oil, and Hogs-Grease mix'd with Lime and Ashes instead of Pitch and Tar: For they found great Plenty of *Spanish* Hogs in this Island, which are supposed to have swam ashore from some Wrecks, and there afterwards increased.

❬ **21.** While these Things were acting in *Bermudas*, Capt. *Smith* being very much burnt by the accidental Firing of some Gun-Powder, as he was upon a Discovery in his Boat, was forced for his Cure sake, and the Benefit of a Surgeon, to take his Passage for *England* in a Ship that was then upon the Point of Sailing.

Several of the Nine Ships that came out with the Three Governours arrived, with many of the Passengers; some of which in their Humours wou'd not submit to the Government there, pretending the New Commission destroy'd the Old one; that Governours were appointed instead of a President, and that they themselves were to be of the Council; and so wou'd assume an independent Power, inspiring the People with Disobedience; by which Means they became frequently exposed in great Parties to the Cruelty of the *Indians;* all sorts of Discipline was laid aside, and their necessary Defence neglected; so that the *Indians* taking Advantage of those Divisions, form'd a Strategem to destroy them Root and Branch, and indeed they did cut many of 'em off, by massacring whole Companies at a time; so that all the Out-Settlements were deserted, and the People that were not destroy'd took Refuge in *James-Town*, except the small Settlement at *Kiquotan*, where they had built themselves a little Fort, and call'd it *Algernoon* Fort: And yet, for all this, they continued their Disorders, wasting their old Provisions, and neglecting to gather others; so that they who remain'd alive were all near famish'd, having brought themselves to that Pass, that they durst not stir from their own Doors to gather the Fruits of the Earth, or the Crabs and Mussels from the Water-side: Much less to hunt or catch wild Beasts, Fish or Fowl, which were found in great Abundance there. They continued in these scanty Circumstances till they were at last reduced to such Extremity, as to eat the very Hides of their Horses, and the Bodies of the *Indians* they had killed; and sometimes also upon a Pinch they wou'd not disdain to dig them up again to make a homely Meal of after they had been buried. And that Time is to this Day remember'd by the Name of the *Starving Time*.

Thus a few Months indiscreet Management brought such an Infamy upon the Country, that to this Day it cannot be wiped away: And the Sicknesses occasion'd by this bad Diet, or rather want of Diet are unjustly remember'd to the Disadvantage of the Country, as a Fault in the Climate; which was only the Foolishness and Indiscretion of those who assumed the Power of Governing. I call it assumed because the New Commission mention'd, by which they pretended to be of the Council, was not in all this time arrived, but remain'd in *Bermudas* with the new Governours.

Here I can't but admire the Care, Labour, Courage and Understanding that Capt. *John Smith* show'd in the Time of his Administration; who not only founded, but also preserved all these Settlements in good Order, while he was amongst them. And without him, they had certainly all been destroy'd, either by Famine, or the Enemy long before; tho' the Country naturally afforded Subsistance enough, even without any other Labour than that of Gathering and Preserving its Spontaneous Provisions.

For the first Three Years that Capt. *Smith* was with them, they never had in that whole Time above Six Months *English* Provisions. But as soon as he had left 'em to themselves, all went to Ruine; for the Indians had no longer any Fear for themselves, or Friendship for the *English*. And Six Months after this Gentleman's Departure, the 500 Men that he left were reduced to Threescore; and they too must of Necessity have starved, if their Relief had been with-held a Week longer.

℄ 22. In the mean time, the Three Governours put to Sea from *Bermudas* in their Two small Vessels, with their Company, to the Number of One Hundred and Fifty, and in Fourteen Days, *viz.* the 25th of *May*, 1610. They arrived both together in *Virginia;* and went with their Vessels up to *James-Town*, where they found the small Remainder of the Five Hundred Men, in that melancholy Way I just now hinted.

℄ 23. Sir *Thomas Gates*, Sir *George Summers*, and Capt. *Newport*, the Governours, were very compassionate of their Condition; and call'd a Council, wherein they inform'd them, that they had but Sixteen Days Provision Aboard; and therefore desired to know their Opinion, whether they would venture to Sea under such a Scarcity: Or if they resolved to continue in the Settlement, and take their Fortunes; they would stay likewise, and share the Provisions among them; but desired that their Determination might be speedy. They soon came to the Conclusion of returning for *England:* But because their Provisions were short, they resolved to go by the Banks of *Newfoundland*, in Hopes of meeting with some of the Fishermen, (this being now the Season) and dividing themselves among their Ships for the greater Certainty of Provision, and for their better Accommodation.

According to this Resolution, they all went aboard, and fell down to *Hog-Island* the 9th of *June* at Night, and the next Morning to *Mulberry-Island* Point, which is Eighteen Miles below *James-Town*, and Thirty above the Mouth of the River; and there they spied a Long-Boat, which the Lord *Delawar* (who was just arrived with Three Ships) had sent before him up the River sounding the Channel. His Lordship was made sole Governour, and was accompanied by several Gentlemen of Condition. He caused all the Men to return again to *James-Town;* resettled them with Satisfaction, and staid with them till *March* following; and then being very sick, he return'd for *England*, leaving about Two Hundred in the Colony.

℄ 24. On the 10th of *May*, 1611, Sir *Thomas Dale* being then made Governour, arriv'd with Three Ships, which brought Supplies of Men, Cattle and Hogs. He found them growing again into the like Disorders as before, taking no Care to plant Corn, and wholly relying upon their Store, which then had but Three Months Provision in it. He therefore set them to work about Corn, and tho' it was the Middle of *May* before they began to prepare the Ground, yet they had an indifferent good Crop.

(25. In *August* the same Year Sir *Thomas Gates* arriv'd at *James-Town* with Six Ships more, and with a plentiful Supply of Hogs, Cattle, Fowls, & c. with a good Quantity of Ammunition, and all other Things necessary for a new Colony, and besides this a Reinforcement of Three Hundred and Fifty chosen Men. In the Beginning of *September* he settled a new Town at *Arrahattuck*, about Fifty Miles above *James-Town*, Paling in the Neck above Two Miles from the Point, from one Reach of the River to the other. Here he built Forts and Centry-Boxes, and in Honour of *Henry* Prince of *Wales*, call'd it *Henrico*. And also run a Palissado on the other Side of the River at *Coxendale*, to secure their Hogs.

(26. *Anno* 1612, Two Ships more arriv'd with Supplies: And Capt. *Argall*, who commanded one of them, being sent in her to *Patowmeck* to buy Corn, he there met with *Pocahontas*, the Excellent Daughter of *Powhatan;* and having prevail'd with her to come Aboard to a Treat, he detain'd her Prisoner, and carried her to *James-Town*, designing to make Peace with her Father by her Release: But on the Contrary, that Prince resented the Affront very highly; and although he loved his Daughter with all imaginable Tenderness, yet he would not be brought to Terms by that unhandsome Treachery; till about Two Years after a Marriage being proposed between Mr. *John Rolfe*, an *English* Gentleman, and this Lady; which *Powhatan* taking to be a sincere Token of Friendship, he vouchsafed to consent to it, and to conclude a Peace.

Intermarriage had been indeed the Method proposed very often by the *Indians* in the Beginning, urging it frequently as a certain Rule, that the *English* were not their Friends, if they refused it. And I can't but think it wou'd have been happy for that Country, had they embraced this Proposal: For, the Jealousie of the *Indians*, which I take to be the Cause of most of the Rapines and Murders they committed, wou'd by this Means have been altogether prevented, and consequently the Abundance of Blood that was shed on both sides wou'd have been saved; the great Extremities they were so often reduced to, by which so many died, wou'd not have happen'd; the Colony, instead of all these Losses of Men on both Sides, wou'd have been encreasing in Children to its Advantage; the Country wou'd have escaped the *Odium* which undeservedly fell upon it, by the Errors and Convulsions in the first Management; and, in all Likelihood, many, if not most, of the *Indians* would have been converted to Christianity by this kind Method; the Country would have been full of People, by the Preservation of the many *Christians* and *Indians* that fell in the Wars between them. Besides, there would have been a Continuance of all those Nations of *Indians* that are now dwindled away to nothing by their frequent Removals, or are fled to other Parts; not to mention the Invitation that so much Success and Prosperity would have been for others to have gone over and settled there, instead of the Frights and Terrors that were produced by all those Misfortunes that happen'd.

(27. *Pocahontas* being thus married in the Year 1613, a firm Peace was concluded with her Father, tho' he would not trust himself at her Wedding. Both the *English* and *Indians* thought themselves intirely secure and quiet. This brought in the *Chicka-homony Indians* also, tho' not out of any Kindness or Respect to the *English*, but out of Fear of being, by their Assistance, brought under *Powhatan's* absolute Subjection, who used now and then to threaten and tyrannize over them.

℄ 28. Sir *Thomas Dale* returning for *England Anno* 1616. took with him Mr. *Rolf* and his Wife *Pocahontas*, who upon the Marriage, was Christen'd, and call'd *Rebecka*. He left Capt. *George Yardly* Deputy-Governour during his Absence, the Country being then intirely at Peace; and arriv'd at *Plimouth* the 12th of *June*.

Capt. *John smith* was at that Time in *England*, and hearing of the Arrival of *Pocahontas* at *Portsmouth*, used all the Means he could to express his Gratitude to her, as having formerly preserv'd his Life by the Hazard of her own: For, when by the Command of her Father, Capt. *Smith's* Head was upon the Block to have his Brains knock'd out, she saved his Head by laying her's close upon it. He was at that Time suddenly to imbark for *New-England*, and fearing he should sail before she got to *London*, he made an humble Petition to the Queen in her Behalf, which I here choose to give you in his own Words, because it will save me the Story at large.

℄ 29. Capt. Smith's PETITION *to Her* Majesty, *in Behalf of* Pocahontas, *Daughter to the* Indian *Emperor* Powhatan.

To the Most High and Vertuous Princess, Queen ANNE, of *Great Britain.*

Most Admir'd Madam,

The Love I bear my God, my King and Country, hath so often embolden'd me in the worst of extream Dangers, that now Honesty doth constrain me to presume thus far beyond my self, to present your Majesty this short Discourse. If Ingratitude be a deadly Poison to all honest Vertues, I must be guilty of that Crime, if I should omit any Means to be thankful.

So it was.

That about Ten Years ago, being in *Virginia*, and taken Prisoner by the Power of *Powhatan*, their chief King, I receiv'd from this great Savage exceeding great Courtesie, especially from his Son *Nantaquaus;* the manliest, comliest, boldest Spirit I ever saw in a Savage; and his Sister *Pocahontas*, the King's most dear and well beloved Daughter, being but a Child of Twelve or Thirteen Years of Age, whose compassionate pitiful Heart of my desperate Estate gave me much Cause to respect her. I being the first *Christian* this proud King and his grim Attendants ever saw, and thus inthrall'd in their barbarous Power; I cannot say I felt the least Occasion of Want, that was in the Power of those my mortal Foes to prevent, notwithstanding all their Threats. After some Six Weeks Fatting amongst those Savage Courtiers, at the Minute of my Execution she hazarded the Beating out of her own Brains to save mine, and not only that, but so prevail'd with her Father, that I was safely conducted to *James-Town*, where I found about Eight and Thirty miserable, poor and sick Creatures to keep Possession for all those large Territories of *Virginia*. Such was the Weakness of this poor Commonwealth, as had not the Savages fed us, we directly had starv'd.

And this Relief, *most Gracious Queen*, was commonly brought us by this Lady *Pocahontas*, notwithstanding all these Passages, when unconstant Fortune turn'd our Peace to War, this tender Virgin would still not spare to dare to visit us; and by her our Jars have been oft appeased, and our Wants still supplied. Were it the Policy of her Father thus to employ her, or the Ordinance of God thus to make her His Instrument, or her extraordinary Affection to our Nation, I know not: But of this I am sure, when her Father, with the utmost of his Policy and Power, sought to surprize me, having but Eighteen with me, the dark Night could not affright her from coming through the irksome Woods, and, with water'd Eyes, give me Intelligence, with her best Advice to escape his Fury; which had he known, he had surely slain her.

James-Town, with her wild Train, she as freely frequented as her Father's Habitation; and during the time of Two or Three Years, she, next under God, was still the Instrument to preserve this Colony from Death, Famine, and utter Confusion, which if, in those Times, had once been dissolv'd, *Virginia* might have lain, as it was at our first Arrival, till this Day. Since then, this Business having been turn'd and varied by many Accidents from what I left it, it is most certain, after a long and troublesome War, since my Departure, betwixt her Father and our Colony, all which Time she was not heard of, about Two Years after she herself was taken Prisoner, being so detain'd near Two Years longer, the Colony by that Means was reliev'd, Peace concluded, and at last, rejecting her barbarous Condition, she was married to an *English* Gentleman, with whom at this Present she is in *England*. The first *Christian* ever of that Nation: The first *Virginian* ever spake *English*, or had a Child in Marriage by an *English* Man. A Matter surely, if my Meaning be truly consider'd and well understood, worthy a Prince's Information.

Thus, *most Gracious Lady*, I have related to your Majesty what at your best Leisure our approv'd Histories will recount to you at large, as done in the Time of your Majesty's Life: And, however this might be presented you from a more worthy Pen, it cannot from a more honest Heart.

As yet I never begg'd any thing of the State, or any; and it is my want of Ability, and her exceeding Desert; your Birth, Means and Authority; her Birth, Vertue, Want and Simplicity, doth make me thus bold, humbly to beseech your Majesty to take this Knowledge of her, tho' it be from one so unworthy to be the Reporter as my self: Her Husband's Estate not being able to make her fit to attend your Majesty.

The most and least I can do, is to tell you this, and the rather because of her being of so great a Spirit, however her Stature. If she should not be well receiv'd, seeing this Kingdom may rightly have a Kingdom by her Means; her present Love to us, and Christianity, might turn to such Scorn and Fury, as to divert all this Good to the worst of Evil: Where finding that so Great a Queen should do her more Honour than she can imagine, for having been kind to her Subjects and Servants, 'twou'd so ravish her with Content, as to endear her dearest Blood to effect that your Majesty and all the King's honest Subjects most earnestly desire. And so I humbly kiss your gracious Hands, &c.

(Sign'd)

Dated June, *1616.*   *John Smith.*

ℭ 30. This Account was presented to her Majesty, and graciously received: But before Captain *Smith* sail'd for *New-England*, the *Indian* Princess arrived at *London*, and her Husband took Lodgings for her at *Branford*, to be a little out of the Smoak of the City, whither Capt. *Smith*, with some of her Friends, went to see her, and congratulate her Arrival, letting her know the Address he had made to the Queen in her Favour.

Till this Lady arrived in *England*, she had all along been inform'd that Capt. *Smith* was dead, because he had been diverted from that Colony by making Settlements in the Second Plantation, now call'd *New-England:* For which Reason, when she see him, she seem'd to think herself much affronted, for that they had dared to impose so gross an

Untruth upon her, and at first Sight of him turn'd away. It cost him a great deal of Intreaty, and some Hours Attendance, before she would do him the Honour to speak to him: But at last she was reconcil'd, and talk'd freely to him. She put him in mind of her former Kindnesses, and then upbraided him for his Forgetfulness of her, shewing by her Reproaches, that even a State of Nature teaches to abhor Ingratitude.

She had in her Retinue a Great Man of her own Nation, whose Name was *Uttamaccomack:* This Man had Orders from *Powhatan,* to count the People in *England,* and give him an Account of their Number. Now the *Indians* having no Letters among them, he at his going ashore provided a Stick, in which he was to make a Notch for every Man he see; but this Accomptant soon grew weary of that tedious Exercise, and threw his Stick away: And at his return, being asked by his King, *How many People there were; He desired him to count the Stars in the sky, the Leaves upon the Trees, and the Sand on the Seashore, for so many People* (he said) *were in* England.

❦ 31. *Pocahontas* had many Honours done her by the Queen upon Account of Capt. *Smith's* Story; and being introduced by the Lady *Delawarr,* she was frequently admitted to wait on her Majesty, and was publickly treated as a Prince's Daughter; she was carried to many Plays, Balls, and other publick Entertainments, and very respectfully receiv'd by all the Ladies about the Court. Upon all which Occasions she behaved her self with so much Decency, and show'd so much Grandure in her Deportment, that she made good the brightest Part of the Character Capt. *Smith* had given of her. In the mean while she gain'd the good Opinion of every Body, so much that the poor Gentleman her Husband had like to have been call'd to an Account for presuming to marry a Princess Royal without the King's Consent; because it had been suggested that he had taken Advantage of her being a Prisoner, and forc'd her to marry him. But upon a more perfect Representation of the Matter, his Majesty was pleased at last to declare himself satisfied.

Every Body paid this young Lady all imaginable Respect; and it is supposed, she wou'd have sufficiently acknowledged those Favours, had she lived to return to her own Country, by bringing the *Indians* to have a kinder Disposition towards the *English.* But upon her Return she was unfortunately taken ill at *Gravesend,* and died in a few Days after, giving great Testimony all the Time she lay sick, of her being a very good Christian. She left Issue one Son, nam'd *Thomas Rolfe,* whose Posterity is at this Day in good Repute in *Virginia.*

❦ 32. Captain *Yardly* made but a very ill Governour, he let the Buildings and Forts go to Ruine; not regarding the Security of the People against the *Indians,* neglecting the Corn, and applying all Hands to plant Tobacco, which promised the most immediate Gain. In this Condition they were when Capt. *Samuel Argall* was sent thither Governour, *Anno* 1617. who found the Number of People reduc'd to something more than Four Hundred, of which not above Half were fit for Labour. In the mean while the *Indians* mixing among 'em, got Experience daily in Fire-Arms, and some of 'em were instructed therein by the *English* themselves, and employ'd to hunt and kill wild Fowl for them. So great was their Security upon this Marriage: But Governour *Argall* not liking those Methods, regulated them on his Arrival, and Capt. *Yardly* return'd to *England.*

❦ 33. Governour *Argall* made the Colony flourish and increase wonderfully, and kept them in great Plenty and Quiet. The next Year, *viz.* Anno 1618, the Lord

Delawarr was sent over again with Two Hundred Men more for the Settlement, with other Necessaries suitable: But Sailing by the Western Islands, they met with contrary Winds, and great Sickness; so that about Thirty of them died, among which the Lord *Delawarr* was one. By which Means the Government there still continued in the Hands of Capt. *Argall.*

℄ 34.   *Powhatan* died in *April* the same Year, leaving his Second Brother *Itopatin* in Possession of his Empire, a Prince far short of the Parts of *Oppechancanough*, who by some was said to be his Elder Brother, and then King of *Chickahomony;* but he having debauch'd them from the Allegiance of *Powhatan*, was disinherited by him. This *Oppechancanough* was a cunning and a brave Prince, who soon grasp'd all the Empire to himself: But at first they jointly renew'd the Peace with the *English*, upon the Accession of *Itopatin* to the Crown.

℄ 35.   Governour *Argall* flourishing thus under the Blessings of Peace and Plenty, and having no Occasion of Fear or Disturbance from the *Indians*, sought new Occasions of incouraging the Plantation. To that End he intended a Coasting Voyage to the Northward, to view the Places where the *English* Ships had so often laded; and if he miss'd them, to reach the Fisheries on the Banks of *Newfoundland*, and so settle a Trade and Correspondence either with the One or the Other. In Accomplishing whereof, as he touch'd at Cape *Codd*, he was inform'd by the *Indians*, That some White People like him were come to inhabit to the Northward of them, upon the Coast of their Neighbouring Nations. Capt. *Argall* not having heard of any *English* Plantation that Way, was jealous that it might be (as it proved) the People of some other Nation. And being very zealous for the Honour and Benefit of *England*, he resolved to make Search according to the Information he had receiv'd, and see who they were. Accordingly he found the Settlement, and a Ship riding before it. This belong'd to some *French* Men, who had fortified themselves upon a small Mount in the North of *New-England.*

℄ 36.   His unexpected Arrival so confounded the *French*, that they cou'd make no Preparation for Resistance on Board their Ship; which Captain *Argall* drew so close to, that with his small Arms he beat all the Men from the Deck, so that they cou'd not use their Guns, their Ship having only a single Deck. Among others, there were Two Jesuits on Board, one of which being more bold than wise, with all that Disadvantage, endeavor'd to fire one of their Cannon, and was shot dead for his Pains.

Capt. *Argall* having taken the Ship, landed and went before the Fort, summoning it to surrender. The Garrison ask'd Time to advise: But that being denied them, they stole privately away, and fled into the Woods. Upon this Capt. *Argall* enter'd the Fort, and lodged there that Night; and the next Day the *French* came to him, and surrender'd themselves. It seems the King of *France* had granted them a Patent for this Settlement, but they gave it up to Capt. *Argall* to be cancell'd. He used them very well, and suffer'd such as had a Mind to return to *France*, to seek their Passage among the Ships of the Fishery: But obliged them to desert this Settlement. And those that were willing to go to *Virginia*, he took with him.

℄ 37.   These People were under the Conduct of Two Jesuits, who upon taking a Pique against their Governour in *Acadia*, named *Biencourt*, had lately separated from a *French* Settlement at *Port-Royal*, lying in the Bay, upon the South-West Part of *Acadia.*

❬ 38. As Governour *Argall* was about to return to *Virginia*, Father *Biard*, the surviving Jesuit (out of Malice to *Biencourt*) told him of this *French* Settlement at *Port-Royal*, and offer'd to Pilot him to it; which Governour *Argall* readily accepted of. With the same Ease he took that Settlement also; where the *French* had sow'd and reap'd, built Barns, Mills, and other Conveniencies, which Capt. *Argall* did no Damage to: But unsettled them, and obliged them to make a Desertion from thence. He gave these the same Leave he had done the Others to dispose of themselves; some whereof return'd to *France*, and others went to settle up the River of *Canada*. After this Governour *Argall* return'd satisfied with the Provision and Plunder he had got in those Two Settlements.

❬ 39. The Report of these Exploits soon reach'd *England;* and whether they were approved or no, being acted without particular Direction, I have not learn'd: But certain it is, that in *April* following there arrived a small Vessel, which did not stay for any Thing, but took on Board Governour *Argall*, and return'd for *England.* He left Captain *Nathaniel Powell* Deputy: And soon after Captain *Yardly* being Knighted, was sent Governour thither again.

❬ 40. Very great Supplies of Cattle and other Provisions were sent there that Year, and likewise 1000 or 1200 Men. They resettled all their old Plantations that had been deserted, made Additions to the Number of the Council, and call'd an Assembly of Burgesses from all Parts of the Country, which were to be elected by the People in their several Plantations.

These Burgesses met the Governour and Council at *James-Town* in *May*, 1620, and sate in Consultation in the same House with them, as the Method of the *Scots* Parliament is, debating Matters for the Improvement and good Government of the Country.

This was the First General Assembly that ever was held there. I heartily wish, tho' they did not unite their Houses again, they wou'd however unite their Endeavours and Affections for the Good of the Country.

❬ 41. In *August* following a *Dutch* Man of War landed Twenty *Negroes* for Sale; which were the First of that kind that were carried into the Country.

❬ 42. This Year they bounded the Corporations, (as they call'd them:) But there does not remain among the Records any one Grant of these Cor[po]rations. There is enter'd a Testimony of Governour *Argall*, concerning the Bounds of the Corporation of *James* City, declaring his Knowledge thereof; and this is in one of the New transcribed Books of Records: But there is not to be found one Word of the Charter or Patent it self of this Corporation.

Then also they apportion'd and laid out Lands in several Allotments, *viz.* to the Company in several Places, to the Governour, to a College, to *Glebes*, and to several particular Persons; many new Settlements were made in *James* and *York* Rivers. The People now knew their own Property, and having the Encouragement of Working for their own Advantage, many became very industrious, and began to vie one with another, in Planting, Building, and other Improvements. Two Gentlemen went over as Deputies to the Company, for the Management of their Lands, and those of the College. All Thoughts of Danger from the *Indians* were laid aside. Several great Gifts were made to the Church and College, and for the Bringing up Young *Indians* at School. Forms were made, and Rules appointed for granting Patents for Land, upon the Condition of importing Goods and Persons to supply and increase the Colony. And all there then began to think themselves the happiest People in the World.

¶ 43.   Thus *Virginia* continued to flourish and increase, great Supplies continually arriving, and new Settlements being made all over the Country. A Salt-Work was set up at Cape *Charles*, on the Eastern Shore; and an Iron-work at *Falling-Creek*, in *James* River, where they made Proof of good Iron Oar, and brought the whole Work so near Perfection, that they writ Word to the Company in *London*, that they did not doubt but to finish the Work, and have plentiful Provision of Iron for them by the next *Easter*. At that time the Fame of the Plenty and Riches in which the *English* lived there, was very great: and Sir *George Yardly* now had all the Appearance of making Amends for the Errors of his former Government. Nevertheless he let them run into the same Sleepyness and Security as before, neglecting all Thoughts of a necessary Defence, which laid the foundations of the following Calamities.

¶ 44.   But the Time of his Government being near expired, Sir *Francis Wyat*, then a young Man, had a Commission to succeed him. The People began to grow numerous, Thirteen Hundred settling there that Year; which was the Occasion of making so much Tobacco, as to overstock the Market. Wherefore his Majesty, out of Pity to the Country, sent his Commands, That they should not suffer their Planters to make above One Hundred Pounds of Tobacco *per* Man; for the Market was so low, that he cou'd not afford to give 'em above Three Shillings the Pound for it. He advised them rather to turn their spare Time towards providing Corn and Stock, and towards the Making of Potash, or other Manufactures.

It was, *October*, 1621, that Sir *Francis Wyat* arrived Governour, and in *November* Capt. *Newport* arrived with Fifty Men imported at his own Charge, besides Passengers; and made a Plantation on *Newport's News*, naming it after himself. The Governour made a Review of all the Settlements, and suffer'd new Ones to be made even as far [as] *Patowmeck* River. This ought to be observed of the Eastern Shore *Indians*, that they never gave the *English* any Trouble, but courted and befriended them from first to last. Perhaps the *English*, by the Time they came to settle those Parts, had consider'd how to rectifie their former Mismanagement, and learn'd better Methods of regulating their Trade with the *Indians*, and of treating them more kindly than at first.

¶ 45.   *Anno*, 1622, Inferior Courts were first appointed by the General Assembly, under the Name of *County Courts*, for Tryal of Minute Causes; the Governour and Council still remaining Judges of the Supream Court of the Colony. In the mean time, by the great Increase of People, and the long Quiet they had enjoy'd among the *Indians*, since the Marriage of *Pocahontas*, and the Accession of *Oppechancanough* to the Imperial Crown; all Men were lull'd into a fatal Security, and became every where familiar with the *Indians*, Eating, Drinking and Sleeping amongst them; by which Means they became perfectly acquainted with all our *English* Strength, and the Use of our Arms: Knowing at all Times, when and where to find our People; whether at Home, or in the Woods; in Bodies, or disperst; in Condition of Defence, or indefencible. This Exposing of their Weekness gave them Occasion to think more contemptibly of them, than otherwise, perhaps, they would have done; for which Reason they became more peevish, and more hardy to attempt any thing against them.

℄ 46.   Thus upon the Loss of one of their leading Men, (a War Captain, as they call him,) who was likewise supposed to be justly kill'd, *Oppechancanough* took Affront, and in Revenge laid the Plot of a general Massacre of the *English*, to be executed on the 22d of *March*, 1622, a little before Noon, at a Time when our Men were all at Work abroad in their Plantations, disperst and unarm'd. This Hellish Contrivance was to take Effect upon all the several Settlements at one and the same Instant, except on the Eastern Shore, whither this Plot did not reach. The *Indians* had been made so familiar with the *English*, as to borrow their Boats and Canoes to cross the Rivers in, when they went to consult with their Neighbouring *Indians* upon this execrable Conspiracy. And, to colour their Design the better, they brought Presents of Deer, Turkies, Fish and Fruits to the *English* the Evening before. The very Morning of the Massacre, they came freely and unarm'd among them, eating with them, and behaving themselves with the same Freedom and Friendship as formerly, till the very Minute they were to put their Plot in Execution. Then they fell to Work all at once every where, knocking the *English* unawares on the Head, some with their Hatchets, which they call *Tommahauks*, others with the Hows and Axes of the *English* themselves, shooting at those who escap'd the Reach of their Hands; sparing neither Age nor Sex, but destroying Man, Woman and Child, according to their cruel Way of leaving none behind to bear Resentment. But whatever was not done by Surprize that Day, was left undone, and many that made early Resistance escaped.

By the Account taken of the *Christians* murder'd that Morning, they were found to be Three Hundred Forty Seven, most of them falling by their own Instruments, and Working-Tools.

℄ 47.   The Massacre had been much more general, had not this Plot been providentially discover'd to the *English* some Hours before the Execution. It happen'd thus:

Two *Indians* that used to be employ'd by the *English* to hunt for them, happen'd to lie together, the Night before the Massacre, in an *English* Man's House, where one of them was employ'd. The *Indian* that was the Guest fell to perswading the other to rise and kill his Master, telling him, that he would do the same by his own the next Day. Whereupon he discover'd the whole Plot that was design'd to be executed on the Morrow. But the other, instead of entering into the Plot, and murdering his Master, got up (under Pretence of going to execute his Comarde's Advice) went into his Master's Chamber, and reveal'd to him the whole Story that he had been told. The Master herupon arose, secur'd his own House, and before Day got to *James-Town*, which, together with such Plantations as cou'd receive Notice time enough, was saved by this Means; the rest, as they happen'd to be watchful in their Defence, also escaped: But such as were surpriz'd, were massacred. Captain *Croshaw* in his Vessel at *Patowmeck*, had Notice also given him by a young *Indian*, by which means he came off untouch'd.

℄ 48.   The Occasion upon which *Oppechancanough* took Affront was this. The War Captain mention'd before to have been kill'd, was called *Nemattanow*. He was an active *Indian*, a great Warriour, and in much Esteem among them; so much, that they believed him to be invulnerable, and immortal, because he had been in very many Conflicts, and escaped untouch'd from them all. He was also a very cunning Fellow, and took great Pride in preserving and increasing this their Superstition concerning him, affecting every thing that was odd and prodigious to work upon their Admiration. For which Purpose he wou'd often dress himself up with Feathers after a fantastick Manner, and by much Use of that Ornament, obtain'd among the *English* the Nickname of *Jack of the Feather*.

This *Nemattanow* coming to a private Settlement of one *Morgan*, who had several Toys which he had a mind to, perswaded him to go to *Pamunky* to dispose of them. He gave him Hopes what mighty Bargains he might meet with there, and kindly offer'd him his Assistance. At last *Morgan* yielded to his Perswasion: But was no more heard of; and it is believ'd, that *Nemattanow* kill'd him by the Way, and took away his Treasure. For within a few Days, this *Nemattanow* return'd to the same House with *Morgan's* Cap upon his Head; where he found Two sturdy Boys, who ask'd for their Master. He very frankly told them, he was dead. But they, knowing the Cap again, suspected the Villain had kill'd their Master, and wou'd have had him before a Justice of Peace: But he refused to go, and very insolently abused them. Whereupon they shot him down, and as they were carrying him to the Governour, he died.

As he was dying, he earnestly press'd the Boys to promise him Two Things; First, That they wou'd not tell how he was kill'd; and, Secondly, That they wou'd bury him among the *English*. So great was the Pride of this vain Heathen, that he had no other Thoughts at his Death, but the Ambition of being esteem'd after he was dead, as he had endeavour'd to make them believe of him while he was alive, *viz.* That he was Invulnerable and Immortal; tho' his increasing Faintness convinc'd himself of the Falsity of both. He imagined that being buried among the *English*, perhaps, might conceal his Death from his own Nation, who might think him translated to some happier Country. Thus he pleased himself to the last Gasp with the Boys Promises to carry on the Delusion. This was reckon'd all the Provocation given to that haughty and revengeful Man *Oppechancanough*, to act this bloody Tragedy, and to take indefatigable Pains to engage in so horrid Villany all the Kings and Nations bordering upon the *English* Settlements, on the Western Shore of *Chesepeak*.

℄ 49.   This gave the *English* a fair Pretence of endeavouring the total Extirpation of the *Indians*, but more-especially of *Oppec[h]ancanough*, and his Nation. Accordingly they set themselves about it, making use of the *Roman* Maxim, (*Faith is not to be kept with Hereticks*) to obtain their Ends. For, after some Months fruitless Pursuit of them, who cou'd too dexterously hide themselves in the Woods, the *English* pretended Articles of Peace, giving them all manner of fair Words and Promises of Oblivion. They design'd thereby (as their own Letters now on Record, and their own Actions thereupon, prove) to draw the *Indians* back, and intice them to plant their Corn on their Habitations nearest adjoining to the *English;* and then to cut it up when the Summer should be too far spent to leave them Hopes of another Crop that Year; by which Means they proposed to bring them to want Necessaries, and starve. And the *English* did so far accomplish their Ends, as to bring the *Indians* to plant their Corn at their usual Habitations, whereby they gain'd an Opportunity of repaying them some part of the Debt in their own Coin; for they fell suddenly upon them, cut to Pieces such of them as could not make their Escape, and afterwards totally destroy'd their Corn.

℄ 50.   Another Effect of the Massacre of the *English*, was the Reducing all their Settlements again to Six or Seven in Number, for their better Defence. Besides, it was such a Disheartening to some good Projects, then just advancing, that to this Day they have never been put in Execution, namely, the Glass-Houses in *James-Town*, and the Iron-Work at *Falling-Creek*, which has been already mention'd. The Massacre fell so hard upon this last Place, that no Soul was saved, but a Boy and a Girl, who, with great Difficulty, hid themselves.

The Superintendent of this Iron-Work had also discover'd a Vein of Lead Oar, which he kept private, and made use of it to furnish all the Neighbours with Bullets and Shot. But he being cut off with the rest, and the Secret not having been communicated, this Lead Mine could never after be found; till Colonel *Byrd*, some few Years ago, prevail'd with an *Indian* under Pretence of Hunting, to give him a Sign, by dropping his *Tomahawk* at the Place, (he not daring publickly to discover it, for fear of being murder'd.) The Sign was accordingly given, and the Company at that Time found several Pieces of good Lead Oar upon the Surface of the Ground, and mark'd the Trees thereabouts: Notwithstanding which, I know not by what Witchcraft it happens, but no Mortal to this Day could ever find that Place again, tho' it be upon part of the Colonel's own Possessions. And so it rests, till Time and thicker Settlements discover it.

¶ 51. Thus the Company of Adventurers having, by those frequent Acts of Mismanagement, met with vast Losses and Misfortunes; Many grew sick of it, and parted with their Shares; and others came into their Places, and promoted the sending in fresh Recruits of Men and Goods. But the chief Design of all parties concern'd was to fetch away the Treasure from thence, aiming more at sudden Gain, than to form any regular Colony, or establish a Settlement in such a Manner, as to make it a lasting Happiness to the Country.

Several Gentlemen went over upon their particular Stocks, separate from that of the Company, with their own Servants and Goods, each designing to obtain Land from the Government, as Capt. *Newport* had done; or, at least, to obtain Patents according to the Regulation for granting Lands to Adventurers. Others sought their Grants of the Company in *London*, and obtain'd Authorities and Jurisdictions, as well as Land, distinct from the Authority of the Government, which was the Foundation of great Disorder, and the Occasion of their following Misfortunes. Among others, one Capt. *Martin*, having made very considerable Preparations towards a Settlement, obtain'd a suitable Grant of Land, and was made of the Council there. But he grasping still at more, hanker'd after Dominion, as well as Possession, and caused so many Differences, that at last he put all Things into Distraction; insomuch, that the *Indians*, still seeking Revenge, took Advantage of these Dissentions, and fell foul again of the *English*, gratifying their Vengence with new Blood-shed.

¶ 52. The fatal Consequences of the Company's Male-Administration cried so loud, that King *Charles* the First, coming to the Crown of *England*, had a tender Concern for the poor People that had been betray'd thither, and lost. Upon which Consideration he dissolv'd the Company in the Year 1626, reducing the Country and Government into his own immediate Direction, appointing the Governor and Council himself, and ordering all Patents and Process to issue in his own Name; reserving only to himself an easie Quit-Rent of Two Shillings for every Hundred Acres of Land, and so *pro rato*.

Ebenezer Cook

(c. 1667–c. 1732)

Whether the title "A Poet Laureat of Maryland" was indeed bestowed on Ebenezer Cook by Lord Baltimore or was only assumed in jest by the poet himself, it is certain that the witty satire of his *The Sot-Weed Factor* has no parallel in early colonial literature. In the rough burlesque of Hudibrastic verse, Cook simultaneously skewers the pretensions of his tobacco merchant ("sot-weed factor") narrator even as he derides the "planting Rabble" with whom he conducts his business. Though Cook's provincial audience would surely have recognized the purposeful absurdity of his portrayals of backwoods life, British readers likely assumed them to be factual.

Probably born in England around 1667, Cook was himself the son of a tobacco farmer. He appears to have divided his time between Maryland and Britain and was in London when *The Sot-Weed Factor* was published in 1708 (evidence suggests it may have been written as early as 1702). He inherited and subsequently sold a share of his family's estate, electing to support himself by practicing law, though it seems that he was barely able to subsist in this profession. Through his association with the public printer William Parks, Cook published a number of other works, most notably "An Elogy on the Death of Thomas Bordley" (1726). "A History of Bacon's Rebellion" (1731), as well as *Sot-weed Redivivus* (1730), in which the same factor of the earlier work narrates a much more serious treatment of agrarian issues of the day. In his later poetry, Cook makes a number of references to his poverty, and after his 1732 verses "In Memory of . . . Benedict Leonard Calvert," he disappears into obscurity.

The Sot-Weed Factor explodes the myth of America as a new Eden, which was so prevalent in promotional literature of the day, and with his comical descriptions of the rustic inhabitants of Maryland who nevertheless easily dupe the pretentious narrator, Cook also serves as a precursor of the Southwestern humorists.

The Sot-Weed Factor, or A Voyage to Maryland

> Condemn'd by Fate to way-ward Curse,
> Of Friends unkind, and empty Purse:
> Plagues worse than fill'd Pandora's Box,
> I took my leave of Albion's Rocks:
> With heavy heart, concern'd that I
> Was forc'd my Native soil to fly.
> And the Old World must bid good-buy.
> But Heav'n ordain'd it should be so.
> And to repine is vain we know:
> Freighted with Fools, from Plymouth sound,
> To Mary-Land our ship was bound.
> Where we arriv'd in dreadful Pain,
> Shock'd by the Terrours of the Main:
> For full three Months, our wavering Boat.
> Did thro' the surley Ocean float.

And furious storms and threat'ning Blasts,
Both tore our Sails and sprung our Masts:
Wearied, yet pleased, we did escape
Such ills, we anchor'd at the Cape.
But weighing soon, we plough'd the Bay,
To Cove it in Piscato-way,
Intending there to open Store
I put myself and Goods a-shore:
Where soon repair'd a numerous Crew,
In Shirts and Drawers of Scotch-cloth Blue.
With neither Stockings, Hat, nor Shooe.
These Sot-weed Planters Crowd the Shoar,
In Hue as tawny as a Moor:
Figures so strange, no God design'd,
To be a part of Humane Kind:
But wanton Nature, void of Rest,
Moulded the brittle Clay in Jest.
At last a Fancy ver odd
Took me. This was the Land of Nod.
Planted at first, when Vagrant Cain,
His Brother had unjustly slain:
then conscious of the Crime he'd done,
From Vengeance dire, he hither run;
And in a Hat supinely dwelt,
The first in Furs and Sot-weed dealt.
And ever since his Time, the Place,
Has harbour'd a detested Race;
Who when they cou'd not live at Home,
For Refuge to these Worlds did roam;
In hopes by Flight they might prevent,
The Devil and his fell intent;
Obtain from Tripple Tree repreive,
And Heav'n and Hell alike deceive:
but e're their Manners I display,
I think it fit I open lay
My Entertainment by the way:
That Strangers well may be aware on,
What homely Diet they must fare on.
To touch that Shoar, where no good Sense is found,
But Conversation's lost, and Manners drown'd.
I crost unto the other side,
A River whose impetuous Tide,
The Savage Borders does divide;
In such a shining odd invention,
I scarce can give its due Dimension.
The Indians call this watery Waggon
Canoo, a Vessel none can brag on;
Cut from a Popular-Tree, or Pine,

And fashioned like a trough for swine:
In this most noble Fishing-Boat,
I boldly put myself afloat:
Standing Erect with legs stretch'd wide,
We paddl'd to the other side:
Where being Landed safe by hap,
As Sol fell into Thetis Lap
A ravenous Gang bent on the stroul,
Of Wolves for Prey, began to howl;
This put me in a pannick Fright,
Least I should be devoured quite:
But as I there a musing stood,
And quite benighted in a Wood.
A Female Voice pierc'd thro' my Ears.
Crying, You Rogue drive home the Steers
I listen'd to th' attractive sound,
And straight a Herd of cattel found
Drove by a Youth, and homewards bound:
Cheer'd with the sight, I straight thought fit,
To ask where I a Bed might get.
The surley Peasant bid me stay,
And ask'd from whom I'de run away.
Surprized at such a saucy Word,
I instantly lugged out my Sword:
Swearing I was no Fugitive.
But from Great-Britain did arrive.
In hopes I better there might Thrive.
To which he mildly made reply
I beg your Pardon, Sir that I
Should talk to you Unmannerly;
But if you please to go with me
To yonder House, you'll welcome be.
Encountring soon the smoaky Seat,
The Planter old did thus me greet:
"Whether you come from Goal or Colledge,
"You're welcome to my certain Knowledge;
"And if you please all Night to stay,
"My Son shall put you in the way."
Which offer I most kindly took.
And for a Seat did round me look:
When presently amongst the rest,
He plac'd his unknown English Guest,
Who found them drinking for a whet,
A Cask of Syder on the Fret,
Till supper came upon the Table,
On which I fed whilst I was able.
So after hearty Entertainment,
Of Drink and Victuals without Payment;

For Planters Tables, you must know,
Are free for all that come and go.
While Pon and Milk, with Mush well stoar'd
In wooden Dishes grac'd the board;
With Homine and Syder-pap,
(Which scarce a hungry Dog would lap)
Well stuff'd with Fat, from Bacon fry'd,
Or with Molossus dulcify'd.
Then out our Landlord pulls a Pouchn,
As greasy as the Leather Couch
On which he sat, and straight begun
To load with Weed his Indian Gun;
In length, scarce longer than one's Finger,
Or that for which the Ladies linger:
His Pipe smoak'd out with aweful Grace,
With aspect grave and solemn pace;
The reverend Sire walks to a Chest,
Of all his Furniture the best,
Closely confin'd within a Room,
Which seldom felt the weight of Broom;
From thence he lugs a Cag of Rum,
And nodding to me, thus begun:
I find, says he, you don't much care,
For this our Indian Country Fare;
But let me tell you, Friend of mine,
You may be glad of it in time,
Tho' now your Stomach is so fine;
And if within this Land you stay,
You'll find it true what I do say.
This said, the Rundlet up he threw,
And bending backwards strongly drew:
I pluck'd as stoutly for my part,
Altho' it made me sick at Heart,
And got so soon into my Head
I scarce cou'd find my way to Bed;
Where I was instantly convey'd
By one who pass'd for Chamber-Maid;
Tho' by her loose and sluttish Dress,
She rather seem'd a Bedlam-Bess.
Curious to know from whence she came,
I prest her to declare her Name
She Blushing seem'd to hide her Eyes,
And thus in Civil Terms replies:
In better Times, e'er to this Land,
I was unhappily Trapann'd,
Perchance as well I did appear,
As any Lord or Lady here,
Not then a Slave for twice two Year.

My Cloaths were fashionably new,
Nor were my Shifts of Linnen Blue
But things are changed now at the Hoie,
I daily work, and Bare-foot go.
In weeding Corn or feeding Swine,
I spend my melancholy Time.
Kidnap'd and Fool'd, I hither fled,
To shun a hated Nuptial Bed.
And to my cost already find,
Worse Plagues than those I left behind.
Whate'er the Wanderer did profess.
Good-faith I cou'd not choose but guess
The Cause which brought her to this place.
Was supping e'er the Priest said Grace,
Quick as my Thoughts, the Slave was fled,
(Her Candle left to shew my Bed)
Which made of Feathers soft and good,
Close in the Chimney-corner stood;
I threw me down expecting Rest,
To be in golden Slumbers blest:
But soon a noise disturb'd my quiet.
And plagu'd me with nocturnal Riot:
A Puss which in the ashes lay,
With grunting Pig began a Fray:
And prudent Dog, that Feuds might cease,
Most strongly bark'd to keep the Peace.
This Qarrel scarcely was decided,
By stick that ready lay provided:
But Reynard arch and cunning Loon.
Broke into my Appartment soon:
In hot pursuit of Ducks and Geese,
With fell intent the same to seize:
Their Cackling Plaints with strange surprize,
Chac'd Sleeps thick Vapours from my eyes:
Raging I jump'd upon the Floar,
And like a Drunken Saylor swore;
With sword I fiercely laid about,
And soon dispers'd the Feather'd Rout:
The Poultry out of Window flew,
And Reynard cautiously withdrew:
The Dogs who this Encounter heard,
Fiercly themselves to aid me rear'd,
And to the Place of Combat run,
Exactly as the Field was won.
Fretting and hot as roasting Capon,
And greasy as a Flitch of Bacon;
I to the Orchard did repair,
To Breathe the cool and open Air,

Expecting there the rising Day,
Extended on a Bank I lay;
But Fortune here, that saucy Whore,
Disturb'd me worse and plagu'd me more,
Than she had done the night before.
Hoarse croaking Frogs did 'bout me ring,
Such Peals the Dead to Life wou'd bring,
A Noise might move their Wooden King.
I stuff'd my ears with Cotten white
For fear of being deaf out-right,
And curst the melancholy Night:
But soon my Vows I did recant,
And Hearing as a Blessing grant;
When a confounded Rattle-Snake,
With hissing made my Heart to ake:
Not knowing how to fly the Foe,
Or whether in the Dark to go;
By strange good Luck, I took a Tree,
Prepar'd by Fate to set me free;
Where riding on a Limb a-stride,
Night and the Branches did me hide,
And I the Devil and Snake defy'd.
Nor yet from Plagues, exempted quite,
The curst Muskitoes did me bite;
Till rising Morn' and blushing Day,
Drove both my Fears and Ills away;
And from Night's Errors set me free.
Discharg'd from hospitable Tree;
I did to Planters Booth repair,
And there at Breakfast nobly Fare,
On rashier broil'd of infant Bear:
I thought the Cub delicious Meat,
Which ne'er did ought but Chesnuts eat,
Nor was young Orsin's flesh the worse,
Because he suck'd a Pagan Nurse.
Our Breakfast done, my Landlord stout,
Handed a Glass of Rum about;
Pleas'd with the Treatment I did find,
I took my leave of Host so kind;
Who to oblige me, did provide,
His eldest Song to be my Guide.
And lent me Horses of his own,
A skittish Colt, and aged rhoan,
The four-leg'd prop of his wife Joan.
Steering our barks in Trot or Pace,
We sail'd directly for a place
In Mary-Land of high renown,
Known by the name of Battle-Town.

To view the Crowds did there resort.
Which Justice made, and Law their sport,
In that sagacious country Court:
Scarce had we enter'd on the way,
Which thro' thick Woods and Marshes lay;
But Indians strange did soon appear,
In hot persuit of wounded deer;
No mortal creature can express,
His wild fantastick Air and Dress;
His painted Skin in colours dy'd,
His sable Hair in Satchel ty'd,
Shew'd Savages not free from Pride:
His tawny Thighs, and Bosom bare,
Disdain'd a useless Coat to wear,
Scorn'd Summer's Heat, and Winters Air;
His manly Shoulders such as please,
Widows and Wives, were bath'd in Grease
Of Cub and Bear, whose supple Oil,
Prepar'd his Limbs 'gainst Heat or Toil.
Thus naked Pict in Battel faught,
Or undisguis'd his Mistress sought;
And knowing well his Ware was good,
Refus'd to screen it with a Hood:
His Visage dun, and chin that ne'er
Did Raizor feel or Scissers bear,
Or knew the ornament of Hair,
Look'd sternly Grim, surpriz'd with Fear,
I spur'd my Horse as he drew near:
But Rhoan who better knew than I,
The little Cause I had to fly;
Seem'd by his solemn steps and pace,
resolv'd I shou'd the Specter face,
Nor faster mov'd, tho' spur'd and lick'd,
Than Balaam's Ass by Prophet kick'd.
Kekicknitop the Heathen cry'd;
How is it Tom. My friend replyd,
Judging from thence the Brute was civel,
I boldly fac'd the Courteous Devil;
And lugging out a Dram of Rum,
I gave his Tawny worship some;
Who in his language as I guess,
(My Guide informing me no less,)
Implored the Devil, me to bless.
I thank'd him for his good Intent,
And forwards on my Journey went,
Discoursing as along I rode,
Whether his Race was framed by God
Or whether some Malignant pow'r,

Contriv'd them in an evil hour
And from his own Infernal Look;
Their Dusky form and Image took:
From thence we fell to Argument
Whence Peopled was the Continent.
My friend suppos'd Tartarians wild,
Or Chinese from their Home exiled;
Wandering thro' Mountains hid with Snow,
and Rills did in the valleys flow,
Far to the South of Mexico:
Broke thro' the Bars which Nature cast,
and wide unbeaten Regions past,
Till near those Streams the humane deludge roll'd,
Which sparkling shin'd with glittering Sands of Gold,
And fetch Pizarro from the Iberian Shoar,
To Rob the Natives of their fatal Stoar.
I Smil'd to hear my young Logician,
Thus Reason like a Politician;
Who ne're by Fathers Pains and Earning
Had got at Mother Cambridge learning;
Where Lubber youth just free from birch
Most stoutly drink to prop the Church:
Nora with Grey Grout had taken Pains
To purge his Head and Cleanse his Reines:
And in obedience to the Colledge
Had pleas'd himself with carnal Knowledge:
And tho' I lik'd the youngester's Wit,
I judg'd the Truth he had not hit;
And could not choose but smile to think
What they could do for Meat and Drink,
Who o'er so many Desarts ran,
With Brats and Wives in Caravan:
Unless perchance they'd got the Trick,
To eat no more than Porker sick;
Or could with well contented Maws.
Quarter like Bears upon their Paws.
Thinking his Reasons to confute,
I gravely thus commenc'd Dispute,
And urg'd that tho' a Chinese Host,
Might penetrate this Indian Coast;
Yet this was certainly most true,
They never cou'd the Isles subdue;
For knowing naot to steer a Boat,
They could not on the Ocean float,
Or plant their Sunburnt Colonies,
In Regions parted by the Seas:
I thence inferr'd Phænicians old,
Discover'd first with Vessels bold

These Western Shoars, and planted here,
Returning once or twice a Year,
With Naval Stoars and Lasses kind,
To comfort those were left behind;
Till by the Winds and Tempest toar,
From their intended Golden Shoar;
They suffer'd Ship-wreck, or were drown'd,
And lost the World so newly found.
But after long and learn'd Contention,
We could not finish our dissention:
And when that both had talk'd their fill,
We had the self same Notion still.
Thus Parson grave well real and Sage,
does in dispute with Priest engage;
The one protests they are not Wise,
Who judge by Sense and trust their Eyes;
And vows he'd burn for it at Stake,
That Man may God his Maker make;
The other smiles at his Religion,
And vows he's but a learned Widgeon:
And when they have empty'd all their stoar
From Books and Fathers, are not more
Convinc'd or wiser than before.
Scarce had we finish'd serious Story,
But I espy'd the Town before me,
And roaring Planters on the ground,
Drinking of Healths in Circle round:
Dismounting Steed with friendly Guide,
Our horses to a Tree we ty'd,
and forwards pass'd amongst the Rout,
To chuse convenient Quarters out:
But being none were to be found,
we sat like others on the ground
Carousing Punch in open Air
Till Cryer did the Court declare;
The planting Rabble being met,
Their Drunken Worships likewise set:
Cryer proclaims that Noise shou'd cease,
And streight the Lawyers broke the Peace:
Wrangling for Plaintif and Defendant,
I thought they ne'er wou'd make an en on't:
With nonsense, stuff, and false quotations,
With brazen Lyes and Allegations;
And in the splitting of the Cause,
They us'd such motion with their Paws,
As shew their zeal was strongly bent,
In Blows to end the Argument.
A reverend Judge, who to the shame

Of all the Bench, cou'd write his Name;
As Petty-fogger took offence,
And wonder'd at his Impudence.
My Neighbour Dash with scorn replies,
And in the face of Justice flies:
The Bench in fury streight divide,
And Scribbles take, or Judges side;
The Jury, Lawyers, and their Clyents,
Contending, fight like earth-born Gyants:
Bust Sheriff wily lay perdue,
Hoping indictments wou'd ensue,
And when . . .
A Hat or Wig fell in the way,
He seiz'd them for the Queen as stray:
The court adjourn'd in usual manner,
In Battle Blood and fractious Clamour;
I thought it proper to provide,
A Lodging for myself and Guide,
So to our Inn we march'd away,
Which at a litle distance lay;
Where all things were in such Confusion,
I thought the World at its conclusion:
A Herd of Planters on the ground,
O'er-whelm'd with Punch, dead drunk we found:
Others were fighting and contending.
Some burnt their Cloaths to save the mending.
A few whose Heads by frequent use,
Could better bare the potent Juice,
Gravely debated State Affairs.
Whilst I most nimbly trip'd up Stairs;
Leaving my Friend discoursing oddly,
And mixing things Prophane and Godly.
Just then beginning to be Drunk,
As from the company I slunk,
To every Room and Nook I crept,
In hopes I might have somewhere slept;
But all the bedding was possest
By one or other drunken Guest:
But after looking long about,
I found an antient Corn-loft out.
Glad that I might in quiet sleep,
And there my bones unfractur'd keep.
I lay'd me down secure from Fray,
And soundly snor'd till break of Day:
When waking fresh I sat upright,
And found my Shoes were vanished quite,
Hat, Wig, and Stocking, all were fled
From this extended Indian Bed:

Vext at the Loss of Goods and Chattel,
I swore I'd give the Rascal battel,
Who had abus'd me in this sort.
And Merchant Stranger made his Sport.
I furiously descended Ladder:
No Hare in March was ever madder:
In vain I search'd for my Apparel.
And did with Host and Servants quarrel;
For one whose Mind did much aspire
To Mischief, threw them in the Fire;
Equip't with neither Hat nor Shooe,
I did my coming hither rue,
And doubtful thought what I should do:
Then looking round, I saw my Friend
Lie naked on a Tables end;
A Sight so dismal to behold,
One wou'd have judg'd him dead and cold;
When wringing of his bloody Nose,
By fighting got we my suppose;
I found him not so fast asleep,
Might give his Friends a cause to weep:
Rise Oronooko, rise, said I,
And from this Hell and Bedlam fly.
My Guide starts up, and in amaze,
With blood-shot Eyes did round him gaze;
At length with many a sigh and groan,
He went in search of aged Rhoan;
But Rhoan, tho' seldom us'd to faulter,
Had fairly this time slipt his Halter;
And not content at Night to stay
Ty'd up from Fodder, ran away:
After my Guide to ketch him ran,
And so I lost both Horse and Man;
Which Disappointment, tho' so great,
Did only Mirth and Jests create:
Till one more Civil than the rest,
In Conversation for the best,
Observing that for want of Rhoan,
I should be left to talk alone;
Most readily did me intreat,
To take a Bottle at his Seat;
A Favour at that time so great,
I blest my kind propitous Fate;
And finding soo a fresh supply,
Of Cloaths from Stoar-house kept hard by,
I mounted streight on such a Steed,
Did rather curb, than whipping need;
And straining at the usual rate,

With spur of Punch which lay in Pate,
E'er long we lighted at the Gate;
Where in an antient Cedar House,
Dwelt my new Friend, a Cokerouse;
Whose Fabrick, tho' 'twas built of Wood,
Had many Springs and Winters stood;
When sturdy Oaks, and lofty Pines
Were level'd with Musmelion Vines,
And Plants eradicated were,
By Hurricanes into the air;
There with good Punch and apple Juice,
We spent our Hours without abuse;
Till Midnight in her sable Vest,
Persuaded Gods and Men to rest;
And with a pleasing kind surprize,
Indulg'd soft Slumbers to my Eyes.
Fierce Æthon courser of the Sun,
Had half his Race exactly run;
And breath'd on me a fiery Ray,
Darting hot Beams the following Day,
When snug in Blanket white I lay:
But Heat and Chinces rais'd the Sinner,
Most opportunely to his Dinner;
Wild Fowl and Fish delicious Meats,
As good as Neptune's Doxy eats,
Began our Hospitable Treat;
Fat Venson follow'd in the Rear,
And Turkies wild Luxurious Chear.
But what the Feast did most commend,
Was hearty welcom from my Friend.
Thus having made a noble Feast,
And eat as well as pamper'd Priest,
Madera strong in flowing Bowls,
Fill'd with extream, delight our Souls;
Till wearied with a purple Flood,
Of generous Wine (the Giant's blood,
As poets feign) away I made,
For some refreshing verdant Shade;
Where musing on my Rambles strange,
And Fortune which so oft did change;
In midst of various Contemplations
Of Fancies ould, and Meditations,
I slumber'd long. . . .
Till hazy Night with noxious Dews,
Did Sleep's unwholsom Fetters lose;
With Vapours chil'd and misty air,
To fire-side I did repair,
Near which a jolly Female Crew

Were deep engag'd at Lanctre-Looe,
In Nighttrails white, with dirty Mein,
Such sights are scarce in England seen:
I thought them first some Witches bent
On Black Designs in dire Convent.
Till one who with affected air,
Had nicely learn'd to Curse and Swear:
Cryid Dealing's lost is but a Flam,
And vow'd by G-d she'd keep her Pam.
When dealing through the board had run,
They ask'd me kindly to make one;
Not staying often to be bid,
I sat me down as others did:
We scarce had play'd a Round about,
But that these Indian Froes fell out.
D-m you, says one, tho' now so brave,
I knew you late a Four-Years Slave;
What if for Planters Wife you go,
Nature design'd you for the Hoe.
Rot you replies the other streight,
The Captain kiss'd you for his Freight;
And if the Truth was known aright,
And how you walk'd the Streets by night,
You'd blush (if one cou'd blush) for shame,
Who from Bridewell or Newgate came.
From Words they fairly fell to Blows,
And being loath to interpose,
Or meddle in the Wars of Punk,
Away to Bed in hast I slunk.
Waking next day, with aking Head,
And Thirst that made me quit my Bed;
I rigg'd myself, and soon got up,
to cool my Liver with a Cup
Of Succahana fresh and clear,
Not half so good as English Beer;
Which ready stood in Kitchin Pail,
And was in fact but Adam's Ale;
For Planters Cellars you must know,
Seldom with good October flow,
But Perry Quince and Apple Juice,
Spout from the Tap like any Sluce;
Until the Cask's grown low and stale,
They're forc'd again to Goad and Pail.
The soathing drought scarce down my throat,
Enough to put a ship a float,
With Cockerouse as I was sitting,
I felt a Feaver Intermitting:
A fiery Pulse beat in my Veins,

From Cold I felt resembling Pains:
This cursed seasoning I remember
Lasted from March to cold December:
Nor would it then its Quarters shift,
Until by Cardus turn'd a drift.
And had my Doctress wanted skill,
Or Kitchin Physick at her will,
My Father's Son had lost his Lands,
And never seen the Goodwin-Sands:
But thanks to fortune and a Nurse
Whose Care depended on my Purse,
I saw myself in good Condition,
Without the help of a Physitian:
At length the shivering ill relieved,
Which long my Head and Heart had grieved;
I then began to think with Care,
How I might sell my British Ware,
That with my freight I might comply,
Did on my Charter party lie:
To this intent, with Guide before,
I tript it to the Eastern Shoar;
While riding near a Sandy Bay,
I met a Quaker, Yea and Nay:
A Pious copnscientious rogue,
As e'er woar Bonnet or a Brogue,
Who neither Swore nor kept his Word.
But cheated in the Fear of God:
And when his Debts he would not pay,
By Light within he ran away.
With this sly Zealot soon I struck
A Bargain for my English Truck,
Agreeing for ten thousand weight,
Of Sot-weed good and fit for freight,
Broad Oronooko bright and sound.
The growth and product of his ground;
In Cask that should contain compleat,
Five hundred of Tobacco neat
The contract thus betwixt us made,
Not well acquainted with the Trade,
My goods I trusted to the Cheat,
Whose crop was then aboard the Fleet;
And going to receive my own,
I found the Bird was newly flown:
Cursing this execrable Slave,
This damn'd pretended Godly Knave;
On due Revenge and Justice ent,
I instantly to Counsel went,
Unto an ambodexter Quack,

Who learnedly had got the knack
Of giving Glisters, making Pills,
Of filling bonds, and forging Wills;
And with a stock of Impudence,
Supply'd his want of Wit and Sense;
With Looks demure, amazing People,
No wiser than a Daw in Steeple;
My Anger flushing in my Face,
I stated the preceeding Case:
And of my Money was so lavish,
That he'd have poyson'd half the Parish,
And hang'd his Father on a Tree,
For such another tempting Fee;
Smiling, said he, the Cause is clear,
I'll manage him you need not fear;
The Case is judg'd, good Sir, but look
In Galen, No—in my Lord Cook,
I vow to God I was mistook:
I'll take out a Provincial Wit;
Upon my Life we'll win the Cause,
With all the ease I cure the Yaws.
Resolv'd to plauge the holy Brother,
I set one Rogue to catch another;
To try the Cause then fully bent,
Up to Annapolis I went,
A City situate on a Plain,
Where scarce a House will keep out Rain;
The buildings fram'd with Cyprus rare,
Resembles much our Southward Fair:
But Stranger here will scarcely meet
With Market-place, Exchange, or Street;
And if the Truth I may report,
'Tis not so large as Tottenham Court.
St. Mary's once was in repute,
Now here the Judges try the Suit,
And Lawyers twice a Year dispute:
As oft the Bench most gravely meet,
Some to get Drunk, and some to eat
A swinging share of Country Treat.
But as for Justice right or wrong,
Not one amongst the numerous throng,
Knows what they mean, or has the Heart,
To give his Verdict on a Stranger's part:
Now Court being call'd by beat of Drum,
The Judges left their Punch and Rum,
When Pettifogger Docter draws,
His Paper forth, and opens Cause:

And least I shou'd the better get,
Brib'd Quack supprest his Knavish Wit.
So Maid upon the downy Field,
Pretends a Force, and Fights to yeild:
The Byast Court without delay,
Adjug'd my Debt in Country Pay:
In Pipe staves, Corn, or Flesh of Boar,
Rare Cargo for the English Shoar:
Raging with Grief, full speed I ran,
To join the Fleet at Kicketan;
Embarqu'd and waiting for a Wind,
I left this dreadful Curse behind.
    May Canniballs transported o'er the Sea
    Prey on these Slaves, as they have done on me:
    May never Merchant's, trading Sails explore
    This Cruel, this Inhospitable Shoar;
    But left abandon'd by the World to starve,
    May they sustain the Fate they well deserve:
    May they turn Savage, or as Indians Wild,
    From Trade, Converse, and Happiness exil'd:
    Recreant to Heaven, may they adore the Sun,
    And into pagan Superstitions run
    For Vengeance ripe . . .
    May Wrath Divine then lay those Regions wast
    Where no Man's Faithful, nor a Woman Chast.

William Byrd II

(1674–1744)

No writer better typified the already sharpening contrast between the Southern temperament and that of the New Englander than did William Byrd, II. Whether his ironic barbs were directed at the "lubbers" of North Carolina or the "saints" to the north, Byrd's wit is reminiscent of the European contemporaries whom he clearly sought to emulate. Evident even in his diaries, Byrd's penchant for irony found its fullest expression in his travelogues *Secret History of the Line* and *History of the Dividing Line*.

Byrd's father migrated to Virginia in 1670, took up residence on 3,000 inherited acres, and in 1673 married Mary Filmer, an eighteen-year-old widow and a daughter of Warham Horsmanden, a Cavalier sympathizer who had fled to the New World during England's civil war. William Byrd, II, was born in 1674, and at the age of seven, he was sent to England for his education. He remained there for most of the next fourteen years, studying first business and then law. During a brief return to Virginia in 1696, he was elected to the House of Burgesses, but he left again almost immediately for England, where he remained until his father's death in 1705. Byrd inherited over 25,000 acres of land from his father, including the plantation of Westover, where he took up residence for the next ten years. His first *Secret Diary*, published in 1941, covers this period of his life. Kept in shorthand, his diaries are hardly literary, but they do establish an intriguing portrait of the Cavalier lifestyle, as Byrd pursued religion, learning, and personal pleasure with equal vigor and without acknowledgment of any conflict between the quests.

Various debts, as well as a dispute with Governor Spotswood, necessitated a return to England in 1715, and he lived there for most of the next eleven years. His first wife, Lucy, died during this interval. Byrd then successfully courted the wealthy young Maria Taylor, whom he married in 1724. In 1726, he returned to Virginia, where he plunged again into political life. In 1727, he was appointed one of three commissioners from Virginia to survey the boundary line with North Carolina. Byrd kept a journal chronicling the experience, later rewritten as *Secret History of the Line* (1929) and *History of the Dividing Line* (1841). Written first, the *Secret History* is the shorter of the two, recounting the exploits of "Steddy" (Byrd), "Firebrand," and "Meanwell" (the latter two, fellow commissioners Richard Fitzwilliam and William Dandridge) in a much more satirical, even sarcastic, tone. The *History*, on the other hand, is clearly intended for a wider audience, extolling Virginia as the Eden of the American colonies, inhabited by a people possessed of both industry and polished sophistication. In both, however, the main targets of Byrd's wit are the pork-eating "lubbers," who, because of their "thorough Aversion to Labor . . . file off to N Carolina, where Plenty and a Warm Sun confirm them in their Disposition to Laziness for their whole Lives." The *History* includes also his observations on Native American religion, summarized for him by Bearskin, the party's Saponi guide. In both histories, as Robert Bain has pointed out, the most interesting character by far is Byrd's own persona, "the Virginia Cavalier and Gentleman equal to any situation."

Byrd wrote accounts of two later expeditions, published as *A Progress to the Mines* and *A Journey to the Land of Eden*. Though plagued by debts in later years, Byrd's wealth continued to grow, and by the time of his death in 1744, he left land holdings that had grown to almost 180,000 acres and the manuscripts that would one day win him literary fame, dispelling much of his era's mistaken conception of the idle Southern aristocrat.

from *Secret History of the Line*

Gentlemen:

We are Sorry we can't have the Pleasure of meeting you in January next as is desired by Your Governour. The Season of the Year in which that is proposed to be done, & the distance of our Habitation from your Frontier, we hope will make our Excuse reasonable. Besides his Majesty's Order marks out our Business so plainly, that we are perswaded that there can be no difficulty in the Construction of it. After this, what imaginable Dispute can arise amongst Gentlemen who meet together with minds averse to Chicane, and Inclinations to do equal Justice both to his Majesty and the Lords Proprietors, in which disposition we make no doubt the Commissioners on both Sides will find each other.

We shall have full powers to agree at our first meeting on what Preliminarys shall be thought necessary, which we hope you will likewise be, that an affair of so great Consequence may have no Delay or Disappointment.

It is very proper to acquaint You in what manner we intend to come provided, that so you, Gentlemen who are appointed in the same Station, may if you please do the same

Honour to Your Government. We shall bring with us about 20 men furnish't with Provisions for 40 days. We shall have a Tent with us & a Marquis for the convenience of ourselves & Servants. We shall be provided with [as] much Wine & Rum as [shall] just enable us, and our men to drink every Night to the Success of the following Day, and because we understand there are many Gentiles on your Frontier, who never had an opportunity of being Baptized, we shall have a chaplain with us to make them Christians. For this Purpose we intend to rest in our Camp every Sunday that there may be leizure for so good a work. And whoever of your Province shall be desirous of novelty may repair on Sundays to our Camp, & hear a Sermon. Of this you may please to give publick notice that the Charitable Intentions of this Government may meet with the happier Success.

Thus much Gentlemen we thought it necessary to acquaint you with and to make use of this first Opportunity of Signifying with how much Satisfaction we receiv'd the News that such able Commissioners are appointed for the Government, with whom we promise our selves we shall converse with prodigious Pleasure, & Execute our Commissions to the full content of those by whom we have the Honour to be employ'd, We are

Gentlemen   Your most humble Servants

FIREBRAND   MEANWELL   STEDDY[1]

March 12 [1728]

Complaint was made to Me this Morning, that the Men belonging to the Periauga, had stole our People's Meat while they Slept. This provoked me to treat them a la Dragon, that is to swear at them furiously; & by the good Grace of my Oaths, I might have past for an Officer in his Majesty's Guards. I was the more out of Humour, because it disappointed us in our early March, it being a standing Order to boil the Pot over Night, that we might not be hinder'd in the Morning. This Accident, & Necessity of drying our Bed-Cloaths kept us from decamping til near 12 a Clock. By this delay the Surveyors found time to plot off their Work, and to observe the Course of the River. Then they past it over against Northern's Creek, the Mouth of which was very near our Line. But the Commissioners made the best of their way to the Bridge, and going ashoar walkt to Mr. Ballance's Plantation. I retir'd early to our Camp at some distance from the House, while my Collegues tarry'd within Doors, & refresh't themselves with a Cheerful Bowl. In the Gaiety of their Hearts, they invited a Tallow-faced Wench that had sprain'd her Wrist to drink with them, and when they had rais'd her in good Humour, they examined all her hidden Charms, and play'd a great many gay Pranks. While Firebrand who had the most Curiosity, was ranging over her sweet Person, he pick't off several Scabs as big as Nipples, the Consequence of eating too much Pork. The pour Damsel was disabled from making any resistance by the Lameness of her Hand; all she cou'd do, was, to sit stil, & make the Fashionable Exclamation of the Country, Flesh a live & tear it, & by what I can understand she never spake so properly in her Life. One of the Representatives of N. Carolina made a Midnight Visit to our Camp, & his Curiosity was so very clamorous that it waked Me, for which I wish't his Nose as flat as any of his Porcivorous Countrymen.[2]

---

[1]Richard Fitzwilliam, William Dandrige, and William Byrd.

[2]Byrd entertained a theory that constant eating of pork "undermined the foundation" of the nose.

From *William Byrd's Histories of the Dividing Line Betwixt Virginia and North Carolina*, edited by W. K. Boyd. The North Carolina Historical Commission, 1929.

from *History of the Dividing Line*

March 6 [1728]

After both Commissions were considered, the first Question was, where the Dividing Line was to begin. This begat a Warm debate; the Virginia Commissioners contending, with a great deal of Reason, to begin at the End of the Spitt of Sand, which was undoubtedly the North Shore of Corautck Inlet. But those of Carolina insisted Strenuously, that the Point of High Land ought rather to be the Place of Beginning, because that was fixt and certain, whereas the Spitt of Sand was ever Shifting, and did actually run out farther now than formerly. The Contest lasted some Hours, with great Vehemence, neither Party receding from their Opinion that Night. But next Morning, Mr. M. . . . , to convince us he was not that Obstinate Person he had been represented, yielded to our Reasons, and found Means to bring over his Collegues.

Here we began already to reap the Benefit of those Peremptory Words in our Commission, which in truth added some Weight to our Reasons. Nevertheless, because positive proof was made by the Oaths of two Credible Witnesses, that the Spitt of Sand had advanced 200 Yards towards the Inlet since the Controversy first began, we were willing for Peace-sake to make them that allowance. Accordingly we fixed our Beginning about that Distance North of the Inlet, and there Ordered a Cedar-Post to be driven deep into the Sand for our beginning. While we continued here, we were told that on the South Shore, not far from the Inlet, dwelt a Marooner, that Modestly call'd himself a Hermit, tho' he forfeited that Name by Suffering a wanton Female to cohabit with Him.

His Habitation was a Bower, cover'd with Bark after the Indian Fashion, which in that mild Situation protected him pretty well from the Weather. Like the Ravens, he neither plow'd nor sow'd, but Subsisted chiefly upon Oysters, which his Handmaid made a Shift to gather from the Adjacent Rocks. Sometimes, too, for Change of Dyet, he sent her to drive up the Neighbour's Cows, to moisten their Mouths with a little Milk. But as for raiment, he depended mostly upon his Length of Beard, and She upon her Length of Hair, part of which she brought decently forward, and the rest dangled behind quite down to her Rump, like one of Herodotus's East Indian Pigmies.

Thus did these Wretches live in a dirty State of Nature, and were mere Adamites, Innocence only excepted.

March 25

The air was chill'd this Morning with a Smart North-west Wind, which favour'd the Dismalities[1] in their Dirty March. They return'd by the Path they had made in coming out, and with great Industry arriv'd in the Evening at the Spot where the Line had been discontinued.

After so long and laborious a Journey, they were glad to repose themselves on their couches of Cypress-bark, where their sleep was as sweet as it wou'd have been on a Bed of Finland Down.

In the mean time, we who stay'd behind had nothing to do, but to make the best observations we cou'd upon that Part of the Country. The Soil of our Landlord's Plantation, tho' none of the best, seem'd more fertile than any thereabouts, where the Ground is near as Sandy as the Desarts of Affrica, and consequently barren. The Road

---

[1]It was necessary to run the survey through the Dismal Swamp.

leading from thence to Edenton, being in distance about 27 Miles, lies upon a Ridge call'd Sandy-Ridge, which is so wretchedly Poor that it will not bring Potatoes.

The Pines in this Part of the country are of a different Species from those that grow in Virginia: their bearded Leaves are much longer and their Cones much larger. Each Cell contains a Seed of the Size and Figure of a black-ey'd Pea, which, Shedding in November, is very good Mast for Hogs, and fattens them in a Short time.

The Smallest of these Pines are full of Cones, which are 8 or 9 Inches long, and each affords commonly 60 or 70 Seeds. This Kind of Mast has the Advantage of all other, by being more constant, and less liable to be nippt by the Frost, or Eaten by the Caterpillars. The Trees also abound more with Turpentine, and consequently yield more Tarr, than either the Yellow or the White Pine; And for the same reason make more durable Timber for building. The Inhabitants hereabouts pick up Knots of Light-wood in Abundance, which they burn into tar, and then carry it to Norfolk or Nansi-mond for a Market. The Tar made in this method is the less Valuable, because it is said to burn the Cordage, tho' it is full as good for all other uses, as that made in Swe-den and Muscovy.

Surely there is no place in the World where the Inhabitants live with less Labour than in N Carolina. It approaches nearer to the Description of Lubberland than any other, by the great felicity of the Climate, the easiness of raising Provisions, and the Slothfulness of the People.

Indian Corn is of so great increase, that a little Pains will Subsist a very large Fam-ily with Bread, and then they may have meat without any pains at all, by the Help of the Low Grounds, and the great Variety of Mast that grows on the High-land. The Men, for their Parts, just like the Indians, impose all the Work upon the poor Women. They make their Wives rise out of their Beds early in the Morning, at the same time that they lye and Snore, till the Sun has run one third of his course, and disperst all the unwholesome Damps. Then, after Stretching and Yawning for half an Hour, they light their Pipes, and, under the Protection of a cloud of Smoak, venture out into the open Air; tho', if it hap-pens to be never so little cold, they quickly return Shivering into the Chimney corner. When the weather is mild, they stand leaning with both their arms upon the corn-field fence, and gravely consider whether they had best go and take a Small Heat at the Hough: but generally find reasons to put it off till another time.

Thus they loiter away their Lives, like Solomon's Sluggard, with their Arms across, and at the Winding up of the Year Scarcely have Bread to Eat.

To speak the Truth, tis a thorough Aversion to Labor that makes People file off to N Carolina, where Plenty and a Warm Sun confirm them in their Disposition to Lazi-ness for their whole Lives.

March 26

Since we were like to be confin'd to this place, till the People return'd out of the Dismal, twas agreed that our Chaplain might Safely take a turn to Edenton, to preach the Gospel to the Infidels there, and Christen their Children. He was accompany'd thither by Mr. Little, One of the Carolina Commissioners, who, to shew his regard for the Church, offer'd to treat Him on the Road with a Fricassee of Rum. They fry'd half a Dozen Rashers of very fat Bacon in a Pint of Rum, both which being disht up to-gether, serv'd the Company at once for meat and Drink.

Most of the Rum they get in this Country comes from New England, and is so bad and unwholesome, that it is not improperly call'd "Kill-Devil." It is distill'd there from forreign molosses, which, if Skilfully manag'd yields near Gallon for Gallon. Their molasses comes from the same country, and has the name of "Long Sugar" in Carolina, I suppose from the Ropiness of it, and Serves all the purposes of Sugar, both in their Eating and Drinking.

When they entertain their Friends bountifully, they fail not to set before them a Capacious Bowl of Bombo, so call'd from the Admiral of that name. This is a Compound of Rum and Water in Equal Parts, made palatable with the said long Sugar. As good Humour begins to flow, and the Bowl to Ebb, they take care to replinish it with Shear Rum, of which there always is a Reserve under the Table. But such Generous doings happen only when that Balsam of life is plenty; for they have often such Melancholy times, that neither Land-graves nor Cassicks can procure one drop for their Wives, when they ly in, or are troubled with the Colick or Vapours. Very few in this Country have the Industry to plant Orchards, which, in a Dearth of Rum, might supply them with much better Liquor.

The Truth is, there is one Inconvenience that easily discourages lazy People from making This improvement: very often, in Autumn, when the Apples begin to ripen, they are visited with Numerous Flights of paraqueets, that bite all the Fruit to Pieces in a moment, for the sake of the Kernels. The Havock they make is Sometimes so great, that whole Orchards are laid waste in Spite of all the Noises that can be made, or Mawkins that can be dresst up, to fright 'em away. These Ravenous Birds visit North Carolina only during the warm Season, and so soon as the Cold begins to come on, retire back towards the Sun. They rarely Venture so far North as Virginia, except in a very hot Summer, when they visit the most Southern Parts of it. They are very Beautiful; but like some other pretty Creatures, are apt to be loud and mischievous.

October 13

This being Sunday, we rested from our Fatigue, and had leisure to reflect on the signal Mercies of Providence.

The great Plenty of Meat herewith Bearskin[2] furnisht us in these lonely Woods made us once more Shorten the men's allowance of Bread, from 5 to 4 Pounds of bisket a week. This was the more necessary, because we knew not yet how long our Business might require us to be out.

In the Afternoon our Hunters went forth, and return'd triumphantly with three brace of wild Turkeys. They told us they cou'd see the Mountains distinctly from every Eminence, tho' the Atmosphere was so thick with Smoak that they appear'd at a greater Distance than they really were.

In the Evening we examin'd our Friend Bearskin, concerning the Religion of his Country and he explain'd it to us, without any of that Reserve to which his Nation is Subject.

He told us he believ'd there was one Supreme God, who had Several Subaltern Deities under Him. And that this Master-God made the World a long time ago. That he told the Sun, the Moon, and Stars, their Business in the Beginning, which they, with good looking after, have faithfully perform'd ever Since.

[2]An Indian guide and hunter whom the party had taken along.

That the same Power that made all things at first has taken care to keep them in the same Method and Motion ever since.

He believ'd God had form'd many Worlds before he form'd this, that those Worlds either grew old and ruinous, or were destroyed for the Dishonesty of the Inhabitants.

That God is very just and very good—ever well pleas'd with those men who possess those God-like Qualities. That he takes good People into his safe Protection, makes them very rich, fills their Bellies plentifully, preserves them from sickness, and from being surpriz'd or Overcome by their Enemies.

But all such as tell Lies, and Cheat those they have Dealings with, he never fails to punish with Sickness, Poverty and Hunger, and, after all that, Suffers them to be knockt on the Head and scalpt by those that fight against them.

He believ'd that after Death both good and bad People are conducted by a strong Guard into a great Road, in which departed Souls travel together for some time, till at a certain Distance this Road forks into two Paths, the one extremely Levil, and the other Stony and Mountainous.

Here the good are parted from the Bad by a flash of Lightening, the first being hurry'd away to the Right, the other to the Left. The Right hand Road leads to a charming warm Country, where the Spring is everlasting, and every Month is May; and as the year is always in its Youth, so are the People, and particularly the Women are bright as Stars, and never Scold.

That in this happy Climate there are Deer, Turkeys, Elks, and Buffaloes innumerable, perpetually fat and gentle, while the Trees are loaded with delicious Fruit quite throughout the four Seasons.

That the Soil brings forth Corn Spontaneously, without the Curse of Labour, and so very wholesome, that None who have the happiness to eat of it are ever Sick, grow old, or dy.

Near the Entrance into this Blessed Land Sits a Venerable Old Man on a Mat richly woven, who examins Strictly all that are brought before Him, and if they have behav'd well, the Guards are order'd to open the Crystal Gate, and let them enter into the Land of Delights.

The left Hand Path is very rugged and uneaven, leading to a dark and barren Country, where it is always Winter. The Ground is the whole year round cover'd with Snow, and nothing is to be seen upon the Trees but Icicles.

All the People are hungry, yet have not a Morsel of any thing to eat, except a bitter kind of Potato, that gives them the Dry-Gripes, and fills their whole Body with loathsome Ulcers, that Stink, and are unsupportably painfull.

Here all the Women are old and ugly, having Claws like a Panther, with which they fly upon the Men that Slight their Passion. For it seems these haggard old Furies are intolerably fond, and expect a vast deal of Cherishing. They talk much and exceedingly Shrill, giving exquisite Pain to the Drum of the Ear, which in that Place of the Torment is so tender, that every Sharp Note wounds it to the Quick.

At the End of this Path sits a dreadful old Woman on a monstrous Toad-Stool, whose head is cover'd with Rattle-Snakes instead of Tresses, with glaring white Eyes, that strike a Terror unspeakable into all that behold her.

This Hag pronounces Sentence of Woe upon all the miserable Wretches that hold up their hands at her Tribunal. After this they are deliver'd over to huge Turkey-Buzzards, like harpys, that fly away with them to the Place above mentioned.

Here, after they have been tormented a certain Number of years, according to their several Degrees of Guilt, they are again driven back into this World, to try if they will mend their Manners, and merit a place the next time in the Regions of Bliss.

This was the Substances of Bearskin's Religion, and was as much to the purpose as cou'd be expected from a meer State of Nature, without one Glimpse of Revelation or Philosophy.

It contain'd, however, the three Great Articles of Natural Religion: The Belief of a God; The Moral Distinction betwixt Good and Evil; and the Expectation of Rewards and Punishments in Another World.

Indeed, the Indian Notion of a Future Happiness is a little Gross and Sensual, like Mahomet's Paradise. But how can it be otherwise, in a People that are contented with Nature as they find Her, and have no other Lights but what they receive from purblind Tradition?

Samuel Davies

(1723–1761)

During his lifetime, Samuel Davies's fame was chiefly a result of his skills as an orator. A contemporary of Jonathan Edwards, whom he would one day succeed as president of the College of New Jersey, Davies fanned the flames of the Great Awakening in Virginia, while the better-known revivalists Edwards and George Whitefield sparked evangelical fervor in the northern colonies. Davies was an exemplar of the dramatic and emotional style of preaching that became a signature of that movement (defended by Edwards in his *Treatise Concerning Religious Affections*), and he fathered a style of "revival preaching" that persists in the South to this day.

Born in New Castle County, Delaware, on November 3, 1723, and raised in a pious household, Davies studied at Reverend Samuel Blair's dissenting academy, or "Log College," in Fagg's Manor, Pennsylvania. Davies was ordained a Presbyterian minister on February 19, 1747, in Hanover County, Virginia, and during the next six years developed his reputation as an orator. In 1753, Davies journeyed to Great Britain on a fund-raising mission for the College of New Jersey, but he returned to Virginia in 1755 to help recruit militia for the French and Indian War. Davies authored a series of essays entitled "The Centinel," which appeared in the *Virginia Gazette* in 1756 and 1757. The best known of these essays, "Centinel No. 10," was highly critical of George Washington's leadership of the Virginia Regiment. In 1758, he succeeded Jonathan Edwards as president of the College of New Jersey and died in New Jersey in 1761.

Davies's poetry is often sentimental, addressing conventional religious themes. Though he was himself quite learned, his poetry is reminiscent of his sermons in that he typically refrains from learned allusions, appealing instead to his readers' emotions and religious fervor. In an age when other writers trumpeted the capacity of human reason to unravel every mystery, Davies sought instead to instill in his readers a sense of awe in the face of a sublime deity.

How Great, How Terrible That God

*The different States of Sinners
and Saints in the Wreck of Nature.*

Isaiah xxiv. 18–20. Long Metre.

I

How great, how terrible that God,
Who shakes Creation with his Nod!
He frowns, and Earth's Foundations shake,
And all the Wheels of Nature break.

II

Crush'd under Guilt's oppressive Weight
The Globe now totters to its Fate,
Trembles beneath its guilty Sons,
And for Deliv'rance loudly groans:

III

And see the glorious dreadful Day
That takes th' enormous Load away!
See Ocean, Earth, all Nature's Frame
Sink in one universal Flame.

IV

Where now, O where shall Sinners seek
For Shelter in the gen'ral Wreck?
Shall falling Rocks be o'er them thrown?
See Rocks, like Snow, dissolving down.

V

In vain for Mercy now they cry;
In Lakes of liquid Fire they lie;
There on the flaming Billows tost,
For ever, O for ever lost!

VI

But, Saints, undaunted and serene
Your Eyes shall view the dreadful Scene;
Your Saviour lives, tho' Worlds expire,
And Earth and Skies dissolve in Fire.

VII

Jesus, the helpless Creature's Friend,
To Thee my All I dare commend:
Thou can'st preserve my feeble Soul,
When Lightnings blaze from Pole to Pole.

Welcome to Earth, Great Son of God

CHRIST *most worthy of Esteem, but*
ungratefully neglected in our World.

Long Metre.

I

WELCOME to Earth, Great Son of GOD!
His best-belov'd, his only Son!
Hail, Thou blest Messenger of Peace
To Sinners helpless and undone!

II

Hail, great Deliv'rer!———Bow the Knee,
Ye Rebel-Nations, and adore!
JESUS, who would not love thy Name?
What Rebel dare offend Thee more?

III

See ev'n this stubborn Heart of mine
Conquer'd by sov'reign Love, submit,
And shall not all the Nations fall
In humble Homage at thy Feet?

IV

[Shall not thy Praise from Tongue to Tongue
Be spread? Thy Love from Breast to Breast?
Thy Name the universal Song
From North to South, from East to West?]

V

But, O my Heart, with Sorrow break,
Mine Eyes pour out incessant Tears!
The Son of GOD, the Sinner's Friend,
Neglected in our World appears.

VI

The Wonders of his dying Love
The Riches of his Grace forgot!———
Strange! *Justice* should behold the Sight,
And yet its Vengeance kindle not.

VII

[O Thou, whose Mercy deign'd to pray
For those who nail'd Thee to the Tree,
The Wonders of thy Pow'r display,
And turn the Hearts of Men to Thee!]

VIII

Make Thyself Room in ev'ry Heart;
Great Savior! welcome into mine;
Welcome, great Conqu'ror, to our World,
To make all Tribes and Nations thine!

Robert Munford

(c. 1737–1783)

The few details known of Robert Munford's life come from a search of public records. His father suffered a series of financial setbacks that eventually cost him all of the family's substantial landholdings, and when he died in 1745, Robert Munford was taken in by William Beverley, the boy's uncle. In 1750, he was taken to England, where he received an exclusive formal education, but when Beverley died in 1756, leaving no provision for Munford, he returned to Virginia, where he pursued a legal education while working in his cousin's law office. He served as an officer in William Byrd, III's, regiment during the French and Indian War, and on his return, he completed his legal studies and married his cousin Anna Beverley. In 1765, he was elected to the House of Burgesses, where he served for the next ten years, but as revolutionary zeal mounted, his moderate sympathies reduced his participation in public life.

Though it is unlikely that either was performed during his lifetime, both of Munford's best-known dramas, *The Candidates* (c. 1770) and *The Patriots* (c. 1777) share a theme that would become quite common in later literature of the South: fear that the "old order" is being overturned by usurpers who neither value nor understand the traditions of the past. Though characterization in the farcical *The Candidates* is less than subtle (the ambitious Wou'dbe, the "worthy" Worthy), its theme is nonetheless ambiguous. In the end, the election is not influenced by the crass self-advancement of the less "worthy" candidates, but the play also evidences the fear of the patrician class that an untutored electorate might betray the common good. *The Patriots*, though in many ways a more mature drama, depends more on a knowledge of local politics, including a number of thinly veiled caricatures of public figures of the day.

The Candidates; or, the Humours of a Virginia Election.

A Comedy, in Three Acts.

DRAMATIS PERSONÆ.

Sir John Toddy,
Mr. Wou'dbe,   Candidates for the office of delegates
Mr. Strutabout,   to the general assembly.
Mr. Smallhopes,

Mr. Julip,   Gentlemen Justices.
Capt. Paunch,

Mr. Worthy, formerly a delegate, but now declines.

Guzzle,
Twist,   }   Freeholders.
Stern,
Prize,

Ralpho, Wou'dbe's servant.
Jack, a tool to Mr. Strutabout.
Ned, the same to Mr. Smallhopes.

Mrs. Guzzle,
Lucy Twist,   }   Freeholder's wives.
Catharine Stern,
Sarah Prize,

Freeholders, Country girls, &c.

PROLOGUE

By a Friend

Ladies and gentlemen, to-night you'll see
A bard delighting in satiric glee;
In merry scenes his biting tale unfold,
And high to Folly's eye the mirror hold:
Here eager candidates shall call for votes,
And bawling voters louder stretch their throats:
Here may you view, in groups diverting, join'd
The poor and wealthy rabble of mankind;
All who deserve the lash, the lash will find.
Here characters, whose names are now unknown,
Shall shine again, as in their spheres they shone;
While some may make malicious explanation,
And know them all still living in the nation.
If any present, say, fie, shameless bard!
Hast thou for decency no more regard
Than at thy betters, thus to make a stand,
And boldly point out meanness, contraband,
Depreciating the wisdom of the land?
Tho' such, the wond'rous sympathy of wits,
That every fool will wear the cap that fits,
I boldly answer, how could he mean you,
Who, when he wrote, about you nothing knew?
The state of things was such, in former times,
'Ere wicked kings were punish'd for their crimes:
When strove the candidates to gain their seats
Most heartily, with drinking bouts, and treats;
The meanest vices all the people stain'd,
And drunkenness, and monarchy both reign'd,

With such strong cause his anger to engage,
How could our Bard restrain satiric rage?
But, God forbid, its edge shou'd now apply,
Or on our race-field, when you cast an eye
You there a home-election—should espy.
Science and virtue, now are wider spread,
And crown with dignity, fair Freedom's head.
We only pray this satire ne'er be just,
Save when apply'd to other times, and trust
Its keenness only, a rememb'rancer,
And guard from future evils, may appear.
If, after this, objections should remain,
The motive's envy, consciousness disdain,
Or any thing, except the poet's want
Of sense, which no true publisher will grant.
Yet virtue is not in our story lost,
E'en then, Virginians could much virtue boast.
With plaudits, therefore, and free laughter own
Virginia's first and only comic son;
Ah! could the bard, rejoicing, raise his head
To hear his praise!—Alas! the bard is dead.

THE
CANDIDATES, & c.

ACT I. SCENE I.

Mr. Wou'dbe's house.

Enter Wou'dbe with a news-paper in his hand.

Wou'dbe. I am very sorry our good old governor Botetourt has left us. He well deserved our friendship, when alive, and that we should for years to come, with gratitude, remember his mild and affable deportment. Well, our little world will soon be up, and very busy towards our next election. Must I again be subject to the humours of a fickle croud? Must I again resign my reason, and be nought but what each voter pleases? Must I cajole, fawn, and wheedle, for a place that brings so little profit?

Enter Ralpho.

Ralpho. Sir John Toddy is below, and if your honour is at leisure, would beg to speak to you.

Wou'dbe. My compliments to Sir John, and tell him, I shall be glad of his company. So—Sir John, some time ago, heard me say I was willing to resign my seat in the house to an abler person, and he comes modestly to accept of it.

Enter Sir John Toddy.

Sir John. Mr. Wou'dbe, your most obedient servant, sir; I am proud to find you well. I hope you are in good health, sir?

Wou'dbe. Very well, I am obliged to you, Sir John. Why, Sir John, you surely are practising the grimace and compliments you intend to make use of among the freeholders in the next election, and have introduced yourself to me with the self-same common-place expressions that we candidates adopt when we intend to wheedle a fellow out of his vote—I hope you have no scheme upon me, Sir John?

Sir John. No, sir, upon my honour, sir, it was punctually to know how your lady and family did, sir, 'pon honour, sir, it was.

Wou'dbe. You had better be more sparing of your honour at present, Sir John; for, if you are a candidate, whenever you make promises to the people that you can't comply with, you must say upon honour, otherwise they won't believe you.

Sir John. Upon honour, sir, I have no thought to set up for a candidate, unless you say the word.

Wou'dbe. Such condescension from you, Sir John, I have no reason to expect: you have my hearty consent to do as you please, and if the people choose you their Representative, I must accept of you as a colleague.

Sir John. As a colleague, Mr. Wou'dbe! I was thinking you did not intend to stand a poll, and my business, sir, was to get the favour of you to speak a good word for me among the people.

Wou'dbe. I hope you have no occasion for a trumpeter, Sir John? If you have, I'll speak a good word to you, and advise you to decline.

Sir John. Why, Mr. Wou'dbe, after you declin'd, I thought I was the next *fittenest* man in the county, and Mr. Wou'dbe, if you would be ungenerous, tho' you are a laughing man, you would tell me so.

Wou'dbe. It would be ungenerous indeed, Sir John, to tell you what the people could never be induced to believe. But I'll be ingenuous enough to tell you, Sir John, if you expect any assistance from me, you'll be disappointed, for I can't think you the *fittenest* man I know.

Sir John. Pray, sir, who do you know besides? Perhaps I may be thought as fit as your honour. But, sir, if you are for that, the hardest fend off: damn me, if I care a farthing for you; and so, your servant, sir.

[*Exit Sir John.*

Wou'dbe. So, I have got the old knight, and his friend Guzzle, I suppose, against me, by speaking so freely; but their interest, I believe, has not weight enough among the people, for me to lose any thing, by making them my enemies. Indeed, the being intimate with such a fool as Sir John, might tend more to my discredit with them, for the people of Virginia have too much sense not to perceive how weak the head must be that is always filled with liquor. Ralpho!—

Enter Ralpho

Ralpho. Sir, what does your honour desire?

Wou'dbe. I'm going into my library, and if any gentleman calls, you may introduce him to me there.

Ralpho. Yes, sir. But, master, as election-times are coming, I wish you would remember a poor servant, a little.

Wou'dbe. What do you want?

Ralpho. Why, the last suit of clothes your honour gave me is quite worn out. Look here, (*shewing his elbows*) the insigns, (as I have heard your honour say, in one of your fine speeches) the insigns of faithful service. Now, methinks, as they that set up for burgesses, cut a dash, and have rare sport, why might not their servants have a little decreation?

Wou'dbe. I understand you, Ralpho, you wish to amuse yourself, and make a figure among the girls this Election, and since such a desire is natural to the young, and innocent if not carried to excess, I am willing to satisfy you; you may therefore, have the suit I pulled off yesterday, and accept this present as an evidence that I am pleased with your diligence and fidelity, and am ever ready to reward it. [*Exit Wou'dbe.*

Ralpho. God bless your honour! what a good master! who would not do every thing to give such a one pleasure? But, e'gad, it's time to think of my new clothes: I'll go and try them on. Gadso! this figure of mine is not reconsiderable in its delurements, and when I'm dressed out like a gentleman, the girls, I'm a thinking, will find me desistible. [*Exit.*

SCENE II.   *A porch of a tavern: a Court-house on one side, and an high road behind.*

Captain Paunch, Ned, and several freeholders discovered.

Ned. Well, gentlemen, I suppose we are all going to the barbecue together.

Capt. Paunch. Indeed, sir, I can assure you, I have no such intention.

Ned. Not go to your friend Wou'dbe's treat! He's such a pretty fellow, and you like him so well, I wonder you won't go to drink his liquor.

Capt. P. Aye, aye, very strange: but your friends Strutabout and Smallhopes, I like so little as never to take a glass from them, because I shall never pay the price which is always expected for it, by voting against my conscience: I therefore don't go, to avoid being asked for what I won't give.

Ned. A very disteress [*sic*] motive, truly, but for the matter of that, you've not so much to boast of your friend Wou'dbe, if what I have been told of him is true; for I have heard say, he and the fine beast of a gentleman, Sir John Toddy, have joined interess. Mr. Wou'dbe, I was creditly 'formed, was known for to say, he wouldn't serve for a burgess, unless Sir John was elected with him.

1st Freeholder. What's that you say, neighbor? has Mr. Wou'dbe and Sir John joined interest?

Ned. Yes, they have; and ant there a clever fellow for ye? a rare burgess you will have, when a fellow gets in, who will go drunk, and be a sleeping in the house! I wish people wouldn't pretend for to hold up their heads so high, who have such friends and associates. There's poor Mr. Smallhopes, who isn't as much attended to, is a very proper gentleman, and is no drunkard, and has no drunken companions.

1st Freeholder. I don't believe it. Mr. Wou'dbe's a cleverer man than that, and people ought to be ashamed to vent such slanders.

2d Freeholder. So I say: and as we are of one mind, let's go strait, and let Mr. Wou'dbe know it. [*Exeunt two Freeholders.*

3d Freeholder. If Mr. Wou'dbe did say it, I won't vote for him, that's sartain.

4th Freeholder. Are you sure of it, neighbour? (*To Ned.*)

Ned. Yes, I am sure of it: d'ye think I'd speak such a thing without having good authority?

4th Freeholder. I'm sorry for't; come neighbour, (*to the 3d Freeholder*) this is the worst news that I've heard for a long time. [*Exeunt 3d & 4th Freeholder.*

5th Freeholder. I'm glad to hear it. Sir John Toddy is a clever open-hearted gentleman as I ever knew, one that wont turn his back upon a poor man, but will take a chearful cup with one as well as another, and it does honour to Mr. Wou'dbe to prefer such a one, to any of your whifflers who han't the heart to be generous, and yet despise poor folks. Huzza! for Mr. Wou'dbe and for Sir John Toddy.

6th Freeholder. I think so too, neighbour. Mr. Wou'dbe, I always thought, was a man of sense, and had larning, as they call it, but he did not love diversion enough, I like him the better for't. Huzza for Mr. Wou'dbe and Sir John Toddy.

Both. Huzza for Mr. Wou'dbe and Sir John Toddy. Wou'dbe and Toddy, for ever, boys!   [*Exeunt.*

Capt. Paunch. The man that heard it is mistaken, for Mr. Wou'dbe never said it.

Ned. I'll lay you a bowl he did.

Capt. P. Done.

Ned. Done, sir, Oh! Jack Sly, Jack Sly.

Jack. (without) Halloa.

Enter Jack, saying, who call'd me? what's your business?

Ned. (winking to Jack). I have laid a bowl with the Captain here, that Mr. Wou'dbe did say, that he would not serve as a burgess, unless Sir John Toddy was elected with him.

Jack. I have heard as much, and more that's little to his credit. He has hurt us more than he'll do us good for one while. It's his doings our levies are so high.

Capt. P. Out upon you, if that's your proof, fetch the bowl. Why gentlemen, if I had a mind, I could say as much and more of the other candidates. But, gentlemen, 'tis not fair play: don't abuse our friend, and we'll let your's alone. Mr. Wou'dbe is a clever gentleman, and perhaps so are the rest: let every man vote as he pleases, and let's raise no stories to the prejudice of either.

Ned. Damn me, if I don't speak my mind. Wou'dbe shan't go if I can help it, by God, for I boldly say, Mr. Wou'dbe has done us more harm, than he will ever do us good, (*raising his voice very high*).   [*Exeunt into the house,*

Jack. So say I.   [*Exit after him.*

Capt. P. Go along: bawl your hearts out: nobody will mind you, I hope. Well, rejoice that Mr. Wou'dbe is determined still to serve us. If he does us no good, he will do us no harm. Mr. Strutabout would do very well if he was not such a coxcomb. As for Smallhopes, I'd as soon send to New-Market, for a burgess, as send him, and old Sir John loves tipple too well: egad, I'll give Wou'dbe my vote, and throw away the other.

                                                                                    [*Exit.*

SCENE III.   *Wou'dbe's house.*

Enter Wou'dbe, looking at a letter.

Wou'dbe. This note gives me information, that the people are much displeased with me for declaring in favour of Sir John Toddy. Who could propagate this report, I know not, but was not this abroad, something else would be reported, as prejudicial to my interest; I must take an opportunity of justifying myself in public.

Enter Ralpho.

Ralpho. Mr. Strutabout waits upon your honour.
Wou'dbe. Desire him to walk in.

Enter Mr. Strutabout.

Strutabout. Mr. Wou'dbe, your servant. Considering the business now in hand, I think you confine yourself too much at home. There are several little reports circulating to your disadvantage, and as a friend, I would advice you to shew yourself to the people, and endeavour to confute them.

Wou'dbe. I believe, sir, I am indebted to my brother candidates, for most of the reports that are propagated to my disadvantage, but I hope, Mr. Strutabout is a man of too much honour, to say anything in my absence, that he cannot make appear.

Strutabout. That you may depend on, sir. But there are some who are so intent upon taking your place, that they will stick at nothing to obtain their ends.

Wou'dbe. Are you in the secret, sir?

Strutabout. So far, sir, that I have had overtures from Mr. Smallhopes and his friends, to join my interest with their's, against you. This, I rejected with disdain, being conscious that you were the properest person to serve the county; but when Smallhopes told me, he intended to prejudice your interest by scatering a few stories among the people to your disadvantage, it raised my blood to such a pitch, that had he not promised me to be silent, I believe I should have chastised him for you myself.

Wou'dbe. If, sir, you were so far my friend, I am obliged to you: though whatever report he is the author of, will, I am certain, gain little credit with the people.

Strutabout. I believe so; and therefore, if you are willing, we'll join our interests together, and soon convince the fellow, that by attacking you he has injured himself.

Wou'dbe. So far from joining with you, or any body else, or endeavouring to procure a vote for you, I am determined never to ask a vote for myself, or receive one that is unduly obtained.

Enter Ralpho.

Ral. Master, rare news, here's our neighbour Guzzle, as drunk as ever Chief Justice Cornelius was upon the bench.

Wou'dbe. That's no news, Ralpho: but do you call it rare news, that a creature in the shape of man, and endued with the faculties of reason, should so far debase the workmanship of heaven, by making his carcase a receptacle for such pollution?

Ralpho. Master, you are hard upon neighbour Guzzle: our Justices gets drunk, and why not poor Guzzle? But sir, he wants to see you.

Wou'dbe. Tell him to come in. *(exit Ralpho).* All must be made welcome now.

Re-enter Ralpho and Guzzle, with an empty bottle.

Guzzle. Ha! Mr. Wou'dbe, how is it?

Wou'dbe. I'm something more in my senses than you, John, tho' not so sensible as you would have me, I suppose.

Guzzle. If I can make you sensible how much I want my bottle filled, and how much I shall love the contents, it's all the senses I desire you to have.

Ralpho. If I may be allowed to speak, neighbour Guzzle, you are wrong; his honour sits up for a burgess, and should have five senses at least.

Guzzle. Five senses! how, what five?

Ralpho. Why, neighbour, you know, eating, drinking, and sleeping are three; t'other two are best known to myself.

Wou'dbe. I'm sorry Mr. Guzzle, you are so ignorant of the necessary qualifications of a member of the house of burgesses.

Guzzle. Why, you old dog, I knew before Ralpho told me. To convince you, eating, drinking, and sleeping, are three; fighting and lying are t'others.

Wou'dbe. Why fighting and lying?

Guzzle. Why, because you are not fit for a burgess, unless you'll fight; suppose a man that values himself upon boxing, should stand in the lobby, ready cock'd and prim'd, and knock you down, and bung up both your eyes for a fortnight, you'd be ashamed to shew your face in the house, and be living at our expence all the time.

Wou'dbe. Why lying?

Guzzle. Because, when you have been at Williamsburg, for six or seven weeks, under pretence of serving your county, and come back, says I to you, what news? none at all, says you; what have you been about? says I,—says you—and so you must tell some damned lie, sooner than say you have been doing nothing.

Wou'dbe. No, Guzzle, I'll make it a point of duty to dispatch the business, and my study to promote the good of my county.

Guzzle. Yes, damn it, you all promise mighty fair, but the devil a bit do you perform; there's Strutabout, now, he'll promise to move mountains. He'll make the rivers navigable, and bring the tide over the tops of the hills, for a vote.

Strutabout. You may depend, Mr. Guzzle, I'll perform whatever I promise.

Guzzle. I don't believe it, damn me if I like you.   [*looking angry.*

Wou'dbe. Don't be angry, John, let our actions hereafter be the test of our inclinations to serve you.   [*Exit Strutabout.*

Guzzle. Agreed, Mr. Wou'dbe, but that fellow that slunk off just now, I've no opinion of.

Wou'dbe. (Looking about) what, is Mr. Strutabout gone? why, surely, Guzzle, you did not put him to flight?

Guzzle. I suppose I did, but no matter, (*holding up his bottle, and looking at it,*) my bottle never was so long a filling in this house, before; surely, there's a leak in the bottom, (*looks at it again*).

Wou'dbe. What have you got in your bottle, John, a lizard?

Guzzle. Yes, a very uncommon one, and I want a little rum put to it, to preserve it.

Wou'dbe. Hav'n't you one in your belly, John?

Guzzle. A dozen, I believe, by their twisting, when I mentioned the rum.

Wou'dbe. Would you have rum to preserve them, too?

Guzzle. Yes, yes, Mr. Wou'dbe, by all means; but, why so much talk about it, if you intend to do it, do it at once, man, for I am in a damnable hurry.

Wou'dbe. Do what? Who are to be burgesses, John?

Guzzle. Who are to be what? (*looking angry*).

Wou'dbe. Burgesses, who are you for?

Guzzle. For the first man that fills my bottle: so Mr. Wou'dbe, your servant.

[*Exit Guzzle.*

Wou'dbe. Ralpho, go after him, and fill his bottle.

Ralpho. Master, we ought to be careful of the rum, else 'twill not hold out, (*aside*) it's always a feast or a famine with us; master has just got a little Jamaica for his own use, and now he must spill it, and spare it till there's not a drop left.   [*Exit.*

Wou'dbe. (pulling out his watch.) 'Tis now the time a friend of mine has appointed for me to meet the freeholders at a barbecue; well, I find, in order to secure a seat in our august senate, 'tis necessary a man should either be a slave or a fool; a slave to the people, for the privilege of serving them, and a fool himself, for thus begging a troublesome and expensive employment.

> To sigh, while toddy-toping sots rejoice,
> To see you paying for their empty voice,
> From morn to night your humble head decline,
> To gain an honour that is justly thine,
> Intreat a fool, who's your's at this day's treat,
> And next another's, if another's meat,
> Is all the bliss a candidate acquires,
> In all his wishes, or his vain desires.

[*Exit.*

END OF THE FIRST ACT.

ACT II. SCENE I.

A race-field, a bullock, and several hogs barbecued.

Twist, Stern, Prize, Lucy, Catharine, and Sarah, sitting on four fence rails.

Twist. Well, gentlemen, what do you think of Mr. Strutabout and Mr. Smallhopes? it seems one of the old ones declines, and t'other, I believe, might as well, if what neighbour Sly says, is true.

Stern. Pray, gentlemen, what plausible objection have you against Mr. Wou'dbe? he's a clever civil gentleman as any, and as far as my poor weak capacity can go, he's a man of as good learning, and knows the punctilios of behaving himself, with the best of them.

Prize. Wou'dbe, for sartin, is a civil gentleman, but he can't speak his mind so boldly as Mr. Strutabout, and commend me to a man that will speak his mind freely;—I say.

Lucy. Well, commend me to Mr. Wou'dbe, I say,—I nately like the man; he's mighty good to all his poor neighbours, and when he comes into a poor body's house, he's so free and so funny, is'nt he, old man? *(speaking to Twist).*

Twist. A little too free sometimes, faith; he was funny when he wanted to see the colour of your garters; wa'nt he?

Lucy. Oh! for shame, husband. Mr. Wou'dbe has no more harm about him, than a sucking babe; at least, if he has, I never saw it.

Twist. Nor felt it, I hope; but wife, you and I, you know, could never agree about burgesses.

Lucy. If the wives were to vote, I believe they would make a better choice than their husbands.

Twist. You'd be for the funnyest—wou'dn't you?

Lucy. Yes, faith; and the wittiest, and prettiest, and the wisest, and the best too; you are all for ugly except when you chose me.

Catharine. Well done, Lucy, you are right, girl. If we were all to speak to our old men as freely as you do, there would be better doings.

Stern. Perhaps not, Kate.

Catharine. I am sure there would; for if a clever gentleman, now-a-days, only gives a body a gingercake in a civil way, you are sullen for a week about it. Remember when Mr. Wou'dbe promised Molly a riband, and a pair of buckles, you would not let the poor girl have 'em: but you take toddy from him;—yes, and you'll drink a little too much, you know, Richard.

Stern. Well, it's none of our costs, if I do.

Catharine. Husband, you know Mr. Wou'dbe is a clever gentleman; he has been a good friend to us.

Stern. I agree to it, and can vote for him without your clash.

Sarah. I'll be bound when it comes to the pinch, they'll all vote for him: won't you old man? he stood for our George, when our neighbor refused us.

Prize. Mr. Wou'dbe's a man well enough in his neighbourhood, and he may have learning, as they say he has, but he don't shew it like Mr. Strutabout.

Enter Guzzle, and several freeholders.

Guzzle. Your servant, gentlemen, (*shakes hands all round*) we have got fine weather, thank God: how are crops with you? we are very dry in our parts.

Twist. We are very dry here; Mr. Guzzle, where's your friend Sir John, and Mr. Wou'dbe? they are to treat to-day, I hear.

Guzzle. I wish I could see it, but there are more treats besides their's; where's your friend Mr. Strutabout? I heard we were to have a treat from Smallhopes and him to-day.

Twist. Fine times, boys. Some of them had better keep their money; I'll vote for no man but to my liking.

Guzzle. If I may be so bold, pray, which way is your liking?

Twist. Not as your's is, I believe; but nobody shall know my mind till the day.

Guzzle. Very good, Mr. Twist; nobody, I hope, will put themselves to the trouble to ask.

Twist. You have taken the trouble already.

Guzzle. No harm, I hope, sir.

Twist. None at all, sir: Yonder comes Sir John, and quite sober, as I live.

Enter Sir John Toddy.

Sir John. Gentlemen and ladies, your servant, hah! my old friend Prize, how goes it? how does your wife and children do?

Sarah. At your service, sir. *(making a low courtsey.)*

Prize. How the devil come he to know me so well, and never spoke to me before in his life? *(aside.)*

Guzzle. *(whispering Sir John)* Dick Stern.

Sir John. Hah! Mr. Stern, I'm proud to see you; I hope your family are well; how many children? does the good woman keep to the old stroke?

Catharine. Yes, an't please your honour, I hope my lady's well, with your honour.

Sir John. At your service, madam.

Guzzle. (whispering Sir John) Roger Twist.

Sir John. Hah! Mr. Roger Twist! your servant, sir. I hope your wife and children are well.

Twist. There's my wife. I have no children, at your service.

Sir John. A pretty girl: why, Roger, it you don't do better, you must call an old fellow to your assistance.

Twist. I have enough to assist me, without applying to you, sir.

Sir John. No offence, I hope, sir; excuse my freedom.

Twist. None at all, sir; Mr. Wou'dbe is ready to befriend me in that way at any time.

Sir John. Not in earnest, I hope, sir; tho' he's a damn'd fellow, I believe.

Lucy. Why, Roger, if you talk at this rate, people will think you are jealous; for shame of yourself.

Twist. For shame of yourself, you mean.

Guzzle. A truce, a truce—here comes Mr. Wou'dbe.

Enter Mr. Wou'dbe.

Wou'dbe. Gentlemen, your servant. Why, Sir John, you have entered the list, it seems; and are determined to whip over the ground, if you are treated with a distance.

Sir John. I'm not to be distanc'd by you, or a dozen such.

Wou'dbe. There's nothing like courage upon these occasions; but you were out when you chose me to ride for you, Sir John.

Sir John. Let's have no more of your algebra, nor proverbs, here.

Guzzle. Come, gentlemen, you are both friends, I hope.

Wou'dbe. While Sir John confined himself to his bottle and dogs, and moved only in his little circle of pot-companions, I could be with him; but since his folly has induced him to offer himself a candidate for a place, for which he is not fit, I must say, I despise him. The people are of opinion, that I favour this undertaking of his; but I now declare, he is not the man I wish the people to elect.

Guzzle. Pray, sir, who gave you a right to choose for us?

Wou'dbe. I have no right to choose for you; but I have a right to give my opinion: especially when I am the supposed author of Sir John's folly.

Guzzle. Perhaps he's no greater fool than some others.

Wou'dbe. It would be ungrateful in you, Mr. Guzzle, not to speak in favour of Sir John; for you have stored away many gallons of his liquor in that belly of you's.

Guzzle. And he's the cleverer gentleman for it; is not he, neighbours?

1st Freeholder. For sartin; it's no disparagement to drink with a poor fellow.

2d Freeholder. No more it is, tho' some of the quality are mighty proud that way.

3d Freeholder. Mr. Wou'dbe shou'd'n't speak so freely against that.

Twist. Mr. Wou'dbe.

Wou'dbe. Sir.

Twist. We have heard a sartin report, that you and Sir John have joined interest.

Wou'dbe. Well; do you believe it?

Twist. Why, it don't look much like it now, Mr. Wou'dbe; but, mayhap, it's only a copy of your countenance.

Wou'dbe. You may put what construction you please upon my behaviour, gentlemen; but I assure you, it never was my intention to join with Sir John, or any one else.

Twist. Moreover, I've heard a 'sponsible man say, he could prove you were the cause of these new taxes.

Wou'dbe. Do you believe that too? or can you believe that it's in the power of any individual member to make a law himself? If a law is enacted that is displeasing to the people, it has the concurrence of the whole legislative body, and my vote for, or against it, is of little consequence.

Guzzle. And what the devil good do you do then?

Wou'dbe. As much as I have abilities to do.

Guzzle. Suppose, Mr. Wou'dbe, we were to want you to get the price of rum lower'd—wou'd you do it?

Wou'dbe. I cou'd not.

Guzzle. Huzza for Sir John! he has promised to do it, huzza for Sir John!

Twist. Suppose, Mr. Wou'dbe, we should want this tax taken off—cou'd you do it?

Wou'dbe. I could not.

Twist. Huzza for Mr. Strutabout! he's damn'd, if he don't. Huzza for Mr. Strutabout!

Stern. Suppose, Mr. Wou'dbe, we that live over the river, should want to come to church on this side, is it not very hard we should pay ferryage; when we pay as much to the church as you do?

Wou'dbe. Very hard.

Stern. Suppose we were to petition the assembly could you get us clear of that expence?

Wou'dbe. I believe it to be just; and make no doubt but it would pass into a law.

Stern. Will you do it?

Wou'dbe. I will endeavour to do it.

Stern. Huzza for Mr. Wou'dbe! Wou'dbe forever!

Prize. Why don't you burgesses, do something with the damn'd pickers? If we have a hogshead of tobacco refused, away it goes to them; and after they have twisted up the best of it for their own use, and taken as much as will pay them for their trouble, the poor planter has little for his share.

Wou'dbe. There are great complaints against them; and I believe the assembly will take them under consideration.

Prize. Will you vote against them?

Wou'dbe. I will, if they deserve it.

Prize. Huzza for Mr. Wou'dbe! you shall go, old fellow; don't be afraid; I'll warrant it.

[*Exeunt severally; some huzzaing for Mr. Wou'dbe—some for Sir John—some for Mr. Strutabout.*

SCENE II.   *Another part of the field.*

Mr. Strutabout, Mr. Smallhopes, and a number of freeholders round them.

1*st Freeholder.* Huzza for Mr. Strutabout!
2*d Freeholder.* Huzza for Mr. Smallhopes!
3*d Freeholder.* Huzza for Mr. Smallhopes and Mr. Strutabout!
4*th Freeholder.* Huzza for Mr. Strutabout and Mr. Smallhopes!

[*Exeunt, huzzaing.*

Enter Guzzle, drunk.

Guzzle. Huzza for Sir John Toddy, the cleverest gentleman—the finest gentleman that ever was (*hickuping.*)

Enter Mrs. Guzzle, drunk.

Mrs. Guzzle. Where's my drunken beast of a husband? (*hickups*) Oh John Guzzle, Oh John Guzzle.

Guzzle. What the devil do you want?

Mrs. Guzzle. Why don't you go home, you drunken beast? Lord bless me, how the gingerbread has given me the hickup.

Guzzle. Why, Joan, you have made too—free with the bottle—I believe.

Mrs. Guzzle. I make free with the bottle—you drunken sot!—Well, well, the gingerbread has made me quite giddy.

Guzzle. Hold up, Joan, don't fall—*(Mrs. Guzzle falls.)* The devil, you will? Joan! Why woman, what's the matter? are you drunk?

Mrs. Guzzle. Drunk! you beast! No, quite sober; but very sick with eating gingerbread.

Guzzle. For shame, Joan get up—*(offers to help her up, and falls upon her.)*

Mrs. Guzzle. Oh Lord! John! you've almost killed me.

Guzzle. Not I—I'll get clear of you as fast as I can.

Mrs. Guzzle. Oh John, I shall die, I shall die.

Guzzle. Very well, you'll die a pleasant death, then.

Mrs. Guzzle. Oh Lord! how sick! how sick!

Guzzle. Oh Joan Guzzle! Oh Joan Guz-zle!—Why don't you go home, you drunken beast. Lord bless me, how the gingerbread has given me the hickup.

Mrs. Guzzle. Pray, my dear John, help me up.

Guzzle. Pray, my dear Joan, get sober first.

Mrs. Guzzle. Pray John, help me up.

Guzzle. Pray, Joan, go to sleep; and when I am as drunk as you, I'll come and take your place. Farewell, Joan. Huzza for Sir John Toddy!   [*Exit huzzaing.*

Scene changes to another part of the field. Strutabout, Smallhopes, and freeholders.

Strutabout. Gentlemen—I'm much obliged to you for your good intentions; I make no doubt but (with the assistance of my friend Mr. Smallhopes) I shall be able to do every thing you have requested. Your grievances shall be redress'd; and all your petitions heard.

Freeholders. Huzza for Mr. Strutabout and Mr. Smallhopes!

Enter Mr. Wou'dbe.

Wou'dbe. Gentlemen, your servant; you seem happy in a circle of your friends, I hope my company is not disagreeable.

Strutabout. It can't be very agreeable to those you have treated so ill.

Smallhopes. You have used me ill, and all this company, by God—

Wou'dbe. If I have, Gentlemen, I am sorry for it; but it never was my intention to treat any person ungenteelly.

Smallhopes. You be damn'd; you're a turn-coat, by God.

Wou'dbe. Your abuse will never have any weight with me: neither do I regard your oaths or imprecations. In order to support a weak cause, you swear to what requires better proof than your assertions.

Smallhopes. Where's your friend, Sir John Toddy? he's a pretty fellow, an't he, and be damn'd to you; you recommend him to the people, don't you?

Wou'dbe. No, sir; I should be as blamable to recommend Sir John, as you, and your friend there *(pointing to Strutabout)* in recommending one another.

Strutabout. Sir, I am as capable of serving the people as yourself; and let me tell you, sir, my sole intention in offering myself is, that I may redress the many and heavy grievances you have imposed upon this poor county.

Wou'dbe. Poor, indeed, when you are believed, or when coxcombs and jockies can impose themselves upon it for men of learning.

1st Freeholder. Well, its no use; Mr. Wou'dbe is too hard for them both.

2d Freeholder. I think so too: why Strutabout! speak up, old fellow, or you'll lose ground.

Strutabout. I'll lay you fifty pounds I'm elected before you.

Wou'dbe. Betting will not determine it; and therefore I shall not lay.

Strutabout. I can lick you, Wou'dbe. *(beginning to strip.)*

Wou'dbe. You need not strip to do it; for you intend to do it with your tongue, I suppose.

Smallhopes. (clapping Strutabout upon the back) Well done Strutabout,— you can do it, by God. Don't be afraid, you shan't be hurt; damn me if you shall, *(strips.)*

Wou'dbe. What! Gentlemen, do they who aspire to the first posts in our county, and who have ambition to become legislators, and to take upon themselves part of the guidance of the state, submit their naked bodies to public view, as if they were malefactors; or, for some crimes, condemned to the whipping-post?

Smallhopes. Come on, damn ye; and don't preach your damn'd proverbs here.

Wou'dbe. Are the candidates to fight for their seats in the house of burgesses? If so, perhaps I may stand as good a chance to succeed, as you.

Smallhopes. I can lick you, by God. Come on, if you dare——*(capering about.)*

1st Freeholder. Up to him—I'll stand by you. *(to Wou'dbe.)*

2d Freeholder. They are not worth your notice, Mr. Wou'dbe; but if you have a mind to try yourself, I'll see fair play.

Wou'dbe. When I think they have sufficiently exposed themselves, I'll explain the opinion I have of them, with the end of my cane.

Smallhopes. Up to him, damn ye, *(pushing Strutabout.)*

Strutabout. You need not push me, I can fight without being pushed to it; fight yourself, if you are so fond of it. *(putting on his cloaths.)*

Smallhopes. Nay, if you are for that, and determined to be a coward, Mr. Strutabout, I can't help it; but damn me if I ever hack. *(putting on his cloaths.)*

Wou'dbe. So you are both scared, gentlemen, without a blow, or an angry look! ha, ha, ha! Well, gentlemen, you have escaped a good caning, and though you are not fit for burgesses, you'll make good soldiers; for you are excellent at a retreat.

1st Freeholder. Huzza for Mr. Wou'dbe!

2d Freeholder. Huzza for Mr. Wou'dbe!

Enter Guzzle.

Guzzle. Huzza for Sir John Toddy! Toddy (*hickups*) forever, boys!

Enter Sir John, drunk.

Guzzle. Here he comes—as fine [a] gentleman, tho' I say it, as the best of them.

Sir John. So I am, John, as clever a fellow (*hickups*) as the famous Mr. Wou'dbe, tho' I (*hickups*) say it.

Strutabout. There's a pretty fellow to be a burgess, gentlemen: lord, what a drunken beast it is.

Sir John. What beast, pray? am I a beast?

Strutabout. Yes, Sir John, you are a beast, and you may take the name of what beast you please; so your servant, my dear.

[*Exeunt Strutabout and Smallhopes.*

Wou'dbe. Except an ass, Sir John, for that he's entitled to.

Sir John. Thank you, sir.

Wou'dbe. A friend in need, Sir John, as the proverb says, is a friend indeed.

Sir John. I thank you, I know you are my friend (*hickups*) Mr. Wou'dbe, if you'd speak your mind—I know you are.

Wou'dbe. How do you know it, Sir John?

Sir John. Did not you take my part just now, Mr. Wou'dbe? (*hickups*) I know it.

Wou'dbe. I shall always take your part, Sir John, when you are imposed upon by a greater scoundrel than yourself, and when you pretend to what you are not fit for, I shall always oppose you.

Sir John. Well, Mr. Wou'dbe, an't I as *fitten* a (*hickups*) man as either of those?

Wou'dbe. More so, Sir John, for they are knaves, and you, Sir John, are an honest blockhead.

Sir John. Is that in my favour, or not, John? *(to Guzzle.)*

Guzzle. In your favour, by all means; for (*hickups*) he says you are honest. Huzza for Mr. Wou'dbe and the honest (*hickups*) Sir John Blockhead.

Enter Ralpho—gives a letter to Wou'dbe.

Wou'dbe. (Reads)—this is good news indeed.

1st Freeholder. Huzza for Mr. Wou'dbe!

2d Freeholder. Huzza for Mr. Wou'dbe!

Guzzle. Huzza for the honest Sir John Block—(*hickups*) head.

Wou'dbe. Silence, gentlemen, and I'll read a letter to you, that (I don't doubt) will give you great pleasure. (*he reads*) Sir, *I have been informed that the scoundrels. who opposed us last election (not content with my resignation) are endeavouring to undermine you in the good opinion of the people: It has warmed my blood, and again call'd my thoughts from retirement; speak this to the people, and let them know I intend to stand a poll, &c. Your's affectionately.*   Worthy

Freeholders. Huzza for Mr. Wou'dbe and Mr. Worthy!

Sir John. Huzza for Mr. Worthy and Mr. Wou'dbe! (*hickups*) I'm not so fitten as they, and therefore gentlemen I recline. (*hickups*) Yes, gentlemen (*staggering about*) I will; for I am not (*hickups*) so fitten as they. (*falls*).

Guzzle. Huzza for the drunken Sir John Toddy. (*hickups*).

Sir John. Help me up John—do, John, help.

Guzzle. No, Sir John, stay, and I'll fetch my wife, Joan, and lay—her along side of you.   [*Exit.*

Wou'dbe. Ralpho.

Ralpho. Sir.

Wou'dbe. Take care of Sir John, least any accident should befall him.

Ralpho. Yes, sir.   [*Exeunt Wou'dbe and freeholders, huzzaing for Wou'dbe and Worthy.*

Enter Guzzle, with his wife in his arms.

Guzzle. Here, Sir John, here's my wife fast asleep, to keep you company, and as drunk as a sow. *(throws her upon Sir John, and returns to one side.)*

Sir John. Oh Lord! You've broke my bones.

Joan. *(waking)* John! John! *(punching Sir John)* get up; *(looking round, sees Sir John)* what have we here? Lord, what would our John give to know this? He would have reason to be jealous of me, then!

Enter Guzzle.

Guzzle. Well, Joan, are you sober?

Joan. *(getting up)* How came that man to be lying with me? It's some of your doings, I'm sure; that you may have an excuse to be jealous of me.

Guzzle. I want no excuse for that, child.

Joan. What brought him there?

Guzzle. The same that brought you, child; rum, sugar, and water.

Joan. Well, well, as I live, I thought it was you, and that we were in our own clean sweet bed. Lord! how I tremble for fear he should have done what you do, sometimes, John.

Guzzle. I never do any thing when I am drunk. Sir John and you have done more than that, I believe.

Joan. Don't be jealous, John; it will ruin us both.

Guzzle. I am very jealous of that.

Joan. If you are, I'll beat the cruel beast that is the cause of it, 'till he satisfies you I am innocent.

Guzzle. Don't, Joan, it will make me more jealous.

Joan. I will, I tell you I will. *(beats Sir John, who all the time cries murder, help, help!)*

Ralpho. Stop, madam, this gentleman is in my care; and you must not abuse him.

Mrs. Guzzle. I will, and you too, you rascal. *(beats him first, and then Sir John.)*

Ralpho. Peace, stop, madam, peace, peace.

Sir John. Oh lord! help, John, for God's sake, help.

Ralpho. Do as you please, madam, do as you please. *(runs off)*.

Joan. *(beating Sir John)* I'll learn you to cuckold a man without letting his wife know it.

Sir John. Help, murder! help.

Guzzle. *(taking hold of Joan)* Stop, Joan, I'm satisfied—quite satisfied.

Joan. What fellow is it?

Guzzle. Sir John Toddy, our good friend; Oh, Joan, you should not have beat poor Sir John, he is as drunk as you and I were, Joan. Oh! poor Sir John. *(cries.)*

Joan. Good lack, why did'nt you tell me? I would have struck you as soon as him, John. Don't be angry, good Sir John, I did not know you.

Sir John. It's well enough: help me out of the mire, neighbours, and I'll forget and forgive.

Guzzle. Yes, Sir John, and so we will. *(they help him up.)* Come, Sir John, let's go home, this is no place for us: come Joan.

[*Exeunt Guzzle and Joan, supporting Sir John.*

SCENE III.   *Another part of the field.*

Enter Wou'dbe and Ralpho.

Wou'dbe. Where's Sir John?

Ralpho. In the hands of a woman, sir, and as I left him in such good hands, I thought there was no farther occasion for my attendance.

Wou'dbe. Are you sure he'll be taken care of?

Ralpho. Yes, the lady, an't please your honour, seemed devilish kind to him.

Wou'dbe. See that you have all ready; it's high time we thought of going home, if we intend there to-night.

Ralpho. All shall be ready, sir.   [*Exit Ralpho.*

Wou'dbe. Well, I've felt the pulse of all the leading men, and find they beat still for Worthy, and myself. Strutabout and Smallhopes fawn and cringe in so abject a manner, for the few votes they get, that I'm in hopes they'll be soon heartily despised.

> The prudent candidate who hopes to rise,
> Ne'er deigns to hide it, in a mean disguise.
> Will, to his place, with moderation slide,
> And win his way, or not resist the tide.
> The fool, aspiring to bright honour's post,
> In noise, in shouts, and tumults oft, is lost.

[*Exit.*

END OF THE SECOND ACT.

ACT III. SCENE I. *Wou'dbe's house.*

Enter Wou'dbe and Worthy.

Wou'dbe. Nothing could have afforded me more pleasure than your letter; I read it to the people, and can with pleasure assure you, it gave them infinite satisfaction.

Worthy. My sole motive in declaring myself was to serve you, and if I am the means of your gaining your election with honour, I shall be satisfied.

Wou'dbe. You have always been extremely kind, sir, but I could not enjoy the success I promised myself, without your participation.

Worthy. I have little inclination to the service; you know my aversion to public life, Wou'dbe, and how little I have ever courted the people for the troublesome office they have hitherto imposed upon me.

Wou'dbe. I believe you enjoy as much domestic happiness as any person, and that your aversion to a public life proceeds from the pleasure you find at home. But, sir, it surely is the duty of every man who has abilities to serve his country, to take up the burden, and bear it with patience.

Worthy. I know it is needless to argue with you upon this head: you are determined I shall serve with you, I find.

Wou'dbe. I am; and therefore let's take the properest methods to insure success.

Worthy. What would you propose?

Wou'dbe. Nothing more than for you to shew yourself to the people.

Worthy. I'll attend you where ever you please.

Wou'dbe. To-morrow being the day of election, I have invited most of the principal freeholders to breakfast with me, in their way to the courthouse, I hope you'll favour us with your company.

Worthy. I will; till then, adieu.   [*Exit Worthy.*

Wou'dbe. I shall expect you. It would give me great pleasure if Worthy would be more anxious than he appears to be upon this occasion; conscious of his abilities and worth, he scorns to ask a vote for any person but me; well, I must turn the tables on him, and solicit as strongly in his favour.

> 'Tis said self-interest is the secret aim,
> Of those uniting under Friendship's name.
> How true this maxim is, let others prove—
> Myself I'd punish for the man I love.

[*Exit Wou'dbe.*

SCENE II.   *Mr. Julip's House.*

Enter Captain Paunch and Mr. Julip.

Capt. Well, neighbour, I have come to see you on purpose to know how votes went at the treat yesterday.

Julip. I was not there; but I've seen neighbour Guzzle this morning, and he says, Sir John gives the matter up to Mr. Worthy and Mr. Wou'dbe.

Capt. Mr. Worthy! does he declare, huzza, my boys! well, I'm proud our county may choose two without being obliged to have one of those jackanapes at the head of it, faith: Who are you for now, neighbour?

Julip. I believe I shall vote for the two old ones, and tho' I said I was for Sir John, it was because I lik'd neither of the others; but since Mr. Worthy will serve us, why, to be sartin its our duty to send Wou'dbe and him.

Capt. Hah, faith, now you speak like a man; you are a man after my own heart: give me your hand.

Julip. Here it is, Wou'dbe and Worthy, I say.

Capt. Done, but who comes yonder? surely, it's not Mr. Worthy! 'Tis, I declare.

Enter Mr. Worthy.

Worthy. Gentlemen, your servant, I hope your families are well.

Capt. At your service, sir.

Worthy. I need not, I suppose, gentlemen, inform you that I have entered the list with my old competitors, and have determined to stand a poll at the next election. If you were in the croud yesterday, my friend Wou'dbe, I doubt not, made a declaration of my intentions to the people.

Capt. We know it, thank heaven, Mr. Worthy, tho' neither of us were there: as I did not like some of the candidates I did not choose to be persecuted for a vote that I was resolved never to bestow upon them.

Julip. My rule is never to taste of a man's liquor unless I'm his friend, and therefore, I stay'd at home.

Worthy. Well, my honest friend, I am proud to find that you still preserve your usual independence. Is it possible Captain, that the people can be so misled, as to reject Wou'dbe, and elect Strutabout in his room?

Capt. You know, Mr. Worthy, how it is, as long as the liquor is running, so long they'll be Mr. Strutabout's friends, but when the day comes, I'm thinking it will be another case.

Worthy. I'm sorry, my countrymen, for the sake of a little toddy, can be induced to behave in a manner so contradictory to the candour and integrity which always should prevail among mankind.

Capt. It's so, sir, you may depend upon it.

Julip. I'm thinking it is.

Worthy. Well, gentlemen, will you give me leave to ask you, how far you think my declaring will be of service to Mr. Wou'dbe?

Capt. Your declaring has already silenced Sir John Toddy; and I doubt not, but Strutabout and Smallhopes will lose many votes by it.

Worthy. Has Sir John declined? poor Sir John is a weak man, but he has more virtues to recommend him than either of the others.

Julip. So I think, Mr. Worthy, and I'll be so bold as to tell you that, had you not set up, Mr. Wou'dbe and Sir John should have had my vote.

Worthy. Was I a constituent, instead of a candidate, I should do the same.

Julip. Well, captain, you see I was not so much to blame.

Capt. Sir John may be honest, but he is no fitter for that place than myself.

Julip. Suppose he was not, if he was the best that offered to serve us, should not we choose him?

Worthy. Yes, surely: Well, my friends, I'm now on my way, to breakfast at Mr. Wou'dbe's, but I hope to meet you at the court-house today.

Both. Aye, aye, depend upon us.   [*Exit Worthy.*

Capt. Well, neighbour, I hope things now go on better; I like the present appearance.

Julip. So do I.

Capt. Do all you can, old fellow.

Julip. I will.

Capt. I hope you will, neighbour. I wish you well.

Julip. You the same.   [*shake hands, and exeunt.*

SCENE III.   *Wou'dbe's house, a long breakfast table set out.*

Wou'dbe, Worthy, Capt. Paunch, Mr. Julip, Twist, Stern, Prize, and other freeholders; several negroes go backwards and forwards, bringing in the breakfast.

1st Freeholder. Give us your hand, neighbour Worthy, I'm extremely glad to see thee with all my heart: So my heart of oak, you are willing to give your time and trouble once more to the service of your country.

Worthy. Your kindness does me honour, and if my labours be productive of good to my country, I shall deem myself fortunate.

2d Freeholder. Still the same sensible man I always thought him. Damn it, now if every county cou'd but send such a burgess, what a noble house we should have?

3d Freeholder. We shall have no polling now, but all will be for the same, I believe. Here's neighbour Twist, who was resolute for Strutabout, I don't doubt, will vote for Mr. Worthy and Mr. Wou'dbe.

Twist. Yes, that I will: what could I do better?

All. Aye, so will we all.

Wou'dbe. Gentlemen, for your forwardness in favour of my good friend Worthy, my sincere thanks are but a poor expression in the pleasure I feel. For my part, your esteem I shall always attribute more to his than my own desert. But come, let us sit down to breakfast, all is ready I believe; and you're heartily welcome to batchelors quarters. *(they all sit down to the table, he asks each of the company which they prefer, coffee, tea, or chocolate, and each chooses to his liking; he pours out, and the servants carry it around.)*

Worthy. Gentlemen, will any of you have a part of this fine salt shad? *(they answer, yes, if you please; and he helps them.)*

Capt. P. This warm toast and butter is very fine, and the shad gives it an excellent flavour.

Mr. Julip. Boy, give me the spirit. This chocolate, me thinks, wants a little lacing to make it admirable. *(the servants bring it.)*

Prize. Mr. Wou'dbe, do your fishing places succeed well this year?

Wou'dbe. Better than they've been known for some seasons.

Stern. I'm very glad of it: for then I can get my supply from you.

Mr. Julip. Neighbour Stalk, how do crops stand with you?

1st Freeholder. Indifferently well, I thank you; how are you?

Mr. Julip. Oh, very well! we crop it gloriously.

Wou'dbe. You have not breakfasted yet, neighbour, give me leave to help you to another dish.

2d Freeholder. Thank ye, sir, but enough's as good as a feast.

Capt. P. (looking at his watch.) I'm afraid we shall be late, they ought to have begun before now.

Wou'dbe. Our horses are at the gate, and we have not far to go.

Freeholders all. Very well, we've all breakfasted. *(they rise from table and the servants take away.)*

1st Freeholder. Come along, my friends, I long to see your triumph. Huzza for Wou'dbe and Worthy!   [*Exit huzzaing.*

SCENE IV.   *The Court-house yard.*

The door open, and a number of freeholders seen crouding within.

1st Freeholder. (to a freeholder coming out of the house) How do votes go, neighbour? for Wou'dbe and Worthy?

2d Freeholder. Aye, aye, they're just come, and sit upon the bench, and yet all the votes are for them. 'Tis quite a hollow thing. The poll will be soon over. The People croud so much, and vote so fast, you can hardly turn around.

1st Freeholder. How do Strutabout and Smallhopes look? very doleful, I reckon.

2d Freeholder. Like a thief under the gallows.

3d Freeholder. There you must be mistaken, neighbour; for two can't be like one.

1st & 2d Freeholders. Ha, ha, ha,—a good joke, a good joke.

3d Freeholder. Not so good neither, when the subject made it so easy.

1st & 2d Freeholders. Better and better, ha, ha, ha. Huzza for Worthy and Wou'dbe! and confusion to Strutabout and Smallhopes.

Enter Guzzle.

Guzzle. Huzza for Wou'dbe and Worthy! and huzza for Sir John Toddy! tho' he reclines.

1st Freeholder. So Guzzle, your friend Sir John reclines, does he? I think he does right.

Guzzle. You think he does right! pray sir, what right have you to think about it? nobody but a fool would kick a fallen man lower.

1st Freeholder. Sir, I won't be called a fool by any man, I'll have you to know, sir.

Guzzle. Then you ought'nt to be one; but here's at ye, adrat ye, if ye're for a quarrel. Sir John Toddy would have stood a good chance, and I'll maintain it, come on, damn ye.

1st Freeholder. Oh! as for fighting, there I'm your servant; a drunkard is as bad to fight as a madman. *(runs off.)*

Guzzle. Houroa, houroa, you see no body so good at a battle as a staunch toper. The milksops are afraid of them to a man.

3d Freeholder. You knew he was a coward before you thought proper to attack him; if you think yourself so brave, try your hand upon me, and you'll find you're mistaken.

Guzzle. For the matter of that, I'm the best judge myself; good day, my dear, good day. Huzza, for Sir John Toddy.   [*Exit.*

3d Freeholder. How weak must Sir John be to be governed by such a wretch as Guzzle!

The Sheriff comes to the door, and says,

Gentlemen freeholders, come into court, and give your votes, or the poll will be closed.

Freeholders. We've all voted.

Sheriff. The poll's closed. Mr. Wou'dbe and Mr. Worthy are elected.

Freeholders without and within. Huzza—huzza! Wou'dbe and Worthy for ever, boys, bring 'em on, bring 'em on, Wou'dbe and Worthy for ever!

Enter Wou'dbe and Worthy, in two chairs, raised aloft by the freeholders.

Freeholders all.—Huzza, for Wou'dbe and Worthy—Huzza for Wou'dbe and Worthy—huzza, for Wou'dbe and Worthy!—*(they traverse the stage, and then set them down.)*

Worthy. Gentlemen, I'm much obliged to you for the signal proof you have given me to-day of your regard. You may depend upon it, that I shall endeavour faithfully to discharge the trust you have reposed in me.

Wou'dbe. I have not only, gentlemen, to return you my hearty thanks for the favours you have conferred upon me, but I beg leave also to thank you for shewing such regard to the merit of my friend. You have in that, shewn your judgment, and a spirit of independence becoming Virginians.

    Capt. P. So we have Mr. Wou'dbe, we have done as we ought, we have elected the ablest, according to the writ.

> Henceforth, let those who pray for wholesome laws,
> And all well-wishers to their country's cause,
> Like us refuse a coxcomb—choose a man—
> Then let our senate blunder if it can.

                                                     [*Exit omnes.*

END OF THE CANDIDATES.

Thomas Jefferson
(1743–1826)

Thomas Jefferson was born on "Shadwell" estate, one of his father's several tobacco plantations in central Virginia. As a youth, he attended the school of the Reverend William Douglas, who first introduced him to the classics. At seventeen he entered the College of William and Mary and was graduated two years later. He began the study of law with George Wythe, a noted law scholar whom he had met in college, and in 1767 he was admitted to the bar. Only a year later, Jefferson began his career in public life as he was elected to the Virginia Assembly. During these years, he was compiling a notebook of writings, which would be published in 1928 as *The Literary Bible of Thomas Jefferson* and which reveals Jefferson's attraction to Greek and Roman ethical thought. In 1774, he published the pamphlet *A Summary View of the Rights of British America*, which attacked the colonial authority of parliament and which articulates clearly his belief in natural rights common to all people. The pamphlet won Jefferson fame as an eloquent proponent of colonial freedom, and when the American Revolution began, he was sent with the delegation from Virginia to the Second Continental Congress in Philadelphia. There he was appointed to a five-man committee assigned to draw up a declaration of independence, and the draft passed by Congress on July 4, 1776, was almost entirely Jefferson's work.

    In 1779, Jefferson was elected governor of Virginia and served for three years. Near the end of his term, in response to inquiries from the Marquis de Barbe-Marbois, a French diplomat gathering data on America, he compiled his *Notes on the State of Virginia*, where he reveals his ideas on art and education, his own personal religious and ethical beliefs, and his (unfortunate) attitudes toward slavery. He also refutes the French naturalist Buffon, who had written that all species, including humans, tended to degenerate in the New World. Jefferson's *Notes* has been called the most important ethical and scientific work of its era, and it established him as the foremost thinker of the American Enlightenment.

    In 1784, he was named an American Commissioner in Paris and the next year succeeded Benjamin Franklin as minister to France. In 1789, as the French Revolution was beginning, Jefferson returned to America, where he was appointed secretary of state in the cabinet of the newly elected president, George Washington. He served as vice president under John Adams and served two terms as president, from 1801 to 1809. After his tenure as president, he retired to Monticello, but one great work remained for him. In 1817, he fulfilled a lifelong dream by founding the University of Virginia, designing many of its buildings and serving as its first rector. He died on July 4, 1826, fifty years to the day after the signing of the *Declaration of Independence* that he had penned.

from *The Autobiography: Notes on the State of Virginia*

A Declaration by the Representatives of the United States of America, in General Congress Assembled.

When in the course of human events it becomes necessary for one people to dissolve the political bands which have connected them with another, and to assume among the powers of the earth the separate & equal station to which the laws of nature and of nature's God entitle them, a decent respect to the opinions of mankind requires that they should declare the causes which impel them to the separation.

 We hold these truths to be self-evident: that all men are created equal; that they are endowed by their creator with <u>inherent and</u> inalienable rights; that among these are life, liberty, & the pursuit of happiness: that to secure these rights, governments are instituted among men, deriving their just powers from the consent of the governed; that whenever any form of government becomes destructive of these ends, it is the right of the people to alter or abolish it, & to institute new government, laying it's foundation on such principles, & organizing it's powers in such form, as to them shall seem most likely to effect their safety & happiness. Prudence indeed will dictate that governments long established should not be changed for light & transient causes; and accordingly all experience hath shown that mankind are more disposed to suffer while evils are sufferable than to right themselves by abolishing the forms to which they are accustomed. But when a long train of abuses & usurpations <u>begun at a distinguished period and</u> pursuing invariably the same object, evinces a design to reduce them under absolute despotism, it is their right, it is their duty to throw off such government, & to provide new guards for their future security. Such has been the patient sufferance of these colonies; & such is now the necessity which constrains them to <u>expunge</u> their former systems of government. The history of the present king of Great Britain is a history of <u>unremitting</u> injuries & usurpations, <u>among which appears no solitary fact to contradict the uniform tenor of the rest but all have</u> in direct object the establishment of an absolute tyranny over these states. To prove this let facts be submitted to a candid world <u>for the truth of which we pledge a faith yet unsullied by falsehood.</u>

 He has refused his assent to laws the most wholesome & necessary for the public good.

 He has forbidden his govenors to pass laws of immediate & pressing importance, unless suspended in their operation till his assent should be obtained; & when so suspended, he has utterly neglected to attend to them.

 He has refused to pass other laws for the accommodation of large districts of people, unless those people would relinquish the right of representation in the legislature, a right inestimable to them, & formidable to tyrants only.

 Underlined passages indicate differences between Jefferson's revision and the Declaration's final adopted text.

He has called together legislative bodies at places unusual, uncomfortable, and distant from the depository of their public records, for the sole purpose of fatiguing them into compliance with his measures.

He has dissolved representative houses repeatedly & continually for opposing with manly firmness his invasions on the rights of the people.

He has refused for a long time after such dissolutions to cause others to be elected, whereby the legislative powers, incapable of annihilation, have returned to the people at large for their exercise, the state remaining in the meantime exposed to all the dangers of invasion from without & convulsions within.

He has endeavored to prevent the population of these states; for that purpose obstructing the laws for naturalization of foreigners, refusing to pass others to encourage their migrations hither, & raising the conditions of new appropriations of lands.

He has suffered the administration of justice totally to cease in some of these states refusing his assent to laws for establishing judiciary powers.

He has made our judges dependant on his will alone, for the tenure of their offices, & the amount & paiment of their salaries.

He has erected a multitude of new offices by a self assumed power and sent hither swarms of new officers to harass our people and eat our their substance.

He has kept among us in times of peace standing armies and ships of war without the consent of our legislatures.

He has affected to render the military independant of, & superior to the civil power.

He has combined with others to subject us to a jurisdiction foreign to our constitutions & unacknowledged by our laws, giving his assent to their acts of pretended legislation for quartering large bodies of armed troops among us; for protecting them by a mock-trial from punishment for any murders which they should commit on the inhabitants of these states; for cutting off our trade with all parts of the world; for imposing taxes on us without our consent; for depriving us [ ] of the benefits of trial by jury; for transporting us beyond seas to be tried for pretended offences; for abolishing the free system of English laws in a neighboring province, establishing therein an arbitrary government, and enlarging it's boundaries, so as to render it at once an example and fit instrument for introducing the same absolute rule into these states; for taking away our charters, abolishing our most valuable laws, and altering fundamentally the forms of our governments; for suspending our own legislatures, & declaring themselves invested with power to legislate for us in all cases whatsoever.

He has abdicated government here withdrawing his governors, and declaring us out of his allegiance & protection.

He has plundered our seas, ravaged our coasts, burnt our towns, & destroyed the lives of our people.

He is at this time transporting large armies of foreign mercenaries to compleat the works of death, desolation & tyranny already begun with circumstances of cruelty and perfidy [ ] unworthy the head of a civilized nation.

He has constrained our fellow citizens taken captive on the high seas to bear arms against their country, to become the executioners of their friends & brethren, or to fall themselves by their hands.

He has [ ] endeavored to bring on the inhabitants of our frontiers the merciless Indian savages, whose known rule of warfare is an undistinguished destruction of all ages, sexes, & conditions of existence.

He has incited treasonable insurrections of our fellow-citizens, with the allurements of forfeiture & confiscation of our property.

He has waged cruel war against human nature itself, violating it's most sacred rights of life and liberty in the persons of a distant people who never offended him, captivating & carrying them into slavery in another hemisphere, or to incur miserable death in their transportation thither. This piratical warfare, the opprobium of INFIDEL powers, is the warfare of the CHRISTIAN king of Great Britain. Determined to keep open a market where MEN should be bought & sold, he has prostituted his negative for suppressing every legislative attempt to prohibit or to restrain this execrable commerce. And that this assemblage of horrors might want no fact of distinguished die, he is now exciting those very people to rise in arms among us, and to purchase that liberty of which he has deprived them, by murdering the people on whom he also obtruded them: thus paying off former crimes committed against the LIBERTIES of one people, with crimes which he urges them to commit against the LIVES of another.

In every stage of these oppressions we have petitioned for redress in the most humble terms: our repeated petitions have been answered only by repeated injuries.

A prince whose character is thus marked by every act which may define a tyrant is unfit to be the ruler of a [ ] people who mean to be free. Future ages will scarcely believe that the hardiness of one man adventured, within the short compass of twelve years only, to lay a foundation so broad & so undisguised for tyranny over a people fostered & fixed in principles of freedom.

Nor have we been wanting in attentions to our British brethren. We have warned them from time to time of attempts by their legislature to extend a jurisdiction over these our states. We have reminded them of the circumstances of our emigration & settlement here, no one of which could warrant so strange a pretension: that these were effected at the expense of our own blood & treasure, unassisted by the wealth or the strength of Great Britain: that in constituting indeed our several forms of government, we had adopted one common king, thereby laying a foundation for perpetual league & amity with them: but that submission to their parliament was no part of our constitution, nor ever in idea, if history may be credited: and, we [ ] appealed to their native justice and magnanimity as well as to the ties of our common kindred to disavow these usurpations which were likely to interrupt our connection and correspondence. They too have been deaf to the voice of justice & of consanguinity, and when occasions have been given them, by the regular course of their laws, of removing from their councils the disturbers of our harmony, they have, by their free election, re-established them in power. At this very time too they are permitting their chief magistrate to send over not only soldiers of our common blood, but Scotch & foreign mercenaries to invade & destroy us. These facts have given the last stab to agonizing affection, and manly spirit bids us to renounce forever these unfeeling brethren. We must endeavor to forget our former love for them, and hold them as we hold the rest of mankind, enemies in war, in peace friends. We might have been a free and a great people together; but a communication of grandeur & of freedom it seems is below their dignity. Be it so, since they will have it. The road to happiness & to glory is open to us too. We will tread it apart from them, and acquiesce in the necessity which denounces our eternal separation [ ]!

We therefore the representatives of the United States of America in General Congress assembled do in the name & by	We therefore the representatives of the United States of America in General Congress assembled, appealing to the

authority of the good people of these states reject & renounce all allegiance & subjection to the kings of Great Britain & all others who may hereafter claim by, through or under them: we utterly dissolve all political connection which may heretofore have subsisted between us & the people or parliament of Great Britain: & finally we do assert & declare these colonies to be free & independent states, & that as free & independent states, they have full power to levy war, conclude peace, contract alliances, establish commerce, & to do all other acts & things which independent states may of right do.

And for the support of this declaration we mutually pledge to each other our lives, our fortunes, & our sacred honor.

supreme judge of the world for the rectitude of our intentions, do in the name, & by the authority of the good people of these colonies, solemnly publish & declare that these united colonies are & of right ought to be free & independent states; that they are absolved from all allegiance to the British crown, and that all political connection between them & the state of Great Britain is, & ought to be, totally dissolved; & that as free & independent states they have full power to levy war, conclude peace, contact alliances, establish commerce & to do all other acts & things which independant states may of right do.

And for the support of this declaration, with a firm reliance on the protection of divine providence we mutually pledge to each other our lives, our fortunes, & our sacred honor.

The Declaration thus signed on the 4th, on paper was engrossed on parchment, & signed again on the 2d. of August.

Query XIV

. . . Many of the laws which were in force during the monarchy being relative merely to that form of government, or inculcating principles inconsistent with republicanism, the first assembly which met after the establishment of the commonwealth appointed a committee to revise the whole code, to reduce it into proper form and volume, and report it to the assembly. This work has been executed by three gentlemen, and reported; but probably will not be taken up till a restoration of peace shall leave to the legislature leisure to go through such a work.

The plan of the revisal was this. The common law of England, by which is meant, that part of the English law which was anterior to the date of the oldest statutes extant, is made the basis of the work. It was thought dangerous to attempt to reduce it to a text: it was therefore left to be collected from the usual monuments of it. Necessary alterations in that, and so much of the whole body of the British statutes, and of acts of assembly, as were thought proper to be retained, were digested into 126 new acts, in which simplicity of stile was aimed at, as far as was safe. The following are the most remarkable alterations proposed:

To change the rules of descent, so as that the lands of any person dying intestate shall be divisible equally among all his children, or other representatives, in equal degree.

To make slaves distributable among the next of kin, as other moveables.

Because the closing passages of the *Declaration* differ substantially from Jefferson's version, he recommended printing the two versions side by side in the *Autobiography*.

To have all public expences, whether of the general treasury, or of a parish or county, (as for the maintenance of the poor, building bridges, court-houses, &c.) supplied by assessments on the citizens, in proportion to their property.

To hire undertakers for keeping the public roads in repair, and indemnify individuals through whose lands new roads shall be opened.

To define with precision the rules whereby aliens should become citizens, and citizens make themselves aliens.

To establish religious freedom on the broadest bottom.

To emancipate all slaves born after passing the act. The bill reported by the revisors does not itself contain this proposition; but an amendment containing it was prepared, to be offered to the legislature whenever the bill should be taken up, and further directing, that they should continue with their parents to a certain age, then be brought up, at the public expence, to tillage, arts or sciences, according to their geniusses, till the females should be eighteen, and the males twenty-one years of age, when they should be colonized to such place as the circumstances of the time should render most proper, sending them out with arms, implements of houshold and of the handicraft arts, feeds, pairs of the useful domestic animals, &c. to declare them a free and independant people, and extend to them our alliance and protection, till they shall have acquired strength; and to send vessels at the same time to other parts of the world for an equal number of white inhabitants; to induce whom to migrate hither, proper encouragements were to be proposed. It will probably be asked, Why not retain and incorporate the blacks into the state, and thus save the expence of supplying, by importation of white settlers, the vacancies they will leave? Deep rooted prejudices entertained by the whites; ten thousand recollections, by the blacks, of the injuries they have sustained; new provocations; the real distinctions which nature has made; and many other circumstances, will divide us into parties, and produce convulsions which will probably never end but in the extermination of the one or the other race.—To these objections, which are political, may be added others, which are physical and moral. The first difference which strikes us is that of colour. Whether the black of the negro resides in the reticular membrane between the skin and scarf-skin, or in the scarf-skin itself; whether it proceeds from the colour of the blood, the colour of the bile, or from that of some other secretion, the difference is fixed in nature, and is as real as if its seat and cause were better known to us. And is this difference of no importance? Is it not the foundation of a greater or less share of beauty in the two races? Are not the fine mixtures of red and white, the expressions of every passion by greater or less suffusions of colour in the one, preferable to that eternal monotony, which reigns in the countenances, that immoveable veil of black which covers all the emotions of the other race? Add to these, flowing hair, a more elegant symmetry of form, their own judgment in favour of the whites, declared by their preference of them, as uniformly as is the preference of the Oranootan for the black women over those of his own species. The circumstance of superior beauty, is thought worthy attention in the propagation of our horses, dogs, and other domestic animals; why not in that of man? Besides those of colour, figure, and hair, there are other physical distinctions proving a difference of race. They have less hair on the face and body. They secrete less by the kidnies, and more by the glands of the skin, which gives them a very strong and disagreeable odour. This greater degree of transpiration renders them more tolerant of heat, and less so of cold, than the whites. Perhaps too a difference of structure in the pulmonary apparatus, which a late ingenious experimentalist has dis-

covered to be the principal regulator of animal heat, may have disabled them from ex-
tricating, in the act of inspiration, so much of that fluid from the outer air, or obliged
them in expiration, to part with more of it. They seem to require less sleep. A black,
after hard labour through the day, will be induced by the slightest amusements to sit
up till midnight, or later, though knowing he must be out with the first dawn of the
morning. They are at least as brave, and more adventuresome. But this may perhaps
proceed from a want of forethought, which prevents their seeing a danger till it be
present. When present, they do not go through it with more coolness or steadiness
than the whites. They are more ardent after their female: but love seems with them to
be more an eager desire, than a tender delicate mixture of sentiment and sensation.
Their griefs are transient. Those numberless afflictions, which render it doubtful
whether heaven has given life to us in mercy or in wrath, are less felt, and sooner forgotten with them. In general, their existence appears to participate more of sensation
than reflection. To this must be ascribed their disposition to sleep when abstracted
from their diversions, and unemployed in labour. An animal whose body is at rest,
and who does not reflect, must be disposed to sleep of course. Comparing them by
their faculties of memory, reason, and imagination, it appears to me, that in memory
they are equal to the whites; in reason much inferior, as I think one could scarcely be
found capable of tracing and comprehending the investigations of Euclid; and that in
imagination they are dull, tasteless, and anomalous. It would be unfair to follow them
to Africa for this investigation. We will consider them here, on the same stage with
the whites, and where the facts are not apocryphal on which a judgment is to be
formed. It will be right to make great allowances for the difference of condition, of
education, of conversation, of the sphere in which they move. Many millions of them
have been brought to, and born in America. Most of them indeed have been confined
to tillage, to their own homes, and their own society: yet many have been so situated,
that they might have availed themselves of the conversation of their masters; many
have been brought up to the handicraft arts, and from that circumstance have always
been associated with the whites. Some have been liberally educated, and all have
lived in countries where the arts and sciences are cultivated to a considerable degree,
and have had before their eyes samples of the best works from abroad. The Indians,
with no advantages of this kind, will often carve figures on their pipes not destitute of
design and merit. They will crayon out an animal, a plant, or a country, so as to prove
the existence of a germ in their minds which only wants cultivation. They astonish
you with strokes of the most sublime oratory; such as prove their reason and sentiment strong, their imagination glowing and elevated. But never yet could I find that a
black had uttered a thought above the level of plain narration; never see even an elementary trait of painting or sculpture. In music they are more generally gifted than
the whites with accurate ears for tune and time, and they have been found capable of
imagining a small catch. Whether they will be equal to the composition of a more extensive run of melody, or of complicated harmony, is yet to be proved. Misery is often
the parent of the most affecting touches in poetry.—Among the blacks is misery
enough, God knows, but no poetry. Love is the peculiar œstrum of the poet. Their
love is ardent, but it kindles the senses only, not the imagination. Religion indeed has
produced a Phyllis Whately; but it could not produce a poet. The compositions published under her name are below the dignity of criticism. The heroes of the Dunciad
are to her, as Hercules to the author of that poem. Ignatius Sancho has approached
nearer to merit in composition; yet his letters do more honour to the heart than the

head. They breathe the purest effusions of friendship and general philanthropy, and shew how great a degree of the latter may be compounded with strong religious zeal. He is often happy in the turn of his compliments, and his stile is easy and familiar, except when he affects a Shandean fabrication of words. But his imagination is wild and extravagant, escapes incessantly from every restraint of reason and taste, and, in the course of its vagaries, leaves a tract of thought as incoherent and eccentric, as is the course of a meteor through the sky. His subjects should often have led him to a process of sober reasoning: yet we find him always substituting sentiment for demonstration. Upon the whole, though we admit him to the first place among those of his own colour who have presented themselves to the public judgment, yet when we compare him with the writers of the race among whom he lived, and particularly with the epistolary class, in which he has taken his own stand, we are compelled to enroll him at the bottom of the column. This criticism supposes the letters published under his name to be genuine, and to have received amendment from no other hand; points which would not be of easy investigation. The improvement of the blacks in body and mind, in the first instance of their mixture with the whites, has been observed by every one, and proves that their inferiority is not the effect merely of their condition of life. We know that among the Romans, about the Augustan age especially, the condition of their slaves was much more deplorable than that of the blacks on the continent of America. The two sexes were confined in separate apartments, because to raise a child cost the master more than to buy one. Cato, for a very restricted indulgence to his slaves in this particular, took from them a certain price. But in this country the slaves multiply as fast as the free inhabitants. Their situation and manners place the commerce between the two sexes almost without restraint.—The same Cato, on a principle of œconomy, always sold his sick and superannuated slaves. He gives it as a standing precept to a master visiting his farm, to sell his old oxen, old waggons, old tools, old and diseased servants, and every thing else become useless. 'Vendat boves vetulos, plaustrum vetus, ferramenta vetera, servum senem, servum morbosum, & si quid aliud supersit vendat.' Cato de re rustica. c. 2. The American slaves cannot enumerate this among the injuries and insults they receive. It was the common practice to expose in the island of Æsculapius, in the Tyber, diseased slaves, whose cure was like to become tedious. The Emperor Claudius, by an edict, gave freedom to such of them as should recover, and first declared, that if any person chose to kill rather than to expose them, it should be deemed homicide. The exposing them is a crime of which no instance has existed with us; and were it to be followed by death, it would be punished capitally. We are told of a certain Vedius Pollio, who, in the presence of Augustus, would have given a slave as food to his fish, for having broken a glass. With the Romans, the regular method of taking the evidence of their slaves was under torture. Here it has been thought better never to resort to their evidence. When a master was murdered, all his slaves, in the same house, or within hearing, were condemned to death. Here punishment falls on the guilty only, and as precise proof is required against him as against a freeman. Yet notwithstanding these and other discouraging circumstances among the Romans, their slaves were often their rarest artists. They excelled too in science, insomuch as to be usually employed as tutors to their master's children. Epictetus, Terence, and Phædrus, were slaves. But they were of the race of whites. It is not their condition then, but nature, which has produced the distinction.—Whether further observation will or will not verify the conjecture, that nature has been less bountiful to them in the endowments of the head, I believe that in those of the heart she will be found to have done them justice. That disposition to theft with which they have been branded, must be ascribed to their situation, and not to any depravity of the moral sense. The man, in whose favour no laws of property exist, probably feels himself less bound to respect those made in favour of others. When arguing for ourselves, we lay it down as a fundamental, that laws, to be just, must give a reciprocation of right: that, without this, they are mere arbitrary rules of conduct, founded in force, and not in conscience: and it is a problem which I give to the master to solve, whether the religious precepts against the violation of property were not framed for him as well as his slave? And whether the slave may not as justifiably take a little from one, who has taken all from him, as he may slay one who would slay him? That a change in the relations in which a man is placed should change his ideas of moral right and wrong, is neither new, nor peculiar to the colour of the blacks. Homer tells us it was so 2600 years ago.

> Ἥμισυ, γαζ τ' ἀρετῆς ἀποαίννλαι εὐρύθπα Ζεὺς
> Ἀνερος, ευτ' ἄν μιν κατὰ δδλιον ἧμαζ ἕλησιν.
> *Od.* 17.323.

Jove fix'd it certain, that whatever day
Makes man a slave, takes half his worth away.

But the slaves of which Homer speaks were whites. Notwithstanding these considerations which must weaken their respect for the laws of property, we find among them numerous instances of the most rigid integrity, and as many as among their better instructed masters, of benevolence, gratitude, and unshaken fidelity.—The opinion, that they are inferior in the faculties of reason and imagination, must be hazarded with great diffidence. To justify a general conclusion, requires may observations, even where the subject may be submitted to the Anatomical knife, to Optical glasses, to analysis by fire, or by solvents. How much more then where it is a faculty, not a substance, we are examining; where it eludes the research of all the senses; where the conditions of its existence are various and variously combined; where the effects of those which are present or absent bid defiance to calculation; let me add too, as a circumstance of great tenderness, where our conclusion would degrade a whole race of men from the rank in the scale of beings which their Creator may perhaps have given them. To our reproach it must be said, that though for a century and a half we have had under our eyes the races of black and of red men, they have never yet been viewed by us as subjects of natural history. I advance it therefore as a suspicion only, that the blacks, whether originally a distinct race, or made distinct by time and circumstances, are inferior to the whites in the endowments both of body and mind. It is not against experience to suppose, that different species of the same genus, or varieties of the same species, may possess different qualifications. Will not a lover of natural history then, one who views the gradations in all the races of animals with the eye of philosophy, excuse an effort to keep those in the department of man as distinct as nature has formed them? This unfortunate difference of colour, and perhaps of faculty, is a powerful obstacle to the emancipation of these people. Many of their advocates, while they wish to vindicate the liberty of human nature, are anxious also to preserve its dignity and beauty. Some of these, embarrassed by the question 'What further is to be done with them?' join themselves in opposition with those who are actuated by sordid avarice only. Among the Romans emancipation required but one effort. The slave, when made free, might mix with, without staining the blood of his master. But with us a second is necessary, unknown to history. When freed, he is to be removed beyond the reach of mixture.

The revised code further proposes to proportion crimes and punishments. This is attempted on the following scale.

I. Crimes whose punishment extends to *Life*.

    1. High treason.   Death by hanging.
Forfeiture of lands and goods to the commonwealth.

    2. Petty treason.   Death by hanging. Dissection.
Forfeiture of half the lands and goods to the representatives of the party slain.

    3. Murder.
        1. by poison   Death by poison.
        Forfeiture of one-half as before.

        2. in Duel.   Death by hanging. Gibbeting, if the challenger.
        Forfeiture of one-half as before, unless it be the party challenged, then the forfeiture is to the commonwealth.

        3. in any other way.   Death by hanging.
        Forfeiture of one-half as before.

    4. Manslaughter. The second offence is murder.

II. Crimes whose punishment goes to *Limb*.

    1. Rape,   ⎱
    2. Sodomy, ⎰   Dismemberment.

    3. Maiming,   ⎫
                ⎬ Retaliation, and the forfeiture of half the lands and goods to the sufferer.
    4. Disfiguring, ⎭

III. Crimes punishable by *Labour*.

1. Manslaughter, 1st offence.	Labour VII. years for the public.	Forfeiture of half as in murder.
2. Counterfeiting money.	Labour VI. years.	Forfeiture of lands and goods to the commonwealth.
3. Arson. 4. Asportation of vessels.	Labour V. years.	Reparation three-fold.
5. Robbery. 6. Burglary.	Labour IV. years.	Reparation double.
7. Housebreaking. 8. Horse-stealing.	Labour III. years.	Reparation.
9. Grand Larcency.	Labour II. years.	Reparation. Pillory.
10. Petty Larcency.	Labour I. year.	Reparation. Pillory.
11. Pretensions to witch-craft, &c.	Ducking.	Stripes.
12. Excusable homicide. 13. Suicide. 14. Apostacy. Heresy.	to be pitied, not punished.	

Pardon and privilege of clergy are proposed to be abolished; but if the verdict be against the defendant, the court in their discretion, may allow a new trial. No attainder to cause a corruption of blood, or forfeiture of dower. Slaves guilty of offences punishable in others by labour, to be transported to Africa, or elsewhere, as the circumstances of the time admit, there to be continued in slavery. A rigorous regimen proposed for those condemned to labour.

Another object of the revisal is, to diffuse knowledge more generally through the mass of the people. This bill proposes to lay off every county into small districts of five or six miles square, called hundreds, and in each of them to establish a school for teaching reading, writing, and arithmetic. The tutor to be supported by the hundred, and every person in it entitled to send their children three years gratis, and as much longer as they please, paying for it. These schools to be under a visitor, who is annually to chuse the boy, of best genius in the school, of those whose parents are too poor to give them further education, and to send him forward to one of the grammar schools, of which twenty are proposed to be erected in different parts of the country, for teaching Greek, Latin, geography, and the higher branches of numerical arithmetic. Of the boys thus sent in any one year, trial is to be made at the grammar schools one or two years, and the best genius of the whole selected, and continued six years, and the residue dismissed. By this means twenty of the best geniusses will be raked from the rubbish annually, and be instructed, at the public expence, so far as the grammer schools go. At the end of six years instruction, one half are to be discontinued (from among whom the grammar schools will probably be supplied with future masters); and the other half, who are to be chosen for the superiority of their parts and disposition, are to be sent and continued three years in the study of such sciences as they shall chuse, at William and Mary college, the plan of which is proposed to be enlarged, as will be hereafter explained, and extended to all the useful sciences. The ultimate result of the whole scheme of education would be the teaching all the children of the state reading, writing, and common arithmetic: turning out ten annually of superior genius, well taught in Greek, Latin, geography, and the higher branches of arithmetic: turning out ten others annually, of still superior parts, who, to those branches of learning, shall have added such of the sciences as their genius shall have led them to: the furnishing to the wealthier part of the people convenient schools, at which their children may be educated, at their own expence.—The general objects of this law are to provide an education adapted to the years, to the capacity, and the condition of every one, and directed to their freedom and happiness. Specific details were not proper for the law. These must be the business of the visitors entrusted with its execution. The first stage of this education being the schools of the hundreds, wherein the great mass of the people will receive their instruction, the principal foundations of future order will be laid here. Instead therefore of putting the Bible and Testament into the hands of the children, at an age when their judgments are not sufficiently matured for religious enquiries, their memories may here be stored with the most useful facts from Grecian, Roman, European and American history. The first elements of morality too may be instilled into their minds; such as, when further developed as their judgments advance in strength, may teach them how to work out their own greatest happiness, by shewing them that it does not depend on the condition of life in which chance has placed them, but is always the result of a good conscience, good health, occupation, and freedom in all just pursuits.— Those whom either the wealth of their parents or the adoption of the state shall destine to higher degrees of learning, will go on to the grammar schools, which constitute the next stage, there to be instructed in the languages. The learning Greek and Latin, I am told, is going into disuse in Europe. I know not what their manners and occupations may call for: but it would be very ill-judged in us to follow their example in this instance. There is a certain period of life, say from eight to fifteen or sixteen years of age, when the mind, like the body, is not yet firm enough for laborious and close operations. If applied to such, it falls an early victim to premature exertion; exhibiting indeed at first, in these young and tender subjects, the flattering appearance of their being men while they are yet children, but ending in reducing them to be children when they should be men. The memory is then most susceptible and tenacious of impressions; and the learning of languages being chiefly a work of memory, it seems precisely fitted to the powers of this period, which is long enough too for acquiring the most useful languages antient and modern. I do not pretend that language is science. It is only an instrument for the attainment of science. But that time is not lost which is employed in providing tools for future operation: more especially as in this case the books put into the hands of the youth for this purpose may be such as will at the same time impress their minds with useful facts and good principles. If this period be suffered to pass in idleness, the mind becomes lethargic and impotent, as would the body it inhabits if unexercised during the same time. The sympathy between body and mind during their rise, progress and decline, is too strict and obvious to endanger our being misled while we reason from the one to the other.—As soon as they are of sufficient age, it is supposed they will be sent on from the grammar schools to the university, which constitutes our third and last stage, there to study those sciences which may be adapted to their views.—By that part of our plan which prescribes the selection of the youths of genius from among the classes of the poor, we hope to avail the state of those talents which nature has sown as liberally among the poor as the rich, but which perish without use, if not sought for and cultivated.—But of all the views of this law none is more important, none more legitimate, than that of rendering the people the safe, as they are the ultimate, guardians of their own liberty. For this purpose the reading in the first stage, where *they* will receive their whole education, is proposed, as has been said, to be chiefly historical. History by apprising them of the past will enable them to judge of the future; it will avail them of the experience of other times and other nations; it will qualify them as judges of the actions and designs of men; it will enable them to know ambition under every disguise it may assume; and knowing it, to defeat its views. In every government on earth is some trace of human weakness, some germ of corruption and degeneracy, which cunning will discover, and wickedness insensibly open, cultivate, and improve. Every government degenerates when trusted to the rulers of the people alone. The people themselves therefore are its only safe depositories. And to render even them safe their minds must be improved to a certain degree. This indeed is not all that is necessary, though it be essentially necessary. An amendment of our constitution must here come in aid of the public education. The influence over government must be shared among all the people. If every individual which composes their mass participates of the ultimate authority, the government will be safe; because the corrupting the whole mass will exceed any private resources of wealth: and public ones cannot be provided but by levies on the people. In this case every man would have to pay his own price. The government of Great-Britain has been corrupted, because but one man in ten has a right to vote for members of parliament. The sellers of the government therefore get nine-tenths of their price clear. It has been thought that corruption is restrained by confining the right of suffrage to a few of the wealthier of the people: but it would be more effectually restrained by an extension of that right to such numbers as would bid defiance to the means of corruption.

Lastly, it is proposed, by a bill in this revisal, to begin a public library and gallery, by laying out a certain sum annually in books, paintings, and statues.

William Wirt

(1772–1834)

When William Wirt published his *Sketches of the Life and Character of Patrick Henry* in 1817, he planned to follow it with a series of such depictions lionizing other heroes of the American Revolution. Though those plans never materialized, even a cursory reading of Wirt's works immediately reveals his motivation for choosing the fiery Henry as the subject of his first portrait. For Wirt, rhetorical eloquence more than any other quality identified the one who possessed it as one of "Nature's noblemen," and he praised parents who trained their children to uphold Virginia's rich oratorical tradition instead of succumbing to a "violent passion for the . . . pleasures of the turf and cock-pit."

Born in Bladensburg, Maryland, on November 8, 1772, Wirt received a classical education before going on to the study of law, and he was licensed to practice in the state of Virginia in 1792, at the age of twenty. Although he was successful in his practice, Wirt began to pursue writing as a sideline during 1803, when he published (anonymously) *The Letters of the British Spy*. Over the next ten years, he refined his skills as an essayist, publishing the collections *The Rainbow* (1804) and *The Old Bachelor* (1814). In 1817, he published his biography of Patrick Henry, over which he had labored for more than twelve years. Even though it made his literary reputation, it is chiefly remembered for its inclusion of Henry's famous speech before the Virginia House of Burgesses in 1775, an oration that was not preserved in writing and that Wirt reconstructed from the memories of Henry's contemporaries. After the publication of *Sketches*, Wirt focused his attention on his political career, serving as U.S. attorney general from 1817 through 1829, longer than any other incumbent. When he died in Washington, D.C., in 1834 while attending a session of the U.S. Supreme Court, both houses of Congress adjourned for his funeral.

Most of Wirt's essays, particularly those of *The Old Bachelor*, decry the passing of a golden age of Virginia, an "age of eloquence," and stress the importance of education for Virginia's "gentlemen," who he believed should be instructed in some "useful trade . . . to prevent the indolent and vicious from contaminating or encumbering the virtuous and industrious."

from *The Old Bachelor*, Essay Number XIX

To Marcellus eris. Virg. En. Lib. VI.
A new Marcellus shall arise in thee. Dryden.

Rosalie and I have just returned from a ride, on horse back, to our neighbor Martin's: and, during the visit, I received a compliment, so truly pleasing, that it poured balm into the wounds of which I complained in my last number, and removed all their anguish.

Mr. Martin is one of those many unfortunate country-men of ours who, with very moderate expectations in point of fortune, are *brought up gentlemen;* that is, directed in their youth to the acquirement of no trade, profession or pursuit of honest industry; but permitted, at least, by the silence and acquiescence of their parents, to believe that they are rich enough to live without the drudgery either of manual or mental labor. The consequences have been the same, in relation to this good gentleman, which we see, every day, to flow from the same wretched management: He learned to dress, to dance, to drink, to smoke, to swear, to game; contracted a violent passion for the very rational, elegant and humane pleasures of the turf and the cock-pit, and was long distinguished for the best horses and game-cocks in the country. Yet he has, in the common current of life, a kind and friendly temper, and when he is out of the region of low debauchery and dissipation, he has the pure and engaging manners of a gentleman. The force of habit, however, is so strong in him, that he seems to have no power to resist the temptation either of a horse race or a cock-fight, and in the indulgence of this master passion of his soul, he has made several very expensive tours of the Continent.

We are told of a custom which prevailed in some of the states of Europe (while there were seperate and independent states in that devoted quarter of the world,) to have even their Princes and the heir apparent of the sovereignty itself, instructed in some useful trade or handicraft. The object, we are informed, was to provide against the caprices of fortune, and put in their hands the means of an honest support in every emergency that might befal them. Why is not this sound and sensible policy adopted by parents in this country? Are we alone, of all the people on earth, exempt from the revolution of Fortune's wheel? Or if parents will not adopt this salutary regulation, does not the power belong to our Legislature to introduce it? Is it not a branch of that power which authorises them to provide for the good morals of society, and to prevent the indolent and vicious from contaminating or encumbering the virtuous and industrious?—But to return to my story:

Mr. Martin, by the aid of a good person, a good temper and that gracefully negligent ease and happy confidence of manner which are said to be so generally pleasing to the fair, has been twice a married man. His first wife was a beauty. Her temper was all sweetness, and her love for her husband was little short of idolatry. She thought nothing wrong which contributed to his pleasure; and their minutes and their money flew "on Angels' wings." At the end of three years, she died, and left him a son, now a young man, who has been formed exactly in his father's model, and is, indeed, his counterpart as well as his companion in every party of pleasure.

Mr. Martin's present wife, although inferior to the first in point of beauty, is, infinitely, her superior in mind and in greatness of character. She is, indeed, one of the finest women I have ever known. With all the captivating softness and gentleness of her sex, she unites an understanding of masculine strength, a genius of the first brilliancy, and above all, a high and heroic cast of character. She displays in conversation all that quickness, nicety and justness of discrimination which belong only to minds of the first order, and her intellectual powers are set off by an expression so flowing, clear and harmonious as might have delighted even Cicero himself to hear.

This lady brought a fortune, in marriage, to Mr. Martin, which came very opportunely. In consideration of which, as well as from the native generosity of his temper, he has refused her no enjoyment which her chaste and elegant taste demanded. She has an excellent library. Their country seat, which belonged to her before marriage, and to which, at her desire, her husband, thereupon, removed, has been highly

adorned under her direction. Its groves, lawns, grottos, garden, fountain, pavilion, orchard, park, fish-pond, clumps of trees, vines, shrubbery and grass-plats are all so disposed as to strike the eye with the finest effect of variety, and to present a most
pleasing combination of beauty and utility. And to crown the whole, there has been
lately finished, on an elevated and commanding scite, a dwelling-house from a plan of
her own drawing, which unites every comfort of modern architecture with all the elegant simplicity of an ancient model.

This lady has a son, about fourteen years of age, an only child, whom she has
called Marcellus; and of whom, unless he shall follow the fate of his illustrious namesake, in Virgil,

"Shall just be shown on earth and snatch'd away,"

I venture to predict, that Fame, at some future day, will give his name to the world in the
loudest notes of her trumpet. His mother is breathing into him the high and magnanimous strain of her own character; and his eyes begin to sparkle, already, at the sound of
glory. But the little fellow never fails to illustrate the ancient notion of a good and evil
soul in the same person, and to betray the secret aspirations of his evil one, whenever
he sees his father and brother equipping themselves for an excursion of pleasure. Such
happened to be the case at the time of our visit; for as we rode up on one side of the
house, Mr. Martin and his eldest son passed off, on the other, without having observed
our arrival. They were going, we were told, to a match race, in the neighborhood, and we
had no disposition to spoil their sport. Poor little Marcellus, after rising and saluting us,
walked to the door from which his father and brother had just departed, and gazing after
them most wistfully, as they rode down the avenue, until they were lost to his view, he
sighed deeply and returned to his chair.—We all understand this little movement of nature, and reciprocally translated it to each other by our looks. And now it was that this
admirable woman displayed her address; showing that she not only knew *when* to hit
the critical minute, but *how* to hit it to the highest advantage.

"Doctor," said she, "Marcellus has been amusing his mother and himself for several
days with a new collection of speeches which Mr. Martin was so good as to bring me
lately from Petersburg. And as I am sure that I cannot entertain either you or my friend
Rosalie more agreeably than with my boy and his book, if you please, he shall read you
a speech of your great favorite Chatham." We were both well enough acquainted with
her to know that there was something in her proposition more than its terms imported,
and that, in fact, she was seizing this auspicious moment to give a lasting lesson to her
son. Expressing, therefore, our thanks to her for the offer, and the obligation which
Marcellus would confer on us by such an entertainment, the noble little fellow forgot
the horse-race in an instant, and flew up stairs, with exulting alacrity, to bring the book.

As soon as he was out of hearing, I could not help murmuring aloud from
my heart—"Happy the mother who has such a son!—Happy, happy the son who has
such a mother!" "Say rather," said she, smiling, yet with an intense suffusion of the
strongest feeling and a voice which faultered, most eloquently, under the suddenness
and force of the excitement—"Say rather, most happy is the mother who has such a
monitor as The Old Bachelor! Such a neighbor and guide and friend as Doctor Cecil!"
I looked at Rosalie to see how she would take this ingenious and beautiful effusion of
nature. Her eyes were swimming with speechless rapture; but Mrs. Martin saw and
understood her heavenly language. O! what a moment was this! Worth an age of com-

mon time—it far overpaid me for all that I have suffered from the busy and officious impertinence of malice and folly.

Marcellus returned with the book; and his mother opened it at a speech which, as we afterwards learned, she had before read and marked, in anticipation of this occasion.—It was Chatham's celebrated speech of the 20th January, 1775, on the plan of absolute co-ercion on the American colonies. She recapitulated to him briefly the points in dispute between the two countries, and having sketched the outline of this famous plan of co-ercion, handed him the book.

The little fellow performed his part most admirably. He read it with an emphasis, which denoted that he not only understood the sense but that he felt and enjoyed the fire of Chatham's "splendid conflagration." His mother had taught him to read with all the vocal graces of an orator; his time and accent were just; the tones of his voice melodious, full and fine; its modulation sweetly and interestingly varied; the words were thrown on the ear with the most delicate and beautifully distinct articulation:— and his panses were natural, yet deeply moving and impressive. For me I confess that I listened with more delight to this embryo statesman and orator, that I have, for several years past, to many of "Nature's Journeymen" of full growth. But if I was thus highly pleased with the general current of the speech, what were my feelings when this young Demosthenes poured out, in a strain of the loftiest enthusiasm, the following noble compliment on the American character:

"When your Lordships have perused the papers transmitted us from America, when you consider the dignity, the firmness and the wisdom with which the Americans have acted, you cannot but respect their cause. History, my Lords, has been my favorite study; and in the celebrated writings of antiquity have I often admired the patriotism of Greece and Rome; but, my Lords, I must declare and avow that in the master states of the world I know not the people nor the Senate who in such a complication of difficult circumstances, can stand in preference to the delegates of America, assembled in General Congress in Philadelphia. I trust it is obvious to your Lordships that all attempts to impose servitude upon such men to establish despotism over such a mighty continental nation, must be vain; must be futile."

Amid the triumph which I felt in this noble eulogy from one of Nature's greatest of noblemen, I could not hinder my mind from glancing, for a moment, at the Edinburgh Reviewers! It was, however, without resentment or contempt, but with a sentiment which, perhaps, they would deem more insulting—it was pity. For while I recollected the very different terms in which they had spoken of my countrymen, I remembered also what Marmontel had-said, in his memoirs, about an attempt of himself and one of his friends to establish a Review, in Paris—"His project of publishing between us a periodical Review, was not so good a thing as he expected—we *had neither gall, nor venom;* and as this Review was neither a faithless, unjust criticism on good works, nor a bitter biting satire on good authors, it had but little sale." The Edinburgh Review, it is said, has a very extensive sale.

This, however, was but the digression of a moment; for I was immediately recalled to Mrs. Martin and her son. As soon as Marcellus had closed the paragraph which I have quoted, he raised his eyes and turned them with delight on his mother. Mine followed them, and never did I see in any face the sublime of sentiment depicted in colors so strong as in that of this admirable woman. Marcellus was struck to the soul with the awful expression of her countenance. The blood which had mantled to his cheek receded;—and while the paleness of terror overspread his face, his eyes reflected the blaze of glory that beamed upon him from his mother's. "Such, my son," cried she with a solemnity of voice which pierced his heart, "such were your ancestors.—Yes! dignity, firmness and wisdom were, indeed, their attributes. No adverse chance of war, no depth of political misfortune, could impair for a moment, the erect and noble dignity of their characters. No perils could daunt their courage; no hardships, however severe and protracted, could shake their constancy and firmness. No ministerial sophistry could entangle, no insidious show of friendship could beguile that wisdom which was forever awake and whose strong and steady light penetrated and scattered even the darkness of futurity.—And how, think you, my son, did they attain this eminence? how did they merit this glorious eulogy of Lord Chatham? Not—trust me—not by giving up the prime and flower of life to indolence and folly; not by listening in their youth to the syren song of sloth and pleasure and thus permitting the divine faculties of the mind to be degraded and brutalized. O! no: widely different was their course. Day after day, and night after night, they kept the holy vigil of study and meditation. If they did not, like Pythagoras, Democratus and Plato, explore the remotest extremities of the globe in quest of knowledge, they retraced, however, the whole route and travel of the human mind; pursued those who had gone before them into every nook and corner of literary adventure, unwound all the mazes of learning and discovery, and followed the towering wing of genius into whatever region of science it shot its bold and daring flight.

"These great men did not in their youth labor under the error so common and so fatal in these days and which many even of its victims most feelingly deplore, that an exemption from toil and study is the greatest good of life. On the contrary, that truth so experimentally certain and infallible, was perpetually inculcated on them, that *"without labor, there is no human excellence."* Hence the vacant ease of the voluptuous couch, and the brilliant festivity of the drawing room or the convivial board had no charms for them. They claimed no participation in the fame either of the racehorse or the game-cock. They sought no renown by discussing the rules of racing in a jockey club, or the laws of war in a council of the main. Leaving these poor and futile pursuits to inferior minds, they soared to objects far beyond them. Their youth was spent in exploring the treasures of recorded wisdom; in making those treasures their own; and increasing their quantity and value by superadding the fruits of their own discoveries. Their Herculean enterprize embraced the whole circle of science. They entered on the career with that sublime enthusiasm without which, glory of the highest order was never yet attained. And not content with giving up their days to the generous pursuit, they were seen to trim the midnight lamp and court the converse of the great dead.

"Illustrious men! Immortal patriots! Where are ye now and who are your successors!!—It is true, indeed, that a few, alas! a very few, of our revolutionary planets still hang above the western horizon! Ah! how does their magnitude and steady splendor show in strong and mournful contrast the poor and feeble specks of light that dimly and faintly twinkle in the gloom of the zenith. Alas! when the glory of those planets shall have set, in what a state of darkness will our hemisphere be left! For now the holy vigils of study and meditation are over; now no generous youth is seen to trim the midnight lamp and court the converse of the illustrious dead. The age of sublime enthusiasm is gone; and the age of great men will soon have passed away. Ah! my son; at this awful moment when darkness and despair threaten to cover our land, could we but see the eastern horizon relumined with the streams of glory from some new ascending orb, what pure and sacred joy would fill our bosoms! Bowing to the earth with more than Persian adoration, how should we bless the beams that gladdened our land!—Marcellus! you are yet below the eastern horizon!"—The little fellow started back at the suggestion; and the ruffle on his bosom which had all along responded to the strong agitation of his heart, began now to bound with encreased violence and rapidity. His mother proceeded—"say now, my boy, is there no prophetic throb in that heart which tells you, that *you* may be that orb of glory?" This was too much for him: the tears gushed from his eyes and he darted out of the room.—His mother's angel smile and blessing followed him.

This animated harangue was rendered doubly affecting by the known motive of the speaker, as well as by the dignity and force of her manner. Rosalie, as much overpowered as Marcellus, took refuge at a window. As for me—I thought of my boys: and fell into a reverie on the present and past state of the country, in reference to its intellectual character, which shall form the subject of some future number. For the present I take my leave.

Mason Locke Weems
(1759–1825)

Though Parson Weems's writings have always been excoriated by critics, it would be difficult to find a writer whose work might be deemed more influential on the popular mind of early nineteenth-century America. An itinerant bookseller and the author of countless tracts, Weems became something of a legendary figure himself as he traveled the Eastern Seaboard, fiddling, preaching, and peddling books, many of which he had written himself. But it was his *Life of Washington*, published first as an eighty-page pamphlet in 1800, the year after Washington's death, that won Weems his fame, a volume that would prove so popular that it was reprinted forty times before his death in 1825 and would go through forty more editions by 1950. The biography, which had grown to over two hundred pages by its sixth edition, was only loosely grounded in fact and created such well-known myths about Washington as the story of his father's ill-fated cherry tree. Weems's tales were appropriated by McGuffey's *Reader* and the works of other children's authors, creating a popular myth that has still not entirely been dispelled.

Born in Maryland's Anne Arundel County in 1759, Weems studied medicine in London and may have served briefly in the British navy. He began preparing for the Anglican priesthood in 1781 and was one of the first Americans ordained in that faith. He abandoned the religious life for the life of a traveling bookseller early on, however, and met his wife, whose father's estate he would eventually inherit, on one of his sales jaunts. Since his vocation gave him a keen insight into popular tastes, he was soon specializing in his own moralistic tracts. When Washington died in 1799, Weems saw his opportunity and leapt on it, to produce his first biography. Later he wrote three more biographies, of Francis Marion, Benjamin Franklin, and William Penn, in the same vein. Critical scorn never seems to have fazed Weems, who died in South Carolina in 1825; he understood well the connection between the religious fervor of many of the new nation's founders and the common citizen's ardent patriotic feelings in the decades following the Revolution.

from *The Life of Washington with Curious Anecdotes*

Chapter II. Birth and Education.

"Children like tender osiers take the bow; "And as they first are form'd, forever grow."

To this day numbers of good Christians can hardly find faith to believe that Washington was, bona fide, a Virginian! "What! a buckskin! say they with a smile. "George Washington a buckskin! pshaw! impossible! he was certainly an European: So great a man could never have been born in America."

So great a man could never have been born in America!—why that's the very prince of reasons why he should have been born here! Nature, we know, is fond of harmonies; and paria paribus, that is, great things to great, is the rule she delights to work by. Where, for example, do we look for the whale, "the biggest born of nature?" not, I trow, in a mill-pond, but in the main ocean. "There go the great ships:" and there are the spoutings of whales amidst their boiling foam.

By the same rule, where shall we look for Washington, the greatest among men, but in America—that greatest Continent, which, rising from beneath the frozen pole, stretches far and wide to the south, running almost "the whole length of this vast terrene," and sustaining on her ample sides the roaring shock of half the watery globe? And equal to its size is the furniture of this vast continent, where the Almighty has reared his cloud-capt mountains, and spread his sea-like lakes, and poured his mighty rivers, and hurled down his thundering cataracts in a style of the sublime, so far superior to any thing of the kind in the other continents, that we may fairly conclude that great men and great deeds are designed for America.

This seems to be the verdict of honest analogy; and accordingly we find America the honoured cradle of Washington, who was born on Pope's creek, in Westmoreland county, Virginia, the 22nd of February, 1732. His father, whose name was Augustin Washington, was also a Virginian: but his grandfather (John) was an Englishman, who came over and settled in Virginia in 1657.

His father, fully persuaded that a marriage of virtuous love comes nearest to angelic life, early stepped up to the altar with glowing cheeks and joy sparkling eyes, while by his side with soft warm hand, sweetly trembling in his, stood the angel-form of the lovely Miss Dandridge.

After several years of great domestic happiness Mr. Washington was separated by death from this excellent woman, who left him with two children to lament her early fate.

Fully persuaded still, that "it is not good for man to be alone," he renewed, for the second time, the chaste delights of matrimonial love. His consort was Miss Mary Ball, a young lady of fortune, and descended from one of the best families in Virginia.

From his intermarriage with this charming girl, it would appear that our hero's father must have possessed either a very pleasing person, or highly polished manners, or perhaps both; for, from what I can learn, he was at that time at least forty years old! while she, on the other hand, was universally toasted as the belle of the Northern Neck, and in the full bloom and freshness of love-inspiring sixteen. This I have from one who tells me that he has carried down many a sett dance with her; I mean that amiable and pleasant old gentleman, John Fitzhugh, Esq. of Stafford, who was, all his life, a neighbour and intimate of the Washington family. By his first wife, Mr. Washington had two children, both sons—Lawrence and Augustin. By his second wife, he had five children, four sons and a daughter—George, Samuel, John, Charles, and Elizabeth. Those over delicate folk, who are ready to faint at thought of a second marriage, might do well to remember, that the greatest man that ever lived was the son of this second marriage.

Little George had scarcely attained his fifth year, when his father left Pope's creek, and came up to a plantation which he had in Stafford, opposite to Fredericksburg. The house in which he lived is still to be seen. It lifts its low and modest front of faded red, over the turbid waters of Rappahannock; whither, to this day, numbers of people repair, and, with emotions unutterable, looking at the weather-beaten mansion, exclaim, "Here's the house where the great Washington was born!"

But it is all a mistake; for he was born, as I said, at Pope's creek, in Westmoreland county, near the margin of his own roaring Potomac.

The first place of education to which George was ever sent, was a little "old field school," kept by one of his father's tenants, named Hobby; an honest, poor old man, who acted in the double character of sexton and schoolmaster. On his skill as a gravedigger, tradition is silent; but for a teacher of youth, his qualifications were certainly of the humbler sort; making what is generally called an A. B. C. schoolmaster. Such was the preceptor who first taught Washington the knowledge of letters! Hobby lived to see his young pupil in all his glory, and rejoiced exceedingly. In his cups—for though a sexton, he would sometimes drink, particularly on the General's birth days—he used to boast that "'twas he, who, between his knees, had laid the foundation of George Washington's greatness."

But though George was early sent to a schoolmaster, yet he was not on that account neglected by his father. Deeply sensible of the loveliness and worth of which human nature is capable, through the virtues and graces early implanted in the heart, he never for a moment, lost sight of George in those all-important respects.

To assist his son to overcome that selfish spirit, which too often leads children to fret and fight about trifles, was a notable care of Mr. Washington. For this purpose, of all the presents, such as cakes, fruit, &c. he received, he was always desired to give a liberal part to his play-mates. To enable him to do this with more alacrity, his father would remind him of the love which he would thereby gain, and the frequent presents which would in return be made to him; and also would tell of that great and good God, who delights above all things to see children love one another, and will assuredly reward them for acting so amiable a part.

Some idea of Mr. Washington's plan of education in this respect, may be collected from the following anecdote, related to me twenty years ago by an aged lady, who was a distant relative, and, when a girl, spent much of her time in the family:

"On a fine morning," said she, "in the fall of 1737, Mr. Washington having little George by the hand, came to the door and asked my cousin Washington and myself to walk with him to the orchard, promising he would show us a fine sight. On arriving at the orchard, we were presented with a fine sight indeed. The whole earth, as far as we could see, was strewed with fruit: and yet the trees were bending under the weight of apples, which hung in clusters like grapes, and vainly strove to hide their blushing cheeks behind the green leaves. Now, George, said his father, look here, my son! don't you remember when this good cousin of yours brought you that fine large apple last spring, how hardly I could prevail on you to divide with your brothers and sisters; though I promised you that if you would but do it, God Almighty would give you plenty of apples this fall. Poor George could not say a word; but hanging down his head, looked quite confused, while with his little naked toes he scratched in the soft ground. Now look up, my son, continued his father, look up, George! and see there how richly the blessed God has made good my promise to you. Wherever you turn your eyes, you see the trees loaded with fine fruit; many of them indeed breaking down; while the ground is covered with mellow apples, more than you could eat, my son, in all your life time."

George looked in silence on the wide wilderness of fruit. He marked the busy humming bees, and heard the gay notes of birds; then lifting his eyes, filled with shining moisture, to his father, he softly said, "Well, Pa, only forgive me this time; and see if I ever be so stingy any more."

Some, when they look up to the oak, whose giant arms throw a darkening shade over distant acres, or whose single trunk lays the keel of a man of war, cannot bear to hear of the time when this mighty plant was but an acorn, which a pig could have demolished. But others, who know their value, like to learn the soil and situation which best produces such noble trees. Thus, parents that are wise, will listen, well pleased, while I relate how moved the steps of the youthful Washington, whose single worth far outweighs all the oaks of Bashan and the red spicy cedars of Lebanon. Yes, they will listen delighted while I tell of their Washington in the days of his youth, when his little feet were swift towards the nests of birds; or when, wearied in the chase of the butterfly, he laid him down on his grassy couch and slept, while ministering spirits, with their roseate wings, fanned his glowing cheeks, and kissed his lips of innocence with that fervent love which makes the Heaven!

Never did the wise Ulysses take more pains with his beloved Telemachus, than did Mr. Washington with George, to inspire him with an early love of truth. "Truth, George," said he, "is the loveliest quality of youth. I would ride fifty miles, my son, to see the little boy whose heart is so honest, and his lips so pure, that we may depend on every word he says. O how lovely does such a child appear in the eyes of every body! his parents doat on him. His relations glory in him. They are constantly praising him to their children, whom they beg to imitate him. They are often sending for him to visit them; and receive him, when he comes, with as much joy as if he were a little angel, come to set pretty examples to their children.

"But, Oh! how different, George, is the case with the boy who is so given to lying, that nobody can believe a word he says! He is looked at with aversion wherever he goes, and parents dread to see him come among their children. Oh, George! my son! rather than see you come to this pass, dear as you are to my heart, gladly would I assist to nail you up in your little coffin, and follow you to your grave. Hard, indeed, would it be to me to give up my son, whose little feet are always so ready to run about with me, and whose fondly looking eyes, and sweet prattle make so large a part of my happiness. But still I would give him up, rather than see him a common liar."

"Pa," said George very seriously, "do I ever tell lies?"

"No, George I thank God you do not, my son; and I rejoice in the hope you never will. At least, you shall never, from me, have cause to be guilty of so shameful a thing. Many parents, indeed, even compel their children to this vile practice, by barbarously beating them for every little fault: hence, on the next offence, the little terrified creature slips out a lie! just to escape the rod. But as to yourself George, you know I have always told you, and now tell you again, that, whenever by accident, you do any thing wrong, which must often be the case, as you are but a poor little boy yet, without experience or knowledge, you must never tell a falsehood to conceal it; but come bravely up; my son, like a little man, and tell me of it: and, instead of beating you, George, I will but the more honour and love you for it, my dear."

This, you'll say, was sowing good seed!—Yes, it was: and the crop, thank God, was, as I believe it ever will be, where a man acts the true parent, that is, the Guardian Angel, by his child.

The following anecdote is a case in point. It is too valuable to be lost, and too true to be doubted; for it was communicated to me by the same excellent lady to whom I am indebted for the last.

"When George," said she, "was about six years old, he was made the wealthy master of a hatchet! of which, like most little boys, he was immoderately fond, and was constantly going about chopping every thing that came in his way. One day, in the garden, where he often amused himself hacking his mother's pea-sticks, he unluckily tried the edge of his hatchet on the body of a beautiful young English cherry-tree, which he barked so terribly, that I don't believe the tree ever got the better of it. The next morning the old gentleman, finding out what had befallen his tree, which, by the by, was a great favourite, came into the house; and with much warmth asked for the mischievous author, declaring at the same time, that he would not have taken five guineas for his tree. Nobody could tell him anything about it. Presently George and his hatchet made their appearance. "George," said his father, "do you know who killed that beautiful little cherry tree yonder in the garden?" This was a tough question; and George staggered under it for a moment; but quickly recovered himself: and looking at his father, with the sweet face of youth brightened with the inexpressible charm of all-conquering truth, he bravely cried out, "I can't tell a lie, Pa; you know I can't tell a lie. I did cut it with my hatchet."—Run to my arms, you dearest boy, cried his father in transports, run to my arms. Glad am I, George, that you killed my tree; for you have paid me for it a thousand fold. Such an act of heroism in my son is more worth than a thousand trees, though blossomed with silver, and their fruits of purest gold."

It was in this way by interesting at once both his heart and head, that Mr. Washington conducted George with great ease and pleasure along the happy paths of virtue. But well knowing that his beloved charge, soon to be a man, would be left exposed to numberless temptations, both from himself and from others, his heart throbbed with the tenderest anxiety to make him acquainted with that great being, whom to know and love, is to possess the surest defence against vice, and the best of all motives to virtue and happiness. To startle George into a lively sense of his Maker, he fell upon the following very curious, but impressive expedient:

One day he went into the garden, and prepared a little bed of finely pulverized earth, on which he wrote George's name at full, in large letters—then strewing in plenty of cabbage seed, he covered them up, and smoothed all over nicely with the roller.—This bed he purposely prepared close along side of a gooseberry walk, which happening at this time to be well hung with ripe fruit, he knew would be honoured with George's visits pretty regularly every day. Not many mornings had passed away before in came George, with eyes wild rolling, and his little cheeks ready to burst with great news.

"O Pa! come here! come here!"

"What's the matter, my son? what's the matter?"

"O come here, I tell you, Pa: come here! and I'll shew you such a sight as you never saw in all your life time."

The old gentleman suspecting what George would be at, gave him his hand, which he seized with great eagerness, and tugging him along through the garden, led him point blank to the bed whereon was inscribed, in large letters, and in all the freshness of newly sprung plants, the full name of

GEORGE WASHINGTON

"There Pa?" said George, quite in an ecstacy of astonishment, "did you ever see such a sight in all your life time?"

"Why it seems like a curious affair, sure enough, George!"

"But, Pa, who did make it there? who did make it there?"

"It grew there by chance, I suppose, my son."

"By chance, Pa! O no! no! it never did grow here by chance, Pa. Indeed that it never did!"

"High! why not, my son?"

"Why, Pa, did you ever see anybody's name in a plant bed before?"

"Well, but George, such a thing might happen, though you never saw it before."

"Yes, Pa; but I did never see the little plants grow up so as to make one single letter of my name before. Now, how could they grow up so as to make all the letters of my name! and then standing one after another, to spell my name so exactly!—and all so neat and even too, at top and bottom!! O Pa, you must not say chance did all this. Indeed somebody did it; and I dare say now, Pa, you did it just to scare me, because I am your little boy."

His father smiled; and said, "Well George, you have guessed right. I indeed did it; but not to scare you, my son; but to learn you a great thing which I wish you to understand. I want, my son, to introduce you to your true Father."

"High, Pa, an't you my true father, that has loved me, and been so good to me always?"

"Yes George, I am your father, as the world calls it: and I love you very dearly too. But yet with all my love for you, George, I am but a poor good-for-nothing sort of a father in comparison of one you have."

"Aye! I know, well enough whom you mean, Pa. You mean God Almighty; don't you?"

"Yes, my son, I mean him indeed. He is your true Father, George."

"But, Pa, where is God Almighty! I did never see him yet."

"True my son; but though you never saw him, yet he is always with you. You did not see me when ten days ago I made this little plant bed, where you see your name in such beautiful green letters: but though you did not see me here, yet you know I was here!!"

"Yes, Pa, that I do. I know you was here."

"Well then, and as my son could not believe that chance had made and put together so exactly the letters of his name, (though only sixteen) then how can he believe, that chance could have made and put together all those millions and millions of things that are now so exactly fitted to his good! That my son may look at every thing around him, see! what fine eyes he has got! and a little pug nose to smell the sweet flowers! and pretty ears to hear sweet sounds! and a lovely mouth for his bread and butter! and O, the little ivory teeth to cut it for him! and the dear little tongue to prattle with his father! and precious little hands and fingers to hold his play-things! and beautiful little feet for him to run about upon! and when my little rogue of a son is tired with running about, then the still night comes for him to lie down: and his mother sings, and the little crickets chirp him to sleep! and as soon as he has slept enough, and jumps up fresh and strong as a little buck, there the sweet golden light is ready for him! When he looks down into the water, there he sees the beautiful silver fishes for him! and up in the trees there are the apples, and peaches, and thousands of sweet fruits for him! and all, all around him, wherever my dear boy looks, he sees everything just to his wants and wishes;—the bubbling springs with cool sweet water for him to drink! and the wood to make him sparkling fires when he is cold! and beautiful horses for him to ride! and strong oxen to work for him! and the good cow to give him milk! and bees to make sweet honey for his sweeter mouth! and the little lambs, with snowy wool, for beautiful clothes for him! Now, these and all the ten thousand thousand other good things more than my son can ever think of, and all so exactly fitted to his use and delight—Now how could chance ever have done all this for my little son? Oh George!—

He would have gone on: but George, who had hung upon his father's words with looks and eyes of all-devouring attention, here broke out—

"Oh, Pa, that's enough! that's enough! It can't be chance, indeed—it can't be chance, that made and gave me all these things."

"What was it then, do you think, my son?"

"Indeed, Pa, I don't know unless it was God Almighty!"

"Yes, George, he it was, my son, and nobody else."

"Well, but Pa, (continued George) does God Almighty give me every thing? Don't you give me some things, Pa?"

"I give you something indeed! Oh how can I give you any thing, George! I who have nothing on earth that I can call my own, no, not even the breath I draw!"

"High, Pa! is'nt that great big house your house, and this garden, and the horses yonder, and oxen, and sheep, and trees, and every thing, is'nt all yours, Pa?"

"Oh no! my son! no! why you make me shrink into nothing, George, when you talk of all these belonging to me, who can't even make a grain of sand! Oh, how could I, my son, have given life to those great oxen and horses, when I can't give life even to a fly?—no! for if the poorest fly were killed, it is not your father, George, nor all the men in the world, that could ever make him alive again!"

At this, George fell into a profound silence, while his pensive looks showed that his youthful soul was labouring with some idea never felt before. Perhaps it was at that moment, that the good Spirit of God ingrafted on his heart that germ of piety, which filled his after life with so many of the precious fruits of morality.

A decade following Thomas Jefferson's *Declaration of Independence*, Southern regional identity came into sharper focus, urging another Virginian, Charles Pinckney, to remark that "when I say Southern, I mean Maryland and the states to the southward of her." The lower South of the colonial period included only two states: South Carolina and Georgia. As mentioned, South Carolina's raison d' être was to support the privileged planter class whose status depended on rice, indigo, and slaves. Thus, South Carolina followed the mercantile impulse found in the Upper South.

Georgia's settlement history was much different, being the focus of a social experiment engineered by visionary reformer James Oglethorpe. In a spirit of altruism uncharacteristic of many other early and wealthy settlers, Oglethorpe envisioned Georgia as a haven for England's oppressed classes. Contrary to the popular misconception, "Oglethorpe didn't bring any convicts to America; he brought the victims of debtors' prison, small impoverished farmers, pensionless sailors, and pennyless storekeepers. To these he added oppressed Protestant minorities, and the ever persecuted Jews."[1] In an effort to ensure his colony's success, Oglethorpe sought a ban on liquor, which he saw as the ruination of colonists in Virginia and South Carolina. He also managed to have slavery outlawed in Georgia in 1735—the first colony to outlaw the practice—as a way of preserving the livelihood of small farmers there. Unfortunately, land speculators transported slaves from other colonies, resulting in the collapse of Oglethorpe's utopian experiment. An additional pressure was Oglethorpe's conflicting military aim of protecting South Carolina from attacks by the Spanish, who would find Georgia a considerable obstacle to their conquests along the seaboard South.

Oglethorpe's conflicting aims are the subject of a prose satire written principally by Patrick Tailfer and two associates, Hugh Anderson and David Douglas. *A True and Historical Narrative of the History of Georgia* (1741) was composed by this trio of malcontents, who were planters in the youngest colony at mid-century, as a lampoon of Oglethorpe's efforts to create a utopian society rooted in the red clay of Georgia. Richard Beale Davis targets the authors' chief motive: "Disillusionment is the key—the potential paradise is but a mismanaged or uncontrolled wilderness, and the fact that the inhabitants are not allowed to import rum or Negroes and do not own their land in fee simple, has resulted in an inability to compete economically with neighboring provinces."[2] The dedication to Oglethorpe is thoroughly droll, an example of what Davis terms "one of the most effectively written satiric passages before the immediate pre-Revolutionary period."

Often imitative of British forms, Southern colonial satire included epigrams based on Latin models and the hitherto-mentioned mock epic. Other instances offered short satiric verses such as Joseph Dumbleton's "A Rhapsody on Rum," published in *South-Carolina Gazette* in March 1740. The poem is a paean to drinking, although particular verses describe how imbibing drams of rum can result in a "fault'ring tongue" and unfinished work in the fields. While emphasizing moderation and the golden mean, Dumbleton makes clear that he harbors no Calvinist prohibitions against drinking.

It is no coincidence that the distinguished tradition of letter writing in Britain, which produced such epistolary novels as Samuel Richardson's *Pamela*, flourished among planter-class ladies and gentlemen of South Carolina. Eliza Lucas Pinckney not only read *Pamela* but also offers keen critical insights about the novel in *The Letterbook of Eliza*

Lucas Pinckney: 1739–1762. Her letters to her "father, brothers, women friends in England and America are vivid pictures of the golden age of Charleston and of an attractive and strong feminine character."[3] In addition to comments about her expansive reading, Pinckney discourses on a variety of subjects: dueling and death, cordials and comets, indigo and Indians. The letters are richly representative of life in colonial South Carolina and of the class distinctions observed there. For instance, Charleston's inhabitants are, in Pinckney's view, "hospitable and honest, and the better sort add to these a polite genteel behavior." However, she scorns the poorer citizenry who "are the most indolent people in the world or they could never be wretched in so plentiful country as this." For all her characteristic class prejudice, Pinckney blends serious metaphysical reflections and a penchant for gossip that characterize later Southern literature.

Notes

1. B. C. Hall and C. T. Wood, *The South* (New York: Simon and Schuster, 1995), 124.
2. Richard Beale Davis, *Intellectual Life in the Colonial South*, Vol. 3 (Knoxville: University of Tennessee Press, 1978), 1399.
3. Davis, 1430.

Patrick Tailfer

(fl. 1741)

Little biographical information about Patrick Tailfer is available. A physician from Edinburgh, Scotland, he arrived in the colony of Georgia in 1734, settling on a plantation there, but after only a short time, he moved to Savannah to practice medicine. There he became associated with several other Georgians who had grown disgruntled over the colony's refusal to import slaves, its prohibition of rum, and its inequitable system of land distribution. Tailfer and his companions (Hugh Anderson, David Douglas, "and others") removed to South Carolina in 1741, and there they published the bitingly satirical *A True and Historical Narrative of the Colony of Georgia*. The dedication of that work is written in imitation of Jonathan Swift, mockingly congratulating James Oglethorpe for almost causing the collapse of his colony.

from *A True and Historical Narrative of the Colony of Georgia*

To His EXCELLENCY JAMES OGLETHORPE, Esq;

General and Commander in Chief of His Majesty's Forces in South Carolina and Georgia; and one of the Honourable Trustees for Establishing the Colony of GEORGIA in AMERICA, &c.

May it please Your Excellency,

As the few surviving Remains of the Colony of *Georgia* find it necessary to present the World (and in particular *Great-Britain*) with a true State of that Province, from its first Rise, to its present Period; Your Excellency (of all Mankind) is best entitled to the Dedication, as the principal Author of its present Strength and Affluence, Freedom and Prosperity: And tho' incontestable Truths will recommend the following *NARRATIVE* to the patient and attentive Reader; yet your Name, *SIR*, will be no little Ornament to the Frontispiece, and may possibly engage some courteous Perusers a little beyond it.

THAT Dedication and Flattery are synonimous, is the Complaint of every Dedicator, who concludes himself ingenuous and fortunate, if he can discover a less trite and direct Method of flattering than is usually practised; but we are happily prevented from the least Intention of this kind, by the repeated Offerings of the *Muses* and *News-Writers* to Your Excellency, in the publick Papers: 'Twere presumptuous even to dream of equalling or encreasing them: We therefore flatter ourselves, that Nothing we can advance will in the least shock Your Excellency's Modesty; not doubting but your Goodness will pardon any Deficiency of Elegance and Politeness, on account of our Sincerity, and the serious Truths we have the Honour to approach you with.

WE have seen the ancient Custom of sending forth Colonies, for the Improvement of any distant Territory, or new Acquisition, continued down to ourselves: but to Your Excellency alone it is owing, that the World is made acquainted with a Plan, highly refined from those of all former Projectors. They fondly imagin'd it necessary to communicate to such young Settlements the fullest Rights and Properties, all the Immunities of their Mother Countries, and Privileges rather more extensive: By such Means, in deed, these Colonies flourish'd with early Trade and Affluence; but Your Excellency's Concern for our perpetual Welfare could never permit you to propose such transitory Advantages for us: You considered Riches like a Divine and Philosopher, as the *Irritamenta Malorum*, and knew that they were disposed to inflate weak Minds with Pride; to pamper the Body with Luxury, and introduce a long Variety of Evils. Thus have you *Protected us from ourselves*, as Mr. *Waller* says, by keeping all Earthly Comforts from us: You have afforded us the Opportunity of arriving at the Integrity of the *Primitive Times*, by intailing a more than *Primitive Poverty* on us: The Toil, that is necessary to our bare Subsistence, must effectually defend us from the Anxieties of any further Ambition: As we have no Properties, to feed Vain-Glory and beget Contention; so we are not puzzled with any System of Laws, to ascertain and establish them: The valuable Virtue of Humility is secured to us, by your Care to prevent our procuring, or so much as seeing any *Negroes* (the only human Creatures proper to improve our Soil) lest our Simplicity might mistake the poor *Africans* for greater Slaves than ourselves: And that we might fully receive the Spiritual Benefit of those wholesome Austerities; you have wisely denied us the Use of such Spiritous Liquors, as might in the least divert our Minds from the Contemplation of our Happy Circumstances.

OUR Subject swells upon us; and did we allow ourselves to indulge our Inclination, without considering our weak Abilities, we should be tempted to launch out into many of Your Excellency's extraordinary Endowments, which do not so much regard the Affair in Hand: But as this would lead us beyond the Bounds of a Dedication; so would it engross a Subject too extensive for us, to the Prejudice of other Authors and Panegyrists; We shall therefore confine ourselves to that remarkable Scene of Your Conduct, whereby *Great-Britain* in general, and the Settlers of *Georgia*, in particular, are laid under such inexpressible Obligations.

BE pleased then, *Great SIR*, to accompany our heated Imaginations, in taking a View of this Colony of *Georgia!* this Child of your auspicious Politicks! arrived at the utmost Vigor of its Constitution, at a Term when most former States have been struggling through the Convulsions of their Infancy. This early Maturity, however, lessens our Admiration, that Your Excellency lives to see (what few Founders ever aspired after) the great Decline and almost final Termination of it. So many have finish'd their Course during the Progress of the Experiment, and such Numbers have retreated from the Fantoms of Poverty and Slavery which their cowardly Imaginations pictur'd to them; that you may justly vaunt with the boldest Hero of them all,

———*Like Death you reign*
O'er silent Subjects and a desart Plain.

Busiris.

YET must your Enemies (if you have any) be reduced to confess, that no ordinary Statesman could have digested, in the like Manner, so capacious a Scheme, such a copious Jumble of Power and Politicks. We shall content ourselves with observing, that all those beauteous Models of Government which the little States of *Germany* exercise, and those extensive Liberties which the Boors of *Poland* enjoy, were design'd to concenter in your System; and were we to regard the Modes of Government, we must have been strangely unlucky to have miss'd of the best, where there was an Appearance of so great a Variety; for, under the Influence of our *Perpetual Dictator*, we have seen something like *Aristocracy*, *Oligarchy*, as well as the *Triumvirate*, *Decemvirate*, and *Consular Authority* of famous Republicks, which have expired many Ages before us: What Wonder then we share the same Fate? Do their Towns and Villages exist but in Story and Rubbish? We are all over Ruins; our Publick-Works, Forts, Wells, High-Ways, Light-House, Store and Water-Mills, &c. are dignified like theirs, with the same venerable Desolation. The Logg-House, indeed, is like to be the last forsaken Spot of Your Empire; yet even this, through the Death, or Desertion of those who should continue to inhabit it, must suddenly decay; the Bankrupt Jailor himself shall be soon denied the Privilege of human Conversation; and when this last Moment of the Spell expires, the whole shall vanish like the Illusion of some *Eastern Magician.*

BUT let not this solitary Prospect impress Your Excellency with any Fears of having your Services to Mankind, and to the Settlers of *Georgia* in particular, buried in Oblivion; for if we diminutive Authors are allow'd to prophesy (as you know Poets in those Cases formerly did) we may confidently presage, That while the Memoirs of *America* continue to be read in *English*, *Spanish*, or the Language of the *Scots* High-Landers, Your Excellency's Exploits and Epocha will be transmitted to Posterity.

SHOULD Your Excellency apprehend the least Tincture of Flattery in any Thing already hinted, we may sincerely assure you, we intended nothing that our Sentiments did not very strictly attribute to your Merit; and, in such Sentiments, we have the Satisfaction of being fortified by all Persons of Impartiality and Discernment.

BUT to trespass no longer on those Minutes, which Your Excellency may suppose more significantly employ'd on the Sequel; let it suffice at present, to assure you, that we are deeply affected with your Favours; and tho' unable of ourselves properly to acknowledge them, we shall embrace every Opportunity of Recommending you to higher Powers, who (we are hopeful) will reward Your Excellency according to your MERIT.

May it please Your Excellency,
Your Excellency's
Most devoted Servants,
The Land-Holders of GEORGIA,
Authors of the following *Narrative.*

Joseph Dumbleton

(fl. 1740)

Other than the fact that he published a number of poems in colonial newspapers between 1740 and 1750, no biographical information about Joseph Dumbleton exists. In fact, it is likely that the name is a pseudonym. His earliest poems appear in the *Virginia Gazette*, and he appears to have been associated with its editor, William Parks. "Ode to St. Patric's Day" appeared in the *South Carolina Gazette* in March 1749, and all of his remaining poems, including "A Rhapsody on Rum" (1749), appeared in that periodical, probably indicating that he was a citizen of South Carolina during at least the later years of his life. Poems like "The Paper Mill" (1744) and "Rhapsody" show a whimsical sense of humor and a flair for satire.

A Rhapsody on Rum

> Great spirit, hail! confusion's angry sire,
> And, like thy parent Bacchus, born of fire:
> The gaol's decoy; the greedy merchant's lure;
> Disease of Money, but Reflection's cure.
>   We owe, great DRAM! the trembling hand to thee,
> The headstrong purpose; and the feeble knee;
> The loss of honour; and the cause of wrong;
> The brain enchanted; and the fault'ring tongue;
> Whilst Fancy flies before thee unconfin'd,
> Thou leav'st disabl'd Prudence far behind.
>   In thy pursuit our fields are left forlorn,
> Whilst giant weeds oppress the pigmy corn
> Thou throw'st a mist before the planter's eyes;
> The plough grows idle, and the harvest dies.
>   By thee refresh'd, no cruel norths we fear;
> 'Tis ever warm and calm, when thou art near:
> On the bare earth for thee expos'd we lie,
> And brave the malice of a frowning skie.
> Like those who did in ancient times repent;
> We sit in ashes, and our cloaths are rent.
>   From thee a thousand flatt'ring whims escape,
> Like hasty births, that ne'er have perfect shape.
> Thine Ideots in gay delusion fair,
> But born in flame, they soon expire in air.
>   O grand deluder! such thy charming art,
> 'Twere good we ne'er should meet, or ne'er should part:
> Ever abscond, or ever tend our call;
> Leave us our sense entire, or none at all.

Eliza Lucas Pinckney

(1722–1793)

The Letterbook of Eliza Lucas Pinckney reveals a woman with a strong, independent spirit, and though she was accorded opportunities very unusual among women of her era, her accomplishments were clearly won through intelligence, hard work, and shrewd management of the plantations left in her charge. The *Letterbook* is divided into three sections; the first demonstrates Pinckney's fierce entrepreneurial spirit in the years before her marriage, as well as a thirst for intellectual endeavors. The second section consists mainly of letters to friends that were written during what seems to have been an idyllic marriage. The third section recounts both her grief at the death of her husband and her own rising patriotic fervor.

Eliza Lucas was born in Antigua, West Indies, in 1722, the oldest of four children. Her father, George Lucas, was a British army officer, and Eliza was educated in England. She returned for a time to Antigua, and in 1738, her father moved the family to a plantation on Wappoo Creek, near Charleston, South Carolina. When Lucas's military duties necessitated his return to Antigua in 1739, he left the management of his South Carolina property to Eliza, who was only seventeen at the time. Over the next five years, Lucas divided her time between the demands of the plantation and rigorous efforts to complete her own education. Encouraged by her father, she experimented with a number of exotic crops, concentrating in the end on the cultivation of indigo, which South Carolina farmers had abandoned more than a generation earlier in favor of rice. Lucas, however, developed a strain of indigo that rivaled the strain produced in the French West Indies, and then she generously distributed the seed to other South Carolina planters. By the 1770s, South Carolina exported more than a million pounds a year of the richly colored dye. Lucas was equally active in cultivating her own intellectual endeavors, studying the works of Virgil, Plutarch, John Milton, Miguel de Cervantes, and Sir Isaac Newton. She also received encouragement to read John Locke's *An Essay Concerning Human Understanding* from her friend Charles Pinckney, whom she would marry in 1744. The marriage produced four children before Charles Pinckney died of malaria in 1758, necessitating Eliza Pinckney's return to the occupation at which she had proven so accomplished before her marriage. The Revolutionary War brought with it financial hardship, but her two sons, Charles Cotesworth and Thomas Pinckney, both won fame in the conflict, and the Pinckney family remained prominent in South Carolina affairs until Eliza Pinckney's death in 1793.

from *The Letterbook of Eliza Lucas Pinckney*

May 3rd, 1741. Wrote to my old friend and school-fellow Miss Parry lamenting the Warr which separates us from my Dear Papa. About the Lottery, &c.

June the 8th, 1741. Wrote again to my father on the subject of the Indigo, Cotton, &c. Also concerning the fall of bills of Exchange. Lamenting the death of his worthy friend Captain Fleming. Acquaint him with Mr. Manigault's great Civility with regard to Lushers taking in his goods.

1741. Wrote to my Aunt on my Grandmama's death, who indeed—to use the Apostle's phrase in another case—might be said to die dayly for many years past. Also on my Cousin Jacob's and Cousin Lucas's death—the latter died at a hundred years of age.

To my Father.

Hon'd Sir   June the 4th, 1741

Never were letters more welcome than yours of Feb. 19th and 20th and March the 15th and 21st, which came almost together. It was near 6 months since we had the pleasure of a line from you. Our fears increased apace and we dreaded some fatal accident befallen, but hearing of your recovery from a dangerous fitt of Illness has more than equaled, great as it was, our former Anxiety. Nor shall we ever think ourselves sufficiently thankful to Almighty God for the continuance of so great a blessing.

I simpathize most sincerely with the Inhabitance of Antigua in so great a Calamity as the scarcity of provisions and the want of the Necessarys of life to the poorer sort. We shall send all we can get of all sorts of provisions particularly what you write for. I wrote this day to Starrat for a barrel [of] butter.

We expect the boat dayly from Garden Hill when I shall be able to give you an account of affairs there. The Cotton, Guiney corn, and most of the Ginger planted here was cutt off by a frost. I wrote you in [a] former letter we had a fine Crop of Indigo Seed upon the ground, and since informed you the frost took it before it was dry. I picked out the best of it and had it planted, but there is not more than a hundred bushes of it come up—which proves the more unlucky as you have sent a man to make it. I make no doubt Indigo will prove a very valuable Commodity in time if we could have the seed from the west Indias [in] time enough to plant the latter end of March, that the seed might be dry enough to gather before our frost. I am sorry we lost this season. We can do nothing towards it now but make the works ready for next year. The Lucern is yet but dwindling, but Mr. Hunt tells me 'tis always so here the first year.

The death of my Grandmama was, as you imagine, very shocking and grievous to my Mama, but I hope the considerations of the misery's that attend so advanced an age will help time to wear it off.

I am very much obliged to you for the present you were so good to send me of the fifty pound bill of Exchange which I duely received.

We hear Carthagene is taken.

Mr. Wallis is dead. Capt. Norberry was lately killed in a duel by Capt. Dobrusee, whose life is dispaired of by the wounds he received. He is much blamed for querreling with such a brawling man as Norberry who was disregarded by every body. Norberry has left a wife and 3 or 4 children in very bad circumstances to lament his rashness.

Mama tenders you her affections and Polly joyns in duty with

My Dr. Papa

Y.m.obt. and ever D[evoted] D[aughter]

E. Lucas

June 1741. Wrote again to my father and sent the provisions he sent for.

1741. Wrote to my Aunt Concerning my dear brother Tommy's illness and my poor Cousen F. Fayweather's deep meloncholy at New England.

Wrote to Mr. Clealand about a bill of Exchange. The 4 wheeled post chaise and wine.

July 1741. Wrote to my Eldest brother upon his going into the Army. After an appoligy for a girl at my early time of life presuming to advise and urge him to beware of false notions of honour. That he makes proper distinctions between Courage and rashness, Justice and revenge. Acknowledged his letter of the 28th of October. Recommended to him upon his first entrance into life to be particularly careful of his duty to his Creator, for nothing but an early piety and steady Virtue can make him happy.

July 23rd, 1741. Wrote to my father concerning the Indigo affair. The report of his having changed Commissions with Major Heron. About Plantation affairs and other business.

July 1741. To Othneil Beale, Esqr., about Starrats affairs.

To Miss F. Fayweather in Boston
My Dear Cousen,   [c. June–July, 1741]
'Tis a great affliction to us to hear what a bad state of health you have in New England; on the other hand we are greatly consoled to hear by Mrs. Pringle with what friendship and tenderness you were received by your Uncle. Mama is very uneasy [because] she has not heard from her dear Fanny for I let her know as little of your illness as I can help. Papa and all our friends in Antigua were well the last time we heard and desired to be remembered to you. Col. Pinckney and Lady desire their Compliments to you and always enquire of your welfair by every one from New England. Mr. Pinckney wrote you a long letter from thence—when he was there and you here—concerning your affairs, but which I believe you never received. Little Polly desires her love to her Cousen and is always talking of you; she never forgets to drink your health every day. Mama desires to be remembered to you in the kindest manner and beg you will let her know if you want anything.

We are obliged to you for the Apples. Potatoes were quite out of Season before we knew by Mr. Fayweather's letter they would be acceptable.

I am so much in the Country I can inform you of nothing new but a few wedings: Mr. Middleton to Miss Williams, Mr. Cooper to Miss Molly Raven, and old Mr. Skoon is dead.

Adieu my dear Fanny. My prayers shall be constant for your happiness. Accept the affections of
                                                              Yr. Sincere friend
                                                              E. Lucas

To Mrs. Pinckney
Dear Madm.
To my great Comfort Mary-Ann informs me you are perfectly recovered of the indisposition you complained of when I was in town. As I then simpathized with you in your pain I would follow the scripture rule and rejoice with you on your recovery at Belmont; but I am afraid to trust myself on that agreeable spott and the Company I meet with there least it should make it too difficult for me to return at the time I ought to be at home.

At my return hither everything appeared gloomy and lonesome. I began to consider what alteration there was in this place that used so agreeably to sooth my (for some time past) pensive humour, and made me indiferent to every thing the gay world could boast; but found the change not in the place but in my self, and it doubtless proceeded from that giddy gayety and want of reflection which I contracted when in town; and I was forced to consult Mr. Lock over and over to see wherein personal Identity consisted and if I was the very same self. I don't affect to appear learned by quoting Mr. Lock, but would let you see what regard I pay to Mr. Pinckney's recommendation of Authors—and, in truth, I understand enough of him to be quite charmed. I recon it will take me five months reading before I have done with him.

I am now returned to my former Gravity and love of solitude and hope you won't conclude me out of my Witts because I am not always gay. I, you know, am not a proper judge in my own Case. I flatter my self you will be favourable in your oppinion of me—tho' 'tis become so much the fashion to say every body that is grave is religiously mad. But be it as it will, those unhappy people have some times intervals, and you may be assured I am in my right Sences when I subscribe my self.

Dear Madm.

Y. m. obt. h. Sert

E. Lucas

Shall send by Capt. Gregory, if it can be got ready in time for him, the Turpintine and neats foot oil.

[To Miss Bartlett]

Dr. Miss B   [c. March–April, 1742]

By your enquiry after the Comett I find your curiosity has not been strong enough to raise you out of your bed so much before your usual time as mine has been. But to answer your querie: The Comett had the appearance of a very large starr with a tail to my sight about 5 or 6 foot long—its real magnitude must then be prodigious. The tale was much paler than the Commet it self and not unlike the milkey way. 'Twas about a fortnight ago that I see it.

The brightness of the Committ was too dazleing for me to give you the information you require. I could not see whether it had petticoats on or not, but I am inclined to think by its modest appearance so early in the morning it wont permitt every Idle gazer to behold its splendour, a favour it will only grant to such as take pains for it—from hence I conclude if I could have discovered any clothing it would have been the female garb. Besides if it is any mortal transformed to this glorious luminary, why not a woman.

The light of the Comitt to my unphilosophical Eyes seems to be natural and all its own. How much it may really borrow from the sun I am not astronomer enough to tell.

Your letter was too long by one sentence, and only one—and that was desireing me to blott out part of your letter.

I now send you the patern of a Cap. 'Tis quite new—which makes me send it to you—and called a whim. You will think the lady that sent it me—who was also the inventor—made a very ill choice when I had so many whims before, more than I could well manage I assure you. But perhaps she thought the head should be all of a peice, the furniture within and the adorning without the same. But as I am of a diferent oppinion I send it to you who have as few as any lady at your time of life.

Our best Compliments attend the Col. and Mrs. Pinckney. I received Mr. Pinckneys favour, but 'tis to[o] late to answer it now. Mrs. P. has been very kind in transacting my little matters. I am most sincerely theirs and

Yr. m o St

Eliza. Lucas

[To Miss Barlett]
Dr. Miss B   [c. March 1742]

All your letters pronounce the contrary of what you lately aserted and I insist you injure my Corrispondant no more with unjust reflections or I shall be greatly offended.

I did not receive your letter in time or should certainly have come to town to hear the Sermon, on a subject so new to me. I am, however, much obliged to you for remembering me on the occasion.

I must beg leave to say the rest to Col. Pinckney. My thanks are due to you also, Sir, for your very obliging invitation to your grand festival. Give me leave now to congratulate you on your Second Prætorship. A Gentleman of your connection informed me you was to be chosen for the ensueing year.

I am with Mamas and my best respects to Mrs. Pinckney, Miss B. and
Yr. m o h St.
E. Lucas

[To Miss Barlett]
Dr. Miss B   [c. March–April, 1742]

I admire your resolution of conquering the Lazey deity Somnus you talk off. I assure you the sight of a commit is not the only pleasure you lose if you lie late a bed in a morning; for this, like every other pernisious custome, gains upon us the more we indulge it. I cant help calling it pernicious, and I devide it into heads like a Sermon; 1st, because by loseing so much of our time we lose so much of life; 2dy because 'tis unhealthy; 3dly and lastly, because we lose by farr the pleasanest part of the day. From all which I could draw some useful inferences, but whether it will be so agreeable to you to hear preaching any where but in a pulpitt I am in doubt.

An old lady in our Neighbourhood is often querrelin with me for riseing so early as 5 o'Clock in the morning, and is in great pain for me least it should spoil my marriage, for she says it will make me look old long before I am so; in this, however, I believe she is mistaking for what ever contributes to health and pleasure of mind must also contribute to good looks. But admiting what she says, I reason with her thus: If I should look older by this practise I really am so; for the longer time we are awake the longer we live. Sleep is so much the Emblem of death that I think it may be rather called breathing than living. Thus then I have the advantage of the sleepers in point of long life, so I beg you will not be frighted by such sort of apprehensions as those suggested above and for fear of your pretty face give up your late pious resolution of early rising.

My Mama joyns with me in Compliments to Mr. and Mrs. Pinckney. I send herewith Colo. Pinckneys books and shall be much obliged to him for Virgils works; notwithstanding this same old Gentlewoman (who I think too has a great friendship for me) has a great spite at my books and had like to have thrown a volume of my Plutarchs lives into the fire the other day. She is sadly afraid, she says, I shall read my self mad and begs most seriously I will never read rather Malbrauch. With this request I believe I shall comply for 'tis very probable I never may. I cant help runing a parrellal between the above lady and my valueable and worthy friend Mrs. Woodward, who I know has as much tenderness for me as any woman in the world, my own good Mama hardly excepted, but she incourages me in every laudable pursuit.

A letter I received yesterd[ay] from my dear papa says their last news from England was that the Czarina of Moscovy was dethroned and princess Elizabeth, daughter of Peter the great, has got the crown through the councils and interest of the French court.

I am

Dr. Miss B

Y m o h St

E. Lucas

[To Miss Barlett]

Dr. Miss B

I was much concerned to hear by our man Togo Mrs. Pinckney was unwell, but as you did not mention it in your letter I am hopeful it was but a slight indisposition.

Why, my dear Miss B, will you so often repeat your desire to know how I triffle away my time in our retirement in my fathers absence. Could it afford you advantage or plea-sure I should not have hesitated, but as you can expect neither from it I would have been excused; however, to show you my readiness in obeying your commands, here it is.

In general then I rise at five o'Clock in the morning, read till Seven, then take a walk in the garden or field, see that the Servants are at their respective business, then to breakfast. The first hour after breakfast is spent at my musick, the next is con-stantly employed in recolecting something I have learned least for want of practise it should be quite lost, such as French and short hand. After that I devote the rest of the time till I dress for dinner to our little Polly and two black girls who I teach to read, and if I have my paps's approbation (my Mamas I have got) I intend [them] for school mistres's for the rest of the Negroe children—another scheme you see. But to pro-ceed, the first hour after dinner as the first after breakfast at musick, the rest of the afternoon in Needle work till candle light, and from that time to bed time read or write. 'Tis the fashion here to carry our work abroad with us so that having company, without they are great strangers, is no interruption to that affair; but I have particular matters for particular days, which is an interruption to mine. Mondays my musick Master is here. Tuesdays my friend Mrs. Chardon (about 3 mile distant) and I are con-stantly engaged to each other, she at our house one Tuesday—I at hers the next and this is one of the happiest days I spend at Woppoe. Thursday the whole day except what the necessary affairs of the family take up is spent in writing, either on the busi-ness of the plantations, or letters to my friends. Every other Fryday, if no company, we go a vizeting so that I go abroad once a week and no oftener.

Now you may form some judgment what time I can have to work my lappets. I own I never go to them with a quite easey conscience as I know my father has an aversion to my employing my time in that poreing work, but they are begun and must be finished. I hate to undertake any thing and not go thro' with it; but by way of relax-ation from the other I have begun a peice of work of a quicker sort which requires nither Eyes nor genius—at least not very good ones. Would you ever guess it to be a shrimp nett? For so it is.

O! I had like to forgot the last thing I have done a great while. I have planted a large figg orchard with design to dry and export them. I have reckoned my expence and the prophets to arise from these figgs, but was I to tell you how great an Estate I am to make this way, and how 'tis to be laid out you would think me far gone in ro-mance. Your good Uncle I know has long thought I have a fertile brain at schemeing. I only confirm him in his opinion; but I own I love the vegitable world extremly. I think it an innocent and useful amusement. Pray tell him, if he laughs much at my project, I never intend to have my hand in a silver mine and he will understand as well as you what I mean.

Our best respects wait on him and Mrs. Pinckney. If my Eyes dont deceive me you in your last [letter] talk of coming very soon by water to see how my oaks grow. Is it really so, or only one of your unripe schemes. While 'tis in your head put it speedily into execution and you will give great pleasure to

Y m o s
E. Lucas

Memdm. Wrote in haste to my father in April 1742.

[To Miss Bartlett]
Dr. Miss B

I have got no further than the first volume of Virgil but was most agreeably disapointed to find my self instructed in agriculture as well as entertained by his charming penn; for I am pursuaded tho' he wrote in and for Italy, it will in many instances suit Carolina. I had never perused those books before and imagined I should imediately enter upon battles, storms and tempest that puts one in a maze and makes one shudder while one reads. But the calm and pleasing diction of pastoral and gardening agreeably presented themselves, not unsuitably to this charming season of the year, with which I am so much delighted that had I but the fine soft language of our poet to paint it properly, I should give you but little respite till you came into the country and attended to the beauties of pure nature unassisted by art. The majestick pine imperceptably puts on a fresher green; the young mirtle joyning its fragrance to that of the Jesamin of golden hue perfumes all the woods and regales the rural wander[er] with its sweets; the daiseys, the honysuckles and a thousand nameless beauties of the woods invite you to partake the pleasures the country affords.

You may wonder how I could in this gay season think of planting a Cedar grove, which rather reflects an Autumnal gloom and solemnity than the freshness and gayty of spring. But so it is. I have begun it last week and intend to make it an Emblem not of a lady, but of a compliment which your good Aunt was pleased to make to the person her partiality has made happy by giving her a place in her esteem and friendship. I intend then to connect in my grove the solemnity (not the solidity) of summer or autumn with the cheerfulness and pleasures of spring, for it shall be filled with all kind of flowers, as well wild as Garden flowers, with seats of Camomoil and here and there a fruit tree—oranges, nectrons, Plumbs, &c., &c.

We are much concerned to hear of Mrs. Pinckneys illness. I have lately found benefit for the pain in my head by keeping my feet a little while every night before I go into bed in hott water. I dare say it would give her present ease if not cure her, but whether it may be hurtful for the spleen or not I can't say. I wish she would mention it to Dr. C.

Pray make our compliments and conclude me

Yr. m. o. St.
E. Lucas

[To Miss Barlett]
Dr. Miss B.

That we were disapointed of seeing you as I expected I hope proceeded from any thing rather than an increase of Mrs. Pinckneys disorder—on whose account we are much concerned.

I suspect David blundered egregiously in delivering his message. Mine was that I would wait on Mrs. Pinckney if I knew when Col. Pinckney left town, to spend a little time with her during his absence. But as my coming depended on that event, I could set no time till I heard from Mrs. Pinckney when he set out. But I have now reason to think David has fixt a time for me and prevented your coming here, and thus we are disapointed both ways—which indeed I deserve for sending verbal messages.

I here inclose you the words of a new song. The tune cant be purchased with any thing but your company. As 'tis past ten o'Clock Saturday night you will give me leave to conclude sooner than usual.

Yr. m o h St
E. Lucas

[To Miss Bartlett]

I am sorry I cant wait on Dear Miss B. on Monday for two reasons: first, the loss I shall have of all your agreeable companies; and the other is my curiosity which you have very much raised must remain unsatisfied. I have so much business on my hands at present I hardly know which to turn my self to first, and most of it such as cant be defered. But pray, cant this important affair be commited to writing, for woman like I shall not rest till I know it. In pity then take penn in hand.

Pray pay my compliments to Col. Pinckney and tell him the ladies of merit have my consent to believe as much as they please of the fine things the Gentlemen say to them, but in this case I claim the previledge of judging for my self, as I do when [I] subscribe my self

Yrs. &c.,
E. Lucas

[To Miss Bartlett]

Dr. Miss B.

The contents of your last concerns us much as it informs us of the accident to Col. Pinckney. I hope Mrs. Pinckney dont apprehend any further danger from the fall than its spoiling him for a horsman. If it only prevents him riding that dancing beauty Chickasaw for the future, I think 'tis not much to be lamented, for he has as many tricks and airs as a dancing bear.

Wont you laugh at me if I tell you I am so busey in providing for Posterity I hardly allow my self time to Eat or sleep and can but just snatch a minnet to write to you and a friend or two now. I am making a large plantation of Oaks which I look upon as my own property, whether my father gives me the land or not; and therefore I design many years hence when oaks are more valueable than they are now—which you know they will be when we come to build fleets. I intend, I say, 2 thirds of the produce of my oaks for a charity (I'll let you know my scheme another time) and the other 3rd for those that shall have the trouble of putting my design in Execution. I sopose according to custom you will show this to your Uncle and Aunt. "She is [a] good girl," says Mrs. Pinckney. "She is never Idle and always means well." "Tell the little Visionary," says your Uncle, "come to town and partake of some of the amusements suitable to her time of life." Pray tell him I think these so, and what he may now think whims and projects may turn out well by and by. Out of many surely one may hitt.

I promised to tell you when the mocking bird began to sing. The little warbler has done wonders; the first time he opened his soft pipe this spring, he inspired me with the spirit of Rymeing, and [I] produced the 3 following lines while I was laceing my stays:

Sing on thou charming mimick of the feathered kind
and let the rational a lesson learn from thee,
to Mimick (not defects) but harmony.

If you let any mortal besides your self see this exquisite piece of poetry, you shall
never have a line more than this specimen; and how great will be your loss you who
have seen the above may jud[g]e as well as

Yr. m. obedt. Servt.

Eliza. Lucas

I hope you never forget to pay my
Mamas and my best respects to Colo.
Pinckney and Lady.

[To Thomas Lucas]   May 22nd, 1742
    I am now set down, my Dear Brother, to obey your commands and give you a
short discription of the part of the world I now inhabit. South Carolina then is a large
and Extensive Country Near the Sea. Most of the settled parts of it is upon a flatt—the
soil near Charles Town sandy, but further distant clay and swamplands. It abounds
with fine navigable rivers, and great quantities of fine timber. The Country at a great
distance, that is to say about a hundred or a hundred and fifty mile from Charles
Town, [is] very hilly.
    The Soil in general [is] very fertile, and there is very few European or American
fruits or grain but what grow here. The Country abounds with wild fowl, Venison and
fish. Beef, veal and motton are here in much greater perfection than in the Islands
[West Indies], tho' not equal to that in England; but their pork exceeds any I ever
tasted any where. The Turkeys [are] extreamly fine, expecially the wild, and indeed
all their poultry is exceeding good; and peaches, Nectrons and mellons of all sorts extreamly fine and in profusion, and their Oranges exceed any I ever tasted in the West
Indies or from Spain or Portugal.
    The people in general [are] hospitable and honest, and the better sort add to these
a polite gentile behaviour. The poorer sort are the most indolent people in the world or
they could never be wretched in so plentiful a country as this. The winters here are very
fine and pleasant, but 4 months in the year is extreamly disagreeable, excessive hott,
much thunder and lightening, and muskatoes and sand flies in abundance.
    Charles Town, the Metropolis, is a neat pretty place. The inhabitants [are] polite
and live in a very gentile manner; the streets and houses regularly built; the ladies and
gentlemen gay in their dress. Upon the whole you will find as many agreeable people
of both sexes for the size of the place as almost any where. St. Phillips church in
Charles Town is a very Eligant one, and much frequented. There are several more
places of publick worship in this town and the generallity of people [are] of a religious turn of mind.
    I began in haste and have observed no method or I should have told you before I
came to Summer that we have a most charming spring in this country, especially for
those who travel through the Country for the scent of the young mirtle and Yellow Jesamin with which the woods abound is delightful.
    The staple comodity here is rice and the only thing they export to Europe. Beef,
pork and lumber they send to the West Indias.

Pray inform me how my good friend Mrs. Boddicott, my Cousen Bartholomew and all my old acquaintance doe.

My Mama and Polly joyn in Love to you with

My dr. brother
Your most affectionately
E. Lucas

Memdm
Wrote to my brother in French.

[To Miss Bartlett]
Dr. Miss B.   [c. June, 1742]

After a pleasant passage of about an hour we arrived safe at home as I hope you and Mrs. Pinckney did at Belmont. But this place appeared much less agreeable than when I left it, having lost the agreeable letters to coppy, but it seems there is a necessity for it—'tis so uncertain whether you will get this.

[To Mrs. Lucas]   So. Ca., Septr. 25th, 1758

With a bleeding heart, Dear Madam, I inform you that since you heard from me the greatest of human Evils has befallen me. Oh, my dear Mother, My dear, dear Mr. Pinckney, the best of men and of husbands is no more! Oh! dreadful reverse of what I was when I last wrote to you.

You were but a short time witness of my happiness. I was for more than 14 year the happiest mortal upon Earth! Heaven had blessed me beyond the lott of mortals and left me nothing to wish for for my self. The Almighty had given every blessing in that dear, that worthy, that valuable man, whose life was one continued course of active Virtue. I had not a desire beyond him, nor had I a petition to make to Heaven but for a continuance of the blessings I injoyed. Think then so truely sensible as I ever was of the happiness I injoyed; for I was truely blessed. Think what I now suffer for my self and for my dear fatherless children! Poor babes. How deplorable is their loss: Their Example, the protector and guide of their youth and the best and tenderest parent that Ever existed is taken from them. God alone, who has promised to be the father of the fatherless, can make up this dreadful loss to them; and I trust he will keep them under his almighty protection and fulfil all their pius fathers prayers upon their heads and will enable the helpless, distressed parent they have left to do them good. Grant, Great God, that I may spend my whole future life in their Service and show my affection and gratitude to their dear father by my care of those precious remains of him, the pledges of the sincerest and tenderest affection that ever was upon Earth.

It was principally for their advantage we returned again to this province, my dear Mr. Pinckney intending as soon as his affairs were disposed of in the manner he approved to return to our Infant Sons. But how much Anguish did the parting with his dear boys give that most affectionate and best of fathers? He parted with life with less pain than with them; for in that awful hour he showed the fruits of a well spent life. His had been the life of a constant steady active Virtue with an habitual trust and confidence in as well as an intire resignation to the Will of the Deity, which made him happy and cheerful through life and made all about him so, for his was true religion free from sourness and superstition; and in his sickness and death the good man and the Christian shined forth in an uncommon resolution and patience, humility, and intire resignation to the Devine Will.—My tears flow too fast. I must have done; 'tis too much, too much, to take a review of that distressful hour!

We left England in March (and did not acquaint you with it least you should be uneasy from apprehensions of our being taken) and arrived here the 19th May after being at Sea ten weeks. One of my dear Mr. Pinckneys first inquirys after his arrival here was for a Vessel to Antigua in order to write to you and my brother. We heard of one but she was stoped by an Embargo till after the 12th of July, the fatal day which deprived me of all my soul held dear and left me in a distress that no language can paint. For his Virtues and aimable quallities are deeply imprinted in my heart, his dear image is ever in my Eye, and the remembrance of his affection and tenderness to me must remain to my latest moment—a remembrance mingled with pleasure and Anguish. The remembrance of what he was sooths and comforts me for a time. With what pleasure I reflect on the clearness of his head, the goodness of his heart, the piety of his mind, the sweetness of his temper, the good Sence and vivacity of his conversation, his fine address, the aimableness of his whole deportment, for I did not know a Virtue he did not posess. This pleases while it pains and may be called the Luxury of grief.

This you know is not a picture drawn by flattery or partialty. Many will subscribe to the justice of it; all that really knew him must. But what anguish is in the reflection that these that were my greatest delights and blessings are taken from me for Ever in this world—for in the next I hope there is a Union of Virtuous souls where there is no more death, no more separation, but virtuous love and friendship to endure to Eternity! And this surely must be one of the greatest degrees of bliss a human soul can injoy, except the injoyment of the Deity himself; and this hope is my comfort for every thing below has lost its relish. Earth has no more charms for me.

I indeed have had a large share of Blessings. How underserving was I, how unexpected was such a treasure, and yet Bounteous Heaven gave him to me! O! Had Heaven but added one blessing more and spared him to see his dear children brought up and let us have gone to the grave hand in hand together, what a heaven had I enjoyed upon Earth! But why these great and uncommon blessings to me? Those already injoyed were beyond desert—vastly beyond desert and expectation.

Great God Almighty, give me thy grace and enable me to drink this bitter cup which Thou hast alloted me, and to submit to Thee however hard the task with that resignation and submission which becomes thy creature and servant, and one that has tasted so largly of thy Bounty as I have done!

How long a letter have I wrote and all on one dismal subject! Forgive me, Oh! my mother, for giving you so much pain while I have indulged my self thus; but my soul is oppressed with bitter anguish and my thoughts intirely taken up with my own meloncholy concerns.

I lately received a letter from good Colo. Talbott to my poor dear Mr. Pinckney with one inclosed from you to me informing us of my brothers being sailed to England. It would have given us great pleasure had it been a year ago. We should then have mett with comfort and pleasure. But my dear boys will rejoyce to see their Uncle, and I hope he will be there before the meloncholy tidings reaches them. My heart is with them and I shall by the Divine permission return as soon as I can consistent with their interest; whether it will be in one, two or three year I cant yet say.

I shall write to you again soon if I am able. I hope you will always command me in every thing wherein I can serve you and be asured it is not more my duty than my inclination to show you in every Instance in my power how much I am

Your Dutiful and affecte. tho'

greatly afflicted daughter

E. Pinckney

[To Mr. Morly]   Sept. 19th, 1759

How, Dr. Sir, shall I thank you sufficiently for leting me hear so often from my dear boys. 'Twas with the utmost gratitude and thankfulness I received your 4 letters by Capt Webb a few days since by way of Bristol. Could you guess the Comfort they give me and with what eager impatience I opened them, you would, I am sure, not repent the trouble you have in doing so charritable a work.

The first letter is the 29th May. I am greatly at a loss to understand a paragraph in the letter as I am quite a stranger to any thing between the Doctor and Col. B. The paragraph is as follows: "Doctor Kirk-patrick is very much obliged to you for mentioning that Col. Barnwels mony is ready for him." My accidentally mentioning Col. B's mony being ready for him (Col. B) immediately after my message to the Doctor must have led to the mistake. I mentioned it for your satisfaction imagining you must know what I meant; but find I was too short. The affair was this: My dear Mr. P. received a sume of mony for Col. B. but as he was to leave England it was necessary he should give security for it. You were that Security. And I must now let you know how the matter stands; I had occation to apply that mony to other uses and the Col. was so good to give me time to pay it inn, but shall hope to pay the whole off this Winter.

I shall be very glad to have it in my power to serve Dr. Kirk-patrick in his affair with Col. B. If it is it will give me pleasure if he will command me. I beg my Compliments and best thanks to him on my dear Childrens account.

I received Mr. Davidsons note inclosed in yours of the 5th June. I my self forwarded a letter of Advice from my brother to him, but by what ship I have intirely forgot.

I thought my Nephew had acquainted you of the Receipt of the Coppy of my dear Mr. Pinckneys Will. I did not know there was any thing necessary to be returned to you as I have not yet looked into those papers, but shall now do it as soon as possible and send you what is Necessary by the first good opportunity.

I am much obliged for the trouble you took with the Turtle, letters, &c., as well as for the letters I received from my good friends Mr. Edwards, Mr. Keate, Mrs. Onslow and Mrs. King—all which I shall answer by the first convoy from hence.

H P Joyns in Compliments to all friends.

Our last accounts from the Cherokees are more agreeable than any we have had [in] a great while.

I am hurryed for my letter and must conclude. And that Heaven may bless, preserve and reward you is the sincere prayer of

Dr. Sir

Yr. M. O[bliged] and O[bedient] St.

E. Pinckney

[To Mr. Keate]   Febr. 1762

A Tedious Illness of seven months succeeded by a long and more tedious weakness prevented me taking the earliest opportunity of acknowledging My Worthy and much esteemed friend Mr. Keats favour of the 3rd of July, a letter that deserved my warmest gratitude and for which you have my sincerest thanks. As it would be no small mortification to me to lose the place in your remembrance I flatter my self to have, you cant imagine what an increase it would be to that mortification was I conscious of being my self the cause of it; and therefore was very desireous you should be made acquainted by my friend Morly (to whom I wrote with many pauses and much difficulty) with my Inability to indulge my self in an Epistolary intercourse with my friends. But as, I thank God, I am much better than I have been for the last 4 year, I please my self with the revival of an imployment which was always agreeable to me, for when I am volontaryly silent 'tis to indulge my friends, not my self. Indeed when I reflect on what a distance from all thats gay or new and can find nothing from within or without to entertain them agreeably, I am ready in pure charity to them to bid adieu to scribling and am only prevented by this one consideration: that I must then bid adieu to hearing of' there welfare, a pleasure I am very loath to part with as long as I live.

Mr. Morly informed me you were so good to give him a letter for me which he inclosed with some others from my friends and forwarded by the Britania, but unluckily for me she was taken by the French and I lost my packet. I regret the loss so much that I look upon my self as one of the greatest sufferers by the Capture, for those that had their wealth on board were insured, and I lie intirely at your mercy to make me amends.

What great doings you have had in England since I left it. You people that live in the great world in the midst of Scenes of' entertainment and pleasure abroad, of improving studies and polite amusement at home, must be very good to think of' your friends in this remote Corner of the Globe. I really think it a great virtue in you; and if I could conceal the selfish principle by which I am actuated I could with a better grace attempt to persuade you that there is so much merrit in seting down at home and writing now and then to an old woman in the Wilds of America that I believe I should take you off an hour some times from attending Matine[e] and the other gay scenes you frequent.

How different is the life we live here; vizeting is the great and almost only amusement of' late years. However, as to my own particular, I live agreeable enough to my own taste, as much so as I can separated from my dear boys.

I love a Garden and a book; and they are all my amusement except I include one of the greatest Businesses of my life (my attention to my dear little girl) under that article. For a pleasure it certainly is to cultivate the tender mind, to teach the young Idea how to shoot, &c., especially to a mind so tractable and a temper so sweet as hers. For, I thank God, I have an excellent soil to work upon, and by the Divine Grace hope the fruit will be answerable to my indeavours in the cultivation.

I know not how to thank you sufficiently for your Notice and kindness to my poor boys, but if my prayers are pius enough to reach Heaven, you and yours are secure of every blessing; for I make none with more sincerity and devotion than those that are offered for them and their friends.

How does good Mr. Hungerford, [illegible] Lutral and their families do?

If you wont think me Romantick I will communicate a scheme I have if I live a few years longer (not purely for the pleasure of scribling a long letter) but because I really want your opinion and advice in it, as your residence at Geneva must make you more capable of judging of the matter than those that never were there. Upon a Peace

(I cant think of crossing the Atlantic before) I intend to See England and after Charles has been two years at Oxford to go with my two boys to finish their studies at Geneva. I must determine upon my plan before I leave this [country]. Be so good, therefore, at your leasure to tell me what you think of it.

Harriott pays her Compliments. She is much ingaged just now with Geography and musick. And 'tis high time to disengage your attention from this tedious Epistle by asureing you that I am, with great truth,

Sir

Your most obliged friend and most obedt.

Servant

E. Pinckney

II

The Rise of the Confederacy and the Civil War (1815–1865)

But for the encroachment of planter class attitudes, Georgia's early example showed that a hospitable agrarian society might have developed in areas south and west of the planter kingdom. Far from thinking and acting alike, as was sometimes supposed by people from outside the region, Southerners were often at odds on social and political issues. Although the grandee class appealed to popular aspirations, the "country gentleman" became more myth than fact as the South expanded beyond mountains and valleys, swamps, and rivers that came to define a formerly unknown area of geographical and cultural extremes. In these hinterlands, the tie to the planter ideal would weaken as backcountry men cultivated frontier-style farming methods, becoming middle-class masters of the new lands.

By the 1830s, the greatest number of Southerners belonged to the middle class, owning or leasing modest farms worked by entire families. Census records show that less than 3 percent of all farms in the South in 1860 comprised more than five hundred acres.[1] Despite their increasing numbers, middle-class Southerners tended to be a tragically untapped resource in the crucial decades before the Civil War:

> Such were two thirds of the Southern peoples: not squires, certainly not poor whites, but rather middle-class Americans bent on getting on in a land of opportunity! The great tragedy of the ante-bellum South lies in the fact that this group failed to assert itself or to greatly influence trends in the section. Gradually, under Northern attack on slavery and slaveholder, it came to defend the interests and institutions of the few aristocrats at the top and to permit them to symbolize all Southern values. For this mistake the middle class eliminated itself from the thinking of most Southern spokesmen and from the attention of Northern enemies. They were thereby lost to a generation of historians and have only been rediscovered in our own time.[2]

Clearly the South did not succeed in creating the kind of social structure that would check exploitation of natural resources or, more importantly, halt the enslavement of African Americans for profit. These failures reinforced the North's perception of Southerners as "haughty nabobs, intemperate and lax in morals, dwelling in great white pillared houses, wringing wealth from those in bondage and sorrow, and seeking to destroy the best government on the face of the earth. Sinners and aristocrats *par excellence!*"[3] The South retaliated in kind by assuming that "all men in the North were Yankees, and that all Yankees were John Browns, [a situation that] did not help matters. Incrimination bred incrimination."[4]

Given increasing sectional tensions, the yeoman farmer, as he is now often called, weathered hardships imposed by Southern aristocrats and Northern intellectuals alike, both groups showing a fondness for mocking the frontier cultivator's "frame house without conveniences," his diet of "hog and hominy," and his lack of literary pursuits but for the Bible.[5] He and his kind were, nonetheless, the backbone of the expanding South and would assume legendary status once Union armies marched onto Southern soil.

Some of that class owned slaves. Most did not. Owning slaves would not have proven profitable for a yeoman family subsisting on relatively small tracts of land while trying to survive in spite of poor soils, fickle weather, and economic upheavals like the widespread rural depression of 1832. Slaves simply would have meant more debt for these small farmers. Planters, too, grudgingly came to realize the unprofitability of a system that required acquisition of more land and slaves for the planter to stay out of debt. Samuel Eliot Morison states that "although cotton growing [in the late eighteenth century] was the most profitable employment for slaves, slave labor was an uneconomical method of growing cotton."[6] We can only speculate what changes in the South's social structure might have resulted had slavery continued to be the spiritually and economically bankrupt system a growing number of people recognized it to be.

All such speculation dissolves with the introduction of the cotton engine, or "gin" as it was popularly called, in 1793. Eli Whitney, an alumnus of Yale and a native of Massachusetts, redesigned an existing machine that would enable a slave to produce up to sixty pounds of cotton fiber a day. Previously, a slave working by hand could produce only a pound. Although cultivation of cotton in the eighteenth century had been restricted largely to a few seaboard areas or offshore islands, cotton could now be profitably grown in the deep South where ambitious dirt farmers soon became plantation owners, manufacturers, and international entrepreneurs. King Cotton, so termed, created a new aristocracy different from the old colonial one. Slavery, too, required a new, more virulent defense.

The first prong of that defense stressed how the South was a final bastion "against the infidelity and heresies of the bourgeois perversion of modernity, which had badly flawed the Enlightenment and brought forth the horrors of the French Revolution, political radicalism, and growing social disorder."[7] A second, more conflicted defense involved a view of progress held by slaveholding intellectuals who argued that the stability of society depended on moderating individual freedom in order to "render progress morally wholesome and socially safe."[8] An unrestrained bourgeois society, like the one in New England, would result in what Southerners believed to be an intolerable system dominated by greed and abstract notions of "freedom." Thus, the moral progress of mankind, many educated Southerners argued, depended on restraints guaranteed by slavery.

That New England intellectuals believed their own views to exhibit "sovereign superiority" over those of Southern thinkers is evident in the New Englanders' refusal to acknowledge that the South had an intellectual position to defend. The most famous apostle for this idea was famed New England intellectual Ralph Waldo Emerson in whose works scholar Louis Simpson finds the consummate distillation of New England values and abolitionist sentiment. Until the outbreak of the Civil War, Emerson refused to consider himself part of the Union because the South belonged to it.

One feature of Emerson's rejection of things Southern was his belief that New England suffered morally by its association with slavery and the slave states. Simpson notes that "the truly monstrous cost of the capture and importation of Africans into America, according to Emerson, [was] the price New England was paying"[9] for taking the South's defense of slavery seriously. Emerson especially deplored the Southerners' habits of mind and "plantation manners," which, he contended, were a means of manipulation that "drove peaceable forgiving New England to emancipation without phrase."[10] Once more, Simpson summarizes Emerson's thought on the subject:

> Obliquely identifying "plantation manners" as a manner of mind or thought, and thus certifying what he said did not exist—a southern intellect—as the enemy, Emerson in effect adopted the strategy of implying that Southerners were merely intellectual "pretenders" and warned against admitting such enemies of thought to the "community of scholars."[11]

A more sanguine view of Emerson is held by Kenneth Stampp, who, while calling Emerson a "kindly philosopher," acknowledges that the Concord sage convinced Southerners that the North not only hated the South but also wanted to obliterate all vestiges of the region.[12] The ideological conflicts between North and South could therefore be viewed as a struggle for the "progress of the culture of mind."[13] Each side sought to impose on the other a form of intellectual and cultural imperialism that would define the nation in a way it had yet to be defined. Unfortunately, mutual distrust and suspicion did not remain at the level of ideas and "theory."

On both sides of the issues, ideas gave rise to violence. Events escalated until the country's citizens could scarcely remain neutral, forced to take sides in a contest about which many were often ambivalent. Perhaps no single event galvanized public opinion more than John Brown's raid on the federal arsenal at Harper's Ferry, Virginia, in October 1859. Even today, historians are rarely dispassionate on the subject of Brown.

Referred to variously as a lunatic or a saint, Brown, an avowed abolitionist, had spent time in "Bleeding Kansas," a territory where proslavery men and abolitionists waged battle in the early 1850s over whether Kansas should be admitted to the Union as a slave or a free state. Known as the instigator of the Pottawatomi Massacre, Brown and his sons had hacked to death five proslavery men with broadswords before escaping the Kansas territory. Obtaining financial and moral support from an influential group of New Englanders calling themselves "friends of freedom" (Emerson numbered himself among the group), Brown turned his attention to a boldly conceived plan described by Samuel Eliot Morison:

> A madman with a method, he [Brown] formed a vague project to establish a republic of fugitive slaves in the Appalachians, whence to wage war on the slave states. From Canadian and New England abolitionists he obtained

money and support, although none were informed as to his exact intentions, and he seems to have had no definite plan. On the night of 16 October 1859, leading an armed troop of thirteen white men and five blacks, John Brown seized the federal arsenal at Harper's Ferry, killed the mayor of the town, and took prisoners from some of the leading people. By daybreak the telegraph was spreading consternation throughout the country.[14]

Brown's raid went hopelessly awry. Slaves did not rise up to help their liberators, but townspeople turned out to exchange volleys of gunfire with Brown and his coconspirators. Later in the evening, federal reinforcements, a company of marines commanded by Colonel Robert E. Lee, arrived from Washington, storming the arsenal and capturing Brown and four surviving insurrectionists.

The ensuing trial was of short duration. On October 31, Brown was convicted of treason against Virginia and sentenced to hang on December 2, 1859. Many in the North saw his death as martyrdom for a just cause. Former slave turned journalist Frederick Douglass praised him, as did Emerson, who compared Brown with Christ. The *New York Tribune* remarked that all people should be "reverently grateful for the privilege of living in a world rendered noble by the daring of heroes, the suffering of martyrs,—among them whom let none doubt that history will accord an honored niche to Old John Brown." Southern newspapers excoriated Brown and his supporters, claiming that Brown's execution had not taken place a moment too soon. Pointing to Brown's avowed desire to murder Southern men, women, and children in their beds, Southern editors wondered how "rabid abolitionists" could support such a man. Politicians were careful to take the middle ground. Lincoln, for instance, repudiated Brown while acknowledging sympathy for the cause he represented. Whatever else John Brown managed to do, he was instrumental in stirring up the feelings of the American people on the issue of slavery. In the South, reactions to him prompted serious talk of secession. In retrospect, he would be considered as one of the catalysts leading to war.

Although Samuel Eliot Morison notes that in 1860, moderate elements existed on both sides of the sectional debate, extremists stirred up sentiment and spread rumors that offered little hope of reconciliation: "Hysteria mounted as rumors of slave insurrection popped up on every side; stories were spread of poisoned wells and the like, creating a feeling that nothing short of . . . secession could protect Southern society from subversion at the hands of vicious agitators."[15]

The debate over slavery intensified in both houses of the United States Congress. On June 4, 1860, Charles Sumner of Massachusetts delivered a speech entitled "The Barbarism of Slavery." In response, Virginia congressman Daniel C. DeJarnette orated on the evils of free labor and unrestrained capitalism in the North, proclaiming that "for every master who cruelly treats his slave, there are two white men at the North who torture and murder their wives," an oblique allusion to John Brown's alleged abuse of his wife.[16]

If there was ever a chance for cool heads to prevail, the volatile presidential election of 1860 squelched any such opportunity. The most devoted of the abolitionists saw Abraham Lincoln's election as a surrender of their most abiding principles, given Lincoln's pledge to respect slavery in those states where it already existed and to enforce fugitive slave laws. "The mind of the lower South"[17] was as fiercely made up. Lincoln's election was an assault on the Southern way of life, and the cotton states, in particular, saw no choice but to secede and establish their own empire free of the taint of New England theocracy and laissez-faire economics. Northern moderates were shouted down in public assemblies in Boston, and upper South pro-Unionists found themselves in the unenviable position of disliking slavery and believing it to be wrong but having to "go along with their neighbors or fight them."[18]

On March 4, 1861, Lincoln was inaugurated as president of the United States. A little more than a month later on April 12, the first shots of the Civil War were fired at Fort Sumter in Charleston Harbor. The provisional Confederate government, under the leadership of newly chosen president Jefferson Davis, believed itself justified in reclaiming Southern territory from federal hands. Lincoln saw the attack on Sumter as a treasonous effort to destroy the Union that he had pledged to preserve, protect, and defend.

Despite its sense of legal and ethical entitlement, along with the assurance that God would see the justness of the Southern cause and supply divinely wrought victories, the South was doomed from the outset to lose the war. In the first place, no states' rights or provisional government could wage war effectively because of the need for centralized authority in planning strategy, raising necessary funds through taxation, and establishing diplomatic ties that would guarantee support of foreign allies. A second reason the South would fail to win independence was the premise on which its government was founded and which Confederate Vice President Alexander Stephens declared in a speech given in March of 1861: "Its [the Confederate government's] foundations are laid, its cornerstone rests, upon the great truth that the Negro is not equal to the white man." Stephens and his new government might have fared better had the advice of another Southerner, James Longstreet, been seriously considered. Referred to as General Robert E. Lee's "war horse," Longstreet often declared that the South should have freed all its slaves before going to war. Indeed, to be for the South and against slavery was often to find oneself in a tragic predicament. The very assumption on which the South's war effort depended would create unendurable tensions within the South, dividing loyalties and diverting energies, and causing the South to fall on its own sword. The Lost Cause, as the struggle for Southern independence has often been called, was lost before it began, though the difficulty lay in convincing Southern partisans and firebrands of the certainty of impending defeat.

The cast of mind that plunged the Southern states into war was the same one that nourished the South's faith in its ability to achieve the impossible. The South made the mistake of assuming the war would be a rout, lasting no more than ninety days once the North perceived the nature of Southern resolve. Perhaps the most fatal error the Confederacy made was its reliance on chivalry and the assumption that the North would fight a "fair" war, forced to recognize Confederate determination as equal to the justness of the Confederate cause. Such characteristic idealism prompted many Southerners to believe, after defeating Northern troops at the battle of First Manassas, that Northern troops would surrender in gentlemanly fashion and leave the South to its own devices. After all, partisans argued, what need was there to make Southerners prove further what they'd already proven? One young Nashville recruit summed it up in a letter: "The scum of the North cannot face the chivalric spirit of the South."[19]

But the North had different plans. Even better than his generals, Lincoln understood that the Union's success depended on controlling the rail junctions in the interior South, what historians now refer to as the Nashville-Chattanooga-Atlanta corridor. Such far-reaching strategy was several removes from the thoughts of the average soldier called on to fight in America's bloodiest war. The motivations of soldiers on both sides were complex, as James McPherson points out in *For Cause and Comrades*. Patriotism certainly played a part as "the initial impulse came from what the French call *rage militaire*—a patriotic furor that swept North and South alike in the weeks after the attack on Fort Sumter."[20]

War fever, as newspapers dubbed it, spread contagion throughout the country, inspired in the North by Lincoln's war proclamation and in the South by the selfsame proclamation. Union soldiers tended to view their enlistment as a necessary check against anarchy and disorder. Invoking the Founding Fathers, Unionists pointed to the sacrifices of that earlier generation of patriots who had bled and died on the battlefield to establish an indissoluble Union. Although few Union soldiers expressly mentioned slavery as the motivation for going to war, the ones who did left little doubt about the intensity of their convictions. McPherson tells of a Massachusetts infantry captain and Harvard alumnus who wrote to his mother in 1861 that "slavery has brought death into our own households already in its wicked rebellion . . . There is but one way [to win the war] and that is emancipation . . . I want to sing *John Brown* in the streets of Charleston, and ram red-hot abolitionism down their unwilling throats at the point of the bayonet."[21]

In contrast, "some Confederate volunteers did indeed avow the defense of slavery as a motive for enlisting," but most believed "they were fighting for liberty as well as slavery"—halting Northern aggression and the ominous possibility of subjugation.[22] Inspired by the same example of the Founding Fathers, Confederate soldiers believed themselves heirs to a legacy of opposing tyranny and unjust government. The reasons they continued to fight, however, may have had little to do with the reasons they enlisted. The abstractness of the Cause and initial jubilation at the prospect of "killing a heap of Yankees" quickly gave way to such practical considerations as durations of campaigns, shortage of supplies, and the desire to see mothers, sweethearts, and wives whom many soldiers never came to see again.

As for Southern women, a good many seemed to oppose slavery, as indicated by numerous diaries, journals, and letters. Yet these same women were willing to sacrifice all they held dear for Confederate independence. Many refused to stay at home, following husbands and sons to battlefields until the impracticality of such a gesture forced them to return home, presumably out of harm's way. Although the South boasted the lion's share of victories during the first two years of war, the women at home suffered unprecedented privation. Walter Sullivan contends that "Southern women had to survive on what they had,"[23] and what they had was severely limited. Sullivan offers a compelling picture of the war that Southern women endured at home and in service in hospitals while their male kin were off fighting.

Women took scores of wounded troops into their homes, treating them as expertise permitted. With medical supplies at a minimum, Southern women "gave their tablecloths and napkins, their good sheets, and their linen undergarments to be folded into bandages."[24] Their generosity resulted in a shortage of clothing, though, as Sullivan reminds us, "not merely Scarlett O'Hara knew the trick of refashioning window curtains into dresses."[25] Ingenuity became the benchmark of the Southern woman called on to make sacrifices for her homeland to which her attachment was anything but abstract. Many of these women lost fathers, husbands, and sons. If, as Glenna Matthew argues, the war gave Northern women the opportunity to act out "scripts in which female efficacy and female valor were brought to bear against the Slave Power,"[26] the war gave Southern women a corresponding opportunity to exhibit unstinting charity and selflessness—spiritual rather than political qualities—for which they have sometimes been criticized, or worse, been seen as lacking in sound judgment for displaying. Nor does it seem likely that Southern women, by and large, lacked the commitment necessary to wage war for the long haul, as has been suggested by Drew Gilpin Faust:

> Historians have wondered in recent years why the Confederacy did not endure longer. In considerable measure, I would suggest, it was because so many women did not want it to. The way in which their interests in the war were publicly denied—gave women little reason to sustain the commitment modern war required. It may well have been because of its women that the South lost the Civil War.[27]

Such a generalization ignores a good many factors and may precipitously place Southern women in the camp with their enemies. This is not to say that Southern women did not want the war to end. They did. Northern women were also dedicated to halting the slaughter. Restricted to petitions in lieu of the ballot, many Northern women, in numbers too imprecise to determine, supported the peace plank of the Democratic party, whose candidate, George B. McClellan, failed to unseat Lincoln for the presidency in 1864. A more balanced view of women's roles thus requires us to acknowledge that while tensions doubtless existed in Southern women's thinking about many issues attached to the war, these women also could have found their enthusiasm dampened by plundering armies, lack of food, and homes burned to the ground. Walter Sullivan records an arresting story of a Georgia mother, Mary Jones, and her pregnant daughter, Mary Jones Mallary, whose efforts to give birth to a fourth child coincided with Sherman's march to the sea:

> And still the Yankees came. Living in Mary Jones' house were three women, one pregnant and expecting daily to go into labor, and five terrified children. The first group of invaders entered the house, broke open the cabinets and chests, took everything that was of value and much that was not, robbed the slaves, and threatened and cursed the women. They took the food they could carry, then ruined what was left. Every day, there was a new group to rifle the already plundered wardrobes, to seize or destroy whatever could be eaten that those who had come before had missed. They demolished the wagons and buggies and carriages. They took the chain from the well to deprive the family of drinking water. While they cursed outside her window, Mary Mallard endured the difficult delivery of her fourth child. The last bit of food on the Jones plantation, a ham belonging to one of the slaves, was seized by a Yankee cavalryman and fed to the dogs. But no one could deprive Mary Jones of her courage. At the end of particularly trying days, she turned to her daughter and her friend Kate King. "Tell me, girls," she would say. "Did I act like a coward?"[28]

Such testimonials are numerous, inviting us to ask not why Southern women's mettle failed to endure in the final analysis but rather why it lasted as long as it did.

Although local dramas reinforced Southern conviction about the sanctity of states' rights, few people doubted that the war was finally about slavery. The phrase "states' rights" became a coded acknowledgment of slavery, given Southern leaders' reluctance to defend openly an institution "with which possibly even a majority of Southerners were not entirely at ease."[29] One East Tennessee newspaper editor put it more bluntly: "We refuse to be hewers of wood for the slave aristocrats west of the Cumberland Mountains."[30]

As long as slavery was couched in abstract social theories that equated slave societies with stable, "progressive" cultures, many Southerners, and a good many Northern "tories," or antiabolitionists, had no trouble accepting slavery in premise or practice. However, facts refuted these theories. Slavery in the South was not based on a model of slaveholding found in ancient and traditional societies, as was often argued. If that were so, then whites would have comprised an equal portion of the existing slave class. Even Southerners sympathetic to the proslavery position of George Fitzhugh found his arguments for including whites as potential slaves too distasteful to accept. The reality of slavery was inescapable: The peculiar institution was based on race, on the presumed inferiority of black people, and, therefore, posed a contradiction, an incompatibility of aims that Swedish scholar Gunnar Myrdal has called an "American dilemma."

Race, as the underlying component of slavery, became the dominant issue forcing Americans in general, and Southerners in particular, to confront glaring contradictions in the American psyche. The war brought these contradictions to the fore. Compelled to recognize the classism and racism inherent in the founding of the government, white Americans paradoxically denied widespread military participation to African Americans, the one group arguably most invested in the outcome of the war. This "accommodation to prejudice,"[31] as Garry Wills terms it, prompted Abraham Lincoln to resist using emancipated blacks in military service. "Over and over," Wills observes, "Lincoln talks of the emancipation as a purely military act he had to resort to in order to restore order in the Southern part of the United States against armed insurrection."[32] Clearly, Lincoln did not want to make the possibility of using black soldiers an issue in border states where support of Confederate aims often wavered. Realizing he would need to govern the Southern people after the Civil War was over, Lincoln upheld the inequality of the races, treating the South's slaves as "commodities of war," while denouncing slavery as an evil. Lincoln also saw the war as a means of fighting for the freedom of African Americans, of doing something for blacks they could not do for themselves. Only late in the war did Lincoln concede the possibility that blacks could fight because they were capable of earning their own freedom on the battlefield.[33]

Still, racism bedimmed any vision of African Americans as troops equal in effectiveness to their white counterparts. Although estimates suggest that some 180,000 African Americans bore arms in the Union army, these soldiers comprised all-volunteer units established briefly near the war's end. T. J. Stiles asserts that throughout the Civil War, "not one company in the standing [Union] Regular Army was open to African-American troops."[34] Only a decade after the war did Congress provide for four infantry and two cavalry regiments composed exclusively of black enlisted men. Even after African Americans were accepted into the Army, "they endured nearly unbearable conditions. They also complained of receiving the worst of everything, including surplus equipment and cast-off horses; many white officers openly bemoaned their assignments and some abused their [black] troops."[35] Incidents such as these showed that it was possible to oppose slavery and still practice racism. Slavery certainly diminished in importance as Lincoln's quest to save the Union intensified. In his now famous letter to journalist Horace Greeley, Lincoln leaves no doubt about his position: "If I could save the Union without freeing any slave, I would do it; if I could save it by freeing all the slaves, I would do it; and if I could save it by freeing some and leaving others alone, I would also do that."[36]

Slavery became a less emotionally potent issue in the South, but for different reasons. In 1865, just a month before the collapse of the Confederate government, Jefferson Davis sent envoys to inform Britain and France that the South was ready to free all its slaves in exchange for diplomatic recognition and European support of the Confederate war effort. This gesture did not represent a change of heart concerning the ethics of slavery so much as it evinced a last-ditch effort to salvage a decimated Confederacy. Certainly, the South's appeal in no way mitigated the racism that held African Americans to be inferior to whites. The North's armies may have convinced the South of the futility of establishing an independent country, but Northern military prowess was incapable of urging the South to accept what the North could not. As a result, "The attitude both of the Union and the Confederacy toward blacks was ambiguous, inconsistent, and even hypocritical, reflecting the unfortunate fact that the average Northern soldier, hardly less than the Southern, disliked any contact with a colored man which implied equality."[37] If the situation had been otherwise, the subsequent era of Reconstruction might have engendered less tumult and widespread violence.

For the Confederacy, the idea of using black troops to fight was initially unthinkable. No one dared arm slaves, even "loyal" ones. Many slaves, however, would be pressed into service as cooks, teamsters, and laborers—some drawing (unequal) army pay. When it was clear that neither Union nor Confederacy could win the war without the moral and physical support of African Americans, General Robert E. Lee urged President Jefferson Davis to accept slave soldiers, provided both slave and owner volunteered. Such may seem an odd occurrence unless we are willing to acknowledge that historical circumstances are often more complex than the speculation afforded by hindsight. Pulitzer nominee William Davis offers insight into the role that African Americans played as Southerners during the war:

> As for slaves in the Confederacy, their activities hardly bear out the story of their resentment of their white rulers. The correspondence of President Jefferson Davis, especially in the early months of 1861, is replete with entreaties from the South's blacks, free and slave, to be allowed to enlist in the Confederate Army and even to raise whole companies for the cause. Others bought treasury bonds and contributed funds and foodstuffs to the war effort and continued doing so. Of course, in the last weeks of the war in 1865 the government actually did start raising black troops and found men willing to join even at that late date. Moreover, the Confederacy could not have survived as long as it did if the black population behind the lines had refused to aid the war effort. With white men mostly off in the armies, trusted slaves ran or helped white women run the large plantations, just as President Davis' own plantation, Brierfield, was run by his slave Isaac Montgomery. Had the blacks mounted a serious resistance or work stoppage, they could have crippled the Confederacy.[38]

Davis's observation does not diminish the horrors of slavery or the passion for freedom that slaves possessed. Obviously, "if asked, maybe a majority [of slaves] would have said they hoped to see the Confederacy fail."[39] Davis's statement does challenge an uncritical view that would lessen the impact African Americans made in the South during the Civil War. Given the nature and extent of their participation, African Americans were indispensable in shaping the South's future—its legacy and possibilities for correction and renewal.

Notes

1. Avery Craven, *The Coming of the Civil War* (Chicago: University of Chicago Press, 1957), 29.
2. Craven, 32.
3. Craven, 18.
4. Craven, 18.
5. Samuel Eliot Morison, *The Oxford History of the American People*, Vol. 2 (New York: Penguin Books, 1972), 256.
6. Morison, 256.
7. Eugene Genovese, *The Slaveholders' Dilemma* (Columbia: University of South Carolina Press, 1992), 7.
8. Genovese, 7.
9. Lewis P. Simpson, *Mind and the American Civil War* (Baton Rouge: Louisiana State University Press, 1989), 75.
10. Simpson, 80.
11. Simpson, 80.
12. Simpson, 52.
13. Simpson, 35.
14. Morison, 372–373.
15. Morison, 377.
16. Morison, 378.
17. Morison, 382.
18. Morison, 381.
19. James M. McPherson, *For Cause and Comrades* (Oxford: Oxford University Press, 1997), 17.
20. McPherson, 17.
21. McPherson, 19.
22. McPherson, 19.
23. Walter Sullivan, *The War the Women Lived* (Nashville: J. S. Sanders and Co., 1995), xvi.
24. Sullivan, xvi.
25. Sullivan, xvi.
26. Glenna Matthews, "Little Women Who Helped Make This Great War," *Why the Civil War Came*, ed. Gabor Borritt (New York: Oxford University Press, 1996), 45.
27. Matthews, 47.
28. Sullivan, xviii.
29. William Davis, *The Lost Cause* (Lawrence: University Press of Kansas, 1996), 182.
30. Thomas Connelly, *Civil War Tennessee* (Knoxville: University of Tennessee Press, 1979), 3.

31. Garry Wills, *Lincoln at Gettysburg* (New York: Simon and Schuster, 1992), 142.
32. Wills, 142.
33. Wills, 142–143.
34. T. J. Stiles, "Buffalo Soldiers," *Smithsonian* (December 1998), 85.
35. Stiles, 85.
36. Wills, 167–168, as quoted.
37. Stiles, 85.
38. Davis, 185.
39. Davis, 185.

UPPER SOUTH

The Upper South was never unilateral in its support of slavery or secession. Tennessee, the last of the Confederate states to secede and the first to rejoin the Union, serves to illustrate this point. On the field of Tennessee's state flag are three white stars representing three "Grand Estates," or geographic divisions, that also delineate important cultural differences.

East Tennessee, particularly the upper mountainous area encompassing the Great Smoky and Cumberland ranges, remains largely Republican to this day because of Unionist sympathies that divided neighbors and families, lending credence to the popular mythology that the Civil War was a contest that found "brother fighting brother." In the early nineteenth century, East Tennesseans owned a reputation for being fiercely independent—the quintessential frontiersmen kowtowing to no one while displaying a rough-hewn spirit embodied in such folk heroes as David Crockett and John Sevier. Under Sevier's leadership, East Tennessee had once declared its independence from North Carolina, establishing in 1785 the short-lived state of Franklin.

At the outbreak of the Civil War, East Tennessee had difficulty determining whether to join sides with Union or with Confederate forces. William Gannaway "Parson" Brownlow, a Methodist preacher and newspaper editor, published anti-Confederate editorials in his *Knoxville Whig* until Confederate faithfuls drove him out of the region. In 1865, Brownlow became Tennessee's governor, the result of political maneuvering that was considered a slap at Confederate loyalists. Although slavery never gained a foothold in the coves and hollows of East Tennessee, the region ultimately gave its support to the Confederate platform. Ironic as it may seem, Union loyalists such as Brownlow often disliked African Americans as fiercely as they opposed secession.

On the eve of the 1864 presidential election, prominent East Tennesseans met in Sale Creek, Tennessee—a rural community thirty miles north of Chattanooga—to sue for entrance back into the Union. Doubting their sincerity, Lincoln rejected their request, letting the petitioners remain disenfranchised for the sins of their fellow statesmen.

Middle Tennessee, an area of rolling hills and defined plateaus, includes all the land west of the Cumberland Plateau extending on to the Tennessee River, which snakes its way northward into the state's interior. Reflecting a self-conscious display of classical values, Nashville, Tennessee's capital, would eventually crown itself the "Athens of the South." At the war's outset, Nashville was a major slave-trading center and a hub of enlistment activity. The Hermitage, home of Andrew Jackson located nearby, is a testimonial to the unadorned architecture representing a populist spirit that infused the Confederate cause.

West Tennessee shares many geographical similarities and cultural ties with northern Mississippi. The alluvial Mississippi Delta made Memphis an economic center for the vast cotton kingdom, where slave labor created unprecedented wealth for planters and their wives. As a result, the cotton aristocrat of West Tennessee often saw himself as a species apart from his fellow citizens in other sections of the state. The reality, more often than not, was that family lists were rewritten to obscure the less than spectacular rise by which a frontiersman of modest origins elevated himself and his family by selling slaves and cotton at a premium never before seen in the South.

Both frontiersmen and horse traders of the Upper South often catapulted themselves into positions of social and political prominence, contributing to the mythic status of the region's self-made men. One such mythic figure was David Crockett, a member of the

United States Congress from West Tennessee. In recounting exploits larger than life in his *A Narrative of the Life of David Crockett* (1834), Crockett focuses on one of the Southern frontiersman's favorite pastimes: hunting. Of course, Crockett's tall-tale approach, including abundant colloquialisms, is designed to entertain rather than to instruct.

Published in the same year as Crockett's *Narrative*, St. George Tucker's *The Poems of St. George Tucker of Williamsburg, Virginia* (1834) shows the continued development of a belletristic tradition in the antebellum South, one serving nationalistic aims while reinforcing strong sectional identification.

Sectional differences are the theme of William Alexander Caruther's *The Kentuckian in New York: or the Adventures of Three Southerners* (1834). This narrative opens with three Upper South Southerners, two whites and a black servant, traveling north on "Southern horses," all the while making observations about the people with whom they come in contact. There are "pretender" gentlemen, poseurs whose manners disappear with the first draught of ale at the inn, as well as Yankees whose rude demeanor is, even by Caruthers's time, an acknowledged cliché. The author offers a valuable sociological insight when he concludes that "the mutual jealousy of the north and south is a decided evidence of littleness in both regions, and ample cause for shame to the educated gentlemen of all parties of this happy country."

The mutual jealousy spills over into the public domain, where scrutiny of slavery and the condition of slaves is unavoidable and where the outbreak of Civil War, given the hostile tenor of the times, seems inevitable. The apologists for slavery are numerous, with George Fitzhugh being one of the most doctrinaire supporters of slaveholding in the Upper South. Proclaiming that "We want no new world!" Fitzhugh supports establishing a stratified society, accomplishing this feat "not [by] a restoration of ancient slavery or medieval serfdom, but [by] the perfection of modern servitude that transformed slavery into a more recognizably Christian and humane system and spread it throughout the world by the force of its example."[1]

What Fitzhugh's stance ignores is a fundamental tenet of the Christianity that he espoused and pledged to practice. By failing to recognize the innate sinfulness of human beings, Fitzhugh poses a Gnostic ideal that allows advocates of slavery to excuse the horrific effects of the institution on the slaves. With "excruciating pomposity,"[2] the South's self-proclaimed social progressives produced theories that exploded in the face of the slaves' own accounts.

Among Upper South slaves cataloguing the horrors of slavery is Harriet Jacobs, whose *Incidents in the Life of a Slave Girl* (1861) suggests how slaveholders distorted Christian doctrine in order to subdue slaves. In response to the slaveholder who complains about the exaggerations of abolitionists, Jacobs asks,

> What does he know of the half-starved wretches toiling from dawn till dark on the plantations? of mothers shrieking for their children, torn from their arms by slave-traders? of young girls dragged down into moral filth? of pools of blood around the whipping post? of hounds trained to tear human flesh? of men screwed into cotton gins to die?

An equally poignant account is offered by Elizabeth Keckley, who displays a remarkable magnanimity as she recounts her days laboring for the wives of both Abraham Lincoln and Confederate president Jefferson Davis. *In Behind the Scenes: Thirty Years a Slave and Four Years in the White House*, Keckley defends Mary Todd Lincoln against negative public perceptions and, as one who had been "punished with the cruel lash," Keckley still finds the generosity of spirit amid the "soul['s] tortures" to offer Jefferson Davis a final benediction: "Peace! You have suffered! Go in peace!"

Peace was not to be had before the crucible of war severed ties between North and South. Edward Pollard, editor of the *Richmond Examiner* and author of *Southern History of the War*, offers a partisan assessment of the causes of the Civil War, insisting that sectional rivalry, not slavery, was the impetus for war and that only after midcentury did "Yankee statesmanship [which] was always intensely sophomorical [sic]" assign slavery as the chief reason for sectional strife.

After war came, it took only two years for the buoyant and hopeful spirit of the South to collapse against forces of overwhelming military resistance. In *I Rode with Stonewall*, Henry Kyd Douglas provides a chronological account of his role as the youngest member of T. J. "Stonewall" Jackson's staff "from the John Brown Raid to the hanging of Mrs. Surratt." Special attention is given to Douglas's incarceration as a prisoner of war at Johnson's Island military prison out in Lake Erie. Despite being "hardly the place Southerners would select as a winter resort," Kyd is almost stoical in his response to the harsh circumstances endured by imprisoned troops in both armies. He concludes that "for some reason not much thought was given to the wants of those in captivity."

Although enlisted men often complained of the superior treatment received by officers, few soldiers in the Army of Northern Virginia doubted the willingness of Robert E. Lee to endure personal sacrifices on behalf of his soldiers. Lee's *Dispatches: Unpublished Letters of Robert E. Lee* provides a glimpse of the aloof Virginia aristocrat who was so beloved of his troops. Lee's willingness to assign blame to himself, even after the debacle at Gettsyburg, made him a cherished figure in the South for decades following the war.

If Lee embodied courage and mastery of personal impulse, John Wilkes Booth carries the stigma of being one of the most cowardly and impetuous men in American history. In *John Wilkes Booth: A Sister's Memoirs* (1874), Asia Booth Clarke defends her illustrious clan, once known as the most celebrated family of actors in America, and she offers a conflicted defense of her brother John Wilkes, whose devotion to his cause, she says, may have forced his mind to lose "its balance between the fall of Richmond and the terrific end." This "justifiable insanity" is one example of the many romantic delusions connected with the Lost Cause.

Perhaps Edgar Allan Poe, more than any other nineteenth-century American writer, anticipated the insanity that is the hallmark of those obsessed with lost causes. Poe's work is unprecedented and psychologically penetrating. His selected poetry, published between 1840 and 1850, often gives voice to the unconscious yearnings of tortured, romantic personae, who, by dramatic example, diminish the role of reason in human affairs. If, as Elizabeth Keckley maintains, slavery was a curse that resulted from rationalist assumptions comprising the cornerstone of Deism, Poe offers a counterpoint to those assumptions, demonstrating the conflicting nature of human motivation and the divided spirit of the times.

Notes

1. Eugene Genovese, *The Slaveholders' Dilemma* (Columbia: University of South Carolina Press, 1992), 13.
2. Genovese, 21.

St. George Tucker

(1752–1827)

Richard Beale Davis has called St. George Tucker a "versatile son of the Enlightenment," and the plays, essays, and more than two hundred poems found in his manuscript papers uphold that assessment. A perfectionist whose unpublished verses often exist in several versions, Tucker seems to have written mostly as an avocation to his career as a jurist, seldom publishing, though he often distributed handwritten copies of his work among his friends.

Born in 1752 near Port Royal, Bermuda, Tucker, along with his two brothers, immigrated to America in 1771. He studied law in Williamsburg, and after serving as an officer in the final years of the Revolutionary War, he began a long and productive career in public life, the success of which was owed, at least in part, to advantageous marriages to widowed heiresses.

Much of Tucker's published works share an anti-Federalist theme; he believed that the policies of Adams, Hamilton, Jay, and others might potentially lead the young nation back to the kind of tyranny they had only recently escaped. Tucker was also an early critic of slavery, and in his *Dissertation on Slavery* (1796), he advocated freeing the children of Virginia slaves once they reached adulthood. He wrote a number of essays for William Wirt's *The Old Bachelor* series, though only one was printed. Most of the belletristic efforts published during his lifetime display his patriotic fervor, exhorting Americans to be ever wakeful in guarding their newfound individual freedoms. However, his manuscripts contain a number of bawdy pieces, and at one time, he planned a Virginia version of *The Canterbury Tales*. During his long career as a lawyer, college professor, and judge, his pen was never still, and when he died in 1827, he left a body of work that is only now receiving its just due.

For the Washington Federalist
A New Federal Song

The Jacobins have got the day
    The Feds are homeward moving;
But when they come again this way,
    There will be desperate shoving.

Yankee doodle, keep it up,
Yankee doodle dandy,
The Feds will never start a peg
Till cider turns to brandy.

Duke Braintree is to Quincy gone,
    To study new defenses,
For spite of all the old he finds,
    The folks have lost their senses.

Yankee doodle, etc.

There's Sedgewick quits his lofty seat
    For better speculation,
Than can be found while surly Smith
    Will print the Fed's orations.

Yankee doodle, etc.

There's Dayton gone to see his lands
    And have them all surveyed, sirs,
But shortly he'll be here again,
    With sword and black cockade, sirs.

Yankee doodle, etc.

There's Wolcott, he gives up the cash,
    To sit upon the bench, sirs:
Like Felix, 'round the Jacobins
    He'll work till he is weary.

Yankee Doodle, etc.

There's Otis leaves seditious laws,
    To be the Fed attorney;
When in your tails he sticks his claws,
    You'll wish the de'il to burn ye.

Yankee doodle, etc.

There's Griswold, he won't condescend,
    To be war secretary;
But if you trust him with the cash
    He'll work till he is weary.

Yankee doodle, etc.

There's Dexter fit for any thing;
    Can preach on any text, sir;
Let John or Jefferson, be king,
    You'll find him Ambidexter.

Yankee doodle, etc.

There's Read, and Green, and Hill, and More
    Are all turned into judges,
For not a Fed, without a place,
    From Congress homeward trudges;

Yankee doodle, etc.

But Bayard, he won't go to France
    To see his gallant cousins,
Lest Heaper's wonderous tales and plots,
Should multiply by dozens,

Yankee doodle, etc.

There's Hamilton, he lies perdue,
    With old sly Pickering, sirs,

In spite of all the fools can do,
    They soon will have a kind, sirs.

Yankee doodle, etc.

Then, we shall sing. "God Save the King";
    Th' aristocrats and Tories,
And placemen all from south to north,
    Will join, in joyful chorus.

Yankee doodle, keep it up,
Yankee doodle dandy,
The Feds will never start a peg
Till cider turns to brandy.

Mar. 3, 1801

The Tobacco Pipe

The wag to mischief who's inclined
To that, alone, gives up his mind,
And sacrifices foes or friends,
Without regret, to gain his ends.
    Where Roanoke rolls its limpid tide
Through fertile fields on either side,
Not long ago there was a wedding,
Where guests were plentier far than bedding.
A stranger, I forget his name,
Who from a distant county came,
At all events must have a bed;
For Robin, Harry, George, and Ned,
A pallet on the floor was spread,
The clock struck twelve—to rest they went,
And till the morning slept content;
But Robin with the lark arose
In haste, and to the garden goes:
Then uprose Harry, George, and Ned,
The stranger, fast asleep, in bed,
Lay all uncovered on his face,
Not dreaming of his foul disgrace;
His hapless case when Harry found
He casts his wicked eyes around.
Takes Robin's pipe from off the shelf
(The stem a reed, the bowl was delft),
And to the stranger's nether eye
The taper point he doth apply,
And shoves it in, up to the bowl,
So well he understood the hole:
Dan Prior's ladle not more quick
In old Corisca's bum did stick;

Then out again the reed he takes,
Before the abused stranger wakes:
But had not time the stem to wipe
When Robin came to seek his pipe,
And presently begun to smoke,
Quoth Harry—"Don't you smell a joke?"
Robin threw down the pipe in haste,
And spitting cried, "Some smell, some taste:
"They're both so strong—so may I thrive,
"They'll last as long as I'm alive."

Nov. 27, 1788

The Faithful Mastiff
A True Story

At lukewarm, or at faithless friends
    I've no design to rail:
An honest, but mistaken zeal,
    The subject of my tale.

Yet think not, with a cynic's eye
    That I regard mankind
Because in men and brutes, alike,
    Some qualities I find.

To err is human—and that dogs
    Can be mistaken too,
Most clearly follows from a tale
    Which I can vouch is true.

Ah! could I but as clearly prove
    That men, like dogs, were true,
Full many a heart would now be blithe,
    Which now their falsehood rue.

In Williamsburg, 'ere party rage
    The capital removed,
Together lived three waggish sparks
    Who mirth, and frolic loved.

Their names are still remembered there;
    For, still, some there remain,
To curse that policy that razed
    Their city to the plain.

The Author's Muse to the Reader
A Monitory Tale

In fair Barbados once there dwelt a dame
Of special note, though I forget her name;
With flatulencies she was oft oppressed,
They soured her temper and disturbed her rest.
At length a grand specific she had found,
'Twas lemonade, with aqua-vitae crowned.
A nutmeg o'er the potion should you grate
'Twould make it punch; and punch the dame did hate.
One morning when the clock had just struck nine
She calls to Betty with a sickly whine.
"This dreadful colic—something I must take."
"A little spirit, madam, shall I add?"
"Yes to be sure! Why sure the girl is mad!
"Can pungent acids with my colic suit
"Unless there's spirit to correct the fruit?"
"A little nutmeg, madam—will you try?"
"Punch in the morning! Gracious God, I die!
"Think you with nasty punch I would get drunk!
"Begone you vile, abominable punk!"
  Now listen reader! punch if thou dost hate
  Shut up the book before it be too late
'Twas wholesome lemonade I meant to brew,
But troth I fear there's nutmeg in it too.
So, gentle reader, if thou dost get tipsy
Pray call me not a saucy wanton gipsy.

Jan. 1, 1790

The Cynic

Whoever to finding fault inclines
Still misconceives the best designs:
Praxiteles in vain might try
To form a statue for his eye;
Appelles too would pain in vain,
And Titian's colors give him pain,
Palladio's best designs displease him,
And Handel's water piece would freeze him,
Not Tully's eloquence can charm,
Nor e'en old Homer's fire warm:
On all occasions still a beast
He frowns upon the genial feast,
Swears that Falernian wine was sour,
And rails at champagne for an hour,

Not Heliogabalus's cook
Could drop a dish at which he'd look.
    Anticipating time and fate
He views all things when past their date,
Destruction in his noodle brewing
Turns palaces to instant ruin:
Speak but of Paris or of London
He tells how Babylon was undone:
Ask him, with Thais if he'll sup
He cries—"The worms will eat her up."
    Once at a merry wedding feast
A cynic chanced to be a guest;
Rich was the father of the bride
And hospitality his pride.
The guests were numerous and the board
With dainties plentifully stored.
There mutton, beef, and vermicelli
Here venison stewed with currant jelly,
Here turkeys robbed of bones and lungs
Are crammed with oysters and with tongues.
There pickled lobsters, prawn, and salmon
And there a stuffed Virginia gammon.
Here custards, tarts, and apple pies
There syllabubs and jellies rise,
Ice creams, and ripe and candied fruits
With comfits and eryngo roots.
Now entered every hungry guest
And all prepared to taste the feast.
Our cynic cries—"How damned absurd
To take such pains to make a —!"

Jan. 1, 1790

David Crockett

(1786–1836)

David Crockett was born on August 17, 1786, near present-day Rogersville, Tennessee. Receiving only a few months' schooling, he learned to read and write at the age of seventeen. Although Crockett attempted several occupations—such as farmer and owner of a grist mill, a powder mill, and a distillery—he found success primarily as a soldier and politician. At the beginning of the Creek War in 1813, he volunteered for service, fighting on occasion under General Andrew Jackson, until the end of the war on March 7, 1814. From 1821 to 1825 he served as a representative in the Tennessee state legislature, and in 1826 he represented Tennessee in the twentieth United States Congress. Even though Crockett also served in the twenty-first and twenty-third Congresses, he was narrowly defeated in his 1834 bid for re-election. Because his loss was primarily due to his break with his former ally Jackson over the Tennessee land bill, Crockett became disillusioned with politics and sought a new beginning in Texas. In 1834, he left for Texas, where in February 1836 he joined the Texans at the Alamo in their struggle for independence. On March 6, 1836, he was killed with the approximately 187 other soldiers who fell during Santa Anna's onslaught. Despite the numerous books that have been attributed to Crockett, including *Sketches and Eccentricities of Colonel David Crockett of West Tennessee* (1833), *The Life of Martin Van Buren, Heir-Apparent to the "Government," and the Appointed Successor of General Jackson* (1835), *An Account of Colonel Crockett's Tour to the North and Down East, etc.* (1835), and *Colonel Crockett's Exploits and Adventures in Texas* (1836), existing evidence suggests that Crockett actually wrote only one work, his autobiography entitled *A Narrative of the Life of David Crockett, of the State of Tennessee* (1834), with the ghost writer Thomas Chilton, congressman from Kentucky. Crockett's *Narrative* is considered by many to be one of the earliest works in the tall-tale tradition of Southwest humorists.

from *A Narrative of the Life of David Crockett:* Hunting in Tennessee

But the reader, I expect, would have no objection to know a little about my employment during the two years while my competitor was in Congress. In this space I had some pretty tuff times, and will relate some few things that happened to me. So here goes, as the boy said when he run by himself.

In the fall of 1825, I concluded I would build two large boats, and load them with pipe staves for market. So I went down to the lake, which was about twenty-five miles from where I lived, and hired some hands to assist me, and went to work; some at boat building, and others to getting staves. I worked on with my hands till the bears got fat, and then I turned out to hunting, to lay in a supply of meat. I soon killed and salted down as many as were necessary for my family; but about this time one of my old neighbours, who had settled down on the lake about twenty-five miles from me, came to my house and told me he wanted me to go down and kill some bears about in his parts. He said they were extremely fat, and very plenty. I know'd that when they were fat, they were easily taken, for a fat bear can't run fast or long. But I asked a bear no favours, no way, further than civility, for I now had *eight* large dogs, and as fierce as painters; so that a bear stood no chance at all to get away from them. So I went home with him, and then went on down towards the Mississippi, and commenced hunting.

We were out two weeks, and in that time killed fifteen bears. Having now supplied my friend with plenty of meat, I engaged occasionally again with my hands in our boat building, and getting staves. But I at length couldn't stand it any longer without another hunt. So I concluded to take my little son, and cross over the lake, and take a hunt there.

[Hunting in Tennessee], from *A Narrative of the Life of David Crockett* by David Crockett. 7th ed. Philadelphia: E. L. Carey and A. Hart, 1834. Rpt. Knoxville: University of Tennessee Press, 1973.

We got over, and that evening turned out and killed three bears, in little or no time. The next morning we drove up four forks, and made a sort of scaffold, on which we salted up our meat, so as to have it out of the reach of the wolves, for as soon as we would leave our camp, they would take possession. We had just eat our breakfast, when a company of hunters came to our camp, who had fourteen dogs, but all so poor, that when they would bark they would almost have to lean up against a tree and take a rest. I told them their dogs couldn't run in smell of a bear, and they had better stay at my camp, and feed them on the bones I had cut out of my meat. I left them there, and cut out; but I hadn't gone far, when my dogs took a first-rate start after a very large fat old *he-bear*, which run right plump towards my camp. I pursued on, but my other hunters had heard my dogs coming, and met them, and killed the bear before I got up with him. I gave him to them, and cut out again for a creek called Big Clover, which wa'n't very far off. Just as I got there, and was entering a cane brake, my dogs all broke and went ahead, and, in a little time, they raised a fuss in the cane, and seemed to be going every way. I listened a while, and found my dogs was in two companies, and that both was in a snorting fight. I sent my little son to one, and I broke for t'other. I got to mine first, and found my dogs had a two-year-old bear down, 'a-wooling away on him; so I just took out my big butcher, and went up and slap'd it into him, and killed him without shooting. There was five of the dogs in my company. In a short time, I heard my little son fire at his bear; when I went to him he had killed it too. He had two dogs in his team. Just at this moment we heard my other dog barking a short distance off, and all the rest immediately broke to him. We pushed on too, and when we got there, we found he had still a larger bear than either of them we had killed, treed by himself. We killed that one also, which made three we had killed in less than half an hour. We turned in and butchered them, and then started to hunt for water, and a good place to camp. But we had no sooner started, than our dogs took a start after another one, and away they went like a thunder-gust, and was out of hearing in a minute. We followed the way they had gone for some time, but at length we gave in the hope of finding them, and turned back. As we were going back, I came to where a poor fellow was grubbing, and he looked like the very picture of hard times. I asked him what he was doing away there in the woods by himself? He said he was grubbing for a man who intended to settle there; and the reason why he did it was, that he had no meat for his family, and he was working for a little.

I was mighty sorry for the poor fellow, for it was not only a hard, but a very slow way to get meat for a hungry family; so I told him if he would go with me, I would give him more meat than he could get by grubbing in a month. I intended to supply him with meat, and also to get him to assist my little boy in packing in and salting up my bears. He had never seen a bear killed in his life. I told him I had six killed then, and my dogs were hard after another. He went off to his little cabin, which was a short distance in the brush, and his wife was very anxious he should go with me. So we started and went to where I had left my three bears, and made a camp. We then gathered my meat and salted, and scaffled it, as I had done the other. Night now came on, but no word from my dogs yet. I afterwards found they had treed the bear about five miles off near to a man's house, and had barked at it the whole enduring night. Poor fellows! many a time they looked for me, and wondered why I didn't come, for they knowed there was no mistake in me, and I know'd they were as good as ever fluttered. In the morning, as soon as it was light enough to see, the man took his gun and went to them, and shot the bear, and killed it. My dogs, however, wouldn't have any thing to say to this stranger; so they left him, and came early in the morning back to me.

We got our breakfast, and cut out again; and we killed four large and very fat bears that day. We hunted out the week, and in that time we killed seventeen, all of them first-rate. When we closed our hunt, I gave the man over a thousand weight of fine fat bear-meat, which pleased him mightily, and made him feel as rich as a Jew. I saw him the next fall, and he told me he had plenty of meat to do him the whole year from his week's hunt. My son and me now went home. This was the week between Christmass and New-year that we made this hunt.

When I got home, one of my neighbours was out of meat, and wanted me to go back, and let him go with me, to take another hunt. I couldn't refuse; but I told him I was afraid the bear had taken to house by that time, for after they get very fat in the fall and early part of the winter, they go into their holes, in large hollow trees, or into hollow logs, or their cane-houses, or the harricanes; and lie there till spring, like frozen snakes. And one thing about this will seem mighty strange to many people. From about the first of January to about the last of April, these varments lie in their holes altogether. In all that time they have no food to eat; and yet when they come out, they are not an ounce lighter than when they went to house. I don't know the cause of this, and still I know it is a fact; and I leave it for others who have more learning than myself to account for it. They have not a particle of food with them, but they just lie and suck the bottom of their paw all the time. I have killed many of them in their trees, which enables me to speak positively on the subject. However, my neighbour, whose name was McDaniel, and my little son and me, went on down to the lake to my second camp, where I had killed my seventeen bears the week before, and turned out to hunting. But we hunted hard all day without getting a single start. We had carried but little provisions with us, and the next morning was entirely out of meat. I sent my son about three miles off, to the house of an old friend, to get some. The old gentleman was much pleased to hear I was hunting in those parts, for the year before the bears had killed a great many of his hogs. He was that day killing his bacon hogs, and so he gave my son some meat, and sent word to me that I must come in to his house that evening, that he would have plenty of feed for my dogs, and some accommodations for ourselves; but before my son got back, we had gone out hunting, and in a large cane brake my dogs found a big bear in a cane-house, which he had fixed for his winter-quarters, as they sometimes do.

When my lead dog found him, and raised the yell, all the rest broke to him, but none of them entered his house until we got up. I encouraged my dogs, and they knowed me so well, that I could have made them seize the old serpent himself, with all his horns and heads, and cloven foot and ugliness into the bargain, if he would only have come to light, so that they could have seen him. They bulged in, and in an instant the bear followed them out, and I told my friend to shoot him, as he was mighty wrathy to kill a bear. He did so, and killed him prime. We carried him to our camp, by which time my son had returned; and after we got our dinners we packed up, and cut for the house of my old friend, whose name was Davidson.

We got there, and staid with him that night; and the next morning, having salted up our meat, we left it with him, and started to take a hunt between the Obion lake and the Red-foot lake; as there had been a dreadful harricane, which passed between them, and I was sure there must be a leap of bears in the fallen timber. We had gone about five miles without seeing any sign at all; but at length we got on some high cany ridges, and, as we rode along, I saw a hole in a large black oak, and on examining more closely, I discovered that a bear had clomb the tree. I could see his tracks going up, but none coming down, and so I was sure he was in there. A person who is acquainted with bear-hunting, can tell easy enough when the varment is in the hollow; for as they go up they don't slip a bit, but as they come down they make long scratches with their nails.

My friend was a little ahead of me, but I called him back, and told him there was a bear in that tree, and I must have him out. So we lit from our horses, and I found a small tree which I thought I could fall so as to lodge against my bear tree, and we fell to work chopping it with our tomahawks. I intended, when we lodged the tree against the other, to let my little son go up, and look into the hole, for he could climb like a squirrel. We had chop'd on a little time and stop'd to rest, when I heard my dogs barking mighty severe at some distance from us, and I told my friend I knowed they had a bear; for it is the nature of a dog, when he finds you are hunting bears, to hunt for nothing else; he becomes fond of the meat, and considers other game as "not worth a notice," as old Johnson said of the devil.

We concluded to leave our tree a bit, and went to my dogs, and when we got there, sure enough they had an eternal great big fat bear up a tree, just ready for shooting. My friend again petitioned me for liberty to shoot this one also. I had a little rather not, as the bear was so big, but I couldn't refuse; and so he blazed away, and down came the old fellow like some great log had fell. I now missed one of my dogs, the same that I before spoke of as having treed the bear by himself sometime before, when I had started the three in the cane break. I told my friend that my missing dog had a bear somewhere, just as sure as fate; so I left them to butcher the one we had just killed, and I went up on a piece of high ground to listen for my dog. I heard him barking with all his might some distance off, and I pushed ahead for him. My other dogs hearing him broke to him, and when I got there, sure enough again he had another bear ready treed; if he hadn't, I wish I may be shot. I fired on him, and brought him down; and then went back, and help'd finish butchering the one at which I had left my friend. We then packed both to our tree where we had left my boy. By this time, the little fellow had cut the tree down that we intended to lodge, but it fell the wrong way; he had then feather'd in on the big tree, to cut that, and had found that it was nothing but a shell on the outside, and all doted in the middle, as too many of our big men are in these days, having only an outside appearance. My friend and my son cut away on it, and I went off about a hundred yards with my dogs to keep them from running under the tree when it should fall. On looking back at the hole, I saw the bear's head out of it, looking down at them as they were cutting. I hollered to them to look up, and they did so; and McDaniel catched up his gun, but by this time the bear was out, and coming down the tree. He fired at it, and as soon as it touch'd ground the dogs were all round it, and they had a roll-and-tumble fight to the foot of the hill, where they stop'd him. I ran up, and putting my gun against the bear, fired and killed him. We now had three, and so we made our scaffold and salted them up.

In the morning I left my son at the camp, and we started on towards the harricane; and when we had went about a mile, we started a very large bear, but we got along mighty slow on account of the cracks in the earth occasioned by the earthquakes. We, however, made out to keep in hearing of the dogs for about three miles, and then we come to the harricane. Here we had to quit our horses, as old Nick himself couldn't have got through it without sneaking it along in the form that he put on, to make a fool of our old grandmother Eve. By this time several of my dogs had got tired and come back; but we went ahead on foot for some little time in the harricane, when we met a bear coming straight to us, and not more than twenty or thirty yards off. I started my tired dogs after him, and McDaniel pursued them, and I went on to where my other dogs were. I had seen the track of the bear they were after, and I knowed he was a screamer. I followed on to about the middle of the harricane; but my dogs pursued him so close, that they made him climb an old stump about twenty feet high. I got in shooting distance of him and fired, but I was all over in such a flutter from fatigue and running, that I couldn't hold steady; but, however, I broke his shoulder, and he fell. I run up and loaded my gun as quick as possible, and shot him again and killed him. When I went to take out my knife to butcher him, I found I had lost it in coming through the harricane. The vines and briers was so thick that I would sometimes have to get down and crawl like a varment to get through at all; and a vine had, as I supposed, caught in the handle and pulled it out. While I was standing and studying what to do, my friend came to me. He had followed my trail through the harricane, and had found my knife, which was mighty good news to me; as a hunter hates the worst in the world to lose a good dog, or any part of his hunting-tools. I now left McDaniel to butcher the bear, and I went after our horses, and brought them as near as the nature of case would allow. I then took our bags, and went back to where he was; and when we had skin'd the bear, we fleeced off the fat and carried it to our horses at several loads. We then packed it up on our horses, and had a heavy pack of it on each one. We now started and went on till about sunset, when I concluded we must be near our camp; so I hollered and my son answered me, and we moved on in the direction to the camp. We had gone but a little way when I heard my dogs make a warm start again; and I jumped down from my horse and gave him up to my friend, and told him I would follow them. He went on to the camp, and I went ahead after my dogs with all my might for a considerable distance, till at last night came on. The woods were very rough and hilly, and all covered over with cane.

I now was compel'd to move on more slowly; and was frequently falling over logs, and into the cracks made by the earthquakes, so that I was very much afraid I would break my gun. However I went on about three miles, when I came to a good big creek, which I waded. It was very cold, and the creek was about knee-deep; but I felt no great inconvenience from it just then, as I was all over wet with sweat from running, and I felt hot enough. After I got over this creek and out of the cane, which was very thick on all our creeks, I listened for my dogs. I found they had either treed or brought the bear to a stop, as they continued barking in the same place. I pushed on as near in the direction to the noise as I could, till I found the hill was too steep for me to climb, and so I backed and went down the creek some distance till I came to a hollow, and then took up that, till I come to a place where I could climb up the hill. It was mighty dark, and was difficult to see my way or any thing else. When I got up the hill, I found I had passed the dogs; and so I turned and went to them. I found, when I got there, they had treed the bear in a large forked poplar, and it was setting in the fork.

I could see the lump, but not plain enough to shoot with any certainty, as there was no moonlight; and so I set in to hunting for some dry brush to make me a light; but I could find none, though I could find that the ground was torn mightily to pieces by the cracks.

At last I thought I could shoot by guess, and kill him; so I pointed as near the lump as I could, and fired away. But the bear didn't come he only clomb up higher, and got out on a limb, which helped me to see him better. I now loaded up again and fired, but this time he didn't move at all. I commenced loading for a third fire, but the first thing I knowed, the bear was down among my dogs, and they were fighting all around me. I had my big butcher in my belt, and I had a pair of dressed buckskin breeches on. So I took out my knife, and stood, determined, if he should get hold of me, to defend myself in the best way I could. I stood there for some time, and could now and then see a white dog I had, but the rest of them, and the bear, which were dark coloured, I couldn't see at all, it was so miserable dark. They still fought around me, and sometimes within three feet of me; but, at last the bear got down into one of the cracks, that the earthquakes had made in the ground, about four feet deep, and I could tell the biting end of him by the hollering of my dogs. So I took my gun and pushed the muzzle of it about, till I thought I had it against the main part of his body, and fired; but it happened to be only the fleshy part of his foreleg. With this, he jumped out of the crack, and he and the dogs had another hard fight around me, as before. At last, however, they forced him back into the crack again, as he was when I had shot.

I had laid down my gun in the dark, and I now began to hunt for it; and, while hunting, I got hold of a pole, and I concluded I would punch him awhile with that. I did so, and when I would punch him, the dogs would jump in on him, when he would bite them badly, and they would jump out again. I concluded, as he would take punching so patiently, it might be that he would lie still enough for me to get down in the crack, and feel slowly along till I could find the right place to give him a dig with my butcher. So I got down, and my dogs got in before him and kept his head towards them, till I got along easily up to him; and placing my hand on his rump, felt for his shoulder, just behind which I intended to stick him. I made a lounge with my long knife, and fortunately stuck him right through the heart; at which he just sank down, and I crawled out in a hurry. In a little time my dogs all come out too, and seemed satisfied, which was the way they always had of telling me that they had finished him.

I suffered very much that night with cold, as my leather breeches, and every thing else I had on, was wet and frozen. But I managed to get my bear out of this crack after several hard trials, and so I butchered him, and laid down to try to sleep. But my fire was very bad, and I couldn't find any thing that would burn well to make it any better; and I concluded I should freeze, if I didn't warm myself in some way by exercise. So I got up, and hollered a while, and then I would just jump up and down with all my might, and throw myself into all sorts of motions. But all this wouldn't do; for my blood was now getting cold, and the chills coming all over me. I was so tired, too, that I could hardly walk; but I thought I would do the best I could to save my life, and then, if I died, nobody would be to blame. So I went to a tree about two feet through, and not a limb on it for thirty feet, and I would climb up it to the limbs, and then lock my arms together around it, and slide down to the bottom again. This would make the insides of my legs and arms feel mighty warm and good. I continued this till daylight in the morning, and how often I clomb up my tree and slid down I don't know, but I reckon at least a hundred times.

In the morning I got my bear hung up so as to be safe, and then set out to hunt for my camp. I found it after a while, and McDaniel and my son were very much rejoiced to see me get back, for they were about to give me up for lost. We got our breakfasts, and then secured our meat by building a high scaffold, and covering it over. We had no fear of its spoiling, for the weather was so cold that it couldn't.

We now started after my other bear, which had caused me so much trouble and suffering; and before we got him, we got a start after another, and took him also. We went on to the creek I had crossed the night before and camped, and then went to where my bear was, that I had killed in the crack. When we examined the place, McDaniel said he wouldn't have gone into it, as I did, for all the bears in the woods.

We took the meat down to our camp and salted it, and also the last one we had killed; intending, in the morning, to make a hunt in the harricane again.

We prepared for resting that night, and I can assure the reader I was in need of it. We had laid down by our fire, and about ten o'clock there came a most terrible earthquake, which shook the earth so, that we were rocked about like we had been in a cradle. We were very much alarmed; for though we were accustomed to feel earthquakes, we were now right in the region which had been torn to pieces by them in 1812, and we thought it might take a notion and swallow us up, like the big fish did Jonah.

In the morning we packed up and moved to the harricane, where we made another camp, and turned out that evening and killed a very large bear, which made *eight* we had now killed in this hunt.

The next morning we entered the harricane again, and in little or no time my dogs were in full cry. We pursued them, and soon came to a thick cane-brake, in which they had stop'd their bear. We got up close to him, as the cane was so thick that we couldn't see more than a few feet. Here I made my friend hold the cane a little open with his gun till I shot the bear, which was a mighty large one. I killed him dead in his tracks. We got him out and butchered him, and in a little time started another and killed him, which now made *ten* we had killed; and we know'd we couldn't pack any more home, as we had only five horses along; therefore we returned to the camp and salted up all our meat, to be ready for a start homeward next morning.

The morning came and we packed our horses with the meat, and had as much as they could possibly carry, and sure enough cut out for home. It was about thirty miles, and we reached home the second day. I now accommodated my neighbour with meat enough to do him, and had killed in all, up to that time, fifty-eight bears, during the fall and winter.

As soon as the time come for them to quit their houses and come out again in the spring, I took a notion to hunt a little more, and in about one month, I killed forty-seven more, which made one hundred and five bears I had killed in less than one year from that time.

William Alexander Caruthers

(1802–1846)

William Alexander Caruthers was born in 1802 in Lexington, Virginia. He attended Washington College (now Washington and Lee University) before going on to medical school at the University of Pennsylvania, receiving a degree in 1823. Shortly after his graduation, he married Louisa Gibson, the daughter of a wealthy Georgia planter, and returned to Lexington to begin his practice. The couple had five children, and though Caruthers was active in Lexington society and politics, he was unsuccessful financially, and by 1829, he had exhausted both Louisa's inheritance and his own. The family moved north and settled in New York City, where they remained for the next five years, weathering the cholera epidemic of 1832. In New York, Caruthers became friends with James Kirke Paulding, with whom he may have collaborated on at least one novel (most likely Paulding's *Westward Ho!*). Near the end of his tenure in New York, he published the first two of his three novels in quick succession, *The Kentuckian in New-York* and *The Cavaliers of Virginia*, both of which were quite popular. The novels did little to ease Caruthers's financial straits, however, and he left New York to return briefly to Lexington before moving again, this time to Savannah, in 1837. There he lived until the end of his life (his final novel, *The Knights of the Horseshoe*, was published by an obscure Alabama press in 1845), which was cut short by tuberculosis in 1846.

Caruthers's fiction is unabashedly sentimental, but it employs a number of themes that would characterize Southern literature for decades, most notably the portrayal of the South as a new Arcadia, the depiction of heroines who exemplify early versions of the Southern belle stereotype, and a pronounced gothic element. *The Kentuckian in New-York* combines narrative and epistolary forms, detailing the escapades of young couples as they travel through Southern and Northern locales, and it includes a portrayal of a Kentucky drover (Montgomery Damon) modeled on the legendary Davy Crockett.

from *The Kentuckian in New-York: or the Adventures of Three Southerns*

Chapter I.

Towards the latter part of the summer of 18—, on one of those cool, delightful, and invigorating mornings which are frequent in the southern regions of the United States, there issued from the principal hotel on the valley-side of Harper's Ferry two travellers, attended by a venerable and stately southern slave. The experienced eye of the old ferryman, as he stood in his flat-bottomed boat awaiting the arrival of this party, discovered at once that our travellers were from the far South.

The first of these, Victor Chevillere, entered the "flat," leading by the bridle a mettlesome southern horse; when he had stationed this fine animal to his satisfaction, he stood directly fronting the prescriptive Charon of the region. This young gentleman, who appeared to be the principal character of the party just entering the boat, was handsomely formed, moderately tall, and fashionably dressed. His face was bold, dignified, and resolute, and not remarkable for any very peculiar fashion of the hair or beard which shaded it. He appeared to be about twenty-three years of age, and though so young, much and early experience of the world had already o'ershadowed his face with a becoming serenity, if not sadness. Not that silly, affected melancholy, however, which is so often worn in these days by young and romantic idle gentlemen, to catch the errant sympathies of some untravelled country beauty.

The next personage of the party (who likewise entered the boat leading a fine southern animal), was a fashionable young gentleman, about the middle size; his face was pale and wan, as if he had but just recovered from an attack of illness. Nevertheless there was a brilliant fire in his eye, and a lurking, but too evident, disposition to fun and humour, which illness had not been entirely able to subdue. Augustus Lamar, for such was his name, was the confidential and long-tried friend of the first-named gentleman: their mutual regard had existed undiminished from the time of their early school days in South Carolina, through their whole college career in Virginia up to the moment of which we speak.

The third and more humble personage of the party bore the time-honoured appellation of Cato. He was a tall old negro, with a face so black as to form a perfect contrast to his white hair and brilliant teeth. He was well dressed and cleanly in his person, and rather solemn and pompous in his manners. Cato had served the father of his present highly honoured young master, and was deeply imbued with that strong feudal attachment to the family, which is a distinguishing characteristic of the southern negroes who serve immediately near the persons of the great landholders.

Our travellers were now smoothly gliding over that most magnificent "meeting of the waters" of the Shenandoah and Potomack, which is usually known by the unpretending name of "Harper's Ferry." It was early morning; the moon was still visible above the horizon, and the sun had not yet risen above those stupendous fragments whose chaotic and irregular position gives token of the violence with which the mass of waters rent for themselves a passage through the mountains, when rushing on to meet that other congregation of rivers, with whose waters they unite to form the Bay of the Chesapeake. The black bituminous smoke from the hundred smithies of the United States' armory, had just begun to rise above the towering crags that seemed, at this early period, to battle with the vapours which are here sent up in thick volumes from the contest of rocks and rivers beneath.

Old Cato had by this time assumed his post at the heads of the three horses, while our southerns stood with folded arms, each impressed with the scene according to his individual impulses. As they approached nearer to the northern shores, Chevillere, addressing Lamar, observed: "An unhappy young lady she must be who arrived at our hotel last evening. I could hear her weeping bitterly as she paced the floor, until a late hour of the night, when finally she seemed to throw herself upon the bed, and fall asleep from mere exhaustion;" and then, turning to the weather-beaten steersman, continued: "I suppose we are the first passengers in the 'flat' this morning?"

"No, sir, you are not; a carriage from the same tavern went over half an hour ago. There was an old gray-headed man, and two young women in it, besides the driver, and the driver told me that they were all the way from York State,—the mail stage, too, went over."

"The same party," said Chevillere, abstractedly; "Did you learn where they were to breakfast, boatman?"

"About ten miles from this, I think I heard say."

They were soon landed and mounted, and cantering away through the fog and vapours of the early morning. Nor were they long in overtaking a handsome travelling-carriage, which was moving at a brisk rate, in accordance with the exertions of two fine, evidently northern, horses. The carriage contained an elderly, grave, formal, and magisterial gentleman; his locks quite gray, and hanging loose upon the collar of his coat; his countenance harsh, austere, and forbidding in the extreme. By his side sat a youthful lady, so enveloped in a large black mantle, and travelling hat and veil, that but little of her form or features could be seen, except a pair of brilliant blue eyes.

It is not to be denied, that these sudden apparitions of young and beautiful females, almost completely shrouded in mantles, drapery, or veils, are the very circumstances fully to arouse the slumbering energies of a lately emancipated college Quixotte. A lovely pair of eyes, brimful of tears,—a "Cinderella" foot and ankle,—a white and beautifully turned hand and tapered fingers, with perhaps a mourning ring or two,—or a bonnet suddenly blown off, so as to dishevel a magnificent head of hair, its pretty mistress meanwhile all confusion, and her snowy neck and temples suffused with blushes,—these are the little incidents on which the real romances of human life are founded. How many persons can look back to such a commencement of their youthful loves! nay, perhaps, refer to it all the little enjoyment with which they have been blessed through life! We venture to say, that those who were so unfortunate as never to bring their first youthful romance to a fortunate denouement, can likewise look back upon such occurrences with many pleasing emotions. A bachelor or a widower, indeed, may not always recur with pleasure to these first passages in the book of life,—but the feelings even of these are not altogether of the melancholy kind. The fairy queens of their spring-tide will sometimes arise in the present tense, until they almost imagine themselves in the possession again of youth and all its raptures,—its brilliant dreams, airy castles, "hair breadth 'scapes," and miraculous deliverances,—cruel fathers, and perverse guardians, and stolen interviews, and lovers' vows and tokens,—winding up finally with a runaway match—all of the imagination.

After the equipage before alluded to had been for some time left behind, our travellers began to descry, at the distance of several miles, the long white portico of the country inn at which they proposed to breakfast. The United States mailcoach for Baltimore was standing at the door, evidently waiting till the passengers should have performed the same needful operation. Servants were running hither and thither, some to the roost, others to the stable, as if a large number of the most distinguished dignitaries of the land had just arrived.

But, behold, when our travellers drew up, they found that all this stir among the servants of the inn was called into being by the real or affected wants of a number of very young gentlemen. We say affected, because we are sorry to acknowledge that it is not uncommon to see very young and inexperienced gentlemen, on such occasions, assume airs and graces which are merely put on as a travelling dress, and which would be thrown aside at the first appearance of an old acquaintance. At such times it is by no means rare to see all the servants of the inn, together with the host and hostess, entirely engrossed by one of these overgrown boys or ill-bred men, while their elders and superiors are compelled either to want or wait upon themselves. At the time we notice, some young bloods of the cities were exercising themselves in their new suit of stage-coach manners.

"Here waiter! waiter!" with an affectedly delicate and foreign voice, cried one of these youths, enveloped in a brown "Petersham box" coat, and with his hands stuck into his pockets over his hips. Under the arm of this person was a black riding-switch, with a golden head, and a small chain of the same precious metal, fastened about six inches therefrom, after the fashion of some old rapier guards. He wore a rakish-looking fur cap, round and tight on the top of his head as a bladder of snuff; this was cocked on one side after a most piratical fashion, so as to show off, in the best possible manner, a great profusion of coarse, shining black hair, which was evidently indebted to art rather than nature for the curls that frizzled out over his ears, while the back part of his head was left as bare and defenceless as if he had already been under the hands of a deputy turnkey. He practised what may be called American puppyism, as technically distinguished from the London species of the same genus. "Here waiter! waiter!" said he, "bring me a gin sling,—and half-a-dozen Bagdad segars,—and a lighted taper,—and a fresh egg,—and a bowl of water,—and a clean towel,—and polish my boots,—and dust my coat,—and then send me the barber, do you hear?"

"O, sir! we has no barber, nor Bagdab segars neither; but we has plenty of the real Baltimores,—real good ones, too,—as I knows very well, for I smokes the old sodgers what the gentlemen throws on the bar-room floor."

"It is one of the most amusing scenes imaginable," said Victor Chevillere to Augustus Lamar, as they sat witnessing this scene, "when the waiter and the master pro tempore are both fools. The fawning, bowing, cringing waiter, with his big lips upon the *qui vive*, his head and shoulders constantly in motion, and rubbing his hands one over the other after the most approved fashion of the men of business. In such a case as that which we have just witnessed, where puppyism comes in contact with the kindred monkey-tricks of the waiter, I can enjoy it. But when it happens, as I have more than once seen, that the waiter is a manly, sensible, and dignified old negro of the loftier sort, such as old Cato,—then you can soon detect the curl of contempt upon his lip,—and he is not long thereafter in selecting the real gentlemen of the party,—always choosing to wait most upon those who least demand it."

"I would bet my horse Talleyrand against an old field scrub, that that fellow is a Yankee," answered Lamar.

"He may be a Yankee," continued Victor Chevillere, "but you have travelled too much and reflected too long upon the nature of man, to ascribe every thing disgusting to a Yankee origin. For my part, I make the character of every man I meet in some measure my study during my travels, and as we have agreed to exchange opinions upon men and things, I will tell you freely what I think of that fellow who has just retreated from our laughter. I have found it not at all uncommon, to see the most undisguised hatred arise between two such persons as he of the stage-coach,—the one from the north, and the other from the south,—when in truth, the actuating impulse was precisely the same in both, but had taken a different direction, and was differently developed by different exciting causes.

"The puppyism of Charleston and that of Boston are only different shades of the same character, yet these kindred spirits can in nowise tolerate each other. As is universally the case, those are most intolerant to others who have most need of forgiveness themselves. The mutual jealousy of the north and south is a decided evidence of littleness in both regions, and ample cause for shame to the educated gentlemen of all parties of this happy country. If pecuniary interest had not been mixed up with this provincial rivalry, the feeling could easily have been so held up to the broad light of intelligence, as to be a fertile source of amusement, and furnish many a subject for comedy and farce in after-times."

This specimen was by no means the only one among the arrivals by the stage-coach. Every waiter in the house was pressed into the service of these coxcombs,—some smoked,—some swaggered through the private rooms,—others adjusted their frizzled locks at the mirrors with brushes carried for the purpose,—and all together created a vast commotion in the quiet country inn.

As our two young southerns sat in the long piazza, eying these stage-coach travellers and waiting for breakfast, the same equipage which they had passed on the road, and containing our northern party, drew up to the door.

Not many minutes had elapsed before a black servant stood in the entry between the double suite of apartments, and briskly swung a small bell to and fro, which seemed to announce breakfast, from the precipitate haste with which the gentlemen of the stage-coach found their way into the long breakfasting-hall of the establishment. Our southerns followed their example, but more quietly, and by the invitation of the host. At the upper end of the table stood the hostess, who, like most of her kind in America, was the wife of a wealthy landholder and farmer, as well as tavern-keeper. She was a genteel and modest-looking woman, and did the honours of the table like a lady at her own hospitable board, and among selected guests. It is owing to a mistake in the character of the host and hostess, that so many foreigners give and take offence at these establishments. They often contumaciously demand as a right, what would have been offered to them in all courtesy after the established usages of the country.

On the right of the hostess sat the youthful lady who had spent such an unhappy night at the ferry,—in the hearing of Victor Chevillere,—and whom they had passed on the road. She was still so enveloped in her travelling dress and veil as to be but partially seen. On the same side, unfortunately, as he no doubt thought, sat Chevillere with Lamar. The grave-looking old gentleman, the companion of the youthful lady mentioned, sat immediately opposite to her. The gentlemen of extreme ton (as they wished to be thought), were ranged along the table, already mangling the dishes, cracking and replacing the eggs, and apparently much dissatisfied with the number of seconds they had remained in heated water. Nor were they long in striking up a conversation, as loud and full of slang as their previous displays had been. During this unseemly and boisterous conduct, some more tender chord seemed to be touched within the bosom of the lovely young female, than would have been supposed from the character of the assailants. Victor Chevillere turned his head in that direction, and saw that her face had become more deadly pale; at the same moment he heard her say, in an under-tone, to the old gentleman her companion, "My dear sir, assist me from this room,—my head grows dizzy, and I feel a deathlike sickness."

Chevillere was upon his feet in an instant, and assisted the lady to rise; by this time, the old gentleman having taken her other arm, they carried rather than led her into one of the adjoining apartments, where, after depositing their beautiful burden upon a sofa, Chevillere left her to the care of the hostess, who had followed, and returned to the breakfast-table.

Let us describe a country breakfast for the uninitiated. At the head of the table was a large salver, or japanned waiter, upon which was spread out various utensils of China-ware,—the only articles of plate being a sugar-dish and cream-pot. On the right of this salver stood a coffee and tea-urn, of some composition metal, resembling silver in appearance. At the other end of the table, under the skilful hands of the host, was a large steak, cut and sawed entirely through the sirloin of the beef. Half-way up the table, on either side, were dishes of broiled game, the intermediate spaces being filled up with various kinds of hot bread, biscuit and pancakes (as they are called in some parts of the north). This custom of eating hot bread at the morning and evening meal, is almost universal at the south. Immediately in the centre stood a pyramid of fresh-churned butter, with a silver butter-knife sticking into the various ornaments of vine-leaves and grapes with which it was stamped.

To this fare Chevillere found his friend Lamar doing the most ample justice, nor was his own keen appetite entirely destroyed by the temporary indisposition of the lady who had so much excited his curiosity and his sympathy. He could have congratulated himself on the little occurrence which had given him some claims to a farther acquaintance, and doubtless could have indulged in delightful reveries as to the fair and youthful stranger,—had not all his gay dreams been put to flight by the boisterous laughter and meager attempts at wit of the other travellers. As he returned towards the table, the one whom we have more particularly described elevated a glass, with a golden handle, to his large, full, and impudent eye. Chevillere returned the gaze until his look almost amounted to a deliberate stare. The "bloods" looked fierce, and exchange pugnacious looks, but all chance of a collision was prevented by the return of the hostess. Notwithstanding the disagreeable qualities of most of the guests at the table, Chevillere found time to turn the little incident of the sudden indisposition and its probable cause several times in his own mind; and, as may be well imagined, his mental soliloquy resulted in no injurious imputation upon the youthful lady,—there was evidently no trait of affectation.

At length the meal was brought to a close,—not however, before the driver of the mail-coach had wound sundry impatient blasts upon his bugle,—general joy seemed to pervade every remaining countenance after the departure of the coxcombs. Both the northern and southern travellers, who were journeying northward, and who had breakfasted at the inn, were soon likewise plodding along at the usual rate of weary travellers by a private conveyance.

Edgar Allan Poe

(1809–1849)

Edgar Allan Poe was born in Boston, the son of itinerant actors who were playing in a stock company there. By the time he was three years old, his father had deserted the family, his mother had died, and the young Poe had been taken in by John Allan, a prosperous merchant of Richmond, Virginia. After living for a time in England, the Allans returned to Virginia in 1820, where Poe demonstrated a love for the classics but little affection for scholarship. At seventeen he entered the newly founded University of Virginia but stayed for only a year, forced to leave because of gambling debts incurred in an effort to supplement the inadequate funds supplied to him by his foster father. Allan refused to pay the young man's debts, a denial that Poe would never forgive.

After leaving home for Boston to enlist in the army, he published *Tamerlane and Other Poems* (1827), his first book of poetry. Released from service in 1829, he published a second volume, *El Aaraaf, Tamerlane, and Minor Poems*. He briefly reconciled with Allan, who helped him secure an appointment to West Point; however, Poe stayed there only eight months, angered by his foster father, who had once again cut him off. He moved to Baltimore in 1831 to live with his aunt, Maria Clemm, and began his literary career in earnest. In 1832, five of his stories were published, and "MS Found in a Bottle" won a short-story contest run by a Baltimore newspaper. Returning to Richmond, he was appointed editor of *The Southern Literary Messenger*, where he published a number of stories, poems, and literary reviews. In 1836, he married his cousin Virginia Clemm, who was only thirteen years old. Less than a year later, he was discharged from the *Messenger*, partly because of his alcoholism but also because the publisher, T. W. White, was embarrassed by the savagery of many of Poe's reviews.

The remaining twelve years of his life were a period of intense creativity marred by fits of black depression and binge drinking. He moved Virginia and her mother, who was living with them, to New York and then to Philadelphia, where he worked in varying capacities for several magazines, most notably *Burton's Gentleman's Magazine* and *Graham's Magazine*. "The Fall of the House of Usher" appeared in *Burton's* in 1839, and later that same year, he published his *Tales of the Grotesque and Arabesque*. In 1844, after leaving *Graham's* as the result of another confrontation brought about by his drinking, he moved his family to New York. There he composed *The Raven and Other Poems* in 1845 and the essay "The Philosophy of Composition" in 1846. By now he was barely eking out an existence, and in 1847, his wife Virginia died. Devastated by her death, Poe nevertheless continued to write, producing the pseudophilosophical essay *Eureka* in 1848 and "The Poetic Principle" in 1849. He also embarked on a series of unsuccessful publishing schemes and unfortunate romances with female literary admirers. In 1849, he returned to Richmond, where he became engaged to a childhood friend, and then set out for another editing job in Philadelphia. For reasons that remain unexplained, he ended up in Baltimore, where he was found unconscious in the street on October 3, 1849. He died in delirium four days later.

from *The Philosophy of Composition*

Charles Dickens, in a note now lying before me, alluding to an examination I once made of the mechanism of "Barnaby Rudge," says—"By the way, are you aware that Godwin wrote his 'Caleb Williams' backwards? He first involved his hero in a web of difficulties, forming the second volume, and then, for the first, cast about him for some mode of accounting for what had been done."

I cannot think this the *precise* mode of procedure on the part of Godwin—and indeed what he himself acknowledges, is not altogether in accordance with Mr. Dickens' idea—but the author of "Caleb Williams" was too good an artist not to perceive the advantage derivable from at least a somewhat similar process. Nothing is more clear than that every plot, worth the name, must be elaborated to its *dénouement* before any thing be attempted with the pen. It is only with the *dénouement* constantly in view that we can give a plot its indispensable air of consequence, or causation, by making the incidents, and especially the tone at all points, tend to the development of the intention.

There is a radical error, I think, in the usual mode of constructing a story. Either history affords a thesis—or one is suggested by an incident of the day—or, at best, the author sets himself to work in the combination of striking events to form merely the basis of his narrative—designing, generally, to fill in which description, dialogue, or autorial comment, whatever crevices of fact, or action, may, from page to page, render themselves apparent.

I prefer commencing with the consideration of an *effect*. Keeping originality always in view—for he is false to himself who ventures to dispense with so obvious and so easily attainable a source of interest—I say to myself, in the first place, "Of the innumerable effects, or impressions, of which the heart, the intellect, or (more generally) the soul is susceptible, what one shall I, on the present occasion, select?" Having chosen a novel, first, and secondly a vivid effect, I consider whether it can best be wrought by incident or tone—whether by ordinary incidents and peculiar tone, or the converse, or by peculiarity both of incident and tone—afterward looking about me (or rather within) for such combinations of event, or tone, as shall best aid me in the construction of the effect.

I have often thought how interesting a magazine paper might be written by any author who would—that is to say, who could—detail, step by step, the processes by which any one of his compositions attained its ultimate point of completion. Why such a paper has never been given to the world, I am much at a loss to say—but, perhaps, the autorial vanity has had more to do with the omission than any one other cause. Most writers—poets in especial—prefer having it understood that they compose by a species of fine frenzy—an ecstatic intuition—and would positively shudder at letting the public take a peep behind the scenes, at the elaborate and vacillating crudities of thought—at the true purposes seized only at the last moment—at the innumerable glimpses of idea that arrived not at the maturity of full view—at the fully matured fancies discarded in despair as unmanageable—at the cautious selections and rejections—at the painful erasures and interpolations—in a word, at the wheels and pinions—the tackle for scene-shifting—the step-ladders and demon-traps—the cock's feathers, the red paint and the black patches, which, in ninety-nine cases out of the hundred, constitute the properties of the literary *histrio*.

I am aware, on the other hand, that the case is by no means common, in which an author is at all in condition to retrace the steps by which his conclusions have been attained. In general, suggestions, having arisen pell-mell, are pursued and forgotten in a similar manner.

For my own part, I have neither sympathy with the repugnance alluded to, nor, at any time, the least difficulty in recalling to mind the progressive steps of any of my compositions; and, since the interest of an analysis, or reconstruction, such as I have considered a *desideratum*, is quite independent of any real or fancied interest in the thing analyzed, it will not be regarded as a breach of decorum on my part to show the *modus operandi* by which some one of my own works was put together. I select "The Raven," as the most generally known. It is my design to render it manifest that no one point in its composition is referrible either to accident or intuition—that the work proceeded, step by step, to its completion with the precision and rigid consequence of a mathematical problem.

Let us dismiss, as irrelevant to the poem *per se*, the circumstance—or say the necessity—which, in the first place, gave rise to the intention of composing a poem that should suit at once the popular and the critical taste.

We commence, then, with this intention.

The initial consideration was that of extent. If any literary work is too long to be read at one sitting, we must be content to dispense with the immensely important effect derivable from unity of impression—for, if two sittings be required, the affairs of the world interfere, and every thing like totality is at once destroyed. But since, *ceteris paribus*, no poet can afford to dispense with *any thing* that may advance his design, it but remains to be seen whether there is, in extent, any advantage to counterbalance the loss of unity which attends it. Here I say no, at once. What we term a long poem is, in fact, merely a succession of brief ones—that is to say, of brief poetical effects. It is needless to demonstrate that a poem is such, only inasmuch as it intensely excites, by elevating, the soul; and all intense excitements are, through a psychal necessity, brief. For this reason, at least one half of the "Paradise Lost" is essentially prose—a succession of poetical excitements interspersed, *inevitably*, with corresponding depressions—the whole being deprived, through the extremeness of its length, of the vastly important artistic element, totality, or unity, of effect.

It appears evident, then, that there is a distinct limit, as regards length, to all works of literary art—the limit of a single sitting—and that, although in certain classes of prose composition, such as "Robinson Crusoe," (demanding no unity,) this limit may be advantageously overpassed, it can never properly be overpassed in a poem. Within this limit, the extent of a poem may be made to bear mathematical relation to its merit—in other words, to the excitement or elevation—again in other words, to the degree of the true poetical effect which it is capable of inducing; for it is clear that the brevity must be in direct ratio of the intensity of the intended effect:—this, with one proviso—that a certain degree of duration is absolutely requisite for the production of any effect at all.

Holding in view these considerations, as well as that degree of excitement which I deemed not above the popular, while not below the critical, taste, I reached at once what I conceived the proper *length* for my intended poem—a length of about one hundred lines. It is, in fact, a hundred and eight.

My next thought concerned the choice of an impression, or effect, to be conveyed: and here I may as well observe that, throughout the construction, I kept steadily in view the design of rendering the work *universally* appreciable. I should be carried too far out of my immediate topic were I to demonstrate a point upon which I have repeatedly insisted, and which, with the poetical, stands not in the slightest need of demonstration—the point, I mean, that Beauty is the sole legitimate province of the poem. A few words, however, in elucidation of my real meaning, which some of my friends have evinced a disposition to misrepresent. That pleasure which is at once the most intense, the most elevating, and the most pure, is, I believe, found in the contemplation of the beautiful. When, indeed, men speak of Beauty, they mean, precisely, not a quality, as is supposed, but an effect—they refer, in short, just to that intense and pure elevation of *soul*—*not* of intellect, or of heart—upon which I have commented, and which is experienced in consequence of contemplating "the beautiful." Now I designate Beauty as the province of the poem, merely because it is an obvious rule of Art that effects should be made to spring from direct causes—that objects should be attained through means best adapted for their attainment—no one as yet having been weak enough to deny that the peculiar elevation alluded to, is *most readily* attained in the poem. Now the object, Truth, or the satisfaction of the intellect, and the object Passion, or the excitement of the heart, are, although attainable, to a certain extent, in poetry, far more readily attainable in prose. Truth, in fact, demands a precision, and Passion, a *homeliness* (the truly passionate will comprehend me) which are absolutely antagonistic to that Beauty which, I maintain, is the excitement, or pleasurable elevation, of the soul. It by no means follows from any thing here said, that passion, or even truth, may not be introduced, and even profitably introduced, into a poem—for they may serve in elucidation, or aid the general effect, as do discords in music, by contrast—but the true artist will always contrive, first, to tone them into proper subservience to the predominant aim, and, secondly, to enveil them, as far as possible, in that Beauty which is the atmosphere and the essence of the poem.

Regarding, then, Beauty as my province, my next question referred to the *tone* of its highest manifestation—and all experience has shown that this tone is one of *sadness*. Beauty of whatever kind, in its supreme development, invariably excites the sensitive soul to tears. Melancholy is thus the most legitimate of all the poetical tones.

The length, the province, and the tone, being thus determined, I betook myself to ordinary induction, with the view of obtaining some artistic piquancy which might serve me as a key-note in the construction of the poem—some pivot upon which the whole structure might turn. In carefully thinking over all the usual artistic effects—or more properly *points*, in the theatrical sense—I did not fail to perceive immediately that no one had been so universally employed as that of the *refrain*. The universality of its employment sufficed to assure me of its intrinsic value, and spared me the necessity of submitting it to analysis. I considered it, however, with regard to its susceptibility of improvement, and soon saw it to be in a primitive condition. As commonly used, the *refrain*, or burden, not only is limited to lyric verse, but depends for its impression upon the force of monotone—both in sound and thought. The pleasure is deduced solely from the sense of identity—of repetition. I resolved to diversify, and so vastly heighten, the effect, by adhering, in general, to the monotone of sound, while I continually varied that of thought: that is to say, I determined to produce continuously novel effects, by the variation *of the application* of the *refrain*—the *refrain* itself remaining, for the most part, unvaried.

These points being settled, I next bethought me of the *nature* of my *refrain*. Since its application was to be repeatedly varied, it was clear that the *refrain* itself must be brief, for there would have been an insurmountable difficulty in frequent variations of application in any sentence of length. In proportion to the brevity of the sentence, would, of course, be the facility of the variation. This led me at once to a single word as the best *refrain*.

The question now arose as to the *character* of the word. Having made up my mind to a *refrain*, the division of the poem into stanzas was, of course, a corollary: the *refrain* forming the close to each stanza. That such a close, to have force, must be sonorous and susceptible of protracted emphasis, admitted no doubt: and these considerations inevitably led me to the long *o* as the most sonorous vowel, in connection with *r* as the most producible consonant.

The sound of the *refrain* being thus determined, it became necessary to select a word embodying this sound, and at the same time in the fullest possible keeping with that melancholy which I had predetermined as the tone of the poem. In such a search it would have been absolutely impossible to overlook the word "Nevermore." In fact, it was the very first which presented itself.

The next *desideratum* was a pretext for the continuous use of the one word "nevermore." In observing the difficulty which I at once found in inventing a sufficiently plausible reason for its continuous repetition, I did not fail to perceive that this difficulty arose solely from the pre-assumption that the word was to be so continuously or monotonously spoken by a *human* being—I did not fail to perceive, in short, that the difficulty lay in the reconciliation of this monotony with the exercise of reason on the part of the creature repeating the word. Here, then, immediately arose the idea of a *non*-reasoning creature capable of speech; and, very naturally, a parrot, in the first instance, suggested itself, but was superseded forthwith by a Raven, as equally capable of speech, and infinitely more in keeping with the intended *tone*.

I had now gone so far as the conception of a Raven—the bird of ill omen—monotonously repeating the one word, "Nevermore," at the conclusion of each stanza, in a poem of melancholy tone, and in length about one hundred lines. Now, never losing sight of the object *supremeness*, or perfection, at all points, I asked myself—"Of all melancholy topics, what, according to the *universal* understanding of mankind, is the *most* melancholy?" Death—was the obvious reply. "And when," I said, "is this most melancholy of topics most poetical?" From what I have already explained at some length, the answer, here also, is obvious—"When it most closely allies itself to *Beauty:* the death, then, of a beautiful woman is, unquestionably, the most poetical topic in the world—and equally is it beyond doubt that the lips best suited for such topic are those of a bereaved lover."

I had now to combine the two ideas, of a lover lamenting his deceased mistress and a Raven continuously repeating the word "Nevermore"—I had to combine these, bearing in mind my design of varying, at every turn, the *application* of the word repeated; but the only intelligible mode of such combination is that of imagining the Raven employing the word in answer to the queries of the lover. And here it was that I saw at once the opportunity afforded for the effect on which I had been depending—that is to say, the effect of the *variation of application*. I saw that I could make the first query propounded by the lover—the first query to which the Raven should reply "Nevermore"—that I could make this first query a commonplace one—the second less so—the third still less, and so on—until at length the lover, startled from his original *nonchalance* by the melancholy character of the word itself—by its frequent repetition—and by a consideration of the ominous reputation of the fowl that uttered it—is at length excited to superstition, and the wildly propounds queries of a far different character—queries whose solution he has passionately at heart—propounds them half in superstition and half in that species of despair which delights in self-torture—propounds them not altogether because he believes in the prophetic or demoniac character of the bird (which, reason assures him, is merely repeating a lesson learned by rote) but because he experiences a phrenzied pleasure in so modeling his questions as to receive from the *expected* "Nevermore" the most delicious because the most intolerable of sorrow. Perceiving the opportunity thus afforded me—or, more strictly, thus forced upon me in the progress of the construction—I first established in mind the climax, or concluding query—that to which "Nevermore" should be in the last place an answer—that in reply to which this word "Nevermore" should involve the utmost conceivable amount of sorrow and despair.

Here then the poem may be said to have its beginning—at the end, where all works of art should begin—for it was here, at this point of my preconsiderations, that I first put pen to paper in the composition of the stanza:

> "Prophet," said I, "thing of evil! prophet still if bird or devil!
> By that heaven that bends above us—by that God we both adore,
> Tell this soul with sorrow laden, if within the distant Aidenn,
> It shall clasp a sainted maiden whom the angels name Lenore—
> Clasp a rare and radiant maiden whom the angels name Lenore."
>   Quoth the raven "Nevermore."

I composed this stanza, at this point, first that, by establishing the climax, I might the better vary and graduate, as regards seriousness and importance, the preceding queries of the lover—and, secondly, that I might definitely settle the rhythm, the metre, and the length and general arrangement of the stanza—as well as graduate the stanzas which were to precede, so that none of them might surpass this in rhythmical effect. Had I been able, in the subsequent composition, to construct more vigorous stanzas, I should, without scruple, have purposely enfeebled them, so as not to interfere with the climacteric effect.

And here I may as well say a few words of the versification. My first object (as usual) was originality. The extent to which this has been neglected, in versification, is one of the most unaccountable things in the world. Admitting that there is little possibility of variety in mere *rhythm*, it is still clear that the possible varieties of metre and stanza are absolutely infinite—and yet, *for centuries, no man, in verse, has ever done, or ever seemed to think of doing, an original thing.* The fact is, originality (unless in minds of very unusual force) is by no means a matter, as some suppose, of impulse or intuition. In general, to be found, it must be elaborately sought, and although a positive merit of the highest class, demands in its attainment less of invention than negation.

Of course, I pretend to no originality in either the rhythm or metre of the "Raven." The former is trochaic—the latter is octameter acatalectic, alternating with heptameter catalectic repeated in the *refrain* of the fifth verse, and terminating with tetrameter catalectic. Less pedantically—the feet employed throughout (trochees) consist of a long syllable followed by a short: the first line of the stanza consists of eight of these feet—the second of seven and a half (in effect two-thirds)—the third of eight—the fourth of seven and a half—the fifth the same—the sixth three and a half. Now, each of these lines, taken individually, has been employed before, and what originality the "Raven" has, is in their *combination into stanza;* nothing even remotely approaching this combination has ever been attempted. The effect of this originality of combination is aided by other unusual, and some altogether novel effects, arising from an extension of the application of the principles of rhyme and alliteration.

The next point to be considered was the mode of bringing together the lover and the Raven—and the first branch of this consideration was the *locale.* For this the most natural suggestion might seem to be a forest, or the fields—but it has always appeared to me that a close *circumscription of space* is absolutely necessary to the effect of insulated incident:—it has the force of a frame to a picture. It has an indisputable moral power in keeping concentrated the attention, and, of course, must not be confounded with mere unity of place.

I determined, then, to place the lover in his chamber—in a chamber rendered sacred to him by memories of her who had frequented it. The room is represented as richly furnished—this in mere pursuance of the ideas I have already explained on the subject of Beauty, as the sole true poetical thesis.

The *locale* being thus determined, I had now to introduce the bird—and the thought of introducing him through the window, was inevitable. The idea of making the lover suppose, in the first instance, that the flapping of the wings of the bird against the shutter, is a "tapping" at the door, originated in a wish to increase, by prolonging, the reader's curiosity, and in a desire to admit the incidental effect arising from the lover's throwing open the door, finding all dark, and thence adopting the half-fancy that it was the spirit of his mistress that knocked.

I made the night tempestuous, first, to account for the Raven's seeking admission, and secondly, for the effect of contrast with the (physical) serenity within the chamber.

I made the bird alight on the bust of Pallas, also for the effect of contrast between the marble and the plumage—it being understood that the bust was absolutely *suggested* by the bird—the bust of *Pallas* being chosen, first, as most in keeping with the scholarship of the lover, and, secondly, for the sonorousness of the word, Pallas, itself.

About the middle of the poem, also, I have availed myself of the force of contrast, with a view of deepening the ultimate impression. For example, an air of the fantastic—approaching as nearly to the ludicrous as was admissible—is given to the Raven's entrance. He comes in "with many a flirt and flutter."

Not the *least obeisance made he*—not a moment stopped or stayed he,
But with mien of lord or lady, perched above my chamber door.

In the two stanzas which follow, the design is more obviously carried out:—

Then this ebony bird beguiling my sad fancy into smiling
By the *grave and stern decorum of the countenance it wore,*

"Though thy *crest be shorn and shaven* thou," I said, "art sure no craven,
Ghastly grim and ancient Raven wandering from the nightly shore—
Tell me what thy lordly name is on the Night's Plutonian shore!"
   Quoth the Raven "Nevermore."

———

Much I marvelled *this ungainly fowl* to hear discourse so plainly,
Though its answer little meaning—little relevancy bore;
For we cannot help agreeing that no living human being
Ever yet was blessed with seeing bird above his chamber door—
Bird or beast upon the sculptured bust above his chamber door,
   With such name as "Nevermore."

———

The effect of the *dénouement* being thus provided for, I immediately drop the fantastic for a tone of the most profound seriousness:—this tone commencing in the stanza directly following the one last quoted, with the line,

But the Raven, sitting lonely on that placid bust, spoke only, etc.

From this epoch the lover no longer jests—no longer sees any thing even of the fantastic in the Raven's demeanor. He speaks of him as a "grim, ungainly, ghastly, gaunt, and ominous bird of yore," and feels the "fiery eyes" burning into his "bosom's core." This revolution of thought, or fancy, on the lover's part, is intended to induce a similar one on the part of the reader—to bring the mind into a proper frame for the *dénouement*—which is now brought about as rapidly and as *directly* as possible.

With the *dénouement* proper—with the Raven's reply, "Nevermore," to the lover's final demand if he shall meet his mistress in another world—the poem, in its obvious phase, that of a simple narrative, may be said to have its completion. So far, every thing is within the limits of the accountable—of the real. A raven, having learned by rote the single word "Nevermore," and having escaped from the custody of its owner, is driven, at midnight, through the violence of a storm, to seek admission at a window from which a light still gleams—the chamber-window of a student, occupied half in poring over a volume, half in dreaming of a beloved mistress deceased. The casement being thrown open at the fluttering of the bird's wings, the bird itself perches on the most convenient seat out of the immediate reach of the student, who, amused by the incident and the oddity of the visitor's demeanor, demands of it, in jest and without looking for a reply, its name. The raven addressed, answers with its customary word, "Nevermore"—a word which finds immediate echo in the melancholy heart of the student, who, giving utterance aloud to certain thoughts suggested by the occasion, is again startled by the fowl's repetition of "Nevermore." The student now guesses the state of the case, but is impelled, as I have before explained, by the human thirst for self-torture, and in part by superstition, to propound such queries to the bird as will bring him, the lover, the most of the luxury of sorrow, through the anticipated answer "Nevermore." With the indulgence, to the utmost extreme, of this self-torture, the narration, in what I have termed its first or obvious phase, has a natural termination, and so far there has been no overstepping of the limits of the real.

But in subjects so handled, however skilfully, or with however vivid an array of incident, there is always a certain hardness or nakedness, which repels the artistical eye. Two things are invariably required—first, some amount of complexity, or more properly, adaptation; and, secondly, some amount of suggestiveness—some under current, however indefinite of meaning. It is this latter, in especial, which imparts to a work of art so much of that *richness* (to borrow from colloquy a forcible term) which we are too fond of confounding with *the ideal*. It is the *excess* of the suggested meaning—it is the rendering this the upper instead of the under current of the theme—which turns into prose (and that of the very flattest kind) the so called poetry of the so called transcendentalists.

Holding these opinions, I added the two concluding stanzas of the poem—their suggestiveness being thus made to pervade all the narrative which has preceded them. The under current of meaning is rendered first apparent in the lines—

"Take thy beak from out *my heart*, and take thy form from off my door!"
Quoth the Raven "Nevermore!"

It will be observed that the words, "from out my heart," involve the first metaphorical expression in the poem. They, with the answer, "Nevermore," dispose the mind to seek a moral in all that has been previously narrated. The reader begins now to regard the Raven as emblematical—but it is not until the very last line of the very last stanza, that the intention of making him emblematical of *Mournful and Neverending Remembrance* is permitted distinctly to be seen:

And the Raven, never flitting, still is sitting, still is sitting,
On the pallid bust of Pallas just above my chamber door;
And his eyes have all the seeming of a demon's that is dreaming,
And the lamplight o'er him streaming throws his shadow on the floor;
And my soul *from out that shadow* that lies floating on the floor
    Shall be lifted—nevermore.

Sonnet—To Science

Science! true daughter of Old Time thou art!
    Who alterest all things with thy peering eyes.
Why preyest thou thus upon the poet's heart,
    Vulture, whose wings are dull realities?
How should he love thee? or how deem thee wise,
    Who wouldst not leave him in his wandering
To seek for treasure in the jewelled skies,
    Albeit he soared with an undaunted wing?
Hast thou not dragged Diana from her car?
    And driven the Hamdryad from the wood
To seek a shelter in some happier star?
    Hast thou not torn the Naiad from her flood,
The Elfin from the green grass, and from me
The summer dream beneath the tamarind tree?

Sonnet—Silence

There are some qualities—some incorporate things,
    That have a double life, which thus is made
A type of that twin entity which springs
    From matter and light, evinced in solid and shade.
There is a two-fold Silence—sea and shore—
    Body and soul. One dwells in lonely places,
    Newly with grass o'ergrown; some solemn graces,
Some human memories and tearful lore,
Render him terrorless: his name's "No More."
He is the corporate Silence: dread him not!
    No power hath he of evil in himself;
But should some urgent fate (untimely lot!)
    Bring thee to meet his shadow (nameless elf,
That haunteth the lone regions where hath trod
No foot of man,) commend thyself to God!

Dream-Land

By a route obscure and lonely,
Haunted by ill angels only,
Where an Eidolon, named NIGHT,
On a black throne reigns upright,
I have reached these lands but newly
From an ultimate dim Thule—
From a wild clime that lieth, sublime,
    Out of SPACE—out of TIME.

Bottomless vales and boundless floods,
And chasms, and caves, and Titan woods,
With forms that no man can discover
For the tears that drip all over;
Mountains toppling evermore
Into seas without a shore;
Seas that restlessly aspire,
Surging, unto skies of fire;
Lakes that endlessly outspread
Their lone waters—lone and dead,—
Their still waters—still and chilly
With the snows of the lolling lily.

By the lakes that thus outspread
Their lone waters, lone and dead,—
Their sad waters, sad and chilly
With the snows of the lolling lily,—
By the mountains—near the river
Murmuring lowly, murmuring ever,—

By the grey woods,—by the swamp
Where the toad and the newt encamp—
By the dismal tarns and pools
    Where dwell the Ghouls,—
By each spot the most unholy—
In each nook most melancholy—
There the traveller meets aghast
Sheeted Memories of the Past—
Shrouded forms that start and sigh
As they pass the wanderer by—
White-robed forms of friends long given,
In agony, to the Earth—and Heaven.

For the heart whose woes are legion
'Tis a peaceful, soothing region—
For the spirit that walks in shadow
'Tis—oh, 'tis an Eldorado!
But the traveller, travelling through it,
May not—dare not openly view it!
Never its mysteries are exposed
To the weak human eye unclosed;
So wills its King, who hath forbid
The uplifting of the fringed lid;
And thus the sad Soul that here passes
Beholds it but through darkened glasses.

By a route obscure and lonely,
Haunted by ill angels only,
Where an Eidolon, named NIGHT,
On a black throne reigns upright,
I have wandered home but newly
From this ultimate dim Thule.

William Wilson

What say of it? what say [of] CONSCIENCE grim,
That spectre in my path?
                                        Chamberlayne's *Pharronida*

Let me call myself, for the present, William Wilson. The fair page now lying before me need not be sullied with my real appellation. This has been already too much an object for the scorn—for the horror—for the detestation of my race. To the uttermost regions of the globe have not the indignant winds bruited its unparalleled infamy? Oh, outcast of all outcasts most abandoned!—to the earth art thou not forever dead? to its honors, to its flowers, to its golden aspirations?—and a cloud, dense, dismal, and limitless, does it not hang eternally between thy hopes and heaven?

I would not, if I could, here or to-day, embody a record of my later years of unspeakable misery, and unpardonable crime. This epoch—these later years—took unto themselves a sudden elevation in turpitude, whose origin alone it is my present purpose to assign. Men usually grow base by degrees. From me, in an instant, all virtue dropped bodily as a mantle. From comparatively trivial wickedness I passed, with the stride of a giant, into more than the enormities of an Elah-Gabalus. What chance—what one event brought this evil thing to pass, bear with me while I relate. Death approaches; and the shadow which foreruns him has thrown a softening influence over my spirit. I long, in passing through the dim valley, for the sympathy—I had nearly said for the pity—of my fellow men. I would fain have them believe that I have been, in some measure, the slave of circumstances beyond human control. I would wish them to seek out for me, in the details I am about to give, some little oasis of fatality amid a wilderness of error. I would have them allow—what they cannot refrain from allowing—that, although temptation may have erewhile existed as great, man was never thus, at least, tempted before—certainly, never thus fell. And is it therefore that he has never thus suffered? Have I not indeed been living in a dream? And am I not now dying a victim to the horror and the mystery of the wildest of all sublunary visions?

I am the descendant of a race whose imaginative and easily excitable temperament has at all times rendered them remarkable; and, in my earliest infancy, I gave evidence of having fully inherited the family character. As I advanced in years it was more strongly developed; becoming, for many reasons, a cause of serious disquietude to my friends, and of positive injury to myself. I grew self-willed, addicted to the wildest caprices, and a prey to the most ungovernable passions. Weak-minded, and beset with constitutional infirmities akin to my own, my parents could do but little to check the evil propensities which distinguished me. Some feeble and ill-directed efforts resulted in complete failure on their part, and, of course, in total triumph on mine. Thenceforward my voice was a household law; and at an age when few children have abandoned their leading-strings, I was left to the guidance of my own will, and became, in all but name, the master of my own actions.

My earliest recollections of a school-life, are connected with a large, rambling, Elizabethan house, in a misty-looking village of England, where were a vast number of gigantic and gnarled trees, and where all the houses were excessively ancient. In truth, it was a dream-like and spirit-soothing place, that venerable old town. At this moment, in fancy, I feel the refreshing chilliness of its deeply-shadowed avenues, inhale the fragrance of its thousand shrubberies, and thrill anew with undefinable delight, at the deep hollow note of the church-bell, breaking, each hour, with sullen and sudden roar, upon the stillness of the dusky atmosphere in which the fretted Gothic steeple lay imbedded and asleep.

It gives me, perhaps, as much of pleasure as I can now in any manner experience, to dwell upon minute recollections of the school and its concerns. Steeped in misery as I am—misery, alas! only too real—I shall be pardoned for seeking relief, however slight and temporary, in the weakness of a few rambling details. These, moreover, utterly trivial, and even ridiculous in themselves, assume, to my fancy, adventitious importance, as connected with a period and a locality when and where I recognise the first ambiguous monitions of the destiny which afterwards so fully overshadowed me. Let me then remember.

The house, I have said, was old and irregular. The grounds were extensive, and a high and solid brick wall, topped with a bed of mortar and broken glass, encompassed the whole. This prison-like rampart formed the limit of our domain; beyond it we saw but thrice a week—once every Saturday afternoon, when, attended by two ushers, we were permitted to take brief walks in a body through some of the neighbouring fields—and twice during Sunday, when we were paraded in the same formal manner to the morning and evening service in the one church of the village. Of this church the principal of our school was pastor. With how deep a spirit of wonder and perplexity was I wont to regard him from our remote pew in the gallery, as, with step solemn and slow, he ascended the pulpit! This reverend man, with countenance so demurely benign, with robes so glossy and so clerically flowing, with wig so minutely powdered, so rigid and so vast,—could this be he who, of late, with sour visage, and in snuffy habiliments, administered, ferule in hand, the Draconian laws of the academy? Oh, gigantic paradox, too utterly monstrous for solution!

At an angle of the ponderous wall frowned a more ponderous gage. It was riveted and studded with iron bolts, and surmounted with jagged iron spikes. What impressions of deep awe did it inspire! It was never opened save for the three periodical egressions and ingressions already mentioned; then, in every creak of its mighty hinges, we found a plenitude of mystery—a world of matter for solemn remark, or for more solemn meditation.

The extensive enclosure was irregular in form, having many capacious recesses. Of these, three or four of the largest constituted the play-ground. It was level, and covered with fine hard gravel. I well remember it had no trees, nor benches, nor anything similar within it. Of course it was in the rear of the house. In front lay a small parterre, planted with box and other shrubs; but through this sacred division we passed only upon rare occasions indeed—such as a first advent to school or final departure thence, or perhaps, when a parent or friend having called for us, we joyfully took our way home for the Christmas or Midsummer holy-days.

But the house!—how quaint an old building was this!—to me how veritably a palace of enchantment! There was really no end to its windings—to its incomprehensible subdivisions. It was difficult, at any given time, to say with certainty upon which of its two stories one happened to be. From each room to every other there were sure to be found three or four steps either in ascent or descent. Then the lateral branches were innumerable—inconceivable—and so returning in upon themselves, that our most exact ideas in regard to the whole mansion were not very far different from those with which we pondered upon infinity. During the five years of my residence here, I was never able to ascertain with precision, in what remote locality lay the little sleeping apartment assigned to myself and some eighteen or twenty other scholars.

The school-room was the largest in the house—I could not help thinking, in the world. It was very long, narrow, and dismally low, with pointed Gothic windows and a ceiling of oak. In a remote and terror-inspiring angle was a square enclosure of eight or ten feet, comprising the sanctum, "during hours," of our principal, the Reverend Dr. Bransby. It was a solid structure, with massy door, sooner than open which in the absence of the "Dominic," we would all have willingly perished by the peine forte et dure. In other angles were two other similar boxes, far less reverenced, indeed, but still greatly matters of awe. One of these was the pulpit of the "classical" usher, one of the "English and mathematical." Interspersed about the room, crossing and recrossing in endless irregularity, were innumerable benches and desks, black, ancient, and time-worn, piled desperately with much-bethumbed books, and so beseamed with initial letters, names at full length, grotesque figures, and other multiplied efforts of the knife, as to have entirely lost what little of original form might have been their portion in days long departed. A huge bucket with water stood at one extremity of the room, and a clock of stupendous dimensions at the other.

Encompassed by the massy walls of this venerable academy, I passed, yet not in tedium or disgust, the years of the third lustrum of my life. The teeming brain of child-hood requires no external world of incident to occupy or amuse it; and the apparently dismal monotony of a school was replete with more intense excitement than my riper youth has derived from luxury, or my full manhood from crime. Yet I must believe that my first mental development had in it much of the uncommon—even much of the outre. Upon mankind at large the events of very early existence rarely leave in mature age any definite impression. All is gray shadow—a weak and irregular remem-brance—an indistinct regathering of feeble pleasures and phantasmagoric pains. With me this is not so. In childhood I must have felt with the energy of a man what I now find stamped upon memory in lines as vivid, as deep, and as durable as the exergues of the Carthaginian medals.

Yet in fact—in the fact of the world's view—how little was there to remember! The morning's awakening, the nightly summons to bed; the connings, the recitations; the periodical half-holidays, and perambulations; the play-ground, with its broils, its pastimes, its intrigues;—these, by a mental sorcery long forgotten, were made to in-volve a wilderness of sensation, a world of rich incident, a universe of varied emo-tion, of excitement the most passionate and spirit-stirring. "Oh, le bon temps, que ce siecle de fer!"

In truth, the ardor, the enthusiasm, and the imperiousness of my disposition, soon rendered me a marked character among my schoolmates, and by slow, but nat-ural gradations, gave me an ascendancy over all not greatly older than myself;—over all with a single exception. This exception was found in the person of a scholar, who, although no relation, bore the same Christian and surname as myself;—a circum-stance, in fact, little remarkable; for, notwithstanding a noble descent, mine was one of those everyday appellations which seem, by prescriptive right, to have been, time out of mind, the common property of the mob. In this narrative I have therefore desig-nated myself as William Wilson,—a fictitious title not very dissimilar to the real. My namesake alone, of those who in school phraseology constituted "our set," presumed to compete with me in the studies of the class—in the sports and broils of the play-ground—to refuse implicit belief in my assertions, and submission to my will—in-deed, to interfere with my arbitrary dictation in any respect whatsoever. If there is on earth a supreme and unqualified despotism, it is the despotism of a master mind in boyhood over the less energetic spirits of its companions.

Wilson's rebellion was to me a source of the greatest embarrassment;—the more so as, in spite of the bravado with which in public I made a point of treating him and his pre-tensions, I secretly felt that I feared him, and could not help thinking the equality which he maintained so easily with myself, a proof of his true superiority; since not to be over-come cost me a perpetual struggle. Yet this superiority—even this equality—was in truth acknowledged by no one but myself; our associates, by some unaccountable blind-ness, seemed not even to suspect it. Indeed, his competition, his resistance, and espe-cially his impertinent and dogged interference with my purposes, were not more pointed than private. He appeared to be destitute alike of the ambition which urged, and of the passionate energy of mind which enabled me to excel. In his rivalry he might have been supposed actuated solely by a whimsical desire to thwart, astonish, or mortify my-self; although there were times when I could not help observing, with a feeling made up of wonder, abasement, and pique, that he mingled with his injuries, his insults, or his contradictions, a certain most inappropriate, and assuredly most unwelcome affectionateness of manner. I could only conceive this singular behavior to arise from a consummate self-conceit assuming the vulgar airs of patronage and protection.

Perhaps it was this latter trait in Wilson's conduct, conjoined with our identity of name, and the mere accident of our having entered the school upon the same day, which set afloat the notion that we were brothers, among the senior classes in the academy. These do not usually inquire with much strictness into the affairs of their juniors. I have before said, or should have said, that Wilson was not, in the most remote degree, connected with my family. But assuredly if we had been brothers we must have been twins; for, after leaving Dr. Bransby's, I casually learned that my namesake was born on the nineteenth of January, 1813—and this is a somewhat remarkable coincidence; for the day is precisely that of my own nativity.

It may seem strange that in spite of the continual anxiety occasioned me by the rivalry of Wilson, and his intolerable spirit of contradiction, I could not bring myself to hate him altogether. We had, to be sure, nearly every day a quarrel in which, yielding me publicly the palm of victory, he, in some manner, contrived to make me feel that it was he who had deserved it; yet a sense of pride on my part, and a veritable dignity on his own, kept us always upon what are called "speaking terms," while there were many points of strong congeniality in our tempers, operating to awake me in a sentiment which our position alone, perhaps, prevented from ripening into friendship. It is difficult, indeed, to define, or even to describe, my real feelings towards him. They formed a motley and heterogeneous admixture;—some petulant animosity, which was not yet hatred, some esteem, more respect, much fear, with a world of uneasy curiosity. To the moralist it will be unnecessary to say, in addition, that Wilson and myself were the most inseparable of companions.

It was no doubt the anomalous state of affairs existing between us, which turned all my attacks upon him, (and they were many, either open or covert) into the channel of banter or practical joke (giving pain while assuming the aspect of mere fun) rather than into a more serious and determined hostility. But my endeavours on this head were by no means uniformly successful, even when my plans were the most wittily concocted; for my namesake had much about him, in character, of that unassuming and quiet austerity which, while enjoying the poignancy of its own jokes, has no heel of Achilles in itself, and absolutely refuses to be laughed at. I could find, indeed, but one vulnerable point, and that, lying in a personal peculiarity, arising, perhaps, from constitutional disease, would have been spared by any antagonist less at his wit's end than myself;—my rival had a weakness in the faucal or guttural organs, which precluded him from raising his voice at any time above a very low whisper. Of this defect I did not fail to take what poor advantage lay in my power.

Wilson's retaliations in kind were many; and there was one form of his practical wit that disturbed me beyond measure. How his sagacity first discovered at all that so petty a thing would vex me, is a question I never could solve; but, having discovered, he habitually practised the annoyance. I had always felt aversion to my uncourtly patronymic, and its very common, if not plebeian praenomen. The words were venom in my ears; and when, upon the day of my arrival, a second William Wilson came also to the academy, I felt angry with him for bearing the name, and doubly disgusted with the name because a stranger bore it, who would be the cause of its twofold repetition, who would be constantly in my presence, and whose concerns, in the ordinary routine of the school business, must inevitably, on account of the detestable coincidence, be often confounded with my own.

The feeling of vexation thus engendered grew stronger with every circumstance tending to show resemblance, moral or physical, between my rival and myself. I had not then discovered the remarkable fact that we were of the same age; but I saw that we were of the same height, and I perceived that we were even singularly alike in general contour of person and outline of feature. I was galled, too, by the rumor touching a relationship, which had grown current in the upper forms. In a word, nothing could more seriously disturb me, although I scrupulously concealed such disturbance, than any allusion to a similarity of mind, person, or condition existing between us. But, in truth, I had no reason to believe that (with the exception of the matter of relationship, and in the case of Wilson himself,) this similarity had ever been made a subject of comment, or even observed at all by our schoolfellows. That he observed it in all its bearings, and as fixedly as I, was apparent; but that he could discover in such circumstances so fruitful a field of annoyance, can only be attributed, as I said before, to his more than ordinary penetration.

His cue, which was to perfect an imitation of myself, lay both in words and in actions; and most admirably did he play his part. My dress it was an easy matter to copy; my gait and general manner were, without difficulty, appropriated; in spite of his constitutional defect, even my voice did not escape him. My louder tones were, of course, unattempted, but then the key, it was identical; and his singular whisper, it grew the very echo of my own.

How greatly this most exquisite portraiture harassed me, (for it could not justly be termed a caricature,) I will not now venture to describe. I had but one consolation—in the fact that the imitation, apparently, was noticed by myself alone, and that I had to endure only the knowing and strangely sarcastic smiles of my namesake himself. Satisfied with having produced in my bosom the intended effect, he seemed to chuckle in secret over the sting he had inflicted, and was characteristically disregardful of the public applause which the success of his witty endeavours might have so easily elicited. That the school, indeed, did not feel his design, perceive its accomplishment, and participate in his sneer, was, for many anxious months, a riddle I could not resolve. Perhaps the gradation of his copy rendered it not so readily perceptible; or, more possibly, I owed my security to the master air of the copyist, who, disdaining the letter, (which in a painting is all the obtuse can see,) gave but the full spirit of his original for my individual contemplation and chagrin.

I have already more than once spoken of the disgusting air of patronage which he assumed toward me, and of his frequent officious interference with my will. This interference often took the ungracious character of advice; advice not openly given, but hinted or insinuated. I received it with a repugnance which gained strength as I grew in years. Yet, at this distant day, let me do him the simple justice to acknowledge that I can recall no occasion when the suggestions of my rival were on the side of those errors or follies so usual to his immature age and seeming inexperience; that his moral sense, at least, if not his general talents and worldly wisdom, was far keener than my own; and that I might, to-day, have been a better, and thus a happier man, had I less frequently rejected the counsels embodied in those meaning whispers which I then but too cordially hated and too bitterly despised.

As it was, I at length grew restive in the extreme under his distasteful supervision, and daily resented more and more openly what I considered his intolerable arrogance. I have said that, in the first years of our connexion as schoolmates, my feelings in regard to him might have been easily ripened into friendship: but, in the latter months of my residence at the academy, although the intrusion of his ordinary manner had, beyond doubt, in some measure, abated, my sentiments, in nearly similar proportion, partook very much of positive hatred. Upon one occasion he saw this, I think, and afterwards avoided, or made a show of avoiding me.

It was about the same period, if I remember aright, that, in an altercation of violence with him, in which he was more than usually thrown off his guard, and spoke and acted with an openness of demeanor rather foreign to his nature, I discovered, or fancied I discovered, in his accent, his air, and general appearance, a something which first startled, and then deeply interested me, by bringing to mind dim visions of my earliest infancy—wild, confused and thronging memories of a time when memory herself was yet unborn. I cannot better describe the sensation which oppressed me than by saying that I could with difficulty shake off the belief of my having been acquainted with the being who stood before me, at some epoch very long ago—some point of the past even infinitely remote. The delusion, however, faded rapidly as it came; and I mention it at all but to define the day of the last conversation I there held with my singular namesake.

The huge old house, with its countless subdivisions, had several large chambers communicating with each other, where slept the greater number of the students. There were, however, (as must necessarily happen in a building so awkwardly planned,) many little nooks or recesses, the odds and ends of the structure; and these the economic ingenuity of Dr. Bransby had also fitted up as dormitories; although, being the merest closets, they were capable of accommodating but a single individual. One of these small apartments was occupied by Wilson.

One night, about the close of my fifth year at the school, and immediately after the altercation just mentioned, finding every one wrapped in sleep, I arose from bed, and, lamp in hand, stole through a wilderness of narrow passages from my own bedroom to that of my rival. I had long been plotting one of those ill-natured pieces of practical wit at his expense in which I had hitherto been so uniformly unsuccessful. It was my intention, now, to put my scheme in operation, and I resolved to make him feel the whole extent of the malice with which I was imbued. Having reached his closet, I noiselessly entered, leaving the lamp, with a shade over it, on the outside. I advanced a step, and listened to the sound of his tranquil breathing. Assured of his being asleep, I returned, took the light, and with it again approached the bed. Close curtains were around it, which, in the prosecution of my plan, I slowly and quietly withdrew, when the bright rays fell vividly upon the sleeper, and my eyes, at the same moment, upon his countenance. I looked;—and a numbness, an iciness of feeling instantly pervaded my frame. My breast heaved, my knees tottered, my whole spirit became possessed with an objectless yet intolerable horror. Gasping for breath, I lowered the lamp in still nearer proximity to the face. Were these—these the lineaments of William Wilson? I saw, indeed, that they were his, but I shook as if with a fit of the ague in fancying they were not. What was there about them to confound me in this manner? I gazed;—while my brain reeled with a multitude of incoherent thoughts. Not thus he appeared—assuredly not thus—in the vivacity of his waking hours. The same name! the same contour of person! the same day of arrival at the academy! And then his dogged and meaningless imitation of my gait, my voice, my habits, and my manner! Was it, in truth, within the bounds of human possibility, that what I now saw was the result, merely, of the habitual practice of this sarcastic imitation? Awe-stricken, and with a creeping shudder, I extinguished the lamp, passed silently from the chamber, and left, at once, the halls of that old academy, never to enter them again.

After a lapse of some months, spent at home in mere idleness, I found myself a student at Eton. The brief interval had been sufficient to enfeeble my remembrance of the events at Dr. Bransby's, or at least to effect a material change in the nature of the feelings with which I remembered them. The truth—the tragedy—of the drama was no more. I could now find room to doubt the evidence of my senses; and seldom called up the subject at all but with wonder at extent of human credulity, and a smile at the vivid force of the imagination which I hereditarily possessed. Neither was this species of scepticism likely to be diminished by the character of the life I led at Eton. The vortex of thoughtless folly into which I there so immediately and so recklessly plunged, washed away all but the froth of my past hours, engulfed at once every solid or serious impression, and left to memory only the veriest levities of a former existence.

I do not wish, however, to trace the course of my miserable profligacy here—a profligacy which set at defiance the laws, while it eluded the vigilance of the institution. Three years of folly, passed without profit, had but given me rooted habits of vice, and added, in a somewhat unusual degree, to my bodily stature, when, after a week of soulless dissipation, I invited a small party of the most dissolute students to a secret carousal in my chambers. We met at a late hour of the night; for our debaucheries were to be faithfully protracted until morning. The wine flowed freely, and there were not wanting other and perhaps more dangerous seductions; so that the gray dawn had already faintly appeared in the east, while our delirious extravagance was at its height. Madly flushed with cards and intoxication, I was in the act of insisting upon a toast of more than wonted profanity, when my attention was suddenly diverted by the violent, although partial unclosing of the door of the apartment, and by the eager voice of a servant from without. He said that some person, apparently in great haste, demanded to speak with me in the hall.

Wildly excited with wine, the unexpected interruption rather delighted than surprised me. I staggered forward at once, and a few steps brought me to the vestibule of the building. In this low and small room there hung no lamp; and now no light at all was admitted, save that of the exceedingly feeble dawn which made its way through the semi-circular window. As I put my foot over the threshold, I became aware of the figure of a youth about my own height, and habited in a white kerseymere morning frock, cut in the novel fashion of the one I myself wore at the moment. This the faint light enabled me to perceive; but the features of his face I could not distinguish. Upon my entering he strode hurriedly up to me, and, seizing me by the arm with a gesture of petulant impatience, whispered the words "William Wilson!" in my ear.

I grew perfectly sober in an instant.

There was that in the manner of the stranger, and in the tremulous shake of his uplifted finger, as he held it between my eyes and the light, which filled me with unqualified amazement; but it was not this which had so violently moved me. It was the pregnancy of solemn admonition in the singular, low, hissing utterance; and, above all, it was the character, the tone, the key, of those few, simple, and familiar, yet whispered syllables, which came with a thousand thronging memories of bygone days, and struck upon my soul with the shock of a galvanic battery. Ere I could recover the use of my senses he was gone.

Although this event failed not of a vivid effect upon my disordered imagination, yet was it evanescent as vivid. For some weeks, indeed, I busied myself in earnest inquiry, or was wrapped in a cloud of morbid speculation. I did not pretend to disguise from my perception the identity of the singular individual who thus perseveringly interfered with my affairs, and harassed me with his insinuated counsel. But who and what was this Wilson?—and whence came he?—and what were his purposes? Upon neither of these points could I be satisfied; merely ascertaining, in regard to him, that a sudden accident in his family had caused his removal from Dr. Bransby's academy on the afternoon of the day in which I myself had eloped. But in a brief period I ceased to think upon the subject; my attention being all absorbed in a contemplated departure for Oxford. Thither I soon went; the uncalculating vanity of my parents furnishing me with an outfit and annual establishment, which would enable me to indulge at will in the luxury already so dear to my heart,—to vie in profuseness of expenditure with the haughtiest heirs of the wealthiest earldoms in Great Britain.

Excited by such appliances to vice, my constitutional temperament broke forth with redoubled ardor, and I spurned even the common restraints of decency in the mad infatuation of my revels. But it were absurd to pause in the detail of my extravagance. Let it suffice, that among spendthrifts I out-Heroded Herod, and that, giving name to a multitude of novel follies, I added no brief appendix to the long catalogue of vices then usual in the most dissolute university of Europe.

It could hardly be credited, however, that I had, even here, so utterly fallen from the gentlemanly estate, as to seek acquaintance with the vilest arts of the gambler by profession, and, having become an adept in his despicable science, to practise it habitually as a means of increasing my already enormous income at the expense of the weak-minded among my fellow-collegians. Such, nevertheless, was the fact. And the very enormity of this offence against all manly and honourable sentiment proved, beyond doubt, the main if not the sole reason of the impunity with which it was committed. Who, indeed, among my most abandoned associates, would not rather have disputed the clearest evidence of his senses, than have suspected of such courses, the gay, the frank, the generous William Wilson—the noblest and most commoner at Oxford—him whose follies (said his parasites) were but the follies of youth and unbridled fancy—whose errors but inimitable whim—whose darkest vice but a careless and dashing extravagance?

I had been now two years successfully busied in this way, when there came to the university a young parvenu nobleman, Glendinning—rich, said report, as Herodes Atticus—his riches, too, as easily acquired. I soon found him of weak intellect, and, of course, marked him as a fitting subject for my skill. I frequently engaged him in play, and contrived, with the gambler's usual art, to let him win considerable sums, the more effectually to entangle him in my snares. At length, my schemes being ripe, I met him (with the full intention that this meeting should be final and decisive) at the chambers of a fellow-commoner, (Mr. Preston,) equally intimate with both, but who, to do him justice, entertained not even a remote suspicion of my design. To give to this a better colouring, I had contrived to have assembled a party of some eight or ten, and was solicitously careful that the introduction of cards should appear accidental, and originate in the proposal of my contemplated dupe himself. To be brief upon a vile topic, none of the low finesse was omitted, so customary upon similar occasions that it is a just matter for wonder how any are still found so besotted as to fall its victim.

We had protracted our sitting far into the night, and I had at length effected the manoeuvre of getting Glendinning as my sole antagonist. The game, too, was my favorite ecarte! The rest of the company, interested in the extent of our play, had abandoned their own cards, and were standing around us as spectators. The parvenu, who had been induced by my artifices in the early part of the evening, to drink deeply, now shuffled, dealt, or played, with a wild nervousness of manner for which his intoxication, I thought, might partially, but could not altogether account. In a very short period he had become my debtor to a large amount, when, having taken a long draught of port, he did precisely what I had been coolly anticipating—he proposed to double our already extravagant stakes. With a well-feigned show of reluctance, and not until after my repeated refusal had seduced him into some angry words which gave a color of pique to my compliance, did I finally comply. The result, of course, did but prove how entirely the prey was in my toils; in less than an hour he had quadrupled his debt. For some time his countenance had been losing the florid tinge lent it by the wine; but now, to my astonishment, I perceived that it had grown to a pallor truly fearful. I say to my astonishment. Glendinning had been represented to my eager inquiries as immeasurably wealthy; and the sums which he had as yet lost, although in themselves vast, could not, I supposed, very seriously annoy, much less so violently affect him. That he was overcome by the wine just swallowed, was the idea which most readily presented itself; and, rather with a view to the preservation of my own character in the eyes of my associates, than from any less interested motive, I was about to insist, peremptorily, upon a discontinuance of the play, when some expressions at my elbow from among the company, and an ejaculation evincing utter despair on the part of Glendinning, gave me to understand that I had effected his total ruin under circumstances which, rendering him an object for the pity of all, should have protected him from the ill offices even of a friend.

What now might have been my conduct it is difficult to say. The pitiable condition of my dupe had thrown an air of embarrassed gloom over all; and, for some moments, a profound silence was maintained, during which I could not help feeling my cheeks tingle with the many burning glances of scorn or reproach cast upon me by the less abandoned of the party. I will even own that an intolerable weight of anxiety was for a brief instant lifted from my bosom by the sudden and extraordinary interruption which ensued. The wide, heavy folding doors of the apartment were all at once thrown open, to their full extent, with a vigorous and rushing impetuosity that extinguished, as if by magic, every candle in the room. Their light, in dying, enabled us just to perceive that a stranger had entered, about my own height, and closely muffled in a cloak. The darkness, however, was now total; and we could only feel that he was standing in our midst. Before any one of us could recover from the extreme astonishment into which this rudeness had thrown all, we heard the voice of the intruder.

"Gentlemen," he said, in a low, distinct, and never-to-be-forgotten whisper which thrilled to the very marrow of my bones, "Gentlemen, I make no apology for this behaviour, because in thus behaving, I am but fulfilling a duty. You are, beyond doubt, uninformed of the true character of the person who has to-night won at ecarté a large sum of money from Lord Glendinning. I will therefore put you upon an expenditious and decisive plan of obtaining this very necessary information. Please to examine, at your leisure, the inner linings of the cuff of his left sleeve, and the several little packages which may be found in the somewhat capacious pockets of his embroidered morning wrapper."

While he spoke, so profound was the stillness that one might have heard a pin drop upon the floor. In ceasing, he departed at once, and as abruptly as he had entered. Can I—shall I describe my sensations?—must I say that I felt all the horrors of the damned? Most assuredly I had little time given for reflection. Many hands roughly seized me upon the spot, and lights were immediately reprocured. A search ensued. In the lining of my sleeve were found all the court cards essential in ecarte, and, in the pockets of my wrapper, a number of packs, facsimiles of those used at our sittings, with the single exception that mine were of the species called, technically, arrondees; the honours being slightly convex at the ends, the lower cards slightly convex at the sides. In this disposition, the dupe who cuts, as customary, at the length of the pack, will invariably find that he cuts his antagonist an honor; while the gambler, cutting at the breadth, will, as certainly, cut nothing for his victim which may count in the records of the game.

Any burst of indignation upon this discovery would have affected me less than the silent contempt, or the sarcastic composure, with which it was received.

"Mr. Wilson," said our host, stooping to remove from beneath his feet an exceedingly luxurious cloak of rare furs, "Mr. Wilson, this is your property." (The weather was cold; and, upon quitting my own room, I had thrown a cloak over my dressing wrapper, putting it off upon reaching the scene of play.) "I presume it is supererogatory to seek here (eyeing the folds of the garment with a bitter smile) for any farther evidence of your skill. Indeed, we have had enough. You will see the necessity, I hope, of quitting Oxford—at all events, of quitting instantly my chambers."

Abased, humbled to the dust as I then was, it is probable that I should have resented this galling language by immediate personal violence, had not my whole attention been at the moment arrested by a fact of the most startling character. The cloak which I had worn was of a rare description of fur; how rare, how extravagantly costly, I shall not venture to say. Its fashion, too, was of my own fantastic invention; for I was fastidious to an absurd degree of coxcombry, in matters of this frivolous nature. When, therefore, Mr. Preston reached me that which he had picked up upon the floor, and near the folding doors of the apartment, it was with an astonishment nearly bordering upon terror, that I perceived my own already hanging on my arm, (where I had no doubt unwittingly placed it,) and that the one presented me was but its exact counterpart in every, in even the minutest possible particular. The singular being who had so disastrously exposed me, had been muffled, I remembered, in a cloak; and none had been worn at all by any of the members of our party with the exception of myself. Retaining some presence of mind, I took the one offered me by Preston; placed it, unnoticed, over my own; left the apartment with a resolute scowl of defiance; and, next morning ere dawn of day, commenced a hurried journey from Oxford to the continent, in a perfect agony of horror and of shame.

I fled in vain. My evil destiny pursued me as if in exultation, and proved, indeed, that the exercise of its mysterious dominion had as yet only begun. Scarcely had I set foot in Paris ere I had fresh evidence of the detestable interest taken by this Wilson in my concerns. Years flew, while I experienced no relief. Villain!—at Rome, with how untimely, yet with how spectral an officiousness, stepped he in between me and my ambition! At Vienna, too—at Berlin—and at Moscow! Where, in truth, had I not bitter cause to curse him within my heart? From his inscrutable tyranny did I at length flee, panic-stricken, as from a pestilence; and to the very ends of the earth I fled in vain.

And again, and again, in secret communion with my own spirit, would I demand the questions "Who is he?—whence came he?—and what are his objects?" But no answer was there found. And then I scrutinized, with a minute scrutiny, the forms, and the methods, and the leading traits of his impertinent supervision. But even here there was very little upon which to base a conjecture. It was noticeable, indeed, that, in no one of the multiplied instances in which he had of late crossed my path, had he so crossed it except to frustrate those schemes, or to disturb those actions, which, if fully carried out, might have resulted in bitter mischief. Poor justification this, in truth, for an authority so imperiously assumed! Poor indemnity for natural rights of self-agency so pertinaciously, so insultingly denied!

I had also been forced to notice that my tormentor, for a very long period of time, (while scrupulously and with miraculous dexterity maintaining his whim of an identity of apparel with myself,) had so contrived it, in the execution of his varied interference with my will, that I saw not, at any moment, the features of his face. Be Wilson what he might, this, at least, was but the veriest of affectation, or of folly. Could he, for an instant, have supposed that, in my admonisher at Eton—in the destroyer of my honor at Oxford,—in him who thwarted my ambition at Rome, my revenge at Paris, my passionate love at Naples, or what he falsely termed my avarice in Egypt,—that in this, my arch-enemy and evil genius, could fail to recognise the William Wilson of my school boy days,—the namesake, the companion, the rival,—the hated and dreaded rival at Dr. Bransby's? Impossible!—But let me hasten to the last eventful scene of the drama.

Thus far I had succumbed supinely to this imperious domination. The sentiment of deep awe with which I habitually regarded the elevated character, the majestic wisdom, the apparent omnipresence and omnipotence of Wilson, added to a feeling of even terror, with which certain other traits in his nature and assumptions inspired me, had operated, hitherto, to impress me with an idea of my own utter weakness and helplessness, and to suggest an implicit, although bitterly reluctant submission to his arbitrary will. But, of late days, I had given myself up entirely to wine; and its maddening influence upon my hereditary temper rendered me more and more impatient of control. I began to murmur,—to hesitate,—to resist. And was it only fancy which induced me to believe that, with the increase of my own firmness, that of my tormentor underwent a proportional diminution? Be this as it may, I now began to feel the inspiration of a burning hope, and at length nurtured in my secret thoughts a stern and desperate resolution that I would submit no longer to be enslaved.

It was at Rome, during the Carnival of 18—, that I attended a masquerade in the palazzo of the Neapolitan Duke Di Broglio. I had indulged more freely than usual in the excesses of the wine-table; and now the suffocating atmosphere of the crowded rooms irritated me beyond endurance. The difficulty, too, of forcing my way through the mazes of the company contributed not a little to the ruffling of my temper; for I was anxiously seeking, (let me not say with what unworthy motive) the young, the gay, the beautiful wife of the aged and doting Di Broglio. With a too unscrupulous confidence she had previously communicated to me the secret of the costume in which she would be habited, and now, having caught a glimpse of her person, I was hurrying to make my way into her presence.—At this moment I felt a light hand placed upon my shoulder, and that ever-remembered, low, damnable whisper within my ear.

In an absolute phrenzy of wrath, I turned at once upon him who had thus interrupted me, and seized him violently by tile collar. He was attired, as I had expected, in a costume altogether similar to my own; wearing a Spanish cloak of blue velvet, begirt about the waist with a crimson belt sustaining a rapier. A mask of black silk entirely covered his face.

"Scoundrel!" I said, in a voice husky with rage, while every syllable I uttered seemed as new fuel to my fury, "scoundrel! impostor! accursed villain! you shall not—you shall not dog me unto death! Follow me, or I stab you where you stand!"—and I broke my way from the ball-room into a small ante-chamber adjoining—dragging him unresistingly with me as I went.

Upon entering, I thrust him furiously from me. He staggered against the wall, while I closed the door with an oath, and commanded him to draw. He hesitated but for an instant; then, with a slight sigh, drew in silence, and put himself upon his defence.

The contest was brief indeed. I was frantic with every species of wild excitement, and felt within my single arm the energy and power of a multitude. In a few seconds I forced him by sheer strength against the wainscoting, and thus, getting him at mercy, plunged my sword, with brute ferocity, repeatedly through and through his bosom.

At that instant some person tried the latch of the door. I hastened to prevent an intrusion, and then immediately returned to my dying antagonist. But what human language can adequately portray that astonishment, that horror which possessed me at the spectacle then presented to view? The brief moment in which I averted my eyes had been sufficient to produce, apparently, a material change in the arrangements at the upper or farther end of the room. A large mirror,—so at first it seemed to me in my confusion—now stood where none had been perceptible before; and, as I stepped up to it in extremity of terror, mine own image, but with features all pale and dabbled in blood, advanced to meet me with a feeble and tottering gait.

Thus it appeared, I say, but was not. It was my antagonist—it was Wilson, who then stood before me in the agonies of his dissolution. His mask and cloak lay, where he had thrown them, upon the floor. Not a thread in all his raiment—not a line in all the marked and singular lineaments of his face which was not, even in the most absolute identity, mine own!

It was Wilson; but he spoke no longer in a whisper, and I could have fancied that I myself was speaking while he said:

"You have conquered, and I yield. Yet, henceforward art thou also dead—dead to the World, to Heaven and to Hope! In me didst thou exist—and, in my death, see by this image, which is thine own, how utterly thou hast murdered thyself."

Harriet Jacobs

(1813–1897)

Though Harriet Jacobs was born a slave in Edenton, North Carolina, she was unaware of that plight in the early years of her life because her parents were allowed to live together in spite of the fact that they had different masters. After her mother's death, however, she was sold to Dr. James Norcom in 1825. Sexually assaulted by Norcom and physically abused by his wife, Jacobs sought help from Samuel Tredwell Sawyer, a white lawyer who she hoped would buy her from Norcom. She began an affair with Sawyer and had two children by him before Norcom finally sent her to a remote plantation in 1835. She escaped back to Edenton and went into hiding for the next seven years before finally fleeing to the North in 1842.

Jacobs went to work for the antislavery office run by her brother in Rochester, New York, and as a nanny for the children of Nathaniel Parker Willis. She grew particularly close to Willis's wife, Cornelia, and in 1853, Cornelia Willis purchased and freed Jacobs. After her emancipation, Jacobs, desiring to do her part for the abolitionist cause, began work on a narrative of her life. She finished it in 1858 but was at first unable to find a publisher. The renowned abolitionist Lydia Maria Child agreed to write a preface and to help Jacobs in editing the manuscript. Thus, in 1861, *Incidents in the Life of a Slave Girl* appeared under the pseudonym Linda Brent. After the outbreak of the Civil War, interest in slave narratives lessened, so that *Incidents* disappeared from notice until the 1980s. Though there is some controversy over the degree to which Child participated in the narrative's composition, *Incidents in the Life of a Slave Girl* has cemented Jacobs's status as a foundational figure in African American literary tradition.

Incidents in the Life of a Slave Girl

XIII. The Church and Slavery

After the alarm caused by Nat Turner's insurrection had subsided, the slaveholders came to the conclusion that it would be well to give the slaves enough of religious instruction to keep them from murdering their masters. The Episcopal clergyman offered to hold a separate service on Sundays for their benefit. His colored members were very few, and also very respectable—a fact which I presume had some weight with him. The difficulty was to decide on a suitable place for them to worship. The Methodist and Baptist churches admitted them in the afternoon; but their carpets and cushions were not so costly as those at the Episcopal church. It was at last decided that they should meet at the house of a free colored man, who was a member.

I was invited to attend, because I could read. Sunday evening came, and, trusting to the cover of night, I ventured out. I rarely ventured out by daylight, for I always went with fear, expecting at every turn to encounter Dr. Flint, who was sure to turn me back, or order me to his office to inquire where I got my bonnet, or some other article of dress. When the Rev. Mr. Pike came, there were some twenty persons present. The reverend gentleman knelt in prayer, then seated himself, and requested all present, who could read, to open their books, while he gave out the portions he wished them to repeat or respond to.

His text was, "Servants, be obedient to them that are your masters according to the flesh, with fear and trembling, in singleness of your heart, as unto Christ."

Pious Mr. Pike brushed up his hair till it stood upright, and, in deep, solemn tones, began: "Hearken, ye servants, Give strict heed unto my words. You are rebellious sinners. Your hearts are filled with all manner of evil. 'Tis the devil who tempts you. God is angry with you, and will surely punish you, if you don't forsake your wicked ways. You that live in town are eye-servants behind your master's back. Instead of serving your masters faithfully, which is pleasing in the sight of your heavenly Master, you are idle, and shirk your work. God sees you. You tell lies. God hears you. Instead of being engaged in worshipping him, you are hidden away somewhere, feasting on your master's substance; tossing coffee-grounds with some wicked fortuneteller, or cutting cards with another old hag. Your masters may not find you out, but God sees you, and will punish you. O, the depravity of your hearts! When your master's work is done, are you quietly together, thinking of the goodness of God to such sinful creatures? No; you are quarrelling, and tying up little bags of roots to bury under the door-steps to poison each other with. God sees you. You men steal away to every grog shop to sell your master's corn, that you may buy rum to drink. God sees you. You sneak into the back streets, or among the bushes, to pitch coppers. Although your masters may not find you out, God sees you; and he will punish you. You must forsake your sinful ways, and be faithful servants. Obey your old master and your young master—your old mistress and your young mistress. If you disobey your earthly master, you offend your heavenly Master. You must obey God's commandments. When you go from here, don't stop at the corners of the streets to talk, but go directly home, and let your master and mistress see that you have come."

The benediction was pronounced. We went home, highly amused at brother Pike's gospel teaching, and we determined to hear him again. I went the next Sabbath evening, and heard pretty much a repetition of the last discourse. At the close of the meeting, Mr. Pike informed us that he found it very inconvenient to meet at the friend's house, and he should be glad to see us, every Sunday evening, at his own kitchen.

I went home with the feeling that I had heard the Reverend Mr. Pike for the last time. Some of his members repaired to his house, and found that the kitchen sported two tallow candles; the first time, I am sure, since its present occupant owned it, for the servants never had any thing but pine knots. It was so long before the reverend gentleman descended from his comfortable parlor that the slaves left, and went to enjoy a Methodist shout. They never seem so happy as when shouting and singing at religious meetings. Many of them are sincere, and nearer to the gate of heaven than sanctimonious Mr. Pike, and other long-faced Christians, who see wounded Samaritans, and pass by on the other side.

The slaves generally compose their own songs and hymns; and they do not trouble their heads much about the measure. They often sing the following verses:

"Old Satan is one busy ole man;
    He rolls dem blocks all in my way;
But Jesus is my bosom friend;
    He rolls dem blocks away.

"If I had died when I was young,
    Den how my stam'ring tongue would have sung;
But I am ole, and now I stand
    A narrow chance for to tread dat heavenly land."

I well remember one occasion when I attended a Methodist class meeting. I went with a burdened spirit, and happened to sit next a poor, bereaved mother, whose heart was still heavier than mine. The class leader was the town constable—a man who bought and sold slaves, who whipped his brethren and sisters of the church at the public whipping post, in jail or out of jail. He was ready to perform that Christian office any where for fifty cents. This white-faced, black-hearted brother came near us, and said to the stricken woman, "Sister, can't you tell us how the Lord deals with your soul? Do you love him as you did formerly?"

She rose to her feet, and said, in piteous tones, "My Lord and Master, help me! My load is more than I can bear. God has hid himself from me, and I am left in darkness and misery." Then, striking her breast, she continued, "I can't tell you what is in here! They've got all my children. Last week they took the last one. God only knows where they've sold her. They let me have her sixteen years, and then————O! O! Pray for her brothers and sisters! I've got nothing to live for now. God make my time short!"

She sat down, quivering in every limb. I saw that constable class leader become crimson in the face with suppressed laughter, while he held up his handkerchief, that those who were weeping for the poor woman's calamity might not see his merriment. Then, with assumed gravity, he said to the bereaved mother, "Sister, pray to the Lord that every dispensation of his divine will may be sanctified to the good of your poor needy soul!"

The congregation struck up a hymn, and sung as though they were as free as the birds that warbled round us,—

"Ole Satan thought he had a mighty aim;
He missed my soul, and caught my sins.
Cry Amen, cry Amen, cry Amen to God!

"He took my sins upon his back;
Went muttering and grumbling down to hell.
Cry Amen, cry Amen, cry Amen to God!

"Old Satan's church is here below.
Up to God's free church I hope to go.
Cry Amen, cry Amen, cry Amen to God!"

Precious are such moments to the poor slaves. If you were to hear them at such times, you might think they were happy. But can that hour of singing and shouting sustain them through the dreary week, toiling without wages, under constant dread of the lash?

The Episcopal clergyman, who, ever since my earliest recollection, had been a sort of god among the slaveholders, concluded, as his family was large, that he must go where money was more abundant. A very different clergyman took his place. The change was very agreeable to the colored people, who said, "God has sent us a good man this time." They loved him, and their children followed him for a smile or a kind word. Even the slaveholders felt his influence. He brought to the rectory five slaves. His wife taught them to read and write, and to be useful to her and themselves. As soon as he was settled, he turned his attention to the needy slaves around him. He urged upon his parishioners the duty of having a meeting expressly for them every Sunday, with a sermon adapted to their comprehension. After much argument and importunity, it was finally agreed that they might occupy the gallery of the church on Sunday evenings. Many colored people, hitherto unaccustomed to attend church, now gladly went to hear the gospel preached. The sermons were simple, and they understood them. Moreover, it was the first time they had ever been addressed as human beings. It was not long before his white parishioners began to be dissatisfied. He was accused of preaching better sermons to the negroes than he did to them. He honestly confessed that he bestowed more pains upon those sermons than upon any others; for the slaves were reared in such ignorance that it was a difficult task to adapt himself to their comprehension. Dissensions arose in the parish. Some wanted he should preach to them in the evening and to the slaves in the afternoon. In the midst of these disputings his wife died, after a very short illness. Her slaves gathered round her dying bed in great sorrow. She said, "I have tried to do you good and promote your happiness; and if I have failed, it has not been for want of interest in your welfare. Do not weep for me; but prepare for the new duties that lie before you. I leave you all free. May we meet in a better world." Her liberated slaves were sent away, with funds to establish them comfortably. The colored people will long bless the memory of that truly Christian woman. Soon after her death her husband preached his farewell sermon, and many tears were shed at his departure.

Several years after, he passed through our town and preached to his former congregation. In his afternoon sermon he addressed the colored people. "My friends," said he, "it affords me great happiness to have an opportunity of speaking to you again. For two years I have been striving to do something for the colored people of my own parish; but nothing is yet accomplished. I have not even preached a sermon to them. Try to live according to the word of God, my friends. Your skin is darker than mine; but God judges men by their hearts, not by the color of their skins." This was strange doctrine from a southern pulpit. It was very offensive to slaveholders. They said he and his wife had made fools of their slaves, and that he preached like a fool to the negroes.

I knew an old black man, whose piety and childlike trust in God were beautiful to witness. At fifty-three years old he joined the Baptist church. He had a most earnest desire to learn to read. He thought he should know how to serve God better if he could only read the Bible. He came to me, and begged me to teach him. He said he could not pay me, for he had no money; but he would bring me nice fruit when the season for it came. I asked him if he didn't know it was contrary to law; and that slaves were whipped and imprisoned for teaching each other to read. This brought the tears into his eyes. "Don't be troubled, uncle Fred," said I. "I have no thoughts of refusing to teach you. I only told you of the law, that you might know the danger, and be on your guard." He thought he could plan to come three times a week without its being suspected. I selected a quiet nook, where no intruder was likely to penetrate, and there I taught him his A, B, C. Considering his age, his progress was astonishing. As soon as he could spell in two syllables he wanted to spell out words in the Bible. The happy smile that illuminated his face put joy into my heart. After spelling out a few words, he paused, and said, "Honey, it 'pears when I can read dis good book I shall be nearer to God. White man is got all de sense. He can larn easy. It ain't easy for ole black man like me. I only wants to read dis book, dat I may know how to live; den I hab no fear 'bout dying."

I tried to encourage him by speaking of the rapid progress he had made. "Hab patience, child," he replied. "I larns slow."

I had no need of patience. His gratitude, and the happiness I imparted, were more than a recompense for all my trouble.

At the end of six months he had read through the New Testament, and could find any text in it. One day, when he had recited unusually well, I said, "Uncle Fred, how do you manage to get your lessons so well?"

"Lord bress you, chile," he replied. "You nebber gibs me a lesson dat I don't pray to God to help me to understan' what I spells and what I reads. And he *does* help me, chile. Bress his holy name!"

There are thousands, who, like good uncle Fred, are thirsting for the water of life; but the law forbids it, and the churches withhold it. They send the Bible to heathen abroad, and neglect the heathen at home. I am glad that missionaries go out to the dark corners of the earth; but I ask them not to overlook the dark corners at home. Talk to American slaveholders as you talk to savages in Africa. Tell *them* it is wrong to traffic in men. Tell them it is sinful to sell their own children, and atrocious to violate their own daughters. Tell them that all men are brethren, and that man has no right to shut out the light of knowledge from his brother. Tell them they are answerable to God for sealing up the Fountain of Life from souls that are thirsting for it.

There are men who would gladly undertake such missionary work as this; but, alas! their number is small. They are hated by the south, and would be driven from its soil, or dragged to prison to die, as others have been before them. The field is ripe for the harvest, and awaits the reapers. Perhaps the great grandchildren of uncle Fred may have freely imparted to them the divine treasures, which he sought by stealth, at the risk of the prison and the scourge.

Are doctors of divinity blind, or are they hypocrites? I suppose some are the one, and some the other; but I think if they felt the interest in the poor and the lowly, that they ought to feel, they would not be so *easily* blinded. A clergyman who goes to the south, for the first time, has usually some feeling, however vague, that slavery is wrong. The slaveholder suspects this, and plays his game accordingly. He makes himself as agreeable as possible; talks on theology, and other kindred topics. The reverend gentleman is asked to invoke a blessing on a table loaded with luxuries. After dinner he walks round the premises, and sees the beautiful groves and flowering vines, and the comfortable huts of favored household slaves. The southerner invites him to talk with these slaves. He asks them if they want to be free, and they say, "O, no, massa." This is sufficient to satisfy him. He comes home to publish a "South-Side View of Slavery," and to complain of the exaggerations of abolitionists. He assures people that he has been to the south, and seen slavery for himself; that it is a beautiful "patriarchal institution;" that the slaves don't want their freedom; that they have hallelujah meetings, and other religious privileges.

What does *he* know of the half-starved wretches toiling from dawn till dark on the plantations? of mothers shrieking for their children, torn from their arms by slave-traders? of young girls dragged down into moral fifth? of pools of blood around the whipping post? of hounds trained to tear human flesh? of men screwed into cotton gins to die? The slaveholder showed him none of these things, and the slaves dared not tell of them if he had asked them.

There is a great difference between Christianity and religion at the south. If a man goes to the communion table, and pays money into the treasury of the church, no matter if it be the price of blood, he is called religious. If a pastor has offspring by a woman not his wife, the church dismiss him, if she is a white woman; but if she is colored, it does not hinder his continuing to be their good shepherd.

When I was told that Dr. Flint had joined the Episcopal church, I was much surprised. I supposed that religion had a purifying effect on the character of men; but the worst persecutions I endured from him were after he was a communicant. The conversation of the doctor, the day after he had been confirmed, certainly gave *me* no indication that he had "renounced the devil and all his works." In answer to some of his usual talk, I reminded him that he had just joined the church. "Yes, Linda," said he. "It was proper for me to do so. I am getting in years, and my position in society requires it, and it puts an end to all the damned slang. You would do well to join the church, too, Linda."

"There are sinners enough in it already," rejoined I. "If I could be allowed to live like a Christian, I should be glad."

"You can do what I require; and if you are faithful to me, you will be as virtuous as my wife," he replied.

I answered that the Bible didn't say so.

His voice became hoarse with rage. "How dare you preach to me about your infernal Bible!" he exclaimed. "What right have you, who are my negro, to talk to me about what you would like, and what you wouldn't like? I am your master, and you shall obey me."

No wonder the slaves sing,—

"Ole Satan's church is here below;
Up to God's free church I hope to go."

When my baby was about to be christened, the former mistress of my father stepped up to me, and proposed to give it her Christian name. To this I added the surname of my father, who had himself no legal right to it; for my grandfather on the paternal side was a white gentleman. What tangled skeins are the genealogies of slavery! I loved my father; but it mortified me to be obliged to bestow his name on my children.

When we left the church, my father's old mistress invited me to go home with her. She clasped a gold chain round my baby's neck. I thanked her for this kindness; but I did not like the emblem. I wanted no chain to be fastened on my daughter, not even if its links were of gold. How earnestly I prayed that she might never feel the weight of slavery's chain, whose iron entereth into the soul!

XV. Continued Persecutions

My children grew finely; and Dr. Flint would often say to me, with an exulting smile, "These brats will bring me a handsome sum of money one of these days."

I thought to myself that, God being my helper, they should never pass into his hands. It seemed to me I would rather see them killed than have them given up to his power. The money for the freedom of myself and my children could be obtained; but I derived no advantage from that circumstance. Dr. Flint loved money, but he loved power more. After much discussion, my friends resolved on making another trial. There was a slaveholder about to leave for Texas, and he was commissioned to buy me. He was to begin with nine hundred dollars, and go up to twelve. My master refused his offers. "Sir," said he, "she don't belong to me. She is my daughter's property, and I have no right to sell her. I mistrust that you come from her paramour. If so, you may tell him that he cannot buy her for any money; neither can he buy her children."

The doctor came to see me the next day, and my heart beat quicker as he entered. I never had seen the old man tread with so majestic a step. He seated himself and looked at me with withering scorn. My children had learned to be afraid of him. The little one would shut her eyes and hide her face on my shoulder whenever she saw him; and Benny, who was now nearly five years old, often inquired, "What makes that bad man come here so many times? Does he want to hurt us?" I would clasp the dear boy in my arms, trusting that he would be free before he was old enough to solve the problem. And now, as the doctor sat there so grim and silent, the child left his play and came and nestled up by me. At last my tormentor spoke. "So you are left in disgust, are you?" said he. "It is no more than I expected. You remember I told you years ago that you would be treated so. So he is tired of you? Ha! ha! ha! The virtuous madam don't like to hear about it, does she? Ha! ha! ha!" There was a sting in his calling me virtuous madam. I no longer had the power of answering him as I had formerly done. He continued: "So it seems you are trying to get up another intrigue. Your new paramour came to me, and offered to buy you; but you may be assured you will not succeed. You are mine; and you shall be mine for life. There lives no human being that can take you out of slavery. I would have done it; but you rejected my kind offer."

I told him I did not wish to get up any intrigue; that I had never seen the man who offered to buy me.

"Do you tell me I lie?" exclaimed he, dragging me from my chair. "Will you say again that you never saw that man?"

I answered, "I do say so."

He clinched my arm with a volley of oaths. Ben began to scream, and I told him to go to his grandmother.

"Don't you stir a step, you little wretch!" said he. The child drew nearer to me, and put his arms round me, as if he wanted to protect me. This was too much for my enraged master. He caught him up and hurled him across the room. I thought he was dead, and rushed towards him to take him up.

"Not yet!" exclaimed the doctor. "Let him lie there till he comes to."

"Let me go! Let me go!" I screamed, "or I will raise the whole house." I struggled and got away; but he clinched me again. Somebody opened the door, and he released me. I picked up my insensible child, and when I turned my tormentor was gone. Anxiously I bent over the little form, so pale and still; and when the brown eyes at last opened, I don't know whether I was very happy.

All the doctor's former persecutions were renewed. He came morning, noon, and night. No jealous lover ever watched a rival more closely than he watched me and the unknown slaveholder, with whom he accused me of wishing to get up an intrigue. When my grandmother was out of the way he searched every room to find him.

In one of his visits, he happened to find a young girl, whom he had sold to a trader a few days previous. His statement was, that he sold her because she had been too familiar with the overseer. She had had a bitter life with him, and was glad to be sold. She had no mother, and no near ties. She had been torn from all her family years before. A few friends had entered into bonds for her safety, if the trader would allow her to spend with them the time that intervened between her sale and the gathering up of his human stock. Such a favor was rarely granted. It saved the trader the expense of board and jail fees, and though the amount was small, it was a weighty consideration in a slave-trader's mind.

Dr. Flint always had an aversion to meeting slaves after he had sold them. He ordered Rose out of the house; but he was no longer her master, and she took no notice of him. For once the crushed Rose was the conqueror. His gray eyes flashed angrily upon her; but that was the extent of his power. "How came this girl here?" he exclaimed. "What right had you to allow it, when you knew I had sold her?"

I answered "This is my grandmother's house, and Rose came to see her. I have no right to turn any body out of doors, that comes here for honest purposes."

He gave me the blow that would have fallen upon Rose if she had still been his slave. My grandmother's attention had been attracted by loud voices, and she entered in time to see a second blow dealt. She was not a woman to let such an outrage, in her own house, go unrebuked. The doctor undertook to explain that I had been insolent. Her indignant feelings rose higher and higher, and finally boiled over in words. "Get out of my house!" she exclaimed. "Go home, and take care of your wife and children, and you will have enough to do, without watching my family."

He threw the birth of my children in her face, and accused her of sanctioning the life I was leading. She told him I was living with her by compulsion of his wife; that he needn't accuse her, for he was the one to blame; he was the one who had caused all the trouble. She grew more and more excited as she went on. "I tell you what, Dr. Flint," said she, "you ain't got many more years to live, and you'd better be saying your prayers. It will take 'em all, and more too, to wash the dirt off your soul."

"Do you know whom you are talking to?" he exclaimed.

She replied, "Yes, I know very well who I am talking to."

He left the house in a great rage. I looked at my grandmother. Our eyes met. Their angry expression had passed away, but she looked sorrowful and weary—weary of incessant strife. I wondered that it did not lessen her love for me; but if it did she never showed it. She was always kind, always ready to sympathize with my troubles. There might have been peace and contentment in that humble home if it had not been for the demon Slavery.

The winter passed undisturbed by the doctor. The beautiful spring came; and when Nature resumes her loveliness, the human soul is apt to revive also. My drooping hopes came to life again with the flowers. I was dreaming of freedom again; more for my children's sake than my own. I planned and I planned. Obstacles hit against plans. There seemed no way of overcoming them; and yet I hoped.

Back came the wily doctor. I was not at home when he called. A friend had invited me to a small party, and to gratify her I went. To my great consternation, a messenger came in haste to say that Dr. Flint was at my grandmother's, and insisted on seeing me. They did not tell him where I was, or he would have come and raised a disturbance in my friend's house. They sent me a dark wrapper; I threw it on and hurried home. My speed did not save me; the doctor had gone away in anger. I dreaded the morning, but I could not delay it; it came, warm and bright. At an early hour the doctor came and asked me where I had been last night. I told him. He did not believe me, and sent to my friend's house to ascertain the facts. He came in the afternoon to assure me he was satisfied that I had spoken the truth. He seemed to be in a facetious mood, and I expected some jeers were coming. "I suppose you need some recreation," said he, "but I am surprised at your being there, among those negroes. It was not the place for *you*. Are you *allowed* to visit such people?"

I understood this covert fling at the white gentleman who was my friend; but I merely replied, "I went to visit my friends, and any company they keep is good enough for me."

He went on to say, "I have seen very little of you of late, but my interest in you is unchanged. When I said I would have no more mercy on you I was rash. I recall my words. Linda, you desire freedom for yourself and your children, and you can obtain it only through me. If you agree to what I am about to propose, you and they shall be free. There must be no communication of any kind between you and their father. I will procure a cottage, where you and the children can live together. Your labor shall be light, such as sewing for my family. Think what is offered you, Linda—a home and freedom! Let the past be forgotten. If I have been harsh with you at times, your wilfulness drove me to it. You know I exact obedience from my own children, and I consider you as yet a child."

He paused for an answer, but I remained silent.

"Why don't you speak?" said he. "What more do you wait for?"

"Nothing, sir."

"Then you accept my offer?"

"No, sir."

His anger was ready to break loose; but he succeeded in curbing it, and replied, "You have answered without thought. But I must let you know there are two sides to my proposition; if you reject the bright side, you will be obliged to take the dark one. You must either accept my offer, or you and your children shall be sent to your young master's plantation, there to remain till your young mistress is married; and your children shall fare like the rest of the negro children. I give you a week to consider of it."

He was shrewd; but I knew he was not to be trusted. I told him I was ready to give my answer now.

"I will not receive it now," he replied. "You act too much from impulse. Remember that you and your children can be free a week from to-day if you choose."

On what a monstrous chance hung the destiny of my children! I knew that my master's offer was a snare, and that if I entered it escape would be impossible. As for his promise, I knew him so well that I was sure if he gave me free papers, they would be so managed as to have no legal value. The alternative was inevitable. I resolved to go to the plantation. But then I thought how completely I should be in his power, and the prospect was apalling. Even if I should kneel before him, and implore him to spare me, for the sake of my children, I knew he would spurn me with his foot, and my weakness would be his triumph.

Before the week expired, I heard that young Mr. Flint was about to be married to a lady of his own stamp. I foresaw the position I should occupy in his establishment. I had once been sent to the plantation for punishment, and fear of the son had induced the father to recall me very soon. My mind was made up; I was resolved that I would foil my master and save my children, or I would perish in the attempt. I kept my plans to myself; I knew that friends would try to dissuade me from them, and I would not wound their feelings by rejecting their advice.

On the decisive day the doctor came, and said he hoped I had made a wise choice.

"I am ready to go to the plantation, sir," I replied.

"Have you thought how important your decision is to your children?" said he.

I told him I had.

"Very well. Go to the plantation, and my curse go with you," he replied. "Your boy shall be put to work, and he shall soon be sold; and your girl shall be raised for the purpose of selling well. Go your own ways!" He left the room with curses, not to be repeated.

As I stood rooted to the spot, my grandmother came and said, "Linda, child, what did you tell him?"

I answered that I was going to the plantation.

"*Must* you go?" said she. "Can't something be done to stop it?"

I told her it was useless to try; but she begged me not to give up. She said she would go to the doctor, and remind him how long and how faithfully she had served in the family, and how she had taken her own baby from her breast to nourish his wife. She would tell him I had been out of the family so long they would not miss me; that she would pay them for my time, and the money would procure a woman who had more strength for the situation than I had. I begged her not to go; but she persisted in saying, "He will listen to *me*, Linda." She went, and was treated as I expected. He coolly listened to what she said, but denied her request. He told her that what he did was for my good, that my feelings were entirely above my situation, and that on the plantation I would receive treatment that was suitable to my behavior.

My grandmother was much cast down. I had my secret hopes; but I must fight my battle alone. I had a woman's pride, and a mother's love for my children; and I resolved that out of the darkness of this hour a brighter dawn should rise for them. My master had power and law on his side; I had a determined will. There is might in each.

XIX. The Children Sold

The doctor came back from New York, of course without accomplishing his purpose. He had expended considerable money, and was rather disheartened. My brother and the children had now been in jail two months, and that also was some expense. My friends thought it was a favorable time to work on his discouraged feelings. Mr. Sands sent a speculator to offer him nine hundred dollars for my brother William, and eight hundred for the two children. These were high prices, as slaves were then selling; but the offer was rejected. If it had been merely a question of money, the doctor would have sold any boy of Benny's age for two hundred dollars; but he could not bear to give up the power of revenge. But he was hard pressed for money, and he revolved the matter in his mind. He knew that if he could keep Ellen till she was fifteen, he could sell her for a high price; but I presume he reflected that she might die, or might be stolen away. At all events, he came to the conclusion that he had better accept the slave-trader's offer. Meeting him in the street, he inquired when he would leave town. "To-day, at ten o'clock," he replied. "Ah, do you go so soon?" said the doctor; "I have been reflecting upon your proposition, and I have concluded to let you have the three negroes if you will say nineteen hundred dollars." After some parley, the trader agreed to his terms. He wanted the bill of sale drawn up and signed immediately, as he had a great deal to attend to during the short time he remained in town. The doctor went to the jail and told William he would take him back into his service if he would promise to behave himself; but he replied that he would rather be sold. "And you *shall* be sold, you ungrateful rascal!" exclaimed the doctor. In less than an hour the money was paid, the papers were signed, sealed, and delivered, and my brother and children were in the hands of the trader.

It was a hurried transaction; and after it was over, the doctor's characteristic caution returned. He went back to the speculator, and said, "Sir, I have come to lay you under obligations of a thousand dollars not to sell any of those negroes in this state." "You come too late," replied the trader; "our bargain is closed." He had, in fact, already sold them to Mr. Sands, but he did not mention it. The doctor required him to put irons on "that rascal, Bill," and to pass through the back streets when he took his gang out of town. The trader was privately instructed to concede to his wishes. My good old aunt went to the jail to bid the children good by, supposing them to be the speculator's property, and that she should never see them again. As she held Benny in her lap, he said, "Aunt Nancy, I want to show you something." He led her to the door and showed her a long row of marks, saying, "Uncle Will taught me to count. I have made a mark for every day I have been here, and it is sixty days. It is a long time; and the speculator is going to take me and Ellen away. He's a bad man. It's wrong for him to take grandmother's children. I want to go to my mother."

My grandmother was told that the children would be restored to her, but she was requested to act as if they were really to be sent away. Accordingly, she made up a bundle of clothes and went to the jail. When she arrived, she found William handcuffed among the gang, and the children in the trader's cart. The scene seemed too much like reality. She was afraid there might have been some deception or mistake. She fainted, and was carried home.

When the wagon stopped at the hotel, several gentlemen came out and proposed to purchase William, but the trader refused their offers, without stating that he was already sold. And now came the trying hour for that drove of human beings, driven away like cattle, to be sold they knew not where. Husbands were torn from wives, parents from children, never to look upon each other again this side the grave. There was wringing of hands and cries of despair.

Dr. Flint had the supreme satisfaction of seeing the wagon leave town, and Mrs. Flint had the gratification of supposing that my children were going "as far as wind and water would carry them." According to agreement, my uncle followed the wagon some miles, until they came to an old farm house. There the trader took the irons from William, and as he did so, he said, "You are a damned clever fellow. I should like to own you myself. Them gentlemen that wanted to buy you said you was a bright, honest chap, and I must git you a good home. I guess your old master will swear to-morrow, and call himself an old fool for selling the children. I reckon he'll never git their mammy back agin. I expect she's made tracks for the north. Good by, old boy. Remember, I have done you a good turn. You must thank me by coaxing all the pretty gals to go with me next fall. That's going to be my last trip. This trading in niggers is a bad business for a fellow that's got any heart. Move on, you fellows!" And the gang went on, God alone knows where.

Much as I despise and detest the class of slave-traders, whom I regard as the vilest wretches on earth, I must do this man the justice to say that he seemed to have some feeling. He took a fancy to William in the jail, and wanted to buy him. When he heard the story of my children, he was willing to aid them in getting out of Dr. Flint's power, even without charging the customary fee.

My uncle procured a wagon and carried William and the children back to town. Great was the joy in my grandmother's house! The curtains were closed, and the candles lighted. The happy grandmother cuddled the little ones to her bosom. They hugged her, and kissed her, and clapped their hands, and shouted. She knelt down and poured forth one of her heartfelt prayers of thanksgiving to God. The father was present for a while; and though such a "parental relation" as existed between him and my children takes slight hold of the hearts or consciences of slaveholders, it must be that he experienced some moments of pure joy in witnessing the happiness he had imparted.

I had no share in the rejoicings of that evening. The events of the day had not come to my knowledge. And now I will tell you something that happened to me; though you will, perhaps, think it illustrates the superstition of slaves. I sat in my usual place on the floor near the window, where I could hear much that was said in the street without being seen. The family had retired for the night, and all was still. I sat there thinking of my children, when I heard a low strain of music. A band of serenaders were under the window, playing "Home, sweet home." I listened till the sounds did not seem like music, but like the moaning of children. It seemed as if my heart would burst. I rose from my sitting posture, and knelt. A streak of moonlight was on the floor before me, and in the midst of it appeared the forms of my two children. They vanished; but I had seen them distinctly. Some will call it a dream, others a vision. I know not how to account for it, but it made a strong impression on my mind, and I felt certain something had happened to my little ones.

I had not seen Betty since morning. Now I heard her softly turning the key. As soon as she entered, I clung to her, and begged her to let me know whether my children were dead, or whether they were sold; for I had seen their spirits in my room, and I was sure something had happened to them. "Lor, chile," said she, putting her arms round me, "you's got de highsterics. I'll sleep wid you to-night, 'cause you'll make a noise, and ruin missis. Something has stirred you up mightily. When you is done cryin, I'll talk wid you. De chillern is well, and mighty happy. I seed 'em myself. Does dat satisfy you? Dar, chile, be still! Somebody vill hear you." I tried to obey her. She lay down, and was soon sound asleep; but no sleep would come to my eyelids.

At dawn, Betty was up and off to the kitchen. The hours passed on, and the vision of the night kept constantly recurring to my thoughts. After a while I heard the voices of two women in the entry. In one of them I recognized the housemaid. The other said to her, "Did you know Linda Brent's children was sold to the speculator yesterday. They say ole massa Flint was mighty glad to see 'em drove out of town; but they say they've come back agin. I 'spect it's all their daddy's doings. They say he's bought William too. Lor! how it will take hold of old massa Flint! Im going roun' to aunt Marthy's to see 'bout it."

I bit my lips till the blood came to keep from crying out. Were my children with their grandmother, or had the speculator carried them off? The suspense was dreadful. Would Betty *never* come, and tell me the truth about it? At last she came, and I eagerly repeated what I had overheard. Her face was one broad, bright smile. "Lor, you foolish ting!" said she. "I'se gwine to tell you all 'bout it. De gals is eating thar breakfast, and missus tole me to let her tell you; but, poor creeter! t'aint right to keep you waitin', and I'se gwine to tell you. Brudder, chillern, all is bought by de daddy! I'se laugh more dan nuff, tinking 'bout ole massa Flint. Lor, how he *vill* swar! He's got ketched dis time, any how; but I must be getting out o'dis, or dem gals vill come and ketch *me*."

Betty went off laughing; and I said to myself, "Can it be true that my children are free? I have not suffered for them in vain. Thank God!"

Great surprise was expressed when it was known that my children had returned to their grandmother's. The news spread through the town, and many a kind word was bestowed on the little ones.

Dr. Flint went to my grandmother's to ascertain who was the owner of my children, and she informed him. "I expected as much," said he. "I am glad to hear it. I have had news from Linda lately, and I shall soon have her. You need never expect to see *her* free. She shall be my slave as long as I live, and when I am dead she shall be the slave of my children. If I ever find out that you or Phillip had any thing to do with her running off I'll kill him. And if I meet William in the street, and he presumes to look at me, I'll flog him within an inch of his life. Keep those brats out of my sight!"

As he turned to leave, my grandmother said something to remind him of his own doings. He looked back upon her, as if he would have been glad to strike her to the ground.

I had my season of joy and thanksgiving. It was the first time since my childhood that I had experienced any real happiness. I heard of the old doctor's threats, but they no longer had the same power to trouble me. The darkest cloud that hung over my life had rolled away. Whatever slavery might do to me, it could not shackle my children. If I fell a sacrifice, my little ones were saved. It was well for me that my simple heart believed all that had been promised for their welfare. It is always better to trust than to doubt.

George Fitzhugh

(1806–1881)

Born in Prince William County, Virginia, in 1806, George Fitzhugh studied law for a time and tried to make a living as a planter in Port Royal. In the mid-1850s, he traveled through the industrial North, where he also met Harriet Beecher Stowe. The visit seems to have cemented his proslavery and anti-industrial views, and he vented those sentiments in the two books that made his reputation, *Sociology for the South* (1854) and *Cannibals All! Or, Slaves Without Masters* (1857).

A leader of the Southern school of proslavery writers, Fitzhugh is something of an intriguing figure because of his incipient Marxist analysis of Northern capitalists, the "cannibals" of the 1857 work's title. However, his contention that the patriarchal system of economy in the South was the answer to capitalism's evils, paired with his assertion that slavery was a necessary universal principle (Fitzhugh actually argued that free Negroes in the South should be made slaves again), served only to confirm the Northern view that Southerners were intolerant despots determined to turn the clock back to the feudal era. Though he opposed secession, Fitzhugh supported the war once it had begun. During the period of Reconstruction following the war, he continued to advocate a paternalistic economy in the South. He died in Texas in 1881.

from *Ante-Bellum Writings of George Fitzhugh and Hinton Rowan Helper on Slavery:*

Cannibals All! Or, Slaves without Masters

Chapter I. The Universal Trade

We are, all, North and South, engaged in the White Slave Trade, and he who succeeds best, is esteemed most respectable. It is far more cruel than the Black Slave Trade, because it exacts more of its slaves, and neither protects nor governs them. We boast, that it exacts more, when we say, "that the *profits* made from employing free labor are greater than those from slave labor." The profits, made from free labor, are the amount of the products of such labor, which the employer, by means of the command which capital or skill gives him, takes away, exacts or "exploitates" from the free laborer. The profits of slave labor are that portion of the products of such labor which the power of the master enables him to appropriate. These profits are less, because the master allows the slave to retain a larger share of the results of his own labor, than do the employers of free labor. But we not only boast that the White Slave Trade is more exacting and fraudulent (in fact, though not in intention,) than Black Slavery; but we also boast, that it is more cruel, in leaving the laborer to take care of himself and family out of the pittance which skill or capital have allowed him to retain. When the day's labor is ended, he is free, but is overburdened with the cares of family and household, which make his freedom an empty and delusive mockery. But his employer is really free, and may enjoy the profits made by others' labor, without a care, or a trouble, as to their well-being. The negro slave is free, too, when the labors of the day are over, and free in mind as well as body; for the master provides food, raiment, house, fuel, and everything else necessary to the physical well-being of himself and family. The master's labors commence just when the slave's end. No wonder men should prefer white slavery to capital, to negro slavery, since it is more profitable, and is free from all the cares and labors of black slave-holding.

Now, reader, if you wish to know yourself—to "descant on your own deformity"—read on. But if you would cherish self-conceit, self-esteem, or self-appreciation, throw down our book; for we will dispel illusions which have promoted your happiness, and shew you that what you have considered and practiced as virtue, is little better than moral Cannibalism. But you will find yourself in numerous and respectable company; for all good and respectable people are "Cannibals all," who do not labor, or who are successfully trying to live without labor, on the unrequited labor of other people:—Whilst low, bad, and disreputable people, are those who labor to support themselves, and to support said respectable people besides. Throwing the negro slaves out of the account, and society is divided in Christendom into four classes: The rich, or independent respectable people, who live well and labor not at all; the professional and skillful respectable people, who do a little light work, for enormous wages; the poor hard-working people, who support every body, and starve themselves; and the poor thieves, swindlers and sturdy beggars, who live like gentlemen, without labor, on the labor of other people. The gentlemen exploitate, which being done on a large scale, and requiring a great many victims, is highly respectable—whilst the rogues and beggars take so little from others, that they fare little better than those who labor.

But, reader, we do not wish to fire into the flock. "Thou art the man!" You are a Cannibal! and if a successful one, pride yourself on the number of your victims, quite as much as any Feejee chieftain, who breakfasts, dines and sups on human flesh.—And your conscience smites you, if you have failed to succeed, quite as much as his, when he returns from an unsuccessful foray.

Probably, you are a lawyer, or a merchant, or a doctor, who have made by your business fifty thousand dollars, and retired to live on your capital. But, mark! not to spend your capital. That would be vulgar, disreputable, criminal. That would be, to live by your own labor; for your capital is your amassed labor. That would be, to do as common working men do; for they take the pittance which their employers leave them, to live on. They live by labor; for they exchange the results of their own labor for the products of other people's labor. It is, no doubt, an honest, vulgar way of living; but not at all a respectable way. The respectable way of living is, to make other people work for you, and to pay them nothing for so doing—and to have no concern about them after their work is done. Hence, white slave-holding is much more respectable than negro slavery—for the master works nearly as hard for the negro, as he for the master. But you, my virtuous, respectable reader, exact three thousand dollars per annum from white labor, (for your income is the product of white labor,) and make not one cent of return in any form. You retain your capital, and never labor, and yet live in luxury on the labor of others. Capital commands labor, as the master does the slave. Neither pays for labor; but the master permits the slave to retain a larger allowance from the proceeds of his own labor, and hence "free labor is cheaper than slave labor." You, with the command over labor which your capital gives you, are a slave owner—a master, without the obligations of a master. They who work for you, who create your income, are slaves, without the rights of slaves. Slaves without a master! Whilst you were engaged in amassing your capital, in seeking to become independent, you were in the White Slave Trade. To become independent, is to be able to make other people support you, without being obliged to labor for *them*. Now, what man in society is not seeking to attain this situation? He who attains it, is a slave owner, in the worst sense. He who is in pursuit of it, is engaged in the slave trade. You, reader, belong to the one or other class. The men without property, in free society, are theoretically in a worse condition than slaves. Practically, their condition corresponds with this theory, as history and statistics every where demonstrate. The capitalists, in free society, live in ten times the luxury and show that Southern masters do, because the slaves to capital work harder and cost less, than negro slaves.

The negro slaves of the South are the happiest, and, in some sense, the freest people in the world. The children and the aged and infirm work not at all, and yet have all the comforts and necessaries of life provided for them. They enjoy liberty, because they are oppressed neither by care nor labor. The women do little hard work, and are protected from the despotism of their husbands by their masters. The negro men and stout boys work, on the average, in good weather, not more than nine hours a day. The balance of their time is spent in perfect abandon. Besides, they have their Sabbaths and holidays. White men, with so much of license and liberty, would die of ennui; but negroes luxuriate in corporeal and mental repose. With their faces upturned to the sun, they can sleep at any hour; and quiet sleep is the greatest of human enjoyments. "Blessed be the man who invented sleep." 'Tis happiness in itself—and results from contentment with the present, and confident assurance of the future. We do not know whether free laborers ever sleep. They are fools to do so; for, whilst they sleep, the wily and watchful capitalist is devising means to ensnare and exploitate them. The free laborer must work or starve. He is more of a slave than the negro, because he works longer and harder for less allowance than the slave, and has no holiday, because the cares of life with him begin when its labors end. He has no liberty, and not a single right. We know, 'tis often said, air and water are common property, which all have equal right to participate and enjoy; but this is utterly false. The appropriation of the lands carries with it the appropriation of all on or above the lands, *usque ad cœlum, aut ad inferos.* A man cannot breathe the air, without a place to breathe it from, and all places are appropriated. All water is private property "to the middle of the stream," except the ocean, and that is not fit to drink.

Free laborers have not a thousandth part of the rights and liberties of negro slaves. Indeed, they have not a single right or a single liberty, unless it be the right or liberty to die. But the reader may think that he and other capitalists and employers are freer than negro slaves. Your capital would soon vanish, if you dared indulge in the liberty and abandon of negroes. You hold your wealth and position by the tenure of constant watchfulness, care and circumspection. You never labor; but you are never free.

Where a few own the soil, they have unlimited power over the balance of society, until domestic slavery comes in, to compel them to permit this balance of society to draw a sufficient and comfortable living from "terra mater." Free society, asserts the right of a few to the earth—slavery, maintains that it belongs, in different degrees, to all.

But, reader, well may you follow the slave trade. It is the only trade worth following, and slaves the only property worth owning. All other is worthless, a mere *caput mortuum,* except in so far as it vests the owner with the power to command the labors of others—to enslave them. Give you a palace, ten thousand acres of land, sumptuous clothes, equipage and every other luxury; and with your artificial wants, you are poorer than Robinson Crusoe, or the lowest working man, if you have no slaves to capital, or domestic slaves. Your capital will not bring you an income of a cent, nor supply one of your wants, without labor. Labor is indispensable to give value to property, and if you owned every thing else, and did not own labor, you would be poor. But fifty thousand dollars means, and is, fifty thousand dollars worth of slaves. You can command, without touching on that capital, three thousand dollars' worth of labor per annum. You could do no more were you to buy slaves with it, and then you would be cumbered with the cares of governing and providing for them. You are a slaveholder now, to the amount of fifty thousand dollars, with all the advantages, and none of the cares and responsibilities of a master.

"Property in man" is what all are struggling to obtain. Why should they not be obliged to take care of man, their property, as they do of their horses and their hounds, their cattle and their sheep. Now, under the delusive name of liberty, you work him, "from morn to dewy eve"—from infancy to old age—then turn him out to starve. You treat your horses and hounds better. Capital is a cruel master. The free slave trade, the commonest, yet the cruellest of trades.

Chapter II. Labor, Skill and Capital

Nothing written on the subject of slavery from the time of Aristotle is worth reading until the days of the modern Socialists. Nobody treating of it thought it worth while to enquire from history and statistics, whether the physical and moral condition of emancipated serfs or slaves had been improved or rendered worse by emancipation. None would condescend to compare the evils of domestic slavery with the evils of liberty without property. It entered no one's head to conceive a doubt as to the actual freedom of the emancipated. The relations of capital and labor, of the property-holders to the non-property-holders, were things about which no one had thought or written. It never occurred to either the enemies or the apologists for slavery, that if no one would employ the free laborer, his condition was infinitely worse than that of actual slavery—nor did it occur to them, that if his wages were less than the allowance of the slave, he was less free after emancipation than before St. Simon, Fourier, Owen, Fanny Wright, and a few others, who discovered and proclaimed that property was not only a bad master, but an intolerable one, were treated as wicked visionaries. After the French and other revolutions in Western Europe in 1830, all men suddenly discovered that the social relations of men were false, and that social, not political, revolutions were needed. Since that period, almost the whole literature of free society is but a voice proclaiming its absolute and total failure. Hence the works of the socialists contain the true defence of slavery.

Most of the active intellect of Christendom has for the last twenty years been engaged in analyzing, detecting and exposing the existing relations of labor, skill and capital, and in vain efforts to rectify those relations. The philosophers of Europe, who have been thus engaged, have excelled all the moral philosophers that preceded them, in the former part of their pursuit, but suggested nothing but puerile absurdities, in the latter. Their destructive philosophy is profound, demonstrative, and unanswerable—their constructive theories, wild, visionary and chimerical on paper, and failures in practice. Each one of them proves clearly enough, that the present edifice of European society is out of all rule and proportion, and must soon tumble to pieces—but no two agree as to how it is to be re-built. "We must (say they all) have a new world, if we are to have any world at all!" and each has a little model Utopia or Phalanstery, for this new and better world, which, having already failed on a small experimental scale, the inventor assures us, is, therefore, the very thing to succeed on a large one. We allude to the socialists and communists, who have more or less tinged all modern literature with their doctrines. In analyzing society; in detecting, exposing, and generalizing its operations and its various phenomena, they are but grammarians or anatomists, confining philosophy to its proper sphere, and employing it for useful purposes. When they attempt to go further— and having found the present social system to be fatally diseased, propose to originate and build up another in its stead—they are as presumptuous as the anatomist, who should attempt to create a man. Social bodies, like human bodies, are the works of God, which man may dissect, and sometimes heal, but which he cannot create. Society was not always thus diseased, or socialism would have been as common in the past as it is now. We think these presumptuous philosophers had best compare it in its healthy state with what it is now, and supply deficiencies or lop off excrescencies, as the comparison may suggest. But our present business is to call attention to some valuable discoveries in the terra firma of social science, which these socialists have made in their vain voyages in search of an ever receding and illusory Utopia. Like the alchymists, although they have signally failed in the objects of their pursuits, they have incidentally hit upon truths, unregarded and unprized by themselves, which will be valuable in the hands of more practical and less sanguine men. It is remarkable, that the political economists, who generally assume labor to be the most just and correct measure of value, should not have discovered that the profits of capital represent no labor at all. To be consistent, the political economists should denounce as unjust all interests, rents, dividends and other profits of capital. We mean by rents, that portion of the rent which is strictly income. The amount annually required for repairs and ultimately to rebuild the house, is not profit. Four per cent, will do this. A rent of ten per cent, is in such case a profit of six per cent. The four per cent, is but a return to the builder of his labor and capital spent in building. "The use of a thing, is only a fair subject of change, in so far as the article used is consumed in the use; for such consumption is the consumption of the labor or capital of the owner, and is but the exchange of equivalent amounts of labor."

These socialists, having discovered that skill and capital, by means of free competition, exercise an undue mastery over labor, propose to do away with skill, capital, and free competition, altogether. They would heal the diseases of society by destroying its most vital functions. Having laid down the broad proposition, that equal amounts of labor, or their results, should be exchanged for each other, they get at the conclusion that as the profits of capital are not the results of labor, the capitalist shall be denied all interest or rents, or other profits on his capital, and be compelled in all cases to exchange a part of the capital itself, for labor, or its results. This would prevent accumulation, or at least limit it to the procurement of the coarsest necessaries of life. They say, "the lawyer and the artist do not work so hard and continuously as the ploughman, and should receive less wages than he—a bushel of wheat represents as much labor as a speech or portrait, and should be exchanged for the one or the other." Such a system of trade and exchange would equalize conditions, but would banish civilization. Yet do these men show, that, by means of the taxation and oppression, which capital and skill exercise over labor, the rich, the professional, the trading and skillful part of society, have become the masters of the laboring masses: whose condition, already intolerable, is daily becoming worse. They point out distinctly the character of the disease under which the patient is laboring, but see no way of curing the disease except by killing the patient.

In the preceding chapter, we illustrated their theory of capital by a single example. We might give hundreds of illustrations, and yet the subject is so difficult that few readers will take the trouble to understand it. Let us take two well known historical instances: England became possessed of two fine islands, Ireland and Jamaica. Englishmen took away, or defrauded, from the Irish, their lands; but professed to leave the people free. The people, however, must have the use of land, or starve. The English charged them, in rent, so much, that their allowance, after deducting that rent, was not half that of Jamaica slaves. They were compelled to labor for their landlords, by the fear of hunger and death—forces stronger than the overseer's lash. They worked more, and did not get half so much pay or allowance as the Jamaica negroes. All the reports to the French and British Parliaments show that the physical wants of the West India slaves were well supplied. The Irish became the subjects of capital— slaves, with no masters obliged by law, self-interest or domestic affections, to provide for them. The freest people in the world, in the loose and common sense of words, their condition, moral, physical and religious, was far worse than that of civilized slaves ever has been or ever can be—for at length, after centuries of slow starvation, three hundred thousand perished in a single season, for want of food. Englishmen took the lands of Jamaica also, but introduced negro slaves, whom they were compelled to support at all seasons, and at any cost. The negroes were comfortable, until philanthropy taxed the poor of England and Ireland a hundred millions to free them. Now, they enjoy Irish liberty, whilst the English hold all the good lands. They are destitute and savage, and in all respects worse off than when in slavery.

Public opinion unites with self-interest, domestic affection and municipal law to protect the slave. The man who maltreats the weak and dependant, who abuses his authority over wife, children or slaves, is universally detested. That same public opinion, which shields and protects the slave, encourages the oppression of free laborers—for it is considered more honorable and praiseworthy to obtain large fees than small ones, to make good bargains than bad ones, (and all fees and profits come ultimately from common laborers)—to live without work, by the exactions of accumulated capital, than to labor at the plough or the spade, for one's living. It is the interest of the capitalist and the skillful to allow free laborers the least possible portion of the fruits of their own labor; for all capital is created by labor, and the smaller the allowance of the free laborer, the greater the gains of his employer. To treat free laborers badly and unfairly, is universally inculcated as a moral duty, and the selfishness of man's nature prompts him to the most rigorous performance of this cannibalish duty. We appeal to political economy; the ethical, social, political and economic philosophy of free society, to prove the truth of our doctrines. As an ethical and social guide, that philosophy teaches, that social, individual and national competition, is a moral duty, and we have attempted to prove that all competition is but the effort to enslave others, without being encumbered with their support. As a political guide, it would simply have government 'keep the peace;' or, to define its doctrine more exactly, it teaches "that it is the whole duty of government to hold the weak whilst the strong rob them"—for it punishes crimes accompanied with force, which none but the weak-minded commit; but encourages the war of the wits, in which the strong and astute are sure to succeed, in stripping the weak and ignorant.

It is time, high time, that political economy was banished from our schools. But what would this avail in free society, where men's antagonistic relations suggest to each one, without a teacher, that "he can only be just to himself, by doing wrong to others." Aristotle, and most other ancient philosophers and statesmen, held the doctrine, "that as money would not breed, interest should not be allowed." Moses, no doubt, saw as the modern socialists do, that all other capital stood on the same grounds with money. None of it is self-creative, or will "breed." The language employed about "usury" and "increase" in 25th Leviticus, and 23d Deuteronomy, is quite broad enough to embrace and prohibit all profits of capital. Such interest or "increase," or profits, might be charged to the Heathen, but not to the Jews. The whole arrangements of Moses were obviously intended to prevent competition in the dealings of the Jews with one another, and to beget permanent equality of condition and fraternal feelings.

The socialists have done one great good. They enable us to understand and appreciate the institutions of Moses, and to see, that none but Divinity could have originated them.* The situation of Judea was, in many respects, anomalous, and we are not to suppose that its political and social relations were intended to be universal. Yet, here it is distinctly asserted, that under certain circumstances, all profits on capital are wrong.

The reformers of the present day are all teetotalists, and attempt to banish evil altogether, not to lessen or restrict it. It would be wiser to assume that there is nothing, in its essence, evil, in the moral or physical world, but only rendered so by the wrongful applications which men make of them. Science is every day discovering that the most fatal poisons, when properly employed, become the most efficacious medicines. So, what appear to be the evil passions and propensities of men, and of societies, under proper regulation, may be made to minister to the wisest and best of purposes. Civilized society has never been found without that competition begotten by man's desire to throw most of the burdens of life on others, and to enjoy the fruits of their labors without exchanging equivalent labor of his own. In all such societies, (outside the Bible,) such selfish and grasping appropriation is inculcated as a moral duty; and he who succeeds best, either by the exercise of professional skill, or by accumulation of capital, in appropriating the labor of others, without laboring in return, is considered most meritorious. It would be unfair, in treating of the relations of capital and labor, not to consider its poor-house system, the ultimate resort of the poor.

The taxes or poor rates which support this system of relief, like all other taxes and values, are derived from the labor of the poor. The able-bodied, industrious poor are compelled by the rich and skillful to support the weak, and too often, the idle poor. In addition to defraying the necessary expenses and the wanton luxuries of the rich, to supporting government, and supporting themselves, capital compels them to support its poor houses. In collection of the poor rates, in their distribution, and in the adminis-

---

*Not only does Moses evince his knowledge of the despotism of capital, in forbidding its profits, but also in his injunction, not to let emancipated slaves "go away empty." Deuteronomy xv. 13, 14.

"And when thou sendest him out free from thee, thou shalt not let him go away empty. Thou shalt furnish him liberally out of thy flock, and out of thy floor, and out of thy wine-press: of that wherewith the Lord thy God hath blessed thee thou shalt give unto him."

People without property exposed to the unrestricted exactions of capital are infinitely worse off after emancipation than before. Moses prevented the exactions of capital by providing property for the new free man.

tration of the poor-house system, probably half the tax raised for the poor is exhausted. Of the remainder, possibly another half is expended on unworthy objects. Masters, in like manner, support the sick, infant and aged slaves from the labor of the strong and healthy. But nothing is wasted in collection and administration, and nothing given to unworthy objects. The master having the control of the objects of his bounty, takes care that they shall not become burdensome by their own crimes and idleness. It is contrary to all human customs and legal analogies, that those who are dependent, or are likely to become so, should not be controlled. The duty of protecting the weak involves the necessity of enslaving them—hence, in all countries, women and children, wards and apprentices, have been essentially slaves, controlled, not by law, but by the will of a superior. This is a fatal defect in the poor-house system. Many men become paupers from their own improvidence or misconduct, and masters alone can prevent such misconduct and improvidence. Masters treat their sick, infant and helpless slaves well, not only from feeling and affection, but from motives of self-interest. Good treatment renders them more valuable. All poor houses, are administered on the penitentiary system, in order to deter the poor from resorting to them. Besides, masters are always in place to render needful aid to the unfortunate and helpless slaves. Thousands of the poor starve out of reach of the poor house, or other public charity.

A common charge preferred against slavery is, that it induces idleness with the masters. The trouble, care and labor, of providing for wife, children and slaves, and of properly governing and administering the whole affairs of the farm, is usually borne on small estates by the master. On larger ones, he is aided by an overseer or manager. If they do their duty, their time is fully occupied. If they do not, the estate goes to ruin. The mistress, on Southern farms, is usually more busily, usefully and benevolently occupied than any one on the farm. She unites in her person, the offices of wife, mother, mistress, housekeeper, and sister of charity. And she fulfills all these offices admirably well. The rich men, in free society, may, if they please, lounge about town, visit clubs, attend the theatre, and have no other trouble than that of collecting rents, interest and dividends of stock. In a well constituted slave society, there should be no idlers. But we cannot divine how the capitalists in free society are to be put to work. The master labors for the slave, they exchange industrial value. But the capitalist, living on his income, gives nothing to his subjects. He lives by mere exploitation.

It is objected that slavery permits or induces immorality and ignorance. This is a mistake. The intercourse of the house-servants with the white family, assimilates, in some degree, their state of information, and their moral conduct, to that of the whites. The house-servants, by their intercourse with the field hands, impart their knowledge to them. The master enforces decent morality in all. Negroes are never ignorant of the truths of Christianity, all speak intelligible English, and are posted up in the ordinary occurrences of the times. The reports to the British Parliament shew, that the agricultural and mining poor of England scarce know the existence of God, do not speak intelligible English, and are generally depraved and ignorant. They learn nothing by intercourse with their superiors, as negroes do. They abuse wives and children, because they have no masters to control them, and the men are often dissipated and idle, leaving all the labor to be done by the women and children—for the want of this same control.

Slavery, by separating the mass of the ignorant from each other, and bringing them in contact and daily intercourse with the well-informed, becomes an admirable educational system—no doubt a necessary one. By subjecting them to the constant control and supervision of their superiors, interested in enforcing morality, it becomes the best and most efficient police system; so efficient, that the ancient Romans had scarcely any criminal code whatever.

The great objections to the colonial slavery of the latter Romans, to serfdom, and all forms of prædial slavery, are: that the slaves are subjected to the cares as well as the labors of life; that the masters become idlers; that want of intercourse destroys the affectionate relations between master and slave, throws the mass of ignorant slaves into no other association but that with the ignorant; and deprives them, as well of the instruction, as the government, of superiors living on the same farm. Southern slavery is becoming the best form of slavery of which we have any history, except that of the Jews. The Jews owned but few slaves, and with them the relation of master and slave was truly affectionate, protective and patriarchal. The master, wife and children were in constant intercourse with the slaves, and formed, in practice as well as theory, affectionate, well-ordered families.

As modern civilization advances, slavery becomes daily more necessary, because its tendency is to accumulate all capital in a few hands, cuts off the masses from the soil, lessen their wages and their chances of employment, and increases the necessity for a means of certain subsistence, which slavery alone can furnish, when a few own all the lands and other capital.

Christian morality can find little practical foothold in a community so constituted, that to "love our neighbor as ourself," or "to do unto others as we would they should do unto us," would be acts of suicidal self-sacrifice. Christian morality, however, was not preached to free competitive society, but to slave society, where it is neither very difficult nor unnatural to practice it. In the various family relations of husband, wife, parent, child, master and slave, the observance of these Christian precepts is often practiced, and almost always promotes the temporal well being of those who observe it. The interests of the various members of the family circle, correctly understood, concur and harmonize, and each member best promotes his own selfish interest by ministering to the wants and interests of the rest. Two great stumbling blocks are removed from the acceptance of Scripture, when it is proved that slavery, which it recognizes, approves and enjoins, is promotive of men's happiness and well-being, and that the morality, which it inculcates, although wholly impracticable in free society, is readily practised in that form of society to which it was addressed.

We do not conceive that there can be any other moral law in free society, than that which teaches "that he is most meritorious who most wrongs his fellow beings:" for any other law would make men martyrs to their own virtues. We see thousands of good men vainly struggling against the evil necessities of their situation, and aggravating by their charities the evils which they would cure, for charity in free society is but the tax which skill and capital levy from the working poor, too often, to bestow on the less deserving and idle poor. We know a man at the North who owns millions of dollars, and would throw every cent into the ocean to benefit mankind. But it is capital, and, place it where he will, it becomes an engine to tax and oppress the laboring poor.

It is impossible to place labor and capital in harmonious or friendly relations, except by the means of slavery, which identifies their interests. Would that gentleman lay his capital out in land and negroes, he might be sure, in whatever hands it came, that it would be employed to protect laborers, not to oppress them; for when slaves are worth near a thousand dollars a head, they will be carefully and well provided for. In any other investment he may make of it, it will be used as an engine to squeeze the largest amount of labor from the poor, for the least amount of allowance. We say allowance, not wages; for neither slaves nor free laborers get wages, in the popular sense of the term: that is, the employer or capitalist pays them from nothing of his own, but allows them a part, generally a very small part, of the proceeds of their own labor. Free laborers pay one another, for labor creates all values, and capital, after taking the lion's share by its taxing power, but pays the so-called wages of one laborer from the proceeds of the labor of another. Capital does not breed, yet remains undiminished. Its profits are but its taxing power. Men seek to become independent, in order to cease to pay labor; in order to become masters, without the cares, duties and responsibilities of masters. Capital exercises a more perfect compulsion over free laborers, than human masters over slaves: for free laborers must at all times work or starve, and slaves are supported whether they work or not. Free laborers have less liberty than slaves, are worse paid and provided for, and have no valuable rights. Slaves, with more of actual practical liberty, with ampler allowance, and constant protection, are secure in the enjoyment of all the rights, which provide for their physical comfort at all times and under all circumstances. The free laborer must be employed or starve, yet no one is obliged to employ him. The slave is taken care of, whether employed or not. Though each free laborer has no particular master, his wants and other men's capital, make him a slave without a master, or with too many masters, which is as bad as none. It were often better that he had an ascertained master, instead of an irresponsible and unascertained one.

There are some startling social phenomena connected with this subject of labor and capital, which will probably be new to most of our readers. Legislators and philosophers often puzzle their own and other people's brains, in vain discussions as to how the taxes shall be laid, so as to fall on the rich rather than the poor. It results from our theory, that as labor creates all values, laborers pay all taxes, and the rich, in the words of Gerrit Smith, "are but the conduits that pass them over to government."

Again, since labor alone creates and pays the profits of capital; increase and accumulation of capital but increase the labor of the poor, and lessen their remuneration. Thus the poor are continually forging new chains for themselves. Proudhon cites a familiar instance to prove and illustrate this theory: A tenant improves a farm or house, and enhances their rents; his labor thus becomes the means of increasing the tax, which he or some one else must pay to the capitalist. What is true in this instance, is true of the aggregate capital of the world: its increase is but an increased tax on labor. A., by trade or speculation, gets hold of an additional million of dollars, to the capital already in existence. Now his million of dollars will yield no profit, unless a number of pauper laborers, sufficient to pay its profits, are at the same time brought into existence. After supporting their families, it will require a thousand of laborers to pay the interest or profits of a million of dollars. It may, therefore, be generally assumed as true, that where a country has gained a millionaire, it has by the same process gained a thousand pauper laborers: Provided it has been made by profits on foreign trade, or by new values created at home—that is, if it be an *addition* of a million to the capital of the nation.

A nation borrows a hundred millions, at six per cent., for a hundred years. During that time it pays, in way of tax, called interest, six times the capital loaned, and then returns the capital itself. During all this time, to the amount of the interest, the people of this nation have been slaves to the lender. He has commanded, not paid, for their labor; for his capital is returned intact. In the abstract, and according to equity, "the use of an article is only a proper subject of charge, when the article is consumed in the use; for this consumption is the consumption of the labor of the lender or hirer, and is the exchange of equal amounts of labor for each other.

A., as a merchant, a lawyer, or doctor, makes twenty dollars a day; that is, exchanges each day of his own labor for twenty days of the labor of common working men, assuming that they work at a dollar a day. In twenty years, he amasses fifty thousand dollars, invests it, and settles it on his family. Without any labor, he and his heirs, retaining all this capital, continue, by its means, to levy a tax of three thousand dollars from common laborers. He and his heirs now pay nothing for labor, but command it. They have nothing to pay except their capital, and that they retain. (This is the exploitation or despotism of capital, which has taken the place of domestic slavery, and is, in fact, a much worse kind of slavery. Hence arises socialism, which proposes to reconstruct society.) Now, this capitalist is considered highly meritorious for so doing, and the poor, self-sacrificing laborers, who really created his capital, and who pays its profits, are thought contemptible, if not criminal. In the general, those men are considered the most meritorious who live in greatest splendor, with the least, or with no labor, and they most contemptible, who labor most for others, and least for themselves. In the abstract, however, that dealing appears most correct, where men exchange equal amounts of labor, bear equal burdens for others, with those that they impose on them. Such is the golden rule of Scripture, but not the approved practice of mankind.

"The worth of a thing is just what it will bring," is the common trading principle of mankind. Yet men revolt at the extreme applications of their own principle, and denunciate any gross and palpable advantage taken of the wants, position and necessities of others as *swindling*. But we should recollect, that in all instances where unequal amounts of labor are exchanged at par, advantage is really taken by him who gets in exchange the larger amount of labor, of the wants, position and necessities of him who receives the smaller amount.

We have said that laborers pay all taxes, but labor being capital in slave society, the laborers or slaves are not injured by increased taxes; and the capitalist or master has to retrench his own expenses to meet the additional tax. Capital is not taxed in free society, but *is* taxed in slave society, because, in such society, labor is capital.

The capitalists and the professional can, and do, by increased profits and fees, throw the whole burden of taxation on the laboring class. Slaveholders cannot do so; for diminished allowance to their slaves would impair their value and lessen their own capital.

Our expose of what the socialists term the exploitation of skill and capital, will not, we know, be satisfactory to slaveholders even; for, although there be much less of such exploitation, or unjust exaction, in slave society; still, too much of it remains to be agreeable to contemplate. Besides, our analysis of human nature and human pursuits, is too dark and sombre to meet with ready acceptance. We should be rejoiced to see our theory refuted. We are sure, however, that it never can be; but equally sure, that it is subject to many modifications and limitations that have not occurred to us. We have this consolation, that in rejecting as false and noxious all systems of moral philosophy, we are thrown upon the Bible, as containing the only true system of morals. We have attempted already to adduce three instances, in which the justification of slavery furnished new and additional evidence of the truth of Christianity. We will now add others.

It is notorious that infidelity appeared in the world, on an extensive scale, only co-temporaneously with the abolition of slavery, and that it is now limited to countries where no domestic slavery exists. Besides, abolitionists are commonly infidels, as their speeches, conventions, and papers daily evince. Where there is no slavery, the minds of men are unsettled on all subjects, and there is, emphatically, faith and conviction about nothing. Their moral and social world is in a chaotic and anarchical state. Order, subordination and adaptation have vanished; and with them, the belief in a Deity, the author of all order. It had often been urged, that the order observable in the moral and physical world, furnished strong evidence of a Deity, the author of that order. How vastly is this argument now strengthened, by the new fact, now first developed, that the destruction of social order generates universal scepticism. Mere political revolutions affect social order but little, and generate but little infidelity. It remained for social revolutions, like those in Europe in 1848, to bring on an infidel age; for, outside of slave society, such is the age in which we live.

If we prove that domestic slavery is, in the general, a natural and necessary institution, we remove the greatest stumbling block to belief in the Bible; for whilst texts, detached and torn from their context, may be found for any other purpose, none can be found that even militates against slavery. The distorted and forced construction of certain passages, for this purpose, by abolitionists, if employed as a common rule of construction, would reduce the Bible to a mere allegory, to be interpreted to suit every vicious taste and wicked purpose.

But we have been looking merely to one side of human nature, and to that side rendered darker by the false, antagonistic and competitive relations in which so-called liberty and equality place man.

Man is, by nature, the most social and gregarious, and, therefore, the least selfish of animals. Within the family there is little room, opportunity or temptation to selfishness—and slavery leaves but little of the world without the family. Man loves that nearest to him best. First his wife, children and parents, then his slaves, next his neighbors and fellow-countrymen. But his unselfishness does not stop here. He is ready and anxious to relieve a famine in Ireland, and shudders when he reads of a murder at the antipodes. He feels deeply for the sufferings of domestic animals, and is rendered happy by witnessing the enjoyments of the flocks, and herds, and carroling birds that surround him. He sympathizes with all external nature. A parched field distresses him, and he rejoices as he sees the groves, and the gardens, and the plains flourishing, and blooming, and smiling about him. All men are philanthropists, and would benefit their fellow-men if they could. But we cannot be sure of benefiting those whom we cannot control. Hence, all actively good men are ambitious, and would be masters, in all save the name.

Benevolence, the love of what is without, and the disposition to incur pain or inconvenience to advance the happiness and well-being of what is without self, is as universal a motive of human conduct, as mere selfishness—which is the disposition to sacrifice the good of others to our own good.

The prevalent philosophy of the day takes cognizance of but half of human nature—and that the worst half. Our happiness is so involved in the happiness and well-being of everything around us, that a mere selfish philosophy, like political economy, is a very unsafe and delusive guide.

We employ the term Benevolence to express our outward affections, sympathies, tastes and feelings; but it is inadequate to express our meaning; it is not the opposite of selfishness, and unselfishness would be too negative for our purpose. Philosophy has been so busy with the worst feature of human nature, that it has not even found a name for this, its better feature. We must fall back on Christianity, which embraces man's whole nature, and though not a code of philosophy, is something better; for it proposes to lead us through the trials and intricacies of life, not by the mere cool calculations of the head, but by the unerring instincts of a pure and regenerate heart. The problem of the Moral World is too vast and complex for the human mind to comprehend; yet the pure heart will, safely and quietly, feel its way through the mazes that confound the head.

Henry Kyd Douglas
(1840–1903)

"Oh, for the presence and inspiration of Old Jack for just one hour!" That sentiment, as expressed by Colonel A. S. "Sandy" Pendleton and reported by Henry Kyd Douglas in his *I Rode with Stonewall*, was shared by all of the South in the campaigns that followed General Stonewall Jackson's accidental shooting death at Chancellorsville. Douglas's memoir of the war provides a portrait of the sainted commander that, although it may be somewhat idealized, is surely more accurate than much of the Jackson legend, describing the general simply as "a soldier of great ability, who left behind a great reverence and tender memory."

Born at Shepherdstown, West Virginia (then Virginia), in 1840, Douglas was educated as a lawyer and admitted to the bar in 1860. He enlisted in the Confederate army in 1861 and served as a private, corporal, and lieutenant, in the Second Virginia Infantry before joining Jackson's staff as assistant inspector general. Some historians believe it may have been Douglas who lost the infamous "Special Orders 191," which fell into Union hands and resulted in the reversal of Lee's invasion of the North at the battle of Antietam. Douglas, who had been wounded a number of times, was captured at Gettysburg on July 3, 1863, after which he spent the following winter in Johnson's Island Prison. Paroled and exchanged in 1864, he was promoted to brigadier general, and his troops fired the last shot at Appomattox. He began keeping the diaries that would become *I Rode with Stonewall* in late 1862, and though he reworked his "Stonewall Papers" to prepare them for publication in 1899, they were not actually published until 1940, by his nephew John Kyd Beckenbaugh.

from *I Rode With Stonewall: Being Chiefly the War Experiences of the Youngest Member of Jackson's Staff from the John Brown Raid to the Hanging of Mrs. Surratt*

22. Wounded and In Prison

I remained at Gettysburg for more than a month. I had nothing to complain of and no sympathy with those who looked for something unpleasant and found it. Dr. Ward, the surgeon in charge, was not only thoroughly qualified for his position, but he did not think it necessary to impress upon his captives that he had an eye on them and was incensed at their iniquity. He was a gentleman, from Indiana I believe. His assistant, who had immediate professional charge of me, was my personal friend, Dr. Harry Leaman of Lancaster, now of Philadelphia. I had known him at college: his brother was in the class before me, he in the one after me. His daily visits, often two or three a day, were a personal pleasure.

And then appeared upon the scene a little Sister from St. Joseph's at Emmittsburg. She looked very young and was very capable; she touched my room so as to make me forget I was in prison; she made me delicate things to eat until I thought peacocks brains would be no delicacy. She was from Mississippi and had a young brother in the Confederate army. Her beauty was her only tinge of mortality—how fresh and beautiful she was! But her devotion to duty, her self-forgetfulness, her gentle manner must have made every man she met her friend and guardian. And then, when no longer needed, she glided away—went to other duties, doubtless, never looking behind. There is no crown in Heaven too good for such an angel!

We had many visitors, some from curiosity, some in kindness. There was a comfortable chair which one man had sent me, and a lady brought the dainty curtains, which my "Little Catholic Sister" hung at the window, gracefully veiling with her deft white hands the blue sky beyond, to which she seemed to belong.

I was furnished with books, too, light and interesting, and one day a young gentleman, Mr. Samuel M. Smucker brought me *Les Miserables*. It was just what I wanted in that place—plenty of reading for plenty of time, full of war and of love, full of wit, wisdom, everything; never before nor since have I enjoyed a book so much. It was translated, I remember, by a lady from Savannah, Georgia, during the war and, being admirably done, was reprinted in the North. Anyone who has read it can well understand what a treat it would be at such a time and in such a place.

Nearby lived two young ladies who were great favorites in the Hospital because their generous hearts did not, apparently, distinguish the color of uniforms—loyal as they were—and on occasional nights, when Dr. Ward was conveniently absent or not visible, I would stroll with them to make visits in the town, the marks on the sleeve of my uninjured arm being artfully concealed by some little female headgear which I was directed to carry just that way; and marching between the sisters—*in medio tutissimus ibis*—we generally landed at Duncan's and made an evening of it. It never seemed to occur to them that they were harboring a Rebel; and nothing occurred to me except their graciousness and attractiveness.

Before I left the Theological Seminary, I entrusted to Dr. Leaman a map which I valued, for it was one of the maps used by General Jackson in his Maryland and Valley campaign, which he had afterwards given to me. Dr. Leaman was to keep it until after the war, and then, if I were living, he was to return it to me, if not living, to keep it as a souvenir of our meeting at Gettysburg. When my imprisonment ended and I got back to Dixie, I was soon active in the army and forgot what had become of the map. After keeping it safely for twenty-nine years Leaman wrote to me that he had lost it twice and rediscovered it, and, in order to relieve himself of the trust, he sent it to me. It is among the few mementoes of the war I have not been persuaded to part with.

I left the ecclesiastical hospital with regrets for I did not again expect to be so well placed, and never was. I was taken to Baltimore and confined in West Buildings Hospital under stricter regulations. The surgeon in charge, Dr. George Rex, tried to make believe, by his growling and unsmiling countenance, that he was an old bear, but there were a lot of us he didn't deceive. He was simply an old gnarled oak with rough bark, sound and all right at the heart. I had a lot of friends in Baltimore who would send me things against the rules. The Doctor would publicly refuse to let me have them and turn them over to the female stewardess, or housekeeper, or whatever she was; and I got them. They were two of a kind, and she was just as much of a fraud in her generous way as he was.

"Douglas, you *must* write to your friend Johnston." (Henry E. Johnston, a banker, whose kindness had no bounds because I had been able to do his brother, Elliott, a small favor when he was wounded and lost a leg at Sharpsburg.) "He ought to know that I couldn't let you have that wine and bottles of brandy and whiskey he sent to you today. I turned it over to the stewardess."

"All right, Doctor, I'll do it"; and I did. I wrote to Johnston not to send me any more such forbidden fruit—until this was gone. When evening came, the stewardess sent for me and told me in the tones of a shrew that she must set her face against such donations—and then gave them to me as I wanted them.

Many a sick and wounded prisoner, who had no friends in Baltimore, found imprisonment and sufferings more tolerable because of the good things to eat and drink that Johnston, his good mother and sister, and others of the same disposition lavished upon me at the West Buildings. Unless they believed I was a hydra-headed cormorant, they never expected me to devour such supplies of high-toned commissary stores. But it was all just like Baltimore in those days, and all days after, when suffering was abroad in the South. And Dr. Rex and his female coadjutor were just like themselves and like no other pair I ever met. As jailors they were trumps. I had books and flowers sent me and a box of dominoes, a Yankee puzzle, and a jewsharp. The last is the only musical instrument I ever studied with any success. I wrestled with it valorously but just as I began to understand its technique and comprehend its expression and realize the beauty of its simplicity, it disappeared. Some people have no ear for music.

I have spoken of the parole given me at Gettysburg by Major Young, Fourth Pennsylvania Cavalry. This is the language of it, written by Major Young:

"Know all men that we the undersigned in consideration of our release from capture by the military authorities of the United States do hereby solemnly pledge our word of honor not to do or undertake any act or to exert any influence for the advantage of the Confederate army or against the Government of the United States during the continuance of the present war or until regularly included in an authorized exchange of prisoners of war." (Here follows the signatures of myself and the wounded in the barn of Mr. Picking.)

"Signed in presence of

"HY. KYD DOUGLAS, Maj. and A. A. Genl.
"S.B.M. YOUNG, Major 4 Penn. Cavl."

In Gettysburg, when well enough, I had sent the paper to General D. N. Couch, United States Army, asking that I be relieved from confinement. After some weeks he returned it, saying he was without authority in the matter and I had better apply to the War Department. On the 27th of September, while at West Buildings, I addressed a communication to General Lorenzo Thomas, Adjutant General, enclosing a copy of the foregoing paper and asking that under its terms I be released from confinement on parole. I stated that I had given my parole in good faith and believed that I was bound by it, that I had strictly observed its provisions, that I had supposed Major Young had a right to require such a parole from me and to take it, that if he had not, I was in no fault, that I had released Major J. H. Whittlesey, Fifth United States Cavalry, when captured, sick in Winchester in May, 1862, in the same way and he was allowed to return to his lines (enclosing a strong letter from Major Whittlesey confirming my statement as to his release and that of other officers), that I had not doubted that I would be released, when sufficiently recovered, upon application, and that now I made the application in accordance with the written parole.

This communication was kindly delivered at the War Department by Captain Horatio C. King of General Samuel Heintzelman's staff. Being referred to Colonel William H. Hoffman, Commissary General of prisoners, it was returned by him to me through General R. C. Schenck's Headquarters with an endorsement: that my parole was "only a personal obligation" between myself and Major Young; that if I had made my "escape while under parole and had again been captured by the U.S. forces," I "could not have been held for break of parole"; that my parole "only remained in force until a superior authority thought proper to set it aside"; that I was simply like any "other prisoner of war." The petition was refused, and from this there was no appeal. While appreciating the grim irony of such reasoning, I knew perfectly well that if I had escaped, got into battle, killed some Union officer, and been recaptured, the same Colonel Hoffman would have given better reasons for shooting or hanging me.

It was then thought I was combative enough to get out of a hospital and should be removed hence. I was started northward, and celebrated my birthday on September 29, 1863, by landing at Johnson's Island military prison, out in Lake Erie, and off from Sandusky, Ohio. I soon found that I was in a much colder temperature, climatic and otherwise. But I had plenty of company, about 1,500 Confederate officers of all ranks, and several hundred privates. Still the 42° of Latitude, North, is hardly the place Southerners would select as a winter resort. Johnson's Island, however, was just the place to convert visitors to the theological belief of the Norwegian that Hell has torments of cold instead of heat.

To a newcomer the outlook was not hopeful. The prison was an oblong, bare piece of ground enclosed by a high fence, and perched up on this fence, or barricade, at intervals, in sentry boxes, were armed sentinels. The barracks or prison houses were long buildings, hastily erected of wood and weatherboard, called wards. The weatherboarding was a single layer nailed to upright beams, and there was no plastering of any kind. The weatherboarding would sometimes warp, and in all rooms there were many knotholes, through which one lying in bed could look out upon the moon or the water; but when the weather got below zero, the scenery was scarcely compensation for the suffering. Bunks were ranged along the walls—if they can be called walls—in three tiers. In my room or ward, there were sixty of these. There was one stove in the middle of the room, which kept the room fairly comfortable within a certain range, except in very cold weather. It was about like living in a canvas tent. Of course out on that lake, the weather became excessively cold, below zero, and not infrequently drove the sentinels from their posts, knowing well enough that no prisoner could escape and live.

On the 9th and 21st of January, 1864—I am not so sure of one of the dates—the thermometer fell to 28° below zero. The former of the two nights I spent in the hospital, which was in the enclosure, nursing a very young fellow from Mobile, who, babbling in his delirium of flowers and fields and playing with his mother and sister in his sunny land, died before morning. During the night Captain Stagg of a Louisiana regiment was frozen so badly that when he was discovered in the morning he was speechless, and it required vigorous measures under a physician's directions to restore him. That same night, as often before or after, two men would squeeze into one bunk so as to double blankets, would wrap themselves up head and feet, and in the morning break through crackling ice, formed by the congealing of the breath that escaped, as one has seen on the blankets of horses in sleighing time.

Poor Captain Stagg had other troubles. His wife was in New Orleans, always used Creole French, and could neither read nor write English. She evidently regarded English with as much disfavor as some of the Pennsylvania Dutch. But as the letter censor could not read French—and all our letters were read—the Captain's letters to and from his wife could not pass that Cerberus. Stagg was in despair until my namesake, Major Henry Douglas, United States Army, whom I did not know, came to the rescue at my request and kindly took charge of that correspondence.

There has been much crimination and recrimination as to the relative treatment of prisoners at Andersonville and Johnson's Island, Libby Prison and Camp Douglas at Chicago. Into this I do not propose to enter. That there was a deal of suffering by those confined in Southern prisons I have no doubt; that the guards and managers of these prisons were often grossly negligent and careless of the health and comfort of their prisoners I do not question. Prisoners therein suffered from the same criminal neglect and ignorance that the Confederate soldiers in the field suffered from. But the conditions of the two peoples were entirely different. The North had everything it wanted and the world to draw from. With a large territory, exposed to invasion on only one border, it could place its prisoners and hospitals where it preferred. The South was cut off from the world; was being invaded on all sides; scarcely knew where it could safely locate its prisons and hospitals; had little in itself and access to nothing it hadn't; medicine and drugs, especially such as are needed as a protection against fever, were contraband— that seems barbarous—and very scarce; and at last had so little food that the soldiers in the field became as emaciated and haggard as their prisoners.

With such a large, protected territory, I do not think any fair man in the North will attempt to defend the selection of Lake Erie as a winter prison for Southern soldiers, any more than he would have excused the selection of the malarial regions of southern Florida or Louisiana as a summer prison for Northern troops. Personally, I believe that the general suffering and ill treatment of prisoners on both sides have been grossly exaggerated, and I do not believe, with exceptions here and there, that there was intentional and willful cruelty on either side as a rule; there were hardships and suffering among prisoners on both sides from neglect, incompetency, and indifference.

If half the statements about the treatment of our soldiers in the Spanish war by their own government are true, its inhumanity exceeds anything that was ever charged against either government during the four terrible years of the Civil War. They were sometimes half-starved for want of food, but they were never poisoned with it. At any rate, when it is known that out of 270,000 prisoners in the South 22,576 died, and out of 220,000 Southern prisoners in the North 26,246 died, it ought to stop a great deal of the wild talk about Libby Prison and Andersonville.

The food we received at Johnson's Island was not, except at times, such as a prisoner had a right to complain of. Then, too, we were allowed to receive boxes of provisions, under reasonable restrictions, from our friends, and we received many such contributions. It may be stated frankly that the Southern people never forgot their soldiers in prison and, however reduced in circumstances, never missed an opportunity to send them what they could; their many friends in the North acted much in the same way. On the contrary, Northern people were singularly indifferent to the fate of their own soldiers and took little pains, individually, to assist them. Of course there were many exceptions where there were sons or brothers in captivity, but I have heard the complaint made time and again by Union soldiers and bitter contrasts drawn. This may be because there were so many foreigners and substitutes in the Federal army and so many others who looked to the government for help; for some reason not much thought was given to the wants of those in captivity.

The hospital arrangements and the medical attendance were good. The officers and guards, with rare exceptions, were civil and considerate. There was a regulation that all lights must be out at 10:00 P.M. and no visiting was allowed between different buildings or wards after 9:00. On one or two occasions drunken sentinels on post fired into wards through the weather-boarding at candles that had been lighted because of the sudden sickness of a prisoner; on another, a man was shot in the thigh running to his ward, after he had overstayed the hour of 9:00 visiting friends.

The regulations limited the length of the letters we wrote or received to one page of note paper, because the censor could not get through such a mass of letters, daily, if there was not some limit to their length. This was plausible, but it was a nuisance all the same. General M. Jefferson Thompson sent for the censor, an excellent fellow, to whom I was indebted for many kindnesses afterwards, and made an arrangement by which he was to put aside all long letters until night and then examine them for the compensation of one-half cent for each and every page over the allowance, to be paid at the end of each week by an order on the Treasurer outside, who kept our money. It was a great scheme all around; the censor, a sergeant, quadrupled his soldier's pay, and we got bulky letters, which we were satisfied he never looked at, except to tear open and count the pages. I had bundles of letters of twenty and more pages, and wrote the same, and hours were spent reading and writing them.

There came a carload of boxes for the prisoners about Christmas which, after reasonable inspection, they were allowed to receive. My box from home contained more cause for merriment and speculation as to its contents than satisfaction. It had received rough treatment on its way, and a bottle of catsup had been broken and its contents very generally distributed through the box. Mince pie and fruit cake saturated with tomato catsup was about as palatable as "embalmed beef" of Cuban memory; but there were other things. Then, too, a friend had sent me in a package a bottle of old brandy. On Christmas morning I quietly called several comrades up into my bunk to taste of the precious fluid—of disappointment. The bottle had been opened outside, the brandy taken and replaced with water, adroitly recorked, and sent in. I hope the Yankee who played that practical joke lived to repent it and was shot before the war ended. But then there came from my same friend, Johnston of Baltimore, a box containing thirty pieces of clothing, for such disposition as I chose to make of them, and another box of hams, chickens, biscuits and cigars for my own mess; and from Mrs. Mary T. Semmes—aunt of the "Alabama" Semmes—another wholesale box of coffee, whiskey, sugar, cigars, gloves, soap, worsted nightcaps, Tennyson's poems, a spinning top (from her grandson), etc. She duplicated it afterwards.

There was nothing about Johnson's Island to resemble the one Robinson Crusoe was cast up on except the absence of the fair sex; but we heard from them. He didn't. News from home told of the death of my horse, "Prince," the one my mother had driven to Gettysburg. He was blind and had fallen over the cliffs into the canal and drowned. I sent my sister a dozen stanzas—in memoriam—which kept up my temperature for a while.

I was surprised about this time to receive a letter from Enoch, whom I have spoken of as my father's colored coachman. He had gone off from home and was living in Harrisburg, Pennsylvania, working for his living, in freedom, but harder than he ever did in his life. He wrote to say that he heard I was wounded and in prison and was having a hard time, and that he had laid aside several hundred dollars and would send it to me, or as much as I wanted, if I were suffering or needed it. His letter was in his own untutored language, but its words were verily apples of gold. I did not need his money, but I hope I wrote him a letter that left no doubt of my appreciation and my gratitude. Poor Enoch, I never saw him again. I do not know that he survived the war; but our old "Aunt Hannah," his companion in slavery, said "he worked hisself to death for a lazy yaller free nigger gal he married up there." In his case, freedom brought him only bondage.

Early in February I was taken with chills which I was advised was a dangerous symptom in that climate at that season of the year. About the middle of the month several hundred of the prisoners were to be taken farther south, but my name was not on the list. My friend the letter censor had become anxious as to the result of my chills, and he undertook upon his own motion to get my name on the list. I was not particularly informed of the method by which it was done, but years afterwards when I heard of men in cities casting their political ballots in dead men's names, I was not as surprised as I might have been. My faithful sergeant took, for humanity's sake, a double risk, for he not only was passing out of that prison one who was expected to remain, but he was perhaps saving the life of a Rebel soldier, who thus with his aid did "live to fight another day." General Jeff Thompson of Missouri was one of those sent out and may be said to have been the leader of that expedition. Arrayed in a black overcoat with a black cape, I looked more like a young clergyman than ever, and it pleased Thompson to refer to me as his chaplain.

We had a prisoners' ovation going through Baltimore and were hustled through that city at a quick step and put on board a steamer for Point Lookout, a point of land in southern Maryland on the west coast of the Chesapeake Bay, on which there was a prison and a hospital. I was rather startled to see the next day in a Philadelphia paper that after passing Harrisburg I had attempted to make my escape by jumping off the train, was thrown under the cars, and had my legs cut off. Some letters of enquiry followed hurriedly, and the rumor disarranged my correspondence for some time. I understood afterwards that some one had attempted that feat and was killed.

I was now in a much milder climate and the place was still different from any other I had seen. I began to look about me and adapt myself to the situation and soon found the change from Johnson's Island an agreeable one. I was soon on pleasant terms with Captain Patterson, the Provost Marshall, an excellent officer who managed to do his duty strictly, but with admirable suavity. His wife and his wife's sister, being Southern women, were not excessively loyal, although very discreet; and the sister saw no harm in furnishing me books and strolling along the beach at times within bounds: and neither did I. We fought over *Vanity Fair*—and I gave her the name of Becky Sharp—but we did not fight over the war, for I was fond of the little suppers I was invited to.

General E. B. Tyler, commanding, with Headquarters at Baltimore, came once to the prison and called to deliver a letter entrusted to him from a friend of mine he knew. He was extremely courteous and then began an acquaintance and friendship which lasted until his death, years after the war. After he left, all my letters were sent to the care of Captain Patterson and I received them unopened. My replies went out with the same security—under the promise of course that I neither would send nor receive any letters not strictly personal. I was in Ward 15, Hammond General Hospital, and there was a surgeon of like civility to whom some of my letters were addressed. One is lying before me now, which contained a photograph I still have after these thirty-five years; and another, containing two pages of rhyme, clever, humorous and a bit satirical; and another accompanying some bottles of peach brandy and a bottle of quaker honey, that I might have "peach-and-honey" as a morning tipple. Although I never could take a breakfast appetizer I, at least, could enjoy the pleasure it gave my wardmates, Colonel Gibson of Georgia, Colonel Leventhrope of North Carolina, and our surgeon, the good Dr. M——.

After a month at Point Lookout, rumors of coming exchange were flying through the air. General B. F. Butler, Federal Commissioner of Exchange at Fortress Monroe, had visited the Hospital and inspected it. "Butcher" Weyler was never more hated by the Cubans, than "Beast" Butler was, at that time, by Confederates. When he passed through our ward, there was death-like silence. He asked if there were any complaints of treatment; no one spoke. That they should be his prisoners added gall to their bitterness.

A few days after, on the 17th of March, a large vessel came steaming up to the Point, sent for prisoners. There was excitement and bustle through prison wards and hospital. Word was sent for those who were to leave to pack up and get ready at once and there was no delay. I slipped over to Captain Patterson's to tell the news of my departure and to get a last lunch in that lovely and hospitable household. When the time came everybody was at the boat and the soldiers quickly crowded aboard. I lingered to talk to those who had been so kind to me and among the last ascended the gang-plank with all my impedimenta.

Just as I touched the boat, a young officer hastily came up and took me off. Orders had come from Brigadier General Gilmon Marston, commanding the post, that I was not to be exchanged, and a private took my black hand trunk and bundle to carry them back to prison. I had met Major John E. Mulford, the Federal agent for exchange of prisoners, on the boat coming from Baltimore and he had been exceedingly civil to me. The young officer who had charge of me, evidently chagrined with his duty, offered his assistance in every way. He asked for Major Mulford; he was not on board. The Captain said he would take a note to him, and I hastily wrote him of what had happened and asked his intervention. The ropes were loosened, the whistle blown, and soon the boat, laden with rejoicing men, was churning the water into foam as it moved toward Dixie. Dejected, in spite of the cheerful attitude of "Becky Sharp" and others, I moved back to my old ward, nearly emptied out; and it did not add buoyancy to my spirits to be told, as I was, that it was rumored at Marston's Headquarters that I was to be put in irons and close confinement in retaliation for someone thus being punished in Richmond. I had a good, long, late supper that night at any rate. But when the Doctor came with me to the gloomy ward, I quickly got into my cot and was soon asleep.

About three o'clock at night there was a flash of light upon my face, and I awoke to see a group of officers standing near. Was it necessary to put a man in irons at this unseemly hour of night? I began to growl; why this infernal haste, etc.? My sleepy mutterings were broken by the cheery voice of Patterson.

"Hurry up, don't swear, dress yourself and get out of this quick if you want to go to Dixie!"

Enough said. I was dressed in a twinkling.

"This is Captain Puffer of General Butler's staff, and the General has sent for you."

In a few minutes we were on the boat and off for Old Point, and on the *Grey-hound*, the General's famous dispatch boat, the fastest one afloat. Major Mulford had received my note, had seen General Butler, and this was the result, in spite of General Marston's order.

What a host on such a boat Captain A. T. Puffer was.

"Breakfast, there, a good one, at daylight and steaming hot," he cried out to a man below.

Upon the first invitation I reversed my decision not to take an "antifogmatic" so early in the morning. There were half a dozen in the party besides Captain Puffer, who was half a dozen more. We took "morning bitters" with one, "an eye-opener" with another, a "pre-prandial" with another, and then an "appetizer" all together, and when breakfast was ready at daylight, so were we.

The little boat ran through the water like a shark, and in the quickest possible time we were under the shadow of Fortress Monroe. A little off rocked the boat which had left me behind at Point Lookout, and in a little while, after saying my thanks and good-by to Captain Puffer and his delightful party, I was on board of her, shaking hands with Major Mulford.

I did not see General Butler, and had no opportunity to ascertain the cause of his extraordinary kindness in taking me out of the clutches of General Marston. Years afterwards, when he was Governor of Massachusetts, he came to Bar Harbor, where I was, for an outing on his yacht *American*, and invited me with several gentlemen to go out one day for some deep-sea fishing. Sitting on deck on our return, over a glass of rum and aerated water, I broached the subject, and ascertained what I wanted to know.

At the time I speak of, it will be remembered that he was in very bad odor with the Confederate government, and he and Judge Ould, the Confederate Commissioner of Exchange, had been carrying on a correspondence so acrid and so full of vituperative heat that their letters would doubtless have set fire to the mails, had they not been carried by water. This was all official and for public consumption and exasperation, whereas between themselves their mutual indignation and hurling of epithets were purely Pickwickian. War was its side lights and byplays. These two frowning officials, who had known each other well before the War and I think had been together in the National Democratic Convention in Charleston, South Carolina, in 1860, when Butler voted fifty-seven ballots to nominate Jefferson Davis as the Democratic candidate for President, had a personal agreement that whatever be the obstacles in Exchange, they would each show courtesy enough to the other to send through any prisoners especially asked for.

It seems that Judge Ould had asked that Captain Cabell Breckinridge, a son of General John C. Breckinridge, Major Buckner, a brother, I think, of Major General Simon B. Buckner, and myself be sent through for exchange, and perhaps others. Of course General Butler could not allow any little plans General Marston might have for my further incarceration to interfere with his promise to Judge Ould! Hence the proceedings I have related, which I could not explain until I saw Governor Butler. I asked him, then, after my convivial friend Captain Puffer and found he had gone to the other side of the inevitable river.

We left Fortress Monroe some time during the day and when we were well under way Major Mulford sent down into the vessel among the prisoners and directed that

Buckner, Breckinridge and myself should join him on deck. He kindly took us into the salon of the boat and introduced us to his wife and sister, by whom we were received most graciously. After this both Breckinridge and Buckner vanish from my recollection, although they doubtless fared just as well. I was given comfortable quarters in a stateroom and the hold of that vessel knew me no more.

To add to the novelty of the situation and its fascinating excitement, I was introduced to Mrs. M. Todd White of Alabama, who was immediately given to my charge to escort to Richmond, which proved to be a most agreeable duty. Mrs. White was a sister, a half-sister, of Mrs. President Lincoln, and now that she is dead at an untimely age I may add, was young, handsome, and of great personal charm of manner. Six weeks before she had gone through the lines, partially on a visit to her sister at the White House, and was now returning.

What she had in the thirteen trunks she now carried was of much curiosity to General Butler, when I saw him. He had not permitted them to be examined at Fortress Monroe, for he suspected there might be some things discovered that were contraband. This discovery would have involved the detention of Mrs. White and her trunks, a public disclosure, his own embarrassment and the especial embarrassment of President Lincoln, who would have released her and brought on himself bombardment from the Democratic press of the North. All this "Old Ben" took in when the Provost Marshall reported to him this mass of luggage, and he shrewdly adopted the wisest and most politic course by letting Mrs. White and her trunks go on their way.

I can account for one of the trunks, for it was turned over to me at Richmond for delivery: it contained the trousseau of Miss Hetty Carey of Baltimore, then in Richmond. She was the most beautiful woman of her day and generation; in January of the next year she became the bride of General John Pegram and was a widow within three weeks. General John Morgan, having escaped from prison, arrived in Richmond just then, and he and his staff might have told the contents of another trunk which was intended for a hospital. But no hospital can successfully compete with a Kentucky woman's hospitality to a Kentucky hero.

At City Point on the 19th we took leave of Major John E. Mulford and his charming family. The name of this courteous and generous gentleman should be held in lasting memory in every Southern household who had a prisoner of war pass through his hands; and it is pleasant to recall that when, after the war, he sought to make Richmond his home, he could have gone nowhere, where he would have been welcomed and received with more cordiality and good-will.

Not knowing the straits to which Richmond had been reduced in matters of luxury since Gettysburg, I telegraphed from City Point for a carriage and baggage wagon to meet me at the wharf on the arrival of our boat, in provision for Mrs. White and her luggage. I wish I had a photograph of the turnout which an old dilapidated Negro, with a burnished, napless silk hat, brought for us: a decaying carriage with two old condemned horses, leaning against each other for mutual support, and a baggage wagon and horses a few shades worse. But they managed to haul us to "The Spotswood," passing the Capitol grounds where President Davis was reviewing the returned prisoners, for which service I paid the polite old darkey, the modest compensation of one hundred dollars, in Confederate money.

The next night, upon invitation of the President, Mrs. White called upon him and Mrs. Davis. I took her in the same turnout, for the same compensation, and met the occupants of the Confederate White House. Mr. Davis who was one of the most dignified and accomplished men that ever occupied a public position, impressed me with the respect and admiration which all men had in his presence, Mrs. Davis with the entertaining cleverness and keen perception that always marked her conversations. Mrs. White, like all her sisters, was a Kentuckian, a Southerner, and a Confederate in every impulse of her nature. Mrs. Lincoln, herself, and Mrs. Grant were loyal to their great husbands and their husbands' cause, but their kindly feelings for their own Southern people were well-known.

Confederate currency had long ceased to maintain any respectable commercial relation with gold; before long it fell below 16 to 1, and gave us warning that a government fiat cannot give value to money. I paid $30 per day for board at "The Spotswood," it cost a friend $300 to give half a dozen of us a night supper at an eating house, and a little later I gave $9.75 (why not $10.00?) for two mint juleps, $1,500 for a uniform, and was offered $5,800 for a horse worth, perhaps, $250. About this time a Confederate cavalryman, being offered $5,000 for a somewhat seedy-looking steed, proudly reined up his bony Bucephalus and explained,

"Five thousand dollars for this horse! Why, I gave a thousand dollars this morning for currying him!"

The Confederate soldier was then serving his country for less than forty cents a month in gold; he was virtually fighting without pay, without bounty, and with no expectation of a pension. Pay day became a sarcasm and a jest. The soldiers' money would buy nothing; it was only good to gamble with.

> *But our boys thought little of price or pay*
> *Or of bills that were over due;*
> *We knew if it bought our bread today*
> *'Twas the best our poor country could do.*
> *I'll keep it—it tells our history o'er*
> *From the birth of our dreams to its last,*
> *Modest and born of an Angel Hope,*
> *Like our hope of success, it passed.*

Edward A. Pollard

(1831–1872)

Edward A. Pollard became editor of the *Daily Richmond Examiner* in 1861. Throughout the years of the Civil War, he used that post to denounce bitterly Jefferson Davis, insisting that he was unfit for his office. One of the most prolific Southern writers of his era, Pollard's style is journalistic and unscientific, and his histories are, in many respects, undependable, though his works were very popular in their day. In 1862, Pollard began publishing his history of the Civil War under the title *The First Year of the War* and followed with other parts year by year, varying the title by *Second, Third,* and *Fourth.* In 1864, he was captured while running the blockade in the steamer *Greyhound,* with the intention of going to England to promote the sale of his books. He was eventually placed in solitary confinement at Fortress Monroe before he was finally exchanged in 1864, when he returned to Richmond. After the war, he combined his four histories under the title *Southern History of the War* (1866) and also rehashed it into another volume, *The Lost Cause; a New Southern History of the War of the Confederates* (1866). All of his histories are notable for his hostility to Davis, whom he identified as the primary cause for the South's defeat.

from *Southern History of the War*

IV.

The peaceful and fortunate career on which Mr. Jefferson's administration launched the country was to meet with a singular interruption. That interruption was the sectional agitation which finally broke the bonds of the Union and plunged North and South into one of the fiercest wars of modern times. The occasion of that conflict was what the Yankees called—by one of their convenient libels in political nomenclature—*slavery;* but what was in fact nothing more than a system of negro servitude in the South; well guarded by laws, which protected the negro laborer in the rights of humanity; moderated by Christian sentiments which provided for his welfare; and, altogether, one of the mildest and most beneficent systems of servitude in the world.

It is not our purpose here to enter upon a moral defence of slavery in the South (using, as we would remind the reader, that opprobrious term, wherever it occurs in these pages, under a constant protest, and simply because it has become the familiar word in the party controversies of America to describe the peculiar institution of labor in the South). Our object in these pages is simply with the political complications of slavery. But as a problem in morals there are but two principles which decide it; and these we may briefly turn our pen to announce, candidly believing them to be the summary of the entire ethics of negro servitude in the South:

1. The white being the superior race, and the black the inferior, subordination, with or without law, must be the status of the African in the mixed society of whites and blacks.

2. It thus becomes the interest of both races, especially of the inferior race, that this status should be fixed and protected by law; and it was simply the declaration and definition of this principle that went by the name of negro slavery in the South.

Slavery (without that moderation of legislative checks and Christian sentiments which were the constant employment of the South) had been planted in America by the direct and persistent action of the British government. It was the common law of the thirteen colonies before their separation from England. The mother country established negro slavery in the colonies. It maintained and protected the institution. It originated and carried on the slave trade. It forbade the colonies permission either to emancipate or export their slaves. It prohibited them from inaugurating any legislation in diminution or discouragement of the institution. Even after the Continental Congress had been assembled, and the battle of Lexington had been fought, the earl of Dartmouth, British Secretary of State, in answer to a remonstrance from the agent of the colonies on the subject of the slave trade, replied: "We cannot allow the colonies to check or discourage in any degree a traffic so beneficial to the nation."

In the constitution of the United States, the slavery question had been singularly accommodated. Two clauses covered it. The first guaranteed to the South its property—it provided for the return of slaves recognized as the property of their Southern masters. Another clause, in the interest of the North, prevented a disturbance of the representative system by an importation of slaves, and provided that the South should not increase her negro population (five of which in the basis of representation were made equal to three white men) by importation after the lapse of twenty years.

The political history of the slavery question in the early periods of the American Union is scarcely more than an enumeration of dates or of measures which were taken as matters of course. The action of the first Congress, in relation to slavery in the territories, was simply to acquiesce in a government for the Northwest territory, based upon a *pre-existing* anti-slavery ordinance—the ordinance of 1781–87. The Fugitive Slave Act of 1793 was passed without opposition and without a division in the Senate; and in the House, by a vote of forty-eight to seven. The slave trade was declared piracy. Petitions upon the slavery question were at first referred to a committee; and afterwards were rejected, and in one instance returned to the petitioner. Louisiana and Florida, both slaveholding countries, were added to our territories without agitation in Congress. Kentucky, Tennessee, Mississippi, and Alabama were admitted into the Union, bringing the institution of slavery with them, without a murmur of opposition.

It is to be remarked, however, that that jealousy of Southern domination which was the characteristic and controlling element of the Northern mind, and which afterwards became singularly associated with the slavery discussion, may be dated with the acquisition of Louisiana. The famous Hartford Convention, held in 1814, aimed two remarkable blows at the power of the South. It proposed to strike down the slave representation in Congress, and to have the representation conformed to the number of free persons in the Union; and as a further restriction upon the power of the South—the extension of our territory being then in that direction—it proposed an amendment to the constitution, to the effect that no new States should be admitted into the Union without the concurrence of two-thirds of both Houses of Congress.

But the slavery question was as yet only incidental to this sectional rivalry, and was scarcely yet developed into a distinct and independent controversy. There was some general discussion as to the policy of the extension of slavery into the new territories; and some political union, without, however, any distinct lines of party organization, had already been occasioned in the North by a proposition to extend the ordinance of 1787 west of the Mississippi River. It is a remarkable circumstance, in connection with these early discussions of the "Free Soil" school, that Mr. Jefferson, notwithstanding his connection with the ordinance of 1787, was in favor of the free and unlimited extension of slavery over the new soil acquired by the United States. And he maintained this view on a very singular and ingenious ground: it was that "the diffusion of the slaves over a greater surface would make them individually happier, and proportionably facilitate the accomplishment of their emancipation, by dividing the burden on a greater number of coadjutors."

It may be said generally—notwithstanding the episode of the Hartford Convention—which fell into early disrepute—that there was nothing in the precedents of the Government to betoken that wild and violent controversy nursed in the selfish mind of the North, which, in 1820, was to break through the bonds of secret jealousy and array the country into two sectional parties struggling for supremacy, on opposite convictions, or perhaps on opposite pretences, with regard to the slavery question.

The Missouri legislation—by which the institution of slavery was bounded by a line of latitude—naturally divided the United States into geographical parties, and tore the country in twain. It created for the first time a distinct political North and a distinct political South. It is to be taken as the proper initial point of that war of sections which raged in America for forty years, and at last culminated in an appeal to arms. The discussion of the Missouri matter awoke the anti-slavery sentiment of the country that had for some years past been almost completely dormant. It was the occasion of a call of a convention of abolitionists at Philadelphia. It fired the passions of the populace, and to the serious statesmen of the country gave unbounded alarm. "From the battle of Bunker's Hill to the treaty of Paris we never had so ominous a question," said Mr. Jefferson. To a friend he wrote: "This momentous question, like a fire-bell in the night, awakened and filled me with terror." After the passage of what was called "a compromise" in Congress, he wrote: "The question sleeps for the present, but is not dead." "A geographical line, coinciding with a marked principle, moral and political, once conceived and held up to the angry passions of men will not be obliterated; and every new irritation will make it deeper and deeper." The Sage of Monticello spoke prophetically, and in one of his letters put on record this remarkable declaration:

"I regret that I am now to die in the belief that the useless sacrifice of themselves, by the generation of 1776, to acquire self-government and happiness to their country, is to be thrown away by the unwise and unworthy passions of their sons; and that my only consolation is to be, I live not to weep over it. If they would but dispassionately weigh the blessings they will throw away, against an abstract principle more likely to be affected by union than by scission, they would pause before they would perpetrate this act of suicide on themselves, and of treason against the hopes of the world."

Mr. Jefferson was right in designating the Missouri Restriction as the preliminary trace of disunion. Thereafter, the slavery question was developed as a well-defined controversy; and for forty years the most ingenious attempts to appease it, and to erase the geographical line, which was drawn in 1820, were worse than ineffectual.

But it is to be remarked that the true causes of sectional animosity between the North and the South were beyond the slavery question, although unavoidably and indissolubly connected with it. If we are to analyze that animosity, we shall discover that its deep-lying causes were certain radical antipathies, which discovered slavery as the most prominent ground of distinction between the two sections, and seized upon it as the readiest point of controversy. We must not fall into the common error of taking occasions for original agents, and confounding as one a number of causes, attached to each other, or even grown out of each other, and yet logically distinct. The war between North and South was essentially a war between two great political schools, and what is more, between two distinct civilizations. Yet in both regards, the slavery question was bound up in the conflict, being, in the first place, an inevitable issue between the States-rights and consolidation schools; and, in the second place, itself being the most prominent cause of the distinction between the civilizations, or social autonomies of North and South.

It is thus that the slavery question, although subordinate—although, so to speak, a smaller question than those with which it was associated—pervaded all of American politics, and played the conspicuous part in the dissolution of the Union. The two great political tendencies in America—that of consolidation and that of State-rights— naturally joined issue on slavery; for the first school, recognizing the authority at Washington as a national one, could easily presume it responsible for what was denounced as "the plague-spot of the country," and deplored as a tarnish of the American name. Again, as the North envied the peculiar intellectual civilization of the

South, its higher sentimentalism, and its superior refinements of scholarship and manners, it would naturally find the leading cause of these things in the peculiar institution of slavery, and concentrate upon it all the unscrupulous rage of jealousy, and that singularly bitter hate, which is inseparable from a sense of inferiority.

Free labor founded in the North a material civilization, a pestilent system of public schools, and that insolent democracy which went by the phrase, "D—n you, I am as good as you." That, and "commercial" politics, made the North prosperous; a showy, glittering mass of all the national elements of civilization, by the side of the apparently scanty, but refined, South. Northern men were apt to sneer at the uncultivated aspects of the South; to point to the slight nets of internal improvements that stretched over tracts of wild timber and swamps; to laugh at the plain architecture in the cities of the South; and to talk, with great self-complacency, of "the want of enterprise" in the slaveholding States. Yet after all, the Yankee trader had a sneaking, irrepressible consciousness that the Southern planter, in his homespun garb, was infinitely his superior as a gentleman; that he could not compete with him in courage, in the sentiment of honor, in the refinements of manners, or in any of the solid and meritorious accomplishments of manhood. The sleek business men of New York, Boston, and Philadelphia might be very impressive in their exteriors, but they never had any manners; they were not even accustomed to the words, "Sir" and "gentleman," in their conversation; they might talk a learned jargon about stocks and markets, but beyond that, in matters of history and literature, many of these well-dressed men were as ignorant as the draymen at their door.

Despite the plainness of the South, and the absence there of the shows and gauds of material prosperity, and the inseparable companion of such prosperity in a *moneyed* aristocracy, there was recognizable, in this slaveholding country, a noble and singularly pure type of civilization. Slavery introduced elements of order and conservatism in the society of the South; and yet, after all, there was no truer democracy in the world than there: the lower white classes recognizing, it is true, certain distinctions in social intercourse; but outside of these, having a manly sense of equality, and claiming, from the more prosperous orders of society, a consideration and measure of respect that the poor man in the North, where society was made up of browbeating on the one hand, and an insolent assertion of equality on the other, in vain contended for. Slavery trained the white race of the South in habits of command; and though, sometimes, these may have degenerated into cruelty and insolence, yet they were generally the occasions of the revival of the spirit of chivalry in the nineteenth century; of the growth of many noble and generous virtues; and of a knightly polish of manners, that the shopkeeping aristocracy of the North, being unable to emulate, was satisfied to ape in its hotels and caravansaries. Slavery relieved the better classes in the South from many of the demands of physical and manual labor; but although in some instances idle or dissolute lives may have been the consequence of this, yet it afforded opportunity for extraordinary intellectual culture in the South, elevated the standards of scholarship and mental cultivation there, and furnishes some explanation of the extraordinary phenomenon in American history, that the *statesmanship* of the country was peculiarly, and almost exclusively, the production of the slaveholding States.

The vulgar North envied the South, even down to the small hands and feet of its people. For the better civilization and higher refinement of slaveholders, the North retaliated that the South was dull and unenterprising, and had to import all of its luxuries, and many of its comforts from Yankee shops. This was true; but it proved nothing, or it might prove more than the Yankee argument might desire, for with Northern luxuries there came into the South Northern vices. It was said, with a coarse wit, but with not a little meaning, that there were "three things" for which the South would always be dependent upon the North, and never could produce for herself; they were "ice, play-actors, and prostitutes." There is a certain exaggeration in every *bon mot;* but the witticism is a good one, as it gives an indication of that coarse, vulgar measure of superiority which the North applied to itself to compensate for its defects in refinement, and in the nobler attributes of national life by the side of the South.

With reference to the singular point of contrast between the North and the South in the exhibitions of statesmanship and political scholarship, we discover the most remarkable feature of American history. Slavery appears, indeed, to have been the school of American statesmanship, for it is from its domains there came by far the most considerable contribution to the political literature of the country. The smallness of Yankee contribution in this respect has been a subject of remark by every impartial historian of America; and there are but few candid persons who will deny that the quality of Yankee statesmanship was always intensely sophomorical. It may have been that slavery afforded to the statesmen of the South certain fields of observation, and applied certain influences of conservatism that qualified them for their peculiar studies; but it is unquestionably true, that to them we must look for the monuments of political literature in America. It has been acutely remarked by a Yankee writer, in the anonymous pages of a magazine, that the public men of the North were generally actuated by an ambition to make a show on what they imagined the theatre of *national* life; that they neglected the obscure theatres, but noble schools, of *State* politics; and that to this shallow, ostentatious ambition is to be attributed much of the Yankee distaste for the severity and exclusiveness of the States-rights school.

Robert E. Lee

(1807–1870)

Many historians consider Robert E. Lee the greatest general of the Civil War, and there is certainly no question that Southerners accorded him that status in the years following the war. Hampered though he was by a lack of adequate resources, his military genius was a principal factor in keeping the Confederacy alive; many of his tactics were years ahead of their time. Even his bitterest enemies acknowledged his admirable moral character. Henry Adams wrote, "I think [Lee] should have been hanged. It was all the worse that he was a good man, had a good character, and acted conscientiously. It's always the good men who do the most harm." Apart from his iconic status in the South (his famous white horse, Traveller, was reportedly half-bald by the war's end from devotees snatching a souvenir of hair as the general passed by) and the vituperations of critics like Adams, the assessment of most of the nation after the war was that Lee, who became president of Washington College (now Washington and Lee University) in the fall of 1865, helped to restore the Union through acceptance of defeat, mediation of sectional differences, and general moderation. Though President Andrew Johnson never granted him the official amnesty for which he applied, until the time of his death, Lee nevertheless urged the people of the South to work for the restoration of peace and harmony in a united country.

from *Lee's Dispatches:*

Unpublished Letters of General Robert E. Lee, CSA

No. 1.

NEAR RICHMOND
3 June, '62

Mʳ PRESIDENT
    I am extremely grateful for your kind offer of your fine horse & feel most sensibly the consideration & thoughtfulness that prompted it. But I really do not require one at this time & would infinitely prefer your retaining him & allow me to enjoy the sense of your kindness & to call for him when I am in want. My gray has calmed down amazingly, gave me a very pleasant ride all day yesterday & I enjoyed his gaits much. My other horses are improving & will soon I hope be ready for service. So I really with my present riding would not know what to do with more. They would not have sufficient exercise & be uncomfortable to me & themselves.
    With a full sense & appreciation of your kindness & great gratitude for your friendship, I must again beg to be allowed to ask you to keep the horse in your service.
    With sentiments of profound respect & esteem
        I am your obliged & humble servt

R. E. LEE

His Excᴰ President DAVIS

No. 59.

[Telegram]

Received at Richmond July 31st. 1863.
    By Telegraph from Culpeper 31st. To Hon. JEFFN. DAVIS President C. S.
    Reports from Scouts indicate movements of Enemy to Fredericksburg. I am making corresponding movements.

R. E. LEE.
Genl.

14/56
    VB.
[Endorsed]
    Telegram from Genl. LEE
        Culpepper C. H.
            July 31st. 1863.

No. 60.

Unofficial

Camp Culpeper 31 July '63

His Exc^y Jeffⁿ Davis
President Confed. States

Mr President

Your note of the 27th enclosing a slip from the Charleston Mercury relative to the battle of Gettysburg is rec^d—I much regret its general censure upon the operations of the army, as it is calculated to do us no good either at home or abroad. But I am prepared for similar criticism & as far as I am concerned the remarks fall harmless. I am particularly sorry however that from partial information & mere assumption of facts that injustice should be done any officer, & that occasion should be taken to asperse your conduct, who of all others are most free of blame, I do not fear that your position in the confidence of the people, can be injured by such attacks, & I hope the official reports will protect the reputation of every officer. These cannot be made at once, & in the meantime as you state much falsehood may be promulgated. But truth is mighty & will eventually prevail. As regards the article in question I think it contains its own contradiction. Although charging Heth with the failure of the battle, it expressly states he was absent wounded. The object of the writer & publisher is evidently to cast discredit upon the operations of the Gov^t & those connected with it & thus gratify feelings more to be pitied than envied—To take notice of such attacks would I think do more harm than good, & would be just what is desired. The delay that will necessarily occur in receiving official reports has induced me to make for the information of the Dept: a brief outline of operations of the army, in which however I have been unable to state the conduct of troops or officers. It is sufficient to show what was done & what was not done. No blame can be attached to the army for its failure to accomplish what was projected by me, nor should it be censured for the unreasonable expectations of the public—I am alone to blame, in perhaps expecting too much of its prowess & valour. It however in my opinion achieved under the guidance of the Most High a general success, though it did not win a victory. I thought at the time that the latter was practicable. I still think if all things could have worked together it would have been accomplished. But with the knowledge I then had, & in the circumstances I was then placed, I do not know what better course I could have pursued. With my present knowledge, & could I have foreseen that the attack on the last day would have failed to drive the enemy from his position, I should certainly have tried some other course. What the ultimate result would have been is not so clear to me. Our loss has been very heavy, that of the enemys is proportionally so. His crippled condition enabled us to retire from the Country, comparatively unmolested. The unexpected state of the Potomac was our only embarrassment. I will not trespass upon your Exc^{ys} time more. With prayers for your health & happiness, & the recognition by your gratified country of your great services.

I remain truly & sincerely yours

R. E. Lee.

No. 82.

HD QRS. DEPT N. VA.
April 7th '64.

To His Excellency
   JEFFERSON DAVIS
      President of the
         Confederate States.

SIR,

I would beg to call your Excellency's attention to the following cases, in which sentences of death have been passed and in which I, having suspended the execution of the sentences, have forwarded the proceedings with the recommendation that the sentences be remitted.

I would ask an early consideration of the cases in as much as in case the recommendations are concurred in, I am desirous of having the men returned to the army in time to take part in the approaching campaign.

Private James F. Haneycutt Co. A. 4th N. C. Regt, recommended on account of his extreme youth.

Private James Arnold Co. D. 50th Va. Regt. recommended on account of his previous character as a soldier, the cheerful discharge of his duty and gallantry, and of the circumstances developed on his trial.

Privates David Ramey, I. W. Ramey and S. H. Bothel of Co. K. and J. W. H. Ramey of G. all of the 12th S. C. Regiment in consideration of their former character as soldiers for gallantry and the faithful discharge of their duties—And in Private David Rameys case, further in consideration of his refusing to listen to the persuasions of his Uncle and quitting the party of deserters and returning to his duty, his extreme youth and the unanimous recommendation of the court.

Private Cyrus Drum Co. G. 38th N. C. Regt in consideration of the patriotic conduct of his wife, who declaring her reluctance to see him as a deserter, induced him to surrender himself the day after he reached his home.

Private Edmund M. Berry Co. H. 22nd N. C. Regt, In consideration of his character as an attentive, obedient and good soldier; his long service and his gallantry at Seven Pines, Mechanicsville, Gaines Mill, Frasiers Farm Malvern Hill and other battles.

Private S. C. Allred Co L. 22nd N. C. Regt, In consideration of his conspicuous gallantry, his general good conduct his voluntary surrender of himself, and the unanimous recommendation of the Court.

Private Peter Treffenstedt Co E 38th N C Regt. In consideration of his extreme youth, his good character as a soldier, his voluntary return to duty and the unanimous recommendation of the Court.

I am with great respect
Your obt. servt.
R. E. LEE
Genl.

No. 83.

[Telegram]

HD QRS. ARMY OF NORTHERN VA.
7th April 1864.

Special Orders No $\frac{96}{v}$

So much of the sentences in the following cases as remains unexecuted are remitted, To wit in the case of

1. Private B. F. Coffman Co "G" 52 Va Regt on account of his youth and the mitigating circumstances developed on the trial

2. Private D. C. Courtney Co "C" 9th Va Cavy on account of the mitigating circumstances developed on the trial, and the unanimous recommendation of the Court

3. Private Thomas Y. Ward Co "H" 44—N. C. Regt on account of the mitigating circumstances developed on the trial

4. Private G. G. Fulcher Co "F"—47 Va Regt on account of his previous good character as a soldier, and the unanimous recommendations of his commanding officers

5. Private Albert Osborn Co "A" 22 Ga Regt on account of the resistance he offered to his elder brother's persuasions to desert and the practical repentance he exhibited after yielding—inducing the party deserting to return to their duty before reaching their homes

6. Pvts. Wm Bracket ⎫ *Graham's Battery*
   Robt Bracket ⎪ *N. C. Troops*
   Joseph Queen ⎪ In consideration of their previous excellent character
   Marada Queen ⎪ and the gallantry they have displayed in action
   Henry Buff ⎬
   James T. Pool ⎪
   Alex Pool ⎪
   John Janeey ⎪
   David W. White ⎭

7. Private John Fisher Co "C" 2—N. C. Regt, on account of his gallantry at the battle of Chancellorsville, his steadfast devotion to the cause and his youthfulness

8. Private W. H. Dorton Co "E" 48 Va Regt, on account of the mitigating circumstances of the case and his previous excellent character as a soldier

9. Private James Dwyer Co "K" 49 Va—Regt, on account of the mitigating circumstances in his case proved subsequent at his trial

10. *Pvts.* Wm. F. Robinson ⎫ Co "K"
    Jno. W. Robinson ⎬ 63—N. C. T.
    On account of their previous excellent character as soldiers and the mitigating circumstances developed on their trial

11. Private W. H. P. Jones Troop Artillery, on account of the mitigating circumstances developed in his case

12. Pvts. Geo M. Gunn ⎫ Co "G"
    Geo W. Phillips ⎬ 31 Va Inf
    Danl J. Sutton ⎭ On account of their previous characters as soldiers, and of the high degree of probability which exists that they were misled by officers, to whom it was natural for them to look to for guidance

13. Private C. B. Pryor Co "K" 53—N. G. Regt on account of his previous character as a soldier and the facts developed subsequently to his trial

14. Private Marion Budges, Rives' Battery on account of his youth and the circumstances in his case tending to mislead one of his inexperience

15. Pvts. J. M. Stricklin ⎱ Co "G"
       Joseph Price ⎰ 55 N. C.
                        Regt
                        On account of events which have occurred since
                        their trial

The foregoing will be returned under guard to their respective commands and
then restored to duty.

In returning to their duty, the Genl Comdg, hopes that the above named will avail
themselves of the approaching campaign to redeem themselves from the stigma of
cowardice, desertion etc. now attached to them and will by their future conduct win
for themselves not only forgetfulness of their past crimes but also a reputation of
which their children and country may be proud. (End) By comd. Genl R E Lee

W. H. TAYLOR, A. A. G.

No. 84.

H^D Q^{RS} ARMY N. VA.
13th April 1864.

His Excy JEFFERSON DAVIS,
    Presdt. Confed. States,
        Richmond,
MR. PRESIDENT,

I have the honor to acknowledge the receipt of the letter of Col Lee written by your
directions, with reference to the case of Privt Jacob Shomore Co. B. 52nd Va. Regt. and
requesting my views as to the policy of extending clemency to other offenders now in
confinement, or undergoing punishment. With regard to prvt. Shomore, my endorsement
expressed the opinion I had formed from reading the application for pardon, and the en-
dorsements of Gens. Ewell & Early. I had not seen, nor have I yet read the record of the
case, it being one of these tried by Gen Ewell's Military court before the late law requiring these proceedings to be reviewed by me. My views are based upon those considerations of policy which experience has satisfied me to be sound, and which are adverse to
leniency, except in cases showing some reason for mitigation. The fact that prvt.
Shomore had been a good soldier previous to his desertion, is insisted upon, as it frequently has been in like cases, as a ground of mitigation, and were he alone concerned, I
would be disposed to give weight to it. But I am satisfied that it would be impolitic and
unjust to the rest of the army to allow previous good conduct alone to atone for an offence most pernicious to the service, and most dangerous as an example. In this connection, I will lay before your Excellency some facts that will assist you in forming your
judgment, and at the same time, present the opinions I have formed on the subject of punishment in the army. In reviewing Court Martial cases, it has been my habit to give the accused the benefit of all extenuating circumstances that could be allowed to operate in
their favor without injury to the service. In addition to those parties whose sentences I
have remitted altogether or in part, or whom, when capitally convicted, I have recom-

mended to pardon or commutation of punishment, I have kept a list during the past winter of certain offenders, whose cases while they could not be allowed to go unpunished altogether, without injury to the service, had some extenuating features connected with them. I confirmed the sentences, and all of them have undergone a part of their punishment, but recently I remitted the remainder in the order of which I enclose a copy.

Beyond this, I do not think it prudent to go, unless some reason be presented which will enable me to be lenient without creating a bad precedent, and encouraging others to become offenders. I have arrived at this conclusion from experience. It is certain that a relaxation of the sternness of discipline as a mere act of indulgence, unsupported by good reasons, is followed by an increase of the number of offenders. The escape of one criminal encourages others to hope for like impunity, and that encouragement can be given as well by a repetition of a general act of amnesty or pardon, as by frequent exercise of clemency towards individuals. If the convicted offenders alone were concerned, there would be no objection to giving them another trial, as we should be no worse off if they again deserted than before. But the effect of the example is the chief thing to be considered, and that it is injurious, I have no doubt. Many more men would be lost to the service if a pardon be extended in a large number of cases, than would be restored to it by the immediate effects of that action.

The military executions that took place to such an extent last autumn, had a very beneficial influence, but in my judgment, many of them would have been avoided had the infliction of punishment in such cases uniformly followed the commission of the offence. But the failure of courts to convict or sentence to death, the cases in which pardon or commutation of punishment had been granted upon my recommendation, and the instances in which the same indulgence was extended by your Excellency upon grounds made known to you by others, had somewhat relaxed discipline in this respect, and the consequences became immediately apparent in the increased number of desertions. I think that a return to the current policy would inevitably be attended with like results. Desertion and absence without leave are nearly the only offences ever tried by our Courts. They appear to be almost the only vices in the army. Notwithstanding the executions that have recently taken place, I fear that the number of those who have escaped punishment in some one of the ways above mentioned has had a bad effect already. The returns for the month of March show 5474 men absent without leave, and 322 desertions during the month. There have been 62 desertions within the present month specially reported, but the whole number I fear considerably exceeds that some of the large number absent without leave, are probably sick men who have failed to report, and some of the deserters are probably absent without leave, but the number is sufficiently great to show the necessity of adhering to the only policy that will restrain the evil, and which I am sure will be found to be truly merciful in the end. Desertions and absence without leave not only weaken the army by the number of offenders not reclaimed, but by the guards that must be kept over those who are arrested. I think therefore that it would not be expedient to pardon & return to duty any of those now under sentence, or release those under charges, except for good cause shown.

I have the honour to be

With great respect

Your obt. servt.

R. E. Lee

Genl.

No. 151.

H^D^Q^RS^ Army N Va.
5th July 1864.

His Excellency Jeff^N^ Davis
Presdt C. States
Mr. President,

The subject of recruiting and keeping up our cavalry force, has occupied much of my thoughts, especially since the opening of the present campaign. The enemy is numerically superior to us in this arm, and possesses greater facilities for recruiting his horses and keeping them in serviceable condition. In the several engagements that have taken place between the cavalry of the two armies, I think great loss has been inflicted upon him, but it has been attended with a diminution of our force which we were less able to bear. Could I sweep his cavalry from the field, or preserve a fair proportion between its numbers and our own, I should feel that our present situation was in a measure secure. But in view of the disparity that exists, and the difficulty of increasing or even maintaining our force, I cannot but entertain serious apprehensions about the safety of our southern communications. Should we be unable to preserve them, I need not point out the consequences. I do not know from what quarter reinforcements can be had. There is one regt. of Georgia Cavalry under Col Anderson which I believe is desirous of joining this army. The War Department can best decide whether it can be spared but if it can be, I beg that it may be ordered to me without delay. You will know whether any can be drawn from Gen Johnston's Dept. That which is in Western Va is needed there and I am aware of no other source of supply. I think that horses might be obtained from Texas, as we have now access to the Mississippi at various points. Those horses would make very serviceable animals for cavalry, and could be brought across the river by swimming, as cattle are higher up the stream and on the Missouri river if only a few can be obtained in this way, it would be of great assistance. It has also occurred to me that horses at least for artillery service could be obtained on the Northern and Western borders of Va. by the system of exchange which is now being successfully carried on for subsistence. If good agents were selected and sent to the Western and Northwestern parts of the State, with authority to exchange cotton and tobacco for horses, the facilities for carrying on the traffic would be greater than that in articles of more difficult transportation, and at the present prices of those commodities in the North, the profits would be a great temptation, and insure the success of the experiment. I think if anything is to be done, now is our most favorable opportunity. I hope your Excellency will be able to devise some means of obtaining an increase of our supply of horses, and recruiting our cavalry, as upon that in a great measure I believe, depends the issue of the campaign in Va.

Very respectfully
Your obt servt
R E Lee
Genl.

Asia Booth Clarke

(1835–1888)

Since its publication in 1938, Asia Booth Clarke's *John Wilkes Booth: A Sister's Memoir* has been acknowledged as an important resource for understanding the personality of Abraham Lincoln's assassin. Clarke was born on the family farm near Bel Air, Maryland, to Junius Brutus Booth, one of America's leading actors, and Mary Ann Holmes. Junius and Mary Booth were both English, having immigrated to the United States in 1821. Asia Booth, named "in remembrance of that country where God first walked with man," was the third of six children; John Wilkes Booth was born three years after his sister, in 1838. Asia, who also wrote a biography of her other well-known sibling, the actor Edwin Booth, composed reminiscences of her younger brother in 1874 and hoped to see them published; however, she was hindered by her husband, John S. Clarke, who had himself been arrested in 1865 on suspicion of association with John Wilkes Booth and who still harbored resentment over the incident. At her death in 1888, the author left the manuscript to friends, who arranged for publication of the memoir fifty years later. The memoir portrays John Wilkes Booth as a study in contrasts: gentle and romantic at times, passionate to the point of fanaticism at others. Though she is horrified at the consequences of her brother's actions, Asia Booth Clarke seeks to understand his "struggles in professional experience and the fiercer struggles with himself."

from *John Wilkes Booth:*

A Sister's Memoir

In November, 1864, the play of "Julius Caesar" was produced at the Winter Garden Theatre, New York. The three brothers assumed the characters of Brutus, Cassius, and Marc Antony. Edwin was nervous; he admired Wilkes and thought that he never beheld a being so perfectly handsome. I think he trembled a little for his own laurels. In the densely packed theater I heard from my standing-place many comments on the merits of the brothers. One voice said delightedly, "*Our Wilkes* looks like a young god."

I turned to see a Southerner with eyes intently watching the play.

This performance and that engagement of one week's duration in 1862 were the only occasions of Wilkes Booth appearing in New York. He enacted "Pescara" for the benefit of John McCullough at Washington, [on March 18, 1865] and that was his last appearance upon the stage.

Fierce scenes of terror and bloodshed, of riots and raids, were daily enacted at this wild time of the war. Wilkes came frequently to me at Philadelphia, or rather, to my husband's house. I saw and heard much that distressed and surprised me, but my husband was a careless steward of his own affairs, and never gave a thought to the direction or management of his own household. Wilkes knew that he could come and go at our house unquestioned and unobserved. He often slept in his clothes on the couch downstairs, having on his long riding boots. Strange men called at late hours, some whose voices I knew, but who would not answer to their names; and others who were perfectly strange to me. They never came farther than the inner sill, and spoke in whispers.

One night, Wilkes was more than usually excited; he looked haggard and worn. I heard him murmur, "Oh, God, grant me to see the end!"

I said, "Do no go South again, my poor brother, do not go."

"Why, where *should* I go then?" he said, opening his eyes wide in astonishment, as if the South held his heartstrings. Then he sang low and distinctly a wild parody, each verse ending with a rhyme to a year, then, "In 1865 when Lincoln shall be king."

I said, "Oh, not that. That will *never* come to pass!"

"No, by God's mercy," he said, springing to his feet.

"Never *that!*" Then he whispered fiercely, "That Sectional Candidate should never have been President, the votes were *doubled* to seat him.* He was smuggled through Maryland to the White House. Maryland is true to the core—every mother's son. Look at the cannon on the heights of Baltimore. It needed just that to keep her quiet. This man's appearance, his pedigree, his coarse low jokes and anecdotes, his vulgar similes, and his policy are a disgrace to the seat he holds. Other brains rule the country. *He* is made the tool of the North, to crush out, or try to crush out slavery, by robbery, rapine, slaughter and bought armies. He is walking in the footprints of old John Brown, but no more fit to stand with that rugged old hero—Great God! No. John Brown was a man inspired, the grandest character of this century! *He* is Bonaparte in one great move, that is, by overturning this blind Republic and making himself a king. This man's re-election which will follow his success, I tell you, will be a reign! The subjects, bastard subjects, of other countries, apostates, are eager to overturn this government. You'll see, you'll see that *re-election* means *succession.* His kin and friends are in every place of office already. Trust the songs of the people. They are the bards, the troubadors. Who make these songs if not the people! 'Vox populi' forever! These false-hearted, unloyal foreigners it is, who would glory in the downfall of the Republic—and that by a half-breed too, a man springing from the ashes of old Assanothime Brown,† a false president yearning for kingly succession as hotly as ever did Ariston."‡

A desperate turn towards the evil had come! I had listened so patiently to these wild tirades, which were the very fever of his distracted brain and tortured heart, that I was powerless to check or soothe. Every person was fierce in condemnation of the South. There was never a relenting word or pity for their terrible loss; only fierce, savage, diabolical joy over every list of defeat and slaughter. The most vindictive and venomous tongues were those of women—not American born women. The North had a serpent tongue and a cruel red hand uppermost.

He had sat late with me on one of these nights—the last—and said to me, "Let me show you the cipher."§

When I understood what he meant, I said, "No, I shall not consent to any knowledge of that kind."

But he added, "I might possibly need to communicate with you about my money affairs, and there is no need to let everyone know what I am worth."

---

*Meaning unclear. There were no irregularities in the count of the 1860 electoral vote.
†So called from his antislavery activities near Osawatomie, Kansas Territory, in 1855.
‡Greek philosopher (d. 87 B.C.) whose ambition led to his becoming tyrant of Athens.
§A "court cipher" or code later found by authorities among Booth's possessions.

I resisted, and then he said, taking a large packet from his breast, "Lock this in your safe for me. I may come back for it, but if anything should happen to me open the packet *alone* and send the letters as directed, and the money and papers give to their owners."

It was not unusual to speak thus of possible accidents, for in these reckless times the travel was rough and incessant, and a traveling actor's life is one of exposure to danger. I promised to lock up the packet. He kissed me many times good-by, and I sat where he had left me looking at the long envelope in my lap, with the one word "Asia" written on it. In a few moments he returned, and said, "Let me *see* you lock up the packet."

Together we unfastened the heavy door, then unbarred the inner iron one, then entered the room of stone and iron, and I stooped and placed the packet in the iron safe. We made all secure, and I hid the last key away. As I sat on the sofa, he came and knelt down at my feet, and laid his head in my lap. After a little time, during which I smoothed his black hair carelessly, he said, looking in my face, "When will your child be born, my girl?"

"In five months, I think, or less."

"I hope you will keep well and get stronger, dear."

Then as we rose together, he kissed me very tenderly and said, "God bless you, sister mine. Take care of yourself, and try to be happy."

"Oh, my boy," I said, with all the anxiety of my heart, "I shall never be happy till I see your face again."

There is no more to add. The rest is horror, fitter for a diary than for these pages. In time the blow fell on us, a loving, united and devoted family. And in time an enraged and furious Government did us much bitter wrong, and some justice. The packet I opened alone and destroyed an envelope with a man's name written upon it. (It is a name since numbered with the dead.) The ashes of this paper I blew about the room for safety, and the letter, with another envelope addressed S. K. Chester,* I handed to my husband and the others who stood near. The packet contained, besides this, bonds or coupons for his mother, a transfer of an oil well to Junius Booth, another for his sister Rosalie. His Boston land was afterwards given by his mother to her son Joseph, and I retained the envelope marked "Asia." This was afterwards taken from me.

Above all his kind love to me, I thanked him most that he left me nothing. Had he done so, it would have put a whip in my foe's hand, to torture my remaining life. Mr. J. S. Clarke thoughtlessly gave that enclosed letter alluding to a kidnapping scheme to Mr. Stockton, his personal friend and the reporter of a daily paper, and, as every shred of news was voraciously accepted, the letter was published, and arrests followed in quick succession.

It was like the days of the Bastille in France. Arrests were made suddenly and in dead of night. No reason or warning given, only let anyone breathe a doubt of the most innocent person and arrest followed swift, and that incarceration meant to wait the law's leisure, innocent or guilty. Detectives, women and men, decoys, and all that vile rabble of human bloodhounds infested the city.

Junius Booth, who was in Cincinnati acting, came to our house. He was arrested, but the officer politely put the handcuffs in his own pocket and allowed the prisoner to walk unmanacled at two o'clock in the morning. A few nights later J. S. Clarke was

---

*Chester (1836–1921), actor, childhood friend of Booth who attempted to lure him into the abduction plot.

arrested, and both were placed in the Old Capitol Prison at Washington. Joseph Booth, who had arrived after three and a half years' trip to Australia, was arrested before landing and placed in jail in New York. Edwin Booth was surrounded by influential friends, but with an outer guard of spies to note his movements.

This unfortunate publication, so useless now when the scheme had failed—and it led to no fresh discoveries—brought a host of miseries, for it not only served for food to newsmongers and enemies, but it directed a free band of male and female detectives to our house. The newspapers called on "servants to be spies upon their employers in the cause of the Government." My house, which was an extensive (*mysteriously built*, it was now called) old mansion, was searched; then, without warning, surprised by a full body of police, surrounded, and searched again. We were under hourly surveillance from outside, and I, left alone, received the visit of a young official who had a carriage and pair at the door to conduct me to Washington. To this young man of twenty-one years perhaps, I was obliged to state my condition of health, and he advised me to procure a certificate to the effect that I was unable to travel. The old doctor who had brought me through much illness could with difficulty be induced to come to my house, but on his telegram being sent to Washington, a polite and assiduous male detective kept me company through the hours that seemed like years. Our letters were few, but they were opened, and no trouble taken to conceal that they had been read first. Every letter that I received was from Edwin Booth, and I handed the same to the attendant officer, who, without asking, seemed to expect this privilege. He was gentle and polite, and although he followed me from room to room he tried not to let me feel myself a prisoner. His greatest annoyance seemed "that I never cried and seldom spoke." He was frequently urging me "to let his wife, who actually cried to think how ill-treated and sick I was, come and stay with me."

"*You* were ordered here by the Government, were you not?" I asked.

"Yes, ma'am, but *she* can come just as well, and I needn't."

"Obey your orders," I said, "but tell your wife I thank her very kindly."

I should rather have been watched by ten men who could keep quiet, than one chattering female.

Edwin Booth wrote frequently to me. From one of his letters the following paragraphs are taken. "Think no more of him as your brother; he is dead to us now, as he soon must be to all the world, but imagine the boy you loved to be in that better part of his spirit, in another world." And, "I have had a heartbroken letter from the poor little girl to whom he had promised so much happiness."

A fearful day! T. J. Hemphill of the Walnut Street Theatre asked to see me. The old man stood steadying himself by the center table; he did not raise his eyes, his face was very pale and working nervously. The attitude and pallor told the news he had been deputed to convey.

"Is it over?"

"Yes, madam."

"Taken?"

"Yes."

"Dead?"

"Yes, madam."

My heart beat like strong machinery, powerful and loud it seemed. I lay down with my face to the wall, thanking God silently, and heard the old man's sobs choking him, heard him go out, and close the street door after him.

Someone sent up, by my servant, a slip from a newspaper with the announcement that "on hearing the news Mrs. J. S. Clarke had gone mad, and was at present confined at the Asylum at West Philadelphia." North, East and West the papers teemed with the most preposterous adventures, and eccentricities, and ill deeds of the vile Booth family. The tongue of every man and woman was free to revile and insult us. Every man's hand was against us. If we had friends they condoled with us in secret; none ventured near. Keeping silent, with the thorn pressed deep, the fury died out in its vehemence. Those who have passed through such an ordeal—if there are any such—may be quick to forgive, slow to resent; they never relearn to trust in human nature, they never resume their old place in the world and they forget only in death.

Among much cruelty and unkindness, the falling off of tried friends, the terror of truculent acquaintances, the device of a young actor named Claud Burroughs,* who came on "a secret mission from Edwin Booth to demand of me, in utter secrecy, *knowledge of the paper which I had placed in my bosom*," the later offer from John S. Clarke, for me to consent to a divorce "which would be *his* only salvation now," the fear of my old doctor to approach my house, the insults of the engaged monthly nurse, and her refusal to attend me—all these and more were doubly, trebly outweighed by the one true womanly letter copied below. The original is treasured as precious gold.

May 3rd, 1865,
Phila.

Mrs. Clarke,
    Dear Madam,
    Although a perfect stranger to you, I take the liberty of offering my sympathy and aid to you in your great sorrow and sickness. If my mother or myself can be of the slightest use to you in any way in this world we should be only too happy. I should have offered before, but illness prevented. May God help and bless you is the
Constant prayer of
EFFIE GERMON†
1129 Race Street.

There is no solidity in love, no truth in friendship, no steadiness in marital faith, and no reason in an angry nation, but above and beyond all this exceeding bitterness, this little token of rare and unsought friendliness is sufficient to set the faithlessness of the world aside, and almost revive belief in human goodness.

After a lapse of many years I spoke of Claud Burroughs to Edwin Booth. He declared, in fearful surprise, "that he *never* sent Burroughs or any other actor, or any human being, to my house, on any mission, or with any message whatsoever." It is as sad to prove that glib-tongued fair-haired young actor only a detective in disguise, as it was delightful to know that beautiful actress a warm, true-hearted woman.

Edwin Booth's letters at this sad time were filled by reiterated suggestions for "Clarke to dissolve all partnership with him." *He* must not be bound in any way to him whose "name and fame were irremediably clouded. He must sever all connection with

---

*Claude Burroughs (1848?–1876), in 1865 an attache at Edwin Booth's Winter Garden Theatre; later an actor.

†Effie Germon (1843?–1914), star actor who had performed with Booth in 1863.

him, theatrically and for ever now." This was a generous offer, made when he, Edwin Booth had all the world against him; but he little knew how ungenerous an offer John S. Clarke was about to make to one whom he had sworn to keep faithful to under more solemn bonds than those of *business*. The incomprehensible words of Wilkes Booth resounded through the years that followed this astounding, heart-sickening proposition: "Bear in mind that you are only a professional stepping-stone."

Amid the happy scenes of our childhood the sensation hunters were actively entertained. There was no surfeit, and Stephen Hooper, the negro, gave valuable testimony of the "doin's of the Booths at the farms." The trench, in which a boy and girl had dug with unremitting toil through the best time of a summer vacation to find a dead Indian chief and relics, was made to appear as an underground store for secreted arms and ammunition. The Hallowe'en raid, although the custom of the country, was exaggerated into "frequent robberies of fowls, cattle and grain by which the idle Booth family were sustained, rather than do a stroke of honest work." Our near neighbor vouched for "the cruelty of Wilkes, who had destroyed valuable game and marketable fowl, destroyed innocent dogs and wild creatures for sport"—nothing was safe that came within range of his gun. He had left for dead a workman whom he had battered with a club, etc., etc. Then, another swore that "the visits of old Ishmael Day"* (who had become a hero of the North) "were only made to try and discover what we rebels were up to, and not for friendship's sake as we supposed." In that time there were no rebels, for there had been no war [yet], but untruth and memory seldom go twinned, and old Ishmael Day had been a casual visitor to the farm before the birth of Wilkes Booth or the young members of our father's family. He was a strange man, with some curse or shame upon him, as he thought, but we regarded him with respect and received him with politeness always.

What is herein written, to be read after my death, is the truth so far as I have been able to understand it, or to transcribe it. That my husband J. S. Clarke was entirely innocent, by knowledge or complicity, in any design whatsoever with Wilkes Booth, no one who ever knew the two men could for an instant doubt. Their temperaments, ideas, dispositions, natures, were widely at variance. The too careless guardian of his own household, being of a heavy, lymphatic temperament, yet to those who mean kindly, his indifference and utter apathy might appear "unsuspecting innocence of evil." Wilkes was an entirely opposite creation. They had no tie in common beyond the accidental one of a marriage connection. That my husband went to prison to save me is a fallacious assertion. The very fact of the summons, and the doctor's certificate for inability, disproves it. Suspicion was directed to his house through the unwise publication of a letter said to have been "secreted on the premises" (but which I promptly and freely produced, reserving to myself the right of destroying a written name that I would have suffered death rather than expose). Probably without this we should have remained untouched, as did Edwin Booth. This latter was an upright honest man, espousing the Northern policy, and had cast his vote for Abraham Lincoln. J. B. Booth and Joseph Booth were neutral.

I loved my brothers devotedly, but Wilkes had grown nearer in those late years at the farm, where we were lonely together. My marriage, which he often urged me to free

---

*Ishmael Day, an elderly Maryland farmer who achieved public notice when he killed a rebel soldier during a Confederate cavalry raid in 1864.

myself from, was become less pleasing to him; this and his professional pursuits separated us at long intervals. He was prudent not to trust me too far, yet he knew that I loved the Marylanders as dearly as himself. Many, many of our young friends had gone down in that unholy war. We glorified Washington and believed in the Constitution. We had many tastes, ideas, and loves in common, but he never even trusted me enough to disclose the whereabouts or meaning of Michael O'Laughlin. Romance and sentiment were woven in those days, and friendships, but no one is the worse for having loved and believed. In the darkness we are happier for once having known the blessing of sight, and the memory of youth is sweet in age. Wilkes never hinted at a scheme, or plot, or any design, legal or illegal. Revenge was a word I never heard from his lips, and I heard many hard epithets for those who tried to subjugate the South. The story of "the bullet which he carried" was concocted at our house, at our table. The origin of it was, "I suppose he was mad enough to carry a bullet in his pocket, with the man's name engraved upon it." This bitter wit was repeated, by lip, and then by pen, and ere long the bullet, so engraved, had been *seen* in different cities, by different persons, who each swore to the truth of the story, and repeated the threat and their conversations with Wilkes.

He who talks loudly of suicide and murder never carries his threats into effect. The thinker is the plotter and the worker; danger is silent. If it cried aloud there would be no danger. Those men, and they are yet increasing in number, who knew him to write his victim's name upon a window pane, and who talked with him while he displayed that famous bullet, were more guilty than he, for either act proclaimed him a madman or themselves accomplices. His was a strongly defined character; looking through all his years it shows consistency. He was a man who could keep a secret, was never a loquacious guest, and was considered abstemious and temperate. The diamond writing on the window glass emanated from the same prolific wit that lashed with scorpions but could do nothing openly.

The little volume of the "Memoir of Booth the Elder" was hurriedly written and arranged for publication in a few months of mental and bodily anguish. It was ready for the press before the 20th of August, 1865, on which day the sad writer gave birth to two babes.

Edwin Booth made several vain requests for possession of his brother's body. The answer was "*to wait*," but the belief of the family and of all interested in the matter was that he had been buried at sea.

Wilkes Booth was not insane; he had a powerful and active brain, and was given to weigh his intents and reflect upon his actions. "Trust to luck is cheerful enough for a song, but I trust to my brains," he said. His was a developed character in boyhood. He did not change much as he matured, only his opinions and principles became more riveted and his friendships stronger. He seldom chattered for pastime, but generally meant what he cared to utter. There are those who judge that men and women who can keep silence, and preserve secrets entrusted to them, are evil essentially, in mind and soul. John S. Clarke abhorred the "secretiveness of the whole Booth race." To his way of thinking it stamped them [as] male and female Iagos. That may be in some measure a truth, and I less than any care to vindicate my character on that score, but my observation has convinced me that Mr. J. S. Clarke's mistakes, which are few, have been the result of a merry and over-indulged loquacity.

Contrasting [Wilkes'] deeds with his peaceful domestic qualities, there seems to have been the impetus of a desperate fate impelling him. We make our destinies, perhaps, but is not each one known to God, and may not the gloom foreshadow us in a greater or lesser degree as our lives partake of sorrow, even as the shadow of the Cross hung over Jesus?

These old diaries keep many trivial records of Wilkes that would sound like fulsome praise. Let another speak of his warm heart and generous nature; there must be those who will do so in fitting time, for he had crowds of friends. The doom that fell on him was not wrought from a maniac brain nor a wicked heart, not from an irreligious soul nor a degraded nature. I believe that with the kidnaping scheme was laid to rest, although with curses, the cherished hope of saving those he would have died to serve. But the fall of Richmond rang in with maddening, exasperating clang of joy, and that triumphant entry into the fallen city (which was not magnanimous) breathed air afresh upon the fire which consumed him.

It was the moan of the religious people, the one throb of anguish to hero-worshipers, that the President had not gone first to a place of worship or have remained at home on this jubilant occasion. It desecrated his idea to have his end come in a devil's den—a theater—in fact. Conquerors cannot be too careful of themselves, as history has ever proved. That fatal visit to the theater had no pity in it; it was jubilation over fields of unburied dead, over miles of desolated homes. It was neither the Te Deum of a noble conqueror nor the Miserere of a Christian nation. It struck the keynote for re-election and re-elections unnumbered. It was defying Washington, contemning the Constitution. It meant to him, to this one desperate man who shouted "Sic semper tyrannis," the fall of the Republic, a dynasty of kings. When he lay dying fast, outside the barn at Bowling Green, the last words uttered, between great gasps for breath, were his will and testament; so firmly did he believe in what he had done, that he declared with his departing strength, "Tell my mother—I died—for my country!"

"He saved his country from a king," but he created for her a martyr. And yet the word *martyr* signifies one who suffers and dies for a belief and a cause. He set the stamp of greatness on an epoch of history, and gave all he had to build this enduring monument to his foe. We regard Boston Corbett* as our deliverer, for by his shot he saved our beloved brother from an ignominious death. He by *his* act gave to his country her first martyr, and to history a hero who would blush to recognize his own posthumous greatness.

I returned Boston Corbett's letter to him; he did not request it exactly, but I thought it honorable to do so and safer at the time not to retain it. I kept a copy of my reply to it. He is still living, but I know he is not happy. He is a brave man and an enthusiast. May he have no regret.

The South avenged the wrongs inflicted by the North. A life inexpressibly dear was sacrificed wildly for what its possessor deemed best. The life best beloved by the North was dashed madly out when most triumphant. Let the blood of both cement the indissoluble union of our country. Slavery is over, white labor omnipotent. Boston Corbett lies without a monument, they tell me, for he is dead now. The North has not immortalized this hero, she had too many perhaps.

If Wilkes Booth was mad, his mind lost its balance between the fall of Richmond and the terrific end. The world will arise from its torpor of hatred. The light of reason will show that success alone makes the hero or the outlaw. It were ill to extol his ac-

*Boston Corbett (1832—?), New York cavalryman who fired the shot which killed Booth at Garrett's farm on April 26, 1865.

tion, as to debase his motive; they were the offspring of his own brain, the creatures of his own terrible will. Both are amenable to a higher justice. But, granting that he died in vain, yet he gave his all on earth, youth, beauty, manhood, a great human love, the certainty of excellence in his profession, a powerful brain, the strength of an athlete, health and great wealth, for "*his cause.*" This man was noble in his life, he periled his immortal soul, and he was brave in death. Already his hidden remains are given Christian burial, and strangers have piled his grave with flowers.

"So runs the world away."*

Elizabeth Keckley

(1818–1907)

Elizabeth Keckley was born a slave in Hillsborough, North Carolina, to parents who were owned by different masters. When she was seven years old, her father's master moved away, and she never saw her father again. Having learned to sew from her mother, she became a skilled seamstress. Keckley was given to her owner's son as a wedding gift, and her only son, George, was the product of a forced relationship with a friend of the owner's son. In 1852, she married James Keckley, but when she found that he was not free and was an alcoholic, she purchased freedom for herself and George through the intervention of a patron who lent her the money needed. After moving to Baltimore, she started a school for young black girls, where they learned sewing and etiquette. When her work on an inaugural ball gown pleased President Abraham Lincoln and Mary Todd Lincoln, she was hired as personal dressmaker for Mrs. Lincoln.

Keckley became Mary Todd Lincoln's friend and confidant. Subsequently, in 1868, she published *Behind the Scenes*, which depicts her years as a slave as well as her four years in the Lincoln White House. Though some literary scholars have speculated that it may have been ghostwritten, *Behind the Scenes* is an interesting combination of memoir, sentimental fiction, and slave narrative that presents a wide range of historical figures and events of the antebellum South.

from *Behind the Scenes:*

Thirty Years a Slave and Four Years in the White House

Preface.

I have often been asked to write my life, as those who know me know that it has been an eventful one. At last I have acceded to the importunities of my friends, and have hastily sketched some of the striking incidents that go to make up my history. My life, so full of romance, may sound like a dream to the matter-of-fact reader, nevertheless everything

---

*Hamlet, act 3, scene 2.

I have written is strictly true; much has been omitted, but nothing has been exaggerated. In writing as I have done, I am well aware that I have invited criticism; but before the critic judges harshly, let my explanation be carefully read and weighed. If I have portrayed the dark side of slavery, I also have painted the bright side. The good that I have said of human servitude should be thrown into the scales with the evil that I have said of it. I have kind, true-hearted friends in the South as well as in the North, and I would not wound those Southern friends by sweeping condemnation, simply because I was once a slave. They were not so much responsible for the curse under which I was born, as the God of nature and the fathers who framed the Constitution for the United States. The law descended to them, and it was but natural that they should recognize it, since it manifestly was their interest to do so. And yet a wrong was inflicted upon me; a cruel custom deprived me of my liberty, and since I was robbed of my dearest right, I would not have been human had I not rebelled against the robbery. God rules the Universe. I was a feeble instrument in His hands, and through me and the enslaved millions of my race, one of the problems was solved that belongs to the great problem of human destiny; and the solution was developed so gradually that there was no great convulsion of the harmonies of natural laws. A solemn truth was thrown to the surface, and what is better still, it was recognized *as a truth* by those who give force to moral laws. An act may be wrong, but unless the ruling power recognizes the wrong, it is useless to hope for a correction of it. Principles may be right, but they are not established within an hour. The masses are slow to reason, and each principle, to acquire moral force, must come to us from the fire of the crucible; the fire may inflict unjust punishment, but then it purifies and renders stronger the principle, not in itself, but in the eyes of those who arrogate judgment to themselves. When the war of the Revolution established the independence of the American colonies, an evil was perpetuated, slavery was more firmly established; and since the evil had been planted, it must pass through certain stages before it could be eradicated. In fact, we give but little thought to the plant of evil until it grows to such monstrous proportions that it overshadows important interests; then the efforts to destroy it become earnest. As one of the victims of slavery I drank of the bitter water; but then, since destiny willed it so, and since I aided in bringing a solemn truth to the surface *as a truth*, perhaps I have no right to complain. Here, as in all things pertaining to life, I can afford to be charitable.

It may be charged that I have written too freely on some questions, especially in regard to Mrs. Lincoln. I do not think so; at least I have been prompted by the purest motive. Mrs. Lincoln, by her own acts, forced herself into notoriety. She stepped beyond the formal lines which hedge about a private life, and invited public criticism. The people have judged her harshly, and no woman was ever more traduced in the public prints of the country. The people knew nothing of the secret history of her transactions, therefore they judged her by what was thrown to the surface. For an act may be wrong judged purely by itself, but when the motive that prompted the act is understood, it is construed differently. I lay it down as an axiom, that only that is criminal in the sight of God where crime is meditated. Mrs. Lincoln may have been imprudent, but since her intentions were good, she should be judged more kindly than she has been. But the world do not know what her intentions were; they have only been made acquainted with her acts without knowing what feeling guided her actions. If the world are to judge her as I have judged her, they must be introduced to the secret history of her transactions. The veil of mystery must be drawn aside; the origin of a fact must be brought to light with the naked fact itself. If I have betrayed confidence in anything I have published, it has been to place Mrs. Lincoln in a better light before the world. A breach of trust—if breach it can be called—of this kind is always excusable. My own character, as well as the character of Mrs. Lincoln, is at stake, since I have been intimately associated with that lady in the most eventful periods of her life. I have been her confidante, and if evil charges are laid at her door, they also must be laid at mine, since I have been a party to all her movements. To defend myself I must defend the lady that I have served. The world have judged Mrs. Lincoln by the facts which float upon the surface, and through her have partially judged me, and the only way to convince them that wrong was not meditated is to explain the motives that actuated us. I have written nothing that can place Mrs. Lincoln in a worse light before the world than the light in which she now stands, therefore the secret history that I publish can do her no harm. I have excluded everything of a personal character from her letters; the extracts introduced only refer to public men, and are such as to throw light upon her unfortunate adventure in New York. These letters were not written for publication, for which reason they are all the more valuable; they are the frank overflowings of the heart, the outcropping of impulse, the key to genuine motives. They prove the motive to have been pure, and if they shall help to stifle the voice of calumny, I am content. I do not forget, before the public journals vilified Mrs. Lincoln, that ladies who moved in the Washington circle in which she moved, freely canvassed her character among themselves. They gloated over many a tale of scandal that grew out of gossip in their own circle. If these ladies could say everything bad of the wife of the President, why should I not be permitted to lay her secret history bare, especially when that history plainly shows that her life, like all lives, has its good side as well as its bad side? None of us are perfect, for which reason we should heed the voice of charity when it whispers in our ears, "Do not magnify the imperfections of others." Had Mrs. Lincoln's acts never become public property, I should not have published to the world the secret chapters of her life. I am not the special champion of the widow of our lamented President; the reader of the pages which follow will discover that I have written with the utmost frankness in regard to her—have exposed her faults as well as given her credit for honest motives. I wish the world to judge her as she is, free from the exaggerations of praise or scandal, since I have been associated with her in so many things that have provoked hostile criticism; and the judgment that the world may pass upon her, I flatter myself, will present my own actions in a better light.

Chapter IV. In the Family of Senator Jefferson Davis

The twelve hundred dollars with which I purchased the freedom of myself and son I consented to accept only as a loan. I went to work in earnest, and in a short time paid every cent that was so kindly advanced by my lady patrons of St. Louis. All this time my husband was a source of trouble to me, and a burden. Too close occupation with my needle had its effects upon my health, and feeling exhausted with work, I determined to make a change. I had a conversation with Mr. Keckley; informed him that since he persisted in dissipation we must separate; that I was going North, and that I should never live with him again, at least until I had good evidence of his reform. He was rapidly debasing himself, and although I was willing to work for him, I was not willing to share his degradation. Poor man; he had his faults, but over these faults death has drawn a veil. My husband is now sleeping in his grave, and in the silent grave I would bury all unpleasant memories of him.

I left St. Louis in the spring of 1860, taking the cars direct for Baltimore, where I stopped six weeks, attempting to realize a sum of money by forming classes of young colored women, and teaching them my system of cutting and fitting dresses. The scheme was not successful, for after six weeks of labor and vexation, I left Baltimore with scarcely money enough to pay my fare to Washington. Arriving in the capital, I sought and obtained work at two dollars and a half per day. However, as I was notified that I could only remain in the city ten days without obtaining a license to do so, such being the law, and as I did not know whom to apply to for assistance, I was sorely troubled. I also had to have some one vouch to the authorities that I was a free woman. My means were too scanty, and my profession too precarious to warrant my purchasing license. In my perplexity I called on a lady for whom I was sewing, Miss Ringold, a member of Gen. Mason's family, from Virginia. I stated my case, and she kindly volunteered to render me all the assistance in her power. She called on Mayor Burritt with me, and Miss Ringold succeeded in making an arrangement for me to remain in Washington without paying the sum required for a license; moreover, I was not to be molested. I rented apartments in a good locality, and soon had a good run of custom. The summer passed, winter came, and I was still in Washington. Mrs. Davis, wife of Senator Jefferson Davis, came from the South in November of 1860, with her husband. Learning that Mrs. Davis wanted a modiste, I presented myself, and was employed by her on the recommendation of one of my patrons and her intimate friend, Mrs. Captain Hetsill. I went to the house to work, but finding that they were such late risers, and as I had to fit many dresses on Mrs. Davis, I told her that I should prefer giving half the day to her, working the other in my own room for some of my other lady patrons. Mrs. D. consented to the proposition, and it was arranged that I should come to her own house every day after 12 M. It was the winter before the breaking out of that fierce and bloody war between the two sections of the country; and as Mr. Davis occupied a leading position, his house was the resort of politicians and statesmen from the South. Almost every night, as I learned from the servants and other members of the family, secret meetings were held at the house; and some of these meetings were protracted to a very late hour. The prospects of war were freely discussed in my presence by Mr. and Mrs. Davis and their friends. The holidays were approaching, and Mrs. Davis kept me busy in manufacturing articles of dress for herself and children. She desired to present Mr. Davis on Christmas with a handsome dressing-gown. The material was purchased, and for weeks the work had been under way. Christmas eve came, and the gown had been laid aside so often that it was still unfinished. I saw that Mrs. D. was anxious to have it completed, so I volunteered to remain and work on it. Wearily the hours dragged on, but there was no rest for my busy fingers. I persevered in my task, notwithstanding my head was aching. Mrs. Davis was busy in the adjoining room, arranging the Christmas tree for the children. I looked at the clock, and the hands pointed to a quarter of twelve. I was arranging the cords on the gown when the Senator came in; he looked somewhat careworn, and his step seemed to be a little nervous. He leaned against the door, and expressed his admiration of the Christmas tree, but there was no smile on his face. Turning round, he saw me sitting in the adjoining room, and quickly exclaimed:

"That you, Lizzie! why are you here so late? Still at work; I hope that Mrs. Davis is not too exacting!"

"No, sir," I answered. "Mrs. Davis was very anxious to have this gown finished tonight, and I volunteered to remain and complete it."

"Well, well, the case must be urgent," and he came slowly towards me, took the gown in his hand, and asked the color of the silk, as he said the gas-light was so deceptive to his old eyes.

"It is a drab changeable silk, Mr. Davis," I answered; and might have added that it was rich and handsome, but did not, well knowing that he would make the discovery in the morning.

He smiled curiously, but turned and walked from the room without another question. He inferred that the gown was for him, that it was to be the Christmas present from his wife, and he did not wish to destroy the pleasure that she would experience in believing that the gift would prove a surprise. In this respect, as in many others, he always appeared to me as a thoughtful, considerate man in the domestic circle. As the clock struck twelve I finished the gown, little dreaming of the future that was before it. It was worn, I have not the shadow of a doubt, by Mr. Davis during the stormy years that he was the President of the Confederate States.

The holidays passed, and before the close of January the war was discussed in Mr. Davis's family as an event certain to happen in the future. Mrs. Davis was warmly attached to Washington, and I often heard her say that she disliked the idea of breaking up old associations, and going South to suffer from trouble and deprivation. One day, while discussing the question in my presence with one of her intimate friends, she exclaimed: "I would rather remain in Washington and be kicked about, than go South and be Mrs. President." Her friend expressed surprise at the remark, and Mrs. Davis insisted that the opinion was an honest one.

While dressing her one day, she said to me: "Lizzie, you are so very handy that I should like to take you South with me."

"When do you go South, Mrs. Davis?" I inquired.

"Oh, I cannot tell just now, but it will be soon. You know there is going to be war, Lizzie?"

"No!"

"But I tell you yes."

"Who will go to war?" I asked.

"The North and South," was her ready reply. "The Southern people will not submit to the humiliating demands of the Abolition party; they will fight first."

"And which do you think will whip?"

"The South, of course. The South is impulsive, is in earnest, and the Southern soldiers will fight to conquer. The North will yield, when it sees the South is in earnest, rather than engage in a long and bloody war."

"But, Mrs. Davis, are you certain that there will be war?"

"Certain!—I know it. You had better go South with me; I will take good care of you. Besides, when the war breaks out, the colored people will suffer in the North. The Northern people will look upon them as the cause of the war, and I fear, in their exasperation, will be inclined to treat you harshly. Then, I may come back to Washington in a few months, and live in the White House. The Southern people talk of choosing Mr. Davis for their President. In fact, it may be considered settled that he will be their President. As soon as we go south and secede from the other States, we will raise an army and march on Washington, and then I shall live in the White House."

I was bewildered with what I heard. I had served Mrs. Davis faithfully, and she had learned to place the greatest confidence in me. At first I was almost tempted to go South with her, for her reasoning seemed plausible. At the time the conversation was closed, with my promise to consider the question.

I thought over the question much, and the more I thought the less inclined I felt to accept the proposition so kindly made by Mrs. Davis. I knew the North to be strong, and believed that the people would fight for the flag that they pretended to venerate so highly. The Republican party had just emerged from a heated campaign, flushed with victory, and I could not think that the hosts composing the party would quietly yield all they had gained in the Presidential canvass. A show of war from the South, I felt, would lead to actual war in the North; and with the two sections bitterly arrayed against each other, I preferred to cast my lot among the people of the North.

I parted with Mrs. Davis kindly, half promising to join her in the South if further deliberation should induce me to change my views. A few weeks before she left Washington I made two chintz wrappers for her. She said that she must give up expensive dressing for a while; and that she, with the Southern people, now that war was imminent, must learn to practise lessons of economy. She left some fine needle-work in my hands, which I finished, and forwarded to her at Montgomery, Alabama, in the month of June, through the assistance of Mrs. Emory, one of her oldest and best friends.

Since bidding them good-by at Washington, early in the year 1860, I have never met any of the Davis family. Years of excitement, years of bloodshed, and hundreds of thousands of graves intervene between the months I spent in the family and now. The years have brought many changes; and in view of these terrible changes even I, who was once a slave, who have been punished with the cruel lash, who have experienced the heart and soul tortures of a slave's life, can say to Mr. Jefferson Davis, "Peace! You have suffered! Go in peace."

In the winter of 1865 I was in Chicago, and one day visited the great charity fair held for the benefit of the families of those soldiers who were killed or wounded during the war. In one part of the building was a wax figure of Jefferson Davis, wearing over his other garments the dress in which it was reported that he was captured. There was always a great crowd around this figure, and I was naturally attracted towards it. I worked my way to the figure, and in examining the dress made the pleasing discovery that it was one of the chintz wrappers that I had made for Mrs. Davis, a short time before she departed from Washington for the South. When it was announced that I recognized the dress as one that I had made for the wife of the late Confederate President there was great cheering and excitement, and I at once became an object of the deepest curiosity. Great crowds followed me, and in order to escape from the embarrassing situation I left the building.

I believe it now is pretty well established that Mr. Davis had on a water-proof cloak instead of a dress, as first reported, when he was captured. This does not invalidate any portion of my story. The dress on the wax figure at the fair in Chicago unquestionably was one of the chintz wrappers that I made for Mrs. Davis in January, 1860, in Washington; and I infer, since it was not found on the body of the fugitive President of the South, it was taken from the trunks of Mrs. Davis, captured at the same time. Be this as it may, the coincidence is none the less striking and curious.

Chapter XI. The Assassination of President Lincoln

I had never heard Mr. Lincoln make a public speech, and, knowing the man so well, was very anxious to hear him. On the morning of the Tuesday after our return from City Point, Mrs. Lincoln came to my apartments, and before she drove away I asked permission to come to the White House that night and hear Mr. Lincoln speak.

"Certainly, Lizabeth; if you take any interest in political speeches, come and listen in welcome."

"Thank you, Mrs. Lincoln. May I trespass further on your kindness by asking permission to bring a friend with me?"

"Yes, bring your friend also. By the way, come in time to dress me before the speaking commences."

"I will be in time. You may rely upon that. Good morning," I added, as she swept from my room, and, passing out into the street, entered her carriage and drove away.

About 7 o'clock that evening I entered the White House. As I went up-stairs I glanced into Mr. Lincoln's room through the half-open door, and seated by a desk was the President, looking over his notes and muttering to himself. His face was thoughtful, his manner abstracted, and I knew, as I paused a moment to watch him, that he was rehearsing the part that he was to play in the great drama soon to commence.

Proceeding to Mrs. Lincoln's apartment, I worked with busy fingers, and in a short time her toilette was completed.

Great crowds began to gather in front of the White House, and loud calls were made for the President. The band stopped playing, and as he advanced to the centre window over the door to make his address, I looked out, and never saw such a mass of heads before. It was like a black, gently swelling sea. The swaying motion of the crowd, in the dim uncertain light, was like the rising and falling of billows—like the ebb and flow of the tide upon the stranded shore of the ocean. Close to the house the faces were plainly discernible, but they faded into mere ghostly outlines on the outskirts of the assembly; and what added to the weird, spectral beauty of the scene, was the confused hum of voices that rose above the sea of forms, sounding like the subdued, sullen roar of an ocean storm, or the wind soughing through the dark lonely forest. It was a grand and imposing scene, and when the President, with pale face and his soul flashing through his eyes, advanced to speak, he looked more like a demi-god than a man crowned with the fleeting days of mortality.

The moment the President appeared at the window he was greeted with a storm of applause, and voices re-echoed the cry, "A light! a light!"

A lamp was brought, and little Tad at once rushed to his father's side, exclaiming: "Let me hold the light, Papa! let me hold the light!"

Mrs. Lincoln directed that the wish of her son be gratified, and the lamp was transferred to his hands. The father and son standing there in the presence of thousands of free citizens, the one lost in a chain of eloquent ideas, the other looking up into the speaking face with a proud, manly look, formed a beautiful and striking tableau.

There were a number of distinguished gentlemen, as well as ladies, in the room, nearly all of whom remarked the picture.

I stood a short distance from Mr. Lincoln, and as the light from the lamp fell full upon him, making him stand out boldly in the darkness, a sudden thought struck me, and I whispered to the friend at my side:

"What an easy matter would it be to kill the President, as he stands there! He could be shot down from the crowd, and no one be able to tell who fired the shot."

I do not know what put such an idea into my head, unless it was the sudden remembrance of the many warnings that Mr. Lincoln had received.

The next day, I made mention to Mrs. Lincoln of the idea that had impressed me so strangely the night before, and she replied with a sigh:

"Yes, yes, Mr. Lincoln's life is always exposed. Ah, no one knows what it is to live in constant dread of some fearful tragedy. The President has been warned so often, that I tremble for him on every public occasion. I have a presentiment that he will meet with a sudden and violent end. I pray God to protect my beloved husband from the hands of the assassin."

Mr. Lincoln was fond of pets. He had two goats that knew the sound of his voice, and when he called them they would come bounding to his side. In the warm bright days, he and Tad would sometimes play in the yard with these goats, for an hour at a time. One Saturday afternoon I went to the White House to dress Mrs. Lincoln. I had nearly completed my task when the President came in. It was a bright day, and walking to the window, he looked down into the yard, smiled, and, turning to me, asked:

"Madam Elizabeth, you are fond of pets, are you not?"

"O yes, sir," I answered.

"Well, come here and look at my two goats. I believe they are the kindest and best goats in the world. See how they sniff the clear air, and skip and play in the sunshine. Whew! what a jump," he exclaimed as one of the goats made a lofty spring. "Madam Elizabeth, did you ever before see such an active goat?" Musing a moment, he continued: "He feeds on my bounty and jumps with joy. Do you think we could call him a bounty-jumper? But I flatter the bounty-jumper. My goat is far above him. I would rather wear his horns and hairy coat through life, than demean myself to the level of the man who plunders the national treasury in the name of patriotism. The man who enlists into the service for a consideration, and deserts the moment he receives his money but to repeat the play, is bad enough; but the men who manipulate the grand machine and who simply make the bounty-jumper their agent in an outrageous fraud are far worse. They are beneath the worms that crawl in the dark hidden places of earth."

His lips curled with haughty scorn, and a cloud was gathering on his brow. Only a moment the shadow rested on his face. Just then both goats looked up at the window and shook their heads as if they would say "How d'ye do, old friend?"

"See, Madam Elizabeth," exclaimed the President in a tone of enthusiasm, "my pets recognize me. How earnestly they look! There they go again; what jolly fun!" and he laughed outright as the goats bounded swiftly to the other side of the yard. Just then Mrs. Lincoln called out, "Come, Lizabeth; if I get ready to go down this evening I must finish dressing myself, or you must stop staring at those silly goats."

Mrs. Lincoln was not fond of pets, and she could not understand how Mr. Lincoln could take so much delight in his goats. After Willie's death, she could not bear the sight of anything he loved, not even a flower. Costly bouquets were presented to her, but she turned from them with a shudder, and either placed them in a room where she could not see them, or threw them out of the window. She gave all of Willie's toys—everything connected with him—away, as she said she could not look upon them without thinking of her poor dead boy, and to think of him, in his white shroud and cold grave, was maddening. I never in my life saw a more peculiarly constituted woman. Search the world over, and you will not find her counterpart. After Mr. Lincoln's death, the goats that he loved so well were given away—I believe to Mrs. Lee, *née* Miss Blair, one of the few ladies with whom Mrs. Lincoln was on intimate terms in Washington.

During my residence in the Capital I made my home with Mr. and Mrs. Walker Lewis, people of my own race, and friends in the truest sense of the word.

The days passed without any incident of particular note disturbing the current of life. On Friday morning, April 14th—alas! what American does not remember the day—I saw Mrs. Lincoln but for a moment. She told me that she was to attend the theatre that night with the President, but I was not summoned to assist her in making her toilette.

Sherman had swept from the northern border of Georgia through the heart of the Confederacy down to the sea, striking the death-blow to the rebellion. Grant had pursued General Lee beyond Richmond, and the army of Virginia, that had made such stubborn resistance, was crumbling to pieces. Fort Sumter had fallen;—the stronghold first wrenched from the Union, and which had braved the fury of Federal guns for so many years, was restored to the Union; the end of the war was near at hand, and the great pulse of the loyal North thrilled with joy. The dark war-cloud was fading, and a white-robed angel seemed to hover in the sky, whispering "Peace—peace on earth, good-will toward men!" Sons, brothers, fathers, friends, sweethearts were coming home. Soon the white tents would be folded, the volunteer army be disbanded, and tranquillity again reign. Happy, happy day!—happy at least to those who fought under the banner of the Union. There was great rejoicing throughout the North. From the Atlantic to the Pacific, flags were gayly thrown to the breeze, and at night every city blazed with its tens of thousand lights. But scarcely had the fireworks ceased to play, and the lights been taken down from the windows, when the lightning flashed the most appalling news over the magnetic wires. "The President has been murdered!" spoke the swift-winged messenger, and the loud huzza died upon the lips. A nation suddenly paused in the midst of festivity, and stood paralyzed with horror—transfixed with awe.

Oh, memorable day! Oh, memorable night! Never before was joy so violently contrasted with sorrow.

At 11 o'clock at night I was awakened by an old friend and neighbor, Miss M. Brown, with the startling intelligence that the entire Cabinet had been assassinated, and Mr. Lincoln shot, but not mortally wounded. When I heard the words I felt as if the blood had been frozen in my veins, and that my lungs must collapse for the want of air. Mr. Lincoln shot! the Cabinet assassinated! What could it mean? The streets were alive with wondering, awe-stricken people. Rumors flew thick and fast, and the wildest reports came with every new arrival. The words were repeated with blanched cheeks and quivering lips. I waked Mr. and Mrs. Lewis, and told them that the President was shot, and that I must go to the White House. I could not remain in a state of uncertainty. I felt that the house would not hold me. They tried to quiet me, but gentle words could not calm the wild tempest. They quickly dressed themselves, and we sallied out into the street to drift with the excited throng. We walked rapidly towards the White House, and on our way passed the residence of Secretary Seward, which was surrounded by armed soldiers, keeping back all intruders with the point of the bayonet. We hurried on, and as we approached the White House, saw that it too was surrounded with soldiers. Every entrance was strongly guarded, and no one was permitted to pass. The guard at the gate told us that Mr. Lincoln had not been brought home, but refused to give any other information. More excited than ever, we wandered down the street. Grief and anxiety were making me weak, and as we joined the outskirts of a large crowd, I began to feel as meek and humble as a penitent child. A gray-haired old man was passing. I caught a glimpse of his face, and it seemed so full of kindness and sorrow that I gently touched his arm, and imploringly asked:

"Will you please, sir, to tell me whether Mr. Lincoln is dead or not?"

"Not dead," he replied, "but dying. God help us!" and with a heavy step he passed on.

"Not dead, but dying! then indeed God help us!"

We learned that the President was mortally wounded—that he had been shot down in his box at the theatre, and that he was not expected to live till morning; when we returned home with heavy hearts. I could not sleep. I wanted to go to Mrs. Lincoln, as I pictured her wild with grief; but then I did not know where to find her, and I must wait till morning. Never did the hours drag so slowly. Every moment seemed an age, and I could do nothing but walk about and hold my arms in mental agony.

Morning came at last, and a sad morning was it. The flags that floated so gayly yesterday now were draped in black, and hung in silent folds at half-mast. The President was dead, and a nation was mourning for him. Every house was draped in black, and every face wore a solemn look. People spoke in subdued tones, and glided whisperingly, wonderingly, silently about the streets.

About eleven o'clock on Saturday morning a carriage drove up to the door, and a messenger asked for "Elizabeth Keckley."

"Who wants her?" I asked.

"I come from Mrs. Lincoln. If you are Mrs. Keckley, come with me immediately to the White House."

I hastily put on my shawl and bonnet, and was driven at a rapid rate to the White House. Everything about the building was sad and solemn. I was quickly shown to Mrs. Lincoln's room, and on entering, saw Mrs. L. tossing uneasily about upon a bed. The room was darkened, and the only person in it besides the widow of the President was Mrs. Secretary Welles, who had spent the night with her. Bowing to Mrs. Welles, I went to the bedside.

"Why did you not come to me last night, Elizabeth—I sent for you?" Mrs. Lincoln asked in a low whisper.

"I did try to come to you, but I could not find you," I answered, as I laid my hand upon her hot brow.

I afterwards learned, that when she had partially recovered from the first shock of the terrible tragedy in the theatre, Mrs. Welles asked:

"Is there no one, Mrs. Lincoln, that you desire to have with you in this terrible affliction?"

"Yes, send for Elizabeth Keckley. I want her just as soon as she can be brought here."

Three messengers, it appears, were successively despatched for me, but all of them mistook the number and failed to find me.

Shortly after entering the room on Saturday morning, Mrs. Welles excused herself, as she said she must go to her own family, and I was left alone with Mrs. Lincoln.

She was nearly exhausted with grief, and when she became a little quiet, I asked and received permission to go into the Guests' Room, where the body of the President lay in state. When I crossed the threshold of the room, I could not help recalling the day on which I had seen little Willie lying in his coffin where the body of his father now lay. I remembered how the President had wept over the pale beautiful face of his gifted boy, and now the President himself was dead. The last time I saw him he spoke kindly to me, but alas! the lips would never move again. The light had faded from his eyes, and when the light went out the soul went with it. What a noble soul was his—noble in all the noble attributes of God! Never did I enter the solemn chamber of death with such palpitating heart and trembling footsteps as I entered it that day. No common mortal had died. The Moses of my people had fallen in the hour of his triumph. Fame had woven her choicest chaplet for his brow. Though the brow was cold and pale in death, the chaplet should not fade, for God had studded it with the glory of the eternal stars.

When I entered the room, the members of the Cabinet and many distinguished officers of the army were grouped around the body of their fallen chief. They made room for me, and, approaching the body, I lifted the white cloth from the white face of the man that I had worshipped as an idol—looked upon as a demi-god. Notwithstanding the violence of the death of the President, there was something beautiful as well as grandly solemn in the expression of the placid face. There lurked the sweetness and gentleness of childhood, and the stately grandeur of godlike intellect. I gazed long at the face, and turned away with tears in my eyes and a choking sensation in my throat. Ah! never was man so widely mourned before. The whole world bowed their heads in grief when Abraham Lincoln died.

Returning to Mrs. Lincoln's room, I found her in a new paroxysm of grief. Robert was bending over his mother with tender affection, and little Tad was crouched at the foot of the bed with a world of agony in his young face. I shall never forget the scene—the wails of a broken heart, the unearthly shrieks, the terrible convulsions, the wild, tempestuous outbursts of grief from the soul. I bathed Mrs. Lincoln's head with cold water, and soothed the terrible tornado as best I could. Tad's grief at his father's death was as great as the grief of his mother, but her terrible outbursts awed the boy into silence. Sometimes he would throw his arms around her neck, and exclaim, between his broken sobs, "Don't cry so, Mamma! don't cry, or you will make me cry, too! You will break my heart."

Mrs. Lincoln could not bear to hear Tad cry, and when he would plead to her not to break his heart, she would calm herself with a great effort, and clasp her child in her arms.

Every room in the White House was darkened, and every one spoke in subdued tones, and moved about with muffled tread. The very atmosphere breathed of the great sorrow which weighed heavily upon each heart. Mrs. Lincoln never left her room, and while the body of her husband was being borne in solemn state from the Atlantic to the broad prairies of the West, she was weeping with her fatherless children in her private chamber. She denied admittance to almost every one, and I was her only companion, except her children, in the days of her great sorrow.

There were many surmises as to who was implicated with J. Wilkes Booth in the assassination of the President. A new messenger had accompanied Mr. and Mrs. Lincoln to the theatre on that terrible Friday night. It was the duty of this messenger to stand at the door of the box during the performance, and thus guard the inmates from all intrusion. It appears that the messenger was carried away by the play, and so neglected his duty that Booth gained easy admission to the box. Mrs. Lincoln firmly believed that this messenger was implicated in the assassination plot.

One night I was lying on a lounge near the bed occupied by Mrs. Lincoln. One of the servants entering the room, Mrs. L. asked:

"Who is on watch to-night?"

"The new messenger," was the reply.

"What! the man who attended us to the theatre on the night my dear, good husband was murdered! He, I believe, is one of the murderers. Tell him to come in to me."

The messenger had overheard Mrs. Lincoln's words through the half-open door, and when he came in he was trembling violently.

She turned to him fiercely: "So you are on guard to-night—on guard in the White House after helping to murder the President!"

"Pardon me, but I did not help to murder the President. I could never stoop to murder—much less to the murder of so good and great a man as the President."

"But it appears that you *did* stoop to murder."

"No, no! don't say that," he broke in. "God knows that I am innocent."

"I don't believe you. Why were you not at the door to keep the assassin out when he rushed into the box?"

"I did wrong, I admit, and I have bitterly repented it, but I did not help to kill the President. I did not believe that any one would try to kill so good a man in such a public place, and the belief made me careless. I was attracted by the play, and did not see the assassin enter the box."

"But you should have seen him. You had no business to be careless. I shall always believe that you are guilty. Hush! I shan't hear another word," she exclaimed, as the messenger essayed to reply. "Go now and keep your watch," she added, with an imperious wave of her hand. With mechanical step and white face the messenger left the room, and Mrs. Lincoln fell back on her pillow, covered her face with her hands, and commenced sobbing.

Robert was very tender to his mother in the days of her sorrow.

He suffered deeply, as his haggard face indicated, but he was ever manly and collected when in the presence of his mother. Mrs. Lincoln was extremely nervous, and she refused to have anybody about her but myself. Many ladies called, but she received none of them. Had she been less secluded in her grief, perhaps she would have had many warmer friends to-day than she has. But far be it from me to harshly judge the sorrow of any one. Could the ladies who called to condole with Mrs. Lincoln, after the death of her husband, and who were denied admittance to her chamber, have seen how completely prostrated she was with grief, they would have learned to speak more kindly of her. Often at night, when Tad would hear her sobbing, he would get up, and come to her bed in his white sleeping-clothes: "Don't cry, Mamma; I cannot sleep if you cry! Papa was good, and he has gone to heaven. He is happy there. He is with God and brother Willie. Don't cry, Mamma, or I will cry too."

The closing appeal always proved the most effectual, as Mrs. Lincoln could not bear to hear her child cry.

Tad had been petted by his father, but petting could not spoil such a manly nature as his. He seemed to realize that he was the son of a President—to realize it in its loftiest and noblest sense. One morning, while being dressed, he looked up at his nurse, and said: "Pa is dead. I can hardly believe that I shall never see him again. I must learn to take care of myself now." He looked thoughtful a moment, then added, "Yes, Pa is dead, and I am only Tad Lincoln now, little Tad, like other little boys. I am not a President's son now. I won't have many presents any more. Well, I will try and be a good boy, and will hope to go some day to Pa and brother Willie, in heaven." He was a brave, manly child, and knew that influence had passed out of their hands with the death of his father, and that his position in life was altered. He seemed to feel that people petted him, and gave him presents, because they wanted to please the President of the United States. From that period forward he became more independent, and in a short time learned to dispense with the services of a nurse. While in Chicago, I saw him get out his clothes one Sunday morning and dress himself, and the change was such a great one to me—for while in the White House, servants obeyed his every nod and bid—that I could scarcely refrain from shedding tears. Had his father lived, I knew it would have been different with his favorite boy. Tad roomed with Robert, and he always took pride in pleasing his brother.

After the Committee had started West with the body of the President, there was quite a breeze of excitement for a few days as to where the remains should be interred. Secretary Stanton and others held frequent conferences with Robert, Mr. Todd, Mrs. Lincoln's cousin, and Dr. Henry, an old schoolmate and friend of Mr. Lincoln. The city authorities of Springfield had purchased a beautiful plat of ground in a prosperous portion of the city, and work was rapidly progressing on the tomb, when Mrs. Lincoln made strenuous objection to the location. She declared that she would stop the body in Chicago before it should be laid to rest in the lot purchased for the purpose by the City of Springfield. She gave as a reason, that it was her desire to be laid by the side of her husband when she died, and that such would be out of the question in a public place of the kind. As is well known, the difficulty was finally settled by placing the remains of the President in the family vault at Oak Ridge, a charming spot for the home of the dead.

After the President's funeral Mrs. Lincoln rallied, and began to make preparations to leave the White House. One day she suddenly exclaimed: "God, Elizabeth, what a change! Did ever woman have to suffer so much and experience so great a change? I had an ambition to be Mrs. President; that ambition has been gratified, and now I must step down from the pedestal. My poor husband! had he never been President, he might be living to-day. Alas! all is over with me!"

Folding her arms for a few moments, she rocked back and forth, then commenced again, more vehemently than ever: "My God, Elizabeth, I can never go back to Springfield! no, never, until I go in my shroud to be laid by my dear husband's side, and may Heaven speed that day! I should like to live for my sons, but life is so full of misery that I would rather die." And then she would go off into a fit of hysterics.

Historian Emory Thomas notes that in the early part of 1863, "the war gods seemed to smile upon the embryo Southern nation."[1] A combined land and naval assault enabled the Confederacy to recapture Galveston, Texas, which had been lost earlier to superior Union forces. A Southern fleet also managed to control river traffic on the Mississippi below Vicksburg. And stalwart Confederates resisted a massive Union assault on Charleston, South Carolina, where commander, Pierre Gustave Toutant Beauregard, dubbed a hero at Fort Sumter and First Manassas, distinguished himself once more. Jefferson Davis and his staff believed Southern independence to be within grasp.[2]

However, by the year's end, the Confederate navy would be rendered ineffectual; Vicksburg would fall to Union forces on July fourth, the day Lee began his retreat from Gettysburg; and P. G. T. Beauregard would be reassigned to peripheral duties in Georgia and South Carolina after a disastrous showing at Shiloh.[3] Depletion of resources, failure to secure European intervention in the war, and abysmal military generalship, particularly in the Army of Tennessee, would sound the death knell for the Confederacy.

Almost at once, the meteoric rise and fall of the Confederate States of America became a story of mythic proportions. With whatever benefits limited hindsight can offer, participants and observers began writing their versions of the war, offering revisions and adjustments as the Lost Cause required. But the myth of the South as a region unto itself, a place with its own distinctive institutions and temperament, rose long before the outbreak of hostilities at Fort Sumter. Craig Werner notes, for example, that "by 1840 the increasing divergence of economic, political, and social conditions had created a specifically Southern literature reflecting the distinctive concerns and attitudes that were to survive as constituting elements of Southern literature in later eras."[4]

Contributing to "the romantic, plantation tradition in fiction"[5] was Caroline Howard Gilman, a Boston native who lived and worked in Charleston, South Carolina, for most of her adult life. A prolific writer, Gilman may be best known for *Recollections of a Southern Matron* (1837). This novel, "sentimental and didactic like most Northern women's fiction of the era, focuses on the experience of a plantation girl growing into womanhood, the first Southern fiction on the theme that would become a standard feature of the tradition."[6]

As the most prominent and prolific writer in the antebellum South, William Gilmore Simms was often compared invidiously with Poe. Influenced by Sir Walter Scott and James Fenimore Cooper, Simms wrote novels in the genre of the historical romance, while also seeking to produce a distinctively Southern literature reflecting the interests of "low-country society, particularly Charleston, with its elegant, caste-conscious aristocracy . . . ,"[7] which simultaneously provided Simms with targets for satire. Although his novels are formulaic in structure and his themes conventional for the time, Simms's short fiction is more original, showing a tendency, in Mary Ann Wimsatt's view, to "experiment with satire, fantasy, whimsy, fairy love, the dream vision, the supernatural"[8] and other stock Gothic features. His story "Confessions of a Murderer" is replete with Gothic stereotypes, among them the inexplicably malevolent narrator and his sympathetically drawn victim, a helpless woman named Emily. With Poe-like verisimilitude, Simms provides a quasi-exploration of the narrator's murky psychological motives in killing a girl who is "most artless, the most innocent of all God's creatures!" Displaying obvious cracks in his facade as a gentleman, the narrator ends by staring out the window of a dungeon, reflecting on the inadequacies of his upbringing.

The desire to observe a code of manners did not keep the Southern gentleman from answering a pugilistic challenge when the occasion required. The "gentleman," especially the frontier variety, often proved a rough-and-ready brawler ready to fight at the first hint of perceived insult or slighted honor. Whereas such contests were regarded as duels or "affairs" among elite Southerners, similar matches pitting backwoodsmen were deemed rude brawls and low-life spectacles by the time of Augustus Baldwin Longstreet's *Georgia Scenes* (1835), considered the first authentic book of Southern humor. Longstreet's "The Fight" offers a no-holds-barred sketch of two north Georgia backwoods titans engaged in a slugfest to decide who is the "better man." Although Longstreet offers a moral censure of such antics, "The Fight" conveys too much enjoyment of its subject for readers to take seriously the author's finger wagging.

Even when striving for humorous effect, most male narrators of the period, being upper-class and white, sought to convey an urbane tenor and genteel style, manifesting tension between the events being described and the authorial voice describing them. Such is the case of Joseph Glover Baldwin in *The Flush Times of Alabama and Mississippi: A Series of Sketches* (1835). Baldwin has no trouble satirizing the insatiable appetite for fritters, small battercakes fried in deep fat, exhibited by an unidentified "Squire," whose elevated opinion of himself is matched only by Baldwin's elevated prose in describing him.

There is little pretense in Augusta Jane Wilson's *Macaria: or Altars of Sacrifice* (1864)—only shrewd humor and protest of existing social conventions. Possessing the distinction of once having been banned by the American Library Association, Wilson initiates a tradition of rule-breaking in *Macaria,* introducing a memorable heroine named Irene, whose independence enables her to declare, "As to what people think, I don't care a cent; as to whether my ancestors did or did not carry their lunch in their own aristocratic hands is a matter of no consequence whatever. I despise all this ridiculous nonsense about aristocracy of family, and I mean to do as I please." Although Wilson's prose is mannered, her sentiments are anything but, making hers a fresh and startlingly unconventional voice announcing new roles for women writers of the period.

It has been argued that the Civil War destroyed the emerging humorist tradition in Southern literature. Closer scrutiny reveals that the impulse toward humor was always moderated by historical tensions ready to surface at any time. The satire inspired by class distinctions presupposed the necessity of slavery in order for such satire to exist. With the approach of war, humor dissipates, and hard-edged polemical prose becomes the order of the day. Efforts to convince, rather than to amuse or to entertain, shape much of the writing, as is the case with John C. Calhoun's *A Disquisition on Government,* an abstruse argument maintaining that inequality is the basic condition of human beings and that Jeffersonian egalitarianism will ultimately result in dangerously unrestrained social impulses. Calhoun further claims that liberty is not an inalienable right but a privilege that must be earned gradually: "The progress of a people rising from a lower to a higher point in the scale of liberty is necessarily slow;—and by attempting to precipitate, we either retard, or permanently defeat it."

A kindred spirit to Calhoun, Jefferson Davis rose to the Confederacy's highest office by wrapping himself in the mantle of states' rights. Davis's "Introduction" to *The Rise and Fall of the Confederate Government* is the most succinct statement of states' rights doctrine and defense that readers are likely to find. Ironically, the exigencies of war and the need for centralization forced Davis to abandon his role as defender of a limited, states' rights government. As a result, critics like Edward Pollard attacked Davis, calling him "King Jeff the First" for making the Confederacy's struggle "a rich man's war and a poor man's fight," a reference to the practice of exempting anyone from military service who owned more than twenty slaves.

Against the arguments that slavery was a Christian and humane system stands the solid opposition of Angelina Emily Grimké, whose *Appeal to the Christian Women of the South* dissects the proslavery position, exposing "excuses and palliations." By a thorough exegesis of biblical passages often used to justify slavery, Grimké shows the incompatibility of slaveholding and Christianity, appealing to Southern women as a potent moral force capable of ending this "most unnatural and unwarrantable power" over the slave. Grimké points out the dissimilarities between ancient and contemporary slaveholding, recognizing the racist nature of slavery that existed in the South from the region's earliest days.

Grimké's voice dies against the thundering patriotism that conferred on Henry Timrod the status of "Laureat of the Confederacy." Novelist and historian Richard Marius acknowledges that the tubercular Timrod "was indeed the best poet of the region at the time of the Civil War." Timrod's poem "Charleston" is a tribute to the city and its people already in the throes of war. In his essay "Literature in the South," Timrod's complaint is a familiar one: the lack of an appreciative audience for authentic literature. The very people who are "forever extolling Southern taste, Southern learning, and Southern civilization," Timrod complains, are the ones who, through "their self-complacency," settle for rubbish when choosing literature. Timrod's essay explores some of the social trends that contribute to the lack of a vital imagination in the South of his time.

Never without its critics from within, the South finds Mary Chesnut an astute diagnostician of the region's ills. Daughter of a South Carolina governor and the wife of a United States senator, Chesnut moved in the highest realms of the Confederacy, her photograph occupying a place on Jefferson Davis's mantel at the Confederate white house in Richmond. Yet her *A Diary from Dixie* (1861), recently edited as *The Private Mary Chesnut: The Unpublished Civil War Diaries*, shows Chesnut's contempt for a patriarchal system that promotes hypocrisy, infidelity, and bastardy, which slaveholders condone as a matter of course: "This *only* I see: like the patriarchs of old our men live all in one house with their wives & their concubines, & the Mulattoes one sees in every family exactly resemble the white children—& every lady tells you who is the father of all the Mulatto children in every body's household, but those in her own, she seems to think drop from the clouds or pretends so to think . . ." Chesnut is especially rankled by what she perceives as the sexually licentious nature of slave mistresses, a complaint frequent among women of Chesnut's social position. Chesnut's resentment is simply a toxic by-product of the system she despises since female slaves had no choice about whether to be promiscuous or not. The body of the black female slave was the master's for the taking, as slaveholders themselves were quick to point out. Notwithstanding her criticisms of the South, Chesnut's diaries are full of the news of war and hopes for the Confederate cause.

Just as Chesnut's entries become increasingly bleak as the war rages, so does Kate Cumming's *A Journal of Hospital Life in the Confederate Army of Tennessee* (1866) reflect the deteriorating state of the Confederate army over time. She writes so that "the southerners may learn a lesson from the superhuman endurance of the glorious dead and mutilated living who so nobly did their duty in their country's hour of peril." Complaining that the North waged an illegal war under false pretenses, Cumming argues that "calling it fighting to the Union is about as false as the love of the abolitionist for the negro, and we all know what that is." Perhaps the strongest feature of Cumming's account is simply the picture she offers of the wounded and dying:

> The men lying all over the house, on their blankets, just as they were brought from the battle-field. They are in the hall, on the gallery, and crowded into very small rooms. The foul air from this mass of human beings at first made me giddy and sick, but I soon got over it. We have to walk, and when we give the men any thing kneel, in blood and water; but we think nothing of it at all. There was much suffering among the patients last night; one old man groaned all the time. He was about sixty years of age, and had lost a leg. He lived near Corinth, and had come there the morning of the battle to see his two sons, who were in the army, and he could not resist shouldering his musket and going into the fight. I comforted him as well as I could. He is a religious man, and prayed nearly all night.

Notes

1. Emory Thomas, *The Confederate Nation: 1861–1865* (New York: Harper and Row, 1979), 215.
2. Thomas, 215.
3. Thomas, 215–277, for complete discussion.
4. Craig Werner. "The Old South, 1815–1840," *The History of Southern Literature*, ed. Louis D. Rubin et al. (Baton Rouge: Louisiana State University Press, 1985), 81.
5. Werner, 87.
6. Werner, 87.
7. Mary Anne Wimsatt, "William Gilmore Simms," in *The History of Southern Literature*, ed. Louis D. Rubin et al. (Baton Rouge: Louisiana State University Press, 1985), 114.
8. Wimsatt, 114.

Caroline Howard Gilman

(1794–1888)

Caroline Howard Gilman was born in Boston in 1794. Both of her parents died by the time she was ten years old. As a result, she spent her teen years moving from town to town in New England until the family finally settled in Cambridge, Massachusetts, where she lived until her marriage at the age of twenty-five to Samuel Gilman, a Unitarian minister. During these years, she began her writing career by publishing a number of pieces in local newspapers, as well as a story in the *North American Review*. Immediately after their marriage, the Gilmans moved to Charleston, South Carolina, where Samuel Gilman took an appointment at the Second Independent Church. In

1832, she began publishing *The Southern Rosebud,* a children's magazine; then, in 1835, she expanded its focus to the entire family, altering the title to *Southern Rose.*

In 1834, she published *Recollections of a Housekeeper,* which she had serialized in her weekly magazine under the pseudonym Clarissa Packard. The success of that work, which humorously related the tribulations of a middle-class, New England wife, led to the publication of *Recollections of a Southern Matron* in 1838. In the second *Recollections,* Gilman clearly demonstrates her support of the Southern cause, portraying plantation life as idyllic and slaves as contented, eager servants of indulgent masters. In her preface to the book, she defends its sentimentality, contending that if its portrayals "have too much sunshine about them, I can only reply, that, to have made different descriptions, I must have resorted to imagination instead of fact, as far as my personal observation is concerned." Gilman hoped that the deepening divisions between North and South might still be bridged if opponents would only recognize that the institution of the family transcended politics. These hopes were dashed by the war, and after its outbreak, she became a strong Southern partisan. Though she made several attempts to revive her literary career after the war, she never regained her former popularity.

from *Recollections of a Southern Matron*

Chapter I. Old Jacque.

> "*Onward,*
> *O'ershadowed more by the green underwood,*
> *Some slight-raised mounds showed where the dead were laid.*
> *Few gravestones told who slept beneath the turf.*
> *(Perchance the heart that deeply mourns needs not*
> *Such poor remembrancer.) The forest flowers*
> *Themselves had fondly clustered there—and white*
> *Azalias with sweet breath stood round about,*
> *Like fair young maidens mourning o'er their dead.*
> *In some sweet solitude like this I would*
> *That I might sleep my last long dreamless sleep.*"
> Anna Maria Wells

> "*He sought him through the bands of fight,*
> *Mid many a pile of slaughtered dead,*
> *Beneath the pale moon's misty light,*
> *With form that shuddered at each tread:*
> *For every step in blood was taken.*"
> W. G. Simms

I write in my paternal mansion. The Ashley, with a graceful sweep, glitters like a lake before me, reflecting the sky and the bending foliage. Occasionally a flat, with its sluggish motion, or a boat, with its urging sail, passes along, and the woods echo to the song or the horn of the negro, waking up life in the solitude. The avenue of noble oaks, under which I sported in childhood, still spread their strong arms, and rustle in the passing breeze. My children are frolicking on the lawn where my first footsteps

were watched by tender parents, and one of those parents rests beneath yonder circling cedars. Change! Sameness! What a perpetual chime those words ring on the ear
of memory! My children love to lead me to the spot where they may spell the inscription on one princely monument to my grandfather, and hear the tale I have to tell of
the fair, the good, and the brave who sleep in that enclosure, sacred to the domestic
dead. There is but one inscription there, for we were as one.

I sometimes feel a joy that all are here—my grandparents; the mother who gave me
being; the baby-sister, who looked like a sunbeam on the world and passed away; my
first-born, he who was twined to my heart's pulses by ties as strong as those which call
up its *natural* vibration; my noble brothers, and my poor cousin Anna, who planted herself the rose that blossoms on her grave! The sun gilds the cedars with his brightest
morning hue; *they* shelter the sleepers from his noonday beams; and when the moon
rises over the cleared fields, showing an amphitheatre of distant woods, the cedar-
mound stands out in full relief, and those dark sentinels seem to guard the dead. I thank
thee, Heaven, that all I love are here!—that stranger-dust mingles not with mine! The tumult of the city rolls not across this sanctuary; careless curiosity treads not on these secluded graves; nor does the idler cull the blossoms that affection has planted, or that
time, with unsparing hand, has hung in graceful wreaths or clustered beauty around. No
rude sound disturbs the silence. The whippoorwill softens, by her melancholy lay, the
mockbird's tale of love and joy. The hare steals lightly over the hillocks, and the serpent
twines his silken folds among the herbage; yet do they not mar, like man, the sacred
relics of memory, nor with jest and profanity disturb the gloom.

My grandfather fell early in our national struggle for liberty, and his bones might
have whitened on the battlefield, had not a locket, containing the fair hair of my
grandmother, suspended from his neck, revealed him to a faithful servant. Good old
Jacque! How often have I climbed his knees to hear his stories of the past! I even love
to recall the peculiar accent with which he beguiled our evenings, when appointed by
our parents to superintend the younger servants in their absence. I can fancy I see
him now, in winter, throwing the oak logs or lightwood knots on the wide hearth,
standing (for he never would sit in the house, even in the presence of the children, unless when holding us on his knees) with a perpetual habit of conscientious trust; or,
in summer, seeking some sunny spot, and, with his blue handkerchief tied round his
head, employing his feeble hands in net or basket making. Rarely could he resist our
Southern entreaty of, *Do, if you please*, daddy Jacque, tell us about grandpapa's
locket, and how he died.

Jacque had been intrusted with the entire control of his young master's household
during the term of his education in Europe; and while the confidence placed in him had
somewhat increased his self-conceit, it never induced him to take a liberty beyond
those which his peculiar situation authorized. Roseland, from the beauty of its location
and its valuable paintings, was frequently visited by strangers in the absence of its orphan proprietor, and it is a singular fact that Jacque was never known to ascend the hall
stairs on such occasions. He pointed out the way with a bow and flourish of profound
respect, and met the guests by a private stairway after they had ascended.

His master returned, married a lovely and highly-educated Southern girl, and the following year Roseland was made doubly beautiful by the birth of a noble boy, the pride of
the house and plantation. This happiness was not of long duration, for the times approached which tried American souls, and the young father was called from the peaceful
sunshine of his home, from the caresses of his wife and the prattle of his child, to the wild

and stormy hardships of war. The night before his departure his wife led him to his likeness by Copley, which still hangs in the hall, and perused his lineaments long and earnestly. She gazed on the manly form beside her, then on the graceful but inanimate representative, took in the loving glance of the living eye, and compared it with its calmer image; then, with a bitter sigh, sank into his arms. The young soldier comforted her with a husband's love, and drew her to the bedside of their sleeping boy. Little Henry started from his repose as they bent over him with whispered words, clung to his father's neck a moment, and then closing his eyes like the bell of a twilight flower, sank upon his pillow.

With his beautiful wife still resting on his arm, the father took from his desk a locket containing her hair, threw the black riband from which it was suspended about his neck, and kissed it fondly. The night passed heavily away, and darkness heavier than night hung over Roseland, when, on the following morning, he departed, attended by Jacque.

In an engagement with the British, Jacque lost sight of his master; the enemy were victorious, and the Americans retreated, leaving their dead unprotected. When the pursuers were exhausted, Jacque searched with anxiety among the living, and, finding no trace of him, returned with sad, cautious, but resolute steps to the field of death. Among the disfigured remains he vainly endeavoured for a long time to distinguish him; he who had so lately reposed in the arms of happy love, had found a cold and bloody bed with the promiscuous slain, among whom not even faithful friendship could detect his semblance. At length Jacque found on a mutilated form a locket, with its braid of auburn hair. He shook his head with an expression of satisfied grief, and wiped the bloody jewel with his coat sleeve. Then bearing the body to a stream, cleansed it reverently, dug a grave, and laid it in its place of rest. Touched and kindled by affectionate remembrance, he knelt on the pliant mould, and offered up an untutored prayer.

It was a dark and stormy evening when he returned, and my grandmother had kept her young son awake, with gentle artifice, for companionship. A footstep was heard in the piazza, and Dash gave a growl between warning and recognition, while Henry, clapping his hands, exclaimed, "Papa! papa!" His mother started as Jacque entered, and exclaimed, "Where is your master?"

Jacque was silent, and stood wiping from his cheeks the streaming tears.

"Tell me, Jacque, for the love of God," cried she, clasping the negro's arm, "where is your master?"

"Jacque got no maussa now," said he, sobbing, "but little Maus Henry."

A long and piercing shriek broke forth from the widow's stricken heart, and she fell senseless on the floor beside her frightened son.

The intelligence spread rapidly through the plantation. Shrieks and lamentations were heard from hut to hut—wild gesticulations were seen by the kindled torchlights among the young, as they cried, "My maussa dead, poor me!"—while the old, rocking on their seats and lifting their hands, responded, "The Lord's will be done. *He* knows."

The following day all was calm but the widow's heart; there the bitter strife of a *new* sorrow raged like a tempest. Even Henry's presence was intolerable. Poor boy! his very step was harsh to her, as, with a paper cap and wooden sword, he marched about her apartment, threatening to revenge his father's death.

Jacque was for several days revolving a measure of importance in his own mind; and at length, determining to give it utterance, went to claim a few moments' attention from his mistress.

She could only shade her eyes, as if to shut out too painful an object, and with one hand pressed closely on her heart, as though to hush its tumult.

"Jacque don't mean no disrespec," said the negro, bowing, as if his errand had something in it of dignity; "my missis know dat as my missis is poorly, and Maussa Henry an't got of no size, Jacque has to turn over what is best to be done for de family; and one great trouble it is on my mind, dat my maussa, what provide like one lord even for niggers, let alone white folks, should lay out mong de wolf and varmin, when we could gie 'em such good commodation here, and keep our eye on him, to say nothing of Christian buryin."

My grandmother was instantly roused; and, starting up, with an animated voice she said, "My dear, good Jacque, can he be brought to me? God bless you for the thought!"

A motive for action was now given her, and her heart seemed lightened of a part of its burden. It was a consolation to her to take Henry by the hand, and go forth in search of an appropriate spot for her husband's grave. It seemed to her excited imagination like preparing an apartment for an absent friend.

"Here, mamma," said her prattling boy, "is a pretty place. Papa used to stand under this tree and throw chips into the pond for Dash to bring to me."

"No, my son," said his mother, musingly; "it is too far. I must see the spot from my window. Look, Henry, at the cluster of cedars on that slightly-rising ground. See how the sun shines on the tree-tops, while all beneath is gloom! Like my hopes," she continued, mentally, "so lately seeming bright when all was darkness. That shall be the spot, Henry," she continued, "and you must see that I am laid there too."

The boy looked wistfully at her, and said, "And where shall I go, mamma?"

He had unconsciously touched the right string; and, as she stooped to kiss his forehead, she patiently resolved to wait God's will, and live for him.

While these scenes of tenderness were beguiling the feelings of the widow, Jacque, with a band of fellow-servants, went on his melancholy errand. Even to the imagination, which only partially illuminated the uneducated mind of the negro, the contrast was strong between the aspect of that now silent field, and the recent period when contending forces, with weapons flashing in the sun, and faces tinged with expectation, and footsteps timed to the march of war, had passed before him. It was a moonlight night, one of those nights which seem to exaggerate brightness and stillness, when Jacque led the way to his master's rude grave.

"'Tis a pretty sight, my young maussas and missis," he used to say, when relating this story, while we stood with inward tremour, almost expecting the pictures of our grandparents to start from their frames; "'tis a pretty thing for see one corpse lay out handsome on he natural bed, wid he head to de east, and he limb straight, and he eye shut, and he white shroud, and de watchers sing psalm; but 'twas altogedder onnatural to see my poor maussa wid de ragiments on, and de varmin busy bout him, and de moonlight shine down, and de owl hoot. Dem niggers (natural fools) get scare when we get to maussa self; den says I, 'My men, how you been let folks say dat we have Christian grave, while our maussa, what fed us and kivered us, was laying mong wolf? It's an ugly job, but to it, my men; and as it is a disrespec to sing "heave ho," one of you strike up a hymn to help us on.'"

There was no ear to listen to those sounds as they rose up on the midnight air, no eye to appreciate that intrepidity which could conquer the dread of superstitious ignorance. I am wrong. He who formed *hearts* in one mould did not disregard them.

They placed the remains of the soldier in the coffin brought for them, and closed it reverently.

The widow, nerved for the obsequies of her husband, reclined in silence, with Henry by her side. Friends from the city and neighbouring plantations sat or stood in whispering circles, shrouded by scarfs, and hoods, and weepers, each holding a sprig of rosemary twined with white paper; the glasses and pictures were turned to the wall, and every article of taste covered with a white cloth. Labour was suspended, the household servants stood in the piazza clothed in mourning, and the field-slaves, with such little testimonials of external respect as they could beg or borrow, arranged themselves below. The coffin was brought to the piazza, its costly ornaments riveted, and little Henry held up to see the inscription. In the city, after a recent decease, the widow would have remained secluded in the formality of grief; but in this case there seemed to be a call for a representative mourner; and, taking Henry's hand, she followed the six negro female *waiters* dressed in white, with napkins pinned over their shoulders, who were preceded by the coffin, which was borne by his people, attended by the pall-bearers, friends of the deceased. The procession passed on, followed by the servants, to Cedar Mound. The coffin was lowered, "dust to dust" was pronounced over it, and the earth fell upon its glittering decorations. Henry clung to his mother, crying, "Papa, come back," while the lamentations and shrieking howl of the negroes filled the air. The widow looked on with zealous scrutiny until the last spadeful of earth was deposited on the swelling mound; then taking her son home, retired to her apartment, where her heart only knew its own bitterness.

The boy soon forgot, in childish blessedness, the funeral of his father, and his notes of happiness rang through the mansion; but how achingly did his mother's thoughts for lingering years dwell in sad revery on her husband's grave. And it is on that spot that my eye now turns. She trained the various vines over its white paling, and planned the monument sacred to her first beloved. There little Henry loved to play with the falling leaves, or gather spring flowers; there his mother laid her head, crowned with reverend honours; there my mother lies; and there may my limbs be borne when God shall call my spirit. But no gloom rests upon it. It has always been a favourite scene for the children of our household. It is not enough that grief should go there and lay down its earthly treasure, or that old age should moralize beneath its shades; happy voices, like Henry's, may still be heard in its enclosure, and the crisp and fresh winter rose that my own Lewis has thrown in my lap he gathered from poor cousin Anna's grave.

William Gilmore Simms

(1806–1870)

The most renowned antebellum Southern writers were Edgar Allan Poe and William Gilmore Simms, but it was Simms who more truly represented the characteristics that have always distinguished Southern literature: a strong sense of place, an awareness of time and the past, and a perception of the South as a distinctive civilization. However, there is no question that only a small portion of his prodigious literary output is of any enduring value. Although modern assessments of his work reveal numerous flaws, it is important to remember that the popular fiction of Sir Walter Scott and of James Fenimore Cooper evince the same flaws, and although much of Simms's oeuvre is forgettable, his best work rivals and even surpasses the works of better-known novelists.

Simms, who was born in Charleston, South Carolina, was educated in that city's public schools. Simms's mother died in childbirth in 1808, and when his father's business failed, necessitating a removal to Mississippi, the young Simms remained behind under the supervision of his maternal grandmother. After spending two years in the College of Charleston, he worked six years as a pharmacist's apprentice before abandoning that endeavor in order to read law. During this same period, he made a number of trips to the Southwest to visit his father, journeys that would provide him with the material for his well-known border romances. He married in 1826 and was admitted to the South Carolina Bar in 1827, but despite these new responsibilities, he was actively pursuing a literary career, publishing four little-remembered books of poetry. In 1829, Simms gave up his law practice to purchase the Charleston *City Gazette*, and in the years in which he headed that paper, he took firm editorial stands against nullification. The newspaper was hurt financially by his unpopular views, and in 1832, he sold it at a heavy loss. Simms's wife had also died in 1832, and later that year, he traveled north, first to Massachusetts and later to New York, where he made a number of contacts, including William Cullen Bryant and Evert Duyckinck. Newly inspired, he returned to Charleston to begin writing fiction.

Over the next twenty-five years, Simms wrote twenty-seven novels, several collections of tales, a history of South Carolina, and four biographies (his biography of Francis Marion is still a respected source for the study of the Revolutionary War general's life). The novels—colonial romances, romances of the Revolution, and border romances—vary greatly in quality. At his best, Simms surpassed Cooper in characterization and ability to sustain a narrative, but many of his efforts, especially imaginative versions of Spanish history, were exceedingly poor and received devastating reviews. *The Yemassee* (1835) is the best of his early novels, and his four Revolutionary romances of the 1850s, beginning with *Katharine Walton* in 1851, are also worthy of attention. Simms himself considered his last romance, *The Cassique of Kiawah*, to be his best, and though the novel is not well-known, his assessment is accurate.

In many ways, Simms's reputation stems from his popular status as the "Dr. Johnson of Charleston." When he remarried in 1836, it was an advantageous match, and his wife's home, The Woodlands, became a gathering place for notable literary figures of the day. He even served a two-year term in the South Carolina legislature and ran, albeit unsuccessfully, for lieutenant governor. An outspoken supporter of slavery and secession, Simms was devastated by the South's defeat and wrote very little in the last years of his life.

"Confessions of a Murderer"

I was born in an obscure country village in D——; the place had not more than ten or twelve families, and that of my parents was one of the most intelligent and respectable. The village was one of that class which is never known to vary its position; it neither increased nor diminished, and my father was one of the principal, if not the only principal man in it. Would he had been less so. Had he thought more of his own and the business of his own family and less of those around, I should not this day recount the history of my own disgrace. But my father was the great man, the lion of the village, and I became no less so of my mama's fireside. I was a spoiled boy even before I could read—so early are the principles of the human mind subject to misdirection. I was perverse, unruly and puerile, and my father mended the matter very considerably by damning at me on all warrantable occasions. To him and to my mother I charge my crime and its punishment, and while they are wondering how so bad a scion should spring from so good a stock, they have been weaving the rope about my neck. I shall render amends to the laws of the land; they are accountable to God, and to his mercies I leave them.

I was a truant from school and exulted in it without punishment. I was brutal while a mere boy to all around me; was a boor in decent society; was insolent to my parents; rude and boisterous at table; savage and ferocious among my associates and received no punishment. Sometimes when I exceeded even the bounds of toleration, tacitly joined to my conduct by my father, I received some such rebuke as—'now my dear how can you do so,' or, 'I will be vexed with you, my son, if you do not behave.'

What was all this to an overgrown boy, nursed in full ideas of his own importance, licentious in his habits, and admitted to all and any irregularities, for which my father furnished an ample model. I bade defiance to threats, and scorned reproaches. I laughed at the soothings of my mother and took her gifts and favors, furnished in order to persuade me to do better, as things of course which she was obliged to give me. I was brought up a brute, and fulfilled to the letter the seeming objects of my education. Their lessons fitted me to be what I have been, and have reduced me to the miserable situation in which I now am. But let that rest.

I was sent to school, but learnt nothing, or what I learnt was entirely obliterated and counteracted by the nature of my education at home. I cared little to learn; my tutor dared not coerce me; he was a poor miserable hireling from the east, who cringed to all for his bread and who considered my father's influence as a matter which would not allow him to restrain or chastise his favorite son. Whatever I did, therefore, went by with impunity. However extravagant, violent or insolent my amusements, I was unpunished. Grown bold and confident, I even ventured to assume the burdens of my companions, announce myself as the offender and get them off free of punishment, while I escaped myself. One day, however, a circumstance occurred which could not pass so easily. It was under the master's own eye, and I was brought up to receive the award which his sense of justice or his lenity might think proper to bestow. He did not even flog me, he spoke to me like a father; as my father never spoke to me; his words were those of kindness, of friendship. I laughed in his face. He was indignant, as well he might be, and gave me a smart blow with his open hand on my face. I looked round upon my companions in order to ascertain if I should be supported, but they were kept in more subjection than myself and dreaded him accordingly. I submitted, though my heart rankled and my spirit burned within me for revenge. I had it—many years afterwards I had it. A deep and dreadful revenge. For the time, however, I contented myself with one more congenial with the little spirit of a bad and brutal boy. He kept me in, as a punishment, after the boys generally had been dismissed. He left me in the schoolroom and retired to his dinner. While in that room shut up, what were my emotions! The spirit of a demon was working in me, and the passion of my heart nearly exhausted my body; I threw myself on the floor and wept; hot, scalding tears. I rose—I strode for a long time to and fro; a sudden thought seized me; a mean and paltry revenge filled my bosom, as I stopt before a couple of large, new and beautiful globes that had just come to my teacher at a vast expense. I now perceived my revenge. Though small in proportion, to what it appeared to me that my wrongs required, I well knew that the injury of his globes would be almost the most severe revenge I could take upon their owner. A jug of ink lay beside them. I opened it carefully and poured its contents upon the beautifully varnished lines of the heavens and the earth. They were ruined, irrevocably ruined. These are trifles you will say, but you are mistaken. To people advanced in years the life of a boy is made up of trifles; but these incidents are developed with the growth of the child to maturity. The same feeling which prompted to the act just related, would prompt an incendiary to the firing of his enemy's dwelling; the same feeling grown mature with my years, prompted me to the commission of a murder—the crime which to-morrow I shall partially expiate upon the gallows.

Weakly could I describe his rage upon discovering what I had done. I was in the school-room, where he had left me, when he returned. For some time he did not perceive them, but walking up and down he spoke to me for a long time in a manner, which, had I not been acted on by something of the spirit of the arch-enemy of man, must have had the effect of compelling me to acknowledge and atone by the only mode in my power for my errors and misconduct. In vain—I was callous alike to reason and kindness. Suddenly, the globes caught his eye—he stopt short; he approached them; passed his hand over his face and actually shed tears. But human passion triumphed; he turned shortly upon me and smote me with his fist upon the face. The blow was a severe one and felled me to the earth. In the first movement of anger, he took me by the arm and with his school strap inflicted upon me a severe but richly deserved flogging. But I thought not so then. I did not for a moment consider the vast robbery I had made from that poor man's small stock of happiness and enjoyment. My feelings were all concentrated in my self—all my own and according with the manner of my education. The revenge of my boyhood did not rest here. A solemn convocation of the chief men of the village, at the head of which stood my father, highly incensed at the indignity, determined upon the offence. The man lost his school and another more indulgent and tractable took his place. What became of the unfortunate man thus turned out of employment by the babble of a boy, for some time I knew not. My revenge contemplated him reduced to necessity, and exulted at the picture which its own desires had presented. He was not the only sufferer. A wife and two infant children—girls—claimed his care. They departed from the village and took a road farther into the country. I did not care to follow them.

Years glided on, and brought something like an improvement to my physical appearance at least. I became manly, and rather graceful and active. My features underwent a considerable change for the better, and perhaps, my manners were less objectionable. My heart, however, remained the same. There was a spell upon it; it seemed seared and while it blighted the fortunes and the feelings of others, partook somewhat of the blight itself. My time, as before, was consumed in idleness. Such amusements as tended to the encouragement of this disposition were always an object of concern with me. Angling, hunting, and frolicking made the day and night of my existence; an existence that I now perceive has been all night. Talk not of the darkness of Greenland; the moral night is the worst of all darkness; the heart and the affections are there, prisoners in a dungeon of space and vacuity.

One morning, with my gun, I had wandered for some time through a part of the country into which I had never before penetrated. The game was plentiful and any thing but shy. I was easily seduced therefore into a long, but encouraging pursuit. I had gone some fourteen or fifteen miles from our village on the opposite river. My way led through a close and umbrageous forest. A grove of dwarf or scrub oaks, woven about with thick and sheltering vines gave a delightful air of quietness to the scene, which while I felt pleased with, my natural inquietude of disposition would not permit me to enjoy. Wheeling to return, I perceived for the first time a clear and sheltered creek, that stole in among the shrubbery and again made its way into the light at a considerable distance beyond. I followed its bendings. It was a sweet place and the hum of the wind among the tree tops alone broke the solemn and mysterious repose of silence. A small arbor arose upon a bank that jutted into the creek so far, that but for a small and narrow neck which united it to the main, might almost be considered an island. I approached it from the point where it was most sheltered, and saw not and was also unseen, by a tall and beautiful girl that reclined on a small hillock beyond it. We both started with surprise at the same moment. I cannot say that our emotions were those of love, but the surprise was productive of pleasure, to me at least, and I feel too much to her. I apologized for my intrusion, and how we grew familiar I cannot now say. My heart has been an Etna and preyed upon its own vitals. Suffice it—we parted, with a hope, though neither of us expressed it, to meet again. We did meet, and every successive day found me with my gun and on the same journey; I killed no birds, however, as before.

That girl was the most artless, the most innocent of all God's creatures! Strange that she should be condemned to a union with the worst and wildest!—need I say, that I, whose touch has contaminated all whose ill fortunes doomed them to any connection with me, blighted and blasted that innocence and changed the smile into the tear and the hope into the fear of that fond and confiding woman. We were both comparatively children; but I— I had lived many, many years of dissipation and crime. I had concentered a long life of wickedness into a few brief years and its concentrated venom fell upon her. But our commerce while it continued was productive of but few sorrows. She gave every thing up to her affection for me: she taught me to love, she loved me, as the young and morning flower has been seen to entwine itself about the deadly and poisonous nightshade.

I had grown to man's estate, my father was returning to a state of second childhood and his principal employment, at this time, was that of looking out a fitting and proper match for his son. Wealth, entered largely into the essentials required of the lady, and his labors were not entirely unavailing. He made a selection. His choice was concurred in by all parties, save myself, and I had, as yet, heard nothing of the matter. But that was no objection. It proved none. I had long been reduced to many straits for ready money. My pursuits rendered much of this necessary; for though my time was greatly given to my intercourse with Emily (such was her name) yet I had not so entirely divested myself of old employments and associates, as to do without this necessary. I saw no difficulty, at the same time, in marrying the heiress, and enjoying as before the society of the poor sweet girl I had dishonored. My resolution was taken, and a few days saw me in preparation for the bridal. For two days I went not to my place of rendesvous. I was too busily employed. On the third a smart but pensive faced boy, arrested me at the door of the mansion house of the lady to whom I was engaged. I recognized her with surprise and apprehension. I took her aside. Emily, said I, what brings you here. Can you ask, she replied; could I fail to see you for two whole days, nor fear every thing. Alas! you know not, I see, how long two days are to me. Where have you been, what has detained you, were you sick. I have been sick, Emily, I replied unhesitatingly, but am not now. Tomorrow you will see me without fail. But where are you going now she continued. Is this the house you live in—'tis very handsome. But Walter, you will come, dear Walter? I will Emily, go now, and expect me. We parted. How like a child, a sweet confiding child, she spoke to me. Yet at the very moment that the accents of her voice were most tender and touching I had begun to hate her. She was in my way. I kept my appointment however. She was in waiting, and seemingly in very bad spirits. Had she heard any thing? She had.

In a few words she gave me to understand that the rumour of my intended marriage had met her ear, and she now enquired of me if it was so. I denied it.

'Walter,' she exclaimed earnestly, 'I believe you, I cannot think for a moment you would wrong me so. But Walter, a something tells me that I shall not live very long, and I would be your wife before the time comes, when my sin will stand embodied before me. You have promised me frequently; say that you will marry me this week, I don't care what time, dear Walter, only let it be this week.'

Her eyes filled as she spoke and her heart palpitated violently as I pressed it against my own. It was the prayer of an apprehensive and almost subdued spirit. Disappointment, for I had long deceived her with promises, had worn and harassed her to a skeleton. But I had no notion of complying. I was inflexible; I was brutally stern, I repulsed and when in the tenderest and most endearing accents she repeated her request, I quickly and pettishly replied that it was impossible.

'It is all true then, as they have said,' she exclaimed passionately. 'Oh, God, now do I feel my infirmity. But think not,' she continued as her face assumed all the majesty and loveliness of inspiration, 'think not thus to injure me unpunished, unpursued. I will go to the village, I will see this lady for whose love mine and my spirit must be sacrificed. She shall know whether it be compatible with her honor or the dignity of the female character, to unite herself with one who has so grievously injured one of her own sex,' and she burst into a passion of tears.

I was alarmed—I had never seen her exhibit so much firmness of purpose on any occasion before. How could I expect it, there had been no occasion whatever for such an exhibition 'till now. I seized her hand. She withdrew it quickly and indignantly. 'Emily,' I exclaimed, while I again took hold of and retained it firmly. She struggled, her strength was opposed to mine and in the heat of the struggle I forgot that victory in such a case would be the greatest shame. I hurled her to the ground, she looked up to me imploringly, apparently strove to speak, but in vain, and she turned her face despairingly upon the still dewy grass and sobbed as if the strings of her heart kept breaking with every motion of her lips. I know not what demon possessed me at that moment. There seemed to be a more than customary silence around me. I knelt beside her, and the fury was in me. My eyes wandered wildly around the forest. I uttered no word, but my left hand grasped her throat, she partly turned her head and exclaimed, while the tones came rattling forth, 'Walter, spare me, do Walter; I am too young, too bad to perish in my sins, dear Walter, I will not reproach you, I will not accuse you, I——O——God!' and she was dead—dead under my hands. I breathed not, I moved not for a minute. My eyes were in the air, on the water, in the woods, but I dared not turn them to the still imploring glance of that fixed and terrified look.

Need I say more, than that I am now about to suffer for that crime? Need I say that Emily Stephenson was the eldest daughter of the poor man, who had been driven from his occupation by the boy, whose manhood had now proved so fatal to him. She was his eldest, most beloved, and tenderly nursed child. I have seen him once since; he spoke not to me; but when he looked upon me, he passed his hands over his eyes as if they had been seared and scathed by a bar of blistering fire. He rushed from my presence but now, and I am alone.

*   *   *   *

I look once more from the window of my dungeon; what a crowd are in waiting. There are parents in that crowd; Alas! is there one whose son's education has been like mine? let him beware!

Augustus Baldwin Longstreet

(1790–1870)

Augustus Baldwin Longstreet held a number of influential positions during his long career, serving at various times as a newspaper editor, judge, clergyman, and university
president. Despite all these achievements, he is remembered mainly for a single book of
humorous sketches, *Georgia Scenes*, which he considered light and inconsequential
and unworthy of an encore. Though Longstreet himself disdained them, these tales
would influence a generation of humorists, including Johnson Jones Hooper and
George Washington Harris, as well as local colorists like Thomas Nelson Page.

Born to a well-to-do Augusta family, Longstreet graduated from Yale in 1813 and
was admitted to the Georgia bar in 1815. In 1822, he was elected a circuit court judge
in Greensboro, Georgia, where he served a three-year term. After moving his family to
Augusta in 1827, Longstreet began writing short sketches of the Southern provincial
life he had witnessed as a lawyer and circuit judge, publishing a series of the pieces in
the *Midgeville Southern Recorder*. When he purchased the *North American Gazette*
in 1834, changing its name to the *State Rights Sentinel*, he published four more of the
sketches before finally collecting nineteen of them to comprise the 1835 edition of
Georgia Scenes. Ordained a Methodist minister in 1838, Longstreet proclaimed his intention to abandon humorous fiction for more serious pursuits, a vow to which he
more or less adhered for the remainder of his career. Although he published a novel,
Master William Mitten, in 1864, it does not approach the quality of his short fiction,
and his other writings were chiefly polemical, best exemplified by his defense of slavery in the 1845 pamphlet *Letters on the Epistle of Paul to Philemon, or the Connection of Apostolical Christianity with Slavery*. Longstreet is remembered chiefly for
Georgia Scenes, however, because with it, as the critic M. Thomas Inge points out,
the "humor of the old Southwest was born."

from *Georgia Scenes*

The Fight

In the younger days of the Republic there lived in the county of ——— two men, who
were admitted on all hands to be the very *best men* in the country; which, in the Georgia
vocabulary, means they could flog any other two men in the county. Each, through
many a hard-fought battle, had acquired the mastery of his own battalion; but they lived
on opposite sides of the Courthouse, and in different battalions: consequently, they
were but seldom thrown together. When they met, however, they were always very
friendly; indeed, at their first interview, they seemed to conceive a wonderful attachment to each other, which rather increased than diminished as they became better acquainted; so that, but for the circumstance which I am about to mention, the question,
which had been a thousand times asked, "Which is the best man, Billy Stallions
(Stallings) or Bob Durham?" would probably never have been answered.

Billy ruled the upper battalion, and Bob the lower. The former measured six feet
and an inch in his stockings, and, without a single pound of cumbrous flesh about him,

weighed a hundred and eighty. The latter was an inch shorter than his rival, and ten pounds lighter; but he was much the most active of the two. In running and jumping he had but few equals in the county; and in wrestling, not one. In other respects they were nearly equal. Both were admirable specimens of human nature in its finest form. Billy's victories had generally been achieved by the tremendous power of his blows, one of which had often proved decisive of his battles; Bob's, by his adroitness in bringing his adversary to the ground. This advantage he had never failed to gain at the onset, and, when gained, he never failed to improve it to the defeat of his adversary. These points of difference have involved the reader in a doubt as to the probable issue of a contest between them. It was not so, however, with the two battalions. Neither had the least difficulty in determining the point by the most natural and irresistible deductions *a priori;* and though, by the same course of reasoning, they arrived at directly opposite conclusions, neither felt its confidence in the least shaken by this circumstance. The upper battalion swore "that Billy only wanted one lick at him to knock his heart, liver, and lights out of him; and if he got two at him, he'd knock him into a cocked hat." The lower battalion retorted, "that he wouldn't have time to double his fist before Bob would put his head where his feet ought to be; and that, by the time he hit the ground, the meat would fly off his face so quick, that people would think it was shook off by the fall." These disputes often led to the *argumentum ad hominem,*[1] but with such equality of success on both sides as to leave the main question just where they found it. They usually ended, however, in the common way, with a bet; and many a quart of old Jamaica (whiskey had not then supplanted rum) were staked upon the issue. Still, greatly to the annoyance of the curious, Billy and Bob continued to be good friends.

Now there happened to reside in the county just alluded to a little fellow by the name of Ransy Sniffle: a sprout of Richmond, who, in his earlier days, had fed copiously upon red clay and blackberries. This diet had given to Ransy a complexion that a corpse would have disdained to own, and an abdominal rotundity that was quite unprepossessing. Long spells of the fever and ague, too, in Ransy's youth, had conspired with clay and blackberries to throw him quite out of the order of nature. His shoulders were fleshless and elevated; his head large and flat; his neck slim and translucent; and his arms, hands, fingers, and feet were lengthened out of all proportion to the rest of his frame. His joints were large and his limbs small; and as for flesh, he could not, with propriety, be said to have any. Those parts which nature usually supplies with the most of this article—the calves of the legs, for example—presented in him the appearance of so many well-drawn blisters. His height was just five feet nothing; and his average weight in blackberry season, ninety-five. I have been thus particular in describing him, for the purpose of showing what a great matter a little fire sometimes kindleth. There was nothing on this earth which delighted Ransy so much as a fight. He never seemed fairly alive except when he was witnessing, fomenting, or talking about a fight. Then, indeed, his deep-sunken gray eye assumed something of a living fire, and his tongue acquired a volubility that bordered upon eloquence. Ransy had been kept for more than a year in the most torturing suspense as to the comparative manhood of Billy Stallings and Bob Durham. He had resorted to all his usual expedients to bring them in collision, and had entirely failed. He had faithfully reported to Bob all that had been said by the people in the upper battalion "agin him," and "he

---

[1] *Argument using an opponent's own words or acts in support of one's views.*

was sure Billy Stallings started it. He heard Billy say himself to Jim Brown, that he could whip him, *or any other man in his battalion;*" and this he told to Bob; adding, "Dod darn his soul, if he was a little bigger, if he'd let any man *put upon* his battalion in such a way." Bob replied, "If he (Stallings) thought so, he'd better come and try it." This Ransy carried to Billy, and delivered it with a spirit becoming his own dignity and the character of his battalion, and with a colouring well calculated to give it effect. These, and many other schemes which Ransy laid for the gratification of his curiosity, entirely failed of their object. Billy and Bob continued friends, and Ransy had begun to lapse into the most tantalizing and hopeless despair, when a circumstance occurred which led to a settlement of the long-disputed question.

It is said that a hundred gamecocks will live in perfect harmony together if you do not put a hen with them; and so it would have been with Billy and Bob, had there been no women in the world. But there were women in the world, and from them each of our heroes had taken to himself a wife. The good ladies were no strangers to the prowess of their husbands, and, strange as it may seem, they presumed a little upon it.

The two battalions had met at the Courthouse upon a regimental parade. The two champions were there, and their wives had accompanied them. Neither knew the other's lady, nor were the ladies known to each other. The exercises of the day were just over, when Mrs. Stallings and Mrs. Durham stepped simultaneously into the store of Zephaniah Atwater, from "down east."

"Have you any Turkey-red?" said Mrs. S.

"Have you any curtain calico?" said Mrs. D. at the same moment.

"Yes, ladies," said Mr. Atwater, "I have both."

"Then help me first," said Mrs. D., "for I'm in a hurry."

"I'm in as great a hurry as she is," said Mrs. S., "and I'll thank you to help me first."

"And, pray, who are you, madam?" continued the other.

"Your better, madam," was the reply.

At this moment Billy Stallings stepped in. "Come," said he, "Nancy, let's be going; it's getting late."

"I'd a been gone half an hour ago," she replied, "if it hadn't a' been for that impudent huzzy."

"Who do you call an impudent huzzy, you nasty, good-for-nothing, snaggle-toothed gaub of fat, you?" returned Mrs. D.

"Look here, woman," said Billy, "have you got a husband here? If you have, I'll *lick* him till he learns to teach you better manners, you *sassy* heifer you." At this moment something was seen to rush out of the store as if ten thousand hornets were stinging it; crying. "Take care—let me go—don't hold me—where's Bob Durham?" It was Ransy Sniffle, who had been listening in breathless delight to all that had passed.

"Yonder's Bob, setting on the Courthouse steps," cried one. "What's the matter?"

"Don't talk to me!" said Ransy. "Bob Durham, you'd better go long yonder, and take care of your wife. They're playing h——l with her there, in Zeph Atwater's store. Dod etarnally darn my soul, if any man was to talk to my wife as Bill Stallions is talking to yours, if I wouldn't drive blue blazes through him in less than no time."

Bob sprang to the store in a minute, followed by a hundred friends; for the bully of a county never wants friends.

"Bill Stallions," said Bob, as he entered, "what have you been saying to my wife?"

"Is that your wife?" inquired Billy, obviously much surprised and a little disconcerted.

"Yes, she is, and no man shall abuse her, I don't care who he is."

"Well," rejoined Billy, "it an't worth while to go over it; I've said enough for a fight: and, if you'll step out, we'll settle it!"

"Billy," said Bob, "are you for a fair fight?"

"I am," said Billy, "I've heard much of your manhood, and I believe I'm a better man than you are. If you will go into a ring with me, we can soon settle the dispute."

"Choose your friends," said Bob; "make your ring, and I'll be in with mine as soon as you will."

They both stepped out, and began to strip very deliberately, each battalion gathering round its champion, except Ransy, who kept himself busy in a most honest endeavour to hear and see all that transpired in both groups at the same time. He ran from one to the other in quick succession; peeped here and listened there; talked to this one, then to that one, and then to himself; squatted under one's legs and another's arms and, in the short interval between stripping and stepping into the ring, managed to get himself trod on by half of both battalions. But Ransy was not the only one interested upon this occasion; the most intense interest prevailed everywhere. Many were the conjectures, doubts, oaths, and imprecations uttered while the parties were preparing for the combat. All the knowing ones were consulted as to the issue, and they all agreed, to a man, in one of two opinions: either that Bob would flog Billy, or Billy would flog Bob. We must be permitted, however, to dwell for a moment upon the opinion of Squire Thomas Loggins; a man who, it was said, had never failed to predict the issue of a fight in all his life. Indeed, so unerring had he always proved in this regard, that it would have been counted the most obstinate infidelity to doubt for a moment after he had delivered himself. Squire Loggins was a man who said but little, but that little was always delivered with the most imposing solemnity of look and cadence. He always wore the aspect of profound thought, and you could not look at him without coming to the conclusion that he was elaborating truth from its most intricate combinations.

"Uncle Tommy," said Sam Reynolds, "you can tell us all about it if you will; how will the fight go?"

The question immediately drew an anxious group around the squire. He raised his teeth slowly from the head of his walking cane, on which they had been resting; pressed his lips closely and thoughtfully together; threw down his eyebrows, dropped his chin, raised his eyes to an angle of twenty-three degrees, paused about half a minute, and replied, "Sammy, watch Robert Durham close in the beginning of the fight; take care of William Stallions in the middle of it; and see who has the wind at the end." As he uttered the last member of the sentence, he looked slyly at Bob's friends, and winked very significantly; whereupon they rushed, with one accord, to tell Bob what Uncle Tommy had said. As they retired, the squire turned to Billy's friends, and said, with a smile, "Them boys think I mean that Bob will whip."

Here the other party kindled into joy, and hastened to inform Billy how Bob's friends had deceived themselves as to Uncle Tommy's opinion. In the meantime the principals and seconds were busily employed in preparing themselves for the combat. The plan of attack and defence, the manner of improving the various turns of the conflict, "the best mode of saving wind," &c., &c., were all discussed and settled. At length Billy announced himself ready, and his crowd were seen moving to the centre of the Courthouse Square; he and his five seconds in the rear. At the same time, Bob's party moved to the same point, and in the same order. The ring was now formed, and for a moment the silence of death reigned through both battalions. It was soon interrupted, however, by the cry of "Clear the way!" from Billy's seconds; when the ring opened in the centre of the upper battalion (for the order of march had arranged the centre of the two battalions on opposite sides of the circle), and Billy stepped into the ring from the east, followed by his friends. He was stripped to the trousers, and exhibited an arm, breast, and shoulders of the most tremendous portent. His step was firm, daring, and martial; and as he bore his fine form a little in advance of his friends, an involuntary burst of triumph broke from his side of the ring; and, at the same moment, an uncontrollable thrill of awe ran along the whole curve of the lower battalion.

"Look at him!" was heard from his friends; "just look at him."

"Ben, how much you ask to stand before that man two seconds?"

"Pshaw, don't talk about it! Just thinkin' about it's broke three o' my ribs a'ready!"

"What's Bob Durham going to do when Billy lets that arm loose upon him?"

"God bless your soul, he'll think thunder and lightning a mint-julep to it."

"Oh, look here, men, go take Bill Stallions out o' that ring, and bring in Phil Johnson's stud horse, so that Durham may have some chance! I don't want to see the man killed right away."

These and many other like expressions, interspersed thickly with oaths of the most modern coinage, were coming from all points of the upper battalion, while Bob was adjusting the girth of his pantaloons, which walking had discovered not to be exactly right. It was just fixed to his mind, his foes becoming a little noisy, and his friends a little uneasy at his delay, when Billy called out, with a smile of some meaning, "Where's the bully of the lower battalion? I'm getting tired of waiting."

"Here he is," said Bob, lighting, as it seemed, from the clouds into the ring, for he had actually bounded clear of the head of Ransy Sniffle into the circle. His descent was quite as imposing as Billy's entry, and excited the same feelings, but in opposite bosoms.

Voices of exultation now rose on his side.

"Where did he come from?"

"Why," said one of his seconds (all having just entered), "we were girting him up, about a hundred yards out yonder, when he heard Billy ask for the bully; and he fetched a leap over the Courthouse, and went out of sight; but I told them to come on, they'd find him here."

Here the lower battalion burst into a peal of laughter, mingled with a look of admiration, which seemed to denote their entire belief of what they had heard.

"Boys, widen the ring, so as to give him room to jump."

"Oh, my little flying wild-cat, hold him if you can! and, when you get him fast, holding lightning next."

"Ned, what do you think he's made of?"

"Steel springs and chicken-hawk, God bless you!"

"Gentlemen," said one of Bob's seconds, "I understand it is to be a fair fight; catch as catch can, rough and tumble: no man touch till one or the other halloos."

"That's the rule," was the reply from the other side.

"Are you ready?"

"We are ready."

"Then blaze away, my game cocks!"

At the word, Bob dashed at his antagonist at full speed; and Bill squared himself to receive him with one of his most fatal blows. Making his calculation, from Bob's velocity, of the time when he would come within striking distance, he let drive with tremendous force. But Bob's onset was obviously planned to avoid this blow; for, contrary to all expectations, he stopped short just out of arm's reach, and, before Billy could recover his balance, Bob had him "all under-hold." The next second, sure enough, "Found Billy's head where his feet ought to be." How it was done no one could tell; but, as if by supernatural power, both Billy's feet were thrown full half his own height in the air, and he came down with a force that seemed to shake the earth. As he struck the ground, commingled shouts, screams, and yells burst from the lower battalion, loud enough to be heard for miles. "Hurra, my little hornet!" "Save him!" "Feed him!" "Give him the Durham physic till his stomach turns!" Billy was no sooner down than Bob was on him, and lending him awful blows about the face and breast. Billy made two efforts to rise by main strength, but failed. "Lord bless you, man, don't try to get up! *Lay* still and take it! you *bleege* to have it!"

Billy now turned his face suddenly to the ground, and rose upon his hands and knees. Bob jerked up both his hands and threw him on his face. He again recovered his late position, of which Bob endeavoured to deprive him as before; but, missing one arm, he failed, and Billy rose. But he had scarcely resumed his feet before they flew up as before, and he came again to the ground. "No fight, gentlemen!" cried Bob's friends; "the man can't stand up! Bouncing feet are bad things to fight in." His fall, however, was this time comparatively light; for, having thrown his right arm round Bob's neck, he carried his head down with him. This grasp, which was obstinately maintained, prevented Bob from getting on him, and they lay head to head, seeming, for a time, to do nothing. Presently they rose, as if by mutual consent; and, as they rose, a shout burst from both battalions. "Oh, my lark!" cried the east, "has he foxed you? Do you begin to feel him? He's only beginning to fight; he ain't got warm yet."

"Look yonder!" cried the west; "didn't I tell you so! He hit the ground so hard it jarred his nose off. Now ain't he a pretty man as he stands? He shall have my sister Sal just for his pretty looks. I want to get in the breed of them sort o' men, to drive ugly out of my kinfolks."

I looked, and saw that Bob had entirely lost his left ear, and a large piece from his left cheek. His right eye was a little discoloured, and the blood flowed profusely from his wounds.

Bill presented a hideous spectacle. About a third of his nose, at the lower extremity, was bit off, and his face so swelled and bruised that it was difficult to discover in it anything of the human visage, much more the fine features which he carried into the ring.

They were up only long enough for me to make the foregoing discoveries, when down they went again, precisely as before. They no sooner touched the ground than Bill relinquished his hold upon Bob's neck. In this he seemed to all to have forfeited the only advantage which put him upon an equality with his adversary. But the movement was soon explained. Bill wanted this arm for other purposes than defence; and he had made arrangements whereby he knew that he could make it answer these purposes; for, when they rose again, he had the middle finger of Bob's left hand in his mouth. He was now secure from Bob's annoying trips; and he began to lend his adversary tremendous blows, every one of which was hailed by a shout from his friends. "Bullets!" "*Hoss*-kicking!" "Thunder!" "That'll do for his face; now feel his short ribs, Billy!"

I now considered the contest settled. I deemed it impossible for any human being to withstand for five seconds the loss of blood which issued from Bob's ear, cheek, nose, and finger, accompanied with such blows as he was receiving. Still he maintained the conflict, and gave blow for blow with considerable effect. But the blows of each became slower and weaker after the first three or four; and it became obvious that Billy wanted the room which Bob's finger occupied for breathing. He would therefore, probably, in a short time, have let it go, had not Bob anticipated his politeness by jerking away his hand, and making him a present of the finger. He now seized Bill again, and brought him to his knees, but he recovered. He again brought him to his knees, and he again recovered. A third effort, however, brought him down, and Bob on top of him. These efforts seemed to exhaust the little remaining strength of both; and they lay, Bill undermost and Bob across his breast, motionless, and panting for breath. After a short pause, Bob gathered his hand full of dirt and sand, and was in the act of grinding it in his adversary's eyes, when Bill cried "ENOUGH!" Language cannot describe the scene that followed; the shouts, oaths, frantic gestures, taunts, replies, and little fights, and therefore I shall not attempt it. The champions were borne off by their seconds and washed; when many a bleeding wound and ugly bruise was discovered on each which no eye had seen before.

Many had gathered round Bob, and were in various ways congratulating and applauding him, when a voice from the centre of the circle cried out, "Boys, hush and listen to me!" It proceeded from Squire Loggins, who had made his way to Bob's side, and had gathered his face up into one of its most flattering and intelligible expressions. All were obedient to the squire's command. "Gentlemen," continued he, with a most knowing smile, "is—Sammy—Reynold—in—this—company—of—gentlemen?"

"Yes," said Sam, "here I am."

"Sammy," said the squire, winking to the company and drawing the head of his cane to his mouth with an arch smile as he closed. "I—wish—you—to tell—cousin—Bobby—and—these—gentlemen here present—what—your—Uncle—Tommy—said—before—the—fight—began?"

"Oh! get away, Uncle Tom," said Sam, smiling (the squire winked), "you don't know nothing about *fighting*." (The squire winked again.) "All you know about it is how it'll begin, how it'll go on, how it'll end; that's all. Cousin Bob, when you going to fight again, just go to the old man, and let him tell you all about it. If he can't, don't ask nobody else nothing about it, I tell you."

The squire's foresight was complimented in many ways by the by-standers; and he retired, advising "the boys to be at peace, as fighting was a bad business."

Durham and Stallings kept their beds for several weeks, and did not meet again for two months. When they met, Billy stepped up to Bob and offered his hand, saying, "Bobby, you've *licked* me a fair fight; but you wouldn't have done it if I hadn't been in the wrong. I oughtn't to have treated your wife as I did; and I felt so through the whole fight; and it sort o' cowed me."

"Well, Billy," said Bob, "let's be friends. Once in the fight, when you had my finger in your mouth, and was pealing me in the face and breast, I was going to halloo; but I thought of Petsy, and knew the house would be too hot for me if I got whipped when fighting for her, after always whipping when I fought for myself."

"Now that's what I always love to see," said a by-stander. "It's true I brought about the fight, but I wouldn't have done it if it hadn't o' been on account of *Miss* (Mrs.) Durham. Bud dod etarnally darn my soul, if I ever could stand by and see any woman put upon, much less *Miss* Durham. If Bobby hadn't been there, I'd o' took it up myself, be darned if I wouldn't, even if I'd o' got whipped for it. But we're all friends now." The reader need hardly be told that this was Ransy Sniffle.

Thanks to the Christian religion, to schools, colleges, and benevolent associations, such scenes of barbarism and cruelty as that which I have been just describing are now of rare occurrence, though they may still be occasionally met with in some of the new counties. Wherever they prevail, they are a disgrace to that community. The peace-officers who countenance them deserve a place in the Penitentiary.

Angelina Emily Grimké

(1805–1879)

Born in Charleston to a prominent South Carolina judge and slave owner, Angelina Grimké and her older sister Sarah opposed slavery from their youth onward. Raised an Episcopalian, Sarah Grimké was converted to Quakerism on a trip to Philadelphia in 1819 and won her sister to that faith on her return to South Carolina. Determined to speak out against slavery, the sisters were forced to move to the North, settling in Philadelphia in the 1820s. After reading William Lloyd Garrison's abolitionist newspaper *The Liberator*, Angelina wrote him a letter, which he published in that periodical in 1835. Inspired, she began work on a pamphlet that was published in 1836 under the title *An Appeal to the Christian Women of the South*. There she attacked the traditional religious justifications of slavery and called on women to fight the institution by freeing slaves that were their own property, by petitioning the legislature for emancipation, and by working to make conditions better for those still in slavery. The fact that the *Appeal* was written by a Southern woman made it especially valuable to the abolitionist cause. In South Carolina, the pamphlet was burned, and authorities threatened to prosecute Grimké if she ever returned.

In 1837, Angelina Grimké published *Appeal to the Women of the Nominally Free States*, where she linked the rights of women to the rights of slaves. She began to win fame as an orator, and in 1838, she became the first woman to address a legislative body when she spoke before the Massachusetts legislative committee on antislavery petitions. That same year, she married Theodore Dwight Weld, himself an active abolitionist, but did not promise "to obey." Weld also renounced his legal rights to own and manage his wife's property. Though she continued to be active in the abolitionist cause, when her husband retired from the movement in 1843 because of poor health, she sharply curtailed her speaking duties and ceased writing altogether.

from *Appeal to the Christian Women of the South*

Then Mordecai commanded to answer Esther, Think not within thyself that thou shalt escape in the king's house more than all the Jews. For if thou altogether holdest thy peace at this time, then shall there enlargement and deliverance arise to the Jews from another place: but thou and thy father's house shall be destroyed: and who knoweth whether thou art come to the kingdom for such a time as this. And Esther bade them return

Mordecai this answer:—and so will I go in unto the king, which is not according to law, and if I perish, I perish."

Esther IV. 13–16.

RESPECTED FRIENDS,

It is because I feel a deep and tender interest in your present and eternal welfare that I am willing thus publicly to address you. Some of you have loved me as a relative, and some have felt bound to me in Christian sympathy, and Gospel fellowship; and even when compelled by a strong sense of duty, to break those outward bonds of union which bound us together as members of the same community, and members of the same religious denomination, you were generous enough to give me credit, for sincerity as a Christian, though you believed I had been most strangely deceived. I thanked you then for your kindness, and I ask you *now*, for the sake of former confidence, and former friendship, to read the following pages in the spirit of calm investigation and fervent prayer. It is because you have known me, that I write thus unto you.

But there are other Christian women scattered over the Southern States, a very large number of whom have never seen me, and never heard my name, and who feel *no* interest whatever in *me*. But I feel an interest in *you*, as branches of the same vine from whose root I daily draw the principle of spiritual vitality—Yes! Sisters in Christ I feel an interest in *you*, and often has the secret prayer arisen on your behalf, Lord "open thou their eyes that they may see wondrous things out of thy Law"—It is then, because I *do feel* and *do pray* for you, that I thus address you upon a subject about which of all others, perhaps you would rather not hear any thing; but, "would to God ye could bear with me a little in my folly, and indeed bear with me, for I am jealous over you with godly jealousy." Be not afraid then to read my appeal; it is *not* written in the heat of passion or prejudice, but in that solemn calmness which is the result of conviction and duty. It is true, I am going to tell you unwelcome truths, but I mean to speak those *truths in love*, and remember Solomon says, "faithful are the *wounds* of a friend." I do not believe the time has yet come when *Christian women* "will not endure sound doctrine," even on the subject of Slavery, if it is spoken to them in tenderness and love, therefore I now address *you*.

To all of you then, known or unknown, relative or strangers, (for you are all *one* in Christ,) I would speak. I have felt for you at this time, when unwelcome light is pouring in upon the world on the subject of slavery; light which even Christians would exclude, if they could, from our country, or at any rate from the southern portion of it, saying, as its rays strike the rock bound coasts of New England and scatter their warmth and radiance over her hills and valleys, and from thence travel onward over the Palisades of the Hudson, and down the soft flowing waters of the Delaware and gild the waves of the Potomac, "hitherto shalt thou come and no further;" I know that even professors of His name who has been emphatically called the "Light of the world" would, if they could, build a wall of adamant around the Southern States whose top might reach unto heaven, in order to shut out the light which is bounding from mountain to mountain and from the hills to the plains and valleys beneath, through the vast extent of our Northern States. But believe me, when I tell you, their attempts will be as utterly fruitless as were the efforts of the builders of Babel; and why? Because moral, like natural light, is so extremely subtle in its nature as to overleap all human barriers, and laugh at the puny efforts of man to control it. All the excuses and palliations of this system must inevitably be swept away, just as other "refuges of lies" have been, by the irresistible torrent of a rectified public opinion. "The *supporters* of the slave system," says Jonathan Dymond in his admirable work on the Principles of Morality, "will *hereafter* be regarded with the *same* public feeling, as he who was an advocate for the slave trade *now is*." It will be, and that very soon, clearly perceived and fully acknowledged by all the virtuous and the candid, that in *principle* it is as sinful to hold a human being in bondage who has been born in Carolina, as one who has been born in Africa. All that sophistry of argument which has been employed to prove, that although it is sinful to send to Africa to procure men and women as slaves, who have never been in slavery, that still, it is not sinful to keep those in bondage who have come down by inheritance, will be utterly overthrown. We must come back to the good old doctrine of our forefathers who declared to the world, "this self evident truth that *all* men are created equal, and that they have certain *inalienable* rights among which are life, *liberty*, and the pursuit of happiness." It is even a greater absurdity to suppose a man can be legally born a slave under *our free Republican* Government, than under the petty despotisms of barbarian Africa. If then, we have no right to enslave an African, surely we can have none to enslave an American; if it is a self evident truth that *all* men, every where and of every color are born equal, and have an *inalienable right to liberty*, then it is equally true that *no* man can be born a slave, and no man can ever *rightfully* be reduced to *involuntary* bondage and held as a slave, however fair may be the claim of his master or mistress through wills and title-deeds.

But after all, it may be said, our fathers were certainly mistaken, for the Bible sanctions Slavery, and that is the highest authority. Now the Bible is my ultimate appeal in all matters of faith and practice, and it is to *this test* I am anxious to bring the subject at issue between us. Let us then begin with Adam and examine the charter of privileges which was given to him. "Have dominion over the fish of the sea, and over the fowl of the air, and over every living thing that moveth upon the earth." In the eighth Psalm we have a still fuller description of this charter which through Adam was given to all mankind. "Thou madest him to have dominion over the works of thy hands; thou hast put all things under his feet. All sheep and oxen, yea, and the beasts of the field, the fowl of the air, the fish of the sea, and whatsoever passeth through the paths of the seas." And after the flood when this charter of human rights was renewed, we find *no additional* power vested in man. "And the fear of you and the dread of you shall be upon every beast of the earth, and every fowl of the air, and upon all that moveth upon the earth, and upon all the fishes of the sea, into your hand are they delivered." In this chapter, although the different kinds of *irrational* beings are so particularly enumerated, and supreme dominion over *all of them* is granted, yet *man* is *never* vested with this dominion *over his fellow man;* he was never told that any of the human species were put *under his feet;* it was only *all things*, and man, who was created in the image of his Maker, *never* can properly be termed a *thing*, though the laws of Slave States do call him "a chattel personal;" *Man* then, I assert *never* was put *under the feet of man*, by that first charter of human rights which was given by God, to the Fathers of the Antediluvian and Postdiluvian worlds, therefore this doctrine of equality is based on the Bible.

But it may be argued, that in the very chapter of Genesis from which I have last quoted, will be found the curse pronounced upon Canaan, by which his posterity was consigned to servitude under his brothers Shem and Japheth. I know this prophecy was uttered, and was most fearfully and wonderfully fulfilled, through the immediate descendants of Canaan, i. e. the Canaanites, and I do not know but it has been through all the children of Ham, but I do know that prophecy does *not* tell us what *ought to be*, but what actually does take place, ages after it has been delivered, and that if we justify America for enslaving the children of Africa, we must also justify Egypt for reducing the children of Israel to bondage, for the latter was foretold as explicitly as the former. I am well aware that prophecy has often been urged as an excuse for Slavery, but be not deceived, the fulfillment of prophecy will *not cover one sin* in the awful day of account. Hear what our Saviour says on this subject; "it must needs be that offences come, but *woe unto that man through whom they come"*— Witness some fulfillment of this declaration in the tremendous destruction of Jerusalem, occasioned by that most nefarious of all crimes the crucifixion of the Son of God. Did the fact of that event having been foretold, exculpate the Jews from sin in perpetrating it; No—for hear what the Apostle Peter says to them on this subject, "Him being delivered by the determinate counsel and foreknowledge of God, *ye* have taken, and by *wicked* hands have crucified and slain." Other striking instances might be adduced, but these will suffice.

But it has been urged that the patriarchs held slaves, and therefore, slavery is right. Do you really believe that patriarchal servitude was like American slavery? Can you believe it? If so, read the history of these primitive fathers of the church and be undeceived. Look at Abraham, though so great a man, going to the herd himself and fetching a calf from thence and serving it up with his own hands, for the entertainment of his guests. Look at Sarah, that princess as her name signifies, baking cakes upon the hearth. If the servants they had were like Southern slaves, would they have performed such comparatively menial offices for themselves? Hear too the plaintive lamentation of Abraham when he feared he should have no son to bear his name down to posterity. "Behold thou hast given me no seed, &c, one born in my house *is mine* heir." From this it appears that one of his *servants* was to inherit his immense estate. Is this like Southern slavery? I leave it to your own good sense and candor to decide. Besides, such was the footing upon which Abraham was with *his* servants, that he trusted them with arms. Are slaveholders willing to put swords and pistols into the hands of their slaves? He was as a father among his servants; what are planters and masters generally among theirs? When the institution of circumcision was established. Abraham was commanded thus; "He that is eight days old shall be circumcised among you, *every* man-child in your generations; he that is born in the house, or bought with money of any stranger which is not of thy seed." And to render this command with regard to his *servants* still more impressive it is repeated in the very next verse; and herein we may perceive the great care which was taken by God to guard the *rights of servants* even under this "dark dispensation." What too was the testimony given to the faithfulness of this eminent patriarch. "For I know him that he will command his children and his *household* after him, and they shall keep the way of the Lord to do justice and judgment." Now my dear friends many of you believe that circumcision has been superseded by baptism in the Church; *Are you* careful to have *all* that are born in your house or bought with money of any stranger, baptized? Are *you* as faithful as Abraham to command *your household to keep the way of the Lord?* I leave it to your own consciences to decide. Was patriarchal servitude then like American Slavery?

But I shall be told, God sanctioned Slavery, yea commanded Slavery under the Jewish Dispensation. Let us examine this subject calmly and prayerfully. I admit that a species of *servitude* was permitted to the Jews, but in studying the subject I have been struck with wonder and admiration at perceiving how carefully the servant was guarded from violence, injustice and wrong. I will first inform you how these servants became servants, for I think this a very important part of our subject. From consulting Horne, Calmet and the Bible, I find there were six different ways by which the Hebrews became servants legally.

1. If reduced to extreme poverty, a Hebrew might sell himself, i. e. his services, for six years, in which case *he* received the purchase money *himself.* Lev. xxv, 39.

2. A father might sell his children as servants, i. e. his *daughters,* in which circumstance it was understood the daughter was to be the wife or daughter-in-law of the man who bought her, and the *father* received the price. In other words, Jewish women were sold as *white women* were in the first settlement of Virginia—as *wives, not* as slaves. Ex. xxi, 7.

3. Insolvent debtors might be delivered to their creditors as servants. 2 Kings iv, 1.

4. Thieves not able to make restitution for their thefts, were sold for the benefit of the injured person. Ex. xxii, 3.

5. They might be born in servitude. Ex. xxi, 4.

6. If a Hebrew had sold himself to a rich Gentile, he might be redeemed by one of his brethren at any time the money was offered; and he who redeemed him, was *not* to take advantage of the favor thus conferred, and rule over his with rigor. Lev. xxv, 47–55.

Before going into an examination of the laws by which these servants were protected, I would just ask whether American slaves have become slaves in any of the ways in which the Hebrews became servants. Did they sell themselves into slavery and receive the purchase money into their own hands? No! Did they become insolvent, and by their own imprudence subject themselves to be sold as slaves? No! Did they steal the property of another, and were they sold to make restitution for their crimes? No! Did their present masters, as an act of kindness, redeem them from some heathen tyrant to whom *they had sold themselves* in the dark hour of adversity? No! Were they born in slavery? No! No! not according to *Jewish Law*, for the servants who were born in servitude among them, were born of parents who had *sold themselves* for six years: Ex. xxi, 4. Were the female slaves of the South sold by their fathers? How shall I answer this question? Thousands and tens of thousands never were, *their* fathers *never* have received the poor compensation of silver or gold for the tears and toils, the suffering, and anguish, and hopeless bondage of *their* daughters. They labor day by day, and year by year, side by side, in the same field, if haply their daughters are permitted to remain on the same plantation with them, instead of being as they often are, separated from their parents and sold into distant states, never again to meet on earth. But do the *fathers of the South ever sell their daughters?* My heart beats, and my hand trembles, as I write the awful affirmative, Yes! The fathers of this Christian land often sell their daughters, *not* as Jewish parents did, to be the wives and daughters-in-law of the man who buys them, but to be the abject slaves of petty tyrants and irresponsible masters. Is it not so, my friends? I leave it to your own candor to corroborate my assertion. Southern slaves then have *not* become slaves in any of the six different ways in which Hebrews became servants, and I hesitate not to say that American masters *cannot* according to *Jewish law* substantiate their claim to the men, women, or children they now hold in bondage.

But there was one way in which a Jew might illegally be reduced to servitude; it was this, he might be *stolen* and afterwards sold as a slave, as was Joseph. To guard most effectually against this dreadful crime of manstealing, God enacted this severe law. "He that stealeth a man and selleth him, or if he be found in his hand, he shall surely be put to death."* As I have tried American Slavery by *legal* Hebrew servitude, and found, (to your surprise, perhaps,) that Jewish law cannot justify the slaveholder's claim, let us now try it by *illegal* Hebrew bondage. Have the Southern slaves then been stolen? If they did not sell themselves into bondage; if they were not sold as insolvent debtors or as thieves; if they were not redeemed from a heathen master to whom *they had sold themselves;* if they were not born in servitude according to Hebrew law; and if the females were not sold by their fathers as wives and daughters-in-law to those who purchased them; then what shall we say of them? what can we say of them? but that according *to Hebrew Law they have been stolen.*

But I shall be told that the Jews had other servants who were absolute slaves. Let us look a little into this also. They had other servants who were procured in two different ways.

1. Captives taken in war were reduced to bondage instead of being killed; but we are not told that their children were enslaved. Deut. xx, 14.

2. Bondmen and bondmaids might be bought from the heathen round about them; these were left by fathers to their children after them, but it does not appear that the *children* of these servants ever were reduced to servitude. Lev. xxv, 44.

I will now try the right of the southern planter by the claims of Hebrew masters over their *heathen slaves.* Were the southern slaves taken captive in war? No! Were they brought from the heathen? No! for surely, no one will *now* vindicate the slave-trade so far as to assert that slaves were bought from the heathen who were obtained by that system of piracy. The only excuse for holding southern slaves is that they were born in slavery, but we have seen that they were *not* born in servitude as Jewish servants were, and that the children of heathen slaves were not legally subjected to bondage even under the Mosaic Law. How then have the slaves of the South been obtained?

I will next proceed to an examination of those laws which were enacted in order to protect the Hebrew and the Heathen servant; for I wish you to understand that *both* are protected by Him, of whom it is said "his mercies are over *all* his works." I will first speak of those which secured the rights of Hebrew servants. This code was headed thus:

1. Thou shalt *not* rule over his with *rigor,* but shalt fear thy God.

2. If thou buy a Hebrew servant, six years shall he serve, and in the seventh year he shall go out free for nothing. Ex. xxi, 2.*

3. If he come in by himself, he shall go out by himself; if he were married, then his wife shall go out with him.

4. If his master have given him a wife and she have borne him sons and daughters, the wife and her children shall be his master's, and he shall go out by himself.

5. If the servant shall plainly say, I love my master, my wife, and my children; I will not go out free; then his master shall bring him unto the Judges, and he shall

---

*And again, "If a man be found stealing any of his brethren of the children of Israel, and maketh merchandise of him, or selleth him; then *that thief shall die;* and thou shalt put away evil from among you." Deut. xxiv, 7.

*And when thou sendest him out free from thee, thou shalt not let him go away empty: Thou shalt furnish him *liberally* out of thy flock and out of thy floor, and out of thy wine-press: of that wherewith the Lord thy God hath blessed thee, shalt thou give unto him. Deut. xv, 13, 14.

bring him to the door, or unto the door-post, and his master shall bore his ear through with an awl, and he shall serve him *forever*. Ex. xxi, 5–6.

6. If a man smite the eye of his servant, or the eye of his maid, that it perish, he shall let him go *free* for his eye's sake. And if he smite out his man servant's tooth or his maid servant's tooth, he shall let him go *free* for his tooth's sake. Ex. xxi, 26, 27.

7. On the Sabbath rest was secured to servants by the fourth commandment. Ex. xx, 10.

8. Servants were permitted to unite with their masters three times in every year in celebrating the Passover, the feast of Pentecost, and the feast of Tabernacles; every male throughout the land was to appear before the Lord at Jerusalem with a gift; here the bond and the free stood on common ground. Deut. xvi.

9. If a man smite his servant or his maid with a rod, and he die under his hand, he shall be surely punished. Notwithstanding, if he continue a day or two, he shall not be punished, for he is his money. Ex. xxi, 20, 21.

From these laws we learn that Hebrew men servants were bound to serve their masters *only six* years, unless their attachment to their employers, their wives and children, should induce them to wish to remain in servitude, in which case, in order to prevent the possibility of deception on the part of the master, the servant was first taken before the magistrate, where he openly declared his intention of continuing in his master's service, (probably a public register was kept of such) he was then conducted to the door of the house, (in warm climates doors are thrown open,) and *there* his ear was *publicly* bored, and by submitting to this operation he testified his willingness to serve him *forever*, i. e. during his life, for Jewish Rabbins who must have understood Jewish *slavery*, (as it is called.) "affirm that servants were set free at the death of their masters and did *not* descend to their heirs:" or that he was to serve him until the year of Jubilee, when *all* servants were set at liberty. To protect servants from violence, it was ordained that if a master struck out the tooth or destroyed the eye of a servant, that servant immediately became *free*, for such an act of violence evidently showed he was unfit to possess the power of a master, and therefore that power was taken from him. All servants enjoyed the rest of the Sabbath and partook of the privileges and festivities of the three great Jewish Feasts; and if a servant died under the infliction of chastisement, his master was surely to be punished. As a tooth for a tooth and life for life was the Jewish law, of course he was punished to death. I know that great stress has been laid upon the following verse: "Notwithstanding, if he continue a day or two, he shall not be punished, for he is his money."

Slaveholders, and the apologists of slavery, have eagerly seized upon this little passage of scripture, and held it up as the masters' Magna Charta, by which they were licensed by God himself to commit the greatest outrages upon the defenceless victims of their oppression. But, my friends, was it designed to be so? If our Heavenly Father would protect by law the eye and the tooth of a Hebrew servant, can we for a moment believe that he would abandon that same servant to the brutal rage of a master who would destroy even life itself. Do we not rather see in this, the *only* law which protected masters, and was it not right that in case of the death of a servant, one or two days after chastisement was inflicted, to which other circumstances might have contributed, that the master should be protected when, in all probability, he never intended to produce so fatal a result? But the phrase "he is his money" has been adduced to show that Hebrew servants were regarded as mere *things*, "chattels personal;" if so, why were so many laws made to *secure their rights as men*, and to ensure their rising into equality and freedom? If they were mere *things*, why were they regarded as responsible beings, and one law made for them as well as for their masters? But I pass on now to the consideration of how the *female* Jewish servants were protected by *law.*

1. If she please not her master, who hath betrothed her to himself, then shall he let her be redeemed: to sell her unto another nation he shall have no power, seeing he hath dealt deceitfully with her.

2. If he have betrothed her unto his son, he shall deal with her after the manner of daughters.

3. If he take him another wife, her food, her raiment, and her duty of marriage, shall he not diminish.

4. If he do not these three unto her, then shall she go out *free* without money.

On these laws I will give you Calmet's remarks; "A father could not sell his daughter as a slave, according to the Rabbins, until she was at the age of puberty, and unless he were reduced to the utmost indigence. Besides when a master bought an Is-raelitish girl, it was *always* with the presumption that he would take her to wife. Hence Moses adds, 'if she please not her master, and he does not think fit to marry her, he shall set her at liberty,' or according to the Hebrew, 'he shall let her be re-deemed.' 'To sell her to another nation he shall have no power, seeing he hath dealt deceitfully with her;' as to the engagement implied, at least of taking her to wife. 'If he have betrothed her unto his son, he shall deal with her after the manner of daughters, i. e. he shall take care that his son uses her as his wife, that he does not despise or maltreat her. If he make his son marry another wife, he shall give her her dowry, her clothes and compensation for her virginity; if he does none of these three, she shall *go out free* without money." Thus were the *rights of female servants carefully secured by law* under the Jewish Dispensation; and now I would ask, are the rights of female slaves at the South thus secured? Are *they* sold only as wives and daughters-in-law, and when not treated as such, are they allowed to *go out free?* No! They have *all* not only been illegally obtained as servants according to Hebrew law, but they are also il-legally *held* in bondage. Masters at the South and West have all forfeited their claims, *(if they ever had any,)* to their female slaves.

We come now to examine the case of those servants who were "of the heathen round about;" Were *they* left entirely unprotected by law? Horne in speaking of the law, "Thou shalt not rule over him with rigor, but shalt fear thy God," remarks, "this law Lev, xxv, 43, it is true speaks expressly of slaves who were of Hebrew descent; but as *alien born* slaves were ingrafted into the Hebrew Church by circumcision, *there is no doubt* but that it applied to *all* slaves;" if so, then we may reasonably sup-pose that the other protective laws extended to them also; and that the only differ-ence between Hebrew and Heathen servants lay in this, that the former served but six years unless they chose to remain longer, and were always freed at the death of their masters; whereas the latter served until the year of Jubilee, though that might include a period of forty-nine years,—and were left from father to son.

There are however two other laws which I have not yet noticed. The one effectually prevented *all involuntary* servitude, and the other completely abolished Jewish servi-tude every fifty years. They were equally operative upon the Heathen and the Hebrew.

1. "Thou shall *not* deliver unto his master the servant that is escaped from his master unto thee. He shall dwell with thee, even among you, in that place which he shall choose, in one of thy gates where it liketh him best: thou shall *not* oppress him." Deut. xxiii, 15, 16.

2. "And ye shall hallow the fiftieth year, and proclaim *Liberty* thoughout *all* the land, unto *all* the inhabitants thereof: it shall be a jubilee unto you." Lev. xxv, 10.

Here, then, we see that by this first law, the *door of Freedom was opened wide to every servant who* had any cause whatever for complaint; if he was unhappy with his master, all he had to do was to leave him, and *no man* had a right to deliver him back to him again, and not only so, but the absconded servant was to *choose* where he should live, and no Jew was permitted to oppress him. He left his master just as our Northern servants leave us; we have no power to compel them to remain with us, and no man has any right to oppress them; they go and dwell in that place where it chooseth them, and live just where they like. Is it so at the South? Is the poor runaway slave protected *by law* from the violence of that master whose oppression and cruelty has driven him from his plantation or his house? No! no! Even the free states of the North are compelled to deliver unto his master the servant that is escaped from his master into them. By *human* law, under the *Christian Dispensation*, in the *nineteenth century we* are commanded to do, what *God* more than *three thousand* years ago, under the *Mosaic Dispensation, positively commanded* the Jews *not* to do. In the wide domain even of our free states, there is not *one* city of refuge for the poor runaway fugitive; not one spot upon which he can stand and say, I am a free man—I am protected in my rights as a *man*, by the strong arm of the law; no! *not one.* How long the North will thus shake hands with the South in sin, I know not. How long she will stand by like the persecutor Saul, *consenting* unto the death of Stephen, and keeping the raiment of them that slew him. I know not; but one thing I do know, the *guilt of the North* is increasing in a tremendous ratio as light is pouring in upon her on the subject and the sin of slavery. As the sun of righteousness climbs higher and higher in the moral heavens, she will stand still more and more abashed as the query is thundered down into her ear, "*Who* hath required *this* at thy hand?" It will be found *no* excuse then that the Constitution of our country required that *persons bound to service* escaping from their masters should be delivered up; no more excuse than was the reason which Adam assigned for eating the forbidden fruit. *He* was *condemned and punished because* he hearkened to the voice of *his wife*, rather than to the command of his Maker; and *we* will assuredly be condemned and punished for obeying *Man* rather than *God*, if we do not speedily repent and bring forth fruits meet for repentance. Yea, are we not receiving chastisement even *now?*

But by the second of these laws a still more astonishing fact is disclosed. If the first effectually prevents *all involuntary servitude*, the last absolutely forbade even *voluntary servitude being perpetual.* On the great day of atonement every fiftieth year the Jubilee trumpet was sounded throughout the land of Judea, and *Liberty* was proclaimed to *all* the inhabitants thereof. I will not say that the servants' *chains* fell off and their *manacles* were burst, for there is no evidence that Jewish servants *ever* felt the weight of iron chains, and collars, and handcuffs; but I do say that even the man who had voluntarily sold himself and the *heathen* who had been sold to a Hebrew master, were set free, the one as well as the other. This law was evidently designed to prevent the oppression of the poor, and the possibility of such a thing as *perpetual servitude* existing among them.

Where, then, I would ask, is the warrant, the justification, or the palliation of American Slavery from Hebrew servitude? How many of the southern slaves would now be in bondage according to the laws of Moses; Not one. You may observe that I have carefully avoided using the term *slavery* when speaking of Jewish servitude; and simply for this reason, that *no such thing* existed among that people; the word translated servant does *not* mean *slave*, it is the same that is applied to Abraham, to Moses, to Elisha and the prophets generally. *Slavery* then *never* existed under the Jewish Dispensation at all, and I cannot but regard it as an aspersion on the character of Him who is "glorious in Holiness" for any one to assert that "*God sanctioned, yea commanded slavery* under the old dispensation." I would fain lift my feeble voice to vindicate Jehovah's character from so foul a slander. If slaveholders are determined to hold slaves as long as they can, let them not dare to say that the God of mercy and of truth *ever* sanctioned such a system of cruelty and wrong. It is blasphemy against Him.

We have seen that the code of laws framed by Moses with regard to servants was designed to *protect them* as *men and women*, to secure to them their *rights* as *human beings*, to guard them from oppression and defend them from violence of every kind. Let us now turn to the Slave laws of the South and West and examine them too. I will give you the substance only, because I fear I shall tresspass too much on your time, were I to quote them at length.

1. *Slavery* is hereditary and perpetual, to the last moment of the slave's earthly existence, and to all his descendants to the latest posterity.

2. The labor of the slave is compulsory and uncompensated; while the kind of labor, the amount of toil, the time allowed for rest, are dictated solely by the master. No bargain is made, no wages given. A pure despotism governs the human brute; and even his covering and provender, both as to quantity and quality, depend entirely on the master's discretion.*

3. The slave being considered a personal chattel may be sold or pledged, or leased at the will of his master. He may be exchanged for marketable commodities, or taken in execution for the debts or taxes either of a living or dead master. Sold at auction, either individually, or in lots to suit the purchaser, he may remain with his family, or be separated from them for ever.

4. Slaves can make no contracts and have no *legal* right to any property, real or personal. Their own honest earnings and the legacies of friends belong in point of law to their masters.

5. Neither a slave nor a free colored person can be a witness against any *white*, or free person, in a court of justice, however atrocious may have been the crimes they have seen him commit, if such testimony would be for the benefit of a *slave;* but they may give testimony *against a fellow slave*, or free colored man, even in cases affecting life, if the *master* is to reap the advantage of it.

6. The slave may be punished at his master's discretion—without trial—without any means of legal redress; whether his offence be real or imaginary; and the master can transfer the same despotic power to any person or persons, he may choose to appoint.

---

*There are laws in some of the slave states, limiting the labor which the master may require of the slave to fourteen hours daily. In some of the states there are laws requiring the masters to furnish a certain amount of food and clothing, as for instance, *one quart* of corn per day, or *one peck* per week, or *one bushel* per month, and *"one* linen shirt and pantaloons for the summer, and a linen shirt and woolen great coat and pantaloons for the winter," &c. But "still," to use the language of Judge Stroud "the slave is entirely under the control of his master,—is unprovided with a protector,—and, especially as he cannot be a witness or make complaint in any known mode against his master, the *apparent* object of these laws may *always* be defeated." Ed.

7. The slave is not allowed to resist any free man under *any* circumstances, *his* only safety consists in the fact that his *owner* may bring suit and recover the price of his body, in case his life is taken, or his limbs rendered unfit for labor.

8. Slaves cannot redeem themselves, or obtain a change of masters, though cruel treatment may have rendered such a change necessary for their personal safety.

9. The slave is entirely unprotected in his domestic relations.

10. The laws greatly obstruct the manumission of slaves, even where the master is willing to enfranchise them.

11. The operation of the laws tends to deprive slaves of religious instruction and consolation.

12. The whole power of the laws is exerted to keep slaves in a state of the lowest ignorance.

13. There is in this country a monstrous inequality of law and right. What is a trifling fault in the *white* man, is considered highly criminal in the *slave;* the same offences which cost a white man a few dollars only, are punished in the negro with death.

14. The laws operate most oppressively upon free people of color.

Shall I ask you now my friends, to draw the *parallel* between Jewish *servitude* and American *slavery?* No! For there is *no likeness* in the two systems; I ask you rather to mark the contrast. The laws of Moses *protected servants* in the *rights* as *men and women*, guarded them from oppression and defended them from wrong. The Code Noir of the South *robs the slave of all his rights* as a *man*, reduces him to a chattel personal, and defends the *master* in the exercise of the most unnatural and unwarrantable power over his slave. They each bear the impress of the hand which formed them. The attributes of justice and mercy are shadowed out in the Hebrew code; those of injustice and cruelty, in the Code Noir of America. Truly it was wise in the slaveholders of the South to declare their slaves to be "chattels personal;" for before they could be robbed of wages, wives, children, and friends, it was absolutely necessary to deny they were human beings. It is wise in them, to keep them in abject ignorance, for the strong man armed must be bound before we can spoil his house—the powerful intellect of man must be bound down with the iron chains of nescience before we can rob him of his rights as a man; we must reduce him to a *thing* before we can claim the right to set our feet upon his neck, because it was only *all things* which were originally *put under the feet of man* by the Almighty and Beneficent Father of all, who has declared himself to be *no respecter* of persons, whether red, white or black.

But some have even said that Jesus Christ did not condemn slavery. To this I reply that our Holy Redeemer lived and preached among the Jews only. The laws which Moses had enacted fifteen hundred years previous to his appearance among them, had never been annulled, and these laws protected every servant in Palestine. If then He did not condemn Jewish servitude this does not prove that he would not have condemned such a monstrous system as that of American *slavery*, if that had existed among them. But did not Jesus condemn slavery? Let us examine some of his precepts. *"Whatsoever ye* would that men should do to you, do *ye even so to them,"* Let every slaveholder apply these queries to his own heart; Am *I* willing to be a slave— Am *I* willing to see *my* wife the slave of another—Am *I* willing to see my mother a slave, or my father, my sister or my brother? If *not*, then in holding others as slaves, I am doing what I would *not* wish to be done to me or any relative I have; and thus have I broken this golden rule which was given *me* to walk by.

But some slaveholders have said, "we were never in bondage to any man," and therefore the yoke of bondage would be insufferable to us, but slaves are accustomed to it, their backs are fitted to the burden. Well, I am willing to admit that you who have lived in freedom would find slavery even more oppressive than the poor slave does, but then you may try this question in another form—Am I willing to reduce *my little child* to slavery? You know that *if it is brought up a slave* it will never know any contrast, between freedom and bondage, its back will become fitted to the burden just as the negro child's does—*not by nature*—but by daily, violent pressure, in the same way that the head of the Indian child becomes flattened by the boards in which it is bound. It has been justly remarked that *"God never made a slave,"* he made man upright; his back was *not* made to carry burdens, nor his neck to wear a yoke, and the *man* must be crushed within him, before *his* back can be *fitted* to the burden of perpetual slavery; and that his back is *not* fitted to it, is manifest by the insurrections that so often disturb the peace and security of slaveholding countries. Who ever heard of a rebellion of the beasts of the field; and why not? simply because *they* were all placed *under the feet of man*, into whose hand they were delivered; it was originally designed that they should serve him, therefore their necks have been formed for the yoke, and their backs for the burden; but *not so with man*, intellectual, immortal man! I appeal to you, my friends, as mothers; Are you willing to enslave *your* children? You start back with horror and indignation at such a question. But why, if slavery is *no wrong* to those upon whom it is imposed? why, if as has often been said, slaves are happier than their masters, free from the cares and perplexities of providing for themselves and their families? why not place *your children* in the way of being supported without your having the trouble to provide for them, or they for themselves? Do you not perceive that as soon as this golden rule of action is applied to *yourselves* that you involuntarily shrink from the test; as soon as *your* actions are weighed in *this* balance of the sanctuary that *you are found wanting?* Try yourselves by another of the Divine precepts, "Thou shalt love thy neighbor as thyself." Can we love a man *as* we love *ourselves* if we do, and continue to do unto him, what we would not wish any one to do to us? Look too, at Christ's example, what does he say of himself, "I came *not* to be ministered unto, but to minister." Can you for a moment imagine the meek, and lowly, and compassionate Saviour, *a slaveholder?* do you not shudder at this thought as much as at that of his being *a warrior?* But why, if slavery is not sinful?

Again, it has been said, the Apostle Paul did not condemn Slavery, for he sent Onesimus back to Philemon. I do not think it can be said he sent him back, for no coercion was made use of. Onesimus was not thrown into prison and then sent back in chains to his master, as your runaway slaves often are—this could not possibly have been the case, because you know Paul as a Jew, was *bound to protect* the runaway, *he had no right* to send any fugitive back to his master. The state of the case then seems to have been this. Onesimus had been an unprofitable servant to Philemon and left him—he afterwards became converted under the Apostle's preaching, and seeing that he had been to blame in his conduct, and desiring by future fidelity to atone for past error, he wished to return, and the Apostle gave him the letter we now have as a recommendation to Philemon, informing him of the conversion of Onesimus, and entreating him as "Paul the aged" "to receive him, *not* now as a *servant*, but *above* a servant, a brother beloved, especially to me, but how much more unto thee, both in the flesh and in the Lord. If thou count *me* therefore as a partner, *receive him as myself."* This then surely cannot be forced into a justification of the practice of returning runaway slaves back to their masters, to be punished with cruel beatings and scourgings as they often are. Besides the word δουλος here translated servant, is the same that is made use of in Matt. xviii, 27. Now it appears that this servant owed his lord ten thousand talents; he possessed property to a vast amount. Onesimus could not then have been a *slave*, for slaves do not own their wives, or children; no, not even their own bodies, much less property. But again, the servitude which the apostle was accustomed to, must have been very different from American slavery, for he says, "the heir (or son), as long as he is a child, differeth *nothing from a servant*, though he be lord of all. But is under *tutors* and governors until the time appointed of the father." From this it appears, that the means of *instruction* were provided for *servants* as well as children; and indeed we know it must have been so among the Jews, because their servants were not permitted to remain in perpetual bondage, and therefore it was absolutely necessary they should be prepared to occupy higher stations in society than those of servants. Is it so at the South, my friends? Is the daily bread of instruction provided for *your slaves?* are their minds enlightened, and they gradually prepared to rise from the grade of menials into that of *free*, independent members of the state? Let your own statute book, and your own daily experience, answer these questions.

If this apostle sanctioned *slavery*, why did he exhort masters thus in his epistle to the Ephesians, "and ye, masters, do the same things unto them (i.e. perform your duties to your servants as unto Christ, not unto me) *forbearing threatening;* knowing that your master also is in heaven, neither is *there respect of persons with him."* And in Colossians, "Masters give unto your servants that which is *just and equal*, knowing that ye also have a master in heaven." Let slaveholders only *obey* these injunctions of Paul, and I am satisfied slavery would soon be abolished. If he thought it sinful even to *threaten* servants, surely he must have thought it sinful to flog and to beat them with sticks and paddles; indeed, when delineating the character of a bishop, he expressly names this as one feature of it, *"no striker."* Let masters give unto their servants that which is *just* and *equal*, and all that vast system of unrequited labor would crumble into ruin. Yes, and if they once felt they had no right to the *labor* of their servants without pay, surely they could not think they had a right to their wives, their children, and their own bodies. Again, how can it be said Paul sanctioned slavery, when, as though to put this matter beyond all doubt, in that black catalogue of sins enumerated in his first epistle to Timothy, he mentions *"menstealers,"* which word may be translated *"slavedealers."* But you may say, we all despise slavedealers as much as any one can; they are never admitted into genteel or respectable society. And why not? Is it not because even you shrink back from the idea of associating with those who make their fortunes by trading in the bodies and souls of men, women, and children? whose daily work it is to break human hearts, by tearing wives from their husbands, and children from their parents? But why hold slavedealers as despicable, if their trade is lawful and virtuous? and why despise them more than the *gentlemen of fortune and standing* who employ them as *their* agents? Why more than the *professors of religion* who barter their fellow-professors to them for gold and silver? We do not despise the land agent, or the physician, or the merchant, and why? Simply because their professions are virtuous and honorable; and if the trade of men-jobbers was honorable, you would not despise them either. There is no difference in *principle*, in *Christian ethics*, between the despised slavedealer and the *Christian* who buys slaves from, or sells slaves to him; indeed, if slaves were not wanted by the respectable, the wealthy, and the religious in a community, there would be no slaves in that community, and of course no *slavedealers*. It is then the *Christians* and the *honorable men* and *women* of the South, who are the *main pillars* of this grand temple built to Mammon and to Moloch. It is the *most enlightened* in every country who are *most* to blame when any public sin is supported by public opinion, hence Isaiah says, *"When* the Lord hath performed his whole work upon mount *Zion* and on *Jerusalem,* (then) I will punish the fruit of the stout heart of the king of Assyria, and the glory of his high looks." And was it not so? Open the historical records of that age, was not Israel carried into captivity B. C. 606, Judah B. C. 588, and the stout heart of the heathen monarchy not punished until B. C. 536, fifty-two years *after* Judah's, and seventy years *after* Israel's captivity, when it was overthrown by Cyrus, king of Persia? Hence, too, the apostle Peter says, "judgment must *begin at the house of God."* Surely this would not be the case, if the *professors of religion* were not *most worthy* of blame.

But it may be asked, why are *they* most culpable? I will tell you, my friends. It is because sin is imputed to us just in proportion to the spiritual light we receive. Thus the prophet Amos says, in the name of Jehovah, *"You only* have I known of all the families of the earth: *therefore* I will punish *you* for all your iniquities." Hear too the doctrine of our Lord on this important subject; "The servant who *knew* his Lord's will and *prepared not* himself, neither did according to his will, shall be beaten with *many* stripes:" and why? "For unto whomsoever *much* is given, *of him* shall *much* be required; and to whom men have committed *much,* of *him* they will ask the *more."* Oh! then that the *Christians* of the south would ponder these things in their hearts, and awake to the vast responsibilities which rest *upon them* at this important crisis.

I have thus, I think, clearly proved to you seven propositions, viz.: First, that slavery is contrary to the declaration of our independence. Second, that it is contrary to the first charter of human rights given to Adam, and renewed to Noah. Third, that the fact of slavery having been the subject of prophecy, furnishes *no* excuse whatever to slavedealers. Fourth, that no such system existed under the patriarchal dispensation. Fifth, that *slavery never* existed under the Jewish dispensation; but so far otherwise, that every servant was placed under the *protection of law,* and care taken not only to prevent all *involuntary* servitude, but all *voluntary perpetual* bondage. Sixth, that slavery in America reduces a *man* to a *thing,* a "chattel personal," *robs him* of *all* his rights as a *human being,* fetters both his mind and body, and protects the *master* in the most unnatural and unreasonable power, whilst it *throws him out* of the protection of law. Seventh, that slavery is contrary to the example and precepts of our holy and merciful Redeemer, and of his apostles.

But perhaps you will be ready to query, why appeal to *women* on this subject? *We* do not make the laws which perpetuate slavery. *No* legislative power is vested in *us; we* can do nothing to overthrow the system, even if we wished to do so. To this I reply, I know you do not make the laws, but I also know that *you are the wives and mothers, the sisters and daughters of those who do;* and if you really suppose *you* can do nothing to overthrow slavery, you are greatly mistaken. You can do much in every way: four things I will name. 1st. You can read on this subject. 2d. You can pray over this subject. 3d. You can speak on this subject. 4th. You can *act* on this subject. I have not placed reading before praying because I regard it more important, but because, in order to pray aright, we must understand what we are praying for; it is only then we can "pray with the understanding and the spirit also."

1. Read then on the subject of slavery. Search the Scriptures daily, whether the things I have told you are true. Other books and papers might be a great help to you in this investigation, but they are not necessary, and it is hardly probable that your Com-

mittees of Vigilance will allow you to have any other. The *Bible* then is the book I want you to read in the spirit of inquiry, and the spirit of prayer. Even the enemies of Abolitionists, acknowledge that their doctrines are drawn from it. In the great mob in Boston, last autumn, when the books and papers of the Anti-Slavery Society, were thrown out of the windows of their office, one individual laid hold of the Bible and was about tossing it out to the ground, when another reminded him that it was the Bible he had in his hand. *"O! 'tis all one,"* he replied, and out went the sacred volume, along with the rest. We thank him for the acknowledgment. Yes, *"it is all one,"* for our books and papers are mostly commentaries on the Bible, and the Declaration. Read the *Bible* then, it contains the words of Jesus, and they are spirit and life. Judge for yourselves whether *he sanctioned* such a system of oppression and crime.

2. Pray over this subject. When you have entered into your closets, and shut to the doors, then pray to your father, who seeth in secret, that he would open your eyes to see whether slavery is *sinful*, and if it is, that he would enable you to bear a faithful, open and unshrinking testimony against it, and to do whatsoever your hands find to do, leaving the consequences entirely to him, who still says to us whenever we try to reason away duty from the fear of consequences, *"What is that to thee, follow thou me."* Pray also for that poor slave, that he may be kept patient and submissive under his hard lot, until God is pleased to open the door of freedom to him without violence or bloodshed. Pray too for the master that his heart may be softened, and he made willing to acknowledge, as Joseph's brethren did, "Verily we are guilty concerning our brother," before he will be compelled to add in consequence of Divine judgment, "therefore is all this evil come upon us." Pray also for all your brethren and sisters who are laboring in the righteous cause of Emancipation in the Northern States, England and the world. There is great encouragement for prayer in these words of our Lord. "Whatsoever ye shall ask the Father *in my name*, he *will give* it to you"—Pray then without ceasing, in the closet and the social circle.

3. Speak on this subject. It is through the tongue, the pen, and the press, that truth is principally propagated. Speak then to your relatives, your friends, your acquaintances on the subject of slavery; be not afraid if you are conscientiously convinced it is *sinful*, to say so openly, but calmly, and to let your sentiments be known. If you are served by the slaves of others, try to ameliorate their condition as much as possible; never aggravate their faults, and thus add fuel to the fire of anger already kindled, in a master and mistress's bosom; remember their extreme ignorance, and consider them as your Heavenly Father does the *less* culpable on this account, even when they do wrong things. Discountenance *all* cruelty to them, all starvation, all corporal chastisement; these may brutalize and *break* their spirits, but will never bend them to willing, cheerful obedience. If possible, see that they are comfortably and *seasonably* fed, whether in the house or the field; it is unreasonable and cruel to expect slaves to wait for their breakfast until eleven o'clock, when they rise at five or six. Do all you can, to induce their owners to clothe them well, and to allow them many little indulgences which would contribute to their comfort. Above all, try to persuade your husband, father, brothers and sons, that *slavery is a crime against God and man*, and that it is a great sin to keep *human beings* in such abject ignorance; to deny them the privilege of learning to read and write. The Catholics are universally condemned, for denying the Bible to the common people, but, *slaveholders must not* blame them, for *they* are doing the *very same thing*, and for the very same reason,

neither of these systems can bear the light which bursts from the pages of that Holy Book. And lastly, endeavour to inculcate submission on the part of the slaves, but whilst doing this be faithful in pleading the cause of the oppressed.

> "Will *you* behold unheeding,
>   Life's holiest feelings crushed,
> Where *woman's* heart is bleeding,
>   Shall *woman's* voice be hushed?"

4. Act on this subject. Some of you *own* slaves yourselves. If you believe slavery is *sinful*, set them at liberty, "undo the heavy burdens and let the oppressed go free." If they wish to remain with you, pay them wages, if not let them leave you. Should they remain teach them, and have them taught the common branches of an English education; they have minds and those minds, *ought to be improved.* So precious a talent as intellect, never was given to be wrapt in a napkin and buried in the earth. It is the *duty* of all, as far as they can, to improve their own mental faculties, because we are commanded to love God with *all our minds*, as well as with all our hearts, and we commit a great sin, if we *forbid or prevent* that cultivation of the mind in others, which would enable them to perform this duty. Teach your servants then to read &c, and encourage them to believe it is their *duty* to learn, if it were only that they might read the Bible.

But some of you will say, we can neither free our slaves nor teach them to read, for the laws of our state forbid it. Be not surprised when I say such wicked laws *ought to be no barrier* in the way of your duty, and I appeal to the Bible to prove this position. What was the conduct of Shiphrah and Puah, when the king of Egypt issued his cruel mandate, with regard to the Hebrew children? *"They* feared *God*, and did *not* as the King of Egypt commanded them, but saved the men children alive." Did these *women* do right in disobeying that monarch? *"Therefore* (says the sacred text), *God dealt well* with them, and made them houses" Ex. i. What was the conduct of Shadrach, Meshach, and Abednego, when Nebuchadnezzar set up a golden image in the plain of Dura, and commanded all people, nations, and languages, to fall down and worship it? "Be it known, unto thee, (said these faithful *Jews*) O king, that *we will not* serve thy gods, nor worship the image which thou hast set up." Did these men *do right in disobeying the law* of their sovereign? Let their miraculous deliverance from the burning fiery furnace, answer; Dan. iii. What was the conduct of Daniel, when Darius made a firm decree that no one should ask a petition of any man or God for thirty days? Did the prophet cease to pray? No! "When Daniel *knew that the writing was signed*, he went into his house, and his windows being *open* towards Jerusalem, he kneeled upon his knees three times a day, and prayed and gave thanks before his God, as he did aforetime." Did Daniel do right thus to *break* the law of his king? Let his wonderful deliverance out of the mouths of the lions answer; Dan. vii. Look, too, at the Apostles Peter and John. When the rulers of the Jews, *"commanded them not* to speak at all, nor teach in the name of Jesus," what did they say? "Whether it be right in the sight of God, to hearken unto you more than unto God, judge ye." And what did they do? "They spake the word of God with boldness, and with great power gave the Apostles witness of the *resurrection* of the Lord Jesus;" although *this* was the very doctrine, for the preaching of which, they had just been cast into prison, and further threatened. Did these men do right? I leave *you* to answer, who now enjoy the benefits of their labors and sufferings, in that Gospel they dared to preach when positively commanded *not to teach any more* in the name of Jesus; Acts iv.

But some of you may say, if we do free our slaves, they will be taken up and sold, therefore there will be no use in doing it. Peter and John might just as well have said, we will not preach the gospel, for if we do, we shall be taken up and put in prison, therefore there will be no use in our preaching. *Consequences*, my friends, belong no more to *you*, than they did to these apostles. Duty is ours and events are God's. If you think slavery is sinful, all *you* have to do is to set your slaves at liberty, do all you can to protect them, and in humble faith and fervent prayer, commend them to your common Father. He can take care of them; but if for wise purposes he sees fit to allow them to be sold, this will afford you an opportunity of testifying openly, wherever you go, against the crime of *manstealing.* Such an act will be *clear robbery*, and if exposed, might, under the Divine direction, do the cause of Emancipation more good, than any thing that could happen, for, "He makes even the wrath of man to praise him, and the remainder of wrath he will restrain."

I know that this doctrine of obeying *God*, rather than man, will be considered as dangerous, and heretical by many, but I am not afraid openly to avow it, because it is the doctrine of the Bible; but I would not be understood to advocate resistance to any law however oppressive, if, in obeying it, I was not obliged to commit *sin.* If for instance, there was a law, which imposed imprisonment or a fine upon me if I manumitted a slave, I would on no account resist that law, I would set the slave free, and then go to prison or pay the fine. If a law commands me to *sin I will break it;* if it calls me to *suffer*, I will let it take its course *unresistingly.* The doctrine of blind obedience and unqualified submission to *any human* power, whether civil or ecclesiastical, is the doctrine of despotism, and ought to have no place among Republicans and Christians.

John C. Calhoun

(1782–1850)

John C. Calhoun was raised on a plantation in the up-country of South Carolina and received little formal education before the age of eighteen, when he entered a classical academy founded by his brother-in-law, the Reverend Moses Waddel. Calhoun spent two years at Yale College and a year at the Tapping Reeve School of Litchfield, Connecticut, and was admitted to the bar in 1807; he was elected to the S.C. state legislature shortly thereafter. In 1810, he was elected to the United States House of Representatives, and in 1811, he solidified his financial situation through an advantageous marriage to a low-country cousin. In Congress he became a leader of the "War Hawks," who helped bring on the war of 1812. Now a figure of national prominence, Calhoun advocated, in the years following the war, a series of federal programs that included the use of protective tariffs to encourage manufacturing.

In 1824, Calhoun was elected vice president in the administration of John Quincy Adams. In 1828, he reversed himself on the tariff issue, drafting what came to be known as the "South Carolina Exposition," a document that was remembered mainly for its advocacy of what Calhoun called interposition, or state veto, but that would come to be known as nullification—the alleged right of a state to suspend operation of a federal law within its boundaries. Overruled by President Jackson (whose administration he now served) on that issue, Calhoun resigned the vice presidency in 1832 and became a member of the Senate, where he served until his death, save only for the years 1844–1845, when he was U.S. Secretary of State. He continued to advocate states' rights and the expansion of slavery, and his 1851 *A Disquisition on Government,* published posthumously, argues that society, especially its substantial economic interests, should take precedence over government.

from *A Disquisition on Government*

To perfect society, it is necessary to develope the faculties, intellectual and moral, with which man is endowed. But the main spring to their development, and, through this, to progress, improvement and civilization, with all their blessings, is the desire of individuals to better their condition. For, this purpose, liberty and security are indispensable. Liberty leaves each free to pursue the course he may deem best to promote his interest and happiness, as far as it may be compatible with the primary end for which government is ordained;—while security gives assurance to each, that he shall not be deprived of the fruits of his exertions to better his condition. These combined, give to this desire the strongest impulse of which it is susceptible. For, to extend liberty beyond the limits assigned, would be to weaken the government and to render it incompetent to fulfil its primary end,—the protection of society against dangers, internal and external. The effect of this would be, insecurity; and, of insecurity,—to weaken the impulse of individuals to better their condition, and thereby retard progress and improvement. On the other hand, to extend the powers of the government, so as to contract the sphere assigned to liberty, would have the same effect, by disabling individuals in their efforts to better their condition.

Herein is to be found the principle which assigns to power and liberty their proper spheres, and reconciles each to the other under all circumstances. For, if power be necessary to secure to liberty the fruits of its exertions, liberty, in turn, repays power with interest, by increased population, wealth, and other advantages, which progress and improvement bestow on the community. By thus assigning to each its appropriate sphere, all conflicts between them cease; and each is made to co-operate with and assist the other, in fulfilling the great ends for which government is ordained.

But the principle, applied to different communities, will assign to them different limits. It will assign a larger sphere to power and a more contracted one to liberty, or the reverse, according to circumstances. To the former, there must ever be allotted, under all circumstances, a sphere sufficiently large to protect the community against danger from without and violence and anarchy within. The residuum belongs to liberty. More cannot be safely or rightly allotted to it.

But some communities require a far greater amount of power than others to protect them against anarchy and external dangers; and, of course, the sphere of liberty in such, must be proportionally contracted. The causes calculated to enlarge the one and contract the other, are numerous and various. Some are physical;—such as open and exposed frontiers, surrounded by powerful and hostile neighbors. Others are moral;—such as the different degrees of intelligence, patriotism, and virtue among the mass of the community, and their experience and proficiency in the art of self-government. Of these, the moral are, by far, that most influential. A community may possess all the necessary moral qualifications, in so high a degree, as to be capable of self-government under the most adverse circumstances; while, on the other hand, another may be so sunk in ignorance and vice, as to be incapable of forming a conception of liberty, or of living, even when most favored by circumstances, under any other than an absolute and despotic government.

The principle, in all communities, according to these numerous and various causes, assigns to power and liberty their proper spheres. To allow to liberty, in any case, a sphere of action more extended than this assigns, would lead to anarchy; and this, probably, in the end, to a contraction instead of an enlargement of its sphere. Liberty, then, when forced on a people unfit for it, would, instead of a blessing, be a curse; as it would, in its reaction, lead directly to anarchy,—the greatest of all curses. No people, indeed, can long enjoy more liberty than that to which their situation and advanced intelligence and morals fairly entitle them. If more than this be allowed, they must soon fall into confusion and disorder,—to be followed, if not by anarchy and despotism, by a change to a form of government more simple and absolute; and, therefore, better suited to their condition. And hence, although it may be true, that a people may not have as much liberty as they are fairly entitled to, and are capable of enjoying,—yet the reverse is unquestionably true,—that no people can long possess more than they are fairly entitled to.

Liberty, indeed, though among the greatest of blessings, is not so great as that of protection; inasmuch, as the end of the former is the progress and improvement of the race,—while that of the latter is its preservation and perpetuation. And hence, when the two come into conflict, liberty must, and ever ought, to yield to protection; as the existence of the race is of greater moment than its improvement.

It follows, from what has been stated, that it is a great and dangerous error to suppose that all people are equally entitled to liberty. It is a reward to be earned, not a blessing to be gratuitously lavished on all alike;—a reward reserved for the intelligent, the patriotic, the virtuous and deserving;—and not a boon to be bestowed on a people too ignorant, degraded and vicious, to be capable either of appreciating or of enjoying it. Nor is it any disparagement to liberty, that such is, and ought to be the case. On the contrary, its greatest praise,—its proudest distinction is, that an all-wise Providence has reserved it, as the noblest and highest reward for the development of our faculties, moral and intellectual. A reward more appropriate than liberty could not be conferred on the deserving;—nor a punishment inflicted on the undeserving more just, than to be subject to lawless and despotic rule. This dispensation seems to be the result of some fixed law;—and every effort to disturb or defeat it, by attempting to elevate a people in the scale of liberty, above the point to which they are entitled to rise, must ever prove abortive, and end in disappointment. The progress of a people rising from a lower to a higher point in the scale of liberty, is necessarily slow;—and by attempting to precipitate, we either retard, or permanently defeat it.

There is another error, not less great and dangerous, usually associated with the one which has just been considered. I refer to the opinion, that liberty and equality are so intimately united, that liberty cannot be perfect without perfect equality.

That they are united to a certain extent,—and that equality of citizens, in the eyes of the law, is essential to liberty in a popular government, is conceded. But to go further, and make equality of *condition* essential to liberty, would be to destroy both liberty and progress. The reason is, that inequality of condition, while it is a necessary consequence of liberty, is, at the same time, indispensable to progress. In order to understand why this is so, it is necessary to bear in mind, that the main spring to progress is, the desire of individuals to better their condition; and that the strongest impulse which can be given to it is, to leave individuals free to exert themselves in the manner they may deem best for that purpose, as far at least as it can be done consistently with the ends for which government is ordained,—and to secure to all the fruits of their exertions. Now, as individuals differ greatly from each other, in intelligence, sagacity, energy, perseverance, skill, habits of industry and economy, physical power, position and opportunity,—the necessary effect of leaving all free to exert themselves to better their condition, must be a corresponding inequality between those who may possess these qualities and advantages in a high degree, and those who may be deficient in them. The only means by which this result can be prevented are, either to impose such restrictions on the exertions of those who may possess them in a high degree, as will place them on a level with those who do not; or to deprive them of the fruits of their exertions. But to impose such restrictions on them would be destructive of liberty,—while, to deprive them of the fruits of their exertions, would be to destroy the desire of bettering their condition. It is, indeed, this inequality of condition between the front and rear ranks, in the march of progress, which gives so strong an impulse to the former to maintain their position, and to the latter to press forward into their files. This gives to progress its greatest impulse. To force the front rank back to the rear, or attempt to push forward the rear into line with the front, by the interposition of the government, would put an end to the impulse, and effectually arrest the march of progress.

These great and dangerous errors have their origin in the prevalent opinion that all men are born free and equal;—than which nothing can be more unfounded and false. It rests upon the assumption of a fact, which is contrary to universal observation, in whatever light it may be regarded. It is, indeed, difficult to explain how an opinion so destitute of all sound reason, ever could have been so extensively entertained, unless we regard it as being confounded with another, which has some semblance of truth;—but which, when properly understood, is not less false and dangerous. I refer to the assertion, that all men are equal in the state of nature; meaning, by a state of nature, a state of individuality, supposed to have existed prior to the social and political state; and in which men lived apart and independent of each other. If such a state ever did exist, all men would have been, indeed, free and equal in it; that is, free to do as they pleased, and exempt from the authority or control of others—as, by supposition, it existed anterior to society and government. But such a state is purely hypothetical. It never did, nor can exist; as it is inconsistent with the preservation and perpetuation of the race. It is, therefore, a great misnomer to call it *the state of nature*. Instead of being the natural state of man, it is, of all conceivable states, the most opposed to his nature—most repugnant to his feelings, and most incompatible with his wants. His natural state is, the social and political—the one for which his Creator made him, and the only one in which he can preserve and perfect his race. As, then, there never was such a state as the, so called, state of nature, and never can be, it follows, that men, instead of being born in it, are born in the social and political state; and of course, instead of being born free and equal, are born subject, not only to parental authority, but to the laws and institutions of the country where born, and under whose protection they draw their first breath. With these remarks, I return from this digression, to resume the thread of the discourse.

It follows, from all that has been said, that the more perfectly a government combines power and liberty,—that is, the greater its power and the more enlarged and secure the liberty of individuals, the more perfectly it fulfils the ends for which government is ordained. To show, then, that the government of the concurrent majority is better calculated to fulfil them than that of the numerical, it is only necessary to explain why the former is better suited to combine a higher degree of power and a wider scope of liberty than the latter. I shall begin with the former.

The concurrent majority, then, is better suited to enlarge and secure the bounds of liberty, because it is better suited to prevent government from passing beyond its proper limits, and to restrict it to its primary end,—the protection of the community. But in doing this, it leaves, necessarily, all beyond it open and free to individual exertions; and thus enlarges and secures the sphere of liberty to the greatest extent which the condition of the community will admit, as has been explained. The tendency of government to pass beyond its proper limits is what exposes liberty to danger, and renders it insecure; and it is the strong counteraction of governments of the concurrent majority to this tendency which makes them so favorable to liberty. On the contrary, those of the numerical, instead of opposing and counteracting this tendency, add to it increased strength, in consequence of the violent party struggles incident to them, as has been fully explained. And hence their encroachments on liberty, and the danger to which it is exposed under such governments.

So great, indeed, is the difference between the two in this respect, that liberty is little more than a name under all governments of the absolute form, including that of the numerical majority; and can only have a secure and durable existence under those of the concurrent or constitutional form. The latter, by giving to each portion of the community which may be unequally affected by its action, a negative on the others, prevents all partial or local legislation, and restricts its action to such measures as are designed for the protection and the good of the whole. In doing this, it secures, at the same time, the rights and liberty of the people, regarded individually; as each portion consists of those who, whatever may be the diversity of interests among themselves, have the same interest in reference to the action of the government.

Such being the case, the interest of each individual may be safely confided to the majority, or voice of his portion, against that of all others, and, of course, the government itself. It is only through an organism which vests each with a negative, in some one form or another, that those who have like interests in preventing the government from passing beyond its proper sphere, and encroaching on the rights and liberty of individuals, can co-operate peaceably and effectually in resisting the encroachments of power, and thereby preserve their rights and liberty. Individual resistance is too feeble, and the difficulty of concert and co-operation too great, unaided by such an organism, to oppose, successfully, the organized power of government, with all the means of the community at its disposal; especially in populous countries of great extent, where concert and co-operation are almost impossible. Even when the oppression of the government comes to be too great to be borne, and force is resorted to in order to overthrow it, the result is rarely ever followed by the establishment of liberty. The force sufficient to overthrow an oppressive government is usually sufficient to establish one equally, or more, oppressive in its place. And hence, in no governments, except those that rest on the principle of the concurrent or constitutional majority, can the people guard their liberty against power; and hence, also, when lost, the great difficulty and uncertainty of regaining it by force.

It may be further affirmed, that, being more favorable to the enlargement and security of liberty, governments of the concurrent, must necessarily be more favorable to progress, development, improvement, and civilization,—and, of course, to the increase of power which results from, and depends on these, than those of the numerical majority. That it is liberty which gives to them their greatest impulse, has already been shown; and it now remains to show, that these, in turn, contribute greatly to the increase of power.

In the earlier stages of society, numbers and individual prowess constituted the principal elements of power. In a more advanced stage, when communities had passed from the barbarous to the civilized state, discipline, strategy, weapons of increased power, and money,—as the means of meeting increased expense,—became additional and important elements. In this stage, the effects of progress and improvement on the increase of power, began to be disclosed; but still numbers and personal prowess were sufficient, for a long period, to enable barbarous nations to contend successfully with the civilized,—and, in the end, to overpower them,—as the pages of history abundantly testify. But a more advanced progress, with its numerous inventions and improvements, has furnished new and far more powerful and destructive implements of offence and defence, and greatly increased the intelligence and wealth, necessary to engage the skill and meet the increased expense required for their construction and application to purposes of war. The discovery of gunpowder, and the use of steam as an impelling force, and their application to military purposes, have for ever settled the question of ascendency between civilized and barbarous communities, in favor of the former. Indeed, these, with other improvements, belonging to the present state of progress, have given to communities the most advanced, a superiority over those the least so, almost as great as that of the latter over the brute creation. And among the civilized, the same causes have decided the question of superiority, where other circumstances are nearly equal, in favor of those whose governments have given the greatest impulse to development, progress, and improvement; that is, to those whose liberty is the largest and best secured. Among these, England and the United States afford striking examples, not only of the effects of liberty in increasing power, but of the more perfect adaptation of governments founded on the principle of the concurrent, or constitutional majority, to enlarge and secure liberty. They are both governments of this description, as will be shown hereafter.

But in estimating the power of a community, moral, as well as physical causes, must be taken into the calculation; and in estimating the effects of liberty on power, it must not be overlooked, that it is, in itself, an important agent in augmenting the force of moral, as well as of physical power. It bestows on a people elevation, self-reliance, energy, and enthusiasm; and these combined, give to physical power a vastly augmented and almost irresistible impetus.

These, however, are not the only elements of moral power. There are others, and among them harmony, unanimity, devotion to country, and a disposition to elevate to places of trust and power, those who are distinguished for wisdom and experience. These, when the occasion requires it, will, without compulsion, and from their very nature, unite and put forth the entire force of the community in the most efficient manner, without hazard to its institutions or its liberty.

All these causes combined, give to a community its maximum of power. Either of them, without the other, would leave it comparatively feeble. But it cannot be necessary, after what has been stated, to enter into any further explanation or argument in order to establish the superiority of governments of the concurrent majority over the numerical, in developing the great elements of moral power. So vast is this superiority, that the one, by its operation, necessarily leads to their development, while the other as necessarily prevents it,—as has been fully shown.

Joseph Glover Baldwin

(1815–1864)

Although Joseph Glover Baldwin was a prolific writer not only of comic fiction but also of serious political history, he is remembered now solely for *The Flush Times of Alabama and Mississippi*. Even though it suffers in comparison with the work of later Southwestern humorists like Augustus Baldwin Longstreet and Johnson Jones Hooper, the collection of "sketches" was popular for more than half a century after its publication and was cited by Abraham Lincoln as one of his favorite books.

Baldwin was born in 1815 in Friendly Grove Factory, Virginia, but his family moved to Winchester in that state before he was a year old. There he was taught by his mother, not beginning formal schooling until 1824, when the family moved again, to the town of Staunton. Though at first the young Baldwin showed little aptitude, as he grew older, he began to demonstrate considerable writing skill. He was forced to leave school at age fourteen to help support the family. He worked as a law clerk and went on to read law himself, qualifying as an attorney when he was twenty-one. During his years as a law student, Baldwin had also begun a career in journalism, and in 1835, he and another man briefly published a newspaper. That enterprise failed, as did a love affair, and in 1836, Baldwin headed for "the territory," settling and establishing a law practice in De Kalb, Mississippi, at the height of the "flush times." The succession of rascals, speculators, and confidence men he would meet there and in the towns of Gainesville, Alabama, and Livingston, Alabama, where he moved in 1837 and 1850, respectively, would provide him with his inspiration for the sketches of *Flush Times*. At about the same time as the move to Livingston, he began publishing short sketches in *The Southern Literary Messenger*, forming a friendship with its editor, John R. Thompson, who helped him arrange for the publication of *The Flush Times of Alabama and Mississippi* in 1853. Baldwin eventually became dissatisfied with life in Alabama, and in 1854, seeking more "flush times," he moved to California, where he would eventually become a state supreme court justice. He died after contracting tetanus from a minor operation in 1864.

The chief criticisms leveled at *Flush Times* over the years have been for its lack of dialect and a genteel prose style seemingly more suited for a European setting than the rough and tumble Southwest, but in it Baldwin sardonically but genially skewers American manners and helps found a tradition that was later inherited by Longstreet, Hooper, and George Washington Harris.

from *The Flush Times of Alabama and Mississippi: A Series of Sketches*

Squire A. and the Fritters

Now, in the times we write of, the flourishing village of M. was in its infancy. She had not dreamed of the great things in store for her when she should have reached her teens, and railroad cars crowded with visitors, should make her the belle-village of all the surrounding country. A few log houses hastily erected and overcrowded with in-

mates, alone were to be seen; nor did the inn, either in the order or style of its architecture, or in the beauty or comfort of its interior arrangements and accommodations, differ from the other and less public edifices about her. In sober truth, it must
be confessed that, like the great man after whom she was named, the promise of her
youth was by no means equal to the respectability of her more advanced age. It was
the season of the year most unpropitious to the development of the resources of the
landlord and the skill of the cook. Fall had set in, and flour made cakes were not set
out. Wheat was not then an article of home growth, and supplies of flour were only to
be got from Mobile, and not from thence, unless the Tombigbee river was up; so, for a
long time, the boarders and guests of the tavern had to rough it on *corn dodger*, as it
was called, greatly to their discontent. At length the joyful tidings were proclaimed,
that a barrel of flour had come from Mobile. Much excitement prevailed. An animated
discussion arose as to the form in which the new aliment should be served up; and on
the motion of A., who eloquently seconded his own resolution, it was determined that
Fritters should be had for supper that night. Supper time dragged its slow length
along: it came, however, at last.

There were a good many borders at the Inn—some twenty or more—and but one
negro waiter, except a servant of J. T., whom he kept about him, and who waited at
table. Now, if Squire A. had any particular weakness, it was in favor of fritters. Fritters were a great favorite, even *per se;* but in the dearth of edibles, they were most especially so. He had a way of eating them with molasses, which gave them a rare and
delectable relish. Accordingly, seating himself the first at the table, and taking a position next the door nearest to the kitchen, he prepared himself for the onslaught. He
ordered a soup-plate and filled it half full of molasses—tucked up his sleeves—
brought the public towel from the roller in the porch, and fixed it before him at the
neck, so as to protect his whole bust—and stood as ready as the jolly Abbot over the
haunch of venison, at the widow Glendinning's, to do full justice to the provant, when
announced.

Now, A. had a distinguished reputation and immense skill in the art and mystery
of fritter eating. How many he could eat at a meal I forget, if I ever heard him say, but
I should say—making allowances for exaggeration in such things—from the various
estimates I have heard, well on to the matter of a bushel—possibly a half a peck or so,
more or less. When right brown and reeking with fresh fat, it would take as many persons to feed him as a carding-machine. Sam Harkness used to say, that if a wick were
run down his throat after a fritter dinner, and lit, it would burn a week—but I don't
believe that.

He used no implement in eating but a fork. He passed the fork through the fritter
in such a way as to break its back, and double it up in the form of the letter W, and
pressing it through and closing up the lines, would flourish it around in the molasses
two or three times, and then convey it, whole, to his mouth—drawing the fork out
with a sort of c-h-u-g.

If A. ever intended to have his daguerreotype taken—that was the time—for a more
hopeful, complacent, benevolent cast of countenance, I never saw than his, when the
door being left a little ajar, the cook could be seen in the kitchen, making time about the
skillet, and the fat was heard cheerfully spitting and spattering in the pan.

"But pleasures are like poppies spread," and so forth. As when some guileless
cock-robin is innocently regaling himself in the chase of a rainbow spangled butterfly,
poising himself on wing, and in the very act of conveying the gay insect to his expectant spouse for domestic use, some ill-omened vulture, seated in solitary state on a

tree hard by unfurls his wing, and swoops in fell destruction upon the hapless warbler, leaving nothing of this scene of peace and innocence but a smothered cry and a
string of feathers. So did J. T. look upon this scene of Squire A.'s expectant and hopeful countenance with a like and kindred malignity and fell purpose. In plain prose,—
confederating and conspiring with three other masterful fritter eaters and Sandy, the
amateur waiter at the Inn, it was agreed that Sandy should station himself at the door,
and, as the waiting-girl came in with the fritters, he should receive the plate, and convey the same to the other confederates for their special behoof, to the entire neglect
of the claim of Squire A. in the premises.

Accordingly the girl brought in the first plate—which was received by Sandy—
Sandy brought the plate on with stately step close by Squire A.—the Squire's fork was
raised to transfix at least six of the smoking cakes with a contingency of sweeping the
whole platter; but the wary Sandy raised the plate high in air, nor heeded he the Squire's
cajoling tones—"Here, Sandy, here, this way, Sandy." Again the plate went and came,
but with no better success to the Squire. Sandy came past a third time—"I say, Sandy,
this way—this way—come Sandy—come now—do—I'll remember you;"—but Sandy
walked on like the Queen of the West unheeding; the Squire threw himself back in his
chair and looked in the puddle of molasses in his plate sourly enough to have fermented
it. Again—again—again and yet again—the plate passed on—the fritters getting
browner and browner, and distance lending enchantment to the view: but the Squire
couldn't get a showing. The Squire began to be peremptory, and threatened Sandy with
all sorts of extermination for his contumacy; but the intrepid servitor passed along as if
he had been deaf and dumb, and his only business to carry fritters to the other end of the
table. At length Sandy came back with an empty plate, and reported that the fritters
were all out. The Squire could contain himself no longer—unharnessing himself of the
towel and striking his fist on the table, upsetting thereby about a pint of molasses from
his plate, he exclaimed in tones of thunder, "I'll quit this dratted house: I'll be eternally
and constitutionally dad blamed, if I stand such infernal partiality!" and rushed out of
the house into the porch, where he met J. T., who, coolly picking his teeth, asked the
Squire how he "liked the fritters?" We need not give the reply—as all *that* matter was afterwards honourably settled by a board of honor.

Augusta Jane Evans Wilson

(1835–1909)

When Nathaniel Hawthorne famously lamented in 1855 that "America is now wholly
given over to a d——d mob of scribbling women," it was the domestic novels of authors like Augusta Jane Evans Wilson that he decried. Domestic novels, which typically feature a young female protagonist whose love redeems a handsome older man
of questionable reputation, who is haunted by secrets from his past, were by far the
most popular form of American literature from 1850 to 1880. Though Wilson, who
was born in Columbus, Georgia, was a fervent advocate of the superiority of the
Southern way (including slavery) and though she believed that women should be subservient to their husbands, she did repeatedly assert that women had an obligation to
explore their talents to the fullest extent, and she often addressed controversial reli-

gious and philosophical issues of the day. *Macaria; or, Altars of Sacrifice*, published in 1863, is dedicated "To the Brave Soldiers of the Southern Army," and it is a tribute to the holiness of the Southern cause. Her writing, especially its florid diction, has not aged well, however, and it is of mainly historical interest for today's reader.

from *Macaria; or, Altars of Sacrifice*

Chapter II.

"Irene, your father will be displeased if he sees you in that plight."

"Pray, what is wrong about me now? You seem to glory in finding fault. What is the matter with my 'plight' as you call it?"

"You know very well your father can't bear to see you carrying your own satchel and basket to school. He ordered Martha to take them every morning and evening, but she says you will not let her carry them. It is just sheer obstinacy in you."

"There it is again! because I don't choose to be petted like a baby, or made a wax doll of, it is set down to obstinacy, as if I had the temper of a heathen. See here, aunt Margaret, I am tired of having Martha tramping eternally at my heels as though I were a two year old child. There is no reason in her walking after me when I am strong enough to carry my own books, and I don't intend she shall do it any longer."

"But, Irene, your father is too proud to have you trudging along the road, like any other beggar, with your books in one arm and a basket swinging in the other. Just suppose the Carters or the Harrisses should meet you? Dear me! they would hardly believe you belonged to a wealthy, aristocratic family like the Huntingdons. Child, I never carried my own dinner to school in my life."

"And I expect that is exactly the reason why you are forever complaining, and scarcely see one well day in the three hundred and sixty-five. As to what people think, I don't care a cent; as to whether my ancestors did or did not carry their lunch in their own aristocratic hands is a matter of no consequence whatever. I dispise all this ridiculous nonsense about aristocracy of family, and I mean to do as I please. I thought that really well-bred persons of high standing and birth could afford to be silent on the subject, and that only *parvenus*, coarse, vulgar people with a little money, put on those kind of airs, and pretended to be shocked at what they had been accustomed to in early life."

"I do not see where you get such plebeian ideas; you positively make me ashamed of you sometimes, when fashionable, genteel persons come to the house. There is such a want of refinement in your notions. You are anything but a Huntingdon."

"I am what God made me, aunt Margaret. If the Huntingdons stand high, it is because they won distinction by their own efforts; I don't want the stepping-stones of my dead ancestry; people must judge me for myself, not from what my grandmother was."

Irene Huntingdon stood on the marble steps of her palatial home, and talked with the maiden aunt who governed her father's household. The girl was about fourteen, tall for her age, straight, finely-formed, slender. The broad straw hat shaded, but by no means concealed her features, and as she looked up at her aunt the sunshine fell upon a face of extraordinary beauty, such as is rarely seen, save in the idealized heads of the old masters. Her hair was of an uncommon shade, neither auburn nor brown, but between gold and bronze; and as the sun shone on it the rippling waves flashed, until their burnished glory seemed a very aureola. It was thick and curling; she wore it parted on her pale, polished forehead, and it hung around her like a gilded veil. The face was an oval; you might measure it by all the rules of art and no imperfection could be found, unless the height of the brow were considered out of proportion. The nose was delicate and clearly cut, and in outline resembled that in the antique medals of Olympias, the wife of Philip of Macedonia. The upper lip was short, and curved like a bow; the lower, thin, firm, and straight. Her eyes were strangely, marvellously beautiful; they were larger than usual, and of that rare shade of purplish blue which borders the white velvet petals of a clematis. When the eyes were uplifted, as on this occasion, long, curling lashes of the bronze hue of her hair rested against her brow. Save the scarlet lines which marked her lips, her face was of that clear, colorlessness which can be likened only to the purest ivory. Though there was an utter absence of the rosy hue of health, the transparency of the complexion seemed characteristic of her type, and precluded all thought of disease. People are powerfully attracted by beauty, either of form, color, or a combination of both; and it frequently happens that something of pain mingles with the sensation of pleasure thus excited. Now, whether it be that this arises from a vague apprehension engendered by the evanescent nature of all sublunary things, or from the inability of earthly types to satisfy the divine ideal which the soul enshrines, I shall not here attempt to decide; but those who examined Irene's countenance were fully aware of this complex emotion; and strangers who passed her in the street felt untuitively that a noble, unsullied soul looked out at them from the deep, calm, thoughtful eyes. Miss Margaret muttered something inaudible in reply to her last remark, and Irene walked on to school. Her father's residence was about a mile from the town, but the winding road rendered the walk somewhat longer; and on one side of this road stood the small house occupied by Mrs. Aubrey. As Irene approached it she saw Electra Grey coming from the opposite direction, and at the cottage gate they met. Both paused; Irene held out her hand cordially—

"Good morning. I have not seen you for a fortnight. I thought you were coming to school again as soon as you were strong enough?"

"No; I am not going back to school."

"Why?"

"Because auntie can't afford to send me any longer. You know her eyes are growing worse every day, and she is not able to take in sewing as she used to do. I am sorry; but it can't be helped."

"How do you know it can't be helped? Russell told me he thought she had cataracts on her eyes, and they can be removed."

"Perhaps so, if we had the means of consulting that celebrated physician in New Orleans. Money removes a great many things, Irie, but unfortunately we have n't it."

"The trip would not cost much; suppose you speak to Russell about it."

"Much or little, it will require more than we can possibly spare. Everything is so high we can barely live as it is. But I must go in, my aunt is waiting for me."

"Where have you been so early, Electra? I hope you will not think me impertinent in asking such a question."

"I carried this waiter full of bouquets to Mr. Carter's. There is to be a grand dinner-party there to-day, and auntie promised as many flowers as she could furnish. However, bouquets pay poorly. Irie, wait one minute; I have a little border of mignonette all my own, and I should like to give you a spray."

She hurried into the garden, and returning with a few delicate sprigs, fastened one in her friend's belt and the remainder in the ribbon on her hat.

"Thank you, Electra; who told you that I love mignonette so well? It will not do for you to stay away from school; I miss you in my class, and besides, you are losing too much time. Something should be done, Electra. Good-by."

They shook hands, and Irene walked on. "Something should be done," she repeated, looking down fixedly yet vacantly at the sandy road. Soon the brick walls of the academy rose grim and uninviting, and taking her place at the desk she applied herself to her books. When school was dismissed in the afternoon, instead of returning home as usual she walked down the principal street, entered Mr. Watson's store, and put her books on the counter. It happened that the proprietor stood near the front door, and he came forward instantly to wait upon her.

"Ah, Miss Irene! happy to see you. What shall I have the pleasure of showing you?"

"Russell Aubrey, if you please."

The merchant stared, and she added:

"I want some kid gauntlets, but Russell can get them for me."

The young clerk stood at the desk in the rear of the store, with his back toward the counter; and Mr. Watson called out—

"Here, Aubrey, some kid gauntlets for this young lady."

He laid down his pen, and taking a box of gloves from the shelves placed it on the counter before her. He had not noticed her particularly, and when she pushed back her hat and looked up at him he started slightly.

"Good-evening, Miss Huntingdon. What number do you wish?"

Perhaps it was from the heat of the day, or from stooping over his desk, or perhaps it was from something else, but his cheek was flushed, and gradually it grew pale again.

"Russell, I want to speak to you about Electra. She ought to be at school, you know."

"Yes."

"But she says your mother can't afford the expense."

"Just now she can not; next year things will be better."

"What is the tuition for her?"

"Five dollars a month."

"Is that all?"

He selected a delicate fawn-colored pair of gloves and laid them before her, while a faint smile passed over his face.

"Russell, has anything happened?"

"What do you mean?"

"What is troubling you so?"

"Nothing more than usual. Do those gloves suit you?"

"Yes, they will fit me, I believe." She looked at him very intently.

He met her gaze steadily, and for an instant his face brightened; then she said, abruptly:

"Your mother's eyes are worse?"

"Yes, much worse."

"Have you consulted Dr. Arnold about them?"

"He says he can do nothing for her."

"How much would it cost to take her to New Orleans and have that celebrated oculist examine them?"

"More than we can afford just now; at least two hundred dollars."

"Oh, Russell! that is not much. Would not Mr. Watson lend you that little?"

"I shall not ask him."

"Not even to restore your mother's sight?"

"Not to buy my own life. Besides, the experiment is a doubtful one."

"Still it is worth making."

"Yes, under different circumstances it certainly would be."

"Have you talked to Mr. Campbell about it?"

"No, because it is useless to discuss the matter."

"It would be dangerous to go to New Orleans now, I suppose?"

"October or November would be better."

Again she looked at him very earnestly, then stretched out her little hand.

"Good-by, Russell; I wish I could do something to help you, to make you less sorrowful."

He held the slight waxen fingers, and his mouth trembled as he answered,

"Thank you, Miss Huntingdon. I am not sorrowful, but my path in life is not quite so flowery as yours."

"I wish you would not call me 'Miss Huntingdon,' in that stiff, far-off way, as if we were not friends. Or maybe it is a hint that you desire me to address you as Mr. Aubrey. It sounds strange, unnatural, to say anything but Russell."

She gathered up her books, took the gloves, and went slowly homeward, and Russell returned to his desk with a light in his eyes which, for the remainder of the day, nothing could quench. As Irene ascended the long hill on which Mr. Huntingdon's residence stood, she saw her father's buggy at the door, and as she approached the steps he came out, drawing on his gloves.

"You are late, Irene. What kept you?"

"I have been shopping a little. Are you going to ride? Take me with you."

"Going to dine at Mr. Carter's."

"Why, the sun is almost down now. What time will you come home? I want to ask you something."

"Not till long after you are asleep."

He took his seat in the buggy, and the spirited horse dashed down the avenue. A servant came forward to take her hat and satchel, and inform her that her dinner had waited some time. Miss Margaret sat crocheting at the front window of the dining-room, and Irene ate her dinner in silence. As she rose and approached her aunt, the door swung open and a youth entered, apparently about Russell's age, though really one year older.

"Irene, I am tired to death waiting for you. What a provoking girl you are. The horses have been saddled at least one hour and a half. Do get on your riding-dress. I am out of all patience."

He rapped his boot heavily with his whip by way of emphasis, and looked hurriedly at his watch.

"I did not promise to ride with you this evening, Hugh," answered his cousin, seating herself on the window-sill and running her fingers lightly over the bars of a beautiful cage where her canary pecked playfully at the fair hand.

"Oh, nonsense! Suppose you did n't promise; I waited for you, and told Grace Harriss and Charlie that we would meet them at the upper bend of the river, just above the factory. Charlie's new horse has just arrived from Vermont—Green Mountain Boy, he calls him—and we have a bet of a half-dozen pairs of gloves that he can't beat my Eclipse. Do come along! Aunt Margaret, make her come."

"I should like to see anybody make her do what she is not in a humor for," said his aunt, looking over her glasses at the lithe, graceful figure on the window-sill.

"Hugh, I would rather stay at home, for I am tired, but I will go to oblige you."

Miss Margaret lifted her eyebrows, and as his cousin left the room Hugh Seymour exclaimed:

"Is n't she the greatest beauty in the United States?"

"She will be a belle when she is grown; just such a one as your mother was, only she lacks her gayety of disposition. She is full of strange notions, Hugh; you don't know the half of her character—her own father does not. Frequently I am puzzled to understand her myself."

"Oh! she will come out of all that. She is curious about some things now, but she will outgrow it."

"I am afraid she will not, for it is as much a part of her as the color of her hair or the shape of her nose. She has always been queen."

Irene appeared at the door with a small silver *porte-monnaie* in her hand. She counted the contents, put it into her pocket, and gathering up the folds of her habit, led the way to the front door. Hugh adjusted the reins, and laying one hand on his, she sprang lightly to her saddle, then stroked her horse's silky mane and said:

"Erebus can leave Green Mountain Boy so far behind that Charlie would find it no easy matter to count the plumes in my hat. Are you ready?"

The beautiful, jetty creature, as if conscious of her praise, tossed his head and sprang off in a canter, but wheeling round she called to the groom who stood watching them:

"Unchain Paragon!"

Five minutes later the cousins were galloping on, with a superb greyhound following close at Erebus' heels, and leaping up now and then in obedience to the motion of Irene's hand. The road ran through a hilly country, now clad in stern, ancestral pines, and now skirted with oak and hickory, and about a mile beyond the town it made a sharp angle, and took the river bank. The sun had set, but the western sky was still aglow; and near the bank, where the current was not perceptible, the changing tints of the clouds were clearly mirrored, but in the middle of the stream a ledge of rock impeded its course, and the water broke over with a dull roar, churning itself into foam and spray as it dashed from shelf to shelf of the stony barrier. Just opposite the Fall, Irene checked her horse, and paused to admire the beauty of the scene; but in another moment the quick tramp of hoofs fell on her ear, and Hugh's young friends joined them. Green Mountain Boy was flecked with foam, and as Irene measured his perfections at one hasty glance she patted her favorite's head and challenged Charlie for a trial of speed.

"No, Charlie and I must have the race. Miss Grace, you and Irene can take care of yourselves for a few minutes. We will wait for you on the edge of town, at the grave yard. Now, Charlie, I am ready."

They took their places in front, and were soon out of sight, as the road followed the curves of the river. Erebus plunged violently at first, not being accustomed to lag behind Eclipse, but by much persuasion and frequent kind touches on his head, Irene managed to reconcile him to the temporary disgrace.

Grace looked at his antics rather fearfully, and observed that no amount of money could tempt her to mount him.

"Why not?"

"He will break your neck yet."

"He is very spirited, but as gentle as Paragon. Come, Grace, it is getting late; they will be waiting for us. Quicken your sober meek little brownie."

"So Electra is not coming back to school. It is a great pity she can't have an education."

"Who told you anything about her?"

"Oh, everybody knows how poor her aunt is; and now to mend matters she is going blind. I would go to see Electra occasionally if the family had not been so disgraced. I like her, but no genteel person recognizes Mrs. Aubrey, even in the street."

"That is very unjust. She is one of the most refined, elegant women I have ever seen. She ought not to be blamed for her husband's misfortune. Poverty is no crime."

If she had been treated to a Hindostanee proverb, Grace could not have looked more stupidly surprised.

"Why, Irene! Mrs. Aubrey wears a bit-calico to church."

"Well, suppose she does? Is people's worth to be determined only by the cost or the quality of their clothes? If I were to give your cook a silk dress exactly like that one your uncle sent you from Paris, and provide her with shawl and bonnet to match, would she be your equal, do you think? I imagine you would not thank me or anybody else who insinuated that Mrs. Harriss' negro cook was quite as genteel and elegant as Miss Grace herself, because she wore exactly the same kind of clothes. I tell you, Grace, it is all humbug! this everlasting talk about fashion, and dress, and gentility! Pshaw! I am sick of it. When our forefathers were fighting for freedom, for a national existence, I wonder whether their wives measured each other's respectability or gentility by their lace collars or the number of flounces on their dresses? Grace Harriss, your great-grandmother, and mine, and probably everybody's else, spun the cotton, and wove the cloth, and cut and made their homespun dresses, and were thankful to get them. And these women who had not even bit-calicoes were the mothers, and wives, and sisters, and daughters of men who established the most glorious government on the face of the broad earth! The way the women of America have degenerated is a crying shame. I tell you, I would blush to look my great-grandmother in the face."

Grace shrugged her shoulders in expressive silence, and, soon after, they reached the spot where the boys were waiting to join them.

"Eclipse made good his name!" cried Hugh, triumphantly, while Charlie bit his lip with chagrin.

"Never mind, Charlie, Erebus can distance Eclipse any day."

"Not so easily," muttered Hugh.

"I will prove it the next time we ride. Now for a canter as far as Grace's door."

On they went, through the main street of the town: Erebus ahead, Paragon at his heels, then all the others. The wind blew Irene's veil over her eyes, she endeavored to put it back, and in the effort dropped her whip. It was dusk; they were near one of the crossings, and a tall well-known form stooped, found the whip, and handed it up. Erebus shied, but the hand touched Irene's as it inserted the silver handle in the slender fingers.

"Thank you, Russell, thank you very much."

He bowed formally, drew his straw hat over his brow, and walked on with two heavy account-books under his arm.

"I can't endure that boy," said Hugh, at the distance of half a square, flourishing his whip energetically as he spoke.

"Nor I," chimed in Charlie.

"Why not? I have known him a long time, and I like him very much."

"He is so confoundedly proud and saintly."

"That exists entirely in your imagination, Hugh. You don't know half his good qualities," returned Irene, a little quickly.

"Bah!"—began her cousin; but here their companions bade them good-night, and, as if disinclined to continue the subject, Irene kept in advance till they reached home. Tea was waiting; Miss Margaret and Hugh talked of various things; Irene sat balancing her spoon upon the edge of her cup. Finally, tired of listening, she glided to the front door and seated herself on the steps. Paragon followed, and laid down at her feet. Everything was quiet, save the distant roar of the river as it foamed over its rocky bed; below, hanging on the bank of the stream, lay the town. From her elevated position she could trace the winding of the streets by the long rows of lamps; and now and then a faint hum rose on the breeze, as it swept up the hill and lost itself in the forest behind the house. Very soon Hugh came out, cigar in hand, and threw himself down besides her.

"What is the matter, Irie?"

"Nothing."

"What are you moping here for?"

"I am not moping at all; I am waiting for father."

"He will not be here for three hours yet. Don't you know that Mr. Carter's dinners always end in card-parties? He is famous for whist and euchre, and doubtless his dinners pay him well. What do you want with uncle?"

"Hugh, do throw away your cigar. It is ridiculous to see a boy of your age puffing away in that style. Betting and smoking seem to be the only things you have learned at Yale. By the way, when do you go back?"

"Are you getting tired of me? I go back in ten days. Irene, do you know that I am not coming home next vacation? I have promised a party of merry fellows to spend it with them in Canada. Then the next summer I go to Europe, for two years at least. Are you listening? Do you understand that it will be four years before I see you again?"

"Yes, I understand."

"I dare say the time will seem longer to me than to you."

"I hope when you do come back we shall not be disappointed in you."

He took her hand, but she withdrew her fingers.

"Irene, you belong to me, and you know it."

"No! I belong to God and myself."

She rose, and, retreating to the library, opened her books and began to study. The night passed very slowly; she looked at the clock again and again. Finally the house became quiet, and at last the crush of wheels on the gravel-walk announced her father's return. He came into the library for a cigar, and, without noticing her, drew his chair to the open window. She approached and put her hand on his shoulder.

"Irene! what is the matter, child?"

"Nothing, sir; only I want to ask you something."

"Well, Queen, what is it?"

He drew her tenderly to his knee, and passed his hand over her floating hair.

Leonard Huntingdon was forty years old; tall, spare, with an erect and martial carriage. He had been trained at West Point, and perhaps early education contributed somewhat to the air of unbending haughtiness which many found repulsive. His black hair was slightly sprinkled with gray, and his features were still decidedly handsome, though the expression of mouth and eyes was, ordinarily, by no means winning. He could seem very fascinating, but rarely deigned to be so; and an intimate acquaintance was not necessary to teach people that he was proud, obstinate, and thoroughly selfish—loving only Hugh, Irene, and himself. She was his only child; her mother had died during her infancy, and on this beautiful idol he lavished all the tenderness of which his nature was capable. His tastes were cultivated, his house was elegant and complete, and furnished magnificently; every luxury that money could yield him he possessed, yet there were times when he seemed moody and cynical, and no one could surmise the cause of his gloom. To-night there was no shadow on his face, however; doubtless the sparkle of the wine-cup still shone in his piercing blue eye, and the girl looked up at him fearing no denial.

"Father, I wish, please, you would give me two hundred dollars."

"What would you do with it, Queen?"

"I do not want it for myself; I should like to have that much to enable a poor woman to recover her sight. She has cataracts on her eyes, and there is a physician in New Orleans who can relieve her. She is poor, and it will cost about two hundred dollars. Father, won't you give me the money?"

He took the cigar from his lips, shook off the ashes, and asked indifferently:

"What is the woman's name? Has she no husband to take care of her?"

"Mrs. Aubrey; she—"

"What!"

The cigar fell from his fingers, he put her from his knee, and rose instantly. His swarthy cheek glowed, and she wondered at the expression of his eyes, so different from anything she had ever seen there before.

"Father, do you know her?"

"What do you know of her? What business is it of yours, whether she goes blind or not? Is it possible Margaret allows you to visit at that house? Answer me; what do you know about her?"

"I know that she is a very gentle, unfortunate woman; that she has many bitter trials; that she works hard to support her family; that she is noble and—"

"Who gave you permission to visit that house?"

"No permission was necessary. I go there because I love her and Electra, and because I like Russell. Why should n't I go there, sir? Is poverty disgrace?"

"Irene, mark me. You are to visit that house no more in future; keep away from the whole family. I will have no such association. Never let me hear their names again. Go to bed."

"Give me one good reason, and I will obey you."

"Reason! My will, my command, is sufficient reason. What do you mean by catechising me in this way? Implicit obedience is your duty."

The calm, holy eyes looked wonderingly into his; and as he marked the startled expression of the girl's pure face his own eyes drooped.

"Father, has Mrs. Aubrey ever injured you?"

No answer.

"If she has not, you are very unjust to her; if she has, remember she is a woman, bowed down with many sorrows, and it is unmanly to hoard up old differences. Father, please give me that money."

"I will bury my last dollar in the Red Sea first! Now are you answered?"

She put her hands over her eyes, as if to shut out some painful vision; and he saw the slight form shudder. In perfect silence she took her books and went up to her room. Mr. Huntingdon reseated himself as the door closed behind her, and the lamp-light showed a sinister smile writhing over his dark features. In the busy hours of day, in the rush and din of active life, men can drown remorseful whispers, and shut their eyes to the panorama which memory strives to place before them; but there come still hours, solemn and inexorable, when struggles are useless, and the phantom-recollections of early years crowd up like bannered armies. He sat there, staring out into the starry night, and seeing by the shimmer of the setting moon only the graceful form and lovely face of Amy Aubrey, as she had appeared to him in other days. Could he forget the hour when she wrenched her cold fingers from his clasp, and, in defi-ance of her father's wishes, vowed she would never be his wife? No; revenge was sweet, very sweet; his heart had swelled with exultation when the verdict of death upon the gallows was pronounced upon the husband of her choice; and now, her poverty, her humiliation, her blindness gave him deep, unutterable joy. The history of the past was a sealed volume to his daughter, but she was now for the first time con-scious that her father regarded the widow and her son with unconquerable hatred; and with strange, foreboding dread she looked into the future, knowing that forgive-ness was no part of his nature; that insult or injury was never forgotten.

Jefferson Davis

(1808–1889)

Jefferson Davis's career was one of contradictions: He became known in Congress in the years before the Civil War as spokesman for the Southern point of view, but he ve-hemently opposed secession from the Union. He was elected president by the provi-sional Congress of the Confederate States in 1861. Although he had been a champion of states' rights as a United States congressman, his tenure as Confederate president was marked by constant conflict with the extreme proponents of that doctrine, as judges of state courts interfered with military matters and state governors fought the centralist policies he attempted to enact to hold the fledgling Confederacy together. Nevertheless, he was responsible for raising the formidable Confederate armies, as well as for the appointment of Robert E. Lee as commander of the Army of Virginia. By 1864, however, Southern newspapers had targeted his administration as the rea-son for the dwindling of Confederate chances, and he became the focus of Southern discontent. Captured at Irwinville, Georgia, a month after Appomattox, he spent two years as a state prisoner. When federal authorities dropped their case against him in 1868, he traveled abroad in an attempt to recover his health and then returned to Mississippi to recover his fortune. Successful in the first attempt but not in the sec-ond, he published *The Rise and Fall of the Confederate Government* in 1881 in de-fense of his actions as president, but it was not well received. Davis died in New Orleans in 1889.

from *The Rise and Fall of the Confederate Government*

Introduction.

A duty to my countrymen; to the memory of those who died in defense of a cause consecrated by inheritance, as well as sustained by conviction; and to those who, perhaps less fortunate, staked all, and lost all, save life and honor, in its behalf, has impelled me to attempt the vindication of their cause and conduct. For this purpose I have decided to present an historical sketch of the events which preceded and attended the struggle of the Southern States to maintain their existence and their rights as sovereign communities—the creators, not the creatures, of the General Government.

The social problem of maintaining the just relation between constitution, government, and people, has been found so difficult, that human history is a record of unsuccessful efforts to establish it. A government, to afford the needful protection and exercise proper care for the welfare of a people, must have homogeneity in its constituents. It is this necessity which has divided the human race into separate nations, and finally has defeated the grandest efforts which conquerors have made to give unlimited extent to their domain. When our fathers dissolved their connection with Great Britain, by declaring themselves free and independent States, they constituted thirteen separate communities, and were careful to assert and preserve, each for itself, its sovereignty and jurisdiction.

At a time when the minds of men are straying far from the lessons our fathers taught, it seems proper and well to recur to the original principles on which the system of government they devised was founded. The eternal truths which they announced, the rights which they declared "*unalienable*," are the foundation-stones on which rests the vindication of the Confederate cause.

He must have been a careless reader of our political history who has not observed that, whether under the style of "United Colonies" or "United States," which was adopted after the Declaration of Independence, whether under the articles of Confederation or the compact of Union, there everywhere appears the distinct assertion of State sovereignty, and nowhere the slightest suggestion of any purpose on the part of the States to consolidate themselves into one body. Will any candid, well-informed man assert that, at any time between 1776 and 1790, a proposition to surrender the sovereignty of the States and merge them in a central government would have had the least possible chance of adoption? Can any historical fact be more demonstrable than that the States did, both in the Confederation and in the Union, retain their sovereignty and independence as distinct communities, voluntarily consenting to federation, but never becoming the fractional parts of a nation? That such opinions should find adherents in our day, may be attributable to the natural law of aggregation; surely not to a conscientious regard for the terms of the compact for union by the States.

In all free governments the constitution or organic law is supreme over the government, and in our Federal Union this was most distinctly marked by limitations and prohibitions against all which was beyond the expressed grants of power to the General Government. In the foreground, therefore, I take the position that those who resisted violations of the compact were the true friends, and those who maintained the usurpation of undelegated powers were the real enemies of the constitutional Union.

Henry Timrod

(1828–1867)

Henry Timrod's most memorable poetry was inspired by the formation of the Confederate States of America and by the Civil War. Dogged by poverty and ill health for much of his life, he struggled desperately to establish himself as an author, but mostly he found only "beggary, starvation, death, bitter grief, [and] utter want of hope," as he wrote in a letter to his friend Paul Hamilton Hayne a year before his death. Perhaps because of his own suffering, Timrod found his poetic voice in praising the tragic beauty of a fallen cause.

Born in Charleston, South Carolina, Timrod was educated in private schools, and he attended the University of Georgia but left in 1846 without taking a degree. After an abortive attempt to read law, he began writing poetry, publishing his work in the *Southern Literary Messenger*, the *Southern Literary Gazette*, and Charleston newspapers. In the 1850s he became associated with a group of Charleston writers led by William Gilmore Simms, which also included his childhood friend Hayne. Meeting in a back room of John Russell's Charleston bookshop, the group established *Russell's Magazine* as a mouthpiece for Southern intellectual opinion and literary expression. Timrod was a constant contributor during the three years of the magazine's existence. He also published three important critical essays in *Russell's*, "The Character and Scope of the Sonnet" (1857), "What Is Poetry?" (1857), and "Literature and the South" (1859). He published his only poetry collection, *Poems*, by subscription in 1859. In 1862, Timrod joined the Confederate Army as a war correspondent for *The Charleston Mercury* but was sent home that same year because of tuberculosis. In 1864, he moved to Columbia to edit *The South Carolinian*, an endeavor that ended disastrously when Sherman burned the city. Timrod succumbed to tuberculosis in 1867.

Charleston

Calm as that second summer which precedes
    The first fall of the snow,
In the broad sunlight of heroic deeds,
    The city bides the foe.

As yet, behind their ramparts, stern and proud,
    Her bolted thunders sleep,—
Dark Sumter, like a battlemented cloud,
    Looms o'er the solemn deep.

No Calpe frowns from lofty cliff or scaur
    To guard the holy strand;
But Moultrie holds in leash her dogs of war
    Above the level sand.

And down the dunes a thousand guns lie couched,
    Unseen, beside the flood,—

Like tigers in some Orient jungle crouched
    That wait and watch for blood.

Meanwhile, through streets still echoing with trade,
    Walk grave and thoughtful men,
Whose hands may one day wield the patriot's blade
    As lightly as the pen.

And maidens, with such eyes as would grow dim
    Over a bleeding hound,
Seem each one to have caught the strength of him
    Whose sword she sadly bound.

Thus girt without and garrisoned at home,
    Day patient following day,
Old Charleston looks from roof and spire and dome,
    Across her tranquil bay.

Ships, through a hundred foes, from Saxon lands
    And spicy Indian ports,
Bring Saxon steel and iron to her hands,
    And Summer to her courts.

But still, along yon dim Atlantic line,
    The only hostile smoke
Creeps like a harmless mist above the brine,
    From some frail, floating oak.

Shall the Spring dawn, and she, still clad in smiles,
    And with an unscathed brow,
Rest in the strong arms of her palm-crowned isles,
    As fair and free as now?

We know not; in the temple of the Fates
    God has inscribed her doom;
And, all untroubled in her faith, she waits
    The triumph or the tomb.

Literature in the South

We think that at no time, and in no country, has the position of an author been beset with such peculiar difficulties as the Southern writer is compelled to struggle with from the beginning to the end of his career. In no country in which literature has ever flourished has an author obtained so limited an audience. In no country, and at no period that we can recall, has an author been constrained by the indifference of the public amid which he lived, to publish with a people who were prejudiced against him. It would scarcely be too extravagant to entitle the Southern author the Pariah of modern literature. It would scarcely be too absurd if we should compare his position to that of the drawer of Shakspeare, who stands in a state of ludicrous confusion between the calls of Prince Hal upon the one side and of Poins upon the other. He is placed, in fact, much in the same relation to the public of the North and the public of the South, as we might suppose a statesman to occupy who should propose to embody in one code a system of laws for two neighbouring people, of one of which he was a constituent, and who yet altogether differed in character, institutions and pursuits. The people among whom the statesman lived would be very indignant upon finding, as they would be sure to find, that some of their interests had been neglected. The people for whom he legislated at a distance would be equally indignant upon discovering, as they would [be] sure to fancy they discovered, that not one of their interests had received proper attention. Both parties would probably unite, with great cordiality and patriotism, in consigning the unlucky statesman to oblivion or the executioner. In precisely the same manner fares the poor scribbler who has been so unfortunate as to be born South of the Potomac. He publishes a book. It is the settled conviction of the North that genius is indigenous there, and flourishes only in a Northern atmosphere. It is the equally firm conviction of the South that genius—literary genius, at least—is an exotic that will not flower on a Southern soil. Probably the book is published by a Northern house. Straightway all the newspapers of the South are indignant that the author did not choose a Southern printer, and address himself more particularly to a Southern community. He heeds their criticism, and of his next book,—published by a Southern printer—such is the secret though unacknowledged prejudice against Southern authors—he finds that more than one half of a small edition remains upon his hands. Perhaps the book contains a correct and beautiful picture of our peculiar state of society. The North is inattentive or abusive, and the South unthankful, or, at most, indifferent. Or it may happen to be only a volume of noble poetry, full of those universal thoughts and feelings which speak, not to a particular people, but to all mankind. It is censured at the South as not sufficiently Southern in spirit, while at the North it is pronounced a very fair specimen of Southern commonplace. Both North and South agree with one mind to condemn the author and forget his book.

We do not think that we are exaggerating the embarrassments which surround the Southern writer. It cannot be denied that on the surface of newspaper and magazine literature there have lately appeared signs that his claims to respect are beginning to be acknowledged. But, in spite of this, we must continue to believe, that among a large majority of Southern readers who devour English books with avidity, there still exists a prejudice—conscious or unconscious—against the works of those authors who have grown up among themselves. This prejudice is strongest, indeed, with a class of persons whose opinions do not find expression in the public prints; but it is on that account more harmful in its evil and insidious influence. As an instance, we may mention that it is not once, but a hundred times, that we have heard the works of the first of Southern authors alluded to with contempt by individuals who had never read anything beyond the title-pages of his books. Of this prejudice there is an easy, though not a very flattering, explanation.

The truth is, it must be confessed, that though an educated, we are a provincial, and not a highly cultivated people. At least, there is among us a very general want of a high critical culture. The principles of that criticism, the basis of which is a profound psychology, are almost utterly ignored. There are scholars of pretension among us, with whom Blair's Rhetoric is still an unquestionable authority. There are schools and colleges in which it is used as a textbook. With the vast advance that has been made in critical science since the time of Blair few seem to be intimately acquainted. The opinions and theories of the last century are still held in reverence. Here Pope is still regarded by many as the most *correct* of English poets, and here, Kaimes, after having been everywhere else removed to the top shelves of libraries, is still thumbed by learned professors and declamatory sophomores. Here literature is still regarded as an epicurean amusement; not as a study, at least equal in importance, and certainly not inferior in difficulty, to law and medicine. Here no one is surprised when some fossil theory of criticism, long buried under the ruins of an exploded school, is dug up, and discussed with infinite gravity by gentlemen who know Pope and Horace by heart, but who have never read a word of Wordsworth or Tennyson, or who have read them with suspicion, and rejected them with superciliousness.

In such a state of critical science, it is no wonder that we are prudently cautious in passing a favourable judgment upon any new candidates for our admiration. It is no wonder that while we accept without a cavil books of English and Northern reputation, we yet hesitate to acknowledge our own writers, until, perhaps, having been commended by English or Northern critics, they present themselves to us with a "certain alienated majesty." There is another class of critics among us—if critics they can be called—which we must not pass over. This class seem disposed to look upon literature as they look upon a Bavarian sour-krout, a Strasbourg paté, or a New Zealand cutlet of "cold clergyman." It is a mere matter of taste. Each one feels himself at liberty to exalt the author—without reference to his real position in the world of letters, as settled by a competent tribunal—whose works afford *him* the most amusement. From such a principle, of course, the most fantastic and discordant opinions result. One regards that fanciful story, the Culprit Fay of Drake, as the greatest of American poems; and another is indignant if Tennyson be mentioned in the same breath with Longfellow. Now, it is good to be independent; but it is not good to be too independent. Some respect is certainly due to the authority of those who, by a careful and loving study of literature, have won the right to speak *ex cathedra*. Nor is that independence, but license, which is not founded upon a wide and deep knowledge of critical science, and upon a careful and respectful collation of our own conclusions, with the impartial philosophical conclusions of others.

In the course of these remarks, we have alluded to three classes of critics, the bigot, the slave, and we cannot better characterize the third, than as the autocratic. There is yet a fourth, which feels, or professes to feel, a warm interest in Southern literature, and which so far is entitled to our respect. But, unfortunately, the critical principles of this class are quite as shallow as those of any of the others; and we notice it chiefly to expose the absurdity of one of its favourite opinions, adopted from a theory which some years ago arose at the North, and which bore the name of Americanism in literature. After the lapse of a period commensurate with the distance it had to travel, it reached the remote South, where it became, with an intensity of absurdity which is admirable indeed, Southernism in literature. Now, if the theory had gone to the depth of that which constitutes true nationality, we should have no objections to urge against it. But to the understandings of these superficial critics, it meant nothing more than that an author should confine himself in the choice of his subjects to the scenery, the history, and the traditions of his own country. To be an American novelist, it was sufficient that a writer should select a story, in which one half the characters should be backwoodsmen, who talked bad Saxon, and the other half should be savages, who talked Choctaw translated into very bombastic English. To be an American poet, it was sufficient either in a style and measure imitated from Pope and Goldsmith, or in the more modern style and measure of Scott and Wordsworth, to describe the vast prairies of the West, the swamps and pine forests of the South, or the great lakes and broad rivers of the North. It signified nothing to these critics whether the tone, the spirit, or the style were caught from European writers or not. If a poet, in genuine Scott, or genuine Byron, compared his hero to a cougar or grisly bear—patriotically ignoring the Asiatic tiger or the African lion—the exclamation of the critic was, "How intensely American!"

We submit that this is a false and narrow criterion, by which to judge of the true nationality of the author. Not in the subject, except to a partial extent, but in the management of the subject, in the tone and bearings of the thought, in the drapery, the colouring, and those thousand nameless touches, which are to be felt rather than expressed, are the characteristics of a writer to be sought. It is in these particulars that an author of original genius—no matter what his subject—will manifest his nationality. In fact, true originality will be always found identical with true nationality. A painter who should paint an American landscape exactly in the style of Salvator or of Claude, ought scarcely to be entitled an American painter. A poet who should write a hymn to Niagara in the blank verse of the Ulysses or the Princess, ought not to be entitled an American poet. In a word, he alone, who, in a style evolved from his own individual nature, speaks the thoughts and feelings of his own deep heart, can be a truly national genius. In the works of such a man, the character which speaks behind and through him—as character does not always speak in the case of men of mere talent, who in some respects are usually more or less under the sway of more commanding minds—will furnish the best and highest types of the intellectual character of his countrymen, and will illustrate most correctly, as well as most subtly—perhaps most correctly because most subtly—the nature of the influences around him. In the poetry of such a man, if he be a poet, whether its scenes be laid in his native country or the land of faery, the pines of his own forests shall be heard to murmur, the music of his own rivers shall swell the diapason, the flowers of his own soil shall bud and burst, though touched perhaps with a more ethereal and lasting grace; and with a brighter and more spiritual lustre, or with a darker and holier beauty, it will be his own skies that look down upon the loveliest landscapes of his creation.

We regard the theory of Southernism in literature as a circumscription, both unnecessary and unreasonable, of the privileges of genius. Shakspeare was not less an Englishman when he wrote Antony and Cleopatra, than when he dramatized the history of the kings of England. Sir Walter was not less a Scotchman when he drew the characters of Louis XI. and Charles the Bold, than when he conceived the characters of Edie Ochiltree and Balfour of Burley. We do not suppose that until this theory germinated in the brain of its foolish originator, it ever occurred to an author that in his selection of subjects, he was to be bounded by certain geographical limits. And if in addition to the many difficulties which he has to overcome, the Southern author be expected, under the penalty of being pronounced un-Southern in tone, and unpatriotic in spirit, never to pass the Potomac on one side, or the Gulf on the other, we shall despair of ever seeing within our borders a literature of such depth and comprehensiveness as will ensure it the respect of other countries, or permanence in the remembrance of posterity. No! the domain of genius is as wide as the world, and as ancient as creation. Wherever the angel of its inspiration may lead, it has the right to follow—and whether exhibited by the light of tropic suns, or of the Arctic morning, whether embodied in the persons of ancient heroes, or of modern thinkers, the eternal verities which it aims to inculcate shall find in every situation, and under every guise, their suitable place, and their proper incarnation.

We should not like to convey the impression that we undervalue the materials for prose and poetry, which may be found in Southern scenery, Southern society, or Southern history. We are simply protesting against a narrow creed, by means of which much injustice may be done to a writer, who, though not less Southern in feeling than another who displays his Southernism on the surface of his books, yet insists upon the right to clothe according to the dictates of his own taste, and locate according to the dictates of his own thoughtful judgment, the creatures of his imagination. At the same time we are not blind to the spacious field which is opened to the Southern author within his own immediate country. The vast aboriginal forests which so weightily oppress us with a sense of antiquity, the mountains, tree-clad to the summit, enclosing unexplored Elysiums, the broad belt of lowland along the ocean, with its peculiar vegetation, the live-oak, stateliest of that stately family, hung with graceful tillandsia, the historical palmetto, and the rank magnificence of swamp and thicket, the blue aureole of the passion flower, the jessamine, with its yellow and fragrant flame, and all the wild luxuriance of a bountiful Flora, the golden carpet which the rice plant spreads for the feet of autumn, and the cotton field white as with a soft, warm snow of summer—these are materials—and these are but a small part of them—from which a poet may draw an inspiration as genuine as that which touched with song the lips of English Thomson, or woke to subtler and profounder utterance the soul of English Wordsworth. Nor is the structure of our social life—so different from that of every other people, whether ancient or modern—incapable of being exhibited in a practical light. There are truths underlying the relations of master and slave; there are meanings beneath that union of the utmost freedom with a healthy conservatism, which, growing out of those relations, is characteristic of Southern thought, of which poetry may avail herself not only to vindicate our system to the eyes of the world, but to convey lessons which shall take root in the hearts of all mankind. We need not commend the poetical themes which are to be found in the history of the South; in the romance of her colonial period; in the sufferings and struggles of her revolution; in the pure patriotism of her warriors and statesmen, the sterling worth of her people, and the grace, the wit, the purity, the dignity, delicacy and self-devotion of her women. He who either in the character of poet or novelist shall associate his name with the South in one or all of the above-mentioned aspects, will have achieved a more enviable fame than any which has yet illustrated the literature of America.

We pass to a brief discussion of an error still more prevalent than the theory just dismissed. We know nothing more discouraging to an author, nothing which more clearly evinces the absence of any profound principles of criticism, than the light in which the labours of the poet and the novelist are very generally viewed at the South. The novel and the poem are almost universally characterized as light reading, and we may say are almost universally estimated as a very light and superficial sort of writing. We read novels and poems indeed, with some pleasure, but at the same time with the tacit conviction that we are engaged in a very trivial occupation; and we promise ourselves that, in order to make up for the precious moments thus thrown away, we shall hereafter redouble our diligence in the study of history or of mathematics. It is the common impression that while there is much practical utility in a knowledge of Euclid and the Calculus, no profit whatever is to be derived from works of poetry and fiction. Of two writers, one of whom should edit a treatise on the conic sections, and the other should give to the world a novel equal in tragic power and interest to the Bride of Lammermoor, the former would be considered the greater man by nine persons out of ten.

It would be from the purpose of this article to go into a minute examination of the prejudices upon which these opinions are founded. But we may be permitted a few words on the subject. What are the advantages which are supposed to result from the study of the mathematics—not, we mean, to those who are to devote their lives to science, but to that more numerous class who, immediately upon graduation, fling aside Playfair, and separate into doctors, lawyers, and politicians? The answer is, we believe, that the study of mathematics is calculated to accustom the student to habits of close reasoning, and to increase his powers of concentration. Some vague generality is usually added about its influence in strengthening the mind.

Now, it is a notorious fact that mathematicians are for the most part bad reasoners out of their particular province. As soon as they get upon topics which do not admit of precise definitions and exact demonstrations, and which they, nevertheless, invariably insist upon subjecting to precise definitions and exact demonstrations, they fall naturally enough into all sorts of blunders and contradictions. They usually beg the question at the outset, and then by means of a most unexceptionable syllogism, they come to a conclusion which, though probably false in fact, is yet, it must be confessed, always logically consistent with their premises.

Now, it will not be denied that such a method of reasoning is the very worst possible which could be employed by a lawyer or a politician. The laws, and their various interpretations, the motives, the objects, the interest in their thousand contradictory aspects, which must form the staple of the arguments of professional and public men, are not to be treated like the squares and circles of geometry. Yet that a familiarity with mathematical modes of proof does not lead to the error of using those modes of proof upon subjects to which they are wholly inapplicable, is evident to anybody who has noticed the style of argument prevalent among the very young orators who have not long cut the apron strings which tied them to a too strictly mathematical Alma Mater. They bristle all over with syllogisms, write notes in the form of captions, invariably open a speech (that is if it be not a fourth of July oration, and if they have anything to prove) with a statement, and end with Q. E. D. corollary and scholium. Not until the last theories have been erased from their memory, or until they shall have learned by repeated reverses the absurdity of which they are guilty, do they begin to reason like men of practical sense.

It must not be inferred that we are arguing against the study of the mathematics. It has its uses—though we think not the uses commonly assigned to it. These we cannot stop to particularize, but we may mention that if it could do nothing but furnish us with the clearest idea we have of the nature of absolute truths, it would still be an important study.

We shall probably be thought paradoxical when we say that we believe that the study of poetry as an art in conjunction with the science of criticism—and this not with the design of writing poetry, but merely to enable the student to appreciate and to judge of it—will afford a better preparative training than all the mathematics in the world, to the legal or political debater. Poetry, as Coleridge well remarks, has a logic of its own; and this logic being more complex, more subtle, and more uncertain than the logic of the demonstrative sciences, is far more akin than the latter can be to the dialectics of common life. And when we consider that while we are mastering this logic, we are at the same time familiarising ourselves with the deepest secrets of the human heart, imbuing our natures with the most refining influences, and storing our minds with the purest thoughts and the loveliest pictures of humanity, the utility of poetry as a study seems to be established beyond a question.

It seems strange, that in this nineteenth century, one should be called upon to vindicate poetry from aspersions which have been repeatedly and triumphantly disproved. Nevertheless, so generally accepted at the South is the prejudice which degrades poetry into a mere servant of our pleasures, that upon most ears, truths, (elsewhere so familiar as to be trite) upon which it bases a loftier pretension, fall with the startling novelty of paradox. How many look upon the imaginative faculty simply as the manufacturer of pretty conceits; how few know it as the power which, by selecting and combining materials never before brought together, in fact, produces pictures and characters in which there shall be nothing untruthful or unnatural, and which shall yet be as new to us as a lately found island in the Pacific. How many of us regard poetry as a mere creature of the fancy; how few appreciate its philosophy, or understand that beneath all the splendour of its diction and imagery, there is in its highest manifestations at least a substratum of profound and valuable thought; how very few perceive the justice of the eloquent definition of Coleridge: "That poetry is the blossom and fragrance of all human wisdom, human passions, learning, and language;" or are prepared to see, as it is expressed in the noble verse of Taylor, that

> Poetry is Reason's self-sublimed;
> Tis Reason's sovereignty, whereunto
> All properties of sense, all dues of wit,
> All fancies, images, perceptions, passions,
> All intellectual ordinance grown up
> From accident, necessity, or custom,
> Seen to be good, and after made authentic;
> All ordinance aforethought, that from science
> Doth prescience take, and from experience law;
> All lights and institutes of digested knowledge,
> Gifts and endowments of intelligence
> From sources living, from the dead bequests,—
> Subserve and minister.

We hurry on to the comparative merits of history and fiction.

It is not generally understood that a novel may be more truthful than a history, in several particulars—but, perhaps, most of all in the delineation of character. The historian, hampered by facts which are not seldom contradictory, is sometimes compelled to touch and retouch his portrait of a character in order to suit those facts. Consequently, he will often give us a character not as it existed, but his idea of that character—a something, the like of which was never in heaven above, nor on the earth beneath. On the other hand, the novelist, whose only obligation is to be true to nature, at least paints us possible men and women, about whose actions we can reason almost with as much accuracy as if they had really lived, loved, acted and died. In doing this, he at once reaches a higher truth than is often attainable by the historians, and imparts to us lessons far more profitable. More of human nature can be learned from the novel of Tom Jones from a History of the whole Roman Empire—written, at least, as histories are commonly written. Again, while it is to history we look for an account of the dynasties, the battles, sieges, revolutions, the triumphs and defeats of a nation, it is from the historical novel that we glean the best idea of that which it is infinitely more important for us to know—of the social state, the manners, morals, opinions, passions, prejudices, and habits of the people. We do not hesitate to say, that of two persons, one of whom has only read Hume's chapter on Richard I., and the other only the Ivanhoe of Scott, the latter will be by far the better acquainted with the real history of the period.

We need not say that we are not quite so silly as to believe that it is possible, by any force of argument, to bring about a reformation in the tastes of the reading community. It is, unfortunately, not in the power of a people to confer together and say, "Come, now, let us arise, and build up a literature." We cannot call meetings, and pass resolutions to this purpose, as we do with respect to turnpikes, railways, and bridges. That genuine appreciation, by which alone literature is encouraged and fostered, is a plant of slow growth. Still, we think something may be done; but in the meanwhile let it not be forgotten that, in spite of every disadvantage, the South already possesses a literature which calls for its patronage and applause. The fate of that literature is a reproach to us. Of all our Southern writers, not one but Poe has received his due measure of fame. The immense resources and versatile powers of Simms are to this day grudgingly acknowledged, or contemptuously denied. There have been writers among us who, in another country, would have been complimented with repeated editions, whose names are now almost forgotten, and whose works it is now utterly impossible to obtain. While our centre-tables are littered with the feeble moralizings of Tupper, done up in very bright morocco; and while the corners of our newspapers are graced with the glibly versified common-places of Mackey, and of writers even more worthless than Mackey, there is, perhaps, scarcely a single bookseller in the United States, on whose face we should not encounter the grin of ignorance, if we chanced to inquire for the Froissart ballads of Philip Pendleton Cooke.

It is not without mortification that we compare the reception which the North gives to its literature to the stolid indifference of the South. There, at least, Genius wears the crown, and receives the tributes which are due to it. It is true, indeed, that not a few Northern authors have owed in part their successes to the art of puffing— an art nowhere carried to such a height of excellence as in the cities of New York and Boston. It is true that through the magic of this art, many a Bottom in literature has been decked with the flowers and fed with the apricots and dewberries of a short-lived reputation. But it is also true, that there is in the reading public of the North a well-founded faith in its capacity to judge for itself, a not inconsiderable knowledge of the present state of Poetry and Art, and a cordial disposition to recognize and reward the native authors who address it.

We are not going to recommend the introduction at the South of a system of puffing. "No quarter to the dunce," whether Southern or Northern, is the motto which should be adopted by every man who has at heart the interests of his country's literature. Not by exalting mediocrity, not by setting dullness on a throne, and putting a garland on the head of vanity, shall we help in the smallest degree the cause of Southern letters. A partiality so mistaken can only serve to depreciate excellence, discourage effort, and disgust the man of real ability. We have regretted to see the tenderness with which a volume of indifferent poetry is sometimes treated—for no other reason that we could discover than that it was the work of a Southerner—by those few clever and well-meaning critics, of whom the South is not altogether destitute. The effect of this ill-judged clemency is to induce those who are indisposed to admit the claims of Southern literature upon their admiration, to look with suspicion upon every verdict of Southern criticism.

We have but one course to suggest to those who are willing, from a painful conviction of the blended servility, superficiality, and antiquated bigotry of criticism among us, to assist in bringing about a reformation. It is to speak the rude truth always. It is to declare war equally against the slaves of English and Northern opinions, and against the salves of the conventional schools of the eighteenth century. If argument fail, perhaps satire may prove a more effective weapon. Everything like old fogyism in literature should be remorselessly ridiculed. That pert license which consults only its own uneducated taste, and that docility which truckles to the *prestige* of a foreign reputation should be alike held up to contempt. It should be shown in plain, unflattering language that the unwillingness with which native genius is acknowledged, is a bitterer slander on the country and its intellect than any of the falsehoods which defile the pages of Trollope, Dickens, Marryatt, or Basil Hall. It would be no injustice to tell those who refuse to credit that the South has done anything in prose or poetry, that in their own shallowness and stupidity they have found the best reasons for their incredulity; and they should be sternly reminded, that because a country annually gives birth to a thousand noodles, it does not follow that it may not now and then produce a man of genius. Nor should any hesitation be felt to inquire boldly into the manner in which the tastes of our youth are educated. Let it be asked on what principle we fill our chairs of belles-lettres; whether to discharge properly the duties of a critical teacher, a thorough acquaintance with English literature be not a rather indispensable requisite, and how it is that in one institution a learned professor shall maintain the Course of Time to be the greatest of English epics, and in another an equally learned professor shall deny, on the ground that he could never read it, save as a very disagreeable task, the transcendent merits of Paradise Lost. Is it not a fact, of which we may feel not unreasonably ashamed, that a student may pass four years under these misleaders of youth, and yet remain ignorant of that most important revolution in imaginative literature—to us of the present day the most important of all literary revolutions—which took place a little more than half a century ago. The influence of the new spiritual philosophy in producing a change from a sensuous to a super-sensuous poetry, the vast difference between the school represented by Wordsworth, and the school represented by Pope, the introduction of that mystical element into our verse which distinguishes it from the verse of the age of Shakespeare, the theory of that analytical criticism which examines a work of art "from the heart outwards, not from surface inwards!" and which deduces its laws from nature and truth, not from the practice of particular writers; these surely are subjects which, in an institution devoted to the purpose of education, may not be overlooked without censure. At the risk of exciting the derisive smiles of those who attach more value to the settlement of a doubtful accent, or a disputed quantity, than to a just definition of the imaginative faculty, or a correct estimation of the scope and objects of poetry, we avow our belief that a systematic study of English literature, under the guidance of proper expounders—even at the expense of the curriculum in other respects—would be attended with the highest benefits to the student and the community. Such a course of study would assist more than anything else in bringing about that improvement in taste which we need so much, and for which we must look especially to the generation now growing up about us. We do not expect much from those whose opinions are already formed. It is next to impossible thoroughly to convert a confirmed papist; and there are no prejudices so difficult to overcome as the prejudices of pedantry and age.

After all, the chief impediment to a broad, deep, and liberal culture is her own self-complacency. With a strange inconsistency, the very persons who decry Southern literature are forever extolling Southern taste, Southern learning, and Southern civilization. There is scarcely a city of any size in the South which has not its clique of amateur critics, poets and philosophers, the regular business of whom is to demonstrate truisms, settle questions which nobody else would think of discussing, to confirm themselves in opinions which have been picked up from the rubbish of seventy years agone, and above all to persuade each other that together they constitute a society not much inferior to that in which figured Burke and Johnson, Goldsmith and Sir Joshua. All of these being oracles, they are unwilling to acknowledge the claims of a professional writer, lest in doing so they should disparage their own authority. It is time that their self-complacency should be disturbed. And we propose satire as the best weapon, because against vanity it is the only effective one. He who shall convince this, and every other class of critics to which we have alluded, that they are not in advance of their age, that they are even a little behind it, will have conferred an incalculable benefit upon them, and upon the South.

We shall not admit that in exposing the deficiencies of the Southern public, we have disparaged in the slightest degree the intellect of the South. Of that intellect in its natural capacity none can conceive more highly than ourself. It is impossible not to respect a people from whom have sprung so many noble warriors, orators and statesmen. And there is that in the constitution of the Southern mind, in the Saxon, Celtic and Teutonic elements of which it is composed, and in the peculiar influences amidst which these elements have been moulded together, a promise of that blending of the philosophic in thought with the enthusiastic in feeling, which makes a literary nation. Even now, while it is in one place trammeled by musty rules and canons, and in another left to its own unguided or misguided impulses, it would be unjust to deny it a quickness of perception, which, if rightly trained, would soon convert this essay into a slander and a falsehood. We will not believe that a people with such a mental character can remain much longer under the dominion of a contracted and illiberal culture. Indeed, we think the signs of a better taste may already be noticed. The circle of careless or prejudiced readers, though large, is a narrowing circle. The circle of thoughtful and earnest students, though a small one, is a widening circle. Young authors are rising up who have won for themselves at least a partial acknowledgment of merit. The time must come at last when the public shall feel that there are ideas characterizing Southern society, as distinguished from Northern and English society, which need the exposition of a new literature. There will be a stirring of the public mind, an expectation aroused which will ensure its own gratification, a demand for Southern prose and poetry, which shall call forth the poet and prose writer from the crowds that now conceal them, and a sympathy established between author and public, which shall infuse inspiration into the one, and heighten the pleasure and profit of the other. Then, indeed, we may look for a literature of which we shall all wear the honours. We shall walk over ground made classic by the imaginations of our poets, the thoughts we speak shall find illustration in verse which has been woven by Southern hearths; and the winds that blow from the land, and the waves that wash our level coast, shall bear to other nations the names of bards who know how to embody the spirit of their country without sinking that universality which shall commend their lessons to all mankind.

Kate Cumming

(1828–1909)

Kate Cumming was born in Edinburgh, Scotland, but moved as a child to Mobile, Alabama, where she attended school and enthusiastically adopted the ways of her new Southern homeland; it is clear from her journal that when the Civil War broke out, she was devoted to the Confederacy. Early in the war, she volunteered her services as a nurse, and she served in a number of hospitals in Alabama, Mississippi, Tennessee, and Georgia. Though the morality of the day prohibited her from duties that might result in improper physical contact with male patients, she helped prepare beds, supervised the kitchens, and did laundry. Other duties included writing letters for patients, reading to them, and sending home to grieving families the personal effects of the dead. Cumming published her work in 1866 as *A Journal of Hospital Life in the Confederate Army of Tennessee*. Though Cumming reveals little of her own thoughts or her life outside the hospital, the journal does provide a straightforward account of life in Confederate hospitals.

from *A Journal of Hospital Life in the Confederate Army of the Tennessee*

Introduction.

For giving the following pages to the public some apology may be due. When the war closed, human nature like, I felt a great thirst for revenge. I should, indeed, not have liked it had I been told so then; but I can look back now and feel how just would have been the charge.

I thought I could hear with calmness, nay, even pleasure, that the French, or any other nation, had desolated the North as the South has been. Since then a better feeling has arisen; and, while arranging my journal for the press, the vivid recollections of what I have witnessed during years of horror have been so shocking, that I have almost doubted whether the past was not all a fevered dream, and, if real, how I ever lived through it.

These notes of passing events, often hurriedly penned amid the active duties of hospital life, but feebly indicate, and only faintly picture, the sad reality. I now pray, and will never cease to pray to the end of my days, that men may beat their swords into plowshares and their spears into pruning-hooks, and that nation may not lift a sword against nation, nor learn war any more.

It is with the hope that the same feeling may be aroused in every reader that I present this volume to the public.

The southerner may learn a lesson from the superhuman endurance of the glorious dead and mutilated living who so nobly did their duty in their country's hour of peril. And the northerner, I trust, when he has brought in review before him the wrongs of every kind inflicted on us, will cry, Enough! they have suffered enough; let their wounds now be healed instead of opening them afresh.

I have another motive in view. At the present moment there are men on trial for ill-treating northern prisoners. This is to me the grossest injustice we have yet suffered. I would stake my life on the truth of every thing which I have related, as an eye-witness, in the following pages. I have used the simplest language, as truth needs no embellishment. May I not hope that what I have related in regard to the manner in which I saw prisoners treated will soften the hearts of the northerners toward the men now undergoing their trial, and make them look a little more to themselves?

We begged, time and again, for an exchange, but none was granted. We starved their prisoners! But who laid waste our corn and wheat fields? And did not we all starve? Have the southern men who were in northern prisons no tales to tell—of being frozen in their beds, and seeing their comrades freeze to death for want of proper clothing? Is there no Wirz for us to bring to trial? But I must stop; the old feeling comes back; these things are hard to bear. People of the North, the southerners have their faults. Cruelty is not one of them. If your prisoners suffered, it was from force of circumstances, and not with design.

I know that the women of the South will think I have said too much against them; but let them remember that I, too, am a woman, and that every slur cast on them falls on me also. Will the neglect of the suffering, which I have but too faintly sketched, not serve to make them resolve in future to do better; and, like the lady in the dream, say

> "The wounds I might have healed—
>   The human sorrow and smart;
> And yet it never was in my soul
>   To play so ill a part:
> But evil is wrought by want of thought,
>   As well as want of heart."

I feel confident that very much of this failure is to be attributed to us. I have said many a time that, if we did not succeed, the women of the South would be responsible. This conclusion was forced upon me by what I could not but see without willful blindness. Not for one moment would I say that there are no women in the South who have nobly done their duty, although there was an adverse current, strong enough to carry all with it. Whole books might be written, recounting heroic deeds and patient suffering, amid trials seemingly impossible to endure. The names of Newsom, Hopkins, Gilmer, Evans, Harrison, Walke, Monroe, and I might mention a host of others, will live in the hearts of the people of the South as long as there is a heart here to beat.

Let us cease to live on the surface; let us do and dare—remembering, if we are true to ourselves, the world will be true to us. There is one very important work before us—a work all will sympathize with and aid. The war has left thousands of our men almost as helpless as they were in infancy. Had we been successful, our government would have done its duty in providing for these men. As the case now stands, there will be very little care bestowed on them. Is nothing to be done for these heroes? It is not charity to care for them, but a sacred duty.

In bringing before the minds of the public, as I have, that I am a native of the "land of the mountain and the flood," there is a motive. All true, honest southerners, I feel confident, will acknowledge that I have not exaggerated the evils that existed in the South. To say I did not feel the wrongs of the South as deeply as any native would be far from the truth. God knows how my heart has bled for them; though many a time, when I have seen her people proving recreant in her hour of trial, I have said that I was thankful I could claim another land; forgetting, in my blindness, that she had her traitors as well as we. And let her not, when she compares the struggle of the two for independence, forget that there is such a thing as comparisons being odious. Were Scotland brought over here and placed in our midst, we should scarcely heed it, from the small surface she would occupy.

We have a territory equal in extent to Great Britain, France, Italy, Germany, and Spain, and not one tenth of the population to defend it. The enemy could come in with his immense armies at any point. That is why the flanking movement succeeded so well.

When the war broke out, I looked around for a parallel, and naturally my native country and her struggle came up first. Since I have been mingling with the southern people, I have found that I was far from being the only one who was claiming that land of romance and chivalry. It was impossible to go any place without meeting her descendants; and, thanks to Walter Scott and Burns, they had any other wish but that of disclaiming her.

I have never seen Scotland to remember her, but have read much about her mountains, glens, and lakes, and I can not see how they can surpass in grandeur and beauty those we have here; and had we only the writers, gifted with the fire to sing, as none but Scotia's bards have done, in her praise, they would find beauties here as boundless as our empire.

Many will say that it is impossible that the South can ever prosper in union with the North. For centuries, not four years, England and Scotland, on the same island, a small rivulet dividing them, fought against each other with a ferocity such as no two nations ever exhibited. In 1608 the throne of England became vacant by the death of Queen Elizabeth. The next and nearest heir was James VI of Scotland. He ascended the English throne. The two nations from that time were united in all save the name. In 1707 the Act of Union was passed, and the two nations formed what is now Great Britain.

Many years have elapsed since that union. Is a Scotchman to-day an Englishman? or, *vice versa*, an Englishman a Scotchman? All know they are as distinct in nationality as the first day they were united. Where is there such a union for harmony? Not on this earth.

Scotland has lost nothing in grandeur or might since then. Her seats of learning can compete with any in the world. Where is there a nation that can boast of more brilliant lights, both civil and military? Is not her literature spread broadcast over the whole earth? But not even in all these does her greatness consist. The "Cotter's Saturday Night" gives them to us in graphic terms, and

"From scenes like these old Scotia's grandeur springs,
   That makes her loved at home, revered abroad:
Princes and lords are but the breath of kings,
   'An honest man's the noblest work of God!'"

Let us learn a lesson from these facts, and, as I said before, look to ourselves.

Many a man, whose name is now a shining light, never would have been heard of had not misfortune come upon him. The misfortunes did not make him great; his greatness was there before, but it had been pampered in luxury. If the southern people ever were a great people they will show it now. In the whole world there is not such a favored spot as the South. It is an

"Empire mightier than the vast domain swayed once by vicious Cæsars!"

That is why the North fought so hard to keep us with her. We have every climate necessary for the well-being of man; we have prairies, mountains, lakes, rivers, and a soil inferior to none. Is this fair heritage to become a howling wilderness, because a people we dislike will have us unite with them whether we will or no? Let us imitate them in what is worthy of imitation. They are enterprising and industrious: we need both. We have much to be proud of. We have men who may be likened to the great Washington, without any disparagement to him: Davis—for I feel certain that not a hair of his head will be harmed—Lee, Johnston, and many others. And have we not our dead? if dead we may call them, for

"To live in hearts we leave behind is not to die!"

O, let us give up this terrible strife! A truly great man does not know revenge; his soul rises above it as something fit for meaner minds. So with nations. Leave our statesmen to settle our difficulties; and let us remember those exquisite lines of Goldsmith, written after he had walked the weary world round in search of happiness, and returned to his native land:

"How small, of all that human hearts endure,
That part which laws or kings can cause or cure!
Still to ourselves in every place consigned,
Our own felicity we make or find;
With secret course, which no loud storms annoy,
Glides the smooth current of domestic joy.
The lifted ax, the agonizing wheel,
Luke's iron crown, and Damien's bed of steel,
To men remote from power but rarely known,
Leave reason, faith, and conscience all our own."

Chapter 1. Okolona—Corinth.

April 7, 1862.—I left Mobile by the Mobile and Ohio Railroad for Corinth, with Rev. Mr. Miller and a number of Mobile ladies. We are going for the purpose of taking care of the sick and wounded of the army.

As news has come that a battle is now raging, there are not a few anxious hearts in the party—my own among the number, as I have a young brother, belonging to Ketchum's Battery, who I know will be in the midst of the fight, and I have also many dear friends there.

A gentleman, Mr. Skates, has heard that his son is among the killed, and is with us on his way to the front to bring back the remains of him who a short time since formed one of his family circle. May God give strength to the mother and sisters now mourning the loss of their loved one! May they find consolation in the thought that he died a martyr's death; was offered up a sacrifice upon the altar of his country; and that, when we have gained our independence, he, with the brave comrades who fought and fell with him, will ever live in the hearts and memories of a grateful people! I can not look at Mr. Skates without asking myself how many of us may ere long be likewise mourners! It is impossible to suppress these gloomy forebodings.

About midnight, at one of the stations, a dispatch was received prohibiting any one from going to Corinth without a special permit from head-quarters. Our disappointment can be better imagined than described. As military orders are peremptory, there is nothing for us to do but to submit. Mr. Miller has concluded to stop at one of the small towns, as near Corinth as he can get, and there wait until receives permission for us to go on.

April 8.—Arrived at Okolona, Miss., this morning. We are still sixty miles from Corinth. When we alighted at the depot, we were told that there were no hotels to go to. As it had been raining for some time very hard, all about us looked as cheerless as possible. Our prospects, as may be supposed, were gloomy enough. While in this perplexity, each one giving an opinion as to what we had best do, word was brought us that the citizens of the place, hearing of our arrival and mission, had opened their houses for our reception, and many sent carriages to take us to their homes.

As the good people of Mobile have provided us with comforts and delicacies of all kinds for the soldiers, our failure to reach Corinth is a sad disappointment. The stories which we hear of the suffering and almost starving condition of our men aggravate it still more.

The people here can tell us little or nothing about the battle, except that one has been fought. How our forces have come out of it, they have not learned.

Several of our party, myself included, are domiciled with an excellent family by the name of Haughton, consisting of an old lady, her young daughter Lucy, and two pretty girls, her granddaughters. They are extending to us true southern hospitality.

We were all exhausted by loss of sleep, disappointment, and anxiety, and hence

How beautiful in death
  The WARRIOR'S corse appears;
Embalmed by fond AFFECTION'S breath,
  And bathed in WOMAN'S tears!

Their loveliest native earth
  Enshrines the fallen brave;
In the dear land that gave them birth,
  They find their tranquil grave."

I spoke to John Maguire, and reminded him of that day, one year ago, when he participated in one of the finest displays of which the city of Mobile boasts—the Firemen's Anniversary.*

*The 9th of April is the anniversary of the organization of the fire department. Two of the companies, the Creole and Neptune, date their origin from 1819. This department has for its members men of the highest standing. On this anniversary, the engines are decked most gorgeously, and dressed with flowers. One year ago to-day the companies vied with each other in their efforts to make the finest display. The whole department exhibited more energy than was its wont. The way spirit had just been aroused on account of the north holding, as a right, what we deemed our own—Fort Sumter—and our people, awakened as if from a lethargy, determined to throw heart and soul into the contest.

A number of ladies have come from Natchez, Miss., to join us. They have also been cared for by the good people of the place.

After we returned to Mrs. Haughton's, I was quite amused in listening to her grand-daughter's account of a visit which they had just made to the hospital. It seems that the surgeons entertain great prejudice against admitting ladies into the hospital in the capacity of nurses. The surgeon in charge, Dr. Caldwell, has carried this so far that he will note even allow the ladies of the place to visit his patients. These young ladies went over with some milk and bouquets, and were not permitted to present them in person to the patients, but had to give them to the doctor. So they told him they knew the reason; he wanted all the *good things* for himself. The doctors, one and all, are getting terrible characters from the ladies; even good Dr. Nott of Mobile is not spared. I only wish that the doctors would let us try and see what we can do! Have we not noble examples of what our women have done? For instance, Mrs. Hopkins, in Virginia, and, I have no doubt, many others. Is the noble example of Miss Nightingale to pass for nothing? I trust not. What one woman has done, another may do. We need not aspire to be Miss Nightingales, or Mrs. Hopkinses; still we can contribute our "two mites."

We have with us two very excellent ladies—Mrs. Hunter and her daughter—refugees from Missouri. They were in a hospital at Nashville when the city was taken possession of by the enemy, and have been relating their experience, which is very interesting.

April 10.—This morning we were informed that we could go to Corinth, as the order did not apply to us. With joy we hailed the news! It was still raining, but we did not mind that. When we reached the depot, Mrs. Ogden informed me that Miss Booth was sick—too much so to leave this morning. As we left Mobile together, I felt it my duty to remain with her.

I met at the depot Dr. Anderson of Mobile; and was quite amused at a remark which he made to some ladies who were telling him how badly Dr. Caldwell had acted, in not permitting us to visit his hospital. In his usual humorous manner, he said, "What can be expected from an old bachelor, who did not appreciate the ladies enough to marry one?" He also said that he did not think any hospital could get along without ladies. So we have one doctor on our side.

I rode in a carriage with Rev. Mr. Clute, the Episcopal minister of the place, to Mrs. Henderson's, where Miss Booth was staying. Mrs. H. was glad to see me. She is a very intelligent lady, and quite handsome. Her sister, Mrs. Young, living with her, is a highly accomplished musician—plays upon the harp and piano beautifully. She sang some very fine Scotch songs for me. We had a long talk about Scotland. They are of Scotch descent. I felt quite proud of the manner in which they spoke of that land of heroes. It is my native land; and although raised in this, and never personally having known any other, I will not forget the country of my forefathers—the land of Wallace and Walter Scott. I have always found that the southern people speak in praise of it, and the noble deeds for which it is famed, and more now than ever, as we are undergoing the same ordeal through which she so nobly passed in her great struggle for independence: all trust that we may show a like spirit, and meet with like success. The husbands of both these ladies are in the army.

This is a very wealthy portion of Mississippi, and food of all kinds seems to be plentiful. At Mrs. Haughton's we had sweet potatoes as a substitute for coffee, and it was very nice. Mrs. H. informed us that she did not intend to use any other kind while the war lasted.

April 11.—Miss Booth and myself arrived at Corinth to-day. It was raining when we left Mrs. Henderson's, and as her carriage was out of repair, she sent us to the depot in an open wagon. We enjoyed the novel ride, and began to feel that we were in the *service* in reality. My heart beat high with expectation as we neared Corinth. As I had never been where there was a large army, and had never seen a wounded man, except in the cars, as they passed, I could not help feeling a little nervous at the prospect of now seeing both. When within a few miles of the place, we could realize the condition of an army immediately after a battle. As it had been raining for days, water and mud abounded. Here and there were wagons hopelessly left to their fate, and men on horseback trying to wade through it. As far as the eye could reach, in the midst of all this slop and mud, the white tents of our brave army could be seen through the trees, making a picture suggestive of any thing but comfort. My thoughts wandered back to the days of ancient Corinth, and the time it was besieged by the brave and warlike Romans, when the heroic Greeks had to succumb through the fault of their commander. I think of this only in contrast; for the Federals are as unlike the former as our fate will be unlike that of the latter. We have not a Diæus commanding, but the dauntless Beauregard and patriotic Bragg, who, knowing their rights, dare and will maintain them, though the whole North be arrayed against them. I am certain of one thing: that neither the Roman nor Greek armies, brave as history has portrayed them, were composed of more high-souled and determined men than those of ours.

Corinth is at the junction of the Memphis and Charleston and the Mobile and Ohio Railroads, about one hundred and twenty miles east from Memphis, and three hundred miles north from Mobile.

The crowd of men at the depot was so great that we found it impossible to get to our place of destination by ourselves. Mr. Miller was not there to meet us. I met Mr. George Redwood of Mobile, who kindly offered to pilot us. We found Mr. Miller and all the ladies busy in attending to the wants of those around them. They had not been assigned to any particular place, but there is plenty for them to do. We are at the Tishomingo Hotel, which, like every other large building, has been taken for a hospital. The yellow flag is fly-ing from the top of each. Mrs. Ogden tried to prepare me for the scenes which I should witness upon entering the wards. But alas! nothing that I had ever heard or read had given me the faintest idea of the horrors witnessed here. I do not think that words are in our vo-cabulary expressive enough to present to the mind the realities of that sad scene. Cer-tainly, none of the glories of the war were presented here. But I must not say that; for if uncomplaining endurance is glory, we had plenty of it. If it is that which makes the hero, here they were by scores. Gray-haired men—men in the pride of manhood—beardless boys—Federals and all, mutilated in every imaginable way, lying on the floor, just as they were taken from the battle-field; so close together that it was almost impossible to walk without stepping on them. I could not command my feelings enough to speak, but thoughts crowded upon me. O, if the authors of this cruel and unnatural war could but see what I saw there, they would try and put a stop to it! To think, that it is man who is work-ing all this woe upon his fellow-man. What can be in the minds of our enemies, who are now arrayed against us, who have never harmed them in any way, but simply claim our own, and nothing more! May God forgive them, for surely they know not what they do.

This was no time for recrimination; there was work to do; so I went at it to do what I could. If I were to live a hundred years, I should never forget the poor suffer-ers' gratitude; for every little thing, done for them—a little water to drink, or the bathing of their wounds—seemed to afford them the greatest relief.

The Federal prisoners are receiving the same attention as our own men; they are lying side by side. Many are just being brought in from the battle-field. The roads are so bad that it is almost impossible to get them moved at all. A great many ladies are below stairs: so I thought that I had better assist above. The first thing which I did was to aid in giving the men their supper, consisting of bread, biscuit, and butter, and tea and coffee, without milk. There were neither waiters nor plates; they took what we gave them in their hands, and were glad to get it. I went with a lady to give some Federal officers their supper, who were in a room by themselves; only one or two of them were wounded. One, a captain from Cincinnati, had a broken arm. Before I went in, I thought that I would be polite, and say as little as possible to them; but when I saw them laughing, and apparently indifferent to the woe which they had been instrumental in bringing upon us, I could not help being indignant; and when one of them told me he was from Iowa, and that was generally called out of the world, I told him that was where I wished him and all like him, so that they might not trouble us any more.

April 12.—I sat up all night, bathing the men's wounds, and giving them water. Every one attending to them seemed completely worn out. Some of the doctors told me that they had scarcely slept since the battle. As far as I have seen, the surgeons are very kind to the wounded, and nurse as well as doctor them.

The men are lying all over the house, on their blankets, just as they were brought from the battle-field. They are in the hall, on the gallery, and crowded into very small rooms. The foul air from this mass of human beings at first made me giddy and sick, but I soon got over it. We have to walk, and when we give the men any thing kneel, in blood and water; but we think nothing of it at all. There was much suffering among the patients last night; one old man groaned all the time. He was about sixty years of age, and had lost a leg. He lived near Corinth, and had come there the morning of the battle to see his two sons, who were in the army, and he could not resist shouldering his musket and going into the fight. I comforted him as well as I could. He is a religious man, and prayed nearly all night.

Another, a very young man, was wounded in the leg and through the lungs, had a most excruciating cough, and seemed to suffer awfully. One fine-looking man had a dreadful wound in the shoulder. Every time I bathed it he thanked me, and seemed grateful. He died this morning before breakfast. Men who were in the room with him told me that he prayed all night. I trust that he is now at rest, far from this dreary world of strife and bloodshed. I could fill whole pages with descriptions of the scenes before me.

Other ladies have their special patients, whom they never leave. One of them, from Natchez, Miss., has been constantly by a young man, badly wounded, ever since she came here, and the doctors say that she has been the means of saving his life. Many of the others are doing the same. Mrs. Ogden and the Mobile ladies are below stairs. I have not even time to speak to them. Mr. Miller is doing much good; he is comforting the suffering and dying, and has already baptized some.

This morning, when passing the front door, a man asked me if I had any thing to eat, which I could give to some men at the depot awaiting transportation on the cars. He said that they had eaten nothing for some days. Some of the ladies assisting me, we took them hot coffee, bread, and meat. The poor fellows ate eagerly, and seemed so thankful. One of the men, who was taking care of them, asked me where I was from. When I replied Mobile, he said that Mobile was the best place in the Confederacy. He was a member of the Twenty-first Alabama Regiment; I have forgotten his name. I have been busy all day, and can scarcely tell what I have been doing; I have not taken time even to eat, and certainly not time to sit down. There seems to be no order. All do as they please. We have men for nurses, and the doctors complain very much at the manner in which they are appointed; they are detailed from the different regiments, like guards. We have a new set every few hours. I can not see how it is possible for them to take proper care of the men, as nursing is a thing that has to be learned, and we should select our best men for it—the best, not physically, but morally—as I am certain that none but good, conscientious persons will ever do justice to the patients.

Sunday, April 13.—Enjoyed a very good night's rest upon some boxes. We all slept below stairs, in the front room—our baggage separating us from the front part of it, which is the clerk's office, and sleeping apartment of some dozen men. It was a laughable sight to see Father Miller fixing our beds for us. Poor man! He tried so hard to make us comfortable. Some slept on shelves. I slept so soundly that I did not even dream, as I was completely worn out with the labor of the day. I could realize how, after a hard day's marching or fighting, a soldier can throw himself upon the ground, and sleep as soundly as if he was on a bed of down. A number of persons arrived last night, looking for their relations. One very pretty lady, with her parents, is in search of her husband, a colonel, who is reported badly wounded. I have since heard that she has found him at a farmhouse, and he is much better off than she had been informed. Her mother, on leaving, presented me with some very nice sperm-candles.

I have just seen my brother. He looks rather the "worse for wear." But, thank God, he is safe! This was his first battle, and I have been told that "he was brave to a fault." The company distinguished itself on that eventful day; and Mobile may well be proud of the gallant men who compose it.

I have been told by a friend that the night of the first day's battle he passed by a wounded Federal, who requested him to bring him some water from a spring near. On going to it, he was much shocked to see three Federals lying with their heads in it. They had dragged themselves to the spring to slake their thirst, and there they had breathed their last. There is no end to the tales of horror related about the battle-field. They fill me with dismay.

> "O shame to men! Devil with Devil damn'd
> Firm concord holds; men only disagree,
> Of creatures rational, though under hope
> Of heavenly grace: and, God proclaiming peace,
> Yet live in hatred, enmity, and strife
> Among themselves, and levy cruel wars,
> Wasting the earth, each other to destroy:
> As if (which might induce us to accord)
> Man had not hellish foes enow besides,
> That, day and night, for his destruction wait."

The confusion and want of order are as great as ever. A great many doctors are here, who came with the men from the different regiments. The amount of good done is not near what it might be, if things were better managed. Some one is to blame for this state of affairs. Many say that it is the fault of Dr. Foard, the medical director. But I suppose that allowance must be made for the unexpected number of wounded. I trust that in a little time things will be better.

One of the doctors, named Little, of Alabama, told me to-day that he had left his young wife on his plantation, with more than a hundred negroes upon it, and no white man but the overseer. He had told the negroes, before he left, if they desired to leave, they could do so when they pleased. He was certain that not more than one or two would go.

I have conversed with some of the wounded prisoners. One of them, quite a young man, named Nott, is very talkative. He says that he dislikes Lincoln and abolitionism as much as we do; declares that he is fighting to save the Union, and nothing more. All of them say the same thing. What a glorious Union it would be!

Quite a number of bunks arrived today, and we are having the most severely wounded placed on them. I am so glad, as we can have some of the filth taken off the floors. A doctor requested me to go down stairs and see if there was a bunk with a Federal upon it, and if so have him taken off, as he had a badly wounded man that needed one. I went and asked Mrs. Royal, from Mobile, whom I had heard talk very bitterly. She knew of one, but would not tell me where it was. Her true woman's nature showed itself, in spite of her dislike. Seeing an enemy wounded and helpless is a different thing from seeing him in health and in power. The first time that I saw one in this condition every feeling of enmity vanished at once. I was curious to find out who the Federal was, and, as Mrs. R. would not tell me, I went in search of him. I found him with but little trouble; went to the men who were upon the bunks, and asked them where they were from. One, quite a youth, with a childish face, told me that he was from Illinois. I knew in a moment that he was the one. I asked him about his mother, and why he had ever left her. Tears filled his eyes, and his lips quivered so that he was unable to speak. I was deeply moved myself, spoke a few words of comfort, and left him. I would not have had him give up his bunk for the world. Poor child! there will be a terrible day of reckoning for those who sent you on your errand, and who are the cause of desolating so many hearts and homes.

As I was passing one of the rooms, a man called me, and begged me to do something for him and others who were with him. No one had been to see them that morning, and they had had no breakfast. I gave them something to eat, and got a nurse to take care of them. About eight were in the room, among them Mr. Regan of Alabama and Mr. Eli Wasson of Texas, both of whom had lost a leg. I paid these special attention, as they were worse than the others. They were very grateful, and thanked me all the time. Mr. W. said that he knew that he would get well now. They are both unmarried, and talk much of their mothers and sisters, as all men do now. "Home, sweet home," is the dearest spot on earth to them, since they are deprived of its comforts. Mother, wife, and sister seem to be sweeter to them than any words in the English language.

We eat in the kitchen, surgeons and all. It is not the cleanest place in the world, and I think, to use a Scotch phrase, would make even Mrs. McClarty "think shame." Hunger is a good antidote for even dirt. I am aware that few will think so except those who have tried it.

April 15.—Enjoyed a very good night's rest in a crowded room. Had part of a mattress upon the floor, but so many were upon it that for half of the night I was under a table.

My patients are doing well. My own health is excellent. While I was down stairs this morning a gentleman requested me to give him something to eat for some fifty or sixty wounded men whom he had in his care. He had nothing for them, but was expecting something from his home in Tennessee. It would be some days before he could get it. Mrs. Ogden gave them what she could. He informed us that his name was Cannon; that he was a doctor, and a clergyman of the Episcopal Church. He said that if our men were not better treated than at the present time, it would be the means of demoralizing them more than the enemy's balls.

While passing through the large ward yesterday, a young man lying upon the floor called me, and asked me if I did not recollect him. His name was Shutterlee; he was from Mobile, and a member of the Twenty-first Alabama Regiment. I remembered that I had often seen him, when a little boy, playing with my brother. Poor fellow! he was badly wounded, and suffered a great deal. I asked him if I could do any thing for him. He told me that Mrs. Lyons of Mobile was taking care of him, but wished me to write to his mother, and inform her where and how he was, which I lost no time in doing.

Mr. Wasson is cheerful, and is doing well; tells me much about his home in Texas and the nice fruit there; says that I must go home with him, as his family would be so glad to see me.

Mrs. Lyons is sitting up day and night, attending to some eight or nine patients. One of them is shot in the face, and has it covered with a cloth, as it is so lacerated that it presents a most revolting aspect. Mrs. L. is also taking care of some prisoners. There is a Federal surgeon named Young waiting on them. I have been told that Dr. Lyle, one of our surgeons, refused to attend them, as he had just lost two brothers in the war, and has heard that his father is a prisoner. His feelings are such that he is fearful he might not do justice to the sufferers. If there were no other surgeons here, he would endeavor to do his duty by them.

April 16.—Mrs. Miller, Mrs. Ogden, and nearly all the ladies from Mobile left for Columbus, Miss. I remained, with Mrs. Glassburn, from Natchez. My brother is here, and I have become so much interested in some of the wounded that I could not leave them. Mrs. Ogden was completely worn out; and it is not much to be wondered at, as she, with the rest of us, has had to sleep in any and every place; and as to making our toilet, that was out of the question. I have not undressed since I came here.

This morning, while the ladies were preparing to leave, as their goods and chattels were all mislaid, much noise prevailed in finding them. I was annoyed, as I knew that many of the wounded were within hearing. I thought that it was not strange that surgeons should prefer to have Sisters of Charity to nurse their sick, for they know how to keep quiet. To add to the noise there were a number of washerwomen who had come from New Orleans. A doctor, who I was informed was Dr. Foard, the medical director, was assigning them to the different places in the hospitals. If Pope had been there, I think that he could have made a few additions to his "Ode to Silence."

I dislike very much to see some of the ladies go, as they have been very kind to the sufferers, and I know that they will miss them very much. They go to Columbus, Miss., where are a great many of the wounded. I daily witness the same sad scenes— men dying all around me. I do not know who they are, nor have I time to learn.

April 17.—I was going round as usual this morning, washing the faces of the men, and had got half through with one before I found out that he was dead. He was lying on the gallery by himself, and had died with no one near him. These are terrible things, and, what is more heart-rending, no one seems to mind them. I thought that my patients were all doing well. Mr. Wasson felt better, and knew that he would soon go home. I asked the surgeon who was attending him about his condition, and was much shocked when I learned that neither he nor Mr. Regan would live to see another day. This was a sad trial to me. I had seen many die, but none of them whom I had attended so closely as these two. I felt toward them as I do toward all the soldiers—as if they were my brothers. I tried to control my feelings before Mr. W., as he was so hopeful of getting well, but it was a hard task. He looked at me once and asked me what was the matter; was he going to die? I asked him if he was afraid. He replied no; but he was so young that he would like to live a little longer, and would like to see his father and mother once more. I did what I could to prepare him for the great change which was soon to come over him, but I could not muster courage to tell him that he was going to die. Poor Mr. Regan was wandering in his mind, and I found it useless to talk to him upon the subject of death. I managed to get him to tell me his mother's address. He belonged to the Twenty-second Alabama Regiment.

About dark a strange doctor was visiting the patients. When he came to Mr. W., I was sitting by his bedside. He asked me if this was a relative. I informed him that he was not, but I had been attending to him for some days, and he now seemed like one. Mr. W. looked at him and said, "Doctor, I wish you to tell me if I am going to die." The doctor felt his pulse and replied, "Young man, you will never see another day in this world." A pallor passed over his countenance, and for a little while he could not speak. When he did, he looked at me and said, "Sister, I want to meet you in heaven," and then requested me to get a clergyman to visit him. There happened to be one in the hospital. I sent for him, and he prayed and talked with him for some time. Mr. W. then asked me if I could not let his brothers know his condition; he had two or three in Corinth. A friend who was with him did all in his power to inform them, so that they could see him before he died, but it was of no avail. They were sick, and we could not ascertain in what hospital they were confined. He was much disappointed in not seeing them. He then asked me to write to his mother, who lives in Grime's County, Texas. He desired me to inform her that he had made his peace with God, and hoped to meet her in that land where all is peace and happiness. He would have rejoiced to have seen her and the rest of his dear relatives before leaving this world, but the Lord had willed it otherwise, and he was resigned.

April 18.—I remained with Mr. Wasson all night. A child could not have been more composed. He told me how good the Lord was in giving him such peace and strength at the last hour. About 4 o'clock A. M. he insisted that I should leave him, as I required rest. He begged so hard that I left him for a little while. When I returned he had breathed his last. One of his companions was with him, and was very attentive—told me that he died as if he was going to sleep. As Bryant has so beautifully expressed it:

"Like one who wraps the drapery of his couch
About him, and lies down to pleasant dreams."

"O, gently close the eye
    That loved to look on you;
O, seal the lip whose earliest sigh,
    Whose latest breath, was true."

Mr. Regan died this morning; was out of his mind to the last.

Since I have been here, I have been more deeply impressed than ever before with the importance of preparing while in health for that great change that must, sooner or later, happen to all. I see that it is almost impossible, while the physical system is suffering, to compose the thoughts on that all-important subject. For days before their final dissolution, many of those we see here are wandering in their minds, so that it is impossible for them to repent; and God has given us but one example of death-bed repentance, but his holy book is filled with denunciations against those who reject the gospel and quench the Holy Spirit. "Therefore will I number you to the sword, and ye shall all bow down to the slaughter: because, when I called, ye did not answer; when I spake, ye did not hear." Isaiah xiii, 12.

It does seem strange that, amid all the terrible scenes of destruction that we are daily witnessing, we think as little of death as ever, and act as if it was something that might happen to others, but never to ourselves.

> "The voice of this instructive scene
>   May every heart obey,
> Nor be the faithful warning vain,
>   Which calls to watch and pray.
>
> O, let us to that Savior fly
>   Whose arm alone can save;
> Then shall our hopes ascend on high,
>   And triumph over the grave."

Mrs. Lyons left this morning for home. She was very sick; and one of the doctors informed her, if she did not leave immediately, she would certainly die. I know the men whom she has been nursing will miss her very much, as she has been so attentive to them.

While I was giving some sermons to the men to read, I met with Dr. Foster of Natchez, Miss., who is here for the purpose of taking home some wounded men. He looked at the sermons. They were preached by Rev. Dr. Pierce on last fast-day, in St. John's Church, Mobile. The first warned us not to put our trust in any thing earthly, but in Him alone who sitteth in the heavens; and, as just as our cause was, if we trusted in man alone, it would come to naught. The other said, as we profess to be a Christian nation, we should act with that forbearance toward our enemies which Christians should always manifest; and, wronged and abused though we be, we must not hate. This task is a hard one; so the author advises us to have hourly upon our lips the language of his text: "Lead us not into temptation, but deliver us from evil." After examining them, Dr. F. asked me to get some copies for him, as he thought that they would be the means of doing much good in the army.

Dr. Smith has taken charge of this hospital. I think that there will be a different order of things now. He is having the house and yard well cleansed. Before this, it was common to have amputated limbs thrown into the yard, and left there.

Mrs. Glassburn and myself started to go to College Hospital, when we met the doctor who spoke to my patient last night, and he went with us. His name is Hughes—is from Lexington, Ky. The walk was very pleasant. Met a general and his staff. The doctor thought it was General Polk—our bishop-general, as he is called. We called at a shed on the way; found it filled with wounded, lying on the floor; some men attending them. All were in the best of spirits. Mrs.G. promised to send them some of our good things. When we arrived at the hospital, we were charmed with the cleanliness and neatness visible on every side. The Sisters of Charity have charge of the domestic part, and, as usual with them, every thing is *parfait*. We were received very kindly by them. One was a friend of Mrs. G. She took us through the hospital. The grounds are very neatly laid out. Before the war it was a female college. I saw, as his mother requested, Mr. John Lyons, who is sick; he is a member of Ketchum's Battery. The wounded seem to be doing very well. One of the surgeons complained bitterly of the bad management of the railroad, and said that its managers should be punished, as they were the cause of a great deal of unnecessary suffering. They take their own time to transport the wounded, and it is impossible to depend upon them. That is the reason why we see so many sick men lying around the depot. Crossing the depot upon our return, we saw a whole Mississippi regiment sick, awaiting transportation. They looked very badly, and nearly all had a cough.

April 19.—Had quite a number of deaths up-stairs to-day. Jesse H. Faught, Walker County, Ala., and John M. Purdy, Morgan County, Tennessee, were of the number. The latter had his brother with him, who is much grieved because he can not inform his mother of the death of her son, as his home is in possession of the enemy. Another man, by the name of Benjamin Smith, from Memphis, Tenn., and a member of the Sixth Tennessee, Volunteers, died. When I went to see him, I found him in the last agonies of death. I was informed that he was a native of Canada. He was scarcely able to speak; when he did so, he asked me to write to his sister, Mrs. H. Hartman, Arovia, Canada West. I regretted that I did not see him sooner, and felt grieved to see him die so far away from home and kindred—I will not say among strangers—none are who are fighting with us in our sacred cause. May his soul rest in peace! He has lost his life in defense of liberty—that of which his own country is so proud—and when maidens come to deck the graves of our southern patriots, they will not forget one who sacrificed all for them. I have only written the names of those who I can recollect; many a poor fellow dies of whom I know nothing.

Mrs. Gilmore is leaving us. I am informed that she has done much for the soldiers, having been in hospitals from the commencement of the war. She returns to her home in Memphis. It is rumored that we are going to evacuate that city, and she wishes to see her family before the enemy reaches it.

I received a letter, and a box filled with eggs, crackers, and nice fresh butter, from Miss Lucy Haughton. She also sends a lot of pickles, which the men relish very much. I hope all the ladies in the Confederacy will be as kind; if they could only witness one-half the suffering that we do, I know they would be. I have sometimes felt like making a vow to eat nothing but what was necessary to sustain life till the war is over, so that our soldiers can have the more. When the men are first brought to the hospital, they eat all they can get, but in a few days their wounds begin to tell upon their systems; their appetites leave them, and it is almost impossible to get them to eat any thing. None but those who are the most severely wounded are left here; all are carried to the rear as soon as they are able to be moved.

A young man, by the name of Farmer, of the Sixth Kentucky Regiment, died down-stairs a day or two ago. He is reported to have been very rich. His brother-in-law, Rev. Mr. Cook, was with him, and intends taking his body to his own home in Tennessee, as the young man's home is in the hands of the enemy. I have made the acquaintance of two of his friends, Mr. Chinn and Lieutenant Minor, both from Kentucky. I feel sorry for all from the state, as it has behaved so badly, and for those who are in our army, as they have given up their all for the cause.

I was shocked at what the men have told me about some dead Federals that they saw on the battle-field. They say that on the bands of their hats was written, "Hell or

Corinth;" meaning, that they were determined to reach one of the places. Heaven help the poor wretches who could degrade themselves thus. I can not but pity them, and pray that God will turn the hearts of their living comrades. Can such a people expect to prosper? Are they really mad enough to think that they can conquer us—a people who shudder at such blasphemy; who, as a nation, have put our trust in the God of battles, and whose sense of the magnanimous would make us scorn to use such language?

I was much amused to-day at an answer that a Federal captain gave to one of our doctors. The doctor asked him how many men the Federals lost at the battle of Shiloh. He answered, not more than eight hundred. The doctor turned away from him without speaking. I laughed, and said that proved them greater cowards than ever; for if that was the case, why did they not take Corinth, as they had come there for that purpose. I do hope that we will let the Federals have the honor of telling all the untruths, and that we will hold to the truth, let the consequences be what they may—remembering that "where boasting ends true dignity begins." The captain is an intelligent man, and was an editor of a newspaper in Cincinnati. The rest of the officers who were in the room with him have left, except a lieutenant, who is sick.

April 22.—All the patients are being sent away on account of the prospects of a battle; at least, those who are able to be moved.

We have had a good deal of cold, wet weather lately. This is the cause of much sickness. Dr. Hereford, chief surgeon of Ruggle's brigade, has just informed me, that nearly our whole army is sick, and if it were not that the Federals are nearly as bad off as ourselves, they could annihilate us with ease. The doctor related an incident to me, which I think worthy of record. Before the battle of Shiloh, as the brigades and divisions were in battle array, with their banners flaunting in the breeze, Dr. H. discovered that General Ruggles's brigade had none. He rode up to him and asked him the reason; just at that moment a rainbow appeared; the general, pointing to it with his sword, exclaimed, "Behold my battle-flag!"

Every one is talking of the impending battle with the greatest indifference. It is strange how soon we become accustomed to all things; and I suppose it is well, as it will do no good to worry about it. Let us do our duty, and leave the rest to God.

It is reported that Fremont is about to reinforce the Federals; I am afraid that it will go hard with us.

April 23.—A young man whom I have been attending is going to have his arm cut off. Poor fellow! I am doing all that I can to cheer him. He says that he knows that he will die, as all who have had limbs amputated in this hospital have died. It is but too true; such is the case. It is said that the reason is that none but the very worst cases are left here, and they are too far gone to survive the shock which the operation gives the frame. The doctors seem to think that the enemy poisoned their balls, as the wounds inflame terribly; but I scarcely think that they are capable of so great an outrage. Our men do not seem to stand half so much as the northerners. Many of the doctors are quite despondent about it, and think that our men will not be able to endure the hardships of camp-life, and that we may have to succumb on account of it; but I trust that they are mistaken. None of the prisoners have yet died; this is a fact that can not be denied; but we have had very few of them in comparison with the number of our own men.

April 24.—Mr. Isaac Fuquet, the young man who had his arm cut off, died to-day. He lived only a few hours after the amputation. The operation was performed by Surgeon Chaupin of New Orleans, whose professional abilities are very highly commended. Dr. Hereford was well acquainted with Mr. F., and intends to inform his mother of his death.

It is reported that an engagement is going on at Monterey. A wounded man has just been brought in.

The amputating table for this ward is at the end of the hall, near the landing of the stairs. When an operation is to be performed, I keep as far away from it as possible. To-day, just as they had got through with Mr. Fuquet, I was compelled to pass the place, and the sight I there beheld made me shudder and sick at heart. A stream of blood ran from the table into a tub in which was the arm. It had been taken off at the socket, and the hand, which but a short time before grasped the musket and battled for the right, was hanging over the edge of the tub, a lifeless thing. I often wish I could become as callous as many seem to be, for there is no end to these horrors.

The passage to the kitchen leads directly past the amputating room below stairs, and many a time I have seen the blood running in streams from it.

There is a Mr. Pinkerton from Georgia shot through the head. A curtain is drawn across a corner where he is lying to hide the hideous spectacle, as his brains are oozing out.

April 25.—A rainy, gloomy day, and well accords with the news just heard. New Orleans is in the hands of the enemy. The particulars have not reached us, but I sincerely trust that it was not given up without a great struggle. What a severe trial this will be to the proud people of that place—to have their fair city desecrated by the tread of such a vandal foe. I trust that the day is not far distant when they will be compelled to leave much quicker than they came into it.

Quite a number of General Price's army came last night. They are from the states of Missouri, Arkansas, Texas, and Louisiana, and as brave and daring a set of men as the world has ever seen. I feel that we are now safe in Corinth, and that Fremont may bring as many of his abolition horde as he pleases; they will meet their match.

Troops are coming in from all quarters. A day or two since a regiment arrived, and camped in front of our windows. The men were nicely dressed, and displayed a flag, of which they appeared very proud. They attracted the attention of a number of ladies—and there was many a conjecture as to where they were from. To-day I learned that it was the Twenty-fourth Alabama Regiment, from Mobile. A number of the officers went to Virginia, as privates, in the Third Alabama.

I am getting along very well now. Miss Henderson from Mobile, and Mrs. Noland from Natchez, and myself are the only ladies attending the men up-stairs. There were two others, but Dr. Smith discovered that they had no business here, and sent them off. Mrs. N. and Miss H. are very devoted nurses. Miss H. is paying a great deal of attention to a young man by the name of Jones. He is badly wounded in the leg, and the doctors think that he will lose it. Mrs. N. has some patients very badly wounded, of whom she has taken as much care as if they were her own children. She has a son in another part of the army, and says that, if any thing happens to him, she knows that some good woman will do the same for him that she is now doing for others.

With a few exceptions, all the ladies are doing good service. It is said that there is always a black sheep in every flock: we have ours. We have been eating our meals lately in a small room opening into a large ward. This morning, while at breakfast, I was not a little astonished to hear a very pretty widow say that she had never enjoyed herself so much as she had since she had been here; that, when she left home, she was told that she must try to catch a beau—and she had succeeded. The doctors, I thought, looked amazed, that any woman, at such a time, and in such a place, should be guilty of such heartlessness. Enjoyed herself! when it was impossible to look one way or the other without seeing the most soul-harrowing scenes that it has ever been the lot of mortals to witness; and at that moment the groans of the suffering and dying were entering the room. I looked at the sentinels who were at the door; they, I thought, looked as shocked as we. I trust that such women are very rare.

April 26.—The day has cleared off beautifully. The news of the fall of New Orleans is confirmed. There was no fighting in the city. The forts were taken, and the gunboats came directly up, and threatened to shell it unless it was immediately surrendered. There were so many women and children in it that the authorities were compelled to surrender without striking a blow in its defense. Its loss is a severe one to us, as it commanded the passage of the Mississippi River, and the gunboats can ascend the river and capture any place they wish. I have been told that our forces destroyed all the sugar in the city at the time of the surrender. I do hope that this is true, as I had rather refrain from its use all my life than that the enemy should have it.

Three men have just had limbs amputated. This is so common that it is scarcely noticed. How my heart sickens in contemplating the horrors with which I am surrounded! Our sins must have been great to have deserved such punishment.

Sunday, April 27.—Mr. Johnson and my brother called on me this morning, and we took a walk round Corinth. The day is very beautiful. Nature is putting forth her glories, and smiling, as if in mockery of the passions which are raging in the heart of man, whom God has made a "little lower than the angels," and who would be so if sin did not deface him. Here are two immense armies, ready at any moment to rush upon each other, and deal death and destruction around them.

We visited one of the hospitals, in a church. Dr. Capers was the surgeon in charge; he is from Mississippi. He was very kind, and took us all through it, and showed us some of the most emaciated human beings that I ever beheld. He informed us that they were thus reduced by drinking poisoned whisky, a sad commentary on the maker and vendor. But what will man not do for the god, Mammon? Ruin his fellow-mortals, soul and body!

The hospital was in good order, and the patients looked cheerful. An Irish lady is in it. She is from Louisiana, and, from all I hear, has done much good in the service. She is a woman of strong nerve. She told me that, on the night following the battle of Shiloh, she visited the battle-field in search of her son, who she thought was killed or wounded, but he was neither.

As we have no chaplain, we have no service. I read the Bible and other books to the men, and they are much pleased to have me do it. I have met with none who have not respect for religion. They are mainly Baptists, Methodists, and Presbyterians, and some few Roman Catholics. A young man by the name of Love is here, badly wounded. He is from Texas, and informed me that he was one of nine brothers in the service. Three, I think, were killed in the battle of Manassas. He wishes that he were better, so that he could go into the army again.

April 29.—About one hundred sick men were brought in last night, on their way to another hospital. We gave them coffee, bread, and meat, with which they were much pleased. Some of them were too sick to eat this, so we gave these the few eggs we had.

General Sterling Price, with a part of his army, has arrived. He is in this hospital. We were all introduced to him. He gave us his left hand, as his right was disabled from a wound received at the battle of Elkhorn. I told him that I felt that we were safe in Corinth now, since he and his brave followers had arrived. He gave me a very dignified bow, and, I thought, looked at me as if he *thought* that I was talking a great deal of nonsense. He was not behind his sex in complimenting the ladies for the sacrifices they are making in doing their duty. I have heard so much of that lately, that I sometimes wonder if the southern women never did their duty before. I meant what I said to the general, and I felt quite proud of the honor I enjoyed in shaking hands with him whose name has become a household word with all admirers of true patriotism, and whose deeds of heroism in the West have endeared him to his followers, so that they look on him more as a father than any thing else.

In the afternoon he visited the patients. Many of them were men who had fought under him, and all were delighted to see him. One of them, Captain Dearing, was wounded at the battle of Shiloh. He was quarter-master in Blythe's Mississippi Regiment, and when the battle came off could not resist the temptation of engaging in it. He is badly wounded in two places, but is doing well. He is from Kentucky, but is a native of the Emerald Isle. I can not help contrasting these men with those born in the South, they seem to be able to endure physically so much more than the southeners. We have had quite a number of them, and I do not recollect that any have died.

April 30.—I saw General Price when he rode to camp. I think he is one of the finest looking men on horseback that I have ever seen. I have a picture of Lord Raglan in the same position, and I think that he and General P. are the image of each other. I showed the picture to some of the doctors, and they agreed with me. General P. is in bad health, but could not be induced to stay longer with us, as his abode is with his soldiers in the camp, where he shares their sorrows and joys. It is this that has so endeared him to them. Missouri may well be proud of her gallant son.

The hospital is nicely fixed up; every thing is as neat and clean as can be in this place.

Mrs. Glassburn has received a great many wines and other delicacies from the good people of Natchez. I believe they have sent every thing—furniture as well as edibles. We have dishes in which to feed the men, which is a great improvement. The food is much better cooked. We have negroes for cooks, a good baker, a nice dining-room, and eat like civilized people. If we only had milk for the patients, we might do very well.

There is a young man here taking care of his brother, who is shot through the jaw. The brother procures milk from one of the farm-houses near, and had it not been for this I believe the sick man would have died of starvation. We have a few more such, and they have to be fed like children. One young man, to whom one of the ladies devotes her whole time, has had his jaw-bone taken out. We have a quantity of arrow-root, and I was told that it was useless to prepare it, as the men would not touch it. I thought that I would try them, and now use gallons of it daily. I make it quite thin, and sometimes beat up a few eggs and stir in while hot; then season with preserves of any kind—those that are a little acid are the best—and let stand until it becomes cold. This makes a very pleasant and nourishing drink; it is good in quite a number of diseases; will ease a cough; and is especially beneficial in cases of pneumonia. With good wine, instead of the preserves, it is also excellent; I have not had one man to refuse it, but I do not tell them of what it is made.

Our army is being reinforced from all quarters. The cars are coming and going constantly, and the noise is deafening. It is a blessing that our men are not nervous, or the noise would kill them. We are strongly fortifying this place. I hope we will soon gain a victory; but our forces can not tempt the Yankees to fight.

We are told by Dr. Smith to do what is necessary for the prisoners, but talk as little as possible to them. The captain from Cincinnati is still here; a very sick lieutenant is in the same room. I believe he is one of the captain's officers. I have to attend him. A few mornings since, when I was visiting him, the captain stated that there was good news in the papers. (He is allowed to read all the southern papers.) I asked what it was. He answered that a proposition had been made for the exchange of prisoners; and that it came from our side. I remarked that all humane proposals came from our side; and that I did not think that his would be magnanimous enough to accept it. He said he hoped they would, so that he could see his home once more. I pray so too, as I know that our men who are prisoners have been enduring extreme hardship.

Every one is still down-hearted about New Orleans, as its fall has divided the Confederacy by opening the Upper Mississippi River to the enemy. All praise the spirited answer given by the mayor when ordered to surrender the city. He said that the citizens of New Orleans yielded to physical force alone, and that they still maintained their allegiance to the Confederate States; and upon refusal to pull down the state flag from the city hall, Commodore Farragut threatened to bombard the city. The mayor replied, the people of New Orleans would not degrade themselves by the humiliating act of lowering their own flag, and that there was no possible way for the women and children to leave; so he would have to do his worst. We can not but admire such spirited behavior; but it is nothing but what I expected from the proud Louisianians. Indeed, I had no idea that they would give up their much-prized city as easily as they did, but thought that it would have to be taken street by street. When all is known, I trust that the people will not be blamed. A number of Louisiana troops are here, who are much enraged about it. General Lovell, who was in command, is severely censured, but I trust he is not in fault.

We are still busy; wounded men are constantly brought in. To-day, two men had each a leg amputated. It is supposed that both will die.

General Van Dorn, with a number of his troops, has just arrived.

May 1.—A bright, beautiful day. I do not feel well. Every one is complaining; quite a number of the ladies and doctors are sick. Corinth is more unhealthy than ever. The cars have just come in, loaded outside and inside with troops. They are Price's and Van Dorn's men, and are from Texas, Arkansas, Louisiana, and Missouri. Poor fellows! they look as if they had seen plenty of hard service, which is true. They are heroes of Oakhill, Elkhorn, and other battles. I have been informed that in their marches through the West they have endured all kinds of hardships; going many days with nothing but parched corn to eat, and walking hundreds of miles, through frost and snow, without shoes. Those on the outside of the cars carried an old shattered flag, of which they seemed to be very proud. I was much astonished that the men who were at the depot did not give these war-worn veterans and their flag one cheer of welcome. I had hard work to keep from giving them one myself. I thought that the southern people were more demonstrative, and I remarked so to a gentleman who was standing near me. He replied that we had become so much accustomed to these things that we did not mind them.

The two men who had their limbs amputated yesterday died during the night. Decatur Benton, from Decatur County, Ala., died to-day. He was wounded at the battle of Shiloh. He had erysipelas upon his head and face, and had been out of his mind some time before his death. He was in his seventeenth year.

May 2.—Mr. Ogden, a member of Captain Ketchum's Battery, called on me this morning. He has been discharged from that company, and is going to Mobile to join the engineering department; the one in which he served while in the British army. From all I can learn, he has been a brave and good soldier.

In the afternoon, Mr. J—— called; he, Miss——, Dr. Herrick, and myself went to pay a visit to the Twenty-first Alabama Regiment. After spending some time in trying to discover its whereabouts, we learned that it was too far distant for us to go. We had a very pleasant ramble in the woods. I had no idea that the country around Corinth was so pretty—it being quite hilly. The woods were arrayed in their summer attire, and the "wind-whispers" through the forest had a soothing effect; like a sweet melody of other years.

"There is music in all things, if men had ears;
The earth is but an echo of the spheres."

The whole wore an air of serenity and peacefulness—a vivid contrast to the fury that is raging in the heart of our remorseless foe. Alas! how "man marks the earth with ruin," and curses "what heaven hath made so glorious."

A company of "dire artillery's clumsy car," not "tugged by sluggish oxen," but drawn by fine-looking horses, passed us. The scene was an impressive one. Nature looked so calm, as if in contrast with the terrible war-monsters before us. I could not look at them without thinking that, ere long, they might be belching forth their iron hail; dealing death and destruction; bringing woe to many a heart and household. General Polk and his staff passed; he looks every inch a soldier. I am told that he is much beloved in camp.

May 3.—A very warm day. I am obliged to stop writing some letters, as I hear heavy cannonading; the sound makes me quite nervous; this is the first time that I have ever heard firing in battle. I suppose my brother is in it.

Seven o'clock P. M., and a number of wounded have just been brought in. There was a skirmish at the intrenchments. My brother is not hurt, or I should have known it by this time.

Sunday morning, May 4.—I have just seen Generals Price and Van Dorn review their troops. They were at too great a distance to distinguish the different regiments; but the sight was quite imposing, as column after column marched along, with their flags flying in the breeze. But little glitter was worn on the dress of the men; they did not need it; we all knew that they carried with them hearts that all the power of the foe could neither bend nor break, and without which all glitter and gold are mere dross. The cavalry appeared splendid; no knights of olden time rode their horses with loftier mien than did these warriors. I enjoyed the scene until the ambulances passed in review, with their white flags, denoting their use. This cast a blight over the whole.

Evening.—Our troops are returning. They offered battle to the foe, but, as usual, it was not accepted. They never will fight when there is any thing like an equal force to oppose them.

It has turned cold and rainy. We have just been looking at some of our troops, who are camping on a hill within sight of the hospital. They have no tents or shelter of any kind, and look very deplorable. It makes us miserable to look at them; but we can not aid them in any way.

I have spent the day talking and reading to the men; they like to hear us read to them, but they do not seem to care much for reading themselves. Mr. McLean of Mo-

bile has given me a number of copies of the Illustrated London News, with a full account of the Crimean war. I thought if any thing would interest them these would; but
they look at the pictures, and throw them down as unworthy of notice. They seem to
have no ambition to know any thing outside of their own country. I regret this, as we
are all creatures of imitation, and if we do not know how others have suffered and
fought for freedom, we will not know how to imitate them. I believe with Longfellow,

> "Lives of great men all remind us
> We can make our lives sublime."

May 5.—Mrs. Ogden is here with four Mobile ladies; the others have returned to
their homes. The ladies who are with her are Mrs. May, Miss Wolf, Miss Murphy, and
Mrs. Millward. They are on their way to Rienzi to attend the patients. I am glad that
they are going, as they will be the means of doing much good.

We have a boy here, named Sloan, from Texas, and a member of the Texas
Rangers. He is only thirteen years of age, and lost a leg in a skirmish. He is as happy
as if nothing was the matter, and he was at home playing with his brothers and sisters. His father is with him, and is quite proud that his young son has distinguished
himself to such a degree, and is very grateful to the ladies for the kind attention which
they bestow upon him.

A few days ago a number of wounded men were brought in. In going round, as
usual, to see if I knew any one, I saw a man who seemed to have suffered a great deal.
His eyes were closed, and while I was looking at him he opened them, and said, with
a feeble voice, "Is not this a cruel war." I requested him to keep quiet. As I left him, a
gentleman approached me and remarked, "I see that you have been talking to my
friend. He is going to die, and we can ill spare such men. He is one of the bravest and
best men in the army." He informed me that his name was Smith, and at the time of
the fight was acting quartermaster of the Twenty-fifth Tennessee Regiment, and that
he was also a Methodist minister. After I had given him a cup of tea, I asked one of
the surgeons what he thought of his condition. He replied that I could do what I
pleased for him, as he could not possibly live more than twenty-four hours. After he
was shot, he carried a wounded man off the battlefield. He himself was then placed
on horseback. The horse, being wild, threw him. He was then placed in a wagon, and
carried some four or five miles, over an extremely rough road. From all this he lost
much blood. Notwithstanding the opinion of the surgeons, he is improving.

I have just received a box of "good things" for the patients from the kind people
of Mobile. My friend, Mr. McLean, has sent his share. I am so grateful for them. If they
only knew or could realize one half the suffering that we daily witness, they would do
more.

Poor Mr. Jones, the young lad whom Miss Henderson is attending, has had a leg
amputated to-day. He conversed very calmly about it before it was done, and seemed
to think that he would not survive the operation. He has told Miss H. all about his people, and what she must tell them if he should die. She has nursed him as carefully as if
she had been his own sister. He loved to have some of us read the Bible to him.

We have no chaplain to attend the sick and dying men; they often ask for one. I
have thought much of this, and wonder why chaplains are not appointed for the hospitals. I think that if there is one place more than another where they should be, it is
one like this; not for the dying alone, but for the moral influence it would exert upon

the living. We profess to be a Christian people, and should see that all the benefits of Christianity are administered to our dying soldiers.

May 6.—Mr. Jones is dead; he was eighteen years of age. He died the death of a Christian; was a brave solider; true to his God and country. Miss H. sat up all night with him. She is endeavoring to procure a coffin for him. We have none now in which to bury the dead, as the Federals have destroyed the factory at which they were made. At one time, I thought that it was dreadful to have the dead buried without them; but there is so much suffering among the living, that I pay little heed to those things now. It matters little what becomes of the clay after the spirit has left it. Men who die as ours do, need "no useless coffin," to enshrine them.

"There honor comes, a pilgrim gray,
To bless the turf that wraps their clay."

May 7.—A beautiful day. The troops are marching in the direction of Rienzi; it is supposed that the enemy are trying to flank our army, but I do not fear while we have such vigilant generals as Beauregard and Bragg to watch them.

I had a slight quarrel with our ward-master. One of the men, lately wounded, was in a room where were some who had occupied it since the battle of Shiloh. One of them—a mere boy—was wasted to a skeleton; his back was covered with bed-sores. Poor child! he was very fretful. I observed that it annoyed the new patient, and requested Dr. Allen, who is very kind to the soldiers, to allow me to have him removed to a room by himself. He kindly gave his consent. While doing it, the ward-master objected; but as I had obtained leave, I had him removed, and he commenced to improve immediately.

I have been through the ward to see if the men are in want of any thing; but all are sound asleep under the influence of morphine. Much of that is administered; more than for their good, and must injure them. I expressed this opinion to one of the doctors; he smiled, and said it was not as bad as to let them suffer.

The moon is shining brightly; the view from my window is really beautiful. A band of music is playing in the distance, which carries my mind back to more peaceful days, and I fervently send up a prayer to Him who sitteth in the heavens, to turn the hearts of our enemies, so they may let us go in peace. I think how many of our brave men, who are now quietly resting, by to-morrow's setting sun may be sleeping their last sleep; and I think of the lonely sentinel, walking his weary rounds, his thoughts on his home and loved ones, and pray that God may lift his thoughts from this weary world, to that paradise on high, where I trust some day will be his home. O, God, be with them all, so that, whether living or dying, they may be thine!

May 8.—A number of men, wounded in a skirmish, have been brought in to-day. The surgeons dressed their wounds; there is always plenty for us to do without that. We wash their hands and faces, which is a great treat to them, as they are covered with dust; we bathe their wounds, which are always inflamed, and give them something refreshing to drink.

O, I do feel so glad that I am here, where I can be of some little service to the poor fellows; and they are so grateful for every little attention paid them.

We get up before sunrise in the morning; take a cup of coffee, as the doctors inform us that unless we do so we will be sick. We then give the men their "toddy;" wash their faces and hands, and then furnish them their breakfast.

May 9.—A great many wounded men, both Federal and Confederate, were brought in to-day. About twenty-five of ours were shot through mistake. A fine-looking Federal captain is wounded in three or four places. His head and face are tied up, and he can not speak. He has a Bible, on the back of which is printed the Union flag. Some of us were looking at it; one of the ladies remarked that it was still sacred in her eyes. This astonished me, after the suffering which we had seen it the innocent cause of. I said that it was the most hateful thing which I could look at; as every stripe in it recalled to my mind the gashes that I had witnessed upon our men. I have conversed with a number of the prisoners; they all express the same opinion as the others, that they dislike Lincoln and the abolitionists as much as we do, but they are fighting for the Union. What a delusion!

I am no politician. I must own to ignorance in regard to federal or state rights; but I think I have a faint idea of the meaning of the word "union." According to Webster and other authorities, it is concord, agreement, and conjunction of mind. We all know how little of that and happiness exists in a forced union of man and wife, where there is neither love nor congeniality of feeling. Can these men really think it when they say it? Are they so blind as to think, even if they succeed, that it can ever bring happiness to them or us? Is it not exactly the same as the case of the marriage state? They must strike out the word union, and have in its stead monarchy or anarchy; one of these, perhaps, would be better. Why, the Czar of Russia lays no higher claim to the right to rule his empire than do these men the right to govern us. Again, supposing they do succeed in subjugating us, have they forgotten that such a thing is not on record, where the Anglo-Saxon race has ever been held in bondage? Why, it would be as much to their disgrace as ours. Are we not the same race? Let them ask themselves what they would do were the case reversed; were we the aggressors, and demanded of them what they now demand of us. I think we all know their answer. It would be that given by the immortal Washington to the haughty monarch of England, when he attempted to make slaves of men who had determined to be free. Grant that we had no lawful right to secede; that I know nothing about, and never was more grieved than when I knew that we had done so; not from any wrong or unlawfulness, but from the fact that, united, we were stronger than we would be when separated; and I also feared the bloodshed which might ensue. If we were sinners in that respect, what were our forefathers when they claimed the right to secede from the British crown? Calling it fighting for the Union, is about as false as the love of the abolitionist for the negro, and we all know what that is. No happiness can exist in union without concord; and there can be no concord where any two people are so diametrically opposed to each other. All this I have repeated to them often, but I might as well have saved myself the trouble, for they are as blind to reason as any bigoted, self-deluded people ever were.

I was introduced to General Hindman, who dined with us to-day. He is still lame from a wound received at the battle of Shiloh. He is a peculiar-looking man; his hair is light and long, floating around his shoulders. I always imagine, when I see a man with his hair so long, that there is a vacancy in his cranium. I believe that it is Shakspeare who says that what a man lacked in brains he had in his hair. As the former is an article that we have much use for, and whose workings are much needed at present among our leading men, I can not but regret that outward indications in this instance were unfavorable. But perhaps this is only my prejudice against foppishness and every thing effeminate in men. General H. may be an exception to this rule, and I trust he is.

May 10.—The hospital is again filled with the badly wounded. There is scarcely an hour during which they are not coming in from skirmishes. I sat up all night to see that the nurses performed their duties properly, and assisted in bathing the wounds of the men. They all rested quite well, excepting one, who was severely wounded in the hand. He suffered a great deal. One died suddenly this morning. I gave him his toddy; he was then quite cheerful; and I went to give him his breakfast, but his bunk was empty—he was dead and gone. He was wounded in the arm. The doctor desired him to have it amputated, which he would on no account permit. The result was hemorrhage ensued, and he bled to death before assistance could be rendered. I did not learn his name, nor any thing about him.

These things are very sad. A few evenings since, Dr. Allen was conversing about the horrors with which we are surrounded. He remarked that it was hard to think that God was just in permitting them. "Shall we receive good at the hands of God, and shall we not receive evil?" We, as a nation, have been so prosperous, that we forget that it was from him that we derived our benefits. He often sends us sorrows to try our faith. He will not send us more than we are able to bear. How patiently the soldiers endure their trials! Who dare say that strength is not given them from on high? Let us do our part, and, whatever happens, not lose trust in him, "for he doeth all things well;" and, in the language of Bishop Wilmer, "May the trials through which we are passing serve to wean us from the world, and move us to set our affections on things above!" "May we bear the rod, and him who hath appointed it!" Dr. A. was some time with General Floyd, in Western Virginia, and remarked that he had seen nothing here to compare with what the men endured there. They were in the mountains, where it was impossible to get any thing for them.

We gained quite a victory yesterday. Price's and Van Dorn's troops were engaged. We saw them as they marched out in the morning. They crossed a bridge opposite our bed-room window.

Sunday, May 11.—A very hot, sultry day. I am very tired, as I have all to attend, the other ladies being sick; many of the nurses are sick also. It is more unhealthy now than ever, and unless some change takes place I fear that we will all die.

As there is much noise and confusion constantly here, it is almost impossible to collect one's thoughts. I miss the calm of the holy Sabbath more than any thing. I have read and talked to the men, and it astonishes me to see how few are members of the Church. They all seem to think and know that it is their duty to belong to it, but still they remain out of it. How much more will they have to answer for than those who have never known God, and have not enjoyed the privileges of the gospel. "He that confesseth me before men, him will I confess before my Father which is in heaven."

May 12.—Two men died this morning, Mr. Adams and Mr. Brennan, from Coffee County, Alabama. Mr. B. was wounded. As a friend, Mr. A. came to nurse him. Both were taken sick this morning, and died after a few hours' illness.

We have the same sad scenes to witness as ever—sick and wounded men lying on the platform at the depot, night and day, and we are not allowed to take them any thing to eat. Dr. Smith is obliged to prohibit it, as it is contrary to orders, and he has not the food to spare for them.

A terrible circumstance happened a few nights since. Our druggist, Dr. Sizemore, went out about 9 o'clock to see some one. When within a short distance from the hospital he heard groans; went to the place from which they proceeded, and found a box-car, that had been switched off the track, filled with wounded men, some dead and others dying, and not a soul with them to do any thing for them. The conductor was censured, but I think whoever sent the men off are in fault for not sending proper persons to take care of them. If this kind of treatment of our brave men continues much longer, I fear that we will have none to fight for us, for such a total disregard of human life must have a demoralizing effect. If we had many more such kind-hearted officers as Dr. Smith, our men would suffer little through neglect. None leave this hospital without he is certain they can go comfortably, and have plenty of nourishment to last them on their journey. I have seen him, many a time, go to the cars himself, to see that they were properly put in. I am informed that he spends every cent of his pay for their comfort. He will reap his reward.

May 13.—Our troops have gone out this morning to endeavor to tempt the enemy to fight, but they will not leave their intrenchments. It is reported that they have been heavily reinforced, but, with all that, I have no doubt that if they would only fight our men would whip them.

We have a member of the Twenty-first Alabama Regiment from Mobile, who was badly wounded at the battle of Shiloh. There is no hope of his recovery. Every thing has been done for him that it is possible to do. He is a sad spectacle; he is so worn and wasted. He is a German, and can not understand any thing said to him by us. He has no relatives in this country.

Conversing with one of the patients, a very intelligent gentleman, I asked him what he thought of President Davis. He thought that he was a good man, but not the one for the place. I did not ask him his reason for this opinion. He is the first man that I have heard say this, and I hope that he is mistaken, as at this time the country needs a great man at its head.

May 15.—Heavy firing was heard to-day, and I felt certain that a battle had commenced. I was in the kitchen when I first heard it, and was compelled to stop what I was doing, as the sound makes me unfit for any thing.

May 16.—The fast-day set apart by the President. I hope that it will be duly observed. I believe that it is well kept in the army. There has been no show of keeping it in this hospital; the old excuse is given—"too much to do."

A few evenings since we came very near being burned out. While the ladies downstairs were making pads for the wounded expected next day—we use hundreds of them daily—the cotton took fire and communicated to some of the ladies' dresses. A gentleman extinguished it before any serious damage occurred. I was attending some patients at the time, and was certain from the noise that the enemy had come to storm the hospital, for which I was laughed at considerably.

Dr. Griffin of Kentucky and Dr. Benedick of New Orleans are both sick.

Sunday, May 18.—A very hot day. Our patients are nearly all gone. Captain Dearing left to-day. He is in a fair way to recover. He was one of the worst of the wounded. Three of the ladies are very sick. Miss Marks is not expected to live. She has made up her mind to that effect, and is perfectly resigned. She is a member of the Episcopal Church.

May 19.—A gloom seems to hang over every body, as if something dreadful was going to happen. No news of a battle yet. It would not surprise me if none took place here. We will be compelled to leave soon, as this place is becoming daily more sickly.

Mr. Smith has just left for one of the hospitals below. He is rapidly improving. So much for the opinions of doctors! but the best of us may be mistaken sometimes.

May 21.—News has just reached us that the battle has commenced in earnest. A number of our surgeons have been ordered to the battle-field. May God give us the victory! I feel confident that if we could gain one here the war would soon be over, and that we would be recognized by foreign nations. I can not see why they do not now recognize us. We certainly can and will be free. My only wish for them to do so is to stop bloodshed, as I think, if they would do it, the North would be compelled to let us alone.

I have just been informed that the Yankee gunboats have passed Fort Morgan. I hope, if true, that Mobile will be laid in ashes before the foot of the vandal foe is permitted to desecrate it. They have not the same excuse that the people of New Orleans had—a large population of women and children; and then we have an outlet which they did not have.

Miss Marks is still very low. I feel very sorry to see her die in this terrible place; but it matters little where we die, so that we are prepared.

May 22.—No battle occurred yesterday. Every one is confident that if the enemy would only fight, we would *whip them soundly*. They are digging intrenchments closer and closer, and could shell Corinth at any hour. Some are not more than two and a half miles from us. We are beginning to feel a little nervous at the prospect of a shell waking us up some morning; certainly not a pleasant one to contemplate.

A prisoner is here, who eats at the table with us. He is a Presbyterian minister. He makes some very provoking remarks. Dr. Smith has advised us to take no notice of them, and say as little as possible. This appears hard, as nearly every one at the table has suffered some wrong at the hands of him and his people; nearly all their homes are in the hands of the enemy.

Dr. Sizemore has just received word of a young brother who has died in a northern prison, and of the ill treatment of the chaplain of his regiment, an inoffensive old man of more than seventy years, who had gone with the regiment more as a father than any thing else. This old man was imprisoned as if he were a common felon. Dr. S., knowing all this, has to endure the presence of this man, and see him treated as if he were one of our best friends. I must say that we are carrying out the commands of our blessed Savior; and how proud I am of it! May we be enabled to do the same to the end; and, above all things, not to retaliate upon the innocent, for God has said, "Vengeance is mine, and I will repay." I was seated next to the prisoner to-day. He says that he is an Englishman. I would like to think that he is telling an untruth, as few Englishmen side with tyranny. But I expect that he has been long enough with the Yankees to imbibe some of their barbarous notions. He expressed the opinion that the southern people were not united. I remarked that if he would go through the state of Mississippi alone, he would change his mind, as I believed that if the men did not fight, the women would. But there will be no need of the latter, as the men will not fail to do their duty.

We requested Dr. Smith to permit us to pay him back for the impertinent remarks he had made to us. He granted permission, and stated that he would reprimand us in his presence. As soon as the foe made his appearance, some of the ladies commenced on him. Dr. S. said, "The ladies are very hard on you." He replied with a very submissive air, "If it pleases them, I have no objection." Mrs. Glassburn, who was at the head of the table, observed, "It does not please us; but I will tell you what will: when we know that every Yankee is laid low in the ground, then we will be pleased indeed." He made no reply, and must have felt the force of the remark. At any other time it would have been a barbarous one; but at the present it was charitable, and one that we all felt, if realized, would not only be a blessing to us, but to humanity.

May 23.—Have had two very nice men here, wounded—a doctor and a captain. They are friends of Mrs. G. Dr. Smith sent them to Rienzi, where the Mobile ladies are. Mrs. G. visited them, and came back perfectly delighted with the hospital arrangements there. She says that Mrs. Ogden is an excellent manager. I am glad of this, as she has had a great deal of opposition from surgeons, as all of the ladies have who have desired to go into hospitals. I can not see what else we can do, as the war is certainly ours as well as that of the men. We can not fight, so must take care of those who do.

I think as soon as surgeons discover that ladies are really of service, that prejudice will cease to exist. The patients are delighted to have us, and say that we can cause them to think of the dearest of places to them now—home.

Miss Marks is a little better, and has been sent to Okolona. The other two ladies who were sick have returned to Mobile.

Every corner of the hospital is clean, and ready for patients. The last of my patients died this morning. He was a German, named Ernest; was wounded at Shiloh. He wandered a good deal in his mind; but just before he died he sent for Dr. Smith, and requested him to write to his wife, and send her all the money he had. She lived on Magazine Street, New Orleans.

One of the saddest sights witnessed are two Federals, who have been here since the battle of Shiloh. One has had his arm, the other his leg amputated. They are seventeen and eighteen years of age, respectively. They look very pitiful, dying among strangers, far away from their homes and relatives. They have been cared for the same as our own; but that is not all that is wanted. They need sympathy, and of that character which it is impossible for us to extend to them, as they came here with the full intention of taking all that is dear to us. They may have been conscientious, and thought that they were doing their duty, but we are of a different opinion, and it will be some time before we change. They will soon die; both are religious. I never look at them without thinking of the thousands of our poor men who are in the same condition in the North. I do sincerely trust that they are as well treated as these poor fellows have been.

Dr. Nott, with several other surgeons, has examined the hospital. He looked well. He has lost a son in the war.

Sunday, May 25.—A bright, beautiful day, but very cold. We have been compelled to have fires in our rooms. Last evening I saw the ubiquitous chieftain, John H. Morgan. He is colonel of a Kentucky regiment, and one of the bravest and most daring of men. It was late when I saw him; so could not judge of his appearance. He had a crowd of admirers following him; he is fairly worshiped. Dr. Smith has just been telling us that he would not be surprised if we had to leave Corinth at a moment's notice, as there is danger of being shelled at any time. For some days back, stores have been moved to the rear in large quantities, which he thinks indicates an evacuation, or important move of some kind.

May 26.—This morning I visited Mrs. Williamson and Mrs. Crocker, who came from Mobile with us. They are in a hospital at the Corinth House. I saw a Mrs. Newsom. I do not recollect that I was ever more struck with a face at first sight than hers. It expressed more purity and goodness than I had ever seen before, and reminded me of a description of one I had seen in a poem. It was

"A face whose every feature telleth
  How light they feel this earthly clod;
A face whose holy beauty showeth
  Their walk is ever close with God."

As I looked upon her, I felt that the verse connected would not be misapplied to her heart:

"A heart that is a casket holy,
  With brightest jewels garnered there;
Gems that sorrow's hand hath polished;
  Richer gems than princes wear."

I asked Mrs. W. who she was. She informed me that she was a rich widow from Arkansas, and had surrendered all the comforts of home to do what she could for the suffering of our army. She had been with it from the commencement of the war, and had spent a great deal of money. Mrs. W. also informed me that her face did not belie the goodness and purity of her heart; and that she was a Christian in the truest sense of the word. I hope that we have many such among us. I can not imagine why it is that I have heard so little about her. Is it because goodness and beauty are so common that Mrs. N. is not worth talking about, or is it that we do not properly appreciate what is good and lovely? As soon as Miss Nightingale went to the Crimean war, the whole world resounded with her praises; and here I have been nearly two months, and have scarcely heard Mrs. N.'s name mentioned.

May 27.—We are all packed up, and intend leaving this morning. Mrs. Glassburn and nearly all the ladies are going to Brookhaven. I intend going to Okolona, and there remain until I learn in which direction the army will move.

We have seen many sad sights and much suffering since we came to this place; still, I shall ever look back on these two months with sincere gratification, and feel that I have lived for something.

The surgeons, one and all, have proved themselves kind and attentive to the brave men whom they have had under their care. The hospital is in perfect order, ready for the reception of patients. I visited Corinth Hospital this morning; they were not thinking of leaving, and had quite a number of wounded men. There I met Mrs. Palmer of Mobile, who had a son in the Twenty-first Alabama Regiment. She had visited the camp the day before with refreshments for the soldiers. She informed me that there were numbers of sick yet in camp, and if we left, she could not conceive how they could be moved.

Mary Boykin Chesnut

(1823–1886)

Mary Boykin Chesnut was the daughter of Stephen Decatur Miller, who had served as a U.S. congressman and senator and who was elected governor of South Carolina when she was three years old. Educated in an exclusive Charleston finishing school, she began reading extensively at a very young age; many who met her assumed she had been tutored in Europe. When she was seventeen, she married James Chesnut, Jr., himself a prosperous planter and also an heir to a South Carolina fortune. Her husband, quickly ascending the political ladder, was elected to the U.S. Senate in 1858. In Washington, the Chesnuts became acquainted with a number of Southern politicians, most notably Jefferson Davis and his wife, Varina, with whom they would become close friends.

After the election of Abraham Lincoln, James Chesnut helped draft South Carolina's ordinance of secession and was elected to the Confederate Congress. As a result, Mary Chesnut found herself in Montgomery, Alabama, for the formation of the Confederacy, in Charleston, South Carolina, for the bombardment of Fort Sumter, and in Richmond, Virginia, at the war's height. Through all of these experiences, she recorded her own thoughts and reactions in a series of diaries. There she revealed her vehement opposition to slavery, as well as a strong feminist sensibility. Her diaries are a candid record of the times, providing observation from an insider's point of view. Though she did extensively revise them in the years before her death, she never published her diaries, which first appeared in 1905 as *A Diary from Dixie*, and later in a more complete and better edited edition as *Mary Chesnut's Civil War.*

from *The Private Mary Chesnut:*

The Unpublished Civil War Diaries

[*March 18, 1861*]

Yesterday on the cars we had a mad woman raving at being separated from her daughter. It excited me so, I quickly took opium, & *that* I kept up. It enables me to retain every particle of mind or sense or brains I ever have, & so quiets my nerves that I can calmly reason & take rational views of things otherwise maddening. Then a *drunken* preacher began to console a "bereaved widow." He quoted more fluently scripture than I ever have heard it—the beast! My book (*after* the opiate) I read diligently. He misses in attempting to describe Yankee character after an elaborate trial, & his women are detestable failures. Still it made the time *glide* rapidly for me. Here I am for Sunday & have refused to accept overtures for peace & forgiveness. After my stormy youth, I did so hope for peace & tranquil domestic happiness. There is none for me in this world. "The peace this world cannot give, which passeth all understanding."

Today the papers say peace again. Yesterday the *Telegraph* & the *Herald* were warlike to a frightful degree. I have just read that Pugh is coming down South—another woman who loved me, & I treated her so badly at first. I have written to Kate that I will go to her if she wants me—dear, dear sister. I wonder if other women shed as bitter tears as I. They *scald* my cheeks & blister my heart. Yet Edward Boykin "wondered & marvelled at my elasticity. Was I always so bright & happy, did ever woman possess such a disposition, life was one continued festival," &c, &c, & Bonham last winter *shortly* said, "it was a *bore* to see any one always in a good humour." *[Following sentence written over unrecoverable erasure:]* Much they know of me—or my power to hide trouble.

> This is full of strange vicissitudes, & in nothing more remarkably than the way people are reconciled, ignore the past, & start afresh in life, to incur more disagreements, & set to bickering again.
>
> *One of Them.*

This long dreary Sunday in Augusta. If I can, I will try to forget it forever.

Mr. Wright traveled with us. I found him quite pleasant. He is a *preacher* & a politician, & he was travelling Sunday, too. Last night at Atlanta I did not leave the cars. The Hotel, it seems, is kept by a Dr. Thompson who married an old school friend of mine, Elizabeth Briggs, & he came down & seemed offended that I did not go up to his house. I was amused. Said Elizabeth was his *present* wife. Whether he had had several before or meant to have several afterwards, I do not know.

I am afraid Mr. C will not please the democracy. He said aloud in the cars he wished we could have separate coaches like the English & get away from those whiskey drinking, tobacca chewing rascals & *rabble.* I was scared somebody might have taken it up, & now every body is armed. The night before we left Montgomery, a man was shot in the street for a trifle, & Mr. Browne expressed his English horror, but was answered—it was only a cropping out of the right temper! The Lord have mercy on our devoted land.

Mrs. Mary Anne Taylor continued her good offices to the last. Sent me a tray of good things to travel on.

I wonder if it be a sin to think slavery a curse to any land. Sumner said not one word of this hated institution which is not true. Men & women are punished when their masters & mistresses are brutes & not when they do wrong—& then we live surrounded by prostitutes. An abandoned woman is sent out of any decent house elsewhere. Who thinks any worse of a Negro or Mulatto woman for being a thing we can't name. God forgive *us,* but ours is a *monstrous* system & wrong & iniquity. Perhaps the rest of the world is as bad. This *only* I see: like the patriarchs of old our men live all in one house with their wives & their concubines, & the Mulattoes one sees in every family exactly resemble the white children—& every lady tells you who is the father of all the Mulatto children in every body's household, but those in her own, she seems to think drop from the clouds or pretends so to think——Good women we have, *but* they talk of all *nastiness*—tho they never do wrong, they talk day & night of *six unrecoverable words, apparently a quote.* My disgust sometimes is boiling over— but they are, I believe, in conduct the purest women God ever made. Thank God for my country women—alas for the men! No worse than men every where, but the lower their mistresses, the more degraded they must be.

My mother in law told me when I was first married not to send my female servants in the street on errands. They were there tempted, led astray—& then she said placidly, "So they told *me* when I came here—& I was very particular, *but you see with what* result." Mr. Harris said it was so patriarchal. So it is—flocks & herds & slaves—& wife Leah does not suffice. Rachel must be *added,* if not *married.* & all the time they seem to think themselves patterns—models of husbands & fathers.

Mrs. Davis told me "every body described my husband's father as an odd character—a Millionaire who did nothing for his son whatever, left him to struggle with poverty," &c. I replied, "Mr. Chesnut Senior thinks himself the best of fathers—& his son thinks likewise. I have nothing to say—but it is true, he has no money but what he makes as a lawyer," &c. Again I say, my countrywomen are as pure as angels—tho surrounded by another race who are—the social evil!

[March 19, 1861]

Arrived at home, found the carriage waiting for us. All hands glad to see us.

Slept & bathed & eat & talked. Heard Kate was better & hope to be spared the journey to Florida. Hope renewed that the Fort may be given up.

19th Really ill with backache & neuralgia of the face. Breakfasted in my room— pure white house linen, cream in coffee, & good coffee, *luxuries* when one comes out of a *den* of abominations such as we have lived in at Montgomery Hall. Make a list of the people I owe calls to in Montgomery.

The snow a foot deep now after a winter like May & June. What a climate.

[*April 13, 1861*]

A lull after a storm. Last night we were jubilant. "No one hurt." No battery even injured—& Anderson has two guns spoiled & his fort injured. To day—the enemy's fort has been repeatedly on fire. Still his guns fire regularly. Still vessels are off the bar—& war is at our doors—but 'tho' we hear the firing we feel so differently—because we feel that our merciful God has so far protected our men—& we pray with faith.

I am miserably ill but run occasionally to Mrs. Wigfall's room & Mrs. Green's.

Mr. Manning seems quite delighted to have found out experimentally that he can be cool under fire. My husband got a good night's rest—poor fellow, he may have to rush off to Montgomery. Jeff Davis has called his Congress together. Alex Taylor & his company are here. What a nation of soldiers we are.

Mr. Chesnut ordered the first gun fired. Saw Wm. Gilmore Simms & did not recognise him in his white beard. Trescot is here with his glasses on the top of the house. *Rumour* that the enemy's ships are firing. Mrs. Green rushes in & out.

[*April 15, 1861*]

Saturday last was a great day. I saw my husband carried by a mob to tell Gen. Beauregard the news that Fort Sumter had surrendered—he followed Louis Wigfall to Fort Sumter after a few minutes' interval, then returned with the news of the surrender & carried fire Engines to Fort Sumter. Our men cheered madly when Anderson continued his firing after he was blazing with houses on fire. Mrs. Cheves McCord & I dined together in the evening. Mrs. Joe Heyward, Mrs. Preston, Mrs. Wigfall & [I] drove on the battery in an open carriage. So gay it was—crowded & the tents & cannons.

Sunday went to Church with Mr. Wm. Bull Pringle & Mr. Appleton of Boston. Mrs. P said I had my mother's eyes. Saw hosts of people. Walked on the battery with Mrs. Joe Heyward. Last night Jack Hamilton called [*one illegible word*] a hero. & Edward Boykin who seemed rather annoyed that I would not give him my undivided attention. That I will never do more to anyone if it is ever lamentable be. Spent the evening gaily with Mrs. Joe Heyward, Mrs. Wigfall, Mrs. Frank Hampton & Hanckel, Dr. Gibbes, &c, &c.

To day talked with Gov. Means. Mrs. Robinson & I called at Quinby's & drove on the battery. John C & Laurence are here. I am now to drive with Sally Rutledge. Had another false alarm & rushed upon the house top.

[*July 9, 1861*]

Battle Summer. The devoted Brewster came back to us—had ever forlorn women such a friend—& he is so *clever* too. Brought a Richmond paper. Terrific threats. Every thing to be confiscated, *our* cotton sold, by our task masters, to England, through our ports! I would fire it myself first—if I hung afterwards for it.

Written home for them to work for our sick soldiers. Wrote to Mr. C to let him know Brewster is with us & so satisfy him as to our safety. Thirty miles from Washington is too near. I will be glad when we leave this, calm & peaceful as it is.

One of our women we call Miss Albina McLush. She is so soft & vapid. They are all so soft & slow & affected—& *wonder* to find us so *fair*. Thought before that *below* N.C. we were as brown as berries.

Miss Hetty Cary had her hands tied behind her in Baltimore & *insults* offered to her person, pretending, the monsters, that they were searching for flags arms. Read a stupid book, *Will He Find Her.* We are all so miserable at Joe Johnston's retreat.

Brewster says *bitter* are the *curses* heaped upon the War department for his want of *men,* arms & ammunition. Oh this fearful red tape.

Brewster says they will not have *Van Dorn* because *he would* fight.

[*July 10, 1861*]

White Sulphur. Yesterday was one of my gloomy days. I felt they *might* over run us. I do not feel so to day. Thank God for a stout heart. It is the darkest hour before day light. I see the Texians have offered their command to Wigfall. I think he will take it. Not a word from my Mother since I saw her in May. Gave Mrs. Ould Mr. Chesnut's carte de visite. Mrs. Preston, Brewster, & Mary Boykin have gone to Warrenton for the *news.* I found Mary transcribing some frantically love sick *farewell* to a lover—so I suppose she still thinks of Edward Cantey. She is so obedient—so kind—so attentive & *withal* so much more sense than I expected that I begin to love her dearly. Oh my country—if I could forget you one moment. What is to become of us all.

> The good die Young.
> But those whose hearts are dry as summer's dust
> Burn to the socket.
>
> Wordsworth

Mrs. Preston says a negro nurse told her once the way to keep young was never to take any more into her heart than she could kick off at the end of her toes.

May, Mrs. P, & Brewster returned. No news—not even a rumour or a report.

Read to day *The Rectory of Moreland—goody* book. Thinks keeping a journal *bad,* morbid, selfish. I do not feel it hurts me. Wrote a long letter to Murray Lang—& must write at once to the Convent in Georgetown.

[*July 11, 1861*]

Yesterday we had no mail—but heard cannon. I read *Rectory of Moreland,* slowly & sadly. Last night a horrible old woman with a wig & *tiara* & red fricked fat arms & black bracelets began telling me how badly Mrs. Davis' ladies dressed in Richmond, in *flats* & gaudy colours. Mrs. Preston got into a *girlish* giggle. There were a bride & groom—the latter a widower, the first sixteen—who played *flute* & piano. The red headed spy rushed in excited & happy that seven hundred were ill in the hospital at Culpepper, that two were dead & thus already speechless, & that Beauregard had sent a flag of *truce* to Washington. Not a word of *truth*—the *fiend.* All night I fancied I heard cannon.

[*July 22, 1861*]

Yesterday after writing I laid so ill. Mrs. Davis came in, sat by me. Kissed me, said a great battle had been fought at Manassas—Jeff Davis led the centre—Beauregard the right wing—Johnston the left. Beauregard's staff safe. What a load from my heart. Wade Hampton wounded—Lieut. Col. Johnson killed—Gen. Bee killed—Kirby Smith killed [*following word added later:*] wounded. Poor Col. Bartow—killed gallantly leading his men into action. President telegraphs we have had a great victory—a thorough *rout*—

dead & dying strewing the fields. Several batteries taken—Sherman's among others—by the Lynchburg regiment which was cut to pieces in doing it. Three hundred of the Legion killed—one U.S.A. flag. Then I lay upon Mrs. Preston's bed—one set of women & men coming in after another. Such miserable wretches, so glad of the victory, so sad for the dead. Those miserable beasts sent a flag of truce to bury their dead. Instead of burying them as they pretended, were throwing up entrenchments.

We are so frantic at this victory. Met Mr. Hunter to day; too busy crying over Mrs. Bartow to say much. Spent the morning with Mrs. Wigfall. She is nearly *mad* to see Louis Wigfall—he has not been here since Tuesday. *Drunk* somewhere—his troop ordered off tomorrow. Miserable woman.

The horrible accident maker, Mrs. Montmolin, is really mad with agitation at the report of her son wounded. She was so angry that she was not allowed to tell the bad news to Mrs. Bartow. Have not dared to face Mrs. Bartow. Met Trescot. Wonder what brings him here. Col. Meyers is so kind. George Deas will not know any thing.

Rain—rain—what is before us. Mrs. Davis has been so devoted to me since my trouble. Mrs. Preston's maid, when I read the papers, said no body talks in them of *S C*—but the number of our *dead* shows we were not backward. Telegraphed Col. Chesnut. Mrs. Johnston told me President Davis said he liked best to have me sit opposite *him;* he liked my style of *chat.* Mrs. McLean introduced her handsome brother in law & her sister—he is to take command somewhere in Western Virginia. Sydney Johnston is expected every day.

We want to go & nurse the soldiers.

Reconstruction and the Rise of the New South

Historians B. C. Hall and C. T. Wood offer the following assessment of the Reconstruction era from 1865 to 1877:

> The Abolitionist North couldn't be satisfied with merely stamping out slavery: it had a seeming determination to imprint the South with the morality of the North (philosophically and economically). Perhaps had the North been somewhat gentler in imposing its will, the South would have changed, but the viciousness of Reconstruction stiffened the South's back and made it look for other answers for its self-imposed guilt.[1]

Similarly, in describing the contributions of a small number of African Americans who fought for the Confederacy, J. K. Obatala concludes that the keen antagonism and division between the races in the South may have resulted more from Reconstruction than from the outcome of the Civil War.[2]

For blacks and whites alike, the question of how to cope with defeat loomed large. The obstacles to survival were many, though Samuel Eliot Morison sees the war itself and the desire of a majority of Southern whites to maintain nostalgic allegiance to the Confederacy as factors every bit as important as Northern policies in determining the South's fate. That the situation was dire can be seen in the following assessment by Morison:

> The economic plight of the South in 1865 was deplorable, far worse than that of central Europe in 1919 or 1945. Unfortunately, the Southern sufferings of that era entered into the reconstruction myth as something deliberately imposed by the North, not the natural result of war and secession. The country had neither capital nor currency. Where Sherman and Sheridan had

passed, almost the entire apparatus of civilized life had been destroyed. In many parts, the white rural underworld swarmed out of swamps and hills to loot the planters whom it envied, and kill the blacks whom it hated. These probably did as much damage as had the Union armies. No Southern bank was solvent, no shop had much to sell. Few schools were left for white children, and none for blacks. Young men of family, who had interrupted their education to fight for Southern independence, had to labor in the fields to keep their families from starving; and a planter's family which still had young men was deemed fortunate.[3]

The effects of this adverse history would be felt well into the twentieth century. The bankrupt state of education, in particular, would result in decades of unfulfilled potential and a lingering perception of the South as anti-intellectual and "unbookish." Before the war, the South boasted of academies and colleges second to none. More white Southerners than white Northerners attended college, and educated aristocrats considered it intellectually fashionable to "embrace Deism and to flaunt a disrespect for the Bible."[4] William and Mary College, the University of North Carolina, Transylvania University in Kentucky, and the University of Georgia were heralded as bastions of free thinking that provided an antidote to the poison of Puritanism distilled in such Northern institutions as Harvard and Yale. Yet, by the war's end, the impact of widespread physical devastation would impede the South's efforts to resurrect an educational system serving even a fraction of the populace. In their 1952 edition of *The Literature of the South*, editors Beatty, Watkins, and Young describe the educational holocaust that occurred in the South following the war, citing numerous documented instances:

> Dr. L. C. Garland, later first Chancellor of Vanderbilt, wrote his father from the University of Alabama in the fall 1865: "The University buildings are all burned." He had returned to teach with a single colleague; one student appeared for registration. At the University of Georgia conditions were no better. Windows and buildings were battered in and Greek columns riddled with gunfire. The University of South Carolina was closed for four years. In 1870, thirty-six students were enrolled at the University of North Carolina, which did not open its doors again until 1875. William and Mary, the oldest Southern college, did not operate between 1881–1887.[5]

A similar account showing the deplorable state of higher education in the post-bellum South is offered by Arthur Ben Chitty, who, in his official capacity as historiographer of the University of the South at Sewanee, Tennessee, notes that the "University was the child of two eras—the rich, confident, aristocratic South of the 1850's and the beaten, emaciated, poverty-stricken South of Reconstruction."[6] With a faculty composed largely of Confederate veterans and with contributions of books—approximately one thousand volumes—made by Oxford and Cambridge Universities in England, the University of the South proved a "forlorn hope for higher education in the South"[7] when state governments were paralyzed and public institutions proved ineffectual in the wake of overwhelming desolation.

The neglect of education was perhaps inevitable, given the more pressing concerns of survival. One Episcopal bishop living in Tennessee wrote a friend traveling in England:

> Bad as things were at the close of our late struggle, they were not to be com-
> pared to the general suffering at the present time. The whites are groaning
> under the task of making a bare subsistence for their families and the blacks
> are compelled to steal or die of pure want. Lord, how long![8]

Politics and the economic fate of the South were inextricably linked to existing conditions. President Andrew Johnson, Lincoln's successor and a pro-Union Southerner
during the war, found himself at odds with his own Cabinet over how Reconstruction
should be carried out in the South. In particular, Johnson saw the increasing need to
broaden his political base by reaching out to Southern Democrats, whose numbers included many of the Old South's planter class.[9] Johnson also refused to support an
edict, issued by Northern Republicans, that recognized Southern state governments
insofar as those governments enfranchised blacks, promoting, in Johnson's earlier
campaign rhetoric, "justice for the colored race."[10] Abandoning his former convictions, Johnson warned in 1867 of the "tyranny" that would result in extending the
"capacity for government" to freedmen.[11] His shift in sentiment caused many Southerners to view him as an ally and a savior. Northerners saw him as a traitor.

     A showdown came when the president demanded the resignation of Secretary of
War Edwin Stanton, a long-time opponent who had argued for extended military occupation of the South after the war. Stanton had believed Johnson's 1864 preelection
promise to "punish and impoverish" the leaders of the Southern rebellion.[12] So
staunch was the president in his earlier claims that, as Eric Foner notes, "The New
York *World* predicted that because of his 'monomania,' Johnson would vigorously enforce the confiscation laws, break up the plantations, and 'create communities of
small freeholders.'"[13] When it became clear that Johnson would not support the
wholesale policies of Stanton and fellow Republicans, the House of Representatives
impeached him on February 24, 1868. Ten of the eleven articles of impeachment referred to Johnson's removal of Stanton. One particularly blatant charge was omitted—that Johnson conspired in the assassination of Abraham Lincoln.

     Although acquitted, America's eighteenth president had no power for the remain-
ing ten months of his term. Radical Republicans had won the day and were not intent
on showing the South any leniency. Carpetbag governments were installed in Southern states, black militia companies were organized to keep order, and taxes were
levied on property, forcing the sale of thousands of farms. The economic recession of
1873 drove down agricultural prices, all but destroying what was left of the South's
agrarian future.

     Doubtless, many in the South counted on Johnson's brief ascendancy to restore
the old order or at least to mitigate intolerable circumstances attributed to Northern
legislators. For the same reasons, the North made clear that it would not be hood-
winked; having won the war, it would not lose the peace by condoning political chicanery designed to aid Southern white men in formulating "their own program of
political, social, and economic readjustment."[14] Above all, the North would not let the
South's leadership ignore the prerogatives of Negro suffrage. The North's plan called
for a "democratic, free labor South, with small farms replacing the great plantations
and Northern capital and migrants energizing the society."[15]

     If the white South was suspicious of the North's mantras for economic progress, it
was because a majority of Southern leaders believed the North had failed to deliver on
many of its own promises. Foner points to the "inequity of protective tariffs, high rail-

road freight rates, and state and federal aid to private corporations"[16] as frequent complaints used to bolster the agrarian agenda and to undermine the success of the North's reform program. Thus, Southern Democrats fumed at a Leviathan of corruption that they saw as having begun with the Lincoln administration's economic policies, which, Southern leaders charged, "enriched Northeastern capitalists at the expense of farmers and laborers, and spawned an enormous group of parasitic nonproducers—notably bondholders and stock market speculators—to the detriment of 'the industrious poor.'"[17] Having recently fought a war in which almost 40 percent of the male population eligible for military duty had been wounded or killed in battle, the South was in no frame of mind to accept the North's progressive platforms, economic or otherwise. Feeling themselves to be a "highly conscious minority within the nation,"[18] many Southerners balked, digging in their heels and refusing to advance along lines leading to acceptance of centralized government and a strong national state. Unwilling to be reconstructed in the image envisioned by the North and demonstrating an engrained habit of defiance, the postwar South resorted to such counter measures as fierce localism and avowed racism that protracted tensions and suffering for decades.

As usual, African Americans were caught in the vice grip of political extremes. In recent decades, revisionist historians have correctly pointed out that the long-term effects of Reconstruction were such as to improve the status of African Americans and to promote social democracy in the South. Such an assertion only underscores the predicament of African Americans at the time, a situation tantamount to setting sail in a lifeboat on stormy seas rather than to remain on a sinking ship.

In the first place, the North tended to behold the mote in the Southern eye while ignoring the beam in its own. While a Joint Committee of the Senate and House of Representatives gathered information on the South's mistreatment of Northerners and blacks during the Johnson years, Northern politicians and businessmen began to worry about the effects of making all freedmen voters. As John Hope Franklin has observed, before the war only three-fifths of all slaves were counted toward congressional representation.[19] If all freedmen were counted as a result of emancipation, then the South would enjoy even greater representation than it had in 1860. The numbers alone frightened Northern political leaders. Franklin acknowledges the gloomy irony of this situation by stating that "even in the matter of enfranchising the Negro the only considerations that seemed to command acceptance of Negroes as voters were the clear mandate of the Congress and the practical necessity of doing so in order to remain in power."[20]

Nor did Northern business leaders greet with open arms the incalculable numbers of former slaves lured by the North's climate of freedom. Determined to keep a firm grip on the future, the North's business plutocracy had profited handsomely from the war, demonstrating how a marriage of government and industry could result in "unprecedented economic activity and prosperity."[21] Indeed, the North had managed to prove about its economy what the South had failed to prove about its own. Still, the North's new millionaire class grew jittery at the prospect of so great an influx of freedmen desperate for economic advantage. Some leaders openly expressed doubts that free labor strategies could accommodate such an influx. As a result, Northern spokesmen began to press with increasing zeal for "home rule" and "black Reconstruction," offering promises of generous help and land ownership that were never kept.[22]

Another important factor arresting the progress of African Americans was the North's desire to invest in the South in the ensuing years of the war. Franklin points out that "the Yankee businessman, his pockets bulging with war profits, saw in the vanquished section a new and highly promising frontier."[23] Even before the war's end, Northern capitalists had begun purchasing land and investing capital in Southern border states. In order to benefit from additional interests there, the North would need the cooperation of white Southerners. Thus, "as preoccupation with material gain increased, zeal for reform declined."[24] Northern businessmen urged government allies to provide "adequate safeguards" for the civil rights of Southern blacks while not interfering in such a way as to threaten new economic alliances with Southern whites. The intensity of antebellum concern for the plight of African Americans soon abated as "new leaders like James G. Blaine of Maine and Roscoe Conkling of New York had less solicitude for humanitarian reform and the difficult problems of political reconstruction than for taking advantage of the peculiar postwar conditions to further the interests of their friends in the industrial and financial community."[25] W. E. B. DuBois would later offer an unequivocal analysis of the postwar period:

> The first decade was merely a prolongation of the vain search for freedom, the boon that seemed ever barely to elude their grasp—like a tantalizing will-o-the-wisp misleading the headless host. The holocaust of war, the terrors of the Ku Klux Klan, the lies of carpetbaggers, the disorganization of industry, and the contradictory advice of friends and foes, left the bewildered serf with no new watchword beyond the old cry for freedom.[26]

If Northern enthusiasm for civil rights evaporated in the face of economic imperatives, Southern hostility lingered, manifesting itself in virulent attacks on citizenship, suffrage, and the lives of Southern blacks. Not only did the South find ways to skirt legislation designed to protect the inalienable rights of African Americans, but also menacing factions arose to ensure that blacks were denied the full privileges of citizenship. Although the issue of war had been officially settled, the terms of peace were anything but certain, resulting in an era of violence that produced what journalists increasingly dubbed as "a war of its own."

Anything less than war would seem inadequate to describe the crimes perpetrated against blacks by the Ku Klux Klan, the most obvious agent of intimidation in the postwar South. Organized by former Confederate officers considered to be "the flower of Southern manhood," the Invisible Empire of the KKK, under the leadership of the Civil War's most controversial figure, Nathan Bedford Forrest, quickly gained a reputation for their dedication to white supremacy. The Klan made clear that the war against African Americans would proliferate across the South. Refusing to recognize the prerogatives of law in the mob-minded, racially ignitable Southland, Klansmen grew strong in numbers, mocking due process while justifying covert violence as an appropriate response to Northern "occupation." Klansmen even organized politically in Tennessee, calling for a constitutional resolution that would be "emphatically in favor of a white man's government and opposed to military despotism and the negro supremacy of the Congressional plan of reconstruction."[27]

However, most of the Ku Klux Klan's activities were terrorist and subterranean in nature. Moving with "the stealth and canniness" of a "wartime cavalry,"[28] Klansmen often rode in small bands, swapping missions so as to minimize recognition by the public. Responding to every rumor of Negro insurrection, Klan raiders targeted blacks indiscriminately, "punishing" as many as possible for the alleged sins of a few.

When violence between blacks and whites actually occurred, as was bound to happen in a South dedicated to preserving the antebellum status quo, the Klan responded swiftly and savagely, resorting to flagrant lawlessness and assassination to achieve the organization's professed aims. The following example is typical of the way Klansmen handled situations regarded as threatening to the general welfare:

> In February 1868, after a white man named Bicknell was robbed and murdered by a black in Maury County [Tennessee], Klansmen attended the funeral in costume; the next day, a party of twenty of them entered the county jail in Columbia and took the black from it, and his body was later found hanging from a tree. Klan raiders in Maury and surrounding counties administered blacks hundreds of lashes with hickory sticks, confiscated guns from Union League and Loyal League members, and ordered teachers at black schools to shutter their institutions and evacuate the area.[29]

In the words of historian Jack Hurst, "the South had become a melting pot of misery."[30]

The Klan's ranks swelled with large numbers of poor whites whose only agenda was the wholesale slaughter of African American freedmen. In May 1867, a black man reported to Memphis authorities that after seeking pay for work done for a white man, the black man had been visited by Klansmen who cut the sinews of his legs and cut off several of his toes.[31] Such accounts became so routine that conservative Democrats began to express alarm at the Klan's activities, which included burning churches and schools, harassing women and children, and lynching aging black men whose only crime was that they were no longer obligated to be slaves. Even Nathan Bedford Forrest soon found the Klan too violent for his tastes, disbanding the organization officially in 1868, lamenting that the Ku Klux Klan was "the greatest blunder our people ever made." Forrest's disavowal of the Klan and his adjuration to halt scourgings and murder did little to stop the Klan's reign of terror. Only with the Ku Klux Klan Act, passed by Congress in 1871, did Klansmen risk federal prosecution for belonging to the Klan and for committing such crimes as murder, arson, and assault. President Grant threatened to send the U.S. Army into states where racially motivated crimes persisted.

Against this backdrop of persistent threat, African Americans were not only expected to survive but also to thrive in positions of leadership for which many were, understandably, unprepared to assume. What experience had African American slaves with the operations of democracy, given that democratic process had been denied them? Also, because "fourteen specified classes [of former white citizens], assumed to be impenitent rebels, were not allowed to vote" under the provisional reconstruction plan, "the effect was to exclude many natural leaders and experienced statesmen from the new state governments."[32] The prospect of governing effectively was dismal in light of innumerable obstacles, many owing to the terrible limitations imposed by slavery:

> A slave existence could hardly be expected to prepare one for the responsibilities of citizenship, especially when there were laws, as there were in all slave states, banning the teaching of slaves. Even if Negroes were free, as were more than 200,000 in the slave states before the war, laws forbade their being taught to read and write. Indeed, when they came out of slavery many

Negroes did not know their own names; many did not even have family names. It goes without saying that a considerable number had not the vaguest notion of what voting and registering meant.[33]

What is remarkable is that large numbers of African Americans were able to assume the obligations of citizenship. Many were ministers. Others taught school. Some had attended colleges in the North or in England. A few, whose fathers had been white men, were given educations equal to those of white children. The notion that all Reconstruction blacks were woefully unprepared for the task of governing was patently false.[34]

Remarkable too was the generosity of spirit shown by a majority of black leaders. In a South Carolina convention assembly, [former slave] Beverly Nash declared, "We must unite with our white fellow-citizens. They tell us that they have been disenfranchised, yet we tell the North that we shall never let the halls of Congress be silent until we remove that disability."[35]

Similarly, "Negroes attempted no revolution of the social relations of the races in the South."[36] Nor did African American leadership seek to wrest economic control from Southern whites. If anything, African Americans understood the necessity of revitalizing the Southern economy by any means necessary, short of the reenslavement of blacks. Without exception, black legislators fought hard for civil rights legislation, understanding that just as the vote had brought on war, the vote could determine a just and reasonable peace. The combination of courage and prudence demonstrated by African American legislators would prompt one of their white contemporaries to note,

The colored men who took their seats in both Senate and House did not appear ignorant or helpless. They were as a rule studious, earnest, ambitious men, whose public conduct would be honorable to any race.[37]

Ambition would be an important trait of survival for both African Americans and whites in an era that Mark Twain would ironically refer to as the Gilded Age, the period from 1865 to 1900. Perhaps at no other time in our country's history was change so drastic. Widespread technological innovations resulted both in unforeseen opportunities and in "problems created by big machines, big business, big labor, big farmers, and big government—problems that were taking shape during this dynamic period."[38] In fact, problems of change may be the key to understanding this pivotal epoch, which shares many similarities with the late twentieth century. According to historians Ari and Olive Hoogenboom, "The machine-made problems of monopoly and automation; the urban problems of slums, transportation, sanitation, and crime; the rural problems of material and cultural poverty; the failure to educate adequately the children of immigrant and African-American minorities; and the world-wide commitment of the United States rooted and matured during the Gilded Age."[39]

The South, with its former reliance on an agrarian economy, found it especially difficult to adapt to the demands of increasing industrialization. Nor did large numbers of Southerners want to adapt, some pointing at once to the problems the new order imposed, others holding tenaciously to myths of the Old South with its special fondness for noble but hopeless causes. Better to live isolated and unreconstructed, many Southerners believed, than to join the godless march of progress that was the truth of Northern victory.

Inevitably, survival demanded that the majority of Southerners be more forward-looking, anticipating future ages. It is no coincidence that on the cusp of a new millennium, Atlanta is heralded as an international city, home to the Olympics and to hundreds of Fortune 500 corporations, including the city's banner enterprise, Coca-Cola. It is also no accident that Atlanta has been for decades the energetic hub for the South's civil rights efforts. Out of the ashes of Sherman's conflagration, Atlanta rose, Phoenixlike, boasting of a population exceeding a million people by 1900. Atlanta may owe its spectacular achievements to a group of visionary business leaders and journalists connected with the *Atlanta Constitution* of the 1880s and 1890s. Among this elite corps of seers and pragmatists stood writer Henry Grady and folklorist Joel Chandler Harris.

Grady is best known for coining the phrase "New South" in a speech given to an audience in New York in 1886:

> Grady proclaimed that his New South had set aside racial hatred as well as its bitter quarrel with the North, and that the only ingredient lacking to bring the South into the Gilded Age was Yankee investment in factories (to be built right next to abundant Southern fields of cotton, corn, and tobacco).[40]

However, as Hall and Wood assert, "Overt democratic racism and patrician rogues running the state capitals blocked any real chance for changing the traditional culture of the South."[41] Atlanta would grow, but not as a promised partnership of Northern industrialists and Southern agrarians. The city's postwar rise would represent business as usual, especially where exploitation of blacks and poor whites was concerned. In *Dixie Rising* (1997), Peter Applebome envisions the possibility of a twenty-first century South that offers "a blend of Yankee hustle and Southern charm with the potential to be not just the nation's economic heart, but its best hope for racial peace as well."[42] On the cusp of the twentieth century, Grady and his peers hoped for the same. What they could not anticipate was the tenacity of old struggles and the failure of new promises to find a way to solve the South's ongoing dilemmas.

Notes

1. B. C. Hall and C. T. Wood, *The South* (New York: Simon and Schuster, 1995), 225.
2. Richard Rollins, *Black Southerners in Gray* (Redondo Beach, CA: Rank and File Publications, 1994), 166.
3. Samuel Eliot Morison, *The Oxford History of the American People*, Vol. 2 (New York: Penguin Books, 1972), 166.
4. Richard Weaver, *The Southern Essays of Richard M. Weaver*, eds. George Curtis and James Thompson (Indianapolis: Liberty Press, 1987), 144.
5. Richmond Beatty, Floyd Watkins, and Thomas Daniel Young, *The Literature of the South* (New York: Scott-Foresman, 1952), 611.
6. Arthur Ben Chitty, *Reconstruction at Sewanee* (Sewanee, TN: Proctor's Hall Press, 1993), 181.
7. Chitty, 105.
8. Chitty, 105.
9. Eric Foner, *Reconstruction* (New York: Harper and Row, 1988), 184.

10. Foner, 178.
11. Foner, 180.
12. Foner, 183.
13. Foner, 183.
14. Kenneth Stampp, *The Era of Reconstruction, 1865–1877* (New York: Random House, 1967), 187.
15. Foner, 29.
16. Foner, 498.
17. Foner, 31.
18. Weaver, 200.
19. John Hope Franklin, *Reconstruction after the Civil War* (Chicago: University of Chicago Press, 1961), 12.
20. Franklin, 196.
21. Franklin, 7.
22. Franklin, 13.
23. Franklin, 9.
24. Franklin, 8.
25. Franklin, 9.
26. W. E. B. DuBois, *The Souls of Black Folk*, ed. Henry Louis Gates, Jr. (New York: Bantam, 1989), 35–36.
27. Jack Hurst, *Nathan Bedford Forrest* (New York: Alfred A. Knopf, 1993).
28. Hurst, 294.
29. Hurst, 294.
30. Hurst, 264.
31. Hurst, 264.
32. Franklin, 87.
33. Franklin, 87.
34. Franklin, 89.
35. Franklin, 90–91.
36. Franklin, 91.
37. Franklin, 137–138.
38. Ari and Olive Hoogenboom, *The Gilded Age* (Englewood Cliffs: Prentice Hall, 1967), I.
39. Hoogenboom and Hoogenboom, I–II.
40. Hall and Wood, 136.
41. Hall and Wood, 136.
42. Peter Applebome, *Dixie Rising* (New York: Harcourt Brace, 1996), 151.

Given tendencies in the Upper South to oppose secession before the war and to switch sides, becoming "homemade Yankees" once the war was under way, denizens of the border South believed they would be treated less severely than pro-Confederate counterparts at the war's end. After all, Lincoln had placed a pro-Union Southerner on the election ticket of 1864, seeking to create a coalition of moderate Republicans and Unionist Democrats, the latter whose loyalty had wavered only for a time and in the face of great pressures. The vast numbers of Confederate deserters from East Tennessee and the westernmost rim of the state offered evidence of a divided South, portions of which were more than ready to reaffirm the Union's prerogatives and to accept the privileges of citizenship that many Southerners had never renounced.

Had Lincoln lived, the Upper South, except Virginia perhaps, might have found itself forgiven, receiving preferential treatment for support of the Union that was at least nominal and often substantive. As it was, Lincoln's assassination and the subsequent debacle over Johnson only confirmed the North's perception that no region of the South was "safe" and that Southerners as a whole could not be trusted to participate faithfully in the government's plans for Reconstruction. In the postwar decades, pro-Union Southerners nurtured resentment for what they perceived as unfair treatment at the hands of a government they had supported, often at great personal risk. The entire state of Tennessee became "one big military prison," complained one former East Tennessee Unionist.

Tennessee represented the worst of the Republican efforts to exercise military might after the fact of war. In March 1865, William G. Brownlow was elected governor by enfranchised Unionists ready to punish fellow statesmen who had opted for secession. Brownlow struck hard, inciting militant Loyal Leagues and promising immunity to any of the Unionist militia men who found a need to shoot ex-Confederates, most assumed by Brownlow to be Ku Kluxers. When one Memphis newspaper editor protested that not all ex-Confederates in the state were Klansmen, Brownlow threatened to have the editor jailed, then shot. Even the governor's allies began to wonder at his sanity, which, by most objective standards, appeared dubious. Brownlow's state of mind seemed, in many ways, to reflect the state of the South itself. Chaos and violence endured long after the war. A region devoted to an Old World order of social relations emphasizing restraint, among other values, found itself straining to accept a perplexing new economic and social agenda that would literally change the Southern landscape. For almost two decades after Appomatox, "the scars of war were evident at [places like] Knoxville and Chattanooga, yet the bustle of activity and factory smoke spoke of the new order."[1]

Such stark contrasts were especially obvious in the postwar Upper South where merchandising partnerships with the North were more enthusiastically embraced than were similar overtures in the Deep South. For all the bitterness that Reconstruction engendered, there was an abiding sense that change was inevitable and certainly preferable to the status quo of devastation that had left portions of the South a physical wasteland. Most Southern leaders, with the notable exception of the unrepentant Jefferson Davis, actually urged "their people to accept the verdict of battle and endeavor to be good citizens in a reunited country."[2] Any residual loyalty to the stars and bars would pass into the celebrated realms of nostalgia. Business was at hand, and for all the South's imperfections, the region was a fortune hunter's paradise. Money was waiting to be made, most especially by Southerners.

Although no one can say for certain, a resurgence of the South's old commercial instincts may have resulted in what few alliances did occur between whites and blacks willing to take advantage of a heretofore unknown spirit of cooperative enterprise. Consenting to open up the whole continent to free labor and Northern enterprise, some white Southerners saw the advantage in regarding blacks as allies instead of enemies.[3] Such may have been the motivation of Nathan Bedford Forrest, notorious Rebel guerilla and first grand wizard of the Ku Klux Klan. For whatever reasons, the ex-frontiersman, who had never successfully fit the mold of the planter-cavalier-aristocrat, "quickly evolved into a forward-looking businessman rather than a backward-looking slaveocrat."[4] That such a man could, in the final eight years of his life, heap "scorn upon the violent racial hatred and oppression epitomized by the Klan," may seem inexplicable, if not patently fraudulent, unless an important historical qualification is considered."[5] In *The Strange Career of Jim Crow*, C. Vann Woodward exposes the fallacy that segregation and the "etiquette of race relations" had existed as a bedrock observance from the earliest days of Southern colonization. He points to a number of "possible areas of contact between the races," noting that not until after Reconstruction and the instituting of the "separate but equal" principle by the federal judiciary, did widespread, culturally sanctioned segregation result.[6] As a slavetrader, Forrest would have known blacks ranging "from brand-new African importees to refined house servants" and would have "had to learn their traits well enough to see both the depth of their longing for liberty and the falsity of prevailing views, that they were more animal than human."[7] A hard-headed pragmatist, Forrest simply might have intuited the best course of survival for his region, a possibility that biographer Jack Hurst is willing to grant, while noting other, more sanguine changes in Forrest that occurred over time.[8] Notwithstanding ideological differences expressed by scholars and other observers about the nineteenth-century South's most problematic figure, Forrest's untitled speech to the African American community in Memphis in 1875 offers an overture of good will and a pledge of support "to elevate every man—to depress none."

Forrest's view in the waning years of his life placed him in a distinct minority of Southern whites. Despite efforts to create a business-driven South in which "towns, cities, and villages enjoyed an early and exciting exposure to the marvels of the nineteenth century,"[9] racism persisted at every level of commercial activity. Although many African Americans succeeded in becoming well-to-do in urban areas where opportunities to accumulate capital were possible, the majority of "ambitious black people confronted heightened frustrations."[10] For all the talk of a New South, the sins of the Old South lingered, albeit in a different form than that earlier described by Frederick Douglass in his *Narrative of the Life of Frederick Douglass, an American Slave* (1845). Unlike Harriet Beecher Stowe, who had seen slavery only once and at a remove, Douglass was born into slavery, having been separated as an infant from his mother, a slaveholding practice Douglass acknowledges as commonplace. In what is universally regarded as the most compelling account of the treatment of slaves in the prewar South, Douglass shatters the proslavery argument that "accepted slavery as neither sinful nor necessarily impolitic" but needing to "be brought up to standards of humanity described . . . as Christian."[11] Douglass points out that the institution of slavery could do nothing less than treat slaves as brutes. His personal history offers numerous examples that he frankly takes pains to understate, making his case all the more convincing and the horrors indubitable to Southern audiences that had been willing to doubt the claims of much abolitionist literature published between 1830 and the Civil War.

Still, the myth of the happy slave stubbornly persisted well into the twentieth century, given support by what has been termed the "plantation school" of white Southern writers, among them Thomas Nelson Page. Just as history tends to become more revisionist the farther it moves from actual events, the plantation school revised circumstances to conform to traditional Southern aims. One of those aims, directly expressed in Page's "Unc' Edinburg's Drowndin'," is to demonstrate the passing of a superior time and culture, an age of gentility that exalted slaves even as it benefited their masters. Edinburg, one of Page's more memorable black voices, laments the times and is "unappreciative of a freedom that only robs him of purpose."[12] At one point, he complains that "Dese heah free-issue niggers don' know what Christmas is." Although Page's intent may have been to reconstruct an idyll of plantation life, "a modern audience perceives, that their [the former slaves'] sad purposelessness in the postbellum present has been caused by a system that never granted them identity as human beings."[13] Ironically, Page played to the expectations of Northern audiences eager to construe the South's past just as the author depicted it.

In fact, the North's literary palate increasingly savored works serving up images of a South replete with noble cavaliers, loyal back retainers, Southern belles, and the omnipresent backdrop of wisteria and magnolias. Writing for Northern audiences became the vogue for Southern writers willing to treat the South as a place apart, a habitat given to producing Gothic oddities and charming eccentricities. If the reality was often darker and more complex, Southern writers largely kept this secret to themselves, a situation reflected in other genres, as well. As Southern musicologist Alan Lomax reminds us, minstrel songs that enjoyed widespread popularity in the North were composed by Southern whites in imitation of plantation melodies created and sung by Southern blacks. Exploiting the South's genuine products in a typically Southern way became the trademark of Mark Twain in *Life on the Mississippi*. Twain dissects the South as an anthropological curiosity, treating his presumed discoveries as novel findings. For instance, Twain focuses on Southern speech, drawing a fine line between parody and appreciation of the South's more easily identifiable dialect features. Southern sports, stemming from agrarian roots, apparently provide different, more curious amusements than do Northern forms of recreation. Southerners also exhibit a penchant for romantic novels and novelists not shared by the rest of the country. The Southern fondness for Sir Walter Scott, for example, may have led directly to the Civil War, a claim that Twain makes only half-jokingly. Twain's persona seems to be that of a Southerner with a dim memory of the South, lending a curiously refracted quality to his observations while granting them the weight of the author's considerable personal authority.

Pulling the North's proverbial leg has always been a favorite pastime of Southern writers, who nonetheless desired to preserve folkways threatened by extinction. Some of the very people most invested in the new South displayed a countertendency to resurrect the Old South in literature. It can be argued that one reason Southerners embraced the New South at all is that they still had access to the Old South through such scribes as George Washington Harris, whose *Sut Lovingood: Yarns Spun by a Nat'ral Born Durn'd Fool; Warped and Wove for Public Wear* was set in East Tennessee's Copper Basin region but was published in New York. A homespun, unpretentious, but shrewd protagonist, Sut would later serve as an inspiration for William Faulkner, a long-time admirer of Sut, who said, "He [Sut] had no illusions about himself, did the best he could; at certain times he was a coward and knew it and wasn't ashamed; he never blamed his misfortunes on anyone and never cursed God for them." In *Stories from Tennessee*, editor Linda Burton Francisco underscores Faulkner's observation, finding in Sut "one who acts confidently in a world filled with hypocrisy and who never questions his own view of this chaotic world."[14] About Sut's status in Harris's "Parson John Bullen's Lizards," Francisco has this to say:

> In "Parson John Bullen's Lizards," Sut never once seriously questions his no-
> tions of right and wrong. For example, after Parson Bullen discovers Sut and
> Sall in a compromising situation in a huckleberry thicket, Sut ostensibly re-
> pents his deed. But in reality he has not been taken in by the self-righteous,
> hypocritical Parson. Setting out both literally and figuratively to unclothe
> the Parson, Sut eventually shows Parson Bullen's nature to his entire con-
> gregation in a story that is one of Harris' most hilarious tales.[15]

Unlike Sut, whose conflicts are largely ethical ones for which the resolutions provide comic relief, Mary Noailles Murfree's protagonists struggle with a harsh and unrelenting physical environment. Offering as her stated purpose to "put Tennessee into literature" and "to let the world know the East Tennessee Mountaineer, before the railroads reached the mountains," Murfree sought to preserve the wealth of tradi-tional customs and verisimilitude of Elizabethan speech, vestiges of which could still be heard in this century in the Cumberland Mountains. In *Stories from Tennessee*, Linda Burton Francisco assesses Murfree's contribution to the genre of local color in what is regarded as Murfree's benchmark story:

> In Murfree's "The 'Harnt' That Walks Chilhowee," first published in William
> Dean Howell's *Atlantic Monthly* in May 1883, Clarsie Giles, the only woman
> protagonist in this section of *Stories From Tennessee*, lives solely by her
> sense of justice, which calls for helping those less fortunate than herself. Re-
> fusing to compromise her values, no matter what the consequences, she
> alone has no doubts about feeding the "ghost" who walks Chilhowee Moun-
> tain. And while solving the mystery of Chilhowee Mountain, Clarsie does not
> succumb to the values of the other mountaineers, who believe rigidly in the
> letter of the law. Instead, confident in her perception of personal morality,
> she defies the community by taking food from herself, but not from her fam-
> ily, to give to the starving "ghost." In part Murfree's creation of such uncom-
> promising Appalachian characters as Clarsie Giles made her extraordinarily
> popular, especially in the Northeast. There readers hungry for stories about
> eccentric mountaineers helped establish Murfree's reputation as one of Ten-
> nessee's most popular writers. It was a reputation that lasted into the twenti-
> eth century when the interest in local color stories finally diminished.[16]

Another New South writer enjoying popularity in the North was Will N. Harben, whose "The Heresy of Abner Calihan" exploits backwoods religion in the mountains of North Georgia. The story focuses on the heretical maunderings of "Abner Calihan, a member of the church and a good industrious citizen . . ." who challenges the doc-trine of salvation through faith by claiming that good deeds also constitute an essen-tial component of saving grace. Believing Abner's views to be dangerous to the "risin' generation" of impressionable children and recalling an incident in which two men swapped wives at a nearby township, the deacons of Big Cabin Church deem it best to "try" Abner, making an example of him. The thick, phonetically rendered dialects and exaggerated actions of the characters—qualities in Harben's work that fascinated Northern audiences of the time—make the author's work slow going for contemporary readers seeking more than an anthropological interest in this and other period pieces by the local colorists.

Still, "the myth of the Old South, the valor of the Lost Cause, and the imagery surrounding the New South elicited an increasingly sympathetic response from other sections. The North, it appeared, had discovered a new and more acceptable South: a region that was loyal, peaceful, and forward-looking as well as exotic."[17] Many writers were indeed making a break with the older Southern order. However, that break did not occur without tensions and attendant anxieties.

One writer dramatizing the struggle to accommodate new social attitudes and changing mores was Amelie Rives, the Richmond-born daughter of a prominent member of Robert E. Lee's staff. Rives's *The Quick or the Dead* (1888) "foreshadowed the direction Southern fiction would take with Faulkner's 'Rose for Emily.'"[18] The novel's heroine is torn between the memory of her dead husband and her feelings for a cousin whose resemblance to her husband proves so striking as to threaten her increasingly fragile state of mind. The plot offers a symbolic duel between the past and the present that is resolved in the final scene when the protagonist "retrieves her wedding ring from the hearth, blows ashes from it, and replaces it on her finger," having "clearly chosen the dead over the quick."[19] A sense of melancholy, even morbidity, hangs redolent over Rives's story, contributing to the Gothic excesses expected of Southern writers by Northern readers.

The Lost Cause continued to offer grist for the Gothic mill, though many Southern writers would have agreed with the observation made by twentieth-century writer Flannery O'Connor, who noted that what was considered Gothic by Northerners was merely realism to Southerners. Even O'Connor's wry disclaimer cannot totally absolve New South writers from exploiting the Civil War as a pervasive theme of the period. After all, the war was the defining event in many people's lives and the source of inspired folklore for a new generation of writers. In characteristic seriocomic style, Twain perhaps put it best by saying,

> In the South, the war is what A.D. is elsewhere; they date from it. All day long you hear things "placed" as having happened since the waw; or du'in' the waw; or befo' the waw; or right after the waw; or 'bout two yeahs or five yeahs or ten yeahs befo' the waw or aftah the waw. It shows how intimately every individual was visited, in his own person, by that tremendous episode.

War was certainly still on the minds of such writers as William P. Trent, a postbellum professor at the University of the South at Sewanee. In his biography entitled *William Gilmore Simms* (1867), Trent showcases the aging South Carolina author and former spokesman for secession and slavery in less than complimentary fashion. Simms becomes a vehicle for Trent's criticism of the entire antebellum South and a system that produced few, if any, original thinkers. In his chapter on Simm's role in the Civil War, Trent draws a zealous conclusion about the disastrous effects of romanticizing the Lost Cause:

> No! The most loyal Southerner may as well make up his mind to face the fact that the cause for which Simms labored, and for which so many thousands of

brave men died, was a losing cause, in consequence of the fact that the people that upheld it were fighting to perpetuate an institution opposed to progress, an institution that blocked the path which a great nation had to take.

Trent was not the only writer in this period critical of the Old South, or of the New South, for that matter. Walter Hines Page was the "acknowledged leader of the new native critics," though "he launched much of his criticism from a vantage point outside the South."[20] Moving from North Carolina to New York and, later, to Boston, Page would represent a growing tradition among Southern writers forced to leave the region in order to write objectively about it. Page's shift in geography let him draw in sharp relief the South of old while offering novel strategies for reform of the New South. Education is a focal point for Page, whose novel *The Southerner* (1909), written under the pseudonym Nicholas Worth, offers a chapter set in a boys' academy where chivalry and honor are just as esteemed as during the war, when many of the boys' fathers fought to preserve "distorted traditions." Although the protagonist of the novel acknowledges that "our fathers were brave," he also recognizes that "we did not become ourselves till they were buried."

A third social critic whose voice echoed throughout the Southland in the journal he founded in 1902, the *South Atlantic Quarterly*, was John Spencer Bassett. According to Fred Hobson, one of Bassett's editorials gave rise to a controversy much greater than any Trent or Page had ever incited. In "Stirring Up the Fires of Race Antipathy" (October 1903), Bassett reminds Southerners of a problem manifested in "restrictions on the negro vote, in the passage of laws for Jim Crow cars, and in a genuine augmentation on the part of Southerners to take fire at the hint of a 'negro outrage.'" Bassett makes clear that the antipathy between the races is really only antipathy of whites toward blacks. However, none of Bassett's social criticisms rankled Southern whites as much as his declaration that Booker T. Washington was "the greatest man, save General Lee, born in the South in a hundred years."

If the war failed to disappear from the minds of many Southerners, neither did its causes evaporate, as Anna Julia Cooper was quick to remind her audience of largely African American women. In *A Voice from the South*, Cooper senses the great challenges and possibilities "in a period of itself transitional and unsettled." Pointing to the unique status that "the colored woman of today occupies," Cooper also notes that "she [the African American woman] is confronted by both a woman question and a race problem, and is as yet an unknown or an unacknowledged factor in both." From the "vantage of a quiet observer" who understands the manipulations and selfishness of American politics, the author urges black women to keep black men solidly in the Republican party, calling the "Democratic Negro . . . a traitor." Cooper's activism, as she points out, is part of a long-standing tradition of work and influence by American women, including such pioneers as Frances Watkins Harper, Charlotte Grimké, Sarah Woodson Early, Martha Briggs, Hallie Quinn Brown, and Fannie Jackson Coppin. As with these women, Cooper sees herself as a crucial agent for moral change at a time ripe for such a possibility.

But such change would come slowly. For instance, Lucinda Mackethan points out that the so-called plantation fiction written between 1865 and 1900 continued to popularize "'black mammy' tales, Negro dialect stories, hillbilly humor, backcountry tales of provincials and reconciliation novels."[21] Some writers even blurred distinctions by "mentioning both colonels and hillbillies," offering an undifferentiated and stereotyped portrait of a South that was, in reality, complex and variegated in social design.[22]

James Lane Allen was a Kentuckian and local colorist determined to prove what the Civil War had not proven: that Kentucky was just as Southerner in outlook and temperament as states more avowedly Confederate. Allen's *The Reign of Law: a Tale of the Kentucky Hemp Fields* traces the history of a single crop, hemp, used for hay-baling until shortly after the Civil War, when cotton production on a large scale disappeared in the South. Lane extols the "Anglo-Saxon" farmers who had no sooner tamed the Kentucky wilderness than they found themselves "sowers of hemp." Hemp production enabled cabin dwellers to become men of means able to acquire both leisure and luxuries associated with the advertised life of a gentleman. Even so, by the time of Allen's writing, that life was close to extinction, a fact that Allen mildly laments.

Changes in the South would ultimately produce changes in the literature. The issues surrounding the war and the South's defeat would assume less potency and engender less nostalgic redolence as time passed. Authors such as William Sydney Porter (pseudonym O. Henry), a native of North Carolina, would use Southern materials less frequently, even "burlesquing Northern misconceptions of the South."[23] Porter's "A Municipal Report" is certainly a Southern story, set in Nashville around the turn of the century. However, the glories of the Old South are few in this piece. Instead, one finds "decaying mansions," "ennuied citizens," and murder associated with urban living. Gone are memories of cherished traditions. Remaining are "the drizzle and monotony of a dreary, eventless Southern town . . . ," a place not even Porter's humorous asides can rescue from the malaise of modern life.

Notes

1. Thomas Connelly, *Civil War Tennessee* (Knoxville: University of Tennessee Press, 1979), 100.
2. Samuel Eliot Morison, *The Oxford History of the American People*, Vol. 2 (New York: Penguin Books, 1972), 500.
3. Eric Foner, *Reconstruction* (New York: Harper and Row, 1988), 29.
4. Jack Hurst, *Nathan Bedford Forrest* (New York: Alfred A. Knopf, 1993), 384–385.
5. Hurst, 385.
6. Lewis M. Killian, *White Southerners* (New York: Random House, 1970), 23.
7. Hurst, 385.
8. Hurst, 385–386.
9. Edward L. Ayers, *The Promise of the New South* (New York: Oxford University Press, 1998), 7.
10. Ayers, 72.
11. Eugene Genovese, *A Consuming Fire* (Athens: University of Georgia Press, 1998), 7.
12. Lucinda Mackethan, "Plantation Fiction, 1865–1900, *The History of Southern Literature*, ed. Louis D. Rubin et al. (Baton Rouge: Louisiana State University Press, 1985), 213.
13. Mackethan, 213.
14. Linda Burton Francisco, *Stories from Tennessee* (Knoxville: University of Tennessee Press, 1983), xi.
15. Francisco, xi–xii.
16. Francisco, xii.

17. Dewey Grantham, "Henry W. Grady and the New South," *The History of Southern Literature*, ed. Louis D. Rubin et al. (Baton Rouge: Louisiana State University Press, 1985), 244.

18. Edgar E. MacDonald, "The Ambivalent Heart: Revival in Richmond," *The History of Southern Literature*, ed. Louis D. Rubin et al. (Baton Route: Louisiana State University Press, 1985), 265.

19. MacDonald, 265.

20. Fred Hobson, "The Rise of the Critical Temper," *The History of Southern Literature*, ed. Louis D. Rubin et al. (Baton Rouge: Louisiana State University Press, 1985), 253.

21. Lucinda Mackethan, 212.

22. Mackethan, 212.

23. Wayne Mixon, "Humor, Romance, and Realism at the Turn of the Century," *The History of Southern Literature*, ed. Louis D. Rubin et al. (Baton Rouge: Louisiana State University Press, 1985), 247.

Frederick Douglass

(1817–1895)

Born Frederick Augustus Washington Bailey in Tuckahoe, Maryland, Frederick Douglass later in life calculated that his birth date was in February 1817. The son of Harriet Bailey and a white man whose name he never learned, Douglass endured countless sufferings during his life as a slave. As a very young child, he was kept in a breeding pen with dogs and pigs, and was fed a diet of corn mush. As he grew older, he served at various times as a house servant, shipyard laborer, and field hand. Taught to read by the wife of one of his masters (instruction that ended abruptly when her husband learned of the deed), Douglass continued his education on his own, using a copy of the *Columbian Orator* that he bought with money he made blacking boots for white men. In 1834, he was turned over to Edward Covey, a paid slave breaker, who beat him constantly until Douglass fought back in a confrontation immortalized in his autobiography. From that day on, he sought an opportunity for escape, and in 1838 he succeeded, using a borrowed sailor's suit. He fled to Philadelphia and then on to New York City, where he married Anna Murray, a Baltimore freedwoman who had helped finance his escape. Taking the surname Douglass, the couple moved to New Bedford, Massachusetts, where Frederick Douglass began attending meetings of William Lloyd Garrison's Abolitionist Society. Encouraged by Garrison, he began his career as an orator, and at the risk of being recaptured, Douglass toured the country, speaking for the abolitionist cause.

In 1845, Douglass published his *Narrative of the Life of Frederick Douglass, American Slave* to convince audiences of the truth of his assertions. After its publication, Douglass fled to England, where friends arranged to purchase his freedom. Returning to America in 1847, he began the newspaper *The North Star* with funds from the same British associates, changing the title in 1851 to *Frederick Douglass's Paper*. When John Brown made his raid on Harper's Ferry in 1859, Douglass was forced once again to flee to England because of his past associations with Brown. He returned early in 1860. Initially an opponent of Abraham Lincoln, Douglass supported him after the Emancipation Proclamation of 1863, and he was called to Washington for a number of meetings with the president during the war. His efforts to influence the South's reconstruction were not well received by Andrew Johnson, but he influenced Ulysses S. Grant to favor the right to vote for American blacks, and he served in various minor posts in government during the Hayes, Garfield, and Arthur administrations.

from *Narrative of the Life of Frederick Douglass, an American Slave*

Chapter I

I was born in Tuckahoe, near Hillsborough, and about twelve miles from Easton, in Talbot county, Maryland. I have no accurate knowledge of my age, never having seen any authentic record containing it. By far the larger part of the slaves know as little of their age as horses know of theirs, and it is the wish of most masters within my knowledge to keep their slaves thus ignorant. I do not remember to have ever met a slave who could tell of his birthday. They seldom come nearer to it than planting-time, harvest-time, cherry-time, spring-time, or fall-time. A want of information concerning my own was a source of unhappiness to me even during childhood. The white children could tell their ages. I could not tell why I ought to be deprived of the same privilege. I was not allowed to make any inquiries of my master concerning it. He deemed all such inquiries on the part of a slave improper and impertinent, and evidence of a restless spirit. The nearest estimate I can give makes me now between twenty-seven and twenty-eight years of age. I come to this, from hearing my master say, some time during 1835, I was about seventeen years old.

My mother was named Harriet Bailey. She was the daughter of Isaac and Betsey Bailey, both colored, and quite dark. My mother was of a darker complexion than either my grandmother or grandfather.

My father was a white man. He was admitted to be such by all I ever heard speak of my parentage. The opinion was also whispered that my master was my father; but of the correctness of this opinion, I know nothing; the means of knowing was withheld from me. My mother and I were separated when I was but an infant—before I knew her as my mother. It is a common custom, in the part of Maryland from which I ran away, to part children from their mothers at a very early age. Frequently, before the child has reached its twelfth month, its mother is taken from it, and hired out on some farm a considerable distance off, and the child is placed under the care of an old woman, too old for field labor. For what this separation is done, I do not know, unless it be to hinder the development of the child's affection toward its mother, and to blunt and destroy the natural affection of the mother for the child. This is the inevitable result.

I never saw my mother, to know her as such, more than four or five times in my life; and each of these times was very short in duration, and at night. She was hired by a Mr. Stewart, who lived about twelve miles from my home. She made her journeys to see me in the night, travelling the whole distance on foot, after the performance of her day's work. She was a field hand, and a whipping is the penalty of not being in the field at sunrise, unless a slave has special permission from his or her master to the contrary—a permission which they seldom get, and one that gives to him that gives it the proud name of being a kind master. I do not recollect of ever seeing my mother by the light of day. She was with me in the night. She would lie down with me, and get me to sleep, but long before I waked she was gone. Very little communication ever took place between us. Death soon ended what little we could have while she lived, and with it her hardships and suffering. She died when I was about seven years old, on one of my master's farms, near Lee's Mill. I was not allowed to be present during her illness, at her death, or burial. She was gone long before I knew any thing about it. Never having enjoyed, to any considerable extent, her soothing presence, her tender and watchful care, I received the tidings of her death with much the same emotions I should have probably felt at the death of a stranger.

Called thus suddenly away, she left me without the slightest intimation of who my father was. The whisper that my master was my father, may or may not be true; and, true or false, it is of but little consequence to my purpose whilst the fact remains, in all its glaring odiousness, that slaveholders have ordained, and by law established, that the children of slave women shall in all cases follow the condition of their mothers; and this is done too obviously to administer to their own lusts, and make a gratification of their wicked desires profitable as well as pleasurable; for by this cunning arrangement, the slaveholder, in cases not a few, sustains to his slaves the double relation of master and father.

I know of such cases; and it is worthy of remark that such slaves invariably suffer greater hardships, and have more to contend with, than others. They are, in the first place, a constant offence to their mistress. She is ever disposed to find fault with them; they can seldom do any thing to please her; she is never better pleased than when she sees them under the lash, especially when she suspects her husband of showing to his mulatto children favors which he withholds from his black slaves. The master is frequently compelled to sell this class of his slaves, out of deference to the feelings of his white wife; and, cruel as the deed may strike any one to be, for a man to sell his own children to human flesh-mongers, it is often the dictate of humanity for him to do so; for, unless he does this, he must not only whip them himself, but must stand by and see one white son tie up his brother, of but few shades darker complexion than himself, and ply the gory lash to his naked back; and if he lisp one word of disapproval, it is set down to his parental partiality, and only makes a bad matter worse, both for himself and the slave whom he would protect and defend.

Every year brings with it multitudes of this class of slaves. It was doubtless in consequence of a knowledge of this fact, that one great statesman of the south predicted the downfall of slavery by the inevitable laws of population. Whether this prophecy is ever fulfilled or not, it is nevertheless plain that a very different-looking class of people are springing up at the south, and are now held in slavery, from those originally brought to this country from Africa; and if their increase will do no other good, it will do away the force of the argument, that God cursed Ham, and therefore American slavery is right. If the lineal descendants of Ham are alone to be scripturally enslaved, it is certain that slavery at the south must soon become unscriptural; for thousands are ushered into the world, annually, who, like myself, owe their existence to white fathers, and those fathers most frequently their own masters.

I have had two masters. My first master's name was Anthony. I do not remember his first name. He was generally called Captain Anthony—a title which, I presume, he acquired by sailing a craft on the Chesapeake Bay. He was not considered a rich slaveholder. He owned two or three farms, and about thirty slaves. His farms and slaves were under the care of an overseer. The overseer's name was Plummer. Mr. Plummer was a miserable drunkard, a profane swearer, and a savage monster. He always went armed with a cowskin and a heavy cudgel. I have known him to cut and slash the women's heads so horribly, that even master would be enraged at his cruelty, and would threaten to whip him if he did not mind himself. Master, however, was not a humane slaveholder. It required extraordinary barbarity on the part of an overseer to affect him. He was a cruel man, hardened by a long life of slaveholding. He would at times seem to take great pleasure in whipping a slave. I have often been awakened at the dawn of day by the most heart-rending shrieks of an own aunt of mine, whom he used to tie up to a joist, and whip upon her naked back till she was literally covered with blood. No words, no tears, no prayers, from his gory victim, seemed to move his iron heart from its bloody purpose. The louder she screamed, the harder he whipped; and where the blood ran fastest, there he whipped longest. He would whip her to make her scream, and whip her to make her hush; and not until overcome by fatigue, would he cease to swing the blood-clotted cowskin. I remember the first time I ever witnessed this horrible exhibition. I was quite a child, but I well remember it. I never shall forget it whilst I remember any thing. It was the first of a long series of such outrages, of which I was doomed to be a witness and a participant. It struck me with awful force. It was the blood-stained gate, the entrance to the hell of slavery, through which I was about to pass. It was a most terrible spectacle. I wish I could commit to paper the feelings with which I beheld it.

This occurrence took place very soon after I went to live with my old master, and under the following circumstances. Aunt Hester went out one night,—where or for what I do not know,—and happened to be absent when my master desired her presence. He had ordered her not to go out evenings, and warned her that she must never let him catch her in company with a young man, who was paying attention to her belonging to Colonel Lloyd. The young man's name was Ned Roberts, generally called Lloyd's Ned. Why master was so careful of her, may be safely left to conjecture. She was a woman of noble form, and of graceful proportions, having very few equals, and fewer superiors, in personal appearance, among the colored or white women of our neighborhood.

Aunt Hester had not only disobeyed his orders in going out, but had been found in company with Lloyd's Ned; which circumstance, I found, from what he said while whipping her, was the chief offence. Had he been a man of pure morals himself, he might have been thought interested in protecting the innocence of my aunt; but those who knew him will not suspect him of any such virtue. Before he commenced whipping Aunt Hester, he took her into the kitchen, and stripped her from neck to waist, leaving her neck, shoulders, and back, entirely naked. He then told her to cross her hands, calling her at the same time a d—d b—h. After crossing her hands, he tied them with a strong rope, and led her to a stool under a large hook in the joist, put in for the purpose. He made her get upon the stool, and tied her hands to the hook. She now stood fair for his infernal purpose. Her arms were stretched up at their full length, so that she stood upon the ends of her toes. He then said to her, "Now, you d—d b—h, I'll learn you how to disobey my orders!" and after rolling up his sleeves, he commenced to lay on the heavy cowskin, and soon the warm, red blood (amid heart-rending shrieks from her, and horrid oaths from him) came dripping to the floor. I was so terrified and horror-stricken at the sight, that I hid myself in a closet, and dared not venture out till long after the bloody transaction was over. I expected it would be my turn next. I t was all new to me. I had never seen any thing like it before. I had always lived with my grandmother on the outskirts of the plantation, where she was put to raise the children of the younger women. I had therefore been, until now, out of the way of the bloody scenes that often occurred on the plantation.

Nathan Bedford Forrest

(1821–1877)

No Southern historical figure has inspired more controversy than Nathan Bedford Forrest. A natural tactician who entered the Confederate army as a private and left as a general, Forrest declared his intention to "put the skeer on [his opponents], an' keep 'em skeered," and he was extremely successful in the endeavor. His exploits have become the stuff of legend, from his refusal to surrender at Fort Donelson, to his single-handed rout of a Union line at Pittsburg Landing (Shiloh). Fierce to the end, he toyed with the idea of continuing to fight in Mexico after Appomatox, and his was the last group of men to surrender east of the Mississippi.

But Forrest's role in the history of racial conflict in America has brought him as much vilification as his military acumen has brought him accolades. After dealing in horses and cattle in Mississippi, he became a slave trader in Memphis, Tennessee, before the war. More significantly, after the war he led a small group of men that acted as enforcers for the Democratic Party in the South, a group that would come to be known as the Ku Klux Klan. However, many historians have ignored the fact that Forrest disbanded the group in 1868, declaring that it had become too violent, calling it "the worst mistake our people ever made." Nevertheless, he was implicated in Klan activities in subsequent Congressional hearings. In the years before his death, he underwent a profound religious conversion, which ameliorated his racial views, and in 1875 he was invited by prominent African Americans in Memphis to speak about racial matters at a civic function. The text of that speech follows.

Speech to the African-American Community of Memphis, 1875

Ladies and Gentlemen—I accept the flowers as a memento of reconciliation between the white and colored races of the southern states. I accept it more particularly as it comes from a colored lady, for if there is any one on God's earth who loves the ladies I believe it is myself. (Immense applause and laughter.) . . . I came here with the jeers of some white people, who think that I am doing wrong. I believe I can exert some influence, and do much to assist the people in strengthening fraternal relations, and shall do all in my power to elevate every man—to depress none. (Applause.) I want to elevate you to take positions in law offices, in stores, on farms, and wherever you are capable of going. I have not said anything about politics today. I don't propose to say anything about politics. You have a right to elect whom you please; vote for the man you think best, and I think, when that is done, you and I are freemen. Do as you consider right and honest in electing men for office. I did not come here to make you a long speech, although invited to do so by you. I am not much of a speaker, and my business prevented me from preparing myself. I came to meet you as friends, and welcome you to the white people. I want you to come nearer to us. When I can serve you I will do so. We have but one flag, one country; let us stand together. We may differ in color, but not in sentiment . . . Many things have been said about me which are wrong, and which white and black persons here, who stood by me through the war, can contradict. I have been in the heat of battle when colored men asked me to protect them. I have placed myself between them and the bullets of my men, and told them they should be kept unharmed. Go to work, be industrious, live honestly and act truly, and when you are oppressed I'll come to your relief. I thank you, ladies and gentlemen, for this opportunity you have afforded me to be with you, and to assure you that I am with you in heart and in hand.

George Washington Harris
(1814–1869)

George Washington Harris was born in Allegheny City, Pennsylvania, on March 20, 1814. In 1819, Harris moved to Knoxville, Tennessee, with his half-brother Samuel Bell, who was considerably older than Harris and to whom the latter eventually served as an apprenticed metalworker. Harris's formal education was scant. Never settling into one profession, Harris was involved throughout his life in a number of occupations, such as metalworker, gentleman farmer, steamship captain, superintendent of the Holston Glass Works, postmaster, and railroad engineer. Regarding his career as a writer, Harris began contributing political articles to the Democratic *Knoxville Argus and Commercial Herald* in 1839, and in 1843 he published several sporting epistles in William T. Porter's New York *Spirit of the Times* under the pseudonym "Mr. Free." In addition, the *Spirit* provided Harris an outlet for his first full-length story, "The Knob Dance—A Tennessee Frolic," which appeared in 1845 under the pseudonym "Sugartail." Of most importance, Harris's first Sut Lovingood story, "Sut Lovingood's Daddy Acting Horse," was printed in the November 4, 1854, issue of the *Spirit*.

In 1858, Harris, a Confederate sympathizer, left Unionist East Tennessee for Confederate Nashville; however, he fled Nashville in 1862—to escape the Union army. Afterwards he lived in several Southern cities, including Chattanooga, Tennessee; Decatur, Alabama; and Trenton, Georgia. In April 1867, Harris's collection of stories, *Sut Lovingood: Yarns Spun by a "Nat'ral Born Durn'd Fool,"* which was set in East Tennessee's Copper Basin area, was published in New York. After Harris's first wife, Mary Emeline Nance, mother of his six children, died in 1867, he married the widowed Mrs. Jane E. Pride on October 19, 1869. Finally, in December 1869, after seeking publication for his new manuscript of stories entitled *High Times and Hard Times* in Lynchburg, Virginia, Harris fell ill on the return train trip home and was taken off the train at Knoxville, where he died on December 11, 1869, after having uttered the word *poisoned*. Although the cause of his death has remained an intriguing mystery, many people believe that Harris died from apoplexy. His unpublished manuscript has never been recovered.

from *Sut Lovingood:*

Yarns Spun by a "Nat'ral Born Durn'd Fool;
Warped and Wove for Public Wear"

Parson John Bullen's Lizards

> *AIT ($8) DULLARS REW-ARD.*
> *"TENSHUN BELEVERS AND KONSTABLES!*
> *KETCH 'IM! KETCH 'IM!*
> This kash wil be pade in korn, ur uther projuce, tu be kolected at ur
> about nex camp-meetin, ur thararter, *by eny wun what ketches him, fur the*
> karkus ove a sartin wun SUT LOVINGOOD, dead ur alive, ur ailin, an'
> safely giv over tu the purtectin care ove Parson John Bullin, ur lef' well
> tied, at Squire Mackjunkins, fur the raisin ove the devil pussonely, an'
> permiskusly discumfurtin the wimen very powerful, an' skeerin ove folks
> generly a heap, an' bustin up a promisin, big warm meetin, an' a making
> the wickid larf, an' wus, an' wus, insultin ove the passun orful.
> Test, JEHU WETHERO.
>> Sined by me,
>> JOHN BULLEN, the passun.

I found written copies of the above highly intelligible and vindictive proclamation, stuck up on every blacksmith shop, doggery, and store door, in the Frog Mountain Range. Its blood-thirsty spirit, its style, and above all, its chirography, interested
me to the extent of taking one down from a tree for preservation.

In a few days I found Sut in a good crowd in front of Capehart's Doggery, and as
he seemed to be about in good tune, I read it to him.

"Yas, George, that ar dockymint am in dead yearnist sartin. Them hard shells
over thar dus want me the wus kine, powerful bad. *But,* I spect ait dullers won't fetch
me, nither wud ait hundred, bekase thar's nun ove 'em fas' enuf tu ketch me, nither is
that hosses by the livin jingo! Say, George, much talk 'bout this fuss up whar yu're
been?" For the sake of a joke I said yes, a great deal.

"Jis' es I 'spected, durn 'em, all git drunk, an' skeer thar fool sefs ni ontu deth, an'
then lay hit ontu me, a poor innersent youf, an' es soun' a believer es they is. Lite, lite,
ole feller an' let that roan ove yourn blow a litil, an' I'll 'splain this cussed misfortnit
affar: hit hes ruinated my karacter es a pius pusson in the s'ciety roun' yere, an' is a
spreadin faster nur meazils. When ever yu hear eny on 'em a spreadin hit, gin hit the
dam lie squar, will yu? I haint dun nuffin tu one ove 'em. Hits true, I did sorter frustrate a few lizzards a littil, but they haint members, es I knows on.

"You see, las' year I went tu the big meetin at Rattlesnake Springs, an' wer a sittin
in a nice shady place convarsin wif a frien' ove mine, intu the huckil berry thickit, jis'
duin nuffin tu nobody an' makin no fuss, when, the fust thing I remembers, I woke up
frum a trance what I hed been knocked inter by a four year old hickory-stick, hilt in
the paw ove ole Passun Bullin, durn his alligator hide; an' he wet standin a striddil ove

"Parson John Bullen's Lizards," by George W. Harris, from *Sut Lovingood Yarns Spun by a*
"Nat'ral Born Durn'd Fool: Warped and Wove for Public Wear." New York: Dick & Fitzgerald, 1867.

me, a foamin at the mouf, a-chompin his teeth—gesterin wif the hickory club—an' a-preachin tu me so you cud a-hearn him a mile, about a sartin sin gineraly, an' my wickedness pussonely; an' mensunin the name ove my frien' loud enuf tu be hearn tu the meetin 'ous. My poor innersent frien' wer dun gone an' I wer glad ove hit, fur I tho't he ment tu kill me rite what I lay, an' I didn't want her tu see me die."

"Who was she, the friend you speak of Sut?" Sut opened his eyes wide.

"Hu the devil, an' durnashun tole *yu* that hit wer a she?"

"Why, you did, Sut"——

"I *didn't*, durn ef I did. Ole Bullin dun hit, an' I'll hev tu kill him yet, the cussed, infernel ole talebarer!"——

"Well, well, Sut who was she?"

"Nun ove y-u-r-e b-i-s-n-i-s-s, durn yure littil ankshus picter! I *sees yu* a lickin ove yure lips. I *will* tell you one thing, George; that night, a neighbor gal got a all fired, overhandid stroppin frum her mam, wif a stirrup leather, an' ole Passun Bullin, hed et supper thar, an' what's wus nur all, that poor, innersent, skeer'd gal hed dun her levil bes' a cookin hit fur 'im. She begged him, a trimblin, an' a-cryin not tu tell on her. He et her cookin, he promised her he'd keep dark—an' then went strait an' tole her mam. Warnt that rale low down, wolf mean? The durnd infunel, hiperkritikal, pot-bellied, scaley-hided, whisky-wastin, stinkin ole groun'-hog. He'd a heap better a stole sum *man's* hoss; I'd a tho't more ove 'im. But I paid him plum up fur hit, an' I means tu keep a payin him, until one ur tuther, ove our toes pints up tu the roots ove the grass.

"Well, yere's the way I lifted that note ove han'. At the nex big meetin at Rattil-snaik—las' week hit wer—I wer on han' es solemn es a ole hat kivver on collection day. I hed my face draw'd out intu the shape an' perporshun ove a tayler's sleeve-board, pint down. I hed put on the convicted sinner so pufeckly that an' ole obsarvin she pillar ove the church sed tu a ole he piller, es I walked up to my bainch:

"'Law sakes alive, ef thar ain't that *orful* sinner, Sut Lovingood, pearced plum thru; hu's nex?'

"Yu see, by golly, George, I *hed* tu promis the ole tub ove soap-greas tu cum an' hev myself convarted, jis' tu keep him frum killin me. An' es I know'd hit wudn't inter-fare wif the relashun I bore tu the still housis roun' thar, I didn't keer a durn. I jis' wanted tu git *ni* old Bullin, onst onsuspected, an' this wer the bes' way tu du hit. I tuk a seat on the side steps ove the pulpit, an' kivvered es much ove my straitch'd face es I could wif my han's, tu prove I wer in yearnis. Hit tuck powerful—fur I hearn a sorter thankful kine ove buzzin all over the congregashun. Ole Bullin hissef looked down at me, over his ole copper specks, an' hit sed jis' es plain es a look cud say hit: 'Yu am thar, ar you—durn yu, hits well fur yu that yu cum.' I tho't sorter different frum that. I tho't hit wud a been well fur *yu*, ef I hadent a-cum, but I didn't say hit jis then. Thar wer a monstrus crowd in that grove, fur the weather wer fine, an' b'levers wer plenty roun' about Rattilsnaik Springs. Ole Bullin gin out, an' they sung that hyme, yu know:

"Thar will be mournin, mournin yere, an' mournin thar,
On that dredful day tu cum."

"Thinks I, ole hoss, kin hit be possibil enybody hes tole yu what's a gwine tu happin; an' then I tho't that nobody know'd hit but me, and I wer cumforted. He nex tuck hisself a tex pow'fly mixed wif brimstone, an' trim'd wif blue flames, an' then he open'd. He cummenced ontu the sinners; he threaten'd 'em orful, tried tu skeer 'em wif all the wust varmints he cud think ove, an' arter a while he got ontu the idear ove Hell-sarpints, and he dwelt on it sum. He tole 'em how the ole Hell-sarpints wud serve em if they didn't repent; how cold they'd crawl over thar nakid bodys, an' how like ontu pitch they'd stick tu 'em as they crawled; how they'd rap thar tails roun' thar naiks chokin clost, poke that tungs up thar noses, an' hiss intu thar years. This wer the way they wer tu sarve men folks. Then he turned ontu the wimmen: tole 'em how they'd quile intu that buzzims, an' how they *wud* crawl down onder thar frock-strings, no odds how tite they tied 'em, an' how sum ove the oldes' an' wus ones wud crawl up thar laigs, an' travil *onder* thar garters, no odds how tight they tied *them*, an' when the two armys ove Hell-sarpents met, then——That las' remark *fotch 'em.* Ove all the screamin, an' hollerin, an' loud cryin, I ever hearn, begun all at onst, all over the hole groun' jis' es he hollered out that word 'then.' He kep on a bellerin, but I got so busy jis' then, that I didn't listen tu him much, fur I saw that my time fur ackshun hed cum. Now yu see, George, I'd cotch seven ur eight big pot-bellied lizzards, an' hed 'em in a littil narrer bag, what I had made a-purpus. Thar tails all at the bottim, an' so crowdid fur room that they cudent turn roun'. So when he wer a-ravin ontu his tip-toes, an' a-poundin the pulpit wif his fis'—onbenowenst tu enybody, I ontied my bag ove reptiles, put the mouf ove hit onder the bottim ove his britches-laig, an' sot intu pinchin thar tails. Quick es gunpowder they all tuck up his bar laig, makin a nise like squirrils a-climbin a shell-bark hickory. He stop'd preachin rite in the middil ove the word 'damnation,' an' looked fur a moment like he wer a listenin fur sumthin—sorter like a ole sow dus, when she hears yu a whistlin fur the dorgs. The tarifick shape ove his feeters stopp't the shoutin an' screamin; instuntly yu cud hearn a cricket chirp. I gin a long groan, an' hilt my head a-twixt my knees. He gin hisself sum orful open-handed slaps wif fust one han' an' then tuther, about the place whar yu cut the bes' steak outen a beef. Then he'd fetch a vigrus ruff rub whar a hosses tail sprouts; then he'd stomp one foot, then tuther, then bof at onst. Then he run his han' atween his waisbun an' his shut an' reach'd way down, an' roun' wif hit; then he spread his big laigs, an' gin his back a good rattlin rub agin the pulpit, like a hog scratches hisself agin a stump, leanin tu hit pow'ful, an' twitchin, an' squirmin all over, es ef he'd slept in a dorg bed, ur ontu a pisant hill. About this time, one ove my lizzards scared an' hurt by all this poundin' an' feelin, an' scratchin, popp'd out his head frum the passun's shut collar, an' his ole brown naik, an' wer a-surveyin the crowd, when ole Bullin struck at 'im, jis' too late, fur he'd dodged back agin. The hell desarvin ole raskil's speech now cum tu 'im, an' sez he, 'Pray fur me brethren an' sisteren, fur I is a-rastlinin wif the great inimy rite now!' an' his voice wer the mos' pitiful, trimblin thing I ever hearn. Sum ove the wimmen fotch a painter yell, an' a young docter, wif ramrod laigs, lean'd toward me monstrus knowin like, an' sez he, 'Clar case ove Delishus Tremenjus.' I nodded my head an' sez I, 'Yas, spechuly the tremenjus part, an' Ise feard hit haint at hits worst.' Ole Bullin's eyes wer a-stickin out like ontu two buckeyes flung agin a mud wall, an' he wer a-cuttin up more shines nor a cockroach in a hot skillet. Off went the clawhammer coat, an' he flung hit ahine 'im like he wer a-gwine intu a fight; he hed no jackid tu take off, so he unbuttoned his galluses, an' vigruslly flung the ainds back over his head. He fotch his shut over-handed a durnd site faster nor I got outen my pasted one, an' then flung hit strait up in the air, like he jis' wanted hit tu keep on up furever; but hit lodged ontu a black-jack, an' I seed one ove my lizzards wif his tail up, a-racin about all over the ole dirty shut, skared too bad tu jump. Then he gin a sorter shake, an' a stompin kine ove twis', an' he cum outer his britches. He tuck 'em by the bottim ove the laigs, an' swung 'em roun' his head a time ur two, an' then fotch 'em down cherall-up over the frunt ove the pulpit. You cud a hearn the smash a quarter ove a mile! Ni ontu fifteen shorten'd biskits, a boiled chicken, wif hits laigs crossed, a big dubbil-bladed knife, a hunk ove terbacker, a cob-pipe, sum copper ore, lots ove broken glass, a cork, a sprinkil ove whisky, a squirt, an' three lizzards flew permiskusly all over that meetin-groun', outen the upper aind ove them big flax britches. One ove the smartes' ove my lizzards lit head-fust intu the buzzim ove a fat 'oman, es big es a skin'd hoss, an' ni ontu es ugly, who sot thuty yards off, a fannin hersef wif a tucky-tail. Smart tu the las', by golly, he imejuntly commenced runnin down the centre ove her breas'-bone, an' kep on, I speck. She wer jis' boun' tu faint; an' she did hit fust rate—flung the tucky-tail up in the air, grabbed the lap ove her gown, gin hit a big histin an' fallin shake, rolled down the hill, tangled her laigs an' garters in the top ove a huckilberry bush, wif her head in the branch an' jis' lay still. She wer interstin, she wer, ontil a serious-lookin, pale-faced 'oman hung a nankeen ridin skirt over the huckilberry bush. That wer all that wer dun to'ards bringin her too, that I seed. Now ole Bullin hed nuffin left ontu 'im but a par ove heavy, low quarter'd shoes, short woolen socks, an' eel-skin garters tu keep off the cramp. His skeer hed druv him plum crazy, fur he felt roun' in the air, abuv his head, like he wer huntin sumthin in the dark, an' he beller'd out, 'Brethren, brethren, take keer ove yerselves, the Hell-sarpints *hes got me!*' When this cum out, yu cud a-hearn the screams tu Halifax. He jis' spit in his han's, an' loped over the frunt ove the pulpid *kerdiff!* He lit on top ove, an' rite amung the mos' pius part ove the congregashun. Ole Misses Chaneyberry sot wif her back tu the pulpit, sorter stoopin forrid. He lit a-stradil ove her long naik, a shuttin her up wif a snap, her head atwix her knees, like shuttin up a jack-knife, an' he sot intu gittin away his levil durndest; he went in a heavy lumberin gallop, like a ole fat waggon hoss, skared at a locomotive. When he jumpt a bainch he shook the yeath. The bonnets, an' fans clar'd the way an' jerked most ove the children wif em, an' the rest he scrunched. He open'd a purfeckly clar track tu the woods, ove every livin thing. He weighed ni ontu three hundred, hed a black stripe down his back, like ontu a ole bridil rein, an' his belly wet 'bout the size, an' color ove a beef paunch, an' hit a-swinging out frum side tu side; he leand back frum hit, like a littil feller a-totin a big drum, at a muster, an' I hearn hit plum tu whar I wer. Thar wer cramp-knots on his laigs es big es walnuts, an' mottled splotches on his shins; an' takin him all over, he minded ove a durnd crazy ole elephant, pussessed ove the devil, rated up on hits hind aind, an' jis' *gittin* frum sum imijut danger ur tribulashun. He did the loudest, an' skariest, an' fussiest runnin I ever seed, tu be no faster nur hit wer, since dad tried tu outrun the ho'nets.

"Well, he disapear'd in the thicket jis' bustin—an' ove all the noises yu ever hearn, wer made thar on that camp groun': sum wimen screamin—they wer the skeery ones; sum larfin—they wer the wicked ones; sum cryin—they wer the fool ones (sorter my stripe yu know); sum trying tu git away wif thar faces red—they wer the modest ones; sum lookin arter ole Bullin—they wer the curious ones; sum hangin clost tu thar sweet-hearts—they wer the sweet ones; sum on thar knees wif thar eyes shot, but facin the way the ole mud turtil wer a-runnin—they wer the 'saitful ones; sum duin nuthin—they wer the waitin ones; an' the mos' dangerus ove all ove em by a durnd long site.

"I tuck a big skeer mysef arter a few rocks, an' sich like fruit, spattered ontu the pulpit ni ontu my head; an' es the Lovingoods, durn em! knows nuffin but tu run, when they gits skeerd, I jis' out fur the swamp on the krick. As I started, a black bottil ove bald-face smashed agin a tree furninst me, arter missin the top ove my head 'bout a inch. Sum durn'd fool professor dun this, who hed more zeal nor sence; fur I say that eny man who wud waste a quart ove even mean sperrits, fur the chance ove knockin a poor ornary devil like me down wif the bottil, is a bigger fool nor ole Squire Mackmullen, an' he tried tu shoot hissef wif a onloaded hoe-handle."

"Did they catch you Sut?"

"Ketch thunder! *No sir!* jis' look at these yere laigs! Skeer me, hoss, jis' skeer me, an' then watch me while I stay in site, an' yu'll never ax that fool question agin. Why, durn it, man that's what the ait dullers am fur.

"Ole Barbelly Bullin, es they calls 'im now, never preached ontil yesterday, an' he hadn't the fust durn'd o'man tu hear 'im; *they hev seed too much ove 'im.* Passuns gin-erly hev a pow'ful strong holt on wimen; but, hoss, I tell yu thar ain't meny ove em kin run stark nakid over an' thru a crowd ove three hundred wimen an' not injure thar karacters *sum.* Enyhow, hits a kind ove show they'd ruther see one at a time, an' pick the passun at that. His tex' wer, 'Nakid I cum intu the world, an' nakid I'm a gwine outen hit, ef I'm spard ontil then.' He sed nakidness warnt much ove a sin, purtickerly ove dark nights. That he wer a weak, frail wum ove the dus', an' a heap more sich truck. Then he totch ontu me; sed I wer a livin proof ove the hell-desarvin nater ove man, an' that thar warnt grace enuf in the whole 'sociation tu saften my outside rind; that I wer 'a lost ball' forty years afore I wer born'd, an' the bes' thing they cud du fur the church, wer tu turn out, an' still hunt fur me ontil I wer shot. An' he never said Hell-sarpints onst in the hole preach. I b'leve, George, the durnd fools am at hit.

"Now, I wants yu tu tell ole Barbelly this fur me, ef he'll let me an' Sall alone, I'll let him alone—a-while; an' ef he don't, ef I don't lizzard him agin, I jis' wish I may be dod durnd! *Skeer him if yu ken.*

"Let's to tu the spring an' take a ho'n.

"Say George, didn't that ar Hell-sarpint sermon ove his'n, hev sumthin like a Hell-sarpint aplicashun?—Hit looks sorter so tu me."

Thomas Nelson Page
(1853–1922)

No author was more responsible for creating the myth of an Edenic antebellum South than Thomas Nelson Page. The noble gentlemen, blushing belles, and contented, happy slaves that populate his fiction inhabit a mythic region that captivated the imaginations not only of Southerners but of those who had been their bitterest foes as well. Thomas Wentworth Higginson, the well-known New England cultural critic and man of letters, is reputed to have broken down and wept over the death of the hero in Page's "Marse Chan." Though his writings obviously do not present accurate histori-cal accounts of postwar life in the South, they do provide valuable insights into the outlook of Page's own generation.

Although his parents were no longer wealthy by the standards of many in the South, Page was raised on a plantation similar to the ones he portrayed in his fiction. The Civil War ended his carefree childhood; his father survived the war, but his farm was ruined. Page entered Washington College in 1869 (during Robert E. Lee's tenure as president) but left because of a lack of funds; he eventually obtained his law de-gree from the University of Virginia in 1874. In 1887 Page published *In Ole Virginia,* which includes "Marse Chan" and "Unc' Edinburg's Drowndin'" and is considered by most to be his best work. He produced a number of similar collections of sentimental fiction, as well as a number of novels, the most ambitious of which was *Red Rock* (1898), a portrayal (and attempted vindication) of the Reconstruction South. In 1893, he moved with his wife to Washington, D.C., and he served for six years as ambassador to Italy in the Woodrow Wilson administration. Page was prolific throughout his long career, and when his works were published in a collected edition in 1912, they comprised eighteen volumes. When he died in 1922, Page left as his legacy an imaginary version of Southern history that for many years stubbornly resisted the efforts of serious historians to provide a more accurate picture.

Unc' Edinburg's Drowndin':

A Plantation Echo

"Well, suh, dat's a fac—dat's what Marse George al'ays said. 'Tis hard to spile Christmas anyways."

The speaker was "Unc' Edinburg," the driver from Werrowcoke, where I was going to spend Christmas; the time was Christmas Eve, and the place the muddiest road in eastern Virginia—a measure which, I feel sure, will, to those who have any experience, establish its claim to distinction.

A half-hour before he had met me at the station, the queerest-looking, raggedest old darky conceivable, brandishing a cedar-staffed whip of enormous proportions in one hand, and clutching a calico letter-bag with a twisted string in the other; and with the exception of a brief interval of temporary suspicion on his part, due to the unfortunate fact that may luggage consisted of only a hand-satchel instead of a trunk, we had been steadily progressing in mutual esteem.

"Dee's a boy standin' by my mules; I got de ker'idge heah for you," had been his first remark on my making myself known to him. "Mistis say as how you might bring a trunk."

I at once saw my danger, and muttered something about "a short visit," but this only made matters worse.

"Dee don' nobody nuver pay short visits dyah," he said, decisively, and I fell to other tactics.

"You couldn' spile Christmas den noways," he repeated, reflectingly, while his little mules trudged knee-deep through the mud. "'Twuz Christmas den, sho' 'nough," he added, the fires of memory smouldering, and then, as they blazed into sudden flame, he asserted, positively: "Dese heah free-issue niggers don' know what Christmas is. Hawg meat an' pop crackers don' meck Christmas. Hit tecks ole times to meck a sho'-'nough, tyahin'-down Christmas. Gord! I's seen 'em! But de wuss Christmas I ever seen tunned out de best in de een," he added, with sudden warmth, "an' dat wuz de Christmas me an' Marse George en' Reveller all got drownded down at Braxton's Creek. You's hearn 'bout dat?"

As he was sitting beside me in solid flesh and blood, and looked as little ethereal in his old hat and patched clothes as an old oak stump would have done, and as Colonel Staunton had made a worldwide reputation when he led his regiment through the Chickahominy thickets against McClellan's intrenchments, I was forced to confess that

I had never been so favored, but would like to hear about it now; and with a hitch of the lap blanket under his outside knee, and a supererogatory jerk of the reins, he began:

"Well, you know, Marse George was jes' eighteen when he went to college. I went wid him, 'cause me an' him wuz de same age; I was born like on a Sat'day in de Christmas, an' he wuz born in de new year on a Chuesday, an' my mammy nussed us bofe at one breast. Dat's de reason maybe huccome we took so to one nurr. He sutney set a heap o' sto' by me; an' I 'ain' nuver see nobody yit wuz good to me as Marse George."

The old fellow, after a short reverie, went on:

"Well, we growed up togerr, jes as to say two stalks in one hill. We cotch ole hyahs togerr, an' we hunted 'possums togerr, an' 'coons. Lord! He wuz a climber! I 'member a fight he had one night up in de ve'y top of a big poplar tree wid a 'coon, whar he done gone up after, en' he flung he hat over he head; an' do' de varmint leetle mo' tyah him all to pieces, he fotch him down dat tree 'live; an' me an' him had him at Christmas. 'Coon meat mighty good when dee fat, you know?"

As this was a direct request for my judgment, I did not have the moral courage to raise an issue, although my views on the subject of 'coon meat are well known to my family; so I grunted something which I doubt not he took for assent, and he proceeded:

"Dee warn' nuttin he didn' lead de row in; he wuz de bes' swimmer I ever see, en' he handled a skiff same as a fish handle heself. An' I wuz wid him constant; wherever you see Marse George, dyah Edinburg sho', jes' like he shadow. So twuz, when he went to de university; 'twarn' nuttin would do but I got to go too. Marster he didn' teck much to de notion, but Marse George wouldn' have it no urr way, en' co'se mistis she teck he side. So I went 'long as he body-servant to teck keer on him an' help meck him a gent'man. An' he wuz, too. From time he got dyah tell he cum 'way he wuz de head man.

"Dee warn' but one man dyah didn' compliment him, an' dat wuz Mr. Darker. But he warn' nuttin! not dat he didn' come o' right good fambly—'cep' dee politics; but he wuz sutney pitted, jes' like sometimes you see a weevly runty pig in a right good litter. Well, Mr. Darker he al'ays 'ginst Marse George; he hate me an him bofe, an' he sutney act mischeevous todes us; 'cause he know he warn' as we all. De Stauntons dee wuz de popularitiest folks in Virginia; an' dee wuz high-larnt besides. So when Marse George run for de medal, an' wuz to meck he gret speech, Mr. Darker he speak 'ginst him. Dat's what Marse George whip him 'bout. 'Ain' nobody nuver told you 'bout dat?"

I again avowed my misfortune; and although it manifestly aroused new doubts, he worked if off on the mules, and once more took up his story.

"Well, you know, dee had been speakin' 'ginst one nurr ev'y Sat'dy night; and ev'ybody knowed Marse George wuz de bes' speaker, but dee give him one mo' sho', an' dee was bofe gwine spread deeselves, an' dee wuz two urr gent'mens also gwine speak. An' dat night when Mr. Darker got up he meck sich a fine speech ev'ybody wuz s'prised; an' some on 'em say Mr. Darker done beat Marse George. But shuh! I know better'n dat; en' Marse George face look so curious; but, suh, when he riz I knowed der wuz somen gwine happen—I wuz leanin' in de winder. He jes step out in front an' throwed up he head like a horse wid a rank kyurb on him, and den he begin; en' twuz jes like de river when hit gits out he bank. He swep' ev'ything. When he fust open he mouf I knowed twuz comin'; he face wuz pale, an' he wuds tremble like a fiddlestring, but he eyes wuz blazin', an' in a minute he wuz jes reshin'. He voice soun' like a bell; an' he jes wallered dat turr man, en' wared him out; an' when he set down dee all yelled en' hollered so you couldn' heah you' ears. Gent'mans, twuz royal!

"Den dee tuck de vote, an' Marse George got it munanimous, en' dee all hollered agin, all 'cep' a few o' Mr. Darker's friends. An' Mr. Darker he wuz de second. An' den dee broke up. An' jes den Marse George walked thoo de crowd straight up to him, an' lookin' him right in de eyes, says to him, 'You stole dat speech you made to-night.' Well, suh, you ought to 'a hearn 'em; hit soun' like a mill-dam. You couldn' heah nuttin 'cep' roarin', an' you couldn' see nuttin 'cep' shovin'; but, big as he wuz, Marse George beat him; an' when dee pull him off, do' he face wuz mighty pale, he stan' out befo' 'em all, dem whar wuz 'ginst him, an' all, an' as straight as an arrow, an' say: 'Dat speech wuz written an' printed years ago by somebody or nurr in Congress, an' this man stole it; had he beat me only, I should not have said one word; but as he has beaten others, I shall show him up!' Gord, suh, he voice wuz clear as a game rooster. I sutney wuz proud on him.

"He did show him up, too, but Mr. Darker ain' wait to see it; he lef' dat night. An' Marse George he wuz de popularest gent'man at dat university. He could handle dem students dyah same as a man handle a hoe.

"Well, twuz de next Christmas we meet Miss Charlotte an' Nancy. Mr. Braxton invite we all to go down to spen' Christmas wid him at he home. An' sich a time as we had!

"We got dyah Christmas Eve night—dis very night—jes befo' supper, an' jes natchelly froze to death," he pursued, dealing in his wonted hyperbole, "an' we jes had time to git a apple toddy or two when supper was ready, an' wud come dat dee wuz waitin' in de hall. I had done fix Marse George up gorgeousome, I tell you; and when he walk down dem stairs in dat swaller-tail coat, an' dem paten'-leather pumps on, dee warn nay one dyah could fetch him; he looked like he own 'em all. I jes rest my mind. I seen him when he shake hands wid 'em all roun', an' I say, 'Um-m-m! he got 'em.'

"But he ain' teck noticement o' none much tell Miss Charlotte come. She didn' live dyah, had jes come over de river dat evenin' from her home, 'bout ten miles off, to spen' Christmas like we all, an' she come down de stairs jes as Marse George finish shakin' hands. I seen he eye light on her as she come down de steps smilin', wid her dim blue dress trainin' behind her, an' her little blue foots peepin' out so pretty, an' holdin' a little hankcher, lookin' like a spider-web, in one hand, an' a gret blue fan in turr, spread out like a peacock tail, an' jes her roun' arms en' th'oat white, an' her gret dark eyes lightin' up her face. I say, 'Dyah 'tis!' and when de ole Cun'l stan' aside an' interduce 'em, an' Marse George step for'ard an' meck he grand bow, an' she sort o' swing back an' gin her curtchy, wid her dress sort o' dammed up 'ginst her, an' her arms so white, an' her face sort o' sunsetty, I say, 'Yes, Lord! Edinburg, dyah you mistis.' Marse George look like he think she done come down right from de top o' de blue sky an' bring piece on it wid her. He ain' nuver took he eyes from her dat night. Dee glued to her, mun! an' she—well, do' she mighty rosy, an' look mighty unconsarned, she sutney ain' hender him. Hit look like kyarn nobody else tote dat fan an' pick up dat hankcher skusin o' him; an' after supper, when dee all playin' blindman's-buff in de hall—I don' know how twuz—but do' she jes as nimble as a filly, an' her ankle jes as clean, an' she kin git up her dress an' dodge out de way o' ev'ybody else, somehow or nurr she kyarn help him ketchin' her to save her life; he al'ays got her corndered; an' when dee'd git fur apart, dat ain' nuttin, dee jes as sure to come togerr agin as water is whar you done run you hand thoo. An' do' he kiss ev'ybody else under de mistletow, 'cause dee be sort o' cousins, he ain' nuver kiss her, nor nobody else nurr, 'cep' de ole Cun'l. I wuz standin' down at de een de hall wid de black folks, an' I notice it 'tic'lar, 'cause I done meck de 'quaintance o' Nancy; she wuz Miss Charlotte's maid; a mighty likely young gal she wuz den, an' jes as impident as a fly. She see it too, do' she ain' 'low it.

"Fust thing I know I seen a mighty likely lightskinned gal standin' dyah by me, wid her hyah mos' straight as white folks, an' a mighty good frock on, an' a clean apron, an' her hand mos' like a lady, only it brown, an' she keep on 'vidin' her eyes twix me an' Miss Charlotte; when I watchin' Miss Charlotte she watchin' me, an' when I steal my eye 'roun' on her she noticin' Miss Charlotte; an' presney I sort o' sidle 'longside her, an' I say, 'Lady, you mighty springhtly to-night.' An' she say she 'bleeged to be sprightly, her mistis look so good; an' I ax her which one twuz, an' she tell me, 'Dat queen one over dyah,' an' I tell her dee's a king dyah too, she got her eye set for; an' when I say her mistis tryin' to set her cap for Marse George, she fly up, an' say she en' her mistis don' have to set dee cap for nobody; dee got to set dee cap an' all dee clo'es for dem, an' den dee ain' gwine cotch 'em, 'cause dee ain' studyin' 'bout no up-country folks whar dee ain' nobody know nuttin 'bout.

"Well, dat oudaciousness so aggrivate me, I lite into dat nigger right dyah. I tell her she ain' been nowhar 'tall ef she don' know we all; dat we wuz de bes' of quality, de ve'y top de pot; an' den I tell her 'bout how gret we wuz; how de ker'idges wuz al'ays hitched up night en' day, en' niggers jes thick as weeds; an' how Unc' Torm he wared he swaller-tail ev'y day when he wait on de table; and Marse George he won' wyah a coat mo'n once or twice anyways, to save you life. Oh! I sutney 'stonish dat nigger, 'cause I wuz teckin up for de fambly, an' I meck out like dee use gold up home like urr folks use wood, an' sow silver like urr folks sow wheat; an' when I got thoo dee wuz all on 'em listenin', an' she 'lowed dat Marse George he were ve'y good, sho 'nough, ef twarn for he nigger; but I ain' tarrifyin' myself none 'but dat, 'cause I know she jes projickin, an' she couldn' help bein' impident ef you wuz to whup de frock off her back.

"Jes den dee struck up de dance. Dee had wheel de pianer out in de hall, and somebody say Jack Forester had come cross de river, an' all on 'em say dee mus' git Jack; an' presney he come in wid he fiddle, grinnin' and scrapin', 'cause he wuz a no-table fiddler, do' I don' think he wuz equal to we all's Tubal, an' I know he couldn' tech Marse George, 'cause Marse George wuz a natchel fiddler, jes like 'coons is natchel pacers, an' mules is natchel kickers. Howsomever, he sutney jucked a jig sweet, an' when he shake dat bow you couldn' help you foot switchin' a leetle—not ef you wuz a member of de chutch. He wuz a mighty sinful man, Jack wuz, en' dat fiddle had done drawed many souls to torment.

"Well, in a minute dee wuz all flyin', an' Jack he wuz rockin' like boat rockin' on de water, an' he face right shiny, an' he teef look like ear o' corn he got in he mouf, an' he big foot set 'way out keepin' time, an' Marse George he was in de lead row dyah too; ev'y chance he git he tunned Miss Charlotte—'petchel motion, right hand across, an' cauli-flower, an' croquette—dee croquette plenty o' urrs, but I notice dee ain' nuver fail to tun one nurr, an' ev'y tun he gin she wrappin' de chain roun' him; once when dee wuz 'prominadin-all' down we all's een o' de hall, as he tunned her somebody step on her dress an' to' it. I heah de screech o' de silk, an' Nancy say, 'O Lord!' den she say, 'Nem mine! now I'll git it!' an' dee stop for a minute for Marse George to pin it up, while turrers went on, an' Marse George wuz down on he knee, an' she look down on him mighty sweet out her eyes, an' say, 'Hit don' meck no difference,' an' he glance up an' cotch her eye, an', jes 'dout a wud, he tyah a gret piece right out de silk an' slipt it in he bosom, an' when he got up, he say, right low, lookin' in her eyes right deep, 'I gwine wyah dis at my weddin',' an' she jes look sweet as candy; an ef Nancy ever wyah dat frock I ain' see it.

"Den presney dee wuz talkin' 'bout stoppin'. De ole Cun'l say hit time to have prars, an' dee wuz beggin' him to wait lettle while; an' Jack Forester lay he fiddle down nigh Marse George, an' he picked 't up an' drawed de bow 'cross it jes to try it, an' den jes projickin' he struck dat chune 'bout 'You'll ermember me.' He hadn' mo'n tech de string when you could heah a pin drap. Marse George he warn noticin', an' he jes lay he face on de fiddle, wid he eyes sort o' half shet, an' drawed her out like he'd do some nights at home in dee moonlight on de gret porch, tell on a sudden he looked up an' cotch Miss Charlotte eye leanin' for'ards so earnest, an' all on 'em list'nin', an' he stops, an' dee all claps dee hands, an' he sudney drapt into a jig, Jack Forester ain' had to play no mo' dat night; even de ole Cun'l ketched de fever, an' he steps out in de flo', in he long-tail coat an' high collar, an' knocked 'em off de 'Snow-bud on de Ash-bank,' an' 'Chicken in de Bread-tray,' right natchel.

"Oh, he could jes plank 'em down!

"Oh, dat wuz a Christmas like you been read 'bout! An' twuz hard to tell which gittin cotch most, Marse George or me; 'cause dat nigger she jes as confusin' as Miss Charlotte. An' she sutney wuz sp'ilt dem days; ev'y nigger on dat place got he eye on her, an' she jes az oudacious an' aggrivatin as jes womens kin be.

"Dees monsus 'ceivin' critters, womens is, jes as onreliable as de hind-leg of a mule; a man got to watch 'em all de time; you kyarn break 'em like you kin horses.

"Now dat off mule dyah" (indicating, by a lazy but not light lash of his whip the one selected for his illustration), "dee ain' no countin' on her at all; she go 'long all day, or maybe a week, jes dat easy an' sociable, an' fust thing you know you ain' know nuttin, she done knock you brains out; dee ain' no 'pendence to be placed in 'em 'tall, suh; she jes as sweet as a kiss one minute, an' next time she come out de house she got her head up in de air, an' her ears backed, an' goin' 'long switchin' herself like I ain' good 'nough for her to walk on.

"'Fox-huntin's?' oh, yes, suh, ev'y day mos'; an' when Marse George didn' git de tail, twuz 'cause twuz a bob-tail fox—you heah me! He play de fiddle for he pastime, but he fotched up in de saddle—dat he cradle!

"De fust day dee went out I heah Nancy quoilin 'bout de tail layin' on Miss Charlotte dressin'-table gittin' hyahs over ev'ything.

"One day de ladies went out too, Miss Charlotte 'mongst 'em, on Miss Lucy gray myah Switchity, an' Marse George he rid Mr. Braxton's chestnut Willful.

"Well, suh, he stick so close to dat gray myah, he leetle mo' los' dat foz; but, Lord! he know what he 'bout—he monsus 'ceivin' 'bout dat—he know de way de fox gwine jes as well as he know heself; an' all de time he leadin' Miss Charlotte whar she kin heah de music, but he watchin' him too, jes as narrow as a ole hound. So, when de fox tun de head o' de creek, Marse George had Miss Charlotte on de aidge o' de flat, an' he de fust man see de fox tun down on turr side wid de hounds right rank after him. Dat sort o' set him back, 'cause by rights de fox ought to 'a double an' come back dis side: he kyarn git out dat way; an' two or three gent'mens dee had see it too, en' wuz jes layin de horses to de groun' to git roun' fust, 'cause de creek wuz heap too wide to jump, an' wuz 'way over you head, an hit cold as Christmas, sho 'nough; well, suh, when dee tunned, Mr. Clarke he wuz in de lead (he wuz ridin' for Miss Charlotte too), an' hit fyah set Marse George on fire; he ain' said but one wud, 'Wait,' an' jes set de chestnut's head straight for de creek, whar de fox comin' wid he hyah up on he back, an' de dogs ravlin mos' on him.

"De ladies screamed, an' some de gent'mens hollered for him to come back, but he ain' mind; he went 'cross dat flat like a wild-duck; an' when he retch de water he horse try to flinch, but dat hand on de bridle, an' dem rowels in he side, an' he 'bleeged to teck it.

"Lord! suh, sich a screech as dee set up! But he wuz swimmin' for life, an' he wuz up de bank an' in de middle o' de dogs time dee fetched ole Gray Jacket; en' when Mr. Clarke got dyah Marse George wuz stan'in' holdin' up de tail for Miss Charlotte to see, turr side de creek, an' de hounds wuz wallerin' all over de body, an' I don' think Mr. Clarke done got up wid 'em yit.

"He cotch de fox, an' he cotch some'n' else besides, in my 'pinion, 'cause when de ladies went upstairs dat night Miss Charlotte had to wait on de steps for a glass o' water, an' couldn' nobody git it but Marse George; an' den when she tell him good-night over de banisters, he couldn' say it good enough; he got to kiss her hand; en' she ain' do nuttin but jes peep upstairs ef anybody dyah lookin'; an' when I come thoo de do' she juck her hand 'way an' ran upstairs jes as farst as she could. Marse George look at me sort o' laughin', an' say: 'Confound you! Nancy couldn' been very good to you.' An' I say, 'She le' me squench my thirst kissin' her hand;' an' he sort o' laugh an' tell me to keep my mouf shet.

"But dat ain' de on'y time I come on 'em. Dee al'ays gittin' corndered; an' de evenin' befo' we come 'way I wuz gwine in thoo de conservity, an' dyah dee wuz sort o' hide 'way. Miss Charlotte she wuz settin' down, an' Marse George he wuz leanin' over her, got her hand to he face, talkin' right low an lookin' right sweet, an' she ain' say nuttin; an' presney he drapt on one knee by her, an' slip he arm roun' her, an' try to look in her eyes, an' she so 'shamed to look at him she got to hide her face on he shoulder, an' I slipt out.

"We come 'way next mornin'. When marster heah 'bout it he didn' teck to de notion at all, 'cause her pa—dat is, he warn' her own pa, 'cause he had married her ma when she wuz a widder after Miss Charlotte pa died—an' he politics warn' same as ourn. 'Why, you kin never stand him, suh,' he said to Marse George. 'We won't mix any mo'n fire and water; you ought to have found that out at college; dat fellow Darker is his son.'

"Marse George he say he know dat; but he on'y de step-brurr of de young lady, an' ain' got a drap a' her blood in he veins, an' he didn' know it when he meet her, an' anyhow hit wouldn' meck any difference; en' when de mistis see how sot Marse George is on it she teck he side, an' dat fix it; 'cause when ole mistis warn marster to do a thing, hit jes good as done. I don' keer how much he rar roun' an' say he ain' gwine do it, you jes well go 'long an' put on you hat; you gwine see him presney doin' it jes peaceable as a lamb. She tun him jes like she got bline-bridle on him, an' he ain' nuver know it.

"So she got him jes straight as a string. An' when de time come for Marse George to go, marster he mo' consarned 'bout it 'n Marse George; he ain' say nuttin 'bout it befo'; but now he walkin' roun' an' roun' axin mistis mo' questions 'bout he cloes en' he horse an' all; an' dat mornin' he gi' him he two Sunday razors, an' gi' me a pyah o' boots an' a beaver hat, 'cause I wuz gwine wid him to kyar he portmanteau, an' git he shavin' water, since marster say ef he wuz gwine marry a Locofoco, he at least must go like a gent'man; an' me an' Marse George had done settle it 'twixt us, cause we al'ays set bofe we traps on de same hyah parf.

"Well, we got 'em, an' when I ax dat gal out on de wood-pile dat night, she say bein' as her mistis gwine own me, an' we bofe got to be in de same estate, she reckon she ain' nuver gwine to be able to git shet o' me; an' den I clamp her. Oh, she wuz a beauty!"

A gesture and guffaw completed the recital of his conquest.

"Yes, suh, we got 'em sho!" he said, presently. "Dee couldn' persist us; we crowd 'em into de fence en' run 'em off dee foots.

"Den come de 'gagement; an' ev'ything wuz smooth as silk. Marse George an' me wuz ridin' over dyah constant, on'y we nuver did git over bein' skeered when we wuz ridin' up dat turpentine road facin' all dem winders. Hit 'pear like ev'ybody in de wull 'mos' wuz lookin' at us.

"One evenin' Marse George say, 'Edinburg, d'you ever see as many winders p'intin' one way in you' life? When I git a house,' he say, 'I gwine have all de winders lookin' turr way.'

"But dat evenin', when I see Miss Charlotte come walkin' out de gret parlor wid her hyah sort o' rumpled over her face, an' some yeller roses on her bres, an' her gret eyes so soft an' sweet, an' Marse George walkin' 'long hinst her, so peaceable, like she got chain roun' him, I say, 'Winders ain' nuttin.'

"Oh, twuz jes like holiday all de time! An' den Miss Charlotte come over to see mistis, an' of co'se she bring her maid wid her, 'cause she 'bleeged to have her maid, you know, an' dat wuz de bes' of all.

"Dat evenin', 'bout sunset, dee come drivin' up in de big ker'idge, wid de gret hyah trunk stropped on de seat behind, an' Nancy she settin' by Billy, an' Marse George settin' inside by he rose-bud, 'cause he had done gone down to bring her up; an' marster he done been drest in he blue coat an' yellow westket ever since dinner, an' walkin' roun', watchin' up de road all de time, en' tellin' de mistis he reckon dee ain' comin', an ole mistis she try to pacify him, an' she come out presney drest, an' rustlin' in her stiff black silk an' all; an' when de ker'idge come in sight, ev'ybody wuz runnin'; an' when dee draw up to de do', Marse George he help her out an' 'duce her to marster an' ole mistis; an' marster he start to meck her a gret bow, en' she jes put up her mouf like a little gal to be kissed, an' dat got him. An' mistis teck her right in her arms an' kiss her twice, an' de servants dee wuz all peepin' an' grinnin'.

"Ev'ywhar you tun you see a nigger teef, 'cause dee all warn see de young mistis whar good 'nough for Marse George. Dee ain' gwine be married tell de next fall, 'count o' Miss Charlotte bein' so young; but she jes good as b'longst to we-all now; en' ole marster en' mistis dee jes as much in love wid her as Marse George. Hi! dee warn pull de house down an' buil' it over for her! An' ev'y hen' on de place he peepin' to try to git a look at he young mistis whar he gwine b'longst to. One evenin' dee all on 'em come roun' de porch en' send for Marse George, an' when he come out, Charley Brown (he al'ays de speaker, 'cause he got so much mouf, kin' talk pretty as white folks), he say dee warn interduce to de young mistis, an' pay dee bespects to her; an' presney Marse George lead her out on de porch laughin' at her, wid her face jes rosy as a wine-sap apple, an' she meck 'em a beautiful bow, an' speak to 'em ev'y one, Marse George namin' de names; an' Charley Brown he meck her a pretty speech, an' tell her we mighty proud to own her; an' one o' dem impident gals ax her to gin her dat white frock when she git married; an' when she say, 'Well, what am I goin' wear?' Sally say, 'Lord, honey, Marse George gwine dress you in pure gol'!' an' she look up at him wid sparks flashin' out her eyes, while he look like dat ain' good 'nough for her. An' so twuz, when she went 'way, Sally Marshall got dat frock, en' proud on it I tell you.

"Oh, yes; he sutney mindin' her tender. Hi! when she go to ride in evenin' wid him, de ain' no horse-block good 'nough for her! Marse George got to have her step in he hand; an' when dee out walkin' he got de umbreller holdin' 't over her all de time, he so feared de sun'll kiss her; an' dee walk so slow down dem walks in de shade you got to sight 'em by a tree to tell ef dee movin' 'tall. She use' to look like she used to it too, I tell you, 'cause she wuz quality, one de white-skinned ones; an' she'd set in dem big cheers, wid her little foots on de cricket whar Marse George al'ays set for her, he so feared dee'd tetch de groun', jes like she on her throne; an' ole marster he'd watch her 'mos' edmirin as Marse George; an' when she went 'way hit sutney was lonesome. Hit look like day-light gone wid her. I don' know which I miss mos', Miss Charlotte or Nancy.

"Den Marse George was 'lected to de Legislature, an' ole Jedge Darker run for de Senator, an' Marse George vote gin him and beat him. An' dat commence de fuss; an' den dat man gi' me de whuppin, an' dat breck 'tup an' breck he heart.

"You see, after Marse George wuz 'lected ('lections wuz 'lections dem days; dee warn' no bait-gode 'lections, wid ev'y sort o' worms squirmin' up 'ginst one nurr, wid piece o' paper d' ain' know what on, drappin' in a chink; didn' nuttin but gent'mens vote den, en' dee took dee dram, en' vote out loud, like gent'mens)—well, arter Marse George wuz 'lected, de parties wuz jes as even balanced as stilyuds, en' wen dee ax Marse George who wuz to be de Senator, he vote for de Whig, 'ginst de old jedge, en' dat beat him, of co'se. An' dee ain' got sense to know he 'bleeged to vote wid he politics. Dat he sprinciple; he kyarn vote for Locofoco, I don' keer ef he is Miss Charlotte pa, much less her steppa. Of co'se de ole jedge ain' speak to him arter dat, nur is Marse George ax him to. But who dat gwine s'pose women-folks got to put dee mouf in too? Miss Charlotte she write Marse George a letter dat pester him mightily; he set up all night answerin' dat letter, an' he mighty solemn, I tell you. An' I wuz gittin' right grewsome myself, cause I studyin' 'bout dat gal down dyah whar I done gi' my wud to, an' when dee ain' no letters come torectly hit hard to tell which one de anxiouser, me or Marse George. Den presney I so 'straughted 'long o' it I ax Aunt Haly 'bouten it: she know all sich things, 'cause she 'mos' a hunderd years ole, an' seed evil sperits, an' got skoripins up her chimley, an' knowed conjure; an' she ax me what wuz de signication, an' I tell her I ain' able nuther to eat nor to sleep, an' dat gal come foolin' 'long me when I sleep jes like as natchel as ef I see her sho 'nough. An' she say I done conjured; dat de gal done tricked me.

"Oh, Gord! dat skeered me!

"You white folks, marster, don' b'lieve nuttin like dat; y' all got too much sense, 'cause y' all kin read; but niggers dee ain' know no better, an' I sutney wuz skeered, 'cause Aunt Haly say my coffin done seasoned, de planks up de chimley.

"Well, I got so bad Marse George ax me 'bout it, an' he sort o' laugh an' sort o' cuss, an' he tell Aunt Haly ef she don' stop dat foolishness skeerin' me he'll sell her an' tyah her ole skoripin house down. Well, co'se he jes talkin', an' he ax me next day how'd I like to go an' see my sweetheart. Gord! suh, I got well torectly. So I set off next evenin', feelin' jes big as ole marster, wid my pass in my pocket, which I warn' to show nobody 'douten I 'bleeged to, 'cause Marse George didn't warn nobody to know he le' me go. An' den dat rascallion teck de shut off my back. But ef Marse George didn' pay him de wuth o' it!

"I done git 'long so good, too.

"When Nancy see me she sutney was 'stonished. She come roun' de cornder in de back yard whar I settin' in Nat's do' (he wuz de gardener), wid her hyah all done un-twist, en' breshed out mighty fine, an' a clean ap'on wid fringe on it, meckin' out she so s'prised to see me (whar wuz all a lie, 'cause some on 'em done notify her I dyah), an' she say, 'Hi! what dis black nigger doin' heah?'

"An' I say, 'Who you callin' nigger, you impident, kercumber-faced thing you?' Den we shake hands, an' I tell her Marse George done set me free—dat I done buy myself; dat's de lie I done lay off to tell her.

"An' when I tole her dat, she bust out laughin', an' say, well, I better go 'long 'way, den, dat she don' warn no free nigger to be comp'ny for her. Dat sort o' set me back, an' I tell her she kickin' 'fo she spurred, dat I ain' got her in my mine; I got a nurr gal at home whar grievin' 'bout me dat ve'y minute. An' after I tell her all sich lies as dat presney she ax me ain' I hongry; an' ef dat nigger didn' git her mammy to gi' me de bes' supter! Umm-m! I kin mos' tas'e it now. Wheat bread off de table, an' zerves, an' fat bacon, tell I couldn' put a nurr mouffil nowhar sep'n I'd teck my hat. Dat night I tote Nancy water for her, an' I tell her all 'bout ev'ything, en' she jes sweet as honey. Next mornin', do', she done sort o' tunned some, an' ain' so sweet. You know how milk gits sort o' bonnyclabberish? An' when she see me she 'gin to 'buse me—say I jes tryin' to fool her, an' all de time got nurr wife at home, or gittin' ready to git one, for all she know, an' she ain' know wherr Marse George ain' jes 'ceivin' as I is; en' nem mine, she got plenty warn marry her; an' as to Miss Charlotte, she got de whole wull; Mr. Darker he ain' got nobody in he way now, dat he deah all de time, an' ain' gwine West no mo'. Well, dat aggravate me so I tell her ef she say dat 'bout Marse George I gwine knock her; en' wid dat she got so oudacious I meck out I gwine 'way, an' lef' fer, an' went up todes de barn; an' up dyah, fust thing I know, I come across dat ar man Mr. Darker. Soon as he see me he begin to cuss me, an' he ax me what I doin' on dat land, an' I tell him nuttin. An' he say, well, he gwine gi' me some'n; he gwine teach me to come prowlin' round gent'men's houses. An' he meck me go in de barn an' teck off my shut, an' he beat me wid he whup tell de blood run out my back. He sutney did beat me scandalous, 'cause he done hate me an' Marse George ever since we wuz at college togurr. An' den he say: 'Now you git right off dis land. Ef either you or you marster ever put you foot on it, you'll git de same thing agin.' An' I tell you, Edinburg he come way, 'cause he sutney had worry me. I ain' stop to see Nancy or nobody; I jes come 'long, shakin' de dust, I tell you. An' as I come 'long de road I pass Miss Charlotte walkin' on de lawn by herself, an' she call me: 'Why, hi! ain' dat Edinburg?'

"She look so sweet, an' her voice soun' so cool, I say, 'Yes'm; how you do, missis?' An' she say, she ve'y well, an' how I been, an' whar I gwine? I tell her I ain' feelin' so well, dat I gwine home. 'Hi!' she say, 'is anybody treat you bad?' An' I tell her, 'Yes'm.' An' she say, 'Oh! Nancy don' mean nuttin by dat; dat you mus'n mine what womens say, an' do, 'cause dee feel sorry for it next minute; an' sometimes dee kyarn help it, or maybe hit you fault; an' anyhow, you ought to be willin' to overlook it; an' I better go back an' wait till tomorrow—ef—ef I ain' 'bleeged to git home to-day.'

"She got mighty mixed up in de een part o' dat, an' she looked mighty anxious 'bout me an' Nancy; an' I tell her, 'No'm, I 'bleeged to git home.'

"Well, when I got home Marse George he warn know all dat gwine on; but I mighty sick—dat man done beat me so; an' he ax me what de marter, an' I upped en' tell him.

"Gord! I nuver see a man in sich a rage. He call me in de office en' meck me teck off my shut, an' he fyah bust out cryin'. He walked up an' down dat office like a caged lion. Ef he had got he hand on Mr. Darker den, he'd 'a kilt him, sho! "He wuz most 'stracted. I don't know what he'd been ef I'd tell him what Nancy tell me. He call for Peter to git he horse torectly, an' he tell me to go an' git sometn' from mammy to put on my back, an' to go to bed torectly, an' not to say nuttin to nobody, but to tell he pa he'd be away for two days, maybe; an' den he got on Reveller an' galloped 'way hard as he could, wid he jaw set farst, an' he heaviest whup clamped in he hand. Gord! I wuz most hopin' he wouldn' meet dat man, 'cause I feared ef he did he'd kill him; an' he would, sho, ef he had meet him right den; dee say he leetle mo' did when he fine him next day, an' he had done been ridin' den all night; he cotch im at a sto' on de road, an' dee say he leetle mo' cut him all to pieces; he drawed a weepin on Marse George, but Marse George wrench it out he hand an' flung it over de fence; an' when dee got him 'way he had weared he whup out on him; an' he got dem whelps on him now, ef he ain' dead. Yes, suh, he ain' let nobody else do dat he ain' do heself, sho!

"Dat done de business!

"He sont Marse George a challenge, but Marse George sont him wud he'll cowhide him agin ef he ever heah any mo' from him, an' he 'ain't. Dat perrify him, so he shet he mouf. Den come he ring an' all he pictures an' things back—a gret box on 'em, and not a wud wid 'em. Marse George, I think he know'd dee wuz comin', but dat ain' keep it from huttin him, 'cause he done been 'gaged to Miss Charlotte, an' got he mine riveted to her; an' do' befo' dat dee had stop writin', an' a riff done git 'twixt 'em, he ain' satisfied in he mine dat she ain't gwine 'pologizee—I know by Nancy; but now he got de confirmation dat he done for good, en' dat de gret gulf fixed 'twix him an' Aberham bosom. An,' Gord, suh, twuz torment, sho 'nough! He ain' say nuttin 'bout it, but I see de light done pass from him, an' de darkness done wrap him up in it. In a leetle while you wouldn' 'a knowed him. Den ole mistis died.

"B'lieve me, ole marster he 'most much hut by Miss Charlotte as Marse George. He meck a 'tempt to buy Nancy for me, so I find out arterward, an' write Jedge Darker he'll pay him anything he'll ax for her, but he letter wuz sont back 'dout any answer. He sutney was mad 'bout it—he say he'd horsewhip him as Marse George did dat urr young puppy, but ole mistis wouldn' le' him do nuttin, and den he grieve heself to death. You see he mighty ole, anyways. He nuver got over ole mistis' death. She had been failin' a long time, en' he ain' terry long 'hinst her; hit sort o' like breckin up a holler—de ole 'coon goes 'way soon arter dat; an' marster nuver could pin he own collar or buckle he own stock—mistis she al'ays do dat; an' do' Marse George do de bes' he kin, an' mighty willin', he kyarn handle pin like a woman; he hand tremble like a p'inter dog; an' anyways he ain' ole mistis. So ole marster foller her dat next fall, when dee wuz gittin in de corn, an' Marse George he ain' got nobody in de wull left; he all alone in dat gret house, an' I wonder sometimes he ain' die too, 'cause he sutney wuz fond o' ole marster.

"When ole mistis wuz dyin, she tell him to be good to ole marster, an' patient wid him, 'cause he ain' got nobody but him now (ole marster he had jes step out de room to cry); an' Marse George he lean over her an' kiss her an' promise her faithful he would. An' he sutney wuz tender wid him as a woman; an' when ole marster die, he set by him an' hol' he hand an' kiss him sorf, like he wuz ole mistis.

"But, Gord! Twuz lonesome arter dat, an' Marse George eyes look wistful, like he al'ays lookin' far 'way; an' Aunt Haly say he see harnts whar walk 'bout in de gret house. She say dee walk dyah constant of nights sence ole marster done alterate de rooms from what dee wuz when he gran'pa buil' em, an' dat dee huntin' for dee ole chambers an' kyarn git no rest 'cause dee kyarn fine 'em. I don't know how dat wuz. I know Marse George he used to walk about heself mightily of nights. All night long, all night long, I'd heah him tell de chickens crowin' dee second crow, en' some mornin's I'd go dyah an' he ain' even rumple de bed. I thought sho he wuz gwine die, but I suppose he done 'arn he days to be long in de land, an' dat save him. But hit sutney wuz lonesome, an' he nuver went off de plantation, an' he got older an' older, tell we all thought he wuz gwine die.

"An' one day come jes befo' Christmas, 'bout nigh two year after marster die, Mr. Braxton ride up to de do'. He had done come to teck Marse George home to spen' Christmas wid him. Marse George warn git out it, but Mr. Braxton won' teck no disapp'int-ment; he say he gwine baptize he boy, an' he done name him after Marse George (he had marry Marse George cousin, Miss Peggy Carter, an' he vite Marse George to de weddin', but he wouldn' go, do I sutney did want him to go, 'cause I heah Miss Charlotte was nom-inated to marry Mr. Darker, an' I warn know what done 'come o' dat bright-skinned nig-ger gal whar I used to know down dyah); an' he say Marse George got to come an' stan' for him, an' gi' him a silver cup en' a gol' rattle. So Marse George he finally promise to come an' spend Christmas Day, an' Mr. Braxton went 'way next mornin', an den hit tun in an' rain so I feared we couldn' go, but hit cler off de day befo' Christmas Eve an' tun cold. Well, suh, we ain' been nowhar for so long I wuz skittish as a young filly; an' den you know twuz de same ole place.

"We didn' git dyah till supper-time, an' twuz a good one too, 'cause seventy miles dat cold a weather hit whet a man's honger jes like a whetstone. "Dee sutney wuz glad to see we all. We rid roun' by de back yard to gi' Billy de horses, an' we see dee wuz havin' gret fixin's; an' den we went to de house, jest as some o' de folks run in en' tell 'em we wuz come. When Marse George steps in de hall, dee all clustered roun' him like dee gwine hug him, dee faces fyah dimplin' wid pleasure, an' Miss Peggy she jes reched up an' teck him in her arms en' hug him.

"Dee tell me in de kitchen dat dee wuz been 'spectin' of Miss Charlotte over to spend Christmas too, but de river wuz so high dee s'pose dee couldn' git 'cross. Chile, dat sutney disapp'int me!

"Well, after supper de niggers had a dance. Hit wuz down in de wash-house, en' de table wuz set in de carpenter shop jes' by. Oh, hit sutney wuz beautiful! Miss Lucy an' Miss Ailsy dee had superintend ev'ything wid dee own hands. So dee wuz down dyah wid dee ap'ons up to dee chins, an' dee had de big silver strandeliers out de house, two on each table, an' some o' ole mistis's best damas' tableclothes, an' ole marster's gret bowl full o' egg-nog; hit look big as a mill-pond settin' dyah in de corn-der; an' dee had flowers out de greenhouse on de table, an' some o' de chany out de gret house, en' de dinin'-room cheers set roun' de room. Oh! oh! nuttin warn too good for niggers dem times; an' de little niggers wuz runnin' roun' right 'stracted, squealin' an' peepin' an' gittin in de way onder you foots; an' de mens dee wuz totin' in de wood—gret hickory logs, look like stock whar you gwine saw—en' de fire so big hit look like you gwine kill hawgs, 'cause hit sutney wuz cold dat night. Dis nigger ain' nuver gwine forgit it! Jack Forester he had come 'cross de river to lead de fiddlers, an' he say he had to put he fiddle onder he coat an' poke he bow in he breeches leg to keep de strings from poppin', en' dat de river would freeze over sho ef twarn so high; but twuz jes snortin', an' he had hard wuck to git over in he skiff, an' Unc' Jeems say he ain' gwine come out he boat-house no mo' dat night—he done tempt Providence often 'nough dat day.

"Den ev'ything wuz ready, en' de fiddlers got dee dram an' chuned up, an' twuz lively, I tell you! Twuz jes as thick in dyah as blackberries on de blackberry bush, 'cause ev'y gal on de plantation wuz dyah shakin' her foot for some young buck, an' back-steppin' for to go 'long. Dem ole sleepers wuz jes a-rockin', an' Jack Forester he wuz callin' de figgers for to wake 'em up. I warn' dancin', 'cause I done got 'ligion an' longst to de chutch since de trouble done tetch us up so rank; but I tell you my foots wuz pintedly eechchin for a leetle sop on it, an' I had to come out to keep from crossin' 'em onst, anyways. Den, too, I had a fetch o' misery in my back, an' I lay off to git a tas'e o' dat egg-nog out dat big bowl, wid snow-drift on it, from Miss Lucy—she al'ays mighty fond o' Marse George; so I slip into de carpenter shop, an' ax her kyarn I do nuttin for her, an' she laugh an' say, yes, I kin drink her health, an' gi' me a gret gobletful, an' jes den de white folks come in to 'spec' de tables, Marse George in de lead, an' dee all fill up dee glasses an' pledge dee health, an' all de servants', an' a merry Christmas; an' den dee went in de wash-house to see de dancin', an' maybe to teck a hand deeself, 'cause white folks' 'ligion ain' like niggers', you know; dee got so much larnin dee kin dance, an' fool de devil too. An' I stay roun' a little while, an' den went in de kitchen to see how supper gittin on, 'cause I wuz so hongry when I got dyah I ain' able to eat 'nough at one time to 'commodate it, en' de smell o' de tuckeys an' de gret saddlers o' mutton in de tin-kitchens wuz mos' 'nough by deeself to feed a right hongry man; an' dyah wuz a whole parcel o' niggers cookin' an' tunnin 'bout for life, an' dee faces jes as shiny as ef dee done bas'e 'em wid gravy; an' dyah, settin' back in a cheer out de way, wid her clean frock up off de flo', wuz dat gal! I sutney did feel curious.

"I say, 'Hi! name o' Gord! whar'd you come from?' She say, 'Oh, Marster! ef heah ain' dat free nigger agin!' An' ev'ybody laughed.

"Well, presny we come out, cause Nancy warn see de dancin', an' we stop a leetle while 'hind de cornder out de wind while she tell me 'bout ev'ything. An' she say dat's all a lie she tell me dat day 'bout Mr. Darker an' Miss Charlotte; an' he done gone 'way now for good 'cause he so low down an' wuthless dee kyarn nobody stand him; an' all he warn marry Miss Charlotte for is to git her niggers. But Nancy say Miss Charlotte nuver could abide him; he so 'sateful, 'spressly sence she fine out what a lie he told 'bout Marse George. You know, Mr. Darker he done meck 'em think Marse George sont me dyah to fine out ef he done come home, an' den dat he fall on him wid he weepin when he ain' noticin' him, an' sort o' out de way too, en' git two urr mens to hold him while he beat him, all 'cause he in love wid Miss Charlotte. D'you ever, ever heah sich a lie? An' Nancy say, do' Miss Charlotte ain' b'lieve it all togerr, hit look so reasonable she done le' de ole jedge an' her ma, who wuz 'pending on what she heah, 'duce her to send back he things; an' dee ain' know no better not tell after de ole jedge die; den dee fine out 'bout de whuppin me, an' all; en' den Miss Charlotte know huc-come I ain 'gwine stay dat day; an' she say dee wuz sutney outdone 'bout it, but it too late den; an' Miss Charlotte kyarn do nuttin but cry 'bout it, an' dat she did, pintedly, 'cause she done lost Marse George, en' done 'stroy he life; en' she nuver keer 'bout no-body else sep Marse George, Nancy say. Mr. Clarke he hangin' on, but Miss Charlotte she done tell him pintedly she ain' nuver gwine marry nobody. An' dee jes done come, she say, 'cause dee had to go 'way round by de rope ferry 'long o' de river bein' so high, an' dee ain' know tell dee done git out de ker'idge an' in de house dat we all wuz heah; an' Nancy say she glad dee ain', 'cause she 'feared ef dee had, Miss Charlotte wouldn' 'a come.

"Den I tell her all 'bout Marse George, cause I know she 'bleeged to tell Miss Charlotte. Twuz powerful cold out dyah, but I ain' mine dat, chile. Nancy she done had to wrop her arms up in her ap'on an' she kyarn meck no zistance 'tall, an' dis nig-ger ain' keerin nuttin 'bout cold den.

"An' jes den two ladies come out de carpenter shop ant went 'long to de wash-house, an' Nancy say, 'Dyah Miss Charlotte now;' an' twuz Miss Lucy an' Miss Char-lotte; an' we heah Miss Lucy coaxin' Miss Charlotte to go, tellin' her she kin come right out; an' jes den dee wuz a gret shout, an' we went in hinst 'em. Twuz Marse George had done teck de fiddle, an' ef he warn' natchelly layin' hit down! he wuz up at de urr een o' de room, 'way from we all, 'cause we wuz at de do', nigh Miss Charlotte whar she wuz standin' 'hind some on 'em, wid her eyes on him mighty timid, like she hidin' from him, an' ev'y nigger in de room wuz on dat flo'. Gord! suh, dee wuz grinnin' so dee warn' a toof in dat room you couldn' git you tweezers on; an' you couldn' heah a wud, dee so proud o' Marse George playin' for 'em.

"Well, dee danced tell you couldn' tell which wuz de clappers an' which de backsteppers; de whole house look like it wuz rockin'; an' presney somebody say supper, an' dat stop 'em, an' dee wuz a spell for a minute, an' Marse George standin' dyah wid de fiddle in he hand. He face wuz tunned away, an' he wuz studyin'—studyin' 'bout dat urr Christmas so long ago—an' sudney he face drapt down on de fiddle, an' he drawed he bow 'cross de strings, an' dat chune begin to whisper right sorf. Hit begin so low ev'ybody had to stop talkin' an' hold dee mouf to heah it; en' Marse George he ain' know nuttin 'bout it, he done gone back, an' standin' dyah in de gret hall playin' it for Miss Charlotte, whar done come down de steps wid her little blue foots an' gret fan, an' standin' dyah in her dim blue dress an' her fyah arms, an' her gret eyes lookin' in he face so earnest, whar he ain' gwine nuver speak to no mo'. I see it by de way he look—an' de fiddle wuz jes pleadin'. He drawed it out jes as fine as a stran' o' Miss Charlotte's hyah.

"Hit so sweet, Miss Charlotte, mun, she couldn' stan' it; she made to de do'; an' jes while she watchin' Marse George to keep him from seein' her he look day way, an' he eyes fall right into hern.

"Well, suh, de fiddle drapt down on de flo'—perlang!—an' he face wuz white as a sycamore limb.

"Dee say twuz a swimmin' in de head he had; an' Jack say de whole fiddle warn' wuff de five dollars.

"Me an' Nancy followed 'em tell dee went in de house, an' den we come back to de shop whar de supper wuz gwine on, an' got we all supper an' a leetle sop o' dat yeller gravy out dat big bowl, an' den we all rejourned to de wash-house agin, an' got onder de big bush o' misseltow whar hangin' from de jice, an' ef you ever see scufflin' dat's de time.

"Well, me an' she had jes done lay off de whole Christmas, when wud, come dat Marse George want he horses.

"I went, but it sutney breck me up; an' I wonder whar de name o' Gord Marse George gwine sen me dat cold night, an' jes as I got to de do' Marse George en' Mr. Braxton come out, en' I know torectly Marse George wuz gwine home. I seen he face by de light o' de lantern, an' twuz set jes rigid as a rock.

"Mr. Braxton he wuz beggin' him to stay; he tell him he ruinin' he life, dat he sho dee's some mistake, en' twill be all right. An' all de answer Marse George meck wuz to swing heself up in de saddle, an' Reveller he look like he gwine fyah 'stracted. He al'ays mighty fool anyways when he git cold, dat horse wuz.

"Well, we come 'long 'way, an' Mr. Braxton an' two mens come down to de river wid lanterns to see us cross, 'cause twuz dark as pitch, sho 'nough.

"An' jes 'fo' I started I got one o' de mens to hol' my horses, an' I went in de kitchen to git warm, an' dyah Nancy wuz. An' she say Miss Charlotte up steairs cryin' right now, 'cause she think Marse George gwine cross de river 'count o' her, en' she whimper a little herself when I tell her good-by. But twuz too late den.

"Well, de river wuz jes natchelly b'ilin', an' hit soun' like a mill-dam roarin' by; an' when we got dyah Marse George tunned to me an' tell me he reckon I better go back. I ax him whar he gwine en' he say, 'Home.' 'Den I gwine wid you!' I says. I wuz mighty skeered but me an' Marse George wuz boys togerr; en' he plunged right in, an' I after him.

"Gord! twuz cold as ice; an' we hadn' got in befo' bofe horses wuz swimmin' for life. He holler to me to byah de myah head up de stream; an' I did try, but what's a nigger to dat water! Hit jes pick me up an' dash me down like I ain' no mo'n a chip, an' de fust thing I know I gwine down de stream like a piece of bark, an' water washin' all over me. I knowed den I gone, an' I hollered for Marse George for help. I heah him answer me not to git skeered but to hold on; but de myah wuz lungin' an' de water wuz all over me like ice, an' den I washed off de myah back, an' got drownded.

"I 'member comin' up an' hollerin' agin for help, but I know den 'tain' no use, dee ain' no help den, an' I got to pray to Gord, an' den some'n hit me an' I went down agin, an'—de next thing I know I wuz in de bed, an' I heah 'em talkin' 'bout wherr I dead or not, en' I ain' know myself tell I taste de whiskey dee po'rin' down my jugular.

"An' den dee tell me 'bout how when I hollered Marse Goerge tun back an' struck out for me for life, an' how jes as I went down de last time he cotch me an' heft on to me tell we wash down to whar de bank curve, an' dyah de current wuz so rapid hit yuck him off Reveller back, but he heft on to de reins tell de horse lunge so he hit him wid he fo' foot an' breck he collar-bone, an' den he had to let him go, an' jes heft on to me; an' jes den we wash up agin de bank an' cotch in a tree, an' de mens got dyah quick as dee could, en' when dee retched us Marse George wuz holdin' on to me, an' had he arm wrapped roun' a limb, an' we wuz lodged in de crotch, an' bofe jes as dead as a nail: an' de myah she got out, but Reveller he wuz drownded, wid his foot cotch in de rein an' de saddle tunned onder he side; an' dee ain' know wherr Marse George ain' dead too, 'cause he not only drownded, but he lef' arm broke up nigh de shoulder.

"An' dee say Miss Charlotte she 'mos' 'stracted; dat de fust thing anybody know 'bout it wuz when some de servants bust in de hall en' holler, an' say Marse George an' me done bofe washed 'way an' drownded, en' dat she drapt down dead on de flo', an' when dee bring her to she 'low to Miss Lucy dat she de 'casion on he death; an' dee say dat when de mens wuz totin' him in de house, an' wuz shuffin' de feets not to meck no noige, an' a little piece o' blue silk drapt out he breast whar somebody picked up en' gin Miss Lucy, Miss Charlotte breck right down agin; an' some on 'em say she sutney did keer for him; an' now when he layin' upstairs dyah dead, hit too late for him ever to know it.

"Well, suh, I couldn' teck it in dat Marse George and Reveller wuz dead, an' jes den somebody say Marse George done comin' to an' dee gi' me so much whiskey I went to sleep.

"An' next mornin' I got up an' went to Marse George room, an' see him layin' dyah in de bed, wid he face so white an' he eyes so tired-lookin', an' he ain' know me no mo' 'n ef he nuver see me, an' I couldn' stan' it; I jes drap down on de flo' an' bust out cryin'. Gord! suh, I couldn' help it, 'cause Reveller wuz drownded, an' Marse George he wuz mos' gone.

"An' he came nigher goin' yit, 'cause he had sich a strain, an' been so long in de water, he heart done got numbed, an' he got 'lirium, an' all de time he thought he tryin' to git 'cross de river to see Miss Charlotte, an' hit so high he kyarn git dyah.

"Hit sutney wuz pitiful to see him layin' dyah tossin' an' pitchin', not knowin' whar he wuz, tell it teck all Mr. Braxton an' me could do to keep him in de bed, an' de doctors say he kyarn hol' out much longer.

"An' all dis time Miss Charlotte she wuz gwine 'bout de house wid her face right white, an' Nancy say she don' do nuttin all day long in her room but cry an' say her pra'rs, prayin' for Marse George, what dyin' upsteairs by 'count o' not knowin' she love him, an' I tell Nancy how he honin' all de time to see her, en' how he constant callin' her name.

"Well, so twuz, tell he mos' done wyah heself out; an' jes lay dyah wid his face white as de pillow, an' he gret pitiful eyes rollin' 'bout so restless, like he still lookin' for he whar he all de time callin' her name, an' kyarn git 'cross dat river to see.

"An' one evenin' 'bout sunset he 'peered to be gwine; he weaker 'n he been at all, he ain' able to scuffle no mo', an' jes layin' dyah so quiet, an' presney he say, lookin' mighty wistful,

"'Edinburg, I'm goin' to-night; ef I don' git 'cross dis time, I'll gin't up.'

"Mr. Braxton wuz standin' nigh de head o' de bed, an' he say, 'Well, by Gord! he shall see her!'—jes so. An' he went out de room, an' to Miss Charlotte do', an' call her, an' tell her she got to come, ef she don't, he'll die dat night; an' fust thing I know, Miss Lucy bring Miss Charlotte in, wid her face right white, but jes as tender as a angel's, an' she come an' stan' by de side de bed, an' lean down over him, an' call he name, 'George!'—jes so.

"An' Marse George he ain' answer; he jes look at her study for a minute, an' den he forehead got smooth, an' he tun he eyes to me, an say, 'Edinburg, I'm 'cross.'"

Samuel Langhorn Clemens

(1835–1910)

Samuel Clemens made his reputation as a humorist, and though he achieved popular fame in the heyday of the Southwestern humorist, his popularity far outstripped that of his contemporaries. For many years, however, critics, unable to look beyond the buffoonery and burlesque that are present in even his best works, did not recognize him as a serious literary talent. Twentieth-century fiction writers, however, have recognized the genius in his use of the vernacular idiom, his mocking portrayals of nineteenth-century gentility, and the underlying sense of alienation that pervades much of his work. Ernest Hemingway remarked, "All modern American literature comes from one book by Mark Twain called *Huckleberry Finn* . . . it's the best book we've had . . . There was nothing before. There has been nothing so good since."

Twain was born and raised in Hannibal, Missouri, the town that would become the "St. Petersburg" of his fiction. After a brief period of schooling, he became a printer's apprentice and moved eastward from city to city. He returned to the Midwest and trained to be a riverboat pilot, a trade he plied until the outbreak of the Civil War effectively ended river traffic. After serving briefly in the Confederate militia, he moved west in 1861 and became a newspaper reporter. A retelling of a tale he first heard in a mining camp, "The Notorious Jumping Frog of Calaveras County," won national acclaim in 1865, launching his literary career. He gathered and revised his irreverent newspaper articles, and in 1869 he published them as *The Innocents Abroad*, following that popular work in quick succession with *Roughing It* (1872), *The Gilded Age* (a collaboration with Charles Dudley Warner, 1873), *The Adventures of Tom Sawyer* (1876), *A Tramp Abroad* (1880), *The Prince and the Pauper* (1882), *Life on the Mississippi* (1883), and *The Adventures of Huckleberry Finn* (1884). This last work achieved a perfect balance between the flippancy of his earlier work and the skepticism that would characterize his last books. Although it is uneven in places, its carefully controlled point of view, masterful use of dialect, and mythic elements have made it the masterpiece of American literature that Hemingway praised.

Twain's later fiction is uneven. He suffered a series of financial setbacks from which he extricated himself through another flurry of publishing, and some of these efforts are little better than hack work. Others, however, display flashes of bitter, cynical brilliance, and many of his writings of this period include scathing attacks on materialism and racial injustice.

from *Life on the Mississippi*

Chapter XL. Castles and Culture

Baton Rouge was clothed in flowers, like a bride—no, much more so; like a greenhouse. For we were in the absolute South now—no modifications, no compromises, no halfway measures. The magnolia trees in the Capitol grounds were lovely and fragrant, with their dense rich foliage and huge snowball blossoms. The scent of the flower is very sweet, but you want distance on it, because it is so powerful. They are not good bedroom blossoms—they might suffocate one in his sleep. We were certainly in the South at last; for here the sugar region begins, and the plantations—vast green levels, with sugar-mill and negro quarters clustered together in the middle distance—were in view. And there was a tropical sun overhead and a tropical swelter in the air.

And at this point, also, begins the pilot's paradise: a wide river hence to New Orleans, abundance of water from shore to shore, and no bars, snags, sawyers, or wrecks in his road.

Sir Walter Scott is probably responsible for the Capitol building; for it is not conceivable that this little sham castle would ever have been built if he had not run the people mad, a couple of generations ago, with his medieval romances. The South has not yet recovered from the debilitating influence of his books. Admiration of his fantastic heroes and their grotesque "chivalry" doings and romantic juvenilities still survives here, in an atmosphere in which is already perceptible the wholesome and practical nineteenth-century smell of cotton factories and locomotives; and traces of its inflated language and other windy humbuggeries survive along with it. It is pathetic enough that a whitewashed castle, with turrets and things—materials all ungenuine within and without, pretending to be what they are not—should ever have been built in this otherwise honorable place; but it is much more pathetic to see this architectural falsehood undergoing restoration and perpetuation in our day, when it would have been so easy to let dynamite finish what a charitable fire began, and then devote this restoration money to the building of something genuine.

Baton Rouge has no patent on imitation castles, however, and no monopoly of them. The following remark is from the advertisement of the "Female Institute" of Columbia, Tennessee:

> The Institute building has long been famed as a model of striking and beautiful architecture. Visitors are charmed with its resemblance to the old castles of song and story, with its towers, turreted walls, and ivy-mantled porches.

Keeping school in a castle is a romantic thing; as romantic as keeping hotel in a castle.

By itself the imitation castle is doubtless harmless, and well enough; but as a symbol and breeder and sustainer of maudlin Middle-Age romanticism here in the midst of the plainest and sturdiest and infinitely greatest and worthiest of all the centuries the world has seen, it is necessarily a hurtful thing and a mistake.

Here is an extract from the prospectus of a Kentucky "Female College." Female college sounds well enough; but since the phrasing it in that unjustifiable way was done purely in the interest of brevity, it seems to me that she-college would have been still better—because shorter, and means the same thing: that is, if either phrase means anything at all:

The president is Southern by birth, by rearing, by education, and by sentiment; the teachers are all Southern in sentiment, and with the exception of those born in Europe were born and raised in the South. Believing the Southern to be the highest type of civilization this continent has seen,[1] the young ladies are trained according to the Southern ideas of delicacy, refinement, womanhood, religion, and propriety; hence we offer a first-class female college for the South and solicit Southern patronage.

What, warder, ho! The man that can blow so complacent a blast as that, probably blows it from a castle.

From Baton Rouge to New Orleans, the great sugar-plantations border both sides of the river all the way, and stretch their league-wide levels back to the dim forest walls of bearded cypress in the rear. Shores lonely no longer. Plenty of dwellings all the way, on both banks—standing so close together, for long distances, that the broad river lying between the two rows becomes a sort of spacious street. A most homelike and happy-looking region. And now and then you see a pillared and porticoed great manor-house, embowered in trees. Here is testimony of one or two of the procession of foreign tourists that filed along here half a century ago. Mrs. Trollope says:

---

[1]Illustrations of it thoughtlessly omitted by the advertiser:

"KNOXVILLE, TENNESSEE, October 19.—This morning, a few minutes after ten o'clock, General Joseph A. Mabry, Thomas O'Connor, and Joseph A. Mabry, Jr., were killed in a shooting affray. The difficulty began yesterday afternoon by General Mabry attacking Major O'Connor and threatening to kill him. This was at the fair-grounds, and O'Connor told Mabry that it was not the place to settle their difficulties. Mabry then told O'Connor he should not live. It seems that Mabry was armed and O'Connor was not. The cause of the difficulty was an old feud about the transfer of some property from Mabry to O'Connor. Later in the afternoon Mabry sent word to O'Connor that he would kill him on sight. This morning Major O'Connor was standing in the door of the Mechanics' National Bank, of which he was president. General Mabry and another gentleman walked down Gay Street on the opposite side from the bank. O'Connor stepped into the bank, got a shotgun, took deliberate aim at General Mabry and fired. Mabry fell dead, being shot in the left side. As he fell O'Connor fired again, the shot taking effect in Mabry's thigh. O'Connor then reached into the bank and got another shotgun. About this time, Joseph A. Mabry, Jr., son of General Mabry, came rushing down the

The unbroken flatness of the banks of the Mississippi continued unvaried for many miles above New Orleans; but the graceful and luxuriant palmetto, the dark and noble ilex, and the bright orange were everywhere to be seen, and it was many days before we were weary of looking at them.

Captain Basil Hall:

The district of country which lies adjacent to the Mississippi, in the lower parts of Louisiana, is everywhere thickly peopled by sugar-planters, whose showy houses, gray piazzas, trig gardens, and numerous slave villages, all clean and neat, gave an exceedingly thriving air to the river scenery.

All the procession paint the attractive picture in the same way. The descriptions of fifty years ago do not need to have a word changed in order to exactly describe the same region as it appears to-day—except as to the "trigness" of the houses. The whitewash is gone from the negro cabins now; and many, possibly most, of the big mansions, once so shining white, have worn out their paint and have a decayed, neglected look. It is the blight of the war. Twenty-one years ago everything was trim and trig and bright along the "coast," just as it had been in 1827, as described by those tourists.

Unfortunate tourists! People humbugged them with stupid and silly lies, and then laughed at them for believing and printing the same. They told Mrs. Trollope that the alligators—or crocodiles, as she calls them—were terrible creatures; and backed up the statement with a blood-curdling account of how one of these slandered reptiles crept into a squatter cabin one night, and ate up a woman and five children. The woman, by herself, would have satisfied any ordinarily impossible alligator; but no, these liars must make him gorge the five children besides. One would not imagine that jokers of this ro-

---

street, unseen by O'Connor until within forty feet, when the young man fired a pistol, the shot taking effect in O'Connor's right breast, passing through the body near the heart. The instant Mabry shot, O'Connor turned and fired, the load taking effect in young Mabry's right breast and side. Mabry fell, pierced with twenty buckshot, and almost instantly O'Connor fell dead without a struggle. Mabry tried to rise, but fell back dead. The whole tragedy occurred within two minutes, and neither of the three spoke after he was shot. General Mabry had about thirty buckshot in his body. A by-stander was painfully wounded in the thigh with a buckshot, and another was wounded in the arm. Four other men had their clothing pierced by buckshot. The affair caused great excitement, and Gay Street was thronged with thousands of people. General Mabry and his son Joe were acquitted only a few days ago of the murder of Moses Lusby and Don Lusby, father and son, whom they killed a few weeks ago. Will Mabry was killed by Don Lusby last Christmas. Major Thomas O'Connor was President of the Mechanics' National Bank here, and the wealthiest man in the State."—*Associated Press Telegram.*

"One day last month Professor Sharpe of the Somerville, Tennessee Female College, 'a quiet and gentlemanly man,' was told that his brother-in-law, a Captain Burton, had threatened to kill him. Burton, it seems had already killed one man and driven his knife into another. The professor armed himself with a double-barreled shotgun, started out in search of his brother-in-law, found him playing billiards in a saloon, and blew his brains out. The Memphis *Avalanche* reports that the professor's course met with pretty general approval in the community; knowing that the law was powerless, in the actual condition of public sentiment, to protect him, he protected himself.

"About the same time, two young men in North Carolina, quarreled about a girl, and 'hostile messages' were exchanged. Friends tried to reconcile them, but had their labor for their pains.

bust breed would be sensitive—but they were. It is difficult, at this day, to understand, and impossible to justify, the reception which the book of the grave, honest, intelligent, gentle, manly, charitable, well-meaning Captain Basil Hall got. Mrs. Trollope's account of it may perhaps entertain the reader: therefore, I have put it in the Appendix.

Chapter XLIV. City Sights

The old French part of New Orleans—anciently the Spanish part—bears no resemblance to the American end of the city: the American end which lies beyond the intervening brick business center. The houses are massed in blocks; are austerely plain and dignified; uniform of pattern, with here and there a departure from it with pleasant effect; all are plastered on the outside, and nearly all have long, iron-railed verandas running along the several stories. Their chief beauty is the deep, warm, varicolored stain with which time and the weather have enriched the plaster. It harmonizes with all the surroundings, and has as natural a look of belonging there as has the flush upon sunset clouds. This charming decoration cannot be successfully imitated; neither is it to be found elsewhere in America.

The iron railings are a specialty, also. The pattern is often exceedingly light and dainty, and airy and graceful—with a large cipher or monogram in the center, a delicate cobweb of baffling, intricate forms, wrought in steel. The ancient railings are handmade, and are now comparatively rare and proportionately valuable. They are become bric-à-brac.

The party had the privilege of idling through this ancient quarter of New Orleans with the South's finest literary genius, the author of *The Grandissimes*. In him the South has found a masterly delineator of its interior life and its history. In truth, I find by experience, that the untrained eye and vacant mind can inspect it and learn of it and judge of it more clearly and profitably in his books than by personal contact with it.

With Mr. Cable along to see for you, and describe and explain and illuminate, a jog through that old quarter is a vivid pleasure. And you have a vivid *sense* as of unseen or dimly seen things—vivid, and yet fitful and darkling; you glimpse salient features, but lose the fine shades or catch them imperfectly through the vision of the imagination: a case, as it were, of an ignorant, near-sighted stranger traversing the rim of wide, vague horizons of Alps with an inspired and enlightened long-sighted native.

On the 24th the young men met in the public highway. One of them had a heavy club in his hand, the other an ax. The man with the club fought desperately for his life, but it was a hopeless fight from the first. A well-directed blow sent his club whirling out of his grasp, and the next moment he was a dead man.

"About the same time, two 'highly connected' young Virginians, clerks in a hardware store at Charlottesville, while 'skylarking,' came to blows. Peter Dick threw pepper in Charles Roads's eyes; Roads demanded an apology; Dick refused to give it, and it was agreed that a duel was inevitable, but a difficulty arose; the parties had no pistols, and it was too late at night to procure them. One of them suggested that butcher-knives would answer the purpose, and the other accepted the suggestion; the result was that Roads fell to the floor with a gash in his abdomen that may or may not prove fatal. If Dick has been arrested, the news has not reached us. He 'expressed deep regret,' and we are told by a Staunton correspondent of the Philadelphia *Press* that 'every effort has been made to hush the matter up.'"—*Extracts from the Public Journals.*

We visited the old St. Louis Hotel, now occupied by municipal offices. There is nothing strikingly remarkable about it; but one can say of it as of the Academy of Music in New York, that if a broom or a shovel has ever been used in it there is no circumstantial evidence to back up the fact. It is curious that cabbages and hay and things do not grow in the Academy of Music; but no doubt it is on account of the interruption of the light by the benches, and the impossibility of hoeing the crop except in the aisles. The fact that the ushers grow their buttonhole bouquets on the premises shows what might be done if they had the right kind of an agricultural head to the establishment.

We visited also the venerable Cathedral, and the pretty square in front of it; the one dim with religious light, the other brilliant with the worldly sort, and lovely with orange trees and blossomy shrubs; then we drove in the hot sun through the wilderness of houses and out onto the wide, dead level beyond, where the villas are, and the waterwheels to drain the town, and the commons populous with cows and children; passing by an old cemetery where we were told lie the ashes of an early pirate; but we took him on trust, and did not visit him. He was a pirate with a tremendous and sanguinary history; and as long as he preserved unspotted, in retirement, the dignity of his name and the grandeur of his ancient calling, homage and reverence were his from high and low; but when at last he descended into politics and became a paltry alderman, the public "shook" him, and turned aside and wept. When he died, they set up a monument over him; and little by little he has come into respect again; but it is respect for the pirate, not the alderman. To-day the loyal and generous remember only what he was, and charitably forget what he became.

Thence, we drove a few miles across a swamp, along a raised shell road, with a canal on one hand and a dense wood on the other; and here and there, in the distance, a ragged and angular-limbed and moss-bearded cypress-top standing out, clear-cut against the sky, and as quaint of form as the apple trees in Japanese pictures—such was our course and the surroundings of it. There was an occasional alligator swimming comfortably along in the canal, and an occasional picturesque colored person on the bank, flinging his statue-rigid reflection upon the still water and watching for a bite.

And by and by we reached the West end, a collection of hotels of the usual light summer-resort pattern, with broad verandas all around, and the waves of the wide and blue Lake Pontchartrain lapping the thresholds. We had dinner on a ground veranda over the water—the chief dish the renowned fish called pompano, delicious as the less criminal forms of sin.

Thousands of people come by rail and carriage to West End and to Spanish Fort every evening, and dine, listen to the bands, take strolls in the open air under the electric lights, go sailing on the lake, and entertain themselves in various and sundry other ways.

We had opportunities on other days and in other places to test the pompano. Notably, at an editorial dinner at one of the clubs in the city. He was in his last possible perfection there, and justified his fame. In his suite was a tall pyramid of scarlet crayfish—large ones; as large as one's thumb; delicate, palatable, appetizing. Also deviled whitebait; also shrimps of choice quality; and a platter of small soft-shell crabs of a most superior breed. The other dishes were what one might get at Delmonico's or Buckingham Palace; those I have spoken of can be had in similar perfection in New Orleans only, I suppose.

In the West and South they have a new institution—the Broom Brigade. It is composed of young ladies who dress in a uniform costume, and go through the infantry drill, with broom in place of musket. It is a very pretty sight, on private view. When they perform on the stage of a theater, in the blaze of colored fires, it must be a fine and fascinating spectacle. I saw them go through their complex manual with grace, spirit, and admirable precision. I saw them do everything which a human being can possibly do with a broom, except sweep. I did not see them sweep. But I know they could learn. What they have already learned proves that. And if they ever should learn, and should go on the war-path down Tchoupitoulas or some of those other streets around there, those thoroughfares would bear a greatly improved aspect in a very few minutes. But the girls themselves wouldn't; so nothing would be really gained, after all.

The drill was in the Washington Artillery building. In this building we saw many interesting relics of the war. Also a fine oil-painting representing Stonewall Jackson's last interview with General Lee. Both men are on horseback. Jackson has just ridden up, and is accosting Lee. The picture is very valuable, on account of the portraits, which are authentic. But like many another historical picture, it means nothing without its label. And one label will fit it as well as another:

First Interview between Lee and Jackson.

Last Interview between Lee and Jackson.

Jackson Introducing Himself to Lee.

Jackson Accepting Lee's Invitation to Dinner.

Jackson Declining Lee's Invitation to Dinner with Thanks.

Jackson Apologizing for a Heavy Defeat.

Jackson Reporting a Great Victory.

Jackson Asking Lee for a Match.

It tells *one* story, and a sufficient one; for it says quite plainly and satisfactorily, "Here are Lee and Jackson together." The artist would have made it tell that this is Lee and Jackson's last interview if he could have done it. But he couldn't, for there wasn't any way to do it. A good legible label is usually worth, for information, a ton of significant attitude and expression in a historical picture. In Rome, people with fine sympathetic natures stand up and weep in front of the celebrated "Beatrice Cenci the Day before Her Execution." It shows what a label can do. If they did not know the picture, they would inspect it unmoved, and say, "Young girl with hay fever; young girl with her head in a bag."

I found the half-forgotten Southern intonations and elisions as pleasing to my ear as they had formerly been. A Southerner talks music. At least it is music to me, but then I was born in the South. The educated Southerner has no use for an *r*, except at the beginning of a word. He says "honah," and "dinnah," and "Gove'nuh," and "befo' the waw," and so on. The words may lack charm to the eye, in print, but they have it to the ear. When did the *r* disappear from Southern speech, and how did it come to disappear? The custom of dropping it was not borrowed from the North, nor inherited from England. Many Southerners—most Southerners—put a *y* into occasional words that begin with the *k* sound. For instance, they say Mr. K'yahtah (Carter) and speak of playing k'yahds or of riding in the k'yahs. And they have the pleasant custom—long ago fallen into decay in the North—of frequently employing the respectful "Sir." Instead of the curt Yes, and the abrupt No, they say "Yes, suh"; "No, suh."

But there are some infelicities, such as "like" for "as," and the addition of an "at" where it isn't needed. I heard an educated gentleman say, "Like the flag-officer did." His cook or his butler would have said, "Like the flag-officer done." You hear gentlemen say, "Where have you been at?" And here is the aggravated form—heard a ragged street Arab say it to a comrade: "I was a-ask'n' Tom whah you was a-sett'n' at." The very elect carelessly say "will" when they mean "shall"; and many of them say "I didn't go to do it," meaning "I didn't mean to do it." The Northern word "guess"—imported from England, where it used to be common, and now regarded by satirical English-men as a Yankee original—is but little used among Southerners. They say "reckon." They haven't any "doesn't" in their language; they say "don't" instead. The unpolished often use "went" for "gone." It is nearly as bad as the Northern "hadn't ought." This re-minds me that a remark of a very peculiar nature was made here in my neighborhood (in the North) a few days ago: "He hadn't ought to have went." How is that? Isn't that a good deal of a triumph? One knows the orders combined in this half-breed's archi-tecture without inquiring: one parent Northern, the other Southern. To-day I heard a schoolmistress ask, "Where is John gone?" This form is so common—so nearly uni-versal, in fact—that if she had used "whither" instead of "where," I think it would have sounded like an affectation.

We picked up one excellent word—a word worth traveling to New Orleans to get; a nice limber, expressive, handy word—"Lagniappe." They pronounce it lanny-yap. It is Spanish—so they said. We discovered it at the head of a column of odds and ends in the *Picayune* the first day; heard twenty people use it the second; inquired what it meant the third; adopted it and got facility in swinging it the fourth. It has a re-stricted meaning, but I think the people spread it out a little when they choose. It is the equivalent of the thirteenth roll in a "baker's dozen." It is something thrown in, gratis, for good measure. The custom originated in the Spanish quarter of the city. When a child or a servant buys something in a shop—or even the mayor or the gover-nor, for aught I know—he finishes the operation by saying:

"Give me something for lagniappe."

The shopman always responds; gives the child a bit of licorice-root, gives the ser-vant a cheap cigar or a spool of thread, gives the governor—I don't know what he gives the governor; support, likely.

When you are invited to drink—and this does occur now and then in New Or-leans—and you say, "What, again?—no, I've had enough," the other party says, "But just this one time more—this is for lagniappe." When the beau perceives that he is stacking his compliments a trifle too high, and sees by the young lady's countenance that the edifice would have been better with the top compliment left off, he puts his "I beg pardon, no harm intended," into the briefer form of "Oh, that's for lagniappe." If the waiter in the restaurant stumbles and spills a gill of coffee down the back of your neck, he says, "F'r lagniappe, sah," and gets you another cup without extra charge.

Chapter XLV. Southern Sports

In the North one hears the war mentioned, in social conversation, once a month; sometimes as often as once a week; but as a distinct subject for talk, it has long ago been relieved of duty. There are sufficient reasons for this. Given a dinner company of six gentlemen to-day, it can easily happen that four of them—and possibly five— were not in the field at all. So the chances are four to two, or five to one, that the war will at no time during the evening become the topic of conversation; and the chances are still greater that if it become the topic it will remain so but a little while. If you add six ladies to the company, you have added six people who saw so little of the dread realities of the war that they ran out of talk concerning them years ago, and now would soon weary of the war topic if you brought it up.

The case is very different in the South. There, every man you meet was in the war; and every lady you meet saw the war. The war is the great chief topic of conversation. The interest in it is vivid and constant; the interest in other topics is fleeting. Mention of the war will wake up a dull company and set their tongues going when nearly any other topic would fail. In the South, the war is what A.D. is elsewhere; they date from it. All day long you hear things "placed" as having happened since the waw; or du'in' the waw; or befo' the waw; or right aftah the waw; or 'bout two yeahs or five yeahs or ten yeahs befo' the waw or aftah the waw. It shows how intimately every individual was visited, in his own person, by that tremendous episode. It gives the inexperienced stranger a better idea of what a vast and comprehensive calamity invasion is than he can ever get by reading books at the fireside.

At a club one evening, a gentleman turned to me and said, in an aside:

"You notice, of course, that we are nearly always talking about the war. It isn't because we haven't anything else to talk about, but because nothing else has so strong an interest for us. And there is another reason: In the war, each of us, in his own person, seems to have sampled all the different varieties of human experience; as a consequence, you can't mention an outside matter of any sort but it will certainly remind some listener of something that happened during the war—and out he comes with it. Of course that brings the talk back to the war. You may try all you want to, to keep other subjects before the house, and we may all join in and help, but there can be but one result: the most random topic would load every man up with war reminiscences, and *shut* him up, too; and talk would be likely to stop presently, because you can't talk pale inconsequentialities when you've got a crimson fact or fancy in your head that you are burning to fetch out."

The poet was sitting some little distance away; and presently he began to speak—about the moon.

The gentleman who had been talking to me remarked in an aside: "There, the moon is far enough from the seat of war, but you will see that it will suggest something to somebody about the war; in ten minutes from now the moon, as a topic, will be shelved."

The poet was saying he had noticed something which was a surprise to him; had had the impression that down here, toward the equator, the moonlight was much stronger and brighter than up North; had had the impression that when he visited New Orleans, many years ago, the moon—

Interruption from the other end of the room:

"Let me explain that. Reminds me of an anecdote. Everything is changed since the war, for better or for worse; but you'll find people down here born grumblers, who see no change except the change for the worse. There was an old negro woman of this sort. A young New-Yorker said in her presence, 'What a wonderful moon you have down here!' She sighed and said, 'Ah, bless yo' heart, honey, you ought to seen dat moon befo' de waw!'"

The new topic was dead already. But the poet resurrected it, and gave it a new start.

A brief dispute followed, as to whether the difference between Northern and Southern moonlight really existed or was only imagined. Moonlight talk drifted easily into talk about artificial methods of dispelling darkness. Then somebody remembered that when Farragut advanced upon Port Hudson on a dark night—and did not wish to assist the aim of the Confederate gunners—he carried no battle-lanterns, but painted the decks of his ships white, and thus created a dim but valuable light, which enabled his own men to grope their way around with considerable facility. At this point the war got the floor again—the ten minutes not quite up yet.

I was not sorry, for war talk by men who have been in a war is always interesting; whereas moon talk by a poet who has not been in the moon is likely to be dull.

We went to a cockpit in New Orleans on a Saturday afternoon. I had never seen a cock-fight before. There were men and boys there of all ages and all colors, and of many languages and nationalities. But I noticed one quite conspicuous and surprising absence: the traditional brutal faces. There were no brutal faces. With no cock-fighting going on, you could have played the gathering on a stranger for a prayer-meeting; and after it began, for a revival—provided you blindfolded your stranger—for the shouting was something prodigious.

A negro and a white man were in the ring; everybody else outside. The cocks were brought in in sacks; and when time was called, they were taken out by the two bottle-holders, stroked, caressed, poked toward each other, and finally liberated. The big black cock plunged instantly at the little gray one and struck him on the head with his spur. The gray responded with spirit. Then the Babel of many-tongued shoutings broke out, and ceased not thenceforth. When the cocks had been fighting some little time, I was expecting them momently to drop dead, for both were blind, red with blood, and so exhausted that they frequently fell down. Yet they would not give up, neither would they die. The negro and the white man would pick them up every few seconds, wipe them off, blow cold water on them in a fine spray, and take their heads in their mouths and hold them there a moment—to warm back the perishing life perhaps; I do not know. Then, being set down again, the dying creatures would totter gropingly about, with dragging wings, find each other, strike a guesswork blow or two, and fall exhausted once more.

I did not see the end of the battle. I forced myself to endure it as long as I could, but it was too pitiful a sight; so I made frank confession to that effect, and we retired. We heard afterward that the black cock died in the ring, and fighting to the last.

Evidently there is abundant fascination about this "sport" for such as have had a degree of familiarity with it. I never saw people enjoy anything more than this gathering enjoyed this fight. The case was the same with old gray-heads and with boys of ten. They lost themselves in frenzies of delight. The "cocking-main" is an inhuman sort of entertainment, there is no question about that; still, it seems a much more respectable and far less cruel sport than fox-hunting—for the cocks like it; they experience, as well as confer enjoyment; which is not the fox's case.

We assisted—in the French sense—at a mule-race, one day. I believe I enjoyed this contest more than any other mule there. I enjoyed it more than I remember having enjoyed any other animal race I ever saw. The grand-stand was well filled with the beauty and the chivalry of New Orleans. That phrase is not original with me. It is the Southern reporter's. He has used it for two generations. He uses it twenty times a day, or twenty thousand times a day, or a million times a day—according to the exigencies. He is obliged to use it a million times a day, if he have occasion to speak of respectable men and women that often; for he has no other phrase for such service except that single one. He never tires of it; it always has a fine sound to him. There is a kind of swell, medieval bulliness and tinsel about it that pleases his gaudy, barbaric soul. If he had been in Palestine in the early times, we should have had no references to "much people" out of him. No, he would have said "the beauty and the chivalry of Galilee" assembled to hear the sermon on the Mount. It is likely that the men and women of the South are sick enough of that phrase by this time, and would like a change, but there is no immediate prospect of their getting it.

The New Orleans editor has a strong, compact, direct, unflowery style; wastes no words, and does not gush. Not so with his average correspondent. In the Appendix I have quoted a good letter, penned by a trained hand; but the average correspondent hurls a style which differs from that. For instance:

The *Times-Democrat* sent a relief-steamer up one of the bayous, last April. This steamer landed at a village, up there somewhere, and the captain invited some of the ladies of the village to make a short trip with him. They accepted and came aboard, and the steamboat shoved out up the creek. That was all there was "to it." And that is all that the editor of the *Times-Democrat* would have got out of it. There was nothing in the thing but statistics, and he would have got nothing else out of it. He would probably have even tabulated them; partly to secure perfect clearness of statement, and partly to save space. But his special correspondent knows other methods of handling statistics. He just throws off all restraint and wallows in them:

> On Saturday, early in the morning, the beauty of the place graced our cabin, and proud of her fair freight the gallant little boat glided up the bayou.

Twenty-two words to say the ladies came aboard and the boat shoved out up the creek, is a clean waste of ten good words, and is also destructive of compactness of statement.

The trouble with the Southern reporter is—Women. They unsettle him; they throw him off his balance. He is plain, and sensible, and satisfactory, until woman heaves in sight. Then he goes all to pieces; his mind totters, becomes flowery and idiotic. From reading the above extract, you would imagine that this student of Sir Walter Scott is an apprentice, and knows next to nothing about handling a pen. On the contrary, he furnishes plenty of proofs, in his long letter, that he knows well enough how to handle it when the women are not around to give him the artificial-flower complaint. For instance:

> At four o'clock ominous clouds began to gather in the southeast, and presently from the Gulf there came a blow which increased in severity every moment. It was not safe to leave the landing then, and there was a delay. The oaks shook off long tresses of their mossy beards to the tugging of the wind, and the bayou in its ambition put on miniature waves in mocking of much larger bodies of water. A lull permitted a start, and homeward we steamed, an inky sky overhead and a heavy wind blowing. As darkness crept on, there were few on board who did not wish themselves nearer home.

There is nothing the matter with that. It is good description, compactly put. Yet there was great temptation, there, to drop into lurid writing.

But let us return to the mule. Since I left him, I have rummaged around and found a full report of the race. In it I find confirmation of the theory which I broached just now—namely, that the trouble with the Southern reporter is Women: Women, supplemented by Walter Scott and his knights and beauty and chivalry, and so on. This is an excellent report, as long as the women stay out of it. But when they intrude, we have this frantic result:

> It will be probably a long time before the ladies' stand presents such a sea of foamlike loveliness as it did yesterday. The New Orleans women are always charming, but never so much so as at this time of the year, when in their dainty spring costumes they bring with them a breath of balmy freshness and an odor of sanctity unspeakable. The stand was so crowded with them that, walking at their feet and seeing no possibility of approach, many a man appreciated as he never did before the Peri's feeling at the Gates of Paradise, and wondered what was the priceless boon that would admit him to their sacred presence. Sparkling on their white-robed breasts or shoulders were the colors of their favorite knights, and were it not for the fact that the doughty heroes appeared on unromantic mules, it would have been easy to imagine one of King Arthur's gala-days.

There were thirteen mules in the first heat; all sorts of mules, they were; all sorts of complexions, gaits, dispositions, aspects. Some were handsome creatures, some were not; some were sleek, some hadn't had their fur brushed lately; some were innocently gay and frisky; some were full of malice and all unrighteousness; guessing from looks, some of them thought the matter on hand was war, some thought it was a lark, the rest took it for a religious occasion. And each mule acted according to his convictions. The result was an absence of harmony well compensated by a conspicuous presence of variety—variety of a picturesque and entertaining sort.

All the riders were young gentlemen in fashionable society. If the reader has been wondering why it is that the ladies of New Orleans attend so humble an orgy as a mule-race, the thing is explained now. It is a fashion freak; all connected with it are people of fashion.

It is great fun, and cordially liked. The mule-race is one of the marked occasions of the year. It has brought some pretty fast mules to the front. One of these had to be ruled out, because he was so fast that he turned the thing into a one-mule contest, and robbed it of one of its best features—variety. But every now and then somebody disguises him with a new name and a new complexion, and rings him in again.

The riders dress in full jockey costumes of bright-colored silks, satins, and velvets.

The thirteen mules got away in a body, after a couple of false starts, and scampered off with prodigious spirit. As each mule and each rider had a distinct opinion of his own as to how the race ought to be run, and which side of the track was best in certain circumstances, and how often the track ought to be crossed, and when a collision ought to be accomplished, and when it ought to be avoided, these twenty-six conflicting opinions created a most fantastic and picturesque confusion, and the resulting spectacle was killingly comical.

Mile heat; time, 2:22. Eight of the thirteen mules distanced. I had a bet on a mule which would have won if the procession had been reversed. The second heat was good fun; and so was the "consolation race for beaten mules," which followed later; but the first heat was the best in that respect.

I think that much the most enjoyable of all races is a steamboat race; but, next to that, I prefer the gay and joyous mule-rush. Two red-hot steamboats raging along, neck-and-neck, straining every nerve—that is to say, every rivet in the boilers—quaking and shaking and groaning from stem to stern, spouting white steam from the pipes, pouring black smoke from the chimneys, raining down sparks, parting the river into long breaks of hissing foam—this is sport that makes a body's very liver curl with enjoyment. A horse-race is pretty tame and colorless in comparison. Still, a horse-race might be well enough, in its way, perhaps, if it were not for the tiresome false starts. But then, nobody is ever killed. At least, nobody was ever killed when I was at a horse-race. They have been crippled, it is true; but this is little to the purpose.

Amelie Rives
(1863–1945)

Amelie Rives was born in Richmond, Virginia, in 1863 at the height of the Civil War. Her father was Colonel Alfred Landon Rives, a member of Robert E. Lee's staff, and Lee himself was her godfather. Her childhood years were spent at the Rives family estate in Albemarle County, Virginia, where she was educated by governesses and perused the library of her grandfather, William Cabell Rives. She began to write very early, but she did not publish any of her work until the manuscript of a short story was discovered by a guest; Rives gave him permission to publish it anonymously, and it appeared in *The Atlantic Monthly* as "A Brother to Dragons" in 1886. She subsequently published a number of other stories, as well as the collection *A Brother to Dragons and Other Old-Time Tales* in 1888.

A celebrated beauty and socialite, Rives married John Armstrong Chanler, a descendant of the millionaire John Jacob Astor, in 1888. In that same year, she also published *The Quick or the Dead?*, which was enormously popular, selling more than 300,000 copies. A Gothic love story that both recalls Poe and anticipates Faulkner, *The Quick or the Dead?* portrays a heroine torn between her love for her dead husband and awakening feelings for his handsome cousin. A sequel, *Barbara Dering*, appeared in 1893. In 1894, Rives and Chanler divorced, and in 1896 she married Prince Pierre Troubetzkoy. She published sixteen novels over the next thirty-five years, and though most have faded into obscurity, *World's End* (1914) and *Shadows of Flames* (1915) have been favorably compared with the works of Henry James and Edith Wharton. Rives died in Charlottesville, Virginia, in 1945.

The Quick or the Dead?

I.

There was a soughing rain asweep that night, with no wind to drive it, yet it ceased and fell, sighed and was hushed incessantly, as by some changing gale. Barbara was a good deal unnerved by the lanternless drive from the station. The shelving road, seamed with abrupt gullies, lay through murk fields and stony hollows, that she well remembered; in the glimpsing lightning she saw scurrying trees against the suave autumn sky, like etchings on bluish paper; the dry, white-brown grasses swirled about the horses' feet in that windless rain; and after what thunderous fashion those horses pounded stableward! They hurled through narrow gate-ways like stones from a cata-pult, rushed past ragged trees whose boles seemed leaping to meet them, spun over large stones as though they had been mere fallen leaves.

The black driver urged his smoking team, as though dissatisfied with their prowess, by sharp, whistling inward breaths, and upward gestures of his bowed el-bows. He was a grotesque figure against the pennons of lightning. Barbara had smiled in spite of her fear, becoming suddenly grave as they just grazed the corner of a slant-ing, half-ruined wall, formed of rough stones and clay, the "Brookfield Barn" of her childhood, and her fears were not calmed by recalling the fact that only twenty yards ahead stretched a long, ramshackle bridge, formed of loose planks held in place by wild grapevine branches and a stone placed here and there. This bridge dipped its lithe middle almost into the waters of a hurling, brown stream, known in the sur-rounding country as "Machunk Creek." There were various legends regarding the ori-gin of this name. The negroes said that a man had crossed it at one time, carrying a chunk of "fat" light-wood; when on the middle of the one plank which then served for bridge, he had dropped his pine-knot, and screamed out desperately, "Oh! my chunk!" Thence the title of the stream. Barbara, who had always unquestioningly believed this story, could almost fancy that she saw this swart, regretful figure poised now above the hurly of rain-swollen waters,—could almost hear his despairing cry. She thought of getting out of the trap and following his example by crossing on foot, when a dull, whirring rumble, followed by a certain rock-a-bye motion, told her that they were upon the bridge. She shut her eyes with an infallible womanly instinct, although it was then absolutely dark, caught a fold of her inner lip between her teeth, and pinched the back of her left hand firmly in the palm of her right. There was a jolt, a spattering scramble from the horses, another of those sharp, unique sounds from Unc' Joshua the driver, and off they sped once more into the ever-increasing gloom.

It was not until the next day that Barbara found there had been lanterns, with candles ready for lighting, on each side of her. She had been finally whirled in upon the gravel of the carriage-drive of Rosemary, and had dodged the familiar arms of the box-trees, that scraped and rattled against the sides of the flying carriage: then came orange blurs of light, between thick, parted curtains, a semicircular glare over the hall door, and little glowing ladders to right and left of it.

Her aunt Fridiswig had rushed to meet her, had embraced her, by leaving a moist splash upon her elastic, night-cool cheek, and some of a pepper-and-salt shawl-fringe caught in the button of her jacket. She had escaped finally, saying that she would like a cup of tea in her bedroom, and that her aunt could come and bid her good-night, but was on no account to sit up past her usual hour for retiring.

She was leaning now in an old, chintz-covered chair in front of a chestnut-wood fire. How vividly that chair recalled other days! She smiled a little drearily as she ran her fingers into a little slit in the stuff, which she had cut there herself, three years ago, while whittling a peg for her easel. She had brought no maid with her, having looked forward with a certain pleasure to the ministrations of the maid of her girl-hood, a dark-brown creature, with a profile like that of Rameses II., and wearing countless slubs of black wool tied up with bits of white string. This person was mov-ing about the room with a light, padding step like that of a cat through wet grass. She was holding up and admiring her mistress's cast-off furs and under-wraps, in the candlelight behind her back, passing her hand up and down the rich sables with a voluptuous ecstasy of appreciation; now tucking them beneath her chin and regarding her reflection in the old-fashioned, gilt-framed toilet-glass, now burying her face in them with a shudderingly delighted movement of her shoulders. Barbara sat listless, her damp hair unwound about her shoulders, tapping the curled ends lightly against the palm of her hand as she dreamed, wide-eyed, in the uncertain firelight. The maid, Martha Ellen, or Rameses, as Barbara called her, came presently and began to warm a pair of red-heeled bedroom slippers by holding them to the blaze, at the same time lifting one of her pretty, yellow-lined hands, palm outward, to protect her face.

The gesture went through Barbara like a knife. How Val used to laugh at it, when Martha Ellen went through the same performance of warming his slippers! She put up both hands to her breast with a movement of anguish. Tears clustered hot and stinging on her lashes, and great breaths that were deeper than sobs thrilled through her from head to foot. Ah, she had been a fool doubtless to come here, for, in the natural course of things, she must expect such painful occurrences twenty times a day; and yet there was a sorrowful sweetness in it, too. She let drop her hands, and, relaxing her tense figure, sent a slow, miserable look around the room. It was spacious, airy, Southern. A delicate, dawn-like mixture of rose and gray characterized its furniture. The large, carved bed, of mahogany, had hangings of rose and white. There were white goat-skins here and there on the gray carpet, and some very good water-colors, by French artists, above the chimney-piece. The chairs and couches were many and capacious. The number of mirrors suggested a certain vanity on the part of its occupant: there were eight in all, none of them small, and all framed heavily in old gilt. A mahogany writing-table near one of the windows had heavy brass handles, awink in the fitful light. Barbara rose suddenly, and, putting back her heavy hair, began to walk up and down the room on soft, slipperless feet.

"Wait, Miss Barb'ra, honey," urged Rameses, approaching her mistress on her knees and holding out the now very-warm slippers. "You'll war out dem pretty stockin's."

Barbara stopped and stared down at her absently, then turned gently away and re-began her long, noiseless stride.

"You can go," she said. "Never mind the slippers. I'll call you presently."

As Rameses left the room, Barbara locked the door through which she had passed, and then, turning, with her hand still on the key, took another long, scrutinizing survey of the room.

Presently she went to one of the windows and drew aside the curtain. The skirt of the sky was strewn from hem to hem with little, flittering, filmy clouds, through which a wet moon shone vaporous; the tulip-trees, nearly stripped of their golden, October leaves, thrust their empty seed-cups out and up, like so many elfin goblets, to be filled with weird mist-wine; the wind blew in puffs, like a thing breathing in its sleep, and the rain had ceased. Barbara's hair made a mellow glow in the wan light, and the already scarlet holly-berries blinked back at her from the frothy gloom of the shadow-waves. A horse neighed impatiently just below, and was answered from a far meadow. She could see the light from her windows streaking the faded grass on the lawn. With a sigh she let the curtain drape itself once more in its accustomed folds, pausing to rest both hands on the mahogany writing-table, and again devouring the room with that slow, absorbing gaze. As her returning eyes fell upon the table on which she leaned, she gave a strange cry, and pressed backward among the window-curtains, still keeping a fixed, horrified look on the table. How bathos will intrude upon pathos! It is the flippant Tweedledum of a most serious Tweedledee. The possible viper from which poor Barbara shrank was nothing more nor less than a half-smoked cigar, which lay in a neat little ash-tray among its ashes, just as the man who had been smoking it had placed it there three years ago. Suddenly she fell on her knees beside the table, and, snatching up the bit of tobacco, kissed it again and again. She was a woman with an almost terrible sense of humor, and presently she began to laugh, not hysterically, but quietly, appreciatively. She saw how ridiculous a thing that act of hers would seem to an on-looker. And then again she kissed it, and, catching her face into her two hands, went into a shuddering passion of sobs, tearless, noiseless, and terrible.

All this will not seem overstrained when one knows its origin.

In this room, among these identical articles, just three years ago, Barbara Pomfret had passed the first three months of an absolutely joyous married life; two years ago her husband had died, and she had come back an utterly unhappy woman to the scene of her former happiness. Every chair, book, knick-knack, rug, in this room, was associated in some way with her husband. The very pictures, the toilet-glass, the ornaments on the mantel-shelf, all held for her some memory which stabbed her as she looked; and yet it was of her own will that she had returned. She did not wish to forget, and she could not better remember than in a place so fraught with memories. She had not, however, calculated the full poignancy of the grief that was about to claim her. As vanished scenes swept across her inner sight, there came with them words and looks and tones innumerable. His arms held her, his breath warmed her, his voice was in her ear, vibrating, actual. She leaped to her feet, stumbling over her heavy gown; her fascinated, dreading eyes sought the vague gloom behind her, as she hurried to the door. The room was full of his voice, of his sighing, of his laughter. She breathed gaspingly, and caught at the key to unlock the door. It was stiff with long disusage, and refused to turn. There again! his laughter, about her, above her, and his lips at her ear. She could hear the words, loving, reckless, impassioned words, not meet for a ghost to utter: "Barbara! Barbara! your curled lips are a cup, and your breath is wine. You make me drunk!—drunk!"

She grasped the key with both hands, panting, sobbing, her eyes strained with a mighty, overwhelming panic. Still the senseless bit of brass resisted. She caught up a fold of her gown and wound it about the handle. Now his very lips were on her: they drew her breath, her life.

"O God, help me! O God, let the door open! let it open!"

Miss Fridiswig, alone with her knitting, in the dining-room just below, heard a sudden noise as of falling, and burst out into the hall, to meet Rameses with her eyes goggling. They made a simultaneous rush up the stairway, and nearly fell over Barbara, who was lying on her face, half in and half out of her room.

Rameses, who was as strong as most men of her size, lifted the poor girl bodily, and laid her upon the bed.

They did all the disagreeable, useless things that people generally do to a fainting woman, and by and by, when it was time for her to return to consciousness, she opened her dark eyes, and drew several short, difficult breaths.

"I know,—I know,—" she said.

"You know what?" coaxed Miss Fridiswig.

"I know,—I know,—" repeated Barbara,—"I know—where I am. Must get—a—new lock—to-morrow. Rameses—sleep—in here—to-night. What's o'clock?"

"Mos' twelve," said Rameses, who was holding Barbara's bare feet in her hands. "You go tuh bade, Miss Fridis. Miss Barb'ra, you go tuh bade too."

"Yes, darling, you must,—for my sake," urged Miss Fridiswig.

"Not yet; not yet," said Barbara.

She tried to sit up, and fell back among the big pillows. A sudden shivering shook her throughout. She made another effort, and got her arm about Rameses' neck.

"Help me—" she panted, "help me—off the bed—quick. That sofa there—"

When they had made her comfortable on the sofa, she closed her eyes and lay so still that they thought she had fainted again; but as Rameses moved to fetch some of the noxious remedies, she pressed down a fair hand on the girl's wool, signifying that she was to remain beside her.

"You go tuh bade, Miss Fridis," said Rameses. "'Tain't no use two on us settin' up."

"No, not a bit," said Barbara. "Please go, Aunt Fridis."

"Ah, let me be of use! let me be of use!" wailed Miss Fridiswig, casting herself on her knees beside Rameses, and leaving another warm splash on Barbara's inert hand.

Barbara, who never willingly hurt the feelings even of a cabman, did not know what to do, until it suddenly occurred to her to faint again. When she came to herself from this simulated swoon, Rameses had packed Miss Fridiswig, willy-nilly, to her virgin slumbers, and was resuscitating the dead fire by breathing on it, after the Biblical method.

Barbara lay watching her, stung again by an almost intolerable pang. How often had she lain on that very sofa and watched Val trying to imitate the negro method of kindling a fire, until his puffed-out cheeks made him into a very excellent likeness of a wind-god couchant!

When the wreathing, lilac flames began to whirr about the fresh logs, she called the girl to her.

"Are you very sleepy?" she said, smiling, a beautiful smile that Martha Ellen remembered. It was associated with countless gifts, and seemed to breathe of the summer, a season endeared above all others to the sensitive little black.

"Lor'! Yuh looks jes' like yuh use tuh!" she exclaimed, regardless of Barbara's question. "I thought yuh done give up smilin' when I seed yuh fust tuh-night."

"Did you?" said Barbara. She smiled again, and yielded her hand graciously to the girl's caresses, repeating her question. Martha Ellen asserted that she didn't feel sleep "nowhar near 'bout her."

"But it must be very late?" Barbara said. "Are all the other servants in bed?"

Martha Ellen thought so, and slipped a lithe arm about her mistress, who stood still for an instant, while the apparent seething of the articles about her subsided. She was tall, and her figure in its silverish dressing-gown of white silk gleamed like a streak of moonlight in the rich dusk. I once saw a stem of white wild-flowers lean against a charred pine as she was now leaning against her dark-skinned waiting-woman.

Presently she moved a step or two. The girl moved with her, bending beneath the bare white arm that rested heavily across her shoulders. As they paused again, she turned her face up, with a sideward, expectant movement.

"I was going to say," Barbara began, "that if you know where the little brass bed is,—the one I used to sleep in as a little girl,—I would help you to get it."

"Naw, you ain't; you ain' gwine he'p me git nuthin'," said Martha Ellen, positively.

Her mistress was as positive. "It is entirely too heavy for you to lift alone," she said. "If you know where it is, I am coming with you to help you."

They went together down a narrow corridor that turned abruptly several times, Martha Ellen in front with a candle that died out to a blue splutter in the many draughts.

Following this elfish light, Barbara found herself at last in the nursery of her childhood. She looked upward and remembered the very cracks in the plaster ceiling: there was the identical one that she had thought resembled the profile of George Washington on the postage-stamps. Underneath it stood the brass cot. It was somewhat tarnished, and the bows of pale-blue ribbon that enlivened its head-piece were decidedly draggled. She untied them mechanically and rolled them around her fingers, while Martha Ellen took off the unsheeted mattresses. How long it was since she had slept in that gay little bed! There is nothing that makes us seem so unreal, so unfamiliar to ourselves, as some pleasant child-possession seen unexpectedly in unhappy womanhood.

She kneeled long beside it that night, with palms pressed hard against her eyes, forgetting to pray, in a great, struggling effort to imagine herself once more a child, pleading for her pony's tail to "grow as long as before the calf chewed it," for "Mammy to be white in heaven," for "Satan to be forgiven after a long, long, long time," for herself to be made a "good little girl and not so cross with Agnes."

At first she was not conscious of any especial emotion, as she bent against the cold linen of the turned-back bedclothes; she had no particular sensation either of happiness or unhappiness; but presently vast waves of passionate regret, and longing, and rebellion, surged over her, each one, as it swelled and formed, more vast and annihilating than the other. The undertow seemed dragging her down, down. God's imagined face took on a horrible grinning. The ministering angels seemed deformed creatures who writhed, and twisted, and uttered wanton gigglings as they circled about the Throne after the fashion of the witches in "Macbeth" about the caldron. Nothing seemed good; nothing seemed kind. She could not even think of her husband as having existed. He was a mere mass of repulsive formlessness in a slimy wedge of earth; perhaps he was not even that. She imagined his ghastly skeleton tricked out in all the mockery of fashionable attire. What delightful, smart, of-the-world-worldly coats he had worn! Why, if he were a skeleton now, one could see his tailor's name in gilt letters through his spinal column! Ha! ha! ha! Ha! ha! ha! She had laughed silently at first, then in a choking whisper, then in a ringing peal of sound that clashed through the silent house, chilling the blood in Martha Ellen's rigid, black body.

It did not occur to her to go to her mistress. She sat up on the pallet where she was sleeping for the night, folded herself in her own embrace, and muttered between her clacking teeth,—

"Miss Barb'ra done gone mad! she done gone mad! *I* dunno what tuh do! Gord knows *I* dunno what tuh do!" Then all as suddenly the laughter ceased.

There seemed to Barbara to be some glowing, resplendent presence about her, lifting up her heart as it were with both hands. She took down her palms from her strained eyes, and stared into the almost absolute gloom. She even reached out her arms into it. The darkness seemed to cling about her. Little, every-day noises distracted her attention,—the snap of the dying fire as it settled among its ashes, the lull and sough of an awakening wind through the branches of the tulip-trees, the noise that a mouse made dragging some little thing along the floor. She rose stiffly to her feet, and cowered shivering down among the icy sheets. Again she held out her arms. The pressure of a warm, curly head against her breast was with her as an actuality.

"Oh, Val," she whispered,—"oh, Val! Oh, darling,—mine!—mine!—mine! Touch me, come to me, here in the darkness,—here where you used to love me. I will not be afraid,—no, not the least, not the least. Oh! God—God! he does not hear me! he cannot hear me! he does not care any more."

She flung herself half out of her childhood's bed upon the large one of carved mahogany near which it stood, sobbing, shuddering, kissing wildly the silken coverlet and pillows that rose softly through the thick firelight, so finally slept, worn out, desolate, chilled to the very core of soul and body.

Mary Noailles Murfree

(1850–1922)

Mary Noailles Murfree was born at Grantland, her family's plantation near Murfreesboro, Tennessee. Having partial paralysis caused by a childhood fever, Murfree spent her summers from 1855 to 1870 at Beersheba Springs, Tennessee, in the Cumberland Mountains, where she came in contact with the mountain people whom she later depicted in her writing. In 1857 the Murfree family moved to Nashville and remained there for more than sixteen years. Murfree enrolled at the Nashville Female Academy, where she was formally educated; and from 1867 to 1869, she attended Chegary Institute, a finishing school in Philadelphia. In 1869, she moved to Nashville but left in 1872 to live at the recently built New Grantland, the old Grantland having been destroyed during the Civil War. During the Murfreesboro years, Murfree's first published essay, "Flirts and Their Ways," appeared in the May 1874 *Lippincott's* under the pseudonym R. Emmet Dembry. Two years later in 1876, Murfree sold her first two mountain stories, "Taking the Blue Ribbon at the County Fair" and "The Panther of Jolton's Ridge," to *Appleton's Weekly*. The publication of these stories, however, did not occur until after the extraordinarily successful reception of "The Dancin' Party at Harrison's Cove," published in May 1878 in the *Atlantic Monthly*, under the pseudonym Charles Egbert Craddock, the name she used for many years. In 1881 the Murfrees moved to St. Louis, Missouri, where Murfree contributed stories to a number of periodicals. In 1884 she published *In the Tennessee Mountains*, her best-known volume of short stories, and a novel, *Where the Battle Was Fought*. During the next thirty years, she published a number of historical novels, the best of which is probably *The Story of Old Fort Loudon* (1899), but her best works were those with prominent local color themes, like *The Prophet of the Great Smoky Mountains* (1885) and *In the "Stranger People's" Country* (1891).

The "Harnt" That Walks Chilhowee

June had crossed the borders of Tennessee. Even on the summit of Chilhowee Mountain the apples in Peter Giles's orchard were beginning to redden, and his Indian corn, planted on so steep a declivity that the stalks seemed to have much ado to keep their

"The 'Harnt' That Walks Chilhowee," by Mary Noailles Murfree, from *In the Tennessee Mountains*. Boston: Houghton Mifflin, 1884. Rpt. Knoxville: University of Tennessee Press, 1970.

footing, was crested with tassels and plumed with silk. Among the dense forests, seen by no man's eye, the elder was flying its creamy banners in honor of June's coming, and, heard by no man's ear, the pink and white bells of the azalea rang out melodies of welcome.

"An' it air a toler'ble for'ard season. Yer wheat looks likely; an' yer gyarden truck air thrivin' powerful. Even that cold spell we-uns hed about the full o' the moon in May ain't done sot it back none, it 'pears like ter me: But, 'cording ter my way o'thinkin', ye hev got chickens enough hyar ter eat off every pea-bloom ez soon ez it opens." And Simon Burney glanced with a gardener's disapproval at the numerous fowls, lifting their red combs and tufted top-knots here and there among the thick clover under the apple-trees.

"Them's Clarsie's chickens,—my darter, ye know," drawled Peter Giles, a pale, listless, and lank mountaineer. "An' she hev been gin ter onderstand ez they hev got ter be kep' out'n the gyarden; 'thout," he added indulgently,—"'thout I'm a-plowin', when I lets 'em foller in the furrow ter pick up worms. But law! Clarsie is so spry that she don't ax no better'n ter be let ter run them chickens off'n the peas."

Then the two men tilted their chairs against the posts of the little porch in front of Peter Giles's log cabin, and puffed their pipes in silence. The panorama spread out before them showed misty and dreamy among the delicate spiral wreaths of smoke. But was that gossamer-like illusion, lying upon the far horizon, the magic of nicotian, or the vague presence of distant heights? As ridge after ridge came down from the sky in ever-graduating shades of intenser blue, Peter Giles might have told you that this parallel system of enchantment was only "the mountings": that here was Foxy, and there was Big Injun, and still beyond was another, which he had hearn tell ran sprang up into Virginny. The sky that bent to clasp this kindred blue was of varying moods. Floods of sunshine submerged Chilhowee in liquid gold, and revealed that dainty outline limned upon the northern horizon; but over the Great Smoky mountains clouds had gathered, and a gigantic rainbow bridged the valley.

Peter Giles's listless eyes were fixed upon a bit of red clay road, which was visible through a gap in the foliage far below. Even a tiny object, that ant-like crawled upon it, could be seen from the summit of Chilhowee. "I reckon that's my brother's wagon an' team," he said, as he watched the moving atom pass under the gorgeous triumphal arch. "He 'lowed he war goin' ter the Cross-Roads terday."

Simon Burney did not speak for a moment. When he did, his words seemed widely irrelevant. "That's a likely gal o'yourn," he drawled, with an odd constraint in his voice,—"a likely gal, that Clarsie."

There was a quick flash of surprise in Peter Giles's dull eyes. He covertly surveyed his guest, with an astounded curiosity rampant in his slow brains. Simon Burney had changed color; an expression of embarrassment lurked in every line of his honest, florid, hard-featured face. An alert imagination might have detected a deprecatory self-consciousness in every gray hair that striped the black beard raggedly fringing his chin.

"Yes," Peter Giles at length replied, "Clarsie air a likely enough gal. But she air mightily sot ter hevin' her own way. An' ef't ain't give ter her peaceable-like, she jes' takes it whether or no."

This statement, made by one presumably fully informed on the subject, might have damped the ardor of many a suitor,—for the monstrous truth was dawning on Peter Giles's mind that suitor was the position to which this slow, elderly widower aspired. But Simon Burney, with that odd, all-prevading constraint still prominently apparent, mildly observed, "Waal, ez much ez I hev seen of her goin's-on, it 'pears ter me ez her way air a mighty good way. An' it ain't comical that she likes it."

Urgent justice compelled Peter Giles to make some amends to the absent Clarissa. "That's a fac'," he admitted. "An' Clarsie ain't no hand ter jaw. She don't hev no words. But then," he qualified, truth and consistency alike constraining him, "she air a toler'ble hard-headed gal. That air a true word. Ye mought as well try ter hender the sun from shining ez ter make that thar Clarsie Giles do what she don't want ter do."

To be sure, Peter Giles had a right to his opinion as to the hardness of his own daughter's head. The expression of his views, however, provoked Simon Burney to wrath; there was something astir within him that in a worthier subject might have been called a chivalric thrill, and it forbade him to hold his peace. He retorted: "Of course ye kin say that, ef so minded; but ennybody ez hev got eyes kin see the change ez hev been made in this hyar place since that thar gal hev been growed. I ain't a-purtendin' ter know that thar Clarsie ez well ez you-uns knows her hyar at home, but I hev seen enough, an' a deal more'n enough, of her goin's-on, ter know that what she does ain't done fur *herself*. An' ef she will hev her way, it air fur the good of the whole tribe of ye. It 'pears ter me ez thar ain't many gals like that thar Clarsie. An' she air a merciful critter. She air mighty savin' of the feelin's of everything, from the cow an' the mare down ter the dogs, an' pigs, an' chickens; always a-feedin' of 'em jes' ter the time, an' never draggin', an' clawin', an' beatin' of 'em. Why, that thar Clarsie can't put her foot out'n the door, that every dumb beastis on this hyar place ain't a-runnin' ter git nigh her. I hev seen them pigs mos' climb the fence when she shows her face at the door. 'Pears 'ter me ez that thar Clarsie could tame a b'ar, ef she looked at him a time or two, she's so savin' o' the critter's feelin's! An' that's that old yaller dog o' yourn," pointing to an ancient cur that was blinking in the sun, "he's older 'n Clarsie, an' no 'count in the worl'. I hev hearn ye say forty times that ye would kill him, 'ceptin' that Clarsie purtected him, an' hed sot her heart on his a-livin' along. An' all the home-folks, an' everybody that kems hyar ter sot an' talk awhile, never misses a chance ter kick that thar old dog, or poke him with a stick, or cuss him. But Clarsie!—I hev seen that gal take the bread an' meat off'n her plate, an' give it ter that old dog, ez 'pears ter me ter be the worst dispositionest dog I ever see, an' no thanks lef' in him. He hain't hed the grace ter wag his tail fur twenty year. That thar Clarsie air surely a merciful critter, an' a mighty spry, likely young gal, besides."

Peter Giles sat in stunned astonishment during this speech, which was delivered in a slow, drawling monotone, with frequent meditative pauses, but nevertheless emphatically. He made no reply, and as they were once more silent there rose suddenly the sound of melody upon the air. It came from beyond that tumultuous stream that raced with the wind down the mountain's side; a great log thrown from bank to bank served as bridge. The song grew momentarily more distinct; among the leaves there were fugitive glimpses of blue and white, and at last Clarsie appeared, walking lightly along the log, clad in her checked homespun dress, and with a pail upon her head.

She was a tall, lithe girl, with that delicately transparent complexion often seen among the women of these mountains. Her lustreless black hair lay along her forehead without a ripple or wave; there was something in the expression of her large eyes that suggested those of a deer,—something free, untamable, and yet gentle. "'T ain't no wonder ter me ez Clarsie is all tuk up with the wild things, an' critters giner-ally," her mother was wont to say. "She sorter looks like 'em, I'm a-thinkin'."

As she came in sight there was a renewal of that odd constraint in Simon Burney's face and manner, and he rose abruptly. "Waal," he said, hastily, going to his horse, a raw-boned sorrel, hitched to the fence, "it's about time I war a-startin' home, I reckons."

He nodded to his host, who silently nodded in return, and the old horse jogged off with him down the road, as Clarsie entered the house and placed the pail upon a shelf.

"Who d'ye think hev been hyar a-speakin' of compli*mints* on ye, Clarsie?" exclaimed Mrs. Giles, who had overheard through the open door every word of the loud, drawling voice on the porch.

Clarsie's liquid eyes widened with surprise, and a faint tinge of rose sprang into her pale face, as she looked an expectant inquiry at her mother.

Mrs. Giles was a slovenly, indolent woman, anxious, at the age of forty-five, to assume the prerogatives of advanced years. She had placed all her domestic cares upon the shapely shoulders of her willing daughter, and had betaken herself to the chimney-corner and a pipe.

"Yes, thar hev been somebody hyar a-speakin' of compli*mints* on ye, Clarsie," she reiterated, with chuckling amusement. "He war a mighty peart, likely boy,—that he war!"

Clarsie's color deepened.

"Old Simon Burney!" exclaimed her mother, in great glee at the incongruity of the idea. "*Old Simon Burney!*—jes' a'sittin' out thar, a-wastin' the time, an' a-burnin' of daylight—jes' ez perlite an' smilin' ez a basket of chips—a-speakin' of compli*mints* on ye!"

There was a flash of laughter among the sylvan suggestions of Clarsie's eyes,—a flash as of sudden sunlight upon water. But despite her mirth she seemed to be unaccountably disappointed. The change in her manner was not noticed by her mother, who continued banteringly,—

"Simon Burney air a mighty pore old man. Ye oughter be sorry fur him, Clarsie. Ye must n't think less of folks than ye does of the dumb beastis,—that ain't religion. Ye knows ye air sorry fur mos' everything; why not fur this comical old consarn? Ye oughter marry him ter take keer of him. He said ye war a merciful critter; now is yer chance ter show it! Why, air ye a-goin' ter weavin', Clarsie, jes' when I wants ter talk ter ye 'bout'n old Simon Burney? But law! I knows ye kerry him with ye in yer heart."

The girl summarily closed the conversation by seating herself before a great hand-loom; presently the persistent thump, thump, of the batten and the noisy creak of the treadle filled the room, and through all the long, hot afternoon her deft, practiced hands lightly tossed the shuttle to and fro.

The breeze freshened, after the sun went down, and the hop and gourd vines were all astir as they clung about the little porch where Clarsie was sitting now, idle at last. The rain clouds had disappeared, and there bent over the dark, heavily wooded ridges a pale blue sky, with here and there the crystalline sparkle of a star. A halo was shimmering in the east, where the mists had gathered about the great white moon, hanging high above the mountains. Noiseless wings flitted through the dusk; now and then the bats swept by so close as to wave Clarsie's hair with the wind of their flight. What an airy, glittering, magical thing was that gigantic spider-web suspended between the silver moon and her shining eyes! Ever and anon there came from the woods a strange, weird, long-drawn sigh, unlike the stir of the wind in the trees, unlike the fret of the water on the rocks. Was it the voiceless sorrow of the sad

earth? There were stars in the night besides those known to astronomers: the stellu-
lar fire-flies gemmed the black shadows with a fluctuating brilliancy; they circled in
and out of the porch, and touched the leaves above Clarsie's head with quivering
points of light. A steadier and an intenser gleam was advancing along the road; and
the sound of languid footsteps came with it; the aroma of tobacco graced the atmosphere, and a tall figure walked up to the gate.

"Come in, come in," said Peter Giles, rising, and tendering the guest a chair. "Ye
air Tom Pratt, ez well ez I kin make out by this light. Waal, Tom, we hain't furgot ye
sence ye done been hyar."

As Tom had been there on the previous evening, this might be considered a joke,
or an equivocal compliment. The young fellow was restless and awkward under it,
but Mrs. Giles chuckled with great merriment.

"An' how air ye a-comin' on, Mrs. Giles?" he asked propitiatorily.

"Jes' toler'ble, Tom. Air they all well ter your house?"

"Yes, they're toler'ble well, too." He glanced at Clarsie, intending to address to
her some polite greeting, but the expression of her shy, half-startled eyes, turned
upon the far-away moon, warned him. "Thar never war a gal so skittish," he thought.
"She'd run a mile, skeered ter death, ef I said a word ter her."

And he was prudently silent.

"Waal," said Peter Giles, "what's the news out your way, Tom? Ennything a-goin' on?"

"Thar war a shower yander on the Backbone; it rained toler'ble hard fur a while,
an' sot up the corn wonderful. Did ye git enny hyar?"

"Not a drap."

"'Pears ter me ez I kin see the clouds a-circlin' round Chilhowee, an' a-rainin' on
everybody's corn-field 'ceptin' ourn," said Mrs. Giles. "Some folks is the favored of the
Lord, an' t'others hev ter work fur everything an' git nothin'. Waal, waal; we-uns will
see our reward in the nex' worl'. Thar's a better worl' than this, Tom."

"That's a fac'," said Tom, in orthodox assent.

"An' when we leaves hyar once, we leaves all trouble an' care behind us, Tom; fur
we don't come back no more." Mrs. Giles was drifting into one of her pious moods.

"I dunno," said Tom. "Thar hev been them ez hev."

"Hev what?" demanded Peter Giles, startled.

"Hev come back ter this hyar yearth. That's a harnt that walks Chilhowee every
night o' the worl'. I knows them ez hev seen him."

Even Clarsie's great dilated eyes were fastened on the speaker's face. There was
a dead silence for a moment, more eloquent with these looks of amazement than any
words could have been.

"I reckons ye remember a puny, shriveled little man, named Reuben Crabb, ez
used ter live yander, eight mile along the ridge ter that thar big sulphur spring," Tom
resumed, appealing to Peter Giles. "He war born with only one arm."

"I 'members him," interpolated Mrs. Giles, vivaciously. "He war a mighty porely,
sickly little critter, all the days of his life. 'T war a wonder he war ever raised ter be a
man,—an' a pity, too. An' 't war powerful comical, the way of his takin' off; a stunted,
one-armed little critter a-ondertakin' ter fight folks an' shoot pistols. He hed the use o'
his one arm, sure."

"Waal," said Tom, "his house ain't thar now, 'kase Sam Grim's brothers burned it ter
the ground fur his a-killin' of Sam. That warn't all that war done ter Reuben fur killin' of
Sam. The sheriff run Reuben Crabb down this hyar road 'bout a mile from hyar,—mebbe

less,—an' shot him dead in the road, jes' whar it forks. Waal, Reuben war in company with another evil-doer—*he* war from the Cross-Roads, an' I furgits what he hed done, but he war a-tryin' ter hide in the mountings, too; an' the sheriff lef' Reuben a-lying thar in the road, while he tries ter ketch up with the t'other; but his horse got a stone in his hoof, an' he los' time, an' hed ter gin it up. An' when he got back ter the forks o' the road whar he had lef' Reuben a-lyin' 'dead, that war nothin' thar 'ceptin' a pool o' blood. Waal, he went right on ter Reuben's house, an' them Grim boys hed burnt it ter the ground; but he seen Reuben's brother Joel. An' Joel, he tole the sheriff that late that evenin' he hed tuk Reuben's body out'n the road an' buried it, 'kase it hed been lin' thar in the road ever sence early in the mornin', an' he could n't leave it thar all night, an' he hed n't no shelter fur it, sence the Grim boys hed burnt down the house. So he war obleeged ter bury it. An' Joel showed the sheriff a new-made grave, an' Reuben's coat whar the sheriff's bullet hed gone in at the back an' kem out'n the breast. The sheriff 'lowed ez they'd fine Joel fifty dollars fur a-buryin' of Reuben afore the cor'ner kem; but they never done it, ez I knows on. The sheriff said that when the cor'ner kem the body would be tuk up fur a 'quest. But thar hed been a powerful big frishet, an' the river 'twixt the cor'ner's house an' Chilhowee could n't be forded fur three weeks. The cor'ner never kem, an' so thar it all stayed. That war four year ago."

"Waal," said Peter Giles, dryly, "I ain't seen no harnt yit. I knowed all that afore."

Clarsie's wondering eyes upon the young man's moonlit face had elicited these facts, familiar to the elders, but strange, he knew, to her.

"I war jes' a-goin' on ter tell," said Tom, abashed. "Waal, ever sence his brother Joel died, this spring, Reuben's harnt walks Chilhowee. He war seen week afore las', 'bout daybreak, by Ephraim Blenkins, who hed been a-fishin', an' war a-goin' home. Eph happened ter stop in the laurel ter wind up his line, when all in a minit he seen the harnt go by, his face white, an' his eyeballs like fire, an' puny an' one-armed, jes' like he lived. Eph, he owed me a haffen day's work; I holped him ter plow las' month, an' so he kem ter-day an' hoed along cornsider'ble ter pay fur it. He say he believes the harnt never seen him, 'kase it went right by. He 'lowed ef the harnt hed so much ez cut one o' them blazin' eyes round at him he could n't but hev drapped dead. Waal, this mornin', 'bout sunrise, my brother Bob's little gal, three year old, strayed off from home while her mother war out milkin' the cow. An' we went a-huntin' of her, mightily worked up, 'kase thar hev been a bar prowlin' round our corn-field twict this summer. An' I went ter the right, an' Bob went ter the lef'. An' he say ez he wat a-pushin' 'long through the laurel, he seen the bushes ahead of him a-rustlin'. An' he jes' stood still an' watched 'em. An' fur a while the bushes war still too; an' then they moved jes' a little, fust this way an' then thar, till all of a suddint the leaves opened, like the mouth of hell mought hev done, an' that he seen Reuben Crabb's face. He say he never seen sech a face! Its mouth war open, an' its eyes war a-startin' out'n its head, an' its skin war white till it war blue; an' ef the devil hed hed it a-hangin' over the coals that minit it could n't hev looked no more skeered. But that war all that Bob seen, 'kase he jes' shet his eyes an' screeched an' screeched like he war *de*stracted. An' when he stopped a second ter ketch his breath he hearn su'thin' a-answerin' him back, sorter weak-like, an' thar war little Peggy a-pullin' through the laurel. Ye know she's too little ter talk good, but the folks down ter our house believes she seen the harnt too."

"My Lord!" exclaimed Peter Giles. "I 'low I could n't live a minit ef I war ter see that thar harnt that walks Chilhowee!"

"I know *I* could n't," said his wife.

"Nor me nuther," murmured Clarsie.

"Waal," said Tom, resuming the thread of his narrative, "we hev all been a-talkin' down yander ter our house ter make out the reason why Reuben Crabb's harnt hev sot out ter walk *jes' sence his brother Joel died,*—'kase it war never seen afore then. An' ez nigh ez we kin make it out, the reason is 'kase thar's nobody lef' in this hyar worl' what believes he warn't ter blame in that thar killin o' Sam Grim. Joel always swore ez Reuben never killed him no more'n nuthin'; that Sam's own pistol went off in his own hand, an' shot him through the heart jes' ez he war a-drawin' of it ter shoot Reuben Crabb. An' I hev hearn other men ez war a-standin' by say the same thing,— though them Grims tells another tale; but ez Reuben never owned no pistol in his life, nor kerried one, it don't 'pear ter me ez what them Grims say air reasonable. Joel always swore ez Sam Grim war a mighty mean man,—a great big feller like him a-rockin' of a deformed little critter, an' a-mockin' of him, an' a-hittin' of him. An' the day of the fight, Sam jes' knocked him down fur nothin' at all; an' afore ye could wink Reuben jumped up suddint, an' flew at him like an eagle, an' struck him in the face. An' then Sam drawed his pistol, an' it went off in his own hand, an' shot him through the heart, an' killed him dead. Joel said that ef he could hev kep' that pore little critter Reuben still, an' let the sheriff arrest him peaceable-like, he war sure the jury would hev let him off; 'kase how war Reuben a-goin' ter shoot ennybody when Sam Grim never left a-holt of the only pistol between them, in life or in death? They tells me they hed ter bury Sam Grim with that thar pistol in his hand; his grip war too tight fur death to unloose it. But Joel said that Reuben war sartain they'd hang him. He hed n't never seen no jestice from enny one man, an' he could n't look fur it from twelve men. So he jes' sot out ter run through the woods, like a painter or a wolf, ter be hunted by the sheriff, an' he war run down an' kilt in the road. Joel said *he* kep' up arter the sheriff ez well ez he could on foot,—fur the Crabbs never hed no horse,—ter try ter beg fur Reuben, if he war cotched, an' tell how little an' how weakly he war. I never seen a young man's head turn white like Joel's done; he said he reckoned it war his troubles. But ter the las' he stuck ter his rifle faithful. He war a powerful hunter; he war out rain or shine, hot or cold, in sech weather ez other folks would think that war n't no use in tryin' ter do nothin' in. I'm mightily afeard o' seein' Reuben, now, that's a fac'," concluded Tom, frankly; "'kase I hev hearn tell, an' I believes it, that ef a harnt speaks ter ye, it air sartain ye're bound ter die right then."

"'Pears ter me," said Mrs. Giles, "ez many mountings ez that air round hyar, he mought hev tuk, ter walkin' some of them, stiddier Chilhowee."

There was a sudden noise close at hand: a great inverted splint-basket, from which came a sound of flapping wings, began to move slightly back and forth. Mrs. Giles gasped out an ejaculation of terror, the two men sprang to their feet, and the coy Clarsie laughed aloud in an exuberance of delighted mirth, forgetful of her shyness. "I declar ter goodness, you-uns air all skeered fur true! Did ye think it war the harnt that walks Chihowee?"

"What's under that thar basket?" demanded Peter Giles, rather sheepishly, as he sat down again.

"Nothin' but the duck-legged Dominicky," said Clarsie, "what air bein' broke up from settin'." The moonlight was full upon the dimpling merriment in her face, upon her shining eyes and parted red lips, and her gurgling laughter was pleasant to hear. Tom Pratt edged his chair a trifle nearer, as he, too, sat down.

"Ye ought n't never ter break up a duck-legged hen, nor a Dominicky, nuther," he volunteered, "'kase they air sech a good kind o' hen ter kerry chickens; but a hen that is duck-legged, an' Dominicky, too, oughter be let ter set, whether or no."

Had he been warned in a dream, he could have found no more secure road to Clarsie's favor and interest than a discussion of the poultry. "I'm a-thinkin'," she said, "that it air too hot fur hens ter set now, an' 't will be till the las' of August."

"It don't 'pear ter me ez it air hot much in June up hyar on Chilhowee,—thar's a differ, I know, down in the valley; but till July, on Chilhowee, it don't 'pear ter me ez it air too hot ter set a hen. An' a duck-legged Dominicky air mighty hard ter break up."

"That's a fac'," Clarsie admitted; "but I'll hev ter do it, somehow, 'kase I ain't got no eggs fur her. All my hens air kerryin' of chickens."

"Waal!" exclaimed Tom, seizing his opportunity, "I'll bring ye some ter-morrer night, when I come agin. We-uns hev got eggs ter our house."

"Thanky," said Clarsie, shyly smiling.

This unique method of courtship would have progressed very prosperously but for the interference of the elders, who are an element always more or less adverse to love-making. "Ye oughter turn out yer hen now, Clarsie," said Mrs. Giles, "ez Tom air a-goin' ter bring ye some eggs ter-morrer. I wonder ye don't think it's mean ter keep her up longer 'n ye air obleeged ter. Ye oughter remember ye war called a merciful critter jes' ter-day."

Clarsie rose precipitately, raised the basket, and out flew the "duck-legged Dominicky," with a frantic flutter and hysterical cackling. But Mrs. Giles was not to be diverted from her purpose; her thoughts had recurred to the absurd episode of the afternoon, and with her relish of the incongruity of the joke she opened upon the subject at once.

"Waal, Tom," she said, "we'll be havin' Clarsie married, afore long, I'm a-thinkin'."

The young man sat bewildered. He, too, had entertained views concerning Clarsie's speedy marriage, but with a distinctly personal application; and this frank mention of the matter by Mrs. Giles had a sinister suggestion that perhaps her idea might be antagonistic. "An' who d'ye think hev been hyar ter-day, a-speakin' of compli*mints* on Clarsie?" He could not answer, but he turned his head with a look of inquiry, and Mrs. Giles continued, "He is a mighty peart, likely boy,—*he* is."

There was a growing anger in the dismay on Tom Pratt's face; he leaned forward to hear the name with a fiery eagerness, altogether incongruous with his usual lacklustre manner.

"Old Simon Burney!" cried Mrs. Giles, with a burst of laughter. "*Old Simon Burney!* Jes' a-speakin' of compli*mints* on Clarsie!"

The young fellow drew back with a look of disgust. "Why, he's a old man; he ain't no fit husband fur Clarsie."

"Don't ye be too sure ter count on that. I war jes' a-layin' off ter tell Clarsie that a gal oughter keep mighty clar o' widowers, 'thout she wants ter marry one. Fur I believes," said Mrs. Giles, with a wild flight of imagination, "ez them men hev got some sort'n trade with the Evil One, an' he gives 'em the power ter witch the gals, somehow, so's ter git 'em ter marry; 'kase I don't think that any gal that's got good sense air a-goin' ter be a man's second ch'ice, an' the mother of a whole pack of step-chil'ren, 'thout she air under some sort'n spell. But them men carries the day with the gals, ginerally, an' I'm a-thinkin' they're banded with the devil. Ef I war a gal, an' a smart, peart boy like Simon Burney kem around a-speakin' of compli*mints*, an' sayin' I war a merciful critter, I'd jes' give it up, an' marry him fur second ch'ice. Thar's one blessin'," she continued, contemplating the possibility in a cold-blooded fashion positively revolting to Tom Pratt: "he ain't got no tribe of chil'ren fur Clarsie ter look arter; nary chick nor child hev old Simon Burney got—He hed two, but they died."

The young man took leave presently, in great depression of spirit,—the idea that the widower was banded with the powers of evil was rather overwhelming to a man whose dependence was in merely mortal attractions; and after he had been gone a little while Clarsie ascended the ladder to a nook in the roof, which she called her room.

For the first time in her life her slumber was fitful and restless, long intervals of wakefulness alternating with snatches of fantastic dreams. At last she rose and sat by the rude window, looking out through the chestnut leaves at the great moon, which had begun to dip toward the dark uncertainty of the western ridges, and at the shimmering, translucent, pearly mists that filled the intermediate valleys. All the air was dew and incense; so subtle and penetrating an odor came from the fir-tree beyond the fence that it seemed as if some invigorating infusion were thrilling along her veins; there floated upward, too, the warm fragrance of the clover, and every breath of the gentle wind brought from over the stream a thousand blended, undistinguishable perfumes of the deep forests beyond. The moon's idealizing glamour had left no trace of the uncouthness of the place which the grayish daylight revealed; the little log house, the great overhanging chestnut-oaks, the jagged precipice before the door, the vague outlines of the distant ranges, all suffused with a magic sheen, might have seemed a stupendous altorilievo in silver repoussé. Still, there came here and there the sweep of the bat's dusky wings; even they were a part of the night's witchery. A tiny owl perched for a moment or two amid the dew-tipped chestnut-leaves, and gazed with great round eyes at Clarsie as solemnly as she gazed at him.

"I'm thankful enough that ye had the grace not ter screech while ye war hyar," she said, after his flight. "I ain't ready ter die yit, an' a screech-ow*el* air the sure sign."

She felt now and then a great impatience with her wakeful mood. Once she took herself to task: "Jes' a-sittin' up hyar all night, the same ez ef I war a fox or that thar harnt that walks Chilhowee!"

And then her mind reverted to Tom Pratt, to old Simon Burney, and to her mother's emphatic and oracular declaration that widowers are in league with Satan, and that the girls upon whom they cast the eye of supernatural fascination have no choice in the matter. "I wish I knowed ef that thar sayin' war true," she murmured, her face still turned to the western spurs, and the moon sinking so slowly toward them.

With a sudden resolution she rose to her feet. She knew a way of telling fortunes which was, according to tradition, infallible, and she determined to try it, and ease her mind as to her future. Now was the propitious moment. "I hev always hearn that it won't come true 'thout ye try it jes' before daybreak, an' a kneelin' down at the forks of the road." She hesitated a moment and listened intently. "They'd never git done a-laughin' at me, ef they fund it out," she thought.

There was no sound in the house, and from the dark woods arose only those monotonous voices of the night, so familiar to her ears that she accounted their murmurous iteration as silence too. She leaned far out of the low window, caught the wide-spreading branches of the tree beside it, and swung herself noiselessly to the ground. The road before her was dark with the shadowy foliage and dank with the dew; but now and then, as long intervals, there lay athwart it a bright bar of light, where the moonshine fell through a gap in the trees. Once, as she went rapidly along her way, she saw speeding across the white radiance, lying just before her feet, the ill-omened shadow of a rabbit. She paused, with a superstitious sinking of the heart, and she heard the animal's quick, leaping rush through the bushes near at hand; but she mustered her courage, and kept steadily on. "'T ain't no use a-goin' back ter git shet o' bad luck," she argued. "Ef old Simon Burney air my fortune, he'll come whether or no,—ef all they say air true."

The serpentine road curved to the mountain's brink before it forked, and there was again that familiar picture of precipice, and far-away ridges, and shining mist, and sinking moon, which was visibly turning from silver to gold. The changing lustre gilded the feathery ferns that grew in the marshy dip. Just at the angle of the divergent paths there rose into the air a great mass of indistinct white blossoms, which she knew were the exquisite mountain azaleas, and all the dark forest was starred with the blooms of the laurel.

She fixed her eyes upon the mystic sphere dropping down the sky, knelt among the azaleas at the forks of the road, and repeated the time-honored invocation:—

"Ef I'm a-goin' ter marry a young man, whistle, Bird, whistle. Ef I'm a-goin' ter marry an old man, low, Cow, low. Ef I ain't a-goin' ter marry nobody, knock, Death, knock."

There was a prolonged silence in the matutinal freshness and perfume of the woods. She raised her head, and listened attentively. No chirp of half-awakened bird, no tapping of woodpecker, or the mysterious death-watch; but from far along the dewy aisles of the forest, the ungrateful Spot, that Clarsie had fed more faithfully than herself, lifted up her voice, and set the echoes vibrating. Clarsie, however, had hardly time for a pang of disappointment. While she still knelt among the azaleas her large, deer-like eyes were suddenly dilated with terror. From around the curve of the road came the quick beat of hastening footsteps, the sobbing sound of panting breath, and between her and the sinking moon there passed an attenuated, one-armed figure, with a pallid, sharpened face, outlined for a moment on its brilliant disk, and dreadful starting eyes, and quivering open mouth. It disappeared in an instant among the shadows of the laurel, and Clarsie, with a horrible fear clutching at her heart, sprang to her feet.

Her flight was arrested by other sounds. Before her reeling senses could distinguish them, a party of horsemen plunged down the road. They reined in suddenly as their eyes fell upon her, and their leader, an eager, authoritative man, was asking her a question. Why could she not understand him? With her nerveless hands feebly catching at the shrubs for support, she listened vaguely to his impatient, meaningless words, and saw with helpless deprecation the rising anger in his face. But there was no time to be lost. With a curse upon the stupidity of the mountaineer, who couldn't speak when she was spoken to, the party sped on in a sweeping gallop, and the rocks and the steeps were hilarious with the sound.

When the last faint echo was hushed, Clarsie tremblingly made her way out into the road; not reassured, however, for she had a frightful conviction that there was now and then a strange stir in the laurel, and that she was stealthily watched. Her eyes were fixed upon the dense growth with a morbid fascination, as she moved away; but she was once more rooted to the spot when the leaves parted and in the golden moonlight the ghost stood before her. She could not nerve herself to run past him, and he was directly in her way homeward. His face was white, and lined, and thin; that pitiful quiver was never still in the parted lips, he looked at her with faltering, beseeching eyes. Clarsie's merciful heart was stirred. "What ails yer, ter come back hyar, an' foller me?" she cried out, abruptly. And then a great horror fell upon her. Was not one to whom a ghost should speak doomed to death, sudden and immediate?

The ghost replied in a broken, shivering voice, like a wail of pain. "I war a-starvin',—I war a-starvin'," he said, with despairing iteration.

It was all over, Clarsie thought. The ghost had spoken, and she was a doomed creature. She wondered that she did not fall dead in the road. But while those beseeching eyes were fastened in piteous appeal on hers, she could not leave him. "I never hearn that 'bout ye," she said, reflectively. "I knows ye hed awful troubles while ye war alive, but I never knowed ez ye war starved."

Surely that was a gleam of sharp surprise in the ghost's prominent eyes, succeeded by a sly intelligence.

"Day is nigh ter breakin','" Clarsie admonished him, as the lower rim of the moon touched the silver mists of the west. "What air ye a-wantin' of me?"

There was a short silence. Mind travels far in such intervals. Clarsie's thoughts had overtaken the scenes when she should have died that sudden terrible death: when there would be no one left to feed the chickens; when no one would care if the pigs cried with the pangs of hunger, unless, indeed, it were time for them to be fattened before killing. The mare,—how often would she be taken from the plow, and shut up for the night in her shanty without a drop of water, after her hard day's work! Who would churn, or spin, or weave? Clarsie could not understand how the machinery of the universe could go on without her. And Towse, poor Towse! He was a useless cumberer of the ground, and it was hardly to be supposed that after his protector was gone he would be spared a blow or a bullet, to hasten his lagging death. But Clarsie still stood in the road, and watched the face of the ghost, as he, with his eager, starting eyes, scanned her open, ingenuous countenance.

"Ye do ez ye air bid, or it'll be the worse for ye," said the "harnt," in the same quivering, shrill tone. "Thar's hunger in the nex' worl' ez well ez in this, an' ye bring me some vittles hyar this time termorrer, an' don't ye tell nobody ye hev seen me, nuther, or it'll be the worse for ye."

There was a threat in his eyes as he disappeared in the laurel, and left the girl standing in the last rays of moonlight.

A curious doubt was stirring in Clarsie's mind when she reached home, in the early dawn, and heard her father talking about the sheriff and his posse, who had stopped at the house in the night, and roused its inmates, to know if they had seen a man pass that way.

"Clarsie never hearn none o' the noise, I'll be bound, 'kase she always sleeps like a log," said Mrs. Giles, as her daughter came in with the pail, after milking the cow. "Tell her 'bout'n it."

"They kem a-bustin' along hyar a while afore day-break, a-runnin' arter the man," drawled Mr. Giles, dramatically. "An' they knocked me up, ter know ef ennybody hed passed. An' one o' them men—I never seen none of 'em afore; they's all valley folks, I'm a-thinkin'—an' one of 'em bruk his saddle-girt' a good piece down the road, an' he kem back ter borrer mine; an' ez we war a-fixin' of it, he tole me what they war all arter. He said that word war tuck ter the sheriff down yander in the valley—'pears ter me them town-folks don't think nobody in the mountings hev got good sense—word war tuk ter the sheriff 'bout this one-armed harnt that walks Chilhowee; an' he sot it down that Reuben Crabb war n't dead at all, an' Joel jes' purtended ter hev buried him, an' it air Reuben hisself that walks Chilhowee. An' thar air two hunderd dollars blood-money reward fur ennybody ez kin ketch him. These hyar valley folks air powerful cur'ous critters,—two hunderd dollars blood-money reward fur that thar harnt that walks Chilhowee! I jes' sot myself ter laughin' when that thar cuss tole it so solemn. I jes' 'lowed ter him ez he could n't shoot a harnt nor hang a harnt, an'

Reuben Crabb hed about got done with his persecutions in this worl'. An' he said that by the time they hed scoured this mounting, like they hed laid off ter do, they would find that that thar puny little harnt war nothin' but a mortal man, an' could be kep' in a jail ez handy ez enny other flesh an' blood. He said the sheriff 'lowed ez the reason Reuben hed jes' taken ter walk Chilhowee since Joel died is 'kase thar air nobody ter feed him, like Joel done, mebbe, in the nights; an' Reuben always war a pore, one-armed, weakly critter, what can't even kerry a gun, an' he air driv by hunger out'n the hole whar he stays, ter prowl round the cornfields an' hencoops ter steal suthin',—an' that's how he kem ter be seen frequent. The sheriff 'lowed that Reuben can't find enough roots an' yerbs ter keep him up; but law!—a harnt eatin'! It jes' sot me off ter laughin'. Reuben Crabb hev been too busy in torment fur the las' four year ter be a-studyin' 'bout eatin'; an' it air his harnt that walks Chilhowee."

The next morning, before the moon sank, Clarsie, with a tin pail in her hand, went to meet the ghost at the appointed place. She understood now why the terrible doom that falls upon those to whom a spirit may chance to speak had not descended upon her, and that fear was gone; but the secrecy of her errand weighed heavily. She had been scrupulously careful to put into the pail only such things as had fallen to her share at the table, and which she had saved from the meals of yesterday. "A gal that goes a-robbin' fur a hongry harnt," was her moral reflection, "oughter be throwed bodaciously off'n the bluff."

She found no one at the forks of the road. In the marshy dip were only the myriads of mountains azaleas, only the masses of feathery ferns, only the constellated glories of the laurel blooms. A sea of shining white mist was in the valley, with glinting golden rays striking athwart it from the great cresset of the sinking moon; here and there the long, dark, horizontal line of a distant mountain's summit rose above the vaporous shimmer, like a dreary, sombre island in the midst of enchanted waters. Her large, dreamy eyes, so wild and yet so gentle, gazed out through the laurel leaves upon the floating gilded flakes of light, as in the deep coverts of the mountain, where the fulvous-tinted deer were lying, other eyes, as wild and as gentle, dreamily watched the vanishing moon. Overhead, the filmy, lace-like clouds, fretting the blue heavens, were tinged with a faint rose. Through the trees she caught a glimpse of the red sky of dawn, and the glister of a great lucent, tremulous star. From the ground, misty blue exhalations were rising, alternating with the long lines of golden light yet drifting through the woods. It was all very still, very peaceful, almost holy. One could hardly believe that these consecrated solitudes had once reverberated with the echoes of man's death-dealing ingenuity, and that Reuben Crabb had fallen, shot through and through, amid that wealth of flowers at the forks of the road. She heard suddenly the faraway baying of a hound. Her great eyes dilated, and she lifted her head to listen. Only the solemn silence of the woods, the slow sinking of the noiseless moon, the voiceless splendor of that eloquent day-star.

Morning was close at hand, and she was beginning to wonder that the ghost did not appear, when the leaves fell into abrupt commotion, and he was standing in the road, beside her. He did not speak, but watched her with an eager, questioning intentness, as she placed the contents of the pail upon the moss at the roadside. "I'm a-comin' agin termorrer," she said, gently. He made no reply, quickly gathered the food from the ground, and disappeared in the deep shades of the woods.

She had not expected thanks, for she was accustomed only to the gratitude of dumb beasts; but she was vaguely conscious of something wanting, as she stood motionless for a moment, and watched the burnished rim of the moon slip down behind the western mountains. Then she slowly walked along her misty way in the dim light of the coming dawn. There was a footstep in the road behind her; she thought it was the ghost once more. She turned, and met Simon Burney, face to face. His rod was on his shoulder, and a string of fish was in his hand.

"Ye air a-doin' wrongful, Clarsie," he said, sternly. "It air agin the law fur folks ter feed an' shelter them ez is a-runnin' from jestice. An' ye'll git yerself inter trouble. Other folks will find ye out, besides me, an' then the sheriff 'll be up hyar arter ye."

The tears rose to Clarsie's eyes. This prospect was infinitely more terrifying than the awful doom which follows the horror of a ghost's speech.

"I can't help it," she said, however, doggedly swinging the pail back and forth. "I can't gin my consent ter starvin' of folks, even ef they air a-hidin' an' a-runnin from jestice."

"They mought put ye in jail, too, I dunno," suggested Simon Burney.

"I can't help that, nuther," said Clarsie, the sobs rising, and the tears falling fast. "Ef they comes an' gits me, an' puts me in the pen'tiary away down yander, some-whars in the valley, like they done Jane Simpkins, fur a-cuttin' of her step-mother's throat with a butcher-knife, while she war asleep,—though some said Jane war crazy,—I can't gin my consent ter starvin' of folks."

A recollection came over Simon Burney of the simile of "hendering the sun from shining."

"She hev done sot it down in her mind," he thought, as he walked on beside her and looked at her resolute face. Still he did not relinquish his effort.

"Doin' wrong, Clarsie, ter aid folks what air a-doin' wrong, an' mebbe *hev* done wrong, air powerful hurtful ter everybody, an' henders the law an' jestice."

"I can't help it," said Clarsie.

"It 'pears toler'ble comical ter me," said Simon Burney, with a sudden perception of a curious fact which has proved a marvel to wiser men, "that no matter how good a woman is, she ain't got no respect fur the laws of the country, an' don't sot no store by jestice." After a momentary silence he appealed to her on another basis. "Some-body will ketch him arter a while, ez sure ez ye air born. The sheriff's a-sarchin' now, an' by the time that word gits around, all the mounting boys'll turn out, 'kase thar air two hunderd dollars blood-money fur him. An' then he'll think, when they ketches him,—an' everybody'll say so, too,—ez ye war constant in feedin' him jes' ter 'tice him ter comin' ter one place, so ez ye could tell somebody whar ter to ter ketch him, an' make them gin ye haffen the blood-money, mebbe. That's what the mounting will say, mos' likely."

"I can't help it," said Clarsie, once more.

He left her walking on toward the rising sun, and retraced his way to the forks of the road. The jubilant morning was filled with the song of birds; the sunlight flashed on the dew; all the delicate enameled bells of the pink and white azaleas were swing-ing tremulously in the wind; the aroma of ferns and mint rose on the delicious fresh air. Presently he checked his pace, creeping stealthily on the moss and grass beside the road rather than in the beaten path. He pulled aside the leaves of the laurel with no more stir than the wind might have made, and stole cautiously through its dense growth, till he came suddenly upon the puny little ghost, lying in the sun at the foot of a tree. The frightened creature sprang to his feet with a wild cry of terror, but before he could move a step he was caught and held fast in the strong grip of the stalwart mountaineer beside him. "I hev kem hyar ter tell ye a word, Reuben Crabb," said Simon Burney. "I hev kem hyar ter tell ye that the whole mounting air a-goin' ter turn out ter sarch fur ye; the sheriff air a-ridin' now, an' ef ye don't come along with me they'll hev ye afore night, 'kase thar air two hunderd dollars reward fur ye."

What a piteous wail went up to the smiling blue sky, seen through the dappling leaves above them! What a horror, and despair, and prescient agony were in the hunted creature's face! The ghost struggled no longer; he slipped from his feet down upon the roots of the tree, and turned that woful face, with its starting eyes and drawn muscles and quivering parted lips, up toward the unseeing sky.

"God A'mighty, man!" exclaimed Simon Burney, moved to pity. "Why n't ye quit this hyar way of livin' in the woods like ye war a wolf? Why n't ye come back an' stand yer trial? From all I've hearn tell, it 'pears ter me ez the jury air obleeged ter let ye off, an' I'll take keer of ye agin them Grims."

"I hain't got no place ter live in," cried out the ghost, with a keen despair.

Simon Burney hesitated. Reuben Crabb was possibly a murderer,—at the best could but be a burden. The burden, however, had fallen in his way, and he lifted it.

"I tell ye now, Reuben Crabb," he said, "I ain't a-goin' ter holp no man ter break the law an' hender jestice; but ef ye will go an' stand yer trial, I'll take keer of ye agin them Grims ez long ez I kin fire a rifle. An' arter the jury hev done let ye off, ye air welcome ter live along o' me at my house till ye die. Ye air no-'count ter work, I know, but I ain't a-goin' ter grudge ye fur a livin' at my house."

And so it came to pass that the reward set upon the head of the harnt that walked Chilhowee was never claimed.

With his powerful ally, the forlorn little spectre went to stand his trial, and the jury acquitted him without leaving the box. Then he came back to the mountains to live with Simon Burney. The cruel gibes of his burly mockers that had beset his feeble life from his childhood up, the deprivation and loneliness and despair and fear that had filled those days when he walked Chilhowee, had not improved the harnt's temper. He was a helpless creature, not able to carry a gun or hold a plow, and the years that he spent smoking his cob-pipe in Simon Burney's door were idle years and unhappy. But Mrs. Giles said she thought he was "a mighty lucky little critter: fust, he hed Joel ter take keer of him an' feed him, when he tuk ter the woods ter purtend he war a harnt; an' they do say now that Clarsie Pratt, afore she war married, used ter kerry him vittles, too; an' then old Simon Burney tuk him up an' fed him ez plenty ez ef he war a good workin' hand, an' gin him clothes an' house-room, an' put up with his jawin' jes' like he never hearn a word of it. But law! some folks dunno when they air well off."

There was only a sluggish current of peasant blood in Simon Burney's veins, but a prince could not have dispensed hospitality with a more royal hand. Ungrudgingly he gave of his best; valiantly he defended his thankless guest at the risk of his life; with a moral gallantry he struggled with his sloth, and worked early and late, that there might be enough to divide. There was no possibility of a recompense for him, not even in the encomiums of discriminating friends, nor the satisfaction of tutored feelings and a practiced spiritual discernment, for he was an uncouth creature, and densely ignorant.

The grace of culture is, in its way, a fine thing, but the best that art can do—the polish of a gentleman—is hardly equal to the best that Nature can do in her higher moods.

Anna Julia Cooper

(1858–1964)

Though she was born into slavery in Raleigh, North Carolina, and though her father was probably her mother's owner, Anna Julia Cooper wrote that she remembered little of her early years as a slave. She was educated at St. Augustine's Normal School and Collegiate Institute, a teachers' training school for newly freed blacks sponsored by the Episcopal Church. In her journals, she describes the difficulties she experienced after expressing interest in mathematics and science, which at the time were considered subjects appropriate mainly for males. She received her teaching certification from St. Augustine's School and in 1877 married George C. Cooper, a candidate for the ministry whom she met there. When her husband died only two years later, she entered Oberlin College, where she received her undergraduate degree in 1884. In 1887 she was hired as a teacher of Latin and mathematics at the M Street High School in Washington, D.C.

Early in her tenure at the M Street School, Cooper became embroiled in a controversy over whether African American students should pursue degrees in liberal arts, a goal that she advocated, or should instead restrict themselves to vocational training, the view promoted by Tuskegee Institute's Booker T. Washington. In response to this ongoing debate, Cooper published *A Voice from the South: By a Black Woman of the South* in 1892. Not only does this work emphasize the "elasticity and hopefulness" of African American youth and their unlimited potential, but it also gives a voice to the "sadly expectant Black Woman," who had been all but ignored by the fledgling feminist movement in the United States. Cooper became principal of M Street High School in 1901 and instituted a rigorous curriculum that for some of her students, won admission in Ivy League universities; however, she was opposed by the school board and so was fired in 1906. She returned to the M Street School in 1910 as a teacher, staying there until she retired in 1930. In 1925, when she was sixty-five years old, she received her doctorate from the Sorbonne, which was conferred in a special ceremony at Howard University.

from *A Voice from the South:*

By a Black Woman of the South

There is to my mind no grander and surer prophecy of the new era and of woman's place in it, than the work already begun in the waning years of the nineteenth century by the W. C. T. U. in America, an organization which has even now reached not only national but international importance, and seems destined to permeate and purify the whole civilized world. It is the living embodiment of woman's activities and woman's ideas, and its extent and strength rightly prefigure her increasing power as a moral factor.

The colored woman of to-day occupies, one may say, a unique position in this country. In a period of itself transitional and unsettled, her status seems one of the least ascertainable and definitive of all the forces which make for our civilization. She is confronted by both a woman question and a race problem, and is as yet an unknown or an unacknowledged factor in both. While the women of the white race can with calm assurance enter upon the work they feel by nature appointed to do, while their men give loyal support and appreciative countenance to their efforts, recognizing in most avenues of usefulness the propriety and the need of woman's distinctive co-operation, the colored woman too often finds herself hampered and shamed by a less liberal sentiment and a more conservative attitude on the part of those for whose opinion she cares most. That this is not universally true I am glad to admit. There are to be found both intensely conservative white men and exceedingly liberal colored men. But as far as my experience goes the average man of our race is less frequently ready to admit the actual need among the sturdier forces of the world for woman's help or influence. That great social and economic questions await her interference, that she could throw any light on problems of national import, that her intermeddling could improve the management of school systems, or elevate the tone of public institutions, or humanize and sanctify the far reaching influence of prisons and reformatories and improve the treatment of lunatics and imbeciles,—that she has a word worth hearing on mooted questions in political economy, that she could contribute a suggestion on the relations of labor and capital, or offer a thought on honest money and honorable trade, I fear the majority of "Americans of the colored variety" are not yet prepared to concede. It may be that they do not yet see these questions in their right perspective, being absorbed in the immediate needs of their own political complications. A good deal depends on where we put the emphasis in this world; and our men are not perhaps to blame if they see everything colored by the light of those agitations in the midst of which they live and move and have their being. The part they have had to play in American history during the last twenty-five or thirty years has tended rather to exaggerate the importance of mere political advantage, as well as to set a fictitious valuation on those able to secure such advantage. It is the astute politician, the manager who can gain preferment for himself and his favorites, the demagogue known to stand in with the powers at the White House and consulted on the bestowal of government plums, whom we set in high places and denominate great. It is they who receive the hosannas of the multitude and are regarded as leaders of the people. The thinker and the doer, the man who solves the problem by enriching his country with an invention worth thousands or by a thought inestimable and precious is given neither bread nor a stone. He is too often left to die in obscurity and neglect even if spared in his life the bitterness of fanatical jealousies and detraction.

And yet politics, and surely American politics, is hardly a school for great minds. Sharpening rather than deepening, it develops the faculty of taking advantage of present emergencies rather than the insight to distinguish between the true and the false, the lasting and the ephemeral advantage. Highly cultivated selfishness rather than consecrated benevolence is its passport to success. Its votaries are never seers. At best they are but manipulators—often only jugglers. It is conducive neither to profound statesmanship nor to the higher type of manhood. Altruism is its *mauvais succes* and naturally enough it is indifferent to any factor which cannot be worked into its own immediate aims and purposes. As woman's influence as a political element is as yet nil in most of the commonwealths of our republic, it is not surprising that with those who place the emphasis on mere political capital she may yet seem almost a nonentity so far as it concerns the solution of great national or even racial perplexities.

There are those, however, who value the calm elevation of the thoughtful spectator who stands aloof from the heated scramble; and, above the turmoil and din of corruption and selfishness, can listen to the teachings of eternal truth and righteousness.

There are even those who feel that the black man's unjust and unlawful exclusion temporarily from participation in the elective franchise in certain states is after all but a lesson "in the desert" fitted to develop in him insight and discrimination against the day of his own appointed time. One needs occasionally to stand aside from the hum and rush of human interests and passions to hear the voices of God. And it not unfrequently happens that the All-loving gives a great push to certain souls to thrust them out, as it were, from the distracting current for awhile to promote their discipline and growth, or to enrich them by communion and reflection. And similarly it may be woman's privilege from her peculiar coigne of vantage as a quiet observer, to whisper just the needed suggestion or the almost forgotten truth. The colored woman, then, should not be ignored because her bark is resting in the silent waters of the sheltered cove. She is watching the movements of the contestants none the less and is all the better qualified, perhaps, to weigh and judge and advise because not herself in the excitement of the race. Her voice, too, has always been heard in clear, unfaltering tones, ringing the changes on those deeper interests which make for permanent good. She is always sound and orthodox on questions affecting the well-being of her race. You do not find the colored woman selling her birthright for a mess of pottage. Nay, even after reason has retired from the contest, she has been known to cling blindly with the instinct of a turtle dove to those principles and policies which to her mind promise hope and safety for children yet unborn. It is notorious that ignorant black women in the South have actually left their husbands' homes and repudiated their support for what was understood by the wife to be race disloyalty, or "voting away," as she expresses it, the privileges of herself and little ones.

It is largely our women in the South to-day who keep the black men solid in the Republican party. The latter as they increase in intelligence and power of discrimination would be more apt to divide on local issues at any rate. They begin to see that the Grand Old Party regards the Negro's cause as an outgrown issue, and on Southern soil at least finds a too intimate acquaintanceship with him a somewhat unsavory recommendation. Then, too, their political wits have been sharpened to appreciate the fact that it is good policy to cultivate one's neighbors and not depend too much on a distant friend to fight one's home battles. But the black woman can never forget— however lukewarm the party may to-day appear—that it was a Republican president who struck the manacles from her own wrists and gave the possibilities of manhood to her helpless little ones; and to her mind a Democratic Negro is a traitor and a time-server. Talk as much as you like of venality and manipulation in the South, there are not many men, I can tell you, who would dare face a wife quivering in every fiber with the consciousness that her husband is a coward who could be paid to desert her deepest and dearest interests.

Not unfelt, then, if unproclaimed has been the work and influence of the colored women of America. Our list of chieftains in the service, though not long, is not inferior in strength and excellence, I dare believe, to any similar list which this country can produce.

Among the pioneers, Frances Watkins Harper could sing with prophetic exaltation in the darkest days, when as yet there was not a rift in the clouds overhanging her people:

> "Yes, Ethiopia shall stretch
> Her bleeding hands abroad;
> Her cry of agony shall reach the burning throne of God.

Redeemed from dust and freed from chains
Her sons shall lift their eyes,
From cloud-capt hills and verdant plains
Shall shouts of triumph rise."

Among preachers of righteousness, an unanswerable silencer of cavilers and objectors, was Sojourner Truth, that unique and rugged genius who seemed carved out without hand or chisel from the solid mountain mass; and in pleasing contrast, Amanda Smith, sweetest of natural singers and pleaders in dulcet tones for the things of God and of His Christ.

Sarah Woodson Early and Martha Briggs, planting and watering in the school room, and giving off from their matchless and irresistible personality an impetus and inspiration which can never die so long as there lives and breathes a remote descendant of their disciples and friends.

Charlotte Fortin Grimke, the gentle spirit whose verses and life link her so beautifully with America's great Quaker poet and loving reformer.

Hallie Quinn Brown, charming reader, earnest, effective lecturer and devoted worker of unflagging zeal and unquestioned power.

Fannie Jackson Coppin, the teacher and organizer, pre-eminent among women of whatever country or race in constructive and executive force.

These women represent all shades of belief and as many departments of activity; but they have one thing in common—their sympathy with the oppressed race in America and the consecration of their several talents in whatever line to the work of its deliverance and development.

Fifty years ago woman's activity according to orthodox definitions was on a pretty clearly cut "sphere," including primarily the kitchen and the nursery, and rescued from the barrenness of prison bars by the womanly mania for adorning every discoverable bit of china or canvass with forlorn looking cranes balanced idiotically on one foot. The woman of to-day finds herself in the presence of responsibilities which ramify through the profoundest and most varied interests of her country and race. Not one of the issues of this plodding, toiling, sinning, repenting, falling, aspiring humanity can afford to shut her out, or can deny the reality of her influence. No plan for renovating society, no scheme for purifying politics, no reform in church or in state, no moral, social, or economic question, no movement upward or downward in the human plane is lost on her. A man once said when told his house was afire: "Go tell my wife; I never meddle with household affairs." But no woman can possibly put herself or her sex outside any of the interests that affect humanity. All departments in the new era are to be hers, in the sense that her interests are in all and through all; and it is incumbent on her to keep intelligently and sympathetically *en rapport* with all the great movements of her time, that she may know on which side to throw the weight of her influence. She stands now at the gateway of this new era of American civilization. In her hands must be moulded the strength, the wit, the statesmanship, the morality, all the psychic force, the social and economic intercourse of that era. To be alive at such an epoch is a privilege, to be a woman then is sublime.

In this last decade of our century, changes of such moment are in progress, such new and alluring vistas are opening out before us, such original and radical suggestions for the adjustment of labor and capital, of government and the governed, of the family, the church and the state, that to be a possible factor though an infinitesimal in such a movement is pregnant with hope and weighty with responsibility. To be a woman in such an age carries with it a privilege and an opportunity never implied before. But to be a woman of the Negro race in America, and to be able to grasp the deep significance of the possibilities of the crisis, is to have a heritage, it seems to me, unique in the ages. In the first place, the race is young and full of the elasticity and hopefulness of youth. All its achievements are before it. It does not look on the masterly triumphs of nineteenth century civilization with that *blasé* world-weary look which characterizes the old washed out and worn out races which have already, so to speak, seen their best days.

Said a European writer recently: "Except the Sclavonic, the Negro is the only original and distinctive genius which has yet to come to growth—and the feeling is to cherish and develop it."

Everything to this race is new and strange and inspiring. There is a quickening of its pulses and a glowing of its self-consciousness. Aha, I can rival that! I can aspire to that! I can honor my name and vindicate my race! Something like this, it strikes me, is the enthusiasm which stirs the genius of young Africa in America; and the memory of past oppression and the fact of present attempted repression only serve to gather momentum for its irrepressible powers. Then again, a race in such a stage of growth is peculiarly sensitive to impressions. Not the photographer's sensitized plate is more delicately impressionable to outer influences than is this high strung people here on the threshold of a career.

What a responsibility then to have the sole management of the primal lights and shadows! Such is the colored woman's office. She must stamp weal or woe on the coming history of this people. May she see her opportunity and vindicate her high prerogative.

William P. Trent

(1862–1939)

William Peterfield Trent's legacy, both as a literary critic and as a historian, can appear paradoxical. In his best-known work, a biography of William Gilmore Simms, he argues that the literature of the South has not received the attention it deserves, while simultaneously contending that Simms himself was a mediocre talent. Trent labored tirelessly to promote the study of Southern history, but his assertion that the cause of the Civil War was slavery, not states' rights, brought him vociferous condemnations from his fellow Southerners. And though he helped found the *Sewanee Review*, his fame as a literary critic was won after he had made a midcareer move from the University of the South to Columbia University in 1900.

Born to a formerly aristocratic family ruined by the Civil War, Trent was educated at Norwood's University School in Richmond and entered the University of Virginia in 1880. After he graduated in 1883, for several years he pursued a law degree before shifting his focus and entering Johns Hopkins University to study history and political science. Trent took his degree from Johns Hopkins in 1888 and then accepted a position at the University of the South. There he and three of his colleagues launched the *Sewanee Review* in 1892, the same year that his biography of William Gilmore Simms appeared. Though his intent was to win more attention for a Southern literature that he felt had been neglected, his description of the cultural condition of the antebellum South won him few friends, and in Charleston he was vilified. A New South liberal, Trent was seen as a progressive by his friends in the North and as a traitor by Southerners; few were willing to accept Trent's own description of himself as "an American who is at the same time a Southerner, proud enough of his section to admit its faults, and yet to proclaim its essential greatness."

from *William Gilmore Simms*

Chapter VII. The War.

"I am here, like a bear with a sore head, and chained to the stake," wrote Simms to Miles on the last day of 1860. "I chafe, and roar, and rage, but can do nothing. Do not be rash, but do not let the old city forget her prestige. Charleston is worth all New England."

But if he could not be up in arms, he could do more than roar and curse New England. He could write letters by the dozen to Jamison and Miles, pointing out mistakes that had been made by those in authority, making military suggestions of all sorts, and showing himself dowered with a large supply of common sense and of genius for affairs, as well as with the poet's "hate of hate, the scorn of scorn, the love of love." Only one of these letters can be given here, but all should some day be published.

Sunday[1] Night, 12 P.M.

I am sleepless, my dear Miles, and must write. If you should be sleepless also, it is not improbable but that my letters will help you to a soporific condition. It seems to me that you will have a little respite. The opening fire upon the Star of the West changes materially the aspect of things to the Federal government, and they will hardly think to send supplies to Sumter except under cover of armed vessels, which is the inauguration of open war upon the State, which the President and cabinet will hardly attempt unless under authority of Congress. Congress alone, I believe, has the power to declare war. There is no telling, however, what may be done when the power is under the hands of a weak administration, counseled and governed, in fact, by a person whose whole training has endowed [him] with military ideas as paramount to all.[2] We must, of course, prepare for two dangers, treachery and assault. But it strikes me that the *unexpected* fire of Fort Morris will compel a pause in the Federal councils, for the better maturing of plans, and some respite for preparation will be allowed you. Not an hour should be lost in preparation. To have numerous guns, to bear equally upon an assailing squadron and Fort Sumter, seems to be the necessity. Looking at the map, I note that Mount Pleasant is distant from Fort Sumter some two miles, while I estimate Moultrie to be some one and a quarter. A battery at Mount Pleasant, cutting the western angle of Sullivan's Island, seems to be in direct range with Sumter, and if within reach of heavy cannon, then a battery of earth at this point, with half a dozen thirty-two pounders, might operate successfully against it, at all events compel a very useful diversion of its fires. So I find that

---

[1]Probably the Sunday that followed the firing on the Star of the West, *i.e.* January 13, 1861.

[2]It seems plain that Simms here alludes to General Winfield Scott. Cass had a military training, but he had resigned from the Cabinet when the above was written.

on the sandhills below Fort Johnson, and on the sandhills at the extreme western verge of Fort Morris, batteries of say three heavy cannon each might face Fort Sumter, framed of logs faced with iron and filled in with sand, which could contribute largely to its distraction, if not its injury. On these sandhills, also, you possess an advantage in their elevation, which will tend to reduce the superiority of Sumter in height. Two or three batteries along these hills and at these points, mere bastions, having two or three guns each of heavy calibre, could be thrown up very suddenly, assuming, as I do, that you can command, from the popular patriotism, any amount of slave labor. I would have them so planted as not to face the portholes of Sumter, yet be able to take them at an angle. Shot entering a porthole obliquely would be more mischievous, perhaps, than if direct, since the zigzag course they would pursue would be likely to kill every man on one side or other of the guns, besides abrading the embrasure very seriously. In reference to Wappoo Cut, let me mention that, as the obvious entrance to that cut is by the Stono, there is an old fort, once thought a pretty strong one, at the mouth of the Stono, on Cole's Island. This might be manned by volunteers from the precinct, officered by some good military man. It covers Bird Key [?] and is very well placed, though still, I think, it would be good policy to stop up Wappoo Cut, or keep an armed schooner in Ashley River, at the mouth of it. I am writing, you perceive, without the slightest knowledge of what *has* been done; and it is quite probable that all my suggestions have been anticipated. If, however, you fancy there is anything in them, communicate with Jamison and any military friends on whose judgment you rely. Ranging timbers properly mortised might be prepared by the mechanics of the city, and the iron bars laid on, if desired, before shipment to the desired points. It is my impression that old Fort Johnson ranges Moultrie in the same line with Sumter. If so, it is a question how far it would be proper to use the former place with heavy cannon with might range across the strait. You should employ all the heavy cannon you can. Jamison told me that you had an abundance. Unless Fort Morris has numerous pieces, she could hardly play any efficient game with many assailing vessels. I do not know where Fort Morris is placed, but suppose it to be fronting equally the Ship and the Twelve-feet channel. In that event, unless the sandhills interpose, it is under the range of Fort Sumter, provided the distance be within three miles, as I suppose it to be. I should have said four, but for the threat of Anderson to fire on Fort Morris. A battery between Fort Morris and the Lighthouse, on the edge of the sandhills, might rake the Ship Channel with a *plunging* fire, yet I should think be out of range and even sight of Fort Sumter. I think I said, in a previous letter, that in sighting the guns for long distances telescopes should be used; of course, I meant only the ordinary ship spyglasses, of which a sufficient number for each battery could be obtained in the city. With another battery to second Fort Morris, each of twelve guns at least, and heavy ones, you could give a telling account of all entering vessels. They might all be sunk with good gunnery. But two shot only taking effect out of eighteen fired, would seem to show that the gunnery was not sufficiently practiced. I write only from report. To-night, I learn that (*on dit*) there has been a mutiny in Fort Sumter, and that Anderson has had to shoot one of his men, and put ten more in irons; and that *this* was the reason why he did *not* fire on Forts Morris and Moultrie. By the "Mercury" it is said that some negotiations are on foot which will prevent bloodshed. The inference is that Fort Sumter will be given up. This is hardly probable. I suspect treachery. We should suspect nothing else. Anderson wishes communication with the city. If opportunity is allowed him to see what we are doing, or to hear of it, or if he is allowed to corrupt mercenaries, we shall have worse mischief. We must not be too confiding, too easy of faith, too courteous, even to an enemy, who, if he had the right feeling, would at once resign his command and throw up his position on the distinct ground of his Southern birth and associations. He should be kept corked up closely, until we are quite ready to draw him off. If he still keep his position, and we are to have an attempt by the war steamers, Fort Sumter must and will take part in it; the vital point is how to neutralize his action in the engagement. I see but the one suggested, to keep as many batteries at work on him, breaching and otherwise, and a cloud of vessels and men ready for scaling, as will effectively divert his regards from those forts which are designed for the defense of the harbor. And unless Fort Morris be made strong in guns, I see that vessels of heavy draft in deep water may shell it *ad libitum*, while the smaller craft passes in. I am very doubtful whether a fort on the east end of Sullivan's can do more than cover the Maffit and Rattlesnake channels, if these. It can hardly do much mischief to vessels entering the Ship Channel. Something will depend upon the calibre of its guns. Do, if you can spare a half hour, write me, in charity, how we stand, and with what degree of preparation, and believe me

W. Gilmore Simms.

To this long letter Simms added a by no means short postscript, in which he detailed a scheme for approaching Fort Sumter by rafts in case an escalade should be attempted, a proceeding which he deprecated upon the whole. The two head rafts were to be covered with thick plank and tin, and to be painted dark. They would thus be protected from hand grenades, and at low water the whole chain of rafts would form an almost solid bridge. But the main point was to wear the garrison out. "So long as we can effect this," he concludes, "and keep them in a state of siege, there is no discredit to the State. We should do nothing rashly now, to the peril of our brave young men, which we can possibly avoid. But you will think me interminable. Once more, good-night."[3]

On February 20, besides his remarks on a copyright law,—a subject which had been discussed by him in the "Southern Literary Messenger" several years before,— he referred as follows to the question of restricting the slave-trade: "We ought to frame no organic law touching the slave-trade. We may express a sentiment, if you please; but no law. Either negro slavery is a beneficent, merciful, God-chartered institution, or it is not. If beneficent, why limit it? Is it better for the negro to be a barbarian and savage in his own country, than to work out his deliverance [sic] in this? If better, why be at the pains to cast censure on the morale of the institution? Regulate the trade, but do not abolish."

In the same letter he asks why the three-fifths rule in regard to the representation of slaves should be adopted,—"a rule forced upon us by a people about to abandon slav-

---

[3]Any elaborate comments upon this letter, or upon the similar ones that succeeded it, would be out of place on the part of a writer who can make no claim to special knowledge of military matters. Yet it would be unfair to Simms not to point out how far he seems to have anticipated in his correspondence the plan of operations subsequently pursued by the State and Confederate authorities in reference to the defenses of Charleston harbor. The floating battery which operated against Sumter, and which Beauregard commended to the Confederate Secretary of War (*The War of the Rebellion*, etc., Series I. vol. i. p. 316), was one of Simms's earliest suggestions. The battery proposed at Fort Johnson was erected, and a second added; a ten-inch mortar was also used at Mount Pleasant. The iron-clad battery at Cummings Point, on the extremity of Morris Island, looking toward Sumter, which was the chief subject of many of his letters, was erected almost entirely in accordance with his plans, as is evident from a comparison of his letters with those which Major Anderson was sending at the time to the authorities at Washington. This battery worked well, but the credit of its conception has been wrongly assigned. *The Charleston Year Book* for 1883 (p. 549) states that "the first

ery, and, in surrendering to which, we gave them the power to conquer us,"—except to conciliate border States like Maryland and Missouri, which will soon hold the relation toward the cotton States, if the latter induce them to enter the new confederacy, which the North formerly held towards the South. He thinks the border States will only weaken the new government, that they had better form a middle confederacy, which they must do if they do not join the cotton States. "Count the votes for yourself," he concludes, "and see where, in a few years, the cotton States would be with such an arrangement. On one hand, Virginia, Maryland, Kentucky, Tennessee, North Carolina, and Missouri, versus South Carolina, Georgia, Florida, Alabama [Mississippi], Arkansas, Louisiana, and Texas. *Verb. sup.* I am sleepy. It is two o'clock in the morning."

He must have been very sleepy if he could have gone to bed without reflecting what a commentary his own predictions were upon his beloved doctrine of secession. Why three groups of States, rather than four, five, or any number? Why not single cotton States after a while, rather than a group of them? And why, if Cotton was king and slavery a divinely appointed institution, should eight States fail to manage six? But he evidently did not think the matter out, for two days later he wrote to emphasize for views, declaring: "If we move steadily forward, they [the border States] cannot help themselves, and must come into our fold and on our own terms. *We should make no organic law, and pass no provision under it, having their case in contemplation at all.* I would rather have a compact empire than a very extensive one, and our future secret of safety and success must depend wholly upon the homogeneity of our society and institutions. Were the territory occupied by the border States an inland sea, a waste of waters, it would please me better." Had this last wish been realized, he would not have had his present biographer pointing out that in the above sentences there is no mention of a union of States holding certain views of the Constitution, but that there is a pretty plain mention of States forming a union to perpetuate slavery. But to continue our extracts. Why, he asks, should we "conciliate States into our alliance whom we shall have to support just as we have supported [sic] New England?" Still they may be of use after all in making "an imposing front which *might* discourage the hostility of the North." And yet he fears that the cotton States will in the future be much more troubled with the question, "Who shall we keep out?" rather than with the question, "How many will come in?" For "in process of time all Mexico is destined to be civilized [sic] through the medium of negro slavery." He further fears that it will be difficult to keep New Jersey and the other Middle States out of his new confederacy, and he prophesies that in three years California will "set up for herself."

---

thought of the modern iron armor now in use originated in Charleston, with the late Col. C. H. Stevens, Twenty-fourth South Carolina Volunteers, who, as a private citizen, in January, 1861, began the erection of an iron-armored battery of two guns, on Morris Island, built with heavy yellow pine timber of great solidity, at an angle of 40°, *and faced with bars of railroad iron.*" The attempt to find in this experiment the germ of the modern iron-clad is, of course, idle, as armor-plated vessels were constructed by the French in the Crimean War. It would seem to be equally erroneous to assign the conception of the idea of the iron-clad battery to Colonel Stevens. The battery was not begun until the last days of January, and it was on February 5 that Major Anderson discovered that it was being covered with railway bars. But at least a month before, Simms had detailed the whole plan of such a battery to Jamison, then acting as Secretary of War to the State of South Carolina. Jamison spoke of the plan to military men, and perhaps Colonel Stevens deserves the credit of having first determined to act upon it. The subject cannot be pursued, but it is at least apparent that Simms's long letters were not without influence, and that he was no mere dabbler in matters outside his sphere.

Let us, then, "not bother our heads to please England and the North on the score of negro slavery and the slave-trade. They have already voted us barbarians. But we have them in our power." It seems a little like the irony of fate that this letter should have been written on Washington's birthday.

In his next letters he urges for low taxes on imports, describes how he is adapting the sword bayonet to the old musket, and refers as follows to his battery: "I find that Jamison has adopted my suggestion of using ranging timbers with facings of railroad iron for batteries; but I am not satisfied with the shape of the battery, nor with the manner in which the iron is laid on. . . . It presents too long a plane surface to a plunging fire. Besides, the rails are not spiked down. I counseled that they should be spiked, but loosely, so as to allow some working of the rail under the shock of shot or shell." And so he went on, giving minute details, illustrating his points by diagrams, and showing at every word how all his faculties were aroused for the defense of the cause he had labored for so long. On April 17, he wrote again about his batteries, concluding with these pathetic words: "To-day, my dear Miles, I am fifty-five! But my gray beard is sixty-five. I have grown very old in two years."

He had been through enough to make him grow gray, and just two weeks before the letter last mentioned was written he had had fresh proof of how hard it was for him to gain any credit for his labors. Certainly one would think that at such a time patriotic services would have been recognized, and that men would have been glad to give credit to one another for any exertion, however small, in behalf of the common cause. And yet we find Simms adding a postscript to his letter to Miles of April 2, which runs as follows:—

"I suppose you have seen how quietly all my agency in the suggestion of the battery of rail iron and ranging timber has been ignored. In my letters to you and to Jamison,—and the letters to you were all transferred to him,—I planned batteries for land and water, went into details, showed all the advantages, showed how the structure should be made easemate, bomb-proof, how the plane should be inclined to the rear, how the '*rat trap*' in the rear might be made to improve upon everything hitherto used. In your letters to me you professed to know nothing of these things, and to have no such intimacy with military men as to justify you in approaching them on the subject. In Jamison's letters, he spoke of the great difficulty which he had in persuading military men to consider the subject; all seemed to doubt and to distrust everything which was novel, and from the hands of a civilian. But gradually, as public opinion *abroad* began to speak of the conception as working a revolution in such structures, I find the battery a subject of great attention, and all my poor agency in it ignored wholly. And yet my plans and suggestions covered this and the floating battery, and covered other schemes for temporary structures, by which I proposed a covered approach to the walls of Sumter, which should be as secure against hand grenades as against cannon—Well! it is not much—More:[4] If there was any strategic device for the relief of Fort Sumter, I argued and anticipated it in my letters to Jamison written almost nightly for months! Enough! Yet one feels a little sore that there should be no record of a patriotism and a devotion to his country, which has left him little time or

---

[4]The effects of his excitement are to be seen in the style of Simms's letters at this time. His ellipses are often confusing, as in the above sentence.

thought for anything else. Ever since the moment of secession, and for years before, in my labors of political literature, I had the same fate."

Poor old man!—but his friend Miles at least stuck by him and declared that to Simms more than to any one else were due the preparations made in Charleston for the reduction of Sumter. And while displaying this intense, but to us misguided patriotism, the zealous partisan was striving to inform himself of all that was being written against his favorite doctrine of the right of secession. In the letter to which the above postscript was added he had written: "I could wish to get every publication which in any degree related to the secession movement. I wish to fortify myself in regard to the controversy, as well from the opposite standpoint as from our own." The results of his studies were seen in editorial after editorial in the "Mercury." For no ignoring of his labors could prevent him from giving up his heart and soul to the cause of his State, and, as we have seen, he did not even stop writing about his batteries.

The war was now fairly begun, and, if his correspondence did not naturally decrease, it is at least certain that few of his letters for the next four years have been preserved. From such as have come to light we see that he was in a constant state of anxiety both for his country and for his family. There was no chance now for summer trips, and although in August, 1861, he wrote to his friend Dr. Porcher that the country about Woodlands was perfectly healthy, there being only one case of fever to seventy negroes, we are inclined to doubt his statement when we find him in the same year losing two of his children from fever of a malignant type. One of these victims was his fifth son, Sydney Hammond, aged two years, the other was Miles's goddaughter Harriet, aged nearly four.

But though mistaken as to the healthfulness of Woodlands, he knew the place well in other respects. Dr. Porcher had just published an essay on the plants of South Carolina and their use in time of war. Here he touched a hobby of Simms's, and the latter wrote him long letters full of suggestions. Sojourns among the Indians and backwoodsmen had enabled our versatile author to pick up much botanical knowledge and many curious recipes for the compounding of medicines and of other useful articles. Soap, cartridge boxes, ink, bonnets, and peanut chocolate, are among the things that can be made easily, the last-named concoction being a very good substitute for coffee, as Porcher can learn for himself if he will run up to Woodlands, where three is no scarcity as yet of "hog and hominy" (April 14, 1863).

If Porcher had made the visit, he would not have found the Woodlands at which Simms had passed so many years of pleasure and of pain. The old house, with its broad piazza, and the study where so many romances had been written, was no more. For about the first of April, 1862, the main house took fire from some unknown cause and burned to the ground; and if its owner had not some months previously built a wing to accommodate his overflowing library, the family would have had no shelter save an outhouse or two.

Simms had driven with General Jamison to Midway, to learn what was happening at the seat of war. They got back about one o'clock at night, and Jamison drove away home, while Simms went quietly to bed, little dreaming that in three hours he would have to flee for his life. Beginning in the attic, the fire made such headway that when it was discovered at four in the morning, there was no chance to save the house. The slaves, however, worked with a will, and in response to Mrs. Simms's urgent cries, "Boys, save my husband's library," the fire was prevented from spreading to the wing. The resulting desolation can be best comprehended from the following letter to Miles:—

WOODLANDS in Ruins, *April* 10.

Thanks, dear friend, for your kind letter. It is the most perfect solace I have, to find gathering to me at this juncture troops of friends. Your words are most precious among them. You have been beside me in previous and, I think, worse trials. Gladly now would I give my dwelling and all that I have saved, for the restoration of my two boys. And since then, a third boy, and a girl, your own protégé, and, I think, one of the most promising and lovely of my children. Truly, I am pursued by a hungry fate! But I will not succumb. It may crush, but shall not subject me, no [sic] more than Yankeedom shall subject our country. I am happy to tell you that I have saved all my manuscripts, and nearly all my library. I fortunately built, only the last year, a wing to the dwelling, connected by a corridor, twenty feet in length. The wing was saved. But for this removal of my books, they must have been all lost. And only a few days before the fire, I gathered up all my manuscripts—matter enough for fifty volumes,—and packed it into trunks, not knowing how soon I should have to fly,—thinking more of the Yankees than of midnight fires, and wishing to be ready. Had I lost my library and manuscripts the blow would have been insupportable. As it is, I mean to die with harness on my back.

My family is occupying my library and two outhouses. I write you this letter from a corner of my carriage house. I am building two rooms in a board house, which will afford me tolerable shelter from the summer, and if the insurance company will pay, as I am promised, seventy-five in the hundred, I shall get enough, with my own bricklayers and workmen, to rebuild the walls and roof of my old mansion. But to restore is impossible. My loss in money is about $10,000. I have lost the best part of my furniture,—every bedstead but one,—half of my bedding, bed and other clothes, drawers, wardrobes, crockery, medicine case, and pictures, statuettes, candelabra, ornaments, and a thousand toys, ornaments, mementos, such as can never be replaced,—the accumulations of two or three families, for five generations. All the stores in my pantry were destroyed. Luckily my meat house and other oathouses were saved. My negroes worked zealously and with a loving devotedness, which was quite grateful to me. I had them on the roofs of corridor, library, and kitchen; narrowly escaped myself by a ladder from an upper window, while the floors overhead were falling in. I do not despair, do not despond, but verily it tasks all my courage and strength to endure such repeated strokes of fortune. . . .

So far he writes of himself; the rest of the letter is occupied with complaints of the neglect of his counsels by the authorities and with new counsels as sure to be disregarded. He asks "why artillerists should not be armed with pikes, instead of with short swords which are of no use," since "pikes in the hands of artillerists could protect a battery against any dash of cavalry." "The art of war," he continues, "is no more perfect than any other art, and is susceptible of a thousand improvements, which are not to be expected from the mere soldiers of drill and routine."

But if his counsels were disregarded by "drill and routine" officials, his losses were not forgotten by his friends, some of whom raised a subscription of three thousand dollars to help him to rebuild. He also tried to make a little money by his pen, which had of late been idle, for he sent the proprietors of the "Southern Illustrated News"—Richmond gentlemen who were rash enough to promise their subscribers original contributions by Dickens and Thackeray—certain poetical "Sketches in Greece," which he had had by him for six years, as well as a serial entitled "Paddy McGann, or The Demon of the Stump,"—a tale of a humorous Irishman who fancies himself haunted by a demon, but who is really worried out of his life by a shrewish spouse. Simms was writing this story at the time of the battle of Fredericksburg, December 13, 1862, and the following sentences, taken from the first chapter, give a vivid picture of the hopes which the victory raised:—

"Even as I write the thunder rolls westward from the east. There is storm along the heights of Virginia. The cry is havoc; the war-dogs are again unleashed! The tempest rages, and the bloody banner of the foe goes down in its own blood. We are victors, and this time the route[5] is complete. Thirty thousand [sic] of the insolent invaders bite the dust. Our triumph is secure, our independence! and Peace, with her beautiful rainbow, plucked from the bosom of the storm, and spread from east to west, from north to south, over all the sunny plains and snowy heights of our beloved Apalachia, sends our gallant sons back once more to the calm blessings of each hospitable home." And the fierceness of his exultation is explained when we read on: "It is not all over, our happy life, my friend! We shall enjoy the old sports of our sweet little river once more, in communion with our noble-hearted companions. It cannot be that God will deliver us into the hands of these atrocious heathens. As between us and the Deity, there is no doubt a sad reckoning to make; but as between us and these accursed Yankees, no reproach lies at our doors, unless that single one of having too long slept within the coil of the serpent. I have faith in God, my friend. He may punish us, and we must suffer, for this is the need of our desert; but he will not let us sink. I have faith in his promise, in his mercy, and I know that after this tribulation, our peace shall return once more, our prosperity, our friends; and the 'song of the turtle shall be heard in the land.'"

It is pathetic to read these heartfelt utterances, committed with such conviction of righteous intention to the worn type and wretched paper familiar to all who have interested themselves in Confederate literature. Those men of the old South felt that their existence as a primitive people was at stake; they felt that the easy, picturesque life they led depended for its perpetuation upon their good swords, and they fought as the soldiers of Charles fought the Saracens at Tours, or as Goth and Roman fought Attila and his Huns at Chalons. In their patriotic songs they spoke of the Northern troops as Huns and Vandals; for they knew too well that a Northern conquest meant the destruction of their peculiar civilization. But they did not and they could not realize that the parallel between themselves and the soldiers of Aetius was apparent only. They did not and they could not realize that they were fighting, not for the true religion and the higher civilization, but for the perpetuation of a barbarous institution and of anarchy disguised.[6] And yet who that sees their mistake to-day would be so rash as to declare that if he had lived in their times and in their environment, he would have acted differently? And who shall deny that they were brave men, pouring out their blood for a cause which to them was true and holy and blessed of God himself? It is idle to deny their bravery, although that, like most of their qualities, was a "survival," and it is equally idle to affirm that a whole people can astonish a world by their heroism in defense of a cause in which they do not believe.

To return, however, to our wrought-up romancer. "Paddy McGann" lies in the dingy pages of the pretentious Richmond weekly, and no one will ever endeavor to

---

[5]One of the numerous typographical errors of which Southern authors were constantly complaining. It is hardly probable that Simms intended to use the obsolete spelling.

[6]It is meant, of course, that this would have been the result of their victory—not that they consciously fought for any such result.

resurrect it. There is no need to do so, unless one wishes to get a pleasant description of the Edisto,—the "sweet little river" of the above extracts,—and of the easy-going life which Simms and Jamison and their neighbors lived on its banks. But all these good men are gathered to their fathers, and few will care to know how Jamison excelled any man in the State in making a cocktail, and Simms in making a punch. The old life is gone, and as Simms felt it going his outcries against the devastating "Northern hordes" became shriller and shriller. As one reads some of the poems he was in the habit of dashing off, as the newspapers brought an account of a new battle, one can fancy that one is listening to the wail of a Romanized Briton telling of the cruel deeds he has seen perpetrated by the yellow-haired barbarians from over sea.

However exaggerated these poems might be, they came from his heart, and were all that he could write. His drama on "Benedict Arnold," which he published in the "Magnolia," another Richmond weekly, bored him greatly, as he confessed to Hayne. "My heart," he continued, "is too full of anxiety to suffer me to write, and though I have a contract for some two hundred dollars' worth of prose, I find myself unable to divert my thoughts from the crisis in which the country trembles in suspense. What I write is in a spasm, a single burst of passion,—hope, or scorn, or rage, or exultation" (July 29, 1863).

Six weeks later a nearer grief assailed him. On September 10, 1863, his wife died, in her forty-seventh year. Not quite a year before, she had given birth to her sixth son and thirteenth child, Charles Carroll, the namesake, probably, of the gentleman in whose office Simms had studied law. For some time previously Simms had mentioned in his letters that his wife was not well; but he had no idea that her condition was critical. He wrote later to Doctor Porcher, that the calamity fell upon him like a bolt out of a clear sky. He was "seized with mental paroxysms of great violence, which threatened the integrity of" his brain. For four days and nights he neither ate nor slept; and but for opiates would have gone mad. This attack was followed by a fever which prostrated him for a month.

Nevertheless, the thought of his children brought him at last to his feet, and he determined for their sakes to battle with the world once more. How the winter was passed is not known, but it appears from a letter to Hayne that early in May he went to Columbia with his eldest son and namesake, whose furlough had just expired. Gilmore was now of age, and whatever his fears for his son's safety, the father was proud to have at least one of his name and blood battling for the Southern cause. The young man went to Virginia, and nearly lost his life at the battle of Trevilian's. A kind lady of the neighborhood nursed him, and sent him home to even harder labors than campaigning had been,—labors of which there will be occasion to speak before long.

While in Columbia Simms saw Timrod, and when he got back to Woodlands, he wrote to Hayne, May 8, 1864, as follows: "I saw Timrod, and was glad to find him in better health and spirits than he has had for years. . . . If his situation lessens his opportunities for verse writing, it at all events gives him the creature comforts, and with a young wife, he has need of all he can earn in these perilous times. Besides, he is making himself a fine prose writer, and the practice in a daily newspaper will improve his energies, without materially disparaging [?] the properties and graces of his style. His tendency is to the tragical, but a daily newspaper will modify this. A daily newspaper in a village like Columbia is far different from that of a great commercial city, and the very limited space accorded by our papers now, lessens the strain upon the mind. The labor is not exhaustive, nor very various. He has only to prepare a couple of dwarf essays, making a single column, and the pleasant public is satisfied. These he does so well that they have reason to be so. Briefly, our friend is in a fair way to fatten and be happy, though his muse becomes costive and complains of his *mésalliances.* . . . I did not meet with Tim's wife, though he gave me an invitation to see her. But the walk was too much for me; I am scarcely good for a mile heat nowadays."

In the same letter he referred to a poem on Stonewall Jackson, which was still unfinished (it remained so), and which he regarded as fine in conception and good in execution. He added: "I should not forget to say that recently I finished what I think a very creditable poem, entitled 'Midnight Chaunt in Autumn.' It was begun several years ago, and shortly after I had lost two noble boys, in one day, by yellow fever. But then after writing a dozen stanzas, my heart failed me, if not my head, and the manuscript was thrown aside. Happening recently upon it, and under similar circumstances of suffering and season, I finished it. It makes some eighty verses, quatrains. You will like it, I think, though whether it sees the printers in a hurry is very questionable. With the plantation upon me, the cares of the family, anxieties without number, tithes and taxes to be provided, and a still heavy burden of correspondence, life seems escaping from me, frittered away in small things and—[?] details." Then follow brief references to the privations of the times. They have enough food at Woodlands, but no variety. Stimulants, too, are wanting,—though Rhett has recently sent him a gallon of whiskey,—and consequently he cannot put a stop to his chills and fever. But the war will end this year, and if Hayne wants to make money he had better desert poetry for a while and turn to prose.

So the days passed. On September 17, 1864, he wrote to Hayne that he was worn out, having just returned from Columbia, whither he had been to attend the funeral of his old friend Jamison, who had died of the yellow fever. The disease was all over Charleston, and so were the enemy's shells. Hood, he hears, has been miserably outgeneraled by Sherman. Unless Johnston or Lee or Beauregard is sent against the latter, the enemy will penetrate to Macon, Augusta, Andersonville, etc. He foresees the end, unless imbecility in office, civil and military, be checked. On November 21, he writes to the same friend that he has been harvesting his sorry crop. Another year of war, and the planters will produce nothing. He has lost two horses and two mules within the year and cannot replace them, and all his agricultural implements are worn out. In literature he does little or nothing. A few short poems are all he has done in eighteen months. And still he has to work for the public, for he goes to Columbia next week as a member of the Board of Visitors of Military Academies.

Whether he stayed at Columbia from this time on, or whether he returned to Woodlands and made arrangements for moving with his younger children to the city, is uncertain; but it seems clear that by the first of the new year, 1865, he was no longer residing at his plantation. The place was not deserted, however, for a Mrs. Pinckney and her family were left as occupants. Simms, of course, thought that Sherman would soon leave Savannah on his northward march; but he probably fancied, as many did, that Charleston would be the object of assault, and that the middle country, in which Columbia lay, would either be fairly safe from the ravages of the main body of the enemy, as lying out of their line of march, or else that the Confederate government would send Johnston to defend South Carolina's capital city. If such were his expectations,—and it is fair to infer from a subsequent publication that he did indulge them,—they were destined to be cruelly disappointed. Barnwell and Midway lay directly in the path taken by the conquerors, and suffered accordingly. Fugitives began to pour into Columbia, bringing heart-rending tales of the desolation that followed every step that Sherman took, and it was not many days after the memorable first of February, when the northward march began, before Simms learned that his newly built house, his library that had but recently escaped so narrowly, and all his out-houses had been completely destroyed by the same element that had so often proved his foe. But his private losses were nothing when contrasted with the horrors that were enacted under his very eyes on that Black Friday (February 17), which saw the beautiful old town of Columbia given up to pillage and the flames.

It is not proposed to give an account here of these horrors or to enter upon any discussion of the much vexed question, "Who burned Columbia?" All who desire to know what Simms saw and what he thought of the conduct of the Northern general and his troops are referred to a pamphlet entitled "Sack and Destruction of the City of Columbia, S. C.," published by our author from the ruined city itself shortly after Sherman left it. Simms never wrote anything more graphic than this account of what he had seen and heard. Doubtless his vehemence induced him to exaggerate in places, but it is hard to read his stirring pages without coming to the conclusion that the sack of Columbia is one of the greatest crimes ever perpetrated by the troops of a civilized country.

Simms himself did not fare badly, but when he saw the magnificent library and scientific collections of his friend Dr. R. W. Gibbes, the antiquarian, fired in the owner's presence amid the jeers of rude soldiers, he doubtless thought of the fate of his own library at Woodlands, and ground his teeth in impotent rage. He saved his watch by his presence of mind, for when accosted by soldiers and asked the time of day, he would look innocently to where the city-hall clock once stood, and reply, "Our city clock is gone, you see, but it must be near—." Twelve hundred less astute citizens, anxious to please, are said to have pulled out their watches only to have them snatched away. Another and pleasanter incident has been recorded by Mr. Aldrich, Simms's neighbor. A young Northern officer knocked at the door of the house where Simms and his children were staying. The novelist answered the summons in person, and after the usual formalities, the visitor said, "Sir, I have enjoyed too much pleasure from your works not to feel grateful. You belong to the Union, and I have come to see if I can render you any service. Simms thanked him and said that he desired only to have his family saved from intrusion. The officer departed, and in a few moments a guard appeared, who were polite and efficient in performing their duty. It is but fair to add that this is by no means the only instance of courtesy on the part of individual officers and soldiers of the Union army to the oppressed inhabitants of Columbia.

Another incident recorded by Mr. Aldrich may be referred to. Shortly after the destruction of Woodlands he met Simms at Columbia, and naturally began to sympathize with him over his losses; but Simms turned around almost fiercely, and exclaimed, "Talk not to me about my losses, when the State is lost." He was not the man, however, to think anything lost for long, and in little over a month after the burning of the city, he had persuaded a printer, Mr. Julian A. Selby, to undertake a tri-weekly newspaper under the appropriate title of the "Columbia Phœnix." Paper, press, and type had to be procured from a distance, but after toilsome trips Selby succeeded in getting the necessary supplies, and on March 21, 1865, the first number made its appearance. Some of the earlier numbers are now before me. Curious, badly printed sheets, they are, about six by eighteen inches, indented to fold so as to give six small pages. *No* subscriptions are taken, but each number retails for one dollar.

After number nine, the paper becomes a daily as well as a triweekly, and persons are allowed to subscribe for a month at twenty and ten dollars respectively, strictly in advance. The veteran editor of nullification times is, of course, at the head of the editorial staff,—probably is the staff,—and is in his element. Through the first twelve numbers runs the account of the sack of Columbia, which has been already mentioned in its pamphlet form. Besides this there are stinging editorials, and, what is more surprising, hopeful prognostications of the future of the war. An occasional telegram makes its appearance, and a fair number of advertisements, among which is one that offers for sale a set of Simms's romances. But an editorial entitled "Woodlands," which appeared in the issue for Wednesday, April 12, 1865, concerns us more narrowly, and we note that just four years have elapsed since that firing on Sumter which Simms so earnestly counseled.[7]

This editorial is nothing more than a long account, evidently from Simm's hand, of the final burning of Woodlands. From it we learn that Mrs. Pinckney, the lady in charge of the place, sent a note to General Blair requesting protection for the dwelling and library. Before an answer could be received, bands of stragglers had entered the house, only six rooms of which had been rebuilt, and begun their work of destruction. In the midst of this turmoil, a guard arrived, which was shortly followed by General Blair himself, in company with other officers. The gentlemen spent some time examining the library, and when they retired they took away with them only some maps of the State and a couple of fowling pieces. While the guard remained, nothing was disturbed, but with the departure of the soldiers, frequent attempts were made to burn the house, and the ladies occupying it fled to Midway for protection. At daybreak the servants discovered that the building was in flames, and that all their labors to preserve it would be fruitless. The library was the first to burn, and not a volume was saved. The larger and better furniture had been previously sent off, and many of the choicer books had been packed in boxes, to be removed whenever transportation could be obtained. Thus the thievish incendiaries, who did not care for books, got little for their pains, and in view of this fact some of the neighbors conceived the idea that the house must have been fired by Simms's own negroes, particularly by his trusted body servant. This man was actually tried by a court of freeholders, but was acquitted. Simms evidently did not believe the charge, but it was repeated by Mr. Aldrich five years later. For the credit of human nature it may be hoped that Simms was right.

Before Simms wrote the description of his losses, which has been abridged above, Lee had surrendered at Appomattox, and the war was practically at an end. Probably it was because he could not bear to think of his people's losses that he occupied himself in writing minutely of his own. He did it with a calmness which it is difficult to imitate. For who shall describe how the old partisan, who had once in his imagination crushed the North like an egg, felt during those last weary months, when the defeat of all his hopes stared him in the face? He had entered the period of struggle with confidence in the justice as well as in the success of his cause; he came out still confident of the justice, but struggling in vain to reconcile the two ideas of a just cause and an unsuccessful one. Many honest people have since his day been trying with equal futility to effect a similar reconciliation. But it will not do. The facts of uni-

---

[7]The *Phœnix* is, I believe, still published in Columbia.

versal history warn them that any such attempt is futile. No people, however brave and true, can wage an eventually successful war with advancing civilization, and this is what the South was trying to do. It is vain to talk of constitutional rights that date from a century back; it is vain to say that deep and honest conviction in the truth of a cause makes a cause true; it is vain to say that mere money and cowardice and wrong are on the successful side, and all bravery and right on the defeated side. Civil wars do not divide a people on such lines; if they did, it would be idle to speak of a nation's fulfilling its destiny under the direction of God. But if nations do not fulfill their destinies under the direction of God, what need is there to speculate about the past or the future at all; what has history to do in such a reign of Chaos and old Night?

No! the most loyal Southerner may as well make up his mind to face the fact that the cause for which Simms labored, and for which so many thousands of brave men died, was a losing cause, in consequence of the fact that the people that upheld it were fighting to perpetuate an institution opposed to progress, an institution that blocked the path which a great nation had to take. In view of this truth, it does not seem necessary to insist upon the part played by the North in the great contest. It is idle to deny that many things were done by her zealous sons, and many things left undone by her lukewarm sons, that tended to hasten the South upon her downward course, and to add to her frenzy and blindness. For it is one of the curses of an institution like slavery that its baleful effects are not confined to its upholders, but react upon its opponents. "Sweetness and light" are virtues that are rarely to be traced in the history of the American people between 1820 and 1865. It could not have been otherwise. "Sweetness and light" had little place in a struggle against slavery; for civilization was never known to go forward in satin slippers. Doubtless many good people, reading the record of these pitiful times, have fancied that if a little "sweetness and light" had appeared, a few more concessions been made, the result would have been different. Such fancies are idle. And old order of things had been planted in a portion of this country by perfectly natural processes; and the time had come for it to give way to a new order of things. But in history there is no beneficent Despot who says, "Let the old order vanish and the new be born." All life is a struggle; and the higher planes of existence, individual as well as national, are reached by toil, by slow degrees, by pain. The war of secession, therefore, having been inevitable, it is not necessary to point out all the false steps made by the North. These false steps delayed the day of change, and made the ordeal through which the South had to pass more bitter and terrible, while reacting, as such steps are sure to do, upon the people that made them. The South, also, took false steps of her own accord, and, as in the case of the North, those false steps were fearfully atoned for. But it was the forces of destiny in the main that placed the South in her direful position; and it was the forces of destiny that made the North the instrument by which the whole country, North and South, was finally saved for what we all believe will be a glorious future.

This view of the matter cannot of course be a popular one, and it has its historical limitations. Most readers prefer the historical method of Carlyle to that of Buckle, because it is pleasanter to praise and blame men than to stand dumb before the inscrutable workings of law. Then again few readers, and few historians, see how it is possible to use both methods at one and the same time. Yet this has to be done. It is just as essential to point out the importance of representative men like Garrison and Simms as to point out the fact that both North and South were merely fulfilling their respective destinies. Law and the individual that embodies its workings are the two foci around which the historian must move; and, if the curve he traces is not a perfect circle, it is not his fault. He is saved at any rate from much erratic wandering; from dropping downwards into the regions of the commonplace, the base, and the low. He is saved, in the particular instance we are considering, from the absurdity of representing two sections of practically the same great race as being entirely the children of light and the children of darkness respectively. He is saved from imagining that all virtue concentrated itself to the north of a certain historic line and all vice to the south of it, or *vice versa*, and that if, since the war, there has been some drifting of the virtues southward or northward, they are promptly recalled and installed in their proper places on the eve of a presidential election. He is saved from all this, and at the same time is allowed to grow eloquent over truly great men like Lincoln and Lee, and also to render the negative service of pointing out that not all the popular heroes of either side are worthy of the homage they are receiving. He can also point out the instructive parallel that exists between the struggle of Cavalier and Puritan on either side of the ocean, can show that the qualities of neither are thoroughly great and lovable, but that in their amalgamation a great people must be produced. But he can also grow tedious.

Yet before this chapter closes, attention should be called once more to the trials that befell Simms during these terrible years. He had done much to bring on the war that ruined him, and yet he had only done what seemed to him to be just and right. If he had been conscious of wrong-doing, it would be time to speak of retribution; but the word would be out of place in connection with an honest man. As a mistaken man he suffered from the natural consequences of his mistakes; but who can recount his losses without feeling that his lot was indeed a pathetic one? His calling gone, his stereotype plates confiscated, his dwelling twice burned down, his books destroyed, friends, two children, and wife taken from him, and his State and section in the dust of humiliation and defeat, who shall say that he was not a sorely tried man? And yet he never proved himself a truer or nobler man than in these days of adversity,—days which to him were hardly cheered by the vision of the new order that was to be.

For out of the ashes of the old South, a new and better South has arisen. A disintegrated and primitive people have become united among themselves and with their former foes, and are moving forward upon the path of progress. Instead of the past, they have the future to look upon; instead of a mere State, they have a nation to trust in and to maintain. They have retained all that was good in the old South, and to their inherited virtues and powers they will add, as the years go by, virtues and powers that must come to any people that move forward with civilization. If they have not yet shaken themselves loose from the clogs of primitive custom which they have inherited from their ancestors; if the slave in the person of the freedman still stands in the way of their progress, they will nevertheless push on, and in the course of years the clogs will fall from them and the freedman will be a help instead of a hindrance. They have the energy of a new people, and they have a territory almost boundless and inexhaustible. They have awakened from their nightmares and gone out into the fresh air of the morning, and the breeze has driven the fever from their brows. They have ceased to lament the tossing hours, the fitful anguish of the night when they called upon God and thought he did not hear them, and the burden of their song of deliverance rolls ever up to his throne:—

"Yet I doubt not thro' the ages one increasing purpose runs,
And the thoughts of men are widened with the process of the suns."

James Lane Allen

(1849–1925)

James Lane Allen's childhood was similar to that of many Southern writers of his era—he was raised in well-to-do circumstances that changed markedly as a result of the Civil War. His mother, an extremely religious woman, insisted that he be educated at home until he was sixteen, after which he enrolled in the preparatory school for Kentucky University (now Transylvania College, affiliated with the Church of Christ) before entering that institution in 1868. After graduating in 1872, he taught in a series of schools in Kentucky and Missouri before accepting an appointment to Bethany College in West Virginia, another church-related school. He returned to Kentucky University to obtain his master's degree, which he obtained in 1877.

Allen began publishing short fiction in the 1880s, and in 1892 he published *Flute and Violin and Other Kentucky Tales and Romances*. In 1895, *A Kentucky Cardinal*, a mixture of local-color sentimentality and romantic idealism, appeared and was followed by two other novels in a similar vein. When *The Reign of Law: A Tale of the Kentucky Hemp Fields* was published in 1900, it caused something of a stir in religious circles. A Hardyesque tale set on a Kentucky hemp plantation, the novel examines the doctrines of evolution and the consequences of circumstance.

from *The Reign of Law: A Tale of the Kentucky Hemp Fields*

The Anglo-Saxon farmers had scarce conquered foothold, stronghold, freehold in the Western wilderness before they became sowers of hemp—with remembrance of Virginia, with remembrance of dear ancestral Britain. Away back in the days when they lived with wife, child, flock in frontier wooden fortresses and hardly ventured forth for water, salt, game, tillage—in the very summer of that wild daylight ride of Tomlinson and Bell, by comparison with which, my children, the midnight ride of Paul Revere, was as tame as the pitching of a rocking-horse in a boy's nursery—on that history-making twelfth of August, of the year 1782, when these two backwoods riflemen, during that same Revolution the Kentuckians then fighting a branch of that same British army, rushed out of Bryan's Station for the rousing of the settlements and the saving of the West—hemp was growing tall and thick near the walls of the fort.

Hemp in Kentucky in 1782—early landmark in the history of the soil, of the people. Cultivated first for the needs of cabin and clearing solely; for twine and rope, towel and table, sheet and shirt. By and by not for cabin and clearing only; not for tow-homespun, fur-clad Kentucky alone. To the north had begun the building of ships, American ships for American commerce, for American arms, for a nation which Nature had herself created and had distinguished as a sea-faring race. To the south had begun the raising of cotton. As the great period of shipbuilding went on—greatest during the twenty years or more ending in 1860; as the great period of cotton-raising and cotton-bailing went on—never so great before as that in that same year—the two parts of the nation looked equally to the one border plateau lying between them, to several counties of Kentucky, for most of the nation's hemp. It was in those days of the North that the *Constitution* was rigged with Russian hemp on one side, with American hemp on the other, for a patriotic test of the superiority of home-grown, home-prepared fibre; and thanks to the latter, before those days ended with the outbreak of the Civil War, the country had become second to Great Britain alone in her ocean craft, and but little behind that mistress of the seas. So that in response to this double demand for hemp on the American ship and hemp on the southern plantation, at the close of that period of national history on land and sea, from those few counties of Kentucky, in the year 1859, were taken well-nigh forty thousand tons of the well-cleaned bast.

What history it wrought in those years, directly for the republic, indirectly for the world! What ineffaceable marks it left on Kentucky itself, land, land-owners! To make way for it, a forest the like of which no human eye will ever see again was felled; and with the forest went its pastures, its waters. The roads of Kentucky, those long lime-stone turnpikes connecting the towns and villages with the farms—they were early made necessary by the hauling of the hemp. For the sake of it slaves were perpetually being trained, hired, bartered; lands perpetually rented and sold; fortunes made or lost. The advancing price of farms, the westward movement of poor families and con-sequent dispersion of the Kentuckians over cheaper territory, whither they carried the same passion for the cultivation of the same plant,—thus making Missouri the second hemp-producing state in the Union,—the regulation of the hours in the Ken-tucky cabin, in the house, at the rope-walk, in the factory,—what phase of life went unaffected by the pursuit and fascination of it. Thought, care, hope of the farmer of-tentimes throughout the entire year! Upon it depending, it may be, the college of his son, the accomplishments of his daughter, the luxuries of his wife, the house he would build, the stock he could own. His own pleasures also: his deer hunting in the South, his fox hunting at home, his fishing on the great lakes, his excursions on the old floating palaces of the Mississippi down to New Orleans—all these depending in large measure upon his hemp, that thickest gold-dust of his golden acres.

With the Civil War began the long decline, lasting still. The record stands that throughout the one hundred and twenty-five odd years elapsing from the entrance of the Anglo-Saxon farmers into the wilderness down to the present time, a few counties of Kentucky have furnished army and navy, the entire country, with all but a small part of the native hemp consumed. Little comparatively is cultivated in Kentucky now. The traveller may still see it here and there, crowning those ever-renewing, self-renewing inexhaustible fields. But the time cannot be far distant when the industry there will have become extinct. Its place in the nation's markets will be still further taken by metals, by other fibres, by finer varieties of the same fibre, by the same vari-ety cultivated in soils less valuable. The history of it in Kentucky will be ended, and, being ended, lost.

Some morning when the roar of March winds is no more heard in the tossing woods, but along still brown boughs a faint, veil-like greenness runs; when every spring, welling out of the soaked earth, trickles through banks of sod unbarred by ice; before a bee is abroad under the calling sky; before the red of apple-buds becomes a sign in the low orchards, or the high song of the thrush is pouring forth far away at wet pale-green sunsets, the sower, the earliest sower of the hemp, goes forth into the fields.

Warm they must be, soft and warm, those fields, its chosen birthplace. Upturned by the plough, crossed and recrossed by the harrow, clodless, levelled, deep, fine, fer-tile—some extinct river-bottom, some valley threaded by streams, some table-land of mild rays, moist airs, alluvial or limestone soils—such is the favorite cradle of the hemp in Nature. Back and forth with measured tread, with measured distance, broadcast the sower sows, scattering with plenteous hand those small oval-shaped fruits, gray-green, black-striped, heavily packed with living marrow.

Lightly covered over by drag or harrow, under the rolled earth now they lie, those mighty, those inert seeds. Down into the darkness about them the sun rays penetrate day by day, stroking them with the brushes of light, prodding them with spears of flame. Drops of nightly dews, drops from the coursing clouds, trickle down to them, moistening the dryness, closing up the little hollows of the ground, drawing the particles of maternal earth more closely. Suddenly—as an insect that has been feigning death cautiously unrolls itself and starts into action—in each seed the great miracle of life begins. Each awakens as from a sleep, as from pretended death. It starts, it moves, it bursts its ashen woody shell, it takes two opposite courses, the white, fibriltapered root hurrying away from the sun; the tiny stem, bearing its lance-like leaves, ascending graceful, brave like a palm.

Some morning, not many days later, the farmer, walking out into his barn lot and casting a look in the direction of his field, sees—or does he not see?—the surface of it less dark. What is that uncertain flush low on the ground, that irresistible rush of multitudinous green? A fort-night, and the field is brown no longer. Overflowing it, burying it out of sight, is the shallow tidal sea of the hemp, ever rippling. Green are the woods now with their varied greenness. Green are the pastures. Green here and there are the fields: with the bluish green of young oats and wheat; with the gray green of young barley and rye: with orderly dots of dull dark green in vast array—the hills of Indian maize. But as the eye sweeps the whole landscape undulating far and near, from the hues of tree, pasture, and corn of every kind, it turns to the color of the hemp. With that in view, all other shades in nature seem dead and count for nothing. Far reflected, conspicuous, brilliant, strange; masses of living emerald, saturated with blazine sunlight.

Darker, always darker turns the hemp as it rushes upward: scarce darker as to the stemless stalks which are hidden now; but darker in the tops. Yet here two shades of greenness: the male plants paler, smaller, maturing earlier, dying first; the females darker, taller, living longer, more luxuriant of foliage and flowering heads.

A hundred days from the sowing, and those flowering heads have come forth with their mass of leaves and bloom and earliest fruits, elastic, swaying six, ten, twelve feet from the ground and ripe for cutting. A hundred days reckoning from the last of March or the last of April, so that it is July, it is August. And now, borne far through the steaming air floats an odor, balsamic, startling: the odor of those plumes and stalks and blossoms from which is exuding freely the narcotic resin of the great nettle. The nostril expands quickly, the lungs swell out deeply to draw it in: fragrance once known in childhood, ever in the memory afterward and able to bring back to the wanderer homesick thoughts of midsummer days in the shadowy, many-toned woods, over into which is blown the smell of the hemp-fields.

Who apparently could number the acres of these in the days gone by? A land of hemp, ready for the cutting! The oats heavy-headed, rustling, have turned to gold and been stacked in the stubble or stored in the lofts of white, bursting barns. The heavy-headed, rustling wheat has turned to gold and been stacked in the stubble or sent through the whirling thresher. The barley and the rye are garnered and gone, the landscape has many bare and open spaces. But separating these everywhere, rise the fields of Indian corn now in blade and tassel; and—more valuable than all else that has been sown and harvested or remains to be—everywhere the impenetrable thickets of the hemp.

Impenetrable! For close together stand the stalks, making common cause for soil and light, each but one of many, the fibre being better when so grown—as is also the fibre of men. Impenetrable and therefore weedless; for no plant life can flourish there, nor animal nor bird. Scarce a beetle runs bewilderingly through those forbidding colossal solitudes. The field-sparrow will flutter away from pollen-bearing to pollen-receiving top, trying to beguile you from its nest hidden near the edge. The crow and the blackbird will seem to love it, having a keen eye for the cutworm, its only enemy. The quail does love it, not for itself, but for its protection, leading her brood into its labyrinths out of the dusty road when danger draws near. Best of all winged creatures it is loved by the iris-eyed, burnish-breasted, murmuring doves, already beginning to gather in the deadened tree-tops with crops eager for the seed. Well remembered also by the long-flight passenger pigeon, coming into the land for the mast. Best of all wild things whose safety lies not in the wing but in the foot, it is loved by the hare for its young, for refuge. Those lithe, velvety, summer-thin bodies! Observe carefully the tops of the still hemp: are they slightly shaken? Among the bases of those stalks a cotton-tail is threading its way inward beyond reach of its pursuer. Are they shaken violently, parted clean and wide to right and left? It is the path of the dog following the hot scent—ever baffled.

A hundred days to lift out of those tiny seed these powerful stalks, hollow, hairy, covered with their tough fibre,—that strength of cables when the big ships are tugged at by the joined fury of wind and ocean. And now some morning at the corner of the field stand the black men with hooks and whetstones. The hook, a keen, straight blade, bent at right angles to the handle two feet from the hand. Let these men be the strongest; no weakling can handle the hemp from seed to seed again. A heart, the doors and walls of which are in perfect order, through which flows freely the full stream of a healthy man's red blood; lungs deep, clear, easily filled, easily emptied; a body that can bend and twist and be straightened again in ceaseless rhythmical movement; limbs tireless; the very spirit of primeval man conquering primeval nature—all these go into the cutting of the hemp. The leader strides to the edge, and throwing forward his left arm, along which the muscles play, he grasps as much as it will embrace, bends the stalks over, and with his right hand draws the blade through them an inch or more from the ground. When he has gathered his armful, he turns and flings it down behind him, so that it lies spread out, covering when fallen the same space it filled while standing. And so he crosses the broad acres, and so each of the big black followers, stepping one by one to a place behind him, until the long, wavering, whitish green swaths of the prostrate hemp lie shimmering across the fields. Strongest now is the smell of it, impregnating the clothing of the men, spreading far throughout the air.

So it lies a week or more drying, dying, till the sap is out of the stalks, till leaves and blossoms and earliest ripened or unripened fruits wither and drop off, giving back to the soil the nourishment they have drawn from it; the whole top being thus otherwise wasted—that part of the hemp which every year the dreamy millions of the Orient still consume in quantities beyond human computation, and for the love of which the very history of this plant is lost in the antiquity of India and Persia, its home—land of narcotics and desires and dreams.

Then the rakers with enormous wooden rakes; they draw the stalks into bundles, tying each with the hemp itself. Following the binders, move the wagon-beds or slides, gathering the bundles and carrying them to where, huge, flat, and round, the stacks begin to rise. At last these are well built; the gates of the field are closed or the bars put up; wagons and laborers are gone; the brown fields stand deserted.

One day something is gone from earth and sky: Autumn has come, season of scales and balances, when the Earth, brought to judgment for its fruits, says, "I have done what I could—now let me rest!"

Fall!—and everywhere the sights and sounds of falling. In the woods, through the cool silvery air, the leaves, so indispensable once, so useless now. Bright day after bright day, dripping night after dripping night, the never-ending filtering or gusty fall of leaves. The fall of walnuts, dropping from bare boughs with muffled boom into the deep grass. The fall of the hickory-nut, rattling noisily down through the scaly limbs and scattering its hulls among the stones of the brook below.

Will N. Harben

(1858–1919)

The optimism of the proponents of a New South found a fictional outlet in the works of Will Harben, who portrayed life in the hill country of his native northern Georgia in thirty novels and nearly sixty short stories. Born in Dalton, Georgia, Harben was a merchant until he was thirty years old but enjoyed little success in that endeavor. In 1888 he moved to New York to try his fortune as a writer, and a year later he published *White Marie*, a tragic tale of slavery and its after-effects. Though he claimed that it was not meant as a hostile commentary, the work won him no friends in the South. During the 1890s, he published nine more books to fairly tepid receptions, but his *Northern Georgia Sketches*, a collection of ten stories previously published in *The Century*, *Lippincott's*, and other magazines, was much more successful. These local-color sketches, which portrayed the dialect, customs, and character of the northern Georgia hillmen Harben knew in his youth, were praised for their realism. For the rest of his career, he published fiction in the same vein; *Abner Daniel* (1902) and *Ann Boyd* (1906) are most notable. *Mam Linda* (1907) is a protest against lynching in the South. Although critics of the day applauded his work (William Dean Howells particularly lauded his characterization of women), Harben's fiction, with its romantic vision of the New South, has only limited appeal for modern readers.

The Heresy of Abner Calihan

Neil Filmore's store was at the crossing of the Big Cabin and Rock Valley roads. Before the advent of Sherman into the South it had been a grist-mill, to which the hardly mountaineers had regularly brought their grain to be ground, in wagons, on horseback, or on their shoulders, according to their conditions. But the Northern soldiers had appropriated the miller's little stock of toll, had torn down the long wooden sluice which had conveyed the water from the race to the mill, had burnt the great wheel and crude wooden machinery, and rolled the massive grinding-stones into the deepest part of the creek.

After the war nobody saw any need for a mill at that point, and Neil Filmore had bought the property from its impoverished owner and turned the building into a store. It proved to be a fair location, for there was considerable travel along the two main roads, and as Filmore was postmaster his store became the general meeting-point for everybody living within ten miles of the spot. He kept for sale, as he expressed it, "a little of everything, from shoe-eyes to a sack of guano." Indeed, a sight of his rough shelves and unplaned counters, filled with cakes of tallow, beeswax and butter, bolts of calico, sheeting and ginghams, and the floor and porch heaped with piles of skins, cases of eggs, coops of chickens, and cans of lard, was enough to make an orderly housewife shudder with horror.

But Mrs. Filmore had grown accustomed to this state of affairs in the front part of the house, for she confined her domestic business, and whatever neatness and order were possible, to the room in the rear, where, as she often phrased it, she did the "eatin' an' cookin', an' never interfeer with pap's part except to lend 'im my cheers when thar is more'n common waitin' fer the mail-carrier."

And her chairs were often in demand, for Filmore was a deacon in Big Cabin Church, which stood at the foot of the green-clad mountain a mile down the road, and it was at the store that his brother deacons frequently met to transact church business.

One summer afternoon they held an important meeting. Abner Calihan, a member of the church and a good, industrious citizen, was to be tried for heresy.

"It has worried me more'n anything that has happened since them two Dutchmen over at Cove Spring swapped wives an' couldn't be convinced of the'r error," said long, lean Bill Odell, after he had come in and borrowed a candle-box to feed his mule in, and had given the animal eight ears of corn from the pockets of his long-tailed coat, and left the mule haltered at a hitching-post in front of the store.

"Ur sence the widder Dill swore she was gwine to sue Hank Dobb's wife fer witchcraft," replied Filmore, in a hospitable tone. "Take a cheer; it must be as hot as a bake-oven out thar in the sun."

Bill Odell took off his coat and folded it carefully and laid it across the beam of the scales, and unbuttoned his vest and sat down, and proceeded to mop his perspiring face with a red bandanna. Toot Bailey came in next, a quiet little man of about fifty, with a dark face, straggling gray hair, and small, penetrating eyes. His blue lean trousers were carelessly stuck into the tops of his clay-stained boots, and he wore a sack-coat, a "hickory" shirt, and a leather belt. Mrs. Filmore put her red head and broad, freckled face out of the door of her apartment to see who had arrived, and the next moment came out dusting a "split-bottomed" chair with her apron.

"How are ye, Toot?" was her greeting as she placed the chair for him between a jar of fresh honey and a barrel of sorghum molasses. "How is the sore eyes over yore way?"

"Toler'ble," he answered, as he leaned back against the counter and fanned himself with his slouch hat. "Mine is about through it, but the Tye children is a sight. Pizen-oak hadn't a circumstance."

"What did ye use?"

"Copperas an' sweet milk. It is the best thing I've struck. I don't want any o' that peppery eye-wash 'bout my place. It'd take the hide off'n a mule's hind leg."

"Now yore a-talkin'," and Bill Odell went to the water-bucket on the end of the counter. He threw his tobacco-quid away, noisily washed out his mouth, and took a long drink from the gourd dipper. Then Bart Callaway and Amos Sanders, who had arrived half an hour before and had walked down to take a look at Filmore's fish-pond, came in together. Both were whittling sticks and looking cool and comfortable.

"We are all heer," said Odell, and he added his hat to his coat and the pile of weights on the scale-beam, and put his right foot on the rung of his chair. "I reckon we mought as well proceed." At these words the men who had arrived last carefully stowed their hats away under their chairs and leaned forward expectantly. Mrs. Filmore glided noiselessly to a corner behind the counter, and with folded arms stood ready to hear all that was to be said.

"Did anybody inform Ab of the object of this meeting?" asked Odell.

They all looked at Filmore, and he transferred their glances to his wife. She flushed under their scrutiny and awkwardly twisted her fat arms together.

"Sister Calihan wuz in here this mornin'," she deposed in an uneven tone. "I 'lowed somebody amongst 'em ort to know what you-uns wuz up to, so I up an' told 'er."

"What did she have to say?" asked Odell, bending over the scales to spit at a crack in the floor, but not removing his eyes from the witness.

"Law, I hardly know what she didn't say! I never seed a woman take on so. Ef the last bit o' kin she had on earth wuz suddenly wiped from the face o' creation, she couldn't 'a' tuk it more to heart. Sally woz with 'er, an' went on wuss 'an her mammy."

"What ailed Sally?"

Mrs. Filmore smiled irrepressibly. "I reckon you ort to know, Brother Odell," she said, under the hand she had raised to hide her smile. "Do you reckon she hain't heerd o' yore declaration that Eph cayn't marry in no heretic family while yo're above ground? It wuz goin' the round at singin'-school two weeks ago, and thar hain't been a thing talked sence."

"I hadn't got a ioty to retract," replied Odell, looking down into the upturned faces for approval. "I'd as soon see a son o' mine in his box. Misfortune an' plague is boun' to foller them that winks at infidelity in any disguise ur gyarb."

"Oh, shucks! don't fetch the young folks into it, Brother Odell," gently protested Bart Callaway. "Them two has been a-settin' up to each other ever sence they wuz knee-high to a duck. They hain't responsible fer the doin's o' the old folks."

"I hain't got nothin' to take back, an' Eph knows it," thundered the tall deacon, and his face flushed angrily. "Ef the membership sees fit to excommunicate Ab Calihan, none o' his stock'll ever come into my family. But this is dilly-dallyin' over nothin'. You fellers'll set thar cocked up, an' chew an' spit, an' look knowin', an' let the day pass 'thout doin' a single thing. Ab Calihan is either fitten or unfitten, one ur t'other. Brother Filmore, you've seed 'im the most, now what's he let fall that's undoctrinal?"

Filmore got up and laid his clay pipe on the counter and kicked back his chair with his foot.

"The fust indications I noticed," he began, in a raised voice, as if he were speaking to some one outside, "wuz the day Liz Wambush died. Bud Thorn come in while I wuz weighing up a side o' bacon fur Ab, an' 'lowed that Liz couldn't live through the night. I axed 'im ef she had made her peace, and he 'lowed she had, entirely, that she wuz jest a-lyin' thar shoutin' Glory ever' breath she drawed, an' that they all wuz glad to see her reconciled, fer you know she wuz a hard case spiritually. Well, it woz right back thar at the fireplace while Ab wuz warmin' hisse'f to start home that he 'lowed that he hadn't a word to say agin Liz's marvelous faith, nur her sudden speritual spurt, but that in his opinion the doctrine o' salvation through faith without actual deeds of the flesh to give it backbone wuz all shucks, an' a dangerous doctrine to teach to a risin' gineration. Them wuz his words as well as I can remember, an' he cited a good many cases to demonstrate that the members o' Big Cabin wuzn't any more ready to help a needy neighbor than a equal number outside the church. He wuz mad kase last summer when his wheat wuz spillin' everybody that come to he'p wuz uv some other denomination, an' the whole lot o' Big Cabin folks made some excuse ur other. He 'lowed that you—"

Filmore hesitated, and the tall man opposite him changed countenance.

"Neil, hadn't you got a bit o' sense?" put in Mrs. Filmore, sharply.

"What did he say ag'in' me—the scamp?" asked Odell, firing up.

Filmore turned his back to his scowling wife, and took an egg from a basket on the counter and looked at it closely, as he rolled it over and over in his fingers.

"Lots that he ortn't to, I reckon," he said, evasively.

"Well, what wuz some of it? I hain't a-keerin' what he says about me."

"He 'lowed, fer one thing, that yore strict adheerance to doctrine had hardened you some, wharas religious conviction, ef thar wuz any divine intention in it, ort, in reason, to have a contrary effect. He 'lowed you wuz money-lovin' an' uncharitable an' unfergivin' an', a heap o' times, un-Christian in yore persecution o' the weak an' helpless—them that has no food an' raiment—when yore crib an' smokehouse is always full. Ab is a powerful talker, an'—"

"It's the devil in 'im a-talkin'," interrupted Odell, angrily, "an' it's plain enough that he ort to be churched. Brother Sanders, you intimated that you'd have a word to say; let us have it."

Sanders, a heavy-set man, bald-headed and red-bearded, rose. He took a prodigious quid of tobacco from his mouth and dropped it on the floor at the side of his chair. His remarks were crisp and to the point.

"My opinion is that Ab Calihan hain't a bit more right in our church than Bob Inglesel. He's got plumb crooked."

"What have you heerd 'im say? That's what we want to git at," said Odell, his leathery face brightening.

"More'n I keered to listen at. He has been readin' stuff he ortn't to. He give up takin' the Advocate, an' wouldn't go in Mary Bank's club when they've been takin' it in his family fer the last five year, an' has been subscribin' fer the True Light sence Christmas. The last time I met 'im at Big Cabin, I think it wuz the second Sunday, he couldn't talk o' nothin' else but what this great man an' t'other had writ somewhar up in Yankeedom, an' that ef we all keep along in our little rut we'll soon be the laughin'-stock of all the rest of the enlightened world. Ab is a slippery sort of a feller, an' it's mighty hard to ketch 'im, but I nailed 'im on one vital p'int."

Sanders paused for a moment, stroked his beard, and then continued: "He got excited sorter, an' 'lowed that he had come to the conclusion that hell warn's no literal, burnin' one nohow, that he had too high a regyard fer the Almighty to believe that He would amuse Hisse'f roastin' an' feedin' melted lead to His creatures jest to see 'em squirm."

"He disputes the Bible, then," said Odell, conclusively, looking first into one face and then another. "He sets his puny self up ag'in' the Almighty. The Book that has softened the pillers o' thousands; the Word that has been the consolation o' millions an' quintillions o' mortals of sense an' judgment in all ages an' countries is a pack o' lies from kiver to kiver. I don't see a bit o' use goin' furder with this investigation."

Just then Mrs. Filmore stepped out from her corner.

"I hain't been axed to put in," she said, warmly; "but ef I wuz you-uns I'd go slow with Abner Calihan. He's nobody fool. He's too good a citizen to be hauled an' drug about like a dog with a rope round his neck. He fit on the right side in the war, an' to my certain knowledge has done more to'ds keepin' peace an' harmony in this community than any other three men in it. He has set up with the sick an' toted medicine to 'em, an' fed the pore an' housed the homeless. Here only last week he got hisse'f stung all over the face an' neck helpin' that lazy Joe Sebastian hive his bees, an' Joe an' his triflin' gang didn't git a scratch. You may see the day you'll regret it ef you run dry shod over that man."

"We simply intend to do our duty, Sister Filmore," said Odell, slightly taken aback; "but you kin see that church rules must be obeyed. I move we go up thar in a body an' lay the case squar before 'im. Ef he is willin' to take back his wild assertions an' go 'long quietly without tryin' to play smash with the religious order of the whole community, he may stay in on probation. What do you-uns say?"

"It's all we kin do now," said Sanders; and they all rose and reached for their hats.

"You'd better stay an' look after the store," Filmore called back to his wife from the outside; "somebody mought happen along." With a reluctant nod of her head she acquiesced, and came out on the little porch and looked after them as they trudged along the hot road toward Abner Calihan's farm. When they were out of sight she turned back into the store. "Well," she muttered, "Abner Calihan may put up with that triflin' layout a-interfeerin' with 'im when he is busy a-savin' his hay, but ef he don't set his dogs on 'em he is a better Christian 'an I think he is an' he's a good un. They are a purty-lookin' set to be a-dictatin' to a man like him."

A little wagon-way, which was not used enough to kill the stubbly grass that grew on it, ran from the main road out to Calihan's house. The woods through which the little road had been cut were so thick and the foliage so dense that the overlapping branches often hid the sky.

Calihan's house was a four-roomed log building which had been weather-boarded on the outside with upright unpainted planks. On the right side of the house was an orchard, and beneath some apple-trees near the door stood an old-fashioned cider-press, a pile of acid-stained rocks which had been used as weights in the press, and numerous tubs, barrels, jugs, and jars, and piles of sour-smelling refuse, over which buzzed a dense swarm of honey-bees, wasps, and yellow-jackets. On the other side of the house, in a chip-strewn yard, stood cords upon cords of wood, and several piles of rich pine-knots and charred pine-logs, which the industrious farmer had on rainy days hauled down from the mountains for kindling-wood. Behind the house was a great log barn and a stable-yard, and beyond them lay the cornfields and the lush green meadow, where a sinuous line of willows and slender cane-brakes marked the course of a little creek.

The approach of the five visitors was announced to Mrs. Calihan and her daughter by a yelping rush toward the gate of half a dozen dogs which had been napping and snapping at flies on the porch. Mrs. Calihan ran out into the yard and vociferously called the dogs off, and with awed hospitality invited the men into the little sitting-room.

Those of them who cared to inspect their surroundings saw a rag carpet, walls of bare, hewn logs, the cracks of which had been filled with yellow mud, a little table in the center of the room, and a cottage organ against the wall near the small window. On the mantel stood a new clock and a glass lamp, the globe of which held a piece of red flannel and some oil. The flannel was to give the lamp color. Indeed, lamps with flannel in them were very much in vogue in that part of the country.

"Me an' Sally wuz sorter expectin' ye," said Mrs. Calihan, as she gave them seats and went around and took their hats from their knees and laid them on a bed in the next room. "I don't know what to make of Mr. Calihan," she continued, plaintively. "He never wuz this away before. When we wuz married he could offer up the best prayer of any young man in the settlement. The Mount Zion meetin'-house couldn't hold protracted meetin' without 'im. He fed more preachers an' the'r bosses than anybody else, an' some 'lowed that he wuz jest too natcherly good to pass away like common folks, an' that when his time come he'd jest disappear body an' all." She was now wiping her eyes on her apron, and her voice had the suggestion of withheld emotions. "I never calculated on him bringin' sech disgrace as this on his family."

"Whar is he now?" asked Odell, preliminarily.

"Down thar stackin' hay. Sally begun on 'im ag'in at dinner about yore orders to Eph, an' he went away 'thout finishin' his dinner. She's been a-cryin' an' a-poutin' en' takin' on fer a week, an' won't tech a bite to eat. I never seed a gal so bound up in anybody as she is in Eph. It has mighty nigh driv her pa distracted, kase he likes Eph, an' Sally's his pet." Mrs. Calihan turned her heard toward the adjoining room: "Sally, oh, Sally! are ye listenin'? Come heer a minute!"

There was silence for a moment, then a sound of heavy shoes on the floor of the next room, and a tall rather good-looking girl entered. Her eyes and cheeks were red, and she hung her head awkwardly, and did not look at any one but her mother.

"Did you call me, ma?"

"Yes, honey; run an' tell yore pa they are all heer,—the last one of 'em, an' fer him to hurry right on to the house an' not keep 'em a-waitin'."

"Yes-sum!" And without any covering for her head the visitors saw her dart across the back yard toward the meadow.

With his pitchfork on his shoulder, a few minutes later Abner Calihan came up to the back door of his house. He wore no coat, and but one frayed suspender supported his patched and baggy trousers. His broad, hairy breast showed through the opening in his shirt. His tanned cheeks and neck were corrugated, his hair and beard long and reddish brown. His brow was high and broad, and a pair of blue eyes shone serenely beneath his shaggy brows.

"Good evenin'," he said, leaning his pitchfork against the door-jamb outside and entering. Without removing his hat he went around and gave a damp hand to each visitor. "It is hard work savin' hay sech weather as this."

No one replied to this remark, though they all nodded and looked as if they wanted to give utterance to something struggling within them. Calihan swung a chair over near the door, and sat down and leaned back against the wall, and looked out at the chickens in the yard and the gorgeous peacock strutting about in the sun. No one seemed quite ready to speak, so, to cover his embarrassment, he looked farther over in the yard to his potato-bank and pig-pens, and then up into the clear sky for indications of rain.

"I reckon you know our business, Brother Calihan," began Odell, in a voice that broke the silence harshly.

"I reckon I could make a purty good guess," and Calihan spit over his left shoulder into the yard. "I hain't heerd nothin' else fer a week. From all the talk, a body'd 'low I'd stole somebody's hawgs."

"We jest had to take action," affirmed the self-constituted speaker for the others. "The opinions you have expressed," and Odell at once began to warm up to his task, "are so undoctrinal an' so p'int blank ag'in' the articles of faith that, believin' as you seem to believe, you are plumb out o' j'int with Big Cabin Church, an' a resky man in any God-feerin' community. God Almighty"—and those who saw Odell's twitching upper lip and indignantly flashing eye knew that the noted "exhorter" was about to become mercilessly personal and vindictive—"God Almighty is the present ruler of the universe, but sence you have set up to run ag'in' Him it looks like you'd need a wider scope of territory to transact business in than jest heer in this settlement."

The blood had left Calihan's face. His eyes swept from one stern, unrelenting countenance to another till they rested on his wife and daughter, who sat side by side, their faces in their aprons, their shoulders quivering with soundless sobs. They had forsaken him. He was an alien in his own house, a criminal convicted beneath his own roof. His rugged breast rose and fell tumultuously as he strove to command his voice.

"I hadn't meant no harm—not a speck," he faltered, as he wiped the perspiration from his quivering chin. "I hain't no hand to stir up strife in a community. I've tried to be law-abidin' an' honest, but it don't seem like a man kin help thinkin'. He—"

"But he kin keep his thinkin' to hisse'f," interrupted Odell, sharply; and a pause came after his words.

In a jerky fashion Calihan spit over his shoulder again. He looked at his wife and daughter for an instant, and nodded several times as if acknowledging the force of Odell's words. Bart Callaway took out his tobacco-quid and nervously shuffled it about in his palm as if he had half made up his mind that Odell ought not to do all the talking, but he remained mute, for Mrs. Calihan had suddenly looked up.

"That's what I told him," she whimpered, bestowing a tearful glance on her husband. "He mought 'a' kep' his idees to hisse'f ef he had to have 'em, and not 'a' fetched calumny an' disgrace down on me an' Sally. When he used to set thar atter supper an' pore over the True Light when ever'body else wuz in bed, I knowed it'd bring trouble, kase some o' the doctrine wuz scand'lous. The next thing I knowed he had lost intrust in prayer-meetin', an' 'lowed that Brother Washburn's sermons wuz the same thing over an' over, an' that they mighty nigh put him to sleep. An' then he give up axin' the blessin' at the table— somethin' that has been done in my family as fur back as the oldest one kin remember. An' he talked his views, too, fer it got out, an' me nur Sally narry one never cheeped it, fer we wuz ashamed. An' then ever' respectable woman in Big Cabin meetin'-house begun to stuff away from us as ef they wuz afeerd o' takin' some dreadful disease. It wuz hard enough on Sally at the start, but when Eph up an' tol' her that you had give him a good tongue-lashin', an' had refused to deed him the land you promised him ef he went any further with her, it mighty nigh prostrated her. She hain't done one thing lately but look out at the road an' pine an' worry. The blame is all on her father. My folks has all been good church members as fur back as kin be traced, an' narry one wuz ever turned out."

Mrs. Calihan broke down and wept. Calihan was deeply touched; he could not bear to see a woman cry. He cleared his throat and tried to look unconcerned.

"What step do you-uns feel called on to take next to—to what you are a-doin' of now?" he stammered.

"We 'lowed," replied Odell, "ef we couldn't come to some sort o' understandin' with you now, we'd fetch up the case before preachin' to-morrow an' let the membership vote on it. The verdict would go ag'in' you, Ab, fer thar hain't a soul in sympathy with you."

The sobbing of the two women broke out in renewed volume at the mention of this dreadful ultimatum, which, despite their familiarity with the rigor of Big Cabin Church discipline, they had up to this moment regarded as a vague contingent rather than a tangible certainty.

Calihan's face grew paler. Whatever struggle might have been going on in his mind was over. He was conquered.

"I am ag'in' bringin' reproach on my wife an' child," he conceded, a lump in his throat and a tear in his eye. "You all know best. I reckon I have been too forward an' too eager to heer myself talk." He got up and looked out toward the towering cliffy mountains and into the blue indefiniteness above them, and without looking at the others he finished awkwardly: "Ef it's jest the same to you-uns you may let the charge drap, an'—an' in future I'll give no cause fer complaint."

"That's the talk" said Odell, warmly, and he got up and gave his hand to Calihan. The others followed his example.

"I'll make a little speech before preachin' in the mornin'," confided Odell to Calihan after congratulations were over. "You needn't be thar unless you want to. I'll fix you up all right."

Calihan smiled faintly and looked shamefacedly toward the meadow, and reached outside and took hold of the handle of his pitchfork.

"I want to try to git through that haystack 'fore dark," he said, awkwardly. "Ef you-uns will be so kind as to excuse me now I'll run down and finish up. I'd sorter set myself a task to do, an' I don't like to fall short o' my mark."

Down in the meadow Calihan worked like a tireless machine, not pausing for a moment to rest his tense muscles. He was trying to make up for the time he had lost with his guests. Higher and smaller grew the great haystack as it slowly tapered toward its apex. The red sun sank behind the mountain and began to draw in its long streamers of light. The gray of dusk, as if fleeing from its darker self, the monster night, crept up from the east, and with a thousand arms extended moved on after the receding light.

Calihan worked on till the crickets began to shrill and the frogs in the marshes to croak, and the hay beneath his feet felt damp with dew. The stack was finished. He leaned on his fork and inspected his work mechanically. It was a perfect cone. Every outside straw and blade of grass lay smoothly downward, like the hair on a well-groomed horse. Then with his fork on his shoulder he trudged slowly up the narrow field-road toward the house. He was vaguely grateful for the darkness; a strange, new, childish embarrassment was on him. For the first time in life he was averse to meeting his wife and child.

"I've been spanked an' told to behave ur it 'ud go wuss with me," he muttered. "I never wuz talked to that away before by nobody, but I jest had to take it. Sally an' her mother never would 'a' heerd the last of it ef I had let out jest once. No man, I reckon, has a moral right to act so as to make his family miserable. I crawfished, I know, an' on short notice; but law me! I wouldn't have Bill Odell's heart in me fer ever' acre o' bottom-lan' in this valley. I wouldn't 'a' talked to a houn' dog as he did to me right before Sally an' her mother."

He was very weary when he leaned his fork against the house and turned to wash his face and hands in the tin basin on the bench at the side of the steps. Mrs. Calihan came to the door, her face beaming.

"I wuz afeerd you never would come," she said, in a sweet, winning tone. "I got yore beans warmed over an' some o' yore brag yam taters cooked. Come on in 'fore the coffee an' biscuits git cold."

"I'll be thar in a minute," he said; and he rolled up his sleeves and plunged his hot hands and face into the cold spring-water.

"Here's a clean towel, pa; somebody has broke the roller." It was Sally. She had put on her best white muslin gown and braided her rich, heavy hair into two long plaits which hung down her back. There was no trace of the former redness about her eyes, and her face was bright and full of happiness. He wiped his hands and face on the towel she held, and took a piece of a comb from his vest pocket and hurriedly raked his coarse hair backward. He looked at her tenderly and smiled in an abashed sort of way.

"Anybody comin' to-night?"

"Yes, sir."

"Eph Odell, I'll bet my hat!"

The girl nodded, and blushed and hung her head.

"How do you know?"

"Mr. Odell 'lowed I mought look fer him."

Abner Calihan laughed slowly and put his arm around his daughter, and together they went toward the steps of the kitchen door.

"You seed yore old daddy whipped clean out to-day," he said, tentatively. "I reckon yo're ashamed to see him sech a coward an' have him sneak away like a dog with his tail tucked 'tween his legs. Bill Odell is a power in this community."

She laughed with him, but she did not understand his banter, and preceded him into the kitchen. It was lighted by a large tallow-dip in the center of the table. There was much on the white cloth to tempt a hungry laborer's appetite—a great dish of greasy string-beans, with pieces of bacon, a plate of smoking biscuits, and a platter of fried ham in brown gravy. But he was not hungry. Slowly and clumsily he drew up his chair and sat down opposite his wife and daughter. He slid a quivering thumb under the edge of his inverted plate and turned it half over, but noticing that they had their hands in their laps and had reverently bowed their heads, he cautiously replaced it. In a flash he comprehended what was expected of him. The color surged into his homely face. He played with his knife for a moment, and then stared at them stubbornly, almost defiantly. They did not look up, but remained motionless and patiently expectant. The dread of the protracted silence, for which he was becoming more and more responsible, conquered him. He lowered his head and spoke in a low, halting tone:

"Good Lord, Father of us all, have mercy on our sins, and make us thankful fer these, Thy many blessings. Amen."

John Spencer Bassett

(1867–1928)

Born in Tarboro, North Carolina, in 1867, John Spencer Bassett entered Trinity College, which in 1886 would become Duke University. He received his degree in 1888 and taught for two years before returning to Trinity in 1890 as an instructor of English. Then he went on to Baltimore to pursue his graduate education at Johns Hopkins University. In 1894, after receiving his degree, Bassett returned to Trinity. Appalled both by the condition of intellectual life in the South and by its atmosphere of political and racial intolerance, Bassett and other members of the 9019 society, a secret

Trinity College organization that he had himself founded during his years there as a student, founded the *South Atlantic Quarterly* in order to provide a forum for liberal Southern thinkers. His article "Stirring up the Fires of Race Antipathy," which appeared in the *Quarterly* in October 1903, attacked both Democratic politicians and editors of Southern newspapers, accusing them of the offense specified in the article's title. Though Bassett stopped short of advocating social equality for blacks, he also opined that the winning of that equality was inevitable. The article was met with vociferous attacks by the editors whom it had condemned, and Josephus Daniels of the *Raleigh News and Observer* managed to precipitate a movement to have Bassett removed from his post at Trinity College. The effort was unsuccessful, and when Bassett left the *Quarterly* in 1905, he stressed his own conviction that the cause of intellectual freedom in the South had been advanced as a result of the brouhaha.

Stirring Up the Fires of Race Antipathy

Whatever be his view of the negro problem the average American knows that in the last five years there has been a notable increase in the general opposition to the negro. This development has occurred in both the South and North. In the South it has manifested itself more strenuously than in the North. We see it there in restrictions on the negro vote, in the passage of laws for "Jim Crow" cars, in an increasing resort to lynching, and in a general augmentation of the sensitive disposition on the part of Southerners to take fire at the hint of a "negro outrage." In the North it is seen, but not nearly so plainly as in the South, and it is especially noticeable because in that section it was supposed formerly not to exist at all. It is manifested in occasional acts of violence, as the recent lynching in Delaware, and in a growing opinion which one finds expressed in newspapers and in private conversation with Northern men. This opinion in the North is most strongly held in the large cities and it is noteworthy that in most of the large Northern cities there is a rapid increase of the negro population.

The causes of this development are perhaps numerous. But there are three facts which lie at its bottom and which are worthy of special consideration. These are; inherent race antipathy, the progress of the negro himself, and the fact that the negro problem is, and has been for a long time, a political matter.

Race antipathy is as old as the negro's residence in America. From the earliest days he has been regarded by the whites as an inferior man, and a man with whom unrestricted communication on the part of the whites is degrading. Eleven years after the landing of the first negro in Virginia this idea received a striking illustration in a decision of the highest court in the colony. It was decreed, says the chronicler, "that Hugh Davis be soundly whipped, before an assembly of negroes and others for abusing himself to the dishonor of God and shame of christians, by defiling his body in lying with a negro; which fault he is to acknowledge next Sabbath day." In 1726 Rev. John Blacknall, of North Carolina, was fined fifty pounds for marrying a white man and a mulatto woman. The commingling which we then set our hearts against in regard to things sexual we have also opposed in regard to most other matters of life. There must be no social equality, no eating together, no joining in amusements, and finally no mingling in religious worship. This feeling has not always appeared on the surface. It has frequently been so well covered over by indifference or opportunism, as to be nearly invisible, but if one will but scratch hard enough he will find it beneath this outer covering.

This antipathy is not mutual. It is not the white man against the negro and the negro against white man. It is not distasteful to the negro to eat his dinner or to go to churches or to theatres, with white men. He is quite willing to have equality. The race feeling is the contempt of the white man for the negro. It is the reaction of the superior against the touch of the inferior; for the white man has no doubt of his own superiority. It is doubtful if the average Southern white farmer would admit that the highest negro in America is superior to the Southern hired man who is white.

The development of the negro since the war has been calculated to intensify this natural race feeling. Singularly enough both his progress and his regression under the regime of freedom have brought down on him the hostility of whites. His regression might well do this because it has stood for his lapse into a lower state after the removal of the supporting hand of the white man. This lapse has not occurred in all sections of the race—perhaps it has not occurred with a majority of the race—but there can be no denial that some negroes today are more worthless than any negroes in slavery. The master was always a restraining hand on the negro, holding back at both extremes. He kept the slave man from going into the higher fields of intellectual development; he confirmed his lack of high moral purpose and he weighed down his self-respect and his individuality, all of which were checks on the best negroes. On the other hand the master was a check on the lowest tendencies of the negro. He restrained his dissipations; he sought to save him from disease; he tried to make him honest and peaceable; and he was very careful that he should not be an idler. The removal of the masters's authority has produced a marked change on each of these extremes. The upper class negro has seized with surprising readiness his new opportunity. No sensible man in the North or in the South who is not blinded by passion will deny that the better negroes of the country have made a remarkable record since the days of emancipation. In the same way the lower class have also made a rapid progress. Among them idleness and shiftlessness have increased; petty crimes and quarrels have increased; coarse ideas have found greater sway; and viciousness has augmented. These good and these bad habits are the fruits of his freedom.

Neither of these two classes, the upper and the lower, are all the negroes; and in forgetting this fact some well intentioned people have fallen into serious error. A man whose mind runs away into baseless optimism is apt to point to Booker T. Washington as a product of the negro race. Now Washington is a great and good man, a Christian statesman, and take him all in all the greatest man, save General Lee, born in the South in a hundred years; but he is not a typical negro. He does not even represent the better class of negroes. He is an exceptional man; and, endowed as he is, it is probable that he would have remained uneducated but for the philanthropic intervention of white men. The race, even the best of them, are so far behind him that we cannot in reason look for his reproduction in the present generation. It is, therefore, too much to hope, for a continued appearance of such men in the near future. It is also too much to set his development up as a standard for his race. To expect it is to insure disappointment.

In the same way some people who are pessimistic in regard to the negro base their opinions on their observations of the negro of the lowest class. Said a gentlemen to me recently: "The negro race will die out within a century." His reason was this: a few years ago there were sixteen negroes in the jail of his county, and the county physician had told him that fifteen of them had venereal diseases. From this he argued that the physical constitution of the race was imperiled. Manifestly, it is illogical to measure either the health, morals, or other quality of the negro by the similar quality of the most depraved. It is true that there is in the race a large lowest class—and a small upper class. And it is true that this lowest class gives the race a certain discouraging tendency. But there is also a strong, and perhaps an increasing, upper class which is ever fighting back its own weakness and shaking off its own shackles.

In this connection I cannot refrain from speaking of a certain false notion in regard to the negro which has caused much error in the opinions of men North and South. I refer to the notion that the ante-bellum negro was a benign old man or a gracious old "mammy," a guardian of the family children, and a dignified expression in ebony of the family honor. The falseness of this notion is due partly to the imaginations of certain novelists and partly to the emotional memories of most Southern women and some Southern men. As to the latter it is pardonable failing. A woman may well remember her old "mammy" and have no recollection of hair-lipped Peter who ran away with a long scar across his forehead, as the advertisements put it. But men who undertake to describe the life of the old South ought to know what it was before they talk about it. Mr. Thomas Nelson Page's castles in Virginia are also castles in the air. The typical ante-bellum negro was the field hand. When we compare the old and the new negro we ought to place the new man by the side of that individual. And if we do not remember what kind of a man the field hand of slavery was—for our novelists have not remembered much about him—we may inform ourselves in the instructive pages of Olmsted, or in Fanny Kemble's interesting "Journal." Nine-tenths of the negroes now in America are descended from this part of the old slave population.

It is important for us to note that the progress of the negro has brought him opposition as well as his regression. Of this the white men who oppose him may not be conscious. They may even fancy that they are the best of friends to the negro. But the advance of the negro in education and in economic conditions brings him ever into new conflicts with the white man. This is true because his advance means a greater degree of comfort—a greater disposition to desire the means of higher life. As long as he was merely a laborer it was not hard to draw the line which divided him from other people. It was at that time not hard for him to be content with inferior hotels, or with accommodations in the kitchens of better hotels. In these days he is becoming too intelligent and too refined to be content with these things. He demands a better place. Formerly, it did not hurt his pride to ride in a "Jim Crow" car; for he had little or no pride of that kind. Now, he considers this law a badge of inferiority, a mark of intolerance which he will some day seek to wipe out.

With most white Americans there is a very definite notion that the negro has his "place." In their minds this notion is a caste feeling. It is an inherited feeling; and it is not difficult to find facts in the negro's life which seem to give it the support of expediency. To make him know his "place," and to make him keep his "place" sum up the philosophy of many people in reference to this intricate and perplexing problem. But we ought to remember that such an idea is neither scientific nor charitable. The "place" of every man in our American life is such one as his virtues and his capacities may enable him to take. Not even a black skin and a flat nose can justly caste in this country.

The most aggravating cause, however, of the present antipathy between the races is the fact that the negro question is in politics. It has been in politics since the day when the negro became the chief factor in American labor. It was so in Georgia in the days of the benevolent Oglethorpe, when the chief political desire of the people was the admission of negro slaves. It appeared in the great constitutional convention of 1787, when certain Southern States spoke darkly of the future in case they should not be allowed to import slaves. It was a political question in the two angry decades which preceded the Civil War, when abolition fires burned fiercely on the one side and pro-slavery fires on the other. It was still in politics in 1860 and 1861, when eleven States seceded from the union rather than run the risk of having the "black republicans" abolish slavery. It was still a political question in the days of constitutional amendment and in the reactionary days of 1875. It has become a political question in another form within the last ten years. Whatever concerns our secular life we undertake to regulate by political action; and it is not strange that we have so often brought law to bear on this question.

But the negro question has gone into politics recently in a party, rather than in a truly political, sense. It has been seized upon by party leaders as a means of winning votes. This has been particularly true in the South. Always since 1875 the Southern democratic campaigners have used the negro issue with good effect. A certain brilliant party leader, who now hold a large share of public attention, used in the early days of his career, to make his best appeal to the gaping audiences at the country cross roads by asking all the men who wanted to vote the white man's ticket to pass to one side of the road and all who would vote the black man's ticket to stay where they were. When the crowd began to move across the road it was hard for a white man to stand in his tracks. That was the worst manifestation of this form of the issue twenty years ago.

Ten years ago the South was in the embrace of the populist movement, designed by its leaders to organize the mass of farmers into a political association. This movement, if successful, would have broken up the democratic party. It was strong enough to make itself dreaded by the party. To fight it down the leaders of the old party were led to seek a strong issue. The negro issue was selected. It lent itself to the exigency because the populists, wherever they triumphed, had been in alliance with the republicans and had brought a few negroes into office. These negroes were usually quietly disposed, but they were frequently unfit for office; and the very fact that they were negroes made it impossible for them to execute their offices on white men. They were also sometimes unduly elated over their success, being merely ignorant negroes. The result was various conflicts. This gave an opportunity to cry "Negro domination." Raising the cry by the one side produced irritation on the other side, and the very denunciation of negroes for "outrages" produced a continuation of the "outrages." From that time to this the negro issue in the South has taken on a new phrase.

In order to ensure its ascendency the old party passed the suffrage amendments. It promised the people that if they would by this means eliminate the negro vote the old condition of a solid white party would disappear and that we should have no more cheating of negroes out of their votes. The success of these campaigns convinced the leaders that the issue was a popular one. Having won a complete success they are loath, in spite of their promise, to give up the means by which they succeeded. It is now good party tactics to keep the negro question before the people. Booker T. Washington's dinner at the White House was seized on for this purpose. The watchful party leaders saw in it an opportunity to make capital with the mass of the people. Not long after this there occurred in Washington what has been known since that time as the "bi-racial reception." This, too, at once suggested itself as a popular means of appealing to the people.

So successful were these two attempts that some political editors have learned to look for similar occasions. At present very inconsiderable affairs are made to do service in the same way. An illustration of how this works is seen in the following incident: In the month of August, 1903, Booker T. Washington and a party of prominent negroes, most of them northern men, were going North after the adjournment of a negro business men's conference in Knoxville, Tenn. He telegraphed to the proprietors of a certain dinner-house on the railroad to know if, on the arrival of the train, he and his party could be given breakfast. The reply was favorable. When the train arrived the regular boarders had been served. The party of negroes, which numbered thirty-eight, were given seats in the regular dining-room. The proprietors understood that there were no white people on the train who desired breakfast, but a few presented themselves and tables were improvised for them in other rooms. The negroes, according to the evidence, bore themselves quietly and unobtrusively. There was no attempt to mix the races. It was not alleged that the accommodations of the one were not as good as those of the other. This incident became in the hands of the politicians a flagrant "outrage." A certain emotional and "yellow" newspaper was conspicuous in its lurid descriptions. Black men, it said, were placed before white men. Formerly a white man ate at the first table and sent the negro's dinner out to the kitchen. Now the negro took the principal seat and the whites took what they could get. It gave a long and hysterical description of this very small affair and ended with the observation that the whole thing was due to the fact that President Roosevelt once had Professor Washington to dine with him. Following the lead of this prominent newspaper a hundred smaller sheets took up the matter in the same vein; and the dinner-house affair now became very much of a sensation. Day after day for more than a fortnight it continually reappeared in the State press, and the echoes of it are still heard.

The effect of such agitation on the people is decided. It unquestionably tends to make votes. The removal of the negro from the voting population has destroyed the oldest and best political capital of the party; and its place is being supplied by these sensational appeals to the race feeling of the white man. But the affair has a more serious side. This political agitation is awaking a demon in the South. There is today more hatred of whites for blacks and of blacks for whites than ever before. Each race seems to be caught in a torrent of passion, which, I fear, is leading the country to an end which I dare not name.

Up in the North a little Southern gentleman with a glib tongue has been going about recently advocating the formation of a black republic in the Philippines to which all the negroes shall be sent. A man who can solve the negro problem in no better way than to advocate deportation has but little capacity to solve problems. Worthy old Hinton Rowan Helper, who still lives to hear the first threatening notes of a new "Impending Crisis," has a more feasible solution, viz: "to fossilize them beneath the American sod." But neither solution will work. The only solution reserved for us is the adoption of these children of Africa into our American life. In spite of our race feeling, of which the writer has his share, they will win equality at some time. We cannot remove them, we cannot kill them, we cannot prevent them from advancing in civilization. They are now very weak; some day they will be stronger. They are now ignorant and passion-wrought; some day they will be wiser and more self-restrained. I do not know just what form the conflict will take. It may be merely a political conflict: it may be more than that. I am persuaded that it is in many respects the old conflict between Roman plebs and Roman patricians over again. It ought to be shorter than that struggle and the issue ought be more fortunate than the issue of the Roman conflict; for American life is richer and better than Roman life.

Some day the white man will beat the negro out of his cowardice, and then "red shirts" will exist no more. Some day the negro will be a great industrial factor in the community; some day he will be united under strong leaders of his own. In that time his struggle will not be so unequal as now. In that time, let us hope, he will have brave and Christian leaders.

The writer has no solution for the negro problem. He does not think that it can be solved by writing magazine articles, or by making speeches. It is the manifestation of a great social force, which will run its course in spite of our laying on of hands. The best we can do is to understand this force as fully as possible, and probably to check in a measure some of its most erratic impulses. We are now just entering the stage of conflict; and this is because the negro is now beginning to be strong enough to make opposition. The conflict will be fiercer in the future than in the present. Lynchings and "outrages" will, perhaps, become more frequent than they now are. As long as one race contends for the absolute inferiority of the other the struggle will go on with increasing intensity. But if some day the spirit of conciliation shall come into the hearts of the superior race the struggle will become less strenuous. The duty of brave and wise men is to seek to infuse the spirit of conciliation into these white leaders of white men. Shall they also be beasts, like the dull-faced black men who stand over against them? Is the white man not superior to the black man—superior in mind, superior in opportunity, superior in obligation to do acts of charity?

William Sydney Porter

(1862–1910)

Though he seldom treated Southern themes in his fiction, William Sydney Porter was a hugely popular fiction writer before he ever published his first book, *Cabbages and Kings*, in 1904. By then he had already written and published (under the legendary pseudonym O. Henry) more than 150 short stories in New York periodicals like *Everybody's*, *McClure's*, and the weekly *New York Sunday World*, stories which offered tantalizing fictive glimpses into Porter's own widely varied life experiences, usually topped off with a trademark (if somewhat artificial at times) surprise ending. Porter would live only six more years, but in that time, he almost doubled his previous literary production, publishing stories that filled eight more volumes before his death, with seven posthumous collections following.

Porter was the second son of a Greensboro, North Carolina, physician who abandoned his practice following his wife's death after the birth of a third child in 1865. Turned over to his grandmother and aunt to be raised and educated, Porter was educated privately (in his aunt's school) and encouraged to read widely. At seventeen he left school to work in an uncle's drugstore, and in 1881 he was himself licensed as a pharmacist. In 1882, he left for Texas, where he worked for the next fifteen years as a cattle hand, bookkeeper, drug clerk, and draftsman. In 1887, he married Athol Estes Roach, who encouraged him to pursue a writing career, an activity which to that point had been only a sideline. His first publications appeared in 1887 in *The Detroit Free Press* and *Truth*. In 1891, he took a job as a teller at the First National Bank of Austin. Then, in 1894 he bought a printing press and the rights to a local scandal sheet that he renamed *The Rolling Stone*. Never a success, *The Rolling Stone* survived only a year, but Porter began embezzling funds from the bank to keep the *Stone* afloat. When he was charged in 1896, he fled to Honduras; however, he returned in 1897 when he learned his wife was incurably ill. She died later that year. Although Porter served three years in the Ohio Penitentiary at Columbus, during his prison years, he continued to publish (and matured as a writer), taking for the first time the pseudonym O. Henry and selling stories based on yarns he heard from fellow prisoners. After being released from prison, Porter made his way to New York, where he would live the rest of his life and which would provide the setting for most of his best-known works. *Cabbages and Kings* appeared in 1904, and *The Four Million* in 1906. "A Municipal Report" was published in 1910, shortly before his death.

A Municipal Report

> *The cities are full of pride,*
>   *Challenging each to each—*
> *This from her mountainside,*
>   *That from her burthened beach.*
>   R. KIPLING.

Fancy a novel about Chicago or Buffalo, let us say, of Nashville, Tennessee! There are just three big cities in the United States that are "story cities"— New York, of course, New Orleans, and, best of the lot, San Francisco.
                                                    —FRANK NORRIS.

East is East, and West is San Francisco, according to Californians. Californians are a race of people; they are not merely inhabitants of a State. They are the Southerners of the West. Now, Chicagoans are no less loyal to their city; but when you ask them why, they stammer and speak of lake fish and the new Odd Fellows Building. But Californians go into detail.

Of course they have, in the climate, an argument that is good for half an hour while you are thinking of your coal bills and heavy underwear. But as soon as they come to mistake your silence for conviction, madness comes upon them, and they picture the city of the Golden Gate as the Bagdad of the New World. So far, as a matter of opinion, no refutation is necessary. But dear cousins all (from Adam and Eve descended), it is a rash one who will lay his finger on the map and say: "In this town there can be no romance—what could happen here?" Yes, it is a bold and a rash deed to challenge in one sentence history, romance, and Rand and McNally.

NASHVILLE.—A city, port of delivery, and the capital of the State of Tennessee, is on the Cumberland River and on the N. C. & St. L. and the L. & N. railroads. This city is regarded as the most important educational centre in the South.

I stepped off the train at 8 P.M. Having searched thesaurus in vain for adjectives, I must, as a substitution, hie me to comparison in the form of a recipe.

Take of London fog 30 parts; malaria 10 parts; gas leaks 20 parts; dewdrops gathered in a brick yard at sunrise, 25 parts; odor of honeysuckle 15 parts. Mix.

The mixture will give you an approximate conception of a Nashville drizzle. It is not so fragrant as a moth-ball nor as thick as pea-soup; but 'tis enough—'twill serve.

I went to a hotel in a tumbril. It required strong self-suppression for me to keep from climbing to the top of it and giving an imitation of Sidney Carton. The vehicle was drawn by beasts of a bygone era and driven by something dark and emancipated.

I was sleepy and tired, so when I got to the hotel I hurriedly paid it the fifty cents it demanded (with approximate lagniappe, I assure you). I knew its habits; and I did not want to hear it prate about its old "marster" or anything that happened "befo' de wah."

The hotel was one of the kind described as "renovated." That means $20,000 worth of new marble pillars, tiling, electric lights and brass cuspidors in the lobby, and a new L. & N. time table and a lithograph of Lookout Mountain in each one of the great rooms above. The management was without reproach, the attention full of exquisite Southern courtesy, the service as slow as the progress of a snail and as good-humored as Rip Van Winkle. The food was worth traveling a thousand miles for. There is no other hotel in the world where you can get such chicken livers *en brochette*.

At dinner I asked a Negro waiter if there was anything doing in town. He pondered gravely for a minute, and then replied: "Well, boss, I don't really reckon there's anything at all doin' after sundown."

Sundown had been accomplished; it had been drowned in the drizzle long before. So that spectacle was denied me. But I went forth upon the streets in the drizzle to see what might be there.

It is built on undulating grounds; and the streets are lighted by electricity at a cost of $32,470 per annum.

As I left the hotel there was a race riot. Down upon me charged a company of freedmen, or Arabs, or Zulus, armed with—no, I saw with relief that they were not rifles, but whips. And I saw dimly a caravan of black, clumsy vehicles; and at the reassuring shouts, "Kyar you anywhere in the town, boss, fuh fifty cents," I reasoned that I was merely a "fare" instead of a victim.

I walked through long streets, all leading uphill. I wondered how those streets ever came down again. Perhaps they didn't until they were "graded." On a few of the "main streets" I saw lights in stores here and there; saw street cars go by conveying worthy burghers hither and yon; saw people pass engaged in the art of conversation, and heard a burst of semi-lively laughter issuing from a soda-water and ice-cream parlor. The streets other than "main" seemed to have enticed upon their borders houses consecrated to peace and domesticity. In many of them lights shone behind discreetly drawn window shades, in a few pianos tinkled orderly and irreproachable music. There was, indeed, little "doing." I wished I had come before sundown. So I returned to my hotel.

In November, 1864, the Confederate General Hood advanced against Nashville, where he shut up a National force under General Thomas. The latter then sallied forth and defeated the Confederates in a terrible conflict.

All my life I have heard of, admired, and witnessed the fine markmanship of the South in its peaceful conflicts in the tobacco-chewing regions. But in my hotel a surprise awaited me. There were twelve bright, new, imposing, capacious brass cuspidors in the great lobby, tall enough to be called urns and so wide-mouthed that the crack pitcher of a lady baseball team should have been able to throw a ball into one of them at five paces distant. But, although a terrible battle had raged and was still raging, the enemy had not suffered. Bright, new, imposing, capacious, untouched, they stood. But, shades of Jefferson Brick: the tile floor—the beautiful tile floor! I could not avoid thinking of the battle of Nashville, and trying to draw, as is my foolish habit, some deductions about hereditary marksmanship.

Here I first saw Major (by misplaced courtesy) Wentworth Caswell. I knew him for a type the moment my eyes suffered from the sight of him. A rat has no geographical habitat. My old friend, A. Tennyson, said, as he so well said almost everything:

Prophet, curse me the blabbing lip,
And curse me the British vermin, the rat.

Let us regard the word "British" as interchangeable *ad lib*. A rat is a rat.

This man was hunting about the hotel lobby like a starved dog that had forgotten where he had buried a bone. He had a face of great acreage, red, pulpy, and with a kind of sleepy massiveness like that of Buddha. He possessed one single virtue—he was very smoothly shaven. The mark of the beast is not indelible upon a man until he goes about with a stubble. I think that if he had not used his razor that day I would have repulsed his advances, and the criminal calendar of the world would have been spared the addition of one murder.

I happened to be standing within five feet of a cuspidor when Major Caswell opened fire upon it. I had been observant enough to perceive that the attacking force was using Gatlings instead of squirrel rifles, so I sidestepped so promptly that the major seized the opportunity to apologize to a noncombatant. He had the blabbing lip. In four minutes he had become my friend and had dragged me to the bar.

I desire to interpolate here that I am a Southerner. But I am not one by profession or trade. I eschew the string tie, the slouch hat, the Prince Albert, the number of bales of cotton destroyed by Sherman, and plug chewing. When the orchestra plays "Dixie" I do not cheer. I slide a little lower on the leather-cornered seat and, well, order another Würzburger and wish that Longstreet had—but what's the use?

Major Caswell banged the bar with his fist, and the first gun at Fort Sumter re-echoed. When he fired the last one at Appomattox I began to hope. But then he began on family trees, and demonstrated that Adam was only a third cousin of a collateral branch of the Caswell family. Genealogy disposed of, he took up, to my distaste, his private family matters. He spoke of his wife, traced her descent back to Eve, and profanely denied any possible rumor that she may have had relations in the land of Nod.

By this time I began to suspect that he was trying to obscure by noise the fact that he had ordered the drinks, on the chance that I would be bewildered into paying for them. But when they were down he crashed a silver dollar loudly upon the bar. Then, of course, another serving was obligatory. And when I had paid for that I took leave of him brusquely; for I wanted no more of him. But before I had obtained my release he had prated loudly of an income that his wife received, and showed a handful of silver money.

When I got my key at the desk the clerk said to me courteously: "If that man Caswell had annoyed you, and if you would like to make a complaint, we will have him ejected. He is a nuisance, a loafer, and without any known means of support, although he seems to have some money most the time. But we don't seem to be able to hit upon any means of throwing him out legally."

"Why no," said I, after some reflection; "I don't see my way clear to making a complaint. But I would like to place myself on record as asserting that I do not care for his company. Your town," I continued, "seems to be a quiet one. What manner of entertainment, adventure, or excitement have you to offer to the stranger within you gates?"

"Well, sire," said the clerk, "there will be a show here next Thursday. It is—I'll look it up and have the announcement sent up to your room with the ice water. Good-night."

After I went up to my room I looked out the window. It was only about ten o'clock, but I looked upon a silent town. The drizzle continued, spangled with dim lights, as far apart as currants in a cake sold at the Ladies' Exchange.

"A quiet place," I said to myself, as my first shoe struck the ceiling of the occupant of the room beneath mine. "Nothing of the life here that gives color and good variety to the cities in the East and West. Just a good, ordinary, humdrum, business town."

Nashville occupies a foremost place among the manufacturing centres of the country. It is the fifth boot and shoe market in the United States, the largest candy and cracker manufacturing city in the South, and does an enormous wholesale dry-goods, grocery, and drug business.

I must tell you how I came to be in Nashville, and I assure you the digression brings as much tedium to me as it does to you. I was traveling elsewhere on my own business, but I had a commission from a Northern literary magazine to stop over there and establish a personal connection between the publication and one of its contributors, Azalea Adair.

Adair (there was no clue to the personality except the handwriting) had sent in some essays (lost art!) and poems that had made the editors swear approvingly over their one o'clock luncheon. So they had commissioned me to round up said Adair and corner by contract his or her output at two cents a word before some other publisher offered her ten or twenty.

At nine o'clock the next morning, after my chicken livers *en brochette* (try them if you can find that hotel), I strayed out into the drizzle, which was still on for an unlimited run. At the first corner I came upon Uncle Cæsar. He was a stalwart Negro, older than the pyramids, with gray wool and a face that reminded me of Brutus, and a second afterwards of the late King Cettiwayo. He wore the most remarkable coat that I ever had seen or expect to see. It reached to his ankles and had once been a Confederate gray in colors. But rain and sun and age had so variegated it that Joseph's coat, beside it, would have faded to a pale monochrome. I must linger with that coat, for it has to do with the story—the story that is so long in coming, because you can hardly expect anything to happen in Nashville.

Once it must have been the military coat of an officer. The cape of it had vanished, but all adown its front it had been frogged and tasseled magnificently. But now the frogs and tassels were gone. In their stead had been patiently stitched (I surmised by some surviving "black mammy") new frogs made of cunningly twisted common hempen twine. This twine was frayed and disheveled. It must have been added to the coat as a substitute for vanished splendors, with tasteless but painstaking devotion, for it followed faithfully the curves of the long-missing frogs. And, to complete the comedy and pathos of the garment, all its buttons were gone save one. The second button from the top alone remained. The coat was fastened by other twine strings tied through the buttonholes and other holes rudely pierced in the opposite side.

There was never such a weird garment so fantastically bedecked and of so many mottled hues. The lone button was the size of a half-dollar, made of yellow horn and sewed on with coarse twine.

This Negro stood by a carriage so old that Ham himself might have started a hack line with it after he left the ark with the two animals hitched to it. As I approached he threw open the door, drew out a feather duster, waved it without using it, and said in deep, rumbling tones:

"Step right in, suh; ain't a speck of dust in it—jus' got back from a funeral, suh."

I inferred that on such gala occasions carriages were given an extra cleaning. I looked up and down the street and perceived that there was little choice among the vehicles for hire that lined the curb. I looked in my memorandum book for the address of Azalea Adair.

"I want to go to 861 Jessamine Street," I said, and was about to step into the hack. But for an instant the thick, long, gorilla-like arm of the Negro barred me. On his massive and saturnine face a look of sudden suspicion and enmity flashed for a moment. Then, with quickly returning conviction, he asked, blandishingly: "What are you gwine there for, boss?"

"What is that to you?" I asked, a little sharply.

"Nothin', suh, jus' nothin'. Only it's a lonesome kind of part of town and few folks ever has business out there. Step right in. The seats is clean—jes' got back from a funeral, suh."

A mile and a half it must have been to our journey's end. I could hear nothing but the fearful rattle of the ancient hack over the uneven brick paving; I could smell nothing but the drizzle, now further flavored with coal smoke and something like a mixture of tar and oleander blossoms. All I could see through the streaming windows were two rows of dim houses.

The city has an area of 10 square miles; 181 miles of streets, of which 137 miles are paved; a system of waterworks that cost $2,000,000 with 77 miles of mains.

Eight-sixty-one Jessamine Street was a decayed mansion. Thirty yards back from the street it stood, outmerged in a splendid grove of trees and untrimmed shrubbery. A row of box bushes overflowed and almost hid the paling fence from sight; the gate was kept closed by a rope noose that encircled the gate post and the first paling of the gate. But when you got inside you saw that 861 was a shell, a shadow, a ghost of former grandeur and excellence. But in the story, I have not yet got inside.

When the hack had ceased from rattling and the weary quadrupeds came to a rest I handed my jehu his fifty cents with an additional quarter, feeling a glow of conscious generosity as I did so. He refused it.

"It's two dollars, suh," he said.

"How's that?" I asked. "I plainly heard you call out at the hotel. 'Fifty cents to any part of the town.'"

"It's two dollars, suh," he repeated obstinately. "It's a long ways from the hotel."

"It is within the city limits and well within them," I argued. "Don't think that you have picked up a greenhorn Yankee. Do you see those hills over there?" I went on, pointing toward the east (I could not see them, myself, for the drizzle); "well, I was born and raised on their other side. You old fool nigger, can't you tell people from other people when you see 'em?"

The grim face of King Cettiwayo softened. "Is you from the South, suh? I reckon it was them shoes of yourn fooled me. They is somethin' sharp in the toes for a Southern gen'l'man to wear."

"Then the change is fifty cents, I suppose?" said I, inexorably.

His former expression, a mingling of cupidity and hostility, returned, remained ten seconds, and vanished.

"Boss," he said, "fifty cents is right; but I *needs* two dollars, suh; I'm *obleeged* to have two dollars. I ain't *demandin'* it now, suh; after I knows whar you's from; I'm jus sayin' that I *has* to have two dollars to-night and business is mighty po'."

Peace and confidence settled upon his heavy features. He had been luckier than he had hoped. Instead of having picked up a greenhorn, ignorant of rates, he had come upon an inheritance.

"You confounded old rascal," I said, reaching down to my pocket, "you ought to be turned over to the police."

For the first time I saw him smile. He knew; *he knew;* HE KNEW.

I gave him two one-dollar bills. As I handed them over I noticed that one of them had seen parlous times. Its upper right-hand corner was missing, and it had been torn through in the middle, but joined again. A strip of blue tissue paper, pasted over the split, preserved its negotiability.

Enough of the African bandit for the present: I left him happy, lifted the rope, and opened the creaky gate.

The house, as I said, was a shell. A paint brush had not touched it in twenty years. I could not see why a strong wind should not have bowled it over like a house of cards until I looked again at the trees that hugged it close—the trees that saw the battle of Nashville and still drew their protecting branches around it against storm and enemy and cold.

Azalea Adair, fifty years old, white-haired, a descendant of the cavaliers, as thin and frail as the house she lived in, robed in the cheapest and cleanest dress I ever saw, with an air as simple as a queen's, received me.

The reception room seemed a mile square, because there was nothing in it except some rows of books, on unpainted white-pine bookshelves, a cracked marble-topped table, a rag rug, a hairless horsehair sofa, and two or three chairs. Yes, there was a picture on the wall, a colored crayon drawing of a cluster of pansies. I looked around for the portrait of Andrew Jackson and the pinecone hanging basket but they were not there.

Azalea Adair and I had conversation, a little of which will be repeated to you. She was a product of the old South, gently nurtured in the sheltered life. Her learning was not broad, but was deep and of splendid originality in its somewhat narrow scope. She had been educated at home, and her knowledge of the world was derived from inference and by inspiration. Of such is the precious, small group of essayists made. While she talked to me I kept brushing my fingers, trying, unconsciously, to rid them guiltily of the absent dust from the half-calf backs of Lamb, Chaucer, Hazlitt, Marcus Aurelius, Montaigne, and Hood. She was exquisite, she was a valuable discovery. Nearly everybody nowadays knows too much—oh, so much too much—of real life.

I could perceive clearly that Azalea Adair was very poor. A house and a dress she had, not much else, I fancied. So, divided between my duty to the magazine and my loyalty to the poets and essayists who fought Thomas in the valley of the Cumberland, I listened to her voice which was like a harpsichord's, and found that I could not speak of contracts. In the presence of the nine Muses and the three Graces one hesitated to lower the topic to two cents. There would have to be another colloquy after I had regained my commercialism. But I spoke of my mission, and three o'clock of the next afternoon was set for the discussion of the business proposition.

"Your town," I said, as I began to make ready to depart (which is the time for smooth generalities) "seems to be a quiet, sedate place. A home town, I should say, where few things out of the ordinary ever happen."

It carries on an extensive trade in stoves and hollow ware with the West and South, and its flouring mills have a daily capacity of more than 2,000 barrels.

Azalea Adair seemed to reflect.

"I have never thought of it that way," she said, with a kind of sincere intensity that seemed to belong to her. "Isn't it in the still, quiet places that things do happen? I fancy that when God began to create the earth on the first Monday morning one could have leaned out one's window and heard the drops of mud splashing from His trowel as He built up the everlasting hills. What did the noisest project in the world—I mean the building of the tower of Babel—result in finally? A page and a half of Esperanto in the *North American Review*."

"Of course," said I, platitudinously, "human nature is the same everywhere; but there is more color—er—more drama and movement and—er—romance in some cities that in others."

"On the surface," said Azalea Adair. "I have traveled many times around the world in a golden airship wafted on two wings—print and dreams. I have seen (on one of my imaginary tours) the Sultan of Turkey bowstring with his own hands one of his wives who had uncovered her face in public. I have seen a man in Nashville tear up his theatre tickets because his wife was going out with her face covered—with rice powder. In San Francisco's Chinatown I saw the slave girl Sing Yee dipped slowly, inch by inch, in boiling almond oil to make her swear she would never see her American lover again. She gave in when the boiling oil had reached three inches above her knee. At a euchre party in East Nashville the other night I saw Kitty Morgan cut dead by seven of her schoolmates and lifelong friends because she had married a house painter. The boiling oil was sizzling as high as her heart; but I wish you could have seen the fine little smile that she carried from table to table. Oh, yes, it is a humdrum town. Just a few miles of red brick houses and mud and stores and lumber yards."

Some one had knocked hollowly at the back of the house. Azalea Adair breathed a soft apology and went to investigate the sound. She came back in three minutes with brightened eyes, a faint flush on her cheeks, and ten years lifted from her shoulders.

"You must have a cup of tea before you go," she said, "and a sugar cake."

She reached and shook a little iron bell. In shuffled a small Negro girl about twelve, barefoot, not very tidy, glowering at me with thumb in mouth and bulging eyes.

Azalea Adair opened a tiny, worn purse and drew out a dollar bill, a dollar bill with the upper right-hand corner missing, torn in two pieces and pasted together again with a strip of blue tissue paper. It was one of those bills I had given the piratical Negro—there was no doubt of it.

"Go up to Mr. Baker's store on the corner, Impy," she said, handing the girl the dollar bill, "and get a quarter of a pound of tea—the kind he always sends me—and ten cents' worth of sugar cakes. Now, hurry. The supply of tea in the house happens to be exhausted," she explained to me.

Impy left by the back way. Before the scrape of her hard, bare feet had died away on the back porch, a wild shriek—I was sure it was hers—filled the hollow house. Then the deep, gruff tones of an angry man's voice mingled with the girl's further squeals and unintelligible words.

Azalea Adair rose without surprise or emotion and disappeared. For two minutes I heard the hoarse rumble of the man's voice; then something like an oath and a slight scuffle, and she returned calmly to her chair.

"This is a roomy house," she said, "and I have a tenant for part of it. I am sorry to have to rescind my invitation to tea. It is impossible to get the kind I always use at the store. Perhaps to-morrow Mr. Baker will be able to supply me."

I was sure that Impy had not had time to leave the house. I inquired concerning street-car lines and took my leave. After I was well on my way I remembered that I had not learned Azalea Adair's name. But to-morrow would do.

That same day I started in on the course of inquiry that this uneventful city forced upon me. I was in the town only two days, but in that time I managed to lie shamelessly by telegraph, and to be an accomplice—after the fact, if that is the correct legal term—to a murder.

As I rounded the corner nearest my hotel the Afrite coachman of the polychromatic, nonpareil coat seized me, swung open the dungeony door of his peripatetic sarcophagus, flirted his feather duster and began his ritual: "Step right in, boss. Carriage is clean—jus' got back from a funeral. Fifty cents to any——"

And then he knew me and grinned broadly. "'Scuse me, boss; you is de gen'l'man what rid out with me dis mawnin'. Thank you kindly, suh."

"I am going out to 861 again to-morrow afternoon at three," said I, "and if you will be here, I'll let you drive me. So you know Miss Adair?" I concluded, thinking of my dollar bill.

"I belonged to her father, Judge Adair, suh," he replied.

"I judge that she is pretty poor," I said, "She hasn't much money to speak of, has she?"

For an instant I looked again at the fierce countenance of King Cettiwayo, and then he changed back to an extortionate old Negro hack driver.

"She ain't gwine to starve, suh," he said, slowly. "She has reso'ces, suh; she has reso'ces."

"I shall pay you fifty cents for the trip," said I.

"Dat is puffeckly correct, suh," he answered, humbly. "I jus' *had* to have dat two dollars dis mawnin', boss."

I went to the hotel and lied by electricity. I wired the magazine: "A. Adair holds out for eight cents a word."

The answer that came back was: "Give it to her quick, you duffer."

Just before dinner "Major" Wentworth Caswell bore down upon me with the greetings of a long-lost friend. I have seen few men whom I have so instantaneously hated, and of whom it was so difficult to be rid. I was standing at the bar when he invaded me; therefore I could not wave the white ribbon in his face. I would have paid gladly for the drinks, hoping thereby, to escape another; but he was one of those despicable, roaring, advertising bibbers who must have brass bands and fireworks attend upon every cent that they waste in their follies.

With an air of producing millions he drew two one-dollar bills from a pocket and dashed one of them upon the bar. I looked once more at the dollar bill with the upper right-hand corner missing, torn through the middle, and patched with a strip of blue tissue paper. It was my dollar bill again. It could have been no other.

I went up to my room. The drizzle and the monotony of a dreary, eventless Southern town had made me tired and listless. I remember that just before I went to bed I mentally disposed of the mysterious dollar bill (which might have formed the clue to a tremendously fine detective story of San Francisco) by saying to myself sleepily: "Seems as if a lot of people here own stock in the Hack-Driver's Trust. Pays dividends promptly, too. Wonder if——" Then I fell asleep.

King Cettiwayo was at his post the next day, and rattled my bones over the stones out to 861. He was to wait and rattle me back again when I was ready.

Azalea Adair looked paler and cleaner and frailer than she had looked on the day before. After she had signed the contract at eight cents per word she grew still paler and began to slip out of her chair. Without much trouble I managed to get her up on the antediluvian horsehair sofa and then I ran out to the sidewalk and yelled to the coffee-colored Pirate to bring a doctor. With a wisdom that I had not suspected in him, he abandoned his team and struck off up the street afoot, realizing the value of speed. In ten minutes he returned with a grave, gray-haired, and capable man of medicine. In a few words (worth much less than eight cents each) I explained to him my presence in the hollow house of mystery. He bowed with stately understanding, and turned to the old Negro.

"Uncle Cæsar," he said, calmly, "run up to my house and ask Miss Lucy to give you a cream pitcher full of fresh milk and half a tumbler of port wine. And hurry back. Don't drive—run. I want you to get back sometime this week."

It occurred to me that Dr. Merriman also felt a distrust as to the speeding powers of the land-pirate's steeds. After Uncle Cæsar was gone, lumberingly, but swiftly, up the street, the doctor looked me over with great politeness and as much careful calculation until he had decided that I might do.

"It is only a case of insufficient nutrition," he said. "In other words, the result of poverty, pride, and starvation. Mrs. Caswell has many devoted friends who would be glad to aid her, but she will accept nothing except from that old Negro, Uncle Cæsar, who was once owned by her family."

"Mrs. Caswell?" said I, in surprise. And then I looked at the contract and saw that she had signed it "Azalea Adair Caswell."

"I thought she was Miss Adair," I said.

"Married to a drunken, worthless loafer, sir," said the doctor. "It is said that he robs her even of the small sums that her old servant contributes toward her support."

When the milk and wine had been brought the doctor soon revived Azalea Adair. She sat up and talked of the beauty of the autumn leaves that were then in season and their height of color. She referred lightly to her fainting seizure as the outcome of an old palpitation of the heart. Impy fanned her as she lay on the sofa. The doctor was due elsewhere, and I followed him to the door. I told him that it was within my power and intentions to make a reasonable advance of money to Azalea Adair on future contributions to the magazine, and he seemed pleased.

"By the way," he said, "perhaps you would like to know that you have had royalty for a coachman. Old Cæsar's grandfather was a king in Congo. Cæsar himself has royal ways, as you may have observed."

As the doctor was moving off I heard Uncle Cæsar's voice inside: "Did he git bofe of dem two dollars from you, Mis' Zalea?"

"Yes, Cæsar," I heard Azalea Adair answer, weakly. And then I went in and concluded business negotiations with our contributor. I assumed the responsibility of advancing fifty dollars, putting it as a necessary formality in binding our bargain. And then Uncle Cæsar drove me back to the hotel.

Here ends all of the story as far as I can testify as a witness. The rest must be only bare statements of facts.

At about six o'clock I went out for a stroll. Uncle Cæsar was at his corner. He threw open the door of his carriage, flourished his duster, and began his depressing formula: "Step right in, suh. Fifty cents to anywhere in the city—hack's puffickly clean, suh—jus' got back from a funeral——"

And then he recognized me. I think his eyesight was getting bad. His coat had taken on a few more faded shades of color, the twine strings were more frayed and ragged, the last remaining button—the button of yellow horn—was gone. A motley descendant of kings was Uncle Cæsar!

About two hours later I saw an excited crowd besieging the front of the drug store. In a desert where nothing happens this was manna; so I wedged my way inside. On an extemporized couch of empty boxes and chairs was stretched the mortal corporeality of Major Wentworth Caswell. A doctor was testing him for the mortal ingredient. His decision was that it was conspicuous by its absence.

The erstwhile Major had been found dead on a dark street and brought by curious and ennuied citizens to the drug store. The late human being had been engaged in terrific battle—the details showed that. Loafer and reprobate though he had been, he had been also a warrior. But he had lost. His hands were yet clinched so tightly that his fingers would not be opened. The gentle citizens who had known him stood about and searched their vocabularies to find some good words, if it were possible, to speak of him. One kind-looking man said, after much thought: "When 'Cas' was about fo'teen he was one of the best spellers in the school."

While I stood there the fingers of the right hand of "the man that was," which hung down the side of a white pine box, relaxed, and dropped something at my feet. I covered it with one foot quietly, and a little later on I picked it up and pocketed it. I reasoned that in his last struggle his hand must have seized that object unwittingly and held it in a death grip.

At the hotel that night the main topic of conversation, with the possible exceptions of politics and prohibition, was the demise of Major Caswell. I heard one man say to a group of listeners:

"In my opinion, gentlemen, Caswell was murdered by some of these no-account niggers for his money. He had fifty dollars this afternoon which he showed to several gentlemen in the hotel. When he was found the money was not on his person."

I left the city the next morning at nine, and as the train was crossing the bridge over the Cumberland River I took out of my pocket a yellow horn overcoat button the size of a fifty-cent piece, with frayed ends of coarse twine hanging from it, and cast it out of the window into the slow, muddy waters below.

I wonder what's doing in Buffalo!

Walter Hines Page

(1855–1918)

Born near Raleigh, North Carolina, Walter Hines Page attended Trinity College (now Duke University), Randolph Macon, and Johns Hopkins University. After receiving his degree from Johns Hopkins in 1878, he taught literature in Louisville, Missouri, for two years before beginning his career as a journalist. After writing for a series of newspapers over the next decade, Page went to work in 1887 for the *Forum*, first as business manager and later as editor. In 1898 he became editor of the *Atlantic Monthly*, reviving what was at the time the declining reputation of that well-known journal. His only novel, *The Southerner*, appeared in 1909 and provides an autobiographical recounting of life in the South following the Civil War. Though as editor of *The Atlantic* Page's influence was substantial, as a critic he was limited. He tended to champion popular taste, denigrating experimental fiction in favor of works more accessible to a general readership.

Politically, Page championed the creed of the New South, denouncing what he saw as the false illusions perpetuated by writers like his own distant cousin, Thomas Nelson Page. In essays like "The Forgotten Man" and "The Rebuilding of Old Commonwealths," Page championed a new future for the South to be won through a commitment to education and industry. *The Southerner* attacks the "ghosts" of racism, religious orthodoxy, and Southern nationalism which he believed hindered necessary and inevitable reforms.

from *The Southerner*

Chapter IV. The Flower of the South

The son of a general, if he were at all a decent fellow, had, of course, a higher social rank among the boys at the Graham school than the son of a colonel. There was some difficulty in deciding the exact rank of a judge or of a governor, as a father; but the son of a preacher had a fair chance of a good social rating, especially of an Episcopalian clergyman. A Presbyterian preacher came next in rank.

I was at first at a social disadvantage. My father had been a Methodist—that was bad enough; but he had had no military title at all. If it had become known among the boys that he had been a "Union man"—I used to shudder at the suspicion in which I should be held. And the fact that my father had had no military title did at last become known; and one day Tom Warren, a boy from the "capital city," twitted me with this unpleasing fact. In a moment or two, we were clinched in a hand-to-hand fight. Of course a crowd gathered, and presently Colonel Graham himself appeared.

"Stand back and see it done fairly," said he, and the boys made the circle wider.

"What is it about?"

"He called me a liar, sir," said Tom.

"Well, no gentleman will take that," said the Colonel.

"I didn't call him a liar, but I do now, and I'll choke him, too," and I made a grasp at Tom's throat; and we were again a whirling mass of swinging arms and dodging heads.

475

"Halt!" Instantly we stood and saluted. My collar was torn and my face was bleeding from Tom's scratches. But we stood erect in silence.

"Sir," said I.

"Speak."

"He cast reflections on my family, sir."

"What have you to say, Tom?"

"I said, sir, that his father was not in the war."

"He said my father was a coward, sir."

Some boy in the crowd cried out, "I'd fight at that."

"Halt!" cried the Colonel, and we kept from clinching again, and again we stood erect, each quivering with anger.

"I see you'll have to fight it out," said the Colonel in a moment, "before you feel better. Square off. Give them room."

Then the fight began again. After we had scratched and pounded one another and torn one another's clothes, I at last threw Tom, and the Colonel called out, "Halt!"

We were on our feet in a second. Each saluted. We were commanded to shake hands. The Colonel explained to the crowd in a sort of oratorical fashion that he had known Mr. Worth, that he had given his time and fortune to his country, and that there was no better man in any part of the Government's service. The incident was over. The crowd of boys went away. The Colonel went back to his office smiling. I was unspeakably grateful to him.

At his office, which was a wooden shanty at one end of the barracks, the Colonel renewed his conversation with a gentleman who had come to plead for his son's reinstatement in the school.

"I cannot tell you, sir," he said, "how deeply I am grieved. But I cannot argue the subject. In fact, I have no power to reinstate your son. I could not keep the honour of the school—I could not even keep the boys, if he were to return. They would appeal to their parents and most of them would be called home. They are the flower of the South, sir."

This boy had cheated on an examination and had been sent home by the first train after his conviction.

That night, a half hour before taps, when my three room-mates were absent, one of my best friends came into my room.

"Worth," he asked, "wasn't your father a colonel?"

"No, but he was in the service of the Confederate Government and he wasn't a coward."

"I didn't mean that he was a coward. But I want to tell you something," and he went on in the sad tone in which we speak of great misfortunes. "You won't tell anybody, Worth, will you? My father—my father isn't a colonel nor nothin'. But I swear he isn't a coward. I saw him whip a man once. Worth, don't you ever tell anybody—he's a good father to me"; and the boy had a sob in his voice. When another fellow came into the room, he warmly shook my hand—since, as he saw it, we had a common misfortune—and he went away.

The rough beds were turned down from their edges whereon they rested all day against the wall of the log room, the poles were drawn that held the blankets and the mattresses in place; and we four room-mates went to bed. Taps were sounded; all lights were out; and the day of my first fight with Tom Warren was done.

The boys said that I had shown my mettle; among my friends I had a day or two of some little glory; and at the beginning of my second year I was made an officer of the battalion, and only "brave" boys were chosen as officers.

Lest you should imagine (and thereby, too, fall into a grave error) that fighting was the only manly art cultivated at the Graham school, you must be informed that, between military exercises, successful onslaughts were made on Latin and mathematics. The master's educational code contained three laws:

A boy must have a sound body, and the more roughly you use him the sounder his body will become and the greater his physical bravery.

A boy must know Latin or he cannot be a gentleman.

A boy must know mathematics or his mind will not be trained.

And the years swiftly passed at these barracked labours, as the years pass swiftly elsewhere at that time of life. Our forced growth—for we had reached the emotional level of manhood while we were yet boys—gave us rapid development.

One high day of school life every year was the parade-day of the battalion at the State Fair. The cadets wore their new gray uniforms of the same colour as the tattered coats in which their fathers and kinsmen had fought on Virginian battlefields. And, on this particular year, the second year of my cadetship, it was a greater day than usual, for a bust of Stonewall Jackson was to be presented to Colonel Graham. Colonel Flint, a veteran of great oratorical power, who also had served under General Jackson, was to make the presentation address; and all the Confederate veterans within reach had been invited. They came from every part of the land, many with armless sleeves, many on crutches, most of them in well-worn, and many in ragged, gray uniforms, in battered hats and caps, and some with remnants of flags. They were the saddest relics of a brave army, I imagine, that were ever seen; for most of them were now but wrecks of men. Years of exposure, of ill-fed fighting, for some of them years of prison life, and years of neglected wounds and injuries since, years of poverty, too, and years of political oppression—these men had borne the physical scourging of the nation for its error of slavery.

They had borne it innocently, too, for they were plain countrymen who were blameless victims of our sectional wrath. But they had borne it also recklessly. They had looked on death—had lived with it, indeed; and they had miraculously survived and crawled to barren homes from the clash and slaughter and from starvation and such deadly vain endeavour as no other men had ever known and lived; and now a brief period was left them to muse on their great adventure, which so filled their minds that thought on other things was impossible.

The little bust was covered and placed on a pedestal which stood on a platform under the trees in the fairground this beautiful October day; and the battalion of cadets stood as a guard of honour about it, in their shining new uniforms.

A bugle was sounded and a drum was heard, and the veterans formed in line at a distance, to march to the benches that had been reserved for them next the standing cadets. A vast crowd filled the few seats farther away and stood all round about.

When the bugle sounded, a mighty shout went up. It was a yell that became a roar, and the crowd took it up, yell after yell, and then the band struck up "Dixie." Every voice in that vast crowd sang. The veterans were by this time in line, limping and leaping rather than marching, coming with more eagerness than precision to the place left for them.

As they came within sight of the crowd every man and woman arose. Hats and handkerchiefs were thrown into the air. They shouted, they clapped, they yelled. The old soldiers bared their heads and limped and leaped along, barely hearing the military commands of their leaders. At last they reached their places; quiet came; and after a long prayer the orator was introduced.

As soon as he stood up every old soldier arose and yell after yell was given in his honour.

"Come down, we want to hug you, Colonel," one man, with stubs of arms, cried out.

But at last the orator began. Even if he did speak almost two hours, nobody in the audience, except the babies, became weary, not even the hundreds of men who stood on the outskirts of the crowd. He was talking about the Lost Cause and Stonewall Jackson, and many of his hearers would have sat till they had dropped asleep from exhaustion, hearing this great adventure praised. It was meat and drink and rest to them.

The climax of Colonel Flint's long speech was the unveiling of the bust. It was covered with a cloth and a cadet stood at either side, who, when the orator gave the cue, was to pull the cords which would remove the covering.

I was one of these. At last Colonel Flint stepped to the very edge of the platform, gave the signal to uncover the bust, and, lifting his great voice to its utmost, said:

"Soldiers, Comrades, Heroes! Behold our immortal commander!"

The band played Dixie again, but nobody now heard it. The old soldiers yelled—yelled—yelled—yell on yell, great folds of shrieking applause; and the crowd echoed every burst of it. The veterans swayed forward.

"God bless old Stonewall!"

"There he is!"

"Get out of my way, boy."

"The immortal leader!"

The cadets presented bayonets to keep them back.

Old soldiers snatched the guns from the boys' hands and, yelling, broke their line. Some were stuck by the bayonets. But no accident nor incident stopped them. The officers who sat on the platform motioned them back. But, with "God bless old Stonewall," on they rushed.

Before anybody knew how the feat was done, one veteran snatched the little bust from its pedestal and, holding it high, kissed it. Another took it and embraced it. It was passed back through the struggling throng. Old men, one after another, grasped the orator by the neck and everybody seemed to be embracing somebody else. As Colonel Graham cried orders to his cadets to re-form their line at the side of the stand, his order was cut short by the shouts of a group who gathered about him and threw their hands wildly in the air.

In a dazed state, I was standing at one side with the cord still in my hand.

"You showed him to us," shouted a gigantic mountaineer, and he seized me and handed me to his neighbour. Thus I was passed from man to man far out into crowd, my cap lost and my coat torn, before I could reach the ground.

I saw my cousin Margaret in the crowd near where I reached the ground. She had been weeping as everybody else wept from such an emotional strain. But she laughed at my plight and waved her hand at me.

After the long railroad ride back to the school that night, I had just life enough left in me, when I pulled my bunk down and recalled the wild scene of the day, to remember that my father had once spoken of the Confederacy as "a foolish enterprise," and I fell asleep wondering if he had been mistaken.

I have since sometimes thought that many of the men who survived that unnatural war unwittingly did us a greater hurt than the war itself. It gave every one of them the intensest experience of his life, and ever afterwards he referred every other experience to this. Thus it stopped the thought of most of them as an earthquake stops a clock. The fierce blow of battle paralyzed the mind. Their speech was in a vocabulary of war; their loyalties were loyalties, not to living ideas or duties, but to old commanders and to distorted traditions. They were dead men, most of them, moving among the living as ghosts; and yet, as ghosts in a play, they held the stage.

Revered, unreasoning, ever-present, some of them became our masters, others became beggars—some masters and beggars, too. We did them honour and we doled them alms, and for years they frightened us into actions that we did not approve, for we feared to offend them. But now, forgetfulness and peace—peace and forgiveness—they are almost all gone; we honour them while we pity them; they were our fathers and they were brave; but we did not become ourselves till they were buried, if indeed we are become ourselves yet; for this was not merely a fierce war—it was a fierce civil war.

Reconstruction resulted in slow and tenuous progress in the Lower South, despite drastic economic and social changes. One obvious deterrant to progress was the continued preoccupation of white Southerners in preserving a segregated society. Elsewhere in this anthology are data compiled by John Shelton Reed, showing the frequency and distribution of lynchings occurring in the South between 1900 and 1930, an era heralded as one of great industrial and agricultural promise. While it is true that by 1900 the black ownership of land was a stunning development in the New South,[1] Reed's conclusions suggest a correlation between areas where lynchings of African Americans (commonly) took place and locales where antebellum cotton production had been highest. The Cotton Kingdom would find ways to preserve segregation and keep the antebellum caste system intact.

The code of honor fostered by these aristocratic notions often produced unprecedented violence. In his landmark study *The Promise of New South: Life After Reconstruction*, Edward Ayers describes the South of the 1880s and 1890s as a cauldron of violent turmoil:

> The New South was a notoriously violent place. Homicide rates among blacks and whites were among the highest in the country, among the highest in the world. Lethal weapons seemed everywhere. Guns as well as life were cheap; two or three dollars would buy a pistol known in the trade as a "nigger killer," or one of its major competitors, the "owl-head" or the "American Bulldog." In a memoir about a Presbyterian picnic, one man recalled that each young gentleman desired to have a "pistol, a jack knife, and a pair of brass knucks," all of which were considered "the proper accouterments of the young blades of the day." One young man working at a cotton compress on the border between the Carolinas wrote a friend for a favor. "I want you to get me a gun if you know where you can get a good one, and send it to me. This is a tough place up here. I am simply afraid to go out at night without one. They shoot about one hundred times every night."[2]

Amazingly, many African Americans in the Lower South chose to weather such turbulence and to remain in the plantation belt rather than follow the lead of Upper South blacks who tended to move to points above the Mason-Dixon line. Ownership of land may have offered incentive for many blacks to remain. Whites, too, were moving in large numbers to cities, abandoning ancestral farms and plantations, leaving "the white-columned porticos" of the once fashionable architecture "mouldering in decay."[3] Indeed, more whites than blacks exited the South, the whites fulfilling their own vision of manifest destiny by settling in Texas or California. Young people of both races stunned their elders by leaving the land behind and adopting the values of urban commerce.[4] This change would prompt older whites to worry "that their sons and grandsons would misunderstand—or worse, target—the struggles of their elders."[5]

One possible feature of such misunderstanding was the desire of a former generation of white males to shelter kinswomen from the harshness of life. Worship of mothers and protection of sisters had been common in antebellum life. However, the war had encouraged women to be far grittier and more independent than it had been imagined they could be. After all, women had tended farms and managed plantations without the aid of male kinfolk. The war had also made widows and orphans of many of these women. Kinlessness, a previously all but unknown phenomenon in the South, was now commonplace. Single, widowed, and divorced women had to support themselves and, often, whole families, and cities and towns offered the most encouraging prospects for employment. Mill towns throughout the South grew in proportion to the large numbers of white women willing to work in the sewing industry. Women's ambition took them into other areas, too, enabling author Rebecca Harding Davis to remark that "they manage plantations and shops; they raise stock, hold office, publish newspapers. Indeed, while Northern women have been clamoring for their rights, Southern women have found their way into more careers than they."[6]

With the decline of the plantation system, a new social structure was emerging. The disinherited and dislocated children of the Old South were turning to commerce and merchandising in a new spirit of enterprise and self-sufficiency. New technologies and products for consumption created new opportunities and restructured existing class lines. Each generation began to expect a higher standard of living than that experienced by the previous generation. Even to regard progress in this way represented a radical shift in Southern consciousness, considering the South's former belief that an absence of change was all that progress demanded.

In the 1880s boosters began promoting the South as a place of cooperation and opportunity.[7] In his speech to the New England Society of New York in 1886, enthusiast Henry Grady, editor of the *Atlanta Constitution*, declared the Old South dead while hyperbolizing the virtues of a new industrial South:

> But what is the sum of our work? We have found out that in the summing up, the free Negro counts more than he did as a slave. We have planted the schoolhouse on the hilltop and made it free to white and black. We have sowed towns and cities in the place of theories, and put business above politics. We have challenged your spinners in Massachusetts and your ironmakers in Pennsylvania. We have learned that the $400,000,000 annually received from our cotton crop will make us rich when the supplies that make it are home-raised. We have reduced the commercial rate of interest from 24 to 6 per cent bonds. We have learned that one northern immigrant is worth fifty foreigners; and have smoothed the path to southward, wiped out the place where Mason and Dixon's line used to be, and hung out latchstring to you and yours.

Grady went so far as to say that "the relations of the Southern people with the Negro are close and cordial," a statement that ignored such entrenched social customs as those forbidding the two races from shaking hands, walking together, or fraternizing in public. Grady's philosophy, while at its core displaying a good measure of wish fulfillment, recognized racial harmony as an essential ingredient of economic progress, and vice versa.

Such was the premise underlying the 1895 Cotton States and International Exposition that was held in Atlanta. Symbolizing Grady's support from the railroads, local manufacturers, and the federal government, the exposition attracted national attention, showcasing the South's phenomenal rise from defeat and its subsequent determination to match the North's industrial prowess. Ironically, the exposition itself was segregated, with white and black spectators forced to sit in separate sections and compelled, as always, to use separate facilities. The only expression of black enterprise to be found was the Negro Building, an edifice located on the outskirts of the exposition. It was hardly the advertisement for racial progress that Grady had envisioned. Nor would such a setting prove anything but controversial for Booker T. Washington, undoubtedly the best-known and most visible African American leader of his day.

In "The Atlanta Exposition Address," later published in *Up From Slavery* (1901), Washington said what white Atlanta business and civic leaders hoped he would say. Recognizing the contempt many Southern whites had for black political activism, Washington adopted a stance of accommodation, urging African Americans to help "cement the friendship of the races" by developing practical rather than political skills. Washington urged the training of blacks for manual and domestic occupations, believing this to be one way of achieving economic progress without causing social upheaval. In the central metaphor of his speech, the author exhorts both races to "cast down your buckets where you are," using all available resources to promote the "business and industrial prosperity of the South. . . ." Acknowledging the validity of the separate but equal principle with regard to social circumstances, Washington shows the impracticality of observing a strict color line where economics are concerned. Washington's policy of conciliation would draw fire from such black leaders as W. E. B. DuBois, who saw Washington's speech as a retreat from the struggles of African Americans, who were still subject to lynchings, disenfranchisement, and the effects of Jim Crow.

Only in music and literature did a blending of cultures and a sharing of traditions occur with relative success. Europeans, Africans, and Native Americans—whatever their feelings for one another—came into repeated contact in the South, trading folklore that would enrich existing oral traditions and would offer opportunities for transcribers to preserve diverse treatments of common materials. Thus, in this section are included African American folktales that share similarities with stories found in the Cherokee oral tradition. (See Appalachia Recognized on page 000). One archetypal figure present in the folklore of both cultures is the hero-god and trickster, represented here by Brer Rabbit and made famous by Joel Chandler Harris. Like Grady, Harris was an editor with the *Atlanta Constitution*, where Brer Rabbit and Uncle Remus first appeared in serial sketches in 1876.

Calling himself an "accidental author," Harris recorded stories he'd heard from Old Harbert and Uncle George Terrell, slaves at the Turnwold plantation, where Harris was sent to work as a printer at age thirteen. Although Harris may not always have been familiar with the levels of irony and linguistic codes shared by African Americans and embedded in the Uncle Remus stories, the author nonetheless served a crucial role as cultural anthropologist. As early as 1922, James Weldon Johnson acknowledged Harris's contribution in keeping alive the secular tradition of African American folktales that was largely ignored by the black intelligentsia of the period. As Johnson points out, the sacred tradition dominated during the several decades following the Civil War. Consequently, the trickster stories, ghost tales, and preacher jokes (often erotic) lost ground among African Americans, who were forced to prove their worth by displaying an exaggerated morality while playing down what Johnson calls their distinctive American products.

The desire to glorify the Old South and its folkways stirred both critics and supporters. Among the more obvious critics of the Deep South plantation system and its excesses was George Washington Cable, whose *The Negro Question* argues for the civil rights of African Americans while urging Southerners to adopt the "National idea" of "safety, order, and progress." As a Confederate veteran, Cable returned to New Orleans, his birthplace and childhood home, in 1884, where he studied Louisiana history and wrote historical sketches for the New Orleans newspaper *Picayune*. Although not a Creole himself, Cable focused literary attention on the fallen aristocrats of the decaying Creole community who symbolized, for the author, the sad, self-destructive plight of the Old South. Cable's "Jean-ah Poquelin" is the story of a once wealthy indigo planter turned slave trader who loses all to the "unkind human world," failing to conceal the secret shame of a long-hidden brother—"a leper, as white as snow" living on the family grounds.

Cable would find his antithesis in Grace Elizabeth King, who proclaimed that Cable had "stabbed New Orleans in the back" in order to augment his status with the Northern press. Enraged by Cable's depiction of the Creoles, King set out to defend New Orleans and uphold its traditions. She "had deep personal feelings about the humiliation suffered by her family after the Civil War," when they were forced to forfeit property and personal fortune to Louisiana's Reconstruction government.[8] A recent reevaluation of King's work maintains that its contribution lies not in simply defending the older social order of the once "brilliant little world of New Orleans"; rather, scholar Anne Jones targets King's treatment of women as an equally important focus of the writer's canon.[9] In "La Grande Demoiselle," King captures the complex circumstances of a woman and her family who experience a reversal of fortune because of the war. Yet, the narrator reminds us of the marginalized status of women in general, observing that ". . . a woman seems the quickest thing forgotten when once the important affairs of life come to men for consideration."

Turn-of-the-century writer Corra Harris of Georgia cocked a sharp eye on her homeland, finding its writers "reactionary, defensive, and greedy," not to mention pathologically enamored of the past. Her fiction, then, demonstrates a successful blend of realism and irony that challenges sentimental notions and rosy depictions of a South too often found in stories written by her contemporaries. Recognizing the hackneyed conventions of Southern romance, Harris begins *The Recording Angel* (1912) with a digression, apologizing to readers "who are accustomed to being humored by the author with a duel or a scandal in the first chapter." Continuing in a satirical vein, Harris describes Ruckersville, Georgia, the setting of her novel, as a "town admirably situated to have developed into a flourishing city." That Ruckersville has not developed along these lines can be attributed to one cause: "But your aristocrat never builds a city. He can ride against one and conquer it, and he can save it from an invading army, but he has neither the patience nor the energy to build one. It takes a parvenu, or at least a Yankee to do that." This feature of social criticism in Harris's work would anticipate a similar focus by latter-day realists.

The social philosophy of Georgia poet Sidney Lanier took a different turn from that of Harris. Having spent four months as a prisoner of war in the Union prison at Point Lookout, Maryland, Harris returned to his native Georgia, where he spent most of his life struggling with tuberculosis. His deeply meditative and lyrical poems (perhaps owing to Lanier's talents as a musician) explore the relationship of nature, art, and philosophy. Like Wordsworth, Coleridge, and other poets in the Romantic tradition, Lanier describes the oppressiveness of a world increasingly motivated by commerce. In "The Symphony," for instance, Lanier apostrophizes the commercial impulse in this vain wish: "O trade! O trade! Would thou wert dead." Elsewhere in the poem, Lanier alludes to the dehumanizing effects of life in the numerous mills springing up in the South. The very nature of what it means to be human in an increasingly machinelike world is the overriding theme of Lanier's work.

A child of privilege much like Elizabeth King, Kate Chopin belonged to a family whose financial reverses occurred in 1878 and 1879. Forced to leave New Orleans and move to her family's plantation near Cloutierville, the burgeoning author "observed the people and customs that she would later chronicle in local-color stories and sketches."[10] However, Chopin did not remain a local colorist but emerged as this period's sharpest-eyed and most controversial realist. Revealing the South's often unspoken shadow side, Chopin explored "a woman's right to question society's expectations of her," broaching such taboo topics as divorce, alcoholism, and extramarital affairs. Perhaps no theme was more volatile to Southern audiences than miscegenation, the scenario offered in Chopin's "Désirée's Baby." In both subject and style, Chopin was a pioneer pointing the direction that much twentieth-century Southern literature would take.

Notes

1. For a thorough and incisive discussion of black land ownership, postbellum migration in the New South, and changing economic conditions, see Edward L. Ayers's *The Promise of the New South* (New York: Oxford University Press, 1992), 26–80.
2. Ayers, 155.
3. Ayers, 25.
4. Ayers, 26.
5. Ayers, 27.
6. Ayers, 28.
7. Ayers, 20.
8. Thomas Richardson, "Local Color in Louisiana," *The History of Southern Literature*, ed. Louis D. Rubin et al. (Baton Rouge: Louisiana State University Press, 1985), 203.
9. Richardson, 204.
10. Anne Rowe, "Kate Chopin," *The History of Southern Literature*, ed. Louis D. Rubin et al. (Baton Rouge: Louisiana State University Press, 1985), 230.

African American Folktales

When Brer Deer and Brer Terrapin Runned a Race

Brer Deer and Brer Terrapin was a-courting of Mr. Coon's daughter. Brer Deer was a peart chap, and have the airs of the quality, no put-on bigoty ways; Brer Deer am a right sure 'nough gentleman, that he is. Well, old Brer Terrapin am a poor, slow, old man; all the creeters wonder how the gal can smile on hisself when Mr. Deer flying round her, but them what knows tells how, when old man Terrapin lay hisself out, he have a mighty taking way with the gals, and the gals in the old times mighty like the gals these here times, and ain't got no sense nohow.

Well, old man Coon he favor Brer Deer, and he powerful set again Brer Terrapin, and he fault him to the gals constant; but the more Brer Coon fault Brer Terrapin, the more the hard-headed gal giggle and cut her eye when Brer Terrapin come 'bout; and old Brer Coon, he just nigh 'bout outdone with her foolishness, and he say he gwine set down on the fooling.

So he say, Brer Coon did, how Brer Deer and Brer Terrapin shall run a seven-mile race, and the one what get there first shall surely have the gal, 'cause he feel that sure in he mind, Brer Coon do, that Brer Deer nat'rally bound to outrun poor old Brer Terrapin.

But I tell you, sah, when old Brer Terrapin pull he head in he house, and shut up all the doors, and just give himself to study, when he do that there way, the old man ain't just dozing away the time. Don't you mind, sah, he have a mighty bright eye, Brer Terrapin have, sah.

Well, Brer Terrapin, he say he run the race, if he can run in the water, 'cause he 'low he mighty slow on the foots. And Brer Deer and Brer Coon, they talk it over to theyselves, and they 'low Brer Deer mighty slow in the water, and so they set the race 'long the river bank. Brer Deer, he gwine run seven miles on the bank, and Brer Terrapin, he gwine run 'long the shore in the water, and he say every mile he gwine raise he head out the water and say, "Oho! here I is."

Den Brer Deer and Brer Coon laugh to burst theyselves, 'cause they lay out for Brer Terrapin done pass the first mile, Brer Deer done win the race.

Well, sah, Brer Terrapin he have six brothers, and he set one in the water every mile, and he set one in the water at the starting-place, and the old man, he set hisself in the water at the seven-mile post. O my, massa, dat old Brer Terrapin, he got a head on hisself, he surely have.

Well, Brer Coon and Brer Deer, they come down to the water, and they see Brer Terrapin out there in the water, an' Brer Coon, he place Brer Deer, and tell him hold on till he get hisself there, 'cause he bound to see the end of the race. So he get on the horse and whip up, and directly Brer Deer and Brer Terrapin start out, and when Brer Deer come to the first milestone he stick his head out the water, and he say, "Oho, here I is!" and Brer Deer, he just set to faster, 'cause he know Brer Terrapin mighty short-winded, but when he git to the two-mile post, sure 'nough, there Brer Terrapin stick he head out and say, "Oho, here I is!" and Brer Deer, he that astonished he nigh 'bout break down, but he set to and do he best, and when he come to the three-mile post, 'fore God if there ain't Brer Terrapin's head come out the water, and he just holler out, "Oho, here I is!"

But Brer Deer he push on, and every mile that there bodacious old Brer Terrapin. Well, when Brer Deer come a-puffing and a-blowing up to the last-most post, and Brer Coon set there on the horse, and just 'fore Brer Deer come up, if there ain't sure 'nough old Brer Terrapin, just where he done been waiting all the time, and just 'fore Brer Deer fotch round *the* bend, he just stick up he head and say, "Oho, Brer Deer, here I is for yourself!"

But Brer Terrapin never tell the gals 'bout his management, and how he get there that soon.

Why Mr. Dog Runs Brer Rabbit

One morning, Mr. Buzzard he say he stomach just hungry for some fish, and he tell Mrs. Buzzard he think he go down to the branch, and catch some for breakfast. So he take he basket, and he sail along till he come to the branch.

He fish right smart, and by sun up he have he basket plum full. But Mr. Buzzard am a powerful greedy man, and he say to hisself, he did, I just catch one more. But while he done gone for this last one, Brer Rabbit he came along, clipity, clipity, and when he see basket plum full of fine whitefish he stop, and he say, "I 'clare to goodness, the old woman just gwine on up to the cabin, 'cause they got nothing for to fry for breakfast. I wonder what she think of this yer fish," and so he put the basket on he head, Brer Rabbit did, and make off to the cabin.

Direc'ly he meet up with Mr. Dog, and he ax him where he been fishing that early in the day, and Brer Rabbit he say how he done sot on the log 'longside of the branch, and let he tail hang in the water and catch all the fish, and he done tell Mr. Dog, the old rascal did, that he tail mighty short for the work, but that Mr. Dog's tail just the right sort for fishing.

So Mr. Dog, he teeth just ache for them whitefish, and he go set on the log and hang he tail in the water, and it mighty cold for he tail, and the fish don't bite, but he mouth just set for them fish, and so he just sot dar, and it turn that cold that when he feel he gin up, sure's you born, Mr. Dog, he tail froze fast in the branch, and he call he chillens, and they come and break the ice.

And then, to be sure, he start off to settle Ole Brer Rabbit, and he get on he track and he run the poor ole man to beat all, and directly he sight him he run him round and round the woods and holler, "Hallelujah! hallelujah!" and the puppies come on behind, and they holler, "Glory! glory!" and they make such a fuss, all the creeters in the woods, they run to see what the matter. Well, sah, from that day, Mr. Dog he run Brer Rabbit, and when they just get gwine on the swing in the big woods, you can hear ole Ben dar just letting hisself out, "Hallelujah! hallelujah!" and them pups just gwine "Glory! glory!" and it surely am the sound what has the music dar, it surely has the music dar.

How Sandy Got His Meat

Brer Rabbit an Brer Coon wuz fishermuns. Brer Rabbit fished fur fish an Brer Coon fished fur f-r-o-g-s.

Arter while de frogs all got so wile Brer Coon couldent ketch em, an he hadn't hab no meat to his house an de chilluns wuz hongry an de ole oman beat em ober de haid wid de broom.

Brer Coon felt mighty bad an he went off down de rode wid he head down wundering what he gwine do. Des den ole Brer Rabbit wuz er skippin down de rode an he seed Brer Coon wuz worried an throwed up his years an say-ed:

"Mornin, Brer Coon."

"Mornin, Brer Rabbit."

"How is yer copperrosity segashuatin, Brer Coon?"

"Porely, Brer Rabbit, porely. De frogs haz all got so wile I caint ketch em an I aint got no meat to my house an de ole oman is mad an de chilluns hongry. Brer Rabbit, I'se got to hab help. Sumthin' haz got to be dun."

Old Brer Rabbit look away crost de ruver long time; den he scratch hiz year wid his hind foot, an say:

"I'll tole ye whut we do Brer Coon. We'll git eber one of dem frogs. You do down on de san bar an lie down an play des lack you wuz d-a-i-d. Don't yer mobe. Be jes as still, jest lack you wuz d-a-i-d."

Ole Brer Coon mosied on down to de ruver. De frogs hear-ed em er comin an de ole big frog say-ed:

"Yer better look er roun. Yer better look er roun. Yer better look er round."

Nother ole frog say-ed:

"Knee deep, knee deep, knee deep."

An "ker-chug" all de frogs went in de water.

But Old Brer Coon lide down on de san an stretched out jest lack he wuz d-a-i-d. De flies got all ober em, but he never moobe. De sun shine hot, but he never moobe; he lie still jest lack he wuz d-a-i-d.

Drectly Ole Brer Rabbit cum er runnin tru de woods an out on de san bar an put his years up high an hollered out:

"Hay, de Ole Coon is d-a-i-d."

De ole big frog out in de ruver say-ed:

"I don't bleve it, I don't bleve it, I don't bleve it." And all de littul frogs roun de edge say-ed:

"I don't bleve it, I don't bleve it, I don't bleve it."

But de ole coon play jes lack he's d-a-i-d an all de frogs cum up out of de ruver an set er roun whare de ole coon lay.

Jes den Brer Rabbit wink his eye an say-ed:

"I'll tell yer what I'de do, Brer Frogs. I'de berry Old Sandy, berry em so deep he never could scratch out."

Den all de frogs gun to dig out de san, dig out de san from under de ole coon. When de had dug er great deep hole wid de ole coon in de middle of it, de frogs all got tired an de ole frog say-ed:

"Deep er nough,—deep er nough,—deep er nough."

An all de littul frogs say-ed:

"Deep er nough,—deep er nough,—deep er nough."

Ole Brer Rabbit was er takin er littul nap in der sun, and he woke up an say-ed:

"Kin you jump out?"

De ole big frog look up to de top of de hole an say-ed:

"Yes I kin. Yes I kin. Yes I kin."

An de littul frogs say-ed:

"Yes I kin. Yes I kin. Yes I kin."

Ole Brer Rabbit tole em:

"Dig it deeper."

Den all de frogs went to wuk an dug er great deep hole way down inside de san wid Old Brer Coon right in de middle jest lack he wuz d-a-i-d. De frogs wuz er gittin putty tired an de ole big frog sung out loud:—

"Deep er nough. Deep er nough. Deep er nough."

An all de littul frogs sung out too:—

"Deep er nough. Deep er nough. Deep er nough."

An Ole Brer Rabbit woke up er gin an axed em:—

"Kin yer jump out?"

"I bleve I kin. I bleve I kin. I bleve I kin."

Ole Brer Rabbit look down in de hole agin an say-ed:—

"Dig dat hole deeper."

Den all de frogs gin to wuk throwin out san, throwin out san, clear till most sun down and dey had er great deep hole way, way down in de san, wid de ole coon layin right in de middle. De frogs wuz plum clean tired out and de ole big frog say-ed:—

"Deep er nough. Deep er nough. Deep er nough."

An all de littul frogs say-ed:—
"Deep er nough. Deep er nough. Deep er nough."
Ole Brer Rabbit peeped down in de hole agin and say:—
"Kin yer jump out?"
An de ole frog say:—
"No I caint. No I caint. No I caint."
An all de littul frogs say:—
"No I caint. No I caint. No I caint."
Den Ole Brer Rabbit jump up right quick an holler out:—
"RISE UP SANDY AN GIT YOUR MEAT."
An Brer Coon had meat fer sepper dat nite.

Joel Chandler Harris (1848–1908)
(Tales told by Harbert and George Terrell)

Joel Chandler Harris was born near Eatonton, Georgia, the illegitimate son of an Irish day laborer who soon deserted his family. Harris was raised by his mother in poor circumstances. When he was thirteen, he went to work at Turnwold plantation as a typesetter's apprentice to Joseph Addison Turner, publisher of a weekly paper called *The Countryman.* Tutored by Turner in literature and grammar, Harris was allowed to peruse the plantation's extensive library. Also at Turnwold, Harris developed a relationship with Harbert and "Uncle" George Terrell, two of Turner's slaves, who regaled him with tales that Harris himself later admitted were the source of many of his hugely successful "Uncle Remus" stories. Turnwold was ransacked by Sherman in 1864, and in 1866, publication of *The Countryman* was suspended. Harris moved on to Macon, where he worked as a typesetter, then to Forsyth, Georgia, where he took an editorial position at the *Monroe Advertiser.* After three years with the *Advertiser,* he was offered an associate editor's position with the *Savannah Morning News,* where he also wrote a daily column. In 1876 he went to work for the *Atlanta Constitution,* and at the request of Evan P. Howell, the *Constitution*'s editor, Harris published a series of sketches narrated in African American dialect. In 1879, Harris first developed the character of Uncle Remus, who entertains his young master with myths and folktales featuring the humorous exploits of the cunning Brer Rabbit. Harris would go on to publish more than a dozen Uncle Remus collections, but before long, folklorists recognized the roots of the stories in African American and Native American legends. Though Harris's work has undeniable racist overtones (Uncle Remus speaks of his plantation days as "laughin' times") and though Harris himself believed slavery had been at least partially beneficial to African Americans, he insisted that he only collected the tales and that his documentation of plot and dialect was accurate. In addition, these tales of a weaker protagonist who constantly gets the better of a more powerful antagonist have been viewed by modern critics as a lovable narrator's subversive wish fulfillment, revealing barely hidden animosity in the only way he can safely do so.

The Wonderful Tar-Baby Story

"Didn't the fox *never* catch the rabbit, Uncle Remus?" asked the little boy the next evening.

"He come mighty nigh it, honey, sho's you born—Brer Fox did. One day atter Brer Rabbit fool 'im wid dat calamus root, Brer Fox went ter wuk en got 'im some tar, en mix it wid some turkentime, en fix up a contrapshun wat he call a Tar-Baby, en he tuck dish yer Tar-Baby en he sot 'er in de big road, en den he lay off in de bushes fer to see what de news wuz gwineter be. En he didn't hatter wait long, nudder, kaze bimeby here comes Brer Rabbit pacin' down de road—lippity-clippity, clippity-lippity—dez ez sassy ez a jay-bird. Brer Fox, he lay low. Brer Rabbit come prancin' 'long twel he spy de Tar-Baby, en den he fotch up on his behime legs like he wuz 'stonished. De Tar-Baby, she sot dar, she did, en Brer Fox, he lay low.

"'Mawnin'!' sez Brer Rabbit, sezee—'nice wedder dis mawnin',' sezee.

"Tar-Baby ain't sayin' nothin', en Brer Fox, he lay low.

"'How duz yo' sym'tums seem ter segashuate?' sez Brer Rabbit, sezee.

"'Brer Fox, he wink his eye slow, en lay low, en de Tar-Baby, she ain't sayin' nothin'.

"'How you come on, den? Is you deaf?' sez Brer Rabbit, sezee. 'Kaze if you is, I kin holler louder,' sezee.

"Tar-Baby stay still, en Brer Fox, he lay low.

"'Youer stuck up, dat's w'at you is,' says Brer Rabbit, sezee, 'en I'm gwineter kyore you, dat's w'at I'm a gwinter do,' sezee.

"Brer Fox, he sorter chuckle in his stummuck, he did, but Tar-Baby ain't sayin' nothin'.

"'I'm gwineter larn you howter talk ter 'specttubble fokes ef hit's de las' ack,' sez Brer Rabbit, sezee. 'Ef you don't take off dat hat en tell me howdy, I'm gwineter bus' you wide open,' sezee.

"Tar-Baby stay still, en Brer Fox, he lay low.

"Brer Rabbit keep on axin' 'im, en de Tar-Baby, she keep on sayin' nothin', twel present'y Brer Rabbit draw back wid his fis', he did, en blip he tuck 'er side er de head. Right dar's whar he broke his merlasses jug. His fis' stuck, en he can't pull loose. De tar hilt 'im. But Tar-Baby, she stay still, en Brer Fox, he lay low.

"'Ef you don't lemme loose, I'll knock you agin,' sez Brer Rabbit, sezee, en wid dat he fotch 'er a wipe wid de udder han', en dat stuck. Tar-Baby, she ain't sayin' nothin', en Brer Fox, he lay low.

"'Tu'n me loose, fo' I kick de natal stuffin' outen you,' sez Brer Rabbit, sezee, but de Tar-Baby, she ain't sayin' nothin'. She des hilt on, en den Brer Rabbit lose de use er his feet in de same way. Brer Fox, he lay low. Den Brer Rabbit squall out dat ef de Tar-Baby don't tu'n 'im loose he butt 'er cranksided. En den he butted, en his head got stuck. Den Brer Fox, he sa'ntered fort', lookin' des ez innercent ez one er yo' mammy's mockin'-birds.

"'Howdy, Brer Rabbit,' sez Brer Fox, sezee. 'You look sorter stuck up dis mawnin',' sezee, en den he rolled on de groun', en laughed en laughed twel he couldn't laugh no mo'. 'I speck you'll take dinner wid me dis time, Brer Rabbit. I done laid in some calamus root, en I ain't gwineter take no skuse,' sez Brer Fox, sezee."

Here Uncle Remus paused, and drew a two-pound yam out of the ashes.

"Did the fox eat the rabbit?" asked the little boy to whom the story had been told.

"Dat's all de fur de tale goes," replied the old man. "He mout, en den agin he moutent. Some say Jedge B'ar come 'long en loosed 'im—some say he didn't. I hear Miss Sally callin'. You better run 'long."

How Mr. Rabbit Saved His Meat

"One time," said Uncle Remus, whetting his knife slowly and thoughtfully on the palm of his hand, and gazing reflectively in the fire—"one time Brer Wolf—"

"Why, Uncle Remus!" the little boy broke in, "I thought you said the Rabbit scalded the Wolf to death a long time ago."

The old man was fairly caught and he knew it; but this made little difference to him. A frown gathered on his usually serene brow as he turned his gaze upon the child—a frown in which both scorn and indignation were visible. Then all at once he seemed to regain control of himself. The frown was chased away by a look of Christian resignation.

"Dar now! W'at I tell you?" he exclaimed as if addressing a witness concealed under the bed. "Ain't I done tole you so? Bless grashus! ef chilluns ain't gittin' so dey knows mo'n ole fokes, en dey'll spute longer you en spute longer you, ceppin der ma call um, w'ich I speck twon't be long 'fo' she will, en den I'll set yere by de chimbly-cornder en git some peace er mine. W'en ole Miss wuz livin'," continued the old man, still addressing some imaginary person, "hit 'uz mo'n enny her chilluns 'ud dast ter do ter come 'sputin' longer me, en Mars John'll tell you de same enny day you ax 'im."

"Well, Uncle Remus, you know you said the Rabbit poured hot water on the Wolf and killed him," said the little boy.

The old man pretended not to hear. He was engaged in searching among some scraps of leather under his chair, and kept on talking to the imaginary person. Finally, he found and drew forth a nicely plaited whip-thong with a red snapper all waxed and knotted.

"I wuz fixin' up a w'ip fer a little chap," he continued, with a sigh, "but, bless grashus! 'fo' I kin git 'er done, de little chap done grow'd up twel he know mo'n I duz."

The child's eyes filled with tears and his lips began to quiver, but he said nothing; whereupon Uncle Remus immediately melted.

"I 'clar' to goodness," he said, reaching out and taking the little boy tenderly by the hand, "ef you ain't de ve'y spit en image er ole Miss w'en I brung 'er de las' news er de war. Hit's des like skeerin' up a ghos' w'at you ain't fear'd un."

Then there was a pause, the old man patting the little child's hand caressingly.

"You ain't mad, is you, honey?" Uncle Remus asked finally, "kaze ef you is, I'm gwine out yere en butt my head 'gin de do' jam'."

But the little boy wasn't mad. Uncle Remus had conquered him and he had conquered Uncle Remus in pretty much the same way before. But it was some time before Uncle Remus would go on with the story. He had to be coaxed. At last, however, he settled himself back in the chair and began:

"Co'se, honey, hit mout er bin ole Brer Wolf, er hit mout er bin er n'er Brer Wolf; it mout er bin 'fo' he got kotch up wid, er it mout er bin atterwards. Ez de tale wer gun to me des dat away I gin it unter you. One time Brer Wolf wuz comin' 'long home fum a fishin' frolic. He s'anter 'long de road, he did, wid his string er fish 'cross his shoulder, wen fus news you know ole Miss Pa'tridge, she hop outer de bushes en flutter 'long right at Brer Wolf nose. Brer Wolf he say ter hisse'f dat ole Miss Pa'tridge tryin' fer ter toll 'im fum her nes', en wid dat he lay his fish down en put out inter de bushes whar ole Miss Pa'tridge come fum, en 'bout dat time Brer Rabbit, he happen 'long. Dar wuz de fishes, en dar wuz Brer Rabbit, en w'en dat de case w'at you speck a sorter innerpen'ent man like Brer Rabbit gwine do? I kin tell you dis, dat dem fishes ain't stay whar Brer Wolf put um at, en w'en Brer Wolf come back dey wuz gone.

"Brer Wolf, he sot down en scratch his head, he did, en study en study, en den hit sorter rush inter his mine dat Brer Rabbit bin 'long dar, en den Brer Wolf, he put out fer Brer Rabbit house, en w'en he git dar he hail 'im. Brer Rabbit, he dunno nuthin' tall 'bout no fishes. Brer Wolf he up'n say he bleedzd ter b'leeve Brer Rabbit got dem fishes. Brer Rabbit 'ny it up en down, but Brer Wolf stan' to it dat Brer Rabbit got dem fishes. Brer Rabbit, he say dat if Brer Wolf b'leeve he got de fishes, den he give Brer Wolf lief fer ter kill de bes' cow he got. Brer Wolf, he tuck Brer Rabbit at his word, en go off ter de pastur' en drive up de cattle en kill Brer Rabbit bes' cow.

"Brer Rabbit, he hate mighty bad fer ter lose his cow, but he lay his plans, en he tell his chilluns dat he gwineter have dat beef yit. Brer Wolf, he bin tuck up by de patter-rollers 'fo' now, en he mighty skeerd un um, en fus news you know, yer come Brer Rabbit hollerin' en tellin' Brer Wolf dat de patter-rollers comin'.

"'You run en hide, Brer Wolf,' sez Brer Rabbit, sezee, 'en I'll stay yer en take keer er de cow twel you gits back,' sezee.

"Soon's Brer Wolf hear talk er de patter-rollers, he scramble off inter de underbresh like he bin shot out'n a gun. En he want mo'n gone 'fo' Brer Rabbit, he whirl in en skunt de cow en salt de hide down, en den he tuck'n cut up de kyarkiss en stow it 'way in de smoke-'ouse, en den he tuck'n stick de een' er de cow-tail in de groun'. Atter he gone en done all dis, den Brer Rabbit he squall out fer Brer Wolf:

"'Run yer, Brer Wolf! Run yer! Yo' cow gwine in de groun'! Run yer!'

"W'en ole Brer Wolf got dar, w'ich he come er scootin', dar wuz Brer Rabbit hol'in' on ter de cow-tail, fer ter keep it fum gwine in de groun'. Brer Wolf, he kotch holt, en dey 'gin a pull er two en up come de tail. Den Brer Rabbit, he wink his off eye en say, sezee:

"'Dar! de tail done pull out en de cow gone,' sezee.

"But Brer Wolf he wer'n't de man fer ter give it up dat away, en he got 'im a spade, en a pick-axe, en a shovel, en he dig en dig fer dat cow twel diggin' wuz pas' all endu'unce, en old Brer Rabbit he sot up dar in his front po'ch en smoke his seegyar. Eve'y time old Brer Wolf stuck de pick-axe in de clay, Brer Rabbit, he giggle ter his chilluns:

"'He diggy, diggy, diggy, but no meat dar! He diggy, diggy, diggy, but no meat dar!'

"Kase all de time de cow wuz layin' pile up in his smoke-'ouse, en him en his chilluns wuz eatin' fried beef en inguns eve'y time dey mouf water.

"Now den, honey, you take dis yer w'ip," continued the old man, twining the leather thong around the little boy's neck, "en scamper up ter de big 'ouse en tell Miss Sally fer ter gin you some un it de nex' time she fine yo' tracks in de sugar-bairl."

Mr. Terrapin Shows His Strength

"Brer Tarrypin wuz de out'nes' man," said Uncle Remus, rubbing his hands together contemplatively, and chuckling to himself in a very significant manner; "he wuz de out'nes' man er de whole gang. He wuz dat."

The little boy sat perfectly quiet, betraying no impatience when Uncle Remus paused to hunt, first in one pocket and then in another, for enough crumbs of tobacco to replenish his pipe. Presently the old man proceeded:

"One night Miss Meadows en de gals dey gun a candy-pullin', en so many er de nabers come in 'sponse ter de invite dat dey hatter put de 'lasses in de wash pot in b'il'de fier in de yard. Brer B'ar, he hope[1] Miss Meadows bring de wood, Brer Fox, he men' de fier, Brer Wolf, he kep' de dogs off, Brer Rabbit, he grease de bottom er de plates fer ter keep de candy fum stickin', en Brer Tarrypin, he klum up in a cheer, en say he'd watch en see dat de 'lasses didn't bile over. Dey wuz all dere, en dey wern't cuttin' up no didos, nudder, kaze Miss Meadows, she done put her foot down, she did, en say dat w'en dey come ter her place dey hatter hang up a flag er truce at de front gate en 'bide by it.

"Well, den, w'iles dey wuz all a settin' dar en de 'lasses wuz a bilin' en a blubberin', dey got ter runnin' on talkin' mighty biggity. Brer Rabbit, he say he de swiffes'; but Brer Tarrypin, he rock 'long in de cheer en watch de 'lasses. Brer Fox, he say he de sharpes', but Brer Tarrypin he rock 'long. Brer Wolf, he say he de mos' suvvigus, but Brer Tarrypin, he rock en he rock 'long. Brer B'ar, he say he de mos' stronges', but Brer Tarrypin he rock, en he keep on rockin'. Bimeby he sorter shet one eye, en say, sezee:

"'Hit look like 'periently dat de ole hardshell ain't nowhars 'longside er dis crowd, yit yer I is, en I'm de same man w'at show Brer Rabbit dat he ain't de swiffes'; en I'm de same man w'at kin show Brer B'ar dat he ain't de stronges',' sezee.

"Den dey all laff en holler, kaze it look like Brer B'ar mo' stronger dan a steer. Bimeby, Miss Meadows, she up'n ax, she did, how he gwine do it.

"'Gimme a good strong rope,' sez Brer Tarrypin, sezee, 'en lemme git in er puddle er water, en den let Brer B'ar see ef he kin pull me out,' sezee.

"Den dey all laff g'in, en Brer B'ar, he ups en sez, sezee: 'We ain't got no rope,' sezee.

"'No,' sez Brer Tarrypin, sezee, 'en needer is you got de strenk,' sezee, en den Brer Tarrypin, he rock en rock 'long, en watch de 'lasses a bilin' en a blubberin'.

"Atter w'ile Miss Meadows, she up en say, she did, dat she'd take'n loan de young men her bed-cord, en w'iles de candy wuz a coolin' in de plates, dey could all go ter de branch en see Brer Tarrypin kyar out his projick. Brer Tarrypin," continued Uncle Remus, in a tone at once confidential and argumentative, "wern't much bigger'n de pa'm er my han', en it look mighty funny fer ter year 'im braggin' 'bout how he kin out-pull Brer B'ar. But dey got de bed-cord atter w'ile, en den dey all put out ter de branch. W'en Brer Tarrypin fine de place he wanter, he tuck one een' er de bed-cord, 'en gun de yuther een' to Brer B'ar.

"'Now den, ladies en gents,' sez Brer Tarrypin, sezee, 'you all go wid Brer B'ar up dar in de woods en I'll stay yer, en w'en you year me holler, den's de time fer Brer B'ar fer ter see ef he kin haul in de slack er de rope. You all take keer er dat ar een',' sezee, 'en I'll take keer er dish yer een',' sezee.

"Den dey all put out en lef' Brer Tarrypin at de branch; en w'en dey got good en gone, he dove down inter de water, he did, en tie de bed-cord hard en fas' ter wunner deze yer big clay-roots, en den he riz up en gin a whoop.

"Brer B'ar he wrop de bed-cord roun' his han', en wink at de gals, en wid dat he gin a big juk, but Brer Tarrypin ain't budge. Den he take bofe han's en gin a big pull,

---

[1]Holp; helped. (Harris's note.)

but, all de same, Brer Tarrypin ain't budge. Den he tu'n 'roun', he did, en put de rope cross his shoulders en try ter walk off wid Brer Tarrypin, but Brer Tarrypin look like he don't feel like walkin'. Den Brer Wolf he put in en hope Brer B'ar pull, but des like he didn't, en den dey all hope 'im, en, bless grashus! w'iles dey wuz all a pullin', Brer Tarrypin, he holler, en ax um w'y dey don't take up de slack. Den w'en Brer Tarrypin feel um quit pullin', he dove down, he did, en ontie de rope, en by de time dey got ter de branch, Brer Tarrypin, he wuz settin' in de aidge er de water des ez natchul ez de nex' un, en he up'n say, sezee:

"'Dat las' pull er yone wuz a mighty stiff un, en a leetle mo'n you'd er had me,' sezee. 'Youer monstus stout, Brer B'ar,' sezee, 'en you pulls like a yoke er steers, but I sorter had de purchis on you,' sezee.

"Den Brer B'ar, bein's his mouf 'gun ter water atter de sweetnin', he up'n say he speck de candy's ripe, en off dey put atter it!"

"It's a wonder," said the little boy, after a while, "that the rope didn't break."

"Break who?" exclaimed Uncle Remus, with a touch of indignation in his tone— "break who? In dem days, Miss Meadow's bed-cord would a hilt a mule."

This put an end to whatever doubts the child might have entertained.

Brother Rabbit and the Mosquitoes

The next night Daddy Jack was still away when the little boy went to see Uncle Remus, and the child asked about him.

"Bless yo' soul, honey! don't ax me 'bout Brer Jack. He look lak he mighty ole en trimbly, but he mighty peart nigger, mon. He look lak he shufflin' 'long, but dat ole nigger gits over groun', sho'. Forty year ergo, maybe I mought er kep' up wid 'im, but I let you know Brer Jack is away 'head er me. He mos' sho'ly is."

"Why, he's older than you are, Uncle Remus!" the child exclaimed.

"Dat w'at I year tell. Seem lak hit mighty kuse, but sho' ez youer bawn Brer Jack is a heap mo' pearter nigger dan w'at ole Remus is. He little, yit he mighty hard. Dat's Brer Jack, up en down."

Uncle Remus paused and reflected a moment. Then he went on:

"Talkin' 'bout Brer Jack put me in min' 'bout a tale w'ich she sho'ly mus' er happen down dar in dat ar country war Brer Jack come fum, en it sorter ketch me in de neighborhoods er de 'stonishment 'kaze he aint done up'n tell it. I 'speck it done wuk loose fum Brer Jack 'membunce."

"What tale was that, Uncle Remus?"

"Seem lak dat one time w'en eve'ything en eve'ybody wuz runnin' 'long des lak dey bin had waggin grease 'pun um, ole Brer Wolf"—

The little boy laughed incredulously and Uncle Remus paused and frowned heavily.

"Why, Uncle Remus! how did Brother Wolf get away from Mammy-Bammy Big-Money?"

The old man's frown deepened and his voice was full of anger as he replied:

"Now, den, is I'm de tale, er is de tale me? Tell me dat! Is I'm de tale, er is de tale me? Well, den, ef I aint de tale en de tale aint me, den how come you wanter take'n rake me over de coals fer?"

"Well, Uncle Remus, you know what you said. You said that was the end of Brother Wolf."

"I bleedz ter 'spute dat," exclaimed Uncle Remus, with the air of one performing a painful duty; "I bleedz ter 'spute it. Dat w'at de tale say. Ole Remus is one nigger en de tale, hit's a n'er nigger. Yit I aint got no time fer ter set back yer en fetch out de oggyments."

Here the old man paused, closed his eyes, leaned back in his chair, and sighed. After a while he said, in a gentle tone:

"So den, Brer Wolf done dead, en yer I wuz runnin' on des same lak he wuz done 'live. Well! well! well!"

Uncle Remus stole a glance at the little boy, and immediately relented.

"Yit," he went on, "ef I'm aint de tale en de tale aint me, hit aint skacely make no diffunce whe'er Brer Wolf dead er whe'er he's a high-primin' 'roun' bodder'n 'longer de yuther creeturs. Dead er no dead, dey wuz one time w'en Brer Wolf live in de swamp down dar in dat ar country whar Brer Jack come fum, en, mo'n dat, he had a mighty likely gal. Look lak all de yuther creeturs wuz atter 'er. Dey 'ud go down dar ter Brer Wolf house, dey would, en dey 'ud set up en court de gal, en 'joy deyse'f.

"Hit went on dis a-way twel atter w'ile de skeeters 'gun ter git monst'us bad. Brer Fox, he went flyin' 'roun' Miss Wolf, en he sot dar, he did, en run on wid 'er en fight skeeters des ez big ez life en twice-t ez natchul. Las' Brer Wolf, he tuck'n kotch Brer Fox slappin' en fightin' at de skeeters. Wid dat he tuck'n tuck Brer Fox by de off year en led 'im out ter de front gate, en w'en he git dar, he 'low, he did, dat no man w'at can't put up wid skeeters aint gwine ter come a-courtin' his gal.

"Den Brer Coon, he come flyin' 'roun' de gal, but he aint bin dar no time skacely 'fo' he 'gun ter knock at de skeeters; en no sooner is he done dis dan Brer Wolf show 'im de do'. Brer Mink, he come en try he han', yit he bleedz ter fight de skeeters, en Brer Wolf ax 'im out.

"Hit went on dis a-way twel bimeby all de creeturs bin flyin' 'roun' Brer Wolf's gal 'ceppin' it's ole Brer Rabbit, en w'en he year w'at kinder treatments de yuther cree-turs bin ketchin' he 'low ter hisse'f dat he b'leeve in he soul he mus' go down ter Brer Wolf house en set de gal out one whet ef it's de las' ack.

"No sooner say, no sooner do. Off he put, en 'twa'n't long 'fo' he fine hisse'f knockin' at Brer Wolf front do'. Ole Sis Wolf, she tuck'n put down 'er knittin' en she up'n 'low, she did:

"'Who dat?'

"De gal, she 'uz stannin' up 'fo' de lookin'-glass sorter primpin', en she choke back a giggle, she did, en 'low:

"'Sh-h-h! My goodness, mammy! dat's Mr. Rabbit. I year de gals say he's a mighty prop-en-tickler[1] gentermun, en I des hope you aint gwine ter set dar en run on lak you mos' allers does w'en I got comp'ny 'bout how much soapgrease you done save up en how many kittens de ole cat got. I gits right 'shame' sometimes, dat I does!'"

The little boy looked astonished.

"Did she talk that way to her mamma?" he asked.

"*Shoo*, chile! 'Mungs' all de creeturs dey aint no mo' kuse creeturs dan de gals. Ole ez I is, ef I wuz ter start in dis minnit fer ter tell you how kuse de gals is, en de Lord wuz ter spar' me plum twel I git done, yo' head 'ud be gray, en Remus 'ud be des twice-t ez ole ez w'at he is right now."

"Well, what did her mamma say, Uncle Remus?"

---

[1]Proper and particular. (Harris's note.)

"Ole Sis Wolf, she sot dar, she did, en settle 'er cap on 'er head, en snicker, en look at de gal lak she monst'us proud. De gal, she tuck'n shuck 'erse'f 'fo' de lookin'-glass a time er two, en den she tipt ter de do' en open' it little ways en peep out des lak she skeer'd some un gwine ter hit 'er a clip side de head. Dar stood ole Brer Rabbit lookin' des ez slick ez a race-hoss. De gal, she tuck'n laff, she did, en holler:

"'W'y law, maw! hit's Mr. Rabbit, en yer we bin 'fraid it 'uz some 'un w'at aint got no business 'roun' yer!'

"Ole Sis Wolf she look over 'er specks, en snicker, en den she up'n 'low:

"'Well, don't keep 'im stannin' out dar all night. Ax 'im in, fer goodness sake.'

"Den de gal, she tuck'n drap 'er hankcher, en Brer Rabbit, he dipt down en grab it en pass it ter 'er wid a bow, en de gal say she much 'blige, 'kaze dat 'uz mo' den Mr. Fox 'ud er done, en den she ax Brer Rabbit how he come on, en Brer Rabbit 'low he right peart, en den he ax 'er wharbouts 'er daddy, en ole Sis Wolf 'low she go fine 'im.

"'Twa'n't long 'fo' Brer Rabbit year Brer Wolf stompin' de mud off'n he foots in de back po'ch, en den bimeby in he come. Dey shuck han's, dey did, en Brer Rabbit say dat w'en he go callin' on he 'quaintunce, hit aint feel natchul 'ceppin' de man er de house settin' 'roun' some'rs.

"'Ef he don't talk none,' sez Brer Rabbit, sezee, 'he kin des set up ag'in' de chimbly-jam en keep time by noddin'.'

"But ole Brer Wolf, he one er deze yer kinder mens w'at got de whimzies,[2] en he up'n 'low dat he don't let hisse'f git ter noddin' front er comp'ny. Dey run on dis a-way twel bimeby Brer Rabbit year de skeeters come zoonin' 'roun', en claimin' kin wid 'im."

The little boy laughed; but Uncle Remus was very serious.

"Co'se dey claim kin wid 'im. Dey claims kin wid folks yit, let 'lone Brer Rabbit. Manys en manys de time w'en I year um sailin' 'roun' en singin' out *'Cousin! Cousin!'* en I let you know, honey, de skeeters is mighty close kin w'en dey gits ter be yo' cousin.

"Brer Rabbit, he year um zoonin'," the old man continued, "en he know he got ter do some mighty nice talkin', so he up'n ax fer drink er water. De gal, she tuck'n fotch it.

"'Mighty nice water, Brer Wolf.' *(De skeeters dey zoon.)*[3]

"'Some say it too full er wiggletails,[4] Brer Rabbit.' *(De skeeters, dey zoon en dey zoon.)*

"'Mighty nice place you got, Brer Wolf.' *(Skeeters dey zoon.)*

"'Some say it too low in de swamp, Brer Rabbit.' *(Skeeters dey zoon en dey zoon.)*

"Dey zoon so bad," said Uncle Remus, drawing a long breath, "dat Brer Rabbit 'gun ter git skeer'd, en w'en dat creetur git skeer'd, he min' wuk lak one er deze yer flutter-mills. Bimeby, he 'low:

"'Went ter town t'er day, en dar I seed a sight w'at I never 'speckted ter see.'

"'W'at dat, Brer Rabbit?'

"'Spotted hoss, Brer Wolf,'

"'*No*, Brer Rabbit!'

"'I mos' sho'ly seed 'im, Brer Wolf.'

---

[2]In these latter days a man with the whimzies, or whimsies, is known simply as a crank. (Harris's note.)

[3]The information in parentheses is imparted in a low, impressive, confidential tone. (Harris's note.)

[4]Is it necessary to say that the wiggletail is the embryo mosquito? (Harris's note.)

"Brer Wolf, he scratch he head, en de gal she hilt up 'er han's en make great 'miration 'bout de spotted hoss. *(De skeeters dey zoon, en dey keep on zoonin'.)* Brer Rabbit, he talk on, he did:

"'Twa'n't des one spotted hoss. Brer Wolf, 't wuz a whole team er spotted hosses, en dey went gallin'-up[5] des lak yuther hosses,' sezee. 'Let 'lone dat, Brer Wolf, my grandaddy wuz spotted,' sez Brer Rabbit, sezee.

"Gal, she squeal en holler out:

"'W'y, Brer Rabbit! aint you 'shame' yo'se'f fer ter be talkin' dat a-way, en 'bout yo' own-'lone blood kin too?'

"'Hit's de naked trufe I'm a-ginin'[6] un you,' sez Brer Rabbit, sezee. *(Skeeter zoon en come closeer.)*

"Brer Wolf 'low 'Well—well—well!' Ole Sis Wolf, she 'low 'Tooby sho'ly, tooby sho'ly!' *(Skeeter zoon en come nigher en nigher.)* Brer Rabbit 'low:

"'Yasser! Des ez sho' ez youer settin' dar, my grandaddy wuz spotted. Spotted all over. *(Skeeter come zoonin' up en light on Brer Rabbit jaw.)* He wuz dat. He had er great big spot right yer!'"

Here Uncle Remus raised his hand and struck himself a resounding slap on the side of the face where the mosquito was supposed to be, and continued:

"No sooner is he do dis dan ne'r skeeter come zoonin' 'roun' en light on Brer Rabbit leg. Brer Rabbit, he talk, en he talk:

"'Po' ole grandaddy! I boun' he make you laff, he look so funny wid all dem spots en speckles. He had spot on de side er de head, whar I done show you, en den he had n'er big spot right yer on de leg,' sezee."

Uncle Remus slapped himself on the leg below the knee, and was apparently so serious about it that the little boy laughed loudly. The old man went on:

"Skeeter zoon en light 'twix' Brer Rabbit shoulder-blades. Den he talk:

"'B'leeve me er not b'leeve me ef you min' to, but my grandaddy had a big black spot up yer on he back w'ich look lak saddle-mark.'

"Blip Brer Rabbit tuck hisse'f on de back!

"Skeeter sail 'roun' en zoon en light down yer beyan de hip-bone. He say he grandaddy got spot down dar.

"Blip he tuck hisse'f beyan de hip-bone.

"Hit keep on dis a-way," continued Uncle Remus, who had given vigorous illustrations of Brer Rabbit's method of killing mosquitos while pretending to tell a story, "twel bimeby ole Brer Wolf en ole Sis Wolf dey lissen at Brer Rabbit twel dey 'gun ter nod, en den ole Brer Rabbit en de gal dey sot up dar en kill skeeters right erlong."

"Did he marry Brother Wolf's daughter?" asked the little boy.

"I year talk," replied Uncle Remus, "dat Brer Wolf sont Brer Rabbit wud nex' day dat he kin git de gal by gwine atter 'er, but I aint never year talk 'bout Brer Rabbit gwine. De day atterwuds wuz mighty long time, en by den Brer Rabbit moughter had some yuther projick on han'."[7]

---

[5]Galloping. (Harris's note.)

[6]G hard as in give. (Harris's note.)

[7]This story, the funniest and most characteristic of all the negro legends, cannot be satisfactorily told on paper. It is full of action, and all the interest centres in the gestures and grimaces that must accompany an explanation of Brother Rabbit's method of disposing of the mosquitos. The story was first called to my attention by Mr. Marion Erwin, of Savannah, and it is properly a coast legend, but I have heard it told by three Middle Georgia negroes. (Harris's note.)

Sidney Lanier

(1842–1881)

Sidney Lanier was born in Macon, Georgia, to Robert Sampson Lanier, a lawyer, and Mary Jane Anderson Lanier, who was an accomplished musician. He demonstrated a passion for music from his earliest childhood, and though he could play many instruments, he settled on the flute. He was educated in private schools until age fourteen, when he entered Oglethorpe University, a small Presbyterian College which he would later admit offered him few challenges. He was graduated from Oglethorpe in 1860 and appointed a tutor there. He planned to continue his studies in Europe, but those plans were interrupted by the outbreak of the Civil War. He enlisted in the Macon Volunteers, and saw action in several battles. After being transferred to the Marine Signal Service, he was captured running blockades and sent to prison at Fort Lookout, Maryland. He was released after a year and returned home, his health ruined. The novel *Tiger Lilies* (1867) is based on his war experiences.

In the years after the war, Lanier spent time clerking in a Montgomery, Alabama, hotel before returning to Macon to practice law with his father. His health continued to deteriorate, however, and in 1873 he settled in Baltimore, determined to devote all his flagging energies to music and literature. He was engaged as first flute for the Peabody Orchestra and held that position for six years. The first of his poems to attract serious critical attention, "Corn," appeared in *Lippincott's Magazine* in 1875, followed by "Florida" in 1876, and in 1877 the slender volume *Poems* appeared. In all of his poetry he explored the interrelationship of music and poetry; "The Symphony" creates musical effects through the use of various poetic devices, and later poems like "The Marshes of Glynn" and "Sunrise" continue to develop his musical style. He published the critical work *The Science of English Verse* in 1880, shortly before his premature death.

The Symphony

"O Trade! O Trade! would thou wert dead!
The Time needs heart—'tis tired of head:
We're all for love," the violins said.
"Of what avail the rigorous tale
Of bill for coin and box for bale?
Grant thee, O Trade! thine uttermost hope:
Level red gold with blue sky-slope,
And base it deep as devils grope:
When all's done, what hast thou won
Of the only sweet that's under the sun?
Ay, canst thou buy a single sigh
Of true love's least, least ecstasy?"
Then, with a bridegroom's heart-beats trembling,
All the mightier strings assembling
Ranged them on the violins' side
As when the bridegroom leads the bride,
And, heart in voice, together cried:

"Yea, what avail the endless tale
Of gain by cunning and plus by sale?
Look up the land, look down the land
The poor, the poor, the poor, they stand,
Wedged by the pressing of Trade's hand
Against an inward-opening door
That pressure tightens evermore:
They sigh a monstrous foul-air sigh
For the outside leagues of liberty,
Where Art, sweet lark, translates the sky
Into a heavenly melody.
'Each day, all day' (these poor folks say),
'In the same old year-long, drear-long way,
We weave in the mills and heave in the kilns,
We sieve mine-meshes under the hills,
And thieve much gold from the Devil's bank tills,
To relieve, O God, what manner of ills?—
The beasts, they hunger, and eat, and die;
And so do we, and the world's a sty;
Hush, fellow-swine: why nuzzle and cry?
Swinehood hath no remedy
Say many men, and hasten by,
Clamping the nose and blinking the eye.
But who said once, in the lordly tone,
Man shall not live by bread alone
But all that cometh from the Throne?
    Hath God said so?
    But Trade saith *No:*
And the kilns and the curt-tongued mills say *Go!*
There's plenty that can, if you can't: we know.
Move out, if you think you're underpaid.
The poor are prolific; we're not afraid;
    Trade is trade.'"
Thereat this passionate protesting
Meekly changed, and softened till
It sank to sad requesting
And suggesting sadder still:
"And oh, if men might some time see
How piteous-false the poor decree
That trade no more than trade must be!
Does business mean, *Die, you—live, I?*
Then 'Trade is trade' but sings a lie:
'Tis only war grown miserly.
If business is battle, name it so:
War-crimes less will shame it so,
And widows less will blame it so.
Alas, for the poor to have some part
In yon sweet living lands of Art,

Makes problem not for head, but heart.
Vainly might Plato's brain revolve it:
Plainly the heart of a child could solve it."

And then, as when from words that seem but rude
We pass to silent pain that sits abrood
Back in our heart's great dark and solitude,
So sank the strings to gentle throbbing
Of long chords change-marked with sobbing—
Motherly sobbing, not distinctlier heard
Than half wing-openings of the sleeping bird,
Some dream of danger to her young hath stirred.
Then stirring and demurring ceased, and lo!
Every least ripple of the strings' song-flow
Died to a level with each level bow
And made a great chord tranquil-surfaced so,
As a brook beneath his curving bank doth go
To linger in the sacred dark and green
Where many boughs the still pool overlean
And many leaves make shadow with their sheen.
    But presently
A velvet flute-note fell down pleasantly
Upon the bosom of that harmony,
And sailed and sailed incessantly,
As if a petal from a wild-rose blown
Had fluttered down upon that pool of tone
And boatwise dropped o' the convex side
And floated down the glassy tide
And clarified and glorified
The solemn spaces where the shadows bide.
From the warm concave of that fluted note
Somewhat, half song, half odor, forth did float,
As if a rose might somehow be a throat:
"When Nature from her far-off glen
Flutes her soft messages to men,
    The flute can say them o'er again;
    Yea, Nature, singing sweet and lone,
Breathes through life's strident polyphone
The flute-voice in the world of tone.
    Sweet friends,
    Man's love ascends
To finer and diviner ends
Than man's mere thought e'er comprehends,
For I, e'en I,
As here I lie,
A petal on a harmony,
Demand of Science whence and why
Man's tender pain, man's inward cry,

When he doth gaze on earth and sky?
I am not overbold:
   I hold
Full powers from Nature manifold.
I speak for each no-tonguéd tree
That, spring by spring, doth nobler be,
And dumbly and most wistfully
His mighty prayerful arms outspreads
Above men's oft-unheeding heads,
And his big blessing downward sheds.
I speak for all-shaped blooms and leaves,
Lichens on stones and moss on eaves.
Grasses and grains in ranks and sheaves;
Broad-fronded ferns and keen-leaved canes,
And briery mazes bounding lanes,
And marsh-plants, thirsty-cupped for rains,
And milky stems and sugary veins;
For every long-armed woman-vine
That round a piteous tree doth twine;
For passionate odors, and divine
Pistils, and petals crystalline;
All purities of shady springs,
All shynesses of film-winged things
That fly from tree-trunks and bark-rings;
All modesties of mountain-fawns
That leap to covert from wild lawns,
And tremble if the day but dawns;
All sparklings of small beady eyes
Of birds, and sidelong glances wise
Wherewith the jay hints tragedies;
All piquancies of prickly burs,
And smoothnesses of downs and furs
Of eiders and of minevers;
All limpid honeys that do lie
At stamen-bases, nor deny
The humming-birds' fine roguery,
Bee-thighs, nor any butterfly;
All gracious curves of slender wings,
Bark-mottlings, fibre-spiralings,
Fern-wavings and leaf-flickerings;
Each dial-marked leaf and flower-bell
Wherewith in every lonesome dell
Time to himself his hours doth tell;
All tree-sounds, rustlings of pine-cones,
Wind-sighings, doves' melodious moans,
And night's unearthly under-tones;
All placid lakes and waveless deeps,
All cool reposing mountain-steeps,

Vale-calms and tranquil lotos-sleeps;—
Yea, all fair forms, and sounds, and lights,
And warmths, and mysteries, and mights,
Of Nature's utmost depths and heights,
—These doth my timid tongue present,
Their mouthpiece and leal instrument
And servant, all love-eloquent.
I heard, when '*All for love*' the violins cried:
So, Nature calls through all her system wide,
Give me thy love, O man, so long denied.
Much time is run, and man hath changed his ways,
Since Nature, in the antique fable-days,
Was hid from man's true love by proxy fays,
False fauns and rascal gods that stole her praise.
The nymphs, cold creatures of man's colder brain,
Chilled Nature's streams till man's warm heart was fain
Never to lave its love in them again.
Later, a sweet Voice *Love thy neighbor* said;
Then first the bounds of neighborhood outspread
Beyond all confines of old ethnic dread.
Vainly the Jew might wag his covenant head:
'*All men are neighbors,*' so the sweet Voice said.
So, when man's arms had circled all man's race,
The liberal compass of his warm embrace
Stretched bigger yet in the dark bounds of space;
With hands a-grope he felt smooth Nature's grace,
Drew her to breast and kissed her sweetheart face:
Yea man found neighbors in great hills and trees
And streams and clouds and suns and birds and bees
And throbbed with neighbor-loves in loving these.
But oh, the poor! the poor! the poor!
That stand by the inward-opening door
Trade's hand doth tighten ever more,
And sigh their monstrous foul-air sigh
For the outside hills of liberty,
Where Nature spreads her wild blue sky
For Art to make into melody!
Thou Trade! thou king of the modern days!
  Change thy ways,
  Change thy ways;
Let the sweaty laborers file
  A little while,
  A little while,
Where Art and Nature sing and smile.
Trade! is thy heart all dead, all dead?
And hast thou nothing but a head?
I'm all for heart," the flute-voice said,
And into sudden silence fled,

Like as a blush that while 'tis red
Dies to a still, still white instead.

    Thereto a thrilling calm succeeds,
Till presently the silence breeds
A little breeze among the reeds
That seems to blow by sea-marsh weeds:
Then from the gentle stir and fret
Sings out the melting clarionet,
Like as a lady sings while yet
Her eyes with salty tears are wet.
"O Trade! O Trade!" the Lady said,
"I too will wish thee utterly dead
If all thy heart is in thy head.
For O my God! and O my God!
What shameful ways have women trod
At beckoning of Trade's golden rod!
Alas when sighs are traders' lies,
And heart's-ease eyes and violet eyes
    Are merchandise!
O purchased lips that kiss with pain!
O cheeks coin-spotted with smirch and stain!
O trafficked hearts that break in twain!
—And yet what wonder at my sisters' crime?
So hath Trade withered up Love's sinewy prime,
Men love not women as in olden time.
Ah, not in these cold merchantable days
Deem men their life an opal gray, where plays
The one red Sweet of gracious ladies'-praise.
Now, comes a suitor with sharp prying eye—
Says, *Here, you Lady, if you'll sell, I'll buy:*
Come, heart for heart—a trade? What! weeping? why?
Shame on such wooers' dapper mercery!
I would my lover kneeling at my feet
In humble manliness should cry, *O sweet!*
I know not if thy heart my heart will greet:
I ask not if thy love my love can meet:
Whate'er thy worshipful soft tongue shall say,
I'll kiss thine answer, be it yea or nay:
I do but know I love thee, and I pray
To be thy knight until my dying day.
Woe him that cunning trades in hearts contrives!
Base love good women to base loving drives.
If men loved larger, larger were our lives;
And wooed they nobler, won they nobler wives."
There thrust the bold straightforward horn
To battle for that lady lorn.
With heartsome voice of mellow scorn.

Like any knight in knighthood's morn.
  "Now comfort thee," said he,
    "Fair Lady.
For God shall right thy grievous wrong,
And man shall sing thee a true-love song,
Voiced in act his whole life long,
  Yea, all thy sweet life long,
    Fair Lady.
Where's he that craftily hath said,
The day of chivalry is dead?
I'll prove that lie upon his head,
  Or I will die instead,
    Fair Lady.
Is Honor gone into his grave?
Hath Faith become a caitiff knave,
And Selfhood turned into a slave
  To work in Mammon's cave,
    Fair Lady?
Will Truth's long blade ne'er gleam again?
Hath Giant Trade in dungeons slain
All great contempts of mean-got gain
  And hates of inward stain,
    Fair Lady?
For aye shall name and fame be sold,
And place be hugged for the sake of gold,
And smirch-robed Justice feebly scold
  At Crime all money-bold,
    Fair Lady?
Shall self-wrapt husbands aye forget
Kiss-pardons for the daily fret
Wherewith sweet wifely eyes are wet—
  Blind to lips kiss-wise set—
    Fair Lady?
Shall lovers higgle, heart for heart,
Till wooing grows a trading mart
Where much for little, and all for part,
  Make love a cheapening art,
    Fair Lady?
Shall woman scorch for a single sin
That her betrayer may revel in,
And she be burnt, and he but grin
  When that the flames begin,
    Fair Lady?
Shall ne'er prevail the woman's plea,
We maids would far, far whiter be
If that our eyes might sometimes see
  Men maids in purity,
    Fair Lady?

Shall Trade aye salve his conscience-aches
With jibes at Chivalry's old mistakes—
The wars that o'erhot knighthood makes
  For Christ's and ladies' sakes,
    Fair Lady?
Now by each knight that e'er hath prayed
To fight like a man and love like a maid,
Since Pembroke's life, as Pembroke's blade,
  I' the scabbard, death was laid,
    Fair Lady,
I dare avouch my faith is bright
That God doth right and God hath might.
Nor time hath changed His hair to white,
  Nor His dear love to spite,
    Fair Lady.
I doubt no doubts: I strive, and shrive my clay,
And fight my fight in the patient modern way
For true love and for thee—ah me! and pray
  To be thy knight until my dying day,
    Fair Lady."
Made end that knightly horn, and spurred away
Into the thick of the melodious fray.

And then the hautboy played and smiled,
And sang like any large-eyed child,
Cool-hearted and all undefiled.
  "Huge Trade!" he said,
"Would thou wouldst lift me on thy head
And run where'er my finger led!
Once said a Man—and wise was He—
Never shalt thou the heavens see,
Save as a little child thou be."
Then o'er sea-lashings of commingling tunes
The ancient wise bassoons,
  Like weird
  Gray-beard
Old harpers sitting on the high sea-dunes,
  Chanted runes:
"Bright-waved gain, gray-waved loss,
The sea of all doth lash and toss,
One wave forward and one across:
But now 'twas trough, now 'tis crest,
And worst doth foam and flash to best,
  And curst to blest.

"Life! Life! thou sea-fugue, writ from east to west,
  Love, Love alone can pore
  On thy dissolving score

Of harsh half-phrasings,
Blotted ere writ,
And double erasings
Of chords most fit.

"Yea, Love, sole music-master blest,
May read thy weltering palimpsest.
To follow Time's dying melodies through,
And never to lose the old in the new,
And ever to solve the discords true—
Love alone can do.
And ever Love hears the poor-folks' crying,
And ever Love hears the women's sighing,
And ever sweet knighthood's death-defying,
And ever wise childhood's deep implying,
But never a trader's glozing and lying.

"And yet shall Love himself be heard,
Though long deferred, though long deferred:
O'er the modern waste a dove hath whirred:
Music is Love in search of a word."

Song of the Chattahoochee

Out of the hills of Habersham,
Down the valleys of Hall,
I hurry amain to reach the plain,
Run the rapid and leap the fall,
Split at the rock and together again,
Accept my bed, or narrow or wide,
And flee from folly on every side
With a lover's pain to attain the plain
Far from the hills of Habersham,
Far from the valleys of Hall.

All down the hills of Habersham,
All through the valleys of Hall,
The rushes cried *Abide, abide*,
The willful waterweeds held me thrall,
The laving laurel turned my tide,
The ferns and the fondling grass said *Stay*,
The dewberry dipped for to work delay,
And the little reeds sighed *Abide, abide*,
Here in the hills of Habersham,
Here in the valleys of Hall.

High o'er the hills of Habersham,
Veiling the valleys of Hall,

The hickory told me manifold
Fair tales of shade, the poplar tall
Wrought me her shadowy self to hold,
The chestnut, the oak, the walnut, the pine,
Overleaning, with flickering meaning and sign,
Said, *Pass not, so cold, these manifold*
    Deep shades of the hills of Habersham,
    These glades in the valleys of Hall.

    And oft in the hills of Habersham,
    And oft in the valleys of Hall,
The white quartz shone, and the smooth brook-stone
Did bar me of passage with friendly brawl,
And many a luminous jewel lone
—Crystals clear or a-cloud with mist,
Ruby, garnet and amethyst—
Made lures with the lights of streaming stone
    In the clefts of the hills of Habersham,
    In the beds of the valleys of Hall.

    But oh, not the hills of Habersham,
    And oh, not the valleys of Hall
Avail: I am fain for to water the plain.
Downward the voices of Duty call—
Downward, to toil and be mixed with the main,
The dry fields burn, and the mills are to turn,
And a myriad flowers mortally yearn,
And the lordly main from beyond the plain
    Calls o'er the hills of Habersham,
    Calls through the valleys of Hall.

The Marshes of Glynn

Glooms of the live-oaks, beautiful-braided and woven
With intricate shades of the vines that myriad-cloven
    Clamber the forks of the multiform boughs,—
        Emerald twilights,—
        Virginal shy lights,
Wrought of the leaves to allure to the whisper of vows,
When lovers pace timidly down through the green colonnades
Of the dim sweet woods, of the dear dark woods,
    Of the heavenly woods and glades,
That run to the radiant marginal sand-beach within
    The wide sea-marshes of Glynn;—

Beautiful glooms, soft dusks in the noon-day fire,—
Wildwood privacies, closets of lone desire,
Chamber from chamber parted with wavering arras of leaves,—

Cells for the passionate pleasure of prayer to the soul that grieves,
Pure with a sense of the passing of saints through the wood,
Cool for the dutiful weighing of ill with good;—

O braided dusks of the oak and woven shades of the vine,
While the riotous noon-day sun of the June-day long did shine
Ye held me fast in your heart and I held you fast in mine;
But now when the noon is no more, and riot is rest,
And the sun is a-wait at the ponderous gate of the West,
And the slant yellow beam down the wood-aisle doth seem
Like a lane into heaven that leads from a dream,—
Ay, now, when my soul all day hath drunken the soul of the oak,
And my heart is at ease from men, and the wearisome sound of the stroke
  Of the scythe of time and the trowel of trade is low,
   And belief overmasters doubt, and I know that I know,
   And my spirit is grown to a lordly great compass within,
That the length and the breadth and the sweep of the marshes of Glynn
Will work me no fear like the fear they have wrought me of yore
When length was fatigue, and when breadth was but bitterness sore,
And when terror and shrinking and dreary unnamable pain
Drew over me out of the merciless miles of the plain,—

Oh, now, unafraid, I am fain to face
  The vast sweet visage of space.
To the edge of the wood I am drawn, I am drawn,
Where the gray beach glimmering runs, as a belt of the dawn,
  For a mete and a mark
   To the forest-dark:—
       So:
Affable live-oak, leaning low,—
Thus—with your favor—soft, with a reverent hand,
(Not lightly touching your person, Lord of the land!)
Bending your beauty aside, with a step I stand
On the firm-packed sand,
      Free
By a world of marsh that borders a world of sea.
  Sinuous southward and sinuous northward the shimmering band
  Of the sand-beach fastens the fringe of the marsh to the folds of the land.
Inward and outward to northward and southward the beach-lines linger and curl
As a silver-wrought garment that clings to and follows the firm sweet limbs of a girl.
Vanishing, swerving, evermore curving again into sight,
Softly the sand-beach wavers away to a dim gray looping of light.
And what if behind me to westward the wall of the woods stands high?
The world lies east: how ample, the marsh and the sea and the sky!
A league and a league of marsh-grass, waist-high, broad in the blade,
Green, and all of a height, and unflecked with a light or a shade,
Stretch leisurely off, in a pleasant plain,
To the terminal blue of the main.

Oh, what is abroad in the marsh and the terminal sea?
    Somehow my soul seems suddenly free
From the weighing of fate and the sad discussion of sin,
By the length and the breadth and the sweep of the marshes of Glynn.

Ye marshes, how candid and simple and nothing-withholding and free
Ye publish yourselves to the sky and offer yourselves to the sea!
Tolerant plains, that suffer the sea and the rains and the sun,
Ye spread and span like the catholic man who hath mightily won
God out of knowledge and good out of infinite pain
And sight out of blindness and purity out of a stain.
As the marsh-hen secretly builds on the watery sod,
Behold I will build me a nest on the greatness of God:
I will fly in the greatness of God as the marsh-hen flies
In the freedom that fills all the space 'twixt the marsh and the skies:
By so many roots as the marsh-grass sends in the sod
I will heartily lay me a-hold on the greatness of God:
Oh, like to the greatness of God is the greatness within
The range of the marshes, the liberal marshes of Glynn.

And the sea lends large, as the marsh: lo, out of his plenty the sea
Pours fast: full soon the time of the flood-tide must be:
Look how the grace of the sea doth go
About and about through the intricate channels that flow
        Here and there,
           Everywhere,
Till his waters have flooded the uttermost creeks and the low-lying lanes,
And the marsh is meshed with a million veins,
That like as with rosy and silvery essences flow
  In the rose-and-silver evening glow.
          Farewell, my lord Sun!
The creeks overflow: a thousand rivulets run
'Twixt the roots of the sod; the blades of the marsh-grass stir;
Passeth a hurrying sound of wings that westward whirr;
Passeth, and all is still; and the currents cease to run;
And the sea and the marsh are one.

How still the plains of the waters be!
The tide is in his ecstasy.
The tide is at his highest height:
         And it is night.
And now from the Vast of the Lord will the waters of sleep
Roll in on the souls of men,
But who will reveal to our waking ken
The forms that swim and the shapes that creep
        Under the waters of sleep?
And I would I could know what swimmeth below when the tide comes in
On the length and the breadth of the marvellous marshes of Glynn.

George Washington Cable

(1844–1925)

Born in New Orleans in 1844 to a mother whose background could be traced to the earliest Puritans of New England and a father who was descended from an established Virginia line, George Washington Cable grew up with a deep affection for Louisiana Creole life, tempered by a deep moral indignation over the issue of slavery. Banished from New Orleans after the city's fall, the young Cable joined the Confederate cavalry and served under Wirt Adams and Nathan Bedford Forrest. After the war, he began writing for the *New Orleans Picayune*, and after researching historical records for newspaper stories, he began writing fiction about life in and around New Orleans. During the next ten years, Cable published a series of local-color stories narrated in Creole dialect and later collected in *Old Creole Days* (1879). In 1880, he published *The Grandissimes*, a novel chronicling the changes experienced by an aristocratic Creole family in the early years of the nineteenth century. *The Grandissimes* also vividly characterizes the rebellious slave Bras Coupe, who escapes from slavery but is eventually recaptured and killed; thus, its publication marks the beginning of Cable's public advocacy of Negro rights, views that would turn the people of his home city against him. *The Creoles of Louisiana* (1884), an informal history, and the novels *Madame Delphine* (1881) and *Dr. Sevier* (1884) all advocated reform, and the essay collection *The Silent South* (1885) cemented Cable's reputation as a progressive.

Alienated from former friends and supporters in the South, Cable moved north in 1885, first to Simsbury, Connecticut, and then to Northampton, Massachusetts, where he would live for the remainder of his life. *Bonaventure* (1888) and *Strange True Stories of Louisiana* (1889) were both sentimental recollections, but with *The Negro Question*, another essay collection published in 1890, Cable returned to his criticisms of the interracial relations in the South. *John March, Southerner*, which appeared in 1894, represented Cable's last effort to address seriously the problems that confronted the land of his boyhood. Though his later efforts never approached the quality of his earlier work, Cable remained prolific to the end of his long life, producing four more novels, three short-story collections, and a guide for Bible study before he died in 1925.

Jean-ah Poquelin

In the first decade of the present century, when the newly established American Government was the most hateful thing in Louisiana—when the Creoles were still kicking at such vile innovations as the trial by jury, American dances, anti-smuggling laws, and the printing of the Governor's proclamation in English—when the Anglo-American flood that was presently to burst in a crevasse of immigration upon the delta had thus far been felt only as slippery seepage which made the Creole tremble for his footing—there stood, a short distance above what is now Canal Street, and considerably back from the line of villas which fringed the riverbank on Tchoupitoulas Road, an old colonial plantation house half in ruin.

It stood aloof from civilization, the tracts that had once been its indigo fields given over to their first noxious wildness, and grown up into one of the horridest marshes within a circuit of fifty miles.

The house was of heavy cypress, lifted up on pillars, grim, solid, and spiritless, its massive build a strong reminder of days still earlier, then every man had been his own peace officer and the insurrection of the blacks a daily contingency. Its dark, weather-beaten roof and sides were hoisted up above the jungly plain in a distracted way, like a gigantic ammunition wagon stuck in the mud and abandoned by some retreating army. Around it was a dense growth of low water willows, with half a hundred sorts of thorny or fetid bushes, savage strangers alike to the "language of flowers" and to the botanist's Greek. They were hung with countless strands of discolored and prickly smilax, and the impassable mud below bristled with *chevaux de frise* of the dwarf palmetto. Two lone forest trees, dead cypresses, stood in the center of the marsh, dotted with roosting vultures. The shallow strips of water were hid by myriads of aquatic plants, under whose coarse and spiritless flowers, could one have seen it, was a harbor of reptiles, great and small, to make one shudder to the end of his days.

The house was on a slightly raised spot, the levee of a draining canal. The waters of this canal did not run; they crawled, and were full of big, ravening fish and alligators that held it against all comers.

Such was the home of old Jean Marie Poquelin, once an opulent indigo planter, standing high in the esteem of his small, proud circle of exclusively male acquaintances in the old city; now a hermit, alike shunned by and shunning all who had ever known him. "The last of his line," said the gossips. His father lies under the floor of the St. Louis Cathedral, with the wife of his youth on one side, and the wife of his old age on the other. Old Jean visits the spot daily. His half brother—alas! there was a mystery; no one knew what had become of the gentle, young half brother, more than thirty years his junior, whom once he seemed so fondly to love, but who, seven years ago, had disappeared suddenly, once for all, and left no clue of his fate.

They had seemed to live so happily in each other's love. No father, mother, wife to either, no kindred upon earth. The elder a bold, frank, impetuous, chivalric adventurer; the younger a gentle, studious, book-loving recluse; they lived upon the ancestral estate like mated birds, one always on the wing, the other always in the nest.

There was no trait in Jean Marie Poquelin, said the old gossips, for which he was so well known among his few friends as his apparent fondness for his "little brother." "Jacques said this," and "Jacques said that"; he "would leave this or that, or any thing to Jacques," for Jacques was a scholar, and "Jacques was good," or "wise," or "just," or "farsighted," as the nature of the case required; and "he should ask Jacques as soon as he got home," since Jacques was never elsewhere to be seen.

It was between the roving character of the one brother, and the bookishness of the other, that the estate fell into decay. Jean Marie, generous gentleman, gambled the slaves away one by one, until none was left, man or woman, but one old African mute.

The indigo fields and vats of Louisiana had been generally abandoned as unremunerative. Certain enterprising men had substituted the culture of sugar; but while the recluse was too apathetic to take so active a course, the other saw larger, and, at that time, equally respectable profits, first in smuggling, and later in the African slave trade. What harm could he see in it? The whole people said it was vitally necessary, and to minister to a vital public necessity—good enough, certainly, and so he laid up many a doubloon, that made him none the worse in the public regard.

One day old Jean Marie was about to start upon a voyage that was to be longer, much longer, than any that he had yet made. Jacques had begged him hard for many days not to go, but he laughed him off, and finally said, kissing him:

"Adieu, 'tit frère."

"No," said Jacques, "I shall go with you."

They left the old hulk of a house in the sole care of the African mute, and went away to the Guinea coast together.

Two years after, old Poquelin came home without his vessel. He must have arrived at his house by night. No one saw him come. No one saw "his little brother"; rumor whispered that he, too, had returned, but he had never been seen again.

A dark suspicion fell upon the old slave trader. No matter that the few kept the many reminded of the tenderness that had ever marked his bearing to the missing man. The many shook their heads. "You know he has a quick and fearful temper"; and "why does he cover his loss with mystery?" "Grief would out with the truth."

"But," said the charitable few, "look in his face; see that expression of true humanity." The many did look in his face, and, as he looked in theirs, he read the silent question: "Where is thy brother Abel?" The few were silenced, his former friends died off, and the name of Jean Marie Poquelin became a symbol of witchery, devilish crime, and hideous nursery fictions.

The man and his house were alike shunned. The snipe and duck hunters forsook the marsh, and the woodcutters abandoned the canal. Sometimes the hardier boys who ventured out there snake-shooting heard a low thumping of oarlocks on the canal. They would look at each other for a moment half in consternation, half in glee, then rush from their sport in wanton haste to assail with their gibes the unoffending, withered old man who, in rusty attire, sat in the stern of a skiff, rowed homeward by his white-headed African mute.

"O Jean-ah Poquelin! O Jean-ah! Jean-ah Poquelin!"

It was not necessary to utter more than that. No hint of wickedness, deformity, or any physical or moral demerit; merely the name and tone of mockery: "Oh, Jean-ah Poquelin!" and while they tumbled one over another in their needless haste to fly, he would rise carefully from his seat, while the aged mute, with downcast face, went on rowing, and, rolling up his brown fist and extending it toward the urchins, would pour forth such an unholy broadside of French imprecation and invective as would all but craze them with delight.

Among both blacks and whites the house was the object of a thousand superstitions. Every midnight, they affirmed, the *feu follet* came out of the marsh and ran in and out of the rooms, flashing from window to window. The story of some lads, whose word in ordinary statements was worthless, was generally credited, that the night they camped in the woods, rather than pass the place after dark, they saw, about sunset, every window blood-red, and on each of the four chimneys an owl sitting, which turned his head three times round, and moaned and laughed with a human voice. There was a bottomless well, everybody professed to know, beneath the sill of the big front door under the rotten veranda; whoever set his foot upon that threshold disappeared forever in the depth below.

What wonder the marsh grew as wild as Africa! Take all the Faubourg Ste. Marie, and half the ancient city, you would not find one graceless daredevil reckless enough to pass within a hundred yards of the house after midnight.

The alien races pouring into old New Orleans began to find the few streets named for the Bourbon princes too strait for them. The wheel of fortune, beginning to whirl, threw them off beyond the ancient corporation lines, and sowed civilization and even trade upon the lands of the Graviers and Girods. Fields became roads, roads streets. Everywhere the leveler was peering through his glass, rodsmen were whacking their way through willow brakes and rose hedges, and the sweating Irishmen tossed the blue clay up with their long-handled shovels.

"Ha! that is all very well," quoth the Jean-Baptistes, feeling the reproach of an enterprise that asked neither cooperation nor advice of them, "but wait till they come yonder to Jean Poquelin's marsh; ha! ha! ha!" The supposed predicament so delighted them, that they put on a mock terror and whirled about in an assumed stampede, then caught their clasped hands between their knees in excess of mirth, and laughed till the tears ran; for whether the streetmakers mired in the marsh, or contrived to cut through old "Jean-ah's" property, either event would be joyful. Meantime a line of tiny rods, with bits of white paper in their split tops, gradually extended its way straight through the haunted ground, and across the canal diagonally.

"We shall fill that ditch, said the men in mud boots, and brushed close along the chained and padlocked gate of the haunted mansion. Ah, Jean-ah Poquelin, those were not Creole boys, to be stampeded with a little hard swearing.

He went to the Governor. That official scanned the odd figure with no slight interest. Jean Poquelin was of short, broad frame, with a bronzed leonine face. His brow was ample and deeply furrowed. His eye, large and black, was bold and open like that of a war horse, and his jaws shut together with the firmness of iron. He was dressed in a suit of Attakapas cottonade, and his shirt unbuttoned and thrown back from the throat and bosom, sailorwise, showed a herculean breast, hard and grizzled. There was no fierceness or defiance in his look, no harsh ungentleness, no symptom of his unlawful life or violent temper; but rather a peaceful and peaceable fearlessness. Across the whole face, not marked in one or another feature, but as it were laid softly upon the countenance like an almost imperceptible veil, was the imprint of some great grief. A careless eye might easily overlook it, but, once seen, there it hung—faint, but unmistakable.

The Governor bowed.

"*Parlez-vous français?*" asked the figure.

"I would rather talk English, if you can do so," said the Governor.

"My name, Jean Poquelin."

"How can I serve you, Mr. Poquelin?"

"My 'ouse is yond'; *dans le marais là-bas.*"

The Governor bowed.

"Dat *marais* billong to me."

"Yes, sir."

"To me; Jean Poquelin; I hown 'im meself."

"Well, sir?"

"He don't billong to you; I get him from me father."

"That is perfectly true, Mr. Poquelin, as far as I am aware."

"You want to make strit pass yond'?"

"I do not know, sir; it is quite probable; but the city will indemnify you for any loss you may suffer—you will get paid, you understand."

"Strit can't pass dare."

"You will have to see the municipal authorities about that, Mr. Poquelin."

A bitter smile came upon the old man's face.

"*Pardon, Monsieur,* you is not *le Gouverneur?*"

"Yes."

"*Mais,* yes. You har *le Gouverneur*—yes. Veh-well. I come to you. I tell you, strit can't pass at me 'ouse."

"But you will have to see—"

"I come to you. You is *le Gouverneur.* I know not the new laws. I ham a Fr-r-rench-a-man! Fr-rench-a-man have something *aller au contraire*—he come at his *Gouverneur.* I come at you. If me not had been bought from me king like *bossals* in the hold time, ze king gof—France would-a-show *Monsieur le Gouverneur* to take care his men to make strit in right places. *Mais,* I know; we billong to *Monsieur le Président.* I want you do somesin for me, eh?"

"What is it?" asked the patient Governor.

"I want you tell *Monsieur le Président,* strit—can't—pass—at—me—'ouse."

"Have a chair, Mr. Poquelin"; but the old man did not stir. The Governor took a quill and wrote a line to a city official, introducing Mr. Poquelin, and asking for him every possible courtesy. He handed it to him, instructing him where to present it.

"Mr. Poquelin," he said, with a conciliatory smile, "tell me, is it your house that our Creole citizens tell such odd stories about?"

The old man glared sternly upon the speaker, and with immovable features said:

"You don't see me trade some Guinea nigga'?"

"Oh, no."

"You don't see me make some smugglin'?"

"No, sir; not at all."

"But, I am Jean Marie Poquelin. I mine me hown bizniss. Dat all right? Adieu."

He put his hat on and withdrew. By and by he stood, letter in hand, before the person to whom it was addressed. This person employed an interpreter.

"He says," said the interpreter to the officer, "he come to make you the fair warning how you muz not make the street pas' at his 'ouse."

The officer remarked that "such impudence was refreshing"; but the experienced interpreter translated freely.

"He says: 'Why you don't want?'" said the interpreter.

The old slave trader answered at some length.

"He says," said the interpreter, again turning to the officer, "the morass is a too unhealth' for peopl' to live."

"But we expect to drain his old marsh; it's not going to be a marsh."

"*Il dit*"—the interpreter explained in French.

The old man answered tersely.

"He says the canal is a private," said the interpreter.

"Oh! *that* old ditch; that's to be filled up. Tell the old man we're going to fix him up nicely."

Translation being duly made, the man in power was amused to see a thunder-cloud gathering on the old man's face.

"Tell him," he added, "by the time we finish, there'll not be a ghost left in his shanty."

The interpreter began to translate, but—

"*J' comprends, j' comprends,*" said the old man, with an impatient gesture, and burst forth, pouring curses upon the United States, the President, the Territory of Orleans, Congress, the Governor and all his subordinates, striding out of the apartment as he cursed, while the object of his maledictions roared with merriment and rammed the floor with his foot.

"Why, it will make his old place worth ten dollars to one," said the official to the interpreter.

" 'Tis not for de worse of de property," said the interpreter.

"I should guess not," said the other, whittling his chair—"seems to me as if some of these old Creoles would liever live in a crawfish hole than to have a neighbor."

"You know what make old Jean Poquelin make like that? I will tell you. You know—"

The interpreter was rolling a cigarette, and paused to light his tinder; then, as the smoke poured in a thick double stream from his nostrils, he said, in a solemn whisper:

"He is a witch."

"Ho, ho, ho!" laughed the other.

"You don't believe it? What you want to bet?" cried the interpreter, jerking himself half up and thrusting out one arm while he bared it of its coat sleeve with the hand of the other. "What you want to bet?"

"How do you know?" asked the official.

"Dass what I goin' to tell you. You know, one evening I was shooting some *grosbec*. I killed three; but I had trouble to find them, it was becoming so dark. When I have them I start' to come home; then I got to pas' at Jean Poquelin's house."

"Ho, ho, ho!" laughed the other, throwing his leg over the arm of his chair.

"Wait," said the interpreter. "I come along slow, not making some noises; still, still—"

"And scared," said the smiling one.

"*Mais*, wait. I get all pas' the 'ouse. 'Ah!' I say; 'all right!' Then I see two thing' before! Hah! I get as cold and humide, and shake like a leaf. You think it was nothing? There I see, so plain as can be (though it was making nearly dark), I see Jean—Marie—Po-que-lin walkin' right in front, and right there beside of him was something like a man—but not a man—white like paint!—I dropp' on the grass from scared—they pass'; so sure as I live 'twas the ghos' of Jacques Poquelin, his brother!"

"Pooh!" said the listener.

"I'll put my han' in the fire," said the interpreter.

"But did you never think," asked the other, "that that might be Jack Poquelin, as you call him, alive and well, and for some cause hid away by his brother?"

"But there har' no cause!" said the other, and the entrance of third parties changed the subject.

Some months passed and the street was opened. A canal was first dug through the marsh, the small one which passed so close to Jean Poquelin's house was filled, and the street, or rather a sunny road, just touched a corner of the old mansion's dooryard. The morass ran dry. Its venomous denizens slipped away through the bulrushes; the cattle roaming freely upon its hardened surface trampled the superabundant undergrowth. The bellowing frogs croaked to westward. Lilies and the flower-de-luce sprang up in the place of reeds; smilax and poison oak gave way to the purple-plumed ironweed and pink spiderwort; the bindweeds ran everywhere blooming as they ran, and on one of the dead cypresses a giant creeper hung its green burden of foliage and lifted its scarlet trumpets. Sparrows and redbirds flitted through the bushes, and dewberries grew ripe beneath. Over all these came a sweet, dry smell of salubrity which the place had not known since the sediments of the Mississippi first lifted it from the sea.

But its owner did not build. Over the willow brakes, and down the vista of the open street, bright new houses, some singly, some by ranks, were prying in upon the old man's privacy. They even settled down toward his southern side. First a woodcutter's hut or two, then a market gardener's shanty, then a painted cottage, and all at once the *faubourg* had flanked and half surrounded him and his dried-up marsh.

Ah! then the common people began to hate him. "The old tyrant!" "You don't mean an old *tyrant?*" "Well, then, why don't he build when the public need demands it? What does he live in that unneighborly way for?" "The old pirate!" "The old kidnaper!" How easily even the most ultra Louisianians put on the imported virtues of the North when they could be brought to bear against the hermit. "There he goes, with the boys after him! Ah! ha! ha! Jean-ah Poquelin! Ah! Jean-ah! Aha! aha! Jean-ah Marie! Jean-ah Poquelin! The old villain!" How merrily the swarming *Américains* echo the spirit of persecution! "The old fraud," they say—"pretends to live in a haunted house, does he? We'll tar and feather him someday. Guess we can fix him."

He cannot be rowed home along the old canal now; he walks. He has broken sadly of late, and the street urchins are ever at his heels. It is like the days when they cried: "Go up, thou baldhead," and the old man now and then turns and delivers ineffectual curses.

To the Creoles—to the incoming lower class of superstitious Germans, Irish, Sicilians, and others—he became an omen and embodiment of public and private ill fortune. Upon him all the vagaries of their superstitions gathered and grew. If a house caught fire, it was imputed to his machinations. Did a woman go off in a fit, he had bewitched her. Did a child stray off for an hour, the mother shivered with the apprehension that Jean Poquelin had offered him to strange gods. The house was the subject of every bad boy's invention who loved to contrive ghostly lies. "As long as that house stands we shall have bad luck. Do you not see our pease and beans dying, our cabbages and lettuce going to seed and our gardens turning to dust, while every day you can see it raining in the woods? The rain will never pass old Poquelin's house. He keeps a fetich. He has conjured the whole Faubourg Ste. Marie. And why, the old wretch? Simply because our playful and innocent children call after him as he passes."

A "Building and Improvement Company," which had not yet got its charter, "but was going to," and which had not, indeed, any tangible capital yet, but "was going to have some," joined the "Jean-ah Poquelin" war. The haunted property would be such a capital site for a market house! They sent a deputation to the old mansion to ask its occupant to sell. The deputation never got beyond the chained gate and a very barren interview with the African mute. The President of the Board was then empowered (for he had studied French in Pennsylvania and was considered qualified) to call and persuade M. Poquelin to subscribe to the company's stock; but—

"Fact is, gentlemen," he said at the next meeting, "it would take us at least twelve months to make Mr. Pokaleen understand the rather original features of our system, and he wouldn't subscribe when we'd done; besides, the only way to see him is to stop him on the street."

There was a great laugh from the Board; they couldn't help it. "Better meet a bear robbed of her whelps," said one.

"You're mistaken as to that," said the President. "I did meet him, and stopped him, and found him quite polite. But I could get no satisfaction from him; the fellow wouldn't talk in French, and when I spoke in English he hoisted his old shoulders up, and gave the same answer to everything I said."

"And that was—?" asked one or two, impatient of the pause.

"That it 'don't worse w'ile?'"

One of the Board said: "Mr. President, this market-house project, as I take it, is not altogether a selfish one; the community is to be benefited by it. We may feel that we are working in the public interest [the Board smiled knowingly], if we employ all possible means to oust this old nuisance from among us. You may know that at the time the street was cut through, this old Poquelann did all he could to prevent it. It was owing to a certain connection which I had with that affair that I heard a ghost story [smiles, followed by a sudden dignified check]—ghost story, which, of course, I am not going to relate; but I *may* say that my profound conviction, arising from a prolonged study of that story, is, that this old villain, John Poquelann, has his brother locked up in that old house. Now, if this is so, and we can fix it on him, I merely *suggest* that we can make the matter highly useful. I don't know," he added, beginning to sit down, "but that it is an action we owe to the community—hem!"

"How do you propose to handle the subject?" asked the President.

"I was thinking," said the speaker, "that, as a Board of Directors, it would be unadvisable for us to authorize any action involving trespass; but if you, for instance, Mr. President, should, as it were, for mere curiosity, *request* someone, as, for instance, our excellent Secretary, simply as a personal favor, to look into the matter—this is merely a suggestion."

The Secretary smiled sufficiently to be understood that, while he certainly did not consider such preposterous service a part of his duties as secretary, he might, notwithstanding, accede to the President's request; and the Board adjourned.

Little White, as the Secretary was called, was a mild, kindhearted little man, who, nevertheless, had no fear of anything, unless it was the fear of being unkind.

"I tell you frankly," he privately said to the President, "I go into this purely for reasons of my own."

The next day, a little after nightfall, one might have descried this little man slipping along the rear fence of the Poquelin place, preparatory to vaulting over into the rank, grass-grown yard, and bearing himself altogether more after the manner of a collector of race chickens than according to the usage of secretaries.

The picture presented to his eye was not calculated to enliven his mind. The old mansion stood out against the western sky, black and silent. One long, lurid pencil stroke along a sky of slate was all that was left of daylight. No sign of life was apparent; no light at any window, unless it might have been on the side of the house hidden from view. No owls were on the chimneys, no dogs were in the yard.

He entered the place, and ventured up behind a small cabin which stood apart from the house. Through one of its many crannies he easily detected the African mute crouched before a flickering pine knot, his head on his knees, fast asleep.

He concluded to enter the mansion, and, with that view, stood and scanned it. The broad rear steps of the veranda would not serve him; he might meet someone midway. He was measuring, with his eye, the proportions of one of the pillars which supported it, and estimating the practicability of climbing it, when he heard a footstep. Someone dragged a chair out toward the railing, then seemed to change his mind and began to pace the veranda, his footfalls resounding on the dry boards with singular loudness. Little White drew a step backward, got the figure between himself and the sky, and at once recognized the short, broad-shouldered form of old Jean Poquelin.

He sat down upon a billet of wood, and, to escape the stings of a whining cloud of mosquitoes, shrouded his face and neck in his handkerchief, leaving his eyes uncovered.

He had sat there but a moment when he noticed a strange, sickening odor, faint, as if coming from a distance, but loathsome and horrid.

Whence could it come? Not from the cabin; not from the marsh, for it was as dry as powder. It was not in the air; it seemed to come from the ground.

Rising up, he noticed, for the first time, a few steps before him a narrow footpath leading toward the house. He glanced down it—ha! right there was someone coming—ghostly white!

Quick as thought, and as noiselessly, he lay down at full length against the cabin. It was bold strategy, and yet, there was no denying it, little White felt that he was frightened. "It is not a ghost," he said to himself. "I *know* it cannot be a ghost"; but the perspiration burst out at every pore, and the air seemed to thicken with heat. "It is a living man," he said in his thoughts. "I hear his footstep, and I hear old Poquelin's footsteps, too, separately, over on the veranda. I am not discovered; the thing has passed; there is that odor again; what a smell of death! Is it coming back? Yes. It stops at the door of the cabin. Is it peering in at the sleeping mute? It moves away. It is in the path again. Now it is gone." He shuddered. "Now, if I dare venture, the mystery is solved." He rose cautiously, close against the cabin, and peered along the path.

The figure of a man, a presence if not a body—but whether clad in some white stuff or naked, the darkness would not allow him to determine—had turned, and now, with a seeming painful gait, moved slowly from him. "Great Heaven! can it be that the dead do walk?" He withdrew again the hands which had gone to his eyes. The dreadful object passed between two pillars and under the house. He listened. There was a faint sound as of feet within a staircase; then all was still except the measured tread of Jean Poquelin walking on the veranda, and the heavy respirations of the mute slumbering in the cabin.

The little Secretary was about to retreat; but as he looked once more toward the haunted house a dim light appeared in the crack of a closed window, and presently old Jean Poquelin came, dragging his chair, and sat down close against the shining cranny. He spoke in a low, tender tone in the French tongue, making some inquiry. An answer came from within. Was it the voice of a human? So unnatural was it—so hollow, so discordant, so unearthly—that the stealthy listener shuddered again from head to foot; and when something stirred in some bushes nearby—though it may have been nothing more than a rat—and came scuttling through the grass, the little Secretary actually turned and fled. As he left the enclosure he moved with bolder leisure through the bushes; yet now and then he spoke aloud: "Oh, oh! I see, I understand!" and shut his eyes in his hands.

How strange that henceforth little White was the champion of Jean Poquelin! In season and out of season—wherever a word was uttered against him—the Secretary, with a quiet, aggressive force that instantly arrested gossip, demanded upon what authority the statement or conjecture was made; but as he did not condescend to explain his own remarkable attitude, it was not long before the disrelish and suspicion which had followed Jean Poquelin so many years fell also upon him.

It was only the next evening but one after his adventure that he made himself a source of sullen amazement to one hundred and fifty boys, by ordering them to desist from their wanton hallooing. Old Jean Poquelin, standing and shaking his cane, rolling out his long-drawn maledictions, paused and stared, then gave the Secretary a courteous bow and started on. The boys, save one, from pure astonishment, ceased; but a ruffianly little Irish lad, more daring than any had yet been, threw a big hurtling clod that struck old Poquelin between the shoulders and burst like a shell. The enraged old man wheeled with uplifted staff to give chase to the scampering vagabond; and—he may have tripped, or he may not, but he fell full length. Little White hastened to help him up, but he waved him off with a fierce imprecation and, staggering to his feet, resumed his way homeward. His lips were reddened with blood.

Little White was on his way to the meeting of the Board. He would have given all he dared spend to have stayed away, for he felt both too fierce and too tremulous to brook the criticisms that were likely to be made.

"I can't help it, gentlemen; I can't help you to make a case against the old man, and I'm not going to."

"We did not expect this disappointment, Mr. White."

"I can't help that, sir. No, sir; you had better not appoint any more investigations. Somebody'll investigate himself into trouble. No, sir; it isn't a threat, it is only my advice, but I warn you that whoever takes the task in hand will rue it to his dying day—which may be hastened, too."

The President expressed himself surprised.

"I don't care a rush," answered little White, wildly and foolishly. "I don't care a rush if you are, sir. No, my nerves are not disordered; my head's as clear as a bell. No, I'm *not* excited."

A Director remarked that the Secretary looked as though he had waked from a nightmare.

"Well, sir, if you want to know the fact, I have; and if you choose to cultivate old Poquelin's society you can have one, too."

"White," called a facetious member, but White did not notice. "White," he called again.

"What?" demanded White, with a scowl.

"Did you see the ghost?"

"Yes, sir; I did," cried White, hitting the table, and handing the President a paper which brought the Board to other business.

The story got among the gossips that somebody (they were afraid to say little White) had been to the Poquelin mansion by night and beheld something appalling. The rumor was but a shadow of truth, magnified and distorted as is the manner of shadows. He had seen skeletons walking, and had barely escaped the clutches of one by making the sign of the cross.

Some madcap boys with an appetite for the horrible plucked up courage to venture through the dried marsh by the cattle path, and come before the house at a spectral hour when the air was full of bats. Something which they but half saw—half a sight was enough—sent them tearing back through the willow brakes and acacia bushes to their homes, where they fairly dropped down, and cried:

"Was it white?" "No—yes—nearly so—we can't tell—but we saw it." And one could hardly doubt, to look at their ashen faces, that they had, whatever it was.

"If that old rascal lived in the country we come from," said certain *Américains*, "he'd have been tarred and feathered before now, wouldn't he, Sanders?"

"Well, now he just would."

"And we'd have rid him on a rail, wouldn't we?"

"That's what I allow."

"Tell you what you *could* do." They were talking to some rollicking Creoles who had assumed an absolute necessity for doing *something*. "What is it you call this thing where an old man marries a young girl, and you come out with horns and—"

"Charivari?" asked the Creoles.

"Yes, that's it. Why don't you shivaree him?" Felicitous suggestion.

Little White, with his wife beside him, was sitting on their doorsteps on the sidewalk, as Creole custom had taught them, looking toward the sunset. They had moved into the lately opened street. The view was not attractive on the score of beauty. The houses were small and scattered, and across the flat commons, spite of the lofty tangle of weeds and bushes, and spite of the thickets of acacia, they needs must see the dismal old Poquelin mansion, tilted awry and shutting out the declining sun. The moon, white and slender, was hanging the tip of its horn over one of the chimneys.

"And you say," said the Secretary, "the old black man has been going by here alone? Patty, suppose old Poquelin should be concocting some mischief; he don't lack provocation; the way that clod hit him the other day was enough to have killed him. Why, Patty, he dropped as quick as *that!* No wonder you haven't seen him. I wonder if they haven't heard something about him up at the drugstore. Suppose I go and see."

"Do," said his wife.

She sat alone for half an hour, watching that sudden going out of the day peculiar to the latitude.

"That moon is ghost enough for one house," she said, as her husband returned. "It has gone right down the chimney."

"Patty," said little White, "the drug clerk says the boys are going to shivaree old Poquelin tonight. I'm going to try to stop it."

"Why, White," said his wife, "you'd better not. You'll get hurt."

"No, I'll not."

"Yes, you will."

"I'm going to sit out here until they come along. They're compelled to pass right by here."

"Why, White, it may be midnight before they start; you're not going to sit out here till then."

"Yes, I am."

"Well, you're very foolish," said Mrs. White in an undertone, looking anxious, and tapping one of the steps with her foot.

They sat a very long time talking over little family matters.

"What's that?" at last said Mrs. White.

"That's the nine-o'clock gun," said White, and they relapsed into a long-sustained, drowsy silence.

"Patty, you'd better go in and go to bed," said he at last.

"I'm not sleepy."

"Well, you're very foolish," quietly remarked little White, and again silence fell upon them.

"Patty, suppose I walk out to the old house and see if I can find out anything."

"Suppose," said she, "you don't do any such—listen!"

Down the street arose a great hubbub. Dogs and boys were howling and barking; men were laughing, shouting, groaning, and blowing horns, whooping, and clanking cowbells, whinnying, and howling, and rattling pots and pans.

"They are coming this way," said little White. "You had better go into the house, Patty."

"So had you."

"No. I'm going to see if I can't stop them."

"Why, White!"

"I'll be back in a minute," said White, and went toward the noise.

In a few moments the little Secretary met the mob. The pen hesitates on the word, for there is a respectable difference, measurable only on the scale of the half century, between a mob and a *charivari*. Little White lifted his ineffectual voice. He faced the head of the disorderly column, and cast himself about as if he were made of wood and moved by the jerk of a string. He rushed to one who seemed, from the size and clatter of his tin pan, to be a leader. *"Stop these fellows, Bienvenu, stop them just a minute, till I tell them something."* Bienvenu turned and brandished his instruments of discord in an imploring way to the crowd. They slackened their pace, two or three hushed their horns and joined the prayer of little White and Bienvenu for silence. The throng halted. The hush was delicious.

"Bienvenu," said little White, "don't shivaree old Poquelin tonight; he's—"

"My fwang," said the swaying Bienvenu, "who tail you I goin' to chahivahi somebody, eh? You sink bickause I make a little playfool wiz zis tin pan zat I am *dhonk?*"

"Oh, no, Bienvenu, old fellow, you're all right. I was afraid you might not know that old Poquelin was sick, you know, but you're not going there, are you?"

"My fwang, I vay soy to tail you zat you ah dhonk as de dev'. I am *shem* of you. I ham ze servan' of *ze publique*. Zese *citoyens* goin' to wickwest Jean Poquelin to give to the Ursuline' two hondred fifty dolla'—"

"Hé quoi!" cried a listener. *"Cinq cent piastres, oui!"*

"Oui!" said Bienvenu, "and if he wiffuse we make him some lit' *musique;* ta-ra-ta!" He hoisted a merry hand and foot, then frowning, added: "Old Poquelin got no bizniz dhink s'much w'isky."

"But, gentlemen," said little White, around whom a circle had gathered, "the old man is very sick."

"My faith!" cried a tiny Creole, "we did not make him to be sick. "W'en we have say we going make *le charivari*, do you want that we hall tell a lie? My faith! 'sfools!"

"But you can shivaree somebody else," said desperate little White.

"Oui!" cried Bienvenu, *"et chahivahi* Jean-ah Poquelin tomo'w'!"

"Let us go to Madame Schneider!" cried two or three, and amid huzzas and confused cries, among which was heard a stentorian Celtic call for drinks, the crowd again began to move.

"Cent piastres pour l'hôpital de charité!"

"Hurrah!"

"One hongred dolla' for Charity Hospital!"

"Hurrah!"

"Whang!" went a tin pan, the crowd yelled, and Pandemonium gaped again. They were off at a right angle.

Nodding, Mrs. White looked at the mantel clock.

"Well, if it isn't away after midnight."

The hideous noise downstreet was passing beyond earshot. She raised a sash and listened. For a moment there was silence. Someone came to the door.

"Is that you, White?"

"Yes. They've gone down to shivaree the old Dutchwoman who married her step-daughter's sweetheart. They say she has got to pay a hundred dollars to the hospital before they stop."

The couple retired, and Mrs. White slumbered. She was awakened by her husband snapping the lid of his watch.

"What time?" she asked.

"Half past three. Patty, I haven't slept a wink. Those fellows are out yet. Don't you hear them?"

"Why, White, they're coming this way!"

"I know they are," said White, sliding out of bed and drawing on his clothes, "and they're coming fast. You'd better go away from that window, Patty! My! What a clatter!"

"Here they are," said Mrs. White, but her husband was gone. Two or three hundred men and boys pass the place at a rapid walk straight down the broad, new street, toward the hated house of ghosts. The din was terrific. She saw little White at the head of the rabble brandishing his arms and trying in vain to make himself heard; but they only shook their heads, laughing and hooting the louder, and so passed, bearing him on before them.

Swiftly they pass out from among the houses, away from the dim oil lamps of the street, out into the broad starlit commons, and enter the willowy jungles of the haunted ground. Some hearts fail and their owners lag behind and turn back, suddenly remembering how near morning it is. But the most part push on, tearing the air with their clamor.

Down ahead of them in the long, thicket-darkened way there is—singularly enough—a faint dancing light. It must be very near the old house; it is. It has stopped now. It is a lantern, and is under a well-known sapling which has grown up on the wayside since the canal was filled. Now it swings mysteriously to and fro. A goodly number of the more ghost-fearing give up the sport; but a full hundred move forward at a run, doubling their devilish howling and banging.

Yes; it is a lantern, and there are two persons under the tree. The crowd draws near—drops into a walk; one of the two is the old African mute; he lifts the lantern up so that it shines on the other; the crowd recoils; there is a hush of all clangor, and all at once, with a cry of mingled fright and horror from every throat, the whole throng rushes back, dropping everything, sweeping past little White and hurrying on, never stopping until the jungle is left behind, and then to find that not one in ten has seen the cause of the stampede, and not one of the tenth is certain what it was.

There is one huge fellow among them who looks capable of any villainy. He finds something to mount on, and, in the Creole *patois*, calls a general halt. Bienvenu sinks down, and, vainly trying to recline gracefully, resigns the leadership. The herd gather round the speaker; he assures them that they have been outraged. Their right peaceably to traverse the public streets has been trampled upon. Shall such encroachments be endured? It is now daybreak. Let them go now by the open light of day and force a free passage of the public highway!

A scattering consent was the response, and the crowd, thinned now and drowsy, straggled quietly down toward the old house. Some drifted ahead, others sauntered behind, but everyone, as he again neared the tree, came to a standstill. Little White sat upon a bank of turf on the opposite side of the way looking very stern and sad. To each newcomer he put the same question:

"Did you come here to go to old Poquelin's?"

"Yes."

"He's dead." And if the shocked hearer started away he would say: "Don't go away."

"Why not?"

"I want you to go to the funeral presently."

If some Louisianian, too loyal to dear France or Spain to understand English, looked bewildered, someone would interpret for him; and presently they went. Little White led the van, the crowd trooping after him down the middle of the way. The gate, that had never been seen before unchained, was open. Stern little White stopped a short distance from it; the rabble stopped behind him. Something was moving out from under the veranda. The many whisperers stretched upward to see. The African mute came very slowly toward the gate, leading by a cord in the nose a small brown bull, which was harnessed to a rude cart. On the flat body of the cart, under a black cloth, were seen the outlines of a long box.

"Hats off, gentlemen," said little White, as the box came in view, and the crowd silently uncovered.

"Gentlemen," said little White, "here come the last remains of Jean Marie Poquelin, a better man, I'm afraid, with all his sins—yes, a better—a kinder man to his blood—a man of more self-forgetful goodness—than all of you put together will ever dare to be."

There was a profound hush as the vehicle came creaking through the gate; but when it turned away from them toward the forest, those in front started suddenly. There was a backward rush, then all stood still again staring one way; for there, behind the bier, with eyes cast down and labored step, walked the living remains—all that was left—of little Jacques Poquelin, the long-hidden brother—a leper, as white as snow.

Dumb with horror, the cringing crowd gazed upon the walking death. They watched, in silent awe, the slow *cortège* creep down the long, straight road and lessen on the view, until by and by it stopped where a wild, unfrequented path branched off into the undergrowth toward the rear of the ancient city.

"They are going to the *Terre aux Lépreux*," said one in the crowd. The rest watched them in silence.

The little bull was set free; the mute, with the strength of an ape, lifted the long box to his shoulder. For a moment more the mute and the leper stood in sight, while the former adjusted his heavy burden; then, without one backward glance upon the unkind human world, turning their faces toward the ridge in the depths of the swamp known as the Leper's Land, they stepped into the jungle, disappeared, and were never seen again.

from *The Negro Question:*

The Answer

I.

As to the Southern people the answer is that, although the Southern master-class now cordially and unanimously admit the folly of slave-holding, yet the fundamental article of political faith on which slavery rested has not been displaced. As to the people of the North the answer is simpler still: the Union is saved.

The Northern cause in our civil war was not primarily the abolition of slavery, although many a Northern soldier and captain fought mainly for this and cared for no other issue while this remained. The Southern cause was not merely for disunion, though many a Southern soldier and captain would never have taken up the sword to defend slave-holding stripped of the disguise of State sovereignty. The Northern cause was pre-eminently the National unity. Emancipation—the emancipation of the negroes—was not what the North fought for, but only what it fought with. The right to secede was not what the South fought for, but only what it fought with. The great majority of the Southern white people loved the Union and consented to its destruction only when there seemed to be no other way to save slavery; the great bulk of the North consented to destroy slavery only when there seemed no other way to save the Union. To put in peril the Union on one side and slavery on the other was enough, when nothing else was enough, to drench one of the greatest and happiest lands on earth with the blood of hundreds of thousands of her own children. Now, what thing of supreme value rested on this Union, and what on this slavery, that they should have been defended at such cost? There rested on, or more truly there underlay, each a fundamental principle, conceived to be absolutely essential to the safety, order, peace, fortune and honor of society; and these two principles were antagonistic.

They were more than antagonistic; they were antipodal and irreconcilable. No people that hold either of these ideas as cardinal in their political creed will ever allow the other to be forced upon them from without so long as blood and lives will buy deliverance. Both were brought from the mother country when America was originally colonized, and both have their advocates in greater or less number in the Northern States, in the Southern, and wherever there is any freedom of thought and speech.

The common subject of the two is the great lower mass of society. The leading thought of the one is that mass's elevation, of the other its subjugation. The one declares the only permanent safety of public society, and its highest development, to require the constant elevation of the lower, and thus of the whole mass, by the free self-government of all under one common code of equal civil rights. It came from England, but it was practically, successfully, beneficently applied on a national scale first in the United States, and Americans claim the right to call it, and it preeminently, the American idea, promulgated and established, not by Northerners or Southerners, one greatly more than another, but by the unsectional majority of a whole new Nation born of the idea. The other principle declares public safety and highest development to require the subjugation of the lower mass under the arbitrary protective supremacy of an untitled but hereditary privileged class, a civil caste. Not, as it is commonly miscalled, an aristocracy, for within one race it takes in all ranks of society, not an aristocracy, for an aristocracy exists, presumably, at least, with the wide consent of all classes, and men in any rank of life may have some hope to attain to it by extraordinary merit and service; but a caste, not the embodiment of a modern European idea, but the resuscitation of an ancient Asiatic one.

That one of these irreconcilable ideas should by-and-by become all-dominant in the formation of public society in one region, and its opposite in the other region, is due to original differences in the conditions under which the colonies were settled. In the South, the corner-stone of the social structure was made the plantation idea—wide lands, an accomplished few, and their rapid aggrandizement by the fostering oversight and employment of an unskilled many. In the North, it was the village and town idea—the notion of farm and factory, skilled labor, an intelligent many, and ultimate wealth through an assured public tranquillity. Nothing could be more natural than for African slavery, once introduced, to flourish and spread under the one idea, and languish and die under the other. It is high time to be done saying that the South retained slavery and the North renounced it merely because to the one it was, and to the other it was not, lucrative. It was inevitable that the most conspicuous feature of one civilization should become the public schoolhouse, and of the other the slave yard. Who could wish to raise the equally idle and offensive question of praise and blame? When Northerners came South by thousands and made their dwelling there, ninety-nine hundredths of them fell into our Southern error up to the eyes, and there is nothing to prove that had the plantation idea, to the exclusion of the village idea, been planted in all the colonies, we should not by this time have had a West Indian civilization from Florida to Oregon. But it was not to be so. Wherever the farm village became the germinal unit of social organization, there was developed in its most comprehensive integrity, that American idea of our Northern and Southern fathers, the representative self-government of the whole people by the constant free consent of all to the frequently reconsidered choice of the majority.

Such a scheme can be safe only when it includes inherently the continual and diligent elevation of that lower mass which human society everywhere is constantly precipitating. But slave-holding on any large scale could not make even a show of public safety without the continual and diligent debasement of its enslaved lower millions. Wherever it prevailed it was bound by the natural necessities of its own existence to undermine and corrode the National scheme. It mistaught the new generations of the white South that the slave-holding fathers of the Republic were approvers and advocates of that sad practice, which by their true histories we know they would gladly have destroyed. It mistaught us to construe the right of a uniform government of all by all, not as a common and inalienable right of man, but as a privilege that became a right only by a people's merit, and which our forefathers bought with the blood of the Revolution in 1776–'83, and which our slaves did not and should not be allowed to acquire. It mistaught us to seek prosperity in the concentration instead of the diffusion of wealth, to seek public safety in a state of siege rather than in a state of peace; it gave us subjects instead of fellow-citizens, and falsely threatened us with the utter shipwreck of public and private society if we dared accord civil power to the degraded millions to whom we had forbidden patriotism. Thus, it could not help but misteach us also to subordinate to its preservation the maintenance of a National union with those Northern communities to whose whole scheme of order slave-holding was intolerable, and to rise at length against the will of the majority and dissolve the Union when that majority refused to give slave-holding the National sanction.

The other system taught the inherent right of all human society to self-government. It taught the impersonal civil equality of all. It admitted that the private, personal inequality of individuals is inevitable, necessary, right and good; but condemned its misuse to set up arbitrary public inequalities. It declared public equality to be, on the one hand, the only true and adequate counterpoise against private inequalities, and, on the other, the best protector and promotor of just private inequalities against unjust. It held that virtue, intelligence and wealth are their own sufficient advantage, and need for self-protection no arbitrary civil preponderance; that their powers of self-protection are never inadequate save when by forgetting equity they mass and exasperate ignorance, vice and poverty against them. It insisted that there is no safe protection but self-protection; that poverty needs at least as much civil equipment for self-protection as property needs; that the right and liberty to acquire intelligence, virtue and wealth are just as precious as the right and liberty to maintain them, and need quite as much self-protection; that the secret of public order and highest prosperity is the common and equal right of all lawfully to acquire as well as retain every equitable means of self-aggrandizement, and that this right is assured to all only through the consent of all to the choice of the majority frequently appealed to without respect of persons. And last, it truly taught that a government founded on these principles and holding them essential to public peace and safety might comfortably bear the proximity of alien neighbors, whose ideas of right and order were not implacably hostile; but that it had no power to abide unless it could put down any internal mutiny against that choice of the majority which was, as it were, the Nation's first commandment.

The war was fought and the Union saved. Fought as it was, on the issue of the consent of all to the choice of the majority, the conviction forced its way that the strife would never end in peace until the liberty of self-government was guaranteed to the entire people, and slavery, as standing for the doctrine of public safety by subjugation, destroyed. Hence, first, emancipation, and then, enfranchisement. And now even the Union saved is not the full measure of the Nation's triumphs; but, saved once by arms, it seems at length to have achieved a better and fuller salvation still; for the people of the once seceded States, with a sincerity that no generous mind can question, have returned to their old love of this saved Union, and the great North, from East to utmost West, full of elation, and feeling what one may call the onus of the winning, side, cries "Enough!" and asks no more.

II.

Thus stands the matter to-day. Old foes are clasping hands on fields where once they met in battle, and touching glasses across the banqueting board, pledging long life to the Union and prosperity to the new South, but at every feast there is one empty seat.

Why should one seat be ever empty, and every guest afraid to look that way? Because the Southern white man swears upon his father's sword that none but a ghost shall ever sit there. And a ghost is there; the ghost of that old heresy of public safety by the mass's subjugation. This is what the Northern people cannot understand. This is what makes the Southern white man an enigma to all the world beside, if not also to himself. To-day the pride with which he boasts himself a citizen of the United States and the sincerity with which he declares for free government as the only safe government cannot be doubted; tomorrow comes an explosion, followed by such a misinterpretation of what free government requires and forbids that it is hard to identify him with the nineteenth century. Emancipation destroyed domestic bondage; enfranchisement, as nearly as its mere decree can, has abolished public servitude; how, then, does this old un-American, undemocratic idea of subjugation, which our British mother country and Europe as well, are so fast repudiating—how does it remain? Was it not founded in these two forms of slavery? The mistake lies just there: They were founded in it, and removing them has not removed it.

It has always been hard for the North to understand the alacrity with which the ex-slaveholder learned to condemn as a moral and economic error that slavery in defense of which he endured four years of desolating war. But it was genuine, and here is the explanation: He believed personal enslavement essential to subjugation. Emancipation at one stroke proved it was not. But it proved no more. Unfortunately for the whole Nation there was already before emancipation came, a defined status, a peculiar niche, waiting for freed negroes. They were nothing new. Nor was it new to lose personal ownership in one's slave. When, under emancipation, no one else could own him, we quickly saw he was not lost at all. There he stood, beggar to us for room for the sole of his foot, the land and all its appliances ours, and he, by the stress of his daily needs, captive to the land. The moment he fell to work of his own free will, we saw that emancipation was even more ours than his; public order stood fast, our homes were safe, our firesides un-invaded; he still served, we still ruled; all need of holding him in private bondage was disproved, and when the notion of necessity vanished the notion of right vanished with it. Emancipation had destroyed private, but it had hardly disturbed public subjugation. The ex-slave was not a free man; he was only a free negro.

Then the winners of the war saw that the great issue which had jeopardized the Union was not settled. The Government's foundation principle was not re-established, and could not be while millions of the country's population were without a voice as to who should rule, who should judge and what should be law. But, as we have seen, the absolute civil equality of privately and socially unequal men was not the whole American idea. It was counterbalanced by an enlarged application of the same principle in the absolute equality of unequal States in the Federal Union, one of the greatest will-ing concessions ever made by stronger political bodies to weaker ones in the history of government. Now manifestly this great concession of equality among the unequal States becomes inordinate, unjust and dangerous when millions of the people in one geo-graphical section, native to the soil, of native parentage, having ties of interest and sym-pathy with no other land, are arbitrarily denied that political equality within the States which obtains elsewhere throughout the Union. This would make us two countries. But we cannot be two merely federated countries without changing our whole plan of gov-ernment; and we cannot be one without a common foundation. Hence the freedman's enfranchisement. It was given him not only because enfranchisement was his only true emancipation, but also because it was, and is, impossible to withhold it and carry on American government on American ground principles. Neither the Nation's honor nor its safety could allow the restoration of revolted States to their autonomy with their pop-ulations divided by lines of status abhorrent to the whole National structure.

Northern men often ask perplexedly if the freedman's enfranchisement was not, as to the South, premature and inexpedient; while Southern men as often call it the one vindictive act of the conqueror, as foolish as it was cruel. It was cruel. Not by intention, and, it may be, unavoidably, but certainly it was not cruel for its haste, but for its tardi-ness. Had enfranchisement come into effect, as emancipation did, while the smoke of the war's last shot was still in the air, when force still ruled unquestioned and civil order and system had not yet superseded martial law, the agonies, the shame and the incalcu-lable losses of the Reconstruction period that followed might have been spared the South and the Nation. Instead there came two unlucky postponements, the slow doling out of re-enfranchisement to the best intelligence of Southern white society and the delay of the freedman's enfranchisement—his civil emancipation—until the "Old South," instead of reorganizing public society in harmony with the National idea, largely returned to its entrenchments in the notion of exclusive white rule. Then, too late to avert a new strike, and as little more than a defensive offset, the freedman was invested with citizenship and the experiment begun of trying to establish a form of public order, wherein, under a political equality accorded by all citizens, to all citizens, new and old, intelligence and virtue would be so free to combine, and ignorance and vice feel so free to divide, as to insure the majority's free choice of rulers of at least enough intelligence and virtue to secure safety, order and progress. This experiment, the North believed, would succeed, and since this was the organic embodiment of the American idea for which it had just shed seas of blood, it stands to reason the North would not have allowed it to fail. But the Old South, still bleeding from her thousand wounds, but as brave as when she fired her first gun, believed not only that the experiment would fail, but also that it was dangerous and dishonorable. And to-day, both in North and South, a widespread impression prevails that this is the experiment which was tried and did in fact fail. Whereas it is just what the Old South never allowed to be tried.

This is the whole secret of the Negro Question's vital force today. And yet the struggle in the Southern States has never been by the blacks for and by the whites against a black supremacy, but only for and against an arbitrary pure white supremacy. From the very first until this day, in all the freedman's intellectual crudity, he has held fast to the one true, National doctrine of the absence of privilege and the rule of all by all, through the common and steadfast consent of all to the free and frequent choice of the majority. He has never rejected white men's political fellowship or leadership because it was white, but only and always when it was unsound in this doctrine. His party has never been a purely black party in fact or principle. The "solid black vote" is only by outside pressure solidified about a principle of American liberty, which is itself against solidity and destroys the political solidity of classes wherever it has free play. But the "solid white vote"—which is not solid by including all whites, but because no colored man can truly enter its ranks, much less its councils, without accepting an emasculated emancipation—the solid white vote is solid, not by outside pressure but by inherent principle. Solid twice over; first, in each State, from sincere motives of self-preservation, solid in keeping the old servile class, by arbitrary classification, servile; and then solid again by a tacit league of Southern States around the assumed right of each State separately to postpone a true and complete emancipation as long as the fear remains that, with full American liberty—this and no more—to all alike, the freedman would himself usurp the arbitrary domination now held over him and plunder and destroy society.

So, then, the Southern question at its root is simply whether there is any real ground sufficient to justify this fear and the attitude taken against it. Only remove this fear, which rests on a majority of the whole white South despite all its splendid, well-proved courage, and the question of right, in law and in morals, will vanish along with the notion of necessity.

Whoever attempts to remove this apprehension must meet it in two forms: First, fear of a hopeless wreck of public government by a complete supremacy of the lower mass; and second, fear of a yet more dreadful wreck of private society in a deluge of social equality.

Henry W. Grady

(1850–1889)

During the 1870s and 1880s, the New South movement, led by journalists, politicians, and educators, gradually gained momentum. Encouraged by a cotton textile boom and more sympathetic Northern attitudes, advocates of a New South trumpeted the benefits of industrial development and agricultural diversification, and insisted that significant progress was being made in race relations. Among the journalists, politicians, and educators leading the movement, none was more prominent than Henry W. Grady of the *Atlanta Constitution*.

Born in Athens, Georgia, Grady was the son of a successful storekeeper who died in 1864 from wounds received at Petersburg, Virginia, and though his family had to sacrifice for the children's education, they were not financially devastated by the war as were many other Southern families. Grady took his degree from the University of Georgia in 1868 and studied law at the University of Virginia. He began his career in journalism as the associate editor of the *Rome Courier* in Georgia and owned interests in two other Rome newspapers before becoming part owner of the *Atlanta Daily Herald* in 1872. Forced to sell the latter paper because of financial difficulties, Grady took a job at the *Atlanta Constitution* in 1876, where he became associated with Evan P. Howell and Joel Chandler Harris. Grady purchased one-fourth interest in the *Constitution* in 1880.

Throughout his career, Grady urged Southerners to forget the Lost Cause and to look to the future. Acknowledging that development in the South could not occur without financial support from the North, he worked toward reconciliation. His best-known effort was his speech "The New South," which was delivered before the New England Society in New York on December 21, 1886. With "a social system compact and closely knitted, less splendid on the surface, but stronger at the core," the New South held a limitless potential, said Grady, and would no longer be confined by "narrow limitations [which] fell forever when the shackles of the Negro slave were broken." As a result of this speech and other activities, Grady's political future seemed bright—he was mentioned as a possible running mate for President Cleveland in 1888—but he died unexpectedly of pneumonia in 1889.

The New South

"There was a South of slavery and secession—that South is dead. There is a South of union and freedom—that South, thank God, is living, breathing, growing every hour." These words, delivered from the immortal lips of Benjamin H. Hill, at Tammany Hall, in 1866, true then and truer now, I shall make my text tonight.

Mr. President and Gentlemen: Let me express to you my appreciation of the kindness by which I am permitted to address you. I make this abrupt acknowledgment advisedly, for I feel that if, when I raise my provincial voice in this ancient and august presence, I could find courage for no more than the opening sentence, it would be well if in that sentence I had met in a rough sense my obligation as a guest, and had perished, so to speak, with courtesy on my lips and grace in my heart. Permitted, through your kindness, to catch my second wind, let me say that I appreciate the significance of being the first Southerner to speak at this board, which bears the substance, if it surpasses the semblance, of original New England hospitality—and honors the sentiment that in turn honors you, but in which my personality is lost, and the compliment to my people made plain.

I bespeak the utmost stretch of your courtesy tonight. I am not troubled about those from whom I come. You remember the man whose wife sent him to a neighbor with a pitcher of milk, and who, tripping on the top step, fell with such casual interruptions as the landings afforded into the basement, and, while picking himself up, had the pleasure of hearing his wife call out: "John, did you break the pitcher?"

"No, I didn't," said John, "but I'll be dinged if I don't."

So, while those who call me from behind may inspire me with energy, if not with courage, I ask an indulgent hearing from you. I beg that you will bring your full faith in American fairness and frankness to judgment upon what I shall say. There was an old preacher once who told some boys of the Bible lesson he was going to read in the morning. The boys, finding the place, glued together the connecting pages. The next morning he read on the bottom of one page, "When Noah was one hundred and twenty years old he took unto himself a wife, who was"—then turning the page—"140 cubits long—40 cubits wide, built of gopher wood—and covered with pitch inside and out." He was naturally puzzled at this. He read it again, verified it, and then said: "My friends, this is the first time I ever met this in the Bible, but I accept this as an evidence of the assertion that we are fearfully and wonderfully made." If I could get you to hold such faith tonight I could proceed cheerfully to the task I otherwise approach with a sense of consecration.

Pardon me one word, Mr. President, spoken for the sole purpose of getting into the volumes that go out annually freighted with the rich eloquence of your speakers—the fact that the Cavalier as well as the Puritan was on the continent in its early days, and that he was "up and able to be about." I have read your books carefully and I find no mention of that fact, which seems to me an important one for preserving a sort of historical equilibrium if for nothing else.

Let me remind you that the Virginia Cavalier first challenged France on the continent—that Cavalier, John Smith, gave New England its very name, and was so pleased with the job that he has been handing his own name around ever since—and that while Myles Standish was cutting off men's ears for courting a girl without her parents' consent, and forbade men to kiss their wives on Sunday, the Cavalier was courting everything in sight, and that the Almighty had vouchsafed great increase to the Cavalier colonies, the huts in the wilderness being as full as the nests in the woods.

But having incorporated the Cavalier as a fact in your charming little books, I shall let him work out his own salvation, as he has always done, with engaging gallantry, and we will hold no controversy as to his merits. Why should we? Neither Puritan nor Cavalier long survived as such. The virtues and good traditions of both happily still live for the inspiration of their sons and the saving of the old fashion. But both Puritan and Cavalier were lost in the storm of the first Revolution, and the American citizen, supplanting both and stronger than either, took possession of the republic bought by their common blood and fashioned to wisdom, and charged himself with teaching men government and establishing the voice of the people as the voice of God.

My friends, Dr. Talmage has told you that the typical American has yet to come. Let me tell you that he has already come. Great types, like valuable plants, are slow to flower and fruit. But from the union of these colonists, Puritans and Cavaliers, from the straightening of their purposes and the crossing of their blood, slow perfecting through a century, came he who stands as the first typical American, the first who comprehended within himself all the strength and gentleness, all the majesty and grace of this republic—Abraham Lincoln. He was the sum of Puritan and Cavalier, for in his ardent nature were fused the virtues of both, and in the depths of his great soul the faults of both were lost. He was greater than Puritan, greater than Cavalier, in that he was American, and that in his honest form were first gathered the vast and thrilling forces of his ideal government—charging it with such tremendous meaning and elevating it above human suffering that martyrdom, though infamously aimed, came as a fitting crown to a life consecrated from the cradle to human liberty. Let us, each cherishing the traditions and honoring his fathers, build with reverent hands to the type of this simple but sublime life, in which all types are honored, and in our common glory as Americans there will be plenty and to spare for your forefathers and for mine.

Dr. Talmage has drawn for you, with a master's hand, the picture of your returning armies. He has told you how, in the pomp and circumstance of war, they came back to you, marching with proud and victorious tread, reading their glory in a nation's eyes! Will you bear with me while I tell you of another army that sought its home at the close of the late war—an army that marched home in defeat and not in victory—in pathos and not in splendor, but in glory that equaled yours, and to hearts as loving as ever welcomed heroes home! Let me picture to you the footsore Confederate soldier, as buttoning up in his faded gray jacket the parole which was to bear testimony to his children of his fidelity and faith, he turned his face southward from Appomattox in April 1865. Think of him as ragged, half-starved, heavy-hearted, enfeebled by want and wounds, having fought to exhaustion, he surrenders his gun, wrings the hands of his comrades in silence, and lifting his tear-stained and pallid face for the last time to the graves that dot old Virginia hills, pulls his gray cap over his brow and begins the slow and painful journey. What does he find—let me ask you who went to your homes eager to find, in the welcome you had justly earned, full payment for four years' sacrifice—what does he find when, having followed the battle-stained cross against overwhelming odds, dreading death not half so much as surrender, he reaches the home he left so prosperous and beautiful? He finds his house in ruins, his farm devastated, his slaves free, his stock killed, his barns empty, his trade destroyed, his money worthless, his social system, feudal in its magnificence, swept away; his people without law or legal status; his comrades slain, and the burdens of others heavy on his shoulders. Crushed by defeat, his very traditions are gone. Without money, credit, employment, material, or training; and beside all this, confronted with the gravest problem that ever met human intelligence—the establishing of a status for the vast body of his liberated slaves.

What does he do—this hero in gray with a heart of gold? Does he sit down in sullenness and despair? Not for a day. Surely God, who had stripped him of his prosperity, inspired him in his adversity. As ruin was never before so overwhelming, never was restoration swifter. The soldier stepped from the trenches into the furrow; horses that had charged Federal guns marched before the plow, and fields that ran red with human blood in April were green with the harvest in June; women reared in luxury cut up their dresses and made breeches for their husbands, and, with a patience and heroism that fit women always as a garment, gave their hands to work. There was little bitterness in all this. Cheerfulness and frankness prevailed. "Bill Arp" struck the key-note when he said: "Well, I killed as many of them as they did of me, and now I'm going to work." Of the soldier returning home after defeat and roasting some corn on the roadside, who made the remark to his comrades: "You may leave the South if you want to, but I am going to Sandersville, kiss my wife and raise a crop, and if the Yankees fool with me any more, I'll whip 'em again." I want to say to General Sherman, who is considered an able man in our parts, though some people think he is a kind of careless man about fire, that from the ashes he left us in 1864 we have raised a brave and beautiful city; that somehow or other we have caught the sunshine in the bricks and mortar of our homes, and have builded therein not one ignoble prejudice or memory.

But what is the sum of our work? We have found out that in the summing up the free Negro counts more than he did as a slave. We have planted the schoolhouse on the hilltop and made it free to white and black. We have sowed towns and cities in the place of theories, and put business above politics. We have challenged your spinners in Massachusetts and your iron-makers in Pennsylvania. We have learned that the $400,000,000 annually received from our cotton crop will make us rich when the supplies that make it are home-raised. We have reduced the commercial rate of interest from 24 to 6 per cent., and are floating 4 per cent. bonds. We have learned that one northern immigrant is worth fifty foreigners; and have smoothed the path to southward, wiped out the place where Mason and Dixon's line used to be, and hung out latchstring to you and yours. We have reached the point that marks perfect harmony in every household, when the husband confesses that the pies which his wife cooks are as good as those his mother used to bake; and we admit that the sun shines as brightly and the moon as softly as it did before the war. We have established thrift in city and country. We have fallen in love with work. We have restored comfort to homes from which culture and elegance never departed. We have let economy take root and spread among us as rank as the crabgrass which sprung from Sherman's cavalry camps, until we are ready to lay odds on the Georgia Yankee as he manufactures relics of the battlefield in a one-story shanty and squeezes pure olive oil out of his cotton seed, against any down-easter that ever swapped wooden nutmegs for flannel sausage in the valleys of Vermont. Above all, we know that we have achieved in these "piping times of peace" a fuller independence for the South than that which our fathers sought to win in the forum by their eloquence or compel in the field by their swords.

It is a rare privilege, sir, to have had part, however humble, in this work. Never was nobler duty confided to human hands than the uplifting and upbuilding of the prostrate and bleeding South—misguided, perhaps, but beautiful in her suffering, and honest, brave and generous always. In the record of her social, industrial and political illustration we await with confidence the verdict of the world.

But what of the Negro? Have we solved the problem he presents or progressed in honor and equity toward solution? Let the record speak to the point. No section shows a more prosperous laboring population than the Negroes of the South, none in fuller sympathy with the employing and land-owning class. He shares our school fund, has the fullest protection of our laws and the friendship of our people. Self-interest, as well as honor, demand that he should have this. Our future, our very existence depend upon our working out this problem in full and exact justice. We understand that when Lincoln signed the emancipation proclamation, your victory was assured, for he then committed you to the cause of human liberty, against which the arms of man cannot prevail—while those of our statesmen who trusted to make slavery the corner-stone of the Confederacy doomed us to defeat as far as they could, committing us to a cause that reason could not defend or the sword maintain in sight of advancing civilization.

Had Mr. Toombs said, which he did not say, "that he would call the roll of his slaves at the foot of Bunker Hill," he would have been foolish, for he might have known that whenever slavery became entangled in war it must perish, and that the chattel in human flesh ended forever in New England when your fathers—not to be blamed for parting with what didn't pay—sold their slaves to our fathers—not to be praised for knowing a paying thing when they saw it. The relations of the Southern people with the Negro are close and cordial. We remember with what fidelity for four years he guarded our defenseless women and children, whose husbands and fathers were fighting against his freedom. To his eternal credit be it said that whenever he struck a blow for his own liberty he fought in open battle, and when at last he raised his black and humble hands that the shackles might be struck off, those hands were innocent of wrong against his helpless charges, and worthy to be taken in loving grasp by every man who honors loyalty and devotion. Ruffians have maltreated him, rascals have misled him, philanthropists established a bank for him, but the South, with the North, protests against injustice to this simple and sincere people. To liberty and enfranchisement is as far as law can carry the Negro. The rest must be left to conscience and common sense. It must be left to those among whom his lot is cast, with whom he is indissolubly connected, and whose prosperity depends upon their possessing his intelligent sympathy and confidence. Faith has been kept with him, in spite of calumnious assertions to the contrary by those who assume to speak for us or by frank opponents. Faith will be kept with him in the future, if the South holds her reason and integrity.

But have we kept faith with you? In the fullest sense, yes. When Lee surrendered—I don't say when Johnson surrendered, because I understand he still alludes to the time when he met General Sherman last as the time when he determined to abandon any further prosecution of the struggle—when Lee surrendered, I say, and Johnson quit, the South became, and has since been, loyal to this Union. We fought hard enough to know that we were whipped, and in perfect frankness accept as final the arbitrament of the sword to which we had appealed. The South found her jewel in the toad's head of defeat. The shackles that had held her in narrow limitations fell forever when the shackles of the Negro slave were broken. Under the old regime the Negroes were slaves to the South; the South was a slave to the system. The old plantation, with its simple police regulations and feudal habit, was the only type possible under slavery. Thus was gathered in the hands of a splendid and chivalric oligarchy the substance that should have been diffused among the people, as the rich blood, under certain artificial conditions, is gathered at the heart, filling that with affluent rapture but leaving the body chill and colorless.

The old South rested everything on slavery and agriculture, unconscious that these could neither give nor maintain healthy growth. The new South presents a perfect democracy, the oligarchs leading in the popular movement—a social system compact and closely knitted, less splendid on the surface, but stronger at the core—a hundred farms for every plantation, fifty homes for every palace—and a diversified industry that meets the complex need of this complex age.

The new South is enamored of her new work. Her soul is stirred with the breath of a new life. The light of a grander day is falling fair on her face. She is thrilling with the consciousness of growing power and prosperity. As she stands upright, full-statured and equal among the people of the earth, breathing the keen air and looking out upon the expanded horizon, she understands that her emancipation came because through the inscrutable wisdom of God her honest purpose was crossed, and her brave armies were beaten.

This is said in no spirit of time-serving or apology. The South has nothing for which to apologize. She believes that the late struggle between the States was war and not rebellion; revolution and not conspiracy, and that her convictions were as honest as yours. I should be unjust to the dauntless spirit of the South and to my own convictions if I did not make this plain in this presence. The South has nothing to take back. In my native town of Athens is a monument that crowns its central hill—a plain, white shaft. Deep cut into its shining side is a name dear to me above the names of men—that of a brave and simple man who died in brave and simple faith. Not for all the glories of New England, from Plymouth Rock all the way, would I exchange the heritage he left me in his soldier's death. To the foot of that I shall send my children's children to reverence him who ennobled their name with his heroic blood. But, sir, speaking from the shadow of that memory which I honor as I do nothing else on earth, I say that the cause in which he suffered and for which he gave his life was adjudged by higher and fuller wisdom than his or mine, and I am glad that the omniscient God held the balance of battle in His Almighty hand and that human slavery was swept forever from American soil, the American Union was saved from the wreck of war.

This message, Mr. President, comes to you from consecrated ground. Every foot of soil about the city in which I live is as sacred as a battle-ground of the republic. Every hill that invests it is hallowed to you by the blood of your brothers who died for your victory, and doubly hallowed to us by the blow of those who died hopeless, but undaunted, in defeat—sacred soil to all of us—rich with memories that make us purer and stronger and better—silent but staunch witnesses in its red desolation of the matchless valor of American hearts and the deathless glory of American arms— speaking an eloquent witness in its white peace and prosperity to the indissoluble union of American States and the imperishable brotherhood of the American people.

Now, what answer has New England to this message? Will she permit the prejudice of war to remain in the hearts of the conquerors, when it has died in the hearts of the conquered? Will she transmit this prejudice to the next generation, that in their hearts which never felt the generous ardor of conflict it may perpetuate itself? Will she withhold, save in strained courtesy, the hand which straight from his soldier's heart Grant offered to Lee at Appomattox? Will she make the vision of a restored and happy people, which gathered above the couch of your dying captain, filling his heart with grace; touching his lips with praise, and glorifying his path to the grave—will she make this vision on which the last sigh of his expiring soul breathed a benediction, a cheat and delusion? If she does, the South, never abject in asking for comradeship, must accept with dignity its refusal; but if she does not refuse to accept in frankness and sincerity this message of good will and friendship, then will the prophecy of Webster, delivered in this very society forty years ago amid tremendous applause, become true, be verified in its fullest sense, when he said: "Standing hand to hand and clasping hands, we should remain united as we have been for sixty years, citizens of the same country, members of the same government, united, all united now and united forever." There have been difficulties, contentions, and controversies, but I tell you that in my judgment,

> "Those opened eyes,
> Which like the meteors of a troubled heaven,
> All of one nature, of one substance bred,

Did lately meet in th' intestine shock,
Shall now, in mutual well beseeming ranks,
March all one way."

Kate Chopin
(1851–1904)

Though Kate Chopin's reputation during her lifetime was as a local colorist of some popularity who later produced a scandalous novel, modern scholars have accorded her a much more important place in the development of American realism, recognizing the boldness of her unflinching depiction of women's roles at the turn of the century. Unfortunately, readers of her day were unprepared for such frankness, and the vehemence of the negative reviews that greeted *The Awakening* when it was published in 1899 probably choked off any further explorations by the formerly prolific writer.

Katherine O'Flaherty was born in St. Louis, Missouri, in 1851 to well-to-do parents, and the stories of French-Creole life related to her by relatives on her mother's side may well have shaped her later literary style. Her father died when she was only four, but Chopin grew up a prototypical "belle," departing from the stereotype only in her maintenance of a commonplace book where she expressed herself in poems and essays, confiding that her social life was an annoying distraction from her true loves of reading and writing. In 1870, she married Oscar Chopin and moved shortly thereafter to New Orleans, where she actively entered into the social life of the city. The Chopins were married twelve years and had six children, and Kate Chopin often summered with her children at Grand isle, the Louisiana island resort she would later depict in *The Awakening*. In 1879, Oscar Chopin suffered a severe financial setback and moved his family to Cloutierville, in the Natchitoches Parish of north central Louisiana. During this time the author was befriended by her obstetrician, Dr. Frederick Kolbenheyer, who influenced her to give up her religious beliefs and to begin writing fiction. In 1883 her husband died of swamp fever, and Chopin moved back to St. Louis to live with her mother, who died shortly thereafter. Faced with a dwindling income, Chopin began her writing career in earnest. She started publishing short stories in periodicals, and in 1890 she published the novel *At Fault* at her own expense. It received some critical attention, but it was the publication of *Bayou Folk* in 1894 that won her national recognition. Its depiction of the folk she had known in Natchitoches—Creole landowners, blacks, and Cajuns—was especially appealing to Northern readers. Another collection, *A Night in Acadie*, followed in 1897 to a somewhat more subdued critical reception, mainly due to Chopin's increasingly frank portrayals of characters' emotional development.

In January 1898 she published *The Awakening*, the story of Edna Pontellier, a young wife who escapes the spiritually stifling confines of her marriage and searches for fulfillment in an extramarital affair before eventually succumbing to despair and suicide. Her refusal to offer a moral commentary on Edna's plight caused a critical storm; and the novel was deemed "poison" by one review and was banned from libraries in St. Louis. Though some reviewers defended her, many of her friends and former connections cut her off, and she seemed never to have fully recovered from the creative paralysis caused by the adverse reviews. She died of a brain hemorrhage in 1904.

Désirée's Baby

As the day was pleasant, Madame Valmondé drove over to L'Abri to see Désirée and the baby.

It made her laugh to think of Désirée with a baby. Why, it seems but yesterday that Désirée was little more than a baby herself; when Monsieur in riding through the gateway of Valmondé had found her lying asleep in the shadow of the big stone pillar.

The little one awoke in his arms and began to cry for "Dada." That was as much as she could do or say. Some people thought she might have strayed there of her own accord, for she was of the toddling age. The prevailing belief was that she had been purposely left by a party of Texans, whose canvas-covered wagon, late in the day, had crossed the ferry that Coton Maïs kept, just below the plantation. In time Madame Valmondé abandoned every speculation but the one that Désirée had been sent to her by a beneficent Providence to be the child of her affection, seeing that she was without child of the flesh. For the girl grew to be beautiful and gentle, affectionate and sincere—the idol of Valmondé.

It was no wonder, when she stood one day against the stone pillar in whose shadow she had lain asleep, eighteen years before, that Armand Aubigny riding by and seeing her there, had fallen in love with her. That was the way all the Aubignys fell in love, as if struck by a pistol shot. The wonder was that he had not loved her before; for he had known her since his father brought him home from Paris, a boy of eight, after his mother died there. The passion that awoke in him that day, when he saw her at the gate, swept along like an avalanche, or like a prairie fire, or like anything that drives headlong over all obstacles.

Madame Valmondé bent her portly figure over Désirée and kissed her, holding her an instant tenderly in her arms. Then she turned to the child.

"This is not the baby!" she exclaimed, in startled tones. French was the language spoken at Valmondé in those days.

"I knew you would be astonished," laughed Désirée, "at the way he has grown. The little *cochon de lait!*[1] Look at his legs, mamma, and his hands and fingernails,—real fingernails. Zandrine had to cut them this morning. Isn't it true, Zadrine?"

The woman bowed her turbaned head majestically, "Mais si, Madame."

"And the way he cries," went on Désirée, "is deafening. Armand heard him the other day as far away as La Blanche's cabin."

Madame Valmondé had never removed her eyes from the child. She lifted it and walked with it over to the window that was lightest. She scanned the baby narrowly, then looked as searchingly at Zandrine, whose face was turned to gaze across the fields.

"Yes, the child has grown, has changed;" said Madame Valmondé, slowly, as she replaced it beside its mother. "What does Armand say?"

Désirée's face became suffused with a glow that was happiness itself.

"Oh, Armand is the proudest father in the parish, I believe, chiefly because it is a boy, to bear his name; though he says not—that he would have loved a girl as well. But I know it isn't true. I know he says that to please me. And mamma," she added, drawing Madame Valmondé's head down to her, and speaking in a whisper, "he hasn't punished one of them—not one of them—since baby is born. Even Négrillon, who

---

[1] Literally "pig of milk"—a big feeder.

pretended to have burnt his leg that he might rest from work—he only laughed, and said Négrillon was a great scamp. Oh, mamma, I'm so happy; it frightens me."

What Désirée said was true. Marriage, and later the birth of his son, had softened Armand Aubigny's imperious and exacting nature greatly. This was what made the gentle Désirée so happy, for she loved him desperately. When he frowned she trembled, but loved him. When he smiled, she asked no greater blessing of God. But Armand's dark, handsome face had not often been disfigured by frowns since the day he fell in love with her.

When the baby was about three months old, Désirée awoke one day to the conviction that there was something in the air menacing her peace. It was at first too subtle to grasp. It had only been a disquieting suggestion; an air of mystery among the blacks; unexpected visits from far-off neighbors who could hardly account for their coming. Then a strange, an awful change in her husband's manner, which she dared not ask him to explain. When he spoke to her, it was with averted eyes, from which the old love light seemed to have gone out. He absented himself from home; and when there, avoided her presence and that of her child, without excuse. And the very spirit of Satan seemed suddenly to take hold of him in his dealings with the slaves. Désirée was miserable enough to die.

She sat in her room, one hot afternoon, in her *peignoir*, listlessly drawing through her fingers the strands of her long, silky brown hair that hung about her shoulders. The baby, half naked, lay asleep upon her own great mahogany bed, that was like a sumptuous throne, with its satin-lined half canopy. One of La Blanche's little quadroon boys—half naked too—stood fanning the child slowly with a fan of peacock feathers. Désirée's eyes had been fixed absently and sadly upon the baby, while she was striving to penetrate the threatening mist that she felt closing about her. She looked from her child to the boy who stood beside him, and back again, over and over. "Ah!" It was a cry that she could not help, which she was not conscious of having uttered. The blood turned like ice in her veins, and a clammy moisture gathered upon her face.

She tried to speak to the little quadroon boy; but no sound would come, at first. When he heard his name uttered, he looked up, and his mistress was pointing to the door. He laid aside the great, soft fan, and obediently stole away, over the polished floor, on his bare tiptoes.

She stayed motionless, with gaze riveted upon her child, and her face the picture of fright.

Presently her husband entered the room, and without noticing her, went to a table and began to search among some papers which covered it.

"Armand," she called to him, in a voice which must have stabbed him, if he was human. But he did not notice. "Armand," she said again. Then she rose and tottered towards him. "Armand," she panted once more, clutching his arm, "look at our child. What does it mean? tell me."

He coldly but gently loosened her fingers from about his arm and thrust the hand away from him. "Tell me what it means!" she cried despairingly.

"It means," he answered lightly, "that the child is not white; it means that you are not white."

A quick conception of all that this accusation meant for her nerved her with unwonted courage to deny it. "It is a lie; it is not true, I am white! Look at my hair, it is brown; and my eyes are gray, Armand, you know they are gray. And my skin is fair," seizing his wrist. "Look at my hand, whiter than yours, Armand," she laughed hysterically.

"As white as La Blanche's," he returned cruelly, and went away leaving her alone with their child.

When she could hold a pen in her hand, she sent a despairing letter to Madame Valmondé.

"My mother, they tell me I am not white. Armand has told me I am not white. For God's sake tell them it is not true. You must know it is not true. I shall die. I must die. I cannot be so unhappy, and live."

The answer that came was as brief:

"My own Désirée: Come home to Valmondé; back to your mother who loves you. Come with your child."

When the letter reached Désirée she went with it to her husband's study, and laid it open upon the desk before which he sat. She was like a stone image: silent, white, motionless after she placed it there.

In silence he ran his cold eyes over the written words. He said nothing. "Shall I go, Armand?" she asked in tones sharp with agonized suspense.

"Yes, go."

"Do you want me to go?"

"Yes, I want you to go."

He thought Almighty God had dealt cruelly and unjustly with him; and felt, somehow, that he was paying Him back in kind when he stabbed thus into his wife's soul. Moreover he no longer loved her, because of the unconscious injury she had brought upon his home and his name.

She turned away like one stunned by a blow, and walked slowly towards the door, hoping he would call her back.

"Good-by, Armand," she moaned.

He did not answer her. That was his last blow at fate.

Désirée went in search of her child. Zandrine was pacing the sombre gallery with it. She took the little one from the nurse's arms with no word of explanation, and descending the steps, walked away, under the live-oak branches.

It was an October afternoon; the sun was just sinking. Out in the still fields the Negroes were picking cotton.

Désirée had not changed the thin white garment nor the slippers which she wore. Her hair was uncovered and the sun's rays brought a golden gleam from its brown meshes. She did not take the broad, beaten road which led to the far-off plantation of Valmondé. She walked across a deserted field, where the stubble bruised her tender feet, so delicately shod, and tore her thin gown to shreds.

She disappeared among the reeds and willows that grew thick along the banks of the deep, sluggish bayou; and she did not come back again.

· · · · · · · ·

Some weeks later there was a curious scene enacted at L'Abri. In the centre of the smoothly swept back yard was a great bonfire. Armand Aubigny sat in the wide hallway that commanded a view of the spectacle; and it was he who dealt out to a half dozen negroes the material which kept this fire ablaze.

A graceful cradle of willow, with all its dainty furbishings, was laid upon the pyre, which had already been fed with the richness of a priceless *layette*. Then there were silk gowns, and velvet and satin ones added to these; laces, too, and embroideries; bonnets and gloves; for the *corbeille*[2] had been of rare quality.

The last thing to go was a tiny bundle of letters; innocent little scribblings that Désirée had sent to him during the days of their espousal. There was the remnant of

---

[2]Basket; linens, clothing, and accessories collected in anticipation of a baby's birth.

one back in the drawer from which he took them. But it was not Désirée's; it was part of an old letter from his mother to his father. He read it. She was thanking God for the blessing of her husband's love:

"But, above all," she wrote, "night and day, I thank the good God for having so arranged our lives that our dear Armand will never know that his mother, who adores him, belongs to the race that is cursed with the brand of slavery."

Booker T. Washington
(1856–1915)

Booker T. Washington was born into slavery in 1856 at Hale's Farm near Roanoke, Virginia. His mother was owned by James Burroughs, and his father was a white man who was likely a member of the Burroughs family. After the war, he moved with his mother to Malden, West Virginia, where he worked in coal mines and salt furnaces until he could afford to further his education. In 1872 he made his way to Hampton Institute, a school for African American students established by the Virginia legislature, walking most of the five-hundred-mile journey. Washington attended Hampton for three years, working as a janitor to pay for his room and board. After graduating in 1875, he taught for two years in Malden, and then attended Wayland Seminary in Washington, D.C., before returning to Hampton as an instructor in 1879. In 1881, he was recommended to head the newly founded Tuskegee Institute, a normal school for black students in Alabama. When he arrived at Tuskegee, he found that neither land nor buildings had been donated for the school, and he was forced to begin his classes in a dilapidated shanty donated by the Methodist church. After borrowing money to purchase a nearby abandoned plantation, Washington moved the school there and instituted an educational program that emphasized industrial skills for male students and domestic training for females. During his thirty-four year tenure, he did eventually expand the school's curriculum to include instruction in professions as well as in trades.

Washington also gained renown as an orator. His speech that was delivered at the 1895 Cotton States and International Exposition in Atlanta was hailed in the white press but condemned by black leaders, particularly W. E. B. DuBois, who argued that higher education and political activism, not economic advancement gained through "accommodation," would better aid African Americans in their struggle to gain equality. Washington produced many published works over the years, but his most influential work by far was *Up from Slavery* (1901), which recounts his own rise from slave to educator and promotes his racial philosophy.

from *Up from Slavery*

Chapter XIV.   The Atlanta Exposition Address

The Atlanta Exposition, at which I had been asked to make an address as a representative of the Negro race, as stated in the last chapter, was opened with a short address from Governor Bullock. After other interesting exercises, including an invocation from Bishop Nelson, of Georgia, a dedicatory ode by Albert Howell, Jr., and addresses by the President of the Exposition and Mrs. Joseph Thompson, the President of the Woman's Board, Governor Bullock introduced me with the words, "We have with us to-day a representative of Negro enterprise and Negro civilization."

When I arose to speak, there was considerable cheering, especially from the coloured people. As I remember it now, the thing that was uppermost in my mind was the desire to say something that would cement the friendship of the races and bring about hearty cooperation between them. So far as my outward surroundings were concerned, the only thing that I recall distinctly now is that when I got up, I saw thousands of eyes looking intently into my face. The following is the address which I delivered:—

Mr. President and Gentlemen of the Board of Directors and Citizens:

One-third of the population of the South is of the Negro race. No enterprise seeking the material, civil, or moral welfare of this section can disregard this element of our population and reach the highest success. I but convey to you, Mr. President and Directors, the sentiment of the masses of my race when I say that in no way have the value and manhood of the American Negro been more fittingly and generously recognized than by the managers of this magnificent Exposition at every stage of its progress. It is a recognition that will do more to cement the friendship of the two races than any occurrence since the dawn of our freedom.

Not only this, but the opportunity here afforded will awaken among us a new era of industrial progress. Ignorant and inexperienced, it is not strange that in the first years of our new life we began at the top instead of at the bottom; that a seat in Congress or the state legislature was more sought than real estate or industrial skill; that the political convention or stump speaking had more attractions than starting a dairy farm or truck garden.

A ship lost at sea for many days suddenly sighted a friendly vessel. From the mast of the unfortunate vessel was seen a signal, "Water, water; we die of thirst!" The answer from the friendly vessel at once came back, "Cast down your bucket where you are." A second time the signal, "Water, water; send us water!" ran up from the distressed vessel, and was answered, "Cast down your bucket where you are." And a third and fourth signal for water was answered, "Cast down your bucket where you are." The captain of the distressed vessel, at last heeding the injunction, cast down his bucket, and it came up full of fresh, sparkling water from the mouth of the Amazon River. To those of my race who depend on bettering their condition in a foreign land or who underestimate the importance of cultivating friendly relations with the Southern white man, who is their next-door neighbour, I would say: "Cast down your bucket where you are"—cast it down in making friends in every manly way of the people of all races by whom we are surrounded.

Cast it down in agriculture, mechanics, in commerce, in domestic service, and in the professions. And in this connection it is well to bear in mind that whatever other sins the South may be called to bear, when it comes to business, pure and simple, it is in the South that the Negro is given a man's chance in the commercial world, and in nothing is this Exposition more eloquent than in emphasizing this chance. Our greatest danger is that in the great leap from slavery to freedom we may overlook the fact that the masses of us are to live by the productions of our hands, and fail to keep in mind that we shall prosper in proportion as we learn to dignify and glorify common labour and put brains and skill into the common occupations of life; shall prosper in proportion as we learn to draw the line between the superficial and the substantial, the ornamental gewgaws of life and the useful. No race can prosper till it learns that there is as much dignity in tilling a field as in writing a poem. It is at the bottom of life we must begin, and not at the top. Nor should we permit our grievances to overshadow our opportunities.

To those of the white race who look to the incoming of those of foreign birth and strange tongue and habits for the prosperity of the South, were I permitted I would repeat what I say to my own race, "Cast down your bucket where you are." Cast it down among the eight millions of Negroes whose habits you know, whose fidelity and love you have tested in days when to have proved treacherous meant the ruin of your firesides. Cast down your bucket among these people who have, without strikes and labour wars, tilled your fields, cleared your forests, builded your railroads and cities, and brought forth treasures from the bowels of the earth, and helped make possible this magnificent representation of the progress of the South. Casting down your bucket among my people, helping and encouraging them as you are doing on these grounds, and to education of head, hand, and heart, you will find that they will buy your surplus land, make blossom the waste places in hour fields, and run your factories. While doing this, you can be sure in the future, as in the past, that you and your families will be surrounded by the most patient, faithful, law-abiding, and unresentful people that the world has seen. As we have proved our loyalty to you in the past, in nursing your children, watching by the sick-bed of your mothers and fathers, and often following them with tear-dimmed eyes to their graves, so in the future, in our humble way, we shall stand by you with a devotion that no foreigner can approach, ready to lay down our lives, if need be, in defence of yours, interlacing our industrial, commercial, civil, and religious life with yours in a way that shall make the interests of both races one. In all things that are purely social we can be as separate as the fingers, yet one as the hand in all things essential to mutual progress.

There is no defence or security for any of us except in the highest intelligence and development of all. If anywhere there are efforts tending to curtail the fullest growth of the Negro, let these efforts be turned into stimulating, encouraging, and making him the most useful and intelligent citizen. Effort or means so invested will pay a thousand per cent interest. These efforts will be twice blessed—"blessing him that gives and him that takes."

There is no escape through law of man or God from the inevitable:—

> *"The laws of changeless justice bind*
> *   Oppressor with oppressed;*
> *And close as sin and suffering joined*
> *   We march to fate abreast."*

Nearly sixteen millions of hands will aid you in pulling the load upward, or they will pull against you the load downward. We shall constitute one-third and more of the ignorance and crime of the South, or one-third its intelligence and progress, we shall contribute one-third to the business and industrial prosperity of the South, or we shall prove a veritable body of death, stagnating, depressing, retarding every effort to advance the body politic.

Gentlemen of the Exposition, as we present to you our humble effort at an exhibition of our progress, you must not expect overmuch. Starting thirty years ago with ownership here and there in a few quilts and pumpkins and chickens (gathered from miscellaneous sources), remember the path that has led from these to the inventions and production of agricultural implements, buggies, steam-engines, newspapers, books, statuary, carving, paintings, the management of drug-stores and banks, has not been trodden without contact with thorns and thistles. While we take pride in what we exhibit as a result of our independent efforts, we do not for a moment forget that our part in this exhibition would fall far short of your expectations but for the constant help that has come to our educational life, not only from the Southern states, but especially from Northern philanthropists, who have made their gifts a constant stream of blessing and encouragement.

The wisest among my race understand that the agitation of questions of social equality is the extremest folly, and that progress in the enjoyment of all the privileges that will come to us must be the result of severe and constant struggle rather than of artificial forcing. No race that has anything to contribute to the markets of the world is long in any degree ostracized. It is important and right that all privileges of the law be ours, but it is vastly more important that we be prepared for the exercise of these privileges. The opportunity to earn a dollar in a factory just now is worth infinitely more than the opportunity to spend a dollar in an opera-house.

In conclusion, may I repeat that nothing in thirty years has given us more hope and encouragement, and drawn us so near to you of the white race, as this opportunity offered by the Exposition; and here bending, as it were, over the altar that represents the results of the struggles of your race and mine, both starting practically empty-handed three decades ago, I pledge that in your effort to work out the great and intricate problem which God has laid at the doors of the South, you shall have at all times the patient, sympathetic help of my race; only let this be constantly in mind, that, while from representations in these buildings of the product of field, of forest, of mine, of factory, letters, and art, much good will come, yet far above and beyond material benefits will be that higher good, that, let us pray God, will come, in a blotting out of sectional differences and racial animosities and suspicions, in a determination to administer absolute justice, in a willing obedience among all clases to the mandates of law. This, coupled with our material prosperity, will bring into our beloved South a new heaven and a new earth.

The first thing that I remember, after I had finished speaking, was that Governor Bullock rushed across the platform and took me by the hand, and that others did the same. I received so many and such hearty congratulations that I found it difficult to get out of the building. I did not appreciate to any degree, however, the impression which my address seemed to have made, until the next morning, when I went into the business part of the city. As soon as I was recognized, I was surprised to find myself pointed out and surrounded by a crowd of men who wished to shake hands with me. This was kept up on every street on to which I went, to an extent which embarrassed me so much that I went back to my boarding-place. The next morning I returned to Tuskegee. At the station in Atlanta, and at almost all of the stations at which the train stopped between that city and Tuskegee, I found a crowd of people anxious to shake hands with me.

The papers in all parts of the United States published the address in full, and for months afterward there were complimentary editorial references to it. Mr. Clark Howell, the editor of the Atlanta *Constitution*, telegraphed to a New York paper, among other words, the following, "I do not exaggerate when I say that Professor Booker T. Washington's address yesterday was one of the most notable speeches, both as to character and as to the warmth of its reception, ever delivered to a Southern audience. The address was a revelation. The whole speech is a platform upon which blacks and whites can stand with full justice to each other."

The Boston *Transcript* said editorially: "The speech of Booker T. Washington at the Atlanta Exposition, this week, seems to have dwarfed all the other proceedings and the Exposition itself. The sensation that it has caused in the press has never been equalled."

I very soon began receiving all kinds of propositions from lecture bureaus, and editors of magazines and papers, to take the lecture platform, and to write articles. One lecture bureau offered me fifty thousand dollars, or two hundred dollars a night and expenses, if I would place my services at its disposal for a given period. To all these communications I replied that my life-work was at Tuskegee; and that whenever I spoke it must be in the interests of the Tuskegee school and my race, and that I would enter into no arrangements that seemed to place a mere commercial value upon my services.

Some days after its delivery I sent a copy of my address to the President of the United States, the Hon. Grover Cleveland. I received from him the following autograph reply:—

Gray Gables
Buzzard's Bay, Mass., October 6, 1895

Booker T. Washington, Esq.:

My Dear Sir: I thank you for sending me a copy of your address delivered at the Atlanta Exposition.

I thank you with much enthusiasm for making the address. I have read it with intense interest, and I think the Exposition would be fully justified if it did not do more than furnish the opportunity for its delivery. Your words cannot fail to delight and encourage all who wish well for your race; and if our coloured fellow-citizens do not from your utterances gather new hope and form new determinations to gain every valuable advantage offered them by their citizenship, it will be strange indeed. Yours very truly,

Grover Cleveland

Grace Elizabeth King

(1852–1932)

Grace King's fiction continues to be read for two main reasons: Her stories provide a window on the travails of Reconstruction in the postwar South, and they present memorable characterizations of women whose own sufferings parallel those of the region where they live. King herself well understood the struggles that she portrays in her fiction; her childhood in New Orleans was a comfortable one, but those comforts evaporated with the onset of the Civil War. Her family fled New Orleans for an outlying plantation, but once there they endured considerable hardship, and she watched as her mother virtually took over management of the farm from her dispirited father. Following the war, her family returned to New Orleans but was forced to live in much humbler circumstances.

While spending summers with friends in Connecticut, King was introduced to William Dean Howells and to Samuel Clemens, who would become a close friend. In 1885, Richard Watson Gilder, editor of the *Century Illustrated Monthly Magazine*, asked King for a reason for the antipathy of New Orleans natives toward George Washington Cable. King's answer was her first published story, "Monsieur Motte," which she later expanded into a novella and published in 1888. In 1892, *Tales of a Time and Place* appeared, the collection containing most of her best work. *Balcony Stories*, published in 1893, was also well received for the most part. King's novels, *The Pleasant Ways of St. Medard* (1916) and *La Dame de Sainte Hermine* (1924), further develop her portrait of postwar Louisiana and achieve an interesting synthesis of local-color sentiment with the predominant literary naturalism of the era.

La Grande Demoiselle

That was what she was called by everybody as soon as she was seen or described. Her name, besides baptismal titles, was Idalie Sainte Foy Mortemart des Islets. When she came into society, in the brilliant little world of New Orleans, it was the event of the season, and after she came in, whatever she did became also events. Whether she went, or did not go; what she said, or did not say; what she wore, and did not wear— all these became important matters of discussion, quoted as much or more than what the president said, or the governor thought. And in those days, the days of '59, New Orleans was not, as it is now, a one-heiress place, but it may be said that one could find heiresses then as one finds type-writing girls now.

Mademoiselle Idalie received her birth, and what education she had, on her parents' plantation, the famed old Reine Sainte Foy place, and it is no secret that, like the ancient kings of France, her birth exceeded her education.

It was a plantation, the Reine Sainte Foy, the richness and luxury of which are really well described in those perfervid pictures of tropical life, at one time the passion of philanthropic imaginations, excited and exciting over the horrors of slavery. Although these pictures were then often accused of being purposely exaggerated, they seem now to fall short of, instead of surpassing, the truth. Stately walls, acres of roses, miles of oranges, unmeasured fields of cane, colossal sugar-house—they were all there, and all the rest of it, with the slaves, slaves, slaves everywhere, whole villages of negro cabins. And there were also, most noticeable to the natural, as well as to the visionary, eye—there were the ease, idleness, extravagance, self-indulgence, pomp, pride, arrogance, in short the whole enumeration, the moral *sine qua non*, as some people considered it, of the wealthy slaveholder of aristocratic descent and tastes.

What Mademoiselle Idalie cared to learn she studied, what she did not she ignored; and she followed the same simple rule untrammeled in her eating, drinking, dressing, and comportment generally; and whatever discipline may have been exercised on the place, either in fact or fiction, most assuredly none of it, even so much as in a threat, ever attainted her sacred person. When she was just turned sixteen, Mademoiselle Idalie made up her mind to go into society. Whether she was beautiful or not, it is hard to say. It is almost impossible to appreciate properly the beauty of the rich, the very rich. The unfettered development, the limitless choice of accessories, the confidence, the self-esteem, the sureness of expression, the simplicity of purpose, the ease of execution—all these produce a certain effect of beauty behind which one really cannot get to measure length of nose, or brilliancy of eye. This much can be said: there was nothing in her that positively contradicted any assumption of beauty on her part, or credit of it on the part of others. She was very tall and very thin with small head, long neck, black eyes, and abundant straight black hair,—for which her hair-dresser deserved more praise than she,—good teeth, of course, and a mouth that, even in prayer, talked nothing but commands; that is about all she had *en fait d'ornements*, as the modistes say. It may be added that she walked as if the Reine Sainte Foy plantation extended over the whole earth, and the soil of it were too vile for her tread. Of course she did not buy her toilets in New Orleans. Everything was ordered from Paris, and came as regularly through the custom-house as the modes and robes to the milliners. She was furnished by a certain house there, just as one of a royal family would be at the present day. As this had lasted from her layette up to her sixteenth year, it may be imagined what took place when she determined to make her début. Then it was literally, not metaphorically, *carte blanche*, at least so it got to the ears of society. She took a sheet of note-paper, wrote the date at the top, added, "I make my début in November," signed her name at the extreme end of the sheet, addressed it to her dressmaker in Paris, and sent it.

It was said that in her dresses the very handsomest silks were used for linings, and that real lace was used where others put imitation,—around the bottoms of the skirts, for instance,—and silk ribbons of the best quality served the purposes of ordinary tapes; and sometimes the buttons were of real gold and silver, sometimes set with precious stones. Not that she ordered these particulars, but the dressmakers, when given *carte blanche* by those who do not condescend to details, so soon exhaust the outside limits of garments that perforce they take to plastering them inside with gold, so to speak, and, when the bill goes in, they depend upon the furnishings to carry out a certain amount of the contract in justifying the price. And it was said that these costly dresses, after being worn once or twice, were cast aside, thrown upon the floor, given to the negroes—anything to get them out of sight. Not an inch of the real lace, not one of the jeweled buttons, not a scrap of ribbon, was ripped off to save. And it was said that if she wanted to romp with her dogs in all her finery, she did it; she was known to have ridden horseback, one moonlight night, all around the plantation in a white silk dinner-dress flounced with Alençon. And at night, when she came from the balls, tired, tired to death as only balls can render one, she would throw herself down upon her bed in her tulle skirts,—on top, or not, of the exquisite flowers, she did not care,—and make her maid undress her in that position; often having her bodices cut off her, because she was too tired to turn over and have them unlaced.

That she was admired, raved about, loved even, goes without saying. After the first month she held the refusal of half the beaux of New Orleans. Men did absurd, undignified, preposterous things for her; and she? Love? Marry? The idea never occurred to her. She treated the most exquisite of her pretenders no better than she treated her Paris gowns, for the matter of that. She could not even bring herself to listen to a proposal patiently; whistling to her dogs, in the middle of the most ardent protestations, or jumping up and walking away with a shrug of the shoulders, and a "Bah!"

Well! Every one knows what happened after '59. There is no need to repeat. The history of one is the history of all. But there was this difference—for there is every shade of difference in misfortune, as there is every shade of resemblance in happiness. Mortemart des Islets went off to fight. That was natural; his family had been doing that, he thought, or said, ever since Charlemagne. Just as naturally he was killed in the first engagement. They, his family, were always among the first killed; so much so that it began to be considered assassination to fight a duel with any of them. All that was in the ordinary course of events. One difference in their misfortunes lay in that after the city was captured, their plantation, so near, convenient, and rich in all kinds of provisions, was selected to receive a contingent of troops—a colored company. If it had been a colored company raised in Louisiana it might have been different; and these negroes mixed with the negroes in the neighborhood,—and negroes are no better than whites, for the proportion of good and bad among them,—and the officers were always off duty when they should have been on, and on when they should have been off.

One night the dwelling caught fire. There was an immediate rush to save the ladies Oh, there was no hesitation about that! They were seized in their beds, and carried out in the very arms of their enemies; carried away off to the sugar-house, and deposited there. No danger of their doing anything but keep very quiet and still in their *chemises de nuit*, and their one sheet apiece, which was about all that was saved from the conflagration—that is, for them. But it must be remembered that this is all hearsay. When one has not been present, one knows nothing of one's own knowledge; one can only repeat. It has been repeated, however, that although the house was burned to the ground, and everything in it destroyed, wherever, for a year afterward, a man of that company or of that neighborhood was found, there could have been found also, without search-warrant, property that had belonged to the Des Islets. That is the story; and it is believed or not, exactly according to prejudice.

How the ladies ever got out of the sugar-house, history does not relate; nor what they did. It was not a time for sociability, either personal or epistolary. At one offensive word your letter, and you, very likely, examined; and Ship Island for a hotel, with soldiers for hostesses! Madame Des Islets died very soon after the accident—of rage, they say; and that was about all the public knew.

Indeed, at that time the society of New Orleans had other things to think about than the fate of the Des Islets. As for *la grande demoiselle,* she had prepared for her own oblivion in the hearts of her female friends. And the gentlemen,—her *preux chevaliers*,—they were burning with other passions than those which had driven them to her knees, encountering a little more serious response than "bahs" and shrugs. And, after all, a woman seems the quickest thing forgotten when once the important affairs of life come to men for consideration.

It might have been ten years according to some calculations, or ten eternities,—the heart and the almanac never agree about time,—but one morning old Champigny (they used to call him Champignon) was walking along his levee front, calculating how soon the water would come over, and drown him out, as the Louisianians say. It was before a seven-o'clock breakfast, cold, wet, rainy, and discouraging. The road was knee-deep in mud, and so broken up with hauling, that it was like walking upon waves to get over it. A shower poured down. Old Champigny was hurrying in when he saw a figure approaching. He had to stop to look at it, for it was worth while. The head was hidden by a green barege veil, which the showers had plentifully besprinkled with dew; a tall, thin figure. Figure! No; not even could it be called a figure: straight up and down, like a finger or a post; high-shouldered, and a step—a step like a plow-man's. No umbrella; no—nothing more, in fact. It does not sound so peculiar as when first related—something must be forgotten. The feet—oh, yes, the feet—they were like waffle-irons, or frying-pans, or anything of that shape.

Old Champigny did not care for women—he never had; they simply did not exist for him in the order of nature. He had been married once, it is true, about a half century before; but that was not reckoned against the existence of his prejudice, because he was *célibataire* to his finger-tips, as any one could see a mile away. But that woman *intrigué'd* him.

He had no servant to inquire from. He performed all of his own domestic work in the wretched little cabin that replaced his old home. For Champigny also belonged to the great majority of the *nouveaux pauvres*. He went out into the rice-field, where were one or two hands that worked on shares with him, and he asked them. They knew immediately; there is nothing connected with the parish that a field-hand does not know at once. She was the teacher of the colored public school some three or four miles away. "Ah," thought Champigny, "some Northern lady on a mission." He watched to see her return in the evening, which she did, of course; in a blinding rain. Imagine the green barege veil then; for it remained always down over her face.

Old Champigny could not get over it that he had never seen her before. But he must have seen her, and, with his abstraction and old age, not have noticed her, for he found out from the negroes that she had been teaching four or five years there. And he found out also—how, is not important—that she was Idalie Sainte Foy Mortemart des Islets. *La grande demoiselle!* He had never known her in the old days, owing to his uncomplimentary attitude toward women, but he knew of her, of course, and of her family. It should have been said that his plantation was about fifty miles higher up the river, and on the opposite bank to Reine Sainte Foy. It seemed terrible. The old gentleman had had reverses of his own, which would bear the telling, but nothing was more shocking to him than this—that Idalie Sainte Foy Mortemart des Islets should be teaching a public colored school for—it makes one blush to name it—seven dollars and a half a month. For seven dollars and a half a month to teach a set of—well! He found out where she lived, a little cabin—not so much worse than his own, for that matter—in the corner of a field; no companion, no servant, nothing but food and shelter. Her clothes have been described.

Only the good God himself knows what passed in Champigny's mind on the subject. We know only the results. He went and married *la grande demoiselle*. How? Only the good God knows that too. Every first of the month, when he goes to the city to buy provisions, he takes her with him—in fact, he takes her everywhere with him.

Passengers on the railroad know them well, and they always have a chance to see her face. When she passes her old plantation *la grande demoiselle* always lifts her veil for one instant—the inevitable green barege veil. What a face! Thin, long, sallow, petrified! And the neck! If she would only tie something around the neck! And her plain, coarse cottonade gown! The negro women about her were better dressed than she.

Poor old Champignon! It was not an act of charity to himself, no doubt cross and disagreeable, besides being ugly. And as for love, gratitude!

Corra Harris

(1869–1935)

Corra Harris was the wife of a minister, and the complaint offered most often by modern readers of her work is that she too spent a great deal of her creative energy on preaching. Born in Farm Hill, Georgia, in 1869, she married a Methodist circuit rider, Lundy Howard Harris, in 1887. When he suffered a breakdown in 1898, she began her literary career to support the family. Harris was highly opinionated, and "novels" like *The Circuit Rider's Wife* (1910) and its sequels, *A Circuit Rider's Widow* (1916) and *My Son* (1921), are little more than fictional frameworks for her own observations about life and morality. Later she would drop all pretenses of fiction writing for autobiographical works like *My Book and Heart* (1924) and *As a Woman Thinks* (1925). Similar to her fiction, these works offer the thinnest underpinning of autobiography as a foundation for Harris's moralizing.

Harris's work might not be worthy of critical attention at all if not for her insightful essays on Southern literature, which she published in national magazines in the early years of the century, and, more importantly, her satire *The Recording Angel* (1912). Her third novel, *The Recording Angel*, is relatively free from the didacticism of *A Circuit Rider's Wife*, and it skewers, sometimes hilariously, small-town Southern culture of the day. Though she criticizes what she believes to be false in Southern tradition, she cherishes what she considers worthy, most notably the region's religious traditions. The style she developed enabled her to be successful for many years, though by the last years of her life, public tastes changed, and her conservative themes were no longer as popular.

from *The Recording Angel*

Chapter I

If you take a certain train at two o'clock in the afternoon, say, at Twenty-third Street Station in New York, and travel steadily southward till you are an hour behind time, you come to the carmine hills of Georgia—round, soft hills that the grasses love. They are all dyed with the blood of heroes, and divided by cotton fields and broken-down "worm" fences and happy, disreputable-looking negro cabins, and an occasional "white folks" house. The hills do not notice you as you pass. They are suckling the grass. They are asleep in the golden sunshine. They are dreaming in the perfume of the cotton blooms. You would not be astonished if one of them should turn over and stretch and show the other breast, they are so very comfortable, so very fertile and lazy. No wonder that every train coming southward in this direction loses time. You cannot "stoke" even a New England engine enough to make it hurry in such an atmosphere of repose and somnambulance. You have missed your dinner at Mount Airy, but it makes no difference. You are not hungry. You are breathing the manna-laden air of imaginary plenty. You begin to feel poetical. You hum an old Southern tune. This is an indication that you are nearing Ruckersville, Georgia, where the scenes of this story are laid.

You will know when the train nears Ruckersville by the cotton warehouses in the suburbs, and the suburbs are only one block from the centre of the town, which you will also recognize by the Daddisman Hotel on one side and the stores on every side, and by a curious, duck-legged statue dedicated to the heroes in gray, which squats in the middle of the square. It—the town—is admirably situated to have developed into a flourishing city. But your aristocrat never builds a city. He can ride against one and conquer it, and he can save it from an invading army, but he has neither the patience nor the energy to build one. It takes a parvenu, or at least a Yankee, to do that. And Ruckersville was settled by a Dublin aristocrat who came over hurriedly with Gen. James Oglethorpe, to avoid offensive financial difficulties at home.

This is how the place grew for three generations merely according to its birth rate. And it was an amazingly large town when you took that fact into consideration. No one moved into it from the outside except by marriage, any more than a business man would move into a dream to speculate. It grew amazingly, like a pumpkin vine, in every direction except the one which led to factories and progress. The first thing a stranger notices is that it was evidently settled first by a set of headstrong families, and then laid off into streets to accommodate the east and west whims of their prejudice and pride. This was due to the fact that these families were nearly all related to one another, each asserting its independence, antagonism, or contempt of the blood bond, after the manner of relatives, who are known to hate each other more than any other class of people in the world. Thus, the Fanning-Rucker residence is built with its back door opening before the distant face of the Rucker-Martin residence, on account of the fact that Mrs. Fanning-Rucker was a Fanning before her marriage and took this means of expressing her contempt for all other Ruckers after the death of her husband because they had objected to his marrying her on the ground that the Fannings "had nothing to recommend them but their money." This elevation of her back-door nose had, in turn, compelled the Rucker-Martins to add a side front to their house and change the direction of the street so that they could go out of the front gate in the morning without smelling Mrs. Fanning-Rucker's breakfast dishes and without seeing her kitchen sink. No street in Ruckersville ever knew the day or the hour when it would be changed to accommodate some outraged emotion. Marriage, in fact, inspired the geometrical topography of the town and accounted for the amazing number of elbows in the streets and for the numerous long forearms of them between dwellings. You may live immediately next door and on a straight fifty-foot line with a stranger or a friend, but when it comes to relatives the situation is different. The dominant Ruckersville instinct was to shrug its architectural shoulders, to build the verandas with averted gaze, and to keep enough distance between its habitations to discourage a gad-about hen in case she fancied the crowing of the rooster in the next door yard. No mixing of chickens was tolerated.

Thus the town stands, insufferably erect, supported by long-shanked verandas, showing a tribal reserve in its distances, shaded by immense trees at irregular intervals, divided by long, crooked, white streets that are magnificently fringed with weeds and goldenrods. And in season it is pervaded by the perfume of cotton blooms from the surrounding cotton fields, and at all seasons by the male odour of tobacco smoke. The only truly busy inhabitants there until quite recently were the bees, who did a thriving business and created annually frightful family disturbances by swarming and deserting one Rucker's hives for another Rucker's hives. This was considered personal by the respective owners of the hives, and gave rise to bitterness, all the more lasting because the Ruckersville bees appeared to have inherited their stings from the original cavaliers, were too quick at the thrust, and too fiercely tempered to be meddled with. They hived where they listed and defended themselves with demoniacal frenzy when any effort was made to ding-dong them back home with their former owner's bell. They were invariably supported in their determination to stay where they were by the Rucker whose hives were complemented by their migratory instinct. There was a devilish old Brigham Young bee drone in the Ruckersville honey business who had in this way alienated some of the best families and nearest relatives. He was said to have descended from an Italian queen bee imported in a cigar box by the grandson of the original settler of Ruckersville. This was Col. Joseph Rucker, who, as I have already intimated, came over with General Oglethorpe, and built his mansion on a grant of land from the king that is now the site of Ruckersville. He was an Irishman, and had a beam in his eye. He was gifted with courage, a poetic genius for "making love," and with a clear-blue optimism. Whatever may be said of Adam, for one I am convinced that Eve was of Irish descent. There was something so naïvely simple and iridescently witty in the way she managed to get Adam out of his innocuous state of innocency and idleness and started in the decent labour of digging and sweating like a proper man for his living. And Col. Joseph Rucker was undoubtedly descended from this maternal line. First, he is recorded as having had a genial genius for inducing others to work and to risk their substance and salvation for his sake. He died, full of honours, at a ripe old age, without ever having put his own hand to the plough, the husband serially of three devoted and industrious women, the father of three sets of children, and the promoter of certain water-power schemes—largely at the expense of others—on Broad River, which flowed like a sweet Jordan close to the town, but which refused to be bridled, in spite of the fact that nearly every man in the community who was not a direct descendant of the Colonel had mortgaged his homestead in the effort to accomplish this.

Another proof of his optimism was the pattern of architecture he set, which was enthusiastically copied by his neighbours. The original Joseph Rucker mansion still stands in a grove of live oaks upon a gentle eminence near the middle of the village, with its back turned hopefully upon the adjacent cemetery and its front facing the rising sun. It is an immense white house with windy chimneys, many rattling windows, a wide veranda, and weather boarding so carelessly put on that it is a monument to the builder's belief in eternal summer. Not, you understand, that there is no winter weather in Ruckersville, but that there was nothing in the animation of the Colonel which corresponded to cold and inclemency or that could forestall providence with a blanket of storm sheeting. His god was a mint julep deity of his own accommodating creation who made the earth for the pleasure of man, for the cradle care of women, for the beauty of every flower that blows, and for the joy of little children.

At the imminent risk of tiring that class of readers who are accustomed to being humoured by the author with a duel or a scandal in the first chapter, I have been obliged to include this digression about the Colonel because he was either the direct or indirect progenitor of so many of the characters who shall figure in this story, and because he left behind him a strain of morning-mindedness in them which they still retain. There is julep in their veins, the highest courage in their imaginations, and every sort of aimless improvidence in their deeds. It is when the leaven of industry, of accomplishment and progress is dropped into such cake-dough humanity as this that comedy, tragedy, and queer adventure result, and it is of these that I shall write in this story.

I say on this particular day—it was Tuesday, the fourteenth of June, 18—, a stranger alighted from the train who was obviously neither a drummer nor a politician. And no one recognized him for a relative. He had a long-horned-steer expression. He wore a wide-brimmed hat with a leather band buckled around the crown. His eyes held you up like a brace of steel-blue pistol barrels. And the deep double crinkle of the skin above them added a steady directness to their aim. The bottom of his face showed through an ugly red stubble, like the jawbone of an apithocanthropoid. His mouth was glued together in a straight line under a nose that insulted you by its mere shape. It was high, thin, and drawn back at the lower corners of the neatly, delicately turned nostrils, as if he smelled you and found the odour disagreeable. His clothes were conventional, but scandalously ill fitting, like the loose, brown hide of an erect animal. He was bow-legged, as it turned out, from having sat in the saddle for so many years. And he straddled in his gait, with his feet set wide apart, like a person who has practised walking straight, even when drunk. Altogether, he did not give the impression of being a good man, but at the same time one inferred that he would not brook having his virtues questioned, provided he was in the mood to claim them. If an immense bald eagle had alighted upon the station platform with three inches of spurs sticking out from his feathery legs it would not have created more excitement, more wondering amazement. He stretched himself, covered the row of idlers leaning against the wall of the station with a glance that left them immediately, as if they were of no consequence, swept out over the town and took in the stores, the Bilfire saloon, the Daddisman Hotel, the squatty statue to the heroes in gray, in the centre of the square, beyond the station. It went on down through the emerald twilight of oaks and poplars on every side, among which the long white legs of the piazzas gleamed and proclaimed the quality of the population. Then he undid his mouth, stretched it at the corners, and snickered. This was the only comment he was ever heard to make upon Ruckersville.

The next moment he lifted one thin, sunburnt hand, shoved back his hat brim till a thick lock of fine dark-red hair showed, drew forth an enormous gold watch that was attached to his waistband by a gold miniature trace chain, looked at it, and straddled off along Elbert Avenue with the air of a man who knew where he was going.

As he turned the first corner and was lost to the view of the astonished group at the station, he came upon Miss Mildred Percey. Their eyes met. He passed without lifting his hat. Miss Mildred pressed her hand to her heart. It was a gesture she had which expressed alarm. She always did it when she met a cow in the road or went into a dark room at night where a man might be concealed under the bed. She went on, wondering who the stranger was. Also, she wondered if he were married. This is the difference between men and women. When a man looks at a woman he knows instinctively at once whether or not she is married, and usually he does not concern himself to register the impression into anything so definite as a thought. But when a woman looks at a man old enough to have a beard on his face, and young enough not to be gray, she cannot tell whether or not he is single, and she always wonders, especially if she is single herself.

Miss Mildred was not married. But she was thirty-five. Therefore, she continued more and more to speculate, as she crimped along with her short, mincing steps, concerning the rude stranger who had not lifted his hat to her. Again she placed her hand upon the fat outer bosom of her heart. She had fallen in love and did not know it. She had often fallen this way before, but no one had ever asked her to marry him. At the same time, no man had ever passed her before without lifting his hat.

It is a fact that she was thirty-five, but she denied it with every art known to Ruckersville femininity. She wore an agonizingly tight corset, a severely firm bust supporter, and beautiful slippers too small for her feet. Her outer garments were loose and sweetly flowing to deny the lacing within. An exquisite and expensive blond braid permitted a few of her own locks to escape negligently in waves about her naturally pretty ears, and they supported a gracefully youthful cherubim hat upon her head, the crown of which was naïvely garlanded with a wreath of wild roses. She had large, prayerful, blue eyes, a tender, lonesome-looking mouth, good teeth, and a lovely chin, round, soft, with a disposition to quiver when she was moved by any kind of emotion. Her nose was not her own. She had merely inherited it, without being strong enough to change it, from a distant male Rucker ancestor, and it really accounted for her not being married. It was too high, too thin, too long. It was a kind of physical libel upon the gentleness of her disposition which she could not conceal as she did the natural ampleness of her bosom. This she did not want or deserve either, and it had also been inherited from her habitual child-bearing forebears. On this particular afternoon she was powdered and painted a little. She was on her way to the regular weekly meeting of the "Woman's Club."

The stranger did not know that he had passed Miss Mildred Percey. He was engaged with his own reflections. He advanced leisurely, insufferably so, along the shaded avenue, looking first at one house, then another. Apparently he recalled the row of ancient boxwood in the Rucker-Martins' garden, or it may have been the ivy on the giant chimneys at either end of the house. He paused before the gate of the Misses Yancey's residence and squinted so insolently at the iron Juliet galleries which surrounded the upstairs windows that the two sadly mature maidens within paused in the preparations they were making at their mirrors, before going to the "Woman's Club," and stood trembling with alarm behind drawn curtains. An awful-looking man standing at their front gate in broad daylight, staring speculatively at their windows and doors, meant that they must look under every bed and in every closet for him before they retired that night. Also, it meant that they would not sleep soundly for thinking about him.

Meanwhile, you will understand, of course, that the stranger at the gate was not thinking of anything so timid as an elderly maiden. He was looking at an immense rose vine that covered the Juliet galleries and flirted a thousand pink-hearted yellow blooms in the soft summer air. He was studying the delicate, feminine, many-branched symmetry of a row of pink crepe trees behind the house, against which it rose like a picture upon an old faded valentine. At last he lifted his folded arms from the gate frame and resumed his walk. The Misses Yancey let go their stifled breaths, resumed their toilets, and knew they would be late at the "Woman's Club," not only because they had been interrupted in their dressing, but because they must delay still longer to lock every door and bar every window lest the dreadful-looking character should return in their absence and enter the place, conceal himself, and be ready to rob and kill them the minute night fell upon their defenceless state.

"The house will be like an oven when we return if we close it," said Miss Agnes, the younger of the sisters, as she dabbled her nose afresh with powder, because the excitement through which she had just passed had caused it to perspire.

"Still, two unmarried women living alone cannot afford to take any chances with a person like that hanging around," said Miss Mary, the elder, as she slammed her wardrobe door and locked it.

"Of course not," returned Agnes, sensitively, as if she thought that her sister thought she wished to take chances at some unimaginable adventure. She had once been secretly in love with an ungainly young blacksmith who was accustomed to pass the house, and she was always afraid her sister would discover her innocent romantic digression.

IV

Renaissance (1925–1960)

In the swelter of July 1925, Clarence Darrow, self-appointed apostle of progress, and William Jennings Bryan, stalwart defender of literalist faith, squared off in the high-ceilinged, newly-lacquered courtroom of Dayton, Tennessee. It was in this setting, amid the arid intellectual topography of a region that would unabashedly relish the distinction of being called the buckle on the Bible Belt, that the fate of opposing mythologies was decided.

As students of history are quick to point out, science did not so much triumph as religion succeeded in losing of its own accord, relying on cliché, equivocal language, and shallow contradictory legends as its only defense in that famous trial between the State of Tennessee and John Thomas Scopes.

As a twenty-six-year-old teacher, Scopes never actually taught Charles Darwin's theory of biological evolution at the high school in Dayton. Urged on by local civic and business representatives who recognized the commercial opportunities that a nationally publicized trial would bring the community, Scopes merely announced his intention to teach evolution, a declaration resulting in his indictment under Tennessee's Butler Bill. The case was a calculated challenge to a statute viewed by Dayton's business faction as an albatross to the community's progress. Thus, by placing evolution and John Scopes on trial, the progressive element might achieve twin aims simultaneously: overturning the repressive antievolution law and enriching the pockets of Dayton's visionary elite. Through a combination of shrewdness and manipulation of the Eastern press, Dayton's cartel succeeded in focusing the nation's attention on an event that was more sideshow spectacle than serious settling of controversy.

This is not to say that Dayton was without its genuine religious advocates and biblical literalists. The outlying landscape was dotted with churches of every possible fundamentalist persuasion, and the "rustic puritans" who attended those churches saw Dayton as a spiritual battleground pitting godless secularism against the claims of the faithful. Refusing to accept that human existence was the result of chance or that man's kinship with higher primates was anything but confabulation, the fundamentalists opposed what they considered "rabidly anti-religious" and "anti-Christian" tendencies culminating in the triumph of materialism. Evolution was just another effort to depose God the creator; it was an expression of man's arrogant desire to remake himself in an image of his own choosing. What fundamentalists found especially amusing was how the evolutionists had chosen to refashion themselves in the image of simians.

The joke would backfire. The entire country came to see the inhabitants of Dayton as benighted "rubes" and "yokels" given to the worst sort of superstition. The visiting press corps placed the "South on trial for terminal ignorance,"[1] dubbing Dayton as "Monkeytown" ever afterward. The progressive element was helpless to combat the stigma of backwardness attaching to the area by the moment. The Scopes Trial merely confirmed every suspicion the North held about the provincial South.

Among the most vitriolic attacks came that from H. L. Mencken, a Baltimore-based journalist, who, after covering the trial, wrote, "Down there, a poet is now almost as rare as an oboe-player, a dry-point etcher or a metaphysician." The South, Mencken claimed, was a cultural wasteland, "the Sahara of the Bozart." He "could not know, of course that at the time he made his statement there was a meeting in the South of a group of poets who were to change the whole course of Southern—and indeed American—literature."[2] This remarkable collection of literary talents came to be known as the Fugitives, so-called after the literary magazine *The Fugitive* that they produced at Vanderbilt University from 1922 to 1925. Important to an understanding of this group and their literary intentions is the preface to the first issue of *The Fugitive* magazine, in which John Crowe Ransom wrote, "The Fugitives flee from nothing faster than high-caste Brahmins of the Old South."[3] A year afterward, Fugitive Donald Davidson elaborated on this statement in an interview with Corra Harris, claiming that "if there is a significance in the title of the magazine, it lies perhaps in the sentiment of the editors (on this point I am sure we all agree) to flee from the extremes of conventionalism, whether old or new. They hope to keep in touch with and to utilize in their work the best qualities of modern poetry, without at the same time casting aside as unworthy all that is established as good in the past."[4]

Louise Cowan's groundbreaking study, *The Fugitive Group*, published in 1959, perhaps best describes the core of the group's beliefs that sparked a poetic renaissance scarcely confined to Nashville and the South:

> It was only through breaking with "Southern literature," as it was then piously conceived, that they could find the way to what they realized years later was the genuine Southern tradition. In its literary practice the South was still split by the two apparently antithetical attitudes which had been defined during the period from 1870 to 1900: Old South versus New South. Defeat had routed authors in two directions, along two paths of escape—one into the golden age of the past, "The sweetest, purest, most beautiful civilization America had produced," according to Thomas Nelson Page; the other into the industrially prosperous Utopia of the future, away from what Walter Hines Page described as the "ghosts" that were strangling the South. Yet, though by the period following the World War the two philosophies still had their separate adherents, they were more and more functioning as one,

since both were based on an uncritical devotion to the South and on a fundamental misunderstanding of the nature of literature.[5]

The Fugitives set out to explore a new literary landscape, realizing there was no middle ground between the "Romantic anti-intellectual aesthetic"[6] fostered by the ancien régime and the spirit of scientific naturalism beginning to define the modern age. The group found a precedent in the work of European poets, among whom numbered such self-imposed American exiles as T. S. Eliot, whose *The Waste Land* (1922) had ushered in a new era of modernist poetry and changed the direction of verse for all time. Recognizing the necessity for "aberrant versification" and avant-garde experiments, Eliot nonetheless lamented the loss of forms and traditions in literature and in civilization. The rupture between form and content in Eliot's work represented an inevitable split in the modern sensibility, producing a consciousness often seen as fragmented, ahistorical, and intensely self-preoccupied. Given the dizzying technological advances in the first two decades of the twentieth century and the despair attending Europe's participation in the First World War, writers and other intellectuals described a civilization in ruins, bereft of the old structures and institutions that had once given the world meaning.

Far from being mere regionalists or local colorists, the Fugitives seized this new cosmopolitan impulse in literature and society and made it their own. However, the group rarely displayed one mind about modernism or anything else. Disagreements soon arose over the extent to which a writer could adopt the techniques of modernism while protesting its excesses. Just as Plato had banished poets from his mythical Republic because of their penchant for irony—saying one thing while meaning another and, therefore, technically lying—so too did the Fugitives wonder how far they might go in creating conceits and verbal dislocations that strained against the morally ordered sensibility of an older world. Allen Tate would try to resolve the issue to his own satisfaction by stating that "perhaps the world as it is doesn't afford accurate correlatives of all the emotional complexes and attitudes; and so the artist, or poet, is justified in not only rearranging (cf. entire English tradition) but remaking, remoulding, in a subjective order, the stuff he must necessarily work with—the material world."[7] Tate's position seemed too extreme for Donald Davidson, who preferred simple descriptive language appealing to "conscious elements of memory."[8] Put another way, Davidson believed in an absolute reality, whereas Tate was willing to acknowledge, within limits, a "reality lying in the consciousness of the protagonist and not in the exterior world."[9] Ransom, too, was not willing to go as far as Tate in the direction of poetic experimentation. To shift the ground of language too much was to threaten to shift the ground of reality itself. Thus, Ransom worked to create ironies and divergences within preexisting structures (e.g., quatrains, odes, sonnets). His experiments dealt largely with diction.

As with Eliot, then, the Fugitives were arriving at both an aesthetic and a metaphysical view of human experience. Literature became a religion of sorts, a way of apprehending ultimate reality. Even adherents to the same basic dogma were likely to find points of controversy.

It was also inevitable that the Fugitives would find common ground. Given Eliot's insistence that a new criticism was needed to explain the nature of the new metaphysical literature being produced by so-called modernists, the Fugitives contributed their own insights about the relationship between aesthetic and social concerns. Just as society needed a literature that could distill the modern age without surrendering to that age's tendency toward chaos and desiccation of the human spirit, civilization also needed to undertake means of preserving values beyond the "dolorless medium of information."[10] Aesthetic theory thus pointed out the direction of a new social theory that did not simply glorify the past, but synthesized past ages with the seemingly incongruous tensions produced by modernity. Seeing the South as a special place, a place like no other in which all the imperfect expressions of the past and the contradictory tendencies of the present converged, the Fugitives regarded their position as unique in showing America the way beyond deification of science and acceptance of the soul-numbing social program fostered by industrialization. John Crowe Ransom perhaps spoke for the entire group when he said, "Our fight (as a region) is for survival; and it's got to be waged not so much against the Yankees as against the exponents of the New South."[11]

The Fugitives' allegiance to the lost cause of agrarianism has often been oversimplified. In fact, the term *agrarianism* is now a loose synonym for agriculture, whereas what the Fugitives meant by *agrarian* had more to do with a complex system of land reform residing in ownership of property by a predominantly yeoman class of farmers. The best and longest-sustaining civilizations had been those rooted in the soil. Many critics understandably suspected that the Fugitive group was calling for the return to the antebellum planter system. The Fugitives denied this allegation, claiming that they opposed slavery of all sorts, including the modern industrial variety that tended to enslave workers in mines, mills, factories, and offices. Independent ownership of land was the antidote to the poison spewing out of America's industrial smokestacks, making workers the mere hollow men of Eliot's designation. The Fugitives' more salient views of society have been summarized as follows:

> All around them the young Southern writers saw a country doing its best to become "modern," "progressive," and "up-to-date," and, as they viewed it, achieving only faddishness, unbelief, and a tawdry commercialism. In the South's eager race to emulate the rest of the country, all the things that they had been taught were good were being cast aside. Business was in the saddle; the chamber of commerce reigned.[12]

About the excesses of the modern industrial society, the Fugitives expressed unequivocal agreement. However, not even with publication of what has been termed a Southern manifesto, written by several prominent Fugitives and other of the region's distinguished authors, would a single consistent social program emerge. *I'll Take My Stand* (1930) inspired the birth of a new Southern agrarianism, though the authors themselves displayed a range of views on such diverse topics as "southern economics, education, history, literature, politics, religion, and tradition, plus some attention to the Negro problem, and . . . the status of women. . . ."[13] In fact, Paul Conkin notes that the "very diversity" of the volume made "any summary suspect."[14] Yet reviewers either focused on key essays, failing to "grasp the diversity of content," or tried to pigeonhole the content and found themselves confused because the book "contained too many unblendable ingredients."[15] Not until more than thirty years later in the politically charged sixties did *I'll Take My Stand* become "a campus bestseller, appealing to campus radicals and to advocates of a counterculture"[16] concerned with the evils of capitalism and the exploitation of alienated workers. This newfound appreciation was just one of the many ironies surrounding the Agrarians in their role as "traditionalists."

Whether because of the absence of a core of prescriptive strategies or the alleged impracticality of the Agrarian agenda, the "movement" lost all momentum in the wake of the Great Depression. The South did not achieve the economic independence from Northern industrialism that the Agrarians had called for. Southern agriculture was hit especially hard, requiring "economic integration and national cooperation with aid from the New Deal."[17] The national perspective on the South was found in Franklin D. Roosevelt's declaration that the region constituted America's "Economic Problem No. 1."[18] Many Southerners bristled at the idea of being a national disgrace, rising up in a "storm of protest when Secretary of Labor Frances Perkins suggested that Southerners needed to start wearing shoes!"[19] Such unflattering stereotypes only made Southerners more determined to dig in their dusty heels in defiant opposition to being refashioned and reconstructed once again. Despite making many Southerners feel marginalized, the depictions of poverty, violence, and coarseness were all too accurate in many cases. Jokes told by poor Southerners about the lack of impact the Depression actually made in areas of the Deep South became a folk genre. For instance, Harry Crews, growing up in the hardscrabble thirties, often heard his home of Bacon County, Georgia, described as the "hookworm capital of the world."

Ironically, out of such privation and hardship sprang some of the finest literature written by Americans in the twentieth century. Contributing to the stereotypes to which their fellow Southerners objected, "Erskine Caldwell, William Faulkner, Carson McCullers, Lillian Smith, Elizabeth Madox Roberts, and others wrote of the South with love" while favoring "a harsh, naturalistic style that laid bare the deficiencies of the region."[20] Belonging to no movement or school, these writers helped Southern regionalism come of age by discovering possibilities in a human situation often devoid of buffers to harsh reality or refinements that concealed a grim status quo. The best writers of the period peeled away the South's soul in layers, exposing the universality of human passions in the particular dilemmas of characters who most often resembled family or friends.

Why was the South fertile ground for such robust literary production? This is a question that has often been asked, and its answer is probably as complex and enigmatic as human nature. Perhaps the South had not yet settled the problem of the human condition in the way the North believed it had—through technological advances and humanitarian "progress." Perhaps the South's many contradictions, not the least of which had been its "peculiar institution" of slavery, provided impetus for dramatic tension and possibilities of resolution. Maybe it is as simple as Walker Percy's terse declaration that "we lost the war." The conquered always have more to ponder than the conquerors have. Like Europe after the First World War, much of the post–Civil War South lay in ruins, a situation inclined to inspire the sort of existential questioning that became the benchmark of the modern age.

Whatever the reasons for the South's illustrious display of literary activity, few can avoid the irony that found so many writers in such inhospitable surroundings. Even in the waning days of the twentieth century, the American South is still, technically speaking, the most illiterate region of the nation. It is also the poorest. Yet, in spite of, or perhaps because of, these conditions, Depression-era writers began to fill the pages of the region's incipient literary journals, the most visible and prestigious one at the time being the *Southern Review*, founded at Louisiana State University in 1935 by Cleanth Brooks and Robert Penn Warren. Offering a venue for the South's best writers, the *Southern Review* was international in scope, attracting contributors from points beyond the South and giving a cosmopolitan cachet to a literature that might otherwise have been regarded as provincial in taste and outlook.

The average Southerner might have cared less for the region's sterling literary achievements, if he or she knew about them at all. Often Southern writers found themselves in the awkward position of being part of a community while also standing apart from it. They assumed a kind of invisibility where friends, family, and neighbors were concerned. Whereas readers outside the region might recognize and appreciate the efforts of the South's literary sons and daughters, an overriding anti-intellectualism within Confederate borders kept many people from knowing about the literary accomplishments often occurring next door. In many instances, this arrangement proved advantageous. A classic example is that of William Faulkner, whose reputation in the world at large would garner him the Nobel Prize in literature in 1949, but whose neighbors simply regarded him as an eccentric, or a "crank," until his status became too obvious to overlook. Still, for several decades Faulkner was able to address the fictional possibilities of his region while remaining virtually anonymous. He was able to plumb the depths of the South's inscrutable psyche with little interference from those living closest to him.

This invisibility should not be sentimentalized, especially when we consider the toll it took on groups already "invisible" to much of the populace. To be unwelcome at home was to be the fate of many writers of this period. A good number of intellectuals and proponents of the region's burgeoning literature proved they were not yet beyond the stranglehold of the South's complex network of social codes and overlay of weary prejudices. Nor were some beyond making their fellow writers feel diminished. One instance, in particular, involving a member of the aforementioned Fugitive group, illustrates "with sad clarity"[21] the racism that was still to be found among the South's literati.

In David Levering Lewis's *When Harlem Was in Vogue*, the author recalls Langston Hughes's famous lecture tour of the South that brought the esteemed poet to Fisk University in Nashville in January 1932. Fisk had been founded and staffed during Reconstruction primarily as an institution for producing black teachers. Its reputation as an intellectual bastion for gifted African American artists and scholars was growing through the efforts of the college's administration to attract such distinguished visiting lecturers as Hughes and, earlier, James Weldon Johnson. The geographical contiguity of the Fugitives at Vanderbilt and members of the Harlem Renaissance visiting Fisk might have been one of the most propitious events in Southern literary history were it not for the incident in question. David Levering Lewis describes what happened:

> In Nashville there was growing social and professional intercourse between the faculties of Fisk and Vanderbilt universities. It was mutually understood that a certain discretion was required of such biracial affairs, that they were exceptions to the local tradition of apartheid, and that only the exceptional should participate in them. When Thomas Mabry, a young member of Vanderbilt's English department, sent out invitations for a small party for Johnson and Hughes in late January 1932, he was surprised to receive a mordant refusal from his colleague Allen Tate. Tate was just establishing his reputation as a member of Vanderbilt's so-called Fugitives, a group of writers espousing southern agrarianism. He would gladly meet these "very interesting writers" in New York, London, or Paris, Tate declared, but he agreed with "the colored man who milks our cow" that there should be no racial inter-

course in the South, "unless we are willing for that to lead to his intermarriage." Tate went on to say that he was sure these people were his "intellectual equals," that Mabry was "disinterested and fine," but common sense dictated accepting the position of Aristotle, "who defined man as a social animal; I do not believe he defined him as an artistic animal."[22]

Lewis reports that Mabry was appalled by Tate's "moral lassitude"[23] and furious on hearing that the renowned Fugitive had stirred additional embers of controversy by sending a letter about the incident to a New York magazine. As a member of a well-connected family from nearby Clarksville, Tennessee, Mabry had received his undergraduate degree from Harvard University before enrolling at Vanderbilt for graduate studies. Receiving the M.A. from Vanderbilt in 1932, the young man had been hired as an instructor in the English department, a position he lost as a result of the aforementioned debacle. Mabry would eventually become executive director of the Museum of Modern Art in New York City, returning to the South in 1958, just ten years before his death. However, the necessity to cancel the meeting between representatives of the Fugitive group and members of the Harlem Renaissance rankled Mabry for years. He had almost certainly never expected the furor, nor was it likely that he anticipated the "modernist" Tate's rabid refusal to meet with fellow writers and "intellectual equals," albeit African American ones. Thus, a crucial opportunity for sharing and healing was lost. It would be decades before such a chance again presented itself.

Nevertheless, the incident is instructive in showing that in matters of race, Southern white intellectuals were at many times divided. Even among the Fugitive-Agrarians, arguments broke out, resulting in "ideological skirmishes."[24] One such skirmish involved Robert Penn Warren's contribution to *I'll Take My Stand*. Disliking the "partisan, politically-loaded implications"[25] of the volume's title, Warren set out to show that African Americans could make important contributions to an agrarian society and would benefit from an agrarian arrangement that stressed land ownership and effective management of small farms. Warren's view was not wholly exceptional. Agrarian contributor and Vanderbilt historian Herman Nixon not only argued for a "Christian social gospel oriented toward the needs of the poor and lowly"[26] but also included African Americans in his reforms and supported "integration and the full equality of blacks."[27] Views such as those held by Warren and Nixon were met with alarm by the "die-hard defenders of segregation and second-class citizenship."[28]

The mere fact of controversy reinforced the second-class status and invisibility of writers struggling to be seen and heard. Yet, by the decade of the 1940s, "fiction in the South was already on its way to becoming largely a woman's province."[29] Obvious exceptions included Faulkner and Thomas Wolfe. However, Southern women were carving out a distinctive domain for themselves and achieving enviable, if undisputed, recognition:

Critics and reviewers in both North and South would probably have ranked Ellen Glasgow along with Faulkner, if not above him, although Glasgow was not to receive the national recognition of a Pulitzer Prize until 1942, and by the time Faulkner achieved that honor, with *A Fable* in 1955, three other Southern women had preceded him: Julia Peterkin for *Scarlet Sister Mann* in 1929, Margaret Mitchell for *Gone With the Wind* in 1937, and Margorie Kinnan Rawlings for *The Yearling* in 1939.[30]

If alienation is a recurring theme in the work of many modern authors, it is especially evident in the writings of Southern women of this era. Carson McCullers explored the many avenues of loneliness; Katherine Anne Porter struggled to chart a course between an ironic past and a perplexing, often nihilistic present; and Caroline Gordon wrestled with the dynastic identifications of family and one's often confusing position in the familial arrangement. Only Eudora Welty and Zora Neale Hurston seemed to have arrived at an almost sublime equanimity of spirit and self-awareness rooted in love. That women of different races and backgrounds could converge at the same place by different routes is testimony to the power of each's imagination to locate the disguised verities of the human condition. Welty and Hurston continue to represent the best of the Southern literary tradition. These authors belong to us because, in a real sense, we belong to them. We are beneficiaries of their power to enrich and heal us.

The decade after World War II showed that "the South was no longer the Sahara that Mencken back in the twenties had declared it to be."[31] The South now had a literature of its own of which it could be justifiably proud. The sheer numbers of successful writers made literature an honorable vocation in the South. As a result of the GI Bill, more and more Southerners attended college, where the premier authors of the region were introduced, read, analyzed, and praised. In 1952, Richmond C. Beaty, Floyd C. Watkins, and Thomas Daniel Young published *The Literature of the South*, an anthology whose Foreword could ask with every measure of intellectual respectability the following questions:

> What is a Southern writer? Is there a Southern literary tradition? What are the distinguishing marks of the Southern mind and the Southern way of life, and consequently of the literature in which the mind and the way of life are reflected? To what extent is Southern literature provincial, and to what extent is the provincialism modified by world influences?[32]

The editors made clear that "there are no categorical answers to these questions, but the student of Southern literature ought to address himself [herself] to such questions and speculate freely upon them."[33] In decades to follow, the encouragement to speculate freely resulted in an expanded Southern canon and a revision of critical perspectives necessary to keep Southern literature alive and thriving. Times changed, and so did perspectives. However, Southern writers of the so-called Renaissance overcame many obstacles (some imposed from within the region, some from outside) in order to give the South a flourishing literature and to plant the seeds of a lush garden where Mencken had earlier detected only an expanse of desert.

Notes

1. B. C. Hall and C. T. Wood, *The South* (New York: Simon and Schuster, 1995), 221.
2. Louise Cowan, *The Fugitive Group* (Baton Rouge: Louisiana State University Press, 1959), 41.
3. Cowan 44, as quoted.
4. Cowan, 44.
5. Cowan, 40–41.
6. Cowan, 40.

7. Cowan, 229.

8. Cowan, 229.

9. Cowan, 229.

10. Cowan, 229.

11. Cowan, 245.

12. Lewis M. Killian, *White Southerners* (New York: Random House, 1970), 29.

13. Paul K. Conkins, *The Southern Agrarians* (Knoxville: University of Tennessee Press, 1988), 57.

14. Conkin, 86.

15. Conkin, 87.

16. Conkin, 87.

17. Richard H. King, *A Southern Renaissance* (New York: Oxford University Press, 1980), 62.

18. Killian, 32.

19. Killian, 32.

20. Killian, 32.

21. David Levering Lewis, *When Harlem Was in Vogue* (New York: Oxford University Press, 1979), 269.

22. Lewis, 269–270.

23. Lewis, 270.

24. Conkin, 72.

25. Conkin, 72.

26. Conkin, 67.

27. Conkin, 73.

28. J. A. Bryant, *Twentieth-Century Southern Literature* (Lexington: University Press of Kentucky, 1997), 137.

29. Bryant, 137.

30. Bryant, 167.

31. R. C. Beatty, Floyd Watkins, and Thomas Daniel Young, *The Literature of the South* (New York: Scott-Foresman, 1952), Foreword, xvii.

32. Beatty, Watkins, and Young, Foreword, xvii.

As a prelude to a collection of his poems,[1] Robert Penn Warren offers the following snippet of remembered conversation:

Old man: "You get old and you can't do anybody any good any more."
Boy: "You do me good, Grandpa. You tell me things."

Much that we need to know about Southern literature can be found in this exchange. Warren reminds us that we are privy to a story connecting generations by word of mouth, by a habit of conversation that includes both the teller and the person being told the story. This is Warren's great "spider web" of history in which every human utterance or act reverberates in unseen ways and with unforeseen consequences. Life is therefore a mysterious proposition not easily deconstructed.

For Warren and many writers of his generation, the field theory of human discovery was a matrix of subtle connections showing time to be anything but linear. As a boy perched in his grandfather's lap and listening to the old man recount his experiences as a Confederate veteran wounded at the battlefield at Shiloh, Warren experienced the immediacy of a war that, for many people living in the 1920s, still remained within the long-arm reach of memory. The last Confederate veteran did not die until 1959, two years after the USSR launched the world's first artificial earth satellite, Sputnik. Hence, the great catastrophic event of the mid–nineteenth century still shaped the lives of people living in the early twentieth century, and almost everyone knew someone who had been touched by the hardships of the Lost Cause, or by slavery, or by both.

For Warren and other contemporaries, then, history was anything but an abstraction. Even the notion of history as comprising past events did not square with the facts of personal experience and certainly not with the "progressive" view of society that increasingly devalued the past, obliterating its significance. What Warren's grandfather implicitly chafes against is the idea that being old or "living in the past" (which is the only place his grandfather, ironically, could have lived) is of no worth. In the boy's declaration "You do me good. . . . You tell me things," we find an acknowledgment of the timelessness of events and the sacramental connection of lives lived and tragedies endured throughout the ages.

That Warren hears stories of which he becomes an inevitable part, from a kinsman whose blood and DNA he shares, reinforces the frequent observation that much Southern literature is about the received pieties of family and home. As a result, Southern writers of the Renaissance often found themselves at odds with an American society that equated (and continues to equate) "moving up with moving out." For most Americans living in the early decades of the new century, success no longer involved a sustained network of family connections rooted in one locale. Instead, success meant moving away from familiar (often rural) surroundings for the purpose of bettering oneself financially (usually in the city). If Southerners remained tied, often nostalgically so, to land and family long after the rest of the country had successfully assimilated into the new industrial society, such attachment may have had less to do with peculiar Southern neuroses as with an abiding conviction that something important was being irretrievably lost. The South continued to be a "problem" to the extent that it failed to recognize the initiatives of progress embraced by the North and its industrial program. Although such opposition may have been viewed as an example of the South's characteristic obstinacy or of its urge to be unreconstructed at all costs, closer examination of Agrarian writings reveals a warning that to reject outright the pieties of home and family was to invite the dangers of unimpeded narcissism. In another context, psychiatrist Robert Coles describes a European culture of the 1930s in which the "fury of self-centeredness"[2] reigned supreme, dividing families and destroying natural affections. Who, if not Southern writers, could have imagined the rise of Nazi secularism and its deification of the individual and his allegiance to the nation-state? As with Thomas Hardy, the Fugitive-Agrarians saw the dangers of cultural dislocation and the emergence of a new industrial human whose only requirement was "that anything and anyone in the proverbial way bend or bow out or be done with."[3] Or as Hardy's own narrator in *Jude the Obscure* intones: "The Egoist is the Son of Himself. He is likewise the Father."[4]

Channeled between the extremes of romanticism (symbolized by the timeworn allegiances of the Deep South) and pragmatic utilitarianism (represented by the North's progressive agenda), Upper South writers sought to navigate between the Scylla and the Charybdis of a modern dilemma. In fleeing the "high caste Brahmins" of the Old Order, they rejected the sentimental attachments to land and family embraced by slaveholders who had thought little of abolishing slave marriages and breaking up slave families. By the same token, the new industrial regime offered its own threats to family, home, and the cohesiveness provided by these once potent forces. It should not be regarded as strange that these writers and thinkers would seek new, albeit imperfect, idioms for expressing alarm at the existing state of change, or that Southern intellectuals would mount a defense of the authentic connections they saw as existing between the individual and his or her community. Slavish acceptance of community norms was not the Fugitive-Agrarian agenda. Preservation of human possibilities in an increasingly inhumane, machine-driven world, was.

What Warren and his colleagues perceived was that unless familial ties and rootedness to place were regarded as sacramental, these "pieties" could not long survive the onslaught of the modern world. Unless religious significance were attached to family, home, and community, these archetypal, other than humanly inspired institutions would be rendered extinct, replaced by an autonomous person and his or her needs-driven, ego complexes. A community, therefore, did not have to believe the same things. It simply had to be a community of believers. For this reason, Allen Tate argued that the real religion of the South should not have been Protestantism, but Roman Catholicism with its invisible and sacramentally connected family of believers. Not even Tate's racial prejudice would have survived intact had everyone in the South been regarded as family.

Thus, uneasiness characterized the approach to aesthetic and social matters adopted by authors whose home states, like Warren's Kentucky, had often been "divided." And while groups like the one at Vanderbilt from 1922 to 1925 expressed embarrassment at the Scopes fiasco, they also found it difficult to accept "an enlightenment which permitted so little of the supernatural to remain, so little of the textural, the unique, the marvelous to stand."[5] Without an appreciation for the mysteries of family and place, the need to tell stories about these human-shared phenomena might disappear. Stories themselves might disappear, and with them, whatever of the human drama had been deemed worthy of preserving. Even the connection to God, some believed, was threatened, since in a culture where reading stories about God was a way of communing directly with Him and where the Son of God was "a spiritually aroused itinerant storyteller,"[6] the story fulfilled a divine and healing function. It was a way of turning the cold, all too sane, calculating modern world on its head. It was a means of showing that the first could indeed be the last.

The fundamentalists at Dayton lived and died by the Bible's stories. Nor were the "Bible thumping" fundamentalists as invested in fundamentalism as their critics preferred to believe. More accurate is to suggest that they were invested in a mythology granting them special status as children—God's own—and, as such, they were not beyond receiving special dispensations or experiencing miracles—what might be termed violations of the natural order. Such divine upheavals assumed the existence of a natural order in the first place. The literalist onlookers at Dayton were not pulling rabbits out of the air. Most were dirt farmers who knew the hard facts of nature. They were, however, corroborating testimony about God's ability to behave in ways no human being could imagine. Special situations like these required special stories, exceptional accounts like the one extolling the ability of a fish to gulp a man whole.

The story of Jonah inspired a dramatic episode that, for the fundamentalist community at Dayton, illuminated the differences between scientific secularism and the mysterious operations of faith. In what was later described as the coup de grâce, the one killing stroke wielded by the literalists in the Evolution Trial (Tennessee Evolution Statutes 1925), William Jennings Bryan explained what appeared beyond Clarence Darrow's ability to grasp:

Darrow—But do you believe He made them—that He made such a fish and that it was big enough to swallow Jonah?

Bryan—Yes, sir. Let me add: One miracle is just as easy to believe as another.

Darrow—Just as hard?

Bryan—It is hard to believe for you, but easy for me. A miracle is a thing performed beyond what man can perform. When you get within the realm of miracles; and it is just as easy to believe the miracle of Jonah as any other miracle in the Bible.

Darrow—Perfectly easy to believe that Jonah swallowed the whale?

Bryan—If the Bible said so; the Bible doesn't make as extreme statements as evolutionists do.

The volleying at Dayton was covered in the national press, whose members found great sport in the spectacle offered there. Among them, H. L. Mencken towers as the warrior most given to attacking a culture he himself admitted already lay in ruins. For what reason or on whose behalf he waged such insulting, or as one fellow reporter described it, "uncivilized," warfare is unclear. In any event, he gave local citizens and New South boosters much to protest in his notorious and oft-quoted "Sahara of the Bozart." In actuality, Mencken cherished Cavalier notions of the South, oddly praising the "late (antebellum) empire." Similarly, he fancied the "urbane instinct and aristocratic manner" of the South's once "superior men," who, unlike the rural folk of Dayton, had been members of the antebellum slaveholding class. Mencken also found it convenient to proclaim that "there are single acres in Europe that house more first-rate men than all the states south of the Potomac." His savagery was declaimed in all quarters of the South, though such an uproar did not stop him from believing "that my attacks had something to do with that revival of Southern letters which followed in the middle 1920's."

Mencken's hubris was excessive. The Fugitives were already under way at Vanderbilt, and writers in other parts of the South were asking ultimate questions that would be answered dramatically in literature—not in philosophy, news reportage, or speculative analysis. Mencken's self-praise was a bit like that of an abusive parent who takes credit for his children's scrupulous behavior.

Mencken's insistence on the South's "philosophical barrenness" indicated his misunderstanding of a fundamental mode of apprehension linked to the Southern mind of the time. As Allen Tate maintained, the Northern mind approached reality through a dialectical mode, whereas the Southern counterpart embraced reality through rhetorical means. The North's approach was primarily abstract and analytical, finding its ultimate expression in the scientific method and its attendant reductionism. The South's approach was largely linguistic and mythopoeic, giving rise to literary expression and preservation of the perceived mystery of human existence. If Mencken had argued that the former Confederate states had produced no first-rate scientists, he would have been right. It was when he asserted that the region was no culture for storytellers that the Fugitives rose up to take their stand against this and the more fractious claim that the South had no stories worth telling. The Fugitives insisted that there was an authentic history beyond the modern prismatic view.

Features of the human history worth preserving found consummate expression in lyric poetry such as that written by John Crowe Ransom. Ransom's poetry is taut, elegant, and modern in its display of irony and paradox. Only by accounting for life's paradoxes could one "develop a sensitive awareness of the past and create a feeling of stability and permanence in the flux of an ever-changing world."[7] It is not that the past is always felicitous; it is that the modern world offers a blitzkrieg of destructive influences so that "purposeless modern man cannot know the redemptive qualities of human love"[8] such as those expressed in "The Equilibrists" (1925). Nor can modern men and women safely conclude that any cause is sacred, since only death imparts such knowledge—the theme of Ransom's "Necrological." Finally, in "Antique Harvesters," the poet examines the role of time in transforming a mythic lady (e.g., the South), thereby enabling Ransom to posit the impossibility of knowing anything accurately or for long.

Not given much to displays of the new style shown by other Fugitives, Donald Davidson worked chiefly in traditional narrative forms. His "Lee in the Mountains" and "The Last Charge" demonstrate the poet's essential fidelity to lost causes. Davidson creates "an imaginative realm where lovers, singers, and others of sensibility and taste can be shielded from the harsh realities of an unsympathetic society."[9] Like the Marxists with whom Davidson would have disagreed on many points, the poet becomes a prophet in proclaiming the destruction of modern industrial society by its own excesses and stratagems.

Allen Tate, the most cerebral of the Fugitives and the one most familiar with the literature of classical antiquity, created a body of poetry that demonstrated a fusion of the formal and vernacular traditions. In "The Swimmers," Tate, who was often ambivalent about racial matters, describes the lynching of a black man and the subsequent indifference of the Kentucky community where the crime occurs. Tate combines folk idiom and Latinate diction, culminating in what Robert Lowell called the finest example of *terza rima* since Dante. Tate's poetry has also been described as dense, opaque, and difficult to penetrate. This opacity is nothing more than the sort of vision afforded by the modern world, with its overlay of conflicting and ironic perspectives. Like Eliot, Tate holds up the past in such poems as "Ode to the Confederate Dead" and "Aeneas in Washington," as a means of showing the fragmentary chaos of the present. In neither poem does the poet blindly glorify the past. Rather, Tate suggests how all human action is undertaken with insufficient knowledge of outcomes. It can never be known whether future ages will understand or appreciate past causes of devotion. It is, furthermore, a tragic feature of modern times that few people are capable of imagining life being lived anywhere but in the "eternal present." Connections are severed, affections lost.

These are recurring themes in the work of Andrew Lytle, a Fugitive equally comfortable and skilled in writing poetry, novels, biography, and criticism. Lytle's short story "Jericho, Jericho, Jericho," first published in the 1936 issue of *The Southern Review*, is, according to Sidney J. Landman, "one of the finest pieces of short fiction to have emerged from the Southern Renaissance of the first half of the twentieth century."[10] The story's protagonist, Mammy, realizes on her deathbed that everything she has believed in for seventy years holds no meaning to anyone else. Least of all does it mean anything to her grandson, who, for the last several years, has lived in town, thereby alienated from Mammy's cherished land, Long Gourd. Expecting to leave her plantation to her grandson, Mammy finds that he is about to marry Eva, an unsuitable woman who will spare no effort in keeping him far from the ancestral home. In one final, desperate gesture, Mammy tries to save the land for her grandson. She dies, however, understanding that the values she believed in for so long and, in fact, based her life on, mean little or nothing to him. In a stunning climax, she hears on her deathbed: "Voices . . . singing, 'Joshua fit the battle of Jericho, Jericho, Jericho— Joshua fit the battle of Jericho, and the wall come a-tumbling down,'" an apt conclusion, since all Mammy's efforts to preserve the past have crumbled.

It is almost universally regarded that of all the Fugitives most concerned with the tensions between past and present, Robert Penn Warren was the most gifted. In what now seems prophetic understatement, Tate wrote to Davidson about Warren in 1924: "That boy's a wonder—has more sheer genius than any of us; watch him: his work from now on can achieve—power."[11] Warren would go on to become the only writer in the twentieth century to win a Pulitzer Prize in two different genres—poetry and fiction. In Warren perhaps resides the best effort of the Fugitives to offer a lasting literature. Published in 1946, Warren's "Blackberry Winter" is a story related by a forty-four-year-old narrator looking back on a particular June day when he was nine years old. Up until that time, the youth-protagonist Seth has lived in a world cushioned from hardships. However, after a disastrous flood, he finds the weather suddenly changed—even cold for June. In talking with a tramp whom his mother has hired to clean up the yard, Seth makes an unsettling discovery, forcing him "to look within, to follow the tramp beyond his own narrow confines and to open himself to experiences which lead to despair, acceptance, wisdom, and courage."[12] The conclusion to this story makes it one of the most powerful in American letters.

For all his talent in fiction, Warren defined himself chiefly as a poet, exploring the ever-shifting axis of a truth shimmering in the distance like a teasing mirage. Warren recognized that the relationship of truth to history was unfathomably complex. As indicated in Warren's poem "Founding Fathers Early Nineteenth Century Style:

Southeast U.S.A.," the present is neither inferior nor superior to the past. What links all ages is an "instinctive awareness of human frailties."[13] The speaker in Warren's poem acknowledges that his ancestors, now dead, have "nothing to tell us for their own complexity of choices." Nor can we do anything but hope "to forgive them their defects," just as we hope our own defects will be forgiven by future generations.

For decades Warren's collaborator in various literary endeavors was Cleanth Brooks, professor of English and critic extraordinaire. With Warren, Professor Brooks wrote some of the most influential college texts published in America, including *Understanding Poetry* (1938), *Understanding Fiction* (1943), and *Understanding Drama* (1945). Each of these works emphasizes an approach to literature based primarily on a close examination of the text itself. This approach came to be known as the New Criticism. Although opponents maintained that the Fugitives and subsequent New Critics often made a political issue of literature, Brooks claimed that the New Critical approach was designed to treat literature as literature, to depoliticize its content, by emphasizing its aesthetic qualities. One of Brooks's chief contributions to Southern literature was to awaken widespread interest in the work of William Faulkner and to provide a critical framework for evaluating Faulkner's canon like the perspective offered in *The Hidden God* (1963). Here Brooks argues for the complexity of Faulkner's religious vision and the author's inability to be pigeonholed with regard to Christian dogma.

The waves of literary influence generated by the Fugitive-Agrarians touched many writers, including Caroline Gordon, who was among the first critics to give the group serious notice:

> Writing for the *Chattanooga News*, Caroline Gordon, who at that time (1932) had never met any of the Fugitives, gave the group more praise than any other reviewer. Under the heading "U.S. Best Poets Here in Tennessee," she surveyed the various little magazines then flourishing in the South, according *The Fugitive* by far the highest laurels.[14]

Gordon's "indirect" relationship with the Fugitives would soon change. In 1924 she met Allen Tate, and the couple were married in New York a short time later. Warren's "spider web" was expanding now beyond the initial group and its purposes. Indeed, talent eclipsed boundaries imposed by culture, race, and gender. Gordon's own influence as a writer and seminal critic shaped the work of such authors as Flannery O'Connor and Walker Percy. Although a stylistically competent novelist, Gordon found her forte in short fiction, offering superbly crafted, psychologically penetrating stories like "Old Red." The tensions between men and women, whites and blacks, parents and children present a tedious and excruciating undercurrent of anxiety in the story. In Gordon's dynastic sagas, the center frequently does not hold, nor can sentimental attachments to home and family withstand the strains created by human imperfection.

A kindred literary spirit to Gordon in many respects, Katherine Anne Porter shows what a potent social force family can be, even when an individual rebels against it. Porter's spare, meticulously crafted prose also reveals keen insight into the relationships between men and women—the tensions between the sexes and the difficulties in resolving those tensions. In "Rope," the roles of protagonist are shared equally between a husband and a wife disagreeing over what seem to be minor domestic arrangements. Very little conversation occurs in this story as each character carries on an interior monologue in response to what the other character must be thinking. The efforts at self-justification by both husband and wife comprise a focal point here. Each assumes the other will understand what each one needs and wants in the relationship. Each also assumes a resolution to a mutual conflict based on a tenuous and assumed knowledge of the other's desires.

The absence of harmony and the presence of incongruity give rise to a literature of social protest important in providing a complete picture of the literary output of this period. Far from adhering to the simplistic creed that all literature of the Renaissance was traditionalist or existed in support of a Southern agenda, the emerging literary practitioners threw off the spell cast by romance, challenging conventional thought and social practices. One such challenge came from one of the finest writers of the period, Ellen Glasgow. Glasgow's *The Battle Ground* (1902) is "a novel about the Civil War, but is by no means an apology for the Confederacy. . . ."[15] The protagonist of this work returns home to find his ancestral plantation leveled and all the past with it. Nevertheless, his wife, embodying a new generation of women willing to challenge traditional values, assures her husband that all will work out, since this time ". . . we will begin together." As Carol Manning's finely tuned observations attest, "Glasgow and other women writers in this time frame progressively demystify the Southern family, romance, and hence the Southern tradition."[16] An additional qualification worth making is that Glasgow expands and re-creates the tradition, exploding clichés about the South's "monolithic" literary achievements generated solely by a small group of men or about the role of Southern women writers in submitting to exclusively patriarchal models.

Nor were Southern women too polite to be politically inspired, as was sometimes argued by critics outside the region. Writing in accord with principles espoused by the American Communist Party of the day, Olive Tilford Dargan protests the conditions created in the South by the Great Depression. In *Call Home the Heart* (1932), the author describes the destructive forces of a class system that makes "burden-bearers" of huge segments of the population. Women, in particular, suffer under the weight of backbreaking toil in the fields, trying to keep families together despite insurmountable odds. Youth and dreams dissolve in a dry, withered landscape where clotted dust obscures the presence of the sun.

The plight of both poor blacks and poor whites is the subject of Paul Green's one-act dramas, including *Hymn to the Rising Sun: A Drama of Man's Waste in One Act* (1936). Having worked in the fields on his father's farm near Lillington, North Carolina, Green gained early exposure to the dispossessed and forgotten, those for whom there was, socially speaking, no room at the inn. Green's plays are social histories rooted in a landscape fraught with hardships. In *Hymn to the Rising Sun*, his characters are, for the most part, convicts subjected to brutality and forced to live without recognition of their status as human beings. Even their names (e.g., Runt, Captain, and Boy) reflect either an absence of genuine identity or the pejorative stereotyped functions these characters serve.

Like Paul Green, Sterling Brown "showed an affinity for people of the soil."[17] The son of a former slave from Tennessee, Brown received his B.A. degree from Williams College and his M.A. from Harvard during the early years of the Harlem Renaissance. Although not physically associated with the movement in Harlem, Brown submitted prize-winning essays to publications devoted to showcasing the increasingly visible talent in Harlem. Brown's attitude toward his native South was anything but ambivalent. In such poems as "Slim in Atlanta" and "Southern Cop," the poet adopts folk materials to help dramatize the absence of a safe haven for African Americans anywhere in the South. His persona named Slim recurs as a voice often comparing the landscape of Dixie with the geography of hell.

The South as a nexus of perpetual conflicts is a theme in the one major work produced by North Carolina journalist Wilbur J. Cash. Cash's *The Mind of the South* (1941) called attention to the region in a way no other treatise ever had. The tone is unmistakable. Cash's purpose is to debunk the existing class arrangement that had previously justified an aristocracy assumed to be "in every case descended from the old gentle folk who for many centuries had made up the ruling classes of Europe." What Cash shows in Chapter Eleven, "The Man at the Center," is how all classes of white Southerners derived from the same basic stock, with a few notable exceptions. The majority of whites were agriculturists who in the early days cleared land and began farming. Then, "as the years passed, they made some money that enabled them to buy more land and bring in some slaves."[18] Well-connected marriages among other "nouveau bluebloods" resulted in more wealth and an increasing sense of entitlement. Genealogical searches for royal ancestors confirmed that almost everyone was related in some way to Alfred the Great. Forgotten was the reality that made all white Southerners kinfolks whether they wanted to be or not. And, of course, many of the South's professed gentry were related by blood to their African American slaves. Cash's ultimate contribution may have been the humbling effect his book engendered among people prone to idealizing the homeland. By helping balance the region's perception of itself, Cash may have provided an opportunity, in his own words, for the South's "virtues to tower ever and conquer its faults" as a prelude to making "the Southern world to come."

Notes

1. Robert Penn Warren, *The Collected Poems of Robert Penn Warren*, ed. John Burt (Baton Rouge: Louisiana State University Press, 1998).
2. Robert Coles, *The Secular Mind* (Princeton: Princeton University Press, 1999), 81.
3. Coles, 81.
4. Coles, 81. Important to note is that we have not only appropriated Professor Coles's line of thinking here, but his example as well. Both seem appropriate to a discussion of the South of the 1920s and 1930s.
5. Louise Cowan, *The Fugitive Group* (Baton Rouge: Louisiana State University Press, 1959), 241.
6. Coles, 25.
7. Thomas Daniel Young, "The Fugitives: Ransom, Davidson, Tate," *The History of Southern Literature*, ed. Louis D. Rubin et al. (Baton Rouge: Louisiana State University Press, 1985), 323.
8. Young, 322.
9. Young, 319.
10. Linda Burton Francisco, *Stories from Tennessee* (Knoxville: University of Tennessee Press, 1982), Introduction, xv, as quoted.
11. Cowan, 107.
12. Francisco, Introduction, xviii.

13. R. C. Beatty, Floyd Watkins, and Thomas Daniel Young, *The Literature of the South* (New York: Scott-Foresman, 1952), 631.

14. Cowan, 98.

15. Edgar E. MacDonald, "The Ambivalent Heart: Literary Revival in Richmond," *The History of Southern Literature*, ed. Louis D. Rubin et al. (Baton Rouge: Louisiana State University Press, 1985), 266.

16. Carol S. Manning, *The Female Tradition in Southern Literature* (Urbana: University of Illinois Press, 1993), 8.

17. Thadious M. Davis, "Southern Standard-Bearers in the New Negro Renaissance," *The History of Southern Literature*, ed. Louis D. Rubin et al. (Baton Rouge: Louisiana State University Press, 1985), 307.

18. B. C. Hall and C. T. Wood, *The South* (New York: Simon and Schuster, 1995), 88.

Tennessee Evolution Statutes

PUBLIC ACTS

OF THE

STATE OF TENNESSEE

PASSED BY THE

SIXTY-FOURTH GENERAL ASSEMBLY

1925

CHAPTER NO. 27

House Bill No. 185

(By Mr. Butler)

AN ACT prohibiting the teaching of the Evolution Theory in all the Universities, Normals and all other public schools of Tennessee, which are supported in whole or in part by the public school funds of the State, and to provide penalties for the violations thereof.

Section 1. *Be it enacted by the General Assembly of the State of Tennessee,* That it shall be unlawful for any teacher in any of the Universities, Normals and all other public schools of the State which are supported in whole or in part by the public school funds of the State, to teach any theory that denies the story of the Divine Creation of man as taught in the Bible, and to teach instead that man has descended from a lower order of animals.

Section 2. *Be it further enacted,* That any teacher found guilty of the violation of this Act, Shall be guilty of a misdemeanor and upon conviction, shall be fined not less than One Hundred ($100.00) Dollars nor more than Five Hundred ($500.00) Dollars for each offense.

Section 3. *Be it further enacted,* That this Act take effect from and after its passage, the public welfare requiring it.

Passed March 13, 1925

W. F. Barry,

Speaker of the House of Representatives

L. D. Hill,

Speaker of the Senate

Approved March 21, 1925.

Austin Peay,

Governor.

PUBLIC ACTS

OF THE

STATE OF TENNESSEE

PASSED BY THE

EIGHTY-FIFTH GENERAL ASSEMBLY

1967

CHAPTER NO. 237

House Bill No. 48

(By Smith, Galbreath, Bradley)

SUBSTITUTED FOR: SENATE BILL NO. 46

(By Elam)

AN ACT to repeal Section 498—1922, Tennessee Code Annotated, prohibiting the teaching of evolution.

Be it enacted by the General Assembly of the State of Tennessee:

Section 1. Section 49—1922, Tennessee Code Annotated, is repealed.

Section 2. This Act shall take effect September 1, 1967.

Passed: May 13, 1967

James H. Cummings

Speaker of the House of Representatives

Frank C. Gorrell,

Speaker of the Senate

Approved: May 17, 1967.

Buford Ellington,

Governor.

State of Tennessee vs. John Scopes

(1925)

The events that culminated in the Scopes trial, or "Monkey Trial" as it came to be known, were set in motion in February 1925 when the state of Tennessee enacted a bill that made it unlawful "to teach any theory that denies the story of divine creation as taught by the Bible and to teach instead that man was descended from a lower order of animals." In Dayton, Tennessee, a group of citizens who opposed the new law approached John Scopes, a science teacher and part-time football coach, and won his agreement to be the defendant in a test case challenging the law. William Jennings Bryan, who had not practiced law in thirty years but who had led the crusade to enact antievolution legislation across the nation, offered to join the prosecution, and the equally well-known Clarence Darrow, a fervent agnostic, volunteered to join Scopes's defense.

The trial opened in July 1925. Dayton was festooned with banners, Anti-Evolution League members hawked Bryan's *Hell and High School* in the streets, and chimpanzees performed in a Main Street sideshow. Journalists from across the country crowded into town, including H. L. Mencken, who was at the time a correspondent for both *The Baltimore Sun* and *The Mercury* and who had already aroused the ire of Southerners with his 1920 essay "The Sahara of the Bozart" (included here in its entirety). The South, Mencken had written, was "almost as sterile, artistically, intellectually, culturally, as the Sahara Desert," and worthwhile art was not to be found "between the Potomac mud flats and the gulf." Mencken welcomed the opportunity to continue his diatribe by providing daily coverage of the Scopes trial.

John T. Raulston, the presiding judge, recommended the trial be held under a revival tent, and when almost one thousand people crowded into the courtroom on July 10, it was moved outside because of fears that the floor would collapse under the weight of the spectators. Before a crowd that grew to over five thousand, William Jennings Bryan was called to the stand by the defense as an "expert on the Bible." Bryan agreed to the stunt, resulting in what the *New York Times* described as "the most amazing court scene in Anglo-Saxon history." Bryan's and Darrow's exchange, a series of questions on literal interpretation of the Bible, has become legendary. In the end, Darrow asked for a verdict of guilty so that the case could be appealed to the Tennessee Supreme Court, a request granted by the court. (The verdict was overturned on appeal, not on constitutional grounds but because of a technicality.) William Jennings Bryan died in Dayton six days after the end of the trial.

from the Scopes Trial Transcripts

Day 7

"Read Your Bible" banner removed from courthouse

Darrow—Your honor, before you send for the jury, I think it my duty to make this motion. Off to the left of where the jury sits a little bit and about ten feet in front of them is a large sign about ten feet long reading "Read Your Bible," and a hand pointing to it. The word "Bible" is in large letters, perhaps, a foot and a half long, and the printing—

The Court—Hardly that long I think, general.

Darrow—What is that?

The Court—Hardly that long.

Darrow—Why, we will call it a foot. . . .

Darrow—I move that it be removed.

The Court—Yes.

McKenzie—If your honor please, why should it be removed?

It is their defense and stated before the court, that they do not deny the Bible, that they expected to introduce proof to make it harmonize. Why should we remove the sign cautioning the people to read the Word of God just to satisfy the others in the case? . . .

Darrow—Let me say something. Your honor, I just want to make this suggestion. Mr. Bryan says that the Bible and evolution conflict. Well, I do not know, I am for evolution, anyway. We might agree to get up a sign of equal size on the other side and in the same position reading, "Hunter's Biology," or "Read your evolution." This sign is not here for no purpose, and it can have no effect but to influence this case, and I read the Bible myself—more or less—and it is pretty good reading in places. But this case has been made a case where it is to be the Bible or evolution, and we have been informed by Mr. Bryan, who himself, a profound Bible student and has an essay every Sunday as to what it means. We have been informed that a Tennessee jury who are not especially educated are better judges of the Bible than all the scholars in the world, and when they see that sign, it means to them their construction of the Bible. It is pretty obvious, it is not fair, your honor, and we object to it. . . .

The Court—The issues in this case, as they have been finally determined by this court is whether or not it is unlawful to teach that man descended from a lower order of animals. I do not understand that issue involved the Bible. If the Bible is involved, I believe in it and am always on its side, but it is not for me to decide in this case. If the presence of the sign irritates anyone, or if anyone thinks it might influence the jury in any way, I have no purpose except to give both sides a fair trial in this case. Feeling that way about it, I will let the sign come down. Let the jury be brought around.

(The sign was thereupon removed from the courthouse wall.)

Darrow's examination of Bryan

Hays—The defense desires to call Mr. Bryan as a witness, and, of course, the only question here is whether Mr. Scopes taught what these children said he taught, we recognize what Mr. Bryan says as a witness would not be very valuable. We think there are other questions involved, and we should want to take Mr. Bryan's testimony for the purpose of our record, even if your honor thinks it is not admissible in general, so we wish to call him now.

The Court—Do you think you have a right to his testimony or evidence like you did these others?

McKenzie—I don't think it is necessary to call him, calling a lawyer who represents a client.

The Court—If you ask him about any confidential matter, I will protect him, of course.

Darrow—On scientific matters, Col. Bryan can speak for himself.

Bryan—If your honor please, I insist that Mr. Darrow can be put on the stand, and Mr. Malone and Mr. Hays.

The Court—Call anybody you desire. Ask them any questions you wish.

Bryan—Then, we will call all three of them.

Darrow—Not at once?

Bryan—Where do you want me to sit?

The Court—Mr. Bryan, you are not objecting to going on the stand?

Bryan—Not at all.

The Court—Do you want Mr. Bryan sworn?

Darrow—No.

Bryan—I can make affirmation; I can say "So help me God, I will tell the truth."

Darrow—No, I take it you will tell the truth, Mr. Bryan.

Examination of W. J. Bryan by Clarence Darrow, of counsel for the defense:

Q—You have given considerable study to the Bible, haven't you, Mr. Bryan?

A—Yes, sir, I have tried to.

Q—Then you have made a general study of it?

A—Yes, I have; I have studied the Bible for about fifty years, or sometime more than that, but, of course, I have studied it more as I have become older than when I was but a boy.

Q—You claim that everything in the Bible should be literally interpreted?

A—I believe everything in the Bible should be accepted as it is given there: some of the Bible is given illustratively. For instance: "Ye are the salt of the earth." I would not insist that man was actually salt, or that he had flesh of salt, but it is used in the sense of salt as saving God's people.

Q—But when you read that Jonah swallowed the whale—or that the whale swallowed Jonah—excuse me please—how do you literally interpret that?

A—When I read that a big fish swallowed Jonah—it does not say whale.

Q—That is my recollection of it. A big fish, and I believe it, and I believe in a God who can make a whale and can make a man and make both what He pleases.

Q—Now, you say, the big fish swallowed Jonah, and he there remained how long—three days—and then he spewed him upon the land. You believe that the big fish was made to swallow Jonah?

A—I am not prepared to say that; the Bible merely says it was done.

Q—You don't know whether it was the ordinary run of fish, or made for that purpose?

A—You may guess; you evolutionists guess. . . .

Q—You are not prepared to say whether that fish was made especially to swallow a man or not?

A—The Bible doesn't say, so I am not prepared to say.

Q—But do you believe He made them—that He made such a fish and that it was big enough to swallow Jonah?

A—Yes, sir. Let me add: One miracle is just as easy to believe as another.

Q—Just as hard?

A—It is hard to believe for you, but easy for me. A miracle is a thing performed beyond what man can perform. When you get within the realm of miracles; and it is just as easy to believe the miracle of Jonah as any other miracle in the Bible.

Q—Perfectly easy to believe that Jonah swallowed the whale?

A—If the Bible said so; the Bible doesn't make as extreme statements as evolutionists do. . . .

Q—The Bible says Joshua commanded the sun to stand still for the purpose of lengthening the day, doesn't it, and you believe it.

A—I do.

Q—Do you believe at that time the entire sun went around the earth?

A—No, I believe that the earth goes around the sun.

Q—Do you believe that the men who wrote it thought that the day could be lengthened or that the sun could be stopped?

A—I don't know what they thought.

Q—You don't know?

A—I think they wrote the fact without expressing their own thoughts.

Q—Have you an opinion as to whether or not the men who wrote that thought . . .

Gen. Stewart—I want to object, your honor; it has gone beyond the pale of any issue that could possibly be injected into this lawsuit, expect by imagination. I do not think the defendant has a right to conduct the examination any further and I ask your honor to exclude it.

The Witness—It seems to me it would be too exacting to confine the defense to the facts; if they are not allowed to get away from the facts, what have they to deal with?

The Court—Mr. Bryan is willing to be examined. Go ahead.

Mr. Darrow—I read that years ago. Can you answer my question directly? If the day was lengthened by stopping either the earth or the sun, it must have been the earth?

A—Well, I should say so.

Q—Now, Mr. Bryan, have you ever pondered what would have happened to the earth if it had stood still?

A—No.

Q—You have not?

A—No; the God I believe in could have taken care of that, Mr. Darrow.

Q—I see. Have you ever pondered what would naturally happen to the earth if it stood still suddenly?

A—No.

Q—Don't you know it would have been converted into molten mass of matter?

A—You testify to that when you get on the stand, I will give you a chance.

Q—Don't you believe it?

A—I would want to hear expert testimony on that.

Q—You have never investigated that subject?

A—I don't think I have ever had the question asked.

Q—Or ever thought of it?

A—I have been too busy on things that I thought were of more importance than that.

Q—You believe the story of the flood to be a literal interpretation?

A—Yes, sir.

Q—When was that Flood?

A—I would not attempt to fix the date. The date is fixed, as suggested this morning.

Q—About 4004 B.C.?

A—That has been the estimate of a man that is accepted today. I would not say it is accurate.

Q—That estimate is printed in the Bible?

A—Everybody knows, at least, I think most of the people know, that was the estimate given.

Q—But what do you think that the Bible, itself says? Don't you know how it was arrived at?

A—I never made a calculation.

Q—A calculation from what?

A—I could not say.

Q—From the generations of man?

A—I would not want to say that.

Q—What do you think?

A—I do not think about things I don't think about.

Q—Do you think about things you do think about?

A—Well, sometimes.

(Laughter in the courtyard.)

Policeman—Let us have order. . . .

Stewart—Your honor, he is perfectly able to take care of this, but we are attaining no evidence. This is not competent evidence.

Witness—These gentlemen have not had much chance—they did not come here to try this case. They came here to try revealed religion. I am here to defend it and they can ask me any question they please.

The Court—All right.

(Applause from the court yard.)

Darrow—Great applause from the bleachers.

Witness—From those whom you call "Yokels."

Darrow—I have never called them yokels.

Witness—That is the ignorance of Tennessee, the bigotry.

Darrow—You mean who are applauding you? (Applause.)

Witness—Those are the people whom you insult.

Darrow—You insult every man of science and learning in the world because he does believe in your fool religion.

The Court—I will not stand for that.

Darrow—For what he is doing?

The Court—I am talking to both of you. . . .

Q—Wait until you get to me. do you know anything about how many people there were in Egypt 3,500 years ago, or how many people there were in China 5,000 years ago?

A—No.

Q—Have you ever tried to find out?

A—No, sir. You are the first man I ever heard of who has been interested in it. (Laughter.)

Q—Mr. Bryan, am I the first man you ever heard of who has been interested in the age of human societies and primitive man?

A—You are the first man I ever heard speak of the number of people at those different periods.

Q—Where have you lived all your life?

A—Not near you. (Laughter and applause.)

Q—Nor near anybody of learning?

A—Oh, don't assume you know it all.

Q—Do you know there are thousands of books in our libraries on all those subjects I have been asking you about?

A—I couldn't say, but I will take your word for it. . . .

Q—Have you any idea how old the earth is?

A—No.

Q—The Book you have introduced in evidence tells you, doesn't it?

A—I don't think it does, Mr. Darrow.

Q—Let's see whether it does; is this the one?

A—That is the one, I think.

Q—It says B.C. 4004?

A—That is Bishop Usher's calculation.

Q—That is printed in the Bible you introduced?

A—Yes, sir. . . .

Q—Would you say that the earth was only 4,000 years old?

A—Oh, no; I think it is much older than that.

Q—How much?

A—I couldn't say.

Q—Do you say whether the Bible itself says it is older than that?

A—I don't think it is older or not.

Q—Do you think the earth was made in six days?

A—Not six days of twenty-four hours.

Q—Doesn't it say so?

A—No, sir. . . .

The Court—Are you about through, Mr. Darrow?

Darrow—I want to ask a few more questions about the creation.

The Court—I know. We are going to adjourn when Mr. Bryan comes off the stand for the day. Be very brief, Mr. Darrow. Of course, I believe I will make myself clearer. Of course, it is incompetent testimony before the jury. The only reason I am allowing this to go on at all is that they may have it in the appellate court as showing what the affidavit would be.

Bryan—The reason I am answering is not for the benefit of the superior court. It is to keep these gentlemen from saying I was afraid to meet them and let them question me, and I want the Christian world to know that any atheist, agnostic, unbeliever, can question me anytime as to my belief in God, and I will answer him.

Darrow—I want to take an exception to this conduct of this witness. He may be very popular down here in the hills. . . .

Bryan—Your honor, they have not asked a question legally and the only reason they have asked any question is for the purpose, as the question about Jonah was asked, for a chance to give this agnostic an opportunity to criticize a believer in the world of God; and I answered the question in order to shut his mouth so that he cannot go out and tell his atheistic friends that I would not answer his questions. That is the only reason, no more reason in the world.

Malone—Your honor on this very subject, I would like to say that I would have asked Mr. Bryan—and I consider myself as good a Christian as he is—every question that Mr. Darrow has asked him for the purpose of bringing out whether or not there is to be taken in this court a literal interpretation of the Bible, or whether, obviously, as these questions indicate, if a general and literal construction cannot be put upon the parts of the Bible which have been covered by Mr. Darrow's questions. I hope for the last time no further attempt will be made by counsel on the other side of the case, or Mr. Bryan, to say the defense is concerned at all with Mr. Darrow's particular religious views or lack of religious views. We are here as lawyers with the same right to our views. I have the same right to mine as a Christian as Mr. Bryan has to his, and we do not intend to have this case charged by Mr. Darrow's agnosticism or Mr. Bryan's brand of Christianity. (A great applause.)

Mr. Darrow:

Q—Mr. Bryan, do you believe that the first woman was Eve?

A—Yes.

Q—Do you believe she was literally made out of Adams's rib?

A—I do.

Q—Did you ever discover where Cain got his wife?

A—No, sir; I leave the agnostics to hunt for her.

Q—You have never found out?

A—I have never tried to find . . .

Q—You have never tried to find?

A—No.

Q—The Bible says he got one, doesn't it? Were there other people on the earth at that time?

A—I cannot say.

Q—You cannot say. Did that ever enter your consideration?

A—Never bothered me.

Q—There were no others recorded, but Cain got a wife.

A—That is what the Bible says.

Q—Where she came from you do not know. All right. Does the statement, "The morning and the evening were the first day," and "The morning and the evening were the second day," mean anything to you?

A—I do not think it necessarily means a twenty-four-hour day.

Q—You do not?

A—No.

Q—What do you consider it to be?

A—I have not attempted to explain it. If you will take the second chapter—let me have the book. (Examining Bible.) The fourth verse of the second chapter says: "These are the generations of the heavens and of the earth, when they were created in the day that the Lord God made the earth and the heavens," the word "day" there in the very next chapter is used to describe a period. I do not see that there is any necessity for construing the words, "the evening and the morning," as meaning necessarily a twenty-four-hour day, "in the day when the Lord made the heaven and the earth."

Q—Then, when the Bible said, for instance, "and God called the firmament heaven. And the evening and the morning were the second day," that does not necessarily mean twenty-four hours?

A—I do not think it necessarily does.

Q—Do you think it does or does not?

A—I know a great many think so.

Q—What do you think?

A—I do not think it does.

Q—You think those were not literal days?

A—I do not think they were twenty-four-hour days.

Q—What do you think about it?

A—That is my opinion—I do not know that my opinion is better on that subject than those who think it does.

Q—You do not think that?

A—No. But I think it would be just as easy for the kind of God we believe in to make the earth in six days as in six years or in 6,000,000 years or in 600,000,000 years. I do not think it important whether we believe one or the other.

Q—Do you think those were literal days?

A—My impression is they were periods, but I would not attempt to argue as against anybody who wanted to believe in literal days.

Q—I will read it to you from the bible: "And the Lord God said unto the serpent, because thou hast done this, thou art cursed above all cattle, and above every beast of the field; upon thy belly shalt thou go and dust shalt thou eat all the days of thy life." Do you think that is why the serpent is compelled to crawl upon its belly?

A—I believe that.

Q—Have you any idea how the snake went before that time?

A—No, sir.

Q—Do you know whether he walked on his tail or not?

A—No, sir. I have no way to know. (Laughter in audience.)

Q—Now, you refer to the cloud that was put in heaven after the flood, the rainbow. Do you believe in that?

A—Read it.

Q—All right, Mr. Bryan, I will read it for you.

Bryan—Your Honor, I think I can shorten this testimony. The only purpose Mr. Darrow has is to slur at the Bible, but I will answer his question. I will answer it all at once, and I have no objection in the world, I want the world to know that this man, who does not believe in a God, is trying to use a court in Tennessee—

Darrow—I object to that.

Bryan—(Continuing) to slur at it, and while it will require time, I am willing to take it.

Darrow—I object to your statement. I am exempting you on your fool ideas that no intelligent Christian on earth believes.

The Court—Court is adjourned until 9 o'clock tomorrow morning.

The Sahara of the Bozart

This produced a ferocious reaction in the South, and I was belabored for months, and even years afterward in a very extravagant manner. The essay in its final form, as it is here reproduced, dates sadly, but I have let it stand as a sort of historical document. On the heels of the violent denunciations of the elder Southerners there soon came a favorable response from the more civilized youngsters, and there is reason to believe that my attack had something to do with that revival of Southern letters which followed in the middle 1920's.

Alas, for the South! Her books have grown fewer—
She never was much given to literature.

In the lamented J. Gordon Coogler, author of these elegiac lines, there was the insight of a true poet. He was the last bard of Dixie, at least in the legitimate line. Down there a poet is now almost as rare as an oboe-player, a dry-point etcher or a metaphysician. It is, indeed, amazing to contemplate so vast a vacuity. One thinks of the interstellar spaces, of the colossal reaches of the now mythical ether. Nearly the whole of Europe could be lost in that stupendous region of worn-out farms, shoddy cities and paralyzed cerebrums: one could throw in France, Germany and Italy, and still have room for the British Isles. And yet, for all its size and all its wealth and all the "progress" it babbles of, it is almost as sterile, artistically, intellectually, culturally, as the Sahara Desert. There are single acres in Europe that house more first-rate men than all the states south of the Potomac; there are probably single square miles in America. If the whole of the late Confederacy were to be engulfed by a tidal wave tomorrow, the effect upon the civilized minority of men in the world would be but little greater than that of a flood on the Yang-tse-kiang. It would be impossible in all history to match so complete a drying-up of a civilization.

I say a civilization because that is what, in the old days, the South had, despite the Baptist and Methodist barbarism that reigns down there now. More, it was a civilization of manifold excellences—perhaps the best that the Western Hemisphere had ever seen—undoubtedly the best that These States have ever seen. Down to the middle of the last century, and even beyond, the main hatchery of ideas on this side of the water was across the Potomac bridges. The New England shopkeepers and theologians never really developed a civilization; all they ever developed was a government. They were, at their best, tawdry and tacky fellows, oafish in manner and devoid of imagination; one searches the books in vain for mention of a salient Yankee gentleman; as well look for a Welsh gentleman. But in the South there were men of delicate fancy, urbane instinct and aristocratic manner—in brief, superior men—in brief, gentry. To politics, their chief diversion, they brought active and original minds. It was there that nearly all the political theories we still cherish and suffer under came to birth. It was there that the crude dogmatism of New England was refined and human-

From *A Mencken Chrestomathy*, 1949. Included in *Prejudices: Second Series*, 1920. Originally printed, in shorter form, in the New York *Evening Mail*, Nov. 13, 1917. Copyright 1920, 1949 by Alfred A. Knopf, Inc. Renewal copyright 1948 by H. L. Mencken.

ized. It was there, above all, that some attention was given to the art of living—that life got beyond and above the state of a mere infliction and became an exhilarating experience. A certain notable spaciousness was in the ancient Southern scheme of things. The *Ur*-Confederate had leisure. He liked to toy with ideas. He was hospitable and tolerant. He had the vague thing that we call culture.

But consider the condition of his late empire today. The picture gives one the creeps. It is as if the Civil War stamped out every last bearer of the torch, and left only a mob of peasants on the field. One thinks of Asia Minor, resigned to Armenians, Greeks and wild swine, of Poland abandoned to the Poles. In all that gargantuan paradise of the fourth-rate there is not a single picture gallery worth going into, or a single orchestra capable of playing the nine symphonies of Beethoven, or a single opera-house, or a single theater devoted to decent plays, or a single public monument that is worth looking at, or a single workshop devoted to the making of beautiful things. Once you have counted James Branch Cabell (a lingering survivor of the *ancien régime:* a scarlet dragon-fly imbedded in opaque amber) you will not find a single Southern prose writer who can actually write. And once you have—but when you come to critics, musical composers, painters, sculptors, architects and the like, you will have to give it up, for there is not even a bad one between the Potomac mudflats and the Gulf. Nor a historian. Nor a philosopher. Nor a theologian. Nor a scientist. In all these fields the South is an awe-inspiring blank—a brother to Portugal, Serbia and Albania.

Consider, for example, the present estate and dignity of Virginia—in the great days indubitably the premier American state, the mother of Presidents and statesmen, the home of the first American university worthy of the name, the *arbiter elegantiarum* of the Western World. Well, observe Virginia today. It is years since a first-rate man, save only Cabell, has come out of it; it is years since an idea has come out of it. The old aristocracy went down the red gullet of war; the poor white trash are now in the saddle. Politics in Virginia are cheap, ignorant, parochial, idiotic; there is scarcely a man in office above the rank of a professional job-seeker; the political doctrine that prevails is made up of hand-me-downs from the bumpkinry of the Middle West—Bryanism, Prohibition, all that sort of filthy claptrap; the administration of the law is turned over to professors of Puritanism and espionage; a Washington or a Jefferson, dumped there by some act of God, would be denounced as a scoundrel and jailed overnight.

Elegance, *esprit,* culture? Virginia has no art, no literature, no philosophy, no mind or aspiration of her own. Her education has sunk to the Baptist seminary level; not a single contribution to human knowledge has come out of her colleges in twenty-five years; she spends less than half upon her common schools, *per capita,* than any Northern state spends. In brief, an intellectual Gobi or Lapland. Urbanity, *politesse,* chivalry? Go to! It was in Virginia that they invented the device of searching for contraband whiskey in women's underwear. . . . There remains, at the top, a ghost of the old aristocracy, a bit wistful and infinitely charming. But it has lost all its old leadership to fabulous monsters from the lower depths; it is submerged in an industrial plutocracy that is ignorant and ignominious. The mind of the state, as it is revealed to the nation, is pathetically naïve and inconsequential. It no longer reacts with energy and elasticity to great problems. It has fallen to the bombastic trivialities of the camp-meeting and the stump. One could no more imagine a Lee or a Washington in the Virginia of today than one could imagine a Huxley in Nicaragua.

I choose the Old Dominion, not because I disdain it, but precisely because I esteem it. It is, by long odds, the most civilized of the Southern states, now as always. It has sent a host of creditable sons northward; the stream kept running into our own time. Virginians, even the worst of them, show the effects of a great tradition. They hold themselves above other Southerners, and with sound pretension. If one turns to such a commonwealth as Georgia the picture becomes far darker. There the liberated lower orders of whites have borrowed the worst commercial bounderism of the Yankee and superimposed it upon a culture that, at bottom, is but little removed from savagery. Georgia is at once the home of the cotton-mill sweater, of the Methodist parson turned Savonarola and of the lynching bee. A self-respecting European, going there to live, would not only find intellectual stimulation utterly lacking; he would actually feel a certain insecurity, as if the scene were the Balkans or the China Coast. There is a state with more than half the area of Italy and more population than either Denmark or Norway, and yet in thirty years it has not produced a single idea. Once upon a time a Georgian printed a couple of books that attracted notice, but immediately it turned out that he was little more than an amanuensis for the local blacks— that his works were really the products, not of white Georgia, but of black Georgia. Writing afterward *as* a white man, he swiftly subsided into the fifth rank. And he is not only the glory of the literature of Georgia; he is, almost literally, the whole of the literature of Georgia—nay, of the entire art of Georgia.[1]

Virginia is the best of the South today, and Georgia is perhaps the worst. The one is simply senile; the other is crass, gross, vulgar and obnoxious. Between lies a vast plain of mediocrity, stupidity, lethargy, almost of dead silence. In the North, of course, there is also grossness, crassness, vulgarity. The North, in its way, is also stupid and obnoxious. But nowhere in the North is there such complete sterility, so depressing a lack of all civilized gesture and aspiration. One would find it difficult to unearth a second-rate city between the Ohio and the Pacific that isn't struggling to establish an orchestra, or setting up a little theater, or going in for an art gallery, or making some other effort to get into touch with civilization. These efforts often fail, and sometimes they succeed rather absurdly, but under them there is at least an impulse that deserves respect, and that is the impulse to seek beauty and to experiment with ideas, and so to give the life of every day a certain dignity and purpose. You will find no such impulse in the South. There are no committees down there cadging subscriptions for orchestras; if a string quartet is ever heard there, the news of it has never come out; an opera troupe, when it roves the land, is a nine days' wonder. The little theater movement has swept the whole country, enormously augmenting the public interest in sound plays, giving new dramatists their chance, forcing reforms upon the commercial theater. Everywhere else the wave rolls high—but along the line of the Potomac it breaks upon a rock-bound shore. There is no little theater beyond. There is no gallery of pictures. No artist ever gives exhibitions. No one talks of such things. No one seems to be interested in such things.

As for the cause of this unanimous torpor and doltishness, this curious and almost pathological estrangement from everything that makes for a civilized culture, I have hinted at it already, and now state it again. The South has simply been drained of all its best blood. The vast hemorrhage of the Civil War half exterminated and wholly paralyzed the old aristocracy, and so left the land to the harsh mercies of the poor white

---

[1] The reference here, of course, was to Joel Chandler Harris.

trash, now its masters. The war, of course, was not a complete massacre. It spared a decent number of first-rate Southerners—perhaps even some of the very best. Moreover, other countries, notably France and Germany, have survived far more staggering butcheries, and even showed marked progress thereafter. But the war not only cost a great many valuable lives; it also brought bankruptcy, demoralization and despair in its train—and so the majority of the first-rate Southerners that were left, broken in spirit and unable to live under the new dispensation, cleared out. A few went to South America, to Egypt, to the Far East. Most came north. They were fecund; their progeny is widely dispersed, to the great benefit of the North. A Southerner of good blood almost always does well in the North. He finds, even in the big cities, surroundings fit for a man of condition. His peculiar qualities have a high social value, and are esteemed. He is welcomed by the codfish aristocracy as one palpably superior. But in the South he throws up his hands. It is impossible for him to stoop to the common level. He cannot brawl in politics with the grandsons of his grandfather's tenants. He is unable to share their fierce jealousy of the emerging black—the cornerstone of all their public thinking. He is anesthetic to their theological and political enthusiasms. He finds himself an alien at their feasts of soul. And so he withdraws into his tower, and is heard of no more. Cabell is almost a perfect example. His eyes, for years, were turned toward the past; he became a professor of the grotesque genealogizing that decaying aristocracies affect; it was only by a sort of accident that he discovered himself to be an artist. The South is unaware of the fact to this day; it regards Woodrow Wilson and John Temple Graves as much finer stylists, and Frank L. Stanton as an infinitely greater poet. If it has heard, which I doubt, that Cabell has been hoofed by the Comstocks, it unquestionably views that assault as a deserved rebuke to a fellow who indulges a lewd passion for fancy writing, and is a covert enemy to the Only True Christianity.

What is needed down there, before the vexatious public problems of the region may be intelligently approached, is a survey of the population by competent ethnologists and anthropologists. The immigrants of the North have been studied at great length, and anyone who is interested may now apply to the Bureau of Ethnology for elaborate data as to their racial strains, their stature and cranial indices, their relative capacity for education, and the changes that they undergo under American *Kultur*. But the older stocks of the South, and particularly the emancipated and dominant poor white trash, have never been investigated scientifically, and most of the current generalizations about them are probably wrong. For example, the generalization that they are purely Anglo-Saxon in blood. This I doubt very seriously. The chief strain down there, I believe, is Celtic rather than Saxon, particularly in the hill country. French blood, too, shows itself here and there, and so does Spanish, and so does German. The last-named entered from the northward, by way of the limestone belt just east of the Alleghenies. Again, it is very likely that in some parts of the South a good many of the plebeian whites have more than a trace of Negro blood. Interbreeding under concubinage produced some very light half-breeds at an early day, and no doubt appreciable numbers of them went over into the white race by the simple process of changing their abode. Not long ago I read a curious article by an intelligent Negro, in which he stated that it is easy for a very light Negro to pass as white in the South on account of the fact that large numbers of Southerners accepted as white have distinctly negroid features. Thus it becomes a delicate and dangerous matter for a train conductor or a hotelkeeper to challenge a suspect. But the Celtic strain is far more obvious than any of these others. It not only makes itself visible in physical stigmata—*e.g.*, leanness and dark coloring—but also in mental traits. For example, the religious thought of the South is almost precisely identical with the religious thought of Wales. There is the same naïve belief in an anthropomorphic Creator but little removed, in manner and desire, from an evangelical bishop; there is the same submission to an ignorant and impudent sacerdotal tyranny, and there is the same sharp contrast between doctrinal orthodoxy and private ethics. Read Caradoc Evans's ironical picture of the Welsh Wesleyans in his preface to "My Neighbors," and you will be instantly reminded of the Georgia and Carolina Methodists. The most booming sort of piety, in the South, is not incompatible with the theory that lynching is a benign institution. Two generations ago it was not incompatible with an ardent belief in slavery.

It is highly probable that some of the worst blood of western Europe flows in the veins of the Southern poor whites, now poor no longer. The original strains, according to every honest historian, were extremely corrupt. Philip Alexander Bruce (a Virginian of the old gentry) says in his "Industrial History of Virginia in the Seventeenth Century" that the first native-born generation was largely illegitimate. "One of the most common offenses against morality committed in the lower ranks of life in Virginia during the Seventeenth Century," he says, "was bastardy." The mothers of these bastards, he continues, were chiefly indentured servants, and "had belonged to the lowest class in their native country." Fanny Kemble Butler, writing of the Georgia poor whites of a century later, described them as "the most degraded race of human beings claiming an Anglo-Saxon origin that can be found on the face of the earth— filthy, lazy, ignorant, brutal, proud, penniless savages." The Sunday-school and the chautauqua, of course, have appreciably mellowed the descendants of these "savages," and their economic progress and rise to political power have done perhaps even more, but the marks of their origin are still unpleasantly plentiful. Every now and then they produce a political leader who puts their secret notions of the true, the good and the beautiful into plain words, to the amazement and scandal of the rest of the country. That amazement is turned into downright incredulity when news comes that his platform has got him high office, and that he is trying to execute it.

In the great days of the South the line between the gentry and the poor whites was very sharply drawn. There was absolutely no intermarriage. So far as I know there is not a single instance in history of a Southerner of the upper class marrying one of the bond-women described by Mr. Bruce. In other societies characterized by class distinctions of that sort it is common for the lower class to be improved by extra-legal crosses. That is to say, the men of the upper class take women of the lower class as mistresses, and out of such unions spring the extraordinary plebeians who rise sharply from the common level, and so propagate the delusion that all other plebeians would do the same thing if they had the chance—in brief, the delusion that class distinctions are merely economic and conventional, and not congenital and genuine. But in the South the men of the upper classes sought their mistresses among the blacks, and after a few generations there was so much white blood in the black women that they were considerably more attractive than the unhealthy and bedraggled women of the poor whites. This preference continued into our own time. A Southerner of good family once told me in all seriousness that he had reached his majority before it ever occurred to him that a white woman might make quite as agreeable a mistress as the octaroons of his jejune fancy. If the thing has changed of late, it is not the fault of the Southern white man, but of the Southern mulatto women. The more sightly yellow girls of the region, with improving economic opportunities, have gained self-respect, and so they are no longer as willing to enter into concubinage as their grand-dams were.

As a result of this preference of the Southern gentry for mulatto mistresses there was created a series of mixed strains containing the best white blood of the South, and perhaps of the whole country. As another result the poor whites went unfertilized from above, and so missed the improvement that so constantly shows itself in the peasant stocks of other countries. It is a commonplace that nearly all Negroes who rise above the general are of mixed blood, usually with the white predominating. I know a great many Negroes, and it would be hard for me to think of an exception. What is too often forgotten is that this white blood is not the blood of the poor whites but that of the old gentry. The mulatto girls of the early days despised the poor whites as creatures distinctly inferior to Negroes, and it was thus almost unheard of for such a girl to enter into relations with a man of that submerged class. This aversion was based upon a sound instinct. The Southern mulatto of today is a proof of it. Like all other half-breeds he is an unhappy man, with disquieting tendencies toward anti-social habits of thought, but he is intrinsically a better animal than the pure-blooded descendant of the old poor whites, and he not infrequently demonstrates it. It is not by accident that the Negroes of the South are making faster progress, culturally, than the masses of the whites. It is not by accident that the only visible esthetic activity in the South is in their hands. No Southern composer has ever written music so good as that of half a dozen white-black composers who might be named. Even in politics, the Negro reveals a curious superiority. Despite the fact that the race question has been the main political concern of the Southern whites for two generations, to the practical exclusion of everything else, they have contributed nothing to its discussion that has impressed the rest of the world so deeply and so favorably as three or four books by Southern Negroes.

Entering upon such themes, of course, one must resign one's self to a vast misunderstanding and abuse. The South has not only lost its old capacity for producing ideas; it has also taken on the worst intolerance of ignorance and stupidity. Its prevailing mental attitude for several decades past has been that of its own hedge ecclesiastics. All who dissent from its orthodox doctrines are scoundrels. All who presume to discuss its ways realistically are damned. I have had, in my day, several experiences in point. Once, after I had published an article on some phase of the eternal race question,[2] a leading Southern newspaper replied by printing a column of denunciation of my father, then dead nearly twenty years—a philippic placarding him as an ignorant foreigner of dubious origin, inhabiting "the Baltimore ghetto" and speaking a dialect recalling that of Weber & Fields—two thousand words of incandescent nonsense, utterly false and beside the point, but exactly meeting the latter-day Southern notion of effective controversy. Another time, I published a short discourse on lynching, arguing that the sport was popular in the South because the backward culture of the region denied the populace more seemly recreations. Among such recreations I mentioned those afforded by brass bands, symphony orchestras, boxing matches, amateur athletic contests, horse races, and so on. In reply another great Southern journal denounced me as a man "of wineshop temperament, brass-jewelry tastes and pornographic predilections." In other words, brass bands, in the South, are classed with brass jewelry, and both are snares of the devil! To advocate setting up symphony orchestras is pornography! . . . Alas, when the touchy Southerner attempts a greater urbanity, the result is often even worse. Some time ago a colleague of mine printed an article deploring the arrested cultural development of Georgia. In reply he received a

[2]"Si Mutare Potest Aethiops Pellum Suam," *Smart Set*, Sept., 1917, pp. 138–42.

number of protests from patriotic Georgians, and all of them solemnly listed the glories of the state. I indulge in a few specimens:

> Who has not heard of Asa G. Candler, whose name is synonymous with Coca-Cola, a Georgia product?
> The first Sunday school in the world was opened in Savannah.
> Who does not recall with pleasure the writings of . . . Frank L. Stanton, Georgia's brilliant poet?
> Georgia was the first state to organize a Boys' Corn Club in the South— Newton county, 1904.
> The first to suggest a common United Daughters of the Confederacy badge was Mrs. Raynes, of Georgia.
> The first to suggest a state historian of the United Daughters of the Confederacy was Mrs. C. Helen Plane (Macon convention, 1896).
> The first to suggest putting to music Heber's "From Greenland's Icy Mountains" was Mrs. F. R. Goulding, of Savannah.

And so on, and so on. These proud boasts came, remember, not from obscure private persons, but from "leading Georgians"—in one case, the state historian. Curious sidelights upon the ex-Confederate mind! Another comes from a stray copy of a Negro paper. It describes an ordinance passed by the city council of Douglas, Ga., forbidding any trousers presser, on penalty of forfeiting a $500 bond, to engage in "pressing for both white and colored." This in a town, says the Negro paper, where practically all of the white inhabitants have "their food prepared by colored hands," "their babies cared for by colored hands," and "the clothes which they wear right next to their skins washed in houses where Negroes live"—houses in which the said clothes "remain for as long as a week at a time." But if you marvel at the absurdity, keep it dark! A casual word, and the united press of the South will be upon your trail, denouncing you bitterly as a scoundrelly damnyankee, a Bolshevik Jew.

Obviously, it is impossible for intelligence to flourish in such an atmosphere. Free inquiry is blocked by the idiotic certainties of ignorant men. The arts, save in the lower reaches of the gospel hymn, the phonograph and the political harangue, are all held in suspicion. The tone of public opinion is set by an upstart class but lately emerged from industrial slavery into commercial enterprise—the class of "bustling" business men, of "live wires," of commercial club luminaries, of "drive" managers, of forward-lookers and right-thinkers—in brief, of third-rate Southerners inoculated with all the worst traits of the Yankee sharper. One observes the curious effects of an old tradition of truculence upon a population now merely pushful and impudent, of an old tradition of chivalry upon a population now quite without imagination. The old repose is gone. The old romanticism is gone. The philistinism of the new type of town-boomer Southerner is not only indifferent to the ideals of the Old South; it is positively antagonistic to them. That philistinism regards human life, not as an agreeable adventure, but as a mere trial of rectitude and efficiency. It is overwhelmingly utilitarian and moral. It is inconceivably hollow and obnoxious. What remains of the ancient tradition is simply a certain charming civility in private intercourse—often broken down, alas, by the hot rages of Puritanism, but still generally visible. The Southerner, at his worst, is never quite the surly cad that the Yankee is. His sensitiveness may betray him into occasional bad manners, but in the main he is a pleasant fellow—hospitable, polite, good-humored, even jovial. . . . But a bit absurd. . . . A bit pathetic.

John Crowe Ransom

(1888–1974)

The son of a minister, John Crowe Ransom grew up in Pulaski, Tennessee, and was educated at Vanderbilt. A Rhodes Scholar, he studied at Oxford University and returned to Vanderbilt to teach in 1914, a position he would hold for the next twenty-three years. Early in his career, he published three volumes of poetry, *Poems about God* (1919), *Chills and Fever* (1924), and *Two Gentlemen in Bonds* (1926), which established him as a leading American poet. Ransom was famed not only as a poet but also as a teacher of poets: He taught all the other poets in the group that came to be known as the Fugitives, most notably Allen Tate, Donald Davidson, and Robert Penn Warren. His style is marked by an interaction of suggestiveness and feeling, treating topics of deep emotion but maintaining a strict, ironic detachment. Like the other Fugitives, he argued against the dominance of modern industrialism, science, and urbanism, standing instead for the virtues of agrarian life. He contributed important essays to *I'll Take My Stand* (1930) and *Who Owns America?* (1936). In the late 1930s, he moved to Kenyon College in Ohio, where he established the influential *Kenyon Review*. His book *The New Criticism* (1941) provided the name for the influential critical movement that stresses close analysis of literary works, uninfluenced by historical or biographical context.

Necrological

The friar had said his paternosters duly
And scourged his limbs, and afterwards would have slept;
But with much riddling his head became unruly,
He arose, from the quiet monastery he crept.

Dawn lightened the place where the battle had been won.
The people were dead—it is easy he thought to die—
These dead remained, but the living all were gone,
Gone with the wailing trumps of victory.

The dead men wore no raiment against the air,
Bartholomew's men had spoiled them where they fell;
In defeat the heroes' bodies were whitely bare,
The field was white like meads of asphodel.

Not all were white; some gory and fabulous
Whom the sword had pierced and then the gray wolf eaten;
But the brother reasoned that heroes' flesh was thus;
Flesh fails, and the postured bones lie weather-beaten.

The lords of chivalry lay prone and shattered,
The gentle and the bodyguard of yeomen;
Bartholomew's stroke went home—but little it mattered,
Bartholomew went to be stricken of other foemen.

Beneath the blue ogive of the firmament
Was a dead warrior, clutching whose mighty knees
Was a leman, who with her flame had warned his tent,
For him enduring all men's pleasantries.

Close by the sable stream that purged the plain
Lay the white stallion and his rider thrown,
The great beast had spilled there his little brain,
And the little groin of the knight was spilled by a stone.

The youth possessed him then of a crooked blade
Deep in the belly of a lugubrious wight;
He fingered it well, and it was cunningly made;
But strange apparatus was it for a Carmelite.

He sat upon a hill and bowed his head
As under a riddle, and in a deep surmise
So still that he likened himself unto those dead
Whom the kites of Heaven solicited with sweet cries.

Antique Harvesters

(SCENE: *Of the Mississippi the bank sinister,*
and of the Ohio the bank sinister.)

Tawny are the leaves turned but they still hold,
And it is harvest; what shall this land produce?
A meager hill of kernels, a runnel of juice;
Declension looks from our land, it is old.
Therefore let us assemble, dry, grey, spare,
And mild as yellow air.

"I hear the croak of a raven's funeral wing."
The young men would be joying in the song
Of passionate birds; their memories are not long.
What is it thus rehearsed in sable? "Nothing."
Trust not but the old endure, and shall be older
Than the scornful beholder.

We pluck the spindling ears and gather the corn.
One spot has special yield? "On this spot stood
Heroes and drenched it with their only blood."
And talk meets talk, as echoes from the horn
Of the hunter—echoes are the old men's arts,
Ample are the chambers of their hearts.

Here come the hunters, keepers of a rite;
The horn, the hounds, the lank mares coursing by
Straddled with archetypes of chivalry;
And the fox, lovely ritualist, in flight
Offering his unearthly ghost to quarry;
And the fields, themselves to harry.

Resume, harvesters. The treasure is full bronze
Which you will garner for the Lady, and the moon
Could tinge it no yellower than does this noon;
But grey will quench it shortly—the field, men, stones.
Pluck fast, dreamers; prove as you amble slowly
Not less than men, not wholly.

Bare the arm, dainty youths, bend the knees
Under bronze burdens. And by an autumn tone
As by a grey, as by a green, you will have known
Your famous Lady's image; for so have these;
And if one say that easily will your hands
More prosper in other lands,

Angry as wasp-music be your cry then:
"Forsake the Proud Lady, of the heart of fire,
The look of snow, to the praise of a dwindled choir,
Song of degenerate specters that were men?
The sons of the fathers shall keep her, worthy of
What these have done in love."

True, it is said of our Lady, she ageth.
But see, if you peep shrewdly, she hath not stooped;
Take no thought of her servitors that have drooped,
For we are nothing; and if one talk of death—
Why, the ribs of the earth subsist frail as a breath
If but God wearieth.

The Equilibrists

Full of her long white arms and milky skin
He had a thousand times remembered sin.
Alone in the press of people traveled he,
Minding her jacinth, and myrrh, and ivory.

Mouth he remembered: the quaint orifice
From which came heat that flamed upon the kiss,
Till cold words came down spiral from the head,
Grey doves from the officious tower illsped.

Body: it was a white field ready for love,
On her body's field, with the gaunt tower above,
The lilies grew, beseeching him to take,
If he would pluck and wear them, bruise and break.

Eyes talking: Never mind the cruel words,
Embrace my flowers, but not embrace the swords.
But what they said, the doves came straightway flying
And unsaid: Honor, Honor, they came crying.

Importunate her doves. Too pure, too wise,
Clambering on his shoulder, saying, Arise,
Leave me now, and never let us meet,
Eternal distance now command thy feet.

Predicament indeed, which thus discovers
Honor among thieves, Honor between lovers.
O such a little word is Honor, they feel!
But the grey word is between them cold as steel.

At length I saw these lovers fully were come
Into their torture of equilibrium;
Dreadfully had forsworn each other, and yet
They were bound each to each, and they did not forget.

And rigid as two painful stars, and twirled
About the clustered night their prison world,
They burned with fierce love always to come near,
But Honor beat them back and kept them clear.

Ah, the strict lovers, they are ruined now!
I cried in anger. But with puddled brow
Devising for those gibbeted and brave
Came I descanting: Man, what would you have?

For spin your period out, and draw your breath,
A kinder sæculum begins with Death.
Would you ascend to Heaven and bodiless dwell?
Or take your bodies honorless to Hell?

In Heaven you have heard no marriage is,
No white flesh tinder to your lecheries,
Your male and female tissue sweetly shaped
Sublimed away, and furious blood escaped.

Great lovers lie in Hell, the stubborn ones
Infatuate of the flesh upon the bones;
Stuprate, they rend each other when they kiss,
The pieces kiss again, no end to this.

But still I watched them spinning, orbited nice.
Their flames were not more radiant than their ice.
I dug in the quiet earth and wrought the tomb
And made these lines to memorize their doom:—

EPITAPH

Equilibrists lie here; stranger, tread light;
Close, but untouching in each other's sight;
Mouldered the lips and ashy the tall skull.
Let them lie perilous and beautiful.

Janet Waking

Beautifully Janet slept
Till it was deeply morning. She woke then
And thought about her dainty-feathered hen,
    To see how it had kept.

One kiss she gave her mother.
Only a small one gave she to her daddy
Who would have kissed each curl of his shining baby;
    No kiss at all for her brother.

"Old Chucky, old Chucky!" she cried,
Running across the world upon the grass
To Chucky's house, and listening. But alas,
    Her Chucky had died.

It was a transmogrifying bee
Came droning down on Chucky's old bald head
And sat and put the poison. It scarcely bled,
    But how exceedingly

And purply did the knot
Swell with the venom and communicate
Its rigor! Now the poor comb stood up straight
    But Chucky did not.

So there was Janet
Kneeling on the wet grass, crying her brown hen
(Translated far beyond the daughters of men)
    To rise and walk upon it.

And weeping fast as she had breath
Janet implored us, "Wake her from her sleep!"
And would not be instructed in how deep
    Was the forgetful kingdom of death.

Donald Davidson

(1893–1968)

Born in 1893 in Campbellsville, Tennessee, Donald Davidson was educated in private
schools and entered Vanderbilt University in 1909. Because of financial difficulties,
he did not receive his undergraduate degree until 1917. In 1920, after a stint in the
army, he began writing for the *Evening Tennessean* and also took an instructor's job
at Vanderbilt as he began pursuing his master's degree. During these years, he joined
the discussion group that would eventually beget the Fugitive movement, and he was
one of the coeditors of *The Fugitive* during the three years of its existence. He pub-

lished *An Outland Piper*, his first volume of poetry, in 1924, followed by *The Tall Men* in 1927. *Lee in the Mountains and Other Poems, Including The Tall Men* appeared in 1938. Davidson died in Nashville in 1968.

When his contemporaries John Crowe Ransom, Allen Tate, and Robert Penn Warren left both the South and the Fugitive movement, Davidson continued to hold fast to the agrarian ideal with an uncompromising devotion. The style of his poetry is reminiscent of the Romantics, not because he was unaware of the artistic currents of his own era but because he saw himself as a throwback to an earlier way of life that was itself dated, standing in opposition to the destructive influence of a modern industrial society. Though his concentration on themes that emphasize a wholesome strength in Old South traditions has resulted in a critical appraisal that is at best mixed, perceptive readers have understood that his poetry and essays advocate not a restoration of the Old South but simply a recognition of the value of a personal and cultural past that was rapidly fading.

Lee in the Mountains

1865–1870

Walking into the shadows, walking alone
Where the sun falls through the ruined boughs of locusts
Up to the president's office. . . .
                  Hearing the voices
Whisper, *Hush, it is General Lee!* And strangely
Hearing my own voice say, *Good morning, boys.*
(Don't get up. You are early. It is long
Before the bell. You will have long to wait
On these cold steps. . . .)
             The young have time to wait.
But soldiers' faces under their tossing flags
Lift no more by any road or field,
And I am spent with old wars and new sorrow.
Walking the rocky path, where steps decay
And the paint cracks and grass eats on the stone.
It is not General Lee, young men. . . .
It is Robert Lee in a dark civilian suit who walks,
An outlaw fumbling for the latch, a voice
Commanding in a dream where no flag flies.

My father's house is taken and his hearth
Left to the candle-drippings where the ashes
Whirl at a chimney-breath on the cold stone.
I can hardly remember my father's look, I cannot
Answer his voice as he calls farewell in the misty
Mounting where riders gather at gates.
He was old then—I was a child—his hand

Held out for mine, some daybreak snatched away,
And he rode out, a broken man. Now let
His lone grave keep, surer than cypress roots,
The vow I made beside him. God too late
Unseals to certain eyes the drift
Of time and the hopes of men and a sacred cause.
The fortunate of the Lees goes with the land
Whose sons will keep it still. My mother
Told me much. She sat among the candles,
Fingering the *Memoirs*, now so long unread.
And as my pen moves on across the page
Her voice comes back, a murmuring distillation
Of old Virginia times now faint and gone,
The hurt of all that was and cannot be.

Why did my father write? I know he saw
History clutched as a wraith out of blowing mist
Where tongues are loud, and a glut of little souls
Laps at the too much blood and the burning house.
He would have his say, but I shall not have mine.
What I do is only a son's devoir
To a lost father. Let him only speak.
The rest must pass to men who never knew
(But on a written page) the strike of armies,
And never heard the long Confederate cry
Charge through the muzzling smoke or saw the bright
Eyes of the beardless boys go up to death.
It is Robert Lee who writes with his father's hand—
The rest must go unsaid and the lips he locked.

If all were told, as it cannot be told—
If all the dread opinion of the heart
Now could speak, now in the shame and torment
Lashing the bound and trampled States—

If a word were said, as it cannot be said—
I see clear waters run in Virginia's Valley
And in the house the weeping of young women
Rises no more. The waves of grain begin.
The Shenandoah is golden with new grain.
The Blue Ridge, crowned with a haze of light,
Thunders no more. The horse is at plough. The rifle
Returns to the chimney crotch and the hunter's hand.
And nothing else than this? Was it for this
That on an April day we stacked our arms
Obedient to a soldier's trust? To lie
Ground by heels of little men,
Forever maimed, defeated, lost, impugned?
And was I then betrayed? Did I betray?

If it were said, as still it might be said—
If it were said, and a word should run like fire,
Like living fire into the roots of grass,
The sunken flag would kindle on wild hills,
The brooding hearts would waken, and the dream
Stir like a crippled phantom under the pines,
And this torn earth would quicken into shouting
Beneath the feet of ragged bands—
                                    The pen
Turns to the waiting page, the sword
Bows to the rust that cankers and the silence.

Among these boys whose eyes lift up to mine
Within gray walls where droning wasps repeat
A hollow reveille, I still must face,
Day after day, the courier with his summons
Once more to surrender, now to surrender all.
Without arms or men I stand, but with knowledge only
I face what long I saw, before others knew,
When Pickett's men streamed back, and I heard the tangled
Cry of the Wilderness wounded, bloody with doom.
The mountains, once I said, in the little room
At Richmond, by the huddled fire, but still
The President shook his head. The mountains wait,
I said, in the long beat and rattle of siege
At cratered Petersburg. Too late
We sought the mountains and those people came.
And Lee is in mountains now, beyond Appomattox,
Listening long for voices that never will speak
Again; hearing the hoofbeats come and go and fade
Without a stop, without a brown hand lifting
The tent-flap, or a bugle call at dawn,
Or ever on the long white road the flag
Of Jackson's quick brigades. I am alone,
Trapped, consenting, taken at last in mountains.

It is not the bugle now, or the long roll beating.
The simple stroke of a chapel bell forbids
The hurtling dream, recalls the lonely mind.
Young men, the God of your fathers is a just
And merciful God Who in this blood once shed
On your green altars measures out all days,
And measures out the grace
Whereby alone we live;
And in His might He waits,
Brooding within the certitude of time,
To bring this lost forsaken valor
And the fierce faith undying
And the love quenchless
To flower among the hills to which we cleave,

To fruit upon the mountains whither we flee,
Never forsaking, never denying
His children and His children's children forever
Unto all generations of the faithful heart.

The Last Charge

Where the road turns between the cedar groves
And the blue waves of hills lap all the distance,
Stop, look northward—all is clear.
Leaves of November are falling on Winstead Hill,
And before us, stark as Franklin field, the past
Is stripped to enduring boughs of memory,
And of glory, what still remains.

No more the sound of guns. The silence drags
Over the sunken breastworks and old graves
Where bones forget their names, and only earth
Utters fragments we know not how to reap.
No sound of guns. A different thunder plagues
The far-off streets where smokes recoil and languor
Dogs the blue cannoneers who now too late
Flinch from the lanyard. For the years take back
The spoils, the laurels that they gave.
The seed of Appomattox blooms; its fruit
Rots where eyes are dazed with a hungry searching,
And ears are deaf with steps that murmur and follow
No command. And no tongue.
Only confusion of tongues, the wrack
Of Babylon that falls, a twilight clutter.
But here a twilight not of dissolution.
In Harpeth valley where they lie the dead
Speak through the dusk, renewing all their vows;
An incantation seized again, by which
This old corruption puts on incorruption.
The lonely graveyard where the searchers brought
The pierced and unknown boys, the old men spent
With wounds and marching, wakes in an hour that brings
Steps of an army, Confederate bugles calling. . . .

Across the field, and red through autumn corn
Their still defiant flags toss to the yell
Of a raveled army breaking the thicket's edge.
This is the last charge of the old brigades
Whose battles rocked the west with thunder-names
On Tennessee waters rolling or the peaks
That looked on Chickamauga and the moon
Of stormy gatherings flung from ridge to ridge
In the red hills of Georgia. These have marched

To the sound of guns in swamps and wilderness,
Bled, retreated, rallied, charged again;
And now the viking arm of Hood, berserk,
Sweeps north at last: One great charge more, my brothers!
Rake the South free from burnt Atlanta's walls
North to Ohio, east to the camps of Lee,
Till the red hand of Sherman marches in vain.
One charge, the last!
                           Well, General, if you say so. . . .
We have riders who know how to lead the way,
And men with guns who can bite a cartridge yet.
Then sound the bugles, dress the ranks, and charge.
The Army of Tennessee knows how to charge.

November sunset reddens their starry banners.
Saint Andrew's Cross towers on Harpeth valley.
Brigades deploy and form their battle line.
The veterans are supple, steady in ranks.
They know their places, they move intent as panthers . . .
The brown necks bare, the rifles poised, the cartridge
Boxes unlatched by the bright-eyed rusty of beard;
And the generals alert in the chieftain's place;
They ride the line; the swords, the hats wave forward.
The skirmishers move out, like hunters
Giving the dare. Ranks march slowly at first,
Guiding center, watching the colors slant.
White and red among dusty trees, the town
Waits in the Federal lines. Batteries open
From hills beyond the river. Figures run
Among the poplars where a cotton gin
Clusters the flags that wave up death.
The charge quickens, they see the enemy now,
And, rushing, fill the valley with their high
Resentful hunt-cry as they mount the slope.
The Army of Tennessee knows how to charge!

Fated, valorous army, who watches you
In this last darkling grapple? Who cheers you on?
Shall you walk in the valley of death without parade,
Knowing the taste of blood and the night too soon?
The hands of mourners will come to gather you
Under the maples of McGavock House,
And presently like you will moulder and sink,
Hearing but pilgrim steps, the pelt of leaves
That cover your ranks . . . your graves. Farewell,
Army of Tennessee! Rough glory, rooted here,
Feeds the lone vow, the lingering touch
Of a late comrade sworn to remember you!
Lights glow from river and town. The darkness stabs.
And winter sweeps the undefended earth.

Allen Tate

(1899–1979)

On November 19, 1899, the poet John Orley Allen Tate was born in Winchester, Kentucky. Tate's formal education was scattered as he attended a number of preparatory schools. In 1923 he completed his B.A. magna cum laude at Vanderbilt University. By the time of his graduation, he was already a published poet and cofounder of *The Fugitive* (1922–1925), the literary magazine that quickly had gained an international reputation. Because of his alienation of important faculty members, Tate failed to receive a scholarship to pursue a master's degree in classical studies. With his formal education ended, he accepted a post teaching high school in Lumberport, West Virginia, in 1924. While spending that summer in Guthrie, Kentucky, with the ailing Robert Penn Warren, who had been his Vanderbilt University roommate, he met the author Caroline Gordon, whom he married on November 2, 1924. Less than a year later, on September 23, 1925, Nancy, their only child, was born. The marriage lasted until the summer of 1959. Until 1928 the Tates lived mostly in New York City, where Tate worked as a critic and free-lance reviewer.

During the winter of 1925, the Tates rented eight rooms of a country house in Patterson, New York, and shared the quarters with their friend Hart Crane. While there, Tate started one of his most famous poems, "Ode to the Confederate Dead," and Crane worked on *The Bridge*. After receiving a Guggenheim Fellowship, Tate spent the next two years in France, where he became friends with the expatriate writers Gertrude Stein, Ernest Hemingway, and John Peale Bishop. Coming back to the United States in 1930, the Tates settled at their farm, Benfolly, near Clarksville, Tennessee, and reestablished ties with Fugitives John Crowe Ransom, Donald Davidson, and Robert Penn Warren. When the controversial agrarian manifesto, *I'll Take My Stand*, was published, Tate had contributed the essay "Remarks on the Southern Religion," later entitled "Religion and the Old South." During the next thirty years, Tate taught at various universities. In addition, he was poet-in-residence at Princeton from 1939 to 1942 and editor of *The Sewanee Review* from 1944 to 1946. His numerous volumes of poetry included *Mr. Pope and Other Poems* (1928), *The Mediterranean and Other Poems* (1936), and *The Swimmers and Other Poems* (1970). In addition, he published a novel, *The Fathers*, in 1938, and two biographies, *Stonewall Jackson, The Good Soldier: A Narrative* (1928) and *Jefferson Davis, His Rise and Fall: A Biographical Narrative* (1929).

Ode to the Confederate Dead

Row after row with strict impunity
The headstones yield their names to the element,
The wind whirrs without recollection;
In the riven troughs the splayed leaves
Pile up, of nature the casual sacrament
To the seasonal eternity of death;
Then driven by the fierce scrutiny
Of heaven to their election in the vast breath,
They sough the rumour of mortality.

Autumn is desolation in the plot
Of a thousand acres where these memories grow
From the inexhaustible bodies that are not
Dead, but feed the grass row after rich row.
Think of the autumns that have come and gone!—
Ambitious November with the humors of the year,
With a particular zeal for every slab,
Staining the uncomfortable angels that rot
On the slabs, a wing chipped here, an arm there:
The brute curiosity of an angel's stare
Turns you, like them, to stone,
Transforms the heaving air
Till plunged to a heavier world below
You shift your sea-space blindly
Heaving, turning like the blind crab.

   Dazed by the wind, only the wind
   The leaves flying, plunge

You know who have waited by the wall
The twilight certainty of an animal,
Those midnight restitutions of the blood
You know—the immitigable pines, the smoky frieze
Of the sky, the sudden call: you know the rage,
The cold pool left by the mounting flood,
Of muted Zeno and Parmenides.
You who have waited for the angry resolution
Of those desires that should be yours tomorrow,
You know the unimportant shrift of death
And praise the vision
And praise the arrogant circumstance
Of those who fall
Rank upon rank, hurried beyond decision—
Here by the sagging gate, stopped by the wall.

   Seeing, seeing only the leaves
   Flying, plunge and expire

Turn your eyes to the immoderate past,
Turn to the inscrutable infantry rising
Demons out of the earth—they will not last.
Stonewall, Stonewall, and the sunken fields of hemp,
Shiloh, Antietam, Malvern Hill, Bull Run.
Lost in that orient of the thick-and-fast
You will curse the setting sun.

   Cursing only the leaves crying
   Like an old man in a storm

You hear the shout, the crazy hemlocks point
With troubled fingers to the silence which
Smothers you, a mummy, in time.

                               The hound bitch
Toothless and dying, in a musty cellar
Hears the wind only.

                      Now that the salt of their blood
Stiffens the saltier oblivion of the sea,
Seals the malignant purity of the flood,
What shall we who count our days and bow
Our heads with a commemorial woe
In the ribboned coats of grim felicity,
What shall we say of the bones, unclean,
Whose verdurous anonymity will grow?
The ragged arms, the ragged heads and eyes
Lost in these acres of the insane green?
The gray lean spiders come, they come and go;
In a tangle of willows without light
The singular screech-owl's tight
Invisible lyric seeds the mind
With the furious murmur of their chivalry.

   We shall say only the leaves
   Flying, plunge and expire

We shall say only the leaves whispering
In the improbable mist of nightfall
That flies on multiple wing;
Night is the beginning and the end
And in between the ends of distraction
Waits mute speculation, the patient curse
That stones the eyes, or like the jaguar leaps
For his own image in a jungle pool, his victim.
What shall we say who have knowledge
Carried to the heart? Shall we take the act
To the grave? Shall we, more hopeful, set up the grave
In the house? The ravenous grave?

                       Leave now
The shut gate and the decomposing wall:
The gentle serpent, green in the mulberry bush,
Riots with his tongue through the hush—
Sentinel of the grave who counts us all!

Aeneas at Washington

I myself saw furious with blood
Neoptolemus, at his side the black Atridae,
Hecuba and the hundred daughters, Priam
Cut down, his filth drenching the holy fires.

In that extremity I bore me well,
A true gentleman, valorous in arms,
Disinterested and honourable. Then fled:
That was a time when civilization
Run by the few fell to the many, and
Crashed to the shout of men, the clang of arms:
Cold victualing I seized, I hoisted up
The old man my father upon my back,
In the smoke made by sea for a new world
Saving little—a mind imperishable
If time is, a love of past things tenuous
As the hesitation of receding love.

(To the reduction of uncitied littorals
We brought chiefly the vigor of prophecy,
Our hunger breeding calculation
And fixed triumphs.)

                    I saw the thirsty dove
In the glowing fields of Troy, hemp ripening
And tawny corn, the thickening Blue Grass
All lying rich forever in the green sun.
I see all things apart, the towers that men
Contrive I too contrived long, long ago.
Now I demand little. The singular passion
Abides its object and consumes desire
In the circling shadow of its appetite.
There was a time when the young eyes were slow,
Their flame steady beyond the firstling fire,
I stood in the rain, far from home at nightfall
By the Potomac, the great Dome lit the water,
The city my blood had built I knew no more
While the screech-owl whistled his new delight
Consecutively dark.

                    Struck in the wet mire
Four thousand leagues from the ninth buried city
I thought of Troy, what we had built her for.

The Swimmers

SCENE: *Montgomery County,*
           Kentucky, July 1911

Kentucky water, clear springs: a boy fleeing
    To water under the dry Kentucky sun,
    His four little friends in tandem with him, seeing

Long shadows of grapevine wriggle and run
   Over the green swirl; mullein under the ear
   Soft as Nausicaä's palm; sullen fun

Savage as childhood's thin harmonious tear:
   O fountain, bosom source undying-dead
   Replenish me the spring of love and fear

And give me back the eye that looked and fled
   When a thrush idling in the tulip tree
   Unwound the cold dream of the copperhead.

—Along the creek the road was winding; we
   Felt the quicksilver sky. I see again
   The shrill companions of that odyssey:

Bill Eaton, Charlie Watson, 'Nigger' Layne
   The doctor's son, Harry Duèsler who played
   The flute; and Tate, with water on the brain.

Dog-days: the dusty leaves where rain delayed
   Hung low on poison-oak and scuppernong,
   And we were following the active shade

Of water, that bells and bickers all night long.
   'No more'n a mile,' Layne said. All five stood still.
   Listening, I heard what seemed at first a song;

Peering, I heard the hooves come down the hill.
   The posse passed, twelve horse; the leader's face
   Was worn as limestone on an ancient sill.

Then, as sleepwalkers shift from a hard place
   In bed, and rising to keep a formal pledge
   Descend a ladder into empty space,

We scuttled down the bank below a ledge
   And marched stiff-legged in our common fright
   Along a hog-track by the riffle's edge:

Into a world where sound shaded the sight
   Dropped the dull hooves again; the horsemen came
   Again, all but the leader: it was night

Momently and I feared: eleven same
   Jesus-Christers unmembered and unmade,
   Whose Corpse had died again in dirty shame.

The bank then levelling in a speckled glade,
   We stopped to breathe above the swimming-hole;
   I gazed at its reticulated shade

Recoiling in blue fear, and felt it roll
   Over my ears and eyes and lift my hair
   Like seaweed tossing on a sunk atoll.

I rose again. Borne on the copper air
　　A distant voice green as a funeral wreath
　　Against a grave: 'That dead nigger there.'

The melancholy sheriff slouched beneath
　　A giant sycamore; shaking his head
　　He plucked a sassafras twig and picked his teeth:

'We come too late.' He spoke to the tired dead
　　Whose ragged shirt soaked up the viscous flow
　　Of blood in which It lay discomfited.

A butting horse-fly gave one ear a blow
　　And glanced off, as the sheriff kicked the rope
　　Loose from the neck and hooked it with his toe

Away from the blood.—I looked back down the slope:
　　The friends were gone that I had hoped to greet.—
　　A single horseman came at a slow lope

And pulled up at the hanged man's horny feet;
　　The sheriff noosed the feet, the other end
　　The stranger tied to his pommel in a neat

Slip-knot. I saw the Negro's body bend
　　And straighten, as a fish-line cast transverse
　　Yields to the current that it must subtend.

The sheriff's Goddamn was a murmured curse
　　Not for the dead but for the blinding dust
　　That boxed the cortège in a cloudy hearse

And dragged it towards our town. I knew I must
　　Not stay till twilight in that silent road;
　　Sliding my bare feet into the warm crust,

I hopped the stonecrop like a panting road
　　Mouth open, following the heaving cloud
　　That floated to the court-house square its load

Of limber corpse that took the sun for shroud.
　　There were three figures in the dying sun
　　Whose light were company where three was crowd.

My breath crackled the dead air like a shotgun
　　As, sheriff and the stranger disappearing,
　　The faceless head lay still. I could not run

Or walk, but stood. Alone in the public clearing
　　This private thing was owned by all the town,
　　Though never claimed by us within my hearing.

Paul Green

(1894–1981)

Paul Green was born in 1894 in Harnett County, North Carolina, and grew up working a mule-drawn plow in the fields on his father's farm. He attended Buies Creek Academy (now Campbell University), graduated in 1914, and then taught in a small country school for two years to save enough money to attend the University of North Carolina. He entered the university in 1916, where he stayed for a year, during which his first play, *Surrender to the Enemy*, was produced on campus. In 1917, during World War I, he enlisted in the army and saw action at the front in France and Belgium. In 1919 he returned to Chapel Hill, where he studied under Edward Koch and married fellow student and dramatist Elizabeth Atkinson Lay. Throughout the 1920s, Green published a series of one-act plays, one of which, *White Dresses*, a tragic story of miscegenation and love, was scheduled for production at Chapel Hill; however, university authorities decided the play should not be staged because of its controversial themes.

In 1926, Green published *Lonesome Road: Six Plays for the Negro Theatre;* among the six was *Abraham's Bosom*, another tragedy of racial themes, which was awarded a Pulitzer prize in May 1927. Besides *Abraham's Bosom*, Green's other best-remembered plays are *The Field God* (1927), *The House of Connelly* (1931), *Roll Sweet Chariot* (1934), and *Hymn to the Rising Sun* (1935). In the mid-1930s, Green moved his plays outdoors, combining music, dance, pageant, and poetry in a form he named "symphonic drama." The best-known of these dramas, *The Lost Colony*, was originally presented at Roanoke Island, North Carolina, in 1937, and has been repeated every summer since.

Hymn to the Rising Sun

A Drama of Man's Waste
In One Act

CHARACTERS

PEARLY GATES
BRIGHT BOY
TWO CONVICTS
RUNT
A WHITE MAN
FIRST GUARD
THE COOK
THE CAPTAIN
SECOND GUARD

First presented by the *Let Freedom Ring* Actors' Troupe at the Civic Repertory Theatre, New York City, January 12, 1936.

HOPPY
CARELESS LOVE
A NEGRO CONVICT
OTHER CONVICTS

TIME: *Some years ago*
PLACE: *Somewhere in the southern part of the United States*

*The rising curtain discloses a convict stockade. It is the hour before sunrise, and
in the gray twilight of the upheaving dawn a tent with the lips of its opening
snarled back stands silhouetted against the paling stars. A line of posts like Indian
palisades passes behind the tent, and stretched across them are the faint horizontal
streaks of close barbed wire. At the left front is a barrel, and beside it a rough
square table, and at the right front a box structure much like a small privy, some
four feet high and about two feet wide. A smoky tin lantern set on top of the box
casts its bilious eye over the scene and into the mouth of the tent where the convicts
are sleeping in their double bunks.*

*For a moment after the curtain rises nothing is heard except the deep breathing of
the sleepers and the occasional clink of a chain as some convict moves his weary
body on a hard shuck mattress. And then far away from the other side of the round
world comes the snug crow of a rooster in salute to the waking day. A huge halfnaked middle-aged Negro lying in the bottom bunk at the left smacks his lips and
mutters in his sleep.*

Pearly Gates *[the sound growling up from the deep cavern of his belly]*. Ah—oom.

*His long arms slide off the bunk and hang limpfully down to the ground. The top
bunk at the right creaks, a chain rattles, and a white* BOY *about seventeen years
old, with shaved head, haggard face, and hollow eyes props himself up on his elbow
and looks over at the Negro. He also is naked from the waist up.*

Boy *[calling in a husky whisper]*.   Pearly Gates. *[But there is no answer from
the Negro. He calls again—softly and with a careful look about him.]* Pearly Gates.

*The Negro stirs in restless fitfulness, pulls his long arms back up across his body,
and with a deep sigh goes on sleeping.*

A Convict's Voice *[from the depths of the tent, angry and guttural]*. Pipe down-n-n!

The BOY *waits a moment and then turns and stares at the box. A long while he
gazes at it as if listening, and then with a sort of moan stretches himself out on his
mattress. For a while everything is quiet again—no rattling of chains, no clank of
iron on iron, cuff on cuff, no muttering is heard. A deep and dreamless sleep once
more seems to pervade the scene. But the sickly rheumy eye of the lantern does not
sleep. Steadily it watches, waits, and watches, while the night gnats and bugs
whirl dizzily around it. Now it begins to wink, for the box on which it sits has*

started shaking. Something is imprisoned there. A scurried drumming is heard inside as if a huge bird were beating at the plank walls with bony featherless wings. The Boy *at the right front raises himself up in his bunk again and stares out at the box, then looks over at the Negro at the left.*

Boy [*in an agonized whisper*]. Pearly Gates, Pearly Gates!

The Negro at the left shakes himself like a huge chained animal, sticks his great hands up, and grasps the side rails of the bunk above him.

Pearly Gates [*muttering*]. Ah—oom.

His hands release the rails and drop to the ground with a thud. The drumming in the box grows louder, and a voice inside is heard calling piteously.

Voice [*in the box, as if embedded in a thick quilt*]. Water—water!
Boy [*now sitting bolt upright and wagging his head in anguish*]. Somebody do something! Oh, do!

A tremulous shaking of iron chains passes through the tent, and the Convicts *turn in their bunks.*

Another Convict's Voice [*from the depths of the tent*]. Go to sleep!
Boy. Yeh—yeh—who can sleep? [*Calling softly again.*] Pearly Gates!
Convict's Voice [*in savage mockery*]. Pearly Gates—Pearly Gates! What can he do?

One of the great hands of the Negro at the left begins waving in the air around his face as if shooing off pestering mosquitoes or flies.

Pearly Gates [*groaning and smacking his lips in his sleep*]. Lemme 'lone, lemme 'lone, I say.
Voice [*in the box.*] Water, water——!
Boy [*moaning*]. Pearly Gates.

In the bunk below the Boy *a dropsical brutal-faced* White Man *of fifty-five turns wrathfully over.*

White Man. Shet your face, Bright Boy, shet it! [*Muttering.*] A man's got to git his sleep, ain't he, if he swings them picks? What with you and the bugs and the heat—— [*He suddenly lunges upward, shoots his hand out around the rail of the* Boy's *bunk, and grabs him fiercely in the side. The* Boy *lets out a low wail and pulls loose from him, and the* White Man *lies down again.*] Next time I get hold of you I'll tear out a whole handful of your guts. [*The* Boy *bends his head on his knees and begins to weep silently. Presently he chokes down his sobs, wipes his eyes with the palm of his hand, and sits staring before him. For an instant everything is silent once more, and then the drumming in the box begins again. The* BOY *moans, and the* WHITE MAN *jerks up his leg to kick at the mattress above him, but a groan bursts from his lips as the shackle bites down on his ankle.*] Great God A'mighty—I've ruint my leg! [*He bends far over and rubs his leg, and then snarls around at the box.*] Stop it, Runt! Stop it!

He turns his face away from the lantern light and stretches himself out for a nap. PEARLY GATES *suddenly sits up in his bunk. He wriggles his fingers in the air, waking them to life, and opens his mouth in great gapes.*

Pearly Gates [*scratching his close-cropped head and staring about him*]. Who that called my name?

Boy. Runt's dying in that box. Oh, he is! Get the Cap'n, I tell you.

Pearly Gates [*thinking a while and then showing his white teeth in a grin*]. How I gonna git the Cap'n and me chained to this here bunk?

Boy. Call him—he'll come.

Pearly Gates. Nunh-unh.

White Man [*turning over on his back and chuckling*]. Reckon when Runt gets out of that box he'll quit going behind the tent to love hisself. [PEARLY GATES *begins to laugh softly.*] What's tickling you?

Pearly Gates. Bull of the woods, he said he was. Ah—oom—a hundred pounds of skin and bones—wimmen's ease.

Runt [*in the box*]. Help me! Help me!

Boy [*vehemently*]. You got to do——

His voice stops dead in the air as the FIRST GUARD *comes in from the left. He is a dissolute-looking fellow about thirty years old, dressed in overalls, a wide field straw hat, and a homespun shirt. He carries a double-barreled shotgun in the crook of his arm. Everybody grows silent, and* PEARLY GATES *lies down again in his bunk.*

First Guard [*quietly*]. Cut out the talking. [*Looking over at the* BOY.] Lie down, sonny. [*He starts on out at the left rear.*]

Boy. Please, sir, please, sir——

First Guard [*stopping*]. What you want?

Boy [*trying to control the trembling in his voice*]. It's the Runt—water—give him a drink.

First Guard [*sauntering back and stopping in front of the tent*]. So Bright Boy don't like the way we treat the Runt, huh?

Boy. Give him some air. [*Raging thoughtlessly out.*] No, I don't like it! Nobody likes it.

First Guard [*peering at the* BOY]. Maybe you forgot what the Cap'n told you yesterday.

Boy. But he's smothering to death in there I tell you.

First Guard. It's Runt in old Aggie's belly, not you.

Boy [*half hysterically*]. And you're killing him—killing——

Pearly Gates [*interposing warningly*]. Heah, heah, boy.

First Guard. So you think this is a Sunday school, huh? [*Suddenly roaring at him.*] Stop that whimpering! [*Then quietly.*] The Cap'n said keep your tongue to yourself, didn't he? Ah-ha, seems like we can't please you, son. But we'll learn to please you.

He turns and saunters on out at the left rear. The Boy *flings himself back on his mattress and stuffs an old ragged blanket over his ears to keep out the low sound of* Runt's *whimpering in the box.*

Pearly Gates [*looking out and whispering*]. Jesus, child, you gonna git hurt if you don't mind. Heah me?

White Man [*whispering likewise up toward the mattress*]. It's hard at first, Bright Boy. But don't you worry. You'll forget your mother's love—song at evening— all of that. Yeah, after while you will. [*Now once more from that other side of the world far away comes the proud crowing of the rooster. The* White Man *mutters to himself.*] Whisht that chicken had a ball and chain around his neck. Oh, God, I do! [*He turns over again and hides his face under his arm.*]

Pearly Gates [*singing in a whisper to himself*].

> Good morning, Mr. Rooster,
> I wisht I had your wing,
> I'd fly across the ocean——

He stops as an alarm clock goes off somewhere at the left, its little sharp daggers of sound stabbing the quiet scene. The Convicts *lie still a moment and then twist and mutter in their bunks, and the rattle and clink of chains accompany them. The* Cook *enters from the left front, carrying a steaming tin tub in his hands which he sets on the table. He is an elderly bent white fellow with a sad monkeylike face. His close- shaven head gives him a strange youthful appearance around his forehead and ears which contrasts sharply with the gnarled eldishness of his mouth and jaw. As the tub thumps down on the table, the prisoner in the box at the right front drums and thunders with a last despairing burst of energy. The lantern reels crazily and falls to the ground, filling the scene with plunging grotesque shadows. A flood of clinking sounds rises from the tent, and the muffled faces and shoulders of the* Convicts *can be seen as they rear up in their bunks to look out. With the slow waddling movement of an old duck the* Cook *goes over, picks up the lantern, and replaces it on top of the box. Then he turns and pokes his way out at the left front, mopping his sweaty face with his apron as he goes. The* Convicts *lay themselves down again to their rest. By this time the slaty gray of the approaching dawn has changed to a pearly gray, and the outlines of the bunks in the tent, fifteen or twenty of them, show up somewhat more distinctly, as do the posts and barbed wire across the rear.*

The convict boss comes walking slowly in from the right front. In the morning gloom he shows to be a heavy-set man, dressed in sombrero, khaki shirt, bow tie, and khaki trousers. Jammed down in one of his heavy boots is the snakelike form of Old Jeff, as the convict lash is called. In a holster at his waist he carries a forty-five automatic.

Stopping by the box a moment he listens and then raps on it with his knuckles.

Captain [*in a husky pleasant voice*]. How is it, old Love Powder?

Runt [*faint and faraway.*] Water, water!

Captain. Sure you're going to get your water—your piece of bread too—at feeding time. [*He walks on toward the mouth of the tent and speaks cheerily as he enters.*] Morning, boys, morning. [*Without waiting for a reply he continues.*] Hope you all slept well. [*Pulling a key from his pocket he begins unlocking the shackles with a cool, deft sound.*] I've let you sleep late today—half an hour extra. Now ain't that nice? I say, ain't that nice?

Several Scattered Voices. Yes, sir, Cap'n, yes, sir.

Captain. In honor of the occasion, I did. Now stir yourselves. [*As each prisoner is unlocked, he slips his shoes on, steps out into the aisle, and stands with his face to the front waiting. The* CAPTAIN *goes on talking pleasantly.*] I've been up an hour. Already had my breakfast. [*Click, click.*] Yes, sir, couldn't sleep. Responsibility, worry, thinking about you fellows—how to handle you, how to keep you happy. [*Chuckling.*] Happy, you heard me. I'm the one that really wears the ball and chain in this camp. [*His voice dropping down into a sudden hard note and then rising to a pleasant pitch again.*] Ha-ha, that's right. Oh, yes, it's right. [*Passing along the tier of bunks to the left he continues unlocking the shackles—click, click.*] I hope Runt's cutting up in that box didn't hinder your beauty sleep. [*He is now unlocking the shackles of* PEARLY GATES.] I say, did it keep you awake?

Pearly Gates [*showing his white teeth in a sudden spasmodic grimace which is meant for a grin*]. No, sir, no, sir.

The CAPTAIN *steps back two or three paces toward the front and draws himself up in a military pose.*

Captain [*his voice barking through the morning air*]. Hep—hep! [*The line of white* CONVICTS *on the right march out and stand facing toward the left. There are ten of them—two elderly men, three middle-aged men, and five boys from seventeen to nineteen years of age. They are all naked to the waist, wearing dirty striped trousers and carrying their jackets and convict caps in their hands. The Negroes led by* PEARLY GATES *come out and join the end of the line. There are eight of these, four young bucks, an old bent mulatto, and three middle-aged fellows. The* CAPTAIN *counts them.*] Two-four-six-eight-ten-twelve-fourteen-sixteen-eighteen—[*Adding with a gesture toward the box behind him.*] nineteen. All right, get over there and purty up your faces. [*They move over to the barrel at the left and begin washing themselves in turn. As each one steps up to the barrel, he sticks his jacket and cap between his knees, lifts out a cupped handful of water, dashes it on his face, and moves on, drying himself with his jacket. The* COOK *brings in a dishpan from the left, sets it on the table by the tub, and returns the way he came. The* CONVICTS *begin putting on their jackets and caps and forming in a line before the table, the ten whites in the same order as before and the Negroes behind them. The* CAPTAIN *pulls out a heavy gold watch, looks at it, snaps the lid to, and sends a brazen shout toward the rear.*] Guard Number One!

First Guard [*answering from the right rear*]. Yay-hoo!

Captain. Guard Number Two!

Second Guard [*from the left rear*]. Yo-ho!

Captain. Four o'clock!

The Cook *comes rolling a wheelbarrow in from the left. It is loaded with tin pans and spoons. He stops it by the table, steps behind the tin tub, and picks up a dipper.*

Cook [*croaking out to the tune of the Army mess call*]. Greasy, greasy, greasy! Greasy, greasy, greasy!

The Convicts *shuffle toward the wheelbarrow, and the white man who is in the lead picks up a plate with a spoon and holds it out for his helping. The* Cook *loads him down with a dipperful of cabbage, fatback, grits, and a hunk of bread. He passes on, goes over to the right rear, squats down on his haunches, and begins eating ravenously. The second man follows with his helping, takes his place by the first, and so on in turn until all have ringed themselves across the scene in a squatting semicircle, showing in the half light like a row of grotesque animals. Some of them eat with the rapacity of dogs—their pewter spoons going scrape, scrape against the bottoms of their tin plates—others slowly and with no interest in their food. The middle-aged and elderly ones seem to have the best appetites. The younger ones eat little, and the* Boy *nothing at all. While the* Convicts *are busy getting their food and settling down, the* Captain *stands watching them indulgently like a circus master with his trained pets. Now he moves over to the right front and leans against the box. As he faces us we get a better view of him in the lantern's glow. His face is swarthy, heavy jowled, clean-shaven and set off with a close-cropped gray mustache. When he is in an easygoing mood as he seems to be now, the pupils of his slumbrous brown eyes are cut across by the drooping curtain of two heavy eyelids. But when he gets mean, these same eyelids have a way of snapping back like the hinged flap of a box, and the gleaming forked light from his eyes looks holes through a man.*

Captain [*scanning the row of figures and listening to the scrape, scrape of the pewter spoons*]. Go to it, boys, I like to hear you eat—and you need it. [*Looking off by the tent toward the horizon where the red of approaching sunrise is beginning to dye the sky.*] It's going to be a fine day. Clear as a bell. And hot—clear and hot. We ought to move many a yard of dirt on that fill, hadn't we? I say hadn't we?
Several Scattered Voices. Yes, sir, Cap'n.
Pearly Gates. Yea, Lord, let the buggies roll!
Captain. That's right, Pearly, old wheelhorse.
Pearly Gates. Just watch me wheel, Cap'n.
Captain [*tapping on the box and addressing the prisoner within*]. And if you'll be a nice boy, Runt, we might give you your shovel back.

The Boy *who is squatted over his untouched food looks joyously up.*

Boy [*his voice half breaking in a fervent sob*]. Thank God!
Captain [*his glance drifting lazily over toward the* Boy]. Son, you hurt my feelings. You oughta thank me—not God. [*His gaze coming back to the box.*] And besides, Runt, we might need this bedroom of yours, who knows? [*The scraping of the spoons suddenly stops. The* Captain *laughs.*] Oh, I'm joking, boys, unless—— [*His voice dies out, and a low aimless whistle begins to sound through his full lips. The scraping of the spoons begins again. Suddenly the air is rent by the sound of two*

shotguns fired off almost simultaneously in the distance. The CONVICTS *spring to their feet with a howl and stand trembling with fear, some of them dropping their pans and food in the dirt. The* CAPTAIN *speaks soothingly to them.*] Never mind, boys, the guards are just celebrating a little. They ain't shooting nobody. [*Calling off in his great voice.*] Ready to ride!

 First Guard [*from the back*]. Yay-hoo!
 Second Guard [*likewise*]. Yo-ho!

The CONVICTS *settle down again on their haunches, some of them holding empty pans disconsolately in their hands. The* CAPTAIN *walks over toward the row of figures. He stops before* PEARLY GATES *who is getting his hunk of fatback out of the dirt.*

 Captain. Why, Pearly, you let a gun firing off scare you, too? I'm surprised.
 Pearly Gates [*grinning and gulping*]. Me too, Cap'n. Seem like I can't help it. [*Now showing his teeth in the same spasmodic grin and with a half-teasing unctuous begging.*] Bet they ain't no seconds for a good boy, is they Cap'n?
 Captain [*to the* COOK]. What say, Greasy?
 Cook [*croakingly, as he stares out before him with his batlike eyes*]. Ain't no seconds.

PEARLY GATES *begins eating his meat, dirt and all. The* CAPTAIN *smiles and moves on.*

 Captain [*stopping in front of the* BOY]. What's the matter, son?
 Boy [*struggling to make his tongue speak and at last getting out a few words*]. Not hungry, Cap'n.
 Captain. Not hungry?
 Boy. No, sir.
 Captain. Sick?
 Boy. Yes, sir, yes, sir.
 Captain. Sorry to hear that. Wish I could fix you up a nice featherbed. Yes, sir, and give you a pretty little nurse to hold your hand and smooth your forehead. But we can't do that, son. [*Suddenly bending over him, his voice chilly as steel.*] Eat them God-damn rations! [*With a terrified look the* BOY *grabs up his plate and begins shoveling down the hated cabbage and side meat. And then suddenly his mouth flies open and he vomits them out again. The* CAPTAIN *backs away from him, bends over with his hands resting on his knees, and peers at him.*] That little shooting upset you, huh?
 Boy [*teetering back and forth on his heels and choking*]. I just can't eat it, Cap'n, I can't.
 Captain. Not good enough, eh?
 Boy [*watching him with ashy face*]. Yes, sir, it's all right, but I just can't eat it—I——
 Captain. And how the hell you 'spect to roll your wheelbarrow, if you don't eat?
 Boy [*his words sputtering from him like a shower of crumbs*]. I'll keep it rolling, Cap'n, I'll keep it turning—I'll——
 Captain [*sorrowfully*]. You didn't do it yesterday, son.
 Boy [*whimpering*]. Yes, sir, yes, sir, I did.

Captain. Well, never mind, may be you did. Anyhow, don't worry over your appetite, son. In a week or two you'll think fatback and cabbage are angel cake. [*He straightens up, laughs quietly as if dismissing the subject, and then addresses them.*] You boys know what today is? [*No one answers.*] Hey, you, Pearly Gates, what is today?

Pearly Gates. Lawd, Cap'n, I don't know.

Captain. What, my right-hand man and he don't know? [*To the bloated-faced white man at his left.*] You, Hoppy, what day is it?

Hoppy. Dunno, sir.

Captain [*to a tall sad-faced young fellow*]. You know, Careless Love?

Careless Love. Thursday, I think.

Captain. I'm ashamed of you fellows. Ain't you got no interest in your country? [*Snarling out to the* BOY, *who jumps nervously.*] What's today, son? What sets it apart from all other days?

Boy [*fearfully*]. It's the Fourth of July.

Captain. That's right, Bright Boy. Independence Day. [*Shouting at them.*] Attenshun! [*They all spring to their feet and stand with their tin pans in their hands.*] Forward, march! [*They move over toward the left and, passing by the wheelbarrow, lay their utensils down, then form in a line as before. The two* GUARDS *enter, one from the left, one from the right. The* SECOND GUARD *is dressed like the first, is about the same age, and also has a double-barreled shotgun in the crook of his arm. They are both gnawing sandwiches. The* CAPTAIN *calls out to them.*] Well, gentlemen, I thought you'd fell into the latrine and got drowned. [*A staccato burst of laughter is fired off among the* CONVICTS *and then dies suddenly away as the* CAPTAIN *looks at them.*] I was just saying that this is the glorious Independence Day, the great day when Old King George got his tail bit off. Hum—hum. I used to shoot thunderbolts in my mammy's yard on Fourth of July. Years ago, years ago, I did. My daddy beat me half to death once for doing it. [*Holding up his left hand from which two fingers are missing.*] Got them fingers blown off that way. [PEARLY GATES *snickers. The* CAPTAIN *looks over at him.*] I forgot you knew all about it, Pearly. [*To the* CONVICTS.] Well, he's right. A nigger bit 'em off long ago when I tried to arrest him for stealing a bushel of corn from old man Tyler. [*Reminiscing as he drops his hand.*] Hum—hum, and when I drilled him with the cold steel, he spit 'em out again—kerdab right in my face. And now, boys, since you know how it happened you needn't keep looking at my hand after this. [*His voice cracking out an order to the* FIRST GUARD.] All right, clean up!

First Guard [*adopting the authority of the* CAPTAIN]. Fall out!

The CONVICTS *fall out of line and begin policing the ground around the tent. The* SECOND GUARD *finishes his sandwich and stands by the box. The* CAPTAIN *wanders toward him.*

Captain [*in a low voice*]. Anything stirring?

Second Guard [*likewise in a low voice*]. Looks like he's got to have it, Cap'n.

Captain. Hum.

Second Guard. Can't seem to quiet him down. Talk—talk—cry, cry. Nobody couldn't sleep last night.

Captain [*softly*]. Bright Boy?

Second Guard. Ah-hah, Bright Boy.

In the background the BOY *bends over for a bit of paper, then stops and looks questioningly around. The* FIRST GUARD *touches him in the rump with the nozzle of his gun.*

First Guard. Step along, Buster.

The BOY *darts forward, grabs up the bit of paper, and begins searching the ground in front of him.*

Second Guard [*to the* CAPTAIN]. Been here a week and worse than ever.
Captain. He wants his mammy.
Second Guard. Three days now and he says he's sick.
Captain. He ain't really sick.
Second Guard. Oh, no, the thermometer said he weren't.
Captain. Ah-hah. He thinks we run a hospital.
Second Guard. It ain't no hospital, is it?
Captain. Hell, no, it ain't that at all.
Second Guard. And he thinks other things too. [*Pulling a spoon from his pocket.*] Found that in his mattress last night.
Captain [*chuckling*]. Thought he'd make him a pewter file, did he?
Second Guard. Looks like it.

The CAPTAIN *takes it and looks at it.*

Captain. They will try them little tricks at first. [*He throws the spoon over into the wheelbarrow.*]
A Negro Convict [*in a high melodious call from the rear*]. Wanter void, Cap'n, wanter void!
Captain [*without looking around*]. You can do it at the job—we're late now.
First Guard [*singing out*]. That's about all, Cap'n!
Captain. Okay, line up! [*The* CONVICTS *who have finished cleaning up resume their places as before. The* CAPTAIN *moves out and stands before them, and the two* GUARDS *stand at the right and left front facing toward the back. For a while everyone waits as the* CAPTAIN'S *eyes study the pitiful motley crew before him. Presently he breaks into a low musical laugh. The* CONVICTS *look at him with a mixture of perplexity and fear. And then he speaks in an easy voice.*] I was just wondering, boys, whether I ought to make you that Fourth of July speech or not. What the hell good will it do? What say, Pearly?
Pearly Gates [*with his everlasting grin*]. Yes, sir, Cap'n, we'd sure like to hear you, suh.
Captain. I ain't had a chance to make you a speech since last Easter when I talked on the Resurrection. But orders from headquarters say I must call your attention to the occasion. [*Clearing his throat.*] Well, boys, orders is orders, as some of you ain't never found out and I take the privilege on our Independence Day of once more addressing a few words unto you. [*He waits a moment and then begins his flow of words.*] According to statute number six hundred and forty-two of the penal code duly proved and entered in the House of Representatives, so I'm told, by a vote of ninety-six to four, the punishment for constant trifling and bellyaching is twenty-nine blows with the whip. [*Stopping and eying them.*] But did I ever whip a man that much? I say, did I?
Pearly Gates. No, sir.

Careless Love. No, Cap'n.

Captain. You're damn right I didn't. Also it prescribes old black Aggie over there, and the goat, and chaining you up for various offenses, such as trying to escape, plotting a mutiny, sex perversion, and crimes against nature. Yes, sir, that's what they tell me to do to you, and I'm nothing but the instrument of the voters' will. The voters say so, and what the voters say is law, ain't it?

Hoppy [*shifting his weight*]. It sure God is.

Some of the others nod their agreement, and all watch the CAPTAIN *with roving blinking eyes, except the* BOY *who stands with his head bowed.*

Captain. Yes, sir, they've got the power, for this is a democracy and democracy means the voice of the people. And the people—well who are the people? Why they are the grand old Daughters of the Revolution, and the Confederacy—and the bishops and ministers of the gospel—Episcopalians, the Baptists, the Methodists, and the Presbyterians, and all the Elks and the Kiwanis Clubs, the Rotarians, the Lions, the college presidents, the professors in the great institutions of learning, the folks that write books, and the lawyers—don't forget them. They are the people. They march to the polls and elect representatives and say pass the laws to keep the peace, and they pass the laws and they hand the laws over to me and say "Twenty-nine blows!" Ain't it so? And they tell me to put Runt there in that sweatbox in solitary confinement for messing with his private organs. Yes, sir, they're the folks that fasten chains and shackles around your legs, ain't it so?

Several Convicts [*with more feeling*]. Yes, sir, Cap'n.

Captain [*with a snarl*]. The hell it is! You fellows put the chains around your own legs. You don't pass the laws, but you break 'em. [*He quiets his voice down and goes on more pleasantly.*] I reckon some of you think I'm hard, that I ain't got no feeling, that I'm a brutal slave driver. Well, I ain't enjoyed beating any one of you the whole time you been here. And I don't enjoy hearing Runt drumming inside that box no better than you do. But you're undergoing a course of training, and I'm the teacher, and I got to call it to your attention again that this ain't no life for a human being to stay in. Behave yourselves, I say. Do what you're told, and get out of here quick as you can. Go back to the other world and start a new life. [*More persuasively.*] Some of you boys have killed folks. You've robbed filling stations, burnt houses, stole, and raped and violated screaming women. Every one of you is in here for some reason. They didn't put you in here just because they liked to go around and ketch you the way boys do birds and wring their necks. The great commonwealth of this state wishes every one of you was out of here. And I do too—wishes you were good upright citizens. Yeh, citizens—you heard me. And that's what you're here for—to see if I can make citizens out of you. And how you going to do that? Not by lying in bed and eating chocolate candy and having a 'lectric fan blowing over you. No, sir. If they made jails like that everybody'd be in jail and there'd be nobody outside of it. [*With a barking laugh.*] Then what'd happen to me? I wouldn't have no job, would I?

The CONVICTS *relax their stony attitude a bit, for now the* CAPTAIN *is feeling his speechmaking power and his voice has grown mellow.*

Voices. Yes, sir, Cap'n, that's right.

Captain. And I try to be a good Cap'n to you, don't I?

Voices [*more heartily*]. Yes, sir, Cap'n.

Captain. You're damn right I do. And I have a hard time of it, 'cause there are a lot of folks on the outside who keep snooping about, messing around, trying to tell me how to run things. Them university fellows come down here and leave their books, and I been reading one of 'em written by a fellow named Green. And what does he say? Why, the man weeps tears, he does. He goes on page after page crying about the po' Negro, how we got to do this and that for him, got to raise him up. A lot of crap, every word of it. A nigger's a nigger. Ain't that so, Pearly Gates?

Pearly Gates [*with his puppetlike spasmodic grin*]. That's the gospel, Cap'n.

Captain. Right. And you niggers that's in here didn't have sense enough to know that, and so you went around trying to stir up trouble, thinking maybe you were just sunburnt white men and could do as you pleased. Well, you got away easy. A lot of you ought to have been strung up to telegraph poles and the limbs of trees, and you know it. Well, when you get out of here, go back home and keep to your place, a nigger's place. And as for you white fellows, look at you. I been bossing convict camps for twenty years. More'n half the prisoners under me has been boys like Bright Boy there—hardly loose from their mother's apron strings, just in the marble stage. What the devil's the matter with you? Well, I reckon it's them same mothers—they didn't know how to train you, petted and spoiled you. Well, I say it again—you won't be petted here. The course of sprouts I'm putting you through is a course of rawhide sprouts, as the Scriptures say. And when I turn you loose you'll be hard as iron, you'll be men. You won't be wanting to go home to suck your mammy's sugar tit, no sir. Hard did I say? You heard me. For when the judge sentenced you here he said at hard labor, and that's what I aim to make it. [*His voice now taking on an oratorical sonorous sweep.*] For this ain't no boat trip on the river, this ain't no little gang of girls playing doll-babies. No, sir, not a bit of it. This ain't no circus full of hootchy-kootchy mommas strutting their hot stuff before your watery mouth. This ain't no riding on a Ferris wheel or eating peanuts and popcorn and drinking cold drinks at a lemonade stand. No it ain't, you bet your life. This is the chain gang, the chain gang. This is the ball and chain, the nine-pound hammer, the wheelbarrow, the shovel, the twenty-nine lashes, the seventy-two lashes, the sweatbox, the steel cage, the rifle and the shotgun. You've heard about them two niggers, Shropshire and Barnes, in the next camp down the road. They didn't want to work. Well, old boss Jackson chained 'em up to the bars till their feet froze and rotted with gangrene, and the doctor had to cut 'em off. Ain't that hard? Yes, that's a little bit hard. Shows you how hard I could be if I wanted to. Compared to that, the Runt is having an easy time of it in that sweatbox. [*The hard note coming suddenly back into his voice.*] But some of you don't think so, do you? Bright Boy there—he says it's killing the Runt. I hear that he lies awake all night making himself sick—worrying and moaning over poor Runt. Why that's a pity, for I'm looking after Runt myself, and there ain't no use of both of us trying to do the same job. Is there? No, sir, there ain't. And Bright Boy will have to learn better. He'll have to get hard. I say it again and that wise old judge he knew. Hard, he said. You heard me. For if you don't get hard you can't make your time, and if you don't make your time you can't pay your debts to the state. And the only way you can pay it is by work. You can't pay by playing sick, by getting beat, by being shut up in the sweatbox, by being chained up till your feet fall off. That don't do nobody no good. It's work we want. Work the state wants. It's for that the great railroad company has hired you from the governor. Yes, sir,

the governor has rented you out the way he would a mule or a shovel or a dragpan—
hired you out to build that railroad. And, boys, you got to build it. 'Cause they need coal
down in Florida, and they need oranges and mushmelons and bananas up there in New
York. And the cotton has to get to the seaport, and the tobacco's got to get to the factory.
And there's a world of shipping and trade got to happen, boys. And it all depends on you.
[*Now his voice drops to a low singing croon.*] I know it's a hell of a life. It's a hell of a
life for all of us—the shackles and the iron pin, the hammer and the ball. But damn your
son-of-a-bitching souls, I'm going to see that you wear 'em till the end! [*His voice dies
out and he stands staring at the* Convicts, *who shift themselves uneasily about. Then
he smiles pleasantly at them.*] Well, boys, that's about all I've got to say. So we'll get on
with the rest of the exercises as per the orders.

> *By this time the light has spread up the sky, and the figures of the raggle-taggle
> crew stand illuminated in it. The* Captain *moves around to the right and begins
> walking slowly behind them, studying each man as he passes. They feel him there
> apprehensively, some of them swaying nervously on their feet like saplings in a
> gentle wind. The* Captain *stops behind* Hoppy.

Captain. Anything to complain of?
Hoppy [*stuttering and like the other* Convicts *staring straight ahead of him*].
No, sir, no, sir, everything's fine.
Captain. Seems like yestiddy that little Georgy buggy needed greasing, huh?
Hoppy [*swallowing and gulping*]. I kept her rolling from sun to sun.
Captain. [*pleasantly*]. Like hell you did! Didn't the wheel get stuck every once in
a while and wouldn't turn?
Hoppy. No, sir, no, sir. But just watch me, boss, watch me today. [*And his great
trembling hand goes up and wipes the popping sweat from his forehead.*]
Captain. Don't mind we'll have to grease it for you, son, the first thing you know.
[*And as he looks at* Hoppy's *shaking form, a half-affectionate smile plays on his
swarthy face. For a moment longer he stares at him and then moves on to the next
man. A sigh, a long half-inaudible sigh escapes from* Hoppy's *lips. The* Captain
turns and gazes at him.] Don't let me scare you, snowbird! [*And now he stops behind the* Boy.] So you're sick, hah?

> *His voice is brittle and steely, a new note in it, and a shiver seems to run the
> length of the dirty gray-striped line. The* Boy *looks out before him with wide
> frightened eyes and face the color of ash-tree wood.*

Boy. Yes, sir, yes, sir, I'm sick.
Captain [*now looming above him*]. Hum. When a man's sick he's got a fever,
ain't he? And when he's got a fever the thermometer says so, don't it? Well, the ther-
mometer says you ain't got no fever. Therefore you ain't sick.
Boy [*in a low agonized pleading*]. Please, sir, please.
Captain. [*suddenly pulling Old Jeff out of the cuff of his boot and touching the*
Boy *on the shoulder*]. This way, son.
Boy [*terror-stricken*]. But I been doing all right, Cap'n. They ain't been any com-
plaint has they, none you've heard of?

Captain [*kindly*]. This way, son.

THE FIRST GUARD *comes up in front of him and touches him in the stomach with his gun.*

First Guard. You heard him.

Boy [*his hands suddenly fluttering aimlessly in the air, his breath sucked through his lips with a gasp*]. Oh, Lord, have mercy! Mercy!

Captain. So, you're callin' on the Lord? Well, the Lord ain't here. The Lord is far away. In fact you might say this ain't no place for the Lord.

Boy [*whispering*]. Cap'n, Cap'n!

Captain. I know you need medicine, son. That's what we're going to give you. Maybe after that you won't be sick. Maybe you won't talk so much either.

Boy [*wailing and bobbing his chin against his breast*]. I'm sick, bad sick, I tell you!

Captain [*snarling*]. And I reckon the man you killed was sick too, when you soused that knife in him.

Boy [gasping]. I didn't kill him. I didn't, I tell you. They put the blame on me!

Captain. Oh, you didn't? But the jury said so. This way, son.

With the lash of the whip clasped against the butt, he reaches out, hooks the loop over the BOY'S *neck and jerks him backward. The* BOY *shakes as if with ague and stands with half-bent knees, about to fall. The* SECOND GUARD *moves through the gap in the line and takes him by the arm.*

Second Guard. Step back! [*He pushes him toward the rear.*]

Captain. Pull your pants down, son.

Boy [*moaning*]. Cap'n, Cap'n!

Captain. Don't call on me—'cause I'm like the Lord. I can't hear you either. Unbutton your pants. [*Snarling.*] I say unbutton your pants! Don't let me tell you thrice, as the Son of God said to the rooster.

With a wild and desperate look around and with a sudden vague gesture in the air, the BOY *slowly begins to undo his belt. The* COOK *at the left front, who has continued cleaning up unconcernedly, piles the tub on the pans in the wheelbarrow and rolls it away to the left. And now the* FIRST GUARD *steps several paces to the front and lays his gun at the menacing ready across his forearm.*

Second Guard. Bend over, son.

The BOY'S *knees sag, he falls forward, and lies with his face in the dirt, his arms outstretched. The* CONVICTS *stand in a stiff line, their eyes staring straight ahead of them, their lips tightly shut.*

Captain [*calling*]. Come hold his feet, Pearly Gates!

Like frightened animals before an approaching storm the CONVICTS *suddenly shrink closer together and the* BOY'S *prone body is hidden from our view.*

Pearly Gates [*twisting his shoulders and flinging his hands together in front of his stomach*]. He'll be good, Cap'n, he'll lie still.

Captain [*yelling*]. Come hold his feet! [PEARLY GATES *leaves his place at the end of the line and goes gingerly around to the rear. The* CONVICTS *stand like a row of stony-faced Indians, outlined against the red light of the approaching sun, the* CAPTAIN'S *head showing above them as he speaks.*] Boys, let this be another warning to you. It's a month now since I had to use the lash. But some of you keep trying to dead-beat me, don't you?

The lids of his eyes are snapped back and his dark brown pupils are filled with a fiery demoniac light. Suddenly like a flash he whirls back toward the recumbent figure, raises himself up on the balls of his feet, and brings the whip down with a whistling tearing sound. Though we don't see it, the BOY'S *body bounds from the ground like a rubber ball, and with a cry* PEARLY GATES *flings himself upon the plunging feet. But no sound comes from the* BOY'S *lips. At this first blow a gust of horror seems to sweep the line of* CONVICTS, *and they waver back and forth and then stand still, their eyes lifted and set toward the vast and empty sky. Once more the* CAPTAIN *brings his whip down, and the* CONVICTS *flinch as if their own backs had felt the lash. Then at the third blow, a wild hysterical scream bursts from the* BOY'S *lips.*

Boy [*with a shriek*]. Mama! Mama!

At the fourth blow he begins to whimper. And at the fifth and sixth blows the wild animal scream tears once more from his body. At the seventh and eighth blows he begins whimpering again like a baby, the sound of his piteous crying rising and then sinking again like a child crying itself to sleep. And then at the tenth blow the CAPTAIN *suddenly stops and doubles up his whip.*

Captain [*curtly*]. Button his diaper. [*Thundering.*] Turn him loose, Pearly Gates!

A moment passes and then the huge Negro backs toward his position at the end of the line, staring hypnotically before him where the gasping figure lies. Presently, the CAPTAIN *comes around to the front, crams the whip into his boot, and stands gazing at them in silence. The* SECOND GUARD *now pushes the shuddering boy back to his place and helps him fasten his belt across his jerking quivering stomach. As he moves away from him, the* BOY *spins drunkenly about, and as he is falling the* GUARD *catches him and steadies him on his feet. The* BOY *stands there moaning and shaking, his eyes closed, the tears wetting his cheeks. The* SECOND GUARD *moves over to the right front, holding his gun before him. For a while the* CAPTAIN *is silent, as if his mind were wrapped away from the scene. Then as the* BOY'S *weeping dies down to an almost inaudible whimper, he looks up.*

Captain. I let him off easy this time, boys, because it's the Fourth of July. [*Gesturing to the two* GUARDS.] All right, gentlemen, give us another little salute to the morning sun. For this is the day the Thirteen Original States freed themselves from the bloody Englishmen. Fee-fi-fo-fum. [*The* GUARDS *raise their guns and fire a volley toward the sunrise. The* CONVICTS *tremble and shudder, their eyes rolling in their haggard faces. The* CAPTAIN *laughs softly, then pulling off his hat gives it a rolling wave around in the air.*] Hooray.

First Guard [*loudly*]. Hooray for the Fourth of July!

Second Guard [*more loudly*]. Hooray for the United States!

Captain. That's right. [*To the* CONVICTS.] Come on, boys, give us a cheer for your country. [*A feeble cheer finally breaks from their pallid lips.*] Damn it, don't you love Uncle Sam better'n that? Come on—once more.

The cheer is given a bit more loudly, but by empty wooden voices.

First Guard [*calling out*]. All right, Bright Boy, we ain't heard from you.

The BOY *tries to control his quivery shoulders.*

Captain. [*interposing*]. Never mind, he'll do it next Fourth of July. [*Pulling a crumpled sheet of paper from his pocket, he smooths it out and looks over at the* CONVICTS *pleasantly.*] Order of the day further certifies that before we set forth to work it shall be the duty of the boss to have a rendition of "America" sung by the prisoners. [*He puts the sheet of paper back into his pocket.*] And you fellows know the tune? [*No one answers.*] I say do any of you know it? [*The* CONVICTS *shake their heads.*] How about you, Bright Boy? [*The* BOY *stands staring at the ground.*] I say do you know the hymn?

The BOY'S *figure gives a spasmodic jerk.*

Boy [*in a muffled voice*]. Yes, sir.

Captain. All right, lead it off.

The boy hesitates, gulps once or twice, and then, lifting his eyes toward the sky, begins to sing in a clear beautiful voice.

Boy.

> My country, 'tis of thee,
> Sweet land of liberty,
> Of thee I sing.

Captain [*thundering at the other* CONVICTS]. Take off your caps!

They pull off their caps. The CAPTAIN *raises his hand in a salute, and the two* GUARDS *present arms. The* BOY *continues singing, some of the* CONVICTS *mumble along with him, and the* CAPTAIN *brays out a stave or two.*

Voices [*led by the* BOY].

> Land where my fathers died,
> Land of the pilgrims' pride,
> From every mountainside
> Let freedom ring.

At the end of the first stanza the CAPTAIN *drops his hand, and two* GUARDS *set their guns down, and the* CONVICTS *stop singing. But the* BOY *continues.*

Boy.

> My native country, thee—
> Land of the noble free,
> Thy name I love.

Captain [*sharply*]. All right, you can stop now. [*The* BOY *stops singing, drops his head on his breast, and stares at the ground again. The* CAPTAIN *turns and goes over to the box at the right front.*] And now, boys, as another honor for the occasion I'm going to do a good turn for Runt. And I'm going to break the law to do it. The voters prescribe twenty-one days for the Runt. Yes, sir, that's what they prescribe in the House of Representatives. But I'm letting him out on the eleventh day. [*He unlocks the door to the box and flings it open.*] All right, Runt, roll out. [*Inside the box we can see a little skinny Negro doubled up like a baby in its mother's womb, his head stuck between his knees.*] Roll out, Runt.

But there is no movement from the doubled-up form. The CAPTAIN *reaches in, takes the Negro by the collar, pulls him out, and drops his head against the ground. The figure lies still. The* CAPTAIN *stares at it. A murmur of fear runs among the* CONVICTS. *The* SECOND GUARD *steps over and peers at the bundle of rags.*

Second Guard [*feeling the bony chest*]. Say, you better——

The CAPTAIN *drops down on his knees, lays his hand on the Negro's heart. He squats there a moment and then rises abruptly to his feet and stands staring thoughtfully at the body.*

Captain. Ain't that a hell of a note!
First Guard [*now coming forward*]. He was okay a few minutes ago.
Captain. Yeh, but he ain't now. Yeh, that's right, I remember—I ain't heard him making no fuss since I first come in. Hum—hum. [*Turning toward the* CONVICTS.] Well, boys, the Runt's gone from us. He's dead. [*A mumble runs through the line, and the prisoners take off their caps in awed respect. But the* BOY's *cap remains on his bowed head, for he is paying no attention to what goes on around him. The* COOK *comes in at the left with a glass of water and a piece of bread held priestlike before him. The* CAPTAIN *looks up.*] Runt won't need his breakfast today, Greasy.

The COOK *stops and gazes impassively down at the body.*

Cook [*croakingly*]. Didn't think he'd make it.
Captain. The hell you say! Then why didn't you tell me he was getting sick in there?
Cook [*impassively*]. I did. Yesterday I said let's take him out—Cap'n, I said.
Captain. You fool! When did you feed him last?
Cook [*with his old man's toothless snicker*]. Feed him, Cap'n?
Captain. Well, give him his bread and water, then?

Cook. Yestiddy—the way the orders say. He cried a little bit and said he was gonna die in that box, and I told him I reckon he would.

Captain. Yeh, and the bastard did. [*He stands thinking a moment.*]

Cook. And he said you could bury him up on the railroad fill, 'cause he didn't have no home and no folks.

Captain. He told you that?

Cook. Yes, sir. And I said I didn't think you would on account of the law.

Captain. What law?

Cook. I dunno, Cap'n, just some law, I reckon.

Captain [*wrathfully*]. I'll bury him where I damn please.

Cook. Yes, sir, he said he wanted to be buried up there so he could hear the trains run at night. [*He turns and goes on out at the left, carrying the glass of water before him.*]

Captain [*to the* CONVICTS]. That's right, boys, you remember how Runt liked to hear the trains blow. What you say? Shall we take him up there and bury him? [*The* CONVICTS *look at him with dull cold eyes.*] Well, I don't blame you for feeling bad over it. I do myself. All right, we will. It's his last wish and the wishes of the dead are sacred. We all know that. [*Now standing over* RUNT *and looking sorrowfully down at him.*] You know me, Runt, I didn't have no grudge against you. It was the law said do it. [*With sudden blinding rage.*] Yeh, the law! [*Then after a moment, more quietly.*] All right, we'll put you away like you wanted. [*With a chuckle.*] But how the hell you gonna hear them trains running at night and your ears packed full of clay? [*Looking pensively beyond the* CONVICTS, *at the light flooding up the eastern sky.*] Yeh, we'll put him up there in a hole. And soon the crossties will be laid—the rails strung out, and the steel-driving men sink the spiks on down. And Runt won't care, will he? Runt won't care. [*Beginning to make his speech again, but this time more lyrically, more singsong, with something of a hedge priest's evangelical fervor.*] Night and day the great trains will be running over old runt's bones, running from the big cities up north to the Floridy pleasure grounds and back again, carrying the President, and his folks maybe, the big bosses from France and Rooshy, and the tobacco kings, pimps and bawds, the gamblers and the bridal couples and the congressmen, the lieutenants and the generals, all pulled along by the fiery iron horse with its one eye. "Hah, hah, hah," it snorts. "Get out of my way. You can harness down the earth and the sun and the moon but you can't put a check rein on me. 'Cause I'm bound for Key West, and I'm going to run right off the deep end and drown the whole God-damned load in the Atlantic Ocean." Yes, by Christ, and I hope it does! [*The* COOK *comes in at the left with a pail of water and a mop and begins to wash off the table. The* CAPTAIN *bends down and picks up* RUNT's *frail little form in his arms. He looks along the line of* CONVICTS *a moment and then steps toward* PEARLY GATES *who draws back with a shudder.*] All right, Pearly, take him. He's crapped all over himself and stinks like a skunk, but he can't hurt you now. [PEARLY GATES *still draws back, but the* CAPTAIN *drapes the crooked body over the huge Negro's shoulder. Pulling a whistle from his belt, he blows two sharp blasts, then barks out.*] R-i-g-h-t face! [*The* CONVICTS *obey, but the* BOY *stands staring at the ground as before.* CARELESS LOVE *pushes him around in line, and we can see the seat of his trousers showing sopping wet with blood.*] Forward, mar-ch! Hep-hep—— [*The* CONVICTS *start marching out at the right, the* SECOND GUARD *going before. The* CAPTAIN *calls back to the* FIRST GUARD.] Better fill out the death certificate.

First Guard [*dropping the butt of his gun lazily to the ground*]. Regular form?

Captain. Hep-hep—— Hell, yes! [*And now* PEARLY GATES, *the last of the line, goes out, carrying* RUNT's *dead body like a sack on his shoulder. The* CAPTAIN *follows after, his heavy boots marching in step, and his voice calling rhythmically.*] Hep-hep-hep!

The COOK *goes on mopping the table. The* FIRST GUARD *yawns and stretches his arms, gun and all, above his head.*

 First Guard. Well, I better get busy on that certificate—old Doc Jones might want it today. Uhm—— And then some sleep. [*He starts out at the left rear, then stops and calls back.*] What was Runt's name?
 Cook [*still intent on his scrubbing*]. Just Runt, I reckon.
 First Guard. I remember now—Johnson. [*With a snicker.*] Vanderbilt Johnson. What you reckon he died of? [*The* COOK *makes no answer.*] Heart failure maybe—— [*With certainty.*] Sure—his heart give out on him—weak heart—natural causes. Hum. [*Looking off toward the east.*] Golly, today's gonna be another scorcher.

He goes on out. The COOK *finishes scouring the table, then brings his utensils over to the sweatbox. Dipping his mop into the pail, he starts cleaning out the fouled insides. In the distance the faint sound of the* CAPTAIN's *"Hep-hep" is heard dying away.*

Cook [*suddenly beginning to sing in a flat froglike voice as he works*].

Land where—my fathers died,
Land of—the pilgrims' pride——

And now peering up over the rim of the world at the back comes the smiling face of the sun.

CURTAIN

Ellen Glasgow
(1873–1945)

The protagonists of Ellen Glasgow's most memorable novels—demonstrating as they do a dogged individual determination in conflict with social pressures—are in many ways autobiographical expressions of her own struggles. Born to a wealthy Richmond, Virginia, family, Glasgow was privately tutored because of ill health, receiving much of her education from the classics in her father's library and being guided in her reading by an attentive brother-in-law. When she was eighteen, she secretly wrote a novel but destroyed it because she knew her family would consider fiction writing an improper activity for a young Southern woman. After her mother's death in 1893, she began more actively to pursue a writing career, and she anonymously published her first novel, *The Descendant*, in 1897. Though she went on to publish eighteen more novels, critics have tended to identify *The Battle Ground* (1902), *Barren Ground* (1925), *Vein of Iron* (1935), and *In This Our Life* (1941), which won a Pulitzer Prize, as her strongest efforts.

In these novels, Glasgow creates strong women characters who struggle to establish themselves in a society dominated by outmoded opinions and manners. Survivors of a dying way of life, these women draw on innate wellsprings of self-reliance and stoic endurance, a "vein of iron" that enables them to win a place for themselves in an increasingly impersonal modern world. Glasgow also wrote an autobiography, *The Woman Within* (1954), which recounted many of the difficulties she experienced as a woman writer but which was withheld from publication at her request until after her death. Although her women characters are not always especially sympathetic, they have a psychological depth unmatched in American fiction before her time.

from *The Battle-Ground*

Chapter I. The Ragged Army

The brigade had halted to gather rations in a corn-field beside the road, and Dan, lying with his head in the shadow of a bush of sumach, hungrily regarded the "roasting ears" that Pinetop had just rolled in the ashes. A malarial fever, which he had contracted in the swamps of the Chickahominy, had wasted his vitality until he had begun to look like the mere shadow of himself; gaunt, unwashed, hollow-eyed, yet wearing his torn gray jacket and brimless cap as jauntily as he had once worn his embroidered waistcoats. His hand trembled as he reached out for his share of the green corn; but weakened as he was by sickness and starvation, the defiant humour shone all the clearer in is eyes. He had still the heart for a whistle, Bland had said last night, looking at him a little wistfully.

As he lay there, with the dusty sumach shrub above him, he saw the ragged army pushing on into the turnpike that led to Maryland. Lean, sun-scorched, half-clothed, dropping its stragglers like leaves by the roadside, marching in borrowed rags, and fighting with the weapons of its enemies, dirty, fevered, choking with the hot dust of the turnpike—it still pressed onward, bending like a blade beneath the hand of Lee. For this army of the sick, fighting slow agues, old wounds, and the sharp diseases that follow on green food, was becoming suddenly an army of invasion. The road led into Maryland, and the brigades swept into it, jesting like schoolboys on a frolic.

Dan, stretched exhausted beside the road, ate his ear of corn, and idly watched the regiment that was marching by—marching, not with the even tread of regular troops, but with scattered ranks and broken column, each man limping in worn-out shoes, at his own pace. They were not fancy soldiers, these men, he felt as he looked after them. They were not imposing upon the road, but when their chance came to fight, they would be very sure to take it. Here and there, a man still carried his old squirrel musket, with a rusted skillet handle stuck into the barrel; but when before many days the skillet would be withdrawn, the load might be relied upon to wing straight home a little later. On wet nights, those muskets would stand upright upon their bayonets, with muzzles in the earth, while the rain dripped off; and on dry days, they would carry aloft the full property of the mess, which had dwindled to a frying-pan and an old quart cup. Though seldom cleaned, they were always fit for service—or if they went foul, what was easier than to pick up a less trusty one upon the field. On the other side hung the blankets, tied at the ends and worn like a sling from the left shoulder. The haversack was gone, and with it the knapsack and the overcoat. When a man wanted a change of linen, he knelt down and washed his single shirt in the brook, sitting in the sun while it dried upon the bank. If it was long in drying, he put it on, wet as it was, and ran ahead to fall in with his company. Where the discipline was easy, each infantryman might become, in case of need, his own commissary.

Dan finished his corn, threw the husks over his head, and sat up, looking idly at the irregular ranks. He was tired and ill, and after a short rest it seemed all the harder to get up and take the road again. As he sat there he began to bandy words with the sergeant of a Maryland regiment that was passing.

"Hello! what brigade?" called the sergeant in friendly tones. He looked fat and well fed, and Dan felt this to be good ground for resentment.

"General Straggler's brigade, but it's none of your business," he promptly retorted.

"General Straggler has a pretty God-forsaken crew," taunted the sergeant, looking back as he stepped on briskly. "I've seen his regiments lining the road clear up from Chantilly."

"If you'd kept your fat eyes open at Manassas the other day, you'd have seen them lining the battle-field as well," Dan pursued pleasantly, chewing a long green blade of corn. "Old Stonewall saw them, I'll be bound. If General Straggler didn't win that battle I'd like to know who did."

"Oh, shucks!" responded the sergeant, and was out of hearing.

The regiment passed by and another took its place. "Was that General Lee you were yelling at down there, boys?" Dan inquired politely, smiling the smile of a man who sits by the roadside and sees another sweating on the march.

"Naw, that warn't Marse Robert," replied a private, limping with bare feet over the border of dried grass. "'Twas a blamed, blank, bottomless well, that's what 'twas. I let my canteen down on a string and it never came back no mo'."

Dan lowered is eyes, and regarded critically the tattered banner of the regiment, covered with the names of the battles over which it had hung unfurled. "Tennessee, aren't you?" he asked, following the flag.

The private shook his head, and stooped to remove a pebble from between his toes. "Naw, we ain't from Tennessee," he drawled. "We've had the measles."

"You show it, by Jove," Dan said, laughing. "Step quickly, if you please—this is the cleanest brigade in the army."

"Huh!" the private exclaimed, eyeing them with contempt. "You look like it, don't you, sonny? Why, I'd ketch the mumps jest to look at sech a set o' rag-a-muffins!"

He went on, still grunting, while Dan rose to his feet and slung his blanket from his shoulder. "Look here, does anybody know where we're going anyway?" he asked of the blue sky.

"I seed General Jackson about two miles up," replied a passing countryman, who had led his horse into the corn-field. "Whoopee! he was going at a God-a'mighty pace, I tell you. If he keeps that up he'll be over the Potomac before sunset."

"Then we are going into Maryland!" Jack Powell cried, jumping to his feet. "Hurrah for Maryland! We're going into Maryland, God bless her!"

The shouts passed down the road, and the Maryland regiment in front sent back three rousing cheers.

"By Jove, I hope I'll find some shoes there," Dan said, shaking the sand from his ragged boots, and twisting the shreds of his socks about his feet. "I've had to punch holes in my soles and lace them with shoe strings to the upper leather, or they'd have dropped off long ago."

"Well, I'll begin by making love to a seamstress when I've over the Potomac," Welch returned, getting upon his feet. "I'm in need of a couple of patches."

"You make love! You!" Jack Powell roared. "Why, you're the kind of thing they set up in Maryland to keep the crows away. Now, if it were Beau, there, I see some sense in it—for, I'll be bound, he's slain more hearts than Yankees in this campaign. The women always drain out their last drop of buttermilk when he goes on a forage."

"Oh, I don't set up to be a popinjay," Welch retorted witheringly.

"Popinjay, the devil!" Dan scowled, "who's a popinjay?"

"Wall, I'd like a pair of good stout breeches," Pinetop interposed. "I've been backin' up agin the fence when I seed a lady comin' for the last three weeks, an' whenever I set down, I'm feared to git up agin. What with all the other things, the Yankees, and the chills, and the measles, it's downright hard on a man to have to be a-feared of his own breeches."

Dan looked round with sympathy. "That's true; it's a shame," he admitted smiling. "Look here, boys, has anybody got an extra pair of breeches?"

A howl of derision went up from the regiment as it fell into ranks.

"Has anybody got a few grape-leaves to spare?" demanded a high chorus.

"Oh shut up," Dan responded promptly. "Come on, Pinetop, we'll clothe ourselves to-morrow."

The brigade formed and swung off rapidly along the road, where the dust lay like a gauze over the sunshine. At the end of a mile somebody stopped and cried out excitedly: "Look here, boys, the persimmons on that tree over thar are gittin' 'mos fit to eat. I can see 'em turnin'," and with the words the column scattered like chaff across the field. But the first man to reach the tree came back with a wry face, and fell to swearing at "the darn fool who could eat persimmons before frost."

"Thar's a tree in my yard that gits ripe about September," Pinetop remarked, as he returned dejectedly across the waste. "Ma she begins to dry 'em 'fo' the frost sets in."

"Oh, well, we'll get a square meal in the morning," Dan responded, growing cheerful as he dreamed of hospitable Maryland.

Some hours later, in the warm dusk, they went into bivouac among the trees, and, in a little while, the campfires made a red glow upon the twilight.

Pinetop, with a wooden bucket on his arm, had plunged off in search of water, and Dan and Jack Powell were sent, in the interests of the mess, to forage through the surrounding country.

"There's a fat farmer about ten miles down, I saw him," remarked a lazy smoker, by way of polite suggestion.

"Ten miles? Well, of all the confounded impudence," Jack retorted, as he strolled off with Dan into the darkness.

For a time they walked in silence, depressed by hunger and the exhaustion of the march; then Dan broke into a whistle, and presently they found themselves walking in step with the merry air.

"Where are your thoughts, Beau?" Jack asked suddenly, turning to look at him by the faint starlight.

Dan's whistle stopped abruptly.

"On a dish of fried chicken and a pot of coffee," he replied at once.

"What's become of the waffles?" Jack demanded indignantly. "I say, old man, do you remember the sinful waste on those blessed Christmas Eves at Chericoke? I've been trying to count the different kinds of meat—roast beef, roast pig, roast goose, roast turkey—"

"Hold your tongue, won't you?"

"Well, I was thinking that if I ever reach home alive I'll deliver the Major a lecture on his extravagance."

"It isn't the Major; it's grandma," Dan groaned.

"Oh, that queen among women!" Jack exclaimed fervently; "but the wines are the Major's, I reckon,—it seems to me I recall some port of which he was vastly proud."

Dan delivered a blow that sent Jack on his knees in the stubble of an old corn-field.

"If you want to make me eat you, you're going straight about it," he declared.

"Look out!" cried Jack, struggling to his feet, "there's a light over there among the trees," and they walked on briskly up a narrow country lane which led, after several turnings, to a large frame house well hidden from the road.

In the doorway a woman was standing, with a lamp held above her head, and when she saw them she gave a little breathless call.

"Is that you, Jim?"

Dan went up the steps and stood, cap in hand, before her. The lamplight fell upon his ragged clothes and upon his pallid face with its strong high-bred lines of mouth and chin.

"I thought you were my husband," the woman said, blushing at her mistake. "If you want food you are welcome to the little that I have—it is very little." She led the way into the house, and motioned, with a pitiable gesture, to a table that was spread in the centre of the sitting-room.

"Will you sit down?" she asked, and at the words, a child in the corner of the room set up a frightened cry.

"It's my supper—I want my supper," wailed the child.

"Hush, dear," said the woman, "they are our soldiers."

"Our soldiers," the child repeated, staring, with its thumb in its mouth and the tear-drops on its cheeks.

For an instant Dan looked at them as they stood there, the woman holding the child in her arms, and biting her thin lips from which hunger had drained all the red. There was scant food on the table, and as his gaze went back to it, it seemed to him that, for the first time, he grasped the full meaning of a war for the people of the soil. This was the real war; not the waving banners, not the bayonets, not the fighting in the ranks.

His eyes were on the woman, and she smiled as all women did when he looked at them.

"My dear madam, you have mistaken our purpose—we are not as hungry as we look," he said, bowing in his ragged jacket. "We were sent merely to ask you if you were in need of a guard for your smokehouse. My Colonel hopes that you have not suffered at our hands."

"There is nothing left," replied the woman mystified, yet relieved. "There is nothing to guard except the children and myself, and we are safe, I think. Your colonel is very kind—I thank him"; and as they went out she lighted them with her lamp from the front steps.

An hour later they returned to camp with aching limbs and empty hands.

"There's nothing above ground," they reported, flinging themselves beside the fire, though the night was warm. "We've scoured the whole country and the Federals have licked it as clean as a plate before us. Bless my soul! what's that I smell? Is this heaven, boys?"

"Licked it clean, have they?" jeered the mess. "Well, they left a sheep anyhow loose somewhere. Beau's darky hadn't gone a hundred yards before he found one."

"Big Abel? You don't say so?" whistled Dan, in astonishment, regarding the mutton suspended on ramrods above the coals.

"Well, suh, 'twuz jes' like dis," explained Big Abel, poking the roast with a small stick. "I know I ain' got a bit a bus'ness ter shoot dat ar sheep wid my ole gun, but de sheep she ain' got no better bus'ness strayin' roun' loose needer. She sutney wuz a dang'ous sheep, dat she wuz. I 'uz jes' a-bleeged ter put a bullet in her haid er she'd er hed my blood sho'."

As the shout went up, he divided the legs of mutton into shares and went off to eat his own on the dark edge of the woods.

A little later he came back to hang Dan's cap and jacket on the branches of a young pine-tree. When he had arranged them with elaborate care, he raked a bed of tags together, and covered them with an army blanket stamped in the centre with the half obliterated letters U. S.

"That's a good boy, Big Abel, go to sleep," said Dan, flinging himself down on the pine-tag bed. "Strange how much spirit a sheep can put into a man. I wouldn't run now if I saw Pope's whole army coming."

Turning over, he lay sleepily gazing into the blue dusk where the campfires were slowly dying down. Around him he heard the subdued murmur of the mess, deep and full, though rising now and then into a clearer burst of laughter. The men were smoking their brier-root pipes about the embers, leaning against the dim bodies of the pines, while they discussed the incidents of the march with the unconquerable humour of the Confederate soldier. Somebody had a fresh joke on the quartermaster, and everybody hoped great things of the campaign into Maryland.

"I pray it may bring me a pair of shoes," Dan muttered as he dropped off into slumber.

The next day, with bands playing "Maryland, My Maryland," and the Southern Cross taking the September wind, the ragged army waded the Potomac, and passed into other fields.

Olive Tilford Dargan

(1869–1968)

Olive Tilford Dargan was born on January 11, 1869, to a pair of Kentucky schoolteachers, and she herself began teaching in a one-room Missouri school when she was only fourteen. At seventeen she won a scholarship to Peabody College in Tennessee and, after graduating two years later, taught for five years in Missouri and Texas. In 1893 she enrolled at Radcliffe College in Boston, where she met Pegram Dargan, a poet from South Carolina who was attending Harvard. They were married in 1898 and moved to New York City, where Olive Dargan began her literary career by publishing a series of verse dramas. In 1906, the Dargans bought a farm in Swain County, North Carolina, but they also began traveling abroad, and Olive Dargan published *The Welsh Pony*, a nonfiction work, and a poetry collection, *Path Flower and Other Verses*, while in England. In 1914, after the drowning death of her husband, she returned to the farm in North Carolina and remained there for the next nine years.

Beginning in 1925, after a move to Asheville, North Carolina, Dargan published a series of works under the pseudonym Fielding Burke. First to appear was *Highland Annals*, a short-story collection, followed by three novels, *Call Home the Heart* (1932), *A Stone Came Rolling* (1935), and *Sons of the Stranger* (1947). All three reflected Dargan's interest in the proletarian movement; the first two are set during the 1929 mill strike in Gastonia, North Carolina, and the third revolves around a coal mine strike in Colorado. *Call Home the Heart*, considered by most critics to be Dargan's best work, portrays a lead character, Ish, caught between love and political involvement, who finally finds peace in a retreat to a tranquil mountain life. Dargan published another collection of poetry and another short-story collection before her death in 1968.

from *Call Home the Heart*

Chapter I. Her Family

Before she was seven, Ishma, the youngest child of Marshall and Laviny Waycaster, had joined the class of burden-bearers. By the time she was thirteen there was little rest for her except on Sunday. That day she kept for herself on the hill-tops. This was after Granny Starkweather's bright, detaining spirit had gone forever from the house. Six days of the week Ishma was merely a family possession, giving herself so effectually that no one suspected she was giving; so entirely that she did not suspect it herself. But channels of being that open so readily outward must, more than those whose gates are tight and rusty, protect their reservoir. With no intuitive hint that she had chanced upon a law of salvation, Ishma found a way of replenishing her fount.

On Sunday morning she would be up early, put some scraps of food into a paper bag, and set off for the high woods. Up there no one came. The travelled trails lay lower down, most of them intersecting at her mother's cabin, making it a popular Sunday rendezvous. All who passed felt that they must stop for friendly speech, if they didn't stay to dinner. But too often they stayed.

High on Lame Goat Ridge Ishma had earth to herself. This was the eastern and highest part of Dancer Ridge, the long line that meandered and dipped and curved between Dancer and Wimble counties. The top of Lame Goat gleamed bonily with cliffs and rocks, but the sides were thickly wooded, enclosing her in a world of tumbling waters and wild odors. In summer there were strange flowers trembling higher than her head, and birds innumerable; creepers, warblers of all kinds; thrushes, chewinks, wood-doves; and sometimes an unknown visitor with a cry thrillingly new. If she went far enough around the mountain on the north-east side she would come to a "bench" big enough for the dashing stream to gather itself into a great pool before creeping to the edge of the bench and shooting a thousand silver arrows downward. She could sit by this pool for hours without wanting to move, feeling within herself a leisurely flow of activity that made her both contented and eager. The fount was filling up.

Her mother, Laviny, had a distorted sense of justice, but could be fair at times, and never remonstrated with Ishma over her Sunday defection. But once when the child came rushing in towards night, saying she had been to Moonfeather Falls, her mother grumbled. "Fer the land's sake, Ishmalee, the strenth ort to be dreened out o' ye, cruisin' so fur, but you look like you could heave a hoss."

Bainie put in a complaint, since Laviny had opened the way. She was Ishma's older sister, and the wearily incompetent mother of four small children. "You shore got out o' work today. I never seen so many folks on the mountain, an' they must 'a' left home 'fore breakfast, measurin' up the way they et. The baby's ailin' too, an' cried till I didn't have no sense."

It was easy to arouse remorse in Ishma's gay heart. "I'm sorry, Bainie," she said. "Maybe I'll stay at home next Sunday."

"Maybe! You know you won't, less'n it's rainin' go-devils! An' if it is, there won't be no company to wait on. I ain't got the pull of a tow string, an' the wash-tub set fer tomorr'."

"I'll do ever' bit of it, Bainie. You needn't wet your hands!"

Bainie knew the child would keep her promise, and her stream of complaint changed somewhat to concern. "Some o' these days you're goin' to plop yer foot down on a rattler an' get bit. You'll lay up there in the woods an' swell till you bust. I don't know what mommie's thinkin' about to let you traipse off thataway." And this set Ishma to laughing again.

Sometimes she would come home late enough to find the tired family in bed. Slipping to the kitchen, she would clean up the supper things, always left for her, then creep into her own little bed which she had made out of split rails and rabbit wire discarded by Jim Wishart, Bainie's husband. This was her happy alternative to sleeping with three of her sister's younguns. A thick layer of "coker" sacks, rescued from the mud around the barn and washed clean in the branch, made her mattress. Over the bed, as a final cover, was spread the pride of her life; a quilt made fifty years before by Granny Starkweather's own hands. Granny had taken it from her hog-hide trunk and given it to Ishma on her tenth birthday. It tinged with glamour the moment of going to bed and the time of getting up. Bainie had never received such a present from grandmother. "She's dauncey an' she's sloven," said candid Granny. "Ishma is clean always, an' she's well always. She'll keep that quilt sweet. It'll last her fer weddin' bed."

The old lady would have sighed then if she hadn't been so determinedly opposed to the sign of dejection. So many marriages and dowerings in her life had left her little to give. Seventeen sons and daughters, going out with this keepsake and that; and here in a bare house was Ishma, whom she would have loved to shower with treasures. Not even John Stark, her wonderful youngest, had been more dear to her than this child who had so surprisingly filled her heart at the end of her time.

A bare house it was; struggling bravely, with crumbling tenacity, to shelter the descendants of Frady Starkweather, its pioneer builder, For ninety odd years the mountain winds had tested their teeth on its big hewn logs. They had held together because so many of them were of winter-cut oak and chestnut. Time and sun had turned the oak to iron, and dried the chestnut to a light, aluminum staunchness. But here and there were logs of poplar, dustily dropping away from the chinking, and yearly widening the cracks in the walls. "No use tackin' boards over doty poplar," Jim Wishart excused himself. "The nails 'll ease right out."

Frady, the great-grandfather of Ishma, had been a young man of twenty, and only two weeks married, when he climbed the unharried slope of Cloudy Knob mountain, his bride and his dog loyal at his heels, and built himself a one-room dwelling with as proud a precision as he could attain with a broad-axe, a giant auger, and huge locust pins. As his family grew, so did his house. Finally there were three rooms, each with its large door and latchstring, opening on the porch that fronted the building its full length, making of it a home with no hint of the decrepit days when again it would be a cabin. The big room on the west became the kitchen, the bigger room toward the east was full of beds, and the middle room evolved into a living centre for the household. This room had windows. Frady put them in for his second wife, so that the light would fall on her loom. Nancy, the first little bride, had succumbed after twenty years of pioneering and childbearing. Sarah, his second—Ishma's own Granny Stark—was a widow of forty when she married handsome Frady. She was trim, slim, wise and witty, with a talent for housewifery that she kept burnished as her own tea-cups. The inadequate fumblings of his gentle first mate had been accepted by Frady as the way of a wife, and it was some time before his astonishment at the competence of Sarah relaxed into surety.

When this desirable woman had been only fifteen, but weirdly mature, she had married a widower with nine children. She wanted a family, she said, and her "druthers" were for a ready-made one. The husband and father died, and she carried on the farm work with more success than masculine direction had attained. When the last of her nine step-children married, she handed over to him her comfortable valley home, and joined Frady on Cloudy Knob, where she found plentiful material, including seven new "steps," for exploiting her restless talent. But Frady himself was her chief reason for ascending the mountain. The union was a love-match, though neither confessed it until after the birth of their son, John. With all of Sarah's preference for ready-mades, and her long-escape from maternity, after a year with Frady she became a dubiously delighted mother. Then their love became shyly communicative. Frady had paid in none of his good looks for the privilege of living so long on the fringe of a wilderness, and Sarah was as piquant as the air of early morning after a sun-drenched frost. This spicy freshness was still with her when she died sixty-seven years later, at the age of one hundred and seven. In her last years she liked to talk of the seventeen sons and daughters she had so earnestly mothered, married, and set on their way. But only John was the actual fruit of her flesh.

This unexpected son of Frady and Sarah became a very promising six-foot youth who married before he was twenty. The following winter was so cold that not even old Gaby Jones ventured to say that he had seen the earth more deeply frozen. "It would shiver the soil to Chiny, an' be a power o' help to next year's crops," the people said, encouraging themselves. But silence fell on them after pneumonia began to pick off its victims. John Starkweather and his young wife, Lindy, were both stricken.

"Too much winter," said the old doctor who came out mule-back from Carson. Mrs. Frady tried to mention the new fresh-air cure, but was suppressed with as much ire as anybody dared exhibit before her. Under the old doctor's stern eyes and direction, the two invalids were placed in the middle room, which was smaller than the others and could be kept sweating warm with a big fire in the fire-place. The windows must be clamped down, and the door opened only for hurried passage.

Lindy's baby was barely a month old. The youthful mother, further weakened by the heat of the room and heavy air, soon gave up her life. Young John's six feet of vitality surrendered to ignorance and grief, and he followed her within twenty-four hours. It did not lessen his mother's sorrow to hear the doctor say, "We have all done our best, my good woman. Let us remember that it is the Lord who has sent this bitter season upon us, and his wisdom is infinite." For the first time in her life she had failed to follow her own lead, and she had forty-seven years of regret before her.

Laviny, the month-old baby of John and Lindy, was left to the care of her grandmother. She grew up quickly, and at seventeen was a slender, sharp-tongued young woman, pretty enough and pert enough to bring the roving feet of Marshall Waycaster to a standstill. Little was known of Marshall except that he was a "roamin' feller" whom everybody liked. Frady was not there to start an investigation. He had died a year before his son. Grandmother didn't start anything, because she liked Waycaster just as he stood in his boots, and felt that perky little Laviny was in luck to get him. "When Laviny wizens up," she had said, "there'll not be much left of her but her tongue." A true prediction. The girl's beauty was very different from her grandmother's which remained vivid long after Laviny's was an incredible memory. Ishma could remember hearing the old lady counsel Laviny after a burst of temper, "Go ahead, my gal. If you make yer face any sharper you can use it to cut yer kindlin' with."

Ishma had the joy of knowing that she pleased grandmother. Children had come rapidly to Marshall and Laviny. Six had preceded Ishma, but only two had lived, Bainie and Steve. Granny detected in the last little girl a strong resemblance to herself. "What ain't me is Marshall," she reflected. "That ought to be a fair mix."

Ishma learned to read by stumbling through the Bible under the old lady's eye, beginning with the chapters that Granny knew by heart. The attentive Frady had read them to her through many rainy day hours, as she sat industrious or idle at her loom, and from memory she could correct the little girl almost to the letter. But Ishma was easily a scholar, and Granny, to her zest and delight, soon found herself led on to less familiar chapters. In fair recompense, she made the child her companion on out-door ventures, and so it was that Ishma learned the way of a wind on the mountain, of water around a rock, of a goat on Devil's Spur.

The last three years of Sarah Starkweather's life she had a "burnin' under her feet" that made walking painful. When she insisted on her periodical visits to her neighbors two and three miles distant she sat in a split-bottomed chair and was carried by any two young men who happened to be available. One on each side, they grasped the rounds of her chair and bore her smoothly up ridge and down, in cove and out, to her chosen destination. Anyone picked for this service was inwardly proud of the honor, but it was the habit of the boys so conscripted to complain about it among themselves. "Come jedgment, Granny Stark 'll send Gabe about his business an' go livin' right on," they said. "She ain't ever meanin' to die."

After grandmother stopped "cruisin' the cliffs" because of her burning feet, Ishma had little time for the low seat at her side. Marshall Waycaster had proved to be a willing worker, but no farmer. "It would be better," said Granny, "if he didn't go at things so hard, sence he goes at 'em back'ards." And she rather encouraged his whistling, dancing, and swapping jokes with the countryside. But Marshall, in the pride of his dancing years, was stricken with paralysis. He who had insisted on an upright position almost day and night throughout his life, spent his last three years supine and speechless.

Laviny's boy, Steve, who, like his grandfather John, was six feet tall at the age of fifteen, ran away in his sixteenth year, and had no trouble in joining the army. Bainie's husband, "coon-huntin' Jim Wishart," was pleased to become the head of the house and master of Cloudy Knob farm, but he saw to it that his honors in no way laid extra duties upon him. Every year his wife presented the tolerant household with a new baby; and every year saw the family scale of living running lower. Granny could stand no longer at her wheel; no longer could she sit treadling at her loom; no more was her voice heard in the big kitchen where she had so long and capably presided over the filling of cans, kraut-tubs and bean-barrels. More and more the family became dependent on Gaffney's store in Beebread, at the foot of the mountain.

Ishma was thirteen when Granny Stark died. The death of her much loved father three years before had been a more bearable sorrow. Hundreds of valley folks climbed the mountain to see the old lady carried to the family graveyard where Frady Starkweather lay, three coves east of the dwelling. Long-faced and conspicuous among the mourners, were the boys who had been so often commandeered to bear Granny Stark's chair.

Ishma had heard that the spirit of the dead sometimes hovered over the grave of its body on the first night after burial, and that night she slipped out of bed to lie in the graveyard with her head on the fresh dirt. But Granny gave no sign. Laviny was awake when the girl came in at dawn, her cheeks wet with tears of disappointment, and later in the day she took her to the spring-house and heckled her until Ishma told where she had been. Then Laviny looked strangely on her daughter, and begged her, for God's sake, never to tell another soul. Of all afflictions that could come to a mountain mother the worst was that of having a child who was not right in the head. It had been hinted that Mrs. Frady had conversed from her early years with invisible counsellors; but this rumor inspired awe rather than fear or aversion. Sarah Starkweather had been superb enough to carry off anything. Poor Laviny couldn't be so sure about her daughter. Sometimes her secret worry would break out in an irritable desire to punish Ishma, but she couldn't forget a scene at Granny's bedside when the dying old lady commanded her never to drop a heavy hand on that child. "If you do, Laviny, I'll not lay quiet, an' you needn't expect it. I'll be hoverin' right over ye." This was merely a threat, for Granny certainly expected to go to Heaven and stay there, but the warning was effective with Laviny.

"In the first place," thought the mother, "the gal knows too much. That sort always dies, er goes wrong, give 'em time." She would slant her eyes disapprovingly on Ishma sitting down to teach the younguns their lessons when she'd never poked her head inside of a school-house. Ever since Sam, Bainie's oldest, had started to school in Beebread, on the outward side of the mountain where the railroad and the new highway ran, Ishma had taken charge of his "home-work." She studied his books carefully, and kept with him through the first, second, third and fourth grades. When he reached the fifth he became stubborn and she had to pull him through. Vainly she drilled him in speech-mending ways according to the rules and examples laid down in his language book. Figures he could endure, and geography was easy, but he couldn't see any sense in learning to talk a new way when the old was just as good. "Pop an' mom an' all the neighbors got along with it." With Ishma's help he memorized enough of the book-stuff to pass examinations, because, he reasoned, he was on the junior basket-ball team, and he'd rather go to school than work anyway, and he hated to let Ish down, but he was going to quit and get a man's job in Carson before long. He was getting too big to wear rags. He wanted *clo's*. The last time that welfare woman frowned at his split shoes he had wanted to sock her one.

Ishma did not share Sam's aversion to the language book. It was a way to power and larger life. She sometimes carried it with her on her days in the woods, and studied the fascinating pages over which Sam would be led the following week. But she found it was pleasanter to do this on her way out to the ridge, stopping to rest for an hour or so. The book was not so entrancing on the home-coming road when her mind was full of the joys of the day.

Her reading was not confined to school matter. She had, indeed, books of her own. In the hog-hide trunk which Granny had left to her she found three volumes that had belonged to Frady. Granny had kept them concealed from the ravaging hands of Bainie's children, who held nothing too good for destruction except the big book on the lam-table, which they thought had power in itself to avenge any disrespect. One of Ishma's inherited volumes was *Pilgrim's Progress*, inscribed with the name of Frady's father and a town in Virginia. Evidently it had trekked with him across Hickory Nut Gap to the wilderness. She read this faithfully, though she thought that the pilgrim was rather stupid. Another volume was Jeremy Taylor's *Holy Living and Dying*, which she liked to read aloud to herself, listening to the words running smoothly along like an endless brook. When they were big and difficult she practiced them until she could read without tripping. And it was true that she was more concerned with her performance than with the matter she fed on. A third book was a thick, small, calf-bound volume in very fine print, entitled *Alonzo and Melissa*. This was a novel, romantic beyond any modern daring, and full of thrills as breathtaking as could be devised out of such material as an underground tunnel, inhuman parent, and the resurrection of the heroine after the hero had wept hours away on her grave. Ishma read it with abandon; incredulous, but grateful for the debauch.

Under the three books when discovered by her, lay something that looked like old magazines with the backs off. Unpromising, but the greatest find of all; a history of England, most bravely illustrated, and told as if the listeners were all men of great adventure and the teller must prove worthy of his famous audience. It had been printed serially, and the missing numbers made aching gaps in Ishma's thrilling advance.

Besides these treasures there was a collection of recipes, which Granny could not read but which she had carefully preserved in the handwriting of numerous and long dead friends. She had been a notable cook, and Frady, under her leading, had become a notable provider. He could bring a ham into her kitchen, a ham cured by himself in hickory ashes, wash it carefully and leave it, knowing it would be boiled in cider, tenderly skinned and given a new covering of baked sugar with just the right number of cloves. He liked to help her can tomatoes. She boiled the sun in them, he said. Long before the Mexican culinary invasion, Granny would cook her tomatoes down to a crimson puree and add a sprinkling of fresh, chipped peppers before applying the tin covers and sealing-wax. In her Frady period, of course, she had the best covers and rubbers obtainable, and in her garden grew every kind of seasoning known to her day. Nothing remained of it but one basil bush in the back yard. Instead of the foresighted Frady with his pungent cellar and full barn, they had Jim, whose idea of providing was limited to fat-back, corn-pone and coffee. Supplementary dishes were entirely the concern of the women, if they cared about such inessentials.

Ishma already knew many of the recipes which she found in the collection, for her grandmother had often consigned them to her verbally; but the books were a different matter. In her struggle with difficult words, whose meaning she had to guess, she received unexpected help. Sam brought home a dictionary which his teacher had compelled him to buy. It had consumed his hoard for cartridges, having cost the price of five 'possum skins. The imposition made him growl and swear, and kick the book into the yard. Ishma picked it up, and finding it so helpful, she paid Sam for it and added it to her treasures.

In time the lock to the trunk was enterprisingly broken, and after that her books gradually disappeared under the brigand hands of Bainie's brats. The English history with its brave pictures was the first seized upon and the first to pass away. Ishma forgave and forgot. Her hunger for reading was appeased from another source. One of the teachers in Sam's school wandered up the mountain. He had thought of staying over Sunday at the farm-house, but revised his plan after casting his eye over sleeping probabilities and sharing a supper served for the entire family, in interlapping relays, with seven pie-tins, two cups and saucers, a few pint cups, three earthen bowls, a broken pitcher, and here and there a knife, fork, or spoon. The food was palatable, for Ishma had cooked it; but his eye became dreamy and a little later he filtered down to Beebread. He was a nice young man, and had been horrified to learn that Ishma had never been in school.

"How could she go?" asked Laviny, virtuously. "She's took keer o' Baine's younguns since she's five year old."

"But the law—" began the young teacher.

"The law don't come up the mountain an' do our work. When it does, I'll send 'em all. Ishmalee don't need larnin'. She's got too much sense now. If she had any more she'd be top-heavy. She'd teeter tryin' to walk."

"The other children go."

"Yes, that's why Ishmalee stays at home mostly. So they can go. They need ever'thing they can git, looks like. An' let me tell you, young man, it's too late to go hornet-huntin' over Ishmalee. She's past fourteen."

The teacher went away with regret brooding in his eyes. That was his last year at Beebread; but for three years thereafter Ishma received a monthly magazine, *Woman at Home*, which may have been an unworthy substitute for the reflecting Jeremy, or the tale of daring souls building the greatest of modern empires, one's own always excepted; but it opened gates to a way of living so enticing in comfort, so engaging in form, so ravishing in color, that it seemed nothing short of celestial to Ishma. Those doorways, those halls, those vistas of bed-rooms, those shimmering bath-rooms, those gleaming floors, those radiant nooks and corners of beauty, with the graceful beings from another world, curving, bending, smiling, always smiling! They took her breath. But the most miraculous of all were the laden eating-tables. Surely they were waiting for angels to sit down at them! Ishma clutched the page to her heart. "He has prepared me a table in the midst of mine enemies," she whispered, with daring misapplication. Sometimes the angels were visible. True they were usually twirling or smoking cigarettes, but how gracefully they did it! How clear-minded and clean of life they looked! Their souls must be as pure as their bodies or they couldn't shine like that.

Once little Nettie came from school trying to tell how a teacher had taken some of the older girls into the 'mestic science room and set a table, then made them do it all over after her. From Nettie's report, Ishma thought that the set-out must have been a very drab affair.

There were times in the woods when she practiced arraying such a table as was in her heart. With a stick she would trace an oval on a bit of mossy ground and mark the line carefully with tiny fern-leaves. Her service set would be of galax. Flattened, the leaves were plates, and she could have them in any size; but she could twist them and pin them with their own stems into cups, bowls, dishes of whatever kind she wished. The food would be made of wild-flower petals and the tender rosy and red-hued baby oaks and maples that had pushed a few inches above the ground.

One Sunday she took her pet rabbit, Dock, with her, a cabbage leaf in her pocket for his dinner. She intended to lose him somewhere, because he had been bothering Laviny's garden. Up by the big pool she prepared her table and looked at it with satisfaction. Never before had she made one so pretty. Dock was invited to be a guest, and very willingly nibbled the cabbage leaf. Ishma was pleased and tired. The night before, neighbors had gathered in for singing and she had been up late. Leaning back against a tree whose roots had been her chair, she slept for a moment. When she opened her eyes a strange little bird was keeping Dock company. It had eaten all of the berries in a galax bowl, and with a whirr of thanks to Dock, flew away. Ishma never set her table again. Nothing nicer than that could happen, she thought.

At eighteen she was tall and strong, with no droop of the shoulders to hint of the burden they carried. Nothing in her face or figure suggested the wiry little Laviny. She had Granny's broad forehead and delicate eyebrows that were almost horizontal until their sudden ending in a down-flung curve. The eyes, too, of twilight grey were direct from grandmother Starkweather. No day had so worn on Granny, guiding the lives of her two families, that her eyes could not keep faith with solitude and deep woods. Ishma's face was open, true to sun and sweet air, but her eyes, with all their level honesty, guarded reserves unknown to herself. Her head was by no means small, though it looked so because of its perfect rondures hugged by short, dark curls. She held it with the light grace of a deer. Derry Unthank, in later days, said that when she looked at him straight and full, he could sniff the woods and see the parted leaves framing her lifted head and neck. At eighteen there was no one around her who could tell her that, though Britt Hensley might have felt it with all of his lithe, happy body.

From Marshall Waycaster Ishma had her correct nose with its thin, breathing nostrils, her large mouth, tenderly curved and marked with an aloof humor, and her straight figure, built for strength; smaller and gentler of mould than his, but larger than the body of most women. "An' well enough," said Laviny, "with all the load she's got to tote."

The girl was almost single-handed in her struggle to make the farm keep them all decently alive. Laviny, bitten and pinched with rheumatism, found it more than she could do to keep up with the garden and patches near the house. Bainie slumped along with the cooking and mending, making occasional gestures toward redding up the rooms. Jim aside from his ploughing, was more of a hindrance than a help, with his chronic mismanagement, his weakness for mastership, and his incurable laziness. During vacation, the children helped uncomplainingly under Ishma's direction, but her busiest times—the seasons of planting and harvest—fell upon her during the school term. Frady's ghost, if ever it hung over the scene of his earthly endeavors, must have found it hard to recognize the briery, outcast fields and the crumbling house with little inside to remind him of his reign of glory. The big corner cupboard of curly maple, which he had lovingly fashioned for Sarah Starkweather, still stood in the kitchen, but Jim, pushed to activity by a cold snap, had threatened to use its doors for kindling. "What's the use o' doors? A curtain is all you want." Laviny had stayed his hand and given him a piece of her bitter mind. "There's dead wood all over the hill, waitin' fer the axe, an' you've kindled up the fence-rails till I kain't find enough fer a calf-pen. You'll be burnin' up the beds next an' put us all on the floor. That's yore idy o' livin', but it ain't mine, Jim Wishart. A body 'ud think you's raised on 'taters an' salt!"

When Laviny finally got through with him, Jim picked up the axe, went up the hill, and brought down enough wood for a Christmas fire. He sat by it, talking of the things he was going to do to make Cloudy Knob a show to the world, but his resolution faded with the fire, and the children picked up chips and brush to cook the next day's dinner.

As Ishma toiled through her crop, she tried to believe that every year was the last for her in the field. She intended to get a little ahead and go away where she could make enough to keep herself and her mother. Jim and his family must shift for themselves. But she loved the children. They were almost her own. On the verge of leaving them she always paused, and every Spring found her back in the field making sure of their bread. She had less time for her forest playground; less time for refilling her fount; and she felt the drouth within her.

But her dream of a more embellished life persisted. She tried to improve her speech by reading aloud and accustoming her ears to something different from the lazily uttered, half-finished words and twisted syntax of those about her. She noticed that visitors in the mountains, who sometimes found their way to Cloudy Knob, and commented on the native speech as "quaint," or "really Shakespearean," were careful to use nothing resembling it. She liked Miss Eller much better. She was a teacher in Beebread who brought the children up the mountain one Autumn day on a chestnut hunt. Miss Eller had shown surprise when she found that Ishma had taught herself. "You talk as well as I do," she said, and promised to send up some books from the library that was having its feeble beginning in the school. She forgot her promise, but Ishma did not forget her encouragement. Attempts to drill the children had been given up, rendered futile by Bainie's sniffs and Laviny's open scorn. For harmony's sake she spoke at home more or less in the family fashion, but she exulted in knowing better. On stormy, cold Sundays she read and practiced in the barn loft, and in bright weather her hills awaited her. Fortunately she did not try to mend her voice; a voice that belonged with her eyes, and bore her words in its flow like a cool, forest brook dripping over shadowy ledges.

We have noted her eighteenth birthday. Radburn Bailey was looking at her with greed and longing in his pleasant blue eyes; but Britton Hensley looked at her with the thrill of ownership. Though she had given him no promise he couldn't imagine any future for himself apart from Ishma Waycaster. Neither of the lovers saw much of her. She had never shared her high trail with anyone. Britt once hardily attempted to follow her, but with lively indirection, dodging and sheltering herself, she outwitted and outclimbed him utterly. When he came in at night he found that she had reached home an hour before him. Both boys felt aggrieved because they had to do their courting in the bosom of the family, but they had no choice except too leave her altogether, which seemed impossible for either of them.

One April day Laviny and Bainie sat on the perilous porch discussing the prospects of the suitors. It was nearing sunset, but Ishma was still in the field getting the land ready for the plough. Ploughing was the only part of the farm work which she refused to do. Jim had become convinced that this perversity must be accepted, and was usually on hand to take hold of the plough when Ishma announced that a field was ready. He felt that this supreme service established him as master of the place and controller of its output. Such trivial work as grubbing, planting, hoeing and harvesting, gave Ishma no special rights as he could see.

"Rad Bailey would make Ish a good livin'," said Bainie, shifting the overalls in her lap to reveal another hole, and threading a big needle. "Nothin' but shoe-thread 'll hold this together, an' they ain't a needleful on the mountain."

"Hit won't be Rad," said Laviny. "Hit'll be Britt."

"Shorely you ain't fer Britt, mommie. His hand is as weak as Jim's in a crop."

"He's a sight better lookin'. Hit'll be Britt."

Laviny reserved her aspirate for emphasis. It's omission showed that her mind had relaxed. It might even indicate resignation. She sighed as if giving up her last bit of energy to the problem of life, then became aggressively alert. "Where's my snuff, Bain' Wishart?" Bainie reached to the window ledge behind her, picked up a box of snuff, and handed it to her mother.

"You've shore been in it! I kain't keep snuff fer ever'body an' only three hens a layin'." Taking a sweet-gum brush from her apron pocket and swabbing it in the box, she placed it far back in her mouth where her lost molars should have been. Her next sigh was resigned, and her third reached contentment. After a few moments she was ready for effort.

"Might as well start the fire an' git the kittle to goin'," she said, entering the house. "Ishmalee 'll be here d'reckly."

Bainie went on patching, not once looking toward her children playing in front of the cabin. Ben, Andy and Nettie had come from school, and were quarrelling about the proper way to build a chimney with rocks they had brought from the branch that ran through the yard. Ellie, three years old, went into the kitchen and, after a consultation with her grandmother, came out nibbling a large piece of corn-bread. She jumped off the porch, and a liver-spotted hound dashed from under it, snapping at the bread. Ellie fought him off with only partial loss of her prize, but she was still insecure in possession. A yellow rooster with a flourishing red and black tail darted to her and pecked at her hand. She screamed, and Ben became interested. The rooster was his.

"Give him a bit, kain't you?" he commanded. Ellie made a careful division and resumed nibbling. But there was a third assault. A very dirty white pig rubbed up, knocked little Ellie over, and ran away with the bread. The fall angered her more than her loss. She scrambled out of the sour-smelling mud and began a determined cry that partially aroused her mother. Without looking up she told Ellie to stop her racket. "I've had enough out o' you fer one day."

At that moment Ishma came around the western end of the porch. She was carrying her field tools—pitchfork, grubbing hoe , and briar scythe. Dropping them all, she went to Ellie.

"Don't cry, honey. I'll wash your dress for you."

"An' what'll she put on while you're washin' it? Tell me that," said Bainie, her eyes still on the patching.

"She wouldn't have got so muddy if you hadn't thrown so much dishwater out here. You promised me you's goin to quit that, Bainie. Looks like shame 's not in you."

Bainie looked and felt too weary to protest. Seven children before she was thirty, and life that had never known a single enthusiasm, had given her a patience more defensive than real. She asked nothing better than to be let alone, with freedom to whine and mutter to her soul's content. Her younger sister's ambitious strength seemed only another oppression.

Ishma took an old sweater from a nail in a porch post. "Here, Ellie, you put this on." She stripped the child of her dress and swathed her in the ragged garment. Ellie flapped her sleeves delighted. "I'm as big as you now, Ishma!"

Ishma was holding up the muddy dress. "I'll do Nettie's too, while I'm washing this—an' Ben's an' Andy's overalls. I was plumb ashamed for them to start off to school this morning fair dripping the dirt."

"What'll *we* put on?" Ben asked doubtfully.

"O, get in there and find something," Ishma ventured with a confidence that Bainie knew was unwarranted. "I've got to have your clothes right now if I do them before slap dark."

The children ran into the house, delighted to have high authority for a rampage. Ishma sat on the floor and began to take off her patched shoes. "Is there a fire in the stove?" she asked.

"Yes, mommie started it, an' the kittle's full, 'cause I didn't wash up after dinner."

Ishma was taking rags off her feet. "You got a flour-poke I can make me some fresh toe-rags out of?"

"No, I hain't. It takes ever' poke I can git aholt of fer the patchin'."

"There!" said Ishma, getting up. "My feet are out of jail and they're not going back till morning. I'll wash at the branch."

She went down to the stream that ran a little distance from the eastern end of the house. There was another, smaller stream on the west side, running from the spring from which they carried water. Between this branch and the house lay a few poles representing a woodpile. Laviny came out, went across to the poles, picked up the axe with grunting effort, and began to cut wood. Bainie protested. Jim would be home in time to get breakfast-wood. *She* wasn't going to do his work. She'd said it and she meant it.

"Takes you a long time to larn you're nothin' but a woman, Bainie. I never seen one, 'scusin Granny, that didn't have to cut wood, if she et her meals halfway reg'lar."

"I'll show Jim!" said Bainie, her voice lifted out of its whine.

"You'll show him like you're doin' this minute. Him out with his gun an' hit ploughin' time! Takin' little Sam at his heels too! Sam could 'a' hacked wood, if he didn't want to go to school."

"You wait, mommie, an' let Ish do it. She's as strong as Sampson's steer. Hit pulled the wind out o' March."

Laviny dropped the axe and gave her words to Bainie straight.

"Ishmalee went to the field 'fore clear daylight this mornin'. She's been cuttin' an' pilin' briers ever sence. Nothin' but a cold snack up by the Birch spring. If she wants to set down, her cheer is bought an' paid fer. But she ain't fer settin' down. She's goin' wash yer brats' clo's."

Laviny returned to the axe. Bainie rolled up the overalls. "Eh-ay," she said, undisturbed, "you're always fer Ish. It's gittin' too duskish to thread a needle."

Ishma came slowly up from the branch on the opposite side of the house. Her head was turned, and she was looking back over her shoulder. West of Cloudy Knob the sun was already hidden, but between it and the south-east where the valley wound along the river, there were no intervening ridges. Reflections from the western sky colored the slow curves of the Little Tennessee as it flowed errantly and golden from its source in the Nantahalas, whose distant peaks were a panting radiance above their dark, blue bodies. When Ishma came up the steps at the end of the porch she turned again and stood looking down on the long stretch of valley, and on out to the horizon where the rolling transparency of the mountains was inundating earth with dream. Her whole body seemed caught in an intent gaze.

Laviny stared across the yard at her daughter. Bainie stared too, but she wasn't silent. "What you seein', Ish?" Her voice was loud enough, but Ishma didn't hear.

"You shet up, Bainie," said her mother. "It *is* purty sunset tonight, dog-gone ef it ain't!"

A little ashamed of her concession to beauty, she resumed her hacking, and Ishma turned at the sound of the axe.

"Mommie!" she called, "I've told you and told you not to do that! Now you'll be hurting all night with your arm!" She crossed to her mother and took the axe. "You go sit down now. Mommie, you *go sit down!*"

Laviny went to a chair on the porch and seated herself, protesting but relieved. Ishma began to cut the wood skillfully, with a man's swinging blow. Andy put his head through the window of the middle room where a pane of glass should have been. He was careful to be visible only from his waist up, being all the way naked. To his complaint that he could find nothing, his mother replied, "Git them overalls I'm usin' fer patches. They's a smart bit of 'em left. In the barrel behind the kitchen door."

"Ben's got *them* on," said Andy.

"You'll have to git yer poppie's best uns then. But don't dirt 'em er he'll tan ye bloody." She ended with a mumble to herself. "Looks like Ish could a let 'em alone till Sat'day."

Nettie, Andy and Ben flopped out of the house and into the yard. Ben's only garment was an unbelievably stripped and tattered pair of overalls. Andy was swallowed in a pair of respectable entirety, the legs rolled into wads about his knees, and the braces tied around his neck. Nettie wore a checked apron pinned over her shoulders and a small red tablecloth for a skirt.

"Now you'll ketch it, Nettie," screamed her mother. "That's the new lamp-table cover Ish bought."

Ishma was coming in with an armful of wood. "Keep out of the mud, Nettie," she said, "and you may wear it till bed-time. Bring me the big tub, Ben." Ben dashed around the house. Ishma left her wood in the kitchen, and came out. Laviny was staring at Nettie, despair mapping her wrinkled face. "Is that youngun scratchin' her head agin?"

"It's nothin' else. That's all school 's fit fer," said Bainie. "To give 'em boogers in the head."

"She's got a power o' hair, an' hit curly. A booger 'd swim a river to git to a head o' hair like that."

Bainie's voice in reply was several depths more disconsolate. "It was jest last week that I bridled the comb an' redd her hair good."

Ishma felt sick. "O, Bainie, stop it!"

"Come ten year you'll have four er five o' yer own to clean up. You won't be so sugar-mouth then."

"Ten years? Ten thousand is more like it!"

Bainie laughed, a silly, vulgar laugh. "Time's the truth-teller," she said.

Ben came back without the tub. Bainie thought the children might have dragged it to their new playhouse above the barn. Ishma set off hastily to find the tub, Ben hurrying after.

"That Ishmalee's a mixtry," said Laviny. "I kain't git aholt o' her. But she's a sight o' help, that's shore. You got to quit throwin' off on her, Bain Wishart. She might up an' leave, an' I reckon we'd all starve without her hand in the crop."

"She'll leave anyhow if she gits married."

"That would be nater. We kain't hep that. 'A gal she must marry, an' a wife she must carry.'"

Ishma returned with Ben, bearing a large wooden tub which she placed on the edge of the porch. "We'll have these rags out in a sawed-off minute," she said to the boy. "I've got a pot full, a kettle full, and a dishpan full of water." She went into the kitchen and swiftly reappeared with a steaming supply. Ben ran to the branch and came back with a bucket of cold water.

"Fine! We'll hurry, Ben. Night sha'n't catch us. Moonlight's not good soap, Granny used to say."

They did hurry, rubbing, wringing, fetching, and in a short time the clothes were ready for rinsing in the branch.

"Eh-law, you never stop," said Laviny. "But you'll stump yer toes some day, like I did."

When the garments were on the fence, Ishma came back, picked up the tub of water and started off with it.

"Why'n't you have decent mercy on yer back? You turn that water out," called her mother.

"I'm not makin' a hogwaller," she answered. "Bainie 'll see to that."

At last she was ready to stop, and sat down on the porch near Laviny's chair. There was no longer any glow in the sky, nor on the distant mountains.

"You be dead tired, I reckon," her mother said.

Ishma accepted the awkward form of speech without a wince, for with her mother "be" was the verb of intimacy and affection.

"No, I'll go help with supper in a minute."

"Let Bainie wrassle it. She's been settin' sence twelve. You're gittin' too much like yer daddy, Ishmalee, goin' ever' minute."

"Tell me about daddy, mommie."

"Law, child, what fer?"

"You never talk about him."

"Well, ain't he dead?"

"You've got children dead too, and you talk about them."

"Yes, I've got four dead, an' they don't give me a minute's trouble."

"Daddy didn't beat you."

"I reckon he didn't! But he was a fidgety man. A fidgety woman is hard to put up with, but a man takes all the peace out o' life."

This was a new picture of her father for Ishma. "But everybody liked him, mommie."

"Yes, he come inter the mountains with the biggest pack o' jokes that anybody ever brought in. He had to have 'em 'cause the only times he could set still was when he's tellin' one. He never got tired. I used to wish he could know what it wuz to feel dog-tired jest once. He wuz never ready fer bed. Looked like it never come night fer him. If there was a dance, er any kind o' shindy doin's, in ten mile of us, he'd walk to it, ay he would, ten year after we's married, an' me with a pack o' younguns. He wore me bone sore. It was a lot easier after he got a stroke an' couldn't leave his cheer. I could make a livin' easier'n I could keep up with him when he wuz goin'. He wuz always beggin' me to leave here an' set out roamin' same as if there wuzn't any younguns to feed."

Ishma looked at the big chair pushed back against the wall and used as a catch-all for corn-baskets, old harness, school books and caps, Laviny's shoe-mending out-fit, ragged quilts, and mail order catalogues. Her father had hired Abe Willis to make it, and the back could be lifted up and let down. Nowadays it was always down so that more things could be piled on it. Ishma's heart bled as she thought of her father lying on that chair for three years.

"Ay, he wuz never satisfied," her mother continued. "Always seekin', an' no name fer it. When he had his stroke the doctors said he'd be gone in three months, but he took a year fer ever' month they give him. I knowed he'd do that. I've wondered some-times why he didn't put out an' leave when he wuz able to walk off. But he thought a sight o' you younguns, pertickly Steve. He wuz a plumb fool about Steve. I reckon that's why he stayed around. Twa'n't me keepin' him."

Ishma was still looking at the chair. She had been six years old when her father was struck down, and nine when he was buried. His prostrate years she tried to for-get, and remembered him walking about, singing gay songs, and teasing her mother.

"I've quit blamin' him," said Laviny, following Ishma's eyes, "fer ever'thing 'cept Steve leavin' me. The only livin' boy I had, an' a grown man at fifteen."

Ishma had proud memories of Steve. "I'll never forget him," she said.

"You ortent. You's eight when he left out. An' you'd mighty nigh see him agin ef you'd look in the bottom of a new dishpan. You're powerful like him, only you've got a gal counternance."

"What did daddy have to do with Steve's leavin' out? You've never told me that."

"I ain't goin' to nuther."

Ishma didn't try persuasion, and Laviny sat in silence, licking old wounds and seeing the past only through her injury. With no intention to speak, her story, as her daughter expected, began to pour through her lips.

"I didn't know his daddy had anything to do with it at first. Steve had been fussin' an' squirmin' fer about a year, like any boy when he's growin' up too fast, an' I'd ketch his daddy lookin' curious at him, like he wanted awful to speak, but his tongue wuz so nigh dead by that time he could only choke an' blow red when he tried to talk. Steve would git out o' bed of a mornin' lookin' holler-eyed an' sayin' he hadn't slep' none. Course the farm was purty heavy on a boy's back, an' him only fifteen. Bainie an' Jim wuz married, an' Jim—"

Laviny stopped loyally, but Ishma took up her words. "And Jim was piling every-thing on Steve."

"Jim wuz doin' fair enough. But I could see yer daddy had Steve on his mind. An' fust I knowed my boy was clear light gone. There I was with a fam'ly an' a farm an' a half-dead man, all waitin' my two hands."

"You had Jim," said Ishma, ashamed of the dig and her suppressed smile.

"Jim!—He had his hands full, you might know, with his own fam'ly, an' Bainie not stout." Again she became silent, nursing her bitterness.

"But what did daddy *do*, mommie?"

"It was about two months after Steve left, I's cuttin' up a pair o' his old overalls that I'd sort o' kep' away from the scissors, 'cause they's the pair he had on the last day he's at home, an' in one o' the pockets, I found a piece o' paper with writin' on it. Pencil marks, mighty shaky, but I made 'em out. *'Go, Steve,'* that's all it said. An' Steve went."

"Daddy wrote it?"

"Ay, he did. An' I didn't know he could move his fingers then. I figgered that he'd looked beggin' at Steve, an' twitched his fingers, an' Steve give him the paper an' pencil. I kain't think of any other way fer it."

"He never found out you knew, did he?"

"I took keer he did! I went right to him an' bust loose. He could hear like a cat to the last, an' I let him have it. There wusn't nothin' I left out. I give it to him on a shovel. An' all at once it come over me that he wuz a laffin'. I wuz plumb beat. Yes, sir, he lay there an' beat me plumb out. I couldn't say another word. My mouth wuz jest sewed up. Him a laffin'!" Laviny paused for a response from Ishma, but no sound came. "An' all I've got left o' my boy is that telegram sayin' he died in the Philippines."

Suddenly she was through with self-pity. "Bainie, why'n't you light the lamp?" she called sharply, and Bainie answered from the kitchen, "Lamp-oil 's out."

"Jim's been usin' it in his huntin' lantern then. We got a whole half a gallon last time. Ishmalee, I saw where some limbs offen that dead chestnut back o' the barn wuz blown down today. They's bone dry, an 'll make a blaze fer us to eat supper by."

Ishma said she would get them, and went off by the path that led around the eastern end of the house then veered north up the hill to the barn. Bainie poked her head out of the kitchen door, and seeing no one but her mother, came out, heavy with mystery.

"Mommie," she whispered, with unnecessary caution, "I've found where Ish keeps her money. I's pullin' splinters off the wall to make a light an' a board come off. There was the money, in the crack. I knowed she's hidin' it. Dimes, nickels an' quarters. There's one fifty-center too! She must a been savin' up fer a year, an' makin' us believe she spent ever' cent! It was tied up in a rag, an' layin' in this little tin box, tight as could be. Fourteen dollars! You reckon she's goin' to buy weddin' clo's?"

Laviny's face had turned a more unhappy grey. "Bainie, you put that board back quick, an' the money behind it! Ishmalee's as much like Steve as a gal child dare to be. You kain't go too fur with her. You put it back right now."

Bainie went in, but there was not time to replace the money before Ishma came up to the porch steps with her arms full of broken sticks. Laviny hurried to meet her.

"Give 'em here, an' I'll start the fire, Ishmalee. You git the younguns things off the fence an' we'll dry 'em by the fire, seein' we've got to have a blaze goin'."

Ishma transferred her armful and started for the fence. A few steps off, she turned back her head. "He was laffin', mother?"

"As I'm standin' here he wuz. An' him nothin' but eyes."

Laviny hastened in and started the fire in the kitchen fireplace. Bainie was still fumbling at the wall.

"Lord, Bainie, lick yer fingers!" warned her mother, hearing Ishma's returning step.

"It's about fixed," said Bainie; but Laviny met Ishma at the door. "I'll spread 'em out," she said, taking the garments, knowing that Ishma would turn back. She never stayed in the house when she could be out of it. A moment later, when Laviny came out on the porch, she was standing at the west end looking at the sky.

"There's a light," she said, "that looks like it might be above Copper Creek. Maybe a fire has started up in Dark Moon Cove."

"Lord hep us, if it's so! I kain't fight fire any more," her mother protested. But Ishma's heart was leaping. She could remember one great forest fire that she had seen when she was five years old. Her father was fighting it. He fought till he fell. The fire got past him and burnt up all of Granny Whitt's hay. Nobody was permitted to forget that fire as long as Granny Whitt lived. But Ishma had not been concerned with the hay. She had broken away from her father and the other men, and had run to a high knob. From there she could see an ocean of flame rolling and twisting in the valley below. That was when Dark Moon had been burnt over. She thought that she had floated high in the air above that fire. Night after night her ecstasy was repeated in her dreams, making it harder to doubt that she had flown over that flaming ocean.

"There's nothing I'd rather see tonight than a big fire," she said, "only I hate for the woods to get burnt up. If they've got to burn though, I want to see it."

"My sakes, child, you'd better be wishin' fer bed an' sleep!"

Ishma came back and stood in the wide kitchen door, watching the blaze made by the dry chestnut in the fire-place. Nothing could be more beautiful than fire, she thought, but what she said, was, "I want to write a letter, and that fire's too hot to sit by."

Bainie looked up from the stove, her face crinkled unpleasantly. "If you want lamp-oil fer a light you'll have to pay fer it yeresef. I'm not goin' to spend another brownie till I buy Nettie a dress. That'n you washed 'll drop offen her 'fore another week. Mommie, if you'd lend me a dollar I'd pay it back soon as we shear the sheep."

"You know that wool money is done took up at Gaffney's store. If I had a dollar I'd know something beter to do with it. I'd git me another bottle of that Indian Bone Cure fer this rheumatiz."

Ishma felt besieged. "You'll poison yourself with that stuff some day," she said to her mother, as she went out the door and off the porch. Laviny called to her to bring the milk and butter from the spring-house. When Ishma reached the spring, she sat down for a moment on the rock wall that guarded it, wondering why she felt cramped and hot when it was so sweet and cool all about her.

Bainie, in the house, was still whining about the money. "She wants to write a letter. I bet she's goin' to order her a dress out o' that new order book. She took it with her to the field yisterday."

"Ain't the bread nearly done?" asked Laviny, uneasy with Bainie's talk.

"No, I made a thick pone." It had grown uncomfortably warm in the kitchen and Bainie had stepped to the door. "I b'lieve that's Aunt Cynthy Webb comin'," she said, peering through the dusk. "This time o' day!"

"Pore Cynthy!" said Laviny. "I reckon Zeke's on a drunk an' she'll stay the night. Howdy, Cynthy!" she called, sending her welcome into the yard. Cynthy Webb, fat and breathless, came on the porch before she returned the salute. She always climbed the steps in terror, expecting them to give way under her two hundred pounds. Laviny put a chair for her guest on one side of the kitchen door, and one for herself on the other side. "Set right down, Cynthy, an' tell me how're y'all."

"Crawlin', crawlin'. Reckon y'all afoot?"

"Ay, about an' about."

Cynthy's affliction was a quarrelling, tippling husband, as everybody knew, but she loyally went through the form of keeping it a secret. She now craned her neck and looked into the kitchen, then drew it back and asked Laviny to let what she was going to tell her go with her to her last bed. Laviny declared that it should freeze in her dead body, and Cynthy disclosed that Zeke had come from Copper Creek drunk.

"I say!" exclaimed Laviny, duly astonished. "They'll make that stuff over there to the end of time, I reckon."

"Long as the mountains don't rock, they will. But the mountains *air* goin' to rock, Laviny, ef folks don't quit peekin' inter hell. Some o' these days they won't git the door shet quick enough, an' the whole lake o' brimstone 'll roll out. I was settin' at home peaceable, readin' my Bible, an' waitin' fer Julie to come up from Beebread. She's helpin' Lu Gaddy down there, puttin' out her garden. An' I looks out an' sees Zeke jest a rockin' the trail. When he got in, ever' side o' the house was hisn. I'd prayed my knees sore astin' the Lord not to let him come home drunk, but looks like my prayers don't git no higher 'n my head. Zeke was rantin' so fierce, I up an' lit out. When Julie comes she'll figger where I am an' come after me."

"You're stayin' right here, Cynthy. Don't you worry more'n a flea can tote in its weskit pocket."

Ishma came from the spring carrying a bowl of butter and a jar of milk. "Howdys" were passed, and the girl added, "You'll stay the night, Aunt Cynthy?"

"Law, child, I got to git home. Zeke might come in an' me gone."

"You let Uncle Zeke take care of himself for one night."

"You won't talk thataway when it's yore man around. That won't be long, I'm thinkin'."

"About as long as never!" Ishma went into the kitchen, her shoulders high. Cynthy watched her put the milk on the table, then go out the back door.

"Tetchy! That means something. Ain't her an' Rad got it fixed up yit?"

"I ain't shore it's Rad. Not gospel shore, I ain't."

"You don't mean she'll take Britt when she can git a steady worker like Rad?"

"I've come to think I don't much keer which un it is. If it's Rad, he'll take her away. But I reckon Britt would have to live right here. He ain't got nothin' but a gittar, an' that's a leetle less than nothin'. He wouldn't take Ishmalee away, an' she's a sight o' help on this place."

"You know how to find the good grain in a sack o' hulls, Laviny. I'd better be startin' down. I know I'll meet Julie, an' save her a step."

"Don't you move, Cynthy. Bainie, lay Aunt Cynthy a plate."

"I've done laid it," called Bainie from the kitchen.

"What's the matter with yer supper?" asked Laviny, starting up and falling back with a groan, saying that her pesterin' knee was stiff again. Cynthy assured her that it couldn't be worse than the stinging she'd had around her neck all the week, an' was botherin' her crazy that minute. Laviny nursed her knee, declaring that it was like an auger borin' in yer bones.

"Mine," insisted Cynthy, "comes jest like a swarm o' sweat-bees settlin' on my neck."

Laviny crowed over her. "A hammer crackin' my bones to the marr' couldn't be wuss," and Cynthy met that with, "A thousand needlepints wouldn't tell it fer *me!*"

They had turned their chairs and faced each other in a duel of ailments, their profiles in hostile outline against the light that poured through the broad door of the kitchen. Ishma, under the apple tree in the front yard, began to laugh softly, listening to their interjections.

"Screwin' right inter the jint—"

"Skin smartin' like it wuz whipped with nettles—"

"Fire a-borin'—"

"Wasps—"

Their voices, growing shriller and running together, were cut off by the sound of a guitar loudly picked by Britt Hensley. He was standing in the path at the western end of the porch. Ishma, when she heard him, slipped around the house at the other end and went into the kitchen by the back door. He might stay to supper, and Bainie always forgot to wipe off the oil-cloth.

Britt came up the steps, singing boldly to the tune of "Rattler."

Two old women talkin',
Night a creepin' round
Make a jay-bird squawkin'
A mighty pleasant sound.

   O, where you goin', Bobby?
   O, where you goin', Bill?
   Goin' to drown my troubles
   At a good old mountain still!

Caroline Gordon
(1895–1981)

Caroline Gordon was born on October 6, 1895, on Merry Mount Farm in Todd County, Kentucky, near Clarksville, Tennessee. Gordon was privately educated at home and then at her father's classical school in Clarksville, where she studied mathematics, Latin, and Greek. She attended high school in Wilmington, Ohio, and received her B.A. degree in 1916 from Bethany College in West Virginia. Following college, she taught high school for three years before taking a job as a reporter with the *Chattanooga News* from 1920 to 1924. In the newspaper's February 10, 1923, issue, she discussed the work of the Fugitives and so was brought to their attention. Through her acquaintance with Robert Penn Warren, she met Allen Tate, whom she married on November 2, 1924. They had one daughter, Nancy, born in 1925. The Tates were divorced in August 1959. In 1924, Gordon went to New York, where she wrote for a newspaper syndicate and performed secretarial duties for Ford Madox Ford. Four years later, she and Tate went to England and France on his Guggenheim Fellowship, and in 1929 she received a Guggenheim and served as Ford Madox Ford's secretary in Paris. In 1931, her first novel, *Penhally*, was published, followed in 1934 by *Aleck Maury, Sportsman*. Two novels, *None Shall Look Back* and *The Garden of Adonis*, were published in 1937. In addition, she became the first writer-in-residence at the University of North Carolina in Greensboro. Throughout the 1940s, Gordon continued to publish fiction, including *Green Centuries* (1941), *The Women on the Porch* (1944), and *The Forest of the South* (1945). For the next three decades, Gordon published such fiction as *The Strange Children* (1951), *The Malefactors* (1956), *Old Red and Other Stories* (1963), and *The Glory of Hera* (1972). Gordon also wrote practical criticism, *How to Read a Novel* (1957), and with Allen Tate, edited *The House of Fiction* (1950). Gordon also served as writer-in-residence at the University of California, Davis (1962–1963), and Purdue University (1963–1964). Moreover, she directed the creative writing program at the University of Dallas in Irving, Texas. Although she preferred to be known as a novelist, her reputation is based primarily on three short stories, "Old Red," "The Captive," and "The Brilliant Leaves," which have been widely anthologized. Gordon died on April 11, 1981.

Old Red

I

When the door had closed behind his daughter, Mr. Maury went to the window and stood a few moments looking out. The roses that had grown in a riot all along that side of the fence had died or been cleared away, but the sun lay across the garden in the same level lances of light that he remembered. He turned back into the room. The shadows had gathered until it was nearly all in gloom. The top of his minnow bucket just emerging from his duffel bag glinted in the last rays of the sun. He stood looking down at his traps all gathered neatly in a heap at the foot of the bed. He would leave them like that. Even if they came in here sweeping and cleaning up—it was only in hotels that a man was master of his own room—even if they came in here cleaning up he would tell them to leave all his things exactly as they were. It was reassuring to see them all there together, ready to be taken up in the hand, to be carried down and put into a car, to be driven off to some railroad station at a moment's notice.

As he moved toward the door he spoke aloud, a habit that was growing on him:

"Anyhow I won't stay but a week. . . . I ain't going to stay but a week, no matter what they say. . . ."

Downstairs in the dining room they were already gathered at the supper table: his white-haired, shrunken mother-in-law; his tall sister-in-law who had the proud carriage of the head, the aquiline nose, but not the spirit of his dead wife; his lean, blond, new son-in-law; his black eyed daughter who, but that she was thin, looked so much like him, all of them gathered there waiting for him, Alexander Maury. It occurred to him that this was the first time he had sat down in the bosom of the family for some years. They were always writing saying that he must make a visit this summer or certainly next summer— ". . . all had a happy Christmas together, but missed you. . . ." They had even made the pretext that he ought to come up to inspect his new son-in-law. As if he hadn't always known exactly the kind of young man Sarah would marry! What was the boy's name? Stephen, yes, Stephen. He must be sure and remember that.

He sat down and, shaking out his napkin, spread it over his capacious paunch and tucked it well up under his chin in the way his wife had never allowed him to do. He let his eyes rove over the table and released a long sigh.

"Hot batter bread," he said, "and ham. Merry Point ham. I sure am glad to taste them one more time before I die."

The old lady was sending the little Negro girl scurrying back to the kitchen for a hot plate of batter bread. He pushed aside the cold plate and waited. She had bridled when he spoke of the batter bread and a faint flush had dawned on her withered cheeks. Vain she had always been as a peacock, of her housekeeping, her children, anything that belonged to her. She went on now, even at her advanced age, making her batter bread, smoking her hams according to that old recipe she was so proud of, but who came here now to this old house to eat or to praise?

He helped himself to a generous slice of batter bread, buttered it, took the first mouthful and chewed it slowly. He shook his head.

"There ain't anything like it," he said. "There ain't anything else like it in the world."

His dark eye roving over the table fell on his son-in-law. "You like batter bread?" he inquired.

Stephen nodded, smiling. Mr. Maury, still masticating slowly, regarded his face, measured the space between the eyes—his favorite test for man, horse, or dog. Yes, there was room enough for sense between the eyes. How young the boy looked! And infected already with the fatal germ, the *cacoëthes scribendi*. Well, their children—if he and Sarah ever had any children—would probably escape. It was like certain diseases of the eye, skipped every other generation. His own father had had it badly all his life. He could see him now sitting at the head of the table spouting his own poetry—or Shakespeare's—while the children watched the preserve dish to see if it was going around. He, Aleck Maury, had been lucky to be born in the generation he had. He had escaped that at least. A few translations from Heine in his courting days, a few fragments from the Greek; but no, he had kept clear of that on the whole. . . .

His sister-in-law's eyes were fixed on him. She was smiling faintly. "You don't look much like dying, Aleck. Florida must agree with you."

The old lady spoke from the head of the table. "I can't see what you do with yourself all winter long. Doesn't time hang heavy on your hands?"

Time, he thought, *time!* They were always mouthing the word, and what did they know about it? Nothing in God's world! He saw time suddenly, a dull, leaden-colored fabric depending from the old lady's hands, from the hands of all of them, a blanket that they pulled about between them, now here, now there, trying to cover up their nakedness. Or they would cast it on the ground and creep in among the folds, finding one day a little more tightly rolled than another, but all of it everywhere the same dull gray substance. But time was a banner that whipped before him always in the wind! He stood on tiptoe to catch at the bright folds, to strain them to his bosom. They were bright and glittering. But they whipped by so fast and were whipping always ever faster. The tears came into his eyes. Where, for instance, had this year gone? He could swear he had not wasted a minute of it, for no man living, he thought, knew better how to make each day a pleasure to him. Not a minute wasted and yet here it was already May. If he lived to the biblical threescore-and-ten, which was all he ever allowed himself in his calculations, he had before him only nine more Mays. Only nine more Mays out of all eternity and they wanted him to waste one of them sitting on the front porch at Merry Point!

The butter plate which had seemed to swim before him in a glittering mist was coming solidly to rest upon the white tablecloth. He winked his eyes rapidly and, laying down his knife and fork, squared himself about in his chair to address his mother-in-law:

"Well, ma'am, you know I'm a man that always likes to be learning something. Now this year I learned how to smell out fish." He glanced around the table, holding his head high and allowing his well-cut nostrils to flutter slightly with his indrawn breaths. "Yes, sir," he said, "I'm probably the only white man in this country knows how to smell out feesh."

There was a discreet smile on the faces of the others. Sarah was laughing outright. "Did you have to learn how or did it just come to you?"

"I learned it from an old nigger woman," her father said. He shook his head reminiscently. "It's wonderful how much you can learn from niggers. But you have to know how to handle them. I was half the winter wooing that old Fanny. . . ."

He waited until their laughter had died down. "We used to start off every morning from the same little cove and we'd drift in there together at night. I noticed how she always brought in a good string, so I says to her: 'Fanny, you just lemme go 'long with you.' But she wouldn't have nothing to do with me. I saw she was going to be a hard nut to crack, but I kept right on. Finally I began giving her presents. . . ."

Laura was regarding him fixedly, a queer glint in her eyes. Seeing outrageous pictures in her mind's eye, doubtless. Poor Laura. Fifty years old if she was a day. More than half her lifetime gone and all of it spent drying up here in the old lady's shadow. She was speaking with a gasping little titter:

"What sort of presents did you give her, Aleck?"

He made his tone hearty in answer. "I give her a fine string of fish one day and I give her fifty cents. And finally I made her a present of a Barlow knife. That was when she broke down. She took me with her that morning. . . ."

"Could she really *smell* fish?" the old lady asked curiously.

"You ought to a seen her," Mr. Maury said. "She'd sail over that lake like a hound on the scent. She'd row right along and then all of a sudden she'd stop rowing." He bent over and peered into the depths of imaginary water. "'Thar they are, White Folks, thar they are. Cain't you smell 'em?'"

Stephen was leaning forward, eyeing his father-in-law intently. "Could you?" he asked.

"I got so I could smell feesh," Mr. Maury told him. "I could smell out the feesh but I couldn't tell which kind they were. Now Fanny could row over a bed and tell just by the smell whether it was bass or bream. But she'd been at it all her life." He paused, sighing. "You can't just pick these things up. . . . Who was it said, 'Genius is an infinite capacity for taking pains'?"

Sarah was rising briskly. Her eyes sought her husband's across the table. She was laughing. "Sir Izaak Walton," she said. "We'd better go in the other room. Mandy wants to clear the table."

The two older ladies remained in the dining room. Mr. Maury walked across the hall to the sitting room, accompanied by Steve and Sarah. He lowered himself cautiously into the most solid-looking of the rocking chairs that were drawn up around the fire. Steve stood on the hearthrug, his back to the fire.

Mr. Maury glanced up at him curiously. "What you thinking about, feller?" he asked.

Steve looked down. He smiled but his gaze was still contemplative. "I was thinking about the sonnet," he said, "in the form in which it first came to England."

Mr. Maury shook his head. "Wyatt and Surrey," he said. "Hey, nonny, nonny. . . . You'll have hardening of the liver long before you're my age." He looked past Steve's shoulder at the picture that hung over the mantelshelf: Cupid and Psyche holding between them a fluttering veil and running along a rocky path toward the beholder. It had been hanging there ever since he could remember; would hang there, he thought, till the house fell down or burned down, as it was more likely to do with the old lady wandering around at night carrying lighted lamps the way she did. "Old Merry Point," he said. "It don't change much, does it?"

He settled himself more solidly in his chair. His mind veered from the old house to his own wanderings in brighter places. He regarded his daughter and son-in-law affably.

"Yes, sir," he said, "this winter in Florida was valuable to me just for the acquaintances I made. Take my friend Jim Yost. Just to live in the same hotel with that man is an education." He paused, smiling reminiscently into the fire. "I'll never forget the first time I saw him. He came up to me there in the lobby of the hotel. 'Professor Maury,' he says, 'you been hearin' about me for twenty years and I been hearin' about you for twenty years. And now we've done met.'"

Sarah had sat down in the little rocking chair by the fire. She leaned toward him now, laughing. "They ought to have put down a cloth of gold for the meeting," she said.

Mr. Maury regarded her critically. It occurred to him that she was, after all, not so much like himself as the sister whom, as a child, he had particularly disliked. A smart girl, Sarah, but too quick always on the uptake. For his own part he preferred a softer-natured woman.

He shook his head. "Nature does that in Florida," he said. "I knew right off the reel it was him. there were half a dozen men standing around. I made 'em witness. 'Jim Yost,' I says, 'Jim Yost of Maysville or I'll eat my hat.'"

"Why is he so famous?" Sarah asked.

Mr. Maury took out his knife and cut off a plug of tobacco. When he had offered a plug to his son-in-law and it had been refused, he put the tobacco back into his pocket. "He's a man of imagination," he said slowly. "There ain't many in this world."

He took a small tin box out of his pocket and set it on the little table that held the lamp. Removing the top, he tilted the box so that they could see its contents: an artificial lure, a bug with a dark body and a red, bulbous head, a hook protruding from what might be considered its vitals.

"Look at her," he said. "Ain't she a killer?"

Sarah leaned forward to look and Steve, still standing on the hearthrug, bent above them. The three heads ringed the light. Mr. Maury disregarded Sarah and addressed himself to Steve. "She takes nine strips of pork rind," he said, "nine strips cut just thick enough." He marked off the width of the strips with his two fingers on the table, then, picking up the lure and cupping it in his palm, he moved it back and forth quickly so that the painted eyes caught the light.

"Look at her," he said, "look at the wicked way she sets forward."

Sarah was poking at the lure with the tip of her finger. "Wanton," she said, "simply wanton. What does he call her?"

"This is his Devil Bug," Mr. Maury said. "He's the only man in this country makes it. I myself had the idea thirty years ago and let it slip by me the way I do with so many of my ideas." He sighed, then, elevating his tremendous bulk slightly above the table level and continuing to hold Steve with his gaze, he produced from his coat pocket the oilskin book that held his flies. He spread it open on the table and began to turn the pages. His eyes sought his son-in-law's as his hand paused before a gray, rather draggled-looking lure.

"Old Speck," he said. "I've had that fly for twenty years. I reckon she's taken five hundred pounds of fish in her day. . . ."

The fire burned lower. A fiery coal rolled from the grate and fell onto the hearthrug. Sarah scooped it up with a shovel and threw it among the ashes. In the circle of the lamplight the two men still bent over the table looking at the flies. Steve was absorbed in them, but he spoke seldom. It was her father's voice that, rising and falling, filled the room. He talked a great deal but he had a beautiful speaking voice. He was telling Steve now about Little West Fork, the first stream ever he put a fly in.

"My first love," he kept calling it. It sounded rather pretty, she thought, in his mellow voice. "My first love. . . ."

II

When Mr. Maury came downstairs the next morning the dining room was empty except for his daughter, Sarah, who sat dawdling over a cup of coffee and a cigarette. Mr. Maury sat down opposite her. To the little Negro girl who presented herself at his elbow he outlined his wants briefly: "A cup of coffee and some hot batter bread, just like we had last night." He turned to his daughter. "Where's Steve?"

"He's working," she said. "He was up at eight and he's been working ever since."

Mr. Maury accepted the cup of coffee from the little girl, poured half of it into his saucer, set it aside to cool. "Ain't it wonderful," he said, "the way a man can sit down and work day after day? When I think of all the work I've done in my time . . . Can he work *every* morning?"

"He sits down at his desk every morning," she said, "but of course he gets more done some mornings than others."

Mr. Maury picked up his saucer, found the coffee cool enough for his taste. He sipped it slowly, looking out of the window. His mind was already busy with his day's program. No water—no running water—nearer than West Fork, three miles away. He couldn't drive a car and Steve was going to be busy writing all morning. There was nothing for it but a pond. The Willow Sink. It was not much, but it was better than nothing. He pushed his chair back and rose.

"Well," he said, "I'd better be starting."

When he came downstairs with his rod a few minutes later the hall was still full of the sound of measured typing. Sarah sat in the dining room in the same position in which he had left her, smoking. Mr. Maury paused in the doorway while he slung his canvas bag over his shoulders. "How you ever going to get anything down if you don't take advantage of the morning hours?" he asked. He glanced at the door opposite as if it had been the entrance to a sick chamber. "What's he writing about?" he inquired in a whisper.

"It's an essay on John Skelton."

Mr. Maury looked out at the new green leaves framed in the doorway. "John Skelton," he said, "God Almighty!"

He went through the hall and stepped down off the porch onto the ground that was still moist with spring rains. As he crossed the lower yard he looked up into the branches of the maples. Yes, the leaves were full-grown already even on the late trees. The year, how swiftly, how steadily it advanced! He had come to the far corner of the yard. Grown up it was in pokeberry shoots and honeysuckle, but there was a place to get through. The top strand of wire had been pulled down and fastened to the others with a ragged piece of rope. He rested his weight on his good leg and swung himself over onto the game one. It gave him a good, sharp twinge when he came down on it. It was getting worse all the time, that leg, but on the other hand he was learning better all the time how to handle it. His mind flew back to a dark, startled moment, that day when the cramp first came on him. He had been sitting still in the boat all day long and that evening when he stood up to get out his leg had failed him utterly. He had pitched forward among the reeds, had lain there a second, face downward, before it came to him what had happened. With the realization came a sharp picture out of his faraway youth. Uncle James, lowering himself ponderously out of the saddle after a hard day's hunting, had fallen forward in exactly the same way, into a knot of yowling little Negroes. He had got up and cursed them all out of the lot. It had scared the old boy to death, coming down like that. The black dog he had had on his shoulder all that fall. But he himself had never lost one day's fishing on account of his leg. He had known from the start how to handle it. It meant simply that he was slowed down that much. It hadn't really made much difference in fishing. He didn't do as much wading but he got around just about as well on the whole. Hunting, of course, had had to go. You couldn't walk all day shooting birds, dragging a game leg. He had just given it up right off the reel, though it was a shame when a man was as good a shot as he was. That day he was out with Tom Kensington, last November, the only day he got out during the bird season. Nine shots he'd had and he'd bagged nine birds. Yes, it was a shame. But a man couldn't do everything. He had to limit himself. . . .

He was up over the little rise now. The field slanted straight down before him to where the pond lay, silver in the morning sun. A Negro cabin was perched halfway up the opposite slope. A woman was hanging out washing on a line stretched between two trees. From the open door little Negroes spilled down the path toward the pond. Mr. Maury surveyed the scene, spoke aloud:

"Ain't it funny now? Niggers always live in the good places."

He stopped under a wild cherry tree to light his pipe. It had been hot crossing the field, but the sunlight here was agreeably tempered by the branches. And that pond down there was fringed with willows. His eyes sought the bright disc of the water, then rose to where the smoke from the cabin chimney lay in a soft plume along the crest of the hill.

When he stooped to pick up his rod again it was with a feeling of sudden keen elation. An image had risen in his memory, an image that was familiar but came to him infrequently of late and that only in moments of elation: the wide field in front of his uncle's house in Albermarle, on one side the dark line of undergrowth that marked the Rivanna River, on the other the blue of Peters' Mountain. They would be waiting there in that broad plain when they had the first sight of the fox. On that little rise by the river, loping steadily, not yet alarmed. The sun would glint on his bright coat, on his quick turning head as he dove into the dark of the woods. There would be hullabaloo after that and shouting and riding. Sometimes there was the tailing of the fox—that time Old Whiskey was brought home on a mattress! All of that to come afterwards, but none of it ever like that first sight of the fox there on the broad plain between the river and the mountain.

There was one fox, they grew to know him in time, to call him affectionately by name. Old Red it was who showed himself always like that there on the crest of the hill. "There he goes, the damn impudent scoundrel. . . ." Uncle James would shout and slap his thigh and yell himself hoarse at Whiskey and Mag and the pups, but they would already have settled to their work. They knew his course, every turn of it, by heart. Through the woods and then down again to the river. Their hope was always to cut him off before he could circle back to the mountain. If he got in there among those old field pines it was all up. But he always made it. Lost 'em every time and dodged through to his hole in Pinnacle rock. A smart fox, Old Red. . . .

He descended the slope and paused in the shade of a clump of willows. The little Negroes who squatted, dabbling in the water, watched him out of round eyes as he unslung his canvas bag and laid it on a stump. He looked down at them gravely.

"D'you ever see a white man that could conjure?" he asked.

The oldest boy laid the brick he was fashioning out of mud down on a plank. He ran the tip of his tongue over his lower lip to moisten it before he spoke. "Naw, suh."

"I'm the man," Mr. Maury told him. "You chillun better quit that playin' and dig me some worms."

He drew his rod out of the case, jointed it up, and laid it down on a stump. Taking out his book of flies, he turned the pages, considering. "Silver Spinner," he said aloud. "They ought to take that . . . in May. Naw, I'll just give Old Speck a chance. It's a long time now since we had her out."

The little Negroes had risen and were stepping quietly off along the path toward the cabin, the two little boys hand in hand, the little girl following, the baby astride her hip. They were pausing now before a dilapidated building that might long ago have been a hen house. Mr. Maury shouted at them: "Look under them old boards. That's the place for worms." The biggest boy was turning around. His treble "Yassuh" quavered over the water. Then their voices died away. There was no sound except the light turning of the willow boughs in the wind.

Mr. Maury walked along the bank, rod in hand, humming: "Bangum's gone to the wild boar's den. . . . *Bangum's* gone to the wild boar's den. . . ." He stopped where a white, peeled log protruded six or seven feet into the water. The pond made a little turn here. He stepped out squarely upon the log, still humming. The line rose smoothly, soared against the blue, and curved sweetly back upon the still water. His quick ear caught the little whish that the fly made when it clove the surface, his eye followed the tiny ripples made by its flight. He cast again, leaning a little backwards as he did sometimes when the mood was on him. Again and again his line soared out over the water. His eye rested now and then on his wrist. He noted with detachment the expert play of the muscles, admired each time the accuracy of his aim. It occurred to him that it was four days now since he had wet a line. Four days. One whole day packing up, parts of two days on the train, and yesterday wasted sitting there on that front porch with the family. But the abstinence had done him good. He had never cast better than he was casting this morning.

There was a rustling along the bank, a glimpse of blue through the trees. Mr. Maury leaned forward and peered around the clump of willows. A hundred yards away Steve, hatless, in an old blue shirt and khaki pants, stood jointing up a rod.

Mr. Maury backed off his log and advanced along the path. He called out cheerfully: "Well, feller, do any good?"

Steve looked up. His face had lightened for a moment but the abstracted expression stole over it again when he spoke. "Oh, I fiddled with it all morning." he said, "but I didn't do much good."

Mr. Maury nodded sympathetically., *"Minerva invita erat,"* he said. "You can do nothing unless Minerva perches on the roof tree. Why, I been castin' here all morning and not a strike. But there's a boat tied up over on the other side. What say we get in it and just drift around?" He paused, looked at the rod Steve had finished jointing up. "I brought another rod along," he said. "You want to use it?"

Steve shook his head. "I'm used to this one," he said.

An expression of relief came over Mr. Maury's face. "That's right," he said, "a man always does better with his own rod."

The boat was only a quarter full of water. They heaved her over and dumped it out, then dragged her down to the bank. The little Negroes had come up, bringing a can of worms. Mr. Maury threw them each a nickel and set the can in the bottom of the boat. "I always like to have a few worms handy," he told Steve, "ever since I was a boy." He lowered himself ponderously into the bow and Steve pushed off and dropped down behind him.

The little Negroes still stood on the bank staring. When the boat was a little distance out on the water the boldest of them spoke:

"You reckon 'at ole jawnboat going to hold you up, Cap'm?"

Mr. Maury turned his head to call over his shoulder. "Go 'way, boy. Ain't I done tole you I's a conjure?"

The boat dipped ominously. Steve changed his position a little and she settled to the water. Sitting well forward, Mr. Maury made graceful casts, now to this side, now to that. Steve, in the stern, made occasional casts but he laid his rod down every now and then to paddle though there was really no use in it. The boat drifted well enough with the wind. At the end of half an hour seven sizable bass lay on the bottom of the boat. Mr. Maury had caught five of them. He reflected that perhaps he really ought to change places with Steve. The man in the bow certainly had the best chance at the fish. "But no," he thought, "it don't make no difference. He don't hardly know where he is now."

He stole a glance over his shoulder at the young man's serious, abstracted face. It was like that of a person submerged. Steve seemed to float up to the surface every now and then, his expression would lighten, he would make some observation that showed he knew where he was, then he would sink again. If you asked him a question he answered punctiliously, two minutes later. Poor boy, dead to the world and would probably be that way the rest of his life. A pang of pity shot through Mr. Maury and on the heels of it a gust of that black fear that occasionally shook him. It was he, not Steve, that was the queer one. The world was full of people like this boy, all of them going around with their heads so full of this and that they hardly knew what they were doing. They were all like that. There was hardly anybody—there was *nobody* really in the whole world like him. . . .

Steve, coming out of his abstraction, spoke politely. He had heard that Mr. Maury was a fine shot. Did he like to fish better than hunt?

Mr. Maury reflected. "Well," he said, "they's something bout a covey of birds rising up in front of you . . . they's something . . . and a good dog. Now they ain't anything in this world that I like better than a good bird dog." He stopped and sighed. "A man has got to come to himself early in life if he's going to amount to anything. Now I was smart, even as a boy. I could look around me and see all the men of my family, Uncle Jeems, Uncle Quent, my father, every one of 'em weighed two hundred by the time he was fifty. You get as heavy on your feet as all that and you can't do any good shooting. But a man can fish as long as he lives. . . . Why, one place I stayed last summer there was an old man ninety years old had himself carried down to the river every morning. Yes, sir, a man can fish as long as he can get down to the water's edge. . . ."

There was a little plop to the right. He turned just in time to see the fish flash out of the water. He watched Steve take it off the hook and drop it on top of the pile in the bottom of the boat. Seven bass that made and one bream. The old lady would be pleased. "Aleck always catches me fish," she'd say.

The boat glided over the still water. There was no wind at all now. The willows that fringed the bank might have been cut out of paper. The plume of smoke hung perfectly horizontal over the roof of the Negro cabin. Mr. Maury watched it stream out in little eddies and disappear into the bright blue.

He spoke softly: "Ain't it wonderful . . . ain't it wonderful now that a man of my gifts can content himself a whole morning on this here little old pond?"

III

Mr. Maury woke with a start. He realized that he had been sleeping on his left side again. A bad idea. It always gave him palpitations of the heart. It must be that that had waked him up. He had gone to sleep almost immediately after his head hit the pillow. He rolled over, cautiously, as he always did since that bed in Leesburg had given down with him and, lying flat on his back, stared at the opposite wall.

The moon rose late. It must be at its height now. That patch of light was so brilliant he could almost discern the pattern of the wallpaper. It hung there, wavering, bitten by the shadows into a semblance of a human figure, a man striding with bent head and swinging arms. All the shadows in the room seemed to be moving toward him. The protruding corner of the washstand was an arrow aimed at his heart, the clumsy old-fashioned dresser was a giant towering above him.

They had put him to sleep in this same room the night after his wife died. In the summer it had been, too, in June; and there must have been a full moon, for the same giant shadows had struggled there with the same towering monsters. It would be like that here on this wall every full moon, for the pieces of furniture would never change their position, had never been changed, probably, since the house was built.

He turned back on his side. The wall before him was dark but he knew every flower in the pattern of the wallpaper, interlacing pink roses with, thrusting up between every third cluster, the enormous, spreading fronds of ferns. The wallpaper in the room across the hall was like it too. The old lady slept there, and in the room next to his own, Laura, his sister-in-law, and in the east bedroom downstairs, the young couple. He and Mary had slept there when they were first married, when they were the young couple in the house.

He tried to remember Mary as she must have looked that day he first saw her, the day he arrived from Virginia to open his school in the old office that used to stand there in the corner of the yard. He could see Mr. Allard plainly, sitting there under the sugar tree with his chair tilted back, could discern the old lady—young she had been then!—hospitably poised in the doorway, hand extended, could hear her voice: "Well, here are two of your pupils to start with. . . ." He remembered Laura, a shy child of nine hiding her face in her mother's skirts, but Mary that day was only a shadow in the dark hall. He could not even remember how her voice had sounded. "Professor Maury," she would have said, and her mother would have corrected her with "Cousin Aleck. . . ."

That day she got off her horse at the stile blocks she had turned as she walked across the lawn to look back at him. Her white sunbonnet had fallen on her shoulders. Her eyes, meeting his, had been dark and startled. He had gone on and had hitched both the horses before he leaped over the stile to join her. But he had known in that moment that she was the woman he was going to have. He could not remember all the rest of it, only that moment stood out. He had won her, she had become his wife, but the woman he had won was not the woman he had sought. It was as if he had had her only in that moment there on the lawn. As if she had paused there only for that one moment and was ever after retreating before him down a devious, a dark way that he would never have chosen.

The death of the first baby had been the start of it, of course. It had been a relief when she took so definitely to religion. Before that there had been those sudden, unaccountable forays out of some dark lurking place that she had. Guerilla warfare and trying to the nerves, but that had been only at first. For many years they had been two enemies contending in the open. . . . Toward the last she had taken mightily to prayer. He would wake often to find her kneeling by the side of the bed in the dark. It had gone on for years. She had never given up hope. . . .

Ah, a stouthearted one, Mary! She had never given up hope of changing him, of making him over into the man she thought he ought to be. Time and again she almost had him. And there were long periods, of course, during which he had been worn down by the conflict, one spring when he himself said, when she had told all the neighbors, that he was too old now to go fishing anymore. . . . But he had made a comeback. She had had to resort to stratagem. His lips curved in a smile, remembering the trick.

It had come over him suddenly, a general lassitude, an odd faintness in the mornings, the time when his spirits ordinarily were at their highest. He had sat there by the window, almost wishing to have some ache or pain, something definite to account for his condition. But he did not feel sick in his body. It was rather a dulling of all his senses. There were no longer the reactions to the visible world that made his days a series of adventures. He had looked out of the window at the woods glistening with spring rain; he had not even taken down his gun to shoot a squirrel.

Remembering Uncle Quent's last days he had been alarmed, had decided finally that he must tell her so that they might begin preparations for the future—he had shuddered at the thought of eventual confinement, perhaps in some institution. She had looked up from her sewing, unable to repress a smile.

"You think it's your mind, Aleck. . . . It's coffee. . . . I've been giving you a coffee substitute every morning. . . ."

They had laughed together over her cleverness. He had not gone back to coffee but the lassitude had worn off. She had gone back to the attack with redoubled vigor. In the afternoons she would stand on the porch calling after him as he slipped down to the creek. "Now, don't stay long enough to get that cramp. You remember how you suffered last time. . . ." He would have forgotten all about the cramp until that moment but it would hang over him then through the whole afternoon's sport and it would descend upon him inevitably when he left the river and started for the house.

Yes, he thought with pride. She was wearing him down—he did not believe there was a man living who could withstand her a lifetime—she was wearing him down and would have had him in another few months, another year certainly. But she had been struck down just as victory was in her grasp. The paralysis had come on her in the night. It was as if a curtain had descended, dividing their life sharply into two parts. In the bewildered year and a half that followed he had found himself forlornly trying to reconstruct the Mary he had known. The pressure she had so constantly exerted upon him had become for him a part of her personality. This new, calm Mary was not the woman he had lived with all these years. She had lain there—heroically they all said—waiting for death. And lying there, waiting, all her faculties engaged now in defensive warfare, she had raised, as it were, her lifelong siege; she had lost interest in his comings and goings, had once even encouraged him to go for an afternoon's sport! He felt a rush of warm pity. Poor Mary! She must have realized toward the last that she had wasted herself in conflict. She had spent her arms and her strength against an inglorious foe when all the time the real, the invincible adversary waited. . . .

He turned over on his back again. The moonlight was waning, the contending shadows paler now and retreating toward the door. From across the hall came the sound of long, sibilant breaths, ending each one on a little upward groan. The old lady. . . . She would maintain till her dying day that she did not snore. He fancied now that he could hear from the next room Laura's light, regular breathing and downstairs were the young couple asleep in each other's arms. . . .

All of them quiet and relaxed now, but they had been lively enough at dinnertime. It had started with the talk about Aunt Sally Crenfew's funeral tomorrow. Living now, as he had for some years, away from women of his family, he had forgotten the need to be cautious. He had spoken up before he thought:

"But that's the day Steve and I were going to Barker's Mill. . . ."

Sarah had cried out at the idea. "Barker's Mill!" she had said. "Right on the Crenfew land . . . well, if not on the very farm, in the very next field. It would be a scandal if he, Professor Maury, known by everybody to be in the neighborhood, could not spare one afternoon, one insignificant summer afternoon, from his fishing long enough to attend the funeral of his cousin, the cousin of all of them, the oldest lady in the whole family connection. . . ."

Looking around the table he had caught the same look in every eye; he had felt a gust of that same fright that had shaken him there on the pond. That look! Sooner or later you met it in every human eye. The thing was to be up and ready, ready to run for your life at a moment's notice. Yes, it had always been like that. It always would be. His fear of them was shot through suddenly with contempt. It was as if Mary were there laughing with him. *She* knew that there was not one of them who could have survived as he had survived, could have paid the price for freedom that he had paid. . . .

Sarah had come to a stop. He had to say something. He shook his head.

"You think we just go fishing to have a good time. The boy and I hold high converse on that pond. I'm starved for intellectual companionship, I tell you. . . . In Florida I never see anybody but niggers. . . ."

They had all laughed out at that. "As if you didn't *prefer* the society of niggers!" Sarah said scornfully.

The old lady had been moved to anecdote:

"I remember when Aleck first came out here from Virginia, Cousin Sophy said: 'Professor Maury is so well educated. Now Cousin Cave Maynor is dead who is there in the neighborhood for him to associate with?' 'Well,' I said, 'I don't know about that. He seems perfectly satisfied with Ben Hooser. They're off to the creek together every evening soon as school is out.'"

Ben Hooser. . . . He could see now the wrinkled face, overlaid with that ashy pallor of the aged Negro, smiling eyes, the pendulous lower lip that, drooping away, showed always some of the rotten teeth. A fine nigger, Ben, and on to a lot of tricks, the only man really that he'd ever cared to take fishing with him.

But the first real friend of his bosom had been old Uncle Teague, the factotum at Hawkwood. Once a week or more likely every ten days he fed the hounds on the carcass of a calf that had had time to get pretty high. They would drive the spring wagon out into the lot; he, a boy of ten, beside Uncle Teague on the driver's seat. The hounds would come in a great rush and rear their slobbering jowls against the wagon wheels. Uncle Teague would wield his whip, chuckling while he threw the first hunk of meat to Old Mag, his favorite.

"Dey goin' run on dis," he'd say. "Dey goin' run like a shadow. . . ."

He shifted his position again, cautiously. People, he thought . . . people . . . so bone ignorant, all of them. Not one person in a thousand realized that a foxhound remains at heart a wild beast and must kill and gorge and then, when he is ravenous, kill and gorge again. . . . Or that the channel cat is a night feeder. . . . Or . . . His daughter had told him once that he ought to set all his knowledge down in a book. "Why?" he had asked. "So everybody else can know as much as I do?"

If he allowed his mind to get active, really active, he would never get any sleep. He was fighting an inclination now to get up and find a cigarette. He relaxed again upon his pillows, deliberately summoned pictures before his mind's eye. Landscapes—and streams. He observed their outlines, watched one flow into another. The Black River into West Fork, that in turn into Spring Creek and Spring Creek into the Withlicoochee. Then they were all flowing together, merging into one broad plain. He watched it take form slowly: the wide field in front of Hawkwood, the Rivanna River on one side, on the other Peters' Mountain. They would be waiting there till the fox showed himself on that little rise by the river. The young men would hold back till Uncle James had wheeled Old Filly, then they would all be off pell-mell across the plain. He himself would be mounted on Jonesboro. Almost blind, but she would take anything you put her at. That first thicket on the edge of the woods. They would break there, one half of them going around, the other half streaking it through the woods. He was always of those going around to try to cut the fox off on the other side. No, he was down off his horse. He was coursing with the fox through the trees. He could hear the sharp, pointed feet padding on the dead leaves, see the quick head turned now and then over the shoulder. The trees kept flashing by, one black trunk after another. And now it was a ragged mountain field and the sage grass running before them in waves to where a narrow stream curved in between the ridges. The fox's feet were light in the water. He moved forward steadily, head down. The hounds' baying grew louder. Old Mag knew the trick. She had stopped to give tongue by that big rock and now they had all leaped the gulch and were scrambling up through the pines. But the fox's feet were already hard on the mountain path. He ran slowly, past the big boulder, past the blasted pine to where the shadow of the Pinnacle Rock was black across the path. He ran on and the shadow swayed and rose to meet him. Its cool touch was on his hot tongue, his heaving flanks. He had slipped in under it. He was sinking down, panting, in black dark, on moist earth while the hounds' baying filled the valley and reverberated from the mountainside.

Mr. Maury got up and lit a cigarette. He smoked it quietly, lying back upon his pillows. When he had finished smoking he rolled over on his side and closed his eyes. It was still a good while till morning, but perhaps he could get some sleep. His mind played quietly over the scene that would be enacted in the morning. He would be sitting on the porch after breakfast, smoking, when Sarah came out. She would ask him how he felt, how he had slept.

He would heave a groan, not looking at her for fear of catching that smile on her face—the girl had little sense of decency. He would heave a groan, not too loud or overdone. "My kidney trouble," he would say, shaking his head. "It's come back on me, daughter, in the night."

She would express sympathy and go on to talk of something else. She never took any stock in his kidney trouble. He would ask her finally if she reckoned Steve had time to drive him to the train that morning. He'd been thinking about how much good the chalybeate water of Estill Springs had done him last year. He might heave another groan here to drown her protests. "No. . . . I better be getting on to the Springs. . . . I need the water. . . ."

She would talk on a lot after that. He would not need to listen. He would be sitting there thinking about Elk River, where it runs through the village of Estill Springs.

He could see that place by the bridge now: a wide, deep pool with plenty of lay-bys under the willows.

The train would get in around one o'clock. That nigger, Ed, would hustle his bags up to the boardinghouse for him. He would tell Mrs. Rogers he must have the same room. He would have his bags packed so he could get at everything quick. He would be into his black shirt and fishing pants before you could say Jack Robinson. . . . Thirty minutes after he got off the train he would have a fly in that water.

Cleanth Brooks

(1906–1994)

Any assessment of literary criticism in the twentieth century must begin with the New Criticism, a critical method pioneered by Cleanth Brooks along with John Crowe Ransom, Allen Tate, and Robert Penn Warren. The New Critics argued that assessing the value of a poem on the basis of any other factors than its own "internal unity"—its success in uniting form and content as well as its value as a part of a larger literary tradition—undercuts its value as an aesthetic object. Many of the critics of Brooks's day objected to the approach, and modern literary theorists have intensified the attacks, asserting that the New Criticism fails to account for the effects of race, class, and gender on the arts. Regardless, few would dispute Brooks's standing as one of the most influential critics of his century.

　　Born the son of a Methodist minister in Murray, Kentucky, Brooks was educated at Vanderbilt University in Tennessee and Tulane University in Louisiana before attending Oxford University in England as a Rhodes Scholar. He taught at Louisiana State University before moving to Yale in 1947, where he finished his career as an educator. *Understanding Poetry*, which he coauthored with Robert Penn Warren in 1938, is considered a foundational text of the New Criticism. *Modern Poetry and the Tradition* (1939), *The Well Wrought Urn* (1947), and *A Shaping Joy* (1971) evidenced the further development of his critical philosophy. Though Brooks first developed this philosophy in relation to poetry, he also applied it to his study of the prose of William Faulkner. His four volumes on Faulkner, *William Faulkner: The Yoknapatawpha Country* (1963), *William Faulkner: Toward Yoknapatawpha and Beyond* (1978), *William Faulkner: First Encounters* (1983), and *On the Prejudices, Predilections, and Firm Beliefs of William Faulkner* (1987), are considered to be among the seminal critiques of that novelist's work. Brooks died at his home in New Haven, Connecticut, in 1994.

from *The Hidden God*

3. William Faulkner: Vision of Good and Evil

Professor Randall Stewart, in his very stimulating little book *American Literature and Christian Doctrine*, asserts that "Faulkner embodies and dramatizes the basic Christian concepts so effectively that he can with justice be regarded as one of the most profoundly Christian writers in our time. There is everywhere in his writings the basic premise of Original Sin: everywhere the conflict between the flesh and the spirit. One finds also the necessity of discipline, of trial by fire in the furnace of affliction, of sacrifice and the sacrificial death, of redemption through sacrifice. Man in Faulkner is a heroic, tragic figure." This is a view with which I am in basic sympathy. I agree heartily with Professor Stewart on the matter of Faulkner's concern with what he calls "original sin," and with Faulkner's emphasis upon discipline, sacrifice, and redemption. But to call Faulkner, "one of the most profoundly Christian writers in our time" seems somewhat incautious. Perhaps it would be safer to say that Faulkner is a profoundly religious writer; that his characters come out of a Christian environment, and represent, whatever their shortcomings and whatever their theological heresies, Christian concerns; and that they are finally to be understood only by reference to Christian premises.

Probably the best place to start is with the term "original sin." The point of reference might very well be T. E. Hulme, one of the profoundly seminal influences on our time, though a critic and philosopher whom Faulkner probably never read. In "Humanism and the Religious Attitude" Hulme argued for a return to orthodox doctrine. His concern with religion, however, had nothing to do with recapturing what he called "the sentiment of Fra Angelico." Rather, "What is important," he asserted, "is what nobody seems to realize—the dogmas like that of Original Sin, which are the closest expression of the categories of the religious attitude. That man is in no sense perfect, but a wretched creature, who can apprehend perfection. It is not, then, that I put up with the dogma for the sake of the sentiment, but that I may possibly swallow the sentiment for the sake of the dogma."

Hulme's position as stated here would seem to smack of scholastic Calvinism rather than of the tradition of Catholic Christianity. His emphasis at least suggests that nature is radically evil and not merely gone wrong somehow—corrupted by a fall. But if Hulme's passage is so tinged, that very fact may make it the more relevant to Faulkner, who shows, in some aspects, the influence of Southern Puritanism.

Be that as it may, Hulme's is not a didactic theory of literature, which stresses some direct preachment to be made. On the contrary, his "classicism" derives from a clear distinction between religious doctrine and poetic structure. It is romantic poetry which blurs that distinction, competing with religion by trying to drag in the infinite. With romanticism we enter the area of "spilt religion," and romantic "damp and fugginess." For Hulme, the classic attitude involves a recognition of man's limitations—his finitude. Since the classical view of man recognizes his limitations and does not presume upon them, the classical attitude, Hulme argues, is a religious attitude. For Hulme is quite convinced that man, though capable of recognizing goodness, is not naturally good. It is only by discipline that he can achieve something of value.

The whole point is an important one, for Faulkner's positive beliefs are often identified with some kind of romantic primitivism. Thus his concern with idiots and children and uneducated rural people, both white and Negro, is sometimes interpreted to mean that man is made evil only by his environment with its corrupting restrictions and inhibitions, and that if man could only realize his deeper impulses, he would be good.[1]

---

[1]Faulkner, a few years ago, in defining his notion of Christianity, called it a "code of behavior by means of which (man) makes himself a better human being than his nature wants to be, if he follows his nature only" (*Paris Review*, Spring 1956, p. 42).

Allied to this misconception is another, namely that Faulkner's characters have no power of choice, being merely the creatures of their drives and needs, and that they are determined by their environment and are helplessly adrift upon the tides of circumstance. It is true that many of his characters are obsessed creatures or badly warped by traumatic experiences, or that they are presented by Faulkner as acting under some kind of compulsion. But his characters are not mere products of an environment. They have the power of choice, they make decisions, and they win their goodness through effort and discipline.

If Faulkner does not believe that man is naturally good and needs only to realize his natural impulses, and if he does believe that man has free will and must act responsibly and discipline himself, then these beliefs are indeed worth stressing, for they are calculated to separate him sharply from writers of a more naturalistic and secularistic temper. But I grant that to attribute to Faulkner a belief in original sin or in man's need for discipline would not necessarily prove him a Christian. The concept of grace, for example, is either lacking or at least not clearly evident in Faulkner's work.

Let us begin, then, by examining Faulkner's criticism of secularism and rationalism. A very important theme in his earlier work is the discovery of evil, which is part of man's initiation into the nature of reality. That brilliant and horrifying early novel *Sanctuary* is, it seems to me, to be understood primarily in terms of such an initiation. Horace Benbow is the sentimental idealist, the man of academic temper, who finds out that the world is not a place of moral tidiness or even of justice. He discovers with increasing horror that evil is rooted in the very nature of things. As an intellectual, he likes to ponder meanings and events, he has a great capacity for belief in ideas, and a great confidence in the efficacy of reason. What he comes to discover is the horrifying presence of evil, its insidiousness, and its penetration of every kind of rational or civilized order. There is in this story, to be sure, the unnatural rape of the seventeen-year-old girl by the gangster Popeye, and the story of Popeye's wanton murder of Tommy, but Horace Benbow might conceivably accept both of these things as the kinds of cruel accidents to which human life is subject. What crumples him up is the moral corruption of the girl, which follows on her rape: she actually accepts her life in the brothel and testifies at the trial in favor of the man who had abducted her. What Horace also discovers is that the forces of law and order are also corruptible. His opponent in the trial, the district attorney, plays fast and loose with the evidence and actually ensures that the innocent man will not only be convicted but burned to death by a mob. And what perhaps Horace himself does not discover (but it is made plainly evident to the reader) is that Horace's betrayal at the trial is finally a bosom betrayal: Horace's own sister gives the district attorney the tip-off that will allow him to defeat her brother and make a mockery of justice. Indeed, Horace's sister, the calm and serene Narcissa, is, next to Popeye, the most terrifying person in the novel. She simply does not want her brother associated with people like the accused man, Lee Goodwin, the bootlegger, and his common-law wife. She exclaims to her brother, "I don't see that it makes any difference who [committed the murder]. The question is, are you going to stay mixed up with it?" And she sees to it with quiet and efficient ruthlessness that the trial ends at the first possible date, even though this costs an innocent man's life.

Sanctuary is clearly Faulkner's bitterest novel. It is a novel in which the initiation which every male must undergo is experienced in its most shattering and disillusioning form. Horace not only discovers the existence of evil: he experiences it, not as an abstract idea but as an integral portion of reality. After he has had his interview with Temple Drake in the brothel, he thinks: "Perhaps it is upon the instant that we realize, admit, that there is a logical pattern to evil, that we die," and he thinks of the expression he had once seen in the eyes of a dead child and in the eyes of the other dead: "the cooling indignation, the shocked despair fading, leaving two empty globes in which the motionless world lurked profoundly in miniature."

One of the most important connections has already been touched upon in what I have said earlier. Horace Benbow's initiation into the nature of reality and the nature of evil is intimately associated with his discovery of the true nature of woman. His discovery is quite typical of Faulkner's male characters. In the Faulknerian notion of things, men have to lose their innocence, confront the hard choice, and through a process of initiation discover reality. The women are already in possession of this knowledge, naturally and instinctively. That is why in moments of bitterness Faulkner's male characters—Mr. Compson in *The Sound and the Fury*, for example—assert that women are not innocent. Mr. Compson tells his son Quentin: "Women are like that[;] they don't acquire knowledge of people[. Men] are for that [. Women] are just born with a practical fertility of suspicion. . . . they have an affinity or evil[—]for supplying whatever the evil lacks in itself[—]drawing it about them instinctively as you do bed clothing in slumber. . . ." Again, "Women only use other people's codes of honour."

I suppose that we need not take these Schopenhauerian profundities of the bourbon-soaked Mr. Compson too seriously. It might on the whole be more accurate to say that Faulkner's women lack the callow idealism of the men, have fewer illusions about human nature, and are less trammeled by legalistic distinctions and niceties of any code of conduct.

Faulkner's view of women, then, is radically old-fashioned—even medieval. Woman is the source and sustainer of virtue and also a prime source of evil. She can be either, because she is, as man is not, always a little beyond good and evil. With her powerful natural drives and her instinct for the concrete and personal, she does not need to agonize over her decisions. There is no code for her to master—no initiation for her to undergo. For this reason she has access to a wisdom which is veiled from man; and man's codes, good or bad, are always, in their formal abstraction, a little absurd in her eyes. Women are close to nature; the feminine principle is closely related to the instinctive and natural: woman typically manifests pathos rather than ethos.

A little later I shall have something more to say about Faulkner's characters in confrontation with nature. At this point, however, I want to go back and refer to another aspect of *Sanctuary*. The worst villains in Faulkner are cut off from nature. They have in some profound way denied their nature, like Flem Snopes in *The Hamlet*, who has no natural vices, only the unnatural vice of a pure lust for power and money. In *Sanctuary* Popeye is depicted as a sort of *ludus naturae*. Everybody has noticed the way in which he is described, as if he were a kind of automaton, with eyes like "two knobs of soft black rubber." As Horace watches him across the spring, Popeye's "face had a queer, bloodless color, as though seen by electric light; against the sunny silence, in his slanted straw hat and his slightly akimbo arms, he had that vicious depthless quality of stamped tin." Faulkner's two figures of speech are brilliantly used here. They serve to rob Popeye of substance and to turn him into a sinister black silhouette against the spring landscape. The phrase "as though seen by electric light" justifies the description of his queer, bloodless color, but it does more than this. Juxtaposed as it is to the phrase "against the sunny silence," it stresses the sense of the contrived, the artificial, as though Popeye constituted a kind of monstrous affront to the natural scene. These suggestions of a shadowy lack of substance are confirmed at the end of the sentence with the closing phrase: "depthless quality of stamped tin." Faulkner relentlessly forces this notion of the unnatural: Popeye deliberately spits into the spring, he cringes in terror from the low swooping owl, he is afraid of the dark.

Popeye has no natural vices either. He cannot drink. Since he is impotent, he is forced to use unnatural means in his rape of Temple. As a consequence, some readers take Popeye to be a kind of allegorical figure, a representation of the inhumanly mechanistic forces of our society. We may say that Popeye is quite literally a monster, remembering that the Latin *monstrum* signifies something that lies outside the ordinary course of nature.

Though Popeye represents an extreme case, in this matter he is typical of all of Faulkner's villains. For example, Thomas Sutpen, in *Absalom, Absalom!*, is a man of great courage and heroic stature, who challenges the role of a tragic protagonist. Yet he has about him this same rigid and mechanical quality. Sutpen, as an acquaintance observes, believes "that the ingredients of morality were like the ingredients of pie or cake and once you had measured them and balanced them and mixed them and put them into the oven it was all finished and nothing but pie or cake could come out."

Sutpen has a great plan in mind, his "design," he calls it—which involves his building a great plantation house and setting up a dynasty. As he tells General Compson, "I had a design. To accomplish it I should require money, a house, and a plantation, slaves, a family—incidentally, of course, a wife." But when he finds later that his wife has a trace of Negro blood, he puts her aside, and he does it with an air of honest grievance. He says "[Her parents] deliberately withheld from me the one fact which I have reason to know they were aware would have caused me to decline the entire matter, otherwise they would not have withheld it from me—a fact which I did not learn until after my son was born. And even then I did not act hastily. I could have reminded them of these wasted years, these years which would now leave me behind with my schedule. . . ." (The last term is significant: Sutpen, modern man that he is, works in accordance with a timetable.) He tells General Compson that when he put aside his wife and child, "his conscience had bothered him somewhat at first but that he had argued calmly and logically with his conscience until it was settled." General Compson is aghast at this revelation of moral myopia. He calls it "innocence," and by the term he means a blindness to the nature of reality. And since the writer is Faulkner, the blindness involves a blindness to the nature of woman. For Sutpen has actually believed that by providing a more than must property settlement he could reconcile his wife to his abandoning her. General Compson had thrown up his hands and exclaimed: "Good God, man . . . what kind of conscience [did you have] to trade with which would have warranted you in the belief that you could have bought immunity from her for no other coin but justice?—"

Evil for Faulkner, then, involves a violation of nature and runs counter to the natural appetites and affections. And yet, as we have seen, the converse is not true; Faulkner does not consider the natural and instinctive and impulsive as automatically and necessarily good. Here I think rests the best warrant for maintaining that Faulkner holds an orthodox view of man and reality. For his men, at least, cannot be content merely with being natural. They cannot live merely by their instincts and natural appetites. They must confront the fact of evil. They are constrained to moral choices. They have to undergo a test of their courage, in making and abiding by the choice. They achieve goodness by discipline and effort. This propositions perhaps most fully and brilliantly illustrated in Faulkner's story "The Bear." Isaac McCaslin, when he comes of age, decides to repudiate his inheritance. He refuses to accept his father's plantation and chooses to earn his living as a carpenter and to live in a rented room. There are two powerful motives that shape this decision: the sacramental view of nature which he has been taught by the old hunter, Sam Fathers, and the discovery of his grandfather's guilt in his treatment of one of his slaves: the grandfather had incestuously begotten a child upon his own half-Negro daughter.

"The Bear" is thus a story of penance and expiation, as also of a difficult moral decision made and maintained, but since it is so well known and has received so much commentary, I want to illustrate Faulkner's characteristic drama of moral choice from a less familiar story, "An Odor of Verbena," which is the concluding section of Faulkner's too little appreciated but brilliant novel *The Unvanquished*. As this episode opens, word has come to Bayard Sartoris, a young man of twenty-four off at law school, that his father has been assassinated by a political enemy. Ringo, the young Negro man of his own age and his boyhood companion, has ridden to the little town where Bayard is at law school to bring the news. Bayard knows what is expected of him—the date is 1874, the tradition of the code of honor still lingers. The devastating Civil War and the Reconstruction have contorted the land with violence, and Bayard knows that the community expects him to call his father's assassin to account. Even the quiet and gentle Judge Wilkins with whom he is studying law expects him to do so, and though he speaks to the boy with pity ("Bayard, my son, my dear son"), he offers him not only his horse but his pistol as well. Certainly also Bayard's father's Civil War troop expect him to avenge his father. Bayard's young stepmother, eight years older than he, expects it. Speaking in a "silvery ecstatic voice" like the priestess of a rite wrought up to a point of hysteria, she offers Bayard the pistols when he returns to the family home. Even Ringo expects it.

Some years before, when Bayard and Ringo were sixteen, at the very end of the Civil War, when the region had become a no-man's land terrorized by bushwhackers, Bayard's grandmother had been killed by a ruffian named Grumby, and Bayard and Ringo had followed him for weeks until finally they had run him down and killed him. Bayard had loved his grandmother, and was resolved that her murderer should be punished. But there was no law and order in this troubled time to which he could appeal; the two sixteen-year-old boys had to undertake the punishment themselves.

Now as the two young men ride back to Jefferson, Ringo says to Bayard, "We could bushwhack him. . . . Like we done Grumby that day. But I reckon that wouldn't suit that white skin you walks around in." Bayard in fact has resolved that he will not kill again.

The motive for this decision is complex. For one thing, he realizes that his father had become a proud and abstracted and ruthless man. Bayard had loved his father but is well aware that his father had pressed his opponent, Redmond, far too hard. George Wyatt, the countryman who had served under his father, earlier had in fact come to Bayard to ask him to restrain his father: "'Right or wrong,' he said, 'us boys and most of the other folks in this county know John's right. But he ought to let Redmond alone. I know what's wrong: he's had to kill too many folks, and that's bad for a man. We all know Colonel's brave as a lion, but Redmond ain't no coward either and they ain't any use in making a brave man that made one mistake eat crow all the time. Can't you talk to him?'"

Another powerful motive is evidently the psychic wound that Bayard has suffered in the killing of Grumby. He has executed vengeance once, and in that instance there were extenuating circumstances to justify his taking the law into his own hands. But this case is different, and as he says to himself before he begins his journey home, "If there [is] anything at all in the Book, anything of hope and peace for [God's] blind and bewildered spawn," the command "'*Thou Shalt not kill*' must be it." Finally, and not least, there is the example of his own father. Even his father had decided that there had been too much killing. Two months before, he had told Bayard: "Now I shall do a little moral house cleaning. I am tired of killing men, no matter what the necessity or the end." Thus Bayard, in resolving not to avenge his father, may be said to be following his father's own resolve.

But Bayard, as a member of a tightly knit community, does not want to be branded as a coward; he respects his community's opinion, and he feels compelled to live up to what the community expects of him. And so he resolves, though the reader does not learn of it until late in the story, to face Redmond, but to face him unarmed.

There is one person who understands his dilemma and can support him in his decision. It is his Aunt Jenny, who tells him when he arrives home that night: "'Yes. All right. Don't let it be Drusilla, poor hysterical young woman. And don't let it be [your father], Bayard, because he's dead now. And don't let it be George Wyatt and those others who will be waiting for you tomorrow morning. I know you are not afraid.' 'But what good will that do?' I said. 'What good will that do?' . . . 'I must live with myself, you see.' 'Then it's not just Drusilla? Not just him? Not just George Wyatt and Jefferson?' 'No,' I said."

It is indeed not just Drusilla and George Wyatt and the other outsiders that are forcing Bayard to take his proposed course of action. As he tells his aunt, it is not enough that *she* knows that he is not afraid. He must prove it to himself. "I must live with myself," he says. This is the situation of many a Faulkner character. He must live with himself. He must prove to himself that he possesses the requisite courage.

Bayard is fortunate. The man that he goes to meet is also brave, also decent. He has decided that, having killed the father, he will not kill the young son. Thus, when Bayard walks up the stairs past the small faded sign "*B. J. Redmond, Atty at Law*" and opens the door, he sees Redmond sitting "behind the desk, not much taller than Father, but thicker as a man gets that spends most of his time sitting and listening to people, freshly shaven and with fresh linen; a lawyer yet it was not a lawyer's face—a face much thinner than the body would indicate, strained (and yes, tragic; I know that now) and exhausted beneath the neat recent steady strokes of the razor, holding a pistol flat on the desk before him, loose beneath his hand and aimed at nothing." Redmond fires twice but Bayard can see that the gun was not aimed at him and that the misses are deliberate. Then Redmond gets up from his desk, blunders down the stairs and walks on out past George Wyatt and the six other members of Colonel Sartoris' old troop. He "walked through the middle of them with his hat on and his head up (they told me how someone shouted at him: 'Have you killed that boy too?' saying no word, staring straight ahead and with his back to them, on to the station where the south-bound train was just in and got on it with no baggage, nothing, and went away from Jefferson and from Mississippi and never came back."

George Wyatt rushes up to Bayard, mistakenly thinking that he had taken Redmond's pistol away from him and then missed him, missed him twice. "Then he answered himself . . . 'No; wait. You walked in here without even a pocket knife and let him miss you twice. My God in heaven.'" But he adds, "'You ain't done anything to be ashamed of. I wouldn't have done it that way, myself. I'd a shot at him once, anyway. But that's your way or you wouldn't have done it.'" And even Drusilla, the wrought-up priestess of violence, before she leaves the house forever to go back to her kinsfolk in Alabama, leaves on Bayard's pillow a sprig of verbena because it is the odor of courage, "that odor which she said you could smell alone above the smell of horses," as a token that she too has accepted his act as brave and honorable.

One further observation: as I have already remarked, it is the men who have to be initiated into the meaning of reality, who have to observe a code of conduct, who have to prove themselves worthy. Aunt Jenny, as a woman, is outside the code. Indeed she sees the code as absurd and quixotic, though she knows that Bayard as a man will have to observe it. And what shall we say of Drusilla, who is a woman, and yet is the very high priestess of the code? Drusilla is the masculinized woman, who as a type occurs more than once in Faulkner. Drusilla's story is that she has lost her fiancé early in the war and finally in her boredom and despair has actually ridden with the Confederate cavalry. She is brave and Faulkner gives her her due, but he is not celebrating her as a kind of Confederate Joan of Arc. Her action exacts its penalty and she ends a warped and twisted woman, truly a victim of the war.

I realize that I am risking oversimplification in pressing some of these issues so hard—for example, the contrast between man and woman, in their relation to nature and to their characteristic roles as active and passive. One may be disposed to doubt that even a traditional writer writing about a traditional society would stylize these relationships as much as I have suggested Faulkner has. Yet I am very anxious to sketch in, even at the risk of overbold strokes, the general nature of Faulkner's conception of good and evil, and so I mean to stand by this summary. Faulkner sees the role of man as active; man makes choices and lives up to the choices. Faulkner sees the role of woman as characteristically fostering and sustaining. She undergirds society, upholding the family and community mores, sending her men out into battle, including the ethical battle. This generalization I believe, is, if oversimplified, basically true. And I should like to relate it to Faulkner's "Calvinistic" Protestantism. In so far as his Calvinism represents a violent repression and constriction of natural impulse, a denial of nature itself, Faulkner tends to regard it as a terrible and evil thing. And the natural foil to characters who have so hardened their hearts in accordance with their notion of a harsh and vindictive God is the feminine principle as exemplified by a person like Lena Grove, the heroine of *Light in August*. Lena has a childlike confidence in herself and in mankind. She is a creature of warm natural sympathies and a deep instinctive commitment to her natural function.

But Faulkner has still another relation to Calvinistic Protestantism. Insofar as the tradition insists that man must be brought up to the urgency of decision, must be set tests of courage and endurance, must have his sinews strung tight for some moral leap or his back braced so as to stand firm against the push of circumstance, Faulkner evidently derives from this tradition. From it may be derived the very necessity that compels his male characters to undergo an initiation. The required initiation may be analogous to the crisis of conversion and the character's successful entrance into knowledge of himself, analogous to the sinner's experiencing salvation.

On the conscious level, Faulkner is obviously a Protestant anticleric, fascinated, but also infuriated, by some of the more violently repressive features of the religion that dominates his country. This matter is easily illustrated. One of his masterpieces,

Light in August, provides a stinging criticism of the harsher aspects of Protestantism. Indeed a basic theme in *Light in August* is man's strained attempt to hold himself up in a rigid aloofness above the relaxed female world. The struggle to do so is, as Faulkner portrays it in this novel, at once monstrous, comic, and heroic, as the various characters take up their special postures.

In a character like old Doc Hines, there is a definite distortion and perversion. His fury at "bitchery and abomination" is the fury of a crazed man. In her conversation with Bunch and Hightower, Mrs. Hines states quite precisely what has happened to her husband: he began "then to take God's name in vain and in pride to justify and excuse the devil that was in him." His attribution of his furies to God is quite literally a taking of God's name in vain, blasphemy. The tendency to call one's own hates the vengeance of a just God is a sin to which Protestantism has always been prone. But not merely Southern Protestantism and, of course, not merely Protestantism as such.

Calvin Burden represents another instance of the militant Protestant, but this man's heartiness and boisterous energy have something of the quality of comedy. He is the son of a Unitarian minister; but when he runs away to the West, he becomes a Roman Catholic and lives for a year in a monastery. Then, on his marriage, he repudiates the Catholic Church, choosing for the scene of his formal repudiation "a saloon, insisting that every one present listen to him and state their objections." Then, though he cannot read the English Bible—he had learned from the priests in California to read Spanish—he begins to instruct his child in the true religion, interspersing his readings to the child in Spanish with "extemporised dissertations composed half of the bleak and bloodless logic which he remembered from his father on interminable New England Sundays and half of immediate hellfire and tangible brimstone." Perhaps he differs from the bulk of doctrinaire hellfire and brimstone Protestants in not being a "proselyter" or a "missionary." But everything else marks him as truly of the breed: his intensity, his stern authoritarianism, and his violence. He has killed a man in an argument over slavery and he threatens to "frail the tar" out of his children if they do not learn to hate what he hates—hell and slaveholders.

The case of the Rev. Gail Hightower is one of the most interesting of all. He is the only one of these Protestants who has had formal theological training. Because of that fact one might expect him to be the most doctrinaire. He is not. He seems at the beginning of the book the most tolerant and pitying of all the characters, the one who recoils in horror at man's capacity for evil and man's propensity to crucify his fellows: he is a man whose only defense against violence is nonresistance. One may be inclined to say that Hightower had rebelled against his Calvinist training and repudiated the jealous and repressive God. Certainly, there is truth in this notion. Hightower is a disillusioned man and a man who has learned something from his sufferings. But there is a sense in which he has never broken out of the mold: he still stresses a God of justice rather than of mercy, for his sincerest belief is that he has somehow "bought immunity." He exclaims: "I have paid. I have paid"—in confidence that God is an honest merchant who has receipted his bill and will honor his title to the precious merchandise he has purchased at such cost.

Lastly there is the case of Joe Christmas, the violent rebel against hellfire Protestantism. His detachment from any kind of human community is shocking. Here is a man who has no family ties, no continuity with the past, no place in any community whatsoever. He is a man who has literally tried to kick the earth out from under his feet. Yet his very alienation and his insistence upon his own individual integrity are touched with the tragically heroic. As a child he is conscious that he is being hounded by old Doc Hines; he resists stubbornly the discipline imposed by his foster father McEachern, whom he finally brains with a chair; and when his paramour, Joanna Burden, threatens him with hell and insists that he kneel with her and pray for forgiveness, he decapitates her. Yet there is a most important sense in which Joe Christmas is the sternest and most doctrinaire Calvinist in the book.

He imbibes more from the training of his foster father than he realizes. For all that he strains in fierce resistance against him, he "could depend" on "the hard, just, ruthless man." It is the "soft kindness" of the woman, his foster mother that he abominates. If one mark of the Calvinists in this novel is their fear and distrust of women and their hatred of the female principle, then Joe Christmas is eminently qualified to take a place among them. He even has affinities with his old childhood ogre, Doc Hines, and Hines' fury at the bitchery of women and the abomination of Negro blood. Joe, hearing the "fecundmellow" voices of Negro women, feels that he and "all other manshaped life about him" had been returned to the "lightless hot wet primogenitive Female" and runs from the scene in a kind of panic.

Christmas too wants not mercy but justice, is afraid of the claims of love and its obligations, and yearns only for a vindication of his identity and integrity—a vindication made the more difficult by his not really knowing precisely what he would vindicate. When he puts aside the temptation to marry Joanna and win ease and security, he does it by saying: "If I give in now, I will deny all the thirty years that I have lived to make me what I chose to be." Finally, Joe is something of a fatalist, and his fatalism is a kind of perversion of Calvinist determinism. On his way to murder Joanna, "he believed with calm paradox that he was the volitionless servant of the fatality in which he believed that he did not believe." But so "fated" is his act of murder that he keeps saying to himself "I had to do it"—using the past tense, as if the act had already been performed.

Lena (along with Eula of *The Hamlet*) has sometimes been called an earth goddess. The description does have a certain aptness when applied to Eula, especially in some of the more rhapsodic passages of *The Hamlet*. But it is a little highfalutin for Lena. It is more accurate to say that Lena is one of Faulkner's several embodiments of the female principle—indeed one of the purest and least complicated of his embodiments. Her rapport with nature is close. She is never baffled as to what course of action to take. She is never torn by doubts and indecisions. There is no painful introspection. This serene composure has frequently been put down to sheer mindlessness, and Lena, to be sure, is a very simple young woman. But Faulkner himself undoubtedly attributes most of Lena's quiet force to her female nature. In this novel the principal male characters suffer alienation. They are separated from the community, are in rebellion against it—and against nature. But Lena moves serenely into the community, and it gathers itself about her with protective gestures. Its response to her, of course, is rooted in a deep and sound instinct: Lena embodies the principle upon which any human community is founded. She is the carrier of life and she has to be protected and nurtured if there is to be any human community at all.

I have said that *Light in August* depicts man's strained attempt to hold himself up in rigid aloofness above the relaxed female world. In terms of the plot, Lena is the direct means by which Byron Bunch and the indirect means by which Hightower are redeemed from their pallid half lives and brought back into the community. This coming back into the community is an essential part of the redemption. Unless the controlling purposes of the individuals are related to those that other men share, and in which the individual can participate, he is indeed isolated, and is forced to fall back upon his personal values, with all the risk of fanaticism and distortion to which such isolation is liable.

The community is at once the field for man's action and the norm by which his action is judged and regulated. It sometimes seems that the sense of an organic community has all but disappeared from modern fiction, and the disappearance accounts for the terrifying self-consciousness and subjectivity of a great deal of modern writing. That Faulkner has some sense of an organic community still behind him is among his most important resources as a writer.

In *Light in August* Faulkner uses Lena to confirm an ideal of integrity and wholeness in the light of which the alienated characters are judged; and this is essentially the function of Dilsey, the Negro servant in *The Sound and the Fury*, regarded by many people as Faulkner's masterpiece. Dilsey's role, to be sure, is more positive than Lena's. She has affinities not with the pagan goddess but with the Christian saint. She is not the young woman and young mother that Lena is. She is an older woman and an older mother, and she is the sustaining force—the only possible sustaining force of a broken and corrupted family.

Yet Dilsey's primary role is generally similar to Lena's: she affirms the ideal of wholeness in a family which shows in every other member splintering and disintegration. *The Sound and the Fury* can be regarded as a study in the fragmentation of modern man. There is Benjy, the idiot brother who represents the life of the instincts and the unreflective emotions; there is Quentin, the intellectual and artistic brother, who is conscious of his own weakness and failure and yet so hagridden by impossible ideals that he finally turns away from life altogether and commits suicide; and there is Jason, the brother who represents an aggressive and destructive rationalism that dissolves all family and community loyalties and attachments. There has been a somewhat strained attempt to portray the brothers in Freudian terms: Benjy as the *id*, Quentin as the tortured *ego*, and Jason as the tyrannical and cruel *super-ego*. Faulkner's own way of regarding the three brothers (as implied in the appendix he supplied for the Modern Library edition) is interesting. Benjy is an idiot, of course; Quentin, in his obsession, is obviously half-mad; and Jason is perfectly sane, the first "sane" Compson for generations. Faulkner's mocking choice of the term "sane" to characterize Jason's coldly monstrous self-serving (all of Faulkner's villains, let me repeat, are characterized by this devouring and destructive rationalism) is highly significant. It is as if Faulkner argued that mere sanity were not enough—indeed that pure sanity was inhuman. The good man has to transcend his mere intellect with some overflow of generosity and love.

But we ought not to confine ourselves to the three brothers, for Dilsey is being contrasted not merely with them but with the whole of the family. There is Mr. Compson, who has been defeated by life and has sunk into whisky and fatalism. There is Mrs. Compson, the mother, whom Faulkner calls a "cold, weak" person. She is the whining, self-centered hypochondriac who has poisoned the whole family relationship. She is evidently a primary cause of her husband's cynicism; she has spoiled and corrupted her favorite son, Jason; and she has withheld her love from the other children. Quentin, on the day of his suicide, can say to himself bitterly, "If I only had a mother." Mrs. Compson is all that Dilsey is not. It is the mother role that she has abandoned that Dilsey is compelled to assume. There is lastly the daughter of the family, Candace, who in her own way also represents the dissolution of the family. Candace has become a wanton. Sex is her particular escape from an unsatisfactory home, and she is subject to her own kind of specialization, the semiprofessionalism of a sexual adventuress.

In contrast with this splintered family, Dilsey maintains a wholeness. Indeed, Dilsey's wholeness constitutes her holiness. (It is well to remember that *whole* and *holy* are related and come from the same root.) In Dilsey the life of the instincts, including the sex drive, the life of the emotions, and the life of ideal values and of rationality are related meaningfully to one another. To say this is to say, of course, that Dilsey is a profoundly religious person. Her life with its round of daily tasks and responsibilities is related to the larger life of eternity and eternal values. Dilsey does not have to strain to make meaningful some particular desire or dream or need. Her world is a solid and meaningful world. It is filled with pain, toil, and difficulty, but it is not wrenched by agonizing doubts and perplexities.

I said a moment ago that Dilsey was sometimes compared to the saint and in what I am going to say I do not mean to deprive her of her properly deserved halo. But we must not allow the term to sentimentalize her. If she treats with compassion the idiot Benjy, saying "You's de Lawd's chile, anyway," she is quite capable of dealing summarily with her own child, Luster, when he needs a rebuke: "Lemme tell you somethin, nigger boy, you got jes es much Compson devilment in you es any of em. Is you right sho you never broke dat window?" Dilsey's earthiness and her human exasperations are very much in evidence in this novel. Because they are, Dilsey's "saintliness" is altogether credible and convincing.

One may say in general of Faulkner's Negroes that they remain close to a concrete world of values—less perverted by abstraction—more honest in recognizing what is essential and elemental than are most of the white people. Faulkner certainly does not assume any inherent virtue in the Negro race. But he does find among his Negro characters less false pride, less false idealism, more seasoned discipline in the elemental human relationships. The Negro virtues which Faulkner praises in "The Bear" are endurance, patience, honesty, courage, and the love of children—white or black. Dilsey, then, is not a primitive figure who through some mystique of race or healthiness of natural impulses is good. Dilsey is unsophisticated and warm-hearted, but she is no noble savage. Her role is in its general dimensions comparable to that of her white sisters such as the matriarchs Aunt Jenny and Mrs. Rosa Millard, fostering and sustaining forces. If she goes beyond them in exemplifying the feminine principle at it's best, still hers is no mere goodness by and of nature, if one means by this a goodness that justifies a faith in man as man. Dilsey does not believe in man; she believes in God.

To try for a summary of a very difficult and complicated topic: Evil for Faulkner involves the violation of the natural and the denial of the human. As Isaac's older kinsman says in "The Bear," "Courage and honor and pride, and pity and love of justice and liberty. They all touch the heart, and what the heart holds to becomes truth, as far as we know truth." A meanness of spirit and coldness of calculation which would deny the virtues that touch the heart is by that very fact proven false. Yet Faulkner is no disciple of Jean-Jacques Rousseau. He has no illusions that man is naturally good or that he can safely trust to his instincts and emotions. Man is capable of evil, and this means that goodness has to be achieved by struggle and discipline and effort. Like T. S. Eliot, Faulkner has small faith in social arrangements so perfectly organized that nobody has to take the trouble to be good. Finally Faulkner's noblest characters are willing to face the fact that most men can learn the deepest truths about themselves and about reality only through suffering. Hurt and pain and loss are not mere accidents to which the human being is subject; nor are they mere punishments incurred by human error; they can be the means to the deeper knowledge and to the more abundant life.

Katherine Anne Porter

(1890–1980)

Katherine Anne Porter was born in Indian Creek, Texas, to a family of hardscrabble farmers much like the ones depicted in "Noon Wine" and "He." Two years after she had left school at the age of fourteen, she married John Henry Koontz and converted to Catholicism for his sake. The marriage did not last, however, and the two divorced in 1915. She would marry three more times and would be involved in countless other painful love affairs. She worked for a time as a movie actress in Chicago. In the 1920s she went to Mexico to study art and became involved in left-wing revolutionary political movements. Her first short story appeared in 1922, and the collection that made her famous, *Flowering Judas and Other Stories*, was published in 1930. A second collection, *Pale Horse, Pale Rider*, appeared in 1939, followed by *The Leaning Tower and Other Stories* in 1944. A voyage to Europe from Mexico in the 1930s provided her with the material for her one novel, *Ship of Fools*, published in 1962. It is her short fiction, however, on which her reputation rests; its most notable feature is the carefully nuanced psychological characterization (particularly in the "Miranda" stories) of heroines escaping the confines of the genteel Southern Catholic background that Porter claimed for herself for many years before astute biographers like Joan Givner provided a more accurate picture.

Rope

On the third day after they moved to the country he came walking back from the village carrying a basket of groceries and a twenty-four-yard coil of rope. She came out to meet him, wiping her hands on her green smock. Her hair was tumbled, her nose was scarlet with sunburn; he told her that already she looked like a born country woman. His gray flannel shirt stuck to him, his heavy shoes were dusty. She assured him he looked like a rural character in a play.

Had he brought the coffee? She had been waiting all day long for coffee. They had forgot it when they ordered at the store the first day.

Gosh, no, he hadn't. Lord, now he'd have to go back. Yes, he would if it killed him. He thought, though, he had everything else. She reminded him it was only because he didn't drink coffee himself. If he did he would remember it quick enough. Suppose they ran out of cigarettes? Then she saw the rope. What was that for? Well, he thought it might do to hang clothes on, or something. Naturally she asked him if he thought they were going to run a laundry? They already had a fifty-foot line hanging right before his eyes? Why, hadn't he noticed it, really? It was a blot on the landscape to her.

He thought there were a lot of things a rope might come in handy for. She wanted to know what, for instance. He thought a few seconds, but nothing occurred. They could wait and see, couldn't they? You need all sorts of strange odds and ends around a place in the country. She said, yes, that was so; but she thought just at that time when every penny counted, it seemed funny to buy more rope. That was all. She hadn't meant anything else. She hadn't just seen, not at first, why he felt it was necessary.

Well, thunder, he had bought it because he wanted to, and that was all there was to it. She thought that was reason enough, and couldn't understand why he hadn't said so, at first. Undoubtedly it would be useful, twenty-four yards of rope, there were hundreds of things, she couldn't think of any at the moment, but it would come in. Of course. As he had said, things always did in the country.

But she was a little disappointed about the coffee, and oh, look, look, look at the eggs! Oh, my, they're all running! What had he put on top of them? Hadn't he known eggs mustn't be squeezed? Squeezed, who had squeezed them, he wanted to know. What a silly thing to say. He had simply brought them along in the basket with the other things. If they got broke it was the grocer's fault. He should know better than to put heavy things on top of eggs.

She believed it was the rope. That was the heaviest thing in the pack, she saw him plainly when he came in from the road, the rope was a big package on top of everything. He desired the whole wide world to witness that this was not a fact. He had carried the rope in one hand and the basket in the other, and what was the use of her having eyes if that was the best they could do for her?

Well, anyhow, she could see one thing plain: no eggs for breakfast. They'd have to scramble them now, for supper. It was too damned bad. She had planned to have steak for supper. No ice, meat wouldn't keep. He wanted to know why she couldn't finish breaking the eggs in a bowl and set them in a cool place.

Cool place! If he could find one for her, she'd be glad to set them there. Well, then, it seemed to him they might very well cook the meat at the same time they cooked the eggs and then warm up the meat for tomorrow. The idea simply choked her. Warmed-over meat, when they might as well have had it fresh. Second best and scraps and makeshifts, even to the meat! He rubbed her shoulder a little. It doesn't really matter so much, does it, darling? Sometimes when they were playful, he would rub her shoulder and she would arch and purr. This time she hissed and almost clawed. He was getting ready to say that they could surely manage somehow when she turned on him and said, if he told her they could manage somehow she would certainly slap his face.

He swallowed the words red hot, his face burned. He picked up the rope and started to put it on the top shelf. She would not have it on the top shelf, the jars and tins belonged there; positively she would not have the top shelf cluttered up with a lot of rope. She had borne all the clutter she meant to bear in the flat in town, there was space here at least and she meant to keep things in order.

Well, in that case, he wanted to know what the hammer and nails were doing up there? And why had she put them there when she knew very well he needed that hammer and those nails upstairs to fix the window sashes? She simply slowed down everything and made double work on the place with her insane habit of changing things around and hiding them.

She was sure she begged his pardon, and if she had had any reason to believe he was going to fix the sashes this summer she would have left the hammer and nails right where he put them; in the middle of the bedroom floor where they could step on them in the dark. And now if he didn't clear the whole mess out of there she would throw them down the well.

Oh, all right, all right—could he put them in the closet? Naturally not, there were brooms and mops and dustpans in the closet, and why couldn't he find a place for his rope outside her kitchen? Had he stopped to consider there were seven God-forsaken rooms in the house, and only one kitchen?

He wanted to know what of it? And did she realize she was making a complete fool of herself? And what did she take him for, a three-year-old idiot? The whole trouble with her was she needed something weaker than she was to heckle and tyrannize over. He wished to God now they had a couple of children she could take it out on. Maybe he'd get some rest.

Her face changed at this, she reminded him he had forgot the coffee and had bought a worthless piece of rope. And when she thought of all the things they actually needed to make the place even decently fit to live in, well, she could cry, that was all. She looked so forlorn, so lost and despairing he couldn't believe it was only a piece of rope that was causing all the racket. What *was* the matter, for God's sake?

Oh, would he please hush and go away, and *stay* away, if he could, for five minutes? By all means, yes, he would. He'd stay away indefinitely if she wished. Lord, yes, there was nothing he'd like better than to clear out and never come back. She couldn't for the life of her see what was holding him, then. It was a swell time. Here she was, stuck, miles from a railroad, with a half-empty house on her hands, and not a penny in her pocket, and everything on earth to do; it seemed the God-sent moment for him to get out from under. She was surprised he hadn't stayed in town as it was until she had come out and done the work and got things straightened out. It was his usual trick.

It appeared to him that this was going a little far. Just a touch out of bounds, if she didn't mind his saying so. Why the hell and he stayed in town the summer before? To do a half-dozen extra jobs to get the money he had sent her. That was it. She knew perfectly well they couldn't have done it otherwise. She had agreed with him at the time. And that was the only time so help him he had ever left her to do anything by herself.

Oh, he could tell that to his great-grandmother. She had her notion of what had kept him in town. Considerably more than a notion, if he wanted to know. So, she was going to bring all that up again, was she? Well, she could just think what she pleased. He was tired of explaining. It may have looked funny but he had simply got hooked in, and what could he do? It was impossible to believe that she was going to take it seriously. Yes, yes, she knew how it was with a man: if he was left by himself a minute, some woman was certain to kidnap him. And naturally he couldn't hurt her feelings by refusing!

Well, what was she raving about? Did she forget she had told him those two weeks alone in the country were the happiest she had known for four years? And how long had they been married when she said that? All right, shut up! If she thought that hadn't stuck in his craw.

She hadn't meant she was happy because she was away from him. She meant she was happy getting the devilish house nice and ready for him. That was what she had meant, and now look! Bringing up something she had said a year ago simply to justify himself for forgetting her coffee and breaking the eggs and buying a wretched piece of rope they couldn't afford. She really thought it was time to drop the subject, and now she wanted only two things in the world. She wanted him to get that rope from underfoot, and go back to the village and get her coffee, and if he could remember it, he might bring a metal mitt for the skillets, and two more curtain rods, and if there were any rubber gloves in the village, her hands were simply raw, and a bottle of milk of magnesia from the drugstore.

He looked out at the dark blue afternoon sweltering on the slopes, and mopped his forehead and sighed heavily and said, if only she could wait a minute for *any-thing*, he was going back. He had said so, hadn't he, the very instant they found he had overlooked it?

Oh, yes, well . . . run along. She was going to wash windows. The country was so beautiful! She doubted they'd have a moment to enjoy it. He meant to go, but he could not until he had said that if she wasn't such a hopeless melancholiac she might see that this was only for a few days. Couldn't she remember anything pleasant about the other summers? Hadn't they ever had any fun? She hadn't time to talk about it, and now would he please not leave that rope lying around for her to trip on? He picked it up, somehow it had toppled off the table, and walked out with it under his arm.

Was he going this minute? He certainly was. She thought so. Sometimes it seemed to her he had second sight about the precisely perfect moment to leave her ditched. She had meant to put the mattresses out to sun, if they put them out this minute they would get at least three hours, he must have heard her say that morning she meant to put them out. So of course he would walk off and leave her to it. She supposed he thought the exercise would do her good.

Well, he was merely going to get her coffee. A four-mile walk for two pounds of coffee was ridiculous, but he was perfectly willing to do it. The habit was making a wreck of her, but if she wanted to wreck herself there was nothing he could do about it. If he thought it was coffee that was making a wreck of her, she congratulated him: he must have a damned easy conscience.

Conscience or no conscience, he didn't see why the mattresses couldn't very well wait until tomorrow. And anyhow, for God's sake, were they living *in* the house, or were they going to let the house ride them to death? She paled at this, her face grew livid about the mouth, she looked quite dangerous, and reminded him that house-keeping was no more her work than it was his: she had other work to do as well, and when did he think she was going to find time to do it at this rate?

Was she going to start on that again? She knew as well as he did that his work brought in the regular money, hers was only occasional, if they depended on what *she* made—and she might as well get straight on this question once for all!

That was positively not the point. The question was, when both of them were work-ing on their own time, was there going to be a division of the housework, or wasn't there? She merely wanted to know, she had to make her plans. Why, he thought that was all arranged. It was understood that he was to help. Hadn't he always, in summers?

Hadn't he, though? Oh, just hadn't he? And when, and where, and doing what? Lord, what an uproarious joke!

It was such a very uproarious joke that her face turned slightly purple, and she screamed with laughter. She laughed so hard she had to sit down, and finally a rush of tears spurted from her eyes and poured down into the lifted corners of her mouth. He dashed towards her and dragged her up to her feet and tried to pour water on her head. The dipper hung by a string on a nail and he broke it loose. Then he tried to pump water with one hand while she struggled in the other. So he gave it up and shook her instead.

She wrenched away, crying out for him to take his rope and go to hell, she had simply given him up: and ran. He heard her high-heeled bedroom slippers clattering and stumbling on the stairs.

He went out around the house and into the lane; he suddenly realized he had a blister on his heel and his shirt felt as if it were on fire. Things broke so suddenly you didn't know where you were. She could work herself into a fury about simply nothing. She was terrible, damn it: not an ounce of reason. You might as well talk to a sieve as that woman when she got going. Damned if he'd spend his life humoring her! Well, what to do now? He would take back the rope and exchange it for something else. Things accumulated, things were mountainous, you couldn't move them or sort them out or get rid of them. They just lay and rotted around. He'd take it back. Hell, why should he? He wanted it. What was it anyhow? A piece of rope. Imagine anybody caring more about a piece of rope than about a man's feelings. What earthly right had she to say a word about it? He remembered all the useless, meaningless things she bought for herself: Why? Because I wanted it, that's why! He stopped and selected a large stone by the road. He would put the rope behind it. He would put it in the tool-box when he got back. He'd heard enough about it to last him a life-time.

When he came back she was leaning against the post box beside the road waiting. It was pretty late, the smell of broiled steak floated nose high in the cooling air. Her face was young and smooth and fresh-looking. Her unmanageable funny black hair was all on end. She waved to him from a distance, and he speeded up. She called out that supper was ready and waiting, was he starved?

You bet he was starved. Here was the coffee. He waved it at her. She looked at his other hand. What was that he had there?

Well, it was the rope again. He stopped short. He had meant to exchange it but forgot. She wanted to know why he should exchange it, if it was something he really wanted. Wasn't the air sweet now, and wasn't it fine to be here?

She walked beside him with one hand hooked into his leather belt. She pulled and jostled him a little as he walked, and leaned against him. He put his arm clear around her and patted her stomach. They exchanged wary smiles. Coffee, coffee for the Ootsum-Wootsums! He felt as if he were bringing her a beautiful present.

He was a love, she firmly believed, and if she had had her coffee in the morning, she wouldn't have behaved so funny . . . There was a whippoorwill still coming back, imagine, clear out of season, sitting in the crab-apple tree calling all by himself. Maybe his girl stood him up. Maybe she did. She hoped to hear him once more, she loved whippoorwills . . . He knew how she was, didn't he?

Sure, he knew how she was.

Sterling Brown

(1901–1989)

Sterling Brown was born the son of a professor of religion at Howard University in a house that would eventually become part of the Howard campus. These were the roots of a loyalty that would later lead him to reject a professorship at Vassar College (an appointment almost unheard of for an African American man at that time) because, as he would later say in an *Ebony* magazine interview, "These are my people and if I had anything to give they would need it more." Brown received his undergraduate degree from Williams College and took a master's from Harvard before returning to Howard in 1929. There he would remain for the next forty years.

Though his first poetry collection, *Southern Road*, was critically well received when it was published in 1932, Brown's second collection, *No Hiding Place*, was rejected by Harcourt, Brace because they felt it would not be profitable. Frustrated, Brown turned to other areas of expression. In a regular column that he wrote for *Opportunity* magazine, he criticized the authors of the agrarian manifesto *I'll Take My Stand*, decrying what he saw as their romanticism, advocating instead a realistic literature that did not "distort black life and character." In 1938 he published two important critical works, *Negro Poetry and Drama* and *The Negro in American Fiction;* and *The Negro Caravan*, a collection he edited with two Howard colleagues, was for many years considered the preeminent anthology of African American literature. In the late 1960s, students involved in the Black Arts movement forced a reassessment of Brown's poetry, and Beacon Press reissued *Southern Road*. His 1938 critical works were also reprinted by Argosy, and, finally, *The Collected Poems of Sterling A. Brown*, which included the rejected "No Hiding Place," was published in 1980. Brown's poetry, with its utter lack of stridency, its consistent humorous element, and its brilliant evocation of dialect, has finally begun to receive the recognition it has so long deserved.

Slim in Atlanta

Down in Atlanta,
    De whitefolks got laws
For to keep all de niggers
    From laughin' outdoors.

        Hope to Gawd I may die
            If I ain't speakin' truth
        Make de niggers do deir laughin'
            In a telefoam booth.

Slim Greer hit de town
    An' de rebs got him told,—
"Dontcha laugh on de street,
    If you want to die old."

        Den dey showed him de booth,
            An' a hundred shines
        In front of it, waitin'
            In double lines.

Slim thought his sides
    Would bust in two,
Yelled, "Lookout, everybody,
    I'm coming through!"

        Pulled de other man out,
            An' bust in de box,
        An' laughed four hours
            By de Georgia clocks.

Den he peeked through de door,
    An' what did he see?
Three hundred niggers there
    In misery.—

        Some holdin' deir sides,
            Some holdin' deir jaws,

To keep from breakin'
De Georgia laws.

An' Slim gave a holler,
An' started again;
An' from three hundred throats
Come a moan of pain.

An' everytime Slim
Saw what was outside,
Got to whoopin' again
Till he nearly died.

An' while de poor critters
Was waitin' deir chance,
Slim laughed till dey sent
Fo' de ambulance.

De state paid de railroad
To take him away;
Den, things was as usural
In Atlanta, Gee A.

Southern Cop

Let us forgive Ty Kendricks.
The place was Darktown. He was young.
His nerves were jittery. The day was hot.
The Negro ran out of the alley.
And so he shot.

Let us understand Ty Kendricks.
The Negro must have been dangerous,
Because he ran;
And here was a rookie with a chance
To prove himself a man.

Let us condone Ty Kendricks
If we cannot decorate.
When he found what the Negro was running for,
It was too late;
And all we can say for the Negro is
It was unfortunate.

Let us pity Ty Kendricks,
He has been through enough,
Standing there, his big gun smoking,
Rabbit-scared, alone,
Having to hear the wenches wail
And the dying Negro to moan.

W. J. Cash

(1900–1941)

W. J. Cash was born in Gaffney, South Carolina, on May 2, 1900. He entered Wofford College in South Carolina in 1919, attended Valparaiso University in Indiana, and was graduated from Wake Forest College in North Carolina in 1922. He taught at George-town College in Kentucky and Hendersonville School for Boys in North Carolina be-fore he turned to journalism. He joined the *Charlotte News* in 1926 and was associate editor from 1937 to 1941.

In July 1929 Cash contributed his first piece to H. L. Mencken's *American Mer-cury*. He married Mary Ross Northrop on December 25, 1940. He gained instant rec-ognition when *The Mind of the South* was published in 1941.

Cash died in Mexico on July 1, 1941.

from *The Mind of the South*

Chapter II. Of the Man at the Center

I have gone into the social origins of the Old South somewhat at length because they are obviously of immense significance in terms of mind. Strike the average of all that I have said, and you get as the basic Southerner, or, rather more exactly, as the core about which most Southerners of whatever degree were likely to be built, an exceed-ingly simple fellow—a backcountry pioneer farmer or the immediate descendant of such a farmer. A man, indeed, who, because of one, two, or more generations in the backcountry was an even more uncomplex sort than had been the original immi-grants from Europe. In some respects, perhaps as simple a type as Western civiliza-tion has produced in modern times.

He had much in common with the half-wild Scotch and Irish clansmen of the sev-enteenth and eighteenth centuries whose blood he so often shared, and from whom, in so far as he remained the product of European influences, he mainly drew his tradi-tion; but with the English squire to whom the legend has always assimilated him, and to whom the Southern Agrarians have recently sought to reassimilate him, not much.

True, both squire and Southerner may be properly described as agrarians. But this word "agrarian" is an extremely loose one; it may be applied to anything from the first settled life of Neolithic man, and from the culture pattern of a Russian muzhik in the time of Peter the Grand, down to, one might almost say, the rustic play of Marie Antoinette and the Duchesse du Maine. And, as a matter of fact, nothing could be more unlike the life of the English squire in its fundamental aspect than that native to the South, nothing could have differed more profoundly from the peculiar coloring with which the squire's world endowed his subconsciousness than that with which the Southerner's endowed his. For the squire's agrarianism was a highly formalized and artificial thing. If it struck its roots in the soil, it lived and had its being only on the medium of a consciously realized tradition—a tradition with a great deal more of the salon than of the earth in it.

The Southerner, however, was primarily a direct product of the soil, as the peasant of Europe is the direct product of the soil. His way of life was his, not—John Crowe Ransom to the contrary notwithstanding—as one "considered and authorized," not because he himself or his ancestors or his class had deliberately chosen it as against something else, not even because it had been tested through centuries and found to be good, but because, given his origins, it was the most natural outcome of the conditions in which he found himself.

The whole difference can be summed up in this: that, though he galloped to hounds in pursuit of the fox precisely as the squire did, it was for quite other reasons. It was not that hoary and sophisticated class tradition dictated it as the proper sport for gentlemen. It was not even, in the first place, that he knew that English squires so behaved, and hungered to identify himself with them by imitation, though this of course was to play a great part in confirming and fixing the pattern. It was simply and primarily for the same reason that, in his youth and often into late manhood, he ran spontaneous and unpremeditated foot-races, wrestled, drank Gargantuan quantities of raw whisky, let off wild yells, and hunted the possum: because the thing was already in his mores when he emerged from the backwoods, because on the frontier it was the obvious thing to do, because he was a hot, stout fellow, full of blood and reared to outdoor activity, because of a primitive and naïve zest for the pursuit in hand.

I do not forget the Virginians and their artificializing influence. I shall have, indeed, presently to report our Southerner as developing a striking self-consciousness and as growing somewhat more complex. But this is what he almost invariably was in the beginning, and what he remained at bottom right down to the end. This simple, rustic figure is the true center from which the Old South proceeded—the frame about which the conditions of the plantation threw up the whole structure of the Southern mind.

2

Inevitably, then, the dominant trait of this mind was an intense individualism—in its way, perhaps the most intense individualism the world has seen since the Italian Renaissance and its men of "terrible fury." The simple man in general invariably tends to be an individualist. Everywhere and invariably his fundamental attitude is purely personal—and purely self-asserting. Only in old, complex, aristocratic societies—in most societies—this tendency in him is likely to be sadly cramped and restricted in its possible development. The close-pressing throng of his fellow men, rigid class distinctions, the yoke of law and government, economic imperatives—all these bear upon him with crushing weight and confine his individualistic activities to a very narrow space indeed. Any genuine scope is possible only to those in the topmost levels of such a society—and even in their case it is not too wide. Even they, for all their prerogatives, cannot really escape the shackles; for against their privileges is usually set off a body of unavoidable obligations—nay, obligations often inhere in the privileges themselves.

Our Southerner, however, was remarkably free from such limits. In so far as he was of the blood of the Scotch and the Irish he had perhaps never been so much subject to them as men of other European groups. But in any case, and whatever his original derivations, the frontier had loosened his bonds as completely as it is possible to imagine them being loosed for man in a social state. The thin distribution of the population over vast reaches of country, the virtual absence of distinctions, and of law and government save in their most rudimentary stages, the fact that at every turn a man was thrown back wholly upon his own resources—all these combined to give his native individualism the widest scope and to spur it on to headlong growth.

And what the frontier had begun, the world which succeeded it—that world which was the creation of the plantation—was admirably calculated to preserve and even greatly to extend. For, to begin with, one of the effects of the plantation system was to perpetuate essentially frontier conditions long after their normal period had run—to freeze solid many of the aspects of the old backwoods which had operated for individualism in the first place. Thus, by drawing the best lands into a relatively few large units, it effectually shooed away the ambitious and desirable immigrant—completely blocked off immigration, in fact—and so carried over and fixed as a permanent feature of the Old South that thin distribution of population which had been the matrix of the backcountry pattern. Now, as before, and despite the striking gregariousness which had long been growing up in counterbalance, the Southerner, whoever and whatever he was, would be likely to be much alone. Or if not strictly alone, then companied only by his slaves and members of his own family, to all of whom his individual will would stand as imperial law.

Again, the plantation tended to find its center in itself: to be an independent social unit, a self-contained and largely self-sufficient little world of its own. In its beginnings, to be sure, it often required some degree of communal effort, particularly if the would-be planter had few or no slaves. But once the forest was cut and the stumps grubbed up, once the seed were in a few times and the harvest home a few times, once he had a Negro or two actually at work—once the plantation was properly carved out and on its way, then the world might go hang. The great part of everything he needed could be and was grown or manufactured on the place, and the rest could be, and, as I have said, often was, imported from the North. Thus, freed from any particular dependence on his neighbors, the planter, as he got his hand in at mastering the slave, would wax continually in lordly self-certainty. More and more, as time went on, he would come to front the world from his borders like a Gael chieftain from his rock-ringed glen, wholly content with his autonomy and jealously guardful that nothing should encroach upon it.

And what is true of the planter is true also, *mutatis mutandis*, for the poorer whites under this plantation order. The farmers and the crackers were in their own way self-sufficient too—as fiercely careful of their prerogatives of ownership, as jealous of their sway over their puny domains, as the grandest lord. No man felt or acknowledged any primary dependence on his fellows, save perhaps in the matter of human sympathy and entertainment—always a pressing one in a wide and lonely land.

The upshot of this is obvious. It made powerfully against the development of law and government beyond the limits imposed by the tradition of the old backcountry. There was in that tradition, of course, a decided feeling that some measure of law and government was necessary. When the Southern backlandsman moved out into the new cotton country west of the Appalachians, he immediately set up the machinery of the State, just as his fathers before him had done in the regions east of the mountains; everywhere he built his courthouse almost before he built anything else. And here in the South, as in all places in all times, the State, once established, inevitably asserted its inherent tendency to growth, to reach out and engross power.

But against this was the fact that the tradition contained also, and as its ruling element, an intense distrust of, and, indeed, downright aversion to, any actual exercise of authority beyond the barest minimum essential to the existence of the social organism. This feeling, common to the American backcountryman in general, had, in truth, reached its apogee in the Southern coon-hunter. On the eve of the Revolution he was refusing to pay, not only the special taxes levied by the Crown, but also—very usually at least—any taxes at all. Hence it fell out in this plantation world that, if the State grew, it grew with remarkable slowness. The South never developed any such compact and effective unit of government as the New England town. Its very counties were merely huge, sprawling hunks of territory, with almost no internal principle of cohesion. And to the last day before the Civil War, the land remained by far the most poorly policed section of the nation.

3

If the yoke of law and government weighed but lightly, so also did that of class. Prior to the last ten or fifteen years before Secession, the Old South may be said, in truth, to have been nearly innocent of the notion of class in any rigid and complete sense. And even when the notion did come into use, it was always something for philosophers bent on rationalizing an economic system to bandy about rather than something which was really an integral part of Southern thinking in general.

Here, manifestly, I do not infer that the Old South was ever egalitarian, as, say, the U.S.S.R. is egalitarian, or that the backcountry's lack of distinctions was brought over into the plantation order without modification. From what I have already recorded, from the reports of every contemporary observer, it is clear that, from an early time, there was a great deal of snobbish feeling; that an overweening pride in the possession of rich lands and slaves, and contempt for those who lacked them, quickly got to be commonplaces; and that the *nouveaux*, fired by the example of the Virginians and their high pride of birth and breeding, were eagerly engaged in heaping distinction upon distinction and establishing themselves in the role of proper gentlemen. Nowhere else in America, indeed, not forgetting even Boston, would class awareness in a certain very narrow sense figure so largely in the private thinking of the master group. And not only in the private thinking of the master group, for that matter. Everybody in the South was aware of, and habitually thought and spoke in terms of, a division of society into Big Men and Little Men, with strict reference to property, power, and the claim to gentility.

Nevertheless, the Southerner's primary approach to his world was not through the idea of class. He never really got around in his subconsciousness to thinking of himself as being, before all else, a member of a caste, with interests and purposes in conflict with the interests and purposes of other castes. And certainly he never felt even the premonitory twinges of class awareness in the full sense—of that state in which the concept of society as divided into rigid layers and orders burrows into the very tissues of the brain and becomes the irresistible magnetic pole for one's deepest loyalties and hates, the all-potent determiner of one's whole ideological and emotional pattern. Rather, he saw with essentially naïve, direct, and personal eyes. Rather, his world, as he beheld it, remained always, in its basic aspect, a simple aggregation of human units, of self-contained and self-sufficient entities, whose grouping along class lines, though it might and would count tremendously in many ways, was yet not a first thing.

Perhaps this will seem amazing in view of what I have already said about the effect of the plantation system in driving back and blocking up poor white and farmer. That might have been expected to generate resentment and even hate—to set off class conflict and make class feeling a prevailing emotion. Yet when one carefully examines the whole of the curious situation which existed in the plantation world, there is nothing amazing here.

The groundwork in this case as elsewhere, it must be borne firmly in mind, was the tradition of the backcountry and the more or less fresh—the never entirely obliterated—remembrance of the community of origins: factors operating, of course, for the preservation of the old basic democratic feeling. It is perfectly plain, indeed, that if, being a poor white or a farmer, you knew that your planter neighbor was a kinsman, you were normally going to find it as difficult to hate him as to think of him as being made of fundamentally different stuff from yourself—a "shining one" begotten by God for the express purpose of ruling you. You might defer to him as a rich man, and you might often feel spite and envy; but to get on to genuine class feeling toward him you would have to have an extraordinarily vivid sense of brutal and intolerable wrong, or something equally compulsive.

Similarly, if you were a planter, and recalled that you had played about a cabin as a boy, that as a youth you had hunted the possum with that slouching fellow passing there, or danced the reel with the girl who had grown unbelievably into the poke-bonneted, sun-faded woman yonder (had maybe kissed her on that moon-burning, unutterable, lost night when you rode away to New Orleans with Andy Jackson), why, the chances were that, for all your forgetfulness when your ambition was involved, for all your pride in your Negroes, and your doctrinaire contempt for incompetence, there was still at the bottom of you a considerable community of feeling with these people—that, in truth, it would unconsciously dominate you and keep class awareness from penetrating below your surface and into the marrow of your bones, so long as those below did not rouse to a sense of wrong and begin to strike back.

But now behold with what precision the plantation conspired—and quite without the intervention of feeble human wit—to see that this sense of wrong did not develop.

4

In the first place, if the plantation system had robbed the common Southern white of much, it had not, you will observe, robbed him completely. Since it was based on Negro slavery, and since Negro slavery was a vastly wasteful system and could be made to pay only on rich soils, it had practically everywhere, as I have implied, left him some sort of land and hence some sort of subsistence. And in doing that, it had exempted him from all direct exploitation, specifically waived all claim to his labor (for the excellent reason, of course, that it had no use for it), and left his independence totally unimpaired. So long, indeed, as the "peculiar institution" prevailed, he might rest here forever, secure in the knowledge that his estate in this respect would never grow worse—after his fashion, as completely a free agent as the greatest planter of the country.

In this regard, it seems to me, the Old South was one of the most remarkable societies which ever existed in the world. Was there ever another instance of a country in which the relation of master and man arose, negligible exceptions aside, only with reference to a special alien group—in which virtually the whole body of the natives who had failed economically got off fully from the servitude that, in one form or another, has almost universally been the penalty of such failure—in which they were *parked*, as it were, and left to go to the devil in the absolute enjoyment of their liberty?

Again, if the Southern social order had blocked in the common Southerner, it had yet not sealed up the exit entirely. If he could not escape *en masse*, he could nevertheless escape as an individual. Always it was possible for the strong, craving lads who still thrust up from the old sturdy root-stock to make their way out and on: to compete with the established planters for the lands of the Southwest, or even—so close to the frontier stage did the whole country remain, so little was the static tendency realized, so numerous were the bankruptcies, with such relative frequency did many estates go on changing hands, and above all, perhaps, so open an opportunity did the profession of law afford—to carve out wealth and honor in the very oldest regions. Thus, of the eight governors of Virginia from 1841 to 1861, only one was born a gentleman, two began their careers by hiring out as plow-hands, and another (the son of a village butcher) as a tailor.

But in their going these emergent ones naturally carried away with them practically the whole effective stock of those qualities which might have generated resentment and rebellion. Those who were left behind were the simplest of the simple men of this country—those who were inclined to accept whatever the day brought forth as in the nature of things—those whose vague ambition, though it might surge up in dreams now and then, was too weak ever to rise to a consistent lust for plantations and slaves, or anything else requiring an extended exercise of will—those who, sensing their own inadequacy, expected and were content with little.

Moreover, they were in general those in whom the frontier tradition was likely to run strongest; which is to say that they were often almost indifferent, even in their dreams, to the possession of plantations and slaves and to the distinctions which such possessions set up. For it is characteristic of the frontier tradition everywhere that it places no such value on wealth and rank as they command in an old and stable society. Great personal courage, unusual physical powers, the ability to drink a quart of whisky or to lose the whole of one's capital on the turn of a card without the quiver of a muscle—these are at least as important as possessions, and infinitely more important than heraldic crests. In the South, if your neighbor overshadowed you in the number of his slaves, you could outshoot him or outfiddle him, and in your own eyes, and in those of many of your fellows, remain essentially as good a man as he.

Once more, the escape of the strong served potently to perpetuate in the weak the belief that opportunity was still wholly free and unlimited. Seeing the success of these, and recalling obscurely that somewhere out there beyond the horizon were fertile lands to be had for the taking, it was the easiest thing for men steeped in the tradition of the frontier to harbor the comfortable, the immensely soothing, faith that if only they chose . . . that if only they chose . . .

But all these considerations are in some sense only negative. And there was in fact a very positive factor at work in the situation. If the plantation had introduced distinctions of wealth and rank among the men of the old backcountry, and, in doing so, had perhaps offended against the ego of the common white, it had also, you will remember, introduced that other vastly ego-warming and ego-expanding distinction between the white man and the black. Robbing him and degrading him in so many ways, it yet, by singular irony, had simultaneously elevated this common white to a position comparable to that of, say, the Doric knight of ancient Sparta. Not only was he not exploited directly, he was himself made by extension a member of the dominant class—was lodged solidly on a tremendous superiority, which, however much the blacks in the "big house" might sneer at him, and however much their masters might privately agree with them, he could never publicly lose. Come what might, he would always be a white man. And before that vast and capacious distinction, all others were foreshortened, dwarfed, and all but obliterated.

The grand outcome was the almost complete disappearance of economic and social focus on the part of the masses. One simply did not have to get on in this world in order to achieve security, independence, or value in one's own estimation and in that of one's fellows.

Hence it happened that pressure never developed within the enclosing walls thrown up by the plantation, that not one in a thousand of the enclosed ever even remotely apprehended the existence of such walls. And so it happened, finally, that the old basic feeling of democracy was preserved practically intact.

5

But I am leaping ahead too rapidly? I am too easily slurring over that narrow class consciousness and that land-and-slave snobbery which I have myself laid down as marked characteristics of the master class? Granted all that I have said, these would still remain—and, remaining, would intolerably wound such men as these common whites—men who, by token of the very things I have predicated of them, by token of their possession of land and independence, by token of their memory of common origin with the planters, would be fiercely self-assertive and sensitive and inordinately resentful of slights and snubs—would be sufficient by themselves to propel such men headlong into class awareness and hate?

So it might seem. But to understand what actually took place here, we must recall again how close the Old South always was to the frontier in time, how late it was before the flux of land-grabbing and fortune-building began to yield place to crystalization, before the planter group or any other acquired even proximate fixity of personnel and character. For this clearly means that distinctions were to the last more in the process of becoming than realized, that such rigidity as they possessed resided more in the concept than in the application.

They might determine, these distinctions, whom one would marry or whom one would have in for dinner, but never with quite the strictness that the legend of the Old South has led us to expect. Behind the normal inclination of property to ally itself only with property, behind the convention that rank must wed only with rank, the backcountry heritage often showed through. Planters very commonly intermarried with yeomen, and alliances between planters and people who were pretty definitely reckoned poor whites were not unheard of. Fully three-quarters of the planters were accustomed to having their farmer neighbors and cousins at their boards now and then; nor was it any rare thing for a great man with political ambitions to seize on a dozen crackers at a camp-meeting or a party rally and bear them off to his home to sleep on his best beds and make merry with his best liquor—or anyhow his second-best liquor. And in all save the oldest districts and the haughtiest of the "big houses," the line at parties and dances was drawn, with discrimination of course, but with scarcely more discrimination than one would normally expect in a farmer community anywhere.

But there was something more important yet, something that I perhaps begin already to suggest. The very marrow of this tradition of the backcountry to which I have referred so often, of the feeling which was basic in the Southern situation, was a sort of immense kindliness and easiness—the kindliness and easiness of men who have long lived together on the same general plane, who have common memories, and who are more or less conscious of the ties of blood. And now, at the exact moment when distinctions were springing up, when land-and-slave pride and the snob spirit were swelling into being, this kindliness and easiness were flowing over to join forces with other factors which I shall discuss presently, to give rise to—to serve as the essential kernel of—the famous Southern manner.

In sober fact, we shall find as we go along that this manner had more than one fault, and was not, as it was practiced by the generality, so altogether lovely as we have been told. But for all that, it served wonderfully for a balance wheel in the Southern social world and so as a barrier against the development of bitterness.

If the common white was scorned, yet that scorn was so attenuated and softened in its passage down through the universal medium of this manner, struck at last so obliquely upon his ego, that it glanced off harmless. When he frequented public gatherings, what he encountered would seldom be naked hauteur. Rather, there would nearly always be a fine gentleman to lay a familiar hand on his shoulder, to inquire by name after the members of his family, maybe to buy him a drink, certainly to rally him on some boasted weakness or treasured misadventure, and to come around eventually to confiding in a hushed voice that that damned nigger-loving scoundrel Garrison, in Boston—in short, to patronize him in such fashion that to his simple eyes he seemed not to be patronized at all but actually deferred to, to send him home, not sullen and vindictive, but glowing with the sense of participation in the common brotherhood of white men.

To sum up, the working code of the Old South, the code which really governed most relations between the classes, was exactly adapted to the exigencies of the Southern order—was adapted above all to the old basic democracy of feeling—was itself, in its peculiar way, simply an embodiment of that feeling. If the common white, with the backcountry hot within him, was likely to carry a haughtiness like that of the Spanish peasant underneath his slouch, very well, so far from challenging and trampling on that, his planter neighbors in effect allowed it, gave it boundless room—nay, even encouraged it and invited it on to growth.

6

In the social situation which I outline here, we have a factor of the first importance for the entire Southern pattern—one which, as we shall see, reached out and wove itself into the Southern mind at many points, and which gave rise, and continues to this day to give rise, to the most striking consequences.

But nowhere was its effect more marked than in the field of that individualism which, as the reader may have forgotten by this time, is the point with which we were immediately engaged. For not only did it do the obvious thing of expanding and extending that individualism in mere quantitative fashion, not only did it provide the perfect ground for the growth of the fundamental Jeffersonian philosophy far beyond anything the rest of the nation was to see—it did even more. In focusing the old backcountry pride upon the ideas of superiority to the Negro and the peerage of white men, and thereby (fully in the masses, and in some basic manner even in the planters) divorcing it from the necessity for achievement, it inevitably shifted emphasis back upon and lent new impulsion to the purely personal and *puerile* attitude which distinguishes the frontier outlook everywhere.

And when to that was added the natural effect on the planters of virtually unlimited sway over their bondsmen, and the natural effect on the common whites of the example of these planters, it eventuated in this: that the individualism of the planta-tion world would be one which, like that of the backcountry before it, would be far too much concerned with bald, immediate, unsupported assertion of the ego, which placed too great stress on the inviolability of personal whim, and which was full of the chip-on-shoulder swagger and brag of a boy—one, in brief, of which the essence was the boast, voiced or not, on the part of every Southerner, that he would knock hell out of whoever dared to cross him.

This character is of the utmost significance. For its corollary was the perpetua-tion and acceleration of the tendency to violence which had grown up in the Southern backwoods as it naturally grows up on all frontiers. Other factors, some of which we shall glance at later on, played their part in perpetuating and elaborating this pattern, too. But none was more decisive than this one. However careful they might be to walk softly, such men as these of the South were bound to come often into conflict. And being what they were—simple, direct, and immensely personal—and their world being what it was—conflict with them could only mean immediate physical clashing, could only mean fisticuffs, the gouging ring, and knife and gun play.

Nor was it only private violence that was thus perpetuated. The Southerner's fun-damental approach carried over into the realm of public offenses as well. What the di-rect willfulness of his individualism demanded, when confronted by a crime that aroused his anger, was immediate satisfaction for itself—catharsis for personal pas-sion in the spectacle of a body dancing at the end of a rope or writhing in the fire—now, within the hour—and not some ponderous abstract justice in a problematic tomorrow. And so, in this world of ineffective social control, the tradition of vigilante action, which normally lives and dies with the frontier, not only survived but grew so steadily that already long before the Civil War and long before hatred for the black man had begun to play any direct part in the pattern (of more than three hundred per-sons said to have been hanged or burned by mobs between 1840 and 1860, less than ten per cent were Negroes) the South had become peculiarly the home of lynching.

But if I show you Southern individualism as eventually in violence, if I imply that the pride which was its root was in some sense puerile, I am very far from suggesting that it ought to be held in contempt. For it reached its ultimate incarnation in the Con-federate soldier.

To the end of his service this soldier could not be disciplined. He slouched. He would never learn to salute in the brisk fashion so dear to the hearts of the professors of mass murder. His "Cap'n" and his "Gin'ral" were likely to pass his lips with a grin—were charged always with easy, unstudied familiarity. He could and did find it in him-self to jeer openly and unabashed in the face of Stonewall Jackson when that austere Presbyterian captain rode along his lines. And down to the final day at Appomattox his officers knew that the way to get him to execute an order without malingering was to flatter and to jest, never to command too brusquely and forthrightly. And yet—and yet—and by virtue of precisely these unsoldierly qualities, he was, as no one will care to deny, one of the world's very finest fighting men.

Allow what you will for *esprit de corps*, for this or for that, the thing that sent him swinging up the slope at Gettysburg on that celebrated, gallant afternoon was be-fore all else nothing more or less than the thing which elsewhere accounted for his vi-olence—was nothing more or less than his conviction, the conviction of every farmer among what was essentially only a band of farmers, that nothing living could cross him and get away with it.

7

But already, by implication, I have been taking you deep into the territory of a second great Southern characteristic which deserves to be examined thoroughly in its own right. I mean the tendency toward unreality, toward romanticism, and, in intimate relation with that, toward hedonism. And rightly to understand this tendency, we cannot begin better than by returning upon the simple figure which I have posed as the center about which the Southern pattern would be built.

A common impression to the contrary notwithstanding, the simple man in general rarely has any considerable capacity for the real. What is ordinarily taken for realism in him is in fact only a sort of biological pragmatism—an intuitive faculty of the practical, like that exhibited by those astounding wasps and bees celebrated by Jean-Henri Fabre—born of the circumstance that he has nearly everywhere and always been the driven slave of the belly, and confined to the narrow sphere of interests and activities marked out by the struggle for mere animal existence.

Relax that drive a little, let him escape a little from this struggle, and the true tenor of his nature promptly appears: he stands before us, has always stood before us in such circumstances, as a romantic and a hedonist. And this, indeed, inheres in the very terms of the equation. To say that he is simple is to say in effect that he necessarily lacks the complexity of mind, the knowledge, and, above all, the habit of skepticism essential to any generally realistic attitude. It is to say that he is inevitably driven back upon imagination, that his world-construction is bound to be mainly a product of fantasy, and that his credulity is limited only by his capacity for conjuring up the unbelievable. And it is to say also that he is the child-man, that primitive stuff of humanity lies very close to the surface in him, that he likes naïvely to play, to expand his ego, his senses, his emotions, that he will accept what pleases him and reject what does not, and that in general he will prefer the extravagant, the flashing, and the brightly colored—in a word, that he displays the whole catalogue of qualities we mean by romanticism and hedonism.

What is thus true of the simple man in general was perhaps even more definitely true of the Southern frontiersman by the time of the coming of the plantation. In the half century and more since he had first begun to enter the backcountry, there had gone on a slow but steady sloughing off of much of even that simple heritage which he had brought from Europe. Ideas that had drifted obscurely within his ken in the old countries faded out here and were lost; his slim stock of knowledge continually dwindled; in time by far the greater number of him were literally in the intellectual status of Lula Vollmer's old mountain woman of our time, who knew of France only that it was "somers yan side of Asheville." And if this plainly does not apply to the better sort, if some of those with the best backgrounds managed heroically to preserve and pass on much, yet they too often lost ground.

It is possible, however, to be more explicit than this. Certain factors which made for a quite positive ripening were in operation here. Thus, there was the unaccustomed freedom of the new country, the glad relief of escape from the European strait-jacket, the vague sense of bright, unlimited vistas opening upon the future. Despite the unquestionable harshness of the life he led, the Southern pioneer (like his congeners elsewhere on the American frontier and in every new country) early began to exhibit a kind of mounting exultancy, which issued in a tendency to frisk and cavort, to posture, to play the slashing hell of a fellow—a notable expansion of the ego testifying at once to his rising individualism and the burgeoning of the romantic and hedonistic spirit.

Moreover, there was the influence of the Southern physical world—itself a sort of cosmic conspiracy against reality in favor of romance. The country is one of extravagant colors, of proliferating foliage and bloom, of flooding yellow sunlight, and, above all perhaps, of haze. Pale blue fogs hang above the valleys in the morning, the atmosphere smokes faintly at midday, and through the long slow afternoon, cloud-stacks tower from the horizon and the earth-heat quivers upward through the iridescent air, blurring every outline and rendering every object vague and problematical. I know that winter comes to the land, certainly. I know there are days when the color and the haze are stripped away and the real stands up in drab and depressing harshness. But these things pass and are forgotten.

The dominant mood, the mood that lingers in the memory, is one of well-nigh drunken reverie—of a hush that seems all the deeper for the far-away mourning of the hounds and the far-away crying of the doves—of such sweet and inexorable opiates as the rich odors of hot earth and pinewood and the perfume of the magnolia in bloom—of soft languor creeping through the blood and mounting surely to the brain. . . . It is a mood, in sum, in which directed thinking is all but impossible, a mood in which the mind yields almost perforce to drift and in which the imagination holds unchecked sway, a mood in which nothing any more seems improbable save the puny inadequateness of fact, nothing incredible save the bareness of truth.

But I must tell you also that the sequel to this mood is invariably a thunderstorm. For days—for weeks, it may be—the land lies thus in reverie, and then . . .

The pattern is profoundly significant—was to enter deeply into the blood and bone of the South—had already entered deeply therein, we may believe, by the time of the coming of the plantation.

8

But all this was as nothing compared to the influence which the conditions created by the plantation were to exert. For here, indeed, reality would retreat to the farthest verge; here, as a corollary to things I have already told you, the very drive of the belly would recede and recede until it operated on our Southerner as gently as it has ever operated on mortal man outside some idyllic Pacific island paradise.

In this world he was to have freedom from labor beyond the wildest dream of the European peasant and the New England farmer wrestling with a meager soil in a bitter, unfriendly climate. If he were a planter, then he—whose ancestors, in likelihood, had for many generations won their daily bread under the primitive curse—found himself free from every necessity of toil, free from all but the grateful tasks of supervision and mastery, free to play the lord at dignified ease. If he were a plain farmer, with few slaves or none, then there was the fact that the growing of cotton (or of corn, for that matter) in this country required no more than three or four months of labor in the year. And finally, if he were a poor white strictly, that was to have to work least of all.

As he escaped toil, so also he escaped that other bane of the European peasant and the Yankee farmer: the haunting specter of want. He would never go actually hungry; for the possession of some sort of land and hence some sort of subsistence, you will recall, was almost universal. And even if, through some mischance, his own larder was empty, a kindly neighborhood communism, brought over from the back-country, saw to it that he was fed, and without harrowing his dignity on the rack of formalized charity. Shelter could be no problem in a land in which pinewoods remained always a nuisance, to be disposed of by wholesale burning. If winter came, it never came so sternly that it could not be banished from the draftiest of huts by a few casual faggots. As for clothing, the little that was wanted need never be ragged, unless, and by exception, his women were lazy; it was too easy for them to grow a bit of cotton for spinning, or even to help themselves to the nearest field of a planter.

In the absolute, certainly, there was much of privation and downright misery in the lot of the poor white, and often in that of the yeoman farmer as well. But these people did not contemplate absolutes. They continued always to reckon their estate in terms established on the frontier. As they themselves would have phrased it from the depths of a great complacency, they found it "tol'able, thankee, tol'able."

But in this complacency itself, of course, we return directly upon the handiwork of the plantation; the loss of social and economic focus on the part of the masses, the divorce of pride from the idea of effort and achievement—the whole complex of extraordinary results proceeding from the curious combination of forces at play in this world.

And that this complex constituted a tragic descent into unreality on the part of these masses I need hardly tell you. Nothing is plainer than that, out of every sensible consideration of his own interest, the common white of the South ought early to have developed some decided awareness of his true position. For these walls which bound him in were very real: they not only barred him off from any advance *en masse;* they also, slowly, obscurely, but certainly and constantly, involved his degradation.

But if this was so, it is also to be noted that the loss of social and economic focus carried his escape from the drive of the belly forward to its ultimate term. His leisure was, as it were, *reamed out.* If he did not come, as has sometimes been charged against him, actually to hold labor as such in contempt (the heritage of the frontier and his laborious European fathers was too potent in him for that; all he ever really despised was "nigger work"—work that smacked of servility or work in gangs under the orders of a boss), he did nevertheless wax vastly indifferent to it, as something in which there was no point. And his energies were freed almost entirely for other ends.

The plantation, however, involved even more than these things. As we know, it had fetched in the Negro. But the Negro is notoriously one of the world's greatest romantics and one of the world's greatest hedonists. I am well aware that, when it is a question of adapting himself to necessity, he is sometimes capable of a remarkable realism. But in the main he is a creature of grandiloquent imagination, of facile emotion, and, above everything else under heaven, of enjoyment.

And in this society in which the infant son of the planter was commonly suckled by a black mammy, in which gray old black men were his most loved story-tellers, in which black stalwarts were among the chiefest heroes and mentors of his boyhood, and in which his usual, often practically his only, companions until he was past the age of puberty were the black boys (and girls) of the plantation—in this society in which by far the greater number of white boys of whatever degree were more or less shaped by such companionship, and in which nearly the whole body of whites, young and old, had constantly before their eyes the example, had constantly in their ears the accent, of the Negro, the relationship between the two groups was, by the second generation at least, nothing less than organic. Negro entered into white man as profoundly as white man entered into Negro—subtly influencing every gesture, every word, every emotion and idea, every attitude.

9

The outcome had all the inevitability of natural law.

In that void of pointless leisure which was his, the poor white turned his energies almost wholly to elaborating the old backcountry pattern of amusement and distinction—became (though it is shocking to say it) one of the most complete romantics and one of the most complete hedonists ever recorded.

To stand on his head in a bar, to toss down a pint of raw whisky at a gulp, to fiddle and dance all night, to bite off the nose or gouge out the eye of a favorite enemy, to fight harder and love harder than the next man, to be known eventually far and wide as a hell of a fellow—such would be his focus. To lie on his back for days and weeks, storing power as the air he breathed stores power under the sun of August, and then to explode, as that air explodes in a thunderstorm, in a violent outburst of emotion—in such fashion would he make life not only tolerable but infinitely sweet.

And what is true of the poor white was true in a fashion of the planter and yeoman farmer as well. In the planter, certainly, the pattern was profoundly modified and disguised by influences which we shall consider more fully later on. And among the more thrifty sort of farmers it was softened and deprived of much of its crude power, not only because they had never so completely lost social and economic focus as the true poor white, not only because they were naturally eager to follow the example of their richer neighbors, but also because the notions of decorum involved in the lower-middle-class heritage from Europe persisted in them with even greater strength than they persisted in the planter.

But the basic fact remains. In every rank men lolled much on their verandas or under their oaks, sat much on fences, dreaming. In every rank they exhibited a striking tendency to build up legends about themselves and to translate these legends into explosive action—to perform with a high, histrionic flourish, and to strive for celebrity as the dashing blade. In every rank they were much concerned with seeing the ponies run, with hearing the band, with making love, with dancing, with extravagant play. And in every rank the essential element about which this arose was the same simple frontier inheritance which the poor white was elaborating so naïvely.

Such is the primary picture. But I must not leave the theme without calling your attention specifically to the stimulation of the tendency to violence which these things obviously involved. Nor must I leave it without pointing to two significant patterns which grew up in the closest association with this romanticism and hedonism and served it as channels of discharge.

The first of these is the Southern fondness for rhetoric. A gorgeous, primitive art, addressed to the autonomic system and not to the encephalon, rhetoric is of course dear to the heart of the simple man everywhere. In its purest and most natural form, oratory, it flourishes wherever he forgathers—and particularly in every new land where bonds are loosed and imagination is vaulting. It flourished over the whole American country in these days of continental expansion, as it has rarely flourished elsewhere at any time.

But in the South, to recapitulate, there was the rising flood of romanticism and hedonism clamoring for expression, and in the South there was the daily impact upon the white man of the example of the Negro, concerning whom nothing is so certain as his remarkable tendency to seize on lovely words, to roll them in his throat, to heap them in redundant profusion one upon another until meaning vanishes and there is nothing left but the sweet, canorous drunkenness of sound, nothing but the play of primitive rhythm upon the secret springs of emotion. Thus rhetoric flourished here far beyond even its American average; it early because a passion—and not only a passion but a primary standard of judgment, the *sine qua non* of leadership. The greatest man would be the man who could best wield it.

But to speak of the love of rhetoric, of oratory, is at once to suggest the love of politics. The two, in fact, were inseparable. Hand in hand they emerged from the frontier tradition, flourished over the swelling territory of the young Republic of the West, and grew into romantic Southern passions.

Of politics, however, it may be objected that I am assuming too much—that, *per se*, it has nothing to do with romanticism and hedonism, and that a conspicuous concern with it might well be the very hallmark of realism. Let us grant it. Let us say that, in the so-called democracies of our Western world at least, one of the proper functions of politics is the resolution of essential conflict in interest among groups and classes. Then the fact stands fast: from such a realistic content the politics of the South was in a peculiarly thorough fashion barred away.

For the end result of all the blindness and complacency bred in the masses by physical and social conditions was the thing which is commonly and somewhat inaccurately called the paternalism of the Old South. I call the term inaccurate because its almost inevitable connotation is the relationship of Roman *patron* and *client*; it suggests, with a force that has led to much confusion, that there existed on the one hand an essential dependence, and on the other a prescriptive right—that it operated through command and obedience and rested finally on compulsion. But, as what we have already seen adequately indicates, there was, in truth, none of this here. The actual fact was simply that, unaware of any primary conflict in interest, and seeing the planter not as an antagonist but as an old friend or kinsman, the common white naturally fell into the habit of honoring him as *primus inter pares*, of deferring to his knowledge and judgment, of consulting him on every occasion, and of looking to him for leadership and opinion—and, above all, for opinion in politics.

Thus the politics of the Old South was a theater for the play of the purely personal, the purely romantic, and the purely hedonistic. It was an arena wherein one great champion confronted another or a dozen, and sought to outdo them in rhetoric and splendid gesturing. It swept back the loneliness of the land, it brought men together under torches, it filled them with the contagious power of the crowd, it unleashed emotion and set it to leaping and dancing, it caught the very meanest man up out of his own tiny legend into the gorgeous fabric of the legend of this or that great hero.

But the only real interest which was ever involved in it was that of the planter. And even in his case the romantic and hedonistic element would grow so potent, so preponderant, that eventually it would bear him outside the orbit of his true interest, would swing him headlong, perhaps against his own more sober judgment, into the disaster of the Civil War.

10

It is to our simple generic figure that we must look also for primary understanding of the South's religious pattern. The legend, of course, has always had it that the land was Anglican—or at least that the ruling class was predominantly so. But in fact there were less than sixty thousand Episcopalians in the South at the outbreak of the Civil

War, and these by no means included the body of the planters. Anglicanism was confined almost entirely to the seaboard districts inhabited by the old aristocracies of colonial days. Here and there it passed over into the cotton country, here and there was to be found a little clump of planters gathered about a St. John's-in-the Wood or a St. Michael's-in-the-Wilderness. But this was the exception and not the rule.

There was a time, to be sure—the period of the ascendancy of the Virginians—when what may be called the Anglican spirit, meaning a fairly easy tolerance in religious matters, was, in sharp contrast to New England, the prevailing rule in the South. There was even a time when atheism and French deism were pretty common both in the older regions and in the backcountry. In 1819 Mr. Jefferson could set up his university on a foundation that, though it was not "godless," as was charged against it, was still remarkable for religious freedom. And Dr. Thomas Cooper, rejected as too skeptical by even this university, could find refuge in the presidency of the College of South Carolina, and at Columbia, first of all places in America, openly apply the so-called Higher Criticism to the Bible.

But this would not and could not last. If the simple backcountryman who was to inherit the great South might sometimes, in his early isolation and engrossment with physical problems, lapse into indifference; if, in the first exuberant self-confidence born of the escape from traditional bonds, he might even be tempted into going all the way, into casting off bonds of every description, into throwing down gods as well as kings—yet, in the long run, he would have to retreat.

As I have said, his chief blood-strain was likely to be the Celtic—of all Western strains the most susceptible to suggestions of the supernatural. Even when he was a sort of native pagan, knowing little of the Bible and hooting contemptuously at parsons, he was nevertheless at bottom religious. Ancestral phobias grappled him toward the old center, and immemorial awes, drawn in with his mother's milk, whispered imperative warning in his ears.

And of the intellectual baggage which he had brought from Europe and managed to preserve on the frontier, the core and the bulk consisted of the Protestant theology of the sixteenth century and the Dissenting moral code of the seventeenth. If he was a hedonist, then, and however paradoxical it may sound, he was also likely to be a Puritan. The sense of sin, if obscured, continued to move darkly in him at every time—not so darkly, not so savagely, not so relentlessly as in the New Englander, it may be, but with conviction nevertheless. The world he knew, the hot sting of the sun in his blood, the sidelong glance of the all-complaisant Negro woman—all these impelled him irresistibly to joy. But even as he danced, and even though he had sloughed off all formal religion, his thoughts were with the piper and his fee.

With this heritage, moreover, the physical world sometimes joined hands. If the dominant mood is one of sultry reverie, the land is capable of other and more somber moods. There are days when the booming of the wind in the pines is like the audible rushing of time—when the sad knowledge of the grave stirs in the subconsciousness and bends the spirit to melancholy; days when the questions that have no answers must insinuate themselves into the minds of the least analytical of men. And there are other days—in July and August—when the nerves wilt under the terrific impact of sun and humidity, and even the soundest grow a bit neurotic; days saturnine and bilious and full of heavy foreboding. And there are those days, too, when the earth whimpers in dread, when the lightning clicks in awful concatenation with continuous thunder, and hurricanes break forth with semi-tropical fury; days when this land which, in its dominant mood, wraps its children in soft illusion, strips them naked before terror.

Nor was it only the physical world. His leisure left the Southerner free to brood as well as to dream—to exaggerate his fears as well as his hopes. And if for practical purposes it is true that he was likely to be complacently content with his lot, and even though it was the lot of white-trash, it is yet not perfectly true. Vaguely, the loneliness of the country, the ennui of long, burning, empty days, a hundred half-perceived miseries, ate into him and filled him with nebulous discontent and obscure longing. Like all men everywhere, he hungered cloudily after a better and a happier world. And if, as was so often the case, this hunger could not move him to toil and battle for the realization of the vision here and now, it could and did impel him to the pursuit of the world beyond the world—could and did combine with everything within and without him to bear him to the sanctuary of religion.

But not to the sanctuary of Anglicanism, surely. An exotic in America which established itself only under royal patronage, it was not simple and vivid enough. Its God "without body, parts, or passions" is an abstraction for intellectuals. It is priestly. It politely ignores hell and talks mellifluously of a God of Love. Its methods, begotten in the relaxing atmosphere of England and refined through centuries, are the methods of understatement. It regards emotion as a kind of moral smallpox.

What our Southerner required, on the other hand, was a faith as simple and emotional as himself. A faith to draw men together in hordes, to terrify them with Apocalyptic rhetoric, to cast them into the pit, rescue them, and at last bring them shouting into the fold of Grace. A faith, not of liturgy and prayer book, but of primitive frenzy and the blood sacrifice—often of fits and jerks and barks. The God demanded was an anthropomorphic God—the Jehovah of the Old Testament: a God who might be seen, a God who *had* been seen. A passionate, whimsical tyrant, to be trembled before, but whose favor was the sweeter for that. A personal God, a God for the individualist, a God whose representatives were not silken priests but preachers risen from the people themselves.

What was demanded here, in other words, was the God and the faith of the Methodists and the Baptists, and the Presbyterians. These personal and often extravagant sects, sweeping the entire American country with their revivals in the first half of the nineteenth century, achieved their greatest success in the personal and extravagant South. And not only among the masses. Fully nine-tenths of the new planters—of the men who were to be masters of the great South—were, and, despite some tendency to fall away to Anglicanism as more high-toned, continued to be, numbered among their adherents.

11

But the spirit of these sects, of course, was essentially Hebraic—their ideal theocratic. And it was characteristic of them all that they asserted, and that their communicants unquestioningly believed, the voice of their ministers to be literally the voice of God.

Thus, as the *nouveaux* came to power, this spirit and this ideal came to power also, and the evangelical ministers armored all too often in ignorance and bitter fanaticism, virtually always in a rigid narrowness of outlook, entered upon that long career of always growing and generally inept sway over public affairs, over the whole mind of the South, which was one day to flower in Bishop Cannon. By the time Andrew Jackson had got to be

President, the old easy tolerance was quite dead. Skepticism of any sort in religion was anathema, and lack of frenetic zeal was being set down for heresy. Before long a Presbyterian minister, named Thornwell, raised a clamor against the "infidelity" of Dr. Cooper, whose pupil he had sometime been, and got the old man turned out of his post and himself elected in his place. And by 1850 almost every non-Anglican seminary of any importance in the South, save only the University of Virginia, was in the hands of evangelical faculties.

The triumph of the evangelical sects also naturally involved the establishment of the Puritan ideal. From the first great revivals onward, the official moral philosophy of the South moved steadily toward the position of that of the Massachusetts Bay Colony. Adherence was demanded, and, with the exception of a handful of recalcitrant colonial aristocrats and stubborn sinners, willingly and even enthusiastically given, to a code that was increasingly Mosaic in its sternness.

And this, mind, coincidentally with the growth of that curious Southern hedonism which was its antithesis. The two streams could and would flow forward side by side, and with a minimum of conflict. The Southerner's frolic humor, his continual violation of his strict precepts in action, might serve constantly to exacerbate the sense of sin in him, to keep his zest for absolution always at white heat, to make him humbly amenable to the public proposals of his preachers, acquiescent in their demands for the incessant extension of their rule; his Puritanism might at a pinch move him to outlaw the beloved fiddle from the church as an instrument of Satan, would indeed lead him habitually to regard pleasure as in its very nature *verboten*. Yet, in the long run, he succeeded in uniting the two incompatible tendencies in his single person, without ever allowing them to come into open and decisive contention.

Hypocrisy? Far from it. There was much of Tartarin in this Southerner, but nothing of Tartufe. His Puritanism was no mere mask put on from cold calculation, but as essential a part of him as his hedonism. And his combination of the two was without conscious imposture. One might say with much truth that it proceeded from a fundamental split in his psyche, from a sort of social schizophrenia. One may say more simply and more safely that it was all part and parcel of that naïve capacity for unreality which was characteristic of him.

Robert Penn Warren

(1905–1989)

Born on April 24, 1905, in Guthrie, Kentucky, Robert Penn Warren graduated *summa cum laude* from Vanderbilt University in Tennessee in 1925. While at Vanderbilt he met Allen Tate, John Crowe Ransom, and Donald Davidson, and in 1922 their poetry magazine, *The Fugitive* (1922–1925), appeared. In 1927, Warren received his M.A. at Berkeley, did graduate work at Yale University from 1927 to 1928, and then, as a Rhodes scholar, went to New College, Oxford, England, where he acquired his B.Litt. degree in 1930.

As one of the four Fugitives who later became Agrarians, Warren contributed "The Briar Patch" to *I'll Take My Stand* (1930), the agrarian manifesto. Throughout the 1930s, Warren taught at universities in the South. While at Louisiana State University, he and Cleanth Brooks founded the *Southern Review* (1935–1942) and collaborated on *Understanding Poetry* (1938).

In 1950, Warren and his first wife, Emma Brescia, were divorced after twenty years of marriage. Two years later Warren married the writer Eleanor Clark, by whom he had two children, Rosanna Phelps and Gabriel Penn. Warren received the Pulitzer Prize for fiction for *All the King's Men* (1947), and for poetry for *Promises* (1957), for which he also received the Edna St. Vincent Millay Prize of the Poetry Society of America and the National Book Award. He was awarded the Bollingen Prize in Poetry for *Selected Poems: New and Old, 1923–1966* (1967), and the publication of *Audubon: A Vision* (1970) brought Warren the National Medal of Literature and the Van Wyck Brooks Award. He was named Poet Laureate in 1986.

Publications include *Night Rider* (1939); *Meet Me in the Green Glen* (1971); *Or Else—Poem/Poems 1968–1974* (1974); *Selected Poems: 1923–1975* (1976); *A Place to Come To* (1977); *Being Here 1977–1980* (1980); *Jefferson Davis Gets His Citizenship Back* (1980); *Rumor Verified* (1981); *Altitudes and Extensions (in New and Selected Poems 1923–1985)* (1986); *Portrait of a Father* (1988); *New and Selected Essays* (1989); and *A Robert Penn Warren Reader* (1987). Warren died on September 15, 1989, in Stratton, Vermont.

Blackberry Winter

It was getting into June and past eight o'clock in the morning, but there was a fire—even if it wasn't a big fire, just a fire of chunks—on the hearth of the big stone fireplace in the living room. I was standing on the hearth, almost into the chimney, hunched over the fire, working my bare toes slowly on the warm stone. I relished the heat which made the skin of my bare legs warp and creep and tingle, even as I called to my mother, who was somewhere back in the dining room or kitchen, and said: "But it's June, I don't have to put them on!"

"You put them on if you are going out," she called.

I tried to assess the degree of authority and conviction in the tone, but at that distance it was hard to decide. I tried to analyze the tone, and then I thought what a fool I had been to start out the back door and let her see that I was barefoot. If I had gone out the front door or the side door she would never have known, not till dinner time anyway, and by then the day would have been half gone and I would have been all over the farm to see what the storm had done and down to the creek to see the flood. But it had never crossed my mind that they would try to stop you from going barefoot in June, no matter if there had been a gully-washer and a cold spell.

Nobody had ever tried to stop me in June as long as I could remember, and when you are nine years old, what you remember seems forever; for you remember everything and everything is important and stands big and full and fills up Time and is so solid that you can walk around and around it like a tree and look at it. You are aware that time passes, that there is a movement in time, but that is not what Time is. Time is not a movement, a flowing, a wind then, but is, rather, a kind of climate in which things are, and when a thing happens it begins to live and keeps on living and stands solid in Time like the tree that you can walk around. And if there is a movement, the movement is not Time itself, any more than a breeze is climate, and all the breeze does is to shake a little the leaves on the tree which is alive and solid. When you are nine, you know that there are things that you don't know, but you know that when you know something you know it. You know how a thing has been and you know that you can go barefoot in June. You do not understand that voice from back in the kitchen which says that you cannot go barefoot outdoors and run to see what has happened and rub your feet over the wet shivery grass and make the perfect mark of your foot in the smooth, creamy, red mud and then muse upon it as though you had suddenly come upon that single mark on the glistening auroral beach of the world. You have never seen a beach, but you have read the book and how the footprint was there.

The voice had said what it had said, and I looked savagely at the black stockings and the strong, scuffed brown shoes which I had brought from my closet as far as the hearth rug. I called once more, "But it's June," and waited.

"It's June," the voice replied from far away, "but it's blackberry winter."

I had lifted my head to reply to that, to make one more test of what was in that tone, when I happened to see the man.

The fireplace in the living room was at the end; for the stone chimney was built, as in so many of the farmhouses in Tennessee, at the end of a gable, and there was a window on each side of the chimney. Out of the window on the north side of the fireplace I could see the man. When I saw the man I did not call out what I had intended, but, engrossed by the strangeness of the sight, watched him, still far off, come along the path by the edge of the woods.

What was strange was that there should be a man there at all. That path went along the yard fence, between the fence and the woods which came right down to the yard, and then on back past the chicken runs and on by the woods until it was lost to sight where the woods bulged out and cut off the back field. There the path disappeared into the woods. It led on back, I knew, through the woods and to the swamp, skirted the swamp where the big trees gave way to sycamores and water oaks and willows and tangled cane, and then led on to the river. Nobody ever went back there except people who wanted to gig frogs in the swamp or to fish in the river or to hunt in the woods, and those people, if they didn't have a standing permission from my father, always stopped to ask permission to cross the farm. But the man whom I now saw wasn't, I could tell even at that distance, a sportsman. And what would a sportsman have been doing down there after a storm? Besides, he was coming from the river, and nobody had gone down there that morning. I knew that for a fact, because if anybody had passed, certainly if a stranger had passed, the dogs would have made a racket and would have been out on him. But this man was coming up from the river and had come up through the woods. I suddenly had a vision of him moving up the grassy path in the woods, in the green twilight under the big trees, not making any sound on the path, while now and then, like drops off the eaves, a big drop of water would fall from a leaf or bough and strike a stiff oak leaf lower down with a small, hollow sound like a drop of water hitting tin. That sound, in the silence of the woods, would be very significant.

When you are a boy and stand in the stillness of woods, which can be so still that your heart almost stops beating and makes you want to stand there in the green twilight until you feel your very feet sinking into and clutching the earth like roots and your body breathing slow through its pores like the leaves—when you stand there and wait for the next drop to drop with its small, flat sound to a lower leaf, that sound seems to measure out something, to put an end to something, to begin something, and you cannot wait for it to happen and are afraid it will not happen, and then when it has happened, you are waiting again, almost afraid.

But the man whom I saw coming through the woods in my mind's eye did not pause and wait, growing into the ground and breathing with the enormous, soundless breathing of the leaves. Instead, I saw him moving in the green twilight inside my head as he was moving at that very moment along the path by the edge of the woods, coming toward the house. He was moving steadily, but not fast, with his shoulders hunched a little and his head thrust forward, like a man who has come a long way and has a long way to go. I shut my eyes for a couple of seconds, thinking that when I opened them he would not be there at all. There was no place for him to have come from, and there was no reason for him to come where he was coming, toward our house. But I opened my eyes, and there he was, and he was coming steadily along the side of the woods. He was not yet even with the back chicken yard.

"Mama," I called.

"You put them on," the voice said.

"There's a man coming," I called, "out back."

She did not reply to that, and I guessed that she had gone to the kitchen window to look. She would be looking at the man and wondering who he was and what he wanted, the way you always do in the country, and if I went back there now she would not notice right off whether or not I was barefoot. So I went back to the kitchen.

She was standing by the window. "I don't recognize him," she said, not looking around at me.

"Where could he be coming from?" I asked.

"I don't know," she said.

"What would he be doing down at the river? At night? In the storm?"

She studied the figure out the window, then said, "Oh, I reckon maybe he cut across from the Dunbar place."

That was, I realized, a perfectly rational explanation. He had not been down at the river in the storm, at night. He had come over this morning. You could cut across from the Dunbar place if you didn't mind breaking through a lot of elder and sassafras and blackberry bushes which had about taken over the old cross path, which nobody ever used any more. That satisfied me for a moment, but only for a moment. "Mama," I asked, "what would he be doing over at the Dunbar place last night?"

Then she looked at me, and I knew I had made a mistake, for she was looking at my bare feet. "You haven't got your shoes on," she said.

But I was saved by the dogs. That instant there was a bark which I recognized as Sam, the collie, and then a heavier, churning kind of bark which was Bully, and I saw a streak of white as Bully tore round the corner of the back porch and headed out for the man. Bully was a big, bone-white bull dog, the kind of dog that they used to call a farm bull dog but that you don't see any more, heavy chested and heavy headed, but with pretty long legs. He could take a fence as light as a hound. He had just cleared the white paling fence toward the woods when my mother ran out to the back porch and began calling, "Here you, Bully! Here you!"

Bully stopped in the path, waiting for the man, but he gave a few more of those deep, gargling, savage barks that reminded you of something down a stone-lined well. The red clay mud, I saw, was splashed up over his white chest and looked exciting, like blood.

The man, however, had not stopped walking even when Bully took the fence and started at him. He had kept right on coming. All he had done was to switch a little paper parcel which he carried from the right hand to the left, and then reach into his pants pocket to get something. Then I saw the glitter and knew that he had a knife in his hand, probably the kind of mean knife just made for devilment and nothing else, with a blade as long as the blade of a frog-sticker, which will snap out ready when you press a button in the handle. That knife must have had a button in the handle, or else how could he have had the blade out glittering so quick and with just one hand?

Pulling his knife against the dogs was a funny thing to do, for Bully was a big, powerful brute and fast, and Sam was all right. If those dogs had meant business, they might have knocked him down and ripped him before he got a stroke in. He ought to have picked up a heavy stick, something to take a swipe at them with and something which they could see and respect when they came at him. But he apparently did not know much about dogs. He just held the knife blade close against the right leg, low down, and kept on moving down the path.

Then my mother had called, and Bully had stopped. So the man let the blade of the knife snap back into the handle, and dropped it into his pocket, and kept on coming. Many women would have been afraid with the strange man who they knew had that knife in his pocket. That is, if they were alone in the house with nobody but a nine-year-old boy. And my mother was alone, for my father had gone off, and Dellie, the cook, was down at her cabin because she wasn't feeling well. But my mother wasn't afraid. She wasn't a big woman, but she was clear and brisk about everything she did and looked everybody and everything right in the eye from her own blue eyes in her tanned face. She had been the first woman in the county to ride a horse astride (that was back when she was a girl and long before I was born), and I have seen her snatch up a pump gun and go out and knock a chicken hawk out of the air like a busted skeet when he came over her chicken yard. She was a steady and self-reliant woman, and when I think of her now after all the years she has been dead, I think of her brown hands, not big, but somewhat square for a woman's hands, with square-cut nails. They looked, as a matter of fact, more like a young boy's hands than a grown woman's. But back then it never crossed my mind that she would ever be dead.

She stood on the back porch and watched the man enter the back gate, where the dogs (Bully had leaped back into the yard) were dancing and muttering and giving sidelong glances back to my mother to see if she meant what she had said. The man walked right by the dogs, almost brushing them, and didn't pay them any attention. I could see now that he wore old khaki pants, and a dark wool coat with stripes in it, and a gray felt hat. He had on a gray shirt with blue stripes in it, and no tie. But I could see a tie, blue and reddish, sticking in his side coat-pocket. Everything was wrong about what he wore. He ought to have been wearing blue jeans or overalls, and a straw hat or an old black felt hat, and the coat, granting that he might have been wearing a wool coat and not a jumper, ought not to have had those stripes. Those clothes, despite the fact that they were old enough and dirty enough for any tramp, didn't belong there in our back yard, coming down the path, in Middle Tennessee, miles away from any big town, and even a mile off the pike.

When he got almost to the steps, without having said anything, my mother, very matter-of-factly, said, "Good morning."

"Good morning," he said, and stopped and looked her over. He did not take off his hat, and under the brim you could see the perfectly unmemorable face, which wasn't old and wasn't young, or thick or thin. It was grayish and covered with about three days of stubble. The eyes were a kind of nondescript, muddy hazel, or something like that, rather bloodshot. His teeth, when he opened his mouth, showed yellow and uneven. A couple of them had been knocked out. You knew that they had been knocked out, because there was a scar, not very old, there on the lower lip just beneath the gap.

"Are you hunting work?" my mother asked him.

"Yes," he said—not "yes, mam"—and still did not take off his hat.

"I don't know about my husband, for he isn't here," she said, and didn't mind a bit telling the tramp, or whoever he was, with the mean knife in his pocket, that no man was around, "but I can give you a few things to do. The storm has drowned a lot of my chicks. Three coops of them. You can gather them up and bury them. Bury them deep so the dogs won't get at them. In the woods. And fix the coops the wind blew over. And down yonder beyond that pen by the edge of the woods are some drowned poults. They got out and I couldn't get them in. Even after it started to rain hard. Poults haven't got any sense."

"What are them things—poults?" he demanded, and spat on the brick walk. He rubbed his foot over the spot, and I saw that he wore a black, pointed-toe low shoe, all cracked and broken. It was a crazy kind of shoe to be wearing in the country.

"Oh, they're young turkeys," my mother was saying. "And they haven't got any sense. I oughtn't to try to raise them around here with so many chickens, anyway. They don't thrive near chickens, even in separate pens. And I won't give up my chickens." Then she stopped herself and resumed briskly on the note of business. "When you finish that, you can fix my flower beds. A lot of trash and mud and gravel has washed down. Maybe you can save some of my flowers if you are careful."

"Flowers," the man said, in a low, impersonal voice which seemed to have a wealth of meaning, but a meaning which I could not fathom. As I think back on it, it probably was not pure contempt. Rather, it was a kind of impersonal and distant marveling that he should be on the verge of grubbing in a flower bed. He said the word, and then looked off across the yard.

"Yes, flowers," my mother replied with some asperity, as though she would have nothing said or implied against flowers. "And they were very fine this year." Then she stopped and looked at the man. "Are you hungry?" she demanded.

"Yeah," he said.

"I'll fix you something," she said, "before you get started." She turned to me. "Show him where he can wash up," she commanded, and went into the house.

I took the man to the end of the porch where a pump was and where a couple of wash pans sat on a low shelf for people to use before they went into the house. I stood there while he laid down his little parcel wrapped in newspaper and took off his hat and looked around for a nail to hang it on. He poured the water and plunged his hands into it. They were big hands, and strong looking, but they did not have the creases and the earth-color of the hands of men who work outdoors. But they were dirty, with black dirt ground into the skin and under the nails. After he had washed his hands, he poured another basin of water and washed his face. He dried his face, and with the towel still dangling in his grasp, stepped over to the mirror on the house wall. He rubbed one hand over the stubble on his face. Then he carefully inspected his face, turning first one side and then the other, and stepped back and settled his striped coat down on his shoulders. He had the movements of a man who has just dressed up to go to church or a party—the way he settled his coat and smoothed it and scanned himself in the mirror.

Then he caught my glance on him. He glared at me for an instant out of the bloodshot eyes, then demanded in a low, harsh voice, "What you looking at?"

"Nothing," I managed to say, and stepped back a step from him.

He flung the towel down, crumpled, on the shelf, and went toward the kitchen door and entered without knocking.

My mother said something to him which I could not catch. I started to go in again, then thought about my bare feet, and decided to go back of the chicken yard, where the man would have to come to pick up the dead chicks. I hung around behind the chicken house until he came out.

He moved across the chicken yard with a fastidious, not quite finicking motion, looking down at the curdled mud flecked with bits of chicken-droppings. The mud curled up over the soles of his black shoes. I stood back from him some six feet and watched him pick up the first of the drowned chicks. He held it up by one foot and inspected it.

There is nothing deader looking than a drowned chick. The feet curl in that feeble, empty way which back when I was a boy, even if I was a country boy who did not mind hog-killing of frog-gigging, made me feel hollow in the stomach. Instead of looking plump and fluffy, the body is stringy and limp with the fluff plastered to it, and the neck is long and loose like a little string of rag. And the eyes have the bluish membrane over them which makes you think of a very old man who is sick about to die.

The man stood there and inspected the chick. Then he looked all around as though he didn't know what to do with it.

"There's a great big old basket in the shed," I said, and pointed to the shed attached to the chicken house.

He inspected me as though he had just discovered my presence, and moved toward the shed.

"There's a spade there, too," I added.

He got the basket and began to pick up the other chicks, picking each one up slowly by a foot and then flinging it into the basket with a nasty, snapping motion. Now and then he would look at me out of the blood-shot eyes. Every time he seemed on the verge of saying something, but he did not. Perhaps he was building up to say something to me, but I did not wait that long. His way of looking at me made me so uncomfortable that I left the chicken yard.

Besides, I had just remembered that the creek was in flood, over the bridge, and that people were down there watching it. So I cut across the farm toward the creek. When I got to the big tobacco field I saw that it had not suffered much. The land lay right and not many tobacco plants had washed out of the ground. But I knew that a lot of tobacco round the country had been washed right out. My father had said so at breakfast.

My father was down at the bridge. When I came out of the gap in the osage hedge into the road, I saw him sitting on his mare over the heads of the other men who were standing around, admiring the flood. The creek was big here, even in low water; for only a couple of miles away it ran into the river, and when a real flood came, the red water got over the pike where it dipped down to the bridge, which was an iron bridge, and high over the floor and even the side railings of the bridge. Only the upper iron work would show, with the water boiling and frothing red and white around it. That creek rose so fast and so heavy because a few miles back it came down out of the hills, where the gorges filled up with water in no time when a rain came. The creek ran in a deep bed with limestone bluffs along both sides until it got within three quarters of a mile of the bridge, and when it came out from between those bluffs in flood it was boiling and hissing and steaming like water from a fire hose.

Whenever there was a flood, people from half the county would come down to see the sight. After a gully-washer there would not be any work to do anyway. If it didn't ruin your crop, you couldn't plow and you felt like taking a holiday to celebrate. If it did ruin your crop, there wasn't anything to do except to try to take your mind off the mortgage, if you were rich enough to have a mortgage, and if you couldn't afford a mortgage you needed something to take your mind off how hungry you would be by Christmas. So people would come down to the bridge and look at the flood. It made something different from the run of days.

There would not be much talking after the first few minutes of trying to guess how high the water was this time. The men and kids just stood around, or sat their horses or mules, as the case might be, or stood up in the wagon beds. They looked at the strangeness of the flood for an hour or two, and then somebody would say that he had better be getting on home to dinner and would start walking down the gray, puddled limestone pike, or would touch heel to his mount and start off. Everybody always knew what it would be like when he got down to the bridge, but people always came. It was like church or a funeral. They always came, that is, if it was summer and the flood unexpected. Nobody ever came down in winter to see high water.

When I came out of the gap in the bodock hedge, I saw the crowd, perhaps fifteen or twenty men and a lot of kids, and saw my father sitting his mare, Nellie Gray. He was a tall, limber man and carried himself well. I always proud to see him sit a horse, he was so quiet and straight, and when I stepped through the gap of the hedge that morning, the first thing that happened was, I remember, the warm feeling I always had when I saw him up on a horse, just sitting. I did not go toward him, but skirted the crowd on the far side, to get a look at the creek. For one thing, I was not sure what he would say about the fact that I was barefoot. But the first thing I knew, I heard his voice calling, "Seth!"

I went toward him, moving apologetically past the men, who bent their large, red or thin, sallow faces above me. I knew some of the men, and knew their names, but because those I knew were there in a crowd, mixed with the strange faces, they seemed foreign to me, and not friendly. I did not look up at my father until I was almost within touching distance of his heel. Then I looked up and tried to read his face, to see if he was angry about my being barefoot. Before I could decide anything from that impassive, high-boned face, he had leaned over and reached a hand to me. "Grab on," he commanded.

I grabbed on and gave a little jump, and he said, "Up-see-daisy!" and whisked me, light as a feather, up to the pommel of his McClellan saddle.

"You can see better up here," he said, slid back on the cantle a little to make me more comfortable, and then, looking over my head at the swollen, tumbling water, seemed to forget all about me. But his right hand was laid on my side, just above my thigh, to steady me.

I was sitting there as quiet as I could, feeling the faint stir of my father's chest against my shoulders as it rose and fell with his breath, when I saw the cow. At first, looking up the creek, I thought it was just another big piece of driftwood streaming down the creek in the ruck of water, but all at once a pretty good-size boy who had climbed part way up a telephone pole by the pike so that he could see better yelled out, "Golly-damn, look at that-air cow!"

Everybody looked. It was a cow all right, but it might just as well have been driftwood; for it was dead as a chunk, rolling and roiling down the creek, appearing and disappearing, feet up or head up, it didn't matter which.

The cow started up the talk again. Somebody wondered whether it would hit one of the clear places under the top girder of the bridge and get through or whether it would get tangled in the drift and trash that had piled against the upright girders and braces. Somebody remembered how about ten years before so much driftwood had piled up on the bridge that it was knocked off its foundations. Then the cow hit. It hit the edge of the drift against one of the girders, and hung there. For a few seconds it seemed as though it might tear loose, but then we saw that it was really caught. It bobbed and heaved on its side there in a slow, grinding, uneasy fashion. It had a yoke around its neck, the kind made out of a forked limb to keep a jumper behind fence.

"She shore jumped one fence," one of the men said.

And another: "Well, she done jumped her last one, fer a fack."

Then they began to wonder about whose cow it might be. They decided it must belong to Milt Alley. They said that he had a cow that was a jumper, and kept her in a fenced-in piece of ground up the creek. I had never seen Milt Alley, but I knew who he was. He was a squatter and lived up the hills a way, on a shirt-tail patch of set-on-edge land, in a cabin. He was pore white trash. He had lots of children. I had seen the children at school, when they came. They were thin-faced, with straight, sticky-looking, dough-colored hair, and they smelled something like old sour buttermilk, not because they drank so much buttermilk but because that is the sort of smell which children out of those cabins tend to have. The big Alley boy drew dirty pictures and showed them to the little boys at school.

That was Milt Alley's cow. It looked like the kind of cow he would have, a scrawny, old, sway-backed cow, with a yoke around her neck. I wondered if Milt Alley had another cow.

"Poppa," I said, "do you think Milt Alley has got another cow?"

"You say 'Mr. Alley,'" my father said quietly.

"Do you think he has?"

"No telling," my father said.

Then a big gangly boy, about fifteen, who was sitting on a scraggly little old mule with a piece of croker sack thrown across the sawtooth spine, and who had been staring at the cow, suddenly said to nobody in particular, "Reckin anybody ever et drownt cow?"

He was the kind of boy who might just as well as not have been the son of Milt Alley, with his faded and patched overalls ragged at the bottom of the pants and the mud-stiff brogans hanging off his skinny, bare ankles at the level of the mule's belly. He had said what he did, and then looked embarrassed and sullen when all the eyes swung at him. He hadn't meant to say it, I am pretty sure now. He would have been too proud to say it, just as Milt Alley would have been too proud. He had just been thinking out loud, and the words had popped out.

There was an old man standing there on the pike, an old man with a white beard. "Son," he said to the embarrassed and sullen boy on the mule, "you live long enough and you'll find a man will eat anything when the time comes."

"Time gonna come fer some folks this year," another man said.

"Son," the old man said, "in my time I et things a man don't like to think on. I was a sojer and I rode with Gin'l Forrest, and them things we et when the time come. I tell you. I et meat what got up and run when you taken out yore knife to cut a slice to put on the fire. You had to knock it down with a carbeen butt, it was so active. That-air meat would jump like a bullfrog, it was so full of skippers."

But nobody was listening to the old man. The boy on the mule turned his sullen sharp face from him, dug a heel into the side of the mule and went off up the pike with a motion which made you think that any second you would hear mule bones clashing inside that lank and scrofulous hide.

"Cy Dundee's boy," a man said, and nodded toward the figure going up the pike on the mule.

"Reckin Cy Dundee's young-uns seen times they'd settle fer drownt cow," another man said.

The old man with the beard peered at them both from his weak, slow eyes, first at one and then at the other. "Live long enough," he said, "and a man will settle fer what he kin git."

Then there was silence again, with the people looking at the red, foam-flecked water.

My father lifted the bridle rein in his left hand, and the mare turned and walked around the group and up the pike. We rode on up to our big gate, where my father dismounted to open it and let me myself ride Nellie Gray through. When he got to the lane that led off from the drive about two hundred yards from our house, my father said, "Grab on." I grabbed on, and he let me down to the ground. "I'm going to ride down and look at my corn," he said. "You go on." He took the lane, and I stood there on the drive and watched him ride off. He was wearing cowhide boots and an old hunting coat, and I thought that that made him look very military, like a picture. That and the way he rode.

I did not go to the house. Instead, I went by the vegetable garden and crossed behind the stables, and headed down for Dellie's cabin. I wanted to go down and play with Jebb, who was Dellie's little boy about two years older than I was. Besides, I was cold. I shivered as I walked, and I had gooseflesh. The mud which crawled up between my toes with every step I took was like ice. Dellie would have a fire, but she wouldn't make me put on shoes and stockings.

Dellie's cabin was of logs, with one side, because it was on a slope, set on limestone chunks, with a little porch attached to it, and had a little whitewashed fence around it and a gate with plow-points on a wire to clink when somebody came in, and had two big white oaks in the yard and some flowers and a nice privy in the back with some honeysuckle growing over it. Dellie and Old Jebb, who was Jebb's father and who lived with Dellie and had lived with her for twenty-five years even if they never had got married, were careful to keep everything nice around their cabin. They had the name all over the community for being clean and clever Negroes. Dellie and Jebb were what they used to call "white-folks' niggers." There was a big difference between their cabin and the other two cabins farther down where the other tenants lived. My father kept the other cabins weatherproof, but he couldn't undertake to go down and pick up after the litter they strewed. They didn't take the trouble to have a vegetable patch like Dellie and Jebb or to make preserves from wild plum, and jelly from crab apple the way Dellie did. They were shiftless, and my father was always threatening to get shed of them. But he never did. When they finally left, they just up and left on their own, for no reason, to go and be shiftless somewhere else. Then some more came. But meanwhile they lived down there, Matt Rawson and his family, and Sid Turner and his, and I played with their children all over the farm when they weren't working. But when I wasn't around they were mean sometimes to Little Jebb. That was because the other tenants down there were jealous of Dellie and Jebb.

I was so cold that I ran the last fifty yards to Dellie's gate. As soon as I had entered the yard, I saw that the storm had been hard on Dellie's flowers. The yard was, as I have said, on a slight slope, and the water running across had gutted the flower beds and washed out all the good black woods-earth which Dellie had brought in. What little grass there was in the yard was plastered sparsely down on the ground, the way the drainage water had left it. It reminded me of the way, the fluff was plastered down on the skin of the drowned chicks that the strange man had been picking up, up in my mother's chicken yard.

I took a few steps up the path to the cabin, and then I saw that the drainage water had washed a lot of trash and filth out from under Dellie's house. Up toward the porch, the ground was not clean any more. Old pieces of rag, two or three rusted cans, pieces of rotten rope, some hunks of old dog dung, broken glass, old paper, and all sorts of things like that had washed out from under Dellie's house to foul her clean yard. It looked just as bad as the yards of the other cabins, or worse. It was worse, as a matter of fact, because it was a surprise. I had never thought of all that filth being under Dellie's house. It was not anything against Dellie that the stuff had been under the cabin. Trash will get under any house. But I did not think of that when I saw the foulness which had washed out on the ground which Dellie sometimes used to sweep with a twig broom to make nice and clean.

I picked my way past the filth, being careful not to get my bare feet on it, and mounted to Dellie's door. When I knocked, I heard her voice telling me to come in.

It was dark inside the cabin, after the daylight, but I could make out Dellie piled up in bed under a quilt, and Little Jebb crouched by the hearth, where a low fire simmered. "Howdy," I said to Dellie, "how you feeling?"

Her big eyes, the whites surprising and glaring in the black face, fixed on me as I stood there, but she did not reply. It did not look like Dellie, or act like Dellie, who would grumble and bustle around our kitchen, talking to herself, scolding me or Little Jebb, clanking pans, making all sorts of unnecessary noises and mutterings like an old-fashioned black steam thrasher engine when it has got up an extra head of steam and keeps popping the governor and rumbling and shaking on its wheels. But now Dellie just lay up there on the bed, under the patch-work quilt, and turned the black face, which I scarcely recognized, and the glaring white eyes to me.

"How you feeling?" I repeated.

"I'se sick," the voice said croakingly out of the strange black face which was not attached to Dellie's big, squat body, but stuck out from under a pile of tangled bedclothes. Then the voice added: "Mighty sick."

"I'm sorry," I managed to say.

The eyes remained fixed on me for a moment, then they left me and the head rolled back on the pillow. "Sorry," the voice said, in a flat way which wasn't question or statement of anything. It was just the empty word put into the air with no meaning or expression, to float off like a feather or a puff of smoke, while the big eyes, with the whites like the peeled white of hard-boiled eggs, stared at the ceiling.

"Dellie," I said after a minute, "there's a tramp up at the house. He's got a knife."

She was not listening. She closed her eyes.

I tiptoed over to the hearth where Jebb was and crouched beside him. We began to talk in low voices. I was asking him to get out his train and play train. Old Jebb had put spool wheels on three cigar boxes and put wire links between the boxes to make a train for Jebb. The box that was the locomotive had the top closed and a length of broom stick for a smoke stack. Jebb didn't want to get the train out, but I told him I would go home if he didn't. So he got out the train, and the colored rocks, and fossils of crinoid stems, and other junk he used for the load, and we began to push it around, talking the way we thought trainmen talked, making a chuck-chucking sound under the breath for the noise of the locomotive and now and then uttering low, cautious toots for the whistle. We got so interested in playing train that the toots got louder. Then, before he thought, Jebb gave a good, loud *toot-toot*, blowing for a crossing.

"Come here," the voice said from the bed.

Jebb got up slow from his hands and knees, giving me a sudden, naked, inimical look.

"Come here!" the voice said.

Jebb went to the bed. Dellie propped herself weakly up on one arm, muttering, "Come closer."

Jebb stood closer.

"Last thing I do, I'm gonna do it," Dellie said. "Done tole you to be quiet."

Then she slapped him. It was an awful slap, more awful for the kind of weakness which it came from and brought to focus. I had seen her slap Jebb before, but the slapping had always been the kind of easy slap you would expect from a good-natured, grumbling Negro woman like Dellie. But this was different. It was awful. It was so awful that Jebb didn't make a sound. The tears just popped out and ran down his face, and his breath came sharp, like gasps.

Dellie fell back. "Cain't even be sick," she said to the ceiling. "Git sick and they won't even let you lay. They tromp all over you. Cain't even be sick." Then she closed her eyes.

I went out of the room. I almost ran getting to the door, and I did run across the porch and down the steps and across the yard, not caring whether or not I stepped on the filth which had washed out from under the cabin. I ran almost all the way home. Then I thought about my mother catching me with the bare feet. So I went down to the stables.

I heard a noise in the crib, and opened the door. There was Big Jebb, sitting on an old nail keg, shelling corn into a bushel basket. I went in, pulling the door shut behind me, and crouched on the floor near him. I crouched there for a couple of minutes before either of us spoke, and watched him shelling the corn.

He had very big hands, knotted and grayish at the joints, with calloused palms which seemed to be streaked with rust with the rust coming up between the fingers to show from the back. His hands were so strong and tough that he could take a big ear of corn and rip the grains right off the cob with the palm of his hand, all in one motion, like a machine. "Work long as me," he would say, "and the good Lawd'll give you a hand lak cass-ion won't nuthin' hurt." And his hands did look like cast iron, old cast iron streaked with rust.

He was an old man, up in his seventies, thirty years or more older than Dellie, but he was strong as a bull. He was a squat sort of man, heavy in the shoulders, with remarkably long arms, the kind of build they say the river natives have on the Congo from paddling so much in their boats. He had a round bullet-head, set on powerful shoulders. His skin was very black, and the thin hair on his head was now grizzled like tufts of old cotton batting. He had small eyes and a flat nose, not big, and the kindest and wisest old face in the world, the blunt, sad, wise face of an old animal peering tolerantly out on the goings-on of the merely human creatures before him. He was a good man, and I loved him next to my mother and father. I crouched there on the floor of the crib and watched him shell corn with the rusty cast-iron hands, while he looked down at me out of the little eyes set in the blunt face.

"Dellie says she's might sick," I said.

"Yeah," he said.

"What's she sick from?"

"Woman-mizry," he said.

"What's woman-mizry?"

"Hit comes on 'em," he said. "Hit just comes on 'em when the time comes."

"What is it?"

"Hit is the change," he said. "Hit is the change of life and time."

"What changes?"

"You too young to know."

"Tell me."

"Time come and you find out everthing."

I knew that there was no use in asking him any more. When I asked him things and he said that, I always knew that he would not tell me. So I continued to crouch there and watch him. Now that I had sat there a little while, I was cold again.

"What you shiver fer?" he asked me.

"I'm cold. I'm cold because it's blackberry winter," I said.

"Maybe 'tis and maybe 'tain't," he said.

"My mother says it is."

"Ain't sayen Miss Sallie doan know and ain't sayen she do. But folks doan know everthing."

"Why isn't it blackberry winter?"

"Too late fer blackberry winter. Blackberries done bloomed."

"She said it was."

"Blackberry winter just a leetle cold spell. Hit come and then hit go away, and hit is growed summer of a sudden lak a gunshot. Ain't no tellen hit will go way this time."

"It's June," I said.

"June," he replied with great contempt. "That what folks say. What June mean? Maybe hit is come cold to stay."

"Why?"

"Cause this-here old yearth is tahrd. Hit is tahrd and ain't gonna perduce. Lawd let hit come rain one time forty days and forty nights, 'cause He wus tahrd of sinful folks. Maybe this-here old yearth say to the Lawd, Lawd, I done plum tahrd, Lawd, lemme rest. And Lawd say, Yearth, you done yore best, you give 'em cawn and you give 'em taters, and all they think on is they gut, and, Yearth, you kin take a rest."

"What will happen?"

"Folks will eat up everthing. The yearth won't perduce no more. Folks cut down all the trees and burn 'em cause they cold, and the yearth won't grow no more. I been tellen 'em. I been tellen folks. Sayen, maybe this year, hit is the time. But they doan listen to me, how the yearth is tahrd. Maybe this year they find out."

"Will everything die?"

"Everthing and everbody, hit will be so."

"This year?"

"Ain't no tellen. Maybe this year."

"My mother said it is blackberry winter," I said confidently, and got up.

"Ain't sayen nuthin' agin Miss Sallie," he said.

I went to the door of the crib. I was really cold now. Running, I had got up a sweat and now I was worse.

I hung on the door, looking at Jebb, who was shelling corn again.

"There's a tramp came to the house," I said. I had almost forgotten the tramp.

"Yeah."

"He came by the back way. What was he doing down there in the storm?"

"They comes and they goes," he said, "and ain't no tellen."

"He had a mean knife."

"The good ones and the bad ones, they comes and they goes. Storm or sun, light or dark. They is folks and they comes and they goes lak folks."

I hung on the door, shivering.

He studied me a moment, then said, "You git on to the house. You ketch yore death. Then what yore mammy say?"

I hesitated.

"You git," he said.

When I came to the back yard, I saw that my father was standing by the back porch and the tramp was walking toward him. They began talking before I reached them, but I got there just as my father was saying, "I'm sorry, but I haven't got any work. I got all the hands on the place I need now. I won't need any extra until wheat thrashing."

The stranger made no reply, just looked at my father.

My father took out his leather coin purse, and got out a half-dollar. He held it toward the man. "This is for half a day," he said.

The man looked at the coin, and then at my father, making no motion to take the money. But that was the right amount. A dollar a day was what you paid them back in 1910. And the man hadn't even worked half a day.

Then the man reached out and took the coin. He dropped it into the right side pocket of his coat. Then he said, very slowly and without feeling: "I didn't want to work on your—farm."

He used the word which they would have frailed me to death for using.

I looked at my father's face and it was streaked white under the sunburn. Then he said, "Get off this place. Get off this place or I won't be responsible."

The man dropped his right hand into his pants pocket. It was the pocket where he kept the knife. I was just about to yell to my father about the knife when the hand came back out with nothing in it. The man gave a kind of twisted grin, showing where the teeth had been knocked out above the new scar. I thought that instant how maybe he had tried before to pull a knife on somebody else and had got his teeth knocked out.

So now he just gave that twisted, sickish grin out of the unmemorable, grayish face, and then spat on the brick path. The glob landed just about six inches from the toe of father's right boot. My father looked down at it, and so did I. I thought that if the glob had hit my father's boot something would have happened. I looked down and saw the bright glob, and on one side of it my father's strong cowhide boots, with the brass eyelets and the leather thongs, heavy boots splashed with good red mud and set solid on the bricks, and on the other side the pointed-toe, broken, black shoes, on which the mud looked so sad and out of place. Then I saw one of the black shoes move a little, just a twitch first, then a real step backward.

The man moved in a quarter circle to the end of the porch, with my father's steady gaze upon him all the while. At the end of the porch, the man reached up to the shelf where the wash pans were to get his little newspaper-wrapped parcel. Then he disappeared around the corner of the house and my father mounted the porch and went into the kitchen without a word.

I followed around the house to see what the man would do. I wasn't afraid of him now, no matter if he did have the knife. When I got around in front, I saw him going out the yard gate and starting up the drive toward the pike. So I ran to catch up with him. He was sixty yards or so up the drive before I caught up.

I did not walk right up even with him at first, but trailed him, the way a kid will, about seven or eight feet behind, now and then running two or three steps in order to hold my place against his longer stride. When I first came up behind him, he turned to give me a look, just a meaningless look, and then fixed his eyes up the drive and kept on walking.

When we had got around the bend in the drive which cut the house from sight, and were going along by the edge of the woods, I decided to come up even with him. I ran a few steps, and was by his side, or almost, but some feet off to the right. I walked along in this position for a while, and he never noticed me. I walked along until we got within sight of the big gate that let on the pike.

Then I said: "Where did you come from?"

He looked at me then with a look which seemed almost surprised that I was there. Then he said, "It ain't none of yore business."

We went on another fifty feet.

Then I said, "Where are you going?"

He stopped, studied me dispassionately for a moment, then suddenly took a step toward me and leaned his face down at me. The lips jerked back, but not in any grin, to show where the teeth were knocked out and to make the scar on the lower lip come white with the tension.

He said: "Stop following me. You don't stop following me and I cut yore throat, you little son-of-a-bitch."

Then he went on to the gate, and up the pike.

That was thirty-five years ago. Since that time my father and mother have died. I was still a boy, but a big boy, when my father got cut on the blade of a mowing machine and died of lockjaw. My mother sold the place and went to town to live with her sister. But she never took hold after my father's death, and she died within three years, right in middle life. My aunt always said, "Sallie just died of a broken heart, she was so devoted." Dellie is dead, too, but she died, I heard, quite a long time after we sold the farm.

As for Little Jebb, he grew up to be a mean and ficey Negro. He killed another Negro in a fight and got sent to the penitentiary, where he is yet, the last I heard tell. He probably grew up to be mean and ficey from just being picked on so much by the children of the other tenants, who were jealous of Jebb and Dellie for being thrifty and clever and being white-folks' niggers.

Old Jebb lived forever. I saw him ten years ago and he was about a hundred then, and not looking much different. He was living in town then, on relief—that was back in the Depression—when I went to see him. He said to me: "Too strong to die. When I was a young feller just comen on and seen how things wuz, I prayed the Lawd. I said, Oh, Lawd, gimme strength and meke me strong fer to do and to in-dure. The Lawd hearkened to my prayer. He give me strength. I was in-duren proud fer being strong and me much man. The Lawd give me my prayer and my strength. But now He done gone off and fergot me and left me alone with my strength. A man doan know what to pray fer, and him mortal."

Jebb is probably living yet, as far as I know.

That is what has happened since the morning when the tramp leaned his face down at me and showed his teeth and said: "Stop following me. You don't stop following me and I cut yore throat, you little son-of-a-bitch." That was what he said, for me not to follow him. But I did follow him, all the years.

Founding Fathers, Early-Nineteenth-Century Style, Southeast U.S.A.

They were human, they suffered, wore long black coat and gold
                                                        watch chain.

They stare from daguerreotype with severe reprehension,
Or from genuine oil, and you'd never guess any pain
In those merciless eyes that now remark our own time's sad declension.

Some composed declarations, remembering Jefferson's language.
Knew pose of the patriot, left hand in crook of the spine or
With finger to table, while right invokes the Lord's just rage.
There was always a grandpa, or cousin at least, who had been a real Signer.

Some were given to study, read Greek in the forest, and these
Longed for an epic to do their own deeds right honor;
Were Nestor by pigpen, in some tavern brawl played Achilles.
In the ring of Sam Houston they found, when he died, one word
                                                        engraved: *Honor.*

Their children were broadcast, like millet seed flung in a wind-flare.
Wives died, were dropped like old shirts in some corner of country.
Said, "Mister," in bed, the child-bride; hadn't known what to find there;
Wept all the next morning for shame; took pleasure in silk; wore the
                                                        keys to the pantry.

"Will die in these ditches if need be," wrote Bowie, at the Alamo.
And did, he whose left foot, soft-catting, came forward, and breath hissed:
Head back, gray eyes narrow, thumb flat along knife-blade, blade low.
"Great gentleman," said Henry Clay, "and a patriot." Portrait by
                                                        Benjamin West.

Or take those, the nameless, of whom no portraits remain,
No locket or seal ring, though somewhere, broken and rusted,
In attic or earth, the long Decherd, stock rotten, has lain;
Or the mold-yellow Bible, God's Word, in which, in their strength,
                                                        they also trusted.

Some wrestled the angel, and took a fall by the corncrib.
Fought the brute, stomp-and-gouge, but knew they were doomed in
                                                        that glory.

All night, in sweat, groaned; fell at last with spit red and a cracked rib.
How sweet then the tears! Thus gentled, they roved the dark land with
                                                                the old story.

Some prospered, had black men and acres, and silver on table,
But remembered the owl call, the smell of burnt bear fat on dusk-air.
Loved family and friends, and stood it as long as able—
"But money and women, too much is ruination, am Arkansas-bound."
                                                                So went there.

One of mine was a land shark, or so the book with scant praise
Denominates him. "A man large and shapeless,
Like a sack of potatoes set on a saddle," it says,
"Little learning but shrewd, not well trusted." Rides thus out of history,
                                                                neck fat and napeless.

One fought Shiloh and such, got cranky, would fiddle all night.
The boys nagged for Texas. "God damn it, there's nothing, God damn it,
In Texas"—but took wagons, went, and to prove he was right,
Stayed a year and a day—"hell, nothing in Texas"—had proved it, came
                                                                back to black vomit,

And died, and they died, and are dead, and now their voices
Come thin, like the last cricket in frost-dark, in grass lost,
With nothing to tell us for our complexity of choices,
But beg us only one word to justify their own old life-cost.

So let us bend ear to them in this hour of lateness,
And what they are trying to say, try to understand,
And try to forgive them their defects, even their greatness,
For we are their children in the light of humanness, and under the
                                                                shadow of God's closing hand.

Andrew Lytle

(1902–1995)

Andrew Lytle was born on December 26, 1902, in Murfreesboro, Tennessee. He was formally educated at Sewanee Military Academy in Sewanee, Tennessee; Exeter College, Oxford, England; and Vanderbilt University in Nashville, where he received his B.A. in 1925. At Vanderbilt, his friends included fellow Fugitives Robert Penn Warren and Allen Tate. With his literary interest primarily in drama, Lytle left Tennessee to attend the Yale School of Drama (1927–1929) and even briefly tried acting in New York City. On June 20, 1938, he married Edna Langdon Barber, with whom he had three daughters, Pamela, Katharine Anne, and Lillie Langdon. His wife passed away in 1963. Lytle spent his career writing and teaching history, English, and creative writing at various universities.

Among Lytle's publications are *Bedford Forrest and His Critter Company* (1931); *The Long Night* (1936); *At the Moon's Inn* (1941); *A Name for Evil* (1947); *The Velvet Horn* (1957); *A Novel, A Novella and Four Stories* (1958); *The Hero with the*

Private Parts: Essays (1966); and *A Wake for the Living: A Family Chronicle* (1975). Lytle was editor of *The Sewanee Review* from 1942 to 1943 and 1961 to 1973.

Lytle's awards include Guggenheim Fellowships (1940, 1941, 1960), a *Kenyon Review* fellowship for fiction (1956), and a National Foundation of Arts and Letters grant (1966–1967). Lytle died on December 12, 1995, in Monteagle, Tennessee.

Jericho, Jericho, Jericho

She opened her eyes. She must have been asleep for hours or months. She could not reckon; she could only feel the steady silence of time. She had been Joshua and made it swing suspended in her room. Forever she had floated above the counterpane; between the tester and the counterpane she had floated until her hand, long and bony, its speckled dried skin drawing away from the bulging blue veins, had reached and drawn her body under the covers. And now she was resting, clear-headed and quiet, her thoughts clicking like a new-greased mower. All creation could not make her lift her thumb or cross it over her finger. She looked at the bed, the bed her mother had died in, the bed her children had been born in, her marriage bed, the bed the General had drenched with his blood. Here it stood where it had stood for seventy years, square and firm on the floor, wide enough for three people to lie comfortable in, if they didn't sleep restless; but not wide enough for her nor long enough when her conscience scorched the cool wrinkles in the sheets. The two footposts, octagonal-shaped and mounted by carved pieces that looked like absurd flowers, stood up to comfort her when the world began to crumble. Her eyes followed down the posts and along the basket-quilt. She had made it before her marriage to the General, only he wasn't a general then. He was a slight, tall young man with a rolling mustache and perfume in his hair. A many a time she had seen her young love's locks dripping with scented oil, down upon his collar . . . She had cut the squares for the baskets in January, and for stuffing had used the letters of old lovers, fragments of passion cut to warm her of a winter's night. The General would have his fun. *Miss Kate, I didn't sleep well last night. I heard Sam Buchanan make love to you out of that farthest basket. If I hear him again, I mean to toss this piece of quilt in the fire.* Then he would chuckle in his round, soft voice; reach under the covers and pull her over to his side of the bed. On a cold and frosting night he would sleep with his nose against her neck. His nose was so quick to turn cold, he said, and her neck was so warm. Sometimes her hair, the loose unruly strands at the nape, would tickle his nostrils and he would wake up with a sneeze. This had been so long ago, and there had been so many years of trouble and worry. Her eyes, as apart from her as the mirror on the bureau, rested upon the half-tester, upon the enormous button that caught the rose-colored canopy and shot its folds out like the rays of the morning sun. She could not see but she could feel the heavy cluster of mahogany grapes that tumbled from the center of the headboard—out of its vines curling down the sides it tumbled. How much longer would these never-picked grapes hang above her head? How much longer would she, rather, hang to the vine of this world, she who lay beneath as dry as any raisin. Then she remembered. She looked at the blinds. They were closed.

"You, Ants, where's my stick? I'm a great mind to break it over your trifling back."

"Awake? What a nice long nap you've had," said Doctor Ed.

"The boy? Where's my grandson? Has he come?"

"I'll say he's come. What do you mean taking to your bed like this? Do you realize, beautiful lady, that this is the first time I ever saw you in bed in my whole life? I
believe you've taken to bed on purpose. I don't believe you want to see me."

"Go long, boy, with your foolishness."

That's all she could say, and she blushed as she said it—she blushing at the
words of a snip of a boy, whom she had diapered a hundred times and had washed as
he stood before the fire in the round tin tub, his little back swayed and his little belly
sticking out in front, rosy from the scrubbing he had gotten. *Mammy, what for I've
got a hole in my stummick; what for, Mammy?* Now he was sitting on the edge of
the bed calling her beautiful lady, an old hag like her, beautiful lady. A good-looker
the girls would call him, with his bold, careless face and his hands with their fine,
long fingers. Soft, how soft they were, running over her rough, skinny bones. He
looked a little like his grandpa, but somehow there was something missing . . .

"Well, boy, it took you a time to come home to see me die."

"Nonsense. Cousin Edwin, I wouldn't wait on a woman who had so little faith in
my healing powers."

"There an't nothing strange about dying. But I an't in such an all-fired hurry. I've
got a heap to tell you about before I go."

The boy leaned over and touched her gently. "Not even death would dispute you
here, on Long Gourd, Mammy."

He was trying to put her at her ease in his carefree way. It was so obvious a pretending, but she loved him for it. There was something nice in its awkwardness, the
charm of the young's blundering and of their efforts to get along in the world. Their
pretty arrogance, their patronizing airs, their colossal unknowing of what was to
come. It was a quenching drink to a sin-thirsty old woman. Somehow his vitality had
got crossed in her blood and made a dry heart leap, her blood that was almost water.
Soon now she would be all water, water and dust, lying in the burying ground between the cedar—and fire. She could smell her soul burning and see it. What a fire it
would make below, dripping with sin, like a rag soaked in kerosene. But she had
known what she was doing. And here was Long Gourd, all its fields intact, ready to be
handed on, in better shape than when she took it over. Yes, she had known what she
was doing. How long, she wondered, would his spirit hold up under the trials of planting, of cultivating, and of the gathering time, year in and year out—how would he
hold up before so many springs and so many autumns. The thought of him giving orders, riding over the place, or rocking on the piazza, and a great pain would pin her
heart to her backbone. She wanted him by her to train—there was so much for him to
know: how the creek field was cold and must be planted late, and where the orchards
would best hold their fruit, and where the frosts crept soonest—that now could never
be. She turned her head—who was that woman, that strange woman standing by the
bed as if she owned it, as if . . .

"This is Eva, Mammy."

"Eva?"

"We are going to be married."

"I wanted to come and see—to meet Dick's grandmother . . ."

I wanted to come see her die. That's what she meant. Why didn't she finish and
say it out. She had come to lick her chops and see what she would enjoy. That's what
she had come for, the lying little slut. The richest acres in Long Gourd valley, so rich

hit'd make yer feet greasy to walk over'm, Saul Oberly at the first tollgate had told the peddler once, and the peddler had told it to her, knowing it would please and make her trade. *Before you die*. Well, why didn't you finish it out? You might as well. You've given yourself away.

Her fierce thoughts dried up the water in her eyes, tired and resting far back in their sockets. They burned like a smothered fire stirred up by the wind as they traveled over the woman who would lie in her bed, eat with her silver, and caress her flesh and blood. The woman's body was soft enough to melt and pour about him. She could see that; and her firm, round breasts, too firm and round for any good to come from them. And her lips, full and red, her eyes bright and cunning. The heavy hair crawled about her head to tangle the poor, foolish boy in its ropes. She might have known he would do something foolish like this. He had a foolish mother. There warn't any way to avoid it. But look at her belly, small and no-count. There wasn't a muscle the size of a worm as she could see. And those hips—

And then she heard her voice: "What did you say her name was, son? Eva? Eva Callahan, I'm glad to meet you, Eva. Where'd your folks come from, Eva? I knew some Callahans who lived in the Goosepad settlement. They couldn't be any of your kin, could they?"

"Oh, no, indeed. My people . . ."

"Right clever people they were. And good farmers, too. Worked hard. Honest—that is, most of 'em. As honest as that run of people go. We always gave them a good name."

"My father and mother live in Birmingham. Have always lived there."

"Birmingham," she heard herself say with contempt. They could have lived there all their lives and still come from somewhere. I've got a mule older'n Birmingham. "What's your pa's name?"

"Her father is Mister E. L. Callahan, Mammy."

"First name not Elijah by any chance? Lige they called him."

"No. Elmore, Mammy."

"Old Mason Callahan had a son they called Lige. Somebody told me he moved to Elyton. So you think you're going to live with the boy here."

"We're to be married . . . that is, if Eva doesn't change her mind."

And she saw his arm slip possessively about the woman's waist. "Well, take care of him, young woman, or I'll come back and ha'nt you. I'll come back and claw your eyes out."

"I'll take very good care of him, Mrs. McCowan."

"I can see that." She could hear the threat in her voice, and Eva heard it.

"Young man," spoke up Doctor Edwin, "you should feel powerful set up, two such women pestering each other about you."

The boy kept an embarrassed silence.

"All of you get out now. I want to talk to him by himself. I've got a lot to say and precious little time to say it in. And he's mighty young and helpless and ignorant."

"Why, Mammy, you forget I'm a man now. Twenty-six. All teeth cut. Long trousers."

"It takes a heap more than pants to make a man. Throw open them blinds, Ants."

"Yes'm."

"You don't have to close the door so all-fired soft. Close it naturally. And you can tip about all you want to—later. I won't be hurried to the burying ground. And keep your head away from that door. What I've got to say to your new master is private."

"Listen at you, mistiss."

"You listen to me. That's all. No, wait. I had something else on my mind—what is it? Yes. How many hens has Melissy set? You don't know. Find out. A few of the old hens ought to be setting. Tell her to be careful to turn the turkey eggs every day. No, you bring them and set them under my bed. I'll make sure. We got a mighty pore hatch last year. You may go now. I'm plumb worn out, boy, worn out thinking for these people. It's that that worries a body down. But you'll know all about it in good time. Stand out there and let me look at you good. You don't let me see enough of you, and I almost forget how you look. Not really, you understand. Just a little. It's your own fault. I've got so much to trouble me that you, when you're not here, naturally slip back in my mind. But that's all over now. You are here to stay, and I'm here to go. There will always be Long Gourd, and there must always be a McCowan on it. I had hoped to have you by me for several years, but you would have your fling in town. I thought it best to clear your blood of it, but as God is hard, I can't see what you find to do in town. And now you've gone and gotten you a woman. Well, they all have to do it. But do you reckon you've picked the right one—you must forgive the frankness of an old lady who can see the bottom of her grave—I had in mind one of the Carlisle girls. The Carlisle place lies so handy to Long Gourd and would give me a landing on the river. Have you seen Anna Belle since she's grown to be a woman? I'm told there's not a better housekeeper in the valley."

"I'm sure Anna Belle is a fine girl. But Mammy, I love Eva."

"She'll wrinkle up on you, Son; and the only wrinkles land gets can be smoothed out by the harrow. And she looks sort of puny to me, Son. She's powerful small in the waist and walks about like she had worms."

"Gee, Mammy, you're not jealous are you? That waist is in style."

"You want to look for the right kind of style in a woman. Old Mrs. Penter Matchem had two daughters with just such waists, but 'twarnt natural. She would tie their corset strings to the bed posts and whip'm out with a buggy whip. The poor girls never drew a hearty breath. Just to please that old woman's vanity. She got paid in kind. It did something to Eliza's bowels and she died before she was twenty. The other one never had any children. She used to whip'm out until they cried. I never like that woman. She thought a whip could do anything."

"Well, anyway, Eva's small waist wasn't made by any corset strings. She doesn't wear any."

"How do you know, sir?"

"Well . . . I . . . What a question for a respectable woman to ask."

"I'm not a respectable woman. No woman can be respectable and run four thousand acres of land. Well, you'll have it your own way. I suppose the safest place for a man to take his folly is to bed."

"Mammy!"

"You must be lenient with your Cousin George. He wanders about night times talking about the War. I put him off in the west wing where he won't keep people awake, but sometimes he gets in the yard and gives orders to his troops. 'I will sweep that hill, General'—and many's the time he's done it when the battle was doubtful— 'I'll sweep it with my iron brooms'; then he shouts out his orders, and pretty soon the dogs commence to barking. But he's been a heap of company for me. You must see that your wife humors him. It won't be for long. He's mighty feeble."

"Eva's not my wife yet, Mammy."

"You won't be free much longer—the way she looks at you, like a hungry hound."

"I was just wondering," he said hurriedly. "I hate to talk about anything like this . . ."

"Everybody has a time to die, and I'll have no maudlin nonsense about mine."

"I was wondering about Cousin George . . . If I could get somebody to keep him. You see, it will be difficult in the winters. Eva will want to spend the winters in town . . ."

He paused, startled, before the great bulk of his grandmother rising from her pillows, and in the silence that frightened the air, his unfinished words hung suspended about them.

After a moment he asked if he should call the doctor.

It was some time before she could find words to speak. "Get out of the room."

"Forgive me, Mammy. You must be tired."

"I'll send for you," sounded the dead voice in the still room, "when I want to see you again. I'll send for you and—the woman."

She watched the door close quietly on his neat square back. Her head whirled and turned like a flying jennet. She lowered and steadied it on the pillows. Four thousand acres of the richest land in the valley he would sell and squander on that slut, and he didn't even know it and there was no way to warn him. This terrifying thought rushed through her mind, and she felt the bed shake with her pain, while before the footboard the specter of an old sin rose up to mock her. How she had struggled to get this land and keep it together—through the War, the Reconstruction, and the pleasanter after days. For eighty-seven years she had suffered and slept and planned and rested and had pleasure in this valley, seventy of it, almost a turning century, on this place; and now that she must leave it . . .

The things she had done to keep it together. No. The one thing . . . From the dusty stacks the musty odor drifted through the room, met the tobacco smoke over the long table piled high with records, reports. Iva Louise stood at one end, her hat clinging perilously to the heavy auburn hair, the hard blue eyes and the voice:

"You promised Pa to look after me"—she had waited for the voice to break and scream—"and you have stolen my land!"

"Now, Miss Iva Louise," the lawyer dropped his empty eyes along the floor, "you don't mean . . ."

"Yes. I do mean it."

Her own voice had restored calm to the room: "I promised your pa his land would not be squandered."

"My husband won't squander my property. You just want it for yourself."

She cut through the scream with the sharp edge of her scorn: "What about that weakling's farm in Madison? Who pays the taxes now?"

The girl had no answer to that. Desperate, she faced the lawyer: "Is there no way, sir, I can get my land from the clutches of this unnatural woman?"

The man coughed; the red rim of his eyes watered with embarrassment. "I'm afraid," he cleared his throat, "you say you can't raise the money . . . I'm afraid—"

That trapped look as the girl turned away. It had come back to her, now trapped in her bed. As a swoon spreads, she felt the desperate terror of weakness, more desperate where there has been strength. Did the girl see right? Had she stolen the land because she wanted it?

Suddenly, like the popping of a thread in a loom, the struggles of the flesh stopped, and the years backed up and covered her thoughts like the spring freshet she had seen so many times creep over the dark soil. Not in order, but as if they were stragglers trying to catch up, the events of her life passed before her sight that had never been so clear.

Sweeping over the mounds of her body rising beneath the quilts came the old familiar odors—the damp, strong, penetrating smell of new-turned ground; the rank, clinging, resistless odor of green-picked feathers stuffed in a pillow by Guinea Nell, thirty-odd years ago; tobacco on the mantel, clean and sharp like smelling salts; her father's sweat, sweet like stale oil; the powerful ammonia of manure turned over in a stall; curing hay in the wind; the polecat's stink on the night air, almost pleasant, a sort of commingled scent of all the animals, man and beast; the dry smell of dust under a rug; the over-strong scent of two-sweet fruit trees blooming; the inhospitable wet ashes of a dead fire in a poor white's cabin; black Rebecca in the kitchen; a wet hound streaming before a fire. There were other odors she could not identify, overwhelming her, making her weak, taking her body and drawing out of it choking longing to hover all that she must leave, the animals, the fences, the crops growing in the fields, the houses, the people in them . . .

It was early summer, and she was standing in the garden after dark—she had heard something after the small chickens. Mericy and Yellow Jane passed beyond the paling fence. Dark shadows—gay full voices. *Where you gwine, gal? I dunno. Jest a-gwine. Where you? To the frolic, do I live. Well, stay off'n yoe back tonight.* Then out of the rich, gushing laughter: *All right, you stay off'n yourn. I done caught de stumbles.* More laughter.

The face of Uncle Ike, head man in slavery days, rose up. A tall Senegalese, he was standing in the crib of the barn unmoved before the bush-whackers. *Nigger, whar is that gold hid? You better tell us, nigger. Down in the well; in the far-place. By God, you black son of a bitch, we'll roast ye alive if you air too contrary to tell. Now listen, ole nigger, Miss McCowan ain't nothen to you no more. You been set free. We'll give ye some of it, a whole sack. Come on, now*—out of the dribbling, leering mouth—*what air it?* Ike's tall form loomed towards the shadows. In the lamp flame his forehead shone like the point, the core of night. He stood there with no word for answer. As she saw the few white beads of sweat on his forehead, she spoke.

She heard her voice reach through the dark—*I know your kind. In better days you'd slip around and set people's barns afire. You shirked the War to live off the old and weak. You don't spare me because I'm a woman. You'd shoot a woman quicker because she has the name of being frail. Well, I'm not frail, and my Navy Six an't frail. Ike, take their guns.* Ike moved and one of them raised his pistol arm. He dropped it, and the acrid smoke stung her nostrils. *Now, Ike, get the rest of their weapons. Their knives, too. One of us might turn our backs.*

On the top of the shot she heard the soft pat of her servants' feet. White eyeballs shining through the cracks in the barn. Then: *Caesar, Al, Zebedee, step in here and lend a hand to Ike.* By sun the people had gathered in the yard. Uneasy, silent, they watched her on the porch. She gave the word, and the whips cracked. The mules strained, trotted off, skittish and afraid, dragging the white naked bodies bouncing and cursing over the sod: *Turn us loose. We'll not bother ye no more, lady. You ain't no woman, you're a devil.* She turned and went into the house. It is strange how a woman gets hard when trouble comes a-gobbling after her people.

Worn from memory, she closed her eyes to stop the whirl, but closing her eyes did no good. She released the lids and did not resist. Brother Jack stood before her, handsome and shy, but ruined from his cradle by a cleft palate, until he came to live only in the fire of spirits. And she understood, so clear was life, down to the smallest things. She had often heard tell of this clarity that took a body whose time was spending on the earth. Poor Brother Jack, the gentlest of men, but because of his mark, made the butt and wit of the valley. She saw him leave for school, where he was sent to separate him from his drinking companions, to a church school where the boys buried their liquor in the ground and sipped it up through straws. His letters: *Dear Ma, quit offering so much advice and send me more money. You send barely enough to keep me from stealing.* His buggy wheels scraping the gravel, driving up as the first roosters crowed. *Katharine, Malcolm, I thought you might want to have a little conversation.* Conversation two hours before sun! And down she would come and let him in, and the General would get up, stir the fire, and they would sit down and smoke. Jack would drink and sing, *If the Little Brown Jug was mine, I'd be drunk all the time and I'd never be sob-er a-gin*—or, *Hog drovers, hog drovers, hog drovers we air, a-courting your darter so sweet and so fair.* They would sit and smoke and drink until she got up to ring the bell.

He stayed as long as the whiskey held out, growing more violent towards the end. She watered his bottles; begged whiskey to make camphor—*Gre't God, Sis Kate, do you sell camphor? I gave you a pint this morning.* Poor Brother Jack, killed in Breckinridge's charge at Murfreesboro, cut in two by a chain shot from an enemy gun. All night long she had sat up after the message came. His body scattered about a splintered black gum tree. She had seen that night, as if she had been on the field, the parties moving over the dark field hunting the wounded and dead. Clyde Bascom had fallen near Jack with a bad hurt. They were messmates. He had to tell somebody; and somehow she was the one he must talk to. The spectral lanterns, swinging towards the dirge of pain and the monotonous cries of *Water*, caught by the river dew on the before-morning air and held suspended over the fields in its acrid quilt. There death dripped to mildew the noisy throats . . . and all the while relief parties, moving, blots of night, sullenly moving in the viscous blackness.

Her eyes widened, and she looked across the foot posts into the room. There was some mistake, some cruel blunder; for there now, tipping about the carpet, hunting in her wardrobe, under the bed, blowing down the fire to its ashes until they glowed in their dryness, stalked the burial parties. They stepped out of the ashes in twos and threes, hunting, hunting, and shaking their heads. Whom were they searching for? Jack had long been buried. They moved more rapidly; looked angry. They crowded the room until she gasped for breath. One, gaunt and haggard, jumped on the foot of her bed; rose to the ceiling; gesticulated, argued in animated silence. He leaned forward; pressed his hand upon her leg. She tried to tell him to take it off. Cold and crushing heavy, it pressed her down to the bowels of the earth. Her lips trembled, but no sound came forth. Now the hand moved up to her stomach; and the haggard eyes looked gravely at her, alert, as if they were waiting for something. Her head turned giddy. She called to Dick, to Ants, to Doctor Ed; but the words struck her teeth and fell back in her throat. She concentrated on lifting the words, and the burial parties sadly shook their heads. Always the cries struck her teeth and fell back down. She strained to hear the silence they made. At last from a great distance she thought she heard . . . *too late* . . . *too late.* How exquisite the sound, like a bell swinging without ringing. Suddenly it came to her. She was dying.

How slyly death slipped up on a body, like sleep moving over the vague boundary. How many times she had laid awake to trick the unconscious there. At last she would know . . . But she wasn't ready. She must first do something about Long Gourd. That slut must not eat it up. She would give it to the hands first. He must be brought to understand this. But the specters shook their heads. Well let them shake. She'd be damned if she would go until she was ready to go. She'd be damned all right, and she smiled at the meaning the word took on now. She gathered together all the particles of her will; the specters faded; and there about her were the anxious faces of kin and servants. Edwin had his hands under the cover feeling her legs. She made to raise her own hand to the boy. It did not go up. Her eyes wanted to roll upward and look behind her forehead, but she pinched them down and looked at her grandson.

"You want to say something, Mammy?"—she saw his lips move.

She had a plenty to say, but her tongue had somehow got glued to her lips. Truly it was now too late. Her will left her. Life withdrawing gathered like a frosty dew on her skin. The last breath blew gently past her nose. The dusty nostrils tingled. She felt a great sneeze coming. There was a roaring; the wind blew through her head once, and a great cotton field bent before it, growing and spreading, the bolls swelling as big as cotton sacks and bursting white as thunder-heads. From a distance, out of the far end of the field, under a sky so blue that it was painful-bright, voices came singing, *Joshua fit the battle of Jericho, Jericho, Jericho—Joshua fit the battle of Jericho, and the walls come a-tumbling down.*

One of the more striking passages found in William Faulkner's *Intruder in the Dust* is the following evocation of a day long past but imagined in all its stunning particularity:

> For every Southern boy fourteen years old, not once but whenever he wants it there is the instant when it's still not yet two o'clock on that July afternoon in 1863, the brigades are in position behind the rail fence, the guns are laid and ready in the woods and the furled flags are already loosened to break out and Pickett himself with his long oiled ringlets and his hat in one hand probably and his sword in the other looking up the hill waiting for Longstreet to give the word and it's all in the balance, it hasn't happened yet, it hasn't even begun yet, it not only hasn't begun yet but there is still time for it not to begin against that position and those circumstances which made more men than Garnett and Kemper and Armstead and Wilcox look grave yet it's going to begin, we all know that, we have come too far with too much at stake and that moment doesn't need even a fourteen-year-old boy to think "This time."[1]

One way to read such a passage is simply to see it as an expression of the narrator's hapless desire to recapture the past, to reassert the prerogatives of a former society characterized by what one writer terms "paternalists' neuroses."[2] In this way, Faulkner can be regarded only as defending the antebellum status quo; his work is therefore limited, in Diane Roberts's estimation, to depicting circumstances that are "particular, historical, and contextualized."[3]

Unfortunately, such a view robs Faulkner of a more universal testimony recognized early by such philosophically disciplined writers as André Malraux and Jean-Paul Sartre. Astute contemporary scholars like the Caribbean author Edouard Glissant also point to Faulkner's use of a particular historical event as a vehicle for elaborating larger, even archetypal, human concerns.[4] And almost a half-century after the author's death, Faulkner's canon continues to be translated into numerous editions for the benefit of increasing numbers of students and scholars in Japan.

What these diverse readers perceive is that Faulkner was not simply bound by "cultural constructs" that impeded his awareness of the "psychosocial dysfunctions" of his region.[5] Faulkner indeed deconstructs his South in such a way as to reveal tensions, contradictions, and oppositions that always existed there. He writes out of the limitations of time and place but presents these limitations in context by reminding us that they are the sad by-products of the human condition. Limitation and hubris are recurring themes in Faulkner. Nor would the author deny that human beings are, in the words of theologian Diedrich Bonhoffer, "separated from one another by an unbridgeable gulf of otherness and strangeness which resists all our attempts to overcome it by means of natural association or emotion or spiritual union."[6] Hence, while some critics wish to find in Faulkner's work a consensus or a psychologically unified "paternalist ideology,"[7] the author may disappoint by displaying an imagination more diverse and expansive than the efforts of the critics to discount that imagination.

Imagination may be the key to appreciating a passage like the aforementioned one. Faulkner contended that imagination, observation, and experience were faculties that the writer must display in abundance if he or she is to create the convincing

illusion that fiction presupposes. An imaginative reading, as opposed to a strictly culturally bound one, of this section of *Intruder in the Dust* finds all the portentous possibilities of the world and of human choice distilled in an instant of time. What is
at stake is not simply Gettsyburg, or the Lost Cause, or even the South, though these
are the vehicles through which the universals of possibility and loss are glimpsed.
Rather, the author suggests through the lens of history how every moment contains
within it the potential for what human beings judge as victory or defeat. The weight of
the sentence, the massive freight behind it, push toward one conclusion, one imperfect
choice that invites inevitable regrets. The sentence itself is a metaphysic for tragedy.

Of special note is how not only the historical event but also the feeling itself can be
revisited in the imagination "whenever he [the boy] wants it." Even the historic battle
scene is subject to the qualifications (and possible inaccuracies) of an imagination that
"probably" recalls Pickett's hat in one hand and that can stall for more time if necessary,
recognizing, like T. S. Eliot's J. Alfred Prufrock, that "In a minute there is time / For decisions and revisions which a minute will reverse." Just as one would never attach
Eliot's declaration about time to a specific man and his predicament, neither should we
be so "culturally bound" as to assume Faulkner is concerned only with the fantasies of
an unreconstructed fourteen-year-old Southern white male who never actually saw
what he is recalling. The more probable lesson here is that the weight of history forces
upon the individual all the tensions, contradictions, conflicted aims, anguished insights,
and collective guilt of his or her forebears and region. Wanting to escape this burden but
being unable to do so are twin facets of the same dilemma.

Faulkner's insistence on the importance of writers' being concerned with "universal truths"[8] by no means indicates that Faulkner believed his own vision of the truth to
be infallible. The contemporary social critic Stephen L. Carter suggests the importance
of this distinction when he says that "the postmoderns have always been right on one
point: information is inherently imperfect. It is not that the real world, the *is* out there,
is contingent and in a sense the creation of our minds, but that our perceptions of that
real world are contingent and in a sense the creation of our minds."[9] Yet Carter warns of
the fallacy of the postmodernist approach and of its failure to make another, equally
crucial distinction: "But here is where the postmoderns go wrong: the contingent nature
of our perceptions does not mean that all perceptions are equally valid. It only means
we make mistakes."[10] Faulkner, like many other writers from this period, would have
understood that the "human heuristic is such that we learn from our errors."[11] He, like
others, also would have seen how "a community that shares a core belief that there is
such a thing as bedrock material truth is able to recognize mistakes and learn from
them. A community that fundamentally disbelieves in the idea of truth will, by definition, make no mistakes, and so it can send undesirables to the gas chambers and teach
that the world is flat and make no apologies."[12] In other words, when all structures of
meaning are eliminated, when truth is splintered into competing "views," all that is left
to ask, as Faulkner pointed out in his Nobel Prize acceptance speech, is, "When will I be
blown up?" Although the South has often been a place of divisive and violent traditions,
many writers in the region have sought the truth of human connectedness that the concept of community imparts, even when that community refused to recognize the legitimate claims of everyone whose right it was to belong.

The ability to transcend traditional categories and to be both a participant in and
an observer of community best describes the genius of Nathan Eugene Toomer. His
Cane (1923) has been heralded variously as a lyrical montage, "an impressionist sym-

phony," and a "prose oratorio of earth, blood and sun."[13] Toomer writes of the "sunset world of the Afro-American serf"[14] in Sparta, Georgia, where the author sought to confront his biracial heritage and the tensions it offered. As a result, he merged "his soul with the present moment and place—and race."[15] Poems such as "Prayer," "Harvest Song," "Portrait in Georgia," and "Cotton Song" are lyrical fragments describing the lives Toomer saw and heard around him in sharecroppers' cabins and weatherboard churches. It is no coincidence that the figure of speech found most often in Toomer's poetry is the synecdoche—a comparison that focuses on a part of something to suggest the whole of that phenomenon. For instance, in "Portrait in Georgia," Toomer provides a picture of an African American woman whose bodily features tell something of her tortured history and of the history of her people. With this approach, Toomer helps us see beyond appearances, training our eyes to discover what, in our ignorance and indifference, we might fail or choose to overlook. Toomer worried that the people whose lives he described as being "rooted in spirit" might one day be forgotten. He prophesied that "a few generations from now, the Negro will still be dark. A portion of his psychology will spring from this fact, but in all else he will be a conformist to the general outline of American civilization, or American chaos."

James Weldon Johnson was determined to preserve the African American folk tradition that included music, plantation tales, dances, and folk sermons. Calling these creations "authentic products" once shared with whites in days before the South had become so unequivocally biracial and slaveholding, Johnson focuses on the sermon as the "mainspring of hope and inspiration for generations of African-Americans." In his preface to *God's Trombones*, Johnson takes up the question of whether Negro dialect can still be an effective poetic and rhetorical technique given the frequent burlesque of that dialect by whites and "the fixing effects of its long association with the Negro only as a happy-go-lucky or a forlorn figure." Johnson elects not to offer his own poetic sermons (e.g., "Listen, Lord") in dialect for these reasons and on the basis of an even "weightier" scholarly consideration: The sermons delivered by "old-time Negro preachers" did not exhibit dialect so much as "a fusion of Negro idioms with Bible English." Johnson's discussion demonstrates the complex system of aesthetics and rich linguistic tradition informing African American oral history and literature. By implication, the author points out that the Southern canon was never limited to the purely literary productions inspired by Aristotle and the Western classical tradition.

African American folkways became a source of fascination for a number of white writers in the 1920s, among them South Carolina author Julia Peterkin. With the pioneering intensity of an anthropologist, Peterkin labored to depict the folk traditions of Gullah blacks living on or near coastal plantations like the one where she was mistress after marrying William Peterkin in 1903. Peterkin's stories often show the almost supernatural power attached to black folk beliefs. In "Ashes," an elderly black woman named Maum Hannah is asked to vacate her tiny cabin sitting adjacent a newly renovated plantation. Having nowhere to go, she asks God for a sign telling her what to do. The sign comes as the morning sky appears "red like fire!" What the old woman does next might be regarded as anything but consonant with Christian dogma. Nevertheless, she is able to return home where she will undoubtedly live out the rest of her days in peace. As for the plantation, the fire that has destroyed it is a "sign" of its own that the new proprietors should find another place to rebuild.

Because of the success of the film *Gone With the Wind*, Atlanta novelist Margaret Mitchell may be the best-known Southern writer in the world. After six decades, people in all corners of the globe continue to name their children after the principal male and female characters in the novel, Rhett Butler and Scarlett O'Hara. Even critics who find the novel's aristocratic ethos repugnant begrudgingly admit the spell that *Gone With the Wind* has cast over readers. As Helen Taylor observes, "Although thousands of books have been written challenging the Southern interpretation of history—many by black authors showing a different side to plantation life—the popular perception of the Civil War continues to be largely determined by *Gone With the Wind*."[16] Doubtless part of the novel's appeal lies in the strength of its characterizations that include the feisty and quintessential Southern belle Scarlett, to whom we are introduced in the very first sentence of Chapter One.

Much has already been written in this introduction about Faulkner and his contributions to Southern literature. The selections offered here—including a portion of the novel *Absalom, Absalom!*, as well as the story "Pantaloon in Black"—are designed to show the range of Faulkner's stylistic achievements and to suggest some recurring themes in Faulkner's canon. According to Cleanth Brooks, Faulkner believed that "a true community (a *gemeinschaft*) is held together by manners and morals deriving from a commonly held view of reality. The common values that bind a given community may be defective, even wrongheaded. In such case, all praise to the individual who tries to amend them."[17] One salient feature of Faulkner's work is the ambivalence that characters demonstrate toward the South, protesting as Quentin Compson does in *Absalom, Absalom!* that "I don't hate it! [the South] I don't hate it!" That Quentin kills himself shortly after making this declaration eliminates any doubt we may have about his true feelings or the potent and contradictory effects the South has often produced in its citizens.

Although written at a time when the South was mired in the deepening effects of the Great Depression, *I'll Take My Stand* warned of the problems inherent in unregulated industrial progress. This iconoclastic volume served, in Richard Weaver's words, as "one of the few effective challenges to a monolithic culture of unredeemed materialism."[18] One contributor, Stark Young, suggests the importance of family, religion, and manners in sustaining a civilized society capable of weathering fads and fashions "whose god is Mutability." Young's "Not in Memoriam, But in Defense" insists that no one would wish to resurrect the "old Southern life," which would prove "intolerable" should it return. Still, the versatile author argues that there are "fruits" of the former Southern civilization worth preserving and that a new order cannot "expect anything to rise higher than the life it comes from." Young worries about the mass media that "have generalized our national thinking." He is especially critical of Southerners' propensity for money-grubbing and for imitating the state of fashions in the North. Richly anecdotal, Young's essay reminds readers of the "catchwords" overheard when advocates of the new industrial program boast of the "progress":

"In our town we've got twenty thousand miles of concrete walks."
"And where do they lead?" I say.

Finally, Young warns of the hubris in assuming that the South is the only region concerned with such matters: "Plenty of people in New England, for example . . . wish to preserve certain elements on the same grounds that we do, and often more coherently and more intelligently." Many Jews also "share our Southern family instinct for the home, the sense of parents, the endless cousins, uncles, and aunts, the nostalgia for one's own blood."

Family and folkways are celebrated features of Zora Neale Hurston's *Their Eyes Were Watching God* (1937). Although Hurston's novel "reflects stylistic innovations associated with the Harlem Renaissance,"[19] her prose is also shaped by aspects of communal life in rural Florida, especially "story swapping, front porch tales, boasts, and other verbal exchanges that characterize the strength, and promise of particular black culture."[20] Strength is the quality that Hurston's heroine Janice Crawford displays in abundance; language for her is power, a spiritual force revealing that "the dream is the truth." Janie's story of "things suffered, things enjoyed, things done and undone" is not an adjunct to her life but an indispensable connection to all that she experiences and becomes. It is no coincidence that the time of day in which the novel opens is sundown:

> It was the time for sitting on porches beside the road. It was the time to hear things and talk. These sitters had been tongueless, earless, eyeless conveniences all day long. Mules and other brutes had occupied their skins. But now, the sun and the bossman were gone, so the skins felt powerful and human. They became lords of sounds and lesser things. They passed notions through their mouths. They sat in judgment.

Against this backdrop of the sadly familiar, Janie's story evolves out of a mythos of love, knowledge, and community. Telling her story not only helps her achieve "authority and autonomy"[21] but also connects her with a community of women whose narratives differ from the men's in one fundamental respect: Men's stories are "mocked to death by time," whereas "women forget all the things they don't want to remember and remember everything they don't want to forget." Telling and listening are ways of growing stronger, and Hurston's Janie is strong enough to resist the limitations imposed on her by her daunting grandmother, three self-assured husbands, and numerous complacent neighbors.

Frustrated love is the theme of much of Carson McCullers's short fiction. In "A Tree, A Rock, A Cloud," a paperboy stopping at an all-night café hears the lament of a man whose wife has left him and whose search for her has led him to conclude that love is a "science." Men, the failed lover points out, "start at the wrong end of love. They begin at the climax." They should instead begin by loving small and ordinary things—"a tree, a rock, a cloud." By this method, a man can learn to love anything or anybody and will not be devastated when the beloved forsakes him. Of course, the storyteller's scientific approach and rational explanations are belied by a sharp-edged urgency bordering on mania. Indeed, the absence of love, as McCullers dramatically asserts, will drive one to craziness and is the source of all the world's ills. That the young recipient of this story is twelve years old and on the cusp of manhood can only suggest the ongoing struggle each generation undertakes to find completion in love. Without realizing it, the boy has heard the one story that will initiate him into the mysteries and disappointments of a quest he has yet to make.

As a member of one of the South's scion families, William Alexander Percy in many ways embodied the aristocratic ideal of *noblesse oblige*. Percy's life was bound up in duty and in civic, historic, and family obligations. Rearing his three orphaned cousins, one of whom included novelist Walker Percy, who gratefully acknowledged the elder Percy's influence on him, William Alexander Percy emerged as a minor poet and major memoirist stressing the virtues of honor and stoic self-denial. Published in the same year as W. J. Cash's *Mind of the South* (1941), Percy's *Lanterns on the Levee* is a defense of the deep South's sharecropping system that many critics viewed as exploitative of land and labor. The author argues that given the agricultural exigencies present in the Depression-era South, sharecropping was by far the most humane arrangement for meeting the material needs of large numbers of people. Percy was also intent on improving the cultural and educational situation in the South, and his home in Greenville, Mississippi, was a gathering place for writers, artists, and musicians. A man who was perhaps never entirely comfortable in the modern world, William Alexander Percy produced writings tinged with the melancholy and romanticism of a former time. Percy's chapter from *Lanterns* entitled "Sewanee" is an evocative remembrance of the author's student days at the University of the South. His praise for Sewanee offers a counterpoint to the more satiric depiction found in Ann Rivers Siddon's *Hill Towns*.

Perhaps no writer in the twentieth-century South has been more affectionately regarded than Eudora Welty, the result, perhaps, of Welty's ability to depict her Mississippi hill people with consummate love and understanding while suspending all judgment of them. Welty never moralizes or offers excuses. Her characters reveal both the worst and the best of the human condition, a condition more akin to comedy than tragedy for the simple reason that Welty manages to penetrate appearances, uncovering as much nobility as baseness of spirit in her characters. The ability to love is a redeeming feature of human nature. Even fantasies, such as those exhibited by Ruby Fisher in "A Piece of News," are less about eroticism than about the need to be loved and desired. Thus, Ruby is a "hitch-hiker" in search of whatever love she can find in casual encounters with men who offer a transcendent glimpse of what her husband Clyde fails to provide her. Love is so important to Ruby that she will die for it—at least in her fantasy life, conjuring a scene in which Clyde murders her in a fit of jealous rage.

A more tempered but expansive view of love informs Welty's "A Worn Path." At Christmas time, an elderly black woman named Phoenix Jackson travels on foot from the country to the city in a ritualistic odyssey undertaken to acquire medicine for her young grandson, who had once swallowed lye but who had miraculously survived. Despite poor eyesight, lapses in concentration, uncertain footing, a harsh landscape, and an encounter with a mean-spirited hunter, Phoenix arrives at the hospital, where she is at once proclaimed a "charity" case. It is, of course, Phoenix's selfless love that offers a lesson in charity, nor will she let herself be defeated, rising, as her name suggests, in a flash of transcendent hope and unbounded compassion. As with Welty's own approach, Phoenix's ways are "too deep, too overflowing, ever to be plumbed outside love."

As the South's best-known playwright of the twentieth century, Tennessee Williams pits sensitive, often tortured individuals against a crass and increasingly brutal modern world. His plays embody "the South's dream of a world of grace and charm that had all but vanished during the Civil War."[22] Williams's female characters, in particular, are quintessential Southern belles—exotic flowers too delicate to withstand the withering effects of society's indifference and harsh treatment. Consequently, Williams's women experience the full range of psychic maladies—from neurotic hypersensitivity to hysteria to full-blown insanity. Williams's characters are people to be pitied, and pathos is the reigning sentiment in all his work.

In Williams's one-act play *Portrait of Madonna*, we encounter Miss Lucretia Collins, a middle-aged spinster who fantasizes about having been raped by a former beau now married to another (Northern) woman and living in Cincinnati. Through the eyes of a crass elevator operator and a more sensitive porter working in the apartment building where Miss Collins lives, we are privy to Miss Collins's unraveling and her thwarted desire to be loved and protected. Ever the lady, she insists that she has been raped and is pregnant with a child who "has a perfect right to its father's name." If we have any doubt about how we are to regard Lucretia Collins and her state of mind, Williams offers an exchange meant to settle the question:

> Elevator Boy: An ole woman like her is disgusting, though, imaginin' somebody's raped her.
> Porter: Pitiful, not disgusting. Watch them cigarette ashes.

Sexual repression is a transparent theme in this play, accounting for symptoms, though probably not the sole source, of the protagonist's anguish. Williams makes clear the difficulty Southern women experience in balancing the demands of being a "lady"—adhering to the idealization of purity and virtue represented by the Madonna, while conveying the sensual allure and coquettishness of a siren. Miss Collins hints at this tension in proclaiming that "your No'then girls receive such excellent domestic training, but in the South it was never considered essential for a girl to have anything but prettiness and charm."

Like Eudora Welty and Tennessee Williams, Richard Wright was a native Mississippian, his formative years spent in Jackson, where he lived with his maternal grandparents. Although *Native Son*, a novel about a Southern black man struggling to stay alive in a Chicago ghetto, is usually considered Wright's major work, *Black Boy* more directly incorporates the author's experiences of growing up in a racist South. As an example of "fictionalized autobiography,"[23] *Black Boy* chronicles Wright's own youth, presenting dramatic episodes of "the black child's hunger, fear, and loneliness, his vulnerability to the content of whites and the harsh discipline imposed by his black elders, presumably to prepare him for life in a world where blacks were expected to know their place, his repeated exploitation by blacks and whites alike, his perpetual humiliation."[24] The selection offered here tells of the young protagonist's intense desire to hear and read stories by which "reality changed, the look of things altered, and the world became peopled with magical presences." However, when the boy writes a story of his own entitled "The Voodoo of Hell's Half-Acre," he encounters the severe religious prohibitions of his elders, who remind him that stories are "lies" and that using the word *hell* in his manuscript is a prelude to damnation. The environment so strangles the boy that he dreams "of going north and writing books, novels." Later, he discovers the mammoth opportunities offered by the public library and even forges a note so as not to arouse suspicion when he wishes to examine some books by H. L. Mencken. *Black Boy* is rarely described as heart-rending, yet the scenes here are arresting in their depiction of the boy's dogged efforts to insist on his humanity despite what amounts to a conspiracy to undermine that humanity at every turn.

Unlike the previous writers, most of whom were concerned with the effects of a tumultuous, disintegrating society, Truman Capote focuses on the self writ large and all the loneliness the self can endure. Even Capote's prose is deliberately lean and pared down, each sentence slicing flesh from the bones of characters whose anguish is exposed with a startling urgency. Often the author's human creations do not want to be reminded of their condition. In Capote's story "A Diamond Guitar," for instance, a fifty-year-old convict named Mr. Schaeffer spends his time carving wooden dolls, not wishing to remember his loneliness because to do so is to feel alive and "he had not wanted to be alive." Yet the arrival of a young Cuban-born convict at the prison farm stirs in Mr. Schaeffer and the other prisoners a hope that they had almost forgotten. Tico Feo is the essence of the life force, his hair shining like gold, his "eyes like strips of sky-blue as the winter evening." He even carries a guitar "studded with glass diamonds." His outrageous lies and sweetly sung tunes transform the men, awakening memories of "brown rivers where the fish run, and sunlight on a lady's hair." However, self-imposed gravity and advancing age prevent Mr. Schaeffer from attempting an escape with Tico. The young man's fate is that of a shooting star destined to impart the knowledge that "what happens to us on earth is lost in the endless shine of eternity."

If Truman Capote was largely interested in the plight of men imprisoned by loneliness and lack of hope, Lillian Smith struck out against the incarceration of women by traditional Southern institutions and culture. In Chapter Four, entitled "Women," from *Killers of the Dream*, Smith explodes the rosy folklore surrounding the Southern white child's "dual Mother-Mammy relationship." With searing psychological insights, Smith discusses the effects of the destructive and "immoral habit" of permitting one's white child to be suckled by a black nanny. The discrimination experienced by both mother and nurse was such as to produce "a secret wound" and a "shameful sore." White women, in particular, felt themselves denied their proper roles as mothers. Unable to give their children maternal nurturing and tenderness, they compensated by stressing an often twisted and rigid moralism. Victims of the "Sacred Institution of Womanhood," these women were forced to deny natural biological processes, resulting in the "sexual erosion of their nature." Is it any wonder, Smith asks, that Southern women would write to end religious, racial, and sexual discrimination? She points out that in 1930, "these women organized an Association of Southern Women for the Prevention of Lynching." The "ladies' valor" also prompted them to attack and in large part subdue the Ku Klux Klan when that group experienced resurgence in the 1920s and 1930s. Smith adds that it was from the KKK that Adolph Hitler doubtless learned much about hatred and intimidation. Smith's account is crucial in illuminating the social commitment of a minority of Southerners who often encountered vicious resistance and whose efforts would not receive proper attention until the Civil Rights movement of the 1960s.

Notes

1. William Faulkner, *Intruder in the Dust* (New York: Random House, 1975), 190.
2. Kevin Railey, "The Social Psychology of Paternalism: *Sanctuary's* Cultural Context," *Faulkner in Cultural Context*, eds. Donald Kartiganer and Ann Abadie (Jackson: University Press of Mississippi, 1997), 85. Crucial to note is that Professor Railey is discussing the "social psychology of paternalism" in Faulkner's *Sanctuary*. Yet, Railey generalizes his thesis to include *Flags in the Dust* and *The Sound and the Fury*. We can therefore assume he would view the cited passage as residing under the aegis of "the aristocratic, paternalist, noblesse oblige world associated with the Old South."
3. Diane Roberts, "French-fried Faulkner" (a review of Edouard Glissant's *Faulkner, Mississippi*), *Brightleaf*, Spring 1999, 13.
4. Edouard Glissant, *Faulkner, Mississippi* (New York: Farrar, Straus, and Giroux, 1999).

5. A number of works use such terminology in presenting theoretical perspectives about Faulkner. See *Faulkner in Cultural Context*, note 2.

6. Dietrich Bonhoeffer, *Dietrich Bonhoeffer: The Modern Spirituality Series* (Springfield, IL: Templegate Publishers, 1990), 39.

7. Railey, 76.

8. William Faulkner, Nobel Prize Acceptance Speech.

9. Stephen L. Carter, *Civility* (New York: Harper Collins, 1998), 202.

10. Carter, 202.

11. Carter, 203.

12. Carter, 203.

13. David Levering Lewis, *When Harlem Was in Vogue* (New York: Oxford University Press, 1979), 64.

14. Lewis, 64.

15. Lewis, 61.

16. Helen Taylor, *Scarlett's Women: Gone With the Wind and Its Female Fans* (New Brunswick, NJ: Rutgers University Press, 1989), 3.

17. Cleanth Brooks, "William Faulkner," *The History of Southern Literature*, ed. Louis D. Rubin et al. (Baton Rouge: Louisiana State University Press, 1985), 338.

18. Richard M. Weaver, *The Southern Essays of Richard M. Weaver*, eds. George M. Curtis and James J. Thompson (Indianapolis: Liberty Press, 1987), 15–16.

19. Lee Green, "Black Novelists and Novels, 1930–1950," *The History of Southern Literature*, ed. Louis D. Rubin et al. (Baton Rouge: Louisiana State University Press, 1985), 384.

20. Thadious Davis, "Southern Standard-Bearers in the New Negro Renaissance," *The History of Southern Literature*, ed. Louis D. Rubin et al. (Baton Rouge: Louisiana State University Press, 1985), 307.

21. Thadious Davis, "Women's Art and Authorship in the Southern Region: Connections," *The Female Tradition in Southern Literature*, ed. Carol Manning (Urbana: University of Illinois Press, 1993), 29.

22. J. A. Bryant, *Twentieth-Century Southern Literature* (Lexington: University Press of Kentucky, 1997), 95.

23. Bryant, 157.

24. Bryant, 157.

Jean Toomer

(1894–1967)

Born in Washington, D.C., on December 26, 1894, Jean Toomer attended the University of Wisconsin–Madison (1914); Massachusetts College of Agriculture, Amherst (1915); American College of Physical Training, Chicago (1916); University of Chicago (1916); New York University (1917); and City College of New York (1917). On October 20, 1931, he married Margery Latimer, who died during the birth of their daughter Margery. On September 1, 1934, he married Marjorie Content.

In 1919, Toomer decided to become a writer and thus associated with other writers in New York. In 1923, he rejected the literary world but continued to write. In 1924, he became a follower of George I. Gurdjieff, Greek spiritual philosopher and leader of the Gurdjieff movement, who advocated a balance of soul, body, and mind. Toomer spent a number of years teaching this philosophy. From 1934 to 1967, he lived on a farm in Doylestown, Pennsylvania.

Among Toomer's writings are *Cane* (1923); *Essentials* (1931); *An Interpretation of Friends Worship* (1947); *The Flavor of Man* (1949); and *The Wayward and the Seeking: A Collection of Writings by Jean Toomer* (1980).

Toomer died in Doylestown on March 30, 1967.

Prayer

My body is opaque to the soul.
Driven of the spirit, long have I sought to temper it unto the spirit's longing,
But my mind, too, is opaque to the soul.
A closed lid is my soul's flesh-eye.
O Spirits of whom my soul is but a little finger,
Direct it to the lid of its flesh-eye.
I am weak with much giving.
I am weak with the desire to give more.
(How strong a thing is the little finger!)
So weak that I have confused the body with the soul,
And the body with its little finger.
(How frail is the little finger.)
My voice could not carry to you did you dwell in stars,
O Spirits of whom my soul is but a little finger . . .

Harvest Song

I am a reaper whose muscles set at sundown. All my oats are
        cradled.
But I am too chilled, and too fatigued to bind them. And I hunger.

I crack a grain between my teeth. I do not taste it.
I have been in the fields all day. My throat is dry. I hunger.

My eyes are caked with dust of oatfields at harvest-time.
I am a blind man who stares across the hills, seeking stack'd fields
    of other harvesters.

It would be good to see them . . . cook'd, split, and iron-ring'd han-
    dles of the scythes. It would be good to see them, dust-
    caked and blind. I hunger.

(Dusk is a strange fear'd sheath their blades are dull'd in.)
My throat is dry. And should I call, a cracked grain like the
    oats . . . eoho—

I fear to call. What should they hear me, and offer me their grain,
    oats, or wheat, or corn? I have been in the fields all day. I
    fear I could not taste it. I fear knowledge of my hunger.

My ears are caked with dust of oatfields at harvest-time.
I am a deaf man who strains to hear the calls of other harvesters
    whose throats are also dry.

It would be good to hear their songs . . . reapers of the sweet-stalk'd
    cane, cutters of the corn . . . even though their throats
    cracked and the strangeness of their voices deafened me.

I hunger. My throat is dry. Now that the sun has set and I am
    chilled, I fear to call. (Eoho, my brothers!)

I am a reaper. (Eoho!) All my oats are cradled. But I am too
    fatigued to bind them. And I hunger. I crack a grain. It
    has no taste to it. My throat is dry . . .

O my brothers, I beat my palms, still soft, against the stubble of my
    harvesting. (You beat your soft palms, too.) My pain is
    sweet. Sweater than the oats or wheat or corn. It will not
    bring me knowledge of my hunger.

Portrait in Georgia

Hair—braided chestnut,
        coiled like a lyncher's rope,
Eyes—fagots,
Lips—old scars, or the first red blisters,
Breath—the last sweet scent of cane,
And her slim body, white as the ash
        of black flesh after flame.

Cotton Song

Come, brother, come. Lets lift it;
Come now, hewit! roll away!
Shackles fall upon the Judgment Day
But lets not wait for it.

God's body's got a soul,
Bodies like to roll the soul,

Cant blame God if we dont roll,
Come, brother, roll, roll!

Cotton bales are the fleecy way
Weary sinner's bare feet trod,
Softly, softly to the throne of God,
"We aint agwine t wait until th Judgment Day!

Nassur; nassur,
Hump.
Eoho, eoho, roll away!
We aint agwine t wait until th Judgment Day!"

God's body's got a soul,
Bodies like to roll the soul,
Cant blame God if we dont roll,
Come, brother, roll, roll!

James Weldon Johnson

(1871–1938)

James Weldon Johnson was born on June 17, 1871, in Jacksonville, Florida. He received his B.A. from Atlanta University (1894) and attended Columbia University (1903–1906). His work is known for being at the crossroads between the nineteenth century and the Harlem Renaissance. He is also remembered for the many songs he wrote with Bob Cole and Rosamond Johnson, his brother. He married Grace Nail on February 10, 1910.

Johnson practiced law in Jacksonville from 1897 to 1901. From 1906 to 1909, he was U.S. consul to Venezuela and to Nicaragua from 1909 to 1912. After joining the staff of the NAACP, he was its executive secretary from 1920 to 1930.

Johnson received numerous awards, including the Springarm Medal (1925); Rosenwald Grant (1929); W. E. B. DuBois Prize for Negro Literature (1933); and the Lewis Carroll Shelf Award for "Lift Every Voice and Sing," (1971), the Negro National Anthem. He edited *The Book of American Negro Poetry* (1922); *The Book of American Negro Spirituals* (1925); and *The Second Book* (1926).

Other publications by Johnson include *The Autobiography of an Ex-Colored Man* (1912); *Fifty Years and Other Poems* (1917); *God's Trombone: Seven Negro Sermons in Verse* (1927); *Black Manhattan* (1930); *Along This Way: The Autobiography of James Weldon Johnson* (1933); *Negro American, What Now?* (1934); and *Saint Peter Relates an Incident: Selected Poems* (1935).

Johnson died in a car-train accident on June 26, 1938.

Preface from *God's Trombones*

A good deal has been written on the folk creations of the American Negro: his music, sacred and secular; his plantation tales, and his dances; but that there are folk sermons, as well, is a fact that has passed unnoticed. I remember hearing in my boyhood sermons that were current, sermons that passed with only slight modifications from preacher to preacher and from locality to locality. Such sermons were, "The Valley of Dry Bones," which was based on the vision of the prophet in the 37th chapter of Ezekiel; the "Train Sermon," in which both God and the devil were pictured as running trains, one loaded with saints, that pulled up in heaven, and the other with sinners, that dumped its load in hell; the "Heavenly March," which gave in detail the journey of the faithful from earth, on up through the pearly gates to the great white throne. Then there was a stereotyped sermon which had no definite subject, and which was quite generally preached; it began with the Creation, went on to the fall of man, rambled through the trials and tribulations of the Hebrew Children, came down to the redemption by Christ, and ended with the Judgment Day and a warning and an exhortation to sinners. This was the framework of a sermon that allowed the individual preacher the widest latitude that could be desired for all his arts and powers. There was one Negro sermon that in its day was a classic, and widely known to the public. Thousands of people, white and black, flocked to the church of John Jasper in Richmond, Virginia, to hear him preach his famous sermon proving that the earth is flat and the sun does move. John Jasper's sermon was imitated and adapted by many lesser preachers.

I heard only a few months ago in Harlem an up-to-date version of the "Train Sermon." The preacher styled himself "Son of Thunder"—a sobriquet adopted by many of the old-time preachers—and phrased his subject, "The Black Diamond Express, running between here and hell, making thirteen stops and arriving in hell ahead of time."

The old-time Negro preacher has not yet been given the niche in which he properly belongs. He has been portrayed only as a semi-comic figure. He had, it is true, his comic aspects, but on the whole he was an important figure, and at bottom a vital factor. It was through him that the people of diverse languages and customs who were brought here from diverse parts of Africa and thrown into slavery were given their first sense of unity and solidarity. He was the first shepherd of this bewildered flock. His power for good or ill was very great. It was the old-time preacher who for generations was the mainspring of hope and inspiration for the Negro in America. It was also he who instilled into the Negro the narcotic doctrine epitomized in the Spiritual, "You May Have All Dis World, But Give Me Jesus." This power of the old-time preacher, somewhat lessened and changed in his successors, is still a vital force; in fact, it is still the greatest single influence among the colored people of the United States. The Negro today is, perhaps, the most priest-governed group in the country.

The history of the Negro preacher reaches back to Colonial days. Before the Revolutionary War, when slavery had not yet taken on its more grim and heartless economic aspects, there were famed black preachers who preached to both whites and blacks. George Liele was preaching to whites and blacks at Augusta, Ga., as far back as 1773, and Andrew Bryan at Savannah a few years later.* The most famous of these earliest preachers was Black Harry, who during the Revolutionary period accompanied Bishop Asbury as a drawing card and preached from the same platform with other founders of the Methodist Church. Of him, John Ledman in his *History of the Rise of Methodism in America* says, "The truth was that Harry was a more popular speaker than Mr. Asbury or almost anyone else in his day." In the two or three

---

*See *The History of the Negro Church*, Carter G. Woodson.

decades before the Civil War Negro preachers in the North, many of them well-educated and cultured, were courageous spokesmen against slavery and all its evils.

The effect on the Negro of the establishment of separate and independent places of worship can hardly be estimated. Some idea of how far this effect reached may be gained by a comparison between the social and religious trends of the Negroes of the Old South and of the Negroes of French Louisiana and the West Indies, where they were within and directly under the Roman Catholic Church and the Church of England. The old-time preacher brought about the establishment of these independent places of worship and thereby provided the first sphere in which race leadership might develop and function. These scattered and often clandestine groups have grown into the strongest and richest organization among colored Americans. Another thought—except for these separate places of worship there never would have been any Spirituals.

The old-time preacher was generally a man far above the average in intelligence; he was, not infrequently, a man of positive genius. The earliest of these preachers must have virtually committed many parts of the Bible to memory through hearing the scriptures read or preached from in the white churches which the slaves attended. They were the first of the slaves to learn to read, and their reading was confined to the Bible, and specifically to the more dramatic passages of the Old Testament. A text served mainly as a starting point and often had no relation to the development of the sermon. Nor would the old-time preacher balk at any text within the lids of the Bible. There is the story of one who after reading a rather cryptic passage took off his spectacles, closed the Bible with a bang and by way of preface said, "Brothers and sisters, this morning—I intend to explain the unexplainable—find out the undefinable—ponder over the imponderable—and unscrew the inscrutable."

*   *   *

The old-time Negro preacher of parts was above all an orator, and in good measure an actor. He knew the secret of oratory, that at bottom it is a progression of rhythmic words more than it is anything else. Indeed, I have witnessed congregations moved to ecstasy by the rhythmic intoning of sheer incoherencies. He was a master of all the modes of eloquence. He often possessed a voice that was a marvelous instrument, a voice he could modulate from a sepulchral whisper to a crashing thunder clap. His discourse was generally kept at a high pitch of fervency, but occasionally he dropped into colloquialisms and, less often, into humor. He preached a personal and anthropomorphic God, a sure-enough heaven and a red-hot hell. His imagination was bold and unfettered. He had the power to sweep his hearers before him; and so himself was often swept away. At such times his language was not prose but poetry. It was from memories of such preachers there grew the idea of this book of poems.

*   *   *

In a general way, these poems were suggested by the rather vague memories of sermons I heard preached in my childhood; but the immediate stimulus for setting them down came quite definitely at a comparatively recent date. I was speaking on a Sunday in Kansas City, addressing meetings in various colored churches. When I had finished my fourth talk it was after nine o'clock at night, but the committee told me there was still another meeting to address. I demurred, making the quotation about the willingness of the spirit and the weakness of the flesh, for I was dead tired. I also protested the lateness of the hour, but I was informed that for the meeting at this church we were in good time. When we reached the church an "exhorter" was just concluding a dull sermon. After his there were two other short sermons. These sermons proved to be preliminaries, mere curtain-raisers for a famed visiting preacher. At last he arose. He was a dark-brown man, handsome in his gigantic proportions. He appeared to be a bit self-conscious, perhaps impressed by the presence of the "distinguished visitor" on the platform, and started in to preach a formal sermon from a formal text. The congregation sat apathetic and dozing. He sensed that he was losing his audience and his opportunity. Suddenly he closed the Bible, stepped out from behind the pulpit and began to preach. He started intoning the old folk-sermon that begins with the creation of the world and ends with Judgment Day. He was at once a changed man, free, at ease and masterful. The change in the congregation was instantaneous. An electric current ran through the crowd. It was in a moment alive and quivering; and all the while the preacher held it in the palm of his hand. He was wonderful in the way he employed his conscious and unconscious art. He strode the pulpit up and down in what was actually a very rhythmic dance, and he brought into play the full gamut of his wonderful voice, a voice—what shall I say?—not of an organ or a trumpet, but rather of a trombone,* the instrument possessing above all others the power to express the wide and varied range of emotions encompassed by the human voice—and with greater amplitude. He intoned, he moaned, he pleaded—he blared, he crashed, he thundered. I sat fascinated; and more, I was, perhaps against my will, deeply moved; the emotional effect upon me was irresistible. Before he had finished I took a slip of paper and somewhat surreptitiously jotted down some ideas for the first poem, "The Creation."

* * *

At first thought, Negro dialect would appear to be the precise medium for these old-time sermons; however, as the reader will see, the poems are not written in dialect. My reason for not using the dialect is double. First, although the dialect is the exact instrument for voicing certain traditional phases of Negro life, it is, and perhaps by that very exactness, a quite limited instrument. Indeed, it is an instrument with but two complete stops, pathos and humor. This limitation is not due to any defect of the dialect as dialect, but to the mould of convention in which Negro dialect in the United States has been set, to the fixing effects of its long association with the Negro only as a happy-go-lucky or a forlorn figure. The Aframerican poet might in time be able to break this mould of convention and write poetry in dialect without feeling that his first line will put the reader in a frame of mind which demands that the poem be either funny or sad, but I doubt that he will make the effort to do it; he does not consider it worth the while. In fact, practically no poetry is being written in dialect by the colored poets of today. These poets have thrown aside dialect and discarded most of the material and subject matter that went into dialect poetry. The passing of dialect as a medium for Negro poetry will be an actual loss, for in it many beautiful things

---

*Trombone: A powerful brass instrument of the trumpet family, the only wind instrument possessing a complete chromatic scale enharmonically true, like the human voice or the violin, and hence very valuable in the orchestra.—Standard Dictionary.

can be done, and done best; however, in my opinion, *traditional* Negro dialect as a form for Aframerican poets is absolutely dead. The Negro poet in the United States, for poetry which he wishes to give a distinctively racial tone and color, needs now an instrument of greater range than dialect; that is, if he is to do more than sound the small notes of sentimentality. I said something on this point in *The Book of American Negro Poetry*, and because I cannot say it better, I quote: "What the colored poet in the United States needs to do is something like what Synge did for the Irish; he needs to find a form that will express the racial spirit by symbols from within rather than by symbols from without—such as the mere mutilation of English spelling and pronunciation. He needs a form that is freer and larger than dialect, but which will still hold the racial flavor; a form expressing the imagery, the idioms, the peculiar turns of thought and the distinctive humor and pathos, too, of the Negro, but which will also be capable of voicing the deepest and highest emotions and aspirations and allow of the widest range of subjects and the widest scope of treatment." The form of "The Creation," the first poem of this group, was a first experiment by me in this direction.

The second part of my reason for not writing these poems in dialect is the weightier. The old-time Negro preachers, though they actually used dialect in their ordinary intercourse, stepped out from its narrow confines when they preached. They were all saturated with the sublime phraseology of the Hebrew prophets and steeped in the idioms of King James English, so when they preached and warmed to their work they spoke another language, a language far removed from traditional Negro dialect. It was really a fusion of Negro idioms with Bible English; and in this there may have been, after all, some kinship with the innate grandiloquence of their old African tongues. To place in the mouths of the talented old-time Negro preachers a language that is a literary imitation of Mississippi cotton-field dialect is sheer burlesque.

Gross exaggeration of the use of big words by these preachers, in fact by Negroes in general, has been commonly made; the laugh being at the exhibition of ignorance involved. What is the basis of this fondness for big words? Is the predilection due, as is supposed, to ignorance desiring to parade itself as knowledge? Not at all. The old-time Negro preacher loved the sonorous, mouth-filling, ear-filling phrase because it gratified a highly developed sense of sound and rhythm in himself and his hearers.

* * *

I claim no more for these poems than that I have written them after the manner of the primitive sermons. In the writing of them I have, naturally, felt the influence of the Spirituals. There is, of course, no way of recreating the atmosphere—the fervor of the congregation, the amens and hallelujahs, the undertone of singing which was often a soft accompaniment to parts of the sermon; nor the personality of the preacher—his physical magnetism, his gestures and gesticulations, his changes of tempo, his pauses for effect, and, more than all, his tones of voice. These poems would better be intoned than read; especially does this apply to "Listen, Lord," "The Crucifixion," and "The Judgment Day." But the intoning practiced by the old-time preacher is a thing next to impossible to describe; it must be heard, and it is extremely difficult to imitate even when heard. The finest, and perhaps the only demonstration ever given to a New York public, was the intoning of the dream in Ridgely Torrence's *Rider of Dreams* by Opal Cooper of the Negro Players at the Madison

Square Theatre in 1917. Those who were fortunate enough to hear him can never, I know, forget the thrill of it. This intoning is always a matter of crescendo and diminuendo in the intensity—a rising and falling between plain speaking and wild chanting. And often a startling effect is gained by breaking off suddenly at the highest point of intensity and dropping into the monotone of ordinary speech.

The tempos of the preacher I have endeavored to indicate by the line arrangement of the poems, and a certain sort of pause that is marked by a quick intaking and an audible expulsion of the breath I have indicated by dashes. There is a decided syncopation of speech—the crowding in of many syllables or the lengthening out of a few to fill one metrical foot, the sensing of which must be left to the reader's ear. The rhythmical stress of this syncopation is partly obtained by a marked silent fraction of a beat; frequently this silent fraction is filled in by a hand clap.

One factor in the creation of atmosphere I have included—the preliminary prayer. The prayer leader was sometimes a woman. It was the prayer leader who directly prepared the way for the sermon, set the scene, as it were. However, a most impressive concomitant of the prayer, the chorus of responses which gave it an antiphonal quality, I have not attempted to set down. These preliminary prayers were often products hardly less remarkable than the sermons.

* * *

The old-time Negro preacher is rapidly passing. I have here tried sincerely to fix something of him.

New York City, 1927.

Listen, Lord

O Lord, we come this morning
Knee-bowed and body-bent
Before thy throne of grace.
O Lord—this morning—
Bow our hearts beneath our knees,
And our knees in some lonesome valley.
We come this morning—
Like empty pitchers to a full fountain,
With no merits of our own.
O Lord—open up a window of heaven,
And lean out far over the battlements of glory,
And listen this morning.

Lord, have mercy on proud and dying sinners—
Sinners hanging over the mouth of hell,
Who seem to love their distance well.
Lord—ride by this morning—
Mount your milk-white horse,
And ride-a this morning—

And in your ride, ride by old hell,
Ride by the dingy gates of hell,
And stop poor sinners in their headlong plunge.

And now, O Lord, this man of God,
Who breaks the bread of life this morning—
Shadow him in the hollow of thy hand,
And keep him out of the gunshot of the devil.
Take him, Lord—this morning—
Wash him with hyssop inside and out,
Hang him up and drain him dry of sin.
Pin his ear to the wisdom-post,
And make his words sledge hammers of truth—
Beating on the iron heart of sin.
Lord God, this morning—
Put his eye to the telescope of eternity,
And let him look upon the paper walls of time.
Lord, turpentine his imagination,
Put perpetual motion in his arms,
Fill him full of the dynamite of thy power,
Anoint him all over with the oil of thy salvation,
And set his tongue on fire.

And now, O Lord—
When I've done drunk my last cup of sorrow—
When I've been called everything but a child of God—
When I'm done travelling up the rough side of the mountain—
O—Mary's Baby—
When I start down the steep and slippery steps of death—
When this old world begins to rock beneath my feet—
Lower me to my dusty grave in peace
To wait for that great gittin' up morning—Amen.

Julia Peterkin

(1880–1961)

Born in Laurens County, South Carolina, on October 31, 1880, Julia Peterkin was graduated from Converse College in 1896. She began teaching in Fort Motte, South Carolina, where she met and married her husband, William Peterkin, on June 3, 1903.

Known for her portrayal of the Gullahs, Peterkin won the Pulitzer Prize for *Scarlet Sister Mary* in 1929. Additional works include *Green Thursday* (1924); *Black April* (1927); *Bright Skin* (1932); *Roll Jordan, Roll* (1933); *A Plantation Christmas* (1934); and *Collected Short Stories of Julia Peterkin* (1970).

Peterkin died on August 10, 1961.

Ashes

An old plantation with smooth-planted fields and rich woodlands and pastures, where little shaded streams run, lies right at the edge of a low wide swamp.

Steep red hills, rising sheer above the slimy mud, lift it out of the reach of two yellow-brown rivers that sprawl drowsily along before they come together to form one stream.

The rivers are hidden by huge trees garlanded with tangled vines, and the swamp seems a soft, undulating, colourful surface that fades into a low line of faint blue hills far away on the other side.

Those hills are the outside world, but the swamp is wide and pathless.

The two rivers commonly lie complacent, but on occasion they rouse and flood low places with furious, yellow water. They lunge and tear at the hillsides that hold the plantation above them until their violence is spent; then they creep back into their rightful channels, leaving other sodden acres desolate and covered with bent, ruined stalks that show where fields of cotton and corn were ripe and ready for harvest.

The old plantation sits always calm. Undisturbed. The rivers can never reach it. And the outside world may wamble and change, but it cannot come any nearer.

Years pass by and leave things unaltered. The same narrow, red roads run through cotton- and cornfields. The same time-grayed cabins send up threads of smoke from their red-clay chimneys. Summer brings the same flowers to bloom round doorways, and china-berry and crape-myrtle blossoms to drop gay petals on little half-clothed black children.

Fields lush with cotton and corn are enlivened by bright-turbaned black women. Sinewy men with soft-stepping bare feet laugh and sing as they guide patient mules up and down the long rows.

When winter browns the fields and brings cold winds up from the swamp, women and children huddle over uncertain fires or gather on sunshiny doorsteps while the men creep down to the swamp in search of food and adventure.

There is nothing to hint that life here could be sweet or that its current runs free and strong. Winter, summer, birth, death, these seem to be all.

The main road on the plantation divides. One straggling, rain-rutted fork runs along the edge of a field to a cluster of low, weather-beaten houses grouped under giant red-oak trees. The Quarters, where most of the black people live.

The other fork bends with a swift, smooth curve and glides into a grove of cedars and live-oaks and magnolias, whose dense evergreen branches hide all beyond them but slight glimpses of white columns and red brick chimneys.

Right where the two roads meet is a sycamore tree. Its milk-white branches reach up to the sky. Its pale, silken leaves glisten and whisper incomplete cadences in the hot summer sunshine.

When frost crisps the leaves and stains them and cuts them away, they flutter down, leaving golden balls to adorn every bough.

There is hardly a sign of the black, twisted roots. There is not a trace to be seen of their silent, tense struggle as they grope deep down in the earth. There is nothing to show how they reach and grapple and hold, or how in the darkness down among the worms they work out mysterious chemistries that change damp clay into beauty.

A little one-roomed log cabin sitting back from the crooked plantation road was gray and weatherstained and its shingled roof was green with moss, but its front was strangely like a cheerful face.

Its narrow open front door made a nose, at each side a small square window with a half-open wooden blind made an eye, and the three rickety steps that led from the door into the front yard made a very good mouth.

The face was warped and cracked with age, but it looked pleasant in the bright morning sun. The gnarled crape-myrtle tree that hugged one corner and almost hid the cabin's red clay chimney was gay with pink blossoms. The front yard, divided in the middle by a clean-swept sandy path, was filled with rich-scented red roses and glossy-leaved gardenia bushes, whose white, waxen blooms perfumed the air.

This was old Maum Hannah's home. Most of the land around her had been sold. But the space she occupied was very small, she was no trouble to anybody, and there was really no reason to disturb her. A few hens, a cow, a patch of peanuts, and a vegetable garden fenced around with hand-split clapboards made her independent. The cross-roads store was not far away, "des a dog's pant" she called it, and there she exchanged well-filled peanuts, new-laid eggs, and frying-size chickens for meal and coffee and plug-cut tobacco. And she was always ready to divide whatever she had with her friends, or with anybody in need.

To a stranger her old arms might look weak and withered, but they were strong enough to wield an ax on the fallen limbs of the trees in the woods back of the house, and the fire in her open fireplace was never allowed to go out, summer or winter.

On this spring morning she sat in a low chair by the fireplace and warmed her crusty bare feet by the charred sticks that burned smokily there among the ashes. She held her breakfast in a pan in her lap and ate slowly while she talked to herself and to the gray cat that lay on the clay hearth by her feet. The cat opened its eyes and purred lazily when she spoke, then drowsed again.

At a sudden rumbling sound outside, the cat jumped up and stretched and walked slowly to the door to look out.

"Who dat?" Maum Hannah asked, and she turned to look out too.

Two strange white men were driving up to the house in a buggy. When they got out, they hitched the horse to the clap-board garden fence.

"A nice house spot," one of them said, looking around him.

"Yes," the other agreed, "and the darkies say there's a fine spring coming out of the hill right behind the house there."

Maum Hannah was a little hard of hearing, but her eyes were keen. She put down her pan of breakfast and stood in the door. Her astonishment made her forget her manners, until one of the men called out sociably:

"Good morning, Auntie." Then she dropped a low curtsey and answered:

"Good mawnin', suh."

"We're just a-lookin' around a little," the man continued in an apologetic tone, for her old eyes, puzzled and alarmed, were fixed on him.

"Yes, suh," she said politely, but she leaned against the door-facing for support.

"It must be a healthy place. That old woman looks like she might be a hundred years old," one said facetiously, and they both chuckled as they walked back into the woods behind the house toward the spring.

Presently Maum Hannah saw them coming back into the front yard. She watched them step off distances. They drove down a few stakes. When they had finished, one of them came to the doorstep and held out a silver coin to her. She bowed gravely as she took it.

"Buy you some tobacco with this, Auntie," he drawled, and he turned away awkwardly. Then he faced her again, and cleared his throat as if embarrassed.

"Auntie," he hesitated, "I hate to tell you this—but you'll have to make arrangements to go somewhere else, I reckon." He did not meet her eyes.

"You see," he continued, "I've done bought this place, and I'm goin' to build my house right here."

Maum Hannah stared at him, but did not reply.

"Well, good-bye," he added, and the two men got into the buggy and drove away.

Maum Hannah watched them until they were out of sight, then she held the coin out in her wrinkled hand and looked at it. It shone bright against the dark-lined palm.

Tears welled up under her shriveled eyelids and hesitated, as if uncertain which path to take through the maze of wrinkles on her cheeks. One shining drop fell with a splash on the silver in her hand. With a sigh she dropped the money into her apron pocket, wiped her eyes with the corner of her apron and turned inside. Taking a handful of meal from a large gourd on the shelf by the door, she scattered it on the ground near the doorstep where a hen with tiny, fluffy chickens around her clucked and scratched.

The very next day, white men with wagonloads of lumber drove into the yard. They had red, sunburned faces, and their shoes and blue overalls were worn and dusty. Maum Hannah looked at them.

"Po-buckra," she said to the cat.

The men sawed and hammered and mixed mortar and smoothed it between red bricks with clinking trowels. Day after day they came. Yellow pine boards made the air fragrant and soon the frame of a new house cast its shadow over Maum Hannah's gardenias and red rose-bushes.

"I 'f'aid dey gwine stop bloomin' now," she said sadly to the cat.

At last the house was finished. One of the men who first came walked up the narrow, clean-swept, sandy path and tapped on the side of Maum Hannah's house with a stick. She came to the door and listened as he drawled nasally:

"Auntie, my house is done now. My folks want to move in next week. You'll have to be movin'. You know I told you that at first. We can't have you a-livin' here in our back yard. Of course, if you was young enough to work, it 'ud be different, but you ain't able to do nothing. I'll need your house anyway to put a cook in. I thought you'd 'a' done been gone before now. I told you in time, you know."

Maum Hannah listened attentively. She heard only part of what he said, but she understood. She must go. She must leave home. It was no longer her home, but *his*.

Her loose old lips trembled as she bowed in answer to him.

She did not go to bed that night. She sat in the low chair by the clay hearth where a pine knot fire wavered and flickered. She filled her cob pipe and puffed at it briskly until it burned red, then she mumbled to herself until it died out and grew cold in her fingers. Rousing up, she'd light it with a fresh coal, smoke for a few puffs, then, absorbed in her trouble, she'd forget it and let it go out.

The cat on the hearth looked up and blinked steepily whenever Maum Hannah repeated:

"He say dis *he* place an' I haffer go f'om heah. Whe' I duh gwine? Who kin tell me dat? Whe' I duh gwine?"

There was Killdee. "My niece," she called him. He was her sister's son and her neighbor. Killdee might come and take her to live with him. But his cabin was very small. Rose's voice was sharp sometimes. No, she could not go there. If Margaret were living—or if she knew where any of her boys were—she might go to them.

She thought of the peaceful graveyard and lifted her old, wrinkled hands above her head in prayer.

"Oh, do, Massa Jedus, he'p me fo' know wha' fo' do. I ain' got no place fo' go. I ain' got nobody fo' tell me. I don' haffer tell You de trouble I got. You know, I ain' got nobody fo' he'p me but You. I know You mus' be gwine he'p me. I eber did been do de bes' I kin. Mebbe sometime I fail.—But, Jedus! Gawd! I know You couldn't hab de hea't to see me suffer! Widout a place to lay my haid." She intoned her prayer and rocked from side to side as she pled for help.

Then she stood up. Tears ran down her cheeks.

"Do gi' me a sign fo' know wha' fo' do. Please, Suh! Do, Massa Jedus! Gi' me a sign! All my chillen's gone an' lef me heah——"

Her bony arms were raised high and her knotted fingers held the cold pipe. Her supplications were emphasized with tense jerks of her arms. With a start she became conscious that ashes from her pipe were trickling down through her fingers and falling on the floor. She stopped and looked at them.

Ashes! Cold ashes! She had asked for a sign and the sign had come! It was *ashes!* Plain as the dawn that steaked the East! There was no doubt of it!

The thought stimulated her like a drug. She went to the door and looked out. A young day reddened the East. The sky was red like fire! "Another sign," she thought. A sign from Heaven.

She lifted her arms and, with tears streaming, said softly:

"Yessuh, Massa Jedus, I understan' You, Suh. You say it mus' be *ashes!* Ashes an' de fiery cloud! Yessuh, I know wha' You tell me fo' do."

Without hesitating, she went to the hearth and took up a smoldering brand of fire. Walking quickly to the front of the new dwelling and stumbling up the steps, she laid it with trembling hands near the front door. Then she went back into the yard and gathered up an apronful of shavings. She sprinkled these carefully on the smoking pine, and knelt and blew until her breath fanned it into flame. Then she went for more shavings and blocks of wood. When the fire grew strong, she left it and went to her own cabin.

She did not sit down but unlocked a trunk in the corner.

Selecting a clean white apron from the clothing there, she put it on, put a stiff-starched white sunbonnet on her head, and tied the strings carefully under her chin. Then she locked the trunk again and put the key in her apron pocket.

The crackle and the roar of the fire outside was startling, but she made herself take time. She closed the wooden blinds of the cabin and latched them on the inside. She pulled the chair away from the hearth, then went out of the door and closed it and locked it behind her. She stepped carefully down the steps, walked past the flaming house, and then on, and on, down the narrow road.

Once she stopped to look back at the flames that already rose high in the sky, but she did not change her steady gait.

"Jedus! It's a long way!" she complained when the road got sandy and her breath became short, but she kept up her pace.

At last the village came in sight. The open spaces became smaller. Low, white-painted cottages huddled close together. She walked slower. Then she stopped and gazed ahead of her, uncertain where to go.

A man driving a team of mules to a wagon was coming. She waited until he reached her, then inquired calmly:

"Son, kin you tell me which-away de sheriff lib?"

"Yes'm," the man answered. He stood up in the wagon and looked toward the houses in the little town.

"You see da' kinder high-lookin' house up yonder on da' hill? De one wid de big white pillar in f'ont ob 'em? Da's de place. De sheriff lib right dere."

Her eyes followed where he pointed.

"T'ank you, son," she said; "Gawd bless you," and started on toward the house he indicated.

The man watched her a minute, then he clucked to his mules to move on. She was a stranger to him. What did she want with the sheriff? Such an old woman. He couldn't imagine.

The sheriff had just finished breakfast when she reached the back door and asked to see him.

"Who is she?" he asked the servant who told him.

"I dunno, suh," was the answer. "A old 'oman. Look lak 'e come a long way. 'E seem out o' breat'."

The sheriff lit a cigar and went to see for himself.

"Good morning, Auntie," he said pleasantly in response to her profound curtsey. "What can I do for you this morning?"

The old woman looked at his kind face, and tears came to her eyes.

"Cap'n sheriff," she began brokenly, "I too troub-led, suh."

Her dry old hands held to each other nervously.

"I dunno wha' you gwine do wid me, suh——" She swallowed a sob. "I reckon you haffer put me on de chain-gang——I done so ol', too——I wouldn't be much 'count at you put me on——"

The sheriff smiled behind his hand.

"Why, Auntie, what have you been doing?"

"A po-buckra man de one done it, suh. He de one. I lib all dis time. I ain' nebber do nobody a hahm t'ing een my life, not tell dis mawnin'. No, suh. You kin ax anybody 'bout me, suh, an' dey'll tell you de same t'ing."

"Well, what have you done now?" the sheriff insisted.

She came nearer to him, encouraged by his gentleness. She spoke in a low tone.

"Dis is how it been, suh." She looked around to see that nobody heard, then began to tell.

"A po-buckra man come an' buil' 'e house right een my front ya'd. 'E say it *he* place, now. 'E say I got to go 'way. I been lib een my house eber sence I kin 'member. Ol' Cap'n sell de plantation, but 'e tell me fo' stay whe' I is. I stay. Dis po-buckra man come an' tell me I mus' go. Whe' I gwine? My peoples is all gone. Mos' o' dem a-layin' een de grabeya'd. I dunno why Jedus see fitten to leab me heah all dis long time——" She lifted her apron to wipe her eyes.

"Las' night I call on Him, up yonder. I beg 'em fo' he'p me. Fo' tell me wha' fo' do. I rassle wid 'em tell 'E gi' me a sign. Yessuh! 'E answer me! 'E gi' me one!"

Her puckered old face lighted up with emotion. Her voice quivered.

"'E gi' me a sign f'om heaben, yessuh. *Ashes! Ashes an' fire!* Him up yonder tell me so!"

Then she leaned forward and whispered: "I put fire to de man house. I bu'n 'em down same lak Jedus tell me fo' do. Yessuh! Den I come right on heah fo' tell you I done 'em."

"Did your house burn too?"

"Oh, no, suh. Jedus sen' a win' fo' blow de spark de udder way."

"Who are you, Auntie?" The sheriff's voice was pitying. Gentle.

"Dis duh me, Hannah Jeems, suh. I one o' ol' Mass' Richard Jeems' niggers, suh. My white folks is all gone. Gone an' lef' me. Times was tight. Dey had to sell de plantation an' go."

She stood before him awaiting sentence with her eyes cast down.

"You walked all the way here from the James plantation this morning?"

"Yessuh. Quick ez I set de house on fire, I come heah fo' tell you, suh."

"Why did you come to tell me?" he asked.

"Well, suh," she hesitated and a far-away look filled her eyes, "when I was a chillen I heah ol' Mass' Richard say de niggers ain' know, but *he* know. De sheriff is de bes' frien' de niggers is got een dis worl', next to Him and Jedus. Mass' Richard been a mighty wise man."

The sheriff looked at the pathetic figure before him. At the mesh of fine wrinkles on her face. At the small, black, frightened hands, clasping and unclasping. At the bare, old, dusty feet. They had walked many a weary mile since life for them first began. His own clear eyes became moist.

"Come on into the kitchen, Auntie. The cook will give you a cup of coffee and some breakfast. Then, we'll talk things over."

"T'ank you, suh," she said gravely as she followed him.

When he reached the door, he faced her again and held up a finger.

"It's best not to talk much, Auntie," he warned her.

She smiled at him brightly.

"Ef da man didn' been a po-buckra 'e wouldn' do me so," she said wistfully.

His brow was knit as if he were uncertain what to say.

"Auntie," he spoke slowly, distinctly, "you believe in the Bible, don't you?"

"Oh, yessuh," she affirmed solemnly, "I can' read 'em, but I b'lieb 'em."

"Did you ever hear how the Bible says you must not let your right hand know what your left hand does?"

"Oh, yessuh," she said reverently.

"Can you remember that passage of Scripture? I think you can."

She looked at him shrewdly, then she smiled and bowed very low.

"T'ank you, suh. T'ank you! An' may Gawd bless you, suh!"

The sheriff was embarrassed. He cleared his throat and awkwardly flicked the ashes off his cigar.

"Auntie," he hesitated, "I'm thinking about riding up that way this morning. I might take you back home." Maum Hannah bowed again.

The distance to the cross-roads store was soon covered by the sheriff's high-powered car. He stopped.

"Jim," he called out to the proprietor, "I hear one of your neighbors lost his new house by fire last night. Did he have any insurance on it?"

"Yes, sir," Jim answered. "Wasn't he lucky to have it?"

"How does he think the house caught?" asked the sheriff.

"He doesn't know, sir, unless it caught from a spark out of Maum Hannah's chimney. It seems she was gone off for the night."

"Yes," said the sheriff, "she came all the way to me hunting for a place to stay. I'm taking her back home now. She may as well stay on there for the present, don't you think so?"

Jim nodded his head confidently.

"I tell you, sheriff, I don't believe anybody'd build a house there again. It's a bad-luck place. It always was."

When Maum Hannah got out of the car in front of her home, a great pile of ashes still smoldered there. She held to the sheriff's hand with both of her quivering ones when she told him good-by.

"Gawd bless you, son! Gawd bless you," she sobbed gratefully, and bright tears followed each other down her old cheeks.

"Come back to me if you ever get in trouble again," the sheriff told her.

"T'ank you kindly, suh," she answered, "but I ain' gwine nebber risk gittin' in trouble no mo'. Not me."

She unlocked her door and fed the cat, and added a few pieces of wood to the fire; then she scattered meal for the frightened hen and little chickens.

When the fire blazed bright, she drew up the little chair before it and sat down. She was tired. She sat still and smoked and nodded. As she dozed, she said softly to the cat: "Ashes is de bes' t'ing eber was fo' roses."

Margaret Mitchell

(1900–1949)

Born in Atlanta, Georgia, on November 8, 1900, Margaret Mitchell is remembered for her novel *Gone With the Wind* (1936). She attended Smith College for one year and began writing for the *Atlanta Journal* in 1922. She married Berrien K. Upshaw in 1922, whom she later divorced, and then married John R. Marsh in 1925. Marsh encouraged her to write the novel on which she spent ten years.

Known for its historical accuracy, *Gone With the Wind* broke all publications records and sold two million copies in a year. It was a Book-of-the-Month Club Selection in 1936 and also won a Pulitzer Prize the same year. On July 30, 1936, Producer David O. Selznick bought the film rights to the novel, paying the highest film fee up to that time. The popular film, starring Clark Gable and Vivian Leigh, was released in 1939.

Mitchell died in Atlanta on August 16, 1949, after she was hit by an automobile while she was crossing the street. *Margaret Mitchell's Gone With the Wind Letters, 1936–1949* was published in 1976.

from *Gone With the Wind*

Chapter I

Scarlett O'Hara was not beautiful, but men seldom realized it when caught by her charm as the Tarleton twins were. In her face were too sharply blended the delicate features of her mother, a Coast aristocrat of French descent, and the heavy ones of her florid Irish father. But it was an arresting face, pointed of chin, square of jaw. Her eyes were pale green without a touch of hazel, starred with bristly black lashes and slightly tilted at the ends. Above them, her thick black brows slanted upward, cutting a startling oblique line in her magnolia-white skin—that skin so prized by Southern women and so carefully guarded with bonnets, veils and mittens against hot Georgia suns.

Seated with Stuart and Brent Tarleton in the cool shade of the porch of Tara, her father's plantation, that bright April afternoon of 1861, she made a pretty picture. Her new green flowered-muslin dress spread its twelve yards of billowing material over her hoops and exactly matched the flat-heeled green morocco slippers her father had recently brought her from Atlanta. The dress set off to perfection the seventeen-inch waist, the smallest in three counties, and the tightly fitting basque showed breasts well matured for her sixteen years. But for all the modesty of her spreading skirts, the demureness of hair netted smoothly into a chignon and the quietness of small white hands folded in her lap, her true self was poorly concealed. The green eyes in the carefully sweet face were turbulent, willful, lusty with life, distinctly at variance with her decorous demeanor. Her manners had been imposed upon her by her mother's gentle admonitions and the sterner discipline of her mammy; her eyes were her own.

On either side of her, the twins lounged easily in their chairs, squinting at the sunlight through tall mint-garnished glasses as they laughed and talked, their long legs, booted to the knee and thick with saddle muscles, crossed negligently. Nineteen years old, six feet two inches tall, long of bone and hard of muscle, with sunburned faces and deep auburn hair, their eyes merry and arrogant, their bodies clothed in identical blue coats and mustard-colored breeches, they were as much alike as two bolls of cotton.

Outside, the late afternoon sun slanted down in the yard, throwing into gleaming brightness the dogwood trees that were solid masses of white blossoms against the background of new green. The twins' horses were hitched in the driveway, big animals, red as their masters' hair; and around the horses' legs quarreled the pack of lean, nervous possum hounds that accompanied Stuart and Brent wherever they went. A little aloof, as became an aristocrat, lay a black-spotted carriage dog, muzzle on paws, patiently waiting for the boys to go home to supper.

Between the hounds and the horses and the twins there was a kinship deeper than that of their constant companionship. They were all healthy, thoughtless young animals, sleek, graceful, high-spirited, the boys as mettlesome as the horses they rode, mettlesome and dangerous but, withal, sweet-tempered to those who knew how to handle them.

Although born to the ease of plantation life, waited on hand and foot since infancy, the faces of the three on the porch were neither slack nor soft. They had the vigor and alertness of country people who have spent all their lives in the open and troubled their heads very little with dull things in books. Life in the north Georgia county of Clayton was still new and, according to the standards of Augusta, Savannah and Charleston, a little crude. The more sedate and older sections of the South looked down their noses at the up-country Georgians, but here in north Georgia, a lack of the niceties of classical education carried no shame, provided a man was smart in the things that mattered. And raising good cotton, riding well, shooting straight, dancing lightly, squiring the ladies with elegance and carrying one's liquor like a gentleman were the things that mattered.

In these accomplishments the twins excelled, and they were equally outstanding in their notorious inability to learn anything contained between the covers of books. Their family had more money, more horses, more slaves than any one else in the County, but the boys had less grammar than most of their poor Cracker neighbors.

It was for this precise reason that Stuart and Brent were idling on the porch of Tara this April afternoon. They had just been expelled from the University of Georgia, the fourth university that had thrown them out in two years; and their older brothers, Tom and Boyd, had come home with them, because they refused to remain at an institution where the twins were not welcome. Stuart and Brent considered their latest expulsion a fine joke, and Scarlett, who had not willingly opened a book since leaving the Fayette-ville Female Academy the year before, thought it just as amusing as they did.

"I know you two don't care about being expelled, or Tom either," she said. "But what about Boyd? He's kind of set on getting an education, and you two have pulled him out of the University of Virginia and Alabama and South Carolina and now Georgia. He'll never get finished at this rate."

"Oh, he can read law in Judge Parmalee's office over in Fayetteville," answered Brent carelessly. "Besides, it don't matter much. We'd have had to come home before the term was out anyway."

"Why?"

"The war, goose! The war's going to start any day, and you don't suppose any of us would stay in college with a war going on, do you?"

"You know there isn't going to be any war," said Scarlett, bored. "It's all just talk. Why, Ashley Wilkes and his father told Pa just last week that our commissioners in Washington would come to—to—an—amicable agreement with Mr. Lincoln about the Confederacy. And anyway, the Yankees are too scared of us to fight. There won't be any war, and I'm tired of hearing about it."

"Not going to be any war!" cried the twins indignantly, as though they had been defrauded.

"Why, honey, of course there's going to be a war," said Stuart. "The Yankees may be scared of us, but after the way General Beauregard shelled them out of Fort Sumter day before yesterday, they'll have to fight or stand branded as cowards before the whole world. Why, the Confederacy—"

Scarlett made a mouth of bored impatience.

"If you say 'war' just once more, I'll go in the house and shut the door. I've never gotten so tired of any one word in my life as 'war,' unless it's 'secession.' Pa talks war morning, noon and night, and all the gentlemen who come to see him shout about Fort Sumter and States' Rights and Abe Lincoln till I get so bored I could scream! And that's all the boys talk about, too, that and their old Troop. There hasn't been any fun at any party this spring because the boys can't talk about anything else. I'm mighty glad Georgia waited till after Christmas before it seceded or it would have ruined the Christmas parties, too. If you say 'war' again, I'll go in the house."

She meant what she said, for she could never long endure any conversation of which she was not the chief subject. But she smiled when she spoke, consciously deepening her dimple and fluttering her bristly black lashes as swiftly as butterflies' wings. The boys were enchanted, as she had intended them to be, and they hastened to apologize for boring her. They thought none the less of her for her lack of interest. Indeed, they thought more. War was men's business, not ladies', and they took her attitude as evidence of her femininity.

Having maneuvered them away from the boring subject of war, she went back with interest to their immediate situation.

"What did your mother say about you two being expelled again?"

The boys looked uncomfortable, recalling their mother's conduct three months ago when they had come home, by request, from the University of Virginia.

"Well," said Stuart, "she hasn't had a chance to say anything yet. Tom and us left home early this morning before she got up, and Tom's laying out over at the Fontaines' while we came over here."

"Didn't she say anything when you got home last night?"

"We were in luck last night. Just before we got home that new stallion Ma got in Kentucky last month was brought in, and the place was in a stew. The big brute—he's a grand horse, Scarlett; you must tell your pa to come over and see him right away—he'd already bitten a hunk out of his groom on the way down here and he'd trampled two of Ma's darkies who met the train at Jonesboro. And just before we got home, he'd about kicked the stable down and half-killed Strawberry, Ma's old stallion.When we got home, Ma was out in the stable with a sackful of sugar smoothing him down and doing it mighty well, too. The darkies were hanging from the rafters, popeyed, they were so scared, but Ma was talking to the horse like he was folks and he was eating out of her hand. There ain't nobody like Ma with a horse. And when she saw us she said: 'In Heaven's name, what are you four doing home again? You're worse than the plagues of Egypt!' And then the horse began snorting and rearing and she said: 'Get out of here! Can't you see he's nervous, the big darling? I'll tend to you four in the morning!' So we went to bed, and this morning we got away before she could catch us and left Boyd to handle her."

"Do you suppose she'll hit Boyd?" Scarlett, like the rest of the County, could never get used to the way small Mrs. Tarleton bullied her grown sons and laid her riding crop on their backs if the occasion seemed to warrant it.

Beatrice Tarleton was a busy woman, having on her hands not only a large cotton plantation, a hundred negroes and eight children, but the largest horse-breeding farm in the state as well. She was hot-tempered and easily plagued by the frequent scrapes of her four sons, and while no one was permitted to whip a horse or a slave, she felt that a lick now and then didn't do the boys any harm.

"Of course she won't hit Boyd. She never did beat Boyd much because he's the oldest and besides he's the runt of the litter," said Stuart, proud of his six feet two. "That's why we left him at home to explain things to her. God'lmighty, Ma ought to stop licking us! We're nineteen and Tom's twenty-one, and she acts like we're six years old."

"Will your mother ride the new horse to the Wilkes barbecue tomorrow?"

"She wants to, but Pa says he's too dangerous. And, anyway, the girls won't let her. They said they were going to have her go to one party at least like a lady, riding in the carriage."

"I hope it doesn't rain tomorrow," said Scarlett. "It's rained nearly every day for a week. There's nothing worse than a barbecue turned into an indoor picnic."

"Oh, it'll be clear tomorrow and hot as June," said Stuart. "Look at that sunset. I never saw one redder. You can always tell weather by sunsets."

They looked out across the endless acres of Gerald O'Hara's newly plowed cotton fields toward the red horizon. Now that the sun was setting in a welter of crimson behind the hills across the Flint River, the warmth of the April day was ebbing into a faint but balmy chill.

Spring had come early that year, with warm quick rains and sudden frothing of pink peach blossoms and dogwood dappling with white stars the dark river swamp and far-off hills. Already the plowing was nearly finished, and the bloody glory of the sunset colored the fresh-cut furrows of red Georgia clay to even redder hues. The moist hungry earth, waiting upturned for the cotton seeds, showed pinkish on the sandy tops of the furrows, vermilion and scarlet and maroon where shadows lay along the sides of the trenches. The whitewashed brick plantation house seemed an island set in a wild red sea, a sea of spiraling, curving, crescent billows petrified suddenly at the moment when the pink-tipped waves were breaking into surf. For here were no long, straight furrows, such as could be seen in the yellow clay fields of the flat middle Georgia country or in the lush black earth of the coastal plantations. The rolling foothill country of north Georgia was plowed in a million curves to keep the rich earth from washing down into the river bottoms.

It was a savagely red land, blood-colored after rains, brick dust in droughts, the best cotton land in the world. It was a pleasant land of white houses, peaceful plowed fields and sluggish yellow rivers, but a land of contrasts, of brightest sun glare and densest shade. The plantation clearings and miles of cotton fields smiled up to a warm sun, placid, complacent. At their edges rose the virgin forests, dark and cool even in the hottest noons, mysterious, a little sinister, the soughing pines seeming to wait with an age-old patience, to threaten with soft sighs: "Be careful! Be careful! We had you once. We can take you back again."

To the ears of the three on the porch came the sounds of hooves, the jingling of harness chains and the shrill careless laughter of negro voices, as the field hands and mules came in from the fields. From within the house floated the soft voice of Scarlett's mother, Ellen O'Hara, as she called to the little black girl who carried her basket of keys. The high-pitched, childish voice answered "Yas'm," and there were sounds of footsteps going out the back way toward the smokehouse where Ellen would ration out the food to the home-coming hands. There was the click of china and the rattle of silver as Pork, the valet-butler of Tara, laid the table for supper.

At these last sounds, the twins realized it was time they were starting home. But they were loath to face their mother and they lingered on he porch of Tara, momentarily expecting Scarlett to give them an invitation to supper.

"Look, Scarlett. About tomorrow," said Brent. "Just because we've been away and didn't know about the barbecue and the ball, that's no reason why we shouldn't get plenty of dances tomorrow night. You haven't promised them all, have you?"

"Well, I have! How did I know you all would be home? I couldn't risk being a wallflower just waiting on you two."

"You a wallflower!" The boys laughed uproariously.

"Look, honey. You've got to give me the first waltz and Stu the last one and you've got to eat supper with us. We'll sit on the stair landing like we did at the last ball and get Mammy Jincy to come tell our fortunes again."

"I don't like Mammy Jincy's fortunes. You know she said I was going to marry a gentleman with jet-black hair and a long black mustache, and I don't like black-haired gentlemen."

"You like 'em red-headed, don't you, honey?" grinned Brent. "Now, come on, promise us all the waltzes and the supper."

"If you'll promise, we'll tell you a secret," said Stuart.

"What?" cried Scarlett, alert as a child at the word.

"Is it what we heard yesterday in Atlanta, Stu? If it is, you know we promised not to tell."

"Well, Miss Pitty told us."

"Miss Who?"

"You know, Ashley Wilkes' cousin who lives in Atlanta, Miss Pittypat Hamilton—Charles and Melanie Hamilton's aunt."

"I do, and a sillier old lady I never met in all my life."

"Well, when we were in Atlanta yesterday, waiting for the home train, her carriage went by the depot and she stopped and talked to us, and she told us there was going to be an engagement announced tomorrow night at the Wilkes ball."

"Oh, I know about that," said Scarlett in disappointment. "That silly nephew of hers, Charlie Hamilton, and Honey Wilkes. Everybody's known for years that they'd get married some time, even if he did seem kind of lukewarm about it."

"Do you think he's silly?" questioned Brent. "Last Christmas you sure let him buzz round you plenty."

"I couldn't help him buzzing," Scarlett shrugged negligently. "I think he's an awful sissy."

"Besides, it isn't his engagement that's going to be announced," said Stuart triumphantly. "It's Ashley's to Charlie's sister, Miss Melanie!"

Scarlett's face did not change but her lips went white—like a person who has received a stunning blow without warning and who, in the first moments of shock, does not realize what has happened. So still was her face as she stared at Stuart that he, never analytic, took it for granted that she was merely surprised and very interested.

"Miss Pitty told us they hadn't intended announcing it till next year, because Miss Melly hasn't been very well; but with all the war talk going around, everybody in both families thought it would be better to get married real soon. So it's to be announced tomorrow night at the supper intermission. Now, Scarlett, we've told you the secret, so you've got to promise to eat supper with us."

"Of course I will," Scarlett said automatically.

"And all the waltzes?"

"All."

"You're sweet! I'll bet the other boys will be hopping mad."

"Let 'em be mad," said Brent. "We two can handle 'em. Look, Scarlett. Sit with us at the barbecue in the morning."

"What?"

Stuart repeated his request.

"Of course."

The twins looked at each other jubilantly but with some surprise. Although they considered themselves Scarlett's favored suitors, they had never before gained tokens of this favor so easily. Usually she made them beg and plead, while she put them off, refusing to give a Yes or No answer, laughing if they sulked, growing cool if they became angry. And here she had practically promised them the whole of tomorrow—seats by her at the barbecue, all the waltzes (and they'd see to it that the dances were all waltzes!) and the supper intermission. This was worth getting expelled from the university.

Filled with new enthusiasm by their success, they lingered on, talking about the barbecue and the ball and Ashley Wilkes and Melanie Hamilton, interrupting each other, making jokes and laughing at them, hinting broadly for invitations to supper. Some time had passed before they realized that Scarlett was having very little to say. The atmosphere had somehow changed. Just how, the twins did not know, but the fine glow had gone out of the afternoon. Scarlett seemed to be paying little attention to what they said, although she made the correct answers. Sensing something they could not understand, baffled and annoyed by it, the twins struggled along for a while, and then rose reluctantly, looking at their watches.

The sun was low across the new-plowed fields and the tall woods across the river were looming blackly in silhouette. Chimney swallows were darting swiftly across the yard, and chickens, ducks and turkeys were waddling and strutting and straggling in from the fields.

Stuart bellowed: "Jeems!" And after an interval a tall black boy of their own age ran breathlessly around the house and out toward the tethered horses. Jeems was their body servant and, like the dogs, accompanied them everywhere. He had been their childhood playmate and had been given to the twins for their own on their tenth birthday. At the sight of him, the Tarleton hounds rose up out of the red dust and stood waiting expectantly for their masters. The boys bowed, shook hands and told Scarlett they'd be over at the Wilkeses' early in the morning, waiting for her. Then they were off down the walk at a rush, mounted their horses and, followed by Jeems, went down the avenue of cedars at a gallop, waving their hats and yelling back to her.

When they had rounded the curve of the dusty road that hid them from Tara, Brent drew his horse to a stop under a clump of dogwood. Stuart halted, too, and the darky boy pulled up a few paces behind them. The horses, feeling slack reins, stretched down their necks to crop the tender spring grass, and the patient hounds lay down again in the soft red dust and looked up longingly at the chimney swallows circling in the gathering dusk. Brent's wide ingenuous face was puzzled and mildly indignant.

"Look," he said. "Don't it look to you like she would of asked us to stay for supper?"

"I thought she would," said Stuart. "I kept waiting for her to do it, but she didn't. What do you make of it?"

"I don't make anything of it. But it just looks to me like she might of. After all, it's our first day home and she hasn't seen us in quite a spell. And we had lots more things to tell her."

"It looked to me like she was mighty glad to see us when we came."

"I thought so, too."

"And then, about a half-hour ago, she got kind of quiet, like she had a headache."

"I noticed that but I didn't pay it any mind then. What do you suppose ailed her?"

"I dunno. Do you suppose we said something that made her mad?"

They both thought for a minute.

"I can't think of anything. Besides, when Scarlett gets mad, everybody knows it. She don't hold herself in like some girls do."

"Yes, that's what I like about her. She don't go around being cold and hateful when she's mad—she tells you about it. But it was something we did or said that made her shut up talking and look sort of sick. I could swear she was glad to see us when we came and was aiming to ask us to supper."

"You don't suppose it's because we got expelled?"

"Hell, no! Don't be a fool. She laughed like everything when we told her about it. And besides Scarlett don't set any more store by book learning than we do."

Brent turned in the saddle and called to the negro groom.

"Jeems!"

"Suh?"

"You heard what we were talking to Miss Scarlett about?"

"Nawsuh, Mist' Brent! Huccome you think Ah be spyin' on w'ite folks?"

"Spying, my God! You darkies know everything that goes on. Why, you liar, I saw you with my own eyes sidle round the corner of the porch and squat in the cape jessamine bush by the wall. Now, did you hear us say anything that might have made Miss Scarlett mad—or hurt her feelings?"

Thus appealed to, Jeems gave up further pretense of not having overheard the conversation and furrowed his black brow.

"Nawsuh, Ah din' notice y'all say anything ter mek her mad. Look ter me lak she sho glad ter see you an' sho had missed you, an' she cheep along happy as a bird, tell 'bout de time y'all got ter talkin' 'bout Mist' Ashley an' Miss Melly Hamilton gittin' mah'ied. Den she quiet down lak a bird w'en de hawk fly ober."

The twins looked at each other and nodded, but without comprehension.

"Jeems is right. But I don't see why," said Stuart. "My Lord! Ashley don't mean anything to her, 'cept a friend. She's not crazy about him. It's us she's crazy about."

Brent nodded an agreement.

"But do you suppose," he said, "that maybe Ashley hadn't told her he was going to announce it tomorrow night and she was mad at him for not telling her, an old friend, before he told everybody else? Girls set a big store on knowing such things first."

"Well, maybe. But what if he hadn't told her it was tomorrow? It was supposed to be a secret and a surprise, and a man's got a right to keep his own engagement quiet, hasn't he? We wouldn't have known it if Miss Melly's aunt hadn't let it out. But Scarlett must have known he was going to marry Miss Melly sometime. Why, we've known it for years. The Wilkes and Hamiltons always marry their own cousins. Everybody knew he'd probably marry her some day, just like Honey Wilkes is going to marry Miss Melly's brother, Charles."

"Well, I give it up. But I'm sorry she didn't ask us to supper. I swear I don't want to go home and listen to Ma take on about us being expelled. It isn't as if this was the first time."

"Maybe Boyd will have smoothed her down by now. You know what a slick talker that little varmint is. You know he always can smooth her down."

"Yes, he can do it, but it takes Boyd time. He has to talk around in circles till Ma gets so confused that she gives up and tells him to save his voice for his law practice. But he ain't had time to get good started yet. Why, I'll bet you Ma is still so excited about the new horse that she'll never even realize we're home again till she sits down to supper tonight and sees Boyd. And before supper is over she'll be going strong and breathing fire. And it'll be ten o'clock before Boyd gets a chance to tell her that it wouldn't have been honorable for any of us to stay in college after the way the Chancellor talked to you and me. And it'll be midnight before he gets her turned around to where she's so mad at the Chancellor she'll be asking Boyd why he didn't shoot him. No, we can't go home till after midnight."

The twins looked at each other glumly. They were completely fearless of wild horses, shooting affrays and the indignation of their neighbors, but they had a wholesome fear of their red-haired mother's outspoken remarks and the riding crop that she did not scruple to lay across their breeches.

"Well, look," said Brent. "Let's go over the Wilkes'. Ashley and the girls'll be glad to have us for supper."

Stuart looked a little discomforted.

"No, don't let's go there. They'll be in a stew getting ready for the barbecue tomorrow and besides—"

"Oh, I forgot about that," said Brent hastily. "No, don't let's go there."

They clucked to their horses and rode along in silence for a while, a flush of embarrassment on Stuart's brown cheeks. Until the previous summer, Stuart had courted India Wilkes with the approbation of both families and the entire County. The County felt that perhaps the cool and contained India Wilkes would have a quieting effect on him. They fervently hoped so, at any rate. And Stuart might have made the match, but Brent had not been satisfied. Brent liked India but he thought her mighty plain and tame, and he simply could not fall in love with her himself to keep Stuart company. That was the first time the twins' interests had ever diverged, and Brent was resentful of his brother's attentions to a girl who seemed to him not at all remarkable.

Then, last summer at a political speaking in a grove of oak trees at Jonesboro, they both suddenly became aware of Scarlett O'Hara. They had known her for years, and, since their childhood, she had been a favorite playmate, for she could ride horses and climb trees almost as well as they. But now to their amazement she had become a grown-up young lady and quite the most charming one in all the world.

They noticed for the first time how her green eyes danced, how deep her dimples were when she laughed, how tiny her hands and feet and what a small waist she had. Their clever remarks sent her into merry peals of laughter and, inspired by the thought that she considered them a remarkable pair, they fairly outdid themselves.

It was a memorable day in the life of the twins. Thereafter, when they talked it over, they always wondered just why they had failed to notice Scarlett's charms before. They never arrived at the correct answer, which was that Scarlett on that day had decided to make them notice. She was constitutionally unable to endure any man being in love with any woman not herself, and the sight of India Wilkes and Stuart at the speaking had been too much for her predatory nature. Not content with Stuart alone, she had set her cap for Brent as well, and with a thoroughness that overwhelmed the two of them.

Now they were both in love with her, and India Wilkes and Letty Munroe, from Lovejoy, whom Brent had been half-heartedly courting, were far in the back of their minds. Just what the loser would do, should Scarlett accept either one of them, the twins did not ask. They would cross that bridge when they came to it. For the present they were quite satisfied to be in accord again about one girl, for they had no jealousies between them. It was a situation which interested the neighbors and annoyed their mother, who had no liking for Scarlett.

"It will serve you right if that sly piece does accept one of you," she said. "Or maybe she'll accept both of you, and then you'll have to move to Utah, if the Mormons'll have you—which I doubt. . . . All that bothers me is that some one of these days you're both going to get lickered up and jealous of each other about that two-faced, little, green-eyed baggage, and you'll shoot each other. But that might not be a bad idea either."

Since the day of the speaking, Stuart had been uncomfortable in India's presence. Not that India ever reproached him or even indicated by look or gesture that she was aware of his abruptly changed allegiance. She was too much of a lady. But Stuart felt guilty and ill at ease with her. He knew he had made India love him and he knew that she still loved him and, deep in his heart, he had the feeling that he had not played the gentleman. He still liked her tremendously and respected her for her cool good breeding, her book learning and all the sterling qualities she possessed. But, damn it, she was just so pallid and uninteresting and always the same, beside Scarlett's bright and changeable charm. You always knew where you stood with India and you never had the slightest notion with Scarlett. That was enough to drive a man to distraction, but it had its charm.

"Well, let's go over to Cade Calvert's and have supper. Scarlett said Cathleen was home from Charleston. Maybe she'll have some news about Fort Sumter that we haven't heard."

"Not Cathleen. I'll lay you two to one she didn't even know the fort was out there in the harbor, much less that it was full of Yankees until we shelled them out. All she'll know about is the balls she went to and the beaux she collected."

"Well, it's fun to hear her gabble. And it'll be somewhere to hide out till Ma has gone to bed."

"Well, hell! I like Cathleen and she is fun and I'd like to hear about Caro Rhett and the rest of the Charleston folks; but I'm damned if I can stand sitting through another meal with that Yankee stepmother of hers."

"Don't be too hard on her, Stuart. She means well."

"I'm not being hard on her. I feel sorry for her, but I don't like people I've got to feel sorry for. And she fusses around so much, trying to do the right thing and make you feel at home, that she always manages to say and do just exactly the wrong thing. She gives me the fidgets! And she thinks Southerners are wild barbarians. She even told Ma so. She's afraid of Southerners. Whenever we're there she always looks scared to death. She reminds me of a skinny hen perched on a chair, her eyes kind of bright and blank and scared, all ready to flap and squawk at the slightest move anybody makes."

"Well, you can't blame her. You did shoot Cade in the leg."

"Well, I was lickered up or I wouldn't have done it," said Stuart. "And Cade never had any hard feelings. Neither did Cathleen or Raiford or Mr. Calvert. It was just that Yankee stepmother who squalled and said I was a wild barbarian and decent people weren't safe around uncivilized Southerners."

"Well, you can't blame her. She's a Yankee and ain't got very good manners; and, after all, you did shoot him and he is her stepson."

"Well, hell! That's no excuse for insulting me! You are Ma's own blood son, but did she take on that time Tony Fontaine shot you in the leg? No, she just sent for old Doc Fontaine to dress it and asked the doctor what ailed Tony's aim. Said she guessed licker was spoiling his marksmanship. Remember how mad that made Tony?"

Both boys yelled with laughter.

"Ma's a card!" said Brent with loving approval. "You can always count on her to do the right thing and not embarrass you in front of folks."

"Yes, but she's mighty liable to talk embarrassing in front of Father and the girls when we get home tonight," said Stuart gloomily. "Look, Brent. I guess this means we don't go to Europe. You know Mother said if we got expelled from another college we couldn't have our Grand Tour."

"Well, hell! We don't care, do we? What is there to see in Europe? I'll bet those foreigners can't show us a thing we haven't got right here in Georgia. I'll bet their horses aren't as fast or their girls as pretty, and I know damn well they haven't got any rye whisky that can touch Father's."

"Ashley Wilkes said they had an awful lot of scenery and music. Ashley liked Europe. He's always talking about it."

"Well—you know how the Wilkes are. They are kind of queer about music and books and scenery. Mother says it's because their grandfather came from Virginia. She says Virginians set quite a store by such things."

"They can have 'em. Give me a good horse to ride and some good licker to drink and a good girl to court and a bad girl to have fun with and anybody can have their Europe. . . . What do we care about missing the Tour? Suppose we were in Europe now, with the war coming on? We couldn't get home soon enough. I'd heap rather go to a war than go to Europe."

"So would I, any day. . . . Look, Brent! I know where we can go for supper. Let's ride across the swamp to Able Wynder's place and tell him we're all four home again and ready for drill."

"That's an idea!" cried Brent with enthusiasm. "And we can hear all the news of the Troop and find out what color they finally decided on for the uniforms."

"If it's Zouave, I'm damned if I'll go in the troop. I'd feel like a sissy in those baggy red pants. They look like ladies' red flannel drawers to me."

"Is y'all aimin' ter go ter Mist' Wynder's? 'Cause ef you is, you ain' gwine git much supper," said Jeems. "Dey cook done died, an' dey ain' bought a new one. Dey got a fe'el han' cookin', an' de niggers tells me she is de wustest cook in de state."

"Good God! Why don't they buy another cook?"

"Huccome po' w'ite trash buy any niggers? Dey ain' never owned mo'n fo' at de mostes'."

There was frank contempt in Jeems' voice. His own social status was assured because the Tarletons owned a hundred negroes and, like all slaves of large planters, he looked down on small farmers whose slaves were few.

"I'm going to beat your hide off for that," cried Stuart fiercely. "Don't you call Able Wynder 'po' white.' Sure he's poor, but he ain't trash; and I'm damned if I'll have any man, darky or white, throwing off on him. There ain't a better man in this County, or why else did the Troop elect him lieutenant?"

"Ah ain' never figgered dat out, mahseff," replied Jeems, undisturbed by his master's scowl. "Look ter me lak dey'd 'lect all de awficers frum rich gempmum, 'stead of swamp trash."

"He ain't trash! Do you mean to compare him with real white trash like the Slatterys? Able just ain't rich. He's a small farmer, not a big planter, and if the boys thought enough of him to elect him lieutenant, then it's not for any darky to talk impudent about him. The Troop knows what it's doing."

The troop of cavalry had been organized three months before, the very day that Georgia seceded from the Union, and since then the recruits had been whistling for war. The outfit was as yet unnamed, though not for want of suggestions. Everyone had his own idea on that subject and was loath to relinquish it, just as everyone had ideas about the color and cut of the uniforms. "Clayton Wild Cats," "Fire Eaters," "North Georgia Hussars," "Zouaves," "The Inland Rifles" (although the Troop was to be armed with pistols, sabers and bowie knives, and not with rifles), "The Clayton Grays," "The Blood and Thunderers," "The Rough and Readys," all had their adherents. Until matters were settled, everyone referred to the organization as the Troop and, despite the high-sounding name finally adopted, they were known to the end of their usefulness simply as "The Troop."

The officers were elected by the members, for no one in the County had had any military experience except a few veterans of the Mexican and Seminole wars and, besides, the Troop would have scorned a veteran as a leader if they had not personally liked him and trusted him. Everyone liked the four Tarleton boys and the three Fontaines, but regretfully refused to elect them, because the Tarletons got lickered up too quickly and liked to skylark, and the Fontaines had such quick, murderous tempers. Ashley Wilkes was elected captain, because he was the best rider in the County and because his cool head was counted on to keep some semblance of order. Raiford Calvert was made first lieutenant, because everybody liked Raif, and Able Wynder, son of a swamp trapper, himself a small farmer, was elected second lieutenant.

Able was a shrewd, grave giant, illiterate, kind of heart, older than the other boys and with as good or better manners in the presence of ladies. There was little snobbery in the Troop. Too many of their fathers and grandfathers had come up to wealth from the small farmer class for that. Moreover, Able was the best shot in the Troop, a real sharpshooter who could pick out the eye of a squirrel at seventy-five yards, and, too, he knew all about living outdoors, building fires in the rain, tracking animals and finding water. The Troop bowed to real worth and moreover, because they liked him, they made him an officer. He bore the honor gravely and with no untoward conceit, as though it were only his due. But the planters' ladies and the planters' slaves could not overlook the fact that he was not born a gentleman, even if their men folks could.

In the beginning, the Troop had been recruited exclusively from the sons of planters, a gentleman's outfit, each man supplying his own horse, arms, equipment, uniform and body servant. But rich planters were few in the young county of Clayton, and, in order to muster a full-strength troop, it had been necessary to raise more recruits among the sons of small farmers, hunters in the backwoods, swamp trappers, Crackers and, in a very few cases, even poor whites, if they were above the average of their class.

These latter young men were as anxious to fight the Yankees, should war come, as were their richer neighbors; but the delicate question of money arose. Few small farmers owned horses. They carried on their farm operations with mules and they had no surplus of these, seldom more than four. The mules could not be spared to go off to war, even if they had been acceptable for the Troop, which they emphatically were not. As for the poor whites, they considered themselves well off if they owned one mule. The backwoods folks and the swamp dwellers owned neither horses nor mules. They lived entirely off the produce of their lands and the game in the swamp, conducting their business generally by the barter system and seldom seeing five dollars in cash a year, and horses and uniforms were out of their reach. But they were as fiercely proud in their poverty as the planters were in their wealth, and they would accept nothing that smacked of charity from their rich neighbors. So, to save the feelings of all and to bring the Troop up to full strength, Scarlett's father, John Wilkes, Buck Munroe, Jim Tarleton, Hugh Calvert, in fact every large planter in the County with the one exception of Angus MacIntosh, had contributed money to completely outfit the Troop, horse and man. The upshot of the matter was that every planter agreed to pay for equipping his own sons and a certain number of the others, but the manner of handling the arrangements was such that the less wealthy members of the outfit could accept horses and uniforms without offense to their honor.

The Troop met twice a week in Jonesboro to drill and to pray for the war to begin. Arrangements had not yet been completed for obtaining the full quota of horses, but those who had horses performed what they imagined to be cavalry maneuvers in the field behind the courthouse, kicked up a great deal of dust, yelled themselves hoarse and waved the Revolutionary-war swords that had been taken down from parlor walls. Those who, as yet, had no horses sat on the curb in front of Bullard's store and watched their mounted comrades, chewed tobacco and told yarns. Or else engaged in shooting matches. There was no need to teach any of the men to shoot. Most Southerners were born with guns in their hands, and lives spent in hunting had made marksmen of them all.

From planters' homes and swamp cabins, a varied array of firearms came to each muster. There were long squirrel guns that had been new when first the Alleghenies were crossed, old muzzle-loaders that had claimed many an Indian when Georgia was new, horse pistols that had seen service in 1812, in the Seminole wars and in Mexico, silver-mounted dueling pistols, pocket derringers, double-barreled hunting pieces and handsome new rifles of English make with shining stocks of fine wood.

Drill always ended in the saloons of Jonesboro, and by nightfall so many fights had broken out that the officers were hard put to ward off casualties until the Yankees could inflict them. It was during one of these brawls that Stuart Tarleton had shot Cade Calvert and Tony Fontaine had shot Brent. The twins had been at home, freshly expelled from the University of Virginia, at the time the Troop was organized and they had joined enthusiastically; but after the shooting episode, two months ago, their mother had packed them off to the state university, with orders to stay there. They had sorely missed the excitement of the drills while away, and they counted education well lost if only they could ride and yell and shoot off rifles in the company of their friends.

"Well, let's cut across country to Able's," suggested Brent. "We can go through Mr. O'Hara's river bottom and the Fontaines' pasture and get there in no time."

"We ain' gwine git nothin' ter eat 'cept possum an' greens," argued Jeems.

"You ain't going to get anything," grinned Stuart. "Because you are going home and tell Ma that we won't be home for supper."

"No, Ah ain'!" cried Jeems in alarm. "No, Ah ain'! Ah doan git no mo' fun outer havin' Miss Beetriss lay me out dan y'all does. Fust place she'll ast me huccome Ah let y'all git expelled agin. An' nex' thing, huccome Ah din' bring y'all home ternight so she could lay you out. An' den she'll light on me lak a duck on a June bug, an' fust thing Ah know Ah'll be ter blame fer it all. Ef y'all doan tek me ter Mist' Wynder's, Ah'll lay out in de woods all night an' maybe de patterollers git me, 'cause Ah heap ruther de patterollers git me dan Miss Beetriss when she in a state."

The twins looked at the determined black boy in perplexity and indignation.

"He'd be just fool enough to let the patterollers get him and that would give Ma something else to talk about for weeks. I swear, darkies are more trouble. Sometimes I think the Abolitionists have got the right idea."

"Well, it wouldn't be right to make Jeems face what we don't want to face. We'll have to take him. But, look, you impudent black fool, if you put on any airs in front of the Wynder darkies and hint that we all the time have fried chicken and ham, while they don't have nothing but rabbit and possum, I'll—I'll tell Ma. And we won't let you go to the war with us, either."

"Airs? Me put on airs fo' dem cheap niggers? Nawsuh, Ah got better manners. Ain' Miss Beetriss taught me manners same as she taught y'all?"

"She didn't do a very good job on any of the three of us," said Stuart. "Come on, let's get going."

He backed his big red horse and then, putting spurs to his side, lifted him easily over the split rail fence into the soft field of Gerald O'Hara's plantation. Brent's horse followed and then Jeems', with Jeems clinging to pommel and mane. Jeems did not like to jump fences, but he had jumped higher ones than this in order to keep up with his masters.

As they picked their way across the red furrows and down the hill to the river bottom in the deepening dusk, Brent yelled to his brother:

"Look, Stu! Don't it seem like to you that Scarlett *would* have asked us to supper?"

"I kept thinking she would," yelled Stuart. "Why do you suppose . . ."

William Faulkner

(1897–1962)

William Faulkner's literary career received a sputtering start with the publication of *Soldier's Pay* in 1926, a manuscript that his friend Sherwood Anderson agreed to help him publish on the condition that he would not have to read it, nor the awkwardly de-rivative *Mosquitoes* in 1927. But in that same year, Faulkner turned his gaze home-ward, to his "own little postage stamp of native soil," the hill country of Northern Mississippi and his hometown of Oxford. The novels he wrote in the next eight years, set in the town of "Jefferson," whose landmarks match those of Oxford and the sur-rounding Yoknapatawpha County, are a tour de force of diverse literary technique, a towering literary accomplishment that explores "the problems of the human heart in conflict with itself" with unparalleled depth, humor, and poignancy.

Faulkner was born William Cuthbert Falkner (he added the "u" when he began to publish) in New Albany, Mississippi, named after his great-grandfather, William Clark Falkner, Civil War Colonel, hero of Second Manassas, builder of railroads, and proto-type for the fictional John Sartoris. When Faulkner was four years old, his family moved to Oxford, where, with the exception of a few brief jaunts to Canada, New Orleans, Hollywood and Charlottesville, he resided for the rest of his life. He never finished high school, and when his childhood sweetheart Estelle Oldham became engaged to another man, he joined the Canadian Air Force, but the war ended before he had received flight training. Back home in Oxford, he frequently wore his uniform and told stories of being wounded in battle. His eccentric habits earned him the nickname "Count No-Count," but he made friends with a local attorney named Phil Stone, who helped him publish a collection of his poetry, *The Marble Faun*, in 1922. In 1925 he spent six months in New Orleans, where he was befriended by Sherwood Anderson.

In 1926 he returned home and published *Soldier's Pay*, a novel of postwar disillu-sionment. *Mosquitoes* followed in 1927, but *Sartoris*, which he completed in 1927 and published in 1929, ignited the aforementioned period of intense creativity that produced, in quick succession, *The Sound and the Fury* (1929), *As I Lay Dying* (1930), *Sanctuary* (1931), *Light in August* (1932), and *Absalom, Absalom!* (1936). With the exception of *Sanctuary*, which Faulkner referred to as a "pot boiler," none of these novels was a popular success (the critical reception was tepid as well). During the next few years, he produced several more novels, including *The Hamlet* (1940) and *Go Down, Moses* (1942), which, though they do not approach the level of excellence achieved in the previous Yoknapatawpha novels, are nevertheless original, innovative works of fiction. In 1930, Estelle Oldham Franklin returned to Oxford, divorced from her first husband, and she and Faulkner were married. Faulkner was struggling, barely able to make enough money to survive; he spent time in Hollywood writing screenplays to keep himself afloat financially, but those efforts prevented him from devoting focused energy to his fiction for sustained periods. The tide turned in 1946, when Malcolm Cowley edited *The Portable Faulkner*, a collection that finally brought him widespread critical attention. *Intruder in the Dust* appeared in 1948, and in 1950 he was awarded the Nobel Prize for Literature. In 1955, *A Fable*, a parable set in World War I, won the Pulitzer Prize. Among the other 1950s novels were *The Town* (1957) and *The Mansion* (1959), which complete the saga of the rise and fall of the Snopes clan. *The Reivers*, a humorous "reminiscence," was published in 1962, only a month before he died.

from *Absalom, Absalom!*

"And so it was the Aunt Rosa that came back to town inside the ambulance," Shreve said. Quentin did not answer; he did not even say, *Miss Rosa*. He just lay there staring at the window without even blinking, breathing the chill heady pure snow-gleamed darkness. "And she went to bed because it was all finished now, there was nothing left now, nothing out there now but that idiot boy to lurk around those ashes and those four gutted chimneys and howl until someone came and drove him away. They couldn't catch him and nobody ever seemed to make him go very far away, he just stopped howling for a little while. Then after awhile they would begin to hear him again. And so she died." Quentin did not answer, staring at the window; then he could not tell if it was the actual window or the window's pale rectangle upon his eyelids, though after a moment it began to emerge. It began to take shape in its same curious, light, gravity-defying attitude—the once-folded sheet out of the wistaria Mississippi summer, the cigar smell, the random blowing of the fireflies. "The South," Shreve said. "The South. Jesus. No wonder you folks all outlive yourselves by years and years and years." It was becoming quite distinct; he would be able to decipher the words soon, in a moment; even almost now, now, now.

"I am older at twenty than a lot of people who have died," Quentin said.

"And more people have died than have been twenty-one," Shreve said. Now he (Quentin) could read it, could finish it—the sloped whimsical ironic hand out of Mississippi attenuated, into the iron snow:

—or perhaps there is. Surely it can harm no one to believe that perhaps she has escaped not at all the privilege of being outraged and amazed and of not forgiving but on the contrary has herself gained that place or bourne where the objects of the outrage and of the commiseration also are no longer ghosts but are actual people to

*be actual recipients of the hatred and the pity. It will do no harm to hope—You see I
have written hope, not think. So let it be hope.—that the one cannot escape the censure which no doubt he deserves, that the other no longer lack the commiseration
which let us hope (while we are hoping) that they have longed for, if only for the
reason that they are about to receive it whether they will or no. The weather was
beautiful though cold and they had to use picks to break the earth for the grave yet
in one of the deeper clods I saw a redworm doubtless alive when the clod was
thrown up though by afternoon it was frozen again.*

"So it took Charles Bon and his mother to get rid of old Tom, and Charles Bon
and the octoroon to get rid of Judith, and Charles Bon and Clytie to get rid of Henry;
and Charles Bon's mother and Charles Bon's grandmother got rid of Charles Bon. So
it takes two niggers to get rid of one Sutpen, dont it?" Quentin did not answer; evidently Shreve did not want an answer now; he continued almost without a pause:
"Which is all right, it's fine; it clears the whole ledger, you can tear all the pages out
and burn them, except for one thing. And do you know what that is?" Perhaps he
hoped for an answer this time, or perhaps he merely paused for emphasis, since he
got no answer. "You've got one nigger left. One nigger Sutpen left. Of course you can't
catch him and you don't even always see him and you never will be able to use him.
But you've got him there still. You still hear him at night sometimes. Don't you?"

"Yes," Quentin said.

"And so do you know what I think?" Now he did expect an answer, and now he
got one:

"No," Quentin said.

"Do you want to know what I think?"

"No," Quentin said.

"Then I'll tell you. I think that in time the Jim Bonds are going to conquer the
western hemisphere. Of course it won't quite be in our time and of course as they
spread toward the poles they will bleach out again like the rabbits and the birds do,
so they won't show up so sharp against the snow. But it will still be Jim Bond; and so
in a few thousand years, I who regard you will also have sprung from the loins of
African kings. Now I want you to tell me just one thing more. Why do you hate the
South?"

"I dont hate it," Quentin said, quickly, at once, immediately; "I dont hate it," he
said. *I dont hate it* he thought, panting in the cold air, the iron New England dark; *I
dont. I dont! I dont hate it! I dont hate it!*

Pantaloon in Black

1.

He stood in the worn, faded clean overalls which Mannie herself had washed only a
week ago, and heard the first clod stride the pine box. Soon he had one of the shovels
himself, which in his hands (he was better than six feet and weighed better than two
hundred pounds) resembled the toy shovel a child plays with at the shore, its half cubic
foot of flung dirt no more than the light gout of sand the child's shovel would have flung.
Another member of his sawmill gang touched his arm and said, "Lemme have hit,
Rider." He didn't even falter. He released one hand in midstroke and flung it backward,

striking the other across the chest, jolting him back a step, and restored the hand to the moving shovel, flinging the dirt with that effortless fury so that the mound seemed to be rising of its own volition, not built up from above but thrusting visibly upward out of the earth itself, until at last the grave, save for its rawness, resembled any other marked off without order about the barren plot by shards of pottery and broken bottles and old brick and other objects insignificant to sight but actually of a profound meaning and fatal to touch, which no white man could have read. Then he straightened up and with one hand flung the shovel quivering upright in the mound like a javelin and turned and began to walk away, walking on even when an old woman came out of the meagre clump of his kin and friends and a few old people who had known him and his dead wife both since they were born, and grasped his forearm. She was his aunt. She had raised him. He could not remember his parents at all.

"Whar you gwine?" she said.

"Ah'm goan home," he said.

"You dont wants ter go back dar by yoself," she said. "You needs to eat. You come on home and eat."

"Ah'm goan home," he repeated, walking out from under her hand, his forearm like iron, as if the weight on it were no more than that of a fly, the other members of the mill gang whose head he was giving way quietly to let him pass. But before he reached the fence one of them overtook him; he did not need to be told it was his aunt's messenger.

"Wait, Rider," the other said. "We gots a jug in de bushes—" Then the other said what he had not intended to say, what he had never conceived of himself saying in circumstances like these, even though everybody knew it—the dead who either will not or cannot quit the earth yet although the flesh they once lived in has been returned to it, let the preachers tell and reiterate and affirm how they left it not only without regret but with joy, mounting toward glory: "You dont wants ter go back dar. She be wawkin yit."

He didn't pause, glancing down at the other, his eyes red at the inner corners in his high, slightly backtilted head. "Lemme lone, Acey," he said. "Doan mess wid me now," and went on, stepping over the three-strand wire fence without even breaking his stride, and crossed the road and entered the woods. It was middle dusk when he emerged from them and crossed the last field, stepping over that fence too in one stride, into the lane. It was empty at this hour of Sunday evening—no family in wagon, no rider, no walkers churchward to speak to him and carefully refrain from looking after him when he had passed—the pale, powder-light, powder-dry dust of August from which the long week's marks of hoof and wheel had been blotted by the strolling and unhurried Sunday shoes, with somewhere beneath them, vanished but not gone, fixed and held in the annealing dust, the narrow, splay-toed prints of his wife's bare feet where on Saturday afternoons she would walk to the commissary to buy their next week's supplies while he took his bath; himself, his own prints, setting the period now as he strode on, moving almost as fast as a smaller man could have trotted, his body breasting the air her body had vacated, his eyes touching the objects—post and tree and field and house and hill—her eyes had lost.

The house was the last one in the lane, not his but rented from Carothers Edmonds, the local white landowner. But the rent was paid promptly in advance, and even in just six months he had refloored the porch and rebuilt and roofed the kitchen, doing the work himself on Saturday afternoon and Sunday with his wife helping him, and bought the stove. Because he made good money: sawmilling ever since he began to get his growth at fifteen and sixteen and now, at twenty-four, head of the timber gang itself because the gang he headed moved a third again as much timber between sunup and sundown as any other moved, handling himself at times out of the vanity of his own strength logs which ordinarily two men would have handled with canthooks; never without work even in the old days when he had not actually needed the money, when a lot of what he wanted, needed perhaps, didn't cost money—the women bright and dark and for all purposes nameless he didn't need to buy and it didn't matter to him what he wore and there was always food for him at any hour of day or night in the house of his aunt who didn't even want to take the two dollars he gave her each Saturday—so there had been only the Saturday and Sunday dice and whiskey that had to be paid for until that day six months ago when he saw Mannie, whom he had known all his life, for the first time and said to himself: "Ah'm thu wid all dat," and they married and he rented the cabin from Carothers Edmonds and built a fire on the hearth on their wedding night as the tale told how Uncle Lucas Beauchamp, Edmonds' oldest tenant, had done on his forty-five years ago and which had burned ever since; and he would rise and dress and eat his breakfast by lamplight to walk the four miles to the mill by sunup, and exactly one hour after sundown he would enter the house again, five days a week, and Saturday. Then the first hour would not have passed noon when he would mount the steps and knock, not on post or doorframe but on the underside of the gallery roof itself, and enter and ring the bright cascade of silver dollars onto the scrubbed table in the kitchen where his dinner simmered on the stove and the galvanised tub of hot water and the baking powder can of soft soap and the towel made of scalded flour sacks sewn together and his clean overalls and shirt waited, and Mannie would gather up the money and walk the half-mile to the commissary and buy their next week's supplies and bank the rest of the money in Edmonds' safe and return and they would eat once again without haste or hurry after five days—the sidemeat, the greens, the cornbread, the buttermilk from the well-house, the cake which she baked every Saturday now that she had a stove to bake in.

But when he put his hand on the gate it seemed to him suddenly that there was nothing beyond it. The house had never been his anyway, but now even the new planks and sills and shingles, the hearth and stove and bed, were all a part of the memory of somebody else, so that he stopped in the half-open gate and said aloud, as though he had gone to sleep in one place and then waked suddenly to find himself in another: "Whut's Ah doin hyar?" before he went on. Then he saw the dog. He had forgotten it. He remembered neither seeing nor hearing it since it began to howl just before dawn yesterday—a big dog, a hound with a strain of mastiff from somewhere (he had told Mannie a month after they married: "Ah needs a big dawg. You's de onliest least thing whut ever kep up wid me one day, leff alone fo weeks.") coming out from beneath the gallery and approaching, not running but seeming rather to drift across the dusk until it stood lightly against his leg, its head raised until the tips of his fingers just touched it, facing the house and making no sound; whereupon, as if the animal controlled it, had lain guardian before it during his absence and only this instant relinquished, the shell of planks and shingles facing him solidified, filled, and for the moment he believed that he could not possibly enter it. "But Ah needs to eat," he said. "Us bofe needs to eat," he said, moving on though the dog did not follow until he turned and cursed it. "Come on hyar!" he said. "Whut you skeered of? She lacked you too, same as me," and they mounted the steps and crossed the porch and entered the house—the dusk-filled single room where all those six months were now crammed and crowded into one instant of time until there was no space left for air to breathe, crammed and crowded about the hearth where the fire which was to have lasted to the end of them, before which in the days before he was able to buy the stove he would enter after his four-mile walk from the mill and find her, the shape of her narrow back and haunches squatting, one narrow spread hand shielding her face from the blaze over which the other hand held the skillet, had already fallen to a dry, light soilure of dead ashes when the sun rose yesterday—and himself standing there while the last of light died about the strong and indomitable beating of his heart and the deep steady arch and collapse of his chest which walking fast over the rough going of woods and fields had not increased and standing still in the quiet and fading room had not slowed down.

Then the dog left him. The light pressure went off his flank; he heard the click and hiss of its claws on the wooden floor as it surged away and he thought at first that it was fleeing. But it stopped just outside the front door, where he could see it now, and the upfling of its head as the howl began, and then he saw her too. She was standing in the kitchen door, looking at him. He didn't move. He didn't breathe nor speak until he knew his voice would be all right, his face fixed too not to alarm her. "Mannie," he said. "Hit's awright. Ah aint afraid." Then he took a step toward her, slow, not even raising his hand yet, and stopped. Then he took another step. But this time as soon as he moved she began to fade. He stopped at once, not breathing again, motionless, willing his eyes to see that she had stopped too. But she had not stopped. She was fading, going. "Wait," he said, talking as sweet as he had ever heard his voice speak to a woman: "Den lemme go wid you, honey." But she was going. She was going fast now, he could actually feel between them the insuperable barrier of that very strength which could handle alone a log which would have taken any two other men to handle, of the blood and bones and flesh too strong, invincible for life, having learned at least once with his own eyes how tough, even in sudden and violent death, not a young man's bones and flesh perhaps but the will of that bone and flesh to remain alive, actually was.

Then she was gone. He walked through the door where she had been standing, and went to the stove. He did not light the lamp. He needed no light. He had set the stove up himself and built the shelves for the dishes, from among which he took two plates by feel and from the pot sitting cold on the cold stove he ladled onto the plates the food which his aunt had brought yesterday and of which he had eaten yesterday though now he did not remember when he had eaten it nor what it was, and carried the plates to the scrubbed bare table beneath the single small fading window and drew two chairs up and sat down, waiting again until he knew his voice would be what he wanted it to be. "Come on hyar, now," he said roughly. "Come on hyar and eat yo supper. Ah aint gonter have no—" and ceased, looking down at his plate, breathing the strong, deep pants, his chest arching and collapsing until he stopped it presently and held himself motionless for perhaps a half minute, and raised a spoonful of the cold and glutinous peas to his mouth. The congealed and lifeless mass seemed to bounce on contact with his lips. Not even warmed from mouth-heat, peas and spoon spattered and rang upon the plate; his chair crashed backward and he was standing, feeling the muscles of his jaw beginning to drag his mouth open, tugging upward the top half of his head. But he stopped that too before it became sound, holding himself again while he rapidly scraped the food from his plate onto the other and took it up and left the kitchen, crossed the other room and the gallery and set the plate on the bottom step and went on toward the gate.

The dog was not there, but it overtook him within the first half mile. There was a moon then, their two shadows flitting broken and intermittent among the trees or slanted long and intact across the slope of pasture or old abandoned fields upon the hills, the man moving almost as fast as a horse could have moved over that ground, altering his course each time a lighted window came in sight, the dog trotting at heel while their shadows shortened to the moon's curve until at last they trod them and the last far lamp had vanished and the shadows began to lengthen on the other hand, keeping to heel even when a rabbit burst from almost beneath the man's foot, then lying in the gray of dawn beside the man's prone body, beside the labored heave and collapse of the chest, the loud harsh snoring which sounded not like groans of pain but like someone engaged without arms in prolonged single combat.

When he reached the mill there was nobody there but the fireman—an older man just turning from the woodpile, watching quietly as he crossed the clearing, striding as if he were going to walk not only through the boiler shed but through (or over) the boiler too, the overalls which had been clean yesterday now draggled and soiled and drenched to the knees with dew, the cloth cap flung onto the side of his head, hanging peak downward over his ear as he always wore it, the whites of his eyes rimmed with red and with something urgent and strained about them. "Whar yo bucket?" he said. But before the fireman could answer he had stepped past him and lifted the polished lard pail down from a nail in a post. "Ah just wants a biscuit," he said.

"Eat hit all," the fireman said. "Ah'll eat outen de yuthers' buckets at dinner. Den you gawn home and go to bed. You dont looks good."

"Ah aint come hyar to look," he said, sitting on the ground, his back against the post, the open pail between his knees, cramming the food into his mouth with his hands, wolfing it—peas again, also gelid and cold, a fragment of yesterday's Sunday fried chicken, a few rough chunks of this morning's fried sidemeat, a biscuit the size of a child's cap—indiscriminate, tasteless. The rest of the crew was gathering now, with voices and sounds of movement outside the boiler shed; presently the white foreman rode into the clearing on a horse. He did not look up, setting the empty pail aside, rising, looking at no one, and went to the branch and lay on his stomach and lowered his face to the water, drawing the water into himself with the same deep, strong, troubled inhalations that he had snored with, or as when he had stood in the empty house at dusk yesterday, trying to get air.

Then the trucks were rolling. The air pulsed with the rapid beating of the exhaust and the whine and clang of the saw, the trucks rolling one by one up to the skidway, he mounting the trucks in turn, to stand balanced on the load he freed, knocking the chocks out and casting loose the shackle chains and with his cant-hook squaring the sticks of cypress and gum and oak one by one to the incline and holding them until the next two men of his gang were ready to receive and guide them, until the discharge of each truck became one long rumbling roar punctuated by grunting shouts and, as the morning grew and the sweat came, chanted phrases of song tossed back and forth. He did not sing with them. He rarely ever did, and this morning might have been no different from any other—himself man-height again above the heads which carefully refrained from looking at him, stripped to the waist now, the shirt removed and the overalls knotted about his hips by the suspender straps, his upper body bare except for the handkerchief about his neck and the cap clapped and clinging somehow over his right ear, the mounting sun sweat-glinted steel-blue on the midnight-colored bunch and slip of muscles until the whistle blew for noon and he said to the two men at the head of the skidway: "Look out. Git out de way," and rode the log down the incline, balanced erect upon it in short rapid backward-running steps above the headlong thunder.

His aunt's husband was waiting for him—an old man, as tall as he was, but lean, almost frail, carrying a tin pail in one hand and a covered plate in the other; they too sat in the shade beside the branch a short distance from where the others were opening their dinner pails. The bucket contained a fruit jar of buttermilk packed in a clean damp towsack. The covered dish was a peach pie, still warm. "She baked hit fer you dis mawin," the uncle said. "She say fer you to come home." He didn't answer, bent forward a little, his elbows on his knees, holding the pie in both hands, wolfing at it, the syrupy filling smearing and trickling down his chin, blinking rapidly as he chewed, the whites of his eyes covered a little more by the creeping red. "Ah went to yo house last night, but you want dar. She sont me. She wants you to come on home. She kept de lamp burnin all last night fer you."

"Ah'm awright," he said.

"You aint awright. De Lawd guv, and He tuck away. Put yo faith and trust in Him. And she kin help you."

"Whut faith and trust?" he said. "Whut Mannie ever done ter Him? Whut He wanter come messin wid me and——"

"Hush!" the old man said. "Hush!"

Then the trucks were rolling again. Then he could stop needing to invent to himself reasons for his breathing, until after a while he began to believe he had forgot about breathing since now he could not hear it himself above the steady thunder of the rolling logs; whereupon as soon as he found himself believing he had forgotten it, he knew that he had not, so that instead of tipping the final log onto the skidway he stood up and cast his cant-hook away as if it were a burnt match and in the dying reverberation of the last log's rumbling descent he vaulted down between the two slanted tracks of the skid, facing the log which still lay on the truck. He had done it before—taken a log from the truck onto his hands, balanced, and turned with it and tossed it onto the skidway, but never with a stick of this size, so that in a complete cessation of all sound save the pulse of the exhaust and the light free-running whine of the disengaged saw since every eye there, even that of the white foreman, was upon him, he nudged the log to the edge of the truckframe and squatted and set his palms against the underside of it. For a time there was no movement at all. It was as if the unrational and inanimate wood had invested, mesmerised the man with some of its own primal inertia. Then a voice said quietly: "He got hit. Hit's off de truck," and they saw the crack and gap of air, watching the infinitesimal straightening of the braced legs until the knees locked, the movement mounting infinitesimally through the belly's insuck, the arch of the chest, the neck cords, lifting the lip from the white clench of teeth in passing, drawing the whole head backward and only the bloodshot fixity of the eyes impervious to it, moving on up the arms and the straightening elbows until the balanced log was higher than his head. "Only he aint gonter turn wid dat un," the same voice said. "And when he try to put hit back on de truck, hit gonter kill him." But none of them moved. Then—there was no gathering of supreme effort—the log seemed to leap suddenly backward over his head of its own volition, spinning, crashing and thundering down the incline; he turned and stepped over the slanting track in one stride and walked through them as they gave way and went on across the clearing toward the woods even though the foreman called after him: "Rider!" and again: "You, Rider!"

At sundown he and the dog were in the river swamp four miles away—another clearing, itself not much larger than a room, a hut, a hovel partly of planks and partly of canvas, an unshaven white man standing in the door beside which a shotgun leaned, watching him as he approached, his hand extended with four silver dollars on the palm. "Ah wants a jug," he said.

"A jug?" the white man said. "You mean a pint. This is Monday. Aint you all running this week?"

"Ah laid off," he said. "Whar's my jug?" waiting, looking at nothing apparently, blinking his bloodshot eyes rapidly in his high, slightly back-tilted head, then turning, the jug hanging from his crooked middle finger against his leg, at which moment the white man looked suddenly and sharply at his eyes as though seeing them for the first time—the eyes which had been strained and urgent this morning and which now seemed to be without vision too and in which no white showed at all—and said,

"Here. Gimme that jug. You dont need no gallon. I'm going to give you that pint, give it to you. Then you get out of here and stay out. Dont come back until—" Then the white man reached and grasped the jug, whereupon the other swung it behind him, sweeping his other arm up and out so that it struck the white man across the chest.

"Look out, white folks," he said. "Hit's mine. Ah done paid you."

The white man cursed him. "No you aint. Here's your money. Put that jug down, nigger."

"Hit's mine," he said, his voice quiet, gentle even, his face quiet save for the rapid blinking of the red eyes. "Ah done paid for hit," turning on, turning his back on the man and the gun both, and recrossed the clearing to where the dog waited beside the path to come to heel again. They moved rapidly on between the close walls of impenetrable cane-stalks which gave a sort of blondness to the twilight and possessed something of that oppression, that lack of room to breathe in, which the walls of his house had had. But this time, instead of fleeing it, he stopped and raised the jug and drew the cob stopper from the fierce duskreek of uncured alcohol and drank, gulping the liquid solid and cold as ice water, without either taste or heat until he lowered the jug and the air got in. "Hah," he said. "Dat's right. Try me. Try me, big boy. Ah gots something hyar now dat kin whup you."

And, once free of the bottom's unbreathing blackness, there was the moon again, his long shadow and that of the lifted jug slanting away as he drank and then held the jug poised, gulping the silver air into his throat until he could breathe again, speaking to the jug: "Come on now. You always claim you's a better man den me. Come on now. Prove it." He drank again, swallowing the chill liquid tamed of taste or heat either while the swallowing lasted, feeling it flow solid and cold with fire, past then enveloping the strong steady panting of his lungs until they too ran suddenly free as his moving body ran in the silver solid wall of air he breasted. And he was all right, his striding shadow and the trotting one of the dog travelling swift as those of two clouds along the hill; the long cast of his motionless shadow and that of the lifted jug slanting across the slope as he watched the frail figure of his aunt's husband toiling up the hill.

"Dey tole me at de mill you was gone," the old man said. "Ah knowed whar to look. Come home, son. Dat ar cant help you."

"Hit done awready hope me," he said. "Ah'm awready home. Ah'm snakebit now and pizen cant hawm me."

"Den stop and see her. Leff her look at you. Dat's all she axes: just leff her look at you—" But he was already moving. "Wait!" the old man cried. "Wait!"

"You cant keep up," he said, speaking into the silver air, breasting aside the silver solid air which began to flow past him almost as fast as it would have flowed past a moving horse. The faint frail voice was already lost in the night's infinitude, his shadow and that of the dog scudding the free miles, the deep strong panting of his chest running free as air now because he was all right.

Then, drinking, he discovered suddenly that no more of the liquid was entering his mouth. Swallowing, it was no longer passing down his throat, his throat and mouth filled now with a solid and unmoving column which without reflex or revulsion sprang, columnar and intact and still retaining the mold of his gullet, outward glinting in the moonlight, splintering, vanishing into the myriad murmur of the dewed grass. He drank again. Again his throat merely filled solidly until two icy rills ran from his mouth-corners; again the intact column sprang silvering, glinting, shivering, while he panted the chill of air into his throat, the jug poised before his mouth while he spoke to it: "Awright. Ah'm ghy try you again. Soon as you makes up yo mind to stay whar I puts you, Ah'll leff you alone." He drank, filling his gullet for the third time and lowered the jug one instant ahead of the bright intact repetition, panting, indrawing the cool of air until he could breathe. He stoppered the cob carefully back into the jug and stood, panting, blinking, the long cast of his solitary shadow slanting away across the hill and beyond, across the mazy infinitude of all the night-bound earth. "Awright,'" he said. "Ah just misread de sign wrong. Hit's done done me all de help Ah needs. Ah'm awright now. Ah doan needs no mo of hit."

He could see the lamp in the window as he crossed the pasture, passing the black-and-silver yawn of the sandy ditch where he had played as a boy with empty snuff-tins and rusted harness-buckles and fragments of trace-chains and now and then an actual wheel, passing the garden patch where he had hoed in the spring days while his aunt stood sentry over him from the kitchen window, crossing the grassless yard in whose dust he had sprawled and crept before he learned to walk. He entered the house, the room, the light itself, and stopped in the door, his head back-tilted a little as if he could not see, the jug hanging from his crooked finger, against his leg. "Unc Alec say you wanter see me," he said.

"Not just to see you," his aunt said. "To come home, whar we kin help you."

"Ah'm awright," he said. "Ah doan needs no help."

"No," she said. She rose from the chair and came and grasped his arm as she had grasped it yesterday at the grave. Again, as on yesterday, the forearm was like iron under her hand. "No! When Alec come back and tole me how you had wawked off de mill and de sun not half down, Ah knowed why and whar. And dat cant help you."

"Hit done awready hope me. Ah'm awright now."

"Dont lie to me," she said. "You aint never lied to me. Dont lie to me now."

Then he said it. It was his own voice, without either grief or amazement, speaking quietly out of the tremendous panting of his chest which in a moment now would begin to strain at the walls of this room too. But he would be gone in a moment.

"Nome," he said, "Hit aint done me no good."

"And hit cant! Cant nothing help you but Him! Ax Him! Tole Him about hit! He wants to hyar you and help you!"

"Efn He God, Ah dont needs to tole Him. Efn He God, He awready know hit. Awright. Hyar Ah is. Leff Him come down hyar and do me some good."

"On yo knees!" she cried. "On yo knees and ax Him!" But it was not his knees on the floor, it was his feet. And for a space he could hear her feet too on the planks of the hall behind him and her voice crying after him from the door: "Spoot! Spoot!"— crying after him across the moon-dappled yard the name he had gone by in his childhood and adolescence, before the men he worked with and the bright dark nameless women he had taken in course and forgotten until he saw Mannie that day and said, "Ah'm thu wid all dat," began to call him Rider.

It was just after midnight when he reached the mill. The dog was gone now. This time he could not remember when nor where. At first he seemed to remember hurling the empty jug at it. But later the jug was still in his hand and it was not empty, although each time he drank now the two icy runnels streamed from his mouthcorners, sopping his shirt and overalls until he walked constantly in the fierce chill of the liquid tamed now of flavor and heat and odor too even when the swallowing ceased. "Sides that," he said, "Ah wouldn't thow nothin at him. Ah mout kick him efn he needed hit and was close enough. But Ah wouldn't ruint no dog chunkin hit."

The jug was still in his hand when he entered the clearing and paused among the mute soaring of the moon-blond lumber-stacks. He stood in the middle now of the unimpeded shadow which he was treading again as he had trod it last night, swaying a little, blinking about at the stacked lumber, the skidway, the piled logs waiting for tomorrow, the boiler-shed all quiet and blanched in the moon. And then it was all right. He was moving again. But he was not moving, he was drinking, the liquid cold and swift and tasteless and requiring no swallowing, so that he could not tell if it were going down inside or outside. But it was all right. And now he was moving, the jug gone now and he didn't know the when or where of that either. He crossed the clearing and entered the boiler shed and went on through it, crossing the junctureless backloop of time's trepan, to the door of the tool-room, the faint glow of the lantern beyond the plank-joints, the surge and fall of living shadow, the mutter of voices, the mute click and scutter of the dice, his hand loud on the barred door, his voice loud too: "Open hit. Hit's me. Ah'm snakebit and bound to die."

Then he was through the door and inside the tool-room. They were the same faces—three members of his timber gang, three or four others of the mill crew, the white night-watchman with the heavy pistol in his hip pocket and the small heap of coins and worn bills on the floor before him, one who was called Rider and was Rider standing above the squatting circle, swaying a little, blinking, the dead muscles of his face shaped into smiling while the white man stared up at him. "Make room, gamblers," he said. "Make room. Ah'm snakebit and de pizen cant hawm me."

"You're drunk," the white man said. "Get out of here. One of you niggers open the door and get him out of here."

"Dass awright, boss-man," he said, his voice equable, his face still fixed in the faint rigid smiling beneath the blinking of the red eyes; "Ah aint drunk. Ah just cant wawk straight fer dis yar money weighin me down."

Now he was kneeling too, the other six dollars of his last week's pay on the floor before him, blinking, still smiling at the face of the white man opposite, then, still smiling, he watched the dice pass from hand to hand around the circle as the white man covered the bets, watching the soiled and palm-worn money in front of the white man gradually and steadily increase, watching the white man cast and win two doubled bets in succession then lose on for twenty-five cents, the dice coming to him at last, the cupped snug clicking of them in his fist. He spun a coin into the center.

"Shoots a dollar," he said, and cast, and watched the white man pick up the dice and flip them back to him. "Ah lets hit lay," he said. "Ah'm snakebit. Ah kin pass wid anything," and cast, and this time one of the negroes flipped the dice back. "Ah lets hit lay," he said, and cast, and moved as the white man moved, catching the white man's wrist before his hand reached the dice, the two of them squatting, facing each other above the dice and the money, his left hand grasping the white man's wrist, his face still fixed in the rigid and deadened smiling, his voice equable, almost deferential: "Ah kin pass even wid missouts. But dese hyar yuther boys—" until the white man's hand sprang open and the second pair of dice clattered onto the floor beside the first two and the white man wrenched free and sprang up and back and reached the hand backward toward the pocket where the pistol was.

The razor hung between his shoulder-blades from a loop of cotton string round his neck inside his shirt. The same motion of the hand which brought the razor forward over his shoulder flipped the blade open and freed it from the cord, the blade opening on until the back edge of it lay across the knuckles of his fist, his thumb pressing the handle into his closing fingers, so that in the second before the half-drawn pistol exploded he actually struck at the white man's throat not with the blade but with a sweeping blow of his fist, following through in the same motion so that not even the first jet of blood touched his hand or arm.

2.

After it was over—it didn't take long; they found the prisoner on the following day, hanging from the bell-rope in a negro schoolhouse about two miles from the sawmill, and the coroner had pronounced his verdict of death at the hands of a person or persons unknown and surrendered the body to its next of kin all within five minutes—the sheriff's deputy who had been officially in charge of the business was telling his wife about it. They were in the kitchen. His wife was cooking supper. The deputy had been out of bed and in motion ever since the jail delivery shortly before midnight of yesterday and had covered considerable ground since, and he was spent now from lack of sleep and hurried food at hurried and curious hours and, sitting in a chair beside the stove, a little hysterical too.

"Them damn niggers," he said. "I swear to godfrey, it's a wonder we have as little trouble with them as we do. Because why? Because they aint human. They look like a man and they walk on their hind legs like a man, and they can talk and you can understand them and you think they are understanding you, at least now and then. But when it comes to the normal human feelings and sentiments of human beings, they might just as well be a damn herd of wild buffaloes. Now you take this one today——"

"I wish you would," his wife said harshly. She was a stout woman, handsome once, graying now and with a neck definitely too short, who looked not harried at all but composed in fact, only choleric. Also, she had attended a club rook-party that afternoon and had won the first, the fifty-cent, prize until another member had insisted on a recount of the scores and the ultimate throwing out of one entire game. "Take him out of my kitchen, anyway. You sheriffs! Sitting around that courthouse all day long, talking. It's no wonder two or three men can walk in and take prisoners out from under your very noses. They would take your chairs and desks and window sills too if you ever got your feet and backsides off of them that long."

"It's more of them Birdsongs than just two or three," the deputy said. "There's forty-two active votes in that connection. Me and Maydew taken the poll-list and counted them one day. But listen—" The wife turned from he stove, carrying a dish. The deputy snatched his feet rapidly out of the way as she passed him, passed almost over him, and went into the dining room. The deputy raised his voice a little to carry the increased distance: "His wife dies on him. All right. But does he grieve? He's the biggest and busiest man at the funeral. Grabs a shovel before they even got the box into the grave they tell me, and starts throwing dirt onto her faster than a slip scraper could have done it. But that's all right—" His wife came back. He moved his feet again and altered his voice again to the altered range: "—maybe that's how he felt about her. There aint any law against a man rushing his wife into the ground, provided he never had nothing to do with rushing her to the cemetery too. But here the next day he's the first man back at work except the fireman, getting back to the mill before the fireman had his fire going, let alone steam up; five minutes earlier and he could even have helped the fireman wake Birdsong up so Birdsong could go home and go back to bed again, or he could even have cut Birdsong's throat then and saved everybody trouble.

"So he comes to work, the first man on the job, when McAndrews and everybody else expected him to take the day off since even a nigger couldn't want no better excuse for a holiday than he had just buried his wife, when a white man would have took the day off out of pure respect no matter how he felt about his wife, when even a little child would have had sense enough to take a day off when he would still get paid for it too. But not him. The first man there, jumping from one log truck to another before the starting whistle quit blowing even, snatching up ten-foot cypress logs by himself and throwing them around like matches. And then, when everybody had finally decided that that's the way to take him, the way he wants to be took, he walks off the job in the middle of the afternoon without by-your-leave or much obliged or goodbye to McAndrews or nobody else, gets himself a whole gallon of bust-skull white-mule whisky, comes straight back to the mill and to the same crap game where Birdsong has been running crooked dice on them mill niggers for fifteen years, goes straight to the same game where he has been peacefully losing a probably steady average ninety-nine percent of his pay ever since he got big enough to read the spots on them miss-out dice, and cuts Birdsong's throat clean to the neckbone five minutes later." The wife passed him again and went to the dining room. Again he drew his feet back and raised his voice:

"So me and Maydew go out there. Not that we expected to do any good, as he had probably passed Jackson, Tennessee, about daylight; and besides, the simplest way to find him would be just to stay close behind them Birdsong boys. Of course there wouldn't be nothing hardly worth bringing back to town after they did find him, but it would close the case. So it's just by the merest chance that we go by his house; I dont even remember why we went now, but we did; and there he is. Sitting behind the barred front door with a open razor on one knee and a loaded shotgun on the other? No. He was asleep. A big pot of field peas et clean empty on the stove, and him laying in the back yard asleep in the broad sun with just his head under the edge of the porch in the shade and a dog that looked like a cross between a bear and a Polled Angus steer yelling fire and murder from the back door. And we wake him and he sets up and says, 'Awright, white folks. Ah done it. Jest dont lock me up,' and Maydew

says, 'Mr Birdsong's kinfolks aint going to lock you up neither. You'll have plenty of
fresh air when they get hold of you,' and he says, 'Ah done it. Jest dont lock me up'—
advising, instructing the sheriff not to lock him up; he done it all right and it's too bad
but it aint convenient for him to be cut off from the fresh air at the moment. So we
loaded him into the car, when here come the old woman—his ma or aunt or something—panting up the road at a dog-trot, wanting to come with us too, and Maydew
trying to explain to her what would maybe happen to her too if them Birdsong kin
catches us before we can get him locked up, only she is coming anyway, and like
Maydew says, her being in the car too might be a good thing if the Birdsongs did happen to run into us, because after all interference with the law cant be condoned even
if the Birdsong connection did carry that beat for Maydew last summer.

"So we brought her along too and got him to town and into the jail all right and
turned him over to Ketcham and Ketcham taken him on up stairs and the old woman
coming too, right on up to the cell, telling Ketcham, 'Ah tried to raise him right. He
was a good boy. He aint never been in no trouble till now. He will suffer for what he
done. But dont let the white folks get him,' until Ketcham says, 'You and him ought to
thought of that before he started barbering white men without using no later first.' So
he locked them both up in the cell because he felt like Maydew did, that her being in
there with him might be a good influence on the Birdsong boys if anything started if
he should happen to be running for sheriff or something when Maydew's term was
up. So Ketcham come on back down stairs and pretty soon the chain gang come in
and went on up to the bull pen and he thought things had settled down for a while
when all of a sudden he begun to hear the yelling, not howling: yelling, though there
wasn't no words in it, and he grabbed his pistol and run back up stairs to the bull pen
where the chain gang was and Ketcham could see into the cell where the old woman
was kind of squinched down in one corner and where that nigger had done tore that
iron cot clean out of the floor it was bolted to and was standing in the middle of the
cell, holding the cot over his head like it was a baby's cradle, yelling, and says to the
old woman, 'Ah aint goan hurt you,' and throws the cot against the wall and comes
and grabs holt of that steel barred door and rips it out of the wall, bricks hinges and
all, and walks out of the cell toting the door over his head like it was a gauze window-
screen, hollering, "'It's awright. It's awright. Ah aint trying to git away.'

"Of course Ketcham could have shot him right there, but like he said, if it wasn't
going to be the law, then them Birdsong boys ought to have the first lick at him. So
Ketcham dont shoot. Instead, he jumps in behind where them chain gang niggers was
kind of backed off from that steel door, hollering, 'Grab him! Throw him down!' except the niggers hung back at first too until Ketcham gets in where he can kick the
ones he can reach, batting at the others with the flat of the pistol until they rush him.
And Ketcham says that for a full minute that nigger would grab them as they come in
and fling them clean across the room like they was rag dolls, saying, 'Ah aint tryin to
git out. Ah aint tryin to git out,' until at last they pulled him down—a big mass of nigger heads and arms and legs boiling around on the floor and even then Ketcham says
every now and then a nigger would come flying out and go sailing through the air
across the room, spraddled out like a flying squirrel and with his eyes sticking out like
car headlights, until at last they had him down and Ketcham went in and begun
peeling away niggers until he could see him laying there under the pile of them, laughing, with tears big as glass marbles running across his face and down past his ears
and making a kind of popping sound on the floor like somebody dropping bird eggs,

laughing and laughing and saying, 'Hit look lack Ah just cant quit thinking. Look lack Ah just cant quit.' And what do you think of that?"

"I think if you eat any supper in this house you'll do it in the next five minutes," his wife said from the dining room. "I'm going to clear this table then and I'm going to the picture show."

Stark Young

(1881–1963)

Stark Young was born on October 11, 1881, in Como, Mississippi. He was educated at the University of Mississippi, where he received his B.A. in 1901, and at Columbia University, where he received his M.A. in 1902. After seventeen years as an English professor, teaching at various colleges including the University of Mississippi, the University of Texas, and Amherst, he left Amherst in 1920 to move to New York where he worked as an editor, a director of plays, and a drama critic. He is known for being a New Critic and was influenced by the Fugitives.

Among Young's works are *Heaven Trees* (1926); *The Torches Flare* (1928); *The River House* (1929); *So Red the Rose* (1934); and "Not in Memoriam, But in Defense" from *I'll Take My Stand* (1930). *So Red the Rose*, which sold well, enhanced the status of the Southern novel. It was adapted for the screen in 1935.

Young died on January 6, 1963, in New York City.

Not in Memoriam, But in Defense

If anything is clear, it is that we can never go back, and neither this essay nor any intelligent person that I know in the South desires a literal restoration of the old Southern life, even if that were possible; dead days are gone, and if by some chance they should return, we should find them intolerable. But out of any epoch in civilization there may arise things worth while, that are the flowers of it. To abandon these, when another epoch arrives, is only stupid, so long as there is still in them the breath and flux of life. In our American life today good things are coming in, which we should try to understand and to share, so far as our natures allow. But it is just as obvious that good things are going out. There was a Southern civilization whose course was halted with those conventions of 1867 by which the negro suffrage in the South—not in the North—was planned, and the pillaging began. But that does not imply that this Southern civilization, once the fine flower of men's lives, is wholly dead; for the core of our humanity lies in the belief that the essence of the soul is its mockery of death. It would be childish and dangerous for the South to be stampeded and betrayed out of its own character by the noise, force, and glittering narrowness of the industrialism and progress spreading everywhere, with varying degrees, from one region to another.

This discussion does not concern the peculiar devotion to their own part of the country, or at least their conscious sense of it, that Southerners exhibit, nor any catalogue or description of certain of our characteristics. What I have to attempt is far less redolent of time's sweetness and the old grace. It is, for a while at least, a problem practical enough: the defense of what we have drawn not from theory but from an actual civilization, and believe it necessary to remember. For us there are certain things, now endangered, that leave a kind of death to follow after them, and so must not be lost.

We cannot, save by an old, indomitable human hope, expect anything to rise higher than the life it comes from. But we may remark that the World War and its aftermath; the churches, trying to keep up with the times or to clinch all the ages; the schools; the moving-pictures; and, most of all, the press—have generalized our national thinking. We are plainly to infer that a hundred million people think the same about everything and that what they think is therefore right. How are we to know, then, what we do think? Not long ago I heard an old gentleman in Mississippi, a doctor of the old school, who has given most of his life to charity and is innocent of all money and business, say that a certain judge in the county ought to have known better than to announce a certain opinion, it would surely displease the man under whom he held office. My old doctor is himself the soul of principle, unable for the life of him to budge an inch from his honor for the sake of any sum of mere money, and yet he spoke like this. It was merely because he had picked up the tone of it from the national air, as it were, with its headlines, bang, boom, and doctrine of making-good, and from the newer riffraff who talk the idle mornings out in front of their little stores around the old town square. He talks the common talk like that at times, but in the midst of such a state of things he is untouched, confused, like a child watching the train passing.

The list of such Southern confusions would be endless, but there is one especially that has always seemed to me full of deadly import about the South; I mean the way in which so many of the Coolidge banalities, crudities, and arid White House silences, turned into virtues by his fortunate press, were accepted by Southern people whose every instinct about culture, manners, and eloquence these things grossly traduced. That such press-agent nonsense about Greatness, Simplicity, Silence, Economy, Fishing, Parallelism to Lincoln, Profundity and Deep Reserve, should be taken seriously by some of the South, simple people on one side and our newer vulgarians on the other, was natural enough; it was the kind of thing that reassures their piety, or soothes their minds, or flatters their origins, and avenges their spites. That Southerners of the older type should have swallowed all this, as many of them did, is a bad sign. The kindest thing to say of them is that they admire virtue and believe print. For a later view we may read a reporter's account of Mr. Coolidge's visit to San Antonio, this spring of 1930. In 1836, for twelve days General Santa Ana besieged the little mission of the Alamo, in which were the hundred and fifty Anglo-Saxon defenders who, refusing the escape that had been arranged for them by the Mexican commander in order to relieve him of this show of patriotism and to clear the way to the rebellious colonies, stayed on. To the last man the garrison died. The Alamo is, then, naturally enough, the shrine of Texas independence and of pride in one of the glorious, inexplicable, heroic moments of all history. Mr. Coolidge, ex-President of the United States and guest of the city, would be sure to be taken there. When he got inside, he had, according to the report, only this to say, "What was the Alamo built for?"

Well, what we can say for that is that, in the first place, he need not have made a trip through Texas in a special coach; there was nothing official about his tour. But since he chose to do so, he was to some extent the guest of the state. Perfect consideration, or even the slimmest fruits of any civilization, indeed, would have led to his finding out ahead of time a few items about the town where he was about—shall we say?—to be met at the train. Or slipping from so high a level of courtesy, he might have waited a little and picked up a thread of information about the Alamo when he got there. At the hotel breakfast in his honor, the reporter said, he was asked if he had enjoyed his trip in Texas. To that effort at mere polite conversation, in favor of which there may have been some local prejudice, he replied, "I thought we had come here to eat." This, I gathered, did not appear to the company as humor, or if to be so taken, as a boorish form indeed, and there was, the account said, some silence afterward. And yet there are Southern people who, reading of this incident, and with the encouragement of a little journalism, may have taken it all as sincerity and rugged worth—people whose fathers were gentlemen and whose servants have good manners. All this might not be worth recording, if it were not so perfect an illustration of the confusion today among Southern people who know better and were born knowing better. It illustrates, too, how powerful words are, meaning different things to different people. To these people in San Antonio the Coolidge press talk about *sincerity* and *simplicity* and *reserve* meant something very different from this they heard when the great man visited their town.

Such instances of confusion and retreat are common all over the South. Among the minor decencies, one good instance is enough; we may take the pictures of Southern women seen—though rarely so far—in the advertisements confessing their addiction to some face cream or some mattress, with boudoir and garden snapshots, and footnotes from the advertisers stating the social importance of these ladies and their ancestors—who would have died at such vulgar exploitation of them. Many European and New York ladies have set the pace for this; many have not. The familiar excuse is money for one's favorite charity; and some at least of the checks paid by the manufacturers doubtless reach a charity; though, under the head of vulgarity, that is not much of a point—one might walk the streets for the benefit of the Marines. But in most cases the $2,500 or $5,000 is not the attraction so much as the strength of an idle, persuasive publicity mania, the wish to be seen, as others are seen. Obviously the entire Southern tradition is against this sort of thing, as it is, or was until lately perhaps, averse to giving the family name to a collar, a physic, hot-water bag, or what not; there was a time when the very servants would have despised you for it.

Well, along with this South, then, where we have much of the old life surviving, the old practices that belong with the land, the old beliefs and standards, the gradual blend of these with later ideas and conditions, the onrush of new powers in money, industry, and communication, and the confusion in what men do think, accept, or decline, as the case may be, there has sprung up these last few years a genuine interest in the South. This has taken the form of research, records, new statistics, fiction dealing with Southern life, written either by Southerners or outsiders, articles in newspapers; an influx, from the North, of touring, wintering and buying up the old places; and—significantly—an ever-growing mass of biographies of famous Southerners and of historical narrative, with a strong slant toward restating accepted accounts and vindicating tarnished causes.

This interest in the South is dictated, I believe, partly by the desire of historians for fresh fields and by the vogue of biographies; partly by the journalist's natural desire to follow where the public leads; and partly by the spreading news of the resources in the South for money-making. This behind-the-times, delightful, lazy land can make one rich, now that is quite another matter. But a good part of this general interest—quite aside from the financial interest—in the South, among people of many sorts, undoubtedly, I think, arises from a certain boredom at the flatness, excitement, and sterility of this American life that they have made for themselves. Not size, not the game of money or success, not even progress, seem to have solved the problem. They like to think of some state of living in which there is less exhaustion, colorless repetition, imitation, and joylessness, fewer well-dressed negligible persons; and, since the thought of Europe as a possibility is no longer satisfying, they ask themselves what, with America the richest country in the world, there is to do about living. Their thoughts turn, accordingly, to the South. In our problem of defense, all this is in our favor.

It is aristocratic to take things for granted, go your own way without comment, apology, defense, or self-consciousness. And, clearly, the greatest, most luminous defense of any point of view is its noble embodiment in persons. This is taking high and, just now, too abstract, ground, however. For such of us as wish to sustain certain elements out of the Southern life, our backs must be against the wall. The diverse and most manifest excellences, such as public improvements, exhilaration, money, and so on, that belong with the new state of things we should be only fools not to see and try to evaluate. But that does not mean that we have to swallow all the jargon, concessions, and simplicity of mind that fill the air. We are not necessarily old-fashioned because we stand by certain guns; it may mean only self-respect, proper pride, and distinguished scorn. But let us have no silence. A more conscious attitude is necessary for us. Not the usual attitude too often met in Southerners, and worse for our cause than silence would be. The mere hauteur, the supercilious, defensive high-headedness, the bursting bitterness, old tales, exclusive sentiment have been used up long ago; and have grown only flat or picturesque and endearing, or impolite or antagonistic, sometimes pathetic. In sum there is a campaign to consider.

At the start I must remember not to let myself disgrace the thing I have set out to defend. I need not forget the grace I celebrate, nor the consideration for others that my boasts imply. This tendency—may I avoid it!—among Southerners at times to drive the shot home arises partly from hurt pride, a defensive tack after years of being poor and shut out from one's inherited way of living; but the display of it is useless and only offends. On the other hand, I should study when to inflame or offend, to be downright and hot, and so bring the opponent into such heat that he will plank down his idea, tell me what he thinks a civilization should be. If he has a solid theory, I can make an honorable argument. If he has only a jumble of puerile catchwords, he may be such as can be led to say:

"In our town we've got twenty thousand miles of concrete walks."

"And where do they lead?" I say.

He will not have thought of that.

I remind myself of diverse things. It is not necessary to make men, foolish or serious, agree with me, no matter what the principle is; they may have different faculties. Nor should I be over-anxious to justify our cause, lest I resemble those who, the more they act out of sheer sensation, the more they claim to live by reason's laws. And I must not make the mistake of saying that any of these qualities that I would promote has reason for its basis; it is based on preference only, and it achieves its consummation, or perfection, in becoming rational. It is then a thing complete in itself, making its own kind of sense.

It is important, too, that we do not make the mistake of thinking we are alone in the whole body of these qualities that we admire and claim as Southern; it is easy thus to be uninformed if not absurd. Plenty of people in New England, for example, though cramped very often by Puritan aridities, resent certain tendencies in American life and wish to preserve certain elements on the same grounds that we do, and often more coherently and more intelligently; indeed, the statement of the New England quality by her nobler authors has won her a fine, solid presentation; and her good fortune in being celebrated in so much bad poetry has made her virtues popular. Many Jews share our Southern family instinct, the home, the sense of parents, the endless cousins, uncles, and aunts, the nostalgia for one's own blood. But such comparative points are too obvious to dwell on, as is the fact that there are gentle things, of course, that gentle people everywhere believe. Though the South, not these other parts of the country, is our subject, we must remember that we are concerned first with a quality itself, not as our own but as found anywhere; and that we defend certain qualities not because they belong to the South, but because the South belongs to them. The intelligent course sees first our Southern culture in relation to other cultures, and then in the light of its own sum.

At the outset we must make it clear that in talking of Southern characteristics we are talking largely of a certain life in the old South, a life founded on land and the ownership of slaves. Of the other people living in the South of that epoch we know less, the people who worked their own farms with their own hands, respectable and sturdy, a fine yeomanry partly, and partly the so-called poor whites, who were more shiftless or less self-respecting. They had certain pioneer virtues, common on all our frontiers, and they sometimes, doubtless, reflected certain traits from the planter class; but it is not they who gave this civilization its peculiar stamp. They have by now, of course, so widely mixed with the other Southern type that—without speaking of the descent and vulgarization of some members of good families which have brought them lower than many over whom they felt their superiority—the line of distinction is long since vague. It is not true, however, as many have said, that the higher class completely lost, along with other things, their social manners and customs. It is true, even at this day in the South, that the manners and customs of the South do not wholly arise from the bottom mass; they have come from the top downward. It is true that our traditional Southern characteristics derive from the landed class.

This leads us to another point. There have developed among us down South—as well as everywhere in the nation—certain of what might have been called in England once, chapel-going virtues. I mean by this a certain degradation of a once austere Puritanism, a whining on certain pious excellences that arise from goodness combined with natural dullness, and a certain half-conscious jealousy of all distinction. You are simple, for example, because you are a mixture of plain thinking and an incapacity for thought, you are praised for a sincerity that consists of boorishness and peasant egotism. There was always in the South a flourishing, social religion if you like. But this middle-class piety, platitude, canting, and ignorant assurance was not common to the better element, however much a certain Scotch-Irish Calvinism was breaking the way for it. In the new South it is rampant. The lack of education after the Civil War, the neglect of ideas, the rise of people whose share in things had been restricted, these are some of the contributing causes to such a state. It is encouraged by democracy—all votes are equal—and is flattered by a commercial society. One of the odious traits of industrialism is that, even where there are men who know better, it defers to the mass, largely in order to exploit them, but partly because most of the leaders have few conceptions—barring business—beyond the mass at large. It is remarkable how far this whine has carried among Southerners born to more noble terms of conduct and the spirit. In my opinion the South should be told flatly and coldly that, with other sections acting as they choose, such moral canting, confidence, and whining belong to a village of cobblers and small traders, and are based on ignorance, commonness, and a sense of what will pay. Such a state may well be within our maudlin possibilities but it is not in our genuine tradition. Politicians may flatter the masses. But the ignorant do not possess every man of any intelligence, who should love and despise rather than indulge them; nor have elemental, narrow, stubborn convictions the right to infringe on private spiritual rights. We can put one thing in our pipes and smoke it—there will never again be distinction in the South until—somewhat contrary to the doctrine of popular and profitable democracy—it is generally clear that no man worth anything is possessed by the people, or sees the world under a smear of the people's wills and beliefs. Of this whining, canting simplicity the Southern quality that we fight to preserve must at the very outset disclaim all defense.

From such a paragraph the great question of education and religion in the South easily evolves. On this subject I would admit almost anything gracefully, trying to show at the same time that education, in the most endowed sense, is making great strides among us. Then I should add that the resounding education in the richer parts of the United States is already by many intelligent observers admitted to be mostly futile, and that I should like to hope that a return of confidence will lead the South to turn toward the general idea, held once in the old South and still in England, that education of the university sort, not professional or technical, is suited to a small number only.

This, at present, un-American idea of education may spread if in our schools and universities a less democratic, mobbed, and imitative course of things should come to be, with less booming and prating, organizing, unrest, babble about equipment, election of trustees from the Stock Exchange—all signs of an adolescent mentality and prosperous innocence of what culture may mean. I shall never forget the encouragement with which I saw for the first time that some of the dormitory doors at the University of Virginia needed paint, so sick was I at the bang-up varnishing, rebuilding, plumbing, endowing, in some of the large Northern institutions. If they learn little at these Virginia halls, it is doubtless as much as they would learn at the others, and they at least escape the poison of the success idea that almost every building is sure to show, the belief that mechanical surface and the outer powers of money are the prime things in living.

Then I should hasten to add, in some further defence of Southern education, that it has suffered from the Civil War, from the poverty due to chaos, bad methods at home and tariffs at Washington. I should also claim for what education we have in the South a few little virtues fairly implicit in it. I have seen hack-drivers at Sewanee, for instance, who showed a nicer sense of consideration toward others and better manners than, on numerous occasions, I have seen by full-fledged graduates of a certain old and famous university; just as I have seen some fellow in that larger institution battle with philosophy and the Lord for hours, where one of my country cousins would have dropped the matter automatically, merely as something beneath him. I had likewise the pleasure once of saying to the dean of a famous old New England college, upon his complaining of the lapses of the students on some matter about which he preached continually, that he should try giving some reason besides the moral wrong of it; there are certain things, I said, that, according to what I had always been taught, belong to decorum, to our *mores* rather than to our morals, and that we refrain from doing as we refrain from bodily odors or obscenity in company. He was too much inured to agreeing with influential alumni or affluent trustees not to agree to this also; but I felt that some faint streak at least had penetrated.

As to religion, I would merely ask what about organized religion in the rest of the country, and would then bewail the low ebb of religion in the South, as is shown by the vast growth of the denominations formerly associated with the most bigoted and ignorant classes, and as the preacher-ridden towns oftener than not confirm. The drift toward such a level is a trait inherent in the Anglo-Saxon, who naturally lacks taste; he is saved, if at all, only by a ruling better class, whose stately or unholy views keep the masses somewhat in awe, or else by an independent middle-class opinion, which we have not at present. We have but to remember that to convert the South to religion is only to convert religion to the Southern; our religion will depend on us. We must then add that we may desire a more modern religious thought for certain kinds of people; for others a chance to fulfill their religious needs without any loss of the old warmth in their hearts, or of the look on their gentle faces; and for the rest, in the organized churches, a return of whatever there was in the old that might lead to dignity, decent formality and tolerant social balance. At present, I may say that, with no great hopefulness either way, my own feeling is that I prefer a certain rude reality in the Southern drift toward religion, to the rude promotion of religiosity as an asset to restraint, production, and mental evasion.

There are kinds of criticism against which you can resort to foreign comparison, colonialism, or snobbery, all legitimate, if lighter, weapons in our campaign. In America the War left us much richer and more sure of ourselves, but we still have a share of colonialism, nevertheless, and such comparisons may have weight. We may, for instance, suggest that the English get on better with Southerners than with other Americans, the better class especially; most Continentals do, the Italians, for example, who have our same family sense and the same proud taste for a friendly, semi-formal, complaisant living. If we are accused of being sentimental, or, at the other extreme, of being cynical and supercilious about the idealistic, sublimated haze in which some persons like to see life, well, the Latins are like us in that. If the Southern culture so often mentioned among us is assailed as perplexingly unlearned, say that the Duke of This or That and many of the English county families have a culture very much the same, and that one of its aspects is a certain indifference to mere attainments, which may be left to the professors, *arrivistes*, and paid performers. If the old habit of sitting back, talking hours on end, is the trouble, the same may be said of the Russian nobility, the Spanish, the French, or of any civilization whose ideal is social existence rather than production, competition, and barter. Nor has any aristocratic life in Europe, though it has its own comfort and an elaborate elegance, ever sought the mechanical perfection in domestic living—the vulgarities in plumbing competitions, for example—that flattens so much of America now, but in the South has never, despite the new progress there, seemed the greatest interest about the home. With the right opponent this foreign citation may prove something of a rout; it is at least a way of checking such as tend to measure everything by their own world, and of forcing them to speak not their own dialect, but Esperanto, a language that is international, whatever else. In the meantime it does us no harm to study our own ideas in the light of tried and ancient civilizations. Such study illumines and dilates our own opinion, not to speak of the mild pleasure of showing what some of our knowers do not know.

But the basis, of course, that all these Southern discussions must at last come to is conceptions. If you have no conceptions on which to base your claims, what you say may seem to others only personal prejudice, with no support beyond your fervor or charm. Certain characteristics we are free to indorse, to exhibit, to feel. But to champion them we must comprehend their grounds, we must know. Otherwise, among the average and incessant, we may be overcome with jargon, progress *clichés*, and views well backed with the arguments of success, which rain upon us from presidential speeches, captains of industry, promoters, journals, pulpits, every speaking source and possibility. Otherwise among the grim, prejudiced and hostile we may be dismissed as only hot and childish. Otherwise, among the courteous and reserved, we may serve only as a Virgilian illustration—

sed argutos inter strepere anser olores

and seem but "to hiss like a goose among the tuneful swans."

We shall have to find grounds, then, for these qualities we indorse—to take an example, provincialism.

Provincialism that is a mere ramification of some insistent egotism is only less nauseous than the same egotism in its purity, raw self without any province to harp upon. But provincialism proper is a fine trait. It is akin to a man's interest in his own center, which is the most deeply rooted consideration that he has, the source of his direction, health and soul. A comparison between New York, the great city, and one's own town or country might mention the petty faults and secret vices of the provinces, the wear and tear, the limited chance, the fellowship of saints, the hairpulling of the wicked, and might also go on, if you like, to the poetry of echoes possible there, the quiet, the stream that reminds you of Carducci's verse where the nymphs' breasts beneath the water were silver like the moon; and then pass to the river of life in the city, the city's protection and privacy, or public stir, whichever you choose; the arts, the lively contacts, the chance to rise into big fortunes, the speed, the variety, or the wonder and enchantment of size and audacious enterprise, for both those who can feel such magic and those who can extract it from magazines. But such comparisons are only possibilities in preference and show how easily the point is missed. Provincialism does not at all imply living in the place on which you base your beliefs and choices. It is a state of mind or persuasion. It is a source. With or without knowing the rest of the world, you can, against all odds, defend your provincialism to yourself quite by simple inner necessity, as you think of your own nature, which you would not at bottom change with anyone else. You need not, for instance, live in the South, but you feel your roots are there. You love even the pain it has given you, and you exasperate some critical citizen elsewhere, who thinks the fact that you would not live in your beloved land a point against you and it, and never discovers that the vacancy in his own heart is partly his forgetfulness of the friendly verdure and first memory of his early years. No matter where you are, in any city or land or on the sea, and some old song suddenly heard again, or a childhood dish tasted, or some fragrance remembered from a garden once, or a voice or word, brings tears to your eyes because of its memory of some place, that place is your country. People who give up their own land too readily need careful weighing, exactly as do those who are so with their convictions. I am not sure that one of the deep mysteries, one of the great, as it were, natural beauties of the heart, does not lie in one's love for his own land. If there is a sadness, or old memory, added to this sense, it may become a part of the substance on which the soul makes its tragic journey.

The discussion of manners, affability, friendliness turns on the salubrity of people's living close together. An at-homeness among others is implied; and a lack of suspicion—the most vulgar and humiliating of traits, I was taught by my elders—with regard to others and their intentions—it was better a thousand times, they said, to be deceived than to be common; a taste for the approval of others—how Southern!—derived from politeness, friendliness, and vanity; the belief that one of our most natural impulses is the wish that the other person may be happy in our company. As to manners and the accusations against Southerners of insincerity, floweriness, gush, and indirection, the answer is that such reproaches are the defensive arguments of selfishness, of meager natures, of self-conscious egotism, of middle-class Puritanism, or of laziness; it is easier not to consider the other man's feelings, or it is sinful to pretend to feelings that we do not feel. In those regions, however, where such non-flowering sincerity is most highly commended, you will not detect any lack of color when they are trying to sell something; it is a sin only when it merely makes life more pleasant for some one.

Manners and sincerity are matters understood only with reference to a state of society that assumes a group welfare and point of view rather than individual whims, a flow among a group of human beings, a life to which each single human being contributes and in which he lives. It is comically true that you may dislike meeting X on Monday, but you say, nevertheless, I'm glad to see you. This declaration may not be true to what you feel toward X on that particular day, but it is true to your feelings for him by the year, feelings that would have been falsified by your not saying on Monday that you were glad to see him; you are, therefore, in X's case, insincere by the moment but sincere by the year; only self-centered boors could think otherwise. As for those judgments and opinions on some person which you try to indicate by your manner toward him, such forms of sincerity are usually ill-bred egotism. "Use every man after his desert," as Hamlet says, "and who shall escape whipping? Use them after your own honor and dignity." Manners are the mask of decency that we employ at need, the currency of fair communication; their flower is a common grace, and their fruit not seldom friendship. To think otherwise than this is only peasant stolidity and middle-class confusion. The stress on the individual in such matters is only barbaric, mere tree-dwelling.

The Southern family sense, often onerous to aliens and not seldom one of our own domestic burdens, is nevertheless a good trait. Our tradition of family involves the fact that so many of our families came from the British Isles, with Scotch clannishness plentiful enough, and remained unmixed with other bloods, as did the French and Spanish of Louisiana, for a long time. And a sense of family followed our connection with the land, a gracious domain where the events of the day began with the sky and light, the bread you ate came from the fields around you, your father's, your own; and life has been led; where you have known man's great desire, that generation of himself in the body of life, of which the earth is the eternal and natural symbol; and where there was, of all occupations, the form of labor in which the mystery and drama of life—the seed, the flower and harvest, the darkness, the renewal— is most represented to us.

As for the notion in general of kin and family, in some men the source of so much proud and tender emotion, it goes back to one of the oldest racial instincts and is rooted in the most human poetry of the imagination. A man's thought of his mother, loving him before he was born, thinking of her own mother during this that has now come to her; his thought of his father, of his father's hopes for him, and of what his father as a young man felt in his warm, restless heart and troubled, glowing brain—And if, then, he loves his father and mother, how can he not love those who brought them into the world and loved them, and those yet farther back, this line of hopes and struggles and love? The nature and course of such love as parents give, no matter what imperfections may appear, is like no other that he will ever receive; and later he may come to say, "What I might have said to them! If only——" As I write I think of my own grandfather's father, whose memory is still so strong in my family, for his reserve and gentleness, his hidden, strong feeling, his authority and control, and find myself wishing that I had some faith by which I could say to him, if he be somewhere now and could hear me, "I know what you felt, I know that you loved me long before I was born, and that your power over me lies in my knowledge of your love and of the passionate gravity of your life." A man's love of these dead is only another love that is also in him: when his blood runs in other veins, not yet born, against the day when the house will be empty, the scene too unbroken; it has the same relation to unceasing life that his pulse has to unending time.

Suppose, as some research has declared, only three Virginia families were of any great importance back in England, there is nothing in that, be it true or false, to throw us off. You need only to say that it was not the memory of the British Isles, it was an attitude and point of view induced by the Southern way of life that we came to mean by *aristocratic*. Suppose your family, like most of the rest, never did anything alarmingly great, was merely a Southern family on Southern land. Be careful here, lest you expose us to the outside scorn of facts, or indulge some of us already too much given to the infirmities of sentiment! You must not begin about the fine house, which, after all, at the very best anywhere in the early American states would have been only pleasantly grand—we had no Caprarola, Strá, or Chenonceaux or Knole—or about china, silver and furniture. Your family lived in a big house, not without elegance, hospitality, and affection; and what made your position was not power necessarily or any eminence in the country's history, but rather your settled connection with the land; it was the fact that your family had maintained a certain quality of living and manners throughout a certain period of time, and had a certain relation to the society of the country. And in the same way, not unlike the British today, our meaning of culture—the Southern culture of which the orators used to spout, adding a dash about chivalry and honor—did not imply, not necessarily as it often did in New England, a learning, perhaps a trifle parochial, in philosophy, the Scriptures, or German, French, and other worthy knowledges. It implied, no doubt, some gentlemanly acquaintance with the classics, a whiff of the poets, or a respect for a polite degree of polish and cultivation, and a genuine taste for oratory, whose large flowers went, perhaps, with white columns and the great white moons of the magnolia. What it did imply is difficult to explain. It was one of those things half of whose mysterious virtue lies in their arbitrariness. Undoubtedly it had to do with a certain fineness of feeling, an indefinable code for yourself and others, and a certain continuity of outlook; but what it inherently implied was something like that which Lord Melbourne, the celebrated Minister to Queen Victoria, meant, when he observed that, of all the coveted orders in England, the one he admired most was that of the Garter—"there was no damn merit about it." In a curious way this defines our Southern notion of the aristocratic. It is a thing forever annoying to those who, from the outside of such traditions, wish to put them into reasonable terms, and it will never be understandable by those born in a different scheme of life.

The aristocratic implied with us a certain long responsibility for others; a habit of domination; a certain arbitrariness; certain ideas of personal honor, with varying degrees of ethics, *amour propre*, and the fantastic. And it implied the possession of no little leisure. Whether that was a good system or not is debatable. I myself think it, if we had to make a choice strictly between either one or the other, better than a society of bankers and bankers' clerks, department-store communities, manufacturers and their henchmen and their semi-slaves, and miserable little middle-class cities, frightened of one's position in the country club, snatching at the daily paper to see if one is all right. Good system or not, from this Southern conception of aristocracy certain ideas arose, about which this book to a fair extent, has been written. This way of life meant mutuality of interests among more people, an innate code of obligations, and a certain openness of life. It meant self-control that implied not the expression of you and your precious personality, not the pleasures of suffering or of denying your own will; you controlled yourself in order to make the society you lived in more decent, affable, and civilized and yourself more amenable and attractive. If in such a life the nature of it made you unhappy, restive under its pattern, you suffered all the more because the people around you were so gentle about it, but you might remember that same fineness and love as in itself some mode of assurance, as some guaranty of goodness, even, reflected from yourself.

In case you have believed lies about your family, which is not so fine and grand as you had thought it, try saying to yourself:

"Is it not better that I should believe lies, believe in my family, desiring its luster for myself, shamed by its ideals and my own unworthiness, touched by the past of its affections and its standards, than to believe another special sort of modern American lie, such a one, for instance as believes Mr. Henry Ford's opinion on art to be of any importance, merely because of his success with wheels in a mechanical system that makes men constantly dryer, more thwarted and less exercised, and Mr. Ford richer and richer?"

It is a sad state of affairs when a Marylander, for example, is pleased merely because a plumber plenipotentiary from afar, or a Broadway broker with his restless wife, likes an old family mansion on the Sound. It is rather generous and pleasant that such persons like what they could never have inherited or created, and what may in time distinguish them from the mob of their successful friends back home. But the final results in the case of any of such patrons must depend on the amount of consideration, refinement, bloated confidence, machine-mindedness, and so on, that he displays; on whether the box walks prove bearable under his meditating feet, whether the ancient quiet is possible to his electric spirit.

As for the pride that people meet in Southerners, sometimes with amazement, and that even old friends and kinsmen at home must now and then be careful of, it is not pride in the boasting sense, though that sort happens in the South as it does everywhere. It is rather a kind of *amour propre*, sometimes a sort of mad self-respect and honor complex, such as the Spanish traditionally have, though as a rule not so strong, foolish, and magnificent as the Spanish. Well, as Byron thought, sheer animal pride is one of the simplest and straightest ways of keeping the human animal decent and superior. I have heard cousins of mine say, "No, I don't do that sort of thing," and let it go at that, like a horse with water that he will not drink. Such pride, though it may take away from your sense of humor, may add to your manner and bearing. What it loses in amiable looseness it may gain in dignity. If it makes enemies it also banishes contempt; and it is sometimes, by its very retreat, capable of drawing others toward you, or by the rankling memory of some surrender they themselves have made, it rouses them in your defence.

This personal honorable, fantastic pride may also have a mad price. I have seen pathetic manifestations of that: a man walking out of an office rather than take some real or fancied slight; a poor cousin giving a third of his day's salary to a negro for a small service, too proud to be thrifty or to resemble the white trash, whom the negro despised and my cousin's family had never invited farther than the front steps. Or shall we take—there are several to be heard of—the poor and unknown writer, coming to New York from the South, uncertain of his work but sure of the vulgar rudeness of this publishing magnate with whom he has been granted an audience. He picks up the manuscript, throwing away his chance before he will accept such patronage, and leaves this publisher, who meant presently to accept the book, somewhat in the lurch and raging at these Southern authors, so huffy and difficult. If these were foolish acts, the glamor of high things, at least, lay upon them, some fine salvation or vain private pomp. Various souls need various nurtures, and there are worse things than refusing to take insults for a mere chance of profit, and worse things than walking out and leaving the dog with the bone.

It is clear that we have come now to where our discussion concerns no outside argument but strictly ourselves. As a matter of fact it has been from the first less a defense of certain Southern qualities than a strengthening of ourselves in them.

The South has long since made a start, now famous indeed, toward that industrialization for which she offers such manifest resources. We are an enthusiastic people and it is certain that, once having turned industrial, we shall be zealous about it. You cannot object to that, for we should be only dull not to respond to the sweep, the live force, the surge of possibility, youthful daring, change, architecture, and invention that America so displays that all other countries may seem to us flat and stale. But at the same time the South has one special advantage.

Voiced in newspapers, in magazines, especially those of success and personality—one and the same thing—and finally in moving pictures, plays, novels, and public utterances, there has arisen in the United States as naïve and limited a mode of thinking as has existed since the primitive epochs. In its simplest form this thought turns on a crude sense of money. But this is the smaller part of it. Our American love of money is both infantile and aimless compared with that of the older countries of Europe; they are far more rapacious than we are, but they have more conceptions of what money does, more wants, systems, and styles of living. What we love is the idea of fortunes, heads of corporations, adventures in competition and material development. Boyish fancy and empty pursuit like that has its lovable side, though it is a little less lovable and heartening when we see the average man produced by it. The primitive man had at least physical strength in his body, and in his mind fear, joy, and wonder at the earth, the elements, the shadows within himself. The type we have created is nervous, busy, softened physically, good-hearted, or easy-going at least, anxious for undisturbing sentiments, without conversation, without much idea of any enjoyment beyond a sort of violent leisure, not much left in him for friendship, too hurried and exhausted for passionate love, and without any taste for the music of women in his life. His wife goes to Europe for months, or with clubs and careers is trying to organize herself into affectionate unconsciousness. His friends compete with him, none of them with a great sense of what it all leads to. He does not care to know anything, but merely to know about it. He is less concerned with the truth than with what people will think. For such a state of civilization as such a man quite generally represents, it is only to be expected that a defensive philosophy, good or bad, should have been developed and that statements the thoughtful mind perceives to be almost comically incredible, time-serving and flattering to the general trend, are widely, eagerly, and fearfully accepted as true, economic, and truly patriotic.

It is just here that our special advantage comes in. Exactly as the factories in the South, erected so recently, are not much encumbered with obsolete types of machines and buildings, so in our passage today into a degree of industrial life we can, if we choose, escape at least some portion of the mentality and point of view that have accompanied the industrial development in so many parts of the United States. We must admit that in some Southern states where industrialism has already taken a foremost place, the public mentality, as events of the last two years have shown, has moved in the dark ages of American industrial history and has made the word "progressive," applied to them, a sickening epithet. There is no reason now that we should pass through quite the state of mind that went, in the rest of the country, with the mechanization of the past decades. We can begin close to where the better sort of thinking and better conditions have by now arrived. We can, if we only would, see industrialism as it spreads in the South, and study it, from the vantage ground of theory, criticism, and error elsewhere developed from experience and from longer observation. We can accept the machine, but create our own attitude toward it.

There is no reason why Southern people, however industrialized, should bolt the whole mess as it stands. Let them concur in whatever extent of industrialism may seem to them advisable, but look sharp to the doctrines they accept, and to the half-unconscious rot, evolved from a dissatisfied, eager and short-sighted state of society, that they blind their own eyes with. Let them remind themselves constantly that the front of this heralded affair is not so solid and unbroken as it may seem, and that there are people, scattered over the country here and there, in some places a good many of them, who watch this confident activity, crass loneliness, and baffled egotism, and its bewildering, rich powers and results, and ask what it is all about and what it will come to. Such people already suspect the childish face-value of this prosperous credo—though it is not so prosperous of late—they suspect the monotony of the American mind. They are bored at the celebrated uniformity of American life, which they may excuse sometimes on the grounds of the rapidity of our development but deplore on the grounds of entertainment, variety, and vital detail in human life. There are people who doubt if two million a year fills a man's head with anything beyond an annual two million, and who puzzle over such a man as delights in mere speed, going faster than anybody for ten miles and unable to think of anything when he gets there except going the next ten miles. And there are those who are saddened at meeting up and down the country the mind and innocence of a child, without that softness and that participation in nature by which the child is divine.

What's more, there are even people quite aware that the reputation of some of the greatest leaders in these industrial times has been created entirely—or else well cleansed—for public consumption, by highly-paid press agents. The press agent looks up stories of former popular heroes and fits them to this monument of progress, or invents fishing tales, biographical tales, charities, pet animals, or other delicate inclinations for the sake of keeping the big name becomingly in the papers. He even invents beguiling things to do; an old magnate, for example, on the point of nationwide disfavor because of some fine scandal, may be instructed by his press agent to give every day a dollar bill to the first red-headed boy he meets; the photographs of which deed, appearing in the papers everywhere and every month or so, after a golf game, a fishing trip, or a banquet to Gold Star Mothers, will soon create the legend of the bounteous heart.

Even so few hints of the reactions of thoughtful people elsewhere should heighten the Southerner's spirits. Besides the more thoughtful virtues, there are in the South plenty of prejudice, pride, and scorn—each with its healthy uses—that will help toward short-cuts to our own position on the new state of things; and that, moreover, will quickly dispose of some of the heroes and superstitions of the day. The simplest way to put it you may often hear ready to hand, as I heard it once from an old Mississippi lady. She was speaking of one of our most headlined millionaires, a semi-comic old creature, whose career of single-mindedness, photography, bonded vulgarity, chicanery, and pious sterility she apparently had observed for a long time: "I don't care. He may have three hundred millions, but he's nothing but trash after all." A very good way to put it. St. Paul said, "Alexander the coppersmith hath done me much harm, the Lord reward him according to his merit"; but it took no divine omniscience to understand what St. Paul meant, and I should have thought him a healthier spirit and a more likable sort if he had sent Alexander to a sound damnation.

This old lady's words were only a whimsical way of relating the new order to our Southern use of it. To have it good for us we shall have to see it in the light of our own tradition, our conceptions, our preferences, the flower of another way of life, more of which is left within us than, in the heat of a new impulse, we may think. It is impossible to believe that a Southerner of good class, with a father who was a gentleman of honorable standards, pride, and formal conceptions, could regard many of our present leaders, however heroic they appear in the tabloids and in the unconscious lapses of great editorial writers, with quite the naïveté of some self-made foreman in a shoe factory, of some Bowery child, born out of a magnificent, ancient spiritual tradition, but muddled with the crass American life around him. For this inheritance of ours, together with all we have learned, all there is outside to profit by, the South must find its own use. It all comes down to the most practical of all points—what is the end of living? What is the end of living that, regardless of all the progress, optimism, and noise, must be the answer to the civilization in the South?

It is a question easy to ask but incorrigibly defensive, even if we lost the fight. It may be that the end of man's living is not mere raw Publicity, Success, Competition, Speed and Speedways, Progress, Donations, and Hot Water, all seen with a capital letter. There are also more fleeting and eternal things to be thought of; more grace, sweetness and time; more security in our instincts, and chance to follow our inmost nature, as Jesus meant when he said he must be about his Father's business; more of that last fine light to shine on what we do, and make the sum of it like some luminous landscape, all the parts of which are equable, distributed, and right. We shall have to think that out for ourselves, and not be fed headlines as seals tallow balls, to keep up the performance.

To arrive, then, at some conception of the end of living, the civilization, that will belong to the South, is our great, immediate problem. But in this case, as always in life, alongside a man's open course there moves a mystery, to him dark and shining at once. The mystery here is change, whose god is Mutability. In the shifting relation between ourselves and the new order lies the profoundest source for our living, I mean change in that almost mystical sense by which, so long as we are alive, we are not the same and yet remain ourselves. All things hate steadfastness and are changed, Spenser wrote, and yet, being rightly weighed:

They are not changéd from their first estate;
But by their change their being do dilate:
And turning to themselves at length again,
Do work their own perfection so by fate.
Then over them change doth not rule and reign,
But they rule over change and do themselves maintain.

That a change is now in course all over the South is plain; and it is as plain that the South changing must be the South still, remembering that for no thing can there be any completeness that is outside its own nature, and no thing for which there is any advance save in its own kind. If this were not so, all nature by now would have dissolved in chaos and folly, nothing in it, neither its own self nor any other.

Zora Neale Hurston

(1903–1960)

Born on January 7, 1891, in Eatonville, Florida, Zora Neale Hurston was a writer and folklorist. She married Herbert Sheen in 1927 (divorced 1931); Albert Price III in 1939 (divorced). She attended Howard University (1923–1924), Barnard College (BA 1928), and did graduate study at Columbia University. Her work in anthropology led to her interest in folklore. She is closely associated with the Harlem Renaissance.

Hurston received a Guggenheim Fellowship in 1936 and 1938. In 1943, she received the Annisfield Award for *Dust Tracks on a Road* (1942). Other works by Hurston include *Jonah's Gourd Vine* (1934); *Mules and Men* (1935); *Their Eyes Were Watching God* (1937); *Moses, Man of the Mountain* (1939); *Seraph on the Suwanee* (1948); *The Complete Stories* (1994); *Folklore, Memoirs, and Other Writings* (1995); and *Novels and Stories* (1995).

from *Their Eyes Were Watching God*

Chapter 1

Ships at a distance have every man's wish on board. For some they come in with the tide. For others they sail forever on the horizon, never out of sight, never landing until the Watcher turns his eyes away in resignation, his dreams mocked to death by Time. That is the life of men.

Now, women forget all those things they don't want to remember, and remember everything they don't want to forget. The dream is the truth. Then they act and do things accordingly.

So the beginning of this was a woman and she had come back from burying the dead. Not the dead of sick and ailing with friends at the pillow and the feet. She had come back from the sodden and the bloated; the sudden dead, their eyes flung wide open in judgment.

The people all saw her come because it was sundown. The sun was gone, but he had left his footprints in the sky. It was the time for sitting on porches beside the road. It was the time to hear things and talk. These sitters had been tongueless, earless, eyeless conveniences all day long. Mules and other brutes had occupied their skins. But now, the sun and the bossman were gone, so the skins felt powerful and human. They became lords of sounds and lesser things. They passed notions through their mouths. They sat in judgment.

Seeing the woman as she was made them remember the envy they had stored up from other times. So they chewed up the back parts of their minds and swallowed with relish. They made burning statements with questions, and killing tools out of laughs. It was mass cruelty. A mood come alive. Words walking without masters; walking altogether like harmony in a song.

"What she doin' coming back here in dem overhalls? Can't she find no dress to put on?—Where's dat blue satin dress she left here in?—Where all dat money her husband took and died and left her?—What dat ole forty year ole 'oman doin' wid her hair swingin' down her back lak some young gal?—Where she left dat young lad of a boy she went off here wid?—Thought she was going to marry?—Where he left *her?*—What he done wid all her money?—Betcha he off wid some gal so young she ain't even got no hairs—why she don't stay in her class?—"

When she got to where they were she turned her face on the bander log and spoke. They scrambled a noisy "good evenin'" and left their mouths setting open and their ears full of hope. Her speech was pleasant enough, but she kept walking straight on to her gate. The porch couldn't talk for looking.

The men noticed her firm buttocks like she had grape fruits in her hip pockets; the great rope of black hair swinging to her waist and unraveling in the wind like a plume; then her pugnacious breasts trying to bore holes in her shirt. They, the men, were saving with the mind what they lost with the eye. The women took the faded shirt and muddy overalls and laid them away for remembrance. It was a weapon against her strength and if it turned out of no significance, still it was a hope that she might fall to their level some day.

But nobody moved, nobody spoke, nobody even thought to swallow spit until after her gate slammed behind her.

Pearl Stone opened her mouth and laughed real hard because she didn't know what else to do. She fell all over Mrs. Sumpkins while she laughed. Mrs. Sumpkins snorted violently and sucked her teeth.

"Humph! Y'all let her worry yuh. You ain't like me. Ah ain't got her to study 'bout. If she ain't got manners enough to stop and let folks know how she been makin' out, let her g'wan!"

"She ain't even worth talkin' after," Lulu Moss drawled through her nose. "She sits high, but she looks low. Dat's what Ah say 'bout dese ole women runnin' after young boys."

Pheoby Watson hitched her rocking chair forward before she spoke. "Well, nobody don't know if it's anything to tell or not. Me, Ah'm her best friend, and *Ah* don't know."

"Maybe us don't know into things lak you do, but we all know how she went 'way from here and us sho seen her come back. 'Tain't no use in your tryin' to cloak no ole woman lak Janie Starks, Pheoby, friend or no friend."

"At dat she ain't so ole as some of y'all dat's talking."

"She's way past forty to my knowledge, Pheoby."

"No more'n forty at de outside."

"She's 'way too old for a boy like Tea Cake."

"Tea Cake ain't been no boy for some time. He's round thirty his ownself."

"Don't keer what it was, she could stop and say a few words with us. She act like we done done something to her," Pearl Stone complained. "She de one been doin' wrong."

"You mean, you mad 'cause she didn't stop and tell us all her business. Anyhow, what you ever know her to do so bad as y'all make out? The worst thing Ah ever knowed her to do was taking a few years offa her age and dat ain't never harmed nobody. Y'all makes me tired. De way you talkin' you'd think de folks in dis town didn't do nothin' in de bed 'cept praise de Lawd. You have to 'scuse me, 'cause Ah'm bound to go take her some supper." Pheoby stood up sharply.

"Don't mind us," Lulu smiled, "just go right ahead, us can mind yo' house for you till you git back. Mah supper is done. You bettah go see how she feel. You kin let de rest of us know."

"Lawd," Pearl agreed, "Ah done scorched-up dat lil meat and bread too long to talk about. Ah kin stay 'way from home long as Ah please. Mah husband ain't fussy."

"Oh, er, Pheoby, if youse ready to go, Ah could walk over dere wid you," Mrs. Sumpkins volunteered. "It's sort of duskin' down dark. De booger man might ketch yuh."

"Naw, Ah thank yuh. Nothin' couldn't ketch me dese few steps Ah'm goin'. Anyhow mah husband tell me say no first class booger would have me. If she got anything to tell yuh, you'll hear it."

Pheoby hurried on off with a covered bowl in her hands. She left the porch pelting her back with unasked questions. They hoped the answers were cruel and strange. When she arrived at the place, Pheoby Watson didn't go in by the front gate and down the palm walk to the front door. She walked around the fence corner and went in the intimate gate with her heaping plate of mulatto rice. Janie must be round that side.

She found her sitting on the steps of the back porch with the lamps all filled and the chimneys cleaned.

"Hello, Janie, how you comin'?"

"Aw, pretty good, Ah'm tryin' to soak some uh de tiredness and de dirt outa mah feet." She laughed a little.

"Ah see you is. Gal, you sho looks *good*. You looks like youse yo' own daughter." They both laughed. "Even wid dem overhalls on, you shows yo' womanhood."

"G'wan! G'wan! You must think Ah brought yuh somethin'. When Ah ain't brought home a thing but mahself."

"Dat's a gracious plenty. Yo' friends wouldn't want nothin' better."

"Ah takes dat flattery offa you, Pheoby, 'cause Ah know it's from de heart." Janie extended her hand. "Good Lawd, Pheoby! Ain't you never goin' tuh gimme dat lil rations you brought me? Ah ain't had a thing on mah stomach today exceptin' mah hand." They both laughed easily. "Give it here and have a seat."

"Ah knowed you'd be hungry. No time to be huntin' stove wood after dark. Mah mulatto rice ain't so good dis time. Not enough bacon grease, but Ah reckon it'll kill hongry."

"Ah'll tell you in a minute," Janie said, lifting the cover. "Gal, it's *too* good! you switches a mean fanny round in a kitchen."

"Aw, dat ain't much to eat, Janie. But Ah'm liable to have something sho nuff good tomorrow, 'cause you done come."

Janie ate heartily and said nothing. The varicolored cloud dust that the sun had stirred up in the sky was settling by slow degrees.

"Here, Pheoby, take yo' ole plate. Ah ain't got a bit of use for a empty dish. Dat grub sho come in handy."

Pheoby laughed at her friend's rough joke. "Youse just as crazy as you ever was."

"Hand me dat wash-rag on dat chair by you, honey. Lemme scrub mah feet." She took the cloth and rubbed vigorously. Laughter came to her from the big road.

"Well, Ah see Mouth-Almighty is still sittin' in de same place. And Ah reckon they got *me* up in they mouth now."

"Yes indeed. You know if you pass some people and don't speak tuh suit 'em dey got tuh go way back in yo' life and see whut you ever done. They know mo' 'bout yuh than you do yo' self. An envious heart makes a treacherous ear. They done 'heard' 'bout you just what they hope done happened."

"If God don't think no mo' 'bout 'em then Ah do, they's a lost ball in de high grass."

"Ah hears what they say 'cause they just will collect round mah porch 'cause it's on de big road. Mah husband git so sick of 'em sometime he makes 'em all git for home."

"Sam is right too. They just wearin' out yo' sittin' chairs."

"Yeah, Sam say most of 'em goes to church so they'll be sure to rise in Judgment. Dat's de day dat every secret is s'posed to be made known. They wants to be there and hear it *all*."

"Sam is *too* crazy! You can't stop laughin' when youse round him."

"Uuh hunh. He says he aims to be there hisself so he can find out who stole his corn-cob pipe."

"Pheoby, dat Sam of your'n just won't quit! Crazy thing!"

"Most of dese zigaboos is so het up over yo' business till they liable to hurry they-self to Judgment to find out about you if they don't soon know. You better make haste and tell 'em 'bout you and Tea Cake gittin' married, and if he taken all yo' money and went off wid some young gal, and where at he is now and where at is all yo' clothes dat you got to come back here in overhalls."

"Ah don't mean to bother wid tellin' 'em nothin', Pheoby. 'Tain't worth de trouble. You can tell 'em what Ah say if you wants to. Dat's just de same as me 'cause mah tongue is in mah friend's mouf."

"If you so desire Ah'll tell 'em what you tell me to tell 'em."

"To start off wid, people like dem wastes up too much time puttin' they mouf on things they don't know nothin' about. Now they got to look into me loving Tea Cake and see whether it was done right or not! They don't know if life is a mess of corn-meal dumplings, and if love is a bed-quilt!"

"So long as they get a name to gnaw on they don't care whose it is, and what about, 'specially if they can make it sound like evil."

"If they wants to see and know, why they don't come kiss and be kissed? Ah could then sit down and tell 'em things. Ah been a delegate to de big 'ssociation of life. Yessuh! De Grand Lodge, de big convention of livin' is just where Ah been dis year and a half y'all ain't seen me."

They sat there in the fresh young darkness close together. Pheoby eager to feel and do through Janie, but hating to show her zest for fear it might be thought mere curiosity. Janie full of that oldest human longing—self revelation. Pheoby held her tongue for a long time, but she couldn't help moving her feet. So Janie spoke.

"They don't need to worry about me and my overhalls long as Ah still got nine hundred dollars in de bank. Tea Cake got me into wearing 'em—following behind him. Tea Cake ain't wasted up no money of mine, and he ain't left me for no young gal, neither. He give me every consolation in de world. He'd tell 'em so too, if he was here. If he wasn't gone."

Pheoby dilated all over with eagerness, "Tea Cake gone?"

"Yeah, Pheoby, Tea Cake is gone. And dat's de only reason you see me back here—cause Ah ain't got nothing to make me happy no more where Ah was at. Down in the Everglades there, down on the muck."

"It's hard for me to understand what you mean, de way you tell it. And then again Ah'm hard of understandin' at times."

"Naw, 'tain't nothin' lak you might think. So 'tain't no use in me telling you somethin' unless Ah give you de understandin' to go 'long wid it. Unless you see de fur, a mink skin ain't no different from a coon hide. Looka heah, Pheoby, is Sam waitin' on you for his supper?"

"It's all ready and waitin'. If he ain't got sense enough to eat it, dat's his hard luck."

"Well then, we can set right where we is and talk. Ah got the house all opened up to let dis breeze get a little catchin'.

"Pheoby, we been kissin'-friends for twenty years, so Ah depend on you for a good thought. And Ah'm talking to you from dat standpoint."

Time makes everything old so the kissing, young darkness became a monstropolous old thing while Janie talked.

Chapter 2

Janie saw her life like a great tree in leaf with the things suffered, things enjoyed, things done and undone. Dawn and doom was in the branches.

"Ah know exactly what Ah got to tell yuh, but it's hard to know where to start at.

"Ah ain't never seen mah papa. And Ah didn't know 'im if Ah did. Mah mama neither. She was gone from round dere long before Ah wuz big enough tuh know. Mah grandma raised me. Mah grandma and de white folks she worked wid. She had a house out in de back-yard and dat's where Ah wuz born. They was quality white folks up dere in West Florida. Named Washburn. She had four gran'chillun on de place and all of us played together and dat's how come Ah never called mah Grandma nothin' but Nanny, 'cause dat's what everybody on de place called her. Nanny used to ketch us in our devilment and lick every youngun on de place and Mis' Washburn did same. Ah reckon dey never hit us ah lick amiss 'cause dem three boys and us two girls wuz pretty aggravatin', Ah speck.

"Ah was wid dem white chillun so much till Ah didn't know Ah wuzn't white till Ah was round six years old. Wouldn't have found it out then, but a man come long takin' pictures and without askin' anybody, Shelby, dat was de oldest boy, he told him to take us. Round a week later de man brought de picture for Mis' Washburn to see and pay him which she did, then give us all a good lickin'.

"So when we looked at de picture and everybody got pointed out there wasn't nobody left except a real dark little girl with long hair standing by Eleanor. Dat's where Ah wuz s'posed to be, but Ah couldn't recognize dat dark chile as me. So Ah ast, 'where is me? Ah don't see me.'

"Everybody laughed, even Mr. Washburn. Miss Nellie, de Mama of de chillun who come back home after her husband dead, she pointed to de dark one and said, 'Dat's you, Alphabet, don't you know yo' ownself?'

"Dey all useter call me Alphabet 'cause so many people had done named me different names. Ah looked at de picture a long time and seen it was mah dress and mah hair so Ah said:

"'Aw, aw! Ah'm colored!'

"Den dey all laughed real hard. But before Ah seen de picture Ah thought Ah wuz just like de rest.

"Us lived dere havin' fun till de chillun at school got to teasin' me 'bout livin' in de white folks' back-yard. Dere wuz uh knotty head gal name Mayrella dat useter git mad every time she look at me. Mis' Washburn useter dress me up in all de clothes her gran'chillun didn't need no mo' which still wuz better'n whut de rest uh de colored chillun had. And then she useter put hair ribbon on mah head fuh me tuh wear. Dat useter rile Mayrella uh lot. So she would pick at me all de time and put some others up tuh do de same. They'd push me 'way from de ring plays and make out they couldn't play wid nobody dat lived on premises. Den they'd tell me not to be takin' on over mah looks 'cause they mama told 'em 'bout de hound dawgs huntin' mah papa all night long. 'Bout Mr. Washburn and de sheriff puttin' de bloodhounds on de trail tuh ketch mah papa for whut he done tuh mah mama. Dey didn't tell about how he wuz seen tryin' tuh git in touch wid mah mama later on so he could marry her. Naw, dey didn't talk dat part of it atall. Dey made it sound real bad so as tuh crumple mah feathers. None of 'em didn't even remember whut his name wuz, but dey all knowed de bloodhound part by heart. Nanny didn't love tuh see me wid mah head hung down, so she figgered it would be mo' better fuh me if us had uh house. She got de land and everything and then Mis' Washburn helped out uh whole heap wid things."

Pheoby's hungry listening helped Janie to tell her story. So she went on thinking back to her young years and explaining them to her friend in soft, easy phrases while all around the house, the night time put on flesh and blackness.

She thought awhile and decided that her conscious life had commenced at Nanny's gate. On a late afternoon Nanny had called her to come inside the house because she had spied Janie letting Johnny Taylor kiss her over the gatepost.

It was a spring afternoon in West Florida. Janie had spent most of the day under a blossoming pear tree in the back-yard. She had been spending every minute that she could steal from her chores under that tree for the last three days. That was to say, ever since the first tiny bloom had opened. It had called her to come and gaze on a mystery. From barren brown stems to glistening leaf-buds; from the leaf-buds to snowy virginity of bloom. It stirred her tremendously. How? Why? It was like a flute song forgotten in another existence and remembered again. What? How? Why? This singing she heard that had nothing to do with her ears. The rose of the world was breathing out smell. It followed her through all her waking moments and caressed her in her sleep. It connected itself with other vaguely felt matters that had struck her outside observation and buried themselves in her flesh. Now they emerged and quested about her consciousness.

She was stretched on her back beneath the pear tree soaking in the alto chant of the visiting bees, the gold of the sun and the panting breath of the breeze when the inaudible voice of it all came to her. She saw a dust-bearing bee sink into the sanctum of a bloom; the thousand sister-calyxes arch to meet the love embrace and the ecstatic shiver of the tree from root to tiniest branch creaming in every blossom and frothing with delight. So this was a marriage? She had been summoned to behold a revelation. Then Janie felt a pain remorseless sweet that left her limp and languid.

After a while she got up from where she was and went over the little garden field entire. She was seeking confirmation of the voice and vision, and everywhere she found and acknowledged answers. A personal answer for all other creations except herself. She felt an answer seeking her, but where? When? How? She found herself at the kitchen door and stumbled inside. In the air of the room were flies tumbling and singing, marrying and giving in marriage. When she reached the narrow hallway she was reminded that her grandmother was home with a sick headache. She was lying across the bed asleep so Janie tipped on out of the front door. Oh to be a pear tree— *any* tree in bloom! With kissing bees singing of the beginning of the world! She was sixteen. She had glossy leaves and bursting buds and she wanted to struggle with life but it seemed to elude her. Where were the singing bees for her? Nothing on the place nor in her grandma's house answered her. She searched as much of the world as she could from the top of the front steps and then went on down to the front gate and leaned over to gaze up and down the road. Looking, waiting, breathing short with impatience. Waiting for the world to be made.

Through pollinated air she saw a glorious being coming up the road. In her former blindness she had known him as shiftless Johnny Taylor, tall and lean. That was before the golden dust of pollen had beglamored his rags and her eyes.

In the last stages of Nanny's sleep, she dreamed of voices. Voices far-off but persistent, and gradually coming nearer. Janie's voice. Janie talking in whispery snatches with a male voice she couldn't quite place. That brought her wide awake. She bolted upright and peered out of the window and saw Johnny Taylor lacerating her Janie with a kiss.

"Janie!"

The old woman's voice was so lacking in command and reproof, so full of crumbling dissolution,—that Janie half believed that Nanny had not seen her. So she extended herself outside of her dream and went inside of the house. That was the end of her childhood.

Nanny's head and face looked like the standing roots of some old tree that had been torn away by storm. Foundation of ancient power that no longer mattered. The cooling palma christi leaves that Janie had bound about her grandma's head with a white rag had wilted down and become part and parcel of the woman. Her eyes didn't bore and pierce. They diffused and melted Janie, the room and the world into one comprehension.

"Janie, youse uh 'oman, now, so—"

"Naw, Nanny, naw Ah ain't no real 'oman yet."

The thought was too new and heavy for Janie. She fought it away.

Nanny closed her eyes and nodded a slow, weary affirmation many times before she gave it voice.

"Yeah, Janie, youse got yo' womanhood on yuh. So Ah mout ez well tell yuh whut Ah been savin' up for uh spell. Ah wants to see you married right away."

"Me, married? Naw, Nanny, no ma'am! Whut Ah know 'bout uh husband?"

"Whut Ah seen just now is plenty for me, honey, Ah don't want no trashy nigger, no breath-and-britches, lak Johnny Taylor usin' yo' body to wipe his foots on."

Nanny's words made Janie's kiss across the gatepost seem like a manure pile after a rain.

"Look at me, Janie. Don't set dere wid yo' head hung down. Look at yo' ole grandma!" Her voice began snagging on the prongs of her feelings. "Ah don't want to be talkin' to you lak dis. Fact is Ah done been on mah knees to mah Maker many's de time askin' *please*—for Him not to make de burden too heavy for me to bear."

"Nanny, Ah just—Ah didn't mean nothin' bad."

"Dat's what makes me skeered. You don't mean no harm. You don't even know where harm is at. Ah'm ole now. Ah can't be always guidin' yo' feet from harm and danger. Ah wants to see you married right away."

"Who Ah'm goin' tuh marry off-hand lak dat? Ah don't know nobody."

"De Lawd will provide. He know Ah done bore de burden in de heat uh de day. Somebody done spoke to me 'bout you long time ago. Ah ain't said nothin' 'cause dat wasn't de way Ah placed you. Ah wanted yuh to school out and pick from a higher bush and a sweeter berry. But dat ain't yo' idea, Ah see."

"Nanny, who—who dat been askin' you for me?"

"Brother Logan Killicks. He's a good man, too."

"Naw, Nanny, no ma'am! Is dat whut he been hangin' round here for? He look like some ole skullhead in de grave yard."

The older woman sat bolt upright and put her feet to the floor, and thrust back the leaves from her face.

"So you don't want to marry off decent like, do yuh? You just wants to hug and kiss and feel around with first one man and then another, huh? You wants to make me suck de same sorrow yo' mama did, eh? Mah ole head ain't gray enough. Mah back ain't bowed enough to suit yuh!"

The vision of Logan Killicks was desecrating the pear tree, but Janie didn't know how to tell Nanny that. She merely hunched over and pouted at the floor.

"Janie."

"Yes, ma'am."

"You answer me when Ah speak. Don't you set dere poutin' wid me after all Ah done went through for you!"

She slapped the girl's face violently, and forced her head back so that their eyes met in struggle. With her hand uplifted for the second blow she saw the huge tear that welled up from Janie's heart and stood in each eye. She saw the terrible agony and the lips tightened down to hold back the cry and desisted. Instead she brushed back the heavy hair from Janie's face and stood there suffering and loving and weeping internally for both of them.

"Come to yo' Grandma, honey. Set in her lap lak yo' use tuh. Yo' Nanny wouldn't harm a hair uh yo' head. She don't want nobody else to do it neither if she kin help it. Honey, de white man is de ruler of everything as fur as Ah been able tuh find out. Maybe it's some place way off in de ocean where de black man is in power, but we don't know nothin' but what we see. So de white man throw down de load and tell de nigger man tuh pick it up. He pick it up because he have to, but he don't tote it. He hand it to his womenfolks. De nigger woman is de mule uh de world so fur as Ah can see. Ah been prayin' fuh it tuh be different wid you. Lawd, Lawd, Lawd!"

For a long time she sat rocking with the girl held tightly to her sunken breast. Janie's long legs dangled over one arm of the chair and the long braids of her hair swung low on the other side. Nanny half sung, half sobbed a running chant-prayer over the head of the weeping girl.

"Lawd have mercy! It was a long time on de way but Ah reckon it had to come. Oh Jesus! Do, Jesus! Ah done de best Ah could."

Finally, they both grew calm.

"Janie, how long you been 'lowin' Johnny Taylor to kiss you?"

"Only dis one time, Nanny. Ah don't love him at all. Whut made me do it is—oh, Ah don't know."

"Thank yuh, Massa Jesus."

"Ah ain't gointuh do it no mo', Nanny. Please don't make me marry Mr. Killicks."

"'Tain't Logan Killicks Ah wants you to have, baby, it's protection. Ah ain't gittin' ole, honey, Ah'm *done* ole. One mornin' soon, now, de angel wid de sword is gointuh stop by here. De day and de hour is hid from me, but it won't be long. Ah ast de Lawd when you was uh infant in mah arms to let me stay here till you got grown. He done spared me to see de day. Mah daily prayer now is tuh let dese golden moments rolls on a few days longer till Ah see you safe in life."

"Lemme wait, Nanny, please, jus' a lil bit mo'."

"Don't think Ah don't feel wid you, Janie, 'cause Ah do. Ah couldn't love yuh no more if Ah had uh felt yo' birth pains mahself. Fact uh de matter, Ah loves yuh a whole heap more'n Ah do yo' mama, de one Ah did birth. But you got to take in consideration you ain't no everyday chile like most of 'em. You ain't got no papa, you might jus' as well say no mama, for de good she do yuh. You ain't got nobody but me. And mah head is ole and tilted towards de grave. Neither can you stand alone by yo'self. De thought uh you bein' kicked around from pillar tuh post is uh hurtin' thing. Every tear you drop squeezes a cup uh blood outa mah heart. Ah got tuh try and do for you befo' mah head is cold."

A sobbing sigh burst out of Janie. The old woman answered her with little soothing pats of the hand.

"You know, honey, us colored folks is branches without roots and that makes things come round in queer ways. You in particular. Ah was born back due in slavery so it wasn't for me to fulfill my dreams of whut a woman oughta be and to do. Dat's one of de hold-backs of slavery. But nothing can't stop you from wishin'. You can't beat nobody down so low till you can rob 'em of they will. Ah didn't want to be used for a work-ox and a brood-sow and Ah didn't want mah daughter used dat way neither. It sho wasn't mah will for things to happen lak they did. Ah even hated de way you was born. But, all de same Ah said thank God, Ah got another chance. Ah wanted to preach a great sermon about colored women sittin' on high, but they wasn't no pulpit for me. Freedom found me wid a baby daughter in mah arms, so Ah said Ah'd take a broom and a cook-pot and throw up a highway through de wilderness for her. She would expound what Ah felt. But somehow she got lost offa de highway and next thing Ah knowed here you was in de world. So whilst Ah was tendin' you of nights Ah said Ah'd save de text for you. Ah been waitin' a long time, Janie, but nothin' Ah been through ain't too much if you just take a stand on high ground lak Ah dreamed."

Old Nanny sat there rocking Janie like an infant and thinking back and back. Mind-pictures brought feelings, and feelings dragged out dramas from the hollows of her heart.

"Dat mornin' on de big plantation close to Savannah, a rider come in a gallop tellin' 'bout Sherman takin' Atlanta. Marse Robert's son had done been kilt at Chickamauga. So he grabbed his gun and straddled his best horse and went off wid de rest of de gray-headed men and young boys to drive de Yankees back into Tennessee.

"They was all cheerin' and cryin' and shoutin' for de men dat was ridin' off. Ah couldn't see nothin' cause yo' mama wasn't but a week old, and Ah was flat uh mah back. But pretty soon he let on he forgot somethin' and run into mah cabin and made me let down mah hair for de last time. He sorta wropped his hand in it, pulled mah big toe, lak he always done, and was gone after de rest lak lightnin'. Ah heard 'em give one last whoop for him. Then de big house and de quarters got sober and silent.

"It was de cool of de evenin' when Mistis come walkin' in mah door. She throwed de door wide open and stood dere lookin' at me outa her eyes and her face. Look lak she been livin' through uh hundred years in January without one day of spring. She come stood over me in de bed.

"'Nanny, Ah come to see that baby uh yourn.'

"Ah tried not to feel de breeze off her face, but it got so cold in dere dat Ah was freezin' to death under the kivvers. So Ah couldn't move right away lak Ah aimed to. But Ah knowed Ah had to make haste and do it.

"'You better git dat kivver offa dat youngun and dat quick!' she clashed at me. 'Look lak you don't know who is Mistis on dis plantation, Madam. But Ah aims to show you.'

"By dat time I had done managed tuh unkivver mah baby enough for her to see de head and face.

"'Nigger, whut's yo' baby doin' wid gray eyes and yaller hair?' She begin tuh slap mah jaws ever which a'way. Ah never felt the fust ones 'cause Ah wuz too busy gittin' de kivver back over mah chile. But dem last lick burnt me lak fire. Ah had too many feelin's tuh tell which one tuh follow so Ah didn't cry and Ah didn't do nothin' else. But then she kept on astin me how come mah baby look white. She asted me dat maybe twenty-five or thirty times, lak she got tuh sayin' dat and couldn't help herself. So Ah told her, 'Ah don't know nothin' but what Ah'm told tuh do, 'cause Ah ain't nothin' but uh nigger and uh slave.'

"Instead of pacifyin' her lak Ah thought, look lak she got madder. But Ah reckon she was tired and wore out 'cause she didn't hit me no more. She went to de foot of de bed and wiped her hands on her handksher. 'Ah wouldn't dirty mah hands on yuh. But first thing in de mornin' de overseer will take you to de whippin' post and tie you down on yo' knees and cut de hide offa yo' yaller back. One hundred lashes wid a raw-hide on yo' bare back. Ah'll have you whipped till de blood run down to yo' heels! Ah mean to count de licks mahself. And if it kills you Ah'll stand de loss. Anyhow, as soon as dat brat is a month old Ah'm going to sell it offa dis place.'

"She flounced on off and let her wintertime wid me. Ah knowed mah body wasn't healed, but Ah couldn't consider dat. In de black dark Ah wrapped mah baby de best Ah knowed how and made it to de swamp by de river. Ah knowed de place was full uh moccasins and other bitin' snakes, but Ah was more skeered uh whut was behind me. Ah hide in dere day and night and suckled de baby every time she start to cry, for fear somebody might hear her and Ah'd git found. Ah ain't sayin' uh friend or two didn't feel mah care. And den de Good Lawd seen to it dat Ah wasn't taken. Ah don't see how come mah milk didn't kill mah chile, wid me so skeered and worried all de time. De noise uh de owls skeered me; de limbs of dem cypress trees took to crawlin' and movin' round after dark, and two three times Ah heered panthers prowlin' round. But nothin' never hurt me 'cause de Lawd knowed how it was.

"Den, one night Ah heard de big guns boomin' lak thunder. It kept up all night long. And de next mornin' Ah could see uh big ship at a distance and a great stirrin' round. So Ah wrapped Leafy up in moss and fixed her good in a tree and picked mah way on down to de landin'. The men was all in blue, and Ah heard people say Sherman was comin' to meet de boats in Savannah, and all of us slaves was free. So Ah run got mah baby and got in quotation wid people and found a place Ah could stay.

"But it was a long time after dat befo' de big Surrender at Richmond. Den de big bell ring in Atlanta and all de men in gray uniforms had to go to Moultrie, and bury their swords in de ground to show they was never to fight about slavery no mo'. So den we knowed we was free.

"Ah wouldn't marry nobody, though Ah could have uh heap uh times, cause Ah didn't want nobody mistreating mah baby. So Ah got with some good white people and come down here in West Florida to work and make de sun shine on both sides of de street for Leafy.

"Mah Madam help me wid her just lak she been doin' wid you. Ah put her in school when it got so it was a school to put her in. Ah was 'spectin' to make a school teacher outa her.

"But one day she didn't come home at de usual time and Ah waited and waited, but she never come all dat night. Ah took a lantern and went round askin' everybody but nobody ain't seen her. De next mornin' she come crawlin' in on her hands and knees. A sight to see. Dat school teacher had done hid her in de woods all night long, and he had done raped mah baby and run on off just before day.

"She was only seventeen, and somethin' lak dat to happen! Lawd a'mussy! Look lak Ah kin see it all over again. It was a long time before she was well, and by dat time we knowed you was on de way. And after you was born she took to drinkin' likker and stayin' out nights. Couldn't git her to stay here and nowhere else. Lawd knows where she is right now. She ain't dead, 'cause Ah'd know it by mah feelings, but sometimes Ah wish she was at rest.

"And, Janie, maybe it wasn't much, but Ah done de best Ah kin by you. Ah raked and scraped and bought dis lil piece uh land so you wouldn't have to stay in de white folks' yard and tuck yo' head befo' other chillun at school. Dat was all right when you was little. But when you got big enough to understand things, Ah wanted you to look upon yo'self. Ah don't want yo' feathers always crumpled by folks throwin' up things in yo' face. And Ah can't die easy thinkin' maybe de menfolks white or black is makin' a spit cup outa you: Have some sympathy fuh me. Put me down easy, Janie, Ah'm a cracked plate."

Chapter 3

There are years that ask questions and years that answer. Janie had had no chance to know things, so she had to ask. Did marriage end the cosmic loneliness of the unmated? Did marriage compel love like the sun the day?

In the few days to live before she went to Logan Killicks and his often-mentioned sixty acres, Janie asked inside of herself and out. She was back and forth to the pear tree continuously wondering and thinking. Finally out of Nanny's talk and her own conjectures she made a sort of comfort for herself. Yes, she would love Logan after they were married. She could see no way for it to come about, but Nanny and the old folks had said it, so it must be so. Husbands and wives always loved each other, and that was what marriage meant. It was just so. Janie felt glad of the thought, for then it wouldn't seem so destructive and mouldy. She wouldn't be lonely anymore.

Janie and Logan got married in Nanny's parlor of a Saturday evening with three cakes and big platters of fried rabbit and chicken. Everything to eat in abundance. Nanny and Mrs. Washburn had seen to that. But nobody put anything on the seat of

Logan's wagon to make it ride glorious on the way to his house. It was a lonesome place like a stump in the middle of the woods where nobody had ever seen. The house was absent of flavor, too. But anyhow Janie went on inside to wait for love to begin. The new moon had been up and down three times before she got worried in mind. Then she went to see Nanny in Mrs. Washburn's kitchen on the day for beaten biscuits.

Nanny beamed all out with gladness and made her come up to the bread board so she could kiss her.

"Lawd a'mussy, honey, Ah sho is glad tuh see mah chile! G'wan inside and let Mis' Washburn know youse heah. Umph! Umph! Umph! How is dat husband uh yourn?"

Janie didn't go in where Mrs. Washburn was. She didn't say anything to match up with Nanny's gladness either. She just fell on a chair with her hips and sat there. Between the biscuits and her beaming pride Nanny didn't notice for a minute. But after a while she found the conversation getting lonesome so she looked up at Janie.

"Whut's de matter, sugar? You ain't none too spry dis mornin'."

"Oh, nothin' much, Ah reckon. Ah come to get a lil information from you."

The old woman looked amazed, then gave a big clatter of laughter. "Don't tell me you done got knocked up already, less see—dis Saturday it's two month and two weeks."

"No'm, Ah don't think so anyhow." Janie blushed a little.

"You ain't got nothin' to be shamed of, honey, youse uh married 'oman. You got yo' lawful husband same as Mis' Washburn or anybody else!"

"Ah'm all right dat way. Ah *know* 'tain't nothin' dere."

"You and Logan been fussin'? Lawd, Ah know dat grass-gut, liver-lipted nigger ain't done took and beat mah baby already! Ah'll take a stick and salivate 'im!"

"No'm, he ain't even talked 'bout hittin' me. He says he never mean to lay de weight uh his hand on me in malice. He chops all de wood he think Ah wants and den he totes it inside de kitchen for me. Keeps both water buckets full."

"Humph! don't 'spect all dat tuh keep up. He ain't kissin' yo' mouf when he carry on over yuh lak dat. He's kissin' yo' foot and 'tain't in uh man tuh kiss foot long. Mouf kissin' is on uh equal and dat's natural but when dey got to bow down tuh love, dey soon straightens up."

"Yes'm."

"Well, if he do all dat whut you come in heah wid uh face long as mah arm for?"

" 'Cause you told me Ah mus gointer love him, and, and Ah don't. Maybe if somebody was to tell me how, Ah could do it."

"You come heah wid yo' mouf full uh foolishness on uh busy day. Heah you got uh prop tuh lean on all yo' bawn days, and big protection, and everybody got tuh tip dey hat tuh you and call you Mis' Killicks, and you come worryin' me 'bout love."

"But Nanny, Ah wants to want him sometimes. Ah don't want him to do all de wantin'."

"If you don't want him, you sho oughta. Heah you is wid de onliest organ in town, amongst colored folks, in yo' parlor. Got a house bought and paid for and sixty acres uh land right on de big road and . . . Lawd have mussy! Dat's de very prong all us black women gits hung on. Dis love! Dat's just whut's got us uh pullin' and uh haulin' and sweatin' and doin' from can't see in de mornin' till can't see at night. Dat's how come de ole folks say dat bein' uh fool don't kill nobody. It jus' makes you sweat. Ah betcha you wants some dressed up dude dat got to look at de sole of his shoe everytime he cross de street tuh see whether he got enough leather dere tuh make it across. You can buy and sell such as dem wid what you got. In fact you can buy 'em and give 'em away."

"Ah ain't studyin' 'bout none of 'em. At de same time Ah ain't takin' dat ole land tuh heart neither. Ah could throw ten acres of it over de fence every day and never look back to see where it fell. Ah feel de same way 'bout Mr. Killicks too. Some folks never was meant to be loved and he's one of 'em."

"How come?"

"'Cause Ah hates de way his head is so long one way and so flat on de sides and dat pone uh fat back uh his neck."

"He never made his own head. You talk so silly."

"Ah don't keer who made it, Ah don't like de job. His belly is too big too, now, and his toe-nails look lak mule foots. And 'tain't nothin' in de way of him washin' his feet every evenin' before he comes tuh bed. 'Tain't nothin' tuh hinder him 'cause Ah places de water for him. Ah'd ruther be shot wid tacks than tuh turn over in de bed and stir up de air whilst he is in dere. He don't even never mention nothin' pretty."

She began to cry.

"Ah wants things sweet wid mah marriage lak when you sit under a pear tree and think. Ah . . ."

"'Tain't no use in you cryin', Janie. Grandma done been long uh few roads her-self. But folks is meant to cry 'bout somethin' or other. Better leave things de way dey is. Youse young yet. No tellin' whut mout happen befo' you die. Wait awhile, baby. Yo' mind will change."

Nanny sent Janie along with a stern mien, but she dwindled all the rest of the day as she worked. And when she gained the privacy of her own little shack she stayed on her knees so long she forgot she was there herself. There is a basin in the mind where words float around on thought and thought on sound and sight. Then there is a depth of thought untouched by words, and deeper still a gulf of formless feelings untouched by thought. Nanny entered this infinity of conscious pain again on her old knees. To-wards morning she muttered, "Lawd, you know mah heart. Ah done de best Ah could do. De rest is left to you." She scuffled up from her knees and fell heavily across the bed. A month later she was dead.

So Janie waited a bloom time, and a green time and an orange time. But when the pollen again gilded the sun and sifted down on the world she began to stand around the gate and expect things. What things? She didn't know exactly. Her breath was gusty and short. She knew things that nobody had ever told her. For instance, the words of the trees and the wind. She often spoke to falling seeds and said, "Ah hope you fall on soft ground," because she had heard seeds saying that to each other as they passed. She knew the world was a stallion rolling in the blue pasture of ether. She knew that God tore down the old world every evening and built a new one by sun-up. It was wonderful to see it take form with the sun and emerge from the gray dust of its making. The familiar people and things had failed her so she hung over the gate and looked up the road towards way off. She knew now that marriage did not make love. Janie's first dream was dead, so she became a woman.

Carson McCullers

(1917–1967)

Carson McCullers was born in Columbus, Georgia, on February 19, 1917. At seventeen, she traveled to New York City to study piano at Juilliard School of Music. Unfortunately, she lost her money and could not attend Juilliard. However, she began devoting herself to writing. She studied creative writing at Columbia and New York University.

In 1937, McCullers married Reeves McCullers, and the couple moved to North Carolina, where she wrote *The Heart Is a Lonely Hunter* (1940). The book was made into a film starring Alan Arkin in 1968. McCullers and her husband separated in 1940, and she returned to New York. They remarried in 1945. She attempted suicide in 1948; her husband killed himself in Paris in 1953. *The Square Root of Wonderful* was published in 1958. After World War II, she lived chiefly in Paris and was a close friend of Truman Capote and Tennessee Williams.

Selected works include *Reflections in a Golden Eye* (1941); *The Member of the Wedding* (1946); *The Ballad of the Sad Café* (1951); *The Novels and the Stories* (1951); *The Clocks Without Hands* (1961); and *The Mortgaged Heart* (1971).

McCullers died in New York on September 29, 1967.

A Tree • A Rock • A Cloud

It was raining that morning, and still very dark. When the boy reached the streetcar café he had almost finished his route and he went in for a cup of coffee. The place was an all-night café owned by a bitter and stingy man called Leo. After the raw, empty street the café seemed friendly and bright: along the counter there were a couple of soldiers, three spinners from the cotton mill, and in a corner a man who sat hunched over with his nose and half his face down in a beer mug. The boy wore a helmet such as aviators wear. When he went into the café he unbuckled the chin strap and raised the right flap up over his pink little ear; often as he drank his coffee someone would speak to him in a friendly way. But this morning Leo did not look into his face and none of the men were talking. He paid and was leaving the café when a voice called out to him:

"Son! Hey Son!"

He turned back and the man in the corner was crooking his finger and nodding to him. He had brought his face out of the beer mug and he seemed suddenly very happy. The man was long and pale, with a big nose and faded orange hair.

"Hey Son!"

The boy went toward him. He was an undersized boy of about twelve, with one shoulder drawn higher than the other because of the weight of the paper sack. His face was shallow, freckled, and his eyes were round child eyes.

"Yeah Mister?"

The man laid one hand on the paper boy's shoulders, then grasped the boy's chin and turned his face slowly from one side to the other. The boy shrank back uneasily.

"Say! What's the big idea?"

The boy's voice was shrill; inside the café it was suddenly very quiet.

The man said slowly: "I love you."

All along the counter the men laughed. The boy, who had scowled and sidled away, did not know what to do. He looked over the counter at Leo, and Leo watched him with a weary, brittle jeer. The boy tried to laugh also. But the man was serious and sad.

"I did not mean to tease you, Son," he said. "Sit down and have a beer with me. There is something I have to explain."

Cautiously, out of the corner of his eye, the paper boy questioned the men along the counter to see what he should do. But they had gone back to their beer or their breakfast and did not notice him. Leo put a cup of coffee on the counter and a little jug of cream.

"He is a minor," Leo said.

The paper boy slid himself up onto the stool. His ear beneath the upturned flap of the helmet was very small and red. The man was nodding at him soberly. "It is important," he said. Then he reached in his hip pocket and brought out something which he held up in the palm of his hand for the boy to see.

"Look very carefully," he said.

The boy stared, but there was nothing to look at very carefully. The man held in his big, grimy palm a photograph. It was the face of a woman, but blurred, so that only the hat and the dress she was wearing stood out clearly.

"See?" the man asked.

The boy nodded and the man placed another picture in his palm. The woman was standing on a beach in a bathing suit. The suit made her stomach very big, and that was the main thing you noticed.

"Got a good look?" He leaned over closer and finally asked: "You ever seen her before?"

The boy sat motionless, staring slantwise at the man. "Not so I know of."

"Very well." The man blew on the photographs and put them back into his pocket. "That was my wife."

"Dead?" the boy asked.

Slowly the man shook his head. He pursed his lips as though about to whistle and answered in a long-drawn way: "Nuuu—" he said. "I will explain."

The beer on the counter before the man was in a large brown mug. He did not pick it up to drink. Instead he bent down and, putting his face over the rim, he rested there for a moment. Then with both hands he tilted the mug and sipped.

"Some night you'll go to sleep with your big nose in a mug and drown," said Leo. "Prominent transient drowns in beer. That would be a cute death."

The paper boy tried to signal to Leo. While the man was not looking he screwed up his face and worked his mouth to question soundlessly: "Drunk?" But Leo only raised his eyebrows and turned away to put some pink strips of bacon on the grill. The man pushed the mug away from him, straightened himself, and folded his loose crooked hands on the counter. His face was sad as he looked at the paper boy. He did not blink, but from time to time the lids closed down with delicate gravity over his pale green eyes. It was nearing dawn and the boy shifted the weight of the paper sack.

"I am talking about love," the man said. "With me it is a science."

The boy half slid down from the stool. But the man raised his forefinger, and there was something about him that held the boy and would not let him go away.

"Twelve years ago I married the woman in the photograph. She was my wife for one year, nine months, three days, and two nights. I loved her. Yes. . . ." He tightened his blurred, rambling voice and said again: "I loved her. I thought also that she loved me. I was a railroad engineer. She had all home comforts and luxuries. It never crept into my brain that she was not satisfied. But do you know what happened?"

"Mgneeow!" said Leo.

The man did not take his eyes from the boy's face. "She left me. I came in one night and the house was empty and she was gone. She left me."

"With a fellow?" the boy asked.

Gently the man placed his palm down on the counter. "Why naturally, Son. A woman does not run off like that alone."

The café was quiet, the soft rain black and endless in the street outside. Leo pressed down the frying bacon with the prongs of his long fork. "So you have been chasing the floozie for eleven years. You frazzled old rascal!"

For the first time the man glanced at Leo. "Please don't be vulgar. Besides, I was not speaking to you." He turned back to the boy and said in a trusting and secretive undertone: "Let's not pay any attention to him. O.K.?"

The paper boy nodded doubtfully.

"It was like this," the man continued. "I am a person who feels many things. All my life one thing after another has impressed me. Moonlight. The leg of a pretty girl. One thing after another. But the point is that when I had enjoyed anything there was a peculiar sensation as though it was laying around loose in me. Nothing seemed to finish itself up or fit in with the other things. Women? I had my portion of them. The same. Afterwards laying around loose in me. I was a man who had never loved."

Very slowly he closed his eyelids, and the gesture was like a curtain drawn at the end of a scene in a play. When he spoke again his voice was excited and the words came fast—the lobes of his large, loose ears seemed to tremble.

"Then I met this woman. I was fifty-one years old and she always said she was thirty. I met her at a filling station and we were married within three days. And do you know what it was like? I just can't tell you. All I had ever felt was gathered together around this woman. Nothing lay around loose in me any more but was finished up by her."

The man stopped suddenly and stroked his long nose. His voice sank down to a steady and reproachful undertone: "I'm not explaining this right. What happened was this. There were these beautiful feelings and loose little pleasures inside me. And this woman was something like an assembly line for my soul. I run these little pieces of myself through her and I come out complete. Now do you follow me?"

"What was her name?" the boy asked.

"Oh," he said. "I called her Dodo. But that is immaterial."

"Did you try to make her come back?"

The man did not seem to hear. "Under the circumstances you can imagine how I felt when she left me."

Leo took the bacon from the grill and folded two strips of it between a bun. He had a gray face, with slitted eyes, and a pinched nose saddled by faint blue shadows. One of the mill workers signaled for more coffee and Leo poured it. He did not give refills on coffee free. The spinner ate breakfast there every morning, but the better Leo knew his customers the stingier he treated them. He nibbled his own bun as though he grudged it to himself.

"And you never got hold of her again?"

The boy did not know what to think of the man, and his child's face was uncertain with mingled curiosity and doubt. He was new on the paper route; it was still strange to him to be out in the town in the black, queer early morning.

"Yes," the man said. "I took a number of steps to get her back. I went around trying to locate her. I went to Tulsa where she had folks. And to Mobile. I went to every town she had ever mentioned to me, and I hunted down every man she had formerly been connected with. Tulsa, Atlanta, Chicago, Cheehaw, Memphis. . . . For the better part of two years I chased around the country trying to lay hold of her."

"But the pair of them had vanished from the face of the earth!" said Leo.

"Don't listen to him," the man said confidentially. "And also just forget those two years. They are not important. What matters is that around the third year a curious thing begun to happen to me."

"What?" the boy asked.

The man leaned down and tilted his mug to take a sip of beer. But as he hovered over the mug his nostrils fluttered slightly; he sniffed the staleness of the beer and did not drink. "Love is a curious thing to begin with. At first I thought only of getting her back. It was a kind of mania. But then as time went on I tried to remember her. But do you know what happened?"

"No," the boy said.

"When I laid myself down on a bed and tried to think about her my mind became a blank. I couldn't see her. I would take out her pictures and look. No good. Nothing doing. A blank. Can you imagine it?"

"Say Mac!" Leo called down the counter. "Can you imagine this bozo's mind a blank!"

Slowly, as though fanning away flies, the man waved his hand. His green eyes were concentrated and fixed on the shallow little face of the paper boy.

"But a sudden piece of glass on a sidewalk. Or a nickel tune in a music box. A shadow on a wall at night. And I would remember. It might happen in a street and I would cry or bang my head against a lamppost. You follow me?"

"A piece of glass . . ." the boy said.

"Anything. I would walk around and I had no power of how and when to remember her. You think you can put up a kind of shield. But remembering don't come to a man face forward—it corners around sideways. I was at the mercy of everything I saw and heard. Suddenly instead of me combing the countryside to find her she begun to chase me around in my very soul. *She* chasing *me*, mind you! And in my soul."

The boy asked finally: "What part of the country were you in then?"

"Ooh," the man groaned. "I was a sick mortal. It was like smallpox. I confess, Son, that I boozed. I fornicated. I committed any sin that suddenly appealed to me. I am loath to confess it but I will do so. When I recall that period it is all curdled in my mind, it was so terrible."

The man leaned his head down and tapped his forehead on the counter. For a few seconds he stayed bowed over in this position, the back of his stringy neck covered with orange furze, his hands with their long warped fingers held palm to palm in an attitude of prayer. Then the man straightened himself; he was smiling and suddenly his face was bright and tremulous and old.

"It was in the fifth year that it happened," he said. "And with it I started my science."

Leo's mouth jerked with a pale, quick grin. "Well none of we boys are getting any younger," he said. Then with sudden anger he balled up a dishcloth he was holding and threw it down hard on the floor. "You draggle-tailed old Romeo!"

"What happened?" the boy asked.

The old man's voice was high and clear: "Peace," he answered.

"Huh?"

"It is hard to explain scientifically, Son," he said. "I guess the logical explanation is that she and I had fleed around from each other for so long that finally we just got tangled up together and lay down and quit. Peace. A queer and beautiful blankness. It was spring in Portland and the rain came every afternoon. All evening I just stayed there on my bed in the dark. All that is how the science come to me."

The windows in the streetcar were pale blue with light. The two soldiers paid for their beers and opened the door—one of the soldiers combed his hair and wiped off his muddy puttees before they went outside. The three mill workers bent silently over their breakfasts. Leo's clock was ticking on the wall.

"It is this. And listen carefully. I meditated on love and reasoned it out. I realized what is wrong with us. Men fall in love for the first time. And what do they fall in love with?"

The boy's soft mouth was partly open and he did not answer.

"A woman," the old man said. "Without science, with nothing to go by, they undertake the most dangerous and sacred experience in God's earth. They fall in love with a woman. Is that correct, Son?"

"Yeah," the boy said faintly.

"They start at the wrong end of love. They begin at the climax. Can you wonder it is so miserable? Do you know how men should love?"

The old man reached over and grasped the boy by the collar of his leather jacket. He gave him a gentle little shake and his green eyes gazed down unblinking and grave.

"Son, do you know how love should be begun?"

The boy sat small and listening and still. Slowly he shook his head. The old man leaned closer and whispered:

"A tree. A rock. A cloud."

It was still raining outside in the street: a mild, gray, endless rain. The mill whistle blew for the six o'clock shift and the three spinners paid and went away. There was no one in the café but Leo, the old man, and the little paper boy.

"The weather was like this in Portland," he said. "At the time my science was begun. I meditated and I started very cautious. I would pick up something from the street and take it home with me. I bought a goldfish and I concentrated on the goldfish and I loved it. I graduated from one thing to another. Day by day I was getting this technique. On the road from Portland to San Diego—"

"Aw shut up!" screamed Leo suddenly. "Shut up! Shut up!"

The old man still held the collar of the boy's jacket; he was trembling and his face was earnest and bright and wild. "For six years now I have gone around by myself and built up my science. And now I am a master, Son. I can love anything. No longer do I have to think about it even. I see a street full of people and a beautiful light comes in me. I watch a bird in the sky. Or I meet a traveler on the road. Everything, Son. And anybody. All stranger and all loved! Do you realize what a science like mine can mean?"

The boy held himself stiffly, his hands curled tight around the counter edge. Finally he asked: "Did you ever really find that lady?"

"What? What say, Son?"

"I mean," the boy asked timidly. "Have you fallen in love with a woman again?"

The old man loosened his grasp on the boy's collar. He turned away and for the first time his green eyes had a vague and scattered look. He lifted the mug from the counter, drank down the yellow beer. His head was shaking slowly from side to side. Then finally he answered: "No, Son. You see that is the last step in my science. I go cautious. And I am not quite ready yet."

"Well!" said Leo. "Well well well!"

The old man stood in the open doorway. "Remember," he said. Framed there in the gray damp light of the early morning he looked shrunken and seedy and frail. But his smile was bright. "Remember I love you," he said with a last nod. And the door closed quietly behind him.

The boy did not speak for a long time. He pulled down the bangs on his forehead and slid his grimy little forefinger around the rim of his empty cup. Then without looking at Leo he finally asked:

"Was he drunk?"

"No," said Leo shortly.

The boy raised his clear voice higher. "Then was he a dope fiend?"

"No."

The boy looked up at Leo, and his flat little face was desperate, his voice urgent and shrill. "Was he crazy? Do you think he was a lunatic?" The paper boy's voice dropped suddenly with doubt. "Leo? Or not?"

But Leo would not answer him. Leo had run a night café for fourteen years, and he held himself to be a critic of craziness. There were the town characters and also the transients who roamed in from the night. He knew the manias of all of them. But he did not want to satisfy the questions of the waiting child. He tightened his pale face and was silent.

So the boy pulled down the right flap of his helmet and as he turned to leave he made the only comment that seemed safe to him, the only remark that could not be laughed down and despised:

"He sure has done a lot of traveling."

William Alexander Percy

(1885–1942)

Born on May 14, 1885, in Greenville, Mississippi, William Alexander Percy read widely in the extensive home library of his parents. He was educated at the University of the South in Tennessee, where he got his B.A. in 1904, and at Harvard University in Massachusetts, where he got his LL.B. in 1908. He was an attorney from 1908 to 1940. Although he remained unmarried, he adopted three orphan cousins, one of whom was writer Walker Percy. In 1918, he was decorated with the Croix de Guerre for distinguished military service in France during World War I.

Percy's works include *Sappho in Levkas, and Other Poems* (1915); *In April Once* (1920); *Enzio's Kingdom and Other Poems* (1924); *Selected Poems* (1930); *Lanterns on the Levee: Recollections of a Planter's Son* (1941); *The Collected Poems of William Alexander Percy* (1943); *Of Silence and of Stars* (1953); and *Sewanee* (1982). Percy died on January 21, 1942, in Greenville, his birthplace.

from *Lanterns on the Levee*

Chapter IX. Sewanee

I had been exposed to enough personalities mellow and magnificent to educate Hottentot and in the process I had somehow received enough formal instruction to condition me for college. Fafar and his brothers had gone to Princeton, Father and his brothers to Sewanee (The University of the South, an Episcopal institution) and to Virginia Law School. Where I should go no one knew, least of all myself, so because it was fairly near and healthy and genteel and inexpensive, Father and Mother drew a long sigh, set me on the train bound for Sewanee, and betook themselves to Europe with Mr. Cook, on their first foreign tour. I was fifteen plus one month, in short trousers, small, weakly, self-reliant, and ignorant as an egg. I had the dimmest notion of how children were born though I knew it required a little co-operation; I had never heard of fraternities, I had never read a football score, I had never known a confidant or been in love. My instructions had been to enter the preparatory school, which was military, but I watched the grammar-school boys in their dusty ill-kept uniforms and I suspected they smelled bad. I developed an antipathy to the military life—which I've never overcome—and so, to the astonishment of the college authorities, I presented myself to them for entrance exams, and passed.

By no means brilliant, I studied hard, often getting up at six, to the scandal of other students, to struggle with Latin and math, and I made excellent grades. I don't know why I studied hard, but I had no shadow of a doubt it was the thing to do. English was my favorite course, whether because of the huge undigested gobs of the best I'd already read or because of Dr. Henneman, it would be hard to guess. He was passionate, black-bearded, bespectacled, with an adoration for *Beowulf*, Chaucer, Shakespeare, a grimace for Dr. Donne and the metaphysical school (oh, woeful unshakable influence), and, much more important, a capacity for furious moral tantrums in which, his beard on end clear out to his ears, he would beat the desk with his fist and roar:

"My God, gentlemen, *do* something!" We earnestly intended to, after such a scene.

And the other great course of those days was Dr. DuBose's Ethics. He was a tiny silver saint who lived elsewhere, being more conversant with the tongues of angels than of men. Sometimes sitting on the edge of his desk in his black gown, talking haltingly of Aristotle, he would suspend, rapt, in some mid air beyond our ken, murmuring: "The starry heavens—" followed by indefinite silence. We, with a glimpse of things, would tiptoe out of the classroom, feeling luminous, and never knowing when he returned to time and space.

It was a small college, in wooded mountains, its students drawn from the impoverished Episcopal gentry of the South, its boarding-houses and dormitories presided over by widows of bishops and Confederate generals. Great Southern names were thick—Kirby-Smith, Elliott, Quintard, Polk, Gorgas, Shoup, Gailor. The only things it wasn't rich in were worldly goods, sociology, and science. A place to be hopelessly sentimental about and to unfit one for anything except the good life.

Until I came to Sewanee I had been utterly without intimates of my own age. I had liked children whose pleasures were my pleasures, but they had not been persons to me and had left no mark. Here I suddenly found myself a social being, among young creatures of charm and humor, more experienced than I, but friendly and fascinating. I was never generally popular, but I had more than my share of friends. I am never surprised at people liking me, I'm always surprised if they don't. I like them and, if they don't like me, I feel they've made a mistake, they've misunderstood something. There's so much backing and filling about getting acquainted—indirection confuses and sometimes deceives me.

Probably because of my size and age and length of trouser I was plentifully adopted. It is a long time now: some of them have gone the journey, others have fallen by the road and can't go on and are just waiting, and a few have won through to autumn. But then the springtime was on them and they taught and tended me in the greenwoods as the Centaurs did Achilles—I don't know how I ever recovered to draw my own bow. Percy Huger, noble and beautiful like a sleepy St. Bernard; Elliott Cage, full of dance-steps and song-snatches, tender and protective, and sad beneath; Paul Ellerbe, who first read me *Dover Beach*, thereby disclosing the rosy mountain-ranges of the Victorians; Harold Abrams, dark and romantic with his violin, quoting the *Rubáiyát* and discoursing Shaw; Parson Masterson, jostling with religion, unexpected and quaint; Sinkler Manning, a knight who met a knight's death at Montfaucon; Arthur Gray, full of iridescence, discovering new paths and views in the woods and the world; Huger Jervey, brilliant and bumptious then, brilliant and wise now, and so human; and more, many more, all with gifts they shared with me, all wastrel creditors who never collected. Peace to them, and endless gratitude.

I suppose crises occurred, problems pressed, decisions had to be made, those four shining years, but for me only one altered the sunlight. Once a month I would ride then miles down the wretched mountain road to Winchester, go to confession, hear mass, and take communion. I had been thinking, I had never stopped thinking, I was determined to be honest if it killed me. So I knelt in the little Winchester church examining my conscience and preparing for confession. How it came about did not seem sudden or dramatic or anything but sad. As I started to the confessional I knew there was no use going, no priest could absolve me, no church could direct my life or my judgment, what most believed I could not believe. What belief remained there was no way of gauging yet. I only knew there was an end, I could no longer pretend to myself or cry: "Mea culpa. Help Thou mine unbelief." It was over, and forever. I rode back to the leafy mountain mournful and unregretful, knowing thenceforth I should breathe a starker and a colder air, with no place to go when I was tired. I would be getting home to the mountain, but for some things there was no haven, the friendly Centaurs couldn't help: from now on I would be living with my own self.

There's no way to tell of youth or of Sewanee, which is youth, directly; it must be done obliquely and by parable. I come back to the mountain often and see with a pang, however different it may be to me, it is no different, though Huger and Sinkler and I are forgotten, Then with humility I try to blend and merge the past and the present, to reach the unchanging essence. To my heart the essence, the unbroken melodic theme, sounds something like this:

The college has about three hundred young men or inmates, or students as they are sometimes called, and besides, quite a number of old ladies, who always were old and ladies, and who never die. It's a long way away, even from Chattanooga, in the middle of woods, on top of a bastion of mountains crenelated with blue coves. It is so beautiful that people who have once been there always, one way or another, come back. For such as can detect apple green in an evening sky, it is Arcadia—not the one that never used to be, but the one that many people always live in; only this one can be shared.

In winter there is a powder of snow; the pines sag like ladies in ermine, and the other trees are glassy and given to creaking. Later, arbutus is under the dead leaves where they have drifted, but unless you look for it betimes, you'll find instead puffs of ghost caught under the higher trees, and that's dogwood, and puffs of the saddest color in the world that's tender too, and that's redbud, which some say is pink and some purple and some give up but simply must write a poem about. The rest of the flowers you wouldn't believe in if I told you, so I'll tell you: anemones and hepaticas and blood-root that troop under the cliffs, always together, too ethereal to mix with reds and yellows or even pinks; and violets everywhere, in armies. The gray and purple and blue sort you'll credit, but not the tiny yellow ones with the bronze throats, nor the jackrabbit ones with royal purple ears and faces of pale lavender that stare without a bit of violet modesty. If you've seen azalea—and miscalled it wild honeysuckle, probably—you still don't know what it is unless you've seen it here, with its incredible range of color from white through shell pink to deep coral (and now and then a tuft of orange that doesn't match anything else in the whole woods), and its perfume actually dangerous, so pagan it is. After it you'd better hunt for a calacanthus with brown petals (what else likes its petal brown?) and a little melancholy in its scent, to sober you. We call our bluets "innocence," for that's what they are. They troop near the iris, which when coarsened by gardens some call fleur-de-lis, and others, who care nothing about names, flags. Our orchids we try to make respectable by christening them "lady-slippers," but they still look as if they had been designed by D. H. Lawrence—only they're rose- and canary-colored.

After Orion has set—in other words, when the most fragile and delicate and wistful things have abandoned loveliness for fructifying—the laurel, rank and magnificent for all its tender pink, starts hanging bouquets as big as hydrangeas on its innumerable bushes. But on moonlight nights there's no use trying to say it isn't a glory and a madness! And so the summer starts—summer, when we're not seraph-eyed enough to see flowers even if there were any. In the fall, when our souls return, a little worse off, a little snively, there are foggy wisps of asters whose quality only a spider would hint at aloud, and in the streams where the iris forgathered there are parnassia, the snowdrop's only kin. Mountain-folk alone have seen their virginal processions, ankle-deep in water, among scarlet leaves, each holding a round green shield and carrying at the end of a spear, no thicker than a broomstraw, a single pale green star. Last, chilly and inaccessible and sorrowful, in the damp of the deep woods, come the gentians, sea-blue and hushed.

Now all these delights the Arcadians not infrequently neglect. You might stroll across the campus and quadrangles of a sunny afternoon and guess from the emptiness and warm quiet there that they had gone out among the trees, lying perhaps in shadow, idly, like fauns, and whistling at the sky. Some may be so unoccupied, though not faun-like to themselves. But more I fear will be amiably and discreetly behind closed doors on the third floor, playing not flutes or lyres or even saxophones, but poker. Still others will be bowed over a table, vexed to the soul with the return of Xenophon or the fall, too long delayed, of a certain empire. A few will be off in the valley bargaining for a beverage called mountain-dew with a splendid virile old vixen who in that way has always earned a pleasant livelihood. Later they will have consumed their purchase to the last sprightly drop and will be bawling out deplorable ballads and pounding tables and putting crockery to uncouth noisy uses in the neighborhood of one or another of the old ladies, who will appear scandalized as expected, but who in the privacy of her own chamber will laugh soundlessly till her glasses fall off on her bosom and have to be wiped with a handkerchief smelling of orris-root.

Yet I would not have you think that the Arcadians are all or always ribald. Even those with a bacchic turn are full of grace and on occasion given to marvels. I myself have witnessed one of them in the ghastly dawn, slippered and unpantalooned, his chaplet a wet towel, sitting in the corner of his room, his feet against the wall, quite alone, reading in a loud boomy voice more beautiful than chimes *Kubla Khan* and the *Ode to a Nightingale*. One afternoon of thick yellow sunshine I was audience to another who stood on an abandoned windlass with tulip trees and a blue vista for backdrop reciting pentameters, which though you may never have heard, we thought too rich and cadenced for the race of men ever to forget. I can remember them even now for you:

> I dreamed last night of a dome of beaten gold
> To be a counter-glory to the Sun.
> There shall the eagle blindly dash himself,
> There the first beam shall strike, and there the Moon
> Shall aim all night her argent archery;
> And it shall be the tryst of sundered stars,
> The haunt of dead and dreaming Solomon;
> Shall send a light upon the lost in hell,
> And flashings upon faces without hope—
> And I will think in gold and dream in silver,
> Imagine in marble and in bronze conceive,
> Till it shall dazzle pilgrim nations
> And stammering tribes from undiscovered lands,
> Allure the living God out of the bliss,
> And all the streaming seraphim from heaven.

Perhaps a poet whose dear words have died should be content if once, no matter how briefly, they have made two lads in a greenwood more shimmery and plumed.

Nights, spring nights in special, temper and tune the Arcadian soul to very gracious tintinnabulations. Three Arcadians on one occasion, I recall, sat through the setting of one constellation after another on a cliff in the tender moonlight with a breathing sea of gray and silver treetops beneath them and discussed the possibility and probability of God. One, upholding the affirmative, announced that he needed no proof of divinity beyond the amethyst smudge on the horns of the moon. This was countered by the fact that this purple lay not in the moon itself but in the observer's eyes. The deist, troubled, at last concluded anyway he'd rather be a god looking out than look out at a god. Only this was all said with humor and a glistening eagerness— a sort of speech I could once fall into, but long ago.

Myself one of these mountain dwellers for four years, I have observed them, off and on, for thirty more. It is to be marveled at that they never change. They may not be quite the same faces or the precise bodies you met a few years back, but the alterations are irrelevant—a brown eye instead of a blue one, a nose set a little more to the left. The lining is the same. Neither from experience nor observation can I quite say what they learn in their Arcadia, though they gad about freely with books and pads. Indeed, many of them attempt to assume a studious air by wearing black Oxford gowns. In this they are not wholly successful, for, no matter how new, the gowns always manage to be torn and insist on hanging from the supple shoulders with something of a dionysiac abandon. Further, even the most bookish are given to pursuing their studies out under the trees. To lie under a tree on your back, overhead a blue and green and gold pattern meddled with by the idlest of breezes, is not—despite the admirable example of Mr. Newton—conducive to the acquisition of knowledge. Flat on your stomach and propped on both elbows, you will inevitably keel and end by doting on the tint of the far shadows, or, worse, by slipping into those delightful oscillations of consciousness known as cat-naps. I cannot therefore commend them for erudition. So it is all the more surprising that in after years the world esteems many of them learned or powerful or godly, and that not infrequently they have been the chosen servitors of the destinies. Yet what they do or know is always less than what they are. Once one of them appeared on the first page of the newspapers because he had climbed with amazing pluck and calculated foolhardiness a hitherto unconquered mountain peak, an Indian boy his only companion. But what we who loved him like best to recall about that exploit is an inch cube of a book he carried along with him and read through—for the hundredth time, likely—before the climb was completed. It was *Hamlet*. Another is immortal for cleansing the world of yellow fever, but the ignorant half-breeds among whom he worked remember him now only for his gentleness, his directness without bluntness, his courtesy which robbed obedience of all humiliation. Still others I understand have amassed fortunes and—to use a word much reverenced by my temporal co-tenants—succeeded. That success I suspect was in spite of their sojourn in our greenwoods. The Arcadians learn here—and that is why I am having such difficulty telling you these things—the imponderables. Ears slightly more pointed and tawny-furred, a bit of leafiness somewhere in the eyes, a manner vaguely Apriline—such attributes though unmistakable are not to be described. When the Arcadians are fools, as they sometimes are, you do not deplore their stupidity, and when they are brilliant you do not resent their intellectuality. The reason is, their manners— the kind not learned or instilled but happening, the core being sweet—are far realer than their other qualities. Socrates and Jesus and St. Francis and Sir Philip Sidney and Lovelace and Stevenson had charm; the Arcadians are of that lineage.

What Pan and Dionysos and the old ladies dower them with is supplemented by an influence which must appear to the uninitiated incompatible. By the aid of a large bell jangled over their sleeping heads from the hands of a perambulating Negro, the Arcadians at seven each morning are driven, not without maledictions, to divine service. A minute before the chapel bell stops ringing, if you happen to be passing, you may imagine the building to be on fire, for young men are dashing to it from every corner of the campus, many struggling with a collar or tie or tightening a belt in their urgent flight. But at the opening of the first hymn you'll find them inside, seated in rows, as quiet as lovebirds on a perch. More quiet, in fact: as the service progresses you might well mistake their vacuity for devotion unless you happen to notice the more nocturnal souls here and there who, sagging decorously, have let the warm sleep in.

Nevertheless, the Arcadians add to their list of benefactors those elderly gentlemen about King James who mistranslated certain Hebrew chronicles and poems into the most magnificent music the human tongue has ever syllabled. In their litanies should be named no less those others (or were they the same?) who wrote the Book of Common Prayer. Each morning these young men hear floating across their semiconsciousness the sea-surge of their own language at its most exalted—clean and thunderous and salty. Some of the wash of that stormy splendor lodges in their gay shallows, inevitably and eternally. Who could hear each morning that phrase "the beauty of holiness" without being beguiled into starrier austerities? If someone daily wished that the peace of God and the fellowship of the Holy Ghost might be with you always, could it help sobering and comforting you, even if God to you were only a gray-bearded old gentleman and the Holy Ghost a dove? Suppose you had never rambled from the divine path farther than the wild-rose hedge along its border, still would not the tide of pity for the illness of things rise in your heart at hearing: "We have wandered and strayed from Thy ways like lost sheep"? Lusty Juventus hereabouts may reflect and forget that there was a modern spiciness in the domestic difficulties of David, but it treasures unforgettably: "The heavens declare the glory of God, and the firmament sheweth His handiwork," and "He maketh me to lie down in green pastures, He leadeth me beside the still waters." Such glistening litter is responsible, perhaps, for the tremulous awe and reverence you find in the recesses of the Arcadian soul—at least you can find them if you are wary and part very gently the sun-spotted greenery of Pan.

Girders and foundations are fine things; and necessary, no doubt. It is stated on authority that the creaking old world would fly into bits without them. But after all what I like best is a tower window. This hankering is an endless source of trouble to me and I like to think to myself, in defense, that it comes from having lived too long among mountain-folk. For they seem always to be leaning from the top of their tower, busy with idle things; watching the leaves shake in the sunlight, the clouds tumble their soundless bales of purple down the long slopes, the seasons eternally up to tricks of beauty, laughing at things that only distance and height reveal humor in, and talking, talking, talking—the enchanting unstained silver of their voices spilling over the bright branches down into the still and happy coves. Sometimes you of the valley may not recognize them, though without introduction they are known of each other. But if some evening a personable youth happens in on your hospitality, greets you with the not irreverent informality reserved for uncles, puts the dowager Empress of Mozambique, your houseguest, at her ease, flirts with your daughter, says grace before the evening meal with unsmiling piety, consumes every variety of food and drink set before him (specializing on hot biscuits) with unabashed gusto, leaves a wake of laughter whenever he dips into the conversation, pays special and apparently delighted attention to the grandmother on his left, enchants the serving maid with two bits and a smile, offers everyone a cigarette, affable under the general disapproval, sings without art a song without merit, sits at last on the doorstep in the moonlight, utterly content, with the dreamy air of the young Hermes (which only means the sense of impending adventure is about his hair like green leaves), and then if that night you dream of a branch of crab-apple blossoms dashed with rain—pursue that youth and entreat him kindly. He hails from Arcady.

Eudora Welty

(1909–   )

Eudora Welty was born on April 13, 1909, in Jackson, Mississippi, where she still lives. She attended Mississippi State College for Women, the University of Wisconsin in Madison, and Columbia University. *The Ponder Heart* (1954) received the William Dean Howells Gold Medal for Fiction, given by the National Institute of Arts and Letters. Her novel *The Optimist's Daughter* (1972) won the Pulitzer Prize for fiction. Welty has also received the Presidential Medal of Freedom.

Welty's publications include *A Curtain of Green, and Other Stories* (1941); *The Robber Bridegroom* (1942); *The Wide Net and Other Stories* (1943); *Delta Wedding* (1946); *Music from Spain* (1948); *The Golden Apples* (1949); *The Bride of the Innisfallen and Other Stories* (1955); *The Shoe Bird* (1964); *Losing Battles* (1970); *One Time, One Place: Mississippi in the Depression; A Snapshot Album* (1971); *The Eye of the Story* (1978); *The Collected Stories of Eudora Welty* (1981); *One Writer's Beginnings* (1984); and *A Writer's Eye: Collected Book Reviews* (1994).

A Worn Path

It was December—a bright frozen day in the early morning. Far out in the country there was an old Negro woman with her head tied in a red rag, coming along a path through the pinewoods. Her name was Phoenix Jackson. She was very old and small and she walked slowly in the dark pine shadows, moving a little from side to side in her steps, with the balanced heaviness and lightness of a pendulum in a grandfather clock. She carried a thin, small cane made from an umbrella, and with this she kept tapping the frozen earth in front of her. This made a grave and persistent noise in the still air, that seemed meditative like the chirping of a solitary little bird.

She wore a dark striped dress reaching down to her shoe tops, and an equally long apron of bleached sugar sacks, with a full pocket: all neat and tidy, but every time she took a step she might have fallen over her shoelaces, which dragged from her unlaced shoes. She looked straight ahead. Her eyes were blue with age. Her skin had a pattern all its own of numberless branching wrinkles and as though a whole little tree stood in the middle of her forehead, but a golden color ran underneath, and the two knobs of her cheeks were illumined by a yellow burning under the dark. Under the red rag her hair came down on her neck in the frailest of ringlets, still black, and with an odor like copper.

Now and then there was a quivering in the thicket. Old Phoenix said, "Out of my way, all you foxes, owls, beetles, jack rabbits, coons and wild animals! . . . Keep out from under these feet, little bob-whites. . . . Keep the big wild hogs out of my path. Don't let none of those come running my direction. I got a long way." Under her small black-freckled hand her cane, limber as a buggy whip, would switch at the brush as if to rouse up any hiding things.

On she went. The woods were deep and still. The sun made the pine needles almost too bright to look at, up where the wind rocked. The cones dropped as light as feathers. Down in the hollow as the mourning dove—it was not too late for him.

The path ran up a hill. "Seem like there is chains about my feet, time I get this far," she said, in the voice of argument old people keep to use with themselves. "Something always take a hold of me on this hill—pleads I should stay."

After she got to the top she turned and gave a full, severe look behind her where she had come. "Up through pines," she said at length. "Now down through oaks."

Her eyes opened their widest, and she started down gently. But before she got to the bottom of the hill a bush caught her dress.

Her fingers were busy and intent, but her skirts were full and long, so that before she could pull them free in one place they were caught in another. It was not possible to allow the dress to tear. "I in the thorny bush," she said. "Thorns, you doing your appointed work. Never want to let folks pass, no sir. Old eyes thought you was a pretty little *green* bush."

Finally, trembling all over, she stood free, and after a moment dared to stoop for her cane.

"Sun so high!" she cried, leaning back and looking, while the thick tears went over her eyes. "The time getting all gone here."

At the foot of this hill was a place where a log was laid across the creek.

"Now comes the trial," said Phoenix.

Putting her right foot out, she mounted the log and shut her eyes. Lifting her skirt, leveling her cane fiercely before her, like a festival figure in some parade, she began to march across. Then she opened her eyes and she was safe on the other side.

"I wasn't as old as I thought," she said.

But she sat down to rest. She spread her skirts on the bank around her and folded her hands over her knees. Up above her was a tree in a pearly cloud of mistletoe. She did not dare to close her eyes, and when a little boy brought her a plate with a slice of marble-cake on it she spoke to him. "That would be acceptable," she said. But when she went to take it there was just her own hand in the air.

So she left that tree, and had to go through a barbed-wire fence. There she had to creep and crawl, spreading her knees and stretching her fingers like a baby trying to climb the steps. But she talked loudly to herself: she could not let her dress be torn now, so late in the day, and she could not pay for having her arm or her leg sawed off if she got caught fast where she was.

At last she was safe through the fence and risen up out in the clearing. Big dead trees, like black men with one arm, were standing in the purple stalks of the withered cotton field. There sat a buzzard.

"Who you watching?"

In the furrow she made her way along.

"Glad this not the season for bulls," she said, looking sideways, "and the good Lord made his snakes to curl up and sleep in the winter. A pleasure I don't see no two-headed snake coming around that tree, where it come once. It took a while to get by him, back in the summer."

She passed through the old cotton and went into a field of dead corn. It whispered and shook and was taller than her head. "Through the maze now," she said, for there was no path.

Then there was something tall, black, and skinny there, moving before her.

At first she took it for a man. It could have been a man dancing in the field. But she stood still and listened, and it did not make a sound. It was as silent as a ghost.

"Ghost," she said sharply, "who be you the ghost of? For I have heard of nary death close by."

But there was no answer—only the ragged dancing in the wind.

She shut her eyes, reached out her hand, and touched a sleeve. She found a coat and inside that an emptiness, cold as ice.

"You scarecrow," she said. Her face lighted. "I ought to be shut up for good," she said with laughter. "My senses is gone. I too old. I the oldest people I ever know. Dance, old scarecrow," she said, "while I dancing with you."

She kicked her foot over the furrow, and with mouth drawn down, shook her head once or twice in a little strutting way. Some husks blew down and whirled in streamers about her skirts.

Then she went on, parting her way from side to side with the cane, through the whispering field. At last she came to the end, to a wagon track where the silver grass blew between the red ruts. The quail were walking around like pullets, seeming all dainty and unseen.

"Walk pretty," she said. "This the easy place. This the easy going."

She followed the track, swaying through the quiet bare fields, through the little strings of trees silver in their dead leaves, past cabins silver from weather, with the doors and windows boarded shut, all like old women under a spell sitting there. "I walking in their sleep," she said, nodding her head vigorously.

In a ravine she went where a spring was silently flowing through a hollow log. Old Phoenix bent and drank. "Sweet-gum makes the water sweet," she said, and drank more. "Nobody know who made this well, for it was here when I was born."

The track crossed a swampy part where the moss hung as white as lace from every limb. "Sleep on, alligators, and blow your bubbles." Then the track went into the road.

Deep, deep the road went down between the high green-colored banks. Overhead the live-oaks met, and it was as dark as a cave.

A black dog with a lolling tongue came up out of the weeds by the ditch. She was meditating, and not ready, and when he came at her she only hit him a little with her cane. Over she went in the ditch, like a little puff of milkweed.

Down there, her senses drifted away. A dream visited her, and she reached her hand up, but nothing reached down and gave her a pull. So she lay there and presently went to talking. "Old woman," she said to herself, "that black dog come up out of the weeds to stall you off, and now there he sitting on his fine tail, smiling at you."

A white man finally came along and found her—a hunter, a young man, with his dog on a chain.

"Well, Granny!" he laughed. "What are you doing there?"

"Lying on my back like a June-bug waiting to be turned over, mister," she said, reaching up her hand.

He lifted her up, gave her a swing in the air, and set her down. "Anything broken, Granny?"

"No sir, them old dead weeds is springy enough," said Phoenix, when she had got her breath. "I thank you for your trouble."

"Where do you live, Granny?" he asked, while the two dogs were growling at each other.

"Away back yonder, sir, behind the ridge. You can't even see it from here."

"On your way home?"

"No sir, I going to town."

"Why, that's too far! That's as far as I walk when I come out myself, and I get something for my trouble." He patted the stuffed bag he carried, and there hung down a little closed claw. It was one of the bob-whites, with its beak hooked bitterly to show it was dead. "Now you go on home, Granny!"

"I bound to go to town, mister," said Phoenix. "The time come around."

He gave another laugh, filling the whole landscape. "I know you old colored people! Wouldn't miss going to town to see Santa Claus!"

But something held old Phoenix very still. The deep lines in her face went into a fierce and different radiation. Without warning, she had seen with her own eyes a flashing nickel fall out of the man's pocket onto the ground.

"How old are you, Granny?" he was saying.

"There is no telling, mister," she said, "no telling."

Then she gave a little cry and clapped her hands and said, "Git on away from here, dog! Look! Look at that dog!" She laughed as if in admiration. "He ain't scared of nobody. He a big black dog." She whispered, "Sic him!"

"Watch me get rid of that cur," said the man. "Sic him, Pete! Sic him!"

Phoenix heard the dogs fighting, and heard the man running and throwing sticks. She even heard a gunshot. But she was slowly bending forward by that time, further and further forward, the lids stretched down over her eyes, as if she were doing this in her sleep. Her chin was lowered almost to her knees. The yellow palm of her hand came out from the fold of her apron. Her fingers slid down and along the ground under the piece of money with the grace and care they would have in lifting an egg from under a setting hen. Then she slowly straightened up, she stood erect, and the nickel was in her apron pocket. A bird flew by. Her lips moved. "God watching me the whole time. I come to stealing."

The man came back, and his own dog panted about them. "Well, I scared him off that time," he said, and then he laughed and lifted his gun and pointed it at Phoenix.

She stood straight and faced him.

"Doesn't the gun scare you?" he said, still pointing it.

"No, sir, I seen plenty go off closer by, in my day, and for less than what I done," she said, holding utterly still.

He smiled, and shouldered the gun. "Well, Granny," he said, "you must be a hundred years old, and scared of nothing. I'd give you a dime if I had any money with me. But you take my advice and stay home, and nothing will happen to you."

"I bound to go on my way, mister," said Phoenix. She inclined her head in the red rag. Then they went in different directions, but she could hear the gun shooting again and again over the hill.

She walked on. The shadows hung from the oak trees to the road like curtains. Then she smelled wood-smoke, and smelled the river, and she saw a steeple and the cabins on their steep steps. Dozens of little black children whirled around her. There ahead was Natchez shining. Bells were ringing. She walked on.

In the paved city it was Christmas time. There were red and green electric lights strung and crisscrossed everywhere, and all turned on in the daytime. Old Phoenix would have been lost if she had not distrusted her eyesight and depended on her feet to know where to take her.

She paused quietly on the sidewalk where people were passing by. A lady came along in the crowd, carrying an armful of red-, green- and silver-wrapped presents; she gave off perfume like the red roses in hot summer, and Phoenix stopped her.

"Please, missy, will you lace up my shoe?" She held up her foot.

"What do you want, Grandma?"

"See my shoe," said Phoenix. "Do all right for out in the country, but wouldn't look right to go in a big building."

"Stand still then, Grandma," said the lady. She put her packages down on the sidewalk beside her and laced and tied both shoes tightly.

"Can't lace 'em with a cane," said Phoenix. "Thank you, missy. I doesn't mind asking a nice lady to tie up my shoe, when I gets out on the street."

Moving slowly and from side to side, she went into the big building, and into a tower of steps, where she walked up and around and around until her feet knew to stop.

She entered a door, and there she saw nailed up on the wall the document that had been stamped with the gold seal and framed in the gold frame, which matched the dream that was hung up in her head.

"Here I be," she said. There was a fixed and ceremonial stiffness over her body.

"A charity case, I suppose," said an attendant who sat at the desk before her.

But Phoenix only looked above her head. There was sweat on her face, the wrinkles in her skin shone like a bright net.

"Speak up, Grandma," the woman said. "What's your name? We must have your history, you know. Have you been here before? What seems to be the trouble with you?"

Old Phoenix only gave a twitch to her face as if a fly were bothering her.

"Are you deaf?" cried the attendant.

But then the nurse came in.

"Oh, that's just old Aunt Phoenix," she said. "She doesn't come for herself—she has a little grandson. She makes these trips just as regular as clockwork. She lives away back off the Old Natchez Trace." She bent down. "Well, Aunt Phoenix, why don't you just take a seat? We won't keep you standing after your long trip." She pointed.

The old woman sat down, bolt upright in the chair.

"Now, how is the boy?" asked the nurse.

Old Phoenix did not speak.

"I said, how is the boy?"

But Phoenix only waited and stared straight ahead, her face very solemn and withdrawn into rigidity.

"Is his throat any better?" asked the nurse. "Aunt Phoenix, don't you hear me? Is your grandson's throat any better since the last time you came for the medicine?"

With her hands on her knees, the old woman waited, silent, erect and motionless, just as if she were in armor.

"You mustn't take up our time this way, Aunt Phoenix," the nurse said. "Tell us quickly about your grandson, and get it over. He isn't dead, is he?"

At last there came a flicker and then a flame of comprehension across her face, and she spoke.

"My grandson. It was my memory had left me. There I sat and forgot why I made my long trip."

"Forgot?" The nurse frowned. "After you came so far?"

Then Phoenix was like an old woman begging a dignified forgiveness for waking up frightened in the night. "I never did go to school, I was too old at the Surrender," she said in a soft voice. "I'm an old woman without an education. It was my memory fail me. My little grandson, he is just the same, and I forgot it in the coming."

"Throat never heals, does it?" said the nurse, speaking in a loud, sure voice to old Phoenix. By now she had a card with something written on it, a little list. "Yes. Swallowed lye. When was it?—January—two, three years ago—"

Phoenix spoke unasked now. "No, missy, he not dead, he just the same. Every little while his throat begin to close up again, and he not able to swallow. He not get his breath. He not able to help himself. So the time come around, and I go on another trip for the soothing medicine."

"All right. The doctor said as long as you came to get it, you could have it," said the nurse. "But it's an obstinate case."

"My little grandson, he sit up there in the house all wrapped up, waiting by himself," Phoenix went on. "We is the only two left in the world. He suffer and it don't seem to put him back at all. He got a sweet look. He going to last. He wear a little patch quilt and peep out holding his mouth open like a little bird. I remembers so plain now. I not going to forget him again, no, the whole enduring time. I could tell him from all the others in creation."

"All right." The nurse was trying to hush her now. She brought her a bottle of medicine. "Charity," she said, making a check mark in a book.

Old Phoenix held the bottle close to her eyes, and then carefully put it into her pocket.

"I thank you," she said.

"It's Christmas time, Grandma," said the attendant. "Could I give you a few pennies out of my purse?"

"Five pennies is a nickel," said Phoenix stiffly.

"Here's a nickel," said the attendant.

Phoenix rose carefully and held out her hand. She received the nickel and then fished the other nickel out of her pocket and laid it beside the new one. She stared at her palm closely, with her head on one side.

Then she gave a tap with her cane on the floor.

"This is what come to me to do," she said. "I going to the store and buy my child a little windmill they sells, made out of paper. He going to find it hard to believe there such a thing in the world. I'll march myself back where he waiting, holding it straight up in this hand."

She lifted her free hand, gave a little nod, turned around, and walked out of the doctor's office. Then her slow step began on the stairs, going down.

A Piece of News

She had been out in the rain. She stood in front of the cabin fireplace, her legs wide apart, bending over, shaking her wet yellow head crossly, like a cat reproaching itself for not knowing better. She was talking to herself—only a small fluttering sound, hard to lay hold of in the sparsity of the room.

"The pouring-down rain, the pouring-down rain"—was that what she was saying over and over, like a song? She stood turning in little quarter turns to dry herself, her head bent forward and the yellow hair hanging out streaming and tangled. She was holding her skirt primly out to draw the warmth in.

Then, quite rosy, she walked over to the table and picked up a little bundle. It was a sack of coffee, marked "Sample" in red letters, which she unwrapped from a wet newspaper. But she handled it tenderly.

"Why, how come he wrapped it in a newspaper!" she said, catching her breath, looking from one hand to the other. She must have been lonesome and slow all her life, the way things would take her by surprise.

She set the coffee on the table, just in the center. Then she dragged the newspaper by one corner in a dreamy walk across the floor, spread it all out, and lay down full length on top of it in front of the fire. Her little song about the rain, her cries of surprise, had been only a preliminary, only playful pouting with which she amused herself when she was alone. She was pleased with herself now. As she sprawled close to the fire, her hair began to slide out of its damp tangles and hung all displayed down her back like a piece of bargain silk. She closed her eyes. Her mouth fell into a deepness, into a look of unconscious cunning. Yet in her very stillness and pleasure she seemed to be hiding there, all alone. And at moments when the fire stirred and tumbled in the grate, she would tremble, and her hand would start out as if in impatience or despair.

Presently she stirred and reached under her back for the newspaper. Then she squatted there, touching the printed page as if it were fragile. She did not merely look at it—she watched it, as if it were unpredictable, like a young girl watching a baby. The paper was still wet in places where her body had lain. Crouching tensely and patting the creases away with small cracked red fingers, she frowned now and then at the blotched drawing of something and big letters that spelled a word underneath. Her lips trembled, as if looking and spelling so slowly had stirred her heart.

All at once she laughed.

She looked up.

"Ruby Fisher!" she whispered.

An expression of utter timidity came over her flat blue eyes and her soft mouth. Then a look of fright. She stared about. . . . What eye in the world did she feel looking in on her? She pulled her dress down tightly and began to spell through a dozen words in the newspaper.

The little item said:

"Mrs. Ruby Fisher had the misfortune to be shot in the leg by her husband this week."

As she passed from one word to the next she only whispered; she left the long word, "misfortune," until the last, and came back to it, then she said it all over out loud, like conversation.

"That's me," she said softly, with deference, very formally.

The fire slipped and suddenly roared in the house already deafening with the rain which beat upon the roof and hung full of lightning and thunder outside.

"You Clyde!" screamed Ruby Fisher at last, jumping to her feet. "Where are you, Clyde Fisher?"

She ran straight to the door and pulled it open. A shudder of cold brushed over her in the heat, and she seemed striped with anger and bewilderment. There was a flash of lightning, and she stood waiting, as if she half thought that would bring him in, a gun leveled in his hand.

She said nothing more and, backing against the door, pushed it closed with her hip. Her anger passed like a remote flare of elation. Neatly avoiding the table where the bag of coffee stood, she began to walk nervously about the room, as if a teasing indecision, an untouched mystery, led her by the hand. There was one window, and she paused now and then, waiting, looking out at the rain. When she was still, there was a passivity about her, or a deception of passivity, that was not really passive at all. There was something in her that never stopped.

At last she flung herself onto the floor, back across the newspaper, and looked at length into the fire. It might have been a mirror in the cabin, into which she could look deeper and deeper as she pulled her fingers through her hair, trying to see herself and Clyde coming up behind her.

"Clyde?"

But of course her husband, Clyde, was still in the woods. He kept a thick brush-wood roof over his whisky still, and he was mortally afraid of lightning like this, and would never go out in it for anything.

And then, almost in amazement, she began to comprehend her predicament: it was unlike Clyde to take up a gun and shoot her.

She bowed her head toward the heat, onto her rosy arms, and began to talk and talk to herself. She grew voluble. Even if he heard about the coffee man, with a Pontiac car, she did not think he would shoot her. When Clyde would make her blue, she would go out onto the road, some car would slow down, and if it had a Tennessee license, the lucky kind, the chances were that she would spend the afternoon in the shed of the empty gin. (Here she rolled her head about on her arms and stretched her legs tiredly be-hind her, like a cat.) And if Clyde got word, he would slap her. But the account in the paper was wrong. Clyde had never shot her, even once. There had been a mistake made.

A spark flew out and nearly caught the paper on fire. Almost in fright she beat it out with her fingers. Then she murmured and lay back more firmly upon the pages.

There she stretched, growing warmer and warmer, sleepier and sleepier. She began to wonder out loud how it would be if Clyde shot her in the leg. . . . If he were truly angry, might he shoot her through the heart?

At once she was imagining herself dying. She would have a nightgown to lie in, and a bullet in her heart. Anyone could tell, to see her lying there with that deep expression about her mouth, how strange and terrible that would be. Underneath a brand-new nightgown her heart would be hurting with every beat, many times more than her tough-ened skin when Clyde slapped at her. Ruby began to cry softly, the way she would be crying from the extremity of pain; tears would run down in a little stream over the quilt. Clyde would be standing there above her, as he once looked, with his wild black hair hanging to his shoulders. He used to be very handsome and strong!

He would say, "Ruby, I done this to you."

She would say—only a whisper—"That is the truth, Clyde—you done this to me."

Then she would die; her life would stop right there.

She lay silently for a moment, composing her face into a look which would be beautiful, desirable, and dead.

Clyde would have to buy her a dress to bury her in. He would have to dig a deep hole behind the house, under the cedar, a grave. He would have to nail her up a pine coffin and lay her inside. Then he would have to carry her to the grave, lay her down and cover her up. All the time he would be wild, shouting, and all distracted, to think he could never touch her one more time.

She moved slightly, and her eyes turned toward the window. The white rain splashed down. She could hardly breathe, for thinking that this was the way it was to fall on her grave, where Clyde would come and stand, looking down in the tears of some repentance.

A whole tree of lightning stood in the sky. She kept looking out the window, suf-fused with the warmth from the fire and with the pity and beauty and power of her death. The thunder rolled.

Then Clyde was standing there, with dark streams flowing over the floor where he had walked. He poked at Ruby with the butt of his gun, as if she were asleep.

"What's keepin' supper?" he growled.

She jumped up and darted away from him. Then, quicker than lightning, she put away the paper. The room was dark, except for the firelight. From the long shadow of his steamy presence she spoke to him glibly and lighted the lamp.

He stood there with a stunned, yet rather good-humored look of delay and patience in his face, and kept on standing there. He stamped his mud-red boots, and his enormous hands seemed weighted with the rain that fell from him and dripped down the barrel of the gun. Presently he sat down with dignity in the chair at the table, making a little tumult of his rightful wetness and hunger. Small streams began to flow from him everywhere.

Ruby was going through the preparations for the meal gently. She stood almost on tiptoe in her bare, warm feet. Once as she knelt at the safe, getting out the biscuits, she saw Clyde looking at her and she smiled and bent her head tenderly. There was some way she began to move her arms that was mysteriously sweet and yet abrupt and tentative, a delicate and vulnerable manner, as though her breasts gave her pain. She made many unnecessary trips back and forth across the floor, circling Clyde where he sat in his steamy silence, a knife and fork in his fists.

"Well, where you been, anyway?" he grumbled at last, as she set the first dish on the table.

"Nowheres special."

"Don't you talk back to me. You been hitchhikin' again, ain't you?" He almost chuckled.

She gave him a quick look straight into his eyes. She had not even heard him. She was filled with happiness. Her hand trembled when she poured the coffee. Some of it splashed on his wrist.

At that he let his hand drop heavily down upon the table and made the plates jump.

"Some day I'm goin' to smack the livin' devil outa you," he said.

Ruby dodged mechanically. She let him eat. Then, when he had crossed his knife and fork over his plate, she brought him the newspaper. Again she looked at him in delight. It excited her even to touch the paper with her hand, to hear its quiet secret noise when she carried it, the rustle of surprise.

"A newspaper!" Clyde snatched it roughly and with a grabbing disparagement. "Where'd you git that? Hussy."

"Look at this-here," said Ruby in her small singsong voice. She opened the paper while he held it and pointed gravely to the paragraph.

Reluctantly, Clyde began to read it. She watched his damp bald head slowly bend and turn.

Then he made a sound in his throat and said, "It's a lie."

"That's what's in the newspaper about me," said Ruby, standing up straight. She took up his plate and gave him that look of joy.

He put his big crooked finger on the paragraph and poked at it.

"Well, I'd just like to see the place I shot you!" he cried explosively. He looked up, his face blank and bold.

But she drew herself in, still holding the empty plate, faced him straightened and hard, and they looked at each other. The moment filled full with their helplessness. Slowly they both flushed, as though with a double shame and a double pleasure. It was as though Clyde might really have killed Ruby, and as though Ruby might really have been dead at his hand. Rare and wavering, some possibility stood timidly like a stranger between them and made them hang their heads.

Then Clyde walked over in his water-soaked boots and laid the paper on the dying fire. It floated there a moment and then burst into flame. They stood still and watched it burn. The whole room was bright.

"Look," said Clyde suddenly. "It's a Tennessee paper. See 'Tennessee'? That wasn't none of you it wrote about." He laughed, to show that he had been right all the time.

"It was Ruby Fisher!" cried Ruby. "My name is Ruby Fisher!" she declared passionately to Clyde.

"Oho, it was another Ruby Fisher—in Tennessee," cried her husband. "Fool me, huh? Where'd you get that paper?" He spanked her good-humoredly across her backside.

Ruby folded her still trembling hands into her skirt. She stood stooping by the window until everything, outside and in, was quieted before she went to her supper.

It was dark and vague outside. The storm had rolled away to faintness like a wagon crossing a bridge.

Tennessee Williams
(1911–1983)

One of the major playwrights of the twentieth century, Thomas Lanier (Tennessee) Williams was born on March 26, 1911, in Columbus, Mississippi. He attended the University of Missouri; Washington University, St. Louis (1936–1937); and the University of Iowa, where he received his B.A. in 1938.

Among Williams's many awards are a Rockefeller Foundation Grant (1940); American Academy of Arts and Letters Award (1944); New York Drama Critics Circle Award, Donaldson Award, and Pulitzer Prize for *A Streetcar Named Desire* (1947); New York Drama Critics Circle Award and Pulitzer Prize for *Cat on a Hot Tin Roof* (1955); National Institute of Arts and Letters Gold Medal (1969); Kennedy Honors Award (1979); and Common Wealth Award for Distinguished Service in Dramatic Arts (1981).

Williams is best known for his plays, which include *The Glass Menagerie* (1945); *Summer and Smoke* (1948); *The Rose Tattoo* (1951); and *The Night of the Iguana* (1961). Four of his plays have been made into movies, and Warner Brothers adapted his novel *The Roman Spring of Mrs. Stone* (1948) into a movie in 1961. His *Memoirs* was published in 1975. Williams died on February 24, 1983.

Portrait of a Madonna

Respectfully dedicated to the talent and charm of Miss Lillian Gish.

CHARACTERS

Miss Lucretia Collins.
The Porter.
The Elevator Boy.
The Doctor.
The Nurse.
Mr. Abrams.

SCENE: *The living room of a moderate-priced city apartment. The furnishings are old-fashioned and everything is in a state of neglect and disorder. There is a door in the back wall to a bedroom, and on the right to the outside hall.*

MISS COLLINS: Richard! *(The door bursts open and Miss Collins rushes out, distractedly. She is a middle-aged spinster, very slight and hunched of figure with a desiccated face that is flushed with excitement. Her hair is arranged in curls that would become a young girl and she wears a frilly negligee which might have come from an old hope chest of a period considerably earlier.)* No, no, no, no! I don't care if the whole church hears about it! *(She frenziedly snatches up the phone.)* Manager, I've got to speak to the manager! Hurry, oh, please hurry, there's a *man*—! *(wildly aside as if to an invisible figure)* Lost all respect, absolutely no respect! . . . Mr. Abrams? *(in a tense bushed voice)* I don't want any reporters to hear about this but something awful has been going on upstairs. Yes, this is Miss Collins' apartment on the top floor. I've refrained from making any complaint because of my connections with the church. I used to be assistant to the Sunday School superintendent and I once had the primary class. I helped them put on the Christmas pageant. I made the dress for the Virgin and Mother, made robes for the Wise Men. Yes, and now this has happened, I'm not responsible for it, but night after night after night this man has been coming into my apartment and—indulging his senses! Do you understand? Not once but repeatedly, Mr. Abrams! I don't know whether he comes in the door or the window or up the fire-escape or whether there's some secret entrance they know about at the church, but he's here now, in my bedroom, and I can't force him to leave, I'll have to have some assistance! No, he isn't a thief, Mr. Abrams, he comes of a very fine family in Webb, Mississippi, but this woman has ruined his character, she's destroyed his respect for ladies! Mr. Abrams? Mr. Abrams! Oh, goodness! *(She slams up the receiver and looks distractedly about for a moment; then rushes back into the bedroom.)* Richard! *(The door slams shut. After a few moments an old porter enters in drab gray cover-alls. He looks about with a sorrowfully humorous curiosity, then timidly calls.)*

PORTER: Miss Collins? *(The elevator door slams open in hall and the Elevator Boy, wearing a uniform, comes in.)*

ELEVATOR BOY: Where is she?

PORTER: Gone in 'er bedroom.

ELEVATOR BOY: *(grinning)* She got him in there with her?

PORTER: Sounds like it. *(Miss Collins' voice can be heard faintly protesting with the mysterious intruder.)*

ELEVATOR BOY: What'd Abrams tell yuh to do?

PORTER: Stay here an' keep a watch on 'er till they git here.

ELEVATOR BOY: Jesus.

PORTER: Close 'at door.

ELEVATOR BOY: I gotta leave it open a little so I can hear the buzzer. Ain't this place a holy sight though?

PORTER: Don't look like it's had a good cleaning in fifteen or twenty years. I bet it ain't either. Abrams'll bust a bloodvessel when he takes a lookit them walls.

ELEVATOR BOY: How come it's in this condition?

PORTER: She wouldn't let no one in.

ELEVATOR BOY: Not even the paper-hangers?

PORTER: Naw. Not even the plumbers. The plaster washed down in the bathroom underneath hers an' she admitted her plumbin' had been stopped up. Mr. Abrams had to let the plumber in with this here pass-key when she went out for a while.

ELEVATOR BOY: Holy Jeez. I wunner if she's got money stashed around here. A lotta freaks do stick away big sums of money in ole mattresses an' things.

PORTER: She ain't. She got a monthly pension check or something she always turned over to Mr. Abrams to dole it out to 'er. She tole him that Southern ladies was never brought up to manage finanshul affairs. Lately the checks quit comin'.

ELEVATOR BOY: Yeah?

PORTER: The pension give out or somethin'. Abrams says he got a contribution from the church to keep 'er on here without 'er knowin' about it. She's proud as a peacock's tail in spite of 'er awful appearance.

ELEVATOR BOY: Lissen to 'er in there!

PORTER: What's she sayin'?

ELEVATOR BOY: Apologizin' to him! For callin' the *police!*

PORTER: She thinks police 're comin'?

MISS COLLINS: *(from bedroom)* Stop it, it's got to stop!

ELEVATOR BOY: Fightin' to protect her honor again! What a commotion, no wunner folks are complainin'!

PORTER: *(lighting his pipe)* This here'll be the last time.

ELEVATOR BOY: She's goin' out, huh?

PORTER: *(blowing out the match)* Tonight.

ELEVATOR BOY: Where'll she go?

PORTER: *(slowly moving to the old gramophone)* She'll go to the state asylum.

ELEVATOR BOY: Holy G!

PORTER: Remember this ole number? *(He puts on a record of "I'm Forever Blowing Bubbles.")*

ELEVATOR BOY: Naw. When did that come out?

PORTER: Before your time, sonny boy. Machine needs oilin'. *(He takes out small oil-can and applies oil about the crank and other parts of gramophone.)*

ELEVATOR BOY: How long is the old girl been here?

PORTER: Abrams says she's been livin' here twenty-five, thirty years, since before he got to be manager even.

ELEVATOR BOY: Livin' alone all that time?

PORTER: She had an old mother died of an operation about fifteen years ago. Since then she ain't gone out of the place excep' on Sundays to church or Friday nights to some kind of religious meeting.

ELEVATOR BOY: Got an awful lot of ol' magazines piled aroun' here.

PORTER: She used to collect 'em. She'd go out in back and fish 'em out of the incinerator.

ELEVATOR BOY: What'n hell for?

PORTER: Mr. Abrams says she used to cut out the Campbell soup kids. Them red-tomato-headed kewpie dolls that go with the soup advertisements. You seen 'em, ain'tcha?

ELEVATOR BOY: Uh-huh.

PORTER: She made a collection of 'em. Filled a big lot of scrapbooks with them paper kiddies an' took 'em down to the Children's Hospitals on Xmas Eve an' Easter Sunday, exactly twicet a year. Sounds better, don't it? *(referring to gramophone, which resumes its faint, wheedling music)* Eliminated some a that crankin' noise . . .

ELEVATOR BOY: I didn't know that she'd been nuts *that* long.

PORTER: Who's nuts an' who ain't? If you ask me the world is populated with people that's just as peculiar as she is.

ELEVATOR BOY: Hell. She don't have brain *one*.

PORTER: There's important people in Europe got less'n she's got. Tonight they're takin' her off 'n' lockin' her up. They'd do a lot better to leave 'er go an' lock up some a them maniacs over there. She's harmless; they ain't. They kill millions of people an' go scot free!

ELEVATOR BOY: An ole woman like her is disgusting, though, imaginin' somebody's raped her.

PORTER: Pitiful, not disgusting. Watch out for them cigarette ashes.

ELEVATOR BOY: What's uh diff'rence? So much dust you can't see it. All a this here goes out in the morning, don't it?

PORTER: Uh-huh.

ELEVATOR BOY: I think I'll take a couple a those ole records as curiosities for my girl friend. She's got a portable in 'er bedroom, she says it's better with music!

PORTER: Leave 'em alone. She's still got 'er property rights.

ELEVATOR BOY: Aw, she's got all she wants with them dreamlovers of hers!

PORTER: Hush up! *(He makes a warning gesture as Miss Collins enters from bedroom. Her appearance is that of a ravaged woman. She leans exhaustedly in the doorway, hands clasped over her flat, virginal bosom.)*

MISS COLLINS: *(breathlessly)* Oh, Richard—Richard . . .

PORTER: *(coughing)* Miss—Collins.

ELEVATOR BOY: Hello, Miss Collins.

MISS COLLINS: *(just noticing the men)* Goodness! You've arrived already! Mother didn't tell me you were here! *(Self-consciously she touches her ridiculous corkscrew curls with the faded pink ribbon tied through them. Her manner becomes that of a slightly coquettish but prim little Southern belle.)* I must ask you gentlemen to excuse the terrible disorder.

PORTER: That's all right, Miss Collins.

MISS COLLINS: It's the maid's day off. Your No'thern girls receive such excellent domestic training, but in the South it was never considered essential for a girl to have anything but prettiness and charm! *(She laughs girlishly.)* Please do sit down. Is it too close? Would you like a window open?

PORTER: No, Miss Collins.

MISS COLLINS: *(advancing with delicate grace to the sofa)* Mother will bring in something cool after while. . . . Oh, my! *(She touches her forehead.)*

PORTER: *(kindly)* Is anything wrong, Miss Collins?

MISS COLLINS: Oh, no, no, thank you, nothing! My head is a little bit heavy. I'm always a little bit—malarial—this time of year! *(She sways dizzily as she starts to sink down on the sofa.)*

PORTER: *(helping her)* Careful there, Miss Collins.

MISS COLLINS: *(vaguely)* Yes, it is, I hadn't noticed before. *(She peers at them nearsightedly with a hesitant smile.)* You gentlemen have come from the church?

PORTER: No, ma'am. I'm Nick, the porter, Miss Collins, and this boy here is Frank that runs the elevator.

MISS COLLINS: *(stiffening a little)* Oh? . . . I don't understand.

PORTER: *(gently)* Mr. Abrams just asked me to drop in here an' see if you was getting along all right.

MISS COLLINS: Oh! Then he must have informed you of what's been going on in here!

PORTER: He mentioned some kind of—disturbance.

MISS COLLINS: Yes! Isn't it outrageous? But it mustn't go any further, you understand. I mean you mustn't repeat it to other people.

PORTER: No, I wouldn't say nothing.

MISS COLLINS: Not a word of it, please!

ELEVATOR BOY: Is the man still here, Miss Collins?

MISS COLLINS: Oh, no. No, he's gone now.

ELEVATOR BOY: How did he go, out the bedroom window, Miss Collins?

MISS COLLINS: *(vaguely)* Yes. . . .

ELEVATOR BOY: I seen a guy that could do that once. He crawled straight up the side of the building. They called him The Human Fly! Gosh, that's a wonderful publicity angle, Miss Collins—"Beautiful Young Society Lady Raped by The Human Fly!"

PORTER: *(nudging him sharply)* Git back in your cracker box!

MISS COLLINS: Publicity? No! It would be so humiliating! Mr. Abrams surely hasn't reported it to the papers!

PORTER: No, ma'am. Don't listen to this smarty pants.

MISS COLLINS: *(touching her curls)* Will pictures be taken, you think? There's one of him on the mantel.

ELEVATOR BOY: *(going to the mantel)* This one here, Miss Collins?

MISS COLLINS: Yes. Of the Sunday School faculty picnic. I had the little kindergardeners that year and he had the older boys. We rode in the cab of a railroad locomotive from Webb to Crystal Springs. *(She covers her ears with a girlish grimace and toss of her curls.)* Oh, how the steam-whistle blew! Blew! *(giggling)* Blewwwww! It frightened me so, he put his arm round my shoulders! But she was there, too, though she had no business being. She grabbed his hat and stuck it on the back of her head and they—they *rassled* for it, they actually *rassled* together! Everyone said it was *shameless!* Don't you think that it was?

PORTER: Yes, Miss Collins.

MISS COLLINS: That's the picture, the one in the silver frame up there on the mantel. We cooled the watermelon in the springs and afterwards played games. She hid somewhere and he took ages to find her. It got to be dark and he hadn't found her yet and everyone whispered and giggled about it and finally they came back together—her hangin' on to his arm like a common little strumpet—and Daisy Belle Huston shrieked out, "Look, everybody, the seat of Evelyn's skirt!" It was—covered with—grass-stains! Did you ever hear of anything as outrageous? It didn't faze her, though, she laughed like it was something very, very amusing! Rather *triumphant* she was!

ELEVATOR BOY: Which one is him, Miss Collins?

MISS COLLINS: The tall one in the blue shirt holding onto one of my curls. He loved to play with them.

ELEVATOR BOY: Quite a Romeo—1910 model, huh?

MISS COLLINS: *(vaguely)* Do you? It's nothing, really, but I like the lace on the collar. I said to Mother, "Even if I don't wear it, Mother, it will be *so* nice for my hope-chest!"

ELEVATOR BOY: How was he dressed tonight when he climbed into your balcony, Miss Collins?

MISS COLLINS: Pardon?

ELEVATOR BOY: Did he still wear that nifty little stick-candy-striped blue shirt with the celluloid collar?

MISS COLLINS: He hasn't changed.

ELEVATOR BOY: Oughta be easy to pick him up in that. What color pants did he wear?

MISS COLLINS: *(vaguely)* I don't remember.

ELEVATOR BOY: Maybe he didn't wear any. Shimmied out of 'em on the way up the wall! You could get him on grounds of indecent exposure, Miss Collins!

PORTER: *(grasping his arm)* Cut that or git back in your cage! Understand?

ELEVATOR BOY: *(snickering)* Take it easy. She don't hear a thing.

PORTER: Well, you keep a decent tongue or get to hell out. Miss Collins here is a lady. You understand that?

ELEVATOR BOY: Okay. She's Shoiley Temple.

PORTER: She's a *lady!*

ELEVATOR BOY: Yeah! *(He returns to the gramophone and looks through the records.)*

MISS COLLINS: I really shouldn't have created this disturbance. When the officers come I'll have to explain that to them. But you can understand my feelings, can't you?

PORTER: Sure, Miss Collins.

MISS COLLINS: When men take advantage of common white-trash women who smoke in public there is probably some excuse for it, but when it occurs to a lady who is single and always com-*pletely* above reproach in her moral behavior, there's really nothing to do but call for police protection! Unless of course the girl is fortunate enough to have a father and brothers who can take care of the matter privately without any scandal.

PORTER: Sure. That's right, Miss Collins.

MISS COLLINS: Of course it's bound to cause a great deal of very disagreeable talk. Especially 'round the *church!* Are you gentlemen Episcopalian?

PORTER: No, ma'am. Catholic, Miss Collins.

MISS COLLINS: Oh. Well, I suppose you know in England we're known as the English Catholic church. We have direct Apostolic succession through St. Paul who christened the Early Angles—which is what the original English people were called—and established the English branch of the Catholic church over there. So when you hear ignorant people claim that our church was founded by—by Henry the *Eighth*—that horrible, *lech*erous old man who had so many wives—as many as *Blue*-beard they say!—you can see how ridiculous it *is* and how thoroughly ob*nox*-ious to anybody who really *knows* and under*stands* Church *His*tory!

PORTER: *(comfortingly)* Sure, Miss Collins. Everybody knows that.

MISS COLLINS: I wish they *did*, but they need to be in*struct*ed! Before he died, my father was Rector at the Church of St. Michael and St. George at Glorious Hill, Mississippi. . . . I've literally grown up right in the very *shadow* of the Episcopal church. At Pass Christian and Natchez, Biloxi, Gulfport, Port Gibson, Columbus and Glorious Hill! *(with gentle, bewildered sadness)* But you know I sometimes suspect that there has been some kind of spiritual schism in the modern church. These northern dioceses have completely departed from the good old church traditions. For instance our Rector at the Church of the Holy Communion has never darkened my door. It's a fashionable church and he's terribly busy, but even so you'd think he might have time to make a stranger in the congregation feel at home. But he doesn't though! Nobody seems to have the time any more. . . . *(She grows more excited as her mind sinks back into illusion.)* I ought not to mention this, but do you know they actually take a malicious de-*light* over there at the Holy Communion—where I've recently transferred my letter—in what's been going on here at night in this apartment? *Yes!!* *(She laughs wildly and throws up her hands.)* They take a malicious de*LIGHT* in it!! *(She catches her breath and gropes vaguely about her wrapper.)*

PORTER: You lookin' for somethin', Miss Collins?

MISS COLLINS: My—handkerchief . . . *(She is blinking her eyes against tears.)*

PORTER: *(removing a rag from his pocket)* Here. Use this, Miss Collins. It's just a rag but it's clean, except along that edge where I wiped off the phonograph handle.

MISS COLLINS: Thanks. You gentlemen are very kind. Mother will bring in something cool after while. . . .

ELEVATOR BOY: *(placing a record on machine)* This one is got some kind of foreign title. *(The record begins to play Tschaikowsky's "None But the Lonely Heart.")*

MISS COLLINS: *(stuffing the rag daintily in her bosom)* Excuse me, please. Is the weather nice outside?

PORTER: *(huskily)* Yes, it's nice, Miss Collins.

MISS COLLINS: *(dreamily)* So wa'm for this time of year. I wore my little astrakhan cape to service but had to *carry* it *home*, as the weight of it actually seemed *oppress*ive to me. *(Her eyes fall shut.)* The sidewalks seem so dreadfully long in summer. . . .

ELEVATOR BOY: This ain't summer, Miss Collins.

MISS COLLINS: *(dreamily)* I used to think I'd never get to the end of that last block. And that's the block where all the trees went down in the big tornado. The walk is simply *glit*-tering with sunlight. *(pressing her eyelids)* Impossible to shade your face and I *do* perspire so freely! *(She touches her forehead daintily with the rag.)* Not a branch, not a leaf to give you a little protection! You simply *have* to en-*dure* it. Turn your hideous red face away from all the front-porches and walk as fast as you decently *can* till you get *by* them! Oh, dear, dear Savior, sometimes you're not so lucky and you *meet* people and have to *smile!* You can't *avoid* them unless you cut *across* and that's so *obvious,* you know. . . . People would say you're pe*cul*iar. . . . His house is right in the middle of that awful leafless block, *their* house, his and *hers*, and they have an automobile and always get home early and sit on the porch and *watch* me walking by—Oh, Father in Heaven—with a ma*lic*ious de*light! (She averts her face in remembered torture.)* She has such *penetrating* eyes, they look straight through me. She sees that terrible choking thing in my throat and the pain I have in *here—(touching her chest)*—and she points it out and laughs and whispers to him, "There she goes with her shiny big red nose, the poor old maid—that *loves* you!" *(She chokes and hides her face in the rag.)*

PORTER: Maybe you better forget all that, Miss Collins.

MISS COLLINS: Never, never forget it! Never, never! I left my parasol once—the one with long white fringe that belonged to Mother—I left it behind in the cloakroom at the church so I didn't have anything to cover my face with when I walked by, and I couldn't turn back either, with all those people behind me—giggling back of me, poking fun at my clothes! Oh, dear, dear! I had to walk straight forward—past the last elm tree and into that *merciless* sunlight. Oh! It beat down on me, *scorching* me! *Whips!* . . . Oh, Jesus! . . . Over my face and my body! . . . I tried to walk on fast but was dizzy and they kept closer behind me—! I stumbled, I nearly fell, and all of them burst out laughing! My face turned so *horribly* red, it got so red and wet, I knew how ugly it was in all that merciless glare—not a single shadow to hide in! And then— *(Her face contorts with fear.)*—their automobile drove up in front of their house, right where I had to pass by it, and *she* stepped out, in white, so fresh and easy, her stomach round with a baby, the first of the *six*. Oh, God! . . . And he stood smiling behind her, white and easy and cool, and they stood there waiting for me. *Waiting!* I had to keep on. What else could I do? I couldn't turn *back*, could I? *No!* I said dear *God*, strike me *dead!* He didn't, though. I put my head way down like I couldn't see them! You know what she did? She stretched out her hand to *stop* me! And *he*—he stepped up straight in front of me, *smiling*, blocking the walk with his terrible big white body! *"Lucretia,"* he said, "Lucretia *Collins!"* I—I tried to speak but I couldn't, the breath went out of my body! I covered my face and—ran! . . . Ran! . . . *Ran! (beating the arm of the sofa)* Till I reached the end of the block—and the elm trees—*started* again. . . . Oh, Merciful Christ in Heaven, how *kind* they were! *(She leans back exhaustedly, her hand relaxed on sofa. She pauses and the music ends.)* I said to Mother, "Mother, we've got to leave town!" We *did* after that. And now after all these years he's finally remembered and come *back!* Moved away from that house and the woman and come *here*—I saw him in the back of the church one day. I wasn't sure—but it *was*. The night after that was the night that he first broke in—and indulged his senses with me. . . . He doesn't realize that I've changed, that I can't feel again the way that I used to feel, now that he's got six children by that Cincinnati girl—three in high-school already! Six! Think of that? Six children! I don't know what he'll say when he knows another one's coming! He'll probably blame *me* for it because a man always *does!* In spite of the fact that he *forced* me!

ELEVATOR BOY: *(grinning)* Did you say—a *baby*, Miss Collins?

MISS COLLINS: *(lowering her eyes but speaking with tenderness and pride)* Yes—I'm expecting a *child*.

ELEVATOR BOY: *Jeez! (He claps his hand over his mouth and turns away quickly.)*

MISS COLLINS: Even if it's not legitimate, I think it has a perfect right to its father's name—don't you?

PORTER: Yes. Sure, Miss Collins.

MISS COLLINS: A child is innocent and pure. No matter how it's conceived. And it must *not* be made to suffer! So I intend to dispose of the little property Cousin Ethel left me and give the child a private education where it won't come under the evil influence of the Christian church! I want to make sure that it doesn't grow up in the shadow of the cross and then have to walk along blocks that scorch you with terrible sunlight! *(The elevator buzzer sounds from the hall.)*

PORTER: Frank! Somebody wants to come up. *(The Elevator Boy goes out. The elevator door bangs shut. The Porter clears his throat.)* Yes, it'd be better—to go off some place else.

MISS COLLINS: If only I had the courage—but I don't. I've grown so used to it here, and people outside—it's always so *hard* to *face* them!

PORTER: Maybe you won't—have to face nobody, Miss Collins. *(The elevator door clangs open.)*

MISS COLLINS: *(rising fearfully)* Is someone coming—here?

PORTER: You just take it easy, Miss Collins.

MISS COLLINS: If that's the officers coming for Richard, tell them to go away. I've decided not to prosecute Mr. Martin. *(Mr. Abrams enters with the Doctor and the Nurse. The Elevator Boy gawks from the doorway. The Doctor is the weary, professional type, the Nurse hard and efficient. Mr. Abrams is a small, kindly person, sincerely troubled by the situation.)*

MISS COLLINS: *(shrinking back, her voice faltering)* I've decided not to—prosecute Mr. Martin . . .

DOCTOR: Miss Collins?

MR. ABRAMS: *(with attempted heartiness)* Yes, this is the lady you wanted to meet, Dr. White.

DOCTOR: Hmmm. *(briskly to the Nurse)* Go in her bedroom and get a few things together.

NURSE: Yes, sir. *(She goes quickly across to the bedroom.)*

MISS COLLINS: *(fearfully shrinking)* Things?

DOCTOR: Yes, Miss Tyler will help you pack up an overnight bag. *(smiling mechanically)* A strange place always seems more homelike the first few days when we have a few of our little personal articles around us.

MISS COLLINS: A strange—place?

DOCTOR: *(carelessly, making a memorandum)* Don't be disturbed, Miss Collins.

MISS COLLINS: I know! *(excitedly)* You've come from the Holy Communion to place me under arrest! On moral charges!

MR. ABRAMS: Oh, no, Miss Collins, you got the wrong idea. This is a doctor who—

DOCTOR: *(impatiently)* Now, now, you're just going away for a while till things get straightened out. *(He glances at his watch.)* Two-twenty-five! Miss Tyler?

NURSE: Coming!

MISS COLLINS: *(with slow and sad comprehension)* Oh. . . . I'm going away. . . .

MR. ABRAMS: She was always a lady, Doctor, such a perfect lady.

DOCTOR: Yes. No doubt.

MR. ABRAMS: It seems too bad!

MISS COLLINS: Let me—write him a note. A pencil? Please?

MR. ABRAMS: Here, Miss Collins. *(She takes the pencil and crouches over the table. The Nurse comes out with a hard, forced smile, carrying a suitcase.)*

DOCTOR: Ready, Miss Tyler?

NURSE: All ready, Dr. White. *(She goes up to Miss Collins.)* Come along, dear, we can tend to that later!

MR. ABRAMS: *(sharply)* Let her finish the note!

MISS COLLINS: *(straightening with a frightened smile)* It's—finished.

NURSE: All right, dear, come along. *(She propels her firmly toward the door.)*

MISS COLLINS: *(turning suddenly back)* Oh, Mr. Abrams!

MR. ABRAMS: Yes, Miss Collins?

MISS COLLINS: If he should come again—and find me gone—I'd rather you didn't tell him—about the baby. . . . I think its better for *me* to tell him *that*. *(gently smiling)* You know how men *are*, don't you?

MR. ABRAMS: Yes, Miss Collins.

PORTER: Goodbye, Miss Collins. *(The Nurse pulls firmly at her arm. She smiles over her shoulder with a slight apologetic gesture.)*

MISS COLLINS: Mother will bring in—something cool—after while . . . *(She disappears down the hall with the Nurse. The elevator door clangs shut with the metallic sound of a locked cage. The wires hum.)*

MR. ABRAMS: She wrote him a note.

PORTER: What did she write, Mr. Abrams?

MR. ABRAMS: "Dear—Richard. I'm going away for a while. But don't worry, I'll be back. I have a secret to tell you. Love—Lucretia." *(He coughs.)* We got to clear out this stuff an' pile it down in the basement till I find out where it goes.

PORTER: *(dully)* Tonight, Mr. Abrams?

MR. ABRAMS: *(roughly to hide his feeling)* No, no, not tonight, you old fool. Enough has happened tonight! *(then gently)* We can do it tomorrow. Turn out that bedroom light—and close the window. *(Music playing softly becomes audible as the men go out slowly, closing the door, and the light fades out.)*

CURTAIN

Richard Wright

(1908–1960)

Richard Wright was born on September 4, 1908, near Natchez, Mississippi. After his father left the family and his mother became ill, the family moved to Jackson, Mississippi, in 1918 to live with his mother's family. From 1925 to 1927, he worked at several jobs in Jackson and in Memphis, Tennessee. While in Memphis, he began to read the works of H. L. Mencken, Theodore Dreiser, and Sinclair Lewis. In 1927, Wright moved to Chicago, eventually working with the Federal Negro Theatre and the Illinois Writers' Project. His first major story, "Superstition," was published in the April 1931 edition of *Abbott's Monthly*.

Wright moved to New York in 1937 and became the Harlem editor of the *Daily Worker*, a Communist newspaper. Four of his stories were published as *Uncle Tom's Children* (1938, enlarged 1940). In 1939 he was awarded a Guggenheim Fellowship to complete *Native Son* (1940), which was chosen as a selection of the Book-of-the-Month Club. He also wrote the screenplay, which was made into a film in 1951. He was married to Dhimah Rose Meadman in August 1939. Following their divorce, he married Ellen Poplar on March 12, 1941, and their daughter Julia was born in 1942. *Black Boy* (1945) was a Book-of-the-Month-Club Selection.

After World War II, Wright lived in Paris. In 1947 he and his family became French citizens. Daughter Rachel was born in 1949. His second novel, *The Outsider*, was published in 1953. Other works include *Savage Holiday* (1954); *Black Power: A Record of Reactions in a Land of Pathos* (1954); *Pagan Spain* (1956); *White Man, Listen!* (1957); and *The Long Dream* (1958). Wright died in Paris on November 28, 1960. *Eight Men* (1960); *Lawd Today* (1963); *American Hunger* (1977); and the *Richard Wright Reader* (1978) were published posthumously.

from *Black Boy*

To help support the household my grandmother boarded a colored schoolteacher, Ella, a young woman with so remote and dreamy and silent a manner that I was as much afraid of her as I was attracted to her. I had long wanted to ask her to tell me about the books that she was always reading, but I could never quite summon enough courage to do so. One afternoon I found her sitting alone upon the front porch, reading.

"Ella," I begged, "please tell me what you are reading."

"It's just a book," she said evasively, looking about with apprehension.

"But what's it about?" I asked.

"Your grandmother wouldn't like it if I talked to you about novels," she told me.

I detected a note of sympathy in her voice.

"I don't care," I said loudly and bravely.

"Shhh— You mustn't say things like that," she said.

"But I want to know."

Black Boy was originally published by Harper & Brothers in 1945.

"When you grow up, you'll read books and know what's in them," she explained.

"But I want to know now."

She thought a while, then closed the book.

"Come here," she said.

I sat at her feet and lifted my face to hers.

"Once upon a time there was an old, old man named Bluebeard," she began in a low voice.

She whispered to me the story of *Bluebeard and His Seven Wives* and I ceased to see the porch, the sunshine, her face, everything. As her words fell upon my new ears, I endowed them with a reality that welled up from somewhere within me. She told how Bluebeard had duped and married his seven wives, how he had loved and slain them, how he had hanged them up by their hair in a dark closet. The tale made the world around me be, throb, live. As she spoke, reality changed, the look of things altered, and the world became peopled with magical presences. My sense of life deepened and the feel of things was different, somehow. Enchanted and enthralled, I stopped her constantly to ask for details. My imagination blazed. The sensations the story aroused in me were never to leave me. When she was about to finish, when my interest was keenest, when I was lost to the world around me, Granny stepped briskly onto the porch.

"You stop that, you evil gal!" she shouted. "I want none of that Devil stuff in my house!"

Her voice jarred me so that I gasped. For a moment I did not know what was happening.

"I'm sorry, Mrs. Wilson," Ella stammered, rising. "But he asked me—"

"He's just a foolish child and you know it!" Granny blazed.

Ella bowed her head and went into the house.

"But, Granny, she didn't finish," I protested, knowing that I should have kept quiet.

She bared her teeth and slapped me across my mouth with the back of her hand.

"You shut your mouth," she hissed. "You don't know what you're talking about!"

"But I want to hear what happened!" I wailed, dodging another blow that I thought was coming.

"That's the Devil's work!" she shouted.

My grandmother was as nearly white as a Negro can get without being white, which means that she was white. The sagging flesh of her face quivered; her eyes, large, dark, deep-set, wide apart, glared at me. Her lips narrowed to a line. Her high forehead wrinkled. When she was angry her eyelids drooped halfway down over her pupils, giving her a baleful aspect.

"But I liked the story," I told her.

"You're going to burn in hell," she said with such furious conviction that for a moment I believed her.

Not to know the end of the tale filled me with a sense of emptiness, loss. I hungered for the sharp, frightening, breath-taking, almost painful excitement that the story had given me, and I vowed that as soon as I was old enough I would buy all the novels there were and read them to feed that thirst for violence that was in me, for intrigue, for plotting, for secrecy, for bloody murders. So profoundly responsive a chord had the tale struck in me that the threats of my mother and grandmother had no effect whatsoever. They read my insistence as mere obstinacy, as foolishness, something that would quickly pass; and they had no notion how desperately serious the tale had made me.

They could not have known that Ella's whispered story of deception and murder had been the first experience in my life that had elicited from me a total emotional response. No words or punishment could have possibly made me doubt. I had tasted what to me was life, and I would have more of it, somehow, someway. I realized that they could not understand what I was feeling and I kept quiet. But when no one was looking I would slip into Ella's room and steal a book and take it back of the barn and try to read it. Usually I could not decipher enough words to make the story have meaning. I burned to learn to read novels and I tortured my mother into telling me the meaning of every strange word I saw, not because the word itself had any value, but because it was the gateway to a forbidden and enchanting land.

. . . The eighth grade days flowed in their hungry path and I grew more conscious of myself; I sat in classes, bored, wondering, dreaming. One long dry afternoon I took out my composition book and told myself that I would write a story; it was sheer idleness that led me to it. What would the story be about? It resolved itself into a plot about a villain who wanted a widow's home and I called it *The Voodoo of Hell's Half-Acre.* It was crudely atmospheric, emotional, intuitively psychological, and stemmed from pure feeling. I finished it in three days and then wondered what to do with it.

The local Negro newspaper! That's it . . . I sailed into the office and shoved my ragged composition book under the nose of the man who called himself the editor.

"What is that?" he asked.

"A story," I said.

"A news story?"

"No, fiction."

"All right. I'll read it," he said.

He pushed my composition book back on his desk and looked at me curiously, sucking at his pipe.

"But I want you to read it *now*," I said.

He blinked. I had no idea how newspapers were run. I thought that one took a story to an editor and he sat down then and there and read it and said yes or no.

"I'll read this and let you know about it tomorrow," he said.

I was disappointed; I had taken time to write it and he seemed distant and uninterested.

"Give me the story," I said, reaching for it.

He turned from me, took up the book and read ten pages or more.

"Won't you come in tomorrow?" he asked. "I'll have it finished then."

I honestly relented.

"All right," I said. "I'll stop in tomorrow."

I left with the conviction that he would not read it. Now, where else could I take it after he had turned it down? The next afternoon, en route to my job, I stepped into the newspaper office.

"Where's my story?" I asked.

"It's in galleys," he said.

"What's that?" I asked; I did not know what galleys were.

"It's set up in type," he said. "We're publishing it."

"How much money will I get?" I asked, excited.

"We can't pay for manuscript," he said.

"But you sell your papers for money," I said with logic.

"Yes, but we're young in business," he explained.

"But you're asking me to *give* you my story, but you don't *give* your papers away," I said.

He laughed.

"Look, you're just starting. This story will put your name before our readers. Now, that's something," he said.

"But if the story is good enough to sell to your readers, then you ought to give me some of the money you get from it," I insisted.

He laughed again and I sensed that I was amusing him.

"I'm going to offer you something more valuable than money," he said. "I'll give you a chance to learn to write."

I was pleased, but I still thought he was taking advantage of me.

"When will you publish my story?"

"I'm dividing it into three installments," he said. "The first installment appears this week. But the main thing is this: Will you get news for me on a space rate basis?"

"I work mornings and evenings for three dollars a week," I said.

"Oh," he said. "Then you better keep that. But what are you doing this summer?"

"Nothing."

"Then come to see me before you take another job," he said. "And write some more stories."

A few days later my classmates came to me with baffled eyes, holding copies of the *Southern Register* in their hands.

"Did you really write that story?" they asked me.

"Yes."

"Why?"

"Because I wanted to."

"Where did you get it from?"

"I made it up."

"You didn't. You copied it out of a book."

"If I had, no one would publish it."

"But what are they publishing it for?"

"So people can read it."

"Who told you to do that?"

"Nobody."

"Then why did you do it?"

"Because I wanted to," I said again.

They were convinced that I had not told them the truth. We had never had any instruction in literary matters at school; the literature of the nation or the Negro had never been mentioned. My schoolmates could not understand why anyone would want to write a story; and, above all, they could not understand why I had called it *The Voodoo of Hell's Half-Acre*. The mood out of which a story was written was the most alien thing conceivable to them. They looked at me with new eyes, and a distance, a suspiciousness came between us. If I had thought anything in writing the story, I had thought that perhaps it would make me more acceptable to them, and now it was cutting me off from them more completely than ever.

At home the effects were no less disturbing. Granny came into my room early one morning and sat on the edge of my bed.

"Richard, what is this you're putting in the papers?" she asked.

"A story," I said.

"About what?"

"It's just a story, granny."

"But they tell me it's been in three times."

"It's the same story. It's in three parts."

"But what is it about?" she insisted.

I hedged, fearful of getting into a religious argument.

"It's just a story I made up," I said.

"Then it's a lie," she said.

"Oh, Christ," I said.

"You must get out of this house if you take the name of the Lord in vain," she said.

"Granny, please . . . I'm sorry," I pleaded. "But it's hard to tell you about the story. You see, granny, everybody knows that the story isn't true, but . . ."

"Then why write it?" she asked.

"Because people might want to read it."

"That's the Devil's work," she said and left.

My mother also was worried.

"Son, you ought to be more serious," she said. "You're growing up now and you won't be able to get jobs if you let people think that you're weak-minded. Suppose the superintendent of schools would ask you to teach here in Jackson, and he found out that you had been writing stories?"

I could not answer her.

"I'll be all right, mama," I said.

Uncle Tom, though surprised, was highly critical and contemptuous. The story had no point, he said. And whoever heard of a story by the title of *The Voodoo of Hell's Half-Acre?* Aunt Addie said that it was a sin for anyone to use the word "hell" and that what was wrong with me was that I had nobody to guide me. She blamed the whole thing upon my upbringing.

In the end I was so angry that I refused to talk about the story. From no quarter, with the exception of the Negro newspaper editor, had there come a single encouraging word. It was rumored that the principal wanted to know why I had used the word "hell." I felt that I had committed a crime. Had I been conscious of the full extent to which I was pushing against the current of my environment, I would have been frightened altogether out of my attempts at writing. But my reactions were limited to the attitude of the people about me, and I did not speculate or generalize.

I dreamed of going north and writing books, novels. The North symbolized to me all that I had not felt and seen; it had no relation whatever to what actually existed. Yet, by imagining a place where everything was possible, I kept hope alive in me. But where had I got this notion of doing something in the future, of going away from home and accomplishing something that would be recognized by others? I had, of course, read my Horatio Alger stories, my pulp stories, and I knew my Get-Rich-Quick Wallingford series from cover to cover, though I had sense enough not to hope to get rich; even to my naïve imagination that possibility was too remote. I knew that I lived in a country in which the aspirations of black people were limited, marked-off. Yet I felt that I had to go somewhere and do something to redeem my being alive.

I was building up in me a dream which the entire educational system of the South had been rigged to stifle. I was feeling the very thing that the state of Mississippi had spent millions of dollars to make sure that I would never feel; I was becoming aware of the thing that the Jim Crow laws had been drafted and passed to keep out of my consciousness; I was acting on impulses that southern senators in the nation's capital had striven to keep out of Negro life; I was beginning to dream the dreams that the state had said were wrong, that the schools had said were taboo.

Had I been articulate about my ultimate aspirations, no doubt someone would have told me what I was bargaining for; but nobody seemed to know, and least of all did I. My classmates felt that I was doing something that was vaguely wrong, but they did not know how to express it. As the outside world grew more meaningful, I became more concerned, tense; and my classmates and my teachers would say: "Why do you ask so many questions?" Or: "Keep quiet."

I was in my fifteenth year; in terms of schooling I was far behind the average youth of the nation, but I did not know that. In me was shaping a yearning for a kind of consciousness, a mode of being that the way of life about me had said could not be, must not be, and upon which the penalty of death had been placed. Somewhere in the dead of the southern night my life had switched onto the wrong track and, without my knowing it, the locomotive of my heart was rushing down a dangerously steep slope, heading for a collision, heedless of the warning red lights that blinked all about me, the sirens and the bells and the screams that filled the air.

One morning I arrived early at work and went into the bank lobby where the Negro porter was mopping. I stood at a counter and picked up the Memphis *Commercial Appeal* and began my free reading of the press. I came finally to the editorial page and saw an article dealing with one H. L. Mencken. I knew by hear-say that he was the editor of the *American Mercury*, but aside from that I knew nothing about him. The article was a furious denunciation of Mencken, concluding with one, hot, short sentence: Mencken is a fool.

I wondered what on earth this Mencken had done to call down upon him the scorn of the South. The only people I had ever heard denounced in the South were Negroes, and this man was not a Negro. Then what ideas did Mencken hold that made a newspaper like the *Commercial Appeal* castigate him publicly? Undoubtedly he must be advocating ideas that the South did not like. Were there, then, people other than Negroes who criticized the South? I knew that during the Civil War the South had hated northern whites, but I had not encountered such hate during my life. Knowing no more of Mencken than I did at that moment, I felt a vague sympathy for him. Had not the South, which had assigned me the role of a non-man, cast at him its hardest words?

Now, how could I find out about this Mencken? There was a huge library near the riverfront, but I knew that Negroes were not allowed to patronize its shelves any more than they were the parks and playgrounds of the city. I had gone into the library several times to get books for the white men on the job. Which of them would now help me to get books? And how could I read them without causing concern to the white men with whom I worked? I had so far been successful in hiding my thoughts and feelings from them, but I knew that I would create hostility if I went about this business of reading in a clumsy way.

I weighed the personalities of the men on the job. There was Don, a Jew; but I distrusted him. His position was not much better than mine and I knew that he was uneasy and insecure; he had always treated me in an offhand, bantering way that barely concealed his contempt. I was afraid to ask him to help me to get books; his frantic desire to demonstrate a racial solidarity with the whites against Negroes might make him betray me.

Then how about the boss? No, he was a Baptist and I had the suspicion that he would not be quite able to comprehend why a black boy would want to read Mencken. There were other white men on the job whose attitudes showed clearly that they were Kluxers or sympathizers, and they were out of the question.

There remained only one man whose attitude did not fit into an anti-Negro category, for I had heard the white men refer to him as a "Pope lover." He was an Irish Catholic and was hated by the white Southerners. I knew that he read books, because I had got him volumes from the library several times. Since he, too, was an object of hatred, I felt that he might refuse me but would hardly betray me. I hesitated, weighing and balancing the imponderable realities.

One morning I paused before the Catholic fellow's desk.

"I want to ask you a favor," I whispered to him.

"What is it?"

"I want to read. I can't get books from the library. I wonder if you'd let me use your card?"

He looked at me suspiciously.

"My card is full most of the time," he said.

"I see," I said and waited, posing my question silently.

"You're not trying to get me into trouble, are you, boy?" he asked, staring at me.

"Oh, no, sir."

"What book do you want?"

"A book by H. L. Mencken."

"Which one?"

"I don't know. Has he written more than one?"

"He has written several."

"I didn't know that."

"What makes you want to read Mencken?"

"Oh, I just saw his name in the newspaper," I said.

"It's good of you to want to read," he said. "But you ought to read the right things."

I said nothing. Would he want to supervise my reading?

"Let me think," he said. "I'll figure out something."

I turned from him and he called me back. He stared at me quizzically.

"Richard, don't mention this to the other white men," he said.

"I understand," I said. "I won't say a word."

A few days later he called me to him.

"I've got a card in my wife's name," he said. "Here's mine."

"Thank you, sir."

"Do you think you can manage it?"

"I'll manage fine," I said.

"If they suspect you, you'll get in trouble," he said.

"I'll write the same kind of notes to the library that you wrote when you sent me for books," I told him. "I'll sign your name."

He laughed.

"Go ahead. Let me see what you get," he said.

That afternoon I addressed myself to forging a note. Now, what were the names of books written by H. L. Mencken? I did not know any of them. I finally wrote what I thought would be a foolproof note: *Dear Madam: Will you please let this nigger boy—*

I used the word "nigger" to make the librarian feel that I could not possibly be the author of the note—*have some books by H. L. Mencken?* I forged the white man's name.

I entered the library as I had always done when on errands for whites, but I felt that I would somehow slip up and betray myself. I doffed my hat, stood a respectful distance from the desk, looked as unbookish as possible, and waited for the white patrons to be taken care of. When the desk was clear of people, I still waited. The white librarian looked at me.

"What do you want, boy?"

As though I did not possess the power of speech, I stepped forward and simply handed her the forged note, not parting my lips.

"What books by Mencken does he want?" she asked.

"I don't know, ma'am," I said, avoiding her eyes.

"Who gave you this card?"

"Mr. Falk," I said.

"Where is he?"

"He's at work, at the M—— Optical Company," I said. "I've been in here for him before."

"I remember," the woman said. "But he never wrote notes like this."

Oh, God, she's suspicious. Perhaps she would not let me have the books? If she had turned her back at that moment, I would have ducked out the door and never gone back. Then I thought of a bold idea.

"You can call him up, ma'am," I said, my heart pounding.

"You're not using these books, are you?" she asked pointedly.

"Oh, no, ma'am. I can't read."

"I don't know what he wants by Mencken," she said under her breath.

I knew now that I had won; she was thinking of other things and the race question had gone out of her mind. She went to the shelves. Once or twice she looked over her shoulder at me, as though she was still doubtful. Finally she came forward with two books in her hand.

"I'm sending him two books," she said. "But tell Mr. Falk to come in next time, or send me the names of the books he wants. I don't know what he wants to read."

I said nothing. She stamped the card and handed me the books. Not daring to glance at them, I went out of the library, fearing that the woman would call me back for further questioning. A block away from the library I opened one of the books and read a title: *A Book of Prefaces*. I was nearing my nineteenth birthday and I did not know how to pronounce the word "preface." I thumbed the pages and saw strange words and strange names. I shook my head, disappointed. I looked at the other book; it was called *Prejudices*. I knew what that word meant; I had heard it all my life. And right off I was on guard against Mencken's books. Why would a man want to call a book *Prejudices?* The word was so stained with all my memories of racial hate that I could not conceive of anybody using it for a title. Perhaps I had made a mistake about Mencken? A man who had prejudices must be wrong.

When I showed the books to Mr. Falk, he looked at me and frowned.

"That librarian might telephone you," I warned him.

"That's all right," he said. "But when you're through reading those books, I want you to tell me what you get out of them."

That night in my rented room, while letting the hot water run over my can of pork and beans in the sink, I opened *A Book of Prefaces* and began to read. I was jarred and shocked by the style, the clear, clean, sweeping sentences. Why did he write like that? And how did one write like that? I pictured the man as a raging demon, slashing with his pen, consumed with hate, denouncing everything American, extolling everything European or German, laughing at the weaknesses of people, mocking God, authority. What was this? I stood up, trying to realize what reality lay behind the meaning of the words . . . Yes, this man was fighting, fighting with words. He was using words as a weapon, using them as one would use a club. Could words be weapons? Well, yes, for here they were. Then, maybe, perhaps, I could use them as a weapon? No. It frightened me. I read on and what amazed me was not what he said, but how on earth anybody had the courage to say it.

Occasionally I glanced up to reassure myself that I was alone in the room. Who were these men about whom Mencken was talking so passionately? Who was Anatole France? Joseph Conrad? Sinclair Lewis, Sherwood Anderson, Dostoevski, George Moore, Gustave Flaubert, Maupassant, Tolstoy, Frank Harris, Mark Twain, Thomas Hardy, Arnold Bennett, Stephen Crane, Zola, Norris, Gorky, Bergson, Ibsen, Balzac, Bernard Shaw, Dumas, Poe, Thomas Mann, O. Henry, Dreiser, H. G. Wells, Gogol, T. S. Eliot, Gide, Baudelaire, Edgar Lee Masters, Stendhal, Turgenev, Huneker, Nietzsche, and scores of others? Were these men real? Did they exist or had they existed? And how did one pronounce their names?

I ran across many words whose meanings I did not know, and I either looked them up in a dictionary or, before I had a chance to do that, encountered the word in a context that made its meaning clear. But what strange world was this? I concluded the book with the conviction that I had somehow overlooked something terribly important in life. I had once tried to write, had once reveled in feeling, had let my crude imagination roam, but the impulse to dream had been slowly beaten out of me by experience. Now it surged up again and I hungered for books, new ways of looking and seeing. It was not a matter of believing or disbelieving what I read, but of feeling something new, of being affected by something that made the look of the world different.

As dawn broke I ate my pork and beans, feeling dopey, sleepy. I went to work, but the mood of the book would not die; it lingered, coloring everything I saw, heard, did. I now felt that I knew what the white men were feeling. Merely because I had read a book that had spoken of how they lived and thought, I identified myself with that book. I felt vaguely guilty. Would I, filled with bookish notions, act in a manner that would make the whites dislike me?

I forged more notes and my trips to the library became frequent. Reading grew into a passion. My first serious novel was Sinclair Lewis's *Main Street*. It made me see my boss, Mr. Gerald, and identify him as an American type. I would smile when I saw him lugging his golf bags into the office. I had always felt a vast distance separating me from the boss, and now I felt closer to him, though still distant. I felt now that I knew him, that I could feel the very limits of his narrow life. And this had happened because I had read a novel about a mythical man called George F. Babbitt.

The plots and stories in the novels did not interest me so much as the point of view revealed. I gave myself over to each novel without reserve, without trying to criticize it; it was enough for me to see and feel something different. And for me, everything was something different. Reading was like a drug, a dope. The novels created moods in which I lived for days. But I could not conquer my sense of guilt, my feeling that the white men around me knew that I was changing, that I had begun to regard them differently.

Whenever I brought a book to the job, I wrapped it in newspaper—a habit that was to persist for years in other cities and under other circumstances. But some of the white men pried into my packages when I was absent and they questioned me.

"Boy, what are you reading those books for?"

"Oh, I don't know, sir."

"That's deep stuff you're reading, boy."

"I'm just killing time, sir."

"You'll addle your brains if you don't watch out."

I read Dreiser's *Jennie Gerhardt* and *Sister Carrie* and they revived in me a vivid sense of my mother's suffering; I was overwhelmed. I grew silent, wondering about the life around me. It would have been impossible for me to have told anyone what I derived from these novels, for it was nothing less than a sense of life itself. All my life had shaped me for the realism, the naturalism of the modern novel, and I could not read enough of them.

Steeped in new moods and ideas, I bought a ream of paper, and tried to write; but nothing would come, or what did come was flat beyond telling. I discovered that more than desire and feeling were necessary to write and I dropped the idea. Yet I still wondered how it was possible to know people sufficiently to write about them? Could I ever learn about life and people? To me, with my vast ignorance, my Jim Crow station in life, it seemed a task impossible of achievement. I now knew what being a Negro meant. I could endure the hunger. I had learned to live with hate. But to feel that there were feelings denied me, that the very breath of life itself was beyond my reach, that more than anything else hurt, wounded me. I had a new hunger.

In buoying me up, reading also cast me down, made me see what was possible, what I had missed. My tension returned, new, terrible, bitter, surging, almost too great to be contained. I no longer *felt* that the world about me was hostile, killing; I *knew* it. A million times I asked myself what I could do to save myself, and there were no answers. I seemed forever condemned, ringed by walls.

I did not discuss my reading with Mr. Falk, who had lent me his library card; it would have meant talking about myself and that would have been too painful. I smiled each day, fighting desperately to maintain my old behavior, to keep my disposition seemingly sunny. But some of the white men discerned that I had begun to brood.

"Wake up there, boy!" Mr. Olin said one day.

"Sir!" I answered for the lack of a better word.

"You act like you've stolen something," he said.

I laughed in the way I knew he expected me to laugh, but I resolved to be more conscious of myself, to watch my every act, to guard and hide the new knowledge that was dawning within me.

If I went north, would it be possible for me to build a new life then? But how could a man build a life upon vague, unformed yearnings? I wanted to write and I did not even know the English language. I bought English grammars and found them dull. I felt that I was getting a better sense of the language from novels than from grammars. I read hard, discarding a writer as soon as I felt that I had grasped his point of view. At night the printed page stood before my eyes in sleep.

Mrs. Moss, my landlady, asked me one Sunday morning:

"Son, what is this you keep on reading?"

"Oh, nothing. Just novels."

"What you get out of 'em?"

"I'm just killing time," I said.

"I hope you know your own mind," she said in a tone which implied that she doubted if I had a mind.

I knew of no Negroes who read the books I liked and I wondered if any Negroes ever thought of them. I knew that there were Negro doctors, lawyers, newspapermen, but I never saw any of them. When I read a Negro newspaper I never caught the faintest echo of my preoccupation in its pages. I felt trapped and occasionally, for a few days, I would stop reading. But a vague hunger would come over me for books, books that opened up new avenues of feeling and seeing, and again I would forge another note to the white librarian. Again I would read and wonder as only the naïve and unlettered can read and wonder, feeling that I carried a secret, criminal burden about with me each day.

That winter my mother and brother came and we set up housekeeping, buying furniture on the installment plan, being cheated and yet knowing no way to avoid it. I began to eat warm food and to my surprise found that regular meals enabled me to read faster. I may have lived through many illnesses and survived them, never suspecting that I was ill. My brother obtained a job and we began to save toward the trip north, plotting our time, setting tentative dates for departure. I told none of the white men on the job that I was planning to go north; I knew that the moment they felt I was thinking of the North they would change toward me. It would have made them feel that I did not like the life I was living, and because my life was completely conditioned by what they said or did, it would have been tantamount to challenging them.

I could calculate my chances for life in the South as a Negro fairly clearly now.

I could fight the southern whites by organizing with other Negroes, as my grandfather had done. But I knew that I could never win that way; there were many whites and there were but few blacks. They were strong and we were weak. Outright black rebellion could never win. If I fought openly I would die and I did not want to die. News of lynchings were frequent.

I could submit and live the life of a genial slave, but that was impossible. All of my life had shaped me to live by my own feelings and thoughts. I could make up to Bess and marry her and inherit the house. But that, too, would be the life of a slave; if I did that, I would crush to death something within me, and I would hate myself as much as I knew the whites already hated those who had submitted. Neither could I ever willingly present myself to be kicked, as Shorty had done. I would rather have died than do that.

I could drain off my restlessness by fighting with Shorty and Harrison. I had seen many Negroes solve the problem of being black by transferring their hatred of themselves to others with a black skin and fighting them. I would have to be cold to do that, and I was not cold and I could never be.

I could, of course, forget what I had read, thrust the whites out of my mind, forget them; and find release from anxiety and longing in sex and alcohol. But the memory of how my father had conducted himself made that course repugnant. If I did not want others to violate my life, how could I voluntarily violate it myself?

I had no hope whatever of being a professional man. Not only had I been so conditioned that I did not desire it, but the fulfillment of such an ambition was beyond my capabilities. Well-to-do Negroes lived in a world that was almost as alien to me as the world inhabited by whites.

What, then, was there? I held my life in my mind, in my consciousness each day, feeling at times that I would stumble and drop it, spill it forever. My reading had created a vast sense of distance between me and the world in which I lived and tried to make a living, and that sense of distance was increasing each day. My days and nights were one long, quiet, continuously contained dream of terror, tension, and anxiety. I wondered how long I could bear it.

Truman Capote
(1924–1984)

Born Truman Streckfus Persons on September 30, 1924, in New Orleans, Louisiana, Truman Capote was brought up in Monroeville, Alabama, where he became the close childhood friend of Harper Lee. In *To Kill a Mockingbird*, Lee bases the character of Dill on Capote. After his parents' divorce, he lived with relatives until his mother married a wealthy businessman, Joseph Capote. At age fifteen, he moved to New York and adopted his stepfather's name. Leaving school at seventeen, Capote began working for *The New Yorker*.

Capote's story "Miriam," first published in *Madamoiselle*, was selected for the O. Henry Memorial Award volume in 1946. *Other Voices, Other Rooms* (1948) earned wide success and became controversial because of its treatment of homosexuality. In 1954, Capote wrote the screenplay for *Beat the Devil*, a John Huston film starring Humphrey Bogart. Capote's *Breakfast at Tiffany's* (1958) was highly acclaimed and made into a film starring Audrey Hepburn in the title role.

Capote attempted what he believed to be a new genre, "creative journalism," with the six years of research and subsequent publication of *In Cold Blood: A True Account of a Multiple Murder and Its Consequences* (1966). *A Christmas Memory* (1966) is considered a classic.

Selected books by Capote are *A Tree of Night and Other Stories* (1950); *Local Color* (1950); *The Grass Harp* (1951); *The House of Flowers* (1954); *The Muses are Heard* (1956); *Observations* (1959); *Selected Writings* (1963); *The Thanksgiving Visitor* (1967); *The Dogs Bark: Public People and Private Places* (1973); *Then It All Came Down* (1976); *Music for Chameleons: New Writing* (1980); *One Christmas* (1982); *Answered Prayers* (1986); and *A Capote Reader* (1987).

Capote died in Los Angeles, California, on August 25, 1984.

A Diamond Guitar

The nearest town to the prison farm is twenty miles away. Many forests of pine trees stand between the farm and the town, and it is in these forests that the convicts work; they tap for turpentine. The prison itself is in a forest. You will find it there at the end of a red rutted road, barbed wire sprawling like a vine over its walls. Inside, there live one hundred and nine white men, ninety-seven Negroes and one Chinese. There are two sleep houses—great green wooden buildings with tarpaper roofs. The white men occupy one, the Negroes and the Chinese the other. In each sleep house there is one large potbellied stove, but the winters are cold here, and at night with the pines waving frostily and a freezing light falling from the moon the men, stretched on their iron cots, lie awake with the fire colors of the stove playing in their eyes.

The men whose cots are nearest the stove are the important men—those who are looked up to or feared. Mr. Schaeffer is one of these. Mr. Schaeffer—for that is what he is called, a mark of special respect—is a lanky, pulled-out man. He has reddish, silvering hair, and his face is attenuated, religious; there is no flesh to him; you can see the workings of his bones, and his eyes are a poor, dull color. He can read and he can write, he can add a column of figures. When another man receives a letter, he brings it to Mr. Schaeffer. Most of these letters are sad and complaining; very often Mr. Schaeffer improvises more cheerful messages and does not read what is written on the page. In the sleep house there are two other men who can read. Even so, one of them brings his letters to Mr. Schaeffer, who obliges by never reading the truth. Mr. Schaeffer himself does not receive mail, not even at Christmas; he seems to have no friends beyond the prison, and actually he has none there—that is, no particular friend. This was not always true.

One winter Sunday some winters ago Mr. Schaeffer was sitting on the steps of the sleep house carving a doll. He is quite talented at this. His dolls are carved in separate sections, then put together with bits of spring wire; the arms and legs move, the head rolls. When he has finished a dozen or so of these dolls, the Captain of the farm takes them into town, and there they are sold in a general store. In this way Mr. Schaeffer earns money for candy and tobacco.

That Sunday, as he sat cutting out the fingers for a little hand, a truck pulled into the prison yard. A young boy, handcuffed to the Captain of the farm, climbed out of the truck and stood blinking at the ghostly winter sun. Mr. Schaeffer only glanced at him. He was then a man of fifty, and seventeen of those years he'd lived at the farm. The arrival of a new prisoner could not arouse him. Sunday is a free day at the farm, and other men who were moping around the yard crowded down to the truck. Afterward, Pick Axe and Goober stopped by to speak with Mr. Schaeffer.

Pick Axe said, "He's a foreigner, the new one is. From Cuba. But with yellow hair."

"A knifer, Cap'n says," said Goober, who was a knifer himself. "Cut up a sailor in Mobile."

"Two sailors," said Pick Axe. "But just a café fight. He didn't hurt them boys none."

"To cut off a man's ear? You call that not hurtin' him? They give him two years, Cap'n says."

Pick Axe said, "He's got a guitar with jewels all over it."

It was getting too dark to work. Mr. Schaeffer fitted the pieces of his doll together and, holding its little hands, set it on his knee. He rolled a cigarette; the pines were blue in the sundown light, and the smoke from his cigarette lingered in the cold, darkening air. He could see the Captain coming across the yard. The new prisoner, a blond young boy, lagged a pace behind. He was carrying a guitar studded with glass diamonds that cast a starry twinkle, and his new uniform was too big for him; it looked like a Halloween suit.

"Somebody for you, Schaeffer," said the Captain, pausing on the steps of the sleep house. The Captain was not a hard man; occasionally he invited Mr. Schaeffer into his office, and they would talk together about things they had read in the newspaper. "Tico Feo," he said as though it were the name of a bird or a song, "this is Mr. Schaeffer. Do like him, and you'll do right."

Mr. Schaeffer glanced up at the boy and smiled. He smiled at him longer than he meant to, for the boy had eyes like strips of sky—blue as the winter evening—and his hair was as gold as the Captain's teeth. He had a fun-loving face, nimble, clever; and, looking at him, Mr. Schaeffer thought of holidays and good times.

"Is like my baby sister," said Tico Feo, touching Mr. Schaeffer's doll. His voice with its Cuban accent was soft and sweet as a banana. "She sit on my knee also."

Mr. Schaeffer was suddenly shy. Bowing to the Captain, he walked off into the shadows of the yard. He stood there whispering the names of the evening stars as they opened in flower above him. The stars were his pleasure, but tonight they did not comfort him; they did not make him remember that what happens to us on earth is lost in the endless shine of eternity. Gazing at them—the stars—he thought of the jeweled guitar and its worldly glitter.

It could be said of Mr. Schaeffer that in his life he'd done only one really bad thing: he'd killed a man. The circumstances of that deed are unimportant, except to say that the man deserved to die and that for it Mr. Schaeffer was sentenced to ninety-nine years and a day. For a long while—for many years, in fact—he had not thought of how it was before he came to the farm. His memory of those times was like a house where no one lives and where the furniture has rotted away. But tonight it was as if lamps had been lighted through all the gloomy dead rooms. It had begun to happen when he saw Tico Feo coming through the dusk with his splendid guitar. Until that moment he had not been lonesome. Now, recognizing his loneliness, he felt alive. He had not wanted to be alive. To be alive was to remember brown rivers where the fish run, and sunlight on a lady's hair.

Mr. Schaeffer hung his head. The glare of the stars had made his eyes water.

The sleep house usually is a glum place, stale with the smell of men and stark in the light of two unshaded electric bulbs. But with the advent of Tico Feo it was as though a tropic occurrence had happened in the cold room, for when Mr. Schaeffer returned from his observance of the stars he came upon a savage and garish scene. Sitting cross-legged on a cot, Tico Feo was picking at his guitar with long swaying fingers and singing a song that sounded as jolly as jingling coins. Though the song was in Spanish, some of the men tried to sing it with him, and Pick Axe and Goober were dancing together. Charlie and Wink were dancing too, but separately. It was nice to hear the men laughing, and when Tico Feo finally put aside his guitar, Mr. Schaeffer was among those who congratulated him.

"You deserve such a fine guitar," he said.

"Is diamond guitar," said Tico Feo, drawing his hand over its vaudeville dazzle. "Once I have a one with rubies. But that one is stole. In Havana my sister work in a, how you say, where make guitar; is how I have this one."

Mr. Schaeffer asked him if he had many sisters, and Tico Feo, grinning, held up four fingers. Then, his blue eyes narrowing greedily, he said, "Please, Mister, you give me doll for my two little sister?"

The next evening Mr. Schaeffer brought him the dolls. After that he was Tico Feo's best friend and they were always together. At all times they considered each other.

Tico Feo was eighteen years old and for two years had worked on a freighter in the Caribbean. As a child he'd gone to school with nuns, and he wore a gold crucifix around his neck. He had a rosary too. The rosary he kept wrapped in a green silk scarf that also held three other treasures: a bottle of Evening in Paris cologne, a pocket mirror and a Rand McNally map of the world. These and the guitar were his only possessions, and he would not allow anyone to touch them. Perhaps he prized his map the most. At night, before the lights were turned off, he would shake out his map and show Mr. Schaeffer the places he'd been—Galveston, Miami, New Orleans, Mobile, Cuba, Haiti, Jamaica, Puerto Rico, the Virgin Islands—and the places he wanted to go to. He wanted to go almost everywhere, especially Madrid, especially the North Pole. This both charmed and frightened Mr. Schaeffer. It hurt him to think of Tico Feo on the seas and in far places. He sometimes looked defensively at his friend and thought, "You are just a lazy dreamer."

It is true that Tico Feo was a lazy fellow. After that first evening he had to be urged even to play his guitar. At daybreak when the guard came to rouse the men, which he did by banging a hammer on the stove, Tico Feo would whimper like a child. Sometimes he pretended to be ill, moaned and rubbed his stomach; but he never got away with this, for the Captain would send him out to work with the rest of the men. He and Mr. Schaeffer were put together on a highway gang. It was hard work, digging at frozen clay and carrying croker sacks filled with broken stone. The guard had always to be shouting at Tico Feo, for he spent most of the time trying to lean on things.

Each noon, when the dinner buckets were passed around, the two friends sat together. There were some good things in Mr. Schaeffer's bucket, as he could afford apples and candy bars from the town. He liked giving these things to his friend, for his friend enjoyed them so much, and he thought, "You are growing; it will be a long time until you are a grown man."

Not all the men liked Tico Feo. Because they were jealous, or for more subtle reasons, some of them told ugly stories about him. Tico Feo himself seemed unaware of this. When the men gathered around him, and he played his guitar and sang his songs, you could see that he felt he was loved. Most of the men did feel a love for him; they waited for and depended upon the hour between supper and lights out. "Tico, play your box," they would say. They did not notice that afterward there was a deeper sadness than there had ever been. Sleep jumped beyond them like a jack rabbit, and their eyes lingered ponderingly on the firelight that creaked behind the grating of the stove. Mr. Schaeffer was the only one who understood their troubled feeling, for he felt it too. It was that his friend had revived the brown rivers where the fish run, and ladies with sunlight in their hair.

Soon Tico Feo was allowed the honor of having a bed near the stove and next to Mr. Schaeffer. Mr. Schaeffer had always known that his friend was a terrible liar. He did not listen for the truth in Tico Feo's tales of adventure, of conquests and encounters with famous people. Rather, he took pleasure in them as plain stories, such as you would read in a magazine, and it warmed him to hear his friend's tropic voice whispering in the dark.

Except that they did not combine their bodies or think to do so, though such things were not unknown at the farm, they were as lovers. Of the seasons, spring is the most shattering: stalks thrusting through the earth's winter-stiffened crust, young leaves cracking out on old left-to-die branches, the falling-asleep wind cruising through all the newborn green. And with Mr. Schaeffer it was the same, a breaking up, a flexing of muscles that had hardened.

It was late January. The friends were sitting on the steps of the sleep house, each with a cigarette in his hand. A moon thin and yellow as a piece of lemon rind curved above them, and under its light, threads of ground frost glistened like silver snail trails. For many days Tico Feo had been drawn into himself—silent as a robber waiting in the shadows. It was no good to say to him, "Tico, play your box." He would only look at you with smooth, under-ether eyes.

"Tell a story," said Mr. Schaeffer, who felt nervous and helpless when he could not reach his friend. "Tell about when you went to the race track in Miami."

"I not ever go to no race track," said Tico Feo, thereby admitting to his wildest lie, one involving hundreds of dollars and a meeting with Bing Crosby. He did not seem to care. He produced a comb and pulled it sulkily through his hair. A few days before this comb had been the cause of a fierce quarrel. One of the men, Wink, claimed that Tico Feo had stolen the comb from him, to which the accused replied by spitting in his face. They had wrestled around until Mr. Schaeffer and another man got them separated. "Is my comb. You tell him!" Tico Feo had demanded of Mr. Schaeffer. But Mr. Schaeffer with quiet firmness had said no, it was not his friend's comb—an answer that seemed to defeat all concerned. "Aw," said Wink, "if he wants it so much, Christ's sake, let the sonofabitch keep it." And later, in a puzzled, uncertain voice, Tico Feo had said, "I thought you was my friend." "I am," Mr. Schaeffer had thought, though he said nothing.

"I not go to no race track, and what I said about the widow woman, that is not true also." He puffed up his cigarette to a furious glow and looked at Mr. Schaeffer with a speculating expression. "Say, you have money, Mister?"

"Maybe twenty dollars," said Mr. Schaeffer hesitantly, afraid of where this was leading.

"Not so good, twenty dollar," Tico said, but without disappointment. "No important, we work our way. In Mobile I have my friend Frederico. He will put us on a boat. There will not be trouble," and it was as though he were saying that the weather had turned colder.

There was a squeezing in Mr. Schaeffer's heart; he could not speak.

"Nobody here can run to catch Tico. He run the fastest."

"Shotguns run faster," said Mr. Schaeffer in a voice hardly alive. "I'm too old," he said, with the knowledge of age churning like nausea inside him.

Tico Feo was not listening. "Then, the world. The world, *el mundo*, my friend." Standing up, he quivered like a young horse; everything seemed to draw close to him—the moon, the callings of screech owls. His breath came quickly and turned to smoke in the air. "Should we go to Madrid? Maybe someone teach me to bullfight. You think so, Mister?"

Mr. Schaeffer was not listening either. "I'm too old," he said. "I'm too damned old."

For the next several weeks Tico Feo kept after him—the world, *el mundo*, my friend; and he wanted to hide. He would shut himself in the toilet and hold his head. Nevertheless, he was excited, tantalized. What if it could come true, the race with Tico across the forests and to the sea? And he imagined himself on a boat, he who had never seen the sea, whose whole life had been land-rooted. During this time one of the convicts died, and in the yard you could hear the coffin being made. As each nail thudded into place, Mr. Schaeffer thought. "This is for me, it is mine."

Tico Feo himself was never in better spirits; he sauntered about with a dancer's snappy, gigolo grace, and had a joke for everyone. In the sleep house after supper his fingers popped at the guitar like firecrackers. He taught the men to cry *olé*, and some of them sailed their caps through the air.

When work on the road was finished, Mr. Schaeffer and Tico Feo were moved back into the forests. On Valentine's Day they ate their lunch under a pine tree. Mr. Schaeffer had ordered a dozen oranges from the town and he peeled them slowly, the skins unraveling in a spiral; the juicier slices he gave to his friend, who was proud of how far he could spit the seeds—a good ten feet.

It was a cold beautiful day, scraps of sunlight blew about them like butterflies, and Mr. Schaeffer, who liked working with the trees, felt dim and happy. Then Tico Feo said, "That one, he no could catch a fly in his mouth." He meant Armstrong, a hog-jowled man sitting with a shotgun propped between his legs. He was the youngest of the guards and new at the farm.

"I don't know," said Mr. Schaeffer. He'd watched Armstrong and noticed that, like many people who are both heavy and vain, the new guard moved with a skimming lightness. "He might could fool you."

"I fool him, maybe," said Tico Feo, and spit an orange seed in Armstrong's direction. The guard scowled at him, then blew a whistle. It was the signal for work to begin.

Sometime during the afternoon the two friends came together again; that is, they were nailing turpentine buckets onto trees that stood next to each other. At a distance below them a shallow bouncing creek branched through the woods. "In water no smell," said Tico Feo meticulously, as though remembering something he'd heard. "We run in the water; until dark we climb a tree. Yes, Mister?"

Mr. Schaeffer went on hammering, but his hand was shaking, and the hammer came down on his thumb. He looked around dazedly at his friend. His face showed no reflection of pain, and he did not put the thumb in his mouth, the way a man ordinarily might.

Tico Feo's blue eyes seemed to swell like bubbles, and when in a voice quieter than the wind sounds in the pinetops he said, "Tomorrow," these eyes were all that Mr. Schaeffer could see.

"Tomorrow, Mister?"

"Tomorrow," said Mr. Schaeffer.

The first colors of morning fell upon the walls of the sleep house, and Mr. Schaeffer, who had rested little, knew that Tico Feo was awake too. With the weary eyes of a crocodile he observed the movements of his friend in the next cot. Tico Feo was unknotting the scarf that contained his treasures. First he took the pocket mirror. Its jellyfish light trembled on his face. For a while he admired himself with serious delight, and combed and slicked his hair as though he were preparing to step out to a party. Then he hung the rosary about his neck. The cologne he never opened, nor the map. The last thing he did was to tune his guitar. While the other men were dressing, he sat on the edge of his cot and tuned the guitar. It was strange, for he must have known he would never play it again.

Bird shrills followed the men through the smoky morning woods. They walked single file, fifteen men to a group, and a guard bringing up the rear of each line. Mr. Schaeffer was sweating as though it were a hot day, and he could not keep in marching step with his friend, who walked ahead, snapping his fingers and whistling at the birds.

A signal had been set. Tico Feo was to call, "Time out," and pretend to go behind a tree. But Mr. Schaeffer did not know when it would happen.

The guard named Armstrong blew a whistle, and his men dropped from the line and separated to their various stations. Mr. Schaeffer, though going about his work as best he could, took care always to be in a position where he could keep an eye on both Tico Feo and the guard. Armstrong sat on a stump, a chew of tobacco lopsiding his face, and his gun pointing into the sun. He had the tricky eyes of a cardsharp; you could not really tell where he was looking.

Once another man gave the signal. Although Mr. Schaeffer had known at once that it was not the voice of his friend, panic had pulled at his throat like a rope. As the morning wore on there was such a drumming in his ears he was afraid he would not hear the signal when it came.

The sun climbed to the center of the sky. "He is just a lazy dreamer. It will never happen," thought Mr. Schaeffer, daring a moment to believe this. But "First we eat," said Tico Feo with a practical air as they set their dinner pails on the bank above the creek. They ate in silence, almost as though each bore the other a grudge, but at the end of it Mr. Schaeffer felt his friend's hand close over his own and hold it with a tender pressure.

"Mister Armstrong, time out . . ."

Near the creek Mr. Schaeffer had seen a sweet gum tree, and he was thinking it would soon be spring and the sweet gum ready to chew. A razory stone ripped open the palm of his hand as he slid off the slippery embankment into the water. He straightened up and began to run; his legs were long, he kept almost abreast of Tico Feo, and icy geysers sprayed around them. Back and forth through the woods the shouts of men boomed hollowly like voices in a cavern, and there were three shots, all highflying, as though the guard were shooting at a cloud of geese.

Mr. Schaeffer did not see the log that lay across the creek. He thought he was still running, and his legs thrashed about him; it was as though he were a turtle stranded on its back.

While he struggled there, it seemed to him that the face of his friend, suspended above him, was part of the white winter sky—it was so distant, judging. It hung there but an instant, like a hummingbird, yet in that time he'd seen that Tico Feo had not wanted him to make it, had never thought he would, and he remembered once thinking that it would be a long time before his friend was a grown man. When they found him, he was still lying in the ankle-deep water as though it were a summer afternoon and he were idly floating on the stream.

Since then three winters have gone by, and each has been said to be the coldest, the longest. Two recent months of rain washed deeper ruts in the clay road leading to the farm, and it is harder than ever to get there, harder to leave. A pair of searchlights has been added to the walls, and they burn there through the night like the eyes of a giant owl. Otherwise, there have not been many changes. Mr. Schaeffer, for instance, looks much the same, except that there is a thicker frost of white in his hair, and as the result of a broken ankle he walks with a limp. It was the Captain himself who said that Mr. Schaeffer had broken his ankle attempting to capture Tico Feo. There was even a picture of Mr. Schaeffer in the newspaper, and under it this caption: "Tried to Prevent Escape." At the time he was deeply mortified, not because he knew the other men were laughing, but because he thought of Tico Feo seeing it. But he cut it out of the paper anyway, and keeps it in an envelope along with several clippings pertaining to his friend: a spinster woman told the authorities he'd entered her home and kissed her, twice he was reported seen in the Mobile vicinity, finally it was believed that he had left the country.

No one has ever disputed Mr. Schaeffer's claim to the guitar. Several months ago a new prisoner was moved into the sleep house. He was said to be a fine player, and Mr. Schaeffer was persuaded to lend him the guitar. But all the man's tunes came out sour, for it was as though Tico Feo, tuning his guitar that last morning, had put a curse upon it. Now it lies under Mr. Schaeffer's cot, where its glass diamonds are turning yellow; in the night his hand sometimes searches it out, and his fingers drift across the strings: then, the world.

Lillian Smith

(1897–1966)

On December 12, 1897, Lillian Smith was born in Jasper, Florida. She attended Piedmont College in Georgia from 1915 to 1916, Peabody Conservatory in Maryland from 1917 to 1922, and Columbia University from 1927 to 1928.

Smith came into prominence with her novel *Strange Fruit* (1944), which described the love of a black woman for a white man. The book was banned "unofficially" in Detroit and Boston, not only for its portrayal of miscegenation but also for its use of a four-letter word and for inclusion of homoeroticity. The book was adapted into a play produced in New York City in 1945. *One Hour* (1959) also deals with a lesbian relationship.

In 1966, Smith resigned from the Congress on Racial Equality (CORE), an organization she had worked with for twenty years, because of its increased-militancy stance. In 1953 she contracted cancer, after which she wrote four books. She died on September 28, 1966, in Atlanta, Georgia. She was the founder, editor, and publisher of the journal successively titled *North Pseudopodia*, then *Georgia Review*, and *South Today* (1936–1946). She won the Southern Award in 1949 for *Killers of the Dream* (1949).

Other works by Smith include *The Journey* (1954); *Now Is the Time* (1955); *Memory of a Large Christmas* (1962); *Our Faces, Our Words* (1964); and *How Am I to Be Heard?: Letters of Lillian Smith* (1993).

from *Killers of the Dream*

4. The Women

Of all the painful and humiliating experiences which southern white women endured, the least easy to accept, I think, was that of a mother who had no choice but to take the husk of a love which her son in his earliest years had given to another woman. She valiantly made jokes about it, telling her friends that her child preferred Mammy to her and that was fine, wasn't it, for it gave her so much more time to attend to all she had to do! "I don't know how I could have done without her," she would say and laugh a light tinkling laugh which sounded like little glass bells about to break into splinters. "Mammy was wonderful," she'd say. "I just don't see how we could do without the colored folks, do you?" she'd say. "I declare! But aren't the younger ones trifling—now look at that Emmy, doing nothing but rolling a dip stick around in her mouth and humming and with her shoes off again! But when I hear men say, 'Send 'em all back to Africa,' I say *they* don't have the housework to do, why we couldn't possibly . . . Oh, my!" sighing and laughing, and trying to forget things she could never forget.

This giving up of one's men and one's childhood to colored women—for the girl-child was shaped as subtly as little boys by the nurse-mother relationship—took on the unreal, shadowy quality of a dream; a recurring dream that southern white women could not rid themselves of. One's self . . . one's father . . . one's husband . . . one's son. . . . Sometimes in the old days it made a pattern like that: a stark dance that all their life long they tread the bleak measures of, with heart too heavy and body too rigid to make of space anything but a thin line to hold to on the way to a death that would not come soon enough.

A secret wound that can never be spoken aloud or shown is not tragedy for tragedy finds its stature on a stage where it can feel beyond it, its audience. To these women their life was only a shameful sore that could not be acknowledged because of its origin in sin.

Sometimes they could weep. A soundless weeping that trickled down into the crevices of personality leaving damp little places for thorns to grow, and sometimes for pale ghostly flowers that gave a fragrance of death to certain women. You remember these women from your childhood, and as you remember you keep thinking of old lost graveyards under oak trees where moss swings in the still air as if to the heartbeat of the dead, and small carved lambs watch over baby mounds; you keep thinking of cape jasmine in your mother's back yard, and the way you felt in the night when you awoke after dreams and smelled the night-blooming cereus below the window. . . .

It was as if these women never quite left the presence of the dead but mourned gently and continuously a loss that they could not bear to know the extent of. Unable to look at the ugly facts of their own life, they learned to see mysterious things the rest of us could never see. I remember how they "felt" premonitions, counting shadows and making of them cryptic answers. They "dreamed" that a beloved one would die and the beloved sometimes died! They "felt" there would be no returning when one left on a long journey and sometimes there was no return! They chanted so sweetly the death-knell of those they loved that I remember how carefully I avoided these friends of my mother's who dwelt serenely among disasters, for I feared that one day a gentle Cassandra might hold the syllables of my name on her tongue.

The little ghost women of small southern towns . . . swishing softly into church, sometimes singing in the choir, slipping like their carefully made custards down the dark maw of life. Their number was few. One remembers them because they roam even now so restlessly through time. I think, however, that most women of my mother's age, though their characters were twisted and shaped by these troubles, retained a more earthy quality and sometimes a firm grasp indeed on things of this world. The pain they felt they denied or tried to displace. Surely this emptiness was the natural way women should feel! Like childbirth pangs and menstrual cramps, the sexual erosion of their nature was "God's way" and hence if you were sensible must be accepted. But some stubbornly called it "female trouble" and went to doctors' offices as often as to church, to moan their misery.

A few "solved it all" by rejecting their womanly qualities. They seemed to hate and envy men for their freedom from pain and their access to pleasure. And sometimes they hated their own Maker too (a blasphemy they carefully hid from their minds) for giving females the long agony of parturition and none of the male's quick ecstasy of procreation. Yet there was usually a curious loyalty to their own father, though every other man was not "fit to be lived with." In later decades, when women were freer, these protesters turned toward the cities, gathering together, a grim little number, cropping their hair short, walking in heavy awkward strides, and acquiring, as do subjugated people everywhere when protesting their chains, the more unpleasant qualities of this enemy who had segregated them from their birthright. Not daring in the secret places of their minds to confess what they really wanted, they demanded to be treated "exactly like men." They were of course a part of the psychosexual, economic, political protest of women arising throughout Western culture, a kind of fibroid growth of sick cells multiplying aggressiveness in an attempt at cure. But there was no comfortable place for such women in the South, though a few of these rebels lived in every town.

The majority of southern women convinced themselves that God had ordained that they be deprived of pleasure, and meekly stuffed their hollowness with piety, trying to believe that the tightness they felt was hunger satisfied. Culturally stunted by a region that still pays nice rewards to simple-mindedness in females, they had no defenses against blandishment. They listened to the round words of men's tribute to Sacred Womanhood and believed, thinking no doubt that if they were not sacred then what under God's heaven *was* the matter with them! Once hoisted up by the old colonels' oratory, they stayed on lonely pedestals and rigidly played "statue" while their men went about more important affairs elsewhere.

These women turned away from the ugliness which they felt powerless to cope with and made for themselves and their families what they called a "normal" life. Their homes, often simple, were gracious and good to live in. The South—if one can forget the shabby milltowns, the rickety Colored Towns, the surrealist city tenements—is full of such homes. Places you remember—if you live on that side of town—of quiet ease and comfort and taste. In these homes, food and flowers were cherished, and old furniture, and the family's past (screened of all but the pleasing and the trivial). Sex was pushed out through the back door as a shameful thing never to be mentioned. Segregation was pushed out of sight also, and this was managed so successfully that until the last twenty years, most white southerners cheerfully said there was no race problem for it had been "solved." Out through the back door went the unpleasant and unmentionable; in through the back door came trays laden with food as delicious as can be found in the world. Though asceticism controlled the regions left out of the physiology books, and Prohibition succeeded sometimes in banishing the bottle, the groaning table was left free.

Whatever the hurt in our lives, there are these memories of food, and flowers, and of southern gardens, filled with our mothers' fantasies that had no other way to creep into life. Ladies and their garden clubs have been made by cartoonists into a national laugh, and sometimes a funny one, but some of us can smile for only a moment. We are always remembering a face we love and the longing in it as plants were set in damp ground and shaded against the sun. . . . A figure stooping, familiar hands feeling around in warm soft dirt to slip a seed out, planting and transplanting little secret dreams, making them live in an azalea, a rose, a camellia, when they could not live in their own arid lives. . . . A voice grown plaintive over a peaked little plant that refused to bloom . . . so softly scolding the flowers for not living their life to its full. In the mornings these old gardens full of lively bugs, and toads hopping among the violets, and new blow-y spider webs that never break in the memory, were like a clear mind filled with bright dewy ideas. But at night in the moonlight, a woman walking alone, up and down prim rows of camellias or in summer among the lilies, even now can make one want to close the gates against the past forever—so hurting is the realization of an anguish that need not have been.

With their gardens and their homes, these women tried to shut out evil, and sometimes succeeded in sheltering their children from it. If you could only keep from them the things of our South that must never be mentioned, all would be well! Innocence, virtue, ignorance, silence were synonyms twining around young lives like smilax. It was not evil but the knowledge of it that injured, these mothers believed.

What you don't hear or read or see surely can never be known to you. And because they did not believe things *could* change or that they should change (though they could not have told you why) they had to shut their own minds against knowledge of evil also. They could not let their imaginations feel the sorrow of a colored mother whose child is shamed from birth, nor once look deep into poverty, nor once touch the agony of a back-door life lived forever and ever, nor once realize what they themselves had been deprived of. They could not have borne it. And because they could not let themselves know, they were terrified at a word, a suggestion, anything that caused them to feel deeply. It was as if one question asked aloud might, like a bulldozer, uproot their garden of fantasies and tear it in a few moments out of time, leaving only naked bleeding reality to live with.

There were others whose minds perhaps were not brighter, but whose natures could not accept life so meekly. They felt compelled to question and to answer their own questions. They would not have used the word "sex" aloud, but their questions and answers told them that all a woman can expect from lingering on exalted heights is a hard chill afterward; that indeed, white women had not profited in the least from the psychosexual profit system which segregation in the South supported so lavishly; and that furthermore, no bargain had been made with them in any of these transactions. They learned that *discrimination* was a word with secret meanings and they did not like its secrets. This much of semantics they understood as clearly as their recipe for beaten biscuits. In the white southern woman's dictionary, *discrimination* could be defined as a painful way of life which too often left an empty place in her bed and an ache in the heart. Whether or not these women had themselves experienced this pain—and we must remember that many had not—they knew segregation in the South had cleaved through white woman's tenderest dreams. They had seen it turn a woman's life drama of child, wife, mother into tragedy, or more often into plain vulgar melodrama. How could they sit in the audience and applaud their own humiliation?

So, learning these answers to their questions, they climbed down from the pedestal when no one was looking and explored a bit. Not as you may think, perhaps. They were conventional, old-fashioned, highly "moral" women, who would not have dreamed of breaking the letter of their marriage vows or, when not married, their technical chastity. But their minds went a-roaming and their sympathies attached themselves like hungry little fibers to all kinds of people and causes while their shrewd common sense kicked old lies around until they were popping like firecrackers.

These ladies went forth to commit treason against a southern tradition set up by men who had betrayed their mothers, sometimes themselves, and many of the South's children white and mixed, for three long centuries. It was truly a subversive affair, but as decorously conducted as an afternoon walk taken by the students of a Female Institute. It started stealthily, in my mother's day. Shyly, these first women sneaked down from their chilly places, did their little sabotage and sneaked up again, wrapping innocence around them like a lace shawl. They set secret time bombs and went back to their needlework, serenely awaiting the blast. They had no lady Lincoln to proclaim their emancipation from southern tradition but they scarcely needed one.

The thing was a spontaneous reaction. Mother in her old age told daughter strange truths that had gnawed on her lonely heart too long. And daughter told other women. Colored and white women stirring up a lemon-cheese cake for the hungry males in the household looked deep into each other's eyes and understood their common past. A mistress, reading the Bible to her colored maid polishing silver, would lay aside Holy Writ and talk of things less holy but of immense importance to both of them.

Insurrection was on. White men were still unaware of it, but the old pedestal on which for so long their women had been safely stowed away, was reeling and rocking. With an emotionally induced stupidity really beneath them, these men went on with their race-economic exploitation, protecting themselves behind rusty shields of as phony a moral cause as the Anglo-American world has ever witnessed. In the name of *sacred womanhood,* of *purity,* of *preserving the home,* lecherous old men and young ones, reeking with impurities, who had violated the home since they were sixteen years old, whipped up lynchings, organized Klans, burned crosses, aroused the poor and ignorant to wild excitement by an obscene, perverse imagery describing the "menace" of Negro men hiding behind every cypress waiting to rape "our" women. In the name of such holiness, they did these things to keep the affairs of their own heart and conscience and home, as well as the community, "under control." And not once did they dream that their women did not believe their lies.

And then it happened. The lady insurrectionists gathered together in one of our southern cities. They primly called themselves church women but churches were forgotten by everybody when they spoke their revolutionary words. They said calmly that they were not afraid of being raped; as for their sacredness, they could take care of it themselves; they did not need the chivalry of a lynching to protect them and did not want it. Not only that, they continued, but they would personally do everything in their power to keep any Negro from being lynched and furthermore, they squeaked bravely, they had plenty of power.

They had more than they knew. They had the power of spiritual blackmail over a large part of the white South. All they had to do was to drop their little bucket into any one of numerous wells of guilt dotting the landscape and splash it around a bit. No one, of thousands of white men, had any notion how much or how little each woman knew about his private goings-on. Some who had never been guilty in act began to equate adolescent fantasies with reality, and there was confusion everywhere.

This was in 1930. These women organized an Association of Southern Women for the Prevention of Lynching. Their husbands, sons, brothers, and uncles often worked proudly by their side; many of them with sincere concern for the state of affairs, others because they had to.

Though it may seem incredible to all but southerners, the custom of lynching had so rarely been questioned that these church women's action gave a genuine shock. For this was a new thing in Dixie. The ladies' valor is not diminished, I think, by reminding ourselves that the movement could not have crystallized so early had not Dr. Will Alexander, and a handful of men and women whom he gathered around him, pushed things off to a good start in 1918 with the first interracial committee in the South. There were other yeasty forces at work: A world war had squeezed and pulled the earth's people apart and squeezed them together again; the Negroes themselves, led by courageous men like Walter White of Atlanta and W. E. B. Du Bois and their northern white friends were making our nation aware that Negroes have rights; the group around Dr. Howard Odum—whose first study of the Negro in 1910 greatly influenced social science's interest in Negro-white patterns of life—were gathering all kinds of facts concerning a region that had been for so long content with its fantasies and fears. The women's role was to bake the first pan of bread made from this rising batter, and to serve it hot as is southern custom.

After this magnificent uprising against the sleazy thing called "chivalry," these women worked like the neat, industrious housewives they really were, using their mops and brooms to clean up a dirty spot here and there but with no real attempt to change this way of life which they dimly realized had injured themselves and their children as much as it had injured Negroes, but which they nevertheless clung to.

Of course the demagogues would have loved to call them "Communists" or "bolsheviks," but how could they? The women were too prim and neat and sweet and ladylike and churchly in their activities, and too many of them were the wives of the most powerful men in town. Indeed, the ladies themselves hated the word "radical" and were quick to turn against anyone who dared go further than they in this housecleaning of Dixie. Few of them had disciplined intellects or giant imaginations and probably no one of them grasped the full implications of this sex-race-religion-economics tangle, but they had warm hearts and powerful energy and a nice technic for bargaining, and many an old cagey politician, and a young one or two, have been outwitted by their soft bending words.

They followed a sound feminine intuition, working as "church women," leaning on the strength of Christ's teachings for support when they needed it. They worked with great bravery but so unobtrusively that even today many southerners know little about them. But they aroused the conscience of the South and the whole country about lynching; they tore a big piece of this evil out of southern tradition, leaving a hole which no sane man in Dixie now dares stuff up with public defenses. They attacked the KKK when few except Julian Harris of the Columbus (Georgia) *Enquirer*, among white southern newspaper men, had criticized this group from whom Hitler surely learned so much. And they have continued this fight (known to demagogues as "northern meddling"), joining their energies with other church women throughout the nation.

But they were not yet done. They had a few more spots to rub out. One had to do with their own souls. They believed that the Lord's Supper is a holy sacrament which Christians cannot take without sacrilege unless they will also break bread with fellow men of other color. Believing, they put on their best bib and tucker and gathered in small groups to eat with colored women, deliberately breaking a taboo that had collected around it as many deep fears as any in southern culture.

It is sometimes difficult for those not reared as white southerners to remember how this eating taboo in childhood is woven into the mesh of things that are "wrong," how it becomes tangled with God and sex, pulling anxieties from stronger prohibitions and attaching them to itself. But we who live here can never forget. One of these church women told me of her experience when she first ate with colored friends. Though her conscience was serene, and her enjoyment of this association with colored women was real, yet she was seized by an acute nausea which disappeared only when the meal was finished. She was too honest to attribute it to anything other than deep-rooted anxiety welling up from the "bottom of her personality," as she expressed it, creeping back from her childhood training. Others have told me similar experiences: of feeling "pangs of conscience," as one put it, "though my conscience was clearly approving"; or suddenly in the night awaking, overwhelmed by "serious doubts of the wisdom of what we are doing."

The white women were not alone in these irrational reactions. Colored women also found it hard, but for different reasons. Sometimes their pride was deeply hurt that white women felt so virtuous when eating with them. They were too sensitive not to be aware of the psychic price the white women paid for this forbidden act, and yet too ignorant of the training given white children to understand why there had to be a price. And sometimes the colored women were themselves almost overcome by a break-through not of guilt but of their old repressed hatred of white people. One of the most charming, sensitive, intelligent Negro women I know, tells me that even now when she is long with white people she grows physically ill and has immense difficulty coming to terms with the resentments of her childhood.

To break bread together as Christians, each group had to force its way through thick psychological barriers, and each did it with little understanding of their own or the other group's feelings. When the seizures came, most of the church women, white and Negro, suppressed them simply and firmly by laying the ponderous weight of the New Testament on their fears and hurts, declaring bravely that "Jesus would have done likewise."

In more recent years this group, united with the church women in all parts of the nation and from most of our denominations, has taken a stand against segregation in the church. The same group in Atlanta whose nucleus is now under Dorothy Tilly's fine leadership—and supported by the Southern Regional Council—has made during the past year a brave strong stand against segregation in our higher schools of learning and in interstate travel. They are daring more these days, doing fewer paint jobs and more carpentry on the old Southern Mansion, adding rooms in it for the rest of the family. And because they are, they are not receiving the indulgence of newspapers and politicians that they once had. Perhaps the old power of spiritual blackmail has waned. Perhaps also, these women are developing new powers, new technics, and are beginning to be feared in new ways. However much or little they have accomplished (and sometimes it seems a small thing set against the size and urgency of the job), these church women found for themselves a sublimation of the deprivations that their culture had exacted of their sex and used their freed energy and love to spread a green-growing cover crop on the South's worn-out spiritual soil. In that strange and lovely and rare way of human nature, they pushed aside their own trouble and somehow grew mature enough to reach out with compassion toward those more miserable. It seemed almost as if they lifted their natures by their own leverage though they would say that it was their faith in the teachings of Jesus that lifted them.

It would be pleasant to stop the story of the South's women here, but there is a more tragic page.

Like their men, most of these deeply hurt women found it easier to cultivate hate than love in their natures. Their own dreams destroyed, they destroyed in cruelty their children's dreams and their men's aspirations.

It was a compulsive thing they did, with no awareness of the unconscious hate compelling them to do it. Most of them felt they were doing "right." Most of them thought it was their duty to watch closely over the morals of their children and husbands. They did not see themselves in the ungracious role of exacting of their family the same obedience to the same Authority that had exacted so much of them. They thought they loved their husbands and children so much that they wanted them to do "right." They would have been horrified had they been accused of setting up their home as a juvenile court and themselves as the judge, though that is what they too often did.

They would have been more deeply shocked had they been accused of hate. They felt nothing but love for their families and sometimes a bit of vexation and disappointment. They nursed them tenderly through illness, planned delicious meals for them, kept the home physically pleasant, were ambitious and proud of their achievements, and felt that they were utterly devoted wives and mothers. They "sacrificed" all their lives long but they never looked clearly at what they were sacrificing.

The little thorns growing deep in secret wounds thrust up sharp points into their conscience, making it a prickly thing, but they covered it with the soft folds of affectionate concern and hid from themselves the thorn tips. When they turned this conscience against their children, or the men in their family, they thought they were doing God's will. And, as is the tragic way of humans, in the name of "what is right" they committed as great evil at home as did their men in the name of Sacred Womanhood over in Colored Town or at the state capitals, or as nations have done in the name of freedom in recent mass wars.

Many a man went into politics, or joined the KKK, had a nervous breakdown or forged checks, got drunk or built up a great industry, because he could no longer bear the police-state set up in his own home. But this would have been a hard thing for these good mothers and wives to believe, and for the men also.

As time passed, mothers went more and more compulsively about the training of their children as if it were a totalitarian discipline: imposing rigidities on spirit and mind, imposing eating schedules as if eating were a duty, elimination schedules as if elimination were a responsibility one owed to one's state, hurrying weaning as if suckling were an immoral habit that babies must give up as soon as possible, binding the curiosity of childhood as the Chinese once bound their little girls' feet.

More and more rigid became this training and more steel-like and impersonal. It was all such a desperate business. If they had been asked what they feared, or to list the evils their children might "find out," they would have been deeply bewildered. They sometimes had tears but no words for their anxiety. They only knew that they must keep their children pure and innocent, they must "make" them good. They felt that inside each little body, inside each mind, there was a powerful force, a kind of atomic energy; if let out, it might blast their children's "morals" to pieces. They were compelled, therefore, to spend their time walling up this danger. With a rigid training they armored their children against their fantasies and sex feelings, preparing them for human relations as if for a cruel medieval battle. Thus they segregated sex from love and tenderness and obligation, and did not see how inevitably it would slip into secret back-door union with hate and guilt.

This training, until recent decades, was often complicated by the child's dual Mother-Mammy relationship. For sometimes Mother would give orders which Mammy, more wise in the ways of childhood, would not carry out. Many a child of my generation was split as deeply in his moral nature as in his first human relationships by a white mother's code that colored nurse intuitively knew was too rigid and unreal for the warm, pliant human spirit to adhere to. Though in many ways it was a thing to be grateful for, sometimes instinctual needs of the body were satisfied at so exorbitant a price exacted by conscience that the personality could not pay it.

We cannot let ourselves forget that their culture had stripped these women of profound biological rights, had ripped off their inherent dignity and made of them silly statues and psychic children, stunting their capacity for rich understanding and enjoyment of husbands and family. It is not strange that they became vigilant guardians of a southern tradition which in guarding they often, unbeknownst to their own minds, avenged themselves on with a Medea-like hatred.

In most of them there was a profound subservience; they dared not question what had injured them so much. It was all wrapped up in one package: sex taboos, race segregation, "the right to make money the way Father made money," the duty to go to church, the fear of new knowledge that would shake old beliefs, the splitting of ideals from actions—and you accepted it all as uncritically as the Communists accept their Stalin-stamped lives. And you insisted on others accepting it also. You dreaded a deviationist, you were in terror lest your children be other than orthodox southerners. You used your conscience as if it were a hypodermic needle, plunging it into the tenderest spots of young spirits, filling them with your guilt, hoping to inoculate them "for their own good" against vague, dread "evils."

But it was a tainted needle that spread through these children a poison that came out in unhealing sores.

It would be as unfair to blame the mothers of two or three generations for a way of life that began twisting and turning and destroying its children long before they were born, as it would be to blame the men. Both men and women were born into it and of it. And because it is a culture that lacks almost completely the self-changing power that comes from honest criticism, because in the past it forced out its children who saw dangers and tried to avert them, who had insight and talents that could have contributed so richly to the South's recovery; because it bruised those who grimly stayed, unwelcomed, until their energies were depleted (we have only to recall Howard Odum's stormy years, and Arthur Raper, H. C. Nixon, William Kilpatrick, and numerous poets, teachers, authors, who were forced into exile or stayed at home under bitter attack)—because it did these things to its own men, it is not difficult to understand why these women, our mothers and perhaps ourselves, could not do other than bend to the system and think it "right" to bend to it. They did not have enough insight—where could they have got it?—to grow wary of a conscience that drives ruthlessly across natural, spontaneous needs. They did not dream that the energy driving this conscience might be hate, not love. They could not have accepted the terrifying fact that their own banned desires had slipped into their conscience giving it its cruel power. They had not questioned life closely enough—for life gave harsh answers to questions—to discover that guilt and ideals are as different sometimes as the insane and the same.

We cannot censure—who would dare!—but we know now with tragic certainty that these women, forced by their culture and their heartbreak, did a thorough job of closing the path to mature genitality for many of their sons and daughters, and an equally good job of leaving little cleared detours that led downhill to homosexual and infantile green pastures, and on to alcoholism, neuroses, divorce, to race-hate and brutality, and to a tight inflexible mind that could not question itself.

They did a thorough job of dishonoring love, of making honesty seem a treasonable thing, of leaving in their children an unquenchable need to feel superior to others, to bow easily to authority, and to value power and money more dearly than human relations and truth.

They did a thorough job of splitting the soul in two. They separated ideals from acts, beliefs from knowledge, and turned their children sometimes into exploiters but more often into moral weaklings who daydream about democracy and human dignity and freedom and integrity, yet cannot find the real desire to bring these dreams into reality; always they keep dreaming and hoping, and fearing, that the next generation will do it.

Sometimes I have grown tired of hearing Mom blamed for all that is wrong with her sons and daughters. After all, we might well ask, who started the grim mess? Who long ago made Mom and her sex "inferior" and stripped her of her economic and political and sexual rights? Who, nearly two thousand years ago, said, "It is good for a man not to touch a woman. . . . But if they cannot contain, let them marry: for it is better to marry than to burn"? Certainly that old misogynist St. Paul was no female apostle. Man, born of woman, has found it a hard thing to forgive her for giving him birth. The patriarchal protest against the ancient matriarch has borne strange fruit through the years. . . .

In speaking of millions of people and their customs, their feelings and values, we have to remind ourselves that many have not shared in experiences that have yet profoundly affected their whole lives. They have, instead, made identification with them. Experiences which others have had link themselves too easily sometimes with our secret fantasies and secret needs until a curious bond is woven of the actual experiences of the few and the unconscious desire of the many to possess them. A generation, free of wounds, will identify itself with the battle scars of a past generation in a masochistic community of daydreams because it needs to feel pain. Hanns Sachs has brilliantly reminded us in *The Creative Unconscious* of man's capacity to daydream in company with others when each has within him a secret fantasy that can be acted out in rhythm with others. Here in the artist is the seed of a dream growing into a book, a painting, a poem, which awakens deep down in the one beholding it another shadowy dream that, like a reflection in a pool, takes on mysterious shape and substance; and suddenly there is a profound communion of dream with dream, not on the bright surface of life but in the secret shadowy places of the spirit. It may be for only a moment in time, or for all of a life, but two fantasies have met, magically bridging time and space, and whispered their secrets to each other. This is art's power over us; and art's terror, for there are dreams we do not want aroused again, ash that must remain ash. And sometimes in blinding anger and fear we turn and rend a poem, a book, a painting, a truth that has blown too steadily on old forgotten graves of memories calling forth ghosts whom we have forbidden to walk the earth again. This is the secret of art. And of a people's myth also. This is the secret of tradition's hypnotic power over the minds of a whole region though most of those minds may know tradition only by hearsay.

Southern tradition, segregation, states' rights have soaked up the secret fears of our people; little private fantasies of childhood have crept there for hiding, unacknowledged arsenals of hate have been stored there, and a loyalty covering up a lack of mature love has glazed the words over with sanctity. No wonder the saying of them aloud can stir anxieties until there are times when it seems that we have lost our grasp of reality.

V

Tradition and Identity
Reevaluated (1960–1980)

In 1961 poet James Dickey wrote in "Notes on the Decline of Outrage," "To be a white Southerner in the mid-twentieth century is to realize the full bafflement and complexity of the human condition."[1] Dickey's statement did not apply exclusively to white Southerners. African American writers in this period were able to demonstrate just how much "bafflement and complexity" they also were experiencing, many reminding white readers of the virulent truth once expressed by French author Simone Weil: "A man loses half his soul the day he becomes a slave."

Novelist Walker Percy put it another way, stating that the South—with all its scenic beauty and natural resources—had been offered something like another opportunity at paradise, another shot at Eden. God's only stipulation this time was that everyone get along and that the white man, in particular, treat his black brother fairly. If the white man could do that, then paradise would be accessible to all. As Percy was quick to point out, the white man flunked the test. Nevertheless, Percy noted, white Southerners were no more inherently evil than white Northerners, who, if the tables had been turned and they had been able to exploit slavery for profit, would have done so: "Slavery was profitable here, not in Massachusetts. It meant that whoever could get slaves got slaves."

The "Revolution of 1861" had ended with Northern victory and the abolition of slavery. However, as the literature of the Reconstruction shows, conflicts and indignation persisted well into the twentieth century, stirring defiance in many writers of the Southern Renaissance who pledged to "exercise autonomy" and "resist conforming to the dictates of others living in other parts of the country."[2] But by the first year of the tumultuous 1960s, Dickey acknowledged that "Southern autonomy, qua Southern, now tends to come out in petty, vindictive acts of ill will toward the Negro, and he [the average white Southerner] wants no part of it."[3]

The average Southern white was "part of it" by virtue of historical imperatives and the residual racism that cast a pall over even the most felicitous Southern traditions. The resulting paradox was the source of Dickey's bafflement and the persistent, gnawing guilt he felt for loving what he should not love—the South with all its unforgivable contradictions:

> All this he knows, but at the same time he recognizes the fact that the South still stands for . . . for something. He has read W. J. Cash, and so has been told the "truth" about the much advertised codes of Southern honor, the cult of Southern womanhood, the Southerner's characteristic extroversion and his "habit of command," the cultural shallowness of the nineteenth-century South, and so on. He knows the verdict of history on his people. He knows one more thing about history too: that it has trapped the Southern white just as securely in his complex of racial attitudes as it has trapped the Southern Negro in his deplorable social, physical, and psychological environment. And he knows that with the increase of industry and "business," with their attendant influx of thousands of people each month from other parts of the country, the "solidarity" of the South, in manners as well as in attitudes about race, is breaking down more and more rapidly, and that when the older patterns of behavior are gone, there will be nothing to put in their place save the empty money-grubbing and soul-killing competitive drives of the Northern industrial concerns. He knows that, as a Southerner, he has only a few things left to him: the intonation of his voice, an appetite for certain kinds of cooking, a vague familiarity with a few quaint folkways far off in the mountains, and his received attitude toward the Negro; and that of these the only one important as a rallying point for his Southerners, as an effective factor in producing sectional assent, as a motivating force in political action, is the last.[4]

To be any sort of Southerner in the 1960s was to witness the old dead causes resurrected as ghoulish reminders of unfinished business. Nor was the South the only area of the country to feel the upheavals and necessary tumult associated with civil rights. Regions that had formerly believed themselves beyond the poisonous touch of racism had the awareness thrust upon them that racism was not simply a malignancy on the Southern landscape but rather a subcutaneous eruption of the body politic that was America itself. Repressing racism in its many guises and relegating it to the status of a problem peculiar to the South had only permitted the existing situation to "fester like a sore," in Langston Hughes's words. Questions of responsibility for this situation found answers in the irreducible logic of violence that was typically Southern and American. Thus, the fallout of racial unrest spread far beyond the epicenter of the ever-explosive South, touching such diverse locales as Detroit and Los Angeles and, later, in the 1970s, Boston—faraway cities that were, like the South, forced to acknowledge a smoldering tension and the "context of [a] failed foundation."[5]

Attempts at sharing the sin do not exonerate the sinner. For Dickey's average white Southerner, then, the plight was twofold: belonging to a community that often refused to condemn racism and intolerance and loving that community nonetheless. As Faulkner had earlier put it, "Loving all of it even while he [the Southerner] had to hate some of it because he knows now that you don't love because: you love despite, not of the virtues, but despite the faults."

Against the most extraordinary opposition, Martin Luther King, Jr., and other civil rights leaders insisted on loving the South despite its faults, loving it enough to tell the truth about it and to demand the best from its people. It was no coincidence that the Civil Rights movement of the sixties originated in the South, the region most resistant to change. Gently but firmly King rejected Faulkner's counsel to blacks that they should "go slow now" concerning integration. Whites made such a strategy impossible, forcing confrontations in such hotspots as Little Rock, Selma, and Oxford, and giving blacks little choice but to protest the justness of their cause in numbers too large to suppress or ignore. Adopting Gandhian strategies of nonviolent resistance and insisting on rights guaranteed by the Declaration of Independence, King and his supporters demonstrated the incompatibility of racial hatred with the teachings of Christ allegedly embraced by a majority of Southerners. By slow degrees, the calcified backbone of racism began to bend in the direction of greater tolerance and acceptance of differences.

However, a muscular defiance persisted in some quarters, causing the South of the sixties to offer a mirror of its bellicose past. Despite being taught the Sunday School anthem that "Jesus loves the little children, all the children of the world," Southern white children were cautioned not to take such idealism seriously. Often, when the threat of integration loomed on the horizon, White Citizens' Councils "manufactured information, spread rumors, gossip and hearsay—and planted the seeds of suspicion that would undermine any effort to break down the walls of segregation."[6]

Children were the special targets of propaganda and direct assault. One poignant example was that of Ruby Bridges, a six-year-old black child who helped initiate school desegregation in New Orleans in 1961. Pulitzer Prize–winning author and psychiatrist Robert Coles describes the difficulties that Ruby encountered while trying to attend elementary school in a fiercely segregated neighborhood: "For days that turned into weeks and weeks that turned into months, this child had to brave murderously heckling mobs, there in the morning and there in the evening, hurling threats and slurs and hysterical denunciations and accusations. Federal marshals took her home. She attended school all by herself for a good part of the school year, owing to a total boycott by white families."[7] Death threats were common, yet Ruby and her family persevered, relying on strong religious convictions to sustain them at a time perhaps best described as the South's "dark night of the soul." At one point, Ruby confided in both Coles and her teacher that she prayed for her tormentors each evening before going to sleep. Asked whether she believed that her prayers would help change the situation, Ruby was quoted as saying, "I'm sure God knows what's happening. He's got a lot to worry about; but there is bad trouble here, and he can't help but notice. He may not rush to do anything; not right away. But there will come a day, just like you hear in church."[8]

Violent extremism persisted throughout the early 1960s, culminating in the bombing of black churches, among them the Sixteenth Street Baptist Church in Birmingham in September 1963. In that explosion, four girls attending Sunday school were killed, reinforcing the savage resistance shown by the Ku Klux Klan and other white supremacist groups to civil rights legislation pending in Congress at the time. Nevertheless, the Birmingham bombing stunned some people, hard-core segregationists, forcing them to rethink support of tactics that had resulted in the murder of children. When Martin Luther King, Jr., went on television to declare that "not even killing our children will keep us from loving you," the region's hate groups suffered a blow from which they would never entirely recover. In response to the savagery in Birmingham and to bombings and burnings of Negro churches throughout the South, selected clergy formed the Committee of Conscience, an interfaith and interdenominational organization that raised $750,000 to rebuild the churches. The chairman of this organization, Harold O'Chester, was a conservative Southern Baptist and a self-proclaimed segregationist who condemned the "burnings, bombings, shootings which have plagued our community in recent weeks."[9]

But the appeals of concerned clergy were not enough to change the sentiments of a large segment of Southern society. Civil rights legislation would be needed to guarantee those rights that were denied to African Americans by segregation. Despite President John Kennedy's support of a civil rights agenda and, in particular, his endorsement of a ban on discrimination in federally funded housing, Kennedy was seen by many African American leaders as little more than a symbolic advocate of basic human rights. Kennedy's tentative approach to the housing issue, for example, prompted King to quip that "if tokenism were our goal, this Administration has moved us adroitly toward its accomplishment." Kennedy displayed more resolve in ordering federal troops to the University of Mississippi, where, in the fall of 1962, James Meredith, a black Air Force veteran, enrolled in classes under a federal court order. The ensuing riot in which two people were killed and hundreds injured came to be known as the Battle of Oxford.

It is difficult to gauge how effective Kennedy's civil rights platform might have proven had the young president not been assassinated on November 22, 1963. What is certain is that his successor, Lyndon Baines Johnson, a Southerner and former majority leader in the Senate, possessed both the connections and the skill necessary to route civil rights legislation through the halls of Congress. Pledging to end poverty and racial injustice, Johnson initiated a hailstorm of new legislation and worked behind the scenes to enact previously stalled bills necessary for the common good. Johnson's success in gaining passage of the Civil Rights Act of 1964 resulted in laws prohibiting discrimination in housing, education, and jobs. Johnson also reinforced the spine of existing voting rights legislation by seeing to it that Congress passed a sterner Voting Rights Act (1965) that eliminated literacy tests for voters and ensured additional controls and protection for blacks registering to vote in the South.

By no means was Johnson a sole crusader in transforming the vision of a just society into a legislative reality. Laws were the result of years of protests, marches, and sit-ins, all designed to dispel the "gradualism" that had so often characterized the South's approach to matters of race. Many lives were also lost on Southern soil as a result of the backlash from whites who were determined to extinguish civil rights support and activities. Assassination of prominent leaders became a mainstay in the arsenal of terrorist persuasion. In 1963, Medgar Evers was gunned down in his driveway in Jackson, Mississippi. Martin Luther King, Jr., was murdered on the balcony of the Lorraine Motel in Memphis in 1968. The unfinished battles of Reconstruction were waged with a ferocity that captured headlines and promised no end in sight. In 1966, newspaper editors in more than one Southern city saw the potential for sweltering heat and race relations to ignite in violence, prompting the editors to warn of "A Long, Hot Summer" for demonstrators and their foes.

One can only speculate how long the "war" in the South would have lasted had not another war vied for the nation's attention, stoking fires of protest against U.S. involvement in Vietnam. Despite his mammoth efforts at social reform and an unstinting desire to realize the dream of a "Great Society," Lyndon Johnson's achievements were, in the words of Martin Luther King, Jr., "shot down on the battlefields of Vietnam." By sending almost half a million troops to Vietnam, the president escalated American involvement to the point where domestic programs suffered irreversible setbacks in the wake of sky-rocketing military appropriations. "Johnson's war" and the unpopularity of the selective service system's draft resulted in widespread opposition, so that by 1968, Johnson and the Democratic party were left floundering. Johnson's decision not to seek reelection paved the way for Richard Nixon's presidency and the latter's policy of détente, a gradual de-escalation of tensions with communist countries.

Nixon's promises of "peace with honor" did not bring about an immediate end to the war. Protests continued well into his presidency, though Southerners, by and large, tended to support U.S. involvement in southeast Asia long after people in other regions of the country began voicing dissent. As early as the First World War, the South had sought to demonstrate its patriotic convictions, perhaps in response to allegations made by the North during the Civil War that Confederate troops were "traitors." Southerners set out self-consciously to prove that was not the case. Every American war in the twentieth century thus found a disproportionate number of Southerners, usually poor, volunteering for military duty. Vietnam was no exception.

Even the South contained pockets of opposition to the ongoing struggle that had placed military advisers in South Vietnam as early as 1955. In the spring of 1969, Richard Nixon ordered the strategic bombing of North Vietnamese supply routes in Laos and Cambodia. Nixon's efforts to intensify a war he had promised to end prompted widespread violence and demonstrations on college campuses throughout the country. Almost no campus was deemed "safe" for a presidential visit. Not even the United States Military Academy at West Point could promise a protest-free commencement should Richard Nixon have insisted on speaking there.

Nixon and his advisors wanted to prove that the president could visit a college campus without generating a firestorm of protest. The campus they proposed was that of the University of Tennessee at Knoxville. The occasion was a crusade sponsored by the Reverend Billy Graham in the spring of 1970. At Graham's invitation, Nixon shared the stage with the famed evangelist, the man whom George Bush would later call "America's pastor." The crusade drew almost 50,000 people to Neyland Stadium, home of the Tennessee Volunteers football team. On being introduced, Nixon stood and gave a brief partisan speech interrupted by a small gathering of protesters brandishing antiwar signs and placards reading "Thou Shalt Not Kill." The protestors, including university faculty from the psychology and history departments, were arrested on site. John Doe warrants were issued later in the week for students who had managed to elude police. Although most of the crusade's attendees favored Nixon and his policies, the event proved that not all Southerners were willing to support a military engagement lasting longer than the Trojan War. Following the Watergate scandal in 1973, Graham, a native of North Carolina, expressed regret at his earlier endorsement of Nixon.

The seventies found the South feeling the country's mood. A tense lull settled over the region, as if all the energy fueling the civil unrest of the sixties was now spent. Not so much a deliberate and collective choice to halt violence, the change at first seemed a fulfillment of the prophecy made by young Ruby Bridges in 1961: "They [the mobs] keep coming and saying the bad words, but my momma says they'll get tired after a while and then they'll stop coming."[10] Whether from lassitude or a shift in the sensibility of a people grown tired but reflective, the fury of the mobs abated: "Gradually scenes also faded off the television screen showing southern whites siccing dogs or using electric cattle prods against southern blacks."[11]

The seventies saw, once more, an intense regional self-consciousness, but that distinctiveness now enabled the South to envision a new role as purveyor of cultural and economic opportunities. Jimmy Carter's election to the presidency in 1976, coinciding with America's bicentennial celebration, was a celebration of things Southern as well. A racially enlightened, born-again Baptist, Carter sought the support of prominent African Americans, filling his cabinet positions with an unprecedented number of minorities. Occupying an especially important position in Carter's inner circle was civil rights leader Andrew Young. Both Carter and Young "shared a deep regional pride and knew that the South could not achieve acceptance on par with other regions of the country until segregation was laid to rest."[12] Well aware of the South's brutal history, Carter made it clear that his administration represented new interests and healing initiatives, citing the South's recent ability to shed its prejudices in providing economic advantages for all. Thus, the economic oasis known as the Sunbelt South attracted a wave of Northern investors, and almost overnight the country fell under the spell of renewed Southern charm:

> Suddenly the national press and media became so fascinated by the South that stereotypes threatened to become institutionalized. All Southerners, like their caricatures on the *Dukes of Hazard*, were quickly assigned downhome residence in imaginary rural counties where the Appalachians and the Bayou swamps were located right next door. During this kitsch outbreak, television also introduced *Roots* to provide a melodramatic mythology for black viewers and revived *Gone With the Wind* to reinstate a melodramatic mythology for Southern white viewers. (As Roy Blount has said, "You got to put the kibble over where even the slow dogs can get some.")[13]

The September 27, 1976, issue of *Time* magazine devoted a special section to the region entitled "The South Today." The tone of the lead article was exultant:

> In what had long been the nation's poorest, most backward-looking region, business booms and economic, social, and political opportunities abound. Cities thrust ever outward and upward. Racial integration proceeds with surprising smoothness. And a Georgian wins the Democratic presidential nomination, the Deep South's first major-party candidate for the presidency in 128 years. Small wonder that the rest of the country is looking to the South to see what it has been missing—and what it might learn.[14]

According to *Time*'s assessment, the South was "surging to prosperity," reversing the brain drain that had previously found Southern professors fleeing to Northern universities, and of most importance, bulldozing the last obstacles to integration.[15] With much to celebrate, James Dickey boasted that Northerners now envied Southerners' music, food, and distinctive mode of talking.

Far less complimentary of the recent achievements of Southern writers, the *Time* article declared that 1964, the year of Flannery O'Connor's death, had signaled the end of a literary era. *Time*'s postmortem analysis found Southern letters "stalled between a glorious past and an uncertain future."[16] The former emphasis on the romantic and the bizarre could scarcely continue to attract readers living in affluent suburbs far from swamps, cotton patches, and sharecroppers' tar shacks. Still, *Time* showcased a number of writers whose work represented current trends in Southern literature.

Receiving qualified praise were Ernest Gaines, whose work dramatized "changes" in the rural Louisiana of his childhood, and Lisa Alther, whose comic depiction of her upper East Tennessee family garnered an appreciative audience above the Mason-Dixon line. Poet Ishmael Reed, a native of Chattanooga, Tennessee, received brief mention for his modern retelling of *Uncle Tom's Cabin*. Likewise, Paul Allen and Harry Crews were tagged as novelists whose books were "technically competent" but whose penchant for the Gothic prompted both authors to write, as Faulkner put it, "not of the heart but of the glands."[17] Only Walker Percy's fiction was deemed notable and only then because Percy moved "steadily away from older Southern atmospheres."[18] A verdict of disappointing failures summed up the literary efforts of the South's new generation of writers.

Other critics of the era voiced agreement, as one particularly trenchant reviewer for the *New York Times Book Review* pronounced all Southern writing to be "local, florid, without distinction."[19] In some quarters, observers were willing to sound the death knell for the Southern literary enterprise, when closer examination revealed only a period of necessary gestation. During the seventies, Pulitzer-winning authors Shirley Ann Grau and Eudora Welty were producing some of their best work, and Walker Percy's *Lancelot* (1977) provoked immediate critical controversy while earning the author a devoted (some would say cult) Southern readership. Other writers beginning their careers in the seventies would come of age in the eighties. Thus, Southern letters, far from dead, were simply experiencing the natural rhythms associated with creative activity.

The fact that a good many writers did not receive the attention due them also may have been linked to a quickly changing political climate. The South's celebration as a region in ascendancy was short-lived, as double-digit inflation, an international oil crisis, and Jimmy Carter's self-described "malaise" dogged the new administration's efforts to show that Southerners possessed a talent for government and politics. Critics leveled accusations of provincialism with which the section's writers had long been familiar. The idea that the South might finally be accepted as a region every bit as Americanized as the Northeast or Midwest proved false, and as Jimmy Carter and his "Georgia Mafia" failed to gain a second term in the White House, some Southerners worried not only about the South's future in politics but also about its ability to sustain a literary tradition fast in eclipse.

Notes

1. James Dickey, *Babel to Byzantium* (New York: Echo Press, 1956), 257.
2. Dickey, 257.
3. Dickey, 262.
4. Dickey, 262–263.
5. Dickey, 262.
6. Will D. Campbell, *And Also With You* (Franklin, TN: Providence House, 1997), 176.

7. Robert Coles, *The Moral Life of Children* (Boston: Houghton Mifflin, 1986), 22.
8. Coles, 24.
9. Campbell, 174.
10. Coles, 24.
11. Doris Betts, "Many Souths and Broadening Scale: A Changing Southern Literature," *The Future South*, eds. Joe P. Dunn and Howard L. Preston (Urbana: University of Illinois Press, 1991), 166.
12. Peter Bourne, *Jimmy Carter* (New York: Scribner, 1997), 296.
13. Betts, 166.
14. *Time* (Sept. 27, 1976), 29.
15. *Time* (Sept. 27, 1976), 29.
16. *Time* (Sept. 27, 1976), 92.
17. *Time* (Sept. 27, 1976), 92.
18. *Time* (Sept. 27, 1976), 93.
19. Betts, 166–167.

In 1960, editors of Chattanooga, Tennessee's, two daily newspapers, the *Chattanooga Times* and *News Free Press*, announced plans for a citywide Civil War centennial celebration scheduled for spring 1961. In collaboration with local television affiliates, the newspapers began advertising a slate of events to include battle reenactments, historical lectures, and full-blown parades honoring the Confederate dead. Many of those gallant gray warriors lay buried in nearby cemeteries, still memorialized with an occasional bouquet placed by representatives of the Daughters of the Confederacy.

"Centennial fever," as it was called, ignited Chattanooga and the surrounding areas. Local schools hosted countless Civil War essay contests. Children gleefully anticipated the annual field trip to Lookout Mountain, site of the decisive "Battle above the Clouds." One local business even sponsored "Little Johnny Rebel" and "Little Suzy Belle" contests. Boys, ages seven to twelve, dressed up in Confederate uniforms, wore painted-on freckles and produced the Rebel yell for an appreciative panel of judges. Girls donned period attire, twirling parasols in their best imitation of Scarlett O'Hara. The winners of these competitions received an all-expense-paid trip to Oz, Kentucky, on a steam locomotive draped with Confederate flags.

Adults found themselves caught up in the frenzy, too. On designated occasions, affluent Chattanoogans hosted "plantation balls," reviving a gloriously idealized past, the aura of which spread quickly to other segments of the population. On an average day in the Chattanooga business district, men strode down the street sporting beards and muttonchops sideburns in the fashion of a century earlier. At the old Tivoli theater, anyone attending a matinee showing of the forties' film *The Southerner* would have been treated to the organist's rousing rendition of "Dixie." African Americans, paying the same admission price as whites, were required to sit in the Tivoli's balcony.

Chattanooga was not the only Southern city to sponsor a centennial celebration. Memphis, Birmingham, and Charleston all hosted similar events, inspiring Hollywood to create what may constitute the worst movie about the South ever made. Filmed in St. Cloud, Florida, in 1964, *2000 Maniacs* is described by one contemporary film guide as a horror cult classic.[1] In the film, the "giggling rednecks of Pleasant Valley, Georgia, trick vacationing Yankees into their small town, planning to make the visitors the guests of honor at the centennial barbeque."[2] The unsuspecting Northerners are then "chopped, crushed, ripped apart, etc. while the ghostly rebels party."[3] Notwithstanding its gratuitous violence and less than realistic special effects, *2000 Maniacs* sought to confirm every Northerner's secret suspicion about Southerners. Even if the film did not accomplish its goal, it reinforced stereotypes about the Gothic insanity, mass hysteria, and potential for violence widespread among Southerners.

If the early 1960s offered a chance for Southerners to wax nostalgic about the region's century-old war of independence, the new decade posed far more realistic and ultimately destructive threats from foreign powers. Perhaps all the centennial hoopla was orchestrated to divert people from the specter of atomic warfare looming on the horizon. In particular, the Cuban Missile Crisis of 1962 presented a special threat to the southeastern United States. In October of that year, U.S. satellite photography revealed the presence of Soviet offensive missiles in Cuba. Armed with atomic warheads, these missiles were directed at American cities, a majority of the urban targets located in the South. At the urging of his advisers and the Joint Chiefs of Staff, President Kennedy opted for a naval quarantine, or blockade, to prevent additional missiles from reaching their destination. In Texas, Georgia, and Florida, missile crews were placed on maximum alert. Fearing that the U.S.S.R. and Cuba would perceive the blockade as too weak a response, Southern senators, facing the prospect of sustaining plus or minus fifty million casualties in a nuclear first-strike situation, urged Kennedy to consider stronger measures. At one point, "the B-52 bomber force was ordered into the air fully loaded with atomic weapons."[4]

For thirteen days, the world stood poised on the brink of atomic holocaust. In Chattanooga, schoolchildren practiced daily civil defense drills, taking cover in hastily constructed fallout shelters after being issued military dog tags as a means of identification following an attack. A hundred miles away in Oak Ridge, Tennessee, one site of U.S. atomic weapons production, jets screeched overhead night and day in what could no longer be termed defense simulations. Describing this period and its aftermath, writer and Cistercian monk Thomas Merton, living at the Trappist monastery in Gethsemane, Kentucky, recalled spotting the blinking red light of a B-52 bomber circling in the night sky, carrying its "egg" of unimaginable destruction.

Even after the crisis was averted and hostilities had subsided for a time, Southerners shivered at the proximity of annihilation. Many citizens lived in fear of glancing at the horizon only to discover a mushroom cloud—the symbol of an apocalyptic end to humankind. Other, more desperate Southerners fortified themselves and their families by building fallout shelters—bunkers actually—on the sides of hills or attached to houses. Unable to explain to small children the purpose of these structures, parents insisted on calling them "playrooms" or "dens."

Thermonuclear war was not the only potentially explosive situation the Upper South faced. A growing movement for civil rights prompted African Americans to claim their birthright as citizens of America and of the region. The official response was predictable. Southern municipalities insisted on providing separate but equal facilities. At Chattanooga's Warner Park, the public swimming pool was restricted for use by whites only on Tuesdays, Thursdays, and Saturdays. Blacks could swim on Mondays, Wednesdays, and Fridays. Despite this accommodation to obvious prejudice, whites soon began complaining about the potential for diseases being spread by black swimmers. As Martin Luther King, Jr., and his supporters reminded Southerners of the irrefutable freedoms guaranteed by the Constitution, even areas where slavery had never gained a foothold bristled with resistance. Kentucky, Tennessee, and Arkansas experienced resurgent Klan activity, and despite federal maneuvering to achieve school desegregation, de facto segregation was prevalent throughout the Border South. Only "King's assassination in April 1968 and a new outbreak of rioting across the country made possible the approval of the Civil Rights Act of 1968."[5]

Changes in the direction of the civil rights movement were inevitable, displaying a "move from a religious to a secular emphasis, from nonviolence and integration to greater militancy and black separatism, from attacking the immorality of segregation to a harsh critique of the economic and social order."[6] In response to this shift, many whites expressed alarm or bewilderment, while others sought to meet force with force. A few attempted to understand the unyielding, revolutionary spirit of the "black power" movement and its repudiation of white society. Such was the case of Fugitive-Agrarian Robert Penn Warren in his collection of recorded conversations and accompanying annotations entitled *Who Speaks for the Negro?* Warren notes that his book is "not a history, a sociological analysis, an anthropological study, or a *Who's Who* of the Negro Revolution. It is a record of my attempt to record what I could find out." Of relevant interest is Warren's interview with Malcolm X, a black power advocate and devotee of Elijah Muhammed and the Black Muslim religion. Calling Martin Luther King, Jr.'s, doctrine of nonviolent resistance "a slave philosophy," Malcolm X does not oppose violence, reserving "the right to do whatever is necessary to exercise complete control." Believing that the white rate is doomed because of its misdeeds, he wants no part of integration, citing the question once asked by Lorraine Hansberry and James Baldwin: "Who wants to integrate with a burning house?" Instead, Malcolm X argues for separatism, contending that "a psychological, cultural, and physical migration back to Africa will solve our problems." On February 20, 1965 (when Warren's book was going to press), Malcolm X was assassinated in Harlem, his alleged assassins reported to be Black Muslims. Writer James Baldwin remarked that "whoever did it was formed in the crucible of the Western World, the American Republic." Warren's own assessment maintains that "Malcolm X had something of the scale of personality and force of will that we associate with the tragic hero."

The shift in cultural sensibilities from the 1960s to the 1970s can be seen in the two introductions (1962 and 1977) to *I'll Take My Stand* offered by Louis D. Rubin, Jr. In his introductory remarks to the Torchback Edition of 1962, Rubin acknowledges the controversial nature of the Agrarian handbook written thirty years earlier and only recently reissued. He asks whether there is anything the volume has to say to the nation that is still worth listening to. Reiterating that mass culture and commercial preoccupations continue to diminish the quality of life and arts in the country, Rubin defends reissuance, noting that *I'll Take My Stand* provided a critique of the "nervous life of cities" that has proven increasingly accurate. As late as 1962, Rubin felt it imperative to defend what many critics believed to be an expression of outmoded social and economic philosophy.

Rubin's 1977 introduction to the Library of Southern Civilization Edition is more relaxed in tone. Basking in the glow of a new era of political and economic ascendancy, the South no longer has so urgent a need to explain and defend. Rubin summarizes the changes:

> Racially, the South has now integrated itself far beyond the most sanguine expectations of 1962, and to an extent that would have seemed inconceivable in 1930. Economically it has all but closed the gap, and there is now even concern in some places about the way in which industries have been moving southward away from the northern and western industrial belt.

Rubin suggests that the appeal of *I'll Take My Stand* for an audience in the 1970s is not the volume's "prescription of a nonindustrialized, unchanged South" but rather a call to "the more spiritual side of a good, full and happy life."

The sacramental status of family has been a feature of both the "good" life and of the Southern literary tradition since the region's settlement. Dysfunctionality has also been part of that tradition. Characterizing Peter Taylor's fiction is the "thin veneer of a social order composed of polite, well-mannered, civilized compassionate people" whose lives display "too many loveless marriages, too much sham and hypocrisy, too many empty and meaningless gestures."[7] In Taylor's "Cousin Aubrey," the well-heeled narrator seeks to understand the family's proverbial black sheep, a cousin named

Aubrey Tucker Bradbury, whose disappearance from the family circle and rejection of all things familial make him an object of enduring fascination. In tracing his cousin's whereabouts, the narrator discovers the ways in which Cousin Aubrey has compensated for his family's rejection of him. The impression Taylor leaves us is that there is more to discover about the family than about the disinherited cousin who bears the burden for all.

Although reared for the most part in Buffalo, New York, Ishmael Reed was born in Chattanooga, Tennessee, the city that serves as the inspiration and title of Reed's collection of verse, *Chattanooga*. Throughout the volume, geographic elevation parallels levels of social stratification. On the brow of Lookout Mountain live the city's wealthiest whites, prompting Reed to recall his own segregated status as a boy attending all-black Howard School at the base of the mountain: "My 6th grade teacher asked me to / Name the highest mountain in the world / I didn't even hesitate, 'Lookout Mountain' I shouted." Local place names such as Cameron Hill, Lincoln Park, and East Ninth Street (later renamed Martin Luther King, Jr., Boulevard) offer rich African American historical associations. Ever mindful that he must survive Chattanooga while living there, Reed invokes the life-sustaining music of "rubboard players and organ grinders" who provide accompaniment for legendary blues singer Bessie Smith, a native Chattanoogan. Reed's "Chattanooga" is a lived history that refuses to be forgotten despite "our a-historical period" that sees Chattanooga "as merely a town in Tennessee."

If the South has often been firm about where it stood in relation to the past, the region has been far more tentative about its role in the present and future. Not only does John Egerton's the *Americanization of Dixie* (1974) analyze the ways that the South has been assimilated into American culture, but the chapter entitled "Culture: Reexploring 'The Sahara of the Bozart'" suggests the ways that the rest of the country has become more "Southernized." Describing Mencken's famous essay of 1920 as a "hatchet job of the first order," Egerton notes that Mencken's criticism was all "the more unbearable . . . because its excesses were interlarded with so much truth." Given "another look fifty years later, Mencken no doubt would have been compelled to acknowledge some remarkable changes." Those changes reflect a process of pluralization, of Americanization to which the South has made significant contributions. Among those contributions is an abiding patriotism that finds expression in "big-time college athletic-school spirit, sportsmanship, character building, national recognition and all the rest." Egerton observes that "segregation, as powerful as it once was, could not forever stand in the way of a conference title or a bowl bid or a spot in the national rankings, and even the most racist fans now appear to accept, however cheerfully, the lofty status of black heroes as well as white ones."

Nor is college athletics the only cultural medium bearing the stamp of Southern approval. In a spirit of "free-enterprise capitalism," Southern entrepreneurs are more than willing to subsidize television shows and movies designed to exploit "manifold forms of physical depravity." In short, the South in most ways mirrors American culture at large. Thus, "what is happening to mass culture in the South is what is happening nationwide, and if there is diversity in it, there is also an element of sameness, of homogenization, of artificiality and shallowness and transcience."

Notes

1. Mike Mayo, *Videohound's Horror Shows* (Detroit: Visible Ink Press, 1998), 367.
2. Mayo, 367.
3. Mayo, 367.
4. Robert F. Kennedy, *Thirteen Days* (New York: W. W. Norton, 1971), 30.
5. Dewey W. Grantham, *The South in Modern America* (New York: Harper Collins, 1994), 256.
6. Grantham, 255.
7. Thomas Daniel Young, "A Second Generation of Novelists," *The History of Southern Literature*, ed. Louis D. Rubin et al. (Baton Rouge: Louisiana State University Press, 1985), 468.

Malcolm X
(interview with Robert Penn Warren)
(1925–1965)

Malcolm X was born as Malcolm Little on May 19, 1925, in Omaha, Nebraska. His father, Earl Little, was a Baptist minister who supported Marcus Garvey's Back-to-Africa movement. The Little family became targets for hostility, resulting in their moving often. Eventually Earl Little was murdered, and his wife Louise was left to rear eight children.

In 1946, Malcolm Little was arrested for robbery and sentenced to ten years in prison. While in prison, he educated himself in the prison library and found the teachings of Elijah Muhammad, the founder and leader of the Black Muslims. He adopted the name Malcolm X. After leaving prison in 1952, he traveled to Chicago to study with Elijah Muhammad. Following a split between the two men, Malcolm X founded the Organization of Afro-American Unity in New York City in 1964, with the objective being to unite blacks from all over the world. He and his wife Betty were the parents of six daughters at the time when he was assassinated on February 21, 1965, in Harlem before an audience of four hundred people.

Most of Malcolm X's publications appeared after his death. Among his published works are *The Autobiography of Malcolm X* with Alex Haley (1965); *Malcolm X Speaks: Selected Speeches and Statements* (1965); *The Speeches of Malcolm X at Harvard* (1968); *Malcolm X and The Negro Revolution: The Speeches of Malcolm X* (1969); and *The End of White World Supremacy: Four Speeches* (1971).

from *Who Speaks for the Negro?* (by Robert Penn Warren)

Foreword

I have written this book because I wanted to find out something, first hand, about the people, some of them anyway, who are making the Negro Revolution what it is—one of the dramatic events of the American story.

This book is not a history, a sociological analysis, an anthropological study, or a *Who's Who* of the Negro Revolution. It is a record of my attempt to find out what I could find out. It is primarily a transcript of conversations, with settings and commentaries. That is, I want to make my reader see, hear, and feel as immediately as possible what I saw, heard, and felt.

No doubt the reader, were he more than the silent spectator which he must here be, would put more probing questions than mine, and would have other, and more significant reactions. But my questions may provide some continuity from interview to interview, and my reactions may give the sense of an involved audience.

Along the way Dr. Anna Hedgeman said to me: "What makes you think that Negroes will tell you the truth?"

I replied: "Even a lie is a kind of truth."

But that is not the only kind that we have here.

The interviews were recorded on tape. In almost all instances the person interviewed checked the transcript for errors. Many of the interviews were long, sometimes several hours, and in a few cases there was more than one conversation. It would have been impossible, and undesirable, to publish all the transcripts. I have chosen the sections which seem to me most significant and exciting, and within these sections have sometimes omitted repetitions and irrelevancies. I have not indicated such omissions. But except for a rare conjunction, transition, or explanatory phrase, I have made no verbal changes.

> *Robert Penn Warren*
> February, 1965.

Interview with Malcolm X

Malcolm Little was born in Omaha, on May 19, 1925, the seventh child of Early Little, a Baptist preacher, a "race man" and a supporter of the Garvey Movement, who did not curry favor with the white people. When Malcolm was very young, the family moved to Lansing, Michigan—really driven from Omaha because of the father's Garveyite principles; but there the same trouble followed, the family's house was fired by the Ku Klux Klan, and the firemen, when they did arrive, merely watched the blaze. "The same fire that burned my father's home still burns my soul," Malcolm X has said.* Later, the father was found on a street-car track with his head crushed and his body cut nearly in two, and the son presumes that he had been murdered and then dumped on the tracks.

After the father's death the family underwent dire poverty, and eventually broke up; and Malcolm, who had been involved in petty thefts, was sent to a detention home to await transfer to the reform school. The matron of the home—apparently the only white person he has ever had any affection or respect for—managed to prevent his being sent to the reformatory; and he entered a regular school.

At school, he was the only Negro—and by both students and faculty was called "the Nigger," but, he says, without meaning "any harm." His grades were "among the highest in the school," and he was, in fact, the president of his class. This account in his *Saturday Evening Post* article is somewhat at variance with the accounts presented by Nat Hentoff, C. Eric Lincoln, and Louis Lomax,† who report that the high grades incurred the resentment of both teachers and students—rather than being rewarded by the office of class president; and that when, in the eighth grade, Malcolm Little said he wanted to be a lawyer he was told that a Negro ought to think about carpentry.

In any case, it was in crime, not carpentry, that he was making a precocious success: in Harlem, still in his teens, "Big Red" was in numbers, bootlegging, dope, hustling, an employer of men, with a $1,000 roll in his pockets. But despite the pay-offs, the law finally had him. He went to prison.

* * *

This morning, in Suite 128 of the Theresa Hotel, he is no longer the heir apparent to Elijah Muhammad, he is merely himself. But that fact—as he stands there across

---

*C. Eric Lincoln, *The Black Muslims in America.*

†Nat Hentoff, "Elijah in the Wilderness," *The Reporter,* August 4, 1960; C. Eric Lincoln, *The Black Muslims in America;* Louis Lomax, *When the Word is Given.*

the expanse of bare, ill-swept floor, conferring with the ominous attendant—is not to be ignored. I am watching him, and he knows I am watching him, but he gives no sign. He has the air of a man who can be himself with many eyes on him.

Finally he beckons to me. The attendant takes my raincoat and hat and hangs them in a little closet, and acknowledges my thanks with a reserved inclination of the head. Minister Malcolm X leads me into a long, very narrow room made by partitioning off the end of the big room where the blackboard is. The only furniture is a small table and two chairs, set face-to-face, under a series of windows that give over the street. Malcolm X tells me that he has only a few minutes, that he has found that you waste a lot of time with reporters and then you don't get much space. It is the same remark that Whitney Young had made to me at our first interview; only he had said, "enough space for the Urban League to justify it."

I begin by asking if the Negro's sense of a lack of identity is the key for the appeal of the Black Muslim religion.

MALCOLM X: Yes. Besides teaching him (the American Negro) that Islam is the best religion, since the main problem that Afro-Americans* have is a lack of cultural identity, it is necessary to teach him that he had some type of identity, culture, civilization before he was brought here. But now, teaching him about his historic and cultural past is not his religion. The two have to be separated.

WARREN: What about the matter of personal identity as distinguished from cultural and blood identity?

MALCOLM X: The religion of Islam actually restores one's human feelings— human rights, human incentives—his talent. It brings out of the individual all of his dormant potential. It gives him the incentive to develop, to be identified collectively in the brotherhood of Islam with the brothers in Islam; at the same time this also gives him the—it has the psychological effect of giving him incentive as an individual.

WARREN: One often encounters among Negroes a deep suspicion of any approach which involves anything like the old phrase "self-improvement" and a Negro's individual responsibility. You take a different line.

MALCOLM X: Definitely. Many of the Negro leaders actually suffer themselves from an inferiority complex, even though they say they don't, and because of this they have subconscious defensive mechanisms, so that when you mention self-improvement, the implication is that the Negro is something distinct and different and therefore needs to improve himself. Negro leaders resent this being said, not because they don't know that it's true but they're

---

*For the Black Muslims, the word *Negro* is a white invention, a badge of slavery. Ordinarily the Muslim will, if he uses the word at all, preface it with "so-called." Afro-Americans or Black Men is preferred. As Malcolm X puts it: "If you call yourself 'white,' why should I not call myself 'black'? Because you have taught me that I am a 'Negro'! Now then, if you ask a man his nationality and he says he is German, that means he comes from a nation called Germany. . . . The term he uses to identify himself connects him with a nation, a language, a culture and a flag. Now if he says his nationality is 'Negro' he has told you nothing—except possibly that he is not good enough to be 'American.' . . . No matter how light or how dark we are, we call ourselves 'black' . . . and we don't feel we have to make apologies about it." (C. Eric Lincoln, *The Black Muslims in America.*)

But in the course of the conversation Malcolm X begins to use "Negro."

thinking—they're looking at it personally, they think the implication is directed at them, and they duck this responsibility, whereas the only real solution to the race problem is a solution that involves individual self-improvement and collective self-improvement.

"Self-improvement," for the Black Muslims, then, carries no stigma of Booker T. Washington or Uncle Tom. And the reason I take to be clear: the purpose of the self-improvement is not to become "worthy" to integrate with the white man, to be "accepted" by him—to integrate with "a burning house"—but to become worthy of the newly discovered self, as well as of a glorious past and a more glorious future. The question asked by Lorraine Hansberry and James Baldwin—"Who wants to integrate with a burning house?"—with its repudiation of white values, has some of the emotional appeal of the Black Muslim prophecy of destruction for the "white devils" and the glory of the Black Kingdom to come. In a more subtle form we find the same appeal in the role that some Negro workers in the Movement assume: the role of being the regenerator of society, not working merely for integration into white society but for the redemption of society—a repudiation, and a transcendence, of white values that gives something of the satisfaction that may be found in the Black Muslim promise of Armageddon, and a perfect world thereafter. It assumes, not equality, but superiority—superiority to, at least, the present-day white man.

I am thinking of the freedom the Black Muslim enjoys in accepting the doctrine of self-improvement, and then of the complex—and sometimes unfree—reaction the white man has to Negro's assumption of the role of regenerator, even as I ask Malcolm X about his own conversion.

MALCOLM X: That was in prison. I was in prison and I was an atheist. In fact, one of the persons who started me to thinking seriously was an atheist—a Negro inmate whom I had heard in discussion with white inmates and who was able to hold his own at all levels; and it was he who switched my reading habits in the direction away from fiction to nonfiction, so that by the time one of my brothers [who had become a Muslim in Detroit] told me about Islam, I was open-minded and I began to read in that direction. One of the things that appealed to me was in Islam a man is honored as a human being and not measured by the color of his skin.

I think of Lolis Elie, back in his office in New Orleans, his voice full of controlled violence as he says: "At what point—when will it be possible for white people to look at black people as human beings?"

Elie had said that he was reading Black Muslim literature. And the thing that drives him is what had driven Malcolm X to his conversion.

WARREN: Was your conversion fast or slow—a flash of intuition?
MALCOLM X: It was fast. I took an about-turn overnight.
WARREN: Really overnight?
MALCOLM X: Yes. And while I was in prison. I was indulging in all types of vice right within the prison, and I never was ostracized as much by the penal authorities while I was participating in all the evils of the prison as they tried to ostracize me after I became a Muslim.

WARREN: If Islam teaches the worth of all men without reference to color, how does this relate to the message of black superiority and the doom of the white race?

MALCOLM X: The white race is doomed not *because* it's white but because of its misdeeds. If people listen to what Muslims declare they will find that, even as Moses told Pharoah, you are doomed if you don't do so-and-so. Always the *if* is there. Well, it's the same way in America. When the Muslims deliver the indictment of the American system, it is not the white man per se that is being doomed.

I discovered that that pale, dull yellowish face that had seemed so veiled, so stony, as though beyond all feeling, had flashed into its merciless, leering life—the sudden wolfish grin, the pale pink lips drawn hard back to show the strong teeth, the unveiled glitter of the eyes beyond the lenses, giving the sense that the lenses were only part of a clever disguise, that the eyes need no help, that they suddenly see everything.

He has made his point.

I study his grin, then say: "There's no blood damnation, then?"

MALCOM X: No, but it's almost impossible to separate the actions—to separate the criminal exploitation and criminal oppression of the American Negro from the color of the skin of the oppressor. So he thinks he's being condemned because of the color of his skin.

WARREN: Can any person of white blood—even one—be guiltless?

MALCOLM X: Guiltless?

WARREN: Yes.

MALCOLM X: You can answer it this way, by turning it around. Can any Negro who is the victim of the system escape the collective stigma that is placed upon all Negroes in this country? And the answer is "No." Well, the white race in America is the same way. As individuals it is impossible to escape the collective crime.

WARREN: Let's take an extreme case—your reaction to it. A white child of three of four—an age below decisions or responsibility—is facing death before an oncoming truck.

MALCOLM X: The white child, although he has not committed any of the deeds that have produced the plight the Negro finds himself in, is he guiltless? The only way you can determine that is to take a Negro child who is only four years old—can he escape, though he's only four years old, can he escape the stigma of segregation? He's only four years old.

WARREN: Let's put the Negro child in front of the truck, and put a white man there who leaps—risks his own life—to save the child. What is your attitude toward him?

MALCOLM X: It wouldn't alter the fact that after the white man saved the little black child he couldn't take that little black child into many restaurants right along with him. That same white man would have to toss that child back into discrimination, segregation.

WARREN: Let's say that white man is willing to go to jail to break segregation. Some white men have. What about him then?

MALCOLM X: My personal attitude is that he has done nothing to solve the problem.

WARREN: But what is your attitude toward his moral nature?

MALCOLM X: I'm not even interested in his moral nature. Until the problem is solved, we're not interested in anybody's moral nature.

How close is this, I wonder, looking back, to what James Forman had said? "It's what the social effect is of what a person is doing that's important," he had said. Does he mean to imply that moral value equates, simply, with consequence? Many people have believed that. Machiavelli, for one; Bishop Paley, who wrote *Evidences of Christianity*, for another; Stalin, for another. I wonder if—and how deeply and in what sense—Forman believes this. I do not need to wonder about Malcolm X.

For behind all his expert illogic there is a frightful, and frightfully compelling, clarity of feeling—one is tempted to say logic. Certainly a logic of history. Of history conceived of as doom.

So, even as I ask Malcolm X if he could call that white man who goes to jail a friend, I know that his answer will be "No."

MALCOLM X: If his own race were being trampled upon as the race of Negroes are being trampled upon, he would use a different course of action to protect his rights [different from going to jail].

WARREN: What course of action?

MALCOLM X: I have never seen white people who would sit—would approach a solution to their own problems nonviolently. It's only when they are so-called fighting for the rights of the Negroes that they nonviolently, passively and lovingly, you know, approach the situation. Those types of whites who are always going to jail with Negroes are the ones who tell Negroes to be loving and kind and patient and be nonviolent and turn the other cheek.

He would not call him a friend. And I think of an article in the *Village Voice*— "View from the Back of the Bus" by Marlene Nadle—reporting the dialogue on a bus to Washington for the March, in August 1963:

Frank Harman (a young man, white, member of the Peace Corps) was asked why, since he was white, he wanted to go to Nigeria. He replied, "I want to help those people because they are human beings."

Suddenly Wayne (a Negro) shouted, "If this thing comes to violence, yours will be the first throat we slit. We don't need your kind. Get out of our organization."

Completely baffled by the outburst, Frank kept repeating the questions, "What's he talking about? What did I say?"

Wayne, straining forward tensely, screamed, "We don't need any white liberals to patronize us!"

Other Negroes joined in. "We don't trust you." "We don't believe you're sincere." "You'll have to prove yourself."

Frank shouted back, "I don't have to prove myself to anyone but myself."

"We've been stabbed in the back too many times."

"The reason white girls come down to civil rights meetings is because they've heard of the black man's reputation of sex."

"The reason white guys come down is because they want to rebel against their parents."

Poor Frank Harman, he doesn't know what kind of test he has to pass. But Malcolm X could tell him.

MALCOLM X: If I see a white man who was willing to go to jail or throw himself in front of a car in behalf of the so-called Negro cause, the test that I would put to him, I'd ask him, "Do you think Negroes—when Negroes are being attacked—they should defend themselves even at the risk of having to kill the one who's attacking them?" If that white man told me, yes, I'd shake his hand.

But what would this mean, this hand-shaking? If the demand Malcolm X makes is merely that the white man recognize his right of self-defense (which the law already defines for him and which the NAACP supports), then he might go around shaking hands all day and not exhaust the available supply. If by "defend themselves" he means the business of Armageddon, then he will find few hands to shake. But in any case, what does the hand-shaking mean if he maintains that the white man, and the white man's system, can't change from the iniquity which he attributes to him?

MALCOLM X: It is the system itself that is incapable of producing freedom for the twenty-two million Afro-Americans. It is like a chicken can't lay a duck egg. A chicken can't lay a duck egg because the system of the chicken isn't constructed in a way to produce a duck egg; and the political and economic system of this country is absolutely incapable of producing freedom and justice and equality and human dignity for the twenty-two million Afro-Americans.
WARREN: You don't see in the American system the possibility of self-regeneration?
MALCOLM X: No.

We come to the separatism, the independent nation, to Africa—the dream or the reality.

MALCOLM X: The solution for the Afro-American is twofold—long-range and short-range. I believe that a psychological, cultural, and philosophical migration back to Africa will solve our problems. Not a physical migration, but a cultural, psychological, philosophical migration back to Africa—which means restoring our common bond—will give us the spiritual strength and the incentive to strengthen our political and social and economic position right here in America, and to fight for the things that are ours by right on this continent. And at the same time this will give incentive to many of our people to also visit and even migrate physically back to Africa, and those who stay here can help those who go back and those who go back can help those who stay here, in the same way as the Jews who go to Israel.
WARREN: What about the short-range?
MALCOLM X: Immediate steps have to be taken to re-educate our people—a more real view of political, economic, and social conditions, and self-

improvement to gain political control over every community in which we predominate, and also over the economy of that same community.

WARREN: That is, you are now thinking of localities—communities in the United States—being operated by Negroes, not of a separate state or nation?

MALCOLM X: No. Separating a section of America for Afro-Americans is similar to expecting a heaven in the sky after you die.

WARREN: You now say it is not practical?

MALCOLM X: To say it is not practical one has to also admit that integration is not practical.

WARREN: I don't follow that.

MALCOLM X: In stating that a separate state is not practical I am also stating that integration—forced integration as they have been making an effort to do for the last ten years—is also just as impractical.

WARREN: To go back—you are thinking simply of Negro-dominated communities?

MALCOLM X: Yes, and once the black man becomes the political master of his own community, it means that the politicians will also be black, which means that he will be sending black representatives even at the federal level.

WARREN: What do you think of the Negroes now holding posts at the federal level?

MALCOLM X: Window dressing.

WARREN: Ralph Bunche too?

MALCOLM X: Any Negro who occupies a position that was given him by the white man—if you analyze his function, it never enables him to really take a firm, militant stand. He opens his mouth only to the degree that the political atmosphere will allow him to do so.

In my opinion, mature political action is the type of action that enables the black people to see the fruits that they should be receiving from the politicians, and thereby determine whether or not the politician is really fulfilling his function, and if he is not they can then set up the machinery to remove him from the position by whatever means necessary. He either produces or not, and he's out one way or another.

WARREN: There's only one way to put a politician out, ordinarily—to vote him out.

MALCOLM X: I think the black people have reached the point where they should reserve the right to do whatever is necessary to exercise complete control over the politicians of their community by whatever means necessary.

I ask him if he believes in political assassination, and he turns the hard, impassive face and veiled eyes upon me, and says: "I wouldn't know anything about that."

He has only said: ". . . reserve the right to do whatever is necessary to exercise complete control . . . by whatever means necessary." What is "reserve the right"? What is "complete control"? What is "whatever means necessary"? Who knows?

Malcolm X has always been a master of the shadowy phrase, the faintly shaken veil, the charged blankness into which the white man can project the images of guilt or fear. He is also a master of parable.

WARREN: What about the matter of nonselective reprisal?

MALCOLM X: Well, I'll tell you, if I go home and my child has blood running down her leg and someone tells me a snake bit her, I'm going out and kill snakes, and when I find a snake I'm not going to look and see if he has blood on his jaws.

WARREN: You mean you'd kill any snake you could find?

MALCOLM X: I grew up in the country, on a farm. And whenever a snake was bothering the chickens, we'd kill snakes. We never knew which was the snake did it.

WARREN: To read your parable, then, you would advocate nonselective reprisals?

MALCOLM X: I'm just telling you about snakes.

* * *

On the Police State:

Whenever you have to pass a law to make a man let me have a house, or you have to pass a law to make a man let me go to school, or you have to pass a law to make a man let me walk down the street, you have to enforce that law—then you'd be living in a police state. America right now is moving toward the police state.

On the Civil Rights Leaders:

I don't think that anyone has been created more by the white press than the civil rights leaders.

On Abraham Lincoln:

He probably did more to trick Negroes than any other man in history.

On Kennedy:

Kennedy I relate right along with Lincoln.

On Roosevelt:

The same thing.

On Eleanor Roosevelt:

The same thing.

* * *

Malcolm X, as we have pointed out, has broken with Elijah Muhammad and lost the succession. But has he lost power? As far as New York is concerned it would seem that he has not lost power; and it would seem that Elijah Muhammad has. When Muhammad appeared in Harlem in early July, 1964, for a rally that had been liberally advertised in advance, the turnout was, by all report, not more than eight thousand. If that was all he could muster, then New York would seem to be Malcolm's parish.

Malcolm X still presents himself as a Muslim—even if not a Black Muslim. He announces that he is opening an official Muslim center in New York. But if he succeeds in this project the key to his future is still in his personality and his instinct for leadership. When he broke with the Black Muslims he said he was able "to approach the whole problem with a broader scope." And he continued: "If you look only through the eye of an organization, you see what the organization wants you to see, you lose your ability to be objective."

With or without the Muslim center, chances are that Malcolm X will continue to be "objective"—that is, to tack with the wind. There is no indication that he will go back on his statement: "The problem is so broad that it's going to take the inner working of all the organizations—going to take a united front of all the organizations—to come up with a solution." And he would, he says to me, even work with Martin Luther King—for they disagree, he says, only on the method.

The remark is, of course, preposterous, for with King the method and the end are inseparable. But the preposterousness appears in other quarters. Shortly after the riots in Harlem and Rochester, in the summer of 1964, a group of leading Negro artists and intellectuals held an informal meeting in New York City. Among them was Clarence B. Jones, legal counsel of Martin Luther King. In the discussions with the press after the meeting, Mr. Jones predicted eventual cooperation between Dr. King and Malcolm X. He said: "I think it an irony and a paradox in terms of the national Negro community that two Negroes of such opposing views as Dr. King and Malcolm X should have such great mass appeal. I personally believe that Malcolm could engender the same feeling in the lumpen proletariat as Dr. King does in other classes of Negroes . . . Malcolm cannot be corrupted, and the Negroes know this and therefore respect him. They also know he comes from the lower depths, as they do, and regard him as one of their own."

The irony and paradox that Mr. Jones remarks on are certainly here, and more deeply set than he indicates; but they may be resolved, and Malcolm X may be even now in the process of resolving them. As early as the spring of 1964, when he was on a visit to the Near East and wrote back to America saying that in Islam color does not matter, he laid the groundwork for the rapprochement with the integrationists, with the white man himself. By the time of the article in the *Saturday Evening Post,* he was saying: "Once I was a racist—yes. But now I have turned my direction away from anything that's racist." Malcolm X is, bit by bit, purging himself of his association with violence and rifle clubs, and as for "snake-killing," proposes only a little guerrilla warfare against the Klan.

With his change of views Malcolm X is in a position to enter into any centralized grouping of the various elements in the Movement that may be managed. He will, in fact, be in a position to be the center of such a centralized grouping.

At the same time, Malcolm X must be aware that the basic appeal he has had is not merely his incorruptibility or his origin in the lower depths; it inheres in his racism, his celebration of blackness, his promise of vengeance. And here is the irony and paradox for Malcolm X himself: Can he maintain that appeal and at the same time move toward a commanding central position?

We may remember that, in the past, even at his most intransigent, Malcolm X has never committed himself. A man like Jesse Gray is committed, and there is no sawdust trail he can take, no matter how much he might bedew the sawdust with tears of repentance. But for Malcolm X there are highroads leading in all directions. In fact, he speaks of his "direction"—and for all his heels-dug-in and grim-jawed intransigence, he also presents himself, in one avatar, as a seeker, a quester, he is "going somewhere," toward some great truth. This fact, this role, has a fundamental appeal, too; we are all "seekers." Therefore his appeal is double. How long can the balancing act continue?

But Malcolm X has, in fact, never had any association with actual violence in behalf of the Negro cause. He has always, by happy accident or clever design, been somewhere else. In the summer of 1964, for instance, when the bad troubles broke, he was not around, he didn't have to put anything on the line—except his trans-Atlantic rhetoric. Perhaps this is what Wyatt Tee Walker meant—and not merely that Malcolm X was a creation of the press—when he said that he is a "paper tiger." James Farmer, as we may remember, said flatly that "Malcolm has done nothing but verbalize—his militancy is a matter of posture . . . he is not an activist, really." And Farmer added: "But there will come a time when Malcolm is going to have to chirp or get off the perch."

That time is, apparently, not yet. And it may not come for a long time, for Malcolm X has, again to quote Farmer, "the footwork to keep pace," and may "be able to survive a long time." He may indeed, for he is a man of great talents and great personal magnetism. He knows that psychologists, and not philosophers, rule the world. He is, like all men of power, a flirt; he flirts with destiny. He conceives of the general situation as fluid and he has made his own situation fluid. He is free to tack, to play the wind. He trusts his magnetism—and his luck. He may end at the barricades or in Congress. Or he might even end on the board of a bank.

Meanwhile Malcolm X, however willing to work with other organizations, and however much he may yearn to enter the world of politics and respectability, still carries over, in his doubleness, some hint of the orthodoxy of the Black Muslims, a weapon and a lure that no other national leader, except the failing Muhammad, can exploit: the stance of total intransigence, the gospel of total repudiation, the promise of hate, the promise of vengeance. Even as late as December 20, 1964, at a Harlem rally, Malcolm X could say: "We need a Mau Mau to win freedom!" With this emotional appeal, which even the coolest-headed and most high-minded Negro, in some deep corner of his being, is apt to admit to responding to, Malcolm X stands prepared to undercut and overreach the leaders of those very organizations which he, with one hand, beckons to a "united front." Beneath all the illogicalities there is the clear logic of feeling: the black powerful current beneath the crazed and brittle ice.

It may be argued that the personal fate of Malcolm X—how much power or what kind of power he attains—is not what is important about him. What is important may be the mere fact of his existence in this moment, his role, his symbolic function.

I may approach this notion by a story told me by Dr. Anna Hedgeman of the National Council of Churches. In a seminar she was conducting on race and religion there was a serious-minded and idealistic young girl, from, I think, Alabama. Among various guests who spoke to the seminar was Malcolm X, who pronounced his usual repudiation of the white devils. The girl asked him if there wasn't anything she could do—not anything—to be acceptable. "Not anything," he said. At that she burst into tears. Later Dr. Hedgeman said to her: "My dear, don't you think it strange that you couldn't stand for one minute to be repudiated by that Negro man, when I, like all other Negroes, have had to spend my whole life being repudiated by the white race?"

There is something of that little white girl in all of us. Everybody wants to be loved. The member of the White Citizens Council always gets around to telling you how Uncle Billie just loved the kids, would have cut off his right hand for 'em, and how Aunt Sukie or Sallie just loved the whole family and they all loved her right back and when she died they all cried and buried her in the family burying ground. But Malcolm X, even now, will have none of this. That stony face breaks into the merciless, glittering leer, and there is not anything, not a thing, you—if you are white—can do, and somewhere deep down in you that little girl is ready to burst into tears. Malcolm X makes you face the absoluteness of the situation.

But Malcolm X, in his symbolic function, does something else, quite paradoxical. Besides the little girl, there is in you too that hard, aggressive, assertive, uncompromising and masculine self that leaps out of its deep inwardness to confront Malcolm X with a repudiation as murderous as his own saying, "OK, OK, so that's the way you want it, let her rip!" We must confront that wild elation in ourselves: "Let her rip!"

So, for the white man, Malcolm X can bring the unseen, even the unsuspected, into light. The white man can know what he has to deal with, in himself.

And it is so for the Negro.

It is reported that Martin Luther King, a few years ago, remarked to a friend: "I just saw Malcolm X on television. I can't deny it. When he starts talking about all that's been done to us, I get a twinge of hate, of identification with him."* This despite the fact that, during Birmingham, Malcolm X had called Martin Luther King "a chump, not a champ," despite the fact that the Muslims called his doctrine "a slave philosophy," despite the fact that the rotten eggs thrown at him in Harlem had, for all intents, come from the hand of Malcolm X. And this despite all of Dr. King's own principles. For principles or no, Malcolm X can evoke, in the Negro, even in Martin Luther King, that self with which he, too, must deal, in shock and fright, or in manic elation.

Malcolm X has one other symbolic function. He is the unspecified conclusion in the syllogism that all of the "responsible" Negro leaders present to the white world: "If you do not take me, then . . ." Then you will have to take Malcolm X, and all he means.

Malcolm X is many things. He is the face not seen in the mirror. He is the threat not spoken. He is the nightmare self. He is the secret sharer.

And we may recall that once, in explaining the "X" in the Muslim name, he said it stands for "the mystery confronting the white man as to what the Negro has become."

Note on the Assassination of Malcolm X

On Sunday, February 20, 1965 (when this book was about to go on press), Malcolm X addressed a meeting of his Organization for Afro-American Unity, in Harlem. He was cut down by a shotgun and two revolvers. One of the alleged assailants was wounded and captured on the spot, and soon two other men, both reported to be Black Muslims, were arrested. Meanwhile, on the night of February 23, while the body of Malcolm lay on view in the Unity Funeral Home, the Black Muslim Mosque Number 7 was burned down, presumably in revenge for the killing of Malcolm X.

In Chicago, addressing the annual meeting of his cult, Muhammad described Malcolm X as "a star gone astray," and said that he had "got just what he preached." At the same meeting, Wallace Muhammad, one of the defecting sons of Muhammad, recanted and begged forgiveness; and two of Malcolm's own brothers denounced him.

In Washington, D.C., Carl Rowan, Director of the United States Information Agency, stated that in Africa and Asia, the death of Malcolm X, despite the efforts of his agency, was being interpreted as the martyrdom of a great integrationist.

*Nat Hentoff, *The New Equality.*

In London, where he had gone to promote the publication of his novel *Another Country*, James Baldwin told the press that no matter who had pulled the trigger, the white community would have to share the blame. "Whoever did it," he said, "was formed in the crucible of the Western World, the American Republic."

Malcolm X had something of the scale of personality and force of will that we associate with the tragic hero. And he finally found himself caught on the horns of the classic dilemma of tragedy.

Louis D. Rubin, Jr.
(1923–   )

Louis D. Rubin, Jr., was born on November 19, 1923, in Charleston, South Carolina. He received his B.A. from the University of Richmond in 1946, his M.A. from Johns Hopkins University in 1949, and his Ph.D. in 1954, also from Johns Hopkins.

Rubin is an editor, a writer, a novelist, and a professor of English. He is most noted for his expansive critical works and edited anthologies. Among his publications are *Thomas Wolfe: The Weather of His Youth* (1955); *The Faraway Country: Writers of the Modern South* (1963); *The Writer in the South* (1972); *A Gallery of Southerners* (1982); *The Mockingbird in the Gum Tree: A Literary Gallimaufry* (1991); *Southern Renascence: The Literature of the Modern South* (1953); *A Biographical Guide to the Study of Southern Literature* (1969); with R. B. Davis and C. Hugh Holman, *Southern Writing 1585–1920* (1970); *The Literary South* (1979); with Robert Bain and Joseph N. Flora, *Southern Writers: A Biographical Dictionary* (1979); *The American South: Portrait of a Culture* (1979); and *The History of Southern Literature* (1985).

Rubin lives in Chapel Hill, North Carolina.

Introductions to *I'll Take My Stand* (1962 and 1977 editions)

Torchbook Edition (1962)

Among those who consider the South, what it has been and what it can be, a book entitled *I'll Take My Stand: The South and the Agrarian Tradition* has for thirty years been the center of constant controversy. Not a single writer about the modern South has failed to mention and discuss it. From the very beginning it has been singled out for praise or blame. Some critics have termed it reactionary, even semi-fascistic. Others have considered it a misguided, romantic attempt to re-create an idyllic utopia that never really existed. Still others have seen it as a voice crying in the wilderness. Ridiculed, condemned, championed, it has been everything except ignored, for that it cannot be by anyone who wants to understand a complex American region.

Published in 1930 in a single printing with a moderate press run, *I'll Take My Stand* has been out of print for most of its history. Now that it becomes available once again it is not amiss to examine this remarkable set of essays with a view toward determining what has kept it so much in the public eye, and held the interest of so many persons at a time when, in order to read it, one has had to borrow a copy from a library or carefully scan the rare book lists until a copy came up for sale. What has given *I'll Take My Stand* its continuing life? What, thirty years and more after publication, does it still have to say about the South and the nation that is worth listening to?

I'll Take My Stand was written by a group of twelve Southerners, many of them associated in some way with Vanderbilt University in Nashville, Tennessee. At the center of the group were four poets who during the early 1920's had been active in one of the most important and influential literary groups ever to exist in American letters, the Nashville Fugitives. For several years this little association of poets published a magazine, *The Fugitive*, whose impact on American writing was far wider than its circulation list. In *The Fugitive*, and in other periodicals of the 1920's, John Crowe Ransom, Allen Tate, Robert Penn Warren and Donald Davidson published the poetry and the criticism of poetry that, along with the work of such writers as Eliot, Pound, Blackmur, Crane and certain others, was to revolutionize the craft of poetry in America.

During the early 1920's, the Fugitives were not particularly interested in their identity as Southerners. Rebelling from the United Daughters of the Confederacy tradition in Southern letters, they found sectional self-consciousness a hindrance to their own literary development. But in the late years of the decade, as they reassessed the role of poetry and the arts in American life, their attitude toward the South changed. The United States of the 1920's seemed increasingly devoted to material things, dedicated to a boom-or-bust economy. Artistic taste was being debased to accommodate the needs of mass culture. Industrial and commercial preoccupations were reducing the fine arts to the status of diversionary, non-essential activities. So overwhelmingly was postwar American life given over to the pursuit of profits that aesthetic and religious considerations were all but ignored.

It was at this point that the four leading Fugitive poets looked to the South. For as poets they were given to the metaphor, and they instinctively resorted to an image for their critique of American society. They saw in the history of their own section the image of a region which had clearly resisted the domination of the machine, persisting in its agricultural ways, even after military defeat, well into the present century, and only now beginning to capitulate fully to the demands of American industrial society.

When measured by the dominant American ideal, the pre-industrial South had been backward, but it had evolved a society, they felt, in which leisure, tradition, aesthetic and religious impulses had not been lost in the pursuit of economic gain. Only now was the South 're-entering the Union'; only now were its old values and beliefs being cast aside as of little use in the rush to industrialize.

Yet in thus bartering away its tranquil ways for the gaudy benefits of industrial American life the South, they felt, was surrendering spiritual sustenance for dubious material gain. What was wrong with the South was not that it was backward and agricultural, but that it was failing to cherish its own highly civilized customs and attitudes. For it was the South, not the industrial Northeast, that still retained a manner of living in which grace, leisure, spiritual, and aesthetic experience were possible. As such it might furnish a needed corrective to America's head-long materialism, and provide an image of the good life. "Suddenly we realized to the full," Donald Davidson has written, "what we had long been dimly feeling, that the Lost Cause might not be wholly lost after all. In its very backwardness the South had clung to some secret which embodied, it seemed, the elements out of which its own reconstruction—and possibly even the reconstruction of America—might be achieved."

Thus the Fugitives became Agrarians. Ransom, Tate, Davidson and Warren were joined by a brilliant group of men with similar ideas about Southern and American life. Two were or would soon be novelists, Stark Young and Andrew Nelson Lytle. Another was a poet, John Gould Fletcher. One was a professor of English, John Donald Wade. Frank Lawrence Owsley and Herman Clarence Nixon were historians, Henry Blue Kline a journalist, Lyle Lanier a psychologist. In 1930, just as the American economy was slumping into the great Depression, they published their Agrarian manifesto.

In the years that followed *I'll Take My Stand*'s publication, the South and the nation cannot be said to have heeded its economic, political and social counsels to any startling effect. The industrialization of the South proceeded apace, with the Depression years representing only a temporary setback in the drive to increase manufactures and commerce. The importance of farm life in the South has steadily diminished, while the cities and towns have expanded relentlessly, until today one-half of all Southerners live in an urban environment. The question that Ransom raised in his essay, of whether the South would let industrialism destroy its traditional identity, or would instead "accept industrialism, but with a very bad grace, and manage to maintain a good deal of her traditional philosophy," has been answered, on the economic plane at any rate, in a most un-agrarian fashion. The South had thrown its lot squarely with the machines and factories; agrarianism as a general pattern of life is largely a dead letter. Today the suburbs of Nashville, Richmond, Charleston, and Mobile are scarcely distinguishable from those of Buffalo, Trenton, Indianapolis, and Hartford. Andrew Lytle's suggestion that the Southern farmer "throw out the radio and take down the fiddle from the wall" has not been followed; instead the radio has been replaced by a television set. Even politically the Solid South is no more; not in 16 years has it voted as a unit. Ransom's proposal that the Democratic Party be renovated in terms of "agrarian, conservative, anti-industrial" principles can hardly be said to have worked out.

In still another respect aspects of *I'll Take My Stand* seem very dated today. For the past decade the chief social issue in the South has been that of Negro rights. While industrialization has steadily gone forward, remodeling the Southern landscape, the attention of most Southerners has been focussed on the desegregation issue. The 1954 decision of the Supreme Court in *Brown v. Board of Education* has resulted in widespread disturbance to countless Southern communities. On this momentous question, the attitude embodied in some of the essays of *I'll Take My Stand* has seemed, to many at least, quite outmoded. Robert Penn Warren's essay on the Negro, entitled "The Briar Patch," was, in his own description, "a defense of segregation," but not only Warren but many other Southerners have changed their minds. A poll taken nowadays might find the surviving Agrarians sharply divided on the desegregation issue. For many of them, and for many Southerners, the attitudes of 1930 will not suffice at all.

If in its economic and social counsel *I'll Take My Stand* has been so little heeded by the South, and if in several important respects its attitude toward crucial issues does not provide a guide for many Southerners, then what accounts for the book's continued influence? Why must every commentator on the region devote paragraphs and pages to a consideration of its arguments? Why do symposia continue to be held about its contents? And why, thirty years later, has this new edition come into being?

For answer, we may turn back to what has already been remarked about this book's genesis. It was a book written, not by economists and sociologists, but by men of letters, of whom the moving spirits were poets. We have noted that as poets they were given to the *image*—the image, as Ransom remarks elsewhere, which is by nature "marvellous in its assemblage of many properties, a manifold of properties, like a mine or a field, something to be explored for the properties."

Just so. For this book of essays, and the vision of an agrarian South depicted within it, can best be considered as an extended metaphor, of which the image of the agrarian community is the figure, standing for and embodying something else. The something else is modern society. Of this society the South is a part, and, for the purposes of the metaphor, the correlative. But this book is about something far more generally important and essential than the economic and social well-being of any one region. It is about man, what he is, what he should be, what he must be. Written in a time when not only the South but the nation seemed given over to a frantic struggle for material possessions, it held up to examination some of the most widely-accepted assumptions of our time.

Man, it said, far from being a godlike genius of unlimited potentialities, is a fallible, finite creature, who functioned best in a society that took account of his limitations. In his zeal for the benefits of modern scientific civilization, he was placing so high a value on material gain that he ignored his own spiritual welfare and his moral obligations to society. Properly controlled, the benefits of science and industry might bolster his human dignity. As it was, he was turning the contrivances of the new industrialism into the objective itself. In place of beauty and truth he had erected a new ideal, Progress. Where properly controlled the benefits of science and industry might bolster his human dignity, he was turning the contrivances of the new industrialism into the objective itself. Caught up in a race to exploit the natural world through applied science, man was becoming an automaton, his entire effort directed toward highly specialized and narrow activities designed to secure immediate material profit.

Man was losing contact with the natural world, with aesthetic and religious reality; his machines were brutalizing and coarsening him, his quest for gain blinding him to all that made life worth living. The tenuous and frail spiritual insights of western civilization, achieved so arduously over the course of many centuries, were being sacrificed. The result, if unchecked, could only be dehumanization and chaos.

This headlong race for mastery over nature, called Progress by some and Industrialism by others, stifled the aesthetic impulse, rendered impotent the religious impulse, and converted man's days into a frantic and frenzied drive for the often tawdry conveniences of modernism. Such, felt the men who wrote *I'll Take My Stand*, was the ruling tendency of American life in the third decade of the twentieth century. As men of letters, dedicated not to Progress but to humanistic values, they felt impelled to protest against it.

The Agrarians were not only men of letters, however; they were Southerners. And in the life of their own region they saw the dehumanizing process going on in a particularly attenuated form. For industrialism had been late in coming to their region, and only now was its impact being felt in full force. In the difference between what the South had been, and the new South that was coming into being, they perceived an image of what had happened to American society. And to indicate the kind of life that they felt Americans should desire, they held up the image of the Old South. Here was what America might have become, but had not. As Robert Penn Warren said of his part in *I'll Take My Stand*, "for me it was a protest . . . against a kind of dehumanizing and disintegrative effect on our notion of what an individual person could be . . . The past is always a rebuke to the present; . . . it's a better rebuke than any dream of the future. It's a better rebuke because you can see what some of the costs were, what frail virtues were achieved in the past by frail men."

The image of the old agrarian South in *I'll Take My Stand* was the image of a society that perhaps never existed, though it resembled the Old South in certain important ways. But it was a society that *should* have existed—one in which men could live as individuals and not as automatons, aware of their finiteness and their dependence upon God and nature, devoted to the enhancement of the moral life in its aesthetic and spiritual dimensions, possessed of a sense of the deep inscrutability of the natural world.

Through their vision of an agrarian community, the authors of *I'll Take My Stand* presented a critique of the modern world. In contrast to the hurried, nervous life of cities, the image of the agrarian South was of a life in which human beings existed serenely and harmoniously. Not driven by lust for gain, they could live free of the tumultuous pace of the modern industrial community. "A farm is not a place to grow wealthy," Andrew Nelson Lytle wrote in his essay, "it is a place to grow corn."

It was the vision of poets, and carried with it certain convictions about living and dying that have held much imaginative appeal to Southerners and many non-Southerners as well.

This, I think, is the essential function of *I'll Take My Stand*, and accounts for the book's continuing hold on the Southern imagination. It is a rebuke to materialism, a corrective to the worship of Progress, and a reaffirmation of man's aesthetic and spiritual needs. And because the South has come so late into the industrial world, it appeals to the lingering memory within the Southerner's mind of the tranquil and leisurely Southern life that existed before the machines and superhighways came. As such the book constitutes both a reminder and a challenge. *What are you losing that you once possessed?* it says to the modern Southerner. *Are you quite sure that you want to discard it entirely?*

That such a life was doomed, that in many respects it was impossible, that many of its actual attributes were neither necessary nor desirable, is not important. What matters is the vision of a more harmonious, aesthetically and spiritually rewarding kind of human existence that the book holds up. That towns have become cities and farms have become suburbs, that fewer Southerners than ever exist on agriculture, matters very little in this respect. *I'll Take My Stand* is not a treatise on economics; it is not a guide to political action; it is not a sociological blueprint. It is a vision of what the good life can be.

Thus the essays in the book that are most appealing now are those that best evoke this image. John Ransom's portrait of the reconstructed but unregenerate Southerner holding fast to his leisurely ways; Donald Davidson's mirror for artistic activity in which he prophetically shows the value of the regional image for the creative artist; Allen Tate's cogent analysis of what religion should mean for the Southerner and the American, and what is wrong with what it now means; Stark Young's definitive commentary on the meaning of manners and customs; above all, John Donald Wade's beautiful sketch of the history of a Southern gentleman whose whole career embodies the good and satisfying life—these and other essays do not date, for what they have to say to the Southerner and to the American is perennially valid. Each of them preaches the gospel of religious humanism, in a compelling metaphor of agrarian life that serves as a rebuke and reminder to the busy modern man who is so caught up in specialization and money-making that he begins to lose sight of what he is living *for*. These essays are the heart of *I'll Take My Stand;* their meaning goes far deeper than the transient issues of economics, politics, social adjustment.

A recent commentator on this book, after castigating the Agrarians at great length for being "abominable advisers on the means of achieving greater material well-being" for the Southern economy, remarks that "as humanists, however, they had (and still have) much to offer in showing all of us how to use the fruits of economic progress, once achieved, as a means to the more spiritual side of a good, full and happy life." As if that were not the whole point of the book! What the Agrarians were telling the South and the nation was a way of life that omits or deemphasizes the "more spiritual side" of existence is necessarily disastrous to *all* phases of life. The Agrarians refused to divide man's life into isolated segments; there was no such thing, they insisted, as economic man, political man, social man; there was only *man*, and his various activities must be considered as parts of one human life. To think and act otherwise was to make him less than human, producing fragmentation, division, chaos.

Some have said that the impact of *I'll Take My Stand* might have been greater, and the amount of misunderstanding reduced, if the book had not been so closely tied in with the South. Indeed, at the time of its preparation several of the contributors wanted to give it a more general title. Tate wished to label it plainly as a defense of religious humanism; Warren proposed it be called *Tracts Against Communism*. Perhaps a more broadly aimed volume might have enjoyed a wider readership, and its purposes been better grasped by readers.

Perhaps so. Yet it is doubtful, I think. For once again, these men were poets, men of letters, to whom the *image* was central. And it is the tangible image of the South that gives the book so much of its compelling quality, its visible, palpable reality. A more abstractly conceived book might have been less topically identified with one region's particular economic and social problems, and therefore less immediately limited, but a great deal of the dramatic power of the book would have been lost. The image of the agrarian South provided the essayists with a rich, complex metaphor, giving body to their arguments, anchoring their perceptions in time and place. To dissociate *I'll Take My Stand* from the South is neither possible nor desirable.

Grounded firmly in the history and social life of one American region, the best essays in this book speak as vividly and as importantly today as ever before. The verdict they pronounce on modern American life has since been echoed by commentator after commentator. What the Agrarians warned about our business civilization is constantly reinforced by such social analysts as Riesman, White, Packard, Warburg, and many others, who nowadays point to the yawning discrepancies between the glittering American social ideal and the human misuse that lies behind it. These men are saying now what the contributors to *I'll Take My Stand* were saying three decades earlier.

One should read this prophetic book, then, not as a treatise on economics and politics, not as a guide to regional social structuring, but as a commentary on the nature of man—man as Southerner, as American, as human being. What the men of letters who composed it said about what man is and where he belongs is for the most part neither outdated nor unimportant. As a human document it is still very much alive; the concerns of 1930 are the concerns of 1962, and will very likely be concerns in the year 2000. They will be so unless human nature changes a great deal in the decades to come. One of the things *I'll Take My Stand* tells us is that human nature never changes very much, and that whatever we do and wherever we live, we had better accept the fact that it doesn't.

Library of Southern Civilization Edition (1977)

The symposium entitled *I'll Take My Stand: The South and the Agrarian Tradition* was first published by Harper in 1930, in a modest edition that was subsequently permitted to go out of print. Except for a small clothbound reprint brought out by Peter Smith, primarily for library use, the book was not again made available to the general public until thirty-two years after its first publication, when Harper reissued it as a paperback to their Torchbook series. For the latter edition I was commissioned to write an introduction. Now that the Agrarian symposium is once again to be reprinted, this time as a volume in LSU Press's Library of Southern Civilization series, I have the privilege of contributing another commentary.

Fifteen years have gone by since the 1962 edition. The South is no more an embattled minority section, attempting to adjust long-standing racial attitudes to the consequences of *Brown* v. *Board of Education*, while also working with great haste to catch up economically with the rest of the country. Racially the South has now integrated itself far beyond the most sanguine expectations of 1962, and to an extent that would have seemed inconceivable in 1930. Economically it has all but closed the gap, and there is now even a growing concern in some places about the way in which industries have been moving southward away from the northern and western industrial belt. With the development of air-conditioning, the more balmy climate of what is now called the Sun Belt rather than the Bible Belt has meant that longer production days and more attractive living conditions and recreational facilities are possible south of the Ohio and Potomac Rivers.

The transformation, it seems to me, was symbolized, during the closing weeks of the bicentennial year in the spectacle of the leading figures in the nation's political and economic establishment converging upon a small community in southwestern Georgia to offer advice about future federal policy to a former peanut farmer who had recently been elected president of the United States. Future historians may well agree that the election of 1976, in which a southern candidate was chosen for the nation's highest office with the strong support of a once-again Solid South and with overwhelming majorities among black voters in the cities of the Northeast and Midwest, in effect signaled the end of the Civil War. It meant an end, surely, to the single issue that had most set apart the states of the South from the nation: segregation, and the attempt to maintain it. Not that the racial issue had been resolved, or black-white tensions eliminated, but no longer were either the issue or the tensions principally a southern problem. Indeed, in important respects they had become less critical in the South than elsewhere, for the South would appear, to a much greater degree at least than most other places, to have achieved a notable measure of genuine public racial integration, without as much of the economic and social polarization that characterized other regions.

Now what has all this to do with a book published forty-seven years earlier, which took for its title words from a song that had once been the anthem of a would-be southern nation whose very reason for being had to do with the desire to maintain and, if possible, to enhance Negro slavery? A book whose announced thesis was opposition to industrialization and urbanization, and advocacy of an agrarian life—a book which was introduced by a statement of principles that deplored the falling off of younger southerners from the southern tradition and that declared itself against the tendency of the South to "join up behind the common or American industrial ideal"?

Surely it must be obvious that if such was the book's objective, then it failed in its objective. The South not only joined up; industrially it has been leading the country in

recent years. Southern cities, with their vast suburbs, have grown by incredible proportions, while the rural hinterlands have been bound into the complexities of an industrial
society to a degree that has thoroughly blurred the once sharp distinction between
countryside and city. As for the retention of the "Southern tradition," to the extent that
that tradition involved what it was once commonly thought to involve—one would be
hard put to identify the South by any such rubric nowadays. Racially the South is the
most genuinely integrated of all American regions.

So, if *I'll Take My Stand* continues to command an audience today, almost half a
century after its publication, the first conclusion to be drawn is that the importance and
the appeal of the Agrarian symposium must not have resided in the efficacy of its prescription of a nonindustrialized, unchanged South as the proper model for the region's
future, but in something else. After all, both before and after its appearance in the
Depression-bound year of 1930, there have been dozens and dozens of books, and many
manifestos, whose economic, political, and racial prescriptions for the South have
proved to be much more accurate. Yet most such books have long since been relegated
to the shelves of the library stacks, whereas the "backward-looking," "cloud-cuckoo
land" manifesto of the twelve southerners has remained alive and in print.

Perhaps a clue to this apparent paradox lies in a remark, quoted in part in my introduction to the 1962 edition, by a distinguished southern economist who had devoted
much effort to demonstrating why an agrarian economy was emphatically what the
South did *not* need. The Agrarians, he said, though "abominable" advisers on ways to
achieve greater material well-being, had much to offer as humanists in suggesting how
the fruits of economic progress could be used as a means to "the more spiritual side of
a good, full and happy life." But the Agrarians were *not* economists. They were humanists, just as Allen Tate said when he envisioned the enterprise as a calculated defense of
religious humanism. And the real values they were asserting in 1930 were not those of
"material well-being" or of neo-Confederate nostalgia, but of thoughtful men who were
very much concerned with the erosion of the quality of individual life by the forces of industrialization and the uncritical worship of material progress as an end in itself. It was
not their assumption that one first achieved material well-being, then used it to further
"the more spiritual side of a good, full and happy life"; on the contrary, they insisted that
any attempt to divorce economics and labor from "the more spiritual side" of one's life
brutalized the labor and cheapened the humanity.

They were writing squarely out of an old American tradition, one that we find
imbedded in American thought almost from the earliest days, and that runs counter
to yet another old American tradition. The tradition out of which they were writing
was that of pastorale; they were invoking the humane virtues of a simpler, more elemental, nonacquisitive existence, as a needed rebuke to the acquisitive, essentially
materialistic compulsions of a society that from the outset was very much engaged in
seeking wealth, power, and plenty on a continent whose prolific natural resources
and vast acres of usable land, forests, and rivers were there for the taking.

The particular pastorale they wrote, however, was given substance and urgency by
their own historical situation. They were southerners, young men born into a society
that had only belatedly experienced the full impact of the industrial dispensation, and
which in their own lifetimes had become caught up in the surge of overwhelming social,
economic, and political change, so that the contrasts between earlier ways and later
were dramatically visible. Nor were they external observers; they felt the change within
themselves, and knew at first hand the problems of definition involved, and could thus

recognize and identify many of the alternatives. Moreover, there was an historical circumstance that bound them together in a community identity and led them to perceive the changes that were altering their community in terms of deeply felt historical loyalties and sectional self-defense. Thus their special version of pastoral rebuke possessed a concrete imagery and an historical depth that imbued it with drama and passion. They did more than merely admonish and prescribe: they "took their stand."

In the introduction to the 1962 edition of *I'll Take My Stand* I described Nashville agrarianism as a metaphor: "an extended metaphor, of which the image of the agrarian community is the figure, standing for and embodying something else. The something else is modern society. Of this society the South is a part, and, for the purposes of the metaphor, the correlative." The Agrarian symposium, I went on to say, was "the vision of poets, and carried with it certain convictions about living and dying that have held much imaginative appeal to Southerners and many non-Southerners as well." I still believe this is essentially true, but I must say that in certain respects the formulation was misleading. For one thing, it suggests a conscious literary strategy, and the extent to which the strategy was conscious and premeditated actually varied from essay to essay and from contributor to contributor. For some—Allen Tate certainly, John Crowe Ransom to an extent, Stark Young, John Wade and Andrew Lytle perhaps—there was at the time of writing a considerable awareness of the metaphoric element involved. But for others—Donald Davidson, Frank Owsley, H. C. Nixon, and (for very different reasons) Robert Penn Warren—it is obvious that at the time the book was being written the enterprise was envisioned as a literal and practical program, a specific course of action. Warren soon changed his mind; Ransom, stung by the criticisms of the venture's "impracticality," proceeded to get much more literally involved in agrarian economics.

Donald Davidson objected strongly to me about the metaphor formulation: "If you say that," he told me, "it's very easy, because you don't have to believe it at all." And that is true. But let it be admitted that, to a very real extent, that was precisely why I *did* describe it as a metaphor. For in the year 1962, when I wrote my original introduction, I was very much concerned with the way that the symposium might be received by the audience for which the Torchbook edition was designed: the academic, intellectual community north and south. There was the chance, even the likelihood, that, as in the early 1930s, the obvious impracticalities of a return to subsistence farming in the age of the tractor, the supermarket, and the television set, as well as the political sectionalism and the defense, implied and stated, of racial segregation, might serve to distract the symposium's readers from what was and is the book's real importance: its assertion of the values of humanism and its rebuke of materialism.

It will also be noted that in the 1962 introduction relatively little is said about racial segregation. So much had happened in the three decades since *I'll Take My Stand* first appeared that many of the racial assumptions in it no longer represented the views of Tate, Ransom, Warren, and certain other contributors to the symposium. It seemed important to me that issues which by 1962 were highly controversial, seen by many southerners then in very different ways than in 1930, should not be permitted to distort the real importance of what the Agrarians had written.*

---

*I did not, however, presume to make this decision alone. Before I forwarded my introduction to the publisher, I sent it to Allen Tate for his approval; and I was heartened when he expressed his entire agreement with what I had done.

But if stressing the "metaphoric" element of *I'll Take My Stand* helped to prevent the anachronistic application of the racial attitudes of the 1960s to the unexamined assumptions of the 1920s, it also had the unfortunate effect of failing to give proper emphasis to the striking "practicality" of another aspect of the Agrarian symposium that not only accounted for much of its continued appeal, but nowadays looms as perhaps the book's most far-sighted and prophetic element. For the critique that *I'll Take My Stand* offered of the social effects of capitalism and industrialism and the dangers they posed to the quality of human life and to the natural environment has become increasingly relevant over the years. The words of John Ransom's essay "Reconstructed but Unregenerate" speak to our economic and our ecological situation with a clarity that can be recognized today as never before:

> Progress never defines its ultimate objective, but thrusts its victims at once into an infinite series. Our vast industrial machine, with its laboratory centers of experimentation, and its far-flung organs of mass production, is like a Prussianized state which is organized strictly for war and can never consent to peace. . . . Our progressivists are the latest version of those pioneers who conquered the wilderness, except that they are pioneering on principle, or from force of habit, and without any recollection of what pioneering was for.

In the 1970s we have learned to worry about such things. We begin to realize that our continent and our planet do not constitute an inexhaustible supply center of natural resources. We are concerned over the destruction of what is left of our wild places, in the name of Progress. We note the economic and social chaos and hardship that result from even temporary dislocations within an industrial system so huge that it can take no cognizance whatever of the needs of individuals, or even of the plight of towns, cities, even regions. We are disturbed at the appetite of our industrialized, electrified, mechanized consumer society, its willingness to use up a disproportionate share of the world's energy at an alarming rate. We begin to suspect that our vaunted material standard of living is being purchased at the cost of others, who now begin to show signs of impatience at their exploitation. And we have the uneasy feeling that there is something to the notion that wars may have played a greater role in our economic well-being than we like to think. What it all means we are not sure, but we begin to perceive that there is more to progress and improvement than had once seemed apparent.

The Nashville Agrarians saw it coming long before most of us. Their critique of 1930, ridiculed at the time by knowing observers who declared smugly that the clock could not be turned back—that, to quote H. L. Mencken, "the South, in point of fact, can no more revive the simple society of the Jefferson era than England can revive that of Queen Anne"—constituted a prophetic warning of what might be in store if the headlong exploitation of natural resources and the unthinking mechanization and dehumanization that accompanied untamed industrialism were not honestly acknowledged and confronted. Doubtless, a return to a preindustrial farming society was unfeasible, but that was the least of what the Agrarians had to say. If not agrarianism, then what? The point was that it was not enough merely to deplore and then look away from unchecked industrialism. In the words of the conclusion to the symposium's Statement of Principles,

> If a community, or a section, or a race, or an age, is groaning under industrialism, and well aware that it is an evil dispensation, it must find the way to

throw it off. To think that this cannot be done is pusillanimous. And if the whole community, section, race, or age thinks it cannot be done, then it has simply lost its political genius and doomed itself to impotence.

What the Agrarians were saying, at a time when few Americans worried about such things, was that if the republic was to live up to its ideals and be what it could be, then it had better look long and hard at what it was in danger of becoming and devote conscious effort to controlling its own destiny, rather than continuing to drift along on the tides of economic materialism. As Allan Tate put it in his essay: "How may the Southerner take hold of his Tradition? The answer is, by violence." How, in other words, can the southerner, as modern American, keep to the heritage of the human community in which men exist as individuals, and thus control and abate the prevailing drift toward mass dehumanization and materialism that seemed to be happening all about him? By an act of resolute, considered will. By refusing to be determined by events rather than attempting to determine them. By thinking in terms of ultimate human values, and then ordering one's economic and social arrangements and one's political actions accordingly, instead of letting the foundations of our values and conduct go unexamined.

For there *was* a southern tradition worthy of preservation, and it had little or nothing to do with racial segregation, Protestant orthodoxy, or states' rights: it was that of the good society, the community of individuals, the security and definition that come when men cease to wage an unrelenting war with nature and enjoy their leisure and their human dignity. If never in the history of the South had that goal been fully realized, and however much it had been largely restricted to only a part of the population, it was not thereby rendered any the less desirable as a standard to be cherished. *At least it had been in men's thoughts.* At least the society had evolved that ideal out of its human circumstance. At least there was the tradition of that kind of human aspiration.

I'll Take My Stand, therefore, was and still is a prophetic book. Its very "impracticality" constituted its strength, for the refusal of the twelve southerners to be bound by what in 1930 was considered "practical" and "inevitable" enabled them to see beneath the surface of Progress and examine the largely unquestioned assumptions on which much of its rhetoric was based. The issue to which the Agrarians addressed themselves was not that of farms versus factories, mules versus tractors, rural play-parties versus radio; it was that of man versus the machine. Their tradition had made it possible for them to believe that human beings could *choose* their course of action.

But is it not possible that in pinning their hopes on the ability of the South somehow to retain the best of its manners and mores, to cherish and retain the humane virtues and refuse to surrender its identity, the Agrarians were not after all backing a lost cause? Is it not possible that the present enviable situation of the South *vis-à-vis* the nation as a whole has come about because in certain vital, nonmaterial respects it has refused to give up its old community identity? May not future historians decide that it was that very "backwardness," that insistence upon retaining the sense of community identity, which made racial integration so difficult at first, but which, once the walls were breached, made it a reality in a way that is now becoming the envy of places where the economic and social forces of an impersonal mass society cannot so readily work such things out on terms of human dignity and individuality?

And if so, then are not recent political developments a testimony to the soundness of what Stark Young was getting at in his essay in *I'll Take My Stand*, that "the

South changing must be the South still," and that "in the shifting relation between ourselves and the new order lies the profoundest source for our living, I mean change in that almost mystical sense by which, so long as we are alive, we are not the same and yet remain ourselves"?

No matter. Such speculations are a dubious business. But this much does seem certain: *I'll Take My Stand*, as it appears in its third edition since its publication almost half a century ago, is very much what Allen Tate wrote to Donald Davidson about it in 1942: "I think it was and *is* a very great success; but then I never expected it to have any political influence. It is a reaffirmation to the humane tradition, and to reaffirm that is an end in itself. Never fear: we shall be remembered when our snipers are forgotten."

Peter Taylor

(1917–1994)

Peter Taylor was born on January 8, 1917, in Trenton, Tennessee. His family later moved to Nashville in 1924, to St. Louis in 1926, and to Memphis in 1932. Taylor entered Southwestern University in Memphis in the spring of 1936, where he studied under Allen Tate. At Tate's suggestion, Taylor transferred to Vanderbilt University in Tennessee to study with John Crowe Ransom. After Ransom left for Kenyon College in Ohio, Taylor followed a year later, entering in the fall of 1938.

From 1941 to 1945, Taylor served in the United States Army at Fort Oglethorpe, Georgia, and at Tidworth Camp in England. In 1943 he married the poet Eleanor Ross, with whom he had two children. For many years Taylor combined the careers of writing and teaching. From 1967 until his death on November 2, 1994, he taught at the University of Virginia at Charlottesville.

Among Taylor's numerous publications are *A Long Fourth* (1948); *The Widows of Thornton* (1954); *Happy Families Are All Alike* (1959); *Miss Leonora When Last Seen and Fifteen Other Stories* (1963); *The Collected Stories of Peter Taylor* (1969); *In the Miro District and Other Stories* (1977); *The Old Forest and Other Stories* (1985); *A Summons to Memphis* (1986); *The Oracle at Stoneleigh Court* (1993); and *In the Tennessee Country* (1994).

Taylor received a Guggenheim Fellowship (1950–1951); National Institute of Arts and Letters grant (1952); Fulbright grant (1955–1956); Ford Foundation Fellowship (1961); Rockefeller Foundation grant (1965); National Academy and Institute of Arts and Letters gold medal for literature (1979); Ritz Paris Hemingway Award and PEN/Faulkner Award for fiction (1983); and the Pulitzer Prize for fiction (1987).

Cousin Aubrey

In the Tennessee country of my forebears it, was not uncommon for a man of good character suddenly to disappear. He might be a young man or a middle-aged man or even sometimes a very old man. Few questions were ever asked. Only rarely was it even speculated that perhaps he had an "ugly situation at home." It was always assumed, moreover, that such a man had gone away of his own volition and that he had good and sufficient reason for resettling himself elsewhere. Such disappearances were especially common in our earliest history, before Tennessee achieved statehood even, but they continued all through the nineteenth century and even into the twentieth. We were brought up on stories of such disappearances. I very early came to think of them as a significant part of our history: the men who had disappeared without leaving behind any explanation of their going.

When in recent years I found myself strangely preoccupied with the possible present whereabouts of one of my mother's aged cousins, one Aubrey Tucker Bradbury, I could not but be mindful of those old stories I had heard about other men who had vanished. By this time I was already a middle-aged man with grown-up children of my own, and my mother herself had been dead for some while. This middle-aged preoccupation of mine would soon develop into what amounted to an obsession. What seemed particularly impressive to me was that this Cousin Aubrey had managed to vanish three times from our midst before his disappearance was complete and permanent, so to speak. Anyhow, I came to find myself wishing above all things, almost, to know what had finally happened to my old cousin and where he might be living out his days. It did not occur to me either that he had had some great good fortune in life or that he had come to an ignominious or perhaps violent end. But somehow I could not rest until I knew what had become of the man. I realized that even as a child I had a good many times wondered what had happened to him. I suppose I had reason enough to wonder, since on every occasion of our meeting before his final departure he had taken particular pains to show a special dislike for the small boy—and later, the adolescent—who was brought forward to meet him, a dislike which seemed totally unwarranted since our meetings were so few and so brief. But all that aside, my sudden and unaccountable preoccupation with finding Cousin Aubrey Bradbury was like some old passion of my youth that had been suppressed and was now in late middle age manifesting itself in a more virulent form.

All the while that I was making the first few tentative inquiries and investigations concerning this missing cousin and even later when we had found him—as a result of my own and my younger son's efforts—I continued to think of those other vanished men who had captured my imagination when I was a boy. I felt that they might offer an explanation of Aubrey's disappearance. I knew how little similarity there could have been between those men and himself—as little as there could also have been between himself and any one of our great achievers, such as my maternal grandfather, for instance, who scaled the great heights of Tennessee politics to end his days in a no less exalted role than that of United States senator and an entrenched power in the capital at Washington. But nonetheless, the names and stories of those other men's disappearances would keep returning to my inflamed and strangely excited mind. My constant reference to them in conversation during this time very nearly drove my wife, Melissa, as well as my son Braxton to distraction. They spoke of this habit I had fallen into as my "mania." But they listened sympathetically, too—they and the rest of the family—as again and again I catalogued the names of vanished Tennesseans. Apparently I spoke of them always in tones of such particular veneration that Braxton especially found it wonderfully amusing. He compared it to the listing of Homeric heroes! At any rate, by all means the most famous name in my said catalogue was that of our old warrior-hero, Governor Sam Houston. Everyone, especially Braxton and his mother, knew the story:

On the morning following the night of Governor Sam Houston's marriage to a Nashville belle, he abandoned his bride and abandoned as well his newly won gubernatorial chair. It is well known that Houston went then for a time to live among the Indians. And afterward, of course, he went on to found the independent Republic of Texas. But, for us, the point is that he never returned to Tennessee. . . . Only somewhat less famous in the annals of the state was a man who had been one of our two Confederate senators and who, after the war, without seeing his family or his constituents again, went off to live in Brazil. From there he sent back photographs of himself posed in opulent surroundings and attired in romantic Portuguese costume. But when some relative, later on, made a point of looking him up, he was found in pathetic rags living in dreadful squalor and quite alone in the slums of Rio de Janeiro.

Not all of our vanished men, however, were public men. They were, some of them, simple, landless men who seemed unable to put down roots anywhere. Sometimes they took their wives right along with them when they went away, as well as whatever children they had and perhaps an old grandmother or some other dependent or relative or, in the earliest time, perhaps a little clutch of black slaves and even an indentured servant or two. But even these rootless men, when they departed, frequently left under the cover of night, as if the act of moving in itself were a disgrace. I am told that in the first quarter of the last century it was indeed quite common in Tennessee to see a crudely lettered sign nailed to a tree trunk in the front yard of an abandoned farmhouse, reading simply GONE TO TEXAS. And that was only a manner of speaking, of course. It was merely a statement that another disenchanted man had put forever behind him the long, green hinterland that is Tennessee, and that he never intended returning to her salubrious clime.

Certainly among my earliest memories is my experience aboard the special funeral train bearing the body of my late grandfather, who was in the United States Senate and who died in Washington in 1916. I was the only grandchild taken along on this journey since the others were of school age and would have been too long absent from classes. Aboard that funeral train the Senator's widow occupied the drawing room in the first of the two Pullman cars. I remember such details not merely because I was present but because I would afterward hear accounts of that train ride repeated endlessly by other members of the family, for whom without exception it was the most important journey of their entire lives. I particularly remember that in the drawing room of the second Pullman car were the late Senator's three daughters by an earlier marriage, one of them being my mother—young matrons they must be called in the language of that day, though despite each being married and the mother of one or more children they were scarcely more than girls, really. And in lower berths nearest to their private compartments would sleep their young husbands, each taking his turn during the long journey to Tennessee at sitting with the dead Senator's corpse up in the baggage car. Among these, also taking his turn at sitting with the corpse, was of course my father. A certain nephew of the Senator, the aforementioned Aubrey Tucker Bradbury, would from time to time offer to relieve one or another of three sons-in-law at his watch. But the sons-in-law regarded their vigil by the Senator's coffin as their exclusive privilege. And the fact was that the very presence on the train of this odd-looking and eccentric kinsman of the Senator's—this Aubrey Tucker Bradbury—was resented by all members of the immediate family. The three sons-in-law agreed among themselves that even the wide black armband on the sleeve of

Aubrey's dark suit was a presumption and an affront. More than anyone else, per-haps, they bore in mind a certain irregularity in Aubrey's very kinship to the family—that is, that he had been born out of wedlock, being, the child of the Senator's deceased elder brother and a "mountain woman" of obscure background. In the eyes of the family there was something infinitely lugubrious, if not sinister, in the young man's very bearing. The eldest of the three sisters was moved to remark (while I, her little nephew, was sitting on her lap in the drawing room) that only by the black mourning band on his sleeve could their cousin Aubrey be distinguished from the long-faced undertakers who had abounded on the scene at the railway platform as they were setting out.

That special train would leave the Union Station in Washington at 2:40 in the af-ternoon on September 18. The year of course was 1916. Although the funeral proces-sion from the Willard Hotel to the station had been led by a horse-drawn hearse bedecked with a mountain of floral wreaths, the rest of the official procession con-sisted of four elegant black limousines and eleven other black motor cars. In the un-covered driver's seat of each of the high-set limousines rode not only a chauffeur uniformed in black but a black-uniformed footman as well. I remember my father's commenting that these funeral vehicles and their funeral attendants were supplied not by the federal government, as one might have supposed, but by the Washington undertaker who would be in charge of all procedure and all protocol until that mo-ment when the Senator's coffin would be lifted into the baggage car.

It must be mentioned that alongside the highly polished limousines rode a number of government-provided plainclothesmen—outriders on horseback, as it were. And it cannot go without mention that these men were present because inside the limousines, among other notables, rode two very great personages indeed. Though the American manners of the day forbade that the bereaved family openly acknowledge the presence of any such person at this solemn occasion, I think it all right, so long afterward and in this latter day, so to speak, for me to make known the rank of those great personages. They were none other than a former president of the United States and the incumbent himself! Their presence is, however, scarcely a significant part of my story. The impor-tant point is that the mounted presidential guards with automatic pistols showing on their belts underneath their jackets seemed impressive to me, at the age of four, and ac-tually frightening to my mother and her two sisters. It gave those young-lady daughters of the dead Senator the uneasy and altogether absurd feeling that the funeral proces-sion might be attacked as it moved along Pennsylvania Avenue.

One of these three sisters who had this irrational response to the armed guards was of course my mother. This youngest daughter of the Senator was of an apprehen-sive and nervous temperament. Already, at earlier events of the funeral, she had kept glancing almost suspiciously in the direction of her eccentric cousin, Aubrey Tucker Bradbury, as if to see if he were experiencing an anxiety similar to her own. (I do think I observed this for myself at the time and was not merely told of it by my mother long afterward.) It was always at Aubrey she glanced during the funeral ser-vice and not at her handsome and youthful husband. The sight of Aubrey Bradbury was somehow reassuring to her during the early period of the funeral, as his presence had often been to her as a child and particularly just after the death of her own mother. Aubrey had actually been her confidant in those earlier times, as he had been also for her sisters during certain times of insecurity in *their* girlhood, and there had even been a period when this cousin had lived in the house with them and served briefly as their papa's private secretary. And at one time or another this same Aubrey had made declarations of undying love to each of the three sisters. (All three of the sisters would in later life give me hints of these outbursts of Aubrey's.) Anyhow, my mother knew of Aubrey's sensitive, serious nature, and though she had since her marriage—and probably through the influence of her husband—come to think of Aubrey as a ridiculous, unmanly sort of creature, she wondered if he were not today imagining, like herself, that outrageous and terrifying things were going to happen to the funeral party. As a matter of fact, I think that without being conscious of it my mother sensed that this occasion marked the end of an era in the life they had all known.

The two other sisters, my two aunts, who were destined to help bring me up after my father's early death, were persons of a far less apprehensive nature than my mother, and so they were able to speak more openly of the absurd anxiety they felt that day. Even as they rode along the avenue between the Willard Hotel and the Union Station and observed total strangers standing at the curb, with hats removed in the old-fashioned way in the presence of death, my Aunt Bertie and Aunt Felicia spoke to each other openly of their anxiety. But my mother, whose name was Gertrude, was of a more introspective and questioning temperament and was unable to speak out about her fear. Her hesitation was due, in part at least, to the peculiar nature of her anxieties. The fantasy she entertained was not merely that those men on horseback would suddenly turn on the procession and perhaps upset the coffin and the precious corpse inside. (*That* was the "crazy feeling" openly confessed to by my aunts and which, as a matter of fact, they would long afterward laughingly tell me about.) But Trudie, as my mother was always called by her older sisters, imagined those armed men as actually forcing open the coffin and revealing to her that her worst fantasy-fear was come true: that it was not Senator Nathan Tucker's body locked in the casket but that of someone known to her but whom she could not quite recognize, someone whose identity somehow eluded her or, rather, whose identity she could not quite bring herself to acknowledge.

My mother knew in reason, of course, that her father's body *was* present, but during the short funeral service in the hotel ballroom it had occurred to her several times that her father was not really dead at all and locked away in the elaborate, brass-trimmed coffin. She would learn in later years that during the very moments when the three sons-in-law, along with her cousin Aubrey Bradbury and two other young kinsmen, were bearing the coffin down a center aisle that was arranged between hotel ballroom chairs—she would learn, that is to say, that other mourners beside herself had had that same fantasy.

Perhaps it seemed to nearly everyone present that day that whatever else might be inside that coffin it could not be the body of Senator Nathan Tucker of Tennessee. The Senator had always seemed to nearly everybody the liveliest and most alive of men. To all present, moreover, the tragedy of the Senator's death seemed almost beyond belief, if only because of the unlikeliness of the circumstance. They could not accept that this noble, gifted, virgorous, healthy man of sixty, who had been more of a gentleman—folk hero than a mere politician, had been brought down by something as ignoble and trivial-sounding as a gallstone operation.

Of far greater and more lasting significance, though, was the shock to the mourners that this ambitious and talented man would be destroyed at the very peak of his illustrious career in public life. (He had served three terms as governor and was at the beginning of his second term in the Senate.) No doubt the most difficult fact to be faced—or perhaps *not* to be faced—was that this distinguished son of an old country family, a family that had been distinguishing itself to an ever greater degree during every generation for more than a hundred years, should now be stricken at the very peak of his family's supreme elevation. Perhaps all the kin and connections assembled at the funeral were in fact saying to themselves, "We have invested so much confidence and hope in this man as chief of our tribe! In him who helped lead us back into the Union and resolved so many other conflicts within us! If he be dead now, to whom shall we turn to bolster our collective ego, and *where* shall we turn?" These Tennessee people were, in 1916, a people who still identified themselves most often in terms of family ties. To them the Senator's achievement represented generations of hanging together in all things. Perhaps everyone present at the funeral service understood this. Perhaps the notables present as well as the fashionable Washington friends of the three daughters were more observing of the antediluvian family feelings than were members of the family themselves. There was something altogether archaic about this family, something that made it seem to step out of an earlier, simpler, nobler age.

Even while riding in the procession to the Union Station and even when the coffin was being hoisted clumsily into the baggage car of the waiting train, Gertrude Tucker Longford, my mother, continued now and again to entertain her ugly fantasy. Her papa's body *could not* lie inside that coffin! It was not her gentle, witty, silver-maned, silver-tongued, her almost beautiful papa who was dead, but some other senator, somebody else's head of family and chief of tribe, or just some other, ordinary man of lower degree and less beloved than her papa. Probably this seemed so to a lesser extent for her two sisters also. Because once the three of them were closeted in their drawing room, there in the second Pullman car of the funeral train, with me sitting on the lap of first one of them then another, each young woman positioned herself in the remotest-seeming corner of the green-upholstered seats, fondling or vaguely trying to entertain me from time to time but totally disregarding her sisters and staring disconsolately into space as if the end of the world had come and she were entirely alone with her grief.

As Trudie Longford, my mother, quietly closed the drawing room door that afternoon, the last face she saw out in the aisle of the Pullman car was that of her cousin Aubrey Bradbury. I was standing close by Mother's side, and Aubrey must have observed the two of us there. I don't recall what my own impression was. But Trudie observed, as she would tell me many times afterward, that Aubrey wore a wounded expression on his heavy but weak-chinned face, and as she closed the door he lowered his eyelids submissively as if acknowledging Trudie's right to shut the door in his face. My own impression was, and remained so ever afterward, that his seemingly lowering his eyes actually represented his glancing down at me with a mixture of ire and resentment. My mother, at any rate, would be confronted by her cousin a good many other times before that journey was over, but she retained her impression always that that was the last time they ever looked directly into each other's eyes, that there was never again the exchange of communicative glances there once had been. After the Senator's lying-in-state in Nashville and after the subsequent burial at the cemetery in Knoxville, Trudie would never in effect look upon Aubrey's countenance again. When he did return rather mysteriously to attend my two aunts' funerals, not too many years later, he was unrecognizable to most people, and Mother had no substantive exchanges with him. His reappearances on those occasions seemed afterward more like apparitions, in most respects. And nobody learned anything of the whereabouts of his present residence or of his present mode of life—not that anybody knew how he learned about the funerals he attended, either. For more than forty years his real whereabouts would remain unknown to any member of the Tucker clan or to anyone in the entire connection. It was, as my mother and her sisters said, as though that day in the Knoxville cemetery the earth of East Tennessee had simply opened up and swallowed Aubrey Bradbury whole. From that moment he was no more among them, no more among us. From that time he became another of those men of good character who disappeared without leaving any explanation of their going.

My points of reference regarding Cousin Aubrey's severance from the world he knew best would not be complete without mention of some other examples that come to mind. My father had a cousin in West Tennessee who set fire to his house and went off with a woman from a neighboring farm. His house was long since heavily insured, perhaps by design, and so he supposed he was not behaving dishonorably or even inconsiderately with his family. He had no concern about the welfare of his wife and children. At a later time word would come that this man wished to return home. But his wife's brothers went to him, wherever he had revealed himself to be, and forbade his coming back or even manifesting his present whereabouts to his wife and children. Most of us never knew where it was he had resettled or whether or not he and the woman from the neighboring farm had stayed together.

And then there was a banker in Nashville whom I would hear about during my childhood who left his office in the middle of one afternoon, without so much as taking his derby hat or his gold-headed cane with his monogram on the crown. They say he went out through the revolving door, like one of the ordinary clerks, with a pencil stuck behind his ear and just as though he were only stepping across the street for a few moments. His whereabouts were not known to us for more than twenty-five years. He did not abscond with any bank funds when he left, and his affairs were in perfect order. His greatest problem was said to be with demon rum. One sad part of the story was that when at last he was found he had altogether rid his life of that difficulty and was regarded as a model citizen in his new location. Sad, though, was not the word for what happened after he was discovered. When he was at last hunted down by a Nashville newspaper reporter ("Just for the story in it," so it was said), the two oldest children of the new family he had started locked themselves in their rooms and put bullets through their heads. It turned out that the banker and his former secretary, whom he had run off with, had opened a small hardware store somewhere in the Northeast and were operating a moderately successful business there. . . . I can assure you there were other instances, all the details of which I once knew as well as I know these. As for my wife and my son Braxton, they have always shown more interest in these stories with unhappy endings than in those that end merely in tantalizing mystery, which are more to my liking. Brax used to predict perversely that to find my cousin Aubrey Bradbury might do him irreparable harm. From the outset I felt that it was likely that the old man's rediscovery by a long-lost cousin, scarcely more than half his own age, might just as easily turn out to be a great boon for the old fellow—and would somehow certainly turn out so for me. Yet in my nightly dreams about him throughout the entire period of my search it would sometimes turn out one way and sometimes another. I cannot even now say for sure what our eventual reunion meant to either Aubrey or to me.

If when I was growing up I asked one of my fragile and ever-ailing aunts or my fragile but long-enduring mother whatever became of Aubrey, she was apt to stare off into space, genuinely bewildered—so it seemed to me—and murmur something like: "We don't know whatever happened to poor Aubrey. I am afraid none of us has kept track of him. Finally he just seemed to have vanished into thin air." They did not want to think about what may have become of him. They only wanted to talk of the trying times they had had with him on the funeral train. If at some other time and in quite another mood I asked if Aubrey had been like my manly father or like my equally manly uncles as a young man, I would likely be answered with a hoot of laughter. They thought my question utterly ridiculous. If all three of these ladies were present when I asked this question, there would come a chorus of "Oh, heavens, no! Not a bit! Not in the least! Not at all like any one of *them!* They were real men, your father and your uncles!" If at still another time I persisted, trying to arrive at some notion of the man, and suggested that perhaps after all he had been rather like those other men who disappeared, I was apt to be given a very straight look. Then there came an emphatic answer: "No *indeed!* Aubrey Tucker Bradbury was most certainly not like one of them! For Aubrey there was no ugly situation at home that *he* had to run away from!"

The phrase "ugly situation at home" was often used in connection with the hero Sam Houston and with our relative in West Tennessee who burned his own house, as well as with a good many others. Once during very recent years I happened to use that very phrase in discussing Cousin Aubrey with my son Brax, and when I quoted my mother to him on this subject I was at first shocked by Brax's burst of laughter. The fact was, Braxton was quite a young man at the time I speak of, and it only recently had been revealed to him that Aubrey Bradbury was actually an "outside cousin" of the Tucker family. I think this had not consciously been concealed from him, but it was rather that Aubrey's irregular kinship was seldom referred to by anyone. I don't recall at what age I stumbled upon the information that Aubrey was the illegitimate son of one of my maternal great-uncles and that Bradbury was actually his mother's surname. Upon my use of the all-too-familiar phrase, Brax, laughing out at me and slapping his thigh in the coarse manner he sometimes exhibits, exclaimed to me, "And you, Daddy—you and your mother and your aunts—you didn't call that 'an ugly situation at home'? Poor Cousin Aubrey! I hope you will never find him again!"

What I then felt I must explain to this son of mine was that in my mother's day—if not quite in my own—an illegitimate child like Aubrey was not put out for adoption and was not left to be brought up in disgrace by his unwed mother. Rather, he was drawn into the extended family, which was a reality in those quaint and distant days in Tennessee, and he was given the family's special protection both at home and abroad in the world. I said this was so, at any rate—or that I had been told so by my forebears—in the really best, the "most long-settled and best-regulated families" in our little up-country corner of the world. As soon as I had insisted upon this to Brax, however, I found myself recalling how my mother and aunts had come at last to regard Aubrey with the condescension and even contempt that their husbands had taught them to feel for him, and that the husbands, in their particular, masculine pride of that period, had always felt. My father and my uncles were all three of them sons of Confederate veterans and were themselves so thoroughly versed in Civil War history that aboard the funeral train they delighted in pointing out the sites of great battles and even small skirmishes. More than once I heard them laughing at Aubrey's ignorance of military history. At Culpepper, my father (whose name, incidentally, was Braxton Bragg Longford) went through the Pullman cars announcing to all that nearby was the spot where "the Gallant Pelham fell," and it had to be explained to Aubrey who that hero had been. Aboard the train there were many whispered conversations about the eccentric cousin's behavior. One night he was discovered in the area between the two Pullman cars, with his face in the crook of his arm, weeping aloud—ostensibly out of grief for his dead benefactor, the Senator. My two uncles discovered him there and led him into the men's smoking room where they administered large doses of whiskey out of their own flasks. And it was at some time on that long journey that I heard Uncle Hobart repeating what was allegedly my grandfather's own account of how he had gone to the simple mountain cabin where Aubrey was being reared until he was about school age and had "rescued" him from the rough people there, had placed him in Mr. Webb's school in Bell Buckle, where he was rather harshly disciplined and received a severely supervised classical education. But I think these incidents and stories did not impress me so strongly as did Cousin Aubrey's own contumelious glances at myself. Very early, though, I began to understand the resentment inspired in him by the mere sight of a boy who enjoyed every protection such a life as mine provided and the affection and even adoration of those three particular women who presided over my every activity. And by the time I was an adolescent I believe I could already conceive that an experience so totally different from mine could have a hardening and corrupting effect upon a being as sensitive to the affection and consideration of others as I believed myself to be.

I must tell you now that when Aubrey Tucker Bradbury resurfaced in my life at last—nearly forty years after his first disappearance—he would resurface little by little, so to speak, inch by inch. That is, I began first of all merely to hear rumors of the existence of a man with a name much like his own, though not exactly like. The surname and the middle name had been reversed. And on the second occasion of my hearing of him it was indicated that the two names had been hyphenated—a most unusual practice for someone hailing from Tennessee. The old Cousin Aubrey in all representations of him had been so modest-sounding and unpretentious that I tended to dismiss the possibility of the two being one and the same. But once I had heard of the existence of this other man it registered indelibly on my mind. After the first report of him I was ever conscious of the remote possibility that this obviously different sort of man might still somehow be Aubrey.

Though it was always some place other than Tennessee that I heard his name spoken, it was inevitably added that his origins were there. It was this that made me first suspect that my mother and my two aunts might have been wrong in their assumption that Aubrey had merely disappeared into the East Tennessee countryside and had there resumed the role of a Tennessee bumpkin. It so happened that the first mention of his name reached my ears not in this country even but when I was traveling in Europe. Since I was not over there on a pleasure trip and was not paying my own expenses, I was put up at a rather better hotel than I normally would have been booked into. (My expenses were being paid by the very generous university where I taught art history in those days and partly by the Italian government, for whom I was helping to direct restoration of art works after the disastrous flood in Florence.) There in the dining room of the great hotel by the Arno I heard someone at the next table pronounce the name of Aubrey Bradbury-Tucker. The people at the table were alternately speaking English, German, and Italian. I listened carefully but was unable to grasp precisely the subject of the conversation. But I heard once again the articulation of that name. The party left the dining room without my ever making out their identity, though I assumed, correctly I think, that they too were involved somehow in the restoration at the Uffizi.

The next time I heard the man's name spoken was on a shuttle flight between New York City and Washington. A garrulous old lady sitting beside me on that short flight insisted on knowing where I was "from." When I told her I was from Charlottesville, she said knowingly that my accent didn't sound like "old Charlottesville" and that I must teach at the university there. (She of course "knew people" there and had often been a visitor.) I confirmed that all she said was so and confessed that I was originally from Tennessee. "Ah, Tennessee," she exclaimed. "Nashville I'll bet it is!" Then she proceeded to tell me about a wonderfully attractive man from Nashville—"so he claimed." She had made his acquaintance aboard a South American cruise ship and he had flirted with her "most scandalously." His name was Mr. Bradbury-Tucker—"hyphenated no less!" she said. And then she laughed her merry laugh again. Suddenly I could see just how attractive she herself had once been, and I could understand how delightful it would have been then to have found oneself on the South American cruise with her. She said that Mr. Bradbury-Tucker had had the most beautiful Vandyke beard she had ever seen on any man. And she said that when she told him so, he replied, with a twinkle in his bewitching brown eyes, that he only wore the beard in order to conceal "a very weak chin." Then she went on to say that Mr. Bradbury-Tucker had deceived her wickedly and that *she* had clearly meant nothing to *him*. Only on the last day of the cruise did she discover that Mr. Bradbury-Tucker was traveling in the company of another woman, a rich woman older than herself who during the voyage had kept mostly to their stateroom. I tried to reassure her—facetiously I suppose—that all Tennesseans were not such rascals, and I told her that my mother's maiden name had been Tucker and she had had a cousin named Bradbury. At this, the lady blushed to the roots of her snow-white hair. She made no further effort at conversation and managed not to hear further questions that it now struck me to ask. I felt she was berating herself for having once again talked too much to a stranger. When she got off the plane she hurried away with the crowd without my learning so much as her name. But it was then that the fantasy first occurred to me that the country bumpkin, the outside cousin, had not disappeared into the countryside of East Tennessee but had been interred with his erstwhile protector, the late Senator Tucker, and that a new Aubrey had been released to make his own way, to take on a new persona and perhaps in that persona take revenge upon the world.

At a party in Charlottesville some two years after that ride on the shuttle, I obtained a really constructive piece of evidence that Mr. Bradbury-Tucker and our Cousin Aubrey Bradbury were indeed one and the same. It was at a men's "smoker"— so called in old-fashioned academic circles—given one afternoon in honor of a visiting lecturer, a man who was being considered for an appointment at the university. Though I was on the selections committee, I felt reasonably certain that he would not accept such an appointment as we would be able to offer. He was too celebrated, too "international" an expert in his field, to be willing to settle down in Charlottesville, Virginia. But he was our guest lecturer of the day and we wished to please him. We happened on the subject of the old days of railways and what a delight traveling had been then. It turned out that our lecturer was a veritable collector of stories about trains. And of course, wishing to please him, we all brought forward our stories on the subject. Perhaps I, more than the others, insisted on being heard and was soon running through my own repertoire. Yet I think everyone present would have acknowledged that our guest more or less urged me on.

When at length I proceeded to tell our lecturer about Grandfather's funeral train, I was careful to speak only of the comic aspects of the journey. In fact, I told him only about how my two uncles ended by getting very drunk and so altogether out of control that they had finally, first one and then a while later the other, to be turned over to the constabulary in the first two county seats where the train stopped after passing over the Tennessee state border.

Indeed I had hardly sketched in my account of those two incidents when our guest lecturer burst out at me, exclaiming "What a strange coincidence this is!" He bent forward and placed his well-manicured hand on my arm. But he was not even looking at me as he spoke. "This is a true story that I have heard before!" he said, bending toward me as he spoke. "How very strange! I do love such stories and most of all how I love to have them turn up in such dissimilar circumstances. I first heard of that train journey from a man by the name of Colonel A. N. Bradbury-Tucker and who himself was present on that funeral train and who was, moreover, a relative of this dead Senator whom you referred to up in the baggage car." (Obviously our guest lecturer had not bothered to catch my own name and my connection to the Senator, though I had already spent a day and a half in his company, squiring him about the university, introducing him to senior professors, deans, and one vice-president. Clearly he did not recall that I had identified the dead Senator as my grandfather.) Presently he continued: "He was a very odd sort of person, this Colonel Bradbury-Tucker who told me his version of the same story. He was a very urbane and distinguished-seeming person. He was more like someone you might meet in Europe. One could not have guessed that his clothes even were American. He had a handsome beard, very beautifully trimmed. Altogether he was wonderfully well groomed in the old-fashioned way. He and I met in the house of a very wealthy old lady in Bristol, Rhode Island. I never knew exactly what *that* relationship was—his and the Rhode Island lady's—but I gathered from little things he let drop that he saw himself as a great lady's man. Anyway, he loved to talk about women—ever so confidingly. Perhaps he had a lot of money. He wished one, at any rate, to think so. Or perhaps he was the sort of man who lives off women. But the thing that interested me most about that funeral train he had been aboard was the presence there of the dead Senator's three young married daughters. I remember his holding up his forefinger and thumb like this and saying, 'They were absolutely delicious.' He was like some very cultivated gourmet describing a variety of his favorite dishes! He made great distinctions and differentiations with regard to the young ladies' three kinds of beauty. He referred to them as innocent young matrons all properly married and perfectly protected, of course, but knowing nothing of the world. 'Genuine provincials!' he said. 'And absolutely delicious!'"

Suddenly I felt deeply offended and wished to hear no more from our lecturer and no more of Colonel Bradbury-Tucker's view of my mother and my aunts. It was undoubtedly my Cousin Aubrey that the lecturer had known, but the picture that this latter-day Colonel Bradbury had painted was so far from what I had received from my mother and my aunts that I felt a kind of electric shock pass through me. When presently our talk was interrupted, I moved away from our guest lecturer and soon took my leave from the smoker. I was afraid that some faculty colleague present might mention to him that my mother's maiden name had been Tucker and that like the colonel, I too originally hailed from Tennessee. . . . I hardly need add that the lecturer did not receive the nomination of the selection committee, and that though I continued to read his distinguished scholarly works I never saw him in person again.

From that day forward I was sure of course that the man I had kept hearing about was my mother's cousin. For a certain period after that I was less sure than formerly that I still wished to come face-to-face with Cousin Aubrey. Yet curiosity about his incredible transformation caused my interest in his whereabouts and his ultimate fate to persist. If the long-ago journey on the Senator's funeral train changed all our lives in some degree and if the significance of those changes was what I longed to understand, then a meeting with Colonel Bradbury-Tucker—surely the most altered of us all—might facilitate my understanding. Only to look upon the man's countenance might solve mysteries about myself.

Very soon Aubrey's resurfacing in my life was destined to come one inch closer. In Charlottesville, Virginia, there are many people, especially among the university faculty, who subscribe to the *Washington Post* as their morning newspaper. But since my wife is a native of a small town in Southside Virginia, we have always read the *Richmond Times-Dispatch* for our morning paper and purchased the *New York Times* at the newsstand on the corner. And that is how I happened to miss—or very nearly miss—seeing the newspaper picture of Colonel Bradbury-Tucker. I first beheld his visage not in a paper that was delivered to my doorstep, and not in one for sale at a newsstand, but in a fragment of newsprint wrapped around a vegetable that my wife brought from the curb market. It was from an issue of the *Washington Post* that was at least three weeks old. Even as the newspaper crossed my vision on its way to the trash can I received an impression of the erect figure and the slightly out-of-focus face that was in the background of the photograph reproduced thereon. I quickly fished it out and spread it on the enamel-topped kitchen table. It purported to be a picture of one of those Washington hostesses whose entertainments one generally avoids unless one is seeking office or has some other self-interested purpose requiring one's presence there. The caption under the picture gave the famously rich hostess's name, of course, describing her as one of Washington's most celebrated socialites. She was apparently so rich and so celebrated that it seemed worthwhile to mention even her slightly out-of-focus escort in the background, one Colonel A. N. Bradbury-Tucker. At last I had a blurred but indubitable image of the man Aubrey Tucker Bradbury had become. Though his beard was white, it seemed to me an absolute facsimile of the streaked gray beard my grandfather had worn in pictures taken not long before his death. And even though the image of his face was blurred, the dark eyes looked out piercingly toward the camera, just as the Senator's had always done in his campaign pictures, those which Mother kept locked away in her leatherbound scrapbook and produced periodically for my admiration and edification. And I had the eerie feeling that indeed it had been the old Cousin Aubrey whose death had come that September day in 1916 and that it was his body that had been substituted for the dead Senator's in the elaborately brass-trimmed coffin that was handed so clumsily onto the special funeral train.

Ishmael Reed

(1938–   )

On February 22, 1938, Ishmael Reed was born in Chattanooga, Tennessee. He grew up in Buffalo, New York, and attended the State University of New York at Buffalo from 1956 to 1960. He moved to New York City and cofounded the newspaper *East Village Other* (1965). Reed's first novel, *The Free-Lance Pallbearers* (1967), illustrated his version of black experimental fiction and the novel as a form of satire and African American folklore.

The year 1972 saw Reed's first major volume of poetry published, which is entitled *Conjure: Selected Poems, 1963–1979*. This volume was followed by *Chattanooga: Poems* (1973) and *A Secretary to the Spirits* (1977). In 1974 he received the Guggenheim Memorial Award for Fiction. *The Last Days of Louisiana Red* (1972) won for Reed the Richard and Hilda Rosenthal Foundation Award and the National Institute of Arts and Letters in 1975.

Other works include *Yellow Black Radio Broke Down* (1969); *Mumbo Jumbo* (1972); *Flight to Canada* (1976); *The Terrible Twos* (1982); *Reckless Eyeballing* (1986); *The Terrible Threes* (1989); and *Japanese by Spring* (1993).

Reed and his wife Carla Blank live in Oakland, California. He is a lecturer at the University of California, Berkeley.

Chattanooga

1

Some say that Chattanooga is the
Old name for Lookout Mountain
To others it is an uncouth name
Used only by the uncivilised
Our a-historical period sees it
As merely a town in Tennessee
To old timers of the Volunteer State
Chattanooga is "The Pittsburgh of
The South"
According to the Cherokee
Chattanooga is a rock that
Comes to a point

They're all right
Chattanooga is something you
Can have anyway you want it
The summit of what you are
I've paid my fare on that
Mountain Incline #2, Chattanooga
I want my ride up
I want Chattanooga

2

Like Nickajack a plucky Blood
I've escaped my battle near
Clover Bottom, braved the
Jolly Roger raising pirates
Had my near miss at Moccasin Bend
To reach your summit so
Give into me Chattanooga
I've dodged the Grey Confederate sharpshooters
Escaped my brother's tomahawks with only
Some minor burns
Traversed a Chickamauga of my own
Making, so
You belong to me Chattanooga

3

I take your East Ninth Street to my
Heart, pay court on your Market
Street of rubboard players and organ
Grinders of Haitian colors rioting
And old Zip Coon Dancers
I want to hear Bessie Smith belt out
I'm wild about that thing in
Your Ivory Theatre
Chattanooga
Coca-Cola's homebase
City on my mind

4

My 6th grade teacher asked me to
Name the highest mountain in the world
I didn't even hesitate, "Lookout Mountain"
I shouted. They laughed
Eastern nitpickers, putting on the
Ritz laughed at my Chattanooga ways
Which means you're always up to it

To get to Chattanooga you must
Have your Tennessee
"She has as many lives as a
cat. As to killing her, even
the floods have failed
you may knock the breath out of
her that's all. She will re-
fill her lungs and draw
a longer breath than ever"
From a Knoxville editorial—
1870s

5

Chattanooga is a woman to me too
I want to run my hands through her
Hair of New Jersey tea and redroot
Aint no harm in that
Be caressed and showered in
Her Ruby Falls
That's only natural
Heal myself in her
Minnehaha Springs
58 degrees F. all year
Around. Climb all over her
Ridges and hills
I wear a sign on my chest
"Chattanooga or bust"

6

"HOLD CHATTANOOGA AT ALL
HAZARDS"—Grant to Thomas

When I tasted your big juicy
Black berries ignoring the rattle-
Snakes they said came to Cameron
Hill after the rain, I knew I
Had to have you Chattanooga
When I swam in Lincoln Park
Listening to Fats Domino sing
I found my thrill on Blueberry
Hill on the loudspeaker
I knew you were mine Chattanooga
Chattanooga whose Howard Negro
School taught my mother Latin
Tennyson and Dunbar
Whose Miller Bros. Department
Store cheated my Uncle out of
What was coming to him
A pension, he only had 6
Months to go
Chattanoooooooooooooooooooga
Chattanoooooooooooooooooooga

"WE WILL HOLD THE TOWN TILL
WE STARVE"—Thomas to Grant

7

To get to Chattanooga you must
Go through your Tennessee
I've taken all the scotsboros

One state can dish out
Made Dr. Shockley's "Monkey Trials"
The laughing stock of the Nation
Capt. Marvel Dr. Sylvanias shazam
Scientists running from light-
ning, so
Open your borders. Tennessee
Hide your TVA
DeSota determined, this
Serpent handler is coming
Through
Are you ready Lookout Mountain?

"Give all of my Generals what he's
drinking." Lincoln said, when the
Potomac crowd called Grant a lush

8

I'm going to strut all over your
Point like Old Sam Grant did
My belly full of good Tennessee
Whiskey, puffing on
A .05 cigar
The campaign for Chattanooga
Behind me
Breathing a spell
Ponying up for
Appomattox!

John Egerton

(1935–   )

John Egerton was born on June 14, 1935, in Atlanta, Georgia. He was graduated from the University of Kentucky, where he earned his B.A. in 1958 and his M.A. in 1960. He received the Weatherford Award in 1983 and the Lillian Smith Award in 1984 for *Generations: An American Family* (1983).

Egerton's publications include *A Mind to Stay Here* (1970); *The Americanization of Dixie* (1974); *Visions of Utopia* (1977); *Southern Food: At Home, on the Road, in History* (1987); *Shades of Gray: Dispatches from the Modern South* (1991); and *Speak Now Against the Day: The Generation Before the Civil Rights Movement in the South* (1994).

Egerton and his wife, Ann Bleidt Egerton, live in Nashville, Tennessee.

from *The Americanization of Dixie:*

The Southernization of America

Culture: Reexploring "The Sahara of the Bozart"

In the style and spirit of the times in which he wrote, Henry Louis Mencken was a perfect embodiment of personal journalism, a slashing and fearless critic of all things sacred and profane. His prejudices were like a sailor's tattoos—visible, irreverent, outrageous. He was a master of invective, a person of deep intellect and insight, a man of wit and humor and cynicism—in short, an immensely talented and colorful and complex character.

Near the mid-point of his career, he wrote a six-volume series of essays which he called, with characteristic bluntness, *Prejudices*, and in the second volume, which came out in 1920, there was an essay called "The Sahara of the Bozart." Its subject was the South as a cultural wasteland, and it is hard to imagine a criticism more unsparingly acerbic and devastating. It was a hatchet job of the first order—made the more unbearable to Southerners, no doubt, because its excesses were interlarded with so much truth.

The South, he wrote, is so large that "nearly the whole of Europe could be lost in that stupendous region of fat farms, shoddy cities and paralyzed cerebrums," and yet "for all its size and all its wealth and all the 'progress' it babbles of, it is almost as sterile, artistically, intellectually, culturally, as the Sahara Desert. There are single acres in Europe that house more first-rate men than all the states south of the Potomac." Indeed, he wrote, it is "amazing to contemplate so vast a vacuity," and it would be "impossible in all history to match so complete a drying-up of a civilization."

Before the Civil War, said Mencken, the South produced "superior men" with "active and original minds"; they were "hospitable and tolerant," they had "the vague thing that we call culture." But not in 1920: "In all that gargantuan paradise of the fourth-rate there is not a single picture gallery worth going into, or a single orchestra capable of playing the nine symphonies of Beethoven, or a single opera-house, or a single theatre devoted to decent plays, or a single public monument . . . that is worth looking at, or a single workshop devoted to the making of beautiful things." With only a couple of exceptions, he went on, there were no poets "above the rank of neighborhood rhymester" and no prose writers "who can actually write," and as for critics, composers, painters, sculptors, architects, historians, sociologists, philosophers, theologians, and scientists, "there is not even a bad one between the Potomac mud-flats and the Gulf."

Mencken called Virginia "the most civilized of southern states, now as always," but he found little there to cheer him: Her politics "are cheap, ignorant, parochial, idiotic . . . a Washington or a Jefferson, dumped there by some act of God, would be denounced as a scoundrel and jailed overnight." And if Virginia "is the best of the south to-day," then Georgia "is perhaps the worst. The one is simply senile; the other is crass, gross, vulgar and obnoxious. Between lies a vast plain of mediocrity, stupidity, lethargy, almost of dead silence. In the north, of course, there is also grossness, crassness, vulgarity. The north, in its way, is also stupid and obnoxious. But nowhere in the north is there such complete sterility, so depressing a lack of all civilized gesture and aspiration."

Having thus warmed up to his subject, Mencken went on for almost twenty pages. Near the end he asserted that

> it is impossible for intelligence to flourish in such an atmosphere. Free inquiry is blocked by the idiotic certainties of ignorant men. The arts, save in the lower reaches of the gospel hymn, the phonograph and the chautauqua harangue, are all held in suspicion. The tone of public opinion is set by an upstart class but lately emerged from industrial slavery into commercial enterprise—the class of "hustling" business men, of "live wires," of commercial club luminaries, of "drive" managers, of forward-lookers and right-thinkers—in brief, of third-rate southerners inoculated with all the worst traits of the Yankee sharper. . . . The southerner, at his worst, is never quite the surly cad that the Yankee is. His sensitiveness may betray him into occasional bad manners, but in the main he is a pleasant fellow—hospitable, polite, good-humored, even jovial. . . . But a bit absurd. . . . A bit pathetic.

Even the most charitable of Southerners must have found such an overdose of verbal vituperation difficult to swallow. The essay is not an outstanding example of Mencken's consummate journalistic skill—it is, in fact, not journalism but cutthroat criticism—but it does illustrate vividly his power to outrage, and part of that power derived from the incapacity of his victims to make an adequate defense against his outpourings of abuse. In point of fact, the South in 1920 did not have much to boast of in the fields of art, music, theater, literature, and the academic disciplines—it was not as barren as Mencken pictured it, but it offered a uniformly unfavorable comparison with other regions of the country. Mencken was looking for what he called in his essay "American *Kultur*"—by which he meant, presumably, the formal manifestations of what was good and true and beautiful. He did not say whose definitions of goodness and truth and beauty should be applied—his own, presumably, or those of some other "higher authority"—but clearly almost nothing he saw in the South satisfied him, and it must have been painful for irate Southerners to have so little to offer in rebuttal.

Had he been around to take another look fifty years later, Mencken no doubt would have been compelled to acknowledge some remarkable changes. There are art galleries and symphony orchestras and theaters of impressive quality in the South now, and there are poets and fiction writers and composers and artists and academicians of national renown. The Sahara, irrigated by indigenous and upcountry fountains, has bloomed and flowered a bit in the past half-century.

It might be of some passing interest to tote up all the blossoms and attempt some quantitative and qualitative comparisons with other regions. But that has already been done very ably by Roger Griffin Hall in a chapter of *You Can't Eat Magnolias*, and in any event, H. L. Mencken's concept of culture (and Hall's) draws too tight a circle to encompass all that belongs in a broader definition, such as Webster's: "the habits, skills, arts, instruments, institutions, etc. of a given people in a given period." Leaving aside the elements of "high culture," there is much in the music, religion, communication arts, life styles, and leisure-time habits of Southerners—and Americans generally—that helps to define them. The manners, tastes, emotions, customs, traditions, social conventions, interests, values, mores, morals, beliefs, proficiencies, and priorities of Americans in the 1970s—in short, the things people devote their time and energy and money to, aside from the basic necessities of life—amount to far more than orchestras and art galleries and academic pursuits, however important those things may be.

In that larger context, the South is certainly not a cultural wasteland. For good and ill, it resembles the rest of America more and more with each passing year. There is developing an increasingly dominant and singular American culture, overlaying myriads of subcultures that struggle constantly for their identity and survival. The subcultures are like the people who comprise them—new ones are born of purposeful union or accidental conjugation, old ones die of neglect or old age. Any examination of elements of the larger culture, or of some of the smaller ones, is apt to show how powerful the process of Americanization has become—and Southern contributions to that process are by no means lacking. Whether or not one approves of these trends, they exist. A caravan crossing Mencken's Sahara in the 1970s can send out picture postcards that will amaze and delight and confuse and disturb and infuriate natives and outlanders alike.

Hemingway Stadium on the campus of the University of Mississippi in Oxford is one of the holy temples of the American Way of Life. On Saturday afternoons in the rust and amber glow of autumn, the religion of the masses is celebrated there with all the ritual and pageantry and spectacle of a High Church ceremony. The sacraments of the faith, the symbols that constitute the religion itself, are paraded before the assembled multitude, and each one is accorded the highest measure of respect.

There is, to begin, Patriotism, symbolized by the waving banners of Mississippi, the Old Confederacy, and the United States, and by the playing of "Dixie" and the National Anthem. There is Militarism, personified by an ROTC honor guard, and perhaps by a visiting astronaut or a returned exprisoner of war. There is Prayer ("May we all be winners in the Game of Life, in Jesus' name we pray, amen"). There is Music, live and in color, performed with skill and precision by the marching bands. There is Conspicuous Consumption—all tickets of admission to the temple are $7 apiece, and most of the 37,500 people there are on a three-day weekend pilgrimage that will cost far more, even seventy times seven. There is Politics, in the person of important public officials and other influential Mississippians, guests of the university president, who sit in special boxes on the 50-yard line. There is Sex: beautiful young cheerleaders and majorettes showing lots of pink flesh, coeds and older women in the crowd dressed to the eyelashes in all the latest fashions. There is White Supremacy, no longer regulated by law but by economics and custom and tradition: the overwhelming whiteness of the crowd, the teams, the coaches, the press, the referees, and the ancient gestures that evoke an unforgotten past—Rebel yells, the waving of the Stars and Bars. And finally, there is Sport—the game itself, the main attraction, the warfare, the applied science of organized violence.

Hemingway Stadium, it should be quickly added, is not the only holy temple, nor is Ole Miss by any means the only keeper of the faith. In fact, the presence of more football coaches than English professors and a long tradition of allowing the athletic tail to wag its academic dog have not been enough to keep the University of Mississippi at the pinnacle of intercollegiate sports. As football has risen to the status of a national folk religion, Southern colleges and universities have been taking it on the chin from the likes of UCLA, Nebraska, Oklahoma, Southern California, and Ohio State. The newest weapon in the arsenal of the gladiators is the black superstar, and the South, being a little late in getting the message, has fallen behind. So it is not the

Mississippi, or the Southern, but the *American* Way of Life that is being celebrated in the coliseums of the land; leave aside the symbols of white supremacy (and they *are* being left aside, with accelerating swiftness, by Southern institutions), and the rest of the pomp and ceremony can be witnessed in hundreds of stadiums across the nation.

Athletics may be doing as much to influence racial attitudes in the United States as the emergence of economic and political black power. The desegregation of higher education, in and out of the South, had been led by the black athlete, and blacks have excelled to such an extent that they very nearly dominate the basketball courts and are more than holding their own on the football fields. Segregation, as powerful as it once was, could not forever stand in the way of a conference title or a bowl bid or a spot in the national rankings, and even the most racist fans now appear to accept, however cheerfully, the lofty status of black heroes as well as white ones. So the Confederate flags are being furled, and the strains of "Dixie" are fading, and not all of the female flesh is pink, and not all of the muscular he-men are blue-eyed blonds, and the South is rising again to athletic prominence.

Notwithstanding the alleged virtues of big-time college athletics—school spirit, sportsmanship, character building, national recognition, and all the rest—there is an unsavory side as well. Intense competition and pressure lead to recruiting violations, manipulation of admissions requirements, cheating in the academic realm, increased violence on the field, and the spread of gambling. The exploitation of athletes has also become a widespread problem, and black athletes in particular appear to have been most affected. "College athletics have grown into a billion-dollar industry, and no one in power wants to let go," wrote the New York *Times*'s veteran sports columnist Arthur Daley in the spring of 1973. "The one simple solution is to stop buying athletes and to use students instead of mercenaries. But since this would mean a return to the horse-and-buggy days, it is manifestly impossible. So college athletics go careening down the road at a breakneck pace, headed for an inevitable crack-up."

The expansion of professional sports and the influence of television on athletics have greatly altered the nature of college competition; what was once legitimately sport is now entertainment, spectacle, and big business, beyond the control of coaches and professors and presidents and susceptible to the influences of corporate and entrepreneurial executives, lawyers, government officials, and gamblers. And since 1960, when Dallas and Houston landed major-league franchises in professional football, pro sports have spread to half a dozen Southern cities. There is as much pennant fever and Super Bowl hysteria in Atlanta and New Orleans and Miami now as there is in Pittsburgh or Los Angeles or Green Bay, Wisconsin.

Sports fanaticism is not a new phenomenon on the American scene, nor is it altogether unhealthy. But the degree of pressure and preoccupation and saturation has risen in the past decade, in parallel with such other developments as the spread of television, the rise in affluence, and the advance of desegregation. There is a seemingly insatiable appetite for fantasy and diversion and high adventure vicariously enjoyed, and the sports extravaganza brings it all together for spectators, whether they are part of the throng on the scene or among the millions who watch the tube.

The ritual that is acted out now with such devotion and seriousness in the nation's stadiums may say as much about the culture and the character of Americans as events in the Colosseum revealed about the Romans nineteen centuries ago. The fascination with violence, the effects of mob psychology, the exhilaration of victory, the element of voyeurism, the sense of liberation from inhibitions, the desire to excel and conquer, the hint of decadence—all are part of the experience encompassed by big-time sports, and that experience is an all-American affair. And if there is legitimacy to the comparison between Romans and Americans, then President Nixon, the nation's number one sports fan, is a modern Nero, having elevated athletics to a level of importance no element of high culture can come close to matching. Nixon may even owe a large measure of his electoral success to his devotion to sports; as a master politician, he could not have failed to notice that University of Texas football coach Darrell Royal is as well known in his state as John Connally, or that George Wallace is no less revered in his home state than the University of Alabama's football coach, Paul "Bear" Bryant.

Football is not the only sport enjoying national popularity. Major-league professional baseball, basketball, golf, and even ice hockey have spread from the North and East through the West and South, drawing large crowds and generating a massive turnover of cash. Automobile racing, once limited mainly to an annual event in Indianapolis, now attracts thousands of devoted followers to tracks all over the country, and Southern stock-car drivers have roared off the backcountry dirt tracks onto the hard-surface ovals to win prominence and prosperity in the sport. Stock-car racing, in fact, is dominated by Southern drivers; it is the best current example of a Southern sport gone national, in contrast to the national sports that have been moving into the South.

One interesting consequence of the elevation of sports in national life has been the emergence of the millionaire athlete. In virtually every sport there are proliferating numbers of men (but not women) whose earnings have put them in a class with corporation executives and businessmen and entertainers and political giants. Many of them are not just rich; they are also national celebrities, heroes who enjoy the adulation of the masses. Horatio Alger stories are as common as athlete's foot among them—every schoolboy knows about the rags-to-riches rise of superstars such as Joe Namath, Willie Mays, Wilt Chamberlain, and Lee Trevino. A story from South Carolina in the fall of 1972 seemed more Algerian than the great Horatio himself could have created. It was written by Jack Bass of the Charlotte *Observer*. Here are parts of it:

> YEMASSE, S.C.—Nick Zeigler interrupted his campaign for the U.S. Senate Tuesday to attend a small candlelight dinner hosted by the new master of Brewton Plantation.
>
> The 368-acre plantation dates back 240 years to a royal grant from King George II of England, and one of the early owners was Charles Pinckney, a signer of the Constitution. George Washington paid a visit there in 1791.
>
> The new owner is Joe Frazier, heavyweight boxing champion of the world and a man whose ancestors were slaves at similar plantations elsewhere in his native Beaufort County.
>
> "He's a delightful person," Zeigler said of Frazier after the dinner, which featured both soul food and wine served by black attendants wearing white jackets.
>
> Zeigler [noted the] "very human story" of Frazier's rise from the 13th child of a poor black family . . . to the owner of a plantation he bought as a place for his mother to live. Zeigler's ancestors were plantation owners and slaveholders before the Civil War.

It takes a little of the edge off the story—but only a little—to note that Frazier subsequently lost his heavyweight crown to another fast riser, George Foreman, and

Ziegler lost his bid for the Senate to incumbent superseg J. Strom Thurmond. Frazier and his arch-foe in the ring, Muhammad Ali, have both been toppled from boxing's mountaintop, but neither of them has been cast back into poverty—and Frazier's sixty-five-year-old mother is still living in the white-columned plantation house that had to be rebuilt more than a hundred years ago after it was burned by General Sherman's troops during the Civil War.

One other story from the world of sports should be mentioned. It was in the newspapers in May 1973, and it is self-explanatory:

> Hank Aaron, the Atlanta Braves' super slugger who is fast approaching Babe Ruth's career record of 714 home runs, says he receives hate mail every day berating him because he is a black man approaching a white man's record.
>
> "Last week I got 416 pieces of mail one day and 600-some-odd the next," the 39-year-old star said. "I'd say that 60 percent of it is of a racist nature.
>
> "If I were a white man, all America would be proud of me. But I'm black. You have to be black in America to know how sick some people are."

The changing life styles of Americans—not just sports heroes but all kinds of people—is a development that reflects both disenchantment with the dominant culture and a fascination with elements of a variety of subcultures. Unprecedented affluence still beckons the majority to the Good Life, and their expenditures for material comforts—cars, boats, appliances, vacation homes—reach new record highs each year, but against that trend the rising consciousness of groups of people coalescing around racial, ethnic, religious, economic, sexual, chronological, or political affinity is very much in evidence. Black Americans, who number almost 25 million and who are in themselves a richly varied group, have had a profound influence on the language, fashions, music, and entertainment tastes of Americans generally, and the assertions of black identity, consciousness, power, nationalism, pride, and solidarity have spawned similar assertions by others, from Indians and Puerto Ricans and Chicanos and white ethnics and mountaineers to women and young people and the elderly.

Yet for all that, the drawing power of the American middle class remains the dominant force. Its capacity for coopting and assimilating tributary movements into the main current of society is both inspiring and frightening—inspiring because of its potential for creating an open and diverse society, and frightening because of its tendency to produce homogenization and conformity. The groups and individuals who pursue life styles that deviate from the cultural mainstream find it more and more difficult to sustain their individuality, whether their aim is radical revolution or benevolent nonconformity.

In its latter-day yearning for equal status in the Union, the South has exhibited a willingness to adopt uncritically the trappings of the dominant culture, and to be intolerant of people who diverge conspicuously from that course. Conformity has long been a tradition in the South, and that tradition persists now, even though there has been a substantial change in the things to which people are expected to conform. Subcultural and countercultural movements and alternative life styles have been visible in the South in recent years, of course, as they have been all over the United States, but they have not thrived there; in fact, the South may be leading the trend toward national cultural homogenization.

If that is so, then the odyssey of Chess McCartney is all the more remarkable. For thirty-five years, McCartney has devoted himself in solitude to a way of life that is the very antithesis of materialism and affluence and upward mobility, and he has stayed at it in spite of ridicule and rejection and abuse.

Born and raised on an Iowa farm, he saw his livelihood washed away by the Depression, and he worked for the WPA until he was crippled by an accident on the job. When he was able to walk—but unable to work—he decided to hit the road with a wagon and a team of goats, and he subsequently traveled well over 100,000 miles through forty-nine states in that unorthodox fashion, using a small plot of land near Jeffersonville, Georgia, as his home base.

The last time I saw McCartney was in the summer of 1971. He had pulled his wagon off the shoulder of U.S. Highway 41 a few miles north of Marietta, Georgia, and stopped it on a gentle slope under some trees. Dusk was approaching, and the goats were tethered and grazing among the weeds, and Chess had a little fire going.

Rushing past with all the other absent-minded motorists, I almost didn't see him, but I turned around at the first opportunity and went back. He hardly looked up when my sons and I got out of the car. To him, I was just one more curious fellow traveler eager to ply him with questions—one too many after a long day on the road. But to me, he was like an apparition from the past.

The first and only time I had ever seen the Goat Man before was on a summer evening in the early 1940s, when he was camped for the night on a river bank just outside the little Kentucky town where I lived. I must have been about eight at the time, and I remember standing watchfully with some of my buddies at a respectful distance from the wagon and the goats. We talked about it for days afterward, about that mysterious and wonderful man with the bushy hair and the long beard and the eyes that had a magician's glint in them, and we daydreamed about tying some clothes on a stick and joining him out there on the open road.

And now I was a middle-aged, middle-class journeyman on another road, and there was old Chess, pushing seventy-five, still on his pilgrimage and looking just the way I remembered him back when I was a kid and life was just a bowl of cherries. I watched my sons gaze in awe and wonderment at the eighteen goats and the ramshackle wagon with its iron wheels and its tin roof and its tiny sleeping compartment and its assortment of tied-on paraphernalia and its PREPARE TO MEET THY GOD sign on top, and I saw a reflection of myself on their faces.

He sold me some postcards picturing himself and his wagon team—the cards are his principal means of income—and a little booklet called "Who the Goat Man Is." In it, he had written:

> I have been called crazy, stupid, ignorant, and many other uncomplimentary names because of my way of life—herding a passel of smelly goats from Florida to Maine to Washington and California. The goats have taught me a lot in the past 30 years. They don't, for example, care how I smell or how I look. They trust me and have faith in me, and this is more than I can say about a lot of people. During my years on the road I have been reviled, cursed, beaten and shot at. I have been denied access to public accommodations, but I have survived. I am an ordained preacher, and I try my best with my limited education to explain God's work to the people. I see a lot of race hate during my travels, both in the South and in the North. And I can see

more of it coming. It will end only when Christ returns to Earth, and I predict that this will be soon. I feel though that preaching about the second coming of Christ is a bit foolish, for too many people haven't yet heard about the first coming.

His supper was ready, and it was time for us to leave. As we started for the car, he pulled one more postcard from the wagon and handed it to me. "You can have this," he said, with the slightest trace of a smile. "One of the goats autographed it." It was a large card with a color photograph of the bib-overalled Goat Man, Bible in hand, standing in a cotton patch. A corner of the card had been bitten off.

No one, least of all Chess McCartney, would suggest that driving a team of goats around America is a viable and attractive alternative life style for people who are disenchanted with the values and the strictures of middle-class society, nor could it be argued convincingly that McCartney has made a valuable contribution to the culture. But his long and solitary journey belongs to a tradition that is as old as the road itself, and it deserves to be remembered. Like the gypsies and the hoboes and the vagabonds, he was one of the early Easy Riders, a forerunner of the beatniks and the hippies and the Jesus freaks. His life as a wanderer may say less about him that it says about the rest of us, for it raises a disturbing question: What is it about life in this country that makes thousands of young people—the spiritual heirs of Chess McCartney—take to the open road?

So there ought to be a monument to the Goat Man in Jeffersonville, Georgia, or somewhere else along the way, and the inscription on it might say something like this: "Chess McCartney, the Goat Man, spent thirty-five years on the road, searching for America. He stayed at it longer than a lot of famous men, including John Gunther, John Steinbeck, Woody Guthrie, Jack Kerouac, Bill Moyers, and Charles Kuralt, and he also outlasted a far larger number who were not so famous. Like all of them, he never found it. Like only a few, he never stopped looking."

This generation's new seekers don't last long as loners. They gravitate to the communes and the cooperatives and the collectives, and still the attrition rate among them is high. The cities of the South—Atlanta, New Orleans, Miami—have had their colonies of transient young people, their drug scene, their counterculture, their waves of runaway teenagers, their young religionists, the same as cities elsewhere have had. In the South as in other places, the rural communes seem less plagued by impermanence than the urban ones, perhaps because they have the advantage of a little land and open space, and at least the potential of a degree of self-sufficiency.

One of the oldest—aside from such religious groups as the Mormons, the Amish, and the Mennonites—is Koinonia Farm near Americus, Georgia. It was started in 1942 by Clarence Jordan, a Southern Baptist minister who wanted to build "an integrated, Christian community" in the heart of the south Georgia black belt. Koinonia survived the threats and violence of white law officers and vigilante groups, grand jury charges of communism, Ku Klux Klan terrorism, and the hostility of the white church, and when Jordan died a few years ago his community was larger than ever and firmly established in a program of home building, farming, and economic development. Incorporated as Koinonia Partners, its goals are to "emancipate" land for low-income farm families to work together in partnership, to create low-overhead, rural-based industries for job opportunity, and to offer no-interest loans to poor families who want to own their own homes. Quoting St. Augustine ("He who possesses a surplus possesses the goods of others"), Jordan used to assert: "That is a polite way of saying that anybody who has too much is a thief. If you are a 'thief,' perhaps you should set a reasonable living standard for your family and restore the 'stolen goods' to humanity through some suitable means."

If that was enough to put conventional churchmen and anticommunist zealots in an orbit of outrage, it was also enough to attract a lot of poor families, white as well as black, and it brought in such people as a wandering prophet named Ashton Jones and a young millionaire named Millard Fuller and a rich assortment of others who understood and accepted Jordan's radical theology. Dallas Lee has written a good account of Clarence Jordan and the Koinonia story in his book *The Cotton Patch Evidence.* As for Jordan himself, his legacy would be rich enough if it were nothing else than the spirit that permeates Koinonia, but there is more: His "Cotton Patch Version" of the New Testament, a modern translation with a Southern accent, is a theological gift to the people he loved—which is to say people everywhere—and while it may make scholars shudder and strict constructionists cringe, it also breathes humor and earthiness and vitality into the ancient words of the Bible. Paul's Epistles to the Romans, the Corinthians, the Ephesians, the Thessalonians, and the Philippians become letters to the Christians in Washington, Atlanta, Birmingham, Selma, and the Alabaster African Church in Smithville, Alabama. A quotation from Matthew 1:18 gives a hint of the tone and flavor:

> The beginning of Jesus the Leader was like this: While his mama, Mary, was engaged to Joseph, but before they had relations, she was made pregnant by the Holy Spirit. Since Joseph, her fiancé, was a considerate man and didn't want to make a public scandal, he decided to quietly break up with her. As he was wondering about the whole situation, a messenger from the Lord came to him in a dream and said, "Joe Davidson, don't be ashamed to marry Mary, because the Holy Spirit has made her pregnant. Now she'll give birth to a boy, who you'll name Jesus, because he will deliver his nation from their errors."

The Cotton Patch Version is no mere parody; it is a painstaking translation of most of the New Testament into the vernacular of the rural South, and as such it is a valuable addition to the culture—not just of the South, but of the nation.

Clarence Jordan was a unique character, and he left an unmistakable imprint with his translation and with Koinonia. There is only one Cotton Patch Version, but there are many communal and cooperative enterprises similar to Koinonia in almost every Southern state, and there is an indigenous Southerness about them that is not found elsewhere. The Highlander Research and Education Center near New Market, in the mountains of Tennessee, is one example, and Providence Farm near Tchula, Mississippi, is another. The Southwest Georgia Project, near Albany, has developed under the able leadership of former SNCC leader Charles Sherrod, and Penn Community Services, in the coastal island region of South Carolina, has been serving the black community of that area since 1862, when it was established as the first school in the South for freed slaves. Under the guidance of John Gadson and Freida Mitchell, Penn has expanded its program to include land reform, housing and economic development, early childhood education, and cultural enrichment.

Each of these cooperative ventures and the others like them are examples of the continuing search for workable alternatives to a dominant culture that has often been inhospitable, oppressive, and repugnant to people it perceived as "different." Another type of communal enterprise, starkly contrasting with these but far more typical of the collectives young people have been forming in recent years, has taken roots near the village of Summertown, Tennessee. It is called The Farm, and its similarities and dissimilarities to places like Koinonia and Penn make an interesting study.

The Farm is a "family monastery" of over 600 adults and children who live on more than 1,500 acres of woods and fields under the watchful eye of a college professor-turned-guru named Stephen Gaskin. It is a commune of like-minded young people who get their spiritual sustenance from Oriental mysticism, Western religions, nature, marijuana, and Gaskin—especially Gaskin. With allowances for some qualification and at the risk of oversimplifying, it is possible to say generally what they are for and what they are against: They are for love, peace, marriage (including group marriage, in multiples of two), cohabitation, nature, organic foods, marijuana, peyote, rock music (some of it), communication, reality, sorghum molasses, soybeans, midwives, education (through the eighth grade), compassion, honesty, manual labor, technology (some of it), and their neighbors. They are against meat, dairy products, fish, poultry, eggs, cheese, birth control, abortion, pornography, materialism, pop art, acid and all chemical drugs, alcohol, tobacco, heroin, political activism, fighting, greed, and "square hairs" (long-haired kids who get into hassles with the police).

Many members of the commune were among several hundred young people who left San Francisco with Gaskin in 1970 in a caravan in search of a rural settling place. The Summertown farm eventually turned out to be the place they were looking for, and they have thrived there, in spite of some setbacks. In 1971, Gaskin and three others were arrested for growing marijuana: their subsequent convictions and one-to-three-year sentences are under appeal on the constitutional ground that the use of the drug is essential to their free exercise of religion. After they got over the shock of seeing so many "long-haired hippie freaks," The Farm's neighbors around Summertown and Lewis County seemed to get used to the idea, and the gentle and unaggressive communards have come to be regarded with tolerance.

The Farm community is made up primarily of white, middle-class casualties of the Affluent Society, young people who dropped out of the rat race but couldn't buy the violence-and-revolution philosophy that so fascinated one wing of the counterculture. Most of them were looking for a spiritual leader who could give them an alternative to the ways of living that had brought them such confusion and alienation and grief, and in Gaskin they found him.

Gaskin is a frail, stoop-shouldered man in his mid-thirties whom one of his admirers once described as "a human energy so powerful that it rushes through your being like a wild wind! You are destroyed, but not hurt. Instead you are magically transformed with him into one great vibration of Joy—all beautiful and bejeweled in the act of touching and knowing . . . the Truth, the Real, the One." That's heavy stuff, and to his near-sycophantic disciples he is a heavy dude. In the commune, he is a benevolent dictator—the rulemaker, teacher, high priest, and judge of last resort—and from every indication, he is all of those things by unanimous and eager acclaim. So much adulation inevitably affects him, and he is given on occasion to considerations of immortality, as in this exchange with a questioner at an off-the-farm appearance:

Question: Does God speak through you?
Gaskin: Sometimes.

Question: Are you a messiah?

Gaskin: I don't know. I ain't done yet. It never hurts to try. You'll have to wait until I'm gone before that can be answered.

Question: What is your long-range goal?

Gaskin: I'm out to save the world.

Question: How?

Gaskin: I don't know yet. I ain't done.

Back when he was teaching creative writing and semantics at San Francisco State College and lecturing among the multitudes in his "Monday Night Class" at a place called the Family Dog, he wrote an article for *Motive* magazine in which he described how he used his "LSD-sharpened perceptions to steer the class into higher vibrational ranges. There is chanting, lecturing and questions and answers on such topics as what to do when stoned, how to make love, what to do about the draft, how to manifest a groovy trip, 'Who is God?' . . ." He added: "Much of the psychic technology we use is in the form of aphorisms learned 'on the hoof' while on LSD." Among the aphorisms: "We are all one." "You can't go anywhere that you can't get back from." "Everyone creates everything that happens to him." "God is love." Although the words of wisdom may seem austere, he wrote, "when it comes to the actual practice, the prime instruction is stay loose, groovy, high, happy and compassionate, to manifest the kingdom here and now, with or without the assistance of drugs."

In Summertown, LSD is a no-no. Aside from their ceremonial uses of pot, which the Lewis County sheriff now says he won't interfere with, the commune members profess to be no longer interested in drugs. They are busy growing crops and building houses. They have formed a nonprofit corporation which has an annual budget of about $250,000, and while their farm products, Gaskin's published writings, their contracted labor for others, and a record their traveling rock band has made bring in some income, the bulk of it comes from the members' contributions of savings, stocks, property, and inheritances. They publish an annual report, including a financial statement.

In many ways, the members of The Farm bear a physical and spiritual resemblance to the Mennonite colony that has long lived nearby. The Gaskinites are said by their neighbors to "have a good name," and be "honest to a fault." Their long hair and beards, their bib overalls and granny dresses and sun bonnets, give them an anachronistic appearance, like nineteenth-century frontier people. They are friendly, generous, peaceful, hard-working, law-abiding and—in their own distinctive manner—pious, moralistic, and orthodox. In fact, what is most astonishing about them after a while is just that orthodoxy, a fundamental conservatism of philosophy and outlook that is the very opposite of the sort of radicalism that has commonly (and inaccurately) been ascribed to almost every movement in the countercultures of the young.

The Summertown commune is vastly different from the Southern cooperative ventures described or mentioned in passing earlier. At places like Koinonia the preoccupations, out of necessity, have revolved around such issues as race, poverty, cultural identity, economic survival, and political unity, and their religious faith often has propelled them into the struggle. The Gaskinites, on the other hand, have had no appreciable involvement in any of those issues, and their spiritual activity has led in the direction of withdrawal rather than engagement.

The Farm has far more in common with the colonies of young people that have been sprinkled across the West in an arc from Colorado and New Mexico up to Oregon and Washington. Like most of them, it is made up principally of refugees from suburban splendor, young immigrants who have renounced the materialism (but not always the money) of their fathers and gone in search of a utopia where life can be simple again, the way it is thought to have been once upon a time. They are mixing a heady potion of idealism and innocence and determination and naïveté and human frailty, and nobody really knows yet what that chemistry will produce. But experiments in group living and pilgrimages to greener pastures and quests for new life styles have been going on since Eden, and utopia still eludes its pursuers like a mirage, and it is hard to imagine that this time will be different. Will The Farm last as long as the Mormons? The Amish? The Mennonites? Koinonia? Chess McCartney? Not even a guru like Stephen Gaskin has the answer. To paraphrase him, they ain't done yet.

Closer to the mainstream, the Jesus freaks have occupied a sort of way station between the mysticism of drug-oriented communes and the materialism of establishment-oriented churches. The South was an especially fertile breeding ground for their brand of fundamentalism, and thousands of young people on the way back up from the drug trip stopped off at the smaller, city-based communes where born-again former hippies and teenie boppers were getting high on Jesus.

Some of those places still exist, but most have either broken up or moved closer to the conventional churches (modifying them in the process) and closer to the crowded right flank of the American religious experience.

Waiting for them there, just outside the doors of the multitude of conservative denominations, were such groups as the Campus Crusade for Christ and the Fellowship of Christian Athletes, and such magnetic evangelical figures as Billy Graham and Oral Roberts. In June of 1972, the Campus Crusade for Christ and its guiding light, a California industrialist named Bill Bright, staged the International Student Congress on Evangelism in the Cotton Bowl in Dallas, and some 80,000 delegates from all fifty states and sixty foreign countries showed up, prompting Graham to call it a "religious Woodstock . . . the greatest religious happening in history."

Most of the participants in Explo '72, as the event was commonly called, were white, middle-class young people. They were served spellbinding sermons by Graham, who told them long hair and beards were okay with God, as long as they stayed clean in mind and body; pep talks by athletes, including Dallas Cowboy quarterback Roger Staubach, who told them "God has given us good field position" in the game of life; amplified music by rock groups in far-out costumes on psychedelic sets, groups like the Armageddon Experience and the Jesus Sound Explosion; and country-pop songs with a spiritual flavor by Johnny Cash and Kris Kristofferson. The response throughout the week-long revival was thunderous applause, reverberating cheers, and a sea of upraised index fingers, signifying that Jesus was Number One.

The basic objective of Explo '72 was scaled to the dimensions of Graham's rhetoric: it was to lay the groundwork for an evangelistic juggernaut that would convert the nation to Jesus Christ by 1976 and the whole world by 1980. The most sophisticated methods of the corporate enterprise, from computer technology and mass communications to the newest techniques of salesmanship, were employed in the training sessions. The delegates paid a $25 registration fee and $50 for room and board, and most of them apparently would have given ten times that much for the experience. The 2,000 or so blacks in attendance seemed equally as taken by it all as their white brothers and sisters.

J. Claude Evans, the chaplain of Southern Methodist University, wrote an account of the event for the newspaper *American Report*, and in it he said: "If Explo is to be faulted, it must be on a deeper level than finances or racial bias." He was critical of its "theological thinness," its slick and oversimplified "how to" techniques, and its "full-blown fundamentalist interpretation of Christianity." The Campus Crusade for Christ, he wrote, "would be more honest if it admitted, both to itself and to the public, that it is really a church denomination of its own."

Whatever it is, the CCC pulled a real coup in Dallas. In one stroke, it probably did more to coopt the Jesus freaks than Billy Graham himself could do even if he took his personal crusade to every commune in the country. And in any event, separating Graham from the CCC would be as difficult as separating him from the Southern Baptists, or the White House, or the television camera. He has long since risen above Baptism and his North Carolina roots to become the nation's unofficial chaplain and a globetrotting messenger of the Lord.

Graham has changed a lot in the thirty-five years since God called him on a golf course in Florida and told him to be a minister. His evangelistic enterprise is now a $15-million-a-year business. He calls on kings and popes and presidents, he draws massive audiences wherever he goes, his voice and image are broadcast to millions by radio and television each week. At fifty-four, he is more than ever the handsome, jutjawed, leonine eminence, God's Golden Boy, a devil-slayer whose sword is his silver tongue. His blond, wavy hair, now streaked with gray and curling fashionably over the collar of his coat, seems a part with his new mod wardrobe.

For more than twenty years, Graham has insisted that his crusades be open to all races and creeds. "Jesus Christ wasn't a white man," he can be heard exclaiming, "and Christianity isn't a white man's religion." Billy is keeping score; he knows what color the world is, and he wants the gospel he proclaims to envelop everybody. He has the instincts of a monopolist, and like the industrial and political and military monopolists of his time, he understands the relationships of numbers and growth and power. He has taken the old-time religion of his native South out into the nation and the world, leaving in his wake such lesser evangelists as Bob Jones and Carl McIntyre, whose ultraconservative approach has been to rail against blacks and Catholics and Jews and Moslems, while Graham's more astute strategy has been to try to convert them.

Graham has identified himself with moderate racial change and with such events as Explo '72 in such a way as to stay in the forefront of the American religious scene. In doing so, he has firmly established himself as the single most influential figure in what can fairly be called the Southernization of American religion, for in spite of his moderate views on race—views the Protestant South does not fully share even yet—virtually everything else he stands for is straight out of the history and traditions of Southern Protestantism.

The Southern Baptist Convention, whose 12 million members make it the largest Protestant denomination in the world, is Billy Graham's mother church, but like Jesus, Graham is too deeply engaged in larger affairs to spend all his time with his mother. "I am a member of the world church first," he says, "and of the Southern Baptist Convention second." Even without full claim to him, though, the SBC has moved beyond the borders of the South, expanding rapidly in the North and West, riding the crest of a conservative wave that is packing the churches that incline in the direction of fundamentalism and emptying the ones that tend to be classified as liberal.

There are at least twenty-five different Baptist bodies in the United States, with an aggregate membership of more than 25 million, and there may be as many as 15 million additional conservative Protestants in a host of denominations who share many of the same theological views. The essential difference between Billy Graham and those institutions is that the institutions cannot envision overcoming their differences to unite under one banner, while Graham can dream of winning them all to the Christ he serves. He is, in a sense, an apostle of conservative ecumenicity. Without the encumbrances of a denominational establishment, he is free to cross the lines of bureaucracy and structure in search of new soldiers for the Lord.

The Southern Baptist Convention and the other Protestant bodies can't do that. At its roots, the SBC is dominated by a strain of conservatism that is not inconsistent with Graham's preachings—it leans to biblical literalism, avoidance of social issues, obedience to authority in the church (but not necessarily in the denomination), personal salvation, patriotism, and proselyting—but the denomination is a bricks-and-mortar institution, and it can't match the maneuverability of a one-man institution like Graham. The SBC, for example, is still racially segregated, in the main, in spite of some efforts in its seminaries, its Christian Life Commission, its urban congregations, and its ranks of young people to change the complexion. Fewer than 1,000 of the denomination's 35,000 churches have even one black member, and the Christian Life Commission, its "conscience watcher" and social concerns arm for the past twenty years, stays constantly in hot water for its efforts to involve Southern Baptists in areas of human service that have more to do with life-serving than with soul-saving.

The second most populous Baptist body after the SBC is the National Baptist Convention, which has more than 5 million members and is the largest black church denomination in the country. The NBC is a reminder of some things about race and religion in the United States that many whites tend to forget, if they ever knew them at all. First, it suggests that black American churchgoers are inclined in general to be as theologically conservative as whites. There are numerous black denominations in addition to the NBC, and most of them can be broadly categorized as conservative. And second, the black church in America has probably grown stronger, not weaker, in the face of desegregation in the larger society; it remains the dominant institution in the black community, while other black institutions have been weakened by the spread of a white-dominated version of integration.

The black church, though it remains essentially segregated, is in far less of a moral quandary about that fact than the white church. Segregation, after all, was a white invention; it was not blacks who imposed it on society, who enforced it, who attempted to elevate it to the status of a cardinal principle ordained by God. White Christians, in and out of the South, now face the paradox of inner division over the issue of race, while their black brothers and sisters, whatever their theological persuasions, are at least united by the fact of their survival and endurance against the injustice and evil of imposed segregation. Black Christians have been bound together and sustained by their faith that God is just, and that his justice will ultimately prevail. White Christians, on the other hand, may be disunited by their belief in a just God, for to some of them, justice would be a vindication, and to others it would be a curse.

The Presbyterian Church in the U.S., a Southern body that broke away from its Northern counterpart in a Civil War split that has never been breached, is one of several predominantly white denominations in which internal tension over racial and social and theological issues has existed for a number of years. One of its ministers, H. Louis Patrick of Trinity Presbyterian Church in Charlotte, North Carolina, has written about Southern religion and culture in a letter published by the *Forum for Contemporary History*.

Southern religion, he wrote, is not simply a reflection of the region's cultural values; it is more nearly the other way around: "Religion is what really makes and keeps the South a separate, solid and stable culture." The South, he said, sees itself as "the true remnant of God's elect," and this "sense of divine election is what makes and keeps the South a region that is both distinct and essentially solid. . . . It removes any troublesome need for repentance, and it makes all change a temporary concession to the powers of evil. Only those elected the way the South is elected are free to glorify the past, sanctify the present and petrify the future." Patrick believes "this mystique has created a Southern Protestant Church absolutely unique in this country. It cuts across denominational lines while at the same time reinforcing the lines of race and class." Its theology, he says, is based on a "belief in the literal inerrancy of the Bible," and its individualism and piety offer "neither an effective way to change society nor any prophetic critique of it. Instead, religion works hand-in-glove with the powers-that-be to conceal the true issues between God and man."

The "New South," asserts Patrick, "does not exist. And as long as the religion of the Southern Protestant Church remains what it is, nothing new will be conceived in, or issue from, the Southern womb." But, he continues, "The South is returning to the mainstream of the nation's life. More than that, in the preservation of a stable society . . . the South is leading the rest of the land." So maybe the nation's newfound interest in the South, and in its religious and cultural life in particular, has come about because (quoting Patrick again) "people at large see in this region the reflection of that status-quo for which they long. Not too long ago the gospel according to Billy Graham was strictly a Southern product. . . . Now, that gospel of individual salvation . . . appeals to persons throughout the land who struggle with the torment of littleness, trying to gain some sense of instant worth and welcome from an indifferent civilization that is too complex for their coping."

The vessels in which culture is created and transmitted and homogenized grow and multiply like hothouse tomatoes. Disney World, the Southern version of Disneyland, is predictably bigger, costlier, and more fantastic than its parent, a monument to gargantuan artificiality, and its imitators sprout everywhere. One of Disney World's neighbors near Orlando, Florida, will be Bible World, a sort of prefabricated New Jerusalem that will feature a walled city, a six-story mosque, museums, shops, acres of parking spaces, an Easter "Passion Week Panorama," and "the only minaret in the Western hemisphere." Fred C. Tallant, president of a land development company with holdings in Georgia and Florida, says Bible World "will be designed for everyone," and its purpose will be to "inform, entertain and inspire." Tallant, who comes from a Baptist family but describes himself as being not particularly religious, says he and a group of religious Atlanta businessmen hope to make a million dollars in profits from Bible World after its first year of operation.

Movies are another medium shaping cultural styles and patterns, and the trends there, reflected in every region of the country, are now dominated by a mixed bag of black films, by hard-core pornography, and by ever more explicit and sophisticated presentations of violence. The moneymakers are films like *The Godfather, A Clock-*

work Orange, Straw Dogs, Oh, Calcutta!, Shaft, Super Fly, and *Deep Throat,* and most of them have enjoyed long runs not only in New York and Los Angeles but in the cities of the Midwest and South and even in the small towns of Middle America. In the spirit of free-enterprise capitalism, entrepreneurs with the keenest instincts for moneymaking have stimulated and exploited a thick seam of public fascination with the manifold forms of physical depravity. Sex-and-violence as a spectator sport is now the movie industry's biggest box office attraction.

Television trails the movies in its treatment of sex and violence, but the lag is not always great; it was TV, after all, that brought the Vietnam war into the nation's living rooms, live and in color, and for blood-and-guts violence, that show was hard to match. Television's continuous image has also blurred the line between the real and the make-believe, giving everything—the war, the news, the commercials, the movies, the network shows—an aura of unreality. As the single most widely used instrument for the continuing education of adults—and for the initiation of children into society—television molds the culture and values and life styles of Americans more than any other thing. And that shaping process is more or less the same everywhere, for the ubiquitous TV screen glows in almost every mansion, apartment, cottage, and cotton-field hovel, and its lights and shadows look the same in New York City and Des Moines and Albuquerque and Holly Springs, Mississippi. Johnny Carson and Barbara Walters and Archie Bunker and Bill Cosby and Walter Cronkite and Dean Martin may have as much to do with what people think and feel and covet as Richard Nixon does, or Billy Graham; each in his own way is an imagemaker and culture shaper. Mighty is the power of the tube.

In the competition for people's time and attention, the print media have yielded ground to television. Newspapers are read as much for their ads and comics and sports and TV listings as for their news and editorials, and among magazines, the death of *Life* and *Look* has left *Reader's Digest* and *TV Guide* at the top of the heap, challenged for readership leadership only by *Playboy* and its imitators, by a host of specialty magazines, and by a dreary profusion of cheap pornography. Regional magazines are also popular: there is *Sunset,* a slick and opulent monthly glorifying the selected virtues of the West, and there is *Southern Living,* which in just eight years has attracted almost a million subscribers with its ad-choked smorgasbord of recipes, fashions, decoration and travel plugs, Old South nostalgia, and New South boosterism.

The South's obeisance to provincialism and piety—the mindset that long kept Prohibition in force, blue laws on the books, *Catcher in the Rye* out of the libraries, and New York magazines off the newsstands—is rapidly eroding. *Jesus Christ Superstar* has packed theaters all over the South, and *Hair* is everywhere; the largest work of art ever created by the late and renowned Pablo Picasso—a 100-foot sculpture entitled *Bust of a Woman*—is being erected at the University of South Florida in Tampa; and *Rolling Stone* gathers no moss among its avid following in the South.

The cultural rites of white Anglo-Saxon Protestants still dominate, but you can find Mexican influences all over Texas, African and Afro-American cultural festivals on dozens of college campuses, a Chinese New Year's parade in Nashville, and a Brazilian Carioca Carnival in Miami, where the Spanish-speaking population now numbers a half-million. In the Cajun country of south Louisiana, where French has traditionally been spoken, about 150 Frenchmen are teaching in the schools in a sort of reverse Peace Corps program jointly financed by France and Louisiana to help preserve the region's linguistic heritage. Even Mississippi has relaxed its border guard: a delegation of Soviet Communist party members visiting Greenville in 1972 was so charmed by Southern hospitality that they chose that Mississippi delta community as their favorite American city. "Here we feel absolutely at home," their leader said.

The magnolia curtain that used to shield the South from cultural breezes is pinned back now, and all sorts of once exotic influences are floating in. There is fire and ice and pollution in those winds—Disney World and Bible World and *Super Fly* and *Deep Throat* and *Hair* and Johnny Carson and *Playboy* and *Rolling Stone* and the Metropolitan Opera and Picasso and the Cubans and the Russians and multitudes of others. The diversity is welcome; certainly it is better to have variety, however mixed its quality may be, than to have a closed and conforming society that regards every stranger as an intruder. But exhilaration would be too strong a response to it all. What is happening to mass culture in the South is what is happening nationwide, and if there is diversity in it, there is also an element of sameness, of homogenization, of artificiality and shallowness and transience.

And finally, there is music. In the perpetuation and diffusion of the many strains of Southern culture, no other instrument carries more force and vitality. The South has been the incubator for most of the indigenous elements in the treasury of American music. It produced jazz and blues and all of their derivations; it spawned country-and-western music, bluegrass, gospel, spirituals; it was a source of rock-'n'-roll, and it has contributed its share of pop and folk and contemporary rock. From W. C. Handy and Louis Armstrong and Bessie Smith and dozens of other giants of an earlier time, through Jimmie Rodgers and Roy Acuff and Bill Monroe and Elvis Presley, and proceeding on to a host of people who are today's superstars, the South can probably claim a longer and more varied roster of nationally influential musicians than any other region of the country.

In almost every one of the major styles of music in America, examples can be found of a substantial Southern contribution, if not of Southern origination. Black Americans—Southerners, more often than not—have enriched the nation's musical heritage out of all proportion to their numbers, and they continue to do so, with more recognition and reward now than ever before. Among instrumental musicians, Earl Scruggs has no peer as a genius of the five-string banjo, Chet Atkins is an acknowledged virtuoso of the guitar, and Guy Carawan, a master of the hammer dulcimer and other instruments of mountain music, is a towering but uncelebrated talent. In the realm of classical music, pianist Van Cliburn, a Texan, has an international reputation, and in the opera, no contemporary star is more luminous than Mississippian Leontyne Price. The rock music and soul music that have so captivated the young in the past decade also have had a Southern flavor; Otis Redding and Janis Joplin are both dead now, but James Brown and Isaac Hayes and the Allman Brothers and many more play on.

And country music, Southern to the core, is warmed by the echoes of ringing applause and ringing cash registers, not only at the Grand Ole Opry in Nashville but on the West coast, the East coast, the vast reaches in between, and even in London and Tokyo. They go for bluegrass, a pure strain of country, at an annual festival in Tokyo's Hibiya Park; at Wembley Stadium in London, the fifth annual International Festival of Country Music in the spring of 1973 drew fans from almost every European and North American country—including a delegation of nearly eighty musicians and music industry representatives from Nashville.

More than 800 American radio stations are devoted exclusively to country music, and another 1,000 program the country sound at least three hours a day. The Country

Music Association, a Nashville-based trade organization, held a meeting of its board of directors in New York's Plaza Hotel in April of 1973, and a few days before that, when country stars Tammy Wynette and George Jones sang in the Lincoln Center's Philharmonic Hall, Mayor John Lindsay proclaimed it "Country Music Day" in New York City. "Country music and New York may not only go together," a newspaper account of the occasion said; "New York may need country music more than country music needs New York."

When the Country Music Association's board was at the Plaza, more than 500 people—most of them Madison Avenue advertising agency executives and media representatives—were treated to a three-hour hoedown under the crystal chandeliers of the Grand Ballroom. "I think it's very refreshing to see this coming in," one guest enthused. "In the fifties and sixties, rock and roll rolled over the country, getting more and more raucous as it went along, especially when the drug aspects got into it. Now there's a swing over to the simple, to the clean, to the healthy. Country music celebrates the goodness of America, faith in America, patriotism." And another, a man whose booking agency, said the New York *Times*, is "not known for its naïveté in the mass-entertainment field," said he thought "the public today is really groping for a new sound, which we haven't had since rock and roll. This could be it."

From the opposite direction—the classics, the so-called serious music—comes the opinion of at least one veteran critic that country and other forms of popular music are so ascendant that classical music will be dead in another fifty years. Henry Pleasants, a native of Philadelphia who has been reviewing symphonic and operatic performances in Europe for the past thirty years, nourishes an open admiration for American jazz and country music, and because he takes them seriously, he is a controversial figure among "serious" music critics.

But Pleasants, and the audiences at the Plaza and the Philharmonic, apparently know which way the wind is blowing. New York used to be the center of the music world and of the recording industry; now the business has gone to Los Angeles and London and most of all to the South, to Nashville and Atlanta and Memphis and Macon and Muscle Shoals, a north Alabama town of 4,000 people. Bill Williams, the country music editor of *Billboard* magazine, estimates that the recording industry in Nashville alone is a $225-million-a-year business—fully one-fourth of the industry's annual gross worldwide—and that the other Southern cities share another one-fourth or more among them. The Southern half of the pie is more than just country music—it's also rhythm and blues, soul, rock, pop, everything but classical. Recording artists as diverse as Perry Como, Joan Baez, Bob Dylan, and the Nitty Gritty Dirt Band are attracted to Nashville by something mystical and evanescent called "the Nashville Sound," an indefinable quality that derives from unexcelled recording studios, superb backup musicians, a cadre of highly professional songwriters and producers and publishers, and an atmosphere that is relaxed and unhurried. "It's a basic style," says Williams. "I can't describe it, but I know it when I hear it. It's been an elixir for a lot of artists, and their coming here has been a real shot in the arm for Nashville."

Most of the more than 300 recording artists who live in and around Nashville are country musicians. Not a few of them are now rich and famous—Grand Ole Opry stars, performers whose records sell millions of copies and whose public appearances are in great demand, musicians with their own syndicated television shows (also made in Nashville). Many of the most successful artists spend most of their time on the road, traveling over the country in customized buses, making one-night stands. It is a hard grind, but highly rewarding. Nobody knows exactly how many millionaires the country music business has made, but the number is high enough to attract thousands of aspiring musicians to Music City, and only a few of them break into the charmed circle.

Country music at its best is down-to-earth, direct, storytelling music. It is about the everyday experiences of ordinary people, about love and faith, playing and praying, working and drinking, living and dying. Down through the years it has been played and sung primarily by and for rural whites who know what poverty is. Of late, its complexion has changed ever so slightly: One of its superstars is a black singer named Charley Pride, and Ray Charles has recorded a double album of country classics, and a few younger performers in the field are black. There is an occasional scattering of blacks in the weekend crowds at the Opry—where, ironically, the first musician to perform almost fifty years ago was a black harmonica player named DeFord Bailey. Pride's blackness is a pigment of the imagination—his style is pure country, not blues or soul—and he has made himself a wealthy man. There is also a popular Mexican American performer, Johnny Davis Rodriguez.

As it has risen in popularity and spread across the country, country music has been modified by new performers, new audiences, and new instruments. The purists, the traditionalists like Roy Acuff and Tex Ritter and Ernest Tubb, are still around and still revered, but they share the stage now with Glen Campbell and Bobby Goldsboro and Kris Kristofferson and Boots Randolph, and the guitars and fiddles have been augmented by electrified instruments and drums and brass and soft strings. The lines that separate country from pop and rock are not always clearly drawn, and as country goes more and more to the city, there is about it a little less twang and a little more slickness. "The music has been increasingly adapted to urban ears," said a story in the New York *Times*. "It has been smoothed out, made more commercially palatable, reduced in twanginess and sometimes crossed with other musical strains to create a contemporary or 'modern' country music sound. . . . The word Western was dropped from the descriptive name 'country and Western' music to reduce its regional identification, and in some places the term 'country' is being dropped in favor of the inclusive designation 'all-American music.'"

In that process of homogenization, country music is finding acceptance and success and affluence such as it has never known. It is a gold mine with a seemingly endless vein, and it is attracting prospectors from every corner of the entertainment world. To many people, it is all too good to be true—if America is looking for a new sound to take the place of rock, and if country is going to be it, this could be the beginning of boom time. But there are others in the field who see something vaguely disquieting in the phenomenon of "modernization." One of the most distinctive things about country music has been the closeness that has existed between the pickers and singers and their audiences. They have shared an intimacy in the music because they also shared a personal knowledge of the experiences it described—poverty and loneliness and all the rest. How much of that intimacy, that authenticity, can be retained when the music goes uptown? When the artists leave the country, when poverty becomes an abstraction in a forgotten past, when the stars live in mansions and drive Cadillacs and belong to the country club—when they are no longer having the experiences they have always sung about—what will it do to the music? And when it is being packaged on Madison Avenue as "all-American music," will it still be country?

Maybe it won't matter. Maybe the best of the musicians will be able to remember what it was like and keep it honest. Or maybe the fans won't care. They keep flocking in undiminished hordes to Nashville to attend the Opry (which, incidentally, is moving out of its ancient holy temple, the Ryman Auditorium, and into a spanking new structure at Opryland, one of the theme parks inspired by Disneyland), and they ride tour buses on Saturday mornings to see the homes of the stars, just like in Hollywood, and they go to the Country Music Hall of Fame on what is called Music Row to look at the old guitars under glass, and the gold records, and all the artifacts of the good old days, and for many of them, it is an unforgettable experience. They will surely keep on coming.

But country music is outgrowing that simple style. It is going big-time, getting into TV specials and advertising contracts and dozens of avenues to wealth. It is putting its slick boot forward, the one without the dust and cow dung on it. The other boot may survive only in the museum, along with the old fiddles and guitars and cowboy hats. Country music, and the people in it, and the people around it, have survived some hard times. Now the test is to see whether they can survive the good times.

In H. L. Mencken's day, culture was seen as something to be reserved for refined and sophisticated people; it had nothing to do with the "crude masses," who were supposedly lacking in "cultivation" and the "finer qualities." In a curious and ironic way, Mencken—the iconoclast, the debunker, the acerbic critic—supported that attitude of haughty elitism. The "American *Kultur*" he castigated the South for lacking in "The Sahara of the Bozart" was high culture—formal, serious, exclusive. It was a standard of quality, taste, and style defined and certified by "experts" and "masters."

That sort of narrow and restricted view of culture no longer dominates American life. There is more latitude and diversity in style and taste and fashion now, and culture is more broadly understood and applied to encompass the lives and interests and endeavors of all people, rather than the pursuits of an elite minority.

Two conflicting and contradictory pressures now influence the shape and substance of culture in the United States, pulling it toward opposite poles. The first is a sort of neoelitism, a fragmentation and splintering of life styles into separate packages that seldom breach the walls dividing them. The vestiges of high culture fit comfortably in that mold, but so do religious cults and communes and suburban walled communities and a great many other self-contained and restricted groups defined by race or sex or age or ideology. Tom Wolfe described the phenomenon in his book *The Pump House Gang;* the esoteric "statuspheres" he wrote about—the surfers, the motorcyclists, the swinging singles—define themselves by their differences. They are, in their own separate ways, elite, exclusive, isolated—they conform to a narrow code, and they are often hostile and suspicious of all that lies outside their sphere.

The other major pressure that is shaping American culture is essentially assimilationist. It is the pressure of homogenization, the force that causes Disneyland to spawn dozens of imitators and country music to be pasteurized to suit the tastes of a wider audience. Television is its ultimate instrument. The impulse to corner the market, to absorb and coopt and swallow up everything, and then to spew it back as "novelty," not only caters to prevalent tastes and fashions—it also creates demand by artificial stimulation.

The South, no less than the nation as a whole, is under the influence of neoelitism and assimilation, being pulled both toward fragmentation and toward homogenization. If there is a middle ground, an integration of cultures that thrives on both unity and diversity, that exalts both relationships and differences, it is not very much in evidence.

In July 1963, folksinger Bob Dylan joined an odyssey of determined civil rights advocates, all traveling to Mississippi for the purpose of rallying behind disfranchised black voters and showing support for black children forced to attend segregated schools. Less than a year earlier in October 1962, the University of Mississippi at Oxford had been the site of a riot in which whites from the surrounding areas seized the campus in response to the enrollment of James Meredith, the university's first black student. Recalling that earlier violence, Dylan penned the lyrics to a song entitled "Oxford Town," a stanza of which describes the resistance encountered by one young social organizer:

> He went down to Oxford Town,
> Guns and clubs followed him down
> All because his face was brown
> Better get away from Oxford Town.

Dylan's ballad in many ways captured the tense spirit of the times in the lower South. Even as the singer was crooning support for civil rights, violence erupted in Greenwood, Mississippi, where the local branch of the Student Nonviolent Coordinating Committee (SNCC) was all but vanquished by repeated episodes of arson and gunfire. A year later in the summer of 1964, the Mississippi Summer Project found hundreds of white Northern college students volunteering to organize black voters and to teach black children in "freedom schools," efforts that resulted in numerous beatings, shootings, and church bombings. Violence culminated in the murders of three SNCC volunteers—James Chaney, Andrew Goodman, and Michael Schwerner—in Philadelphia, Mississippi.[1]

The deaths of the young civil rights workers struck a sympathetic chord with many otherwise ambivalent Mississippians, some recalling vividly the murder of Emmett Till a decade before in 1955. Till, a fourteen-year-old Chicago black youth visiting his aunt in Leflore County, Mississippi, was lynched for allegedly whistling at a white woman. Till's killing prompted William Faulkner to remark that "if we in America have reached that point in our desperate culture when we must murder children no matter for what reason or what color, we don't deserve to survive, and, probably won't." However, Till's murderers evaded prosecution, demonstrating that Mississippi justice of the era was anything but colorblind.

But if the Deep South has tended to be a region of dramatic historical confrontations, then perhaps the most dramatic of these has been one frequently overlooked—the challenge to racist politics offered by the religious traditions that once sanctioned racial injustice. Indeed, ideological appeals probably did little to change the hearts of Southern white citizens in the 1960s. If anything, many people resisted legislative efforts to end segregation, embittered by the efforts of the federal government to ignore the earlier *Southern Manifesto* (1956), a document drafted by a majority of Southern legislators who asserted states' rights over federally sanctioned desegregation. Even the Voting Rights Act of 1965 seemed to many whites to be targeted at the lower South, where resistance to black voter registration had been strongest. Obviously, laws were needed as a means of overturning segregationist practices. Harder to change was the collective mind of the South that had often sabotaged efforts at federal intervention and social reform.

Southern clergy may have been the deciding factor urging compliance with new legislation designed to end discrimination. Appealing to the consciences of Southerners and to Judeo-Christian dogma and its emphasis on loving one's neighbor despite the color of that neighbor's skin, priests, ministers, and rabbis throughout the South worked to bring about justice for all. Not coincidentally, many key figures in the Civil Rights movement were clergy. Dr. Martin Luther King, Jr., Jesse Jackson, Andrew Young, and John Lewis were all ordained African American ministers from the lower South. To the aforementioned list of those championing equal rights can be added the names of Will Campbell, a race-relations troubleshooter for the National Council of Churches in the 1950s and 1960s, and Duncan Gray, the Episcopal Bishop of Mississippi and, later, chancellor of the University of the South (Sewanee). Both Campbell and Gray are white.

Although most of the clerical civil rights reformers were Protestants, a small but vocal number were Roman Catholics. Seen largely as a vehicle of social reform and as a repository for "immigrants," the Catholic Church had never gained a solid foothold in the South except in coastal areas and a few larger cities such as Savannah, Charleston, and New Orleans. Those Catholics who did settle and stay made deep inroads into the region's literature, constituting something of a radical influence on Southern letters, particularly in the revolutionary era of the 1960s. One such writer was Thomas Merton.

Although born in Prades, France, in 1915, Merton spent almost half of his fifty-three years as a Trappist monk at the Abbey of Our Lady of Gethsemane outside Bardstown, Kentucky. At home in his Southern surroundings, Merton spoke often of "my Kentucky." Devoting his life to contemplation, Merton wrote two hours each day for a lay audience hungering for social justice, equality, and peace. A great admirer of Flannery O'Connor (also a Roman Catholic), Merton offers special tribute to the novelist and short-story writer in "Flannery O'Connor: A Prose Elegy." Beginning with O'Connor's assertion that the problem for the writer with Christian preoccupations is that the language of Christianity is worn-out, Merton suggests that O'Connor examines all the spurious reverences associated with the term *respect*. She shows in her stories that although people say that they respect "everything good," the reality is that "we have lost the most elementary respect even for ourselves." Merton praises O'Connor for her unflinching courage in showing how Southerners, in particular, tend to make a cliché of religious experience, trivializing what they claim to "respect."

Exposing all the tricks of self-deception and demonstrating all the ways people avoid their quests for salvation are twin purposes that inform Flannery O'Connor's work. Recognizing O'Connor's avowed desire to let "Christian preoccupations" serve as the underpinnings of her fiction, Margaret Early Whit offers the following insight:

> O'Connor suggests that the modern age lacks a religious sense, and when the age appears to shift with the moment, effective allegory will not work. The serious novelist writes about people in a world where something is missing, and for that writer the greatest drama is "the salvation or loss of the soul." When an audience does not believe in the soul, "there is very little drama."[2]

The ways people choose not to believe does, however, provide comedy of the most serious sort in O'Connor's fiction. In "Revelation," O'Connor places the central character, Mrs. Turpin, smack in the center of a doctor's waiting room, where she immediately begins classifying those assembled according to social class. Unable to see that the people there are more than "white trash" or "niggers," Mrs. Turpin, for all her privileged views, is herself an example of the spiritually impoverished. Only grace will provide the "revelation" she needs in order to see herself as she really is.

O'Connor spelled out her belief in the inextricably woven connection between belief and art in such essays as "The Catholic Novelist in the Protestant South," a lecture delivered at Georgetown University in 1963 and published in *Viewpoint* in 1966. Here she argues that "belief can be made believable" not by stressing dogma but by emphasizing art that draws inspiration from the well of sacramental mystery. Mystery is at the heart of fiction; moreover, the Roman Catholic liturgy reveals the drama of salvation. Although being a Catholic novelist in the South forces O'Connor to "follow the spirit into strange places," the writer acknowledges that "the opportunities for the potential Catholic writer in the South are so great as to be intimidating."

Tending, as O'Connor did, to incorporate themes about the ultimate meaning of life, Shirley Ann Grau also managed to draw on a stock of familiar Southern motifs: "family, miscegenation, strong women, and revenge."[3] In Grau's novel, *Keepers of the House*, for instance, "even the most taboo subject is open: in that novel the relationship between a white man and a black woman emphasizes their need for each other, not their affront to white society."[4] In "The Black Prince," Grau's focus is on the rural African American folk of southern Louisiana, "the poorest part of the smallest and worst county in the state." At the story's outset, Alberta Lacy encounters the stranger Stanley Albert Thompson, who just "walked straight out of the morning" woods, appearing before her. Intrigued by his strength and good looks, Alberta keeps track of the rumors circulating about Stanley. For one thing, he is a formidable brawler at the nearby tavern. He carries money and is a drinker of good whiskey. Assuming larger-than-life status, Stanley also inspires fear and jealousy among the locals. The story's climax reinforces the almost supernatural, electric effect he produces in the community.

Depression-era Monroeville, Alabama, provides the historical setting for Harper Lee's acclaimed novel *To Kill a Mockingbird*. Like Grau, Lee works with familiar Southern materials, presenting an explosive racial scenario in which a black man is falsely accused of raping a white woman. Lee's only novel showcases a small-town white lawyer's unsuccessful efforts to defend his client. Told from the point of view of the lawyer's young daughter, Scout, *To Kill a Mockingbird* offers the frankness of a child's perspective in commenting on matters of race and class. Writer Truman Capote, Harper Lee's childhood friend, is said to have served as the inspiration for the character Dill. Lee's novel was later adapted by screenwriter Horton Foote as an Oscar-winning film (1962), one of the best of the emerging Southern genre. Gregory Peck also won an Oscar for his performance as Atticus Finch, Scout's father and the attorney whose unswerving moral sense points to the possibility of rising above prejudice and defusing violence.

Martin Luther King, Jr.'s, civil rights initiative was based on the notion of bearing the cross for one's neighbors. In a tireless crusade of self-sacrifice, King traveled throughout the country, emphasizing that "we must have compassion and understanding for those who hate us." King's approach owed much to the Christian teachings of Leo Tolstoy and to the satyagraha philosophy of Mahatma Gandhi—the latter system of beliefs stressing "nondirect resistance" and "creative tension" to achieve desired results. Adopting such strategies as boycotts, sit-ins, and peaceful demonstrations, King and his supporters forced elements of the population to confront racist tendencies and contradictions in their professed beliefs. Only by enabling a racist society to see the consequences of its racism could change be permanent.

Consonant with King's endorsement of nonviolent protest, the civil rights leader traveled to Memphis in 1968, where he led a march in support of striking sanitation workers, most of whom were African Americans. When a riot subsequently erupted, the national media accused King of violating his own avowed principles. King answered his critics in a speech entitled "I've Been to the Mountaintop." In the homiletic style of most of his speeches, King's address employs such characteristic devices as anaphora (repetition), antithesis, and rhetorical balance to reiterate the principles underlying the Civil Rights movement in the South. His speech echoes the history of recent protests, citing abuse of demonstrators by police in such cities as Birmingham. King nonetheless reaffirms his faith in "our nonviolent movement." The speech reaches a crescendo at the instant King announces his arrival at a summit of spiritual awareness, "the mountaintop," from which he has glimpsed the "promised land" of a just America. King's declaration that he might not live to inhabit the promised land with his supporters is eerily prescient in light of his subsequent assassination.

The turbulent sixties prompted many writers in the American South to experience a crisis of meaning. Describing the Kennedy assassination as a pivotal event in his life, inspiring a year or more of lassitude and depression, Walker Percy emerged as a proponent of Christianity, not through orthodox avenues but through the crucible of personal experience, or subjectivity, as one of the great influences on Percy's work, Soren Kierkegaard, described it. Coming to fiction writing by an indirect route—reading the French existentialists rather than soaking up stories on the front porch—Percy focuses on the isolation of the wayfarer in search of "love or death." The obstacles to this quest are many, and as with O'Connor, Percy describes all the tricks of self-deception that people master in order to avoid being authentic.

But it is the inauthentic that plagues Percy's protagonist, Will Barrett, in *The Last Gentleman*. A twenty-five-year-old native of Ithaca, Mississippi, Will has spent time in New York "employed as humidification engineer at Macy's." He suffers from a "nervous condition," ostensibly resulting from his father's suicide and his own inability to connect with the people around him. Women pose a special problem for him, despite his falling in love at one point with Kitty Vaught, a young ballet dancer. Will's malaise is all too characteristic of modern society. Only when he experiences a series of "shocks" does Will discover a way to transcend "everydayness" and affirm life on terms that make it somewhat meaningful. Although Percy's character is melancholic, the author's tone is anything but. Moreover, Will is a sly observer, poking fun at himself with the same relish that he spoofs those around him.

Regarded by many as the South's foremost Civil War historian, Shelby Foote is the author of six novels rooted firmly in the alluvial soil of northern Mississippi. Sharing similar concerns as those of his lifelong friend Walker Percy, Foote explores the effects of alienation on people living in a world devoid of love. Nowhere is this theme more apparent than in an early story by Foote entitled "Rain Down Home." Foote's protagonist, Paul Green, has returned from the Second World War only to find his hometown of Bristol changed almost beyond recognition. New traffic lights, a new department store, and new parking meters indicate that the town has grown considerably. More disturbing is that some of the town's citizens no longer recognize Green. This "invisibility" makes him feel isolated, hopeless. As a soldier, however, Green sees it as his duty not to live in a meaningless world, one in which suffering is intolerably evident and love is intolerably absent. Unfortunately, he is viewed as crazy by those who lack his sensitivity and understanding.

The character as misfit is a stock device of Southern fiction. From the very first sentence of John Kennedy Toole's *A Confederacy of Dunces*, a posthumously published novel awarded the Pulitzer Prize for fiction in 1981, we are treated to the delightful "pseudophilosopher Ignatius Reilly, and a splendid cast of minor characters such as the delightfully senile Miss Trixie."[5] Ignatius possesses the physical dimensions and robust humor of a Falstaff. His barbed wit finds all New Orleans a suitable target for satire. Underlying all the humor is the sadness of a genuine eccentric isolated from society. That Toole's novel is often thinly veiled autobiography can perhaps be gleaned in Walker Percy's Foreword explaining the circumstances by which *A Confederacy of Dunces* came to be published.

If Southern literature in the 1960s and 1970s tended to be more existential than in the past, it also clung to the oral tradition in ways that expanded existing genres, combining memoir, fiction, and history to create compelling narratives like Margaret Walker's *Jubilee* (1965). Based on a story told to the author by her grandmother, *Jubilee* recounts episodes in the life of a slave woman named Vyry, whose day-to-day existence provides an ironic counterpoint to what many people consider the momentous events of the age: Lincoln's election, Southern secession, and the firing on Fort Sumter. Although Walker has been charged with creating in Vyry a character who shows too much "loyalty to her white mistress" and who fails to represent "a broader cast of defiant slaves," the author's protagonist is not flat, mindless, or caricatured.[6] Indeed, Walker recognizes the need to avoid stereotypes. Thus, what Vyry sees is just as important as what she does. The crucial ordering of details in the narrative offers a means for the reader to see what Vyry sees. For instance, Marse John, the plantation owner, is described at one point as having an infected leg that may require amputation. This detail later resonates symbolically as Marse John rails against Northern radicals, claiming that "I don't see where they have a leg to stand on. . . ." By letting the slaveholders defend themselves so assiduously, Walker demonstrates the defenselessness of their position. Details pushed far enough become symbolic in Walker's fiction.

In her essay entitled "A Brief Introduction to Southern Literature," Walker reiterates a well-argued position that the Southern writer, black or white, "cannot escape the ever present factor of race and the problems of race as they have grown out of the southern society and affected all of America." She offers a critique of earliest days, noting that two segregated societies produced not merely a literature of polarization but also one of warfare: "The battle and the conflict [of disparate aims] can be seen in the literature."

Walker evaluates the contributions of numerous writers to this struggle, pointing out, among other things, the role of black folk expression in influencing politically conscious postbellum white writers. One such writer was William Faulkner. In "Faulkner and Race," Walker notes that "Faulkner was, in fact, a racist." However, she offers some key qualifications, among them Faulkner's recognition that he was a racist and his refusal to believe that this recognition absolved him of guilt or responsibility. At the core of Faulkner's work, then, is a moral dilemma. And although

Faulkner tried to "avoid the old stereotypes about race brought over from the plantation tradition," Walker acknowledges that he created new stereotypes.

If controversy has always been at the heart of Southern writing, perhaps no writer of the period elicited more passionate and extreme reaction than James Dickey. Reviving what some people saw as the cult of the Hemingwayesque, man's man sort of writer, Dickey was known for his public persona that included drinking, brawling, and womanizing. Behind the persona, however, resided a poet, novelist, and critic extraordinaire. As Richard J. Calhoun points out, Dickey was often seen as a "hatchet man," decrying the excesses of the Northern establishment, particularly the Northern literary establishment with its self-indulgent displays of political and social fadism.[7] In a similar analysis, Ronald Baughman, writing while Dickey was still alive, observes that Dickey "hates the dishonesty of false sufferers, and he abhors the condescension of intellectual elitism."[8] Baughman further notes that the writer's "uncompromising honesty was bound to draw fire" from others whose limitations Dickey spared no effort in exposing. Yet, being a large target himself afforded Dickey celebrity status, enabling him, as unofficial laureate of the Carter administration, to "barnstorm" for poetry.

"The Strength of Fields" is an occasional poem that was written specifically for Jimmy Carter's inaugural festivities and that was delivered by Dickey on national television. The poem opens as the speaker is "alone with his thoughts on the eve of his assuming office."[9] Drawing on his rural roots and the reverent traditions of his homeland, the speaker seeks help from a higher power—"Dear Lord of the fields." He wants only to know what "I can give" to those who have chosen him to lead a nation. The answer comes in the form of "the simplest things," echoing the need for "more kindness" that will "save every sleeping one" of us.

Saving what can be lost in an instant of careless inattention is the theme of Dickey's "The Bee." Frightened by a stinging insect, the speaker's son panics, running from the site of a family's roadside picnic into the "sheer/Murder of California traffic." Calling on the voices of dead coaches to help him "get the lead out," the speaker snatches the child amid "the traffic blasting past us" in time to save the boy. After retreating into the woods, the child sleeps while his father acknowledges the long-dead gift givers whose silent efforts have aided in rescuing his son. Employing what Dickey termed a split-line technique, "The Bee" exhibits a series of broken lines and gaps between words that mimic the uncertain motion of the father who emerges as his son's "savior."

Notes

1. Andria Lisle, "Bob Dylan's Mississippi," *The Oxford American*, Summer 1999 (Music Issue), ed. Marc Smirnoff (Oxford: The Oxford American Press, 1999), 117.
2. Margaret Earley Whitt, *Understanding Flannery O'Connor* (Columbia: University of South Carolina Press, 1995), 184.
3. John Shelton Reed and Dale Volberg Reed, *1001 Things Everyone Should Know about the South* (New York: Doubleday, 1996), 155.
4. Lewis A. Lawson, *Another Generation: Southern Fiction Since World War II* (Jackson: University Press of Mississippi, 1984), 17.
5. Martha E. Cook, "Old Ways and New Ways," *The History of Southern Literature*, ed. Louis D. Rubin et al. (Baton Rouge: Louisiana State University Press, 1985), 534.

6. Trudier Harris, "Black Writers in a Changed Landscape, Since 1950," *The History of Southern Literature*, ed. Louis D. Rubin et al. (Baton Rouge: Louisiana State University Press, 1985), 567.
7. Ronald Baughman, *Understanding James Dickey* (Columbia: University of South Carolina Press, 1985), 144.
8. Baughman, 145–146.
9. Baughman, 134.

Thomas Merton

(1915–1968)

On January 31, 1915, Thomas Merton was born in Prades, Pyrénées-Orientales, France. He became a naturalized citizen of the United States in 1951. Merton attended Clare College, Cambridge, England, from 1933 to 1934. He received his B.A. in 1938 and his M.A. in 1939 from Columbia University. He converted to Catholicism in 1938.

Merton was ordained as a Roman Catholic priest in 1949. From 1941 until his death, he was a Trappist Monk (Roman Catholic Monk of Cistercians of Strick Observance), living at the abbey of Our Lady of Gethsemane near Bardstown, Kentucky. Merton's first book of poetry, *Thirty Poems*, was published in 1944. His autobiography, *The Seven Storey Mountain* (1948), was an instant success. Merton's works are often divided into early Merton and later Merton, with his increasingly social activism present in his later writings.

Merton died on December 10, 1968, in Bangkok, Thailand. He is buried in the monastic cemetery near Bardstown, Kentucky. Bellarmine College in Kentucky is the repository of his writings. In 1969 the college established the Thomas Merton Center. Dozens of his works have been published posthumously, and centers in which to study Merton have been established throughout the world. The International Thomas Merton Society was founded in 1987.

Selected works by Merton include *The Sign of Jonas* (1953); *No Man Is an Island* (1955); *New Seeds of Contemplation* (1962); *Conjectures of a Guilty Bystander* (1966); *Mystics and Zen Masters* (1967); *The Collected Poems of Thomas Merton* (1977); *The Literary Essays of Thomas Merton* (1981); *A Vow of Conversation: Journals, 1964–65* (1988); *Ways of the Christian Mystics* (1994); *Passion for Peace: The Social Essays* (1955); and *Thoughts on the East* (1995).

Flannery O'Connor:

A Prose Elegy

Now Flannery is dead and I will write her name with honor, with love for the great slashing innocence of that dry-eyed irony that could keep looking the South in the face without bleeding or even sobbing. Her South was deeper than mine, crazier than Kentucky, but wild with no other madness than the crafty paranoia that is all over the place, including the North! Only madder, craftier, hung up in wilder and more absurd legends, more inventive of more outrageous lies! And solemn! Taking seriously the need to be respectable when one is an obsolescent and very agile fury.

The key word to Flannery's stories probably is "respect." She never gave up examining its ambiguities and its decay. In this bitter dialectic of half-truths that have become endemic to our system, she probed our very life—its conflicts, its falsities, its obsessions, its vanities. Have we become an enormous complex organization of spurious reverences? Respect is continually advertised, and we are still convinced that we respect "everything good"—when we know too well that we have lost the most elementary respect even for ourselves. Flannery saw this and saw, better than others, what it implied.

She wrote in and out of the anatomy of a word that became genteel, then self-conscious, then obsessive, finally dying of contempt, but kept calling itself "respect." Contempt for the child, for the stranger, for the woman, for the Negro, for the animal, for the white man, for the farmer, for the country, for the preacher, for the city, for the world, for reality itself. Contempt, contempt, so that in the end the gestures of respect they kept making to themselves and to each other and to God became desperately obscene.

But respect had to be maintained. Flannery maintained it ironically and relentlessly with a kind of innocent passion long after it had died of contempt—as if she were the only one left who took this thing seriously. One would think (if one put a Catholic chip on his shoulder and decided to make a problem of her) that she could not look so steadily, so drily and so long at so much false respect without herself dying of despair. She never made any funny faces. She never said: "Here is a terrible thing!" She just looked and said what they said and how they said it. It was not she that invented their despair, and perhaps her only way out of despair herself was to respect the way they announced the gospel of contempt. She patiently recorded all they had got themselves into. Their world was a big, fantastic, crawling, exploding junk pile of despair. I will write her name with honor for seeing it so clearly and looking straight at it without remorse. Perhaps her way of irony was the only possible catharsis for a madness so cruel and so endemic. Perhaps a dry honesty like hers can save the South more simply than the North can ever be saved.

Flannery's people were two kinds of very advanced primitives: the city kind, exhausted, disillusioned, tired of imagining, perhaps still given to a grim willfulness in the service of doubt, still driving on in fury and ill will, or scientifically expert in nastiness; and the rural kind: furious, slow, cunning, inexhaustible, living sweetly on the verge of the unbelievable, more inclined to prefer the abyss to solid ground, but keeping contact with the world of contempt by raw insensate poetry and religious mirth: the mirth of a god who himself, they suspected, was the craftiest and most powerful deceiver of all. Flannery saw the contempt of primitives who admitted that they would hate to be saved, and the greater contempt of those other primitives whose salvation was an elaborately contrived possibility, always being brought back into question. Take the sweet idiot deceit of the fury grandmother in "A Good Man Is Hard to Find" whose respectable and catastrophic fantasy easily destroyed her urban son with all his plans, his last shred of trust in reason, and his insolent children.

The way Flannery O'Connor made a story: she would put together all these elements of unreason and let them fly slowly and inexorably at one another. Then sometimes the urban madness, less powerful, would fall weakly prey to the rural madness and be inexorably devoured by a superior and more primitive absurdity. Or the rural madness would fail and fall short of the required malice and urban deceit would compass its destruction, with all possible contempt, cursing, superior violence and fully implemented disbelief. For it would usually be wholesome faith that left the rural primitive unarmed. So you would watch, fascinated, almost in despair, knowing that in the end the very worst thing, the least reasonable, the least desirable, was what would have to happen. Not because Flannery wanted it so, but because it turned out to *be* so in a realm where the advertised satisfaction is compounded of so many lies and of so much contempt for the customer. She had seen too clearly all that is sinister in our commercial paradise, and in its rural roots.

Flannery's people were two kinds of trash, able to mix inanity with poetry, with exuberant nonsense, and with the most profound and systematic contempt for reality.

Her people knew how to be trash to the limit, unabashed, on purpose, out of self-contempt that has finally won out over every other feeling and turned into a parody of freedom in the spirit. What spirit? A spirit of ungodly stateliness and parody—the pomp and glee of arbitrary sports, freaks not of nature but of blighted and social will-fulness, rich in the creation of respectable and three-eyed monsters. Her beings are always raising the question of *worth*. Who is a good man? Where is he? He is "hard to find." Meanwhile you will have to make out with a bad one who is so respectable that he is horrible, so horrible that he is funny, so funny that he is pathetic, but so pathetic that it would be gruesome to pity him. So funny that you do not dare to laugh too loud for fear of demons.

And that is how Flannery finally solved the problem of respect: having peeled the whole onion of respect layer by layer, having taken it all apart with admirable patience, showing clearly that each layer was only another kind of contempt, she ended up by seeing clearly that it was funny, but not merely funny in a way that you could laugh at. Humorous, yes, but also uncanny, inexplicable, demonic, so you could never laugh at it as if you understood. Because if you pretended to understand, you, too, would find yourself among her demons practicing contempt. She respected all her people by searching for some sense in them, searching for truth, searching to the end and then suspending judgment. To have condemned them on moral grounds would have been to connive with their own crafty arts and their own demonic imagination. It would have meant getting tangled up with them in the same machinery of unreality and of contempt. The only way to be saved was to stay out of it, not to think, not to speak, just to record the slow, sweet, ridiculous verbalizing of Southern furies, working their way through their charming lazy hell.

That is why when I read Flannery I don't think of Hemingway, or Katherine Anne Porter, or Sartre, but rather of someone like Sophocles. What more can be said of a writer? I write her name with honor, for all the truth and all the craft with which she shows man's fall and his dishonor.

Flannery O'Connor
(1925–1964)

Mary Flannery O'Connor was born in Savannah, Georgia, on March 25, 1925. During her brief writing career, she established herself as one of the most important modern American writers. She was a graduate of Georgia State College for Women (1945) and the State University of Iowa (1947).

O'Connor, a Roman Catholic, spent most of her life in Milledgeville, Georgia, where she died from lupus on August 3, 1964. Her novel *Wise Blood* (1952) was made into a film directed by John Huston (1980). Other published works include *The Violent Bear It Away* (1960); *Three by Flannery O'Connor* (1964); *The Complete Short Stories* (1971); *The Habit of Being: Letters* (1979); and *Collected Works* (1988).

O'Connor won first place in the O. Henry Memorial Awards in 1957, 1963, and 1965. In 1972, *The Flannery O'Connor Bulletin* was established. In that same year, *The Complete Short Stories* won the National Book Award.

The Catholic Novelist in the Protestant South

In the past several years I have gone to speak at a number of Catholic colleges, and I have been pleased to discover that fiction seems to be important to the Catholic student in a way it would not have been twenty, or even ten, years ago. In the past, Catholic imagination in this country has been devoted almost exclusively to practical affairs. Our energies have gone into what has been necessary to sustain existence, and now that our existence is no longer in doubt, we are beginning to realize that an impoverishment of the imagination means an impoverishment of the religious life as well.

I am concerned that future Catholics have a literature. I want them to have a litera-ture that will be undeniably theirs, but which will also be understood and cherished by the rest of our countrymen. A literature for ourselves alone is a contradiction in terms. You may ask, why not simply call this literature Christian? Unfortunately, the word Christian is no longer reliable. It has come to mean anyone with a golden heart. And a golden heart would be a positive interference in the writing of fiction.

I am specifically concerned with fiction because that is what I write. There is a certain embarrassment about being a storyteller in these times when stories are con-sidered not quite as satisfying as statements and statements not quite as satisfying as statistics; but in the long run, a people is known, not by its statements or its statistics, but by the stories it tells. Fiction is the most impure and the most modest and the most human of the arts. It is closest to man in his sin and his suffering and his hope, and it is often rejected by Catholics for the very reasons that make it what it is. It es-capes any orthodoxy we might set up for it, because its dignity is an imitation of our own, based like our own on free will, a free will that operates even in the teeth of di-vine displeasure. I won't go far into the subject of whether such a thing as a Catholic novel is possible or not. I feel that this is a bone which has been picked bare without giving anybody any nourishment. I am simple going to assume that novelists who are deeply Catholic will write novels which you may call Catholic if the Catholic aspects of the novel are what interest you. Such a novel may be characterized in any number of other ways, and perhaps the more ways the better.

In American Catholic circles we are long on theories of what Catholic fiction should be, and short on the experience of having any of it. Once when I spoke on this subject at a Catholic university in the South, a gentleman arose and said that the con-cept *Catholic novel* was a limiting one and that the novelist, like Whitman, should be alien to nothing. All I could say to him was, "Well, I'm alien to a great deal." We are lim-ited human beings, and the novel is a product of our best limitations. We write with the whole personality, and any attempt to circumvent it, whether this be an effort to rise above belief or above background, is going to result in a reduced approach to reality.

But I think that in spite of this spotty and suspect sophistication, which you find here and there among us, the American Catholic feels the same way he has always felt toward the novel: he trusts the fictional imagination about as little as he trusts anything. Before it is well on its feet, he is worrying about how to control it. The young Catholic writer, more than any other, is liable to be smothered at the outset by theory. The Catholic press is constantly broken out in a rash of articles on the failure of the Catholic novelist: the Catholic novelist is failing to reflect the virtue of hope, failing to show the Church's interest in social justice, failing to portray our beliefs in a light that will make them desirable to others. He occasionally writes well, but he al-ways writes wrong.

We have recently gone through a period of self-criticism on the subject of Catholics and scholarship, which for the most part has taken place on a high level. Our scholarship, or lack of it, has been discussed in relation to what scholarship is in itself, and the discussion—when it has been most valuable—has been conducted by those who are scholars and who know from their own experience what the scholar is and does.

But when we talk about the Catholic failure to produce good fiction in this country, we seldom hear from anyone actively engaged in trying to produce it, and the discussion has not yielded any noticeable returns. We hear from editors, schoolteachers, moralists, and housewives; anyone living considers himself an authority on fiction. The novelist, on the other hand, is supposed to be like Mr. Jarrell's pig that didn't know what bacon was. I think, though, that it is occasionally desirable that we look at the novel—even the so-called Catholic novel—from some particular novelist's point of view.

Catholic discussions of novels by Catholics are frequently ridiculous because every given circumstance of the writer is ignored except his Faith. No one taking part in these discussions seems to remember that the eye sees what it has been given to see by concrete circumstances, and the imagination reproduces what, by some related gift, it is able to make live.

I collect articles from the Catholic press on the failures of the Catholic novelist, and recently in one of them I came upon this typical sentence: "Why not a positive novel based on the Church's fight for social justice, or the liturgical revival, or life in a seminary?"

I take it that if seminarians began to write novels about life in the seminary, there would soon be several less seminarians, but we are to assume that anybody who can write at all, and who has the energy to do some research, can give us a novel on this or any needed subject—and can make it positive.

A lot of novels do get written in this way. It is, in fact, the traditional procedure of the hack, and by some accident of God, such a novel might turn out to be a work of art, but the possibility is unlikely.

In this same article, the writer asked this wistful question: "Would it not seem in order now for some of our younger men to explore the possibilities inherent in certain positive factors which make Catholic life and the Catholic position in this country increasingly challenging?"

This attitude, which proceeds from the standpoint of what it would be good to do or have to supply a general need, is totally opposite from the novelist's own approach. No serious novelist "explores possibilities inherent in factors." Conrad wrote that the artist "descends within himself, and in that region of stress and strife, if he be deserving and fortunate, he finds the terms of his appeal."

Where you find the terms of your appeal may have little or nothing to do with what is challenging in the life of the Church at the moment. And this is particularly apparent to the Southern Catholic writer, whose imagination has been molded by life in a region which is traditionally Protestant. The two circumstances that have given character to my own writing have been those of being Southern and being Catholic. This is considered by many to be an unlikely combination, but I have found it to be a most likely one. I think that the South provides the Catholic novelist with some benefits that he usually lacks, and lacks to a conspicuous degree. The Catholic novel can't be categorized by subject matter, but only by what it assumes about human and divine reality. It cannot see man as determined; it cannot see him as totally depraved. It will see him as incomplete in himself, as prone to evil, but as redeemable when his own efforts are assisted by grace. And it will see this grace as working through nature, but as entirely transcending it, so that a door is always open to possibility and the unexpected in the human soul. Its center of meaning will be Christ; its center of destruction will be the devil. No matter how this view of life may be fleshed out, these assumptions form its skeleton.

But you don't write fiction with assumptions. The things we see, hear, smell, and touch affect us long before we believe anything at all, and the South impresses its image on us from the moment we are able to distinguish one sound from another. By the time we are able to use our imaginations for fiction, we find that our senses have responded irrevocably to a certain reality. This discovery of being bound through the senses to a particular society and a particular history, to particular sounds and a particular idiom, is for the writer the beginning of a recognition that first puts his work into real human perspective for him. What the Southern Catholic writer is apt to find, when he descends within his imagination, is not Catholic life but the life of this region in which he is both native and alien. He discovers that the imagination is not free, but bound.

For many young writers, Catholic or other, this is not a pleasant discovery. They feel that the first thing they must do in order to write well is to shake off the clutch of the region. They would like to set their stories in a region whose way of life seems nearer the spirit of what they think they have to say, or better, they would like to eliminate the region altogether and approach the infinite directly. But this is not even a possibility.

The fiction writer finds in time, if not at once, that he cannot proceed at all if he cuts himself off from the sights and sounds that have developed a life of their own in his senses. The novelist is concerned with the mystery of personality, and you cannot say much that is significant about this mystery unless the characters you create exist with the marks of a believable society about them. The larger social context is simply left out of much current fiction, but it cannot be left out by the Southern writer. The image of the South, in all its complexity, is so powerful in us that it is a force which has to be encountered and engaged. The writer must wrestle with it, like Jacob with the angel, until he has extracted a blessing. The writing of any novel worth the effort is a kind of personal encounter, an encounter with the circumstances of the particular writer's imagination, with circumstances which are brought to order only in the actual writing.

The Catholic novel that fails is usually one in which this kind of engagement is absent. It is a novel which doesn't grapple with any particular culture. It may try to make a culture out of the Church, but this is always a mistake because the Church is not a culture. The Catholic novel that fails is a novel in which there is no sense of place, and in which feeling is, by that much, diminished. Its action occurs in an abstracted setting that could be anywhere or nowhere. This reduces its dimensions drastically and cuts down on those tensions that keep fiction from being facile and slick.

The Southern writer's greatest tie with the South is through his ear, which is usually sharp but not too versatile outside his own idiom. With a few exceptions, such as Miss Katherine Anne Porter, he is not too often successfully cosmopolitan in fiction, but the fact is that he doesn't need to be. A distinctive idiom is a powerful instrument for keeping fiction social. When one Southern character speaks, regardless of his station in life, an echo of all Southern life is heard. This helps to keep Southern fiction from being a fiction of purely private experience.

Alienation was once a diagnosis, but in much of the fiction of our time it has become an ideal. The modern hero is the outsider. His experience is rootless. He can go anywhere. He belongs nowhere. Being alien to nothing, he ends up being alienated from any kind of community based on common tastes and interests. The borders of his country are the sides of his skull.

The South is traditionally hostile to outsiders, except on her own terms. She is traditionally against intruders, foreigners from Chicago or New Jersey, all those who come from afar with moral energy that increases in direct proportion to the distance from home. It is difficult to separate the virtues of this quality from the narrowness which accompanies and colors it for the outside world. It is more difficult still to reconcile the South's instinct to preserve her identity with her equal instinct to fall eager victim to every poisonous breath from Hollywood or Madison Avenue. But good and evil appear to be joined in every culture at the spine, and as far as the creation of a body of fiction is concerned, the social is superior to the purely personal. Somewhere is better than anywhere. And traditional manners, however unbalanced, are better than no manners at all.

The writer whose themes are religious particularly needs a region where these themes find a response in the life of the people. The American Catholic is short on places that reflect his particular religious life and his particular problems. This country isn't exactly cut in his image. Where he does have a place—such as the Midwestern parishes, which serve as J. F. Powers' region, or South Boston, which belongs to Edwin O'Connor—these places lack the significant features that result in a high degree of regional self-consciousness. They have no great geographical extent, they have no particularly significant history, certainly no history of defeat; they have no real peasant class, and no cultural unity of the kind you find in the South. So that no matter what the writer brings to them in the way of talents, they don't bring much to him in the way of exploitable benefits. Where Catholics do abound, they usually blend almost imperceptibly into the general materialistic background. If the Catholic faith were central to life in America, Catholic fiction would fare better, but the Church is not central to this society. The things that bind us together as Catholics are known only to ourselves. A secular society understands us less and less. It becomes more and more difficult in America to make belief believable, but in this the Southern writer has the greatest possible advantage. He lives in the Bible Belt.

It was about 1919 that Mencken called the South the Bible Belt and the Sahara of the Bozarts. Today Southern literature is known around the world, and the South is still the Bible Belt. Sam Jones' grandma read the Bible thirty-seven times on her knees. And the rural and small-town South, and even a certain level of the city South, is made up of the descendants of old ladies like her. You don't shake off their influence in even several generations.

To be great storytellers, we need something to measure ourselves against, and this is what we conspicuously lack in this age. Men judge themselves now by what they find themselves doing. The Catholic has the natural law and the teachings of the Church to guide him, but for the writing of fiction, something more is necessary.

For the purposes of fiction, these guides have to exist in a concrete form, known and held sacred by the whole community. They have to exist in the form of stories which affect our image and our judgment of ourselves. Abstractions, formulas, laws will not serve here. We have to have stories in our background. It takes a story to make a story. It takes a story of mythic dimensions, one which belongs to everybody, one in which everybody is able to recognize the hand of God and its descent. In the Protestant South, the Scriptures fill this role.

The Hebrew genius for making the absolute concrete has conditioned the Southerner's way of looking at things. That is one of the reasons why the South is a story-telling section. Our response to life is different if we have been taught only a definition of faith than if we have trembled with Abraham as he held the knife over Isaac. Both of these kinds of knowledge are necessary, but in the last four or five centuries, Catholics have overemphasized the abstract and consequently impoverished their imaginations and their capacity for prophetic insight.

Nothing will insure the future of Catholic fiction so much as the biblical revival that we see signs of now in Catholic life. The Bible is held sacred in the Church, we hear it read at Mass, bits and pieces of it are exposed to us in the liturgy, but because we are not totally dependent on it, it has not penetrated very far into our consciousness nor conditioned our reactions to experience. Unfortunately, where you find Catholics reading the Bible, you find that it is usually a pursuit of the educated, but in the South the Bible is known by the ignorant as well, and it is always that *mythos* which the poor hold in common that is most valuable to the fiction writer. When the poor hold sacred history in common, they have ties to the universal and the holy, which allows the meaning of their every action to be heightened and seen under the aspect of eternity. The writer who views the world in this light will be very thankful if he has been fortunate enough to have the South for his background, because here belief can still be made believable, even if for the modern mind it cannot be made admirable.

Religious enthusiasm is accepted as one of the South's more grotesque features, and it is possible to build upon that acceptance, however little real understanding such acceptance may carry with it. When you write about backwoods prophets, it is very difficult to get across to the modern reader that you take these people seriously, that you are not making fun of them, but that their concerns are your own and, in your judgment, central to human life. It is almost inconceivable to this reader that such could be the case. It is hard enough for him to suspend his disbelief and accept an anagogical level of action at all, harder still for him to accept its action in an obviously grotesque character. He has the mistaken notion that a concern with grace is a concern with exalted human behavior, that it is a pretentious concern. It is, however, simply a concern with the human reaction to that which, instant by instant, gives life to the soul. It is a concern with a realization that breeds charity and with the charity that breeds action. Often the nature of grace can be made plain only by describing its absence.

The Catholic writer may be immersed in the Bible himself, but if his readers and his characters are not, he does not have the instrument to plumb meaning—and specifically Christian meaning—that he would have if the biblical background were known to all. It is what writer, character, and reader share that makes it possible to write fiction at all.

The circumstances of being a Southerner, of living in a non-Catholic but religious society, furnish the Catholic novelist with some very fine antidotes to his own worst tendencies. We too much enjoy indulging ourselves in the logic that kills, in making categories smaller and smaller, in prescribing attitudes and proscribing subjects. For the Catholic, one result of the Counter-Reformation was a practical overemphasis on the legal and logical and a consequent neglect of the Church's broader tradition. The need for this emphasis has now diminished, and the Church is busy encouraging those biblical and liturgical revivals which should restore Catholic life to its proper fullness. Nevertheless the scars of this legalistic approach are still upon us. Those who are long on logic, definitions, abstractions, and formulas are frequently short on a sense of the concrete, and when they find themselves in an environment where their own principles have only a partial application to society, they are forced, not to abandon the principles, but in applying them to a different situation, to come up with fresh reactions.

I often find among Catholics a certain impatience with Southern literature, sometimes a fascinated impatience, but usually a definite feeling that with all the violence and grotesqueries and religious enthusiasm reflected in its fiction, the South—that is, the rural, Protestant, Bible Belt South—is a little beyond the pale of Catholic respect, and that certainly it would be ridiculous to expect the emergence in such soil of anything like a literature inspired by Catholic belief. But for my part, I don't think that this is at all unlikely. There are certain conditions necessary for the emergence of Catholic literature which are found nowhere else in this country in such abundance as in the Protestant South; and I look forward with considerable relish to the day when we are going to have to enlarge our notions about the Catholic novel to include some pretty odd Southern specimens.

It seems to me that the Catholic Southerner's experience of living so intimately with the division of Christendom is an experience that can give much breadth and poignance to the novels he may produce. The Catholic novelist in the South is forced to follow the spirit into strange places and to recognize it in many forms not totally congenial to him. He may feel that the kind of religion that has influenced Southern life has run hand in hand with extreme individualism for so long that there is nothing left of it that he can recognize, but when he penetrates to the human aspiration beneath it, he sees not only what has been lost to the life he observes, but more, the terrible loss to us in the Church of human faith and passion. I think he will feel a good deal more kinship with backwoods prophets and shouting fundamentals than he will with those politer elements for whom the supernatural is an embarrassment and for whom religion has become a department of sociology or culture or personality development. His interest and sympathy may very well go—as I know my own does—directly to those aspects of Southern life where the religious feeling is most intense and where its outward forms are farthest from the Catholic, and most revealing of a need that only the Church can fill. This is not because, in the felt superiority of orthodoxy, he wishes to subtract one theology from another, but because, descending within himself to find his region, he discovers that it is with these aspects of Southern life that he has a feeling of kinship strong enough to spur him to write.

The result of these underground religious affinities will be a strange and, to many, perverse fiction, one which serves no felt need, which gives us no picture of Catholic life, or the religious experiences that are usual with us, but I believe that it will be Catholic fiction. These people in the invisible Church make discoveries that have meaning for us who are better protected from the vicissitudes of our own natures, and who are often too lazy and satisfied to make any discoveries at all. I believe that the Catholic fiction writer is free to find his subject in the invisible Church and that this will be the vocation of many of us brought up in the South. In a literature that tends naturally to extremes, as Southern literature does, we need something to protect us against the merely extreme, the merely personal, the merely grotesque, and here the Catholic, with his older tradition and his ability to resist the dissolution of belief, can make his contribution to Southern literature, but only if he realizes first that he has as much to learn from it as to give it. The Catholic novelist in the South will bolster the South's best traditions, for they are the same as his own. And the South will perhaps lead him to be less timid as a novelist, more respectful of the concrete, more trustful of the blind imagination.

The opportunities for the potential Catholic writer in the South are so great as to be intimidating. He lives in a region where there is a thriving literary tradition, and this is always an advantage to the writer, who is initially inspired less by life than by the work of his predecessors. He lives in a region which is struggling, in both good ways and bad, to preserve its identity, and this is an advantage, for his dramatic need is to know manners under stress. He lives in the Bible Belt, where belief can be made believable. He has also here a good view of the modern world. A half-hour's ride in this region will take him from places where the life has a distinctly Old Testament flavor to places where the life might be considered post-Christian. Yet all these varied situations can be seen in one glance and heard in one conversation.

I think that Catholic novelists in the future will be able to reinforce the vital strength of Southern literature, for they will know that what has given the South her identity are those beliefs and qualities which she has absorbed from the Scriptures and from her own history of defeat and violation: a distrust of the abstract, a sense of human dependence on the grace of God, and a knowledge that evil is not simply a problem to be solved, but a mystery to be endured.

If all that is missing in this scene is the practical influence of the visible Catholic Church, the writer will find that he has to supply the lack, as best he can, out of himself; and he will do this by the way he uses his eyes. If he uses them in the confidence of his Faith, and according to the needs of what he is making, there will be nothing in life too grotesque, or too "un-Catholic," to supply the materials of his work. Certainly in a secular world, he is in a particular position to appreciate and cherish the Protestant South, to remind us of what we have and what we must keep.

Revelation

The doctor's waiting room, which was very small, was almost full when the Turpins entered and Mrs. Turpin, who was very large, made it look even smaller by her presence. She stood looming at the head of the magazine table set in the center of it, a living demonstration that the room was inadequate and ridiculous. Her little bright black eyes took in all the patients as she sized up the seating situation. There was one vacant chair and a place on the sofa occupied by a blond child in a dirty blue romper who should have been told to move over and make room for the lady. He was five or six, but Mrs. Turpin saw at once that no one was going to tell him to move over. He was slumped down in the seat, his arms idle at his sides and his eyes idle in his head; his nose ran unchecked.

Mrs. Turpin put a firm hand on Claud's shoulder and said in a voice that included anyone who wanted to listen, "Claud, you sit in that chair there," and gave him a push down into the vacant one, Claud was florid and bald and sturdy, somewhat shorter than Mrs. Turpin, but he sat down as if he were accustomed to doing what she told him to.

Mrs. Turpin remained standing. The only man in the room besides Claud was a lean stringy old fellow with a rusty hand spread out on each knee, whose eyes were closed as if he were asleep or dead or pretending to be so as not to get up and offer her his seat. Her gaze settled agreeably on a well-dressed grey-haired lady whose eyes met hers and whose expression said: if that child belonged to me, he would have some manners and move over—there's plenty of room there for you and him too.

Claud looked up with a sigh and made as if to rise.

"Sit down," Mrs. Turpin said. "You know you're not supposed to stand on that leg. He has an ulcer on his leg," she explained.

Claud lifted his foot onto the magazine table and rolled his trouser leg up to reveal a purple swelling on a plump marble-white calf.

"My!" the pleasant lady said. "How did you do that?"

"A cow kicked him," Mrs. Turpin said.

"Goodness!" said the lady.

Claud rolled his trouser leg down.

"Maybe the little boy would move over," the lady suggested, but the child did not stir.

"Somebody will be leaving in a minute," Mrs. Turpin said. She could not understand why a doctor—with as much money as they made charging five dollars a day to just stick their head in the hospital door and look at you—couldn't afford a decent-sized waiting room. This one was hardly bigger than a garage. The table was cluttered with limp-looking magazines and at one end of it there was a big green glass ash tray full of cigaret butts and cotton wads with little blood spots on them. If she had had anything to do with the running of the place, that would have been emptied every so often. There were no chairs against the wall at the head of the room. It had a rectangular-shaped panel in it that permitted a view of the office where the nurse came and went and the secretary listened to the radio. A plastic fern in a gold pot sat in the opening and trailed its fronds down almost to the floor. The radio was softly playing gospel music.

Just then the inner door opened and a nurse with the highest stack of yellow hair Mrs. Turpin had even seen put her face in the crack and called for the next patient. The woman sitting beside Claud grasped the two arms of her chair and hoisted herself up; she pulled her dress free from her legs and lumbered through the door where the nurse had disappeared.

Mrs. Turpin eased into the vacant chair, which held her tight as a corset. "I wish I could reduce," she said, and rolled her eyes and gave a comic sigh.

"Oh, *you* aren't fat," the stylish lady said.

"Ooooo I am too," Mrs. Turpin said. "Claud he eats all he wants to and never weighs over one hundred and seventy-five pounds, but me I just look at something good to eat and I gain some weight," and her stomach and shoulders shook with laughter. "You can eat all you want to, can't you, Claud?" she asked, turning to him.

Claud only grinned.

"Well, as long as you have such a good disposition," the stylish lady said, "I don't think it makes a bit of difference what size you are. You just can't beat a good disposition."

Next to her was a fat girl of eighteen or nineteen, scowling into a thick blue book which Mrs. Turpin saw was entitled *Human Development*. The girl raised her head and directed her scowl at Mrs. Turpin as if she did not like her looks. She appeared annoyed that anyone should speak while she tried to read. The poor girl's face was blue with acne and Mrs. Turpin thought how pitiful it was to have a face like that at that age. She gave the girl a friendly smile but the girl only scowled the harder. Mrs. Turpin herself was fat but she had always had good skin, and, though she was forty-seven years old, there was not a wrinkle in her face except around her eyes from laughing too much.

Next to the ugly girl was the child, still in exactly the same position, and next to him was a thin leathery old woman in a cotton print dress. She and Claud had three sacks of chicken feed in their pump house that was in the same print. She had seen from the first that the child belonged with the old woman. She could tell by the way they sat—kind of vacant and white-trashy, as if they would sit there until Doomsday if nobody called and told them to get up. And at right angles but next to the well-dressed pleasant lady was a lank-faced woman who was certainly the child's mother. She had on a yellow sweat shirt and wine-colored slacks, both gritty-looking, and the rims of her lips were stained with snuff. Her dirty yellow hair was tied behind with a little piece of red paper ribbon. Worse than niggers any day, Mrs. Turpin thought.

The gospel hymn playing was, "When I looked up and He looked down," and Mrs. Turpin, who knew it, supplied the last line mentally, "And wona these days I know I'll we-eara crown."

Without appearing to, Mrs. Turpin always noticed people's feet. The well-dressed lady had on red and grey suede shoes to match her dress. Mrs. Turpin had on her good black patent leather pumps. The ugly girl had on Girl Scout shoes and heavy socks. The old woman had on tennis shoes and the white-trashy mother had on what appeared to be bedroom slippers, black straw with gold braid threaded through them—exactly what you would have expected her to have on.

Sometimes at night when she couldn't go to sleep, Mrs. Turpin would occupy herself with the question of who she would have chosen to be if she couldn't have been herself. If Jesus had said to her before he made her, "There's only two places available for you. You can either be a nigger or white-trash," what would she have said? "Please, Jesus, please," she would have said, "just let me wait until there's another place available," and he would have said, "No, you have to go right now and I have only those two places so make up your mind." She would have wiggled and squirmed and begged and pleaded but it would have been no use and finally she would have said, "All right, make me a nigger then—but that don't mean a trashy one." And he would have made her a neat clean respectable Negro woman, herself but black.

Next to the child's mother was a red-headed youngish woman, reading one of the magazines and working a piece of chewing gum, hell for leather, as Claud would say. Mrs. Turpin could not see the woman's feet. She was not white-trash, just common. Sometimes Mrs. Turpin occupied herself at night naming the classes of people. On the bottom of the heap were most colored people, not the kind she would have been if she had been one, but most of them; then next to them—not above, just away from— were the white-trash; then above them were the home-owners, and above them the home-and-land owners, to which she and Claud belonged. Above she and Claud were people with a lot of money and much bigger houses and much more land. But here the complexity of it would begin to bear in on her, for some of the people with a lot of money were common and ought to be below she and Claud and some of the people who had good blood had lost their money and had to rent and then there were colored people who owned their homes and land as well. There was a colored dentist in town who had two red Lincolns and a swimming pool and a farm with registered white-face cattle on it. Usually by the time she had fallen asleep all the classes of people were moiling and roiling around in her head, and she would dream they were all crammed in together in a box car, being ridden off to be put in a gas oven.

"That's a beautiful clock," she said and nodded to her right. It was a big wall clock, the face encased in a brass sunburst.

"Yes, it's very pretty," the stylish lady said agreeable. "And right on the dot too," she added, glancing at her watch.

The ugly girl beside her cast an eye upward at the clock, smirked, then looked directly at Mrs. Turpin and smirked again. Then she returned her eyes to her book. She was obviously the lady's daughter because, although they didn't look anything alike as to disposition, they both had the same shape of face and the same blue eyes. On the lady they sparkled pleasantly but in the girl's seared face they appeared alternately to smolder and to blaze.

What if Jesus had said, "All right, you can be white-trash or a nigger or ugly"!

Mrs. Turpin felt an awful pity for the girl, though she thought it was one thing to be ugly and another to act ugly.

The woman with the snuff-stained lips turned around in her chair and looked up at the clock. Then she turned back and appeared to look a little to the side of Mrs. Turpin. There was a cast in one of her eyes. "You want to know wher you can get you one of themther clocks?" she asked in a loud voice.

"No, I already have a nice clock," Mrs. Turpin said. Once somebody like her got a leg in the conversation, she would be all over it.

"You can get you one with green stamps," the woman said. "That's most likely wher he got hisn. Save you up enough, you can get you most anythang. I got me some joo'ry."

Ought to have got you a wash rag and some soap, Mrs. Turnpin thought.

"I get contour sheets with mine," the pleasant lady said.

The daughter slammed her book shut. She looked straight in front of her, directly through Mrs. Turpin and on through the yellow curtain and the plate glass window which made the wall behind her. The girl's eyes seemed lit all of a sudden with a peculiar light, an unnatural light like night road signs give. Mrs. Turpin turned her head to see if there was anything going on outside that she should see, but she could not see anything. Figures passing cast only a pale shadow through the curtain. There was no reason the girl should single her out for her ugly looks.

"Miss Finley," the nurse said, cracking the door. The gum-chewing woman got up and passed in front of her and Claud and went into the office. She had on red high-heeled shoes.

Directly across the table, the ugly girl's eyes were fixed on Mrs. Turpin as if she had some very special reason for disliking her.

"This is wonderful weather, isn't it?" the girl's mother said.

"It's good weather for cotton if you can get the niggers to pick it," Mrs. Turpin said, "but niggers don't want to pick cotton any more. You can't get the white folks to pick it and now you can't get the niggers—because they got to be right up there with the white folks."

"They gonna *try* anyways," the white-trash woman said, leaning forward.

"Do you have one of those cotton-picking machines?" the pleasant lady asked.

"No," Mrs. Turpin said, "they leave half the cotton in the field. We don't have much cotton anyway. If you want to make it farming now, you have to have a little of everything. We got a couple of acres of cotton and a few hogs and chickens and just enough white-face that Claud can look after them himself."

"One thang I don't want," the white-trash woman said, wiping her mouth with the back of her hand. "Hogs. Nasty stinking things, a-gruntin and a-rootin all over the place."

Mrs. Turpin gave her the merest edge of her attention. "Our hogs are not dirty and they don't stink," she said. "They're cleaner than some children I've seen. Their feet never touch the ground. We have a pig-parlor—that's where you raise them on concrete," she explained to the pleasant lady, "and Claud scoots them down with the hose every afternoon and washes off the floor." Cleaner by far than that child right there, she thought. Poor nasty little thing. He had not moved except to put the thumb of his dirty hand into his mouth.

The woman turned her face away from Mrs. Turpin. "I know I wouldn't scoot down no hog with no hose," she said to the wall.

You wouldn't have no hog to scoot down, Mrs. Turpin said to herself.

"A-gruntin and a-rootin and a-groanin," the woman muttered.

"We got a little of everything," Mrs. Turpin said to the pleasant lady. "It's no use in having more than you can handle yourself with help like it is. We found enough niggers to pick our cotton this year but Claud he has to go after them and take them home again in the evening. They can't walk that half a mile. No they can't. I tell you," she said and laughed merrily, "I sure am tired of buttering up niggers, but you got to love em if you want em to work for you. When they come in the morning, I run out and I say, 'Hi yawl this morning?' and when Claud drives them off to the field I just wave to beat the band and they just wave back." And she waved her hand rapidly to illustrate.

"Like you read out of the same book," the lady said, showing she understood perfectly.

"Child, yes," Mrs. Turpin said. "And when they come in from the field, I run out with a bucket of icewater. That's the way it's going to be from now on," she said. "You may as well face it."

"One thang I know," the white-trash woman said. "Two thangs I ain't going to do: love no niggers or scoot down no hog with no hose." And she let out a bark of contempt.

The look that Mrs. Turpin and the pleasant lady exchanged indicated they both understood that you had to *have* certain things before you could *know* certain things. But every time Mrs. Turpin exchanged a look with the lady, she was aware that the ugly girl's peculiar eyes were still on her, and she had trouble bringing her attention back to the conversation.

"When you got something," she said, "you got to look after it." And when you ain't got a thing but breath and britches, she added to herself, you can afford to come to town every morning and just sit on the Court House coping and spit.

A grotesque revolving shadow passed across the curtain behind her and was thrown palely on the opposite wall. Then a bicycle clattered down against the outside of the building. The door opened and a colored boy glided in with a tray from the drug store. It had two large red and white paper cups on it with tops on them. He was a tall, very black boy in discolored white pants and a green nylon shirt. He was chewing gum slowly, as if to music. He set the tray down in the office opening next to the fern and stuck his head through to look for the secretary. She was not in there. He rested his arms on the ledge and waited, his narrow bottom stuck out, swaying slowly to the left and right. He raised a hand over his head and scratched the base of his skull.

"You see that button there, boy?" Mrs. Turpin said. "You can punch that and she'll come. She's probably in the back somewhere."

"Is thas right?" the boy said agreeably, as if he had never seen the button before. He leaned to the right and put his finger on it. "She sometime out," he said and twisted around to face his audience, his elbows behind him on the counter. The nurse appeared and he twisted back again. She handed him a dollar and he rooted in his pocket and made the change and counted it out to her. She gave him fifteen cents for a tip and he went out with the empty tray. The heavy door swung to slowly and closed at length with the sound of suction. For a moment no one spoke.

"They ought to send all them niggers back to Africa," the white-trash woman said. "That's wher they come from in the first place."

"Oh, I couldn't do without my good colored friends," the pleasant lady said.

"There's a heap of things worse than a nigger," Mrs. Turpin agreed. "It's all kinds of them just like it's all kinds of us."

"Yes, and it takes all kinds to make the world go round," the lady said in her musical voice.

As she said it, the raw-complexioned girl snapped her teeth together. Her lower lip turned downwards and inside out, revealing the pale pink inside of her mouth. After a second it rolled back up. It was the ugliest face Mrs. Turpin had ever seen anyone make and for a moment she was certain that the girl had made it at her. She was looking at her as if she had known and disliked her all her life—all of Mrs. Turpin's life, it seemed too, not just all the girl's life. Why, girl, I don't even know you, Mrs. Turpin said silently.

She forced her attention back to the discussion. "It wouldn't be practical to send them back to Africa," she said. "They wouldn't want to go. They got it too good here."

"Wouldn't be what they wanted—if I had anything to do with it," the woman said.

"It wouldn't be a way in the world you could get all the niggers back over there," Mrs. Turpin said. "They'd be hiding out and lying down and turning sick on you and wailing and hollering and raring and pitching. It wouldn't be a way in the world to get them over there."

"They got over here," the trashy woman said. "Get back like they got over."

"It wasn't so many of them then," Mrs. Turpin explained.

The woman looked at Mrs. Turpin as if here was an idiot indeed but Mrs. Turpin was not bothered by the look, considering where it came from.

"Nooo," she said, "they're going to stay here where they can go to New York and marry white folks and improve their color. That's what they all want to do, every one of them, improve their color."

"You know what comes of that, don't you?" Claud asked.

"No, Claud, what?" Mrs. Turpin said.

Claud's eyes twinkled, "White-faced niggers," he said with never a smile.

Everybody in the office laughed except the white-trash and the ugly girl. The girl gripped the book in her lap with white fingers. The trashy woman looked around her from face to face as if she thought they were all idiots. The old woman in the feed sack dress continued to gaze expressionless across the floor at the high-top shoes of the man opposite her, the one who had been pretending to be asleep when the Turpins came in. He was laughing heartily, his hands still spread out on his knees. The child had fallen to the side and was lying now almost face down in the old woman's lap.

While they recovered from their laughter, the nasal chorus on the radio kept, the room from silence.

> *"You go to blank blank*
> *And I'll go to mine*
> *But we'll all blank along*

To-geth-ther,
And all along the blank
We'll hep eachother out
Smile-ling in any kind of
Weath-ther!"

Mrs. Turpin didn't catch every word but she caught enough to agree with the spirit of the song and it turned her thoughts sober. To help anybody out that needed it was her philosophy of life. She never spared herself when she found somebody in need, whether they were white or black, trash or decent. And of all she had to be thankful for, she was most thankful that this was so. If Jesus had said, "You can be high society and have all the money you want and be thin and svelte-like, but you can't be a good woman with it," she would have had to say, "Well don't make me that then. Make me a good woman and it don't matter what else, how fat or how ugly or how poor!" Her heart rose. He had not made her a nigger or white-trash or ugly! He had made her herself and given her a little of everything. Jesus, thank you! she said. Thank you thank you thank you! Whenever she counted her blessings she felt as buoyant as if she weighed one hundred and twenty-five pounds instead of one hundred and eighty.

"What's wrong with your little boy?" the pleasant lady asked the white-trashy woman.

"He has a ulcer," the woman said proudly. "He ain't give me a minute's peace since he was born. Him and her are just alike," she said, nodding at the old woman, who was running her leathery fingers through the child's pale hair. "Look like I can't get nothing down them two but Co' Cola and candy."

That's all you try to get down em, Mrs. Turpin said to herself. Too lazy to light the fire. There was nothing you could tell her about people like them that she didn't know already. And it was not just that they didn't have anything. Because if you gave them everything, in two weeks it would all be broken or filthy or they would have chopped it up for lightwood. She knew all this from her own experience. Help them you must, but help them you couldn't.

All at once the ugly girl turned her lips inside out again. Her eyes were fixed like two drills on Mrs. Turpin. This time there was no mistaking that there was something urgent behind them.

Girl, Mrs. Turpin exclaimed silently, I haven't done a thing to you! The girl might be confusing her with somebody else. There was no need to sit by and let herself be intimidated. "You must be in college," she said boldly, looking directly at the girl. "I see you reading a book there."

The girl continued to stare and pointedly did not answer.

Her mother blushed at this rudeness. "The lady asked you a question, Mary Grace," she said under her breath.

"I have ears," Mary Grace said.

The poor mother blushed again. "Mary Grace goes to Wellesley College," she explained. She twisted one of the buttons on her dress. "In Massachusetts," she added with a grimace. "And in the summer she just keeps right on studying. Just reads all the time, a real book worm. She's done real well at Wellesley; she's taking English and Math and History and Psychology and Social Studies," she rattled on, "and I think it's too much. I think she ought to get out and have fun."

The girl looked as if she would like to hurl them all through the plate glass window.

"Way up north," Mrs. Turpin murmured and thought, well, it hasn't done much for her manners.

"I'd almost rather to have him sick," the white-trash woman said, wrenching the attention back to herself. "He's so mean when he ain't. Look like some children just take natural to meanness. It's some gets bad when they get sick but he was the opposite. Took sick and turned good. He don't give me no trouble now. It's me waitin to see the doctor," she said.

If I was going to send anybody back to Africa, Mrs. Turpin thought, it would be your kind, woman. "Yes, indeed," she said aloud, but looking up at the ceiling, "it's a heap of things worse than a nigger." And dirtier than a hog, she added to herself.

"I think people with bad dispositions are more to be pitied than anyone on earth," the pleasant lady said in a voice that was decidedly thin.

"I thank the Lord he has blessed me with a good one," Mrs. Turpin said. "The day has never dawned that I couldn't find something to laugh at."

"Not since she married me anyways," Claud said with a comical straight face.

Everybody laughed except the girl and the white-trash.

Mrs. Turpin's stomach shook. "He's such a caution," she said, "that I can't help but laugh at him."

The girl made a loud ugly noise through her teeth.

Her mother's mouth grew thin and tight. "I think the worst thing in the world," she said, "is an ungrateful person. To have everything and not appreciate it. I know a girl," she said, "who has parents who would give her anything, a little brother who loves her dearly, who is getting a good education, who wears the best clothes, but who can never say a kind word to anyone, who never smiles, who just criticizes and complains all day long."

"Is she too old to paddle?" Claud asked.

The girl's face was almost purple.

"Yes," the lady said, "I'm afraid there's nothing to do but leave her to her folly. Some day she'll wake up and it'll be too late."

"It never hurt anyone to smile," Mrs. Turpin said. "It just makes you feel better all over."

"Of course," the lady said sadly, "but there are just some people you can't tell anything to. They can't take criticism."

"If it's one thing I am," Mrs. Turpin said with feeling, "it's grateful. When I think who all I could have been besides myself and what all I got, a little of everything, and a good disposition besides, I just feel like shouting, 'Thank you, Jesus, for making everything the way it is!' It could have been different!" For one thing, somebody else could have got Claud. At the thought of this, she was flooded with gratitude and a terrible pang of joy ran through her. "Oh thank you, Jesus, Jesus, thank you!" she cried aloud.

The book struck her directly over her left eye. It struck almost at the same instant that she realized the girl was about to hurl it. Before she could utter a sound, the raw face came crashing across the table toward her, howling. The girl's fingers sank like clamps into the soft flesh of her neck. She heard the mother cry out and Claud shout, "Whoa!" There was an instant when she was certain that she was about to be in an earthquake.

All at once her vision narrowed and she saw everything as if it were happening in a small room far away, or as if she were looking at it through the wrong end of a telescope. Claud's face crumpled and fell out of sight. The nurse ran in, then out, then in again. Then the gangling figure of the doctor rushed out of the inner door. Magazines flew this way and that as the table turned over. The girl fell with a thud and Mrs. Turpin's vision suddenly reversed itself and she saw everything large instead of small. The eyes of the white-trashy woman were staring hugely at the floor. There the girl, held down on one side by the nurse and on the other by her mother, was wrenching and turning in their grasp. The doctor was kneeling astride her, trying to hold her arm down. He managed after a second to sink a long needle into it.

Mrs. Turpin felt entirely hollow except for her heart which swung from side to side as if it were agitated in a great empty drum of flesh.

"Somebody that's not busy call for the ambulance," the doctor said in the off-hand voice young doctors adopt for terrible occasions.

Mrs. Turpin could not have moved a finger. The old man who had been sitting next to her skipped nimbly into the office and made the call, for the secretary still seemed to be gone.

"Claud!" Mrs. Turpin called.

He was not in his chair. She knew she must jump up and find him but she felt like some one trying to catch a train in a dream, when everything moves in slow motion and the faster you try to run the slower you go.

"Here I am," a suffocated voice, very unlike Claud's, said. He was doubled up in the corner on the floor, pale as paper, holding his leg. She wanted to get up and go to him but she could not move. Instead, her gaze was drawn slowly downward to the churning face on the floor, which she could see over the doctor's shoulder.

The girl's eyes stopped rolling and focused on her. They seemed a much lighter blue than before, as if a door that had been tightly closed behind them was now open to admit light and air.

Mrs. Turpin's head cleared and her power of motion returned. She leaned forward until she was looking directly into the fierce brilliant eyes. There was no doubt in her mind that the girl did know her, knew her in some intense and personal way, beyond time and place and condition. "What you got to say to me?" she asked hoarsely and held her breath, waiting, as for a revelation.

The girl raised her head. Her gaze locked with Mrs. Turpin's. "Go back to hell where you came from, you old wart hog," she whispered. Her voice was low but clear. Her eyes burned for a moment as if she saw with pleasure that her message had struck its target.

Mrs. Turpin sank back in her chair.

After a moment the girl's eyes closed and she turned her head wearily to the side.

The doctor rose and handed the nurse the empty syringe. He leaned over and put both hands for a moment on the mother's shoulders, which were shaking. She was sitting on the floor, her lips pressed together, holding Mary Grace's hand in her lap. The girl's fingers were gripped like a baby's around her thumb. "Go on to the hospital," he said. "I'll call and make the arrangements."

"Now let's see that neck," he said in a jovial voice to Mrs. Turpin. He began to inspect her neck with his first two fingers. Two little moon-shaped lines like pink fish bones were indented over her windpipe. There was the beginning of an angry red swelling above her eye. His fingers passed over this also.

"Lea' me be," she said thickly and shook him off. "See about Claud. She kicked him."

"I'll see about him in a minute," he said and felt her pulse. He was a thin grey-haired man, given to pleasantries. "Go home and have yourself a vacation the rest of the day," he said and patted her on the shoulder.

Quit your pattin me, Mrs. Turpin growled to herself.

"And put an ice pack over that eye," he said. Then he went and squatted down beside Claud and looked at his leg. After a moment he pulled him up and Claud limped after him into the office.

Until the ambulance came, the only sounds in the room were the tremulous moans of the girl's mother, who continued to sit on the floor. The white-trash woman did not take her eyes off the girl. Mrs. Turpin looked straight ahead at nothing. Presently the ambulance drew up, a long dark shadow, behind the curtain. The attendants came in and set the stretcher down beside the girl and lifted her expertly onto it and carried her out. The nurse helped the mother gather up her things. The shadow of the ambulance moved silently away and the nurse came back in the office.

"That there girl is going to be a lunatic, ain't she?" the white-trash woman asked the nurse, but the nurse kept on to the back and never answered her.

"Yes, she's going to be a lunatic," the white-trash woman said to the rest of them.

"Po' critter," the old woman murmured. The child's face was still in her lap. His eyes looked idly out over her knees. He had not moved during the disturbance except to draw one leg up under him.

"I thank Gawd," the white-trash woman said fervently, "I ain't a lunatic."

Claud came limping out and the Turpins went home.

As their pick-up truck turned into their own dirt road and made the crest of the hill, Mrs. Turpin gripped the window ledge and looked out suspiciously. The land sloped gracefully down through a field dotted with lavender weeds and at the start of the rise their small yellow frame house, with its little flower beds spread out around it like a fancy apron, sat primly in its accustomed place between two giant hickory trees. She would not have been startled to see a burnt wound between two blackened chimneys.

Neither of them felt like eating so they put on their house clothes and lowered the shade in the bedroom and lay down, Claud with his leg on a pillow and herself with a damp washcloth over her eye. The instant she was flat on her back, the image of a razor-backed hog with warts on its face and horns coming out behind its ears snorted into her head. She moaned, a low quiet moan.

"I am not," she said tearfully, "a wart hog. From hell." But the denial had no force. The girl's eyes and her words, even the tone of her voice, low but clear, directed only to her, brooked no repudiation. She had been singled out for the message, though there was trash in the room to whom it might justly have been applied. The full force of this fact struck her only now. There was a woman there who was neglecting her own child but she had been overlooked. The message had been given to Ruby Turpin, a respectable, hard-working, church-going woman. The tears dried. Her eyes began to burn instead with wrath.

She rose on her elbow and the washcloth fell into her hand. Claud was lying on his back, snoring. She wanted to tell him what the girl had said. At the same time, she did not wish to put the image of herself as a wart hog from hell into his mind.

"Hey, Claud," she muttered and pushed his shoulder.

Claud opened one pale baby blue eye.

She looked into it warily. He did not think about anything. He just went his way.

"Wha, whasit?" he said and closed the eye again.

"Nothing," she said. "Does your leg pain you?"

"Hurts like hell," Claud said.

"It'll quit terreckly," she said and lay back down. In a moment Claud was snoring again. For the rest of the afternoon they lay there. Claud slept. She scowled at the ceiling. Occasionally she raised her fist and made a small stabbing motion over her chest as if she was defending her innocence to invisible guests who were like the comforters of Job, reasonable-seeming but wrong.

About five-thirty Claud stirred. "Got to go after those niggers," he sighed, not moving.

She was looking straight up as if there were unintelligible handwriting on the ceiling. The protuberance over her eye had turned a greenish-blue. "Listen here," she said.

"What?"

"Kiss me."

Claud leaned over and kissed her loudly on the mouth. He pinched her side and their hands interlocked. Her expression of ferocious concentration did not change. Claud got up, groaning and growling, and limped off. She continued to study the ceiling.

She did not get up until she heard the pick-up truck coming back with the Negroes. Then she rose and thrust her feet in her brown oxfords, which she did not bother to lace, and stumped out onto the back porch and got her red plastic bucket. She emptied a tray of ice cubes into it and filled it half full of water and went out into the back yard. Every afternoon after Claud brought the hands in, one of the boys helped him put out hay and the rest waited in the back of the truck until he was ready to take them home. The truck was parked in the shade under one of the hickory trees.

"Hi yawl this evening?" Mrs. Turpin asked grimly, appearing with the bucket and the dipper. There were three women and a boy in the truck.

"Us doin nicely," the oldest woman said. "Hi you doin?" and her gaze stuck immediately on the dark lump on Mrs. Turpin's forehead. "You done fell down, ain't you?" she asked in a solicitous voice. The old woman was dark and almost toothless. She had on an old felt hat of Claud's set back on her head. The other two women were younger and lighter and they both had new bright green sun hats. One of them had hers on her head; the other had taken hers off and the boy was grinning beneath it.

Mrs. Turpin set the bucket down on the floor of the truck. "Yawl hep yourselves," she said. She looked around to make sure Claud had gone. "No. I didn't fall down," she said, folding her arms. "It was something worse than that."

"Ain't nothing bad happen to you!" the old woman said. She said it as if they all knew that Mrs. Turpin was protected in some special way by Divine Providence. "You just had you a little fall."

"We were in town at the doctor's office for where the cow kicked Mr. Turpin," Mrs. Turpin said in a flat tone that indicated they could leave off their foolishness. "And there was this girl there. A big fat girl with her face all broke out. I could look at that girl and tell she was peculiar but I couldn't tell how. And me and her mama were just talking and going along and all of a sudden WHAM! She throws this big book she was reading at me and . . ."

"Naw!" the old woman cried out.

"And then she jumps over the table and commences to choke me."

"Naw!" they all exclaimed, "naw!"

"Hi come she do that?" the old woman asked. "What ail her?"

Mrs. Turpin only glared in front of her.

"Somethin ail her," the old woman said.

"They carried her off in an ambulance," Mrs. Turpin continued, "but before she went she was rolling on the floor and they were trying to hold her down to give her a shot and she said something to me." She paused. "You know what she said to me?"

"What she say?" they asked.

"She said," Mrs. Turpin began, and stopped, her face very dark and heavy. The sun was getting whiter and whiter, blanching the sky overhead so that the leaves of the hickory tree were black in the face of it. She could not bring forth the words. "Something real ugly," she muttered.

"She sho shouldn't said nothin ugly to you." the old woman said. "You so sweet. You the sweetest lady I know."

"She pretty too," the one with the hat on said.

"And stout," the other one said. "I never knowed no sweeter white lady."

"That's the truth befo' Jesus," the old woman said. "Amen! You des as sweet and pretty as you can be."

Mrs. Turpin knew just exactly how much Negro flattery was worth and it added to her rage. "She said," she began again and finished this time with a fierce rush of breath, "that I was an old wart hog from hell."

There was an astounded silence.

"Where she at?" the youngest woman cried in a piercing voice.

"Lemme see her, I'll kill her!"

"I'll kill her with you!" the other one cried.

"She b'long in the sylum," the old woman said emphatically. "You the sweetest white lady I know."

"She pretty too," the other two said. "Stout as she can be and sweet. Jesus satisfied with her!"

"Deed he is," the old woman declared.

Idiots! Mrs. Turpin growled to herself. You could never say anything intelligent to a nigger. You could talk at them but not with them. "Yawl ain't drunk your water," she said shortly. "Leave the bucket in the truck when you're finished with it. I got more to do than just stand around and pass the time of day," and she moved off and into the house.

She stood for a moment in the middle of the kitchen. The dark protuberance over her eye looked like a miniature tornado cloud which might any moment sweep across the horizon of her brow. Her lower lip protruded dangerously. She squared her massive shoulders. Then she marched into the front of the house and out the side door and started down the road to the pig parlor. She had the look of a woman going single-handed, weaponless, into battle.

The sun was a deep yellow now like a harvest moon and was riding westward very fast over the far tree line as if it meant to reach the hogs before she did. The road was rutted and she kicked several good-sized stones out of her path as she strode along. The pig parlor was on a little knoll at the end of a lane that ran off from the side of the barn. It was a square of concrete as large as a small room, with a board fence about four feet high around it. The concrete floor sloped slightly so that the hog wash could drain off into a trench where it was carried to the field for fertilizer. Claud was standing on the outside, on the edge of the concrete, hanging onto the top board, hosing down the floor inside. The hose was connected to the faucet of a water trough nearby.

Mrs. Turpin climbed up beside him and glowered down at the hogs inside. There were seven long-snouted bristly shoats in it—tan with liver-colored spots—and an old sow a few weeks off from farrowing. She was lying on her side grunting. The shoats were running about shaking themselves like idiot children, their little slit pig eyes searching the floor for anything left. She had read that pigs were the most intelligent animal. She doubted it. They were supposed to be smarter than dogs. There had even been a pig astronaut. He had performed his assignment perfectly but died of a heart attack afterwards because they left him in his electric suit, sitting upright throughout his examination when naturally a hog should be on all fours.

A-gruntin and a-rooting and a-groanin.

"Gimme that hose," she said, yanking it away from Claud. "Go on and carry them niggers home and then get off that leg."

"You look like you might have swallowed a mad dog," Claud observed, but he got down and limped off. He paid no attention to her humors.

Until he was out of earshot, Mrs. Turpin stood on the side of the pen, holding the hose and pointing the stream of water at the hind quarters of any shoat that looked as if it might try to lie down. When he had had time to get over the hill, she turned her head slightly and her wrathful eyes scanned the path. He was nowhere in sight. She turned back again and seemed to gather herself up. Her shoulders rose and she drew in her breath.

"What do you send me a message like that for?" she said in a low fierce voice, barely above a whisper but with the force of a shout in its concentrated fury. "How am I a hog and me both? How am I saved and from hell too?" Her free fist was knotted and with the other she gripped the hose, blindly pointing the stream of water in and out of the eye of the old sow whose outraged squeal she did not hear.

The pig parlor commanded a view of the back pasture where their twenty beef cows were gathered around the haybales Claud and the boy had put out. The freshly cut pasture sloped down to the highway. Across it was their cotton field and beyond that a dark green dusty wood which they owned as well. The sun was behind the wood, very red, looking over the paling of trees like a farmer inspecting his own hogs.

"Why me?" she rumbled. "It's no trash around here, black or white, that I haven't given to. And break my back to the bone every day working. And do for the church."

She appeared to be the right size woman to command the arena before her. "How am I a hog?" she demanded. "Exactly how am I like them?" and she jabbed the stream of water at the shoats. "There was plenty of trash there. It didn't have to be me.

"If you like trash better, go get yourself some trash then," she railed. "You could have made me trash. Or a nigger. If trash is what you wanted why didn't you make me trash?" She shook her fist with the hose in it and a watery snake appeared momentarily in the air. "I could quit working and take it easy and be filthy," she growled. "Lounge about the sidewalks all day drinking root beer. Dip snuff and spit in every puddle and have it all over my face. I could be nasty.

"Or you could have made me a nigger. It's too late for me to be a nigger," she said with deep sarcasm, "but I could act like one. Lay down in the middle of the road and stop traffic. Roll on the ground."

In the deepening light everything was taking on a mysterious hue. The pasture was growing a peculiar glassy green and the streak of highway had turned lavender. She braced herself for a final assault and this time her voice rolled out over the pasture. "Go on," she yelled, "call me a hog! Call me a hog again. From hell. Call me a wart hog from hell. Put that bottom rail on top. There'll still be a top and bottom!"

A garbled echo returned to her.

A final surge of fury shook her and she roared, "Who do you think you are?"

The color of everything, field and crimson sky, burned for a moment with a transparent intensity. The question carried over the pasture and across the highway and the cotton field and returned to her clearly like an answer from beyond the wood.

She opened her mouth but no sound came out of it.

A tiny truck, Claud's, appeared on the highway, heading rapidly out of sight. Its gears scraped thinly. It looked like a child's toy. At any moment a bigger truck might smash into it and scatter Claud's and the niggers' brains all over the road.

Mrs. Turpin stood there, her gaze fixed on the highway, all her muscles rigid, until in five or six minutes the truck reappeared, returning. She waited until it had had time to turn into their own road. Then like a monumental statue coming to life, she bent her head slowly and gazed, as if through the very heart of mystery, down into the pig parlor at the hogs. They had settled all in one corner around the old sow who was grunting softly. A red glow suffused them. They appeared to pant with a secret life.

Until the sun slipped finally behind the tree line, Mrs. Turpin remained there with her gaze bent to them as if she were absorbing some abysmal life-giving knowledge. At last she lifted her head. There was only a purple streak in the sky, cutting through a field of crimson and leading, like an extension of the highway, into the descending dusk. She raised her hands from the side of the pen in a gesture hieratic and profound. A visionary light settled in her eyes. She saw the streak as a vast swinging bridge extending upward from the earth through a field of living fire. Upon it a vast horde of souls were rumbling toward heaven. There were whole companies of white-trash, clean for the first time in their lives, and bands of black niggers in white robes, and battalions of freaks and lunatics shouting and clapping and leaping like frogs. And bringing up the end of the procession was a tribe of people whom she recognized at once as those who, like herself and Claud, had always had a little of everything and the God-given wit to use it right. She leaned forward to observe them closer. They were marching behind the others with great dignity, accountable as they had always been for good order and common sense and respectable behavior. They alone were on key. Yet she could see by their shocked and altered faces that even their virtues were being burned away. She lowered her hands and gripped the rail of the hog pen, her eyes small but fixed unblinkingly on what lay ahead. In a moment the vision faded but she remained where she was, immobile.

At length she got down and turned off the faucet and made her slow way on the darkening path to the house. In the woods around her the invisible cricket choruses had struck up, but what she heard were the voices of the souls climbing upward into the starry field and shouting hallelujah.

Shirley Ann Grau

(1929–   )

Born on July 8, 1929, in New Orleans, Louisiana, Shirley Ann Grau is known for her realistic portrayal of the South. She was graduated from Tulane University in 1950. In 1955, she published *The Black Prince and Other Stories*, which received critical acclaim. In 1965, she won the Pulitzer Prize for fiction with the novel *The Keepers of the House* (1964). *The Condor Passes* (1971) was a Book-of-the-Month-Club Selection.

Other works include *The Hard Blue Sky* (1958); *The House on Coliseum Street* (1961); *The Wind Shifting West* (1973); *Evidence of Love* (1977); *Nine Women* (1985); and *Roadwalkers* (1994).

Grau and her husband James Kern Feibleman are the parents of four children. Grau continues to write in her home, New Orleans.

The Black Prince

"How art thou fallen from heaven,
O Lucifer, son of the morning!"

Winters are short and very cold; sometimes there is even a snow like heavy frost on the ground. Summers are powdery hot; the white ball sun goes rolling around and around in a sky behind the smoke from the summer fires. There is always a burning somewhere in summer; the pines are dry and waiting; the sun itself starts the smoldering. A pine fire is quiet; there is only a kind of rustle from the flames inside the trunks until the branches and needles go up with a whistling. A whole hill often burns that way, its smoke rising straight up to the white sun, and quiet.

In the plowed patches, green things grow quickly: the ground is rich and there are underground rivers. But there are no big farms: only patches of corn, green beans, and a field or two of cotton (grown for a little cash to spend on Saturdays at Luther's General Store or Willie's Café; these are the only two places for forty miles in any direction). There is good pasture: the green places along the hillsides with pines for shade and sure water in the streams that come down from the Smokies to the north; even in the burnt-out land of five seasons back, shrubs are high. But in the whole country there are only fifty cows, gone wild most of them and dry because they were never milked. They are afraid of men and feed in the farthest ridges and the swamps that are the bottoms of some littlest of the valleys. Their numbers are slowly increasing because no one bothers them. Only once in a while some man with a hankering for cow meat takes his rifle and goes after them. But that is not often; the people prefer pork. Each family keeps enough razorbacks in a run of bark palings.

It is all colored people here, and it is the poorest part of the smallest and worst county in the state. The place at the end of the dirt road leading from the state highway, the place where Luther's Store and Willie's Café stand, does not even have a name in the county records.

The only cool time of the summer day is very early, before the mists have shriveled away. There is a breeze then, a good stiff one out of the Smokies. During the day there is no sound: it is dead hot. But in the early mornings, when the breeze from the north is blowing, it is not so lonesomely quiet: crickets and locusts and the birds that flutter about hunting them, calling frantically as if they had something of importance to settle quick before the heat sets in. (By seven they are quiet again, in the invisible places they have chosen to wait out the day.)

A pine cone rattled down on Alberta's head and bounced from her shoulder. She scooped it from the ground and threw it upward through the branches. "You just keep your cone, mister birds. I got no cause to want it." With a pumping of wings the birds were gone, their cries sliding after them, back down the air. "You just yell your head off. I can hit you any time I want. Any time I want." There was a small round piece of granite at her feet and she tossed it, without particular aim, into the biggest of the bay trees: a gray squirrel with a thin rattail tumbled from the branches and peeped at her from behind the trunk with a pointed little rat face. She jammed her hands in the pockets of her dress and went on, swaggering slightly, cool and feeling good.

She was a handsome girl, taller than most people in her part of the county, and light brown—there had been a lot of white blood in her family, back somewhere, they'd forgot where exactly. She was not graceful—not as a woman is—but light on her feet and supple as a man. Her dress, which the sun had bleached to a whitish color, leaving only a trace of pink along the seams, had shrunk out of size for her: it pulled tight across her broad, slightly hunched, muscled back, even though she had left all the front buttons open down to the waist.

As she walked along, the birds were making even more of a row, knocking loose cones and dry pine needles and old broad bay leaves, and twice she stopped, threw back her head, and called up to them: "Crazy fool birds. Can't do nothing to me. Fool jackass birds." Up ahead, a couple of minutes' walk, was the field and the cotton, bursting white out of the brown cups and waiting to be picked. And she did not feel like working. She leaned against a tree, stretching so that the bark crumbled in her fingers, listening to the birds.

Something different was in their calling. She listened, her head bent forward, her eyes closed, as she sorted the sounds. One jay was wrong: its long sustained note ended with the cluck of a quail. No bird did that. Alberta opened her eyes and looked slowly around. But the pines were thick and close and full of blue night shadow and wrapped with fog that moved like bits of cloth in the wind. Leaving the other bird calls, the whistle became distinct, high, soaring, mocking, like some rare bird, proudly, insolently.

Alberta moved a few steps out from the tree and turned slowly on her heels. The whistle was going around her now, in slow circles, and she turned with it, keeping her eye on the sound, seeing nothing. The birds were still calling and fluttering in the branches, sending bits of twig and bark tumbling down.

Alberta said: "A fool thing you doing. A crazy fool jackass thing." She sat down on a tumbled pile of bricks that had been the chimney of a sugarhouse burned during the Civil War. She spoke in her best tone, while the whistling went round and round her faster. "I reckon you got nothing better to do than go around messing up folks. You got me so riled up I don't reckon I know what way I'm heading in." The sound went around her and around her, but she held her head steady, talking to the pine directly in front of her. "I don't reckon there's nothing for me but set here till you tires out and goes away." The whistle circled her twice and then abruptly stopped, the last high clear note running off down the breeze. Alberta stood up, pulling down her faded dress. "I am mighty glad you come to stopping. I reckon now I can tell what direction I got to go in."

He was right there, leaning on the same pine she had been staring at, cleaning his front teeth with a little green twig and studying her, and she told him to his face: "That was a crazy mean thing, and you ain't got nothing better to do."

"Reckon not," he said, moving the little green twig in and out of the hole between his lower front teeth.

She pushed her hands in the pockets of her dress and looked him over. "Where you come from?"

"Me?" The little green twig went in and out of his teeth with each breath. "I just come straight out the morning."

She turned and walked away. "I be glad to see you go."

He stood in front of her: he had a way of moving without a sound, of popping up in places. "I be sorry to see you go, Alberta Lacy."

She studied him before she answered: tall, not too big or heavy, and black (no other blood but his own in him, she thought). He was dressed nice—a leather jacket with fringe on the sleeves, a red plaid shirt, and new blue denim pants. "How you know what I'm called?" she asked him politely.

He grinned, and his teeth were white and perfect. "I done seen it in the fire," he said. "I done seen it in the fire and I read it clear: Alberta Lacy."

She frowned. "I don't see as how I understand."

He blew the little green twig out of his mouth. "I might could be seeing you again real soon, Alberta Lacy." Then he slipped around the tree like the last trail of night shadow and disappeared.

Alberta stood listening: only the birds and the insects and the wind. Then everything got quiet, and the sun was shining white all around, and she climbed down the slope to the field.

A little field—just a strip of cotton tucked in between two ridges. Her father and her two biggest brothers had planted it with half a morning's work, and they hadn't gone back to tend it once. They didn't even seem to remember it: whatever work they did was in the older fields closer to home. So Alberta had taken it over. Sometimes she brought along the twins: Sidney and Silvia; they were seven: young enough for her to order around and big enough to be a help. But usually she couldn't find them; they were strange ones, gone out of the house for a couple of days at a time in summer, sleeping out somewhere, always sticking together. They were strange little ones and not worth trouble looking for. So most times Alberta worked with Maggie Mary Evans, who was Josh Evans's daughter and just about the only girl her age she was friendly with. From the field there'd be maybe three bales of real early stuff; and they'd split the profit. They worked all morning, pulling off the bolls and dropping them in the sacks they slung crosswise across their shoulders. They worked very slowly, so slowly that at times their hands seemed hardly to move, dozing in the heat. When it got to be noon, when they had no shadow any more, they slipped off the sacks, leaving them between the furrows, and turned to the shade to eat their lunch.

He was waiting for them there, stretched out along the ground with his head propped up on the slender trunk of a little bay tree. He winked lazily at Alberta; his eyes were big and shiny black as oil. "How you, Miss Alberta Lacy?"

Alberta looked down at him, crooking her lips. "You got nothing to do but pester me?"

"Sure I got something to do, but ain't nothing nice like this."

Alberta looked at him through half-closed lids, then sat down to the lunch.

"You hungry, mister?" Maggie Mary asked. She had stood watching, both hands jammed into the belt of her dress, and her eyes moving from one to the other with the quickness and the color of a sparrow.

The man rolled over and looked up at her. "Reckon I am."

"You can have some of our lunch," Maggie Mary said.

Crazy fool, Alberta thought, standing so close with him on the ground like that. He must can see all the way up her. And from the way he lay there, grinning, he must be enjoying it.

"That real nice," he said to Maggie Mary, and crawled over on his stomach to where the lunch bucket was.

Alberta watched his smooth, black hand reaching into the bucket and suddenly she remembered. "How you called?"

He put a piece of corn bread in his mouth, chewed it briefly, and swallowed it with a gulp. "I got three names."

"No fooling," Maggie Mary said, and giggled in her hand. "I got three names, too."

"Stanley Albert Thompson."

"That a good-sounding name," Alberta said. She began to eat her lunch quickly, her mouth too full to talk. Stanley Albert was staring at her, but she didn't raise her eyes. Then he began to sing, low, pounding time with the flat of his hand against the ground.

"Alberta, let you hair hang low,
Alberta, let you hair hang low,
I'll give you more gold than you apron can hold
If you just let you hair hang low."

Alberta got up slowly, not looking at him. "We got work to finish."

Stanley Albert turned over so that his face was pressed in the grass and pine needles. "All you get's the muscles in you arm."

"That right." Maggie Mary nodded quickly. "That right."

"Maggie Mary," Alberta said, "iffen you don't come with me I gonna bop you so hard you land in the middle of tomorrow."

"Good-by, Mr. Stanley Albert Thompson," Maggie Mary said, but he had fallen asleep.

By the time they finished work he was gone; there wasn't even a spot in the pine needles and short grass to show where he had been.

"Ain't that the strangest thing?" Maggie Mary said.

Alberta picked up the small bucket they carried their lunch in. "I reckon not."

"Seemed like he was fixing to wait for us."

"He ain't fixing to wait for nobody, that kind." Alberta rubbed one hand across her shoulders, sighing slightly. "I got a pain fit to kill."

Maggie Mary leaned one arm against a tree and looked off across the little field where they had spent the day. "You reckon he was in here most all morning watching us?"

"Maybe." Alberta began to walk home. Maggie Mary followed slowly, her head still turned, watching the field.

"He musta spent all morning just watching."

"Nothing hard about doing that, watching us break our back out in the sun."

Maggie Mary took one long, loping step and came up with Alberta. "You reckon he coming back?"

Alberta stared full at her, head bent, chewing on her lower lip. "Maggie Mary Evans," she said, "you might could get a thought that he might be wanting you and you might could get a thought that you be wanting him—"

Maggie Mary bent down and brushed the dust off her bare feet carefully, not answering.

"You a plain crazy fool." Alberta planted both hands on her hips and bent her body forward slightly. "A plain crazy fool. You wouldn't be forgetting Jay Mastern?" Jay Mastern had gone off to Ramsey to work at the mill and never come back, but left Maggie Mary to have his baby. So one day Maggie Mary took her pa's best mule and put a blanket on it for a saddle and rode over to Blue Goose Lake, where the old woman lived who could tell her what to do. The old woman gave her medicine in a beer can: whisky and calomel and other things that were a secret. Maggie Mary took the medicine in one gulp, because it tasted so bad, waded way out into Blue Goose Lake so that the water came up to her neck, then dripping wet got up on the mule and whipped him up to a good fast pace all the way home. The baby had come off all right: there wasn't one. And Maggie Mary nearly died. It was something on to three months before she was able to do more than walk around, her arms hanging straight down and stiff and her black skin overtinged with gray.

"You wouldn't be forgetting Jay Mastern?"

"Sure," Maggie Mary said, brushing the dust off her bare feet lightly. "I clean forgot about him."

"Don't you be having nothing to do with this here Stanley Albert Thompson."

Maggie Mary began to walk again, slowly, smiling just a little bit with one corner of her mouth. "Sounds like you been thinking about him for yourself."

Alberta jammed both hands down in the pockets of her dress. "I been thinking nothing of the sort."

"Willie'll kill him."

Alberta chewed on one finger. "I reckon he could care for himself."

Maggie Mary smiled to herself softly, remembering. "I reckon he could; he's real fine-appearing man."

"He was dressed good."

"Where you reckon he come from?" Maggie Mary asked.

Alberta shrugged. "He just come walking out of the morning fog."

That was how he came into this country: he appeared one day whistling a bird call in the woods in high summer. And he stayed on. The very first Saturday night he went down to Willie's and had four fights and won them all.

Willie's was an ordinary house made of pine slabs, older than most of the other houses, but more solid. There were two rooms: a little one where Willie lived (a heavy scrolled ironwork bed, a square oak dresser, a chest, a three-footed table, and on its cracked marble top a blue-painted mandolin without strings). And a big room: the café. Since anybody could remember, the café had been there with Willie's father or his grandfather, as long as there had been people in these parts. And that had been a long while: long before the Civil War even, runaways were settling here, knowing they'd be safe and hidden in the rough, uneven hills and the pines.

Willie had made some changes in the five or six years since his father died. He painted the counter that was the bar with varnish; that had not been a good idea: the whisky took the varnish off in a few weeks. And he painted the walls: bright blue. Then he went over them again, shaking his brush so that the walls were flecked like a mockingbird's eggs. But Willie used red to fleck—red against blue. And the mirror, gilt-edged, and hanging from a thick gold cord: that had been Willie's idea, too. He'd found it one day, lying on the shoulder alongside the state highway; it must have fallen from a truck somehow. So he took it home. It was cracked in maybe two dozen pieces. Anyone who looked into it would see his face split up into a dozen different parts, all separate. But Willie hung it right over the shelves where he kept his whisky and set one of the kerosene lamps in front of it so that the light should reflect yellow-bright from all the pieces. One of them fell out (so that Willie had to glue it back with flour and water) the night Stanley Albert had his fourth fight, which he won like the other three. Not a man in the country would stand up like that, because fighting at Willie's on Saturday night is a rough affair with razors, or knives, or bottles.

Not a man in the country could have matched the way Stanley Albert fought that night, his shirt off, and his black body shining with sweat, the muscles along his neck and shoulders twisting like grass snakes. There wasn't a finer-looking man and there wasn't a better: he proved that.

The first three fights were real orderly affairs. Everybody could see what was coming minutes ahead, and Willie got the two of them out in the yard before they got at each other. And everybody who was sober enough to walk went out on the porch and watched Stanley Albert pound first Ran Carey's and then Henry Johnson's head up and down in the dust. Alberta sat on the porch (Willie had brought her a chair from inside) and watched Stanley Albert roll around the dust of the yard and didn't even blink an eye, not even during the third fight when Tim Evans, who was Maggie Mary's brother, pull a razor. The razor got Stanley Albert all down one cheek, but Tim didn't have any teeth left and one side of his face got punched in so that it looked peculiar always afterward. Maggie Mary went running down into the yard, not bothering with her brother, to press her finger up against the little cut across Stanley Albert's cheek.

The fourth fight came up so suddenly nobody had time hardly to get out of the way: Joe Turner got one arm hooked around Stanley Albert's neck from behind. There wasn't any reason for it, except maybe that Joe was so drunk he didn't see who he had and that once there's been a couple of fights there's always more. Stanley Albert swung a bottle over his shoulder to break the hold and then nobody could see exactly what was happening: they were trying so hard to get clear. Willie pulled Alberta over the bar and pushed her down behind it and crouched alongside her, grinning. "That some fighter." And when it was all over they stood up again; first thing they saw was Joe Turner down on the floor and Stanley Albert leaning on a chair with Maggie dabbing at a cut on his hand with the edge of her petticoat.

He got a reputation from that Saturday night, and everybody was polite to him, and he could have had just about any of the girls he wanted. But he didn't seem to want them; at least he never took to coming to the houses to see them or to taking them home from Willie's. Maggie Mary Evans swore up and down that he had got her one day when she was fishing in Scanos River, but nobody paid her much attention. She liked to make up stories that way.

He had a little house in a valley to the east. Some boys who had gone out to shoot a cow for Christmas meat said they saw it. But they didn't go close even if there was three of them with a shotgun while Stanley Albert only carried a razor. Usually people only saw him on Saturday nights, and after a while they got used to him, though none of the men ever got to be friendly with him. There wasn't any mistaking the way the girls watched him. But after four or five Saturdays, by the time the summer was over, everybody expected him and waited for him, the way you'd wait for a storm to come or a freeze: not liking it, but not being able to do anything either. That's the way it went along: he'd buy his food for the coming week at Luther's Store, and then he'd come next door to Willie's.

He never stood up at the counter that was the bar. He'd take his glass and walk over to a table and sit down, and pull out a little bottle from his pocket, and add white lightning to the whisky. There wasn't anything could insult Willie more. He made the whisky and it was the best stuff in the county. He even had some customers drive clear out from Montgomery to buy some of his corn, and, being good stuff, there wasn't any call to add anything: it had enough kick of its own; raw and stinging to the throat. It was good stuff; nobody added anything to it—except Stanley Albert Thompson, while Willie looked at him and said things under his breath. But nothing ever came of it, because everybody remembered how good a job Stanley Albert had done the first night he came.

Stanley Albert always had money, enough of it to pay for the groceries and all the whisky he wanted. There was always the sound of silver jingling in his trouser pocket. Everybody could hear that. Once when Willie was standing behind the bar, shuffling a pack of cards with a wide fancy twirl—just for amusement—Stanley Albert, who had had a couple of drinks and was feeling especially good, got up and pulled a handful of coins out of his pocket. He began to shuffle them through the air, the way Willie had done with the cards. Stanley Albert's black hands flipped the coins back and forth, faster and faster, until there was a solid silver ring hanging and shining in the air. Then Stanley Albert let one of his hands drop to his side and the silver ring poured back into the other hand and disappeared with a little clinking sound. And he dropped the money into his pocket with a short quick laugh.

That was the way Stanley Albert used his money: he had fun with it. Only thing, one night when Stanley Albert had had maybe a bit too much and sat dozing at his table, Morris Henry slipped a hand into the pocket. He wouldn't have ever dared to do that if Stanley Albert hadn't been dozing, leaning back in his chair, the bottle of white lightning empty in one hand. And Morris Henry slipped his little hand in the pocket and felt all around carefully. Then he turned his head slowly in a circle, looking at everybody in the room. He was a little black monkey Negro and his eyes were shiny and flat as mirrors. He slipped his hand back and scurried out into the yard and hid in the blackberry bushes. He wouldn't move until morning came; he just sat there, chewing on his little black fingers with his wide flaring yellow teeth. Anybody who wanted to know what was happening had to go out there and ask him. And ever afterwards Morris Henry swore that there hadn't been anything at all in Stanley Albert Thompson's pocket. But then everybody knew Morris Henry was crazy because just a few minutes later when Stanley Albert woke up and walked across to the bar, the change jingled in the pocket and he laid five quarters on the counter. And the money was good enough because Willie bounced it on the counter and it gave the clear ring of new silver.

Stanley Albert had money all right and he spent it; there wasn't anything short about him. He'd buy drinks for anybody who'd come over to his table; the only ones who came were the girls. And he didn't seem to care how much they drank. He'd just sit there, leaning way back in his chair, grinning, his teeth white and big behind his black lips, and matching them drink for drink, and every now and then running his eye up and down their length just to let them know he was appreciating their figures. Most often it was Maggie Mary who would be sitting there, warning all the other girls away with a little slanting of her eyes when they got near. And sometimes he'd sing a song: a song about whisky that would make everyone forget they didn't like him and laugh; or a song about poor boys who were going to be hanged in the morning. He had a good voice, strong and clear, and he pounded time with the flat of his hand on the table. And he'd always be looking at Alberta when he was singing until she'd get up, holding her head high and stiff, and march over to where Willie was and take hold of his arm real sweet and smile at him. And Willie would give Stanley Albert a quick mean look and then pour her a drink of his best whisky.

Stanley Albert had a watch, a big heavy gold one, round almost as a tomato, that would strike the hours. (That was how you could tell he was around sometimes— hearing his watch strike.) It was attached to a broad black ribbon and sometimes he held it up, let it swing before the eyes of whatever girl it happened to be at the time, let it swing slowly back and forth, up and down, so that her head moved with it. He had a ring too, on his right little finger: a white-colored band with a stone big as a chip of second coal and dark green. And when he fought, the first time he came into Willie's, the ring cut the same as a razor in his hand; it was maybe a little more messy, because its edges were jagged.

Those were two things—the watch and the ring—that must have cost more than all the money around here in a year. That was why all the women liked him so; they kept thinking of the nice things he could give them if he got interested. And that was why the men hated him. Things can go as smooth as glass if everybody's got about the same things and the same amount of money knocking around in a jean pocket on Saturday night. But when they don't, things begin happening. It would have been simpler maybe if they could have fought Stanley Albert Thompson, but there wasn't any man keen to fight him. That was how they started fighting each other. A feud that no-body'd paid any mind to for eight or ten years started up again.

It began one Sunday morning along toward dawn when everyone was feeling tired and leaving Willie's. Stanley Albert had gone out first and was sitting aside the porch railing. Jim Mastern was standing on the lowest step not moving, just staring across the fields, not being able to see anything in the dark, except maybe the bright-colored patterns the whisky set shooting starwise before his eyes. And Randall Stevens was standing in the doorway, looking down at his own foot, which he kept moving in a little circle around and around on the floor boards. And Stanley Albert was looking hard at him. Randall Stevens didn't lift his head; he just had his razor out and was across the porch in one minute, bringing down his arm in a sweeping motion to get at Jim Mastern's neck. But he was too drunk to aim very straight and he missed; but he did cut the ear away so that it fell on the steps. Jim Mastern was off like a bat in the daylight, running fast, crashing into things, holding one hand to the side of his head. And Randall Stevens folded up the razor and slipped it back in his pocket and walked off slowly, his head bent over, as if he was sleepy. There wasn't any more sense to it than that; but it started the feud again.

Stanley Albert swung his legs over the railing and stretched himself and yawned. Nobody noticed except Alberta, they were so busy listening to the way Jim Mastern was screaming and running across the fields, and watching Randall Stevens march off, solemnly, like a priest.

And the next night Randall Stevens tumbled down the steps of his cabin with his head full of scatter shot. It was a Monday night in November. His mother came out to see and stepped square on him, and his blood spattered on the hoarfrost. Randall Stevens had six brothers, and the next night they rode their lanky burred horses five miles south and tried to set fire to the Mastern house. That was the beginning; the fighting kept up, off and on, all through the winter. The sheriff from Gloverston came down to investigate. He came driving down the road in the new shiny white state police patrol car—the only one in the county—stopped in Willie's Café for a drink and went back taking two gallons of home brew with him. That wasn't exactly right, maybe, seeing that he had taken an oath to uphold the law; but he couldn't have done much, except get killed. And that was certain.

The Stevenses and their friends took to coming to Willie's on Friday nights; the Masterns kept on coming on Saturday. That just made two nights Willie had to keep the place open and the lamps filled with kerosene; the crowd was smaller; shotguns were leaning against the wall.

That's the way it went all winter. Everybody got on one side or the other—everybody except Stanley Albert Thompson. They both wanted him: they had seen what he could do in a fight. But Stanley Albert took to coming a night all by himself: Sunday night, and Willie had to light all the lamps for just him and stand behind the counter and watch him sit at the table adding lightning to the whisky.

Once along toward the end of February when Cy Mastern was killed and the roof of his house started burning with pine knots tossed from the ground, Stanley Albert was standing just on the rim of the light, watching. He helped the Masterns carry water, but Ed Stevens, who was hiding up in top of a pine to watch, swore that the water was like kerosene in his hands. Wherever he'd toss a bucketful, the fire would shoot up, brighter and hotter than before.

By March the frosts stopped, and there weren't any more cold winds. The farmers came out every noon, solemnly, and laid their hands on the bare ground to see if it was time to put in their earliest corn and potatoes. But the ground stayed cold a long time that year so that there wasn't any plowing until near May. All during that time from March till May there wasn't anything doing; that was the worst time for the fighting. In the winter your hand shakes so with the cold that you aren't much good with a gun or knife. But by March the air is warmer and you don't have any work to get you tired, so you spend all the time thinking.

That spring things got bad. There wasn't a crowd any more at Willie's though he kept the place open and the lights on for the three nights of the week-end. Neither the Stevenses nor the Masterns would come; they were too easy targets in a house with wall lamps burning. And on Sunday night the only person who ever came was Stanley Albert Thompson. He'd sit and drink his whisky and lightning and maybe sing a song or two for the girls who came over to see him. By the end of April that was changed too. He finally got himself the girl he wanted; the one he'd been waiting around nearly all winter for. And his courting was like this:

Thomas Henry Lacy and his sons, Luke and Tom, had gone for a walk, spoiling for a fight. They hadn't seen anything all evening, just some of the cows that had gone wild and went crashing away through the blueberry bushes. Alberta had taken herself along with them, since she was nearly as good as a man in a fight. They had been on the move all night but keeping in the range of a couple of miles and on the one side of the Scanos River. They were for Stevens and there was no telling what sort of affair the Masterns had rigged up on their ground. They rested for a while on the bluff of the river. Tom had some bread in his pocket and they ate it there, wondering if there was anybody in the laurels across the river just waiting for them to show themselves. Then they walked on again, not saying very much, seeing nothing but the moon flat against the sky and its light shiny on the heavy dew.

Alberta didn't particularly care when they left her behind. She turned her head to listen to the plaintive gargling call of a night quail, and when she looked again her father and the boys were gone. She knew where she was: on the second ridge away from home. There was just the big high ridge there to the left. The house was maybe twenty minutes away, but a hard walk, and Alberta was tired. She'd been washing all day, trying to make the clear brook water carry off the dirt and grease from the clothes, her mother standing behind her, yelling at each spot that remained, her light face black almost as her husband's with temper, and her gray fuzzy hair tied into knots like a pickaninny's. The boys had spent the whole day dozing in the shed while they put a new shoe on the mule.

Alberta listened carefully; there was nothing but night noises; her father and the boys would be halfway home by now, scrambling down the rain-washed sides of the ridge. For a moment she considered following them. "Ain't no raving rush, girl," she told herself aloud. The night was cool, but there wasn't any wind. With her bare feet she felt the dry pine needles, then sat down on them, propping her back against a tree. She slipped the razor from the cord around her neck and held it open loosely in the palm of her hand; then she fell asleep.

She woke when the singing started, opening her eyes but not moving. The moon was right overhead, shining down so that the trunks of the pines stuck straight up out of the white shiny ground. There wasn't a man could hide behind a pine, yet she didn't see him. Only the singing going round and round her.

> *"Alberta, what's on you mind,*
> *Alberta, why you treat me so unkind?*
> *You keep me worried; you keep me blue*
> *All the time,*
> *Alberta, why you treat me so unkind?"*

She pushed herself up to a sitting position, still looking straight ahead, not following the song around and around. She let the hand that held the razor fall in her lap, so that the moon struck on the blade.

> *"Alberta, why you treat me so unkind?"*

Nothing grows under pines, not much grass even, not any bushes big enough to hide a man. Only pine trees, like black matches stuck in the moonlight. Black like matches, and thin like matches. There wasn't a man could hide behind a pine under a bright moon. There wasn't a man could pass a bright open space and not be seen.

> *"Alberta, let you hair hang low,*
> *Alberta, let you hair hang low,*
> *I'll give you more gold*
> *Than you apron can hold."*

"That ain't a very nice song," she said.

"I'll give you more gold
Than you apron can hold."

She lifted her right hand and turned the razor's edge slowly in the light. "I got silver of my own right here," she said. "That enough for me."

The song went round in a circle, round and round, weaving in and out of the pines, passing invisible across the open moon filled spaces.

"Alberta, let you hair hang low,
I'll give you more gold
Than you apron can hold
If you just let you hair hang low."

There wasn't a man alive could do that. Go round and round.

"Alberta, why you treat me so unkind?"

Round and round, in and out the thin black trees. Alberta stood up, following the sound, turning on her heel.

"You keep me worried, you keep me blue
All the time."

"I plain confused," she said. "I don't reckon I understand."

"I'll give you more gold
Than you apron can hold."

"I ain't got no apron," she said.

"Alberta, let you hair hang low,
Just let you hair hang low."

The song stopped and Stanley Albert Thompson came right out of a patch of bright moon ground, where there were only brown pine needles.

Alberta forgot she was tired; the moon-spotted ground rolled past her feet like the moon in the sky—effortless. She recognized the country they passed through: Blue Goose Lake, Scanos River, and the steeper rough ground of the north part of the country, toward the Tennessee border. It was a far piece to walk and she wondered at the lightness of her feet. By moonset they had got there—the cabin that the boys had seen one day while they were hunting cows. She hesitated a little then, not afraid, not reluctant, but just not sure how to go on. Stanley Albert Thompson had been holding her hand all evening; he still held it. Right at the beginning when he had first taken her along with him, she'd shook her head, no, she could walk; no man needed to lead her. But he'd grinned at her, and shook his head, imitating her gesture, so that the moon sparkled on his black curly hair, and his black broad forehead, and he took her hand and led her so that the miles seemed nothing and the hours like smooth water.

He showed her the cabin, from the outside first: mustard color, trimmed with white, like the cabins the railroad company builds. One room with high peaked roof.

"A real fine house," she said. "A real fine house. You work for the railroad?"

"No."

He took her inside. "You light with candles," she said.

"I ain't ever been able to stand the smell of lamps," he said.

"But it's a real nice house. I might could learn to like it."

"No might could about it." He smoothed the cloth on the table with his fingers. "You going to like it."

She bent her head and looked at him through her eyelashes. "Now I don't rightly know. Seems as how I don't know you."

"Sure you do," he said. "I'm standing right here."

"Seems as how I don't know nothing. You might could have a dozen girls all over this here state."

"I reckon there's a dozen," he said.

She glared at him, hands on hips. "You old fool jackass," she said. "I reckon you can just keep everything."

He jammed his hands into the back pockets of his denim pants and bent backward staring at the ceiling.

"Ain't you gonna try to stop me?"

"Nuh-uh."

She leaned against the doorjamb and twisted her neck to look at him. "Ain't you sorry I going?"

"Sure." He was still staring upward at the ceiling with its four crossed beams. "Sure, I real sorry."

"I don't see as how I could stay though."

"Sure you could." He did not look at her.

"I don't see as how. You ain't give me none of the things you said."

"You a driving woman," he said, and grinned, his mouth wide and white in the dark of his face.

Then he sat down at the table. There were five candles there, stuck in bottles, but only one was lighted, the one in the center. Wax had run all down the side of the candle and down the bottle in little round blobs, nubby like gravel. He picked one off, dirty white between his black fingers. He rolled it slowly between his flat palms, back and forth. Then he flipped it toward Alberta. It flashed silvery through the circle of lamplight and thudded against her skirt. She bent forward to pick it up: a coin, new silver. As she bent there, another one struck her shoulder, and another. Stanley Albert Thompson sat at the table, grinning and tossing the coins to her, until she had filled both pockets of her dress.

He pushed the candle away from him. "You all right, I reckon, now."

She held one coin in her hands, turning it over and over.

"That ain't what you promised. I remember how you came and sang:

'I give you more gold
Than you apron can hold.'"

"Sure," he said and lifted a single eyebrow, very high. "I can do that all right, iffen you want it. I reckon I can do that."

She stood for a moment studying him. And Stanley Albert Thompson, from where he still sat at the table, curled up one corner of his mouth.

And very slowly Alberta began to smile. "I might could like it here," she said. "If you was real nice."

He got up then and rubbed her cheek very gently with his first finger. "I might could do that," he said. "I don't reckon it would be too heavy a thing to do."

The candle was on the table to one side. It caught the brightness of Alberta's eyes as she stood smiling at Stanley Albert Thompson. The steady yellow light threw her shadow over his body, a dark shadow that reached to his chin. His own shadow was on the wall behind. She glanced at it over his shoulder and giggled. "You better do something about your shadow there, Mr. Thompson. That there is a ugly shadow, sure."

He turned his head and glanced at it briefly. "Reckon so," he said.

It was an ugly shadow, sure. Alberta looked at Stanley Albert Thompson and shook her head. "I can't hardly believe it," she said. "You a right pretty man."

He grinned at her and shook himself so that the shadow on the wall spun around in a wild turn.

"I don't reckon you can do anything about it?"

"No," he said briefly. "I can't go changing my shadow." He hunched his back so that the figure on the wall seemed to jump up and down in anger.

She stepped over to him, putting her hands behind her, leaning backward to see his face. "If he don't do any more than dance on a wall, I ain't complaining."

Stanley Albert stood looking down at her, looking down the length of his face at her, and rocking slowly back and forth on his heels. "No," he said. "He ain't gonna do more than wiggle around the wall sometimes. But you can bet I am."

The coins weighed down the pockets of her dress, and his hands were warm against her skin. "I reckon I'm satisfied," she said.

That was the way it began. That was the courting. The woman was young and attractive and strong. The man could give her whatever she wanted. There were other courtings like that in this country. Every season there were courtings like that.

People would see them around sometimes; or sometimes they'd only hear them when they were still far off. Sometimes it would be Stanley Albert Thompson singing:

"Alberta, let you hair hang low,
Alberta, let you hair hang low.
I'll give you more gold
Than you apron can hold
If you just let you hair hang low."

He had a strong voice. It could carry far in a quiet day or night. And if any of the people heard it, they'd turn and look at each other and nod their heads toward it, not saying anything, but just being sure that everyone was listening. And whenever Willie heard it, he'd close his eyes for a minute, seeing Alberta; and then he'd rub his hands all over his little black kinky head and whistle: "Euuuu," which meant that he was very, very sorry she had left him.

And sometimes all you could hear of them would be the chiming of Stanley Albert's watch every quarter-hour. One night that August, when the moon was heavy and hot and low, Maggie Mary was out walking with Jack Belden. She heard the clear high chime and remembered the nights at Willie's and the dangling gold watch. And she turned to Jack Belden, who had just got her comfortable in one arm, and jammed her fingers in his eyes and ran off after the sound. She didn't find them; and it wouldn't have much mattered if she had. Stanley Albert was much too gone on Alberta to notice any other woman in more than a passing appraising way.

And sometimes people would come on them walking alone, arms around each other's waist; or sitting in a shady spot during the day's heat, his head on her lap and both of them dozing and smiling a little. And everybody who saw them would turn around and get out of there fast; but neither of them turned a head or looked up: there might not have been anyone there.

And then every night they'd go down to Willie's. The first night they came—it was on a Thursday—the place was closed up tight. There wasn't ever anybody came on Thursday. Stanley Albert went around back to where Willie lived and pounded on the door, and when Willie didn't answer he went around to the front again where Alberta was waiting on the steps and kicked in the front panel of the wood door. Willie came scuttling out, his eyes round and bewildered like a suckling's and saw them sitting at one of the tables drinking his home brew, only first putting lightning into it. After that they came every night, just them. It was all most people could do to afford a drink on Saturday or the week-end, but some of them would walk over to Willie's just to look at Stanley Albert and Alberta sitting there. They'd stand at the windows and look in, sweating in the hot summer nights and looking. Maybe a few of them would still be there waiting when Stanley and Alberta got ready to go, along toward morning.

That's what they did every single night of the year or so they were together. If they fell asleep, Willie would just have to stand waiting. They'd go out with their arms around each other's waist, staggering some, but not falling. And an hour or so later, people who were going out before dawn to get a little work done in the cool would see them clear over on the other side of the county, at Goose Lake, maybe, a good three hours' walk for a man cold sober. Willie had his own version of how they got around. They just picked up their feet, he said, and went sliding off down the winds. Once, he said, when they were sitting over on the bench against the wall, Stanley Albert flat on it with his head on her lap, when the whisky made the man in him come up sudden, so he couldn't wait, they went straight out the window, up the air, like a whistle sound. Willie had the broken glass to show the next morning, if you wanted to believe him.

Willie hated them, the two of them, maybe because they broke his glass, maybe because they made him stay up late every single night of the week, so that he had to hold his eyes open with his fingers, and watch them pour lightning into his very best whisky, maybe because he had wanted Alberta mighty bad himself. He'd been giving her presents—bottles of his best stuff—but he just couldn't match Stanley Albert. Those are three reasons; maybe he had others. And Maggie Mary hated them; and she had only one reason.

Once Pete Stokes shot at Stanley Albert Thompson. He hadn't wanted to: he was scared like everybody else. But Maggie Mary Evans talked him into it. She was a fine-looking girl: she could do things like that. He hid behind the privy and got a perfect bead on Stanley Albert as he came out the door. The bullet just knocked off a piece of Willie's doorframe. When Pete saw what happened he dropped the gun and began to run, jumping the rail fence and crashing face-first through the thick heavy berry bushes. Stanley Albert pursed his lips together and rubbed his hands on his chin, slow, like he was deciding what to do. Then he jumped down from the porch and went after Pete. He ran through the hackberries too; only with him it did not seem difficult: none of the crackling and crashing and waving arms. Stanley Albert just put his head down and moved his legs, and the sprays of the bushes, some of them thick as a roosters spur, seemed to pull back and make way. Nobody saw the fight: the brave ones were too drunk to travel fast; and the sober ones didn't want to mix with a man like Stanley Albert, drunk and mad. Alberta, she just ran her hand across her mouth and then wiped it along the side of her green satin dress, yawning like she was tired. She stood listening for a while, her head cocked a little, though there wasn't anything to hear, then walked off, pulling down the dress across her hips. And the next night she and Stanley Albert were back at Willie's, and Pete never did turn up again. Willie used to swear that he ended up in the Scanos River and that if the water wasn't so yellow muddy, that if you could see to the bottom, you would see Pete lying there, along with all the others Stanley Albert had killed.

At the last it was Willie who got the idea. For a week, carefully, he put aside the coins Stanley Albert gave him. There were a lot of them, all new silver, because Stanley Albert always paid in silver. Then one morning very early, just after Stanley Albert and Alberta left, Willie melted the coins down, and using the molds he kept for his old outsized pistol, he cast four bullets.

He made a special little shelf for the pistol under the counter so that it would be near at hand. And he waited all evening, sometimes touching the heavy black handle with the tips of his fingers; and he waited, hoping that Stanley Albert would drink enough to pass out. But of course nothing like that happened. So Willie poured himself three or four fingers of his best stuff and swallowed it fast as his throat would stand, then he blinked his little eyes fast for a second or so to clear his vision, and he reached for the gun. He got two shots over the bar, two good ones: the whole front of Stanley Albert's plaid shirt folded together and sank in, after the silver bullets went through. He got up, holding the table edge, unsteady, bending over, looking much smaller, his black skin gray-filmed and dull. His eyes were larger: they reached almost across his face— and they weren't dark any more; they were silver, two polished pieces of silver. Willie was afraid to fire again; the pistol shook where he held it in his two hands.

Then Stanley Albert walked out, not unsteady any more, but bent over the hole in his chest, walked out slowly with his eyes shining like flat metal, Alberta a few steps behind. They passed right in front of Willie, who still hadn't moved; his face was stiff with fear. Quietly, smoothly, in a single motion, almost without interrupting her step, Alberta picked up a bottle (the same one from which he had poured his drink moments before) and swung it against Willie's head. He slipped down in a quiet little heap, his legs folded under him, his black kinky head on top. But his idea had worked: over by Stanley Albert's chair there was a black pool of blood.

All that was maybe eight or ten years ago. People don't see them any more—Stanley and Alberta. They don't think much about them, except when something goes wrong— like weevils getting in the cotton, or Willie's burning down and Willie inside it—then they begin to think that those two had a hand in it. Brad Tedrow swore that he had seen Stanley Albert that night, just for a second, standing on the edge of the circle of light, with a burning faggot in his hand. And the next morning Brad went back to look, knowing that your eyes play tricks at night in firelight; he went back to look for footprints or some sign. All he found was a burnt-out stick of pine wood that anybody could have dropped.

And kids sometimes think they hear the jingle of silver in Stanley Albert's pocket, or the sound of his watch. And when women talk—when there's been a miscarriage or a stillbirth—they remember and whisper together.

And they all wonder if that's not the sort of work they do, the two of them. Maybe so; maybe not. The people themselves are not too sure. They don't see them around any more.

Harper Lee

(1926–   )

Nelle Harper Lee, a descendent of Robert E. Lee, was born on April 28, 1926, in Monroeville, Alabama. She attended Huntingdon College in Alabama from 1944 to 1945, then studied law at the University of Alabama from 1945 to 1949. She was an exchange student at Oxford University in England from 1949 to 1950.

Lee's only published novel, *To Kill a Mockingbird* (1960), won the Pulitzer Prize in 1961 and became an international bestseller. The book has never been out of print. In 1995, HarperCollins published the thirty-fifth anniversary edition. The novel was made into a 1962 film, which starred Gregory Peck, who received an Oscar for Best Actor for his portrayal of Atticus Finch, a character based on Lee's father, Amasa Lee. The character Dill is based on Lee's lifelong friend Truman Capote.

Lee divides her time between New York City and Monroeville, where she lives with her sister Alice, a retired attorney.

from *To Kill a Mockingbird*

1

When he was nearly thirteen, my brother Jem got his arm badly broken at the elbow. When it healed, and Jem's fears of never being able to play football were assuaged, he was seldom self-conscious about his injury. His left arm was somewhat shorter than his right; when he stood or walked, the back of his hand was at right angles to his body, his thumb parallel to his thigh. He couldn't have cared less, so long as he could pass and punt.

When enough years had gone by to enable us to look back on them, we sometimes discussed the events leading to his accident. I maintain that the Ewells started it all, but Jem, who was four years my senior, said it started long before that. He said it began the summer Dill came to us, when Dill first gave us the idea of making Boo Radley come out.

I said if he wanted to take a broad view of the thing, it really began with Andrew Jackson. If General Jackson hadn't run the Creeks up the creek, Simon Finch would never have paddled up the Alabama, and where would we be if he hadn't? We were far too old to settle an argument with a fist-fight, so we consulted Atticus. Our father said we were both right.

Being Southerners, it was a source of shame to some members of the family that we had no recorded ancestors on either side of the Battle of Hastings. All we had was Simon Finch, a fur-trapping apothecary from Cornwall whose piety was exceeded only by his stinginess. In England, Simon was irritated by the persecution of those who called themselves Methodists at the hands of their more liberal brethren, and as Simon called himself a Methodist, he worked his way across the Atlantic to Philadelphia, thence to Jamaica, thence to Mobile, and up the Saint Stephens. Mindful of John Wesley's strictures on the use of many words in buying and selling, Simon made a pile practicing medicine, but in this pursuit he was unhappy lest he be tempted into doing what he knew was not for the glory of God, as the putting on of gold and costly apparel. So Simon, having forgotten his teacher's dictum on the possession of human chattels, bought three slaves and with their aid established a homestead on the banks of the Alabama River some forty miles above Saint Stephens. He returned to Saint Stephens only once, to find a wife, and with her established a line that ran high to daughters. Simon lived to an impressive age and died rich.

It was customary for the men in the family to remain on Simon's homestead, Finch's Landing, and make their living from cotton. The place was self-sufficient: modest in comparison with the empires around it, the Landing nevertheless produced everything required to sustain life except ice, wheat flour, and articles of clothing, supplied by river-boats from Mobile.

Simon would have regarded with impotent fury the disturbance between the North and the South, as it left his descendants stripped of everything but their land, yet the tradition of living on the land remained unbroken until well into the twentieth century, when my father, Atticus Finch, went to Montgomery to read law, and his younger brother went to Boston to study medicine. Their sister Alexandra was the Finch who remained at the Landing: she married a taciturn man who spent most of his time lying in a hammock by the river wondering if his trot-lines were full.

When my father was admitted to the bar, he returned to Maycomb and began his practice. Maycomb, some twenty miles east of Finch's Landing, was the county seat of Maycomb County. Atticus's office in the courthouse contained little more than a hat rack, a spittoon, a checkerboard and an unsullied Code of Alabama. His first two clients were the last two persons hanged in the Maycomb County jail. Atticus had urged them to accept the state's generosity in allowing them to plead Guilty to second-degree murder and escape with their lives, but they were Haverfords, in Maycomb County a name synonymous with jackass. The Haverfords had dispatched Maycomb's leading blacksmith in a misunderstanding arising from the alleged wrongful detention of a mare, were imprudent enough to do it in the presence of three witnesses, and insisted that the-son-of-a-bitch-had-it-coming-to-him was a good enough defense for anybody. They persisted in pleading Not Guilty to first-degree murder, so there was nothing much Atticus could do for his clients except be present at their departure, an occasion that was probably the beginning of my father's profound distaste for the practice of criminal law.

During his first five years in Maycomb, Atticus practiced economy more than anything; for several years thereafter he invested his earnings in his brother's education. John Hale Finch was ten years younger than my father, and chose to study medicine at a time when cotton was not worth growing; but after getting Uncle Jack started, Atticus derived a reasonable income from the law. He liked Maycomb, he was Maycomb County born and bred; he knew his people, they knew him, and because of Simon Finch's industry, Atticus was related by blood or marriage to nearly every family in the town.

Maycomb was an old town, but it was a tired old town when I first knew it. In rainy weather the streets turned to red slop; grass grew on the sidewalks, the courthouse sagged in the square. Somehow, it was hotter then: a black dog suffered on a summer's day; bony mules hitched to Hoover carts flicked flies in the sweltering shade of the live oaks on the square. Men's stiff collars wilted by nine in the morning. Ladies bathed before noon, after their three-o'clock naps, and by nightfall were like soft teacakes with frostings of sweat and sweet talcum.

People moved slowly then. They ambled across the square, shuffled in and out of the stores around it, took their time about everything. A day was twenty-four hours long but seemed longer. There was no hurry, for there was nowhere to go, nothing to buy and no money to buy it with, nothing to see outside the boundaries of Maycomb County. But it was a time of vague optimism for some of the people: Maycomb County had recently been told that it had nothing to fear but fear itself.

We lived on the main residential street in town—Atticus, Jem and I, plus Calpurnia our cook. Jem and I found our father satisfactory: he played with us, read to us, and treated us with courteous detachment.

Calpurnia was something else again. She was all angles and bones; she was nearsighted; she squinted; her hand was wide as a bed slat and twice as hard. She was always ordering me out of the kitchen, asking me why I couldn't behave as well as Jem when she knew he was older, and calling me home when I wasn't ready to come. Our battles were epic and one-sided. Calpurnia always won, mainly because Atticus always took her side. She had been with us ever since Jem was born, and I had felt her tyrannical presence as long as I could remember.

Our mother died when I was two, so I never felt her absence. She was a Graham from Montgomery; Atticus met her when he was first elected to the state legislature. He was middle-aged then, she was fifteen years his junior. Jem was the product of their first year of marriage; four years later I was born, and two years later our mother died from a sudden heart attack. They said it ran in her family. I did not miss her, but I think Jem did. He remembered her clearly, and sometimes in the middle of a game he would sigh at length, then go off and play by himself behind the car-house. When he was like that, I knew better than to bother him.

When I was almost six and Jem was nearly ten, our summertime boundaries (within calling distance of Calpurnia) were Mrs. Henry Lafayette Dubose's house two doors to the north of us, and the Radley Place three doors to the south. We were never tempted to break them. The Radley Place was inhabited by an unknown entity the mere description of whom was enough to make us behave for days on end; Mrs. Dubose was plain hell.

That was the summer Dill came to us.

Early one morning as we were beginning our day's play in the back yard, Jem and I heard something next door in Miss Rachel Haverford's collard patch. We went to the wire fence to see if there was a puppy—Miss Rachel's rat terrier was expecting—instead we found someone sitting looking at us. Sitting down, he wasn't much higher than the collards. We stared at him until he spoke:

"Hey."

"Hey yourself," said Jem pleasantly.

"I'm Charles Baker Harris," he said. "I can read."

"So what?" I said.

"I just thought you'd like to know I can read. You got anything needs readin' I can do it. . . ."

"How old are you," asked Jem, "four-and-a-half?"

"Goin' on seven."

"Shoot no wonder, then," said Jem, jerking his thumb at me. "Scout yonder's been readin' ever since she was born, and she ain't even started to school yet. You look right puny for goin' on seven."

"I'm little but I'm old," he said.

Jem brushed his hair back to get a better look. "Why don't you come over, Charles Baker Harris?" he said. "Lord, what a name."

" 's not any funnier'n yours. Aunt Rachel says your name's Jeremy Atticus Finch."

Jem scowled. "I'm big enough to fit mine," he said. "Your name's longer'n you are. Bet it's a foot longer."

"Folks call me Dill," said Dill, struggling under the fence.

"Do better if you go over it instead of under it," I said. "Where'd you come from?"

Dill was from Meridian, Mississippi, was spending the summer with his aunt, Miss Rachel, and would be spending every summer in Maycomb from now on. His family was from Maycomb County originally, his mother worked for a photographer in Meridian, had entered his picture in a Beautiful Child contest and won five dollars. She gave the money to Dill, who went to the picture show twenty times on it.

"Don't have any picture shows here, except Jesus ones in the courthouse sometimes," said Jem. "Ever see anything good?"

Dill had seen *Dracula*, a revelation that moved Jem to eye him with the beginning of respect. "Tell it to us," he said.

Dill was a curiosity. He wore blue linen shorts that buttoned to his shirt, his hair was snow white and stuck to his head like duckfluff; he was a year my senior but I towered over him. As he told us the old tale his blue eyes would lighten and darken; his laugh was sudden and happy; he habitually pulled at a cowlick in the center of his forehead.

When Dill reduced Dracula to dust, and Jem said the show sounded better than the book, I asked Dill where his father was: "You ain't said anything about him."

"I haven't got one."

"Is he dead?"

"No . . ."

"Then if he's not dead you've got one, haven't you?"

Dill blushed and Jem told me to hush, a sure sign that Dill had been studied and found acceptable. Thereafter the summer passed in routine contentment. Routine contentment was: improving our treehouse that rested between giant twin chinaberry trees in the back yard, fussing, running through our list of dramas based on the works of Oliver Optic, Victor Appleton, and Edgar Rice Burroughs. In this matter we were lucky to have Dill. He played the character parts formerly thrust upon me—the ape in *Tarzan*, Mr. Crabtree in *The Rover Boys*, Mr. Damon in *Tom Swift*. Thus we came to know Dill as a pocket Merlin, whose head teemed with eccentric plans, strange longings, and quaint fancies.

But by the end of August our repertoire was vapid from countless reproductions, and it was then that Dill gave us the idea of making Boo Radley come out.

The Radley Place fascinated Dill. In spite of our warnings and explanations it drew him as the moon draws water, but drew him no nearer than the light-pole on the corner, a safe distance from the Radley gate. There he would stand, his arm around the fat pole, staring and wondering.

The Radley Place jutted into a sharp curve beyond our house. Walking south, one faced its porch; the sidewalk turned and ran beside the lot. The house was low, was once white with a deep front porch and green shutters, but had long ago darkened to the color of the slate-gray yard around it. Rain-rotted shingles drooped over the eaves of the veranda; oak trees kept the sun away. The remains of a picket drunkenly guarded the front yard—a "swept" yard that was never swept—where johnson grass and rabbit-tobacco grew in abundance.

Inside the house lived a malevolent phantom. People said he existed, but Jem and I had never seen him. People said he went out at night when he moon was down, and peeped in windows. When people's azaleas froze in a cold snap, it was because he had breathed on them. Any stealthy small crimes committed in Maycomb were his work. Once the town was terrorized by a series of morbid nocturnal events: people's chickens and household pets were found mutilated; although the culprit was Crazy Addie, who eventually drowned himself in Barker's Eddy, people still looked at the Radley Place, unwilling to discard their initial suspicions. A Negro would not pass the Radley Place at night, he would cut across to the sidewalk opposite and whistle as he walked. The Maycomb school grounds adjoined the back of the Radley lot; from the Radley chickenyard tall pecan trees shook their fruit into the schoolyard, but the nuts lay untouched by the children: Radley pecans would kill you. A baseball hit into the Radley yard was a lost ball and no questions asked.

The misery of that house began many years before Jem and I were born. The Radleys, welcome anywhere in town, kept to themselves, a predilection unforgivable in Maycomb. They did not go to church, Maycomb's principal recreation, but worshiped at home; Mrs. Radley seldom if ever crossed the street for a mid-morning coffee break with her neighbors, and certainly never joined a missionary circle. Mr. Radley walked to town at eleven-thirty every morning and came back promptly at twelve, sometimes carrying a brown paper bag that the neighborhood assumed contained the family groceries. I never knew how old Mr. Radley made his living—Jem said he "bought cotton," a polite term for doing nothing—but Mr. Radley and his wife had lived there with their two sons as long as anybody could remember.

The shutters and doors of the Radley house were closed on Sundays, another thing alien to Maycomb's ways: closed doors meant illness and cold weather only. Of all days Sunday was the day for formal afternoon visiting: ladies wore corsets, men wore coats, children wore shoes. But to climb the Radley front steps and call, "He-y," of a Sunday afternoon was something their neighbors never did. The Radley house had no screen doors. I once asked Atticus if it ever had any; Atticus said yes, but before I was born.

According to neighborhood legend, when the younger Radley boy was in his teens he became acquainted with some of the Cunninghams from Old Sarum, an enormous and confusing tribe domiciled in the northern part of the county, and they formed the nearest thing to a gang ever seen in Maycomb. They did little, but enough to be discussed by the town and publicly warned from three pulpits: they hung around the barbershop; they rode the bus to Abbottsville on Sundays and went to the picture show; they attended dances at the county's riverside gambling hell, the Dew-Drop Inn & Fishing Camp; they experimented with stumphole whiskey. Nobody in Maycomb had nerve enough to tell Mr. Radley that his boy was in with the wrong crowd.

One night, in an excessive spurt of high spirits, the boys backed around the square in a borrowed flivver, resisted arrest by Maycomb's ancient beadle, Mr. Conner, and locked him in the courthouse outhouse. The town decided something had to be done; Mr. Conner said he knew who each and every one of them was, and he was bound and determined they wouldn't get away with it, so the boys came before the probate judge on charges of disorderly conduct, disturbing the peace, assault and battery, and using abusive and profane language in the presence and hearing of a female. The judge asked Mr. Conner why he included the last charge; Mr. Conner said they cussed so loud he was sure every lady in Maycomb heard them. The judge decided to send the boys to the state industrial school, where boys were sometimes sent for no other reason than to provide them with food and decent shelter: it was no prison and it was no disgrace. Mr. Radley thought it was. If the judge released Arthur, Mr. Radley would see to it that Arthur gave no further trouble. Knowing that Mr. Radley's word was his bond, the judge was glad to do so.

The other boys attended the industrial school and received the best secondary education to be had in the state; one of them eventually worked his way through engineering school at Auburn. The doors of the Radley house was closed on weekdays as well as Sundays, and Mr. Radley's boy was not seen again for fifteen years.

But there came a day, barely within Jem's memory, when Boo Radley was heard from and was seen by several people, but not by Jem. He said Atticus never talked much about the Radleys: when Jem would question him Atticus's only answer was for him to mind his own business and let the Radleys mind theirs, they had a right to; but when it happened Jem said Atticus shook his head and said, "Mm, mm, mm."

So Jem received most of his information from Miss Stephanie Crawford, a neighborhood scold, who said she knew the whole thing. According to Miss Stephanie, Boo was sitting in the livingroom cutting some items from *The Maycomb Tribune* to paste in his scrapbook. His father entered the room. As Mr. Radley passed by, Boo drove the scissors into his parent's leg, pulled them out, wiped them on his pants, and resumed his activities.

Mrs. Radley ran screaming into the street that Arthur was killing them all, but when the sheriff arrived he found Boo still sitting in the livingroom, cutting up the *Tribune*. He was thirty-three years old then.

Miss Stephanie said old Mr. Radley said no Radley was going to any asylum, when it was suggested that a season in Tuscaloosa might be helpful to Boo. Boo wasn't crazy, he was high-strung at times. It was all right to shut him up, Mr. Radley conceded, but insisted that Boo not be charged with anything: he was not a criminal. The sheriff hadn't the heart to put him in jail alongside Negroes, so Boo was locked in the courthouse basement.

Boo's transition from the basement to back home was nebulous in Jem's memory. Miss Stephanie Crawford said some of the town council told Mr. Radley that if he didn't take Boo back, Boo would die of mold from the damp. Besides, Boo could not live forever on the bounty of the county.

Nobody knew what form of intimidation Mr. Radley employed to keep Boo out of sight, but Jem figured that Mr. Radley kept him chained to the bed most of the time. Atticus said no, it wasn't that sort of thing, that there were other ways of making people into ghosts.

My memory came alive to see Mrs. Radley occasionally open the front door, walk to the edge of the porch, and pour water on her cannas. But every day Jem and I would see Mr. Radley walking to and from town. He was a thin leathery man with colorless eyes, so colorless they did not reflect light. His cheekbones were sharp and his mouth was wide, with a thin upper lip and a full lower lip. Miss Stephanie Crawford said he was so upright he took the word of God as his only law, and we believed her, because Mr. Radley's posture was ramrod straight.

He never spoke to us. When he passed we would look at the ground and say, "Good morning, sir," and he would cough in reply. Mr. Radley's elder son lived in Pensacola; he came home at Christmas, and he was one of the few persons we ever saw enter or leave the place. From the day Mr. Radley took Arthur home, people said the house died.

But there came a day when Atticus told us he'd wear us out if we made any noise in the yard and commissioned Calpurnia to serve in his absence if she heard a sound out of us. Mr. Radley was dying.

He took his time about it. Wooden sawhorses blocked the road at each end of the Radley lot, straw was put down on the sidewalk, traffic was diverted to the back street. Dr. Reynolds parked his car in front of our house and walked to the Radley's every time he called. Jem and I crept around the yard for days. At last the sawhorses were taken away, and we stood watching from the front porch when Mr. Radley made his final journey past our house.

"There goes the meanest man ever God blew breath into," murmured Calpurnia, and she spat meditatively into the yard. We looked at her in surprise, for Calpurnia rarely commented on the ways of white people.

The neighborhood thought when Mr. Radley went under Boo would come out, but it had another thing coming: Boo's elder brother returned from Pensacola and took Mr. Radley's place. The only difference between him and his father was their ages. Jem said Mr. Nathan Radley "bought cotton," too. Mr. Nathan would speak to us, however, when we said good morning, and sometimes we saw him coming from town with a magazine in his hand.

The more we told Dill about the Radleys, the more he wanted to know, the longer he would stand hugging the light-pole on the corner, the more he would wonder.

"Wonder what he does in there," he would murmur. "Looks like he'd just stick his head out the door."

Jem said, "He goes out, all right, when it's pitch dark. Miss Stephanie Crawford said she woke up in the middle of the night one time and saw him looking straight through the window at her . . . said his head was like a skull lookin' at her. Ain't you ever waked up at night and heard him, Dill? He walks like this—" Jem slid his feet through the gravel. "Why do you think Miss Rachel locks up so tight at night? I've seen his tracks in our back yard many a mornin', and one night I heard him scratching on the back screen, but he was gone time Atticus got there."

"Wonder what he looks like?" said Dill.

Jem gave a reasonable description of Boo: Boo was about six-and-a-half feet tall, judging from his tracks; he dined on raw squirrels and any cats he could catch, that's why his hands were bloodstained—if you ate an animal raw, you could never wash the blood off. There was a long jagged scar that ran across his face; what teeth he had were yellow and rotten; his eyes popped, and he drooled most of the time.

"Let's try to make him come out," said Dill. "I'd like to see what he looks like."

Jem said if Dill wanted to get himself killed, all he had to do was go up and knock on the front door.

Our first raid came to pass only because Dill bet Jem *The Gray Ghost* against two Tom Swifts that Jem wouldn't get any farther than the Radley gate. In all his life, Jem had never declined a dare.

Jem thought abut it for three days. I suppose he loved honor more than his head, for Dill wore him down easily: "You're scared," Dill said, the first day. "Ain't scared, just respectful," Jem said. The next day Dill said, "You're too scared even to put your big toe in the front yard." Jem said he reckoned he wasn't, he'd passed the Radley Place every school day of his life.

"Always runnin'," I said.

But Dill got him the third day, when he told Jem that folks in Meridian certainly weren't as afraid as the folks in Maycomb, that he'd never seen such scary folks as the ones in Maycomb.

This was enough to make Jem march to the corner, where he stopped and leaned against the light-pole, watching the gate hanging crazily on its homemade hinge.

"I hope you've got it through your head that he'll kill us each and every one, Dill Harris," said Jem, when we joined him. "Don't blame me when he gouges your eyes out. You started it, remember."

"You're still scared," murmured Dill patiently.

Jem wanted Dill to know once and for all that he wasn't scared of anything. "It's just that I can't think of a way to make him come out without him gettin' us." Besides, Jem had his little sister to think of.

When he said that, I knew he was afraid. Jem had his little sister to think of the time I dared him to jump off the top of the house: "If I got killed, what'd become of you?" he asked. Then he jumped, landed unhurt, and his sense of responsibility left him until confronted by the Radley Place.

"You gonna run out on a dare?" asked Dill. "If you are, then—"

"Dill, you have to think about these things," Jem said. "Lemme think a minute . . . it's sort of like making a turtle come out . . ."

"How's that?" asked Dill.

"Strike a match under him."

I told Jem if he set fire to the Radley house I was going to tell Atticus on him.

Dill said striking a match under a turtle was hateful.

"Ain't hateful, just persuades him—'s not like you'd chunk him in the fire," Jem growled.

"How do you know a match don't hurt him?"

"Turtles can't feel, stupid," said Jem.

"Were you ever a turtle, huh?"

"My stars, Dill! Now lemme think . . . reckon we can rock him. . . ."

Jem stood in thought so long that Dill made a mild concession: "I won't say you ran out on a dare an' I'll swap you *The Gray Ghost* if you just go up and touch the house."

Jem brightened. "Touch the house, that all?"

Dill nodded.

"Sure that's all, now? I don't want you hollerin' something different the minute I get back."

"Yeah, that's all," said Dill. "He'll probably come out after you when he sees you in the yard, then Scout'n' me'll jump on him and hold him down till we can tell him we ain't gonna hurt him."

We left the corner, crossed the side street that ran in front of the Radley house, and stopped at the gate.

"Well go on," said Dill, "Scout and me's right behind you."

"I'm going," said Jem, "don't hurry me."

He walked to the corner of the lot, then back again, studying the simple terrain as if deciding how best to effect an entry, frowning and scratching his head.

Then I sneered at him.

Jem threw open the gate and sped to the side of the house, slapped it with his palm and ran back past us, not waiting to see if his foray was successful. Dill and I followed on his heels. Safely on our porch, panting and out of breath, we looked back.

The old house was the same, droopy and sick, but as we stared down the street we thought we saw an inside shutter move. Flick. A tiny, almost invisible movement, and the house was still.

2

Dill left us early in September, to return to Meridian. We saw him off on the five o'clock bus and I was miserable without him until it occurred to me that I would be starting to school in a week. I never looked forward more to anything in my life. Hours of wintertime had found me in the treehouse, looking over at the schoolyard, spying on multitudes of children through a two-power telescope Jem had given me, learning their games, following Jem's red jacket through wriggling circles of blind man's buff, secretly sharing their misfortunes and minor victories. I longed to join them.

Jem condescended to take me to school the first day, a job usually done by one's parents, but Atticus had said Jem would be delighted to show me where my room was. I think some money changed hands in this transaction, for as we trotted around the corner past the Radley Place I heard an unfamiliar jingle in Jem's pockets. When we slowed to a walk at the edge of the schoolyard, Jem was careful to explain that during school hours I was not to bother him, I was not to approach him with requests to enact a chapter of *Tarzan and the Ant Men*, to embarrass him with references to his private life, or tag along behind him at recess and noon. I was to stick with the first grade and he would stick with the fifth. In short, I was to leave him alone.

"You mean we can't play any more?" I asked.

"We'll do like we always do at home," he said, "but you'll see—school's different."

It certainly was. Before the first morning was over, Miss Caroline Fisher, our teacher, hauled me up to the front of the room and patted the palm of my hand with a ruler, then made me stand in the corner until noon.

Miss Caroline was no more than twenty-one. She had bright auburn hair, pink cheeks, and wore crimson fingernail polish. She also wore high-heeled pumps and a red-and-white-striped dress. She looked and smelled like a peppermint drop. She boarded across the street one door down from us in Miss Maudie Atkinson's upstairs front room, and when Miss Maudie introduced us to her, Jem was in a haze for days.

Miss Caroline printed her name on the blackboard and said, "This says I am Miss Caroline Fisher. I am from North Alabama, from Winston County." The class murmured apprehensively, should she prove to harbor her share of the peculiarities indigenous to that region. (When Alabama seceded from the Union on January 11, 1861, Winston County seceded from Alabama, and every child in Maycomb County knew it.) North Alabama was full of Liquor Interests, Big Mules, steel companies, Republicans, professors, and other persons of no background.

Miss Caroline began the day by reading us a story about cats. The cats had long conversations with one another, they wore cunning little clothes and lived in a warm house beneath a kitchen stove. By the time Mrs. Cat called the drugstore for an order of chocolate malted mice the class was wriggling like a bucketful of catawba worms. Miss Caroline seemed unaware that the ragged, denim-shirted and floursack-skirted first grade, most of whom had chopped cotton and fed hogs from the time they were able to walk, were immune to imaginative literature. Miss Caroline came to the end of the story and said, "*Oh*, my, wasn't that nice?"

Then she went to the blackboard and printed the alphabet in enormous square capitals, turned to the class and asked, "Does anybody know what these are?"

Everybody did; most of the first grade had failed it last year.

I suppose she chose me because she knew my name; as I read the alphabet a faint line appeared between her eyebrows, and after making me read most of *My First Reader* and the stock-market quotations from *The Mobile Register* aloud, she discovered that I was literate and looked at me with more than faint distaste. Miss Caroline told me to tell my father not to teach me any more, it would interfere with my reading.

"Teach me?" I said in surprise. "He hasn't taught me anything, Miss Caroline. Atticus ain't got time to teach me anything," I added, when Miss Caroline smiled and shoot her head. "Why, he's so tired at night he just sits in the livingroom and reads."

"If he didn't teach you, who did?" Miss Caroline asked good-naturedly. "Somebody did. You weren't born reading *The Mobile Register*."

"Jem says I was. He read in a book where I was a Bullfinch instead of a Finch. Jem says my name's really Jean Louise Bullfinch, that I got swapped when I was born and I'm really a—"

Miss Caroline apparently thought I was lying. "Let's not let our imaginations run away with us, dear," she said. "Now you tell your father not to teach you any more. It's best to begin reading with a fresh mind. You tell him I'll take over from here and try to undo the damage—"

"Ma'am?"

"Your father does not know how to teach. You can have a seat now."

I mumbled that I was sorry and retired meditating upon my crime. I never deliberately learned to read, but somehow I had been wallowing illicitly in the daily papers. In the long hours of church—was it then I learned? I could not remember not being able to read hymns. Now that I was compelled to think about it, reading was something that just came to me, as learning to fasten the seat of my union suit without looking around, or achieving two bows from a snarl of shoelaces. I could not remember when the lines above Atticus's moving finger separated into words, but I had stared at them all the evenings in my memory, listening to the news of the day, Bills to Be Enacted into Laws, the diaries of Lorenzo Dow—anything Atticus happened to be reading when I crawled into his lap every night. Until I feared I would lose it, I never loved to read. One does not love breathing.

I knew I had annoyed Miss Caroline, so I let well enough alone and stared out the window until recess when Jem cut me from the covey of first-graders in the schoolyard. He asked how I was getting along. I told him.

"If I didn't have to stay I'd leave. Jem, that damn lady says Atticus's been teaching me to read and for him to stop it—"

"Don't worry, Scout," Jem comforted me. "Our teacher says Miss Caroline's introducing a new way of teaching. She learned about it in college. It'll be in all the grades soon. You don't have to learn much out of books that way—it's like if you wanta learn about cows, you go milk one, see?"

"Yeah Jem, but I don't wanta study cows, I—"

"Sure you do. You hafta know about cows, they're a big part of life in Maycomb County."

I contented myself with asking Jem if he'd lost his mind.

"I'm just trying to tell you the new way they're teachin' the first grade, stubborn. It's the Dewey Decimal System."

Having never questioned Jem's pronouncements, I saw no reason to begin now. The Dewey Decimal System consisted, in part, of Miss Caroline waving cards at us on which were printed "the," "cat," "rat," "man," and "you." No comment seemed to be expected of us, and the class received these impressionistic revelations in silence. I was bored, so I began a letter to Dill. Miss Caroline caught me writing and told me to tell my father to stop teaching me. "Besides," she said. "We don't write in the first grade, we print. You won't learn to write until you're in the third grade."

Calpurnia was to blame for this. It kept me from driving her crazy on rainy days, I guess. She would set me a writing task by scrawling the alphabet firmly across the top of a tablet, then copying out a chapter of the Bible beneath. If I reproduced her penmanship satisfactorily, she rewarded me with an open-faced sandwich of bread and butter and sugar. In Calpurnia's teaching, there was no sentimentality: I seldom pleased her and she seldom rewarded me.

"Everybody who goes home to lunch hold up your hands," said Miss Caroline, breaking into my new grudge against Calpurnia.

The town children did so, and she looked us over.

"Everybody who brings his lunch put it on top of his desk."

Molasses buckets appeared from nowhere, and the ceiling danced with metallic light. Miss Caroline walked up and down the rows peering and poking into lunch containers, nodding if the contents pleased her, frowning a little at others. She stopped at Walter Cunningham's desk. "Where's yours?" she asked.

Walter Cunningham's face told everybody in the first grade he had hookworms. His absence of shoes told us how he got them. People caught hookworms going barefooted in barnyards and hog wallows. If Walter had owned any shoes he would have worn them the first day of school, and then discarded them until mid-winter. He did have on a clean shirt and neatly mended overalls.

"Did you forget your lunch this morning?" asked Miss Caroline.

Walter looked straight ahead. I saw a muscle jump in his skinny jaw.

"Did you forget it this morning?" asked Miss Caroline. Walter's jaw twitched again.

"Yeb'm," he finally mumbled.

Miss Caroline went to her desk and opened her purse. "Here's a quarter," she said to Walter. "Go and eat downtown today. You can pay me back tomorrow."

Walter shook his head. "Nome thank you ma'am," he drawled softly.

Impatience crept into Miss Caroline's voice: "Here Walter, come get it."

Walter shook his head again.

When Walter shook his head a third time someone whispered, "Go on and tell her, Scout."

I turned around and saw most of the town people and the entire bus delegation looking at me. Miss Caroline and I had conferred twice already, and they were looking at me in the innocent assurance that familiarity breeds understanding.

I rose graciously on Walter's behalf: "Ah—Miss Caroline?"

"What is it, Jean Louise?"

"Miss Caroline, he's a Cunningham."

I sat back down.

"What, Jean Louise?"

I thought I had made things sufficiently clear. It was clear enough to the rest of us: Walter Cunningham was sitting there lying his head off. He didn't forget his lunch, he didn't have any. He had none today nor would he have any tomorrow or the next day. He had probably never seen three quarters together at the same time in his life.

I tried again: "Walter's one of the Cunninghams, Miss Caroline."

"I beg your pardon, Jean Louise?"

"That's okay, ma'am, you'll get to know all the county folks after a while. The Cunninghams never took anything they can't pay back—no church baskets and no scrip stamps. They never took anything off of anybody, they get along on what they have. They don't have much, but they get along on it."

My special knowledge of the Cunningham tribe—one branch, that is—was gained from events of last winter. Walter's father was one of Atticus's clients. After a dreary conversation in our livingroom one night about his entailment, before Mr. Cunningham left he said, "Mr. Finch, I don't know when I'll ever be able to pay you."

"Let that be the least of your worries, Walter," Atticus said.

When I asked Jem what entailment was, and Jem described it as a condition of having your tail in a crack, I asked Atticus if Mr. Cunningham would ever pay us.

"Not in money," Atticus said, "but before the year's out I'll have been paid. You watch."

We watched. One morning Jem and I found a load of stovewood in the back yard. Later, a sack of hickory nuts appeared on the back steps. With Christmas came a crate of smilax and holly. That spring when we found a crokersack full of turnip greens, Atticus said Mr. Cunningham had more than paid him.

"Why does she pay you like that?" I asked.

"Because that's the only way he can pay me. He has no money."

"Are we poor, Atticus?"

Atticus nodded. "We are indeed."

Jem's nose wrinkled. "Are we as poor as the Cunninghams?"

"Not exactly. The Cunninghams are country folks, farmers, and the crash hit them hardest."

Atticus said professional people were poor because the farmers were poor. As Maycomb County was farm country, nickels and dimes were hard to come by for doctors and dentists and lawyers. Entailment was only a part of Mr. Cunningham's vexations. The acres not entailed were mortgaged to the hilt, and the little cash he made went to interest. If he held his mouth right, Mr. Cunningham could get a WPA job, but his land would go to ruin if he left it, and he was willing to go hungry to keep his land and vote as he pleased. Mr. Cunningham, said Atticus, came from a set breed of men.

As the Cunninghams had no money to pay a lawyer, they simply paid us with what they had. "Did you know," said Atticus, "that Dr. Reynolds works the same way? He charges some folks a bushel of potatoes for delivery of a baby. Miss Scout, if you give me your attention I'll tell you what entailment is. Jem's definitions are very nearly accurate sometimes."

If I could have explained these things to Miss Caroline, I would have saved myself some inconvenience and Miss Caroline subsequent mortification, but it was beyond my ability to explain things as well as Atticus, so I said, "You're shamin' him, Miss Caroline. Walter hasn't got a quarter at home to bring you, and you can't use any stovewood."

Miss Caroline stood stock still, then grabbed me by the collar and hauled me back to her desk. "Jean Louise, I've had about enough of you this morning," she said. "You're starting off on the wrong foot in every way, my dear. Hold out your hand."

I thought she was going to spit in it, which was the only reason anybody in Maycomb held out his hand: it was a time-honored method of sealing oral contracts. Wondering what bargain we had made, I turned to the class for an answer, but the class looked back at me in puzzlement. Miss Caroline picked up her ruler, gave me half a dozen quick little pats, then told me to stand in the corner. A storm of laughter broke loose when it finally occurred to the class that Miss Caroline had whipped me.

When Miss Caroline threatened it with a similar fate the first grade exploded again, becoming cold sober only when the shadow of Miss Blount fell over them. Miss Blount, a native Maycombian as yet uninitiated in the mysteries of the Decimal System, appeared at the door hands on hips and announced: "If I hear another sound from this room I'll burn up everybody in it. Miss Caroline, the sixth grade cannot concentrate on the pyramids for all this racket!"

My sojourn in the corner was a short one. Saved by the bell, Miss Caroline watched the class file out for lunch. As I was the last to leave, I saw her sink down into her chair and bury her head in her arms. Had her conduct been more friendly toward me, I would have felt sorry for her. She was a pretty little thing.

3

Catching Walter Cunningham in the schoolyard gave me some pleasure, but when I was rubbing his nose in the dirt Jem came by and told me to stop. "You're bigger'n he is," he said.

"He's as old as you, nearly," I said. "He made me start off on the wrong foot."

"Let him go, Scout. Why?"

"He didn't have any lunch," I said, and explained my involvement in Walter's dietary affairs.

Walter had picked himself up and was standing quietly listening to Jem and me. His fists were half cocked, as if expecting an onslaught from both of us. I stomped at him to chase him away, but Jem put out his hand and stopped me. He examined Walter with an air of speculation. "Your daddy Mr. Walter Cunningham from Old Sarum?" he asked, and Walter nodded.

Walter looked as if he had been raised on fish food: his eyes, as blue as Dill Harris's, were red-rimmed and watery. There was no color in his face except at the tip of his nose, which was moistly pink. He fingered the straps of his overalls, nervously picking at the metal hooks.

Jem suddenly grinned at him. "Come on home to dinner with us, Walter," he said. "We'd be glad to have you."

Walter's face brightened, then darkened.

Jem said, "Our daddy's a friend of your daddy's. Scout here, she's crazy—she won't fight you any more."

"I wouldn't be too certain of that," I said. Jem's free dispensation of my pledge irked me, but precious noontime minutes were ticking away. "Yeah Walter, I won't jump on you again. Don't you like butterbeans? Our Cal's a real good cook."

Walter stood where he was, biting his lip. Jem and I gave up, and we were nearly to the Radley Place when Walter called, "Hey, I'm comin'!"

When Walter caught up with us, Jem made pleasant conversation with him. "A hain't lives there," he said cordially, pointing to the Radley house. "Ever hear about him, Walter?"

"Reckon I have," said Walter. "Almost died first year I come to school and et them pecans—folks say he pizened 'em and put 'em over on the school side of the fence."

Jem seemed to have little fear of Boo Radley now that Walter and I walked beside him. Indeed, Jem grew boastful: "I went all the way up to the house once," he said to Walter.

"Anybody who went up to the house once oughta not to still run every time he passes it," I said to the clouds above.

"And who's runnin', Miss Priss?"

"You are, when ain't anybody with you."

By the time we reached our front steps Walter had forgotten he was a Cunningham. Jem ran to the kitchen and asked Calpurnia to set an extra plate, we had company. Atticus greeted Walter and began a discussion about crops neither Jem nor I could follow.

"Reason I can't pass the first grade, Mr. Finch, is I've had to stay out ever' spring an' help Papa with the choppin', but there's another'n at the house now that's field size."

"Did you pay a bushel of potatoes for him?" I asked, but Atticus shook his head at me.

While Walter piled food on his plate, he and Atticus talked together like two men, to the wonderment of Jem and me. Atticus was expounding upon farm problems when Walter interrupted to ask if there was any molasses in the house. Atticus summoned Calpurnia, who returned bearing the syrup pitcher. She stood waiting for Walter to help himself. Walter poured syrup on his vegetables and meat with a generous hand. He would probably have poured it into his milk glass had I not asked what the sam hill he was doing.

The silver saucer clattered when he replaced the pitcher, and he quickly put his hands in his lap. Then he ducked his head.

Atticus shook his head at me again. "But he's gone and drowned his dinner in syrup," I protested. "He's poured it all over—"

It was then that Calpurnia requested my presence in the kitchen.

She was furious, and when she was furious Calpurnia's grammar became erratic. When in tranquility, her grammar was as good as anybody's in Maycomb. Atticus said Calpurnia had more education than most colored folks.

When she squinted down at me the tiny lines around her eyes deepened. "There's some folks who don't eat like us," she whispered fiercely, "but you ain't called on to contradict 'em at the table when they don't. That boy's yo' comp'ny and if he wants to eat up the table cloth you let him, you hear?"

"He ain't company, Cal, he's just a Cunningham—"

"Hush your mouth! Don't matter who they are, anybody sets foot in this house's yo' comp'ny, and don't you let me catch you remarkin' on their ways like you was so high and mighty! Yo' folks might be better'n the Cunninghams but it don't count for nothin' the way you're disgracin' 'em—if you can't act fit to eat at the table you can just set here and eat in the kitchen!"

Calpurnia sent me through the swinging door to the diningroom with a stinging smack. I retrieved my plate and finished dinner in the kitchen, thankful, though, that I was spared the humiliation of facing them again. I told Calpurnia to just wait, I'd fix her: one of these days when she wasn't looking I'd go off and drown myself in Barker's Eddy and then she'd be sorry. Besides, I added, she'd already gotten me in trouble once today: she had taught me to write and it was all her fault. "Hush your fussin'," she said.

Jem and Walter returned to school ahead of me: staying behind to advise Atticus of Calpurnia's iniquities was worth a solitary sprint past the Radley Place. "She likes

Jem better'n she likes me, anyway," I concluded, and suggested that Atticus lose no time in packing her off.

"Have you ever considered that Jem doesn't worry her half as much?" Atticus's voice was flinty. "I've no intention of getting rid of her, now or ever. We couldn't operate a single day without Cal, have you ever thought of that? You think about how much Cal does for you, and you mind her, you hear?"

I returned to school and hated Calpurnia steadily until a sudden shriek shattered my resentments. I looked up to see Miss Caroline standing in the middle of the room, sheer horror flooding her face. Apparently she had revived enough to persevere in her profession.

"It's alive!" she screamed.

The male population of the class rushed as one to her assistance. Lord, I thought, she's scared of a mouse. Little Chuck Little, whose patience with all living things was phenomenal, said, "Which way did he go, Miss Caroline? Tell us where he went, quick! D.C.—" he turned to a boy behind him—"D.C., shut the door and we'll catch him. Quick, ma'am, where'd he go?"

Miss Caroline pointed a shaking finger not at the floor nor at a desk, but to a hulking individual unknown to me. Little Chuck's face contracted and he said gently, "You mean him, ma'am? Yessum, he's alive. Did he scare you some way?"

Miss Caroline said desperately, "I was just walking by when it crawled out of his hair . . . just crawled out of his hair—"

Little Chuck grinned broadly. "There ain't no need to fear a cootie, ma'am. Ain't you ever seen one? Now don't you be afraid, you just go back to your desk and teach us some more."

Little Chuck Little was another member of the population who didn't know where his next meal was coming from, but he was a born gentleman. He put his hand under her elbow and led Miss Caroline to the front of the room. "Now don't you fret, ma'am," he said. "There ain't no need to fear a cootie. I'll just fetch you some cool water."

The cootie's host showed not the faintest interest in the furor he had wrought. He searched the scalp above his forehead, located his guest and pinched it between his thumb and forefinger.

Miss Caroline watched the process in horrid fascination. Little Chuck brought water in a paper cup, and she drank it gratefully. Finally she found her voice. "What is your name, son?" she asked softly.

The boy blinked. "Who, me?" Miss Caroline nodded.

"Burris Ewell."

Miss Caroline inspected her roll-book. "I have a Ewell here, but I don't have a first name . . . would you spell your first name for me?"

"Don't know how. They call me Burris't home."

"Well, Burris," said Miss Caroline, "I think we'd better excuse you for the rest of the afternoon. I want you to go home and wash your hair."

From her desk she produced a thick volume, leafed through its pages and read for a moment. "A good home remedy for—Burris, I want you to go home and wash your hair with lye soap. When you've done that, treat your scalp with kerosene."

"What fer, missus?"

"To get rid of the—er, cooties. You see, Burris, the other children might catch them, and you wouldn't want that, would you?"

The boy stood up. He was the filthiest human I had ever seen. His neck was dark gray, the backs of his hands were rusty, and his fingernails were black deep into the quick. He peered at Miss Caroline from a fist-sized clean space on his face. No one had noticed him, probably, because Miss Caroline and I had entertained the class most of the morning.

"And Burris," said Miss Caroline, "please bathe yourself before you come back tomorrow."

The boy laughed rudely. "Yo ain't sendin' me home, missus. I was on the verge of leavin'—I done done my time for this year."

Miss Caroline looked puzzled. "What do you mean by that?"

The boy did not answer. He gave a short contemptuous snort.

One of the elderly members of the class answered her: "He's one of the Ewells, ma'am," and I wondered if this explanation would be as unsuccessful as my attempt. But Miss Caroline seemed willing to listen. "Whole school's full of 'em. They come first day every year and then leave. The truant lady gets 'em here 'cause she threatens 'em with the sheriff, but she's give up tryin' to hold 'em. She reckons she's carried out the law just gettin' their names on the roll and runnin' 'em here the first day. You're supposed to mark 'em absent the rest of the year . . ."

"But what about their parents?" asked Miss Caroline, in genuine concern.

"Ain't got no mother," was the answer, "and their paw's right contentious."

Burris Ewell was flattered by the recital. "Been comin' to the first day o' the first grade fer three year now," he said expansively. "Reckon if I'm smart this year they'll promote me to the second. . . ."

Miss Caroline said, "Sit back down, please, Burris," and the moment she said it I knew she had made a serious mistake. The boy's condescension flashed to anger.

"You try and make me, missus."

Little Chuck Little got to his feet. "Let him go, ma'am," he said. "He's a mean one, a hard-down mean one. He's liable to start somethin', and there's some little folks here."

He was among the most diminutive of men, but when Burris Ewell turned toward him, Little Chuck's right hand went to his pocket. "Watch your step, Burris," he said. "I'd soon's kill you as look at you. Now go home."

Burris seemed to be afraid of a child half his height, and Miss Caroline took advantage of his indecision: "Burris, go home. If you don't I'll call the principal," she said. "I'll have to report this, anyway."

The boy snorted and slouched leisurely to the door.

Safely out of range, he turned and shouted: "Report and be damned to ye! Ain't no snot-nosed slut of a schoolteacher ever born c'n make me do nothin'! You ain't' makin' me go nowhere, missus. You just remember that, you ain't' makin' me go nowhere!"

He waited until he was sure she was crying, then he shuffled out of the building.

Soon we were clustered around her desk, trying in our various ways to comfort her. He was a real mean one . . . below the belt . . . you ain't called on to teach folks like that . . . them ain't Maycomb's ways, Miss Caroline, not really . . . now don't you fret, ma'am. Miss Caroline, why don't you read us a story? That cat thing was real fine this mornin'. . . .

Miss Caroline smiled, blew her nose, said, "Thank you, darlings," dispersed us, opened a book and mystified the first grade with a long narrative about a toadfrog that lived in a hall.

When I passed the Radley Place for the fourth time that day—twice at a full gallop—my gloom had deepened to match the house. If the remainder of the school year were as fraught with drama as the first day, perhaps it would be mildly entertaining, but the prospect of spending nine months refraining from reading and writing made me think of running away.

By late afternoon most of my traveling plans were complete; when Jem and I raced each other up the sidewalk to meet Atticus coming home from work, I didn't give him much of a race. It was our habit to run meet Atticus the moment we saw him round the post office corner in the distance. Atticus seemed to have forgotten my noontime fall from grace; he was full of questions about school. My replies were monosyllabic and he did not press me.

Perhaps Calpurnia sensed that my day had been a grim one: she let me watch her fix supper. "Shut your eyes and open your mouth and I'll give you a surprise," she said.

It was not often that she made crackling bread, she said she never had time, but with both of us at school today had been an easy one for her. She knew I loved crackling bread.

"I missed you today," she said. "The house got so lonesome 'long about two o'clock I had to turn on the radio."

"Why? Jem'n me ain't ever in the house unless it's rainin'."

"I know," she said, "But one of you's always in callin' distance. I wonder how much of the day I spend just callin' after you. Well," she said, getting up from the kitchen chair, "it's enough time to make a pan of cracklin' bread, I reckon. You run along now and let me get supper on the table."

Calpurnia bent down and kissed me. I ran along, wondering what had come over her. She had wanted to make up with me, that was it. She had always been too hard on me, she had at last seen the error of her fractious ways, she was sorry and too stubborn to say so. I was weary from the day's crimes.

After supper, Atticus sat down with the paper and called, "Scout, ready to read?" The Lord sent me more than I could bear, and I went to the front porch. Atticus followed me.

"Something wrong, Scout?"

I told Atticus I didn't feel very well and didn't think I'd go to school any more if it was all right with him.

Atticus sat down in the swing and crossed his legs. His fingers wandered to his watchpocket; he said that was the only way he could think. He waited in amiable silence, and I sought to reinforce my position: "You never went to school and you do all right, so I'll just stay home too. You can teach me like Granddaddy taught you 'n' Uncle Jack."

"No I can't," said Atticus. "I have to make a living. Besides, they'd put me in jail if I kept you at home—dose of magnesia for you tonight and school tomorrow."

"I'm feeling all right, really."

"Thought so. Now what's the matter?"

Bit by bit, I told him the day's misfortunes. "—and she said you taught me all wrong, so we can't ever read any more, ever. Please don't send me back, please sir."

Atticus stood up and walked to the end of the porch. When he completed his examination of the wisteria vine he strolled back to me.

"First of all," he said, "if you can learn a simple trick, Scout, you'll get along a lot better with all kinds of folks. You never really understand a person until you consider things from his point of view—"

"Sir?"

"—until you climb into his skin and walk around in it."

Atticus said I had learned many things today, and Miss Caroline had learned several things herself. She had learned not to hand something to a Cunningham, for one thing, but if Walter and I had put ourselves in her shoes we'd have seen it was an honest mistake on her part. We could not expect her to learn all Maycomb's ways in one day, and we could not hold her responsible when she knew no better.

"I'll be dogged," I said. "I didn't know no better than not to read to her, and she held me responsible—listen Atticus, I don't have to go to school!" I was bursting with a sudden thought. "Burris Ewell, remember? He just goes to school the first day. The truant lady reckons she's carried out the law when she gets his name on the roll—"

"You can't do that, Scout," Atticus said. "Sometimes it's better to bend the law a little in special cases. In your case, the law remains rigid. So to school you must go."

"I don't see why I have to when he doesn't."

"Then listen."

Atticus said the Ewells had been the disgrace of Maycomb for three generations. None of them had done an honest day's work in his recollection. He said that some Christmas, when he was getting rid of the tree, he would take me with him and show me where and how they lived. They were people, but they lived like animals. "They can go to school any time they want to, when they show the faintest symptom of wanting an education," said Atticus. "There are ways of keeping them in school by force, but it's silly to force people like the Ewells into a new environment—"

"If I didn't go to school tomorrow, you'd force me to."

"Let us leave it at this," said Atticus dryly. "You, Miss Scout Finch, are of the common folk. You must obey the law." He said that the Ewells were members of an exclusive society made up of Ewells. In certain circumstances the common folk judiciously allowed them certain privileges by the simple method of becoming blind to some of the Ewells' activities. They didn't have to go to school, for one thing. Another thing, Mr. Bob Ewell, Burris's father, was permitted to hunt and trap out of season.

"Atticus, that's bad," I said. In Maycomb County, hunting out of season was a misdemeanor at law, a capital felony in the eyes of the populace.

"It's against the law, all right," said my father, "and it's certainly bad, but when a man spends his relief checks on green whiskey his children have a way of crying from hunger pains. I don't know of any landowner around here who begrudges those children any game their father can hit."

"Mr. Ewell shouldn't do that—"

"Of course he shouldn't, but he'll never change his ways. Are you going to take out your disapproval on his children?"

"No sir," I murmured, and made a final stand: "But if I keep on goin' to school, we can't ever read any more. . . ."

"That's really bothering you, isn't it?"

"Yes sir."

When Atticus looked down at me I saw the expression on his face that always made me expect something. "Do you know what a compromise is?" he asked.

"Bending the law?"

"No, an agreement reached by mutual concessions. It works this way," he said. "If you'll concede the necessity of going to school, we'll go on reading every night just as we always have. Is it a bargain?"

"Yes sir!"

"We'll consider it sealed without the usual formality," Atticus said, when he saw me preparing to spit.

As I opened the front screen door Atticus said, "By the way, Scout, you'd better not say anything at school about our agreement."

"Why not?"

"I'm afraid our activities would be received with considerable disapprobation by the more learned authorities."

Jem and I were accustomed to our father's last-will-and-testament diction, and we were at all times free to interrupt Atticus for a translation when it was beyond our understanding.

"Huh, sir?"

"I never went to school," he said, "but I have a feeling that if you tell Miss Caroline we read every night she'll get after me, and I wouldn't want her after *me*."

Atticus kept us in fits that evening, gravely reading columns of print about a man who sat on a flagpole for no discernible reason, which was reason enough for Jem to spend the following Saturday aloft in the treehouse. Jem sat from after breakfast until sunset and would have remained overnight had not Atticus severed his supply lines. I had spent most of the day climbing up and down, running errands for him, providing him with literature, nourishment and water, and was carrying him blankets for the night when Atticus said if I paid no attention to him, Jem would come down. Atticus was right.

Martin Luther King, Jr.

(1929–1968)

Martin Luther King, Jr., was born on January 15, 1929, in Atlanta, Georgia. On February 25, 1948, he was ordained as a Baptist minister. In June 1948 he was graduated from Morehouse College in Atlanta. The next year he began his study at Crozer Theological Seminary in Chester, Pennsylvania. While there, he learned about the teachings of Mahatma Gandhi. In 1951 he was graduated from Crozer with a Bachelor of Divinity degree. King began the doctoral program in theology at Boston University in 1951. In 1953 he married Coretta Scott, with whom he had four children, Yolanda, Martin Luther King, III, Dexter Scott, and Bernice Albertine.

In May 1954, King accepted a pastoral position at the Dexter Avenue Baptist Church in Montgomery, Alabama. One year later, he received his Ph.D. from Boston University. King and more than sixty other black ministers formed the Southern Christian Leadership Conference (SCLC) at a meeting in Atlanta on January 9 and 10, 1957. In 1959 he became a co-pastor with his father of Ebenezer Baptist Church in Atlanta. On August 28, 1963, King delivered his famous "I Have a Dream" speech before 250,000 participants of the March on Washington. In 1964 he was selected as *Time Magazine*'s "Man of the Year." On December 10, 1964, he received the Nobel Peace Prize.

King was assassinated in Memphis, Tennessee, on April 4, 1968.

I've Been to the Mountaintop

Thank you very kindly, my friends. As I listened to Ralph Abernathy in his eloquent and generous introduction and then thought about myself, I wondered who he was talking about. It's always good to have your closest friend and associate say something good about you. And Ralph is the best friend that I have in the world.

I'm delighted to see each of you here tonight in spite of a storm warning. You reveal that you are determined to go on anyhow. Something is happening in Memphis, something is happening in our world.

As you know, if I were standing at the beginning of time, with the possibility of general and panoramic view of the whole human history up to now, and the Almighty said to me, "Martin Luther King, which age would you like to live in?"—I would take my mental flight by Egypt through, or rather across the Red Sea, through the wilderness on toward the promised land. And in spite of its magnificence, I wouldn't stop there. I would move on by Greece, and take my mind to Mount Olympus. And I would see Plato, Aristotle, Socrates, Euripides and Aristophanes assembled around the Parthenon as they discussed the great and eternal issues of reality.

But I wouldn't stop there. I would go on, even to the great heyday of the Roman Empire. And I would see developments around there, through various emperors and leaders. But I wouldn't stop there. I would even come up to the day of the Renaissance, and get a quick picture of all that the Renaissance did for the cultural and esthetic life of man. But I wouldn't stop there. I would even go by the way that the man for whom I'm named had his habitat. And I would watch Martin Luther as he tacked his ninety-five theses on the door at the church in Wittenberg.

But I wouldn't stop there. I would come on up even to 1863, and watch a vacillating president by the name of Abraham Lincoln finally come to the conclusion that he had to sign the Emancipation Proclamation. But I wouldn't stop there. I would even come up to the early thirties, and see a man grappling with the problems of the bankruptcy of his nation. And come with an eloquent cry that we have nothing to fear but fear itself.

But I wouldn't stop there. Strangely enough, I would turn to the Almighty, and say, "If you allow me to live just a few years in the second half of the twentieth century, I will be happy." Now that's a strange statement to make, because the world is all messed up. The nation is sick. Trouble is in the land. Confusion all around. That's a strange statement. But I know, somehow, that only when it is dark enough, can you see the stars. And I see God working in this period of the twentieth century in a way that men, in some strange way, are responding—something is happening in our world. The masses of people are rising up. And wherever they are assembled today, whether they are in Johannesburg, South Africa; Nairobi, Kenya; Accra, Ghana; New York City; Atlanta, Georgia; Jackson, Mississippi; or Memphis, Tennessee—the cry is always the same—"We want to be free."

And another reason that I'm happy to live in this period is that we have been forced to a point where we're going to have to grapple with the problems that men have been trying to grapple with through history, but the demands didn't force them to do it. Survival demands that we grapple with them. Men, for years now, have been talking about war and peace. But now, no longer can they just talk about it. It is no longer a choice between violence and nonviolence in this world; it's nonviolence or nonexistence.

That is where we are today. And also in the human rights revolution, if something isn't done, and in a hurry, to bring the colored peoples of the world out of their long years of poverty, their long years of hurt and neglect, the whole world is doomed. Now, I'm just happy that God has allowed me to live in this period, to see what is unfolding. And I'm happy that he's allowed me to be in Memphis.

I can remember, I can remember when Negroes were just going around as Ralph has said, so often, scratching where they didn't itch, and laughing when they were not tickled. But that day is all over. We mean business now, and we are determined to gain our rightful place in God's world.

And that's all this whole thing is about. We aren't engaged in any negative protest and in any negative arguments with anybody. We are saying that we are determined to be men. We are determined to be people. We are saying that we are God's children. And that we don't have to live like we are forced to live.

Now, what does all of this mean in this great period of history? It means that we've got to stay together. We've got to stay together and maintain unity. You know, whenever Pharaoh wanted to prolong the period of slavery in Egypt, he had a favorite, favorite formula for doing it. What was that? He kept the slaves fighting among themselves. But whenever the slaves get together, something happens in Pharaoh's court, and he cannot hold the slaves in slavery. When the slaves get together, that's the beginning of getting out of slavery. Now let us maintain unity.

Secondly, let us keep the issues where they are. The issue is injustice. The issue is the refusal of Memphis to be fair and honest in its dealings with its public servants, who happen to be sanitation workers. Now, we've got to keep attention on that. That's always the problem with a little violence. You know what happened the other day, and the press dealt only with the window-breaking. I read the articles. They very seldom got around to mentioning the fact that one thousand, three hundred sanitation workers were on strike, and that Memphis is not being fair to them, and that Mayor Loeb is in dire need of a doctor. They didn't get around to that.

Now we're going to march again, and we've got to march again, in order to put the issue where it is supposed to be. And force everybody to see that there are thirteen hundred of God's children here suffering, sometimes going hungry, going through dark and dreary nights wondering how this thing is going to come out. That's the issue. And we've got to say to the nation: we know it's coming out. For when people get caught up with that which is right and they are willing to sacrifice for it, there is no stopping point short of victory.

We aren't going to let any mace stop us. We are masters in our nonviolent movement in disarming police forces; they don't know what to do. I've seen them so often. I remember in Birmingham, Alabama, when we were in that majestic struggle there we would move out of the 16th Street Baptist Church day after day; by the hundreds we would move out. And Bull Connor would tell them to send the dogs forth and they did come; but we just went before the dogs singing, "Ain't gonna let nobody turn me round." Bull Connor next would say, "Turn the fire hoses on." And as I said to you the other night, Bull Connor didn't know history. He knew a kind of physics that somehow didn't relate to the transphysics that we knew about. And that was the fact that there was a certain kind of fire that no water could put out. And we went before the fire hoses; we had known water. If we were Baptist or some other denomination, we had been immersed. If we were Methodist, and some others, we had been sprinkled, but we knew water.

That couldn't stop us. And we just went on before the dogs and we would look at them; and we'd go on before the water hoses and we would look at it, and we'd just go on singing "Over my head I see freedom in the air." And then we would be thrown in the paddy wagons, and sometimes we were stacked in there like sardines in a can. And they would throw us in, and old Bull would say, "Take them off," and they did; and we would just go in the paddy wagon singing, "We Shall Overcome." And every now and then we'd get in the jail, and we'd see the jailers looking through the windows being moved by our prayers, and being moved by our words and our songs. And there was a power there which Bull Connor couldn't adjust to; and so we ended up transforming Bull into a steer, and we won our struggle in Birmingham.

Now we've got to go on to Memphis just like that. I call upon you to be with us Monday. Now about injunctions: We have an injunction and we're going into court tomorrow morning to fight this illegal, unconstitutional injunction. All we say to America is, "Be true to what you said on paper." If I lived in China or even Russia, or any totalitarian country, maybe I could understand the denial of certain basic First Amendment privileges, because they hadn't committed themselves to that over there. But somewhere I read of the freedom of assembly. Somewhere I read of the freedom of speech. Somewhere I read of the freedom of the press. Somewhere I read that the greatness of America is the right to protest for right. And so just as I say, we aren't going to let any injunction turn us around. We are going on.

We need all of you. And you know what's beautiful to me, is to see all of these ministers of the Gospel. It's a marvelous picture. Who is it that is supposed to articulate the longings and aspirations of the people more than the preacher? Somehow the preacher must be an Amos, and say, "Let justice roll down like waters and righteousness like a mighty stream." Somehow, the preacher must say with Jesus, "The spirit of the Lord is upon me, because he hath anointed me to deal with the problems of the poor."

And I want to commend the preachers, under the leadership of these noble men: James Lawson, one who has been in this struggle for many years; he's been to jail for struggling; but he's still going on, fighting for the rights of his people. Rev. Ralph Jackson, Billy Kiles; I could just go right on down the list, but time will not permit. But I want to thank them all. And I want you to thank them, because so often, preachers aren't concerned about anything but themselves. And I'm always happy to see a relevant ministry.

It's alright to talk about "long white robes over yonder," in all of its symbolism. But ultimately people want some suits and dresses and shoes to wear down here. It's alright to talk about "streets flowing with milk and honey," but God has commanded us to be concerned about the slums down here, and his children who can't eat three square meals a day. It's alright to talk about the new Jerusalem, but one day, God's preacher must talk about the New York, the new Atlanta, the new Philadelphia, the new Los Angeles, the new Memphis, Tennessee. This is what we have to do.

Now the other thing we'll have to do is this: Always anchor our external direct action with the power of economic withdrawal. Now, we are poor people, individually, we are poor when you compare us with white society in America. We are poor. Never stop and forget that collectively, that means all of us together, collectively we are richer than all the nations in the world, with the exception of nine. Did you ever think about that? After you leave the United States, Soviet Russia, Great Britain, West Germany, France, and I could name the others, the Negro collectively is richer than most nations of the world. We have an annual income of more than thirty billion dollars a year, which is more than all of the exports of the United States, and more than the national budget of Canada. Did you know that? That's power right there, if we know how to pool it.

We don't have to argue with anybody. We don't have to curse and go around acting bad with our words. We don't need any bricks and bottles, we don't need any Molotov cocktails, we just need to go around to these stores, and to these massive industries in our country, and say, "God sent us by here, to say to you that you're not treating his children right. And we've come by here to ask you to make the first item on your agenda—fair treatment, where God's children are concerned. Now, if you are not prepared to do that, we do have an agenda that we must follow. And our agenda calls for withdrawing economic support from you."

And so, as a result of this, we are asking you tonight, to go out and tell your neighbors not to buy Coca-Cola in Memphis. Go by and tell them not to buy Sealtest milk. Tell them not to buy—what is the other bread?—Wonder Bread. And what is the other bread company, Jesse? Tell them not to buy Hart's bread. As Jesse Jackson has said, up to now, only the garbage men have been feeling pain; now we must kind of redistribute the pain. We are choosing these companies because they haven't been fair in their hiring policies; and we are choosing them because they can begin the process of saying, they are going to support the needs and the rights of these men who are on strike. And then they can move on downtown and tell Mayor Loeb to do what is right.

But not only that, we've got to strengthen black institutions. I call upon you to take your money out of the banks downtown and deposit your money in Tri-State Bank—we want a "bank-in" movement in Memphis. So go by the savings and loan association. I'm not asking you something that we don't do ourselves at SCLC. Judge Hooks and others will tell you that we have an account here in the savings and loan association from the Southern Christian Leadership Conference. We're just telling you to follow what we're doing. Put your money there. You have six or seven black insurance companies in Memphis. Take out your insurance there. We want to have an "insurance-in."

Now these are some practical things we can do. We begin the process of building a greater economic base. And at the same time, we are putting pressure where it really hurts. I ask you to follow through here.

Now, let me say as I move to my conclusion that we've got to give ourselves to this struggle until the end. Nothing would be more tragic than to stop at this point, in Memphis. We've got to see it through. And when we have our march, you need to be there. Be concerned about your brother. You may not be on strike. But either we go up together, or we go down together.

Let us develop a kind of dangerous unselfishness. One day a man came to Jesus; and he wanted to raise some questions about some vital matters in life. At points, he wanted to trick Jesus, and show him that he knew a little more than Jesus knew, and through this, throw him off base. Now that question could have easily ended up in a philosophical and theological debate. But Jesus immediately pulled that question from mid-air, and placed it on a dangerous curve between Jerusalem and Jericho. And he talked about a certain man, who fell among thieves. You remember that a Levite and a priest passed by on the other side. They didn't stop to help him. And finally a man of another race came by. He got down from his beast, decided not to be compassionate by proxy. But with him, administered first aid, and helped the man in need. Jesus ended up saying, this was the good man, this was the great man, because he had the capacity to project the "I" into the "thou," and to be concerned about his brother. Now you know, we use our imagination a great deal to try to determine why the priest and the Levite didn't stop. At times we say they were busy going to church meetings—an ecclesiastical gathering—and they had to get on down to Jerusalem so they wouldn't be late for their meeting. At other times we would speculate that there was a religious law that "One who was engaged in religious ceremonials was not to touch a human body twenty-four hours before the ceremony." And every now and then we begin to wonder whether maybe they were not going down to Jerusalem, or down to Jericho, rather to organize a "Jericho Road Improvement Association." That's a possibility. Maybe they felt that it was better to deal with the problem from the casual root, rather than to get bogged down with an individual effort.

But I'm going to tell you what my imagination tells me. It's possible that these men were afraid. You see, the Jericho road is a dangerous road. I remember when Mrs. King and I were first in Jerusalem. We rented a car and drove from Jerusalem down to Jericho. And as soon as we got on that road, I said to my wife, "I can see why Jesus used this as a setting for his parable." It's a winding, meandering road. It's really conducive for ambushing. You start out in Jerusalem, which is about 1200 miles, or rather 1200 feet above sea level. And by the time you get down to Jericho, fifteen or twenty minutes later, you're about 2200 feet below sea level. That's a dangerous road. In the days of Jesus it came to be known as the "Bloody Pass." And you know, it's possible that the priest and the Levite looked over that man on the ground and wondered if the robbers were still around. Or it's possible that they felt that the man on the ground was merely faking. And he was acting like he had been robbed and hurt, in order to seize them over there, lure them for quick and easy seizure. And so the first question that the Levite asked was, "If I stop to help this man, what will happen to me?" But then the Good Samaritan came by. And he reversed the question: "If I do not stop to help this man, what will happen to him?"

That's the question before you tonight. Not, "If I stop to help the sanitation workers, what will happen to all of the hours that I usually spend in my office every day and every week as a pastor?" The question is not, "If I stop to help this man in need, what will happen to me?" "If I do not stop to help the sanitation workers, what will happen to them?" That's the question.

Let us rise up tonight with a greater readiness. Let us stand with a greater determination. And let us move on in these powerful days, these days of challenge to make America what it ought to be. We have an opportunity to make America a better nation. And I want to thank God, once more, for allowing me to be here with you.

You know, several years ago, I was in New York City autographing the first book that I had written. And while sitting there autographing books, a demented black woman came up. The only question I heard from her was, "Are you Martin Luther King?"

And I was looking down writing, and I said yes. And the next minute I felt something beating on my chest. Before I knew it I had been stabbed by this demented woman. I was rushed to Harlem Hospital. It was a dark Saturday afternoon. And that blade had gone through, and the X-rays revealed that the tip of the blade was on the edge of my aorta, the main artery. And once that's punctured, you drown in your own blood—that's the end of you.

It came out in the *New York Times* the next morning, that if I had sneezed, I would have died. Well, about four days later, they allowed me, after the operation, after my chest had been opened, and the blade had been taken out, to move around in the wheel chair in the hospital. They allowed me to read some of the mail that came in, and from all over the states, and the world, kind letters came in. I read a few, but one of them I will never forget. I had received one from the President and the Vice-

President. I've forgotten what those telegrams said. I'd received a visit and a letter from the Governor of New York, but I've forgotten what the letter said. But there was another letter that came from a little girl, a young girl who was a student at the White Plains High School. And I looked at that letter, and I'll never forget it. It said simply, "Dear Dr. King: I am a ninth-grade student at the White Plains High School." She said, "While it should not matter, I would like to mention that I am a white girl. I read in the paper of your misfortune, and of your suffering. And I read that if you had sneezed, you would have died. And I'm simply writing you to say that I'm so happy that you didn't sneeze."

And I want to say tonight, I want to say that I am happy that I didn't sneeze. Because if I had sneezed, I wouldn't have been around here in 1960, when students all over the South started sitting-in at lunch counters. And I knew that as they were sitting in, they were really standing up for the best in the American dream. And taking the whole nation back to those great walls of democracy which were dug deep by the Founding Fathers in the Declaration of Independence and the Constitution. If I had sneezed, I wouldn't have been around in 1962, when Negroes in Albany, Georgia, decided to straighten their backs up. And whenever men and women straighten their backs up, they are going somewhere, because a man can't ride your back unless it is bent. If I had sneezed, I wouldn't have been here in 1963, when the black people of Birmingham, Alabama, aroused the conscience of this nation, and brought into being the Civil Rights Bill. If I had sneezed, I wouldn't have had a chance later that year, in August, to try to tell America about a dream that I had had. If I had sneezed, I wouldn't have been down in Selma, Alabama, to see the great movement there. If I had sneezed, I wouldn't have been in Memphis to see a community rally around those brothers and sisters who are suffering. I'm so happy that I didn't sneeze.

And they were telling me, now it doesn't matter now. It really doesn't matter what happens now. I left Atlanta this morning, and as we got started on the plane, there were six of us, the pilot said over the public address system, "We are sorry for the delay, but we have Dr. Martin Luther King on the plane. And to be sure that all of the bags were checked, and to be sure that nothing would be wrong with the plane, we had to check out everything carefully. And we've had the plane protected and guarded all night."

And then I got into Memphis. And some began to say the threats, or talk about the threats that were out. What would happen to me from some of our sick white brothers?

Well, I don't know what will happen now. We've got some difficult days ahead. But it doesn't matter with me now. Because I've been to the mountaintop. And I don't mind. Like anybody, I would like to live a long life. Longevity has its place. But I'm not concerned about that now. I just want to do God's will. And He's allowed me to go up to the mountain. And I've looked over. And I've seen the promised land. I may not get there with you. But I want you to know tonight, that we, as a people will get to the promised land. And I'm happy, tonight. I'm not worried about anything. I'm not fearing any man. Mine eyes have seen the glory of the coming of the Lord.

Walker Percy

(1916–1990)

Walker Percy was born on May 28, 1916, in Birmingham, Alabama. Following the untimely death of his father in 1929, he began living with his father's first cousin, William Alexander Percy, in Greenville, Mississippi. His mother died in 1932 in an automobile accident.

Percy was graduated in 1937 from the University of North Carolina at Chapel Hill, and in 1941 he was graduated with the M.D. degree from Columbia University. In 1946 he married Mary Bernice Townsend and then converted to Catholicism in 1947. In 1950 he moved to Covington, Louisiana, where he lived until his death on May 10, 1990.

In 1961 he published *The Moviegoer*, which won the National Book Award in 1962. Other books published include *The Last Gentleman* (1966); *Love in the Ruins* (1971); *The Message in the Bottle* (1975); *Lancelot* (1977); *The Second Coming* (1980); *Lost in the Cosmos* (1983); and *The Thanatos Syndrome* (1987).

from *The Last Gentleman*

3.

The next morning he walked the levee into Ithaca, curving into town under a great white sky. New grass, killed by the recent frost, had whitened and curled like wool. Grasshoppers started up at his feet and went stitching away. Below where the town was cradled in the long curving arm of the levee, the humpy crowns of oaks, lobules upon lobules, were broken only by steeples and the courthouse cupola. There arose to him the fitful and compassed sound of human affairs, the civil morning sounds of tolerable enterprise, the slap of lumber, a back-door slam, the chunk of an engine, and the routine shouts of a work crew: ho; ho; *ho now!*

Here he used to walk with his father and speak of the galaxies and of the expanding universe and take pleasure in the insignificance of man in the great lonely universe. His father could recite "Dover Beach," setting his jaw askew and wagging his head like F.D.R.:

> *for the world which seems*
> *To lie before us like a land of dreams,*
> *So various, so beautiful, so new,*
> *Hath really neither joy, nor love, nor light,*
> *Nor certitude, nor peace, nor help for pain—*

or else speak of the grandfather and the days of great deeds: "And so he looked down at him where he was sitting in his barber chair and he said to him: 'I'm going to tell you one time, you son of a bitch, and that's all, so hear me well; if anything happens to Judge Hampton, I'm not asking any questions, I'm not calling the police, I'm coming to look for you, and when I find you I'm going to kill you.' Nothing happened to Judge Hampton."

Beyond the old brown roiled water, the bindings and lacings of water upon water, the Louisiana shore stretched misty and perfunctory. When he came abreast of the quarterboat of the U.S. Engineers, his knee began to leap and he sat down in the tall grass under a river beacon and had a little fit. It was not a convulsion, but his eyes twittered around under his eyeballs. He dreamed that old men sat in a circle around him, looking at him from the corners of their eyes.

"Who's that?" he cried, jumping to his feet and brushing off his Macy's Dacron. Someone had called to him. But there was no one and nothing but the white sky and the humpy lobuled oaks of the town.

He went down into Front Street, past the Syrian and Jewish dry goods and the Chinese grocery, and turned quickly into Market and came to the iron lion in front of the bank. It was a hollow lion with a hole between his shoulders which always smelled of pee.

Spicer CoCo and Ben Huger, two planters his own age, stood in line behind him at the teller's window and began to kid him in the peculiar reflected style of the deep Delta.

"Reckon he's going to get all his money out and go on back off up there?" said Spicer CoCo.

"I notice he got his box-back coat on. I think he be here *for a while*," said Ben Huger.

He had to grin and fool with them, fend them off, while he asked the teller about the check. "Doris," he said to the pretty plump brunette, remembering her before he could forget, "can I stop payment on a certified check?"

She gave him a form to fill in. "Hello, Will. It's good to see you."

"Just fine." He scratched his head. "No, ah— You see, it's not my check and it's not on this bank. It was a check endorsed to me. I—it was misplaced." He hoped he didn't have to tell the amount.

"Then have the payer make a stop-payment order," she said, gazing at him with an expression both lively and absent-minded. "How long ago did you lose it?"

"I don't remember—ah, two days."

"Same old Will."

"What?"

"You haven't changed a bit."

"I haven't?" he said, pleased to hear it. "I thought I was worse." I'll call Poppy then, he said to himself and fell to wondering: how strange that they seem to know me and that I never supposed they could have, and perhaps that was my mistake.

"You know why he taking his money out," said Spicer.

"No, why is that?" asked Ben.

The two were standing behind him, snapping their fingers and popping their knees back and forth inside their trousers. They were talking in a certain broad style which was used in Ithaca jokingly; it was something like Negro talk but not the same.

"He on his way to the game Saddy. You can tell he come on into town to get his money—look, he done took off his regular walking shoes which he hid under a bridge and done put on his town slippers"—pointing down to the engineer's suède oxfords.

"That had slipped my notice," said Ben. "But look how he still th'ows his foot out like Cary Middlecoff, like he fixin' to hit a *long ball*."

"He come over here to draw his money out and make a bet on the game and take our money because he thinks we don't know they number one."

"What are you talking about," cried the engineer, laughing and shaking his head, all but overcome by an irritable sort of happiness—and all the while trying to tell Doris Mascagni about his savings account. "Yall are number one on the U.P." he told them, turning around nervously.

"What you say there, Will." They shook hands with him, still casting an eye about in the oblique Ithaca style.

What good fellows they were, he thought, as Doris counted out his money. Why did I ever go away? Ben Huger detained him and told a story about a man who bought a golf-playing gorilla. The gorilla had been taught to play golf by the smartest trainer in the world. This man who bought the gorilla was also a hard-luck gambler but for once he seemed to have hit on a sure thing. Because when he took the gorilla out to a driving range and handed him a driver and a basket of balls, each ball flew straight down the middle for five hundred yards. So he entered the gorilla in the Masters at Augusta. On the first tee, a par five hole, the gorilla followed Nicklaus and Palmer. He addressed his ball with assurance and drove the green four hundred and ninety yards away. Great day in the morning, thought the gambler, who was acting as the gorilla's caddy, I got it made this time for sure. Already he had plans for the P.G.A. and the British Open after collecting his fifty thousand in first prize money. But when the threesome reached the green and the gambler handed the gorilla his putter to sink the one-footer, the gorilla took the same full, perfected swing and drove the ball another four hundred and ninety yards. Then—

Here's what I'll do, thought the engineer who was sweating profusely and was fairly beside himself with irritable delight. I'll come back here and farm Hampton, my grandfather's old place, long since reclaimed by the cockleburs, and live this same sweet life with these splendid fellows.

"You gon' be home for a while, Will?" they asked him.

"For a while," he said vaguely and left them, glad to escape this dread delight.

Hardly aware that he did so, he took Kemper Street, a narrow decrepit boulevard which ran as string to the bow of the river. It still had its dusty old crape myrtles and chinaberries and horse troughs and an occasional tile marker set in the sidewalk: *Travelers Bicycle Club 1903.* The street changed to a Negro district. The old frame houses gave way to concrete nightclubs and shotgun cottages, some of which were converted to tiny churches by tacking on two square towers and covering the whole with brick paper. He sat on a trough which was choked with dry leaves and still exhaled the faint sunny tart smell of summer, and studied the Esso map, peering closely at the Gulf Coast, New Orleans, Houston, and points west. It came over him suddenly that he didn't live anywhere and had no address. As he began to go through his pockets he spied a new outdoor phone in a yellow plastic shell—and remembered Kitty. Lining up quarters and dimes on the steel shelf, he gazed down Kemper to the old city jail at the corner of Vincennes. Here on the top step stood his great-uncle the sheriff, or high sheriff, as the Negroes called him, on a summer night in 1928.

The telephone was ringing in the purple castle beside the golf links and under the rosy temple of Juno.

The sheriff put his hands in his back pockets so that the skirt of his coat cleared his pistol butt. "I respectfully ask yall to go on back to your homes and your families. There will be no violence here tonight because I'm going to kill the first sapsucker who puts his foot on that bottom step. Yall go on now. Go ahead on."

"Hello." It was David.

"Hello. David."

"Yes suh." He would be standing in the narrow hall between the pantry and the big front hall, the receiver held as loosely in his hand as if it had fallen into the crotch of a small tree.

"This is, ah, Will Barrett." It sounded strange because they didn't, the Negroes, know him by a name.

"Who? Yes *suh!* Mist' Billy!" David, feeling summoned, cast about for the right response—was it surprise? joy?—and hit instead on a keening bogus cheeriness, then, seeing it as such, lapsed into hilarity: *"Ts-ts-ts."*

"Is Miss Kitty there?"

"No suh. She *been* gone."

"Where?" His heart sank. She and Rita had gone to Spain.

"School."

"Oh yes." Today was Monday. He reflected.

"Yes suh," mused David, politely giving shape and form to the silence. "I notice the little bitty Spite was gone when I got here. And I got here on time."

"Is anyone else there?"

"Nobody but Miss Rita."

"Never mind. Give Miss Kitty a message."

"Oh yes suh."

"Tell her I got hurt at the college, got hit in the head, and had a relapse. She'll understand. Tell her I've been sick but I feel better."

"Yes suh. I'll sho tell her. *Sick?*" David, aiming for the famous Negro sympathy, hit instead on a hooting incredulity. David, David, thought the engineer, shaking his head, what is going to happen to you? You ain't white nor black nor nothing.

"I'm better now. Tell her I'll call her."

"Yes suh."

"Goodbye, David."

"Goodbye, Mist' Billy!" cried David, stifling his hilarity. He reached Mr. Vaught at Confederate Chevrolet.

"Billy boy!" cried the old fellow. "You still at school?"

"Sir? Well, no sir. I—"

"You all right, boy?"

"Yes sir. That is, I was hurt—"

"How bad is it down there now?"

"Down here?"

"How did you get out? They didn't want to let Kitty leave. I had to go get her myself last night. Why, they kept them down in the basement of the sorority house all night. Man, they got the army in there."

"Yes, sir," said the engineer, understanding not a single word save only that some larger catastrophe had occurred and that in the commotion his own lapse had been set at nought, remitted.

"You sure you all right?"

"I was knocked out but I got away the next morning," said the engineer carefully. "Now I'm on my way to find—" He faltered.

"Jamie. Good."

"Yes. Jamie. Sir," he began again. This one thing he clearly perceived: the ruckus on the campus dispensed him and he might say what he pleased.

"Yes?"

"Sir, please listen carefully. Something has happened that I think you should know about and will wish to do something about."

"If you think so, I'll do it."

"Yes sir. You see, Kitty's check has been lost or stolen, the check for one hundred thousand dollars."

"What's that?" Mr. Vaught's voice sounded as if he had crept into the receiver. All foolishness aside: this was money, Chevrolets.

The engineer had perceived that he could set forth any facts whatever, however outrageous, and that they would be attended to, acted upon and not held against him.

"My suggestion is that you stop payment, if it is possible."

"It is possible," said the old man, his voice pitched at perfect neutrality. The engineer could hear him riffling through the phone book as he looked up the bank's number.

"It was endorsed over to me, if that is any help."

"It was endorsed over to you," repeated the other as if he were taking it down. *Very well then, it is understood this time, what with one thing and another, that it is for you to tell me and for me to listen. This time.*

"I tried to reach Kitty but couldn't. Tell her that I'll call her."

"I'll tell her."

"Tell her I'll be back."

"You'll be back."

After he hung up, he sat gazing at the old jail and thinking about his kinsman, the high sheriff. Next to the phone booth was the Dew Drop Inn, a rounded corner of streaked concrete and glass brick, a place he knew well. It belonged to a Negro named Sweet Evening Breeze who was said to be effeminate. As he left and came opposite the open door, the sound came: *pssssst!*—not four feet from his ear.

"Eh," he said, pausing and frowning. "Is that you, Breeze?"

"Barrett!"

"What?" He turned, blinking. A pair of eyes gazed at him from the interior darkness.

"Come in, Barrett."

"Thank you all the same, but—"

Hands were laid on him and he was yanked inside. By the same motion a shutter of memory was tripped: it was not so much that he remembered as that, once shoved out of the wings and onto stage, he could then trot through his part perfectly well.

"Mr. Aiken," he said courteously, shaking hands with his old friend, the pseudo-Negro.

"Come in, come in, come in. Listen, I don't in the least blame you—" began the other.

"Please allow me to explain," said the engineer, blinking around at the watery darkness which smelled of sweet beer and hosed-down concrete—there were others present but he could not yet make them out. "The truth is that when I saw you yesterday I did not place you. As you may recall, I spoke to you last summer of my nervous condition and its accompanying symptom of amnesia. Then yesterday, or the day before, I received a blow on the head—"

"Listen," cried the pseudo-Negro. "Yes, right! You have no idea how glad I am to see you. Oh, boy. God knows you have to be careful!"

"No, you don't understand—"

"Don't worry about it," said the pseudo-Negro.

The engineer shrugged. "What you say, Breeze?" He caught sight of the proprietor, a chunky shark-skinned Negro who still wore a cap made of a Nylon stocking rolled and knotted.

"All right now," said Breeze, shaking hands but sucking his teeth, not quite looking at him. He could tell that Breeze remembered him but did not know what to make of his being here. Breeze knew him from the days when he, the engineer, used to cut through the alley behind the Dew Drop on his way to the country club to caddy for his father.

"Where's Mort?" asked the engineer, who began to accommodate to the gloom.

"Mort couldn't make it," said the pseudo-Negro in a voice heavy with grievance, and introduced him to his new friends. There were two men, a Negro and a white man, and a white woman. The men, he understood from the pseudo-Negro's buzzing excitement, were celebrities, and indeed even to the engineer, who did not keep up with current events, they looked familiar. The white man, who sat in a booth with a beautiful sullen untidy girl all black hair and white face and black sweater, was an actor. Though he was dressed like a tramp, he wore a stern haughty expression. A single baleful glance he shot at the engineer and did not look at him again and did not offer his hand at the introduction.

"This is the Merle you spoke of?" the actor asked the pseudo-Negro, indicating the engineer with a splendid one-millimeter theatrical inclination of his head.

"Merle?" repeated the puzzled engineer. "My name is not Merle." Though the rudeness and haughtiness of the actor made him angry at first, the engineer was soon absorbed in the other's mannerisms and his remarkable way of living from one moment to the next. This he accomplished by a certain inclination of his head and a hitching around of his shoulder while he fiddled with a swizzle stick, and a gravity of expression which was aware of itself as gravity. His lips fitted together in a rich conscious union. The sentient engineer, who had been having trouble with his expression today, now felt his own lips come together in a triumphant fit. Perhaps he should be an actor!

"You're here for the festival, the, ah, morality play," said the engineer to demonstrate his returning memory.

"Yes," said the pseudo-Negro. "Do you know the sheriff here?"

"Yes," said the engineer. They were standing at the bar under a ballroom globe which reflected watery specters of sunlight from the glass bricks. The pseudo-Negro introduced him to the other celebrity, a playwright, a slender pop-eyed Negro who was all but swallowed up by a Bulldog Drummond trenchcoat and who, unlike his white companion, greeted the engineer amiably and in fact regarded him with an intense curiosity. For once the engineer felt as powerful and white-hot a radar beam leveled at him as he leveled at others. This fellow was not one to be trifled with. He had done the impossible!—kept his ancient Negro radar intact and added to it a white edginess and restiveness. He fidgeted around and came on at you like a proper Yankee but unlike a Yankee had this great ear which he swung round at you. Already he was onto the engineer: that here too was another odd one, a Southerner who had crossed up his wires and was something betwixt and between. He drank his beer and looked at the engineer sideways. Where the actor was all self playing itself and triumphantly succeeding, coinciding with itself, the playwright was all eyes and ears and not in the least mindful of himself—if he had been, he wouldn't have had his trenchcoat collar turned up in great flaps around his cheeks. The Negro was preposterous-looking, but he didn't care if he was. The actor did care. As for the poor engineer, tuning in both, which was he, actor or playwright?

"You really did not remember him, did you?" the Negro asked the engineer.

"No, that's right."

"He's not conning you, Forney," the playwright told the pseudo-Negro.

"I knew that," cried the pseudo-Negro. "Barrett and I are old shipmates. Aren't we?"

"That's right."

"We went through the Philadelphia thing together, didn't we?"

"Yes." It seemed to the engineer that the pseudo-Negro said "Philadelphia" as if it were a trophy, one of a number of campaign ribbons, though to the best of the engineer's recollection the only campaign which had occurred was his getting hit on the nose by an irate housewife from Haddon Heights, New Jersey.

"Do you think you could prevail upon the local fuzz to do something for you?" the pseudo-Negro asked him.

"What?"

"Let Bugs out of jail."

"Bugs?"

"Bugs Flieger. They put him in jail last night after the festival, and our information is he's been beaten up. Did you know Mona over there is Bug's sister?"

"Bugs Flieger," mused the engineer.

The actor and the white girl looked at each other, the former popping his jaw muscles like Spencer Tracy.

"Tell—ah—Merle here," said the actor, hollowing out his throat, "that Bugs Flieger plays the guitar a little."

"Merle?" asked the mystified engineer, looking around at the others. "Is he talking to me? Why does he call me Merle?"

"You really never heard of Flieger, have you?" asked the playwright.

"No. I have been quite preoccupied lately. I never watch television," said the engineer.

"Television," said the girl. "Jesus Christ."

"What have you been preoccupied with?" the playwright asked him.

"I have recently returned to the South from New York, where I felt quite dislocated as a consequence of a nervous condition," replied the engineer, who always told the truth. "Only to find upon my return that I was no less dislocated here."

"I haven't been well myself," said the playwright as amiably as ever and not in the least sarcastically. "I am a very shaky man."

"Could you speak to the sheriff?" the pseudo-Negro asked him.

"Sure."

Breeze brought more beer and they all sat in the round booth at the corner under the glass bricks.

"Baby, are you really from around here?" the playwright asked the engineer.

"Ask Breeze." The engineer scowled. Why couldn't these people call him by his name?

But when the playwright turned to Breeze the latter only nodded and shrugged. Breeze, the engineer perceived, was extremely nervous. His, the engineer's, presence, disconcerted him. He didn't know what footing to get on with the engineer, the old one, the old ironic Ithaca style: "Hey, Will, where you going?" "Going to caddy." "How come your daddy pays you five dollars a round?" "He don't pay no five dollars"—or the solemn fierce footing of the others. But finally Breeze said absently and to no one and from no footing at all: "This here's Will Barrett, Lawyer Barrett's boy. Lawyer Barrett help many a one." But it was more than that, the engineer then saw, something else was making Breeze nervous. He kept opening the door a crack and looking out. He was scared to death.

But the pseudo-Negro wanted to talk about more serious matters. He asked the others some interview-type questions about racial subjects, all the while snapping pictures (only the engineer noticed) from his tie-clasp camera.

"It's a moral issue," said the actor, breaking the swizzle stick between his fingers, breaking it the way actors break swizzle sticks and pencils. The pseudo-Negro explained that the actor had flown in from Hollywood with Mona his companion to assist in the present drive at great cost to himself, both financially and emotionally, the latter because he was embroiled in a distressing custody suit in the course of which his wife had broken into his bedroom and pulled Mona's hair.

"Of course it's a moral issue," said the playwright. Now the engineer remembered seeing one of his plays with Midge Auchincloss. It was about an artist who has gone stale, lost his creative powers, until he musters the courage to face the truth within himself, which is his love for his wife's younger brother. He puts a merciful end to the joyless uncreative marriage in favor of a more meaningful relationship with his friend. The last scene shows the lovers standing in a window of the artist's Left Bank apartment looking up at the gleaming towers of Sacre-Coeur. "There has been a loss of the holy in the world," said the youth. "Yes, we must recover it," replies the artist. "It has fallen to us to recover the holy." "It has been a long time since I was at Mass," says the youth, looking at the church. "Let's have our own Mass," replies the artist as softly as Pelleas and, stretching forth a shy hand, touches the youth's golden hair.

Sweet Evening Breeze, the engineer noticed, was growing more nervous by the minute. His skin turned grayer and more sharklike and he had fallen into a complicated way of snapping his fingers. Once, after peering through the cracked door, he called the pseudo-Negro aside.

"Breeze says the fuzz is on its way over here," the pseudo-Negro told them gravely.

"How do you know?" the playwright asked Breeze.

"I know."

"How do they know we're here?"

"Ask Merle," said the actor.

"Don't be ridiculous," said the pseudo-Negro, frowning. "I pulled him in here, remember. Barrett's all right."

"The man done pass by here twice," said Breeze, rattling off a drumroll of finger-snaps. "The next time he's coming in."

"How do you know?" asked the pseudo-Negro with his lively reporters' eyes.

"I knows, that's all."

"Wonderful," said the playwright. The playwright's joy, the engineer perceived, came from seeing life unfold in the same absurd dramatic way as a Broadway play—it was incredible that the one should be like the other after all.

"Bill," said the pseudo-Negro earnestly. "We've got to get Mona out of here. You know what will happen to her?"

The engineer reflected a moment. "Do you all want to leave town?"

"Yes. Our business here is finished except for Bugs."

"What about your Chevrolet?"

"They picked it up an hour ago."

"Why not get on a bus?"

"That's where they got Bugs, at the bus station."

"Here they come," said Breeze.

Sure enough, there was a hammering at the door. "Here's what you do," said the engineer suddenly. Upside down as always, he could think only when thinking was impossible. It was when thinking was expected of one that he couldn't think. "Take my camper. Here." He quickly drew a sketch of the highway and the old river road.

"It's over the levee here. I'll talk to the police. Go out the back door. You drive," he said to Mona, handing her the key. The actor was watching him with a fine gray eye. "The others can ride in the back." The hammering became deafening. "Now if I don't meet you at the levee," shouted the engineer, "go to my uncle's in Louisiana. Cross the bridge at Vicksburg. Mr. Fannin Barrett of Shut Off. I'll meet you there." From his breast pocket he took out a sheaf of road maps, selected a Conoco state map, made an X, and wrote a name and gave it to Mona. "Who are they?" he asked Breeze, who stood rooted at the heaving door.

"That's Mist' Ross and Mist' Gover," said Breeze eagerly, as if he were already smoothing things over with the police.

"Do you know them, Merle?" asked the actor, with a new appraising glint in his eye. "Yes."

"How are they?"

"Gover's all right."

"Open the door, Breeze." The voice came through the door.

"Yes suh."

"No, hold it—" began the engineer.

"The man said unlock it." It was too late. The doorway was first flooded by sunlight, then darkened by uniforms.

"What do you say, Beans. Ellis," said the engineer, coming toward them.

"Where's the poontang?" asked Beans Ross, a strong, tall, fat man with a handsome tanned face and green-tinted sunglasses such as highway police wear, though he was only a town deputy.

"This is Will Barrett, Beans," said the engineer, holding out his hand. "Mister Ed's boy."

"What," said Beans, shoving his glasses onto his forehead. He even took the other's hand and there was for a split second a chance of peace between them. "What the hell are you doing here?" Beans took from his pocket a small blackjack as soft and worn as skin.

"I'll explain, but meanwhile there is no reason to hit Breeze." He knew at once what Beans meant to do.

"All right, Breeze," said Beans in a routine voice, not looking at him.

Sweet Evening Breeze, knowing what was expected of him, doffed his stocking cap and presented the crown of his head. Hardly watching but with a quick outward flick of his wrist, Beans hit Breeze on the forehead with the blackjack. Breeze fell down.

"Goddamn it, Beans," said the engineer. "That's no way to act."

"You got something to say bout it?"

"Yes."

"Where's the poontang?" asked Beans, and with a gesture at once fond and conspiratorial—enlisting him—and contemptuous, he leaned across and snapped his middle finger on the engineer's fly.

"Augh," grunted the engineer, bowing slightly and seeming to remember something. Had this happened to him as a boy, getting snapped on the fly? The humiliation was familiar.

"Don't do that, Beans," said Ellis Gover, coming between them and shaking his head. "This is a real good old boy."

By the time the engineer's nausea had cleared, Beans had caught sight of Mona in the booth. Without taking his eyes from her, he pulled Ellis close and began to whisper. The engineer had time to straighten himself and to brace his foot in the corner of the jamb and sill of the front door. For once in his life he had time and position and a good shot, and for once things became as clear as they used to be in the old honorable days. He hit Beans in the root of his neck as hard as he ever hit the sandbag in the West Side Y.M.C.A. Beans's cap and glasses flew off and he sat down on the floor. "Now listen here, Ellis," said the engineer immediately, turning to the tall, younger policeman. "Yall go ahead," he told the others casually, waving them over Beans's outstretched legs and out the front door. "Catch a Bluebird cab at the corner."

"Wait a minute," said Ellis, but he did not stop them.

"Don't worry about it, Ellis. They haven't done anything. They're leaving town and that's what you want."

"But, shit, man," said Ellis, who could not take his eyes from the fallen policeman. "You done hit Beans."

"I know, but look at Breeze," said the engineer by way of answer, and nodded to the Negro, who was laid out straight as a corpse. Standing next to Ellis, he took him by the elbow just as he used to touch him in a football huddle. Ellis was all-state halfback and the engineer, who was quarterback (not all-state), had called the plays in huddle. Ellis was a bit slow in catching the signals and the engineer used to squeeze him so, just above the elbow.

"Yeah, but hailfire, Will."

"Listen, Ellis," said the engineer, already moving. "You bring charges against me to clear yourself, do you understand? Tell Beans the others got in behind you. You got it?"

"Yeah, but—"

"Now give Beans a hand and tell him to come after me, O.K.?" He said this though Beans was still out cold, and giving Ellis a final huddle sort of squeeze and nod, the engineer walked quickly to the back door and out into Heck's Alley.

"Will," cried Ellis again, feeling that all was not well. But the other had already crossed the alley to a certain board in a fence which had been eroded into the shape of Illinois and which he knew, now fifteen years later, to swing free on a single nail, was through it and into Miss Mamie Billups' back yard. Miss Mamie was sitting on her side porch when he stooped to pass under her satsuma tree.

"How do you do, Miss Mamie," said the courteous engineer, bowing and putting his tie inside his coat.

"Who is that?" called out the old woman sharply. Everyone used to steal her satsumas.

"This is Will Barrett, Miss Mamie."

"Will Barrett! You come on up here, Will!"

"I can't right now, Miss Mamie," said the engineer, turning Theard Street. "I'll be right back!"

4.

His friends waited for him but not long enough. By the time he rounded the lower curve of Milliken Bend, having walked the inner shoulder of the levee out of sight of highway and town, the Trav-L-Aire had already lumbered out of the willows and started up the levee—at an angle! The cabin teetered dangerously. He forgot to tell Mona not to do this. He covered his face with his hands: Mona, thinking to spare the

G.M.C. the climb straight up, was in a fair way to turn her plumb over. When he looked up, however, the levee was clear.

It was two o'clock. He was hungry. At the levee end of Theard Street he bought a half dozen tamales from a street vendor (but not the same whose cry *Rayed hot!* used to echo up and down the summer night in the 1950's). Now finding a patch of waist-high elephant grass past the towhead and out of sight of anyone standing on the levee behind him, he rolled to and fro and made a hollow which was tilted like a buttercup into the westering sun. It was warm enough to take off his coat and roll up his sleeves. He ate the tamales carefully, taking care not to stain his clothes. The meat was good but his tooth encountered a number-eight shot: rabbit or possibly squirrel. Afterwards he washed his hands in river water, which still thrashed through the lower level of the towhead, and dried them with his handkerchief. Returning to his hollow, he sat cross-legged for a while and watched a towboat push a good half acre of sulphur barges up the dead water on the Louisiana side. Then he curled up and, using his coat folded wrong-side-out for a pillow, went to sleep.

Cold and stiffness woke him. It was a moonless overcast night, but he could make out Scorpio writhing dimly over Louisiana, convulsed around great bloody Antares. Buttoning all three buttons of his jacket, he ran along the inner shoulder of the levee, out of sight of town, until he got warm. When he came abreast of the stacks of the gypsum mill, he went quickly over and down into Blanton Street and took the Illinois Central tracks, which went curving away behind the high school. It was pitch dark under the stadium, but his muscles remembered the spacing of the ties. The open rear of the bleachers exhaled a faint odor of cellar earth and urine. At the China-man's he took the tangent of Houston Street, which ran through a better Negro neighborhood of neat shotgun cottages and flower gardens, into the heavy humming air and ham-rich smell of the cottonseed oil mill, and out at De Ridder.

He stood in the inky darkness of the water oaks and looked at his house. It was the same except that the gallery had been closed by glass louvers and a flagpole stuck out of a second-story window. His aunts were sitting on the porch. They had moved out, television and all. He came closer and stood amid the azaleas. They were jolly and fit, were the aunts, and younger than ever. Three were watching "Strike It Rich," two were playing canasta, and one was reading *Race and Reason* and eating Whitman's Sampler. He remembered now that Sophie wrote love letters to Bill Cullen. What a tough hearty crew they were! hearty as muzhiks, and good haters, yet not ill-natured—they'd be honestly and unaffectedly glad to see him walk in, would kiss him and hold him off and make over him—rosy-skinned, easy in their consciences, arteries as supple as a girl's, husbands dead and gone these forty years, pegged out so long ago that he could not remember anyone ever speaking of them; Christian ladies every one, four Protestant, Presbyterian, and Scotch-Irish, two Catholic and Creole, but long since reconciled, ecumenized, by bon appétit and laughter and good hearty hatred.

It was here under the water oaks that his father used to stroll of a summer night, hands in his pockets and head down, sauntering along the sidewalk in his old Princeton style of sauntering, right side turning forward with right leg. Here under the water oaks or there under the street light, he would hold parley with passers-by, stranger and friend, white and black, thief and police. The boy would sit on the front steps, close enough to speak with his father and close enough too to service the Philco which played its stack of prewar 78's but always had trouble doing it. The mechanism creaked and whirred and down came the record plop and round it went for a spell, hissing under the voyaging needle. From the open window came Brahms, nearly always Brahms. Up and down the sidewalk went his father, took his turn under the street light sometimes with a client, sometimes alone. The clients, black and white and by and large the sorriest of crews but of course listening now with every eager effort of attention and even of a special stratospheric understanding. Between records the boy could hear snatches of talk: "Yassuh, that's the way it is now! I have notice the same thing myself!"—the father having said something about the cheapness of good intentions and the rarity of good character—"I'm sho gon' do like you say"—the passer-by working him of course for the fifty cents or five dollars or what, but working him as gracefully as anyone ever worked, they as good at their trade as he at his. The boy listening: what was the dread in his heart as he heard the colloquy and the beautiful terrible Brahms which went abroad into the humming summer night and the heavy ham-rich air?

The aunts let out a holler. Bill Cullen had given away a cabin cruiser to a lady from Michigan City, Indiana.

It was on such an evening—he passed his hand over his eyes and stretching it forth touched the sibilant corky bark of the water oak—that his father had died. The son watched from the step, old Brahms went abroad, the father took a stroll and spoke to a stranger of the good life and the loneliness of the galaxies. "Yes suh," said the stranger. "I have heard tell it was so" (that the closest star was two light years away).

When the man came back the boy asked him:

"Father, why do you walk in the dark when you know they have sworn to kill you?"

"I'm not afraid, son."

To the west the cars of the white people were nosing up the levee, headlights switched first to parking, then out altogether. From the east, beyond the cottonseed-oil mill, came the sound of Negro laughter.

The man walked until midnight. Once a police car stopped. The policeman spoke to the man.

"You've won," said the youth when the man came back. "I heard the policeman. They've left town."

"We haven't won, son. We've lost."

"But they're gone, Father."

"Why shouldn't they leave? They've won."

"How have they won, Father?"

"They don't have to stay. Because they found out that we are like them after all and so there was no reason for them to stay."

"How are we like them, Father?"

"Once they were the fornicators and the bribers and the takers of bribes and we were not and that was why they hated us. Now we are like them, so why should they stay? They know they don't have to kill me."

"How do they know that, Father?"

"Because we've lost it all, son."

"Lost what?"

"But there's one thing they don't know."

"What's that, Father?"

"They may have won, but I don't have to choose that."

"Choose what?"

"Choose them."

This time, as he turned to leave, the youth called out to him. "Wait."

"What?"

"Don't leave."

"I'm just going to the corner."

But there was a dread about this night, the night of victory. (Victory is the saddest thing of all, said the father.) The mellowness of Brahms had gone overripe, the victorious serenity of the Great Horn Theme was false, oh fake fake. Underneath, all was unwell.

"Father."

"What?"

"Why do you like to be alone?"

"In the last analysis, you are alone." He turned into the darkness of the oaks.

"Don't leave." The terror of the beautiful victorious music pierced his very soul.

"I'm not leaving, son," said the man and, after taking a turn, came back to the steps. But instead of stopping to sit beside the youth, he went up past him, resting his hand on the other's shoulder so heavily that the boy looked up to see his father's face. But the father went on without saying anything: went into the house, on through the old closed-in dogtrot hall to the back porch, opened the country food press which had been converted to a gun cabinet, took down the double-barrel twelve-gauge Greener, loaded it, went up the back stairs into the attic, and, fitting the muzzle of the Greener into the notch of his breastbone, could still reach both triggers with his thumbs. That was how it had to happen, the sheriff told the youth, that was the only way it could have happened.

The sound came crashing through the music, louder than twenty Philcos, a single sound, yet more prolonged and thunderous than a single shot. The youth turned off the Philco and went upstairs.

"—and Anacin does not upset your stummick," said Bill Cullen.

Again his hand went forth, knowing where it was, though he could not see, and touched the tiny iron horsehead of the hitching post, traced the cold metal down to the place where the oak had grown round it in an elephant lip. His fingertips touched the warm finny whispering bark.

Wait. While his fingers explored the juncture of iron and bark, his eyes narrowed as if he caught a glimmer of light on the cold iron skull. *Wait.* I think he was wrong and that he was looking in the wrong place. No, not he but the times. The times were wrong and one looked in the wrong place. It wasn't even his fault because that was the way he was and the way the times were, and there was no other place a man could look. It was the worst of times, a time of fake beauty and fake victory. *Wait.* He had missed it! It was not in the Brahms that one looked and not in solitariness and not in the old sad poetry but—he wrung out his ear—but here, under your nose, here in the very curiousness and drollness and extraness of the iron and the bark that—he shook his head—that—

The TV studio audience laughed with its quick, obedient, and above all grateful Los Angeles laughter—once we were lonesome back home, the old sad home of our fathers, and here we are together and happy at last.

A Negro came whistling toward him under the street light, a young man his own age. Entering the darkness of the water oaks, the Negro did not at first see him (though it had been his, the Negro's, business, and until now, to see him first), then did see him two yards away and stopped for a long half second. They looked at each other. There was nothing to say. Their fathers would have had much to say: "In the end, Sam, it comes down to a question of character." "Yes suh, Lawyer Barrett, you right about that. Like I was saying to my wife only this evening—" But the sons had nothing to say. The engineer looked at the other as the half second wore on. You may be in a fix and I know that but what you don't know and won't believe and must find out for yourself is that I'm in a fix too and you got to get where I am before you even know what I'm talking about and I know that and that's why there is nothing to say now. Meanwhile I wish you well.

It was only then, belatedly, and as if it were required of him, that the Negro shuddered and went his way.

As he watched his aunts, a squad car came slowly down De Ridder and stopped not twelve feet beyond the iron horse. A policeman, not Ross or Gover, went up to the porch and spoke to Aunt Sophie. She shook her head four or five times, hand to her throat, and when the policeman left, turned off the television and in her excitement stumbled a little as she told the others. Aunt Bootie forgot the Whitman's Sampler in her lap, stood up and scattered nougats and bird eggs in all directions. No one noticed.

Without taking much care about it, he walked through the azaleas and around to the back screen door, which was locked and which he opened, without knowing that he remembered, by wedging the door back against its hinges so that the bolt could be forced free of its worn wooden mortise, and went straight up the two flights to the attic and straight into the windowless interior room built into the peak of the house. His uplifted hand felt for and found the string. The old clear-glass 25-watt bulb shed a yellow mizzling light, a light of rays, actual striae. The room had not been touched, they were still here; the grandfather's army blanket, Plattsburg issue, the puttees, a belt of webbing, the Kaiser Bill helmets, the five-pound binoculars with an artillery scale etched into one lens. He picked up the Greener, broke the breech and sighted at the yellow bulb. The bore was still speckled with powder grains. And the collapsible boat: an English contraption of silvery zeppelin fabric with varnished spruce spars to spring it into shape. It lay as it had lain ten years ago, half disassembled and hastily packed from a duck hunt he and his father had taken on the White River in the early fifties. Now, as if it were the very night of their return, he knelt absently and repacked the boat, remembering the feel and fit of the spar-ends and the brass sockets and even the goofy English directions: "—Don't be discouraged if spar L does not fit immediately into socket J—patience is required."

After he repacked the boat, he lay on the cot and, propping himself against the wall, drew the hard scratchy army blanket up to his armpits. For two hours he sat so, wakeful and alert, while his eyes followed the yellow drizzle of light into every corner of the attic room.

It was eight o'clock when he went downstairs, English boat slung over one shoulder, artillery binoculars over the other. The aunts had not gotten up. Hearing D'lo shuffling about the kitchen, he took care not to startle her: he slipped out the back door and came in noisily again.

"Law, if it ain't Mr. Billy," said D'lo, rolling her eyes conventionally and noticing the wall clock as she did so. She was no more surprised by the doings of white folks than he was.

D'lo stirred steaming boilers of grits and batter, fist sunk deep into her side, knees driven together by her great weight and bare heels ridden off her old pink mules and onto the floor. It crossed his mind that D'lo had somehow known he was here. He asked her not to tell his aunts.

"I ain't gon' tell them nothing!"

"I'm surprised you're still here."

"Where I'm going!"

"They still fight?"

"Fight! You don't know, fight."

"The police are looking for me."

"Uh-oh," said D'lo. This was serious. Yet he could not have sworn she did not know all about it.

D'lo found him his father's Rolls razor and, while he washed and shaved in the downstairs bathroom, fixed him a big breakfast of grits and sausage and batter cakes. When he left, he gave her twenty dollars.

"I thank you," said D'lo formally and twisted the bill into the stocking roll below her fat old knee, which curved out in six different arcs of rich cinnamon flesh.

A step creaked. "Here *she* come," said D'lo. Sophie was *she*, ole miss, the one who gave the orders.

"I'll be seeing you, D'lo," he said, shouldering the boat.

"All right now, Mist' Billy," she cried politely, socking down the grits spoon on the boiler and curling her lip in a rich and complex acknowledgment of his own queerness and her no more than mild sympathy and of the distance between them, maybe not even sympathy but just a good-humored letting him be. (All right now, you was a good little boy, but don't mess with me too much, go on, get out of my kitchen.)

Ten minutes later he was up and over the levee and down into the willows, where he assembled the boat and the two-bladed paddle. It was a sparkling day. The river was ruffled by glittering steel wavelets like a northern lake. Shoving off and sitting buttoned up kayak style in the aft hole, he went dropping away in the fast water, past the barrow pits and blue holes, and now beginning to paddle, went skimming over the wide river, which seemed to brim and curve up like a watchglass from the great creamy boils that shed tons of cold bottom water, down past old Fort Ste. Marie on the Louisiana side, its ramparts gone back to blackberries and honeysuckle. He knew every tunnel, embrasure, magazine room, and did not bother to look. Two Negroes in a skiff were running a trotline under the caving bank. They watched him a second longer than they might have. Now they were watching him again, under their arms as they handed the line along. He frowned, wondering how he looked in the face, then recollected himself: it was after all an uncommon sight, a man fully dressed in coat and necktie and buttoned up in a tiny waterbug of a boat and at nine o'clock of a Tuesday morning. They could not encompass him; he was beyond their reckoning. But hold on, something new! As he drifted past the fort, he rubbed his eyes. A pennant fluttered from the parapet, the Stars and Bars! And the entire fort was surrounded by a ten-foot-high hurricane fence. But of course! This very month marked the hundredth anniversary of the reduction of the fort by Admiral Foote's gunboats. It was part of the preparation for the Centennial! No doubt they would, at the proper time, imprison the "Confederates" behind the fence.

But as he dropped past the fort, he was surprised to see "sentinels" patrolling the fence and even a few prisoners inside, but as unlikely a lot of Confederates as one could imagine—men and women! The men bearded properly enough, but both sexes blue-jeaned and sweat-shirted and altogether disreputable. And Negroes! And yonder, pacing the parapet—God Lord!—was Milo Menander, the politician, who was evidently playing the role of Beast Banks, the infamous federal commandant of the infamous federal prison into which the fort was converted after its capture. Capital! And hadn't he got himself up grandly for the occasion: flowing locks, big cigar, hand pressed Napoleonically into his side, a proper villainous-looking old man if ever there was one.

But hold on! Something was wrong. Were they not two years late with their celebration? The fort was captured early in the war, and here it was 19—What year was this? He wrang out his ear and beat his pockets in vain for his Gulf calender card. Another slip: if Beast Banks had reduced and occupied the fort, why was the Stars and Bars still flying?

It was past figuring even if he'd a stomach for figuring. Something may be amiss here, but then all was not well with him either. Next he'd be hearing singing ravening particles. Besides, he had other fish to fry and many a mile to travel. British wariness woke in him and, putting his head down, he dropped below the fort as silently as an Englishman slipping past Heligoland.

He put in at the old ferry landing, abandoned when the bridge at Vicksburg was built and now no more than a sloughing bank of mealy earth honeycombed by cliff swallows. Disassembling and packing his boat, he stowed it in a cave-in and pulled dirt over it and set out up the sunken ferry road, which ran through loess cuts filled now as always with a smoky morning twilight and the smell of roots (here in Louisiana across the river it was ever a dim green place of swamps and shacks and Negro graveyards sparkling with red and green medicine bottles; the tree stumps were inhabited by spirits), past flooded pin-oak flats where great pileated woodpeckers went ringing down the smoky aisles. Though it was only two hundred yards from home, Louisiana had ever seemed misty and faraway, removed in time and space. Over yonder in the swamps lived the same great birds Audubon saw. Freejacks, Frenchmen, and river rats trapped muskrat and caught catfish. It was a place of small and pleasant deeds.

"Hey, Merum!"

Uncle Fannin was walking up and down the back porch, his face narrow and dark as a piece of slab bark, carrying in the crook of his arm the Browning automatic worn to silver, with bluing left only in the grooves of the etching. The trigger guard was worn as thin as an old man's wedding ring.

"Mayrom! Where's that Ma'am?"

He was calling his servant Merriam but he never called him twice by the same name.

It was characteristic of the uncle that he had greeted his nephew without surprise, as if it were nothing out of the ordinary that he should come hiking up out of nowhere with his artillery binoculars, and after five years. He hardly stopped his pacing.

"We're fixing to mark some coveys up on Sunnyside," he said, as if it were he who owed the explanations.

The engineer blinked. They might have been waiting for him.

The Trav-L-Aire was nowhere in sight and Uncle Fannin knew nothing about it or any company of "actors," as the engineer called them (calculating that a mixture of blacks and whites was somehow more tolerable if they were performers).

Merriam came round the corner of the house with two pointers, one an old liver-and-white bitch who knew what was what and had no time for foolery, trotting head down, dugs rippling like a curtain; the other pointer was a fool. He was a young dog named Rock. He put his muzzle in the engineer's hand and nudged him hard. His head was heavy as iron. There were warts all over him where Uncle Fannin had shot him for his mistakes. Merriam, the engineer perceived, was partial to Rock and was afraid the uncle was going to shoot him again. Merriam was a short heavy Negro whose face was welted and bound up through the cheeks so that he was muffle-jawed in his speech. Blackness like a fury seemed to rush forward in his face. But the engineer knew that the fury was a kind of good nature. He wore a lumpy white sweater with stuffing sticking out of it like a scarecrow.

It was not a real hunt they were setting out on. Uncle Fannin wanted to mark coveys for the season. Later in the fall, businessmen would come down from Memphis and up from New Orleans and he would take them out. The engineer refused the gun offered to him, but he went along with them. They drove into the woods in an old high-finned De Soto whose back seat had been removed to make room for the dogs. A partition of chicken wire fenced off the front seat. The dogs stuck their heads out the windows, grinning and splitting the wind, their feet scrabbling for purchase on the metal seat bed. The car smelled of old bitter car metal and croker sacks and the hot funky firecracker smell of dry bird dogs.

Merriam sat with the two Barretts on the front seat, but swiveled around to face them to show he was not sitting with them, not quite on or off the seat, mostly off and claiming, in a nice deprecation, not more than an inch of seat, not through any real necessity but only as the proper concession due the law of gravity. It was not hard to believe that Merriam could have sat in the air if it had been required of him.

The De Soto plunged and roared, crashing into potholes not with a single shock but with a distributed and mediated looseness, a shambling sound like throwing a chain against a wall, knocking the dogs every whichway. When Uncle Fannin slammed on the brakes, the dogs were thrust forward, their chins pushing against the shoulders of the passengers, but already back-pedaling apologetically, their expressions both agrieved and grinning.

They hunted from an old plantation dike long since reclaimed by the woods and now no more than a high path through thickets. The engineer, still dressed in Dacron suit and suède oxfords, followed along, hands in pockets. Rock got shot again, though with bird shot and from a sufficient distance so that it did no more harm than raise a new crop of warts.

"Meroom!"

"Yassuh."

Merriam was carrying a brand-new single-shot nickel-plated sixteen-gauge from Sears Roebuck which looked like a silver flute.

"Look at that son of a bitch."

"I see him."

Below and ahead of them the bitch Maggie was holding a point, her body bent like a pin, tail quivering. Rock had swung wide and was doubling back and coming up behind her, bounding up and down like a springbok to see over the grass. He smelled nothing.

"He's sho gon' run over her," said the uncle.

"No suh, he ain't," said Merriam, but keeping a fearful weather eye on Rock.

"What's he doing then?"

The engineer perceived that the uncle was asking the question ironically, taking due notice of the magic and incantatory faculty that Negroes are supposed to have—they know what animals are going to do, for example—but doing it ironically.

"Goddamn, he *is* going to run over her!"—joking aside now.

"He ain't stuttn it," said Merriam.

Of course Rock, damn fool that he was, did run over Maggie, landing squarely in the middle of the covey and exploding quail in all directions—it coming over him in mid-air and at the last second, the inkling of what lay below, he braking and back-pedaling wildly like Goofy. Uncle Fannin shot three times, twice at quail and once at Rock, and, like all dead shots, already beginning to talk as he shot as if the shooting itself were the least of it. "Look at that cock, one, two, and—" *Wham*. He got three birds, one with one shot and two crossing with the other shot. The third shot hit Rock. The engineer opened his mouth to say something but a fourth shot went off.

"Lord to God," groaned Merriam. "He done shot him again." Merriam went to look after Rock.

The uncle didn't hear. He was already down the levee and after a single who had gone angling off into the woods, wings propped down, chunky, teetering in his glide. Uncle Fannin went sidling and backing into the underbrush, reloading as he went, the vines singing and popping around his legs. When he couldn't find the single, even though they had seen where he landed, Merriam told the two Barretts that the quail had hidden from the dogs.

"Now how in the hell is he going to hide from the dogs," said the disgusted uncle.

"He hiding now," said Merriam, still speaking to the engineer. "They has a way of hiding so that no dog in the world can see or smell them."

"Oh, Goddamn, come on now. You hold that dog."

"I seen them!"

"How do they hide, Merriam?" the engineer asked him.

"They hits the ground and grab ahold of trash and sticks with both feets and throws theyselfs upside down with his feets sticking up and the dogs will go right over him ever' time."

"Hold that goddamn dog now, Mayrim!"

After supper they watched television. An old round-eyed Zenith and two leatherette recliners, the kind that are advertised on the back page of the comic section, had been placed in a clearing that had been made long ago by pushing Aunt Felice's good New Orleans furniture back into the dark corners of the room. Merriam watched from a roost somewhere atop a pile of chairs and tables. The sentient engineer perceived immediately that the recliner he was given was Merriam's seat, but there was nothing he could do about it. Uncle Fannin pretended the reclinder had been brought out for the engineer (how could it have been?) and Merriam pretended he always roosted high in the darkness. But when they, Uncle Fannin and Merriam, talked during the programs, sometimes the uncle, forgetting, would speak to the other recliner:

"He's leaving now but he be back up there later, don't worry about it."

"Yes suh," said Merriam from the upper darkness.

"He's a pistol ball now, ain't he?"

"I mean."

"But Chester, now. Chester can't hold them by himself."

"That Mist' Chester is all right now," cried Merriam.

"Shoot."

Whenever a commercial ended, Uncle Fannin lifted himself and took a quick pluck at his seat by way of getting ready.

"That laig don't hold him!"

"It ain't his leg that's holding him now," said the uncle, and, noticing that it was his nephew who sat beside him, gave him a wink and a poke in the ribs to show that he didn't take Merriam seriously.

Merriam didn't mind. They argued about the Western heroes as if they were real people whose motives could be figured out. During a commercial, Merriam told the engineer of a program they had seen last week. It made a strong impression on him because the hero, their favorite, a black knight of a man, both gentleman and a brawler, had gotten badly beat up. It was part one of a series and so he was still beat up.

"I told Mist' Fanny"—Merriam spoke muffle-jawed and all in a rush as if he hoped to get the words out before they got bound up in his cheeks—"that the onliest way in the world they can catch him is to get in behind him. Mist' Fanny, he say they gon' stomp him. I say they got to get in behind him first. What happened, some man called his attention, like I say 'look here!' and he looked and they did get in behind him and Lord, they stomped him, bad, I mean all up in the head. He lay out there in the street two days and folks scared to help him, everybody scared of this one man, Mister errerr—, errerr—" Merriam snapped his fingers. "It slips my mind, but he was a stout man and low, lower than you or Mist' Fanny, he brush his hair up in the front like." Merriam showed them and described the man so that the engineer would recognize him if he happened to see him. "They taken his money and his gun and his horse and left him out there in the sun. Then here come this other man to kill him. And I said to Mist' Fanny, there is one thing this other man don't know and that is he got this little biddy pistol on him and they didn't take it off him because he got it hid in his bosom."

"Man, how you going to go up against a thirty-thirty with a derringer," said the uncle disdainfully, yet shyly, watchful of the engineer lest he, the engineer, think too badly of Merriam. His uncle was pleading with him!

"I'd like to see how that comes out," said the engineer. "Is the second part coming on tonight?" he asked Merriam.

"Yessuh."

"That fellow's name was Bogardus," said the uncle presently. "He carried a carbine with a lever action and he can work that lever as fast as you can shoot that automatic there."

"Yessuh," said Merriam, but without conviction.

Still no sign of the Trav-L-Aire, and at midnight the engineer went to bed—without taking thought about it, going up to the second-floor room he used to have in the summertime, a narrow cell under the eaves furnished with an armoire, a basin and ewer and chamber pot, and an old-style feather bed with bolster. The skull was still there on the shelf of the armoire, property of his namesake, Dr. Williston Barrett, the original misfit, who graduated from old Jefferson Medical College, by persuasion an abolitionist but who nevertheless went to fight in Virginia and afterwards having had enough, he said, of the dying and the dead and the living as well, the North and the South, of men in sum, came home to the country and never practiced a day in his life, took instead to his own laudanum and became a philosopher of sorts, lived another sixty years, the only long-lived Barrett male. The skull had turned as yellow as ivory and was pencil-marked by ten generations of children; it was sawed through the dome and the lid securely fastened by silver hinges; undo that and the brain pan was itself sectioned and hinged, opening in turn into an airy comb of sinus cells.

It was cold but he knew the feather bed, so he stripped to his shorts, and after washing his T-shirt in the ewer and spreading it on the marble stand to dry, he climbed into bed. The warm goosedown flowed up around him. It was, he had always imagined, something like going to bed in Central Europe. He pulled the bolster up to his shoulders and propped Sutter's casebook on its thick margin.

R.R., white male, c. 25, well-dev. but under-nour. 10 mm. entrance wound in right temporal, moderate powder tattooing and branding, right exophthalmus and hematoma; stellate exit wund left mastoidal base, approx 28 mm diam. Cops say suicide.

From Lt. B.'s report: R.R., b. Garden City, Long Island; grad LIU and MIT last June. Employed Redstone Arsenal since June 15. Drove here after work yesterday, July 3, purchased S & W .38 rev. from Pioneer Sports, rented room at Jeff D. Hotel, found on bed clothed 9 a.m., approx time of death, 1 a.m., July 4.

Lt. B.: "His life before him, etc." "One of the lucky ones, etc." "No woman trouble, liquor or drugs or money, etc." "? ? ?"

Suicide considered as consequence of the spirit of abstraction and of transcendence; lewdness as sole portal of reentry into world demoted to immanence; reentry into immanence via orgasm; but post-orgasmic transcendence 7 devils worse than first.

Man who falls victim to transcendence as the spirit of abstraction, i.e., elevates self to posture over and against world which is *pari passu* demoted to immanence and seen as examplar and specimen and coordinate, and who is not at same time compensated by beauty of motion of method of science, has no choice but to seek reentry into immanent world *qua* immanence. But since no avenue of reentry remains save genital and since reentry coterminus $\bar{c}$ orgasm, post-orgasmic despair without remedy. Of my series of four suicides in scientists and technicians, 3 post-coital (spermatozoa at meatus), 2 in hotel room. Hotel room = site of intersection of transcendence and immanence: room itself, a triaxial coordinate ten floors above street; whore who comes up = pure immanence to be entered. But entry doesn't avail: one skids off into transcendence. *There is no reentry from the orbit of transcendence.*

Lt. B.: "Maybe they're so shocked by what they've turned loose on the world—" Pandora's Box theory, etc. "Maybe that's why he did it," etc.

I say: "Bullshit, Lt., and on the contrary. This Schadenfreude is what keeps them going," etc.

What I cannot tell Lt.: If R.R. had been a good pornographer, he would not have suicided. His death was due, not to lewdness, but to the failure of lewdness.

I say to Val: Re Sweden: increase in suicides in Sweden due not to increase in lewdness but to decline of lewdness. When Sweden was post-Christian but had not yet forgotten Cx (circa 1850–1914), Swedish lewdness intact and suicides negligible. But when Swedes truly post-Christian (not merely post-Christian but also post-memory of Cx), lewdness declined and suicides rose in inverse relation.

Val to me: Don't sell Sweden short. (I notice that her language has taken on the deplorable and lapsed slanginess found in many religious, priests and nuns, and in *Our Sunday Visitor.*) The next great saint must come from Sweden, etc. It is only from desolation of total transcendence of self and total descent of world of immanence that a man can come who can recover himself and world under God, etc. Give me suicidal Swede, says she, over Alabama Christian any day, etc.

I say: Very good, very good talk, but it is after all only that, that is the kind of talk we have between us.

The bar turned in his head, synapses gave way, and he slept ten hours dreamlessly and without spansules.

Still no sign of the Trav-L-Aire the next morning, but after a great steaming breakfast of brains and eggs and apple rings served in front of the Zenith. (Captain Kangaroo: Uncle Fannin and Merriam cackled like maniacs at the doings of Captain K. and Mr. Greenjeans, and the engineer wondered, how is it that uncle and servant, who were solid 3-D persons, true denizens of this misty Natchez Trace country, should be transported by these sad gags from Madison Avenue? But they were transported. They were merry as could be, and he, the engineer, guessed that was all right: more power to Captain K.)

After he had transacted his oil-lease business with his uncle, the telephone rang. It was the deputy sheriff in Shut Off. It seemed a little "trailer" had been stolen by a bunch of niggers and outside agitators and that papers and books in the name of Williston Bibb Barrett had been found therein. Did Mr. Fannin know anything about it? If he did and if it was his property or his kin's, he might reclaim the same by coming down to Shut Off and picking it up.

The uncle held the phone and told his nephew.

"What happened to the, ah, Negroes and the outside agitators?" asked the latter calmly.

Nothing, it seemed. They were there, at this moment, in Shut Off. It needed but a word from Mr. Fannin to give the lie to their crazy story that they had borrowed the trailer from his kinsman and the lot of them would be thrown in jail, if not into the dungeon at Fort Ste. Marie.

"The dungeon. So that's it," said the nephew, relieved despite himself. "And what if the story is confirmed?" he asked his uncle.

Then they'd be packed off in twenty minutes on the next bus to Memphis.

"Confirm the story," said the nephew. "And tell him I'll be there in an hour to pick up my camper." He wanted his friends free, clear of danger, but free and clear of him too, gone, by the time he reached Shut Off.

After bidding his uncle and Merriam farewell—who were only waiting for him to leave to set off with the dogs in the De Soto—he struck out for the old landing, where he retrieved his boat and drifted a mile or so to the meadows, which presently separated the river from Shut Off. So it came to be called Shut Off: many years ago one of the meanderings of the river had jumped the neck of a peninsula and shut the landing off from the river.

Shelby Foote

(1916–   )

Shelby Foote was born on November 17, 1916, in Greenville, Mississippi. From 1935 to 1937 he attended the University of North Carolina before joining the Mississippi National Guard in 1939. Foote then served in the United States Army from 1940 to 1944 and in the Marine Corps during 1945. When World War II ended, he held various odd jobs, such as a reporter for the *Delta Democrat-Times* and as a construction worker. In 1949, Foote completed his first novel, *Tournament,* and within the next five years, four more novels were published: *Follow Me Down* (1950), *Love in a Dry Season* (1951), *Shiloh* (1952), and *Jordan County: A Landscape in Narrative* (1954). In addition, in 1954, Foote began his nonfiction Civil War trilogy entitled *The Civil War: A Narrative.* In 1958, Volume 1, *Fort Sumter to Perryville,* was published; Volume II, *Fredericksburg to Meridian,* was published in 1963; and Volume III, *Red River to Appomattox,* was published in 1974. Although Foote moved briefly to Alabama in 1964, he has lived primarily in Memphis since 1953. Foote has been writer-in-residence at the University of Virginia in 1963, Memphis State University from 1966 to 1967, and Hollins College during 1968. Furthermore, as playwright-in-residence at Arena Stage, Washington, D.C., he wrote the play *Jordan County,* based on the novel of the same name, which was produced in 1964. Over the years, Foote has received numerous awards, including three Guggenheim Fellowships (1955, 1956, 1957), the Ford Fellowship for drama (1963), and the Fletcher Pratt Award for nonfiction (1964). His sixth novel, *September, September,* was published in 1978.

Foote's role in Ken Burns's documentary *The Civil War,* first shown on television in 1990, created renewed interest in Foote's work. *The Correspondence of Shelby Foote and Walker Percy* was published in 1997.

Rain Down Home

Dawn broke somewhere up the line, pearly under a drizzle of rain, but presently the rain left off and the flat eastern rim of earth was tinted rose. The sun came up fast, dark red while still half hidden, the color of blood, then fiery as it bounced clear of the landline, shining on the picked-over cotton that hung in bluing skeins on dead brown stalks. Ahead the engine was rounding a curve and suddenly a plume of steam was balanced on the whistle; it screamed, much as a hound will bay once in full course for no reason at all; then the plume disappeared and it hushed. The rain returned but the sun still shone, pale yellow through the mizzle. "I ought to watch," the young man told himself. He spoke aloud. But that was the last he remembered. He slid back into drowsiness and slumber, taking with him only the present sensations of dusty plush and cinders and vibration.

"Dont," he said. The hand nudged at his shoulder again and the voice came back, as if from a long way off.

"Bristol," it said. "All out."

He saw the hand, the black cuff with its gold-thread stars and bars of longterm service toward retirement, and looking up he saw the conductor himself, the face with its halo of white hair, the broken veins of the nose, the jowls and dewlap. "Hey?"

"End of the line. All out for Bristol."

Then he woke. It was there, outside the window, in broad open daylight. He had stayed awake all night, riding south out of Memphis through the hundred-odd miles of blackness, with only the soft gold gleam of cabin lanterns scattered at random across the fields and the infrequent sudden garish burst of streetlights announcing towns, and then had slept through the arrival. "Thanks," he said.

Rising—he was about twenty-five, rumpled and unshaven after the all-night train-ride—he took his suitcase from the overhead rack and carried it down the aisle of the empty coach. At the door onto the rear platform he turned suddenly, looking back, and saw what he had known he would see. The conductor stood there, watching him, the ticket punch in his left hand glinting highlight. He narrowed his eyes and pulled his chin down. "Whats the matter?" he said. "You think I'm drunk or something?" The conductor shrugged and turned away. He smiled, swung the door ajar, and stepped onto the platform.

Brilliant early morning sunlight struck him across the eyes as he came down the iron steps to where the flagman stood on the concrete quay, the brass buttons on his coat as bright as the sun itself. "Mississippi, hey?" the young man cried. He smiled as he spoke.

"That's right," the flagman said. "Home again."

"Jordan County. You think itll rain?"

"Oh sure. Cotton's all in: why not?"

"Why not," he said, waving his hand, and went into the depot.

He intended to leave his bag with the ticket agent, but the agent was busy at his window with three Negroes. Grave-faced, they wore funeral clothes, dark suits with heavy watch chains and boiled collars. The agent was scratching his head, grave-faced too. They had accompanied a dead friend to the station; they wanted to ship him to Vicksburg in his coffin. That was easy enough. The problem was they wanted him sent back two days later for a second funeral. He had lived both in Vicksburg and in Bristol, with lodge brothers and relatives in each, and since the widow insisted on burial here, they figured it would be cheaper, more convenient all around, that is, to send him to Vicksburg so his friends could see him there, laid out in style, than it would be for all those people to leave their jobs and buy railroad tickets to come up here and see him. Then they would ship him back to Bristol for the second funeral and the burial. That made sense; the trouble lay in the question of fares. First-class was the normal rate, but the agent was not so sure about the propriety of selling a round-trip ticket to a corpse. His friends maintained he was entitled to it, but the agent was doubtful; he was not even sure but what it might be sacrilegious. "I'll call the office and get a ruling," he was saying, still scratching his head, as the young man left with the suitcase.

Again in brilliant sunlight he walked westward down the main street of the town. Cars went past or paused at intersections, obedient to the traffic lights suspended between poles, the lidless glare of red and green, the momentary blink of amber, relaying the orders of some central brain, peremptory, electric, and unthinking. The young man frowned. When he had gone two blocks he stopped and gazed across the street at a department store with a new façade of imitation marble that was mottled like a pinto; *Goodblood's* it said in a flowing script across the pony-colored front. He shook his head. Then as he stood looking down the line of bright new parking meters, each with its clockwork entrails ticking off the time between now and the red flag of violation, he saw a man coming toward him. The man walked with his head tipped forward, a worried expression on his face. He stopped, patting his pockets, preoccupied, and the young man spoke.

"They changed it," he said to the man. "They changed it on me while my back was turned."

"How's that?" The worried look did not leave the man's face.

"The town. They changed it. It's all new."

"Yes; it's growing," the man said. He nodded once and hurried on, preoccupied, patting his pockets.

"Hey!" The man did not glance back; he was already out of earshot. "You didnt know me, did you?" the young man said, standing at the curb with the suitcase held against his leg. "You didnt know little Pauly Green that used to deliver your paper. Did you, Mr. Nowell?"

Just then a cloud blew past the sun. The glitter left the rain-washed streets but then came back as bright as ever; the cloud was gone and the parking meters twinkled in steady metallic progression along the curb. He turned to go, swinging the suitcase clear of his leg, and as he turned he saw an envelope lying face-down on the sidewalk. Something was written on the flap. Bending forward Pauly read the almost childish script. *Write soon!* PS. *I am seventeen now. My birthday was Fri 13, I hope not bad luck.* He picked it up. When he turned it over he saw that the stamp had not been canceled and the address, damp from contact with the sidewalk, was written in the same adolescent scrawl. *Miss Norma Jean Purdy, Box 221, Route 7, Indemnity, Miss.* He turned it over again. The flap had come unglued, so he opened it and took out a sheet of blue-lined paper with three loose-leaf holes down the left margin. Another cloud blew past the sun while he read. The paper went from dazzling white to gray, then back to dazzling.

> *Dear Norma Jean:*
>
> *I was glad to get your letter. I am sorry I havent written you before now. I guess my letter got pretty dull, no exciting news. But I will try to write more interesting letters so you wont mind writing.*
>
> *I had a grand time at Ole Miss. If you had been there it would have been complete.*
>
> *We went Fri morning, got there about 10:00. We rehersed to much I cant hardly talk now. There was a party at the gym Friday night. I had a good time. I met a boy from Isstabula I think you spell it. He asked me to walk back to the dormitory but I refused because I do not like to go with just anybody. Saturday I had a real good time but made my self so tired walking and see-ing everything on the campus. The boys were so nice, college boys. Some-times we would be walking down the side walk and they would whistle at us.*
>
> *I wish you could come see me sometimes, I sure would enjoy your visit. It wont be long until Xmas. I hope you can come and stay with me some. We could go on a shopping spree or something, so please come to see me when you can.*
>
> *Hope you have good luck with your new boy friend. Hope you will get or got to go on the hay ride with him. Write me real soon. Love,*
>
> *ALICE*
>
> *Please write soon!! I am trying to make my letters more interesting.*
> *Love & xxxx.*
> PS. *Went to the revile last night. That sure is a good preacher that is holding it. His name is Juny Lynch. He is a Methodist.*

Pauly smiled. The post office was one block farther; as he went past the mailbox he sealed the sticky flap again and dropped the letter into the slot. "Go where you belong, where youre not wanted," he told it as it fell from sight. As always, when he turned it loose there was the sense of having done something irretrievable. Another cloud went over the sun, but this time it did not pass. Rain began to fall and he hurried to the door of a café in the middle of the block. Inside, he sat on a stool at the counter, the suitcase upended on the floor beside him. "What will it be?" the waitress said.

"Whats good?"

"You want breakfast?"

"Breakfast." He nodded and the waitress watched him across the glass of water she had brought. "Whats good?" He smiled but she did not smile back. Her nails were coral; they looked detachable, like earrings bought in a shop. She was no longer young and crow's feet were etched at the outward corners of her eyes.

"It's all good."

"Is the bacon good?"

"It's all good," she said mournfully.

"O.K. Give me ham and eggs. Coffee now."

"How you want the eggs?"

"What?"

"How you want them fixed?"

"Mm—I dont care. Looking at me, I reckon."

"Two!" she cried over her shoulder, in the direction of the order window. "Straight up, with ham!"

"Yao," a voice said from the kitchen.

When she returned from the coffee urn and set the thick white cup and saucer on the counter, he was waiting. He leaned forward and asked her, stiff-lipped with the steam from the coffee rising about his face: "Why doesnt everybody love each other?"

"Do what?"

"Love each other. Why don't they love each other?"

"Say, what are you anyhow? Some kind of a nut?"

"No—really. Why not?" He was not discouraged. He spoke stiff-lipped, his face wreathed with steam. "Were you ever wrapped in wet sheets, wrapped up tight? Thats what they need, and then theyd love each other. I'm telling you. Wrap them up, good and tight, leave them there for a while like that, then turn them loose, and believe me theyd love each other."

"Look," she said. "I'm busy."

She went on down the counter and did not come near him again until she brought the ham and eggs. Then she only set them down in passing; she kept moving, out of reach. He ate hungrily, all of it, including three slices of toast, and when he had finished he took up the suitcase and started for the door. The Greek proprietor stood at the cash register. He had the drawer open, looking at his money. Pauly paid for the meal and turned to leave. Then he turned back. He was blond and short, with wide shoulders, small gray eyes, and an aggressive chin. "Say," he said. The Greek looked up from the cash drawer. "Could I leave this here for a while?" He raised the suitcase and lowered it again.

"All right," the Greek said. "Put back here. But not responsible, unnerstand?"

"Sure. I'll be right back."

"Ho K."

When he had put the suitcase behind the plywood partition he went to the front door and stood looking through the glass. A fine rain was still falling but there were pale gray shadows on the sidewalk. Pauly opened the door and saw the sun through the mizzling rain. "What do you know," he cried over his shoulder. "The devil is beating his wife."

He turned up the collar of his coat and went out into the rain, going west still, toward the river. The levee was a block and a half away, with the veterans' sign in front of it, blue and white except for the red stars and stripes on the flag in the middle. He walked fast and soon he stood in front of it, holding his collar with both hands at his throat. The sign had words in big letters on both sides of the flag. To the left it said: IN MEMORY OF THOSE WHO SERVED IN WORLD WAR TWO, and on the opposite side, in balance: MAY THE SPIRIT OF OUR BOYS WHO FELL IN BATTLE LIVE FOREVER. He had heard about that. Originally it was intended to put the names of the war dead on the signboard, the whites down one side and the Negroes down the other, with the American flag between. But the notion of having them all on one board caused so much ugly feeling—there was even some talk of dynamite, for example—that the service club whose project it was took a vote and decided that it would be better just to say something fitting about the spirit of our boys. That was what they did, and already it had begun to look a bit weathered around the edges. Pauly stood in the rain, looking at it and holding his collar close at the throat. His hair was all the way wet by now and the rain ran in trickles down his face.

Presently he walked around the sign and climbed the levee, no easy job for the grass was slippery and under it there was mud. When he reached the crest the rain stopped as if by signal; his shadow darkened on the grass, and below him lay the river, the Mississippi. Tawny, wide, dimpled and swirled by eddies, it sparkled in the sunlight as it swept along to the south. Pauly was alone up here and a cold wind blew against his face. Behind him Bristol thrust its steeples through the overarching trees. "Hello, big river," he said. He felt better now. He came down, slipping and smiling. "That's one big river," he said.

He did not stop at the base of the levee; he kept going east, back past the café where he had left his suitcase, past the depot—wondering if the corpse had got its round-trip ticket—past the courthouse where the Confederate soldier watched from his marble shaft, past the ramped tracks of the C & B, and on out that same street, until finally he came to a park: WINGATE PARK it was called on a wrought-iron arch above the entrance. Sunlight glittered on the rain-washed gravel paths; the grass was still green after the first cold snap of late November. He entered the park and sat on a circular bench that was built around the trunk of a big oak. Despite the coolness he took off his damp coat and sat with it folded across his lap. The stubble of beard was more obvious now, with a coppery glint in the sunshine. His clothes were even more rumpled. The whites of his eyes were threaded with red and each lid showed the edge of its red lining. He leaned back against the tree, and almost immediately he was asleep.

Singing woke him. At first he did not know where he was, nor then how long he had been there. The singer was a little girl who was playing with two dolls about five yards from the bench. She wore a short wool skirt, a beret, and a corduroy jacket. "Hello," Pauly said. She did not hear him. He leaned forward, hands on his knees, and said it again. "Hel-lo."

Turning her head she looked at him and her eyes were large and dark. She was very pretty. "Hello," she said.

"What are you playing?"

"Dolls."

"Oh. Have they got names?"

"Yes."

"Tell me, are they nice names?"

"Nice," she said.

"What, for instance?"

"I'm sorry. Mummy says I mustnt talk to strangers."

"Well, you just tell your mummy I said she's wrong. Some of the nicest people I ever knew were strangers."

She smiled at this and he smiled back. Then: "Sal Ann," they heard a flat voice say, and Pauly saw a young Negress sitting on a nearby bench, holding a multicolored booklet in both hands. She wore loafers with new pennies in the flaps and bright green socks. "Come play over here," she said. Her voice was expressionless; she did not look at Pauly. Sally Ann took up her dolls.

"I have to go."

"You do?"

"Oh, yes. She's my nurse."

"I know," he said. "Ive had them myself. Goodbye."

"Goodbye."

He watched her go, and suddenly feeling the chill he put his coat on. Presently, when the nurse had finished her comic book—*Bat Man* was its title; she seemed to have derived small pleasure from it—she rose and beckoned to the little girl. "Time for your nap," she said. Leaving by way of the arch they passed a man who walked bent forward, leaning on a cane. As he drew closer Pauly saw that he was old and there was pain in his face. Then he saw Pauly and turned aside, taking the bench where the nurse had read through *Bat Man*. He sat with the cane planted stiffly between his shoes, both hands on the crook, and his face was empty except for the lines of pain.

The sun was past the overhead. Pauly rose abruptly and went to the old man's bench. From closer he saw that he was poor as well as old. His shoes were broken and there were holes in the ankles of his cotton socks. The cuffs of his shirt were badly frayed, as was the collar, and where the button was missing the points bunched forward, overlapping the knot of his tie, which had been tied and re-tied so often in the same place that the knot looked as tight and hard as a little piece of gravel. His coat, loose-fitting and almost as rumpled as Pauly's own, gave him a scarecrow aspect. When he turned his head Pauly saw that the pain was old, like the rest of him; he had lived with it for years. "How do," he said.

"Hello. Could I sit down and talk?"

"All right."

Pauly sat beside him on the bench, and again that stiff-lipped expression came onto his face. "Ive been trying to figure," he said. He paused and the old man watched him, unsurprised. "I came back from the war and all, back here where I was born and raised, and people don't even know me on the street. I see things all around me and it tears me up inside. A letter on the sidewalk, say, from a teen-age girl reaching out for love and already knowing she wont find it . . . Sad things, terrible things happen to people! Do you realize that right this minute there are people all over the world crying, weeping, lying awake in their beds at night, smoking cigarettes till their gums are sore, and looking up at the ceiling like they thought theyd find the answer written there? Kicked in the teeth, insulted, full of misery the way a glass can get so full it bulges at the brim with surface tension—what does it mean? What does it mean? It's got to mean something, all that suffering."

"It's just people, the way they are," the old man said. For a moment he was quiet. Then he added: "They got away from God."

"God? Whats God got to do with it? What does He care?"

"Maybe they just werent meant to be happy, then."

"No! That's not true!" Pauly jerked his hands as he spoke, clenching and un-clenching his fists. "I want to live in the world but I don't understand, and until I can understand I cant live. Why wont people be happy? Not cant: *wont*."

"I dont know," the old man said. He looked away, across the park. "Ive been here going on eighty-seven years and I don't know. My wife died of a cancer until finally all that was left was teeth and eyes and yelling, like some animal. I asked myself all those things: 'What does it mean? What does it mean?' Then she died. She'd been a beautiful woman in her day, and she wound up like a run-over cat. I asked myself, again and again: 'What does it mean? What does it mean?' And you know, I finally found the an-swer; one answer, anyhow. It dont mean a thing. Nothing. Why should it mean any-thing? I stopped thinking about it is what I finally did. It's what you better do, too. Dont think about it. They'll lock you up, you keep at it too long. They wanted to lock me up, down at Whitfield, but I quit thinking about it and they let me alone. Now they say I'm harmless. And I am."

The stiff-lipped expression had turned to horror; Pauly jumped up. He was about to speak, but then instead he turned and walked away. Near the entrance he looked back. The old man was just sitting there, his hands on the crook of the cane; he looked out across the park, the graveled paths glittering in the sunlight; he sat there, empty-eyed, and the young man might never have spoken to him at all. Pauly went under the wrought-iron arch. He walked three blocks fast, then three blocks slow, and by that time he was back in front of the courthouse, looking up at the Confeder-ate, the blank stone eyeballs under the wide-brimmed hat. Within the next three blocks he passed the depot and was within sight of the post office. He went past it, walking fast again, and re-entered the café.

He took a booth this time, one in back. The same waitress came with a glass of water as before, still wearing the detachable-looking nails and the crow's feet at the corners of her eyes. "Hello," he said.

"What will it be?"

"Look: I'm sorry about all that other. I meant it, but I'm sorry I bothered you with it's what I mean. I was lonesome."

"I'm real busy. What will it be?"

This was not true. There were only a few people in the place, three men drinking beer in a booth across the way and three others seated singly on the stools along the counter. It was two oclock, the postlunch lull. "O.K. Whats good?" he asked. She was about to speak but he held up one hand, pontifical. "It's *all* good," he said mournfully. "Bring me liver and onions. Coffee. Apple pie. Can you do that?"

"All right," she said.

He went back to the men's room, the walls of which were penciled with obscenities so crowded that the later entries had had to be squeezed into the margins and even be-tween the lines of the earlier ones. Pauly tried to close his eyes to them, pictures and text, just as he tried to close his nostrils against the stench of creosote and urine, but the two attempts were equally unsuccessful. *Kilroy was here* was scrawled in several places, opposite one of which someone had written: *A good place for him.*

When Pauly returned to the booth he saw through the front window that the rain had come on again, no drizzle now, but true rain, big drops pattering hard against the glass. Outside, the street was darkened and the buildings were hidden across the way.

"Say, thats *rain*," he said to the waitress as she set the food in front of him.

"Yes," she said, and left.

While he ate he heard one of the beer drinkers in the adjoining booth tell the other two a story. He was a young businessman but he broadened his accent, pretending to be more country than he was. "There was this scratch farmer, a white man working about sixty acres. But it was a wet year and the weeds began to get out of control, so he brought in some help, a dozen hoe-hands, and went down to the field to work alongside them. One of the women was brown-skinned, not yet middle aged, and he took him a notion. So he called her aside where the cotton was high, and the two of them lay down between the rows. Well, his wife came to the field about this time, bringing a pail of water, and she walked right up on them in the act. When he saw her he jumped up and began to run. She yelled after him: 'You, Ephraim! It aint no use to run. You know I caught you!' 'Yessum,' he said, 'I know you did. But I believe I'll run a little ways anyhow.'"

There was laughter, including the laughter of the man who told the story, and when it died down, one of the other beer drinkers said, "I can see how that might help." They laughed again.

Pauly frowned. He motioned to the waitress and she came over, still with the mistrustful look. "Bring me another cup of coffee with that," he told her, pointing at the pie. She brought it, and as she set it down in front of him he said, "I was wrong, baby, wrong and never wronger. It's not love they need. I know what they need. And I'm the one can give it to them, too. Wait till I drink this." He put three big spoonfuls of sugar into the coffee and stirred in the jug of cream. The waitress went away but he did not notice. His face was not stiff-lipped now. He looked happy, with a peculiar glint to his eyes.

When he had finished the coffee he rose from the booth and went up front, where the Greek stood looking into the register. "Hand me my suitcase, will you, bud?"

"Here," the Greek said, and held the swing door ajar.

"Thanks." Pauly leaned inside and took up the suitcase.

He came back to the booth with it. The waitress was still there, removing the dishes, all except the uneaten pie, but he did not look at her. He set the suitcase on the floor and opened it. From the jumbled disorder of faded khaki and books and shaving gear he took out an Army .45 and four loaded clips. He set them on the table, then turned back to close the bag. "Wait," he said. "Lets do this right." He rooted in the suitcase until he found what he was looking for—an Expert marksmanship badge, the maltese cross inclosed in a silver wreath, with three bars suspended beneath it like a ladder; *Pistol, Pistol, Pistol,* it said on the rungs. He pinned the badge to the rumpled lapel of his coat, and took up the pistol, drawing back the slide. It went back with a dry, thick, deadly sound, then forward with a snick, the hammer cocked. "Now," he said. He was talking to himself by then, for the waitress was nowhere in sight.

The first shot hit the coffee urn dead center and a half-inch amber stream came spouting from the hole the bullet made. He swung on to the right where the Greek stood round-eyed, his hands on the open drawer, looking toward the sound of the explosion. "You and your goddam money," Pauly said. "You wouldnt even hand a man a suitcase." He took careful aim and shot him in the head. As the Greek went down he pushed with both hands, closing the cash drawer. So Pauly took two shots at the register. The second hit something vital and the drawer ran out again, ringing a bell. "Cigar!" he cried, and turned to look for other targets.

He found plenty of them—the light fixtures, the mirror behind the counter, the glasses racked along the wall, even the little cream jugs arranged on a tray beside a spigot. Each gave off its particular brand of fireworks when hit. The cream jugs were especially amusing, for they flew in all directions. He had thirty-five shots and he took his time, replacing the empty clips methodically. "This is doing me a lot of good," he said at one point, and indeed it seemed to be true; he appeared to enjoy the whole display, from start to finish. The beer drinkers had disappeared, along with the three men who had sat at the counter. He had the place to himself. It was very quiet between shots. Between the sharp, popping explosions of cartridges he heard the rain murmur against the plate glass window and the low moans of the Greek proprietor from somewhere down behind the open register.

Though it seemed considerably longer to those who crouched beneath the tables and behind the counter, the whole affair took less than five minutes by the clock. The thing that frightened them most, they said when they told about it later, was the way the shooter kept laughing between shots. He was sitting there eating the pie, quite happy, with the empty pistol and the four empty clips on the table in front of him, when the police arrived. He even smiled when they shook him, roughed him up. "Do your duty, men," he said, "just like I did mine."

Next day it was in all the papers, how he shot up the place for no reason at all. The Greek proprietor, whose injury had been more bloody than serious—all he lost was the lobe from one of his ears—used that day to date things from, the way old people once spoke of falling stars. The waitress was quoted too: "I knew it was something wrong with that one from the minute I laid eyes on him." DERANGED VETERAN the headlines called him, and the stories gave a list of the various institutions he had been in and out of since the war. Everyone agreed that that was what he was, all right, deranged.

John Kennedy Toole

(1937–1969)

John Kennedy Toole was born in New Orleans in 1937. When he was sixteen, he enrolled at Tulane University in his home state, where he was graduated cum laude. He then attended Columbia University.

While Toole was in Puerto Rico in the armed services, he wrote *A Confederacy of Dunces* (1980), which won the Pulitzer Prize for Fiction in 1981. After serving in the U.S. Army, he taught at Hunter College in New York, the University of Southwestern Louisiana, and St. Mary's Dominican in Louisiana. In 1969, Toole left New Orleans. On March 26 of that year, he committed suicide in Biloxi, Mississippi. *The Neon Bible*, written when he was sixteen, was published in 1989.

from *A Confederacy of Dunces*

Foreword

Perhaps the best way to introduce this novel—which on my third reading of it astounds me even more than the first—is to tell of my first encounter with it. While I was teaching at Loyola in 1976 I began to get telephone calls from a lady unknown to me. What she proposed was preposterous. It was not that she had written a couple of chapters of a novel and wanted to get into my class. It was that her son, who was dead, had written an entire novel during the early sixties, a big novel, and she wanted me to read it. Why would I want to do that? I asked her. Because it is a great novel, she said.

Over the years I have become very good at getting out of things I don't want to do. And if ever there was something I didn't want to do, this was surely it: to deal with the mother of a dead novelist and, worst of all, to have to read a manuscript that she said was *great*, and that, as it turned out, was a badly smeared, scarcely readable carbon.

But the lady was persistent, and it somehow came to pass that she stood in my office handing me the hefty manuscript. There was no getting out of it; only one hope remained—that I could read a few pages and that they would be bad enough for me, in good conscience, to read no farther. Usually I can do just that. Indeed the first paragraph often suffices. My only fear was that this one might not be bad enough, or might be just good enough, so that I would have to keep reading.

In this case I read on. And on. First with the sinking feeling that it was not bad enough to quit, then with a prickle of interest, then a growing excitement, and finally an incredulity: surely it was not possible that it was so good. I shall resist the temptation to say what first made me gape, grin, laugh out loud, shake my head in wonderment. Better let the reader make the discovery on his own.

Here at any rate is Ignatius Reilly, without progenitor in any literature I know of—slob extraordinary, a mad Oliver Hardy, a fat Don Quixote, a perverse Thomas Aquinas rolled into one—who is in violent revolt against the entire modern age, lying in his flannel nightshirt, in a back bedroom on Constantinople Street in New Orleans, who between gigantic seizures of flatulence and eructations is filling dozens of Big Chief tablets with invective.

His mother thinks he needs to go to work. He does, in a succession of jobs. Each job rapidly escalates into a lunatic adventure, a full-blown disaster: yet each has, like Don Quixote's, its own eerie logic.

His girlfriend, Myrna Minkoff of the Bronx, thinks he needs sex. What happens between Myrna and Ignatius is like no other boy-meets-girl story in my experience.

By no means a lesser virtue of Toole's novel is his rendering of the particularities of New Orleans, its back streets, its out-of-the-way neighborhoods, its odd speech, its ethnic whites—and one black in whom Toole has achieved the near-impossible, a superb comic character of immense wit and resourcefulness without the least trace of Rastus minstrelsy.

But Toole's greatest achievement is Ignatius Reilly himself, intellectual, ideologue, deadbeat, goof-off, glutton, who should repel the reader with his gargantuan bloats, his thunderous contempt and one-man war against everybody—Freud, homosexuals, heterosexuals, Protestants, and the assorted excesses of modern times. Imagine an Aquinas gone to pot, transported to New Orleans whence he makes a wild foray through the swamps to LSU at Baton Rouge, where his lumber jacket is stolen in the faculty men's room where he is seated, overcome by mammoth gastrointestinal problems. His pyloric valve periodically closes in response to the lack of a "proper geometry and theology" in the modern world.

I hesitate to use the word *comedy*—though comedy it is—because that implies simply a funny book, and this novel is a great deal more than that. A great rumbling farce of Falstaffian dimensions would better describe it; *commedia* would be closer to it.

It is also sad. One never quite knows where the sadness comes from—from the tragedy at the heart of Ignatius's great gaseous rages and lunatic adventures or the tragedy attending the book itself.

The tragedy of the book is the tragedy of the author—his suicide in 1969 at the age of thirty-two. Another tragedy is the body of work we have been denied.

It is a great pity that John Kennedy Toole is not alive and well and writing. But he is not, and there is nothing we can do about it but make sure that this gargantuan tumultuous human tragicomedy is at least made available to a world of readers.

WALKER PERCY

One

A green hunting cap squeezed the top of the fleshy balloon of a head. The green earflaps, full of large ears and uncut hair and the fine bristles that grew in the ears themselves, stuck out on either side like turn signals indicating two directions at once. Full, pursed lips protruded beneath the bushy black moustache and, at their corners, sank into little folds filled with disapproval and potato chip crumbs. In the shadow under the green visor of the cap Ignatius J. Reilly's supercilious blue and yellow eyes looked down upon the other people waiting under the clock at the D. H. Holmes department store, studying the crowd of people for signs of bad taste in dress. Several of the outfits, Ignatius noticed, were new enough and expensive enough to be properly considered offenses against taste and decency. Possession of anything new or expensive only reflected a person's lack of theology and geometry; it could even cast doubts upon one's soul.

Ignatius himself was dressed comfortably and sensibly. The hunting cap prevented head colds. The voluminous tweed trousers were durable and permitted unusually free locomotion. Their pleats and nooks contained pockets of warm, stale air that soothed Ignatius. The plaid flannel shirt made a jacket unnecessary while the muffler guarded exposed Reilly skin between earflap and collar. The outfit was acceptable by any theological and geometrical standards, however abstruse, and suggested a rich inner life.

Shifting from one hip to the other in his lumbering, elephantine fashion, Ignatius sent waves of flesh rippling beneath the tweed and flannel, waves that broke upon buttons and seams. Thus rearranged, he contemplated the long while that he had been waiting for his mother. Principally he considered the discomfort he was beginning to feel. It seemed as if his whole being was ready to burst from his swollen suede desert boots, and, as if to verify this, Ignatius turned his singular eyes toward his feet. The feet did indeed look swollen. He was prepared to offer the sight of those bulging boots to his mother as evidence of her thoughtlessness. Looking up, he saw the sun beginning to descend over the Mississippi at the foot of Canal Street. The Holmes clock said almost five. Already he was polishing a few carefully worded accusations designed to reduce his mother to repentance or, at least, confusion. He often had to keep her in her place.

She had driven him downtown in the old Plymouth, and while she was at the doctor's seeing about her arthritis, Ignatius had bought some sheet music at Werlein's for his trumpet and a new string for his lute. Then he had wandered into the Penny Arcade on Royal Street to see whether any new games had been installed. He had been disappointed to find the miniature mechanical baseball game gone. Perhaps it was only being repaired. The last time that he had played it the batter would not work and, after some argument, the management had returned his nickel, even though the Penny Arcade people had been base enough to suggest that Ignatius had himself broken the baseball machine by kicking it.

Concentrating upon the fate of the miniature baseball machine, Ignatius detached his being from the physical reality of Canal Street and the people around him and therefore did not notice the two eyes that were hungrily watching him from behind one of D. H. Holmes' pillars, two sad eyes shining with hope and desire.

Was it possible to repair the machine in New Orleans? Probably so. However, it might have to be sent to some place like Milwaukee or Chicago or some other city whose name Ignatius associated with efficient repair shops and permanently smoking factories. Ignatius hoped that the baseball game was being carefully handled in shipment, that none of its little players was being chipped or maimed by brutal railroad employees determined to ruin the railroad forever with damage claims from shippers, railroad employees who would subsequently go on strike and destroy the Illinois Central.

As Ignatius was considering the delight which the little baseball game afforded humanity, the two sad and covetous eyes moved toward him through the crowd like torpedoes zeroing in on a great woolly tanker. The policeman plucked at Ignatius's bag of sheet music.

"You got any identification, mister?" the policeman asked in a voice that hoped that Ignatius was officially unidentified.

"What?" Ignatius looked down upon the badge on the blue cap. "Who are you?"

"Let me see your driver's license."

"I don't drive. Will you kindly go away? I am waiting for my mother."

"What's this hanging out your bag?"

"What do you think it is, stupid? It's a string for my lute."

"What's that?" The policeman drew back a little. "Are you local?"

"Is it the part of the police department to harass me when this city is a flagrant vice capital of the civilized world?" Ignatius bellowed over the crowd in front of the store. "This city is famous for its gamblers, prostitutes, exhibitionists, anti-Christs, alcoholics, sodomites, drug addicts, fetishists, onanists, pornographers, frauds, jades, litterbugs, and lesbians, all of whom are only too well protected by graft. If you have a moment, I shall endeavor to discuss the crime problem with you, but don't make the mistake of bothering *me*."

The policeman grabbed Ignatius by the arm and was struck on his cap with the sheet music. The dangling lute string whipped him on the ear.

"Hey," the policeman said.

"Take that!" Ignatius cried, noticing that a circle of interested shoppers was beginning to form.

Inside D. H. Holmes, Mrs. Reilly was in the bakery department pressing her maternal breast against a glass case of macaroons. With one of her fingers, chafed from many years of scrubbing her son's mammoth, yellowed drawers, she tapped on the glass case to attract the saleslady.

"Oh, Miss Inez," Mrs. Reilly called in that accent that occurs south of New Jersey only in New Orleans, that Hoboken near the Gulf of Mexico. "Over here, babe."

"Hey, how you making?" Miss Inez asked. "How you feeling, darling?"

"Not so hot," Mrs. Reilly answered truthfully.

"Ain't that a shame." Miss Inez leaned over the glass case and forgot about her cakes. "I don't feel so hot myself. It's my feet."

"Lord, I wisht I was that lucky. I got arthuritis in my elbow."

"Aw no!" Miss Inez said with genuine sympathy. "My poor old poppa's got that. We make him go set himself in a hot tub fulla berling water."

"My boy's floating around in our tub all day long. I can't hardly get in my own bathroom no more."

"I thought he was married, precious."

"Ignatius? Eh, la la," Mrs. Reilly said sadly. "Sweetheart, you wanna gimme two dozen of them fancy mix?"

"But I thought you told me he was married," Miss Inez said while she was putting the cakes in a box.

"He ain't even got him a prospect. The little girl friend he had flew the coop."

"Well, he's got time."

"I guess so," Mrs. Reilly said disinterestedly. "Look, you wanna gimme half a dozen wine cakes, too? Ignatius gets nasty if we run outta cake."

"Your boy likes his cake, huh?"

"Oh, Lord, my elbow's killing me," Mrs. Reilly answered.

In the center of the crowd that had formed before the department store the hunting cap, the green radius of the circle of people, was bobbing about violently.

"I shall contact the mayor," Ignatius was shouting.

"Let the boy alone," a voice said from the crowd.

"Go get the strippers on Bourbon Street," an old man added. "He's a good boy. He's waiting for his momma."

"Thank you," Ignatius said haughtily. "I hope that all of you will bear witness to this outrage."

"You come with me," the policeman said to Ignatius with waning self-confidence. The crowd was turning into something of a mob, and there was no traffic patrolman in sight. "We're going to the precinct."

"A good boy can't even wait for his momma by D. H. Holmes." It was the old man again. "I'm telling you, the city was never like this. It's the communiss."

"Are you calling me a communiss?" the policeman asked the old man while he tried to avoid the lashing of the lute string. "I'll take you in, too. You better watch out who you calling a communiss."

"You can't arress me," the old man cried. "I'm a member of the Golden Age Club sponsored by the New Orleans Recreation Department."

"Let that old man alone, you dirty cop," a woman screamed. "He's prolly somebody's grampaw."

"I am," the old man said. "I got six granchirren all studying with the sisters. Smart, too."

Over the heads of the people Ignatius saw his mother walking slowly out of the lobby of the department store carrying the bakery products as if they were boxes of cement.

"Mother!" he called. "Not a moment too soon. I've been seized."

Pushing through the people, Mrs. Reilly said, "Ignatius! What's going on here? What you done now? Hey, take your hands off my boy."

"I'm not touching him, lady," the policeman said. "Is this here your son?"

Mrs. Reilly snatched the whizzing lute string from Ignatius.

"Of course I'm her child," Ignatius said. "Can't you see her affection for me?"

"She loves her boy," the old man said.

"What you trying to do my poor child?" Mrs. Reilly asked the policeman. Ignatius patted his mother's hennaed hair with one of his huge paws. "You got plenty business picking on poor chirren with all the kind of people they got running in this town. Waiting for his momma and they try to arrest him."

"This is clearly a case for the Civil Liberties Union," Ignatius observed, squeezing his mother's drooping shoulder with the paw. "We must contact Myrna Minkoff, my lost love. She knows about those things."

"It's the communiss," the old man interrupted.

"How old is he?" the policeman asked Mrs. Reilly.

"I am thirty," Ignatius said condescendingly.

"You got a job?"

"Ignatius hasta help me at home," Mrs. Reilly said. Her initial courage was failing a little, and she began to twist the lute string with the cord on the cake boxes. "I got terrible arthuritis."

"I dust a bit," Ignatius told the policeman. "In addition, I am at the moment writing a lengthy indictment against our century. When my brain begins to reel from my literary labors, I make an occasional cheese dip."

"Ignatius makes delicious cheese dips," Mrs. Reilly said.

"That's very nice of him," the old man said. "Most boys are out running around all the time."

"Why don't you shut up?" the policeman said to the old man.

"Ignatius," Mrs. Reilly asked in a trembling voice, "what you done, boy?"

"Actually, Mother, I believe that it was he who started everything." Ignatius pointed to the old man with his bag of sheet music. "I was simply standing about, waiting for you, praying that the news from the doctor would be encouraging."

"Get that old man outta here," Mrs. Reilly said to the policeman. "He's making trouble. It's a shame they got people like him walking the streets."

"The police are all communiss," the old man said.

"Didn't I say for you to shut up?" the policeman said angrily.

"I fall on my knees every night to thank my God we got protection," Mrs. Reilly told the crowd. "We'd all be dead without the police. We'd all be laying in our beds with our throats cut open from ear to ear."

"That's the truth, girl," some woman answered from the crowd.

"Say a rosary for the police force." Mrs. Reilly was now addressing her remarks to the crowd. Ignatius caressed her shoulders wildly, whispering encouragement. "Would you say a rosary for a communiss?"

"No!" several voices answered fervently. Someone pushed the old man.

"It's true, lady," the old man cried. "He tried to arrest your boy. Just like in Russia. They're all communiss."

"Come on," the policeman said to the old man. He grabbed him roughly by the back of the coat.

"Oh, my God!" Ignatius said, watching the wan little policeman try to control the old man. "Now my nerves are totally frayed."

"Help!" the old man appealed to the crowd. "It's a takeover. It's a violation of the Constitution!"

"He's crazy, Ignatius," Mrs. Reilly said. "We better get outta here, baby." She turned to the crowd. "Run, folks. He might kill us all. Personally, I think maybe *he's* the communiss."

"You don't have to overdo it, Mother," Ignatius said as they pushed through the dispersing crowd and started walking rapidly down Canal Street. He looked back and saw the old man and the bantam policeman grappling beneath the department store clock. "Will you please slow down a bit? I think I'm having a heart murmur."

"Oh, shut up. How you think I feel? I shouldn't haveta be running like this at my age."

"The heart is important at any age, I'm afraid."

"They's nothing wrong with your heart."

"There will be if we don't go a little slower." The tweed trousers billowed around Ignatius's gargantuan rump as he rolled forward. "Do you have my lute string?"

Mrs. Reilly pulled him around the corner onto Bourbon Street, and they started walking down into the French Quarter.

"How come that policeman was after you, boy?"

"I shall never know. But he will probably be coming after us in a few moments, as soon as he has subdued that aged fascist."

"You think so?" Mrs. Reilly asked nervously.

"I would imagine so. He seemed determined to arrest me. He must have some sort of quota or something. I seriously doubt that he will permit me to elude him so easily."

"Wouldn't that be awful! You'd be all over the papers, Ignatius. The disgrace! You musta done something while you was waiting for me, Ignatius. I know you, boy."

"If anyone was ever minding his business, it was I," Ignatius breathed. "Please. We must stop. I think I'm going to have a hemorrhage."

"Okay," Mrs. Reilly looked at her son's reddening face and realized that he would very happily collapse at her feet just to prove his point. He had done it before. The last time that she had forced him to accompany her to mass on Sunday he had collapsed twice on the way to the church and had collapsed once again during the sermon about sloth, reeling out of the pew and creating an embarrassing disturbance. "Let's go in here and sit down."

She pushed him through the door of the Night of Joy bar with one of the cake boxes. In the darkness that smelled of bourbon and cigarette butts they climbed onto two stools. While Mrs. Reilly arranged her cake boxes on the bar, Ignatius spread his expansive nostrils and said, "My God, Mother, it smells awful. My stomach is beginning to churn."

"You wanna go back on the street? You want that policeman to take you in?"

Ignatius did not answer; he was sniffing loudly and making faces. A bartender, who had been observing the two, asked quizzically from the shadows, "Yes?"

"I shall have a coffee," Ignatius said grandly. "Chicory coffee with boiled milk."

"Only instant," the bartender said.

"I can't possibly drink that," Ignatius told his mother. "It's an abomination."

"Well, get a beer, Ignatius. It won't kill you."

"I may bloat."

"I'll take a Dixie 45," Mrs. Reilly said to the bartender.

"And the gentleman?" the bartender asked in a rich, assumed voice. "What is his pleasure?"

"Give him a Dixie, too."

"I may not drink it," Ignatius said as the bartender went off to open the beers.

"We can't sit in here for free, Ignatius."

"I don't see why not. We're the only customers. They should be glad to have us."

"They got strippers in here at night, huh?" Mrs. Reilly nudged her son.

"I would imagine so," Ignatius said coldly. He looked quite pained. "We might have stopped somewhere else. I suspect that the police will raid this place momentarily anyway." He snorted loudly and cleared his throat. "Thank God my moustache filters out some of the stench. My olfactories are already beginning to send out distress signals."

After what seemed a long time during which there was much tinkling of glass and closing of coolers somewhere in the shadows, the bartender appeared again and set the beers before them, pretending to knock Ignatius's beer into his lap. The Reillys were getting the Night of Joy's worst service, the treatment given unwanted customers.

"You don't by any chance have a cold Dr. Nut, do you?" Ignatius asked.

"No."

"My son loves Dr. Nut," Mrs. Reilly explained. "I gotta buy it by the case. Sometimes he sits himself down and drinks two, three Dr. Nuts at one time."

"I am sure that this man is not particularly interested," Ignatius said.

"Like to take that cap off?" the bartender asked.

"No, I wouldn't!" Ignatius thundered. "There's a chill in here."

"Suit yourself," the bartender said and drifted off into the shadows at the other end of the bar.

"Really!"

"Calm down," his mother said.

Ignatius raised the earflap on the side next to his mother.

"Well, I will lift this so that you won't have to strain your voice. What did the doctor tell you about your elbow or whatever it is?"

"It's gotta be massaged."

"I hope you don't want me to do that. You know how I feel about touching other people."

"He told me to stay out the cold as much as possible."

"If I could drive, I would be able to help you more, I imagine."

"Aw, that's okay, honey."

"Actually, even riding in a car affects me enough. Of course, the worst thing is riding on top in one of those Greyhound Scenicruisers. So high up. Do you remember the time that I went to Baton Rouge in one of those? I vomited several times. The driver had to stop the bus somewhere in the swamps to let me get off and walk around for a while. The other passengers were rather angry. They must have had stomachs of iron to ride in that awful machine. Leaving New Orleans also frightened me considerably. Outside of the city limits the heart of darkness, the true wasteland begins."

"I remember that, Ignatius," Mrs. Reilly said absently, drinking her beer in gulps. "You was really sick when you got back home."

"I felt better *then*. The worst moment was my arrival in Baton Rouge. I realized that I had a round-trip ticket and would have to return on the bus."

"You told me that, babe."

"The taxi back to New Orleans cost me forty dollars, but at least I wasn't violently ill during the taxi ride, although I felt myself beginning to gag several times. I made the driver go very slowly, which was unfortunate for him. The state police stopped him twice for being below the minimum highway speed limit. On the third time that they stopped him they took away his chauffeur's license. You see, they had been watching us on the radar all along."

Mrs. Reilly's attention wavered between her son and the beer. She had been listening to the story for three years.

"Of course," Ignatius continued, mistaking his mother's rapt look for interest, "that was the only time that I had ever been out of New Orleans in my life. I think that perhaps it was the lack of a center of orientation that might have upset me. Speeding along in that bus was like hurtling into the abyss. By the time we had left the swamps and reached those rolling hills near Baton Rouge, I was getting afraid that some rural red-necks might toss bombs at the bus. They love to attack vehicles, which are a symbol of progress, I guess."

"Well, I'm glad you didn't take the job," Mrs. Reilly said automatically, taking *guess* as her cue.

"I couldn't possibly take the job. When I saw the chairman of the Medieval Culture Department, my hands began breaking out in small white bumps. He was a totally soulless man. Then he made a comment about my not wearing a tie and made some smirky remark about the lumber jacket. I was appalled that so meaningless a person would dare such effrontery. That lumber jacket was one of the few creature comforts to which I've ever been really attached, and if I ever find the lunatic who stole it, I shall report him to the proper authorities."

Mrs. Reilly saw again the horrible, coffee-stained lumber jacket that she had always secretly wanted to give to the Volunteers of America along with several other pieces of Ignatius's favorite clothing.

"You see, I was so overwhelmed by the complete grossness of that spurious 'chairman' that I ran from his office in the middle of one of his cretinous ramblings and rushed to the nearest bathroom, which turned out to be the one for 'Faculty Men.' At any rate, I was seated in one of the booths, having rested the lumber jacket on top of the door of the booth. Suddenly I saw the jacket being whisked over the door. I heard footsteps. Then the door of the restroom closed. At the moment, I was unable to pursue the shameless thief, so I began to scream. Someone entered the bathroom and knocked at the door of the booth. It turned out to be a member of the campus security force, or so he said. Through the door I explained what had just happened. He promised to find the jacket and went away. Actually, as I have mentioned to you before, I have always suspected that he and the 'chairman' were the same person. Their voices sounded somewhat similar."

"You sure can't trust nobody nowadays, honey."

"As soon as I could, I fled from the bathroom, eager only to get away from that horrible place. Of course, I was almost frozen standing on that desolate campus trying to hail a taxi. I finally got one that agreed to take me to New Orleans for forty dollars, and the driver was selfless enough to lend me his jacket. By the time we arrived here, however, he was quite depressed about losing his license and had grown rather surly. He also appeared to be developing a bad cold, judging by the frequency of his sneezes. After all, we were on the highway for almost two hours."

"I think I could drink me another beer, Ignatius."

"Mother! In this forsaken place?"

"Just one, baby. Come on, I want another."

"We're probably catching something from these glasses. However, if you're quite determined about the thing, get me a brandy, will you?"

Mrs. Reilly signaled to the bartender, who came out of the shadows and asked, "Now what happened to you on that bus, bud? I didn't get the end of the story."

"Will you kindly tend the bar properly?" Ignatius asked furiously. "It is your duty to silently serve when we call upon you. If we had wished to include you in our conversation, we would have indicated it by now. As a matter of fact, we are discussing rather urgent personal matters."

"The man's just trying to be nice, Ignatius. Shame on you."

"That in itself is a contradiction in terms. No one could possibly be nice in a den like this."

"We want two more beers."

"One beer and one brandy." Ignatius corrected.

"No more clean glasses," the bartender said.

"Ain't that a shame," Mrs. Reilly said. "Well, we can use the ones we got."

The bartender shrugged and went off into the shadows.

*

In the precinct the old man sat on a bench with the others, mostly shoplifters, who composed the late afternoon haul. He had neatly arranged along his thigh his Social Security card, his membership card in the St. Odo of Cluny Holy Name Society, a Golden Age Club badge, and a slip of paper identifying him as a member of the American Legion. A young black man, eyeless behind spaceage sunglasses, studied the little dossier on the thigh next to his.

"Whoa!" he said, grinning, "Say, you mus belong to everthin."

The old man rearranged his cards meticulously and said nothing.

"How come they draggin in somebody like you?" The sunglasses blew smoke all over the old man's cards. "Them po-lice mus be gettin desperate."

"I'm here in violation of my constitutional rights," the old man said with sudden anger.

"Well, they not gonna believe that. You better think up somethin else." A dark hand reached for one of the cards. "Hey, wha this mean, 'Colder Age'?"

The old man snatched the card and put it back on his thigh.

"Them little card not gonna do you no good. They throw you in jail anyway. They throw everbody in jail."

"You think so?" the old man asked the cloud of smoke.

"Sure." A new cloud floated up. "How come you here, man?"

"I don't know."

"You don't know? Whoa! That crazy. You gotta be here for somethin. Plenty time they pickin up color peoples for nothing, but, mister, you gotta be here for somethin."

"I really don't know," the old man said glumly. "I was just standing in a crowd in front of D. H. Holmes."

"And you lif somebody wallet."

"No, I called a policeman a name."

"Like wha you callin him?"

"Communiss."

"Cawmniss! Ooo-woo. If I call a po-lice a cawmniss, my ass be in Angola right now for sure. I like to call one of them mother a cawmniss, though. Like this afternoon I standin aroun in Woolsworth and some cat steal a bag of cashew nuts out the 'Nut House' star screaming like she been stab. Hey! The nex thing, a flo'walk grabbin me, and then a po-lice mother draggin me off. A man ain got a chance. Whoa!" His lips sucked at the cigarette. "Nobody findin them cashews on me, but that po-lice still draggin me off. I think that flo'walk a cawmniss. Mean motherfucker."

The old man cleared his throat and played with his cards.

"They probly let you go," the sunglasses said. "Me, they probly gimma a little talk think it scare me, even though they know I ain got them cashews. They probly try to prove I got them nuts. They probly buy a bag, slip it in my pocket. Woolsworth probly try to send me up for life."

The Negro seemed quite resigned and blew out a new cloud of blue smoke that enveloped him and the old man and the little cards. Then he said to himself, "I wonder who lif them nuts. Probly that flo'walk hisself."

A policeman summoned the old man up to the desk in the center of the room where a sergeant was seated. The patrolman who had arrested him was standing there.

"What's your name?" the sergeant asked the old man.

"Claude Robichaux," he answered and put his little cards on the desk before the sergeant.

The sergeant looked over the cards and said, "Patrolman Mancuso here says you resisted arrest and called him a communiss."

"I didn't mean it," the old man said sadly, noticing how fiercely the sergeant was handling the little cards.

"Mancuso says you says all policeman are communiss."

"Oo-wee," the Negro said across the room.

"Will you shut up, Jones?" the sergeant called out.

"Okay," Jones answered.

"I'll get to you next."

"Say, I didn call nobody no cawmniss," Jones said. "I been frame by that flo'walk in Woolsworth. I don even like cashews."

"Shut your mouth up."

"Okay," Jones said brightly and blew a great thundercloud of smoke.

"I didn't mean anything I said," Mr. Robichaux told the sergeant. "I just got nervous. I got carried away. This patrolman was trying to aress a poor boy waiting for his momma by Holmes."

"What?" the sergeant turned to the wan little policeman. "What were you trying to do?"

"He wasn't a boy," Mancuso said. "He was a big fat man dressed funny. He looked like a suspicious character. I was just trying to make a routine check and he started to resist. To tell you the truth, he looked like a big prevert."

"A pervert, huh?" the sergeant asked greedily.

"Yes," Mancuso said with new confidence. "A great big prevert."

"How big?"

"The biggest I ever saw in my whole life," Mancuso said, stretching his arms as if he were describing a fishing catch. The sergeant's eyes shone. "The first thing I spotted was this green hunting cap he was wearing."

Jones listened in attentive detachment somewhere within his cloud.

"Well, what happened, Mancuso? How come he's not standing here before me?"

"He got away. This woman came out the store and got everything mixed up, and she and him run around the corner into the Quarter."

"Oh, two Quarter characters," the sergeant said, suddenly enlightened.

"No, sir," the old man interrupted. "She was really his momma. A nice, pretty lady. I seen them downtown before. This policeman frightened her."

"Oh, listen, Mancuso," the sergeant screamed. "You're the only guy on the force who'd try to arrest somebody away from his mother. And why did you bring in grampaw here? Ring up his family and tell them to come get him."

"Please," Mr. Robichaux pleaded. "Don't do that. My daughter's busy with her kids. I never been arrested in my whole life. She can't come get me. What are my granchirren gonna think? They're all studying with the sisters."

"Get his daughter's number, Mancuso. That'll teach him to call us communiss!"

"Please!" Mr. Robichaux was in tears. "My granchirren respect me."

"Jesus Christ!" the sergeant said. "Trying to arrest a kid with his momma, bringing in somebody's grampaw. Get the hell outta here, Mancuso, and take grampaw with you. You wanna arrest suspicious characters? We'll fix you up."

"Yes, sir," Mancuso said weakly, leading the weeping old man away.

"Ooo-wee!" Jones said from the secrecy of his cloud.

*

Twilight was settling around the Night of Joy bar. Outside, Bourbon Street was beginning to light up. Neon signs flashed off and on, reflecting in the streets dampened by the light mist that had been falling steadily for some time. The taxis bringing the evening's first customers, midwestern tourists and conventioneers, made slight splashing sounds in the cold dusk.

A few other customers were in the Night of Joy, a man who ran his finger along a racing form, a depressed blonde who seemed connected with the bar in some capacity, and an elegantly dressed young man who chainsmoked Salems and drank frozen daiquiris in gulps.

"Ignatius, we better go," Mrs. Reilly said and belched.

"What?" Ignatius bellowed. "We must stay to watch the corruption. It's already beginning to set in."

The elegant young man spilled his daiquiri on his bottle-green velvet jacket.

"Hey, bartender," Mrs. Reilly called. "Get a rag. One of the customers just spilled they drink."

"That's *quite* all right, darling," the young man said angrily. He arched an eyebrow at Ignatius and his mother. "I think I'm in the wrong bar anyway."

"Don't get upset, honey," Mrs. Reilly counseled. "What's that you drinking? It looks like a pineapple snowball."

"Even if I described it to you, I doubt whether you'd understand what it is."

"How dare you talk to my dear, beloved mother like that!"

"Oh, hush, you big thing," the young man snapped. "Just look at my jacket."

"It's totally grotesque."

"Okay, now. Let's be friends," Mrs. Reilly said through foamy lips. "We got enough bombs and things already."

"And your son seems to delight in dropping them, I must say."

"Okay, you two. This is the kinda place where everybody oughta have themselves some fun." Mrs. Reilly smiled at the young man. "Let me buy you another drink, babe, for the one you spilled. And I think I'll take me another Dixie."

"I really must run," the young man sighed. "Thanks anyway."

"On a night like this?" Mrs. Reilly asked. "Aw, don't pay no mind to what Ignatius says. Why don't you stay and see the show?"

The young man rolled his eyes heavenward.

"Yeah," The blonde broke her silence. "See some ass and tits."

"Mother," Ignatius said coldly. "I do believe that you are encouraging these preposterous people."

"Well, you're the one wanted to stay, Ignatius."

"Yes, I did want to stay as an observer. I am not especially anxious to mingle."

"Honey, to tell you the truth, I can't listen to that story about that bus no more tonight. You already told it four times since we got here."

Ignatius looked hurt.

"I hardly suspected that I was boring you. After all, that bus ride was one of the more formative experiences of my life. As a mother, you should be interested in the traumas that have created my worldview."

"What's with the bus?" the blonde asked, moving to the stool next to Ignatius. "My name's Darlene. I like good stories. You got a spicy one?"

The bartender slammed the beer and the daiquiri down just as the bus was starting off on its journey in the vortex.

"Here, have a clean glass," the bartender snarled at Mrs. Reilly.

"Ain't that nice. Hey, Ignatius, I just got a clean glass."

But her son was too preoccupied with his arrival in Baton Rouge to hear her.

"You know, sweetheart," Mrs. Reilly said to the young man, "me and my boy was in trouble today. The police tried to arress him."

"Oh, my dear. Policemen are always so adamant, aren't they?"

"Yeah, and Ignatius got him a master's degree and all."

"What in the world was he doing?"

"Nothing. Just standing waiting for his poor, dear momma."

"His outfit is a little bizarre. I thought he was a performer of some sort when I first came in, although I tried not to imagine the nature of his act."

"I keep on telling him about his clothes, but he won't listen." Mrs. Reilly looked at the back of her son's flannel shirt and at the hair curling down the back of his neck. "That's sure pretty, that jacket you got."

"Oh, this?" the young man asked, feeling the velvet on the sleeve. "I don't mind telling you it cost a fortune. I found it in a dear little shop in the Village."

"You don't look like you from the country."

"Oh, my," the young man sighed and lit a Salem with a great click of his lighter. "I meant Greenwich Village in New York, sweetie. By the way, where did you ever get that hat? It's truly fantastic."

"Aw, Lord, I had this since Ignatius made his First Communion."

"Would you consider selling it?"

"How come?"

"I'm a dealer in used clothing. I'll give you ten dollars for it."

"Aw, come on. For this?"

"Fifteen?"

"Really?" Mrs. Reilly removed the hat. "Sure, honey."

The young man opened his wallet and gave Mrs. Reilly three five dollar bills. Draining his daiquiri glass, he stood up and said, "Now I really must run."

"So soon?"

"It's been perfectly delightful meeting you."

"Take care out in the cold and wet."

The young man smiled, placed the hat carefully beneath his trench coat, and left the bar.

"The radar patrol," Ignatius was telling Darlene, "is obviously rather foolproof. It seems that the cab driver and I were making small dots on their screen all the way from Baton Rouge."

"You was on radar," Darlene yawned. "Just think of that."

"Ignatius, we gotta go now," Mrs. Reilly said. "I'm hungry."

She turned toward him and knocked her beer bottle to the floor where it broke into a spray of brown, jagged glass.

"Mother, are you making a scene?" Ignatius asked irritably. "Can't you see that Miss Darlene and I are speaking? You have some cakes with you. Eat those. You're always complaining that you never go anywhere. I would have imagined that you would be enjoying your night on the town."

Ignatius was back on radar, so Mrs. Reilly reached in her boxes and ate a brownie.

"Like one?" she asked the bartender. "They nice. I got some nice wine cakes, too."

The bartender pretended to be looking for something on his shelves.

"I smell wine cakes," Darlene cried, looking past Ignatius.

"Have one, honey," Mrs. Reilly said.

"I think that I shall have one, too," Ignatius said. "I imagine that they taste rather good with brandy."

Mrs. Reilly spread the box out on the bar. Even the man with the racing form agreed to take a macaroon.

"Where you bought these nice wine cakes, lady?" Darlene asked Mrs. Reilly. "They're nice and juicy."

"Over by Holmes, sugar. They got a good selection. Plenty variety."

"They are rather tasty," Ignatius conceded, sending out his flabby pink tongue over his moustache to hunt for crumbs. "I think that I shall have a macaroon or two. I have always found coconut to be good roughage."

He picked around in the box purposefully.

"Me, I always like some good cake after I finish eating." Mrs. Reilly told the bartender, who turned his back on her.

"I bet you cook good, huh?" Darlene asked.

"Mother doesn't cook," Ignatius said dogmatically. "She burns."

"I used to cook too when I was married," Darlene told them. "I sort of used a lot of that canned stuff, though. I like that Spanish rice they got and that spaghetti with the tomato gravy."

"Canned food is a perversion," Ignatius said. "I suspect that it is ultimately very damaging to the soul."

"Lord, my elbow's starting up again," Mrs. Reilly sighed.

"Please, I am speaking," her son told her. "I never eat canned food. I did once, and I could feel my intestines starting to atrophy."

"You got a good education," Darlene said.

"Ignatius graduated from college. Then he stuck around there for four more years to get him a master's degree. Ignatius graduated smart."

"'Graduated smart,'" Ignatius repeated with some pique. "Please define your terms. Exactly what do you mean by 'graduated smart.'"

"Don't talk to your momma like that," Darlene said.

"Oh, he treats me bad sometimes," Mrs. Reilly said loudly and began to cry. "You just don't know. When I think of all I done for that boy . . ."

"Mother, what are you saying?"

"You don't appreciate me."

"Stop that right now. I'm afraid that you've had too much beer."

"You treat me like garbage. I been good," Mrs. Reilly sobbed. She turned to Darlene. "I spent all his poor Grammaw Reilly's insurance money to keep him in college for eight years, and since then all he's done is lay around the house watching television."

"You oughta be ashamed," Darlene said to Ignatius. "A big man like you. Look at your poor momma."

Mrs. Reilly had collapsed, sobbing, on the bar, one hand clenched around her beer glass.

"This is ridiculous. Mother, stop that."

"If I knew you was so crool, mister, I wouldna listened to your crazy story about that Greyhound bus."

"Get up, Mother."

"You look like a big crazyman anyway," Darlene said. "I shoulda known. Just look how that poor woman's crying."

Darlene tried to push Ignatius from his stool but sent him crashing into his mother, who suddenly stopped crying and gasped, "My elbow!"

"What's going on here?" a woman asked from the padded chartreuse leatherette door of the bar. She was a statuesque woman nearing middle age, her fine body covered with a black leather overcoat that glistened with mist. "I leave this place for a few hours to go shopping and look what happens. I gotta be here every minute, I guess, to watch out you people don't ruin my investment."

"Just two drunks," the bartender said. "I've been giving them the cold shoulder since they come in, but they've been sticking like flies."

"But you, Darlene," the woman said. "You're big friends with them, huh? Playing games on the stools with these two characters?"

"This guy's been mistreating his momma," Darlene explained.

"Mothers? We got mothers in here now? Business already stinks."

"I beg your pardon," Ignatius said.

The woman ignored him and looked at the broken and empty cake box on the bar, saying, "Somebody's been having a picnic in here. Goddamit. I already told you people about ant and rats."

"I beg your pardon," Ignatius said again. "My mother is present."

"It's just my luck to have this crap broken all over here just when I'm looking for a janitor." The woman looked at the bartender. "Get these two out."

"Yes, Miss Lee."

"Don't you worry," Mrs. Reilly said. "We're leaving."

"We certainly are," Ignatius added, lumbering toward the door, leaving his mother behind to climb off her stool. "Hurry along, Mother. This woman looks like a Nazi commandant. She may strike us."

"Wait!" Miss Lee screamed, grabbing Ignatius's sleeve. "How much these characters owe?"

"Eight dollars," the bartender said.

"This is highway robbery!" Ignatius thundered. "You will hear from our attorneys."

Mrs. Reilly paid with two of the bills the young man had given her and, as she swayed past Miss Lee, she said, "We know when we not wanted. We can take our trade elsewheres."

"Good," Miss Lee answered. "Beat it. Trade from people like you is the kiss of death."

After the padded door had closed behind the Reillys, Miss Lee said, "I never liked mothers. Not even my own."

"My mother was a whore," the man with the racing form said, not looking up from his paper.

"Mothers are full of shit," Miss Lee observed and took off her leather coat. "Now let's you and me have a little talk, Darlene."

Outside, Mrs. Reilly took her son's arm for support, but, as much as they tried, they moved forward very slowly, although they seemed to move sideward more easily. Their walking had developed a pattern: three quick steps to the left, pause, three quick steps to the right, pause.

"That was a terrible woman," Mrs. Reilly said.

"A negation of all human qualities," Ignatius added. "By the way, how far is the car? I'm very tired."

"On St. Ann, honey. Just a few blocks."

"You left your hat in the bar."

"Oh, I sold it to that young man."

"You sold it? Why? Did you ask me whether I wanted it to be sold? I was very attached to that hat."

"I'm sorry, Ignatius. I didn't know you liked it so much. You never said nothing about it."

"I had an unspoken attachment to it. It was a contact with my childhood, a link with the past."

"But he gave me fifteen dollars, Ignatius."

"Please. Don't talk about it anymore. The whole business is sacrilegious. Goodness knows what degenerate uses he will find for that hat. Do you have the fifteen dollars on you?"

"I still got seven left."

"Then why don't we stop and eat something?" Ignatius pointed to the cart at the corner. It was shaped like a hot dog on wheels. "I believe that they vend foot-long hot dogs."

"Hot dogs? Honey, in all this rain and cold we gonna stand outside and eat weenies?"

"It's a thought."

"No," Mrs. Reilly said with somewhat beery courage. "Let's get home. I wouldn't eat nothing outta one of them dirty wagons anyway. They all operated by a bunch of bums."

"If you insist," Ignatius said, pouting. "Although I am rather hungry, and you have, after all, just sold a memento of my childhood for thirty pieces of silver, so to speak."

They continued their little pattern of steps along the wet flagstones of Bourbon Street. On St. Ann they found the old Plymouth easily. Its high roof stood above all the other cars, its best feature. The Plymouth was always easy to find in supermarket parking lots. Mrs. Reilly climbed the curb twice trying to force the car out of the parking place and left the impression of a 1946 Plymouth bumper in the hood of the Volkswagen in the rear.

"My nerves!" Ignatius said. He was slumped down in the seat so that just the top of his green hunting cap appeared in the window, looking like the tip of a promising watermelon. From the rear, where he always sat, having read somewhere that the seat next to the driver was the most dangerous, he watched his mother's wild and in-expert shifting with disapproval. "I suspect that you have effectively demolished the small car that someone innocently parked behind this bus. You had better succeed in getting out of this spot before its owner happens along."

"Shut up, Ignatius. You making me nervous," Mrs. Reilly said, looking at the hunt-ing cap in the rearview mirror.

Ignatius got up on the seat and looked out of the rear window.

"That car is a total wreck. Your driver's license, if you do indeed have one, will doubtlessly be revoked. I certainly wouldn't blame them."

"Lay down there and take a nap," his mother said as the car jerked back again.

"Do you think that I could sleep now? I'm afraid for my life. Are you sure that you're turning the wheel the right way?"

Suddenly the car leaped out of the parking spot and skidded across the wet street into a post supporting a wrought-iron balcony. The post fell away to one side, and the Plymouth crunched against the building.

"Oh, my God!" Ignatius screamed from the rear. "What have you done now?"

"Call a priest!"

"I don't think that we're injured, Mother. However, you have just ruined my stom-ach for the next few days." Ignatius rolled down one of the rear windows and studied the fender that was pressed against the wall. "We shall need a new headlight on this side, I imagine."

"What we gonna do?"

"If I were driving, I would put the auto in reverse and back gracefully away from the scene. Someone will certainly press charges. The people who own this wreck of a build-ing have been waiting for an opportunity like this for years. They probably spread grease on the street after nightfall hoping that motorists like you will spin toward their hovel." He belched. "My digestion has been destroyed. I think that I am beginning to bloat!"

Mrs. Reilly shifted the worn gears and inched slowly backward. As the car moved, the splintering of wood sounded over their heads, a splintering that changed into splitting of boards and scraping of metal. Then the balcony was falling in large sections, thundering on the roof of the car with the dull, heavy thud of grenades. The car, like a stoned human, stopped moving, and a piece of wrought-iron decoration shattered a rear window.

"Honey, are you okay?" Mrs. Reilly asked wildly after what seemed to be the final bombardment.

Ignatius made a gagging sound. The blue and yellow eyes were watering.

"Say something, Ignatius," his mother pleaded, turning round just in time to see Ignatius stick his head out of a window and vomit down the side of the dented car.

Patrolman Mancuso was walking slowly down Chartres Street dressed in ballet tights and a yellow sweater, a costume which the sergeant said would enable him to bring in genuine, bona fide suspicious characters instead of grandfathers and boys waiting for their mothers. The costume was the sergeant's punishment. He had told Mancuso that from now on he would be strictly responsible for bringing in suspicious characters, that police headquarters had a costume wardrobe that would permit Man-cuso to be a new character every day. Forlornly, Patrolman Mancuso had put on the tights before the sergeant, who had pushed him out of the precinct and told him to shape up or get off the force.

In the two hours that he had been cruising the French Quarter, he had captured no one. Twice things had looked hopeful. He had stopped a man wearing a beret and asked for a cigarette, but the man had threatened to have him arrested. Then he accosted a young man in a trench coat who was wearing a lady's hat, but the young man had slapped him across the face and dashed away.

As Patrolman Mancuso walked down Chartres rubbing his cheek, which still smarted from the slap, he heard what seemed to be an explosion. Hoping that a suspicious character had just thrown a bomb or shot himself, he ran around the corner onto St. Ann and saw the green hunting cap emitting vomit among the ruins.

Margaret Walker Alexander

(1915–1998)

Born on July 7, 1915, in Birmingham, Alabama, Margaret Walker Alexander was expected to achieve academically by her highly educated parents. When she was sixteen, she enrolled at New Orleans University, and in 1935 she completed her B.A. at Northwestern University, where she met W. E. B. DuBois, who published her early poems. In 1940 she was awarded her M.A. from the University of Iowa; she would return later for further study, receiving her Ph.D. in 1965. In 1942 she married Firnist James Alexander. They were the parents of four children.

Walker's first collection of poetry, *For My People* (1942), won the Yale Younger Poets Prize. She began teaching English in 1942 at West Virginia State College. She taught at Jackson State University in Mississippi from 1949 to 1979, where she also directed the Institute for the Study of the History, Life, and Culture of Black People. She received the Rosenwald Fellowship for Creative Writing in 1944 and a Ford Fellowship at Yale University in 1954. Her novel *Jubilee* (1966) won the Houghton Mifflin Literary Fellowship (1966).

Walker's other works include *Prophets for a New Day* (1970); *Richard Wright: Daemonic Genius* (1987); and *This Is My Century: New and Collected Poems* (1989). Walker died on November 30, 1998.

from *Jubilee*

Mine eyes have seen the glory of the coming of the Lord.

19. "John Brown's body lies a-mouldering in the grave"

John Morris Dutton was fifty-seven years old and he had been in the House of Representatives of the Georgia Legislature for fifteen years. During those years he watched several developments in Georgia which coincided with his personal life and interests. First, he watched the elevation of three of Georgia's greatest statesmen: Alexander Stephens, Robert Toombs, and Howell Cobb. Although he could not claim these men as his closest friends and cronies, he had more than a speaking acquaintance with them, and his deep admiration of their policies, personalities, and philosophies was well known. Second, he was in total agreement with their belief that Georgia and the pro-slavery South should gird on its armor and enter the throes of a political battle in order to preserve their sacred states' rights. Georgia's property rights and fundamental religious beliefs as free men and citizens in a free country were being threatened by the unconstitutional actions of that Anti-Slavery party now coming into power in the North. It behooved every loyal southerner to battle this party to its just and certain death. Third, there were many changes at home on his plantation. At least a half-dozen of his slaves had died or disappeared during those stormy years of the fifties when he was very busy in Milledgeville. Sometimes he blamed his wife, Missy Salina, and their zealous overseer, Ed Grimes, for this deplorable state of affairs. Often he blamed himself. With these exceptions, however, he was fairly content with his personal life. His son, Johnny, was doing well at West Point. His daughter, Lillian, was married and had two children, Robert and Susan. She and her husband, Kevin, made their home in Milledgeville at Oglethorpe University and he saw them frequently. Once he had seriously thought of running for the Senate. The Senate was a natural stepping-stone to Washington. Howell Cobb had gone from the Senate to Washington, and Dutton had thought in time he would do the same. Now all that was changed.

He was riding home from Montgomery, Alabama. He was ending a long journey on the Central of Georgia Railroad and he was weary in body and mind. Sam would meet him at the station and then there would be a long jostling ride through the swamp woods on the old wagon road. They would be lucky to get home before dark and in time for supper. Vyry would have a good meal ready and Salina would be eager to know the news. He felt half-hearted in spirit, not burning with the same enthusiasm with which he had left home. Perhaps it was a natural reaction to feel let down after so much excitement. This was his third long journey out of the state in the past six months. No wonder his body felt weary to the bone. Last year during the summer he had attended two conventions, both Democratic. The first one was held in the North, where the South felt insulted and infuriated with the compromising tactics used to discourage slavery in the territories. The second was held in Baltimore, where loyal southerners took a bold stand against those radical anti-slavery northerners and nominated Breckinridge as their states' rights candidate. Splitting the Democratic party was, of course, disastrous, and for the first time since its origin a brief eight years before, the Anti-Slavery party of Radical Republicans won the national elections.

In four short years people learned much about their successful candidate. Ever since Fremont was defeated in 1856 and the controversy over slavery and states' rights had verged on secession this man, who was a tool of the Republicans, kept breathing thunder against the slave states. They really heard more about him during his debate with Stephen Douglas, who finally made a poor candidate for the northern Democrats. In 1857 the South won a moral victory with the Dred Scott case, but then came 1858 and that threatening speech of Seward's about the rising of an "irrepressible conflict" and the dire imminence of a social revolution. It was still 1858 when Abraham Lincoln, the candidate, declared that the country could not remain half slave and half free but would have to be one or the other. As John Dutton told his wife, Salina, at the time, "The northern abolitionists and free-soilers have finally got themselves a man. They say he is from the poor people—a backwoodsman of low origin from Kentucky. He has been first one thing and then another. I believe I heard once he made his living splitting rails, and just lately has been a lawyer of sorts who got himself elected to the Illinois Legislature. He is obviously nothing but a willing tool for those northern radicals."

Then came elections and the Republicans won with Abraham Lincoln. South Carolina saw the handwriting on the wall and immediately seceded from the Union, but in Georgia they waited, chiefly on the advice of Howell Cobb, who was still in Washington. But on January 19 when the legislature met, Georgia seceded. Now during the month of February in Montgomery, Alabama, seven southern states formed the Confederate States of America: South Carolina, Alabama, Mississippi, Georgia, Louisiana, Florida, and Texas. Jefferson Davis and Alexander Stephens, both good men, were elected to lead the new southern nation. *We couldn't have chosen better men. Salina will be pleased.* Both Alex Stephens and Howell Cobb like Robert Toombs had honored them with a visit to the plantation. The South would be in good hands. This was the trip he had just made, and the historic events he had witnessed.

Now he looked out at the sky apprehensively. From the time he left Alabama it had been raining steadily. The rain was turning to sleet and the temperature was rapidly falling. He looked forward to his home-coming with a warm supper, a hot bath before bed, and a stiff toddy. He felt a cold coming on and the weather was surely getting worse. The train was stopping at Dawson. He looked out and was relieved when he saw Sam, right on time.

"Hello Sam! Good to see you."

"Evening sir, glad to see you too. Kinda nasty out and Missy been wondering would you be late."

"No, looks like we're right on time."

"I'll take your bag, sir."

"Never mind. I can manage. Just anxious to be getting on. Sky looks bad. See if we can't make it home before dark."

"Yessir. I sure hope so, sir."

Darkness was coming on fast, and the cold rain was slowly freezing. They started out with the horses moving in a quick trot until Sam paced them faster and then they were racing at a clip.

Marse John, warm in his carriage robes, was dozing when he suddenly felt a sharp jolt as though they had struck a large rock in the road and the horses had stumbled. He looked out and saw the horses rearing. He heard them neighing nervously and just at that moment he was thrown forward as the carriage rose in the air and fell over on its side. In the whirling split second he saw Sam thrown from his high coachman's seat. The harness snapped and the frightened horses ran off leaving their master and his coachman on the old wagon road with the cold February night rapidly closing on them.

For a long moment Marse John felt stunned, then he tried to get out of the carriage, but his right leg was doubled back under him and when he tried to move, the sharp pain sickened him and sweat popped from his forehead. He saw he was pinned inside while the carriage lay on its side. He could see Sam lying still on the icy road, but when he called to him, Sam did not answer.

When the harnessed horses trotted into the stable of Marse John's plantation a general alarm was sounded throughout the Big House. Big Missy quickly ordered Jim, the houseboy, and Grimes to fetch old Doc, while a wagon and another carriage with fresh horses were quickly harnessed for the rescue. Darkness had now fallen and the winter night was frigid. In the Big House the fireplaces were blazing with cheerful fires. Supper was waiting and Vyry tried to keep the food hot without burning it in the midst of all this excitement and impending gloom. Big Missy wanted to join the searching party but the servants in the Big House persuaded her against such foolhardiness.

The hours seemed much longer than the time actually elapsed before the party returned. Sam's cold body lay stiff in the wagon with his neck broken, but Marse John was still conscious and they lifted him into the house after warming him first against the chill of the night with a stiff shot of brandy.

Supper was very late for they kept it waiting while Doc examined Marster's leg and found it broken in two places. Big Missy agreed with the doctor that her husband would be better off downstairs, so they put him to bed in the room where he often worked over his accounting books and legislative papers. The room had a huge fireplace, books, a desk, and family portraits. It was comfortable, warm, and familiar, and here it was hoped he could make a speedy recovery as pleasantly as possible.

Vyry carried supper to the Marster, once he was as comfortable as they could make him, and she was startled at the sight of him in repose with the leg in splints and his huge hulk of flesh dominating the room in this strange fashion. He lay on a large black-leather couch with an improvised feather bed under him and pillows piled up to elevate his leonine head. He looked paler than usual, his graying blond hair faded or washed out, but his blue eyes were sharp as ever and his mouth had a twisted smile. When she had placed the tray of food on a table within his arm's reach, she looked up to find his eyes on her face. Her eyes dropped and she stepped backward toward the open door. He looked up at the pictures over the mantel and flanking the sides of the fireplace before he spoke to her, "See that man up there, Vyry? He was my grandfather, and on both sides of him are my parents, my mother and father."

The portrait over the mantel showed a man in colonial dress with a powdered wig. His face was stern and his mouth was a thin straight line, but his eyes looked kind and they seemed to be staring down upon the occupants of the room. The faces on either side were younger and were in full-length portraits. The man looked a dandy with his high hat in his hand. The lady was dressed in a full-length ruffled hooped skirt with an open parasol held over her shoulder. Her bodice had a priscilla collar crisscrossed in a fichu. Vyry studied them curiously, wondering why he was telling her this, while he went on talking:

"Every time I took at them I think they are telling me to uphold the honor of this house. I have inherited their responsibility just as my son will inherit the honor of this house when I am dead."

Vyry thought of Miss Lillian, who was more devoted to her father than Johnny, who worshipped his mother, but she said nothing.

"He must be a little tipsy from all that brandy," she thought, and sure enough, looking at him, she saw his eyes swimming and his head nodding. She heard Big Missy coming down the hall and she hastened back to her kitchen.

We shall meet but we shall miss him,
There will be one vacant chair
We shall linger to caress him,
When we breathe our evening prayer.

20. This pot is boiling over and the fat is in the fire

On March 4, 1861, Abraham Lincoln was inaugurated the sixteenth President of the United States. On that same day in Montgomery, and for the first time, the Confederate flag of seven stars and three bars on a field of gray was unfurled and hung on the

Capitol of the Confederacy. Marse John had been confined to his library for two weeks, and he was chafing with enforced confinement. He could see that his swollen leg was slightly inflamed. He listened quietly enough to Big Missy, who was reading the newspapers to him, and he was delighted to hear in a letter from Lillian that she was bringing the children for a nice long visit, but he confided to old Doc that he was about to go out of his mind with inaction.

"I can't remember ever being sick in bed a day in my life."

"Well, you can sit up in a chair, and rest yourself from the bed to the chair, but you're going to be in this room a long while."

"How long, Doc, two more weeks?"

"At least. Maybe more or less, I can't tell right now."

"When will you know?"

"Well, barring accidents, if this inflammation only continues and doesn't spread, if the fever doesn't get too high, or you contract pneumonia, and the bone continues to knit properly and fast, you could be on crutches in six weeks."

"Six weeks! You must be out of your mind. I'll die first!"

"Let's hope not, but that's a limited possibility."

Then he changed the subject.

"You notice these black frosts we're having here in March? Had one this morning. Wouldn't be surprised if they didn't hold up spring planting quite a while, don't you think?"

Marse John did not answer. He was muttering and fuming while old Doc was closing his bag and preparing to leave. The doctor glanced at him and then spoke again. "Just wouldn't be surprised when your hands can get on with spring plowing, not with all these black frosts." And he shut his bag and went out.

By the middle of March, however, Marse John was suffering from a great deal more pain in his leg. Miss Lillian was home with her two young children and she was trying to tempt her father's appetite with special dishes and tidbits such as custards and calf's-foot jelly and other delicacies. Instead of eating he was drinking more heavily, and as his temper grew worse and his cursing grew more vociferous, his horrified family left him more and more to the strict care of the servants. The doctor still refused to admit any worry over the growing amount of inflammation and swelling and the possibility that the leg might be gangrenous. He suggested rather tentatively and timidly the possibility of amputation. Marse John's reaction to this was such a wrathful explosion that old Doc retreated without further discussion:

"Amputate? You mean cut off my leg? Are you out of your mind? Why, I would die of the very pain. What will you use, a hatchet or an axe? I saw a poor fellow lose his leg like that once. The howling wretch was full of whiskey too, but it didn't dull his senses one whit and he died in a matter of hours."

One day without warning, a delegation of seven men from the Georgia Assembly descended in a body upon their colleague. Big Missy thought this was sure to cheer him and make him more like his flippant self, but his cohorts were either too jolly or too morose and their visit put such a strain on his weakened sensibilities that late in the afternoon when they departed, after much liquid refreshment, he subsided into a gloomy silence and drank himself into a stupor.

He had too much time to think. First, he reflected on the state of affairs of his beloved Georgia and the whole Southland. Big Missy read the news to him and he chafed with the way things were going. He hated the name of Lincoln. As for his slaves, when he thought of how Sam had died that night, how Aunt Sally and Vyry had cooked so many years in his kitchen, he concluded that if the northern radicals only knew and understood his nigra slaves the way he did, they would not carry on such foolishness about *containing* slavery and not letting it spread to the territories.

"They must take us for big fools if they thought we would stay in their Union and let them control congress and dictate to us against our interests. If it has come to war, then let it come. But they are nothing but cowards and they won't dare fight us. They know we would whip them so fast it would be pathetic. The Bible is a witness to the benefits of slavery. The Church defends our system and the Constitution protects it. I don't see where they have a leg to stand on, but I wish I were out of this bed."

In the ensuing days he was less coherent. His leg was steadily growing worse and his temperature rose higher at night. In the morning he always seemed better. Old Miss would find him wet with perspiration and sleeping after a restless night of tossing with fever.

Jim, the houseboy, and Caline, now growing more aged but still active and haughty, were given the difficult task of nursing Marse John. Vyry carried his meals to him and May Liza cleaned his room. At first Missy Salina read the daily mail and newspapers to him, but after those first four weeks she realized he wasn't listening. Alexander Stephens delivered an important speech in her beloved Savannah on March 21, 1861, and his words were inspiring to her, especially when he said, "The new Southern Nation is founded upon the great truth that the Negro is not equal to the white man; subordination to the superior race is his natural and moral condition." But when she tried to read the speech in the newspapers to her husband he was too sick to pay any attention.

Marster loved his good old jamaica,
His good old jamaica, his good old jamaica,
Marster loved his good old jamaica
Down in Georgia Land.

21. The Vernal Equinox of 1861

Spring came late to Georgia in 1861. Cold rain, black, killing frosts, and temperatures as low as freezing delayed the usual spring plowing and spring planting. With Marse John ill in bed and the 1860 crop still bulging in the barns, nobody seemed to worry too much about the weather. The field hands were glad to have rest, and so was Grimes. He offered his help to Missy Salina as soon as he saw how it was with Marse John. She gravely thanked him for his offer, but said, "There's nothing you can do that you haven't already done." Grimes had little faith in old Doc, but then he was the only doctor they had used around the plantation for all these years, and surely now he would do his best for the master.

It was Missy Salina who first noticed the turn for the worse in Marse John. He continued to call for whiskey and he was steadily drinking more and more. When his eyes began to glaze she thought it was from too much liquor; but his mind, too, seemed to wander. And then she noticed the peculiar odor that subtly began to cling to the room. She ordered May Liza and Jim to use more carbolic acid in the scrubbing and cleaning water which afforded a high degree of disinfectant. At first she thought the odor was due to the fever and liquor but gradually she realized it was coming from his badly swollen and inflamed leg, which now clearly showed signs of gangrene. For the first time, fearful about this turn of events, Missy Salina took old Doc aside.

"I think he's getting worse, Doctor. Is he going to die?"

The doctor looked at her for a long moment, as though he were trying to assess the amount of hysteria she could generate. She looked strong and tough enough, but then you can never tell about a woman, so he looked off and let his eyes wander in the distance.

"Ma'am, that's something a doctor never knows. You know life and death are in the hands of our God."

"Yes, I know that. I shouldn't have said die, but I mean is he going to get well?"

The doctor did not smile nor did he have a quick answer ready for her, but he was determined to dismiss her fears at this stage in her husband's illness.

"It's a possibility, but not a certain fact. He has a strong constitution and he has already withstood the worst, I think. He has had a lot of laudable pus which I think is good, if only the gangrene doesn't take a firm hold. I suggested amputation, but you remember he wouldn't hear of it."

"Maybe we should go ahead with amputation anyway."

"Not without his consent. And every day we wait may lessen his chances to survive amputation."

Missy Salina carried such a solemn and sanctimonious expression into Marse John's sickroom, he quickly read her face. She approached the difficult subject as tactfully as she knew how.

"Why won't you let Doc amputate that leg? Can't you see it won't be much use to you like that?"

"Damn you, no! When did you ever hear of anybody my age recovering from amputation? Or is it, that I'm not dying fast enough for you? Don't count on my death, Salina! I may live yet to stand over your open grave."

"You ought to be ashamed of yourself talking like that! You ought to pray and stop cursing everybody out when all we are trying to do is help you. Do you want me to read to you from the Bible?"

"Hell, no. Why should you start something now you never have done before? And get out of here, standing over me like a vulture. I'm tired of your sham piety and all your pretenses about your concern for me. Your solicitude would be touching if it weren't so false. Get on out, get out I say!" And when she hesitated, he picked up a book and hurled it after her. Startled at his action, and considerably shaken over his condition, she ran from the room. Tearfully she reported this scene to Miss Lillian, who was awfully upset and kept saying, "Poor papa, poor papa!" And that very day they sent a telegram to young Marster Johnny in West Point.

According to the field hands and the old slaves in the Quarters, Marse John was dying "hard." They declared they could hear him yelling and cursing in the night, and indeed, Jim, the houseboy, admitted he found it hard to hold him down on his bed when the fever was raging at night, the liquor no longer having any effect, and the pain in the gangrenous and rotting leg driving the master out of his mind.

In the morning when Caline and May Liza entered the place to straighten and clean the room the odor made them hold their breath. Old Missy and young Missy scarcely went farther than the door, sometimes to speak if he were affable and conscious, but mostly to see what further changes had taken place in him. They prayed that the liquor and the opiates the doctor administered would sink him into a dying stupor but he raged through these until too exhausted to do more than lie and mumble in his troubled sleep which was also broken with pain.

At the full moon Brother Zeke told Vyry that he doubted the master could live another two weeks. "When the new moon come, he be gone." The weather was changing and as the folks in the Quarters muttered, "March come in like a lion, she going out like a lamb." In the night Vyry heard the honking of geese flying north, and in the swamp woods she saw the spring flowers blooming. Under the pines on Baptist Hill there were dogtooth violets, sheep sorrel, and may hops, and in the barns the cows were calving. The winter weather had broken and the long stormy weeks were ending.

Vyry could tell by the untouched tray that Marster was getting weaker. Except for liquids he took little nourishment, had no appetite, and lost interest in what was going on around him. He made a great effort to rouse himself when his small grandchildren came to his door to speak to him, or Lillian brought him a vase of spring flowers. Now his days were divided into three periods. Early in the morning he slept hard, sometimes not rousing or opening his eyes until noonday. Afternoon was his best time. The fever was at low ebb, he drank water and whiskey, often let himself be shaved and washed, and carried on a little conversation with Jim, but now he was growing more listless in the afternoons and noticing those about him in the room less and less. As the darkness drew on and the fever began to rise to interminable heights he began to rave and scream. Then began the unbearable hours. In those first days of April almost nobody in the Big House closed their eyes at night except the small children. The doctor now gave sedatives to Missy Salina and Miss Lillian so that they, too, slept late in the mornings.

One afternoon, a few days before the new moon, Vyry was surprised to have the Marster recognize her when she carried his tray. There was little on it except clear hot broth and coffee and soda crackers, but he showed no inclination to eat. She could see that he had wasted away to nothing since that first night when they had brought him into this room. His eyes were sunken in his head and they glittered strangely. His hands were unsteady and they pushed the cover alternately back and forth, sometimes plucking at the coverlets or pulling them closer. She was surprised when he spoke to her.

"So you're still here, hanh? And you not afraid to come in here, hanh?"

Startled at his hoarse voice, her eyes widened, but she did not speak, only nodded and shook her head in agreement.

"Think I forgot what I told you? I promised to set you free when I die, didn't I? Got it in my will, right here!" And he patted the books and papers beside his bed. "But I ain't dead yet!" And he rose up from the couch as though he would strike her, so that she hurriedly backed out of the room, but as she fled down the hall to the kitchen she could still hear him saying, "You ain't free till I die, and I ain't dead yet!"

That night he died. Early in the evening they heard him screaming and hollering in pain as usual, but shortly around midnight his howling stopped. Jim, the houseboy, was with him at the end, but he decided to say nothing to Big Missy until morning, that is, unless she came down to inquire, and she did not come down until morning. It was May Liza, Caline, and Jim who washed his dead body and dressed him for burial, while Missy Salina began to put into operation the elaborate plans she had made weeks in advance for her husband's funeral.

Southrons, hear your country call you
Up! lest worse than death befall you!
To arms! To arms! To arms! in Dixie!
                    ALBERT PIKE—*1861*

22. Don't make them come and get you! Volunteer!

When young Marster Johnny first heard of his father's accident he did not have the slightest idea that it would prove fatal. When he received his mother's first telegram, he was still loath to go home, but when her final message came that his father was dead he knew he had to go home at once. He had never especially admired his father but he respected his position. There was only one matter about his father's death that disturbed his thoughts, whether his mother would expect him to come home and run the plantation. This he did not want to do. Things were happening in the East and when he graduated in June he would be a commissioned officer in the army. He wanted nothing to interfere with that appointment.

Kevin MacDougall came to his wife and children before young Marster Johnny arrived from school. He found the two mistresses in deep sorrow and planning the costumes of mourning. Even the children must wear black armbands for their grand-father. Kevin had never felt that Marse John especially liked him, but he had been able to maintain good relationships with all his wife's people. In a way, he was se-cretly relieved when he heard that his father-in-law had passed. He missed his wife and children and needed them at home. He steeled himself, however, for the ordeal of the long obsequies, and tried to think of comforting words to say to his wife, Lillian, whom he truly adored.

The final rites for John Dutton occupied a week. His coffin was sealed and re-mained shut in the legislature, the church, his house, and at the graveside. Big Missy regretted this necessity, but she realized it was physically impossible to do otherwise. There were two sermons and three speeches eulogizing the dead legislator. The music was supplied by a black-robed choir singing hymns, a group of slaves singing spirituals, a white soloist who sang the perennial favorite, "Flee as a bird to your mountain" and a black fiddler who played plaintive notes at the grave.

Big Missy ran the gamut of her emotions at her husband's death. She told all the servants and neighbors who came to call, the friends and distinguished legislators, "My husband has suffered so greatly, I rejoice that he is out of his pain and misery even though death has taken my companion of twenty-five years." She maintained her stoic poise and the dignity demanded of her in the public eye, and wept only before her children and grandchildren. She was annoyed with Lillian, who sobbed audibly during all the services. She was proud of Johnny, who wore his dress uniform as a West Pointer, and she was even pleased with Kevin because of his tender devotion to his wife and small children. At the graveside she faltered only once. There swept back over her mind all the memories of her youth and early marriage, her wedding journey to this backwoods place, her children's births and their childhood, the acute embar-rassment she felt over her husband's attachment to a nigger woman, the bastards he had brought in his house to rear as servants, the distinguished career he had carved out for himself in the state house of Georgia, and now this lingering death that had re-duced his big handsome body to a bony frame. She bit back her sobs and stifled her tears, for they were not for him but entirely for herself. She was not so stupid as not to realize that she was burying a large part of her life now that her married life had ended, and she would leave this grave with the new status of a widow-woman. But when Johnny wondered about running the place, she laughed. "Your father never gave this plantation a passing thought. Mister Grimes, the overseer, and I have always run this plantation. I guess we can continue."

Johnny was proud of his capable mother and along with admiration he felt a surge of relief that the tiresome job of being a farmer was not required of him.

John Morris Dutton was buried in the same family plot where his parents lay buried and where many of his slaves were also interred. Over the master's grave, however, was a significant monument. It was chiselled of marble and rose high enough to be discerned from the road. There was space in that grave lot for six more bodies.

The April sun was shining when the preacher said his last words over Marse John and as the mourners turned away from the grave, relatives, friends, and slaves, they could hear the mockingbirds making merry in the trees. Even as they turned away, the Winston boys startled young Marster Johnny and Kevin MacDougall with the news that the guns of Charleston, South Carolina, had fired on the Federal flag at Fort Sumter, and Abraham Lincoln, President of the United States of America, had declared the seceded states of the Confederacy to be in a state of rebellion which must be put down if the Union were to be preserved. He had called for seventy-five thousand volunteers and a state of war now existed between the Federal Union and the Confederacy. Johnny's face—especially his eyes—lighted up when he heard the news, but Kevin, more cautious and unwilling to believe such news, asked, "Are you sure?"

"Of course I'm sure. My father received a telegram from Montgomery this morning, and I would have told you then, but I promised not to say anything to you all about it until after the funeral. Now what are you going to do?"

Johnny hastened to speak. "My mind is already made up. I would enlist immediately because I intend to fight for our Cause, but I've got to go back to school and get my commission first. Kevin, what will you do?"

"I honestly don't know. You know how I hate the thought of war but I won't be called a traitor to our Cause nor a coward. I'll probably fight, but I've got to get myself together and think about it first."

When the subject came up at the dinner table, Big Missy Salina was shocked with the news and she remembered her husband's words. "John said they wouldn't fight, that they are cowards."

Johnny said, "It's not written they'll fight long. They don't have the fighting spirit, and that shows they are cowards."

But Miss Lillian was terribly distressed. "First papa, and then this! Oh, Kevin, you don't have to go, do you?"

Johnny's lips curled as he looked at her. "What kind of southerner are you? Is that your patriotism?"

Lillian wept and said, "But I don't *feel* patriotic."

"Nonsense," said their mother, "we will all do our patriotic duty and fight for the Cause however we are called upon to serve."

The death of Marse John set up a chain of mixed emotions and reactions in Vyry. On his very last day of life he had taunted her with the promise of her freedom, something he knew she wanted more than anything else in the world. If he had really emancipated her in his will, would Big Missy free her? She knew better than to believe it. According to Aunt Sally and all the stories she had heard around the planta-tion from Mammy Sukey and other slaves, Marse John was her natural father. She was as much his child as Miss Lillian and she looked as much like him. But she was also his slave as her mother had been before her, and now her children were slaves. When she saw Miss Lillian weeping in grief over the death of her father, Vyry felt no sympathetic emotion. He had never once acknowledged her as his child and she had no tears to shed for him. True enough, he had never been as cruel to her as Big Missy, but neither had he ever showed her any parental love. Her condition was peculiar; her color was a badge of shame and her children, like herself, were bound in servitude to the household of John Morris Dutton. He did not prevent the guards from whipping her, he would not give her permission to marry, and now in stone-cold death she know he had taunted her with the promise of freedom. She could not help recalling with bitterness his speech that first night about the honor of his house.

There were almost as many guests in the house for the funeral as there had been for the wedding. Big Missy Salina's folks came from Savannah and all Marse John's relatives came from far and near, mostly poor kinfolk. This meant Vyry was cooking whole sides of beef and hams and baking pies and cakes. She worked her worry down, for that was what Marse John's death brought to her, a new measure of worry.

It was late when she lay down on her own pallet and then she could not sleep. Her babies were sleeping beside her, but she was wakeful, too tired to sleep, and brooding over many troubled thoughts. She thought she heard a bird cry, but then she wondered if she had only imagined it. It seemed too faint and distant for her to be sure. Fully another fifteen minutes passed before she heard the whippoorwill much closer. She jumped up and threw a shawl around her shoulders against the night dew, then she waited almost breathless for another cry from the bird. Sure enough, soon she could detect the low, shrill cry of a whippoorwill behind her cabin and she quickly moved in her bare feet around the side of the shanty. There crouched a boy whom she had never seen before, and when he stood up he was as tall as a man. He was dressed in dirty rags but his eyes were keen and in the darkness they searched her face for the answers he needed before he gave her his message. He had a written note but neither he nor she could read it. He told her, "A man brung it from the North this morning, say get it here by night." Then he was gone as quickly as he had come.

Vyry felt sure that this was a note from her free man, Randall Ware, but she was unable to read a word. She was fascinated by the piece of paper and she turned it over and over before she thrust it inside her bosom to keep it until Brother Ezekiel could read it to her. A thousand hopes sprang suddenly to birth. Perhaps this time she would escape. After all Lucy tried twice before she succeeded and Vyry was willing to try more than twice if she thought she could ever succeed. Perhaps he had another plan to help her. But the next afternoon her hopes died when she learned the con-tents of the note. The door to freedom was still closed in her face and she did not know the magic password to open the door. Brother Ezekiel read, "There's going to be a war to set the black slaves free. When the war is over I will come and get you. Wait for me." Vyry burst into bitter, angry tears of disappointment. "A war to set us niggers free? What kind of crazy talk is that?"

James Dickey

(1923–1997)

Born in the Buckhead suburb of Atlanta on February 2, 1923, James Dickey is one of the major figures in modern American literature. He entered Clemson College in South Carolina in 1942 and then enlisted in the U.S. Army Air Corps, where he spent his free time reading literature. He was decorated for his military service.

After the end of World War II, Dickey enrolled at Vanderbilt University in Tennessee, where he earned his B.A. in 1949 and his M.A. in 1950. In 1948 he married Maxine Syerson, with whom he had two children, Christopher and Kevin. After she died in 1976, he married Deborah Dodson. Their daughter is Bronwen.

Dickey's first book, *Into the Stone*, won for him a Guggenheim Fellowship. *Drowning With Others* (1962); *Helmets* (1964); *Buckdancer's Choice* (1965); and *Poems 1957–1967* (1967) followed his first book. He received the National Book Award and was Consultant in Poetry to the Library of Congress from 1966 to 1968.

Dickey was appointed to the Department of English at the University of South Carolina in 1969. His novel *Deliverance* (1970), which was a best-seller, was made into a major film starring Burt Reynolds. In 1972 he read a poem at President Jimmy Carter's inauguration, which he had written for the occasion.

Additional books include *Puella* (1982); *Alnilam* (1987); *The Eagle's Mile* (1990); *The Whole Motion: Collected Poems, 1945–1992* (1992); and *To the White Sea* (1993). Dickey was inducted into the American Academy and Institute of Arts and Letters in 1988. He died in Columbia, South Carolina, on January 19, 1997.

The Bee

To the football coaches of Clemson College, 1942

One dot
Grainily shifting   we at roadside and
The smallest wings coming   along the rail fence out
Of the woods   one dot   of all that green. It now
Becomes flesh-crawling   then the quite still
Of stinging. I must live faster for my terrified
Small son   it is on him. Has come. Clings.

Old wingback, come
To life. If your knee action is high
Enough, the fat may fall in time   God damn
You, Dickey, *dig*   this is your last time to cut
And run   but you must give it everything you have
Left, for screaming near your screaming child is the sheer
Murder of California traffic: some bee hangs driving

Your child
Blindly onto the highway. Get there however
Is still possible. Long live what I badly did
At Clemson   and all of my clumsiest drives

For the ball   all of my trying to turn
The corner downfield   and my spindling explosions
Through the five-hole over tackle. O backfield

Coach Shag Norton,
Tell me as you never yet have told me
To get the lead out   scream whatever will get
The slow-motion of middle age off me   I cannot
Make it this way   I will have to leave
My feet   they are gone   I have him where
He lives   and down we go singing with screams into

The dirt,
Son-screams of fathers   screams of dead coaches turning
To approval   and from between us the bee rises screaming
With flight   grainily shifting   riding the rail fence
Back into the woods   traffic blasting past us
Unchanged, nothing heard through the air-
conditioning glass   we lying at roadside full

Of the forearm prints
Of roadrocks   strawberries on our elbows as from
Scrimmage with the varsity   now we can get
Up   stand   turn away from the highway   look straight
Into trees. See, there is nothing coming out   no
Smallest wing   no shift of a flight-grain   nothing
Nothing. Let us go in, son, and listen

For some tobacco-
mumbling voice in the branches   to say "That's
a little better,"   to our lives still hanging
By a hair. There is nothing to stop us   we can go
Deep   deeper   into elms, and listen to traffic die
Roaring, like a football crowd from which we have
Vanished. Dead coaches live in the air, son   live

In the ear
Like fathers, and *urge*   and *urge*. They want you better
Than you are. When needed, they rise and curse you   they scream
When something must be saved. Here, under this tree,
We can sit down. You can sleep, and I can try
To give back what I have earned by keeping us
Alive, and safe from bees: the smile of some kind

Of savior—
Of touchdowns, of fumbles, battles,
Lives. Let me sit here with you, son
As on the bench, while the first string takes back
Over, far away   and say with my silentest tongue, with the man-
creating bruises of my arms   with a live leaf a quick
Dead hand on my shoulder, "Coach Norton, I am your boy."

The Strength of Fields

> *. . . a separation from the world,*
> *a penetration to some source of power*
> *and a life-enhancing return . . .*
> Van Gennep: *Rites de Passage*

Moth-force a small town always has,

Given the night.

        What field-forms can be,
Outlying the small civic light-decisions over
    A man walking near home?

               Men are not where he is
Exactly now, but they are around him around   him like the strength

Of fields.   The solar system floats on
Above him in town-moths.

           Tell me, train-sound,

With all your long-lost grief,

         what I can give.

   Dear Lord of all the fields

         what am I going to *do?*
     Street-lights, blue-force and frail
As the homes of men, tell me how to do it   how
   To withdraw   how to penetrate and find the source
    Of the power you always had

         light as a moth, and rising
   With the level and moonlit expansion
Of the fields around, and the sleep of hoping men.

   You?   I?   What difference is there?   We can all be saved

   By a secret blooming. Now as I walk
The night   and you walk with me   we know simplicity
   Is close to the source that sleeping men
    Search for in their home-deep beds.

   We know that the sun is away   we know that the sun can be conquered
   By moths, in blue home-town air.
     The stars splinter, pointed and wild. The dead lie under
The pastures.   They look on and help.   Tell me, freight-train,
       When there is no one else
   To hear.   Tell me in a voice the sea
   Would have, if it had not a better one: as it lifts,
    Hundreds of miles away, its fumbling, deep-structured roar
     Like the profound, unstoppable craving
     Of nations for their wish.

                             Hunger, time and the moon:
The moon lying on the brain

                         as on the excited sea   as on
   The strength of fields.   Lord, let me shake

   With purpose.   Wild hope can always spring
   From tended strength.   Everything is in that.
     That and nothing but kindness.   More kindness, dear Lord
Of the renewing green.

                   That is where it all has to start:
 With the simplest things.   More kindness will do nothing less
      Than save every sleeping one
       And night-walking one

   Of us.
        My life belongs to the world. I will do what I can.

VI

Appalachia Recognized

Perhaps no region of the country has been more stigmatized than Southern Appalachia, the highland realm covering an area larger than New England and stretching from the western rim of Virginia southward to northern Alabama. Part of this stigma arises from a tradition of self-conscious isolation that makes Appalachia, in the estimate of many observers, a place akin to a foreign country. The region's people, too, have long inspired extreme reactions ranging from admiration to the less than favorable judgment of Edgar Allan Poe, who viewed the Southern highlanders as "an uncouth and fierce race of men" about whom almost nothing was known in the mid–nineteenth century.

The abysmal lack of knowledge about the mountains and valleys, coves, and hollows that define what scholar J. W. Williamson terms "Hillbillyland"[1] has continued down to our own time, giving rise both to stereotypes and to an abiding sense of Appalachia's being a place apart, an embarrassing but tantalizing repository of cultural Neanderthals scarcely to be imagined in an age of urban sprawl, unprecedented affluence, and Internet connectedness. In fact, Allen Batteau has remarked that Appalachia is now more image than substance, "a creature of the urban imagination" designed to serve the "economic opportunism, political creativity, or passing fancy of urban elites."[2] Similarly, in his award-winning study entitled *Two Worlds in the Tennessee Mountains: Exploring the Origins of Appalachian Stereotypes*, David C. Hsiung notes that the word *Appalachia* is a potent semiotic, evoking in the popular imagination "a host of images and stereotypes involving feuds, individualism, moonshine, subsistence farming, quilting bees, illiteracy, dueling banjos, and many other things."[3]

Stereotypes, often lurid and derogatory, are never far from "the nature and meaning of Appalachian otherness."[4] Consider the archetypal hillbilly, "provoking a range of responses, from an odd kind of comfort to a real terror."[5] He is our "symbolic American country cousin,"[6] the slack-jawed yokel at whom we poke fun from a distance but who terrifies us at close range. He symbolizes "an uncomfortable and unwelcome opening into a history we have tried to forget, our conflict memory of the pain and heartache of living in the dirt on the frontier."[7] Even his rude, spare accessories are inseparable from his image as a figure of folk legend. His squirrel rifle, outhouse, and moonshine whisky jug are the stuff of innumerable caricatures reinforcing our cultural and economic superiority at his expense. His wife, the rock-faced "maw" found in such comic strips as *L'il Abner* and *Snuffy Smith*, provides an additional "decorative snapshot" in a family album too often characterized by "coarseness, brutality, and unspeakable possibilities spawned in the darkest corners of our consciousness."[8] The hillbilly's backwardness—his aversion to civilized amenities and to a way of life ratified by the cities—offers a "useful negative object lesson, a keep-away sign"[9] pointing to the superiority of mainstream, which is to say *urban*, culture and the comforts offered there.

Yet, the mountaineer, the hillbilly, is ironically the most democratic and fiercely individualistic of our longstanding cultural icons. In many ways, he represents the best traditions of the South and of the nation. At first glance, there is little of the romance about him that we associate with such Southern types as the Cavalier or Planter. He has almost nothing in common with either, having had little inclination for rewriting his family's lists or for owning other human beings as a way of getting work done that the hillbilly can do himself.

Suspicious of pseudoaristocrats and people who put on airs, the early Appalachian mountaineer rejected the coastal Southerner's obsession with genealogy. As John Rice Irwin, founder and Director of the Museum of Appalachia in Norris, Tennessee, points out, people of the Southern Appalachian mountains "were reflective, philosophical, and even studious, when it came to unwritten history; but in referring to the 'old' family members they never got beyond 'Virginia, North Carolina, or Pennsylvania.'"[10] The reason, Rice contends, was that rural mountain folk considered themselves foremost to be "all Americans, and if pushed as to where one's family was from, the patriarch might say 'they was Irish or they was Scotch-Irish,' or that 'they come from across the waters.'"[11] Appalachian scholar Billy Kennedy identifies a similar tendency, suggesting that the Scots-Irish emigrant families who settled in the American frontier during the eighteenth century "were a unique breed of people with an independent spirit which boldly challenged the arbitrary power of monarchs and established church prelates."[12] Consequently, "almost everyone, it seems, who has written about this region refers admirably [to its inhabitants] as a brave, hard working, independent, self-reliant, and fiercely honest people."[13]

Yet these very qualities, coupled with ongoing cultural and geographical isolation, have often made the mountaineer a living artifact, subject both to ridicule and to culturally sanctioned caricature. One explanation for this phenomenon may lie in the Appalachian mountain people's tendency to go their own way, eschewing "progress" and the politics associated with various social programs and reforms. Undeniably, rural Appalachia has resisted change for almost three centuries, often in ways detrimental to the people there. For instance, Southern Appalachian counties are still among the poorest in the country. Health care is often substandard or lacking in rural Appalachia, and education lags sadly behind the rest of the nation. The coal industry, a traditional source of livelihood for many inhabitants of the region, represents one of the most ambivalent, bitter choices that mountain people have been forced to make in order to supplement inadequate farming incomes. No one can accurately assess the human toll that mining has exacted in the Southern Appalachians.

Too often, what the rest of the country sees when regarding Appalachia is the people's habitual recalcitrance and their unreasonable resistance to social improvements. Consequently, there is sometimes a conflicting response by mainstream America to refashion Southern Appalachia into something more culturally acceptable or to reject Appalachia out of hand as a region of bumpkins and misfits, often "abnormal, degenerative, and pathological."[14] Our "romanticized awe" for the mountains and for the simplicity of mountain life is countered by a "deeply ingrained aversion [that has] never disappeared and is the key to our modern ambiguity."[15]

This ambiguity makes it easier for Americans not to take seriously Appalachia itself or its contributions to our national life. A much easier task is to paint the region's citizens in broad strokes, equating their traditional "multicolored patchwork dress" with the motley of court jesters and fools.[16] Again, J. W. Williamson points to this oft-made connection. The "hillbilly as fool," as Williamson points out, is a cultural archetype. Even English etymology bears out this pejorative link. *Clown*, for example, "originally meant a peasant, a rustic, a farm worker."[17] Likewise, the "word *idiot* derives from Greek *idiotes*, meaning 'a private person,' one who dwells outside the pale, presumably because of foolish or unnerving behavior."[18] The word *fool* itself describes "a scapegoat, one visually stigmatized by either outright deformity or outlandish dress."[19] These are some of the lingering images that attach to the hill people of Appalachia, a people who have somehow managed to "survive and even thrive despite our low opinion of their worth."[20]

Fortunately, not everyone has been content to regard the mountaineer and his family in such derogatory terms. Several attempts to present an authentic portrait of the "multitude of little farmers living up the branches and on the steep hillsides" date back to Horace Kephart's classic *Our Southern Highlanders*, published in 1913 and reissued in subsequent editions.[21] Although novelists Mary Noilles Murfree, John Fox, and Alice McGowan had written earlier accounts of "typical" highlanders, Kephart's sympathetic and thorough portrayal went far in correcting misinformation and in exploding cruel stereotypes. Noting how the topography of the Great Smoky Mountains reinforces the inhabitants' "amazing isolation from all that lies beyond the blue, hazy outline of their mountains,"[22] Kephart also acknowledges the sort of community that necessarily arose amid such isolated circumstances. Time indeed stood still for mountain folk "so long detached from the life and movement of modern times."[23] Thus, those traits that enabled frontiersmen to settle in such a remote, inhospitable region were ones Kephart found unchanged since "the days of Daniel Boone."[24] "The map" and its omnipresent barriers provided all the impetus needed for mountaineers to live just as their rough-and-ready Scots-Irish ancestors had lived in the early eighteenth century.

As for particulars of that life, Kephart finds that "it is a patriarchal existence" in which "the man of the house is lord. He takes no orders from anybody at home or abroad. Whether he shall work or visit or roam the woods with dog or gun is nobody's affair but his own. About family matters he consults his wife, but in the end his word is law."[25] Moreover, the mountain farmer's wife "is not only a household drudge, but a field-hand as well. She helps to plant, hoe corn, gather fodder, sometimes either blows or splits rails. It is the commonest of sights for a woman to be awkwardly hacking up firewood with a dull axe."[26] Neighbors, though sometimes living at a remote distance, are important allies since they often possess talents and trades necessary to the mountain community's survival. In short, harsh conditions foster pragmatic, rather than social, ties among the highland people. Nevertheless, the mountain code of conduct is a "curious mixture of savagery and civility, creating sometimes vengeful and cruel behavior" but also a pronounced hospitality considered a "sacred duty toward wayfarers of any degree."[27] Admitting that Southern Appalachia contains natives both "trifling and immoral,"[28] Kephart finds much that can excite admiration and hope. Despite their much advertised aversion to progress, the people possess "certain sterling qualities . . . that our nation can ill afford to waste."[29]

Harry M. Caudill's *Night Comes to the Cumberlands: A Biography of a Depressed Area*, first published in 1962, is equally sympathetic but far less optimistic about modern mountaineers and the communities in which they live. An ex-Kentucky legislator, Caudill recognizes how culture and history have conspired to produce a "land of economic, social, and political blight without parallel in the nation."[30] The problematic status of Southern Appalachia finds validation in Caudill's account as the author focuses on the poverty and squalor created by the exploitative coal industry:

> Coal has always cursed the land in which it lies. When men begin to wrest it from the earth, it leaves a legacy of foul streams, hideous slagheaps and polluted air. It peoples this transformed land with blind and crippled men and with widows and orphans. It is an extractive industry which takes all away and restores nothing. It mars but never beautifies. It corrupts but never purifies.[31]

Caudill's central thesis is that an unregulated coal industry has depleted the physical and human resources of a people already forced to live a marginal existence. As the rest of the country progresses economically and socially, the Appalachian Mountain regions remain "hopelessly bogged in politics."[32] Yet even Caudill finds hope in "localized efforts at revival" and in the inherent qualities that "show what brave men and women can accomplish in the face of adverse circumstances."[33]

As has often been the case, the people of Southern Appalachia have transformed their perceived weaknesses into strengths designed to help their homeland. The qualities of independence, self-reliance, a capacity for hard and patient work, and a passion for justice have enabled people in the region to cling to indispensable traditions while embracing vital changes. Oddly, Appalachia, more than any other region of the nation, may teach us the value of returning to a place with renewed vision and enlarged action. Such efforts find inspiration in projects like the Drinko Symposium currently sponsored by Marshall University in Huntington, West Virginia. Under the leadership of program director Shirley Lumpkin, selected students, all natives of Appalachia, examine their communities with an eye for balancing the demands of tradition and change. The most familiar with the region are thus able to undertake efforts at "Re-membering, Re-weaving, and Re-visioning Other Ways" of considering Appalachia. One special focus of the symposium is to recognize the extraordinary diversity of Appalachian experience. Race and gender stereotypes are challenged, social classifications are critically examined, and the boundaries of Appalachia are expanded to account for the complexities of the place and people.

Publications in Southern Appalachia also contribute to a growing awareness of the region's complex history, traditions, and potential. Recognizing that Appalachia is a place where computers can contribute to a farmer's livelihood, where women enjoy professions as surgeons and lawyers, and where the stock market is often analyzed as carefully as the weather, Appalachia's magazines and journals offer new ways of looking at an old region. No longer a literary terra incognita, the Southern mountain area is favorable soil to a flowering of publications including *Now and Then*, *Appalachian Journal*, *Appalachian Heritage*, *Sow's Ear*, *Iron Mountain Review*, and *Mossy Creek Reader*, among many others. What is remarkable is the diversity these publications represent and the wealth of insights they offer about a region whose original settlers were never restricted to the Scots-Irish but once included the largest Native American tribe in the South—the Cherokees.

Appalachia's first people were 20,000 to 25,000 members of the Cherokee tribe scattered throughout areas including present-day North Carolina, Tennessee, and Georgia. The Cherokees were further "divided into clans composed of individuals who believed that all [of the Cherokees] were descended from a common ancestor."[34] Each clan took its name from the natural world, specifically from the animal kingdom, so that Deer, Wolf, and Bird were common forms of clan identification. The Cherokees "viewed most affairs having to do with themselves and the world around them in a spiritual context. They thought that most objects and occurrences in nature had spiritual counterparts."[35] The result of this cosmology was that "everything and every occurrence had natural and religious overtones for these people."[36] Because of the initial absence of native written languages, the Cherokees passed down their accumulated knowledge and traditions orally from one generation to the next in the form of myths. These myths can be classified according to several types: "sacred myths, animal stories, local legends, and historical traditions."[37] In the case of sacred myths, only the priests, myth-keepers, and conjurers knew this class of stories. Animal stories, in contrast, belonged to all members of the tribe. As with their human counterparts, the animals "had chiefs, councils, and townhouses," and all "spoke the same language."[38] Each animal was assigned a specific role in the society of creatures. For instance, the rabbit was a trickster and mischief maker, a character also appearing in African American folk legends. Among the selections included here are myths accounting for the origin of the world and for the origin of game and corn. Localized versions of the race between the Terrapin and the Rabbit and the familiar narrative of the Rabbit and the Tar Wolf are offered as well.

One unfortunate result of the racially motivated class system in the South was that the Cherokees sometimes followed the lead of white Southerners in demonstrating prejudice toward African Americans. For instance, "Indian slaveholders took steps to restrict the rights of the blacks they acquired. . . . In 1824 the Cherokee Nation forbade its citizens to intermarry with Negroes and prohibited black slaves from owning horses, cattle, or hogs."[39] Thus, groups whose common experience of oppression should have made them allies were often conquered and divided by the South's white ruling elites. Also, when any disenfranchised group received additional "rights," or enhanced status, divisiveness often grew, and a fierce competitiveness resulted. With resources often at a scarce premium, the poor and exploited frequently debated claims of entitlement.

Such was the case of Rebecca Harding Davis, who, while belying "the stereotypes of languid Southern womanhood"[40] and demonstrating women's ability to succeed in post–Civil War commercial enterprises, may have underestimated the difficulties that former slaves faced in earning a living. In "The Black North," Davis acknowledges that the "negro workman" has had "to contend against an absurd and cruel prejudice," but she argues that it is in the South, rather than in the North, that the black man will find opportunities of employment. Echoing the sentiments of Booker T. Washington, Davis praises the capitalist spirit of the New South where "you will scarcely find a town or village . . . that has not its industrious, shrewd, successful negro—a mechanic, a trader; an employer of other men, self-respecting neighbors." Pointing out that trade unions in the North shut out black workers, Davis affirms her faith in the South's steady economic progress and need for labor. Yet, as Edward Ayers asserts, "Even the South's greatest drawing card for every industry—cheap and plentiful labor—hurt the iron and steel industry in the long run, delaying the adoption of new techniques . . ." and creating "work in the mills at rates far below Northern wages."[41] In Southern Appalachia, the "very foundations of the mountain social order" were shaken to the ground with the "expanding industrial capitalism."[42] Between 1880 and 1930, "mountain agriculture went into serious decline."[43] Whereas in the 1880s, the size of the average mountain farm was approximately 187 acres, by the 1930s, "the average Appalachian farm contained only 76 acres."[44]

Such changes have always been regarded with ambivalence by the inhabitants of Appalachia. There is perhaps no more controversial term than *progress* for those people confronted with the choice of leaving Appalachia in order to seek a "better" way of life. This theme is exquisitely dramatized in Elizabeth Madox Roberts's story "On the Mountainside." A native Kentuckian, Roberts describes the conflict of a young man named Newt Reddix whose passion for "learnen" and exposure to a spell-binding teacher prompt him to explore the world beyond his mountain home. He fantasizes about finding "men having things done by machinery; lovely girls not yet imagined; and things to know beyond anything he could recall, and not one of them too fine or too good for him." Setting out for the region of lights in the lowland settlements that extend to "the other end of this old globe," Newt encounters a stranger who ironically would give anything to return to his native mountains. "You may go far and see a heap in life," the stranger tells Newt, "but mark me as I say it, the places you knowed when you was a little tad will be the strongest in your remembrance. . . . Your whole insides is made outen what you done first."

Born in Branwell, West Virginia, but making her home in Lynchburg, Virginia, for most of her life, Anne Spencer "is typical of a group of Southerners, in particular Jonathan Brooks and George Leonard Allen, who contributed to the [New Negro] renaissance [of the 1920s and 1930s] from their homes in the South."[45] With a focus on finely wrought craft, Spencer "wrote in response to things that moved her personally, but her poems are not primarily topical and are rarely controversial."[46] The poet explores and preserves the sacred mystery associated with particular places in such poems as "Substitution" and "For Jim, Easter Eve." In both poems, a garden is the recurring motif, a place of "wordless patterns" in which opposites are reconciled. Although Spencer's literary production was small when compared with that of many other Appalachian poets, her naturalness of idiom and subtle lyricism combine to offer stunning effects.

Place and its operations on the soul are the focus of much of the fiction written by Asheville, North Carolina, native Thomas Wolfe. Wolfe's challenge to such traditional Southern pieties as home and family can be seen in *Of Time and River*, subtitled *A Legend of a Man's Hunger in His Youth*, published in 1935. The novel is sprawling and episodic in detailing the semiautobiographical experiences of a young protagonist named Eugene Gant, a self-imposed exile from a stifling middle-class Southern community with its undue emphasis on conformity. Gant's travels have taken him far from home—first to Harvard as a student, then to New York City as a schoolteacher, and finally to Europe as an observer—a participant of the literary scene. Yet it is his father's death at home that serves as the major dramatic premise of the story: the young man's "search to find a father, not merely the lost father of his youth, but the image of a strength and wisdom external to his need and superior to his hunger, to which the belief and power of his own life could be united." However, at the time of his father's death, Eugene Gant can only envision a dark and answerless time inseparable from our common mortality:

> October has come again, has come again . . . I have come home again, and found my father dead, . . . and that was time . . . time . . . time . . . Where shall I go now? What shall I do? For October has come again, but there has gone some richness from the life we knew, and we are lost.

Born in rural Green County, Kentucky, poet Jesse Stuart is "essentially a teller of tales, a writer one step away from the oral tradition in which he grew up in the dark hollows of Kentucky."[47] Acknowledging in his prose poem "Kentucky Is My Land" that "I didn't have any choice as to where I was born," Stuart nonetheless declares that he would have "chosen Kentucky" as his place of nurture. For "even the drab hills of winter" there are "filled with music." Stuart's creativity is inextricable from the natural cycles and rhythms of the place he calls home, enabling him to "put poems on paper [that] wrote themselves for they were ripe / And ready for harvest . . ." Stuart's poems entitled "Her Work Is Done" and "Prayer for My Father" offer loving tributes to his parents. Against the backdrop of such love and caring stand the efforts of pioneers long forgotten in the quest for "Modernity," itself a specious concept robbing us of our independence and native strengths. Like Thoreau before him, Stuart recognizes in such poems as "Stand Out and Count" that our real treasures in this fleeting life are "those things of beauty you have known from birth." Similarly, in "Summer Has Faded," each season is its own "book" that can only be read with "living eyes."

As in Wolfe's *Of Time and the River*, a dead father is the catalyst for the protagonist's self-discovery in James Agee's *A Death in the Family*. The autobiographical novel begins with a prologue, "Knoxville, Summer 1915," considered by many to be one of the most lyrical prose passages in American literature. Indeed, the prologue amounts to a prose poem with its lush and sensory-laden impressions of a life lived in the early 1900s at 1505 Highland Avenue in Knoxville, Tennessee. The prologue ends with the young narrator Rufus being put to bed by those who treat him "as one familiar and well-beloved in that home." However, in Chapter One, we sense an almost compulsive desire on the narrator's part to remember details about his father—the man's eyes, which were "calm and grave," and his mouth, which was "strong and more quiet than Rufus had ever seen." By the end of the chapter, we realize the importance of this intense recollection, for the boy awakens in the morning to discover that his father has died in a car accident the night before. In an instant, Rufus's world is shattered, his life altered irrevocably. Even Agee's prose mirrors the change, displaying fewer lyrical flourishes and syntactical variations while substituting utterances as blunt and direct as a death sentence. Agee makes clear that a part of Rufus dies with his father, just as Agee himself never stopped grieving over the loss of his own father in identical circumstances—a car accident on the Clinton Highway just outside Knoxville.

Family is the focus of George Scarbrough's brilliantly crafted poetry, though the natural world serves as an equally important source of inspiration. As Scarbrough maintains, "home was the place of my altar, poor as the trappings of the house may have been. But outside were the earth itself and the blue wall of the sky. Which was only another house, only larger and more inclusive." Home for Scarbrough is the intellectually arid geography of Polk County in southeastern Tennessee, the region settled by his grandfather in 1850. Here a boy's impressions are never distinct from his experiences. Both land and season conspire to result in larger metaphysical discoveries like the ones made in "The Winter Mole." In this example of long-lined free verse, the speaker confronts a cold landscape that reinforces his loneliness but also offers a glimpse of the "small truths" with which he is most comfortable. In fact, he remarks, "the smaller the better." In "Death Is A Short Word," Scarbrough begins his series of quatrains with a simile drawn from the natural world: "Like a sparrow sitting in a wide walk, / I myself grew small and precise inside / In exact proportion to how much he died." Inspired by the death of the poet's father, this poem articulates the stunned speechlessness that accompanies the death of someone close. Clarity of vision and sureness of form characterize the effect created in "Blackberry Winter." Here the speaker climbs to higher ground in order to ask, "What love is there in all that country, wonder?" Yet, as before, the speaker stands alone in a spot where "No feet but mine impede the berry flowers." One of the most striking features of Scarbrough's talent is his ability to combine what William Butler Yeats called the best of the folk and classical traditions. Perhaps no living poet, and certainly no poet since Allen Tate, has been able to use the vernacular and the formal to more heightened effect than Scarbrough.

The woven stories of a community comprise much of the short fiction written by Gurney Norman. Born in Grundy, Virginia (the birthplace of Lee Smith, as well), Norman moved in infancy with his family to Kentucky. There he became acquainted with the numerous kinfolks who people his stories, their lives providing a continuous thread tying one generation to the next. In Norman's story "The Revival," the protagonist named Wilgus visits his alcoholic uncle, who sits on the couch holding "an open Bible in his lap and a king-size beer in his hand." Taunted by the demons of drink, Uncle Delmer is pondering his spiritual fate. At one point, he concludes that "My soul's blacker'n a piece of coal." Wilgus tries to convince his uncle otherwise, cleaning him up in preparation for the return home of Delmer's wife and children, who had earlier been driven away by Delmer's drinking. The story is actually an episode in a larger pattern of interrelated narratives; thus, Delmer's fate is still uncertain by the end of "Revival." Norman is a literary realist who refuses to serve up sentimental niceties in lieu of a hard-edged truth. His characters, like Uncle Delmer, are often caught between the extremes of damnation and salvation. Despite their spiritual poverty, Norman's people find reassurance in the love given by family and neighbors.

Family and neighbors are what Gertie Nevels must leave behind in Harriette Simpson Arnow's *The Dollmaker*. "The most popular of her four novels," *The Dollmaker* is the story of a woman whose plight in moving with her family from Kentucky to Detroit represents "the saga of all displayed, uprooted individuals suddenly shoved into a cold, seemingly ruthless environment."[48] The migration of Southern Appalachian families to Northern cities was a common phenomenon during the first half of the twentieth century. Even today, dialectologists can identify vestiges of mountain speech in suburban neighborhoods outside Detroit and Flint, Michigan. Far from being the suburbs, Gertie's new home is an urban housing project in which tenants live in "alleys." So harsh and unfamiliar are these surroundings that the homesick Gertie "resumes wood carving (a mountain craft) as a means of creating and finding order and a chance to understand the paradoxical nature of the world."[49] Gertie cannot, however, reconcile the paradox of death she confronts when her young daughter Cassie is killed by a train in a nearby rail-yard. In one of the most arresting scenes in all of Appalachian fiction, we witness not only Cassie's death but also Gertie's excruciating helplessness. And yet, all of Gertie's experiences are a catalyst by which she is transformed, discovering her own indomitable qualities of courage and love. In the words of Wendell Berry, she refuses to let all she cares about "die a second, more final time."

Preserving what is loved and valued has been the task of many Appalachian writers, including Kentucky Poet Laureate James Still. Most of Still's novels, short fiction, and poetry record events in the lives of people residing in a remote pocket of Knott County known as Troublesome Creek. Here traditions of mountain life have persisted to the present. One such tradition is that of the isolated mountain farm. In Still's poem entitled "Farm," the speaker notes all the living presences anticipating a much-awaited harvest. Reminiscent of Robert Frost's "Design," Still's "Pattern for Death" reminds us of the underlying logic of nature that results in a "pattern" of life and death. The spider in the poem weaves a "quiet design" that will ensnare the "crane fly" in "a ladder of silk." The lines themselves reveal a delicate and skillful handling of sound devices. This music underscores the theme of Still's "When the Dulcimers are Gone" in which one of the oldest of mountain instruments offers its "mellow voice" to be heard in the "pennyroyal meadow." In the selfsame spirit as Coleridge's "The Eolian Harp," Still's poem mimics the harmonies of the dulcimer, imploring us to ask what we stand to lose "when the dulcimers are gone."

As the editor of both an anthology of Appalachian literature and *The Wolfpen Poems*, the collected poems of James Still, Jim Wayne Miller was one of the region's most respected scholars and teachers. In addition to six volumes of poetry, Miller wrote a novel, *Newfound* (1989), the story of a boy growing up in his grandparents' house in the Tennessee hills. Young Robert Wells is the beneficiary of stories told by a family of powerful voices. There are stories about raccoon hunts, tumultuous marriages, and squirrels falling from the sky. Offered here are some of the benchmark episodes in the protagonist's life, including his decision to leave home and attend Berea College in Kentucky. At one point, Robert delivers a speech to students at his former high school, expressing a decided ambivalence about leaving a place he loved: "I talked about the hundreds of thousands of people who had left our Appalachian region over the years to seek work in other places. I asked why we had to leave a place that was so beautiful; why the natural beauty that attracted tourists from all over the country was being destroyed in many places, by strip-mining." Robert is quick to point out that his whole family was present in the audience.

The spiritual life of a particular family is the dramatic situation underlying Lee Smith's novel *Saving Grace*. Smith's focal character, Florida Grace Shepherd, possesses the dubious distinction of being a snake-handler's daughter. The practice of snake-handling as a religious observance originated around the turn of the twentieth century when an itinerant preacher named George Hensley stunned attendees at a small church service by handling poisonous snakes and, later, by drinking poison. Accounts vary as to whether Hensley first handled the vipers at a church in Sale Creek or a tabernacle in Dolly Pond, both communities in southeastern Tennessee. Hensley was never clear in his recollections about the event. What is known is that he was inspired by Mark 16:17–18: ". . . and they shall be able to handle serpents, and they shall be able to drink deadly poison without harm, and the sick upon whom they lay their hands shall recover."

Smith's Grace describes the unfavorable publicity surrounding her father's activities and the subsequent embarrassment she experiences. Realizing that snakehandling, drinking poison, laying on of hands, and speaking in tongues are bizarre rituals, even by Southern standards, Grace sets out to discover a spirituality that is uniquely her own. Her past drives her into an uncertain future, but one that enables her to return home with an awareness achieved by heroic struggles and the operations of divine grace. The demons she exorcises during her quest are the tensions and anxieties rising up from the depths of an unresolved childhood. Out of such a childhood, Grace finds the motivation to come to terms with all she becomes and has known.

Perhaps no contemporary writer in Appalachia is more respected than Wendell Berry, for his unswerving vision and consummate workmanship. Berry's inseparable habits of writing and being stem from his fidelity to the rural community he calls home, Port Royal, Kentucky. As a farmer, Berry's attachment to the land is authentic. He is no abstract "ecologist" but a steward of the land and a defender of human prerogatives in the face of growing threats to our humanity. Recognizing the dangers offered to the human spirit by our blind devotion and uncritical approaches to technology, Berry sounds a clarion alarm in his poems, essays, and novels. He demonstrates the commitment and work necessary to sustain communities, households, marriages, and friendships. The work becomes more difficult, the challenges greater, as we rely increasingly on machines to relieve us from "drudgery." In fact, Berry warns, we have developed an entire economy designed to divorce the worker from the consequences of his or her work. This is one of the benchmark themes of Berry's essay "Why I Am Not Going to Buy a Computer." Here Berry notes that far from creating better writers, computers simply create the *illusion* of producing better writing. When writing becomes solely a matter of convenience, utilitarian in the extreme, the prerogatives of writing are undermined, if not destroyed. What we need is not faster, more conveniently produced prose—a quick and ready product. What is required are writers who are more careful and respectful of language and audience.

Berry's care in choosing words can be seen in his approach to poetry. In his collection of essays *What Are People For?* the author clarifies the role of both poem and poet:

> By its formal integrity a poem reminds us of the formal integrity of other words, creatures, and structures of the world. The form of a good poem is, in a way perhaps not altogether explainable or demonstrable, an analogue of the forms of other things. By its form it alludes to other forms, evokes them, resonates with them, and so becomes a part of the system of analogies or harmonies by which we live. Thus the poet affirms and collaborates in the formality of the Creation. This, I think, is a matter of supreme, and mostly unacknowledged, importance.[50]

Berry's selected poetry from his volume *Sabbaths* demonstrates his assertion that "a poem reminds us also of the spiritual elation that we call 'inspiration' or 'gift.'"[51] Composed on successive Sundays over several years, the poems show us, among other things, the necessary relationship between labor and rest, reaffirming an awareness of the "good and perfect gift" that is our lives. These elegant, carefully crafted poems are prayerful in their recognition of all that we humans touch and leave behind "in our few troubled days" here.

The ability of a good poem to serve as "an analogue of the form of other things" is especially apparent in the work of North Carolinian Fred Chappell. A versatile and accomplished writer in several genres, Chappell is perhaps best known as a poet able to create and sustain poignant and meaningful metaphors like those found in his series of baseball poems: "Third Base Coach," "Fast Ball," "Spitballer," "Junk Ball," and "Strike Zone." An agrarian pastime, baseball does not depend on technology so much as it does on "grass raw and electric as the cat's whiskers." In addition, the similarities between poetry and baseball suggest that both activities require control and chance to produce startling effects. As with his suite of baseball poems, Chappell's "Song of Seven" depends, in part, on athletic imagery in personifying the seven deadly sins. This poem is both serious and whimsical in its contemporary depiction of transgressions that the speaker has fun in toppling.

Notes

1. J. W. Williamson, *Hillbillyland*, (Chapel Hill: University of North Carolina Press, 1995), 1.
2. David C. Hsiung, *Two Worlds in the Tennessee Mountains* (University Press of Kentucky, 1997), 1.
3. Hsiung, 1.
4. Hsiung, 2.
5. Williamson, 1.
6. Williamson, 2.
7. Williamson, 3.
8. Williamson, 5.
9. Williamson, 5.
10. Billy Kennedy, *The Scot-Irish in the Hills of Tennessee* (Greenville, SC: Emerald House, 1995), 10.
11. Kennedy, 10.
12. Kennedy, 19.
13. Kennedy, 9–10.
14. Williamson, 19.
15. Williamson, 19.
16. Williamson, 22.
17. Williamson, 21.
18. Williamson, 21–22.
19. Williamson, 22.
20. Williamson, 20.
21. Horace Kephart, *Our Southern Highlanders* (New York: Macmillan, 1913), 17.
22. Kephart, 17.
23. Kephart, 18.
24. Kephart, 18.
25. Kephart, 330.
26. Kephart, 331.
27. Kephart, 267.
28. Kephart, 465.
29. Kephart, 465.
30. Harry Caudill, *Night Comes to the Cumberlands* (Boston: Atlantic Monthly Press: 1962), ix–x.

31. Caudill, x.

32. Caudill, 336.

33. Caudill, 334.

34. Ronald Satz, *Tennessee's Indian Peoples* (Knoxville: University of Tennessee Press, 1979), 19.

35. Satz, 32.

36. Satz, 36.

37. James Mooney, *Myths of the Cherokee and Sacred Formulas of the Cherokees* (Nashville: Elder Publishers, 1982), 229.

38. Mooney, 231.

39. Satz, 85.

40. Edward Ayers, *The Promise of the New South* (New York: Oxford University Press, 1992), 28.

41. Ayers, 110.

42. Ronald Eller, *Miners, Millhands, and Mountaineers* (Knoxville: University of Tennessee Press, 1982), xvii–xix.

43. Eller, xix.

44. Eller, xix.

45. Thadious M. Davis, "Southern Standard Bearers in the New Negro Renaissance" *The History of Southern Literature*, eds. Louis D. Rubin et al. (Baton Rouge: Louisiana State University Press, 1985), 294–295.

46. Davis, 295.

47. Herschel Gower, "Regions and Rebels," *The History of Southern Literature*, eds. Louis D. Rubin et al. (Baton Rouge: Louisiana State University Press, 1985), 403.

48. Gower, 405.

49. Gower, 405.

50. Wendell Berry, *What Are People For?* (Berkeley: North Point Press, 1990), 89.

51. Berry, 89–90.

Cherokee Myths and Legends

The Cherokee, a branch of the Iroquois nation, trace their history back more than a thousand years. Originally their society was based on hunting, trading, and agriculture. By the time European explorers and traders arrived, Cherokee lands covered a large part of what is now the southeastern United States.

By traditional law, tales or stories like the ones included here were told only to other Cherokee and were passed down from generation to generation. They were recited in a small, dome-shaped earthen-covered hut in a gathering that lasted all night and into the morning, until the sun appeared in the east.

How the World Was Made

The earth is a great island floating in a sea of water, and suspended at each of the four cardinal points by a cord hanging down from the sky vault, which is of solid rock. When the world grows old and worn out, the people will die and the cords will break and let the earth sink down into the ocean, and all will be water again. The Indians are afraid of this.

When all was water, the animals were above in Gălûñ'lătĭ, beyond the arch; but it was very much crowded, and they were wanting more room. They wondered what was below the water, and at last Dâyuni'sĭ, "Beaver's Grandchild," the little Water-beetle, offered to go and see if it could learn. It darted in every direction over the surface of the water, but could find no firm place to rest. Then it dived to the bottom and came up with some soft mud, which began to grow and spread on every side until it became the island which we call the earth. It was afterward fastened to the sky with four cords, but no one remembers who did this.

At first the earth was flat and very soft and wet. The animals were anxious to get down, and sent out different birds to see if it was yet dry, but they found no place to alight and came back again to Gălûñ'lătĭ. At last it seemed to be time, and they sent out the Buzzard and told him to go and make ready for them. This was the Great Buzzard, the father of all the buzzards we see now. He flew all over the earth, low down near the ground, and it was still soft. When he reached the Cherokee country, he was very tired, and his wings began to flap and strike the ground, and wherever they struck the earth there was a valley, and where they turned up again there was a mountain. When the animals above saw this, they were afraid that the whole world would be mountains, so they called him back, but the Cherokee country remains full of mountains to this day.

When the earth was dry and the animals came down, it was still dark, so they got the sun and set it in a track to go every day across the island from east to west, just overhead. It was too hot this way, and Tsiska'gĭlĭ', the Red Crawfish, had his shell scorched a bright red, so that his meat was spoiled; and the Cherokee do not eat it. The conjurers put the sun another hand-breadth higher in the air, but it was still too hot. They raised it another time, and another, until it was seven handbreadths high and just under the sky arch. Then it was right, and they left it so. This is why the conjurers call the highest place Gûlkwâ'gine Di'gălûñ'lătiyûñ', "the seventh height," because it is seven hand-breadths above the earth. Every day the sun goes along under this arch, and returns at night on the upper side to the starting place.

There is another world under this, and it is like ours in everything—animals, plants, and people—save that the seasons are different. The streams that come down from the mountains are the trails by which we reach this underworld, and the springs at their heads are the doorways by which we enter it, but to do this one must fast and go to water and have one of the underground people for a guide. We know that the seasons in the underworld are different from ours, because the water in the springs is always warmer in winter and cooler in summer than the outer air.

When the animals and plants were first made—we do not know by whom—they were told to watch and keep awake for seven nights, just as young men now fast and keep awake when they pray to their medicine. They tried to do this, and nearly all were awake through the first night, but the next night several dropped off to sleep, and the third night others were asleep, and then others, until, on the seventh night, of all the animals only the owl, the panther, and one or two more were still awake. To these were given the power to see and to go about in the dark, and to make prey of the birds and animals which must sleep at night. Of the trees only the cedar, the pine, the spruce, the holly, and the laurel were awake to the end, and to them it was given to be always green and to be greatest for medicine, but to the others it was said: "Because you have not endured to the end you shall lose your hair every winter."

Men came after the animals and plants. At first there were only a brother and sister until he struck her with a fish and told her to multiply, and so it was. In seven days a child was born to her, and thereafter every seven days another, and they increased very fast until there was danger that the world could not keep them. Then it was made that a woman should have only one child in a year, and it has been so ever since.

Kana'tĭ and Selu: The Origin of Game and Corn

When I was a boy this is what the old men told me they had heard when they were boys.

Long years ago, soon after the world was made, a hunter and his wife lived at Pilot knob with their only child, a little boy. The father's name was Kana'tĭ (The Lucky Hunter), and his wife was called Selu (Corn). No matter when Kana'tĭ went into the wood, he never failed to bring back a load of game, which his wife would cut up and prepare, washing off the blood from the meat in the river near the house. The little boy used to play down by the river every day, and one morning the old people thought they heard laughing and talking in the bushes as though there were two children there. When the boy came home at night his parents asked him who had been playing with him all day. "He comes out of the water," said the boy, "and he calls himself my elder brother. He says his mother was cruel to him and threw him into the river." Then they knew that the strange boy had sprung from the blood of the game which Selu had washed off at the river's edge.

Every day when the little boy went out to play the other would join him, but as he always went back again into the water the old people never had a chance to see him. At last one evening Kana'tĭ said to his son, "Tomorrow, when the other boy comes to play, get him to wrestle with you, and when you have your arms around him hold on to him and call for us." The boy promised to do as he was told, so the next day as soon as his playmate appeared he challenged him to a wrestling match. The other agreed at once, but as soon as they had their arms around each other, Kana'tĭ's boy began to scream for his father. The old folks at once came running down, and as soon as the Wild Boy saw them he struggled to free himself and cried out, "Let me go; you threw me away!" but his brother held on until the parents reached the spot, when they seized the Wild Boy and took him home with them. They kept him in the house until they had tamed him, but he was always wild and artful in his disposition, and was the leader of his brother in every mischief. It was not long until the old people discovered that he had magic powers, and they called him I'nage-utăsŭñ'hĭ (He-who-grew-up-wild).

Whenever Kana'tĭ went into the mountains he always brought back a fat buck or doe, or maybe a couple of turkeys. One day the Wild Boy said to his brother, "I wonder where our father gets all that game; let's follow him next time and find out." A few days afterward Kana'tĭ took a bow and some feathers in his hand and started off toward the west. The boys waited a little while and then went after him, keeping out of sight until they saw him go into a swamp where there were a great many of the small reeds that hunters use to make arrowshafts. Then the Wild Boy changed himself into a puff of bird's down, which the wind took up and carried until it alighted upon Kana'tĭ's shoulder just as he entered the swamp, but Kana'tĭ knew nothing about it. The old man cut reeds, fitted the feathers to them and made some arrows, and the Wild Boy—in his other shape—thought, "I wonder what those things are for?" When Kana'tĭ had his arrows finished he came out of the swamp and went on again. The wind blew the down from his shoulder, and it fell in the woods, when the Wild Boy took his right shape again and went back and told his brother what he had seen. Keeping out of sight of their father, they followed him up the mountain until he stopped at a certain place and lifted a large rock. At once there ran out a buck, which Kana'tĭ shot, and then lifting it upon his back he started for home again. "Oho!" exclaimed the boys, "he keeps all the deer shut up in that hole, and whenever he wants meat he just lets one out and kills it with those things he made in the swamp." They hurried and reached home before their father, who had the heavy deer to carry, and he never knew that they had followed.

A few days later the boys went back to the swamp, cut some reeds, and made seven arrows, and then started up the mountain to where their father kept the game. When they got to the place, they raised the rock and a deer came running out. Just as they drew back to shoot it, another came out, and then another and another, until the boys got confused and forgot what they were about. In those days all the deer had their tails hanging down like other animals, but as a buck was running past the Wild Boy struck its tail with his arrow so that it pointed upward. The boys thought this good sport, and when the next one ran past the Wild Boy struck its tail so that it stood straight up, and his brother struck the next one so hard with his arrow that the deer's tail was almost curled over his back. The deer carries his tail this way ever since. The deer came running past until the last one had come out of the hole and escaped into the forest. Then came droves of raccoons, rabbits, and all the other four-footed animals—all but the bear, because there was no bear then. Last came great flocks of turkeys, pigeons, and partridges that darkened the air like a cloud and made such a noise with their wings that Kana'tĭ, sitting at home, heard the sound like distant thunder on the mountains and said to himself, "My bad boys have got into trouble; I must go and see what they are doing."

So he went up the mountain, and when he came to the place where he kept the game he found the two boys standing by the rock, and all the birds and animals were gone. Kana'tĭ was furious, but without saying a word he went down into the cave and kicked the covers off four jars in one corner, when out swarmed bedbugs, fleas, lice, and gnats, and got all over the boys. They screamed with pain and fright and tried to beat off the insects, but the thousands of vermin crawled over them and bit and stung them until both dropped down nearly dead. Kana'tĭ stood looking on until he thought they had been punished enough, when he knocked off the vermin and made the boys a talk. "Now, you rascals," said he, "you have always had plenty to eat and never had to work for it. Whenever you were hungry all I had to do was to come up here and get a deer or a turkey and bring it home for your mother to cook; but now you have let out all the animals, and after this when you want a deer to eat you will have to hunt all over the woods for it, and then maybe not find one. Go home now to your mother, while I see if I can find something to eat for supper."

When the boys got home again they were very tired and hungry and asked their mother for something to eat. "There is no meat," said Selu, "but wait a little while and I'll get you something." So she took a basket and started out to the storehouse. This storehouse was built upon poles high up from the ground, to keep it out of the reach of animals, and there was a ladder to climb up by, and one door, but no other opening. Every day when Selu got ready to cook the dinner she would go out to the storehouse with a basket and bring it back full of corn and beans. The boys had never been inside the storehouse, so wondered where all the corn and beans could come from, as the house was not a very large one; so as soon as Selu went out of the door the Wild Boy said to his brother, "Let's go and see what she does." They ran around and climbed up at the back of the storehouse and pulled out a piece of clay from between the logs, so that they could look in. There they saw Selu standing in the middle of the room with the basket in front of her on the floor. Leaning over the basket, she rubbed her stomach—*so*—and the basket was half full of corn. Then she rubbed under her armpits—*so*—and the basket was full to the top with beans. The boys looked at each other and said, "This will never do; our mother is a witch. If we eat any of that it will poison us. We must kill her."

When the boys came back into the house, she knew their thoughts before they spoke. "So you are going to kill me?" said Selu. "Yes," said the boys, "you are a witch." "Well," said their mother, "when you have killed me, clear a large piece of ground in front of the house and drag my body seven times around the circle. Then drag me seven times over the ground inside the circle, and stay up all night and watch, and in the morning you will have plenty of corn." The boys killed her with their clubs, and cut off her head and put it up on the roof of the house with her face turned to the west, and told her to look for her husband. Then they set to work to clear the ground in front of the house, but instead of clearing the whole piece they cleared only seven little spots. This is why corn now grows only in a few places instead of over the whole world. They dragged the body of Selu around the circle, and wherever her blood fell on the ground the corn sprang up. But instead of dragging her body seven times across the ground they dragged it over only twice, which is the reason the Indians still work their crop but twice. The two brothers sat up and watched their corn all night, and in the morning it was full grown and ripe.

When Kana'tĭ came home at last, he look around, but could not see Selu anywhere, and asked the boys where was their mother. "She was a witch, and we killed her," said the boys; "there is her head up there on top of the house." When he saw his wife's head on the roof, he was very angry, and said, "I won't stay with you any longer; I am going to the Wolf people." So he started off, but before he had gone far the Wild Boy changed himself again to a tuft of down, which fell on Kana'tĭ's shoulder. When Kana'tĭ reached the settlement of the Wolf people, they were holding a council in the townhouse. He went in and sat down with the tuft of bird's down on his shoulder, but he never noticed it. When the Wolf chief asked him his business, he said: "I have two bad boys at home, and I want you to go in seven days from now and play ball against them." Although Kana'tĭ spoke as though he wanted them to play a game of ball, the Wolves knew that he meant for them to go and kill the two boys. They promised to go. Then the bird's down blew off from Kana'tĭ's shoulder, and the smoke carried it up through the hole in the roof of the townhouse. When it came down on the ground outside, the Wild Boy took his right shape again and went home and told his brother all that he had heard in the townhouse. But when Kana'tĭ left the Wolf people, he did not return home, but went on farther.

The boys then began to get ready for the Wolves, and the Wild Boy—the magician—told his brother what to do. They ran around the house in a wide circle until they had made a trail all around it excepting on the side from which the Wolves would come, where they left a small open space. Then they made four large bundles of arrows and placed them at four different points on the outside of the circle, after which they hid themselves in the woods and waited for the Wolves. In a day or two a whole party of Wolves came and surrounded the house to kill the boys. The Wolves did not notice the trail around the house, because they came in where the boys had left the opening, but the moment they went inside the circle the trail changed to a high brush fence and shut them in. Then the boys on the outside took their arrows and began shooting them down, and as the Wolves could not jump over the fence they were all killed, excepting a few that escaped through the opening into a great swamp close by. The boys ran around the swamp, and a circle of fire sprang up in their tracks and set fire to the grass and bushes and burned up nearly all the other Wolves. Only two or three got away, and from these have come all the wolves that are now in the world.

Soon afterward some strangers from a distance, who had heard that the brothers had a wonderful grain from which they made bread, came to ask for some, for none but Selu and her family had ever known corn before. The boys gave them seven grains of corn, which they told them to plant the next night on their way home, sitting up all night to watch the corn, which would have seven ripe ears in the morning. These they were to plant the next night and watch in the same way, and so on every night until they reached home, when they would have corn enough to supply the whole people. The strangers lived seven days' journey away. They took the seven grains and watched all through the darkness until morning, when they saw seven tall stalks, each stalk bearing a ripened ear. They gathered the ears and went on their way. The next night they planted all their corn, and guarded it as before until daybreak, when they found an abundant increase. But the way was long and the sun was hot, and the people grew tired. On the last night before reaching home they fell asleep, and in the morning the corn they had planted had not even sprouted. They brought with them to their settlement what corn they had left and planted it, and with care and attention were able to raise a crop. But ever since the corn must be watched and tended through half the year, which before would grow and ripen in a night.

As Kana'tĭ did not return, the boys at last concluded to go and find him. The Wild Boy took a gaming wheel and rolled it toward the Darkening land. In a little while the wheel came rolling back, and the boys knew their father was not there. He rolled it to the south and to the north, and each time the wheel came back to him, and they knew their father was not there. Then he rolled it toward the Sunland, and it did not return. "Our father is there," said the Wild Boy, "let us go and find him." So the two brothers set off toward the east, and after traveling a long time they came upon Kana'tĭ walking along with a little dog by his side. "You bad boys," said their father, "have you come here?" "Yes," they answered, "we always accomplish what we start out to do—we are men." "This dog overtook me four days ago," then said Kana'tĭ, but the boys knew that the dog was the wheel which they had sent after him to find him. "Well," said Kana'tĭ, "as you have found me, we may as well travel together, but I shall take the lead."

Soon they came to a swamp, and Kana'tĭ told them there was something danger-ous there and they must keep away from it. He went on ahead, but as soon as he was out of sight the Wild Boy said to his brother, "Come and let us see what is in the swamp." They went in together, and in the middle of the swamp they found a large panther asleep. The Wild Boy got out an arrow and shot the panther in the side of the head. The panther turned his head and the other boy shot him on that side. He turned his head away again and the two brothers shot together—*tust, tust, tust!* But the pan-ther was not hurt by the arrows and paid no more attention to the boys. They came out of the swamp and soon overtook Kana'tĭ, waiting for them. "Did you find it?" asked Kana'tĭ. "Yes," said the boys, "we found it, but it never hurt us. We are men." Kana'tĭ was surprised, but said nothing, and they went on again.

After a while he turned to them and said, "Now you must be careful. We are coming to a tribe called the Anăda'dûñtăskĭ ("Roasters," i.e., cannibals), and if they get you they will put you into a pot and feast on you." Then he went on ahead. Soon the boys came to a tree which had been struck by lightning, and the Wild Boy directed his brother to gather some of the splinters from the tree and told him what to do with them. In a little while they came to the settlement of the cannibals, who, as soon as they saw the boys, came running out, crying, "Good, here are two nice fat strangers. Now we'll have a grand feast!" They caught the boys and dragged them into the townhouse, and sent word to all the people of the settlement to come to the feast. They made up a great fire, put water into a large pot and set it to boiling, and then seized the Wild Boy and put him down into it. His brother was not in the least frightened and made no attempt to escape, but quietly knelt down and began putting the splinters into the fire, as if to make it burn better. When the cannibals thought the meat was about ready they lifted the pot from the fire, and that instant a blinding light filled the townhouse, and the lightning began to dart from one side to the other, striking down the cannibals until not one of them was left alive. Then the lightning went up through the smokehole, and the next moment there were the two boys standing outside the townhouse as though nothing had happened. They went on and soon met Kana'tĭ, who seemed much surprised to see them, and said, "What! are you here again?" "O, yes, we never give up. We are great men!" "What did the cannibals do to you?" "We met them and they brought us to their townhouse, but they never hurt us." Kana'tĭ said nothing more, and they went on.

*   *   *   *   *   *   *

He soon got out of sight of the boys, but they kept on until they came to the end of the world, where the sun comes out. The sky was just coming down when they got there, but they waited until it went up again, and then they went through and climbed up on the other side. There they found Kana'tĭ and Selu sitting together. The old folk received them kindly and were glad to see them, telling them they might stay there a while, but then they must go to live where the sun goes down. The boys stayed with their parents seven days and then went on toward the Darkening land, where they are now. We call them Anisga'ya Tsunsdi' (The Little Men), and when they talk to each other we hear low rolling thunder in the west.

    *   *   *   *   *   *   *

After Kana'tï's boys had let the deer out from the cave where their father used to keep them, the hunters tramped about in the woods for a long time without finding any game, so that the people were very hungry. At last they heard that the Thunder Boys were now living in the far west, beyond the sun door, and that if they were sent for they could bring back the game. So they sent messengers for them, and the boys came and sat down in the middle of the townhouse and began to sing.

At the first song there was a roaring sound like a strong wind in the northwest, and it grew louder and nearer as the boys sang on, until at the seventh song a whole herd of deer, led by a large buck, came out from the woods. The boys had told the people to be ready with their bows and arrows, and when the song was ended and all the deer were close around the townhouse, the hunters shot into them and killed as many as they needed before the herd could get back into the timber.

Then the Thunder Boys went back to the Darkening land, but before they left they taught the people the seven songs with which to call up the deer. It all happened so long ago that the songs are now forgotten—all but two, which the hunters still sing whenever they go after deer.

How the Terrapin Beat the Rabbit

The Rabbit was a great runner, and everybody knew it. No one thought the Terrapin anything but a slow traveler, but he was a great warrior and very boastful, and the two were always disputing about their speed. At last they agreed to decide the matter by a race. They fixed the day and the starting place and arranged to run across four mountain ridges, and the one who came in first at the end was to be the winner.

The Rabbit felt so sure of it that he said to the Terrapin, "You know you can't run. You can never win the race, so I'll give you the first ridge and then you'll have only three to cross while I go over four."

The Terrapin said that would be all right, but that night when he went home to his family he sent for his Terrapin friends and told them he wanted their help. He said he knew he could outrun the Rabbit, but he wanted to stop the Rabbit's boasting. He explained his plan to his friends and they agreed to help him.

When the day came all the animals were there to see the race. The Rabbit was with them, but the Terrapin was gone ahead toward the first ridge, as they had arranged, and they could hardly see him on account of the long grass. The word was given and the Rabbit started off with long jumps up the mountain, expecting to win the race before the Terrapin could get down the other side. But before he got up the mountain he saw the Terrapin go over the ridge ahead of him. He ran on, and when he reached the top he looked all around, but could not see the Terrapin on account of the long grass. He kept on down the mountain and began to climb the second ridge, but when he looked up again there was the Terrapin just going over the top. Now he was surprised and made his longest jumps to catch up, but when he got to the top there was the Terrapin away in front going over the third ridge. The Rabbit was getting tired now and nearly out of breath, but he kept on down the mountain and up the other ridge until he got to the top just in time to see the Terrapin cross the fourth ridge and thus win the race.

The Rabbit could not make another jump, but fell over on the ground, crying *mĭ*, *mĭ*, *mĭ*, *mĭ*, as the Rabbit does ever since when he is too tired to run any more. The race was given to the Terrapin and all the animals wondered how he could win against the Rabbit, but he kept still and never told. It was easy enough, however, because all the Terrapin's friends looked just alike, and he had simply posted one near the top of each ridge to wait until the Rabbit came in sight and then climb over and hide in the long grass. When the Rabbit came on he could not find the Terrapin and so thought the Terrapin was ahead, and if he had met one of the other terrapins he would have thought it the same one because they looked so much alike. The real Terrapin had posted himself on the fourth ridge, so as to come in at the end of the race and be ready to answer questions if the animals suspected anything.

Because the Rabbit had to lie down and lose the race the conjurer now, when preparing his young men for the ball play, boils a lot of rabbit hamstrings into a soup, and sends some one at night to pour it across the path along which the other players are to come in the morning, so that they may become tired in the same way and lose the game. It is not always easy to do this, because the other party is expecting it and has watchers ahead to prevent it.

The Rabbit and the Tar Wolf

Once there was such a long spell of dry weather that there was no more water in the creeks and springs, and the animals held a council to see what to do about it. They decided to dig a well, and all agreed to help except the Rabbit, who was a lazy fellow, and said, "I don't need to dig for water. The dew on the grass is enough for me." The others did not like this, but they went to work together and dug their well.

They noticed that the Rabbit kept sleek and lively, although it was still dry weather and the water was getting low in the well. They said, "That tricky Rabbit steals our water at night," so they made a wolf of pine gum and tar and set it up by the well to scare the thief. That night the Rabbit came, as he had been coming every night, to drink enough to last him all next day. He saw the queer black thing by the well and said, "Who's there?" but the tar wolf said nothing. He came nearer, but the wolf never moved, so he grew braver and said, "Get out of my way or I'll strike you." Still the wolf never moved and the Rabbit came up and struck it with his paw, but the gum held his foot and it stuck fast. Now he was angry and said, "Let me go or I'll kick you." Still the wolf said nothing. Then the Rabbit struck again with his hind foot, so hard that it was caught in the gum and he could not move, and there he stuck until the animals came for water in the morning. When they found who the thief was they had great sport over him for a while and then got ready to kill him, but as soon as he was unfastened from the tar wolf he managed to get away.

Rebecca Harding Davis

(1831–1910)

Rebecca Harding Davis was born in Washington, Pennsylvania, on June 24, 1831, and spent her first five years in Big Springs, Alabama. In 1836, her family moved to Wheeling in what would become West Virginia. When she was fourteen, she was sent to the Washington Female Seminary in Pennsylvania. In 1848 she returned to Wheeling and joined the staff of the Wheeling *Intelligencer*.

In 1861 Davis submitted "Life in the Iron Mills" to the *Atlantic Monthly*, where it was published. Davis's first novel, *Margaret Howth*, was published in 1862. In 1863 she married Clarke Davis, an attorney who corresponded with her after reading "Life in the Iron Mills." In 1864, the first of their three children was born. They lived in Philadelphia, where her husband was editor of the *Inquirer*.

Davis published more than ten novels. Her autobiography, *Bits of Gossip*, was published in 1904. The Feminist Press published a new edition of "Life in the Iron Mills" (1972), for which Tillie Olsen wrote the Introduction. Davis died on September 29, 1910, at the home of her son, Richard Harding Davis, in Mount Kisco, New York.

The "Black North"

Mr. W. E. Burghardt du Bois has lately finished his series of advisory lectures to the negroes. Just now our poor black brother is the most advised man in Christendom. First of all, he has as counselor Booker T. Washington, whom God has sent to pull him out of the slough as surely as he sent Moses to bring his people to the promised land. The next generation may appreciate the common sense, the piercing sagacity, the moderation of this black leader, but his race do not appreciate it now. Each man among them who has achieved any kind of an education shouts out a differing order to the struggling dumb hosts below him.

"Aim at the highest," cries one. "Get a college education; get Greek, mathematics, logic, tho you have to earn your bread as a barber or a baker."

"Learn a trade," commands another.

"Go to the North."

"Stay in the South."

"Make friends of your old masters. To follow peace with all men is Christian and expedient."

"Fight for your rights! Organize! Drill! Form into companies. Be ready to strike when the hour comes!"

Is it any wonder that the negro, dazed and perplexed by this multitude of counsel, staggers this way and that on his upward road? The miracle is that he goes up it at all.

White men are equally noisy concerning him. "The negro" is the one theme on which every American feels competent to pronounce a final judgment. Down to the unwashed emigrant limping on shore in his rags each one of them is ready to decide the place and future of the negro. Is he not black? Are they not white? What other authority do you want? The ignorant white finds down among his squalid mean thoughts a dislike to a dark skin—just as he may dislike a harelip or a hunchback. But he parades it as "a racial instinct," God-given, irremovable, and because he has this puerile prejudice demands that a whole nation, noble in their high aim, their courage and their patience, shall be sentenced to perpetual defeat and ignominy. Could anything have been more ludicrous than the spasm which convulsed the country the other day when the President asked Mr. Washington to dinner? Your white American will sit calmly every day while a negro shaves him, rubs his face and hair, touches his eyes and lips with his black fingers; or he will eat bread kneaded by other black fingers, or meat which they have seasoned and cooked: he will put his child into the arms of a black nurse; he will come, in a word, into the closest personal contact with the ignorant and often unclean low class of negro, and yet, when Mr. Roosevelt asks one of the foremost leaders of thought and action among Americans, a gentleman by instinct and habit, to sit down near him and be helped to the same mutton and potatoes he shrieks with dismay the Republic is in peril! Unimaginable horrors will follow this recognition of the fact that a man with a dark skin is a leader in thought or a gentleman in instinct and habit.

The most absurd explanation of this action was given by certain Southern editors who gravely assured us that as soon as the negro was admitted to the table of the white, general miscegenation would follow! Nothing could stop the white woman of the South from marrying him. The white woman of the South certainly had no reason that day to thank her champion for his defense!

It is a significant fact that the negro journals were much more calm and temperate in their comments on this incident than were those of their white brethren. They were not unduly uplifted by the invitation to dinner from the President to one of their race. The fact is, the negro is less excited by the desire for social recognition than the whites imagine. This is partly due to a dignified self respect common to the upper class of colored people, and perhaps to a certain funny trait of self-esteem common to the lower class—a vanity which makes them ridiculous, perhaps, but which comforts them enormously in their desperate climb upward. It is like the conceit and self-confidence of a child which carries him over obstacles in youth, but which he outgrows, and at which he laughs when it is no longer necessary to him.

Mr. Du Bois in the papers lately finished takes his usual pessimistic view of the fortunes of his race, but his advice to them is good, except as it seems to me, when, after acknowledging that the negro can find work in the South, which he cannot find in the North, he insists that he must not for that reason remain there. "A certain sort of soul," he says, "a certain kind of spirit finds the narrow repression, the provincialism of the South almost unbearable."

This may be true of the young educated negro who has ambitions and longings in him for—he scarcely knows what—altho Booker T. Washington and my friend the venerable Dr. Crummles and many other black men whom I am proud to call friends, who are doing steady, vigorous work for their race in the South, are apparently not tormented by any such vague discontent.

These sentimental objections to "the provincialism of the South" fade into nothingness in the face of the great fact that the negro to live must find work, and that his old masters will give him work, and his new friends in the North will not. The trades unions here shut him out. But there is not a town in the South to-day where a black mason or carpenter or blacksmith cannot find work and wages. The real difficulty there in his way is that, as a rule, he will not work steadily. Every capitalist who has operated in the Southern States will tell the same story of the negroes who would work for a week and as soon as they were paid would "lay off to rest up" for a fortnight. It is this unconquerable habit of the negro workman that has closed factories and phosphate works from Carolina to the Gulf.

On the other hand, you will scarcely find a town or village in the South that has not its industrious, shrewd, successful negro—a mechanic, a trader; an employer of other men, self-respecting and respected by his white neighbors.

The sum of the whole matter is, that both the white and black leaders of the race have fallen too much into the habit of considering it as a unit, of urging it here and there, and of prophesying defeat or victory of it as a whole people.

The fact is that the defeat or success of the negro, as of the white, depends upon himself as an individual. He has, it is true, to contend against an absurd and cruel prejudice. But every man has to contend against some difficulty—a dull brain, or deafness, or a tendancy bequeathed by his grandfathers to drink, or to lie, or to steal. Whoever he is, be sure that he has his fight to make.

The negro, almost without a fight, has gained freedom, suffrage and education—now he wants work and has difficulty in getting it, just as women had thirty years ago. *They have it now.*

In spite of this difficulty, I should like to show him that he can succeed, if he keeps his head, works steadily to his purpose, trusts in God, and deserves success.

I have in mind now a freed slave who came to Philadelphia in the sixties. He had only learned to read and write; he had not a dollar, nor a friend in the city. But he was honest, he had keen mother wit, unflagging capacity for work, and that fine natural courtesy in which his race so far surpasses ours. He began work as a waiter, then became a caterer; then employed other men and women and made his establishment a universal aid to housekeepers. He laid your carpets, he draped your curtains, he cooked and served your meals, he took charge of your moving and carried you from one house to the other as quietly as if you were on a magic carpet. In word and work he never was known to be slack. His business increased rapidly. He took enormous buildings into his care, his huge vans were seen in every street. When the town fell asleep in summer he went to a seaside resort and opened a great *café*. When he died he left a comfortable fortune to his children and an honorable name. Everybody felt that Philadelphia had lost one of her most useful and worthy citizens.

What one man has done others may do. It is a significant fact, however, that there was not an educated young negro in Philadelphia ready or willing to take the good will of this man's business or to carry it on when he died.

I have known other freed slaves in the same town who unaided made their way to comfort, even luxury, as purveyors, coal dealers, even brokers. Success waits for the black or white man who works for it. No man is the sport of any god. The negro leaders do irreparable damage to their people by their incessant melancholy wails of complaint and defeat.

Elizabeth Madox Roberts

(1881–1941)

Elizabeth Madox Roberts was born in Perryville, Kentucky, on October 30, 1881. She began college in 1900 at the University of Kentucky but withdrew because of illness. When she was thirty-six, she enrolled at the University of Chicago, where she was graduated in 1921. She was awarded the Fiske Poetry Prize of the University of Chicago.

Roberts's publication *The Time of Man* (1926) afforded her an international reputation. Other books followed: *My Heart and My Flesh* (1927); *Jingling in the Wind* (1928); *The Great Meadow* (1930); *A Buried Treasure* (1931); *The Haunted Mirror* (1932); *He Sent Forth a Raven* (1935); *Black Is My Truelove's Hair* (1938); *Song in the Meadow* (1940); and *Not by Strange Gods* (1941). After a lifetime of suffering from illnesses, Roberts died on March 13, 1941.

On the Mountainside

There was a play-party at the schoolhouse at the bottom of the cove. Newt Reddix waited outside the house, listening to the noises as Lester Hunter, the teacher, had listened to them—a new way for Newt. Sound at the bottom of a cove was different from sound at the top, he noticed, for at the top voices spread into a wide thinness. Before Lester came, Newt had let his ears have their own way of listening. Sounds had then been for but one purpose—to tell him what was happening or what was being said. Now the what of happenings and sayings was wrapped about with some unrelated feeling or prettiness, or it stood back beyond some heightened qualities.

"Listen!" Lester had said to him one evening, standing outside a house where a party was going forward. "Listen!" And there were footsteps and outcries of men and women, happy cries, shrill notes of surprise and pretended anger, footsteps on rough wood, unequal intervals, a flare of fiddle playing and a tramp of dancing feet. Down in the cove the sounds from a party were different from those that came from a house on the side of a hill, the cries of men bent and disturbed, distorted by the place, by the sink and rise of land. While he listened, the knowledge that Lester Hunter would soon go out of the country, the school term being over, brought a loneliness to his thought.

He went inside the schoolhouse and flung his hat on the floor beside the door; he would take his part now in the playing. His hat was pinned up in front with a thorn and was as pert a hat as any of those beside the door, and no one would give it dishonor. The schoolteacher was stepping about in the dance, turning Corie Yancey, and the fiddle was scraping the top of a tune. For him the entire party was filled with the teacher's impending departure.

"Ladies change and gents the same," the fiddler called, his voice unblended with the tune he played. Newt fell into place when an older man withdrew in his favor and gave him Ollie Mack for his partner. The teacher danced easily, bent to the curve of the music, neglectful and willing, giving the music the flowing lightness of his limp body.

Newt wanted to dance as the teacher did, but he denied himself and kept the old harsh gesture, pounding the floor more roughly now and then with a deeply accented step. He wanted to tread the music lightly, meeting it halfway, but he would not openly imitate anybody. While he danced he was always, moment by moment, aware of the teacher, aware of him standing to wait his turn, pulling his collar straight, pushing his hands into the pockets of his coat, looking at Ollie Mack when she laughed, looking full into her face with pleasure, unafraid. The teacher had given an air to the dance, and had made it, for him, more bold in form, more like itself or more true to its kind, more gentle in courtesy. Lester had come from one of the low counties of the rolling plain where the curving creeks of the Pigeon River spread slowly, winding broadly to gather up many little rills. Newt had learned somewhere, in his own blood, to hate the lower country for its pleasantness. There the fields rolled out smoothly and the soil was deep. The grass of any roadside was bluegrass mingled, perhaps, with rich weeds. Fat cattle, fine beasts, ate in the mythical pastures. Smooth roads ran between the farms. Dancing, shaking his body stiffly with the beat of the fiddle, Newt saw that Lester took his partner's hand lightly, that he gave equal courtesy to all the women, calling them ladies. He wanted to be as the teacher was, but he could not. The dance drawing to an end, he realized again that in two days more the teacher would go, for he had set his head upon some place far away, down in the settlements, among the lower counties from which he had come six months earlier.

There was pie for a treat, baked by Marthy Anne Sands and brought to the schoolhouse in a great hickory basket. Standing about eating the pie, all were quiet, regretting the teacher's going. Newt wove a vagrant path in and out among them, hearing the talk of the older men and women.

"My little tad, the least one, Becky, is plumb bereft over 'im," one said, a woman speaking.

"Last year at the school there wasn't hardly anybody would go, and look at this. I had to whop Joel to make him stay on the place one day to feed and water the property whilst I had to go. Hit appears like Joel loves book-sense since Les Hunter come up the mountain."

"What makes you in such a swivet to go nohow?" one asked.

"Did you come up the gorge to borrow fire you're in such a swivet to get on?"

"There's a big meeten over to Kitty's branch next light moon. Why don't you stay? No harm in you to be broguen about a small spell."

"You could loafer around a spell and wait for the meeten."

"Big meeten. And nohow the meeten needs youens to help sing."

"What's he in such a swivet to go off for?"

"I got to go. I got to see the other end of the world yet."

"What's he a-sayen?"

"I got to go to the other end of the world."

"That's too far a piece."

"That surely undoubtedly is a right smart piece to go."

"He could stay a spell at my place and welcome. I'd be real proud to have him stay with my folks a spell. And Nate, he'd keep youens a week, that I right well know. Youens could loafer around awhile as well as not."

"He always earns his way and more, ever since he kem up the mountain, always earns his keep, anyhow."

"I've got to go. I'm bound for the other end of this old globe. I'm obliged all the same, but I got a heap to see yet. I'm bound to go."

Newt plowed the corn in the rocky field above the house where he lived, one horse to the plow, or he hoed where the field lay steepest. The teacher was gone now.

On Sunday Newt would put on his clean shirt his mother had washed on Friday, and climb up the gorge to the head of the rise and meet there Tige English and Jonathan Evans. Then they would go to see Lum Baker's girls. He would contrive to kiss each girl before the night fell and Lum would cry out: "Come on, you gals now, and milk the cow brutes." Or sometimes they would go down the way to see Corie Yancey and Ollie Mack. To Newt all the place seemed still since the teacher had left, idle, as if it had lost its uses and its future. Going to the well for water he would stare at the winch, at the soft rot of the bucket, at the stones inside the well curb, or he would listen intently to the sounds as the vessel struck the water or beat against the stones.

The noises gave him more than the mere report of a bucket falling into a well to get water; they gave him some comprehension of all things that were yet unknown. The sounds, rich with tonality, as the bucket struck, the water, rang with some strange sonority and throbbed with a beat that was like something he could not define, some other, unlike fiddle playing but related to it in its unlikeness. A report had come to him from an outside world and a suspicion of more than he could know in his present state haunted him. He cried out inwardly for the answer, or he looked about him and listened, remembering all that he could of what Lester Hunter had taught—capitals of countries, seaports, buying and selling, nouns, verbs, numbers multiplied together to make other numbers. Now he looked intently and listened. He detected a throb in sound, but again there was a beat in the hot sun over a moist field. One day he thought that he had divined a throb in numbers as he counted, a beat in the recurrences of kinds, but this evaded him. He listened and looked at the well happenings, at the house wall, at the rail fence, at the barn, at the hills going upward toward the top of the gorge.

On every side were evasions. These sights and sounds could not give him enough; they lay flat against the air; they were imbedded within his own flesh and were sunk into his own sense of them. He would stare at the green and brown moss on the broken frame of the well box and stare again at the floating images in the dark of the well water. The rope would twine over the axle as he turned the wooden handle, and the rounds of the rope would fall into orderly place, side by side, as he knew too casually and too well. Since the teacher had gone the place had flattened to an intolerable staleness that gave out meager tokens of withheld qualities and beings—his mother leaning from the door to call him to dinner, his sister dragging his chair to the table and setting his cup beside his place, the old dog running out to bark at some varmint above in the brush. He could hardly separate the fall of his own bare foot from the rock door-step over which he had walked since he could first walk at all. His thirst and his water to drink were one now. His loneliness, as he sat to rest at noon beside the fence, merged and was identified with the still country from brush-grown slope to brush-grown slope.

His father began to clear a new patch below the house; they grubbed at the roots all day when the corn was laid by. One morning in September, when the sun, moving south, was just getting free of Rattlesnake Hill, it came to him that he would go down to the settlements, that he would go to Merryman. All summer he had known that there was a school at Merryman, but he had not thought to go there, for he had no money. It came to him as a settled fact that he would go there and look about at the place. Three high ridges with numberless breaks and gorges intervened; he had heard this said by men who knew or had heard of what lay beyond. The determination to set forth and the wish to go came to him at one instant. "My aim, hit's to go there," he said. "I lay off to do that-there, like I say."

He remembered the teacher more clearly at this moment, saw him in a more sharply detailed picture; his own breath jerked deeply inward as he was himself related, through his intended departure, to the picture. Hunter was remembered cutting wood for the schoolhouse fire, sweethearting the girls and turning them lightly in the dance, or sitting by the fire at night, reading his book, holding the page low to the blaze. He was remembered hallooing back up the mountain the day he left, his voice calling back as he went down the ridge and he himself answering until there was not even a faint hollow whoopee to come up the slope. By the fire Newt had often taken Hunter's book into his hands, but he could never read the strange words nor in any way know what they meant when they were read, for they had stood four-square and hostile against his understanding. His father's voice would fall dully over the slow clearing: "You could work on this-here enduren the while that I cut the corn patch."

He knew that he would go. His determination rejected the clearing, knowing that he would be gone before the corn was ready to cut. It rejected the monotonous passing of the days, the clutter of feet on the stones by the door, the dull, inconspicuous corn patch above. He would walk, taking the short cut over the mountains. Two ridges to go and then there would be a road for his feet, some one had said. He announced his plan to his father one day while they leaned over their grub hoes. There was no willingness offered, but his mind was set, and three days later he had established his plan. His mother had washed his shirts clean and had rolled them into a bundle with his spare socks, and she had baked him bread and a joint of ham. She and his sister stood by the doorway weeping after he had driven back the dog and had shouted his goodbye.

It was a mid-afternoon and the sun beat down into the cove where he traveled. He worked his way through the thick-set laurel, struggling to keep his bundle tied to his shoulders where the brush stood most dense.

The dry clatter of the higher boughs came to his ears, but it was so mingled with the pricking snarls of the twigs on his face that the one sense was not divided from the other. "This durned ivy," he said when the laurel held him back. He matched his strength against boughs or he flashed his wits against snarls and rebounds, hot and weary, tingling with sweat and with the pricking twigs. Pushed back at one place where he tried to find an opening, he assailed another and then another, throwing all his strength angrily against the brush and tearing himself through the mesh with *goddamns* of relief. A large shaded stone that bulged angrily out of the mountainside gave him a space of rest. He stretched himself on the slanting rock, his face away from the sun, and lay for an hour, thinking nothing, feeling the weariness as it beat heavily upon his limbs.

"I'm bodaciously tired," he said, after a long period of torpor. "Could I come by a spring branch, I'd drink me a whole durned quart of it."

Another tree-grown mountain arose across the cove, misty now in the afternoon and in the first haze of autumn, and beyond lay other blue mountains, sinking farther and farther into the air. Back of him it was the same; he had been on the way two weeks now. Before him he knew each one would be dense with laurel until he came to the wagon road. He took to the pathless way after his hour of rest, going forward. When the sun was setting behind Bee Gum Mountain, he saw a house down in the cove, not far as the crow would fly but the distance of two hours' going for him. When he saw the cabin he began to sing, chanting:

Right hands across and howdy-do,
Left and back and how are you.

Oh, call up yo' dog, oh, call up yo' dog,
Ring twang a-whoddle lanky day.

The sight of the house quickened his desire for Merryman and the cities and counties in the settlements, and this desire had become more definite in his act of going. His wish was for sure, quick gestures and easy sayings that would come from the mouth as easily as breath. There were for him other things, as yet unrelated to any one place—men playing ball with a great crowd to watch, all the crowd breaking into a laugh at one time; men racing fine horses on a hard, smooth track; music playing; men having things done by machinery; lovely girls not yet imagined; and things to know beyond anything he could recall, and not one of them too fine or too good for him. He sang as he went down the slope, his song leaping out of him. He had heard it said that the lights of Merryman could be seen from Coster Ridge on a clear night, and Coster was now visible standing up in the pale air, for a man had pointed him the way that morning. Singing, he set himself toward the house at the bottom of the cove.

Night was falling when he called "Hello" at the foot of Bee Gum Mountain. The man of the house asked his name and told his own, making him welcome. Supper was over, but the host, whose name was Tom Bland, ordered Nance, his woman, to give the stranger a snack of biscuit bread and bacon, and this Newt ate sitting beside the fire. Another stranger was sitting in the cabin, an old man who kept very still while Nance worked with the utensils, his dim eyes looking into the fire or eyeing Newt, who stared back and searched the looks of the stranger. Then Tom told Nance how they would sleep that night, telling her to give the old man her place in the bed beside himself.

"You could get in bed along with the young ones," he said to her. "The boy here, he could sleep on a shakedown alongside the fireplace."

From gazing into the fire the old stranger would fall asleep, but after a moment he would awake, opening dim, ashamed eyes that glanced feebly at Newt, faintly defying him. Then Nance put some children to bed, her own perhaps, and sat quietly in the corner of the hearth, her hands in her lap. Newt had looked at the host, acquainting himself with him. He was a strong man, far past youth, large-boned and broad-muscled. His heavy feet scraped on the floor when he moved from his chair to the water bucket on the window sill. Newt saw that he on his side had been silently searching out the old stranger. After a while the host and the old man began to talk, Tom speaking first.

"There's a sight of travel now."

"Hit's a moven age."

Between each speech there was a slow pause as each saying was carefully probed before the reply was offered.

Tom said: "Two in one night, and last week there was one come by." And then after a while he asked: "Where might youens be bound for, stranger?"

"I'm on my way back," the man said.

There was a long season of quiet. The ideas were richly interspersed with action, for Nance softly jolted back and forth in her chair, her bare feet tapping lightly on the boards of the floor.

"You been far?" Tom asked.

"I been a right far piece. I been to the settlements in Froman county, and then I been to the mines around Tateville and Beemen."

Newt bit nervously at his knuckles and looked at the man, taking from him these signs of the world. The fire burned low, and breaking the long silence Tom said once or twice: "There's a sight of travel now." Newt looked at the old man's feet in their patched shoes, feet that had walked the streets in towns. Indefinite wonders touched the man's feet, his crumpled knees, and his crooked hands that were spread on his lap.

Then Tom said: "Froman, I reckon that's a prime good place to be now."

"Hit may be so, but I wouldn't be-nasty my feet with the dust of hit no longer. Nor any other place down there. I'm on my way back."

The old man's voice quavered over his words toward the close of this speech, and after a little while he added, his voice lifted: "Hit's a far piece back, but a man has a rather about where he'd like to be." Finally he spoke in great anger, his arm raised and his hand threatening: "I've swat my last drop of sweat in that-there country and eat my last meal's victuals. A man has a rather as to the place he likes to be."

This thought lay heavily over the fireplace, shared by all but uncomprehended by Nance, whose skin was rich with blood and life. She sat complacently rocking back and forth in her small chair.

After the long quiet which surrounded this thought the old man began to speak softly, having spent his passion: "I'm on my way back. I been in a study a long time about goen back but seems like I couldn't make hit to go. Work was terrible pressen. But now I'm on my way back where I was borned and my mammy and pappy before me. I was a plumb traitor to my God when I left the mountains and come to the settlements. Many is the day I'd study about that-there and many is the night I lay awake to study about the way back over Coster Ridge, on past Bear Mountain, past Hog Run, past Little Pine Tree, up and on past Louse Run, up, then on over Long Ridge and up into Laurel, into Grady Creek and on up the branch, past the Flat Rock, past the saw-mill, past the grove of he-balsams, and then the smoke a-comen outen the chimney and the door open and old Nomie's pup a-comen down the road to meet me. I'd climb the whole way whilst I was a-layen there, in my own mind I would, and I'd see the ivy as plain as you'd see your hand afore your face, and the coves and the he-balsams. In my own mind I'd go back, a step at a time, Coster, Bear Mountain and the Bee Gum, Little Pine Tree, Louse Run, Grady, and I'd see the rocks in the way to go, and a log stretched out in my way maybe. I wouldn't make hit too easy to go. Past Bear Mountain, past Hog Run and the cove, scratchen my way through ivy brush. Then I'd come to myself and there I'd be, a month's travel from as much as a sight of the Flat Rock, and I'd groan and shake and turn over again. I was a traitor to my God."

Nance laid a little stick on the fire, with a glance at Tom, he allowing it without protest. Then she sat back in her stiff chair with a quick movement, her bare feet light on the boards. The old man was talking again.

"Where my mammy was borned before me and her mammy and daddy before again. And no water in all Froman or Tateville but dead pump waters, no freestone like you'd want. How could a man expect to live? Many's the night I've said, could I be on the shady side of the Flat Rock, up past the saw-mill, up past the grove of he-balsams, where the spring branch runs out over the horse-shoe rock, and could I get me one drink of that-there cold crystal water I'd ask ne'er thing more of God Almighty in life."

"I know that-there very spring branch," Newt now said. He was eager to enter the drama of the world, and his time now had come. "I know that-there very place. You come to a rock set on end and a hemlock bush set off to the right, she-balsams all off to the left like."

"Mankind, that's just how hit's set. I believe you been right there!"

"A mountain goes straight up afore you as you stand, say this-here is the spring, and the water comes out and runs off over a horse-shoe rock."

"Makind, that's just how hit's set. I do believe you know that-there very place. You say hit's there just the same?"

"I got me a drink at that-there very spring branch Tuesday 'twas a week ago."

"You drank them waters!" And then he said after a period of wonder: "To think you been to that very spring branch! You been there!"

"We can burn another stick," Tom said, as if in honor of the strange event, and Nance mended the fire again. Outside Newt heard dogs howling far up the slope and some small beast cried.

"To think you been there! You are a-setten right now in hearen of my voice and yet a Tuesday 'twas a week ago you was in the spot I call home. Hit's hard to study over. You come down the mountain fast. That country is powerful hard goen."

"Yes, I come right fast."

"I couldn't make hit back in twice the time and more. Hard goen it was. What made you travel so hard, young man?"

"I'm a-maken hit toward the settle-ments."

"And what you think to find in the settle-ments, God knows! What you think to see, young man?"

"Learnen. I look to find learnen in the settle-ments."

In the pause that followed the old man gazed at the hearth as if he were looking into time, into all qualities, and he fell momentarily asleep under the impact of his gaze. But presently he looked at Newt and said: "And to think you tasted them waters Tuesday 'twas a week ago!"

"You come to a rock set on end, and here's the hemlock off to the right like, and here to the left goes the gorge."

The old man was asleep, his eyes falling away before the fire. But he waked suddenly and said with kindling eyes, his hand uplifted: "You come from there at a master pace, young man, come from the place I hope to see if God Almighty sees fitten to bless me afore I lay me down and die. You walked, I reckon, right over the spot I pined to see a many is the year, God knows, and it was nothing to you, but take care. The places you knowed when you was a little shirt-tail boy won't go outen your head or outen your recollections."

Then he said, another outbreak after a long pause, his hand again uplifted: "I reckon you relish learnen, young man, and take a delight in hit, and set a heap of store by the settle-ments. But the places you knowed when you was a little tad, they won't go outen your remembrance. Your insides is made that way, and made outen what you did when you was a shirt-tail boy, and you'll find it's so. Your dreams of a night and all you pine to see will go back. You won't get shed so easy of hit. You won't get shed."

Newt looked into the fire and a terror grew into his thought. He saw minutely the moss on the well curb and the shapes in which it grew, and saw the three stones that lay beside the well, that lifted his feet out of the mud. The sound made by the bucket in the well as it rocked from wall to wall, as it finally struck the water, rolled acutely backward into his inner hearing. He saw the rope twine over the beam as he turned the wooden handle, drawing the full bucket to the top. Three long steps then to the door of the house, the feel of the filled bucket drawing at his arm. Up the loft ladder to his room, his hands drawing up his body, the simple act of climbing, of emerging from some lower place to a higher, and he was buried in the act, submerged in a deep sense of it.

"You may go far and see a heap in life," the old stranger said, slowly, defiantly prophetic, "you may go far, but mark me as I say it, the places you knowed when you was a little tad will be the strongest in your remembrance. It's true, whoever you are and whatever land you come from. Your whole insides is made outen what you done first."

Newt saw in terror what he saw as he gazed into the sinking embers. His mother calling him from the house door, calling him to come to his dinner, her hand uplifted to the door frame. His sister, a little girl, dragging his chair in place and pushing his cup up against the plate. His tears for them dimmed the fire to a vague, red, quivering glow. The floating images in the dark of the well water, the bright light of the sky in the middle as a picture in a frame, and his own head looking into the heart of the picture—these were between him and the fire, moving more inwardly and dragging himself with them as they went. He as bereft, divided, emptied of his every wish, and he gazed at the fire, scarcely seeing it.

There was moving in the room, figures making a dim passage of shadows behind him. Presently he knew that the old man had gone to his sleeping place and that Nance was spreading quilts on the floor to the side of the fireplace. Her strong body was pleasant to sense as she flung out the covers and pulled them into line, and a delight in the strange room, the strange bed, welled over him. His breath was then set to a fluted rhythm as he drew suddenly inward a rich flood of air, a rhythm flowing deeply until it touched the core of his desire for the settlements, laid an amorous pulse on his determination to go there. Learning was the word he cherished and kept identified with his quickened breath. He remembered that the lights of Merrymen and the settlements would be brightly dusted over the low valley when he reached Coster.

By the end of the week he would, his eager breath told him, be looking down on to the farther valleys.

Anne Bethel Spencer

(1882–1975)

On February 6, 1882, Anne Bethel Spencer was born. In 1893 she traveled to Lynchburg, Virginia, where she entered Virginia Theological Seminary and College, graduating from high school and college. While in school, she met Edward A. Spencer, who became her husband and father of their children, Bethel, Alroy, and Chauncey. Edward built a sanctuary named Edankraal for her in the backyard.

Working as a librarian during the day, Spencer wrote poetry in her free time. Her hospitality was well known, and among those who visited her were Martin Luther King, Jr., and Thurgood Marshall. She died in Lynchburg, Virginia, on July 27, 1975.

Substitution

Is Life itself but many ways of thought,
How real the tropic storm or lambent breeze
Within the slightest convolution wrought
Our mantled world and men-freighted seas?
God thinks . . . and being comes to ardent things:
The splendor of the day-spent sun, love's birth,—
Or dreams a little, while creation swings
The circle of His mind and Time's full girth . . .
As here within this noisy peopled room
My thought leans forward . . . quick! you're lifted clear
Of brick and frame to moonlit garden bloom,—
Absurdly easy, now, our walking, dear,
Talking, my leaning close to touch your face . . .
His All-Mind bids us keep this sacred place!

For Jim, Easter Eve

If ever a garden was a Gethsemane,
with old tombs set high against
the crumpled olive tree—and lichen,
this, my garden has been to me.
For such as I none other is so sweet:
Lacking old tombs, here stands my grief,
and certainly its ancient tree.

Peace is here and in every season
a quiet beauty.
The sky falling about me
evenly to the compass . . .
What is sorrow but tenderness now
in this earth-close frame of land and sky
falling constantly into horizons
of east and west, north and south;
what is pain but happiness here
amid these green and wordless patterns,—
indefinite texture of blade and leaf:

Beauty of an old, old tree,
last comfort in Gethsemane.

Thomas Clayton Wolfe

(1900–1938)

Thomas Wolfe was born on October 3, 1900, in Asheville, North Carolina. When he was almost sixteen, he entered the University of North Carolina at Chapel Hill. He became editor of the *Tar Heel*, the student newspaper. After graduating at twenty, Wolfe went to Harvard University, where he studied playwriting and received his M.A. From 1924 to 1930, Wolfe taught English at New York University.

Look Homeward, Angel was published in 1929 and became immediately successful. In 1930 he received a Guggenheim Fellowship and visited Europe. When he returned, he developed a friendship with Maxwell Perkins, his editor at Scribners. *Of Time and the River* was published in 1935, followed by *The Web and the Rock* (1939); *You Can't Go Home Again* (1940); and *The Party at Jack's* (1995).

Wolfe died on September 15, 1938, and was buried in Asheville, North Carolina.

from *Of Time and the River*

XXXI

The dying man himself was no longer to be fooled and duped by hope; he knew that he was done for, and he no longer cared. Rather, as if that knowledge had brought him a new strength—the immense and measureless strength that comes from resignation, and that has vanquished terror and despair—Gant had already consigned himself to death, and now was waiting for it, without weariness or anxiety, and with a perfect and peaceful acquiescence.

The complete resignation and tranquillity of a man whose life had been so full of violence, protest, and howling fury stunned and silenced them, and left them helpless. It seemed that Gant, knowing that often he had lived badly, was now determined to die well. And in this he succeeded. He accepted every ministration, every visit, every stammering reassurance, or frenzied activity, with a passive gratefulness which he seemed to want every one to know. On the evening of the day after his first hemorrhage, he asked for food and Eliza, bustling out, pathetically eager to do something, killed a chicken and cooked it for him.

And as if, from that infinite depth of death and silence from which he looked at her, he had seen, behind the bridling brisk activity of her figure, forever bustling back and forth, saying confusedly—"Why, yes! The very thing! This very minute, sir!"—had seen the white strained face, the stricken eyes of a proud and sensitive woman who had wanted affection all her life, had received for the most part injury and abuse, and who was ready to clutch at any crust of comfort that might console or justify her before he died—he ate part of the chicken with relish, and then looking up at her, said quietly:

"I tell you what—that was a good chicken."

And Helen, who had been sitting beside him on the bed, and feeding him, now cried out in a tone of bantering and good-humored challenge:

"What! Is it better than the ones *I* cook for you! You'd better not say it is—I'll beat you if you do."

And Gant, grinning feebly, shook his head, and answered:

"Ah-h! Your mother is a good cook, Helen. You're a good cook, too—but there's no one else can cook a chicken like your mother!"

And stretching out his great right hand, he patted Eliza's worn fingers with his own.

And Eliza, suddenly touched by that word of unaccustomed praise and tenderness, turned and rushed blindly from the room at a clumsy bridling gait, clasping her hands together at the wrist, her weak eyes blind with tears—shaking her head in a strong convulsive movement, her mouth smiling a pale tremulous smile, ludicrous, touching, made unnatural by her false teeth, whispering over and over to herself, "Poor fellow! Says, 'There's no one else can cook a chicken like your mother.' Reached out and patted me on the hand, you know. Says 'I tell you what, there's no one who can cook a chicken like your mother.' I reckon he wanted to let me know, to tell me, but says, 'The rest of you have all been good to me, Helen's a good cook, but there's no one else can cook like your mother.'"

"Oh, here, here, here," said Helen, who, laughing uncertainly had followed her mother from the room when Eliza had rushed out, and had seized her by the arms, and shook her gently, "good heavens! *Here!* You mustn't carry on like this! You mustn't take it this way! Why, he's all right!" she cried out heartily and shook Eliza again. "Papa's going to be all right! Why, what are you crying for?" she laughed. "He's going to get well now—don't you know that?"

And Eliza could say nothing for a moment but kept smiling that false trembling and unnatural smile, shaking her head in a slight convulsive movement, her eyes blind with tears.

"I tell you what," she whispered, smiling tremulously again and shaking her head, "there was something about it—you know, the way he said it—says, 'There's no one who can come up to your mother'—there was something in the way he said it! Poor fellow, says, 'None of the rest of you can cook like her'—says, 'I tell you what, that was certainly a good chicken'—Poor fellow! It wasn't so much what he said as the way he said it—there was something about it that went through me like a knife—I tell you what it did!"

"Oh, here, here, here!" Helen cried again, laughing. But her own eyes were also wet, the bitter possessiveness that had dominated all her relations with her father, and that had thrust Eliza away from him, was suddenly vanquished. At that moment she began to feel an affection for her mother that she had never felt before, a deep and nameless pity and regret, and a sense of sombre satisfaction.

"Well," she thought, "I guess it's all she's had, but I'm glad she's got that much to remember. I'm glad he said it: she'll always have that now to hang on to."

And Gant lay looking up from that sunken depth of death and silence, his great hands of living power quiet with their immense and passive strength beside him on the bed.

XXXII

Towards one o'clock that night Gant fell asleep and dreamed that he was walking down the road that led to Spangler's Run. And although he had not been along that road for fifty years everything was as fresh, as green, as living and familiar as it had ever been to him. He came out on the road from Schaefer's farm, and on his left he passed by the little white frame church of the United Brethren, and the graveyard about the church where his friends and family had been buried. From the road he could see the line of family gravestones which he himself had carved and set up after he had returned from serving his apprenticeship in Baltimore. The stones were all alike: tall flat slabs of marble with plain rounded tops, and there was one for his sister Susan, who had died in infancy, and one for his sister Huldah, who had died in childbirth while the war was on, and one for Huldah's husband, a young farmer named Jake Lentz who had been killed at Chancellorsville, and one for the husband of his oldest sister, Augusta, a man named Martin, who had been an itinerant photographer and had died soon after the war, and finally one for Gant's own father. And since there were no stones for his brother George or for Elmer or for John, and none for his mother or Augusta, Gant knew that he was still a young man, and had just recently come home. The stones which he had put up were still white and new, and in the lower right hand corner of each stone, he had carved his own name: W. O. Gant.

It was a fine morning in early May and everything was sweet and green and as familiar as it had always been. The graveyard was carpeted with thick green grass, and all around the graveyard and the church there was the incomparable green velvet of young wheat. And the thought came back to Gant, as it had come to him a thousand times, that the wheat around the graveyard looked greener and richer than any other wheat that he had ever seen. And beside him on his right were the great fields of the Schaefer farm, some richly carpeted with young green wheat, and some ploughed, showing great bronze-red strips of fertile nobly swelling earth. And behind him on the great swell of the land, and commanding that sweet and casual scene with the majesty of its incomparable lay was Jacob Schaefer's great red barn and to the right the neat brick house with the white trimming of its windows, the white picket fence, the green yard with its rich tapestry of flowers and lilac bushes and the massed leafy spread of its big maple trees. And behind the house the hill rose, and all its woods were just greening into May, still smoky, tender and unfledged, gold-yellow with the magic of young green. And before the woods began there was the apple orchard halfway up the hill; the trees were heavy with the blossoms and stood there in all their dense still bloom incredible.

And from the greening trees the bird-song rose, the grass was thick with the dense gold glory of the dandelions, and all about him were a thousand magic things that came and went and never could be captured. Below the church, he passed the old frame house where Elly Spangler, who kept the church keys, lived, and there were apple trees behind the house, all dense with bloom, but the house was rickety, unpainted and dilapidated as it had always been, and he wondered if the kitchen was still buzzing with a million flies, and if Elly's half-wit brothers, Jim and Willy, were inside. And even as he shook his head and thought, as he had thought so many times "Poor Elly," the back door opened and Willy Spangler, a man past thirty wearing overalls, and with a fond, foolish witless face, came galloping down across the yard toward him, flinging his arms out in exuberant greeting, and shouting to him the same welcome that he shouted out to every one who passed, friends and strangers all alike—"I've been lookin' fer ye! I've been lookin' fer ye, Oll," using, as was the custom of the friends and kinsmen of his Pennsylvania boyhood, his second name—and then, anxiously, pleadingly, again the same words that he spoke to every one: "Ain't ye goin' to stay?"

And Gant, grinning, but touched by the indefinable sadness and pity which that kind and witless greeting had always stirred in him since his own childhood, shook his head, and said quietly:

"No, Willy. Not to-day. I'm meeting some one down the road"—and straightway felt, with thudding heart, a powerful and nameless excitement, the urgency of that impending meeting—why, where, with whom, he did not know—but all-compelling now, inevitable.

And Willy, still with wondering, foolish, kindly face followed along beside him now, saying eagerly, as he said to every one:

"Did ye bring anythin' fer me? Have ye got a chew?"

And Gant, starting to shake his head in refusal, stopped suddenly, seeing the look of disappointment on the idiot's face, and putting his hand in the pocket of his coat, took out a plug of apple-tobacco, saying:

"Yes. Here you are, Willy. You can have this."

And Willy, grinning with foolish joy, had clutched the plug of tobacco and, still kind and foolish, had followed on a few steps more, saying anxiously:

"Are ye comin' back, Oll? Will ye be comin' back real soon?"

And Gant, feeling a strange and nameless sorrow, answered:

"I don't know, Willy"—for suddenly he saw that he might never come this way again.

But Willy, still happy, foolish, and contented, had turned and galloped away toward the house, flinging his arms out and shouting as he went:

"I'll be waitin' fer ye. I'll be waitin' fer ye, Oll."

And Gant went on then, down the road, and there was a nameless sorrow in him that he could not understand, and some of the brightness had gone out of the day.

When he got to the mill, he turned left along the road that went down by Spangler's run, crossed by the bridge below, and turned from the road into the wood-path on the other side. A child was standing in the path, and turned and went on ahead of him. In the wood the sunlight made swarming moths of light across the path, and through the leafy tangle of the trees: the sunlight kept shifting and swarming on the child's gold hair, and all around him were the sudden noises of the wood, the stir, the rustle, and the bullet thrum of wings, the cool broken sound of hidden water.

The wood got denser, darker as he went on and coming to a place where the path split away into two forks, Gant stopped, and turning to the child said, "Which one shall I take?" And the child did not answer him.

But some one was there in the wood before him. He heard footsteps on the path, and saw a footprint in the earth, and turning took the path where the footprint was, and where it seemed he could hear some one walking.

And then, with the bridgeless instancy of dreams, it seemed to him that all of the bright green-gold around him in the wood grew dark and sombre, the path grew darker, and suddenly he was walking in a strange and gloomy forest, haunted by the brown and tragic light of dreams. The forest shapes of great trees rose around him, he could hear no bird-song now, even his own feet on the path were soundless, but he always thought he heard the sound of some one walking in the wood before him. He stopped and listened: the steps were muffled, softly thunderous, they seemed so near that he thought that he must catch up with the one he followed in another second, and then they seemed immensely far away, receding in the dark mystery of that gloomy wood. And again he stopped and listened, the footsteps faded, vanished, he shouted, no one answered. And suddenly he knew that he had taken the wrong path, that he was lost. And in his heart there was an immense and quiet sadness, and the dark light of the enormous wood was all around him; no birds sang.

XXXIII

Gant awoke suddenly and found himself looking straight up at Eliza who was seated in a chair beside the bed.

"You were asleep," she said quietly with a grave smile, looking at him in her direct and almost accusing fashion.

"Yes," he said, breathing a little hoarsely, "what time is it?"

It was a few minutes before three o'clock in the morning. She looked at the clock and told him the time: he asked where Helen was.

"Why," said Eliza quickly, "she's right here in this hall room: I reckon she's asleep, too. Said she was tired, you know, but that if you woke up and needed her to call her. Do you want me to get her?"

"No," said Gant. "Don't bother her. I guess she needs the rest, poor child. Let her sleep."

"Yes," said Eliza, nodding, "and that's exactly what you must do, too, Mr. Gant. You try to go on back to sleep now," she said coaxingly, "for that's what we all need. There's no medicine like sleep—as the fellow says, it's Nature's sovereign remedy," said Eliza, with that form of sententiousness that she was very fond of—"so you go on, now, Mr. Gant, and get a good night's sleep, and when you wake up in the morning, you'll feel like a new man. That's half the battle—if you can get your sleep, you're already on the road to recovery."

"No," said Gant, "I've slept enough."

He was breathing rather hoarsely and heavily and she asked him if he was comfortable and needed anything. He made no answer for a moment, and then muttered something under his breath that she could not hear plainly, but that sounded like "little boy."

"Hah? What say? What is it, Mr. Gant?" Eliza said. "Little boy?" she said sharply, as he did not answer.

"Did you see him?" he said.

She looked at him for a moment with troubled eyes, then said:

"Pshaw, Mr. Gant, I guess you must have been dreaming."

He did not answer, and for a moment there was no sound in the room but his breathing, hoarse, a little heavy. Then he muttered:

"Did some one come into the house?"

She looked at him sharply, inquiringly again, with troubled eyes:

"Hah? What say? Why, no, I think not," she said doubtfully, "unless you may have heard Gilmer come in an' go up to his room."

And Gant was again silent for several moments, breathing a little heavily and hoarsely, his hands resting with an enormous passive strength, upon the bed. Presently he said quietly:

"Where's Bacchus?"

"Hah? Who's that?" Eliza said sharply, in a startled kind of tone. "Bacchus? You mean Uncle Bacchus?"

"Yes," said Gant.

"Why, pshaw, Mr. Gant!" cried Eliza laughing—for a startled moment she had wondered if "his mind was wanderin'," but one glance at his quiet eyes, the tranquil sanity of his quiet tone, reassured her——

"Pshaw!" she said, putting one finger up to her broad nose-wing and laughing slyly. "You must have been havin' queer dreams, for a fact!"

"Is he here?"

"Why, I'll vow, Mr. Gant!" she cried again. "What on earth is in your mind? You know that Uncle Bacchus is way out West in Oregon—it's been ten years since he came back home last—that summer of the reunion at Gettysburg."

"Yes," said Gant. "I remember now."

And again he fell silent, staring upward in the semi-darkness, his hands quietly at rest beside him, breathing a little hoarsely, but without pain. Eliza sat in the chair watching him, her hands clasped loosely at her waist, her lips pursed reflectively, and a puzzled look in her eyes: "Now I wonder what ever put that in his mind?" she thought. "I wonder what made him think of Bacchus. Now his mind's not wanderin'—that's one thing sure. He knows what he's doing just as well as I do—I reckon he must have dreamed it—that Bacchus was here—but that's certainly a strange thing, that he should bring it up like this."

He was so silent that she thought he might have gone to sleep again, he lay motionless with his eyes turned upward in the semi-darkness of the room, his hands immense and passive at his side. But suddenly he startled her again by speaking, a voice so quiet and low that he might have been talking to himself.

"Father died the year before the war," he said, "when I was nine years old. I never got to know him very well. I guess Mother had a hard time of it. There were seven of us—and nothing but that little place to live on—and some of us too young to help her much—and George away at war. She spoke pretty hard to us sometimes—but I guess she had a hard time of it. It was a tough time for all of us," he muttered, "I tell you what, it was."

"Yes," Eliza said, "I guess it was. I know she told me—I talked to her, you know, the time we went there on our honeymoon—whew! what about it?" she shrieked faintly, and put her finger up to her broad nose-wing with the same sly gesture—"it was all I could do to keep a straight face sometimes—why, you know, the way she had of talkin'—the expressions she used—oh! came right out with it, you know—sometimes I'd have to turn my head away so she wouldn't see me laughin'—says, you know, 'I was left a widow with seven children to bring up, but I never took charity from no one; as I told 'em all, I've crawled under the dog's belly all my life; now I guess I can get over its back.'"

"Yes," said Gant with a faint grin. "Many's the time I've heard her say that."

"But she told it then, you know," Eliza went on in explanatory fashion, "about your father and how he'd done hard labor on a farm all his life and died—well, I reckon you'd call it consumption."

"Yes," said Gant. "That was it."

"And," Eliza said reflectively, "I never asked—of course, I didn't want to embarrass her—but I reckon from what she said, he may have been—well, I suppose you might say he was a drinkin' man."

"Yes," said Gant, "I guess he was."

"And I know she told it on him," said Eliza, laughing again, and passing one finger slyly at the corner of her broad nose-wing, "how he went to town that time—to Brant's Mill, I guess it was—and how she was afraid he'd get to drinkin', and she sent you and Wes along to watch him and to see he got home again—and how he met up with some fellers there and, sure enough, I guess he started drinkin' and stayed away too long—and then, I reckon he was afraid of what she'd say to him when he got back—and that was when he bought the clock—it's that very clock upon the mantel,

Mr. Gant—but that was when he got the clock, all right—I guess he thought it would pacify her when she started out to scold him for gettin' drunk and bein' late."

"Yes," said Gant, who had listened without moving, staring at the ceiling, and with a faint grin printed at the corners of his mouth, "well do I remember: that was it, all right."

"And then," Eliza went on, "he lost the way comin' home—it had been snowin', and I reckon it was getting dark, and he had been drinkin'—and instead of turnin' in on the road that went down by your place he kept goin' on until he passed Jake Schaefer's farm—an' I guess Wes and you, poor child, kept follerin' where he led, thinkin' it was all right—and when he realized his mistake he said he was tired an' had to rest a while and—I'll vow! to think he'd go and do a thing like that," said Eliza, laughing again—"he lay right down in the snow, sir, with the clock beside him—and went sound to sleep."

"Yes," said Gant, "and the clock was broken."

"Yes," Eliza said, "she told me about that too—and how she heard you all come creepin' in real quiet an' easy-like about nine o'clock that night, when she and all the children were in bed—an' how she could hear him whisperin' to you and Wes to be quiet—an' how she heard you all come creepin' up the steps—and how he came tip-toein' in real easy-like an' laid the clock down on the bed—I reckon the glass had been broken out of it—hopin' she'd see it when she woke up in the morning an' wouldn't scold him then for stayin' out——"

"Yes," said Gant, still with the faint attentive grin, "and then the clock began to strike."

"Whew-w!" cried Eliza, putting her finger underneath her broad nose-wing—"I know she had to laugh about it when she told it to me—she said that all of you looked so sheepish when the clock began to strike that she didn't have the heart to scold him."

And Gant, grinning faintly again, emitted a faint rusty cackle that sounded like "E'God!" and said: "Yes, that was it. Poor fellow."

"But to think," Eliza went on, "that he would have no more sense than to do a thing like that—to lay right down there in the snow an' go to sleep with you two children watchin' him. And I know how she told it, how she questioned you and Wes next day, and I reckon started in to scold you for not takin' better care of him, and how you told her, 'Well, Mother, I thought that it would be all right. I kept steppin' where he stepped, I thought he knew the way.' And said she didn't have the heart to scold you after that— poor child, I reckon you were only eight or nine years old, and boy-like thought you'd follow in your father's footsteps and that everything would be all right."

"Yes," said Gant, with the faint grin again, "I kept stretchin' my legs to put my feet down in his tracks—it was all I could do to keep up with him. . . . Ah, Lord," he said, and in a moment said in a faint low voice, "how well I can remember it. That was just the winter before he died."

"And you've had that old clock ever since," Eliza said. "That very clock upon the mantel, sir—at least, you've had it ever since I've known you, and I reckon you had it long before that—for I know you told me how you brought it South with you. And that clock must be all of sixty or seventy years old—if it's a day."

"Yes," said Gant, "it's all of that."

And again he was silent, and lay so still and motionless that there was no sound in the room except his faint and labored breathing, the languid stir of the curtains in the cool night breeze, and the punctual tocking of the old wooden clock. And presently, when she thought that he might have gone off to sleep again, he spoke, in the same remote and detached voice as before:

"Eliza,"—he said—and at the sound of that unaccustomed word, a name he had spoken only twice in forty years—her white face and her worn brown eyes turned toward him with the quick and startled look of an animal—"Eliza," he said quietly, "you have had a hard life with me, a hard time. I want to tell you that I'm sorry."

And before she could move from her white stillness of shocked surprise, he lifted his great right hand and put it gently down across her own. And for a moment she sat there bolt upright, shaken, frozen, with a look of terror in her eyes, her heart drained of blood, a pale smile trembling uncertainly and foolishly on her lips. Then she tried to withdraw her hand with a clumsy movement, she began to stammer with an air of ludicrous embarrassment, she bridled, saying—"Aw-w, now, Mr. Gant. Well, now, I reckon,"—and suddenly these few simple words of regret and affection did what all the violence, abuse, drunkenness and injury of forty years had failed to do. She wrenched her hand free like a wounded creature, her face was suddenly contorted by that grotesque and pitiable grimace of sorrow that women have had in moments of grief since the beginning of time, and digging her fist into her closed eye quickly with the pathetic gesture of a child, she lowered her head and wept bitterly:

"It was a hard time, Mr. Gant," she whispered, "a hard time, sure enough. . . . It wasn't all the cursin' and the drinkin'—I got used to that. . . . I reckon I was only an ignorant sort of girl when I met you and I guess," she went on with a pathetic and unconscious humor, "I didn't know what married life was like . . . but I could have stood the rest of it . . . the bad names an' all the things you called me when I was goin' to have another child . . . but it was what you said when Grover died . . . accusin' me of bein' responsible for his death because I took the children to St. Louis to the Fair—" and at the words as if an old and lacerated wound had been re-opened raw and bleeding, she wept hoarsely, harshly, bitterly—"that was the worst time that I had—sometimes I prayed to God that I would not wake up—he was a fine boy, Mr. Gant, the best I had—like the write-up in the paper said he had the sense an' judgment of one twice his age . . . an' somehow it had grown a part of me, I expected him to lead the others—when he died it seemed like everything was gone . . . an' then to have you say that I had—" her voice faltered to a whisper, stopped: with a pathetic gesture she wiped the sleeve of her old frayed sweater across her eyes and already ashamed of her tears, said hastily:

"Not that I'm blamin' you, Mr. Gant. . . . I reckon we were both at fault . . . we were both to blame . . . if I had it to do all over I know I could do better . . . but I was so young and ignorant when I met you, Mr. Gant . . . knew nothing of the world . . . there was always something strange-like about you that I didn't understand."

Then, as he said nothing, but lay still and passive, looking at the ceiling, she said quickly, drying her eyes and speaking with a brisk and instant cheerfulness, the undaunted optimism of her ever-hopeful nature:

"Well, now, Mr. Gant, that's all over, and the best thing we can do is to forget about it. . . . We've both made our mistakes—we wouldn't be human if we didn't—but now we've got to profit by experience—the worst of all this trouble is all over— you've got to think of getting well now, that's the only thing you've got to do, sir," she said pursing her lips and winking briskly at him—"just set your mind on getting well—that's all you've got to do now, Mr. Gant—and the battle is half won. For half our ills and troubles are all imagination," she said sententiously, "and if you'll just make up your mind now that you're going to get well—why, sir, you'll do it," and she looked at him with a brisk nod. "And we've both got years before us, Mr. Gant—for all we know, the best years of our life are still ahead of us—so we'll both go on and profit by the mistakes of the past and make the most of what time's left," she said. "That's just exactly what we'll do!"

And quietly, kindly, without moving, and with the impassive and limitless regret of a man who knows that there is no return, he answered:

"Yes, Eliza. That is what we'll do."

"And now," she went on coaxingly, "why don't you go on back to sleep now, Mr. Gant? There's nothin' like sleep to restore a man to health—as the feller says, it's Nature's sovereign remedy, worth all the doctors and all the medicine on earth," she winked at him, and then concluded on a note of cheerful finality, "so you go on and get some sleep now, and tomorrow you will feel like a new man."

And again he shook his head in an almost imperceptible gesture of negation:

"No," he said, "not now. Can't sleep."

He was silent again, and presently, his breath coming somewhat hoarse and labored, he cleared his throat, and put one hand up to his throat, as if to relieve himself of some impediment.

Eliza looked at him with troubled eyes and said:

"What's the matter, Mr. Gant? There's nothing hurtin' you?"

"No," he said. "Just something in my throat. Could I have some water?"

"Why, yes, sir! That's the very thing!" She got up hastily, and looking about in a somewhat confused manner, saw behind her a pitcher of water and a glass upon his old walnut bureau, and saying "This very minute, sir!" started across the room.

And at the same moment, Gant was aware that some one had entered the house, was coming towards him through the hall, would soon be with him. Turning his head towards the door he was conscious of something approaching with the speed of light, the instancy of thought, and at that moment he was filled with a sense of inexpressible joy, a feeling of triumph and security he had never known. Something immensely bright and beautiful was converging in a flare of light, and at that instant, the whole room blurred around him, his sight was fixed upon that focal image in the door, and suddenly the child was standing there and looking towards him.

And even as he started from his pillows, and tried to call his wife he felt something thick and heavy in his throat that would not let him speak. He tried to call to her again but no sound came, then something wet and warm began to flow out of his mouth and nostrils, he lifted his hands up to his throat, the warm wet blood came pouring out across his fingers; he saw it and felt joy.

For now the child—or some one in the house was speaking, calling to him; he heard great footsteps, soft but thunderous, imminent, yet immensely far, a voice well-known, never heard before. He called to it, and then it seemed to answer him; he called to it with faith and joy to give him rescue, strength, and life, and it answered him and told him that all the error, old age, pain and grief of life was nothing but an evil dream; that he who had been lost was found again, that his youth would be restored to him and that he would never die, and that he would find again the path he had not taken long ago in a dark wood.

And the child still smiled at him from the dark door; the great steps, soft and powerful, came ever closer, and as the instant imminent approach of that last meeting came intolerably near, he cried out through the lake of jetting blood, "Here, Father, here!" and heard a strong voice answer him, "My son!"

At that instant he was torn by a rending cough, something was wrenched loose in him, the death gasp rattled through his blood, and a mass of greenish matter foamed out through his lips. Then the world was blotted out, a blind black fog swam up and closed above his head, some one seized him, he was held, supported in two arms, he heard some one's voice saying in a low tone of terror and of pity, "Mr. Gant! Mr. Gant! Oh, poor man, poor man! He's gone!" And his brain faded into night. Even before she lowered him back upon the pillows, she knew that he was dead.

Eliza's sharp scream brought three of her children—Daisy, Steve, and Luke, and the nurse, Bessie Gant, who was the wife of Gant's nephew Ollie—running from the kitchen. At the same moment Helen, who had taken an hour's sleep—her first in two days—in the little hall-bedroom off the porch, was wakened by her mother's cry, the sound of a screen-door slammed, and the sound of footsteps running past her window on the porch. Then, for several minutes she had no consciousness of what she did, and later she could not remember it. Her actions were those of a person driven by a desperate force, who acts from blind intuition, not from reason. Instantly, the moment that she heard her mother scream, the slam of the screen-door, and the running feet, she knew what had happened, and from that moment she knew only one frenzied desire; somehow to get to her father before he died.

The breath caught hoarse and sharp in her throat in a kind of nervous sob, it seemed that her heart had stopped beating and that her whole life-force was paralyzed; but she was out of her bed with a movement that left the old springs rattling, and she came across the back-porch with a kind of tornado-like speed that just came instantly from nowhere: in a moment she was standing in the open door with the sudden bolted look of a person who has been shot through the heart, staring at the silent group of people, and at the figure on the bed, with a dull strained stare of disbelief and horror.

All the time, although she was not conscious of it, her breath kept coming in a kind of hoarse short sob, her large big-boned face had an almost animal look of anguish and surprise, her mouth was partly open, her large chin hung down, and at this moment, as they turned towards her she began to moan, "Oh-h, oh-h, oh-h, oh-h!" in the same unconscious way, like a person who has received a heavy blow in the pit of the stomach. Then her mouth gaped open, a hoarse and ugly cry was torn from her throat—a cry not of grief but loss—and she rushed forward like a mad woman. They tried to stop her, to restrain her, she flung them away as if they had been rag dolls and hurled herself down across the body on the bed, raving like a maniac.

"Oh, Papa, Papa. . . . Why didn't they tell me? . . . Why didn't they let me know? . . . Why didn't they call me? . . . Oh, Papa, Papa, Papa! . . . dead, dead, dead . . . and they didn't tell me . . . they didn't let me know . . . they let you die . . . and I wasn't here! . . . I wasn't here!"—and she wept harshly, horribly, bitterly, rocking back and forth like a mad woman, with a dead man in her arms. She kept moaning, ". . . They didn't tell me . . . they let you die without me . . . I wasn't here . . . I wasn't here . . ."

And even when they lifted her up from the bed, detached her arms from the body they had held in such a desperate hug, she still kept moaning in a demented manner, as if talking to the corpse, and oblivious of the presence of these living people:

"They never told me . . . they never told me. . . . They let you die here all by yourself . . . and I wasn't here . . . I wasn't here."

All of the women, except Bessie Gant, had now begun to weep hysterically, more from shock, exhaustion, and the nervous strain than from grief, and now Bessie

Gant's voice could be heard speaking to them sharply, coldly, peremptorily, as she tried to bring back order and calmness to the distracted scene:

"Now, you get out of here—all of you! . . . There's nothing more any of you can do—I'll take care of all the rest of it! . . . Get out, now . . . I can't have you in the room while there's work to do. . . . Helen, go on back to bed and get some sleep. . . . You'll feel better in the morning."

"They never told me! . . . They never told me," she turned and stared stupidly at Bessie Gant with dull glazed eyes. "Can't you do something? . . . Where's McGuire? Has any one called him yet?"

"No," said the nurse sharply and angrily, "and no one's going to. You're not going to get that man out of bed at this hour of the night when there's nothing to be done. . . . Get out of here, now, all of you," she began to push and herd them towards the door. "I can't be bothered with you. . . . Go somewhere—anywhere—get drunk—only don't come back in here."

The whole house had come to life; in the excitement, shock, and exhaustion of their nerves the dead man still lying there in such a grotesque and twisted position, was forgotten. One of Eliza's lodgers, a man named Gilmer, who had been in the house for years, was wakened, went out, and got a gallon of corn whiskey; every one drank a great deal, became, in fact, somewhat intoxicated; when the undertakers came to take Gant away, none of the family was present. No one saw it. They were all in the kitchen seated around Eliza's battered old kitchen table, with the jug of whiskey on the table before them. They drank and talked together all night long until dawn came.

XXXIX

October had come again, and that year it was sharp and soon: frost was early, burning the thick green on the mountain sides to massed brilliant hues of blazing colors, painting the air with sharpness, sorrow and delight—and with October. Sometimes, and often, there was warmth by day, an ancient drowsy light, a golden warmth and pollenated haze in afternoon, but over all the earth there was the premonitory breath of frost, an exultancy for all the men who were returning, a haunting sorrow for the buried men, and for all those who were gone and would not come again.

His father was dead, and now it seemed to him that he had never found him. His father was dead, and yet he sought him everywhere, and could not believe that he was dead, and was sure that he would find him. It was October and that year, after years of absence and of wandering, he had come home again.

He could not think that his father had died, but he had come home in October, and all the life that he had known there was strange and sorrowful as dreams. And yet he saw it all in shapes of deathless brightness—the town, the streets, the magic hills, and the plain prognathous faces of the people he had known. He saw them all in shapes of deathless brightness, and everything was instantly familiar as his father's face, and stranger, more phantasmal than a dream.

Their words came to him with the accents of an utter naturalness, and yet were sorrowful and lost and strange like voices speaking in a dream, and in their eyes he read a lost and lonely light, as if they were all phantoms and all lost, or as if he had re-visited the shores of this great earth again with a heart of fire, a cry of pain and ecstasy, a memory of intolerable longing and regret for all the glorious and exultant life that he had known and which he must visit now forever as a fleshless ghost, never to touch, to hold, to have its palpable warmth and substance for his own again. He had come home again, and yet he could not believe his father was dead, and he thought he heard his great voice ringing in the street again, and that he would see him striding toward him across the Square with his gaunt earth-devouring stride, or find him waiting every time he turned the corner, or lunging toward the house bearing the tremendous provender of his food and meat, bringing to them all the deathless security of his strength and power and passion, bringing to them all again the roaring message of his fires that shook the fire-full chimney throat with their terrific blast, giving to them all again the exultant knowledge that the good days, the magic days, the golden weather of their lives would come again, and that this dreamlike and phantasmal world in which they found themselves would waken instantly, as it had once, to all the palpable warmth and glory of the earth, if only his father would come back to make it live, to give them life, again.

Therefore, he could not think that he was dead, and yet it was October, and that year he had come home again. And at night, in his mother's house, he would lie in his bed in the dark, hearing the wind that rattled dry leaves along the empty pavement, hearing far-off across the wind, the barking of a dog, feeling dark time, strange time, dark secret time, as it flowed on around him, remembering his life, this house, and all the million strange and secret visages of time, dark time, thinking, feeling, thinking:

"October has come again, has come again.... I have come home again, and found my father dead ... and that was time ... time ... time.... Where shall I go now? What shall I do? For October has come again, but there has gone some richness from the life we knew, and we are lost."

Storm shook the house at night—the old house, his mother's house—where he had seen his brother die. The old doors swung and creaked in darkness, darkness pressed against the house, the darkness filled them, filled the house at night, it moved about them soft and secret, palpable, filled with a thousand secret presences of sorrowful time and memory, moving about him as he lay below his brother's room in darkness, while storm shook the house in late October, and something creaked and rattled in the wind's strong blast. It was October, and he had come home again: he could not believe that his father was dead.

Wind beat at them with burly shoulders in the night. The darkness moved there in the house like something silent, palpable—a spirit breathing in his mother's house, a demon and a friend—speaking to him its silent and intolerable prophecy of flight, of darkness and the storm, moving about him constantly, prowling about the edges of his life, ever beside him, with him, in him, whispering:

"Child, child—come with me—come with me to your brother's grave tonight. Come with me to the places where the young men lie whose bodies have long since been buried in the earth. Come with me where they walk and move again tonight, and you shall see your brother's face again, and hear his voice, and see again, as they march toward you from their graves the company of the young men who died, as he did, in October, speaking to you their messages of flight, of triumph, and the all-exultant darkness, telling you that all will be again as it was once."

October had come again, and he would lie there in his mother's house at night, and feel the darkness moving softly all about him, and hear the dry leaves scampering on the street outside, and the huge and burly rushes of the wind. And then the wind would rush away with huge caprice, and he could hear it far off roaring with remote demented cries in the embraces of great trees, and he would lie there thinking:

"October has come again—has come again"—feeling the dark around him, not believing that his father could be dead, thinking: "The strange and lonely years have come again. . . . I have come home again . . . come home again . . . and will it not be with us all as it has been?"—feeling the darkness as it moved about him, thinking, "Is it not the same darkness that I knew in childhood, and have I not lain here in bed before, and felt this darkness moving all about me? . . . Did we not hear dogs that barked in darkness, in October?" he then thought. "Were not their howls far broken by the wind? . . . And hear dry leaves that scampered on the streets at night . . . and the huge and burly rushes of the wind . . . and hear huge limbs that stiffly creak in the remote demented howlings of the burly wind . . . and something creaking in the wind at night . . . and think, then, as we think now, of all the men who have gone and never will come back again, and of our friends and brothers who lie buried in the earth? . . . Oh, has not October now come back again?" he cried. "As always—as it always was?"—and hearing the great darkness softly prowling in his mother's house at night, and thinking, feeling, thinking, as he lay there in the dark:

"Now October has come again which in our land is different from October in the other lands. The ripe, the golden month has come again, and in Virginia the chinkapins are falling. Frost sharps the middle music of the seasons, and all things living on the earth turn home again. The country is so big you cannot say the country has the same October. In Maine, the frost comes sharp and quick as driven nails, just for a week or so the woods, all of the bright and bitter leaves, flare up: the maples turn a blazing bitter red, and other leaves turn yellow like a living light, falling about you as you walk the woods, falling about you like small pieces of the sun so that you cannot say where sunlight shakes and flutters on the ground, and where the leaves.

"Meanwhile the Palisades are melting in massed molten colors, the season swings along the nation, and a little later in the South dense woodings on the hill begin to glow and soften, and when they smell the burning wood-smoke in Ohio children say: 'I'll bet that there's a forest fire in Michigan.' And the mountaineer goes hunting down in North Carolina, he stays out late with mournful flop-eared hounds, a rind of moon comes up across the rude lift of the hills: what do his friends say to him when he stays out late? Full of hoarse innocence and laughter, they will say: 'Mister, yore ole woman's goin' to whup ye if ye don't go home.'"

Oh, return, return!

"October is the richest of the seasons: the fields are cut, the granaries are full, the bins are loaded to the brim with fatness, and from the cider-press the rich brown oozings of the York Imperials run. The bee bores to the belly of the yellowed grape, the fly gets old and fat and blue, he buzzes loud, crawls slow, creeps heavily to death on sill and ceiling, the sun goes down in blood and pollen across the bronzed and mown fields of old October.

"The corn is shocked: it sticks out in hard yellow rows upon dried ears, fit now for great red barns in Pennsylvania, and the big stained teeth of crunching horses. The indolent hooves kick swiftly at the boards, the barn is sweet with hay and leather, wood and apples—this, and the clean dry crunching of the teeth is all: the sweat, the labor, and the plow is over. The late pears mellow on a sunny shelf; smoked hams hang to the warped barn rafters; the pantry shelves are loaded with 300 jars of fruit. Meanwhile the leaves are turning, turning, up in Maine, the chestnut burrs plop thickly to the earth in gusts of wind, and in Virginia the chinkapins are falling.

"There is a smell of burning in small towns in afternoon, and men with buckles on their arms are raking leaves in yards as boys come by with straps slung back across their shoulders. The oak leaves, big and brown, are bedded deep in yard and gutter: they make deep wadings to the knee for children in the streets. The fire will snap and crackle like a whip, sharp acrid smoke will sting the eyes, in mown fields the little vipers of the flame eat past the black coarse edges of burned stubble like a line of locusts. Fire drives a thorn of memory in the heart.

"The bladed grass, a forest of small spears of ice, is thawed by noon: summer is over but the sun is warm again, and there are days throughout the land of gold and russet. But summer is dead and gone, the earth is waiting, suspense and ecstasy are gnawing at the hearts of men, the brooding prescience of frost is there. The sun flames red and bloody as it sets, there are old red glintings on the battered pails, the great barn gets the ancient light as the boy slops homeward with warm foaming milk. Great shadows lengthen in the fields, the old red light dies swiftly, and the sunset barking of the hounds is faint and far and full of frost: there are shrewd whistles to the dogs, and frost and silence—this is all. Wind stirs and scuffs and rattles up the old brown leaves, and through the night the great oak leaves keep falling.

"Trains cross the continent in a swirl of dust and thunder, the leaves fly down the tracks behind them: the great trains cleave through gulch and gulley, they rumble with spoked thunder on the bridges over the powerful brown wash of mighty rivers, they toil through hills, they skirt the rough brown stubble of shorn fields, they whip past empty stations in the little towns and their great stride pounds its even pulse across America. Field and hill and lift and gulch and hollow, mountain and plain and river, a wilderness with fallen trees across it, a thicket of bedded brown and twisted undergrowth, a plain, a desert, and a plantation, a mighty landscape with no fenced niceness, an immensity of folded and convolution that can never be remembered, that can never be forgotten, that has never been described—weary with harvest, potent with every fruit and ore, the immeasurable richness embrowned with autumn, rank, crude, unharnessed, careless of scars or beauty, everlasting and magnificent, a cry, a space, an ecstasy!—American earth in old October.

"And the great winds howl and swoop across the land: they make a distant roaring in great trees, and boys in bed will stir in ecstasy, thinking of demons and vast swoopings through the earth. All through the night there is the clean, the bitter rain of acorns, and the chestnut burrs are plopping to the ground.

"And often in the night there is only the living silence, the distant frosty barking of a dog, the small clumsy stir and feathery stumble of the chickens on limed roosts, and the moon, the low and heavy moon of autumn, now barred behind the leafless poles of pines, now at the pine-woods' brooding edge and summit, now falling with ghost's dawn of milky light upon rimed clods of fields and on the frosty scurf on pumpkins, now whiter, smaller, brighter, hanging against the steeple's slope, hanging the same way in a million streets, steeping all the earth in frost and silence.

"Then a chime of frost-cold bells may peal out on the brooding air, and people lying in their beds will listen. They will not speak or stir, silence will gnaw the darkness like a rat, but they will whisper in their hearts:

"'Summer has come and gone, has come and gone. And now—?' But they will say no more, they will have no more to say: they will wait listening, silent and brooding as the frost, to time, strange ticking time, dark time that haunts us with the briefness of our days. They will think of men long dead, of men now buried in the earth, of frost and silence long ago, of a forgotten face and moment of lost time, and they will think of things they have no words to utter.

"And in the night, in the dark, in the living sleeping silence of the towns, the million streets, they will hear the thunder of the fast express, the whistles of great ships upon the river.

"What will they say then? What will they say?"

Only the darkness moved about him as he lay there thinking, feeling in the darkness: a door creaked softly in the house.

"October is the season for returning: the bowels of youth are yearning with lost love. Their mouths are dry and bitter with desire: their hearts are torn with the thorns of spring. For lovely April, cruel and flowerful, will tear them with sharp joy and wordless lust. Spring has no language but a cry; but crueller than April is the asp of time.

"October is the season for returning: even the town is born anew," he thought. "The tide of life is at the full again, the rich return to business or to fashion, and the bodies of the poor are rescued out of heat and weariness. The ruin and horror of the summer is forgotten—a memory of hot cells and humid walls, a hell of ugly sweat and labor and distress and hopelessness, a limbo of pale greasy faces. Now joy and hope have revived again in the hearts of millions of people, they breathe the air again with hunger, their movements are full of life and energy. The mark of their summer's suffering is still legible upon their flesh, there is something starved and patient in their eyes, and a look that has a child's hope and expectation in it.

"All things on earth point home in old October: sailors to sea, travellers to walls and fences, hunters to field and hollow and the long voice of the hounds, the lover to the love he has forsaken—all things that live upon this earth return, return: Father, will you not, too, come back again?

"Where are you now, when all things on the earth come back again? For have not all these things been here before, have we not seen them, heard them, known them, and will they not live again for us as they did once, if only you come back again?

"Father, in the night time, in the dark, I have heard the thunder of the fast express. In the night, in the dark, I have heard the howling of the winds among great trees, and the sharp and windy raining of the acorns. In the night, in the dark, I have heard the feet of rain upon the roofs, the glut and gurgle of the gutter spouts, and the soaking gulping throat of all the mighty earth, drinking its thirst out in the month of May—and heard the sorrowful silence of the river in October. The hill-streams foam and welter in a steady plunge, the mined clay drops and melts and eddies in the night, the snake coils cool and glistening under dripping ferns, the water roars down past the mill in one sheer sheetlike plunge, making a steady noise like wind, and in the night, in the dark, the river flows by us to the sea.

"The great maw slowly drinks the land as we lie sleeping: the mined banks cave and crumble in the dark, the earth melts and drops into its tide, great horns are baying in the gulph of night, great boats are baying at the river's mouth. Thus, darkened by our dumpings, thickened by our stains, rich, rank, beautiful, and unending as all life, all living, the river, the dark immortal river, full of strange tragic time is flowing by us—by us—by us—to the sea.

"All this has been upon the earth, and will abide forever. But you are gone; our lives are ruined and broken in the night, our lives are mined below us by the river, our lives are whirled away into the sea and darkness, and we are lost unless you come to give us life again.

"Come to us, Father, in the watches of the night, come to us as you always came, bringing to us the invincible sustenance of your strength, the limitless treasure of your bounty, the tremendous structure of your life that will shape all lost and broken things on earth again into a golden pattern of exultancy and joy. Come to us, Father, while the winds howl in the darkness, for October has come again bringing with its huge prophecies of death and life and the great cargo of the men who will return. For we are ruined, lost, and broken if you do not come, and our lives, like rotten chips, are whirled about us onward in darkness to the sea."

So, thinking, feeling, speaking, he lay there in his mother's house, but there was nothing in the house but silence and the moving darkness: storm shook the house and huge winds rushed upon them, and he knew then that his father would not come again, and that all the life that he had known was now lost and broken as a dream.

Jesse Stuart

(1907–1984)

Born on August 8, 1907, in Greenup, Kentucky, Jesse Hilton Stuart, inspired by his high school English teacher "Hattie" Hatton, enrolled at Lincoln Memorial University in Harrogate, Tennessee. After LMU, Stuart taught high school in Greenup and then attended Vanderbilt University in Tennessee and Peabody College in Tennessee for graduate school. He then went back to farming. At the age of twenty-four, he was asked to become superintendent of Greenup County Schools. Stuart was later to become the Poet Laureate of Kentucky.

In 1934, Stuart's first book of poems, *Man with a Bull-Tongue Plough,* was published. After receiving a Guggenheim Fellowship, he traveled abroad. He married Naomi Deane, and in 1942 their child, Jessica Jane, was born. *Taps for Private Tussie* was published in 1943, right before Stuart joined the U.S. Navy. After World War II, he returned to Kentucky. His book *The Thread That Runs So True* (1940) was selected as best book by the National Education Association.

Stuart wrote more than sixty books. Other works by him include *Harvest of Youth* (1930); *Head O' W-Hollow* (1936); *Men of the Mountain* (1941); *Album of Destiny* (1944); *Kentucky Is My Land* (1952); *Hold April* (1962); and *A Jesse Stuart Reader: Stories and Poems Selected and Introduced by Jesse Stuart* (1963). He died on February 17, 1984.

Kentucky Is My Land

Kentucky is my land.
It is a place beneath the wind and sun
In the very heart of America.
It is bounded on the east, north and west by rivers

And on the south by mountains.
Only one boundary line is not a natural one,
It is a portion of southern boundary
That runs westward from the mountains
Across the delta lowlands to the Mississippi.

Within these natural boundaries is Kentucky,
Shaped like the mouldboard on a hillside turning-plow.
Kentucky is neither southern, northern, eastern or western,
It is the core of America.
If these United States can be called a body,
Kentucky can be called its heart.

I didn't have any choice as to where I was born,
But if I had had my choice,
I would have chosen Kentucky.
And if I could have chosen wind to breathe,
I would have chosen a Kentucky wind
With the scent of cedar, pinetree needles,
Green tobacco leaves, pawpaw, persimmon and sassafras.
I would have chosen too,
Wind from the sawbriar and greenbriar blossoms.

If I could have chosen the spot in Kentucky,
I would have chosen W-Hollow,
The place where I was born,
Where four generations of my people have lived,
And where they still live.
Here, too, I have always lived where
The hills form a semicircle barrier against roads
And there is only one way to get out.

This way is to follow the stream.
Here, I first saw Kentucky light.
Here, I first breathed Kentucky air.
And here I grew from childhood to manhood
Before I had been away to see what lay beyond
The rim of hills that closed my world.

I followed the little streams
That flowed over rocks between the high hills to the rivers
And then somewhere into the unknown world.
I hunted the wild game in the hunting seasons
Skillful as an Indian.
And I ran wild over the rock-ribbed hills
Enjoying this land of lonesome waters, sunlight,
Tobacco, pine, pawpaw, persimmon, sawbriar, greenbriar and sassafras.
I enjoyed the four seasons,
Sections of time my father used to divide his work for the year,
As much as any boy in America ever enjoyed them.

For Kentucky has four distinct seasons.
I learned this in childhood
And I didn't get it from a book.
Each season I learned was approximately three months.
Kentucky wasn't all summer, all autumn, all winter or spring.
The two seasons that I wanted to be longer and longer
Were the Kentucky spring and autumn.

When winter began to break, snow melted
And ran down the little channels on the high hills.
Spring was in the wind.
I could feel it.
I could taste it.
I could see it.
And it was beautiful to me.
Then came the sawbriar and the greenbriar leaves
And the trailing arbutus on the rock-ribbed hills.

Next came the snowwhite blossoms of percoon in the coves,
Then came the canvas-topped tobacco beds,
White strips of fortune on each high hill slope.
Then came the dogwood and the wild crabapple blossoms,
White sails in the soft honey-colored wind of morning
And red sails of the flowering redbud,
Stationary fire hanging in the soft mellow wind
Of evening against the sunset . . .
The weeping willow, stream willow, and pussy-willow
Loosed their long fronds to finger the bright wind tenderly.
Then came soft avalanches of green beech tops
In the deep hollows that hid the May-apple,
Yellowroot, ginseng, wild sweet williams, babytear and phlox.
When I learned Kentucky springs
Could not go on forever,
I was sick at heart.

For summer followed with work on the high hills.
I plowed the earth on steep slopes
And hoed corn, tobacco, cane, beside my strong mother
With a bright-worn gooseneck hoe.
Summer brought good earthy smells
Of tobacco, cane and corn and ferny loam and growing roots.
Summer brought berries too
That grew wild in the creviced rocks,
On the loamy coves and in the deep valleys.
Here grew the wild blackberries, strawberries, raspberries and dewberries.
All I had to do was take my bucket and pick them.

Then came the autumn with hazelnuts ripening on the pasture bluffs
Along the cattle paths and sheep trails.
The black walnuts, white walnuts, hickory nuts, beech nuts

Fell from the trees in little heaps.
And the canopy of leaves turned many colors
After the first sharp frost had fallen
And the soft summer wind turned cool and brittle
And the insect sounds of summer became a lost murmur
Like the dwindling streams.
Autumn brought sweet smells of the wild possum grapes
And the mountain tea berries
And the blood-red sassafras and persimmon leaf . . .
Autumn brought the mellow taste of the persimmon
That after frost did not pucker my mouth with summer bitterness.
October pawpaws with purple-colored skins,
I found in heaps beneath the trees when I went after cows.
I opened them to find the cornmeal-mush softness,
Yellow-gold in color and better than bananas to taste.

These things are my Kentucky.
They went into the brain, body, flesh and blood of me.
These things, Kentucky-flavored, grown in her dirt,
Helped build my body strong and shape my brain.
They laid foundations for my future thoughts.
They made me a part of Kentucky.
They made Kentucky a part of me.
These are the inescapable things,
Childhood to boyhood to manhood.
Even the drab hills of winter were filled with music.
The lonesome streams in the narrow-gauged valleys
Sang poetic songs without words.
And the leafless trees etched on gray winter skies
Were strong and substantial lines of poetry.

When I was compelled to put poems on paper
They wrote themselves for they were ripe
And ready for harvest
As the wild berries, the persimmons and the pawpaws
As the yellow leaves and nuts falling from the trees.
Then I went for the first time into other states
And I knew my Kentucky was different.

As I observed the closeness of the tombstones
In the eastern cemeteries
This gave me a feeling that land was scarce.
I saw the tall smokestacks of industry
Etched against the eastern skies
And cities that were a pillar of fire by night
And clouds of rolling smoke by day . . .
I saw New York, a city so large it frightened me,
Cliff dwellings as high as Kentucky mountains,
The streets and avenues were deep gorges

Between high walls of multicolored stone.
And while it interested me
To see how fellow Americans lived,
I longed for Kentucky sunlight, sights and sounds
And for logshacks and the lonesome waters.
I was homesick for the land of the fox
And spring's tender bud, bloom and leaf,
For white sails of the dogwood and the crabapple
And the flame of redbud in the sunset.
I knew that my Kentucky was different
And something there called me home.
The language too was different,
Not that it was softer
But it was more musical with the hard "g"s
Left automatically from the spoken word
And the prefix "a" supplemented . . .
I knew more than ever before my brain
Had been fashioned by the sights and sounds
And beauties of wildgrowth and life of the hills
That had nurtured my flesh from infancy to full growth.

Then I went beyond the hills to see
America's South of which I had always thought
We were a distinct part.
But I learned we were different from the South
Though our soils grew cane, cotton and tobacco . . .
We moved faster and we spoke differently.

The West I visited where land
Was level as a floor,
Where the endless field of growing corn
Was a dark cloud that hugged the earth,
Where the single field of growing wheat was endless, endless,
And the clouds always in the distance
Came down and touched the earth.
No matter how fast the train or the car ran,
It never reached the spot where the clouds came down to earth.
The people moved quickly,
They talked with the speed of the western wind.
They were "doers," not talkers.
I knew this was not the heart of America:
This was the West, the young strong man of America.

I visited the North where industry
Is balanced with agriculture
And where a man is measured by what he can do.
I did not find the softness of the pawpaw and the persimmon,
The lusty morning smell of green growing tobacco,
The twilight softness of Kentucky spring

But I did find the endless fields of corn and wheat
Where machinery did the work . . .
Beyond the cornfields and wheatfields
I saw the smokestacks of industry,
Belching fire and smoke toward the sky.
Highways were filled with traffic that shot past me like bullets.
And I found industrial city streets filled
With the fast tempo of humanity . . .
Then I was as positive as death Kentucky
Was not east, west, south or north
But it was the heart of America
Pulsing with a little bit of everything.

. . . The heart of America
A land of even tempo,
A land of mild traditions,
A land that has kept its traditions of horse racing,
Ballad, song, story and folk music.
It has held steadfast to its pioneer tradition
Of fighting men, fighting for America
And for the soil of Kentucky,
That is filled with bluegrass beauty
That is not akin to poetry
But is poetry . . .
And when I go beyond the border,
I take with me growth and beauty of the seasons,
The music of wind in pine and cedar tops,
The wordless songs of snow-melted water
When it pours over the rocks to wake the spring.
I take with me Kentucky embedded in my brain and heart,
In my flesh and bone and blood
Since I am of Kentucky
And Kentucky is part of me.

Her Work Is Done

I thought my mother was a forceful river
When as a child I walked along beside;
I thought that life for her would be forever,
That she would give me counsel, be my guide.
She gave me counsel as the years went by;
She taught me how to use a heavy hoe
On mountain slopes that shouldered to the sky
In stalwart corn and long tobacco row . . .
And as I grew in strength to meet the years,
Among the clouds, up with the mountain wind

She would not have me bow to petty fears,
She taught me courage that was hard to bend . . .
Now time has passed with many seasons flown,
On mountain slopes my mother's work is done;
That forceful stream that was my mother's own
Flowed quietly toward the set of sun.

Prayer for My Father

Be with him, Time, extend his stay some longer,
He fights to live more than oaks fight to grow;
Be with him, Time, and make his body stronger
And give his heart more strength to make blood flow.
He's cheated Death for forty years and more
To walk upon the crust of earth he's known;
Give him more years before you close the door.
Be kind to him—his better days were sown
With pick and shovel deep in dark coal mine
And laying railroad steel to earn us bread
To carry home upon his back to nine.
Be with him, Time, delay the hour of dread.
Give him the extra time you have to spare
To plod upon his little mountain farm;
He'll love some leisure days without a care
Before Death takes him gently by the arm.

Stand Out and Count

Stand out and count tonight the winds that blow,
Stand out and count the times the green leaves stir
While earth is liquid-green and stars seem low . . .
Stand out and count, it does not matter where.
And you will see as often as wind blows
Are segments of clean beauty on this earth . . .
High clouds, moon, stars, mist, river, fern and rose.
    These things of beauty you have known from birth.
    More often than you count earth's heart pumps blood
    Through tight veins of the many rough-barked trees
    To give them life, leaf, beauty, bloom and bud,
    To give their rugged bodies symmetry . . .
    Feel in the vibrant wind earth's beating heart,
    Rejoice for life, love and eternity;
    And know that all of this you are a part
    Of everything there is and is to be.

Modernity

Before the hard roads came my legs were strong.
I walked on paths through bracken and the fern,
And five to thirty miles were not too long
On paths I knew by tree and rock and turn.
I knew in March where trailing arbutus
Bloomed under hanging cliffs and dogwood groves
And thin-leafed willows were wind-tremulous.
I knew where April percoon bloomed in coves.
But since I drive, my legs are losing power,
For clutch and brake are not leg exercise.
I cannot drive contented by the hour,
For driving is not soothing to the eyes.
The road's grown old that I am forced to see
Above the stream where water churns to foam,
Where great green hills slant up in mystery . . .
I sometimes see a bird or bee fly home.

Summer Has Faded

Summer has faded from all living eyes.
It is a written book that we have read
With sentences of green beneath blue skies.
Each word is now a leaf of dying red.
We stand to watch birds gather for the south,
We watch them rise in this bright autumn weather;
And with joy in the heart, song in the mouth,
They are off through boundless skies together.
Above the thistle furze that floats on wind,
Above the leaves of scarlet-red and gold,
Above treetops the autumn winds have thinned
They rise to sing before their autumn blood grows cold.
We stand below to listen and to look
And wait the season of another book.

James Agee

(1909–1955)

James Agee was born on November 27, 1909, in Knoxville, Tennessee, where he spent his early childhood. Three years following the death of his father in 1916, Agee enrolled at St. Andrew's School near Sewanee, Tennessee, where he remained through 1924. In 1924 he returned to Knoxville to attend high school. A year later, he left Knoxville to further his education at Phillips Exeter Academy in New Hampshire. Entering Harvard University in 1928, he became editor of the *Harvard Advocate* from 1931 to 1932, to which he contributed poetry, book reviews, and fiction. After graduating from Harvard in 1932, Agee went to work for *Fortune*. In 1934 he published *Permit Me Voyage*, a book of poetry that was part of the Yale Series of Younger Poets.

In 1936, Agee and photographer Walker Evans lived in Alabama for eight weeks to record the lives of tenant farmers. Five years later, in September 1941, Agee and Evans's monumental study, *Let Us Now Praise Famous Men*, was published. While working at *Fortune*, Agee married Olivia Saunders in 1933. After their divorce in 1939, he married Alma Mailman, who was to become the mother of his son Joel. Following their divorce in 1944, he married Mia Fritsch, by whom he had three children, Teresa, Andrea Maria, and John Alexander.

Gaining success as a film critic, Agee began to write original screenplays such as *Noa Noa*, and adaptations such as *The Blue Hotel* (1948–1949), *The African Queen* (1950) with John Huston, and *The Night of the Hunter* (1954). Agee died on May 16, 1955. Two years later his posthumously published novel, *A Death in the Family* (1957), received the Pulitzer Prize, as did the dramatic version, entitled *All the Way Home*, which was made into a movie in 1962.

from *A Death in the Family*

Knoxville: Summer, 1915

We are talking now of summer evenings in Knoxville, Tennessee, in the time that I lived there so successfully disguised to myself as a child. It was a little bit mixed sort of block, fairly solidly lower middle class, with one or two juts apiece on either side of that. The houses corresponded: middle-sized gracefully fretted wood houses built in the late nineties and early nineteen hundreds, with small front and side and more spacious back yards, and trees in the yards, and porches. These were softwooded trees, poplars, tulip trees, cottonwoods. There were fences around one or two of the houses, but mainly the yards ran into each other with only now and then a low hedge that wasn't doing very well. There were few good friends among the grown people, and they were not poor enough for the other sort of intimate acquaintance, but everyone nodded and spoke, and even might talk short times, trivially, and at the two extremes of the general or the particular, and ordinarily nextdoor neighbors talked quite a bit when they happened to run into each other, and never paid calls. The men were mostly small businessmen, one or two very modestly executives, one or two worked with their hands, most of them clerical, and most of them between thirty and forty-five.

But it is of these evenings, I speak.

Supper was at six and was over by half past. There was still daylight, shining softly and with a tarnish, like the lining of a shell; and the carbon lamps lifted at the corners were on in the light, and the locusts were started, and the fire flies were out, and a few frogs were flopping in the dewy grass, by the time the fathers and the children came out. The children ran out first hell bent and yelling those names by which they were known; then the fathers sank out leisurely in crossed suspenders, their collars removed and their necks looking tall and shy. The mothers stayed back in the kitchen washing and drying, putting things away, recrossing their traceless footsteps like the lifetime journeys of bees, measuring out the dry cocoa for breakfast. When they came out they had taken off their aprons and their skirts were dampened and they sat in rockers on their porches quietly.

It is not of the games children play in the evening that I want to speak now, it is of a contemporaneous atmosphere that has little to do with them: that of the fathers of families, each in his space of lawn, his shirt fishlike pale in the unnatural light and his face nearly anonymous, hosing their lawns. The hoses were attached at spiggots that stood out of the brick foundations of the houses. The nozzles were variously set but usually so there was a long sweet stream of spray, the nozzle wet in the hand, the water trickling the right forearm and the peeled-back cuff, and the water whishing out a long loose and low-curved cone, and so gentle a sound. First an insane noise of violence in the nozzle, then the still irregular sound of adjustment, then the smoothing into steadiness and a pitch as accurately tuned to the size and style of stream as any violin. So many qualities of sound out of one hose: so many choral differences out of those several hoses that were in earshot. Out of any one hose, the almost dead silence of the release, and the short still arch of the separate big drops, silent as a held breath, and the only noise the flattering noise on leaves and the slapped grass at the fall of each big drop. That, and the intense hiss with the intense stream; that, and that same intensity not growing less but growing more quiet and delicate with the turn of the nozzle, up to that extreme tender whisper when the water was just a wide bell of film. Chiefly, though, the hoses were set much alike, in a compromise between distance and tenderness of spray (and quite surely a sense of art behind this compromise, and a quiet deep joy, too real to recognize itself), and the sounds therefore were pitched much alike; pointed by the snorting start of a new hose; decorated by some man playful with the nozzle; left empty, like God by the sparrow's fall, when any single one of them desists: and all, though near alike, of various pitch; and in this unison. These sweet pale streamings in the light lift out their pallors and their voices all together, mothers hushing their children, the hushing unnaturally prolonged, the men gentle and silent and each snail-like withdrawn into the quietude of what he singly is doing, the urination of huge children stood loosely military against an invisible wall, and gentle happy and peaceful, tasting the mean goodness of their living like the last of their suppers in their mouths; while the locusts carry on this noise of hoses on their much higher and sharper key. The noise of the locust is dry, and it seems not to be rasped or vibrated but urged from him as if through a small orifice by a breath that can never give out. Also there is never one locust but an illusion of at least a thousand. The noise of each locust is pitched in some classic locust range out of which none of them varies more than two full tones: and yet you seem to hear each locust discrete from all the rest, and there is a long, slow, pulse in their noise, like the scarcely defined arch of a long and high set bridge. They are all around in every tree, so that the noise seems to come from nowhere and everywhere at once, from the whole shell heaven, shivering in your flesh and teasing your eardrums, the boldest of all the sounds of night. And yet it is habitual to summer nights, and is of the great order of noises, like the noises of the sea and of the blood her precocious grandchild, which you realize you are hearing only when you catch yourself listening. Meantime from low in the dark, just outside the swaying horizons of the horses, conveying always grass in the damp of dew and its strong green-black smear of smell, the regular yet spaced noises of the crickets, each a sweet cold silver noise three-noted, like the slipping each time of three matched links of a small chain.

But the men by now, one by one, have silenced their hoses and drained and coiled them. Now only two, and now only one, is left, and you see only ghostlike shirt with the sleeve garters, and sober mystery of his mild face like the lifted face of large cattle enquiring of your presence in a pitchdark pool of meadow; and now he too is gone; and it has become that time of evening when people sit on their porches, rocking gently and talking gently and watching the street and the standing up into their sphere of possession of the trees, of birds hung havens, hangars. People go by; things go by. A horse, drawing a buggy, breaking his hollow iron music on the asphalt; a loud auto; a quiet auto; people in pairs, not in a hurry, scuffling, switching their weight of aestival body, talking casually, the taste hovering over them of vanilla, strawberry, pasteboard and starched milk, the image upon them of lovers and horsemen, squared with clowns in hueless amber. A street car raising its iron moan; stopping, belling and starting; stertorous; rousing and raising again its iron increasing moan and swimming its gold windows and straw seats on past and past and past, the bleak spark crackling and cursing above it like a small malignant spirit set to dog its tracks; the iron whine rises on rising speed; still risen, faints; halts; the faint stinging bell; rises again, still fainter, fainting, lifting, lifts, faints forgone: forgotten. Now is the night one blue dew.

> *Now is the night one blue dew, my father has drained, he has coiled the hose.*
> *Low on the length of lawns, a frailing of fire who breathes.*
> *Content, silver, like peeps of light, each cricket makes his comment over*
>   *and over in the drowned grass.*
> *A cold toad thumpily flounders.*
> *Within the edges of damp shadows of side yards are hovering children nearly*
>   *sick with joy of fear, who watch the unguarding of a telephone pole.*
> *Around white carbon corner lamps bugs of all sizes are lifted elliptic, solar*
>   *systems. Big hardshells bruise themselves, assailant: he is fallen on*
>   *his back, legs squiggling.*
> *Parents on porches: rock and rock: From damp strings morning glories:*
>   *hang their ancient faces.*
> *The dry and exalted noise of the locusts from all the air at once enchants*
>   *my eardrums.*

On the rough wet grass of the back yard my father and mother have spread quilts. We all lie there, my mother, my father, my uncle, my aunt, and I too am lying there. First we were sitting up, then one of us lay down, and then we all lay down, on our stomachs, or on our sides, or on our backs, and they have kept on talking. They are not talking much, and the talk is quiet, of nothing in particular, of nothing at all in particular, of nothing at all. The stars are wide and alive, they seem each like a smile of great sweetness, and they seem very near. All my people are larger bodies than mine, quiet, with voices gentle and meaningless like the voices of sleeping birds. One is an artist, he is living at home. One is a musician, she is living at home. One is my mother who is good to me. One is my father who is good to me. By some chance, here they are, all on this earth; and who shall ever tell the sorrow of being on this earth, lying, on quilts, on the grass, in a summer evening, among the sounds of night. May God bless my people, my uncle, my aunt, my mother, my good father, oh, remember them kindly in their time of trouble; and in the hour of their taking away.

After a little I am taken in and put to bed. Sleep, soft smiling, draws me unto her: and those receive me, who quietly treat me, as one familiar and well-beloved in that home: but will not, oh, will not, not now, not ever; but will not ever tell me who I am.

Chapter 1

At supper that night, as many times before, his father said, "Well, spose we go to the picture show."

"Oh, Jay!" his mother said. "That horrid little man!"

"What's wrong with him?" his father asked, not because he didn't know what she would say, but so she would say it.

"He's so *nasty!*" she said, as she always did. "So *vulgar!* With his nasty little cane; hooking up skirts and things, and that nasty little walk!"

His father laughed, as he always did, and Rufus felt that it had become rather an empty joke; but as always the laughter also cheered him; he felt that the laughter enclosed him with his father.

They walked downtown in the light of mother-of-pearl, to the Majestic, and found their way to seats by the light of the screen, in the exhilarating smell of stale tobacco, rank sweat, perfume and dirty drawers, while the piano played fast music and galloping horses raised a grandiose flag of dust. And there was William S. Hart with both guns blazing and his long, horse face and his long, hard lip, and the great country rode away behind him as wide as the world. Then he made a bashful face at a girl and his horse raised its upper lip and everybody laughed, and then the screen was filled with a city and with the sidewalk of a side street of a city, a long line of palms and there was Charlie; everyone laughed the minute they saw him squattily walking with his toes out and his knees wide apart, as if he were chafed; Rufus' father laughed, and Rufus laughed too. This time Charlie stole a whole bag of eggs and when a cop came along he hid them in the seat of his pants. Then he caught sight of a pretty woman and he began to squat and twirl his cane and make silly faces. She tossed her head and walked away with her chin up high and her dark mouth as small as she could make it and he followed her very busily, doing all sorts of things with his cane that made everybody laugh, but she paid no attention. Finally she stopped at a corner to wait for a streetcar, turning her back to him, and pretending he wasn't even there, and after trying to get her attention for a while, and not succeeding, he looked out at the audience, shrugged his shoulders, and acted as if *she* wasn't there. But after tapping his foot for a little, pretending he didn't care, he became interested again, and with a charming smile, tipped his derby; but she only stiffened, and tossed her head again, and everybody laughed. Then he walked back and forth behind her, looking at her and squatting a little while he walked very quietly, and everybody laughed again; then he flicked hold of the straight end of his cane and, with the crooked end, hooked up her skirt to the knee, in exactly the way that disgusted Mama, looking very eagerly at her legs, and everybody laughed loudly; but she pretended she had not noticed. Then he twirled his cane and suddenly squatted, bending the cane and hitching up his pants, and again hooked up her skirt so that you could see the panties she wore, ruffled almost like the edges of curtains, and everybody whooped with laughter, and she suddenly turned in rage and gave him a shove in the chest, and he sat down straight-legged, hard enough to hurt, and everybody whooped again; and she walked haughtily away up the street, forgetting about the streetcar, "mad as a hornet!" as his father exclaimed in delight; and there was Charlie, flat on his bottom on the sidewalk, and the way he looked, kind of sickly and disgusted, you could see that he suddenly remembered those eggs, and suddenly you remembered them too. The way his face looked, with the lip wrinkled off the teeth and the sickly little smile, it made you feel just the way those broken eggs must feel against your seat, as queer and awful as that time in the white pekay suit, when it ran down out of the pants-legs and showed all over your stockings and you had to walk home that way with people looking; and Rufus' father nearly tore his head off laughing and so did everybody else, and Rufus was sorry for Charlie, having been so recently in a similar predicament, but the contagion of laughter was too much for him, and he laughed too. And then it was even funnier when Charlie very carefully got himself up from the sidewalk, with that sickly look even worse on his face, and put his cane under one arm, and began to pick at his pants, front and back, very carefully, with his little fingers crooked, as if it were too dirty to touch, picking the sticky cloth away from his skin. Then he reached behind him and took out the wet bag of broken eggs and opened it and peered in; and took out a broken egg and pulled the shell disgustedly apart, letting the elastic yolk slump from one half shell into the other, and dropped it, shuddering. Then he peered in again and fished out a whole egg, all slimy with broken yolk, and polished it off carefully on his sleeve, and looked at it, and wrapped it in his dirty handkerchief, and put it carefully into the vest pocket of his little coat. Then he whipped out his cane from under his armpit and took command of it again, and with a final look at everybody, still sickly but at the same time cheerful, shrugged his shoulders and turned his back and scraped backward with his big shoes at the broken shells and the slimy bag, just like a dog, and looked back at the mess (everybody laughed again at that) and started to walk away, bending his cane deep with every shuffle, and squatting deeper, with his knees wider apart, than ever before, constantly picking at the seat of his pants with his left hand, and shaking one foot, then the other, and once gouging deep into his seat and then pausing and shaking his whole body, like a wet dog, and then walking on; while the screen shut over his small image a sudden circle of darkness: then the player-piano changed its tune, and the ads came in motionless color. They sat on into the William S. Hart feature to make sure why he had killed the man with the fancy vest—it was as they had expected by her frightened, pleased face after the killing; he had insulted a girl and cheated her father as well—and Rufus' father said, "Well, reckon this is where we came in," but they watched him kill the man all over again; then they walked out.

It was full dark now, but still early; Gay Street was full of absorbed faces; many of the store windows were still alight. Plaster people, in ennobled postures, stiffly wore untouchably new clothes; there was even a little boy, with short, straight pants, bare knees and high socks, obviously a sissy: but he wore a cap, all the same, not a hat like a baby. Rufus' whole insides lifted and sank as he looked at the cap and he looked up at his father; but his father did not notice; his face was wrapped in good humor, the memory of Charlie. Remembering his rebuff of a year ago, even though it had been his mother, Rufus was afraid to speak of it. His father wouldn't mind, but she wouldn't want him to have a cap, yet. If he asked his father now, his father would say no, Charlie Chaplin was enough. He watched the absorbed faces pushing past each other and the great bright letters of the signs: "Sterchi's." "George's." I can read them now, he reflected. I even know how to say "Sturkeys." But he thought it best not to say so; he remembered how his father had said, "Don't you brag," and he had been puzzled and rather stupid in school for several days, because of the stern tone in his voice.

What was bragging? It was bad.

They turned aside into a darker street, where the fewer faces looked more secret, and came into the odd, shaky light of Market Square. It was almost empty at this hour, but here and there, along the pavement streaked with horse urine, a wagon stayed still, and low firelight shone through the white cloth shell stretched tightly on its hickory hoops. A dark-faced man leaned against the white brick wall, gnawing a turnip; he looked at them low, with sad, pale eyes. When Rufus' father raised his hand in silent greeting, he raised his hand, but less, and Rufus, turning, saw how he looked sorrowfully, somehow dangerously, after them. They passed a wagon in which a lantern burned low orange; there lay a whole family, large and small, silent, asleep. In the tail of one wagon a woman sat, her face narrow beneath her flare of sunbonnet, her dark eyes in its shade, like smudges of soot. Rufus' father averted his eyes and touched his straw hat lightly; and Rufus, looking back, saw how her dead eyes kept looking gently ahead of her.

"Well," his father said, "reckon I'll hoist me a couple."

They turned through the swinging doors into a blast of odor and sound. There was no music: only the density of bodies and of the smell of a market bar, of beer, whiskey and country bodies, salt and leather; no clamor, only the thick quietude of crumpled talk. Rufus stood looking at the light on a damp spittoon and he heard his father ask for whiskey, and knew he was looking up and down the bar for men he might know. But they seldom came from so far away as the Powell River Valley; and Rufus soon realized that his father had found, tonight, no one he knew. He looked up his father's length and watched him bend backwards tossing one off in one jolt in a lordly manner, and a moment later heard him say to the man next him, "That's my boy"; and felt a warmth of love. Next moment he felt his father's hands under his armpits, and he was lifted, high, and seated on the bar, looking into a long row of huge bristling and bearded red faces. The eyes of the men nearest him were interested, and kind; some of them smiled; further away, the eyes were impersonal and questioning, but now even some of these began to smile. Somewhat timidly, but feeling assured that this father was proud of him and that he was liked, and liked these men, he smiled back; and suddenly many of the men laughed. He was disconcerted by their laughter and lost his smile a moment; then, realizing it was friendly, smiled again; and again they laughed. His father smiled at him. "That's my boy," he said warmly. "Six years old, and he can already read like I couldn't read when I was twice his age."

Rufus felt a sudden hollowness in his voice, and all along the bar, and in his own heart. But how does he fight, he thought. You don't brag about smartness if your son is brave. He felt the anguish of shame, but his father did not seem to notice, except that as suddenly as he had lifted him up to the bar, he gently lifted him down again. "Reckon I'll have another," he said, and drank it more slowly; then, with a few good nights, they went out.

His father proffered a Life Saver, courteously, man to man; he took it with a special sense of courtesy. It sealed their contract. Only once had his father felt it necessary to say to him, "I wouldn't tell your mama, if I were you"; he had known, from then on, that he could trust Rufus; and Rufus had felt gratitude in this silent trust. They walked away from Market Square, along a dark and nearly empty street, sucking their Life Savers; and Rufus' father reflected, without particular concern, that Life Savers were not quite life saver enough; he had better play very tired tonight, and turn away the minute they got in bed.

The deaf and dumb asylum was deaf and dumb, his father observed very quietly, as if he were careful not to wake it, as he always did on these evenings; its windows showed black in its pale brick, as the nursing woman's eyes, and it stood deep and silent among the light shadows of its trees. Ahead, Asylum Avenue lay bleak beneath its lamps. Latticed in pawnshop iron, an old saber caught the glint of a street lamp, a mandolin's belly glowed. In a closed drug store stood Venus de Milo, her golden body laced in elastic straps. The stained glass of the L&N Depot smoldered like an exhausted butterfly, and at the middle of the viaduct they paused to inhale the burst of smoke from a switch engine which passed under; Rufus, lifted, the cinders stinging his face, was grateful no longer to feel fear at this suspension over the tracks and the powerful locomotives. Far down the yard, a red light flicked to green; a moment later, they heard the thrilling click. It was ten-seven by the depot clock. They went on, more idly than before.

If I could fight, thought Rufus. If I were brave; he would never brag how I could read: Brag. Of course. "Don't you brag." That was it. What it meant. Don't brag you're smart if you're not brave. You've got nothing to brag about. Don't you brag.

The young leaves of Forest Avenue wavered against street lamps and they approached their corner.

It was a vacant lot, part rubbed bare clay, part over-grown with weeds, rising a little from the sidewalk. A few feet in from the sidewalk there was a medium-sized tree and, near enough to be within its shade in daytime, an outcrop of limestone like a great bundle of dirty laundry. If you sat on a certain part of it the trunk of the tree shut off the weak street lamp a block away, and it seemed very dark. Whenever they walked downtown and walked back home, in the evenings, they always began to walk more slowly, from about the middle of the viaduct, and as they came near this corner they walked more slowly still, but with purpose; and paused a moment, at the edge of the sidewalk; then, without speaking, stepped into the dark lot and sat down on the rock, looking out over the steep face of the hill and at the lights of North Knoxville. Deep in the valley an engine coughed and browsed; couplings settled their long chains, and the empty cars sounded like broken drums. A man came up the far side of the street, walking neither slow nor fast, not turning his head, as he paused, and quite surely not noticing them; they watched him until he was out of sight, and Rufus felt, and was sure that his father felt, that though there was no harm in the man and he had as good a right as they did to be there, minding his own business, their journey was interrupted from the moment they first saw him until they saw him out of sight. Once he was out of sight they realized more pleasure in their privacy than before; they really relaxed in it. They looked across the darkness at the lights of North Knoxville. They were aware of the quiet leaves above them, and looked into them and through them. They looked between the leaves into the stars. Usually on these evening waits, or a few minutes before going on home, Rufus' father smoked a cigarette through, and when it was finished, it was time to get up and go on home. But this time he did not smoke. Up to recently he had always said something about Rufus' being tired, when they were still about a block away from the corner; but lately he had not done so, and Rufus realized that his father stopped as much because he wanted to, as on Rufus' account. He was just not in a hurry to get home, Rufus realized; and, far more important, it was clear that he liked to spend these few minutes with Rufus. Rufus had come recently to feel a quiet kind of anticipation of the corner, from the moment they finished crossing the viaduct; and, during the ten to twenty minutes they sat on the rock, a particular kind of contentment, unlike any other that he knew. He did not know what this was, in words or ideas, or what the reason was; it was simply all that he saw and felt. It was, mainly, knowing that his father, too, felt a particular kind of contentment, here, unlike any other, and that their kinds of contentment were much alike, and depended on each other. Rufus seldom had at all sharply the feeling that he and his father were estranged, yet they must have been, and he must have felt it, for always during these quiet moments on the rock a part of his sense of complete contentment lay in the feeling that they were reconciled, that there was really no division, no estrangement, or none so strong, anyhow, that it could mean much, by comparison with they unity that was so firm and assured, here. He felt that although his father loved their home and loved all of them, he was more lonely than the contentment of this family love could help; that it even increased his loneliness, or made it hard for him not to be lonely. He felt that sitting out here, he was not lonely; or if he was, that he felt on good terms with the loneliness; that he was a homesick man, and that here on the rock, though he might be more homesick than ever, he was well. He knew that a very important part of his well-being came of staying a few minutes away from home, very quietly, in the dark, listening to the leaves if they moved, and looking at the stars; and that his own, Rufus' own presence, was fully as indispensable to this well-being. He knew that each of them knew of the other's well-being, and of the reasons for it, and knew how each depended on the other, how each meant more to the other, in this most important of all ways, than anyone or anything else in the world; and that the best of this well-being lay in this mutual knowledge, which was neither concealed nor revealed. He knew these things very distinctly, but not, of course, in any such way as we have of suggesting them in words. There were no words, or even ideas, or formed emotions, of the kind that have been suggested here, no more in the man than in the boy child. These realizations moved clearly through the senses, the memory, the feelings, the mere feeling of the place they paused at, about a quarter of a mile from home, on a rock under a stray tree that had grown in the city, their feet on undomesticated clay, facing north through the night over the Southern Railway tracks and over North Knoxville, towards the deeply folded small mountains and the Powell River Valley, and above them, the trembling lanterns of the universe, seeming so near, so intimate, that when air stirred the leaves and their hair, it seemed to be the breathing, the whispering of the stars. Sometimes on these evenings his father would hum a little and the humming would break open into a word or two, but he never finished even a part of a tune, for silence was even more pleasurable, and sometimes he would say a few words, of very little consequence, but would never seek to say much, or to finish what he was saying, or to listen for a reply; for silence again was even more pleasurable. Sometimes, Rufus had noticed, he would stroke the wrinkled rock and press his hand firmly against it; and sometimes he would put out his cigarette and tear and scatter it before it was half finished. But this time he was much quieter than ordinarily. They slackened their walking a little sooner than usual and walked a little more slowly, without a word, to the corner; and hesitated, before stepping off the sidewalk into the clay, purely for the luxury of hesitation; and took their place on the rock without breaking silence. As always, Rufus' father took off his hat and put it over the front of his bent knee, and as always, Rufus imitated him, but this time his father did not roll a cigarette. They waited while the man came by, intruding on their privacy, and disappeared, as someone nearly always did, and then relaxed sharply into the pleasure of their privacy; but this time Rufus' father did not hum, nor did he say anything, nor even touch the rock with his hand, but sat with his hands hung between his knees and looked out over North Knoxville, hearing the restive assemblage of the train; and after there had been silence for a while, raised his head and looked up into the leaves and between the leaves into the broad stars, not smiling, but with his eyes more calm and grave and his mouth strong and more quiet, than Rufus had ever seen his eyes and his mouth; and as he watched his father's face, Rufus felt his father's hand settle, without groping or clumsiness, on the top of his bare head; it took his forehead and smoothed it, and pushed the hair backward from his forehead, and held the back of his head while Rufus pressed his head backward against the firm hand, and, in reply to that pressure, clasped over his right ear and cheek, over the whole side of the head, and drew Rufus' head quietly and strongly against the sharp cloth that covered his father's body, through which Rufus could feel the breathing ribs; then relinquished him, and Rufus sat upright, while the hand lay strongly on his shoulder, and he saw that his father's eyes had become still more clear and grave and that the deep lines around his mouth were satisfied; and looked up at what his father was so steadily looking at, at the leaves which silently breathed and at the stars which beat like hearts. He heard a long, deep sigh break from his father, and then his father's abrupt voice: "*Well . . .*" and the hand lifted from him and they both stood up. The rest of the way home they did not speak, or put on their hats. When he was nearly asleep Rufus heard once more the crumpling of freight cars, and deep in the night he heard the crumpling of subdued voices and the words, "Naw: I'll probly be back before they're asleep"; then quick feet creaking quietly downstairs. But by the time he heard the creaking and departure of the Ford, he was already so deeply asleep that it seemed only a part of a dream, and by next morning, when his mother explained to them why his father was not at breakfast, he had so forgotten the words and the noises that years later, when he remembered them, he could never be sure that he was not making them up.

George Scarbrough

(1915–   )

Born to a sharecropping family in Patty, Tennessee, on October 20, 1915, George Scarbrough describes himself as an early, avid reader. He attended the University of Tennessee from 1935 to 1936 and the University of the South at Sewanee, Tennessee, from 1942 to 1943. In 1947 he was graduated with a B.A. from Lincoln Memorial University in Harrogate, Tennessee. In 1954 he received the M.A. from the University of Tennessee.

Scarbrough's poetry includes *Tellico Blue* (1948); *The Course Is Upward* (1951); *Summer So-Called* (1956); *New and Selected Poems* (1977); and *Invitation to Kim* (1989). His novel *A Summer Ago* was published in 1986.

Scarbrough lives and writes in Oak Ridge, Tennessee.

The Winter Mole

Behind me in my tract, reamed from the southern
slope, the mole freezes, slowly. It is snowing.
My horses turn dappled shoulders at the end of
furrows black as the tarpaper roof on my
house there, below me, in the swale. My house is
stubborn. It floats there in the winding snow
like a fly stuck in a glass of milk. I am happy.
I know black is hotter than white, and white is
colder than black. And I am cold, so very cold.
But I am also delighted with myself, being
comfortable with small truths. The smaller the
better. For instance, the off-horse relieves
himself. Piss, but he is beautiful, straddling
his streaked hams to make water! Piss is
beautiful, a stinking hot straw-lemon in the
odorless snow. We wait, his mate and I, in the
vast politeness engendered, not by great cold
but by great horses, for his suggestion to work.
Sanctioned by him, we are, pissing, every whit as
beautiful as he. It is beautiful to be doing the
same thing. Finished, we step on, round and
round the shining hole where my house is, in
ever-narrowing gyres bringing a black relief to
the captured fly. Such patent counterpoint as
the whirling snow, that does not fall from the
invisible sky but rises centrifugally from the
black-eyed swale, is an aspect of truth I can
labor by, a minuscule verity my mind can ingest
without strain or torpor. My mind balks at the
warmer fact of a blind pocket of earth. Too much
of implication denies the act of inference. This
restraint is my salvation. The smooth landfall
of my art, the spinning reference of my dream,
the wild convolution of a season made for a close
port of call—these are the matters I can speak
to. Not even in my coldest reverie will the great
icy point of a plow depend into my sleepingroom,
under my black roof hang the glittering stalactite
of a truth larger than these; never, with groaning
speed, drag from my walls the roots of shoring
weeds. O I am blessed! Oceanic ruin of lapping
light and sparkle will never interrupt the long
run of my peace, nor alter my blind content. I
was born for the less imposing certainties, and
am acclimatized this noon to dapper fields, and
furrows that run out in sweet procession, shorter
and shorter, to the end of light.

Death Is a Short Word

Like a sparrow sitting in a wide walk,
I myself grew small and precise inside
In exact proportion to how much he died;
And it was thus it affected my talk.

For if he sank and wrestled in a sound,
I said immaculately thrifty words,
The beautiful, voweled speeches of birds
That love short sound,

As if in the projection of clean speech,
The bright impossible face of death
Was set backward by my careful breath,
Him I retrieved, restored. But let him reach

Pertness again, be lively, learn to smile
In some way I remembered, order died
And my amazing tongue became untied
And roar arose and lingered for a while,

Till he subsided into pale and pallid,
Closing his shining eyes: then I perceived
The catastrophic tongue again believed
Only the monosyllable finally valid.

Blackberry Winter

In the valley below there is no wind.
I know it is so there, for I came
Through still, blue air upward this quarter hour.
There is no wind there, only a blue mist rising.

Here where I stand to halt the first clean lover,
A white wind blows among the berry flowers,
Out of the north a wind with a drop of rain is blowing.
But the chimney swifts are glad with the spring and dusk.

Swung to the fine rib-coils, a cup of salt and water,
Ready as new nests and brave as wing-swept ground,
Teases the honest mind with firm, delineate dreaming.
What love is there in all that country, wonder?

The scented musk of the flower is odd as prayer.
But wind, involved with rain, springs tall and lonely
And black as ripeness to this novel land.
How slowly does the blue heart of the valley rise!

In the valley below there is no wind.
I know it is so there. . . . Where I stand
A white wind blows and chimney swifts are flying,
No feet but mine impede the berry flowers.

Gurney Norman

(1937–   )

Gurney Norman was born on July 22, 1937, in Grundy, Virginia. His family moved to Allais, Kentucky, when he was a small child. He was graduated from the University of Kentucky in 1959 and studied creative writing at Stanford University on a Stegner Fellowship during 1960 and 1961.

Norman's first novel, *Divine Right's Trip* (1972), was published originally in *The Last Whole Earth Catalog.* His second book, *Kinfolks* (1977), is a collection of short stories. Two of these stories have been made into films.

Norman lives in Lexington, Kentucky, where he teaches at the University of Kentucky.

The Revival

Wilgus found his Uncle Delmer sitting on the couch in the living room, staring at the wavy lines and falling snow on the silent television screen. Delmer held an open Bible in his lap and a king-size beer in his hand.

"Delmer old buddy, how you doing?" Wilgus asked as he sat down next to his uncle.

Delmer waited a long time before he answered. Without taking his eyes off the TV screen he said, "I ain't doing no good."

"You know who I am, don't you?"

Slowly, like an old turtle, Delmer turned his head. After studying his nephew's face a minute he said, "You're Wilgus, ain't you?"

Wilgus laughed and gave his uncle's knee a squeeze. "You're not as bad off as they said you were, Delmer."

But Delmer didn't laugh with Wilgus. He felt too awful to laugh. And he looked every bit as bad as he felt. Delmer was only forty-three, but after twenty-one straight days of hard drinking he looked like a sick old man. His eyes were red and rheumy. The flesh around his nose was moist and raw-looking. Apparently he hadn't shaved since he'd started drinking. His cheeks were covered by a scraggly gray beard. His hair lay across his head in a tangle of oily gray matted strings.

"I'm bad off, all right," Delmer sighed.

"Well," said Wilgus. "I'm glad to see you sitting up, anyhow. From what they all said, I was afraid I'd find you stretched out on the floor or something."

Delmer sipped his beer, then sipped it again, each time carefully returning the hand that held the can back to the arm rest of the old stuffed couch.

Delmer and Wilgus watched TV a while without saying anything. Finally Delmer looked at his nephew and said, "I guess you know I'm hell-bound, don't you?"

"No," said Wilgus. "I didn't know that."

"I am," said Delmer. "My soul's blacker'n a piece of coal."

"Aw, Delmer. You don't mean that."

Delmer's eyes filled up with tears as he said, "I'm afraid Jesus ain't going to let me in."

Delmer turned his head away so Wilgus wouldn't see his tears. In order to pretend he hadn't, Wilgus got to his feet and said, "It's cold in here, Delmer. I'm going to build us a fire."

Before he could build a fire Wilgus had to clean the ashes out of the bottom pan of the living room heater and carry them out to the ash pile in the back yard. While he was outside he split some kindling and filled a bucket with coal. As the wood and coal caught fire Wilgus went around the room picking up the empty beer cans and whiskey bottles that lay scattered across the floor and led away in trails toward the bedrooms and the kitchen. He filled a cardboard box five times with the litter, emptying it each time outside by the ash pile. By the time he'd swept the living room and kitchen floors the fire was going good in the heater and the room was beginning to warm.

"Delmer, how about something to eat?" Wilgus asked. "Little soup, or something."

Delmer shook his head forlornly.

"Food in your stomach might make you feel better."

"I don't *deserve* to feel no better," Delmer moaned. His voice collapsed in a fit of weeping as soon as the words were out of his mouth. He cried hard this time, not even trying to hide it. Wilgus turned and went back to the kitchen and began to rummage around for something to eat.

The only edible food in the house turned out to be a can of bean soup and two old heels of bread, plus a solitary beer in the far corner of the refrigerator. Looking around to be sure Delmer didn't see him, Wilgus opened the beer and took a drink. He hid the can under a paper bag next to the breadbox and sipped from it as he worked in the kitchen, cooking soup and washing dishes. When the soup was ready he poured two coffee cups full and carried them into the living room.

"Delmer, here's some hot soup if you want it."

Delmer was staring at the TV screen again. He seemed to have forgotten all about his nephew being there with him. The Bible lay open on his lap now, and his hand rested on the page as if he'd been tracing words with his finger. When Wilgus thrust the cup in front of his face, Delmer dropped his eyes to look at it. Carefully he closed the Bible and laid it on the couch next to his leg. Then he accepted the steaming cup of soup with both hands.

They sipped their soup without talking. When the broth was gone they ate the beans with spoons. Delmer ate a lot slower than Wilgus but gradually he got it all down. When Wilgus offered him a second cup and a piece of hard bread to go with it, he took it, dipped it into the soup, then bit off the soggy end and chewed it slowly. When he swallowed he looked across at Wilgus and said, "I guess you heard about Pauline leaving me."

"Yeah, I heard about that, Delmer."

"Just up and went," said Delmer. "Took the children, took her clothes. Gone!"

"How come 'em to leave, do you reckon?" asked Wilgus.

"Ay, Lord," Delmer sighed. "'Cause I'm so goddamn sorry, I reckon."

"You're not sorry, Delmer," said Wilgus.

"It's a punishment is what it is," said Delmer.

Wilgus asked Delmer who he thought was punishing him.

Delmer looked at his nephew through fresh tears. "God!" he said.

Wilgus scraped the remaining beans from his cup and ate them. As he stood up he said, "Well Delmer, I don't think God's going to punish you much longer. My feeling is, Pauline and the children'll be coming home before long. In fact, I wouldn't be surprised if they didn't come back some time tomorrow. The thing for me and you to do is clean the house up some before they get here. I've already started washing the dishes."

Wilgus took Delmer's empty cup and without further word went back to the kitchen where he went to work again on the great mound of dishes in the sink.

It took Delmer a full ten minutes to work his way off the couch and stagger into the kitchen to ask Wilgus what he'd said. He fell back twice, trying to rise. He finally had to get down on his knees and crawl along the floor a ways before he could maneuver his long body to a vertical position. But at last he made it. Supporting himself on the furniture as he walked, leaning against the walls and then the door frame at the entrance to the kitchen, Delmer at last arrived. His beer can was empty now, but he raised it to his lips and after blinking his eyes and stammering and stuttering awhile, he said, "What was that you said?"

"About what, Delmer?"

"About my wife Pauline."

"I just said she's coming home tomorrow, and me and you ought to straighten the house up some before she gets here."

"Coming here?"

"Yep. Be here in the morning. Going to bring the kids."

"Lord God." Delmer turned around and started back toward the couch in the living room. But half way there he turned again, nearly falling in the process, and went back to lean against the door frame.

"She ain't coming here?"

"Sure is," said Wilgus. "They'll all be here tomorrow."

"Lord God."

Delmer's face turned green as his beans bolted out of his stomach and flooded his throat and mouth. Pitching and falling, he lurched through the living room and down the short hallway to the bathroom, letting go of the beer can to hold both hands to his mouth as he ran. Some of the vomit went on the bathroom floor and some went down his shirt front. But most of it went in the commode as Delmer knelt in front of it and held his head close to the water.

Wilgus went on washing dishes as long as Delmer was authentically vomiting. But when his uncle's dry heaves started he went to the bathroom and without a word set about scrubbing the dirty ring from the sides of the tub.

"Lorrd Gahd!" Delmer wailed between heaves.

"You'll be all right," Wilgus reassured him.

"Oh Lorrd Jesus Gahd!"

As the tub filled, Wilgus helped his uncle to his feet and out of his filthy clothes. All Delmer could say as he stepped into the steaming water was "Lorrd Gahd!"

But as Delmer began to wash himself in the tub, he found other things to say. "My children's like little angels to me," he said.

"They're good kids," said Wilgus.

"But what have they got for a daddy but a damned old devil."

"You're not a devil," said Wilgus. "You're a good man."

Wilgus was shampooing Delmer's hair now, scrubbing the scalp with his finger tips and running his fingers through the thickly lathered hair. The force of Wilgus' hands bent Delmer's head over until his chin nearly touched his chest. Yelling in order to be heard above the running water, Delmer shrieked, "I been reading the Bible!"

"I noticed you had it open," Wilgus yelled back.

"You know what it's been telling me to do?" Delmer yelled.

"What's that, Delmer?"

"It's been telling me to straighten up and do right!"

"That sounds like pretty good advice," said Wilgus.

He maneuvered his uncle to the front of the tub where he rinsed his head under the faucet. As Wilgus soaped his hair again and went on scrubbing, Delmer yelled, "I mean, a man's got to do *right*."

"He's got to try to, anyway," said Wilgus.

"If a man don't do right, he can't get no peace. Ain't that right?"

"That's right," said Wilgus.

He held Delmer's head under the faucet again. When he emerged, looking like a wet pup, Delmer looked up at Wilgus and said, "You know Jesus is the Prince of Peace, don't you?"

"Yeah, I know that," said Wilgus.

Wilgus had turned away to find Delmer's shaving gear. The razor was so full of gunk it took him a few minutes to get it clean in the sink, and to find a new blade. While he searched Delmer exclaimed, "Jesus offered peace to anybody that's got sense enough to take it, and brother I'll tell you now, them that don't take it's lost, ain't that right?"

"That's right," said Wilgus.

"I mean, they're gone!"

Wilgus covered Delmer's face with shaving cream. Yelling through the white foam, Delmer said, "I mean, you get to the forks of the road, you got to go one way or the other, you can't go but one way. You go down one road toward the devil, or down the other where Jesus is, ain't that right?"

"Amen," said Wilgus.

"Amen is right," said Delmer. "The devil's down one road, walking around like an old lion, ready to eat you. It says that in the Bible. But down the other road is Jesus, calling out to us to come home. He's *calling* us, brother. And when you feel the call you either go or you don't go, ain't that right?"

"That's right," said Wilgus. "Hold still now, I'm getting ready to shave off that beard."

Wilgus shaved one side of Delmer's face, then twisted his head around so he could shave the other.

"I've been hearing the call," said Delmer. "But I've just been too drunk to *answer*."

"Well, you're going to sober up now," said Wilgus.

"I'm going to sober up, and I'm going to start doing right," said Delmer. "Yes, sir. I am."

After Wilgus finished the shave he helped Delmer out of the tub and handed him a towel. While his uncle dried himself Wilgus looked for clean underwear in the bedroom. He found some white longhandles in the bottom of the bureau and carried them in to Delmer. Dressed in them, his wet hair combed, his face smooth and shiny clean, Delmer looked like a brand new man.

But a very tired new man. His eyes were drooping shut as he waited for Wilgus to put clean sheets on his bed. As Wilgus tucked him in, Delmer blinked and moved his lips to say something. But sleep was coming over him too fast for him to do more than mutter a faint amen.

Wilgus said amen.

Then he went in the living room to telephone his Aunt Pauline, and try to persuade her to come on home.

Harriette Simpson Arnow

(1908–1986)

Born on July 7, 1908, in Wayne County, Kentucky, Harriette Simpson Arnow enrolled at Berea College in Kentucky in 1926 and attended through 1928. Following two years of teaching, she returned to school at the University of Louisville, where her writing was encouraged. After graduating in 1930, she taught for two years and then moved to Cincinnati in 1934 to pursue a writing career.

Arnow's first novel, *Mountain Path*, was published in 1936. In 1939 she married Harold B. Arnow. Five years later they moved to Detroit, where Arnow worked for the *Detroit Times*. Later moving to a farm near Ann Arbor, Michigan, they became the parents of two children, Marcella and Thomas. *The Dollmaker* (1954) established Arnow's reputation and became a bestseller, receiving in 1955 the award from the Friends of American Writers. The novel was made into a 1983 film starring Jane Fonda.

Arnow's additional books include *Hunter's Horn* (1949); *Seedtime on the Cumberland* (1960); *Flowering of the Cumberland* (1963); *The Weedkiller's Daughter* (1970); *The Kentucky Trace: A Novel of the American Revolution* (1974); and *Old Burnside* (1977). Arnow died on March 22, 1986.

from *The Dollmaker*

Chapter Twenty-Six

There was disappointment in the alley when, after all their troubles with her children, Mrs. Daly did not get her picture in the paper. It was homecoming time for day-shift workers when a blurry-voiced, too stately stepping Mr. Daly, dressed in his Sunday best, announced to all who wanted to hear that he was on his way to see his wife, who had been delivered of a daughter in St. Theresa's Hospital at two fifty-seven that afternoon. He had gone high-stepping it out of the alley and, according to Mrs. Bommarita, who'd listened through her wall, he hadn't got home until almost three in the morning; she knew because he'd wakened Maggie, and Maggie's crying by the wall had wakened her.

However, next morning, when Maggie stopped by on her way home from mass— she was staying out of school to mind the children but had to leave them long enough for mass—she was her usual smiling self as she offered Gertie a fifty-cent ticket to a bingo party with door prizes of china dinner plates.

Gertie shook her weary head against the dishes, and closed her door with relief. It seemed that she had run into the alley a thousand times to see about the little Dalys, two of whom had gone several blocks as stowaways on a milk truck and might have been gone all day had not the driver discovered them and hastily as well as angrily returned them to the alley.

She forgot about the Dalys when her own came home for lunch. Clytie was angry, splattered from head to foot with mud. "An, boy, did them guys laugh when they whooshed right by th curb in that ole clunker an made us girls jump an scream."

Worse than Clytie's trouble was Gertie's realization that Cassie was no place in sight. Frightened, she had run down the alley hunting, before she found her fooling along by the railroad fence. "Your dinner'ull be cold," she called in sharp scolding.

"I ain't hungry, Mom. Cain't I jist stay outside?"

Gertie, more troubled than angry now, hurried up to her, and saw that she had been crying, and at her, "What's th matter, honey?" Cassie dissolved in weak hopeless tears, such as she had never shed.

Gertie picked her up as if she were a baby, and learned as they walked home that: "I wet on myself, Mom. I done it right where all th youngens could see." And the shamed and sobbing whisper, coming up from the face buried on her shoulder: "An all th youngens they laughed at me. Don't tell Clytie, Mom."

"Lots a little youngens has done sich at school. Don't feel so bad now, even if that ole Miz Huffacre did talk mean to you. One a these days . . ." She shut her mouth into a straight hard line. Promises, that was all she'd ever given Reuben.

"Oh, Miz Huffacre," Cassie said, "she said lots a little youngens had done sich when they didn't feel good er somethen. But, Mom, she asked me did you git her note. Mom, do you recken she's mad at me?" And Cassie cried again.

She continued to cry with a weary sobbing as Gertie changed her clothing, telling a little lie to the others that Cassie had fallen into a puddle. She was so miserable, not wanting any lunch, that Gertie picked her up and for want of a rocking chair sat on a straight-backed chair in the living room, and tipping back and forth, sang one of Cassie's favorites: "'I've reached the land of corn and wine; and all its riches freely mine; here shines undimmed one blissful day . . .'" Her voice, at first low, grew louder as the child snuggled against her, drowsing with half closed eyes, and on the chorus, "'Oh, Beulah land, sweet Beulah land,'" her voice was forgetful, booming out as in the old days.

Enoch, eating a sandwich in snatches crouched by the radio, began complaining: "Mom, you're a maken so much racket I cain't hear Silver Sam. Sing in her bedroom."

"I'd mebbe wake Sophronie er your pop."

"Well, sing in mine."

"Victor's got to have his sleep, too."

Clytie was calling in a shus-shushing, chiding voice: "Mom, you're already a waken Pop. I can hear him a groanen."

Gertie sat for an instant like one ready to rise. Let Clovis wake up and go now and see Miss Huffacre and learn what was this trouble with Cassie. She looked at the child, and began rocking her again, soundlessly, moving only her body now. Her face down in the crook of her own big arm looked so little and pale and tired, or lonesome, more lonesome than tired, she decided. Maybe she'd doze off and wake up happier; but if they all started talking about Miss Huffacre now she'd start crying again. Gertie continued to rock silently, looking down at the drowsing child, and wanting nothing except the privilege of holding her. But in only a few minutes Cassie came wide awake and looked wildly about her. She slid from her mother's lap, yawning, but asking, "Can I go outside, Mom?"

Gertie cleaned her tear-smudged glasses. "Whyn't you stay inside, mebbe take a little nap? It's so cold and raw outside, like a January thaw back home; er if," she coaxed, "you cain't sleep, you could show me how good you can read. You ain't read for me in days and days."

Cassie shook her head, glanced at the block of wood. "That wouldn't be no fun. I hafta play. Cain't I, Mom?"

Gertie pondered, studying her; maybe a little running about would make her hungry, take her mind from what had happened at school. She said nothing as Cassie struggled into her snow pants, put on her boots, hurrying a little, her tired sleepy face determined, hard-pressed somehow, like Sophronie's on her overtime days, when she slept too late and had to fight the clock until time to go to work again.

Gertie, busy with a washing, saw her in the alley now and then, sometimes with Amos, but mostly alone, playing the game of airplane she had learned in kindergarten or singing little songs. The afternoon shift of school was over, and still Cassie played, in front of her own door now, where she and the smaller Dalys and Georgie built a school. Cassie became Miss Huffacre, the side of the coalhouse a blackboard, a piece of kindling wood a pointer. Cassie would point to a knothole and cry: "That word is 'skip.' Now, children, show what it tells you to do." There were many words: "run," "jump," "skip," "sing"; and the children amid much laughter and many shouts did the bidding of each word.

The fun attracted a little crowd; even Wheateye, eating what looked to be a quarter of a large-sized head of cabbage, watched critically for a time, but at last cried: "That ain't no blackboard. An yu ain't no teacher—cuckoo."

The bigger Dalys took up the cry of, "Cuckoo, cuckoo," and Cassie, after standing a moment, red-faced and silent, Miss Huffacre's smile frozen on her face, dropped the kindling-wood pointer and ran away. Wheateye immediately seized it, and holding it in one hand and the cabbage in the other, continued the school, amid much chewing of and at times strangling on cabbage.

The Dalys, weary of being pupils, repeated Wheateye's cry of, "That ain't no blackboard, yu cuckoo kid," turning it on Wheateye, who quickly crammed the remainder of the cabbage into her mouth, and so having both hands free, bopped the kindling-wood pointer hard against the seat of Jimmy Daly's pants, and then on the stove wrecker's head.

"I'm the principal, sillies," she yelled, as they turned in retreat.

"Yu don't know nutten," Jimmy cried. "Youse don't learn nutten ata ole public school but communism. Da good sisters, dey hitcha ona hands. Come on, kids; da devil'll gitcha fu goen tuda public school—cuckoo—crazy."

"Yu're expelled," Wheateye cried. "Git out," she screamed, ducking dirt from Jimmy, a tin can from the stove wrecker, and at the same time getting in two good licks with the kindling wood, good enough that the Dalys retreated. She saw the Miller children of kindergarten and first-grade size, and called to them to come and play school, then looked about calling: "Cassie, hey, Cassie, come on an play. Yu can be teacher an I'll be the principal. An bring yu girl friend, what's her name—Callie Lou. She can be th bad kid, an we'll make her stand in a corner like we done th other day. An these Millers can be th good kids. Ana Dalys can be th real bad kids wot comes an breaks th winder lights an throws th books ona floor when we're gone. Come on, Cassie."

Cassie's smile at being called back to play was like a light across her eyes. Her mittened hand went out, seizing the witch child's hand, and her voice held the old burbling. "Come on, yu mean youngen. Miss Huffacre's gonna make yu stand in the corner."

Jimmy Daly watched her jealously. "Nuts inu bean, hillbilly. Talks to herself. Nuts inu bean."

Georgie, coming down his steps, his vigor renewed with a vitamin pill, a rest period, and the prescribed midafternoon snack, took up the cry, "Nuts inu bean."

Cassie dropped her hand and stood red-faced, looking uncertainly at Wheateye, who was only now swallowing the last of her mouthful of cabbage, tossing her head, wriggling her neck to make it go down in a hurry. The cabbage down, she twirled her kindling wood and cried to Cassie: "Run, honey, run. Them wild mean kids wanta hurt yu little kid. Yu gotta stand up fu yer kid."

The hand flew out, protective now, but Cassie, when almost opposite the door, looked up and saw Gertie watching, listening. Her mother was stern-faced and frowning, for she had been wondering for the last five minutes if she oughtn't to tell Wheateye to be quiet, or else go somewhere else to play. They'd waken Victor again—and Clovis, too.

Cassie's hand dropped, her smile faded, as her mother's glance touched her, and ever an obedient child, she mumbled to Wheateye, her voice choked and guilty, "They ain't no Callie Lou." She ran then, and did not stop until she was out of sight around Max's corner.

No one came to Wheateye's calling, "Come back, come back; we gotta have Callie Lou."

Gertie went back into her kitchen to turn down the gas flame under the boiling beans. She bumped her head on the high shelf as she turned, but never noticed it for thinking on Callie Lou, smiling. All this business of doing away with Callie Lou had been a mistake. Suppose Miss Huffacre had heard the child talking to herself and felt about it the way Mrs. Anderson did? Cassie could have Callie Lou at home. She, Gertie, couldn't kill her when already she lived in the alley.

She waited a moment on the steps, watching for Cassie, and when she did not come went to the end of the building and around Max's unit hunting her, smiling. She'd call out, "Lady, lady, bring that black-headed child in out a this raw cold," or some such, and Cassie couldn't talk for giggling, and then she'd feel so good she'd eat a great big supper.

Cassie was not in the paper-littered water-soaked strip of earth between the front of their building and the front of the next, nor was she by the railroad fence. Gertie stood in the alley by the fence and looked about her, uncertain whether to go looking in the next alley or back to the other side of her own building. Quick-footed Cassie had most likely run all the way around as she often did. She wouldn't stay here in all this smoke, for on the other side of the fence a train stood on the side track. The switch engine was still in front of a long string of boxcars, broken apart at the through street. It had dropped off cars for the steel mill and was waiting, with smoke and steam flying up, to back across the street and pick up the caboose and the other cars.

The purring, steaming engine was far away and made but little sound. Fainter, like the buzzing of a horsefly, was the buzzing of an airplane, still high above, and almost hidden from sight, but she knew from experience that it would in a moment come in low for a landing in swooping circles of head-hurting sound. She savored for a moment the silence, when all Detroit seemed sleeping, and even the big engine was like something sighing and whispering in its sleep.

She had walked a few steps over the muddy gravel, still smiling thinking on how pleased Cassie would be to have Callie Lou back again, when she heard the word, hardly more than a louder whisper of the engine, but Cassie's voice, soft, yet warning, "Callie Lou." Gertie stopped dead still, puzzled. Memories of old tales of witches and warnings of names called down from the sky or up from a river came back to her. The wind, she'd always said, for the wind in leaves and by water had many voices. There was a little wind today, but the brassy-voiced Detroit wind could never whisper so. Machinery? A radio? She was still an instant longer, listening, looking about her, then walked on, for the airplane had swooped, circling, drowning even the sound of the engine.

She turned slowly about for a last look around before starting home. In turning, her glance, moving swiftly by the railroad fence—for Cassie was plainly not by it—stopped, held by some strangeness about a crack between two of the eight-foot perpendicular boards—red-colored it had looked to be. It was a narrow crack, but wide enough for her to see, with one eye against it, Cassie's red babushka on the other side, so close she could have touched it could her glance have been her hand. Cassie stood between the main line and the fence, one hand holding Callie Lou's hand. Her head was turned sideways, cheek toward Gertie while her lips moved, laughing as she shook her head in some argument with Callie Lou, then nodded toward the boxcar on the next track.

Gertie called to her, "Git away, Cassie, git away," but the airplane kept her words from Cassie as if she'd been a mile away. Her calling more a screaming now, she could only watch the moment's argument that followed. Cassie shook her head violently and even shook the stubborn Callie Lou, who yielded at last and let Cassie step onto the shining rail of the main track. She stepped off it onto the crosstie and then walked the few steps to the next rail, on which she stood for an instant, looking down at the silvery shine below her boots.

She did not stop again until she had reached the boxcar on the next track, dull red, empty, with its sliding door invitingly open. Still swinging onto Callie Lou, she stood on tiptoe, peeping, but it was too high for much looking into, though she could touch it with the tips of her fingers. She found the great wheel, its shining roundness, almost as high as her head, more interesting. And unable to hear the terror-filled voice on the other side of the fence: "Cassie, git back! Thet car's on a engine. It could move!" she put her hand on it.

Once she turned and looked about her, her eyes for an instant seemed like on the crack behind which Gertie pounded, but the airplane was low now, smothering the world with its crying. Cassie looked up at it briefly, for she hated the noise, then turned, put her hands on the edge of the boxcar by the wheel, arched her body as much as possible, shielding, Gertie realized, the smaller, more timid Callie Lou from the sound.

Gertie, still screaming, whirled away from the crack. Somewhere there was the hole through which Cassie had crawled. She hadn't time to run to the through street and around. She ran up and down, searching, calling, beating on the fence. She found the hole at last, so small and low she had twice run past it. She shoved her head through, though its lowness forced her to her knees; but heave with her shoulders, claw with her hands behind her as she would, she could not get her wide shoulders through, for the hole was the width of a board, broken off at the bottom and no higher than the stringer to which it was nailed on the other side.

She could only try to send her screams above the airplane that circled ever lower. Cassie had dropped to her knees on the end of a crosstie under the boxcar, and was holding out her hand, her lips moving in some reassuring burbling chuckle, her hair fallen across her eyes, as with a reassuring smile to Callie Lou she pointed to the boxcar above her head.

Gertie screamed more loudly, certain at last that Cassie had heard her, for the child seemed suddenly afraid, and sprang up. She looked once toward the fence, then down the track toward something Gertie had neither seen nor heard. It was the through train for which the switch engine had been waiting. Cassie stood an instant, her mouth open, her startled eyes bright with fright. Then, swiftly, she dropped to the ground, and as if hunting sanctuary from the oncoming train, crawled onto the rail and sat huddled close to the great wheel, waiting, her eyes squinched, Callie Lou cradled in her arms.

Gertie jerked her head from the hole. Cassie could never hear in all the racket. Why hadn't she thought to throw something—a pebble, a stick, anything would do to make her move away? She was little. She'd be safe between the trains. Why—why—hadn't she let Callie Lou live in the alley? Why hadn't she known that sooner or later she'd go away with Callie Lou? Why—why was there nothing to throw to make her move? The swampy earth held no rock—nothing. Callie Lou, you make her move. Feet away she saw a rusty tin can. She could jerk off her shoe quicker than she could run for the can. The can would have been quicker. The shoe was an oxford laced on her foot. Why hadn't she worn high-heeled pumps like Mrs. Bommarita? Cassie had always wanted her to wear high-heeled shiny shoes. She jerked and jerked, turned at last toward the low hole, the shoe in her hand. She'd have to take good aim to throw through that low hole sideways to hit Cassie, and not able to get her head and arm through at the same time.

She bent far down and threw, and for an instant saw Cassie. Her legs were now over the rail, as she tried to get as far as possible from the oncoming train. Then the train shot past her, but still Gertie screamed for a moment longer, her head through the hole again, her shoulders fighting the wood. She knew Cassie couldn't hear, but still she screamed: "Thet other train'ull move, too! Git *away*, honey! Git *between* em!"

She jerked her head back, turned, and ran down the alley toward the through-street railroad crossing. She had never run so slowly or so awkward seeming as in the one shoe. Her hair, jerked down from her struggles to get through the little hole, had fallen across her face. Blood oozed from her forehead, her neck, her shoulders, her ears, from her battle with the wood and her torn hands dripped more blood.

It was her eyes, she knew, made everything look blurry past the speeding train, like another train was moving on the other side, slowly, like the switching train. The switch engine tried to do as much as it could when another train was passing. Clovis had said that once when she complained because Cassie had to stand so long in the cold; but never so long as this while the train flew by. Something hit hard against her hip. She stared about her, unaware of pain, angry at being stopped. She saw the high dirt-spattered iron of a truck bumper, and wondered why it was there, and why did a red-faced man behind and above it glare down at her, his lips moving as if he yelled.

She turned to look at the train. Maybe if she looked away again it would be gone. Cassie had waited between the trains and would come running behind it. She would grab her up and carry her home, and they'd have school with Callie Lou and she'd send for ice cream for their supper.

There was a hard pull on her arm, and the same face that had glared at her was now looking up at her, the lips moving, but the eyes not hunting her eyes, fixed on the blood running down her coat. She realized even as she jerked her arm free that she had been out in the street running back and forth in front of the stopped cars. She ought to be ashamed acting so crazy, for Cassie would be all right. It was just that she had to be certain. She couldn't wait any longer. Why hadn't she thought of the place where the board fence stopped? It cornered so close to the tracts there was no room for a body to squeeze between it and a train. But she could crawl—there would be room between the fence and the wheels.

The man behind her was tearing her coat off, and around her there seemed suddenly a crowd of people, mostly children, but she was getting into the opening, like diving into a pool of noise. She could get through. Why hadn't she thought of it sooner? Then the last car shot past, and she sprang onto the track. Cassie would be on it—if she hadn't already gone back through the hole in the fence.

She was dazedly aware of cries and calls behind her, and from the other side of the fence, "Wotsa matter? Who?" But mostly, as she ran down the track, she was aware of silence. The airplanes were still, only one going high and far away with a faint moaning so that after the roaring of the through train the world seemed still, so still that if she listened hard she'd hear again the low-voiced, "Callie Lou," and with it the burbling laughter. The backward-moving switch engine rolled slowly, so very slowly it made but little noise. Somewhere close behind her were pounding feet and a voice insisting, "Easy now, da kid's gonna be awright."

Then the switch engine stopped with a jerk that sent shivering knocks through all the cars. A man leaped down from the engine, crying to someone between her and the through street, "Where, Chuck, where?"

She had come almost opposite the place where she had first seen Cassie, when the man who had cried out began running, his eyes fixed on something behind her. She turned and saw near the rail a child's boot, looked away from it, searching for Cassie.

The man's eyes, bulging, frightened, were fixed on nothing but the boot. She turned and stared at it again, a little boot that looked to be stuffed with something: torn cloth, oozing, soggy. She sprang toward it. The man behind her who had dragged her out of the street was crying, "No—no, lady—please, lady!"

She heard then the frightened whimper. Cassie was safe. She was scared, that was all. The blood-oozing boot had nothing to do with Cassie. She, the trainmen, and the truck driver dropped by the sound together, and under the train she saw Cassie, white-faced, strange-looking, whimpering little begging cries of "Mommie, Mommie." Cassie was alive, moving on her hands and knees. Many hands reached, and there was begging, "Please, lady." But Gertie's arms were longer than the men's and she caught Cassie by the shoulders, her hungry hands gripping, pulling. She was alive, alive.

The truck driver was whispering "Jesus," and lifting carefully with the tips of his gloved fingers something else from under the train that dragged after Cassie as Gertie lifted her out. Gertie did not look at the bloody dragging thing, but laid Cassie across her knees. She squatted a moment holding her, looked down into her face, white, the eyes wide, straining, hunting, perspiration like a rain on her forehead. Her eyes tried to hold Gertie's face, but the head kept flinging itself about like the arms, flailing, striking her mother's chest with aimless beatings, while she cried in a choked, unnatural voice, "It hurts, Mommie—oh, *Mommie!*"

The words ended in a gasping, inhuman scream, and Gertie sprang up, rocking her back and forth in her arms as she had done when she cried at noon; the twin streams of blood from the severed legs were like red fountains gushing down her apron, the blood-filled boot dangled, the toe turned backward knocking against her thigh.

Gertie looked once at the streams of blood, then dropped again to the ground, letting Cassie's head and shoulders fall into her lap while she caught the stubs of the legs, one in either hand, and sat holding them. She looked once at Cassie's white twisting face, touched now with blood from the frothing uplifted legs, then up at what seemed to be a whole forest of faces above her. "Hep me, somebody, hep me try an keep down th bleeden. We've got tu stop it."

There were cries and running behind her for cops, firemen, an ambulance; but no one stepped forward. The trainman's face was white, his glance unable to stay on the blood, spreading ever more over Cassie's body, congealing in bright lumps and sheets on Gertie's apron. He was not even able to look at Cassie's head, fallen backward across her mother's lap, the top brushing the cinders, twisting, writhing, the mouth open but no longer screaming, the whimper of "Mommie" muffled, as if she had been running. No, not running, that would never make Cassie lose her breath—laughing did it—gasping from laughter and chattering and running all at one time.

"Here, lemme." It was Victor, reaching for Cassie's legs. "Yu git up," he said. "Start moving, quick! Cops, ambulance, somebody gotta take yu quick tuda hospital."

Gertie held the child's body and Victor walked with her, holding the bloody stumps, one just below the knee, one just above, but even so the blood was still like brightly frothing fountains leaping over his hands.

Gertie tried to hurry, stumbling at times with eyes for nothing but Cassie, gasping more and more, no breath left now for screaming, each cry of "Mommie" shorter, lower than the last.

The railroad tracks and the sidewalk were black and thick with people; many turned pale and looked away; many stood on tiptoe hunting blood, but all were silent, moving back, making a lane for Victor and Gertie as they hurried through. There was soon, from somewhere, the same wild screaming that had come for Mrs. Daly. Gertie kept walking, hurrying, seemed like they walked forever to meet it, held up as it was by the train-bound traffic and the crowds of people.

She looked at the scout car surrounded by swarms of children, and shook her head, her voice thick. "We need a ambulance with that stuff like blood."

The man by the wheel in the scout car shook his head; the other, outside, pushed her a little. "If it's plasma yu mean, a ambulance wouldn't have it. Yu ain't got no time tu argue—you gotta git quick to da hospital." He helped her into the car, looked down at her feet as he did so, both bare now—the shoe she'd jerked first must have come off. "Yu gotta go all away downtown—s'emergency."

"I've got money," she cried, but they never seemed to hear her. She never looked at the dangling boot or the blood again, still bubbling up, but more slowly, between Victor's clenched, unmoving fingers. She had Cassie, her forever straggling hair over her arms, one hand with a mitten, one without.

They were all alone together. Seemed like the first time they had been alone, the two of them, since she'd made the golden doll by the Tipton spring. Cassie whimpered less and less; she was only gasping now, looking straight up, her eyes wide, frightened. Gertie looked into them, smiling, whispering: "You're goen to be all right, Cassie Marie. We'll set all day, Cassie Marie, an have school an tea parties when you're gitten well—an ever day an ever minnit you can play with Callie Lou."

James Still

(1906–   )

Born on July 16, 1906, in Lafayette, Alabama, James Still has lived in Hindman, Kentucky, since 1932. He attended Lincoln Memorial University in Harrogate, Tennessee. At the beginning of his junior year, Still had no money to continue college. A professor found a sponsor who paid for Still's education at Lincoln Memorial, where he received his B.A. in 1929, and also at Vanderbilt University in Tennessee, where he received his M.A. in 1930. He received his B.S. from the University of Illinois in 1931.

Still received an O. Henry Memorial Prize and the Southern Authors' Award for *River of Earth* (1940). Other works include *On Troublesome Creek* (1941); *Patterns of a Man and Other Stories* (1976); *The Run for the Elberta's* (1980); *The Wolfpen Poems* (1986); and *The Man in the Bushes: The Notebooks of James Still, 1935–1987* (1988).

Farm

In the deep moist hollows, on the burnt acres
Suspended upon the mountain side, the crisp green corn
Tapers blunt to the fruiting tassel;
Long straight shafts of yellow poplar
Strike upward like prongs of lightning at the field's edge,
Dwarfing the tender blades, the jointed growth;
Crows haggle their dark feathers, glare beady eyes
Surveying the slanted crop from the poplar boughs,
Opening purple beaks to cry the ripening feast,
And flow from their perch in heavy pointless flight.
A lizard, timid and tremulous, swallowing clots of air
With pulsing throat, pauses at the smooth trunk
And runs up the sky with liquid feet.

Pattern for Death

The spider puzzles his legs and rests his web
On aftergrass. No winds stir here to break
The quiet design, nothing protests the weaving
Of taut threads in a ladder of silk:
He is clever, he is fastidious, and intricate;
He is skilled with his cords of hate.

Who can escape through the grass: The crane-fly
Quivers its body in paralytic sleep;
The giant moths shed their golden dust
From fettered wings, and the spider speeds his lust.

Who reads the language of direction? Where may we pass
Through the immense pattern sheer as glass?

When the Dulcimers Are Gone

When the dulcimers are mingled with the dust
Of flowering chestnut, and their lean fretted necks
Are slain maple stalks, their strings dull threads of rust,
Where shall the mellow voice be heard upon the hills,
Upon what pennyroyal meadow, beside what rills?

Where shall the gentle words in mild abandon sing
With sweet design in loitering melody
As flights of swallows aimless on the wing,

Yet skilled as scythes that curve through yellow grain
And fragment as jasmine after freshening rain?

Or may the heart's breath on the slender reed
Sing bright virelays to match the oriole?—
The tulip tree the lyre that one must heed
When the dulcimers are gone, when afternoons attend
The silver underleaf of poplars in the wind?

Jim Wayne Miller
(1936–1996)

Jim Wayne Miller was born in Liecester, North Carolina, on October 21, 1936. In 1954 Miller enrolled at Berea College in Kentucky. After graduating in 1958, he married May Ellen Yates. In 1960 he enrolled at Vanderbilt University in Tennessee on a scholarship. Two sons were born while in Nashville. In 1963 he began teaching at Western Kentucky University and completed the Ph.D. at Vanderbilt in 1965. His daughter was born in 1967.

Among his numerous publications are *Copperhead Cane* (1964); *The More Things Change The More They Stay The Same* (1971); *The Mountains Have Come Closer* (1980); *Nostalgia for 70* (1986); *Brier, His Book* (1988); and *His First, Best Country* (1993).

Miller died on August 18, 1996.

from *Newfound*

29

Soon after I began my senior year at West Madison I got a big brown envelope from Aunt Vi. The envelope had a lot of papers and brochures in it, and a letter from Aunt Vi written on the letterhead of the college where she taught in Pennsylvania. At first I thought she was saying I should come to her college. But she was explaining about a college in Kentucky, where I could go to school even though I didn't have much money. At Berea College, students could work to pay for all their school expenses. The envelope full of papers and brochures explained all about Berea College. One of the places where students could work was Fireside Industries. That sounded cozy.

I showed Grandma Wells the things Aunt Vi had sent me. She smiled. Yes, by all means, I should apply, Grandma Wells said, for it would be a wonderful opportunity. She added that she had asked Aunt Vi to see that the materials about Berea College were sent to me.

In Mountain City—I rode there with Grandpa Wells—I went by Dad's office and told him about Berea College. He made a quick telephone call and we went to lunch in a nearby restaurant. A pretty blond woman came and sat down at the table with us. Dad introduced us. Her name was Flora, and she smiled and smelled good. While we ate, she talked to Dad and kept putting her hand on his. I thought about her name—Flora. It rhymed with Mom's name—Nora.

Dad told Flora I was thinking about going to college. He showed Flora the brochures. He had gone to Sevier College before he quit, but he knew about Berea College, and he agreed with Grandma Wells that I should apply. Flora thought I should apply, too. Outside the restaurant she kissed Dad on the cheek and gave me a hug.

"That's Flora—Flora Addington," Dad said as we walked back to his office. "I wanted you to meet her."

I figured it had been Flora he had called just before we left his office.

"Did you like her?" Dad asked.

He was trying to tell me Flora was his girlfriend, but I knew that just by the way she came in and sat down with us. I said I liked her fine. Dad said he did, too.

"Mom has a boyfriend," I said.

"Old Walter Lee," Dad said. "How do you like him?"

I said I liked him fine. Grandma and Grandpa Smith liked Walter Lee, too. When he came by to see Mom, Walter Lee would talk to Grandma about his folks, and then to Grandpa about fox hunting. Walter Lee and Mom looked funny together because he was so much taller. He had gray hair in his sideburns, but from the back he sometimes looked like a knot-headed boy. "His ears stick out," Eugene said once. "Looks like he's about to fly."

"Hush!" Mom said. She said Walter Lee might look like he was about to fly, but she had never known anybody who had his feet more solidly on the ground than he did.

Walter Lee carried a big wallet in his hip pocket. A plaited leather thong connected the wallet to his belt. Jeanette asked Mom if she knew how much money Walter Lee had in his wallet. She bet he had a thousand dollars in it.

Mom grinned. She didn't know, but however much it was, she bet the first dollar Walter Lee ever made was in there. Walter Lee was as close as he was slow, Mom said.

"Nothing wrong with being close," Grandma Smith said. Anyway, all the Rogerses were saving.

Walter Lee was always saying funny things and making Jeanette laugh. He made Jeanette laugh even when she felt bad. Once when Walter Lee came by to see Mom, Jeanette had had a shot at school and felt grumpy. She wouldn't laugh at anything Walter Lee said—until Walter Lee was telling Mom he'd just bought his new hunting license. He winked at Jeanette, showed her the new license, and said it was his vaccination against game wardens.

     *   *   *   *   *   *

Mrs. Simpson, the counselor at West Madison, gave me some tests Berea College sent her. I filled out the application forms and wrote an essay about why I wanted to attend Berea College. Early in the spring I got a letter saying I was accepted. As soon as I read the letter, I began to leave Newfound Creek and my family. I read and reread all the papers and brochures and catalogues Berea College sent me, studied the pictures, and imagined what it would be like in Kentucky. I got some books out of the library and read more about Kentucky. I got a map and figured out the route from Newfound Creek to Berea College. I knew what the map said, I knew it was where Mom and Dad had gone to get married, but in my mind college lay up ahead, a country where everyone spoke a foreign language.

"Reckon what kind of country it is up there in Kentucky?" Grandpa Smith wondered one evening after supper. We were all sitting out under the maples. A bobwhite was calling from the orchard grass below the barn.

I said I'd be finding out and I'd tell him the first time I came home.

"They have horses," Jeanette said. "And the grass is blue."

"It is not," Eugene said. "Bluegrass is just the name of it. Clifford Shelton has got bluegrass in his pasture, and it's not blue. It's green like any other grass."

"I was only kidding, dopey," Jeanette said.

Grandma Smith said she'd always heard that some of her people went to Kentucky, back years ago, but she didn't know where they settled.

Mom said she thought Uncle Clinton knew; he'd had a letter from a Ponder in Kentucky.

I thought of the man in the dim tintype behind Great-grandfather Leland's picture, on the wall inside the house.

The bobwhite called again from below the barn.

Grandma Smith said they would all miss me.

"I'm not gone yet, Grandma," I said.

But I was gone, in my mind. The winter had been mild, we didn't miss any days because of snow, and so graduation came in late May. I was astonished to learn that I was salutatorian, with the second-highest grade average in my class. Before I gave my speech, Mr. Bennett said a few words about West Madison Consolidated High School and about the value of preserving traditions of the smaller schools we students had attended before West Madison brought us all together. In the smaller schools students had been encouraged to tell stories and present recitations before their schoolmates. Mr. Bennett thought this was a tradition worth preserving and he encouraged storytelling and public speaking at West Madison. Then he introduced me as a graduate who had come from the Newfound School to West Madison.

I gave a speech called "Citizens of Somewhere." Mr. Bennett and Mrs. Slone had read it twice and made corrections and suggestions. I told how, when I knew I would be going to college, Grandma Smith had said so many young people from Newfound left home after school and became "citizens of nowhere." I talked about the hundreds of thousands of people who had left our Appalachian region over the years to seek work in other places. I asked why we had to leave a place that was so beautiful; why the natural beauty that attracted tourists from all over the country was being destroyed, in many places, by strip-mining. I recited a poem that Mr. Bennett had read to us, a poem called "Heritage," that described the hills toppling their heads to level earth and forests sliding out of the sky. I talked about the Sutherlands and the baskets and chairs they made, about old-fashioned ways and modern ways, about mules and missiles. I said I thought I was somebody from somewhere, from a place I would be leaving to attend college, but hoped to return to.

My whole family was in the audience—Mom with Walter Lee Rogers, Dad with Flora Addington, Eugene and Jeanette sitting with Grandma and Grandpa Smith and Grandma and Grandpa Wells. I watched them while I spoke and thought especially of Grandpa Wells, who had not much favored the idea when he'd first heard I would be going off to college. He'd wanted me to think about staying and helping him run the farm and store. But Grandma Wells had put a stop to that talk. And after graduation Grandpa Wells shook my hand and said I had "spizzerinctum." Dad said my speech was *almost* as good as the one he'd given the time he won the medal. Grandma Wells said she would be hard pressed to say which was better, for they were both good talks.

*   *   *   *   *   *   *

I helped George Hawkins haul watermelons again that summer, and spent most of the time coming and going from Mountain City to Florida, Georgia, and South Carolina. I saved the money George paid me, and thought about how soon I would be going north to Berea College.

I would come home to Newfound Creek for a day or an evening, before we'd head south for another load, and catch up on the news. Home from one trip, I learned that Eugene was working in timber and saving his money to buy a car. When I came home another time, Eugene had already bought the car—a Mercury convertible—and he and Selma Austin had been to Jewell Hill to the drive-in. I was really surprised when I came home about a week after that and found out that now Eugene was teaching Mom to drive. She drove Eugene's car out to the barn, turned, and came back to the house while we all stood in the yard watching her. Jeanette and I clapped when she set the emergency brake carefully and got out. Grandpa Smith just stood with a funny little smile on his face. He said mountain people just naturally knew always to set the emergency brake when they got out of their cars.

I was home one Saturday in July when Jeanette came running up the road from Grandma and Grandpa Wells's. Jeanette was working three days a week now for Grandma Wells. She came huffing into the kitchen—I was drinking coffee, Mom was stirring cake batter—and held out a carpenter's level to Mom.

"Grandpa Wells said to give this to you," Jeanette said, still breathing hard. "He said you'd understand. I hope you do, because I don't!"

Mom set down the cake batter and, looking puzzled, took the level from Jeanette. "Where did this come from?" she asked.

Jeanette said Grandpa Wells and Willard Sexton had torn away the old porch steps that morning and were building new ones. Grandpa Wells had found the level under the old steps. He'd called Jeanette from her cleaning in the house and told her to take the level straight to Mom.

Mom just stood there holding the level with a look of great satisfaction on her face. "That's the level!" Mom said, looking first at me, then at Jeanette. "The very level!"

Then I remembered.

"That's the level your Grandma Wells said I lost!" Mom said. "And Papa believed it, too, and whipped me." Mom kept standing there turning the level over and over in her hands.

Jeanette had to go back down to Grandma and Grandpa Wells's to finish cleaning.

"You tell Mr. Wells I understand," Mom said, "and say I thank him. Mr. Wells never did believe I lost that level," she said to me. "He said it didn't make any difference if I did."

When Grandma Smith came in from the barn with a basket of eggs, Mom showed her the level and retold the whole story. "I'll declare!" Grandma Smith said. Mom sent me down to the tobacco patch, where Grandpa Smith and Eugene were pulling suckers from the tobacco, to fetch Grandpa Smith to the house. Grandpa Smith didn't remember the level, so Mom reminded him of how, years ago, he'd switched her for losing it.

Grandpa Smith grinned and cocked his head to one side, like a bird. "And this level was under the steps all that time?" he asked.

Yes, Mom said, and Grandpa was actually the one who'd lost it, by building the steps around it.

Grandpa Smith said he was sorry he'd switched her legs and ankles for losing the level. He figured that must have been thirty years ago.

"That's right," Mom said. "I wasn't more than four or five years old." But the way she talked about it made it seem like only yesterday. She sat in the living room, her legs crossed, holding the level across her lap.

"One time you whipped me for something Robert did," Eugene told Mom.

"Is this your cake you've started?" Grandma Smith said from the kitchen.

Mom seemed not to hear either of them. Wiggling her foot contentedly inside her shoe, she said, "I knew all the time I never lost that level."

"What are you going to do with it?" Eugene said.

Mom said, "I think I'll frame it!"

*   *   *   *   *   *   *

I had planned to get Eugene to drive me to Jewell Hill in his Mercury and then catch the bus from there to Berea College. But when I got to talking about it with George Hawkins, he said, "Pshaw, I'll drive you up there." George said he'd like to see what the country looked like up that way. So at five o'clock one morning in September George came to the house in his truck, the same one I'd ridden in two summers hauling watermelons. George always liked to get an early start, and since he didn't believe there was better water than what he had at home, he always brought his own jug of water.

Everyone had been up since four, knowing I was leaving early. I joked with Mom. "Hold it in the road!" I said to her. I hugged Jeanette, who was sitting in her gown, trying to keep her eyes open. "Go back to bed!" I told her. I shook Eugene's hand and told him to try to watch the movie at the drive-in. I hugged Grandma Smith and put my arm around Grandpa Smith. Out on the porch, where I picked up the suitcases Dad had bought for me in Mountain City, tears came in my eyes. I fumbled with the suitcases until I got hold of myself, then carried them to the truck that waited, idling, with all its amber running lights glowing in the thinning darkness. Still, I wasn't ready to go. I went to the dog lot in the stand of pines and said goodbye to my foxhound, Lady. I kissed her right on her cold nose.

*   *   *   *   *   *   *

I wrote home and told what George Hawkins had said when we got to Berea. He looked all around, his hands jammed in his pockets, and said, "They've got more sky up here!" I wrote again to tell Grandpa Smith what I'd found out about squirrels. "Remember you told me once about hunting back on the Bearwallow and all these squirrels, hundreds of them, came past you, leaping through the trees?" I said I never had believed that story, but I had read in a magazine that zoologists from the Smithsonian Institution's Center for Short-lived Phenomena were hurrying to the Appalachian Mountains, where large numbers of squirrels were on the move. These scientists were observing gray squirrels crossing highways, scurrying across fields, swimming lakes. They were trying to figure out what caused these mass movements of squirrels, but as yet they didn't understand. I told Grandpa I believed him now. Mom answered for Grandpa on her typewriter. She said all Grandpa said was, "It happened."

I wrote letters to Eugene and Jeanette. Eugene didn't write back. Instead, he asked Jeanette to include his news in her letter: Mom was getting better and better at driving. He was teaching her to parallel park. He had taken Mom out on the Newfound Creek road to practice, but she was afraid of the curves; she wanted to stop the car, get out, and look around the curve to see if a car was coming before she drove on. Jeanette said she was pretty sure Mom and Walter Lee Rogers were going to get married. Because Walter Lee was Mom's boss at Blue Ridge Manufacturing, Jeanette had thought Mom probably didn't have to work hard, but Mom had said she had to work harder because she worked for Walter Lee. Jeanette was already thinking about having a bridal shower for Mom when they got married. That would be neat—giving your own mother a bridal shower!

In another letter home I told Jeanette she would have to come to Berea College, too. She would fit right in at Fireside Industries, where they made quilts and baskets and wove coverlets. She would do well in the college, too. Hadn't Grandma Smith always said Jeanette was "good in her books"? Jeanette and I agreed that Eugene probably wouldn't go to college. He and Selma Austin would get married as soon as they finished high school.

I told Jeanette about meeting a girl at Berea, Rebecca Sterling, who was from over on Beaverdam. She'd sat across from me during orientation when we took all sorts of tests—a whole week of them—and I knew I had seen her somewhere but I couldn't remember where. At first I thought maybe she was from Florida, or Georgia, or South Carolina, and I had seen her on one of those trips I'd made with George Hawkins. I was sure I had been riding a truck when I saw her, whenever or wherever it was. When I found out she was from Beaverdam I knew how it was I remembered her.

"Do you remember," I asked her, "how you used to meet the rolling store on Saturdays?"

How did I know that? she wanted to know.

I told her I had been on the rolling store with Kermit Worley once when we came around a turn and saw her standing on the limb of an apple tree.

"That was you?" she said. "You don't look the same!"

"You do," I said.

I wrote to tell Grandma Smith I'd always thought, when she warned me about "spread natters" in the pine woods, that the real word was "adder," not "natter." But I had found out in a book I had to read that the word was "natter" before it ever became "adder."

I wrote Grandma and Grandpa Wells a letter, but I didn't mention I'd found out, from a girl who'd also had a job there, that Aunt Alma had worked that past summer at Opryland, in Nashville. I figured they knew that, and since they hadn't said anything about it, it wasn't my place to mention it.

I could write home about all sorts of things, but there was so much else I couldn't say in letters: how I remembered that time over on Beaverdam so clearly I could even tell Rebecca Sterling what she'd been wearing that Saturday morning—jeans and a yellow blouse. And she'd brought butter and strawberries, and the butter had the shape of maple leaves impressed on it. There'd been a new barn in a clearing close to the apple tree Rebecca had been standing in, and I could still smell the bitter fragrance of the green lumber, could see the dazzle of the tin roof, and the glint of new nails.

I couldn't write in a letter, either, about how I dreamed one night that fall of Grandma Smith, running under a cloud of swarming bees, beating an empty pie pan with a spoon till the swarm settled, black on a drooping pine bough. I wanted to say those things, but I hadn't found a way. And I had so many questions: I wanted to know why Gerald Scott left Newfound and never came home again; why people like Junior Crumm and Wiley Woods kept trying to leave and couldn't.

Still, the more I learned about other places, the more interesting, even mysterious, my home in the mountains grew. I had lived on Newfound Creek, and now, I was discovering, Newfound Creek lived on in me, and would live in me, no matter how far away I might travel.

Lee Smith

(1942–)

Born in Grundy, Virginia, on November 1, 1944, Lee Smith has returned to Appalachian settings for many of her stories. She attended Hollins College in Virginia, studying creative writing with Louis Rubin, a major influence on her development as a writer. After graduating from Hollins in 1967, Smith married James Seay and moved to Tuscaloosa, Alabama. While there, she finished her second novel, *Something in the Wind* (1971). *Fancy Strut*, her third (1973), was set in Alabama. The couple moved to Chapel Hill, North Carolina, and in 1981 Smith accepted a full-time teaching position in creative writing at North Carolina State University in Raleigh. With *Black Mountain Breakdown* (1980), Smith returned to Appalachia for the setting. In 1982, Smith and Seay divorced. In 1985, Smith married Harold B. Crowther, Jr.

In 1984, Smith received both the Sir Walter Raleigh Award and the John Dos Passos Award. In 1991, she received the Robert Penn Warren Prize for Fiction and in 1994 received the Lila Wallace Reader's Digest Fund award. She retired in 1999 from North Carolina State University.

Works by Smith include *Cakewalk* (1981); *Oral History* (1983); *Family Linen* (1985); *Fair and Tender Ladies* (1988); *Bob, a Dog* (1988); *Me and My Baby View the Eclipse* (1990); *The Devil's Dream* (1992); *Saving Grace* (1995); *The Christmas Letters* (1996); and *News of the Spirit* (1997).

from *Saving Grace*

Daddy healed others, including a woman who cried all the time because her nerves had gone bad, a baby that wouldn't suck, a man with a sore on his leg that wouldn't stop running, another man that couldn't hold a job because of his headaches, a girl possessed by the Devil, and many more. So there was a lot of wonder and joy in the Jesus Name Church. Daddy did not handle the serpents at every service, not even after the other saints began to take them up too. It was done only at the meeting on Sundays, after the preaching, and when a crusade was going on, where it could convince an unbeliever like nothing else. Often serpents were not present in meeting at all, and sometimes when they were present, the Lord didn't move on them, and nobody was blessed to take them up. It was only *one* of the signs that followed believers, as Daddy used to remind everybody. He hardly ever preached on those verses anyway, often letting the Bible just fall open willy-nilly and getting Mama to read out loud from whatever page the Lord had picked. Daddy could preach a good sermon on any verse. People marveled at him.

But when the time was right, and the Lord blessed him to do it, why then Daddy did take up the serpents, as did the other saints, including of course Ruth and Carlton Duty and Rufus Graybeal and Dillard Jones and the Cline sisters, and many more. Sometimes the Spirit would be so strong that the whole congregation appeared to catch it, shouting "Hallelujah" and jumping up in joy to dance, and passing the serpents from hand to hand.

People in the Spirit will often act like children—laughing out loud, giggling, patting their feet or clapping, sometimes talking baby talk. I saw old Mrs. Duke Watson, who had to be almost carried into meeting whenever she came, get up and dance the hula. I saw Lily's mama get up and throw her new baby at the nearest woman she could find, then grasp a copperhead in each hand. I saw my own sister Evelyn dance right down the aisle with a yellow rattler, popping her gum and grinning. Later, she wouldn't talk about it much. "*You* do it, Sissy," she said. "Then you'll see."

But I had never been anointed, and prayed that I never would be.

I always sat way in the back with Lily, watching what all went on. We played tic-tac-toe on a little pad of paper when things got boring. A lot of the time I got to stay home and keep Troy Lee anyway. Meeting was not really the place for children. God would send for you when He was ready for you.

There were several teenagers active in the Jesus Name congregation though, besides Evelyn. There was Evelyn's best friend Patsy Manier, a plump funny girl that everybody liked—Patsy would talk your ear off—and Darlene Knott who wore harlequin eyeglasses, the first I ever saw, and her brother Robbie Knott, who played drums sometimes in meeting, and Doyle Stacy, the thin boy with a thin mustache who played electric guitar and lived with his sick mother and worked for the Appalachian Power Company. I had a little crush on Doyle Stacy. I had a little crush on beautiful Rhonda Rose too, who had quit cheerleading in ninth grade because God told her to. This amazed me.

If I *ever* made cheerleader, I wouldn't quit for anything. I used to plan how I would hide my cheerleading outfit in my locker at the high school and just get it out when I had to wear it, so Mama and Daddy would never have to know. But this was pure fantasy, and by the time I was old enough to be a cheerleader, I was long gone from Scrabble Creek anyway.

Of course people did get bit in meeting sometimes, but nobody ever died of it. As Daddy liked to point out, the Bible says, "They shall take up serpents," *not* "They shall not bite you." Daddy himself had been bit over two hundred times, so often he had quit counting. Whenever it happened, he cried out "Glory to God," for he believed always in the perfect will of God, and turned himself over to it. He said that God has His reasons, which we know naught of. Sometimes He's just testing you. And when the serpent bites, you have to keep your mind directly on the Lord, and He will recover you. If you let your mind get off the Lord, you'll swell up.

Carlton Duty swore this was true, for he was hurt bad by a copperhead that he attempted to handle when he was thinking about buying a new truck. "The Lord taught me a good lesson," he said later, "and I thank Him for it!" though he was laid up in the bed for months afterward.

Whenever anyone was bit, we'd all go to their house and pray over them night and day, as long as it took to get them out of danger. I liked going to the people's houses, since we didn't get out much. I also liked it when they came to our house, though I couldn't stand to see Daddy get bit. It made me get the worst feeling deep in my stomach, like *I* might die. I saw this happen many times as a child, and I never got used to it, though frequently Daddy was back at church for the very next meeting, his faith was so strong.

Once I saw a rattler strike the upper part of his arm so hard it actually hung there swinging until some other men pulled it off, but by the next day you could scarcely see its fang marks. Then there was old Lonnie Ratchett, who swore that getting bit had helped his arthritis, and recommended it.

Many were healed at the Jesus Name Church, and many were baptized, and signs and wonders, such as speaking in tongues, were commonplace. Tongues of fire were seen to come down on Ruth Duty, and several people saw golden wings in the air over Daddy's head.

      *   *   *   *   *   *   *

This was before all the bad things started happening. I always thought that a lot of the trouble had to do with the size of Daddy's ministry. At first it was small, so that the church the men had built near the old brush arbor held everybody just fine. The whole congregation came from right around there and had known each other most all their lives, so the meetings were filled with love and unity, and God was always present, and sent His anointing down accordingly.

But after Rhonda Rose's mother flew into a panic and took her to the big hospital in Waynesville for serpent bite, we got written up in the newspapers, and the crowds started getting real big. They tore one wall out of the church and added on to make it bigger, and then added on again. People were coming from miles and miles away to worship at the Jesus Name Church, believers and unbelievers alike, and troublemakers too.

Then came the time when Daddy was hurt bad. There were a lot of unbelievers present, a lot of people we didn't know, and the very air in the church house felt wrong. I don't know how to describe it. It felt to me like it does before a thunderstorm, I could smell it the way you can smell lightning. I was watching Daddy real close to see if he could feel it too, but it seemed that he could not. He was preaching and playing his guitar to lead the singing just as usual, when some of the people in the back started to yell out and heckle him.

"Hey, preacher man!" they yelled. "Where's them snakes?" And such as that.

Daddy tried to ignore them, but people in the congregation kept turning around to look, and the Spirit was slow to move among them. My heart sank when one of the men in the back hollered, "Hey, preacher! Let's get to it! We've brung a big un for you!" For I knew that they would torment the serpent before they brought him in, and sometimes put red pepper on him so he'd be ready to bite. This had happened before, and Daddy had amazed all, but tonight it didn't feel good.

"Get to it, preacher!" they yelled.

Then finally the Lord moved on the congregation, and Rufus Graybeal, always the first, brought out two rattlesnakes, and Carlton Duty took off his shoes to tread on one of them, and Doyle Stacy put his face down in his serpent box, something he had taken to doing which bothered me a lot. People were crying out and singing and dancing as usual, having forgotten about the strangers.

Suddenly a heavyset man ran up from the back, past me and Lily, and flung a huge cottonmouth onto the floor in the midst of everybody. The Spirit fled. People began screaming and trying to get away.

Daddy had to come forward then and try to grab the serpent up, and I saw it bury its fangs deep in the fleshy part of his right hand, between his thumb and index finger, and then rear back and strike his leg before he could even try again to pick it up. Carlton Duty had to help Daddy get it off his leg.

Then Daddy held the cottonmouth—the biggest one I had ever seen—up above his head with both hands, and cried out, "Glory to God!" in a strong deep voice before putting him into a sack. Daddy went on preaching to those that remained, but he had been hurt, I could tell. His speech grew slower and more halting, and he stumbled as he walked. Finally he sat down on a chair and slumped sideways.

The service was over.

Rufus and Carlton rushed to catch Daddy before he fell on the floor, and they supported him out the door and into Carlton's truck and brought him home. It would be the next day before we would learn that in all the confusion, Doyle had also suffered a serpent bite on the cheek.

By the time we got home, Mama was crying at Daddy's side and his whole arm was swelled up like a ham. His hand was black. The skin on his leg was black too, with red streaks fanning out around the serpent bite. Mama had cut his pants leg off above the knee. "Pray, children, pray!" Mama told us, so we fell to our knees and prayed and prayed, but as the night wore on, Daddy seemed to get worse instead of better. He lost consciousness and vomited blood. We understood that Daddy had been hurt because he was not anointed when he worked the signs, and we knew that he would die if it was God's will to take him on home.

Along with others from the Jesus Name Church, we prayed all night long, and it was noon of the next day before it grew clear that Daddy would live. In fact Daddy astonished everybody by going back to church that very night and handling the same serpent, the giant cottonmouth, which was now gentle as a little kitten in his arms. Doyle Stacy was not so lucky. The whole left side of his face was paralyzed, so that one eyelid drooped shut and he drooled out of the left side of his mouth. It also affected his vocal cords. He sounded real funny when he talked, and now it would be hard for him to become a preacher as he'd hoped. But you had to admire Doyle's attitude. He said that God had been testing his faith, and he thanked God that he was equal to the test.

Around this time, Rufus Graybeal was going more and more out of control. This happens sometimes. He gathered up serpents from the mountains until he had a roomful of them at his house, it was said. His wife left him one day while he was gone to meeting. She took both his little girls. They went down to Florida on a Greyhound bus, to where her people lived. Then Rufus got fired from his job at the highway department. After this, he was over at the Jesus Name Church all the time, night and day. He practically lived there.

He took money out of the bank and ordered off for some exotic serpents from a place in Florida—coral snakes, bamboo vipers, a python. They came in a special wooden box on a cargo plane. Rufus had to drive to the Asheville airport to get them. Afterward, he was real proud of those serpents, and drove around showing them to people. He had them in coolers in the back of his truck. I know that Daddy was very worried about Rufus, and talked to him many times about the sin of self-exaltation, and told him he was setting himself up to get bit if he could not rid himself of it.

So nobody was surprised when it happened, nor when he died, though we were all real sorry. Carlton Duty, speaking at the funeral, said that maybe Rufus had gotten too puffed up in the Lord. Then Daddy said that while this seemed to be the case, we were not to second-guess God, and reminded us of Jesus' words, "He that loses his life for my sake and the Gospel shall find it." Daddy said that while the ways of God are mysterious and passeth understanding, he had no doubt that Rufus Graybeal was in the heavenly kingdom of the Lord right now, having found that perfect peace which he was so far from having on this earth.

Serpents were handled at Rufus's funeral, of course, where everybody outdid themselves preaching.

They ran a picture of Daddy on page one of the *Waynesville Times*, plus a picture of Rufus in his open coffin with quarters on his eyes and a rattlesnake coiled up on his stomach. After the funeral, his brothers snatched him up and carried him to West Virginia to be buried and then came back and started talking against Daddy and the Jesus Name Church. An editorial against the church appeared in the Asheville paper, mentioning Daddy in particular. I hated that. For I had a real hard time at school anyway, without us making the paper.

In elementary school, I had gotten used to them all teasing me and leaving garter snakes in the top of my desk, and to not ever being elected to anything and not making good grades because I had to miss school so much, taking care of Troy Lee or praying over those who were sick or had gotten bit. I fought a lot too, just like a boy, though Mama said not to. Mama said to ignore them for they know not what they do, but I just couldn't. I'd get mad as fire, and when somebody did something like stick out their foot to trip me as I went by, I'd turn around and kick them as hard as I could. I didn't even care if the teachers spanked me for it, which they did.

But this one year was going to be different. This year I had the chance to start all over, and I meant to do it right. I had been assigned to a new school closer to town because of redistricting, and I had already made one true friend there named Marie Royal, a regular girl from a regular family.

I thought Marie was the most beautiful girl. She had long jet-black hair, like Rose Red in my fairy-tale book, and skin as white as snow, and delicate features. When she giggled, which was often, deep dimples appeared in her cheeks. She had long willowy legs, like a deer.

I felt awkward and country around Marie. In fact I stumbled over a stool when we met, the second day of seventh grade. Our teacher was showing us how to use the school library. I was real excited, since I had never gone to a school that had a library. I had noticed Marie because she was so pretty and because she looked different from all the rest of us, but of course I hadn't said anything to her, and didn't plan to. For I had determined not to talk to *anybody*, so nobody would find out about me and tease me.

I planned to be a girl of mystery in the seventh grade.

Billie Jean was a year behind me in the new school because she had flunked twice, and I had already sworn her to secrecy. This was not hard, as she was too shy to talk to anybody anyway. Lily went to a different school because of where she lived, and Evelyn had dropped out of school altogether in order to sing with Daddy when he went out street preaching and evangelizing, which was all the time now. So the coast was clear. I was off to a great new start.

I had even gotten Mama to cut me some bangs, which I wore long, right to my eyebrows. I kept my eyes down and didn't say anything to anybody, thinking, *Girl of mystery, girl of mystery. I am a girl of mystery.*

But I got so excited in the library that I forgot myself and made a beeline for the little display of horse books on a table. I didn't even see the stool until I had knocked it into Marie.

"Ooh!" she said, hopping on one foot and clutching the other.

"I'm sorry," I mumbled, eyes down. Actually I didn't care. I couldn't wait to check out as many of those Walter Farley Black Stallion books as I could get at one time. I reached past Marie to grab.

"That one's real good," she said with authority. "That's where he goes down in these secret caves at the ocean. I'm going to get this one." She took *My Friend Flicka* off the table.

I could feel her looking at me, though I tried to hide under my bangs.

"Aren't you in Miss Black's room too?" she asked, and I said I was, and then she said, "What's your name?"

"Gracie Shepherd." I held my breath, but it was clear from the way she nodded that she had never heard of us.

"I'm Marie Royal," she said. "I can draw horses. I can draw a horse that looks just like this." She pointed at the stallion on the cover of *The Island Stallion*, which I stood there holding.

"Can't," I said immediately.

"Can," Marie said. "Look, I'll show you." She pulled one of the little wooden chairs up to a table and motioned for me to sit down on it next to her, and I did. Then she opened up a pink plastic three-ring notebook I would have given anything to own, and took several colored pencils out of a clear plastic pouch that fitted right onto the rings. I watched while she bit her tongue, concentrating, and drew the best horse's head I had ever seen. I couldn't believe it. "My mother's an artist," Marie said without looking up. "She's giving me lessons." Then she went on to draw the horse's body, which was not as good as the head, and four legs that were too short. "Here," she said, ripping out a sheet of paper for me and giving me a purple pencil. "You try it." My purple horse's head looked like a dog's head, which made me admire Marie's even more.

"Girls!" Miss Black, our teacher, bore down on us from her great skinny height. "Marie! Florida Grace! What are you doing? I've been looking everywhere for you all!" She grabbed our horses and crumpled them up. "That'll be ten minutes out of lunch for you young ladies." Miss Black talked through her nose.

"She *sounds* like a horse," I whispered to Marie as Miss Black jerked us along the hall to our room, and Marie giggled, and then we were friends.

When Miss Black kept us in at lunch, we drew four horses apiece and named them. Marie's were Jumping Jack, Hot Potato, Queen of England, and Blackie. Mine were Shadrach, Meshach, Abednego, and Judas. "Wow! Neat names," Marie said. She had never heard them before because her family didn't go to church, not *ever*, as I would learn.

"Can you come home with me one afternoon?" she asked later that day, and though I wanted to go so bad, I had to say no.

"I don't know how I'd get back to my house," I said, "if I was to miss the bus. We live way out of town on Scrabble Creek."

"Oh, Mama will drive you home," Marie said instantly, to my amazement. I couldn't imagine a mother who even knew how to drive, but Marie's mother turned out to have a car of her very own, and she was perfectly willing to drive it anyplace Marie wanted her to. Marie got to call the shots around her house. For she had been adopted, like a princess in a story. She was an only child, which seemed to make her extra generous, instead of spoiled. For lunch her mother always packed two sandwiches for her, as well as potato chips in a waxed paper bag and an apple and a peppermint patty or maybe a cupcake or some cookies. I was embarrassed about my own lunch, which was nothing but a piece of cornbread usually, and sometimes a mason jar of buttermilk to break the cornbread up in, or maybe a biscuit. Some days I didn't have any lunch at all, and then I always said I was on a diet, but Marie would put half of her lunch on my desk anyway, and not say a word when I ate it up. Sometimes she had pickle loaf sandwiches, which I had never heard of, and sometimes she had peanut butter and marshmallow whip sandwiches, which were wonderful. It took a long time of begging Mama, though, before she'd ever let me go home with Marie. I knew better than to ask Daddy about it, of course. I was sure he would say no, and that would be the end of it. At first Mama said no too, but I kept at her about it.

"Why not?" I asked one day in late September. "Her mama will bring me home by dinner. She's got a red station wagon, I've seen it. She's our room mother. She's real nice. I'll do all the wash," I said. "I'll do anything. I'll be real good."

"Oh, Gracie honey—" Mama sighed while I was going on and on about it. She stroked my hair and played with my new bangs. "You *are* good, honey. It's just that— oh, it's better if . . ." Mama stared out over my head, beyond me, at the blue fall sky and the yellow leaves tumbling across our yard in the wind. She set her jaw. "Don't ask me no more." Her voice sounded funny, and when I looked at her, she turned her face away.

I waited another week or so, until Daddy went on a crusade to Tennessee, taking Evelyn with him. Then I cleaned up our room and washed all the floors in the whole house and asked Mama again. She was just coming in the door with Ruth Duty. Mama always seemed stronger, somehow, when she was with Ruth Duty, as if Ruth's good spirits and pluck had rubbed off on her too. She had this effect on everybody.

"Why, look here!" Ruth exclaimed. "I wish you'd just look at what all this child has got done! Aren't you something, Florida Grace. I know you're real proud of your girls," Ruth said to Mama, who nodded and beamed, taking off her hat, and so I popped up and asked her again if I couldn't go home one day after school with Marie.

Mama looked at Ruth.

"Honey, I'd let her, if it was me," Ruth said. "I'll swear I can't see no harm in it."

So I got to be picked up after school by Marie's mother in the red Chevrolet station wagon and driven in toward Waynesville to Marie's house. She lived in a white brick ranch house with grass in the yard and a picture window that bowed out from the living room and had about a million little panes of glass in it. Inside, the entire house looked like a magazine, with everything matching.

Marie's mother gave us olive and cream cheese sandwiches on white bread with the crusts cut off, set out on plates at the kitchen table, and Coca-Colas. At home we were not allowed to have Coca-Colas. I thought I had never tasted anything in all the world as good as those sandwiches, and I loved how the Coca-Cola fizzed on my tongue. I tried to drink it real slow, so this would go on for a long time.

Marie's mother, whose first name was Irene, sat at the kitchen table with us and smoked Salem cigarettes, which she held at an angle that I admired. I admired the way she blew the smoke out too, in a thin stream toward the ceiling, pursing her mouth. Mrs. Royal had a pixie haircut, which was popular then. Her made-up eyes pointed out at the end, like a cat's eyes. She wore pale pink lipstick and tight black pants, and her hands were stained with paint because she was an artist. I did not think much of her paintings, which were mostly just blocks of color with black lines running every which way between them. I thought Marie's horses were a lot better, and said so when Mrs. Royal asked me what I thought of her work. She threw back her head and laughed. She told me, in her strange hard Northern voice, that she found me "very refreshing." I was surprised to learn that Marie's dad was at home too, reading a book. Mr. Royal was called Dr. Royal, but he wasn't a real doctor, he just worked over at the college in Cullowhee. It must not be much of a job, I thought, for him to be home in the afternoon. He asked me a lot of questions and listened hard, nodding seriously, to my answers. I wasn't used to being asked questions, or listened to. I knew I had to be real careful about what I said, and though I told them all about my brothers and sisters, I just said that my daddy traveled, which was true. Dr. Royal nodded in a way that made me feel grown-up, and sucked on his pipe. I felt like I got drunk on smoke in that house every time I went over there, and I resolved to start smoking myself, the first chance I got, and hold my cigarette at an angle like Mrs. Royal.

Marie had a big dollhose and a closet full of dolls, a shelf of books, a pink-and-white indoors bathroom with a lacy cover on the toilet seat and—best of all—a television set! This was the first television I had ever seen, and I will never forget the chill which came over me that day as we sat down before it and watched Kate Smith sing "When the Moon Comes over the Mountain" in grainy black-and-white. I started crying, I was so surprised! And then I got tickled, and Marie got tickled too.

That afternoon passed so fast I couldn't believe it when Mrs. Royal said it was time to go. Marie and I sat in the backseat and giggled while her mother smoked Salems and played the radio. Sometimes she sang along.

I had to pay attention and give directions for the last part of the drive. "Are you *sure* this is the road?" Mrs. Royal kept asking when we left the pavement and took the gravel road up to Scrabble Creek. "Yes ma'am, I'm sure, yes ma'am, this is right," I kept saying, and then I was home and she stopped the car and we all stared up the hill at my house, which looked so poor to me suddenly, like a picture in a book about olden times.

"Oh neat, look at the creek!" Marie said, and Mrs. Royal said, "Is that your mother on the porch?" and then Marie was saying, "Mama, can we go in for a minute? Can we, can we?"

I looked up the hill and saw my mother stand up and go in the house, closing the door behind her. She did not wave.

"I've got to go," I said. "Thanks a lot, I'll see you tomorrow, Marie." I slammed the car door and ran up the hill as fast as my legs would carry me, stumbling over rocks and roots on the way because my eyes were stinging with wind and tears.

*   *   *   *   *   *   *

Mama let me go home with Marie once a week from then on throughout the fall, but she never let me spend the night or the weekend, though the Royals asked me to. I couldn't miss meeting, Mama said. I told Marie that I had to stay home and keep Troy Lee because Mama worked, which turned out to be sort of true, after Mama started helping out at Dutys' grocery. Mama never came down to the car to meet Mrs. Royal, or told me to invite her in. Mama did not go to PTA, or come to the school on Parent Day. Billie Jean was real jealous of my friendship with Marie, and whined about it, accusing me of being stuck-up. She asked me lots and lots of questions at first about the Royals' house and what all Marie had—what toys, what dolls—but I wouldn't say. I wanted to keep it all to myself, just for me, though I knew it was a sin to be selfish. I didn't care. I wanted something just for myself, and I wouldn't tell Billie Jean a thing. Finally she quit asking.

I didn't tell Billie Jean that she was invited to go the Halloween fair at the Waynesville Lions Club with me and Marie in late October. I just told Mrs. Royal that Billie couldn't go. "Billie Jean has asthma," I said. I knew about asthma because of Lily. "She has to rest a lot." "Oh dear," Mrs. Royal said, and at the Halloween fair she bought a gumball necklace for me to take home to Billie Jean, but I kept it. I didn't care if I went to Hell or not.

Marie and her family were *mine*.

One thing Marie and I always did together was write horse books—that is, I'd write the story, and Marie would draw the pictures. We had made up a talking roan named Spice and a girl named Melinda who owned him. Nobody except Melinda knew that he could talk. They solved mysteries together, and the names of the books were the names of the mysteries—*The Secret in the Hollow Tree, The Clue of the Broken Flower, Melinda Saves the Day,* and *What Went On in the Meadow,* which was Mrs. Royal's favorite. She was just crazy about our books, and used to bring lemonade for us into the dining room, where we got to work on our books at the big table under the fancy hanging light.

While I was visiting, Mrs. Royal was usually in the kitchen cooking, or reading magazines and smoking cigarettes, or sewing. She made a lot of Marie's clothes, but you could never tell that they were homemade. I didn't understand why she did this. "If I could buy my little girl any dress she wanted at Wilson's, I would," I said to Marie one day. "I'd *never* make it!" Wilson's Department store was the biggest store in downtown Waynesville. I had stood on the street corner outside it with Daddy while he preached.

"Oh, Mama just likes to sew," Marie said.

I still thought it was stupid to make something if you could afford to buy it.

Then one day Mrs. Royal showed me some sky-blue corduroy and a matching piece of cotton with flowers all over it. "I thought I might make you and Marie both some jumpers out of this," she said, kind of offhand but watching me, "and blouses to match. What do you think of that idea?"

"I wouldn't mind," I said, though my heart was jumping right out of my chest. The only time I'd ever had anything brand-new to wear in my whole life was when Ruth and Carlton Duty gave each one of us an outfit the Christmas before. So Mrs. Royal spread the blue corduroy out on the carpet in the living room, covered it with crinkly pattern pieces, and started cutting. The next time I went there, Mrs. Royal asked me what Mama had said about us having the matching jumpers, and I said Mama was tickled to death. This was a lie. I kept the jumpers secret from Mama, just as I kept other things secret from Marie and Mrs. Royal.

I had a lot of secrets that fall, so many that sometimes I thought my head would burst and they would all fly out into the room like hornets from a nest, stinging everybody.

Wendell Berry

(1934–   )

Wendell Berry's literary achievements place him as one of America's foremost writers. Born on August 5, 1934, in New Castle, Kentucky, Berry has received acclaim for his poetry, novels, and essays, which embrace agrarianism and small-scale farming.

Berry was graduated from the University of Kentucky with a B.A. in 1956, and he received his M.A. there in 1957. From 1958 to 1960, he attended Stanford University. He traveled to Italy and France on a Guggenheim fellowship from 1961 to 1962 and taught at New York University from 1962 to 1964. In 1964, he accepted a faculty position at the University of Kentucky. In 1965, he moved to his present home, a small farm at Port Royal, Kentucky, with his wife Tanya and their two children.

The recipient of numerous awards, Berry has received the National Institute of Arts and Letters Literary award (1971); the Friends of American Writers Award (1975) for *The Memory of Old Jack* (1974); and the T. S. Eliot Award, Ingersoll Foundation (1994).

Berry's works include *Nathan Coulter: A Novel* (1960); *The Broken Ground* (1965); *A Place on Earth: A Novel* (1967); *Farming: A Handbook* (1973); *The Hidden Wound* (1970); *A Continuous Harmony: Essays Cultural and Agricultural* (1972); *The Country of Marriage* (1973); *The Memory of Old Jack* (1974); *Sayings and Doings: An Eastward Look* (1975); *The Unsettling of America: Culture and Agriculture* (1977); *The Collected Poems, 1957–1983* (1985); *Sabbath: Poems* (1987); *Home Economics: Fourteen Essays* (1987); *Remembering* (1988); *Entries: Poems* (1994); *The Farm* (1995); and *A Timbered Choir: The Sabbath Poems, 1979–1997* (1998).

Why I Am Not Going to Buy a Computer

Like almost everybody else, I am hooked to the energy corporations, which I do not admire. I hope to become less hooked to them. In my work, I try to be as little hooked to them as possible. As a farmer, I do almost all of my work with horses. As a writer, I work with a pencil or a pen and a piece of paper.

My wife types my work on a Royal standard typewriter bought new in 1956 and as good now as it was then. As she types, she sees things that are wrong and marks them with small checks in the margins. She is my best critic because she is the one most familiar with my habitual errors and weaknesses. She also understands, sometimes better than I do, what *ought* to be said. We have, I think, a literary cottage industry that works well and pleasantly. I do not see anything wrong with it.

A number of people, by now, have told me that I could greatly improve things by buying a computer. My answer is that I am not going to do it. I have several reasons, and they are good ones.

The first is the one I mentioned at the beginning. I would hate to think that my work as a writer could not be done without a direct dependence on strip-mined coal. How could I write conscientiously against the rape of nature if I were, in the act of writing, implicated in the rape? For the same reason, it matters to me that my writing is done in the daytime, without electric light.

I do not admire the computer manufacturers a great deal more than I admire the energy industries. I have seen their advertisements, attempting to seduce struggling or failing farmers into the belief that they can solve their problems by buying yet another piece of expensive equipment. I am familiar with their propaganda campaigns that have put computers into public schools in need of books. That computers are expected to become as common as TV sets in "the future" does not impress me or matter to me. I do not own a TV set. I do not see that computers are bringing us one step nearer to anything that does matter to me: peace, economic justice, ecological health, political honesty, family and community stability, good work.

What would a computer cost me? More money, for one thing, than I can afford, and more than I wish to pay to people whom I do not admire. But the cost would not be just monetary. It is well understood that technological innovation always requires the discarding of the "old model"—the "old model" in this case being not just our old Royal standard, but my wife, my critic, my closest reader, my fellow worker. Thus (and I think this is typical of present-day technological innovation), what would be superseded would be not only something, but somebody. In order to be technologically up-to-date as a writer, I would have to sacrifice an association that I am dependent upon and that I treasure.

My final and perhaps my best reason for not owning a computer is that I do not wish to fool myself. I disbelieve, and therefore strongly resent, the assertion that I or anybody else could write better or more easily with a computer than with a pencil. I do not see why I should not be as scientific about this as the next fellow: when somebody has used a computer to write work that is demonstrably better than Dante's, and when this better is demonstrably attributable to the use of a computer, then I will speak of computers with a more respectful tone of voice, though I still will not buy one.

To make myself as plain as I can, I should give my standards for technological innovation in my own work. They are as follows:

1. The new tool should be cheaper than the one it replaces.

2. It should be at least as small in scale as the one it replaces.

3. It should do work that is clearly and demonstrably better than the one it replaces.

4. It should use less energy than the one it replaces.

5. If possible, it should use some form of solar energy, such as that of the body.

6. It should be repairable by a person of ordinary intelligence, provided that he or she has the necessary tools.

7. It should be purchasable and repairable as near to home as possible.

8. It should come from a small, privately owned shop or store that will take it back for maintenance and repair.

9. It should not replace or disrupt anything good that already exists, and this includes family and community relationships.

1987

After the foregoing essay, first published in the *New England Review and Bread Loaf Quarterly*, was reprinted in *Harper's*, the *Harper's* editors published the following letters in response and permitted me a reply.   W.B.

Letters

Wendell Berry provides writers enslaved by the computer with a handy alternative: Wife—a low-tech energy-saving device. Drop a pile of handwritten notes on Wife and you get back a finished manuscript, edited while it was typed. What computer can do that? Wife meets all of Berry's uncompromising standards for technological innovation: she's cheap, repairable near home, and good for the family structure. Best of all, Wife is politically correct because she breaks a writer's "direct dependence on strip-mined coal."

History teaches us that Wife can also be used to beat rugs and wash clothes by hand, thus eliminating the need for the vacuum cleaner and washing machine, two more nasty machines that threaten the act of writing.

Gorden Inkeles
Miranda, Calif.

I have no quarrel with Berry because he prefers to write with pencil and paper; that is his choice. But he implies that I and others are somehow impure because we choose to write on a computer. I do not admire the energy corporations, either. Their shortcoming is not that they produce electricity but how they go about it. They are poorly managed because they are blind to long-term consequences. To solve this problem, wouldn't it make more sense to correct the precise error they are making rather than simply ignore their product? I would be happy to join Berry in a protest against strip mining, but I intend to keep plugging this computer into the wall with a clear conscience.

James Rhoads
Battle Creek, Mich.

I enjoyed reading Berry's declaration of intent never to buy a personal computer in the same way that I enjoy reading about the belief systems of unfamiliar tribal cultures. I tried to imagine a tool that would meet Berry's criteria for superiority to his old manual typewriter. The clear winner is the quill pen. It is cheaper, smaller, more energy-efficient, human-powered, easily repaired, and non-disruptive of existing relationships.

Berry also requires that this tool must be "clearly and demonstrably better" than the one it replaces. But surely we all recognize by now that "better" is in the mind of the beholder. To the quill pen aficionado, the benefits obtained from elegant calligraphy might well outweigh all others.

I have no particular desire to see Berry use a word processor; if he doesn't like computers, that's fine with me. However, I do object to his portrayal of this reluctance as a moral virtue. Many of us have found that computers can be an invaluable tool in the fight to protect our environment. In addition to helping me write, my personal computer gives me access to up-to-the-minute reports on the workings of the EPA and the nuclear industry. I participate in electronic bulletin boards on which environmental activists discuss strategy and warn each other about urgent legislative issues. Perhaps Berry feels that the Sierra Club should eschew modern printing technology, which is highly wasteful of energy, in favor of having its members handcopy the club's magazines and other mailings each month?

Nathaniel S. Borenstein
Pittsburgh, Pa.

The value of a computer to a writer is that it is a tool not for generating ideas but for typing and editing words. It is cheaper than a secretary (or a wife!) and arguably more fuel-efficient. And it enables spouses who are not inclined to provide free labor more time to concentrate on *their* own work.

We should support alternatives both to coal-generated electricity and to IBM-style technocracy. But I am reluctant to entertain alternatives that presuppose the traditional subservience of one class to another. Let the PCs come and the wives and servants go seek more meaningful work.

Toby Koosman
Knoxville, Tenn.

Berry asks how he could write conscientiously against the rape of nature if in the act of writing on a computer he was implicated in the rape. I find it ironic that a writer who sees the underlying connectedness of things would allow his diatribe against computers to be published in a magazine that carries ads for the National Rural Electric Cooperative Association, Marlboro, Phillips Petroleum, McDonnell Douglas, and yes, even Smith-Corona. If Berry rests comfortably at night, he must be using sleeping pills.

Bradley C. Johnson
Grand Forks, N.D.

Wendell Berry Replies:

The foregoing letters surprised me with the intensity of the feelings they expressed. According to the writers' testimony, there is nothing wrong with their computers; they are utterly satisfied with them and all that they stand for. My correspondents are certain that I am wrong and that I am, moreover, on the losing side, a side already relegated to the dustbin of history. And yet they grow huffy and condescending over my tiny dissent. What are they so anxious about?

I can only conclude that I have scratched the skin of a technological fundamentalism that, like other fundamentalisms, wishes to monopolize a whole society and, therefore, cannot tolerate the smallest difference of opinion. At the slightest hint of a threat to their complacency, they repeat, like a chorus of toads, the notes sounded by their leaders in industry. The past was gloomy, drudgery-ridden, servile, meaningless, and slow. The present, thanks only to purchasable products, is meaningful, bright, lively, centralized, and fast. The future, thanks only to more purchasable products, is going to be even better. Thus consumers become salesmen, and the world is made safer for corporations.

I am also surprised by the meanness with which two of these writers refer to my wife. In order to imply that I am a tyrant, they suggest by both direct statement and innuendo that she is subservient, characterless, and stupid—a mere "device" easily forced to provide meaningless "free labor." I understand that it is impossible to make an adequate public defense of one's private life, and so I will only point out that there are a number of kinder possibilities that my critics have disdained to imagine: that my wife may do this work because she wants to and likes to; that she may find some use and some meaning in it; that she may not work for nothing. These gentlemen obviously think themselves feminists of the most correct and principled sort, and yet they do not hesitate to stereotype and insult, on the basis of one fact, a woman they do not know. They are audacious and irresponsible gossips.

In his letter, Bradley C. Johnson rushes past the possibility of sense in what I said in my essay by implying that I am or ought to be a fanatic. That I am a person of this century and am implicated in many practices that I regret is fully acknowledged at the beginning of my essay. I did not say that I proposed to end forthwith all my involvement in harmful technology, for I do not know how to do that. I said merely that I want to limit such involvement, and to a certain extent I do know how to do that. If some technology does damage to the world—as two of the above letters seem to agree that it does—then why is it not reasonable, and indeed moral, to try to limit one's use of that technology? *Of course*, I think that I am right to do this.

I would not think so, obviously, if I agreed with Nathaniel S. Borenstein that "'better' is in the mind of the beholder." But if he truly believes this, I do not see why he bothers with his personal computer's "up-to-the-minute reports on the workings of the EPA and the nuclear industry" or why he wishes to be warned about "urgent legislative issues." According to his system, the "better" in a bureaucratic, industrial, or legislative mind is as good as the "better" in his. His mind apparently is being subverted by an objective standard of some sort, and he had better look out.

Borenstein does not say what he does after his computer has drummed him awake. I assume from his letter that he must send donations to conservation organizations and letters to officials. Like James Rhoads, at any rate, he has a clear conscience. But this is what is wrong with the conservation movement. It has a clear conscience. The guilty are always other people, and the wrong is always somewhere else. That is why Borenstein finds his "electronic bulletin board" so handy. To the conservation movement, it is only production that causes environmental degradation; the consumption that supports the production is rarely acknowledged to be at fault. The ideal of the run-of-the-mill conservationist is to impose restraints upon production without limiting consumption or burdening the consciences of consumers.

But virtually all of our consumption now is extravagant, and virtually all of it consumes the world. It is not beside the point that most electrical power comes from strip-mined coal. The history of the exploitation of the Appalachian coal fields is long, and it is available to readers. I do not see how anyone can read it and plug in any appliance with a clear conscience. If Rhoads can do so, that does not mean that his conscience is clear; it means that his conscience is not working.

To the extent that we consume, in our present circumstances, we are guilty. To the extent that we guilty consumers are conservationists, we are absurd. But what can we do? Must we go on writing letters to politicians and donating to conservation organizations until the majority of our fellow citizens agree with us? Or can we do something directly to solve our share of the problem?

I am a conservationist. I believe wholeheartedly in putting pressure on the politicians and in maintaining the conservation organizations. But I wrote my little essay partly in distrust of centralization. I don't think that the government and the conservation organizations alone will ever make us a conserving society. Why do I need a centralized computer system to alert me to environmental crises? That I live every hour of every day in an environmental crisis I know from all my senses. Why then is not my first duty to reduce, so far as I can, my own consumption?

Finally, it seems to me that none of my correspondents recognizes the innovativeness of my essay. If the use of a computer is a new idea, then a newer idea is not to use one.

from *Sabbath: Poems*

I (1979)

I go among trees and sit still.
All my stirring becomes quiet
around me like circles on water.
My tasks lie in their places
where I left them, asleep like cattle.

Then what is afraid of me comes
and lives a while in my sight.
What it fears in me leaves me,
and the fear of me leaves it.
It sings, and I hear its song.

Then what I am afraid of comes.
I live for a while in its sight.
What I fear in it leaves it,
and the fear of it leaves me.
It sings, and I hear its song.

After days of labor,
mute in my consternations,
I hear my song at last,
and I sing it. As we sing
the day turns, the trees move.

VIII (1979)

I go from the woods into the cleared field:
A place no human made, a place unmade
By human greed, and to be made again.
Where centuries of leaves once built by dying
A deathless potency of light and stone
And mold of all that grew and fell, the timeless
Fell into time. The earth fled with the rain,
The growth of fifty thousand years undone
In a few careless seasons, stripped to rock
And clay—a "new land," truly, that no race
Was ever native to, but hungry mice
And sparrows and the circling hawks, dry thorns
And thistles sent by generosity
Of new beginning. No Eden, this was
A garden once, a good and perfect gift;
Its possible abundance stood in it
As it then stood. But now what it might be
Must be foreseen, darkly, through many lives—
Thousands of years to make it what it was,
Beginning now, in our few troubled days.

III (1984)

The crop must drink, we move the pipe
To draw the water back in time
To fall again upon the field,
So that the harvest may grow ripe,
The year complete its ancient rhyme
With other years, and a good yield
Complete our human hope. And this
Is Sunday work, necessity
Depriving us of needed rest.
Yet this necessity is less,
Being met, not by one, but three.
Neighbors, we make this need our feast.

IV (1984)

The summer ends, and it is time
To face another way. Our theme
Reversed, we harvest the last row
To store against the cold, undo
The garden that will be undone.
We grieve under the weakened sun
To see all earth's green fountains dried,
And fallen all the works of light.
You do not speak, and I regret
This downfall of the good we sought
As though the fault were mine. I bring
The plow to turn the shattering
Leaves and bent stems into the dark.
From which they may return. At work,
I see you leaving our bright land,
The last cut flowers in your hand.

Fred Chappell

(1936–   )

Fred Chappell was born on May 28, 1936, in Canton, North Carolina. He earned his
B.A. from Duke University in 1961, where he began a lifetime friendship with
Reynolds Price. He completed his M.A. at Duke in 1964, the same year he began
teaching creative writing at the University of North Carolina at Greensboro, a position he has held since that time. In 1959, Chappell married Susan Nicholls, with whom
he has a son, Heath.

Both a poet and a novelist, Chappell published *It Is Time, Lord* in 1963. This first
novel was followed quickly by the second, *The Inkling* (1965). His first book of
poems, *The World Between His Eyes* (1971), received the Roanoke-Chowan Poetry
Cup of the North Carolina Literary and Historical Association. In 1981 he published a
book of meditative poems, *Midquest: A Poem*, often seen as the greatest achievement
of his work.

Chappell continues to publish fiction with *Moments of Light* (1979), a short story
collection. In 1985 he received the Bollingen Prize. In 1987 *The Fred Chappell Reader*
was published, which includes selected earlier works. Other works by Chappell are
The Gaudy Place (1973); *Bloodfire: A Poem* (1979); *Castle Tzingal* (1984); *Brighten
the Corner Where You Are* (1989); *C: Poems* (1993); *Spring Garden: New and Selected Poems* (1995); *Farewell, I'm Bound to Leave You* (1996); and *Look Back All the
Green Valley: A Novel* (1999).

Third Base Coach

He commands as mysteriously as
the ghost of Hamlet's father.

Shuffles & tugs & yawns & spits.
Like a steeplejack he itches weirdly and continually.

Dances on his grave plot.
Prophetic flame at the wiped lip.

The fouls go by him like tracer bullets.
Writes runes with his toe, healthy spells.

Like an Aeschylean tragedy he's static; baffling;
Boring; but.
                                    Urgent with import.

Fast Ball

for Winston Watson

The grass raw and electric
as the cat's whiskers.

3 and 2.

At second the runner: loiters:
nervous as the corner
junkie: loitering for a connection.

Hunched like the cat, the batter;
his prehensile
bat he curls and uncurls.

The pitcher hitches & hitches.

At last the hitcher pitches.

"It gets about as big," Ty
Cobb said, "as a watermelon seed.
It hisses at you as it passes."

The outfielders prance like kittens
back to the dugout.
They've seen what they're glad *they*
don't have to worry about.

Spitballer

A poet because his hand goes first
to his head & then to his heart.

The catcher accepts the pitch
as a pool receives a dripping diver;
soaks up the curve like
cornflakes in milk.

The hitter makes great
show of wringing out his bat.

On the mound he grins, tiger
in a tree, when the umpire
turns round & round the ball
magically dry as alum.

He draws a second salary as maintenance man.
Since while he pitches he waters the lawn.

Junk Ball

By the time it gets to the plate
it's got weevils and termites.

Trying to hit Wednesday with a bb gun.

Sunday.

Or curves like a Chippendale leg or
flutters like a film unsprocketed or
plunges like Zsa Zsa's neckline or
sails away as coy as Shirley Temple

                                        (or)

Not even Mussolini could make
the sonofabitch arrive on time.

Strike Zone

for Joe Nicholls

Like the Presidency its size
depends upon the man.

Paneless window he doesn't want to smash,
the pitcher whittles at the casement.

The batter peers
into it like a peeping tom.
Does he like what he sees?

The limits get stricter
as they get less visible:

throwing at yards & yards of McCovey,
an inch or so
of Aparicio,
the pitcher tries not to go
bats.
The umpire knows a secret.
But he gives no sign.

Ball 2.

Song of the Seven

I saw the seven deadly sins
        Sitting all in a pretty row
And twittering like blackbirds
        Above new-fallen snow.

Avarice clothed in gold-red fishscale
        Hoarded itself for moth and rust
And a voice like a naughty French postcard said
        "Trust Lust."

Hate was gnawing its beshitted tail
        Down to the bitter bone
And baleful Envy, with a leer,
        Uttered a bitter groan.

Gluttony gorged itself on mud.
        Shaped like a basketball
It couldn't budge; merely a mouth
        To chew and slobber all.

And Blasphemy was a stupid mouth
        A voice like a fetid fart.
Eyeless Despair shuffled searching, searching
        For its unremembered heart,

Shuffling and searching in the holy light
        Darkening holy air
Whining its genuine pity
        For eyeless forsaken Despair.

I took up stones round comfy stones,
        I knocked them over, one by one,
I watched them topple like political excuses.
        Lord Jesus it was fun.

VII

Postmodern South (1980–Present)

Is the postmodern South a world unto itself, a cultural "island" even more separate and distinctive than other identifiable islands in the American archipelago? How has the South contributed to its own institutionalized stereotypes that continue to make the region an enigma, thwarting efforts at interpretation? These questions are at the root of Southern literature and experience in our time and suggest ways that the South has historically offered a challenge to American ideals and identity.

This challenge has traditionally been perceived as one of a peculiar social malignancy requiring government aid to eradicate related economic, racial, and health-related maladies. Sociologist Larry Griffin summarizes the ills plaguing the South in the first decades of the modern era:

> In the first half of the twentieth century, the South, more than the rest of the nation, was understood to be economically impoverished: too many of its children, black and white, were uneducated and suffering from hunger, pellagra, hookworm; too many of its adults, white and black, were unskilled and trapped in a vicious cycle of sharecropping, debt peonage, and poverty. Only in the South were conditions of life so brutal and dispiriting that almost ten million of its citizens escaped the region through migration to the North, one of the largest voluntary mass movements of human beings ever witnessed. Only in the South was the use of thousands of U.S. Army troops required to get its public schools and colleges to open their doors to members of a minority race.[1]

Griffin acknowledges that his list is a partial one, the "inventory" of "serious problems . . . virtually as long and damning" as the perpetual "register of Southern outrages."[2] Fueling the Southern habit of outrage are the numerous depictions of the

South as a problematic region, a place in need of "fixing" by social engineers, academics, and specialists of the talk-show variety.

Obvious enough is that the South still owns its share of social problems "amenable to solution."[3] In 1999, for example, the former eleven Confederate states comprised slightly less than one-third of the country's population while accounting for almost 40 percent of the nation's homicides. The South's large cities have earned a reputation for being especially murderous. Juvenile crime of a repugnant and lethal nature is on the upswing, too. Whereas in the past, hatemongers found time-honored allegiance with such groups as the Ku Klux Klan, "the new direction of intolerance lies with the [younger] skinheads and the neo-Nazis."[4] Even these groups are not exclusive to the South, however. Morris Dees, civil rights advocate and founder of Klanwatch (1981), notes a current tendency for militant racist organizations to spring up outside the South, finding followers in such states as Idaho, Oregon, and Washington. Uncertain is whether the South is becoming more tolerant or whether other sections are developing their own distinctively virulent strains of prejudice.

What may at first seem less problematic and more inspiring are recent advances in the Southern economy. As late as 1980, a small percentage of domiciles in the South lacked indoor plumbing, and medical care in some rural areas was lacking or substandard. Although the South still retains pockets of severe poverty, a dearth of material resources is far less obvious than in the past, and the region now boasts of communities ranking among the country's most affluent. In preferred locales, Southern property values exceed the national average, while the cost of living tends to be about 10 percent lower.[5] The preponderance of shopping malls, restaurants, bookstores, museums, country clubs, and vacation resorts all attest to the South's urgency not only to realize the American dream but also to demonstrate that Southern enterprise is second to none. Fortune 500 corporations find the South a hospitable environs, and business interests all but obliterate race and class distinctions in many computer-driven Southern cities. Accounting for this newfound harmony, writer Harry Crews targets the major source of inspiration: "In the South, money is more important than death."

Yet affluence has created unanticipated problems. Southerners now spend almost as much time commuting to work as their counterparts in more exclusively urban sections of the nation; and according to traffic engineers in Atlanta, that metropolis may outrank Los Angeles as the most congested American city of the twenty-first century. Atlantans know, say the engineers, that so-called "rush hour"—the time it takes to exit the city's glass towers for the suburban outskirts of Dunwoody, Decatur, and Snellville—is, in actuality, a bracketed juggernaut lasting from approximately two o'clock in the afternoon until seven or eight o'clock each evening. Against the Atlanta sunset stretches a shimmering northbound caravan of bumper-locked traffic. With few exceptions, the drivers are all journeying back to the relative calm and security of neighborhoods where neighbors spend little time getting to know each other. There is no porch talk, because there are no porches. Amid the countless "tract" mansions and within the confines of gated communities, neighborhood associations compensate for the lack of geniality by sponsoring occasional parties where uneasy talk centers on work, school, golf, and the value of real estate. In short, the suburban South takes stubborn pride in being no different from any other place else in America. Or as Marshall Frady describes it, "The South has become etherized in all those ways a people are subtly rendered memoryless, blank of identity, by assimilation into chrome and asphalt and plastic."

Detaching themselves from the glowing screens of the Internet, Southerners may at times feel a nagging compulsion to ask just what problem the American South now poses that the rest of the country does not. If the South is just as affluent, as violent, as rude, as urbanized, as homogenized as everywhere else, then what precisely is the problem that defines the South and its oppositional relation to the rest of the country? In the past, the South stood apart, often embarrassingly so. No longer a brooding pterodactyl casting a shadow over the nation's progress, the region has achieved cultural assimilation more speedily than could have been imagined several decades ago. In response to this dizzying phenomenon, some baby boom Southerners display an overriding nostalgia that finds outlets in genealogical research, historical reenactment, and architectural reclamation. A fear seems to exist that, without this frenzy of activity, the South will cease to remember itself as it was—both for its good and bad qualities. Moreover, some say that this anxiety is justified, given the tendency of increasingly ahistorical generation X Southerners not to be concerned with Southern identity at all. For many of these younger Southerners, the South is simply an artifact of the pop culture, a mythic region of stereotypes created in Hollywood and New York.

As has often been the case, stereotypes about the South cling with a potent tenacity. The genre of Southern films, for instance, owes its life to such identifiable character types as "pitifully poor farmers, unrepentent bigots, sadistic rednecks, sex objects, and greedy, ambitious members of a corrupt upper class."[6] Nor has Hollywood's depiction of these types evolved much since 1945. One reason is that it is often easier to accept formulaic assumptions about a people and a place than to acknowledge the more complex social realities operating beneath the surface of appearances. Another reason is the lingering suspicion that not all stereotypes are invalid and may even prove useful. An examination of such 1980s-era films as *Southern Comfort* (1981), *The Lords of Discipline* (1982), *The Color Purple* (1985), and *Mississippi Burning* (1988) reveals situations that do not fall short of fact in depicting some Southerners and some kinds of Southern experience.

Not even Hollywood's obvious historical inaccuracies and grating caricatures seem to diminish a fondness for the timeworn Southern trinity of race, class, and religion—a fact seen in the popularity of such 1990s films as *Driving Miss Daisy*, *Fried Green Tomatoes*, *A Gathering of Old Men*, and *The Apostle*. Because Southerners tend to equate virtue with simplicity (even simplemindedness), few people could ask for more satisfying displays of this sentimental indulgence than the ones found in *Nell*, *Forrest Gump*, and *Swingblade*. In retrospect, popular films of the 1980s and 1990s could not have been more accommodating in reinforcing salient features of the Southern myth.

If Southerners themselves failed to rise up in protest against the media creations they were supposed to represent, that may have been the case because those stereotypes had not yet disappeared from the Southern landscape. Some were gaining prominence in the national political arena, showing a talent for statesmanship while shaping a broad cultural agenda. For this reason, historian and American studies specialists B. C. Hall and economist and sociologist C. T. Wood kept track of the South's end-of-the-century goings-on by monitoring the activities of three varieties of the "species" of Southern white male. In recent films, literature, and life, these three types have emerged full-blown from W. J. Cash's "man at the center," the yeoman farmer whose industry and chicanery accounted for the evolution of the South's aristocracy. Hall and Wood's descriptions of these "evolutionary cousins" are tart, characteristically irreverent, and arguably offensive.[7] Nevertheless, the scholars maintain that their taxonomy and nomenclature are essential to an understanding of the postmodern South. As with the antebellum caste system, Hall and Wood's classifications exist as a hierarchy predicated on notions of class. At the apex of this class pyramid resides the Redneck Aristocrat:

> With him resides the hope of the Neo-South. Much is expected of him when he is born into a family of the genteel poor. The Redneck Aristocrat attends the right Protestant church and is encouraged to keep company with only the right people; he is invited to the social affairs of the local baron as the lesser friend of the baronial spawn. In his adolescence he was a Methodist or a Baptist lay speaker and was eaten up with the Calvinist dogma of guilt. His attitude toward women is from the Old Testament vision of women as vessels of wrath, a chalice of original sin issuing from Eve. The Redneck Aristocrat was an ROTC cadet in high school, an honor graduate, salutatorian perhaps but hardly ever valedictorian (a role reserved for the daughter of the local nabob). He attended a private university—Vanderbilt or Duke or even the Ivy League—on a combination of loans and academic or athletic scholarships. One or two of his number even achieved the dizzying heights of a Fulbright or Wilson or Rhodes fellowship.[8]

Hall and Wood point out that with notable exceptions, military experience is a "must" for the redneck aristocrat. Working hard to establish all the right social connections, he marries into a prominent family, adopting a mantle of social responsibility while promoting his own career. The seedier side to this sort of Southerner is the deception with which he passes himself off as a family man while keeping a "mistress at the condo he owns at the state capital."[9]

The second type of white Southern male casting a shadow of influence in the new South is what Hall and Wood term the Good Old Boy:

> The eldest male child born of a family as poor as frogs living in a posthole, the Good Old Boy has forever been known in the South as a horse trader. He's good at everything. He does things with his hands that a lot of men can't. He's got what's known down here as "a little bit of wit, a little bit of grit, and a whole lot of shit." He's funny and he's a trickster, and he'll get his hand in your back pocket faster than his granddaddy, the snake-oil pitchman. He'll beat you at horse, nine-ball, or straight poker. He's got the best coon dogs in the region and knows where to get the best moonshine in four states. He's been around the world once and to two county fairs. His sweet little sister gave him his name as her first word, "Bubber."[10]

The comic manifestations of this type are obvious until we consider his inherent racism and belief in "white supremacy." Nevertheless, he loves "his wife, his children, and his dogs!"[11] He will fight for his principles and to protect his family. With the good old boy, honor is everything. He is the source of the Southern adage that a man's handshake is his word.

At the bottom of the list is the most detestable and fearful of Anglo-Saxon descendants, the Mean Sumbitch:

> No redeeming factor involved here. This one is dangerous, in a particularly low, mean, Southern way. The Mean Sumbitch grew up believing that fighting is the way to prove everything—manhood, values, worth, character. He treats women like sewer water.[12]

Although the mean sumbitch is usually a loner, he somehow manages to locate equally demented associates who join him in his often racially motivated criminal activities. Historically, "he's the one standing beside his trophy, the body of a black man beaten and scoured, still showing a little fire and blood [while hanging] from a rope drawn from the ground."[13]

Although most people will find these stereotypes repugnant, few can deny that they continue to be stock features of postmodern film and literature—powerful semiotic stimuli that often coax charged emotions from viewers and readers alike. If, as theologian Harvey Cox maintains, people are becoming more intuitive and less logical, then the unconscious effect of Hall and Wood's types is to reinforce images that have already been culturally sanctioned. Few Southern stories in our time do not rely at least somewhat on these depiction, if for no other reason but to parody or debunk them. Stereotypes of the Southern white male are not the only persistent manifestations of regional consciousness. The Southern belle is a fixture every bit as established as other Southern types. For all her hackneyed and reactionary status, the belle remains a compelling archetype—especially for audiences outside the region where perceptions sometimes substitute for facts and where the South more often exists as a state of mind than a reality. In defining the belle, Florence King points out that she is a "product of the Deep South, which is a product of the nineteenth century and the Age of Romanticism."[14]

The belle did not die in the century of her birth. Hollywood kept her alive in numerous twentieth-century cinematic depictions—the most obvious being Scarlett O'Hara in *Gone With the Wind*—and television more recently resuscitated her flagging image in the Southern-inspired sitcom *Designing Women* (1986–1993). Even this program's title played on the allegedly dissembling and manipulative nature of the belle who survives "by her beauty, her spirited veneer, and her ability to manage men without seeming to do so."[15] The series was enormously popular, owing not only to the viewing audience's fascination with the type but also with writer Linda Bloodworth-Thomason's ability to let the major characters play off against the roles created for them. The ability to invoke a stereotype while at the same time mocking it has been a chief feature of Southern aesthetics both in the past and in recent times. In fact, it is the collapse of the stereotype under the weight of its own assumptions that creates convincing situations like those found in the fiction of such postmodern writers as Lisa Alther, Bobbie Ann Mason, and Ann Rivers Siddons.

Some critics warn that there is a danger in perpetuating stereotypes of any fashion. For instance, while the Southern belle may at times be naively "charming," other types such as Mammies and Daisy Maes are more destructive in the social messages they convey. Stereotypes may also disguise or distort a complex web of relationships like the ones noted by sociologist Barbara Ellen Smith:

Southern women of different races and classes live in complex relationship to one another. Young white women in Mississippi who fashion themselves Southern belles unknowingly rest their delicacy on the cultural representations of their African-American peers. Working-class women in eastern Kentucky, once dependent on the wages of their coal miner husbands, now support their families by charging twenty-five dollars a day to take care of others' children, thus making it feasible for middle-class mothers to pursue their careers. Women who are midlevel bankers and stockbrokers in Atlanta, frustrated by the acts of sexism and the glass ceiling they encounter each day, nonetheless enjoy the accouterments of privilege made possible by, among many others, the Cambodian women who dust and vacuum their offices at night. This web of relationships stretches wide far beyond the South: women workers in a Philips electronic factory in Tennessee are unemployed because their employer just moved their plant to the U.S. Mexican border, where he hires Latinas for the same reason—low wages—that he once hired Southern women.[16]

Smith is correct in noting that the social network of feminine relationships in the South represents an intricate matrix with far-reaching consequences never entirely circumscribed by geography. By implication, Southern writers need to account for this complexity rather than relying on stock situations and caricatures.

Unfortunately, even out of the most complex social realities emerge typologies that only reinforce the omnipresent problem of Southern identity. *Southern Cultures* coeditor Harry Watson explains: "Most any southerner can tell you about some time or another when he or she felt labeled with an unwelcome stereotype, and felt the urge to deny that southerness could be summed up in any particular trait or image."[17] Yet, Watson notes, "Without batting an eye at the contradiction, many of us are just as ready to complete the sentence 'all southerners are ———,' resorting to such familiar images as poor, dumb, bigoted, aristocratic, violent, polite."[18] Thus, it may be more difficult than imagined to shake off stereotypes that history and the ongoing quest for identity conspire to reinforce, especially when the national impulse is to suggest that only in the South do stereotypes actually apply.

Conscious effort to reject some types often invites the introduction of other unintended ones. Over time, a favorable type can also undergo an unfavorable transformation, given shifting historical awareness. Who would have anticipated that a much admired, even lauded, species of Southern white male in the 1960s would become the subject of such searing excoriation as that offered by historian Nash Boney in the mid-1980s? Defending the "redneck" as a maligned figure in history and literature, Boney targets the redneck's self-righteous detractors, taking aim at their hypocrisy masquerading as virtue:

The redneck's privileged, well-to-do critics preach truth and beauty, brotherhood and integration, but often they lead a very different private life. The scenario is all too familiar. The classic liberal male—the kind of guy who jogs all the way to his vasectomy—and his equally trendy wife surge out into the rotten world at dawn. They emerge from a luxury, highrise apartment that stands in the heart of a great city but is totally removed from the real life of the urban masses, or more likely they drive into the inner city from a comfortable, sheltered suburb. On the way to work they drop off their precious children at a properly sanitized private or parochial school—not lily white, of course, but ivory white with only a few token middle-class black students. Then they speed on downtown past several rundown public schools swarming with the great unwashed black and white and brown masses. These committed crusaders hardly notice; they have a busy day ahead, including afternoon conferences with reform groups dedicated to eradicating America's many ills, especially racism. Then finally the workday ends and they quickly return to their ivory tower apartment or, more likely, to their safe suburb, which is just about as meaningfully integrated as their children's school.[19]

Even Boney's passion for this "lost cause" seems dated now. Yet his defense of one Southern social type at the expense of another shows a draconian shift in regional sensibility characteristic of the South since its earliest days.

The problem with stereotypes and what to do with familiar, often recycled Southern materials is not a new one. Recognizing in 1967 that the well of inspiration had dried up for Southern writers continuing to exploit the "magnolias and mint julep school," novelist Walker Percy exhorted his colleagues to embrace present realities rather than indulge in a nostalgic past. Contemporary fiction, Percy maintained, had to account for the "highway culture," skyscrapers, and the "average" person in the suburbs or on the golf course. Percy's dictum was so sedulously obeyed that, by 1988, Josephine Humphreys began to complain about these overworked topics: "Too many writers have milked the condo-golf resort scene; too many books have pointed out that the South continues to become more like the North every day."[20] Concluding that "a purely urban setting" was "hard ground for a novelist," Humphreys opted for the small town since "town alone is that community in which community itself is discernible."[21] Humphreys's declaration demonstrates how Southern writers have been willing to shift terrains in order to find what they were looking for. If they didn't always know what they were looking for, they sometimes shifted anyway.

The constantly shifting landscape of the postmodern world finds a new generation of writers confronting changes and embracing challenges posed by yet another "highway culture"—that of the information highway. If, in the past, stereotypes militated against the Southern writer's efforts to locate new territory to explore, the dawn of the twenty-first century reveals an ever-shrinking South in which old and new images alike risk quick assimilation, overexposure, and subsequent discarding. The New South will need to be created newer and newer by the moment, no small task for writers living at digital speed.

Ironically, as our technology becomes more complex, the "messages" we receive about the South may become simpler, given the need for speed that our attention spans have come to expect. The slowly woven syntax of relations characterizing Southern literature and history may be streamlined beyond recognition into a network of inevitable links, sites, and bytes. If Southern writers have learned anything over the past four hundred years, however, it is that change is inevitable, nor is all change bad. The trick has always been to let the present mediate between the extremes of the past and the future, between tradition and transition.

Even at a time when older Southern writers wonder where new writers and readers will come from, it is risky to proclaim that the South and Southern literature are artifacts suited only for anthropological exploration. As in the past, the South may have plenty left to say to the nation—even in the information age. As for an overriding fear that the region will be swallowed up by a Leviathan of technological excesses, we may do well to recall a mantra once offered by George Tindall: "The Vanishing South has staged one of the most prolonged disappearing acts since the decline and fall of the Roman Empire."[22]

Already there are signs of new vitality on the Southern landscape. As usual, these signs are being found in what may seem unusual places until we consider the power of the "messages" in art and the penchant for shrewd marketing practices displayed by many Southerners. In 1997 in Charleston, South Carolina, two aspiring entrepreneurs, Cuban-born Angel Quintero and his African American partner Sherman Evans, opened NuSouth Apparel, specializing in unusual clothing and "racial reconciliation." Bridging a gulf between the past and the present, the two market a "lifestyle" in the form of "clothing with a message." In particular, Quintero and Evans embroider a new and improved version of the Confederate flag on T-shirts and sweaters. John Edge summarizes the changes:

> The bones of the design are the stars and bars of the old battle flag of the Confederacy albeit with a change in colors from white and blue to green and black. The background is now bloodred rather than maroon. In short, the flag associated with secession, slavery, states' rights, and white supremacy has been reclaimed and reworked, incorporating the colors often associated with African liberation. The effects are subtle; the intent is to elicit comment, conversation, and commerce.[23]

Quintero and Evans admit that "the NuSouth message is an odd amalgam of sound bite-sized profundity and sloganeering."[24] What may not be as obvious is how they have merged the Old and New South in such a way as to remind us of the best of both. In their own words, "NuSouth offers an opportunity for dialogue. That's the real solution to race relations: dialogue. It's like our new campaign says, 'For the sons and daughters of former slaves. For the sons and daughters of former slave owners. Threads that connect us. Words that free us.'"[25]

May it always be so.

Notes

1. Larry J. Griffin, *The South as an American Problem*, eds. Larry J. Griffin and Don H. Doyle (Athens: University of Georgia Press, 1995), 12.
2. Griffin, 12–13.
3. Griffin, 14.
4. B. C. Hall and C. T. Wood, *The South* (New York: Simon and Schuster, 1995), 171.
5. John Shelton Reed and Dale Volberg Reed, *1001 Things Everyone Should Know about the South* (New York: Doubleday, 1996), 56.
6. Edward D. C. Campbell, *The Celluloid South*, (Knoxville: University of Tennessee Press, 1980), 143.
7. Hall and Wood, 160.
8. Hall and Wood, 159.
9. Hall and Wood, 160.

10. Hall and Wood, 161.
11. Hall and Wood, 161.
12. Hall and Wood, 162.
13. Hall and Wood, 163.
14. Florence King, *On the Night the Hogs Ate Willie*, eds. Barbara Binswanger and Jim Charlton (New York: Penguin Books, 1994), 33.
15. King, 35.
16. Barbara Ellen Smith, *Neither Separate Nor Equal* (Philadelphia: Temple University Press, 1999), 13.
17. Harry Watson, *Southern Cultures*, Vol 4, no. 2 (Chapel Hill: University of North Carolina Press, 1998), 2.
18. Watson, 2.
19. F. N. Boney, *Southerners All* (Macon: Mercer University Press, 1984), 35.
20. Josephine Humphreys, *The Prevailing South*, ed. Dudley Clendinen (Marietta, GA: Longstreet Press, 1988), 214.
21. Humphreys, 216.
22. George Tindall, *On the Night the Hogs Ate Willie*, eds. Barbara Binswanger and Jim Charlton (New York: Penguin Books, 1994), 144.
23. John Edge, *The Oxford American*, Jan/Feb 1999, ed. Marc Smirnoff, *Magazine* (Oxford: The Oxford American Press, 1999), 76.
24. Edge, 76.
25. Edge, 76.

The most significant event in the Upper South in the last decade of the twentieth century was the election of an Arkansan, William Jefferson Clinton, as president, and of a Tennessean, Albert Gore, Jr., as vice president, of the United States. Not being from the Deep South seemed advantageous to both men. John Shelton Reed and Dale Volberg Reed describe the felicitous arrangement:

> Bill Clinton was liberal enough to overcome non–Southern Democrats' reservations about a governor of Arkansas, but he wasn't seen as a "typical Democrat," so he could still appeal to some conservative white voters. Clinton's choice of a running mate, Senator Al Gore of Tennessee, produced the so-called double-Bubba ticket, the first time since before the Civil War that a major party had nominated two Southerners.[1]

Despite the reference to Clinton and Gore as bubbas, each was a quintessential example of what Hall and Wood term the Redneck Aristocrat. Ostensibly small-town boys, a generation removed from Southern agricultural roots, both spent time at elite Eastern schools (Clinton at Yale Law School, Gore at Harvard) in the habit of past generations of would-be Southern aristocrats. Both practiced law (a gentleman's profession in the South) and married women who could offer social and political advantages. Both were Protestant in a particularly inoffensive way. Whenever the occasion called for it, each could invoke a "plainfolks" appeal designed to put people at ease and remind audiences of the penchant for humble origins shared by Southerners. But, as Julia Reed pointed out in the November 1998 issue of *The Oxford American* magazine, "The president is not naturally a good ole boy."[2] Even his folksy locutions, said Reed, were designed to trick Northerners rather than to demonstrate the *copia* of colorful Southern colloquialisms.

Yet labels confirming the "good old boy" stereotype continue to attach. For example, after the Clinton-Gore victory of 1992, Gore Vidal, America's brilliant twentieth-century wag, wrote an essay for *GQ* entitled "Goin' South."[3] In characteristic satirical style, Vidal compared the victorious political duo with Huck Finn and Tom Sawyer, noting the roguish similarities between the newly elected president and vice president and Twain's fictional mischief makers. It scarcely mattered that Vidal's analogy quickly broke down or that his portraits of Clinton and Gore were largely caricatures. Significant was the handiness with which Vidal reached for a literary comparison and found one. Southern literature provided both the source and inspiration, a fact pointing to the inextricable relationship between Southern politics and a literary tradition dating back to Colonial times.

For a people given to taking their literature seriously, the leap in making a comparison like Vidal's is almost effortless. After all, Clinton and Gore were characters in our nation's serialized narrative, their status mythic in an age when political celebrities embody larger-than-life dimensions. At the core of their success lay a version of Southern adversity overcome. In a land of storytellers, their ascendancy was—just as Vidal intuited—a story worth telling.

In many ways, the South still invites expansion of a storytelling tradition shared with the past. Because the South's story is ongoing, even "problematic," the region continues seeking ways to account for the complexities, contradictions, and paradoxical status that literature has always mirrored. This quest finds Upper South writers exploring questions of race, class, gender, and religion in numerous regional magazines and journals. A count reveals that of the more than one thousand publications listed in the 1999 edition of *Poet's Market*, a third are published in the South. Of that number, more than half originate in the Upper South. In a region where literacy rates are often lowest, the devotion to literary activities is keen, reflecting an awareness of a revered tradition and the potential for future accomplishments. A tally of individual states shows that the number of publications devoted to publishing poetry in Virginia is 32; in Maryland, 28; in North Carolina, 24; in Tennessee, 17; and in Kentucky, 16. Kentucky ties with Connecticut in the number of journals given to poetry in each state.

Even magazines not devoted exclusively to literature often focus on Southern writing, providing the region's authors with a way of showcasing some of their best contemporary work. Such was the case of *Southern Magazine*, published in Little Rock, Arkansas, in the 1980s. Devoted to the changing South while focusing on numerous unchanging traditions (e.g., grits, quail hunting, and church attendance), *Southern Magazine* featured fiction by such postmodern authors as Bobbie Ann Mason, Harry Crews, and Will Campbell. Also included were articles like "Robinson Crusoe Reading," which polled Southern writers about which books they would ask for if they suddenly found themselves stranded on a desert island. In one such installment, Madison Smartt Bell summed up the dilemma of both the postmodern Southern writer and his or her reader:

> If it's true . . . that Western Civilization is in the process of fragmenting into utter chaos, then we're really all island dwellers already. When no one can agree on what's important to know and prize, then everyone's system of thought is already insular enough. And the picture of everyone floating off alone on his own cultural asteroid is one of the things that any desert island books agenda represents.[4]

Despite the privatization of experience so common to the postmodern world, Bell indulges in the fantasy of being an "island dweller" long enough to select works that answer the mythological requirements of (qualified) meaning in our time. Predictably, a number of those works are written by authors found in this anthology: William Faulkner, Andrew Lytle, Shelby Foote, Eudora Welty, Flannery O'Connor, Peter Taylor, Wendell Berry, and Robert Penn Warren. Recognizing that a list can be "a fence to keep my ideas in and yours out," Bell suggests that the ideal "is for books to foster and support a community of thought."[5]

Emphasis on community and a shared interest in literature have given rise to numerous literary conferences in the Upper South. Few regions can boast the number and quality of events designed to bring writers and readers in close association. For instance, the University of the South at Sewanee, Tennessee, sponsors the annual Sewanee Writers' Conference, a prestigious gathering of writers, readers, and literary aficionados who labor in workshop settings with Nobel Laureates and Pulitzer Prize winners. The Southern Conference on Literature, held in Chattanooga, Tennessee, features presentations and panel discussions by some of the South's most illustrious novelists, playwrights, poets, and critics. Similarly, the Southern Book Festival, a fall celebration staged on the mall adjacent the Tennessee capitol building in Nashville, is a three-day conference honoring the contributions of the South's premier authors and publishers. While the Sewanee-Chattanooga-Nashville axis offers an important impetus to contemporary Southern literature, other Upper South cities host similar occasions, giving citizens an opportunity to savor literature in hospitable surroundings. The atmosphere is often described as familial, and attendees compare the experience to a family reunion where family members display none of the characteristic Southern dysfunctionality.

No event brings families together in closer dysfunctional proximity than the death of a "loved one." "The Art of Dying Well," a chapter from Lisa Alther's serio-comic novel *Kinflicks*, is a delightfully irreverent dissection of the Southern habit of dying. Almost no one dies better or more theatrically than a particular class of Southerner, ever conscious of good manners and tasteful displays of grief. The protagonist of the novel, a young woman named Ginny Hull, recalls her mother's fascination with "dying properly." A gallery of family photos is a reminder of the inevitability of death and of the need to exit this vale of tears with aplomb. Some of Ginny's relatives have not always accomplished this goal:

> [There was] Great-uncle Lester, a druggist in Sow Gap, who became addicted to cough syrup and one night threw himself under the southbound train to Chattanooga. Cousin Lovella, who dove into a nest of water moccasins in an abandoned stone quarry at a family reunion in 1932. Another cousin who stuck his head out of a car window to read a historical marker about the Battle of Lookout Mountain and was sideswiped by a Mason-Dixon transport truck.

Although sometimes accused of creating characters that are stereotypes, Alther scarcely exaggerates the complex dynamics of Southern families in which the roles of patriarch and matriarch are solidly defined.

The family in need of healing is a key theme of Maya Angelou's "On the Pulse of Morning." However, the family here is not merely the South with its history of divided relations, but rather the entire nation living "too long in the bruising darkness." The speaker is the anima of the country, its soul, that finds ultimate expression in the elemental voices of "A Rock, A River, A Tree." Each voice offers its own particular strength, its own urging. Yet, each reminds us that we are wedded to the past and to each new hour that "holds new chances / For a new beginning." What we are not wedded to is "fear, yoked eternally / To brutishness." In this powerful lyric, Angelou suggests that only a nation courageous enough to confront its past can hope to face the uncertainties of the present and future. "On the Pulse of Morning" was written at the request of President-elect Bill Clinton and was read by Angelou at Clinton's inauguration on January 20, 1993.

As with Angelou's work, rocks, trees, and water provide both the literal and metaphysical imagery in A. R. Ammons's taut, elegant poetry. Although Ammons's status as a Southerner is not an indispensable influence on his writing, his early training as a botanist figures prominently in shaping the themes of his work. Like any good scientist, Ammons pays close attention to details, and the ability to see clearly beyond boundaries that ordinarily limit our perception is a recurring motif in poems such as "Classic," "Periphery," and "Clarity." In "Classic," for instance, Ammons addresses the paradox that occurs between the observer and the thing being observed, in this case, a mountain. The mountain reminds the poet that the poet's perceptions are an inescapable part of whatever description he offers. In "Periphery," Ammons complains about intrusions that disrupt his tidy way of seeing things, his "paradigm" of meaning that risks "meaningless" each second with the introduction of new data and new objects in the visual field. The need for unchanging vision in a constantly changing world is the conundrum Ammons addresses in "Clarity." There a rockslide changes an expected scene, causing the poet to lament mildly that the "sight will never be the same." Yet even turmoil can reveal "scores of knowledge / now obvious and quiet."

Hearing is just as important as seeing in the life of a community like Bourbonville, Tennessee, the fictional locale of several novels by Richard Marius, author of *After the War* (1992). Reminding us that portions of the South have always been, in Shelby Foote's phrase "a great melting pot," Marius traces the history of a Greek immigrant family in rural East Tennessee following World War I. The problems of assimilation can be seen early in the novel when an immigrant named Bernal warns the narrator, "You should never listen to stories about the place. They will make you forget ours."

But the narrator does listen to the community's lore of fact and fiction. One such narrative is a tall-tale account of the marriage and subsequent breakup of Molly Montgomery Clanton and Roy Tom Blankenship, both doomed to absurdly comic destinies resulting from Roy Tom's tendency to produce vulgar "abdominal convulsions" during the act of sexual union. Rumor and gossip contribute to Roy Tom's ordeal. The story ignites with the townspeople's frequently repeated phrase "I heard" and is fanned by a long-winded utterance growing more outrageous and inventive by the instant. Marius's exquisitely controlled sentence is a Faulknerian tour de force of more than eleven hundred words and almost two pages of text. *After the War* confirms the author's reputation as an eminent historian and a superb raconteur.

Like Marius, Cormac McCarthy is sometimes viewed by critics as a writer's writer, someone given to stylistic experiments in which the hypnotic lilts and sways of the language are just as important as the story itself. McCarthy has generated a cult of admirers in the South who believe him to be a novelist every bit as innovative as Faulkner while possessing a genius of his own. Critics such as Charles McGrath, however, fault McCarthy for his stylistic excesses, McGrath going so far as to call McCarthy the last of the "thesaurus-thumbing tribe" of Southern writers, a reference to the latter's use of arcane vocabulary. McCarthy's exploitation of grotesque characters and situations has also raised critical eyebrows at times. In *Suttree* (1979), for example, one character is jailed for raiding the local farmers' gardens, a prelude to raping the watermelons he steals. Other characters include convicted felons, prostitutes, alcoholics, and former inmates of the local asylum. For all of McCarthy's "excesses," his brilliance is unmistakable in *Suttree*, which is set in Knoxville, Tennessee, in the 1950s. Even if a thesaurus is needed to guide a reader through the lush thickets of McCarthy's prose, the effort is small compared with the sheer indulgent beauty of language for language's sake.

Reynolds Price's long and illustrious career finds that he, like McCarthy, "has survived criticism."[6] Compared invidiously with Faulkner at times, Price has emerged as an exceptional talent given to sustained accomplishment in a number of genres. Fiction, often thinly veiled autobiography, is still Price's forte, and his almost casual gifts as a storyteller can be seen in a novel like *The Tongues of Angels* (1990). Here the narrator recalls his experiences as a counselor at a boys' camp near Asheville, North Carolina. With his friend Kevin, a "Yankee" from Rhode Island, the protagonist must figure out how to spend Sunday, their one free day. They decide to visit the home of writer Thomas Wolfe, now "a manicured historical site operated by the state." With youthful enthusiasm, the narrator has earlier devoured Wolfe's work, having heard that "Wolfe wrote a lot about sex, whores, and body crabs." What the young counselors find at the Wolfe home is a situation more disarmingly human that they could have imagined. "A pretty young woman with a snotty baby on her hip" offers them an unforgettable lesson in humility.

Women writers in the contemporary South are the focus of Doris Betts's comprehensive and insightful essay, "Daughters, Southerners, and Daisy." Challenging the convenient labels often used to describe Southern women's writing and the oversimplified explanation about how that writing arose, Betts reminds readers that "the South reflected in women's fiction today differs from that portrayed during the much-touted renaissance of the twenties and thirties." The South that women writers currently confront is "urban, mobile, transient, electronic." Nor is all Southern women's writing confessional. Almost none of it finds its inspiration in the Lost Cause or in any of the feminine types that the Civil War engendered as romantic legacy. What can be said about the postmodern situation in the South is that "the usual literary motifs historically classified as 'Southern' are being modified by contemporary male and female, black and white, Southern writers." And while all the old themes linger—"race, religion, concreteness, family, a sense of evil, history"—Betts notes that contemporary literature must account for the fact that "in the K-Mart checkout line, Dilsey's descendants and those from the Compson and Sartoris clans are all wearing jeans."

Once described by Walker Percy as a "Yankee's sort of Southern writer," William Styron has spent little of his adult life in the South, belonging instead to that class of regional expatriates who must leave the South in order to write about it. The effect is often to intensify the memory of youth's experiences like those revealed in Styron's powerful memoir-story "Shadrach." Set in 1935 in the Tidewater area of Virginia, "Shadrach" derives its title from the name of a former slave "of unbelievable antiquity" who has returned home to die. "Home" is actually a homestead owned by the once venerable Dabney family, now fallen on hard times. The narrator, ten-year-old Paul Whitehurst, is a neighbor of the Dabneys but would prefer to be a Dabney himself, envying the family their shabby gentility and "that total absence in them of bourgeois aspirations." The story unfolds as Paul describes how the ruined Dabneys respond to Shadrach's sudden appearance and insistence on being buried on Dabney property, also his "home." With no money to provide Shadrach with a decent burial, Mr. and Mrs. Dabney confront their own conflicting feelings, discovering a grief born of unexpected compassion.

Referred to by one writer as the South's preeminent "Dixieologist," John Shelton Reed brings a sociologist's research methods and a novelist's flair to our understanding of the contemporary South. In *My Tears Spoiled My Aim*, Reed offers inestimable insights and data about who Southerners are, where they have been, and where they might be going. Ever aware that "the South is more than just a collection of unfavorable statistics," Reed observes that "it has also been home to several populations, black and white, whose intertwined cultures have set them off from other Americans as well as each other. Some of us, in fact, have suggested that Southerners ought to be viewed as an American ethnic group, like Italian- or Polish-Americans." What, then, are some of the distinctive features that define the South and Southern experience? Reed isolates a number of them: weather, cotton, kudzu, voting patterns, illiteracy rates, and birthplaces of country music notables. Although some writers have complained that the last thing the South needs is another academic specialist confirming stereotypes about the region, Reed provides evidence for what were previously only suspicions. In doing so, he not only lends credibility to the enterprise of

Southern studies but also confers on such activities the status of respectability long craved by Southerners throughout their checkered history.

History and the vaunted Southern literary tradition are no longer the major concerns of many contemporary writers living in the region. Such writers are more inclined to be "conditioned by television, movies, rock music, and other manifestations of popular culture."[7] In particular, "the fictional world of Bobbie Ann Mason is the superficial present-day South—a South of mobile homes, plastic restaurants, and Parthenon-like shopping malls."[8] True to Doris Betts's assertion that Southern women now find themselves standing in the K-Mart checkout line while wearing jeans, Mason's women characters stand on both sides of the checkout line when, and if, the women can find work. In Mason's "Still Life with Watermelon," the central character, Louise Milsap, has lost her job at Kroger's and must now occupy a place in the unemployment line. In her spare time, she paints pictures of watermelons in response to a rumor that "a rich collector from Paducah [Kentucky] will buy the pictures." The story proceeds as Louise discovers the "sudden yearnings" that motivate her to paint while confronting the "absurd idea" that anyone would actually be interested in the paintings. As with a number of Mason's characters, Louise must acknowledge the ordinariness and seeming lack of significance of her life in the "plastic" South. Nowhere to be found are either the cult of chivalry or Southern belles. Mason's women protagonists are the frequently overlooked and overworked faces in the South's innumerable checkout lines.

Mason's choice of characters points to an unsettling reality recently noted by Elizabeth Anne Payne: "In polite conversation in many of the region's academic halls, it is still acceptable to refer to poor whites as 'trash,' 'trailer trash,' and 'rednecks.'"[9] Novelist Will D. Campbell has spent his life countering the harshness of these "acceptable" stereotypes. Showing that poor white Southerners have often been despised, insulted, and misunderstood, Campbell writes with expansive sympathy and keen understanding about the religious practices of Pentecostal and holiness worshipers in his novel *The Glad River*. Campbell's focus is on snake-handling sects, the often legally harassed and socially mocked outcasts whose theology distills down to a single verse of scripture, Mark 16:17: "They shall speak with new tongues; they shall take up serpents; and if they drink any deadly thing, it shall not hurt them; they shall lay hands on the sick, and they shall recover."

Campbell's focal character, a writer named Doops who is reporting on a snake-handling assembly in the East Tennessee hills, never mocks what he doesn't understand. Nevertheless, his journalistic objectivity is shattered by the power and authenticity of the service that includes faith healing, speaking in tongues, and handling venomous snakes. So transformative is the experience that Doops feels an immediate compulsion to be baptized, proclaiming that "I feel like I just learned something I never knew before." Campbell's characters often exhibit dramatic changes associated with the mysterious operations of grace in their lives.

Notes

1. John Shelton Reed and Dale Volberg Reed, *1001 Things Everyone Should Know about the South* (New York: Doubleday, 1996), 120–121.
2. Julia Reed, *The Oxford American*, Nov/Dec 1998, ed. Marc Smirnoff (Oxford: The Oxford American Press, 1998), 34.

3. Gore Vidal, "Goin' South," *G.Q.*, Vol, 62, no. 11 (New York: GQ Press, 1992), 226ff.

4. Madison Smartt Bell, "Robinson Crusoe Reading," *Southern Magazine*, Dec 1988, ed. Linton Weeks (Little Rock: Southern Limited Partnership, 1988), 22–25.

5. Bell, 25.

6. Michael Kreyling, "Reynolds Price," *The History of Southern Literature*. ed. Louis D. Rubin et al. (Baton Rouge: Louisiana State University Press, 1985), 519.

7. Dewey W. Grantham, *The South in Modern America* (New York: Harper Collins, 1994), 330.

8. Grantham, 330.

9. Elizabeth Anne Payne, "The Lady Was a Sharecropper," *Southern Cultures*, Vol. 2, no. 2, eds. John Shelton Reed and Harry L. Watson (Chapel Hill: University of North Carolina Press, 1998), 25.

Lisa Alther

(1944–   )

Born in Kingsport, Tennessee, on July 23, 1944, Lisa Alther left Kingsport for Wellesley College in Massachusetts. After graduating in 1966 with a B.A. in English literature, she worked for Atheneum Publishers in New York. For more than thirty years, her home has been Hinesburg, Vermont. She married Richard Philip Alther and has one daughter, Sara Halsey.

Beginning with *Kinflicks* (1975), Alther's novels have appeared on the bestseller lists. *Kinflicks*, *Original Sins* (1981), and *Other Women* (1984) were chosen as featured books of the Book-of-the-Month Club. *Bedrock* was published in 1990, followed in 1995 by *Five Minutes in Heaven*.

from *Kinflicks*

1 The Art of Dying Well

My family has always been into death. My father, the Major, used to insist on having an ice pick next to his placemat at meals so that he could perform an emergency tracheotomy when one of us strangled on a piece of meat. Even now, by running my index fingers along my collarbones to the indentation where the bones join, I can locate the optimal site for a trachial puncture with the same deftness as a junky a vein.

The Major wasn't always a virtuoso at disaster prediction, however. When I was very young, he was all brisk efficiency, and made no room whatsoever for the unscheduled or the unexpected. "Ridiculous!" he would bark at Mother as she sat composing drafts of her epitaph. "Do you want to turn the children into a bunch of psychotics like the rest of your crazy family?" Perhaps, like my southern mother, you have to be the heiress to a conquered civilization to take your own vulnerability seriously prior to actually experiencing it. At least if you were born, as was the Major, in 1918 B.B. (Before the Bomb).

Whatever the reason, the Major's Cassandra complex developed late in life. He was a carpetbagger by profession, brought to Hullsport, Tennessee, from Boston to run the chemical plant that is the town's only industry. During the Korean War the plant, with its acres of red brick buildings and forests of billowing smoke stacks, was converted from production of synthetic fabrics to munitions; there were contracts from the federal government and top-secret contacts with the laboratories at Oak Ridge. On summer evenings, the Major used to take us kids out for cones of soft ice cream dipped in chocolate glaze, and then to the firing range where the new shell models were tested. Licking our dripping cones, we would watch proudly as the Major, tall and thin and elegant, listing forward on the balls of his feet, signaled the blasts with upraised arms, like an orchestra conductor cuing cymbal crashes.

Shortly after the conversion of the plant to munitions, the Major experienced his own personal conversion, and in a fashion that even an experienced aficionado of calamity like Mother could never have foreseen: He caught his platinum wedding band on a loose screw on a loaded truck bed at the factory and was dragged along until his ring finger popped out of its socket like a fried chicken wing being dismembered. Then his legs were run over by the rear wheels. There he lay, a fallen industrial cowboy, his boot caught in a stirrup, trampled by his own horse. Truckloads of hams and cakes and casseroles began arriving at the house from bereaved admirers/employees. All the downtown churches offered up hours of prayers for his recovery.

Ira was hurt, in the early days of our marriage, when I wouldn't wear my wedding band. He considered it symbolic of the tepidity of my response to him. Maybe he was right, but Ira had never seen a hand with only the bloody remains of a knuckle socket where the ring finger used to be. He merely assumed, until the day he ran me out of his house in Vermont with a rifle, that I was frigid. Well, he had to find some rational explanation for the failure of our union, because it was impossible for him to entertain the notion that he, Ira Braithwaite Bliss IV, might simply have picked a lemon from the tree of life. But more later of my refusal to share Ira's bed.

When the Major emerged from his casts, a metamorphosis had occurred: He was no longer bold and brash. In fact, the first project he undertook was to renovate the basement family room into a bomb shelter as a surprise for Mother's birthday. *Her* reaction to the atmospheric nuclear tests going on all over the world then was to join a group in Hullsport called Mothers' Organization for Peace. MOP consisted of a dozen housewives, mostly wives of chemical plant executives who'd been exiled to Hullsport for a dreary year as grooming for high managerial posts in Boston. MOP meetings consisted of a handful of women with abrasive Yankee accents who sipped tea and twisted handkerchief corners and insisted bravely that Russian mothers *must* feel the same about strontium 90 in *their* babies' bones.

The Major, sneering at MOP, kept going with his bomb shelter. We kids were delighted. I took my girl friends down there to play house; and we confronted such ethical issues as whether or not to let old Mr. Thornberg next door share our shelter when the bomb dropped, or whether to slam the door in his miserly face, as he did to us on Halloween nights. Later we girls took Clem Cloyd and the acned boys from Magnolia Manor development down there to play Five Minutes in Heaven. While the others counted outside, the designated couple went into the chemical toilet enclosure to execute the painful grinding of braces that left us all with raw and bruised mouths . . . but in love. And in high school I brought dates down for serious sessions of heavy petting. In fact, I broke the heart of Joe Bob Sparks, star tailback of the Hullsport Pirates and body beautiful of Hullsport Regional High School, by forfeiting my maidenhead to Clem Cloyd one night on the altarlike wooden sleeping platform, double-locked behind the foot-thick steel door, while Mother and the Major slept on blissfully unaware upstairs. But more about the many charms of Joe Bob and Clem later.

Soon, no situation was too safe for the Major to be unable to locate its potential for tragedy. Death to him was not the inevitable companion of one's later years, the kindly warden who freed each soul from its earthly prison. Death to him was a sneak and a cheat who was ever vigilant to ambush the unwary, of whom the Major was determined not to be one. In contrast to Mother, who regarded Death as some kind of demon lover. The challenge, as she saw it, was to be ready for the assignation, so that you weren't distracted during consummation by unresolved earthly matters. The trick was in being both willing to die and able to at the same time. Dying properly was like achieving simultaneous orgasm.

Mother had many photographs, matted in eggshell white and framed in narrow black wood, on the fireplace mantel in her bedroom. As I was growing up, she would sit me on her lap and take down these yellowed cracked photos and tell me about the people in them, people who had already experienced, prepared for it or not, this ultimate fuck with Death. Her grandmother, Dixie Lee Hull, in a blouse with a high lace neck, who had cut her finger on a recipe card for spoon bread and had died of septicemia at age twenty-nine. Great-uncle Lester, a druggist in Sow Gap, who became addicted to cough syrup and one night threw himself under the southbound train to Chattanooga. Cousin Louella, who dove into a nest of water moccasins in an abandoned stone quarry at a family reunion in 1932. Another cousin who stuck his head out of a car window to read a historical marker about the Battle of Lookout Mountain and was sideswiped by a Mason-Dixon transport truck. It was always so unsatisfying to rage at her in a tantrum, as children do, "I *hate* you! I hope you *die!*" She'd reply calmly, "Don't worry, I will. And so will you."

At spots in our decor where lesser women would have settled for Audubon prints or college diplomas, Mother hung handsomely framed and matted rubbings of the tombstones of our forebears, done in dark chalk on fine rice paper. The Major always planned family vacations around business conferences so the expenses would be tax deductible and so that he wouldn't have to spend long stretches trapped with his family. Mother used to coordinate his meetings with trips for the rest of us to unvisited gravesites of remote relations. I spent most of my first seventeen summers weeding and edging and planting around obscure ancestral crypts. Mother considered these pilgrimages to burying plots around the nation as didactic exercises for us children, far superior to the overworked landmarks, like the Statue of Liberty, on the American Freedom Trail.

Apparently a trait like fascination with eschatology is hereditary. At any rate, it seems to run in *our* family. Mother's ancestors, however humble their circumstances (and most of them were in very humble circumstances, being dirt farmers and coal miners), invested a great deal of thought and money in their memorials to themselves. In any given cemetery, the most elaborately carved urns and weeping willows and hands pointing confidently to heaven invariably belong to my ancestors. Also the most catchy epitaphs: "Stop and look as you pass by. / As you are now, so once was I. / As I am now, so you will be. / Prepare to die and follow me." Mother considered that one, by a great-great-aunt named Hattie, the pinnacle of our family's achievement. Mother had dozens of trial epitaphs for herself, saved up in a small black looseleaf notebook. The prime contender when I left home for college in Boston was, "The way that is weary, dark and cold / May lead to shelter within the fold. / Grieve not for me when I am gone. / The body's dark night: the soul's dawn."

When Mother wasn't working on her epitaph, she was rewriting her funeral ceremony. "Let's see—" she'd say to me as I sat on the floor beside her mahogany Chippendale desk dressing my doll in black crepe for a wake. "Do you think 'A Mighty Fortress Is Our God' should go before or after 'Deus Noster Refugium'?" I'd look up from my doll's funeral. "You won't forget, will you, dear?" she'd inquire sternly. "The agenda for my memorial service will be in my upper right-hand desk drawer."

Or she'd repolish her obituary and worry over whether or not the Knoxville *Sentinel* would accept it for publication. I have since come to understand her agony. When my classmates were taking frantic notes on penile lengths in first term Physiology 110 at Worthley College, I was diligently preparing the wording of my engagement announcement in the margin of my notebook: "Major and Mrs. Wesley Marshall Babcock IV of Hullsport, Tennessee, and Hickory, Virginia, take pleasure in announcing the engagement of their daughter Virginia Hull Babcock to Clemuel Cloyd. . . ." Years later, when the time finally came to dust off this draft and replace the name of

Clemuel Cloyd with Ira Bliss, I discovered that the Boston *Globe* wouldn't print it, in spite of the fact that I'd read their damned paper dutifully every Sunday for the two years I'd been in college there. What could bring more posthumous humiliation than to have your obituary rejected by a paper like the Knoxville *Sentinel?*

Maya Angelou

(1928–)

Born in St. Louis, Missouri, on April 4, 1928, Maya Angelou moved to Stamps, Arkansas, when she was three years old, to live with her grandmother. She is best known for her autobiographical books. Her first book, *I Know Why the Caged Bird Sings* (1970), chronicles her early life. She married Tosh Angelou (divorced 1952) and Paul Du Feu in December 1973 (divorced). She has one son, Guy Johnson.

Angelou's second volume of autobiography, *Gather Together in My Name* (1974), begins when she was seventeen. *Singin' and Swingin' and Gettin' Merry Like Christmas* (1976) is the third book in the series. The 1950s and 1960s are chronicled in *The Heart of a Woman* (1981). In 1993, she read her poem "On the Pulse of Morning" at President Bill Clinton's inauguration.

Angelou has also written poetry, plays, and television and film scripts. Her works include *All God's Children Need Traveling Shoes* (1986); *Poems: Maya Angelou* (1986); and *I Shall Not Be Moved* (1990).

On the Pulse of Morning

A Rock, A River, A Tree
Hosts to species long since departed,
Marked the mastodon,
The dinosaur, who left dried tokens
Of their sojourn here
On our planet floor,
Any broad alarm of their hastening doom
Is lost in the gloom of dust and ages.

*   *   *

There is a true yearning to respond to
The singing River and the wise Rock.
So say the Asian, the Hispanic, the Jew
The African, the Native American, the Sioux,
The Catholic, the Muslim, the French, the Greek,
The Irish, the Rabbi, the Priest, the Sheik,
The Gay, the Straight, the Preacher,
The privileged, the homeless, the Teacher.
They hear. They all hear
The speaking of the Tree.

*   *   *

Here on the pulse of this new day
You may have the grace to look up and out
And into your sister's eyes,
And into your brother's face,
Your country,
And say simply
Very simply
With hope—
Good morning.

A. R. Ammons

(1926–   )

A. R. Ammons was born on February 18, 1926, on a farm near Whiteville, North Carolina. He joined the U.S. Navy and served in the South Pacific during World War II. Ammons received his B.S. degree from Wake Forest College in North Carolina in 1949. After marrying Phyllis Plumbo, he studied literature for three semesters at the University of California, Berkeley. In 1964, Ammons moved to Ithaca, New York, to teach at Cornell University, where he has lived and worked since that time. He holds the Goldwin Smith Professorship in Poetry.

Following in the American Romantic tradition of Emerson, Thoreau, and Whitman, Ammons published his first book, *Ommateum with Doxology*, in 1955. He received the National Book Award and the Bollingen Prize for *Collected Poems, 1951–1971* (1972). In 1994, he won a second National Book Award for *Garbage* (1993).

Other works include *Expressions of Sea Level* (1963); *Coursons Inlet: A Book of Poems* (1965); *Tape for the Turn of the Year* (1965); *Northfield Poems* (1966); *Uplands* (1970); *Briefings: Poems Small and Easy* (1971); *Sphere: The Form of a Motion* (1974); *Diversification: Poems* (1975); *The Snow Poems* (1977); *Road* (1977); *Suite* (1978); *Selected Longer Poems* (1980); *Things* (1981); *A Coast of Trees* (1981); *Worldly Hopes* (1982); *Lake Effect Country* (1983); *Sumerian Vistas* (1987); *The Really Short Poems of A. R. Ammons* (1980); *The North Carolina Poems* (1994); *Brink Road* (1996); and *Strip* (1997).

Classic

I sat by a stream in a
perfect—except for willows—
emptiness
and the mountain that
was around,

scraggly with brush &
rock

said
I see you're scribbling again:

accustomed to mountains,
their cumbersome intrusions,
I said

well, yes, but in a fashion very
like the water here
uncapturable and vanishing:

but that
said the mountain does not
excuse the stance
or diction

and next if you're not careful
you'll be
arriving at ways
water survives its motions.

Periphery

One day I complained about the periphery
that it was thickets hard to get around in
    or get around for
an older man: it's like keeping charts

of symptoms, every reality a symptom
where the ailment's not nailed down:
    much knowledge, precise enough,
but so multiple it says this man is alive

or isn't: it's like all of a body answering
all of pharmacopoeia, a too
    adequate relationship:
so I complained and said maybe I'd brush

deeper and see what was pushing all this
periphery, so difficult to make any sense
    out of, out:
with me, decision brings its own

hesitation, a symptom, no doubt, but open
and meaningless enough without paradigm:
    but hesitation
can be all right, too: I came on a spruce

thicket full of elk, gushy snow-weed,
nine species of lichen, four pure white
    rocks and
several swatches of verbena near bloom.

Clarity

After the event the rockslide
realized,
in a still diversity of completion,
grain and fissure,
declivity
&
force of upheaval,
whether rain slippage,
ice crawl, root
explosion or
stream erosive undercut:

well I said it is a pity:
one swath of sight will never
be the same: nonetheless,
this
shambles has
relieved a bind, a taut of twist,
revealing streaks &
scores of knowledge
now obvious and quiet.

Richard Marius

(1933–1999)

Richard Marius was born on July 29, 1933, in Martel, Tennessee, and grew up on a farm near Lenoir City, Tennessee. He attended the University of Tennessee, where he received his B.S. in 1954. The next year Marius married Gail Smith, with whom he had two sons. After their divorce, he married Lanier Smythe, with whom he had one son.

Marius was awarded a B.D. from Southern Baptist Theological Seminary in Kentucky in 1958. He received his M.A. in 1959 and his Ph.D. in history in 1962 from Yale University. After teaching history at the University of Tennessee, he left in 1978 for Harvard University, where he was appointed director of expository writing.

Marius's first published novel, *The Coming of Rain* (1969), was selected as the best first novel (1969) by Friends of American Writers and was designated an alternate selection of the Book-of-the-Month Club in 1970. Marius adapted *The Coming of Rain* into a play in 1996 as part of the Southern Writers' Project. He also published biography: *Luther* (1974) and *Thomas More: A Biography* (1984).

Other books by Marius include *A Writer's Companion* (1985) and *After the War* (1992). Marius died in Cambridge, Massachusetts, on November 5, 1999.

from *After the War*

28

I had never tasted anything like Hub's whiskey. It looked like water, but it burned all the way down. After a while the burning felt good. We sat in rocking chairs before the fire. The talk went on to the accompaniment of a rhythmic thumping of wood against wood. A comfortable sound.

I knew that Guy and Bernal were behind me in the shadows. I refused to turn around. Brian and Hub talked languidly after the energy of their first meeting was spent. After all the years of their friendship, they had little new to tell, and they were often silent, looking into the fire, puffing their pipes, sipping the whiskey, listening to the wind sing in the chimney. If Dr. Youngblood had not been there, they might have sat away the afternoon and perhaps the night as well in the thoughtless and peaceful intimacy of wind, fire, tobacco, whiskey, and silence.

Dr. Youngblood provoked them to talk. He seemed content to listen to their stories and to tell none of his own. I was a new audience; by being present I made something new of old tales. He was a man without the simplest envy, and he delighted in the people he loved as some might have delighted in jewels or in coins or in stocks and bonds. He wanted to give his friends to me with a generosity that might have caused others to give food to strangers, the act being a hospitality that, he felt, he owed as much as he owed his medical powers to the sick and the maimed. He had long since heard all the stories that Brian and Hub could tell, and he could have told them himself. He wanted me to hear them, but he wanted Brian and Hub to tell them.

So he said "Tell Paul the one about . . ." and the two old men leaped to draw up their tales from that great pool where all our stories lie patiently still, one old voice beginning, the other adding, the first adding again, sometimes disputing, a squeaking of old ropes and pulleys, tugging upward until a time and place stood solid in the room.

Dr. Youngblood sat puffing softly at his pipe, his round and kindly face red with whiskey and contentment, and he laughed in his languorous way with the anticipation some feel when a singer begins a dear old song.

"You should never listen to stories about this place," Bernal whispered at the back of my neck. "They will make you forget ours." His whisper fell into the wind gusting in the chimney and sighing beyond the cabin walls and in the forest beyond waving for miles in its dance with the cold air.

So while the last of the afternoon light thinned and paled and faded into a dusk that slowly extinguished the trees beyond the window of the cabin, I heard of the black midnight when Buster Abernathy's wife, Abigail, became convinced that Buster had a woman hiding in the outdoor privy and how she took a ten-gauge shotgun and blazed away at the outhouse with buckshot and filled it full of holes so that a decent man could not relieve himself there without being on public display to anybody who passed by in the road, and how Buster did indeed have a woman but how she hid in the hay in the barn at milking time and how once in their thrashing around they stirred up the fresh milk so much that they churned it into butter and how Buster explained to his wife that the cow had run around all over the place that day and churned it inside herself so that milking her had taken twice as long as it usually did since what came out of her teats was pure butter in long strips.

I heard how Molly Montgomery Clanton, daughter of the preacher at the Tabernacle Baptist Church on Second Avenue, eloped in the spring of '93 with Roy Tom
Blankenship and how she discovered, after they had said the proper words and signed
the proper papers before a proper justice of the peace in Rossville, Georgia, where you
could get married without having to wait three days after procuring a marriage license,
and after they had checked into room 238 of the Grand Plaza Hotel in Chattanooga, Tennessee, and locked and chained the door and pinned their brand-new Georgia marriage
license to the flowered wallpaper over the bed—how Molly Montgomery Clanton
learned that Roy Tom, when seized by great excitement, as, for example, in the anticipation of sexual union, was afflicted by abdominal convulsions that in some people produce the hiccups but that in Roy Tom produced uncontrollable and suffocating farts,
and how Molly Montgomery Clanton's undying love for Roy Tom, who sported a fine little mustache, dissolved like sugar in castor oil and made the marriage bed and the marital experience repulsive and how she leaped out of bed and grabbed her clothes and
covered her thin nakedness as best she could and ran away, still less than half dressed,
out into the empty streets and came home sobbing from Chattanooga in a caboose because there were no eastbound passenger trains at one o'clock in the morning, and how
she walked all the way from the depot to her father's house behind the church whence
she had run off with a cardboard suitcase on the previous afternoon, and wept on her
forgiving father's loving shoulder and told him that she could never, never bear the children of a man who cared so little for her as to lose all control of his lower abdominal
functions and produce the foul-smelling gunpowder blasts of Roy Tom Blankenship but
that because she had seen Roy Tom's nakedness (a nakedness reported to be unremarkable by others unknown to Molly Montgomery Clanton but experienced in the
matter) and because he had seen her nakedness and had devoured her with his lustful
eyes, she could never, she said, never honorably live with another man in Christian mat-
rimony because she had been defiled and her virgin conscience deflowered so that she
could *never* bring the purity the Lord Jesus Christ demanded to the marriage sheets of
a deserving and fartless man, so she became a spinster missionary schoolteacher and
went out with the China Inland Mission to Nanking, China, and never came back to
Bourbonville again, and the two old men, taking turns with the lines, told how Preacher
George Montgomery Clanton, her father, had explained and excused his daughter by
declaiming the real true facts of the case in a sermon to the biggest Sunday-morning
congregation that the Tabernacle Baptist Church had ever held within its sagging walls
and how he had given a private and much more detailed account of the story to others
who for unaccountable reasons did not make it to preaching that day, including Hub
Delaney, then sheriff of Bourbon County, who never went to church but who received a
visit from Preacher George Montgomery Clanton so that Hub could spread the truth
around on his official business just in case anyone asked, and how the tale provoked
Bourbon Countians to indecent laughter in the presence of pale, angry, silent Roy Tom
Blankenship who, they said, would be the only man since Creation to get his heavenly
reward for sending to the heathens his very own missionary, paying for her with an in-
testinal malfunction that had been used by the merciful and mysterious providence of
God to be the instrument of salvation for untold thousands and perhaps millions of Chinamen who on the Great White Throne Judgment Day would mill around Roy Tom
Blankenship and sniff at his nether parts with abject Oriental gratitude, joyfully chattering in their heavenly China talk, exalting him as the divine censer pot of all the ages,
and they told how Roy Tom finally in frustration and in exasperation and in incandes-

cent fury at the unanimous, unceasing, and inescapable mockery of the town one morning during the July heat wave of '03 took the early train to Knoxville where resided the nearest known (though tiny) congregation of Chinamen and walked into the Wong Lee Laundry on Market Square and introduced himself as if his name—Roy Tom Blankenship—pronounced at the top of his voice and with a marked separation of the syllables, would bring a flash of instant recognition to the yellow face of any Chinaman in the world and how, having shouted his name a second time as though in explanation sufficient for what he was about to do, proceeded to try to dunk the laundry's head Chinaman, Mr. Wong Lee himself, into a galvanized iron washtub full of boiling bedsheets from the King Cotton Hotel, and how the Chinaman's wife picked up a hot flat iron and commenced to beat Roy Tom in the head with it, and how he didn't even feel it, he said later, and how the Knoxville police had to come rushing to rescue the squawking and indignant and thoroughly terrified Chinaman, and how they dragged Roy Tom bleeding and bruised and partly scalded himself and still shouting and unapologetic off to jail and kept him overnight and fined him ten dollars for public drunkenness the next morning in court, and how he risked contempt by protesting to the baffled judge that he had never swallowed so much as a drop of liquor in his entire life and how his defense was his decision to become a missionary for the Hindoo religion and to baptize Chinamen in scalding water to save them from ignorant East Tennessee Christianity, and how after it was all in the newspapers, he had to leave town, and how he ended (so some said) in Detroit, Michigan, where he went to work for Henry Ford and was never heard of again—except that Brian Ledbetter swore that when you got three brand-new Ford cars together, you could sniff very carefully, and something indefinable, so faint under the new-car smell you could scarcely tell it was there, something maybe in the cloth upholstery Henry was putting in some of his cars now, would hover in the air, and whatever it was just made you naturally think of Roy Tom Blankenship.

And Dr. Youngblood, who had heard the story a dozen or maybe three dozen times, laughed and laughed and turned a deeper shade of red and shut his eyes down until they became fine, straight lines in his face and, as he always did at the end, asked the only question that a Harvard-educated man from Baltimore, Maryland, a man who remembered (as he told me) the ordered brick streets and the ordered brick houses built wall to wall with the white marble steps and the black maids in white dresses scrubbing the steps in the morning light so that the world seemed rectangular and precise as a brick abacus, *had* to ask in Bourbon County, Tennessee, where nothing was exactly straight at the corners and where the world, except for the brick courthouse, was wood and all the clocks told a different time: "Is it really true? Is that damned story *really* true?"

And Brian Ledbetter, looking solemn and venerable, lifted his big right hand as if to take an oath binding his immortal soul, and he nodded gravely, slowly, and he said in a low and reverent voice, "That's gospel, Doc. I swear it's gospel. On my sacred mother's honor, it's gospel."

"I don't believe it," Dr. Youngblood said. "I never believe it."

Brian solemnly shook his head. "Doc, you think I could make up a story like that? You think I could make up all them *details?* You think somebody like old Hub there could make up a story like *that?*"

"It makes me want to be a Christian," Dr. Youngblood said. "Anybody that can believe that story can believe anything."

"By faith you can move mountains," Hub said solemnly. And as he spoke he sat up straight and motioned for silence. "Listen!" he said.

Cormac McCarthy

(1933–   )

Born in Providence, Rhode Island, on July 20, 1933, Cormac McCarthy moved with his family to Knoxville, Tennessee, at the age of four. His father was an attorney with the Tennessee Valley Authority. McCarthy was reared a Roman Catholic and was graduated from Knoxville Catholic High School in 1951. He attended the University of Tennessee from 1951 to 1952, spent four years in the U.S. Air Force from 1953 to 1957, and returned to the university in 1957, where he received the Ingram-Merrill Award for creative writing for the 1959–60 school year. He left in the summer of 1960 to pursue a writing career.

McCarthy married Lee Holleman in January 1961, and their son Cullen was born in 1962. They later divorced. His first book, *The Orchard Keeper*, was published in 1965. The novel won the William Faulkner Foundation award in 1965 for the best first novel. In May 1996 he married Anne DeLisle, a British singer and ballet dancer. From 1966 to 1968, the two traveled on a grant from the Rockefeller Foundation. Then in 1967, they moved to Rockford, Tennessee. In 1969 McCarthy received a Guggenheim Fellowship.

The couple separated in 1976 and divorced in 1980. Since 1976, El Paso, Texas, has served as McCarthy's home base, and at present he resides there. With his move from Tennessee to Texas, McCarthy has also changed his physical settings for his fiction from the Eastern Tennessee area to Texas, New Mexico, and Mexico. In 1981, McCarthy received a grant from the MacArthur Foundation. His most critically acclaimed novel, *All the Pretty Horses* (1992), won the National Book Award and the National Book Critics Circle Award. In 1998, McCarthy completed the third novel in what has been described as the Border Trilogy.

Among his novels are *The Orchard Keeper* (1965); *Outer Dark* (1968); *Child of God* (1974); *Suttree* (1979); *Blood Meridian or The Evening Redness in the West* (1985); *The Crossing* (1994); and *Cities of the Plain* (1998).

from *Suttree*

Dear friend now in the dusty clockless hours of the town when the streets lie black and steaming in the wake of the watertrucks and now when the drunk and the homeless have washed up in the lee of walls in alleys or abandoned lots and cats go forth highshouldered and lean in the grim perimeters about, now in these sootblacked brick or cobbled corridors where lightwire shadows make a gothic harp of cellar doors no soul shall walk save you.

Old stone walls unplumbed by weathers, lodged in their striae fossil bones, limestone scarabs rucked in the floor of this once inland sea. Thin dark trees through yon iron palings where the dead keep their own small metropolis. Curious marble architecture, stele and obelisk and cross and little rainworn stones where names grow dim with years. Earth packed with samples of the casketmaker's trade, the dusty bones and rotted silk, the deathwear stained with carrion. Out there under the blue lamplight the trolleytracks run on to darkness, curved like cockheels in the pinchbeck dusk. The steel leaks back the day's heat, you can feel it through the floors of your shoes. Past these corrugated warehouse walls down little sandy streets where blownout autos sulk on pedestals of cinderblock. Through warrens of sumac and pokeweed and withered honeysuckle giving onto the scored clay banks of the railway. Gray vines coiled leftward in this northern hemisphere, what winds them shapes the dogwhelk's shell. Weeds sprouted from cinder and brick. A steamshovel reared in solitary abandonment against the night sky. Cross here. By frograils and fishplates where engines cough like lions in the dark of the yard. To a darker town, past lamps stoned blind, past smoking oblique shacks and china dogs and painted tires where dirty flowers grow. Down pavings rent with ruin, the slow cataclysm of neglect, the wires that belly pole to pole across the constellations hung with kitestring, with bolos composed of hobbled bottles or the toys of the smaller children. Encampment of the damned. Precincts perhaps where dripping lepers prowl unbelled. Above the heat and the improbable skyline of the city a brass moon has risen and the clouds run before it like watered ink. The buildings stamped against the night are like a rampart to a farther world forsaken, old purposes forgot. Countrymen come for miles with the earth clinging to their shoes and sit all day like mutes in the marketplace. This city constructed on no known paradigm, a mongrel architecture reading back through the works of man in a brief delineation of the aberrant disordered and mad. A carnival of shapes upreared on the river plain that has dried up the sap of the earth for miles about.

Factory walls of old dark brick, tracks of a spur line grown with weeds, a course of foul blue drainage where dark filaments of nameless dross sway in the current. Tin panes among the glass in the rusted window frames. There is a moonshaped rictus in the streetlamp's globe where a stone has gone and from this aperture there drifts down through the constant helix of aspiring insects a faint and steady rain of the same forms burnt and lifeless.

Here at the creek mouth the fields run on to the river, the mud deltaed and baring out of its rich alluvial harbored bones and dread waste, a wrack of cratewood and condoms and fruitrinds. Old tins and jars and ruined household artifacts that rear from the fecal mire of the flats like landmarks in the trackless vales of dementia praecox. A world beyond all fantasy, malevolent and tactile and dissociate, the blown lightbulbs like shorn polyps semitranslucent and skullcolored bobbing blindly down and spectral eyes of oil and now and again the beached and stinking forms of foetal humans bloated like young birds mooneyed and bluish or stale gray. Beyond in the dark the river flows in a sluggard ooze toward southern seas, running down out of the rainflattened corn and petty crops and riverloam gardens of upcountry landkeepers, grating along like bonedust, afreight with the past, dreams dispersed in the water someway, nothing ever lost. Houseboats ride at their hawsers. The neap mud along the shore lies ribbed and slick like the cavernous flitch of some beast hugely foundered and beyond the country rolls away to the south and the mountains. Where hunters and woodcutters once slept in their boots by the dying light of their thousand fires and went on, old teutonic forebears with eyes incandesced by the visionary light of a massive rapacity, wave on wave of the violent and the insane, their brains stoked with spoorless analogues of all that was, lean aryans with their abrogate semitic chapbook reenacting the dramas and parables therein and mindless and pale with a longing that nothing save dark's total restitution could appease.

We are come to a world within the world. In these alien reaches, these maugre sinks and interstitial wastes that the righteous see from carriage and car another life dreams. Illshapen or black or deranged, fugitive of all order, strangers in every land.

*The night is quiet. Like a camp before battle. The city beset by a thing unknown
and will it come from forest or sea? The murengers have walled the pale, the gates
are shut, but lo the thing's inside and can you guess his shape? Where he's kept or
what's the counter of his face? Is he a weaver, bloody shuttle shot through a time-
warp, a carder of souls from the world's nap? Or a hunter with hounds or do bone
horses draw his deadcart through the streets and does he call his trade to each?
Dear friend he is not to be dwelt upon for it is by just suchwise that he's invited in.*

*The rest indeed is silence. It has begun to rain. Light summer rain, you can see it
falling slant in the town lights. The river lies in a grail of quietude. Here from the
bridge the world below seems a gift of simplicity. Curious, no more. Down there in
grots of fallen light a cat transpires from stone to stone across the cobbles liquid black
and sewn in rapid antipodes over the raindark street to vanish cat and countercat in
the rifted works beyond. Faint summer lightning far downriver. A curtain is rising
on the western world. A fine rain of soot, dead beetles, anonymous small bones. The
audience sits webbed in dust. Within the gutted sockets of the interlocutor's skull a spider sleeps and the jointed ruins of the hanged fool dangle from the flies, bone pendulum in motley. Fourfooted shapes go to and fro over the boards. Ruder forms survive.*

Peering down into the water where the morning sun fashioned wheels of light, coronets
fanwise in which lay trapped each twig, each grain of sediment, long flakes and blades
of light in the dusty water sliding away like optic strobes where motes sifted and spun.
A hand trails over the gunwale and he lies athwart the skiff, the toe of one sneaker
plucking periodic dimples in the river with the boat's slight cradling, drifting down beneath the bridge and slowly past the mudstained stanchions. Under the high cool arches
and dark keeps of the span's undercarriage where pigeons babble and the hollow flap of
their wings echoes in stark applause. Glancing up at these cathedraled vaultings with
their fossil woodknots and pseudomorphic nailheads in gray concrete, drifting, the
bridge's slant shadow leaning the width of the river with that headlong illusion postu-
late in old cupracers frozen on photoplates, their wheels elliptic with speed. These
shadows form over the skiff, accommodate his prone figure and pass on.

With his jaw cradled in the crook of his arm he watched idly surface phenomena,
gouts of sewage faintly working, gray clots of nameless waste and yellow condoms
roiling slowly out of the murk like some giant form of fluke or tapeworm. The
watcher's face rode beside the boat, a sepia visage yawning in the scum, eyes veering
and watery grimace. A welt curled sluggishly on the river's surface as if something unseen had stirred in the deeps and small bubbles of gas erupted in oily spectra.

Below the bridge he eased himself erect, took up the oars and began to row
toward the south bank. There he brought the skiff about, swinging the stern into a
clump of willows, and going aft he raised up a heavy cord that ran into the water from
an iron pipe driven into the mud of the bank. This he relayed through an open oarlock
mounted on the skiff's transom. Now he set out again, rowing slowly, the cord coming up wet and smooth through the lock and dipping into the river again. When he
was some thirty feet from shore the first dropper came up, doubling the line until he
reached and cast it off. He went on, the skiff lightly quartered against the river's drift,
the hooks riding up one by one into the oarlock with their leached and tattered gob-
bets of flesh. When he felt the weight of the first fish he shipped the dripping oars and
took hold of the line and brought it in by hand. A large carp broke water, a coarse
mailed flank dull bronze and glinting. He braced himself with one knee and hefted it

into the boat and cut the line and tied on a fresh hook with a chunk of cutbait and dropped it over the side and went on, sculling with one oar, the carp warping heavily against the floorboards.

When he had finished running the line he was on the other side of the river. He rebaited the last drop and let the heavy cord go, watching it sink in the muddy water among a spangled nimbus of sunmotes, a broken corono up through which flared for a moment the last pale chunk of rancid meat. Shifting the oars aboard he sprawled himself over the seats again to take the sun. The skiff swung gently, drifting in the current. He undid his shirt to the waist and put one forearm to his eyes. He could hear the river talking softly beneath him, heavy old river with wrinkled face. Beneath the sliding water cannons and carriages, trunnions seized and rusting in the mud, keelboats rotted to the consistency of mucilage. Fabled sturgeons with their horny pentagonal bodies, the cupreous and dacebright carp and catfish with their pale and sprueless underbellies, a thick muck shot with broken glass, with bones and rusted tins and bits of crockery reticulate with mudblack crazings. Across the river the limestone cliffs reared gray and roughly faceted and strung with grass across their face in thin green faults. Where they overhung the water they made a cool shade and the surface lay calm and dark and reflected like a small white star the form of a plover hovering on the updrafts off the edge of the bluff. Under the seat of the skiff a catfish swam dry and intransigent with his broad face pressed to the bulkhead.

Passing the creek mouth he raised one hand and waved slowly, the old blacks all flowered and bonneted coming about like a windtilted garden with their canes bobbing and their arms lifting dark and random into the air and their gaudy and barbaric costumes billowing with the movement. Beyond them the shape of the city rising wore a wrought, a jaded look, hammered out dark and smoking against a china sky. The grimy river littoral lay warped and shimmering in the heat and there was no sound in all this lonely summer forenoon.

Below the railway trestle he set to running his other line. The water was warm to the touch and had a granular lubricity like graphite. It was full noon when he finished and he stood in the skiff for a moment looking over the catch. He came back upriver rowing slowly, the fish struggling in a thin gray bilge in the floor of the boat, their soft barbels fingering with dull wonder the slimed boards and their backs where they bowed into the sunlight already bleached a bloodless pale. The brass oarlocks creaked in their blocks and the riverwater curled from the bowplanks with a viscid quality and lay behind the skiff in a wake like plowed mire.

He rowed up from under the shadow of the bluffs and past the sand and gravel company and then along by barren and dusty lots where rails ran on cinder beds and boxcars oxidized on blind sidings, past warehouses of galvanized and corrugated tin set in flats gouged from the brickcolored earth where rhomboid and volute shapes of limestone jutted all brindled with mud like great bones washed out. He had already started across the river when he saw the rescue boats against the bank. They were trolling in the channel while a small crowd watched from the shore. Two white boats lightly veiled in the heat and the slow blue smoke of their exhaust, a faint chug of motors carrying the calm of the river. He crossed and rowed up the edge of the channel. The boats had come alongside each other and one of them had cut the engine. The rescue workers wore yachting caps and moved gravely at their task. As the fisherman passed they were taking aboard a dead man. He was very stiff and he looked like a windowdummy save for his face. The face seemed soft and bloated and wore a grappling hook in the side of it

and a crazed grin. They raised him so, gambreled up by the bones of his cheek. A pale in-
cruent wound. He seemed to protest woodenly, his head awry. They lifted him onto the
deck where he lay in his wet seersucker suit and his lemoncolored socks, leering
walleyed up at the workers with the hook in his face like some gross water homunculus
taken in trolling that the light of God's day had stricken dead instanter.

The fisherman went past and pulled the skiff into the bank upriver from the
crowd. He rolled a stone over the rope and walked down to watch. The rescue boat
was coming in and one of the workers was kneeling over the corpse trying to pry the
grapnel loose. The crowd was watching him and he was sweating and working at the
hook. Finally he set his shoe against the dead man's skull and wrenched the hook
with both hands until it came away trailing a stringy piece of blanched flesh.

They brought him ashore on a canvas litter and laid him in the grass where he
stared at the sun with his drained eyes and his smile. A snarling clot of flies had already accrued out of the vapid air. The workers covered the dead man with a coarse
gray blanket. His feet stuck out.

The fisherman had made to go when someone in the crowd took his elbow. Hey
Suttree.

He turned. Hey Joe, he said. Did you see it?

No. They say he jumped last night. They found his shoes on the bridge.

They stood looking at the dead man. The squad workers were coiling their ropes
and seeing to their tackle. The crowd had come to press about like mourners and the
fisherman and his friend found themselves going past the dead man as if they'd pay
respects. He lay there in his yellow socks with the flies crawling on the blanket and
one hand stretched out on the grass. He wore his watch on the inside of his wrist as
some folks do or used to and as Suttree passed he noticed with a feeling he could not
name that the dead man's watch was still running.

That's a bad way to check out, said Joe.

Let's go.

They walked along the cinders by the edge of the railroad. Suttree rubbed the
gently pulsing muscle in his speculative jaw.

Which way do you go? said Joe.

Right here. I've got my boat.

Are you still fishin?

Yeah.

What made you take that up?

I don't know, Suttree said. It seemed like a good idea at the time.

You ever get uptown?

Sometimes.

Why don't you come out to the Corner some evenin and we'll drink a beer.

I'll get out there one of these days.

You fishin today?

Yeah. A little.

Joe was watching him. Listen, he said. You could get on up at Miller's. Brother
said they needed somebody in men's shoes.

Suttree looked at the ground and smiled and wiped his mouth with the back of
his wrist and looked up again. Well, he said. I guess I'll just stick to the river for a
while yet.

Well come out some evenin.

I will.

They lifted each a hand in farewell and he watched they boy go on up the tracks and then across the fields toward the road. Then he went down to the skiff and pulled the rope up and tossed it in and pushed off into the river again. The dead man was still lying on the bank under his blanket but the crowd had begun to drift away. He rowed on across the river.

He swung the skiff in beneath the bridge and shipped the oars and sat looking down at the fish. He selected a blue cat and fetched it up by the gillslots, his thumb resting in the soft yellow throat. It flexed once and was still. The oars dripped in the river. He climbed from the skiff and tied up at a stob and labored up the slick grassless bank toward the arches where the bridge went to earth. Here a dark cavern beneath the vaulted concrete with rocks piled about the entrance and a crudely lettered keep out sign slashed in yellow paint across a boulder. A fire burned in a stone cairn on the rank and sunless clay and there was an old man squatting before it. The old man looked up at him and looked back at the fire again.

I brought you a catfish, Suttree said.

He mumbled and waved his hand about. Suttree laid the fish down and the old man squinted at it and then poked among the ashes of the fire. Set down, he said.

He squatted.

The old man watched the thin flames. Slow traffic passed above them in a muted rumble. In the fire potatoes blistered and split their charred jackets with low hissing sounds like small organisms expiring on the coals. The old man speared them from the ashes, one, two, three black stones smoking. He grouped them in a rusty hubcap. Get ye a tater, he said.

Suttree lifted a hand. He did not answer because he knew that the old man would offer three times and he must parcel out his words of refusal. The old man had tilted a steaming can and was peering inside. A handful of beans boiled in riverwater. He raised his ruined eyes and looked out from under the beam of tufted bone that shaded them. I remember you now, he said. From when you was just little. Suttree didnt think so but he nodded. The old man used to go from door to door and he could make the dolls and bears to talk.

Go on and get ye a tater, he said.

Thanks, said Suttree. I've already eaten.

Raw steam rose from the mealy pith of the potato he broke in his hands. Suttree looked out toward the river.

I like a hot dinner, dont you? the old man said.

Suttree nodded. Arched sumac fronds quivered in the noon warmth and pigeons squabbled and crooned in the bridge's ribbed spandrels. The shadowed earth in which he squatted bore the stale odor of a crypt.

You didnt see that man jump, did you? Suttree said.

He shook his head. An old ragpicker, his thin chops wobbling. I seen em draggin, he said. Did they find him?

Yes.

What did he jump for?

I dont guess he said.

I wouldnt do it. Would you?

I hope not. Did you go over in town this morning?

No, I never went. I been too poorly to go.

What's the matter?

Lord I dont know. They say death comes like a thief in the night, where is he? I'll hug his neck.

Well dont jump off the bridge.

I wouldnt do it for nothin.

They always seem to jump in hot weather.

They's worse weather to come, said the ragpicker. Hard weather. Be foretold.

Did that girl come out to see you?

Aint been nobody to see me.

He was eating the beans from the tin with a brass spoon.

I'll talk to her again, said Suttree.

Well. I wish ye'd get ye one of these here taters.

Suttree rose. I've got to get on, he said.

Dont rush off.

Got to go.

Come back.

All right.

A slight wind had come up and going back across the river he braced his feet against the uprights in the stern and pulled hard. The skiff had shipped enough water through her illjoined planks to float the morning's catch and they wandered over the cupped and paintchipped floorboards colliding dumbly. Rag ends of caulkingstring flared from the seams and ebbed in the dirty water among bits of bait and paper and the sweeps dipped and rose and a constant sipe of riverwater sang from under the tin of one patched blade. Half awash as she was the skiff wallowed with a mercurial inertia and made heavy going. He turned upriver close to shore and went on. Black families in bright Sunday clothes fishing at the river's brim watched somberly his passage. Dinner pails and baskets adorned the grass and dark infants were displayed on blankets kept at their corners by stones against the wind.

When he reached the houseboat he shipped the oars and the skiff slewed to a stall and settled ponderously against the tirecasings nailed there. He swung himself up with the rope in one hand and made fast. The skiff bobbed and slid heavily and the bilgewater surged. The fish sculled sluggishly. Suttress stretched and rubbed his back and eyed the sun. It was already very hot. He went along the deck and pushed open the door and entered. Inside the shanty the boards seemed buckled with the heat and beads of pitch were dripping from the beams under the tin roof.

He crossed the cabin and stretched himself out on the cot. Closing his eyes. A faint breeze from the window stirring his hair. The shantyboat trembled slightly in the river and one of the steel drums beneath the floor expanded in the heat with a melancholy bong. Eyes resting. This hushed and mazy Sunday. The heart beneath the breastbone pumping. The blood on its appointed rounds. Life in small places, narrow crannies. In the leaves, the toad's pulse. The delicate cellular warfare in a waterdrop. A dextrocardiac, said the smiling doctor. Your heart's in the right place. Weathershrunk and loveless. The skin drawn and split like an overripe fruit.

He turned heavily on the cot and put one eye to a space in the rough board wall. The river flowing past out there. Cloaca Maxima. Death by drowning, the ticking of a dead man's watch. The old tin clock on Grandfather's table hammered like a foundry. Leaning to say goodbye in the little yellow room, reek of lilies and incense. He arched his neck to tell to me some thing. I never heard. He wheezed my name, his grip belied the frailty of him. His caved and wasted face. The dead would take the living with them if they could, I pulled away. Sat in an ivy garden that lizards kept with constant leather slitherings. Hutched hares ghost pale in the shade of the carriagehouse wall. Flagstones in a rosegarden, the terraced slope of the lawn above the river, odor of boxwood and mossmold and old brick in the shadow of the springhouse. Under the watercress stones in the clear flowage cluttered with periwinkles. A salamander, troutspeckled. Leaning to suck the cold and mossy water. A rimpled child's face watching back, a watery isomer agoggle in the rings.

In my father's last letter he said that the world is run by those willing to take the responsibility for the running of it. If it is life that you feel you are missing I can tell you where to find it. In the law courts, in business, in government. There is nothing occurring in the streets. Nothing but a dumbshow composed of the helpless and the impotent.

From all old seamy throats of elders, musty books, I've salvaged not a word. In a dream I walked with my grandfather by a dark lake and the old man's talk was filled with incertitude. I saw how all things false fall from the dead. We spoke easily and I was humbly honored to walk with him deep in that world where he was a man like all men. From the small end of a corridor in the autumn woods he watched me go away to the world of the waking. If our dead kin are sainted we may rightly pray to them. Mother Church tells us so. She does not say that they'll speak back, in dreams or out. Or in what tongue the stillborn might be spoken. More common visitor. Silent. The infant's ossature, the thin and brindled bones along whose sulcate facets clove old shreds of flesh and cerements of tattered swaddle. Bones that would no more than fill a shoebox, a bulbous skull. On the right temple a mauve halfmoon.

Suttree turned and lay staring at the ceiling, touching a like mark on his own left temple gently with his fingertips. The ordinary of the second son. Mirror image. Gauche carbon. He lies in Woodlawn, whatever be left of the child with whom you shared your mother's belly. He neither spoke nor saw nor does he now. Perhaps his skull held seawater. Born dead and witless both or a terratoma grisly in form. No, for we were like to the last hair. I followed him into the world, me. A breech birth. Hind end fore in common with whales and bats, life forms meant for other mediums than the earth and having no affinity for it. And used to pray for his soul days past. Believing this ghastly circus reconvened elsewhere for alltime. He in the limbo of the Christless righteous, I in a terrestrial hell.

Through the thin and riven wall sounds of fish surging in the sinking skiff. The sign of faith. Twelfth house of the heavens. Ushering in the western church. St Peter patron of fishmongers. St Fiacre that of piles. Suttree placed one arm across his eyes. He said that he might have been a fisher of men in another time but these fish now seemed task enough for him.

It was late evening before he woke. He did not stir, lying there on the rough army blanket watching the licking shapes of light from the river's face lapse and flare over the ceiling. He felt the shanty tilt slightly, steps on the catwalk and a low trundling sound among the barrels. No shade, this. Through the cracks he could see someone coming along the walk. A timorous tapping, once again.

Come in, he said.

Buddy?

He turned his head. His uncle was standing in the doorway. He looked back at the ceiling, blinked, sat up and swung his feet to the floor. Come in, John, he said.

The uncle came through the door, looking about, hesitant. He stopped in the center of the room, arrested in the quadrate bar of dusty light davited between the window and its skewed replica on the far wall, a barren countenance cruelly lit, eyes watery and half closed with their slack pendules of flesh hanging down his cheeks. His hands moved slightly with the wooden smile he managed. Hey boy, he said.

Suttree sat looking at his shoes. He folded his hands together, opened them again and looked up. Sit down, he said.

The uncle looked about, pulled the one chair back and sat carefully in it. Well, he said. How are you Buddy?

Like you see. How are you?

Fine. Fine. How is everything going?

All right. How did you find me?

I saw John Clancy up at the Eagles and he said that you were living in a houseboat or something so I looked along the river here and found you.

He was smiling uncertainly. Suttree looked at him. Did you tell them where I was?

He stopped smiling. No no, he said. No. That's your business.

All right.

How long have you been down here?

Suttree studied with a cold face the tolerant amusement his uncle affected. Since I got out, he said.

Well, we hadnt heard anything. How long has it been?

Who's we?

I hadnt heard. I mean I didnt know for sure if you were even out or not.

I got out in January.

Good, good. What, do you rent this or what?

I bought it.

Well good. He was looking about. Not bad. Stove and all.

How have you been John?

Oh, I cant complain. You know.

Suttree watched him. He looked made up for an older part, hair streaked with chalk, his face a clay mask cracked in a footman's smile.

You're looking well, said Suttree. A tic jerked his mouthcorner.

Well thanks, thanks. Try to keep fit you know. Old liver not the best. He put the flat of his hand to his abdomen, looked up toward the ceiling, out the window where the shadows had grown long toward night. Had an operation back in the winter. I guess you didnt know.

No.

I'm pulling out of it, of course.

Suttree could smell him in the heat of the little room, the rank odor of his clothes touched with a faint reek of whiskey. Sweet smell of death at the edges. Behind him in the western wall of candled woodknots shone blood red and incandescent like the eyes of watching fiends.

I dont have a drink or I'd offer you one.

The uncle raised a palm. No, no, he said. Not for me, thanks.

He lowered one brow at Suttree. I saw your mother, he said.

Suttree didnt answer. The uncle was pulling at his cigarettes. He held out the pack. Cigarette? he said.

No thanks.

He shook the pack. Go ahead.

I dont smoke.

You used to.

I quit.

The uncle lit up and blew smoke in a thin blue viper's breath toward the window. It coiled and diffused in the yellow light. He smiled. I'd like to have a dollar for every time I quit, he said. Anyway, they're all fine. Thought I'd let you know.

I didnt think you saw them.

I saw your mother uptown.

You said.

Well. I dont get out there much, of course. I went at Christmas. You know. They left word at the Eagles for me to call one time and I dont know. Come to dinner sometime. You know. I didnt want to go out there.

I dont blame you for that.

The uncle shifted a little in his chair. Well, it's not that I dont get along with them really. I just . . .

You just cant stand them nor them you.

A funny little smile crossed the uncle's face. Well, he said. I dont think I'd go so far as to say that. Now of course they've never done me any favors.

Tell me about it, said Suttree dryly.

I guess that's right, the uncle said, nodding his head. He sucked deeply on his cigarette, reflecting. I guess you and me have a little in common there, eh boy?

He thinks so.

You should have known my father. He was a fine man. The uncle was looking down at his hands uncertainly. Yes, he said. A fine man.

I remember him.

He died when you were a baby.

I know.

The uncle took another tack. You ought to come up to the Eagles some night, he said. I could get you in. They have a dance on Saturday night. They have some good-looking women come up there. You'd be surprised.

I guess I would.

Suttree had leaned back against the raw plank wall. A blue dusk filled the little cabin. He was looking out the window where nighthawks had come forth and swifts shied chittering over the river.

You're a funny fella, Buddy. I cant imagine anyone being more different from your brother.

Which one?

What?

I said which one.

Which what?

Which brother.

The uncle chuckled uneasily. Why, he said, you've just got the one. Carl.

Couldnt they think of a name for the other one?

What other one? What in the hell are you talking about?

The one that was born dead.

Who told you that?

I remembered it.

Who told you?

You did.

I never. When did I?

Year ago. You were drunk.

I never did.

All right. You didnt.

What difference does it make?

I dont know. I just wondered why it was supposed to be a secret. What did he die of?

He was stillborn.

I know that.

I dont know why. He just was. You were both premature. You swear I told you?

It's not important.

You wont say anything will you?

No. I was just wondering about it. What the doctor says for instance. I mean, you have to take them both home, only one you take in a bag or a box. I guess they have people to take care of these things.

Just dont say anything.

Suttree was leaning forward looking down at his cheap and rotting shoes where they lay crossed on the floor. God, John, dont worry about it. I wont.

Okay.

Dont tell them you saw me.

Okay. Fair enough. That's a deal.

Right John. A deal.

I dont see them anyway.

So you said.

The uncle shifted in the chair and pulled at his collar with a long yellow forefinger. He could have helped me, you know. I never asked him for anything. Never did, by God. He could have helped me.

Well, said Suttree, he didnt.

The uncle nodded, watching the floor. You know, he said, you and me are a lot alike.

I dont think so.

In some ways.

No, said Suttree. We're not alike.

Well, I mean . . . the uncle waved his hand.

That's his thesis. But I'm not like you.

Well, you know what I mean.

I do know what you mean. But I'm not like you. I'm not like him. I'm not like Carl. I'm like me. Dont tell me who I'm like.

Well now look, Buddy, there's no need . . .

I think there is a need. I dont want you down here either. I know they dont like you, he doesnt. I dont blame you. It's not your fault. I cant do anything.

The uncle narrowed his eyes at Suttree. No need to get on your high horse with me, he said. At least I was never in the goddamned penitentiary.

Suttree smiled. The workhouse, John. It's a little different. But I am what I am. I dont go around telling people that I've been in a T B sanitarium.

So? I dont claim to be a teetotaler, if that's what you're getting at.

Are you an alcoholic?

No. What are you smiling at? I'm no goddamned alcoholic.

He always called you a rummy. I guess that's not quite as bad.

I dont give a damn what he says. He can . . .

Go ahead.

The uncle looked at him warily. He flipped the tiny stud of his cigarette out the door. Well, he said. He dont know everything.

Look, said Suttree, leaning forward. When a man marries beneath him his children are beneath him. If he thinks that way at all. If you werent a drunk he might see me with different eyes. As it is, my case was always doubtful. I was expected to turn out badly. My grandfather used to say Blood will tell. It was his favorite saying. What are you looking at? Look at me.

I dont know what you're talking about.

Yes you do. I'm saying that my father is contemptuous of me because I'm related to you. Dont you think that's a fair statement?

I dont know why you try and blame me for your troubles. You and your crackpot theories.

Suttree reached across the little space and took his uncle's willowing hands and composed them. I dont blame you, he said. I just want to tell you how some people are.

I know how people are. I should know.

Why should you? You think my father and his kind are a race apart. You can laugh at their pretensions, but you never question their right to the way of life they maintain.

He puts his pants on the same way I do mine.

Bullshit, John. You dont even believe that.

I said it didnt I?

What do you suppose he thinks of his wife?

They get along okay.

They get along okay.

Yeah.

John, she's a housekeeper. He has no real belief even in her goodness. Cant you guess that he sees in her traces of the same sorriness he sees in you? An innocent gesture can call you to mind.

Dont call me sorry, said the uncle.

He probably believes that only his own benevolent guidance kept her out of the whorehouse.

That's my sister you're talking about, boy.

She's my mother, you maudlin sot.

Sudden quiet in the little cabin. The uncle rose shaking, his voice was low. They were right, he said. What they told me. They were right about you. You're a vicious person. A nasty vicious person.

Suttree sat with his forehead in his hands. The uncle moved warily to the door. His shadow fell across Suttree and Suttree raised his head.

Maybe it's like colorblindness, he said. The women are just carriers. You are colorblind, arent you?

At least I'm not crazy.

No, Suttree said. Not crazy.

The uncle's narrowed eyes seemed to soften. God help you, he said. He turned and stepped onto the catwalk and went down the boards. Suttree rose and went to the door. The uncle was crossing the fields in the last of the day's light toward the darkening city.

John, he called.

He looked back. But that old man seemed so glassed away in words of his own contrivance that Suttree only raised his hand. The uncle nodded like a man who understood and then went on.

The cabin was almost dark and Suttree walked around on the little deck and kicked up a stool and sat leaning back against the wall of the houseboat with his feet propped on the railing. A breeze was coming off the river bearing a faint odor of oil and fish. Night sounds and laughter drifted from the yellow shacks beyond the railspur and the river spooled past highbacked and hissing in the dark at his feet like the seething of sand in a glass, wind in a desert, the slow voice of ruin. He wedged his knuckles in his eyesockets and rested his head against the boards. They were still warm from the sun, like a faint breath at his nape. Across the river the lights of the lumber company lay foreshort and dismembered in the black water and downriver the strung bridgelamps hung in catenary replica shore to shore and softy guttering under the wind's faint chop. The tower clock in the courthouse tolled the half hour. Lonely bell in the city. A firefly there. And there. He rose and spat into the river and went down the catwalk to the shore and across the field toward the road.

He walked up Front Street breathing in the cool of the evening, the western sky before him still a deep cyanic blue shot through with the shapes of bats crossing blind and spastic like spores on a slide. A rank smell of boiled greens hung in the night and a thread of radio music followed him house by house. He went by yards and cinder gardens rank with the mutes of roosting fowls and by dark grottos among the shacks where the music flared and died again and past dim windowlights where shadows reeled down cracked and yellowed paper shades. Through reeking clapboard warrens where children cried and craven halfbald watchdogs yapped and slank.

He climbed the hill toward the edge of the city, past the open door of the negro meetinghouse. Softly lit within. A preacher that looked like a storybook blackbird in his suit and goldwire spectacles. Suttree coming up out of this hot and funky netherworld attended by gospel music. Dusky throats titled and veined like the welted flanks of horses. He has watched them summer nights, a pale pagan sat on the curb without. One rainy night nearby he heard news in his toothfillings, music softly. He was stayed in a peace that drained his mind, for even a false adumbration of the world of the spirit is better than none at all.

Up these steep walkways cannelured for footpurchase, the free passage of roaches. To tap at this latched door leaning. Jimmy Smith's brown rodent teeth just beyond the screen. There is a hole in the rotten fabric which perhaps his breath has made over the years. Down a long hallway lit by a single sulphurcolored lightbulb hung from a cord in the ceiling. Smith's shuffling slippers rasp over the linoleum. He turns at the end of the hall, holding the door there. The slack yellow skin of his shoulders and chest so bloodless and lined that he appears patched up out of odd scraps and remnants of flesh, tacked with lap seams and carefully bound in the insubstantial and foul gray web of his undershirt. In the little kitchen two men are sitting at a table drinking whiskey. A third leans against a stained refrigerator. There is an open door giving onto a porch, a small buckled portico of gray boards that hangs in the dark above the river. The rise and fall of cigarettes tells the occupants. There are sounds of laughter and a bloated whore looks out into the kitchen and goes away again.

What'll you have, Sut.

A beer.

The man leaning against the refrigerator moves slightly to one side. What say Bud, he says.

Hey Junior.

Jimmy Smith has opened a can of beer and holds it toward Suttree. He pays and the owner deals up change out of his loathsome breeks and counts the coins into Suttree's palm and shuffles away.

Who's back in the back?

Bunch of drunks. Brother's back there.

Suttree tipped a swallow of the beer against the back of his throat. It was cold and good. Well, he said. Let me go back there and see him.

He nodded to the two men at the table and went past and down the corridor and entered an enormous old drawing room with high sliding doors long painted fast in their tracks. Five men sat at a card table, none looked up. The room was otherwise barren, a white marble fireplace masked with a sheet of tin, old varnished wainscoting and a high stamped rococo ceiling with parget scrolls and beaded drops of brazing about the gasjet where a lightbulb now burned.

Surrounded as they were in this crazed austerity by the remnants of a former grandeur the poker players seemed themselves like shades of older times or rude imposters on a stage set. They drank and bet and muttered in an air of electric transiency, old men in gaitered sleeves galvanized from some stained sepia, posting time at cards prevenient of their dimly augured doom. Suttree passed on through.

In the front room was a broken sofa propped on bricks, nothing more. One wonky spring reared from the back with a beercan seized in its coils and deeply couched in the mousecolored and napless upholstery sat a row of drunks.

Hey Suttree, they called.

Goddamn, said J-Bone, surging from the bowels of the couch. He threw an arm around Suttree's shoulders. Here's my old buddy, he said. Where's the whiskey? Give him a drink of that old crazy shit.

How you doing, Jim?

I'm doin everybody I can, where you been? Where's the whiskey? Here ye go. Get ye a drink, Bud.

What is it?

Early Times. Best little old drink in the world. Get ye a drink, Sut.

Suttree held it to the light. Small twigs, debris, matter, coiled in the oily liquid. He shook it. Smoke rose from the yellow floor of the bottle. Shit almighty, he said.

Best little old drink in the world, sang out J-Bone. Have a drink, Bud.

He unthreaded the cap, sniffed, shivered, drank.

J-Bone hugged the drinking figure. Watch old Suttree take a drink, he called out.

Suttree's eyes were squeezed shut and he was holding the bottle out to whoever would take it. Goddamn. What is that shit?

Early Times, called J-Bone. Best little old drink they is. Drink that and you wont feel a thing the next mornin.

Or any morning.

Whoo lord, give it here. Hello Early, come to your old daddy.

Here, pour some of it in this cup and let me cut it with Coca-Cola.

Cant do it, Bud.

Why not?

We done tried it. It eats the bottom out.

Watch it Suttree. Dont spill none on your shoes.

Hey Bobbyjohn.

When's old Callahan gettin out? said Bobbyjohn.

I dont know. Sometime this month. When have you seen Bucket?

He's moved to Burlington, the Bucket has. He dont come round no more.

Come set with us, Sut.

J-Bone steered him by the arm. Set down, Bud. Set down.

Suttree eased himself down on the arm of the sofa and sipped his beer. He patted J-Bone on the back. The voices seemed to fade. He waved away the whiskeybottle with a smile. In this tall room, the cracked plaster sootstreaked with the shapes of laths beneath, this barrenness, this fellowship of the doomed. Where life pulsed obscenely fecund. In the drift of voices and the laughter and the reek of stale beer the Sunday loneliness seeped away.

Aint that right Suttree?

What's that?

About there bein caves all in under the city.

That's right.

What all's down there in em?

Blind slime. As above, so it is below. Suttree shrugged. Nothing that I know of, he said. They're just some caves.

They say there's one that runs plumb underneath the river.

That's the one that comes out over in Chilhowee Park. They was supposed to of used it in the Civil War to hide stuff down there.

Wonder what all's down in there now.

Shit if I know. Ast Suttree.

You reckon you can still get down in them Civil War caves, Sut?

I dont know. I always heard there was one ran under the river but I never heard of anybody that was ever in it.

There might be them Civil War relics down there.

Here comes one of them now, said J-Bone. What say, Nigger.

Suttree looked toward the door. A graylooking man in glasses was watching them. I caint say, he said. How you boys? What are ye drinkin?

Early Times, Jim says it is.

Get ye a drink, Nig.

He shuffled toward the bottle, nodding to all, small eyes moving rapidly behind the glasses. He seized the whiskey and drank, his slack gullet jerking. When he lowered it his eyes were closed and his face a twisted mask. Pooh! He blew a volatile mist toward the smiling watchers. Lord God what is that?

Early Times, Nig, cried J-Bone.

Early tombs is more like it.

Lord honey I know they make that old splo in the bathtub but this here is made in the toilet. He was looking at the bottle, shaking it. Bubbles the size of gooseshot veered greasily up through the smoky fuel it held.

It'll make ye drunk, said J-Bone.

Nig shook his head and blew and took another drink and handed over the bottle with his face averted in agony. When he could speak he said: Boys, I've fought some bad whiskey but I'm a dirty nigger if that there aint almost too sorry to drink.

J-Bone waved the bottle toward the door where Junior stood grinning. Brother, dont you want a drink?

Junior shook his head.

Boys, scoot over and let the old Nigger set down.

Here Nig, set here. Scoot over some, Bearhunter.

Lord boys if I aint plumb give out. He took off his glasses and wiped his weepy eyes. What you been up to, Nig?

I been trying to raise some money about Bobby. He turned and looked up at Suttree. Dont I know you? he said.

We drank a few beers together.

I thought I remembered ye. Did you not know Bobby?

I saw him a time or two.

Nigger shook his head reflectively. I raised four boys and damned if they aint all in the penitentiary cept Ralph. Of course we all went to Jordonia. And they did have me up here in the workhouse one time but I slipped off. Old Blackburn was guard up there knowed me but he never would say nothin. Was you in Jordonia? Clarence says they aint nothin to it now. Boys, when I was in there it was rougher'n a old cob. Course they didnt send ye there for singin in a choir. I done three year for stealin. Tried to get sent to T S I where they learn ye a trade but you had to be tardy to get in down there and they said I wasnt tardy. I was eighteen when I come out of Jordonia and that was in nineteen and sixteen. I wisht I could understand them boys of mine. They have costed me. I spent eighteen thousand dollars gettin them boys out. Their grandaddy was never in the least trouble that you could think of and he lived to be eighty-seven year old. Now he'd take a drink. Which I do myself. But he was never in no trouble with the law.

Get ye a drink, Sut.

Nigger intercepted the bottle. You know Jim? He's a fine boy. Dont think he aint. I wisht McAnally Flats was full of em just like him. I knowed his daddy. He was smaller than Junior yonder. Just a minute. Whew. Damn if that aint some whiskey. He wouldnt take nothin off nobody, Irish Long wouldnt. I remember he come over on what they used to call Woolen Mill Corners there one time. You know where it's at Jim. Where Workers Cafe is at. Come over there one Sunday mornin huntin a man and they was a bunch of tush hogs all standin around out there under a shed used to be there, you boys wouldnt remember it, drinkin whiskey and was friends of this old boy's, and Irish Long walked up to em and wanted to know where he's at. Well, they wouldnt say, but they wasnt a one of them tush hogs ast what he wanted with him. He would mortally whip your ass if you messed with him, Irish Long would. And they wasnt nobody in McAnally no betterhearted. He give away everything he owned. He'd of been rich if he wanted. Had them stores. Nobody didnt have no money, people couldnt buy their groceries. You boys dont remember the depression. He's tell em just go on and get what they needed. Flour and taters. Milk for the babies. He never turned down nobody, Irish Long never. They is people livin in this town today in big houses that would of starved plumb to death cept for him but they aint big enough to own it.

Better get ye a drink there Sut, fore Nigger drinks it all.

Give Bearhunter a drink, Suttree said.

How about givin Bobbyjohn a drink, said Bobbyjohn.

There's a man'll take a drink, said Nigger. Dont think he wont.

Which I will myself, said J-Bone.

Which I will my damnself, said Nigger.

Jimmy Smith was moving through the room like an enormous trained mole collecting the empty cans. He shuffled out, his small eyes blinking. Kenneth Hazelwood stood in the doorframe watching them all with a sardonic smile.

Come in here, Worm, called J-Bone. Get ye a drink of this good whiskey.

Hazelwood entered smiling and took the bottle. He tilted it and sniffed and gave it back.

The last time I drank some of that shit I like to died. I stunk from the inside out. I laid in a tub of hot water all day and climbed out and dried and you could still smell it. I had to burn my clothes. I had the dry heaves, the drizzlin shits, the cold shakes and the jakeleg. I can think about it now and feel bad.

Hell Worm, this is good whusk.

I pass.

Worm's put down my whiskey, Bud.

I think you better put it down before it puts you down. You'll find your liver in your sock some morning.

But J-Bone had turned away with a whoop. Early Times, he called. Make your liver quiver.

Hazelwood grinned and turned to Suttree. Cant you take no better care of him than that? he said.

Suttree shook his head.

Me and Katherine's goin out to the Trocadero. Come on go with us.

I better get home, Kenneth.

Come ride out there with us. We'll bring you back.

I remember the last time I went for a ride with you. You got us in three fights, kicked some woman's door in, and got in jail. I ran through some yards and like to hang myself on a clothesline and got a bunch of dogs after me and spotlights zippin around and cops all over the place and I wound up spendin the night in a corrugated conduit with a cat.

Worm grinned. Come on, he said. We'll just have a drink and see what all's goin on out there.

I can't, Kenneth. I'm broke anyway.

I didnt ast ye if you had any money.

Hey Worm, did you see old Crumbliss in the paper this mornin?

What's he done now?

They found him about six oclock this mornin under a tree in a big alfalfa field. He found the only tree in the whole field and run into it. They said when the cops come and opened the door old Crumbliss fell out and just laid there. Directly he looked up and seen them blue suits and he jumped up and hollered, said: Where is that man I hired to drive me home?

Suttree rose grinning.

Dont run off, Sut.

I've got to go.

Where you goin?

I've got to get something to eat. I'll see you all later.

Jimmy Smith fell in with him to see him to the door, down the long corridor, mole and guest, an unlatching of the screendoor and so into the night.

It is overcast with impending rain and the lights of the city wash against the curdled heavens, lie puddled in the wet black streets. The watertruck recedes down Locust with its footmen in their tattered oilskins wielding brooms in the flooded gutters and the air is rich with the odor of damp paving. Through the midnight emptiness the few sounds carry with amphoric hollow and the city in its quietude seems to lie under edict. The buildings lean upon the dim and muted corridors where the watchman's heels click away the minutes. Past black and padlocked shopfronts. A poultry-dresser's window where halfnaked cockerels nod in a constant blue dawn. Clockchime and belltoll lonely in the brooding sleepfast town. The gutted rusting trucks on Market Street with their splayed tires pooling on the tar. The flowers and fruit are gone and the sewer grates festooned with wilted greens. Under the fanned light of a streetlamp a white china cuphandle curled like a sleeping slug.

In the lobbies of the slattern hotels the porters and bellmen are napping in the chairs and lounges, dark faces jerking in their sleep down the worn wine plush. In the rooms lie drunken homecome soldiers sprawled in painless crucifixion on the rumpled counterpanes and the whores are sleeping now. Small tropic fish start and check in the moss-green deeps of the eyedoctor's shopwindow. A lynx rampant with a waxen snarl. Gouts of shredded wood sprout from the sutures in his leather belly and his glass eyes bulge in agony. Dim tavern, an alleymouth where ashcans gape and where in a dream I was stopped by a man I took to be my father, dark figure against the shadowed brick. I would go by but he has stayed me with his hand. I have been looking for you, he said. The wind was cold, dreamwinds are so, I had been hurrying. I would draw back from him and his bone grip. The knife he held severed the pallid lamplight like a thin blue fish and our footsteps amplified themselves in the emptiness of the streets to an echo of routed multitudes. Yet it was not my father but my son who accosted me with such rancorless intent.

On Gay Street the traffic lights are stilled. The trolleyrails gleam in their beds and a late car passes with a long slish of tires. In the long arcade of the bus station footfalls come back like laughter. He marches darkly toward his darkly marching shape in the glass of the depot door. His fetch come up from life's other side like an autoscopic hallucination, Suttree and Antisuttree, hand reaching to the hand. The door swung back and he entered the waiting room. The shapes of figures sleeping on the wooden benches lay like laundry. In the men's room an elderly pederast leaning against a wall.

Suttree washed his hands and went out past the pinball machines to the grill. He took a stool and studied the menu. The waitress stood tapping her pencil against the pad of tickets she held.

Suttree looked up. Grilled cheese and coffee.

She wrote. He watched.

She tore off the ticket and placed it facedown on the marble counter and moved away. He watched the shape of her underclothes through the thin white uniform. In the rear of the cafe a young black labored in a clatter of steaming crockery. Suttree rubbed his eyes.

She came with the coffee, setting it down with a click and the coffee titling up the side of the pink plastic cup and flooding the saucer. He poured it back and sipped. Acridity of burnt socks. She returned with napkin, spoon. Ring of gold orangeblossoms constricting her puffy finger. He took another sip of the coffee. In a few minutes she came with the sandwich. He held the first wedge of it to his nose for a minute, rich odor of toast and butter and melting cheese. He bit off an enormous mouthful, sucked the pickle from the toothpick and closed his eyes, chewing.

When he had finished he took the quarter from his pocket and laid it on the counter and rose. She was watching him from beyond the coffee urn.

You want some more coffee? she said.

No thank you.

Come back, she said.

Suttree shoved the door with his shoulder, one hand in his pocket, the other working the toothpick. A face rose from a near bench and looked at him blearily and subsided.

He walked along Gay Street, pausing by storewindows, fine goods kept in glass. A police cruiser passed slowly. He moved on, from out of his eyecorner watching them watch. Past Woodruff's, Clark and Jones, the threatres. Corners emptied of their newspedlers and trash scuttling in the wind. He went down to the end of the town and walked out on the bridge and placed his hands on the cool iron rail and looked at the river below. The bridgelights trembled in the black eddywater like chained and burning supplicants and along the riverfront a gray mist moved in over the ashen fields of sedge and went ferreting among the dwellings. He folded his arms on the rail. Out there a jumbled shackstrewn waste dimly lit. Kindlingwood cottages, gardens of rue. A patchwork of roofs canted under the pale blue cones of lamplight where moths aspire in giddy coils. Little plots of corn, warped purlieus of tillage in the dead spaces shaped by constriction and want like the lives of the dark and bitter husbandmen who have this sparse harvest for their own out of all the wide earth's keeping.

Small spills of rain had started, cold on his arm. Downstream recurving shore currents chased in deckle light wave on wave like silver spawn. To fall through dark to darkness. Struggle in those opaque and fecal deeps, which way is up. Till the lungs suck brown sewage and funny lights go down the final corridors of the brain, small watchmen to see that all is quiet for the advent of eternal night.

The courthouse clock tolled two. He raised his face. There you can see the illumined dial suspended above the town with not even a shadow to mark the tower. A cheshire clock hung in the void like a strange hieroglyphic moon. Suttree palmed the water from his face. The smoky yellow windowlight in the houseboat of Abednego Jones went dark. Below he could make out the shape of his own place where he must go. High over the downriver land lightning quaked soundlessly and ceased. Far clouds rimlit. A brimstone light. Are there dragons in the wings of the world? The rain was falling harder, falling past him toward the river. Steep rain leaning in the lamplight, across the clock's face. Hard weather, says the old man. So may it be. Wrap me in the weathers of the earth, I will be hard and hard. My face will turn rain like the stones.

Reynolds Price

(1933–   )

Born on February 1, 1933, Reynolds Price was educated at Duke University in North Carolina. He is a teacher, poet, essayist, novelist, playwright, and writer of short fiction. He was a Rhodes Scholar and attended Merton College, Oxford, England, receiving his B.Litt. in 1958. In the same year, he returned to Duke, where he has remained part of the English faculty. In 1977, he was named to the position of James B. Duke Professor of English.

A Long and Happy Life (1962) won for Price the William Faulkner Award and the Sir Walter Raleigh Award. In 1976 he received the Lillian Smith Award for *The Surface of Earth* (1975). *Kate Varden* (1986) won the National Book Critics Circle Award. In 1971 he received from the National Institute of Arts and Letters the Award in Literature.

His works include *The Names and Faces of Heroes* (1963); *A Generous Man* (1966); *Love and Work* (1968); *Permanent Errors* (1970); *Early Dark* (1977); *The Source of Light* (1981); *Good Hearts* (1988); *The Tongues of Angels* (1990); *Blue Calhoun* (1992); *Full Moon* (1993); *A Whole New Life: An Illness and a Healing* (1994); *The Promise of Rest* (1995); *Three Gospels* (1996); *The Collected Poems* (1997); *Roxanna Slade* (1998); and *Learning a Trade: A Craftsman's Notebooks, 1955–1997* (1998).

from *The Tongues of Angels*

The Saturday morning was cleanup time. Each counselor spread all his cabin's mattress pads out to sun. And it was only then that I realized how successfully my threatened bedwetter had deceived me and his cabin mates. His mattress pad was a swamp of concentric circles of never-dried pee. I hauled it far up into the woods and abandoned it, with a real shudder for the boy who suffered five weeks of cold sodden nights rather than confess.

Sunday was free. I haven't mentioned previous such days. One day a week, once we'd seen our boys through breakfast, we were free till reveille the next morning. Kevin and I usually managed to take the same day off. Since neither one of us had a car, we'd catch a ride into Asheville with some older staff member or we'd hitch.

Now the whole city has been leveled, homogenized and defaced. But back then the pocket-sized town had the irregular charm of a real place. It felt like one whole single thing that had grown in slow response to various needs of people and the land. And in the case of Asheville, the charm was all the greater because of the mountain terrain. A small busy downtown square was overwatched by a ring of still wild mountains, with only the tan stone hulk of the Grove Park Inn staring down. Even the streets were humped here and there by an uncertain grounding.

Kev and I would get there a little after ten. We'd part and do personal errands. Then we'd meet at a particularly generous cafeteria and gorge on what we never got at camp. I remember craving fried eggplant and country-style steak. In the afternoon together we'd hunt through the several old bookstores, then the cafeteria again for supper, a movie, then the trip back to camp. Neither Kevin nor I was a night owl, but it was vital to the notion of a day off that we stay in town till our boys were asleep.

Those few free days have a distinct sweetness in my memory. It comes partly from the fact that, since I'd never had a job before, I'd never known the joy of *not* working. Mostly though the pleasure comes from remembering the long hours of talk with Kevin. Americans in their early twenties then were still fairly wild to learn their way forward into the world. They'd talk a whole night just to learn some scrap of useful news that they could have found in an almanac in fourteen seconds—say, the manner of death of Catherine the Great, and did it involve her suffocation by an amorous donkey? Kevin and I were in that boat but mainly me. I knew he was further along than me in everything.

Kev's answers to me on a big range of subjects were wide, deep and well-seasoned with wit. They were also land-mined with unexpected questions that kept me constantly on guard. A thoroughly typical case was this. Over strawberry shortcake one day at lunch, I made the strategic error of owning up to a little less than half my ambition for greatness. Kevin heard it straight through with no trace of a smile, and then he asked "What will the world do if you die tonight?" No trace of an edge on his question either. He was just asking for the sake of the news, so he'd know if I croaked.

If I meant then to lay out my wares for Kev, I had to be damned sure they were strong enough to handle and were laid down carefully. You couldn't just tell him that, say, Picasso was greater than Gilbert Stuart. You had to prove it and mostly I couldn't. So breakage was high in any such dialogue. Kev would hold back politely and let you choose the topic. But once you invited him in, he *jumped*. I've said that, because of the recent Depression and war, Americans hadn't traveled much for twenty-five years; and the country was strictly divided into regions. If you'd grown up in Rockford, Illinois, you barely knew anybody from Chicago, much less Winston-Salem.

And Kevin Hawser was the first real Yankee I'd spent time with. I enjoyed the speed and fresh air of our talks, but I also knew what a heavy brake his urban cynicism put on me. I could never let him see the full gleam of my intentions or my plans for reaching them. My sort of dream, in those early days, melted in the presence of laughter. That midsummer Sunday though, Kev set the pace. He asked me the night before if I'd like to join him tomorrow for a "pilgrimage"—the quotation marks were his—to Thomas Wolfe's home. I gladly agreed, though with reservations that will soon appear.

* * *

As a native North Carolinian, I knew that the state's most famous artist of any sort was born in Asheville in 1900 and died from tuberculosis of the brain before he was forty. My father, exactly Wolfe's age, had met him briefly in the early twenties. A lot of painters are big readers; so when I began consuming fiction in my teens, Father suggested that I notice his friend Tom Wolfe. In some brand of adolescent truculence, I didn't. Then early in high school, several of my male friends began to echo Father—Thomas Wolfe had apparently solved the mysteries of human longing or had at least captured them in words forever. They confided also that Wolfe wrote a lot about sex, whores and body crabs.

That knocked me off-center, and I rushed out to find him. But the book wasn't in our school library, being thought unfit for innocent eyes. The old dragons at the Public downtown were sleeping for once, so I managed to check out *Look Homeward, Angel*. But even at age sixteen, pitching and tossing in the very flames Wolfe described—youthful sex and vaulting ambition—I thought I knew bad prose when I saw it. And I stopped for good at page fifty.

That didn't keep me from wanting to see his home. Now I hear it's a manicured historical site operated by the state. But in the early fifties, with Wolfe not twenty years dead, it was still owned by members of the family. A rambling white barn of no architectural distinction, it had till fairly recently been a busy boardinghouse run by Wolfe's feisty mother right through his childhood, youth, fame and death.

The front door was open. We knocked on the screen and were met by a pretty young woman with a snotty baby on her hip. We asked if this really was the Wolfe house. She nodded yes, said it cost a quarter and took our money. Then she stepped aside and let us in. Her voice had the high blackboard-scraping harshness of the born mountaineer, but then her prematurely exhausted face broke into a quick smile that I'd still give a lot to paint. It was as good an emblem as I've ever seen for hanging on when the sky's against you.

But she didn't look any the worse for wear. To me, she wore whatever pain she'd borne like an invitation to take one short step and save her life, hers and the smiling girl-baby's she held.

She said "I'm right busy, with the baby and whatnot. And since I ain't been here but a week, I don't know much nohow. So if y'all want to look around, make yourself at home. Just try not to touch things more than you have to. They're precious and all."

We pretty much made ourselves at home. It hadn't dawned on me to wonder what no-nonsense Kevin was seeking here at this font of wind. But it was soon clear that he'd come along in hopes of a postcard to send a professor friend and Wolfe fan. Kev had at least read *Look Homeward, Angel*; but he kept most of his knowledge to himself as always. Since I couldn't say what had happened in the many rooms of the dim upper warrens, it was pretty much a musty old boardinghouse to me. But there were little hand-lettered cards, saying "Tom's Boyhood Room," "Tom's Boyhood Shakespeare" by a thick black book or "Brother Ben's Deathbed." And even Kevin, an English major, seemed muffled so I stayed respectful. I had to admit to myself that it did have a certain pregnant air, as if a big artist hadn't yet been born but was going to be, here and soon. I used the word *artist* a lot in those days. I thought it would help me grow. But my only clear memory of the house itself is of a huge black pay-phone by the door in a back hallway.

It was the old kind that had so many different comforting odors—one for the metal of the chassis, one for the heavy Bakelite handset, one for the breathed-on mouthpiece, another for the thick stiff cord. And it had names and phone numbers still gouged in the plaster around it, old-timey numbers in pencil or scratched with a key, just three digits—*Ethel 468* or *Mamie 300*. I stroked a finger down the cool plaster and thought I could see a crowd of faces, all waiting alone in rented rooms for the bell to ring, for life to strike.

When we'd used up the space, we could hear the young woman knocking around in the kitchen. We found our way there and thanked her. She said shoot, she hadn't done nothing but rob us to see a dirty old house. She rushed on to add that she had a husband in the Army who was maybe coming home in two weeks, but I still doubt it. She had on the kind of cheap left-hand ring that girls have been known to buy from the dime store.

By then she was very much a girl to my eyes. And she had too lost a look in her eyes. This girl had been abandoned. When she told us that she'd have give us some dinner if she'd knowed we was coming, I felt like we ought to get out fast and neat. But Kevin kept asking her questions till it was clear she'd told the truth in one respect anyhow. She knew very little about the place—just that one of the Wolfes was famous and all, mostly up north as far as she could tell from the people that came, maybe ten on a weekday.

In fact as we finally turned to go, she asked me "Who was this fellow you're aiming at?" Though the visit was Kev's idea and he'd done most of the talking, she aimed her question straight at my eyes. And she seemed to be referring to Tom, as most native Tar Heels still call him, like a family member. I'd mentioned him at the start; and thinking she must admire him, I'd also said I was hoping to be as good at painting as Wolfe was at fiction. In fact I was hoping to be a lot better. So now I told her "He was one Asheville boy that wrote a famous book and died too soon."

She nodded as if she'd put that aside for further thought. Then she said "You find what you're looking for?"

I said "Well, it proves famous men can be born anywhere."

She said "Even stables." But then she laughed and apologized for the dust. "Seems like dust just dogs my tracks, every house I'm in. You could eat off'n my mama's floor, no plate. But look at all this." On its own, her hand indicated the floor—dust curled at our feet. Then she managed a smile, thanked us for coming and followed us to the door. The baby was no longer in sight. And when we were on the outside of the screen door, she stayed behind the rusty mesh. But she made a last try. She laughed again, harder and covering her teeth. Then she said "You must not of gone to church either."

I confessed and said "Ain't it awful?" Back then in the South, if you missed Sunday church, you had you a good alibi before sunrise.

She stood there and genuinely fought with herself. It tortured her eyes. Then she said "They throwed me *out*, down there at Hog Elk—fine Christian souls!" Her last word flung on past us, towards the road.

Kev was plainly at a loss. This was a deeply Southern transaction, even though she was mountaineer and I was piedmont. Many Americans would die naked in the road before they'd tell you what's hurt them the worst. But born Southerners will show you the cell in their heart that burns the hardest. They'll hold it right towards you, in their bare right hand. This girl had done that for me, Lord God. So what could I say but "That's all they know. You're far better off"?

Her thanks were deep and they welled in her eyes. But right away she said "Look, if you want to come back next week—both of you—and eat a good dinner I cook and all, you could read me some from that book he wrote. Then I'd know better what to tell folks. I feel real ignorant now." She dredged up her smile again, and this time it lasted so long I was ready to go back and better her lot by whatever means. With Father's death so raw in my heart, how could I leave a needy magnetic soul that pretty and lonesome?

Kevin was Yankee-polite about it—you know, you tell somebody the hard truth; but you tell it a little to the right of their eyes. Still he told her it just couldn't be. We were both tied up from here on out till summer ended. Then he took my elbow and steered me around.

Once I'd turned my back on her face, I couldn't look again. I might cave in and do something wild. Kev had seen that and done the right thing by me, mean as it seemed.

I can hear her voice though, clear as my own, right to this minute. "I hope people want to see your house someday."

We spent the rest of Sunday eating and seeing two movies. I said before that Kev was a true Yankee, from Rhode Island. He could no more ask you a personal question than flap his arms and fly unaided. Southerners ask intimate questions in the way monkeys groom each other for lice, not to pry but to make you feel cared for. Kev though could sit and stare, just past your ear for maybe five minutes, and not say a word. I could have robbed a bank vault and be wearing the Hope diamond in plain view, and he would have died before asking me about it. Since all my campers were children, and since their self-entrapment ruled out curiosity into lives older than their own, I was running a good two quarts low on close attention. So over the breaded veal cutlet at lunch, I said "I would have married that girl on the spot."

Kev said "So I noticed—girl and baby. Hope you didn't mind the rescue."

"Not a bit." But I did. I just slightly did.

Kevin said "I figured old Chief might be a little flummoxed if we got back tonight with a wife and baby." On other days off I'd told Kev a little about my presence at Father's death and, as I said, my ambitions. He'd heard me patiently and with what seemed genuine interest. He was hoping for a diplomatic career and would need a working knowledge of all brands of human folly. But as usual he asked no further questions.

So now I asked if he thought I was crazy.

He looked out the street window, in fact at the blinding sunlight, and said "Yes."

When I finished laughing I told him not to worry, that I was a little dizzy still from my hospital duties with Father, plus five weeks of boys, and would pipe down soon.

Kev waited and said "Don't get me wrong. You're beyond me now. You've seen a man die. And with no brothers or sisters, you're the last person in line in your family. That makes you the hitter and backstop and pitcher and all. You're rightly scared stiff."

It still seems a real piece of understanding. That it came from a twenty-one-year-old unmarried man, as protected as me, is hard to believe. I've never heard the same from anyone since, but I've noticed its accuracy in dozens of lives. Once you're the next member of your family in line for death, you become a new person. And for quite a while, you can easily fly off the handle and make entangling commitments or else you can run. We didn't say more on the subject that day, but I thought through it many times in the remainder of the summer. And I think it guided my subsequent actions. Which is not the same thing as blaming Kevin for my ignorant error.

When we got back to camp past midnight, the air was actually cold. I walked into Cabin 16 thinking I'd be asleep in two minutes. But when I stripped and lay down, my mind was howling ahead. It mainly told me that the whole experience of the tawdry Wolfe house and the lost madonna and child and Kevin's insight was a single shaft aimed at my heart. I'd got both a big new wound and a gift—a broad leap of knowledge that would show in my life, beginning tomorrow. I had a fairly decent heart and a worthy aim. But oh, I was loose in the world and must *work*.

My canvas was locked downhill in the crafts cabin, safe. But at one in the morning, I halfway dressed and went down there in the near freezing dark to study the drawing. At night you tried to remember never to walk without a flashlight and to step high to avoid rattlers. So far this year nobody had been bit. The week before though, the hardy boys from Tsali brought a full and squirming gunnysack down the mountain. They said it was a dozen live rattlers they'd trapped. They wanted undamaged skins to make hatbands and belts, so they'd come up with the idea of gassing the snakes by cranking the camp station wagon and tying the mouth of the sack over the tailpipe. Without Chief's permission somehow they got the key, and the project very nearly worked.

When the sack stopped moving, they turned off the engine, untied the sack and dumped the contents out on the ground. I was there to see it. Sure enough, eleven dead snakes. But the boys were sure there'd been twelve to start with. They tried to recrank the engine and force the stray out but the engine was dead. It turned out that the twelfth snake had climbed up the tailpipe and got himself far forward in the exhaust system before dying in place. Chief made the boys pool their spending money to get the station wagon towed to Asheville where some brave fool located the snake and fished it out. Of course all us city-slicker counselors rejoiced at the downfall of the hardscrabble Tsali boys. But the gunnysack reminded me anyhow what kind of world was underfoot here, by day and night.

I got all the way to the crafts cabin safely and found the door unlocked. To rest his bowed legs, Uncle Mike kept a cot in the Indian lore room next door. I took the flashlight and went in to Mike's cot, propped my canvas on a chair and lay on my belly to study it. Even in black and white pencil line, I thought I could almost read the meaning of so much rock against so much sky. It was yearning to speak, the way a good dog—a setter or retriever—will meet your eyes and grieve, pure grieve, not to know your language.

If you think such thoughts are incompatible with good art, then you haven't read Michelangelo's poems or especially van Gogh's letters. They meant every picture as a forthright message, to change men's souls. Anyhow that night I was suddenly surer than ever that—if I was good and daring enough as a painter—I'd finish the summer with a picture that would also be a real gift of beauty and useful knowledge, for myself and every patient onlooker. Finally the whole good day fell on me. And lying under Mike's dusty Navaho blanket, I slid off to sleep and rested deeper than dreams or fears till cold first light.

Then Mike came limping through the door. With his stiff shock of white hair and his broad seamed face, he looked more than a little like pictures of God. And though he was older than Chief, he made at least as big a presence. When he finally saw me, he said "O Wise One, arise and dress. Seven new immortal souls await thee!" I had sat in on some of his Indian talks. He was genuinely informed on the subject, not just a half-baked enthusiast. And he'd taken to calling me Wise One because I also knew some Indian history.

I won't describe our many long talks. But from here looking back, I can see that Mike Dorfman was one of that summer's really good influences on my life. He'd graduated from Juilliard "back before God," as he said. Then he'd taken an M.A. in anthropology from Columbia, with fieldwork among two bands of the Sioux. And all this was forty years ago, just one generation after Wounded Knee and the Custer massacre. But the plight of the Indians disturbed him too deeply. So he turned aside, had a nervous breakdown—which he freely admitted to me—and spent his life teaching composition, piano, violin and "everything else but gynecology" at various conservatories and colleges. His wife had died young, leaving him with a daughter who was now somewhere with the Red Cross in Africa.

He'd met Chief in the late twenties, when he came down here to the Smokies to convalesce from TB. And once he retired from teaching, he decided to spend his summers at Juniper. That was mainly because it was so near the Cherokees. And also, he told me, because he had a whole lifetime of guilt to repay. He'd never forgiven himself for turning aside from the Sioux. He thought he could make some recompense by teaching white boys what a wrong we'd done, destroying the Indians. Since beginning to read I'd also consumed every word I could find on the same people, and I shared his guilt. If God is just, this country may never finish paying for their death—though maybe Vietnam was part of the payment, more or less exactly a century after our red version of a Final Solution. If so, at fifty thousand dead boys, we got off light.

Anyhow it was the first morning of second session and I'd overslept. I raced to shower and dress in my whites. Parents and new boys were driving towards us already from every corner of the South and a few from the Northeast. For the first time, I resented their droning nearness and my own renewed commitment to five more weeks of babysitting. A mind hot as mine, and aimed as narrowly, thought it needed whole days and weeks free to *see* and to translate. Or so I told myself, as I poised upright and old enough to know much better, on the doorsill of launching what may be the real piece of harm I've done the world.

Doris Betts

(1934–   )

Born in Statesville, North Carolina, on June 4, 1932, Doris Betts has published fiction since 1953. She attended the University of North Carolina-Greensboro (1953) and The University of North Carolina-Chapel Hill in 1954. In 1952, she married Lowry Betts, with whom she lives in Pittsboro, North Carolina. They are the parents of three children.

Betts's first novel, *Tall Houses in Winter* (1957), was selected for the Historical Book Club of North Carolina's Sir Walter Raleigh Award for fiction. In 1966, Betts began teaching at UNC-Chapel Hill, and in 1998 the Doris Betts Professorship in Creative Writing was established in her honor.

Among Betts's publications are *The Gentle Insurrection* (1954); *The Scarlet Thread* (1964); *The Astronomer and Other Stories* (1966); *The River to Pickle Beach* (1972); *Beasts of the Southern Wild and Other Stories* (1973); *Heading West* (1981); *Souls Raised from the Dead* (1994); and *The Sharp Teeth of Love* (1997).

Daughters, Southerners, and Daisy

On the content of *Little Women*, Louisa Mae Alcott said, "We really lived most of it."[1]

Many of us women writers seem more willing than men to admit to practicing that very partnership we used to read off the cover of a typical high school textbook, *Literature and Life*. Women writers often endorse Gail Godwin's statement: "I believe our lives shape our fiction just as much as our fiction gives shape to our lives. . . . All my protagonists—slapstick, allegorical, disguised by gender, species, occupation, social class, or hardly disguised at all—are parts of myself" (75).

Born the year before Thomas Wolfe died and with memories of a rather different Asheville, North Carolina, Godwin recalls writing her first story at age eight or nine, about a henpecked Ollie McGonnigle who, after falling into a manhole, climbs out and whacks a guffawing spectator with his umbrella; but later learns he must dine that very evening with that very same spectator who turns out to be—Gasp!—THE MAYOR OF THE TOWN! When she wrote this story, the Godwin household was entirely female; her knowledge of henpecked husbands was derived from Jiggs and Dagwood in the comics, and the rebellious little man facing embarrassment represented her own insecure self wearing trousers. In later stories, she continued to assign male names to young Gail as well as to small rebellions—sometimes her protagonist was even a male dog—until she reached adolescence. Then, overly restricted young women determined despite society to make independent choices surfaced in Gail Godwin's plots and began standing up there for themselves (71–72).

Because misuse and oversimplification are so likely ("Clearly Edgar Allen Poe *is* Arthur Gordon Pym"), autobiographical criticism has an uncertain reputation. While Adrienne Rich stresses the importance of writing as an act of looking back to see one's life with fresh eyes, feminist critics remain wary of emphasizing women's backward looks at perhaps restricted lives, lest this method congeal for male readers their work into limited (even boring) domestic fiction and poetry. Colette concluded that men make fun of women's writings because women "can't help being autobiographical," as in Woolf's *To the Lighthouse* St. Ives becomes the Hebrides while Leslie and Julia Stephen become the Ramsays. But when male writers use direct experience, as Ernest Hemingway does in rewriting his marriages and friendships, many male critics consider their content reveals greater breadth or meaning. Even in literary criticism there are better-half assumptions, such as the way one would read Anaïs Nin in order to get to Henry Miller, Aline Bernstein and Zelda Fitzgerald for glimpses of Thomas Wolfe and Scott, or the wife's eye view of Jean Stafford on Robert Graves, Mary McCarthy on Edmund Wilson, Caroline Gordon on Allen Tate, and so on. As Mary Gordon has warned, readers and book reviewers sometimes assume that "Hemingway writing about boys in the woods is major; Mansfield writing about girls in the house is minor" ("The Parable of the Cave" 132–33).

Specific girl characters in their fictional houses certainly can be traced directly on the writer herself. Jean Rhys always called her work autobiographical; Rita Mae Brown describes Molly in *Ruby Fruit Jungle* as "a nice version of me." Joan Williams's novel *The Wintering* fictionalized her love affair with William Faulkner. Evelyn Scott's first two novels are clearly autobiographical. Laura Wilder began her "Little House" stories at the age of sixty-three, but they recall her own remembered pioneer childhood. Surely Mary Lee Settle's protagonist, novelist Hannah McKarkle, is at least a kissing cousin. Elizabeth Bowen called *Seven Winters* a "fragment of autobiography," adding that after early childhood no subsequent years ever proved "so acute."

Other creative women have found candid exploration of their own lives difficult or unappealing. Anne Tyler writes for the pleasure of living *other* lives, she says, not reliving her own; and Jayne Anne Phillips agrees that a writer's goal is to get beyond oneself. She thinks having one's work called autobiographical is basically the praise of a responsive reader convinced that the author has "really lived" the work. There are women, too, who, because they are still embedded in family life, postpone recording it and exposing its dark side; especially do they delay satirizing it. Women writers with husbands, children, parents, and the extended web of kinfolk still typical in the South seldom enjoy that light of exposé in whose glare a writer like Erica Jong turns her best profile toward the lens.

Very few contemporary writers, male or female, however, can entirely elude contemporary speculation about the mixture of their private lives, public roles, and published fiction, as Salinger and Pynchon have done. Today's Emily Dickinson will be followed to her upstairs drawing room by reporters; Christina Rossetti's love poems would today be tried on for size by various lover-candidates. Even if, like the reserved Anne Tyler, today's woman writer writes at home and abstains from public appearances, nobody's privacy can be renewed long-term like copyright. As Merle Oberon and Cornell Wilde once hyped on film the love life of George Sand, Meryl Streep has popularized Izak Dinesen's in a technicolor Africa. Would Virginia Woolf have told Leon Edel her dreams; can we imagine Willa Cather answering Barbara Walters's prying speculations about Edith Lewis?

And in a world inhabited not only by exploiters but also by earnest graduate students, once a writer is safely dead, any wall of privacy will probably crash more loudly than at Jericho, and whatever autobiography she may have consciously omitted from her fictions will get dredged and applied nonetheless. When Joyce Carol Oates reviewed for the *New York Times* a 1988 biography of Jean Stafford, for instance, she commented on the new literary genre, "pathography," her term for writers' biographies so "cruel and merciless that the only surviving mystery is 'How did a distinguished body of work emerge from so undistinguished a life?'" ("Adventures" 3).

One Southern woman writer, Eudora Welty, avoids dichotomy between art and life by making clear that what happened in her past was only a springboard for the imagination, that memory became attached to her later vision, that while she *was* an optimist's daughter, she was never identical to Laurel McKelva. Though she had always been writing about "the structure of the family" (Welty 86), her fiction does not merely record life experiences nor make them prettier for public display nor even rearrange them for emotional effect; Welty insists that fiction results after the artist's imagination has acted upon raw material both lived and observed. While Welty acknowledges her own "literal memory" of specific sights and sounds, she adds quickly that her work is not autobiographical, just "very personal; they aren't the same thing at all." When, from the decade of her seventies, she looks back on her life and that of both parents, she sees continuities invisible when her parents were still alive, and admits that writing fiction has "developed in me an abiding respect for the *unknown* in human life" (90, italics mine).

When the known facts of the lives of other women writers are laid alongside their best imaginative work, their work, too, is seen as "personal"—not private, not merely autobiographical nor confessional. For example, a young North Carolina novelist, Kaye Gibbons, credits her own writing urge to her mother, Shine, a "good country women who kept crocheted doilies pinned to the backs of chairs," and who coped with her husband's drinking by "going and doing despite my father's Snopesian not going and not doing." Gibbons admits that she writes under the burden of memory; but when as a University of North Carolina undergraduate she showed Professor Louis Rubin thirty pages of manuscript that began, "When I was little, I would think of ways to kill my daddy," her verisimilitude of memories was already being altered by imagination into the themes of her first novel, *Ellen Foster*; and in 1989 her second, *A Virtuous Woman*, transformed by imagination Shine from Gibbons' mother into a fictional character larger than life.

Coleridge called imagination that creative function of the intellect by which the small jigsaw parts of human experience get synthesized into a new whole, different from and transcending its small components, into, for instance, a poem as personal (but not autobiographical) as "Kubla Khan." When Hortense Calisher defined the novel as "rescued life," she might have added that what rescues life is not video nor audio nor print reproduction, but the transforming imagination that can reveal the very truths, as Jessamyn West added, "that reality obscures." Jayne Anne Phillips, who wrote about, never fought in, Vietnam, has said that what fiction does for history is "to make what happened real."

Welty put it this way:

> Writing a story or a novel is one way of discovering *sequence* in experience, of stumbling upon cause and effect in the happenings of a writer's own life. This has been the case with me. Connections slowly emerge. Like distant landmarks you are approaching, cause and effect begin to align themselves, draw closer together. Experiences too indefinite of outline in themselves to be recognized for themselves connect and are identified as a larger shape. And suddenly a light is thrown back, as when your train makes a curve, showing that there has been a mountain of meaning rising behind you on the way you've come, is rising there still, proven now through retrospect. (90)

Thus, any fascination with writers' childhoods is not concerned with those molehills of old events, but with that mountain of meaning later to be discerned in the work.

I had not yet realized this when, as a child planning to grow up and be a writer myself, I started on the other end through avid reading to learn from the trivial details of writers' biographies what decisive childhood preparations I should undertake. If Amy Lowell had smoked cigars I planned to try them; it might be worth infections to become Katherine Mansfield or Elizabeth Barrett Browning. I did not really pay attention, then, to the advice of writers to apply imagination to whatever childhood was at hand. Katherine Anne Porter was not much interested in anyone's personal history after the tenth year: "Whatever one was going to be was all prepared before that." Willa Cather would have added five more years; she believed that a writer's basic material was acquired before the age of fifteen.

Perhaps it is just as well that the details of many writers' lives remained unknown to me and beyond my imitation. During those formative years that Porter and Cather cite, for instance: Louise Bogan survived a household of quarrels with a mother who had love affairs and periodically disappeared; Sara Teasdale, a late child, felt smothered by worried, overprotective, controlling parents; Nadine Gordimer, at ten, became a cardiac semi-invalid (and became as voracious a reader as Walker Percy had after tuberculosis); Maya Angelou was raped at age eight by her mother's boyfriend; Olive Higgins Prouty's nervous breakdown at age twelve foreshadowed the future of her future protégée Sylvia Plath; and Phyllis Wheatley, probably from Senegal, sold as a slave in 1760 in Boston, opened her mouth to an owner who estimated by her teeth that her age was seven.

Writers as Daughters

The easy assumption for those doing biographical study of women writers has usually been that women writers—like Alcott's Jo March, like Kaye Gibbons—became creative almost by default, because their lives did not reveal to them that creativity was normally assigned to males. Supposedly they had strong role-model mothers or grandmothers, weak or absent fathers; the cultural pattern became distorted for them in houses where women had rooms of their own.

Some biographies of women writers do, of course, reflect this pattern. Anne Sexton's father was alcoholic; Diane Wakoski's father was almost continually absent. Marianne Moore's father abandoned the family; so did Kate Millett's, and her mother sold insurance to support them. The poet Anne Spencer of Virginia, illegitimate daughter of a slave woman and a Reynolds family tobacco heir, was reared by her mother, who finally left her Seminole husband. In contrast, Ellen Glasgow had a strong father who "never changed his mind or admitted he was wrong," but she became disillusioned with him when as a teenager she watched her mother have a breakdown after learning of his black mistress.

Among writers with strong role-model women in the family: At sixty-seven Sara Teasdale sighed that her superwoman mother still seemed to have "as much strength in her little finger as I have in my whole body." Gail Godwin's spunky mother was a writer. Mary Mebane's strong woman was her Aunt Jo, without whom she could never have gone to college nor written her story of growing up poor and black near Durham, North Carolina. For Josephine Humphreys, the strong woman was her grandmother Nita. Bobbie Ann Mason and her mother traveled together as groupie fans of recording stars during the 1950s. Margaret Mitchell's bright and humorous mother worked for women's suffrage. Four generations of women reared Kate Chopin, whose handsome father died in a train wreck when she was four. After Rita Mae Brown left the orphanage, her mother kept them going on hambone soup cooked and recooked for days; now her mother crusades for gay rights. And the mother of Edna St. Vincent Millay got rid of her gambler husband when Edna was seven and supported her three daughters by working as a practical nurse. She was such a vivid role model that in 1920 Edmund Wilson said she had anticipated the Bohemianism of her daughters, smoked heavily, and though she looked like a New England school teacher, "sometimes made remarks that were startling from the lips of a little old lady."

Some biographers can even claim that women in the family had a direct influence on the woman writer's career or writing. Lillian Hellman modeled most of her characters on her mother and her mother's family. For Katherine Anne Porter, the grandmother in Kyle, Texas, who reared her from the age of two became the heroine of many stories. Alice Walker, eighth child of a sharecropper father who earned three hundred dollars a year, has said, "Many of the stories that I write are my mother's stories," and she enlarges this life experience to a general black woman's aesthetic in *In Search of Our Mothers' Gardens.* Ellen Douglas (Josephine Haxton) uses as her pseudonym the name of her unpublished writer-grandmother. Elizabeth Madox Roberts, a frail girl nurtured on family stories, especially loved those about her great-grandmother who had come to Kentucky by the wilderness road. Elizabeth Spencer's mother encouraged her to write; her father wanted the whole nonsense stopped. Mona Simpson was given a typewriter by her mother, the financing to write a novel by her grandmother. Florence King, Pamela Frankeau, Rachel Carson have all acknowledged their debts to their mothers.

Other researchers have explained women writers' creativity by whatever positions in the family constellation would produce independence and self-reliance. While a student at Radcliffe, Rosellen Brown did research showing that female achievers were often the oldest or only daughters in families. Eudora Welty's memoir shows how with Edward, three years younger, and then Walter, three years younger still, she acquired an audience. And consider: Willa Cather, oldest of seven; Margaret Mead, oldest of five; Jessamyn West, oldest of four; Elinor Wylie, oldest of five; and only children Madeline L'Engle, Mabel Luhan, Flannery O'Connor, May Sarton, Ann Beattie.

The tunnel vision that produces such easy patterns is surely one reason biographical criticism needs to be read with a whole box full of salt. In 1988, Leo Schneiderman's *The Literary Mind* placed nine modern writers, including Southern women Lillian Hellman and Flannery O'Connor, on his own procrustean bed and demonstrated that "deep personal suffering is an essential ingredient in creating great literature" (jacket copy). O'Connor's Catholicism becomes here merely the expression of Freudian parental conflicts; all the words written by Lillian Hellman (another only child) spring from chronic rage resulting from maternal deprivation, and so on. Remember those "little did they know" biographies we read in childhood, in which 20-20 hindsight spotted, like some omniscient Paul Harvey, the pimply boy with an earache who would grow up to write the Ninth Symphony?

No, the easy post hoc effects of writers' girlhoods must allow for pro-daddy patterns, too. Adrienne Rich, born into a household of books with a father who encouraged her to read and write, wrote for twenty years with him as her chief audience. Nancy Leman traces her love of eccentrics to her father. Mary McCarthy's father taught her to read before she went to school, and when he died, her father had been reading to her a long fairy story that they never finished and she never forgot. There were favored academic upbringings with two supportive parents for Alice Adams, Ursula K. Le Guin, Anne Morrow Lindbergh, and Anne Tyler. Caroline Gordon was tutored by her father until she was ten, then attended his all-boys classical school. Gene Stratton Porter spent her youth outdoors with father and brothers. Harper Lee, like her fictional Scout, watched proudly from a courtroom balcony the jury speeches of her lawyer father. Grandfathers were important for Mississippi writers Berry Morgan and Elizabeth Spencer.

When Toni Morrison wrote *Song of Solomon*, she was in a rage because her father was dead and she wanted to figure out "what he may have known." Her own view of memory as it informs fiction is similar to Welty's:

> The act of imagination is bound up with memory. You know, they straightened out the Mississippi River in places, to make room for houses and livable acreage. Occasionally the river floods these places. "Floods" is the word they use, but in fact it is not flooding; it is remembering. Remembering where it used to be. All water has a perfect memory and is forever trying to get back to where it was. Writers are like that: remembering where we were, what valley we ran through, what the banks were like, the light that was there and the route back to our original place. It is emotional memory—what the nerves and the skin remember as well as how it appeared. And a rush of imagination is our "flooding." (119)

Out of good and bad memories of the past, imagination produces art. Mary Gordon has written: "Everywhere I have been I have thought at least once a day of my dead father. He has been dead for over thirty years. In a book he inscribed for me are these words, in his handwriting, a translation of a line of Virgil: 'Among the dead there are so many thousands of the beautiful'" ("Notes from California" 198).

Southern Girlhoods

History, of course, is memory on a larger scale—and in the South those thousands of the beautiful dead have been assumed to be Confederate forefathers, the famous Lost Cause of the Civil War a standard stimulus for the imagination of regional writers. In *A Writer's America*, Alfred Kazin has said that no Southern boy or girl becoming a writer would ever lose that intervention into history that Faulkner wrote about near the end of his career:

> For every Southern boy fourteen years old, not once but whenever he wants it, there is the instant when it's still not two o'clock on that July afternoon in 1863, the brigades are in position behind the rail fence, the guns are laid and ready in the woods, and the furled flags are already loosened to break out and Pickett himself with his long oiled ringlets and his hat in one hand probably and his sword in the other looking up the hill waiting for Longstreet to give the word and it's all in the balance, it hasn't happened yet. (quoted in Kazin 144)

If women writers apply their imaginations to wildly varied girlhoods, perhaps in the South their individual memories might nonetheless share an overarching and archetypal regional history? There is little indication that female Southern writers sat on moss-draped verandas and listened to veterans' grisly recollections of Pickett's charge; perhaps the sisters of Faulkner's deep-South audience were out in the detached kitchens baking pies at storytime. Eudora Welty, for example, says she hates the Civil War, claims to be ignorant about it, and had kinfolks fighting on both sides. She has written only one Civil War story, "The Burning." Bobbie Anne Mason's characters go to Shiloh today for reasons unlike Shelby Foote's.

If their personal histories fit no universal pattern, their gender histories will spill out of the usual file folders marked "Fugitives" or "Agrarians." Mary Lee Settle has made her own Yoknapatawpha in the coal-mining region of West Virginia and traced it back into prehistory, but she is not much interested in slaveowner guilt. In her introduction to *Women Writers of the Contemporary South*, Peggy Prenshaw notes that the South reflected in women's fiction today differs from that portrayed during the much-touted renaissance of the twenties and thirties. The South that contemporary women remember was less rural than the one Ransom and Tate and Porter and Faulkner recalled; the South they grew into is urban, mobile, transient, electronic. They may have a sense of place and community, but it is a woman's place, often a woman from the middle or lower economic class, the granddaughter of yeoman farmers or slaves rather than plantation owners—not the same South as that where Donald Davidson and Cleanth Brooks spent their childhoods. These women grew up reading the large body of serious Southern literature that came out of the period between two world wars, but the youngest ones also grew up under the shadow of another war with guilts of its own and Saigon as its Appomattox, and more extensive lost causes in national racism and environmental filth.

Since Appomattox, too, the age of puberty has dropped from seventeen to thirteen. Near-babies know where babies come from now, and their older sisters are off the pedestal and on the pill. Since Hiroshima, one Southern Democrat has become president while the solid South has solidly switched parties. The land of cotton is the integrated, urbanized, crowded land of the computer. In the K—Mart checkout line, Dilsey's descendants and those from the Compson and Sartoris clans are all wearing jeans.

The usual literary motifs historically classified as "Southern" are being modified by contemporary male and female, black and white, Southern writers: race, religion, nature, concreteness, family, a sense of evil, history, and so on. *Oldest Living Confederate Widow Tells All*, a first novel by Allan Gurganus, recalls the Civil War with horror more than pride, and ends with the very old lady flying over today's Georgia, still able to see from her airplane window the lightning zig-zag line of greener vegetation stretching down to Atlanta that marks the route of Sherman's army and its 1865 torches. In most Southern literature today, the mark of that great conflict may still be visible from far enough aloft, but as the passenger across the airplane aisle remarks when he points out the scar upon the land, "They claim it'll fade on us in a few years." The fact is, as the elderly widow observes, "people recover."

That very optimism—perhaps better described as stoicism with its teeth in view—seems one of the characteristics of the heroines of Southern novels by many women, all the way from Scarlett O'Hara's "Tomorrow will be better" at the end of *Gone with the Wind* to the identical mood of Maggie Moran at the end of Anne Tyler's *Breathing Lessons* and, indeed, at the end of most of her novels, or Laurel McKelva's at the end of Welty's *The Optimist's Daughter*, understanding the confluence of rivers and of life.

How do Southern women writers handle other themes thought to be specific to their region? The natural setting is still a meaningful locale for Annie Dillard's speculations, for characters like Sylvia Wilkinson's Cary or Ramy, or Lee Smith's mountain women. At the end of Smith's *Oral History*, the unsullied human spirit of the mountain people has been vandalized and Hoot Owl Holler is being sold out to a commercial theme park called Ghostland. Even so, the "ghost" of the dead granny still haunts the commercialized despoilment and invisibly moves her old rocking chair on the artificial porch. The regional emphasis on nature seems for many current women writers linked now to feminism, to the traditions of earth goddess folk wisdom, instinct—and in this area a trust in concrete experience rather than abstraction or fact seems to fuse the frequent preoccupations of writers who are Southerners, blacks, and feminists.

Religion? Though the Bible Belt appears to be more religious still than northeastern metropolitan America, and while a recent biographical dictionary of Southern writers cited the church denomination of many, Walker Percy was correct in setting *The Second Coming* in Linwood, North Carolina, a spiritual wasteland surrounded by a plethora of busy bee churches. Not many Southern choirgirls have grown up to profess in 1980s' novels the commitments of Flannery O'Connor.

Though racial conflict and pain remain a Southern subject for women writers, too, many of these writers are also black. Those genteel Southern guilts lived out by fine old families whose sons went to Sewanee, where they worried like Hawthorne about inherited sin, have proved irrelevant to black anger, energy, and ambition. Nor do the Southern Agrarians have many white female counterparts. Though Gail Godwin is correct in asking whoever heard of a Northern or Midwestern "belle," young Southern women today talk more like Belle Watling than Aunt Pitty Pat, and have their best girlfriends at the economic levels portrayed by Harriet Arnow, Jill McCorkle, and Lee Smith. "Today's Southern women," says Reynolds Price, are "Mack trucks disguised as powder puffs."

If the South itself is no longer defined by its Delta or low-country plantation subsouth, if Southern history has shifted to include women's history and slave narratives, the new stereotype for women—and for many female characters in novels—is the equally oversimplified category of Sharon McKern's title, *Redneck Mothers, Good Ol' Girls, and Other Southern Belles*. McKern sees modern Southern women as stage managers who apply only those parts of feminism that suit their machinations. Daphne Athas in her essay, "Why There Are No Southern Writers," says these are the new characters of Southern women's fiction, from the farm, the mill, the new city, named Vicki or Elizabeth rather than Norma Rae, in novels by Lisa Alther, Rita Mae Brown, Bertha Harris, Shirley Ann Grau, and others. She thinks there is little similarity in content or theme in Southern women's writing; what they may still have in common is a particular prose style, sometimes musical, usually oblique, increasingly plebian.

There may be one other distinctive quality in Southern women's fiction, even when it deals in its local drawl with broader American themes such as feminism. Flannery O'Connor put her finger on "the business of being a storyteller" when, on a panel with Caroline Gordon, Madison Jones, and Louis Rubin at Wesleyan College in 1960, she said that language alone did not correlate with Southern identity in literature. "I have Boston cousins and when they come South they discuss problems, they don't tell stories," she said. "We tell stories" (71).

In its early stages, the women's movement understandably dissected problems and produced thesis fiction. Marilyn French's *Women's Room* seems as didactic as

any of the illustrative homilies Charles Dwight Moody invented to illustrate his sermons. And Southerners who grew up reading the Bible knew how often sermons
needed an accompanying pious anecdote, since the mysterious Bible stories themselves were often morally ambiguous and strange. You might get a rags-to-riches
story in which the hero was a cheat and liar, like Jacob; by turning a few pages you
could leave the Good Samaritan behind and watch Jael pound a tent peg through a
sleeping man's skull. Even today, when fewer of the South's women writers look back
on girlhoods spent memorizing verses in Sunday School, something must survive of
the puzzlement with which children tried to grasp why Jepthah needed to pacify God
by killing his own daughter and why this story now was meant to produce their moral
edification. Whatever the source, to an audience nurtured on television's disease-of-
the-week documentaries—where "theme" is defined as the suggested social solution
to AIDS, Drug Abuse, or Apartheid—Southerners of both genders still seem to know
that a story is not a prescription, that the artist reveals with amazement how things
are, rather than sending the world telegrams about how things should be.

Stories, novels, poems do not solve problems so much as gaze upon mysteries
and secrets. In Welty's memoir, she recalls long weeks of pestering her mother to tell
her in detail where babies came from. Then one day she found a small cardboard box
containing two polished buffalo nickels, and learned these had weighted the cold eyelids of a stillborn baby brother years before. "She'd told me the wrong secret," Welty
writes—"not how babies could come but how they could die, how they could be forgotten about" (17).

For Southern boys, the discovery that ordinary lives were full of secrets might have
been made about slavery or Gettysburg or Pickett's charge. Battles as time-worn as
Adam's with Eve and Mom's with Dad stirred mystery for others, since imagination always stretches toward those parts of any story somebody lived but could never fully
tell. The three parts of Welty's memoir seem to summarize this process of the boyhoods
and girlhoods of future writers: "Listening." "Learning to See." "Finding a Voice."

Daisy

For me, at the heart of a happy childhood, lay one such secret, first to overhear as
fact, then to see and now to tell as story.

Like so many future writers, I was before first grade already reading feverishly,
making bad rhymes, acting out long, complicated dramas with a neighborhood cast,
and spying on adult mystery. Unlike my playmates, I had three grandmothers—two
with the usual surnames, and a more mysterious third stranger who visited us rarely
from another city and whose coming made my parents polite and tense. Daisy
Cloninger Turner was a plump, red-haired woman who stayed an occasional afternoon and stared too hard at me and each time left a limp dollar bill hidden under my
dresser scarf. In separate conversations, my parents told me with anxiety and warning, "She writes poems, too!" as if poetry could develop into a debilitating, possibly
genetic, disease.

Years passed before I learned that Daisy was my father's "real" mother, that he
had been born out of wedlock in 1911, adopted in 1915 by childless sharecroppers,
the Waughs of Iredell County, North Carolina, who then were promptly surprised by
four successive babies of their own.

"Well, so what?" was my half defensive, half-delighted reaction. I could not wait for Daisy's next visit to see if something dissolute showed between the wrinkles of her face.

My mother, fearing that since I owned scrapbooks of passionate poems I might also become like Daisy in other ways, gave me her version of a lecture on sex hygiene; she read me the first confusing six verses of Psalm 51.

Thereafter, in steamy holiday kitchens, I slowly picked up crumbs of the story from judgmental women; the family males were down by the barn discussing Hitler and baseball and hay. They only had one Civil War story, involving family treasures buried for fear of Sherman and the location then lost; after a century, this wealth had grown vast somewhere underground. I was more interested in Daisy Cloninger, sixteen, who had named her baby boy William Elmore after her own father, had kept him until age four when her money ran out. There had never been a legal adoption, just an agreement among farm people used to raising calves, foals, and sons able to pick cotton. The Waughs took Will asleep, from Daisy in the middle of the night, so that he woke crying in a strange place, and strangers gave him jar lids to play with.

A hole in the story occurs here partly because, from delicacy, I never asked my father what he remembered from his boyhood on that farm. I wanted Grandmother Waugh to be the unreliable narrator—tired, overworked, poor, overwhelmed by a late flux of babies.

When Will is school age, he begins to stutter. He develops a temper, too—inherited, everybody thinks. Though small for his age, and destined always to be short, he fights boys who say bad things. His adopted mother breaks a cake of hot cornbread over his head because she has heard that such a shock is a guaranteed cure for stuttering.

Another hole, years-long, intrudes. Then, when he has at last become a happy farm boy, speaking smoothly without a snag, well adjusted, age twelve and black-haired, eldest of five, four of whom have red hair and blue eyes, his Mama says to him abruptly one day, "Your *real* mother is in the front room; wash your hands and go see her."

He edges in, holding clean hands away from his field overalls, to stare at a young woman unknown to him. He will remember nothing of their struggle to converse. Afterwards, his stuttering recurs.

But, no, Daisy was not just a sentimental betrayed country virgin from solid peasant stock. Despite even larger holes in her story, I know she also bore a second child out of wedlock, a girl, and by a different father. My own natural grandfather was said to have been a traveling machinery salesman out of Greensboro, married and with sons of his own, very different from Daisy's struggling kinsmen farming these red clay fields in piedmont North Carolina.

Meantime, William Elmore Waugh, who nowadays would have been aborted in the first trimester after a brief clinic conference, grew up poor and working hard, finally joined the Navy at sixteen, where he injured his back, and after discharge came home to marry in August 1931 a shy, religious girl from a neighboring farm, Mary Ellen Freeze, who had a cleft palate. The Freezes were also poor, but at least they owned their seventy acres.

Because she was unwilling to say much in her nasal, noticeable voice, Mary Ellen had made a youthful promise—like Hannah's in the Old Testament—that if God ever gave her a child she would return that child, like Samuel, to His service; perhaps that child, like the voluble Aaron, would become an orator for God? The bride and groom were not quite twenty. The next June, God sent her me.

Now my loving, only-child girlhood begins, with William being to me the devoted father he'd never had, with Mary Ellen marveling that words seemed essential to the daughter of one who spoke them only timidly, who disliked being asked if she had a terrible cold, who, in fact, hated to get thirsty in public and cope with fountains that sent their icy water streaming from her nostrils. And she puzzled, perhaps, over why those words seemed destined for secular purposes, verses and stories. *Entertainment*—not what she nor Hannah had had in mind.

Dad worked hard, in the Depression as a cotton weaver, later as a post office maintenance man. I suppose we were poor, though well-loved children seldom feel poor. Both parents were thrifty enough and inspiring enough to guide me toward the college opportunity they had lacked. They saved as much of the tuition and costs as possible, my mother by then working in the mill herself in a metallic din that would eventually cost her hearing. It bothered her that William Elmore would not join her in steady church attendance, but her prayers and example wore him down. In the end Dad became a Sunday School teacher, an elder in the conservative Associate Reformed Presbyterian Church in Statesville, the church treasurer.

As the years passed he finally rediscovered Daisy, who had married and lived in Lincolnton. Though he began visiting her regularly, I was by then in college, later married, then a mother living across the state, and did not share this new relationship, though Daisy and I did occasionally correspond. She sent me her picture—a rather homely woman in a flowered hat with teeth that had not been tended in time. With age she had grown so deeply religious that even my mother felt uneasy, and now instead of poems wrote regular letters about Jesus to convicts in Central Prison. She had also begun, rather tentatively in case I might mind, to tell people I was her granddaughter, a writer. I did not mind. Once my father had been bitter because she had given him away. Now he no longer minded, either.

A widow and a non-smoker, Daisy had beaten lung cancer after surgery in her sixties and lived on. When finally she died in her late eighties, the boy she hadn't been able to keep kept vigil by her hospital bed. He grieved for her. He gave to me what little and unremarkable furniture she had left. And all these years he remained a devoted son to his adopted mother as well.

Not until after Dad's death in 1983 did distant kin send me a browning early photograph of Daisy, age fifteen, taken the year before my father was born to her, taken three months before she was even pregnant. She stands there forever—and stands there for no time at all, as Anne Tyler and Rainer Maria Rilke know—young and beautiful in her pure white dress. She looks like me. Her very dark eyes look like mine, like my children's.

I set forth, then, to locate and identify the unknown salesman who had changed so many lives, whose name Daisy had finally told me in a letter. After a surprisingly simple search through newspapers and death certificates, I finally stood in High Point, North Carolina, by the grave of the grandfather who never even dreamed of me, much less of my children and grandchildren farther along. My father had never even gotten his true surname right, perhaps because he was outdoors listening to menfolk argue over squirrel hunts and war, while indoors we women spelled things out for one another.

Though I had expected to feel some feminist anger, by then I knew too much— how the obituary showed he and my Dad had died of the same heart ailment, the son's life prolonged by medication maybe eight years longer; how volunteer firemen had been his pallbearers; where his legitimate sons had lived and worked; that they became parents, too.

This late, who could be blamed? Is blame even a question? So do most omniscient novelists conclude if their stories cover enough time and lives, or if they work long enough at their trade.

But the true secret of any human life is not what happened during its span, not mere facts or names or dates; the true secret here and everywhere remains emotionally as unsolved as ever. Unknown feelings rise up off history like vapors and evaporate like steam. Did Daisy hate him? Did he even know there was a boy in the world who maybe had his temper? Was her next man a cure, a revenge, a despair, a triviality? Her eventual marriage an economic compromise or a joy? How did she remember her twelve-year-old son with a changed face and fresh-washed hands? And the grandfather—how did his marriage turn out, and those of his children? And me—Do I favor free choice on abortion? If I had been Daisy, I would have chosen no. But then I have the 20-20 hindsight that knows how the story ended; Daisy had no choice at all.

Though this is my first time to mention Daisy Cloninger in print or in public, my stories have drawn on her mysterious life for years. In the first novel, *Tall Houses in Winter*, as Jessica, she bears a boy named Fenwick whose fatherhood is ambiguous. In *The Scarlet Thread* Esther is betrayed, perhaps pregnant, runs away North and vanishes for years but makes a success of her unknown life. In a short novel, "The Astronomer," she is like Eva whose abortion causes guilt and a possible religious conversion based on the book of *Hosea*. In *Heading West* Nancy Finch is the daughter of an older Daisy, this one embittered, who confides that premarital sex was never that important after all.

Yet of course none of these characters is Daisy; all are only my response to her mystery. I agree with Welty, "Writing fiction has developed in me an abiding respect for the unknown in a human lifetime" (90).

The Chinese have a saying, "It is easier to paint a dragon than a horse." We have seen so many horses; seen pictures of horses; people have told us far too much about horses. But the imagination is still able to act on mystery, on the idea of a dragon.

Whether our childhoods were lived through in the North or South, one crucial element for potential writers is that their maps of memory contain uncharted terrain, secret treasure, mystery, possible dragons. For certain Southern writers, the mystery lay in Vicksburg, Chicamaugua; the mystery lay in owning slaves, or being them. Women growing up in the same latitude heard in the kitchen less of battles or emancipation, more of fevers and bastard babies and deathbed sayings. Even the Sunday School teachers who told us stories of Goliath perishing before a shepherd boy's slingshot throw, and hurried past our questions about why God wanted Abraham to sacrifice Isaac in the first place, lingered longer on King David wandering through his palace crying, "Absalom, my son. My son, Absalom!"

And so we concentrated less on Saul's contest for the throne than on Bathsheba's feelings when a very patriarchal God killed her baby for spite. Or we imagined how Mrs. Jefferson Davis managed. Facts are like horses everybody's seen, but the dragon's lair is the heart. Welty says it is our "inward journey that leads us through time—forward or back, seldom in a straight line, most often spiraling. As we discover, we remember; remembering, we discover, and most intensely do we experience this when our separate journeys converge. Our living experience at those meeting points is one of the charged dramatic fields of fiction" (102).

The girl still smiling in her white dress in 1910 could have been me as a teenager, and then my daughter; and soon she will stand fixed there the age and size of my grandchildren; and still I cannot rescue her from anything nor whisper to her that it all turned out all right, that people do recover, that even the scorched long scar to Atlanta has healed over now with green. "All that is remembered," wrote Welty at the end of her memoir, "joins, and lives—the old and the young, the past and the present, the living and the dead" (104). Writers claim access by means of imagination even to all they cannot directly remember but seem to know, as I seem to know how it was to be a pretty black-haired teenager named Daisy Cloninger during that long night she packed everything that belonged to her four-year-old son and watched him sleep for the last time.

Note

1. I have not documented every brief quotation because the sources are so varied that constant notation would be less an aid than a hindrance. Instead, I cite sources used extensively and sources for substantial quotations. In a separate list I indicate additional sources consulted but generally omit sources for biographical information readily available in standard reference guides or in a number of places.

Works Cited

Athas, Daphne. "Why There Are No Southern Writers." In *Women Writers of the Contemporary South*. Ed. Peggy Whitman Prenshaw. Jackson: University Press of Mississippi, 1984. 295–306.

Godwin, Gail. "The Uses of Autobiography." In *The Writer's Handbook*. Ed. Sylvia K. Burack. Boston: The Writer, 1988. 71–75.

Gordon, Mary. "Notes from California." *Antaeus* 61, no. 2 (1988): 196–98.

———. "The Parable of the Cave or: In Praise of Watercolors." In *First Person Singular: Writers on Their Craft*. Comp. Joyce Carol Oates. Princeton: Ontario Review Press, 1983. 132–35.

Gurganus, Allan. *Oldest Living Confederate Widow Tells All*. New York: Alfred A. Knopf, 1989.

Kazin, Alfred. *A Writer's America*. New York: Alfred A. Knopf, 1988.

McKern, Sharon. *Redneck Mothers, Good Ol' girls, and Other Southern Belles*. New York: Viking Penguin, 1979.

Morrison, Toni. "The Site of Memory." In *Inventing the Truth: The Art and Craft of Memoir*. Ed. William Zinsser. New York: Houghton Mifflin, 1987. 101–24.

Oates, Joyce Carol. "Adventures in Abandonment." *New York Times* 28 Aug. 1988, sec. 7: 3+.

O'Connor, Flannery. "Recent Southern Fiction: A Panel Discussion." In *Conversations with Flannery O'Connor*. Ed. Rosemary M. Magee. Jackson: University Press of Mississippi, 1987. 61–78.

Prenshaw, Peggy Whitman. Introduction. *Women Writers of the Contemporary South*. Ed. Peggy Whitman Prenshaw Jackson. University Press of Mississippi, 1984. vii–xii.

Scheniderman, Leo. *The Literary Mind*. New York: Human Sciences Press, 1988.

Welty, Eudora. *One Writer's Beginnings*. Cambridge: Harvard University Press, 1984.

Additional Works Consulted

Faust, Langdon L., ed. *American Women Writers*. Abr. ed. New York: Frederick Ungar, 1988.

Jones, John Griffin, interviewer and ed. *Mississippi Writers Talking*. 2 vols. Jackson: University Press of Mississippi, 1982–1983. (Interviews of Ellen Douglas, Margaret Walker, Elizabeth Spencer, and others.)

McCaffery, Larry, and Sinda Gregory, eds. *Alive and Writing*. Urbana: University of Illinois Press, 1987. (Information on Ursula Le Guinn and others.)

Oates, Joyce Carol, comp. *First Person Singular: Writers on Their Craft*. Princeton: Ontario Review Press, 1983. (Information on Adrienne Rich, Mary Gordon, Anne Tyler, and Joyce Carol Oates.)

Polak, Maralyn Lois, ed. *The Writer as Celebrity*. New York: M. Evans, 1986. (Interview of Rita Mae Brown and others.)

Paris Review. Interview Series.

Prenshaw, Peggy Whitman, ed. *Women Writers of the Contemporary South*. Jackson: University Press of Mississippi, 1984. (Information on Lisa Alther, Shirley Ann Grau, Mary Lee Settle, Elizabeth Spencer, Anne Tyler, Ellen Douglas, Gail Godwin, Lee Smith, and others.)

Profile of Kay Gibbons in Chapel Hill *Triangle News Leader*. December 1988.

Schumacher, Michael, ed. *Reasons to Believe: New Voices in American Fiction*. New York: St. Martin's Press, 1988. (Information on Jayne Anne Phillips, Nancy Leman, Mona Simpson.)

Todd, Janet, ed. *Women Writers Talking*. New York: Holmes & Meier, 1983. (Information on Alison Lurie, Grace Paley, and others.)

William Styron

(1925–   )

On June 11, 1925, William Styron was born in Newport News, Virginia. He studied at Davidson College and in 1943 transferred to Duke University, both in North Carolina, following his enlistment in the Marine Corps to attend the V-12 officer-training program. He was graduated from Duke with a B.A. and moved to New York in 1947 to work at McGraw-Hill.

Styron moved to Paris, France, in the early 1950s, where he, George Plimpton, and Peter Matthiessen founded *The Paris Review*. Styron returned to the United States in 1953 and married Rose Burgunder. They now reside in Roxbury, Connecticut. In 1970, he received the William Dean Howell Medal of the American Academy of Arts and Letters. President Bill Clinton awarded Styron the National Medal of the Arts in 1993. His book *The Confessions of Nat Turner* (1967) won the Pulitzer Prize in fiction for 1968. *Sophie's Choice* (1979) earned the 1980 American Book Award and was made into a film in 1982 starring Meryl Streep.

Among Styron's other works are *Lie Down in Darkness* (1951); *The Long March* (1956); *Set This House on Fire* (1960); *In the Clap Shack* (1973); *This Quiet Dust and Other Writing* (1982); *Darkness Visible: A Memoir of Madness* (1991); and *A Tidewater Morning: Three Tales from Youth* (1993).

Shadrach

My tenth summer on earth, in the year 1935, will never leave my mind because of Shadrach and the way he brightened and darkened my life then and thereafter. He turned up as if from nowhere, arriving at high noon in the village where I grew up in Tidewater Virginia. He was a black apparition of unbelievable antiquity, palsied and feeble, blue-gummed and grinning, a caricature of a caricature at a time when every creaky, superannuated Negro grandsire was (in the eyes of society, not alone the eyes of a small southern white boy) a combination of Stepin Fetchit and Uncle Remus. On that day when he seemed to materialize before us, almost out of the ether, we were playing marbles. Little boys rarely play marbles nowadays but marbles were an obses-sion in 1935, somewhat predating the yo-yo as a kids' craze. One could admire these elegant many-colored spheres as potentates admire rubies and emeralds; they had a sound yet slippery substantiality, evoking the tactile delight—the same aesthetic yet opulent pleasure—of small precious globes of jade. Thus, among other things, my memory of Shadrach is bound up with the lapidary feel of marbles in my fingers and the odor of cool bare earth on a smoldering hot day beneath a sycamore tree, and still another odor (ineffably a part of the moment): a basic fetor which that squeamish decade christened B.O., and which radiated from a child named Little Mole Dabney, my opponent at marbles. He was ten years old, too, and had never been known to use Lifebuoy soap, or any other cleansing agent.

Which brings me soon enough to the Dabneys. For I realize I must deal with the Dabneys in order to try to explain the encompassing mystery of Shadrach—who after a fashion was a Dabney himself. The Dabneys were not close neighbors; they lived nearby down the road in a rambling weatherworn house that lacked a lawn. On the grassless, graceless terrain of the front yard was a random litter of eviscerated Frigidaires, electric generators, stoves, and the remains of two or three ancient auto-mobiles, whose scavenged carcasses lay abandoned beneath the sycamores like huge rusted insects. Poking up through these husks were masses of weeds and hollyhocks, dandelions gone to seed, sunflowers. Junk and auto parts were a sideline of Mr. Dabney's. He also did odd jobs, but his primary pursuit was bootlegging.

Like such noble Virginia family names as Randolph and Peyton and Tucker and Harrison and Lee and Fitzhugh and a score of others, the patronym Dabney is an illus-trious one, but with the present Dabney, christened Vernon, the name had lost almost all of its luster. He should have gone to the University of Virginia; instead, he dropped out of school in the fifth grade. It was not his fault; nor was it his fault that the family had so declined in status. It was said that his father (a true scion of the distinguished old tree but a man with a character defect and a weakness for the bottle) had long ago slid down the social ladder, forfeiting his F.F.V. status by marrying a half-breed Mattaponi or Pamunkey Indian girl from the York River, which accounted perhaps for the black hair and sallowish muddy complexion of the son.

Mr. Dabney—at this time, I imagine he was in his forties—was a runty, hyperac-tive entrepreneur with a sourly intense, purse-lipped, preoccupied air and a some-times rampaging temper. He also had a ridiculously foul mouth, from which I learned my first dirty words. It was with delectation, with the same sickishly delighted appre-hension of evil that beset me about eight years later when I was accosted by my first prostitute, that I heard Mr. Dabney in his frequent transports of rage use those words forbidden to me in my own home. His blasphemies and obscenities, far from scaring me, caused me to shiver with their splendor. I practiced his words in secret, deriving from their amalgamated filth what, in a dim pediatric way, I could perceive was erotic inflammation. "Son of a bitch whorehouse bat shit Jesus Christ pisspot asshole!" I would screech into an empty closet, and feel my little ten-year-old pecker rise. Yet as ugly and threatening as Mr. Dabney might sometimes appear, I was never really daunted by him, for he had a humane and gentle side. Although he might curse like a stevedore at his wife and children, at the assorted mutts and cats that thronged the place, at the pet billy goat, which he once caught in the act of devouring his new three-dollar Thom McAn shoes, I soon saw that even his most murderous fits were largely bluster. This would include his loud and eccentric dislike of Franklin D. Roosevelt. Most down-and-out people of the Tidewater revered F.D.R., like poor people everywhere; not Mr. Dabney. Much later I surmised that his tantrums probably derived from a pining to return to his aristocratic origins.

Oh, how I loved the Dabneys! I actually wanted to *be* a Dabney—wanted to change my name from Paul Whitehurst to Paul Dabney. I visited the Dabney homestead as often as I could, basking in its casual squalor. I must avoid giving the impression of Tobacco Road; the Dabneys were of better quality. Yet there were similarities. The mother, named Trixie, was a huge sweaty generous sugarloaf of a woman, often drunk. It was she, I am sure, who propagated the domestic sloppiness. But I loved her passionately, just as I loved and envied the whole Dabney tribe and that total absence in them of the bourgeois aspirations and gentility which were my own inheritance. I envied the sheer teeming multitude of the Dabneys—there were seven children—which made my status as an only child seem so effete, spoiled, and lonesome. Only illicit whiskey kept the family from complete destitution, and I envied their near poverty. Also their religion. They were Baptists: as a Presbyterian I envied that. To be totally immersed—how wet and natural! They lived in a house devoid of books or any reading matter except funny papers—more envy. I envied their abandoned slovenliness, their sour unmade beds, their roaches, the cracked linoleum on the floor, the homely cur dogs leprous with mange that foraged at will through house and yard. My perverse longings were—to turn around a phrase unknown at the time—downwardly mobile. Afflicted at the age of ten by *nostalgie de la boue*, I felt deprived of a certain depravity. I was too young to know, of course, that one of the countless things of which the Dabneys were victims was the Great Depression.

Yet beneath this scruffy façade, the Dabneys were a family of some property. Although their ramshackle house was rented, as were most of the dwellings in our village, they owned a place elsewhere, and there was occasionally chatter in the household about "the Farm," far upriver in King and Queen County. Mr. Dabney had inherited the place from his dissolute father and it had been in the family for generations. It could not have been much of a holding, or else it would have been sold years before, and when, long afterward, I came to absorb the history of the Virginia Tidewater—that primordial American demesne where the land was sucked dry by tobacco, laid waste and destroyed a whole century before golden California became an idea, much less a hope or a westward dream—I realized that the Dabney farm must have been as nondescript and as pathetic a relic as any of the scores of shrunken, abandoned "plantations" scattered for a hundred miles across the tidelands between the Potomac and the James. The chrysalis, unpainted, of a dinky, thrice-rebuilt farmhouse with a few mean acres in corn and second-growth timber—that was all. Nonetheless it was to this ancestral dwelling that the nine Dabneys, packed like squirming eels into a fifteen-year-old Model T Ford pockmarked with the ulcers of terminal decay, would go forth for a month's sojourn each August, as seemingly bland and blasé about their customary estivation as Rockefellers decamping to Pocantico Hills. But they were not entirely vacationing. I did not know then but discovered later that the woodland glens and lost glades of the depopulated land of King and Queen were every moonshiner's dream for hideaways in which to decoct white lightning, and the exodus to "the Farm" served a purpose beyond the purely recreative: each Dabney, of whatever age and sex, had at least a hand in the operation of the still, even if it was simply shucking corn.

All of the three Dabney boys bore the nickname Mole, being differentiated from each other by a logical nomenclature—Little, Middle, and Big Mole; I don't think I ever knew their real names. It was the youngest of the three Moles I was playing marbles with when Shadrach made his appearance. Little Mole was a child of stunning ugliness, sharing with his brothers an inherited mixture of bulging thyroid eyes, mashed-in spoonlike nose, and jutting jaw that (I say in retrospect) might have nicely corresponded to Cesare Lombroso's description of the criminal physiognomy. Something more remarkable—accounting surely for their collective nickname—was the fact that save for their graduated sizes they were nearly exact replicas of each other, appearing related less as brothers than as monotonous clones, as if Big Mole had reproduced Middle, who in turn had created Little, my evil-smelling playmate. None of the Moles ever wished or was ever required to bathe, and this accounted for another phenomenon. At the vast and dismal consolidated rural school, we attended, one could mark the presence of any of the three Dabney brothers in a classroom by the ring of empty desks isolating each Mole from his classmates, who, edging away without apology from the effluvium, would leave the poor Mole abandoned in his aloneness, like some species of bacterium on a microscope slide whose noxious discharge has destroyed all life in a circle around it.

By contrast—the absurdity of genetics!—the four Dabney girls were fair, fragrant in their Woolworth perfumes, buxom, lusciously ripe of hindquarter, at least two of them knocked up and wed before attaining full growth. Oh, those lost beauties . . .

That day Little Mole took aim with a glittering taw of surreal chalcedony; he had warts on his fingers, his odor in my nostrils was quintessential Mole. He sent my agate spinning into the weeds.

Shadrach appeared then. We somehow sensed his presence, looked up, and found him there. We had not heard him approach; he had come as silently and portentously as if he had been lowered on some celestial apparatus operated by unseen hands. He was astoundingly black. I had never seen a Negro of that impenetrable hue: it was blackness of such intensity that it reflected no light at all, achieving a virtual obliteration of facial features and taking on a mysterious undertone that had the blue-gray of ashes. Perched on a fender, he was grinning at us from the rusted frame of a demolished Pierce-Arrow. It was a blissful grin, which revealed deathly purple gums, the yellowish stumps of two teeth, and wet mobile tongue. For a long while he said nothing but, continuing to grin, contentedly rooted at his crotch with a hand warped and wrinkled with age: the bones moved beneath the black skin in clear skeletal outline. With his other hand he firmly grasped a walking stick.

It was then that I felt myself draw a breath in wonder at his age, which was surely unfathomable. He looked older than all the patriarchs of Genesis whose names flooded my mind in a Sunday school litany: Lamech, Noah, Enoch, and that perdurable old Jewish fossil Methuselah. Little Mole and I drew closer, and I saw then that the old man had to be at least partially blind; cataracts clouded his eyes like milky cauls, the corneas swam with rheum. Yet he was not entirely without sight. I sensed the way he observed our approach; above the implacable sweet grin there were flickers of wise recognition. His presence remained worrisomely biblical; I felt myself drawn to him with an almost devout compulsion, as if he were the prophet Elijah sent to bring truth, light, the Word. The shiny black mohair mail-order suit he wore was baggy and frayed, streaked with dust; the cuffs hung loose, and from one of the ripped ankle-high clodhoppers protruded a naked black toe. Even so, the presence was thrillingly ecclesiastical and fed my piety.

It was midsummer. The very trees seemed to hover on the edge of combustion; a mockingbird began to chant nearby in notes rippling and clear. I walked closer to the granddaddy through a swarm of fat green flies supping hungrily on the assorted offal carpeting the Dabney yard. Streams of sweat were pouring off the ancient black face. Finally I heard him speak, in a senescent voice so faint and garbled that it took moments for it to penetrate my understanding. But I understood: "Praise de Lawd. Praise his sweet name! Ise arrived in Ole Virginny!"

He beckoned to me with one of his elongated, bony, bituminous fingers; at first it alarmed me but then the finger seemed to move appealingly, like a small harmless snake. "Climb up on ole Shad's knee," he said. I was beginning to get the hang of his gluey diction, realized that it was a matter of listening to certain internal rhythms; even so, with the throaty gulping sound of Africa in it, it was nigger talk I had never heard before. "Jes climb up," he commanded. I obeyed. I obeyed with love and eagerness; it was like creeping up against the bosom of Abraham. In the collapsed old lap I sat happily, fingering a brass chain which wound across the grease-shiny vest; at the end of the chain, dangling, was a nickel-plated watch upon the face of which the black mitts of Mickey Mouse marked the noontime hour. Giggling now, snuggled against the ministerial breast, I inhaled the odor of great age—indefinable, not exactly unpleasant but stale, like a long-unopened cupboard—mingled with the smell of unlaundered fabric and dust. Only inches away the tongue quivered like a pink clapper in the dark gorge of a cavernous bell. "You jes a sweetie," he crooned. "Is you a Dabney?" I replied with regret, "No," and pointed to Little Mole. "That's a Dabney," I said.

"You a sweetie, too," he said, summoning Little Mole with the outstretched forefinger, black, palsied, wiggling. "Oh, you jes de sweetest thing!" The voice rose joyfully. Little Mole looked perplexed. I felt Shadrach's entire body quiver; to my mystification he was overcome with emotion at beholding a flesh-and-blood Dabney, and as he reached toward the boy I heard him breathe again: "Praise de Lawd! Ise arrived in Ole Virginny!"

Then at that instant Shadrach suffered a cataclysmic crisis—one that plainly had to do with the fearful heat. He could not, of course, grow pallid, but something enormous and vital did dissolve within the black eternity of his face; the wrinkled old skin of his cheeks sagged, his milky eyes rolled blindly upward, and uttering a soft moan, he fell back across the car's ruptured seat with its naked springs and its holes disgorging horsehair.

"Watah!" I heard him cry feebly, "*Watah!*" I slid out of his lap, watched the scrawny black legs no bigger around than pine saplings begin to shake and twitch. "Watah, please!" I heard the voice implore, but Little Mole and I needed no further urging; we were gone—racing headlong to the kitchen and the cluttered, reeking sink. "That old cullud man's dying!" Little Mole wailed. We got a cracked jelly glass, ran water from the faucet in a panic, speculating as we did: Little Mole ventured the notion of a heat stroke; I theorized a heart attack. We screamed and babbled; we debated whether the water should be at room temperature or iced. Little Mole added half a cupful of salt, then decided that the water should be hot. Our long delay was fortunate, for several moments later, as we hurried with the terrible potion to Shadrach's side, we found that the elder Dabney had appeared from a far corner of the yard and, taking command of the emergency, had pried Shadrach away from the seat of the Pierce-Arrow, dragged or carried him across the plot of bare earth, propped him up against a tree trunk, and now stood sluicing water from a garden hose into Shadrach's gaping mouth. The old man gulped his fill. Then Mr. Dabney, small and fiercely intent in his baggy overalls, hunched down over the stricken patriarch, whipped out a pint bottle from his pocket, and poured a stream of crystalline whiskey down Shadrach's gorge. While he did this he muttered to himself in tones of incredulity and inwardly tickled amazement: "Well, kiss my ass! Who are you, old uncle? Just who in the goddamned hell *are* you?"

We heard Shadrach give a strangled cough; then he began to try out something resembling speech. But the word he was almost able to produce was swallowed and lost in the hollow of his throat.

"What did he say? What did he say?" Mr. Dabney demanded impatiently.

"He said his name is Shadrach!" I shouted, proud that I alone seemed able to fathom this obscure Negro dialect, further muddled by the crippled cadences of senility.

"What's he want, Paul?" Mr. Dabney said to me.

I bent my face toward Shadrach's, which looked contented again. His voice in my ear was at once whispery and sweet, a gargle of beatitude: "Die on Dabney ground."

"I think he said," I told Mr. Dabney at last, "that he wants to die on Dabney ground."

"Well, I'll be goddamned," said Mr. Dabney.

"Praise de Lawd!" Shadrach cried suddenly, in a voice that even Mr. Dabney could understand. "Ise arrived in Ole Virginny!"

Mr. Dabney roared at me: "Ask him where he came from!"

Again I inclined my face to that black shrunken visage upturned to the blazing sun; I whispered the question and the reply came back after a long silence, in fitful stammerings. At last I said to Mr. Dabney: "He says he's from Clay County down in Alabama."

"*Alabama!* Well, kiss my ass!"

I felt Shadrach pluck at my sleeve and once more I bent down to listen. Many seconds passed before I could discover the outlines of the words struggling for meaning on the flailing, ungovernable tongue. But finally I captured their shapes, arranged them in order.

"What did he say now, Paul?" Mr. Dabney said.

"He said he wants you to bury him."

"*Bury him!*" Mr. Dabney shouted. "How can I bury him? He ain't even dead yet!"

From Shadrach's breast there now came a gentle keening sound which, commencing on a note of the purest grief, startled me by the way it resolved itself suddenly into a mild faraway chuckle; the moonshine was taking hold. The pink clapper of a tongue lolled in the cave of the jagged old mouth. Shadrach grinned.

"Ask him how old he is, Paul," came the command. I asked him. "Nimenime" was the glutinous reply.

"He says he's ninety-nine years old," I reported, glancing up from the ageless abyss.

"*Ninety-nine!* Well, I'll be goddamned!"

Now other Dabneys began to arrive, including the mother, Trixie, and the two larger Moles, along with one of the older teenage daughters, whalelike but meltingly beautiful as she floated on the crest of her pregnancy, and accompanied by her hulking, acne-cratered teenage spouse. There also came a murmuring clutch of neighbors—sun-reddened shipyard workers in cheap sport shirts, scampering towhead children, a quartet of scrawny housewives in sacklike dresses, bluish crescents of sweat beneath their arms. In my memory they make an aching tableau of those exhausted years. They jabbered and clucked in wonder at Shadrach, who, immobilized by alcohol, heat, infirmity, and his ninety-nine Augusts, beamed and raised his rheumy eyes to the sun. "Praise de Lawd!" he quavered.

We hoisted him to his feet and supported the frail, almost weightless old frame as he limped on dancing tiptoe to the house, where we settled him down upon a rumpsprung glider that squatted on the back porch in an ambient fragrance of dog urine, tobacco smoke, and mildew. "You hungry, Shad?" Mr. Dabney bellowed. "Mama, get Shadrach something to eat!" Slumped in the glider, the ancient visitor gorged himself like one plucked from the edge of critical starvation: he devoured three cantaloupes, slurped down bowl after bowl of Rice Krispies, and gummed his way through a panful of hot cornbread smeared with lard. We watched silently, in wonderment. Before our solemnly attentive eyes he gently and carefully eased himself back on the malodorous pillows and with a soft sigh went to sleep.

Some time after this—during the waning hours of the afternoon, when Shadrach woke up, and then on into the evening—the mystery of the old man's appearance became gradually unlocked. One of the Dabney daughters was a fawn-faced creature of twelve named Edmonia; the fragile beauty (especially when contrasted with ill-favored brothers) and her precocious breasts and bottom had caused me—young as I was—a troubling, unresolved itch. I was awed by the ease and nonchalance with which she wiped the drool from Shadrach's lips. Like me, she possessed some inborn gift of interpretation, and through our joint efforts there was pieced together over several hours an explanation for this old man—for his identity and his bizarre and inescapable coming.

He stayed on the glider; we put another pillow under his head. Nourishing his dragon's appetite with Hershey bars and, later on, with nips from Mr. Dabney's bottle, we were able to coax from those aged lips a fragmented, abbreviated, but reasonably coherent biography. After a while it became an anxious business for, as one of the adults noticed, old Shad seemed to be running a fever; his half-blind eyes swam about from time to time, and the clotted phlegm that rose in his throat made it all the more difficult to understand anything. But somehow we began to divine the truth. One phrase, repeated over and over, I particularly remember: "Ise a Dabney." And indeed those words provided the chief clue to his story.

Born a slave on the Dabney plantation in King and Queen County, he had been sold down to Alabama in the decades before the Civil War. Shadrach's memory was imperfect regarding the date of his sale. Once he said "fifty," meaning 1850, and another time he said "fifty-five," but it was an item of little importance; he was probably somewhere between fifteen and twenty-five years old when his master—Vernon Dabney's great-grandfather—disposed of him, selling him to one of the many traders prowling the worn-out Virginia soil of that stricken bygone era; and since in his confessional to us, garbled as it was, he used the word "coffle" (a word beyond my ten-year-old knowledge but one whose meaning I later understood), he must have journeyed those six hundred miles to Alabama on foot and in the company of God knows how many other black slaves, linked together by chains.

So now, as we began slowly to discover, this was Shadrach's return trip home to Ole Virginny—three quarters of a century or thereabouts after his departure from the land out of which he had sprung, which had nurtured him, and where he had lived his happy years. Happy? Who knows? But we had to assume they were his happy years— else why this incredible pilgrimage at the end of his life? As he had announced with such abrupt fervor earlier, he wanted only to die and be buried on "Dabney ground."

We learned that after the war he had become a sharecropper, that he had married three times and had had many children (once he said twelve, another time fifteen; no matter, they were legion); he had outlived them all, wives and offspring. Even the grandchildren had died off, or had somehow vanished. "Ah was dibested of all mah plenty" was another statement I can still record verbatim. Thus divested and (as he cheerfully made plain to all who gathered around him to listen) sensing mortality in his own shriveled flesh and bones, he had departed Alabama on foot—just as he had come there—to find the Virginia of his youth.

Six hundred miles! The trip, we were able to gather, took over four months, since he said he set out from Clay County in the early spring. He walked nearly the entire way, although now and then he would accept a ride—almost always, one can be sure, from the few Negroes who owned cars in the rural South of those years. He had saved up a few dollars, which allowed him to provide for his stomach. He slept on the side of the road or in barns; sometimes a friendly Negro family would give him shelter. The trek took him across Georgia and the Carolinas and through Southside Virginia. His itinerary is still anyone's conjecture. Because he could not read either road sign or road map, he obviously followed his own northward-questing nose, a profoundly imperfect method of finding one's way (he allowed to Edmonia with a faint cackle), since he once got so far astray that he ended up not only miles away from the proper highway but in a city and state completely off his route—Chattanooga, Tennessee. But he circled back and moved on. And how, once arrived in Virginia with its teeming Dabneys, did he discover the only Dabney who would matter, the single Dabney who was not merely the proprietor of his birthplace but the one whom he also unquestioningly expected to oversee his swiftly approaching departure, laying him to rest in the earth of their mutual ancestors? How did he find *Vernon Dabney*? Mr. Dabney was by no means an ill-spirited or ungenerous man (despite his runaway temper), but was a soul nonetheless beset by many woes in the dingy threadbare year 1935, being hard pressed not merely for dollars but for dimes and quarters, crushed beneath an elephantine and inebriate wife, along with three generally shiftless sons and two knocked-up daughters, plus two more likely to be so, and living with the abiding threat of revenue agents swooping down to terminate his livelihood and, perhaps, get him sent to the Atlanta penitentiary for five or six years. He needed no more cares or burdens, and now in the hot katydid-shrill hours of summer night I saw him gaze down at the leathery old dying black face with an expression that mingled compassion and bewilderment and stoppered-up rage and desperation, and then whisper to himself: "He wants to die on Dabney ground! Well, kiss my ass, just kiss my ass!" Plainly he wondered how, among all his horde of Virginia kinfolk, Shadrach found *him*, for he squatted low and murmured; "Shad! Shad, how come you knew who to look for?" But in his fever Shadrach had drifted off to sleep, and so far as I ever knew there was never any answer to that.

The next day it was plain that Shadrach was badly off. During the night he had somehow fallen from the glider, and in the early morning hours he was discovered on the floor, leaking blood. We bandaged him up. The wound just above his ear was superficial, as it turned out, but it had done him no good; and when he was replaced on the swing he appeared to be confused and at the edge of delirium, plucking at his shirt, whispering, and rolling his gentle opaque eyes at the ceiling. Whenever he spoke now, his words were beyond the power of Edmonia or me to comprehend, faint high-pitched mumbo jumbo in a drowned dialect. He seemed to recognize no one. Trixie, leaning over the old man as she sucked at her first Pabst Blue Ribbon of the morning, decided firmly that there was no time to waste. "Shoog," she said to Mr. Dabney, using her habitual pet name (diminutive form of Sugar), "you better get out the car if we're goin' to the Farm. I think he ain't gone last much longer." And so, given unusual parental leave to go along on the trip, I squeezed myself into the backseat of the Model T, privileged to hold in my lap a huge greasy paper bag full of fried chicken which Trixie had prepared for noontime dinner at the Farm.

Not all of the Dabneys made the journey—the two older daughters and the largest Mole were left behind—but we still composed a multitude. We children were packed sweatily skin to skin and atop each other's laps in the rear seat, which reproduced in miniature the messiness of the house with this new litter of empty RC Cola and Nehi bottles, funny papers, watermelon rinds, banana peels, greasy jack handles, oil-smeared gears of assorted sizes, and wads of old Kleenex. On the floor beneath my feet I even discerned (to my intense discomfort, for I had just learned to recognize such an object) a crumpled, yellowish used condom, left there haphazardly, I was certain, by one of the older daughters' boyfriends who had been able to borrow the heap for carnal sport. It was a bright summer day, scorchingly hot like the day preceding it, but the car had no workable windows and we were pleasantly ventilated. Shadrach sat in the middle of the front seat. Mr. Dabney was hunched over the wheel, chewing at a wad of tobacco and driving with black absorption; he had stripped to his undershirt, and I thought I could almost see the rage and frustration in the tight bunched muscles of his neck. He muttered curses at the balky gearshift but otherwise said little, rapt in his guardian misery. So voluminous that the flesh of her shoulders fell in a freckled cascade over the back of her seat, Trixie loomed on the other side of Shadrach; the corpulence of her body seemed in some way to both enfold and support the old man, who nodded and dozed. The encircling hair around the shiny black head was, I thought, like a delicate halo of the purest frost or foam. Curiously, for the first time since Shadrach's coming, I felt a stab of grief and achingly wanted him not to die.

"Shoog," said Trixie, standing by the rail of the dumpy little ferry that crossed the York River, "what kind of big birds do you reckon those are behind that boat there?" The Model T had been the first car aboard, and all of us had flocked out to look at the river, leaving Shadrach to sit there and sleep during the fifteen-minute ride. The water was blue, sparkling with whitecaps, lovely. A huge gray naval tug with white markings chugged along to the mine depot at Yorktown, trailing eddies of garbage and a swooping flock of frantic gulls. Their squeals echoed across the peaceful channel.

"Seagulls," said Mr. Dabney. "Ain't you never recognized seagulls before? I can't believe such a question. Seagulls. Dumb greedy bastards."

"Beautiful things," she replied softly, "all big and white. Can you eat one?"

"So tough you'd like to choke to death."

We were halfway across the river when Edmonia went to the car to get a ginger ale. When she came back she said hesitantly: "Mama, Shadrach has made a fantastic mess in his pants."

"Oh, Lord," said Trixie.

Mr. Dabney clutched the rail and raised his small, pinched, tormented face to heaven. "Ninety-nine years old! Christ almighty! He ain't nothin' but a ninety-nine-years-old *baby!*"

"It smells just awful," said Edmonia.

"Why in the goddamned hell didn't he go to the bathroom before we left?" Mr. Dabney said. "Ain't it bad enough we got to drive three hours to the Farm without—"

"Shoosh!" Trixie interrupted, moving ponderously to the car. "Poor ol' thing, he can't help it. Vernon, you see how you manage your bowels fifty years from now."

Once off the ferry we children giggled and squirmed in the backseat, pointedly squeezed our noses, and scuffled amid the oily rubbish of the floorboards. It *was* an awful smell. But a few miles up the road in the hamlet of Gloucester Court House, drowsing in eighteenth-century brick and ivy, Trixie brought relief to the situation by bidding Mr. Dabney to stop at an Amoco station. Shadrach had partly awakened from his slumbrous trance. He stirred restlessly in his pool of discomfort, and began to make little fretful sounds, so softly restrained as to barely give voice to what must have been his real and terrible distress. "There now, Shad," Trixie said gently, "Trixie'll look after you." And this she did, half-coaxing, half-hoisting the old man from the car and into a standing position, then with the help of Mr. Dabney propelling his skinny scarecrow frame in a suspended tiptoe dance to the rest room marked COLORED, where to the muffled sound of rushing water she performed some careful rite of cleansing and diapering. Then they brought him back to the car. For the first time that morning Shadrach seemed really aroused from that stupor into which he had plunged so swiftly hours before. "Praise de Lawd!" we heard him say, feebly but with spirit, as the elder Dabneys maneuvered him back onto the seat, purified. He gazed about him with glints of recognition, responding with soft chuckles to our little pats of attention. Even Mr. Dabney seemed in sudden good humor. "You comin' along all right now, Shad?" he howled over the rackety clattering sound of the motor. Shadrach nodded and grinned but remained silent. There was a mood in the car of joy and revival. "Slow down, Shoog," Trixie murmured indolently, gulping at a beer, "there might be a speed cop." I was filled with elation, and hope tugged at my heart as the flowering landscape rushed by, green and lush with summer and smelling of hay and honeysuckle.

The Dabney country retreat, as I have said, was dilapidated and rudimentary, a true downfall from bygone majesty. Where there once stood a plantation house of the Palladian stateliness required of its kind during the Tidewater dominion in its heyday, there now roosted a dwelling considerably grander than a shack yet modest by any reckoning. Boxlike, paintless, supported by naked concrete blocks, and crowned by a roof of glistening sheet metal, it would have been an eyesore almost anywhere except in King and Queen County, a bailiwick so distant and underpopulated that the house was scarcely ever viewed by human eyes. A tilted privy out back lent another homely note; junk littered the yard here too. But the soft green acres that surrounded the place were Elysian; the ancient fields and the wild woods rampant with sweet gum and oak and redbud had reverted to the primeval glory of the time of Pocahontas and Powhatan. Grapevines crowded the emerald-green thickets that bordered the house on every side, a delicious winey smell of cedar filled the air, and the forest at night echoed with the sound of whippoorwills. The house itself was relatively clean, thanks not to any effort on the part of the Dabneys but to the fact that it remained unlived in by Dabneys for most of the year.

That day after our fried chicken meal we placed Shadrach between clean sheets on a bed in one of the sparsely furnished rooms, then turned to our various recreations. Little Mole and I played marbles all afternoon just outside the house, seeking the shade of a majestic old beech tree; after an hour of crawling in the dirt our faces were streaked and filthy. Later we took a plunge in the millpond, which, among other things, purged Little Mole of his B.O. The other children went fishing for perch and bream in the brackish creek that ran through the woods. Mr. Dabney drove off to get provisions at the crossroads store, then vanished into the underbrush to tinker around his well-hidden still. Meanwhile Trixie tramped about with heavy footfalls in the kitchen and downed half a dozen Blue Ribbons, pausing occasionally to look in on Shadrach. Little Mole and I peered in, too, from time to time. Shadrach lay in a deep sleep and seemed to be at peace, even though now and then his breath came in a ragged gasp and his long black fingers plucked convulsively at the hem of the sheet, which covered him to his breast like a white shroud. Then the afternoon was over. After a dinner of fried perch and bream we all went to bed with the setting of the sun. Little Mole and I lay sprawled naked in the heat on the same mattress, separated by a paper-thin wall from Shadrach's breathing, which rose and fell in my ears against the other night sounds of this faraway and time-haunted place: katydids and crickets and hoot owls and the reassuring cheer—now near, now almost lost—of a whippoorwill.

Late the next morning the county sheriff paid a visit on Mr. Dabney. We were not at the house when he arrived, and so he had to wait for us; we were at the graveyard. Shadrach still slept, with the children standing watch by turns. After our watch Little Mole and I had spent an hour exploring the woods and swinging on the grapevines, and when we emerged from a grove of pine trees a quarter of a mile or so behind the house, we came upon Mr. Dabney and Trixie. They were poking about in a bramble-filled plot of land which was the old Dabney family burial ground. It was a sunny, peaceful place, where grasshoppers skittered in the tall grass. Choked with briars and nettles and weeds and littered with tumbledown stone markers, unfenced and untended for countless decades, it had been abandoned to the encroachments of summer after summer like this one, when even granite and marble had to give way against the stranglehold of spreading roots and voracious green growing things.

All of Mr. Dabney's remote ancestors lay buried here, together with their slaves, who slept in a plot several feet off to the side—inseparable from their masters and mistresses, but steadfastly apart in death as in life. Mr. Dabney stood amid the tombstones of the slaves, glaring gloomily down at the tangle of vegetation and at the crumbling lopsided little markers. He held a shovel in his hand but had not begun to dig. I peered at the headstones, read the given names, which were as matter-of-fact in their lack of patronymic as the names of spaniels or cats: *Fauntleroy, Wake-*

field, Sweet Betty, Mary, Jupiter, Lulu. Requiescat in Pace. Anno Domini 1790 . . . 1814 . . . 1831. All of these Dabneys, I thought, like Shadrach.

"I'll be goddamned if I believe there's a square inch of space left," Mr. Dabney observed to Trixie, and spat a russet gob of tobacco juice into the weeds. "They just crowded all the old dead uncles and mammies they could into this piece of land here. They must be shoulder to shoulder down there." He paused and made his characteristic sound of anguish—a choked dirgelike groan. "Christ Almighty! I hate to think of diggin' about half a ton of dirt!"

"Shoog, why don't you leave off diggin' until this evenin'?" Trixie said. She was trying to fan herself with a soggy handkerchief, and her face—which I had witnessed before in this state of drastic summer discomfort—wore the washed-out bluish shade of skim milk. It usually preceded a fainting spell. "This sun would kill a mule."

Mr. Dabney agreed, saying that he looked forward to a cool glass of iced tea, and we made our way back to the house along a little path of bare earth that wound through a field glistening with goldenrod. Then, just as we arrived at the back of the house we saw the sheriff waiting. He was standing with a foot on the running board of his Plymouth sedan; perched on its front fender was a hulkingly round, intimidating silver siren (in those days pronounced si-*reen*). He was a potbellied middle-aged man with a sunscorched face fissured with delicate seams, and he wore steel-rimmed spectacles. A gold-plated star was pinned to his civilian shirt, which was soaked with sweat. He appeared hearty, made an informal salute and said: "Mornin', Trixie. Mornin', Vern."

"Mornin', Tazewell," Mr. Dabney replied solemnly, though with an edge of suspicion. Without pause he continued to trudge toward the house. "You want some ice tea?"

"No, thank you," he said. "Vern, hold on a minute. I'd like a word with you."

I was knowledgeable enough to fear in a vague way some involvement with the distillery in the woods, and I held my breath, but then Mr. Dabney halted, turned, and said evenly: "What's wrong?"

"Vern," the sheriff said, "I hear you're fixin' to bury an elderly colored man on your property here. Joe Thornton down at the store said you told him that yesterday. Is that right?

Mr. Dabney put his hands on his hips and glowered at the sheriff. Then he said: "Joe Thornton is a god-damned incurable blabbermouth. But that's right. What's wrong with that?"

"You can't," said the sheriff.

There was a pause. "Why not?" said Mr. Dabney.

"Because it's against the law."

I had seen rage, especially in matters involving the law, build up within Mr. Dabney in the past. A pulsing vein always appeared near his temple, along with a rising flush in cheeks and brow; both came now, the little vein began to wiggle and squirm like a worm. "What do you mean, it's against the law?"

"Just that. It's against the law to bury anybody on private property."

"*Why* is it against the law?" Mr. Dabney demanded.

"I don't *know* why, Vern," said the sheriff, with a touch of exasperation. "It just *is*, that's all."

Mr. Dabney flung his arm out—up and then down in a stiff, adamant, unrelenting gesture, like a railroad semaphore.

"Down in that field, Tazewell, there have been people buried for nearabout two hundred years. I got an old senile man on my hands. He was a slave and he was born on this place. Now he's dyin' and I've got to bury him here. And I am."

"Vern, let me tell you something," the sheriff said with an attempt at patience. "You will not be permitted to do any such a thing, so please don't try to give me this argument. He will have to be buried in a place where it's legally permitted, like any of the colored churchyards around here, and he will have to be attended to by a licensed colored undertaker. That's the *law*, Commonwealth of Virginia, and there ain't any which, whys, or wherefores about it."

Trixie began to anticipate Mr. Dabney's fury and resentment even before he erupted. "Shoog, keep yourself calm—"

"*Bat shit!* It is an *outrage!*" he roared. "Since when did a taxpaying citizen have to answer to the gov'ment in order to bury a harmless sick old colored man on his own property! It goes against every bill of rights I ever heard of—"

"Shoog!" Trixie put in. "*Please—*" She began to wail.

The sheriff put out placating hands and loudly commanded: "*Quiet!*" Then when Mr. Dabney and Trixie fell silent he went on: "Vern, me an' you have been acquainted for a long time, so please don't give me no trouble. I'm tellin' you for the last time, this. Namely, you have *got* to arrange to get that old man buried at one of the colored churches around here, and you will also have to have him taken care of by a licensed undertaker. You can have your choice. There's a well-known colored undertaker in Tappahannock and also I heard of one over in Middlesex, somewhere near Urbanna or Saluda. If you want, I'll give them a telephone call from the courthouse."

I watched as the red rage in Mr. Dabney's face was overtaken by a paler, softer hue of resignation. After a brooding long silence, he said: "All right then. *All right!* How much you reckon it'll cost?"

"I don't know exactly, Vern, but there was an old washerwoman worked for me and Ruby died not long ago, and I heard they buried her for thirty-five dollars."

"*Thirty-five dollars!*" I heard Mr. Dabney breathe. "Christ have mercy!"

Perhaps it was only his rage that caused him to flee, but all afternoon Mr. Dabney was gone and we did not see him again until that evening. Meanwhile, Shadrach rallied for a time from his deep slumber, so taking us by surprise that we thought he might revive completely. Trixie was shelling peas and sipping beer while she watched Little Mole and me at our marbles game. Suddenly Edmonia, who had been assigned to tend to Shadrach for an hour, came running from the house. "Come here, you all, real quick!" she said in a voice out of breath. "Shadrach's wide awake and talking!" And he was: when we rushed to his side we saw that he had hiked himself up in bed, and his face for the first time in many hours wore an alert and knowing expression, as if he were at least partially aware of his surroundings. He had even regained his appetite. Edmonia had put a daisy in the buttonhole of his shirt, and at some point during his amazing resurrection, she said, he had eaten part of it.

"You should have heard him just now," Edmonia said, leaning over the bed. "He kept talking about going to the millpond. What do you think he meant?"

"Well, could be he just wants to go see the millpond," Trixie replied. She had brought Shadrach a bottle of RC Cola from the kitchen and now she sat beside him, helping him to drink it through a paper straw. "Shad," she asked in a soft voice, "is that what you want? You want to go see the millpond?"

A look of anticipation and pleasure spread over the black face and possessed those old rheumy eyes. And his voice was high-pitched but strong when he turned his head to Trixie and said: "Yes, ma'am, I does. I wants to see de millpond."

"How come you want to see the millpond?" Trixie said gently.

Shadrach offered no explanation, merely said again: "I wants to see de millpond."

And so, in obedience to a wish whose reason we were unable to plumb but could not help honoring, we took Shadrach to see the millpond. It lay in the woods several hundred yards to the east of the house—an ageless murky dammed-up pool bordered on one side by a glade of moss and fern, spectacularly green, and surrounded on all its other sides by towering oaks and elms. Fed by springs and by the same swiftly rushing stream in which the other children had gone fishing, its water mirrored the overhanging trees and the changing sky and was a pleasurable ordeal to swim in, possessing the icy cold that shocks a body to its bones. For a while we could not figure out how to transport Shadrach down to the place; it plainly would not do to let him try to hobble that long distance, propelled, with our clumsy help, on his nearly strengthless legs in their dangling gait. Finally someone thought of the wheelbarrow, which Mr. Dabney used to haul corn to the still. It was fetched from its shed, and we quickly made of it a not unhandsome and passably comfortable sort of a wheeled litter, filling it with hay and placing a blanket on top.

On this mound Shadrach rested easily, with a look of composure, as we moved him gently rocking down the path. I watched him on the way: in my memory he still appears to be a half-blind but self-possessed and serene African potentate being borne in the fullness of his many years to some longed-for, inevitable reward.

We set the wheelbarrow down on the mossy bank, and there for a long time Shadrach gazed at the millpond, alive with its skating waterbugs and trembling beneath a copper-colored haze of sunlight where small dragonflies swooped in nervous filmy iridescence. Standing next to the wheelbarrow, out of which the shanks of Shadrach's skinny legs protruded like fragile black reeds, I turned and stared into the ancient face, trying to determine what it was he beheld now that created such a look of wistfulness and repose. His eyes began to follow the Dabney children, who had stripped to their underdrawers and had plunged into the water. That seemed to be an answer, and in a bright gleam I was certain that Shadrach had once swum here too, during some unimaginable August nearly a hundred years before.

I had no way of knowing that if his long and solitary journey from the Deep South had been a quest to find this millpond and for a recaptured glimpse of childhood, it might just as readily have been a final turning of his back on a life of suffering. Even now I cannot say for certain, but I have always had to assume that the still-young Shadrach who was emancipated in Alabama those many years ago was set loose, like most of his brothers and sisters, into another slavery perhaps more excruciating than the sanctioned bondage. The chronicle has already been a thousand times told of those people liberated into their new and incomprehensible nightmare: of their poverty and hunger and humiliation, of the crosses burning in the night, the random butchery, and, above all, the unending dread. None of that madness and mayhem belongs in this story, but without at least a reminder of these things I would not be faithful to Shadrach. Despite the immense cheerfulness with which he had spoken to us of being "dibested of mah plenty," he must have endured unutterable adversity. Yet his return to Virginia, I can now see, was out of no longing for the former bondage, but to find an earlier innocence. And as a small boy at the edge of the millpond I saw Shadrach not as one who had fled darkness, but as one who had searched for light refracted within a flashing moment of remembered childhood. As Shadrach's old clouded eyes gazed at the millpond with its plunging and calling children, his face was suffused with an immeasurable calm and sweetness, and I sensed that he had recaptured perhaps the one pure, untroubled moment in his life. "Shad, did you go swimming here too?" I said. But there was no answer. And it was not long before he was drowsing again; his head fell to the side and we rolled him back to the house in the wheelbarrow.

On Saturday nights in the country the Dabneys usually went to bed as late as ten o'clock. That evening Mr. Dabney returned at suppertime, still sullen and fretful by saying little, still plainly distraught and sick over the sheriff's mandate. He did not himself even pick up a fork. But the supper was one of those ample and blessed meals of Trixie's I recall so well. Only the bounty of a place like the Tidewater backcountry could provide such a feast for poor people in those hard-pressed years: ham with red-eye gravy, grits, collard greens, okra, sweet corn, huge red tomatoes oozing juice in a salad with onions and herbs and vinegar. For dessert there was a delectable bread pudding drowned in fresh cream. Afterward, a farmer and bootlegging colleague from down the road named Mr. Seddon R. Washington arrived in a broken-down pickup truck to join with Mr. Dabney at the only pastime I ever saw him engage in—a game of dominoes. Twilight fell and the oil lanterns were lit. Little Mole and I went back like dull slugs to our obsessive sport, scratching a large circle in the dust beside the porch and crouching down with our crystals and agates in a moth-crazed oblong of lantern light, tiger-yellow and flickering. A full moon rose slowly out of the edge of the woods like an immense, bright, faintly smudged balloon. The clicking of our marbles alternated with the click-click of the dominoes on the porch bench.

"If you wish to know the plain and simple truth about whose fault it is," I heard Mr. Dabney explain to Mr. Washington, "you can say it is the fault of your Franklin D-for-Disaster Roosevelt. The Dutchman millionaire. And his so-called New Deal ain't worth diddley squat. You know how much I made last year—legal, that is?"

"How much?" said Mr. Washington.

"I can't even tell you. It would shame me. They are colored people sellin' deviled crabs for five cents apiece on the streets in Newport News made more than me. There is an injustice somewhere with this system." He paused. "Eleanor's near about as bad as he is." Another pause. "They say she fools around with colored men and Jews. Preachers mainly."

"Things bound to get better," Mr. Washington said.

"They can't get no worse," said Mr. Dabney. "I can't get a job anywhere. I'm un-qualified. I'm only qualified for making whiskey."

Footsteps made a soft slow padding sound across the porch and I looked up and saw Edmonia draw near her father. She parted her lips, hesitated for a moment, then said: "Daddy, I think Shadrach has passed away."

Mr. Dabney said nothing, attending to the dominoes with his expression of pinched, absorbed desperation and muffled wrath. Edmonia put her hand lightly on his shoulder. "Daddy, did you hear what I said?"

"I heard."

"I was sitting next to him, holding his hand, and then all of a sudden his head—it just sort of rolled over and he was still and not breathing. And his hand—it just got limp and—well, what I mean, cold." She paused again. "He never made a sound."

Mr. Washington rose with a cough and walked to the far edge of the porch, where he lit a pipe and gazed up at the blazing moon. When again Mr. Dabney made no response, Edmonia lightly stroked the edge of his shoulder and said gently: "Daddy, I'm afraid."

"What're you afraid about?" he replied.

"I don't know," she said with a tremor. "Dying. It scares me. I don't know what it means—death. I never saw anyone—like that before."

"Death ain't nothin' to be afraid about," he blurted in a quick, choked voice. "It's life that's fearsome! *Life!*" Suddenly he arose from the bench, scattering dominoes to the floor, and when he roared *"Life!"* again, I saw Trixie emerge from the black hollow of the front door and approach with footfalls that sent a shudder through the porch timbers. "Now, *Shoog*—" she began.

"Life is where you've got to be terrified!" he cried as the unplugged rage spilled forth. "Sometimes I understand why men commit suicide! Where in the god-damned hell am I goin' to get the money to put him in the ground? Niggers have always been the biggest problem! Goddamnit, I was brought up to have a certain respect and say 'colored' instead of 'niggers' but they are always a problem. They will always just drag you down! I ain't got thirty-five-dollars! I ain't got *twenty-five* dollars! I ain't got *five* dollars!"

"Vernon!" Trixie's voice rose, and she entreatingly spread out her great creamy arms. "Someday you're goin' to get a *stroke!*"

"And one other thing!" He stopped.

Then suddenly his fury—or the harsher, wilder part of it—seemed to evaporate, sucked up into the moonlit night with its soft summery cricketing sounds and its scent of warm loam and honeysuckle. For an instant he looked shrunken, runtier than ever, so light and frail that he might blow away like a leaf, and he ran a nervous, trembling hand through his shock of tangled black hair. "I know, I know," he said in a faint, unsteady voice edged with grief. "Poor old man, he couldn't help it. He was a decent, pitiful old thing, probably never done anybody the slightest harm. I ain't got a thing in the world against Shadrach. Poor old man."

Crouching below the porch I felt an abrupt, smothering misery. The tenderest gust of wind blew from the woods and I shivered at its touch on my cheek, mourning for Shadrach and Mr. Dabney, and slavery and destitution, and all the human discord swirling around me in a time and place I could not understand. As if to banish my fierce unease, I began to try—in a seizure of concentration—to count the fireflies sparkling in the night air. Eighteen, nineteen, twenty . . .

"And anyway," Trixie said, touching her husband's hand, "he died on Dabney ground like he wanted to. Even if he's got to be put away in a strange graveyard."

"Well, he won't know the difference," said Mr. Dabney. "When you're dead nobody knows the difference. Death ain't much."

John Shelton Reed

(1942–)

John Shelton Reed, a native of Kingsport, Tennessee, was born on January 8, 1942. He received his B.S. from Massachusetts Institute of Technology in 1964. In 1970 he received his Ph.D. from Columbia University.

Reed is the Director of the Institute for Research in Social Science and the William Rand Kenan Jr. Professor of Sociology at the University of North Carolina at Chapel Hill. He coedits the quarterly *Southern Cultures*.

His books include *Whistling Dixie: Dispatches from the South* (1992); *My Tears Spoiled My Aim and Other Reflections on Southern Culture* (1993); *Surveying the South: Studies in Regional Sociology* (1993); and *Kicking Back: Further Dispatches from the South* (1995).

Reed received the 1995 Prize for Non-Fiction from the Fellowship of Southern Writers.

The South

What Is It? Where Is It?

So you've moved, or been moved, to the South. Or maybe you're thinking about it. You're wondering: What is this place? What's different about it? *Is* it different, anymore?

Good questions. Old ones, too. People have been asking them for decades. Some of us even make our livings by asking them, but we still don't agree about the answers. Let's look at what might seem to be a simpler question: Where is the South?

That's easy enough, isn't it? People more or less agree about which parts of the United States are in the South and which aren't. If I gave you a list of states and asked which are "Southern," all in all, chances are you'd agree with some of my students, whose answers are summarized in Figure 1. I don't share their hesitation about Arkansas, and I think too many were ready to put Missouri in the South, but there's not a lot to argue with here.

That tells us something. It tells us that the South is, to begin with, a concept— and a shared one. It's an idea that people can talk about, think about, use to orient themselves and each other. People know whether they're in it or not. As a geographer would put it, the South is a "vernacular" region.

Stop and think about that. Why should that be? Why can I write "South" with some assurance that you'll know I mean Richmond and don't mean Phoenix? What is it that the South's boundaries enclose?

Well, for starters, it's not news that the South has been an economically and demographically distinctive place—a poor, rural region with a biracial population, reflecting the historic dominance of the plantation system. One thing the South's boundaries have set off is a set of distinctive problems, growing out of that history. Those problems may be less and less obvious, but most are still with us to some extent, and we can still use them to locate the South.

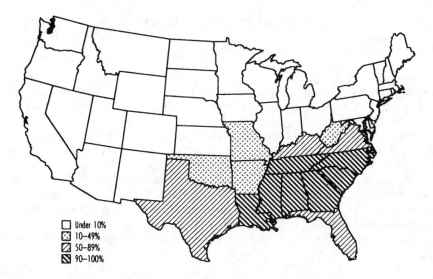

Figure 1   Percentage Who Say Each State Is Southern, "All in All"
Source: Sixty-eight students at the University of North Carolina at Chapel Hill.

But the South is more than just a collection of unfavorable statistics. It has also been home to several populations, black and white, whose intertwined cultures have set them off from other Americans as well as from each other. Some of us, in fact, have suggested that Southerners ought to be viewed as an American ethnic group, like Italian- or Polish-Americans. If we can use distinctive cultural attributes to find Southerners, then we can say that the South is where they are found.

Southerners are also like immigrant ethnic groups in that they have a sense of group identity based on their shared history and their cultural distinctiveness in the present. If we could get at it, one of the best ways to define the South would be with what Hamilton Horton calls the "Hell, yes!" line: where people begin to answer that way when asked if they're Southerners.

Finally, to the considerable extent that people do have a sense of the South's existence, its distinctiveness, and its boundaries, regional institutions have contributed. Southern businesses, Southern magazines, Southern voluntary associations, colleges, and universities—many such have at least aspired to serve the South as a whole. We can map the South by looking at where the influence of such enterprises extends.

All of these are plausible ways to go about answering the question of where the South is. For the most part, they give similar answers, which is reassuring. But it's where they differ (as they sometimes do) that they're most likely to tell us something about what the South has been, and is becoming. Nobody would exclude Mississippi from the South. But is Texas now a Southern state? Is Florida, anymore? How about West Virginia?

Allow me a homely simile. The South is like my favorite pair of blue jeans. It's shrunk some, faded a bit, got a few holes in it. There's always the possibility that it might split at the seams. It doesn't look much like it used to, but it's more comfortable, and there's probably a lot of wear left in it.

The Socioeconomic South

"Let us begin by discussing the weather," wrote U. B. Phillips in 1929. The weather, that distinguished Southern historian asserted, "has been the chief agency in making the South distinctive. It fostered the cultivation of the staple crops, which promoted the plantation system, which brought the importation of negroes, which not only gave rise to chattel slavery but created a lasting race problem. These led to controversy and regional rivalry for power, which . . . culminated in a stroke for independence." Phillips and the many who have shared his views see almost everything of interest about the South as emanating from this complex of plantation, black population, Civil War—thus, ultimately, from the weather.

You may have noticed that it's hot here in the summer, and humid. Some vegetable life loves that. Kudzu, for instance: that rampant, loopy vine needs long, moist summers, and gets them in the South. "Where kudzu grows" (Figure 2) isn't a bad definition of the South (and notice that it doesn't grow in southern Florida or West Texas).

But another plant has been far more consequential for the South. That plant, of course, is cotton. Dixie *was* "the land of cotton," and Figure 3 shows that in the early years of this century Southerners grew cotton nearly everywhere they could grow it: everywhere with two hundred or more frost-free days, annual precipitation of twenty-three inches or more, and soil that wasn't sand.

Certainly cotton culture affected the racial makeup of the South and slowed the growth of Southern cities. Figure 4 shows what the region looked like, demographically, in 1920. Few cities interrupted the countryside. A band of rural counties with

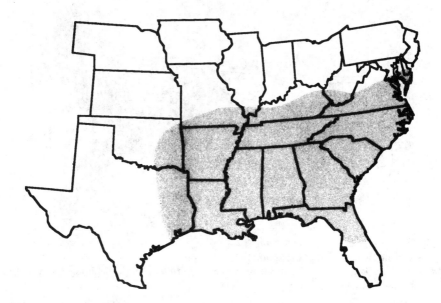

Figure 2 Where Kudzu Grows
Source: John J. Winberry and David M. Jones, "Rise and Decline of the 'Miracle Vine': Kudzu in the Southern Landscape," *Southeastern Geographer* 13 (November 1973): 62.

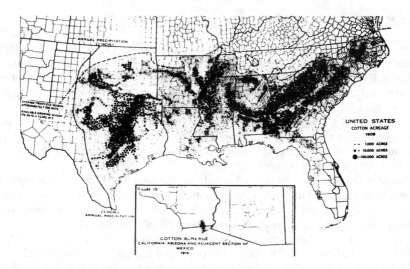

Figure 3   Acres of Cotton Cultivation, 1909
Source: U.S. Department of Agriculture, Bureau of Agricultural Economics.
Note: Map also shows gradients for precipitation and frost-free days.

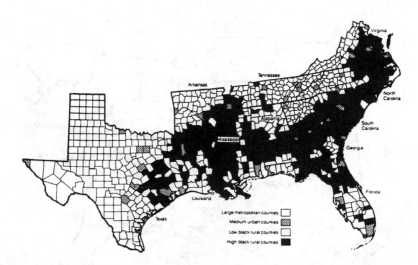

Figure 4   The Demography of the South, 1920
Source: Earl Black and Merle Black, *Politics and Society in the South* (Cambridge: Harvard University Press, 1987), 36.

substantial black populations (solidly shaded on the map) traced the area of cotton cultivation and plantation agriculture, in a long arc from southeastern Virginia down and across to eastern Texas, with arms north and south along the Mississippi River.

This is the *Deep* South—what a geographer would call the "core area" of the region defined by its staple-crop economy. Here some Southern characteristics and phenomena were found in their purest, most concentrated form. Lynchings, for example (Figure 5). Or peculiar, single-issue politics (that issue, as a politician once put it, "spelled n-i-g-g-e-r"), reflected in support for third-party or unpopular major-party presidential candidates (Figure 6). For decades the Deep South shaped Southern culture and politics and, still more, shaped people's image of what the South was all about.

Two out of three Southerners are now urban folk, and most rural Southerners work in industry anyway, but the fossil remains of this old South can still be found as concentrations of poor, rural black Southerners (compare Figure 7, for 1980, to Figure 4). This population, together with poor, rural *white* Southerners in the Southern highlands, means that most Southern states are still at the bottom of the U.S. per capita income distribution. (Virginia, Texas, and Florida—barely involved in plantation agriculture, and with little or no mountain population—are exceptions.) This means, in turn, that almost any problem of poor people, or of poor states, can still be used to map the South. Everything from outdoor toilets (Figure 8) to illiteracy (Figure 9) to bad teeth (Figure 10) costs money to put right, and many Southern people and most Southern states still don't have much.

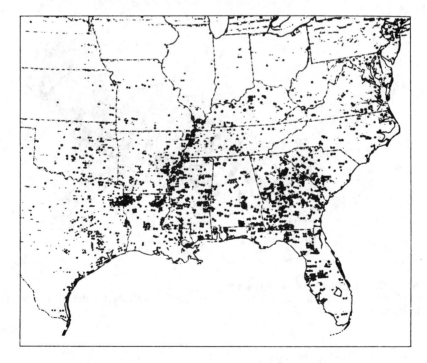

Figure 5 Lynchings, 1900–1930
Source: Southern Commission on the Study of Lynching.

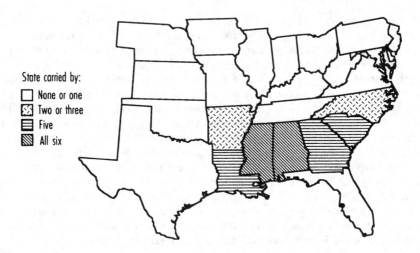

Figure 6   Unusual Voting in Presidential Elections, 1928–1968
Note: Unusual voting is defined as majorities for the following candidates: Al Smith (Democrat, 1928); Strom Thurmond (States' Rights, 1948); Adlai Stevenson (Democrat, 1952, 1956); Barry Goldwater (Republican, 1964); George Wallace (American Independent, 1968).

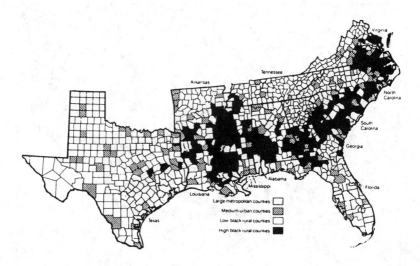

Figure 7   The Demography of the South, 1980
Source: Earl Black and Merle Black, *Politics and Society in the South* (Cambridge: Harvard University Press, 1987), 38.

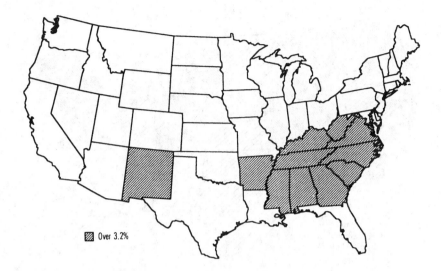

Figure 8   Housing Units without Complete Plumbing, 1980
Source: Data from *Statistical Abstract of the United States, 1982–83*, 755.
Note: Complete plumbing is defined as a flush toilet, a bathtub or shower, and hot and cold running water.

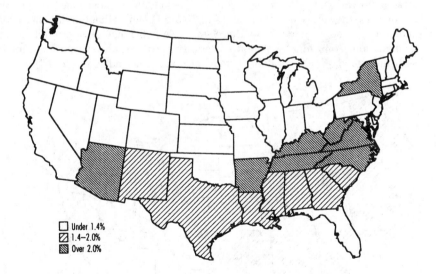

Figure 9   Illiteracy Rates, 1970
Source: Data from *Statistical Abstract of the United States, 1981*, 143.

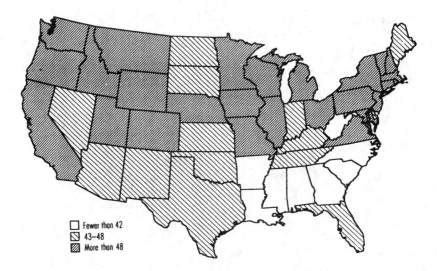

Figure 10   Active Dentists per 1,000 Residents, 1982
Source: Data from *Statistical Abstract of the United States, 1986*, 104.

Poverty is bad news, in general, and I certainly don't suggest that we get nostalgic about it, but it has had one or two good points. Burglary rates, for example, are strikingly correlated with states' average incomes—presumably not because rich people steal but because they have more *to* steal—and Figure 11 shows that burglary has been less common in all but the richest Southern states. (A policeman once offered me another explanation. Going in other people's windows is a more dangerous occupation in the South, he argued. "You're more likely to meet something lead coming out.")

Figure 11   High Burglary Rates, 1984
Source: Data from *Statistical Abstract of the United States, 1986*, 167.

In any case, now, the shadow of the plantation is giving way to the light of the "Sunbelt." The South may still be on the bottom of the socioeconomic heap, but the difference between top and bottom is smaller than it used to be. (In a few respects, South and non-South have traded places: the Southern birthrate, for instance, historically higher, is now lower than the national average.) Consequently, those who view the South primarily in economic terms are likely to believe that the region is disappearing. "Southern characteristics" that simply revealed that the South was a poor, rural region are more and more confined to pockets of poverty within the region—or, more accurately, the statistics increasingly reflect the presence of air-conditioned pockets of affluence, particularly in Texas, Florida, and a few metropolitan areas elsewhere. If we map the South with the same criteria people used even fifty years ago, what we get these days looks more like a swiss cheese than a coherent region.

The Cultural South

But suppose we don't define the South in economic and demographic terms. What if we somehow identify Southerners, and then define the South as where they come from? We could say, for example, that people who eat grits, listen to country music, follow stock-car racing, support corporal punishment in the schools, hunt possum, go to Baptist churches, and prefer bourbon to scotch (if they drink at all) are likely to be Southerners. It isn't necessary that all or even most Southerners do these things, or that other people not do them; if Southerners just do them more often than other Americans, we can use them to locate the South.

Look at the geographical distribution of Baptists, for example (Figure 12). Early on, members of that faith established their dominance in the Southern backcountry, in numbers approached only by those of Methodists. As Southerners moved on to the west and south, they took their religion with them. The map shows a good many Baptists in New York, to be sure, but New York has lots of everything. Not many people live in West Texas, but they're likely to be Baptists. In this respect, the mountain South, too, is virtually indistinguishable from the rest of the region.

And when it comes to Southern music, the mountains and the Southwest are right at the heart of things. Figure 13 shows where country music–makers come from: a fertile crescent extending from southwest Virginia through Kentucky and Tennessee to Arkansas, Oklahoma, and Texas. Musically, what is sometimes called the "peripheral" South is in fact the region's core. The *Deep* South is peripheral to the country–music scene, although it's not a vacuum like New England, and a similar map for traditional black musicians would almost certainly fill some of the gap. Country musicians' origins are reflected in the songs they produce, too: in Figure 14, the size of the states is proportional to the number of times they're mentioned in country–music lyrics. Notice Florida's role as a sort of appendix to the South.

Those lyrics also suggest a regional propensity for several sorts of violence, and FBI statistics show that this isn't just talk. The South has had a higher homicide rate than the rest of the United States for as long as reliable records have been kept, and the mountains and Southwest share fully in this pattern. Southern violence, however, isn't directed inward. Around the world, societies with high homicide rates tend to have low suicide rates, and the same is true for American states. It very much looks as if there is some sort of trade-off at work. Figure 15 shows where homicide

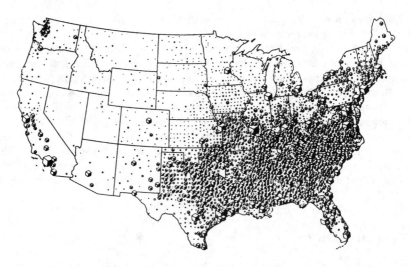

Figure 12   Members of Baptist Churches, 1952
Source: Wilbur Zelinsky, "An Approach to the Religious Geography of the United States: Patterns of Church Membership in 1952," *Annals of the Association of American Geographers* 51 (June 1961): 172.

Figure 13   Birthplaces of Country Music Notables, 1870–1960
Source: George O. Carey, "T for Texas, T for Tennessee: The Origins of American Country Music Notables," *Journal of Geography* 78 (November 1979): 221.

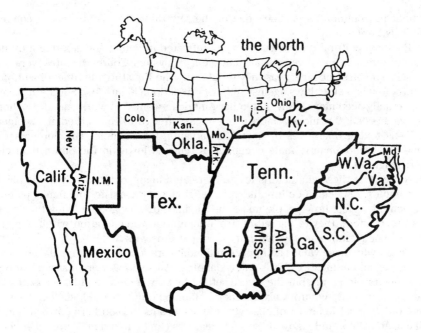

Figure 14 States Mentioned in Country-Music Lyrics
Source: Ben Marsh, "A Rose-Colored Map," *Harper's*, July 1977, 80. Used by permission.
Note: The size of each state is proportional to the number of times it is mentioned.

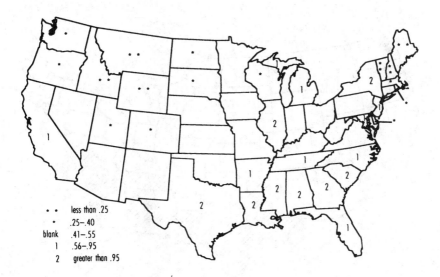

Figure 15 Ratio of Homicides to Suicides, 1983
Source: Data from *Statistical Abstract of the United States, 1987*, 77.

is about as common as suicide—one of the few things the South has in common with New York.

Regional cultural differences are also reflected in family and sex-role attitudes. These differences have even surfaced in the legal system: Southern states were slow to enact women's suffrage; most never did ratify the Equal Rights Amendment; until recently few had state laws against sex discrimination (Figure 16). Southern women have actually been more likely than other American women to work outside the home (they've needed the money more), but most often they've worked in "women's jobs"—as textile operatives or domestic servants, for example. The percentage of women in predominantly male occupations remains lower in the South than elsewhere (Figure 17).

Notice that these characteristics aren't related in any obvious way to the plantation complex. Aspects of culture like diet, religion, sports, music, and family patterns don't simply reflect how people make their livings, or how good a living they make. To a great extent, they're passed on from generation to generation within families. Usually, when families move they carry these patterns with them.

That's why these values and tastes and habits are found in the Appalachians and the Ozarks, and in most of Texas and Oklahoma. Those areas were marginal, at best, to the plantation South, but they were settled by Southerners, and by measures like these they are quite comfortably Southern. Mapping things like this makes it easy to figure out who settled most of Missouri, too, as well as the southern parts of Illinois, Indiana, and Ohio. And many of the same features can be found in scattered enclaves of Southern migrants all around the United States—among auto workers in Ypsilanti, for instance, or the children and grandchildren of Okies in Bakersfield. And we can't expect the demise of the plantation to make these characteristics go away. So if we define the South as a patch of territory somehow different from the rest of the United

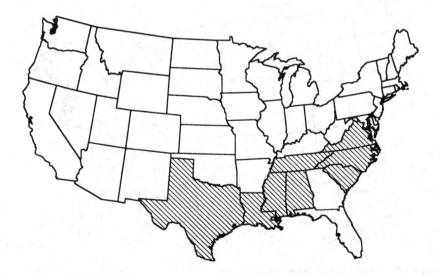

Figure 16   No State Law against Sex Discrimination, 1972

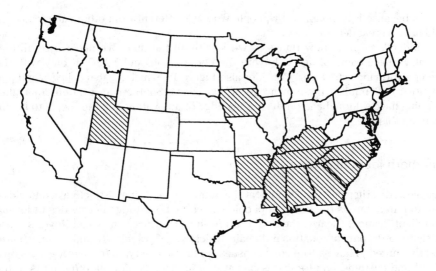

Figure 17 Low Percentage of White Women Employed in Traditionally White Male Occupations, 1985
Source: Data from Southern Labor Institute.
Note: The bottom ten states are shaded.

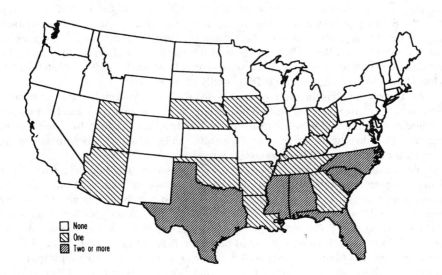

Figure 18 Colleges and Universities That Publish Sports Magazines, 1982
Source: Data from *Chronicle of Higher Education*, September 15, 1982, 17.

States because it is inhabited by people who are different from other Americans, we still have a great deal to work with.

Indeed, we have new things to work with all the time. We need to recall that country music came of age only with the phonograph, and NASCAR only with the high-performance stock car. Consider also Figure 18, which locates colleges and universities that publish their own sports magazines. Southern institutions of higher learning have seldom been on the cutting edge of innovation, but they seem to be out front on this one.

Southern Identification

I suggested earlier that we can look at the South, not as just a distinctive economic or cultural area, but as the home of people somehow bound together by ties of loyalty and identification. Clearly, the South has been a "province," in Josiah Royce's sense of that word: "part of a national domain which is, geographically and socially, sufficiently unified to have a true consciousness of its own unity, to feel a pride in its own ideals and customs, and to possess a sense of its distinction from other parts of the country."

Not long ago, the regional patriotism of most white Southerners was based on the shared experience of Confederate independence and defeat. There are still reminders of this past in the South's culture and social life. Figure 19, for example, shows where to find chapters of the Kappa Alpha Order, a college fraternity with an explicitly Confederate heritage.

For many, the word *Dixie* evokes that same heritage, and Figure 20 shows where people are likely to include that word in the names of their business enterprises. Notice that the Appalachian South, which wasn't wild about Dixie in 1861, still isn't. Now the Southwest, too, has largely abandoned Dixie (turn about: the Confederacy largely abandoned the Southwest, once). Most of Florida would probably be gone as well if there were no Dixie Highway to keep the word in use. Even in the city of Atlanta, Dixie seems to be gone with the wind—or at least on the way out. Only in what is left of the old plantation South is Dixie really alive and well.

As a basis for identification, obviously, symbols of the Confederate experience necessarily exclude nearly all black Southerners, as well as many Appalachian whites and migrants to the region who are so recent that they haven't forgotten that they're migrants. Fortunately, however, regional loyalty can be based on other things among them cultural differences like those we've already examined.

We can ask, in other words, not "where do people display Southern ways?" but "where do people assert the superiority of Southern ways?" Figure 21, for example, shows where people are likely to say that they like to hear Southern accents, prefer Southern food, and believe that Southern women are better looking than other women. (The Gallup Poll hasn't asked these questions lately, so the data are a little old, but I doubt that the patterns would be much different now.) The South defined this way naturally coincides pretty well with the area where one is actually apt to encounter Southern accents, Southern food, and Southern women—a bigger region than what remains of the Confederate South, just as the cultural South extends well beyond the domain of the old plantation system.

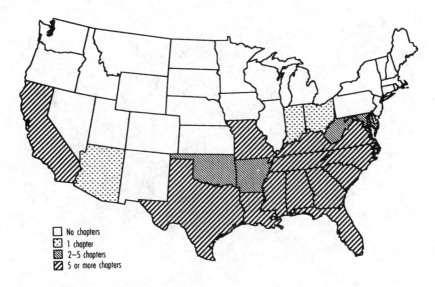

Figure 19   Chapters of the Kappa Alpha Order, 1988
Source: Data from Upsilon of Kappa Alpha.

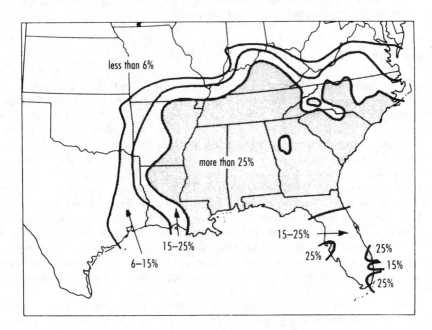

Figure 20   "Dixie" Listings as Percentage of "American" Listings in Telephone Directories, ca. 1975
Source: J. S. Reed, "The Heart of Dixie: An Essay in Folk Geography," *Social Forces* 54 (June 1976): 932.

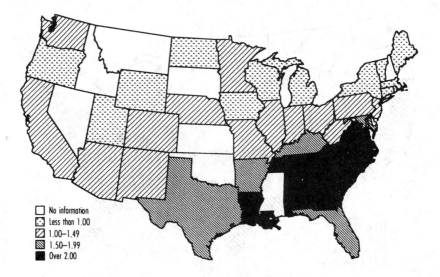

Figure 21   Average Scores on "Index of Southern Preference," 1957
Source: J. S. Reed, *The Enduring South: Subcultural Persistence in Mass Society* (Chapel Hill: University of North Carolina Press, 1974), 18.
Note: One point each for liking a Southern accent, liking Southern cooking, and thinking Southern women are better looking than other American women.

Regional Institutions

Regional institutions play a part in sustaining the South, as both idea and reality, tying the region together economically and socially and contributing to a sense of distinctiveness and solidarity. Here, too, we find a close analogy to the life of American ethnic groups. Like some of those groups, Southerners have their own social and professional organizations, organs of communication, colleges and universities, and so forth. In fact, they probably have more of them now than they ever did before. When Karl Marx said scornfully of the Confederacy that it wasn't a nation at all, just a battle cry, he was referring to the absence of this sort of institutional apparatus, and until recently the South couldn't *afford* much in the way of regional institutions.

But now the Southern Historical Association, the Southern Railway, the Southern Baptist Convention, the Southern Growth Policies Board—these and other, similar institutions establish channels of communication and influence within the region, making it more of a social reality than it would be otherwise. At the same time, even the names of organizations like these serve to reinforce the idea that the South exists, that it means something, that it is somehow a fact of nature.

Southern Living magazine, for instance, implies month after month that there is such a thing as Southern living, that it is different and (by plain implication) better. Figure 22 shows where that message falls on fertile ground. Notice that Floridians are relatively uninterested in it. So are Texans, despite heroic efforts by the magazine (including a special Southwestern edition). Here we see plainly a development that regional sociologists were predicting fifty years ago, something maps of regional

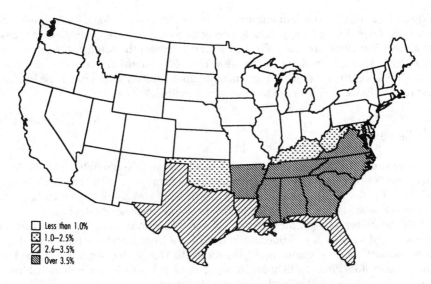

Figure 22 *Southern Living* Readers as Percentage of White Population, 1981
Source: Data from Marketing Department, *Southern Living.*

culture and regional identification only hint at: the bifurcation of the South into a "Southeast" centered on Atlanta and a "Southwest" that is, essentially, greater Texas. (Texas has its own magazines.)

We find something similar when we look at one of the South's regional universities. The University of North Carolina, in Chapel Hill, has long been a center for the

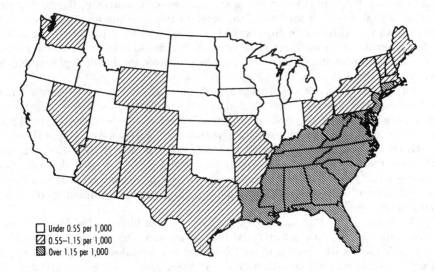

Figure 23 Alumni of the University of North Carolina at Chapel Hill as Estimated Proportion of All Residents with 1–4 Years of College, 1985
Source: Data from Alumni Office, University of North Carolina at Chapel Hill.

study and nurture of Southern culture. It has also helped to educate a regional elite. Figure 23 shows where an appreciable percentage of all college graduates are Chapel Hill alumni. Tar Heels are thick on the ground throughout the southeastern states, but (aside from some brain drain to the New York City suburbs) that's the only place they're thick on the ground. In particular, Chapel Hill has little market penetration west of the Mississippi. (Texas has its own universities.)

So Where Is It?

So where is the South? Well, that depends on which South you're talking about. Some places are Southern by anybody's reckoning, to be sure, but at the edges it's hard to say where the South is because people have different ideas about *what* it is. And most of those ideas are correct, or at least useful, for some purpose or other.

The South is no longer the locus of a distinctive economic system, exporting raw materials and surplus population to the rest of the United States while generating a variety of social and economic problems for itself. That system's gone, and good riddance. Some of its effects still linger, though, and a few—such as a genuinely biracial population—will be with us for the foreseeable future.

The South is also set apart by its people and their distinctive ways of doing things. Mass society has made some inroads, but Southerners still do many things differently. Some are even inventing new ways to do things differently. And the persistence of the cultural South doesn't require that Southerners stay poor and rural. Indeed, poor folks can't afford some of its trappings: bass boats and four-wheel drive vehicles, for instance.

Because its history and its culture are somewhat different from the run of the American mill, the South also exists as an idea—an idea, moreover, that people can have feelings about. Many are fond of the South (some even love it); others have been known to view it with disdain. In either case, the South exists in people's heads and in their conversations. From this point of view, the South will exist for as long as people think and talk about it, and as for its boundaries—well, the South begins wherever people agree that it does.

Finally, the South is a social system, perhaps more now than ever before. A network of institutions exists to serve it, and an ever-increasing number of people have a crass, pecuniary interest in making sure that it continues to exist. Here, the brute facts of distance and diversity conspire to reduce the South to a southeastern core.

Given all these different Souths, obviously, we can't just draw a line on a map and call it the South's border. As Southerners are fond of saying: it depends. But, what the hell, if I had to do it, my candidate would be the line in Figure 24 that shows where "Southern" entries begin to be found in serious numbers in urban telephone directories (the one at 35 percent).

The South below that line makes a lot of sense. It includes the eleven former Confederate States, minus all of Texas but the eastern edge. It also includes Kentucky, which had a wishful star in the Rebel flag, but not Missouri, which did too. A corner of Oklahoma makes it in as well: we get Muskogee.

Figure 24 shows variation within the South that also makes sense. It follows some of the stress lines we've already looked at. Kentucky and much of Virginia, East Texas and part of Arkansas, most of peninsular Florida—all these areas on the edges

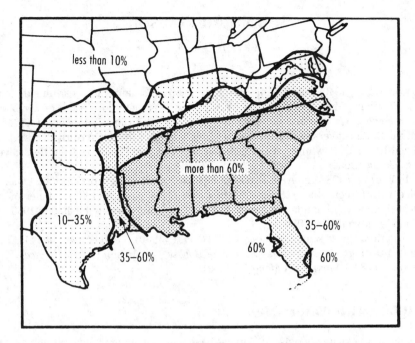

Figure 24 "Southern" Listings as Percentage of "American" Listings in Telephone Directories, ca. 1975
Source: J. S. Reed, "The Heart of Dixie: An Essay in Folk Geography," *Social Forces* 54 (June 1976): 929.

of the South are less "Southern" than the regional heartland, by this measure as by others we've examined. On the other hand, a Southern sphere of influence takes in Maryland, West Virginia, Oklahoma, much of Texas, and the southern parts of the states from Ohio west to Missouri. Few would include most of these areas in the South proper, but fewer would deny their Southern cultural flavor.

This one statistic indicates the presence of the sort of regional institutions I mentioned earlier, as well as the kind of regional enthusiasm that leads an entrepreneur to call a newsstand, say, the Southern Fruit and News. It shows, that is, where the idea of the South is vital, where its social reality extends, or both.

In other words, if you want to know whether you're in the South, you could do worse than to look in the phone book.

Bobbie Ann Mason

(1940–   )

Born on May 1, 1940, Bobbie Ann Mason grew up on a dairy farm just outside May-field, Kentucky. Mason entered the University of Kentucky in the fall of 1958, and after receiving her B.A. in 1962, she moved to New York City. She received her M.A. from the State University of New York at Binghamton in 1966. On April 12, 1969, she married Roger B. Rawlings. In 1972, Mason was awarded her Ph.D. from the University of Connecticut.

In February 1980, the *New Yorker* published "Offering," a short story that was included with fifteen other stories in *Shiloh and Other Stories* (1982), winner of the Ernest Hemingway Foundation Award in 1983. *In Country* was published in 1985 and was made into a film in 1989.

Additional works include *Love Life: Stories* (1989); *Feather Crowns: A Novel* (1993); *Midnight Magic: Selected Stories of Bobbie Ann Mason* (1998); *Spence + Lila* (1998); and *Clear Springs: A Memoir* (1999).

Still Life with Watermelon

For several weeks now, Louise Milsap has been painting pictures of watermelons. The first one she tried looked like a dark-green basketball floating on an algae-covered pond. Too much green, she realized. She began varying the backgrounds, and sometimes now she throws in unusual decorative objects—a few candles, a soap dish, a pair of wire pliers. She tried including other fruits, but the size of the melons among apples and grapes made them appear odd and unnatural. When she saw a photograph of a cornucopia in a magazine, she imagined a huge watermelon stuck in its mouth.

Louise's housemate, Peggy Wilson, insists that a rich collector from Paducah named Herman Priddle will buy the pictures. Peggy and her husband, Jerry, had rented an apartment from him, but Jerry ran away with Priddle's mistress and now Peggy lives with Louise. Peggy told her, "That man's whole house is full of them stupid watermelons." When Peggy said he would pay a fortune for anything with a watermelon in it, Louise bought a set of paints.

Peggy said, "He's got this one cute picture of these two little colored twins eating a slice of watermelon. One at each end, like bookends. I bet he paid at least thirty dollars for it."

Louise has lost her job at Kroger's supermarket, and she lies to the unemployment office about seeking a new job. Instead, she spends all day painting on small canvas boards in her canning room. Her husband, Tom, is in Texas with Jim Yates, a carpenter who worked for him. A month before, Tom suddenly left his business and went out West to work on Jim's uncle's ranch. Louise used to like Tom's impulsiveness. He would call up a radio program and dedicate love songs to her, knowing it both embarrassed and pleased her to hear her name on the radio. Tom never cared about public opinion. Before he went to Texas, he bought a cowboy hat from Sam's Surplus. He left in his pickup, his "General Contracting" sign still painted on the door, and he didn't say when he would return. Louise said to him, "If you're going to be a born-again cowboy, I guess you'll want to get yourself all bunged up on one of them bull machines."

"That ain't necessarily what I'm aiming to do," he said.

"Go ahead. *See* if I care."

Louise, always a practical person, is determined to get along without Tom. She should look for a job, but she doesn't want to. She paints a dozen pictures in a row. She feels less and less practical. For two dollars and eighty-nine cents she buys a watermelon at Kroger's and paints a picture of it. It is a long, slender melon the color of a tobacco worm, with zigzag stripes. She went to Kroger's from force of habit, and then felt embarrassed to be seen at her old checkout lane.

"Old man Priddle would give you a hundred dollars for that," says Peggy, glancing at the painting when she comes home from work. Louise is just finishing the clouds in the background. Clouds had been a last-minute inspiration.

Peggy inserts a Dixieland tape into Louise's tape deck and opens a beer. Beer makes Peggy giggly, but Dixieland puts her in a sad mood because her husband once promised to take her to New Orleans to hear Al Hirt in person. Louise stands there with her paintbrush, waiting to see what will happen.

Peggy says, "He's got this big velvet tapestry on his wall? It's one big, solid watermelon that must have weighed a ton." Laughing, she stretches her arms to show the size. The beer can tilts, about to spill. Three slugs of beer and Peggy is already giggly.

Louise needs Peggy's rent money, but having her around is like having a grown child who refuses to leave home. Peggy reads Harlequin romances and watches TV simultaneously. She pays attention when the minister on *The 700 Club* gives advice on budgets. "People just aren't *smart* about the way they use credit cards," she informs Louise. This is shop talk from her job in customer services at the K Mart. Peggy keeps promising to call Herman Priddle, to make an appointment for Louise to take her paintings to Paducah, but Peggy has a thing about using the telephone. She doesn't want to tie up the line in case her husband tries to call. She frowns impatiently when Louise is on the telephone. One good thing about living with Peggy—she does all the cooking. Sometimes she pours beer into the spaghetti sauce—"to give it a little whang," she says.

"You shouldn't listen to that tape," Louise says to Peggy later. The music is getting to Peggy by now. She sits in a cross-legged, meditative pose, the beer can balanced in her palm.

"I just don't know what he sees in a woman who's twenty years older than him," says Peggy. "With a face-lift."

"How long can it last, anyhow?"

"Till she needs another face-lift, I reckon."

"Well, that can't be long. I read they don't last," says Louise.

"That woman's so big and strong, she could skin a mule one-handed," says Peggy, lifting her beer.

Louise puts away her paints and then props the new picture against a chair. Looking at the melon, she can feel its weight and imagine just exactly how ripe it is.

While she paints, Louise has time to reflect on their situation: two women with little in common whose husbands are away. Both men left unconscionably. Sudden yearnings. One thought he could be a cowboy (Tom had never been on a horse); the other fell for an older woman. Louise cannot understand either compulsion. The fact that she cannot helps her not to care.

She tried to reason with Tom—about how boyish his notion was and how disastrous it would be to leave his business. Jim Yates had lived in Denver one summer, and in every conversation he found a way to mention Colorado and how pure the air was there. Tom believed everything Jim said. "You can't just take off and expect to pick up your business where you left it when you get back," Louise argued. "There's plenty of guys waiting to horn in. It takes *years* to get where you've got." That was Louise being reasonable. At first Tom wanted her to go with him, but she wouldn't dream of moving so far away from home. He accused her of being afraid to try new things, and over a period of weeks her resistance turned to anger. Eventually Louise, to her own astonishment, threw a Corning Ware Petite Pan at Tom and made his ear bleed. He and Jim took off two days later. The day they left, Tom was wearing a T-shirt that read: "You better get in line now 'cause I get better-looking every day." Who did he think he was?

Peggy does not like to be reminded of the watermelon collector, and Louise has to probe for information. Peggy and her husband, Jerry ("Flathead") Wilson, had gone to live in Paducah, forty miles away, and had had trouble finding work and a place to live, but an elderly man, Herman Priddle, offered them three identical bedrooms on the third floor of his house. "It was a mansion," Peggy told Louise. Then Priddle hired Jerry to convert two of the rooms into a bathroom and a kitchen. Peggy laid vinyl tiles and painted the walls. The old man, fascinated, watched them work. He let Peggy and Jerry watch his TV and he invited them to eat with him. His mistress, a beautician named Eddy Gail Moses, slept with him three nights a week, and while she was there she made enough hamburger-and-macaroni casseroles to last him the rest of the week. She lived with her father, who disapproved of her behavior, despite her age.

Before Peggy knew what was happening, her husband had become infatuated with the woman, and he abruptly went to live with her and her father, leaving Peggy with Herman Priddle. Although Peggy grew suspicious of the way he looked at her, she and Priddle consoled each other for a while. Peggy started making the casseroles he was used to, and she stayed in Paducah for a few months, working at a pit barbecue stand. Gradually, Peggy told Louise, the old man began collecting pictures of watermelons. He looked for them in flea markets, at antique shops, and in catalogs; and he put ads in trade papers. When he hung one of the pictures in her bedroom, Peggy moved out. The watermelon was sliced lengthwise and it resembled a lecherous grin, she said, shuddering.

"Peggy's still in shock from the way Jerry treated her," Louise tells Tom in a letter one evening. She writes him in care of a tourist home in Amarillo, Texas. She intends to write only perfunctory replies to his postcards so he will know she is alive, but she finds herself being more expressive than she ever was in the four years they were face to face. Hitting him seemed to release something in her, but she won't apologize. She won't beg him to come back. He doesn't know she has lost her job. And if he saw her paintings, he would laugh.

When Louise seals the letter, Peggy says to her, "Did I tell you I heard Jim Yates is queer?"

"No."

"Debbie Potts said that at work. She used to know Jim Yates back in high school."

"Well, I don't believe it. He's too overbearing."

"Debbie Potts has been to Europe," says Peggy, looking up from the kitchen counter, where she is making supper. "Did you know that?"

"Hooray for her."

"That don't mean she's an expert on anything," Peggy says apologetically. "I'm sure she don't know what she's talking about."

"For crying out loud."

"I'm sorry, Louise. I'm always putting my big foot in it. But you know, a lot of guys are coming right out now and saying they're gay? It's amazing." She laughs wildly. "They sure wouldn't be much use where it counts, would they? At least Flathead ran off with a woman—knock on wood." Peggy taps a wooden spoon against the counter.

"How can you love a guy called Flathead?" says Louise, irritated. Apparently Jerry Wilson's nickname has nothing to do with his appearance. Louise has read that the Flathead Indians used to tie rocks to their heads to flatten them—why, she cannot imagine.

Peggy says, "It's just what I know him by. I never thought about it."

Peggy is making a casserole, probably one of Eddy Gail Moses's recipes. The Dixieland tape is playing full blast. Peggy says, "The real reason he run off with that floozy was she babied him."

"I wouldn't baby a man if my life depended on it," says Louise.

She rummages around for a stamp. Too late, she wonders if she should have told Tom about the trouble with the air conditioner. He will think she is hinting for him to come home. Tom was always helpful around the house. He helped choose the kitchen curtains, saying that a print of butterflies she wanted was too busy and suggesting a solid color. She always admired him for that. It was so perceptive of him to say the curtains were busy. But that didn't mean anything abnormal. In fact, after he started hanging out with Jim Yates, Tom grew less attentive to such details. He and Jim Yates had a Space Invaders competition going at Patsy's Dairy Whip, and sometimes they stayed there until midnight. Jim, who hit six thousand long before Tom, several times had his name on the machine as high scorer of the day. Once Tom brought Jim over for supper, and Louise disliked the way Jim took charge, comparing her tacos to the ones he'd had in Denver and insisting that she get up and grate more cheese. It seemed to Louise that he was still playing Space Invaders. Tom didn't notice. The night, weeks later, when Louise threw the Corning Ware at Tom, she knew she was trying to get his attention.

Late one evening, Peggy tells Louise that she saw her husband at the K Mart. He didn't realize that Peggy worked there. "He turned all shades when he saw me," Peggy says. "But I wasn't surprised. I had a premonition."

Peggy believes in dreams and coincidences. The night before she saw him, she had read a romance story about a complicated adoption proceeding. Louise doesn't get the connection and Peggy is too drunk to explain. She and Jerry have been out drinking, talking things over. Louise notices that Peggy already has a spot on her new pants suit, which she managed to buy even though she owes Louise for groceries.

"Would you take him back?" Louise wants to know.

"If he's good." Peggy laughs loudly. "He's coming over again one day next week. He had to get back to Paducah tonight."

"Is he still with that woman?"

"He *said* he wasn't." Peggy closes her eyes and does a dance step. Then she says exuberantly, "Everything Flathead touches turns to money. He cashed this check at the K Mart for fifty dollars. He sold a used hot-water heater and made a twenty-dollar profit on it. Imagine that."

When Peggy sees Louise polishing her toenails, she says abruptly, "Your second toe is longer than your big toe. That means you dominate your husband."

"Where'd you get that idea?"

"Didn't you know that? Everybody knows that."

Louise says, "Are any of them stories you read ever about women who beat up their husbands?"

Peggy laughs. "What an idea!"

Louise is thinking of Tom's humiliation the night she struck him with the dish. Suddenly in her memory is a vague impression that the lights flickered, the way it was said the electricity used to do on certain midnights when the electric chair was being used at the state penitentiary, not far away.

If Peggy goes back to her husband, Louise will have to earn some extra money. It dawns on her that the paintings are an absurd idea. Childish. For a few days she stays out of the canning room, afraid to look at the pictures. Halfheartedly she reads the want ads. They say: salesclerk, short-order cook, secretarial assistant, salesclerk.

On the day she is scheduled to sign up for her weekly unemployment check, Louise arranges the paintings in the living room, intending to decide whether to continue with them. The pictures are startling. Some of the first ones appear to be optical illusions—watermelons disappearing like black holes into vacant skies. The later pictures are more credible—one watermelon is on a table before a paned window, with the light making little windows on the surface of the fruit; another, split in half, is balanced against a coffee percolator. Louise pretends she's a woman from Mars and the paintings are the first things she sees on earth. They aren't bad, but the backgrounds worry her. They don't match the melons. Why would a watermelon be placed against a blue sky? One watermelon on a flowered tablecloth resembles a blimp that has landed in a petunia bed. Even the sliced melons are unrealistic. The red is wrong—too pale, like a tongue. Tom sent her a picture postcard of the Painted Desert, but Louise suspects the colors in *that* picture are too brilliant. No desert could look like that.

On her way to the unemployment office, Louise picks up a set of acrylics on discount at Big-D. Acrylics are far more economical than oils. In the car, Louise, pleased by the prospect of the fresh tubes of paint, examines the colors: scarlet, cobalt blue, Prussian blue, aquamarine, emerald, yellow ochre, orange, white, black. She doesn't really need green. The discovery that yellow and blue make green still astonishes her; when she mixes them, she feels like a magician. As she drives toward the unemployment office she wonders recklessly if the green of the trees along the street could be broken down by some scientific process into their true colors.

At the unemployment office the line is long and the building stuffy. The whole place seems wound up. A fat woman standing behind Louise says, "One time it got so hot here I passed out, and not a soul would help. They didn't want to lose their place in line. Look at 'em. Lined up like cows at a slaughterhouse. Ever notice how cows follow along, nose to tail?"

"Elephants have a cute way of doing that," says Louise, in high spirits. "They grab the next one's tail with their trunk."

"Grab," the woman says. "That's all people want to do. Just grab." She reaches inside her blouse and yanks her bra strap back onto her shoulder. She has yellow hair and blue eyes. She could turn green if she doesn't watch out, Louise thinks. The line moves slowly. No one faints.

When Louise arrives at home, Peggy's husband is there, and he and Peggy are piling her possessions into his van. Peggy has happy feet, like Steve Martin on TV. She is moving to Paducah with Jerry. Calmly Louise pours a glass of iced tea and watches the ice cubes crack.

"I already up and quit work," Peggy calls to Louise from her bedroom.

"I got us a place in a big apartment complex," says Jerry with an air of satisfaction.

"It's got a swimming pool," says Peggy, appearing with an armload of clothes on hangers.

"I saved twenty dollars a month by getting one without a dishwasher," says Jerry. "I'm going to put one in myself."

Peggy's husband is tall and muscular, with a sparse mustache that a teenager might grow. He looks amazingly like one of the Sha Na Na, the one in the sleeveless black T-shirt. Louise notices that he can't keep his hands off his wife. He holds on to her hips, her elbows, as she tries to pack.

"Tell what else you promised," Peggy says.

"You mean about going to New Orleans?" Jerry says.

"Yeah."

Louise says, "Well, don't you go off without setting me up with that watermelon man. I was counting on you."

"I'll give him a call tomorrow," says Peggy.

"Could you do it right now, before I lose track of y'all?"

Louise's sharp tone works. Peggy pulls away from Jerry and goes to the telephone.

While she is trying to find the number, she says, "I hate to mention it, Louise, but I gave you a whole month's rent and it's only been a week. Do you think . . . ?"

While Peggy is on the telephone, Louise writes a check for seventy-five dollars. She writes boldly and decisively, with enlarged numbers. Her new bank balance is twelve dollars and eleven cents. If Flathead Wilson were *her* husband, she would show him the road.

"He said come over Tuesday afternoon," says Peggy, taking the check. "I just know he's going to love your pictures. He sounded thrilled."

After Peggy and Jerry leave, Louise notices the mail, which Peggy has left on a lamp table—a circular, the water-and-light bill, and a letter from Tom, postmarked ten days before. Louise laughs with relief when she reads that Jim Yates went to Mexico City with a woman he met in Amarillo. Jim plans to work in adobe construction. "Can you imagine going to Mexico to work?" Tom writes. "Usually it's the other way around."

Happily Louise plays a Glen Campbell tape and washes the dishes Peggy has left. Peggy gave Louise all her cooking utensils—the cracked enamel pans and scratched Teflon. "Flathead's going to buy me all new," she said. Louise wishes Peggy hadn't left before hearing the news from Tom. But she's glad to be alone at last. While Glen Campbell sings longingly of Galveston, Louise for the first time imagines Tom doing chores on a ranch. Something like housework, no doubt, except out of doors.

She paints through the weekend, staying up late, eating TV dinners at random. It thrills her to step back from a picture and watch the sea of green turn into a watermelon. She loves the way the acrylics dry so easily; they are convenient, like Perma-Press clothing. After finishing several pictures, she discovers a trick about backgrounds: If she makes them hazier, the watermelons stand out in contrast, look less like balloons floating in space. With the new paints, she hits upon the right mix for the red interiors, and now the watermelon slices look good enough to eat.

On the day of Louise's appointment with Herman Priddle, Tom suddenly walks in the door. Louise freezes. She's standing in the center of the living room, as though she had been standing there all during his absence, waiting for his return. She can tell how time has passed by the way his jeans have faded. His hair has grown shaggy and he has a deep tan.

"Surprise!" he says with a grin. "I'm home."

Louise manages to say, "What are you doing back here?"

"And why ain't you at work?" Tom says.

"Laid off."

"What's going on here?" he asks, seeing the pictures.

Suddenly Louise is ashamed of them. She feels confused. "You picked a *fine* time to show up," she says. She tries to explain about the paintings. Her explanation makes no sense.

For a long time Tom studies her pictures, squatting to see the ones on the floor. His jeans strain at the seams. He reaches out to touch one picture, as though for a moment he thought the watermelon might be real. Louise begins taking the paintings to her car, snatching them from under his gaze. He follows her, carrying some of the paintings.

Tom says, "I couldn't wait to get back home."

"You didn't have to go off like that."

"I've been thinking things over."

"So have I." She slams the rear hatch door of her car. "Where's the pickup?"

"Totaled it north of Amarillo."

"What? I thought all the roads were flat and straight out there."

He shrugs. "I reckon they are."

"Where'd you get the junk heap?" she asks. The car he has brought home is a rusted-out hulk.

"In Amarillo. It was the best I could do—cost me two hundred dollars. But it drives good."

He opens the door of his car and takes out a McDonald's sack from the front seat. "I brought you a Big Mac," he says.

Later, when he insists on driving her in her car to Paducah, Louise doesn't try to stop him. She sits still and glum beside him, like a child being escorted to a school recital. On the way, she says, "That postcard you sent of the Painted Desert was mailed in Amarillo. I thought the Painted Desert was in Arizona."

"I didn't mail it till I got back to Amarillo."

"I thought maybe you hadn't even been there."

"Yes, I was."

"I thought maybe you sent it just to impress me."

"Why would I do that?"

"So I wouldn't think the West was just dull, open spaces."

"Well, it wasn't. And I did go to the Painted Desert."

"What else did you do out there?"

"Different things."

"Look—John Wayne's dead. Don't think you have to be the strong, silent type just 'cause you went out West."

Louise wants to know about the colors of the Painted Desert, but she can't bring herself to ask Tom about them. Tom is driving the car with his forearms loosely draped over the wheel and his elbows sticking out. He drives so casually. Louise imagines him driving all the way to Texas like this, as if he had nothing better to do.

"I did a lot of driving around," Tom says finally, after smoking a cigarette all the way down. "Just to see what there was to see."

"Sounds fascinating." Louise doesn't know why she wants to give him such a hard time. She realizes that she is shaking at the thought of him wrecking his pickup, alone in some empty landscape. The ear she hit is facing her—no sign of damage. His hair is growing over it and she can't really see where she hit him. His sideburn, shaped like the outline of Italy, juts out onto his jaw. Tom is home and she doesn't know what that means.

Herman Priddle's house has a turret, a large bay window, and a wraparound porch, which a woman is sweeping.

"Would you say that's a mansion?" Louise asks Tom.

"Not really."

"Peggy said it was."

Louise makes Tom wait in the car while she walks up to the house. She thinks the woman on the porch must be Eddy Gail Moses, but she turns out to be Priddle's niece. She has on a turquoise pants suit and wears her hair up in sculptured curls. When Louise inquires, the woman says, "Uncle Herman's in the hospital. He had a stroke a-Sunday and he's real bad, but they pulled him off the critical list today."

"I brought some pictures for him to see," says Louise nervously.

"Watermelons, I bet," says the woman, eyeing Louise.

"He was supposed to buy my pictures."

"Well, the thing of it *is*—what are we to do with the ones he's got? He'll have to be moved. He can't stay by hisself in this big old place." The woman opens the door. "Look at these things."

Louise follows her into the dim room cluttered with antiques. The sight of all the watermelons in the room is stunning. The walls are filled, and other paintings are on the floor, leaning against the wall. Louise stands and stares while the woman chatters on. There are so many approaches Louise has not thought of—close-ups, groupings, unusual perspectives, floral accompaniments. All her own pictures are so prim and tidy. The collection includes oils, drawings, watercolors, even a needlepoint chair cover and a china souvenir plate. The tapestry Peggy described is a zeppelin floating above the piano. Louise has the feeling that she is witnessing something secret and forbidden, something of historical importance. She is barely aware that Tom has entered and is talking to Herman Priddle's niece. Louise feels foolish. In sixth grade the teacher had once pointed out to the class how well Louise could draw, and now—as if acting at last on the basis of that praise—Louise has spent two months concocting an elaborate surprise for an eccentric stranger. What could she have been thinking of?

"Looks like somebody's crazy about watermelons," Tom is saying politely.

"They won't bring a thing at auction," the woman replies with a laugh. In a hushed voice then, she says, "He sure had me fooled. He was here by hisself so much I didn't know whatall was going on. Now it seems like he was always collecting these things. It suited him. Do you ever have people do you that way? You think things are one way and then they get turned around and you lose track of how they used to be?"

"I know what you mean," says Tom, nodding with enthusiasm.

On the way home Louise is in tears. Tom, perplexed, tries to console her, telling her that her pictures are as good as any of the old man's watermelons.

"Don't worry about him," he says, holding her hand. "It won't matter that you lost your job. I thought I'd go see about getting a small-business loan to get started again. We'll get straightened out somehow."

Louise, crying, cannot reply. She doesn't feel like arguing.

"I didn't even know you could draw," Tom says.

"I'm not going to paint any more watermelons," she says.

"You won't have to."

Louise blows her nose and dries her eyes. Tom's knuckles are tapping a tune against the steering wheel and he seems to be driving automatically. His mind could be somewhere else, like someone in an out-of-body experience. But Louise is the one who has been off on a crazy adventure. She knows now that she painted the watermelons out of spite, as if to prove to Tom that she could do something as wild as what he was doing. She lost her head during the past weekend when she was alone, feeling the glow of independence. Gazing at the white highway line, she tries to imagine the next steps: eating supper with Tom, going to bed together, returning to old routines. Something about the conflicting impulses of men and women has gotten twisted around, she feels. She had preached the idea of staying home, but it occurs to her now that perhaps the meaning of home grows out of the fear of open spaces. In some people that fear is so intense that it is a disease, Louise has read.

At the house, Louise reaches the door first, and she turns to see Tom coming up the walk. His face is in shadow against the afternoon sun. His features aren't painted in; she wouldn't recognize him. Beyond him is a vacant lot—a field of weeds and low bushes shaped like cupcakes. Now, for the first time, Louise sees the subtle colors— amber, yellow, and deep shades of purple—leaping out of that landscape. The empty field is broad and hazy and dancing with light, but it fades away for a moment when Tom reaches the doorway and his face thrusts out from the shadow. He looks scared. But then he grins slowly. The coastline of Italy wobbles a little, retreats.

Will Davis Campbell

(1926–)

Will Davis Campbell was born in Amite County, Mississippi, and grew up in Liberty, Mississippi. He received his B.A. degree at Wake Forest College in North Carolina and his B.D. from Yale University in Connecticut. From 1954 to 1956, he was the director of religious life at the University of Mississippi. A participant in the Civil Right movement, Campbell was forced to leave the university because of his activities. He served on the National Council of Churches as a race relations consultant. He lives in Mount Juliet, Tennessee, where he continues his work.

Campbell's awards include the Lillian Smith Prize, the Christopher Award, and a National Book Award nomination for *Brother to a Dragonfly* (1977). Among his other published works are the *The Glad River* (1982); *Cecelia's Sin: A Novella* (1983); *Chester & Chun Ling* (1989); and *Forty Acres and a Goat: A Memoir* (1988).

from *The Glad River*

18

"Dr. Jamison is coming up from the seminary to preach on Sunday," Doops's mother said. "Are you going to be back?" Doops was packing to go to east Tennessee to begin a story for *The Southern Supposer.* Kingston was going along for the ride. Since the trial, Doops had tried to write at least one story a week and had made a sharecropping arrangement with his mother so that he would get a larger percentage of the crops. Kingston had moved to Baton Rouge to work for the Ethyl Corporation. He and Doops were saving their money to take the verdict through all possible appeals even though Mr. Corbitt had told them not to worry about the money, that he was going to do everything that could be done whether they paid him or not.

It had been six months since the trial. They had a schedule: Doops visited Model T on Tuesday, Kingston drove from Baton Rouge to Cummings on Thursday evening, and on Sunday afternoon they both went to see him.

"You going to be back?" his mother asked again when he didn't answer.

"I doubt it, Mamma. This story is going to take me through the weekend. There will be services Friday night and Saturday night. They never meet in the daytime. Kingston and I have arranged to see Model T on Monday instead of Sunday. No. I'm sure I won't be back."

"Services? What kind of services? You writing a story about something civil for a change? Is it a church service?" She asked all the questions all at once, not waiting for him to answer.

"It's a story about a church service," he said. "But it won't be civil. It's a different kind of church. It won't be civil."

"What kind of church? Is it a Baptist church?"

"Naw, that would be civil, I'm afraid," Doops said. "It's called the Church of the Almighty in Jesus Name Amen." As she started to leave the room, he called after her. "They're a cult. They lift up serpents."

His mother did not turn around, walked on down the hall to the kitchen. In less than a minute she was back. The same brown-skinned woman who had worked for them for years was with her. "I just want Ina to hear this. I just want her to hear what you said, where you said you were going." When he continued to throw things in the Gladstone bag he was packing, she moved to the opposite side of the bed, the woman right beside her.

"Ina, do ya'll pick up snakes in your church?" she said in a tone of ridicule.

The woman giggled nervously, pushed her hands out, and moved backward. "No ma'am," the woman said. "I done a lot of things the preacher told me to do. But he better not ax me to pick up no snake. Mr. Doops, you gon' git yoreself killed." The woman was still snickering as she hurried back toward the kitchen.

"You see," his mother said, standing with her hands on her hips. "Not even the most ignorant darkies do that sort of crazy thing. And I've seen them do some crazy things, too, in their church, moaning and screaming and all that business."

Doops did not answer her.

She had not mentioned getting baptized to him since she had made the offer about signing the bond for Model T if he would agree to join the church. Doops knew that she was about to do it now. She moved to the dresser and began helping him with his toilet articles.

"Do you have your toothbrush?" she asked, no longer defiant. Doops pointed to it in the corner of the bag, wrapped in a washcloth.

"Honey," she said, pleading, placing her hand on his shoulder. "I know you still have it in your craw that I wouldn't put the place up to get your little friend out of jail. But, honey, this place is all we have. Your daddy worked himself to death to make it the good farm it is, to leave it for us. And, well, I just think it was too much to ask to risk it for somebody like that. I mean, you don't ever know what someone like that will do."

"I do," Doops said, moving out of her reach. "I know. But it's all right. I guess I really didn't expect you to know."

"Honey, I didn't come in here to argue with you. I know you think a lot of the boy, know you were in that terrible war together and all that. But have you ever really looked at him? Honey, he looks like something in a carnival. What would somebody like that have to lose? Looking like that and staring the electric chair in the face. I mean, don't you know that he would have just disappeared if we had got him out of jail? And there we'd be, left in the road. I just think you're being unreasonable. And what do you think the people around here would have thought of me, what kind of a woman do you think they would have thought I was, putting my husband's place up for somebody who had done what he did?"

"He didn't *do* anything," Doops sighed, snapping the bag shut and starting to leave the room, his mother following as he headed for the kitchen.

"How can you say he didn't *do* anything, honey?" she said, trying to hide her annoyance. "Twelve of the finest men in that county. They said he did it. They had his fingerprints, honey. And even you said that you couldn't account for the half hour, when he was supposed to have been going to the store. How can you say he didn't do it?" She was talking louder and faster, her face red.

Doops sat at the table and Ina brought him coffee. "You want some more coffee, Miss Christine?" she asked.

"No, Ina. I don't," she said, sitting down across the table from Doops. "But I tell you what I do want."

"What's that, Miss Christine?" She said it as if they had rehearsed the lines before.

"I want this old precious boy of ours here to experience Christ in baptism."

"Yes, ma'am. I reckon you told me that a million times. But I reckon we all gonna do what we gonna do."

Doop's mother looked at her as if she had missed her cue.

"No, Ina. We can do the right thing. We can be baptized and live a Christian life the way you and I do. I've done a lot of things these past few years that I feel good about. I went back to school and finished my education when I was too old to be going to school. And I'm proud of that, proud of the fact that I wasn't satisfied to sit around and be a simple country woman. But the thing that makes me the happiest is to know I'm a Christian. You know Christian people, black or white, are the happiest people in the world. Don't you agree?"

The woman seemed uncomfortable, scampering about the kitchen with busy-work, as if she knew what was coming next and dreaded it. Doops sat sipping his coffee, looking through the *Jackson Clarion-Ledger*.

"Now, come over here and sit down at the table with us," his mother said to the woman. "In the eyes of the Lord, you're just as good as we are. I really do believe that. I know you're a Christian because you've been too good to me when I needed you to be anything else but a Christian. I want you to join us in prayer that Doops will accept Christ as his personal Savior and follow Him in baptism. Come on." She motioned to the chair she wanted her to sit in. "Sit down right here with us. Put your paper down, honey." The woman untied her apron, hung it on a nail by the door, and sat down. His mother began to pray the bedtime prayer she had used every night when he was little.

"Now I lay me down to sleep. I pray Thee, Lord, my soul to keep. If I should die before I wake, I pray Thee, Lord, my soul to take."

Doops and the woman said amen but his mother continued to pray. "And our dear heavenly Father, thou knowest all the burdens of our hearts. Thou knowest our deepest secrets."

Without meaning, without thinking, Doops murmured, "Yesss, Lord."

His mother seemed baffled but went on. "Thou knowest the love we have for those Thou hast given us. And, our dear heavenly Father, we are weak, but Thou art strong. Thou canst do all things and without Thee we can do nothing. We pray that Thou wilt touch the heart of the unsaved, and dear heavenly Father, we just pray that they will know no peace until they give their heart to Thee."

Doops sat casually but respectfully. Occasionally he opened his eyes enough to see if Ina had her eyes closed. She seemed to be sitting more through duty than participation. His mother prayed by name for several people with minor problems or illnesses. She talked about how we never know the day nor the hour when the Lord would come back to earth, and of the awful day of judgment. "And dear heavenly Father, we never know when we lay our weary bodies in the bed at night if we will wake in the morning. And the traveler knows not what peril lies in store." Once he thought she was going to mention Model T when she began praying for those in bonds, but she was talking about the bondage of sin.

"That shore was a mighty pretty prayer, Miss Christine," the woman said when the prayer was over.

"Thank you, Ina. You know, God does answer prayer. I know that for a fact."

"Yes, ma'am. That's the truth. 'Course, sometimes he answers in funny ways. My old man say he prayed for the Lord to teach him patience and the Lord give him me to put up with." She laughed and slapped her hands as she reached for her apron. She turned back as she tied the strings in place, glancing quickly at Doops as she did. Doops winked lightly, grinning behind his coffee cup.

They were going through Cummings to see Model T before they headed north to the mountains. Kingston picked him up on time and they got to the jail in Cummings a little after ten o'clock. The deputy told them Model T was in the exercise yard and they would have to wait. Only one of the sheriff's deputies bothered to search them anymore when they came, and Kingston said he thought that was more because he liked to touch men's bodies then because he was expecting to find contraband. The deputy on duty let them wait in Model T's cell. Prisoners awaiting execution were kept in a special cell adjoining the office. The cell opened onto a hallway that went the length of the jail. There were no windows and little ventilation, but Model T could see through the front door of the jail when it was open. It was a small room, six feet wide and ten feet long. There was no movable furniture in it. A heavy metal bunk, made of one solid piece, was welded to the steel wall. There was a small washbasin with one faucet and a lidless toilet. When Model T was first placed in the cell, the toilet ran over whenever it was flushed. The only way Kingston could get it fixed was to bring his grandfather's tractor with a front-end loader and dig up the septic tank and feeder lines. He simply showed up one day and did it.

When the sheriff drove up just as he was finishing and told him he couldn't do work on county property without authorization, Kingston asked him if he wanted him to unfix it.

The bunk in the cell had a thin cotton pad on it and at first there was no pillow. The sheriff said they could not bring him sheets because prisoners sometimes hanged themselves with sheets. He did agree for them to bring him a pillow.

Model T was cheerful when the deputy locked the door and walked away. He slapped them both on the back, rubbed his hand across Doop's cowlick, which he had cut short again, and teased Kingston. "Which fountain you drinking out of these days?" he asked him. "Whichever is closest," Kingston said.

"Did they give you your cap yet?" Doops asked.

"Not yet," Model T said. "I don't think they're going to give it to me. I asked the sheriff about it again last week. He just laughed. Said, 'You'll get your cap all right.'"

"That lousy sonofabitch," Kingston said. *"Sacré misère!"*

"I guess he's just doing his job," Model T said.

"Yeah, I guess so," Kingston said. "So was Hitler."

"And so was Judas," Doops added.

The cap was the only thing Model T had asked for after they brought him to death row. His sister, Cécile, had sent it to him before they left New Caledonia to go to Guadalcanal. She'd seen an advertisement in a *Grit* newspaper saying that, for selling twenty-four boxes of White Cloverine Salve from Tyrone, Pennsylvania, you could get your choice of prizes. She chose the Chesapeake captain's cap. It was quite ordinary looking, made of white twill with a black bill and band around it. She bought three of the boxes of salve herself with money she had made helping their daddy pick moss and gave them to school friends for Christmas presents. A Syrian merchant in Mermentau bought the other twenty-one boxes when she went to his dry-goods store and told him that she wanted to send a cap to her brother who was overseas. Model T treasured it and kept it with him wherever they went.

The day they brought the cap to the jail the sheriff said he would have to look at it, that men on death row were required to wear clothing issued by the jail. He said he was not sure that he wanted to set a precedent by letting him have the cap. When Doops questioned him on just what sort of a precedent he would be setting by letting Model T wear a ship captain's cap, the sheriff said he had to take unusual precaution with men sentenced to die because there was always the possibility that they would try to kill themselves.

"Just leave it here with me. I'll look at it. I have to make sure there isn't a poison needle in it, dope, nothing like that. Just leave it here." But he never gave it to him.

"Don't worry about the cap," Model T told them. So they talked about trivial things and then about Mr. Corbitt's motion for a new trial. Model T said that if the storekeeper and his wife would come to the jail to see him, he was sure they would change their testimony. Kingston asked if he would take the oath if he did get a new trial. He and Doops had agreed that his refusal to swear on the Bible had hurt him with the jury.

"Oh, no," Model T said. "Couldn't do that. I'd have to do it the same way again. I told them everything I knew. If they didn't believe me then, they won't believe me next time."

"And why the hell not? You crazy coonass," Kingston said. "Why can't you *swear* you're going to tell the truth? You know you are."

"I told you already," Model T said. "I read the Bible. And it said not to swear. Remember that book?" He grinned at Doops and did his awkward wink. "That's one of the ones we read in the hospital when we were waiting for Doops. Remember? It said not to swear."

"Look," Kingston said, his voice a mixture of concern and pride. "The Bible says a lot of things. It says let your conversation be yea, yea and nay, nay. Now, when we're talking you don't just sit around babbling, 'Yea, yea. Nay, nay. Yea, yea. Nay, nay.' Jesus! They'd haul you out of here and take you over to Whitfield in a straitjacket. Talk to him, Doops. This crazy coonass wants to help them bastards kill him." Doops did not answer.

Model T moved to the cell door and faced the hallway, holding on to the bars with both hands. "Maybe he shouldn't have given me the book," he said, shaking the bars slightly as he spoke. "The other book, I mean."

"Book? Which book? I've brought you a hundred books. What book?"

"You guys ever do this kind of exercises?" Model T asked, pressing his hands toward each other. "One of the deputies took a Charles Atlas class. He told me how to do them. I do a lot of them these days. Clears the head."

Doops sat on the far end of the bunk, his head down, still saying nothing.

Kingston moved beside Model T and leaned backward against the bars, trying to see his face. "What book?" he asked again. "What the hell you talking about? What's come over you, T? Where's the coonass boy from Mermentau I used to run with? What book you talking about?"

"Doops's book," Model T said, almost matter-of-factly. "You know . . . Cecelia. The book he wrote. I guess I've read it fifteen times since the prosecutor gave it to me. I asked him for it one day when he was here to see the sheriff and he sent it to me. Said he was supposed to give it back to Doops's mamma."

He turned around and looked down at Doops, who continued to sit with his head bowed. "They were up to something, Doops," he said, sitting down beside him. "Those folks. They were up to something. I guess it never hit me before. I mean, when the nurse read it to us that time on the beach, I just thought it was pretty words. I liked it but I thought it was because you had written it. I would have liked anything I was so glad we were back together." He reached under the bunk and picked up the crinkled and faded manuscript and held it on his lap, snapping the wide rubber band that held it together. "They knew something, Doops," he said. "Those folks knew something. And you know it too, don't you."

"One of us does," Doops said, his voice sounding faraway. "But I'm not sure I'm the one."

"It's a good book, *mon ami*," Model T said, placing the manuscript in Doops's hands. "I'm glad the nurse didn't let you burn it. I've read a lot of things now. Since you birds came along and told me there were things in the world besides muskrats and Jax beer." He stood up and began to pace the length of the cell. "You've been good teachers, neighbors," he said as he walked back and forth. "Real good teachers. And I appreciate it. I just wanted to tell you."

The deputy came to the cell door and told them it was time for them to leave. "Two minutes," he said, tapping his billy club on the bars as if playing a xylophone.

"We'll see you on Monday," Kingston said. "When we get back from Doops's holy-roller meeting. That's if we don't get snake-bit." He spoke as if he had not heard what Model T had said to them.

Model T sat down and motioned for them to sit down beside him. The deputy was waiting to unlock the door for them to leave. "You want to hear something funny?" Model T said.

Neither of them answered.

"They're talking about killing me for rape." He whispered so the deputy could not hear him, leaning over to Kingston and then to Doops. "And I'm still a virgin."

When he saw that they were not going to answer, he began to laugh, nodding for the deputy to unlock the cell.

"Now all I have to figure out is whether I'm a wise virgin or a foolish virgin."

"I think you trimmed your lamp," Doops managed to say, still not laughing.

"I guess we're going to have to talk about it," Kingston said as they walked toward the car from the jail. They had never discussed the possibility of it actually happening.

The closest they had come to talking about it was the day the judge pronounced the sentence. After the sheriff had led him back to his cell and Doops had come in to see him, Model T stood up and faced him squarely as he entered.

"Will you go with me?" he asked, a seeming acceptance in his voice.

"Yes," Doops replied.

They had embraced and turned to talking of other things.

"This thing is starting to hit me," Kingston said to Doops as they were driving out of town, heading for Tennessee. "Looks like time is running out on us. I mean, good God! We can't let it happen to him."

"We'll keep doing everything we can. That's all he expects from us," Doops said.

"The thing that tears my guts is that he doesn't even expect *that* from us," Kingston said, looking back until the jail faded from sight.

"Get the map," Doops said. "You'll have to navigate. I've never been farther in this direction than Corinth."

It was late afternoon when they left the U.S. highway in Sanborn, Tennessee, and asked directions to the village of Zion Mountain. Doops's editor had told him that the preacher's name was Edward Vinsang and that he worked at a cannery in Zion Mountain. He was friendly and would let them go to the service. The editor wanted a story on primitivity in America.

Primitivity? Doops thought. "Primitivity in America," he mumbled, thinking of Model T.

They found the preacher operating a forklift at a little cannery built beside a mountain stream. He remembered the exchange of letters with Doops's editor but said a lot of things had happened since then and he was not sure what the service would be like that night. He was cordial enough, but a bit suspicious too.

"You boys ain't from the government, are you?"

Doops showed him his press card, explained to him that they had their own problems with the government. He told him about Model T and when he finished, the man got off the forklift, closed the doors of the big tractor truck he was loading with cartons of canned string beans, and motioned them to a darkened area in the corner of the big warehouse. He sat down on a stack of wooden pallets and began telling them of his own troubles, appearing to trust them fully.

"Three weeks ago tonight. That's when they come in and arrested me and Brother Busby. He's from North Carolina and was in here preaching a revival for me. They busted right in on us while we was worshiping and praising God, handcuffed the two of us together and hauled us off to jail. Wouldn't even let us finish the service or tell our women folks good-bye. 'Course, we was just in jail overnight, but if a body can't pray to his God in a free country . . ." His voice trailed off and he gazed into the last of the mountain sun.

Doops, making rapid notes on a small pad, asked him why they arrested them.

"Well, we believe in the Bible. We read it and whatever it says we believe." He pulled a small New Testament from his shirt pocket and began to read.

And these signs shall follow them that believe; In my name shall they cast our devils; they shall speak with new tongues; They shall take up serpents; and if they drink any deadly thing, it shall not hurt them; they shall lay hands on the sick, and they shall recover.

He closed the little book gently and put it back in his pocket, stood up, and began prancing around where Doops and Kingston were standing. "Now we believe that. And we practice it. But they got a law in this state that says you can't pick up snakes, which we don't do in the first place for the Bible don't say nothing about snakes. It don't even mention snakes. It says 'take up serpents.' Anyway, this law says you can't do that and you can't tempt or harass anybody else into doing that. Of course, we don't do that neither. I never preached a sermon in my life when I didn't warn the people, when I didn't exhort them in just the direct opposite direction. I tell them not to touch them deadly devils until they are anointed by the Spirit to lift them up 'cause they will flat kill you. But that's what they arrested us for. In court I told the judge that. He told us he would just let us go with a fine if we would promise not to handle any more snakes. I told him we didn't handle snakes, that we took up serpents. Like the Bible says. The Bible don't mention snakes. It says serpents. And I told him we don't do that unless we are anointed by the Spirit. He sent this feller, the bailiff I think you call him, out to get a dictionary. Said, 'Now boys, let's us see what Mr. Webster says *anoint* means.' Then he read out of the dictionary and then said, 'Now boys, that's what Mr. Webster says *anoint* means. Is that what happens to you before you do whatever it is you do with the snakes . . . the serpents?' I said, 'But judge, we don't live by Mr. Webster. We live by the Bible. And we already know what anoint means.' Well, he got powerful mad then and that's when he sentenced me to thirty days in jail and Brother Busby to twenty days. I don't mind telling you I can't afford to spend no month in jail. I got a family to feed and if I don't work they don't eat."

"Don't you get a salary from the church?" Doops asked, continuing to write on the note pad.

"Oh, nosirree. We don't hold with that. That was when the trouble started with most churches. When they started paying one another to preach and pray. When they started talking about 'full-time Christian service.' Can you tell me how in the world somebody can be in part-time Christian service? Either you're saved by the blood of the lamb or you ain't. And if you are, well, then you're saved full-time. You can't be a Christian part of the time and a heathen part of the time. That's like saying I'm Edward Vinsang part of the time and somebody else the rest of the time. I got to be Edward Vinsang all the time, for that's who I am."

Doops had stopped writing and was following him around the area as he talked, listening, studying his person. "But Paul and Silas went to jail for preaching the Gospel," he went on. "And I don't reckon we're any better than they were."

"Why did you say you don't know what kind of service you will have tonight?" Doops asked him.

"Well, I said it because a lot of people around here are scared. I mean folks don't know what to make of it when the law comes in their church houses and drags their preachers off to jail. But we'll be there. Brother Busby will be back and I'll be there

and my family will be there. I can't predict how many people will come but the faithful ones will be there all right. So y'all come if you want to."

Kingston had moved to the pallets. "Will you be picking up any . . . lifting up serpents?" he asked.

The preacher came over and sat down beside him. "When somebody tells us
they're telling the truth, I believe them," he said. "You say you're not from the government and I believe you're not from the government. But that's the same question a
deputy came out here and asked me yesterday. He brought some papers, said it was
an injunction. Said the judge sent them. He read it out loud to me. Like I can't read.
My mamma said I was a-readin' before I went to school. Anyway, what they said was
that if we lift up serpents while the case is going through the appeals, we'll be in contempt of court. I'm going to answer you the way I answered him. We're going to do
what the Spirit leads us to do. And that's all I can tell you."

"Look, Brother Vinsang," Doops said. "I don't want to do anything to disturb your
service. I respect you. I respect your beliefs. And your rights. If our coming to the service will be in any way unsettling to any of your congregation, will be disruptive in
any way . . . well, we just won't go. I don't have to write this article. We can get back
in the car, go over the mountain, and forget it."

The preacher walked over and put his hand on Doops's shoulder and looked him
directly in the eye. "You saluted me as 'brother.' When a man does that I know that he
is after the truth. And that's all we want. There has been a lot of lies told about us in
the newspapers. And on the radio. In Third John we read, 'For I rejoiced greatly,
when the brethren came and testified of the truth that is in thee, even as though walk-
est in the truth.' That's all I ask. That you walk in the truth, that you write the truth
you find in our midst. No sir. You won't interfere. Some folks say because our little
church is way down at the very end of a mountain trail we hide out to worship. Well,
we built it there because one of our members gave us some land and that's where the
land was. Some folks have to walk across the mountain to get there or drive thirty
miles around on the road to get to a place that ain't no more than a mile from where
they live. The county won't build a road so we can get in and out and then they say we
hide out. You see what kind of lies I'm talking about."

The man told them how to get to the church and said he would be on down as
soon as he went home and cleaned up. Doops drove past the First Baptist Church of
Zion Mountain and turned at the second road to the right, the way the preacher had
told him. Just before that road came to a dead end at a row of tobacco barns, there
was a descending wagonway veering to the left. They followed it across a shallow
ford and Kingston opened a barbed-wire gap stretched across the trail. Doops told
him the man had said to leave it open.

The church was a small, one-room structure with buckeye siding of random
widths and lengths. There was one door at the front and the wooden shutters were
propped open. There were no glass windows. There was a graveled parking area but
theirs was the only car there. Doops turned around and parked the car so that it was
heading back in the direction they had come from.

"Think you might want to be the first to leave?" Kingston said.

"Never can tell," Doops said.

Above the door was a neatly painted sign: THE CHURCH OF THE ALMIGHTY IN JESUS
NAME AMEN. The pulpit was a slanted stand made of the same wood as the siding on
the building. It was on a slightly elevated stage. On one side of it was a quart bottle
half filled with a clear fluid.

"That'll be strychnine," Doops said.

"How you know?" Kingston asked him.

"And that one will be arsenic," Doops said, pointing to a glass jar on the other side of the pulpit.

"How the hell . . . uh . . ." He glanced quickly about the room. "How you know that?"

"I've read about them," Doops said. "And didn't you hear the preacher read to us? 'If they drink any deadly thing, it shall not hurt them.'"

"You're shittin' . . . whoops . . . you're kidding me!" Kingston said. "You telling me they actually drink that stuff?"

"So they tell me," Doops said. "My first trip, too."

"And my last," Kingston said. "What the hell . . . God damn it . . . I keep forgetting we're in a church house. Let's get out of here."

"I've got to get a story. Got to write about primitivity in America. Well, here it is. I can't leave until it happens."

"I don't mean for always. I just mean let's go out of here for right now. So I can talk right. I keep forgetting where we are, that we're in a church house."

"That's because you're a bigot," Doops said. "Bet you wouldn't forget if you smelled incense."

They walked back outside and stood beside the car.

"Looks like it's going to be a slim congregation," Kingston said.

"Can't tell yet," Doops said. "The preacher said they didn't start at any certain time."

They heard talking from the direction of the main road and several people moved into view. When they saw the car and Doops and Kingston standing beside it, they stopped walking and stood silent, watching. Then a car pulled alongside the little group and the driver said something, and they began to move on in the direction of the building.

"That must be the preacher," Doops said. The car drove to the door and parked. Preacher Vinsang walked toward them carrying two small boxes crudely constructed of pine lumber and glass. "Don't be nervous," he said, smiling at them. "They can't get out. These in this box never had a handle on them."

They could tell the boxes were heavy and he dropped them clumsily on the ground. Both of them looked at the box closest to them. Through the glass they could see a coiled and tangled mass of slithering, glistening, tremoring diamondback rattlesnakes.

"Those folks left their cars somewhere else," he said, ignoring the continuous buzzing of the rattlers inside the cage, motioning to the group continuing to move toward them. "Don't want the law to be gettin' their tag numbers. I told them who you were. Be more coming along soon and we'll get started."

He picked up the two cages and moved through the door.

"What the . . . what does that mean? Never had a handle on them?" Kingston asked when he had disappeared.

"Means no one has ever handled them before," Doops said. "I suppose that's what it means. I told you it's my first trip too. I guess it means they have never been lifted up."

They watched as several other small groups drifted down the hill. A few cars, moving almost as cautiously as the pedestrians, pulled onto various spots about the parking area. A panelbody truck with *Cherokee Plumbing* lettered on the side drove off again after three men got out, two carrying guitars and one a double bass fiddle. Doops and Kingston continued to mull around in the shadows of the trees, listening to the men tuning the instruments inside. When they heard them singing, they moved inside and sat on one of the benches about halfway down the single aisle.

"Canaan land is far away
    Will I see you there?
There will be so many joys
    You and I will share."

"I could improve on those lyrics," Doops whispered to Kingston, who looked confused. They played in peppy ragtime, their voices sometimes a whole beat behind the music. Doops wondered if Kingston had ever attended any kind of religious service other than Catholic and what he was thinking. The preachers sat in the front row with the congregation. There were several ladderback chairs on the platform but no one sat on them. There seemed to be no particular order to the service. Sometimes the people sang along with the band and sometimes they sat and listened. A few clapped their hands with the rhythm of the music but most of them seemed subdued. For nearly an hour, the singing continued, the enthusiasm mounting gradually as they went along. Occasionally one of the preachers would jump to the pulpit and say a few words, speaking of the lack of unity in the church. And of coldness. Once they stood up together and talked to each other, meaning for the people to hear what they were saying.

"You know, a fellow, I believe he was a Methodist, asked me the other day if we lifted up serpents before the sermon or afterwards," one of them said, laughing loudly.

"And I wonder if you told him what I would have told him," the other one said.

"Yeah, I bet I did. I told him we don't have a printed bulletin that's sent to the printer on Tuesday for next Sunday's service. You know what I'm a-talking about!" he screamed to the applauding congregation. "They'll have all this fancy stuff. Processional. Call to Worship. Invocation. Or whatever they call it when the preacher gets up and reads something out of a book. Congregational Hymn. Offertory. First Lesson. Second Lesson. Responsive Reading. And all that. Sermon. Recessional. Prayers of Intercession. All that. I just told him, 'Now brother, we don't write it down in advance because we don't know what the Spirit has in mind for us to do until He leads us to do it. We don't have printed on a piece of paper Processional, Call to Worship, Hymn, Sermon, Lift up Serpents! We lift up serpents when the Spirit of the living God tells us to lift up serpents! Not when some elder or bishop or pope tells us to. You know what I'm a-talking about out there!" Most of the people were on their feet, laughing, clapping their hands, and some dancing in the aisle.

"Don't you think we ought to clear out of here!" Kingston said.

"Not yet," Doops whispered.

Doops wondered how he would respond if they really did start handling the snakes and passing them around the room, for snakes had been one of his worst fears as a child. He had expected the service to be pitched at a much more frenzied level and wondered if they were subdued because of his and Kingston's presence. Or perhaps because they feared the officers would come back.

One of the preachers invited the worshipers to come forth and give their testimony. Some of them told of being delivered from drunkenness, from various illnesses and vices. One woman said the Lord had rescued her from certain divorce and restored her husband's love. Her husband, a very bald and very fat man with no bottom teeth, stood beside her, holding her hand. There was more handclapping, cheers, and cries of

"Amen!" "Praise God!" and "Hallelujah!" but still not the frenetic outpouring that Doops had anticipated. The other preacher asked if there were any sick in their midst who desired to be healed. A few came forward with an assortment of minor complaints. The preachers placed hands on their heads, exhorting them to total and unconditional belief, chiding the demons that possessed them to depart, and then declaring them whole. But this too seemed stilted and routine, if not downright contrived.

But then it happened. A slender woman of about forty had moved out of the congregation and seated herself at an old upright piano with yellowing keys and no front panel. The band moved in around her. She was wearing a full-length velveteen dress, solid white with half-sleeves and a close-fitting collar that covered her neck completely. Her hair was a moderate brown, gathered in two half-buns over each shoulder. She paused for a moment as she sat down, opening and closing her hands, stretching her fingers. As she began to play, the movement of her fingers, hands, and arms gave a stroboscopic effect, moving from one end of the keyboard to the other in rapid succession. She followed her hands with the upper part of her body, leaning to the left as her fingers moved, her torso stretching as far as her arms did. Then swaying back to the right as her hands moved to the opposite end of the keyboard. Doops did not recognize what she was playing and the people did not sing. Only Doops and Kingston remained seated. The others were shouting, sighing, dancing in place, their bodies divested of all control, their cares released.

As soon as she started to play, a young man who looked no more than twenty ran to the raised platform and flipped open the two cages, threw his head straight back so that he could not even see inside, reached his hands into each of the boxes, and when he stood up he was holding three of the snakes in one hand and two in the other. The three in his right hand were cottonmouth moccasins. The other two were rattlers. There was a sort of faraway, glazed look in his eyes. It was not fear. Nor was Doops afraid as the man strolled up and down the aisle, passing a few feet from where he and Kingston remained seated, flinging the serpents over his head and waving them round and round, occasionally clutching them to his chest, sometimes looking at one or another as he exposed his neck and head to their fangs. The sounds coming from the congregation now were indescribable, aspects of rushing water, the whimper of a newborn baby, the fury of a tornado, the fragility of a lullaby, the frenzy of a giant airplane about to leave the ground.

"But judge, we don't live by Mr. Webster. We live by the Bible." The words kept running through Doops's mind.

"Great God!"

The young man with the snakes was the center. Sometimes some of them formed a circle about him as he moved. The woman at the piano continued with the same tune as when she began. Suddenly the music stopped as if by some prearranged signal. When it did the young man let one of the moccasins slither from his hand onto the floor, and one of the rattlers onto the huge Bible resting on the pulpit, then dropped the others in the box. He kicked his unlaced shoes off and stood victoriously, massaging the lengthy spine of the cottonmouth with his toes. The big rattler lay on the open Bible, moving only its tongue, a rhythmic in-and-out oscillation possible only among the cursed ophidians. There was no more music, no shouts, dancing, or handclapping in the aisle. Only the silence. The man began to speak.

"They say it takes music for us to do this—what I been a-doing." Apparently he was not unmindful of the skeptics who tried to explain their behavior. "Well there ain't no music now. And look at them!" He spoke slowly and softly. "Only God can do that. I can't do it. You can't do it. *Them things'll kill ya!*" he screamed. "Only God can do that. I can't. You can't. That's the devil lying there. Oh, he won in the Garden of Eden. But just like God said, 'Upon thy belly shalt thou go, and dust shalt thou eat all the days of thy life.' Look at the devil eat the dust and go on his belly. Oh, he's powerful all right. He's strong. And he's dangerous!" He reached down and picked up the moccasin again, leaving the rattler wriggling in place. "But he's second best. But *look out!*" He jumped straight at the congregation, all seated now, exhausted. "Look out," he said again, whispering. "'Cause he *is* second best. He's the next most powerful thing to God. But just look at him now. He's helpless. He didn't bite me and if he had of, it wouldn't of hurt me. He's conquered. The devil is conquered. *Hallelujah! Hallelujah! Hallelujah!*" The people were on their feet again, shouting with him.

He flung both snakes in the box, secured the latch, and sat down. As soon as he did the woman at the piano stood up, moved forward, and began to speak. She wandered in and out among the congregation, not looking at the people, up and down the aisle, giving the impression that she did not care if they saw her, heard her or not.

"Ah 'ach ma hah moora, ay *doopsgesinde*
andorra ay ach-ah ha moora
Ammtee muhr ah had melah, ay *doopsgesinde*
ah nahah mahah murch *doopsgesinde* mahlan."

At first Doops tried to write down the ciphers. But as the tongues continued his pen dropped from his hand to the floor. Kingston picked it up and tried to hand it back to him but he did not move to take it.

"You getting the symptoms?" Kingston asked him.

"Afraid so," he muttered panting heavily.

"Let's go," Kingston said, taking him by the arm and standing up.

As they moved toward the door, Doops stumbling along behind, some of the people smiled and waved cordially. The same young man was speaking again as they left the building.

"If they take me to jail tonight, for being here tonight, for doing what I'm a-doing tonight, they can keep me there forever and I won't pay no fine. I ain't got no fine money for Caesar. I give my money to the Lord. If they come and put a padlock on the church door tonight while I'm a-sleeping, I'll come saw it off in the morning and go on confirming the mighty acts of God like the Bible tells me."

Kingston pushed Doops into the car and got in on the driver's side.

"You feeling better?" he asked, driving away. "You look like a ghost."

"Maybe I am," Doops said.

"No, you're not. Now tell me how you feel."

"I feel like I just learned something I never knew before."

"Like what?" Kingston snapped. "Hell, I was scared of those vipers. What the devil did you learn in there?"

"My name," Doops said. "But never mind. Drive this thing. We have to get back."

"You mean tonight? What's the hurry?"

"I've got to get Model T to baptize me. It's time for me to get baptized."

Kingston answered him but not right away.

LOWER SOUTH

Understanding that Southern literature possesses its own distinctive conventions and themes, Pat Conroy once offered the following quip in helping define the genre: "My mother, Southern to the bone, once told me, 'All Southern literature can be summed up in these words: "On the night the hogs ate Willie, Mama died when she heard what Daddy did to sister.'" Conroy acknowledges an impulse in the popular imagination to view the Deep South as a place of "delightful ambiguities" at the least, and of schizophrenic polarities in the most extreme cases. It is a place wreathed in ironies—where the best and the worst sit side by side in stark juxtaposition. A mile in any direction may find the astute observer encountering near-Gothic extremes: antebellum mansions and mobile home parks; family values and families who rank lowest in the United States in caring for their children; numerous churches dotting the landscape and an abiding racial intolerance; politeness and a proliferation of firearms. It is as if the Deep South remains, just as Morris Dees says, "a separate country," a microcosm of exaggerated traits defining the American character. Whatever exists here will find its antithesis, its shadowy counterpart, hovering nearby. If, as it has sometimes been argued, the North corresponds to the country's "head," valuing intellect and the knowledge acquired by scientific rationalism, the South is the country's "heart," seeking a deeper, more intuitive understanding whose dialectic is largely conflict.

Even the effort to locate the geographical center of this "heart" has inspired controversy at times. Alabama's license plates traditionally proclaimed that state to be the "Heart of Dixie." Mississippi boasts of being the "Most Southern Place on Earth." Georgia beams with pride at Atlanta's status as the gateway to the new technological South. Doggedly partisan to the end, South Carolina supports legislation to honor both Martin Luther King, Jr., and Afro-Confederate soldiers. Natives of Louisiana need only bask in the aura of accolades once supplied by Mark Twain, who observed, while visiting, that "Baton Rouge was clothed in flowers like a bride—no, much more so; like a greenhouse. For we were in the absolute South now—no modifications, no compromises, no halfway measures."

Nor does halfhearted enthusiasm characterize the region's current regard for literature. Not even William Gilmore Simms's 1847 declaration that "the South don't care a damn for literature and art" has eclipsed efforts by the Lower South to sponsor world-class literary conferences and to publish first-rate literary periodicals. Some states even have their own literature anthologies, showcasing writers with national and, in some cases, international reputations. Intra-South competition for literary preeminence is almost as fierce as collegiate gridiron rivalries. The ongoing vitality of the Southern tradition in literature can be seen in such nationally distributed publications as *The Oxford American*, which bills itself as a "Southern magazine of good writing." In an age when technological ascendancy and cultural dislocation threaten to dismantle existing traditions, the South's hold on literature seems as secure as ever, generating an unequivocal pride in the literary arts produced by the region's poets, novelists, playwrights, screenwriters, and essayists.

In the 1980s, such pride contributed to a species of regional literature dubbed as "grit lit." In the words of writer Fred Chappell, grit lit is "Southern literature that defiantly makes itself known as Southern." Rather than focusing on a new generation of genteel folk, many of whom had been the beneficiaries of racial enlightenment, grit lit took as its unabashed subject matter the "rednecks" and, in some instances, "mean sumbitches" of Hall and Woods's classification. In the work of such grit lit practition-ers as Harry Crews, Barry Hannah, and Larry Brown, the fictional characters are often the overlooked, scorned, and despised—poor whites and poor blacks trying to discover the terms by which life can be made more livable. As characters, they repre-sent the numerous unnamed Southerners standing in the Wal-Mart checkout line. Their status as celebrities is often restricted to a few sentences in the local obituary.

Ironically, grit lit's focus on such people drew critical censure from outside the region. John Gardner, for instance, complained that such an avowedly defiant brand of Southern literature only reinforced regional prejudices and exalted the worst char-acteristics of provincialism. Robert Bly suggested that the most appalling impulses in Southern society (e.g., militarism and the blood lust associated with hunting) were being glorified by some influential grit writers. Some writers in the popular media rose to the defense of "rednecks" and their recent exposure in Southern fiction. As late as 1995, author Gail Gilchrist wrote and published *Bubbas and Beaus*, a popular treatment designed to topple the "last bastions of socially acceptable prejudice" that reinforce the image of "good old boys" as "wife-beating racist illiterates."

Even when stereotypes breathe inspiration from real-life counterparts, writers such as Dorothy Allison are careful to make distinctions that can prove crucial to one's survival. Just as not all good old boys are bad, not all are good, either. In *Bas-tard Out of Carolina*, Allison chronicles the plight of a young girl whose raw exis-tence includes exposure to numerous male relations who qualify as good old boys and, in particular cases, "mean sumbitches." For Ruth Anne Boatwright, nicknamed Bones, so-called "affection" becomes sexual abuse in a culture where psychological and physical boundaries often go unobserved. Terror is the weapon that Bones's step-father uses to subdue her until the stunning climax of the novel. Yet even those un-cles whom Bones admires offer a disturbing picture all too common in the annals of the Southern poor: "They were all big men with wide shoulders, broken teeth, and sunken features. . . . Only when they were drunk or fighting with each other did they seem as dangerous as they were supposed to be."

A landscape of harsh realities is the setting for Larry Brown's fiction and, specifi-cally, for his award-winning short story "Facing the Music." In this story, the male pro-tagonist no longer experiences sexual attraction for his wife, the result of a mastectomy that she has earlier been forced to endure. Although despising himself for feeling as he does, the narrator makes excuses and avoids intimacy until his wife prompts him to ac-knowledge that ". . . you don't want me since the operation." The suffocating closeness between them is intensified by Brown's blunt dialogue and lean style.

Southerners have always known that the brutishness of life can be moderated by religion. However, Southerners are most comfortable when religion takes the form of platitudinous certainty, a buttress for the existing status quo. Let someone take the gospel message seriously and the results can be unpredictable, producing itinerant misfits and "prophets" like Grandpa Wingo in Pat Conroy's *The Prince of Tides*. The story of Tom Wingo and his efforts to help his troubled sister, Conroy's novel also ex-amines the extended Southern family as an "obsessive theme." Taking pride in his grandfather's eccentricity, Tom describes how the old man celebrated Good Friday by standing at a congested intersection with a makeshift cross on his back. Oblivious to the "admixture of scorn and awe of his townsmen," Amos Wingo "was a figure of majesty to some, a perfect jackass to others." Nevertheless, when Amos dies, "the whole town knew it had lost something exquisite and irreplaceable." For "nothing so affects a southern family as the death of the man who lent it balance and fragility in a world askew with corrupt values."

Fragility best describes the hand-to-mouth existence of Depression-era tenant farmers like those found in Harry Crews's brilliant and searing memoir, *A Childhood*. Underscoring that the only certainty was the prospect of pain and uncertainty, Crews depicts the lives of several black and white sharecropping families, all living in close proximity and all sharing similar fates under the scorching Georgia sun. Farming is ritual, as Crews points out, and one such ritual was that of the annual hog killing. In one of the most terrifying and understated episodes of Crews's narrative, the author describes how, as a child, he ended up in a pot of boiling water next to "a scalded floating hog." With "the knowledge of death upon me," Crews notes that he "reached over and touched my right hand with my left, and the whole thing came off like a wet glove . . . I could see my fingernails lying in the little puddle my flesh made on the ground in front of me." Rushed to a hospital more than thirty miles away, Crews was treated by a doctor as one of innumerable "charity" cases. As with Dorothy Allison, Crews offers a portrait of childhood as harrowing as any other in contemporary literature.

Despite its reputation for intolerance, the South has routinely made a place for people deemed eccentric or "odd." Aberrant behavior is both scorned and revered in the South, giving rise to the oft-quoted adage that although "a man may be a son-of-a bitch, he's our son-of-a-bitch." During the Civil War, loyalty to the region and loyalty to the Lost Cause were far more important considerations than a man's sexual preference. Thus, although homosexuality was publicly scorned, it was privately overlooked and even condoned in some all-male bastions. In Barry Hannah's "Knowing He Was Not My Kind Yet I Followed," the narrator, a Confederate soldier whom the "Creator made . . . strange," displays both bravery and loyalty while serving under Jeb Stuart's command. Recognizing their mutual differences, the narrator and Stuart nonetheless exhibit admiration for each other. Only once do the two soldiers experience a conflict whose resolution leaves both men with their separate "natures" intact. Indeed, the narrator's aversion to killing and his insistence that "we are not defending our beloved Dixie anymore [but only looting and marauding]" offer an important counterpoint to Stuart's cavalier disregard for life.

Despite occasional efforts to embrace differences in other people, contemporary American culture is all too often, in William Styron's words, "dominated by hostility and suspicion, by doctrinaire attitudes in matters of gender and race, by an ugly spirit of partisanship and exclusion, and by an all-around failure of mutual generosity." A volatile milieu has been a commonplace occurrence in the South's history. Yet, efforts to solve controversies and conflicts have been frequent, too. Exposing "the confluence of past and present, the day-to-day mingling of the dark ghosts and the better angels of our nature," Mississippi writer Willie Morris stares unflinchingly at "my home state's more virulent strains of racism," while recording some of the "salubrious changes" that have taken place.[1] In *The Courting of Marcus Dupree*, Morris examines the role of collegiate athletics in promoting integration in the South. Demonstrating that the South's martial impulse and desire for glory outweigh its enthusiasm for segregation, Morris chronicles the plight of one gifted African American athlete who was recruited by colleges throughout the country. What the author discovers is exploitation, broken promises, and utter disregard for young athletes once they have fulfilled their required functions.

Fellow Mississippian Elizabeth Spencer draws inspiration from rural settings in which characters often reveal secret motivations and multilayered dimensions not always visible at first glance. Past and present blend easily in Spencer's fiction, as a re-sult of "several modernist techniques—irregular chronology, flashbacks, [and] multi-ple point of view. . . ."[2] But, as Peggy Whitman Prenshaw asserts, Spencer's greatest gift is the ability to create "vital, credible characters" like the male and female protag-onists in "First Dark."[3] Here a man and a woman fall in love as a result of both's hav-ing seen the same "ghost" out along the Jackson Road at twilight. The only potential obstacle to this burgeoning romance is the young woman's ailing mother, who nonetheless refuses to stand in the way of her daughter's happiness. The mother's sacrifice offers a stunning solution to the couple's mutual problem. However, the story does not end there. The couple must decide what to do about all the "ghosts"—memories not easily left behind. Ironically, it is the house that the newlyweds abandon that provides the final commentary, an "unconscious" indictment of the characters and their irrevocable choices.

Whereas setting is a daunting and an inescapable feature of the lives of Spencer's characters, it is place in Alice Walker's poetry and fiction that "goes beyond pure evo-cation to a striking emphasis on the South as an African-American homeland."[4] One recurring notion in Walker's canon is that of a "black reclamation of the South."[5] Re-fusing to create a "universalized portrait of black southern life," Walker explores in her characters all the possibilities of spiritual transformation that contribute to a view of community transcending exclusively white perspectives.[6] Revolutionary in both theme and techniques, Walker's fiction (including such acclaimed works as *The Color Purple*) shares similarities with her poetry, which is often underrepresented in literary anthologies. Nevertheless, the seeds of Walker's extraordinary novels can be found in early poems from such collections as *Revolutionary Petunias and Other Poems*. In "J, My Good Friend (Another Foolish Innocent)," Walker's narrator re-claims Jesus and his revolutionary spirit that ". . . worries greatness / to an early grave." Just as innocence is a requirement of spiritual awareness and change, the poem's speaker anticipates a time when she will grow old, singing "In my cracked and ugly voice / Of Jesus my good / Friend." The music found in Walker's short-lined verse is especially resonant in "Women," where "My mama's generation Husky of voice" possesses an elemental power belying stereotypes and ignoring qualifications. For their children, these women "battered down / Doors / And ironed / Starched white / Shirts" in an effort to provide "A place for us." That place is one where the children can "discover books." The speaker expresses amazement at the women's ability to recognize what the children needed without "knowing a page / Of it / Themselves." One related theme in Walker's poem "Eagle Rock" is the way society works to explain away and to diminish the power of authentic people and places. Mentioning the "town where I was born," the speaker notes the existence of a mound "the Cherokees raised. . . ." However, the contemporary inhabitants, exhibiting a convenient histori-cal amnesia, regard the mound only as "piled up stones." What they fail to recognize is that the mound "lives" with a power that cannot be circumscribed by "Jolly con-querors" wearing cameras.

Like Walker, whose novel *The Color Purple* was made into an award-winning film (1985), Ernest Gaines has written fiction that has been adapted to screen and television. His highly acclaimed novel *Gathering of Old Men* (produced under the video title *Murder on the Bayou*) is a poignant drama about a group of elderly Louisiana black men who step forward to take responsibility for killing a notorious white racist. Less well known, but equally powerful, is Gaines's short fiction, in which "with great warmth, he celebrates the indomitable strength and resilience and moral reserve of black people."[7] As for setting, Gaines acknowledges that "I've always thought the idea of having things in a single setting and limited to twenty-four hours was the ideal way of telling stories."[8] Such is the case in "The Sky Is Gray," the story of a young boy facing the ordeal of visiting the dentist. Encouraged by his mama not to be a "crybaby," he endures the pain of a toothache, even submitting to "Catholic prayers," though the only prayers he really knows are "Baptist." The story unfolds as a quest in which voices heard in passing reveal the inequities between the black and the white worlds occupying the same geographical locale. The child's innocent perspective reveals anything but innocent circumstances. The boy is unwittingly part of all he meets and experiences. In this way, the author's fiction offers, in his own words, "as many facets as possible."[9]

Because Southern literature has been so successfully appropriated by the popular media, distinctions between commercial and literary fiction have all but disappeared. Ann Rivers Siddons proves that one can be both a best-selling author and a Southern novelist extraordinaire. The Southern landscape is a shifting oasis for Siddons, who finds hospitable settings in the Outer Banks of North Carolina, in the low country of South Carolina, or on a mountaintop in Tennessee. In fact, it is the fictional "Morgan's Mountain in south Tennessee," home of "Trinity College," that provides the initial setting for Siddons's novel *Hill Towns*. Siddons's protagonist, an attractive, middle-aged woman named Catherine Compton, experiences panic attacks even at the thought of leaving her beloved mountain. Yet, when she and her husband travel, as part of her therapy, to the Tuscan hills of Rome, Catherine discovers the source of her anxieties and emerges as a profoundly strong woman, confident in her ability to meet any challenge. Siddons's choice of setting is just as important as her choice of character in the story's development. Readers familiar with Monteagle Mountain and the University of the South at Sewanee will find satirical descriptions of both in Siddons's novel. Her tongue-in-cheek depictions offer a whimsical counterpoint to an earlier selection by William Alexander Percy entitled "Sewanee."

Notes

1. Willie Morris, *The Ghosts of Medgar Evers* (New York: Random House, 1998), 7.
2. Peggy Whitman Prenshaw, "Elizabeth Spencer," *The History of Southern Literature*, ed. Louis D. Rubin et al. (Baton Rouge: Louisiana State University Press, 1985), 497.
3. Prenshaw, 498.
4. Linda Tate, *A Southern Weave of Women* (Athens: University of Georgia Press, 1994), 158.
5. Tate, 158.
6. Tate, 158.
7. Theodore R. Hudson, "Ernest J. Gaines," *The History of Southern Literature*, ed. Louis D. Rubin et al. (Baton Rouge: Louisiana State University Press, 1985), 514.
8. Jennifer Levasseur and Kevin Rabalais, "An Interview with Ernest Gaines," *Missouri Review*, Vol. XXII, no. 1, 1999, 109.
9. Levasseur and Rabalais, 104.

Dorothy Allison

(1949–   )

Dorothy Allison was born on April 11, 1949, in Greenville, South Carolina. She earned her B.A. from Florida Presbyterian College in 1971. Allison writes, in particular, about the struggle for survival. She received acclaim for her novel *Bastard Out of Carolina* (1992).

Other works include *The Women Who Hate Me: Poetry, 1980–1990* (1991); *Two or Three Things I Know for Sure* (1995); and *Cavedweller* (1998). She lives in northern California.

from *Bastard Out of Carolina*

2

Greenville, South Carolina, in 1955 was the most beautiful place in the world. Black walnut trees dropped their green-black fuzzy bulbs on Aunt Ruth's matted lawn, past where their knotty roots rose up out of the ground like the elbows and knees of dirty children suntanned dark and covered with scars. Weeping willows marched across the yard, following every wandering stream and ditch, their long whiplike fronds making tents that sheltered sweet-smelling beds of clover. Over at the house Aunt Raylene rented near the river, all the trees had been cut back and the scuppernong vines torn out. The clover grew in long sweeps of tiny white and yellow flowers that hid slender red-and-black-striped caterpillars and fat gray-black slugs—the ones Uncle Earle swore would draw fish to a hook even in a thunderstorm. But at Aunt Alma's, over near the Eustis Highway, the landlord had locked down the spigots so that the kids wouldn't cost him a fortune in water bills. Without the relief of a sprinkler or a hose the heat had burned up the grass, and the combined efforts of dogs and boys had reduced the narrow yard to a smoldering expanse of baked dirt and scattered rocks.

"Yard's like a hot griddle," Aunt Alma complained. "Catches all the heat of that tin roof and concentrates it. You could just about cook on that ground."

"Oh, it's hot everywhere." Granny never agreed with Aunt Alma, and particularly not that summer when she was being paid a lot less than she wanted to watch Alma's kids. And the little Mama threw in to pay her for keeping Reese and me didn't sweeten her attitude. Granny loved all her grandchildren, but she was always announcing that she didn't have much use for her daughters.

"My three boys worship me," she'd tell everybody, "but my girls, Lord! I've got five girls and they never seem to appreciate me. It's how girls are, though, selfish and full of themselves. I shouldn't expect any better."

"Your granny means well," Mama told me before dropping us off to stay the day over at Aunt Alma's, "but don't pay too much attention to the things she says. She's always loved her boy children more. It's just the way some women are." I nodded. I believed anything that Mama said was so.

Almost the first thing I remember is Aunt Alma's house and yard, back behind the tiny roadside store she and Uncle Wade were trying to manage. It was the summer after Reese was born, which means I must have been about five years old, only slightly bigger than Little Earle, Alma's youngest. But Little Earle was a fat toddler still chafing in rubber pants and grabbing at everything with his unfailingly sticky hands, while I was a solemn watchful child with long thin bones and a cloud of wild black hair. I looked down on Little Earle as a lesser creature and stayed well out of reach of his grubby fingers and pushed-out baby lips. That was the summer it was so hot the katydids failed to sing and everyone spent their evenings out on the porch with large glasses of ice tea and damp hand towels to cool the back of the neck. Alma wouldn't even start cooking until after the sun had gone down. Twilight came on early, though, a long-drawn-out dimming of the heat and glare that made everything soft and magical, brought out the first fireflies, and added a cool enchantment to the metallic echoes of the slide guitar playing on Alma's kitchen radio. Granny would plant herself in the porch rocker, leaving Alma's girls to pick through snap beans, hope for a rainstorm, and tease her into telling stories.

I always positioned myself behind Granny, up against the wall next to the screen door, where I could listen to Kitty Wells and George Jones, the whine of that guitar and what talk there was in the kitchen, as well as the sound of Aunt Alma's twin boys thumping their feet against the porch steps and the girls' giggles as their fingers slipped through the cool, dusty beans. There I was pretty much safe from Little Earle as he ran back and forth from Granny's apron pockets to the steps, where his brothers pitched pennies and practiced betting against each other. Little Earle would lope like a crippled crawfish, angling to the side, swaying unsteadily, and giggling his own wet croupy babble. The boys would laugh at him, Granny would just smile. Oblivious and happy, Little Earle would pound his fists on Grey's shoulders and then twirl himself around to run all out toward Granny, Temple, and Patsy Ruth. Naked, dimpled all over, fat and brown and wide, his stubborn little body bulged with determination, and his little-boy prick bounced like a rubber toy between his bowlegged thighs as he whooped and ran, bumping his head on Granny's hip. He was like a windup toy spinning itself out, and his delight only increased when everyone started laughing at him as he jumped up again after falling plop on his behind next to the tub of snap beans.

Granny covered her mouth with one hand to hide her teeth. "You ugly little boy," she teased Little Earle, almost laughing between her words. "You ugly, ugly, ugly little thing."

Earle paused, crowed like a hoot owl, and rocked back and forth as if his momentum were too strong for him to come to a full stop without falling over. Temple and Patsy Ruth shook their wet fingers at his fat little belly while Grey and Garvey smacked their lips and joined in with Granny.

"Ugly, ugly, ugly, ugly! You so ugly you almost pretty!"

Earle squealed and jumped and laughed full out. "Ug-ly," he parroted them. "Uggg-lly!" His face was bright and smiling, and his hands flew up and down like bumblebees, fast and wild up near his ears.

"Ugly. Ugly. Ugly."

"You are just the ugliest thing!" Granny rocked forward and caught her hands under Little Earle's arms, swinging him up off his feet and directly before her face. "You dimple-belly," she called him, "you little dimple-butt." She pressed her mouth against his midriff and blew fiercely so that her lips vibrated against Little Earle's navel—a bubble-bubble roar that made him shriek and bounce and giggle a high-pitched wail of hysterical laughter. He drew his knees up and cupped his little hands around his sex, which only made Temple and Patsy Ruth laugh louder. Granny swung him back and forth a few times and then dropped him down on his feet. He took off immediately for the shelter of his older brother's armpit.

"Dimple-butt," Grey snorted, but pulled his little brother in tight to his side. "An't so ugly maybe." He rubbed his knuckles across Little Earle's nearly bald head and sang out, "You just tall, that's all." Grey laughed at that while Granny wiped her eyes and the girls poured cool water across the beans.

I edged forward until I could put my hand on Granny's chair, fingers sliding over the smooth, worn trellis of woven slats to feel the heat of her body through her cotton dress. The laughter echoed around me, the music, truck brakes ground up on the highway, and somebody started shouting far off as the dark descended and the fire-flies began to flicker past the boys' heads. Granny put her arm down and squeezed my wrist. She leaned over and spat a stream of brown snuff off the side of the porch. I heard the dull plopping sound it made as it landed in the dusty yard. I slipped under her shoulder, leaned across the side of the rocker, and put my face close to her breast. I could smell wet snap beans, tobacco, lemon juice on her neck, a little sharp piss scent, and a little salt.

"Ugly," I repeated, and buried my face in her dress, my smile so wide the warm cotton rubbed my teeth.

"Pretty ugly," Granny whispered above me, her fingers sliding across the back of my head, untangling my hair and lifting it up off my neck. "Almost pretty. Oh, you're a Boatwright all right, a Boatwright for sure."

I laughed up into her neck. Granny was ugly herself, she said so often enough, though she didn't seem to care. Her wide face was seamed and spotted with freckles and long deep lines. Her hair was thin and gray and tied back with one of the little black strings that came off a snuff pouch. She smelled strong—bitter and salt, sour and sweet, all at the same time. My sweat disappeared into her skirt, my arms wrapped around her waist, and I breathed her in like the steam off soup. I rocked my-self against her, as happy and safe as Little Earle had felt with her teeth on his belly.

"You know, Bone, your mama's gonna be late," Temple told me. "These hot nights, they take forever to clean up down at the diner, and old Glen's gonna be there hanging over the counter and slowing her down. He's pure crazy where your mama's concerned."

I nodded solemnly, hanging on to Granny. The radio sounded louder, the boys started to fight. Everybody was busy, everybody was talking, but I was perfectly happy at Granny's side, waiting for Mama to come home late from the diner, take Reese and me back to the tiny duplex she had rented downtown. If the heat contin-ued into the night Mama would put us out on the screened porch on a makeshift mat-tress of couch cushions and sheets. She would sit up by us out there, humming and smoking in the quiet dark, while the radio played so soft we couldn't make it out.

The world that came in over the radio was wide and far away and didn't touch us at all. We lived on one porch or another all summer long, laughing at Little Earle, teas-ing the boys and picking over beans, listening to stories, or to the crickets beating out their own soft songs. When I think of that summer—sleeping over at one of my aunts' houses as easily as at home, the smell of Mama's neck as she bent over to hug us in the dark, the sound of Little Earle's giggle or Granny's spit thudding onto the dry ground, and that country music playing low everywhere, as much a part of the evening as crickets and moonlight—I always feel safe again. No place has ever seemed so sweet and quiet, no place ever felt so much like home.

I worshiped my uncles—Earle, Beau, and Nevil. They were all big men with wide shoulders, broken teeth, and sunken features. They kept dogs trained for hunting and drove old trucks with metal toolboxes bolted to the reinforced wood sides. They worked in the mills or at the furnace repair business, or sometimes did roofing or construction work depending on how the industry was going. They tinkered with cars together on the weekends, standing around in the yard sipping whiskey and talking dirty, kicking at the greasy remains of engines they never finished rebuilding. Their eyes were narrow under sunbleached eyebrows, and their hands were forever working a blade or a piece of wood, or oiling some little machine part or other.

"You hold a knife like this," they told me. "You work a screwdriver from your shoulder, swing a hammer from your hip, and spread your fingers when you want to hold something safe."

Though half the country went in terror of them, my uncles were invariably gentle and affectionate with me and my cousins. Only when they were drunk or fighting with each other did they seem as dangerous as they were supposed to be. The knives they carried were bright, sharp, and fascinating, their toolboxes were massive, full of every imaginable metal implement. Even their wallets bulged with the unknown and the mysterious—outdated ID cards from the air base construction crew, passes for the racetrack, receipts for car repairs and IOUs from card games, as well as little faded pictures of pretty women who were not their wives. My aunts treated my uncles like overgrown boys—rambunctious teenagers whose antics were more to be joked about than worried over—and they seemed to think of themselves that way too. They looked young, even Nevil, who'd had his teeth knocked out, while the aunts—Ruth, Raylene, Alma, and even Mama—seemed old, worn-down, and slow, born to mother, nurse, and clean up after the men.

Men could do anything, and everything they did, no matter how violent or mistaken, was viewed with humor and understanding. The sheriff would lock them up for shooting out each other's windows, or racing their pickups down the railroad tracks, or punching out the bartender over at the Rhythm Ranch, and my aunts would shrug and make sure the children were all right at home. What men did was just what men did. Some days I would grind my teeth, wishing I had been born a boy.

I begged my aunts for Earle's and Beau's old denim work-shirts so I could wear them just the way they did when they worked on their trucks, with the front tucked in and the tail hanging out. Beau laughed at me affectionately as I mimicked him. Earle and Nevil raked their calloused fingers through my black hair and played at catching my shirttail as I ran past them, but their hands never hurt me and their pride in me was as bright as the coals on the cigarettes they always held loosely between their fingers. I followed them around and stole things from them that they didn't really care about—old tools, pieces of chain, and broken engine parts. I wanted most of all a knife like the ones they all carried—a Buck knife with a brass-and-stained-wood handle or a jackknife decorated with mother-of-pearl. I found a broken jackknife with a shattered handle that I taped back together around the bent steel tang. I carried that knife all the time until my cousin Grey took pity and gave me a better one.

Uncle Earle was my favorite of all my uncles. He was known as black Earle for three counties around. Mama said he was called Black Earle for that black black hair that fell over his eyes in a great soft curl, but Aunt Raylene said it was for his black black heart. He was a good-looking man, soft-spoken and hardworking. He told Mama that all the girls loved him because he looked like Elvis Presley, only skinny and with muscles. In a way he did, but his face was etched with lines and sunburned a deep red-brown. The truth was he had none of Elvis Presley's baby-faced innocence; he had a devilish look and a body Aunt Alma swore was made for sex. He was a big man, long and lanky, with wide hands marked with scars. "Earle looks like trouble coming in on greased skids," my uncle Beau laughed. All the aunts agreed, their cheeks wrinkling around indulgent smiles while their fingers trailed across Uncle Earle's big shoulders as sweetly and tenderly as the threadlike feet of hummingbirds.

Uncle Earle always seemed to have money in his pockets, some job he was just leaving and another one he was about to take up. His wife had left him around the time Lyle Parsons died, because of what she called his lying ways. He wouldn't stay away from women, and that made her mad. Teresa was Catholic and took her vows seriously, which Earle had expected, but he had never imagined she would leave him for messing around with girls he would never have married and didn't love. His anger and grief over losing her and his three daughters gave him an underlying bitterness that seemed to make him just that much more attractive.

"That Earle's got the magic," Aunt Ruth told me. "Man is just a magnet to women. Breaks their hearts and makes them like it." She shook her head and smiled at me. "All these youngsters playing at being something, imagining they can drive women wild with their narrow little hips and sweet baby smiles, they never gonna have the gift Earle has, don't even know enough to recognize it for what it is. A sad wounded man who genuinely likes women—that's what Earle is, a hurt little boy with just enough meanness in him to keep a woman interested."

She pushed my hair back off my face and ran her thumb over my eyebrows, smoothing down the fine black hairs. "Your real daddy . . ." She paused, looked around, and started again. "He had some of that too, just enough, anyway, to win your mama. He liked women too, and that's something I can say for him. A man who really likes women always has a touch of magic."

There weren't any pictures of my real daddy, and Mama wouldn't talk to me about him—no more than she would about the rest of the family. It was Granny who told me what a pissant he was; told me he lived up near Blackburn with a wife and six children who didn't even know I existed; said he sold insurance to colored people out in the county and had never been in jail a day in his life. "A sorry excuse for a man," she called him, making me feel kind of wretched until Aunt Alma swore he hadn't been that bad, just pissed everybody off when he wouldn't come back and ask Granny's forgiveness after she ran him off.

"Eight days after you were born," Aunt Alma told me, "he came around while Granny was over at the mill to settle some trouble with one of the boys. Anney wasn't sure she wanted to see him at all, but Raylene and I persuaded her to let him see you while she stayed in the back bedroom. That boy was scared shitless, holding you in hands stained dark green where he'd been painting his daddy's flatbed truck. You just looked at him with your black Indian eyes like he wasn't nothing but a servant, lifting you up for some air or something. Then you let loose and pissed a pailful all down his sleeves, the front of his shirt, and right down his pants halfway to his knees! You peed all over the son of a bitch!"

Aunt Alma hugged me up onto her lap. Her grin was so wide it made her nose seem small. She looked like she'd been waiting to tell me this story since I was born, waiting to praise and thank me for this thing I didn't even know I had done.

"It's like you were putting out your mama's opinion, speaking up for her there on his lap. And that boy seemed to know just what it meant, with your baby piss stinking up his clothes for all to smell. He passed you right over to me like you were gonna go on to drown him if he didn't hurry. Took off without speaking to your mama and never came back again. When we heard he'd married another little girl was already carrying his baby, Earle joked that the boy was just too fertile for his own good, that he couldn't plow a woman without making children, and maybe it's true. With the six he's got legal, and you, and the others people say he's got scattered from Spartanburg to Greer, he's been a kind of one-man population movement. You got family you an't ever gonna know is your own—all of you with that dark dark hair he had himself." She grinned at me, reaching out to push my midnight-black hair back off my face.

"Oh, Bone!" she laughed. "Maybe you should plan on marrying yourself a blond just to be safe. Huh?"

Granny wouldn't talk much about my real daddy except to curse his name, but she told me just about everything else. She would lean back in her chair and start reeling out story and memory, making no distinction between what she knew to be true and what she had only heard told. The tales she told me in her rough, drawling whisper were lilting songs, ballads of family, love, and disappointment. Everything seemed to come back to grief and blood, and everybody seemed legendary.

"My granddaddy, your great-great-granddaddy, he was a Cherokee, and he didn't much like us, all his towheaded grandchildren. Some said he had another family down to Eustis anyway, a proper Indian wife who gave him black-haired babies with blue eyes. Ha! Blue eyes an't that rare among the Cherokee around here. Me, I always thought it a shame we never turned up with them like his other babies. Of course, he was a black-eyed bastard himself, and maybe he never really made those other babies like they say. What was certain was my grandma never stepped out on him. Woman was just obsessed with that man, obsessed to the point of madness. Used to cry like a dog in the night when he was gone. He didn't stay round that much either, but every time he come home she'd make another baby, another red-blond child with muddy brown eyes that he'd treat like a puppydog or a kitten. Man never spanked a child in his life, never hit Grandma. You'd think he would have, he didn't seem to care all that much. Quiet man, too. Wouldn't fight, wouldn't barely talk. Not a Boatwright, that's for sure.

"But we loved him, you know, almost as much as Grandma. Would have killed to win his attention even one more minute than we got, and near died to be any way more like him, though we were as different from him as children can be. None of us quiet, all of us fighters. None of us got those blue eyes, and no one but you got that blue-black hair. Lord, you were a strange thing! You were like a fat red-faced doll with all that black black hair—a baby doll with a full head of hair. Just as quiet and sweet-natured as he used to be. You didn't even cry till you took croup at four months. I've always thought he'd have liked you, Granddaddy would. You even got a little of the shine of him. Those dark eyes and that hair when you was born, black as midnight. I was there to see."

"Oh, hell," Earle laughed when I repeated some of Granny's stories. "Every third family in Greenville County swears it's part of Cherokee Nation. Whether our great-granddaddy was or wasn't, it don't really make a titty's worth of difference. You're a Boatwright, Bone, even if you are the strangest girl-child we got."

I looked at him carefully, keeping my Cherokee eyes level and my face blank. I could not have said a word if Great-Great-Granddaddy had been standing there looking back at me with my own black eyes.

Mama wore her hair cut short, curled, and bleached. Every other month she and Aunt Alma would get together and do each other's hair, rinsing Aunt Alma's in beer or lemon juice to lighten it just a little, trimming Mama's back and bleaching it that dark blond she liked. Then they'd set pin curls for each other, and while those dried they would coax Reese into sitting still long enough that her baby-fine red locks could be tied up in rags. I would tear up the rags, rinse pins, strain the juice through a cloth happily enough, but I refused the perm Mama was always insisting she wanted to give me.

"Stinks and hurts," I complained. "Do it to Reese."

"Oh, Reese don't need it. Look at this." And Aunt Alma tugged a few of Reese's springy long curls free from the rags. Like soft corkscrews, the curls bounced and swung as if they were magical. "This child has the best hair in the world, just like yours, Anney, when you were a baby. Yours had a little red to it too, seems to me."

"No." Mama shook her head while she pulled more rags out of Reese's curls. "You know my hair was just blond. You had the red touch, you and Ruth. Remember how you used to fight over whose was darker?"

"Oh, but you had the prettiest hair!" Aunt Alma turned to me. "Your mama had the prettiest hair you ever saw. Soft? Why, it would make Reese's feel like steel wire. It was the softest hair in Greenville County, and gold as sunlight on sheets. It didn't go dark till she had you girls, a little bit with you and all dark with Reese. Hair will do that, you know, darken in pregnancy. An't nothing that will stop it once it starts."

Mama laughed. "Remember when Carr first got pregnant and swore she'd shave her head if it looked like it was gonna go dark?"

Aunt Alma nodded, her dark brown pin curls bobbing. "Rinsed it in piss, she did, every Sunday evening, Tommy Lee's baby piss that she begged off Ruth. All 'cause Granny swore baby-piss rinses would keep her blond."

"Didn't she stink?" I bit at the rubber tip of a hairpin, peeling the coating off the metal so I could taste the sweet iron tang underneath.

"Baby piss don't stink," Aunt Alma told me, "unless the baby's sick, and Tommy Lee wasn't never sick a day in his life. Carr didn't smell no different than she ever did, but her hair went dark anyway. It's the price of babies."

"Oh, it an't that." Mama pulled me up onto her lap and started the arduous process of brushing out my hair. "All us Boatwrights go dark as we get older. It's just the way it goes. Blond goes red or brown, and darker and darker. An't none of us stays a blond once we're grown."

"'Cept you, honey," Aunt Alma grinned.

"Yeah, but I got Clairol, don't I?" Mama laughed and hugged me. "What you think, Alma? Should I cut this mop or not? She can't keep it neat to save her life, hates me pulling on it when I try to brush it out."

"Hell yes, cut it. I'll get the bowl. We'll trim it right down to her neck."

"*Noooo!*" I howled, and wrapped my hands around my head. "I want my hair. I want my hair."

"But you won't let us do nothing with it, honey."

"No! No! No! It's my hair and I want it. I want it long and tangled and just the way it is."

Aunt Alma reached over and took the hairpin out of my mouth. "Lord, look at her," she said. "Stubborn as the day is long."

"Uh-huh." Mama put both hands on my shoulders and squeezed. She didn't sound angry. I raised my head to look at her. Her brown eyes were enormous close up, with little flecks of light in the pupils. I could almost see myself between the flashes of gold.

"Well, what you expect, huh?"

I looked back at Aunt Alma. Her eyes were the same warm brown, deep and shining with the same gold lights, and I realized suddenly that she had the same cheekbones as Mama, the same mouth.

"She's just like you."

My mouth wasn't like that, or my face either. Worse, my black eyes had no gold. I didn't look like anybody at all.

"You, you mean," said Mama.

She and Aunt Alma nodded together above me, grinning at each other in complete agreement. I loosened my hands from around my skull slowly, letting Mama start brushing out my hair. Reese put her pudgy little fingers in her mouth and stared at me solemnly. "B-Bone," she stammered.

"Yes," Aunt Alma agreed, hefting Reese up in her arms. "Our stubborn Bone is just like her mama, Reesecup. Just like her aunts, just like a Boatwright, and just like you."

"But I don't look like nobody," I wailed.

Aunt Alma laughed. "Why, you look like our Bone, girl."

"I don't look like Mama. I don't look like you. I don't look like nobody."

"You look like me," Mama said. "You look like my own baby girl." She put her fingers delicately on my cheeks, pressing under my eyes. "You got the look, all right. I can see it, see what it's gonna be like when you grow bigger, these bones here." Her fingers slipped smoothly down over my mouth and chin. "And here. You gonna look like our granddaddy, for sure. Those Cherokee cheekbones, huh, Alma?"

"Oh yes, for sure. She's gonna be another one, another beauty to worry about."

I smiled wide, not really believing them but wanting to. I held still then, trying not to flinch as Mama began to brush relentlessly at my knotted hair. If I got a permanent, I would lose those hours on Mama's lap sitting in the curve of her arm while she brushed and brushed and smoothed my hair and talked soft above me. She always seemed to smell of buttery flour, salt, and fingernail polish—a delicate insinuating aroma of the familiar and the astringent. I would breathe deep and bite my lips to keep from moaning while my scalp ached and burned. I would have cut off my head before I let them cut my hair and lost the unspeakable pleasure of being drawn up onto Mama's lap every evening.

"Do I look like my daddy?" I asked.

There was silence. Mama brushed steadily while Aunt Alma finished pulling the rags from Reese's hair.

"Do I? Like my daddy, Mama?"

Mama gathered all my hair up in one hand and picked at the ends with the side of the brush. "Alma, get me some of that sweet oil, honey, just a little for my palm. That's enough."

The brush started again in long sweeping strokes. Aunt Alma started to hum. I dropped my head. It wasn't even that I was so insistent on knowing anything about my missing father. I wouldn't have minded a lie. I just wanted the story Mama would have told. What was the thing she wouldn't tell me, the first thing, the place where she had made herself different from all her brothers and sisters and shut her mouth on her life?

Mama brushed so hard she pulled my head all the way back. "You just don't know how to sit still, Bone."

"No, Mama."

I closed my eyes and let her move my head, let her pull and jerk my hair until she relaxed a little. Aunt Alma was humming softly. The smell of sweet oil on Mama's fingers hung in the air. Reese's singsong joined Aunt Alma's hum. I opened my eyes and looked into Mama's. You could see Reese's baby smile in those eyes. In the pupils gold flecks gleamed and glittered, like pieces of something bright reflecting light.

Larry Brown

(1951–   )

Larry Brown was born in Oxford, Mississippi, on July 9, 1951. On August 17, 1974, he married Mary Annie Coleman. They are the parents of Billy Ray, Shane, and LeAnne. Brown attended the University of Mississippi in 1982. An enthusiastic reader, Brown is a self-taught writer who studied the works of Raymond Carver, Flannery O'Connor, Stephen King, and William Faulkner.

Facing the Music (1988) won an award for literature from the Mississippi Institute of Arts and Letters in 1990. Other books include *Dirty Work* (1989); *Big Bad Love* (1990); *Joe* (1991); *On Fire* (1995); and *Father and Son* (1997). Brown's home is Oxford, Mississippi.

Facing the Music

For Richard Howorth

I cut my eyes sideways because I know what's coming. "You want the light off, honey?" she says. Very quietly.

I can see as well with it as without it. It's an old movie I'm watching, Ray Milland in *The Lost Weekend.* This character he's playing, this guy will do anything to get a drink. He'd sell children, probably, to get a drink. That's the kind of person Ray's playing.

Sometimes I have trouble resting at night, so I watch the movies until I get sleepy. They show them—all-night movies—on these stations from Memphis and Tupelo. There are probably a lot of people like me, unable to sleep, lying around watching them with me. I've got remote control so I can turn it on or off and change channels. She's stirring around the bedroom, doing things, doing something—I don't know what. She has to stay busy. Our children moved away and we don't have any pets. We used to have a dog, a little brown one, but I accidentally killed it. Backed over its head with the station wagon one morning. She used to feed it in the kitchen, right after she came home from the hospital. But I told her, no more. It hurts too much to lose one.

"It doesn't matter," I say, finally, which is not what I'm thinking.

"That's Ray Milland," she says. "Wasn't he young then." Wistful like.

So he was. I was too once. So was she. So was everybody. But this movie is forty years old.

"You going to finish watching this?" she says. She sits on the bed right beside me. I'm propped up on the TV pillow. It's blue corduroy and I got it for Christmas last year. She said I was spending so much time in the bed, I might as well be comfortable. She also said it could be used for other things, too. I said what things?

I don't know why I have to be so mean to her, like it's her fault. She asks me if I want some more ice. I'm drinking whiskey. She knows it helps me. I'm not so much of a bastard that I don't know she loves me.

Actually, it's worse than that. I don't mean anything against God by saying this, but sometimes I think she worships me.

"I'm okay," I say. Ray has his booze hanging out the window on a string—hiding it from these booze-thieves he's trying to get away from—and before long he'll have to face the music. Ray can never find a good place to hide his booze. He gets so drunk he can't remember where he hid it when he sobers up. Later on, he's going to try to write a novel, pecking the title and his name out with two fingers. But he's going to have a hard time. Ray is crazy about that booze, and doesn't even know how to type.

She may start rubbing on me. That's what I have to watch out for. That's what she does. She gets in bed with me when I'm watching a movie and she starts rubbing on me. I can't stand it. I especially can't stand for the light to be on when she does it. If the light's on when she does it, she winds up crying in the bathroom. That's the kind of husband I am.

But everything's okay, so far. She's not rubbing on me yet. I go ahead and mix myself another drink. I've got a whole bottle beside the bed. We had our Christmas party at the fire station the other night and everybody got a fifth. My wife didn't attend. She said every person in there would look at her. I told her they wouldn't, but I didn't argue much. I was on duty anyway and couldn't drink anything. All I could do was eat my steak and look around, go get another cup of coffee.

"I could do something for you," she says. She's teasing but she means it. I have to smile. One of those frozen ones. I feel like shooting both of us because she's fixed her hair up nice and she's got on a new nightgown.

"I could turn the lamp off," she says.

I have to be very careful. If I say the wrong thing, she'll take it the wrong way. She'll wind up crying in the bathroom if I say the wrong thing. I don't know what to say. Ray's just met this good-looking chick—Jane Wyman?—and I know he's going to steal a lady's purse later on; I don't want to miss it. I could do the things Ray Milland is doing in this movie and worse. Boy. Could I. But she's right over here beside my face wanting an answer. Now. She's smiling at me. She's licking her lips. I don't want to give in. Giving in leads to other things, other givings.

I have to say something. But I don't say anything.

She gets up and goes back over to her dressing table. She picks up her brush. I can hear her raking and tearing it through her hair. It sounds like she's ripping it out by the roots. I have to stay here and listen to it. I can understand why people jump off bridges.

"You want a drink?" I say. "I can mix you up a little bourbon and Coke."

"I've got some," she says, and she lifts her can to show me. Diet Coke. At least a six-pack a day. The refrigerator's crammed full of them. I can hardly get to my beer for them. I think they're only one calorie or something. She thinks she's fat and that's the reason I don't pay enough attention to her, but it isn't.

She's been hurt. I know she has. You can lie around the house all your life and think you're safe. But you're not. Something from outside or inside can reach out and get you. You can get sick and have to go to the hospital. Some nut could walk into the station one night and kill us all in our beds. You can read about things like that in the paper any morning you want to. I try not to think about it. I just do my job and then come home and try to stay in the house with her. But sometimes I can't.

Last week, I was in this bar in town. I'd gone down there with some of these boys we're breaking in, rookies. Just young boys, nineteen or twenty. They'd passed probation and wanted to celebrate, so a few of us older guys went with them. We drank a few pitchers and listened to the band. It was a pretty good band. They did a lot of Willie and Waylon stuff. I'm thinking about all this while she's getting up and moving around the room, looking out the windows.

I don't go looking for things—I don't—but later on, well, there was this woman in there. Not a young woman. Younger than me. About forty. She was sitting by herself. I was in no hurry to go home. All the boys had gone, Bradshaw, too. I was the only one of the group left. So I said what the hell. I went up to the bar and bought two drinks and carried them over to her table. I sat down with them and I smiled at her. And she smiled back. In an hour we were over at her house.

I don't know why I did it. I'd never done anything like that before. She had some money. You could tell it from her house and things. I was a little drunk, but I know that's no excuse. She took me into her bedroom and she put a record on, some nice slow orchestra or something. I was lying on the bed the whole time, knowing my wife was at home waiting up on me. This woman stood up in the middle of the room and started turning. She had her arms over her head. She had white hair piled up high. When she took off her jacket, I could tell she had something nice underneath. She took off her shirt, and her breasts were like something you'd see in a movie, deep long things you might only glimpse in a swimming suit. Before I knew it, she was on the bed with me, putting one of them in my mouth.

"You sure you don't want a drink?" I say.

"I want you," she says, and I don't know what to say. She's not looking at me. She's looking out the window. Ray's coming out of the bathroom now with the lady's purse under his arm. But I know they're all going to be waiting for him, the whole club. I know what he's going to feel. Everybody's going to be looking at him.

When this woman got on top of me, the only thing I could think was: God.

"What are we going to do?" my wife says.

"Nothing," I say. But I don't know what I'm saying. I've got these big soft nipples in my mouth and I can't think of anything else. I'm trying to remember exactly how it was.

I thought I'd be different somehow, changed. I thought she'd know what I'd done just by looking at me. But she didn't. She didn't even notice.

I look at her and her shoulders are jerking under the little green gown. I'm always making her cry and I don't mean to. Here's the kind of bastard I am: my wife's crying because she wants me, and I'm lying here watching Ray Milland, and drinking whiskey, and thinking about putting another woman's breasts in my mouth. She was on top of me and they were hanging right over my face. It was so wonderful, but now it seems so awful I can hardly stand to think about it.

"I understand how you feel," she says. "But how do you think I feel?"

She's not talking to me; she's talking to the window and Ray is staggering down the street in the hot sunshine, looking for a pawnshop so he can hock the typewriter he was going to use to write his novel.

A commercial comes on, a man selling dog food. I can't just sit here and not say anything. I have to say something. But, God, it hurts to.

"I know," I say. It's almost the same as saying nothing. It doesn't mean anything.

We've been married for twenty-three years.

"You don't know," she says. "You don't know the things that go through my mind."

I know what she's going to say. I know the things going through her mind. She's seeing me on top of her with her legs over my shoulders, her legs locked around my back. But she won't take her gown off anymore. She'll just push it up. She never takes her gown off, doesn't want me to see. I know what will happen. I can't do anything about it. Before long she'll be over here rubbing on me, and if I don't start, she'll stop and wind up crying in the bathroom.

"Why don't you have a drink?" I say. I wish she'd have a drink. Or go to sleep. Or just watch the movie with me. Why can't she just watch the movie with me?

"I should have just died," she says. "Then you could have gotten you somebody else."

I guess maybe she means somebody like the friendly woman with the nice house and the nice nipples.

I don't know. I can't find a comfortable place for my neck. "You shouldn't say that."

"Well it's true. I'm not a whole woman anymore. I'm just a burden on you."

"You're not."

"Well you don't want me since the operation."

She's always saying that. She wants me to admit it. And I don't want to lie anymore, I don't want to spare her feelings anymore, I want her to know I've got feelings too and it's hurt me almost as bad as it has her. But that's not what I say. I can't say that.

"I do want you," I say. I have to say it. She makes me say it.

"Then prove it," she says. She comes close to the bed and she leans over me. She's painted her brows with black stuff and her face is made up to where I can hardly believe it.

"You've got too much makeup on," I whisper.

She leaves. She's in the bathroom scrubbing. I can hear the water running. Ray's got the blind staggers. Everybody's hiding his whiskey from him and he can't get a drink. He's got it bad. He's on his way to the nuthouse.

Don't feel like a lone ranger, Ray.

The water stops running. She cuts the light off in there and then she steps out. I don't look around. I'm watching a hardware store commercial. Hammers and Skilsaws are on the wall. They always have this pretty girl with large breasts selling their hardware. The big special this week is garden hose. You can buy a hundred feet, she says, for less than four dollars.

The TV is just a dim gray spot between my socks. She's getting on the bed, setting one knee down and pulling up the hem of her gown. She can't wait. I'm thinking of it again, how the woman's breasts looked, how she looked in her shirt before she took it off, how I could tell she had something nice underneath, and how wonderful it was to be drunk in that moment when I knew what she was going to do.

It's time now. She's touching me. Her hands are moving, sliding all over me. Everywhere. Ray is typing with two fingers somewhere, just the title and his name. I can hear the pecking of his keys. That old boy, he's trying to do what he knows he should. He has responsibilities to people who love him and need him; he can't let them down. But he's scared to death. He doesn't know where to start.

"You going to keep watching this?" she says, but dreamy-like, kissing me, as if she doesn't care one way or the other.

I don't say anything when I cut the TV off. I can't speak. I'm thinking of how it was on our honeymoon, in that little room at Hattiesburg, when she bent her arms behind her back and slumped her shoulders forward, how the cups loosened and fell as the straps slid off her arms. I'm thinking that your first love is your best love, that you'll never find any better. The way she did it was like she was saying, here I am, I'm all yours, all of me, forever. Nothing's changed. She turns the light off, and we reach to find each other in the darkness like people who are blind.

Pat Conroy

(1945–   )

Pat Conroy, the first child of seven, was born on October 26, 1945, in Atlanta, Georgia. His father, a career military officer, moved the family to various military bases in the South. Conroy attended the Citadel Military Academy in Charleston, South Carolina. After graduation, he taught English in Beaufort, South Carolina, where he married Barbara Bolling. He then taught English on Daufuskie Island (located off the coast of South Carolina); however, he was fired for his innovative teaching practices. In *The Water Is Wide* (1972), he describes the conditions that the students experienced. For this work, he won an award from the National Education Association, and the book was made into the film *Conrack*.

Conroy and his wife moved to Atlanta, following the birth of their daughter, Megan. They were divorced in 1977 after the publication of *The Great Santini* (1976). This novel and *The Lords of Discipline* (1980) were both made into movies. Conroy moved to Rome, Italy, to write *The Prince of Tides* (1986). The novel was made into a film starring Nick Nolte, for which he received an Oscar nomination. *Beach Music* was published in 1995. Conroy lives in San Francisco and South Carolina.

from *The Prince of Tides*

I grew up loathing Good Fridays. It was a seasonal aversion that had little to do with theology but everything to do with the rites of worship and the odd slant my grandfather brought to his overenthusiastic commemoration of Christ's passion.

Good Friday was the day when Amos Wingo each year walked to the shed behind his house in Colleton proper and dusted off the ninety-pound wooden cross he had made in a violent seizure of religious extravagance when he was a boy of fourteen. From noon to three on that commemorative day he would walk up and down the length of the Street of Tides to remind the backsliding, sinful citizenry of my hometown of the unimaginable suffering of Jesus Christ on that melancholy hill above Jerusalem so long ago. It was the summit and the Grand Guignol of my grandfather's liturgical year; it embodied characteristics of both the saints and the asylum. There was always a lunatic beauty to his walk.

I would have preferred that my grandfather celebrated Good Friday in a quieter, more contemplative fashion. It embarrassed me deeply to watch his gaunt, angular body bent under the weight of the cross, trudging through the congested traffic, stopping at intersections, oblivious to the admixture of scorn and awe of his townsmen, sweat discoloring his costume, and his lips moving continuously in the inaudible worship of his Creator. He was a figure of majesty to some, a perfect jackass to others.

Each year the sheriff would issue a ticket for obstructing traffic and each year the parishioners of the Baptist church would take up a special collection to pay the fine. Through the years, his offbeat spiritual trek of remembrance had become something of a venerated annual phenomenon and had begun to attract a sizable in-gathering of pilgrims and tourists who collected along the Street of Tides to pray and read the Bible as Grandpa Wingo huffed and puffed his way through his solemn reenactment of the single walk that changed the history of the Western soul. Each year the *Colleton Gazette* published a photograph of his walk the week following Easter Sunday.

When we were children, both Savannah and I would beg him to take his act to Charleston or Columbia, cities we considered to be far more gaudy and reprehensible in the eyes of the Lord than small, mild Colleton could ever be. My grandmother expressed her own mortification by retreating to her bedroom with a full bottle of Beefeater gin and a collection of back issues of *Police Gazette* that she had commandeered from Fender's barbershop. When the walk was completed at three, so was the bottle, and my grandmother would be comatose until late the next morning. When she awoke to her memorial headache, she would find my grandfather on his knees, praying for her sweet, boozy soul.

During the entire Easter vigil, Amos would watch over the recumbent, motionless body of his wife, who had elaborated her own ritual as an act of self-defense to protest the ceremony of observance he insisted on performing. There was a bizarre euphony in the counterbalance of their spirits. On Sunday morning, sickened by her debauch but having made her annual point, my grandmother, as she put it, "rose from the goddamn dead" in time to accompany my grandfather to Easter Sunday services. It was her only church appearance of the year and, in its own way, became as traditional in the spiritual life of the town as my grandfather's walk.

In my junior year, on the Wednesday before Easter, I walked to my grandfather's house after school with Savannah. We stopped by Long's Pharmacy for a cherry Coke and took it out by the river and drank it sitting on the sea wall, watching the fiddler crabs wave their claws in the mud below us.

"Good Friday is coming up again," I said to my sister. "I hate that day."

She grinned and punched me on the arm, saying, "It's good for a family to face total humiliation once a year. It's character-building to have a whole town laugh at your grandfather, then laugh at you."

"I wouldn't mind it if I didn't have to be there," I answered, my eyes fixed on the hypnotic movement of the crabs beneath us. They were like quarters scattered randomly across the mud. "Dad's putting you on the lemonade stand this year. He's going to film the major highlights of the walk again."

"Oh, grotesque," she said. "He's filmed it for the past five years. He's got five years of film to prove to any court that grandpa's a lunatic."

"Dad says it's for the family archives and that we'll thank him one day for making a record of our childhood."

"Oh, sure," she said. "That's all I want. A photographic history of Auschwitz. Of course, you think this is a normal family."

"I don't know if it's a normal family or not," I said. "It's the only family I've ever lived in."

"It's a nut-house factory. Mark my words."

My grandfather's house in Colleton was a simple one-story frame house, painted white with red trim, built on a half acre of land beside the Colleton River. When we entered the house we found our grandmother in the kitchen watching my grandfather work on his cross in the back yard.

"There he is," she said in a weary, exasperated voice, nodding toward the back yard as she saw us enter. "Your grandpa. My husband. The village idiot. He's been working on his prop all day."

"What's he doing to it, Tolitha?" I asked, calling her by her given name according to her own desires.

"A wheel," Savannah said, laughing as she ran to the window.

"He said folks won't mind a sixty-year-old man putting a wheel on his cross. He said that Jesus was only thirty-three when he took a walk up that hill, so no one should expect a sixty-year-old man to do much better. He gets softer in the head each year. I'm going to have to put him in a home soon. No question about it. The highway patrol was out here again this week trying to get him to hand in his driver's license. They say he's a danger on the road every time he takes his Ford for a spin."

"Why did you marry him, Tolitha?" Savannah asked. "It seems ridiculous that two people so different in every way could live together."

My grandmother looked out toward the yard again, the window reflected off her glasses in a trapezoid of light, repeating in glass what she saw from the window. The question had taken her by surprise and I realized Savannah had asked one of those forbidden questions, one with daunting implications, whose mystery predated our own birth.

"Let me get you some iced tea," Tolitha said finally. "He'll dawdle in here in a while and I don't get a chance to visit with you so much now that you're grown and out spoonin' and such."

She poured three huge glasses of tea, then floated mint leaves above the chipped ice. When she sat on her stool, she adjusted her eyeglasses over her nose.

"I knew your grandpa was a Christian man when I first met him. That's because everybody in town was Christian then. I was a Christian, too, only I was fourteen when we got married, too young to know anything one way or the other. It wasn't until later that I realized he was a fanatic. He kind of hid it from me when we were courting because he was so riled up and eager to get at me."

"Tolitha," I said, totally embarrassed.

"You're such a child sometimes, Tom," Savannah said. "You act like you were snake-bit every time the subject of sex comes up."

My grandmother laughed and continued. "I stirred him up good when I was a girl-child, and I never heard nothing much about Jesus when I had him beneath the sheets in those early years."

"Tolitha, please, for God's sake," I begged. "We don't want to hear all that."

"Yes, we do," Savannah disagreed. "It's fascinating."

"Who but a weirdo like you wants to hear a play-by-play description of sex between their grandparents?"

"Then, as the years passed, he got tired of me as all men do and he started praying to our Lord on what you might call a twenty-four-hour basis until he got kind of soft in the head about it. Never made a decent living in his life. Just cut hair, sold a few Bibles, and ran his mouth about heaven and hell and everything in between."

"But he's such a good man," I interjected.

She turned and gazed out the window at my grandfather. There was no ardor in her gaze, but there was softness and an abiding affection. He was still hunched over his cross, attaching a rubber tricycle wheel to its base. "People ask me all the time what it's like being married to a saint. Boring, I tell them. Better to marry a devil. I've tasted a little bit of heaven in my life and a little bit of hell and I'll take hell every time. But what you say is true, Tom. He is a mighty fine man."

"Why did you leave him during the Depression?" Savannah asked, encouraged by her openness, the guileless spillage of old secrets. "Dad won't even talk about it."

"I guess you're old enough to know," she said, turning toward us, her voice suddenly despondent, almost dreamy. "In the middle of the Depression, he quit his job and started preaching the Lord's word down in front of Baitery's Pharmacy. That paid even less money than barbering. He got it into his head that the Depression was a sign that the world was going to end. It was easy to think that. A lot of boys got the same idea about that time. We were starving or close to it. I didn't cotton too much to starving. I told Amos I was leaving him. Of course, he didn't believe me because folks didn't divorce in those days. I told him to take care of your father or I'd come back and kill him, and I hitched a ride and headed for Atlanta. I got a job at Rich's department store the same week. After a while, I met Papa John and married him a couple of days later."

"That's horrible, Tolitha," I said. "That's the worst thing I ever heard."

"That's the saint out in the back yard, Tom," she said, her eyes narrowing behind the glasses, her eyebrows touching like two slightly mismatched caterpillars. "The woman is here in the kitchen. I'm not proud of everything I did, but I'll tell you everything I did."

"No wonder Dad's so screwed up," I said, whistling.

"Shut up, Tom. You're such a traditionalist," Savannah said archly. "You don't understand a thing about survival."

"I did the best I could under the circumstances. Seemed like the whole world went a little crazy around that time and I didn't get no exemption."

"Go on," I said, "before Grandpa gets in here."

"Don't worry about Grandpa. He'll be playing with that cross until dinnertime. Well, it was hardest on your father. I'll admit that. He was only eleven or so when I brought him up to Atlanta, and he hadn't seen me in maybe five years. He hardly even knew me and couldn't understand either why I had left or why he had to call me Tolitha and not Mama. He used to cry out in his sleep, 'Mama, Mama, Mama,' and Papa John used to hear it and it liked to break his sweet heart. He would go in and sing Greek songs to your daddy until he went back to sleep. Your daddy didn't know no Tolitha and didn't want to know her. I'd do it differently now. Honestly, I would. But now isn't then. And there's no returning to then."

"It's hard to see Dad as a tragic figure," Savannah said., "Especially a tragic child. I can't even imagine him as a little kid."

"Did you have other husbands, Tolitha?" I asked.

"Ha," she laughed. "Your mother's been talking again."

"No," I said quickly, "I've just heard rumors around town."

"After Papa John died I was half crazy with grief. I took the money he left me, and it was a fair sum, I mean to tell you, and lit out for all these places I heard about. Hong Kong, Africa, India. I went around the world, traveling by ship. First class from port to port. And I had this problem. Everybody's always loved me. Especially men. I'm just that kind of person. Men just love to buzz around me like there was a sweet smell coming from me. I just sat there and watched 'em line up trying to make me laugh or buy me a couple of drinks. I married a couple of those old boys. The longest lasted about six months. That marriage lasted exactly the time it took to sail from Madagascar to Capetown. He wanted me to do unmentionable, filthy things to him."

"What unmentionable, filthy things?" Savannah asked breathlessly, leaning toward my grandmother.

"No. No. don't ask her that," I pleaded. "Don't ask her."

"Why?" Savannah asked me.

"Because she'll tell us, Savannah. She'll tell us and it will be something horrible and embarrassing."

"He wanted me to suck the area where his legs met," my grandmother explained, rather primly for her, I had to admit. She always told you a bit more than you ever wanted to hear.

"How disgusting," Savannah said.

"He had animal appetites," Tolitha said. "It was a nightmare."

"Why did you come back to Grandpa?" I asked, wanting to steer the conversation from animal appetites.

She turned her gaze toward me and lifted her glass of tea to her lips. For a moment I thought she wasn't going to answer, or couldn't.

"I got tired, Tom. Real tired. And I was starting to get old, to look old, to feel old. I knew Amos would always be here by the river and always be waiting for me. I knew I could light down here and he would never say a word to me. He'd just be thankful I came back. Your Daddy's the same way about Lila. He's only been interested in a single woman his whole life. Just like his father. It just goes to show you that it's easier for blood to carry a fanatic down to a new generation than whatever it was that made everyone love me."

"But everyone loves Grandpa, too," I said, suddenly feeling sorry for the man in the background.

"They love him because he's a fanatic, Tom. Because he picks up that cross each year. But I say who needs a saint? I'd rather have a drink and a couple of laughs."

"But you love Grandpa, don't you, Tolitha?" I insisted.

"Love." She turned the word over in her mouth like a flavorless lozenge. "Yes, I suppose I do love him. You have to love what you can always come back to, what's home waiting for you. I was thinking about time the other day. Not love, but time, and they're related somehow but I'm not smart enough to know how exactly. I was married to your grandfather and to Papa John for about the same amount of time. But when I look back at my life it seems I was married to Papa John for a few days. That's how happy I was. Seems like I was married to your grandpa for a thousand years."

"This is an adult conversation," Savannah announced proudly. "I've been waiting for a long time to have a truly adult conversation."

"Your parents are just trying to protect you from things they don't think children should know, Savannah. They don't approve of the life I've led. But since it's an adult conversation, I don't think they need to know anything about it."

"I'd never tell," Savannah said. "But Tom can be such a child sometimes."

I ignored Savannah and asked Tolitha, "Do you think Dad ever got over being left when he was a little boy?"

"Do you mean do I think he's forgiven me, Tom?" she said. "I think so. In family matters you can get over anything. That's one thing you'll learn as an adult. There's a lot you have to learn which is a lot worse than that. You'd never think of forgiving a friend for some of the things your parents did to you. But with friends it's different. Friends aren't the roll of the dice."

"I need to help Grandpa fix up his cross," I said.

"Yeah, and I need to get to the liquor store," Tolitha said.

"You plan to get liquored up again on Good Friday?" I asked.

"Tom, you are so rude," Savannah said.

Tolitha laughed and said, "That's the only civilized response to his walk I can think of. It also reminds him that he doesn't own me and never will. It's my way of telling him how ridiculous the whole thing is. Of course, he talked it over with God a few days ago and got the go-ahead, so there's no talking sense into him."

"He's just being a good Christian. That's what he told me," I said. "He said if the world was acting right, the whole town of Colleton would be out there with crosses walking with him."

"Then they'd lock the whole town up. No, Tom. I'm not saying anything against being a good Christian. Believe me. I want you to be a good Christian man; just don't take it so goddamn seriously."

"Are you a good Christian, Tolitha?" asked Savannah. "Do you think you're going to heaven?"

"I've never done one thing in my life that makes me deserve to burn in hell for all eternity. Any god that does that isn't deserving of the name. I've tried hard to live an interesting life and I don't see any harm that comes from that."

"Don't you think Grandpa's led an interesting life, too?" I said.

"Tom, you ask the silliest questions," Savannah scolded.

"Remember, Tom, whenever you consider what makes up an interesting life, think of this. When your grandpa was cutting hair and your mom and dad were picking crabs and heading shrimp, I was coming through the Khyber Pass, riding into Afghanistan disguised as an Afghan warrior. I'm probably the only person you'll meet who's ever done that."

"But you're back here, Tolitha. What good did it do you if you have to end up back here in Colleton? Back where you started?" I asked.

"It means that I ran out of money," she said. "It means I failed to do what I set out to do."

"I think you're the only success our family has produced, Tolitha," Savannah said. "I really do. You're the only reason I know I can escape from all this."

"You got Tolitha written all over you, Savannah. You have ever since you were a little girl. But play it smarter than me. I had the wildness in me. I didn't have the smarts. It was harder for women back then. Much harder. But try to get out if you can. Colleton's a sweet poison, but poison nonetheless. Once it gets into a soul it can never wash out. It's funny. But all the places I saw in Europe, Africa, and Asia, some were so beautiful it would make you cry. But none of them was more beautiful than Colleton and that's the truth. None of them could make me forget the marsh and the river right out yonder. The smell of this place rides in the bones wherever you go. I don't know if that's a good or a bad thing."

She rose and lit the fire in the stove. The afternoon was still and the air was cool and silken in the late afternoon. A barge, laden with a cargo of timber, urged upriver, and we saw my grandfather wave at the bargemen. The barge answered with a deep-throated salute from its horn and simultaneously the bridge across the river began its slow, ponderous division in the middle.

"Go out and talk to your grandpa, kids," she said. "I'll get us a little dinner, but first, why don't you go gather a couple of dozen oysters from the river and I'll fix 'em up while we're waiting for the chicken to bake."

We walked out into the back yard and into the very different world of Grandpa Wingo. He was lifting up the cross now and, laying it on his shoulder and walking it across the grass, testing the new wheel. The wheel squeaked slightly as it rolled across the grass.

"Hello, children," he said, smiling when he saw us. "I can't quite get the squeak out of this wheel."

"Hello, Grandpa," we said, and both of us ran to kiss him beneath the cross.

"How do you think the cross looks, children?" he asked, worriedly. "Be honest now. Don't be afraid to hurt your grandpa's feelings. Do you think the wheel looks all right?"

"It looks fine, Grandpa," Savannah said, "but I've never seen a cross with a wheel on it before."

"I was in bed for a week last year after the last walk," he explained. "I thought the wheel would make it easier, but I'm worried that folks'll get the wrong impression."

"They'll understand, Grandpa," I said.

"The cross got rained on this winter, and it's starting to rot in the center beam. I may have to build a new one for next year. Maybe a lighter model if I can find the right kind of wood."

"Why don't you retire, Grandpa?" Savannah said. "Let a younger man in the church take over."

"I've thought a lot about that, child," he said. "I've always hoped Luke or Tom would take over after I'm gone. That's what I pray to the good Lord for. It'd be nice to keep it in the family, don't you think?"

"I'm sure Tom would love to do it," Savannah offered graciously. "In fact, I've been praying to the good Lord for the same thing."

I pinched Savannah on the back of the arm and said, "Tolitha wants us to go across the river and pick some oysters, Grandpa. You want to go with us?"

"I'd be mighty pleased to go, children. Tom, could you just walk this cross over to the garage? I've got to find out where this squeak is coming from."

"He'd be glad to," Savannah said. "It'll also give him a little practice for when he takes over the job."

I took the cross from my grandfather and laid it over my right shoulder and began moving it quickly across the yard. I could hear my grandmother hooting at me from the kitchen.

"Just a minute, child," my grandfather said. "I see where that squeak is coming from."

He bent down and applied oil to the wheel from a rusted can.

"I think that might do it. Try it again."

I resumed my surly walk, trying to ignore Savannah's grinning face and the chuckling image of my grandmother framed in the kitchen window. My grandfather, of course, was oblivious to all occasions of mirth and humiliation.

"I think that cross looks good on him, don't you, child?" my grandfather said to Savannah.

"I think it looks divine, Grandpa," Savannah agreed. "That boy was born to carry that cross."

"It's heavy," I said miserably.

"You ought to carry it without the wheel. It's a man's work. But when I think of the Lord's suffering and all he went through for me," Grandpa said.

"Yeah, Tom. Quit complaining. Think of what the Lord went through for you," Savannah chided.

"Just walk it this way one more time, child," said my grandfather. "I want to make sure I got that squeak."

After returning the cross to the garage, the three of us loaded into Grandpa's small green boat. He hand-cranked the motor and I gathered in the ropes and we headed across the Colleton River toward the oyster bank near the *Hardeville* wreck on St. Stephen's Island. The *Hardeville* was an old paddlewheel ferry that had sunk during the same hurricane when Savannah and I were born. Its great wheel lay buried in the mud and from a distance it looked like a half-made clock. Thousands of oysters clustered around the base of the hull and at full tide it was one of the most productive, bountiful fishing holes in the county. A family of otters lived in the brown encrusted hull of the ship, and had ever since I could remember. Tradition made those otters sacrosanct and inviolable and no hunter had ever attempted to trap them. Two otter pups were pursuing each other between the ribs of the foundered ship when my grandfather killed the motor and we slid into the flats exposed by the receding tide.

    *   *   *   *   *   *   *

At noon on Good Friday, my grandfather lifted the wooden cross and laid it upon his right shoulder. He was dressed in a white choir robe and he was wearing a pair of sandals he had bought at a K Mart in Charleston. Luke made last-minute adjustments on the wheel with a set of pliers.

Mr. Fruit directed traffic and waited for my grandfather to signal that the walk was about to begin. Since Mr. Fruit directed traffic and led all parades, he always had to perform double duty on Good Friday. For reasons known only to him, Mr. Fruit considered my grandfather's walk a parade. A small parade, and not much fun, but a parade nonetheless.

Mr. Fruit put the whistle to his lips and my grandfather nodded his head. Mr. Fruit blew the whistle and strutted up the Street of Tides, high-stepping it like a drum major, his knees pumping as high as his chin. My grandfather followed ten yards behind. I heard a couple of people laugh when they saw the wheel. Up by Baitery's Pharmacy, I watched my father filming the first part of the walk.

About halfway down the street, my grandfather fell for the first time. It was a spectacular fall and he hit the street hard, with the cross falling on him. He loved the falls best of anything in the three-hour walk. They always surprised the crowd, and besides, he was a good faller. My father was zooming in when my grandfather fell and it was evident that the two of them had worked out a system of signals whenever the highlights of the walk were coming up. Amos was also a good staggerer, and his knees buckled under him when he tried to rise. My grandfather knew nothing about the theater of the absurd, but he managed to invent it for himself year after year.

After the first hour, the wheel broke and had to be discarded. Sheriff Lucas appeared at the traffic light by the bridge and wrote out the annual citation for obstruction of traffic. Mr. Fruit stopped marching and directed cars through the intersection as some of the crowd booed the sheriff. Mr. Kupcinet, a deacon at Grandpa's church, read aloud from the Bible about the walk of Jesus through the streets of Jerusalem, his crucifixion on Calvary flanked by two thieves, the darkness over the city, the great cry of agony *Eli, Eli lama sabachthani* ("My God, my God, why hast thou forsaken me?"), and the centurion saying again as he would say for all the centuries that would pass, "Truly this is the Son of God."

And my grandfather would walk back and forth between stores that sold shoes and real estate and lingerie, sweat pouring from his face but his eyes serene, knowing he was serving his God as best as he knew how. Savannah and I sold lemonade in front of Sarah Poston's dress shop and Luke had the job of stopping my grandfather in the middle of his walk and forcing a Dixie cup of vinegar between Amos's lips. Then Luke played the part of Simon of Cyrene and helped bear the weight of the cross for one whole transit of the street. By the third hour, my grandfather would be staggering for real. When he fell the last time, he could not rise to his feet until Luke reached him and lifted the cross off his body. There was blood in a thin strip along the shoulder of the choir robe. He rose, smiled, and thanked Luke, promising to cut my brother's hair later on in the day. Then he continued down the street, lurching and weaving from side to side.

I did not know then and do not know now what to make of my grandfather's awesome love of the Word of God. As a teenager I found his walk humiliating. But Savannah would write about his walk in poems of uncommon beauty. She would celebrate the "shy Oberammergau of the itinerant barber."

And when Amos Wingo's walk ended that day and we caught him as he fell and carried him to the lemonade stand, where we rubbed his face with ice and made him drink a cup of lemonade, I had a feeling that sainthood was the most frightening and incurable disease on earth.

He was trembling and delirious as we laid him out on the sidewalk. People pressed forward to get Grandpa to sign their Bibles and my father filmed his collapse.

Luke and I got him to his feet, and with his arms around our shoulders, we bore his weight and carried him home, with Luke saying the whole way: "You're so beautiful, Grandpa. You're so beautiful."

     *   *   *   *   *   *   *

Chapter 25

A year later Tolitha sent Amos out shopping for a pound of self-rising flour and a bottle of A-1 steak sauce. He had almost made it to the aisle with the steak sauce when he stopped suddenly, gave out with a small cry, and pitched forward into a canned goods display of turnip greens flavored with pork. Amos Wingo was dead when he hit the ground even though Patrolman Sasser tried vainly to revive him with mouth-to-mouth resuscitation. They said that Sasser cried like a baby when the ambulance squad drove off to the hospital with my grandfather's body. But Sasser was only the first in Colleton to weep that night. The whole town knew it had lost something exquisite and irreplaceable. Nothing so affects a small town as the loss of its rarest and finest man. Nothing so affects a southern family as the death of the man who lent it balance and fragility in a world askew with corrupt values. His faith had always been a form of splendid madness and his love affair with the world was a hymn of eloquent praise to the lamb who made him. There would be no more letters to the *Colleton Gazette* with word-by-word transcriptions of the Lord's gossipy chats with Amos. Now those dialogues would be face-to-face as Amos cut the Lord's hair in a mansion sweet with the birdsong of angels. Those were the words of Preacher Turner Ball that rang through the white clapboard church on the day they buried my grandfather.

The South died for me that day, or at least I lost the most resonant and eminent part of it. It lost that blithe magic I associate with earned incongruity. He had caught flies and mosquitoes in jars and set them free in the back yard because he could not bear to kill one of God's creatures.

"They're part of the colony," he had said. "They're part of the design."

His death forced me to acknowledge the secret wisdom that issues naturally from the contemplative life. His was a life of detachment from the material and the temporal. As a boy I was embarrassed by the undiluted ardor he brought to worship. As an adult I would envy forever the simplicity and grandeur of his vision of what it was to be a complete and contributing man. His whole life was a compliance and a donation to an immaculate faith. When I wept at his funeral, it was not because of my own loss. You carry a man like Amos with you, a memory of immortal rose in the garden of the human ego. No, I cried because my children would never know him and I knew that I was not articulate enough in any language to describe the perfect solitude and perfect charity of a man who believed and lived every simple word of the book he sold door to door the length and breadth of the American South. The only word for goodness is goodness, and it is not enough.

Amidst the shouts of "Hallelujah" and "Praise be the Lord" six men with newly made wooden crosses began thumping the bases of the crosses against the wooden floor of the church as a gesture of homage to my grandfather. They drummed the crosses in unison, creating a palsied, unfathomable tattoo, the dark music of crucifixionists. My father rose up with Tolitha leaning against him and he walked his mother down the center aisle, where she faced Amos for the last time. In the open casket, with his hair swept back in a pompadour and a slight bedeviled smile on his face (indelible signature of the undertaker, Winthrop Ogletree), Amos looked like a choirboy gone to seed. A white Bible was opened to the page where Jesus spoke the red words, "I am the Resurrection and the Life." The organist played "Blessed Be the Tie that Binds" and the congregation sang the words as Tolitha leaned down and kissed my grandfather's lips for the last time.

We walked from the church to the cemetery. I held Sallie's hand and Luke walked with my mother. Savannah helped my father with Tolitha. The whole town, black and white, moved in solemn processional silence behind us. The men with the crosses dragged them down the center of the street. Mr. Fruit led the entourage, tooting his whistle with tears streaming down his face. Patrolman Sasser was one of the pallbearers.

We buried him in the paltry light of an overcast day. After they lowered Amos into his grave, Luke, Savannah, and I stayed behind to shovel the dirt ourselves. It took us an hour to get it right. When we had finished we sat beneath the water oak that shaded the Wingo family plot. We cried and we told stories about Amos and his role in our childhood. Our grandfather, in dreamless sleep beneath us, spoke to us from the singing hive of memory. There is an art to farewell, but we were too young to have mastered it. We simply told stories about the man who had cut our hair since we were children and who had fashioned out of his life an incorruptible psalm to the God who made him.

Harry Crews

(1935–   )

Harry Crews was born in Bacon County, Georgia, on June 7, 1935. His father, Ray Crews, died when Harry was twenty-one-months old. His mother, Myrtice, remarried and later moved the family away from her husband and his severe drinking problem to Jacksonville, Florida, where Crews spent his adolescent years. In 1953, he joined the U.S. Marine Corps, where he began reading extensively. In 1956, he enrolled at the University of Florida, left after two years to ride a motorcycle around the country, and returned to the university in 1958, where Andrew Lytle became his mentor. In addition, Crews has credited Graham Greene as being a major influence on his fiction-writing processes. In 1960, Crews married Sally Ellis, the mother of his son Patrick Scott. Another son, Byron Jason, was born in 1960. Crews and his wife later divorced. He received a B.A. in 1960 and an M.S. in education in 1962. In July 1961, Patrick Crews drowned in a neighbor's swimming pool. In 1968, Crews returned to the University of Florida as a faculty member in the English department and taught creative writing until his retirement in 1997.

Crews's fiction is described as being in the vein of Southern Gothic. His humor is often grim, and his characters, who are generally deformed, on occasion find redemption. His autobiography, *A Childhood: The Biography of a Place*, was published in 1978.

Books include *The Gospel Singer* (1968); *Naked in Garden Hills* (1969); *This Thing Don't Lead to Heaven* (1970); *Karate Is a Thing of the Spirit* (1971); *Car* (1973); *The Hawk Is Dying* (1973); *The Gypsy's Curse* (1974); *A Feast of Snakes* (1976); *Blood and Grits* (1979); *Florida Frenzy* (1982); *Two* (1984); *All We Need of Hell* (1987); *The Knockout Artist* (1988); *Body* (1990); *Madonna at Ringside* (1991); *Scar Lover* (1992); *Classic Crews: A Harry Crews Reader* (1993); *The Mulching of America* (1995); *The Gospel Singer & Where Does One Go When There's No Place Left to Go?* (1995); and *Celebration* (1998).

from *A Childhood: The Biography of a Place*

As winter grew deeper and we waited for hog-killing time, at home the center was not holding. Whether it was because the crops were in and not much work was to be done or whether it was because of my having just spent so long a time crippled in the bed, daddy had grown progressively crazier, more violent. He was gone from home for longer and longer periods of time, and during those brief intervals when he was home, the crashing noise of breaking things was everywhere about us. Daddy had also taken to picking up the shotgun and screaming threats while he waved it about, but at that time he had not as yet fired it.

While that was going on, it occurred to me for the first time that being alive was like being awake in a nightmare.

I remember saying aloud to myself: "Scary as a nightmare. Jest like being awake in a nightmare."

Never once did I ever think that my life was not just like everybody else's, that my fears and uncertainties were not universal. For which I can only thank God. Thinking so could only have made it more bearable.

My sleepwalking had become worse now that I could get out of bed on my unsure legs. I woke up sometimes in the middle of the night in the dirt lane by the house or sometimes sitting in my room in a corner chewing on something. It didn't matter much what: the sleeve of my gown or the side of my hand or even one time the laces of a shoe. And when I would wake up, it was always in terror, habitually remembering now what Auntie had said about the birds spitting in my mouth. No, more than *remembering* what she had said. Rather, seeing what she had said, the image of a bird burned clearly on the backs of my eyelids, its beak hooked like the nose of a Byzantine Christ, shooting spit thick as phlegm on a solid line into my open and willing mouth. With such dreams turning in my head it came time for us to all help kill and butcher hogs. Daddy was laid up somewhere drunk; we had not seen him in four days. So he did not go with us to Uncle Alton's to help with the slaughter. Farm families swapped labor at hog-killing time just as they swapped labor to put in tobacco or pick cotton. Early one morning our tenant farmers, mama, my brother, and I walked the half mile to Uncle Alton's place to help put a year's worth of meat in the smokehouse. Later his family would come and help us do the same thing.

Before it was over, everything on the hog would have been used. The lights (lungs) and liver—together called haslet—would be made into a fresh stew by first pouring and pouring again fresh water through the slit throat—the exposed throat called a goozle—to clean the lights out good. Then the fat would be trimmed off and put with the fat trimmed from the guts to cook crisp into cracklins to mix with cornbread or else put in a wash pot to make soap.

The guts would be washed and then turned and washed again. Many times. After the guts had been covered with salt overnight, they were used as casings for sausage made from shoulder meat, tenderloin, and—if times were hard—any kind of scrap that was not entirely fat.

The eyes would be removed from the head, then the end of the snout cut off, and the whole thing boiled until the teeth could be picked out. Whatever meat was left, cheeks, ears, and so on, would be picked off, crushed with herbs and spices and packed tightly into muslin cloth for hog's headcheese.

The fat from the liver, lungs, guts, or wherever was cooked until it was as crisp as it would get and then packed into tin syrup buckets to be ground up later for cracklin cornbread. Even the feet were removed, and after the outer layer of split hooves was taken off, the whole thing was boiled and pickled in vinegar and peppers. If later in the year the cracklins started to get rank, they would be thrown into a cast-iron wash pot with fried meat's grease, any meat for that matter that might have gone bad in the smokehouse, and some potash and lye and cooked into soap, always made on the full of the moon so it wouldn't shrink. I remember one time mama out in the backyard making soap when a chicken for some reason tried to fly over the wash pot but didn't make it. The chicken dropped flapping and squawking into the boiling fat and lye. Mama, who was stirring the mixture with an old ax handle, never missed a beat. She just stirred the chicken right on down to the bottom. Any kind of meat was good for making soap.

By the time we got to Uncle Alton's the dirt floor of the smokehouse had been covered with green pine tops. After the pork stayed overnight in tubs of salt, it would be laid on the green pine straw all night, sometimes for two nights, to get all the water out of it. Then it was taken up and packed again in salt for three or four days. When it was taken out of the salt for the last time, it was dipped in plain hot water or else in a solution of crushed hot peppers and syrup or wild honey. Then it was hung over a deep pile of smoldering hickory spread across the entire floor of the smokehouse. The hickory was watched very carefully to keep any sort of blaze from flaring up. Day and night until it was over, light gray smoke boiled continuously from under the eaves and around the door where the meat was being cured. It was the sweetest smoke a man was ever to smell.

It was a bright cold day in February 1941, so cold the ground was still frozen at ten o'clock in the morning. The air was full of the steaming smell of excrement and the oily, flatulent odor of intestines and the heavy sweetness of blood—in every way a perfect day to slaughter animals. I watched the hogs called to the feeding trough just as they were every morning except this morning it was to receive the ax instead of slop.

A little slop *was* poured into their long communal trough, enough to make them stand still while Uncle Alton or his boy Theron went quietly among them with the ax, using the flat end like a sledgehammer (shells were expensive enough to make a gun out of the question). He would approach the hog from the rear while it slopped at the trough, and then he would straddle it, one leg on each side, patiently waiting for the hog to raise its snout from the slop to take a breath, showing as it did the wide bristled bone between its ears to the ax.

It never took but one blow, delivered expertly and with consummate skill, and the hog was dead. He then moved with his hammer to the next hog and straddled it. None of the hogs ever seemed to mind that their companions were dropping dead all around them but continued in a single-minded passion to eat. They didn't even mind when another of my cousins (this could be a boy of only eight or nine because it took neither strength nor skill) came right behind the hammer and drew a long razor-boned butcher knife across the throat of the fallen hog. Blood spurted with the still-beating heart, and a live hog would sometimes turn to one that was lying beside it at the trough and stick its snout into the spurting blood and drink a bit just seconds before it had its own head crushed.

It was a time of great joy and celebration for the children. We played games and ran (I gimping along pretty well by then) and screamed and brought wood to the boiler and thought of that night, when we would have fresh fried pork and stew made from lungs and liver and heart in an enormous pot that covered half the stove.

The air was charged with the smell of fat being rendered in tubs in the backyard and the sharp squeals of the pigs at the troughs, squeals from pure piggishness at the slop, never from pain. Animals were killed but seldom hurt. Farmers took tremendous precautions about pain at slaughter. It is, whether or not they ever admit it when they talk, a ritual. As brutal as they sometimes are with farm animals and with themselves, no farmer would ever eat an animal he had willingly made suffer.

The heel strings were cut on each of the hog's hind legs, and a stick, called a gambreling stick, or a gallus, was inserted into the cut behind the tendon and the hog dragged to the huge cast-iron boiler, which sat in a depression dug into the ground so the hog could be slipped in and pulled out easily. The fire snapped and roared in the depression under the boiler. The fire had to be tended carefully because the water could never quite come to a boil. If the hog was dipped in boiling water, the hair would set and become impossible to take off. The ideal temperature was water you could rapidly draw your finger through three times in succession without being blistered.

Unlike cows, which are skinned, a hog is scraped. After the hog is pulled from the water, a blunt knife is drawn over the animal, and if the water has not been too hot, the hair slips off smooth as butter, leaving a white, naked, utterly beautiful pig.

To the great glee of the watching children, when the hog is slipped into the water, it defecates. The children squeal and clap their hands and make their delightfully obscene children's jokes as they watch it all.

On that morning, mama was around in the back by the smokehouse where some hogs, already scalded and scraped, were hanging in the air from their heel strings being disemboweled. Along with the other ladies she was washing out the guts, turning them inside out, cleaning them good so they could later be stuffed with ground and seasoned sausage meat.

Out in front of the house where the boiler was, I was playing pop-the-whip as best I could with my brother and several of my cousins. Pop-the-whip is a game in which everyone holds hands and runs fast and then the leader of the line turns sharply. Because he is turning through a tighter arc than the other children, the line acts as a whip with each child farther down the line having to travel through a greater space and consequently having to go faster in order to keep up. The last child in the line literally gets *popped* loose and sent flying from his playmates.

I was popped loose and sent flying into the steaming boiler of water beside a scalded, floating hog.

I remember everything about as clearly as I remember anything that ever happened to me, except the screaming. Curiously, I cannot remember the screaming. They say I screamed all the way to town, but I cannot remember it.

What I remember is John C. Pace, a black man whose daddy was also named John C. Pace, reached right into the scalding water and pulled me out and set me on my feet and stood back to look at me. I did not fall but stood looking at John and seeing in his face that I was dead.

The children's faces, including my brother's, showed I was dead, too. And I knew it must be so because I knew where I had fallen and I felt no pain—not in that moment—and I knew with the bone-chilling certainty most people are spared that, yes, death does come and mine had just touched me.

John C. Pace ran screaming and the other children ran screaming and left me standing there by the boiler, my hair and skin and clothes steaming in the bright cold February air.

In memory I stand there alone with the knowledge of death upon me, watching steam rising from my hands and clothes while everybody runs and, after everybody has gone, standing there for minutes while nobody comes.

That is only memory. It may have been but seconds before my mama and Uncle Alton came to me. Mama tells me she heard me scream and started running toward the boiler, knowing already what had happened. She has also told me that she could not bring herself to try to do anything with that smoking ghostlike thing standing by the boiler. But she did. They all did. They did what they could.

But in that interminable time between John pulling me out and my mother arriving in front of me, I remember first the pain. It didn't begin as bad pain, but rather like maybe sandspurs under my clothes.

I reached over and touched my right hand with my left, and the whole thing came off like a wet glove. I mean, the skin on the top of the wrist and the back of my hand, along with the fingernails, all just turned loose and slid on down to the ground. I could see my fingernails lying in the little puddle my flesh made on the ground in front of me.

Then hands were on me, taking off my clothes, and the pain turned into something words cannot touch, or at least my words cannot touch. There is no way for me to talk about it because when my shirt was taken off, my back came off with it. When my overalls were pulled down, my cooked and glowing skin came down.

I still had not fallen, and I stood there participating in my own butchering. When they got the clothes off me, they did the worst thing they could have done; they wrapped me in a sheet. They did it out of panic and terror and ignorance and love.

That day there happened to be a car at the farm. I can't remember who it belonged to, but I was taken into the backseat into my mama's lap—God love the lady, out of her head, pressing her boiled son to her breast—and we started for Alma, a distance of about sixteen miles. The only thing that I can remember about the trip was that I started telling mama that I did not want to die. I started saying it and never stopped.

The car we piled into was incredibly slow. An old car and very, very slow, and every once in a while Uncle Alton, who was like a daddy to me, would jump out of the car and run alongside it and helplessly scream for it to go faster and then he would jump on the running board until he couldn't stand it any longer and then he would jump off again.

But like bad beginnings everywhere, they sometimes end well. When I got to Dr. Sharp's office in Alma and he finally managed to get me out of the sticking sheet, he found that I was scalded over two-thirds of my body but that my head had not gone under the water (he said that would have killed me), and for some strange reason I have never understood, the burns were not deep. He said I would probably even out-grow the scars, which I have. Until I was about fifteen years old, the scars were puckered and discolored on my back and right arm and legs. But now their outlines are barely visible.

The only hospital at the time was thirty miles away, and Dr. Sharp said I'd do just as well at home if they built a frame over the bed to keep the coves off me and also kept a light burning over me twenty-four hours a day. (He knew as well as we did that I couldn't go to a hospital anyway, since the only thing Dr. Sharp ever got for taking care of me was satisfaction for a job well done, if he got that. Over the years, I was his most demanding and persistent charity, which he never mentioned to me or mama. Perhaps that is why in an age when it is fashionable to distrust and hate doctors, I love them.)

So they took me back home and put a buggy frame over my bed to make it re-semble, when the sheet was on it, a covered wagon, and ran a line in from the Rural Electrification Administration so I could have the drying light hanging just over me. The pain was not nearly so bad now that I had for the first time in my life the miracle of electricity close enough to touch. The pain was bad enough, though, but relieved to some extent by some medicine Dr. Sharp gave us to spray out of a bottle onto the burns by pumping a black rubber ball. When it dried, it raised to form a protective, cooling scab. But it was bad to crack. The bed was always full of black crumbs, which Auntie worked continually at. When they brought me home, Auntie, without anybody saying a word to her, came back up the road to take care of me.

The same day Hollis Toomey came, too. He walked into the house without knock-ing or speaking to anyone. Nobody had sent for him. But whenever anybody in the county was burned, he showed up as if by magic, because he could talk the fire out of you. He did not call himself a faith healer, never spoke of God, didn't even go to church, although his family did. His was a gift that was real, and everybody in the county knew it was real. For reasons which he never gave, because he was the most reticent of men and never took money or anything else for what he did, he was drawn to a bad burn the way iron filings are drawn to a magnet, never even saying, "You're welcome," to those who thanked him. He was as sure of his powers and as implacable as God.

When he arrived, the light had not yet been brought into the house, and the buggy frame was not yet over my bed and I was lying in unsayable pain. His farm was not far from ours, and it was unlike any other in the county. Birds' nests made from gourds, shaped like crooked-necked squash with a hole cut in one side with the seeds taken out, hung everywhere from the forest of old and arching oak trees about his house. Undulating flocks of white pigeons flew in and out of his hayloft. He had a blacksmith shed, black as smut and always hot from the open hearth where he made among other things iron rims for wagon wheels. He could handcraft a true-shooting gun, including the barrel which was not smooth-bore but had calibrated riflings. He owned two oxen, heavier than mules, whose harness, including the double yoke, he had made himself. His boys were never allowed to take care of them. He watered them and fed them and pulled them now and again to stumps of trees. But he also had the only Belgian draft horse in the county. The horse was so monstrously heavy that you could hitch him to two spans of good mules—four of them—and he would walk off with them as though they were goats. So the oxen were really useless. It just pleased him to keep them.

He favored very clean women and very dirty men. He thought it was the natural order of things. One of the few things I ever heard him say, and he said it looking off toward the far horizon, speaking to nobody: "A man's got the *right* to stink."

His wife always wore her hair tightly bunned at the back of her head under a stiffly starched white bonnet. Her dresses were nearly to her ankles, and they always looked and smelled as if they had just come off the clothesline after a long day in the sun.

Hollis always smelled like his pockets were full of ripe chicken guts, and his overalls were as stiff as metal. He didn't wear a beard; he wore a stubble. The stubble was coal black despite the fact he was over sixty, and it always seemed to be the same length, the length where you've got to shave or start telling everybody you're growing a beard. Hollis Toomey did neither.

When I saw him in the door, it was as though a soothing balm had touched me. This was Hollis Toomey, who was from my county, whose boys I knew, who didn't talk to God about your hurt. He didn't even talk to *you;* he talked to the *fire.* A mosquito couldn't fly through a door he was standing in he was so wide and high, and more, he was obviously indestructible. He ran on his own time, went where he needed to go. Nobody ever thought of doing anything for him, helping him. If he wanted something, he made it. If he couldn't make it, he took it. Hollis Toomey was not a kind man.

My daddy had finally come home, red-eyed and full of puke. He was at the foot of the bed, but he didn't say a word while Hollis sat beside me.

Hollis Toomey's voice was low like the quiet rasping of a file on metal. I couldn't hear most of what he had to say, but that was all right because I stopped burning before he ever started talking. He talked to the fire like an old and respected adversary, but one he had beaten consistently and had come to beat again. I don't remember him once looking at my face while he explained: "Fire, this boy is mine. This bed is mine. This room is mine. It ain't nothing here that's yours. It's a lot that is, but it ain't nothing here that is."

At some point while he talked he put his hands on me, one of them spread out big as a frying pan, and I was already as cool as spring water. But I had known I would be from the moment I had seen him standing in the door. Before it was over, he cursed the fire, calling it all kinds of sonofabitch, but the words neither surprised nor shocked me. The tone of his voice made me know that he was locked in a real and terrible conflict with the fire. His hands flexed and hurt my stomach, but it was nothing compared to the pain that had been on me before he came.

I had almost dozed off when he suddenly got up and walked out of the room. My daddy called, "Thank you," in a weak, alcohol-spattered voice. Hollis Toomey did not answer.

When they finally got the buggy frame up, it was not as terrible as I at first thought it was going to be. I was, of course, by then used to the bed and that was no problem and the buggy frame gave a new dimension, a new feeling to the sickbed. With the frame arching over me it was a time for fantasy and magic because I lived in a sort of playhouse, a kingdom that was all mine.

At least I pretended it was a kingdom, pretended it in self-defense. I did not want to be there, but there was no help for it, so I might as well pretend it was a kingdom as anything else. And like every child who owns anything, I ruled it like a tyrant. There was something very special and beautiful about being the youngest member of a family and being badly hurt.

Since it pleased me to do so, I spent a lot of time with the Sears, Roebuck catalogue, started writing and nearly finished a detective novel, although at that time I had never seen a novel, detective or otherwise. I printed it out with a soft-lead pencil on lined paper, and it was about a boy who, for his protection, carried not a pistol but firecrackers. He solved crimes and gave things to poor people and doctors. The boy was also absolutely fearless.

I was given a great deal of ginger ale to drink because the doctor or mama or somebody thought that where burns were concerned, it had miraculous therapeutic value. This ginger ale was the store-bought kind, too, not some homemade concoction but wonderfully fizzy and capped in real bottles. Since Hoyet and I almost never saw anything from the store, I drank as much of it as they brought me, and they brought me a lot. I never learned to like it but could never get over my fascination with the bubbles that rose in the bottle under the yellow light hanging from the buggy frame.

But I was tired of being alone in bed, and since I was going into my second major hurt back to back, I decided I might as well assert myself.

Old Black Bill had sired several kids the previous spring, and one of them was himself black and a male, so I named him Old Black Bill, too, and he grew up with me under the buggy frame. No animal is allowed in a farmhouse in Bacon County, at least to my knowledge. Dogs stay in the yard. Cats usually live in the barn catching rats, and goats, well, goats only get in the house if they have first been butchered for the table.

But I had been scalded and I was special. And I knew even then that an advantage unused becomes no advantage at all. So I insisted Old Black Bill's kid be brought to my bed. I was only about three weeks into my recovery, and I thought that a goat would be good company.

They brought him in, and I fed him bits of hay and shelled corn under the buggy frame. We had long conversations. Or rather, I had long monologues and he, patiently chewing, listened.

The two tall windows at the foot of my bed opened onto a forty-acre field. Through the long winter days Old Black Bill and I watched it being prepared to grow another crop. First the cornstalks were cut by a machine with revolving blades, pulled by a single mule. Then two mules were hitched to a big rake, so big a man could ride on it. When all the stalks were piled and burned, the land had to be broken, completely turned under, the single hardest job on a farm for the farmer and his mules.

Every morning, when the light came up enough for me to see into the field, Willalee's daddy, Will, would already be out there behind a span of mules walking at remarkable speed, breaking the hard, clayish earth more than a foot deep. Sometimes daddy was out there plowing, too. Most of the time he was not.

Willalee's daddy would mark off an enormous square, fifteen acres or better, then follow that square around and around, always taking about a fourteen-inch bite with the turnplow so that when he went once around on each of the four sides of the square, the land still to be broken would have been reduced by fourteen inches on a side.

A man breaking land would easily walk thirty miles or more every day, day in and day out, until the entire farm was turned under. Even though the mules were given more corn and more hay than they were used to, they still lost weight. Every night when they were brought to the barn, they had high stiff ridges of salt outlining where their collars and backbands and trace chains and even their bridles had been.

With only my head out from under the buggy frame, continually dried and scabbed by the burning light, I watched the plows drag on through the long blowing days, Willalee's daddy moving dim as a ghost in the sickly half-light of the winter sun. Then after the longest, hardest time, the turnplow was taken out of the field, and the row marker brought in to lay off the lines in the soft earth where the corn would finally begin to show in the springtime. The row marker was made out of a trunk of a tree, sometimes a young oak, more often a pine, made by boring holes thirty-six inches apart and inserting a straight section of limb into each of the holes. Two holes were bored into the top of the log for handles and two holes in the front of the log for the shaves, between which the mule was hitched to drag the whole rig across the turned-under field, marking off four rows at a time.

Some farmers always had crops that grew in rows straight as a plumb line. Others didn't seem to care about it much, one way or the other. It was not unusual for a farmer bumping along in a wagon behind a steaming mule in the heat of summer to comment on how the rows were marked off on each farm he passed.

"Sumbitch, he musta been drunk when he laid them off."

"I bet he has to git drunk again ever time he plows that mess."

"I guess he figgers as much'll grow in a crooked row as a straight one."

For reasons I never knew, perhaps it was nothing more complicated than pride of workmamship, farmers always associated crooked rows with sorry people. So much of farming was beyond a man's control, but at least he could have whatever nature allowed to grow laid off in straight rows. And the feeling was that a man who didn't care enough to keep his rows from being crooked couldn't be much of a man.

In all the years in Bacon County, I never saw any rows straighter than the ones Willalee's daddy put down. He would take some point of reference at the other end of the field, say, a tree or a post, and then keep his eye on it as the mule dragged the row marker over the freshly broken ground, laying down those first critical rows. If the first four rows were straight, the rest of the field would be laid off straight, because the outside marker would always run in the last row laid down.

It didn't hurt to have a good mule. As was true of so many other things done on the farm, it was much easier if the abiding genius of a good mule was brought to bear on the job. There were mules in Bacon County that a blind man could have laid off straight rows behind. Such mules knew only one way to work: the right way. To whatever work they were asked to do, they brought a lovely exactitude, whether it was walking off rows, snaking logs, sledding tobacco without a driver, or any of the other unaccountable jobs that came their way during a crop year.

After the field was marked in a pattern of rows, Willalee's daddy came in with the middlebuster, a plow with a wing on both sides that opens up the row to receive first the fertilizer and then the seed. When all the rows had been plowed into shallow trenches, Will appeared in the field early one morning with a two-horse wagon full of guano, universally called *gyou-anner*. It was a commercial fertilizer sold in 200-pound bags, and Will had loaded the wagon before daylight by himself and brought it at sunup into the field where he unloaded one bag every three rows across the middle of the field.

Shortly after he left with the wagon, he came back with the guano strower and Willalee Bookatee. Willalee had a tin bucket with him. He plodded sleepily behind his daddy, the bucket banging at his knees. The guano strower was a kind of square wooden box that got smaller at the bottom, where there was a metal shaft shaped like a corkscrew and over which the guano had to fall as it poured into the trench opened by the middlebuster. The corkscrew shaft broke up any lumps in the fertilizer and made sure it kept flowing. Two little tongue-shaped metal plows at the back of the guano strower were set so that one ran on each side of the furrow. They covered up the thin stream of fertilizer the instant after it was laid down.

Willalee was out there to fill up the guano strower for his daddy, a bad, boring job and one reserved exclusively for small boys. Willalee would open one of the bags, fill the strower, and his daddy would head for the end of the row. As soon as he was gone, Willalee would go back to the sack, and since he could not pick up anything that heavy, he would have to dip the bucket full with his hands. Then he had nothing to do but shift from foot to foot, the fertilizer burning his arms and hands and before long his eyes, and wait for his daddy to come back down the row. When he did, Willalee would fill up the strower and the whole thing would be to do over again.

10

By the time the field was covered with corn about an inch high I was able to do without the buggy frame and the constantly burning light. Dr. Sharp also said I could stay out of bed all I wanted to if the pain was not too bad.

Then two things happened in the same day: I saw my first grapefruit, and daddy went briefly crazy. I always remember the two things together. They got mixed and twisted in such a way that in the months to come, my nose would sometimes fill with the oily, biting smell of grapefruit.

My brother was going to the schoolhouse a half mile away on the same dirt road as our farm, and every other Thursday the federal government sent out a big truck filled with food of one kind or another, mostly in cans, for the children to take home.

"What all was it in the commodities truck?" I asked immediately upon seeing my brother's face when he came home from school.

"It was everything it ever was. And something else besides, too."

Mama had come in the room where we were. She stood wiping her hands on her apron.

"Did you git your commodity?" I asked, knowing he would never have come gloating into my room like that if he had not. But I'd really asked just so I could say the word *commodity*. All of us loved the word and put some pretty good mileage on it every other Thursday during the school year. I didn't have the slightest notion of what *commodity* meant. To me it meant: free food that comes on a truck. I've since managed to find the several definitions of the word, but in my secret heart I'll always know what commodity means: *free food that comes on a truck.*

"What did you git, son?" mama asked.

"Oh, I got my commodity," Hoyet said, drawing the whole thing out for as long as he could.

"You lost it. You lost your damn commodity," I said in a choked, accusing voice, hoping that saying he'd lost it would make him produce it. Which he did. While mama scowled and warned me about cursing—a habit I'd developed with some vigor because my early mortal hurts made everybody spoil me, even mama—my brother whipped his hand from behind his back.

"Godamighty," I said. "Is it a orange or just what?"

"That commodity right there," said my brother in a voice suddenly serious as death, "is a grapefruit."

The words *grape* and *fruit* did not seem to me to cover it. We all stood silently staring at the round golden thing in his hand, so strange there in a tag end of winter, when everything in Bacon County was burned brown with cold and broken in the field. Then I began to smell it, *really* smell it, a smell full of the sun and green leaves and a sweet tongue and a delightfully cool bellyful of juice.

"See," he said. "We could have a can of Campbell's pork and beans or one of these."

"And you took this," I said.

"It don't look like pork and beans, do it?" he said. Then: "It's just like a orange, only bigger."

We knew all about oranges, or not all about them, but we did see them from time to time, little, shriveled, discolored things. But this was orange to the tenth power, which was precisely the way we thought about it even though obviously we could not have said it.

We all smelled it, pressing it against our noses, and felt it and held it longer than was necessary. Mama had brought the butcher knife from the kitchen.

"You reckon we ought to wait for daddy?" I said, a genuinely optimistic question since we hadn't seen him in almost a week.

"Ain't no use to wait," Hoyet said. His expression did not change. He raised the plump grapefruit to his face and peeled it back. Then we halved it and lifted off carefully and deliberately one slice at a time. The slices, which we called slisures, were dripping and yellow as flowers.

But I only had to touch my lips to my piece to know that something was wrong, bad wrong. "Damn if I don't believe my slisure's ruint," I said.

"Do taste a little rank, don't it?" Hoyet said.

Mama made me come over to her so she could hit me. She said: "Come over here so I can slap your head, boy. You cain't talk like that in my house." She liked to make you come to her to get your lick sometimes because she knew the humiliation made it worse. Soon as she had my head ringing like a bell tower she gently and sadly explained the bitter truth about certain grapefruit. "But they tell me," she said, "grapefruits is real good for you. Howsomever, to me they do taste a lot like a green persimmon."

We stood there in the room and gagged down that whole sour thing, slice by slice. It wouldn't do to let a commodity go to waste. The federal government had hauled it all the way to the schoolhouse, and Hoyet had deliberately chosen it over pork and beans and then brought it home in the empty syrup bucket with the wire bale on top he used to carry his lunch to school. That was why it had to be eaten, as mama carefully explained, while we chewed and swallowed, swallowed and chewed.

Finally, it was over. All that remained were a few seeds, a little pulp, and the skin. As soon as I could do it without either of them knowing, I went outside, leaned over the fence, and threw up. When I finally raised my head, I saw Willalee. His back was to me, down in the dirt lane by his house, too far to call him. It was the last time I ever saw him because that night daddy shot the mantelshelf off the fireplace with a twelve-gauge shotgun.

I heard the pickup truck and heard him when he came in and knew without thinking it was going to be a bad night. For about an hour, things were bad in the way they had been bad before: incredibly imaginative cursing between mama and daddy delivered at the top of their voices; pots and pans bouncing off the walls of the kitchen, where daddy had gone to feed the long bout he'd had with whiskey; dishes breaking; the dull unmistakable thump of flesh on flesh. The old house was shaking and I was shaking and my brother, who had started sleeping in the same bed with me again now that my burn had pretty much healed, my brother was shaking too.

Then the shotgun, the eye-rattling blast of a twelve-gauge, so unthinkably loud that it blew every other sound out of the house, leaving a silence scarier than all the noise that preceded it. The sound we had all waited for and expected for so long had finally come. It literally shattered our lives in fact and in memory.

Barry Hannah

(1942–   )

Barry Hannah was born on April 23, 1942, in Clinton, Mississippi. In 1964 he received his B.A. from Mississippi College, and in 1966 he was awarded his M.A. by the University of Arkansas. His formal education was completed in 1967 when he earned a Master of Fine Arts in Creative Writing from the University of Arkansas. He taught creative writing at Clemson University in South Carolina from 1967 to 1973. In 1983, he returned to the University of Mississippi, where he still teaches today.

Hannah's first novel, *Geronimo Rex* (1972), won the William Faulkner Prize for writing. In 1979 he received the Award for Literature from the American Institute of Arts and Letters.

Publications include *Nightwatchmen* (1973); *Ray* (1980); *The Tennis Handsome* (1983); *Captain Maximus* (1983); *Hey Jack!* (1987); *Boomerang* (1989); *Never Die* (1991); *Airships* (1978); *Bats Out of Hell* (1993); and *High Lonesome* (1996).

Knowing He Was Not My Kind, Yet I Followed

It makes me sick when we kill them or ride horses over them. My gun is blazing just like the rest of them, but I hate it.

One day I rode up on a fellow in blue and we were both out of ammunition. He was trying to draw his saber and I was so outraged I slapped him right off his horse.

The horseman behind me cheered. He said I'd broken the man's neck. I was horrified. Oh, life, life—you kill what you love. I have seen such handsome faces with their mouths open, their necks open to the Pennsylvania sun. I love stealing for forage and food, but I hate this murdering business that goes along with it.

Some nights I amble in near the fire to take a cup with the boys, but they chase me away. I don't scold, but in my mind there are the words: All right, have your way in this twinkling mortal world.

Our Jeb Stuart is never tired. You could wake him with a message any time of night and he's awake on the instant. He's such a bull. They called him "Beauty" at West Point. We're fighting and killing all his old classmates and even his father-in-law, General Philip St. George Cooke. Jeb wrote about this man once when he failed to join the Confederacy: "He will regret it but once, and that will be continuously."

Gee, he can use the word, Jeb can. I was with him through the ostrich feathers in his hat and the early harassments, when we had nothing but shotguns and pretty horses. He was always a fool at running around his enemy. I was with him when we rode down a lane around a confused Yank picket, risking the Miniés. But he's a good family man too, they say.

I was with him when he first went around McClellan and scouted Porter's wing. That's when I fell in love with burning and looting. We threw ourselves on railroad cars and wagons, we collected carbines, uniforms and cow steaks that we roasted on sticks over the embers of the rails. Jeb passed right by when I was chewing my beef and dipping water out of the great tank. He had his banjo man and his dancing nigger with him. Jeb has terrific body odor along with his mud-spattered boots, but it rather draws than repels, like the musk of a woman.

When we were celebrating in Richmond, even I was escorted by a woman out into the shadows and this is why I say this. She surrendered to me, her hoop skirt was around her eyebrows, her white nakedness lying under me if I wanted it, and I suppose I did, because I went laboring at her, head full of smoke and unreason. I left her with her dress over her face like a tent and have no clear notion of what her face was like, though my acquaintance Ruppert Longstreet told me in daylight she was a troll.

That was when young Pelham set fire to the Yank boat in the James with his one Napoleon cannon. We whipped a warship from the shore. Pelham was a genius about artillery. I loved that too.

It's killing close up that bothers me. Once a blue-suited man on the ground was holding his hands out after his horse fell over. This was at Manassas. He seemed to be unclear about whether this was an actual event; he seemed to be asking for directions back to his place in a stunned friendly way. My horse, Pardon Me, was rearing way high and I couldn't put the muzzle of my shotgun at him. Then Jeb rode in, plumes shivering. He slashed the man deep in the shoulder with his saber. The man knelt down, closing his eyes as if to pray. Jeb rode next to me. What a body odor he had. On his horse, he said:

"Finish that poor Christian off, soldier."

My horse settled down and I blew the man over. Pardon Me reared at the shot and tore away in his own race down a vacant meadow—fortunate for me, since I never had to look at the carnage but only thought of holding on.

After McClellan placed himself back on the York, we slipped through Maryland and here we are in Pennsylvania. We go spying and cavorting and looting. I'm wearing out.

Pardon Me, I think, feels the lunacy even in this smooth countryside. We're too far from home. We are not defending our beloved Dixie anymore. We're just bandits and maniacal. The gleam in the men's eyes tells this. Everyone is getting crazier on the craziness of being simply too far from home for decent return. It is like Ruth in the alien corn, or a troop of men given wings over the terrain they cherished and taken by the wind to trees they do not know.

Jeb leads us. Some days he has the sneer of Satan himself.

Nothing but bad news comes up from home, when it comes.

Lee is valiant but always too few.

All the great bullies I used to see out front are dead or wounded past use.

The truth is, not a one of us except Jeb Stuart believes in anything any longer. The man himself the exception. There is nobody who does not believe in Jeb Stuart. Oh, the zany purposeful eyes, the haggard gleam, the feet of his lean horse high in the air, his rotting flannel shirt under the old soiled grays, and his heroic body odor! He makes one want to be a Christian. I wish I could be one. I'm afraid the only things I count on are chance and safety.

The other night I got my nerve up and asked for him in his tent. When I went in, he had his head on the field desk, dead asleep. The quill was still in his hand. I took up the letter. It was to his wife, Flora. A daguerreotype of her lay next to the paper. It was still wet from Jeb's tears. At the beginning of the letter there was small talk about finding her the black silk she'd always wanted near Gettsyburg. Then it continued: "After the shameful defeat at Gettysburg," etc.

I was shocked. I always thought we won at Gettysburg. All the fellows I knew thought we had won. Further, he said:

"The only thing that keeps me going on my mission is the sacred inalienable right of the Confederacy to be the Confederacy, Christ Our Lord, and the memory of your hot hairy jumping nexus when I return."

I placed the letter back on the table. This motion woke him.

I was incredulous that he knew my first name. He looked as if he had not slept a second.

The stories were true.

"Corporal Deed Ainsworth," he said.

"Sorry to wake you, General."

"Your grievance?" he said.

"No one is my friend," I mumbled.

"Because the Creator made you strange, my man. I never met a chap more loyal in the saddle than you. God made us different and we should love His differences as well as His likenesses."

"I'd like to kiss you, General," I said.

"Oh, no. He made me abhor that. Take to your good sleep, my man. We surprise the railroad tomorrow."

"Our raids still entertain you?" I asked.

"Not so much. But I believe our course has been written. We'll kill ten and lose two. Our old Bobbie Lee will smile when we send the nigger back to him with the message. I'll do hell for Lee's smile."

The nigger came in the tent about then. He was high-falutin, never hardly glanced at me. They had a magnificent bay waiting for the letters. Two soldiers came in and took an armload of missives from General Stuart's trunk, pressing them into the saddlebags. The nigger, in civilian clothes, finally looked at me.

"Who dis?" he said.

"Corporal Deed Ainsworth; shake hands," said General Stuart.

I have a glass shop in Biloxi. I never shook hands with any nigger. Yet the moment constrained me to. He was Jeb's best minstrel. He played the guitar better than anything one might want to hear, and the banjo. His voice singing "All Hail the Power" was the only feeling I ever had to fall on my knees and pray. But now he was going back down South as a rider with the messages.

"Ain't shaking hands with no nancy," said the nigger. "They say he lay down with a Choctaw chief in Mississippi, say he lick a heathen all over his feathers."

"You're getting opinions for a nigger, George," said Jeb, standing. "I don't believe Our Lord has room for another nigger's thoughts. You are tiring God when you use your mouth, George."

"Yessuh," said George.

"Do you want to apologize to Corporal Ainsworth?"

"I real sorry. I don't know what I say," the nigger said to me. "General Jeb taught me how to talk and sometimes I just go on talking to try it out."

"Ah, my brother George," Jeb suddenly erupted.

He rushed to the nigger and threw his arms around him. His eyes were full of tears. He embraced the black man in the manner of my dreams of how he might embrace me.

"My chap, my chum. Don't get yourself killed," said Jeb to George. "Try to look ignorant when you get near the road pickets, same as when I found you and saved you from drink."

"I loves you too, General Jeb. I ain't touched nothing since you saved me. Promise. I gon look ignorant like you say, tills I get to Richmond. Then I might have me a beer."

"Even Christ wouldn't deny you that. Ah, my George, there's a heaven where we'll all prosper together. Even this sissy, Corporal Ainsworth."

They both looked at me benevolently. I felt below the nigger.

George got on the horse and took off South.

At five the next morning we came out of a stand of birches and all of us flew high over the railroad, shooting down the men. I had two stolen repeaters on my hip in the middle of the rout and let myself off Pardon Me. A poor torn Yank, driven out of the attack, with no arm but a kitchen fork, straggled up to me. We'd burned and killed almost everything else.

Stuart rode by me screaming in his rich bass to mount. The blue cavalry was coming across the fire toward us. The wounded man was stabbing me in the chest with his fork. Jeb took his saber out in the old grand style to cleave the man from me. I drew the pistol on my right hip and put it almost against Jeb's nose when he leaned to me.

"You kill him, I kill you, General," I said.

There was no time for a puzzled look, but he boomed out: "Are you happy, Corporal Ainsworth? Are you satisfied, my good man Deed?"

I nodded.

"Go with your nature and remember our Savior!" he shouted, last in the retreat.

I have seen it many times, but there is no glory like Jeb Stuart putting spurs in his sorrel and escaping the Minié balls.

They captured me and sent me to Albany prison, where I write this.

I am well fed and wretched.

A gleeful little floorwipe came in the other day to say they'd killed Jeb in Virginia. I don't think there's much reservoir of self left to me now.

This earth will never see his kind again.

Willie Morris

(1934–1999)

Willie Morris, a native of Mississippi, was born on November 29, 1934, in Jackson and moved to Yazoo City in that state when he was six months old. At seventeen, he enrolled in the University of Texas at Austin, where he wrote for the student newspaper, the *Daily Texan*. After graduating with a B.A. in 1956, he went to New College, Oxford University, in England, where he studied on a Rhodes Scholarship for the next few years. In 1958, Morris received a B.A. from Oxford. In 1960, he was graduated with an M.A., also from Oxford.

In 1960, Morris moved back to Texas and became the editor of the *Texas Observer*, a position he held from 1960 to 1962 before relocating to New York. In 1963 he became associate editor of *Harper's*, and then in 1967 he assumed the position of editor-in-chief. His memoir, *North Toward Home*, was published in 1967 and won the Houghton Mifflin Literary Award. He left in 1971 to pursue a writing career. In 1980, he accepted the position of writer-in-residence at the University of Mississippi. In 1990, he moved to Jackson, Mississippi.

Morris's nonfiction books also include *Yazoo: Integration in a Deep-Southern Town* (1971); *A Southern Album: Recollections of Some People and Places and Times Gone By* (1975); *James Jones: A Friendship* (1978); *The Courting of Marcus Dupree* (1983); *Faulkner's Mississippi* (1990); *New York Days* (1993); *My Dog Skip* (1995); and *The Ghosts of Medgar Evers: A Tale of Race, Murder, Mississippi, and Hollywood* (1998). His novel, *The Last of the Southern Girls*, was published in 1973. Additionally, he published two children's books and numerous essay collections.

Morris died in Jackson, Mississippi, on August 2, 1999.

from *The Courting of Marcus Dupree*

We were Southerners, of course, and in 1981 we knew a little of the drama and intricacy of relying upon the black athlete in the colleges of the native South. We knew where the future lay, and also something of the irony of our past.

Kentucky, in 1967, was the first Southeastern Conference school to have a black football player.* Bear Bryant and Alabama came along fairly late in 1971. Southern Cal visited Birmingham in the first game of the 1970 season and defeated all-white Al-

---

*The first black athlete in the Southeastern Conference, embracing the states of Mississippi, Tennessee, Kentucky, Alabama, Louisiana, Georgia, and Florida, was a basketball player named Perry Wallace. He played for Vanderbilt in 1966. On road games, especially in Mississippi and Alabama, he suffered untold abuse. *The Los Angeles Times* recently asked him if he would

abama, 42–21. The black fullback for Southern Cal, Sam "The Bam" Cunningham, scored three touchdowns that night and gained over two hundred yards. One of Bryant's assistant coaches remarked to him that Sam Cunningham did more for integration in the South in sixty minutes than Martin Luther King had in twenty years. After Bryant integrated his Alabama teams, he said, "I don't believe you are better because you're black or because you're white. But some of the blacks now are like I was when I came out of Arkansas. They don't want to go back to what they came from." Bo Schembechler, the coach at Michigan, advised Bryant before he began seeking black players, "They won't quit you. They got nothing to go to."

Bear Bryant began recruiting blacks after the Southern Cal game of '70. He played two blacks in 1971 and a few more with each passing season. His teams won fifty-three regular-season games and lost two over this five-year span.

After Bryant's retirement and shortly before his death in 1983, Howell Raines of *The New York Times*, a native of Alabama and a graduate of the university, wrote a moving, introspective article in *The New Republic* in which he posed the question: If the Bear were such a saint and hero, why did he wait until 1971 to integrate his teams?

Before he is enshrined forever as an Icon of Sports, it is worth remembering that Paul William Bryant, Jr., was also a public man who lived in a poor and troubled state at a grim time. The year 1958, when Bryant fielded his first Alabama team, was also the year in which George C. Wallace made his first campaign for governor. Throughout the 1960s and 1970s, these two men were the dominant figures of public life in Alabama and the state's main representatives to the nation. In that time, they so dominated the consciousness of the state that it is only in relation to Wallace that we can understand the service that Bear Bryant did Alabama and how, like so many lesser men, he also failed that state in the midnight of its humiliation.

Nonetheless, Raines said, the record was fairly strong that Bryant felt contempt for Wallace's brutalizing racist politics. He worked behind the scenes with the university president to try to soften some of Wallace's behavior. In 1963 he warned Bull Connor, the police chief of Birmingham who had become a television celebrity when he turned the fire hoses on children, that if tickets were not made available to blacks at Alabama games in Birmingham, and if they were not treated with courtesy, then 'Bama would not play any more games in Birmingham. "Bryant and his teams provided a diversion from the old compulsions. They gave the state at least one thing to be proud of when Wallace was making it an object of approbrium. If Bryant never stood up to Wallace as he might have, he at least forced the little man to share center stage, and the coach's huge, calm presence made Wallace look small and shrill."

The early 1970s, coinciding with the massive integration of the Southern public schools, were revolutionary for college sports in Dixie. The exodus of black players going

---

do it again. "I don't know. Probably not. But a son of mine? God, no. Never. I'd never put him through something like that."

Seven years later, in 1973, Coach C. M. Newton of Alabama had four black starters on his basketball team. In 1982 in the Southeastern Conference, considered by many the best basketball league in the country, forty-two out of the fifty starting players were black.

from the South to the North was ending. The all-white colleges had suddenly opened to blacks. States like Mississippi, Georgia, Alabama, Louisiana, Tennessee, and Texas, which in the recent past had permitted their native blacks to perform on the West Coast or in the Midwest, were now inducing them to remain at home, not at the smaller all-black schools like Alcorn, Jackson State, Tennessee State, and Grambling, but at the principal state universities. The white fans cheered their black players, who became authentic campus heroes and began to be held in as much affection as their white contemporaries. The first black football player at Ole Miss, for instance, Ben Williams of my hometown Yazoo City who would later go on to the Buffalo Bills of the National Football League, in his senior year was elected by the student body "Colonel Rebel," the highest honor for a male student. There was a perfunctory query in Mississippi in our day regarding any promising high school player. "Is he white, or black?" Marcus Dupree of Philadelphia, Mississippi, would be a foremost legacy of those indwelling changes of the seventies.

It was indicative of the importance of the Southern black schools athletically before those changes that 197 alumni of Grambling in Louisiana went on to play professional football over the years. The record of Jackson State, Alcorn, Tennessee State, Southern University, and the others was also impressive. The professional football scouts were spending less and less time at the black schools. In 1968 the National Football League drafted eleven players from Jackson State. Eleven years later the entire Southwestern Athletic Conference, of which Jackson State was one of seven members, had only five players selected.

Eddie Robinson, the coach at Grambling for more than four decades who in 1981 was second only to Bear Bryant in his number of victories, understood the implications of this newly integrated South. "There was a time when a black player worried about being recruited just by a Grambling or a Jackson State or an Alcorn," he said. "Now, he's got a lot of schools interested in him. Yes, it's tough on the coaches. But more than anything, it's tough on the athlete. Now that same black player worries about adjusting to a predominantly black school because he probably came up through an integrated system." Marino Casem, the coach at Alcorn, which was located in the woodlands north of Natchez not far from the Mississippi River, also remembered the days before integration: "Quite naturally when we had carte blanche with the black athletes in our area, if a kid wanted to stay in the state he stayed with us. We had more players to choose from and we got the cream of the crop. Now the predominantly white schools are recruiting the cream of the crop. And the recruiting is more intense." One never sees more blacks than whites sitting on the bench at the primarily white colleges, he would add. Jake Gaither, who coached for years at Florida A&M in Tallahassee, predicted those transformations a long time ago. "Kids used to hitch rides in here," he said. "Now I have to go out and pay air fare for them."

The trend at the three predominantly white universities in Mississippi was obvious. In 1981 the Mississippi State and Ole Miss football rosters were roughly half white and half black. Southern Mississippi had established itself as a football power by persuading black players to come there rather than to the traditional black schools.* The enticements of expensive facilities and playing before large audiences had not been lost on those outstanding young blacks. Johnnie Cooks, a black line-

---

*I am very grateful to Jerry Potter of *The Jackson Clarion-Ledger* for his help and writings in this largely neglected area, as well as to Temple Drake and other knowledgeable recruiters.

backer from the Delta town of Leland, Mississippi, who was an all-American at Mississippi State in 1981 and a first-round choice in the professional draft, had been recruited by several black colleges before he decided on State. "I've got to live with white people," he said. "I went to high school with them. I've lived with them all my life. I didn't see why I should make a big jump and go to an SWAC school. If you have the ability and go to the big-time schools, you'll do well. And you'll get more publicity than you'd get if you'd gone to the black schools. That's going to give you a big edge."

The descriptions of the college recruiters going into the homes of poor black families were heartrending and legend. Every recruiter in America had his stories about those experiences. At one conference in a bar near the Mississippi River in western Tennessee, Temple Drake told me he once almost cried in front of a recruit and his family. He was sitting in a straight-backed chair in a tenant shack talking with a big tackle. It was a few days before Christmas and the house was cold. There was cardboard in the windows. The grandmother was wandering about in a torn nightgown and old tennis sneakers with holes in the toes. The little brothers and sisters were sitting on the bare floor looking up at him and saying nothing. They had just had a dinner of cornbread and water. They all slept on blankets on the floor in two rooms in the back. The father was in one of the back rooms coughing. The mother was out somewhere working as a maid. "I felt so sorry for them I didn't know what to do," he said. "I'd seen a lot of bad places, but it was Christmas, and there wasn't a toy in the house for those kids. There wasn't even a television. I talked to the boy for a while, but my heart wasn't in it. When I got up to leave I looked in my wallet. I had seventy-five dollars and needed twenty-five dollars to get home. I went into the back room and gave the father a fifty-dollar bill for Christmas. Sure it violated the rules. Some payoff! To hell with the damned NCAA. You're a human before you're a coach."

John Merritt, the football coach at Tennessee State in Nashville, had three brothers named Richardson who played for him when he was coaching at Jackson State:

> There was Willie Richardson, who played for Baltimore for a while, and one played with the Cleveland Browns and Kansas City, and the other played with New England. They lived in one of these shotgun houses, a slender house with one room right behind the next one. You got a living room and right behind that is a bedroom and right behind that is a kitchen and right behind that is the outdoor toilet. And, of course, those boys were able to build their mother and father a new home and give them and that family a whole new outlook. Their brothers and sisters, who weren't athletes, got a college education. Before that, college wasn't even in their future. To me, this is the wonderful thing that happens in football. But it's depressing at the time, when you see it recruiting. And, oh Lord, there's so much of it, so many people living like that, more than most people can ever imagine. Most people are sheltered from that kind of thing. They don't know it's even going on. They never see it.

One recruiter told me of the young man who had large blisters on his feet because he was wearing his older brother's discarded shoes, which were three or four sizes too big. His mother said she hoped the facilities at the university were good ones; her son had used an indoor toilet for the first time in the Head Start Program.

Bill Canty of Ole Miss described the shack on the Gulf Coast that was so crowded with people the boy had to go out to an abandoned car in the backyard and study his schoolbooks by flashlight. Eddie Crawford spoke of a boy with alcoholic parents and six or seven brothers and sisters in a tiny house. He had a sleeping bag and slept in the back seat of an old car. The tales abounded among the recruiters of going into the bare cold-water apartments in the city ghettos and being both saddened and afraid.

A gentleman named Bill "Bull" Bolton told a story about basketball recruiting. Bolton was an assistant coach at Florida State. He was from a small town in Tennessee and had played for Ole Miss during the Meredith times. He went to New York to recruit a six-foot-eleven black boy who lived in an impoverished ghetto of the Bronx. He decided to buy a long leather jacket so he might blend into the environment. He wandered through the crumbling neighborhoods but could not find the prospect's apartment. As he stood dubiously on a street corner, six large young black men approached him. One was carrying a portable radio of the type known as a "ghetto-blaster." "I'm in trouble," Bolton said to himself.

The young blacks came up to him and began touching his new leather jacket. "Hey, man, we like this coat," one of them said.

"Bull" Bolton told them he was a basketball coach at Florida State University and gave them the name of the young man he was looking for. "We want him to play basketball in Florida," he said. "I'm trying to get him out of here."

The six blacks escorted him to the apartment and introduced him to his man.

One assistant coach in the South recounted visiting a little concrete-block house and sitting next to the young athlete in front of a wood fire. He remembered it was during the off-season, and the fire was not big enough to heat the whole house. While they talked, the boy's stomach kept growling.

"When was the last time you had anything to eat?" the coach asked.

"Yesterday."

"What did you have?"

"A bologna sandwich."

"What about your brothers and sisters?"

"Yesterday too."

The coach took all of them to a restaurant for hamburgers. The bill came to about twenty dollars, which was also against the rules.

The coach was prompted to add a footnote. "The kid's father was about six feet two and 140 pounds, thin as death, with only four front teeth that went in all directions. When I saw the father again a month later he had gained about twenty pounds and had a new set of teeth. I knew then I'd lost the kid."

One young man from a poor family, a promising cornerback, arrived as a freshman at the school he had chosen. He was an immediate disappointment. He was running slower than his recorded speed and he could not lift weights very well. The coaches sent him for another physical examination. The doctors discovered that his mouth was riddled with abscesses. He had never been to a dentist.

A few years ago in a dilapidated house in Vicksburg, Mississippi, the father of the athlete did not like what a recruiter from Mississippi State was saying. He drew a pistol on the visitor and ordered him to leave, which the recruiter did with no further encouragement.

A Texas coach remembered waiting for two hours for a top prospect to meet an appointment. He sat in a sad little shack watching television with the parents and a number of younger children. While an infant urinated in his lap, two dogs began using his legs as sexual objects. When the young athlete finally arrived, he said, "Coach, I'll be back in a few minutes." From a window, the recruiter saw him drive off in a car with "Texas A&M" on the door. "That's when I decided to retire," the coach said.

One coach, whom I knew to be a consummately straightforward man not given to exaggeration, brought in a junior college player from Los Angeles and met him at the Memphis airport. "I decided to take the scenic route down to school, kind of show him the area. We were driving along on a back road around Sardis and he asked, 'What's that?' I told him it was a cow. He said he'd never seen a cow before. He was amazed." He also went somewhere else, the coach explained.

In one black family in Mississippi, several of the sons had grown up picking cotton and had gone on to excel in sports. The youngest, a senior in high school, was a superb football player. The word around the recruiter's network was that an out-of-state school had offered a substantial amount of cash. A Mississippi recruiter, who knew and admired the father, discussed this with him. "Coach," the father said, "I've raised seven boys, and I ain't sold any of 'em yet."

We were getting into a day in the South and elsewhere, one must add, in which black assistant coaches were beginning to go into white households and recruit white athletes. There would be a literature to that, too, for I had learned that the best people among the recruiters were not least of all chroniclers of the heart.

I would get to know a black man in Philadelphia, Marcus' Cub Scout leader and Little League coach, who in smaller measure had been the "Marcus Dupree" of his time there. He was an excellent running back for Booker T. Washington High School. He missed by less than a year the integration of the public schools, and the integration of the football teams at the majority white universities of Mississippi by two or three. He came from a poor family and decided on East Central Junior College, where he got hurt and languished with injuries. Yet even had he been as superlative an athlete as his protégé was to become, the options of his day in the South were few. Much had happened since the late sixties.

The alternatives available to Marcus at age seventeen would be exceptionally varied, encompassing not just Mississippi or the South but the whole of America. His mother was a graduate of Alcorn University. Coach W. C. Gordon of Jackson State, which only a few years before had produced the great running back Walter Payton of the Chicago Bears, was earnestly pursuing him. With all the methodical encouragement that he remain in his native state, would the black Mississippi schools make a provocative argument? Or, in 1981, was it too late for that?

* * *

In 1981 there were approximately seven hundred black students at Ole Miss out of an enrollment of ten thousand, or 7 percent. The University actively recruited blacks and encouraged their participation in extracurricular activities. Whites and blacks strolled across the campus greenswards together, and sat on the grass studying their books together in the Grove. Yet the subtleties abounded and required the discerning eye. There were only seven full-time undergraduate black professors. Money was one problem, and black professors and administrators were often lost to larger schools. The rural backdrop was another, as was the absence of a sizable middle-class black community here. The Black Student Union and the Associated Student Body, which, in effect, had been the student government, had recently merged. But the pervasive sorority and fraternity system remained segregated; the blacks had their own chapters.

Many black students complained that they did not feel they were a significant part of campus life, and that there were in fact two cultures juxtaposed here. I witnessed this emotion in a small class I taught. I had encouraged the young whites and blacks to be candid about the realities of their relationships here. Everyone began talking at once, as if an ancient burden had been lifted. The blacks said they found it difficult to consider this *their* university. The whites said they were trying to understand. One white young-ster was especially disarming. "I have nothing against you," he said. "In fact, I like you. I think if there were *more* of you the situation would be better."

I had heard other stories. In a freshman zoology class of thirty-six students, mostly white sorority girls, with only one black male student, no one chose to be the black's laboratory partner. Finally, after an embarrassing interval, a white girl who was not in a sorority volunteered. In a history class which was discussing the Meredith Riots, a black student argued: "Only the vocabulary has changed. How many black professors are there? How many administrators?" A white private academy graduate replied: "If things are so bad, why are you here?" During this discussion, it was noted, two white sorority girls were thumbing through *Vogue* magazine.

It was a sensitive dialogue, enveloped with consequence. Both the white and black students were largely the "aristocrats" of their races in the state, and they were imbued with a fierce pride. "There are only five or six black students I can call by name," a young white said. "I average one black a semester in my classes." Another said: "It's like they separate themselves from us." A graduate student argued: "The blacks on this campus permit tokenism and the whites promote it." A professor cited the products of the rigorously ideological private academies which emerged after the integration of the public schools—roughly 20 to 25 percent of the student body by his calculations. "They don't even know their black contemporaries the way we did in the *segregated* South," he said. A black teacher said: "For many whites and blacks, rap-port is not the natural thing it may seem. People have to learn it."

A final contention lay in the traditional symbols of the Old South. Many blacks com-plained of the school fight song "Dixie," the mascot "Colonel Rebel," and the waving of the Confederate flag at athletic events; the flag was by far the most inflammatory. The first black cheerleader in Ole Miss history attracted considerable attention by announcing he would not carry the flag on the field. His wishes were understood by both the administra-tion and most of the students, although he was the recipient of considerable hate mail. Na-tional reporters, who swiftly came down believing Mississippi was on the brink of another Armageddon, were impressed by the dignity of the young black man. A columnist in *The Daily Mississippian*, young Dan Turner of Philadelphia, Mississippi, addressing himself to a few disgruntled alumni, wrote: "I have one piece of advice to all those amazed with our selection of cheerleaders. Grow up. We did." As for "Dixie," the Ole Miss band, which had many black performers, had perfected a song called "From Dixie with Love," which was a stirring blend of both "Dixie," and "The Battle Hymn of the Republic." This rendi-tion, played at all games, would have touched the soul of a Massachusetts abolitionist.

The institution was a blend of everything the Deep South was and is. Many of the white students lived the most sheltered of lives. Their proximity with their black con-temporaries seemed both mystifying and exhilarating. They were both grown-up and rowdy children. They still got hopelessly drunk at the Gin or the Warehouse or the Abby, and I sometimes wondered how many of them read books.* Yet others of them

---

*It was interesting to note, however, that Ole Miss had produced twenty-two Rhodes Schol-ars, eighth among American public universities, compared with one for Mississippi State and none for the University of Southern Mississippi.

came to the Hoka at midnight for coffee to discuss those things which were inherent to a university town—literature and history, the human race. Allison Brown, daughter of an old Mississippi family, honor student and campus beauty who was the editor of the Meredith anniversary issue of the *Ole Miss Magazine*, would write in her editorial: "We are of a generation in Mississippi that knows first-hand that blacks and whites can actually work together, grow up together, and share common experiences. Even at Ole Miss, where tradition hangs on until the very last thread, much progress has been made ... Our generation can do something about it. We can work toward the inevitable changes that will make Ole Miss a better place for people of all races."

In the spring of 1983, however, as I was finishing this book about Marcus, a number of sorrowful events served to cut through the assumptions many of us had had about racial enlightenment at the state university. In three years I had learned much from my young black students. The Ole Miss blacks, in response to the publishing of several photographs of the Ku Klux Klan in the new yearbook, came out with a set of fourteen demands, including the abolition of the Confederate flag, the mascot "Colonel Rebel," and "Dixie." (The Chancellor, Porter Fortune, had already decided to withdraw any official sanction of the flag, and made that announcement later in the week. He received several death threats.) One night several hundred white students, a thousand of them by some estimates, marched on a tiny black fraternity house, in such contrast to the palatial white sorority and fraternity residences, where one of the black student leaders, young John Hawkins, the cheerleader who had refused to wave the Rebel flag at ball games, lived. The ten or twelve black youngsters in the fraternity house were confronted by this mob, which yelled "Nigger night!" and "Save the flag!" An Ole Miss spokesman later called this an expression of "spring fever." The police arrived in time to surround the house. In the days following, many white students taunted the blacks on the campus and the streets of town by waving the flag in their faces and demanding to know why they were not at Jackson State. "What kind of people must have raised these kids?" someone asked.

The party-loving sorority and fraternity students, representatives of an entrenched social system rife with philistinism, were at the core of this shameful outbreak, and of the emotions which prompted it. It was an exercise in penultimate nihilistic Mississippi self-destruction, as if these young whites neither knew of nor cared for the delicate progress of twenty years, neither understood nor even acknowledged the presence of an outside world, of Auschwitz and the choice Sophie had to make, or Selma or Neshoba in '64, or the Tet Offensive, or all the assassinations, or the very flow of human history; or the reluctant American civilization itself trying to deal with our darker impulses. "The girls are gorgeous and the boys are sleek young hounds," a friend of mine who knew and was concerned for them said. "Their disaffection is frivolous and unearned. We've failed them somehow." "It's a time warp," commented Leon Daniel, a much-traveled wire service reporter who had covered the Meredith Riots and the Vietnam war. "I haven't seen kids like these since the 1950s." Dean Faulkner Wells, the novelist's niece, herself a writer and a graduate of Ole Miss, said: "It takes a certain kind of human being to come here and stay happy. It's a haven from the rest of the world. A very safe place. Moonlight and magnolias. They really do believe that *Gone With the Wind* was real. It was real to their mamas and real to their grandmamas. This is a continuation of the security they've had all their lives. All of the clichés come to mind; 'Daddy's rich and mama's good-looking.' Unless they're crossed they're perfectly harmless."

In the autumn of 1981 Ole Miss was anxious to have Marcus Dupree. "Is he going to come here?" everyone asked me. "He should."

The Ole Miss football team was roughly half white and half black. The Rebel partisans cheered their black players as enthusiastically as they did the whites, and the outstanding ones were campus heroes—Hammerhead and Buford, Michael and Carlos, Freddy Joe and Chico. It was one of the endless ironies of this complicated setting that the white fraternity boys with their Rebel flags who might march on a dozen unsuspecting blacks would show an unqualified pride in the black athletes and appreciate their friendship. What manner of state was ours? "We all love Mississippi," the historian David Sansing once said to me, "but sometimes she does not love us back."

Michael Harmon, a pass receiver who had played in high school against Marcus Dupree, grew up in Kosciusko. He was one of nine children. "We all picked cotton growing up," he said. "It's pretty rough work, but we did it together as a family. We didn't mind. A lot of times we'd get up at dawn and pick cotton until school started. We'd go to school and then come home and pick cotton until dark. I used to miss twenty or twenty-five days of school a year picking cotton. On Saturdays we'd take a radio to the fields and listen to the games. I liked Ole Miss and I liked Coach Sloan," he said. He was a good student and he married the first girl he dated on the campus. "I wouldn't change anything about it, except maybe what people think about Ole Miss," he said. He actually had black football recruits ask him if they beat black players at Ole Miss with chains. "Can you believe that? Chains!"

This touched upon an interesting point, germane to this narrative. The competition for high school football players in Mississippi between Mississippi State, Southern Mississippi, and Ole Miss had become suicidal. In the successful days of Ole Miss football under Johnny Vaught, when the team was consistently one of the national powers, Ole Miss got most of the Mississippi players it wanted. "When I was coaching at Alabama," Coach Steve Sloan of Ole Miss said in the summer before Marcus' senior year in high school, "Coach Bryant used to tell us that we had to get at least 75 percent of the players in the state of Alabama to be a great football team. This is true of any state in the Southeast and especially in Mississippi, where we don't have as many people as most states. Prior to integration, Ole Miss did this in Mississippi. After integration, we began to split the players. In some years, especially before the seventies, we were dominant in this state. That's why I refer to Ole Miss football in terms of B.I. and A.I., before integration and after integration."

The problem athletically at Ole Miss had much to do with recruiting the great black players from the state. The rival recruiters from other schools, especially Southern Mississippi, were telling the black players and their parents that Ole Miss was a slave factory, harkening to the plantation days. The traditional symbols of the older South at the state university were only a part of this campaign. This systematic elaboration of the alleged treatment of black students at Ole Miss was relentless and often persuasive.

All three schools, naturally, were avid to have Marcus. Herschel Walker, after all, had made the University of Georgia a national contender almost overnight. And Marcus was a Mississippian. State and Southern had been fielding winning football teams, and both had excellent coaches and good small-town environments; Ole Miss had been losing. I myself admired much about the people of State and Southern; the jousting among the three schools for the young athlete was a source for me of a nearly obsessive fascination.

In the summer of '81, the case could be made that Ole Miss had an inside track. Marcus had attended the Ole Miss summer football camps in his high school years. From these he knew the coaches and the coaches knew him. His two closest friends had chosen to attend Ole Miss on football scholarships. And there was the additional challenge, in the language of the world of football, of "turning the program around."

But all this, of course, was involved with something broader.

James Meredith had always intrigued me. He was a mystic, I sensed; one could not fault him his courage. It was gratifying that Ole Miss invited him back to give the keynote speech at the observance of the twentieth anniversary of his stormy entrance to the university. When I was living on the Upper West Side of Manhattan in the late 1960s and he was a student at Columbia, by exceptional fate my telephone number was identical to his except for the last digit, which was one different. I got more than a few of his calls and I presume he got some of mine.

Not too long ago he said:

Man, let me tell you something. It's true I was born in Mississippi, but that's not why I'm here. Mississippi is the center point, the apex of the system that brought blacks and whites together. Mississippi is the perfection of the merging of blacks and whites. The merger took place because of economics. The system was slavery. No place was this system more perfected than in Mississippi. That means this is the turn-around point. This is where the turn-around has got to come. That makes Mississippi a land of opportunity. That's why I'm here.

In terms of just living, Mississippi is by far the best place in America to be. You have more integration in Mississippi than you have anywhere else by far, North or South. You can go anywhere in Jackson, Mississippi, tonight and see blacks and whites eating, dancing and having a good time together.

But that doesn't mean there's anything to celebrate. I think Mississippi has decided to standardize the social pattern in this state. They want to set the standard for the South and for the nation. And that's going to take place. The only question is what that standard is going to be.

The most horrific specters of the state had always been racism and poverty. Ed Perry, the chairman of the Appropriations Committee of the Mississippi House of Representatives who had accompanied me to see Marcus play in Philadelphia, recalled what his grandfather, who was a farmer down in the hard land of Choctaw County not far from Neshoba, once told him: "Mississippi was the first state the Depression hit. It was so poor people didn't even know they were in a Depression. They were in a Depression before there was a Depression."

The returning son needed little to remind him. The shacks and the unpainted façades still abounded, and although the paved streets and public housing in the older black sections of the towns seemed prolific in contrast to the 1940s, a random drive through the rural land or the larger cities revealed much of that same abject impoverishment, mainly black but white as well. Out in the Delta, where time often seems not to have moved, the extremes haunted one as they always did (the homes of many of the rich white planters, it must be said, would be cottages in East Hampton, Long Island), but the very land itself seemed bereaved with the countless half-collapsed, abandoned tenant shacks set against the boundless horizon.

Near the end of his life Martin Luther King had stopped in the town of Marks in the Delta. In *Let the Trumpet Sound* Stephen B. Oates described the visit:

> He saw scores of Negro children walking barefoot in the streets, their stomachs protruding from hunger. Their mothers and fathers were trying to get funds from Washington, but nothing had come through yet. They raised a little money here and there trying to feed their children, trying to teach them something. Some parents were unemployed and had no source of income—no pensions, no welfare checks, nothing. "How do you live?" King asked, incredulous. "Well," they said, "we go around—go around to the neighbors and ask them for a little something. When the berry season comes, we pick berries; when the rabbit season comes, we hunt and catch a few rabbits, and that's about it." Sometimes, though, it was really bad. Sometimes they couldn't get any food at all, not even for the children . . . When King heard that, he broke down and cried.

On a recent drive through the upper Delta, I saw a number of haphazard concrete-block structures, now used for storage in the flat fields. These were the rural Negro schools which had been built in the late 1940s in an effort to give substance to the doctrine of "separate but equal." I came upon the hamlet of Falcon, an all-black town which had recently been incorporated and had a brand-new water tower and hydrants—a municipal water system constructed under the Carter administration with federal money. It was a Sunday afternoon, and I drove down the dirt main street paralleling the railroad. The lean-to shacks, the sagging stores, the people reminded me of Haiti.

Signs of the economic recession of the early 1980s were everywhere in the state. White and black tramps carrying their pathetic bundles hitchhiked on the roads between Oxford and Philadelphia. I stopped in one small town en route to Philadelphia to buy something in a drugstore; two drugstores on the main street were closed in the middle of the afternoon. When I asked a fireman sitting in front of the firehouse why they were not open, he said: "Because they ain't doin' no business." At the corner of Mill and Amite in Jackson, a scene I remembered from my childhood in the Depression was re-enacted in our day—the dozens of black men, seated on buckets, waiting for people to drive by looking for day laborers, indicating with their fingers how many workers were needed, and the scramble that ensued.

"Since the Civil War," John Emmerich, one of the state's perceptive editors, wrote not too long ago, "the history of Mississippi has been the story of two races of people—black and white—trying with difficulty to live together, one dominant, the other suppressed, the two often in conflict. Both really have been disadvantaged—first by military defeat, ultimately by economic decline, recession, depression, rural poverty, and enormous social, educational,* and economic problems beyond our ability to overcome. That is why Mississippi today is the poorest, the worst educated, the

---

*Governor William Winter of Mississippi, one of the most enlightened leaders of the modern South, steered through the legislature in 1982 his Education Reform Act. Among other things it established a compulsory school attendance law (more than 40 percent of those who started school in the state did not finish) and public school kindergartens. Mississippi had been the only state without public kindergartens.

most dependent on the federal government of all the states—and the list on which Mississippi is at the bottom goes on and on . . . It's an old story in the history of mankind: economic greed perpetuated oppression. Today we continue to pay for the sins of our forefathers."

The figures were there to see, and they were emphatic—unemployment for blacks in the state running two or three times higher than for whites, most black families existing below the recognized poverty level, more than one fourth of all black families fatherless (compared with 56 percent nationally). Mississippi was last among all the states in black median family income, which was less than half that of Mississippi whites.

Yet in Marcus' lifetime one was witness to the decline in the urban civilization of the North. The black riots of the late 1960s led in city after city to the continuing massive flight to white suburbia and the white abandonment of the public schools. The statistics on this exodus of the 1970s were remarkable. Examining them, Theodore H. White would conclude: "Big-city schools are now more segregated in fact (though integrated in law) than ever before." One of the ironies of contemporary America was that institutionalized racial integration among the young, with all its human implications, was working best in the small to middle-sized towns of Dixie. Who would have predicted it?

What had happened in many of these places of the South? I had posed the question to my friend the night we left the earthen dam in Neshoba. The cup of bitterness at last drained? The old basic decency freeing itself before it was too late? What would Faulkner make of these changes in Mississippi and much of the South since his death less than two months before the Meredith confrontations of '62? If I chanced across him on the Square in Oxford tomorrow in his old tweed jacket with the leather elbows in front of Shine Morgan's Furniture Store and he said, "Let's go sit on the front porch, Morris, and drink some whiskey . . . I want to know what's been goin' on"—what would I tell him?

I believed I would begin with his sixteen-year old great-nephew whom we know as "The Jaybird," grandson of his younger brother Dean. One night recently I was sitting at the old table in the house on South Lamar where Dean Faulkner Wells, The Jaybird's mother, and her husband, Larry Wells—publisher, editor, and janitor of the Yoknapatawpha Press, located over the Sneed Ace Hardware Store, now lived. Much of *Absalom, Absalom* had been written on this table, during Faulkner's grief over his brother's death. The Jaybird had just departed to play in the high school basketball game. I was talking with Miss Louise—Faulkner's sister-in-law, Dean's widow. "Miss Louise," I asked, "if Mr. Bill were sitting here tonight and knew that The Jaybird was the only white boy on the starting five for Oxford High School, what would he think?" Miss Louise thought for a while. "I think," she finally replied, "he'd be honored that The Jaybird made the team."

To me The Jaybird's warm comradeship and day-to-day proximity under the official auspices of the public schools of Mississippi with Topcat, The Hawk, Toad, Scott, Calvin, and the others went to the heart of a different South.

Sitting on the front porch with Mr. Bill, I would have to go from there. I would suggest that since his departure the very context of our dialogue—the dialogue itself—had altered drastically. Public kindness, courtesy, and regard were surely not inconsequential qualities, and much of the malevolence of the language had disappeared, and the rhetoric of the most belligerent of the white supremacists was no longer fashionable. Would I advise him that the immense tide of legislative accomplishment and judicial decree which emerged from the struggles of the 1960s—the Second Reconstruction, as C. Vann Woodward and others called it—had helped save the South from itself? The Civil Rights Act of 1964, the Voting Rights Act of 1965, the whole crescendo of decisions from the federal courts, such as Judge Frank Johnson's in Alabama, and Judge William Keady's in Mississippi, had achieved results that were tangible now.

The author of *Go Down, Moses* and *The Unvanquished* would be intrigued, yet by no means surprised, to learn of one of the most splendid periods in our history when the bravery of the black Southerners of the 1960s and those of The Movement—in Neshoba County and elsewhere—demanded equality under the law for themselves and their progeny, and their traditional allies among the white Southerners grew in number and derived an incalculable sustenance from their example. Leaders like Martin Luther King, as a young black once said, "made it possible for them to believe they *could* overcome."

In 1965, writing in a special issue of *Harper's* on the one-hundredth anniversary of Appomattox, Walker Percy, I might have told Mr. Bill, described Mississippi as "a fallen paradise," which had spurned all civility. What Percy found tragically absent in Mississippi, and implicitly in much of the lower South of the mid 1960s, was a sense of "public space" in which people might let one another alone for the sake of civilizing values. I believed Mississippi and the South in the years which followed rediscovered the necessity of such a noncombat zone. For whatever reason, the flourishing of independent expression here in recent times—the tolerance of the hopes and fears of others, the awareness that words used carelessly can be the most inflammatory of instruments—and with this the articulated recognition in the broader context of the necessity of universal access to public institutions—had served our deepest traditions well. On the front porch, sipping the sour mash, Mr. Bill may have been listening, so that I might have asked him to drive down to Philadelphia with Pete and me the following week to watch Marcus Dupree.

Elizabeth Spencer

(1921–   )

The writing career of Elizabeth Spencer, who was born on July 19, 1921, in Carrollton, Mississippi, spans decades. In 1942 she was graduated from Belhaven College in Jackson, Mississippi, and in 1943 she received an M.A. from Vanderbilt University in Tennessee, where she studied under Donald Davidson. She has taught English at Northwest Mississippi Junior College (1943–1944); Ward-Belmont (1944–1945); University of Mississippi (late 1940s); Concordia University in Montréal (1976–1986); and the University of North Carolina, Chapel Hill. She was married to John Rusher in 1956, moved to Montréal in 1958, and now lives in Chapel Hill, North Carolina.

Spencer's novels explore inner and outer conflicts. Whereas the first novels were set in the rural South, she has used other backdrops, in particular Europe, to explore the psychology of human actions and reactions. *Fire in the Morning*, her first novel, was published in 1948. While in Italy on a Guggenheim grant in 1953, she wrote most of *The Voice at the Back Door*, which was published in 1956. Critics have particularly praised the novella, *The Light in the Piazza*, which was made into a movie. Among her numerous awards is the 1996–1997 John William Corrington Award for Literary Excellence.

Books also include *This Crooked Way* (1952); *The Knights and Dragons* (1965); *No Place for an Angel* (1967); *Ship Island and Other Stories* (1968); *The Snare* (1972); *Marilee* (1981); *The Stories of Elizabeth Spencer* (1981); *The Mules* (1982); *The Salt Line* (1984); *Jack of Diamonds and Other Stories* (1988); *Innocence Betrayed* (1989); *Conversations with Elizabeth Spencer* (1991); *On the Gulf* (1991); *The Night Travellers* (1991); and *Landscapes of the Heart: A Memoir* (1997).

First Dark

When Tom Beavers started coming back to Richton, Mississippi, on weekends, after the war was over, everybody in town was surprised and pleased. They had never noticed him much before he paid them this compliment; now they could not say enough nice things. There was not much left in Richton for him to call family—just his aunt who had raised him, Miss Rita Beavers, old as God, ugly as sin, deaf as a post. So he must be fond of the town, they reasoned; certainly it was a pretty old place. Far too many young men had left it and never come back at all.

He would drive in every Friday night from Jackson, where he worked. All weekend, his Ford, dusty of flank, like a hard-ridden horse, would sit parked down the hill near Miss Rita's old wire front gate, which sagged from the top hinge and had worn a span in the ground. On Saturday morning, he would head for the drugstore, then the post office; then he would be observed walking here and there around the streets under the shade trees. It was as though he were looking for something.

He wore steel taps on his heels, and in the still the click of them on the sidewalks would sound across the big front lawns and all the way up to the porches of the houses, where two ladies might be sitting behind a row of ferns. They would identify him to one another, murmuring in their fine little voices, and say it was just too bad there was nothing here for young people. It was just a shame they didn't have one or two more old houses, here, for a Pilgrimage—look how Natchez had waked up.

One Saturday morning in early October, Tom Beavers sat at the counter in the drugstore and reminded Totsie Poteet, the drugstore clerk, of a ghost story. Did he remember the strange old man who used to appear to people who were coming into Richton along the Jackson road at twilight—what they called "first dark"?

"Sure I remember," said Totsie. "Old Cud'n Jimmy Wiltshire used to tell us about him every time we went 'possum hunting. I could see him plain as I can see you, the way he used to tell it. Tall, with a top hat on, yeah, and waiting in the weeds alongside the road ditch, so'n you couldn't tell if he wasn't taller than any mortal man could be, because you couldn't tell if he was standing down in the ditch or not. It would look like he just grew up out of the weeds. Then he'd signal to you."

"Them that stopped never saw anybody," said Tom Beavers, stirring his coffee. "There were lots of folks besides Mr. Jimmy that saw him."

"There was, let me see . . ." Totsie enumerated others—some men, some women, some known to drink, others who never touched a drop. There was no way to explain it. "There was that story the road gang told. Do you remember, or were you off at school? It was while they were straightening the road out to the highway—taking the curves out and building a new bridge. Anyway, they said that one night at quitting time, along in the winter and just about dark, this old guy signaled to some of 'em. They said they went over and he asked them to move a bulldozer they had left across the road, because he had a wagon back behind on a little dirt road, with a sick nigger girl in it. Had to get to the doctor and this was the only way. They claimed they knew didn't nobody live back there on that little old road, but niggers can come from anywhere. So they moved the bulldozer and cleared back a whole lot of other stuff, and waited and waited. Not only didn't no wagon ever come, but the man that had stopped them, he was gone, too. They was right shook up over it. You never heard that one?"

"No, I never did." Tom Beavers said this with his eyes looking up over his coffee cup, as though he sat behind a hand of cards. His lashes and brows were heavier than was ordinary, and worked as a veil might, to keep you away from knowing exactly what he was thinking.

"They said he was tall and had a hat on." The screen door flapped to announce a customer, but Totsie kept on talking. "But whether he was a white man or a real light-colored nigger they couldn't say. Some said one and some said another. I figured they'd been pulling on the jug a little earlier than usual. You know why? I never heard of *our* ghost *saying* nothing. Did you, Tom?"

He moved away on the last words, the way a clerk will, talking back over his shoulder and ahead of him to his new customer at the same time, as though he had two voices and two heads. "And what'll it be today, Miss Frances?"

The young woman standing at the counter had a prescription already out of her bag. She stood with it poised between her fingers, but her attention was drawn toward Tom Beavers, his coffee cup, and the conversation she had interrupted. She was a girl whom no ordinary description would fit. One would have to know first of all who she was: Frances Harvey. After that, it was all right for her to be a little odd-looking, with her reddish hair that curled back from her brow, her light eyes, and her high, pale temples. This is not the material for being pretty, but in Frances Harvey it was what could sometimes be beauty. Her family home was laden with history that nobody but the Harveys could remember. It would have been on a Pilgrimage if Richton had had one. Frances still lived in it, looking after an invalid mother.

"What were you-all talking about?" she wanted to know.

"About that ghost they used to tell about," said Totsie, holding out his hand for the prescription. "The one people used to see just outside of town, on the Jackson road."

"But why?" she demanded. "Why were you talking about him?"

"Tom, here—" the clerk began, but Tom Beavers interrupted him.

"I was asking because I was curious," he said. He had been studying her from the corner of his eye. Her face was beginning to show the wear of her mother's long illness, but that couldn't be called change. Changing was something she didn't seem to have done, her own style being the only one natural to her.

"I was asking," he went on, "because I saw him." He turned away from her somewhat too direct gaze and said to Totsie Poteet, whose mouth had fallen open, "It was where the new road runs close to the old road, and as far as I could tell he was right on the part of the old road where people always used to see him."

"But when?" Frances Harvey demanded.

"Last night," he told her. "Just around first dark. Driving home."

A wealth of quick feeling came up in her face. "So did I! Driving home from Jackson! I saw him, too!"

For some people, a liking for the same phonograph record or for Mayan archaeology is enough of an excuse to get together. Possibly, seeing the same ghost was no more than that. Anyway, a week later, on Saturday at first dark, Frances Harvey and Tom Beavers were sitting together in a car parked just off the highway, near the spot where they agreed the ghost had appeared. The season was that long, peculiar one between summer and fall, and there were so many crickets and tree frogs going full tilt in their periphery that their voices could hardly be distinguished from the background noises, though they both would have heard a single football in the grass. An edge of autumn was in the air at night, and Frances had put on a tweed jacket at the last minute, so the smell of moth balls was in the car, brisk and most unghostlike.

But Tom Beavers was not going to forget the value of the ghost, whether it put in an appearance or not. His questions led Frances into reminiscence.

"No, I never saw him before the other night," she admitted. "The Negroes used to talk in the kitchen, and Regina and I—you know my sister Regina—would sit there listening, scared to go and scared to stay. Then finally going to bed upstairs was no relief, either, because sometimes Aunt Henrietta was visiting us, and *she'd* seen it. Or if she wasn't visiting us, the front room next to us, where she stayed, would be empty, which was worse. There was no way to lock ourselves in, and besides, what was there to lock out? We'd lie all night like two sticks in bed, and shiver. Papa finally had to take a hand. He called us in and sat us down and said that the whole thing was easy to explain—it was all automobiles. What their headlights did with the dust and shadows out on the Jackson road. 'Oh, but Sammie and Jerry!' we said, with great big eyes, sitting side by side on the sofa, with our tennis shoes flat on the floor."

"Who were Sammie and Jerry?" asked Tom Beavers.

"Sammie was our cook. Jerry was her son, or husband, or something. Anyway, they certainly didn't have cars. Papa called them in. They were standing side by side by the bookcase, and Regina and I were on the sofa—four pairs of big eyes, and Papa pointing his finger. Papa said, 'Now, you made up these stories about ghosts, didn't you?' 'Yes, sir,' said Sammie. 'We made them up.' 'Yes, sir,' said Jerry. 'We sho did.' 'Well, then, you can just stop it,' Papa said. 'See how peaked these children look?' Sammie and Jerry were terribly polite to us for a week, and we got in the car and rode up and down the Jackson road at first dark to see if the headlights really did it. But we never saw anything. We didn't tell Papa, but headlights had nothing whatever to do with it."

"You had your own *car* then?" He couldn't believe it.

"Oh, no!" She was emphatic. "We were too young for that. Too young to drive, really, but we did anyway."

She leaned over to let him give her cigarette a light, and saw his hand tremble. Was he afraid of the ghost or of her? She would have to stay away from talking family.

Frances remembered Tommy Beavers from her childhood—a small boy going home from school down a muddy side road alone, walking right down the middle of the road. His old aunt's house was at the bottom of a hill. It was damp there, and the yard was always muddy, with big fat chicken tracks all over it, like Egyptian writing. How did Frances know? She could not remember going there, ever. Miss Rita Beavers was said to order cold ham, mustard, bread, and condensed milk from the grocery store. "I doubt if that child ever has anything hot," Frances's mother had said once. He was always neatly dressed in the same knee pants, high socks, and checked shirt, and sat several rows ahead of Frances in study hall, right in the middle of his seat. He was three grades behind her; in those days, that much younger seemed very young indeed. What had happened to his parents? There was some story, but it was not terribly interesting, and, his people being of no importance, she had forgotten.

"I think it's past time for our ghost," she said. "He's never out so late at night."

"He gets hungry, like me," said Tom Beavers. "Are you hungry, Frances?"

They agreed on a highway restaurant where an orchestra played on weekends. Everyone went there now.

From he moment they drew up on the graveled entrance, cheerful lights and a blare of music chased the spooks from their heads. Tom Beavers ordered well and danced well, as it turned out. Wasn't there something she had heard about his being "smart"? By "smart," Southerners mean intellectual, and they say it in an almost condescending way, smart being what you are when you can't be anything else, but it is better, at least, than being nothing. Frances Harvey had been away enough not to look at things from a completely Southern point of view, and she was encouraged to discover that she and Tom had other things in common besides a ghost, though all stemming, perhaps, from the imagination it took to see one.

They agreed about books and favorite movies and longing to see more plays. She sighed that life in Richton was so confining, but he assured her that Jackson could be just as bad; *it* was getting to be like any Middle Western city, he said, while Richton at least had a sense of the past. This was the main reason, he went on, gaining confidence in the jumble of commonplace noises—dishes, music, and a couple of drinkers chattering behind them—that he had started coming back to Richton so often. He wanted to keep a connection with the past. He lived in a modern apartment, worked in a soundproof office—he could be in any city. But Richton was where he had been born and raised, and nothing could be more old-fashioned. Too many people seemed to have their lives cut in two. He was earnest in desiring that this should not happen to him.

"You'd better be careful," Frances said lightly. Her mood did not incline her to profound conversation. "There's more than one ghost in Richton: You may turn into one yourself, like the rest of us."

"It's the last thing I'd think of you," he was quick to assure her.

Had Tommy Beavers really said such a thing, in such a natural, charming way? Was Frances Harvey really so pleased? Not only was she pleased but, feeling warmly alive amid the music and small lights, she agreed with him. She could not have agreed with him more.

*   *   *

"I hear that Thomas Beavers has gotten to be a very attractive man," Frances Harvey's mother said unexpectedly one afternoon.

Frances had been reading aloud—Jane Austen this time. Theirs was one house where the leather-bound sets were actually read. In Jane Austen, men and women seesawed back and forth for two or three hundred pages until they struck a point of balance; then they got married. She had just put aside the book, at the end of a chapter, and risen to lower the shade against the slant of afternoon sun. "Or so Cud'n Jennie and Mrs. Giles Antley and Miss Fannie Stapleton have been coming and telling you," she said.

"People talk, of course, but the consensus is favorable," Mrs. Harvey said. "Wonders never cease; his mother ran away with a brush salesman. But nobody can make out what he's up to, coming back to Richton."

"Does he have to be 'up to' anything?" Frances asked.

"Men are always up to something," said the old lady at once. She added, more slowly, "In Thomas's case, maybe it isn't anything it oughtn't to be. They say he reads a lot. He may just have taken up with some sort of idea."

Frances stole a long glance at her mother's face on the pillow. Age and illness had reduced the image of Mrs. Harvey to a kind of caricature, centered on a mouth that Frances could not help comparing to that of a fish. There was a tension around its rim, as though it were outlined in bone, and the underlip even stuck out a little. The mouth ate, it took medicine, it asked for things, it gasped when breath was short, it commented. But when it commented, it ceased to be just a mouth and became part of Mrs. Harvey, that witty tyrant with the infallible memory for the right detail, who was at her terrible best about men.

"And what could he be thinking of?" she was wont to inquire when some man had acted foolishly. No one could ever defend accurately the man in question, and the only conclusion was Mrs. Harvey's; namely, that he wasn't thinking, if, indeed, he could. Although she had never been a belle, never a flirt, her popularity with men was always formidable. She would be observed talking marathons with one in a corner, and could you ever be sure, when they both burst into laughter, that they had not just exchanged the most shocking stories? "Of course, *he*—" she would begin later, back with the family, and the masculinity that had just been encouraged to strut and preen a little was quickly shown up as idiotic. Perhaps Mrs. Harvey hoped by this method to train her daughters away from a lot of sentimental nonsense that was their birthright as pretty Southern girls in a house with a lawn that moonlight fell on and that was often lit also by Japanese lanterns hung for parties. "Oh, he's not like that, Mama!" the little girls would cry. They were already alert for heroes who would ride up and cart them off. "Well, then, you watch," she would say. Sure enough, if you watched, she would be right.

Mrs. Harvey's younger daughter, Regina, was a credit to her mother's long campaign; she married well. The old lady, however, never tired of pointing out behind her son-in-law's back that his fondness for money was ill-concealed, that he had the longest feet she'd ever seen, and that he sometimes made grammatical errors.

Her elder daughter, Frances, on a trip to Europe, fell in love, alas! The gentlemen was of French extraction but Swiss citizenship, and Frances did not marry him, because he was already married—that much filtered back to Richton. In response to a cable, she had returned home one hot July in time to witness her father's wasted face and last weeks of life. That same September, the war began. When peace came, Richton wanted to know if Frances Harvey would go back to Europe. Certain subtly complicated European matters, little understood in Richton, seemed to be obstructing Romance; one of them was probably named Money. Meanwhile, Frances's mother took to bed, in what was generally known to be her last illness.

So no one crossed the ocean, but eventually Tom Beavers came up to Mrs. Harvey's room one afternoon, to tea.

Though almost all her other faculties were seriously impaired, in ear and tongue Mrs. Harvey was as sound as a young beagle, and she could still weave a more interesting conversation than most people who go about every day and look at the world. She was of the old school of Southern lady talkers; she vexed you with no ideas, she tried to protect you from even a moment of silence. In the old days, when a bright company filled the downstairs rooms, she could keep the ball rolling amongst a crowd. Everyone—all the men especially—got their word in, but the flow of things came back to her. If one of those twenty-minutes-to-or-after silences fell—and even with her they did occur—people would turn and look at her daughter Frances. "And what do you think?" some kind-eyed gentleman would ask. Frances did not credit that she had the sort of face people would turn to, and so did not know how to take advantage of it. What did she think? Well, to answer that honestly took a moment of reflection—a fatal moment, it always turned out. Her mother would be up instructing the maid, offering someone an ashtray or another goody, or remarking outright, "Frances is so timid. She never says a word."

Tom Beavers stayed not only past teatime that day but for a drink as well. Mrs. Harvey was induced to take a glass of sherry, and now her bed became her enormous throne. Her keenest suffering as an invalid was occasioned by the absence of men. "What is a house without a man in it?" she would often cry. From her eagerness to be charming to Frances's guest that afternoon, it seemed that she would have married Tom Beavers herself if he had asked her. The amber liquid set in her small four-sided glass glowed like a jewel, and her diamond flashed; she had put on her best ring for the company. What a pity no longer to show her ankle, that delicious bone, so remarkably slender for so ample a frame.

Since the time had flown so, they all agreed enthusiastically that Tom should wait downstairs while Frances got ready to go out to dinner with him. He was hardly past the stair landing before the old lady was seized by such a fit of coughing that she could hardly speak. "It's been—it's been too much—too *much* for me!" she gasped out.

But after Frances had found the proper sedative for her, she was calmed, and insisted on having her say.

"Thomas Beavers has a good job with an insurance company in Jackson," she informed her daughter, as though Frances were incapable of finding out anything for herself. "He makes a good appearance. He is the kind of man"—she paused—"who would value a wife of good family." She stopped, panting for breath. It was this complimenting a man behind his back that was too much for her—as much out of character, and hence as much of a strain, as if she had got out of bed and tried to tap-dance.

"Heavens, Mama," Frances said, and almost giggled.

At this, the old lady, thinking the girl had made light of her suitor, half screamed at her, "Don't be so critical, Frances! You can't be so critical of men!" and fell into an even more terrible spasm of coughing. Frances had to lift her from the pillow and hold her straight until the fit passed and her breath returned. Then Mrs. Harvey's old, dry, crooked, ineradicably feminine hand was laid on her daughter's arm, and when she spoke again she shook the arm to emphasize her words.

"When your father knew he didn't have long to live," she whispered, "we discussed whether to send for you or not. You know you were his favorite, Frances. 'Suppose our girl is happy over there,' he said. 'I wouldn't want to bring her back on my account.' I said you had to have the right to choose whether to come back or not. You'd never forgive us, I said, if you didn't have the right to choose."

Frances could visualize this very conversation taking place between her parents; she could see them, decorous and serious, talking over the fact of his approaching death as though it were a piece of property for agreeable disposition in the family. She could never remember him without thinking, with a smile, how he used to come home on Sunday from church (he being the only one of them who went) and how, immediately after hanging his hat and cane in the hall, he would say, "Let all things proceed in orderly progression to their final confusion. How long before dinner?" No, she had had to come home. Some humor had always existed between them—her father and her—and humor, of all things, cannot be betrayed.

"I meant to go back," said Frances now. "But there was the war. At first I kept waiting for it to be over. I still wake up at night sometimes thinking, I wonder how much longer before the war will be over. And then—" She stopped short. For the fact was that her lover had been married to somebody else, and her mother was the very person capable of pointing that out to her. Even in the old lady's present silence she heard the unspoken thought, and got up nervously from the bed, loosing herself from the hand on her arm, smoothing her reddish hair where it was inclined to straggle. "And then he wrote me that he had gone back to his wife. Her family and his had always been close, and the war brought them back together. This was in Switzerland—naturally, he couldn't stay on in Paris during the war. There were the children, too—all of them were Catholic. Oh, I do understand how it happened."

Mrs. Harvey turned her head impatiently on the pillow. She dabbed at her moist upper lip with a crumpled linen handkerchief; her diamond flashed once in motion. "War, religion, wife, children—yes. But men do what they want to."

Could anyone make Frances as angry as her mother could? "Believe what you like then! You always know so much better than I do? *You* would have managed things somehow. Oh, you would have had your way!"

"Frances," said Mrs. Harvey, "I'm an old woman." The hand holding the handkerchief fell wearily, and her eyelids dropped shut. "If you should want to marry Thomas Beavers and bring him here, I will accept it. There will be no distinctions. Next, I suppose, we will be having his old deaf aunt for tea. I hope she has a hearing aid. I haven't got the strength to holler at her."

"I don't think any of these plans are necessary, Mama."

The eyelid slowly lifted. "None?"

"None."

Mrs. Harvey's breathing was as audible as a voice. She spoke, at last, without scorn, honestly. "I cannot bear the thought of leaving you alone. You, nor the house, nor your place in it—alone. I foresaw Tom Beavers here! What has he got that's better than you and this place? I knew he would come!"

Terrible as her mother's meanness was, it was not half so terrible as her love. Answering nothing, explaining nothing, Frances stood without giving in. She trembled, and tears ran down her cheeks. The two women looked at each other helplessly across the darkening room.

In the car, later that night, Tom Beavers asked, "Is your mother trying to get rid of me?" They had passed an unsatisfactory evening, and he was not going away without knowing why.

"No, it's just the other way around," said Frances, in her candid way. "She wants you so much she'd like to eat you up. She wants you in the house. Couldn't you tell?"

"She once chased me out of the yard," he recalled.

"Not really!"

They turned into Harvey Street (that was actually the name of it), and when he had drawn the car up before the dark front steps, he related the incident. He told her that Mrs. Harvey had been standing just there in the yard, talking to some visitor who was leaving by inches, the way ladies used to—ten minutes' more talk for every forward step. He, a boy not more than nine, had been crossing a corner of the lawn where a faint path had already been worn; he had had nothing to do with wearing the path and had taken it quite innocently and openly. "You, boy!" Mrs. Harvey's fan was an enormous painted thing. She had furled it with a clack so loud he could still hear it. "You don't cut through my yard again! Now, you stop where you are and you go all the way back around by the walk, and don't you ever do that again." He went back and all the way around. She was fanning comfortably as he passed. "Old Miss Rita Beavers' nephew," he heard her say, and though he did not speak of it now to Frances, Mrs. Harvey's rich tone had been as stuffed with wickedness as a fruitcake with goodies. In it you could have found so many things: that, of course, he didn't know any better, that he was poor, that she knew his first name but would not deign to mention it, that she meant him to understand all this and more. Her fan was probably still somewhere in the house, he reflected. If he ever opened the wrong door, it might fall from above and brain him. It seemed impossible that nowadays he could even have the chance to open the wrong door in the Harvey house. With its graceful rooms and big lawn, its camellias and magnolia trees, the house had been one of the enchanted castles of his childhood, and Frances and Regina Harvey had been two princesses running about the lawn one Saturday morning drying their hair with big white towels and not noticing when he passed.

There was a strong wind that evening. On the way home, Frances and Tom had notice how the night was streaming, but whether with mist or dust or the smoke from some far-off fire in the dry winter woods they could not tell. As they stood on the sidewalk, the clouds raced over them, and moonlight now and again came through. A limb rubbed against a high cornice. Inside the screened area of the porch, the swing jangled in its iron chains. Frances's coat blew about her, and her hair blew. She felt herself to be no different from anything there that the wind and blowing on, her happiness of no relevance in the dark torrent of nature.

"I can't leave her, Tom. But I can't ask you to live with her, either. Of all the horrible ideas! She'd make demands, take all my time, laugh at you behind your back—she has to run everything. You'd hate me in a week."

He did not try to pretty up the picture, because he had a feeling that it was all too accurate. Now, obviously, was the time she should go on to say there was no good his waiting around through the years for her. But hearts are not noted for practicality, and Frances stood with her hair blowing, her hands stuck in her coat pockets, and did not go on to say anything. Tom pulled her close to him—in, as it were, out of the wind.

"I'll be coming by next weekend, just like I've been doing. And the next one, too," he said. "We'll just leave it that way, if it's O.K. with you."

"Oh yes, it is, Tom!" Never so satisfied to be weak, she kissed him and ran inside.

He stood watching on the walk until her light flashed on. Well, he had got what he was looking for; a connection with the past, he had said. It was right upstairs, a splendid old mass of dictatorial female flesh, thinking about him. Well, they could go on, he and Frances, sitting on either side of a sickbed, drinking tea and sipping sherry with streaks of gray broadening on their brows, while the familiar seasons came and went. So he thought. Like Frances, he believed that the old lady had a stranglehold on life.

Suddenly, in March, Mrs. Harvey died.

A heavy spring funeral, with lots of roses and other scented flowers in the house, is the worst kind of all. There is something so recklessly fecund about a south Mississippi spring that death becomes just another word in the dictionary, along with swarms of others, and even so pure and white a thing as a gardenia has too heavy a scent and may suggest decay. Mrs. Harvey, amid such odors, sank to rest with a determined pomp, surrounded by admiring eyes.

While Tom Beavers did not "sit with the family" at this time, he was often observed with the Harveys, and there was whispered speculation among those who were at the church and the cemetery that the Harvey house might soon come into new hands, "after a decent interval." No one would undertake to judge for a Harvey how long an interval was decent.

Frances suffered from insomnia in the weeks that followed, and at night she wandered about the spring-swollen air of the old house, smelling now spring and now death. "Let all things proceed in orderly progression to their final confusion." She had always thought that the final confusion referred to death, but now she began to think that it could happen any time; that final confusion, having found the door ajar, could come into a house and show no inclination to leave. The worrisome thing, the thing it all came back to, was her mother's clothes. They were numerous, expensive, and famous, and Mrs. Harvey had never discarded any of them. If you opened a closet door, hatboxes as big as crates towered above your head. The shiny black trim of a great shawl stuck out of a wardrobe door just below the lock. Beneath the lid of a cedar chest, the bright eyes of a tippet were ready to twinkle at you. And the jewels! Frances's sister had restrained her from burying them all on their mother, and had even gone off with a wad of them tangled up like fishing tackle in an envelope, on the ground of promises made now and again in the course of the years.

("Regina," said Frances, "what else where you two talking about besides jewelry?" "I don't remember," said Regina, getting mad.

"Frances makes me so mad," said Regina to her husband as they were driving home. "I guess I can love Mama and jewelry, too. Mama certainly loved *us* and jewelry, too.")

One afternoon, Frances went out to the cemetery to take two wreaths sent by somebody who had "just heard." She drove out along the winding cemetery road, stopping the car a good distance before she reached the gate, in order to walk through the woods. The dogwood was beautiful that year. She saw a field where a house used to stand but had burned down; its cedar trees remained, and two bushes of bridal wreath marked where the front gate had swung. She stopped to admire the clusters of white bloom massing up through the young, feathery leaf and stronger now than the leaf itself. In the woods, the redbud was a smoke along shadowy ridges, and the dogwood drifted in layers, like snow suspended to give you all the time you needed to wonder at it. But why, she wondered, do they call it bridal *wreath?* It's not a wreath but a little bouquet. Wreaths are for funerals, anyway. As if to prove it, she looked down at the two she held, one in each hand. She walked on, and such complete desolation came over her that it was more of a wonder than anything in the woods—more, even, than death.

As she returned to the car from the two parallel graves, she met a thin, elderly, very light-skinned Negro man in the road. He inquired if she would mind moving her car so that he could pass. He said that there was a sick colored girl in his wagon, whom he was driving in to the doctor. He pointed out politely that she had left her car right in the middle of the road. "Oh, I'm terribly sorry," said Frances, and hurried off toward the car.

That night, reading late in bed, she thought, I could have given her a ride into town. No wonder they talk about us up North. A mile into town in a wagon! She might have been having a baby. She became conscience-stricken about it—foolishly so, she realized, but if you start worrying about something in a house like the one Frances Harvey lived in, in the dead of night, alone, you will go on worrying about it until dawn. She was out of sleeping pills.

She remembered having bought a fresh box of sedatives for her mother the day before she died. She got up and went into her mother's closed room, where the bed had been dismantled for airing, its wooden parts propped along the walls. On the closet shelf she found the shoe box into which she had packed away the familiar articles of the bedside table. Inside she found the small enameled-cardboard box, with the date and prescription inked on the cover in Totsie Poteet's somewhat prissy handwriting, but the box was empty. She was surprised, for she realized that her mother could have used only one or two of the pills. Frances was so determined to get some sleep that she searched the entire little store of things in the shoe box quite heartlessly, but there were no pills. She returned to her room and tried to read, but could not, and so smoked instead and stared out at the dawn-blackening sky. The house sighed. She could not take her mind off the Negro girl. If she died . . . When it was light, she dressed and got into the car.

In town, the postman was unlocking the post office to sort the early mail. "I declare," he said to the rural mail carrier who arrived a few minutes later, "Miss Frances Harvey is driving herself crazy. Going back out yonder to the cemetery, and it not seven o'clock in the morning."

"Aw," said the rural deliveryman skeptically, looking at the empty road.

"That's right. I was here and seen her. You wait there, you'll see her come back. She'll drive herself nuts. Them old maids like that, left in them old houses—crazy and sweet, or crazy and mean, or just plain crazy. They just ain't locked up like them that's down in the asylum. That's the only difference."

"Miss Frances Harvey ain't no more than thirty-two, -three years old."

"Then she's just got more time to get crazier in. You'll see."

That day was Friday, and Tom Beavers, back from Jackson, came up Frances Harvey's sidewalk, as usual, at exactly a quarter past seven in the evening. Frances was not "going out" yet, and Regina had telephoned her long distance to say that "in all probability" she should not be receiving gentlemen "in." "What would Mama say?" Regina asked. Frances said she didn't know, which was not true, and went right on cooking dinners for Tom every weekend.

In the dining room that night, she sat across one corner of the long table from Tom. The useless length of polished cherry stretched away from them into the shadows as sadly as a road. Her plate pushed back, her chin resting on one palm, Frances stirred her coffee and said, "I don't know what on earth to do with all of Mama's clothes. I can't give them away, I can't sell them, I can't burn them, and the attic is full already. What can I do?"

"You look better tonight," said Tom.

"I slept," said Frances. "I slept and slept. From early this morning until just 'while ago. I never slept so well."

Then she told him about the Negro near the cemetery the previous afternoon, and how she had driven back out there as soon as dawn came, and found him again. He had been walking across the open field near the remains of the house that had burned down. There was no path to him from her, and she had hurried across ground uneven from old plowing and covered with the kind of small, tender grass it takes a very skillful mule to crop. "Wait!" she had cried. "Please wait!" The Negro had stopped and waited for her to reach him. "Your daughter?" she asked, out of breath.

"Daughter?" he repeated.

"The colored girl that was in the wagon yesterday. She was sick, you said, so I wondered. I could have taken her to town in the car, but I just didn't think. I wanted to know, how is she? Is she very sick?"

He had removed his old felt nigger hat as she approached him. "She a whole lot better, Miss Frances. She going to be all right now." Then he smiled at her. He did not say thank you, or anything more. Frances turned and walked back to the road and the car. And exactly as though the recovery of the Negro girl in the wagon had been her own recovery, she felt the return of a quiet breath and a steady pulse, and sensed the blessed stirring of a morning breeze. Up in her room, she had barely time to draw an old quilt over her before she fell asleep.

"When I woke, I knew about Mama," she said now to Tom. By the deepened intensity of her voice and eyes, it was plain that this was the important part. "It isn't right to say I *knew*," she went on, "because I had known all the time—ever since last night. I just realized it, that's all. I realized she had killed herself. It had to be that."

He listened soberly through the story about the box of sedatives. "But why?" he asked her. "It maybe looks that way, but what would be her reason for doing it?"

"Well, you see—" Frances said, and stopped.

Tom Beavers talked quietly on. "She didn't suffer. With what she had, she could have lived five, ten, who knows how many years. She was well cared for. Not hard up, I wouldn't say. Why?"

The pressure of his questioning could be insistent, and her trust in him, even if he was nobody but old Miss Rita Beavers' nephew, was well-nigh complete. "Because of you and me," she said, finally. "I'm certain of it, Tom. She didn't want to stand in our way. She never knew how to express love, you see." Frances controlled herself with an effort.

He did not reply, but sat industriously balancing a match folder on the tines of an unused serving fork. Anyone who has passed a lonely childhood in the company of an old deaf aunt is not inclined to doubt things hastily, and Tom Beavers would not have said he disbelieved anything Frances had told him. In fact, it seemed only too real to him. Almost before his eyes, that imperial, practical old hand went fumbling for the pills in the dark. But there had been much more to it than just love, he reflected. Bitterness, too, and pride, and control. And humor, perhaps, and the memory of a frightened little boy chased out of the yard by a twitch of her fan. Being invited to tea was one thing; suicide was quite another. Times had certainly changed, he thought.

But, of course, he could not say that he believed it, either. There was only Frances to go by. The match folder came to balance and rested on the tines. He glanced up at her, and a chill walked up his spine, for she was too serene. Cheek on palm, a lock of reddish hair fallen forward, she was staring at nothing with the absorbed silence of a child, or of a sweet, silver-haired old lady engaged in memory. Soon he might find that more and more of her was vanishing beneath this placid surface.

He himself did not know what he had seen that Friday evening so many months ago—what the figure had been that stood forward from the roadside at the tilt of the curve and urgently waved an arm to him. By the time he had braked and backed, the man had disappeared. Maybe it had been somebody drunk (for Richton had plenty of those to offer), walking it off in the cool of the woods at first dark. No such doubts had occurred to Frances. And what if he told her now the story Totsie had related of the road gang and the sick Negro girl in the wagon? Another labyrinth would open before her; she would never get out.

In Richton, the door to the past was always wide open, and what came in through it and went out of it had made people "different." But it scarcely ever happens, even in Richton, that one is able to see the precise moment when fact becomes faith, when life turns into legend, and people start to bend their finest loyalties to make themselves bemused custodians of the grave. Tom Beavers saw that moment now, in the profile of this dreaming girl, and he knew there was no time to lose.

He dropped the match folder into his coat pocket. "I think we should be leaving, Frances."

"Oh well, I don't know about going out yet," she said. "People criticize you so. Regina even had the nerve to telephone. Word had got all the way to her that you came here to have supper with me and we were alone in the house. When I tell the maid I want biscuits made up for two people, she looks like 'What would yo' mama say?'"

"I mean," he said, "I think it's time we left for good."

"And never came back?" It was exactly like Frances to balk at going to a movie but seriously consider an elopement.

"Well, never is a long time. I like to see about Aunt Rita every once in a great while. She can't remember from one time to the next whether it's two days or two years since I last came."

She glanced about the walls and at the furniture, the pictures, and the silver. "But I thought you would want to live here, Tom. It never occurred to me. I know it never occurred to Mama . . . This house . . . It can't be just left."

"It's a fine old house," he agreed. "But what would you do with all your mother's clothes?"

Her freckled hand remained beside the porcelain cup for what seemed a long time. He waited and made no move toward her; he felt her uncertainty keenly, but he believed that some people should not be startled out of a spell.

"It's just as you said," he went on, finally. "You can't give them away, you can't sell them, you can't burn them, and you can't put them in the attic, because the attic is full already. So what are you going to do?"

Between them, the single candle flame achieved a silent altitude. Then, politely, as on any other night, though shaking back her hair in a decided way, she said, "Just let me get my coat, Tom."

She locked the door when they left, and put the key under the mat—a last obsequy to the house. Their hearts were bounding ahead faster than they could walk down the sidewalk or drive off in the car, and, mindful, perhaps, of what happened to people who did, they did not look back.

Had they done so, they would have seen that the Harvey house was more beautiful than ever. All unconscious of its rejection by so mere a person as Tom Beavers, it seemed, instead, to have got rid of what did not suit it, to be free, at last, to enter with abandon the land of mourning and shadows and memory.

Alice Walker

(1944–   )

Born on February 9, 1944, in Eatonton, Georgia, to sharecropping parents, Alice Walker excelled in school and became high school valedictorian. Part of her success has been attributed to an unfortunate accident that occurred when Walker was eight. Playing cowboys and Indians with her brothers, she was blinded in the eye with a BB gun pellet and became even more immersed in schoolwork. She attended Spelman College in Atlanta, where she was involved in the Civil Rights movement and met Dr. Martin Luther King, Jr. Then she transferred to Sarah Lawrence College, in Bronxville, New York, for her junior year and was graduated in 1965.

In March 1967, Walker married Melvyn Leventhal, a Jewish civil rights lawyer whom she met while registering voters in Mississippi. She accepted a teaching position at Jackson State University, and her daughter Rebecca was born in 1969. The marriage ended in 1975. Influenced by her travels in Africa, she also was affected by the Civil Rights movement and the fiction of Flannery O'Connor and of Zora Neale Hurston, the latter a member of the Harlem Renaissance whose book *Their Eyes Were Watching God* (1937) was "discovered" by Walker. Walker's first novel, *The Third Life of Grange Copeland*, was published in 1970. *The Color Purple* (1982), which won both the Pulitzer Prize and the American Book Award, was made into a popular film by director Steven Spielberg.

Walker's themes deal with the definition of self that comes from within and exists outside of race and gender. Published books include *Once: Poems* (1968); *In Love and Trouble: Stories of Black Women* (1973); *Revolutionary Petunias and Other Poems* (1973); *Langston Hughes: American Poet* (1974); *Meridian* (1976); *Good Night, Willie Lee, I'll See You in the Morning* (1979); *You Can't Keep a Good Woman Down* (1981); *In Search of Our Mothers' Gardens* (1983); *Horses Make a Landscape Look More Beautiful: Poems* (1984); *Living by the Word: Selected Writings, 1973–1987* (1988); *To Hell with Dying* (1988); *The Temple of my Familiar* (1989); *Her Blue Body Everything We Know: Earthling Poems, 1965–1990 Complete* (1991); *Possessing the Secret of Joy* (1992); *The Same River Twice: Honoring the Difficult* (1995); and *By the Light of My Father's Smile* (1998).

Walker now lives in Mendocino, California.

Women

They were women then
My mama's generation
Husky of voice—Stout of
Step
With fists as well as
Hands
How they battered down
Doors
And ironed
Starched white

Shirts
How they led
Armies
Headragged Generals
Across mined
Fields
Booby-trapped
Ditches
To discover books
Desks
A place for us
How they knew what we
Must know
Without knowing a page
Of it
Themselves.

Eagle Rock

In the town where I was born
There is a mound
Some eight feet high
That from the ground
Seems piled up stones
In Georgia
Insignificant.

But from above
The lookout tower
Floor
An eagle widespread
In solid gravel
Stone
Takes shape
Below;

The Cherokees raised it
Long ago
Before westward journeys
In the snow
Before the
National Policy slew
Long before Columbus knew.

I used to stop and
Linger there
Within the cleanswept tower stair
Rock Eagle pinesounds

Rush of stillness
Lifting up my hair.

Pinned to the earth
The eagle endures
The Cherokees are gone
The people come on tours.
And on surrounding National
Forest lakes the air rings
With cries
The silenced make.

Wearing cameras
They never hear
But relive their victory
Every year
And take it home
With them.
Young Future Farmers
As paleface warriors
Grub
Live off the land
Pretend Indian, therefore
Man,
Can envision a lake
But never a flood
On earth
So cleanly scrubbed
Of blood:
They come before the rock
Jolly conquerors.

They do not know the rock
They love
Lives and is bound
To bide its time
To wrap its stony wings
Around
The innocent eager 4-H Club.

J, My Good Friend
(another foolish innocent)

It is too easy not to like
Jesus,
It worries greatness
To an early grave
Without any inkling
Of what is wise.

So when I am old,
And so foolish with pain
No one who knows
me
Can tell from which
Senility or fancy
I deign to speak,
I may sing
In my cracked and ugly voice
Of Jesus my good
Friend;
Just as the old women
In my home town
Do now.

Ernest J. Gaines

(1933–   )

Born on River Lake Plantation near Oscar, Louisiana, on January 15, 1933, Ernest J. Gaines moved to Vallejo, California, when he was fifteen. In 1957, Gaines entered Stanford University on a creative writing fellowship. Eventually he served in the armed forces from 1953 to 1955. He attended Vallejo Junior College; San Francisco State College, where he received his B.A. in 1957; and undertook graduate study at Stanford University during 1958 to 1959.

Considered to be one of the most prominent African American writers, Gaines has published *Catherine Carmier* (1964); *Of Love and Dust* (1967); *Bloodline* (1968); *A Long Day in November* (1971); *The Autobiography of Miss Jane Pittman* (1971); *In My Father's House* (1978); *A Gathering of Old Men* (1983); and *A Lesson Before Dying* (1993). For *A Lesson Before Dying*, he received the following awards: Southern Writers' Conference, Louisiana Library, John Dos Passos, Langston Hughes, and Amistad awards. This novel was also included in the Oprah Winfrey Book Club, September 1997, and won the National Book Critics Circle Award for 1993. *The Autobiography of Miss Jane Pittman*, "The Sky is Gray" from *Bloodline*, and *A Gathering of Old Men* have all been made into television dramas.

Gaines acknowledges the influences of William Faulkner, Ernest Hemingway, Ivan Turgenev, Leo Tolstoy, and Nikolay Gogol. Most of his fiction is set in the mythical community of Bayonne, Louisiana, where he looks to find the richness of the human experience. Gaines is writer-in-residence at Southwestern Louisiana University.

The Sky Is Gray

Go'n be coming in a few minutes. Coming 'round that bend down there full speed. And I'm go'n get out my handkercher and I'm go'n wave it down and us go'n get on it and go.

I keep on looking for it, but Mama don't look that way no more. She looking down the road where us jest come from. It's a long old road, and far's you can see you don't see nothing but gravel. You got dry weeds on both sides, and you got trees on both sides, and fences on both sides, too. And you got cows in the pastures and they standing close together. And when us was coming out yer to catch the bus I seen the smoke coming out o' the cow's nose.

I look at my mama and I know what she thinking. I been with Mama so much, jest me and her, I know what she thinking all the time. Right now it's home—Auntie and them. She thinking if they got 'nough wood—if she left 'nough there to keep 'em warm till us get back. She thinking if it go'n rain and if any of 'em go'n have to go out in the rain. She thinking 'bout the hog—if he go'n get out, and if Ty and Val be able to get him back in. She always worry like that when she leave the house. She don't worry too much if she leave me there with the smaller ones 'cause she know I'm go'n look after 'em and look after Auntie and everything else. I'm the oldest and she say I'm the man.

I look at my mama and I love my mama. She wearing that black coat and that black hat and she looking sad. I love my mama and I want to put my arm 'round her and tell her. But I'm not s'pose to do that. She say that's weakness and that's cry-baby stuff, and she don't want no cry-baby 'round her. She don't want you to be scared neither. 'Cause Ty scared of ghosts and she always whipping him. I'm scared of the dark, too. But I make 'tend I ain't. I make 'tend I ain't cause I'm the oldest, and I got to set a good sample for the rest. I can't ever be scared and I can't ever cry. And that's the reason I didn't never say nothing 'bout my teef. It been hurting me and hurting me close to a month now. But I didn't say it. I didn't say it 'cause I didn't want act like no cry-baby, and 'cause I know us didn't have 'nough money to have it pulled. But, Lord, it been hurting me. And look like it won't start till at night when you trying to get little sleep. Then soon's you shet your eyes—umm-umm, Lord. Look like it go right down to your heart string.

"Hurting, hanh?" Ty'd say.

I'd shake my head, but I wouldn't open my mouth for nothing. You open your mouth and let that wind in, and it almost kill you.

I'd just lay there and listen to 'em snore. Ty, there, right 'side me, and Auntie and Val over by the fireplace. Val younger 'an me and Ty, and he sleep with Auntie. Mama sleep 'round the other side with Louis and Walker.

I'd just lay there and listen to 'em, and listen to that wind out there, and listen to that fire in the fireplace. Sometime it'd stop long enough to let me get little rest. Sometime it just hurt, hurt, hurt. Lord, have mercy.

II

Auntie knowed it was hurting me. I didn't tell nobody but Ty, 'cause us buddies and he ain't go'n tell nobody. But some kind o' way Auntie found out. When she asked me, I told her no, nothing was wrong. But she knowed it all the time. She told me to mash up a piece o' aspirin and wrap it in some cotton and jugg it down in the hole. I did it, but it didn't do no good. It stopped for a little while, and started right back again. She wanted to tell Mama, but I told her Uh-uh. 'Cause I knowed it didn't have no money, and it jest was go'n make her mad again. So she told Monsieur Bayonne, and Monsieur Bayonne came to the house and told me to kneel down 'side him on the fireplace. He put his finger in his mouth and made the Sign of the Cross on my jaw. The tip of Monsieur Bayonne finger is some hard, 'cause he always playing on that guitar. If us sit outside at night us can always hear Monsieur Bayonne playing on his guitar. Sometime us leave him out there playing on the guitar.

He made the Sign of the Cross over and over on my jaw, but that didn't do no good. Even when he prayed and told me to pray some, too, that teef still hurt.

"How you feeling?" he say.

"Same," I say.

He kept on praying and making the Sign of the Cross and I kept on praying, too.

"Still hurting?" he says.

"Yes, sir."

Monsieur Bayonne mashed harder and harder on my jaw. He mashed so hard he almost pushed me on Ty. But then he stopped.

"What kind o' prayers you praying, boy?" he say.

"Baptist," I say.

"Well, I'll be—no wonder that teef still killing him. I'm going one way and he going the other. Boy, don't you know any Catholic prayers?"

"Hail Mary," I say.

"Then you better start saying it."

"Yes, sir."

He started mashing again, and I could hear him praying at the same time. And, sure 'nough, afterwhile it stopped.

Me and Ty went outside where Monsieur Bayonne two hounds was, and us started playing with 'em. "Let's go hunting," Ty say. "All right," I say; and us went on back in the pasture. Soon the hounds got on a trail, and me and Ty followed 'em all cross the pasture and then back in the woods, too. And then they cornered this little old rabbit and killed him, and me and Ty made 'em get back, and us picked up the rabbit and started on back home. But it had started hurting me again. It was hurting me plenty now, but I wouldn't tell Monsieur Bayonne. That night I didn't sleep a bit, and first thing in the morning Auntie told me go back and let Monsieur Bayonne pray over me some more. Monsieur Bayonne was in his kitchen making coffee when I got there. Soon's he seen me, he knowed what was wrong.

"All right, kneel down there 'side that stove," he say. "And this time pray Catholic. I don't know nothing 'bout Baptist, and don't want know nothing 'bout him."

III

Last night Mama say: "Tomorrow us going to town."

"It ain't hurting me no more," I say. "I can eat anything on it."

"Tomorrow us going to town," she say.

And after she finished eating, she got up and went to bed. She always go to bed early now. 'Fore Daddy went in the Army, she used to stay up late. All o' us sitting out on the gallery or 'round the fire. But now, look like soon's she finish eating she go to bed.

This morning when I woke up, her and Auntie was standing 'fore the fireplace. She say: "'Nough to get there and back. Dollar and a half to have it pulled. Twenty-five for me to go, twenty-five for him. Twenty-five for me to come back, twenty-five for him. Fifty cents left. Guess I get a little piece o' salt meat with that."

"Sure can use a piece," Auntie say. "White beans and no salt meat ain't white beans."

"I do the best I can," Mama say.

They was quiet after that, and I made 'tend I was still sleep.

"James, hit the floor," Auntie say.

I still made 'tend I was sleep. I didn't want 'em to know I was listening.

"All right," Auntie say, shaking me by the shoulder. "Come on. Today's the day."

I pushed the cover down to get out, and Ty grabbed it and pulled it back.

"You, too, Ty," Auntie say.

"I ain't getting no teef pulled," Ty say.

"Don't mean it ain't time to get up," Auntie say. "Hit it, Ty."

Ty got up grumbling.

"James, you hurry up and get in your clothes and eat your food," Auntie say. "What time y'all coming back?" she say to Mama.

"That 'leven o'clock bus," Mama say. "Got to get back in that field this evening."

"Get a move on you, James," Auntie say.

I went in the kitchen and washed my face, then I ate my breakfast. I was having bread and syrup. The bread was warm and hard and tasted good. And I tried to make it last a long time.

Ty came back there, grumbling and mad at me.

"Got to get up," he say. "I ain't having no teef pulled. What I got to be getting up for."

Ty poured some syrup in his pan and got a piece of bread. He didn't wash his hands, neither his face, and I could see that white stuff in his eyes.

"You the one getting a teef pulled," he say. "What I got to get up for. I bet you if I was getting a teef pulled, you wouldn't be getting up. Shucks; syrup again. I'm getting tired of this old syrup. Syrup, syrup, syrup. I want me some bacon sometime."

"Go out in the field and work and you can have bacon," Auntie say. She stood in the middle door looking at Ty. "You better be glad you got syrup. Some people ain't got that—hard's time is."

"Shucks," Ty say. "How can I be strong."

"I don't know too much 'bout your strength," Auntie say; "but I know where you go'n be hot, you keep that grumbling up. James, get a move on you; your mama waiting."

I ate my last piece of bread and went in the front room. Mama was standing 'fore the fireplace warming her hands. I put on my coat and my cap, and us left the house.

IV

I look down there again, but it still ain't coming. I almost say, "It ain't coming, yet," but I keep my mouth shet. 'Cause that's something else she don't like. She don't like for you to say something just for nothing. She can see it ain't coming, I can see it ain't coming, so why say it ain't coming. I don't say it, and I turn and look at the river that's back o' us. It so cold the smoke just raising up from the water. I see a bunch of pull-doos not too far out—jest on the other side the lilies. I'm wondering if you can eat pull-doos. I ain't too sure, 'cause I ain't never ate none. But I done ate owls and black birds, and I done ate red birds, too. I didn't want kill the red birds, but she made me kill 'em. They had two of 'em back there. One in my trap, one in Ty trap. Me and Ty was go'n play with 'em and let 'em go. But she made me kill 'em 'cause us needed the food.

"I can't," I say. "I can't."

"Here," she say. "Take it."

"I can't," I say. "I can't. I can't kill him, Mama. Please."

"Here," she say. "Take this fork, James."

"Please, Mama, I can't kill him," I say.

I could tell she was go'n hit me. And I jecked back, but I didn't jeck back soon enough.

"Take it," she say.

I took it and reached in for him, but he kept hopping to the back.

"I can't, Mama," I say. The water just kept running down my face. "I can't."

"Get him out o' there," she say.

I reached in for him and he kept hopping to the back. Then I reached in farther, and he pecked me on the hand.

"I can't Mama," I say.

She slapped me again.

I reached in again, but he kept hopping out of my way. Then he hopped to one side, and I reached there. The fork got him on the leg and I heard his leg pop. I pulled my hand out 'cause I had hurt him.

"Give it here," she say, and jecked the fork out my hand.

She reached and got the little bird right in the neck. I heard the fork go in his neck, and I heard it go in the ground. She brought him out and helt him right in front o' me.

"That's one," she say. She shook him off and gived me the fork. "Get the other one."

"I can't, Mama. I do anything. But I can't do that."

She went to the corner o' the fence and broke the biggest switch over there. I knelt 'side the trap crying.

"Get him out o' there," she say.

"I can't, Mama."

She started hitting me cross the back. I went down on the ground crying.

"Get him," she say.

"Octavia," Auntie say.

'Cause she had come out o' the house and she was standing by the tree looking at us.

"Get him out o' there," Mama say.

"Octavia," Auntie say; "explain to him. Explain to him. Jest don't beat him. Explain to him."

But she hit me and hit me and hit me.

I'm still young. I ain't no more'an eight. But I know now. I know why I had to. (They was so little, though. They was so little. I 'member how I picked the feathers off 'em and cleaned 'em and helt 'em over the fire. Then us all ate 'em. Ain't had but little bitty piece, but us all had little bitty piece, and ever'body jest looked at me, 'cause they was so proud.) S'pose she had to go away? That's why I had to do it. S'pose she had to go away like Daddy went away? Then who was go'n look after us? They had to be somebody left to carry on. I didn't know it then, but I know it now. Auntie and Monsieur Bayonne talked to me and made me see.

V

Time I see it, I get out my handkercher and start waving. It still 'way down there, but I keep waving anyhow. Then it come closer and stop and me and Mama get on. Mama tell me go sit in the back while she pay. I do like she say, and the people look at me. When I pass the little sign that say White and Colored, I start looking for a seat. I jest see one of 'em back there, but I don't take it, 'cause I want my mama to sit down herself. She come in the back and sit down, and I lean on the seat. They got seats in the front, but I know I can't sit there, 'cause I have to sit back o' the sign. Anyhow, I don't want sit there if my mama go'n sit back here.

They got a lady sitting 'side my mama and she look at me and grin little bit. I grin back, but I don't open my mouth, 'cause the wind'll get in and make that teef hurt. The lady take out a pack o' gum and reach me a slice, but I shake my head. She reach Mama a slice, and Mama shake her head. The lady jest can't understand why a little boy'll turn down gum and she reached me a slice again. This time I point to my jaw. The lady understand and grin little bit, and I grin little bit, but I don't open my mouth, though.

They got a girl sitting 'cross from me. She got on a red overcoat, and her hair plaited in one big plait. First, I make 'tend I don't even see her. But then I start looking at her little bit. She make 'tend she don't see me neither, but I catch her looking that way. She got a cold, and ever' now and then she hist that little handkercher to her nose. She ought to blow it, but she don't. Must think she too much a lady or something.

Ever' time she hist that little handkercher, the lady 'side her say something in her yer. She shake her head and lay her hands in her lap again. Then I catch her kind o' looking where I'm at. I grin at her. But think she'll grin back? No. She turn up her little old nose like I got some snot on my face or something. Well, I show her both o' us can turn us head. I turn mine, too, and look out at the river.

The river is gray. The sky is gray. They have pull-doos on the water. The water is wavey, and the pull-doos go up and down. The bus go 'round a turn, and you got plenty trees hiding the river. Then the bus go 'round another turn, and I can see the river again.

I look to the front where all the white people sitting. Then I look at that little old gal again. I don't look right at her, 'cause I don't want all them people to know I love her. I jest look at her little bit, like I'm looking out that window over there. But she know I'm looking that way, and she kind o' look at me, too. The lady sitting 'side her catch her this time, and she lean over and say something in her yer.

"I don't love him nothing," that little old gal say out loud.

Ever'body back there yer her mouth, and all of 'em look at us and laugh.

"I don't love you, neither," I say. "So you don't have to turn up your nose, Miss."

"You the one looking," she say.

"I wasn't looking at you," I say. "I was looking out that window, there."

"Out that window, my foot," she say. "I seen you. Ever' time I turn 'round you look at me."

"You must o' been looking yourself if you seen me all them times," I say.

"Shucks," she say. "I got me all kind o' boyfriends."

"I got girlfriends, too," I say.

"Well, I just don't want you to get your hopes up," she say.

I don't say no more to that little old gal, 'cause I don't want have to bust her in the mouth. I lean on the seat where Mama sitting, and I don't even look that way no more. When us get to Bayonne, she jugg her little old tongue out at me. I make 'tend I'm go'n hit her, and she duck down side her mama. And all the people laugh at us again.

VI

Me and Mama get off and start walking in town. Bayonne is a little bitty town. Baton Rouge is a hundred times bigger 'an Bayonne. I went to Baton Rouge once—me, Ty, Mama, and Daddy. But that was 'way back yonder—'fore he went in the Army. I wonder when us go'n see him again. I wonder when. Look like he ain't ever coming home. . . . Even the pavement all cracked in Bayonne. Got grass shooting right out the sidewalk. Got weeds in the ditch, too; jest like they got home.

It some cold in Bayonne. Look like it colder 'an it is home. The wind blow in my face, and I feel that stuff running down my nose. I sniff. Mama say use that hand-kercher. I blow my nose and put it back.

Us pass a school and I see them white children playing in the yard. Big old red school, and them children jest running and playing. Then us pass a café, and I see a bunch of 'em in there eating. I wish I was in there 'cause I'm cold. Mama tell me keep my eyes in front where they blonks.

Us pass stores that got dummies, and us pass another café, and then us pass a shoe shop, and that baldhead man in there fixing on a shoe. I look at him and I butt into that white lady, and Mama jeck me in front and tell me stay there.

Us come to the courthouse, and I see the flag waving there. This one yer ain't like the one us got at school. This one yer ain't got but a handful of stars. One at school got a big pile of stars—one for ever' state. Us pass it and us turn and there it is—the dentist office. Me and Mama go in, and they got people sitting ever' where you look. They even got a little boy in there younger 'an me.

Me and Mama sit on that bench, and a white lady come in there and ask me what my name. Mama tell her, and the white lady go back. Then I yer somebody hollering in there. And soon's that little boy hear him hollering, he start hollering, too. His mama pat him and pat him, trying to make him hush up, but he ain't thinking 'bout her.

The man that was hollering in there come out holding his jaw.

"Got it, hanh?" another man say.

The man shake his head.

"Man, I thought they was killing you in there," the other man say. "Hollering like a pig under a gate."

The man don't say nothing. He jest head for the door, and the other man follow him.

"John Lee," the white lady say. "John Lee Williams."

The little boy jugg his head down in his mama lap and holler more now. His mama tell him go with the nurse, but he ain't thinking 'bout her. His mama tell him again, but he don't even yer. His mama pick him up and take him in there, and even when the white lady shet the door I can still hear him hollering.

"I often wonder why the Lord let a child like that suffer," a lady say to my mama. The lady's sitting right in front o' us on another bench. She got on a white dress and a black sweater. She must be a nurse or something herself, I reckoned.

"Not us to question," a man say.

"Sometimes I don't know if we shouldn't," the lady say.

"I know definitely we shouldn't," the man say. The man look like a preacher. He big and fat and he got on a black suit. He got a gold chain, too.

"Why?" the lady say.

"Why anything?" the preacher say.

"Yes," the lady say. "Why anything?"

"Not us to question," the preacher say.

The lady look at the preacher a little while and look at Mama again.

"And look like it's the poor who do most the suffering," she say. "I don't understand it."

"Best not to even try," the preacher say. "He works in mysterious ways. Wonders to perform."

Right then Little John Lee bust out hollering, and ever'body turn they head.

"He's not a good dentist," the lady say. "Dr. Robillard is much better. But more expensive. That's why most of the colored people come here. The white people go to Dr. Robillard. Y'all from Bayonne?"

"Down the river," my mama say. And that's all she go'n say, 'cause she don't talk much. But the lady keep on looking at her, and so she say: "Near Morgan."

"I see," the lady say.

VII

"That's the trouble with the black people in this country today," somebody else say. This one yer sitting on the same side me and Mama sitting, and he kind o'sitting in front of that preacher. He look like a teacher or somebody that go to college. He got on a suit, and he got a book that he been reading. "We don't question is exactly the trouble," he say. "We should question and question and question. Question everything."

The preacher jest look at him a long time. He done put a toothpick or something in his mouth, and he jest keep turning it and turning it. You can see he don't like that boy with that book.

"Maybe you can explain what you mean," he say.

"I said what I meant," the boy say. "Question everything. Every stripe, every star, every word spoken. Everything."

"It 'pears to me this young lady and I was talking 'bout God, young man," the preacher say.

"Question Him, too," the boy say.

"Wait," the preacher say. "Wait now."

"You heard me right," the boy say. "His existence as well as everything else. Everything."

The preacher jest look cross the room at the boy. You can see he getting madder and madder. But mad or no mad, the boy ain't thinking 'bout him. He look at the preacher jest's hard's the preacher look at him.

"Is this what they coming to?" the preacher say. "Is this what we educating them for?"

"You're not educating me," the boy say. "I wash dishes at night to go to school in the day. So even the words you spoke need questioning."

The preacher jest look at him and shake his head.

"When I come in this room and seen you there with your book, I said to myself, There's an intelligent man. How wrong a person can be."

"Show me one reason to believe in the existence of a God," the boy say.

"My heart tell me," the preacher say.

"My heart tells me," the boy say. "My heart tells me. Sure, my heart tells me. And as long as you listen to what your heart tells you, you will have only what the white man gives you and nothing more. Me, I don't listen to my heart. The purpose of the heart is to pump blood throughout the body, and nothing else."

"Who's your paw, boy?" the preacher say.

"Why?"

"Who is he?"

"He's dead."

"And your mom?"

"She's in Charity Hospital with pneumonia. Half killed herself working for nothing."

"And 'cause he's dead and she sick, you mad at the world?"

"I'm not mad at the world. I'm questioning the world. I'm questioning it with cold logic, sir. What do words like Freedom, Liberty, God, White, Colored mean? I want to know. That's why *you* are sending us to school, to read and to ask questions. And because we ask these questions, you call us mad. No, sir, it is not us who are mad."

"You keep saying 'us'?"

"'Us' . . . why not? I'm not alone."

The preacher jest shake his head. Then he look at ever'body in the room—ever'body. Some of the people look down at the floor, keep from looking at him. I kind o' look 'way myself, but soon's I know he done turn his head. I look that way again.

"I'm sorry for you," he say.

"Why?" the boy say. "Why not be sorry for yourself? Why are you so much better off than I am? Why aren't you sorry for these other people in here? Why not be sorry for the lady who had to drag her child into the dentist office? Why not be sorry for the lady sitting on that bench over there? Be sorry for them. Not for me. Some way or other I'm going to make it."

"No, I'm sorry for you," the preacher say.

"Of course. Of course," the boy say, shaking his head. "You're sorry for me because I rock that pillar you're leaning on."

"You can't ever rock the pillar I'm leaning on, young man. It's stronger than anything man can ever do."

"You believe in God because a man told you to believe in God. A white man told you to believe in God. And why? To keep you ignorant, so he can keep you under his feet."

"So now, we the ignorant?"

"Yes," the boy say. "Yes." And he open his book again.

The preacher jest look at him there. The boy done forgot all about him. Ever'body else make 'tend they done forgot 'bout the squabble, too.

Then I see that preacher getting up real slow. Preacher a great big old man, and he got to brace hisself to get up. He come 'cross the room where the boy is. He jest stand there looking at him, but the boy don't raise his head.

"Stand up, boy," preacher say.

The boy look up at him, then he shet his book real slow and stand up. Preacher jest draw back and hit him in the face. The boy fall 'gainst the wall, but he straighten hisself up and look right back at that preacher.

"You forgot the other cheek," he say.

The preacher hit him again on the other side. But this time the boy don't fall.

"That hasn't changed a thing," he say.

The preacher jest look at the boy. The preacher breathing real hard like he jest run up a hill. The boy sit down and open his book again.

"I feel sorry for you," the preacher say. "I never felt so sorry for a man before."

The boy make 'tend he don't even hear that preacher. He keep on reading his book. The preacher go back and get his hat off the chair.

"Excuse me," he say to us. "I'll come back some other time. Y'all, please excuse me."

And he look at the boy and go out the room. The boy hist his hand up to his mouth one time, to wipe 'way some blood. All the rest o' the time he keep on reading.

VIII

The lady and her little boy come out the dentist, and the nurse call somebody else in. Then little bit later they come out, and the nurse call another name. But fast's she call somebody in there, somebody else come in the place where we at, and the room stay full.

The people coming in now, all of 'em wearing big coats. One of 'em say something 'bout sleeting, and another one say he hope not. Another one say he think it ain't nothing but rain. 'Cause, he say, rain can get awful cold this time o' year.

All 'cross the room they talking. Some of 'em talking to people right by 'em, some of 'em talking to people clare 'cross the room, some of 'em talking to anybody'll listen. It's a little bitty room, no bigger 'an us kitchen, and I can see ever'body in there. The little old room's rull of smoke, 'cause you got two ole men smoking pipes. I think I feel my teef thumping me some, and I hold my breath and wait. I wait and wait, but it don't thump me no more. Thank God for that.

I feel like going to sleep, and I lean back 'gainst the wall. But I'm scared to go to sleep: Scared 'cause the nurse might call my name and I won't hear her. And Mama might go to sleep, too, and she be mad if neither us heard the nurse.

I look up at Mama. I love my mama. I love my mama. And when cotton come I'm go'n get her a newer coat. And I ain't go'n get a black one neither. I think I'm go'n get her a red one.

"They got some books over there," I say. "Want read one of 'em?"

Mama look at the books, but she don't answer me.

"You got yourself a little man there," the lady say.

Mama don't say nothing to the lady, but she must 'a' grin a little bit, 'cause I seen the lady grinning back. The lady look at me a little while, like she feeling sorry for me.

"You sure got that preacher out here in a hurry," she say to that other boy.

The boy look up at her and look in his book again. When I grow up I want to be jest like him. I want clothes like that and I want keep a book with me, too.

"You really don't believe in God?" the lady say.

"No," he say.

"But why?" the lady say.

"Because the wind is pink," he say.

"What?" the lady say.

The boy don't answer her no more. He jest read in his book.

"Talking 'bout the wind is pink," that old lady say. She sitting on the same bench with the boy, and she trying to look in his face. The boy make 'tend the old lady ain't even there. He jest keep reading. "Wind is pink," she say again. "Eh, Lord, what children go'n be saying next?"

The lady 'cross from us bust out laughing.

"That's a good one," she say. "The wind is pink. Yes, sir, that's a good one."

"Don't you believe the wind is pink?" the boy say. He keep his head down in the book.

"Course I believe it, Honey," the lady say. "Course I do." She look at us and wink her eye. "And what color is grass, Honey?"

"Grass? Grass is black."

She bust out laughing again. The boy look at her.

"Don't you believe grass is black?" he say.

The lady quit laughing and look at him. Ever'body else look at him now. The place quiet, quiet.

"Grass is green, Honey," the lady say. "It was green yesterday, it's green today, and it's go'n be green tomorrow."

"How do you know it's green?"

"I know because I know."

"You don't know it's green. You believe it's green because someone told you it was green. If someone had told you it was black you'd believe it was black."

"It's green," the lady say. "I know green when I see green."

"Prove it's green."

"Surely, now," the lady say. "Don't tell me it's coming to that?"

"It's coming to just that," the boy say. "Words mean nothing. One means no more than the other."

"That's what it all coming to?" that old lady say. The old lady got on a turban and she got on two sweaters. She got a green sweater under a black sweater. I can see the green sweater 'cause some of the buttons on the other sweater missing.

"Yes, ma'am," the boy say. "Words mean nothing. Action is the only thing. Doing. That's the only thing."

"Other words, you want the Lord to come down here and show Hisself to you?" she say.

"Exactly, ma'am."

"You don't mean that, I'm sure?"

"I do, ma'am."

"Done, Jesus," the old lady say, shaking her head.

"I didn't go 'long with that preacher at first," the other lady say; "but now—I don't know. When a person say the grass is black, he's either a lunatic or something wrong."

"Prove to me that it's green."

"It's green because the people say it's green."

"Those same people say we're citizens of the United States."

"I think I'm a citizen."

"Citizens have certain rights. Name me one right that you have. One right, granted by the Constitution, that you can exercise in Bayonne."

The lady don't answer him. She jest look at him like she don't know what he talking 'bout. I know I don't.

"Things changing," she say.

"Things are changing because some black men have begun to follow their brains instead of their hearts."

"You trying to say these people don't believe in God?"

"I'm sure some of them do. Maybe most of them do. But they don't believe that God is going to touch these white people's hearts and change them tomorrow. Things change through action. By no other way."

Ever'body sit quiet and look at the boy. Nobody say a thing. Then the lady 'cross from me and Mama jest shake her head.

"Let's hope that not all your generation feel the same way you do," she say.

"Think what you please, it doesn't matter," the boy say. "But it will be men who listen to their heads and not their hearts who will see that your children have a better chance than you had."

"Let's hope they ain't all like you, though," the old lady say. "Done forgot the heart absolutely."

"Yes, ma'am, I hope they aren't all like me," the boy say. "Unfortunately I was born too late to believe in your God. Let's hope that the ones who come after will have your faith—if not in your God, then in something else, something definitely that they can lean on. I haven't anything. For me, the wind is pink; the grass is black."

IX

The nurse come in the room where us all sitting and waiting and say the doctor won't take no more patients till one o'clock this evening. My mama jump up off the bench and go up to the white lady.

"Nurse, I have to go back in the field this evening," she say.

"The doctor is treating his last patient now," the nurse say. "One o'clock this evening."

"Can I at least speak to the doctor?" my mama say.

"I'm his nurse," the lady say.

"My little boy sick," my mama say. "Right now his teef almost killing him."

The nurse look at me. She trying to make up her mind if to let me come in. I look at her real pitiful. The teef ain't hurting me a tall, but mama say it is, so I make 'tend for her sake.

"This evening," the nurse say, and go back in the office.

"Don't feel 'jected, Honey," the lady say to Mama. "I been 'round 'em a long time—they take you when they want to. If you was white, that's something else; but you the wrong shade."

Mama don't say nothing to the lady, and me and her go outside and stand 'gainst the wall. It's cold out there. I can feel that wind going through my coat. Some of the other people come out of the room and go up the street. Me and Mama stand there a little while and start to walking. I don't know where us going. When us come to the other street us jest stand there.

"You don't have to make water, do you?" Mama say.

"No, ma'am," I say.

Us go up the street. Walking real slow. I can tell Mama don't know where she going. When us come to a store us stand there and look at the dummies. I look at a little boy with a brown overcoat. He got on brown shoes, too. I look at my old shoes and look at his'n again. You wait till summer, I say.

Me and Mama walk away. Us come up to another store and us stop and look at them dummies, too. Then us go again. Us pass a café where the white people in there eating. Mama tell me keep my eyes in front where they blonks, but I can't help from seeing them people eat. My stomach start to growling 'cause I'm hungry. When I see people eating, I get hungry; when I see a coat, I get cold.

A man whistle at my mama when us go by a filling station. She make 'tend she don't even see him. I look back and I feel like hitting him in the mouth. If I was bigger, I say. If I was bigger, you see.

Us keep on going. I'm getting colder and colder, but I don't say nothing. I feel that stuff running down my nose and I sniff.

"That rag," she say.

I git it out and wipe my nose. I'm getting cold all over now—my face, my hands, my feet, ever'thing. Us pass another little café, but this'n for white people, too, and us can't go in there neither. So us jest walk. I'm so cold now. I'm 'bout ready to say it. If I knowed where us was going, I wouldn't be so cold, but I don't know where us going. Us go, us go, us go. Us walk clean out o' Bayonne. Then us cross the street and us come back. Same thing I seen when I got off the bus. Same old trees, same old walk, same old weeds, same old cracked pave—same old ever'thing.

I sniff again.

"That rag," she say.

I wipe my nose real fast and jugg that handkercher back in my pocket 'fore my hand get too cold. I raise my head and I can see David hardware store. When us come up to it, us go in. I don't know why, but I'm glad.

It warm in there. It so warm in there you don't want ever leave. I look for the heater, and I see it over by them ba'ls. Three white men standing 'round the heater talking in Creole. One of 'em come to see what Mama want.

"Got any ax handle?" she say.

Me, Mama, and the white man start to the back, but Mama stop me when us come to the heater. Her and the white man go on. I hold my hand over the heater and look at 'em. They go all the way in the back, and I see the white man point to the ax handle 'gainst the wall. Mama take one of 'em and shake it like she trying to figure how much it weigh. Then she rub her hand over it from one end to the other. She turn it over and look at the other side, then she shake it again, and shake her head and put it back. She get another one and she do it jest like she did the first one, then she shake her head. Then she get a brown one and do it that, too. But she don't like this one neither. Then she get another one, but 'fore she shake it or anything, she look at me. Look like she trying to say something to me, but I don't know what it is. All I know is I done got warm now and I'm feeling right smart better. Mama shake this ax handle jest like she done the others, and shake her head and say something to the white man. The white man jest look at his pile of ax handle, and when Mama pass by him to come to the front, the white man jest scratch his head and follow her. She tell me come on, and us go on out and start walking again.

Us walk and walk, and no time at all I'm cold again. Look like I'm colder now 'cause I can still remember how good it was back there. My stomach growl and I suck it in to keep Mama from yering it. She walking right 'side me, and it growl so loud you can yer it a mile. But Mama don't say a word.

X

When us come up to the courthouse, I look at the clock. It got quarter to twelve. Mean us got another hour and a quarter to be out yer in the cold. Us go and stand side a building. Something hit my cap and I look up at the sky. Sleet falling.

I look at Mama standing there. I want stand close 'side her, but she don't like that. She say that's cry-baby stuff. She say you got to stand for yourself, by yourself.

"Let's go back to that office," she say.

Us cross the street. When us get to the dentist I try to open the door, but I can't. Mama push me on the side and she twist the knob. But she can't open it neither. She twist it some more, harder, but she can't open it. She turn 'way from the door. I look at her, but I don't move and I don't say nothing. I done seen her like this before and I'm scared.

"You hungry?" she say. She say it like she mad at me, like I'm the one cause of ever'thing.

"No, ma'am," I say.

"You want eat and walk back, or you rather don't eat and ride?"

"I ain't hungry," I say.

I ain't jest hungry, but I'm cold, too. I'm so hungry and I'm so cold I want cry. And look like I'm getting colder and colder. My feet done got numb. I try to work my toes, but I can't. Look like I'm go'n die. Look like I'm go'n stand right here and freeze to death. I think about home. I think about Val and Auntie and Ty and Louis and Walker. It 'bout twelve o'clock and I know they eating dinner. I can hear Ty making jokes. That's Ty. Always trying to make some kind o' joke. I wish I was right there listening to him. Give anything in the world if I was home 'round the fire.

"Come on," Mama say.

Us start walking again. My feet so numb I can't hardly feel 'em. Us turn the corner and go back up the street. The clock start hitting for twelve.

The sleet's coming down plenty now. They hit the pave and bounce like rice. Oh, Lord; oh, Lord, I pray. Don't let me die. Don't let me die. Don't let me die, Lord.

XI

Now I know where us going. Us going back o' town where the colored people eat. I don't care if I don't eat. I been hungry before. I can stand it. But I can't stand the cold.

I can see us go'n have a long walk. It 'bout a mile down there. But I don't mind. I know when I get there I'm go'n warm myself. I think I can hold out. My hands numb in my pockets and my feet numb, too, but if I keep moving I can hold out. Jest don't stop no more, that's all.

The sky's gray. The sleet keeps falling. Falling like rain now—plenty, plenty. You can hear it hitting the pave. You can see it bouncing. Sometimes it bounce two times 'fore it settle.

Us keep going. Us don't say nothing. Us jest keep going, keep going.

I wonder what Mama thinking. I hope she ain't mad with me. When summer come I'm go'n pick plenty cotton and get her a coat. I'm go'n get her a red one.

I hope they make it summer all the time. I be glad if it was summer all the time—but it ain't. Us got to have winter, too. Lord, I hate the winter. I guess ever'body hate the winter.

I don't sniff this time. I get out my handkercher and wipe my nose. My hand so cold I can hardly hold the handkercher.

I think us getting close, but us ain't there yet. I wonder where ever'body is. Can't see nobody but us. Look like us the only two people moving 'round today. Must be too cold for the rest of the people to move 'round.

I can hear my teefes. I hope they don't knock together too hard and make that bad one hurt. Lord, that's all I need, for that bad one to start off.

I hear a church bell somewhere. But today ain't Sunday. They must be ringing for a funeral or something.

I wonder what they doing at home. They must be eating. Monsieur Bayonne might be there with his guitar. One day Ty played with Monsieur Bayonne guitar and broke one o' the string. Monsieur Bayonne got some mad with Ty. He say Ty ain't go'n never 'mount to nothing. Ty can go jest like him when he ain't there. Ty can make ever'body laugh mocking Monsieur Bayonne.

I used to like to be with Mama and Daddy. Us used to be happy. But they took him in the Army. Now, nobody happy no more. . . . I be glad when he come back.

Monsieur Bayonne say it wasn't fair for 'em to take Daddy and give Mama nothing and give us nothing. Auntie say, Shhh, Etienne. Don't let 'em yer you talk like that.

Monsieur Bayonne say, It's God truth. What they giving his children? They have to walk three and a half mile to school hot or cold. That's anything to give for a paw? She's got to work in the field rain or shine jest to make ends meet. That's anything to give for a husband? Auntie say, Shhh Etienne, shhh. Yes, you right, Monsieur Bayonne say. Best don't say it in front of 'em now. But one day they go'n find out. One day. Yes, s'pose so, Auntie say. Then what, Rose Mary? Monsieur Bayonne say. I don't know, Etienne, Auntie say. All us can do is us job, and leave ever'thing else in His hand. . . .

Us getting closer, now. Us getting closer. I can see the railroad tracks.

Us cross the tracks, and now I see the café. Jest to get in there, I say, Jest to get in there. Already I'm starting to feel little better.

XII

Us go in. Ahhh, it good. I look for the heater; there 'gainst the wall. One of them little brown ones. I jest stand there and hold my hand over it. I can't open my hands too wide 'cause they almost froze.

Mama standing right 'side me. She done unbuttoned her coat. Smoke rise out the coat, and the coat smell like a wet dog.

I move to the side so Mama can have more room. She open out her hands and rub 'em together. I rub mine together, too, 'cause this keeps 'em from hurting. If you let 'em warm too fast, they hurt you sure. But if you let 'em warm jest little bit at a time, and you keep rubbing 'em, they be all right ever' time.

They got jest two more people in the café. A lady back o' the counter, and a man on this side the counter. They been watching us ever since us come in.

Mama get out the handkercher and count the money. Both o' us know how much money she got there. Three dollars. No, she ain't got three dollars. 'Cause she had to pay us way up here. She ain't got but two dollars and a half left. Dollar and a half to get my teef pulled, and fifty cents for us to go back on, and fifty cents worse o' salt meat.

She stir the money 'round with her finger. Most o' the money is change 'cause I can hear it rubbing together. She stir it and stir it. Then she look at the door. It still sleeting. I can yer it hitting 'gainst the wall like rice.

"I ain't hungry, Mama," I say.

"Got to pay 'em something for they heat," she say.

She take a quarter out the handkercher and tie the handkercher up again. She look over her shoulder at the people, but she still don't move. I hope she don't spend the money. I don't want her spend it on me. I'm hungry, I'm almost starving I'm so hungry, but I don't want her spending the money on me.

She flip the quarter over like she thinking. She must be thinking 'bout us walking back home. Lord, I sure don't want walk home. If I thought it done any good to say something, I say it. But my mama make up her own mind.

She turn way from the heater right fast, like she better hurry up and do it 'fore she change her mind. I turn to look at her go to the counter. The man and the lady look at her, too. She tell the lady something and the lady walk away. The man keep on looking at her. Her back turn to the man, and Mama don't even know he standing there.

The lady put some cakes and a glass o' milk on the counter. Then she pour up a cup o' coffee and set it side the other stuff. Mama pay her for the things and come back where I'm at. She tell me sit down at that table 'gainst the wall.

The milk and the cakes for me. The coffee for my mama. I eat slow, and I look at her. She looking outside at the sleet. She looking real sad. I say to myself, I'm go'n make all this up one day. You see, one day, I'm go'n make all this up. I want to say it now. I want to tell how I feel right now. But Mama don't like for us to talk like that.

"I can't eat all this," I say.

They got just three little cakes there. And I'm so hungry right now, the Lord know I can eat a hundred times three. But I want her to have one.

She don't even look my way. She know I'm hungry. She know I want it. I let it stay there a while, then I get it and eat it. I eat jest on my front teefes, 'cause if it tech that back teef I know what'll happen. Thank God it ain't hurt me a tall today.

After I finish eating I see the man go to the juke box. He drop a nickel in it, then he jest stand there looking at the record. Mama tell me keep my eyes in front where they blonks. I turn my head like she say, but then I yer the man coming towards us.

"Dance, Pretty?" he say.

Mama get up to dance with him. But 'fore you know it, she done grabbed the little man and done throwed him 'side the wall. He hit the wall so hard he stop the juke box from playing.

"Some pimp," the lady back o' the counter say. "Some pimp."

The little man jump off the floor and start towards my mama. 'Fore you know it, Mama done sprung open her knife and she waiting for him.

"Come on," she say. "Come on. I'll cut you from you neighbo to your throat. Come on."

I go up to the little man to hit him, but Mama make me come and stand 'side her. The little man look at me and Mama and go back to the counter.

"Some pimp," the lady back o' the counter say. "Some pimp." She start laughing and pointing at the little man. "Yes, sir, you a pimp, all right. Yes sir."

XIII

"Fasten that coat. Let's go," Mama say.

"You don't have to leave," the lady say.

Mama don't answer the lady, and us right out in the cold again. I'm warm right now—my hands, my yers, my feet—but I know this ain't go'n last too long. It done sleet so much now you got ice ever'where.

Us cross the railroad tracks, and soon's us do, I get cold. That wind go through this little old coat like it ain't nothing. I got a shirt and a sweater under it, but that wind don't pay 'em no mind. I look up and I can see us got a long way to go. I wonder if us go'n make it 'fore I get too cold.

Us cross over to walk on the sidewalk. They got jest one sidewalk back here. It's over there.

After us go jest a little piece, I smell bread cooking. I look, then I see a baker shop. When us get closer, I can smell it more better. I shet my eyes and make 'tend I'm eating. But I keep 'em shet too long and I butt up 'gainst a telephone post. Mama grab me, and see if I'm hurt. I ain't bleeding or nothing and she turn me loose.

I can feel I'm getting colder and colder, and I look up to see how far us still got to go. Uptown is 'way up yonder. A half mile, I reckoned. I try to think of something. They say think and you won't get cold. I think of that poem, *Annabel Lee*. I ain't been to school in so long—this bad weather—I reckoned they done passed *Annabel Lee*. But passed it or not, I'm sure Miss Walker go'n make me recite it when I get there. That woman don't never forget nothing. I ain't never seen nobody like that.

I'm still getting cold. *Annabel Lee* or no *Annabel Lee*, I'm still getting cold. But I can see us getting closer. Us getting there gradually.

Soon's us turn the corner, I see a little old white lady up in front o' us. She the only lady on the street. She all in black and she got a long black rag over her head.

"Stop," she say.

Me and Mama stop and look at her. She must be crazy to be out in all this sleet. Ain't got but a few other people out there, and all of 'em men.

"Yall done ate?" she say.

"Jest finished," Mama say.

"Yall must be cold then?" she say.

"Us headed for the dentist," Mama say. "Us'll warm up when us get there."

"What dentist?" the old lady say. "Mr. Bassett?"

"Yes, ma'am," Mama say.

"Come on in," the old lady say. "I'll telephone him and tell him yall coming."

Me and Mama follow the old lady in the store. It's a little bitty store, and it don't have much in there. The old lady take off her head piece and fold it up.

"Helena?" somebody call from the back.

"Yes, Alnest?" the old lady say.

"Did you see them?"

"They're here. Standing beside me."

"Good. Now you can stay inside."

The old lady look at Mama. Mama waiting to hear what she brought us in here for. I'm waiting for that, too.

"I saw yall each time you went by," she say. "I came out to catch you, but you were gone."

"Us went back 'o town," Mama say.

"Did you eat?"

"Yes, ma'am."

The old lady look at Mama a long time, like she thinking Mama might be jest saying that. Mama look right back at her. The old lady look at me to see what I got to say. I don't say nothing. I sure ain't going 'gainst my mama.

"There's food in the kitchen," she say to Mama. "I've been keeping it warm."

Mama turn right around and start for the door.

"Just a minute," the old lady say. Mama stop. "The boy'll have to work for it. It isn't free."

"Us don't take no handout," Mama say.

"I'm not handing out anything," the old lady say. "I need my garbage moved to the front. Ernest has a bad cold and can't go out there."

"James'll move it for you," Mama say.

"Not unless you eat," the old lady say. "I'm old, but I have my pride, too, you know."

Mama can see she ain't go'n beat this old lady down, so she jest shake her head.

"All right," the old lady say. "Come into the kitchen."

She lead the way with that rag in her hand. The kitchen is a little bitty thing, too. The table and the stove jest about fill it up. They got a little room to the side. Somebody in there laying cross the bed. Must be the person she was talking with: Alnest or Ernest—I forget what she call him.

"Sit down," the old lady say to Mama. "Not you," she say to me. "You have to move the cans."

"Helena?" somebody say in the other room.

"Yes, Alnest?" the old lady say.

"Are you going out there again?"

"I must show the boy where the garbage is," the old lady say.

"Keep that shawl over your head," the old man say.

"You don't have to remind me. Come boy," the old lady say.

Us go out in the yard. Little old back yard ain't no bigger 'an the store or the kitchen. But it can sleet here jest like it can sleet in any big back yard. And 'fore you know it I'm trembling.

"There," the old lady say, pointing to the cans. I pick up one of the cans. The can so light I put it back down to look inside o' it.

"Here," the old lady say. "Leave that cap alone."

I look at her in the door. She got that black rag wrapped 'round her shoulders, and she pointing one of her fingers at me.

"Pick it up and carry it to the front," she say. I go by her with the can. I'm sure the thing's empty. She could 'a' carried the thing by herself, I'm sure. "Set it on the sidewalk by the door and come back for the other one," she say.

I go and come back, Mama look at me when I pass her. I get the other can and take it to the front. It don't feel no heavier 'an the other one. I tell myself to look inside and see just what I been hauling. First, I look up and down the street. Nobody coming. Then I look over my shoulder. Little old lady done slipped there jest's quiet 's mouse, watching me. Look like she knowed I was go'n try that.

"Ehh, Lord," she say. "Children, children. Come in here, boy, and go wash your hands."

I follow her into the kitchen, and she point, and I go to the bathroom. When I come out, the old lady done dished up the food. Rice, gravy, meat, and she even got some lettuce and tomato in a saucer. She even got a glass o' milk and a piece o' cake there, too. It look so good. I almost start eating 'fore I say my blessing.

"Helena?" the old man say.

"Yes Alnest?" she say.

"Are they eating?"

"Yes," she say.

"Good," he say. "Now you'll stay inside."

The old lady go in there where he is and I can hear 'em talking. I look at Mama. She eating slow like she thinking. I wonder what's the matter now. I reckoned she think 'bout home.

The old lady come back in the kitchen.

"I talked to Dr. Bassett's nurse," she say. "Dr. Bassett will take you as soon as you get there."

"Thank you, ma'am," Mama say.

"Perfectly all right," the old lady say. "Which one is it?"

Mama nod towards me. The old lady look at me real sad. I look sad, too.

"You're not afraid, are you?" she say.

"No'm," I say.

"That's a good boy," the old lady say. "Nothing to be afraid of."

When me and Mama get through eating, us thank the old lady again.

"Helena, are they leaving?" the old man say.

"Yes, Alnest."

"Tell them I say good-by."

"They can hear you. Alnest."

"Good-by both mother and son," the old man say. "And may God be with you."

Me and Mama tell the old man good-by, and us follow the old lady in the front. Mama open the door to go out, but she stop and come back in the store.

"You sell salt meat?" she say.

"Yes."

"Give me two bits worse."

"That isn't very much salt meat," the old lady say.

"That'll all I have," Mama say.

The old lady go back o' the counter and cut a big piece off the chunk. Then she wrap it and put it in a paper bag.

"Two bits," she say.

"That look like awful lot of meat for a quarter," Mama say

"Two bits," the old lady say. "I've been selling salt meat behind this counter twenty-five years. I think I know what I'm doing."

"You got a scale there," Mama say.

"What?" the old lady say.

"Weigh it," Mama say.

"What?" the old lady say. "Are you telling me how to run my business?"

"Thanks very much for the food," Mama say.

"Just a minute," the old lady say.

"James," Mama say to me. I move towards the door.

"Just one minute, I said," the old lady say.

Me and Mama stop again and look at her. The old lady take the meat out the bag and unwrap it and cut 'bout half o' it off. Then she wrap it up again and jugg it back in the bag and give it to Mama. Mama lay the quarter on the counter.

"Your kindness will never be forgotten," she say. "James," she say to me.

Us go out, and the old lady come to the door to look at us. After us go a little piece I look back, and she still there watching us.

The sleet's coming down heavy, heavy now, and I turn up my collar to keep my neck warm. My mama tell me turn it right back down.

"You not a bum," she say. "You a man."

Anne Rivers Siddons

(1938–)

A native of Georgia, Anne Rivers Siddons was graduated from Auburn University in Alabama in 1958. In 1964 she became a senior editor for *Atlanta* magazine. Siddons was named Georgia author of the year in 1988. She relocated from Atlanta, where the author had lived in the same house for more than thirty years, to Charleston, South Carolina, in 1998. She divides her time between Charleston and Haven Colony, Brooklin, Maine.

Siddons is a prolific, best-selling writer who has received literary acclaim. Beginning in 1976 with the publication of *Heartbreak Hotel* (fiction) and *John Chancellor Makes Me Cry* (nonfiction), Siddons has received recognition for *The House Next Door* (1978); *Go Straight on Peachtree* (1978); *Fox's Earth* (1981); *Homeplace* (1987); *Peachtree Road* (1988); *King's Oak* (1990); *Outer Banks* (1991); *Colony* (1992); *Hill Towns* (1993); *Down Town* (1994); *Fault Lines* (1995); *Up Island* (1997); and *Low Country* (1998). *Heartbreak Hotel* was adapted into the film *Heart of Dixie* by Orion Pictures in 1989.

Siddons's fiction, with its lush description, has been described as residing in the Southern Gothic tradition. Her strong, female protagonists often discover their true beings during midlife when they undergo crises that thrust them into a new reality.

from *Hill Towns*

Trinity College crowns the flat summit of Morgan's Mountain in south Tennessee like a mortarboard or a forage cap, or perhaps a bishop's miter, apt similes all. It was born just after the Civil War (referred to on the Mountain as the War for Southern Independence) expressly to serve the southern dioceses of the Episcopal Church in the Christian education of its young gentlemen. It was modeled, as perfectly as human frailty allowed, after the venerable Anglican colleges of England and held together during its hardscrabble early years by the unspent passion of a great many unemployed Confederate officers. Many southern bishops blessed it, and not a few came to teach there. Several still do. Widows of Confederate officers or Episcopal clergymen were its first housemothers. Early on, it became an indulgent little joke that "Trinity" in the college's case referred to God the Father, God the Son, and General Robert E. Lee.

Succeeding generations of Trinitarians have found no cause to scuttle the joke. God the Father and God the Son are still manifestly present in the mellow gray dimness of All Souls Chapel and Compton Seminary, and General Lee's portrait, flanked by draped Confederate flags and crossed dress sabers, still hangs in Commons.

The education presided over by these eminences is unalterably classical liberal arts and generally first rate in spite of it, and for that reason many undergraduates are now drawn from all parts of the country and even the world. Very few these days come to be molded by God and Robert E. Lee for life and service in the vanished world of the Christian gentlemen's South, and many new students come up the Mountain for the first time prepared to jeer. Even those of us whose permanent world it is often laugh at Trinity's sheer hubris of intent and tradition; the "Trinity experience" no longer fits one to live anywhere but Trinity, it's often said at faculty doings on the Mountain.

But those who remain do not wish to leave. And the young who enter laughing and stay to graduate almost always go out into the world off the Mountain taking with them the swish of invisible academic gowns and a set of near-chivalric values. There is enormous power in these old gray stones, cloistered away up here on Morgan's Mountain. They bend reality and stop time. I do not wonder that Trinity produces so few successful junk bond salesmen and politicians. The daily subliminal infusions of honor are an effective lifelong purgative for a great many contemporary ambitions. I sometimes imagine that the last sound new graduates hear as they roll out under the stone arch that marks the southernmost boundary of the Domain, as we call it, is the triumphant laughter of long-dead bishops and generals.

Much of Trinity's power lies in its sheer beauty. The Mountain and the village of Montview are almost phantasmagorical in their loveliness. There are to me no mountains on earth so beautiful as these. They are among the oldest in the world, smoothed now to the curves of a sleeping woman's body. They roll across the middle South in symmetrical soft, misted waves. Morgan's Mountain sits a little apart from the rest, a last convulsion that marks the dying of the Appalachian chain. And green: green everywhere, always, all the greens of the entire earth, each to its own season. The top of Morgan's Mountain is a globe of pure green swimming suspended in the thin, clear blue air of the southern highlands. It comes eventually to be the only air where permanent Trinitarians can thrive. We are unfit, I have always thought, to breathe other richer, ranker air for long.

That dreaming old beauty is the snare, of course. Those who do not need it do not stay. A high percentage of freshmen and sophomores do not return. Some flunk out, but many simply bolt back to the rich, comforting stench of the world. Those who stay need bells in their ears, and plainsong, and countless angels dancing always on the heads of pins. And after all, the world is lucky that relatively few do stay; what would we do with all those elite young philosopher princelings if their numbers were legion? Where would we fit all those languorous, learned young Anglophiles?

But the ones who do stay . . . ah the old mossy stones and the flying dark gowns and the ranked pennons in chapel looking for all the world like medieval banners, and the slow turn of the burnished seasons in the great hardwood forest, and the mists of autumn and the white snowfall of spring dogwoods and the world spread out at one's feet all around off the Mountain, and the bittersweet smoke of wood fires and the drunkenness of poetry and mathematics and the flow of bourbon and the night music of concerts and dances through new green leaves, and the delicately bawdy laughter of young girls and the sheen of their flesh and hair, and the special trembling awareness of cold dew and dawn breaking on monumental hangovers after you have talked all night of wonderful or terrible things and sung many songs and perhaps made out by the lake or on the Steep: these things are golden barbs in the flesh and will hold always. Trinity is eccentric and elitist and chauvinistic and innocent and arrogant and very, very particular, and it claims its own like a great gray raptor.

My grandfather Cash was a janitor there.

"What did that feel like?" Joe asked me when he learned that one grandfather used to clean the structure that bore the other's name. Not for long; Papaw Cash refused to enter Compton Seminary with his mops and brooms once the Compton of it entered his family. Everyone at Trinity understood.

Joe was powerfully attracted to my family's bizarre history. He found none of it amusing and all of it profound. Joe was a born teacher of literature.

"It's pure American tragedy," he said, over and over. "It's all of folklore and literature, really: the Montagues and the Capulets, the Medicis, most of Faulkner—"

"And the Hatfields and the McCoys, maybe?" I said. "Or the Jukes and the Kallikaks?"

I was in his senior Southern Literature seminar that winter. It was how we met. I knew he knew the story of my provenance on the Mountain before he knew me; everyone at Trinity did. I had stopped minding long before. Such was Trinity's ecclesiastical, liberal-arts predilection for wounded birds and fascination with its own redolently Gothic milieu that I was a campus favorite from the days I used to come to work with my grandfather Cash and sit docilely on the steps of whatever structure he was cleaning, Mamaw Cash being practically certifiable by then. Somehow I never felt an outsider in the Domain. Everyone knew and felt sorry for me, the strange little hybrid of gown and town. And I suppose I was an appealing child; I heard it often. I was slight and grave and long-limbed, with a cap of curls like a little Greek boy's, only fair, and fine thin features. I looked for all the world like my father and still do, save for the very dark eyes that were my mother's. Except for the fine dry lines around my eyes and mouth, I could pass now for a rather androgynous late teen. My father had the same look in the photographs taken just before he died, and it is there in the portrait of my great-grandfather Compton, in the seminary. Unworldly and dreaming, patrician as an overbred collie. It has, I think, served all us Comptons well, even my poor father. It both enabled and excused him a great deal.

"What did it feel like?" I answered Joe when he first asked. "To tell you the truth, it made me feel rather special. Everybody bent over backward to make me feel accepted, not to feel . . . singled out because my grandfather was a campus janitor, and not even the head honcho at that. I think I was pretty much Trinity's poster child for a long time. Papaw wouldn't even speak my father's name by then, but I knew the name on the seminary was mine, and somehow I knew that half of me, anyway, was connected to the college in an important way. After a while Mrs. Pierce, the provost's wife, put her foot down and said it was a disgrace for Bishop Compton's great-granddaughter to sit on the steps with the mops and brooms all day, and she took me into her own house with her housekeeper. I pretty much grew up there weekdays; I went to the little Trinity kindergarten, and the faculty children came to play with me, and it got so I went to all the right little Mountain birthday parties and play groups and then to Montview Day. I know my Compton grandparents paid my tuition and probably kicked in a good bit more in those earliest days, but I think they must have sent it straight to the Pierces, or maybe there was a discreet little fund established at the school. The bequest came much later, after they died. I know if they'd sent money to my Cash grandparents' house, Mamaw Cash would have given it all to her church. She was practically handling snakes by that time."

Joe's eyes shone behind his rimless round glasses. More Faulkner; this was beyond his wildest dreams. I could practically see a monograph taking shape inside his long, elegant skull: "The Survival of the Gothic Tradition in the American Southern Highlands."

"Too bad it all had such an ordinary happy ending." I said.

He wouldn't surrender so easily.

"That's not the way I heard it," he said. "I heard you went through a god-awful time with your Cash grandparents before they died. Christ, no wonder you don't want to leave this place. It must seem like the only refuge you ever had."

I didn't bother to ask who had told him about the other side of my childhood, the side that prevailed when I went home each afternoon with Papaw Cash. Anyone could have. It was part of the cherished Legend of Catherine Compton. I heard much later that another professor, a pale young man in the music school who much admired the ballads of John Jacob Niles, had made up a folk song about me once while drunk on jug wine at a faculty party: "The Ballad of Cat Compton." It amused me when I finally heard it, in my early thirties and safe in my stone house on the Steep overlooking the entire valley, with Joe and our daughter Lacey. But it would have embarrassed me no end if I had learned about it at the time. Back then I wanted only to put every vestige of my life in the dark vine-strangled shack on the other side of the Mountain behind me and melt into the body of Trinity.

Dark . . . dear Lord, the darkness around that house and in it! Not only the darkness of the enshrouding kudzu and creeper vines that finally came to hold the black weathered boards together; not only the darkness of the encircling pines and the wet gray lip of pure mountain granite that beetled over it, so that between trees and rock you never saw the sun or the blue of the sky unless you went outside and stood in the front yard. No, the darkness in the house of Burrell and Mattie Cash seeped from the very walls and canted floors; from the stained rag rugs and cracked linoleum and the few pieces of scarred old dark fumed oak furniture; from the black iron stove and the wash pot in the kitchen and the listing moss-slick outhouse in the pines behind; from the mean small fireplaces in the four rooms that lay cold and dank and empty except in the very dead of winter; from, it seemed to me, the very stuff of my grandparents' shapeless lye-boiled clothing, to which my own clothing was nearly identical; from their dark closed faces and shuttered, black Cash eyes.

I never knew why my grandparents were so cold and angry; it was not entirely at my father, and at my mother's shameful death with him on the chain bridge, for they were silent and angry even before that. I remember distinctly that I really feared going to their house when my parents were alive, and was always cold there, and finally my mother did not take me anymore. None of Rosellen Cash's older brothers and sisters lived in their parents' house that I can remember. All of them had fled it as soon as they could find sustenance for themselves elsewhere. Three Cash aunts had married when they were sixteen and could legally do so and moved to the flatlands, where they raised what seemed to me entire phalanxes of dark, jeering Cash cousins. Two Cash uncles had also fled to the flats but did not marry and seemed to spend most of their time raising hell. They were said by Papaw to be sorry and by Mamaw to be damned, and I did not see them at all, even after I went to live in their childhood home.

I think now that the darkness in that house—the metaphorical darkness, not the physical, which was entirely corporeal—had its genesis in the madness of my grandmother Mattie Cash. I believe it was that madness that I smelt when I was small, like a young animal smells hidden blood, and feared her house as if it had been a charnel house. And I think it is an apt measure of the terrible fear of randomness, of murdering chance, that was born in me when my parents died that I chose that house rather than the benign house of my Compton kin. Mattie Cash was obliquely mad then; an outlander might mistake it for simple mountain reclusiveness, the queerness of old ways, and perhaps a long skein of inbreeding in the blood. There was more than a little of that in those hills then, born of proximity and inaccessibility and sheer xenophobia. But the skewedness that poured from the old house like invisible smoke was madness pure and simple, and in my grandmother's case it chose, as its object, God.

My grandmother was a religious fanatic from the day she was converted by a hellfire-screaming, circuit-riding preacher in her sixteenth year on the other side of the Mountain from Trinity College. By the time her daughter died naked in her lust and I came to her, she was drunk on God. By the time my grandfather began taking me to work with him, she was so deeply possessed by the Holy Ghost that even he, stone-cold man that he was himself, feared she would harm me if I were left alone with her. Mamaw never ceased trying, with cries and threats and apocalyptic quotes from the Old Testament or Revelation, to convert anyone who came within range of her terrible God.

And he *was* terrible. He was a God of fire and blood and vengeance, who demanded of his followers flesh and fealty and money and whatever else they had. He took and he judged and he damned. In my grandmother's ruined mind, he left it up to her to save and instructed her to do it with her tongue and her hands and her broom and even the occasional kitchen knife, if the occasion for that arose. She murdered one of Papaw's two prized heifers, destined to fatten and thrive and keep us all in milk and butter for winters to come, because her God demanded of her, one steaming July day, the sacrifice of a fatted calf. She went after the social worker from the county, who heard about the calf and came to see how I was faring, with the same knife. Only the intervention of the pastor of the church to which my grandmother was indentured, and my grandfather's promise to keep me away from her, saved her from being committed then and there to the state mental facility in Knoxville.

Papaw wasn't stupid or mean, only frozen in his bitterness. He could see the trouble my slender fairness and the betraying chocolate eyes of my mother portended for me. As for Pastor Elkins, he was indeed a snake handler and half mad himself, but he was a consummate fund raiser. His ramshackle prophecy-haunted tabernacle in a tangled hollow at the base of the Mountain owed half its provenance to the money Mamaw appropriated from Papaw's wages, money kept aside to feed and clothe us. Even more largesse flowed from the sums my Compton grandparents sent regularly for my schooling and general well-being. I don't doubt that those gentle, cultivated Anglicans financed the upkeep of more than one thick, sluggish, deadly Mountain rattlesnake or water moccasin. Pastor Elkins looked upon his handmaiden's rapt, mad face and saw there many more years of affluence from the Tidewater before I attained my majority. He smiled his bleached feral smile at the country folks and promised there would not be any more unpleasantness from Sister Cash.

"She is God's daughter in her heart," he said. "She's only just got so full of the Holy Spirit that it runs over sometimes."

"Holy Spirit, my behind. That old bat is as crazy as a bedbug," I heard the young woman from the county say to her supervisor as they got back into the battered county sedan and bumped out of our yard.

The next morning I went for the first time up the winding road to Trinity College with my grandfather in his old truck and passed for the first time under the arch and into the Domain.

"Yes," the small part of me deep inside that knew about such things whispered. "This is right. This is the place."

And when the first of the faculty members passed me, sitting quietly, as my grandfather had bidden me, on the gray stone steps of Lawler Hall, where the college's administrative offices were, I raised my head and looked straight at them and smiled.

"It's a pretty morning, isn't it?" I said, and when they invariably stopped and asked me my name and whose little girl I was, I said my name was Catherine Rose Compton, and my mama and daddy were dead, and I lived now with Papaw, who made the college clean. And smiled again.

I was six years old, then, and on that day saved myself.

"And the rest, as they say, is history," I told Joe soon after I met him. I told Joe everything about me soon after we met, except the manner of my parents' death. And that came just a little later, for it was only months after we met that I knew we would marry and I might, with luck, stay forever on the Mountain. Only then did I feel I could trust Joe with the thing at the heart of my fear of leaving the Mountain, though I knew from the beginning I would have to explain.

I told him, finally, on a day when he had asked me to go with him down off the Mountain and over to Chattanooga, to hear an organ concert in one of the big Episcopal churches there. Like many other new converts to Trinity's Oxbridgian magic, Joe had fallen in love with all things Anglican and wanted passionately for me to go with him and hear Bach and Palestrina played on the new organ at St. Anselm's. I simply could not do it, but no excuse would serve. I was abundantly healthy, lived in one of the dormitories and would have been warmly encouraged by my housemother to attend the concert, and by that time was seeing no one but him.

"I have all the God up here I need," I said finally. "I don't need a dose of anybody else's."

He looked at me in thinly veiled alarm. Joe was a good Congregationalist boy from a poor, rocky little village in rural Vermont; he was both beguiled by and still a bit wary of the lush half-mystic eccentricities of the Domain. I think some buried puritan part of him expected me suddenly to forsake the orderly, dreaming gray and green spell of Trinity and start handling serpents myself.

"I've often wondered what you must have made of God, after those early years," he said. "I mean, your grandmother's fanaticism, and then up here, all this, your great-grandfather and Compton Hall. God must have confused you terribly. Nothing about him was consistent for you."

"I don't think I was confused, exactly," I said. "What did I know about consistency? I just concluded there were two of him. One for up here and another one for . . . you know. Out there. Down there."

"Cat," Joe said. "What is this out-there down-there business? Why won't you leave this mountain? What are you afraid of?"

And so I told him. And he wept. And I knew I would marry him if he asked me, and he probably would. And he did, not long after that day.

I fell in love with him on the first day of his seminar, in the winter of my senior year, when he came into class wearing a gray flat-topped Confederate officer's forage cap. Atop his thick fair hair, with his silky, full mustache and short golden beard, the cap looked wonderfully easy and contemporary; it was like meeting Jeb Stuart himself, or someone equally mythic and dashing. His academic gown was flung carelessly over a worn Harris tweed jacket, his blue oxford-cloth collar was unbuttoned, and his tie was jammed into a hip pocket. His eyes were blue and full of a kind of swimming light behind the round wire glasses, and his features were narrow and sharp and tanned by whatever he had been doing the previous summer, before he had come to Trinity. We heard he had been snatched away from somewhere like Yale or Williams and was considered a great asset to Trinity. He was the first of the influx of young

Ivy-League-educated faculty Trinity managed to lure south at the start of the seventies, that decade of greatest change, and those of us who had qualified for his elite senior seminar sat silently and stared at him. He did not speak, only stood still, hipshot, in the forage cap and looked back at us. He was tall and very thin.

"Hey, y'all," he said, in a truly terrible parody of a southern drawl. His voice was flat, nasal, and harsh, with two hundred years of New England in it. He fairly honked. We burst into laughter and he grinned, and I caught my breath sharply.

He was the image of my father when he smiled, of my young father as he smiled down at my mother and me on a long-ago sunny day on the edge of the Steep, in the only photograph I had of him. Mamaw had searched out and burned all the others.

"My name is Joe Gaillard," he said. "Josiah Peabody Gaillard. The Josiah and the Peabody are Vermont Yankee from back to Adam, but the Gaillard is a Cajun merchant marine who met my mother in Boston on her high school class trip and married her three hours before I was born. I just figured I'd get things off on the right foot and let you guys know you didn't have the lock on Gothic down here."

We laughed again, and I was lost.

Acknowledgments

Text Credits

John Crowe Ransom, "Janet Waking," "Necrological," "Antique Harvesters," and "The Equilibrists" from *Selected Poems*. Copyright 1924, 1927, 1934, 1939, 1945, © 1962, 1963 by Alfred A. Knopf, Inc. Reprinted with the permission of Alfred A. Knopf, a division of Random House, Inc.

Donald Davidson, "The Last Charge" and "Lee in the Mountains" from *Poems 1922–1961*. Copyright 1924, 1927, 1934, 1935, 1938, 1952, © 1961, 1966 by Donald Davidson. Reprinted with the permission of the University of Minnesota Press.

Allen Tate, "Ode to the Confederate Dead," "Aeneas at Washington," and "The Swimmers" from *Collected Poems 1919–1976*. Copyright © 1976 by Allen Tate. Reprinted with the permission of Farrar, Straus & Giroux, LLC.

Paul Green, "Hymn to the Rising Sun" from *Five Plays of the South*. Copyright © 1963 by Paul Green. Reprinted with the permission of Hill and Wang, a division of Farrar, Straus and Giroux, LLC.

Fielding Burke [Olive Tilford Dargan], "Her Family" from *Call Home the Heart*. Copyright 1932 in the name of the author, renewed 1983. Reprinted with the permission of The Feminist Press at The City University of New York.

Caroline Gordon, "Old Red" from *Old Red and Other Stories*. Copyright © 1963 by Caroline Gordon. Reprinted with the permission of Farrar, Straus & Giroux, LLC.

Cleanth Brooks, "William Faulkner: Vision of Good and Evil" from *The Hidden God: Studies in Hemingway, Faulkner, Yeats, Eliot, and Warren*. Copyright © 1963 by Yale University. Reprinted with the permission of Yale University Press.

Katherine Anne Porter, "Rope" from *Flowering Judas and Other Stories*. Copyright 1930 and renewed © 1958 by Katherine Anne Porter. Reprinted with the permission of Harcourt, Inc.

Sterling A. Brown, "Slim in Atlanta" and "Southern Cop" from *The Collected Poems of Sterling A. Brown*, edited by Michael S. Harper. Copyright 1932 by Harcourt Brace & Co., renewed © 1960 by Sterling A. Brown. Copyright © 1980 by Sterling A. Brown. Reprinted with permission of HarperCollins Publishers, Inc.

W. J. Cash, excerpt from *The Mind of the South*. Copyright 1941 by Alfred A. Knopf, Inc. and renewed © 1969 by Mary R. Maury. Reprinted with the permission of Alfred A. Knopf, a division of Random House, Inc.

Robert Penn Warren, "Founding Fathers, Early-Nineteenth-Century Style, Southeast U.S.A." from *New and Selected Poems, 1923–1985* (New York, Random House, 1985). Copyright © 1985 by Robert Penn Warren. Reprinted by permission of William Morris Agency, Inc. on behalf of the author. "Blackberry Winter" from *The Circus in the Attic and Other Stories*. Copyright 1947 by Robert Penn Warren. Reprinted with the permission of Harcourt, Inc.

Andrew Lytle, "Jericho, Jericho, Jericho" from *The Southern Review*, I (1935–36). Copyright 1936, renewed © 1958 by Andrew Lytle. Reprinted by permission.

Jean Toomer, "Harvest Song," "Prayer," "Portrait in Georgia," and "Cotton Song" from *Cane*. Copyright 1923 by Boni & Liveright, renewed 1951 by Jean Toomer. Reprinted with the permission of Liveright Publishing Corporation.

James Weldon Johnson, "Preface" and "Listen, Lord—A Prayer" from *God's Trombones*. Copyright 1927 The Viking Press, Inc., renewed © 1955 by Grace Nail Johnson. Reprinted with the permission of Viking Penguin, a division of Penguin Putnam Inc.

Julia Peterkin, "Ashes" from *Collected Short Stories of Julia Peterkin*. Reprinted with the permission of the University of South Carolina Press.

Margaret Mitchell, "Chapter I" from *Gone With the Wind*. Copyright 1936 by Margaret Mitchell. Reprinted with the permission of the William Morris Agency on behalf of the Estate of Margaret Mitchell.

William Faulkner, excerpt from *Absalom, Absalom!* Copyright 1936 by William Faulkner and renewed © 1964 by Estelle Faulkner and Jill Faulkner Summers. Excerpt from *Go Down, Moses*. Copyright 1940, 1942 by William Faulkner and renewed © 1968, 1970 by Estelle Faulkner and Jill Faulkner Summers. Both reprinted with the permission of Random House, Inc.

Stark Young, "Not in Memoriam, But in Defense" from *I'll Take My Stand: The South and the Agrarian Tradition*. Reprinted with the permission of Louisiana State University Press.

Zora Neal Hurston, excerpt from *Their Eyes Were Watching God*. Copyright 1937 by Harper & Row, Publishers, Inc., renewed © 1965 by John C. Hurston and Joel Hurston. Reprinted with the permission of HarperCollins Publishers, Inc.

Carson McCullers, "A Tree, A Rock, A Cloud" from *The Ballad of the Sad Café and Collected Short Stories*. Copyright 1936, 1941, 1942, 1950, © 1955 by Carson McCullers, © renewed 1979 by Floria V. Lasky. Reprinted with the permission of Houghton Mifflin Company. All rights reserved.

William Alexander Percy, excerpt from *Lanterns on the Levee*. Copyright 1941 by Alfred A. Knopf, Inc. and renewed 1969 by LeRoy Pratt Percy. Reprinted with the permission of Alfred A. Knopf, a division of Random House, Inc.

Eudora Welty, "A Piece of News" and "A Worn Path" from *A Curtain of Green and Other Stories*. Copyright 1937 and renewed © 1965 by Eudora Welty. Reprinted with the permission of Harcourt, Inc.

Tennessee Williams, "Portrait of a Madonna" from *27 Wagons Full of Cotton*. Copyright 1945 by University of the South. Reprinted with the permission of New Directions Publishing Corporation.

Richard Wright, excerpt from *Black Boy*. Copyright 1937, 1942, 1944, 1945 by Richard Wright, renewed © 1973 by Ellen Wright. Reprinted with the permission of HarperCollins Publishers, Inc.

Michel Fabre, notes from *Richard Wright Reader*. Copyright © 1978 by Michel Fabre. Reprinted with the permission of John Hawkins & Associates, Inc.

Truman Capote, "A Diamond Guitar" from *Breakfast at Tiffany's*. Copyright 1950 by Truman Capote. Reprinted with the permission of Random House, Inc.

Lillian Smith, "The Women" from *Killers of the Dream*. Copyright 1949, © 1961 by Lillian Smith. Reprinted with the permission of W. W. Norton & Company, Inc.

of The Feminist Press at The City University of New York. "Faulkner and Race" from *The Maker and the Myth*. Reprinted with the permission of the University Press of Mississippi. "Southern Song" and "Sorrow Home" from *This is My Century: New and Collected Poems*. Copyright © 1989 by Margaret Walker Alexander. Reprinted with the permission of The University of Georgia Press.

James Dickey, "The Strength of Fields" from *The Strength of Fields*. Copyright © 1979 by James Dickey. Reprinted with the permission of Doubleday, a division of Random House, Inc., "The Bee" from *Collected Poems 1945–1992* (Hanover, NH: Wesleyan University Press). Copyright © 1967 by James Dickey. Reprinted with the permission of University Press of New England.

Elizabeth Madox Roberts, "On The Mountainside" from *The Haunted Mirror*. Copyright 1932 by Elizabeth Madox Roberts; renewed © 1960 by Ivor S. Roberts. Reprinted with the permission of Viking Penguin, a division of Penguin Putnam, Inc.

Anne Spencer, "Substitution" and "For Jim, Easter Eve" from J. Lee Greene, ed., *Time's Unfading Garden: Anne Spencer's Life and Poetry* (Baton Rouge: Louisiana State University Press, 1977). Reprinted with the permission of J. Lee Greene.

Thomas Wolfe, excerpts from *Of Time and the River*. Copyright 1935 by Charles Scribner's Sons, renewed © 1963 by Paul Gitlin, Administrator, C.T.A. Reprinted with the permission of Scribner, a division of Simon & Schuster, Inc.

Jesse Stuart, "Kentucky Is My Land," "Her Work Is Done," "Prayer for My Father," "Stand Out and Count," "Modernity," and "Summer Has Faded" from *Kentucky Is My Land* by Jesse Stuart. Copyright © 1980 by The Jesse Stuart Foundation. Reprinted by permission of The Jesse Stuart Foundation.

James Agee, "Knoxville: Summer 1915" and "Chapter One" from *A Death in the Family*. Copyright © 1957 by The James Agee Trust, renewed 1985 by Mia Agee. Reprinted with the permission of Grosset & Dunlap, Inc., a division of Penguin Putnam, Inc.

George Scarbrough, "The Winter Mole," "Death Is A Short Word," and "Blackberry Winter" from *George Scarbrough: New and Selected Poems* (Binghamton, NY: Iris Press, 1977). Reprinted with the permission of the author.

Gurney Norman, "The Revival" from *Kinfolks, The Wilgus Stories* (Frankfort, KY: The Gnomon Press, 1977). Reprinted by permission.

Harriet Arnow, excerpt from *The Dollmaker*. Copyright 1954 and renewed © 1982 by Harriet Simpson Arnow. Reprinted with the permission of Scribner, a division of Simon & Schuster, Inc.

James Still, "Farm," "Pattern For Death," and "When the Dulcimers Are Gone" from *The Wolfpen Poems* (Berea, KY: The Berea College Press, 1986). Copyright © 1986 by James Still. Reprinted by permission.

Jim Wayne Miller, "Chapter 29" from *Newfound*. Copyright © 1989 by Jim Wayne Miller. Reprinted with the permission of Orchard Books, a division of Franklin Watts, Inc.

Lee Smith, excerpt from *Saving Grace*. Copyright © 1995 by Lee Smith. Reprinted with the permission of Putnam Berkeley, a division of Penguin Putnam, Inc.

Wendell Berry, "I" ["I go among trees and sit still"], "III" ["To sit and look at light-filled leaves"], "IV" ["The bell calls in the town"], and "VIII" ["I go from the woods into the cleared field"] from *Sabbaths*. Copyright © 1987 by Wendell Berry. "Why I Am

Index

✧